SIR BANISTER FLETCHER'S

A HISTORY OF ARCHITECTURE

SIR BANISTER FLETCHER'S A HISTORY OF ARCHITECTURE

TWENTIETH EDITION

EDITED BY
DAN CRUICKSHANK

Consultant Editors
ANDREW SAINT
PETER BLUNDELL JONES
KENNETH FRAMPTON

Assistant Editor
FLEUR RICHARDS

ARCHITECTURAL PRESS

Architectural Press
An imprint of Butterworth-Heinemann
Linacre House, Jordan Hill, Oxford OX2 8DP
A division of Reed Educational and Professional Publishing Ltd

A member of the Reed Elsevier plc group

OXFORD BOSTON JOHANNESBURG
MELBOURNE NEW DELHI SINGAPORE

First published 1896
Twentieth edition 1996

Under the terms of the Will of Sir Banister Fletcher, the Royal Institute of British Architects and the University of London became the joint beneficiaries of a Trust Fund, of which one of the principal assets is the copyright in *A History of Architecture*. The income from this Fund, which is shared by the Institute and the University, is to be devoted to the furtherance of architectural teaching and appreciation in accordance with the various intentions expressed by Sir Banister Fletcher in his Will

British Library Cataloguing in Publication Data
A catalogue record for this book is available from the British Library

Library of Congress Cataloguing in Publication Data
A catalogue record for this book is available from the Library of Congress

ISBN 0 7506 2267 9

Composition by Genesis Typesetting, Rochester, Kent
Printed and bound in Great Britain

CONTENTS

LIST OF CONTRIBUTORS

EDITOR
Dan Cruickshank, *Honorary Fellow of the Royal Institute of British Architects, Visiting Professor in the Department of Architecture, Sheffield University, and author of* London: The Art of Georgian Building *and* Life in the Georgian City

CONSULTANT EDITORS
Andrew Saint, *Honorary Fellow of the Royal Institute of British Architects, Professor in the Department of Architecture, Cambridge University, and author of the biography* Richard Norman Shaw
Peter Blundell Jones, *Professor in the Department of Architecture, Sheffield University, and author of the biographies* Hans Scharoun *and* Hugo Häring
Kenneth Frampton, *Ware Professor of Architecture, Columbia University, New York, and author of* Modern Architecture 1851–1945 *and* Modern Architecture: A Critical History

CONTRIBUTORS
Chris Abel, *Senior Lecturer in Architecture, University of Nottingham, and author of* Architecture and Identity: Towards a Global Eco-culture
Chapters 55 and 56
Gautam Bhatia, *architect based in Delhi and author of* Punjabi Baroque *and* Silent Spaces
Chapter 57
Dr Charles A. Burney, *Department of Archaeology, University of Manchester*
Chapters 3 and 4
Dr Kim Choung Ki, *Director, National Institute of Cultural Properties of Korea*
Chapters 25 and 39
Dr Catherine Cooke, *architect, chair of course on Design Principles and Practice, Open University, and author of* Russian Avant-Garde: Theories of Art, Architecture and the City
Chapter 47
Colin Davies, *architect, Senior Lecturer in Architectural History, University of North London*
Chapter 51
Dr Caroline Elam, *formerly of the Department of Architecture, Westfield College, University of London, and editor of the* Burlington Magazine
Chapters 29–33 (assisted by Paul Davies, David Hemsoll, Patrick Sweeney and Neil Macgregor)
Professor Dr sc. phil Hubert Faensen, *Section Aesthetic und Kunstwissenschaften, Humboldt University, Berlin*
Chapter 12
Professor Wu Guang-zu, *Department of Architecture, Tongji University, Shanghai*
Chapters 38 and 53
Professor Daiheng Guo, *Department of Architecture, Tsinghua University, Beijing*
Chapter 24
Dr Julienne Hanson, *Bartlett School of Graduate Studies, University College London*
Chapters 2, 5, 9 and 22
Dr Adam Hardy, *Director of Practice, Research and Advancement in South Asian Design and Architecture (PRASADA), De Montfort University, Leicester*
Chapter 26

Stephen Heywood, *historian with Norfolk County Council*
Chapter 13
Eizo Inagaki, *Department of Architecture, University of Tokyo*
Chapters 25 and 39
Eitan Karol, *architect and historian based in Israel*
Chapter 48
Dr Peter Kidson, *Courtauld Institute of Art, University of London*
Chapter 14 (assisted by Lindy M. Grant, Allan Brodie and Christopher Welander)
Dr Jon Lim, *School of Architecture, National University of Singapore*
Chapter 40 (assisted by Budi A. Sukada)
Dr Derek Linstrum, *formerly of the Institute of Advanced Architectural Studies, University of York*
Chapters 36 and 49
Professor Richard Longstreth, *American Studies Program, George Washington University, Washington, DC*
Chapter 50
Professor H. Stanley Loten, *School of Architecture, Carleton University, Ottawa*
Chapter 23
Dr Otakar Macel, *Technische Hogeschool, Delft*
Chapter 46
Dr Rowland J. Mainstone, *author of the definitive study of Hagia Sophia, Istanbul*
Chapters 10 and 11
Anthony McIntyre, *architectural critic, teacher and author of several books on historic and contemporary European architecture*
Chapter 45
Louise Noelle Mereles, *Instituto de Investigaciones Esteticas, Universidad Nacional Autonoma de Mexico*
Chapter 37
Dr Stefan Muthesius, *School of World Art Studies and Museology, University of East Anglia*
Chapter 34
Dr Mary Neighbour Parent, *Department of Architecture, University of Tokyo*
Chapters 25 and 39
Dr Suha Ozkan, *architect, former vice-president of the Middle East Technical University (METU), Ankara, and currently Secretary-General of the Aga Khan Award for Architecture*
Chapter 48
Professor Andrew Saint, *Department of Architecture, University of Cambridge*
Chapters 37 and 44 (a major revision and extension of earlier text by David Dunster)
Professor David Saunders, *formerly of the Department of Architecture, University of Adelaide*
Chapter 42
Dennis Sharp, *architect, University of Nottingham*
Chapter 46
Dr Roland Silva, *Director General, Central Cultural Fund, Colombo*
Chapter 41
Jennifer Taylor, *Associate Professor, Department of Architecture, University of Sydney*
Chapter 58
Helen Thomas, *architect*
Chapter 52
Professor Richard A. Tomlinson, *Director, British School at Athens*
Chapters 6 and 7
Dr Christopher Wakeling, *Centre for Adult and Continuing Education, University of Keele*
Chapter 34
John C. T. Warren, *architect and co-author of a study of traditional houses in Baghdad*
Chapters 15–20
Thomas Weaver, *Princeton University*
Chapter 54

ILLUSTRATIONS
Dr Mark Gelernter, *Lecturer, Bartlett School of Architecture and Planning,* prepared 23 sheets of drawings
Ken Waas and **Alick Newman,** *Department of Geography, University College London,* revised the maps

BIBLIOGRAPHY
Julian Osley, *RIBA Library*

SOURCES OF ILLUSTRATIONS

The publishers wish to express their thanks to the great number of institutions, commercial firms and private persons who have supplied photographs for use in this book or who have given permission for copyright material to be used in the preparation of plans and drawings.

Where acknowledgement is made to published works mentioned in the bibliography at the end of the book the date of the publication is given.

ABBREVIATIONS

RCHME The Royal Commission on the Historical Monuments of England

RIBA Royal Institute of British Architects

CHAPTER 1

8A, from Stobart, 1964.
8B, from D. Stronach, 1978.
23A,C, from A. K. Orlandos, 1966.
23B, from R. S. Young, *Three Great Early Tumuli*, 1981.

CHAPTER 3

46A, after Emery, 1939.
46B, after J. Garstang, *Mahasna and Bêt Khallâf*, 1902.
46C, after A. Badawy, *A History of Egyptian Architecture*, vol. i, 1954.
46D, after (i) F. Benoit, *L'Architecture d'antiquité*, 1911, (ii) A. Rowe, *Museum Journal of the University of Philadelphia*, xxii, No. I, 1931, (iii) A. Schaff, *Handbuch der Archaeologie, Aegypten*, 1939.
46G, after Lange and Hirmer, 1968.
46H, after L. Borchardt, *Die Enstehung der Pyramide an der Baugeschichte der Pyramide bei Mejdum nachgewiesen*, 1928.
46J, after Reisner.
46K,L, after (i) D. Hölscher, *Das Grabdenkmal des Königs Chephren*, 1912, (ii) A. Badawy, (iii) Edwards, 1961.
46N, after L. Borchardt, *Das Grabdenkmal des Königs Sahu-Ré*, 1910–13, and Edwards.
47, drawings and reconstructions by J. P. Lauer.
48, after E. Droton, J. P. Lauer, C. M. Firth and J. E. Quibell.
50F, in part after Edwards.
51A, 63A, Aerofilms Ltd.
51B, from G. Jequier, *Les Temples memphites et thébains des origines à la XVIIIe dynastie*, 1920.
56A, after H. Ricke, *Beiträge zur Aegyptischen Bauforschung und Altertumskunde*, 1950, and Baedeker, *Egypt and the Sudan*, 1908.
56B, after A. M. Calverley, *The Temple of King Sethos I at Abydos*, 1933, by permission of the Egypt Exploration Society and the Oriental Institute, University of Chicago.
56C–F, after Baedeker, *Egypt and the Sudan*, 1908 and 1929 editions.
56G, after Lange and Hirmer.
59A, Metropolitan Museum of Art, New York, bequest of Levi Hale Willard, 1883.
59B, 64B, Lehnert and Landrock, Cairo.
60A, from Lange and Hirmer.
61B, Courtauld Institute of Art.
63B,C, 65B, 66B, A. F. Kersting.
64A, Oriental Institute, University of Chicago.
67, from Emery, 1965.

CHAPTER 4

72A, after (i) Parrot, 1946, (ii) Frankfort, 1954, (iii) Noldeke *et al., Vorläufiger Bericht über die Ausgrabungen in Uruk-Warka*, 1937.
72B, after Parrot, 1946 and Sir Leonard Woolley, *Ur Excavations V, The Ziggurat and its Surroundings*, 1939.
72C, R. Ghirshman.
75A, Oriental Institute, University of Chicago, reconstruction by Hamilton Darby.
75B, Oriental Institute, University of Chicago, reconstruction by H. D. Hill.
76A,B, 77A,B, after Mallowan, 1966.
77C, from D. Oates, *Iraq XXIX*, 1967.
80C, after Loud, by permission of the Oriental Institute, University of Chicago.

81F, after Luschan *et al.*.
81G, after *Mitteilungen aus den Orientalischen Sammlungen, Heft XXV; Ausgrabungen in Sendschirli IV*, Königliches Museum, Berlin, 1911.
83A, Vorderasiatisches Museum, Berlin, by permission of Generalverwaltung der Staatlichen Museen zu Berlin.
83B, from Mallowan, 1966.
83C, from Loud, by permission of the Oriental Institute, University of Chicago.
84A, after Seton Lloyd, *Early Anatolia*, 1956, and Puchstein.
84B, after Gurney and Puchstein.
84C, Oriental Institute, University of Chicago.
84D, after K. Bittel, R. Naumann, H. Otto, *Yazilikaya*, 1941.
84E, after K. Bittel, *Die Ruinen von Bogazköy*, 1937.
89A, courtesy of Altan Cilingiroglu.
89B, C. Burney.
90A, from B. B. Piotrovskii, *Urartu: the Kingdom of Van and its art*, 1967.
90B, from C. Nylander, 1971.
90C, from C. P. E. Haspels, 1971.
91A, from T. Özgüc, 'The Urartian Architecture on the Summit of Altintepe', *Anatolia VII*, 1963.
91B, from *Anatolian Studies XVI*.
91C, from E. Bilgiç and B. Oğun, 'Excavations at Kefkalesi, 1964', *Anatolia VIII*, 1964.
94C, after Schmidt, by permission of the Oriental Institute, University of Chicago.
95A,B, Oriental Institute, University of Chicago.
95C, from Ghirsham, 1954.
95D, David Stronach.

CHAPTER 6

108A, after Sir Arthur Evans, *Palace of Minos at Knossos*, 1928.
108B, after Pendlebury.
110C, 126C, 146A,B, William Taylor.
111A,B, after Dinsmoor, and Piet de Jong.
111C, 132A, after Lawrence, 1957 ed.
113F, after Dinsmoor.
118A,B, after Dinsmoor, and W. J. Anderson and R. P. Spiers, *Architecture of Ancient Greece and Rome*, 1907.
126A,B, 129A, Agora Excavations, American School of Classical Studies/photo Alison Frantz.
130A, 136A, N. Hiscock.
130B, A. F. Kersting.
130C, 147C, Agora Excavations, American School of Classical Studies, Athens.
132B, 133A, 133B, after Berve, Gruben and Hirmer, by permission of Hirmer Verlag München.
135E, 136B, after A. Furtwängler *et al. Aegina: das Heiligtum der Aphaia*, 1906.
139, in part after Dinsmoor.
140B,C, in part after Lawrence, 1957 ed., and F. Krischen, *Die Griechische Stadt*, 1938.
141, in part after Dinsmoor, and T. Wiegand, *Achter vorläufiger Bericht über die von den Staatlichen Museen in Milet und Didyma unternommenen Ausgrabungen*, 1924.
147A, from Berve, Gruben and Hirmer.
147B, Trustees of the British Museum.

CHAPTER 7

156N, after T. Wiegand (as 130).
157A, R. A. Tomlinson.
157B, 161A, William Taylor.
157C, from T. Wiegand, *et al., Milet: Die Ergebnisse der Ausgrabungen und Untersuchungen*, 1906.
161B, from Martin.
163, after T. Homolle, *et al., Exploration archéologique de Délos*, 1902, by permission of the Ecole française, Athens, and Editions Boccard, Paris.

CHAPTER 8

175A, Museum of Antiquities, University and Society of Antiquaries, Newcastle upon Tyne.
175B, Alinari.
175C, Giraudon.
186, copyright St Gallen Library
187, from Conant, 1959 ed.

CHAPTER 9

218A, Crown Copyright, reproduced by permission of the Scottish Development Dept.
218B, National Museum of Archaeology, Malta.

CHAPTER 10

231A, 265, from Boethius and Ward-Perkins, Istituto di Etruscologia e di Antichita Italiche, Rome University.
231B, 233A, 239B, 248B, 259C, 264C, 268A, Alinari.
233B,C, 235A, 239A, 244A,B, 248A, 252B,C, 256A–F, 264A,B, 267A, 270B, 271A,B,C, 273B, 276A, 277A, 280A–E, R. Mainstone.
234A,B, Alterocca, Terni.
235B, Josephine Powell.
244C, 251B,C, 259B, 267B, Fototeca Unione, Rome.
244A, Leonard von Matt.
259A, 276B, A. F. Kersting.
270A, from D. S. Robertson, by permission of Staatsbibliothek Bildarchiv, Berlin.
273A, from Wheeler, 1964, drawing by William Suddaby.

CHAPTER 11

291B, 294B,C,E, 298B,C, 301A, 304A,B, 312A, 313A,B, 315A,D, 316A, 318A,B, R. Mainstone.
292A, Fototeca Unione, Rome.
292B, 296B, Alinari.
294A, Foto Marburg.

298A, G. H. Forsyth, Kelsey Museum, University of Michigan/reproduced courtesy of the Michigan-Princeton-Alexandria Expedition to Mount Sinai.
301B, from D. Talbot Rice, *The Art of Byzantium*, 1959.
302, from Fossati.
305, from M. Hürlimann, *Istanbul*, 1958.
312B, Foto Marburg.
313C, Antonello Perissinotto.
316B, Testolini.

CHAPTER 12
324A, Courtauld Institute of Art.
324B, 325A, courtesy The Byzantine Collection/photo C. Mango, copyright Dumbarton Oaks, Trustees of Harvard University.
325B–D, 327A–C, 328, 330A–C, 336, 337A–D, 340A–D, 341A,B, 342A–D, Klaus G. Beyer.
333, after H. Faensen and V. Ivanov, 1975.

CHAPTER 13
353A,C, 354A,C, 357B, 358A,C, 360A, Alinari.
353B, Courtauld Institute of Art.
357A, Omniafoto, Turin.
359, Fototeca Unione, Rome.
366A, Combier Imp. Mâcon.
366B, Giraudon.
371A, Archives photographiques, Paris.
371B, Courtauld Institute of Art/photo G. C. Druce.
371D, 375B,C, 385B, 399B, S. Heywood.
371E, 386A,B, 387B, 392B,C, 400, A. F. Kersting.
375A,D, Foto Marburg.
382A, after K. J. Conant, *The Early Architectural History of the Cathedral of Santiago de Compostela*, copyright 1926 by the President and Fellows of Harvard College/1954 by Kenneth J. Conant.
382B,D,E, after Bevan, 1938.
382C, after Clapham.
384A,C, 385A, C–E, 386C,D, 387A, Foto Mas.
384B, Courtauld Institute of Art.
392A, H. E. Stutchbury.
392D, 406B–E, 407A,C, Aerofilms Ltd.
397C, E–G, after Webb.
399A, photograph by J. R. H. Weaver.
406A, Thomas H. Mason and Sons Ltd.
407B, Crown Copyright, RCHME.
412A, Royal Norwegian Embassy, London.
412B, Swedish Tourist Traffic Association, Stockholm.
412C,D, 414C, Riksantikvaren.
413A, The Danish Tourist Board, London.
413B, Refot.
414A,B, after Clapham.
414D, after Paulssen.

CHAPTER 14
427A,C, 431A,B, 441B,D, 442C,D, 445A, 446B, 447A,C,D, 448A,B, 476B, 493A,B, 494A–D, 498A, 504A,B, 510A–E, 512A,C, 513A,B, 525A,B,D, 528C, 529A,D, 530A–C, 538B, 540B, 556C, Courtauld Institute of Art.
429, 442A, 456B, 459B, 466, 468A, 469A, 473C, 474B,C, 476C, 518D, 526A,B, 538A, 550B,C, 551A,B, A. F. Kersting.
431C,D, 433C, 493C,D, 498B,C, 503, 504C,D, Foto Marburg.
439, Roger-Viollet.
4441A, 525C, Foto Mas.
445C, J. Austin.
447B, 451A, Archives photographiques, Paris.
455A, 456D, School of Architecture, University of Manchester.
455B, 470A–D, 471A, 473B, 474A, 475A, 476A, 477B, 479A,B, 487A,C, Crown Copyright, RCHME.
456A, from Braun, 1970.
459A, 460A,B, 468B, 473A, 479C, 481A,B, 482A, Aerofilms Ltd.
471B, Gordon Fraser Gallery/photo Edwin Smith.
477A, Perfecta Publications/photo S. Newberg.
481C, Crown Copyright, reproduced by permission of HM Stationery Office/Alan Sorrell reconstruction drawing.
482B, from J. Nash, *The Mansions of England in the Olden Time*, 1839.
485H, after Garner and Stratton.
487B, F. C. Morgan.
512B,D, 515A, Rijksdienst voor de Monumentenzorg.
513C, 528B, copyright ACL Brussels.
518A,B, 528B, Courtauld Institute of Art/C. Welander.
504A,C, 538C, 541A,B, 543A, 550A, 552A–C, 554B, 556A, Alinari.

CHAPTER 15
570A, From G.Michell, 1978.
570B, From G. Michell, 1978.
570C, From R. Lewcock and Z. Freeth, 1978
572, From G. Michell, 1978

CHAPTER 16
576A, J. Warren.
576B, J. Warren.
577B, J. Warren.
577C, J. Warren.

CHAPTER 17
582A, Middle East Archive, London
583A, A. F. Kersting.
583B, J. Warren.
589A, J. Warren.
589B, A. F. Kersting.
589C, A. F. Kersting.
592A, J. Warren.
592B, A. F. Kersting.
592C, A. F. Kersting.
592D, J. Warren.

595, F. Kersting.
597A, A. F. Kersting.
597B, A. F. Kersting.
597C, Foto Mas.
597D, Foto Mas.

CHAPTER 18
601A, A. F. Kersting.
601B, Thames and Husdon/photo Roger Wood, London.
601C, Yolande Crowe.
601D, Office of the Press Counsellor, Turkish Embassy, London.
603A, Yolande Crowe.
603B, Novosti Press Agency.
604A, Office of the Press Counsellor, Turkish Embassy, London.
604B, A. F. Kersting.
604C, A. F. Kersting.
604D, J. Warren.
608A, Novosti Press Agency.
608B, A. F. Kersting.
609, Yolande Crewe.

CHAPTER 19
612A, Roger Wood, London.
612B, Douglas Dickens.
612C, Office of the Press Counsellor, Turkish Embassy, London.
612D, Godfrey Goodwin.
614A, J. Warren.
614B, J. Warren.
614C, J. Warren.
615A, J. Warren.
615B, J. Warren.
615C, J. Warren.
619A, Office of the Press Counsellor, Turkish Embassy, London.
619B, A. F. Kersting.
622A, Douglas Dickens.
622C, A. F. Kersting.
623A, Douglas Dickens.
623B, J. Warren.
623C, A. F. Kersting.
627B, A. F. Kersting.

CHAPTER 20
630A, J. Warren.
630B, From F. Stark, *The Southern Gates of Arabia*, 1971.
631A, J. Warren.
631B, J. Warren.

CHAPTER 21
648A, 663C,E, J. Musgrove.
658A,B, from M. Meister, Vol. 1, 1983.
658C, after Liang Ssu Cheng, 1984.
663A, Lou Qingxi.
663B,D, 648B, Dept. of Architecture, Tsinghua University.

CHAPTER 23
673, 675, 677A, 678A–D, 681A,B, 682A,B, 683A,B, 684B,C, 686A,B, 687A, 689A,B, 690A, 691A, H. Stanley Loten.
677B, from T. Proskouriakoff, 1963.
684A, Unesco/photo R. Garraud.
687B, Douglas Dickins.
690B, Victor Kennett.
690C, Grace Line Inc..
690D, L. Hervé.
691B, Courtauld Institute of Art.

CHAPTER 24
695A, 703A, 705A,C, 706D, 709A, 711A–C, 712A–C, 713A,D, Dept. of Architecture, Tsinghua University.
695B,C, 705B, 706C, 710B,C, Daiheng Guo.
695D, 696A,B, 697A–D, 698A,B, 703B, 704A,B,D, 705D, 706A,B, 710A, 713B,C, Lou Qingxi.
701, 702, Virondra Rawat.
704C, 709B, Chinese Photograph Agency.

CHAPTER 25
718–20, 722, Kim Choung Ki.
725, 727–9, 730, 733, 734, 736, 739, 740, 743–5, Eizo Inagaki.

CHAPTER 26
749B, Adam Hardy.
749C, Unesco/photo Cart.
751A, Archaeological Department, Government of Sri Lanka.
752A–G, Virendra Rawat
753A, Adam Hardy
753B, Adam Hardy
753C, Adam Hardy
756A, Adam Hardy
756B, Adam Hardy
756C, Adam Hardy
759A–E, Virendra Rawat
760A, A. F. Kersting.
763A–F, Virendra Rawat.
764A, Adam Hardy.
764B, Adam Hardy.
764C, Adam Hardy.
766A–C, Virendra Rawat
767A–L, Virendra Rawat
768A, Adam Hardy.
768B, Adam Hardy.
768C, Adam Hardy.
768D, Adam Hardy.
771A, Adam Hardy.
771B, Adam Hardy.
771C, Adam Hardy.
772A, Adam Hardy.
772B, Adam Hardy.
773A, From M. Meister, Vol. 2, 1983.
773B, Adam Hardy.
773C, Adam Hardy.
775A, Adam Hardy.

775B, Adam Hardy.
776A, Victor Kennett.
776B, From M. Meister, Vol. 2, 1983.
777A, From P. Brown, 1959.
777B, Adam Hardy.
778A, Adam Hardy.
778B, From J. Fergusson, Vol. 2, 1910.
778C, Adam Hardy.
778D, From J. Fergusson, Vol. 2, 1910.
778E, From M. Meister, Vol. 2, 1983.
780A, From P. Brown, 1959.
780B, From M. Meister, Vol. 2, 1983.
783A, Adam Hardy.
783B, Adam Hardy.
783C, Adam Hardy.
784A, Archaeological Department, Government of Sri Lanka.
784B, Archaeological Department, Government of Sri Lanka.
785A, From J. Fergusson, Vol. 2, 1910.
785B, From E. B. Havell, 1915.
785C, British Museum.

CHAPTER 27

791A, 792A, 801B, from Hugo Munsterberg, *Art of India and Southeast Asia*, 1970.
791B, copyright RIBA.
791C, 792B, 793A–C, 795A,B, 797C, 800B–D, 801C, from J. Fergusson, Vol. 2, 1910.
795C, 797B, 798A, Unesco/photo C. Baugey.
796B, 797A, 798B, 800A, Douglas Dickins.
801A,D, Unesco/photo D. Davies.
801E, Unesco/photo Cart.

CHAPTER 28

813A,B, Alinari.
816B, A.F. Kersting.

CHAPTER 29

852A,B,D, 856B,C,E, 857C, 861, 863C, 868B, 877A,B, 885B,C, 889A,B, 890A–C, 897A–C, 899A,C, 900A,B, 902A–C, 903A,D, 906A,B,D, 909A,B, 911B, 912A–C, 916A, 917A,B, Alinari.
852C, Christopher Wilson.
856A, A. F. Kersting.
856D, 857A,B, 863A,B, 868A, 885A, 889C, 899B, 900C, 906C, 908A,B, 911C,D, 916B, 917C, 918B, Courtauld Institute of Art.
868C, Courtauld Institute of Art/Piranesi.
870E,F, after P. M. Letarouilly, *The Vatican*, I, 1953.
880A,E,G–J, after Haupt.
890, Dan Cruickshank.
913, from *Architettura*, 6, 1960.
914, from *Architettura*, 7, 1961.

CHAPTER 30

928A, 936A, 941C, 950A, 957C, Giraudon.
932B, 936B, 939A, 941A, 942A, 950B, 952C,D, 954A, 971A,B,C, 972, 973C, Courtauld Institute of Art.
933B, Archives photographiques, Paris.
936C, 937B, 939B, 942B, 950C, 952A,B, 953A, Foto Marburg.
937A, Roger-Viollet.
945B, Aero-photo.
946B, 957B, 969A, A. F. Kersting.
947A, after Ward, 1926.
947B, after Blondel.
953B, French Government Tourist Office.
957A, *Country Life*.
962A–C, 963A,B, 965A,C,D, 969B,C,D, 970A,B, Foto Mas.
966, after Prentice.
973A, Alvão, Oporto.
973B, Mario Novaes.

CHAPTER 31

978A,B, 991A,B, Courtauld Institute of Art.
978C, 984A,C, 986A,C, 987B, 990A,B, 994A,C, 995A,C, 996A, Foto Marburg.
984B, 987A, Bundesdenkmalamt, Vienna/photo Eva Frodl-Kraft.
986B, C. N. P. Powell.
987C, 996B, Deutsche Fotothek Dresden.
988, 991C, 994B, A. F. Kersting.
995B, Deutsche Fotothek Dresden/photo Handrick.

CHAPTER 32

1002A,B, 1003A,B, 1005A,C, copyright ACL Brussels.
1002C, Press Bureau, Belgian Embassy.
1003C, 1005B,D, 1007A–C, Rijksdienst voor de Monumentenzorg.
1005E, Rijksmuseum, Amsterdam.
1014B, 1020A, 1028C, 1040C, 1048A, 1059E, Courtauld Institute of Art.
1014C, 1021C–E, 1028A,B, 1044A, 1045A, 1053A, 1054B, 1056C, 1058A–C, 1059A,C, Crown Copyright, RCHME.
1016A, 1021A,B, 1032A, 1039C, 1040B, 1044B,C, 1048B, 1056A, 1059D, 1060A, 1063A,B,D, A. F. Kersting.
1020B, 1023B, 1051A,B, *Country Life*.
1023A, Crown Copyright, reproduced by permission of the Controller of HM Stationery Office.
1039B, Birmingham Post and Mail Ltd.
1045B, J. B. Price.
1047A, Raphael Tuck and Sons Ltd.
1047B, B. T. Batsford Ltd.
1047C, Aerofilms Ltd.
1048C, 1062A, Christopher Wilson.
1053B, 1054A, Judges Ltd, Hastings.
1056B, RIBA Library.
1059B, Francis Milsom.
1060B, Radio Times Hulton Picture Library.
1060C, British Museum.
1062B, from A. E. Richardson, *Monumental Classical Architecture in Great Britain*, 1914.
1063C, NBR/photo Gerald Cobb.

CHAPTER 33

1067A, 1071C, 1072B, Bernard Cox.
1067B,C, 1072A,C, Novosti Press Agency.
1069A,B, 1070A–C, Allan Braham.
1071B, 1080B, Courtauld Institute of Art.
1075A, 1077A, 1080C, 1086A,B, Nationalmuseet, Copenhagen.
1075B, Nationalhistoriske Museum, Frederiksborg.
1077B, 1078B, 1079A, B, Refot.
1078A, Stockholms Stadsmuseum.
1078C, 1080A, 1081, 1085A,B, Ronald Sheridan.
1083A,B, Norsk Folkemuseum, Oslo.
1083C, Eric de Maré.
1086C, 1087A, B, Riksantikvaren.
1087C, 1088A,C, 1089A, Finnish Embassy, London.
1088B, A. F. Kersting.

CHAPTER 34

1097A, S. Muthesius.
1097B, Thorwaldsen Museum, Copenhagen.
1097C, 1098B, 1099S,B, 1103A, 1104A,B, 1113A< 1118B, 1117B, 1121C, 1123A,C, 1128A, 1131, 1133A, 1136B, 1148C, 1154A, 1155A, A. F. Kersting.
1098A, Periklis Papahatzidakis, Athens.
1098C, after Barry.
1102A, 1123B, 1137A, Alinari.
1102B, 1103C, 1104C, 1133B, C. Wakeling.
1102C, from *Survey of London*, vol. XXX, 1960, by permission of London County Council;
plan after *Civil Engineer and Architect's Journal*, Dec. 1840.
1103B, 1110B, 1111A, 1114A,B, 1119A,C, 1127B, 1130B, 1132B, 1139, 1141A, 1147C, 1150B, 1153C, Crown Copyright, RCHME.
1106A, 1125A, 1127A, 1130C, 1145A, Archives photographiques, Paris.
1106B, by permission of the British Transport Commission.
1107A, from W. H. Pyne, *The History of the Royal Residences*, vol. iii, 1819.
1107B, J. Austin.
1107C, 1122A, 1142B, Bulloz.
1109A, 1113C, 1156A, 1150A, *Country Life*.
1109B, Sir John Summerson.
1110C, after A. W. Pugin, *The Present State of Ecclesiastical Architecture in England*, 1843.
1111B, Fox Photos Ltd.
1113B, Staatliche Landesbildstelle Hamburg.
1114B, Dan Cruickshank.
1114C, 1134B, Roger-Viollet.
1115A, 1137B, J. Allan Cash.
1117A, Leeds Metropolitan District Council.
1117C, 1144A, copyright ACL Brussels.
1118A, Manchester Central Library.
1118C, Elsam, Mann and Cooper.
1121B, from J. Guadet, *Eléments et Théorie de l'Architecture, 1901–4.*
1122B,C, 1126A, 1144C, 1145B, 1148A, 1149, Chevojon/copyright by SPADEM, Paris;
1125B, 1140A–C, 1128D, T. and R. Annan.
1125C, Eric de Maré.
1126B,C, from Giedion, 1954.
1127C, from P. Lavedan, *Architecture française*, 1944.
1128C, Austrian Embassy, London.
1130A, from Eastlake.
1132A, from Pevsner.
1132C, after M. H. and C. H. B. Quennell, *A History of Everyday Things in England*, 1934.
1133C, 1150C, 1154B, RIBA Drawings Collection.
1134A, Crown Copyright, Victoria and Albert Museum.
1134C, Austrian Embassy, London/photo Bildarchiv d. Oest. Nationalbibliothek.
1136A, Netherlands Government Information Service/aero-photo Nederland.
1140D, from H. Muthesius, *Die Englische Baukunst der Gegenwart*, 1900.
1145C, RIBA Library.
1156B, Andrew Saint.
1142A, Rheinisches Bildarchiv, Cologne.
1144B, Netherlands Government Information Service/photo E. M. van Ojen.
1147A, Netherlands Government Information Service.
1147B, Birmingham Post and Mail Ltd.
1148B, 1155B, Foto Mas.
1148D, Robert Roskrow Photography.
1151A, after Girouard.
1151B, after Hitchcock, 3rd ed., 1970.
1153A, from *The British Architect*, vol. 30, 1888.
1153B, RIBA Library, by permission of C. Cowles-Voysey.
1141B, from Pevsner, 1960.
1157A, Chris Wakeling.

CHAPTER 36

1173A, Royal Commonwealth Society.
1173B, Courtauld Institute of Art.
1178A, E, 1179B, 1182A–C, 1183A–D, 1186A–E, 1187B,C, 1188A–C, 1190A–E, D. Linstrum.
1178B, John Linstrum.
1178C, 1179C, T. N. Watson.
1178D, 1179A, Flemming Aalund.
1187A, 1191A,B, SATOUR.

CHAPTER 37

1196A–C, 1197A,B, 1205B,D,E, 1207A,B, 1209B, 1212A,B, 1215A, 1216A, 1218B, 1221B, 1223B, Wayne Andrews.
1197C, from Kelemen.
1197D, 1200A, 1204B, from T. E. Sanford, *The Story of Architecture in Mexico*, 1947.
1197E, G. E. Kidder Smith.
1200B, Sawders from Cushing.
1204C, Brazilian Embassy, London.

1205A, Library of Congress.
1201, 1203A–C, Louise Noelle Mercles.
1205C, Alexandra Casserley.
1208, 1215D,E, City of Philadelphia.
1209A, photo by Abbie Rowe, courtesy National Park Service.
1216B, from Kimball.
1218A, Public Archives of Canada.
1221A,C, 1222B,C, 1223A, Chicago Architectural Photo Co.
1222A, US Department of the Interior.
1223C, from A. Bush-Brown, *Louis Sullivan*, 1960.
1224, Hedrich-Blessing.

CHAPTER 38
1229A, from *Landscape of Peking*, 1930.
1229B, 1230A, Lou Qingxi.
1229C, 1230D, 1231B, 1232BE, 1234A, 1235A,B, Editorial Board of Chinese Architectural History (EBCAH).
1229D, 1230C, 1234B, 1236C, from *A Brief History of Chinese Architecture*, Book Two, 1962.
1229E, 1230B, 1232C,D, Wu Guang-zu.
1231A, Wu Jiang.
1232A, Deng Qing-yao.

CHAPTER 39
1241–1243, Eizo Inagaki.
1244, Kim Choung Ki.

CHAPTER 40
1247A, Pinna Indorf.
1247B, Lai Chee Kian.
1249A, Jon Lim.
1249B, Jon Lim.
1249C, Jon Lim.
1250A, Jon Lim.
1250B, Jon Lim.
1250C, Jon Lim.
1250D, Jon Lim.
1252A, Office of The Istana, Singapore.
1252B, J. Musgrove.
1252C, Ian Lloyd.
1252D, Office of the Istana.
1253A, Budi A. Sukada.
1253D, Yong Hock Seng, Raymond Woo & Associates.
1254B, Dept. of Tourism, Embassy of Thailand, Singapore.

CHAPTER 41
1258A,B, from *Marg*, vol. XXXV, No. 3.
1258C, 1275A,B,D, 1276A,B,D.
1258D,E, 1260C, 1262B,C, 1263A,C–F, 1264A,B, 1267A,B, 1268A,B, 1269A–C, 1271A–C, 1272A,B, 1273A–D, 1275C, 1276C, 1277A, 1278B, 1279A–C, by permission of the British Library.
1260A,B, from W. A. Nelson, *Dutch Forts in Sri Lanka*, 1984.
1260D,E, 1262A, Derek Linstrum.
1263B, 1268C, India Office, London.
1277B, Dan Cruickshank.

CHAPTER 42
1280A,B, 1291A–E, 1292A–D, 1296A,B, 1297A,B, 1304A,C, Max Dupain.
1282A, Archives, Alexander Turnbull Library, Wellington.
1282B, 1308A, Archives, Auckland Institute and Museum.
1287A, 1305A,D, Fox.
1287B,C, 1299D, 1310B, 1304B,C,E,D. Saunders.
1294A, John Stacpoole/photo Clifton Firth Ltd.
1294B, drawing by Neil Harrap and Margaret Alington.
1296C, 1298, 1299A,B, 1300B Richard Stringer.
1299C, Richard Stringer, after Pearson.
1300A, Australian Information Service, London.
1307A, John Stacpoole/photo Mannering and Associates Ltd, Christchurch.
1307B,C, John Fields.
1308B, Archives.
1309A, Archives, Otago Early Settlers Association.
1309B, John Stacpoole.
1309C, John Stacpoole/photo John Fields.

CHAPTER 44
1322A, Kunstgewerbemuseum, Zurich.
1322B, ACL, Brussels.
1325A, RIBA Library.
1325B, SPADEM, Paris
1325C, Martin Charles.
1325D, E, from *Le Corbusier and Pierre Jeanout,* Vol. II, ed. W. Boesigen, 1935.
1326A, SPADEM, Paris.
1326B, SPADEM, Paris.
1326C, Martin Charles.
1326D, SPADEM, Paris.
1328B, SPADEM, Paris.
1328C, Edifice/Lewis.
1328D, from *Pierre Chareau*, by B. Taylor, 1992.
1331A, Foto Marburg.
1331B, Dyckerhoff & Widman.
1331C, From Pevsner.
1333A, SPADEM, Paris.
1333B, The Architects Collaborative.
1337A, RIBA Library.
1337B, Dan Cruickshank.
1337C, David Dunster.
1337D, Dan Cruickshank.
1339A, A. F. Kersting.
1339B, Dan Cruickshank.
1339C, Dan Cruickshank.
1339D, Dan Cruickshank.
1339E, Dan Cruickshank.
1340B, Kodak Ltd.
1340C, A. F. Kersting.
1341A, Robert Roddam.

1341B, David Wrightson.
1343A, Lucinda Lambton/Arcaid.
1343B, Peter Inskip.
1344A, From Howarth.
1344B, From Pevsner.
1345C, Elsam, Mann and Cooper.
1345D, John Archer.
1347B, Dan Cruickshank.
1347C, from *Survey of London,* vol. xxx, 1960, by permission of the Archives Department, Westminster City Library.
1348A, Manchester Central Library.
1349A, RCHME/copyright *The Architect.*
1349B, Kenneth Prater/RIBA Press Office.
1349C, Dell and Wainwright/*Architectural Review.*
1350A, RIBA Library.
1350B, Newbery/*Architectural Review.*
1350C, London Transport.
1350D, *Daily Express.*
1352A, The National Trust.
1352B, Fry, Drew and Partners/*Architectural Review.*
1353A, *The Field.*
1353B, Dell and Wainwright/*Architectural Review.*
1354A, Skinner and Bailey.
1354B, Dell and Wainwright/*Architectural Review.*
1357A, Dell and Wainwright/*Architectural Review.*
1357B, RIBA Library.
1357C, E. M. van Ojen/Netherlands Government Information Service.
1359A, Wigfusson/Swedish Tourist Traffic Association.
1359B, Heurlin/Swedish Tourist Traffic Association.
1359C, Heurlin/Swedish Tourist Traffic Association.
1360A, Strüwing.
1360B, Martin Charles.
1360C, Martin Charles.
1363A, Martin Charles.
1363B, G. Welin/Finnish Embassy, London.
1363C, RIBA Library.
1364A, Tim Benton.
1364B, Foto Mas.
1364C, Foto Mas.

CHAPTER 45

1367A, David Dunster.
1367B, Alvar Aalto Museo.
1371A, SPADEM, Paris.
1371D, Phaidon.
1373A, Lucien Hervé.
1373B, Lucien Hervé.
1374A, Dan Cruickshank.
1374B, Martin Charles/Richard Rogers Partnership.
1374C, Richard Rogers Partnership.
1374D, RIBA Library.
1374E, Foster Associates.
1377A, Dennis Gilbert.
1377B, Dan Cruickshank.
1377C, Museum of Modern Art, New York.
1379A, Richard Bryant/Arcaid.
1379B, Peter Walser.
1379C, Christian Richters.
1379D, Wilford Stirling.
1381A, Dennis Gilbert.
1381B, Bill Toomey.
1381C, Dan Cruickshank.
1381D, David Dunster.
1381E, Peter Baistow.
1384A, Richard Einzig/Arcaid.
1384B, Richard Bryant/Arcaid.
1384C, Wilford Stirling.
1384D, Wilford Stirling.
1384E, Richard Einzig/Arcaid.
1385A, Dennis Gilbert.
1385B, MacCormac, Jamieson and Prichard.
1385C, Radio Times Hulton Picture Library.
1385D, Barry Gasson.
1385E, Barry Gasson.
1385F, Barry Gasson.
1387A, Foster Associates.
1387B, Foster Associates.
1387C, Sir Michael Hopkins.
1387D, Dave Bower.
1387E, Sir Michael Hopkins.
1388A, Richard Bryant/Arcaid.
1388B, Sir Richard Rogers.
1388C, Sir Richard Rogers.
1389A, Richard Davies.
1389B, Richard Davies.
1389C, Foster Associates.
1389D, Foster Associates.
1389E, Foster Associates.
1392A, Paolo Portoghesi.
1392B, Paolo Portoghesi.
1392C, Richard Murphy.
1392D, Richard Murphy.
1393A, Publifoto.
1393B, Renzo Piano.
1393C, Renzo Piano.
1393D, Willem Dispraam.
1393E, Bruno Krapp.
1393F, Architectuurstudio Herman Hertzberger.

CHAPTER 46

1403A, RIBA Library.
1403B, From *Modern Architecture in Czechoslovakia*, 1970.
1404A, Otakar Macel.
1404B, RIBA Library.
1404C, Dan Cruickshank.
1404D, Dan Cruickshank.
1406A, Dan Cruickshank.
1406B, From *Modern Architecture in Czechoslovakia*, 1970.
1406C, RIBA Library.
1408A, RIBA Library.
1408B, Otakar Macel.
1408C, Otakar Macel.

1409A, RIBA Library.
1409B, RIBA Library.
1409C, Otakar Macel.
1411A, Dan Cruickshank.
1411B, Dan Cruickshank.
1411D, Dan Cruickshank.
1412A, Dan Cruickshank.
1412B, Dan Cruickshank.
1413A, Dan Cruickshank.
1413C, Otakar Macel.
1415A, Otakar Macel.
1415B, Otakar Macel.
1416A, Dennis Sharp.
1416B, Dennis Sharp.
1416C, Dan Cruickshank.
1418A, Dennis Sharp.
1418B, Otakar Macel.
1420A, Otakar Macel.
1420B, Alan Blanc.
1420C, Alan Blanc.

CHAPTER 47

1428A–C, Catherine Cooke.
1430A–D, Catherine Cooke.
1432A–C, Catherine Cooke.
1433A–D, Catherine Cooke.
1435A–D, Catherine Cooke.
1436A, B, Catherine Cooke.
1437A–D, Catherine Cooke.
1439A, B, Catherine Cooke.
1439C, D, Otakar Macel.
1440A–C, Catherine Cooke.
1442A, Catherine Cooke.
1442B, Valve Pormeister.
1442C, Abdulla Akhmedov.
1442D, Ilya Cherniavsky.
1443A, Alexander Velikanov.
1443B, Vakhtang Davitaia.

CHAPTER 48

1447A, Yildirim Yavuz.
1447B, Yildirim Yavuz.
1447C, Yildirim Yavuz.
1448A, Yildirim Yavuz.
1448B, Yildirim Yavuz.
1448C, Yildirim Yavuz.
1448D, Yildirim Yavuz.
1449A, Yildirim Yavuz.
1449B, Yildirim Yavuz.
1449C, Yildirim Yavuz.
1450A, Santar.
1450B, Cengiz Bektas.
1450C, Cengiz Bektas.
1450D, A. Dundar.
1452A, Makiya Associates.
1452B, R. Chadirji.
1452C, S & J Lindström.
1452D, TAC.
1452E, Urbahn and Coile.
1454A, Omramia.
1454B, SOM.
1454C, Kenzo Tange.
1454D, Caudil, Rowlett and Scott.
1455A, H. R. Gunny.
1455B, Kamal el-Kafrawl.
1458, T. Technikum, Haifa.
1459A, Dan Cruickshank.
1459B, Dan Cruickshank.
1459C, Dan Cruickshank.
1459D, Dan Cruickshank.
1461A, The Israel Museum.
1462A, Dan Cruickshank.
1462B, Dan Cruickshank.
1462C, Dan Cruickshank.
1462D, Z. Rechter.
1463A, Dan Cruickshank.
1463B, Richard Bryant/ARCAID.
1464A, Ram Karmi and Ada Karmi-Melamede.
1464B, Ram Karmi and Ada Karmi-Melamede.

CHAPTER 49

1468A, SATOUR.
1469A, SATOUR.
1469B, SATOUR.
1469C, Udo Kultermann.
1469D, Architectural Press/EMAP.
1473A, Udo Kultermann.
1473B, Architectural Press/EMAP.
1473C, Udo Kultermann.
1473D, Abdelhalim Seray.
1475C, D, Murphy Jahn.
1476C, Aga Khan Award for Architecture.
1479A, B, Aga Khan Award for Architecture.
1479D, Aga Khan Award for Architecture/photo C. Avedissian/Concept Media Pte and Architectural Press/EMAP.
1481A, Aga Khan Award for Architecture.
1481B, Aga Khan Award for Architecture.

CHAPTER 50

1485A, Richard Longstreth.
1485B, *American Architect and Building News*, 23 August 1902.
1485C, Brown Brothers.
1485D, Brown Brothers.
1487A, David Hyde/Kalmbach Publishing Company.
1487B, William Middleton.
1488A, Charles Phelps Cushing.
1488B, Museum of Modern Art, New York.
1488C, Irving Underhill/Museum of City of New York.
1490A, Chicago Architectural Photographing Company, Theatre Historical Society.
1490B, D. R. Goff/Quicksilver Photography, courtesy Columbus Association for the Performing Arts.
1492, *Monograph of the Work of Charles A. Platt*.
1493A, Farrell Grenan/Arcaid.

1493B, Athenaeum of Philadelphia.
1493C, Fello Atkinson/Architectural Association.
1493D, Philip Turner/Historic American Buildings Survey.
1493E, Wayne Andrews.
1495A, Chicago Architectural Photographing Company.
1495B, Chicago Architectural Photographing Company.
1497A, David Gebhard.
1497B, Richard Longstreth.
1497C, Richard Longstreth.
1497D, Colonial Williamsburg Foundation.
1498A, State Historical Society of Nebraska.
1498B, Tennessee Valley Authority.
1500A, Andrew Holmes/Architectural Association.
1500B, Empire State Building Corporation.
1501A, Thomas Airviews.
1501B, Rockefeller Center.
1503A, Hedrich-Blessing/Albert Kahn Associates.
1503B, Dione Neutra.
1504A, Julius Shulman.
1504B, Roger Sturtevant/Wurster, Bernardi and Emmons
1504C, Hedrich-Blessing
1506A, Joe Price/Shin'en Kan, Inc
1506B, *Architectural Forum*, January 1938.
1506C, Richard Longstreth.
1506D, Geoffrey Smythe/Architectural Association.
1507A, Hedrich-Blessing.
1507B, Museum of Modern Art, New York.
1508A, Hazel Cook/Architectural Association.
1508B, Philip Johnson.

CHAPTER 51

1513A, Wayne Andrews.
1513B, Museum of the City of New York.
1513C, RIBA Library.
1514A, Ezra Stoller.
1516A, RIBA Library.
1516B, Ezra Stoller.
1518A, Cervin Robinson.
1518B, RIBA Library.
1518C, RIBA Library.
1518D, RIBA Library.
1520B, Cervin Robinson.
1520D, Richard Longstreth.
1522A, Kevin Roche, John Dinkeloo and Associates.
1522B, Kevin Roche, John Dinkeloo and Associates.
1522C, Kevin Roche, John Dinkeloo and Associates.
1522D, Kevin Roche, John Dinkeloo and Associates.
1523A, Timothy Hursely.
1523B, SOM.
1523C, SOM.
1524A, Pei Cobb Freen and Partners.
1524B, Esto Photographics.
1524C, Gruen Associates.
1526A, Rollin La France.
1526B, Robert Venturi.
1526C, Robert Venturi.
1526D, Rollin La France.
1526E, RIBA Library.
1528A, Proto Acme.
1528B, Michael Graves.
1528C, RIBA Library.
1530A, Esto Photographics.
1530B, Esto Photographics.
1530C, Esto Photographics.
1530D, Joshua White.
1530E, Frank Gehry.

CHAPTER 52

1533A, Amanda Holmes.
1533C, Helen Thomas.
1533D, Helen Thomas.
1533E, Helen Thomas.
1536A, Carl Frank/Black Star.
1536C, From H.-R. Hitchcock, 1955.
1537A, From H.-R. Hitchcock, 1955.
1537B, Armin Haab/Black Star.
1539A, Eladio Disle.
1539B, M. L. Cetto.
1539C, M. L. Cetto.
1539D, Sarah Wigglesworth and Jeremy Till.
1541A, Paolo Gasparini/*Punto 59*.
1541B, Paolo Gasparini/*Punto 59*.
1542A, National Museum of Anthropology and History, Mexico City.
1542B, National Museum of Anthropology and History, Mexico City.
1542C, National Museum of Anthropology and History, Mexico City.
1542D, National Museum of Anthropology and History, Mexico City.
1542E, National Museum of Anthropology and History, Mexico City.
1543A, Paolo Gasparini/*Punto 59*.
1543B, RIBA Library/A. C. Cooper.
1543C, Souvenir Brasilia Ltda.
1543D, Souvenir Brasilia Ltda.
1544A, M. L. Cetto.
1544B, Cristiano Mascaro.
1547A, Ricardo Legoretta.
1547B, Ricardo Legoretta.
1547C, Helen Thomas.
1547D, Davilla.
1548A, Sacha Mirzoeff.

CHAPTER 53

1553A, Wu Ghang-zu.
1553B, Wu Guang-zu.
1553C, Wu Guang-zu.
1554A, Wu Guang-zu.
1554B, Wu Guang-zu.

1554C, Editorial Board of Chinese Architectural History.
1554D, Chen Hao-kai.
1554E, Chen Hao-kai.
1556A, Zhang Shao-yuan.
1556B, Zhang Shao-yuan.
1556C, *A Landscape of Peking*, 1930.
1557A, Zhou Jing-ping.
1557B, *A Brief History of Chinese Architecture*, Book Two.
1558A, Wu Guang-zu.
1558B, Wu Guang-zu.
1558C, Wu Jiang.
1558D, Editorial Board of Chinese Architectural History.
1559A, *A Brief History of Chinese Architecture*, Book Two.
1559B, Editorial Board of Chinese Architectural History.
1561A, Wu Guang-zu.
1561B, Wu Guang-zu.
1562A, *Ten Years of Architectural Design*.
1562B, Wu Guang-zu.
1564A, Wu Guang-zu.
1564B, Wu Guang-zu.
1564C, Wu Guang-zu.
1564D, Zhang Shao-yuan.
1565A, Mo Bo-zhi.
1565B, Wu Guang-zu.
1566A, Luo Xiao-wei.
1566B, Zhang Jin-qin.
1566C, *Chinese Architecture 1949–1989*.
1566D, Li Gao-lan.
1566E, Wu Guang-zu.
1568A, Zhang-Jin-quin.
1568B, Wu Guang-zu.
1568C, Huang Han-min.
1568D, Wu Guang-zu.
1568E, Gong De-Shan.
1570A, Ma Guo-fin.
1570B, Wu Guang-zu.
1570C, Lu Ji-wei.
1570D, Wu Liang-yong.

CHAPTER 54

1573B, Eizo Inagaki.
1574A, From V. Lampugnani (Ed.) 1986.
1574B, From V. Lampugnani (Ed.) 1986.
1574C, From V. Lampugnani (Ed.) 1986.
1574D, Eizo Inagaki
1575A, From H. Suzuki, R. Banham and K. Kobayashi, 1985.
1575B, From R. Boyd, 1968.
1578A, From H. Suzuki, R. Banham and K. Kobayashi, 1985.
1578B, From E. Tempel, 1969.
1578C, From H. Suzuki, R. Banham and K. Kobayashi, 1985.
1579A, From H. Suzuki, R. Banham and K. Kobayashi, 1985.
1579B, From H. Suzuki, R. Banham and K. Kobayashi, 1985.
1579C, From H. Suzuki, R. Banham and K. Kobayashi, 1985.
1580A, From H. Suzuki, R. Banham and K. Kobayashi, 1985.
1580B, From H. Suzuki, R. Banham and K. Kobayashi, 1985.
1581A, Tomio Ohashi.
1581B, From K. Kurokawa, *Metabolism in Architecture*, 1977.
1581C, From H. Suzuki, R. Banham and K. Kobayashi, 1985.
1581D, From R. Boyd, 1968.
1583A, From H. Suzuki, R. Banham and K. Kobayashi, 1985.
1583B, From H. Suzuki, R. Banham and K. Kobayashi, 1985.
1583C, From H. Suzuki, R. Banham and K. Kobayashi, 1985.
1585A, From H. Suzuki, R. Banham and K. Kobayashi, 1985.
1585B, K. Shinohara.
1585C, Terutaka Hoashi.
1586A, From H. Suzuki, R. Banham and K. Kobayashi, 1985.
1586B, Tadeo Ando.
1586C, From H. Suzuki, R. Banham and K. Kobayashi, 1985.
1586D, Tadeo Ando.
1587A, RIBA Library.
1587B, Katsuhisa Kida.
1587C, Ushida Findlay.
1587D, Ushida Findlay.
1589A, Tadeo Ando.
1589B, Tadeo Ando.
1589C, Tadeo Ando.
1590A, Tadeo Ando.
1590B, Tadeo Ando.
1591A, Renzo Piano.
1591B, Yoshio Hata.
1591C, Riba Library.
1591D, Valentine Ames.

CHAPTER 55

1595A, C, Abel.
1595B, C, Abel.
1595C, C, Abel.
1595D, C, Abel.
1597A, HDB.
1597B, C, Abel.
1597C, Design Partnership.
1599A, Paul Rudolph.
1599C, Albert Links.
1601B, C, Abel.
1603A, C, Abel.
1603C, Cesar Pelli.

1605A, Helen Jessup.
1605C, Paul Rudolph.
1605D, Profile.
1608A, Kawasumi.
1608B, Shinfuku-Kutokyo.

CHAPTER 56

1613A, Sir Norman Foster.
1613B, Ian Lambot.
1613C, Sir Norman Foster.
1614, Ian Lambot
1615B, I. M. Pei.
1615C, Peter Aaron/Esno.
1617D, Terry Farrell

CHAPTER 57

1621A, British Library.
1621B, British Library.
1622A, Country Life
1623A, Dan Cruickshank.
1623B, Dan Cruickshank.
1623C, Dan Cruickshank.
1623D, Dan Cruickshank.
1624A, British Library.
1624B, Dan Cruickshank.
1624C, Dan Cruickshank.
1624D, Dan Cruickshank.
1626A, From S. Nilsson, 1973.
1626B, From Le Corbusier, *Oeuvres Complètes*.
1627A, From Le Corbusier, *Oeuvres Complètes*.
1627B, Dan Cruickshank.
1629A, Habib Rahman
1629C, Jatinder Singh
1630A, B. V. Doshi.
1630B, Raj Rewal.
1630C, Hosur (1900).
1633B, Gautam Bhatia.
1633C, Krishna Menon.
1633D, Krishna Menon.
1633E, Krishna Menon.
1634A, Dan Cruickshank.
1634B, Dan Cruickshank.
1634C, Dan Cruickshank.
1634D, B. V. Doshi.
1636A, Dinesh Mehta.
1636B, Dan Cruickshank.
1637A, Dan Cruickshank.
1637B, Raj Rewal.
1637C, Madan Mehta.
1638A, Uttam C. Jain.
1638B, Uttam C. Jain.
1638D, Uttam C. Jain.
1640A, B. Taylor/*MIMAR 6*.
1640B, From R. Giurgola and J. Mehta, 1975.
1640C, From R. Giurgola and J. Mehta, 1975.
1641A, Ranjit Sabikhi and Ajoy Choudhury, The Design Group/*MIMAR 14*.
1641B, Charles Correa/*MIMAR 17*.
1641C, *Process Architecture*, No. 20, 1980.
1641D, Raj Rewal.
1643B, Laurie Baker.
1643C, Laurie Baker.
1643D, Laurie Baker.
1643E, Laurie Baker.
1644B, Gerard de Cunha.
1644C, Dulal Mukherjee.

CHAPTER 58

1649A, Richard Stringer,
1649B, Wolfgang Sievers.
1650A, Max Dupain.
1650B, David Moore.
1650C, Fritz Kos.
1650D, Adrian Boddington.
1651A, Ashton and Raggatt.
1651B, John Gollings.
1651C, John Gollings.
1653A, David Moore.
1653B, John Dabron/Ross Thorne.
1653C, David Moore.
1653D, Adrian Boddington.
1654A, Patrick Bingham-Hall.
1654B, Max Dupain.
1656A, Wolfgang Sievers.
1656B, Richard Stringer.
1656C, Max Dupain.
1658A, Max Dupain.
1658B, Max Dupain.
1659A, Max Dupain.
1659B, Max Dupain.
1660A, Wolfgang Sievers.
1660B, J. Taylor.
1660C, Max Dupain.
1661A, David Moore.
1662A, G. Poole.
1662C, Edmond and Corrigan.
1664A, Profimage.
1664B, Clifton Firth/Melva Firth.
1664C, Profimage.
1666A, Profimage.
1666B, J. Taylor.
1666C, Euan Sorginson.
1667A, Gillian Chaplin.
1667B, Julie Stout.
1667C, J. Taylor.
1667D, Architects Pacific.
1667E, Kevin Murray.
1669A, J. Taylor.
1669B, Peter Johnson.
1669C, Peter Johnson.

PREFACE

The twentieth edition of Banister Fletcher's *A History of Architecture* marks the one hundredth year of publication. During this period the aims and appearance of the book have, naturally, changed significantly but few changes were more dramatic than those which took place between the eighteenth edition and the nineteenth, which was published in 1987. The nineteenth edition was, in effect, a rethink of the Banister Fletcher structure in which the time-honoured approach of considering different architectures, periods and locations by the 'comparative method' was replaced with a system of 'Background' chapters, each introducing one of the book's seven sections. These Background chapters set the architecture discussed in the section in its social, economic and political context and sought to provide useful basic information. The nineteenth edition also strove to redress the imbalance between the coverage of European pre-twentieth-century architecture (which has traditionally enjoyed a large proportion of the Banister Fletcher pages) and non-European and contemporary architecture.

The twentieth edition is, necessarily, an extensive revision and extension of the nineteenth rather than a major overhaul or exercise in restructuring. Nevertheless, around 35 per cent of the text is new, the book is nearly 200 pages longer, and a significant series of chapters have been recast, extended or introduced. Of the book's 37 contributors, 14 are new to the project.

The central aim behind this edition reflects and continues certain of the key directions established in the nineteenth edition. The scope has been widened to include more coverage of architecture from non-European regions and to contain more information about vernacular buildings and engineered structures and works by architect/engineers such as bridges and fortifications. There is also more attention paid, in the part dealing with the twentieth century, to urban design.

In their presentation these additions and reorganisations seek to reinforce what are, in the end, the cardinal virtues of Banister Fletcher – it is an-easy-to use reference book, it is objective and authoritative with all the major examples of world architecture described and explained and, in many cases, fully illustrated, and all contained within one volume. To make clear the nature of the alterations and additions which are contained within this edition it is most convenient to resort to a list.

The first and, in many ways the most significant change in this edition is the fact that the survey of world architecture of the twentieth century has been greatly enlarged and updated to include buildings completed as late as the year of publication – 1996. For the first time the architecture of the twentieth century can be considered as a whole and assessed in historic perspective.

This increase in the coverage of twentieth-century architecture includes a new chapter on the Middle East, incorporating Israel, by Suha Ozkan and Eitan Karol; new chapters on South-east Asia and on Hong Kong by Chris Abel; on the Indian subcontinent by Gautam Bhatia; on Russia and the Soviet Union by Dr Catherine Cooke and on Eastern Europe by Dennis Sharp and Otakar Macel. Western Europe has been divided into two chapters with new texts by Andrew Saint on the pre-World War II period and Anthony McIntyre on the post-war period. The chapter on the Americas has been divided into three chapters with new texts on the post-1950 architecture of North America by Colin Davies and on Latin America by Helen Thomas. The chapter on Japan and Korea has been rewritten by Thomas Weaver.

The coverage of pre-twentieth century architecture has also been increased and strengthened. This includes the creation of an entire part on the architecture of Islam with six new chapters written by John Warren. In addition, the chapter on the architecture of the Americas before 1900 has been largely rewritten by Andrew Saint with Louise Noelle Mereles; the chapter on the traditional architecture of the Indian subcontinent has been rewritten by Dr Adam Hardy, and there is a new chapter on South-east Asia by Dr Jon Lim.

This edition also contains new, specially commissioned drawings of the traditional architecture of the Indian subcontinent and China. There is an entire part devoted to the Bibliography which acts as a key source of information on all periods of world architecture.

Producing the twentieth edition has been a complex team effort. Key members of the team are the three Consultant Editors who have read and offered comments on the new texts and on whose advice (including recommendations for new contributors) I have acted with much gratitude. However, final points of editing rest with me and if there are errors or misrepresentations of fact, dubious interpretations or strange inclusions or omissions of buildings the responsibility is mine. The Consultant Editors are Andrew Saint, Professor of Architecture at the University of Cambridge, Peter Blundell Jones, Professor in the School of Architecture at the University of Sheffield and Kenneth Frampton, Ware Professor of Architecture at Columbia University, New York.

As well as the main consultants many others have given help with the commissioning, editing and production of this edition. First and foremost I would like to thank the Banister Fletcher Trustees – Ruth Kamen of the Royal Institute of British Architecture and Peter Holwell and Robin Thomas of the University of London – for many useful discussions about the project and for their unfailing support, and my Assistant Editor Fleur Richards for her tireless efforts to produce an accurate text on time. The publisher, Neil Warnock Smith, of Butterworth-Heinemann has given often complex proceedings a positive direction and air of calm, ably supported by his Editorial Assistant Zoë A. Youd. The sub-editor, James Shepherd, has been a pivotal figure in the production of this edition, patient, enthusiastic and informed, and I am grateful to Alexandra Casserley for her help with correcting page proofs. Much useful advice on authors and texts has been offered, and gratefully received, from Dr Adrian Forty and Dr Gavin Stamp, and excellent new drawings of traditional Indian and Chinese buildings have been produced by Virendra Rawat. At the Royal Institute of British Architects, Julian Osley has laboured hard and successfully to revise and extend the Bibliography and Robert Elwell has provided invaluable help with the location and selection of photographs. The staff in the RIBA library have been exceptionally prompt and professional. Finally, I would like to thank Keith Macqueen for compiling the Index.

Dan Cruickshank

INTRODUCTION

The twentieth edition of Sir Banister Fletcher's *A History of Architecture* continues the format pioneered in the nineteenth edition. But this format has been revised and developed by the addition of new chapters from new authors, as described in the Preface. The current edition is explained below in the context of the earlier development of the book.

Content and classification

From the first edition of 1896, published under the joint names of Professor Banister Fletcher and his son, Banister Flight Fletcher (later Sir Banister), there was a degree of broad classification of the contents of the book. This was achieved by inserting a 'General Introduction' at the beginning of each series of chapters dealing with one style. For example, there is a chapter called 'Renaissance Architecture in Europe: General Introduction', and one each for Romanesque, Gothic and so on; the chapters dealing with each style, country by country, follow. The introductions served to divide up the book, which, in addition to the ancient world and the Classical period, covered mainly the traditionally accepted West European styles. After the death of Professor Fletcher, Banister *fils* revised and extended the book for the fourth edition of 1901. He divided it into two parts. The first, containing all the material from earlier editions, he called the Historical Styles, and he added a new, much shorter second part, called the Non-Historical Styles, comprising '. . . the Indian, Chinese, Japanese and Saracenic . . .', keeping them '. . . apart from the Historical Styles with which they are but little connected, as they cannot be said to form part of the evolution of Western Architecture. Nevertheless, a history of architecture as a whole is bound to take account of these Eastern styles, whose interrelationships and individual characteristics are of no little interest' (Preface to the fourth edition, p. vi). The new part amounted to about 15 per cent of the book at that stage, but the proportion (if not the coverage in real terms) diminished through the editions which followed; the separation of Part II was retained up to and including the seventeenth edition (1961) edited by Professor R. A. Cordingley, in which Parts I and II were retitled Ancient Architecture and the Western Succession, and Architecture in the East, respectively.

However, the internal divisions in Part I became less evident in the Cordingley edition, and in the eighteenth edition (1975) James Palmes eschewed broad classifications and opted for a straight run of forty chapters. He added some new and some revised chapters on the architecture of South-east Asia and the Far East, all of them still quite brief. These covered mostly ancient 'indigenous' buildings and were placed near the beginning of the book immediately after the chapters on Egypt and the ancient Near East. Palmes also reclassified by chapter the post-Renaissance period and introduced a much-expanded final chapter, 'International Architecture since 1914'.

For the nineteenth edition, edited by Professor John Musgrove, it was decided that the international coverage should be extended. Taking this into account, and having established that Sir Banister himself had begun to move towards general divisions, a classification of chapters was devised in preference to the undifferentiated run of the eighteenth edition.

This reorganisation proved to be somewhat radical, with information reorganised and reclassified to allow for the inclusion of more non-European architecture. This change gave the book a distinctly different form but, as Professor Musgrove explained in the nineteenth edition: 'on the evidence of the development of the book it can be argued that Sir Banister would have supported reclassification'. However, Professor Musgrove admitted that 'there remains the ethical question as to how far it may be permissible to depart from the *intentions* of the original author which, if we are to judge from the book, were primarily the provision of descriptive material about buildings against their historical and physical background'.

This question as to the extent of change that was possible without fundamentally undermining the traditions of the book was in part answered by Sir Banister's own definition of architecture: 'Essentially a human art as well as an affair of material, Architecture is governed and limited by many practical requirements which do not apply to the work of painters, sculptors and musicians. It also provides a key to the habits, thoughts and aspirations of the people, and without a knowledge of this art the history of any period lacks that human interest with which it should be invested; . . . The study of Architecture opens up the enjoyment of buildings with an appreciation of their purpose, meaning and charm . . .'

(Preface to the tenth edition, 1938, pp. viii and ix). As Professor Musgrove pointed out, 'this definition describes quite accurately in general terms the content' of the nineteenth edition and 'not only argues for expanded coverage, but also accentuates the need for a classification of the book's contents in which significant buildings of every culture may be accommodated'.

Consequently in the nineteenth edition a comprehensive classification was attempted for the first time with the history of world architecture being divided into seven parts. The classification was essentially chronological, but overlaid with other factors affecting the character of the architecture in any given location at any time. The coverage was influenced by the nature and volume of surviving material, although in many instances reference to seminal but lost buildings was essential.

Each of the parts in the nineteenth edition was organised to start with a Background chapter containing all those elements previously included in each chapter individually under the sub-heading 'Influences'. This edition also travelled back in time to cover prehistoric buildings – a subject area that had been omitted from the eighteenth edition,

Recent scholarship suggests that there were a number of distinctly separate starts to civilisation (J. M. Roberts, *The Pelican History of the World*, 1980), thus Parts 1 to 4 of the nineteenth edition related to these several beginnings, with each covering the prehistoric architecture of the region concerned. Developing the framework established by Professor Musgrove, the twentieth edition continues the division of the subject into seven parts, but the parts have generally been enlarged and reorganised, with existing chapters overhauled and updated and new ones added.

Part 1 includes the architecture of Greece and its empire as well as that of Egypt and the ancient Near East. This does not denigrate the vital nature of the influence of Greece upon the development of Roman culture, but draws attention to the Greek achievement as the culmination of early western Asiatic and eastern Mediterranean cultures. It has to be remembered that, in terms of architectural influence, Alexander the Great's eastern empire (established within a century of the end of the Peloponnesian wars) stretched from Macedonia to the Indus. And as late as the end of the Punic wars, the Hellenistic world reached to the Caspian Sea, and the Graeco-Bactrian Kingdom from the Oxus to modern Pakistan. Of course, the forms of Hellenistic architecture from the fourth to the second centuries BC influenced both Etruscan and Roman architecture, the latter especially from the end of the third century BC with the active involvement of Rome with the Hellenistic world. In a sense, however, Rome provides the vigorous and obvious models from which stemmed the development of European architecture for the next 1500 years. This part also includes a chapter on Early Asian Cultures.

In Part 2 the early European settlements are shown to precede the beginnings of significant architectural development in central Italy, the Roman ascendancy and the growth of the Roman empire throughout Europe and the Mediterranean. In Europe and the Mediterranean basin there was a clear line of development from Rome through early Christian and Byzantine to Romanesque and Gothic architecture. All these, along with Early Russian architecture, are included in Part 2, which runs to the end of the mediaeval period, the emergence of European humanism, and the return to earlier models. The direct lines of development engendered by Roman conquest and colonisation provide many remarkable examples of the radical changes wrought upon the future character of architecture in the countries concerned. Eventually such influences also determined the styles of architecture exported to those areas of the world colonised by Europeans right up to the beginning of the twentieth century.

Part 3 focuses on the architecture of Islam and is new in this edition of Banister Fletcher. Islamic architecture covers a wide geographic, cultural and time span but the information has been grouped to emphasise the interconnections and to allow a narrative to be developed. It should be pointed out that this section does not represent the book's entire coverage of Islamic architecture with references appearing also in Chapter 24 on China and in several chapters in Part 7.

Part 4 includes all the significant cultures which predated the earliest European settlements worldwide, including Africa and the Americas as well as feudal China and Japan. It brings the remainder of the world's civilisations up to approximately the same date as that reached for Europe, the Mediterranean, western Asia and the Levant in Parts 1, 2 and 3.

From Part 5 onwards the book moves into periods when the volume of building began to increase exponentially, first in Europe and later elsewhere in the world (Part 6), and cultural traditions were subjected to increasingly diverse influences. Part 5, covering the Renaissance in Europe, includes also the post-Renaissance period, industrial architecture, the introduction of new building techniques, and the *fin de siècle* transitional styles and links to the Modern Movement in architecture.

Part 6 extends the Renaissance and post-Renaissance coverage during the period of European colonial dominance worldwide. As the European powers settled in areas all over the world either to exploit resources or for political or military advantage, they took with them European architectural models, and reproduced them as they remembered them, from New England to Singapore and from Buenos Aires to Shanghai. They have become subjects of increasing architectural interest over the last few years.

In Part 7 twentieth-century architecture is covered in a number of separate chapters, classified by country or region. Here, of course, not only has the stage been reached when the volume of architecture has become so great that significant buildings inevitably must be omitted, but also the selection of examples and presentation of material gave authors much greater freedom within the framework to determine how best to describe twentieth-century architectural developments in areas for which they were responsible. Thus diversity in the attitudes of authors and in the presentation of material is more evident in Part 7 than elsewhere in the book.

The coverage of twentieth-century architecture has been greatly expanded in the twentieth edition. This is not only because there are a greater number of buildings to choose from and which demand recognition but also because a number of new chapters have been created. These both expand on the areas in the nineteenth edition (for example, there are now two chapters each on Western Europe and North America rather than one each as in the nineteenth edition) and cover areas previously omitted, such as the Middle East.

Up to and including the seventeenth edition, the title of the book was *A History of Architecture on the Comparative Method*. The method was devised from the first edition with a 'diagram' for the 'system of classification for each style' taking the form of influences, architectural character, examples, comparative table and reference books. For the eighteenth edition the 'comparative table' was omitted from each chapter and reference to the Comparative Method was deleted from the title of the book. Palmes asserted that the Comparative Analysis section in the 'majority of chapters' repeated matters dealt with under the sub-heading Architectural Character, and as he wished to extend the geographical coverage of the book, he needed to reduce the length of the existing text if it was to retain its single-volume format.

But merely to remove the word 'comparative' from the standard chapter sub-headings does not automatically eliminate the Comparative Method, and indeed a good deal of the comparative material remained in the eighteenth edition, including all the standard chapter sub-headings other than that mentioned above. While the comparative table was important to the original system, the repetition of chapter sub-headings contributed to the comparative method, and most of these remained in the eighteenth edition.

In the nineteenth edition a framework was devised in which contextual and technological information could be collected for each part of the book while the description of architectural character or some other form of introductory analysis could remain with the examples in each of the substantive chapters. This system has been continued in the twentieth edition.

The Background chapters for each part follow a series of standardised sub-headings which can be read separately: they relate historical and socio-cultural context to the human and physical resources and technological processes by means of which buildings are realised. These headings, listed below, form a new basis for the comparative analysis of all those factors which affect and contribute to the development of architecture as described and explained in the substantive chapters themselves.

Extended Description gives a more detailed description of the part and explains its formation as a division of the book.

Physical Characteristics covers the climate, topography and geology of the region.

History includes social, political and economic history with the emphasis placed where it most clearly illuminates the architectural development of the period or place.

Culture places architecture within the cultural development of the society generally.

Resources covers the availability of those human and material resources which have a marked effect upon the character and morphology of buildings. Human resources relate to the level of social and technological development of the society which, in turn, determines the ability to locate and process naturally occurring materials such as clay, timber, sand and gravel, and metal ores.

Building Techniques and Processes also relates to the availability of resources, which is reciprocally linked to the development of skills in the society in response to human needs and aspirations. V. Gordon Childe's proposed definition of technology is apposite to the analysis of these factors: 'Technology should mean the study of those activities, directed to the satisfaction of human needs, which produce alterations in the material world . . . Any technology in this sense, like human life itself, involves the regular and habitual co-operation of members of a human group, of society. The character of the co-operating group is profoundly affected at any time by its size, by the needs that are socially recognised, and by the relations between its members' (Early Forms of Society, in *Oxford History of Technology*, Vol. 1, 1956, p. 38).

It should be stressed that the standard arrangement of the Background chapters is no more than a framework. When appropriate, only some elements may be selected; for example in Chapter 28 a section dealing with architectural education follows those on resources and techniques. In other chapters the headings may be abandoned in part or as a whole, except as a guide to coverage, where some of the elements have already been dealt with in earlier chapters, or for other editorial reasons.

Format and character

This edition continues the format established for the nineteenth edition which, in its time, represented a major change in the appearance of the book. But, contrary to popular belief, the book's appearance has been altered frequently since it was first published.

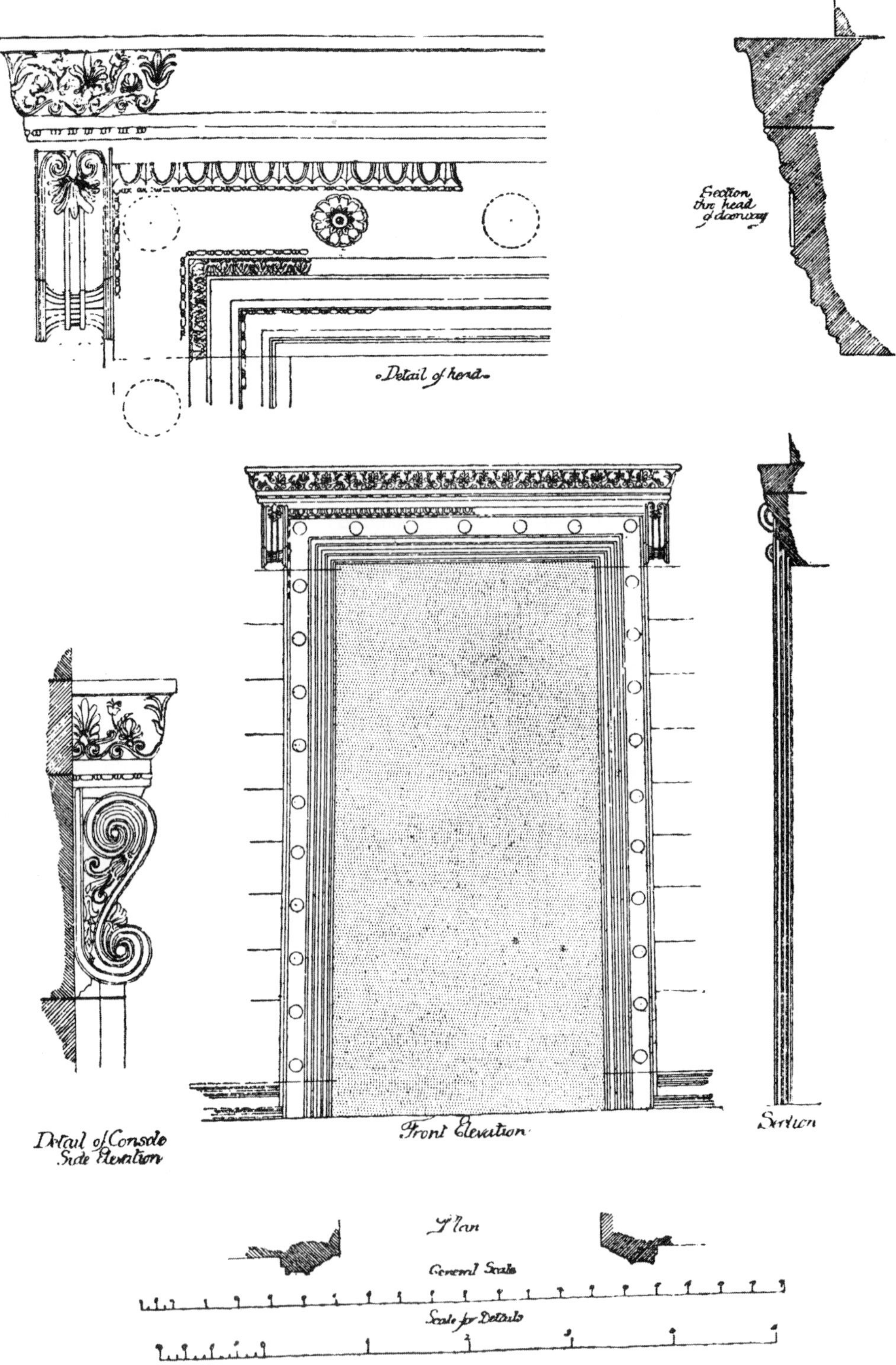

Banister F. Fletcher del

COMPARATIVE EXAMPLES OF GREEK AND ROMAN DOORWAYS.
METAL GRILLE
METAL DOORS.
A.
ELEVATION.
SCALE 5 0 5 10 15 FEET.
DOORWAY FROM THE PANTHEON, ROME.
DETAIL OF PILASTERS AND CORNICE OVER.
B.
12 6 0 1 2 FEET
SCALE FOR DETAILS.
C.
DETAIL OF ARCHITRAVE AND CORNICE.
D.
ELEVATION.
SCALE 1 0 1 2 3 4 5 6 7 8 9 10 FEET.
DOORWAY FROM THE NORTH PORTICO, ERECHTHEION, ATHENS.
E.
DETAIL OF HEAD OF DOORWAY.
F.
SIDE ELEVATION OF CONSOLE.
G.
SECTION THRO' CONSOLE
H.
SECTION THRO HEAD OF DOORWAY.
SCALE 12 9 6 3 0 1 FEET.

GREEK ARCHITECTURE

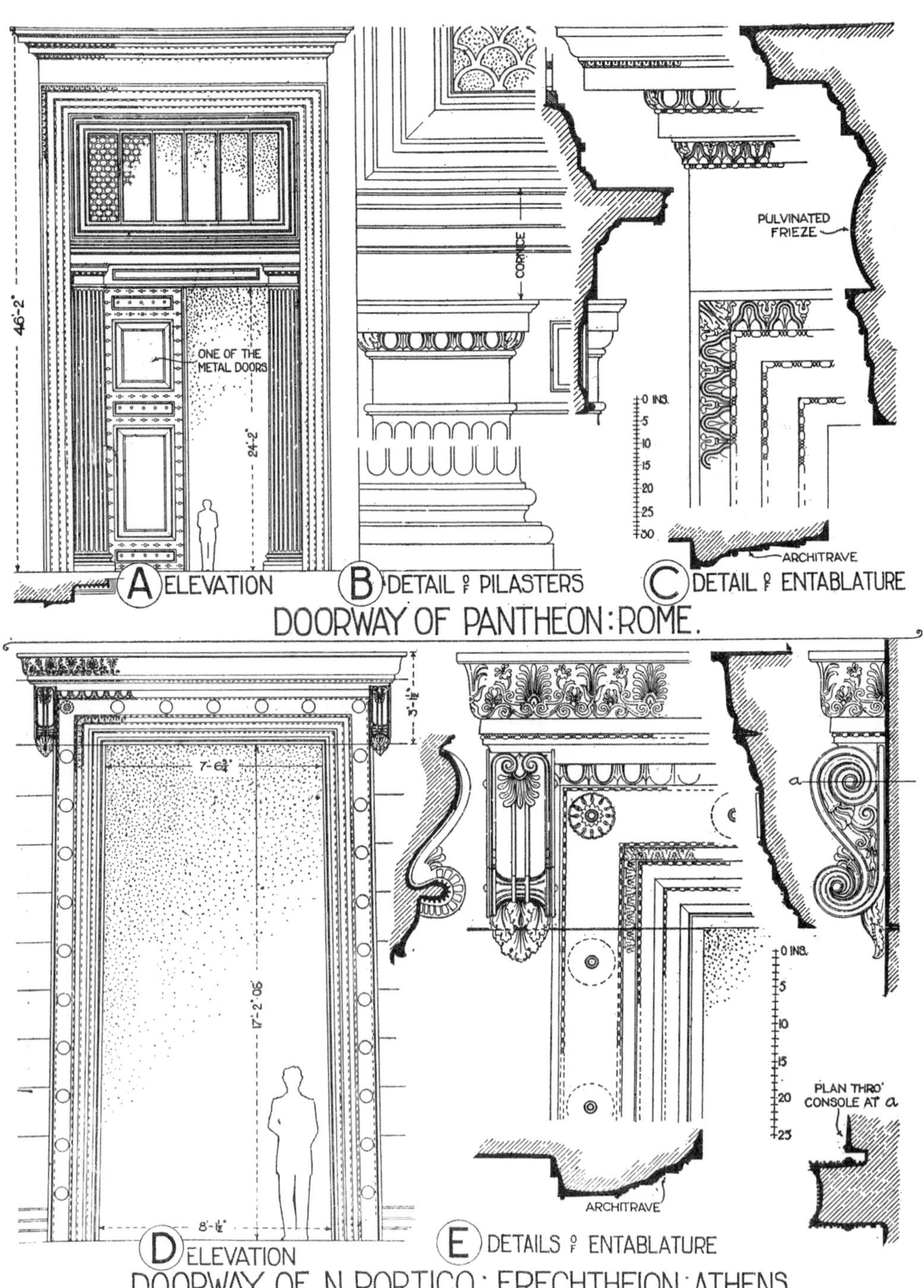
46'-2"
ONE OF THE METAL DOORS
24'-2"
CORNICE
PULVINATED FRIEZE
0 INS. 5 10 15 20 25 30
ARCHITRAVE
A ELEVATION
B DETAIL OF PILASTERS
C DETAIL OF ENTABLATURE
DOORWAY OF PANTHEON: ROME.
3'-1½"
7'-6¾"
a
17'-2.05"
0 INS. 5 10 15 20 25
PLAN THRO' CONSOLE AT a
ARCHITRAVE
8'-1½"
D ELEVATION
E DETAILS OF ENTABLATURE
DOORWAY OF N. PORTICO: ERECHTHEION: ATHENS

The first edition (1896) had a small page size, approximately 180 mm × 120mm, which had been increased to 210 mm × 140 mm by the time the fourth edition appeared in 1901. It remained at this size for the fifth edition and until after World War I: the next edition appeared in 1921 when the size again increased to 230 mm × 140 mm. When the tenth edition (also a long-running version of the book) was published in 1938, the page size had grown again to 240 mm × 150 mm, and there it remained until the eighteenth edition (1975) when it was reduced slightly to about 220 mm × 145 mm. The new page size (245 mm × 190 mm) and double-column layout of the nineteenth edition, continued in this edition, was designed to allow a significant increase in the contents of the book, while retaining the single-volume format.

Although the layout of the book is an important element in establishing its image, it is the character and style of the illustrations which have always determined its visual impact. The first edition of 1896 contained 159 illustrations in a total of 293 pages. With the exception of a few of the smaller line drawings which were set within text pages, all the illustrations covered a full page of the book. The photographic illustrations were collotypes of remarkable quality. The proportion of text to illustrations was established from the beginning, although the book has gradually shed the character of a late Victorian textbook which it first assumed – even to the point of publishing a photograph of the lecture room at King's College, London, where both authors were teachers at the time of publication (Plate 32, facing p. 49 of the first edition).

But it is the development of the 'study-sheet' line illustrations which above all indicates the changing image and character of the book. Taking as an example the signed drawing of the Erechtheion doorway from the first edition (p. xxviii), the original measured drawing was partly redrawn and completely rearranged to be combined with a drawing of the Pantheon doorway for comparison in the Fourth Edition (1901), for which the drawings were captioned and annotated with mannered freehand lettering (p. xxix) throughout the book. For the sixth edition twenty years later (1921) the Erechtheion drawing, with all the others, was revised in both character and content: the mannered lettering was largely removed, and the more familiar outline Roman titles appeared for the first time (p. xxx) and have been retained ever since, although the example referred to above was cut in half for the eighteenth edition and the drawing of the Erechtheion doorway was combined on the same page with halftones. Sir Banister, however, apparently saw nothing sacrosanct about either the character or the specific arrangements of the drawings, even those which carried his own signature.

The nineteenth edition had an enlarged page size so drawings were reproduced to a larger size than ever before. This generosity of scale has been continued in the twentieth edition. A substantial number of new drawings have been made, notably for Chapter 26, while a great many architects' drawings have been used in Part 7. This is something of a departure, but, as pointed out above, the drawing style has been far from consistent over the years. In addition, an architect's drawing of a building can have a particular interest and reveal more than a draughtman's rendering. New halftones have also been introduced in support of new and revised chapters. Chronological tables are placed at the end of this Introduction; they consist of an outline general chronology and a small number of specialised tables for periods and dynasties with which readers may be unfamiliar.

The twentieth edition

The decision to maintain the format established by the ninetenth edition, along with a number of the same authors and chapters, may make the twentieth edition appear no more than a mere revision. But, as outlined in the Preface, if this is a revision, it is a very thorough one. All the retained chapters have been corrected and brought up to date to reflect new scholarship and, where relevant, to include the discussion of newly completed buildings. In addition, 24 chapters have been added or thoroughly revised which means that around 35 per cent of this edition is effectively new material.

Most significant are the dedication of an entire section – Part 3 – to the pre-twentieth-century architecture of Islam, the compilation of an entirely new chapter on the pre-colonial architecture of the Indian subcontinent, and the overhaul and expansion of Part 7 – the architecture of the twentieth century.

This revision and extension of the book has involved significant contributions from 14 new authors as well as from most of the authors of the nineteenth edition. Three consultant editors have also assisted publication by suggesting authors and reading articles before publication. However, their role has been only advisory and if responsible for many of the good points of the new edition these consultants cannot be held accountable for any errors or omissions which might be thought to disfigure the text.

BARRACLOUGH, G. *The Times Concise Atlas of World History.* London 1982. Gazetteer, maps and historical bibliography in *Chambers's Encyclopaedia.* 15 vols. Oxford, 1966.

MCEVEDY, C. and JONES, R. *Atlas of World population History.* Harmondsworth, 1980.

PLACZEK, A. K. (Ed.) *Macmillan Encyclopaedia of Architects.* 4 vols. London, 1982.

ROBERTS, J. M.X The Pelican History of the World. Harmondsworth, 1980.

Chronological Table 1: Northern Europe and Mediterranean – general archaeology and economy, and key

	Archaeology/economy/geology	*Key buildings*	*Key to tables*
BC 9000	**Paleolithic** (↑) Pleistocene ends (↑)		
8000	**Mesolithic** (↓) Holocene begins (↓)		
7000			
6000	Hunters, fishermen, collectors	Catal Hüyük (*c.* 7000–6000)	
5000			
4000	**Neolithic** (↓)		
3000	Farmers	Step Pyramid, Sakkara (2778) Great Pyramids, Cairo Ur, Royal Tombs Indus Civilization: Mohenjodaro Harappa	Egypt and ancient Near East (CT3) (↓)
2000	**Bronze Age** (↓)		Persia and Greece (CT2) (↓) China (CT4) (↓)
1000	Birth of Confucius (550) Birth of Buddha (560)	The Parthenon (432) Great Stupa, Sanchi (first century)	
AD 0	Birth of Christ **Iron Age** (↓) Birth of Mohammed (570)	S. Sophia, Constantinople (532–7)	Japan (CT5) (↓) Islam (CT6) (↓)
1000		Great Temple, Tanjore (1000) S. Denis, Paris (1135–44) S. Peter, Rome (1506–1626)	
2000			

Chronological Table 2: Persia and Greece

	Persia		*Greece*	
	Dynasties/rulers		*Periods, etc.*	
BC 2000				
1800				
1600			**Minoan**	
1400			Palace of Minos (destroyed *c.*1400)	**Mycenaean**
1200				Lion Gate (*c.*1250)
1000			**'Dark Age'**	
800			Rome founded (753)	
600	**Medes**			
	Cyrus's victory over Medes (550)	Cyrus (550–530)	Persian wars	
	Persian	Darius (522–486)	Peloponnesian wars (431–404)	
400		Xerxes (450–465)	**Hellenic**	The Parthenon (432)
	Death of Alexander the Great (323)			
200			**Hellenistic**	Temple of Athena Polias, Priene (334)
			Siege of Corinth: Roman control of Greece (147)	
0	**Parthian** (247BC–226AD)			
AD 200				
400	**Sassanian** (226–651)			
600				
800				
1000				

Chronological Table 3: Egypt and the ancient Near East

	Egypt		*Southern Mesopotamia*
	Period	*Dynasty/rulers*	*Period/dynasty/rulers*
BC 3200	Predynastic		
		Menes (*c.* 3200)	
3000			
2800	Archaic	I–II	
2600		Seneferu Cheops	**Kish** (Mesilim) **Ur** (Messanipada)
2400	Old Kingdom	III–VI	Sargon I (2371)
2200			**Lagash** (Gudra, 2230–2113)
2000	First Intermediate	VII–XI	**Ur** (Third Dynasty) (2113–2006)
1800	Middle Kingdom	XII	**Babylon** (First Dynasty) (1894–1595) Hammurabi (1792–1750)
1600	Second Intermediate	XIII–XVII	
1400		Thotmes I (1530)	**Kassite rule** Kurigalzu II (1345–1324)
1200	New Kingdom	XVIII–XX Rameses II (1304–1237)	
1000		XXI	Nebuchadnezzar I (1124–1103)
800			
600		XXVI (Saite) Persian conquest (525)	End of Assyrian rule (626) Persian conquest (539)
400			
200		Alexander the Great (336–323)	
0		**Ptolemies**	
		Roman province	
AD 200			

	Assyria	*Hatti/Urartu*	*Israel*	*Judah*
	Rulers	*Rulers*		
BC 3200				
3000				
2800				
2600				
2400				
2200				
2000				
1800	Shamshi-Adad I (1813–1781)			
1600				
1400		Shuppiluliumash I Mattusilish III Tudhaliyash IV } Hatti		
1200	Shalmaneser I (1274–1245) Tiglath-Pileser (1115–1077)			
1000			David Solomon (965–931)	
800	Ashurnasirpal II (883–859) Shalmaneser II (858–824) Tiglath-Pileser III (745–727) Sargon II (721–705) Sennacherib (705–681)	Arame (?858–844) Menua (810–786) Sarduri II (764–735) Rusa II (680–640) } Urartu	Jeroboam I (931–910) Ahab (874–852)	Jehosophat (876–848) Josiah (?–609)
600	Fall of Nineveh (612)			Exile (586)
400			Seleucid Empire (312–64) West of Euphrates only, after 140.	
200				
0			Roman conquest	
AD 200				

Chronological Table 4: China

BC	*Social system*	*Main period*		
	Primitive society			
2000	Slave society	Xia (2100–1600)		
1800				
1600		Shang (1600–1028)		
1400				
1200				
1000		Zhou	Western Zhou (1027–771)	
800			Eastern Zhou (770–256)	Spring and Autumn Period (770–476)
600				
400	Feudal society			Warring States Period (475–221)
200		Qin (221–206)		
		Han	Western Han (206 BC–AD 8)	
0				

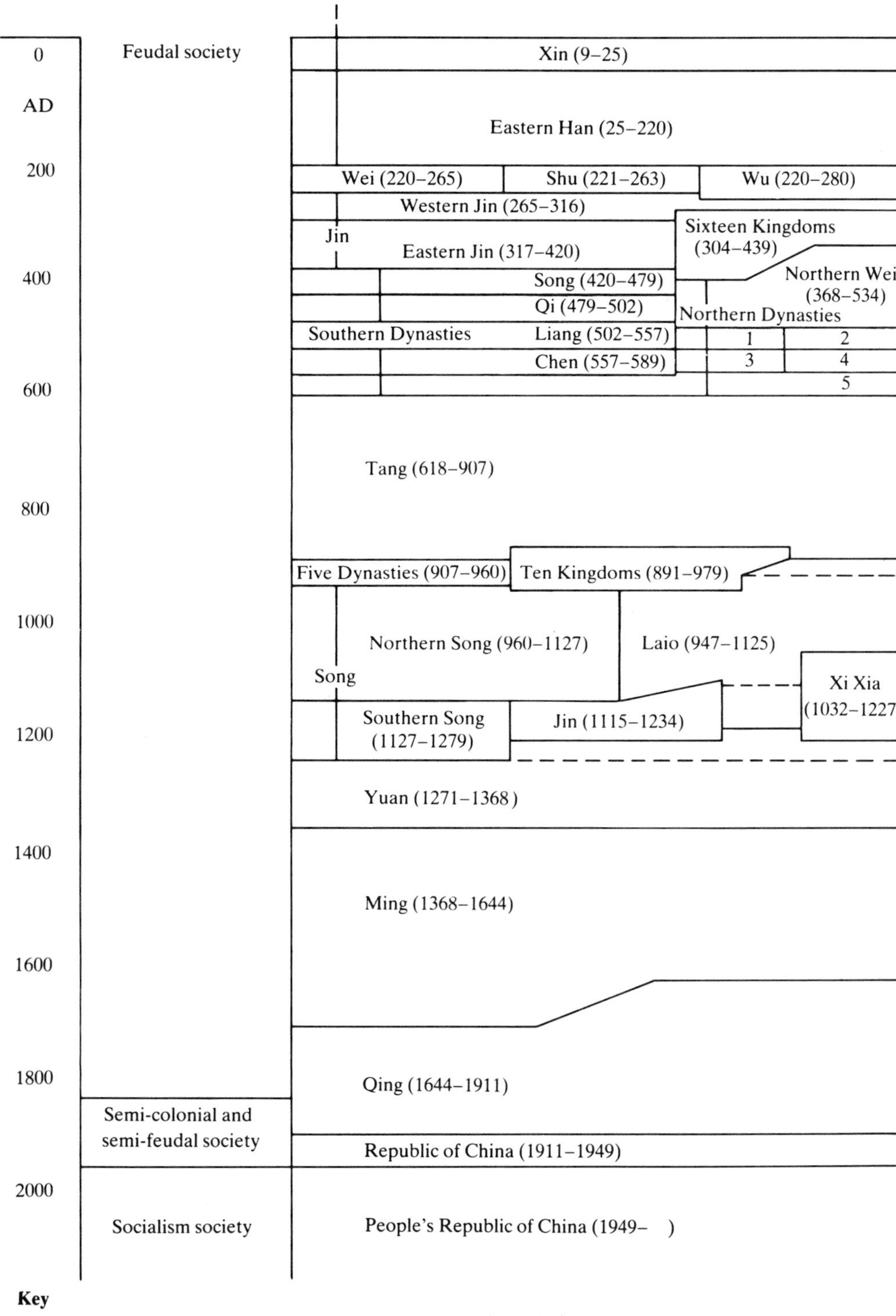

Key

1 Eastern Wei (534–550)
2 Western Wei (535–556)
3 Northern Qi (550–557)
4 Northern Zhou (557–581)
5 Sui (581–618)

Chronological Table 5: Japan

Prehistoric	
Jomon	*c.* 10,000–300 BC
Yayoi	300 BC–AD 300
Tumulus (Kofun)	AD 300–538/552
Ancient	
Asuka	552–645
Early Nara (Hakuho)	645–710
Late Nara (Tempyo)	710–785
Heian	785–1185
Mediaeval	
Kamakura	1185–1333
Nambokucho	1333–1392
Muromachi	1392–1568
Pre-modern	
Momoyama	1568–1615
Edo (Tokugawa)	1615–1867
Modern	1868–present

Chronological Table 6: Islam (showing principal dynasties)

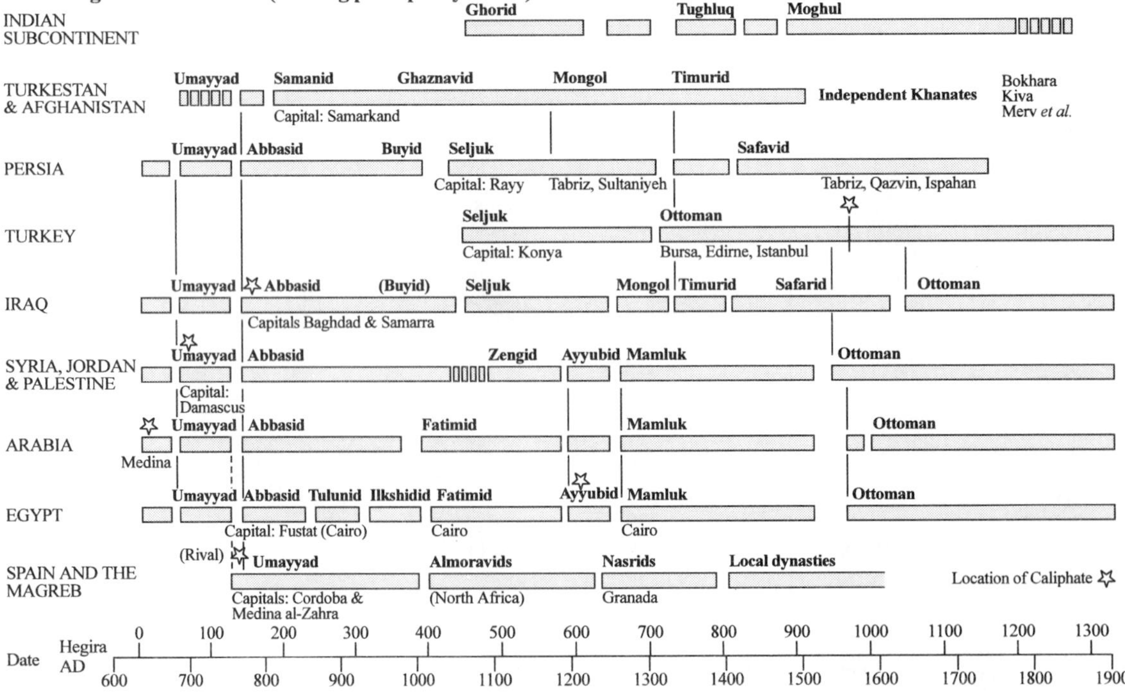

Part One

THE ARCHITECTURE OF EGYPT, THE ANCIENT NEAR EAST, ASIA, GREECE AND THE HELLENISTIC KINGDOMS

Chapter 1
BACKGROUND

Extended Description

Egypt and the Ancient Near East

Archaeological sites from the late Pleistocene (*c.* 20,000–16,000 BC) show the region to have been inhabited by bands of hunter-gatherers. But little of architectural interest predated the beginnings of agriculture about 9000 BC, when the first buildings appeared with the more settled communities of the Natufian culture. It stretched from southern Turkey to the Nile delta. The transition to permanent agricultural villages with a mud-brick architecture took place between 7500 BC and 6000 BC, and by the latter date south-west Asia was dotted with thousands of these villages. The Neolithic period in Anatolia and the Levant produced some of the largest, and architecturally the most impressive, towns. The period 6000–3500 BC was a formative one, marked by a succession of cultures; Hassuna (*c.* 6000–4500 BC), Samarran (*c.* 5500 BC), Halafian (*c.* 5000 BC), Eridu (*c.* 5400 BC) and Ubaid (*c.* 4500–3500 BC). By the end of the period, in Mesopotamia there were the beginnings of small, independent city-states ruled by councils and assemblies.

The Nile valley was occupied from the late Pleistocene Age, but early evidence of occupation has been buried under deep deposits of silt. A proto-agricultural economy developed in some areas as early as 12,000 BC but, for the most part, hunting and gathering were the basis of human existence in Lower Egypt until about 6000 BC, and in Upper Egypt until 4000 BC. In the fifth millennium distinct settled cultural groups appeared, but the local Neolithic period began much later, around 3000 BC. Lower Egypt produced the Faiyum (*c.* 5000 BC) and Mermida (*c.* 4000 BC) cultures, and Upper Egypt the Badarian (*c.* 4000 BC), Amratian (*c.* 3800 BC) and Gerzean (*c.* 3600 BC) cultures. Around 3200 BC unification was achieved under the god-king, and the historical (dynastic) period began.

The earliest villages, towns and cities of the world, with the developments therefrom, are in themselves of great significance, spanning nearly five millennia in some parts of the Near East, much less in other parts. The ancient Near East, with Egypt, provides much of the background to Western civilisation. The term 'Near East' is here used to cover the Arab states, Israel, Cyprus, Turkey, Iran and the Trans-Caucasian republics of the former USSR (Georgia, Armenia and Azerbaijan), as well as Egypt. This part of the book comprehends also the Aegean region, closely linked at first with the Levant and later with the Phoenicians and with the far-flung Persian empire.

From walled Jericho, Catal Hüyük with its painted shrines, and the seasonal communities of the first settlers in the Zagros highlands of western Iran to the gradual emergence of urban life in Mesopotamia, the construction of city temples and palaces and the rise of the first empires, the story of the ancient Near East should not be over-simplified.

Standing in some sense on one side was Egypt, relatively isolated by geography, though less so than some specialists have seemed to imply. Its precise relations with the rest of the Near East are initially obscure, and not known in detail before the mid-second millennium BC. The panorama of Egyptian state, society and civilisation extends, however, over more than three thousand years until its absorption into the Graeco-Roman world, beginning with the meteoric career of Alexander the Great.

Early Asian Cultures

China

The earliest inhabitants of China so far discovered lived at Lantian (Shaanxi province) 600,000 years ago. But the first forms of civilised life emerge during the Neolithic era. There were two major cultures, the Yangshao based in west China and the Longshan to the east. The Longshan culture seems to have outlived, indeed to a degree superseded, the Yangshao. The Longshan also pioneered constructional characteristics which were to be developed during the subsequent Bronze Age. They surrounded their settlements with walls formed by layers of pounded earth (pisé) – a technique which was also used in the construction of buildings.

The first identifiable dynasty is the Xia (2100–1600 BC), of which no cultural remains have, as yet, been discovered but which was probably a late Longshan foundation. The succeeding Shang period (*c.* 1850–1027 BC) is divided into three distinct phases, each represented by a major site – early Shang at Erlitou, middle Shang at Zhengzhou and late Shang at Anyang, all in Hanan province. The Shang are sometimes called Yin in Chinese.

Shang rulers were dedicated builders creating walled settlements around their palaces and suburbs for the use of specific industries, such as the manufacture of bronze implements and pottery. Construction still involved the use of pounded earth although stone columns were used, sometimes clad in bronze plates. The Shang rulers also constructed enormous subterranean tombs. It was during the Shang dynasty that China began its remarkable pioneering technological development. First there was the development of a sophisticated bronze industry, then the production of cast iron, porcelain and paper.

The Shang rulers were finally overthrown around 1028 BC by the Zhou from Shaanxi province. The Zhou period (1027–256 BC) is complicated to chronicle. Around 770 BC the Zhou came under intense presssure from warlike nomadic tribes and moved their capital east from the Wei Valley to Luoyang. This move divides the dynasty into two distinct periods – the Western Zhou (1060–770 BC) and the Eastern Zhou (770–256 BC). This later phase is in turn subdivided to reflect the political complexion of the time; the Spring and Autumn Period of 722–481 BC and the Warring States Period of 403–221 BC. During this later period Zhou power broke down as individual fiefdoms asserted their independence. Unification came with the Qin who by 221 BC had conquered all the other states. Standardisation became a paramount concern – a process which laid the foundation for great advances in Chinese civilisation: weights and measures were unified, standard copper coins were issued, the Qin writing style was imposed, the road and canal system was initiated, the Great Wall began to protect the northern frontier, and to 'unify' thought all texts – except those on medicine, agriculture and divination – were burnt. Such authoritarian rule naturally caused a revolt and in 206 BC the Qin army was defeated and the Han dynasty established. It was to rule until AD 220. During this period China enjoyed one of its 'Golden Ages' during which Chinese culture and commerce flourished and the centralised bureaucratic government was based on the Confucian ideal of paternalistic rule by educated and moral men.

India

The Indus civilisation, which flourished in the third and second millennia BC, produced great cities – notably Mohenjodaro and Harappa – which were of sophisticated design and construction with regularly laid-out streets, brick buildings and a variety of civic amenities. However, this civilisation was in a state of collapse by the middle of the second millennium BC when Aryan peoples entered India through the mountain passes in the north-west. From this period onwards India's history can be characterised as a series of repeated invasions by peoples from the north-west, their dispersal across the plains and gradual absorption into the established population. Alexander the Great entered India from this direction in 326 BC, the Kushanas in the first century AD, the Hunas in the sixth century and, most significantly, waves of Muslims from the end of the 12th century onwards.

The religion practised in the Indus civilisation remains unclear. Cult figurines, especially of 'goddesses', have been discovered as well as fertility emblems but the scripts associated with these objects are as yet undeciphered. The Aryan invaders introduced an independent religion which was expounded in a body of writings known as the *Vedas*. The *Rig Veda*, the oldest Aryan text, is regarded as the source for later Hindu literature. The Buddha, born in 563 BC and who lived in the plains below the Himalayan foothills, was a leading exponent of a reform movement that was in reaction against the Aryan social system. By the third century BC it became one of the state doctrines of the Maurya dynasty when the Emperor Ashoka who ruled from Pataliputra (modern Patna) in eastern India was converted to Buddhism in 262 BC.

Greece and the Greek World

The first major civilisation in Europe developed around the Aegean Sea and has proved to be a great influence on all subsequent European civilisation. The architecture of ancient Greece was the essential origin of European architecture, through its influence on the architecture of the Roman Empire and so, indirectly, of mediaeval Europe.

Greek architecture itself did not develop in isolation. In the more remote prehistoric period distinct regional vernacular styles are discernible, in the east and north Aegean, on the mainland, and in the southern Aegean islands, especially Crete. The geography of the Aegean area stimulated navigation. Seafaring traders from the eastern Mediterranean were attracted to the Aegean by way of the southern coasts of Asia Minor, and brought knowledge of Near Eastern and Egyptian forms. An important civilisation developed on the island of Crete, and in its turn spread to the mainland, stimulating the communities adjacent to the Aegean. By the fourteenth century BC the centre of power and influence had shifted to the Greek-speaking mainland, only to collapse in disarray and poverty by the end of the twelfth century BC. During this period Greeks had migrated from the mainland, across the Aegean to the coastal regions of Asia Minor, and to Cyprus; in the period of revival which followed, a more extensive movement overseas took the Greeks to North Africa (Cyrenaica), to the coasts of the Black Sea, and above all to southern Italy and Sicily. These communities contributed to the development of Classical Greek architecture, often forming distinctive regional variations, that of Sicily and Italy being in its turn influential on the forms developed in Italy in the Etruscan cities and, eventually, Rome. Subsequently, the establishment of Macedonian supremacy over Aegean Greece by Philip II and the conquest by his son, Alexander, of the Persian Empire greatly extended the area of Greek political – and thus intellectual and artistic – domination. Greek architecture, stimulated by Egypt and the Near East, was itself the stimulator of Roman and later European architecture. To all the arts, to literature, and to science, the Greeks brought to bear remarkable qualities of intellect and aesthetic judgement; the architecture of ancient Greece fully demonstrates the levels of their achievement.

Physical Characteristics

Egypt and the Near East

Three broad zones comprise the greater part of the Near East. To the south lies the Arabian peninsula, with its desert extending northwards into Syria, though with fertile highlands in its southernmost region, the Yemen; in a great arc stretching from the Mediterranean coastal plain and the hill country of Palestine through north Syria and Iraq to the head of the Gulf, lies the zone of grasslands, steppes, the Piedmont (foothills) and alluvial river plains known as the Fertile Crescent; and for 2400 km (1500 miles) from west to east extends a chain of mountains and plateaux from the Taurus range and central plateau of Anatolia through the mountains and lakes of eastern Turkey and north-western Iran to the parallel ranges of the Zagros highlands, dividing the wide Iranian plateau from the plains of Mesopotamia. The coastal regions of the Aegean, southern Turkey and the Levant are typically Mediterranean, once forested but now largely denuded of trees. A heavily forested belt stretches along the Pontic coast, the south Black Sea littoral, the south coast of the Caspian Sea being subtropical in vegetation. To the north the Caucasus range forms a clearly defined frontier of the Near East, both environmentally and culturally.

The environment of Egypt was uniquely favourable to early settlement and the development and survival of a centralised state, comprising as it did the long, narrow valley of the Nile, its rich alluvial soil bounded on each side by the arid desert, beginning either with a gentle slope or with a marked escarpment. Whatever the precise local topography, the line between the 'Black Land' of the valley and the extensive delta and the 'Red Land' of the desert was sharp and clear. The reason for this was the lack of any other water supply than that provided by the Nile, a majestic, slow-flowing river, supremely reliable from one year to the next, yet carrying only one-fifth of the volume of silt brought down in a good year by the River Tigris. One outcome of the distinctive form of the settled zone of Egypt was that towns and villages were strung out over long distances, comprising loosely connected compounds. Physical environment and political security alike rendered densely concentrated, walled cities, characteristic of Mesopotamia, inappropriate. Outside the Nile delta (Lower Egypt) these never developed significantly, while evidence of early periods of occupation in the delta lies buried beneath later deposits. Indeed the record of ancient Egypt is overwhelmingly that of the long Nile valley (Upper Egypt), the two regions retaining the memory of their prehistoric existence as separate political entities. In antiquity Egypt proper ended at the First Cataract, where the Nile descends over a band of granite at Aswan; upstream lay Lower Nubia, as far as the Second Cataract, a far more formidable natural barrier and a readily defensible frontier, the present-day border between Egypt and the Sudan.

The climate of the Near East, the Aegean region and Egypt can largely be described in terms of present-day conditions, as changes over the past five millennia or so have been for the most part localised. In the closing phases of the Pleistocene era and following the last glaciation the Near East was, on the evidence provided by analyses of pollen traces in sedimentary deposits, rather colder and drier than today and the tree line was at a lower altitude. In the Levant, sheltered from the effects of the glaciation, thriving stands of trees survived.

There are indications of a climatic optimum in western Iran and Mesopotamia, if not throughout the Near East, round about the middle of the fourth millennium BC. Conditions became rather warmer and more humid, encouraging wider distribution of settlements. The level of the Persian Gulf, and thus by implication general sea levels, rose to about one metre above present-day levels. The tree cover in highland areas rapidly extended. To what degree, if any, this can be seen as a factor directly favouring the rise of towns and cities in southern Mesopotamia is perhaps still a matter for speculation. Rather would such a climatic improvement have stimulated wider distribution of settlements, not their concentration in larger but fewer communities; in other words, the growth of villages rather than towns. In fact such a development is discernible slightly earlier in Mesopotamia, during the fifth millennium BC, preceding the so-called Urban Revolution.

Much of the Near East is balanced on a knife-edge between adequate and insufficient rainfall: in the highland regions this is supplemented by snow, occurring as far south as the hills above Petra, in southern Jordan.

Natural regeneration of forests has been curtailed as a result of over-grazing over a long period. Slash-and-burn agriculture, so common in tropical Africa, was probably never significant in the Near East. The worst destruction of forests has of course occurred with the felling of timber for building or shipbuilding purposes, a process hardly extensive enough to have had significant effects before Classical times.

The development of a settled way of life took place around this 'fertile' crescent. The earliest villages appeared on the foothills of the Piedmont, where rainfall was adequate and the grazing good. Human occupation of the Zagros and Taurus regions was sparse, but their natural resources played a major role in early agricultural economies. In the northern Mesopotamian plains the climate was more arid, and rainfall was not sufficient for crop-growing without irrigation except between the Euphrates and the Tigris. But it was on the southern Mesopotamian alluvium, inhospitable though fertile if irrigated, that the first complex societies of south-west Asia evolved.

Habitation in the Epipaleolithic (20,000–10,000 BC) was in caves and impermanent open campsites. Most structures were of a perishable nature. The Natufians of the Mesolithic period moved seasonally to exploit a wide range of natural resources. Certain sites served as more permanent bases for recurrent visits over many years and it was here that more permanent buildings were developed. Neolithic settlements prior to 5000 BC were located with regard to the availability of local resources.

Predynastic Egypt was shaped by its more stable climate and the dominance of the Nile. The Nile valley, a narrow strip of alluvial plain bordered by desert, was one of the world's richest ecological niches. Above Cairo, the strip varied from 3 km to 22 km (2–14 miles) across, with a sharp division between the desert and the alluvium. North of Cairo extended the delta, 165 km to 250 km (103–155 miles) across, lush, well-watered and fertile. Temperatures rarely exceeded 38°C, but rainfall was sparse, and irrigation was required for agricultural production. The heat and humidity were suitable for a wide range of plants. The deserts were rich in natural building stone and minerals and shielded Egypt from external influences, but the river was an efficient means of internal communication. Settlement took place around the head of the delta, and along the river banks in the less hospitable environment of Upper Egypt.

Unlike Egypt, Mesopotamia lacks natural defensive boundaries: on the west it shades gradually into the undulating steppes of the Arabian desert, while on the east the valleys and foothills of the Zagros ranges were fertile enough to nurture neighbouring peoples watchfully envious of the richer living offered by the Mesopotamian plains. After the melting of the snows in the highlands to the north, the Tigris, though not always reliable, floods in the spring and the Euphrates a few weeks later, in May. The gentler current of the Euphrates made an easier means of communication and trade and a more favourable setting for the early rise of urban communities. The two great rivers deposited their silt over the flat plain, forming natural banks or levées and frequently changing their courses: thus a network of watercourses divided the plain. It was these secondary channels which were tapped as sources for irrigation in the earliest periods of settlement from the mid-sixth millennium BC onwards, but which steadily decreased as the main rivers were progressively brought under control by the cities and towns. From about the same time the Gulf ceased its relatively rapid expansion northward and a slower retreat began, leaving a fringe of marshes round the head of the Gulf.

Between the early city-states with their fertile agricultural lands lay barren stretches of steppe, providing natural frontiers: not all the land represented on maps as low-lying in Mesopotamia is necessarily fertile, or ever has been. Conditions range from those akin to the Aegean region, as in western Anatolia, to the harsh continental extremes of eastern Anatolia and to the arid interior of Iran, its mountain ranges enclosing two deserts. Centres of population tended to be concentrated in certain more fertile plains, including that of Erevan in the Araxes valley, the river now forming the frontier between Turkey and Armenia.

Syria was open to influences from all directions in that it had access to the maritime trade across the Mediterranean; it was also on the highway from the Anatolian plateau to Egypt and lay athwart the middle reaches of the Euphrates, thus being accessible to and from the cities of Mesopotamia. Much of Syria is very fertile, along the coast and inland, east of the mountain ranges of Lebanon, Anti-Lebanon and Amanus; but further east the landscape shades into desert, green only briefly after seasonal rains.

Until our own century the annual inundation of the Nile from July to October enriched the black land, as the ancient Egyptians called the valley and delta, with fresh deposits of silt, maintaining the quality of the soil. In recent years dams have undoubtedly affected local climate. Just as the disappearance millennia ago of extensive inland lakes, as from the Konya plain of Anatolia, must have reduced annual precipitation, the creation of artificial lakes in the form of reservoirs on the whole has the opposite effect.

Agricultural activities based on the longer perspective are generally beneficial to the environment, as exemplified by the terrace-building so characteristic of much of Syria and Palestine from Canaanite and Phoenician times onwards. It prevented erosion, which has so widely stripped the hillsides down to the bedrock, rendering them useless for food-production.

Egypt was uniquely protected from foreign incursions, with but one route from the Red Sea and another into the eastern delta. Successive Pharaohs organised expeditions to exploit the mineral resources (copper and gold) of the Sinai peninsula and the eastern desert.

The geology of the Near East is immensely varied, having a far-reaching effect both on the vegetation cover and on the character of public and even vernacular architecture, through the availability or absence of suitable building stone. Limestone dominates the landscape of northern Egypt, much of the Levant and parts of the highland zone, where, for example, the citadel of Van is built on a mile-long ridge of hard crystalline limestone. In Upper Egypt sandstone predominates. Basalt formations extend over wide areas of Jordan and also of eastern Anatolia, resulting in extensive tracts of stony desert or barren uplands. Recent volcanoes have occurred across the Anatolian plateau as far east as Mount Ararat. The Van region exemplifies the great variety of geological formations in Anatolia, with andesite, limestone, schist, basalt and red volcanic tuff. Across northern Anatolia, from east to west, extends a zone all too often liable to suffer severe earthquakes. Regions of inland drainage create salt pans and heavily salty lakes, notably the Dead Sea, Lake Urmia in north-western Iran and the Salt Lake in central Anatolia, while the Dasht-i-Lut (Salt Desert) and the Dasht-i-Kavir (Great Desert) extend over much of the interior of central and eastern Iran. Perhaps the greatest impact of local geology on human settlement in the Near East is an indirect one related to the location of water supplies, especially springs.

Early Asian Cultures

China

Chinese civilisation originated in the Neolithic period in the cool temperate provinces of the north-east. The primary locus was in the Huanghe valley, and later around the Changjiang. China was geographically isolated throughout this period, and its culture developed autochthonously. The region was a rich zone of marshes, lakes and alluvial plains with little natural forest cover. Rainfall was sparse and the winters harsh, but the cold, arid climate was well-suited to the farming, hunting, fishing and foraging the region supported from about 3500 BC.

The slash and burn techniques of cultivation used earlier were superseded by permanent field systems during the Xia period (2100–1600 BC), which also saw the transition from seasonal sites to large and permanent villages scattered over much of northern China. In the expansion into the Changjiang basin and to the coastal regions of southern China farming was adapted to higher temperatures and levels of rainfall. The Shang period (1600–1028 BC) was confined to the northern plains of Henan and its immediate surroundings, and the heartland of Zhou China (1027–256 BC) was along the Wei valley. The extent of Zhou territory fluctuated with the pressure from northern nomads but the density of settlement increased and the pace of urbanisation quickened. Under the Qin (221–206 BC) the empire spread west to Sichuan (Szechwan) and south to the Guangzhou delta.

India

Cut off from Asia by the Himalayas, the flow of ideas and peoples into India came mainly from the north-west, but trade routes linked north-east India with the Far East, and there was sea-borne trade along India's extensive coastline. The great riverine cultures of the Indus and the Ganges were geographically well sited to receive such diverse cultural influxes. The fertile Indus plain, even with its hot, dry climate, was capable of supporting several crops a year and the foothills of Pakistan, Afghanistan and Iran to the west were sources of minerals, metals and animal products. The Himalayas provided a formidable barrier to external influences and the Great Indian Desert limited contact with the remainder of the sub-continent. The Indus was navigable over most of its length but the surrounding plains were liable to flooding and this influenced the form and appearance of Harappan cities. It has been suggested that the Harappan civilisation ended in catastrophic flooding brought about by a major shift in the earth's crust near the mouth of the Indus.

Greece and the Greek World

The climate enjoyed by most Greek cities is, of course, that of the Mediterranean. Winters are short, and severe periods limited in duration though more extreme in the mountains of central Greece, the north Aegean, Thrace and the Black Sea. Rainfall is generally adequate, and occurs in autumn, winter and spring, often in heavy storms – the summers are hot and dry so that the resulting clear air and intense summer sunshine made it possible to appreciate the

Olympia: Valley of the Alpheus. See p.9

Pasargadae: detail of west facade. See p.26

fine details of Greek buildings, enhanced by carving and colour. The interiors of buildings were designed to provide relief from the intense light and heat of summer; temples received light only through their doors, while in other buildings windows were generally small, and normally opened not to the street but onto inner courtyards which were frequently surrounded by roofed porticoes. Much public activity took place in the open air, even in the winter months. Shade from the summer sun, shelter from the winter rains were desirable but not essential, and the structures which provided them were luxuries, and developed late. Nevertheless, if the temple was the building for which Greek architectural forms were originally developed, it was the extended roofed portico or stoa which became the most widespread and numerous by the end of the Classical period, and particularly during the final Hellenistic period.

The Greek lands are mountainous, and prone to earthquake. The present geography was formed by the sinking of the Aegean basin through earth movements; the islands of the Aegean are, most often, formed from the tops of submerged mountains. The mainland is indented by long inlets of the sea, particularly the substantial eastward-facing Gulfs of Argos and the Saronikos (Saronic); the latter is separated only by the narrow Isthmus of Corinth from the long westward-facing Gulf of Corinth, which provides sheltered navigation for a considerable distance, and certainly stimulated the development of western trade, so that the city of Corinth flourished as a result. There are few substantial rivers, and these are not navigable; their benefit is rather for irrigation. In southern Greece, south of the Isthmus of Corinth (the Peloponnese), the important rivers are the Eurotas and the Alpheius, which rise in the central plateau of Arcadia and flow, respectively, to the south, through the district of Laconia and past the city of Sparta, and to the west, through Elis and past the sanctuary of Olympia (p. 8). North of the Isthmus the important rivers are in the west (the Mornos and Achelous) and to the north: the Peneus, which drains the plain of Thessaly and then flows through the spectacular gorge, the 'Vale' of Tempe; and the large rivers of Macedonia and Thrace, the Haliacmon, the Axius and the Strymon. The valleys of the last two give access to the Balkan peninsula. The eastern Greek settlements were on the coast of Anatolia, mostly where the substantial rivers flowing from the Anatolian plateau to the Aegean, the Caicus, the Hermus and the Maeander, broaden out into wide, rich alluvial valleys. The homelands of the Greeks are divided by inlets of the sea and mountain barriers into distinctive regions, each with its own area of cultivable plain which provided the basic livelihood for the inhabitants. The size and importance of the community depended first, on the area of its cultivable land, second, on the ease with which adjacent communities could amalgamate into larger units. (The important city-states of the Classical period were all amalgamations of this type.) In their overseas settlements the Greeks most naturally selected a region of similar geography, and, until the conquests of Alexander, never at any distance from the sea.

History

Egypt and the Ancient Near East

The scale of society in the Mesolithic age was small. Natufians lived in groups of three or four households, with no marked differentiations in wealth or status. They engaged in small-scale trade or barter for luxury items like shell ornaments and obsidian for salt. The wide distribution of the culture was not mirrored by political unity. In the Neolithic period there were villages with populations numbered in hundreds, but village life was still largely self-sufficient, and politically and economically independent. The lack of a public architecture has been taken as evidence of the absence of a centralised polity. During the period 8000–6000 BC, population densities increased. The settling of nomadic populations may have played some part, but the absolute increase in numbers was also due to increased agricultural productivity. The period 6000–3500 BC was a formative one, during which population densities again increased; pottery and other artefacts emerged, and trade prospered.

The colonisation of the southern Mesopotamian alluvium after 5300 BC, with the need for irrigation, may have led to increased social complexity in this region and to the creation of greater surpluses and greater occupational specialisation. At any rate, by 4500 BC public architecture and cities characteristic of more complex civilisations had arrived. The Ubaid period produced a uniform architecture over most of the alluvium, and its influence extended throughout the surrounding regions. Settlements were located on reliable watercourses and almost all were at least 10 ha (25 acres) in extent. The temples of the Ubaid period were evidence of increasing cultural complexity in the diversion of resources into public architecture, and by the close of the prehistoric period some towns were approaching the status of city-states.

In Egypt, the proto-agricultural period of 12,500–9500 BC did not lead to agriculture. To all intents and purposes Egypt was two independent kingdoms, with the northern capital at Buto and the southern capital at Hierakonpolis. The kingdoms were virtually autonomous politically and administratively. Towards the end of the predynastic period, however, there were moves towards political unity brought about by the development of the institution of kingship. There is evidence that artefacts and craft techniques were imported from Egypt and the Near East.

Although it was in the Nile valley that the oldest major continuing and highly centralised monarchy emerged around 3200 BC to be ruled by the Pharaohs of Egypt for nearly three millennia, it was in the cities of southern Mesopotamia in Sumer in the middle of the fourth millennium BC that writing first seems to have been developed and that the longest historical records can be found. The archaeological evidence suggests that the Sumerians had been occupying the land from the first settlement of Eridu, by historical tradition the oldest city of Sumer, for two millennia before the earliest writing appeared. With the seizure of political control by Sargon of Agade (*c.* 2340 BC), the Akkadian dynasty was established, ruling over indigenous Sumerians and incoming Semitic Akkadians alike. Three new developments occurred: first, political unity was imposed by force on the warring city-states; second, the status of the ruler was deliberately exalted, the king claiming divinity in his lifetime and provincial governors being appointed and styling themselves 'slaves of the god'; third, trade beyond the confines of Mesopotamia – first developed in the later fourth millennium BC (Late Uruk period) – was revived by expeditions led by the king, their purpose as much economic as military. Moreover, the Akkadian language steadily extended its hold on Mesopotamia and in due course became the language of diplomacy as far afield as Egypt until the rise of Aramaic in the last century of the Assyrian empire. The Sumerian language and literature left a widespread legacy: for example, the links with the scribal schools of Mesopotamia apparent in the archives of the burnt palace of Ebla in northern Syria. There was a final revival of Sumerian civilisation in its homeland under the powerful Third Dynasty of Ur, at the end of the third millennium BC.

Contemporary archives from the age of Hammurabi of Babylon (1792–1750 BC) have been recovered in enough cities to demonstrate the brief phenomenon of an international balance of power, recognised as such at the time. The famous code of Hammurabi sheds light on the rules governing trade, land tenure, feudal service, taxation, slavery and the organisation of labour, and emphasises the growth of the power of the secular ruler or palace in relation to that of the temples, whose role in trade was also in decline. Restoration of older buildings rather than construction of new ones was typical of this, the Old Babylonian period. Of the city of Babylon itself at this time little is known: its political supremacy was quite short-lived, control of the marshes at the head of the Gulf, and thus of access to the lucrative maritime trade, being lost soon after the death of Hammurabi. Meanwhile two groups of newcomers, the Hurrians and Kassites, were becoming prominent in northern and central Mesopotamia respectively, until the latter took over political control in the Mesopotamian plain. Kassite rule lasted over four centuries (*c.* 1595–1155 BC).

Egypt witnessed its greatest prosperity, military aggrandisement and territorial expansion, both in Asia and in the African hinterland of Nubia, under the New Kingdom, approximately contemporary with Kassite rule in Mesopotamia. With the expulsion of the Hyksos invaders following their occupation of Egypt (*c.* 1674–1567 BC), the land of Egypt had reverted to the crown. But with the subsequent progressive reversal of this process, imperial expeditions became a necessity. These were abandoned in the reign of the luxury-loving Amenhotep III (*c.* 1417–1379 BC), when vassal lands in Asia were left to their fate. The ensuing religious innovation, personified by the king Akhenaten and his family and symbolised by the sun disc of his god Aten, was a political move designed to destroy the power of the priests of the orthodox cult of Amun-Ra. After the brief reign of the young king Tutankhamun, far more famous in death than ever he was in life, orthodoxy was restored to the Egyptian court, and with it the military tradition of the earlier New Kingdom. Attempts to regain control of Syria and Palestine were, however, less successful: most of Syria fell under Hittite rule after the indecisive battle of Kadesh (1299 BC), when Rameses II (1304–1237 BC) narrowly escaped disaster. Sixteen years later a treaty between Egypt and Hatti (the Hittite kingdom centred on the Anatolian plateau) established an international peace which was to last a full century. The complex, unsettled political climate of the Amarna period – in the earlier fourteenth century BC, in the reign of Akhenaten – gave way to a tripartite division of power, between Egypt, Hatti and the growing power of Assyria, a kingdom whose origins dated back into the third millennium BC. A fourth power, the kingdom of Mitanni, in the Khabur valley of north-eastern Syria, ruled by an Indo-Aryan dynasty with a class of knights (maryannu), lacked naturally defensible frontiers, and inevitably vanished.

The plateau of Iran was overrun from the mid-second millennium BC onwards by Iranian newcomers, most probably arriving from their old homeland in north-eastern Iran and another group perhaps coming via the Caucasus. These were the ancestors of the Medes and Persians of the historical period, and from the beginning may have introduced the essentials of the Zoroastrian religion, now thought to antedate the lifetime of Zoroaster himself.

The end of the established order of the Bronze Age in Anatolia and the Levant, as far as the border of Egypt, came abruptly in the early twelfth century BC, with the invasion of the 'Sea Peoples' – known principally from the reliefs and inscriptions on the temple of Rameses III at Medinet Habu, Thebes – the Philistines, who occupied much of the fertile coastal plain of the land which has ever since retained their name, Palestine. Many cities then destroyed, including the great mercantile centre of Ugarit on the Syrian coast, were never rebuilt, and the Hittite state vanished.

The resulting vacuum in the power politics of the ancient Near East lasted some three centuries until the rise of the Late Assyrian state. In Syria several great cities rose to prosperity, most notably Carchemish and Hamath, culturally the heirs of Hatti. There was an admixture of influence from the Aramaean groups which had been penetrating the settled lands from the pastoral fringes of the desert zone for some time – at least from the twelfth century BC. To the south the united kingdom of Israel flourished under David and Solomon. After the division of the kingdom, there was a revival of prosperity in the northern kingdom of Israel under Ahab (*c.* 874–852 BC), and the building of a new capital at Samaria by his father Omri (*c.* 880 BC). A religious reaction under Jehu led to military and cultural decline.

From the late tenth century BC the Assyrians, whose small but tenacious population was only partly Semitic, re-emerged from the domination of their homeland by Aramaean tribes. Babylon had declined likewise, under pressure from Chaldaean tribes. Not until the reign of Ashurnasirpal II (883–859 BC) was there time for major building activity, with the removal of the seals of government up the Tigris, from Ashur to Nimrud (Kalhu). The Assyrian kings showed great energy in scientific and literary pursuits, culminating in the establishment of a library in the final capital at Nineveh. After another period of decline, the throne was seized by Tiglath-Pileser III (745–727 BC), an outstanding campaigner and administrative reformer who transformed the Assyrian territories from a ring of vassal principalities around the homeland in the upper Tigris valley into an efficiently controlled empire under governors appointed by the king: regular taxes replaced tribute. The army came to depend upon regular units backed up by auxiliaries reunited from the conquered peoples. Sennacherib (705–681 BC), who rebuilt Nineveh, curbed Egyptian intrigues in Asia by his campaign against Hezekiah of Judah by laying siege to Jerusalem and Lachish (700 BC) and endeavoured (with limited success) to solve the complexities of Babylonian politics in the face of interference by Elam, the ancient state in south-west Iran. Sennacherib eventually lost patience with the hitherto respected city of Babylon and destroyed it (689 BC) – an act whose repercussions led to his assassination (681 BC). Assyria overreached itself in the short-lived annexation of Egypt by Esarhaddon (681–669 BC). Early in the reign of Ashurbanipal (668–627 BC) Egypt reasserted its independence under Dynasty XXVI (663–525 BC), the so-called Saite Period, during which the rulers originated in the city of Sais in the Nile delta. Loss of control of the north-eastern frontier and a costly civil war with Babylon left the way open to the new and formidable coalition of the Medes, and reduced the manpower of the Assyrian army. Babylonia had been too populous ever to be effectively subjugated; and the sack of Susa (*c.* 640 BC), though for ever eliminating Elam, removed a buffer state. The major cities of Assyria had become artificially extended, supported by the dues paid from the countryside and the conquered lands. Once the machinery of state collapsed, as it did very suddenly in the years leading up to the destruction of Nineveh (612 BC), the cities withered and the countryside was abandoned. Thus Assyria disappeared almost immediately and without trace, bringing an era to an end.

Among the contempories of Assyria, the highland kingdom of Urartu, founded in the ninth century BC but with its roots in earlier tribal confederacies, was centred on Van. Urartu reached its zenith in the early eighth century BC; suffered defeats at the hand of Assyria; enjoyed a renaissance in the early seventh century BC under Rusa II (*c.* 685–645 BC); and survived a few years after the fall of Assyria, ultimately succumbing to the Medes. Phrygia, which attained wide if rather short-lived power under Mita (Midas) in the eighth century BC, had its capital at Gordion in north-western Anatolia. Gordion fell to attack by northern nomads from the plains of southern Russia, the Cimmerians (*c.* 696 BC), who went on to assault the more westerly kingdom of Lydia and its capital of Sardis (652 BC).

The Phoenician cities of the east Mediterranean seaboard, which lived by trade and industry, survived relatively unscathed until the advent of the heir to the Assyrian empire, the Neo-Babylonian state (*c.* 626–539 BC). The brief history of the latter was marked by a deliberate cultural archaism, manifested in the restoration of the Sumerian city of Ur: this trend was paralleled at the same time in Egypt, where Saite sculptors looked back to the Old Kingdom for their inspiration. Under Nebuchadnezzar II (605–563 BC) Babylon was rebuilt on a far grander scale than before and economic factors led to westward expansion which led to the destruction of the small kingdom of Judah (587 BC) and of the island city of Tyre (572 BC). Nabonidus, last of the Neo-Babylonian kings, suffered the hatred of the established priesthood of the national god Marduk for his devotion to the moon god Sin and contributed to the ease with which Cyrus the Persian occupied Babylon (539 BC).

The defeat by Cyrus king of the Persians of the king of the Medes (his own grandfather, Astyages) marked the foundation of the Persian empire, called Achaemenid after the ancestor of the royal house (550 BC). The westward expansion of the empire was secured by the defeat of Croesus, the king of Lydia, and the capture of Sardis (546 BC). Babylon fell without resistance, and with it the Babylonian possessions in the Levant. Eastward expansion proved harder, however, and Cyrus died in battle beyond the River Oxus. Preparations for the conquest of Egypt had to be carried through by Cambyses II (525 BC). It seems that the impression produced by the buildings of Memphis and Thebes, perhaps even more than the sight of the Greek cities of the Ionian coast, popularised columnar architecture among the Persians. After the civil war Darius I (522–486 BC) built the network of arterial roads and reorganised the empire into satrapies or provinces, twenty in all, each under a satrap or governor. The Persian empire, the widest in the ancient world, then extended from the Danube to the Indus. Persian rule was not harsh; the customs and cults of the conquered peoples were respected. The first serious reverses were suffered in efforts to conquer Greece, which met with final failure under Xerxes at the battles of Salamis and Plataea, on sea and land respectively (480–479 BC). Persian gold was later more effective in manipulating the rival Greek cities.

After the rise of Macedon under Philip and his subjugation of the Greek cities, the way lay open to his son Alexander the Great (336–323 BC) to carry the war into Asia, where his name is still remembered. The empire founded by Cyrus the Great thus fell into Alexander's hands and Greek civilisation began to spread its influence even to Bactria (Afghanistan) and the Indus valley.

While Egypt fell to the Ptolemies with the partition of the vast empire after Alexander's death in Babylon (323 BC), the gods and temples of Egypt were lavishly endowed, with new temples built to the traditional design. The centre of Greek culture was the new city of Alexandria. But the greater part of Alexander's empire was under the Seleucid dynasty, including Iran (312–247 BC), which later passed successively under the Parthian (247 BC–AD 226) and Sassanian (AD 226–561) dynasties, and was finally conquered by the armies of Islam. From the first century BC onwards the Mediterranean lands of the Near East, as well as Anatolia as far as the upper Euphrates, came by stages under the grip of Rome.

Early Asian Cultures

China

The earliest peasants of the prehistoric period were subsistence farmers with little craft specialisation. Communication between villages was poor and there was little differentiation of roles or of the status of individuals. The absence of walls and fortifications has been taken as an indication of the peaceful nature of the society and the lack of specialised buildings as a reflection of an egalitarian society. Later, Xia peasants practised more intensive forms of agriculture, and supported larger and more permanent villages. There was some craft specialisation, but economically and politically villages were still relatively autonomous. As the Shang dynasty emerged gradually from these roots the major transformation was that subsistence agriculture was augmented by forms of craft and social specialisation, and an organised polity began to emerge.

The Shang dynasty held sway within a restricted territory and the emperor's position as one of a number of petty chiefs was tenuous. A vertically stratified society was formed and local exchange economies were replaced by an institutionalised redistribution system, whereas outside of Shang rule China remained predominantly at a Neolithic level of development. The emergence of the large capital city has been cited as a conspicuous manifestation of this change. The Shang capital was moved several times from Erlitou (*c.* 1850–1600 BC) to Zhengzhou (*c.* 1600–1400 BC) and then to Anyang (*c.* 1400–1027 BC). In the Erlitou phase, the techniques of bronze metallurgy were mastered; during the Zhengzhou period, urbanisation began to take place. Shang cities were centres of production, exchange and political control. Life in the villages continued on a subsistence basis but the villagers were gradually coordinated into the system of commerce. Late Shang culture extended over an immense territory under the leadership of emperors who governed with the aid of a complex hierarchy of nobles with considerable authority in their homelands, but also with obligations to central government for defence, conscription, public works and tax-collection.

The Zhou political system consisted of a hierarchy of nobles, intellectuals, warriors, artisans, peasants and slaves under an emperor and a royal court, although the basis of power was unstable as the loose alliances of nobles formed and reformed. The pace of urbanisation quickened and the cities became the loci of an emergent merchant class. Trade was considerable and was facilitated by the adoption of a standardised coinage. Iron-working became important to the economy.

Under the Qin a new system of administration was introduced and brought the provinces under centralised control. A programme of road-building, canal construction, and defence building on the northern frontiers was implemented by central government. Conscription to the army and for service on large public projects was introduced.

India

There were earlier settlements in the Indus basin than those of the Harappan civilisation. These were at Mehrgarh in Baluchistan (*c.* 6000–2600 BC) and others were found below Harappan levels, at Amri, Kalibangan and Kot Diji. These showed a continuity of settlement form and material culture with the Harappans, but the earlier villages appear to have been economically and politically autonomous. By contrast the Harappan culture was notable for its sheer spatial and physical scope. It unified an area of 1,300,000 square kilometres (502,000 square miles) – considerably larger in extent than any of the Old World civilisations of the period. Throughout the region more than 200 settlement sites have been found, including six metropolitan centres, twenty towns and over 200 villages, large and small.

There was a high degree of uniformity in all aspects of Harappan material culture, including architecture and urban form. The latter usually consisted of a defended citadel, residential districts and an associated cemetery. The regularity of the arrangement is such that the provision of public utilities and services have been taken to indicate a highly developed form of social coordination, but no monumental buildings have been discovered which could be associated with dynastic rule or centralised power.

The dominant feature of the Harappan urban economy was an extensive and highly specialised division of labour, which some archaeologists have suggested gave Harappan society internal cohesion and was a precursor of the caste system. Craftsmen produced high-quality, well-finished goods. They depended upon the rural hinterland for foodstuffs. Raw materials were acquired, and finished products were exported through an extensive sea-borne trade which included Sumer through an entrepôt on the Persian Gulf. Large granaries in the metropolitan centres have been taken as evidence of a redistribution economy.

Suggested causes for the decline of the Harappan civilisation have included the onset of a period of drought in about 1800 BC, a dramatic rise in the water table throughout the region, deforestation and soil erosion, and invasion. Evidence of the decline is found in the buildings themselves, which became progressively poorer in quality in the most recent levels of excavation.

Greece and the Greek World

The civilisation of Greece and the Aegean can be divided, broadly, into the prehistoric, of the second millennium BC and earlier, and the historical or Classical, which emerged after a period of poverty and retrogression around 1000 BC. At neither period is the area a political or historical unity. The earliest phases are certainly pre-Greek, that is, the people of these times spoke languages which are not Greek in form. The most important early phase centres on the island of Crete; its discovery is the work of modern archaeologists, in particular the excavator of Knossos, Sir Arthur Evans, who gave this civilisation the conventional name of Minoan (after Minos, who in Greek legend was King at Knossos). It is divided, in accordance with the development of pottery styles, into Early Minoan (roughly third millennium BC), Middle (early second millennium) and Late (the second half of the second millennium); more significant, perhaps, is the architectural division into pre-palatial, down to the early second millennium, and palatial, characterised by architecturally complex administrative centres ('palaces'), again typified by that at Knossos (p. 108) and influenced by east Mediterranean political concepts, though it must be emphasised that the development of architectural forms is local and continuous, from pre-palatial to palatial. The palatial period was literate, using, at least for record purposes, a linear syllabic script, of which there are two versions, the earlier (Linear A) being used for the (undeciphered) Cretan language, the later (Linear B) for an early form of Greek.

The palaces of Bronze Age Crete were more than the residences of the rulers. Besides the recognisable domestic quarters they included on their ground floors substantial areas for storage, as well as work rooms. Later Greek tradition had a memory of King Minos's fleet controlling the Aegean (much in the way that in historical times the Athenian fleet dominated the seas) but this may be something of an anachronism or distortion; overseas contacts seem to be much more a matter of trade than of empire, and there is no evidence for executive Minoan domination of the mainland. There is little evidence for the social and political structure, beyond the undoubted hierarchic and presumably autocratic element. Each palace (the size varies from large to small, depending on the size of the community) must have represented a separate centre of administration; whether the smaller were in any way subordinate to the larger, or, in the late Minoan period at least, to the largest of them all, at Knossos, is quite uncertain. The general impression is of peacefulness. There are no fortifications of any note, and the prosperity of the palace communities is demonstrated by their size, and the luxuriousness of building construction and appurtenances. Smaller but still substantial houses or villas suggest the extension of wealth through the urban community, at least. Women are frequently depicted in the art of the palaces, participating in or observing the religious rituals. Representation of priestesses is frequent, but, again, it is difficult to build a secure interpretation of the general status of women from this, and the existence of an exploited rural population may lurk behind the brilliance of the palace forms.

Around 1400 BC the Cretans were overcome by people from the mainland. The archaeology of the mainland communities is distinctive, though linked to that of Crete and the islands; the modern, conventional term used to describe it is Helladic. The early Bronze Age is probably pre-Greek, Greek settlers arriving towards the end of the third millennium BC (there were still areas where pre-Greek languages were spoken even in the historical period, and these have left their traces in the place-names, many of which, such as Athens or Corinth, have no sensible meaning in Greek). Early Bronze Age settlements are small, though few have been excavated, and the important ones were in places where extensive subsequent occupation makes the recovery of the early settlements plans difficult. There are distinct signs of chaos and disintegration towards the end of the early Bronze Age, which may be coincidental with the arrival of Greek-speaking peoples.

The mainland developed particularly in the Late Bronze Age. The major settlements are characterised by the possession of citadels, more and more strongly fortified, and enclosing palaces clearly influenced by those of Crete, but not Cretan in plan and arrangement (p. 110A).

The social organisation of the mainland communities seems to have followed that of Crete; there is clear evidence for a ruling class, the kings, who were buried in particularly sumptuous tombs, with wealthy grave goods, much more lavish than the forms of burial found in Crete. They were an aggressive people, extending their influence in the Aegean more by raiding, plundering and, eventually, subjugation, than by trade. Late Bronze Age pottery of the mainland is finely made, and is found widely distributed through the Mediterranean, indicating that the mainland Greeks took over the trade which previously had been centred on the Minoan palaces. It was probably at mainland-occupied Knossos that the Linear A syllabary was adapted (Linear B) to the writing of Greek; Linear B tablets (but not Linear A) have been found on the mainland.

Around 1200 BC this flourishing civilisation entered into a period of severe decline. During this Dark Age, Greece underwent some depopulation, whole groups of people moving across or even out of the Aegean altogether, either as sea-raiders or settlers. In turn, other Greeks from the mountains and from less prosperous northern regions took advantage of weakness and depopulation in the south to migrate to these more fertile regions. These Dark Age movements formed the basis for the principal dialect divisions of Greek. Central Peloponnese (Arcadia) was unscathed by these movements, and continued the form of Greek spoken in the Bronze Age; but another branch of the same dialect is found in Cyprus, indicating a common origin for peoples completely separate in the historical period. The northern migrants brought with them the dialect known as Dorian, spoken in Messenia, Laconia, the Argolid, Corinthia and adjacent areas as well as Crete and Rhodes. Migrants to the eastern Aegean spoke Ionian Greek, which, in a variant form, survived on the mainland as the Athenian dialect. Other forms of northern Greek (Aeolic) were spoken on the mainland north of Athens, and in the northern parts of the Asia Minor coast. These dialect terms are also equated with the principal geographical divisions, and so (Ionic, Doric, Aeolic) with the characteristic architectural forms which evolved in them. It is important to note that these geographical and architectural divisions did not precisely coincide with the dialect divisions. Doric, for example, is the essential style of the entire mainland, even Athens.

The revival of the Greek world was fitful. Poverty was exacerbated by virtual isolation from the rest of the Mediterranean world. Some communities, such as Athens, flourished earlier than others, but the real revival did not begin until the eighth century BC, when there is evidence of the renewal of overseas trading contacts. Not all Greek communities traded, but those that did grew richer, and, by amalgamating forcibly or voluntarily with their neighbours, formed larger states, the polis (city-state) being the natural and desirable political entity in the ensuing Classical period. Early examples are Athens, Corinth, Argos and Sparta, on the Greek mainland, while in the eastern Aegean Samos, Chios, Smyrna, Ephesus and Miletus also grew (the last three, being on the mainland of Asia Minor rather than islands, were not confined, and came to control extended regions inhabited largely by people of non-Greek origin). During this period, the 'Archaic', which extended from the eighth to the sixth century BC, Greek artists broke away from the abstract, geometric forms which had been inherited from the Late Bronze Age, and introduced oriental motifs, decorative patterns and representations of animals and human beings which were all parts of the common repertoire in the Levant communities. The Levantine origin of what is termed the 'orientalising' phase of Greek art is emphasised by the development of the new, alphabetic system of writing adapted from the Phoenician script, Linear B having disappeared during the Dark Age except in a modified form in Cyprus.

Each city-state was jealous of its autonomy and independence. Even so the Greeks were conscious of a degree of unity, fostered by a unity of language which was recognised above the variant dialect forms, and particularly by shared religious concepts, belief in the same gods who thus acquired both local (city) and universal (Greek) significance. Politically, this archaic phase of Classical Greece was dominated by the leading aristocratic families in each city, either acting in concert or squabbling among themselves for supremacy. At times individual aristocrats, taking advantage of popular dissatisfaction, and putting themselves forward as leaders, managed to seize authoritarian power. Such rulers were called tyrants, from a borrowed (Asiatic) word meaning king. Their regimes were, at this time, usually beneficent; only later, as their power was challenged, did they become harsher and thus warrant the change in the meaning of the word. The arts were most greatly stimulated by aristocratic or tyrant patronage. The movement of Greeks to colonies overseas (Italy, Sicily, North

Africa, the Black Sea), for the encouragement of trade and to relieve pressure of population, was caused as much by readjustment of the economy in favour of the ruling families, as by natural population growth.

This development was challenged by the rise of major states in the east. Asia Minor passed to the dynasty of Gyges and his successors, who were based on Sardis in Lydia. This dominion seems not to have been oppressive and the Greeks benefited from the support of the Lydian kings, particularly the last of them, Croesus, whose financial contributions made possible the grandiose temple of Artemis at Ephesus. In 546 BC, however, the Lydian kingdom was overwhelmed by the rising power of Persia which rapidly extended to include the whole of the Near East and Egypt, as well as the Iranian plateau. Some Greek cities came under immediate Persian control (those on the mainland of Asia Minor); the offshore islands were conquered later. Persian authority extended into the Balkans, and a rebellion of the Ionian Greeks, though supported by Athens, failed. Miletus was destroyed, together with the temple of Apollo at Didyma; the free Greek cities saw the threat that was developing, and prepared for resistance. A seaborne expedition to Athens, where the Persians hoped to install a cooperative tyrant, was heroically defeated at Marathon in 490 BC; the subsequent death of the Persian king, Darius, and the rebellion of Egypt put off the expected retribution until 480 BC, when the invasion was led by the new Persian king Xerxes. By now the Greeks were ready. Sinking their differences, they formed a grand alliance under the leadership of aristocratic Sparta. Athens, which had developed a truly democratic constitution late in the sixth century, built a large fleet, and the Persian invasion was comprehensively repulsed in 479 BC. The alliance had to be maintained, however, if the Persian empire were not to pick off the Greek cities piecemeal; Sparta had turned its back on naval activity, which gave political muscle to the poorer sections of the population, and the Greeks of the Aegean turned to Athens for leadership. Gradually the alliance was transformed into an empire, though the Persians were successfully kept at bay, and the Athenians, under the leadership of Pericles, felt justified in turning the defence revenue into temples as thank-offerings to the gods for victory. Athens thus reached the height of its power and prosperity, but all this was thrown away in a senseless war with Sparta, which dragged on fitfully until Athens lost its fleet and was starved into submission. The struggle was essentially between the democratic, revolutionary spirit of Athens, supreme in the arts of peace but unfitted for the control of a major war, and aristocratic, reactionary Sparta, less brilliant in the arts and architecture, but militarily far more successful.

Greece gradually slipped into political chaos, so that the weakened Persian empire was able to dictate terms, and this was accompanied by a marked, though not catastrophic, economic decline. Sculpture still flourished, particularly at Athens, but less money was now available for building. Few temples were built (though of course most important sanctuaries were now well enough endowed with temples), but there was some development in the construction of buildings for more ordinary human use. There was some revival of architecture at Athens at about the middle of the fourth century BC, which may indicate the existence of Persian support. If so, it was aimed at countering the new rising power of Macedon in the north. This had been a backward and largely negligible border state in the fifth century, and in the early fourth was no less chaotic than the rest of Greece. The transformation of Macedon was due largely to the efforts of one man, Philip, who became king on the death of his brother in 359 BC. Relying on the fighting skills of the Macedonians, coupled with his own brilliance as soldier and diplomat, he rapidly extended Macedonian power and wealth, until at the battle of Chaeronea in 338 BC he defeated a coalition of the major Greek cities, Athens and Thebes, and created a new federation of all the Greeks, theoretically free, but in practice controlled by Philip as its appointed leader. To achieve a unity of purpose he proclaimed a crusade against the Persians, originally proposed many years previously by Isocrates; and though he was assassinated before he could do more than make the preliminary moves, his son and heir, Alexander, carried through the crusade with complete success and established himself as the ruler of the former Persian empire.

Alexander's short life was almost entirely taken up with campaigns, and at his death in 323 BC he had not achieved the permanent organisation of his empire or made proper provision for the succession. In default of an effective heir, the empire was divided among the Macedonian generals, who carved out of it separate kingdoms for themselves. Those of Ptolemy in Egypt and of Seleucus in the Near East were the more important and durable. Macedon passed to a new dynasty, that of Antigonus. The Greek cities established their freedom for the Achaean and Aetolian confederations. Asia Minor reverted to its traditional pattern of local dynasts, those of Pergamum making an especial contribution to the architecture of the period.

During this period, the Hellenistic age, Greek forms of art and civic life were transplanted into the newly conquered areas, though always subordinated to the control and policies of the ruling kings. Greeks migrated to the cities founded in the new territories, of which the most important and durable were Alexandria-by-Egypt, founded by Alexander, and Antioch in Syria, founded by Seleucus. These attained levels of wealth unprecedented in earlier, Classical Greece. There was considerable expenditure on ephemeral show (particularly religious processions), but the arts and architecture also flourished. Although the concept of Graeco-Macedonian supremacy (which grew weaker as a result of bickering between the kingdoms during the third century BC) ensured the introduction of Greek architectural concepts in the new cities, and prevented the direct and wholesale copying of local art and architecture by the Greeks, the majority of the population in these kingdoms was not Greek but, for example, Egyptian or Syrian, and for them the old styles and tastes and religious beliefs continued. Influences between groups are discernible; as far as the Greeks were concerned, this was largely a matter of taste or fashion rather than deliberate adoption of the local forms, but there can be no doubt that this had some modifying effect on the architecture. In the end, the eastern areas, the Iranian plateau and most of Mesopotamia were lost to the resurgent oriental kingdom of the Parthians. Egypt, Syria and Hellenistic Asia Minor were rescued by the Romans, who gradually took over responsibility for them, receiving Pergamum by the bequest of its ruler Attalus III in 133 BC, and, finally, Egypt on the death of Cleopatra VII in 30 BC.

Culture

Egypt and the Ancient Near East

Sickles, querns, mortars, pestles, pounders and other ground stone tools have been found in abundance at Natufian sites in the Near East. Vessels made of limestone and marble have been recovered but there is no evidence of pottery. Carved figurines of animals and women occur at many sites, and cave paintings of the period have been found. Burials were in simple graves set in the floors of houses. Grave goods were infrequent and took the form of decorative objects. At some sites, cemeteries suggested more protracted periods of habitation.

In the Neolithic period, stone tools, mainly flint, were supplemented by artefacts made of bone. Art took the form of decoration on beads, carved animal heads on knife handles and stone carvings. Small ornaments were produced in turquoise, marble and alabaster. Burials were frequently under floors, but hoards of human skulls have been recovered with faces modelled in plaster and eyes indicated by shells. Pottery was produced widely from about 6500 BC. It appears to have had multiple places of origin, and the technique spread rapidly throughout south-west Asia. The first sophisticated and uniform pottery styles appeared about 5500 BC with Samarran and Halafian wares. Pots were hand made, fired at high temperatures and decorated in polychrome geometric designs. The pottery Neolithic period in Anatolia was marked by a richness in material goods, and developments in the sphere of art and religion: shrine-rooms were decorated with paintings and reliefs representing women and the heads and horns of bulls. The numbers and size of these rooms are suggestive of domestic rituals. The Ubaid period produced both hand-made and wheel-turned pots, and copper tools supplemented the older lithic technology. The growing importance of religious practices was indicated by developments in building temples, some of the facades of which were decorated with friezes. One of these depicted dairying scenes.

Some of the most striking products of the material culture of the Neolithic Age in predynastic Egypt are the rock paintings and engravings at Tassili in the Sahara Desert. Faiyumi sites have yielded flint and bone tools, coarse pottery and a variety of woven artefacts including textiles, mats and baskets. Mermidan sites differed only in that the dead were buried among the dwellings. The Badarians made advances in stoneworking, and produced articles of personal adornment including stone beads, necklaces, girdles and cosmetics. Copper appeared in the form of beads. Thin-walled, burnished pottery was produced by the Badarians, and the Amratians made a red, burnished ware, line-decorated with white slip. Stone vases, a characteristic product of ancient Egypt, date from this period. Gerzean pottery developed from Amratian ware. A greater range of vessel types was produced, and decorative motifs included stylised animals, humans, and scenes from everyday life, as well as geometric designs. Faience was produced, copper came into widespread use, and hieroglyphic writing also dates from this period. It is possible that mud-brick architecture was introduced at this time from abroad. Burial in cemetery sites became more elaborate, with an increasing differentiation of the structure and contents of graves, pointing to an increasing emphasis on the after-life.

Religion is more clearly reflected in the architecture of the ancient Near East than social structure and development, if only because of the disproportionate ratio of religious to secular buildings among those excavated. In the Neolithic period the cellular layout of houses and shrines at Catal Hüyük, on the Anatolian plateau, may reflect the growth of extended families; but not enough of the site has been uncovered for definitive conclusions to be drawn.

From around 5000 BC the temple, first discernible at Eridu, emerged as the outward and visible sign of the cohesion of the Sumerian city, of its control by a ruling elite and of its growing attachment to cultural traditions. This conservatism was reinforced by the introduction of writing, making it possible to refer back to precedents. The Mesopotamian temple, at first relatively accessible to the populace, as time passed, seems to have become more a palace for the sovereign protector of the city, than the house of the patron god or goddess. As the secular influence of the temple declined (partly as the result of growing literacy in the mercantile class), access to the temples was more and more restricted to the priesthood.

In Egypt the close connection between religion and architecture is everywhere manifest; the priesthood was powerful and equipped with all the learning of the age. Egyptian religious rights were mysterious and virtually unchangeable, characteristics reflected faithfully in the architecture of tombs and temples. Egyptian mythology was in effect polytheistic and complicated by the multiplicity of local gods in different places. The royal cult was essentially that of the sun, while the worship of Osiris, god of death and resurrection to eternal life, became ever more popular as the centuries passed. Elaborate preparations were made for the preservation of the body after death. The earthly dwelling-house was regarded as the temporary lodging and the tomb as the permanent abode: hence the enduring pyramid tombs of the Old Kingdom and the description of the duration of the royal rock-cut tombs of the kings west of Thebes, in the New Kingdom, as 'of millions of years'. The kings of Egypt were both gods and priests, while the gods themselves were invested with superhuman and therefore with inventive powers, as when the art of writing was regarded as the invention of the god Thoth. The gods were often associated in triads: thus Amun the sun-god, Mut his wife, the mother of all things and Khons their son, the moon-god, were the great triad of Thebes; while Ptah, a creator and craftsman, Sekhmet, goddess of war, and Nefertum, their son, formed the triad of Memphis. These and many hundreds more divinities occur singly or in combination. Much was added to the religion of Egypt: nothing was ever taken away.

Spatial analysis, in the sense of detection of an overall layout of buildings in relation one to another, is seldom possible in the ancient Near East, for one of two reasons. Either the city grew over successive generations or excavations do not reveal the whole layout. On the whole the dominant tradition in the architecture of the Near East was that of the inward-looking plan, with rooms opening off one or more courtyards, allowing for light and air, but likewise privacy and security: this applied to palaces and town houses alike, especially in Mesopotamia. But a very different tradition becomes evident at Pasargadae, the earliest Achaemenid Persian royal residence, where buildings were dotted about the highland plain like the scattered tents of a great army.

Religion reflected the peculiarities of each zone of the Near East, perhaps being least dominant in the commercial and industrial ethos of the Phoenician homeland and colonies, though the old Canaanite cults survived and were exported to Carthage, from its traditional foundation date (814 BC). The clashes between the austere religion of Yahveh, with its desert background, and the priests of Ba'al are familiar from the Old Testament. Priest and prophet were uneasy partners: both Zadok the priest and Nathan the prophet officiated at Solomon's coronation. It is the priestly legacy which is more relevant to the history of art and architecture, however, than the prophetic.

The Hittite kings, as chief priests, spent much of their time in peregrinations from one shrine or sacred city to the next. The origins of their status lay in their Indo-European ancestry; but contact with the older civilisations of the Near East in the last two centuries of the Hittite kingdom brought its kingship more closely in line with oriental charisma. The Hittite king became 'The sun', the winged sun disc of Egyptian origin hovering over his head.

In his famous rock inscription of Bisitun (Behistun), Darius the Great emphasised his adherence to a simple ethical code, to cling to the Truth and to abjure the Lie, and to be a good horseman. Whether or not Darius was an adherent, the religion of Zoroaster, as well as the associated cult of fire, had its beginnings well back in early Iranian history.

Early Asian Cultures

China

During the pre-Xia period the foundations of Chinese traditions of ceramics, decoration, calligraphy and pictorial art appear to have been laid down. Pottery was a kiln-fired red ware brush-painted in black or purple with stylised human and animal forms and geometric designs. Polished stone and bone tools were produced, including a variety of axes, hoes and knives. Textile crafts included the making of mats and baskets, and weaving, possibly including silk. Burial was in cemeteries accompanied by food and pottery. The subsequent Xia period was distinguished by the production of wheel-turned, thin-walled pottery with a plain, black burnished surface. Crafts diversified to include jade carving, and the manufacture of weapons. Literacy was limited to scapulimancy, the art of inscribing and interpreting oracle bones.

Shang pottery mainly took the form of grey-walled vessels, but some pots were manufactured from white kaolin, a precursor of porcelain. Bronze ritual vessels were cast in multiple clay moulds, and were elaborately ornamented in deep relief modelled on the inner face of the moulds. Both crafts used techniques of high-temperature firing under controlled conditions. Sculpture featured kneeling or squatting human forms, animals and monsters in jade, limestone and marble. Large numbers of weapons were produced including lightly-built wooden chariots with fine, spoked wheels. Bronze was used as a decorative finish for chariots, harness, weapons and armour. The art of scapulimancy continued to be practised. Oracle bones were inscribed with phonetic, ideographic and pictographic characters. Tortoise carapaces were also used in divination. Ancestor worship was practised, and religious practices combined animistic elements with ceremonies designed to buttress the institution of kingship. The Shang period was marked by an elaborate funerary architecture, at least for high-ranking members of society.

Under the Zhou the basic forms of pottery, bronze-working, art, sculpture and weapons found in the Shang period were continued. The range of pottery styles was smaller, and explicit human and animal motifs were replaced by geometrical figures. Bronze bells were used in ceremonial music. Lacquer work and iron tools came into widespread use. Literacy expanded, and the teachings of philosophers like Confucius and Mencius in provincial academies laid the foundations for the education of an official bureaucracy which encouraged social stability through doctrines emphasising tolerance, deference and accord. Little artistic or literary development took place under the Qin which was an intensely practical regime, during which evidence suggests intellectuals were persecuted.

The Indus Civilisation

Cultural uniformity throughout the Harappan realm was encouraged by a standardised system of weights and measures. The main linear units were the foot (330–335 mm) and the cubit (515–528 mm). The granaries of Harappa were ten cubits wide and thirty cubits long. The system seems to have been based on multiples of sixteen. Writing extended to the use of pictographic inscriptions on steatite seals. These have never been deciphered but seem to have been of commercial use in identifying goods, rather than of literary significance. Seal and stamp carvings, although produced for mundane purposes, were delicate and refined. The seals were normally square, varying from 20 mm to 45 mm wide, with a perforated boss at the back for hanging and handling. Decorative motifs on seals included intaglio designs depicting men, animals and grotesques as well as pictographs. The same care was expended upon the production of jewellery – mainly bangles and nose-ornaments, and leisure objects such as gaming pieces. Pottery was wheel-turned pinkish ware using red slip, decorated in black with a variety of geometric and stylised designs. Stone sculpture was limited to a few representations of men or gods, frequently in a squatting position, and a few bronzes have been recovered, mainly of dancing girls and buffalo. Popular sculpture was in terracotta, notably of men and buffalo, but large numbers of standing females heavily ornamented with jewellery have been found, as well as toy carts and human and animal grotesques. The hallmark of Harappan craft industry was the efficient mass-production of artefacts. There is little evidence that the Harappans had a highly evolved religious life. No major temple or shrine-like building groups have been found, nor any material evidence of household ritual. Burial took the form of inhumation in cemetery sites.

Greece and the Greek World

The ritual of prehistoric religion in Greece cannot be properly reconstructed on the archaeological evidence, and modern interpretations are inevitably controversial. In Crete there was a contrast between ritual in the palaces, which included processions and bull-leaping in the courtyards, and ritual in the rural shrines, on mountain tops and, above all, associated with sacred caves. Figurines have been identified as goddesses, while representations of bulls and bull-leaping, together with later Greek legends of the Minotaur, emphasise the place that animals had in Cretan cults.

On the mainland, shrines and cult rooms have been identified at Mycenae, Tiryns and elsewhere. Small shrines outside the palace areas, and often in the vicinity of the gates, suggest a protecting role. It is quite uncertain whether or not, among the main rooms of the palace, the megaron and its hearth served a religious function (despite the superficial similarity in plan to the later temples of the Classical period).

In Classical Greece, the polis, the city-state community, was of paramount importance and the individual was subordinated to it. Maintenance of the community depended on the maintenance of the families, the households (oikoi). All aspects of life were under the protection of the gods, who were regarded as all-powerful, but similar to ordinary humans in their passions, desires and appetites. The origins of Greek religion are lost in the remoteness of prehistory, though it is clear that there is no single line of development. Despite hostility toward innovation, religious belief was constantly changing and developing, reflecting changes in human circumstances. New cults were introduced from time to time, so long as they did not challenge the essential polytheistic, anthropomorphic nature of religious belief, while existing cults developed or changed their emphasis in response to human needs.

The essential concept in religious practice was that of contract, of obligation and the paying of obligations. Humans – primarily as a community – called on the gods for protection, and made offerings to the gods to secure this. Foremost was the regular ritual of sacrifice, the offering of food, and religious practices centred on this. Sacrifices took place throughout the year, but there was always one principal annual ceremony or festival for each god in every community, in the sanctuary set aside for that cult. The offering included animals, which were brought to the sanctuary and slaughtered. Those parts – generally the less edible – offered to the god were burned on an altar; the remaining meat was cooked, rather than burned, and distributed to human worshippers, who consumed it in the sanctuary (there was frequently a prohibition on the removal of sacrificial meat from the sanctuary). Other offerings comprised durable objects, essentially those whose acquisition was desirable in ordinary life. Statues commemorating periods of service to the gods, as priest or priestess, might be set up; not only did they commemorate former service, but continued it, the statue constituting a perpetual servant. The sanctuary was the estate of the god: he required a house where he might live and keep his belongings safe.

Thus a Greek sanctuary comprised essentially an open space, marked off as the god's property but not necessarily closed off from the outside world by a physical barrier. There was an entrance, so that one knew the point at which one left the mundane world and entered the god's property. There had to be enough space to accommodate the worshippers at the festival. Some cults had limited support, but the chief protecting deities of the city-state might attract the entire population, so large sanctuaries were needed. Cult focused on the open-air altar, at which the sacrifice was made. This was the only real essential. The god was represented in the sanctuary by an image (which by the Classical period generally meant a realistic, representational statue); this might be wooden (the earliest images seem to have been invariably of wood) or of stone or bronze, while the most expensive were made from plaques of gold and ivory attached to a wooden frame. Some shelter was necessary, particularly for wooden and gold and ivory images. Whether this reached a level of architectural interest depended on various factors – the importance of the cult, the availability of funds in the worshipping community and so forth. Buildings were themselves offerings, and there was therefore pressure on the worshipping community to provide them, as magnificently executed and decorated as possible, in order to please the god. It was this that led to the building of temples, rather than any functional purpose as congregational buildings. The earliest sanctuaries had none – they were merely places for festival and sacrifice, and even the altar need be no more than the pile of ashes left by former sacrifice. In the Dark Age, shrine or temple buildings were virtually non-existent (there is one temple-like building at Lefkandi on the island of Euboea, of about 1000 BC, but this is an embellishment of a grave, not a structure, it would seem, dedicated to a god). Otherwise the building of temples is first securely attested in the eighth century BC, at the period when east Mediterranean influences were making themselves felt on Greek society and its artistic achievement.

Other categories of building responded to the particular conventions of Greek society. Political systems depended on gatherings. This idea developed at village level, and a place had to be provided where the citizen body might be gathered together, if necessary, to make the vital decisions on war and peace. The gathering place might be a field outside, but with the growth of organised towns, the central gathering place or agora was an essential element in the town plan (and had to be large enough to accommodate, in theory at least, all the adult male population). The agora was essentially a space, not a building, though the structures required for the functioning of the polis might be placed at its edge. Such buildings did not have to be as magnificent as the temples, or as solidly constructed. In the wealthier cities stone buildings were put up, but even Athens in the fifth century constructed buildings of unbaked mud brick in its agora.

Public life was for the male citizens. Women lived a more secluded life, mostly in the privacy of the home (though they attended the religious festivals). If anything, restrictions on their lives seem to have become more severe in the historical period, and the forms of domestic architecture reflect this. Houses turned their backs on the outside world, looking inward to the enclosed courtyard. Even inside the house, there was a division between the men's room (andron) where male guests participated in dinner and drinking parties, and the women's quarters, to which the female members of the family were banished on these occasions.

These circumstances created the essential architectural principles which are discernible in the arrangements of a Classical Greek city. The first, the temple principle, is that the simple rectangular, roofed structure – in essence an embellished and improved hut – was built as an offering to the god and was designed to be admired from outside. Its architectural interest is therefore concentrated on the exterior. The second is that of building around a space or courtyard – an architectural effect which can be appreciated only from within the court. The enclosing structures need not be continuous – a series of separate buildings, perhaps – but very often they were given porticoes on the side that faced the court, the tendency being to run porticoes or colonnades continuously along each side of the court, with only occasional gaps or, eventually, with no gaps at all. These enclosed, colonnaded courts are a particular feature of Hellenistic cities.

Resources

Egypt and the Ancient Near East

Only truly local materials were available for building purposes in the Near East, including Egypt, from prehistoric times until the stage (at varying dates in each region) when the necessary political advances had occurred so that long-distance trade and the extraction of resources became possible. The labour for construction must be assumed to have been local except for documented instances when foreign craftsmen are known to have been brought in to execute the work.

In the alluvial plains of the Tigris and Euphrates stone and timber suitable for building were rare or unobtainable unless imported. There was, however, a plentiful supply of soil which, mixed with water into mud, poured into moulds and either sun-dried or kiln-fired, provided bricks for every kind of structure. Kiln-fired bricks were used only for drains, pavements and the facing of certain major buildings, such as the ziggurat at Ur; it was not until the Neo-Babylonian period, in the sixth century BC, that kiln-fired brick became the standard building material in Mesopotamia. The Assyrian kings were much concerned to receive reports of the harvest, partly because of its direct effect on the royal building programme for the coming year, since without enough straw to mix with the mud, bricks could not be made, as the Hebrews pointed out in their well-known complaint to Pharaoh. The Assyrians were masters of the art of deploying large labour forces to build new palaces, temples and defensive walls or to repair old ones: it has been estimated that mud bricks could be laid at the rate of one hundred per man per day. Mud brick is the most important of ancient Near Eastern building materials, because of its ubiquity. Many sites in the highland zone might seem to have been built only of stone but excavation often reveals remains of mud-brick superstructure above the masonry, as in the Urartian fortresses. The precise measurements of mud bricks tended to become standardised for each region in a given period, the limit on size being the weight readily handled by one man, as is still the case today.

Reeds, papyrus (a plant now almost extinct) and palm-branch ribs, plastered over with clay, were tractable materials readily available in the Nile valley, where they were used in the buildings of predynastic Egypt. A roughly comparable tradition flourished in Mesopotamia, particularly in the Sumerian south, where it is perpetuated to this day by the Marsh Arabs, who construct large halls of reeds and live on low platforms very close to water level, much as depicted in the palace at Nineveh in reliefs of Sennacherib's largely abortive campaign into the marshes near the head of the Gulf. Reed matting was used between mud-brick courses as reinforcement in Mesopotamia and Egypt alike.

One material available in Mesopotamia and the neighbouring plain of Susa (in due course the heart of the kingdom of Elam) was bitumen, which was obtainable from natural springs. It was first used in Neolithic times as a mastic, especially for setting flint sickle-blades into hafts of bone. Eventually its water-proofing qualities were realised, and it was employed for lining drains and to reduce the erosion of mud-brick walls.

In Egypt abundant labour was available for the transportation of stone blocks from quarry to building site, by raft on the Nile and laboriously up ramps from the river bank, especially in the summer season of the annual inundation, without resort to slavery.

Egypt shared with Mesopotamia a lack of timber for major building work, though the date palm could be used for houses, largely for roofing. From the earliest dynasties the Egyptian kings imported cedar-wood by ship from Byblos, the ancient port just north of Beirut, for building purposes, coffins and some ship-building, though papyrus was the local material. The cedar forests of the Lebanon mountains were thus exploited for the Egyptian market, while the rulers of Mesopotamia from the middle of the third millennium BC onwards obtained their cedar from the Amanus range, close to the north-east corner of the Mediterranean. The Assyrian kings listed with pride and in considerable detail the materials used for the construction, embellishment and furnishing of their palaces and temples: cedar and fir were favoured for roof beams and doors. Cedar was used by Darius the Great and his successors in roofing the columned halls of Parsa (Persepolis).

Foreign peoples might be employed, more or less forcibly, by an imperial power for the construction of great public buildings, especially since Near Eastern kings were always anxious to complete their temples or tombs in their own lifetime. The Assyrian king Sennacherib recounts his removal of over 200,000 people from Judah: the fate of such deportees is vividly portrayed at Nineveh in the relief showing workmen toiling up the steep side of the foundation platform of the new 'Palace Without a Rival', to empty their baskets of earth and rubble, watched over by the royal guard. A clay tablet found in a palace of Darius at Susa mentions masons from Ionia and Sardis and woodworkers also from Sardis, making inlays; the Babylonians were still the most skilled workers in mud brick. Cambyses is said to have deported many craftsmen from Egypt.

Early Asian Cultures

China

Throughout the prehistoric periods, local materials were used in construction. Mud walls, reinforced with timber rods, were replaced by compacted earth walls during the Shang dynasty. From the Shang dynasty onwards, rammed-earth platforms supported timber-framed buildings of post and beam construction, with roofs of thatch or reeds. The use of stone was restricted to column footings, pavements and defences. Bricks and tiles do not appear to have been in use before the Zhou period. From the Shang dynasty onwards, conscription provided the labour resources needed for large building projects: it has been estimated that the walls of Zhengzhou took a labour force of 10,000 approximately eighteen years to build. The excavation of shaft-tombs also demanded massive labour resources: the digging of a grave shaft is thought to have taken up to 7000 days.

India

The Indus basin was rich in timber for building and fuel, but there was no local building stone, and baked or kiln-fired brick was the standard building material. The discovery of fired brick played an important role in Harappan urban development, particularly in counteracting the effects of flooding. Harappan architecture has been described by archaeologists as drab and utilitarian, but it required large numbers of skilled bricklayers. It has been suggested that the facades of Harappan buildings may have been elaborated in timber which has not survived.

Greece and the Greek World

The Greek world in general has abundant sources of high quality building stone, particularly limestone and marble, which can be quarried without undue difficulty. There are good sources of clay. In much of the Greek mainland timber is by comparison scarce or stunted in growth. The characteristic trees are pine and cypress; substantial hardwoods are not available. There is thus a severe restriction on building imposed by the difficulty of roofing wide spaces. The greatest width that can be spanned without intermediate support is about 10 m (33 ft); only the most important buildings, for which timber could be imported, such as the Parthenon, exceed this, and even then only by one or two metres. The shortage of timber for firing meant also that bricks were of unbaked clay: fired terracotta was employed only for tiles (which might also be made of marble on important buildings) and the decorative revetments.

The volcanic activity in the Aegean (Santorini), Sicily (Etna), and southern Italy (Vesuvius) indicates the presence of metamorphic rocks; the other contributory geological factor is that of sedimentary deposition. Thus, much of Greece is hard limestone or marble, in various forms, though there are other areas (noticeably Olympia) where the rock is a poor quality conglomerate. In general it was the hard limestones and marbles which were exploited for building purposes, and created the distinctive appearance of Greek architecture. There are many types of marble, generally variegated and often coloured. Coloured marble was used for the architecture of the mainland in the prehistoric period, and was again much appreciated by Roman architects, by whom it was exported over a wide area; Classical Greek architecture preferred, almost exclusively, the white marbles, that of the islands of Paros and Naxos being first exploited in the seventh and sixth centuries BC for both architecture and sculpture. (As the quarries are close to the sea it was easily transported to other parts of Greece.) In the fifth century BC the Athenians developed the quarries of Mount Pentelikos (Pentelic marble). There are numerous other sources of white marble, especially in Asia Minor.

Proconnesian marble from the Propontis (Sea of Marmara) was exported widely; other types tended to be used more in their immediate locality. Gypsum was quarried in Crete and used, in the form of saw-cut blocks, for walls in the buildings of the prehistoric period.

The western Greek communities in Sicily and Italy, and those in Cyrenaica, did not have marble, and their architecture is invariably created in limestone; even in Aegean Greece limestone is more commonly used than marble, particularly for the more mundane structures. Limestone was also burnt to provide mortar, though in most parts of Greece the relative shortage of timber made this an expensive process, and its use was limited to providing a fine finish (mixed with marble dust) for limestone buildings of importance. It was used also as a hydraulic cement, for submerged works and industrial structures. There are good sources of clay which were exploited for unbaked brick, and for terracotta for tiles and decorative revetments.

Skilled architects and craftsmen were in demand, and frequently travelled from state to state. Systems of employment and methods of payment in the early period are uncertain; coined money was not developed until the sixth century BC, but by the fifth century there are records giving the wages or piecework rates for builders. Financial resources thus became an important factor in building, whether provided by the state, the sanctuaries themselves, or private individuals. Architects and craftsmen usually were free men, though not necessarily citizens of the community in which they undertook work. Slave labour was employed and there is evidence in the building records of the Erechtheion at Athens of payments to slave owners for the work done. It is wrong to give this undue emphasis and there is no evidence for the corvée, or forced labour, in Classical Greek building, though it may have been used in the prehistoric period.

An important factor in Greek building was the part played by the financial guarantor, who came between the employer (the state, or religious officials) and the builder. This role was regarded as a duty to be undertaken on behalf of the community by its wealthy members. It was their responsibility to see that the work contracted for in all aspects of building, from the quarrying and gathering of material to the finishing touches, was properly carried out; the guarantor, not the contractor or craftsmen, paid any penalty for inadequate work.

Building Techniques and Processes

Egypt and the Ancient Near East

The Natufians used simple drystone techniques to a limited extent, but building was predominantly in mud brick. After careful selection and preparation of the clay, the main bricks were formed by hand or occasionally moulded and then sun-dried; alternatively the clay was used as a plastic material by building up wet mud in courses and allowing each to dry before adding the next. Fixed features such as storage bins, platforms, hearths and seats were modelled *in situ*. Occasionally the mud was mixed with straw, and foundations were sometimes of stone to ensure that the building did not stand on a wet base. Roofs were generally flat, and made of timber beams covered with matting plastered with clay. Thatched roofs were used sometimes and walls buttressed to support the roof timbers. Doorways were lined with timber reveals and thresholds. Plastered floors and walls were common. Mud or lime plaster was finished in a variety of ways including painting, burnishing or setting with terrazzo.

Egypt made the transition from insubstantial vegetable materials like reeds, papyrus, palm fronds and matting to the tectonic forms of mud brick and stone in Late Gerzean times, possibly influenced by contact with Mesopotamia. Timber and matting linings were used in grave construction.

In each region techniques and processes developed through a blend of local resources. Care was often lavished more on decoration and finish than on structure: this is especially true of Egypt, where metallurgy lagged behind that of Asia – bronze did not appear until the Middle Kingdom. In a sense, Egypt also lagged behind in building technology. For example, although in the roughly finished stone-work of the Royal Cemetery at Ur the true arch and vault appeared, they seem to have been unknown to the stonemasons of Egypt of the same period. However, there is no denying the superior stone-dressing and sheer mass of the contemporary pyramids of Gizeh.

In pre-dynastic Egypt there is evidence that bundles of reeds were set vertically side by side and lashed to bundles placed horizontally near the top, to make walls or fences. Alternatively, palm-leaf ribs were planted in the ground at short intervals, with others laced in a diagonal network across them and secured to a horizontal member near the top, the whole being finally daubed with mud. The pressure of flat reed-and-mud roofs against the tops of the wall reeds may have produced the characteristic Egyptian 'gorge' cornice, while the 'kheker' cresting less frequently appearing in later architecture may have originated in the terminal tufts of a papyrus-stalk wall (p. 41B). The horizontal binders and angle bundles survived in the roll moulding of stone cornices and wall angles of the historical period (p. 41J).

Dearth of pictorial representations as much as meagreness of archaeological evidence in the form of building remains makes it harder to describe with any certainty the earliest building techniques of the Near East outside Egypt. The round houses of Pre-Pottery 'Neolithic A' Jericho, three millennia older than the earliest village remains in the Nile valley, doubtless had flimsy domical roofs. At Catal Hüyük a typical Near Eastern conservatism is in evidence. The original purely timber construction survived in the timber-frame houses and shrines revealed by the excavations, and only in the latest levels was it supplanted by construction entirely in mud brick.

The essentially arcuated architecture of Mesopotamia was the outcome of the constraints imposed by the structural demands of brick vaulting (p. 25E). Rooms had to be narrow in relation to their length, with massively thick walls: a similar constraint applied in the Assyrian palaces as a result of the use of cedar beams for roof-construction. The true arch with radiating voussoirs was known by the third millennium BC. For want of stone of the right quality and size, free-standing columns were not much used, although very massive examples occurred as early as the Late Uruk period (mid-fourth millennium BC) in the Pillar Hall of Eanna IV, the main sacred and governmental precinct of Warka (Uruk), in the Sumerian homeland; and there are a few examples in Late Assyrian and Neo-Babylonian work. Even in prehistoric times in the Near East some temples were built with quite thin mud-brick walls, reinforced by buttresses, sometimes of elaborately recessed design, allowing shadows to break up the harsh glare of the sun. This architectural tradition in mud brick was somehow transmitted, by a route as yet unknown, to Egypt at the beginning of dynastic times, when there are other parallels with Late Uruk-period Mesopotamia, to form the prototype of the serekh (palace) facade of the tombs of the Archaic period (Dynasties I-II), and thus also the public buildings in the Nile valley, unfortunately no longer preserved.

In Egypt, sun-dried mud-brick walling never went out of use; it was only for the finest buildings of religious character that cut stone became normal. Even palaces remained relatively frail. For stability, walls of Egyptian buildings diminished course by course towards the top, chiefly because of the alternate shrinkage and expansion of the soil caused by the annual inundations. Since the inner face of the walls had to be vertical for ordinary convenience, it was the outer face only which showed this inward inclination, or 'batter', which remained one of the

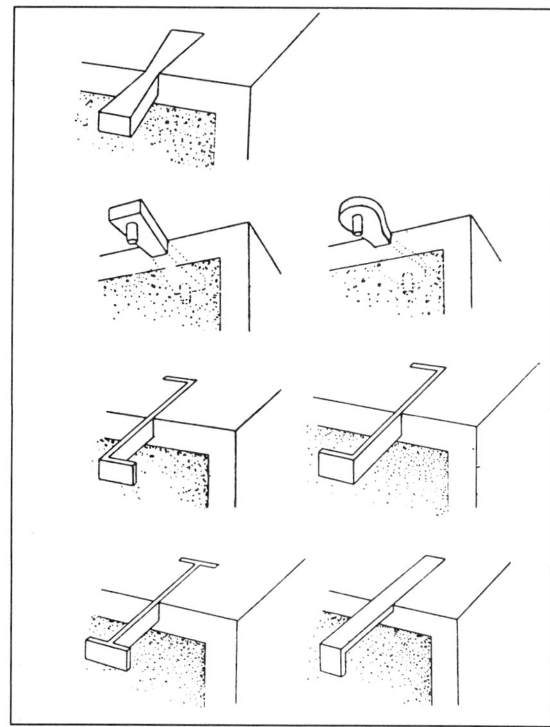

Various forms of clamp-iron set in lead, except top left, which is generally of wood. See p.24

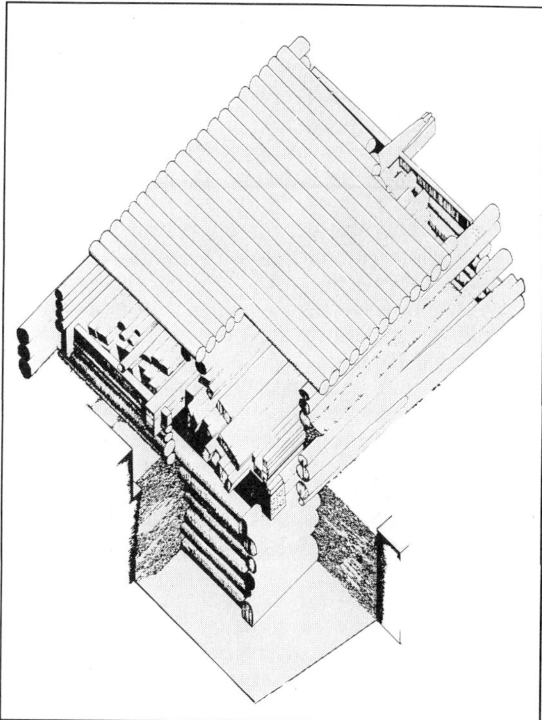

Tumulus MM: isometric view of tomb chamber, from NW. See p.24

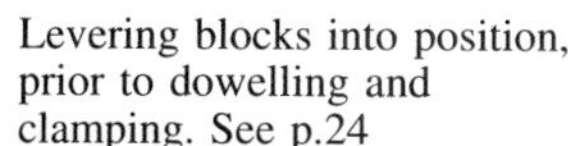

Levering blocks into position, prior to dowelling and clamping. See p.24

principal characteristics of Egyptian architecture whether in brick or stone. Sometimes fibre or reed mats were placed between the brick courses at intervals up the walls to reinforce them, particularly at the angels; and a late development was the use of sagging concave courses, for alternate lengths of a long wall, built in advance of the intervening stretches. This allowed the drying out of the inner brickwork of walls such as those round the great temple enclosures which were between 9 m (30 ft) and 24.5 m (80 ft) thick. Though the true arch was never used in Egyptian monumental stonework, the principle became known and there are brick vaults as early as the beginning of the Third Dynasty. Frequently the arch rings were built in sloping courses, so that no temporary support centering was needed; usually there were two or more arched rings arranged concentrically, the one lying upon the other.

Many of the building techniques and processes used by the stonemasons of the Old Kingdom in Egypt were demonstrated in the construction of the royal pyramids. They were built on the bedrock which was levelled to receive them, and the sides scrupulously oriented with the cardinal points. Pyramids were built in a series of concentric sloping slices or layers around a steep pyramidal core: this method of ensuring downward, centripetal thrust achieved the stability essential for these massive structures, although apparently not before at least one serious mishap. The whole mass of the pyramid was first constructed in step-like tiers, until the true pyramidal form was completed. The steps were then filled with packing blocks and brought to their ultimate shape with finely dressed facings, placed at the chosen angle of inclination. The final meticulous dressing of the finished faces was inevitably from top to bottom. The blocks of the Great Pyramid of Cheops at Gizeh, near Cairo, weighing on average 2500 kg (2½ tons), are thickly bedded in lime mortar, used as a lubricant during fixing rather than as an adhesive. Corbelling and flat stone beams were used to cover the interior chambers and in no two pyramids were the same.

The Egyptians did not know of the pulley: their principal tool for raising and turning stone blocks was the lever. To transport blocks overland, wooden sledges were used, with or without the aid of rollers. Blocks of stone for the pyramids were hauled up great broad-topped sloping ramps of sand or earth, reinforced with crude brick walls. The Egyptian mason had at his disposal copper chisels with flanged blades and saws which were work-hardened and therefore brittle: neither bronze nor iron tools were available.

In the temples of the New Kingdom, with their pylons and columned halls, there is considerable evidence of haste, especially from the time of Rameses II onwards; less care was taken with foundations and with finishing than in earlier times. Perhaps the most vivid evidence of sheer effort is in the obelisks – vast granite monoliths laboriously quarried at Aswan by the patient use of wedges, pounders and fire. Sandstone from the quarries at Gebel Silsileh was the standard building material for the temples of Upper Egypt. It was less suitable for relief-carving than limestone but capable of spanning greater widths for roofing purposes. The influence of the less durable forms of Egyptian architecture is clearly demonstrated both by the imitation of corner and cross-poles in the pylons and by their cornices, derived from the bending of palm leaves above the cross-pole, metamorphosed into the toros moulding. Egyptian columns likewise have vegetable origins, their shafts indicative of bundles of plant stems, gathered in at the base, and with capitals seemingly derived from the lotus bud (p. 41G), the papyrus flower (p. 41C) or the ubiquitous palm. As an economy of material and labour, no doubt, the massive roofing slabs of the New Kingdom temples, at first laid on edge for maximum strength, came to be laid flat. By the reign of Rameses II, the elegant columns had become bulbous monstrosities covered with inscriptions which detracted from their essential form.

The Canaanites and their Phoenician descendants in the Levant were skilled stonemasons, whose carefully dressed and finely jointed masonry laid in even, horizontal courses is first manifest on a large scale in the thirteenth-century BC palace at Ugarit (Ras Shamra), the prosperous commercial city on the Syrian coast. The same fine quality of masonry occurs at Samaria in its first two phases at the time of Omri and Ahab (*c.* 880–852 BC).

The Anatolian tradition of building was radically different from those of Mesopotamia and the Levant, largely owing to the ample supplies of timber lengths and girths no longer available today after centuries of deforestation. Stone was used for footings, timber for reinforcement or to build a structural framework, and mud brick for walls in one and the same building. An echo of vanished wooden structures is discernible in the massive tomb chambers of the burial mounds of the city of Gordion, capital of the Phrygian kingdom. The double-pitched roof of the chamber of the great Tumulus MM (p. 23) was supported by three gables, one in the centre and one at each end, its planks carefully squared and mortised. The walls of this tomb chamber were enclosed in an outer casing of juniper logs, two feet square in section, with a layer of rubble outside the logs supported by a strong retaining wall. A capping of stones and a massive tumulus mound of clay were superimposed and survived till excavated: this, the largest of over seventy tumuli at Gordion, stood about 50 m (166 ft) high. The workmanship was native Phrygian or north-west Anatolian of the Iron Age (*c.* 700 BC) but the tradition of burial in tumuli derived from south Russia.

The standard of dressing of masonry in Urartu varied widely, the finest ashlar being almost entirely

A. Mohenjodaro: brick wall of house. See p.26

B. Mohenjodaro: Great Granary: upper part of podium. See p.26

C. Mohenjodaro: drain of great bath; corbelled vault. See p.26

D. Mohenjodaro: street with drains. See p.26

E. The palace at Ctesiphon. See p.22

limited to temples, built most often of basalt, which was favoured also for inscriptions and reliefs. At least one temple retains its complete stone footings but none of the mud-brick superstructures survive. One distinctive technique widespread in Urartu was the cutting of foundation ledges, resembling steps, in the steep rock hillsides, to provide a firm foundation for the masonry. The construction of massive terraces was an essential part of the building of Urartian fortresses and citadels, and demanded a large labour force. Even in the best-quality works fortress walls were built with slightly irregular courses, each block being individually cut to fit its neighbours. No doubt iron tools were employed: chisel marks are to be seen over much of Van citadel. There are, moreover, Assyrian references to cutting channels through the rock with iron picks.

The background to Achaemenid Persian columnar architecture is now believed to be in Median sites and even earlier and further north at Hasanlu in the Iron II period (*c.* 1100–800 BC). Wider horizons are also evident at Pasargadae, where foreign stonemasons were undoubtedly employed by Cyrus the Great and his immediate successors. Rusticated masonry is a feature of the great terrace of the citadel (Takht-i-Suleiman), and another characteristic of Achaemenid construction was the use of swallowtail clamps of lead and iron, as structurally superfluous reinforcement for the great blocks, accurately cut, smoothly dressed and laid without mortar. At least two technical features of the stonework at Pasargadae point to Greek inspiration (p. 8). There are traces, on the early works at Pasargadae, of the use of chisels with plain cutting edges; but thereafter, from the accession of Darius the Great (552 BC), the multi-toothed chisel left its imprint on the masonry of Pasargadae and likewise at Persepolis, having first appeared in Greece some fifty years earlier.

Early Asian Cultures

China

Chinese buildings of the prehistoric period were characterised by a tripartite division into rammed-earth podium, timber-columniated superstructure and pitched and gabled roof. After the Shang period all important buildings were set upon rammed-earth podia, built up in layers 80–100 mm (3–4 in) thick to a height of about 600 mm (2 ft), which supported a superstructure of simple, single-storey post and beam construction, infilled with lightweight screens. Separately-roofed galleries surrounded pavilion-like buildings with pitched and gabled roofs. Tiles replaced thatch during the Zhou period, but the roofs of Chinese buildings had not yet acquired their characteristic curved form. Ridge and eaves, however, were decorated with ceramic tiles depicting birds and mythical beasts. It has been suggested that terreplein building, in which a stepped core of earth was surrounded by galleries, was used to give an appearance of height.

India

Bricks were moulded or sawn and laid with alternate courses of headers and stretchers (p. 25A,B). A standard sized 280 mm × 140 mm × 70 mm (11 in × 5½ in × 3 in) brick was used. The use of unbaked brick was confined to the brick platforms upon which the major buildings were supported. Some of them were laced with timbers. The true arch was unknown, but corbelled arches in brick were frequent (p. 25C). Internally, mud plaster was used as a finish.

Harappan bathrooms had fine floors of sawn brick. Flat roofs were constructed in timber with square-section members spanning up to 4 m (13 ft). The large public granaries of Mohenjodaro were built entirely of timber resting on massive brick podia. Intricate water supply and sewerage systems were built in the metropolitan centres (p. 25C,D). Covered baked-brick drains with neat inspection holes were characteristic of the settlements of the Indus basin, as were public wells, which were executed in fine brickwork.

Greece and the Greek World

Cut stone was used in the prehistoric period, in Crete (where soft gypsum, which can be sawn to shape, was often preferred) and on the mainland, for important buildings, palaces and substantial houses, and the built 'tholos' tombs. Timber frameworks were normal. In the Dark Age all knowledge of sophisticated building technique appears to have been lost, and the few buildings discovered have unworked stone footings with mud-brick superstructures and simple wooden posts supporting roofs which were probably covered with reed thatch. Similar techniques were used in the earliest temples of the eighth century. But development in building technique was considerable during the seventh century. Quarried and shaped stone was used in substantial buildings (for example, the Temple of Poseidon at Isthmia, built before the middle of the seventh century), and terracotta tiles and revetments were developed. In the second half of the century the Greeks secured direct access to Egypt, and thus acquired knowledge of Egyptian stone-working techniques. It became possible to quarry large pieces of stone for monolithic columns, and to turn the blocks on a lathe to secure a truly circular section.

By the Classical period the processes of design and construction had become traditional and fixed. It is doubtful whether drawings were made in detail.

Papyrus was limited in size, and expensive, while scaled measuring instruments were not known. It might have been possible to make general drawings and plans on waxed board, but since buildings were traditional in type these were not really necessary. It is more likely that the design was created *in situ*, by measuring out the foundations from which the remaining dimensions could be calculated, in accordance with traditional proportions, though it is clear these were gradually modified. More intricate details would be executed on full-scale models, from which the measurements would be taken (by dividers rather than rulers) for repetition during construction.

Blocks of stone were ordered from the quarry, to be delivered trimmed to size and, where possible, shape (the function of the blocks having been specified). Columns, which had been made with monolithic shafts in the sixth century, were built up from the separate drums dowelled together (except for small-scale work) in the fifth and subsequent centuries. In the quarries at Agrileza which supplied the temple of Poseidon at Sounion it can be seen that column drums were cut to their circular section during the quarrying, rather than turned. Surfaces were left rough (hammer faced) to avoid damage in transit. The blocks were given their final preparation at the building site, where the resulting chippings are often found. Contact surfaces were given final and accurate treatment before being placed in position. Overall dimensions of the building and its elements were worked to a fine degree of accuracy, but there are variations in the measurements of constituent parts; for example, blocks in a wall course may vary from each other in length, but not height or width. Non-contact surfaces were left with a preliminary finish only, except for vital guidelines for future reference which were fully finished. Concealed vertical surfaces (between blocks in a course) were slightly hollowed on their central parts (anathyrosis) to reduce the cost of making an accurate, smoothed contact face.

Blocks were relatively large and retained their position by their own mass and weight; it was not necessary to fix them together in any way, and, in general, foundations and stepped bases were not fixed. Above the base, in important buildings such as temples, it was usual to fix the blocks to each other, to guard against the dangers of earthquake, though the systems employed would never guarantee safety against major tremors. Blocks in wall courses were clamped together with iron clamps set in lead (which was poured round them) (p. 23). Generally there was one clamp at each end, though larger blocks might be given pairs of clamps. Courses were dowelled to each other with rectangular dowels, placed at the centre of the block in the lower course, and at the junction of two blocks in the upper. Column drums (and the capitals) were fixed together with metal dowels set in wood, or leaded in. Blocks were lifted by cranes and pulleys, and then levered into their final positions with crowbars (p. 23). Some entablatures, particularly in the larger temples, were of considerable dimension and were often made from double stonework, a facer and a backer, or even three blocks, with an additional block between facer and backer, as in the Parthenon. Walls were usually constructed of single blocks giving the required thickness, but in Hellenistic times the architects of Pergamum constructed walls with inner and outer faces, leaving a space between them which was filled with dry rubble. Single walls were normally formed in Classical temples from ashlar blocks of regular height (isodomic), but varied patterns, particularly alternating high and low courses (pseudisodomic), are known: for example, the temple of Poseidon at Sounion. In their rubble-filled walls Pergamene architects usually alternated the upright pairs of facing stones with low throughstones (headers).

Roofs normally depended on wooden beams and rafters, which were cut to square sections. There are a few buildings with roofs of wide span (the fourth temple of Athena at Delphi, the large dining rooms in the palace at Vergina in Macedon), where beams were made from two long timbers fixed side by side to each other. The ridge beam and other longitudinal beams were supported either on props or on the walls or colonnades, and there is no evidence for the use of fixed, triangular trusses. Roofs may have been fully boarded. Tiles were not nailed in position, but rested under their own weight; it follows that roof pitches were always low, usually about 13–17°.

The ceilings of temples were constructed over the horizontal cross beams. In major temples the cella ceilings were invariably wooden and are totally lost, but that between walls and outer colonnade would be stone, with coffer grids resting on stone beams, apparently recalling wooden forms. Exceptionally, the halls of the gateway building (Propylaea) to the Athenian Acropolis had stone beams and ceilings. Here the span and weight were so great that iron reinforcing beams were set in the marble, but this is unique.

Only after the roof was complete would the finishing processes be applied. Some carved decoration (pediment groups or metope panels in Doric buildings, for example) would be carved on the ground, and incorporated in the structure when finished. Other elements, such as decorative mouldings, were only roughed out during construction, and finished off *in situ*. Finally, the non-contact surfaces on walls and bases, which had been left with a protecting unfinished surface during construction, were carved and polished to the final surfaces and levels indicated by the guidelines. Thus an important Greek building, such as a major temple, was carved into its final form. Stone was selected for the quality it would give to the final finish of the building, and for this purpose marble was preferred. Stone of inferior quality was finished in stucco in imitation of polished marble, and stucco was also used to conceal unbaked mud brick.

Classical, fifth-century Greek architects preferred to work their blocks so finely that the hairline jointing between them was hardly visible: the impression desired was that walls appeared to be made out of solid single slabs of stone. In contrast, individual blocks might be emphasised by drafting their edges, perhaps leaving the inner section with a less finely worked surface. Later architecture took this form of decoration to extremes by leaving the main field of the block quite rusticated. The lower courses of a wall, the dado, orthostates and covering courses, had surfaces projecting slightly from the plane formed by the remainder of the wall, an echo of the contrast between stone footing and mud brick.

Colour work rarely survives. Traces of it were noted on the Parthenon in the nineteenth century, though the colour tones were faded and distorted; perfectly preserved colour work survives more considerably in the Macedonian tombs. The colours – washes of simple, rather harsh tones or in detailed patterns – were not applied to the total surface, but only to emphasise details, such as mouldings, friezes, and the separate rhythm of triglyph and metope in Doric architecture. Stuccoed wall surfaces were usually given monochrome washes, generally an ochre. It has been argued that even the marble walls of buildings such as the Parthenon were given an exterior ochre wash, perhaps to tone down the dazzling brightness of the newly polished stone, but this is not certain. In Doric it was the entablature which was painted. The taenia and regulae of the architrave were painted red; triglyphs were generally blue. Mouldings, which in Ionic were given carved patterns, in Doric had similar patterns in paint. The band over the frieze in the Macedonian tombs was picked out with a golden-yellow meander. This paintwork serves to emphasise the articulation of the different elements in the design. In addition to this, terracotta revetments, particularly the gutters (cymas), provided a strong contrast to the lighter tones of the stonework. It must be remembered that this colour work, though now lost from most buildings, was a vital ingredient in Classical design. It occasionally passed into the stonework itself. The Propylaea and the Erechtheion on the Athenian acropolis made use of a dark grey limestone from Eleusis to give a contrast to the white of the Pentelic marble: in the Erechtheion it formed the background of the continuous frieze, to which were attached carved figures in white marble.

In the Hellenistic period greater importance was attached to the decoration of interior walls. In some Classical buildings, such as the various temples at Epidaurus, interior colonnades were placed against walls to serve decorative rather than structural purposes, though the walls themselves were left plain, or served as backgrounds for attached panel paintings. More complex schemes of decorative painting evolved for walls, enhancing moulded stucco work. This is found, for example, in the houses at Delos, and is similar to the decorative forms on the painted walls of Pompeii. Some walls in Hellenistic Alexandria, in the tombs, had patterns, which stemmed from Egyptian architecture. Another Hellenistic development was the attachment to walls built in cruder stone of thin veneer panels of polished stone, often with patterning or made of alabaster or coloured marbles. This technique was taken up by Roman architects.

An important technical innovation, developed in the fourth century BC, was the keystone tunnel vault. There are occasional examples in Egyptian architecture of vaults which approach the true keystone technique (see above), but where the crucial upper sections remain corbelled. The keystone arch and vault were adopted (behind facades preserving the forms of conventional Greek architecture) for the Macedonian royal tombs at Aegeae, including that which almost certainly was the burial place built by Alexander the Great for his father, Philip II, in 336 BC. These early Macedonian vaults antedate any proven use of vaulting in Etruscan Italy. They were subsequently employed in fortifications, and, by Pergamene architects, to strengthen terrace walls.

Chapter 2
PREHISTORIC

Architectural Character

Permanent buildings in pre-dynastic Egypt and the ancient Near East were of two kinds, possibly derived from earlier temporary shelters. They were either of the single-cell type, beehive-shaped, round or oval in plan, or multi-celled collections of rectangular rooms.

Early housing of the Natufian (middle Mesolithic) period was circular in plan and was widely distributed throughout south-west Asia, where the transition to houses with rectangular rooms took place between 9000 and 7000 BC. In most regions, evolution was from semi-subterranean drystone huts, to apsidal houses in mud or stone, and finally to rectangular houses in tauf (loaf-shaped bricks of mud and straw) or mud brick. The development of moulded mud bricks encouraged precision of construction and the use of features such as external buttresses for visual effect. In Egypt the transition took place much later (*c.* 3400 BC).

Architectural character in the Neolithic period in the Near East derives from houses of similar size superimposed one above the other. They were constructed of mud, and rebuilt by each generation, the earlier buildings being absorbed into settlement mounds or tells.

Early tells were simply organised with no palaces, rich houses or non-residential buildings. In the ancient Near East (*c.* 8000–6000 BC) small communities were composed of single-roomed houses with flat roofs, built of mud and stone, with walls and floors buttressed and mud-plastered internally and painted in a variety of earth colours.

Most villages consisted of contiguous dwellings, with access by way of the roofs, but some villages had narrow alleys and courtyards. With the exception of Catal Hüyük (p. 36G–K), where large numbers of elaborate shrines were found, architecture was usually limited to fortification-walls within which settlements were housed, as at Jericho (p. 36A), or to stone pavements, as at Munhata.

During the Neolithic period, the character of these simple villages changed in four ways: through improvements in construction and planning which resulted in multi-roomed, thin-walled houses of mud brick; through the emergence of non-residential buildings for work, storage and ritual purposes, culminating in the monumental temple architecture of the Ubaid period in Mesopotamia; through more open forms of village layout, including streets; and through the more widespread construction of walls for many purposes, including defence.

By the end of the Ubaid period (*c.* 4000 BC) the numbers of villages had increased dramatically in many areas, and there was great regional diversity in the layout and spatial forms of domestic buildings. The trend everywhere was to larger townships, many of them fortified.

Storage buildings often consisted of rectangular rooms disposed on either side of a central corridor. By contrast, shrines were planned with rooms in sequence and occasionally followed a megaron-like plan. Both types of building tended towards regular and symmetrical layouts. At first, specialised buildings were contiguous with houses within the settlement but later they were free-standing. Occasionally temples or storage blocks were grouped around three sides of a courtyard.

The most striking monuments of the Neolithic period in the Near East were the temples of the Ubaid. They were rectangular mud-brick buildings erected on platforms of clay or imported stone, forerunners of the Sumerian ziggurats. As in houses, a central rectangular chamber was flanked on the long sides by small cells, but temples were larger and more elaborately decorated. A flight of stairs to a door in the long side led to a room about 10 m (33 ft) long with a broad platform at one end and a table or small altar at the other. Ladders in the smaller rooms occasionally gave access to an upper floor or to the roof. Buttresses were designed to articulate patterns of light and shade. Terracotta scale models appear to have been used as aids to design. Late temples had friezes decorated with coloured ceramic cones and bitumen.

In Egypt, the transition to rectangular, mud-built town houses took place in late Gerzean times, at the end of the Mesolithic period. These were constructed from wattle and daub, occasionally on rough stone

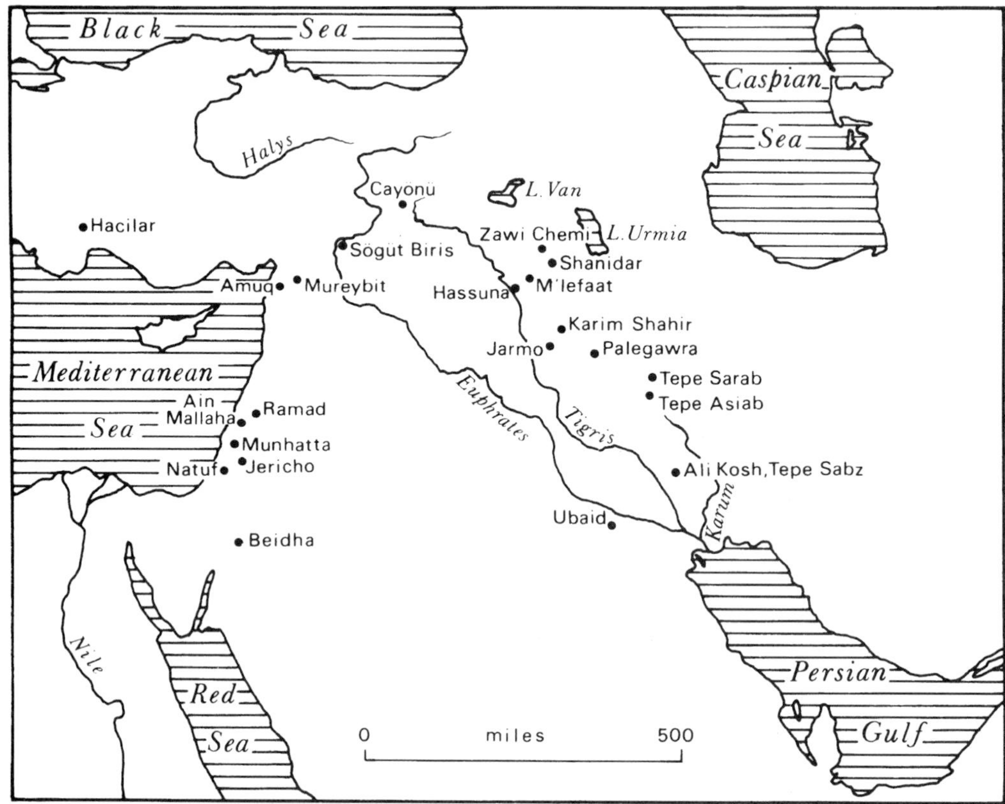

The Prehistoric Near East

foundations. Houses were two-roomed, with walled open courts adjoining the street. Graves became increasingly elaborate.

Examples

The Late Mesolithic and Early Neolithic Periods

Natufian dwellings were of two types: flimsy brushwood shelters or windbreaks built in front of caves on stone pavements, or more frequently round or oval drystone huts built in open settlements near water sources in the limestone uplands. The transition to rectangular, mud-brick houses also began in this period and continued into the Neolithic period.

At **Ain Mallaha**, near Lake Hulen, Israel (*c.* 9000–8000 BC) (p. 32D), there were about fifty drystone huts on an open site of some 2000 m^2 (21,500 ft^2), most of them circular, semi-subterranean and rock-lined, from 3 m (10 ft) to 9 m (30 ft) in diameter. The beehive forms were constructed of reeds or matting and were probably supported on posts. The huts were dug into the bank on the upper side to a depth of about 1.3 m (4 ft), and the entrances were located on the lower side. Some of the huts had stone-paved floors, and one had walls finished with lime plaster painted with red ochre. The settlement had a population of between two and three hundred. Similar huts were found at **Wadi Fallah** and **Nahal Oren**, and at **Beidha** (p. 32A) in southern Jordan.

The Khirokitia culture, of the aceramic Neolithic period in Cyprus (*c.* 5650 BC), built round houses 3 m to 8 m (10 ft to 26 ft) in diameter. The village of **Khirokitia** (p. 32C) comprised about a thousand houses, and was approached by a stone-paved road. The lower parts of the walls were made of local limestone, and the domed superstructure of pisé or mud brick. Some houses had double walls, the outer leaf acting as a retaining wall. Some examples had lofts supported on stone pillars, and a number of outbuildings used for grinding corn, storage, cooking and workshops. Most houses gave onto walled courtyards.

Beehive-shaped tholoi were built in the Mesopotamian lowlands during the Halaf period (Neolithic). At **Arpachiyah** (*c.* 5000 BC) (p. 32E) dwellings which were keyhole-shaped in plan had walls up to

2 m (7 ft) thick. Rectangular anterooms were up to 19 m (62 ft) long and the domed chambers up to 10 m (33 ft) across. The walls were of plastered tauf, occasionally painted red, and roofs were thatched.

Houses of the Shulaveri culture at **Imiris Gora** (*c.* 4660–3955 BC) (p. 32B), in Transcaucasia, were round or oval, 3 m to 4.5 m (10 ft to 15 ft) in diameter, and were built of mud brick on stone foundations. As in Natufian dwellings, many were semi-subterranean. Several of the houses had keyhole-shaped plans, with internal buttresses to take the thrust where the domes abutted, and others had out-houses arranged round courtyards. Later in the period, two-roomed houses evolved with buttressed walls and flat roofs supported on timber posts. The village had a population estimated at 200–250.

At **Faiyum** (*c.* 6000–5000 BC), in Lower Egypt, only storage pits have survived, but at **Merimde** (*c.* 4500 BC) a century or so later, on the western edge of the Delta in Lower Egypt, there is evidence of a village of huts which were oval or horseshoe on plan, 5 m to 6 m (16 ft to 20 ft) across. They were constructed from a framework of posts and covered with reed matting. The huts were aligned in rows and some of them may have had fenced yards.

Badarian and Amratian sites in Upper Egypt are also known to have had beehive-shaped huts of grass and reeds. The Badarian site of **Hammamiya** (*c.* 4000 BC) consisted of a number of hut circles which included storage and living rooms up to 2 m (7 ft) in diameter, and sunk into the ground to a depth of about 1 m (3 ft). **Naqada** (*c.* 3600 BC), an Amratian site in Upper Egypt, consisted of a similar group of mud and reed huts.

The early Neolithic period (*c.* 7500–6000 BC) was marked almost everywhere by a change from round to rectangular buildings built of mud. Rectangular houses were sometimes built on top of earlier round drystone buildings. Speed and mode of construction varied profoundly from region to region, and culturally distinct areas have been identified in the Levant, Anatolia, the Zargos region, the Transcaspian lowlands, and Transcaucasia, Mesopotamia and Egypt. These are dealt with separately below. Where shrine-like buildings emerged early in the evolutionary sequence they were usually planned in the same way as dwellings, but were made larger and were more elaborately decorated. By the end of the Neolithic period these shrines had evolved as precursors of Mesopotamian temple architecture. In Egypt, the design of tombs had become more elaborate, and already possessed many of the essential features of later monumental funerary architecture.

The Levant

The architecture of the Levant during the early pre-pottery Neolithic period was primarily domestic, but shrines, workshops and storage buildings have also been found. At the beginning of the sixth millennium, however, many of these early pre-pottery townships were deserted and, within the ceramic Neolithic period, Anatolian and Mesopotamian architecture became more significant.

RESIDENTIAL BUILDINGS

Many round and oval houses spreading over 4 ha (10 acres) were found in the lowest Neolithic levels of **Jericho** (*c.* 8350–7350 BC). Each was about 5 m (16 ft) in diameter and had evolved from the Natufian drystone tradition, but they were built of loaf-shaped mud-bricks with indentations on the convex face to give a key to the clay mortar. The bricks supported domed superstructures of branches covered with clay.

The round houses at Jericho lay under a pre-pottery Neolithic township (*c.* 7350 BC) encircled by a stone wall 3 m (10 ft) thick, 4 m (13 ft) high and over 700 m (2300 ft) in circumference. The fortifications underwent a complex sequence of rebuilding, including the erection of cisterns and storage chambers with roof entry set against the base of an apsidal watch-tower. Here the houses were of cigar-shaped mud bricks with thumb-print keys on the upper surface. They had solid walls and wide doorways with rounded jambs; some had stone foundations and some may have had upper floors made of timber. The houses were closely packed, but seem to have intercommunicated through screen walls and courtyards. They had highly burnished lime plaster floors laid on gravel and stained red, pink or orange, and plastered walls with red-painted dados. Some of the walls were also decorated with geometric designs. Similar houses dating from the same period have been found at **Munhata**, further up the Jordan Valley.

At **Mureybet** in north Syria the first two levels (*c.* 8640 BC and *c.* 8142 BC) consisted of round or oval huts with red clay walls supporting a light timber superstructure. In level three (*c.* 7954–7542 BC) there were rectangular houses as well as round huts. Both were constructed from loaf-shaped pieces of soft limestone laid in a clay and pebble mortar. By the end of the period, the plan had evolved to include multi-roomed houses, possibly with access through the roofs. A wall-painting showing a zigzag pattern in black on a buff ground was found in one of the houses at Mureybet.

Similar houses have been discovered nearby at **Tell Abu Hureyra**, on the southern bank of the Euphrates in north Syria. Natufian remains were covered in the aceramic Neolithic period (late eighth and early seventh millennium BC) by rectangular mud-brick and tauf houses. Floors were made of stamped earth finished with red or black burnished plaster and walls of white plaster decorated with red lines.

EVOLUTION OF HOUSES

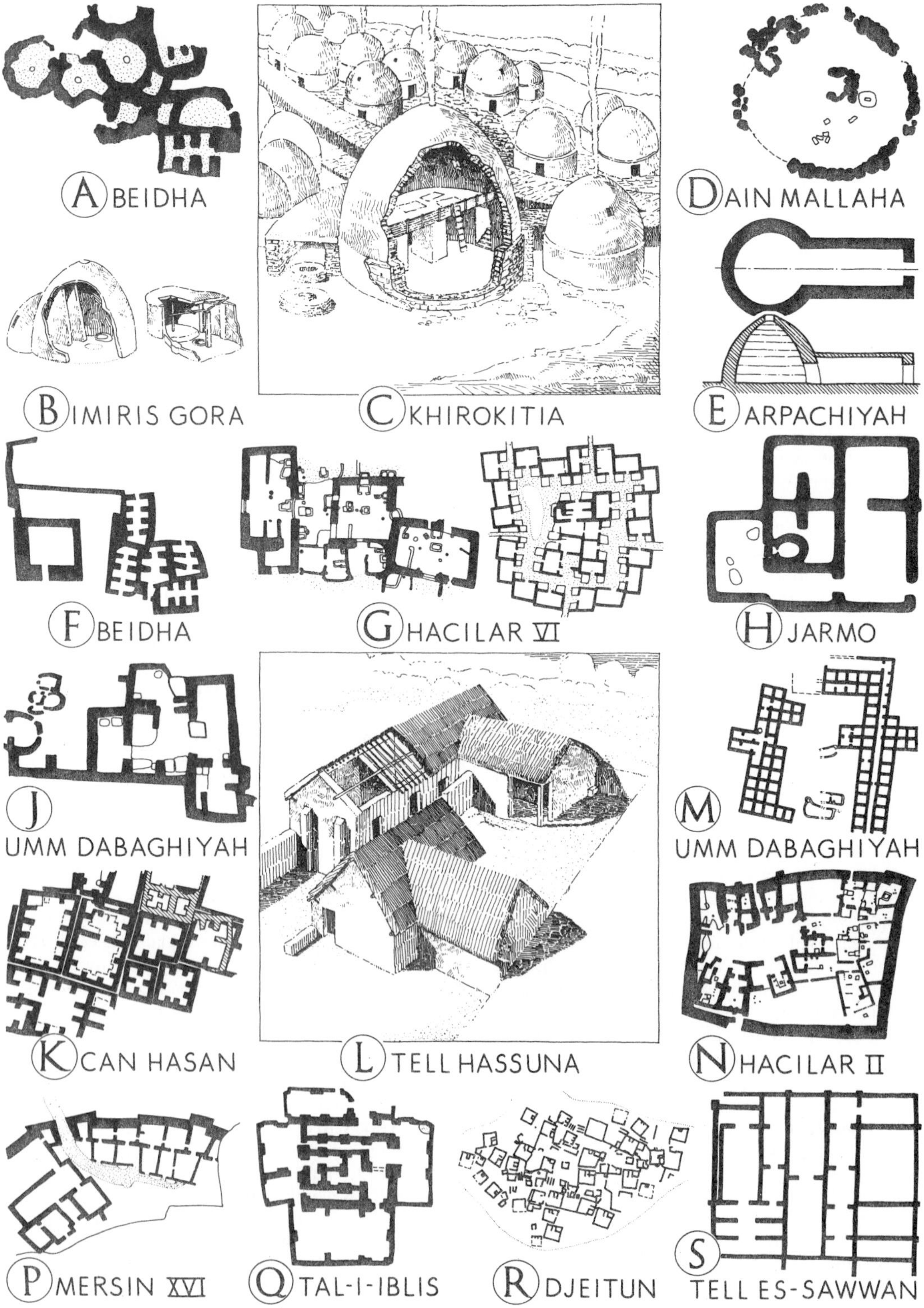

A BEIDHA

B IMIRIS GORA

C KHIROKITIA

D AIN MALLAHA

E ARPACHIYAH

F BEIDHA

G HACILAR VI

H JARMO

J UMM DABAGHIYAH

K CAN HASAN

L TELL HASSUNA

M UMM DABAGHIYAH

N HACILAR II

P MERSIN XVI

Q TAL-I-IBLIS

R DJEITUN

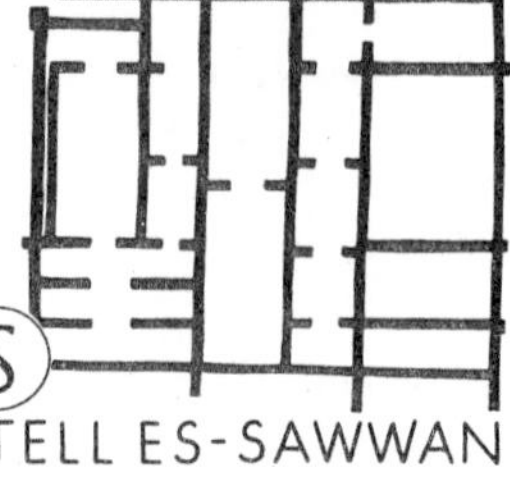

S TELL ES-SAWWAN

The first huts at **Beidha** (*c.* 7000–6000 BC), in southern Jordan, were curvilinear in the Natufian tradition. They were semi-subterranean, and up to 4 m (13 ft) in diameter. The dwellings and storerooms were grouped in clusters within walled courtyards, and the whole village was surrounded by a stone wall.

Later, in the aceramic Neolithic period, this post-house style was accompanied at Beidha by free-standing polygonal houses with rounded corners. These were followed by rectangular stone houses, and finally by clusters of stone-built houses and workshops. Each house had one room measuring 7 m × 9 m (23 ft × 30 ft), with floor and walls of white burnished plaster decorated with a red stripe at floor level. Outside was an L-shaped, walled courtyard and each had several workshops about 8 m (26 ft) long, clustered together (p. 32F).

The lowest levels of the site for which floor plans could be reconstructed at **Cayonu** (*c.* 7500–6800 BC), in northern Syria, contained substantial rectangular stone buildings 5 m × 10 m (16 ft × 33 ft) in area. A multi-roomed building with a hall and a square room, with two flanking rows of three cubicles, and plastered floors, had grid-like foundations which may have supported a suspended, timber-joisted floor.

The top levels of Cayonu yielded a workshop measuring 5 m × 8 m (16 ft × 26 ft) overall, made up of six or seven small cubicles, each containing a set of tools. The first mud-brick buildings were of similar date and were simple square or rectangular one-roomed houses measuring about 5 m × 9 m (16 ft × 30 ft). A model recovered at Cayonu indicated that houses had doorways with curved jambs located at the narrow end and were flat-roofed.

At **Tell Ramad** (*c.* 6000 BC), south-west of Damascus, round or oval semi-subterranean houses were superseded late in the aceramic Neolithic period by rectangular one-roomed houses of mud brick on stone foundations, which were separated by narrow alleys.

SHRINES

A number of shrine-like buildings were found at **Jericho** (*c.* 7000 BC) (p. 36A). A small room, with a niche in which was placed a standing stone, may have been a cult room. Another had a portico, which led to a vestibule and inner chamber containing a pair of stone pillars symmetrically disposed about the axis of entry.

Outside the village at **Beidha** (*c.* 7000 BC) there was a group of three buildings approached by a paved path. The earliest was round, with a door facing east, and a flagstone floor; a flat slab of white sandstone was set outside, against the east wall. This was followed by an oval building 6 m × 3.5 m (20 ft × 11 ft) with a paved floor, in the centre of which was a large flat sandstone block, and another large slab with a parapet was placed against the south wall. A third block lay outside the building, against the north-west corner of the wall, and to the south lay a basin 3.8 m × 2.65 m × 0.25 m (12 ft × 9 ft × 10 in).

At **Munhata** (*c.* 7000 BC), there is a vast circular structure over 300 m^2 in area, the function of which is not known. It consists of a platform of large basalt blocks carved with water channels at the centre and surrounded by a zone of paved basins, open areas, plaster floors and hearths.

Cayonu (*c.* 7000 BC) had a shrine-like building 9 m × 10 m (30 ft × 33 ft) with internally buttressed stone walls. The highly burnished tessellated floor was paved with salmon-pink pebbles between 100 mm (4 in) and 300 mm (12 in) long, set in red mortar. Across each side of the room were areas of white marble pebbles 500 mm (29 in) wide and 4 m (13 ft) long.

Anatolia

Some of the most remarkable architectural evidence pointing to the evolution of a highly complex society has come from Neolithic sites in Anatolia. The dwellings, particularly at **Catal Hüyük**, displayed an unusual degree of standardisation, and the inhabitants seem to have taken part in highly organised rituals. Late in the period, many settlements were heavily fortified, and at least one fortress has been identified.

RESIDENTIAL BUILDINGS

In the aceramic Neolithic period at **Hacilar** (*c.* 7500–6000 BC) in Anatolia, rectangular dwellings were built of mud bricks on stone foundations. No complete house plans have survived, but they appear to have been multi-roomed, plastered internally and painted in cream and red bands. The dwellings were close-packed with access by way of the roofs.

Later in the period at Hacilar (*c.* 5400 BC) more substantial rectangular mud-brick houses 10 m × 4 m (33 ft × 13 ft) were built with walls over a metre thick (p. 32G). Some houses had vestibules flanked by lean-to brushwood and plaster cooking areas. Doorways were normally in the centre of the long sides, and had timber thresholds and jambs designed to take wooden double doors. Cupboards were let into the walls, and lightweight partitions of sticks and plaster screened off the storage area. Ceilings of stout timber beams were supported on a pair of centre posts and were reinforced at the corners by cross-bracing. The posts may have carried a lightweight upper storey of wood and plaster, consisting of a verandah and a row of small rooms.

In its final stages (*c.* 5400–5000 BC), Hacilar was fortified with a stone wall, which enclosed an area 70 m × 35 m (230 ft × 115 ft) (p. 32N). Within it the settlement consisted of houses, a granary, a guard-house, potters' workshops, and shrines. Before it was abandoned in *c.* 4800 BC, Hacilar was heavily fortified and its central courtyard was ringed by blocks of two-storey houses, with roof access and separated from each other by small fenced yards.

At **Can Hasan** (p. 32K), at **Asikli** and at **Suberde** (7500–6000 BC) in Anatolia during the aceramic period the houses were close-packed and square or rectangular in plan. Later buildings (*c.* 4950 BC) were thick-walled and built of mud brick reinforced with timber. Here also some houses had lightweight upper storeys.

The city of **Catal Hüyük** (p. 36G–K), at the foot of the Taurus Mountains in Anatolia (6250–5400 BC), was continuously occupied. It extended over 13 ha (32 acres) and supported a population of 4000–6000 people. Some 138 buildings have been excavated, and they are mainly rectangular single-roomed houses, each about 25 m^2 (270 ft^2), with plastered walls and floors. They were densely packed and contiguous, with occasional open courtyards, but each house had its own walls. The floors were covered with straw mats and the walls were decorated with simple geometric designs. Access was by ladder from the roof.

The fortress of **Mersin** (*c.* 4500–4200 BC) (p. 32P), in the plain of Cilicia, was entered by a tiered gateway with projecting towers. The garrison's quarters, which surrounded a central open courtyard, had flat roofs, and comprised rows of barrack-like rooms which abutted the defensive walls at the rear and had small walled yards to the front. Originally intercommunicating but later self-contained, the rooms had slit windows, and contained grindstones, mud platforms and hearths. To the right of the main gate was a larger and more elaborate house for the commander of the garrison.

SHRINES

Excavations at **Catal Hüyük** (*c.* 6250–5400 BC) revealed richly furnished and decorated buildings which seem to have been shrines (p. 36G). They were laid out in the same way as the residences, and were intermingled with them, but differed in that they were decorated with paintings, reliefs and engravings on themes connected with fertility and death.

The shrines at **Hacilar** (*c.* 5400 BC) were usually simple square rooms with niches containing standing stones, in front of which were libation holes, but one was planned like a megaron with a porch and anteroom. Here, too, shrines were decorated with geometric wall paintings.

Zagros

The Zagros region has yielded evidence of early settlement from the **Shanidar Cave** and other associated prehistoric sites such as **Zawi Chemi** (*c.* 9000 BC). This region did not produce shrines, although large, multi-roomed dwellings were found.

RESIDENTIAL BUILDINGS

At **Ali Kosh** (*c.* 8000–6500 BC) in the Khuzistan plain, small single-storey, thin-walled houses of rectangular plan were built from local red clay bricks roughly 250 mm × 150 mm × 100 mm (10 in × 6 in × 4 in). Larger, multi-roomed houses came later and had rooms up to 3 m × 3 m (10 ft × 10 ft) and walls built of untempered clay slabs 400 mm × 250 mm × 100 mm (16 in × 10 in × 4 in). There were open courtyards, and alleys separated the houses.

At **Ganjdareh** (*c.* 7289–7000 BC) in western Iran, a substantial mud-brick village was built, with walls of tauf. The houses were made up of small rectangular rooms, close-packed and with roof access. Roofs were made of beams supporting reeds daubed with clay, and walls and floors were finished internally with mud plaster.

Tepe Guran (*c.* 6500–5500 BC) in Luristan began as a winter camp of wooden huts, each with two or three small rooms. Later (*c.* 6200 BC) similar houses were constructed in mud brick and contained built-in mud benches and tables. Floors and walls were finished with white or red plaster, courtyards with terrazzo made from white felspar chippings set in red clay.

Jarmo (*c.* 6000–5000 BC) (p. 32H), in the Zagros Mountains, had a population of about 150 people and was made up of 20–30 small, rectangular mud houses. The lower levels of occupation dating from 6500–6000 BC were built of tauf with mud floors laid on reeds. Each house had an open courtyard measuring roughly 3 m × 4 m (10 ft × 13 ft) and comprised several small rectangular rooms, packed into a space about 5 m × 6 m (16 ft × 20 ft).

At **Tal-i-Iblis** (*c.* 4000 BC) (p. 32Q) in the Zagros, houses were built with thick-walled, heavily buttressed storerooms grouped at the centre, and surrounded by larger living rooms with red plaster floors. One of the houses had an elaborate arch, and contained infant burials. Similar houses were found at **Tepe Yahya.**

At **Siyalik** (*c.* 5500 BC), south of Kashan, light structures of branches, mud and reeds were superseded by houses with tauf walls and mud floors, and then by rectangular tauf structures on mud brick foundations.

Transcaspian and Transcaucasian Regions

These regions produced simple, standardised one-roomed houses, and larger shrine-like buildings decorated with wall-paintings. Of particular interest is the variety of village layouts ranging from open, irregular free-standing groups, to contiguous clumps (each with a shrine, and separated from the others by street-like spaces), and finally to walled settlements containing blocks of dwellings and shrines.

RESIDENTIAL BUILDINGS

Houses at **Djeitun** (*c.* 5600 BC), on the margins of the Kara-kan Desert in Turkmenia, were built in mud and sun-dried brick tempered with straw (p. 32R). The village had about thirty households and a population of about 150 people. Houses were rectangular in plan, each with one room about 5 m × 6 m (16 ft × 20 ft). Some houses had plain interiors with a hearth located centrally on one wall, while others were more elaborate. The walls were coated with mud plaster and were occasionally painted red or black. Each house had a courtyard and outbuildings, sometimes shared with a neighbour. In the open space of the village there were timber grain-drying platforms supported on parallel mud brick walls. There were also shrine-like buildings in Djeitun.

The village of **Hajji Fruz** (*c.* 5319–4959 BC) in the province of Azerbaijan in the north-west corner of modern Iran was an open village of single-roomed detached houses separated by lanes and courtyards. The yards contained outbuildings constructed of packed mud. Houses were 6.5 m × 4 m (21 ft × 13 ft) and built of mud brick and mortar. Internal mud brick buttresses and wooden posts supported a roof of beams, reeds and clay which may have been of pitched shape. There were similar houses at **Yanki Tepe** in the same province.

Monjukli Depe (*c.* 5000 BC) had houses with interiors in the Djeitun tradition, but the buildings were separated by a lane into two groups. The houses, unlike those at Djeitun, were contiguous. The village of **Chakmakli Depe** of similar date was also divided by a lane into two groups. The houses were made of large mud bricks, 200 mm × 500 mm × 100 mm (8 in × 29 in × 4 in). The houses had two rooms – small kitchens and larger living rooms in sequence – and in each group of dwellings there was one with red walls and floors which may have served as a shrine.

Dashliji Depe (*c.* 5000 BC), in the Geoksyur oasis, was a fortified settlement 45 m × 38 m (148 ft × 124 ft) in which stood small mud-brick houses like those at Djeitun, and a larger shrine-like structure. The nearby site of **Yalangach Depe** (*c.* 4500 BC) was enclosed by a massive defensive wall with round towers. In the north-west corner of the township was an arrangement of houses surrounding a central, larger space, possibly a shrine. **Mullali Depe**, in the same oasis, was also walled and had round towers, and a shrine at its centre.

SHRINES

A shrine-like building, similar in layout but twice as large as the houses, was found at **Djeitun** (*c.* 5600 BC) (p. 36F), and there were similar houses and shrines at **Pessejik**, where the floors and walls were decorated with polychrome paintings of animals, and with geometric motifs.

There was a more elaborate shrine at **Yasa Depe** (*c.* 5000 BC) (p. 36B) in the foothills of the Kopet Dagh. This was larger and had two rooms. The outer room was decorated with wall-paintings and contained a ritual hearth. The inner room had colonnades of wooden pillars on the flank walls. The doorway was opposite the altar, which was decorated with geometric wall paintings in brown, red and white. The shrine at **Dashliji Depe** (*c.* 5000 BC) (p. 36D) was also painted in black and red.

Mesopotamia

In the region between the rivers there was a succession of cultures, Hassuna, Samarra, Halaf, Eridu and Ubaid; there was even an earlier occupation of the region at Umm Dabaghiya which predated the first of these. Mud-brick dwellings of the Hassuna and Samarra periods were large and rectangular, with several rooms. Those of the Halaf period reverted to a tholos-like design. Settlements of the Eridu and Ubaid periods in the southern Mesopotamian alluvium have yielded little direct evidence of dwelling types. However, representations on cylinder-seals depict reed-built structures characteristic of later southern Mesopotamian sites. By contrast, ritual buildings of the period were executed in a simple but dignified mud-brick style. Temple buildings of the Ubaid period are in the direct line of development of the monumental temple architecture of the Sumerian dynasties.

RESIDENTIAL BUILDINGS

At **Umm Dabaghiya**, where evidence was found of the earliest culture (*c.* 5500 BC) west of the Tigris, there was a pre-Hassuna mound 100 m × 85 m (330 ft × 280 ft) by 4 m (13 ft) high in the northern plain of Iraq. Occupation passed through the evolutionary stages of small, oval temporary shelters and storage pits, tauf-built houses, houses and storage blocks ranged around central courtyards, and finally unplastered storage cubicles with roof access, linked internally by corridors. The domestic architecture of Umm Dabaghiyah (p. 32J) was exceptionally neat. Houses were oriented north-south, and were close-packed, although each had its own walls. Each house comprised a living room, kitchen and one or two further rooms 1.2 m to 2 m (4 ft to 7 ft) square, constructed in tauf without stone foundations. The walls were buttressed internally and some houses had access from the roof. Usually one room was divided by an arch spanning its width, one of the earliest uses of this form of construction. Houses were decorated

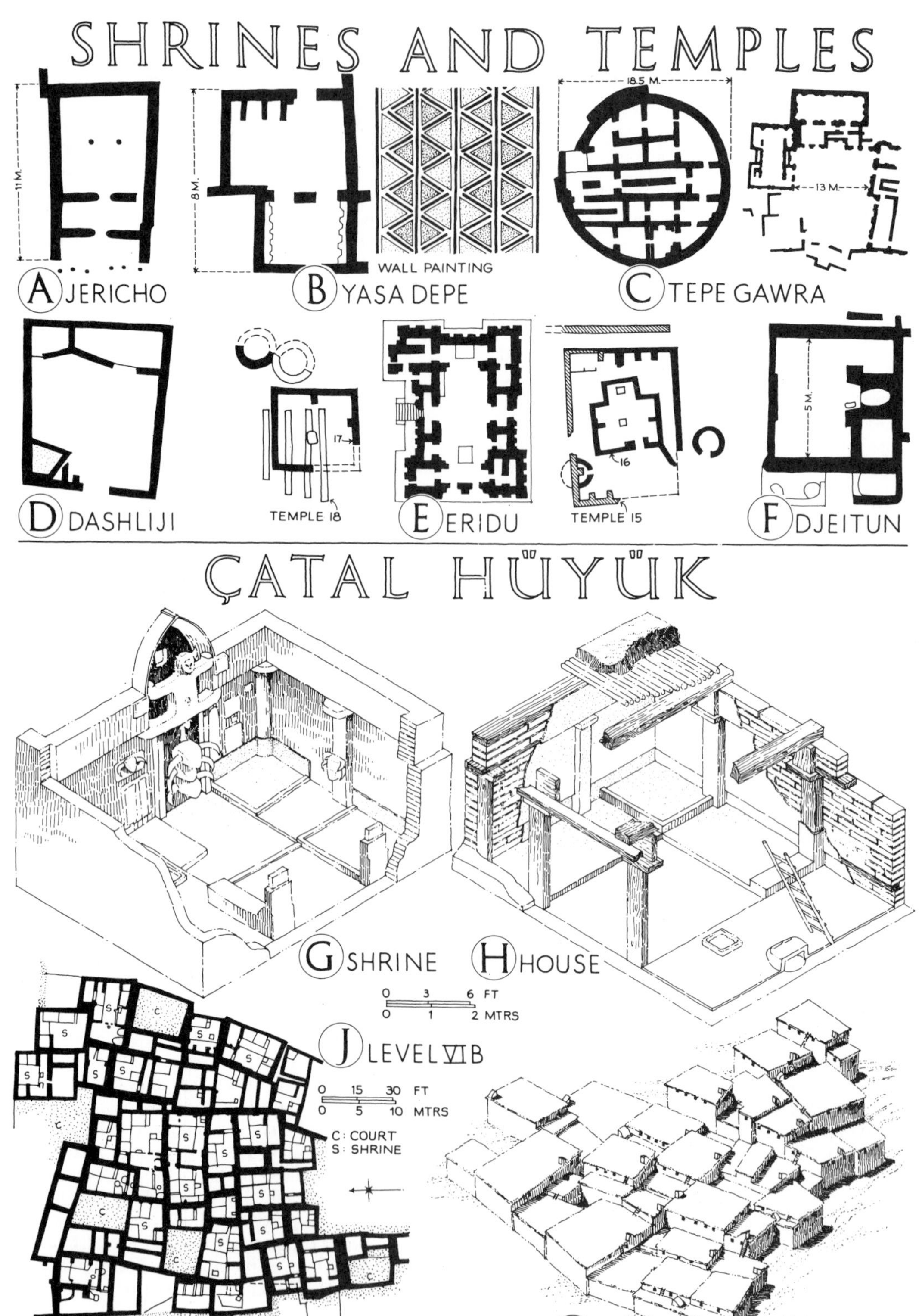
SHRINES AND TEMPLES
11 M.
A JERICHO
8 M.
WALL PAINTING
B YASA DEPE
18.5 M.
13 M.
C TEPE GAWRA
D DASHLIJI
17
TEMPLE 18
E ERIDU
16
TEMPLE 15
5 M.
F DJEITUN
ÇATAL HÜYÜK
G SHRINE
H HOUSE
0 3 6 FT
0 1 2 MTRS
J LEVEL VIB
0 15 30 FT
0 5 10 MTRS
C: COURT
S: SHRINE
AERIAL VIEW K

internally with plaster and red paint, and wall-paintings in black, red and yellow showed hunting scenes. At a later stage, storage blocks were built around open U-shaped courtyards (p. 32M). The buildings were single-storey, with roofs of branches and reeds covered in plaster and furnished with trapdoors. The small-scale construction may have been necessitated by the lack of timber locally.

There was a mound 200 m × 150 m (660 ft × 490 ft) with many levels of buildings at **Tell Hassuna** (*c.* 5500–5000 BC) south-west of Mosul. Round structures 2.5 m to 6 m (8 ft to 20 ft) across, and rectangular dwellings 10 m × 2.5 m (33 ft × 8 ft) in plan, were found together in the lowest levels of the site (p. 32L). More recent levels yielded larger and more sophisticated buildings in which passages and courtyards finished with gypsum plaster separated large, single-storey, multi-roomed houses with flat roofs and interior courtyards.

Yarim Tepe, also dated to the Hassuna period in Sinjar, comprised some 60 to 70 houses with an estimated population of about 400. The mud-brick houses were uniform in shape, size and character, and were arranged in parallel rows.

The Samarran settlement of **Tell-es-Sawwan** on the east bank of the Tigris covered an area 220 m × 110 m (720 ft × 360 ft). The lowest levels of the site, from about 5600–5300 BC, showed Tell-es-Sawwan to have been a farming village of several hundred people. The residential character differed from villages of similar date in that the houses had stone foundations. They were uniform in size and were constructed of moulded mud bricks (p. 32S). Walls and floors were coated in mud plaster, and were externally buttressed to take beams supporting a roof of reeds and clay. The village was surrounded by a large ditch or moat, which cut into the bedrock on which the village was built.

Choga Mami (*c.* 5500 BC) was enclosed by buttressed walls. Houses were rectangular and multicellular: for example, one of them had twelve rooms packed into an area of 9 m × 7 m (30 ft × 23 ft). The construction was similar to that used at Tell-es-Sawwan.

Al'Ubaid (*c.* 4500–4200 BC), set on a low mound of river silt in the Euphrates valley, consisted of dwellings with flat roofs and walls formed of reed mats suspended between palm stems and plastered with mud, and partly of houses with roofs formed by bending bundles of reeds to form arches. The dwellings were reminiscent of modern Marsh Arab guest-houses.

TEMPLES

At **Tell-es-Sawwan** (*c.* 5300 BC), a large T-shaped building with fourteen rooms was discovered immediately overlying a cemetery. Several rooms contained alabaster idols. Although architecturally similar to other buildings on the site, it contained no domestic artefacts, and may have been a small temple.

Eridu (*c.* 5400 BC) (p. 36E) is the oldest known settlement on the southern Mesopotamian alluvium. Seventeen temples have survived and are superimposed one upon another, thus raising the later buildings to a considerable height. The earliest of these was a small room, about 3 m (10 ft) square, constructed of sun-dried bricks; it contained a cult-niche and a central offering-table. Temple XV was approached by a ramp, and was a small, nearly square room about 3.5 m × 4.5 m (11 ft × 15 ft). An altar in a niche in the rear wall faced the entrance, and a pedestal at the centre served as an offering place. In Temples XI to IX this scheme evolved into a tripartite plan, with a central cella and projecting lateral wings. The remainder of the Ubaid period was notable for the development of more sophisticated buildings, with central cellae, entered via vestibules flanked by rows of small rooms.

In the Ubaid period, **Tepe Gawra** (*c.* 3600 BC) (p. 36C) also boasted an important sequence of temple buildings similar to those at Eridu. There was also a round building 18 m (59 ft) in diameter containing seventeen rooms within its outer walls, which were over a metre thick. Its purpose is not known, but it had possibly been used for rituals in a local tradition which existed alongside those of the Ubaid, who raised a group of three temples round a large courtyard, onto which other minor buildings faced. The eastern shrine was the earliest of the group. The temples were similar in plan to those of Eridu XI to IX but lacked ritual objects. Later temples had rectangular sanctuaries, and were entered by way of open porticoes, usually with two lateral chambers on either side.

Egypt

Evidence of dwellings in pre-dynastic Egypt is sparse, and graves and cemeteries are the main architectural remains. Flimsy, insubstantial reed and timber dwellings were replaced in late Gerzean times by new ones built in mud.

RESIDENTIAL BUILDINGS

Houses at **El-Badari** and **Hierakonpolis** (*c.* 3200 BC) had two rooms, facing open-walled courtyards, and larger inner living-rooms about 2 m square. A pottery model of a town-house from the late Gerzean period shows a substantial, rectangular, wattle and daub structure with battered walls and a roof of thatch and mud.

FUNERARY ARCHITECTURE

The cemetery at **Badari** contains several hundred burials grouped in dense clusters. No superstructures survive to mark the graves, but they are thought to have been marked originally by cairns.

Early tombs at **Naqada** resembled those at Badari, but later Naqada II tombs were more substantial. The walls of graves were strengthened by sticks and matting, or wood-panelled chambers were constructed. Some chambers had an upper compartment, designed to carry grave goods. Both types of structure were roofed with mud-plastered sticks and matting or planks. These were the precursors of the wood-panelled central chambers found at the Royal Tombs at Abydos, and the Sakkaran mastaba tombs. One of these tombs had a stone superstructure in the form of a four-tiered step pyramid, on a square base over 20 m × 20 m (66 ft × 66 ft) in area. The stones were undressed and roughly coursed, and beneath the pyramid a pit had been dug into the sand to hold the corpse and grave goods.

Chapter 3
EGYPT

Architectural Character

The primitive architecture in the valley of the Nile consisted of readily available tractable materials like reeds, papyrus (now practically extinct) and palm-branch ribs, plastered over with clay. With bundles of stems placed vertically side by side and lashed to a bundle placed horizontally near the top, walls or fences could be made. Alternatively, palm-leaf ribs were planted in the ground at short intervals, with others laced in a diagonal network across them and secured to a horizontal member near the top, the whole being daubed with mud afterwards. Buildings with circular plans could have domical coverings of similar construction, or, if rectangular, could have a tunnel-shaped covering or a flat roof. The pressure of the flat reed-and-mud roofs against the tops of the wall reeds may have produced the characteristic Egyptian 'gorge' cornice (p. 41J), while the 'Kheker' cresting less frequently appearing in later architecture may have originated in the terminal tufts of a papyrus-stalk wall (p. 41B). The horizontal binders and angle bundles survived in the roll moulding of stone cornices and wall angles of the historic period (p. 41J).

A type of pavilion or kiosk which came to have a special religious significance in connection with the 'Heb-sed' or jubilee festivals of the Pharaohs – though originally commonly used on Nile boats as well as on land – consisted of a light, rectangular structure, open-fronted and with a porch carried on two slender angle-shafts and having a slab-like roof arching from the back to the front. In the Heb-sed ceremony, held at definite intervals of years in the king's reign, the Pharaoh seated himself on a throne beneath such an awning, raised on a high podium and approached by a flight of steps at the front.

Timber, once quite plentiful, was used for the better buildings, in square, heavy vertical plates, lapping one in front of the other and producing an effect of composite buttresses joined at the head and enframing narrow panels, in the upper parts of which window-vents might occur. Palm logs, rounded on the underside, were sometimes used for roofs.

All these various forms of construction produced their effects on matured art and architecture, and apart from timber, which had become scarce by dynastic times, never entirely went out of use.

Stone was not much employed before the Third Dynasty, except as rubble and as a stiffening or foundation to solid mud walls. Sun-dried mud-brick walling never ceased to be employed, for it was only for the finest buildings of religious character that cut stone became normal. Even palaces remained always relatively frail. Made of Nile mud and mixed with chopped straw or sand, and thoroughly matured by exposure to the sun, the mud bricks were very long lasting, and large, about 356 mm (14 in) long, 178 mm (7 in) wide and 102 mm (4 in) thick. For stability, walls diminished course by course towards the top, chiefly because of the alternate shrinkage and expansion of the soil caused by the annual inundation. As the inner face of the walls had to be vertical for ordinary convenience, it was the outer face only which showed this inward inclination, or 'batter', which remained throughout one of the principal characteristics of Egyptian architecture whether in brick or stone. Sometimes fibre or reed mats were placed between the brick courses at intervals up the walls, to reinforce them, particularly at a building's angles; and a late development was the use of sagging concave courses, for alternate lengths of a long wall, built in advance of the intervening stretches, to allow the drying out of the inner brickwork, since walls such as those around the great temple enclosures were very thick, between 9 m (30 ft) and 24.5 m (80 ft).

Though the true arch was never used in monumental stonework, the principle was known very early on: there are brick vaults as early as the beginning of the Third Dynasty. Frequently, the arch rings were built in sloping courses, so that no 'centering' or temporary support was needed, and usually there were two or more arched rings arranged concentrically, the one lying upon the other. The Romans adopted the method of building arches in concentric, superposed rings, though they did not slope them but used centering in the normal way.

The surface decoration of the masonry walls is held to have been derived from the practice of scratching

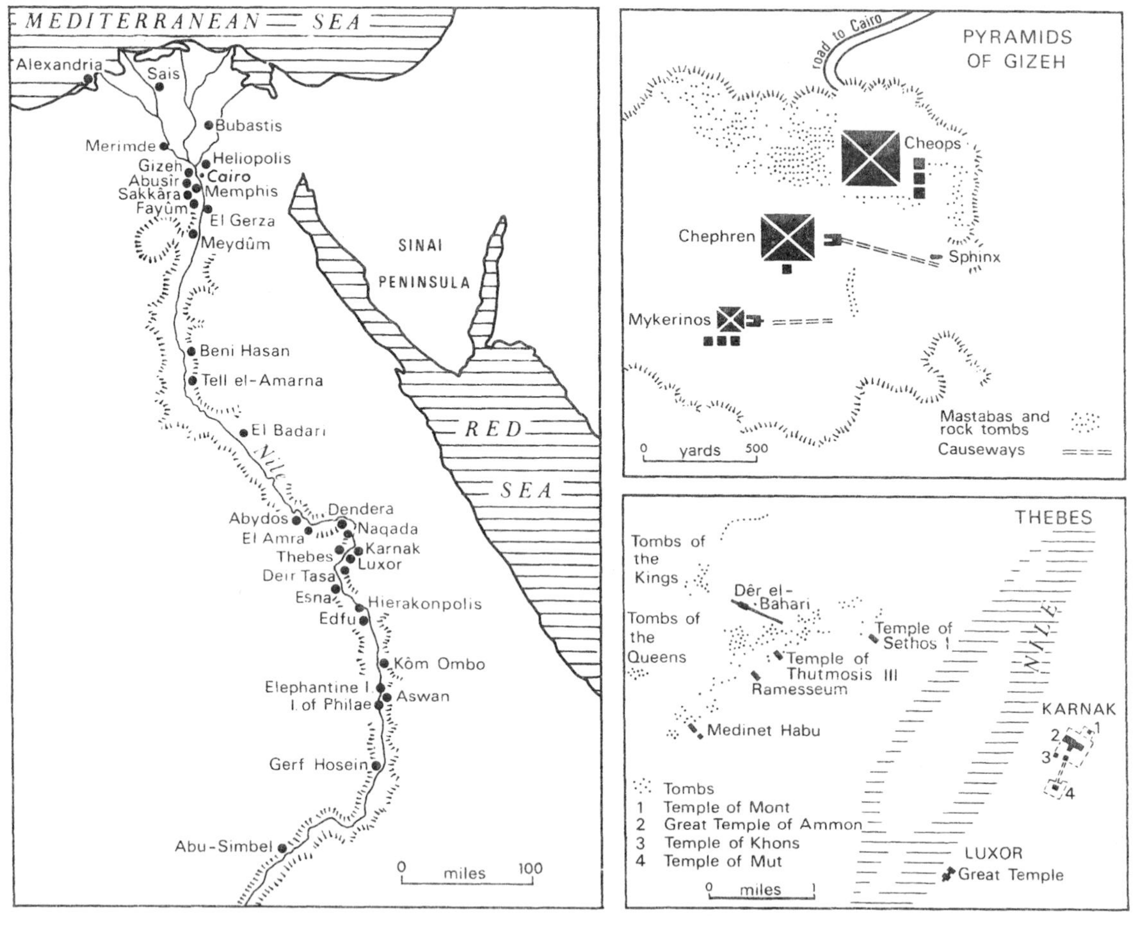

Ancient Egypt; the Great Pyramids; Thebes

pictures on the early mud-plaster walls, which manifestly did not lend themselves to modelled or projecting ornament, though their flat and windowless surfaces were eminently suitable for incised relief and explanatory hieroglyphs (pp. 42, 43) – a method of popular teaching which has its parallel in the sculptured facades and stained-glass windows of mediaeval cathedrals.

Egyptian columns (p. 41) have a distinctive character, and a very large proportion of them plainly advertise their vegetable origin, their shafts indicative of bundles of plant stems, gathered in a little at the base, and with capitals seemingly derived from the lotus bud (p. 41G), the papyrus flower (p. 41C), or the ubiquitous palm.

Egyptian monumental architecture, which is essentially a columnar and trabeated style, is expressed mainly in pyramids and other tombs and in temples, in contrast to the Near Eastern, its nearest in age, in which tombs are insignificant and spacious palaces assume an importance rivalling that of temple structure. Egyptian temples (p. 55), approached by impressive avenues of sphinxes – mythical monsters, each with the body of a lion and the head of a man, hawk, ram or woman – possess in their massive pylons, great courts, hypostyle halls, inner sanctuaries and dim, secret rooms, a special character; for typically, temples grew by accretion or replacement according to the increasing requirements of a powerful priesthood, or to satisfy the pious ambition of successive kings. Greek temples were each planned as one homogeneous whole, and the component parts were all essential to the complete design, while some of the greatest Egyptian temples were but a string of successive buildings diminishing in height behind their imposing pylons (p. 55E).

Egyptian architecture persistently maintained its traditions, and when necessity dictated a change in methods of construction or in the materials used, the traditional forms, hallowed by long use, were perpetuated in spite of novel conditions. It is impressive because of its solemnity and gloom as well as its

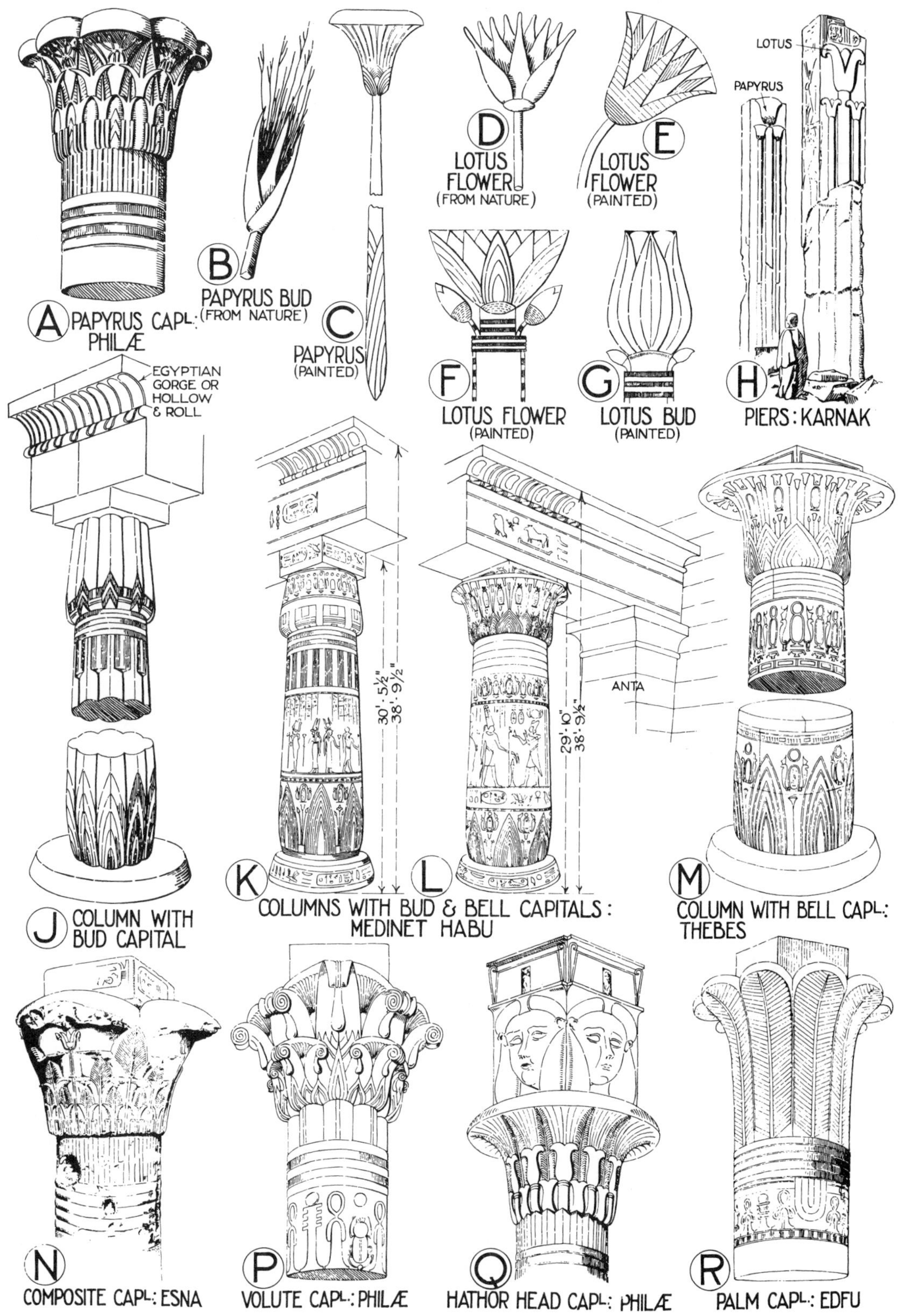
A PAPYRUS CAPL.: PHILÆ
B PAPYRUS BUD (FROM NATURE)
C PAPYRUS (PAINTED)
D LOTUS FLOWER (FROM NATURE)
E LOTUS FLOWER (PAINTED)
F LOTUS FLOWER (PAINTED)
G LOTUS BUD (PAINTED)
LOTUS
PAPYRUS
H PIERS: KARNAK
EGYPTIAN GORGE OR HOLLOW & ROLL
J COLUMN WITH BUD CAPITAL
30' 5½"
38' 9½"
29' 10"
38' 9½"
ANTA
K L COLUMNS WITH BUD & BELL CAPITALS: MEDINET HABU
M COLUMN WITH BELL CAPL.: THEBES
N COMPOSITE CAPL.: ESNA
P VOLUTE CAPL.: PHILÆ
Q HATHOR HEAD CAPL.: PHILÆ
R PALM CAPL.: EDFU

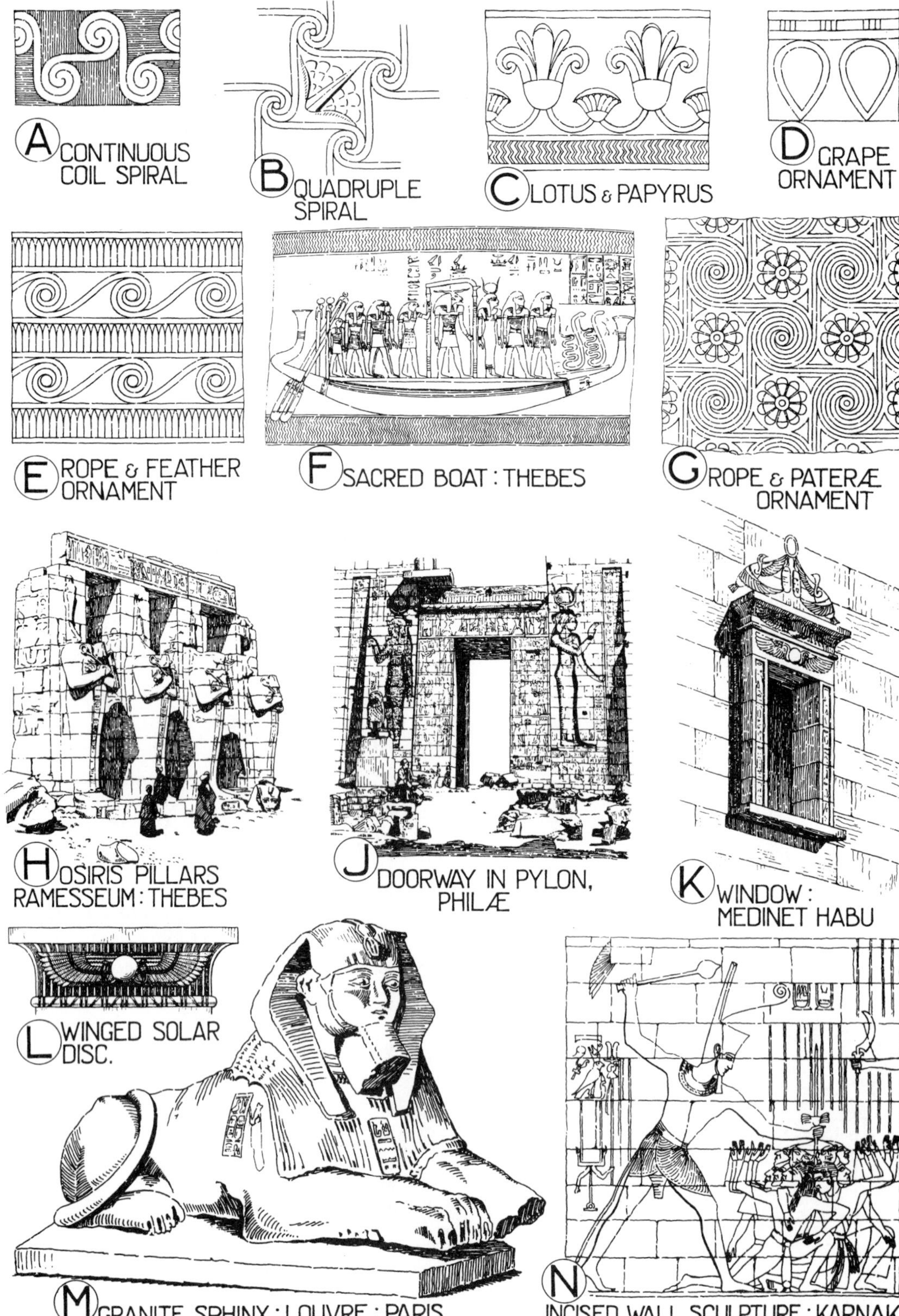
A CONTINUOUS COIL SPIRAL
B QUADRUPLE SPIRAL
C LOTUS & PAPYRUS
D GRAPE ORNAMENT
E ROPE & FEATHER ORNAMENT
F SACRED BOAT : THEBES
G ROPE & PATERÆ ORNAMENT
H OSIRIS PILLARS RAMESSEUM : THEBES
J DOORWAY IN PYLON, PHILÆ
K WINDOW : MEDINET HABU
L WINGED SOLAR DISC.
M GRANITE SPHINX : LOUVRE : PARIS
N INCISED WALL SCULPTURE : KARNAK

A. Wall sculptures, Temple of Hatshepsut, Dêr el-Bahari (*c.* 1520 BC). See p.58

B. Wall sculptures, Temple of Seti I, Abydos (*c.* 1312 BC). See p.62

ponderous solidity, which suggests that the buildings were intended to last eternally. The idea is not without foundation when we realize that the avowed purpose of the pyramids was not only to preserve the mummy of the Pharaoh for the return of the soul in the infinite hereafter, but also to be the centre of the cult of the royal dead, and as a consequence, the dominant element of the vast monumental complex.

Examples

Tomb Architecture

The tombs were of three main types: mastabas, royal pyramids and rock-hewn tombs.

Mastabas

Since the Ancient Egyptians believed so strongly in an after-life, they did their utmost, each according to his means, to build lasting tombs, to preserve the body, and to bury with it the finest commodities that might be needed for the sustenance and eternal enjoyment of the deceased. As early as the First Dynasty bands of linen were used to wrap round the limbs of the body, to aid its preservation, though embalming was not fully developed until the New Kingdom. In the Archaic period (Dynasties I – II) the king and other leading personages normally had two tombs, one in Lower Egypt and the other in Upper Egypt, the two kingdoms united by Menes, the first of the Pharaohs. Only one tomb, of course, could take the real burial, the other being a cenotaph. The royal cenotaphs were at Sakkâra, overlooking the capital Memphis, the tombs being far to the south at Abydos. Until the closing years of the First Dynasty these tombs and cenotaphs were surrounded by rows of burials, evidently those of retainers sacrificed to accompany their masters: this custom soon died out in Egypt proper.

By the First Dynasty, the more elaborate graves had come to simulate house plans of several small rooms, a central one containing the sarcophagus and others surrounding it to receive the abundant funerary offerings (p. 46A). The whole was constructed in a broad pit below ground, the wooden roof being supported by wooden posts or crude brick pillars, and the entire area covered by a rectangular, flat-topped mound of the spoil from the excavation, retained in place by very thick brick walls. The outer faces were either serrated with alternate buttress-like projections and narrow recesses – the so-called 'palace facade' arrangement – or plain, and sloped backwards at an angle of about 75°. The 'palace facade' design, perhaps derived from timber panelling equally had its origins in the mud-brick architecture of Mesopotamia in the Uruk and Jemdet Nasr periods; Mesopotamian influences on Egyptian civilisation, then in its formative phase, have long been recognised. Frequently these facades were painted in bright colours, represented by splashes of paint on the plinths at their base and hinted at by the decoration of later wooden coffins. Such tombs are nowadays known as mastabas, from their resemblance to the low benches built outside the modern Egyptian house. Closely surrounding them was an enclosure wall. Subsequent changes in the design of the mastaba may be summarised as the attempt to achieve greater security for the body of the dead owner and the goods buried with him by concentrating resources on cutting even deeper into the rock, abandoning the elaborate layout of rooms in the superstructure found in the First Dynasty tombs.

Typical of the Second and Third Dynasties is the 'stairway' mastaba, the tomb chamber, with its attendant magazines, having been sunk much deeper and cut in the rock below (p. 46B). Normally, the main axis of the tomb lay north and south, and steps and ramps led from the north end of the top of the mastaba to connect with a shaft which descended to the level of the tomb chamber. After the burial, heavy stone portcullises were dropped across the approach from slots built to receive them, and this was then filled in and all surface traces removed. Externally, the imitation of panelling was usually abandoned in favour of the plain battered sides, except that there were two well-spaced recesses on the long east side. This was the front towards the Nile. The southernmost of the two recesses was a false door (p. 46E), allowing the spirit of the deceased to enter or leave at will, and in front of it was a table for the daily offerings of fresh food.

It was here that about the Fourth Dynasty a small offering chapel developed, tacked on to the mastaba, or an offering room was constructed within the mastaba itself (p. 46C). Tomb chambers were sunk more deeply still, approached by a short horizontal passage from a vertical shaft sunk from the north end of the top of the superstructure. There are many such 'shaft' mastabas at Gizeh (p. 46D). By this time the majority of the mastabas were of limestone, which had been used only sparingly for floors and wall linings in the finest of the brick mastabas of early dynastic times. With the Fifth and Sixth Dynasties the offering room or chapel at ground level tended to become increasingly elaborate (p. 46F,G). In the most sumptuous examples, there might be a group of rooms, within or adjacent to the mastaba mound, including a columned hall, the walls lined with vividly-coloured reliefs, depicting scenes from the daily life of the deceased. Important among the rooms was the 'serdab' – sometimes there was more than one – completely enclosed except for a slot opposite the head of a statue of the deceased contained within.

In the offering room was a 'stele', an upright stone slab inscribed with the name of the deceased, funerary texts and relief carvings intended to serve in the event of failure in the supply of daily offerings. An offering-table stood at its foot.

The **Mastaba K.1 at Beit Khallaf** (p. 46B) is a massive 'stairway' tomb of crude brick, typical of the Third Dynasty. The stairs and ramp, guarded by five stone portcullises, lead to a rock-cut, stone-lined tomb chamber surrounded by a knot of magazines for the funerary offerings. Above ground, the mastaba is plain and virtually solid.

The **Mastabas at Gizeh**, mostly of the Fourth and Fifth Dynasties, number two or three hundred, arranged in orderly ranks, and adjoin the famous pyramids there (pp.46C,D, 51A). Fourth Dynasty examples illustrate, on the one hand, the development of the offering chapel (p. 46C), and on the other, the typical 'shaft' mastaba (p. 46D) with deep, underground tomb chambers and a sloping-sided superstructure having two widely spaced recesses on the long east side, the southern one of which served as a false door (p. 46E) and for offerings.

The **Mastaba of Thi, Sakkâra** (p. 46G), a high dignitary of the Fifth Dynasty, has all the elaboration of its time. A large pillared court is attached to the north end of the east side, approached from the north by a portico which has a serdab alongside. A passage connects the court with a small chamber and an offering-room, with two pillars, lying inside the mastaba itself. This is equipped with two stelae and an offering-table against the west wall; and south of it is a second serdab, with three slots through the intervening wall corresponding to the three duplicate statues of Thi enclosed there. The low-relief sculptures of this tomb are among the finest and most interesting in Egypt (p. 46F). The actual tomb chamber is below the south end of the mastaba, behind the west wall of the offering-room but at a much lower level. It is reached from a passage slanting diagonally to connect with a stairway emerging in the centre of the court.

Royal Pyramids

The great pyramids of the Third to Sixth Dynasties are on sites distributed intermittently along the west side of the Nile for about fifty miles southward of the apex of the Delta, standing on the rocky shelf clear of the cultivated land. Early royal tombs were of the mastaba type, from which the true pyramid evolved, the most important stages being demonstrated by the early Third Dynasty 'Step' pyramid of the Pharaoh Zoser at Sakkâra (pp. 47, 48). Further stages of development are marked by one at Meydûm and by two at Dahshûr by Seneferu, first king of the Fourth Dynasty, including the so-called 'Bent' pyramid. The finest true pyramids are the famous three at Gizeh, built by the Fourth Dynasty successors of Seneferu.

Pyramids did not stand in solitary isolation but were the primary part of a complex of buildings. They were surrounded by a walled enclosure and had an offering chapel, with a stele, usually abutting the east side of the pyramid but occasionally on the north; a mortuary temple for the worship of the dead and deified Pharaoh, on the north side in Zoser's complex but normally projecting from the enclosure on the east side; and a raised and enclosed causeway leading to the nearer, western edge of the cultivation where there stood a 'Valley Building' in which embalmment was carried out and interment rites performed. A canal was built to connect the Valley Building with the Nile, by which the funeral cortège magnificently arrived.

Pyramids were built with immense outlay in labour and material, in the lifetime of the Pharaohs concerned, to secure the preservation of the body after death till that time should have passed when, according to their belief in immortality, the soul would once more return to the body. Infinite pains were taken to conceal and protect the tomb chamber and its contents, as well as the approach passages, but all precautions proved to be vain, for they were successively rifled first in the period of chaos which followed the Sixth Dynasty and again in the Persian, Roman and Arab periods. Pyramids were founded on the living rock, levelled to receive them, and were of limestone quarried in their locality, faced with the finer limestone coming from Tura on the opposite, eastern, side of the Nile. Granite, in limited use for such as the linings of the chambers and passages, was brought from up-river at Aswan. Tomb chambers and their approaches were either cut in the rock below the monument or were in its constructed core. Entrances normally were from the north side, and the sides were scrupulously oriented with the cardinal points.

In all known cases, pyramids were built in a series of concentric sloping slices or layers around a steep pyramidal core, so that the whole mass first appeared in step-like tiers, until, in the case of the true pyramidal form, the steps had been filled in with packing blocks and brought with finely finished facings to their ultimate shape, at the chosen angle of inclination. Nevertheless, all the inner layers were built more or less at the same time, course by course, so that as work proceeded the top was always approximately level. The final meticulous dressing of the finished faces was from top to bottom, and the apex stone probably was gilded.

The Egyptians did not know of the pulley, and their principal tool for raising and turning stone blocks was the lever. To transport them overland, wooden sledges were used, with or without the aid of rollers dropped in turn in front of a sledge and picked up again behind. Blocks for the pyramids were hauled up great broad-topped, sloping ramps of sand or earth, reinforced with crude brick walls, such ramps being placed at right angles to the most convenient of the faces.

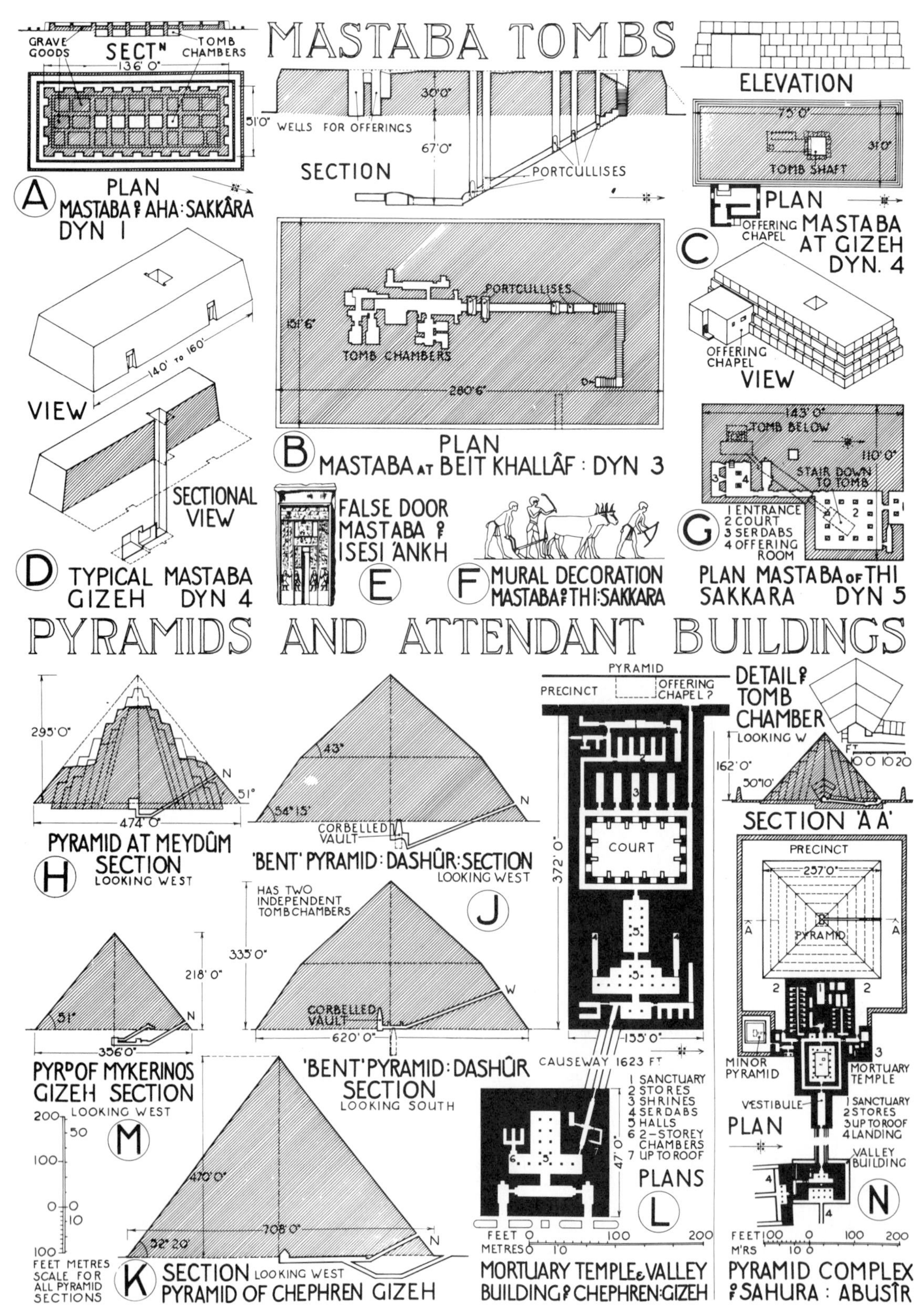
MASTABA TOMBS
GRAVE GOODS
SECTN
TOMB CHAMBERS
136' 0"
51'0"
A PLAN MASTABA OF AHA : SAKKÂRA DYN 1
WELLS FOR OFFERINGS
30'0"
67'0"
SECTION
PORTCULLISES
ELEVATION
75'0"
31'0"
TOMB SHAFT
PLAN
OFFERING CHAPEL
C MASTABA AT GIZEH DYN. 4
OFFERING CHAPEL
VIEW
151'6"
PORTCULLISES
TOMB CHAMBERS
280'6"
B PLAN MASTABA AT BEIT KHALLÂF : DYN 3
VIEW
140' to 160'
SECTIONAL VIEW
D TYPICAL MASTABA GIZEH DYN 4
FALSE DOOR MASTABA OF ISESI ÁNKH
E
F MURAL DECORATION MASTABA OF THI : SAKKARA
143' 0"
TOMB BELOW
110'0"
STAIR DOWN TO TOMB
1 ENTRANCE
2 COURT
3 SERDABS
4 OFFERING ROOM
G PLAN MASTABA OF THI SAKKARA DYN 5
PYRAMIDS AND ATTENDANT BUILDINGS
295'0"
51°
474'0"
PYRAMID AT MEYDÛM SECTION LOOKING WEST
H
43°
54°15'
CORBELLED VAULT
'BENT' PYRAMID : DASHÛR : SECTION LOOKING WEST
J
HAS TWO INDEPENDENT TOMB CHAMBERS
335'0"
CORBELLED VAULT
620'0"
'BENT' PYRAMID : DASHÛR SECTION LOOKING SOUTH
218'0"
51°
356'0"
PYRD OF MYKERINOS GIZEH SECTION LOOKING WEST
M
470'0"
708'0"
52°20'
K SECTION LOOKING WEST PYRAMID OF CHEPHREN GIZEH
FEET METRES SCALE FOR ALL PYRAMID SECTIONS
PYRAMID
PRECINCT
OFFERING CHAPEL?
COURT
372'0"
155'0"
CAUSEWAY 1623 FT
47'0"
1 SANCTUARY
2 STORES
3 SHRINES
4 SERDABS
5 HALLS
6 2-STOREY CHAMBERS
7 UP TO ROOF
PLANS
L
FEET
METRES
MORTUARY TEMPLE & VALLEY BUILDING OF CHEPHREN : GIZEH
DETAIL OF TOMB CHAMBER
LOOKING W
162'0"
50°10'
SECTION 'A A'
PRECINCT
257'0"
PYRAMID
MINOR PYRAMID
MORTUARY TEMPLE
VESTIBULE
1 SANCTUARY
2 STORES
3 UP TO ROOF
4 LANDING
PLAN
VALLEY BUILDING
N
M'RS
PYRAMID COMPLEX OF SAHURA : ABUSÎR

Step Pyramid of Zoser, Sakkâra (2778 BC.) See p.49

A. (*above*) Restored view of the pyramid and enclosure from the flooded Nile valley

B. (*left*) Aerial view of the pyramid and enclosure

C. Processional corridor (restored)

D. Angle of Great Court

STEP PYRAMID OF ZOSER: SAKKARA

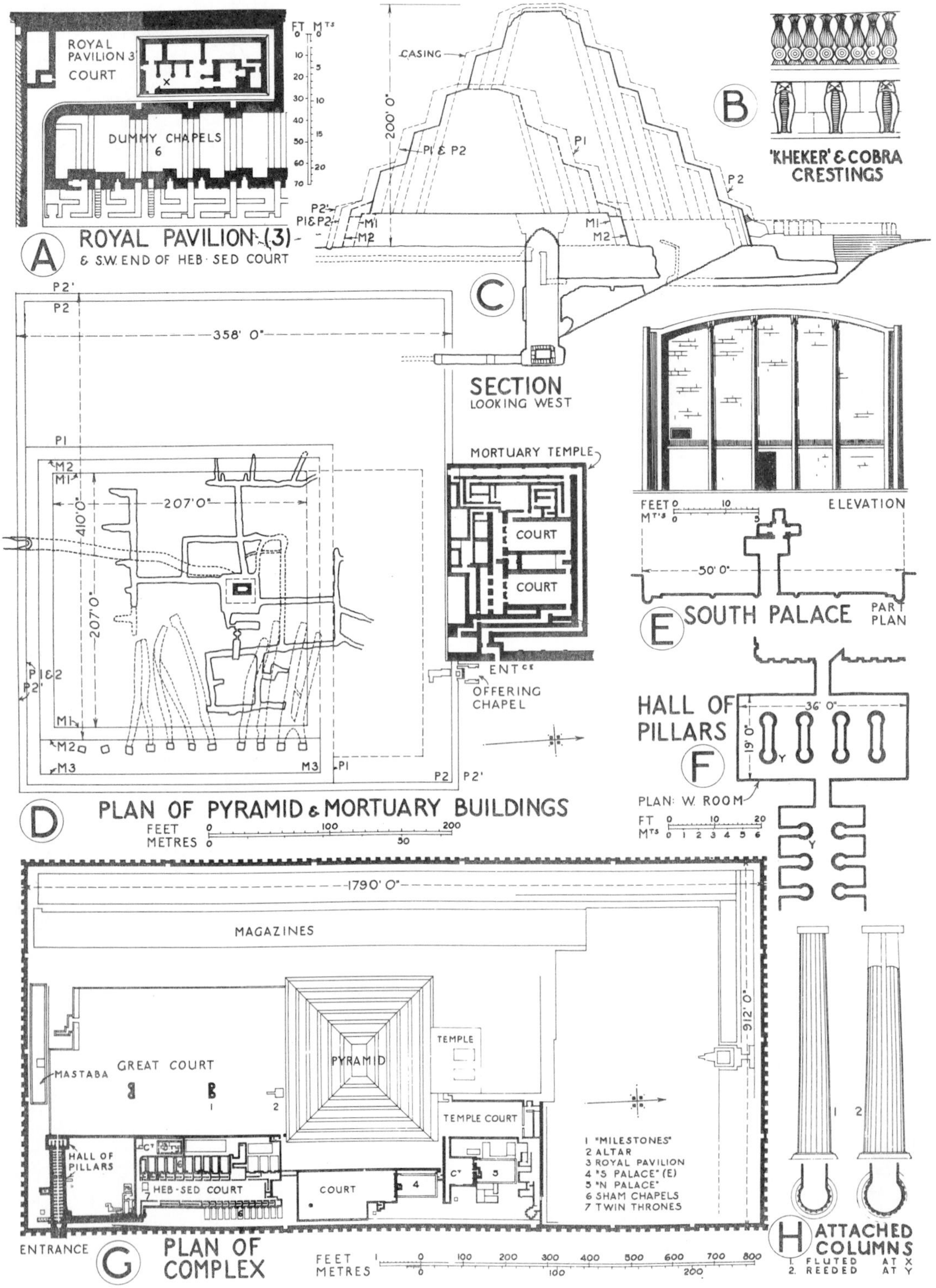

ROYAL PAVILION 3
COURT
X
DUMMY CHAPELS
6
FT MTS
0 0
10 5
20
30 10
40
50 15
60 20
70

(A) ROYAL PAVILION (3)
& S.W. END OF HEB-SED COURT

CASING
200' 0"
P1 & P2
P1
P2
P2'
P1 & P2
M1
M2
M1
M2

(C) SECTION
LOOKING WEST

(B) 'KHEKER' & COBRA CRESTINGS

P2'
P2
358' 0"
P1
M2
M1
207' 0"
410' 0"
207' 0"
P1 & 2
P2'
M1
M2
M3
M3
P1
P2
P2'

MORTUARY TEMPLE
COURT
COURT
ENTCE
OFFERING CHAPEL

(D) PLAN OF PYRAMID & MORTUARY BUILDINGS
FEET 0 100 200
METRES 0 50

FEET 0 10
MT'S 0 5
ELEVATION
50' 0"
(E) SOUTH PALACE PART PLAN

HALL OF PILLARS
36' 0"
19' 0"
Y
(F)
PLAN: W. ROOM
FT 0 10 20
MTS 0 1 2 3 4 5 6
Y

1790' 0"
MAGAZINES
MASTABA
GREAT COURT
1
2
PYRAMID
TEMPLE
TEMPLE COURT
912' 0"
HALL OF PILLARS
C'
HEB-SED COURT
7
6
COURT
4
C'
5

1 "MILESTONES"
2 ALTAR
3 ROYAL PAVILION
4 "S PALACE" (E)
5 "N PALACE"
6 SHAM CHAPELS
7 TWIN THRONES

ENTRANCE
(G) PLAN OF COMPLEX
FEET 0 100 200 300 400 500 600 700 800
METRES 0 100 200

1 2
(H) ATTACHED COLUMNS
1. FLUTED AT X
2. REEDED AT Y

The **Step Pyramid of Zoser, Sakkâra** (2778 BC, beginning of Third Dynasty) (pp.47, 48) is remarkable as being the world's first large-scale monument in stone. King Zoser's architect, Imhotep, was greatly revered both in his own and later times, and in the Twenty-sixth Dynasty was deified. The pyramid itself shows no less than five changes of plan in the course of building. It began as a complete mastaba, 7.9 m (26 ft) high, unusual in having a square plan, with sides of 63 m (207 ft). It was then twice extended, first by a regular addition of 4.3 m (14 ft) to each of its sloping sides and next by an extension eastwards of 8.5 m (28 ft). At this stage the whole was used as a basis for a four-stepped pyramid, made up of layers inclined against a steep-sided core, and again enlarged at the same time so that its plan became a rectangle of about 83 m × 75 m (272 ft × 244 ft). A further enormous addition on the north and west, followed by a comparatively slight one all round, brought it to its final dimensions of 125 m (410 ft) from east to west by 109 m (358 ft) wide and 60 m (200 ft) high, and added two more steps to the height, making six in all. In this stepped form it remained. Usually, underground tomb chambers were finished before the superstructure had been begun, but here there were two stages owing to the successive enlargements above. A pit of 7.3 m (24 ft) side and 8.5 m (28 ft) deep was the counterpart of the first mastaba, approached by a horizontal tunnel emerging at the north side in an open ramp. This pit was deepened to 28 m (92 ft) at the pyramid stage of development, and had an Aswan granite tomb chamber at the bottom, above which was a limestone-walled room containing a granite plug to stop a hole at the top of the tomb chamber when the burial had been completed. The approach tunnel too was deepened and converted to a ramp entering the pit at a point some 21.5 m (70 ft) above its base. From the bottom of the pit four corridors extend irregularly towards the four cardinal points, connecting to galleries running approximately parallel with the four sides of the pyramid, and having spur galleries thrusting from them. Independent of the main subterranean system is a series of eleven separate pits, 32 m (106 ft) deep, on the east side of the original mastaba. These were tombs of members of the royal family. The tomb entrances were sealed by the third extension of the mastaba.

Surrounding the pyramid was a vast rectangular enclosure, 547 m (1790 ft) from north to south and 278 m (912 ft) wide, with a massive Tura limestone wall, 10.7 m (35 ft) high, indented in the manner of the earlier mastaba facades. Around the walls were bastions, fourteen in all, and each had stone false doors. The only entrance was in a broader bastion near the southern end of the eastern face. In the fact that there is a small offering chapel (with stelae, offering table and a statue of Zoser) and a well-developed mortuary temple, containing two courts, a maze of corridors and many rooms, the buildings inside the enclosure show some relation to earlier developments of the mastaba; but these two buildings abut the north face of the pyramid, instead of the east as was to be the common practice, and all the rest of the structures are quite exceptional and unique to this complex. They are dummy representations of the palace of Zoser and the buildings used in connection with the celebration of his jubilee in his lifetime. Most of them therefore are solid, or almost so, comprised of earth or debris faced with Tura limestone. They are grouped around courts.

The entrance to the great enclosure leads to a long processional corridor lined with reeded columns – this site provides the only known instances of the type – which bore architraves and a roof of long stones shaped on the underside like timber logs (p. 47). At the inner end of the corridor is a pillared hall, with reeded columns attached in pairs, beyond which is the Great Court (p. 47), where there are two low B-shaped pedestals, used in the royal ceremonial, an altar near the pyramid south face and, on the south side of the court, a mastaba, unusually aligned east-west. Just inside the enclosure entrance a narrow corridor runs deviously northwards to the Heb-sed Court, the principal scene of this festival, lined with sham chapels, each with its small forecourt, those on the western side representing the provinces or 'nomes' of Upper Egypt and those on the eastern, of Lower Egypt. These virtually solid structures had segmental-arched roofs, as also had two similarly solid large halls of unequal size farther north, each facing southwards into its own court; the halls might have symbolised the two kingdoms. The facades of all of them, chapels and halls, bore three slender, attached columns. Near to the Heb-sed Court, to the west, is the so-called 'Royal Pavilion', within which are three fluted, attached columns. In Zoser's complex as a whole, the masonry technique and the almost total absence of free-standing columns, together with the small spans of the stone beam roofs, indicates the novelty of stone as a building material at this time. The architectural forms show clearly their derivation from earlier structures in reeds, timber or sun-dried brick.

The **Pyramid at Meydûm** (p. 46H) is attributed to Huni, last king of the Third Dynasty. Though eventually completed as a true pyramid, at one stage it was a seven-stepped structure, contrived by building six thick layers of masonry, each faced with Tura limestone, against a nucleus with sides sloping steeply at 75°; there was then an addition of a fresh layer all round, raising the number of steps to eight. These again were faced with Tura limestone, dressed only where the faces showed. Thus both the seven- and the eight-step pyramids had at the time been regarded as finished. But there was yet a further development, in which the steps were packed out and the sides made smooth with finely-dressed Tura

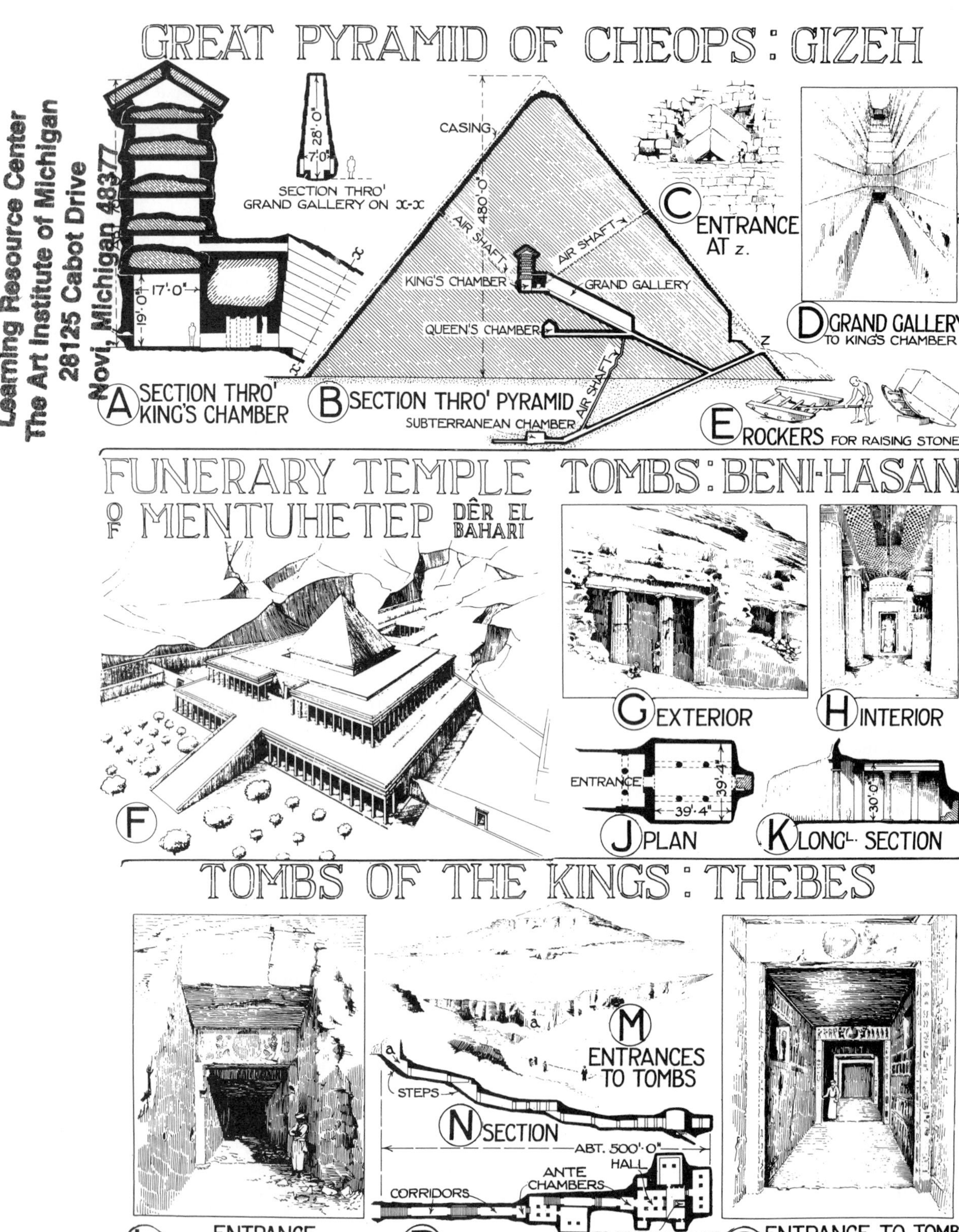
GREAT PYRAMID OF CHEOPS : GIZEH
SECTION THRO' GRAND GALLERY ON x-x
28'·0"
7'·0"
17'·0"
19'·0"
CASING
480'·0"
AIR SHAFT
KING'S CHAMBER
GRAND GALLERY
QUEEN'S CHAMBER
SUBTERRANEAN CHAMBER
A SECTION THRO' KING'S CHAMBER
B SECTION THRO' PYRAMID
C ENTRANCE AT z.
D GRAND GALLERY TO KING'S CHAMBER
E ROCKERS FOR RAISING STONES
FUNERARY TEMPLE OF MENTUHETEP DÊR EL BAHARI
F
TOMBS : BENI-HASAN
G EXTERIOR
H INTERIOR
ENTRANCE
39'·4"
J PLAN
30'·0"
K LONGL. SECTION
TOMBS OF THE KINGS : THEBES
L ENTRANCE TO A TOMB : THEBES
M ENTRANCES TO TOMBS
STEPS
N SECTION
ABT. 500'·0"
HALL
ANTE CHAMBERS
CORRIDORS
TO MUMMY SHAFT
P PLAN : TOMB OF SETI·I
Q ENTRANCE TO TOMB OF RAMESES·IX

A. The Pyramids, Gizeh: aerial view from SE, with the Sphinx and Valley Building of Chephren in the middle foreground (*c.* 2723–2563 BC)., See p.52

B. Tombs at Beni Hasan (2130–1785 BC). See p.54

stone. Of this ultimate true pyramid, 144.5 m (474 ft) square on base and 90 m (295 ft) high, with sides sloping at 51°, the lower portion still survives, but the upper part has been oddly denuded into a shouldered, tower-like structure. The simple, corbel-roofed tomb chamber was at ground-level in the heart of the masonry. Around the pyramid was a stone enclosure wall, 233 m (764 ft) from north to south, by 209 m (686 ft), within which were a small pyramid on the south side and a mastaba on the north. Abutting the centre of the east face of the pyramid was a small offering-chapel, with an offering-table, flanked by two stelae, in its inner small court. There was no mortuary temple, but a causeway from the eastern wall led to the Valley Building, now submerged.

The **Bent or South Pyramid of Seneferu, Dahshûr** (2723 BC) (p. 46J) has the peculiarities, first, that the angle of inclination of the sides changes about halfway up from 54° 15 minutes in the lower part to 43° in the upper, where it shows hasty completion; and second, that it has two entirely independent tomb chambers, reached one from the north side and one from the west. The change in slope had the object of lightening the weight of the upper masonry, as the walls of chambers and passages began to show fissures. The plan is square, 187 m (620 ft), and the height about 102 m (335 ft), the materials being the usual local stone with Tura limestone facing, well preserved. The tomb-chambers are covered by corbelled roofs with gradually in-stepping courses from all four sides, that over the lower chamber concluding with a 305 mm (12 in) span some 24 m (80 ft) above the floor. Corbelling, as instanced here and at Meydûm, is thus one of the earliest experimental devices for constructing a stone vault. Around the pyramid there was a double-walled rectangular enclosure, an offering chapel and a mortuary temple on the east side and a causeway leading to the Valley Building. The subsidiary structures here probably provide the first instance of what was to be the customary complement and arrangement.

The **North Pyramid of Seneferu, Dahshûr**, made after the abandonment of the Bent Pyramid, was the actual place of burial of Seneferu, for nearby are tombs of the royal family and officiating priests; it was designed and completed as a true pyramid, the earliest known. The pitch of its sides, however, is unusually low: 43° 36 minutes, instead of the usual 52° or so, and thus very similar to that of the upper part of the Bent Pyramid. For the rest the pyramid is normal.

The **Great Pyramid of Cheops** (Khufu), **near Cairo** (pp.50A–E, 51A). Cheops was the son of Seneferu, and the second king of the Fourth Dynasty. His pyramid, largest of the famous three on this site, was originally 146.4 m (480 ft) high and 230.6 m (756 ft) square on plan, with an area of about 13 acres, or more than twice that of S. Peter, Rome. The four sides, which, as in all periods with only a minor exception, face the cardinal points, are nearly equilateral triangles and make an angle of 51° 52 minutes with the ground. There are three separate internal chambers, due to changes of plan in the course of building. The subterranean chamber and the so-called 'Queen's Chamber' are discarded projects, abandoned in turn in favour of the 'King's Chamber' where the granite sarcophagus is located. The entrance is 7.3 m (24 ft) off-centre on the north side, and 17 m (55 ft) above ground level, measured vertically, leading to a corridor descending at about 26° to the original rock-cut chamber. In this descending corridor, after the first change of plan, an ascending corridor was cut in the ceiling, about 18.3 m (60 ft) along, rising to some 21 m (70 ft) above ground, at which level the Queen's Chamber was constructed. But before it was entirely completed, the approach was sealed off and the ascending corridor extended into what is now known as the Grand Gallery (p. 50D), a passage 2.1 m (7 ft) wide and 2.3 m (7 ft 6 in) high, covered by a ramped, corbelled vault of seven great courses, rising to a height of 8.5 m (28 ft) vertically from the floor, where the surviving span of 1.1 m (3 ft 6 in) is closed by stone slabs. At the top, the Grand Gallery gave on to the King's Chamber, 5.2 m (17 ft 2 in) from north to south, 10.5 m (34 ft 4 in) long and 5.8 m (19 ft) high, which like its vestibule is lined in granite. In the vestibule there were originally three massive granite slabs, let down in slots in the side walls to seal the chamber after the burial. The covering of the chamber is most elaborate. Five tiers of great stone beams, nine to a tier and together weighing about 406 tonnes (400 tons), are ranged one above the other, with a void space between the layers. Above them all is an embryonic vault of pairs of great stones inclined against one another. This latter device occurs also over the Queen's Chamber and again over the pyramid entrance, where just within the former casing there are pairs of inclined stones superposed in two tiers (p. 50C). Two shafts, 203 mm × 152 mm (8 in × 6 in), leading from the King's Chamber to the outer face of the pyramid, may have been for ventilation or to allow the free passage of the Ka or spirit of the dead king. There are similar shafts from the Queen's Chamber, left incomplete like the chamber itself.

Built solidly of local stone, the pyramid originally was cased in finely dressed Tura limestone blocks and the apex stone perhaps gilded, but only a few casing stones at the base now survive. The average weight of blocks is 2500 kg (2½ tons); they are bedded in a thin lime-mortar, used as a lubricant during fixing rather than as an adhesive, and are laid with amazingly fine joints. Little trace of the pyramid enclosure wall now exists, nor does much remain of the customary attendant buildings. The offering chapel abutted the centre of the pyramid east face, and the mortuary temple stood axially in front of it, joined by a causeway which led askew eastwards towards the

Valley Building. Flanking the temple on east and west are two boat-shaped pits cut in the rock, and there is a third alongside the north flank of the causeway. Whether these actually contained wooden boats for the king's transport in his afterlife is not definitely known. In 1954 two more pits were discovered adjacent to the south side of the pyramid, covered with stone beams as originally the others had been, in which wooden boats, 35.5 m (115 ft) long, were disclosed intact and in a remarkably fine state of preservation. At a little distance south-east of the east face of the pyramid are three subsidiary pyramids, with chapels on their own east sides, tombs of Cheops' queens.

The **Pyramid of Chephren** (Khafra) (Fourth Dynasty) (pp. 46K,L, 51A) is the second of the three at Gizeh and only a little less large than the Great Pyramid, 216 m (708 ft) side and 143 m (470 ft) high, but has a steeper slope (52° 20 minutes). There is only one chamber at the core, partly in the rock and partly built-up, but two approaches to it from the north: one through the stonework and the other subterranean, these joining halfway. Near the apex of the pyramid much of the original limestone casing is preserved, and there are fragments to show that the two base courses of the facing were of granite. The remaining buildings of the complex, too, are better preserved than in other cases. The offering chapel and the mortuary temple were in the normal positions axial on the east face. The latter, 113.3 m (372 ft) from east to west and 47.2 m (155 ft) wide, was of limestone, lined internally on the north. It was extremely solid and barren of features externally. To the west of a great open court, with twelve statues against the piers between the many openings leading to a surrounding corridor, were five deep chambers for statues of the Pharaoh, the central one wider than the rest, while behind them were corresponding stores, serdabs, and the only entrance to the pyramid enclosure. East of the court was a fore-temple, very similar in plan to the Valley Building, with two pillared halls and long serdabs on the wings. From an entrance corridor there opened in the north-east-corner of the block a series of four rooms in alabaster, where there were alabaster chests containing elements of the viscera, and in the south-east corner were two rooms in granite which received the two royal crowns. Despite the essential symmetry of the plan, the entrance was insignificant and off-centre, leading aslant to the causeway from the Valley Building, which survives substantially intact.

The Valley Building (p. 46L) is 44.8 m (147 ft) square and battered outside and vertical within. In this building and on its roof, various ceremonies of purification, mummification and 'opening of the mouth' were conducted. Dual entrances lead from a landing place to a transverse vestibule, and thence to a T-shaped granite-pillared hall, around which were ranged twenty-three statues of the king, the hall being lit by slots in the angle of the wall and ceiling (as p. 57E). Off the southern arm of the hall, there are three chambers in two tiers, while on the opposite flank an alabaster stair turns through angles to the roof, cutting across the approach to the causeway in the process.

A little to the north-west of the Valley Building is the **Great Sphinx of Chephren** (p. 51A), the colossal enigmatic monster carved from a spur of rock left by Cheops' quarry-masons. It bears the head of Chephren, wearing the royal head-dress, false beard and cobra brow ornament, and has the body of a recumbent lion. The sculpture is 73.2 m (240 ft) long and 20 m (66 ft) maximum height, the face being 4.1m (13 ft 6 in) across. Deficiencies in the rock were made good in stonework. Between the forepaws is a large, inscribed granite stele, recording a restoration made by Thothmes IV (1425 BC), of the Eighteenth Dynasty.

The **Pyramid of Mykerinos** (Menkaura) (Fourth Dynasty) (pp. 46M, 51A) is much smaller than its two predecessors at Gizeh, 109 m (356 ft) square and 66.5 m (218 ft) high, with sides sloping at 51°. Much of the casing is preserved, and is mainly Tura limestone but includes sixteen base courses in granite.

The principal pyramids of the Fifth and Sixth Dynasties (2563–2263 BC), all built at Abusîr and Sakkâra, were inferior in size and construction to those of the previous dynasty, and tomb chambers and their corridors were simpler and more sterotyped in arrangement.

The **Pyramid of Sahura, Abusîr** (Fifth Dynasty) (p. 46N), is remarkable for the triple series of enormous paired-stone false arches which cover its tomb chamber. It is representative of Fifth and Sixth Dynasty practice in several important particulars. Its complex still has the old elements of valley building, causeway and mortuary temple, but the offering chapel is now incorporated in the temple. A subsidiary small pyramid is included in the south-east angle of the enclosure; this was not a burial place for a queen but had a ritual significance. Relative to the Fourth Dynasty, there is a considerable increase in the number of store-chambers, which tend to enlarge and complicate the plan of the mortuary temple. In decoration, wall reliefs are profuse – a feature which applies also to contemporary mastabas, for example the Mastaba of Thi (p. 46F). Particularly important architecturally was the use now of granite, free-standing columns, with reeded or plain shafts, and lotus, papyrus or palm capitals, replacing the wholly plain and square pillars of Fourth Dynasty buildings.

Rock-hewn Tombs

These are rare before the Middle Kingdom, and even at that time they served for the nobility rather than royalty; pyramids, though of indifferent construction, remained the principal form of royal tomb.

The **Tombs, Beni Hasan**, numbering thirty-nine, are of the Eleventh and Twelfth Dynasties (2130–1785 BC) and belonged to a provincial great family. They are wholly rock-hewn; each consists of a chamber behind a porticoed facade plainly imitating wooden construction in the character of the eight- or sixteen-sided, slightly fluted and tapered columns, their trabeation and the rafter ends above (p. 50G–K, 51B). Some tombs, like that of Khnemhetep, have slightly-vaulted rock ceilings, supported on fluted or reeded columns, and walls in general were lightly stuccoed and painted with pastoral, domestic and other scenes.

The **Tombs of the Kings, Thebes** (p. 50L–Q) are in the arid mountains on the west side of the Nile. They witness a complete abandonment of the royal pyramid tomb during the New Kingdom in favour of a corridor type, in which stairs, passages and chambers extend as much as 210 m (690 ft) into the mountain side and up to 96 m (315 ft) below the valley floor. The sarcophagus usually lay in a concluding rock-columned hall, and the walls were elaborately painted with ceremonial funerary scenes and religious texts. The most important tombs are those of Seti I and Rameses III, IV and IX. The tombs served only for the sarcophagus and funerary deposits; the mortuary temples stood completely detached (for example, the Ramesseum, that at Medînet-Habu and Queen Hatshepsut's temple at Dêr el-Bahari), sited in the necropolis adjacent to the western, cultivated land, where there were similar but smaller tombs of high-ranking persons. The temple of Mentuhetep II at Dêr el-Bahari (Middle Kingdom) is transitional, being conjoined with the rock-cut tomb, while also having a small pyramid in its confines.

Temples

Temples were of two main classes; the mortuary temples, for ministrations to deified Pharaohs; and the cult temples, for the popular worship of the ancient and mysterious gods. The mortuary temples developed from the offering chapels of the royal mastabas and pyramids, assuming early permanence and ever greater importance. In the Middle Kingdom, when royal burials began to be made in the hillside, they became architecturally the more important of the two elements; and in the New Kingdom they stood quite detached from the then-customary corridor tombs. Thereafter, their special character tended increasingly to merge into that of the cult temples, and distinction between the two types was eventually lost.

Cult temples began in the worship of multifarious local deities. The original essentials were a rectangular palisaded court, entered from a narrow end flanked by pennon-poles and having centrally within them an emblem of the deity. Inside the further end of the court was a pavilion, comprising vestibule and sanctuary. Owing to successive rebuildings upon these ancient sites, the stages of development are difficult to trace. Apparently, little but the sanctuary and attendant apartments was being built in stone at the opening of the Eighteenth Dynasty, but somewhat later in the New Kingdom, the influx of wealth and universal spread of favoured cults brought the cult temples into full flower.

By this time, mortuary and cult temples had most features in common, yet still bore a resemblance of arrangement to the most venerable shrines. Along a main axis, not specifically oriented, there was a walled open court, with colonnades around, leading to a covered structure, comprising a transverse columned vestibule or 'hypostyle hall' and a sanctuary beyond (or more than one if the temple had a multiple dedication) attended by chapels and other rooms needed by the priesthood. An impressive axial gateway to the court was traditional; it now was extended across the whole width of the court to form a towering, sloping-sided pair of pylons, with tall portal between, equipped with pennon-masts, gorge cornice and roll-moulded outer angles. Temple services were held thrice daily, with none but the priesthood admitted to them, though privileged persons might sometimes be admitted to the court for certain ceremonies. In the cult temples, processions were a feature, particularly during the periodic festivals, so free circulation was required through or around the sanctuary. Numerous festivals were celebrated during the year, some of which might last for days; at times, shrines of the gods were carried by land or water to other temples or sacred sites in the neighbourhood, and it was only on such occasions that the populace in general took any kind of part. The whole temple itself stood within a great enclosure, and about it were houses of the priests, official buildings, stores, granaries and a sacred pool or lake (p. 65A).

The **Temple of Khons, Karnak** (1198 BC) pp. 55E–H, 57A), a cult temple, may be taken as the usual type, characterised by entrance pylons, court hypostyle hall, sanctuary, and various chapels, all enclosed by a high girdle wall. The entrance pylons, fronted by obelisks, were approached through an imposing avenue of sphinxes. The portal gave on to the open court, surrounded on three sides by a double colonnade and leading to the hypostyle hall, to which light was admitted by a clerestory, formed by the increased height of the columns of the central aisle. Beyond was the sanctuary, with openings front and rear and a circulating passage around, and beyond this again was a four-columned hall. The smaller rooms flanking the sanctuary and at its rear were mostly chapels or served for purposes of the ritual. The temple was protected by a great wall of the same height as the halls themselves, and like them the wall decreased in height towards the sanctuary end.

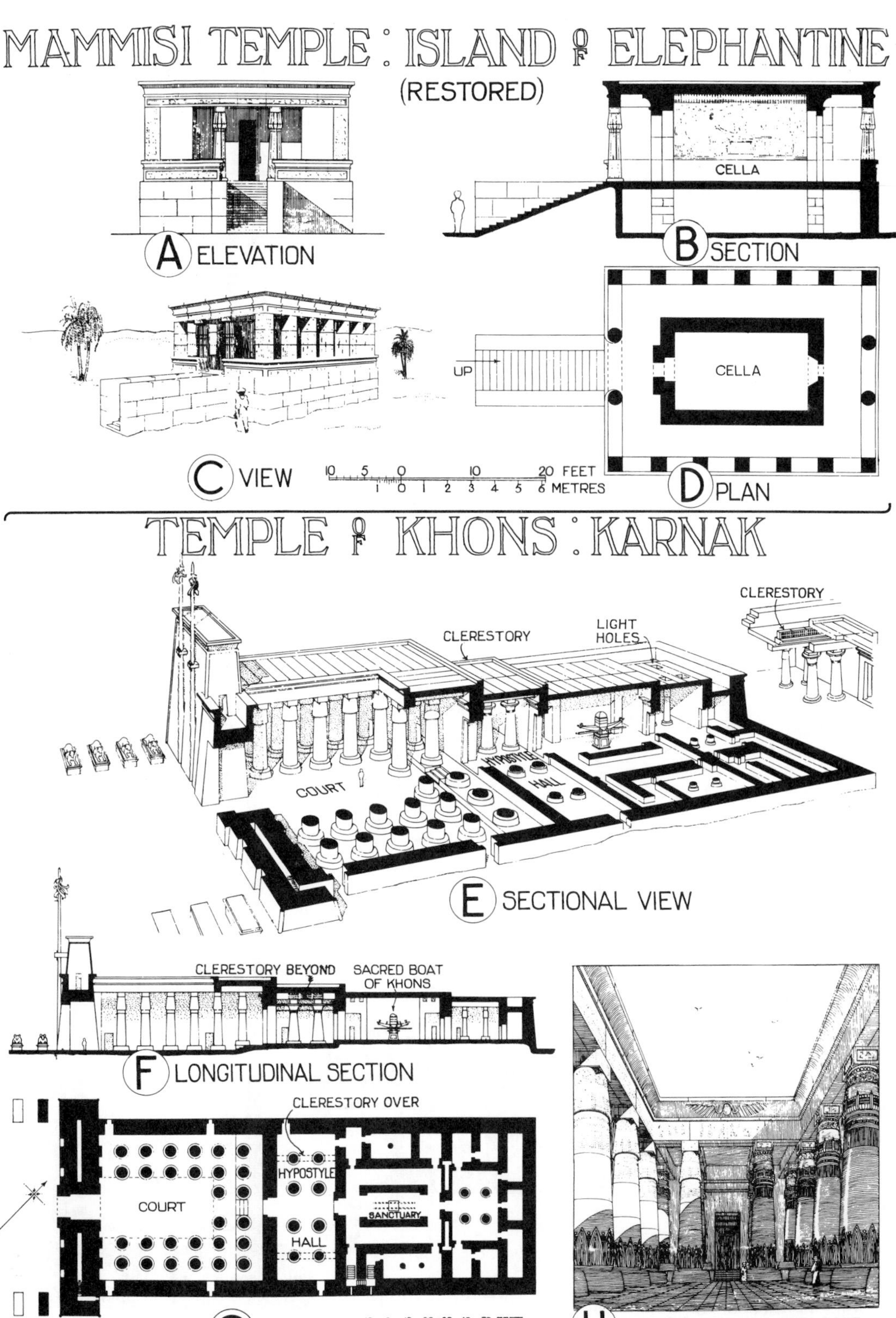
MAMMISI TEMPLE: ISLAND OF ELEPHANTINE
(RESTORED)
CELLA
A ELEVATION
B SECTION
UP
CELLA
C VIEW
10 5 0 10 20 FEET
1 0 1 2 3 4 5 6 METRES
D PLAN
TEMPLE OF KHONS: KARNAK
CLERESTORY
CLERESTORY
LIGHT HOLES
COURT
HYPOSTYLE
HALL
E SECTIONAL VIEW
CLERESTORY BEYOND
SACRED BOAT OF KHONS
F LONGITUDINAL SECTION
CLERESTORY OVER
HYPOSTYLE
COURT
SANCTUARY
HALL
G PLAN
10 0 10 20 30 40 50 FEET
5 0 5 10 15 METRES
H COURT FROM ENTRANCE

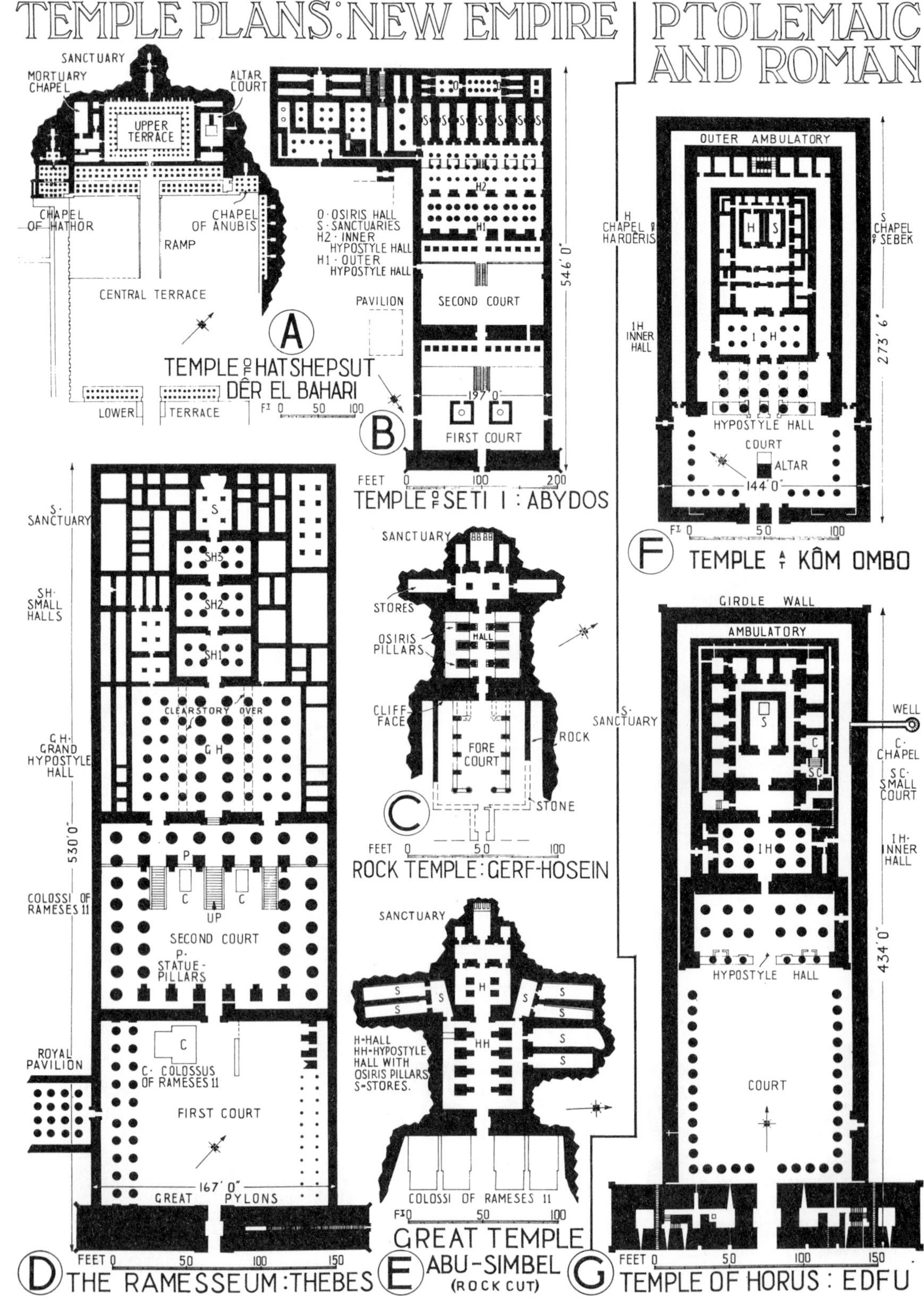
TEMPLE PLANS: NEW EMPIRE
PTOLEMAIC AND ROMAN
SANCTUARY
MORTUARY CHAPEL
ALTAR COURT
UPPER TERRACE
CHAPEL OF HATHOR
CHAPEL OF ANUBIS
RAMP
CENTRAL TERRACE
LOWER TERRACE
A
TEMPLE OF HATSHEPSUT DÊR EL BAHARI
FT 0 50 100
O · OSIRIS HALL
S · SANCTUARIES
H2 · INNER HYPOSTYLE HALL
H1 · OUTER HYPOSTYLE HALL
PAVILION
SECOND COURT
546' 0"
197' 0"
FIRST COURT
B
FEET 0 100 200
TEMPLE OF SETI I : ABYDOS
OUTER AMBULATORY
H CHAPEL OF HAROERIS
S CHAPEL OF SEBEK
IH INNER HALL
273' 6"
HYPOSTYLE HALL
COURT
ALTAR
144' 0"
FT 0 50 100
F
TEMPLE AT KÔM OMBO
S · SANCTUARY
SH · SMALL HALLS
GH · GRAND HYPOSTYLE HALL
CLEARSTORY OVER
530' 0"
COLOSSI OF RAMESES II
UP
SECOND COURT
P · STATUE-PILLARS
ROYAL PAVILION
C · COLOSSUS OF RAMESES II
FIRST COURT
167' 0"
GREAT PYLONS
FEET 0 50 100 150
D
THE RAMESSEUM : THEBES
SANCTUARY
STORES
OSIRIS PILLARS
HALL
CLIFF FACE
FORE COURT
ROCK
STONE
C
FEET 0 50 100
ROCK TEMPLE : GERF-HOSEIN
SANCTUARY
H-HALL
HH-HYPOSTYLE HALL WITH OSIRIS PILLARS
S-STORES.
COLOSSI OF RAMESES II
FT 0 50 100
GREAT TEMPLE
E
ABU-SIMBEL
(ROCK CUT)
GIRDLE WALL
AMBULATORY
S · SANCTUARY
WELL
C · CHAPEL
SC · SMALL COURT
IH · INNER HALL
434' 0"
HYPOSTYLE HALL
COURT
FEET 0 50 100 150
G
TEMPLE OF HORUS : EDFU

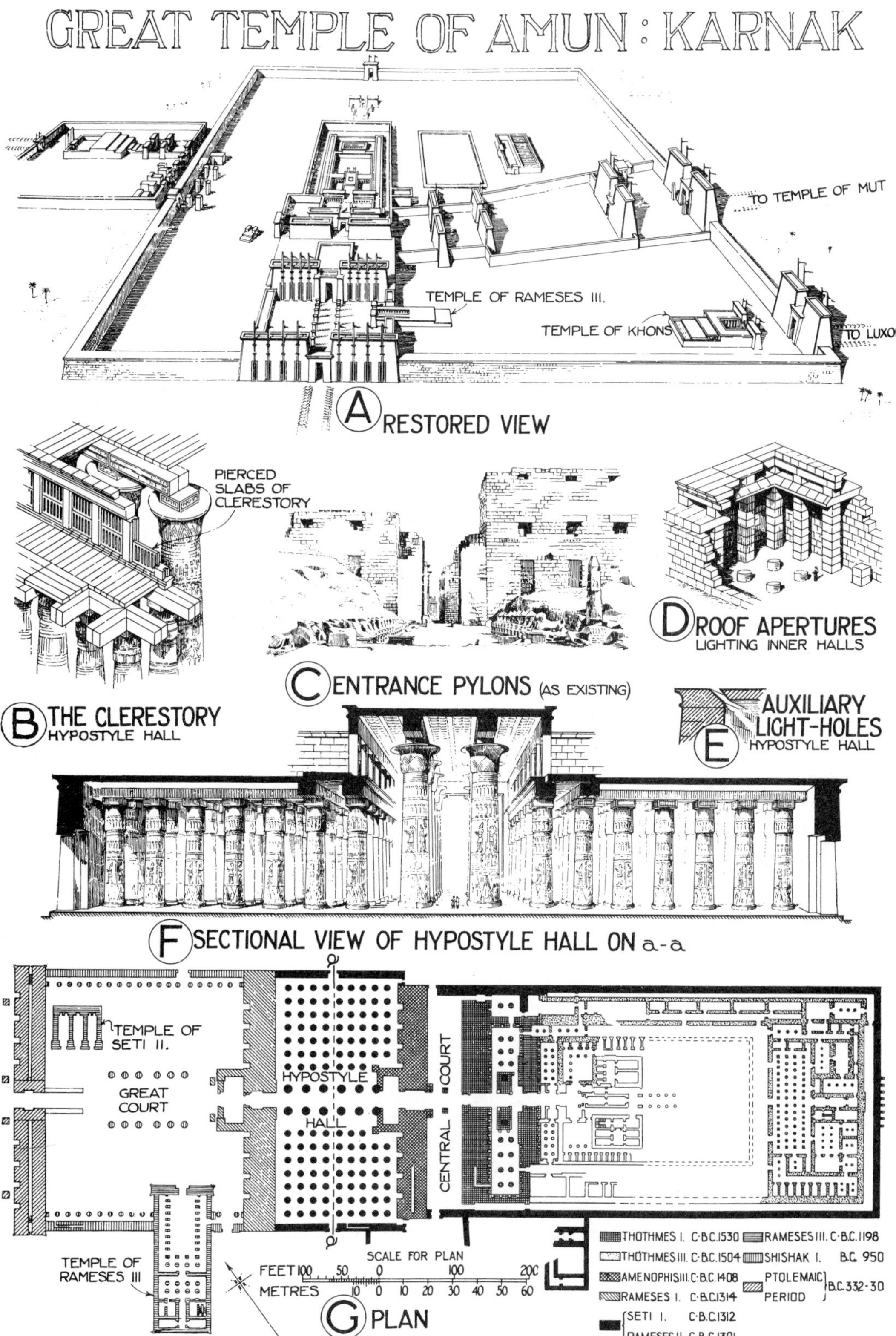
GREAT TEMPLE OF AMUN : KARNAK
TO TEMPLE OF MUT
TEMPLE OF RAMESES III.
TEMPLE OF KHONS
TO LUXOR
(A) RESTORED VIEW
PIERCED SLABS OF CLERESTORY
(B) THE CLERESTORY
HYPOSTYLE HALL
(C) ENTRANCE PYLONS (AS EXISTING)
(D) ROOF APERTURES
LIGHTING INNER HALLS
(E) AUXILIARY LIGHT-HOLES
HYPOSTYLE HALL
(F) SECTIONAL VIEW OF HYPOSTYLE HALL ON a-a
TEMPLE OF SETI II.
GREAT COURT
HYPOSTYLE HALL
CENTRAL COURT
TEMPLE OF RAMESES III
SCALE FOR PLAN
FEET 100 50 0 100 200
METRES 10 0 10 20 30 40 50 60
(G) PLAN
THOTHMES I. C·B.C.1530
THOTHMES III. C·B.C.1504
AMENOPHIS III. C·B.C.1408
RAMESES I. C·B.C.1314
SETI I. C·B.C.1312
RAMESES II. C·B.C.1301
RAMESES III. C·B.C.1198
SHISHAK I. B.C. 950
PTOLEMAIC PERIOD B.C.332-30

The examples which follow are arranged in approximate chronological order.

Middle Kingdom (2130–1580 BC)

The **Temple of Mentuhetep, Dêr el-Bahari, Thebes** (2065 BC) (p. 50F) is exceptional in that it is a mortuary temple directly related to a corridor tomb. It is terraced in two main levels, at the base of steep cliffs. The upper terrace, faced with double colonnades, is approached from a tree-planted forecourt by an inclined way. On the upper terrace a small, completely solid pyramid, raised aloft on a high podium, is wholly surrounded by a walled, hypostyle hall which has further double colonnades outside it. The pyramid is really a cenotaph, for in the rock below it is a dummy burial chamber, approached by an irregular passage from the forecourt. In the rear of the temple is another pillared hall, recessed into the rock face, preceded by an open court from the centre of which a ramp leads down to Mentuhetep's 152.5 m (500 ft) long corridor tomb. Like the Old Kingdom pyramids, this temple had a causeway, shielded by walls, leading down to a Valley Building three-quarters of a mile away.

New Kingdom (1580–332 BC)

The **Temple of Hatshepsut, Dêr el-Bahari, Thebes** (1520 BC) (pp. 43A, 56A, 60A) was built by her architect, Senmut, alongside that of Mentuhetep, of 500 years previously. It is terraced similarly, but her place of burial lay far away in a corridor tomb in the mountains beyond, and this was solely a mortuary temple, dedicated to Amun and other gods. A processional way of sphinxes connected the temple with the valley. The terraces, approached by ramps, are in three levels, mounting towards the base of the cliffs, their faces lined with double colonnades. The upper terrace is a walled court, lined with a further double colonnade, flanked on the left by the queen's mortuary chapel and on the right by a minor court containing an enormous altar to the sun god Ra. The chief sanctuary lies axially in the rear of the upper court, cut deep in the rock. To right and left of the face of the middle terrace are sanctuaries of Hathor and Anubis. The wall reliefs in this temple are exceptionally fine, and include representations of the queen's trade expedition to Punt (p. 43A), and of her allegedly divine birth. Many pillars are of the eight- or or sixteen-sided types reminiscent of the Greek Doric.

The **Great Temple of Amun, Karnak, Thebes** (1530–323 BC) (pp. 57, 59A,B), the grandest of all Egyptian temples, was not built upon one complete plan, but owes its size, disposition and magnificence to the work of many kings. Originally it consisted of a modest shrine constructed early in the Middle Kingdom, about 2000 BC; the first considerable enlargement was made by Thothmes I (1530 BC). It occupies a site of 366 m × 110 m (1200 ft × 360 ft), and is placed in an immense enclosure along with other temples and a sacred lake, surrounded by a girdle wall 6.1 m to 9 m (20 ft to 30 ft) thick, while it was connected by an avenue of sphinxes with the temple at Luxor. The temple had six pairs of pylons, added by successive rulers, and consists of various courts and halls leading to the sanctuary, and a large ceremonial hall by Thothmes III in the rear. A great court, 103 m × 84 m (338 ft × 275 ft) deep, gives entrance to the vast hypostyle hall, by Seti I and Rameses II, some 103 m × 52 m (338 ft × 170 ft) internally. The roof of enormous slabs of stone is supported by 134 columns in sixteen rows; the central avenues are about 24 m (78 ft) in height and have columns 21 m (69 ft) high and 3.6 m (11 ft 9 in) in diameter, with capitals of the papyrus-flower or bell type, while, in order to admit light through the clerestory, the side avenues are lower, with columns 13 m (42 ft 6 in) high and 2.7 m (8 ft 9 in) in diameter, with papyrus-bud capitals (pp. 57B–F, 59A) – a method of clerestory lighting more fully developed during the Gothic period in Europe. The effect produced by this forest of columns is most awe-inspiring; the eye is led from the smaller columns of the side avenues, which gradually vanish into semi-darkness and give an idea of unlimited extent, to the larger columns of the central avenues. Incised inscriptions and reliefs in colour, which cover the walls, column shafts and architraves, give the names and exploits of the royal personages who contributed to its grandeur, and praise the gods to whom it was dedicated. In these ancient carvings we find the germ of the idea which, centuries later, led in Christian churches to the employment of coloured mosaics and frescos, stained-glass windows and mural statues to record incidents of Bible history and the lives of saints and heroes.

The **Temple at Luxor, Thebes** (1408–1300 BC) (p. 60B), though founded on an older sanctuary and, like most temples, altered and repaired subsequently, is substantially the work of Amenophis III, apart from a great forecourt, with pylons, added by Rameses II. It was dedicated to the Theban triad, Amun, Mut and Khons. The illustration shows remains of the forecourt, with papyrus-bud capitals and a seated colossus of Rameses, connected by twin colonnades, 53 m (174 ft) long, to a lesser court by Amenophis in the distance. The twin colonnades of bell-capital columns, 12.8 m (42 ft) high, were the only part ever built of a grand hypostyle hall projected by Amenophis, or by the last king of his dynasty, Horemheb. Amenophis III also built a mortuary temple on the west bank at Thebes, but little survives except the twin seated statues of himself, originally 20.8 m (68 ft) high, famous from ancient time as the **Colossi of Memnon**.

A. Great Temple of Amun, Karnak: Hypostyle Hall (restored model) (*c.* 1312–1301 BC). See p.58

B. Great Temple of Amun, Karnak: view across Hypostyle Hall

C. Temple of Seti, Abydos: second Hypostyle Hall (*c.* 1312 BC). See p.62

A. Temple of Queen Hatshepsut, Dêr el-Bahari (*c.* 1520 BC). See p.58

B. Temple of Amun, Luxor (*c.* 1408–1300 BC). See p.58

A. Great Temple, Abu-Simbel (*c.* 1301 BC). See p.62

B. Great Temple, Abu-Simbel

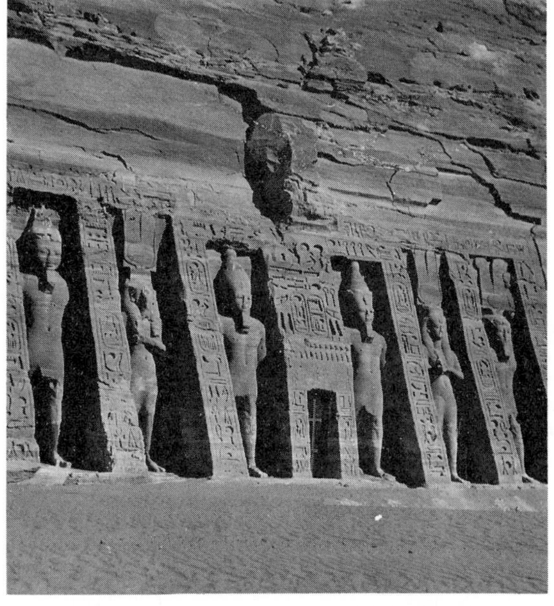

C. Small Temple, Abu-Simbel (*c.* 1301 BC). See p.62

The **Temple, Island of Elephantine** (1408 BC) (p. 55), destroyed in 1922, was one of the small so-called Mammisi temples or Birth Houses which often stood in the outer enclosures of large temples and were subsidiary to them. They were sanctuaries perpetuating the tradition of the divine birth of a Pharaoh from a union of the god Horus and a mortal mother, and Hathor, the mother-goddess, or the god Bes, protector of the newly born, usually attended the event. The Birth Houses comprise a single room, or little more, surrounded by a portico of pillars or columns and sometimes stand on a raised podium, approached by a flight of steps from one end. Design for external effect is not typical of Egyptian buildings, but there are instances from the early Eighteenth Dynasty onwards, and the tendency increases in the Ptolemaic and Roman periods.

The **Temple of Seti I, Abydos** (1312 BC) (pp. 43B, 56B, 59C) has two pylons, two forecourts and two hypostyle halls, and is unique in having seven sanctuaries side by side, each roofed with stone, corbelled courses cut in the shape of a segmental arch on the underside. Another unusual feature of the temple is a wing of chambers projecting at right angles to the main structure, following the shape of the eminence on which the temple stands. The reliefs on the walls of close-grained limestone are among the finest in Egypt (p. 43B). Seti I built a second mortuary temple on the west bank at Thebes; his successor, Rameses II, added the finishing touches to both.

The **Ramesseum, Thebes** (1301 BC) (pp. 42H, 56D) by Rameses II, is as typical of New Kingdom mortuary temples as that of Khons, Karnak, is of the cult type, though the differences of principle are not very great. In such temples the Pharaoh was worshipped and offerings were made, while his tomb lay far in the mountains behind. The front pylons were 67 m (220 ft) wide, and led to two columned courts, the second having Osiris pillars on the front and rear walls; and so to a grand hypostyle hall, succeeded by three smaller columned halls, which preceded the sanctuary at the far end of the building. There are no arrangements for processional circulation around the sanctuaries of mortuary temples. The hypostyle hall is much smaller than that at Karnak, 30 m × 60 m (98 ft × 196 ft), possessing only forty-eight columns, including twelve with bell capitals, but like it had an elevated roof over the three axial avenues and an equally well-developed clerestory. Around the temple, ruins of the temenos walls and the brick-built priests' houses, granaries, stores, etc., still survive. There are fragmentary remains of another mortuary temple by Rameses II at Abydos; and one by Rameses III (1198 BC) at **Medînet-Habu** which closely resembles the Ramesseum, and similarly still has evidences of its temenos and brick-built subsidiary buildings surviving (p. 65A).

The **Great Temple, Abu-Simbel** (*c.* 1301 BC) (pp. 56E, 61A,B) is one of two rock-hewn temples at this place commanded by the indefatigable Rameses II, and quite the most stupendous and impressive of its class. An entrance forecourt leads to the imposing facade, 36 m (119 ft) wide and 32 m (105 ft) high, formed as a pylon, immediately in front of which are four rock-cut seated colossal statues of Rameses, over 20 m (65 ft) high. The hall beyond, 9 m (30 ft) high, has eight Osiris pillars and vividly coloured wall reliefs. Eight smaller chambers open off asymmetrically to right and left, while on the main axis is a smaller hall with four pillars, leading to a vestibule serving three apartments, the central one being the sanctuary and containing four statues of gods and a support for a sacred boat. The temple has been moved from its original site on the Nile to a higher level.

The **Small Temple, Abu-Simbel** (*c.* 1301 BC) (p. 61C), by Rameses II, close to the Great Temple, was dedicated to his deified Queen, Nefertari, and the goddess Hathor. The facade here is 27.4 m (90 ft) wide and 12.2 m (40 ft) high, and comprises six niches recessed in the face of the rock and containing six colossal statues, 10 m (33 ft) high; two represent Rameses and one Nefertari on each side of the portal, which leads to a vestibule and a hall, 10.4 m × 8.2 m (34 ft × 27 ft), with six pillars bearing the sculptured head of Hathor.

The **Rock-cut Temple at Gerf Hosein** (*c.* 1301 BC) (p. 56C) is yet another example due to Rameses II. It is of interest in that it retains a considerable portion of its forecourt, the walls of which are in part rock-cut.

Ptolemaic and Roman Periods (332 BC–first century AD)

The **Temple of Isis, on the Island of Philae** (pp. 42J, 63, 64) marks an ancient sacred site. Minor parts of the surviving buildings belong to the Thirtieth Dynasty (378–341 BC) but most are by the Ptolemies II–XIII (283–47 BC). The irregularities of the plan are due to piecemeal building. The principle of arrangement, however, remains much the same as at the height of the New Kingdom period, a thousand years earlier – a progressive concentration of effect from outer and inner courts and pylons to the ultimate sanctuary in the temple nucleus. Such changes as there are, largely concern details. Column capitals are coarser and more ornate, varied in design from column to column, and have very deep abacus blocks; colonnades appear more frequently on the exterior of buildings, their columns linked by screen walls reaching about half-way up (p. 63B). Such characteristics are notable in the 'Birth House' or Mammisi temple on the west side of the inner court, and also in a pavilion known as the 'Kiosk' or 'Pharaoh's Bed', standing on the east side of the island, though this is of Roman date (*c.* 96) (pp. 63A, 64A). The Kiosk is

A. Island of Philae, aerial view from E when not submerged: Kiosk in foreground (*c.* 96); pylons, Temple of Isis and Mammisi Temple on further side of island (283–47 BC). See p.62

B. Temple of Isis, Philae: columns

C. Temple of Isis, Philae: second pylon

A. Temple of Isis, Philae (283–47 BC), with Kiosk (*c.* 96) partly submerged. See p.62

B. Temple of Isis, Philae: entrance court, showing pylons

A. Mortuary Temple of Rameses III, Medinet-Habu (1198 BC) showing surrounding brick-built buildings in temenos. See p.62

B. Temple of Hathor, Dendera (110 BC–AD 68). See p.68

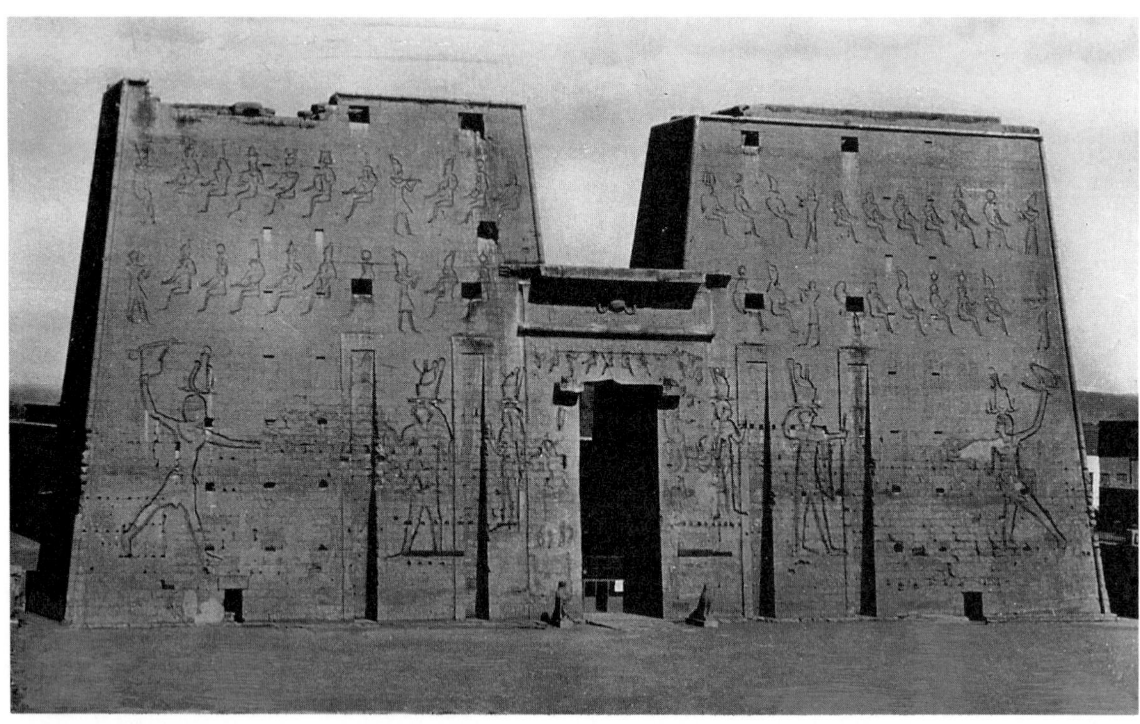

A. Temple of Horus, Edfu (237–57 BC). See p.68

B. Temple of Horus, Edfu: portico with screen between columns

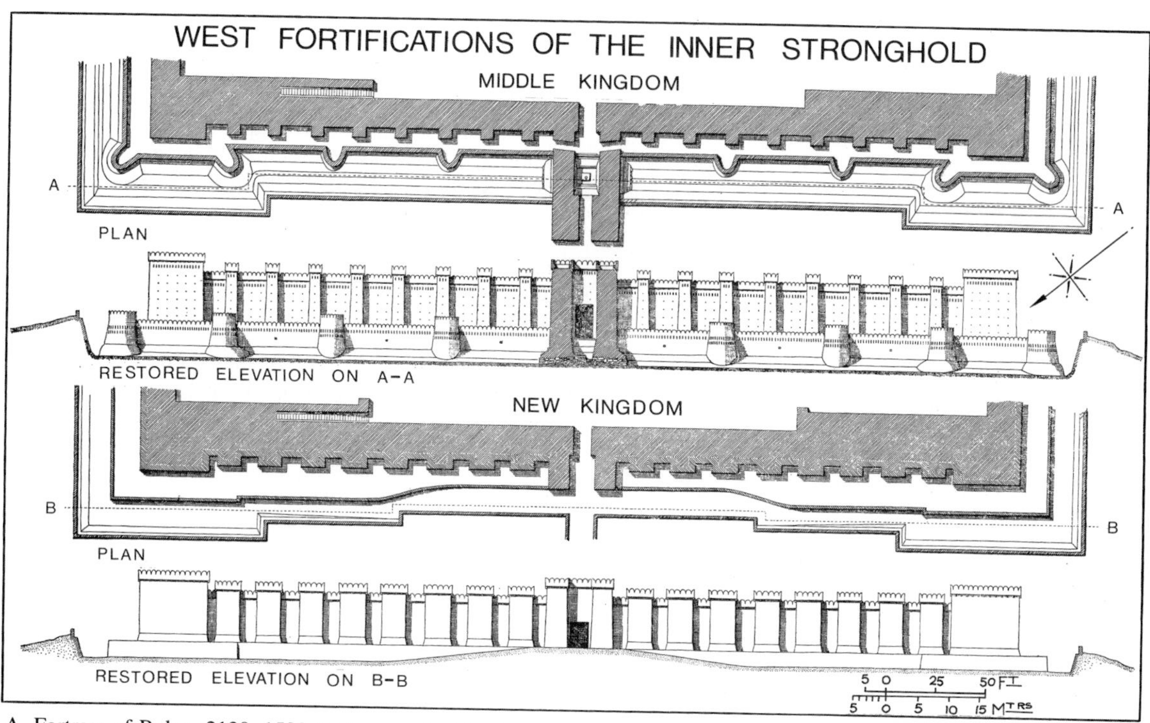

A. Fortress of Buhen 2130–1580 BC): west fortification of the inner stronghold. See p.69

B. Fortress of Buhen: reconstruction of West Gate

C. Buhen Fortress: west fortification

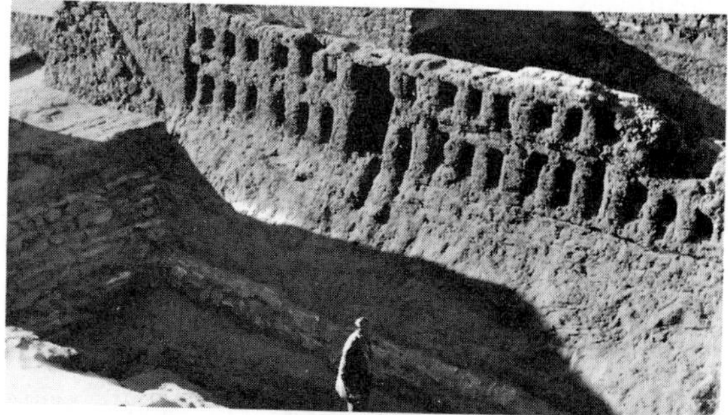

D. Buhen Fortress: loopholes of the lower ramparts

roofless, and has four columns on the ends and five on the flanks. The two portals axial on the short sides are designed without a central part to the lintels, so as to permit the passage of banners and effigies carried in procession. The whole island is now submerged during part of each year, and the temple has been relocated at a higher level.

The **Temple of Horus, Edfu** (237–57 BC) (pp. 56G, 66A,B), is a fine, well-preserved example of the period. It was built in three stages, with protracted intervals between: first the temple proper by Ptolemy III, then the outer hypostyle hall (140–124 BC), and finally the perimeter wall and pylons. It is plainly a processional cult temple. There is a passage surrounding the sanctuary, which serves also to give access to thirteen small chapels, and another completing the entire circuit of the enclosing wall. All the inner rooms were completely dark and windowless. The grand pylons are some 62.6 m (205 ft) across and 30.5 m (100 ft) high. Though in the main the temple demonstrates the tenacity of the ancient traditions, there are here again those distinguishing features of the period, particularly notable in the main hypostyle hall: the foliated or palm capitals, varying in design in pairs astride the axis, the deep abaci, the screen walls between the columns, and the 'broken' lintel of the central portal.

The **Mammisi Temple, Edfu** (116 BC), standing in the outer enclosure of the Temple of Horus, is typical of all externally colonnaded birth-houses, and similar to others at Elephantine, Philae (see above) and Dendera, where there are two, one Ptolemaic and the other Roman.

The **Temple of Hathor, Dendera** (110 BC–AD 68) (p. 65B) is most imposing, standing in a brick-walled temenos 290 m (951 ft) by 280 m (918 ft) wide. Except in lacking pylons, it closely resembles that at Edfu, and, as there, the hypostyle hall was added to the Ptolemaic nucleus in Roman times, along with the peripheral wall, which stands sufficiently clear of the temple to allow a complete processional circuit. The four-sided, Hathor-headed capitals of the hypostyle hall, carrying a conventional representation of the birth-house on the deep abaci above, are typical of the period. Many narrow chambers are concealed in the thickness of the massive outer walls, and stairs lead to the roof, where ceremonies took place.

The **Temple of Sebek and Haroeris at Kôm Ombo** (145 BC–AD 14) (p. 56F) is peculiar in having a double approach to its twin sanctuaries and two peripheral processional circuits.

Obelisks

The obelisks, originating in the sacred symbol of the sun god of Heliopolis, usually stood in pairs astride temple entrances. They are huge monoliths, square on plan and tapering to an electrum-capped pyramidion at the summit, which was the sacred part. They have a height of nine or ten times the diameter at the base, and the four sides are cut with hieroglyphs. The granite for obelisks was quarried by the very laborious method of pounding trenches around the tremendous block with balls of dolerite, a very hard stone, as the more normal method of splitting from the parent rock by means of timber wedges, which expanded after soaking, was too hazardous for so long a unit. Mural reliefs show that obelisks were transported on sledges and river-barges, and erected on their foundations by hauling them up earthen ramps, and then tilting them into position. Many were removed from Egypt by the Roman Emperors, and there are at least twelve in Rome alone.

The **Obelisk** in the Piazza of S. Giovanni in Laterano was brought to Rome from the Temple of Amun at Karnak, Thebes (q.v.), where it was originally erected by Thothmes III, and is the largest known. It is a monolith of red granite from Aswan, 32 m (105 ft) high without the added pedestal, 2.7 m (9 ft) square at the base and 1.9 m (6 ft 2 in) at the top, and weighs about 230 tons.

'Cleopatra's Needle', the obelisk on the Thames Embankment, London, originally at Heliopolis, was brought to England from Alexandria in 1878. It bears inscriptions of Thothmes III and Rameses II. It is 20.9 m (68 ft 6 in) high, 2.4 m × 2.3 m (8 ft × 7 ft 6 in) at the base, and weighs 180 tons.

Dwellings

Clay models deposited in tombs indicate that ordinary dwellings were of crude brick, one or two storeys high, with flat or arched ceilings and a parapeted roof partly occupied by a loggia. Rooms looked towards a north-facing court. Remains of barrack-like dwellings for workers exist at the pyramid sites of Chephren at Gizeh (Fourth Dynasty) and of Sesostris II at Kahun (Twelfth Dynasty) on the eastern edge of the Fayûm; and again at Tell el-Amarna, where the Pharaoh Akhnaten (Eighteenth Dynasty) built his ephemeral new town, occupied only for about fifteen years (*c.* 1366–1351 BC). Each workers' establishment constituted a considerable village, laid out on rigidly formal lines. More freely planned was a village at Dêr el-Medina, which was constructed for those engaged upon the Theban royal corridor-tombs, and which endured for four centuries.

Though in the towns even the better houses were on constricted plots and therefore might be three or four storeys high, where space allowed mansions stood in their own grounds, laid out formally with groves, gardens, pools and minor structures surrounding the rectangular, crude-brick dwelling, this having its door and window openings dressed around in stone. Columns and beams, doors and window frames were made from precious timber. Typically, there was a central hall or living-room, raised sufficiently high with the help of columns to allow clerestory light on one or more sides, for first floors were only partial. Regularly there were three fundamental parts: a reception suite, on the cooler, north side of the house; service; and private quarters.

Archaic palaces were faced with overlapping vertical timbers, giving the so-called 'palace facade' effect which left its decorative impress upon funerary stone architecture for some time. The 'white walls' of Memphis, famed in later records, were perhaps more probably of mud brick faced with mud plaster and whitewashed, although the long tradition of stone-working at Memphis may suggest they were of limestone, thus being glaring white in the strong Egyptian sun.

Relatively little is known of later dynastic palaces, of which the most impressive was perhaps that of Amenhotep III at **Malkata**, on the west bank of Thebes and south of the temple of Medînet-Habu. The whole complex comprised a number of large, rambling buildings facing on to wide courts or parade grounds, without any easily discernible plan for the whole: stone was used only sparingly, for column-bases, door-sills and the flooring of baths; mud brick was the material used for walls, with wood for columns and roofing beams. Tomb paintings reveal the gorgeously canopied thrones in the audience halls of this period; and at Malkata lavish use was made of painted decoration, including plants and water birds around a rectangular pool, on the floors, and likewise on the walls and ceilings. The central palace at Amarna shows development in the reign of Akhnaten from his father's palace at Malkata, being laid out on a more monumental scale and with greater use of stone in the state rooms. It is, however, significant that in the reign of Amenhotep III, at the height of the Eighteenth Dynasty, the king's chief palace was of brick rather than stone. The pictures at Tell el-Amarna of the royal palace and temples provide very useful evidence for correlation with the excavated remains. Later New Kingdom palaces include those of Mer-neptah at Memphis and the modest palace of Rameses III within his mortuary temple complex at Medînet-Habu, at a time when the chief centre of government had been moved from Thebes to Lower Egypt.

Fortresses

Egyptian penetration of Nubia is now known, through excavations carried out before the completion of the High Dam at Aswan, to have begun by the Fourth Dynasty, a town site of the Old Kingdom having been excavated near the later **Fortress of Buhen** (p. 67A-D). The best preserved of the architectural monuments of the Twelfth Dynasty, the Middle Kingdom, are not in Egypt proper but in Nubia. Here great fortresses were built by successive kings, especially Senusret III, in whose reign Egyptian control of Lower Nubia, between the First and Second Cataracts, was finally made secure. Most of the fortresses were on the west bank of the Nile or on the islands. There was close communication between one fortress and the next, with the headquarters at Buhen, the largest stronghold.

The military architecture revealed here and at the other fortresses shows an astonishing sophistication. At Buhen the main wall stood 4.8 m (15 ft 8 in) thick and 11 m (36 ft) high, reinforced along its exterior by projecting rectangular towers. At wider intervals along the revetment of the paved rampart beneath the main wall there were semicircular bastions, having triple loopholes with single embrasures, through which archers could cover the ditch below them by cross-fire (p. 67D). This ditch was dry, with a scarp, and about 9 m (30 ft) wide by 7 m (23 ft) deep. On the outer side of the ditch was a counterscarp surmounted by a narrow covered way of brickwork, beyond which was a glacis sloping down to the natural ground level. The great West Gate (p. 67B), facing the desert and the long roads leading to the mines and quarries, was especially strongly fortified. The use of the scarp or glacis must have been primarily to hinder the advance of an attacking force, and also to prevent undermining of the massive walls. There is no question of its being designed against chariotry, since the horse was not introduced into Egypt from Asia until the Hyksos conquest in the seventeenth century BC. The organisation and skill of the local tribes must have been formidable, to necessitate such fortresses.

After the collapse of Egyptian rule in Nubia in the period following the Twelfth Dynasty, control was re-established without much difficulty in the early Eighteenth Dynasty. The fortifications of Buhen, once again probably the military and governmental headquarters of Nubia, were rebuilt on a larger scale but of irregular shape, with wide salients, the largest being on the west side. Within them was a great gatehouse with a rock-cut causeway across the ditch, the main entrance to the fortress, facing the desert.

The fortress on Uronarti Island had a gate at each end, with an administrative building with storerooms inside each, and there were houses for the garrison and their families. The best use was made of the restricted space, and little change took place with the reoccupation in the New Kingdom.

Chapter 4
THE ANCIENT NEAR EAST

Architectural Character

In the alluvial plains of the Tigris and Euphrates stone and timber suitable for building were rare or unobtainable except by importation. There was, however, an abundance of clay which, compressed in moulds and either dried in the sun or kiln-fired, provided bricks for every kind of structure. Besides massive, towered fortifications, the outstanding constructions were temple-complexes or palaces, temples being typical of Babylonian architecture and palaces of Assyrian. Buildings were raised on mud-brick platforms, and the chief temples had sacred 'ziggurats' (p. 72), artificial mountains made up of tiered, rectangular stages which rose in number from one to seven in the course of Mesopotamian history. Apart from the fortifications and the ziggurats, buildings of all types were arranged round large and small courts, the rooms narrow and thick-walled, carrying brick barrel vaults and sometimes domes. The roofs were usually flat outside, except where domes protruded. Alternatively, in early or commonplace buildings, palm logs supported rushes and packed clay served for coverings, or, for the best work, cedar and other fine timber was laboriously imported. Burnt brick was used sparingly for facings or where special stress was expected. Walls were whitewashed or, as with the developed ziggurat, painted in colour.

Essentially, architecture was arcuated, the true arch with radiating voussoirs having been known by the third millennium BC. For want of stone, columns were not used, except in a few instances in late Assyrian and Neo-Babylonian work. Towers or flat buttress strips were commonly vertically panelled and finished in stepped battlements above and stone plinths below, with colossal winged bulls guarding the chief portals; in palaces the alabaster plinths or dadoes of state courts and chambers bore low-relief carving, the walls above them being painted internally with bands of continuous friezes on the thin plaster coverings. Facing with polychrome glazed bricks, introduced by the Assyrians, was another mode of decoration, especially favoured by the Neo-Babylonians in lieu of sculptured stone slabs, since in Babylonia stone was scarcer than in Assyria.

The architecture of the Persians was columnar, and thus vastly different from the massive arcuated architecture of the Mesopotamian peoples they conquered. Flat timber roofs rather than vaults served for coverings, which allowed columns to be slender and graceful, while with their help rooms could be large where necessary, and of square proportions rather than elongated as the Mesopotamian brick vaults demanded. For ceilings, wooden brackets and beams carried by the columns supported a covering of clay on a bedding of reeds on logs or planks (p. 94). The use of double mud-brick walls for stability, as at Persepolis, may have allowed small windows just below ceiling level without their appearing on the severe external facades. Stone was plentiful on the upland sites, but used sparingly for such purposes as fire-temples and palace platforms, door and window surrounds, and for richly ornate columns and relief sculpture, often with figures on a modest scale. The Persians were at first relatively inexperienced craftsmen, and drew upon the superior skills of the peoples of their empire; many of the usages and features demonstrate derivation from Egyptian, Mesopotamian, Syrian, Ionian, Greek and other sources.

It would be accurate to claim that the architectural character of the major buildings erected during many centuries in Mesopotamia, and during the Achaemenian period in Iran, exemplify the two main traditions of the Near East as a whole, that of the alluvial river plains and that of the whole highland zone respectively. These were the traditions of clay and wood.

Examples

The architecture of the ancient Near East is considered under the following headings:

Early Mesopotamian (fifth to second millennia BC)
Assyrian and Neo-Babylonian (*c.* 1859–539 BC)
Early Anatolian and Hittite (*c.* 3250–*c.* 1170 BC)
Canaanite, Phoenician and Israelite (*c.* 3250–587 BC)

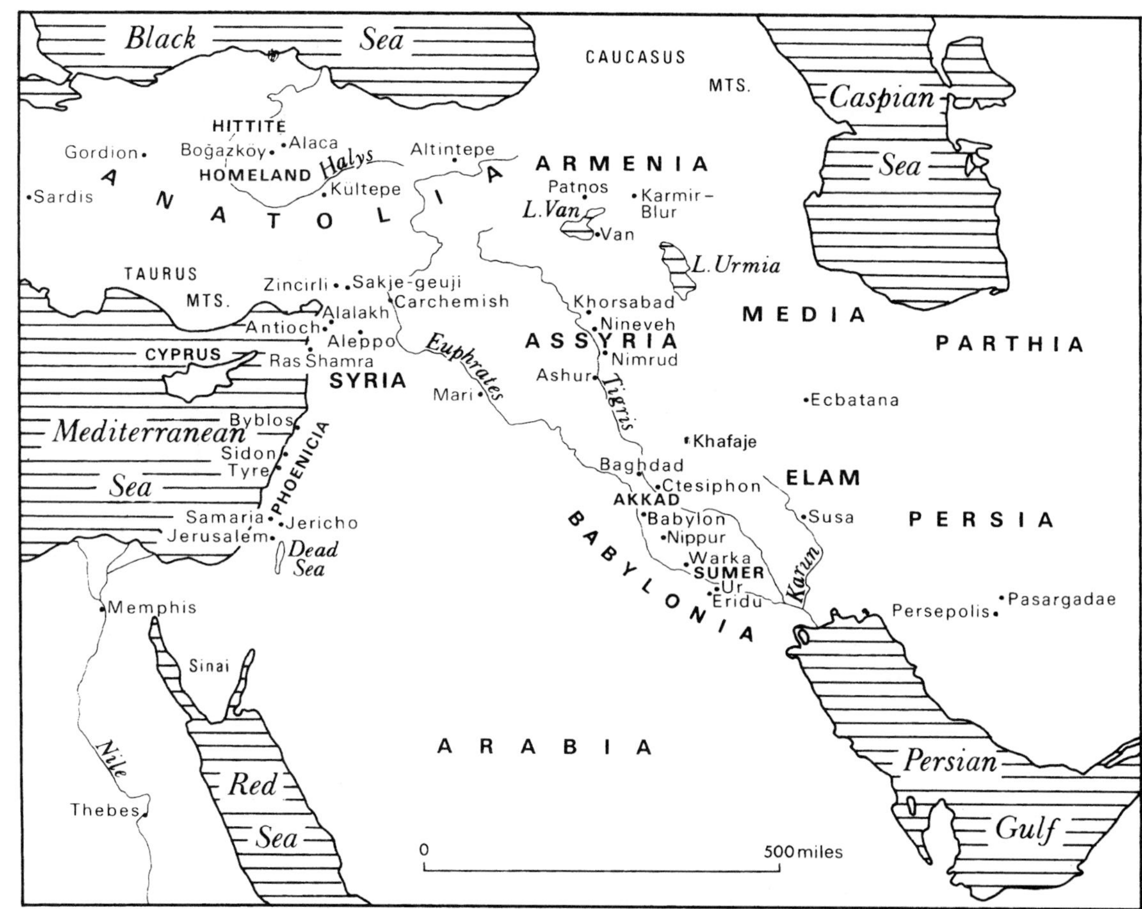

The ancient Near East

Syro-Hittite (*c.* 1170–745 BC)
Urartian (*c.* 850–*c.* 600 BC)
Phrygian (*c.* 750–*c.* 650 BC)
Median and Persian (*c.* 750–*c.* 350 BC)
Seleucid, Parthian and Sassanian (312 BC–AD 641)

Early Mesopotamian Architecture

Eridu is the first significant example of the initial association of the Mesopotamian tradition in architecture with that of the Sumerians. A succession of remains of temples has been excavated dating back probably earlier than any yet known elsewhere in Sumer. Temple XVI, the earliest to be uncovered in its entirety, already reveals the central feature of the typical Mesopotamian temple, the 'cella' or sanctuary, with an altar in a niche and a central offering-table with traces of burning. The later temples in this sequence at Eridu are on a much larger scale, with the emergence of the tripartite plan, having subsidiary rooms on either side of the cella: this plan was to become standard. Here too was first manifested the embellishment of the exterior by alternating niches and buttresses. The exact orientation of a Mesopotamian temple was of great religious significance from this time onward. The predilection for established sites led to enduring continuity in the sites of temples, themselves the nucleus each of its own city.

Warka (Uruk: the Biblical Erech) was by far the largest of the Sumerian cities which eventually, in the Early Dynastic Period (*c.* 2900–2340 BC), had a perimeter of over 9 km (6 miles). About one-third of this great area was occupied by temples and other public buildings. The two major areas of the city with important buildings were the Eanna and the Anu precincts, associated with the mother goddess and the sky god respectively, and dating back to the late fifth millennium BC. By the late Uruk (or Protoliterate A and B) period the Eanna precinct had become an impressive grouping of temples, larger than any

ZIGGURATS

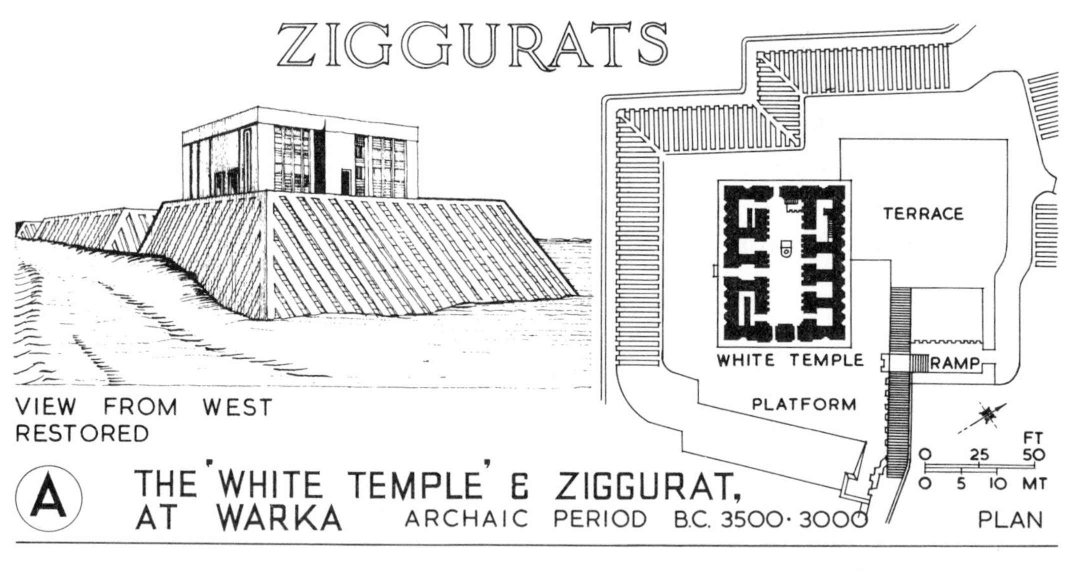

A THE 'WHITE TEMPLE' & ZIGGURAT, AT WARKA ARCHAIC PERIOD B.C. 3500-3000

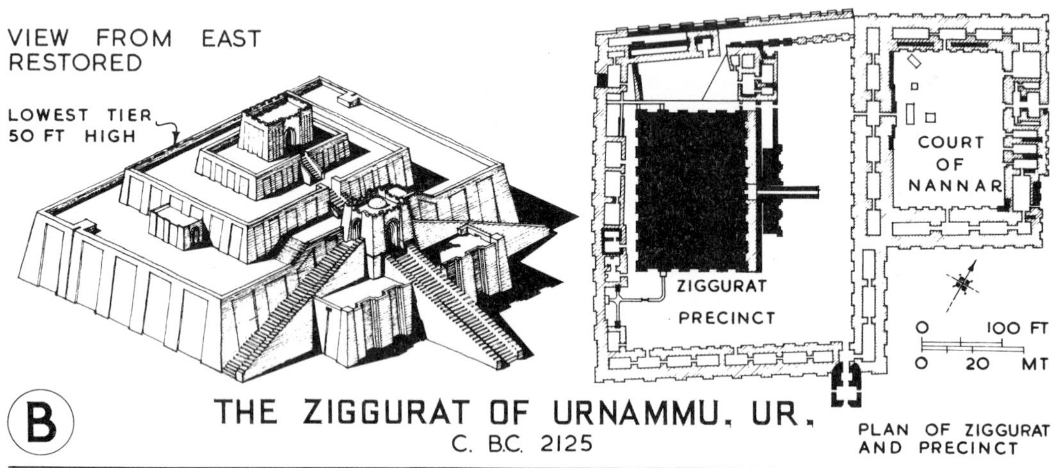

B THE ZIGGURAT OF URNAMMU, UR, C. B.C. 2125

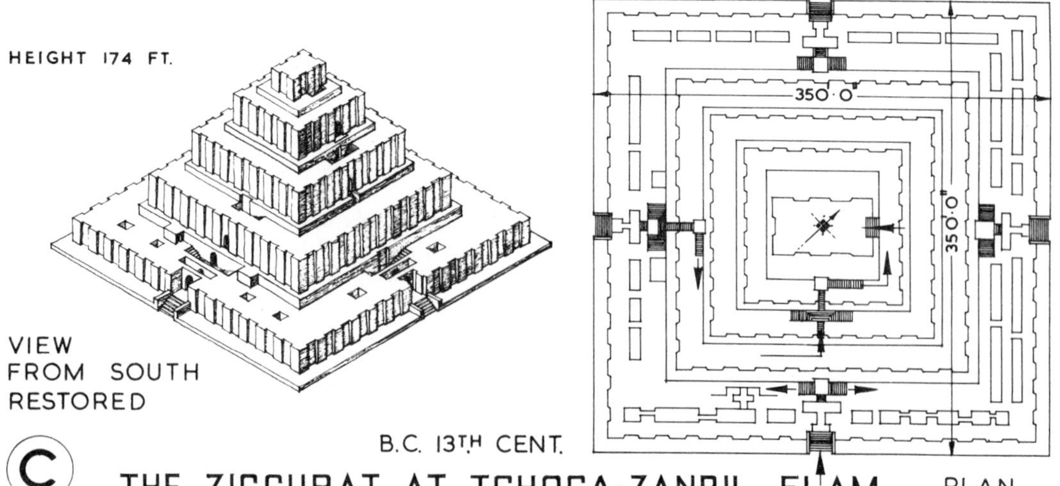

C THE ZIGGURAT AT TCHOGA-ZANBIL ELAM

previously built. Cones of baked clay were set in mud plaster over many of the wall faces in the Eanna precinct temples, forming a distinctive mosaic decoration. One of the most striking examples of this is the so-called **Pillar Temple**, which stood on a terrace or platform and included two rows of massive columns, 2.6 m (8 ft 6 in) in diameter. Their great girth and the primitive way in which they are constructed, with bricks laid radially to form an approximate circle, suggest a hesitant and experimental approach to an advance in building techniques, this being the oldest surviving evidence of free-standing columns. However, the pattern of cone mosaics clearly suggests imitation of a palm trunk. The Anu 'ziggurat' is more typically Mesopotamian in its tripartite plan for the temple: it is in fact not a ziggurat at all, but a series of temples, each built on top of the preceding one and each on a high platform.

The **White Temple** (p. 72A), the best preserved in the Anu series, may be said to illustrate the origin of the ziggurat, or temple-tower, in the prehistoric Mesopotamian temple set on its platform. The concept of the ziggurat may well have combined two separate functions, the religious one being the recreation of a sacred mountain in the flat alluvial plain, and the secular one being to provide a permanent reminder to the populace of the political, social and economic pre-eminence of the temple. The White Temple platform had sloping sides, three of which had flat buttresses; a subsidiary broad square platform of similar height overlapped the north corner, served by a long flight of easy steps from which a circuitous ramp led off from an intermediate landing. The temple, originally whitewashed, had an end-to-end hall with a span of 4.5 m (15 ft), flanked on both sides by a series of smaller rooms, three of which contained stairways leading to the roof. Of four entrances, the chief was placed asymmetrically on one long side, giving a 'bent-axis' approach to the sanctuary, marked by an altar platform 1.2 m (4 ft) high, in the north corner of the hall. Centrally nearby was a brick offering table, adjoined by a low semicircular hearth. Shallow buttresses formed the principal decoration of the hall and external walls. The platform stood 13 m (42 ft 6 in) high, an impressive podium.

The **Ziggurat and Precinct of Ur** (p. 72B), already very old, were extensively remodelled by Urnammu (*c.* 2125 BC) and his successors. The complex comprised the ziggurat and its court, a secondary court attached to it, and three great temples. All these stood on a great rectangular platform at the heart of an oval-shaped walled city, itself about 6.1 m (20 ft) above the surrounding plain. The ziggurat, 62 m × 43 m (205 ft × 141 ft) at its base, and about 21 m (70 ft) high, carried the usual temple on its summit and had the normal orientation. The ziggurat at Ur had a solid core of mud brick, covered with a skin of burnt brickwork 2.4 m (8 ft) thick, laid in bitumen and with layers of matting at intervals to improve cohesion. Its sides were slightly convex, giving an added effect of mass, with broad shallow corner buttresses. Weeper-holes through the brickwork allowed for drainage and the slow drying out of the interior: this is a likelier explanation than the theory of the excavator, Woolley, that trees were planted on the stages of the ziggurat as the sacred mountain, and required regular watering.

Close to the ziggurat precinct at Ur stood a building with rooms corbel-vaulted in kiln-fired brick and approached down long flights of steps. The floors had to be raised hurriedly, to avoid the Euphrates flood water. This is usually described as the **mausoleum** of the kings of the powerful **Third Dynasty of Ur**, although there is no proof that they were buried in the city.

The **Temple Complex, Ischali** (p. 75B), of the early second millennium BC, was of the terrace type, without a ziggurat. It was rectangular in plan, with a large main terrace court and an upper one in which the temple lay at right angles to the chief axis. On the corresponding side of the main court there were two minor courts, and all were lined with rooms.

The **Temple Oval at Khafaje** (p. 75A), north-east of Baghdad, was an unusual complex, dating from the Early Dynastic and subsequent periods. Within the ovals the layout was rectilinear, the corners oriented to the four cardinal points. Of three ascending terrace levels, the lowest made a forecourt approached through an arched and towered gateway from the town, with a many-roomed building on one side, either administrative or a dwelling for the chief priest. The second terrace, wholly surrounded by rooms used as workshops and stores, had at its further end the temple platform about 3.6 m (12 ft) high. Near its staircase, against the side of the temple terrace, was an external sacrificial altar, while elsewhere in the court were a well and two basins for ritual ablutions. Some special sanctity seems to have attached to the Temple Oval, for before its construction the whole area was dug down to virgin soil, through the accumulated depth of earlier building levels, and then filled with clean sand; foundations of a depth greater than structually requisite were laid in the sand, and clay packed down against the walls. Thus the purity of the soil beneath the temple was assured. The later temple at Ischali had largely similar arrangements, though not within an oval perimeter. Just north-east of the Temple Oval stood the Temple of the moon god Sin at Khafaje, with ten successive phases, five dating to the late prehistoric (Jemdet Nasr) period and five to the three phases of the Early Dynastic period. Thus Khafaje illustrates the northward extension of urban life centred upon the city temple, from its first beginnings in Sumer.

The hallmark of Sumerian architecture in the Early Dynastic period, but neither before nor after, was the plano-convex mud brick: these were laid in herring-bone pattern, or sometimes with three diagonally laid courses, all leaning in one direction, followed by two or three courses laid flat, with their convex sides upwards, thus acting as an imperfect bonding.

At **Tepe Gawra** in northern Mesopotamia, at a time approximately contemporary with the earliest levels at Warka, the first important manifestation of monumental religious architecture appeared, where in Level XIII three contiguous temples, the Northern Temple, the Central Temple and the Eastern Shrine, formed a group unique at that early date. Bricks of a special size were used for these three temples.

The **Royal Cemetery at Ur** (Early Dynastic III period) displays at its best the engineering skills of Sumerian architects. The stone used in the royal tombs, at a time when brickwork was more and more superseding stone, was limestone, never dressed and only roughly split after quarrying. This use of rubble masonry makes all the more remarkable the ability of the Sumerian builders to roof a tomb chamber with a vault or dome. The true arch was known, and so too was the true barrel-vault, in stone, mud brick and burnt brick. Where the tomb itself, set at the foot of a shaft, had more than one room, the connecting doors were often spanned by an arch. However, no chronological sequence of the royal tombs at Ur can be drawn up on the basis of the construction of their roofs: corbel-vaulting, a more primitive method than the true barrel-vault, was used not only for some of the royal tombs but also very extensively in the Third Dynasty of Ur. In one of the royal tombs of the Early Dynastic III cemetery at Ur a wooden frame was found on the floor, perhaps used as centering. Two examples of the use of an apse were found. The dome is best exemplified by one tomb chamber found intact: just as the principle of the true arch had been mastered by the Sumerian architects, so too had the use of pendentives.

At **Tell Asmar** (Eshnunna), in the Diyala valley, three sequences of temples span the Early Dynastic period. In the Early Dynastic II period the **Square Temple** was designed round an interior court with two shrines added to the original one. Here a large cache of statues of provincial Sumerian style had been preserved.

The usual plan of Mesopotamian temples before the end of the Early Dynastic period had an indirect or 'bent axis' approach, with the entrance in one of the longer walls. But later it became normal to have the entrance at one end, giving a long, straight approach to the altar.

The **Palace at Mari** was founded in the late third millennium BC and endured until its destruction by Hammurabi of Babylon (*c.* 1757 BC). This great building combined within its walls the functions of royal residence, centre for receptions and audiences, offices and a school for the civil service, servants' quarters and numerous store-rooms; in some rooms were found the thousands of cuneiform tablets constituting the royal archives, one of the major sources of historical evidence uncovered in the ancient Near East. There was the indirect access characteristic of palaces in the ancient Near East, preventing the shooting of missiles from without into the great forecourt. The section of the palace devoted to the private apartments of the royal family was embellished with mural paintings displaying contacts with the Minoan civilisation of Crete, then at its height. Next to this section were the offices of the civil service, including two rooms with brick benches and yielding tablets showing that here the young recruits were taught the slow, painful mastery of the Akkadian syllabary. The layout of the palace as a whole exemplifies the typical Mesopotamian arrangement of rooms round a succession of courtyards, providing light, air and means of access. Rooms must have been gloomy inside, but doorways were high and only partially covered with matting; most of the palace was probably of one storey only.

The four centuries of Kassite rule in Babylonia (*c.* 1595–1171 BC) were undistinguished in art and architecture generally, being marked by restorations at Ur and elsewhere, but at the new capital of **Dur Kurigalzu**, 32 km (20 miles) west of present-day Baghdad, the royal palace has some new features, including a court bordered on two sides by an ambulatory with square pillars. To the east lay the kingdom of Elam, with its capital at Susa. Nearby was the **Ziggurat of Tchoga-Zanbil** (p. 72C), of the thirteenth century BC, built by Untash-Gal. The remarkably complete remains give a fuller and more authentic picture of the upper parts of a ziggurat than were previously available. There were five tiers, the lowest shallower than the rest, each mounted on a plinth. The base is 107 m (350 ft) square and the total height was about 53 m (174 ft). Flights of stairs, recessed in the mass, led to the top of the first tier on the centre of each front, but only that on the south-west led to the second tier, while the rest of the height had to be scaled on the south-east, the principal facade.

Assyrian Architecture

In the second millennium BC, covering the Old Assyrian and Middle Assyrian periods, Assyria had to struggle for its existence. Though its art and architecture were closely bound to those of the south, distinctive traits began to manifest themselves. Polychrome ornamental brickwork, introduced by the Assyrians, had its origins in these early centuries, although the second great innovation, the use of high plinths or dadoes of great stone slabs placed on edge and usually carved with low-relief sculpture, did not appear until the reign of Ashurnasirpal II (*c.* 883–859 BC). Temples both with and without ziggurats were built in Assyria, but by the Late Assyrian

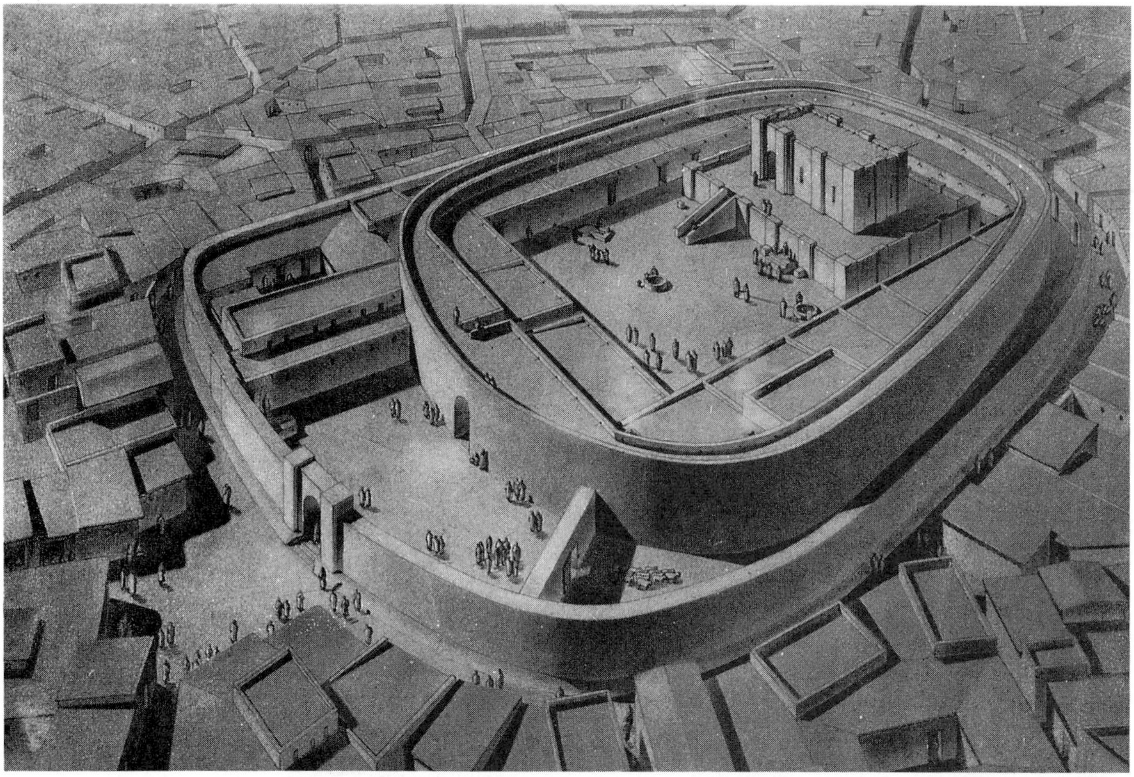

A. (*above*)
The Temple Oval at Khafaje.Third millennium BC. See p.73

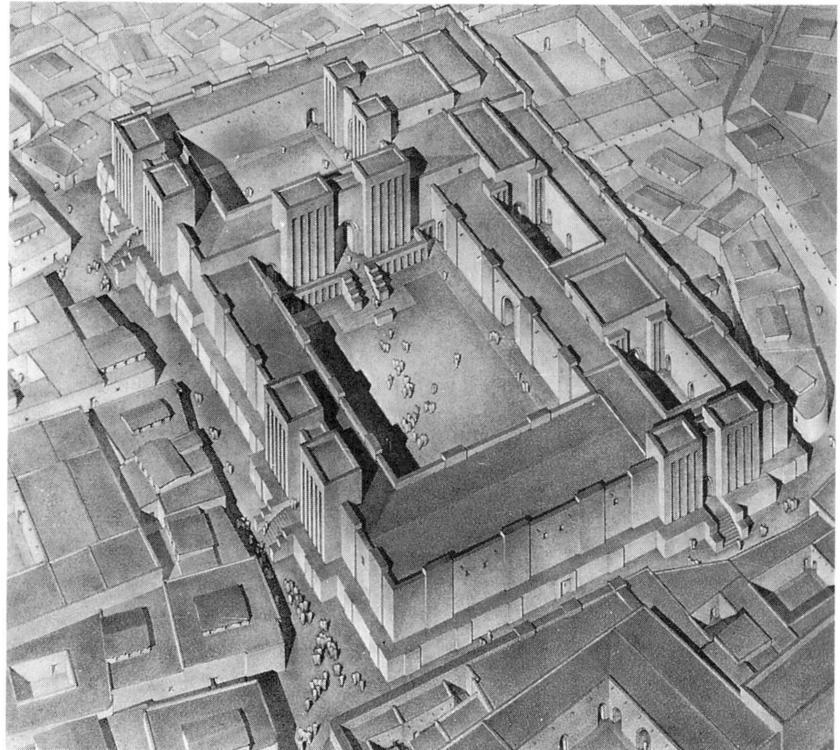

B. (*right*)
The Temple Complex at Ischali. Early second millennium BC. See p.73

A. Gypsum relief from throne room at NW Palace, Nimrud (*c.* 879 BC). See p.78

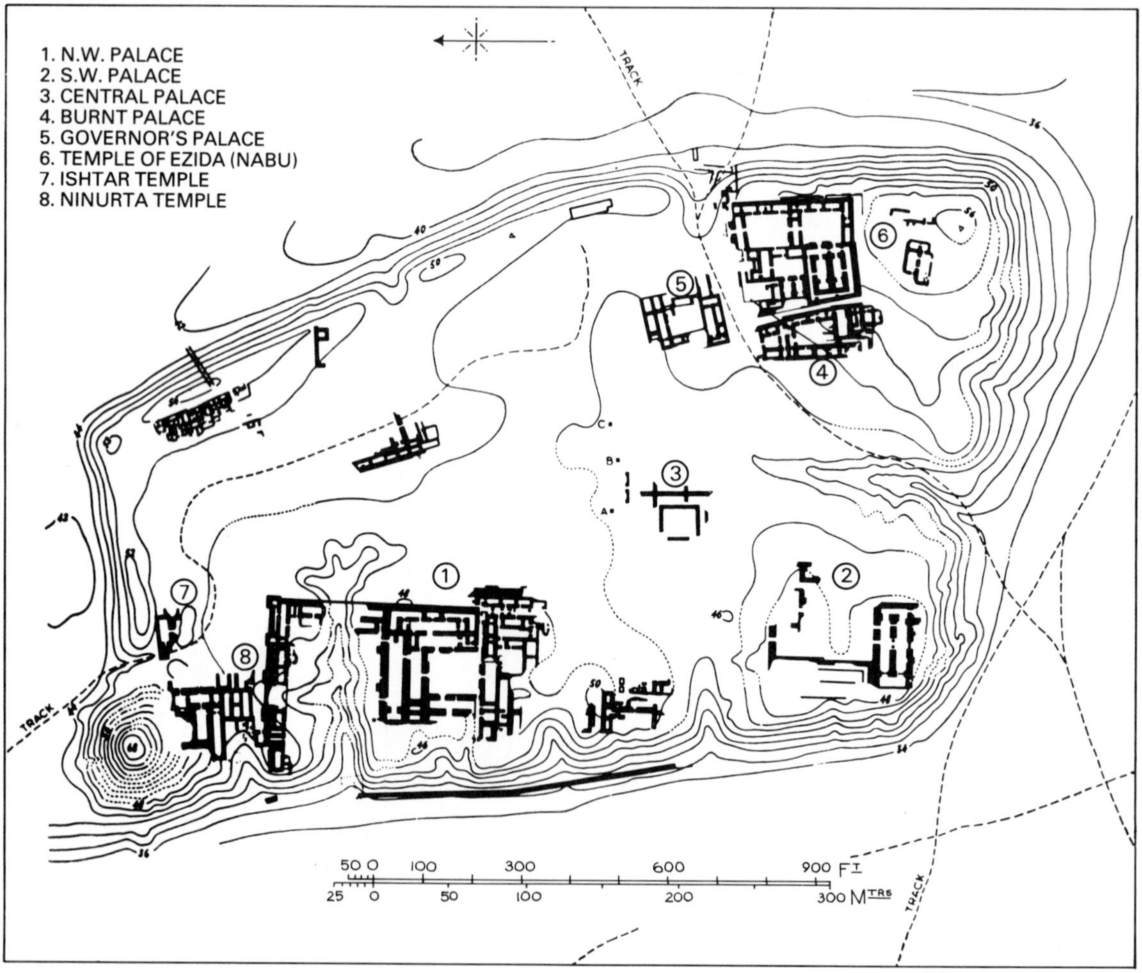

1. N.W. PALACE
2. S.W. PALACE
3. CENTRAL PALACE
4. BURNT PALACE
5. GOVERNOR'S PALACE
6. TEMPLE OF EZIDA (NABU)
7. ISHTAR TEMPLE
8. NINURTA TEMPLE

TRACK

50 0 100 300 600 900 FT

25 0 50 100 200 300 MTRS

B. Nimrud: plan of the citadel. See p.78

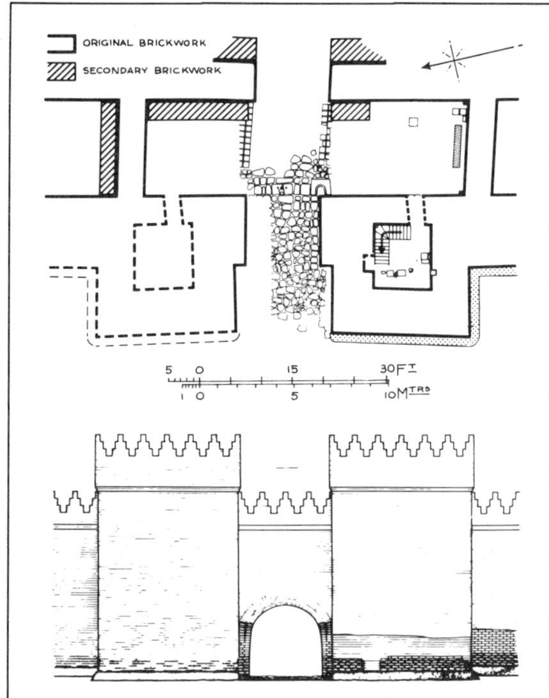

A. Fort Shalmaneser, Nimrud (mid-ninth century B): plan and elevation of west gate. See p.78

C. Tell Rimah: spiral column decoration of brickwork. See p.78

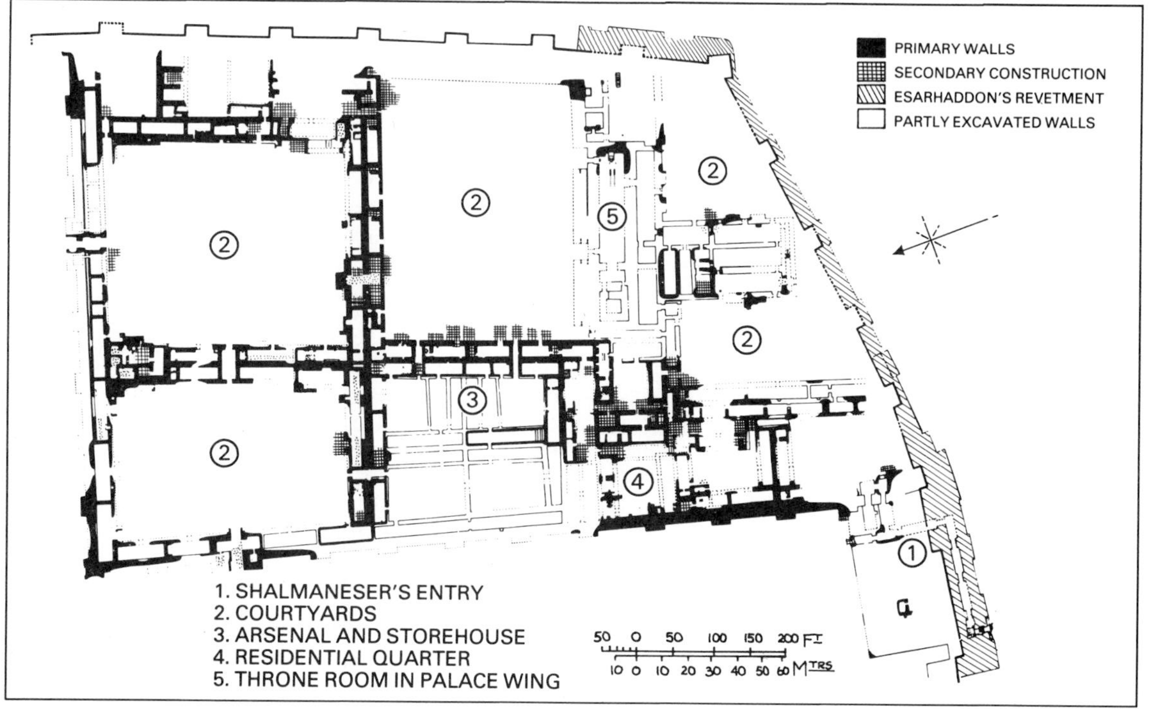

B. Fort Shalmaneser, Nimrud: plan of west fort

period (911–612 BC) palaces were much more numerous and important, emphasising the central role of the monarchy. Excavations at Tell Rimah have revealed the use of brick barrel-vaulting on a considerable scale.

The **City of Ashur** was the ancient religious and national centre of the Assyrian state, always important wherever the administrative capital might be. It was built on a high rocky promontory above the Tigris, being surrounded during the second millennium BC by a strong defensive wall. An outer wall was added in the ninth century BC with a further extension to protect a residential suburb, the frontage along the Tigris becoming 3 km (1.8 miles). But the first shrine on the site of a temple dedicated to Ishtar, goddess of both love and war, was built in the Early Dynastic period. The ziggurat temple of Ashur, the national god, was restored by Tukulti-Ninurta I (*c.* 1244–1208 BC). In his reign and in subsequent generations Ashur displayed the ability of the Assyrian architects to experiment with architectural combinations in a way which demonstrated intentional divergences from the Babylonian prototypes. The double temple of Anu and Adad had twin ziggurats, with their related temples spanning between them. There were two further temples without ziggurats and two enormous palaces, one being primarily for administrative purposes.

At **Tell Rimah**, in the Sinjar district west of Mosul, an area densely settled throughout prehistoric times, Shamshi-Adad I, the strongest ruler of Assyria in the early second millennium BC, built a temple of imposing proportions and distinctive design overlying earlier building remains constituting a citadel mound; and in the next generation a palace was built that has yielded archives of tablets listing issues of wine rations, foreshadowing the wine lists of Nimrud, a millennium later. This palace is paralleled in its plan not at Mari but at more distant Ur. There was also an outer town. The necessarily restricted area of excavations on the south side of the central mound, in levels preceding the temple, revealed three main phases of buildings with remarkably sophisticated 'pitched-brick' vaulting, a domical vault of the second phase being especially well preserved. The bricks used were smaller and thinner than those in the walls, clearly in order that they could be supported by the adhesion of the mud mortar for the requisite length of time during construction. This technique is better known, in rather simpler form, in the arch of Ctesiphon, near Baghdad, of the sixth century. Whereas in the more usual technique the voussoirs are laid radially, here the bricks are laid with their faces along the long axis of the vault, each ring of bricks being slanted for partial support by its predecessor. Construction usually continued from both ends, supported by each end wall. Fans of brickwork from each corner supported these vaults, with their very flat profile, and resembled pendentives. These 'pitched-brick' vaulted buildings can be dated to the late third millennium BC (Third Dynasty of Ur). By the early second millennium BC, however, the temple was built entirely with radial vaulting.

The close relationship between the ziggurat and the temple at its foot is typically Assyrian, a precursor of the tradition best known at Nimrud and Khorsabad. But the ornamentation of the facades is unique in its virtuosity of craftsmanship and design. In all there were 277 engaged columns, single or in groups, the fifty large columns being made of carved bricks laid in complex palm-trunk and spiraliform patterns (p. 77C). The temple itself was of Babylonian plan, the technical expertise in mud brick according with this southern origin.

The **City of Nimrud** (Calah) (pp. 76, 77, 79), was restored and enlarged by Ashurnasirpal II (*c.* 883–859 BC), who made it the capital of his kingdom. Excavations at Nimrud have been mostly within the citadel (p. 76B), which had an area 550 m × 320 m (1800 ft × 1050 ft) and was situated at the south-west corner of the outer town, whose wall had a perimeter of no less than 7.5 km (4¾ miles), enclosing an area of 358 hectares (895 acres). The North-West Palace (p. 76A,B) was built by Ashurnasirpal II as his chief residence; it comprised a large public court, flanked on the north side by a modest ziggurat with associated temples, and by a row of rooms later used to house administrative records, and on the south side by the huge throne-room and the private wing of the palace. This was to become the traditional plan of Assyrian palaces, for the first time adorned with slabs carved with scenes of war and the chase and domestic scenes (pp. 76A, 79).

Fort Shalmaneser, Nimrud (p. 77A,B) was built by Shalmaneser III (859–824 BC) outside the citadel, which he used as the administrative capital: the Fort served as palace, barracks, arsenal and storehouse. The palace wing included the usual vast throne-room, and, though in this reign relief sculpture was much less in evidence, there was a magnificent panel of glazed bricks (p. 83B) depicting the king twice, on either side of the sacred tree, a favourite motif of Assyrian art. The rest of Fort Shalmaneser consisted of four courtyards, one entirely of store-rooms and the others surrounded by quarters for the royal guard, including ablutions and 'garages' for the army's chariots.

At **Imgur-Enlil** (Balawat), 40 km (25 miles) west of Mosul, Ashurnasirpal II and his son Shalmaneser III built themselves a country residence, with a palace and temple. Here three pairs of massive wooden gates were embellished with bronze bands decorated in relief in the repoussé technique, illustrating ninth-century BC Assyrian campaigns. Among the details provided is the earliest known representation of Urartian fortresses.

The **Temple of Ezida, Nimrud** (p. 76B) was built towards the end of the ninth century BC, and included

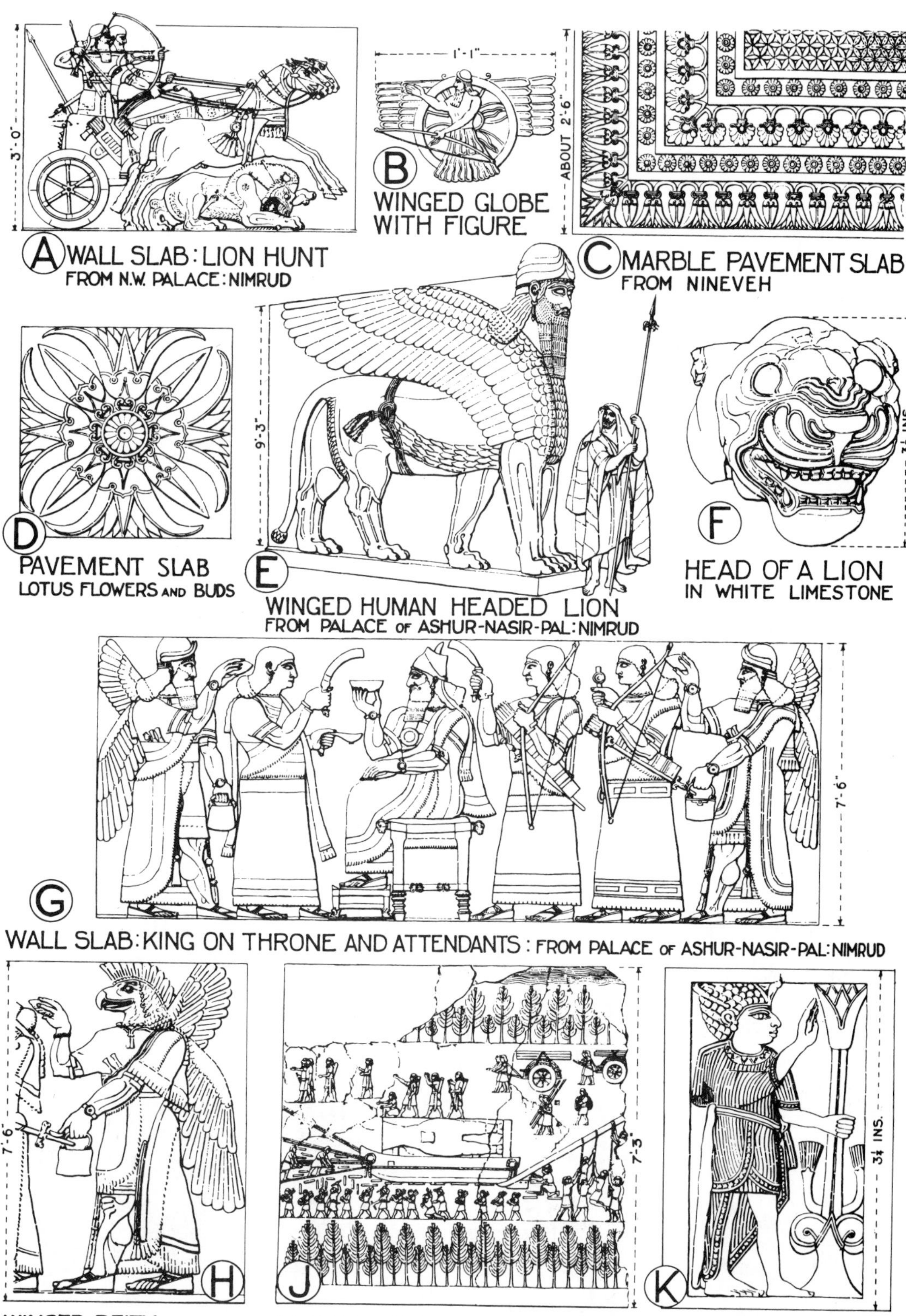

A WALL SLAB: LION HUNT FROM N.W. PALACE: NIMRUD

B WINGED GLOBE WITH FIGURE

C MARBLE PAVEMENT SLAB FROM NINEVEH

D PAVEMENT SLAB LOTUS FLOWERS AND BUDS

E WINGED HUMAN HEADED LION FROM PALACE OF ASHUR-NASIR-PAL: NIMRUD

F HEAD OF A LION IN WHITE LIMESTONE

G WALL SLAB: KING ON THRONE AND ATTENDANTS: FROM PALACE OF ASHUR-NASIR-PAL: NIMRUD

H WINGED DEITY: NIMRUD

J TRANSPORT OF A BULL: NINEVEH

K EGYPTIAN KING IN IVORY

PALACE OF SARGON : KHORSABAD

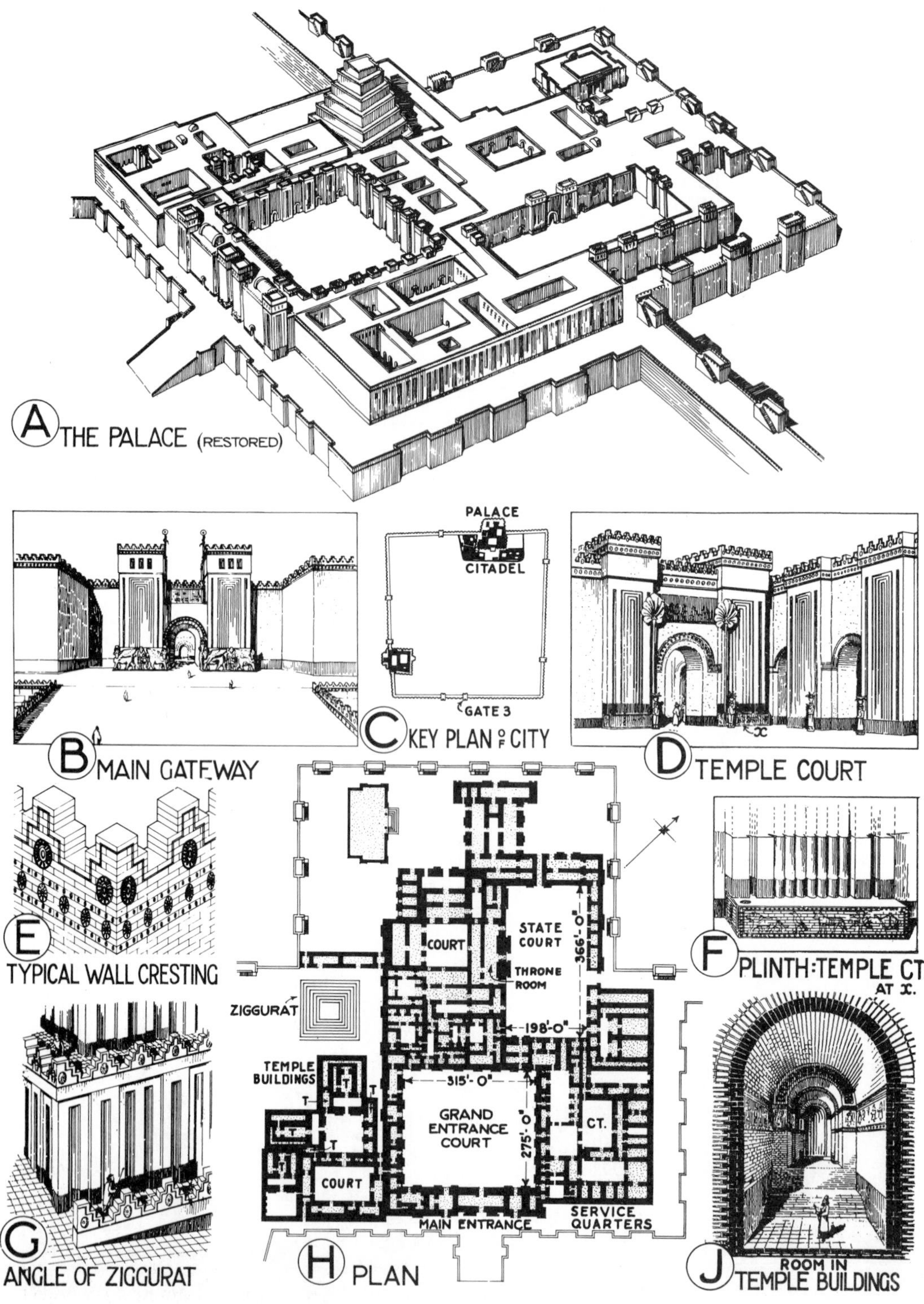
A THE PALACE (RESTORED)
PALACE
CITADEL
GATE 3
B MAIN GATEWAY
C KEY PLAN OF CITY
D TEMPLE COURT
E TYPICAL WALL CRESTING
F PLINTH: TEMPLE CT. AT X.
STATE COURT
366'-0"
COURT
THRONE ROOM
ZIGGURAT
198'-0"
TEMPLE BUILDINGS
315'-0"
GRAND ENTRANCE COURT
275'-0"
CT.
COURT
SERVICE QUARTERS
MAIN ENTRANCE
G ANGLE OF ZIGGURAT
H PLAN
J ROOM IN TEMPLE BUILDINGS

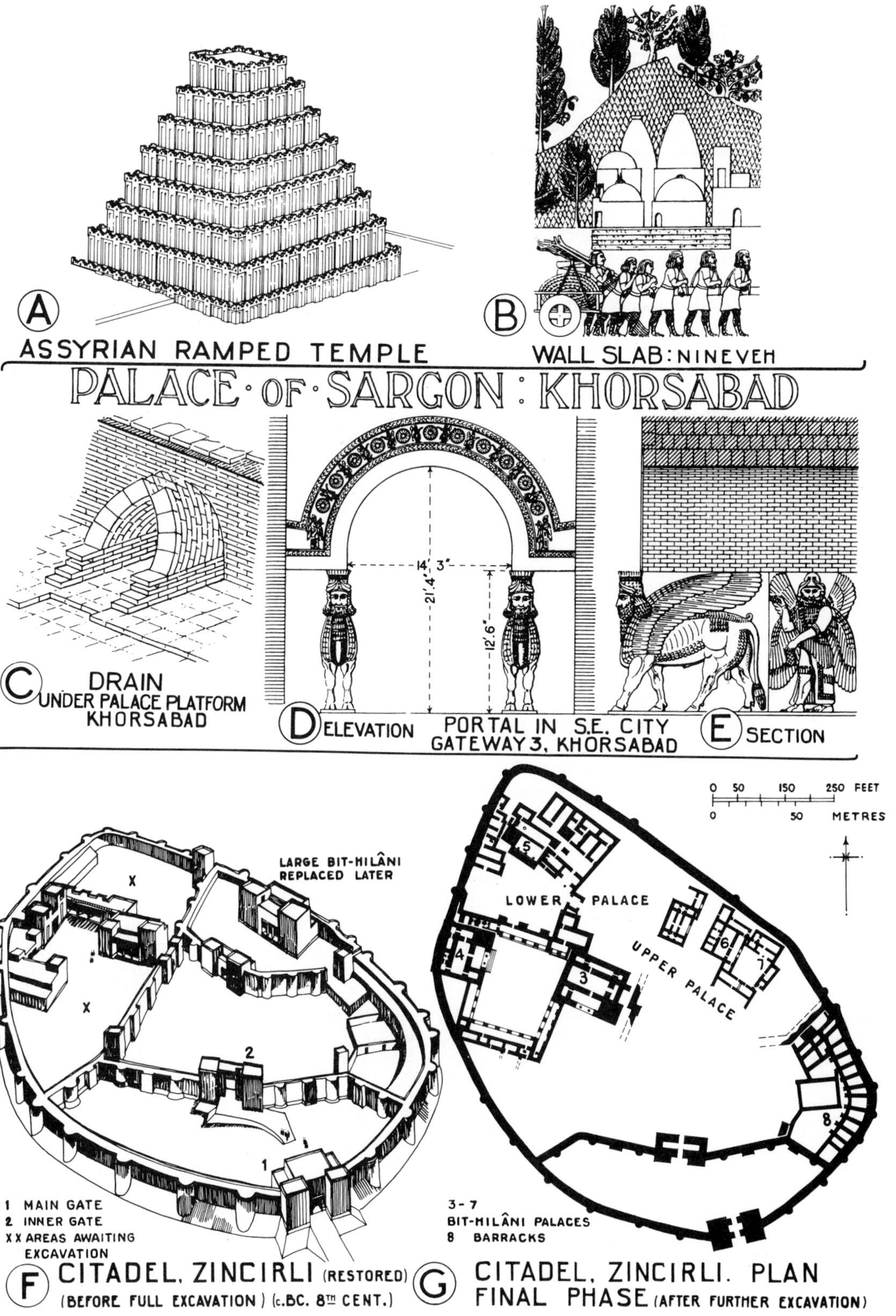
A
ASSYRIAN RAMPED TEMPLE
B
WALL SLAB: NINEVEH
PALACE · OF · SARGON : KHORSABAD
C
DRAIN
UNDER PALACE PLATFORM
KHORSABAD
14' 3"
21' 4"
12' 6"
D ELEVATION
PORTAL IN S.E. CITY
GATEWAY 3, KHORSABAD
E SECTION
LARGE BIT-HILÂNI
REPLACED LATER
X
X
2
1
1 MAIN GATE
2 INNER GATE
X X AREAS AWAITING
EXCAVATION
F CITADEL, ZINCIRLI (RESTORED)
(BEFORE FULL EXCAVATION) (c.BC. 8TH CENT.)
0 50 150 250 FEET
0 50 METRES
LOWER PALACE
UPPER PALACE
5
4
3
6
7
8
3-7
BIT-HILÂNI PALACES
8 BARRACKS
G CITADEL, ZINCIRLI. PLAN
FINAL PHASE (AFTER FURTHER EXCAVATION)

in its main wing the double sanctuary of Nabu (god of writing) and his consort. Off the court in front of this sanctuary was a well, interpreted as the source of water to be mixed with the very fine clay used for the tablets for writing by the scribes in cuneiform. There was a north wing, with comparable double sanctuary, used for the rituals of the New Year festival each spring.

The **City of Khorsabad** (p. 80C) contained the next important buildings in Assyria; it was built by Sargon II (722–705 BC) and abandoned at his death. It was square-planned, with a defensive perimeter, and covered nearly one square mile, but this area was never entirely occupied by buildings. There were two gateways in each tower-serrated wall (p. 81D,E), except where the place of one of them on the north-west wall was taken by an extensive citadel enclosure, containing all but one of the town's chief buildings. These comprised a palace for the king's brother, who was his vizier; a temple to Nabu; several official buildings, and, dominating them all, the **Palace of Sargon**, a complex of large and small courts, corridors and rooms, covering 23 acres (p. 80). Each of the buildings was raised upon a terrace, that of the palace of Sargon reaching to the level of the town walls, which the palace site bestrode, and was approached by broad ramps. The main entrance to the palace grand court was flanked by great towers and guarded by man-headed winged bulls, nearly 3.8 (12 ft 6 in) high, supporting a bold, semi-circular arch decorated with brilliantly coloured glazed bricks.

The palace had three main parts, each abutting the grand court. On the left on entering was a group of three large and three small temples; on the right, service quarters and administrative offices; and opposite, the private and residential apartments, with the state chambers behind. The state chambers had their own court, almost as large as the first, round which were dado slabs over 2.1 m (7 ft) high bearing reliefs of the king and his courtiers. The lofty throne-room, about 49 m × 10.7 m (160 ft × 35 ft), was the outermost of the state suite planned around its own internal court. It was probably one of the few apartments to have a flat timber ceiling, for fine timber was rare and costly. The plastered walls bore a painted decoration of a triple band of friezes, framed in running ornament, about 5.5 m (18 ft) high overall, around the room above a stone dado or reliefs (p. 83C). Walls were thick, about 6 m (20 ft) on average. In the Grand and Temple Courts decoration was contrived by sunken vertical panelling on the whitewashed walls and towers, finishing in stepped battlements above and stone plinths below, plain or carved (p. 80D).

Within the mud-brick platforms of the palace there were jointed terracotta drains to carry away rainwater, joining larger drains of burnt brick covered with vaults which were slightly pointed and in which the brick courses were laid obliquely, to avoid using wood centering (p. 81C). This device was well known to the Egyptians too.

Only stone dadoes so far have been mentioned; at the foot of the facade of the three chief temples there were high plinths projecting from the wall, faced in polychrome glazed bricks portraying sacred motifs and serving as pedestals for high cedar masts probably ringed with ornamental bronze bands, on the most likely reconstruction (p. 80F). The wall behind was panelled with a series of abutted half-columns, a revival of an ancient motif originating in the imitation of palm logs.

It is worth noting that the only ziggurat of the city is associated with the palace temples, as at Nimrud, and not with the large Nabu temple nearby. On a square base of 45 m (148 ft) side, the seven-tiered ziggurat rose to the same height (45 m, including the shrine at the top), ascended by a winding ramp 1.8 m (6 ft) wide. The successive tiers were panelled and battlemented and were painted in different colours on the plastered faces (p. 80A,G).

A structural peculiarity of Khorsabad was that the mud bricks were not left to dry hard in the sun but were laid in a pliable state, with mortar rarely used, surely indicating a certain urgency about this building programme. Probably this is explicable on internal political grounds, the consolidation of royal bureaucracy against the old power of the aristocracy, through the abandonment of Nimrud (Kalhu) by Sargon II, in favour of a virgin site. Kiln-fired bricks were used liberally for facings and pavements. Stone blocks up to 23 tonnes in weight and 2.7 m (9 ft) long were used for the palace platform. Within the palace the relief-carved orthostats were set in place and carved, remarkably, before the brick superstructure was built. Cedar, cypress, juniper and maple were used for the palace roofs, sometimes with painted beams: timber seems to have been plentiful. The perimeter wall of the city was over 20 m (66 ft) thick, with a dressed stone footing of 1.1 m (3 ft 6 in) and mud-brick superstructure.

The **City of Nineveh** was made the capital of the Assyrian empire by Sargon's son Sennacherib (705–681 BC) who spent the first two years of his reign on the work of raising mighty walls and, on the citadel now called Kuyunjik, building his 'Palace without a Rival' (the South-West Palace). Long inscriptions describing this palace were recovered during the excavations made in the nineteenth century, and the considerable labour of the building operations, especially that of making a secure foundation platform on the mound formed by successive levels of earlier occupation, is stressed therein; it is also depicted in reliefs now in the British Museum (pp. 79J, 81B). Other reliefs show campaigns and hunting in greater detail than ever before. More palaces were built at Nineveh by Sennacherib's immediate successors, Esarhaddon and Ashurbanipal. In the latter's reign relief sculpture in Assyria attained

A. (*right*)
The Ishtar Gate, Babylon (rebuilt by Nebuchadnezzar II, 605–563 BC). See p.85

B. Glazed brick panel from throne room suite, Fort Shalmaneser, Nimrud. See p.78

C. Wall painting, Palace of Sargon II, Khorsabad (722–705 BC). See p.82

A KINGS GATE, BOGHAZKÖY: OUTER SIDE (c.B.C.1360)

B PART PLAN OUTER TOWN WALLS & A GATE BOGHAZKÖY (c.B.C.1360)

C COLUMN BASE TELL TAYANAT (B.C. 8th CENT)

D OPEN AIR SANCTUARY & TEMPLE YASILIKAYA (c.B.C. 13TH CENT)

E TEMPLE I & MAGAZINES, BOGHAZKÖY (c.B.C. 14TH-13TH CENTS.)

its apogee in scenes of lion hunting and of the bloody campaigns against the kingdom of Elam, culminating in the destruction of Susa (*c.* 640 BC). Soon before the fall of Assyria, Nineveh was given an extra rampart along its vulnerable east side, but this was never finished. The city fell finally only after a prolonged attack by the Medes and Babylonians in 612 BC, and was never to rise again.

Water supply had long been a major concern of the Assyrian kings: Ashurnasirpal II dug a canal from the river Zab to irrigate the land close to Nimrud, while an arched aqueduct of stone construction, built by Sennacherib at Jerwan, may be said to anticipate Roman achievements of this class.

Neo-Babylonian Architecture

Neo-Babylonian architecture was naturally descended from that of the earlier centuries in Mesopotamia, but it derived much also from the architecture of the Assyrians.

The **City of Babylon**, whose ruins differ from those of earlier cities largely because of the use of burnt brick, was rebuilt by Nebuchadnezzar II (605–563 BC), for it had been thoroughly destroyed by Sennacherib (689 BC). It had an inner and outer part, each heavily fortified. The inner town was approximately square in plan, of about 1300 m (4350 ft) sides, containing the principal buildings, the Euphrates river forming the west side. The few main streets intersected starkly at right angles, terminating in tower-framed bronze gates where they met the walls. Between the main streets tiered dwellings, business houses, temples, chapels and shrines jostled in lively disorder. The principal sites lined the river front, and behind them ran a grand processional way, its vista closed on the north by the Ishtar Gate (p. 83A), glowing in coloured glazed bricks, patterned with yellow and white bulls and dragons in relief upon a blue ground. Hereabouts there were palace-citadels, and connected with Nebuchadnezzar's great palace complex on the water side was that marvel of the ancient world, the Hanging Gardens, 275 m × 183 m (900 ft × 600 ft) overall; among its maze of rooms was a vast throne-room, 52 m × 17 m (170 ft × 56 ft), its long facade decorated with polychrome glazed bricks. The central sites on the river front were occupied by the chief temple of the god of the city, Marduk, and, to the north of it, the expansive precinct where rose the associated ziggurat, the 'Tower of Babel'. The celebrated ziggurat appears to have been one combining the triple stairway approach and massive lower tier customary in early Mesopotamia, with upper stages arranged spirally according to Assyrian practice. The plan was square, of 90 m (295 ft) sides, and there were seven stages in all, the summit temple being faced with blue glazed bricks.

Early Anatolian and Hittite Architecture

The Hittites, although the best-known of the ancient peoples of Anatolia, were not the earliest inhabitants: they inherited on their arrival (*c.* 2000 BC) a long tradition of building. In contrast to Mesopotamia, both stone and timber were available in abundance, and in the most densely forest-covered areas timber-frame construction must have been normal. One simple unit which seems to have been Anatolian in origin and which appeared very early was the 'megaron', a rectangular room with central hearth and door at one end, set in a deep porch formed by the prolongation of the side walls to make 'antae'. This unit is too simple not to have been evolved independently in different regions, though it was suited to the extremes of the Anatolian climate. The best-known examples have been found at Troy, from the First Settlement (*c.* 3500–3100 BC) onwards, and at Beycesultan, in south-western Anatolia. Village houses in much of Turkey today are of mud brick with extensive use of timber, especially for the flat roofs; and where of two storeys, these houses have their living-rooms upstairs, the ground floor being principally for kitchens and store-rooms, and often also for animals. A largely comparable arrangement has been found in the merchant colony established by traders from Ashur at Kanesh (Kultepe), whose houses included an archive for their business records, kept on clay tablets baked in an oven.

Most of the surviving monuments of Hittite architecture date from the fourteenth and thirteenth centuries BC, the period of the 'Empire'. Mesopotamian influences were strong in Hittite building, but there was much that was individual. In important structures massive stone masonry was used, though the upper parts of walls, even of highland town fortifications, were commonly of sun-dried bricks in timber framing; the chief remains are of town walls and temples.

The **Palace of Beycesultan**, Level V (*c.* 1900–1750 BC) is an outstanding example of the use of timber as reinforcement for walls constructed of mud brick with footings of limestone. Some resemblance to the palaces of Minoan Crete is discernible, though not a close one. As in pottery and other artefacts so in architecture this fertile region of south-western Anatolia maintained a tradition distinct from that of the Hittite homeland in central Anatolia.

At **Büyükkale** (Turkish: 'great castle'), **Boğazköy**, the ingenuity of the German excavators over many seasons has made it possible to gain a sound grasp of the layout of the citadel of the Hittite capital of Hattušas. A fortified double gateway admitted to an entrance court crossed by red marble flagstones and thence through a hall to a lower court. At its north-east end was a gate building with triple gateway, admitting to a middle and upper court, the private sector. A large audience hall, almost 32 m (104 ft) square, opened on to the middle court: this seems to have had five rows of five wooden columns, supported by parallel walls. There were three archives, in the smallest of which were labels indicating the original cataloguing of the tablets. By the thirteenth century BC the entire citadel rock was occupied by these governmental and residential buildings, an area of up to 250 m × 150 m (810 ft × 490 ft), the upper part being denuded to the bare rock.

The outer **Town Walls of Boğazköy** (*c.* 1360 BC) (p. 84B) enclosed some 300 acres. They were of casemate construction, like those of Mesopotamia, being double and connected by cross-walls, the compartments thus formed being packed with rubble. Square towers projected at frequent intervals, and some 6 m (20 ft) in front was a lesser wall, with its own minor towers. The outer shell of the main wall was particularly strong, built of large, rock-faced, close-jointed stones up to 1.5 m (5 ft) long, varying in shape from the rectangular to the polygonal. The upper parts of the walls were of brick, and fragments of models provide good evidence that towers and walls finished in crenellations similar to the Mesopotamian. Five gateways partially survive. These were flanked by great towers and had peculiar elliptical openings of which the corbellated upper parts stood on pairs of enormous monolithic stone jambs (p. 84A). Broad archivolts surrounded the portals, and ornamenting the jambs of three of the gates were boldly projecting sculptures. On the 'King's Gate' was an armed figure on the reveal, not in fact a warrior but a god; on the 'Lion Gate' were foreparts of lions on the face of the jambs; and on the 'Sphinx Gate' sphinxes not only project forward but show the full body-length on the reveals, thus anticipating the monsters of Assyrian times by some five centuries.

Temple I, Boğazköy (p. 84E) is the largest and oldest of many identified there, which have no regular orientation but show other principal features in common. They consist of a number of rooms arranged round a central court, with cloister or corridor access on two or more sides. In Temple I the building is girdled by a paved road beyond which are numerous magazines, many still filled with great pottery jars and one containing cuneiform tablets constituting the temple records. Asymmetrically placed was a special unit of several rooms, the largest of all being a sanctuary, only to be reached circuitously through adjacent smaller rooms. The sanctuary projected at one end, so that windows might give side illumination to the cult statue. Unlike Mesopotamian temples, light to most rooms came from deep windows on the external walls. The entrance was also asymmetrical, whether through a simple recessed porch on the flank or, as in Temple I, on the front opposite the sanctuary unit. To one side of the court in Temple I stood a cell built of granite, as was the sanctuary unit, the building elsewhere being of limestone. There was a similar temple at Alaca Hüyük.

The **Open-air Sanctuary, Yazilikaya** (p. 84D), about 1.6 km (1 mile) north-east of Boğazköy, is a deep re-entrant in an almost sheer limestone face, with processions of some seventy gods and goddesses, about 1 m (3 ft) high, carved at eye level on the faces, converging on a rear panel. A lesser sanctuary with reliefs adjoined on the east. Screening the groves was a temple, comprising three buildings in a series, linked by walls: a deep propylaeum; the temple proper, with rooms on three sides of a court in which stood a walled cell and from which a lefthand turn was made towards the sacred groves through a second, pillared propylaeum; and a large sanctuary, independently approached. The propylaeum unit occurs also in the architecture of Minoan Crete and Mycenaean Greece (q.v.).

Canaanite, Phoenician and Israelite Architecture

The architecture of the Levant in the second millennium BC, of the regions now included within the south-eastern fringes of Turkey, Syria, Lebanon, Jordan and Israel, cannot strictly be described under the above heading. Indeed, the Hurrians formed an important element in the population, especially in north Syria.

The two **Palaces at Tell Atchana** (ancient Alalakh), in the plain of Antioch, may be ascribed to the Hurrians more than to any other group. The earlier of these was built by Yarim-Lim, ruler of the minor kingdom of Yamkhad and a contemporary of Hammurabi. It is in essence a private house, with the public rooms in the north wing and the private rooms in the south, including traces of wall paintings from the upper storey. Perhaps the most interesting feature of Yarim-Lim's palace is the use of basalt orthostats in the north wing, the earliest example of a tradition later occurring, as mentioned above, in Hittite and Assyrian buildings. In its extensive use of timber to reinforce the mud-brick superstructure this palace was more in the Anatolian than the Mesopotamian tradition. The larger palace of Niqmepa, built almost three centuries later, represents a refinement of the design of the earlier palace and a larger, more public building.

The **Palace at Ras Shamra** (ancient Ugarit), the prosperous city on the north Syrian coast, seems to be transitional in plan between the palaces of Yarim-Lim and Niqmepa, being less advanced than the latter, although Ugarit was a much more important city than Alalakh. The undoubted achievements of the city-states of the Levant were never adequately reflected in their architecture, at least as hitherto revealed by excavations. It is noteworthy that a group of fourteen family vaults at Ugarit, all with a short dromos with descending stairway and a rectangular funerary chamber with a corbel-vaulted roof, and outstanding in design and execution, can undoubtedly be ascribed to an Aegean element in the city's population, presumably merchants. Rather earlier (probably of the fifteenth century BC) were the fortifications of Ugarit, of rough stone masonry and including a well-built postern tunnel for sorties in time of siege. To the thirteenth century BC belong palace buildings in dressed stone, which provide the earliest parallel with the better type of masonry used in Palestine, first in the United Kingdom of David and Solomon and later especially in Israel, from the tenth century BC onwards. The missing link between these two periods was through the Phoenicians, for whose achievement reliance has still largely to be placed on the Old Testament; the Phoenician cities, mostly concealed beneath remains of Graeco-Roman cities and Crusader castles, have yet to be extensively investigated.

At **Samaria**, founded by Omri (*c.* 880 BC) and captured by the Assyrians (*c.* 720 BC), when the kingdom of Israel was absorbed into the Assyrian empire, excavations have given the most coherent record of the material civilisation of Israel, of which it was the capital. Six architectural phases have been distinguished for this period, the first two being marked by the use of finely jointed and dressed masonry, the courses even and horizontal.

At **Jerusalem** nothing has survived of the Temple of Solomon, built by Phoenician craftsmen, with cedar beams imported from the Lebanon. However, the excavations have revealed much of the long and complex succession of defences of the city in the Jebusite period and after David made it the centre of his kingdom, although little has been found surviving of the buildings within the city's walls. Hezekiah's tunnel in the city and cisterns in the barren Negev testify to the continuing concern of the Judaean kings for water supply, a serious weakness of Samaria.

Megiddo and **Hazor** in the northern kingdom, and **Lachish** and **Tell Beit Mersim** in the southern, were among the major sites. At **Ezion-Geber**, later called Elath, situated at the head of the Gulf of Aqaba, a smelter for refining the copper from the Wadi Arabah was built, surrounded by workers' quarters and by a protective wall, this being originally founded in the time of Solomon. He is said in the Bible to have fortified Hazor, Megiddo and Gezer, at all of which have been found gateways of similar multi-chambered design, at Megiddo continuing through several subsequent phases: these comprise some of the few remains attributable with any certainty to his reign.

Syro-Hittite Architecture

The porched house, or 'bit-hilâni', so characteristic of Syria, may have had its origin as early as the palace of Yarim-Lim at Alalakh, although it is not until the early first millennium BC that this unit can be discerned in developed form in the context of Syro-Hittite civilisation. Cultural continuity in Syria was never entirely broken after the end of the Hittite empire; unfortunately, however, the excavations at Carchemish, which had a strong Hittite element in the population, have been sufficient only to establish the sequence of the town's defences and the relative chronology of several groups of relief-sculptured orthostats. The Long Wall of sculptures depicts the victory procession of the ruler of Carchemish at that time, Katuwas (*c.* 900 BC).

At the **Citadel of Zincirli** (p. 81F,G), because far more excavated, the layout is much clearer. It was of oval plan, standing centrally on a mound in a walled town which, like so many in ancient West Asia, was completely circular. The construction of the citadel walls was typical of the period in being timber-framed with sun-dried brick infill, standing on two courses of cut masonry on rubble foundations. Internally the citadel was divided into defensive zones by cross-walls, securing the approaches to an 'Upper' and a 'Lower' Palace, of about the eighth century BC. Each comprised bit-hilâni, two of which are particularly plain in the plan of the Lower Palace (p. 81G). These stood on opposite sides of a large cloistered court, and each had a two-columned porch, with a stair on the right, leading to a transverse hall or throne room, beyond which was a range of smaller rooms including bedroom and bathroom. In front of the throne was a circular hearth, while a hall in the Upper Palace had a movable iron hearth on bronze wheels. The porch columns were of wood, with stone bases shaped either as a pair of lions or monsters, or in triple ornamented stone cushions having some likeness to the earliest versions of the bases of the Classical Greek Ionic Order (q.v.). Instances of both occur at Tell Tayanat, west of Antioch (p. 84C). Following the old Hittite tradition and partly contemporary Assyrian practice, gates were protected by stone monsters and decorated by orthostats carved in relief.

The **City of Hamath** was distinguished during its most prosperous period (*c.* 900–720 BC) by monumental buildings on the citadel, including two gateways, a probable temple and two palaces, only one of which (Building II) has been entirely uncovered. The main gate (Building I) had a long staircase, with a landing on the threshold, but the plan is simpler than in the cities of north Syria, such as Carchemish. Though there is the same use of orthostats, they are plain, the work of the sculptors at Hamath being almost confined to the provision of guardian lions. There are no guard rooms on either side, though there are flanking towers. The palace had a buttressed facade notably lacking a columned portico. Traces of gold leaf and fragments of red, blue and white plaster give a hint of the richness of decoration in the living quarters of the palace, on the upper floor; from here too probably came the throne and window grille, both carved in basalt, found thrown into the central court. The staircase evidently had two flights, only the lower one surviving, which gave the main evidence for the excavators' reconstruction of the height of the palace as some 14.4 m (47 ft), with the upper storey being 7 m (23 ft) high; a fallen pier of brickwork from the upper storey was of 48 courses. Hamath is a good example of many sites in the ancient Near East whose poor preservation makes it difficult to grasp immediately the achievements of their architects. Hamath was then, as now, one of the leading cities of inland Syria. Its prosperity, and that of Syro-Hittite cities in general, rapidly declined with the growth of Assyrian power after 745 BC.

Urartian Architecture

The origins of the architecture of the Kingdom of Van, known to its Assyrian enemies as Urartu (Ararat), are as obscure as those of the kingdom itself.

Fortresses

The most typical buildings so far known in Urartu are the numerous fortresses, many of them strategically sited round Lake Van, others being further afield, round Lake Urmia in north-west Iran, and especially in the Araxes valley. Massive stone masonry of cyclopean character was used for the lower parts of the fortress walls, with buttresses or towers at regular intervals (p. 89A), while mud brick was used for the superstructure. Timber was available for roofing, though not so abundant as in Anatolia. Store-rooms containing huge jars of wine, oil or corn are also a usual feature.

The **Citadel of Van**, the capital of Urartu, must have been impregnable; it has a cliff along the south side, and some 90 m (300 ft) of the Urartian walls (*c.* 800 BC) (p. 89A) survives among much later work. At the foot of the west end of the citadel of Van stands a massive stone podium, perhaps a shrine but more probably a form of barbican protecting the entrance to the citadel and its water supply from a spring: this was built by Sarduri I, the founder of Van as capital of the kingdom, and some of the blocks are 5.2 m (17 ft) long, being about 1.2 m × 1.2 m (4 ft × 4 ft) in section. The fortifications of the citadel above, like many of the fortresses of Urartu, were almost certainly the work of Menua, whose reign (*c.* 810–786 BC), together with that of Rusa II (*c.* 685–645 BC) saw the two main periods of building activity that seem to have occurred in the history of Urartu.

At **Çavuştepe**, south-east of Van, there stands a long, narrow citadel crowning the summit of a rocky ridge in the middle of the Hoşap valley. This is one of the few buildings which show that, although massiveness rather than finesse seems the chief characteristic of Urartian architecture, it does include examples of a higher standard than the average Urartian building indicates. Blind windows carved on basalt monoliths, represented on a bronze model from Toprakkale (Van), have been found tumbled down the hillside. At Çavuştepe the perimeter wall is of limestone masonry whose joints are largely oblique, but which is finely dressed throughout. With its temple, this site belongs to the reign of Sarduri II who, before his defeats by Tiglath-Pileser III of Assyria, had brought Urartu to the zenith of its power.

Karmir-Blur (ancient Teishebaini) (p. 90A), just outside Erevan, is an outstanding example of an Urartian fortress and governmental centre, with towered and buttressed perimeter wall, massive gateway, parade ground within the wall and ground floor entirely occupied by store-rooms.

The **Citadel of Kefkalesi**, above Adilcevaz on the north-west shore of Lake Van, is of similar date (seventh century BC). Less typical is the large fortified enclosure at the foot of Anzavur, near Patnos, whose situation makes it all the more likely to have been a military compound. This is of the time of Menua (*c.* 810–786 BC).

The **Citadel of Bastam**, near the north-west extremity of Iran, was built by Rusa II (*c.* 685–645 BC) to guard an approach road to Van. The greater part comprises massively terraced structures on a steep, rocky hillside, which on the further side falls precipitously from its ridge to the valley below. Among major structures are gateways at the north and south ends, a columned hall and a large stable block in the plain outside the walls.

Temples

The most characteristic manifestation of Urartian architecture is the temple, whose original appearance must have resembled a tall, fortified tower. There is a standard plan, square and with shallow corner buttresses; the footings are usually of very fine, smoothly dressed basalt ashlar, of an altogether finer quality than the walls of the fortresses.

The **Temple at Kayalidere**, which is of rougher masonry, has a facade over 12 m (40 ft) long, with walls 3.2 m (10 ft 6 in) thick, while the interior of the sanctuary is barely 5 m (16 ft 4 in) square. Such massive walls themselves imply great height, and although an Assyrian relief depicting the temple of Haldi, chief god of Urartu, at the city of Musasir, suggests much squatter proportions, this was due to the confined space of the register in the relief. The Achaemenian **Fire Temple at Naksh-i-Rustam** (p. 95C) suggests that the proportions of the standard Urartian temple may well have been a double cube,

A. Urartian masonry, Citadel of Van (*c.* 800 BC). See p.88

B. The Temple, Alintepe (seventh century BC). See p.92

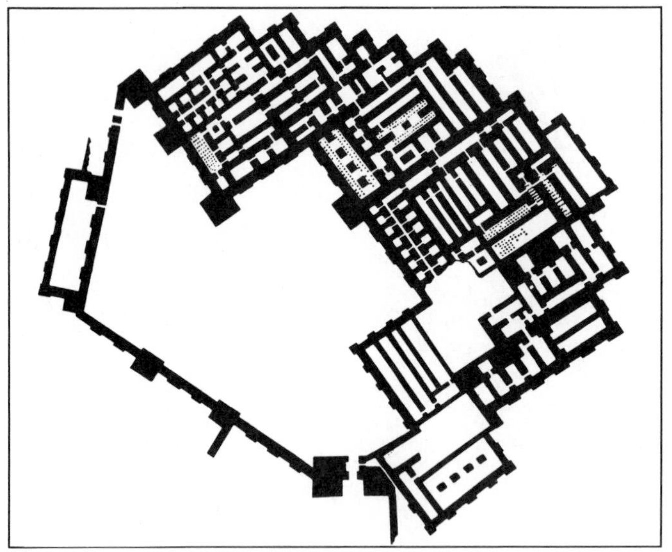

A. Karmir-Blur: plan of citadel (*c.* 685–645 BC). See p.88

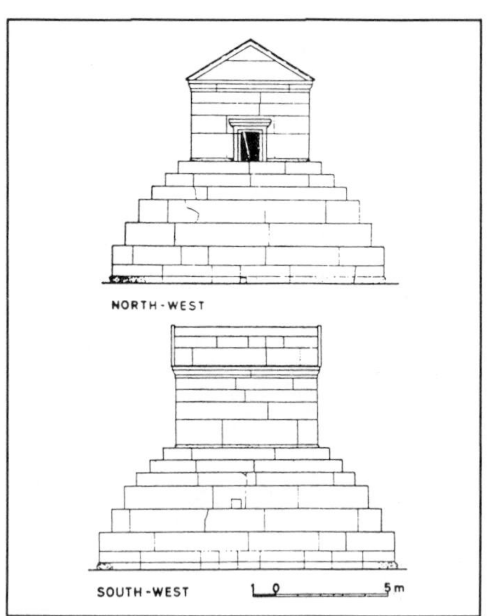

B. The Cyrus Tomb: NW and SW elevations. See p.93

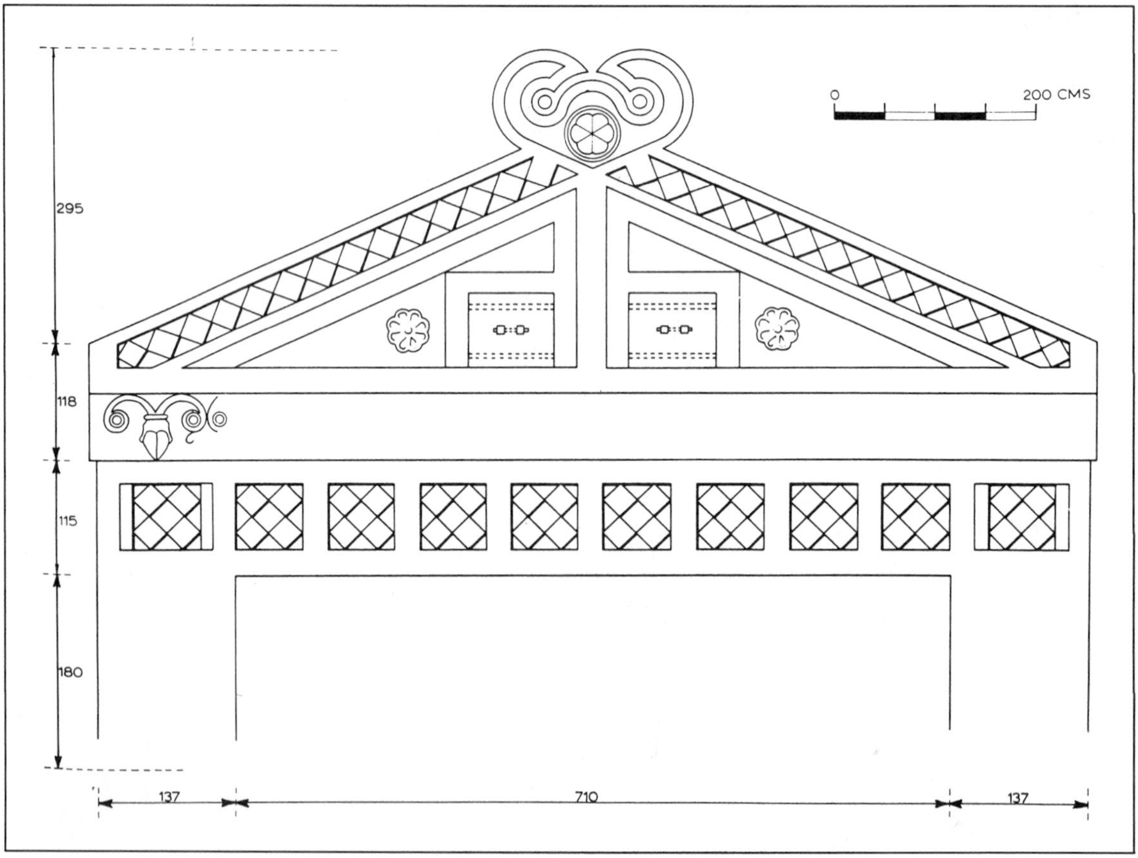

C. Phrygia: unfinished monument. See p.92

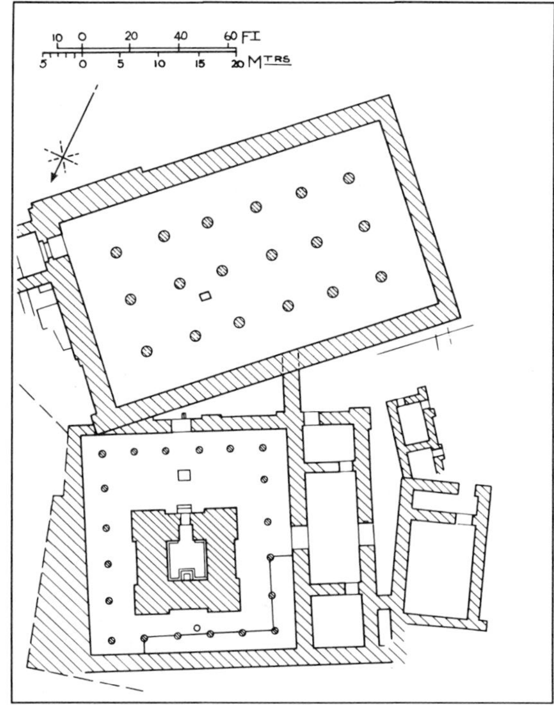

A. Altintepe: plan of temple and audience hall (seventh century BC). See p.92

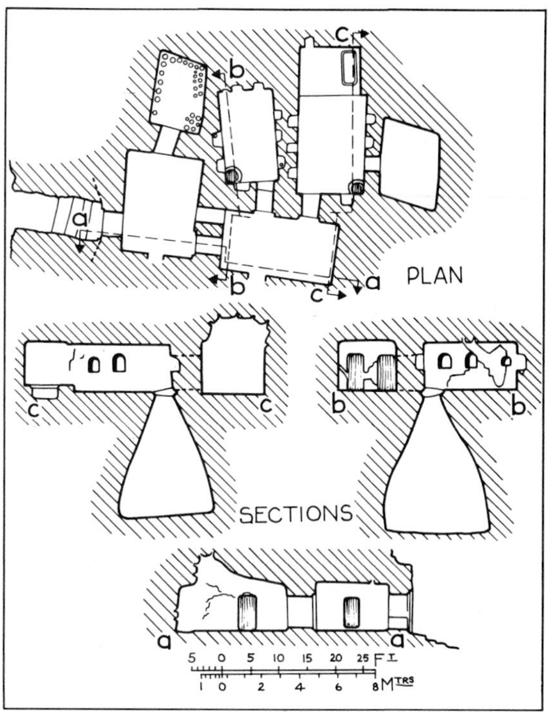

B. Kayalidere: plan and sections of tomb (*c.* 700 BC). See p.92

C. Kefkalesi: Urartian relief with inscription of Rusa II (*c.* 685–645 BC) and background of battlemented fortress. See p.92

and if, as the relief of the Musasir temple suggests, the Urartian temples had gabled roofs, these may have resembled that of the Tomb of Cyrus at Pasargadae (q.v.), though in wood instead of stone.

Apart from the temple at Kayalidere, there are temples of the standard plan at **Anzavur** (with the annals inscription of Menua), **Çavuştepe, Toprakkale** and **Altintepe** (pp. 89B, 91A) (with a colonnade running round the court in which the temple stands). Open-air rock-cut shrines occur at Van and elsewhere.

The **Temple at Toprakkale** is also worthy of mention for its rusticated masonry, the centre of each block being left rough and the joints recessed and smooth. Though this occurs at Ugarit in the second millennium BC, there seems no adequate evidence to suggest that the Urartians did not develop this independently. At Toprakkale stones of different colours, limestone and basalt, were used inlaid to achieve a contrast.

The characteristic **Urartian tomb** was cut out of the solid rock, with niches in the walls for lamps or offerings: such are the tombs in the south side of the citadel of Van and at Kayalidere. At Altintepe there are tombs of comparable design, but of masonry and built into the hillside just beneath the summit of the citadel. False vaults occur in the Altintepe tombs; at **Kayalidere** there are bottle-shaped shafts accessible only through an opening in the floor of the chamber above (p. 91B).

The **Shamiram Su** (Semiramis Canal) is the most famous of the canals and cisterns which formed a major part of the works of the successive Urartian kings, and was constructed by Menua to bring water from the valley of the Hoşap river south-east of Van to the fields and gardens round the capital. This canal is largely visible to this day.

Sculpture was little manifest in Urartu and late in appearance. At Kefkalesi a relief (p. 91C) includes a representation of battlements, windows of narrow slit form and doorways. A bronze model from Toprakkale provides similar evidence of the mud-brick superstructure typical of an architectural tradition of which the stone footings alone normally survive, except where fire (as at Kefkalesi and Karmir-Blur) has preserved some of the brickwork.

Palaces

The **Palace of Argishti I** (*c.* 786–764 BC) at **Arin-Berd** (ancient Erebuni), the city which he founded close to the later Karmir-Blur, is the most important Urartian palace known. It was decorated with mural paintings in the formal court style adapted from that of Assyria, with some examples of a freer genre, owing little or nothing to outside influences. This palace included a throne room with two entrances and a courtyard with a wooden gallery supported by fourteen wooden columns on stone bases.

At **Giriktepe**, close to Patnos, a smaller palace has been excavated: its large hall, decorated with doubly recessed niches, shows similarities to the architecture of the large **citadel of Hasanlu** (*c.* 1100–800 BC), a major site just south of Lake Urmia, in a region from which the expanding kingdom of Urartu may have drawn some inspiration for its architecture, at least in mud brick.

At **Altintepe** (p. 91A), near Erzincan, situated by the north-west frontier of Urartu, a palace has been excavated with an audience hall 43.7 m × 24.7 m (143 ft × 81 ft), with six rows of three columns having their superstructure of mud brick, not wood. The diameter of the column bases of stone was almost 1.5 m (5 ft), and they are spaced nearly 5.2 m (17 ft) apart. This hall seems to date from the seventh century BC, a period of revival in Urartu not long before its final eclipse.

Phrygian Architecture

At **Gordion**, the Phrygian capital, the architecture uncovered by excavations includes houses built on the 'megaron' plan, with its essential features of a front porch flanked by antae prolonging the line of the main walls, and leading into a large room with a hearth at or near its centre. This was suited to the extremes of the Anatolian climate. At one time, perhaps through comparisons with modern Turkish village houses, it was doubted whether these ancient megara had anything but flat roofs. The great width and absence of central pillars might alone have suggested otherwise; the proof of gabled roofs is provided by graffiti on walls of megara, by the roof of the timber tomb chamber of the great tumulus at Gordion, supported by three gables, one in the middle and one at each end, and by at least ten of the rock monuments of Phrygia (p. 90C), including those of the so-called Midas City. This group of monuments comprises not tombs but shrines, since the Phrygians had introduced the custom of burial in tumuli. The great gateway of Gordion has a pronounced batter to its facade, and, with the absence of niches and buttresses at regular intervals and the relatively small size of the stones used, these fortifications are quite different in style and construction from the Urartian.

At **Midas City** the carved facades show the timbers crossing at the apex of the gable, as on the graffiti at Gordion, and reveal other architectural features too. One chamber is carved to imitate a house built of logs; in the so-called Tomb of Midas's Wife there are two shuttered windows carved in the gable; doors are represented as opening inwards; the so-called Broken Tomb has a large chamber hewn out of the rock to represent the interior of a house, with benches along three sides, and in the Lion Grave there is a carved bed inside the chamber.

A distinctive feature of Phrygian architecture was the use of terracotta tiles as ornament, represented by examples from Gordion and from Pazarli, in central Anatolia; they may also be rendered as geometric patterns on the facades of two of the shrines of Midas City. These tiles seem to have been used as a frieze beneath the pediment of gabled buildings. Vertical and horizontal beams and cross-ties were used in the wooden framework of some of the Phrygian buildings of Gordion. Together with the chamber of the great tumulus and the ornate furniture found there they attest to the wide variety of Phrygian wood-working and the high level of skill achieved in an essentially Anatolian civilisation, owing much to Assyria, and perhaps also to Urartu, but at the same time preserving its own identity.

Median and Persian Architecture

The architectural achievements of the Medes and Persians before the reign of Cyrus the Great have recently been recognised in buildings of the eighth-seventh century BC excavated in western Iran, at Godin Tepe, Baba Jan and Nush-i Jan.

At **Godin Tepe**, Level II, the upper citadel originally comprised a fortified manor, or minor palace, which centred around a larger and a smaller columned hall, with additional smaller rooms and rows of magazines; the whole was protected by a fortification wall with bastions, a tower and arrow slots.

At **Baba Jan**, in Levels II and I, the manor must have presented a formidable facade, being defended by eight rectangular towers, one of which was replaced in Level I by a columned portico as the main entrance; the space within the towered wall comprised a rectangular court, later roofed, with a long room on either side. A contemporary building in another part of the same site had one room decorated in a style unknown elsewhere, with heavy painted wall tiles. Columns were also a feature of a large citadel building, approximately contemporary with the manor of Baba Jan, at Haftavan Tepe, in the Urmia basin of north-west Iran.

At **Tepe Nush-i-Jan**, near Hamadan (Ecbatana), well-preserved mud-brick buildings of Median date have been uncovered in Level I (*c.* 700–550 BC) (p. 95D). In one building the earliest known example of a fire altar has been discovered. Unusual mural decorations, suggesting long experience in the use of mud brick, include recessed crosses, blind windows, and holes with the appearance of serving to support a scaffold. Another building was a fort, with a ramp leading to a staircase, turning round a central pier and roofed with a mud-brick corbel-vault. The palaces and tombs of the Persians show that many features of their remarkable columnar architecture were derived from the older civilisations: the gorge moulding from Egypt; the sculptured monsters, relief-carved orthostats and polychrome glazed brickwork from Mesopotamia; the style of masonry indirectly perhaps from Urartu.

The site of **Pasargadae** comprises four groups of structures scattered over a plain, centred round the citadel, the residential palace, the tomb of Cyrus and the sacred precinct respectively. Rusticated masonry is a feature of the great platform of the citadel (Takht-i-Suleiman), whose ambitious plan was abandoned, presumably at the death of Cyrus (530 BC), in favour of a more modest scheme in mud brick. The **Tomb of Cyrus** (p. 90B), a simple box-like monument of limestone 3.2 m × 2.3 m (10 ft 6 in × 7 ft 6 in), gabled, and standing on a platform of six steps, is typically Achaemenian in its use of large blocks, accurately cut, smoothly dressed, without mortar but reinforced by swallowtail clamps of lead and iron. Its design, based on an early type of gabled house, is paralleled in the southern Zagros highlands by the tomb of Gur-i-Dokhtar, and has possible antecedents in the underground tombs with gabled roofs in Luristan and in central Iran at Tepe Sialk, near Kashan. A continuing tradition of gabled roofs is suggested by their occurrence in all the finished chambers of the rock-cut tomb of Darius I.

Susa, ancient city of Elam, became the Persian capital in succession to Babylon with the building there of a citadel and palace complex by Darius I (522–486 BC). A most illuminating building inscription tells how the resources and skills of the whole empire were utilised in the construction of the palace buildings. Cedar was brought from Lebanon, teak from the Zagros mountains and southern Persia, while the baked bricks were made by the Babylonian method. Most significant of all, craftsmen were drawn from the Assyrians, Babylonians, Egyptians and Ionian Greeks. The remarkable compound of features which constitute the unique and gracious architecture of Persia is thus explained. From this palace and a later one by Artaxerxes II (404–358 BC) come the famous glazed-brick decorations, portraying processions of archers, lions, bulls or dragons (p. 94F,G).

The **Palace of Persepolis** (pp. 94A–E, 95A), begun in 518 BC by Darius I, was mostly executed by Xerxes I (486–465 BC) and finished by Artaxerxes I about 460 BC. The various buildings stood on a platform, partly built up and partly excavated, faced in well-laid local stone bound with iron clamps, about 460 m × 275 m (1500 ft × 900 ft) in extent and rising 15 m (50 ft) above the plain at the base of a rocky spur. The approach on the north-west was by a magnificent flight of steps, 6.7 m (22 ft) wide, shallow enough for horses to ascend. A gatehouse by Xerxes had mud-brick walls, faced with polychrome bricks, and front and rear portals guarded by stone bulls. A third doorway on the south led towards the 'Apadana', a grand audience hall, 76.2 m (250 ft) square and with thirty-six columns within its 6 m

A. Persepolis: Hall of the Hundred Columns (restored) (*c.* 518–460 BC). Other details of the palaces at Perseoplis are given below. See p.93

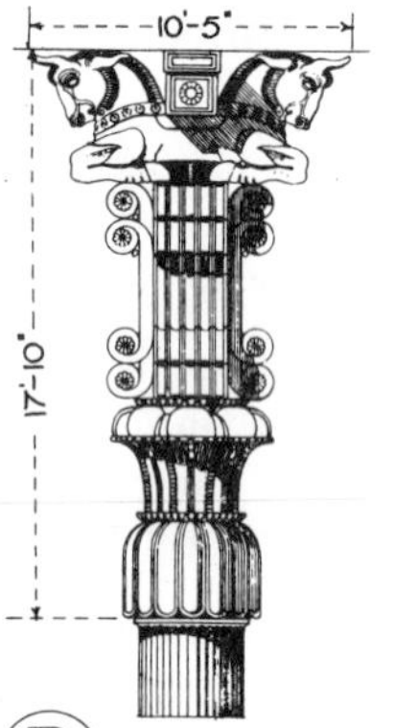

10'-5"

17'-10"

B DOUBLE "BULL" CAP: APADANA OF XERXES

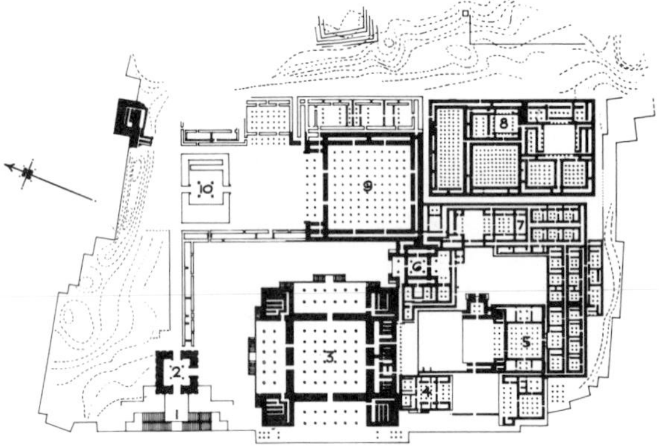

1. STAIRWAY TO TERRACE
2. GATEHOUSE OF XERXES
3. APADANA OF DARIUS I
4. PALACE OF DARIUS I
5. PALACE OF XERXES
6. TRIPYLON
7. HAREM
8. TREASURY
9. HALL OF 100 COLUMNS
10. INNER GATEHOUSE

100 0 100 300 500 700 FEET
0 100 200 METRES

C PLAN OF PALACE PLATFORM.

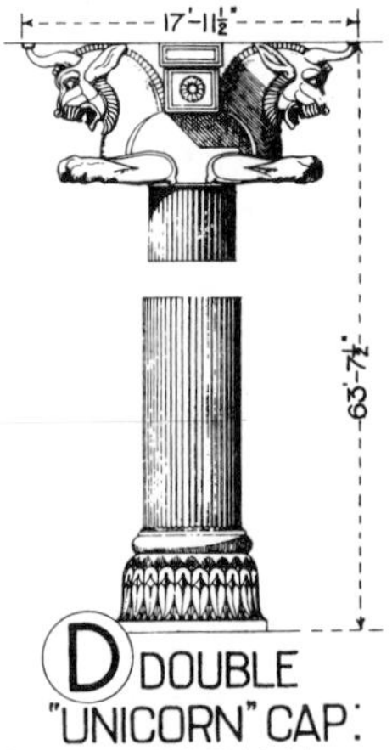

17'-11½"

63'-7½"

D DOUBLE "UNICORN" CAP: APADANA OF XERXES

ABT 7.10"

E BAS-RELIEF: PERSEPOLIS.

ABT 4.0"

F LION FRIEZE: SUSA.

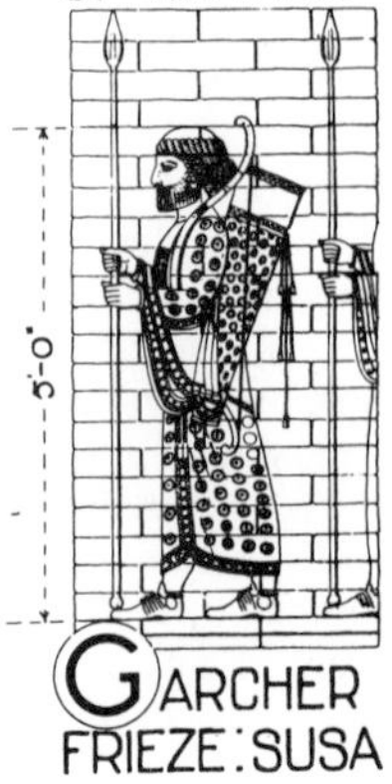

5'-0"

G ARCHER FRIEZE: SUSA

A. Stairway of Tripylon, Persepolis (518–486 BC). See p.93

B. Tomb of Darius, Naksh-i-Rustam (485 BC). See p.97

C. Fire Temple, Naksh-i-Rustam. See p.97

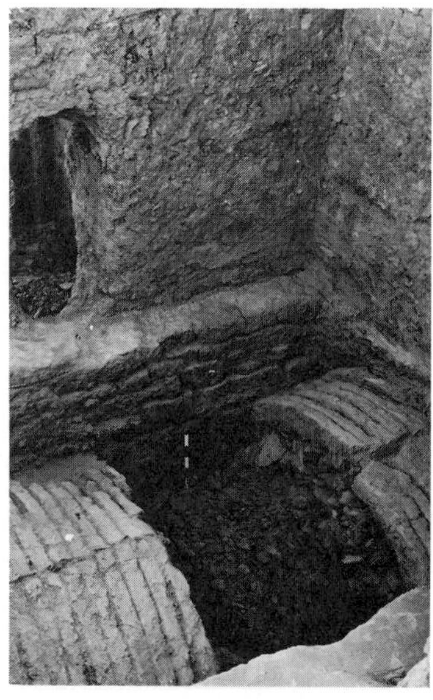

D. Tepe Nush-i-Jan: shale-filled antechamber. See p.93

PALACE AT FERUZ-ABAD

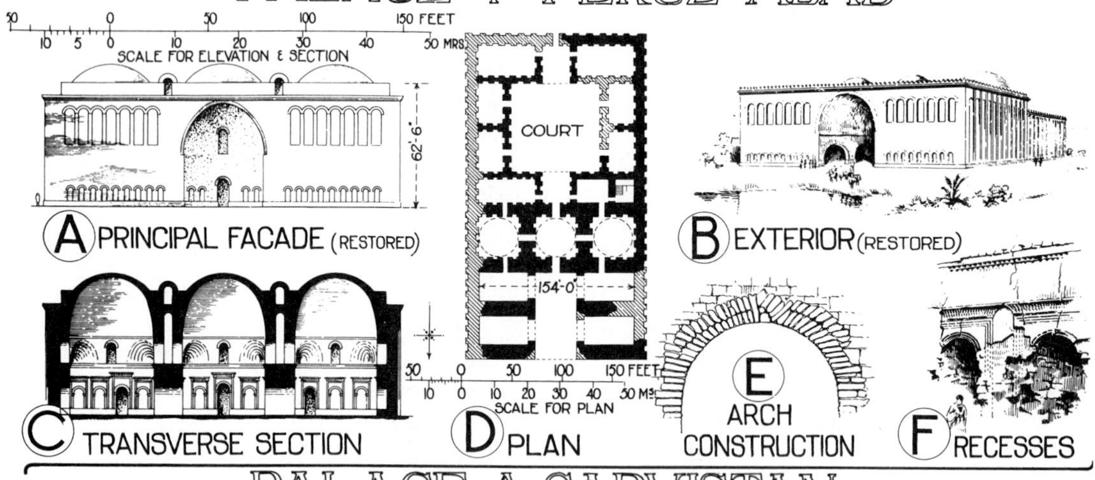
50 0 50 100 150 FEET
10 5 0 10 20 30 40 50 MRS
SCALE FOR ELEVATION & SECTION
62'-6"
COURT
154'-0"
50 0 50 100 150 FEET
10 0 10 20 30 40 50 MRS
SCALE FOR PLAN
A PRINCIPAL FACADE (RESTORED)
B EXTERIOR (RESTORED)
C TRANSVERSE SECTION
D PLAN
E ARCH CONSTRUCTION
F RECESSES

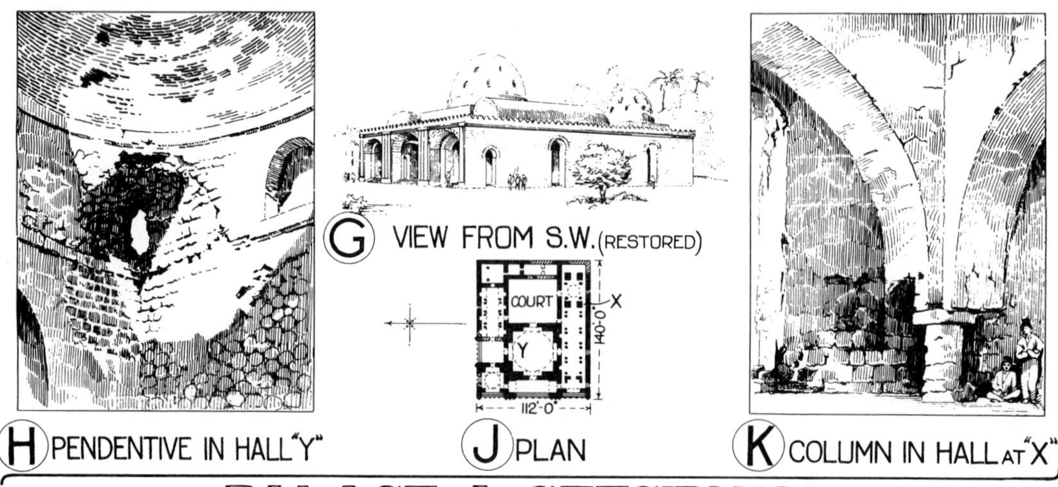
PALACE AT SARVISTAN
G VIEW FROM S.W. (RESTORED)
COURT
Y
X
140'-0"
112'-0"
H PENDENTIVE IN HALL "Y"
J PLAN
K COLUMN IN HALL AT "X"

PALACE AT CTESIPHON
112'-6"
16'-6"
83'-0"
60'-0"
170'-0"
312'-0"
L RESTORATION ONE BAY
M VIEW OF EXISTING RUINS
N RUINS FROM S.
P PLAN

(20 ft) thick walls, begun by Darius but completed by his two successors. It stood on its own terrace, 3 m (10 ft) high; had three porticoes, each with double colonnades; stairways on the north and east sides; and minor rooms across the south side and in the four angle towers. The Palace of Darius, small by comparison, lay immediately south of the Apadana, near the west terrace wall. This might have been finished in his lifetime, as also the terraced 'Tripylon', which lay centrally among the buildings and acted as a reception chamber and guard-room for the more private quarters of the palace group. Also by Darius was the 'Treasury', in the south-east angle of the site, a double-walled administrative and storehouse building with columned halls of different sizes and only a single doorway. The buildings of Darius were arranged in the loose fashion of earlier times. Xerxes added his in between. He built his own palace near the south-west angle, connected with an L-shaped building, identified as the women's quarters (harem) which completed the enclosure of a court south of the Tripylon. He also commenced the famous 'Hall of the Hundred Columns' (finished by Artaxerxes I); this is a Throne Hall, 68.6 m (225 ft) square, with columns 11.3 m (37 ft) high, supporting a flat, cedar roof (p. 94A,C). The walls were double, except on the north side, where a portico faced a forecourt, with its own gatehouse, separated from the Apadana forecourt by a stout wall. The Throne Hall had two doorways and seven windows on the entrance wall, matched on the other three sides except that niches replaced the windows. All were framed in stone surrounds in the 3.4 m (11 ft) thick brick wall.

From Persepolis have been recovered many wonderful architectural sculptures. All the monumental stairs were lined with reliefs, as also the Apadana terrace, where they were arranged in triple tiers or 'registers', separated by bands of rosettes. Nobles, courtiers, chieftains, tribute-bearers and guardsmen advanced in dignified procession, and traditional subjects filled the awkward angles of the stairways and the deep jambs of the doorways (p. 94E). Stepped battlements crowned the parapet walls. All these sculptures were originally in brilliant colour. Columns of the lesser apartments had wooden shafts, thickly plastered and decoratively painted, but those of the Halls were of stone throughout. They have a character all their own, with moulded bases, fluted shafts and curious, complex capitals with vertical Ionic-like volutes and twin bulls or dragons supporting the roof beams (p. 94B,D).

The **Tomb of Darius, Naksh-i-Rustam** (485 BC) (p. 95B), 13 km (8 miles) north of Persepolis, is one of four rock-hewn sepulchres of the great Achaemenian kings. Its facade, 18.3 m (60 ft) wide, appears to reproduce the south front of Darius' palace at Persepolis, with four columns of the double-bull type, central doorway with Egyptian-like cornice, and upper compartment in which an elaborate throne, 2.7 m (9 ft) high, is supported by two rows of figures, above which the king stands before a fire altar. Near the tomb stands a **Fire Temple**, a stone square tower containing a single room, approached by an outside stairway (p. 95C).

Seleucid, Parthian and Sassanian Architecture

The Seleucid Empire, founded in 312 BC after the death of Alexander, began to disintegrate about 247 BC, and after 140 BC was confined to the region west of the Euphrates, finally giving way to the Romans in 64 BC. Meanwhile there was a considerable influx of Macedonian and Greek settlers, who built many new towns, including Seleucia, near Babylon, and Antioch, in Syria. In Bactria, on the eastern border, they spread Greek civilisation to India; but in general their influence was uneven, and in art and architecture it was sometimes the Hellenistic and sometimes the local Persian character that prevailed. The Parthians, who wrested the eastern and Mesopotamian territories piecemeal from the Seleucids, respected the Hellenistic culture and institutions and under their long rule the new Greek cities flourished. Yet as integration proceeded, the arts profoundly declined. With the Sassanian dynasty (226–642), when the principal city was Ctesiphon, near Babylon, vigour sprang anew and a number of fine buildings were erected which form a connecting link between the old Mesopotamian architecture on the one hand and Byzantine on the other. Palaces were the dominant type.

The **Palace, Feruz-abad** (south of Persepolis) (*c.* 250) (p. 96), built of stone rubble faced with plaster, has a deep, open-fronted arched entrance leading to three domed halls, forming a reception suite, beyond which is a court surrounded by private chambers. The domes are seated over the three square halls with the help of 'squinch' arches thrown across the angles (p. 96C), while the internal walls below them are ornamented with niches having plaster archivolts and enframements of a classical complexion but capped with cornices of the Egyptian 'gorge' type (p. 96C,F).

The **Palace of Shapur I, Bishapur** (west of Persepolis) (*c.* 260), was a remarkable building built of plastered stone rubble, with a cruciform plan, dominated by a central dome of elliptical section springing from floor level. The coloured-plaster wall-decoration of modelled architectural features again had a classical character.

The **Palace, Sarvistan** (vicinity of Persepolis) (*c.* 350) (p. 96) was fronted by the typical deep barrel-vaulted porches, behind which rose a beehive dome, carried on squinch arches (p. 96H), marking the principal apartment. The dome was pierced with openings for light and ventilation. Two long side chambers had barrel vaults supported on massive piers which themselves stood on pairs of stumpy columns (p. 96K), a most ingenious method of reducing the effective span and obtaining powerful abutment to the vaults.

At Feruz-abad and Bishapur there were towered fire-temples, used in connection with open-air ceremonies, similar to that at Naksh-i-Rustam (see above).

The **Palace, Ctesiphon** (p. 96) is usually attributed to Chosroes I (531–579) but is probably of the fourth century. As it is in the Mesopotamian plain, it is of brick. The principal part surviving is a vast banqueting hall, open-fronted like the reception tents of tribal sheiks in nomadic days, with flanking private wings screened by an enormous wall, 34.4 m (112 ft 6 in) high. The latter is ornamented with tiers of attached columns and arcades, an arrangement betraying Roman influence. One wing of the facade fell in 1909 after an exceptional Tigris flood. The elliptical barrel vault over the hall, 7.3 m (24 ft) thick at the base and rising 36.7 m (120 ft) from the floor to cover the 25.3 m (83 ft) span, equalled if it did not surpass the mightiest structural achievements of Ancient Rome. The lower part of the vault is constructed in horizontal courses – Sassanian domes were usually constructed wholly in this manner – but substantially the vault is made up of arch rings sloped against an end wall, so as to avoid the necessity of temporary wood centering. This was a practice adopted for brick vaults equally in Ancient Egypt and in Assyrian architecture.

Chapter 5

EARLY ASIAN CULTURES

Architectural Character

India

During the Paleolithic and early Mesolithic periods, people lived mainly in caves, rock shelters and open campsites; late in the Mesolithic period, the transition to round, stone-paved huts with wattle and daub walls was made at Chopani-Mando in the Kaimur hills and in Andhra Pradesh. Early in the Neolithic era, rectangular houses were built in pressed earth and sun-dried bricks, but the earliest significant buildings in brick come from west of the Indus valley, on the edge of the Iranian plateau. The forerunners of the domestic architecture of the Indus civilisation, however, seem to be the buildings at Mehrgarh in the Baluchistan region of central Pakistan. Simultaneously, sites in the Indus valley itself also showed advances in town planning, and some of the groups even had small monumental buildings.

At major sites such as Mohenjodaro and Harappa, and also at some smaller urban centres like Chanhu-Daro, Kot Diji, Kalibangan and Lothal, the city was divided into a tightly packed chequerboard of artisans' dwellings. To the west and separated by open ground there was a higher citadel mound, walled and fortified with square towers and bastions, which contained plain but massive public buildings and installations set on mud-brick podia and oriented north–south. Among the most important were communal granaries, and at some sites a cemetery associated with (but separate from) the town and citadel.

The residential areas of Harappan cities were oriented north–south and east–west in regular, rectangular blocks separated by streets which contained what may have been the world's most advanced public water supply and sewerage system, which served both the private houses and public wells and privies. Within the urban blocks were shops and single- and two-storey courtyard houses with flat roofs; these were entered by way of narrow, winding alleys which cut through the regular rectangular blocks. Blank, windowless walls faced the main streets.

Contemporary buildings in other parts of India continued earlier Neolithic practices, but were adapted to local climate and materials. Those on Iron Age sites in the Ganges plain were less sophisticated than in the Indus Valley, and did not include monumental public buildings.

During the Iron Age, provincial capitals were established under the Persians and Greeks in northern India, either *de novo* or as extensions to existing settlements. Indigenous, irregularly planned towns were replaced by new towns on gridiron plans.

The Iron Age (*c.* 1000–100 BC) in the subcontinent generally was notable for its megalithic burials. These took a number of forms: urns, rock-cut chambers, pit circle-graves, and stone cist graves. Contemporary with megalithic burials were sites with standing stones, aligned in square or diagonal arrangements.

China

China has been contrasted with other comparable civilisations of the ancient world because of a lack of monumental architecture, particularly during the period up to the beginning of the Xia and into the early Shang periods, and also because of the relatively late appearance of cities. Before the beginning of the Xia period (2100–1600 BC) peasants lived in small villages of pit-houses, constructed from wattle and daub. Individual houses were round or rectangular, about 5 m (16 ft) in diameter, with pitched and thatched roofs carried on four stout vertical centre-posts. The eaves reached almost to the ground. Lightweight walls which defined recessed or projecting, porch-like entrances and floors were either of stamped earth or were plastered. The arrangement of villages and the orientation of dwellings appear to have been systematic, and some villages had centrally placed communal houses.

Xia villages were larger and many were enclosed by walls of pounded earth. Dwellings, and their disposition around a central longhouse, remained broadly similar to those of the earlier prehistoric period.

The Shang dynasty (*c.* 1850–1027 BC) was marked by the building of cities. Each had an aristocratic centre delineated by a walled enclosure of rammed earth, within which were set palaces and ceremonial buildings. An outer unwalled region contained industrial zones and farming villages. Rectangular post-and-beam houses set on rammed earth podia and with pitched roofs gradually replaced pit-houses. Symmetrically planned palace buildings date from this period. Typically, tombs were about 10 m (33 ft) deep, with a burial chamber 4 m (13 ft) high and about 20 m (66 ft) square, with ramps extending a further 15 m to 20 m (51 ft to 66 ft). The chamber was lined with close-set squared timbers and contained a timber coffin. Smaller Shang tombs consisted of a simple shaft without ramps, which after burial was refilled with earth. There were no superstructures.

During the Zhou period (1028–256 BC), many large, walled cities were built. Most were square or rectangular in plan, and their main buildings stood on platforms of rammed earth. Towards the close of the Zhou period, the density of the settlements within the walled areas became greater, and suburbs of thatched clay dwellings grew up around them. A nucleus of ceremonial buildings was frequently walled off within the heart of the city.

During the Qin period (221–206 BC) large public works projects were executed, including the Great Wall along China's northern frontier which replaced earlier defences of rammed earth. In its present form it is constructed from stone blocks, and is 2250 km (1397 miles) long, and 6 m to 10 m (20 ft to 33 ft) high. The wall is crenellated with watch- and garrison-towers at frequent intervals. Most of the surviving wall, however, dates from the Ming dynasty (1368–1644). Qin cities retained a rectangular or square plan oriented on the cardinal points, and were walled in pisé earth. Public buildings set on earth platforms were aligned along the north–south axis.

Examples

India

Residential Architecture

Mehrgarh, in the Baluchistan region of Pakistan, was made up of small villages known as Mehrgarh I to VII, each of which was established on new ground after the previous site had been abandoned. Mehrgarh I and II were sizable and permanent villages, whose architecture included symmetrical, multi-roomed buildings, and what seem to have been granaries. **Mehrgarh I** (*c.* 5000 BC) consisted of rectangular, multi-roomed mud-brick dwellings some 8 m × 4 m (26 ft × 13 ft) in area, with between six and nine rooms on either side of a central corridor. The houses were built with distinctive mud bricks, with rounded ends and finger imprints on the upper face to give a key to the mortar. **Mehrgarh II** (*c.* 4500 BC) had a similar arrangement of rectangular mud-brick buildings. By the final stages of **Mehrgarh VI** (*c.* 3000–2700 BC) and **VII** (*c.* 1700–2600 BC), which were contemporary with the early Indus civilisation, house plans had become more complex. Some were two storeys high with upper-storey living rooms carried on timber-joisted floors, and one metre high undercrofts used for storage.

Mundigak (*c.* 2500 BC) in south-east Afghanistan had defensive walls and square bastions of sun-dried bricks. Similar remains of monumental buildings – including a colonnaded palace and one which may have been a temple – have been found at **Damb Sadaat** in the **Quetta valley**.

Mud-brick houses have been discovered below Harappan buildings at three widely separated sites in the Indus basin at **Amri** (*c.* 2500 BC), where the mud brick was combined with stone, at **Kalibangan** and at **Kot Diji**. The settlements were surrounded by massive ramparts, precursors of Harappan forms. At **Rahman Dheri** (*c.* 2500 BC), in the western Indus plain, there is evidence of an early attempt at town planning on Harappan lines: the walled town, 550 m × 400 m (1700 ft × 1300 ft) in area, was divided by a main street running from north-west to south-east and was laid out on a regular grid.

The city of **Mohenjodaro** (*c.* 2500–1700 BC) (p. 101C–F) near the River Indus in Sind province, was commanded by an artificial citadel mound some 15 m (49 ft) high, situated 150 m (490 ft) to the north-west of the town. The land between it and the town may have been flooded. The citadel (p. 101C) was fortified by a baked-brick wall with solid towers and was dominated by a 13 m (43 ft) high brick platform, thought to have been a refuge in times of flood. The functions of many of the public buildings on the citadel remain obscure, but among those which have been positively identified are the Great Bath and the Granary. The town occupied an area of some 2.5 km^2. The residential district was made up of rectangular blocks each approximately 365 m × 182 m (1197 ft × 597 ft), oriented north and south and subdivided by lanes. The main streets were about 14 m (46 ft) wide, and the central north–south street was flanked by open drainage ditches.

The domestic architecture of **Mohenjodaro** (p. 101D) consisted of substantial flat-roofed single- and two-storey houses built in fired brick, organised around open courtyards, and with high featureless walls facing the surrounding streets. Plain doorways with timber lintels led to courtyards, off which the household rooms opened. Dwellings varied considerably in size, from one-room tenements to houses with over a dozen rooms ranged around multiple courtyards. Nearly all houses had private wells,

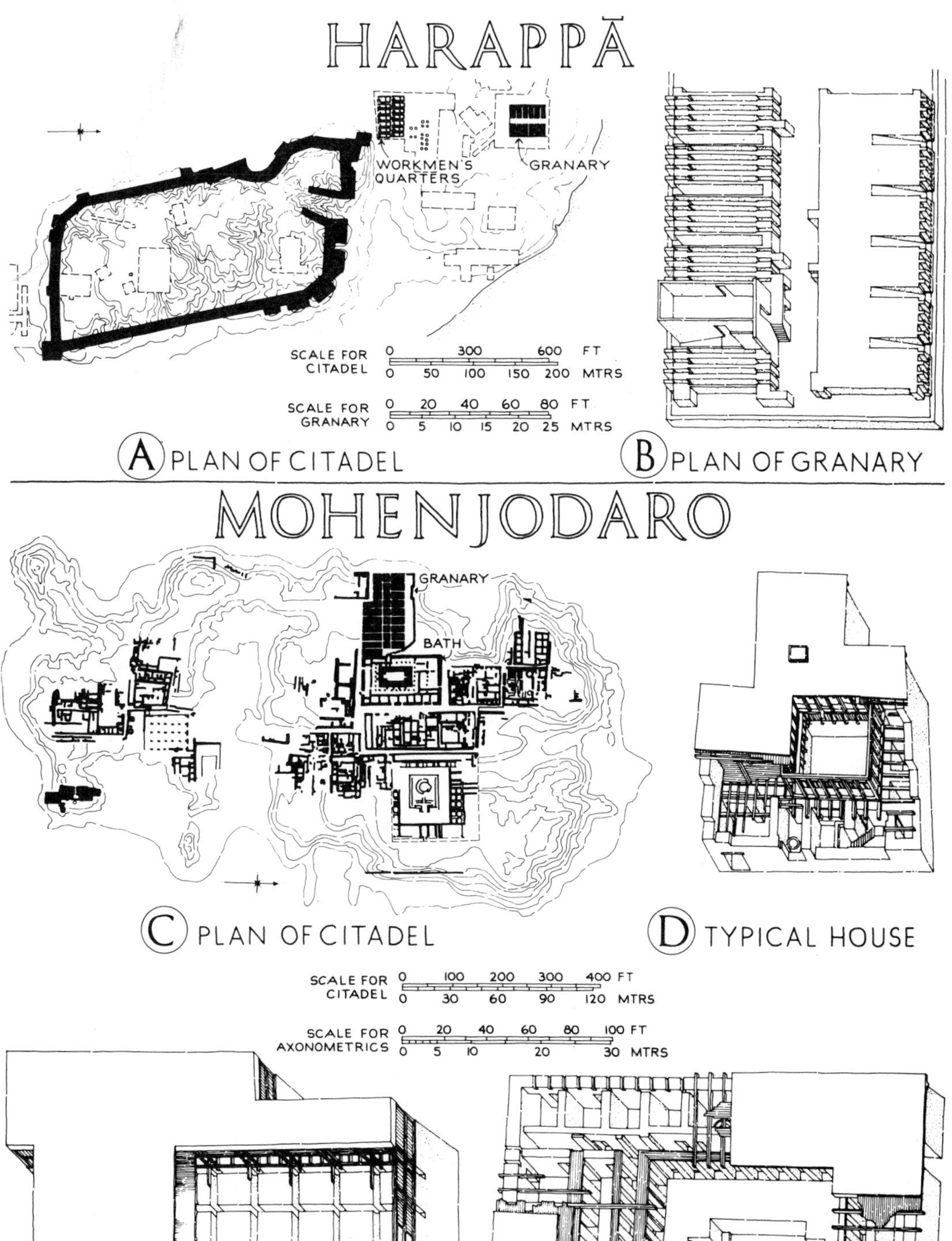

A PLAN OF CITADEL

B PLAN OF GRANARY

C PLAN OF CITADEL

D TYPICAL HOUSE

E GRANARY

F GREAT BATH

hearths, and bathrooms with finely sawn brick pavements connected by drains to shafts built within the walls to sewers in the main street. Some houses had flights of brick stairs giving access to a first floor or roof. Temples or shrine-like buildings have not been clearly identified, but one 'house', in which a large U-shaped building was approached through an outer gateway, may have had some ritual function. A block of cells opposite is believed to have been either a priests' college or a police station.

The layout of **Harappa** (p. 101A), on the Ravi, a tributary of the Indus in the Punjab, appears to have been similar to that of Mohenjodaro, although the city was all but destroyed in the nineteenth century by railway engineers who plundered the site for bricks. The general outline of the citadel and a few fragments of the residential layout have survived. The citadel mound was fortified with mud-brick ramparts tapering upwards from a 12 m (39 ft) thick base, with an external revetment of baked brick. Between the citadel and the town was a barrack-like block of workmen's quarters, together with circular brick floors on which grain was pounded. Two lines of small rectangular dwellings were separated by lanes about a metre wide, the whole enclosed within a compound wall.

The town of **Lothal**, on the sea plain of Kathiawar, south-east of Mohenjodaro at the head of the Gulf of Cambay, had a typical Harappan plan with a citadel and lower town. On the citadel mound was a podium of mud brick, 48.5 m × 42.5 m (159 ft × 139 ft), subdivided into blocks, each some 3.6 m (12 ft) square and penetrated by ventilation ducts. This is thought to have been the foundation of a communal granary similar to that at Mohenjodaro.

The city of **Kalibangan** overlooked the valley of the River Ghaggar in Rajasthan, south of Harappa. The visible remains comprised two square settlement mounds, each about 120 m (390 ft) wide. On one of a series of mud-brick platforms was a row of seven 'fire altars', together with a pit containing animal remains which seems to have served some ritual purpose. The platforms were contained within an oblong mud-brick wall fortified with rectangular bastions, smoothed to a battered face and finished with mud plaster. An entrance of baked brick was located on the southern side. The eastern mound was unfortified.

Similar towns have been located at **Chanhu-Daro**, south of Mohenjodaro, and at **Kot Diji**.

Sites north of the Indus plain, at Burzahom (*c.* 2920 BC) in Kashmir, have revealed pit-houses up to 4 m (13 ft) deep and 4 m (13 ft) wide at the bottom narrowing to about 2.7 m (9 ft) at the rim, with timber posts supporting conical roofs. These appear to have been a local adaptation to cold-climate conditions.

At the same time as Harappan cities were constructed, but further south at **Ahar** and **Gillund** (*c.* 2000–1600 BC) in southern Rajasthan, settlements of rectangular houses were built with mud walls resting on stone foundations. Contemporary villages in southern India (*c.* 2500–2000 BC) consisted of oblong or round lightweight wooden structures of which little trace remains; at **Tekkalakota**, structures of this kind were supported on drystone foundations, and had central hearths and floors coated with mud or cow dung. At **Pirak** in Afghanistan (*c.* 1500 BC) there are one- and two-roomed brick houses with wall niches.

At the Iron Age sites of **Bhagawanpura** and **Jakhera**, in the Ganges basin, circular timber-framed huts were panelled with wattle and daub. Early houses at **Hastinapura** (*c.* 800–500 BC), on the upper Ganges, were also timber-framed with mud walls, but baked brick became the standard building material at a later date (*c.* 500–200 BC).

Excavations at **Charsada**, north-east of Peshawar, and at **Taxila**, north-west of Rawalpindi, have revealed settlement mounds dating from Persian and Greek occupations. At Charsada, there was an earlier settlement, but in the second century BC the town was moved to a new site to the north-east and set out on a regular grid. At Taxila, a similar transformation took place. An earlier irregularly planned settlement was abandoned and a new one laid out along a north–south axis which survived until Parthian times (*c.* 100). Most of the buildings lining the main street were shops, raised slightly above street level with houses densely packed behind them.

Monumental Buildings

The **Great Bath at Mohenjodaro** (p. 101F) was an open-air pool, about 12 m × 7 m (39 ft × 23 ft) in plan, and 2.5 m (8 ft) deep. It was constructed in sawn bricks set on edge in a gypsum mortar and sealed with bitumen. At the north and south ends were brick steps with timber treads set in bitumen. The bath was drained from a corbel-vaulted drain fed from an outlet at the south-west corner. Surrounding the bath was a covered colonnade, and beyond it on three sides were changing rooms, staggered to give privacy. Some of the changing rooms had toilets and private baths. The bath may have featured in ritual activity.

The **Granary at Mohenjodaro** (p. 101E) was a timber building carried on a tiered brick-lined podium. The upper tier was made up of twenty-seven blocks of brickwork intersected by ventilation channels. The lower tier was of mud brick reinforced with 125 mm (5 in) square timbers. It was later enlarged and partially rebuilt with a brick stair leading to an upper-level timber superstructure. Its sloped external walls gave it a grim fortress-like appearance.

Other buildings on the citadel mound at **Mohenjodaro** have been variously interpreted as granaries, assembly halls, a garrison, and a priestly official's residence. The assembly hall was rectangular in plan, with four rows of five-brick plinths which may have supported timber columns. The floor was of finely sawn brickwork. Rooms to the west contained statues and part of a ritual stone column. The building thought to have been an official's residence measured 70 m × 24 m (230 ft × 79 ft) and had an open courtyard 10 m (33 ft) square, surrounded on three sides by verandahs.

The **Granary at Harappa** (p. 101B) was unusual in that it did not form part of the public installations on the citadel mound. It was situated between the citadel and the river, and was set on a shallow brick podium about 1 m (3 ft) high approached from the north. The granaries, twelve in all, each measured 16 m × 6 m (52 ft × 20 ft) and were aligned in two rows separated by a wide central passage. The total floorspace occupied by the granaries was some 800 m^2 (8608 ft^2) – about the same as that of the granary at Mohenjodaro before enlargement.

China

Chinese architecture during the prehistoric period was mainly residential. Monumental architecture was confined to palace buildings and royal tombs.

Residential Architecture

Banpocun (Pan-p'o-ts'un) (*c.* 4000 BC) was a typical pre-Xia (Yang-shao) village in the Shanxi province. Planned as an irregular oval, oriented north–south, it covered an area of approximately 7 ha (17 acres) and housed a population of two to three hundred. The houses were clustered at the centre of the village in an area of some 3 ha (7 acres), demarcated by a ditch about 6 m (20 ft) deep and 6 m (20 ft) wide. Banpocun comprised scores of circular semi-subterranean wattle and daub houses, about 5 m (16 ft) in diameter and sunk about 600 mm (24 in) into the ground (p. 104E). Each had a central hearth defined by four centreposts which supported a conical wattle and daub roof; this sloped almost to the ground at the eaves and was supported by a ring of slender posts outside the walls. In the centre of the village was a larger and more substantial rectangular structure, about 160 m^2 (1720 ft^2) in area, similarly constructed but built on foundations of rammed earth. This is thought to have been a meeting house, or possibly the dwelling of the headman. Analogous buildings have been found at the contemporary site of **Jiangzhai**, also in Shanxi, where all the houses opened towards the centre of the village, and at **Dahezhuang** (*c.* 2000 BC) in Gansu province, where there was a later, local Neolithic period.

At the early Shang city of **Erlitou** (*c.* 1800 BC) there were few monumental buildings or elaborate tombs. The residents lived in wattle and daub pit-houses, but they were larger and more elaborately constructed that those of earlier date.

The Shang city of **Zhengzhou** (*c.* 1600 BC), in northern Henan, was rectangular and earth-walled extending over 3.2 ha (8 acres), with perimeter walls 7.2 km (4.5 miles) long, 9 m (30 ft) high, and 3 m to 6 m (10 ft to 20 ft) thick at the base. The central area within the wall was laid out in a chequerboard pattern and oriented north and south; it is thought to have been the royal residence and ceremonial centre of the court, the buildings of which were rectangular and built mainly of wood on platforms of rammed earth. The houses had pitched and gabled roofs supported on stout timber posts, some of which were carried on stone bases. The smallest dwellings were 9 m × 5 m (30 ft × 16 ft) and the largest 52 m × 25 m (170 ft × 82 ft). Walls and floors were finished with lime plaster. Parallel houses at **Ming Kung Su** were large and had lime-washed walls and floors, while others at **Tzu-Ching** had walls of compacted earth up to a metre thick. There is no sign of courtyard housing during the Shang period. Surrounding the walled enclosure at Zhengzhou were thousands of pit-houses with pounded earth floors, up to 3 m × 1.5 m (10 ft × 5 ft) in area and sunk about 500 mm (20 in) into the ground.

Excavations at **Xiaotun**, north-west of Anyang in Henan province, have uncovered a large ceremonial and administrative centre of the Shang period (*c.* 1400 BC), surrounded by smaller dependent hamlets and craft centres. Parts of the town were laid out on a chequerboard pattern, with nearly parallel rows of rectangular dwellings built on rammed-earth podia, although, as noted earlier, at this time the majority of residents still lived in pit-houses of traditional construction. The centre of Xiaotun contained a group of over fifty timber-framed buildings with pitched and gabled roofs set on rammed-earth podia and arranged in three clusters (p. 104C).

The Zhou capital at **Louyang**, in Henan province (eighth to seventh century BC), also had a rectangular plan. Parts of the walls have survived. Most Zhou cities dating from the period of the Warring States (475–221 BC) have more than one earth-walled enclosure. **Jiang**, in Shanxi province, for example, had a rectangular walled enclosure, 2.7 km × 1.6 km (1.7 mile × 1 mile), oriented north–south and surrounded by a moat, and a smaller enclosure, about 800 m (2620 ft) square, located centrally inside the perimeter wall at the northern end. **Wo-kuo** in Shanxi province had two concentric enclosures: the inner one was square, with sides of about 1.1 km (0.7 mile), while the outer measured 3.1 km × 2.6 km (1.9 mile × 1.6 mile). The city of **Anyi** in Shanxi province had two L-shaped enclosures containing between them a small square in which the palace stood. At **Handan** in Hebei province, there were two adjoining walled enclosures: the larger of the two was square and contained the city proper; the smaller was rectangular

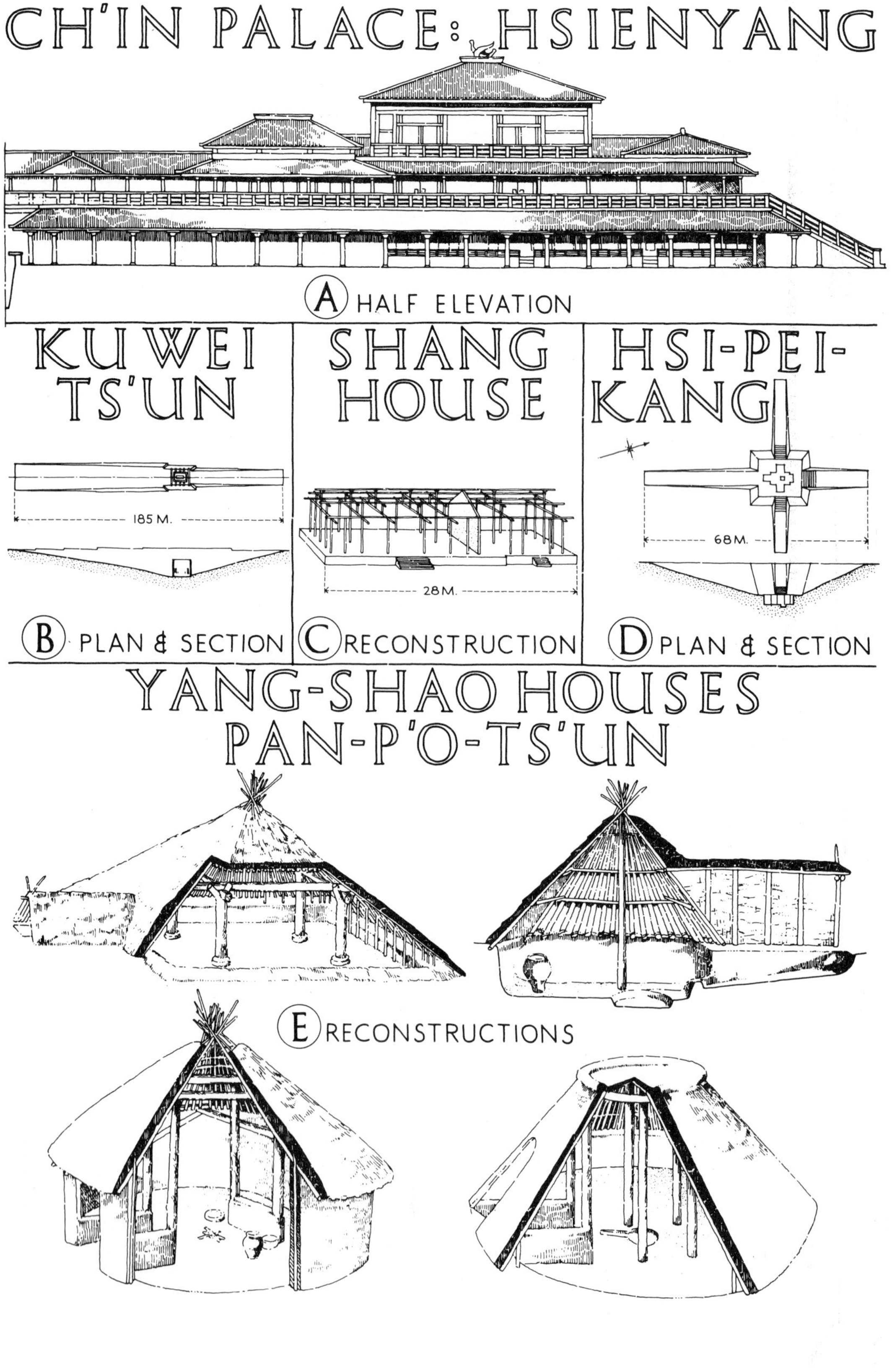

A HALF ELEVATION

KU WEI TS'UN

185 M.

B PLAN & SECTION

SHANG HOUSE

28 M.

C RECONSTRUCTION

HSI-PEI-KANG

68 M.

D PLAN & SECTION

YANG-SHAO HOUSES PAN-P'O-TS'UN

E RECONSTRUCTIONS

and abutted it to the east. The capital of the Qin empire at **Xianyang** (221–206 BC) consisted of a rectangular enclosure with a rammed-earth wall surrounding a palace and substantial houses built on rammed-earth platforms. Little remains to indicate the character of the architecture of Zhou and Qin cities, but the tradition of courtyard building in China probably dates from this period.

Palaces

The Shang city of **Erlitou** contains the foundations of a palace which is the earliest known monumental building in Chinese history. An earth platform measuring 108 m × 100 m (354 ft × 328 ft), and oriented on a north–south axis, was surrounded by a pisé wall, against which were erected roofed galleries of wattle and daub reinforced with timber. The compound was entered from the south. Within the walled area was a pavilion on a rammed-earth podium. The pavilion was constructed in reinforced wattle and daub and had pitched roofs supported by a separate internal structure of stout timber posts resting on boulders. A similar Shang palace from **Banlongzheng**, 38 m × 11 m (125 ft × 36 ft), stood on a rammed-earth platform and comprised four chambers under a pitched and gabled main roof surrounded by separately roofed galleries. A late Shang palace at **Xiaotun**, Anyang, was a rectangular building of trabeated construction with a ridged and thatched roof spanning from wall to wall.

The **Dragon Terrace** in the Zhou city of Handan (fourth to third century BC) was set on a stepped podium of rammed earth, 430 m × 280 m (1410 ft × 920 ft) and aligned on the axis leading to the main gate in the south wall. The superstructure is thought to have been two storeys high.

The **Qin (Ch'in) palace at Xianyang (Hsienyang)** (p. 104A) has been reconstructed as a three-storey galleried building, with pitched, gabled and tiled roofs, a post and beam structure and possibly a terreplein core. The walls and floors were internally finished with plaster and decorated with frescos.

Tombs

The cemetery of **Xibeigang (Hsi-pei-kang)**, Anyang, contained examples of Shang funerary architecture (p. 104D). The royal dead were buried in shaft graves up to 14 m × 19 m (46 ft × 62 ft) in area and 10 m (33 ft) deep, and were approached by a cruciform arrangement of ramps, with the principal access from the south. The burial chambers were constructed with a double lining of jointed timber. In an exceptionally well-preserved tomb, the chamber was covered by a painted and inlaid wooden canopy.

Early Zhou graves at **Louyang** were similar to the Shang burial shafts. Graves at **T'angshan** in Hebei province were boxes lined with thin stone slabs set on edge and large enough to take a wooden coffin. Similar cist graves were found at the frontier site of **Hsit'uan-shan-tzu**, near **Kirin**. A later Zhou grave at **Guweicun (Ku Wei Ts'un)** in Henan province (p. 104B) was 200 m (660 ft) long, with wide ramps leading down to a central pit from the north and south, with the latter, ceremonial entrance being considerably wider and longer. The Zhou tomb at **Xiadu** was marked only by a burial mound.

The tomb of the Qin emperor **Shihuangdi at Lishan**, east of Xian in Shanxi province, was covered by an imposing square rammed-earth mound 1.4 km (0.9 mile) in circumference and 46 m (150 ft) high. It was surrounded by two (concentric) rectangular walled enclosures oriented north–south. Bushes and trees were planted on the mound to give it a rural appearance, and the approach roads to the tomb were lined with 4 m (13 ft) high stone animals. The tomb was plundered after the collapse of the Qin dynasty. Vaults nearby yielded life-size terracotta figures of warriors and horses.

Chapter 6
GREECE

Prehistoric Architecture

In the Aegean, during the prehistoric period, there were two distinct architectural traditions which can be seen clearly in the domestic buildings of the Early Bronze Age: one in which the typical house was a free-standing hut with just a single room, and the other in which houses consisted of an apparently random and totally asymmetrical agglomeration of rooms. The differences are, as much as anything, geographical. The first is found in mainland Greece and the north-east regions, most notably at Early Bronze Age Troy, the second in Asia Minor and in Crete. Few buildings in this period were monumental, with the exception of those on the **citadel of Troy** which included a large rectangular hall (**Building IIA**), consisting of a room which was nearly square with a deep porch formed by prolonging the side walls: this is the so-called megaron plan, which was to be the basis of the Classical Greek temple.

In the second millenium BC there were important developments in the agglomerated buildings of Crete. Maritime contact with the eastern Mediterranean had created increased wealth there, and this was reflected in the building of 'palaces', the residences of powerful rulers who controlled the towns in which they were situated. But in addition they housed the administration and served as places of manufacture and storage. An essential feature, adopted from the Near East and Egypt, was the arrangement of rooms (at this time still quite asymmetrical) round a courtyard, which might well be totally enclosed. The first palaces were built in the nineteenth century BC but were obliterated about 1625 BC in a series of catastrophic earthquakes. They were then rebuilt in a more sumptuous manner, but all were destroyed (along with country houses and the towns) in the mid-fifteenth century BC, the only known exception being the greatest, Knossos, which survived until about 1375 BC. During its last years Knossos was occupied by Greek-speaking peoples; it is not certain whether the whole of Crete was ruled from Knossos, since there may have been other palaces not yet excavated in western Crete, but it is clear that Knossos dominated the eastern half of the island.

The **Palace of Knossos** (p. 108) was arranged round an open court measuring 170 × 82.5 'Minoan' feet of 0.3036 m. The buildings covered 122 m (400 ft) square (approximately 1.6 hectares, 4 acres). Outside was another paved court (the west court) crossed by raised walks, a typical feature of Minoan architecture, and overlooked by the monumental west facade, with the principal entrance at its southern end. Characteristically for Minoan architecture, this entrance, to the western state rooms, was indirect and dog-leg in form. The buildings of the palace had at least two storeys. The ground floor consisted mostly of storage rooms. Those in the west wing contained oil jars, whereas others on the north side were probably granaries. The most important room at this level in the west side was the so-called throne room, approached from an anteroom, at a level lower than the court, from which it opened by four pairs of folding doors. The throne room itself was dark and mysterious: the stone throne was against the north wall, and flanked by benches, the walls decorated with frescos. The purpose is religious rather than royal.

On the principal (first) floor of the west wing were probably more spacious rooms. The restored piano nobile illustrates the way in which rooms in the palace were arranged for functional purposes (here clearly ceremonial) rather than for reasons of symmetry. On the north side of the court was a separate entrance, approached from the 'theatral area' outside the palace. To the east of this were rooms for industrial activity. Centrally in the east wing, at the upper level, was a further hall of state. Near the south-east corner of the central court the slope was cut away to accommodate the three-storey royal apartments. The uppermost storey was on a level with the court; the other two are below court level, and faced eastwards over terraced gardens. The rooms here were thus isolated from the court, though connected with each other. Passages were cool and the area was lit by three light wells. Rooms were approached through rows of double doors, so that they could be opened, or totally or partially shut off; everything was designed to permit the circulation of cool air, to counteract the intense heat of the Cretan summer. The stairways, light wells, and colonnades

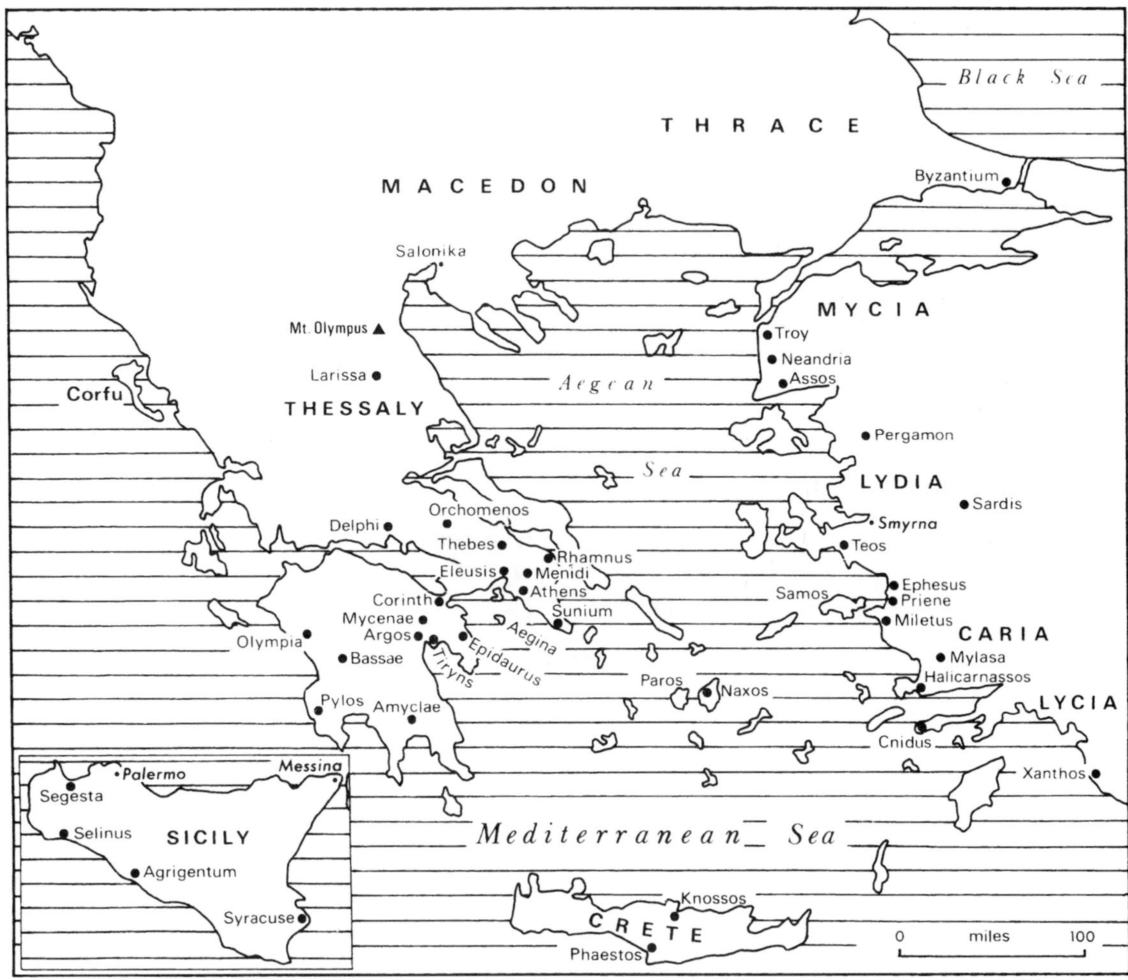

The central lands of the Greek world

of downward-tapering cypress-wood columns were typically Minoan, as were the elaborate and developed sanitation and drainage. In plan, particularly, the palace appears at a first glance to be chaotic, but its layout was the result of organic growth; this can best be appreciated from within, particularly in those domestic quarters which Sir Arthur Evans restored in order to give a proper impression of their character. Other Cretan palaces (such as Phaistos, Mallia and Zakro) were smaller but similar in style.

More ordinary domestic architecture of the Minoans is represented by a **house at Pyrgos**, in the south-west of Crete, built of gypsum blocks, with a first-floor verandah (with three Minoan columns) placed directly over the porch; the effect is of a smaller-scale version of the domestic quarters of the palaces. Particularly well preserved are the **town houses at Akrotiri**, on the island of Thera, buried during the eruption of the volcano in the fifteenth century; these too are typified by their irregular agglomeration of rooms, with large window openings and balconies.

The tombs of Minoan Crete are not monumental. Some are rectangular structures subdivided into small rooms, whereas others are simple rock-cut chambers.

On the mainland of Greece, the buildings of the early second millennium BC were free-standing megaron houses. In the second half of the millennium, Cretan influences and political developments led to the evolution of palaces, and the introduction of the courtyard. In these palaces, however, the megaron, even when flanked by other rooms, remained the essential feature.

The **Palace at Tiryns** (p. 110) is on a low, rocky citadel hill, in prehistoric times situated by the edge of the sea. There are traces of Early Bronze Age buildings (including an enigmatic circular structure of

PALACE OF KING MINOS: KNOSSOS. CRETE

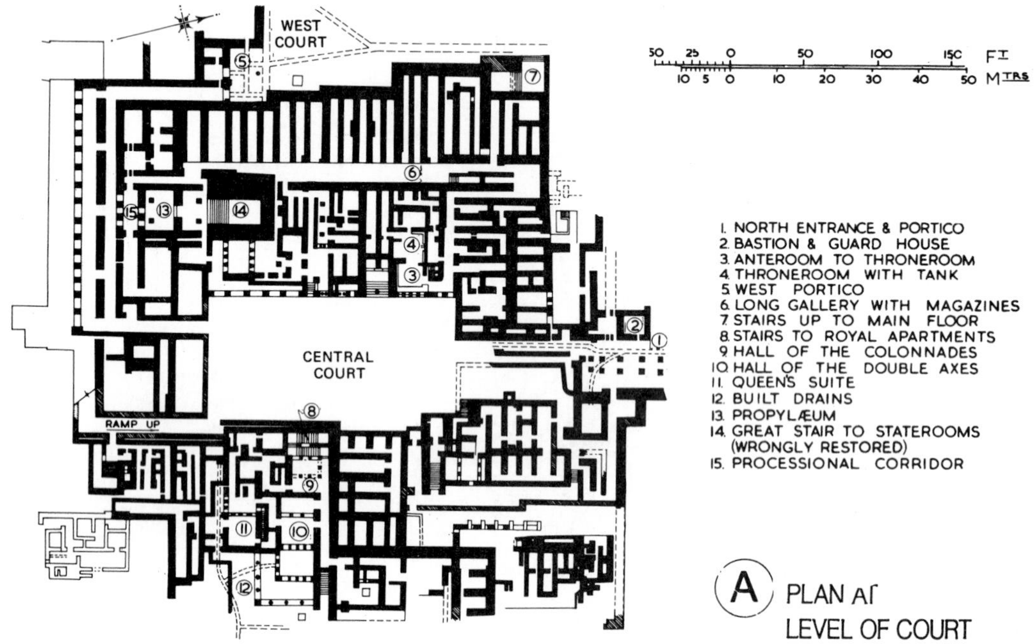

(A) PLAN AT LEVEL OF COURT

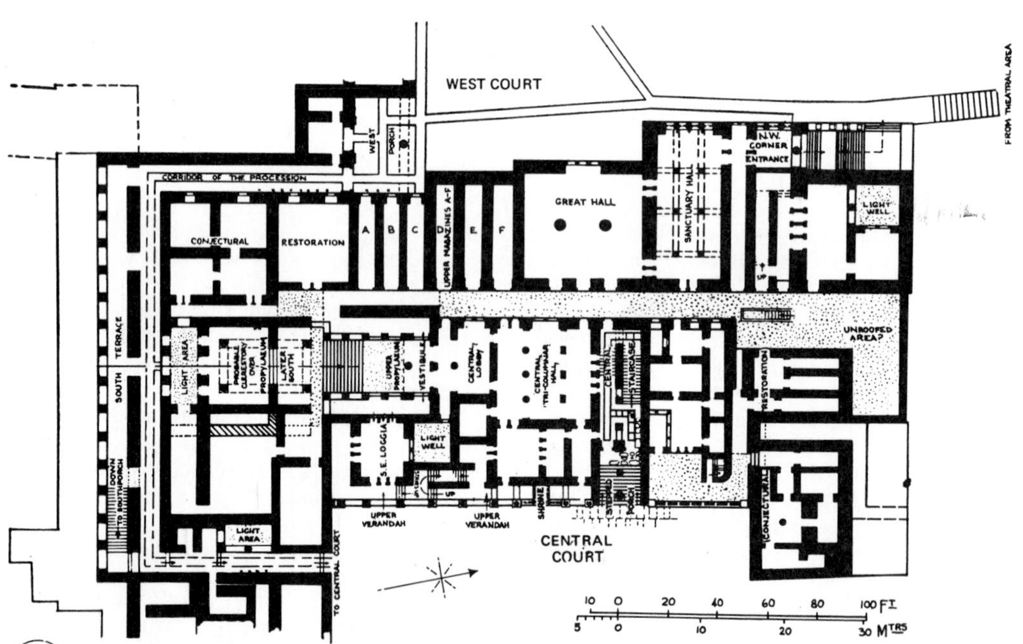

(B) PLAN (RESTORED) OF ENTRANCE SYSTEM AND PIANO NOBILE OF WEST PALACE SYSTEM

baked brick) but the visible remains are of the Late Bronze Age. Massive fortifications to the upper part of the citadel were constructed in the second half of the fourteenth century BC in the irregular style of masonry termed cyclopean by the Greeks of the Classical period. Later additional walls included a slightly lower terrace to the north, and a long, narrow approach on the east side provided with two gates, which could be barred. Towards the end of the thirteenth century BC the area of the fortification was doubled by enclosing yet another terrace to the north. Such defences are in direct contrast to the more open character of the Minoan palaces.

The palace at Tiryns was on the upper part of the citadel. When the fortifications were strengthened the original gateway on the east side was replaced by a decorative propylon, H-shaped in plan, with a single door in the cross-wall and columns between the side walls, at front and back. In front of this was a forecourt with a colonnade along the outer wall, containing a row of magazines, built of massive blocks and roofed by means of corbelled vaults; there was a similar row of magazines at the south end. The propylon led to an outer court, on the north side of which a second propylon, similar in plan, led to an inner court, flanked on the east, south and west sides by wooden colonnades; at the centre on the north side was the colonnaded porch of the principal megaron. This porch gave access to an anteroom through a triple opening comparable with those in Minoan palaces. Behind this the main, inner room contained a large circular decorated hearth in a group of four columns which probably supported a lantern. The floor of this room was plastered and painted, with a space, presumably for a throne, on the east side. The walls of the anteroom were decorated at the base with an alabaster frieze, with a pattern of two semicircles, back to back, between vertical rectangular panels each divided into three vertical bands; it has been suggested, plausibly, that this design is the origin of the triglyph and metope pattern of the Doric order.

The **Palace at Mycenae** is essentially similar. Vast fortifications were constructed at the same time as those of neighbouring Tiryns, probably by the same workmen and certainly in the same style. The principal feature is the entrance, which is protected by a flanking bastion. The gate is at the inner end: great upright stone jambs 3.1 m (10 ft) high support an immense lintel 4.9 m long × 1.06 m high × 2.4 m deep (16 ft × 3 ft 6 in × 8 ft) over an opening 3 m (10 ft) wide. Above is a triangular-shaped, corbelled opening filled with a stone panel, bearing a carved relief depicting two rampant lions facing a central column of the downward-tapering type. This is the **Lion Gate** (pp.110C, 111H), which takes its name from this carving. Inside the fortification, by the gateway, is a circular enclosure formed by an inner and outer row of continuous upright stones with horizontal slabs over them; this surrounded the shaft graves of the burial place of kings who ruled before the fortifications were built (a second grave circle always remained outside the fortified area). Further inside the citadel were houses, and among them a shrine, the 'house with the idols', distinguished by fresco paintings depicting a goddess, and containing terracotta cult figures. The palace proper at the top of the citadel was simpler than at Tiryns: a plastered court led to the megaron, consisting of a porch, an antechamber entered by a single door, and a main room 13 m × 12 m (42 ft 6 in × 39 ft 3 in).

The **Palace at Pylos** had a courtyard leading to a megaron porch, but the inner room with central hearth and columns was set to the side, more in the Minoan manner. To the east of this another, smaller court led to the main megaron, which was conventionally aligned, and an anteroom with a single central door. This palace was not heavily fortified.

The most impressive and substantial tombs of Late Bronze Age Greece (about 1600 BC) are the 'tholoi', circular chambers cut into the hillside, approached by an open passage or 'dromos' and lined with masonry. The chambers were corbel-vaulted structures shaped like old-fashioned beehives, the upper part of which emerged above ground level, and were covered with a mound. After the final burial the dromos was filled in.

The most splendid tholos is at Mycenae, the so-called **'Treasury of Atreus'** (or **'Tomb of Agamemnon'**, both names being applied to it in later, Classical times) (p. 111). It was built after 1350, but before 1250 BC. Here the stone lining is of excellent quality masonry throughout. The dromos is about 6 m (20 ft) wide and 36 m (118 ft) long, its side walls rising to a maximum of 13.7 m (45 ft) at the entrance to the chamber. The chamber itself is 14.5 m (47 ft 6 in) in diameter and 13.2 m (43 ft) high, made up of thirty-four circular courses of masonry, cut during construction to give the final curvature, and capped with a single block of stone. There are clear indications that decoration, probably metal, was attached to the walls. A lateral rock-cut chamber 8.2 m (27 ft) square and 5.8 m (19 ft) high, possibly once lined with masonry, was the actual place of burial. The facade to the main chamber is over 10.3 m (34 ft) high, with a doorway 5.4 m (17 ft 9 in) high. The entrance passage is 5.4 m long, and roofed by two enormous limestone lintels, one of them weighing more than 100 tons. On either side of the door were two green limestone half-columns (large portions of which are preserved in the British Museum). They are of the usual tapering form, and decorated with bands of chevron ornament in relief. The triangle over the lintel contained slabs of deep red stone, carved with horizontal bands of connected spirals, separated by mouldings, with plain bands between them. A strip of green stone, carved with a row of discs and surmounted by rising spirals and the triglyph and metope pattern, appears on the lintel.

THE CITADEL OF TIRYNS

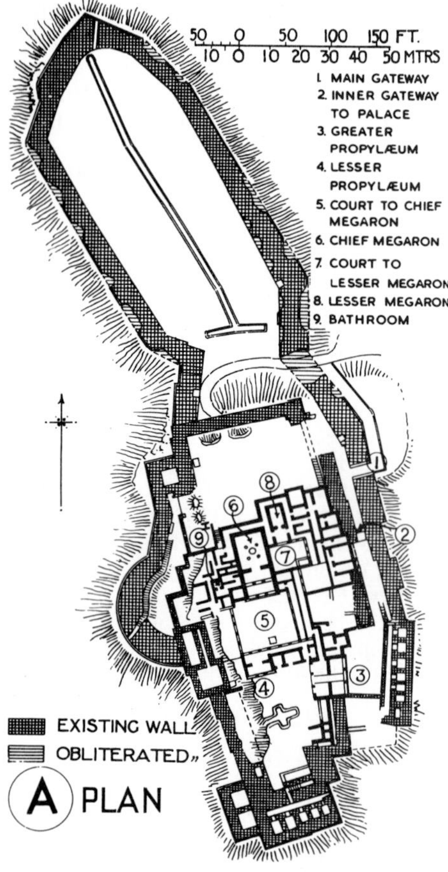

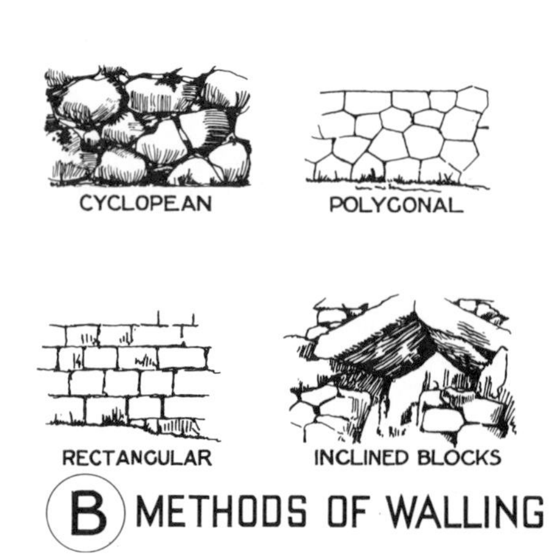

C. (*right*) The Lion Gate, Mycenae (*c.* 1250 BC). See p.109

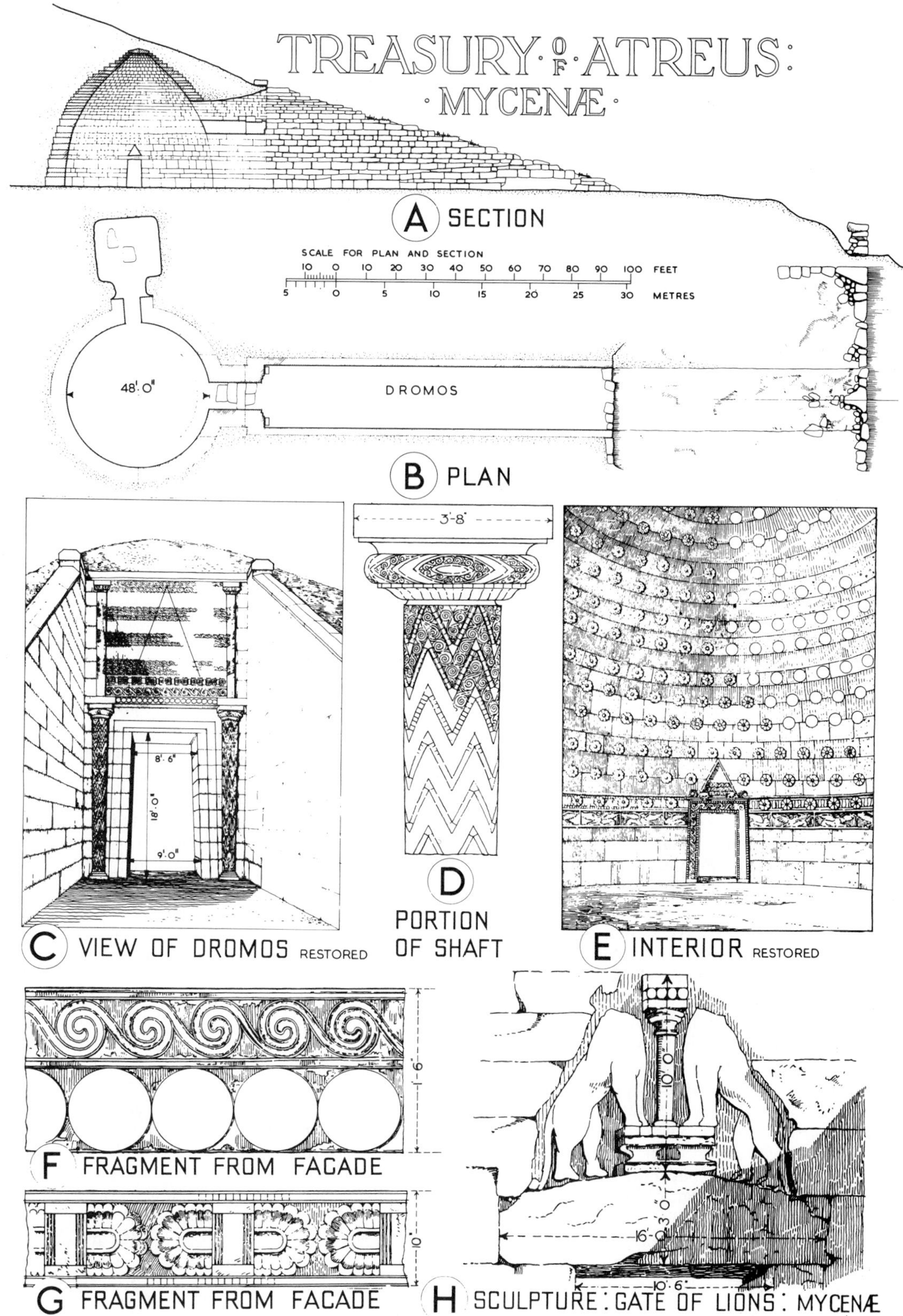
TREASURY OF ATREUS: MYCENÆ
A SECTION
SCALE FOR PLAN AND SECTION
10 0 10 20 30 40 50 60 70 80 90 100 FEET
5 0 5 10 15 20 25 30 METRES
48'.0"
DROMOS
B PLAN
3'-8"
8'-6"
18'-0"
9'-0"
C VIEW OF DROMOS RESTORED
D PORTION OF SHAFT
E INTERIOR RESTORED
1'-6"
F FRAGMENT FROM FACADE
10"
G FRAGMENT FROM FACADE
10'-0"
3'-0"
16'-0"
10'-6"
H SCULPTURE: GATE OF LIONS: MYCENÆ

Other important tholos tombs are the **'Tomb of Clytemnestra', Mycenae**, the door of which had fluted shafts, and the **'Treasury of Minyas', Orchomenos in Boeotia**.

The 'Dark Age'

The only known substantial building from the Dark Age which followed the collapse of the Late Bronze Age states is the **Heroon at Lefkandi**, of the tenth century BC. This was of unbaked brick, apsidal in plan, measuring 10 m by at least 45 m (33 ft × 148 ft). It had a surrounding colonnade of wooden posts. Despite its resemblance to later temples, it was a funerary monument built over a grave, and so short-lived that it is unlikely to have influenced later buildings. Otherwise, buildings which can be recognised as temples are not found before the eighth century BC. These are simple, horseshoe-shaped structures with porches at the end, built of mud brick on rubble footings (as at Perachora near Corinth) or wooden framing with wattle infill over timber sleepers (as at Eretria). The roofs of both buildings were of thatch.

The Classical Period

The principal orders of Classical Greek architecture, the Doric and Ionic, were first used for temples.

The Doric Order

The Doric column (p. 113) stands without a base directly on a crepis (or crepidoma), conventionally of three steps in temples, though other buildings, such as stoas, may have only one.

The earliest columns are very slender, but later ones are excessively thick, with a height no more than four times the diameter at the base. In the fifth century BC this was lightened to 5½ to 5¾ diameters, while in the Hellenistic period columns over seven times their diameter in height are known.

The circular shaft, diminishing at the top to between ¾ and ⅔ of the diameter at the base, is usually divided into twenty shallow flutes or channels separated by sharp 'arrises', but sometimes there are twelve, sixteen, eighteen or, as at Paestum, twenty-four (p. 114C). The shaft has normally a slightly convex profile called the entasis, to counteract the concave appearance produced by straight-sided columns (p. 115). The shaft terminates in the 'hypotrachelion', usually formed of three grooves in archaic examples and later of one groove; immediately above, on the block which forms the capital, is the continuation of the fluted shaft known as the 'trachelion' or necking. The distinctive capital consists of abacus and echinus. Near the base of the echinus are 'annulets' or horizontal fillets, from three to five in number, which stop the vertical lines of the arrises and flutes of the shaft. The form of the echinus varies with the date of the building. In the earlier temples at Paestum (p. 114B,C) it projects considerably and is fuller in outline, whereas in mature examples, such as the Parthenon (p. 114F), the projection is less and the profile more subtle; in Hellenistic work, when the column has become more slender, the whole capital is shallower and narrower and the curve of the echinus approaches a straight line. The abacus, which forms the upper member of the capital, is a square slab, unmoulded until the Hellenistic period when it sometimes acquired a small moulding at the top.

The Doric entablature (p. 113) has three main divisions. (a) The architrave or principal beam, which in larger temples usually is made up of two or three slabs in the depth, the outermost showing a vertical face in one plane. Capping it is a flat projecting band called the taenia, and under this, at intervals corresponding to the triglyphs, are strips known as the regulae, each with six guttae or small conical drops below it. (b) The frieze, which is formed of triglyphs with two vertical channels (glyphs), and two half channels at each side (so 'three glyphs') alternating with metopes or square spaces sometimes ornamented with fine relief sculpture, as in the Parthenon (pp. 113, 126). A triglyph is aligned over each column and another centrally over each intercolumniation. At the angles of the temple, however, two triglyphs meet with a bevelled edge. It is a general rule that Doric friezes must end with a triglyph, which may be moved outwards from its proper position over the centre of the end column: to achieve this, the columns are brought closer together at the corners. (c) The cornice or geison, which is the upper or crowning part. The soffit or underside has an inclination approximating to the slope of the roof, and has flat blocks or mutules, which suggest the ends of sloping rafters. A mutule occurs over each triglyph and each metope, and is usually ornamented with eighteen guttae, in three rows of six each. The vertical face, or corona, has an overhanging drip at the bottom. The top is occasionally surmounted by a continuous cyma or gutter (for example the Temple of Zeus at Olympia) but this is often omitted (as in the Parthenon). In the latter case the ends of the cover tiles are stopped by antefixae. The sima always crowns the raking cornice of the pediment, which is not provided with mutules, and is identical in profile to that of the Ionic order. Indeed, the first recorded use of the word Ionic as an architectural technical term is to describe the raking cornice of the Doric porch to the Telesterion

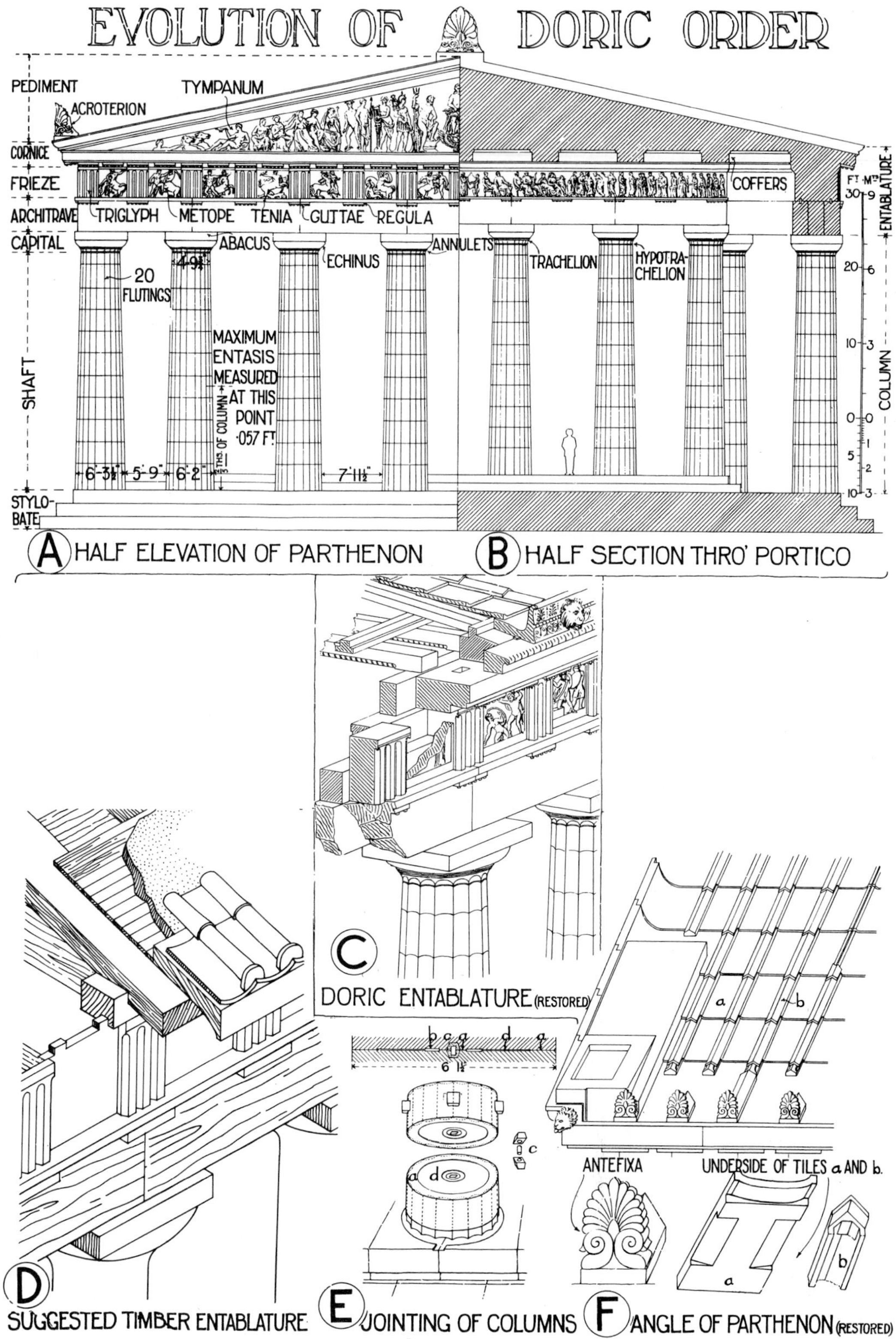
EVOLUTION OF DORIC ORDER
PEDIMENT
TYMPANUM
ACROTERION
CORNICE
FRIEZE
ARCHITRAVE
TRIGLYPH
METOPE
TENIA
GUTTAE
REGULA
CAPITAL
ABACUS
ECHINUS
ANNULETS
TRACHELION
HYPOTRACHELION
COFFERS
20 FLUTINGS
MAXIMUM ENTASIS MEASURED AT THIS POINT ·057 FT.
SHAFT
STYLOBATE
ENTABLATURE
COLUMN
A HALF ELEVATION OF PARTHENON
B HALF SECTION THRO' PORTICO
C DORIC ENTABLATURE (RESTORED)
ANTEFIXA
UNDERSIDE OF TILES a AND b.
D SUGGESTED TIMBER ENTABLATURE
E JOINTING OF COLUMNS
F ANGLE OF PARTHENON (RESTORED)

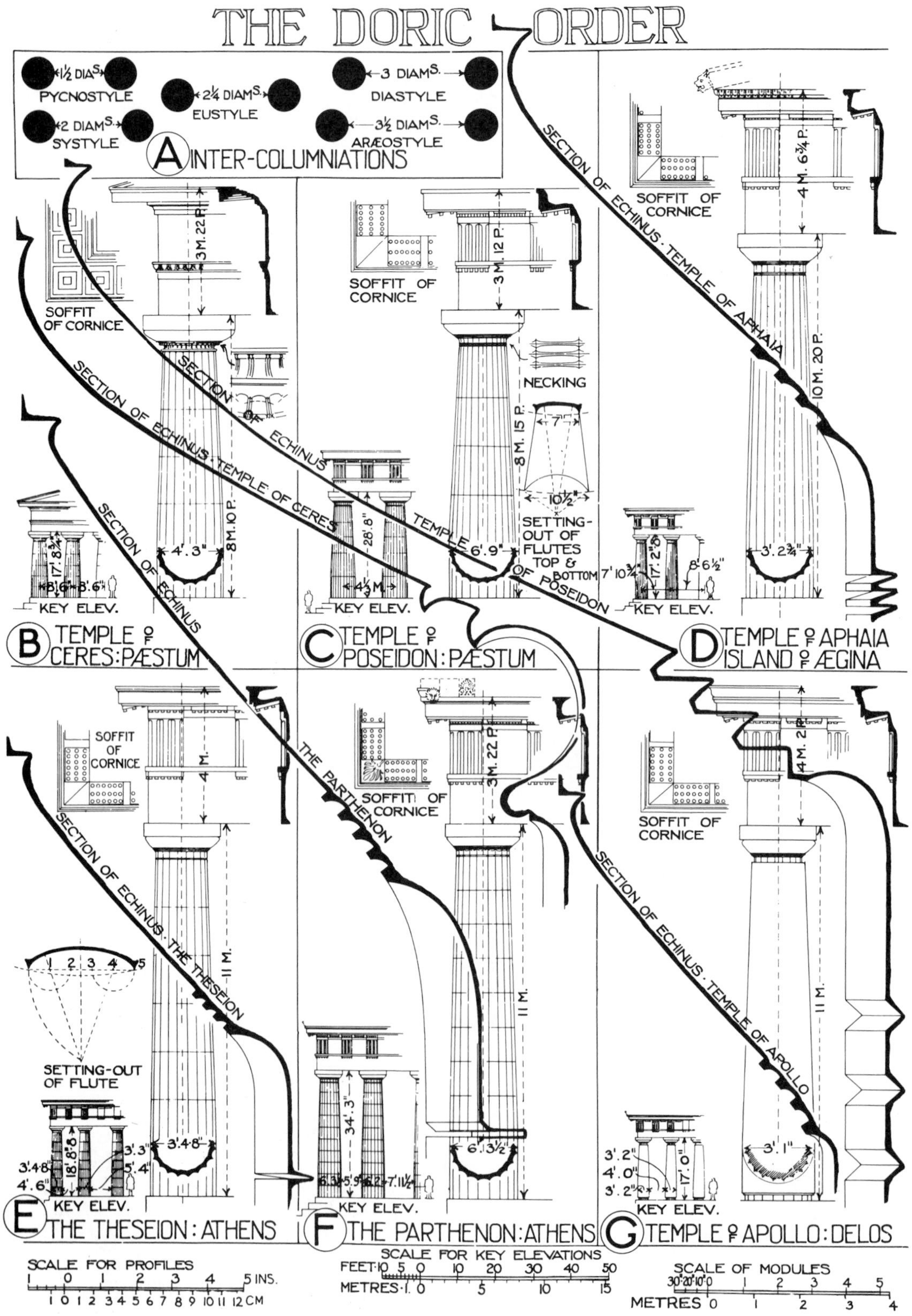
THE DORIC ORDER
1½ DIAS.
PYCNOSTYLE
2 DIAMS.
SYSTYLE
2¼ DIAMS.
EUSTYLE
3 DIAMS.
DIASTYLE
3½ DIAMS.
ARÆOSTYLE
A INTER-COLUMNIATIONS
SOFFIT OF CORNICE
SECTION OF ECHINUS · TEMPLE OF CERES
SECTION OF ECHINUS · TEMPLE OF POSEIDON
SECTION OF ECHINUS · TEMPLE OF APHAIA
NECKING
SETTING-OUT OF FLUTES TOP & BOTTOM
KEY ELEV.
B TEMPLE OF CERES: PÆSTUM
C TEMPLE OF POSEIDON: PÆSTUM
D TEMPLE OF APHAIA ISLAND OF ÆGINA
SECTION OF ECHINUS · THE THESEION
SECTION OF ECHINUS · THE PARTHENON
SECTION OF ECHINUS · TEMPLE OF APOLLO
SETTING-OUT OF FLUTE
E THE THESEION: ATHENS
F THE PARTHENON: ATHENS
G TEMPLE OF APOLLO: DELOS
SCALE FOR PROFILES
INS.
CM
SCALE FOR KEY ELEVATIONS
FEET
METRES
SCALE OF MODULES
METRES

OPTICAL CORRECTIONS IN ARCHITECTURE

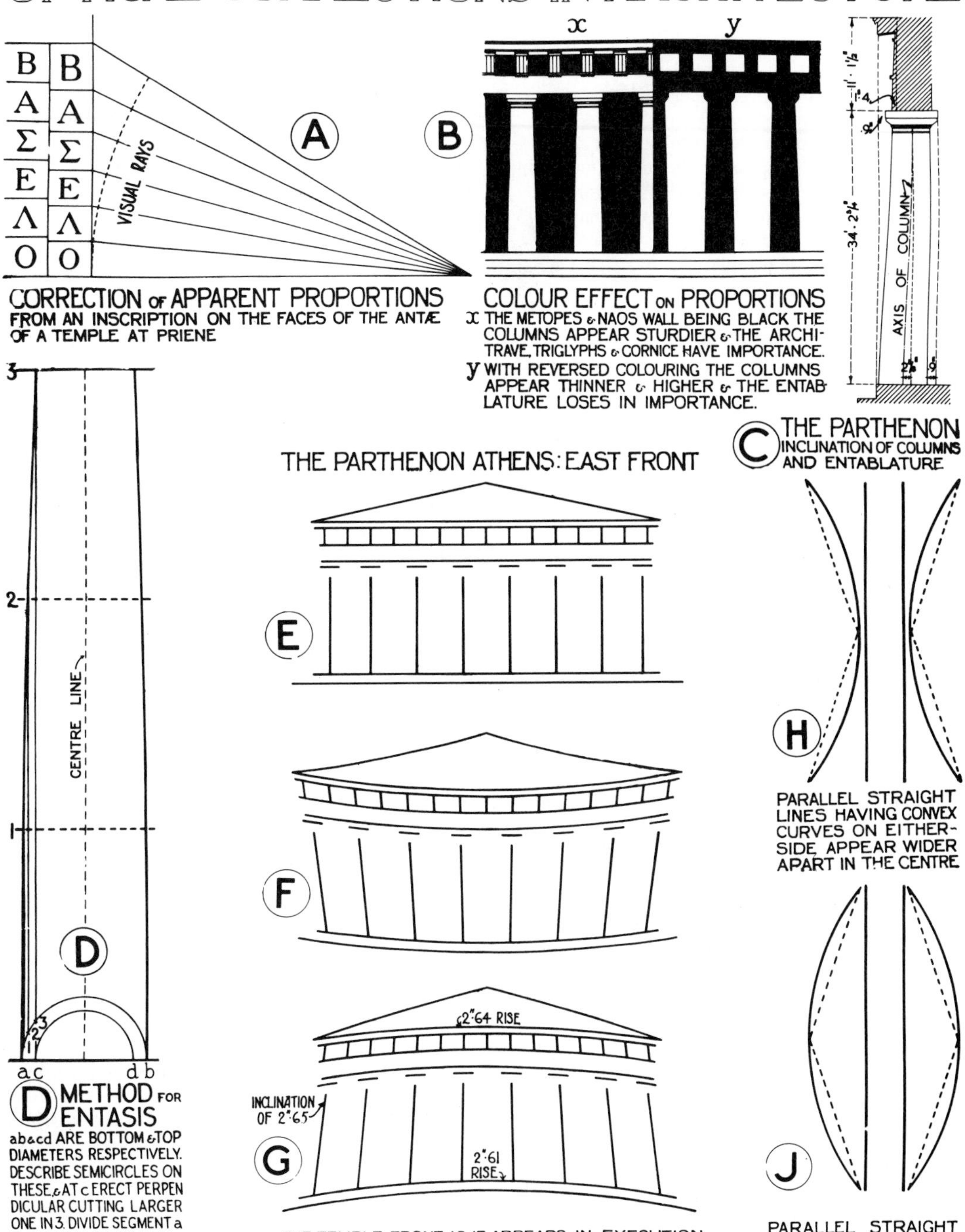

CORRECTION OF APPARENT PROPORTIONS
FROM AN INSCRIPTION ON THE FACES OF THE ANTÆ OF A TEMPLE AT PRIENE

COLOUR EFFECT ON PROPORTIONS
x THE METOPES & NAOS WALL BEING BLACK THE COLUMNS APPEAR STURDIER & THE ARCHITRAVE, TRIGLYPHS & CORNICE HAVE IMPORTANCE.
y WITH REVERSED COLOURING THE COLUMNS APPEAR THINNER & HIGHER & THE ENTABLATURE LOSES IN IMPORTANCE.

C THE PARTHENON
INCLINATION OF COLUMNS AND ENTABLATURE

D METHOD FOR ENTASIS
ab & cd ARE BOTTOM & TOP DIAMETERS RESPECTIVELY. DESCRIBE SEMICIRCLES ON THESE & AT c ERECT PERPENDICULAR CUTTING LARGER ONE IN 3. DIVIDE SEGMENT a 3 & HEIGHT OF COLUMN INTO ANY NUMBER OF EQUAL PARTS - SAY 3 - & NUMBER BOTH 1, 2, 3 FROM a. THRO' POINTS 1, 2, 3 IN SEGMENT ERECT PERPENDICULARS CUTTING CORRESPONDING DIVISIONS OF THE HEIGHT. THRO' THE POINTS THUS OBTAINED DRAW CURVE.

E THE TEMPLE FRONT AS IT APPEARS IN EXECUTION WITH CURVED HORIZONTAL LINES AND INCLINED VERTICAL FEATURES AS AT G.

F THE TEMPLE FRONT AS IT WOULD APPEAR IF BUILT AS AT E WITHOUT OPTICAL CORRECTIONS.

G THE TEMPLE FRONT ARRANGED WITH VERTICAL AXES INCLINING & WITH CONVEX STYLOBATE, ARCHITRAVE - ENTABLATURE & PEDIMENT PRODUCING RESULT AS AT E.

PARALLEL STRAIGHT LINES HAVING CONVEX CURVES ON EITHER SIDE APPEAR WIDER APART IN THE CENTRE

PARALLEL STRAIGHT LINES HAVING CONCAVE CURVES ON EITHER - SIDE APPEAR CLOSER TOGETHER IN THE CENTRE.

A SIMILAR EFFECT PRODUCED BY INCLINED LINES AS INDICATED IN H & J BY DOTTED LINES

at Eleusis, of the mid-fourth century BC, on the inscription which records the specification for that structure.

The Ionic Order

Ionic columns, including capital and base, are usually between nine and ten times their lower diameter in height and have twenty-four flutes separated by flattened arrises. Early examples, however, may have as many as forty, forty-four or forty-eight flutes, which then are shallow and separated by a sharp arris. The Ionic columns of southern mainland Greece (the Peloponnese) usually have only twenty flutes, with flattened arrises. There are different forms of base, principally that used in the eastern Greek area, and that developed in the fifth century BC in Athens, which eventually prevailed over the eastern form. The capital has two pairs of volutes or spirals, about two-thirds the diameter in height, one pair on the front of the column, the other on the back, and joined at the sides by a concave cushion, sometimes plain but usually ornamented with numerous flutes, fillets and beads. The volute scroll rests on an echinus, circular in plan, carved with an egg-and-dart moulding and resting on a bead moulding, usually with running palmettes where it disappears under the volutes (p. 117R,S). Above the volute scrolls is a shallow abacus. The Ionic capital presented difficulties at the corners of a rectangular building, and in such positions a canted angle volute was used (p. 118). The four-fronted capital of Peloponnesian Ionic, as in the Order of the Temple at Bassae, is exceptional in Classical Greek architecture though it became increasingly common in the Hellenistic period.

The Ionic entablature (p. 117) passed through various stages of development. As evolved in the eastern Greek area, it had only two main parts, architrave and cornice, the latter supported by a frieze of large dentils. It was therefore very light in relation to the columns, being as little as one-sixth of their height, though in some temples, such as the archaic temple of Artemis at Ephesus, it was increased by a high vertical-faced 'parapet' sima, with carved decoration as for a frieze. A high entablature, with frieze and dentils under the cornice, was first used about 340 BC (for the 'temenos' at Samothrace) but did not become general until well into the third century BC. The order was soon used on the mainland too, at first only in treasuries built at Delphi by eastern Greek cities (p. 146B) or in unusual monuments such as the 'throne' (actually a decorated altar) at Amyclae near Sparta. In the fifth century BC it was adopted by the Athenians (who claimed Athens to be the mother city of the Ionians) for temples such as the Erechtheion (p. 128) and the Temple of Athena Nikè, Athens (p. 146A), which are the finest examples of the style. On the mainland, generally, a frieze was inserted in the entablature, but the dentils were omitted. The Ionic architrave, normally with three fasciae, is capped by two mouldings, a low astragal and a high ovolo, until the time of Hermogenes. The frieze, when present, is often decorated with a continuous band of sculpture. Ionic temples do not have antefixae on the flanks; instead, the sima or gutter moulding of the raking cornices at the ends of the temple is carried along the side cornices, too, and is often ornamented with an acanthus scroll. Carved lion heads at intervals serve to throw rainwater from the roof.

The Corinthian Order

The Corinthian order made its first appearance in Greek architecture in the fifth century BC as a decorative variant of the Ionic, the difference lying almost entirely in the column capital. It was first used only for internal colonnades (Bassae, Epidaurus, the tholos at Delphi) or for fanciful monuments (the Choragic monument of Lysicrates, Athens). Its use in external colonnades was a Hellenistic development. The distinctive capital is much deeper than the Ionic and, though of variable height at first, settled down to a proportion of about one and one-third diameters high (p. 120). Vitruvius records the fable (*De Architectura*, Bk. IV, Chap. i) that the invention of the capital was due to Callimachus, a famous Athenian sculptor in bronze, who obtained the idea from observing a basket over the grave of a Corinthian maiden, covered with a tile to protect the offerings it contained. Accidentally, the basket was placed over the root of an acanthus plant, the stems and foliage of which grew and turned into volutes at the angle of the tile. The perfected type has a deep, inverted bell, the lower part of which is surrounded by two tiers of eight acanthus leaves, and from between the leaves of the upper row rise eight caulicoli (caulis = stalk), each surmounted by a calyx from which emerge volutes or helices supporting the angles of the abacus and the central foliated ornaments. Each face of the moulded abacus is curved outwards to the corners, where it either ends in a point or is chamfered.

The Corinthian entablature is not distinguishable from the developed Ionic until the later Hellenistic period; in the earliest known instance of the order, in the Temple of Apollo Epicurius at Bassae, Corinthian and Ionic internal columns share the same entablature.

Evolution of the Orders

The developments which led to the evolution of the Classical Greek orders belong to the seventh century BC. Larger temples were built, of more durable form and more interestingly decorated. The inspiration is probably to be sought in the cities of the Levant, with

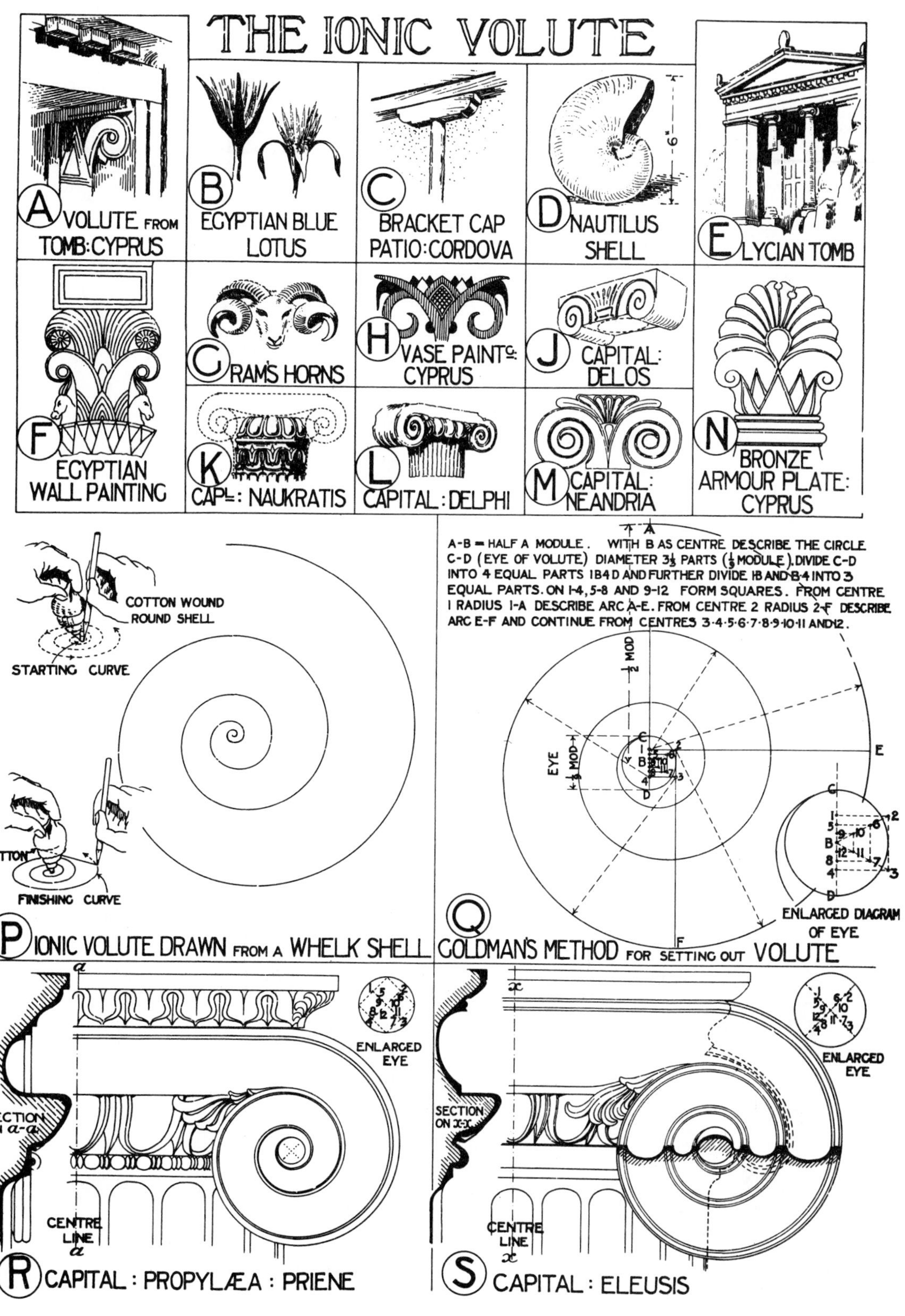
THE IONIC VOLUTE
A VOLUTE FROM TOMB: CYPRUS
B EGYPTIAN BLUE LOTUS
C BRACKET CAP PATIO: CORDOVA
D NAUTILUS SHELL
6"
E LYCIAN TOMB
F EGYPTIAN WALL PAINTING
G RAM'S HORNS
H VASE PAINTG: CYPRUS
J CAPITAL: DELOS
K CAPL: NAUKRATIS
L CAPITAL: DELPHI
M CAPITAL: NEANDRIA
N BRONZE ARMOUR PLATE: CYPRUS
COTTON WOUND ROUND SHELL
STARTING CURVE
COTTON
FINISHING CURVE
P IONIC VOLUTE DRAWN FROM A WHELK SHELL
A-B = HALF A MODULE. WITH B AS CENTRE DESCRIBE THE CIRCLE C-D (EYE OF VOLUTE) DIAMETER 3½ PARTS (⅛ MODULE). DIVIDE C-D INTO 4 EQUAL PARTS 1B4D AND FURTHER DIVIDE 1B AND B4 INTO 3 EQUAL PARTS. ON 1-4, 5-8 AND 9-12 FORM SQUARES. FROM CENTRE 1 RADIUS 1-A DESCRIBE ARC A-E. FROM CENTRE 2 RADIUS 2-F DESCRIBE ARC E-F AND CONTINUE FROM CENTRES 3·4·5·6·7·8·9·10·11 AND 12.
½ MOD
EYE
⅛ MOD
ENLARGED DIAGRAM OF EYE
Q GOLDMAN'S METHOD FOR SETTING OUT VOLUTE
ENLARGED EYE
SECTION ON a-a
CENTRE LINE
R CAPITAL : PROPYLÆA : PRIENE
SECTION ON x-x
S CAPITAL : ELEUSIS

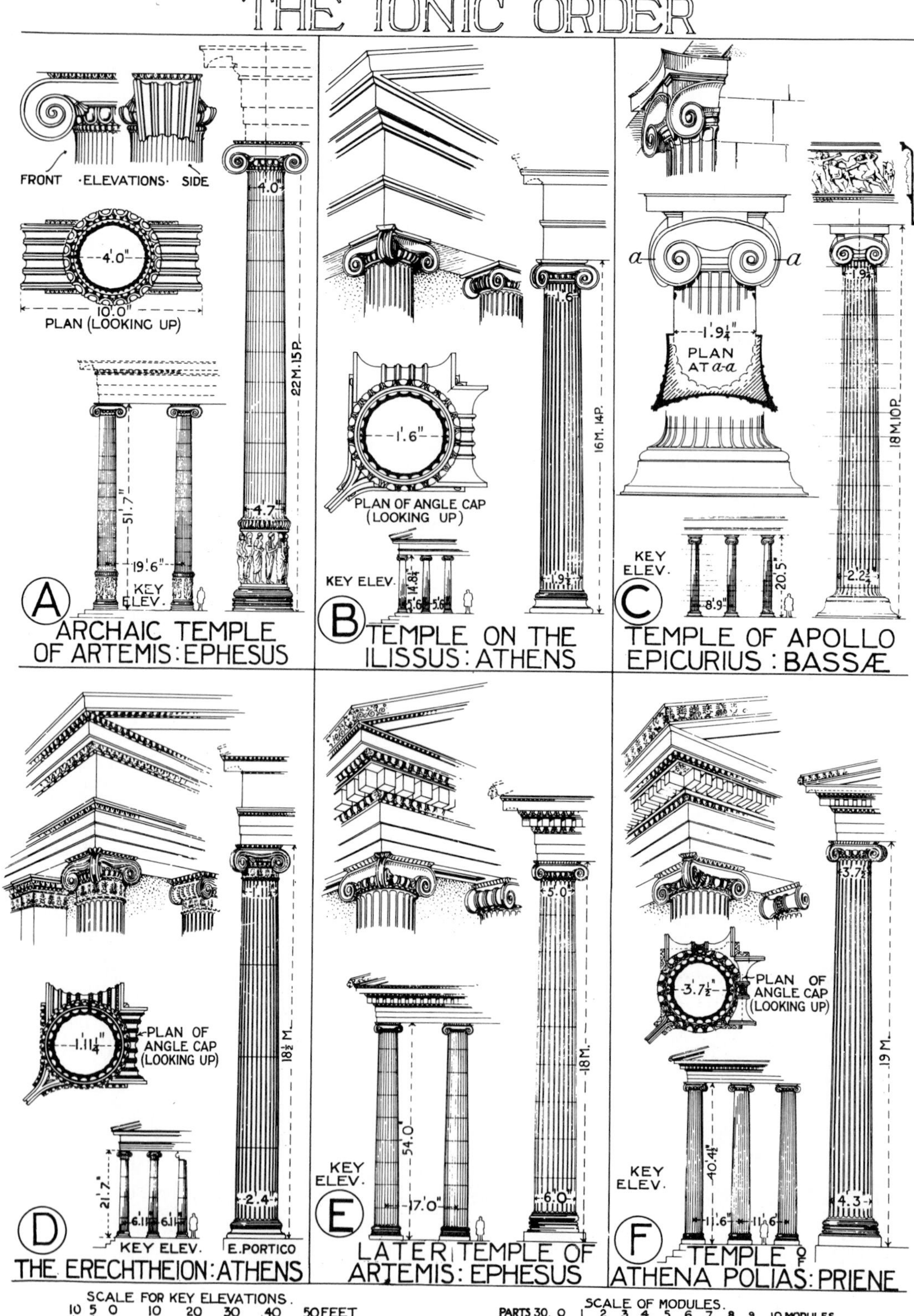
THE IONIC ORDER
FRONT ·ELEVATIONS· SIDE
4'.0"
10'.0"
PLAN (LOOKING UP)
22M.15P.
4'.0"
4'.7"
51'.7"
19'.6"
KEY ELEV.
A
ARCHAIC TEMPLE OF ARTEMIS: EPHESUS
1'.6"
PLAN OF ANGLE CAP (LOOKING UP)
KEY ELEV.
14'.8¼"
5'.6"
5'.6"
16M.14P.
B
TEMPLE ON THE ILISSUS: ATHENS
a
a
1'.9¼"
PLAN AT a-a
18M.10P.
KEY ELEV.
20'.5"
8'.9"
C
TEMPLE OF APOLLO EPICURIUS: BASSÆ
1'.11¼"
PLAN OF ANGLE CAP (LOOKING UP)
18½ M.
21'.7"
6'.11"
6'.11"
KEY ELEV.
E.PORTICO
2'.4"
D
THE ERECHTHEION: ATHENS
5'.0"
18M.
54'.0"
17'.0"
6'.0"
KEY ELEV.
E
LATER TEMPLE OF ARTEMIS: EPHESUS
3'.7½"
PLAN OF ANGLE CAP (LOOKING UP)
19M.
40'.4½"
11'.6"
11'.6"
4'.3"
KEY ELEV.
F
TEMPLE OF ATHENA POLIAS: PRIENE
SCALE FOR KEY ELEVATIONS.
10 5 0 10 20 30 40 50FEET
SCALE OF MODULES.
PARTS 30 0 1 2 3 4 5 6 7 8 9 10 MODULES

which the Greeks were now trading. The orders reflect the geographic divisions of the Greek world at that time, Doric evolving in the mainland communities, and Ionic in the eastern Greek area of the Aegean islands and the coast of Asia Minor. The structural improvements include the increasing use of stone in regularly trimmed blocks to form the bases of colonnades and walls, and the introduction of terracotta for tiles and revetments. These meant heavier roofs, which required the support either of stone walls or walls with massive timber framing. Woodwork therefore became more substantial and included external colonnades either in porches or completely surrounding the buildings. The plans of temples are similar in mainland and eastern Greek areas; it is the form of the columns and their entablature which distinguishes eastern Greek from mainland architecture. The eastern Greek versions (pp. 117, 118) are clearly related to Levantine prototypes, particularly the capital with two outward-turning volutes (the 'lily capitals', found in Jewish and Phoenician architecture long before they were introduced to Greece). Stone versions of this are not found in Greece until the sixth century BC; earlier examples may have existed in wood. There are two variants, that of the northern Aegean and coastal region (Aeolic), which is closer to the oriental prototype, the volutes rising from separate stems, and that of the southern Aegean, the Cyclades and adjacent coastal regions, where the volutes are linked (Ionic). The Aeolic style died out in the fifth century BC.

The origins of the Doric order are more obscure. It was probably developed in Dorian Corinth, which gives the order its name, though it was also the traditional architectural form in non-Dorian mainland cities, such as Athens. The capital echoes the Bronze Age type, though there is no evidence for the downward tapering shafts, and it is doubtful whether any Bronze Age columns survived at the time of the eighth and seventh centuries BC, except those stone examples on the facades of the Tholos tombs, of which, at least, the Treasury of Atreus was cleared and known at this time. The entablature with the triglyph and metope frieze reflects the pattern used to decorate prehistoric structures including the Treasury of Atreus – but similar patterns were used to decorate other objects, such as painted vases, and are found on ivory work made in Syria. Any of these may have been the inspiration of the Doric order. It is important to emphasise that the system is decorative, rather than structural in inspiration. These early decorative schemes were undoubtedly worked out in wood. The Temple of Poseidon at Isthmia, near Corinth, has stone walls (patterned to imitate a structure of wooden framing with brick infill) and a stone stylobate, but nothing survives of columns or entablature, which were presumably wooden. There were terracotta tiles, arranged to form a hipped rather than a pedimented roof. This dates to the first half of the seventh century BC. The temple of Apollo at Thermon, of about 620 BC, had metopes of terracotta, with painted decoration. In plan these early temples have a cella in the form of a megaron, with rectangular ends, and surrounded by a rectangular colonnade. Both mainland and eastern Greek examples (such as the early temple of Hera on the island of Samos) are long and narrow, and do not have the near square plans of the main room of the Bronze Age megaron, making it unlikely that there is a direct connection: the megaron plan still formed the traditional house type in Dark Age Greece.

The conversion of the Doric order from wood to stone took place towards the end of the seventh century BC. There is a contemporary stone Aeolic temple at Smyrna, which was destroyed, unfinished, in the last decade of the century. The earliest stone versions of Ionic are found in the island of Delos (the 'oikos of the Naxians', probably the first temple of Apollo there), which was embellished and improved in the early sixth century BC. The details of the Doric order clearly suggest the timber prototypes, particularly the series of strips under the projecting band at the top of the architrave, the regulae, with circular drops (guttae) beneath, surely reflecting the nails and pegs used to fix triglyphs and metopes in place. There are similar, but wider, blocks (mutules) fixed with pegs under the cornice, to secure the roof.

The earliest stone Doric temples are those of Athena at Delphi and Artemis at Corfu, of about 600 and 590 BC. The contemporary temple of Hera at Olympia still had mud-brick walls and timber columns, which were only gradually replaced in stone.

Sanctuaries and Temples

The Greeks recognised separate areas as sacred to a god, both in their towns and villages, and in the surrounding countryside. Some were on sites occupied in the late Bronze Age, where presumably visible remains of earlier walls, or even some continuity of cult, led to their selection for religious purposes. Others were chosen because of natural distinctions, such as the proximity of springs. In eastern Greece, certain low-lying sanctuaries (Hera on Samos, Artemis at Ephesus) were probably places used for cult practices inherited by the Greek settlers from earlier inhabitants. In towns some sanctuaries were in walled citadels, although in several Greek cities the major sanctuary was not in the town at all, but outside in the countryside (the sanctuaries of Hera at Argos and on Samos, for example). Unless they were on citadels, they were rarely walled, and formal gateways are surprisingly infrequent.

Even if it was not absolutely necessary to the religious practice, all sanctuaries of any pretension included a temple. By the Classical period these

EVOLUTION OF THE CORINTHIAN CAPITAL

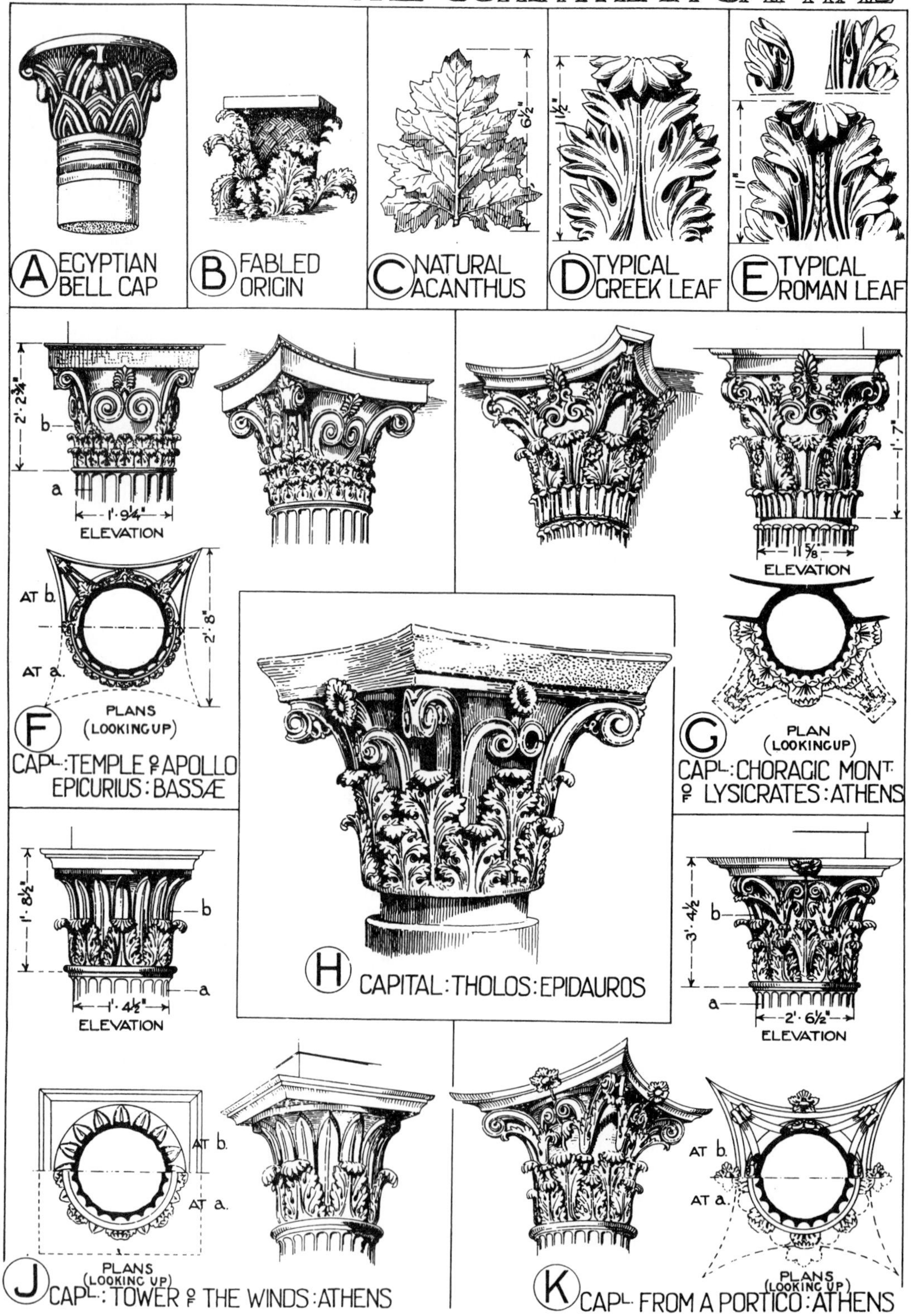

(A) EGYPTIAN BELL CAP

(B) FABLED ORIGIN

(C) NATURAL ACANTHUS

6½"

(D) TYPICAL GREEK LEAF

1½"

(E) TYPICAL ROMAN LEAF

11"

2'·2¾"
b
a
1'·9¼"
ELEVATION

AT b.
AT a.
2'·8"
PLANS (LOOKING UP)

(F) CAPL.: TEMPLE OF APOLLO EPICURIUS: BASSÆ

1'·7"
11⅝"
ELEVATION

PLAN (LOOKING UP)

(G) CAPL.: CHORAGIC MONT. OF LYSICRATES: ATHENS

(H) CAPITAL: THOLOS: EPIDAUROS

1'·8½"
b
a
1'·4½"
ELEVATION

3'·4½"
b
a
2'·6½"
ELEVATION

AT b.
AT a.
PLANS (LOOKING UP)

(J) CAPL.: TOWER OF THE WINDS: ATHENS

AT b.
AT a.
PLANS (LOOKING UP)

(K) CAPL. FROM A PORTICO: ATHENS

THE ACROPOLIS: ATHENS

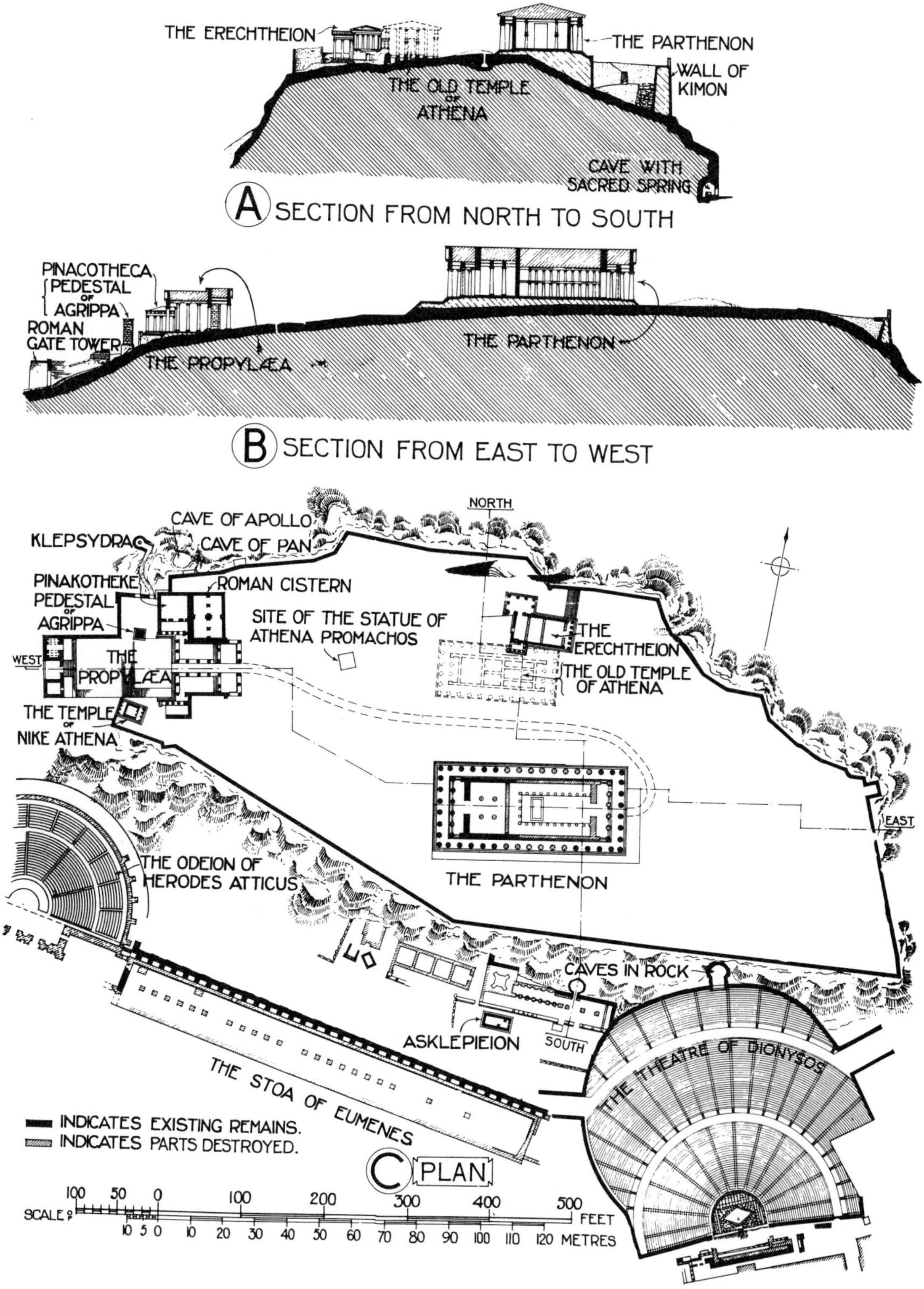

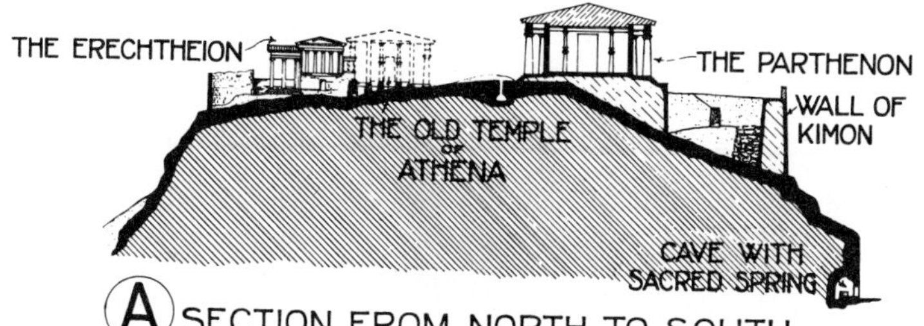

THE ERECHTHEION
THE PARTHENON
WALL OF KIMON
THE OLD TEMPLE OF ATHENA
CAVE WITH SACRED SPRING
A SECTION FROM NORTH TO SOUTH
PINACOTHECA
PEDESTAL OF AGRIPPA
ROMAN GATE TOWER
THE PROPYLÆA
THE PARTHENON
B SECTION FROM EAST TO WEST
NORTH
CAVE OF APOLLO
KLEPSYDRA
CAVE OF PAN
PINAKOTHEKE
PEDESTAL OF AGRIPPA
ROMAN CISTERN
SITE OF THE STATUE OF ATHENA PROMACHOS
WEST
THE PROPYLÆA
THE ERECHTHEION
THE OLD TEMPLE OF ATHENA
THE TEMPLE OF NIKE ATHENA
EAST
THE ODEION OF HERODES ATTICUS
THE PARTHENON
CAVES IN ROCK
ASKLEPIEION
SOUTH
THE THEATRE OF DIONYSOS
THE STOA OF EUMENES
INDICATES EXISTING REMAINS.
INDICATES PARTS DESTROYED.
C PLAN
SCALE
100 50 0 100 200 300 400 500 FEET
10 5 0 10 20 30 40 50 60 70 80 90 100 110 120 METRES

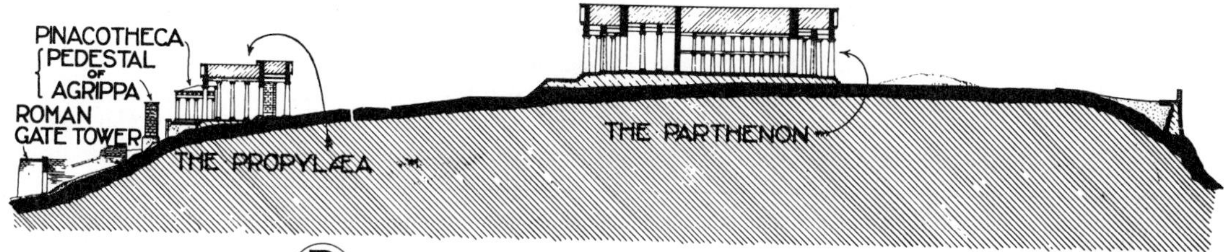

temples varied in detail, though almost all consisted essentially of simple rectangular buildings to hold statues of gods. The statue stood in the cella or naos, the width of which was limited by the restricted sizes of roof timbers, though inner colonnades made wider rooms possible. The side walls usually extended forward to form the porch, so that the traditional megaron plan survives. Porches, in all but the smallest buildings, were embellished with columns, placed either between the ends of the side walls (in antis) or in a row in front of them (prostyle).

The conventional description of the numbers of columns consists of a Greek numeral plus the word 'style' (stylos, the Greek for column). Thus distyle (two columns), tetrastyle (four), hexastyle (six), octastyle (eight) and decastyle (ten). Odd numbers, three (tristyle), five (pentastyle), seven (heptastyle), nine (enneastyle) are unusual, and found chiefly in early buildings, of the sixth century BC. The commonest simple temples (apart from those which are mere unembellished rooms) are distyle in antis. The same terms are used for the numbers of columns forming the facade of peripteral temples, that is, those where the cella is surrounded by columns. In such temples the number of columns along the flanks is variable. In Doric temples of the fifth century BC the number on the flank usually is twice the number on the facade plus one, but the length of a temple reflects its internal arrangements, where there may be extra rooms, or false porches at the back.

Externally, temples might be made larger and more impressive by using double rows of external columns (dipteral) or even three rows (tripteral) along each end. The outer colonnade might be spaced as though there were a second, internal row which is in fact omitted (pseudodipteral). Colonnaded false porches in non-peripteral temples are rare and restricted to prostyle examples; they are called amphiprostyle and are either tetrastyle (the temple of Athena Nikè on the Athenian Acropolis) or hexastyle (the fourth century BC temple of Athena, Delphi).

Sanctuaries might well contain more than one temple and include those of lesser importance than the principal building (such as the temple of Artemis in the sanctuary of Asklepios at Epidaurus), or temples constructed at different periods, but apparently of equal importance (as at Selinus in Sicily). Altars were often monumental, generally rectangular and embellished with architectural motifs and mouldings such as triglyph-and-metope friezes, or screens of columns. All sanctuaries had altars, even if there was no temple. In sanctuaries which commanded the support of all Greek cities (Zeus at Olympia, Apollo at Delphi) individual cities might offer to the god a building resembling a small non-peripteral temple, termed a 'treasury' (thesauros); these were not mere storage places but offerings in their own right, often lavishly decorated with sculpture, and generally commemorating some important event, such as a victory in war (the **Athenian treasury at Delphi**, p. 146) or the discovery of a rich vein of silver (the treasury of the Siphnians, also at Delphi). Buildings may have been peculiar to a particular cult. For example Asklepios at Epidaurus (who was regarded as a mortal who became deified) had a circular building, the Thymele, which may have served as a cenotaph: in Greek architecture circular buildings are never temples, but serve commemorative purposes. The tholos at Delphi and the Philippeion at Olympia are other examples. All were decorated with Corinthian colonnades internally. There was also a building for the healing ritual of incubation, the abaton, where patients would pass the night in the sanctuary in the hope of a miraculous visit from the god. Most sanctuaries became full of monuments, statues and other offerings, often placed on elaborate high bases, and exhedrae, rectangular or semicircular seats and recesses. In many sanctuaries it is possible to distinguish between the most sacred area near to the temple and altar and the other, less holy area devoted to the human involvement in cult and ritual. In these outer areas are to be found buildings such as a theatre for the religious dramatic festivals, the stadium and hippodrome for athletic contests and chariot racing, and exercise grounds, palaistrai and gymnasia (often attached to or close to a stadium). There may also be special buildings for the sacred banquets, in which privileged worshippers consumed their share of the sacrificial meat, while reclining on couches in the Greek manner.

The **Acropolis at Athens** (p. 121) is the supreme example of a Greek sanctuary. It was originally a Late Bronze Age citadel, with massive fortifications similar to those at Tiryns and Mycenae, and with a western entrance gate flanked by a projecting bastion like the Lion gate at Mycenae (q.v.). These fortifications remained in use until the sixth century BC. On the summit there was undoubtedly a palace, destroyed presumably early in the Dark Age. Nothing more is known until the eighth century BC, by which time there was an altar on its highest point, and possibly a simple nondescript temple to Athena. The temple was rebuilt and improved on several occasions. The core of it became a double cella, one part facing east, the other, an anteroom, facing west, with two side-by-side inner rooms. There were tetrastyle prostyle porches at each end, and, probably not later than the later seventh century BC, a peripteral colonnade in the Doric order. This temple (the 'old temple') was finally rebuilt, with the same plan, in about 525 BC, but this was burnt by the Persians in 480 BC. The west cella was then patched up as a storeroom and parts of the entablature were set into the renewed north wall of the Acropolis, probably as a war memorial.

Early in the fifth century BC (perhaps to celebrate the victory at Marathon in 490) it was decided to add new buildings to the Acropolis. The old Bronze Age gateway was demolished, and a new propylon designed to replace it. It was H-shaped in plan, possibly with five doors in the cross-wall and four columns in antis to each facade, the antae being formed by returns along front and back from the side walls. To the south of the 'old temple' a larger Doric temple, also to be dedicated to Athena, was begun, but this too was burnt, unfinished, by the Persians.

The Athenians merely tidied up the ruins when the Persians withdrew. Only when the Persians were forced to accept peace in 449 BC was the work renewed. The old propylon was replaced by a more complex structure called the **Propylaea** (a plural term, indicating that it is more than a simple propylon entrance) (p. 124), the architect of which was Mnesicles. Its central element is again an H-shaped gateway building, now turned so that it is on the east–west axis of the Acropolis. The inner hall is at a higher level, and the cross-wall, with five doors, is closer to the back. It is preceded by a flight of seven steps, except to the central (and largest) door, through which passes a continuous slope, providing access for processions and sacrificial animals. Both facades are Doric hexastyle prostyle. Inner and outer halls had different roof levels. The roof of the outer hall was supported by two rows of three Ionic columns, flanking the central passageway. The ceiling was of marble (as was the rest of the structure except for contrasting elements in Eleusinian limestone) with gilded stars in the coffer squares. The outer facade is flanked by two wings, placed against walls which run out from the sides of the main hall to north and south. Both are tristyle in antis with Doric columns smaller than those of the main gate halls. Behind the north wing is a rectangular room, the front wall of which has an off-centre door with flanking windows. This indicates that the room had couches placed around the walls and functioned as a formal dining room. The walls were decorated with panel paintings, which give it the name of Pinacotheca, picture gallery. The south wing was truncated and had only a wall behind its colonnade. It corresponds to a similar-shaped area which flanked the earlier propylon, and gave access to the Nikè Bastion.

An interesting feature of Mnesicles' Propylaea is the way in which it was built up from separate building masses, each with its own roof line – the two wings on the west front, the outer entrance hall and the inner entrance hall – and the manner in which the separate elements of the earlier arrangement (gate house, dining room, inner rooms and L-shaped area) were now assembled into a more coherent composition. The Propylaea was started in 436 BC and left incomplete on the outbreak of the Peloponnesian War in 431 BC.

The main building on the Acropolis is the revived large temple to Athena, the **Parthenon**, started in 447 BC and completed in 436 BC (pp. 113A,B, 125, 126). The existing massive south foundations were re-used, but the temple was made wider by extending it towards the centre of the Acropolis. The facade was now given eight, rather than six, columns, while there were seventeen along the flanks, the approved fifth-century ratio. The architects were Ictinus and Callicrates: it is not known how the work was shared between them. Phidias was the master sculptor, and may have been responsible for general supervision of the work on the Acropolis.

The temple stands on the conventional three steps, below which the foundation platform originally created for its predecessor remained visible on the west, south and east sides of the building. Dimensions at the top step are 30.9 m × 69.5 m (101 ft × 228 ft). The steps, with a height of 508 mm (29 in), were too high to use, so intermediate steps were provided at the centre of each of the short sides. The cella consisted of two rooms end to end with hexastyle prostyle porches. The eastern room was 29.8 m long by 19.2 m wide (98 ft × 63 ft), with internal Doric colonnades in two tiers, structurally necessary to support the roof timbers. Inside the colonnades, towards the end, there stood the gold and ivory statue of Athena Parthenos, the work of Phidias, representing Athena fully armed with spear, helmet, aegis and shield, accompanied by a snake, and holding in her extended right arm a statue of victory. The ceiling was of wood, with painted and gilded decoration. Light was admitted, as normally in Greek temples through the doorway when the great doors were opened, but it is now known that there were also windows high in the walls on either side of the door. To the west, with its own porch, was a square chamber, the Parthenon or Virgin's chamber, a depository for valuable offerings. Here the roof was probably supported by a group of four Ionic columns. The spaces between the antae and porch columns, at either end, were closed by metal grilles.

On the exterior, the Doric columns measure 1.9 m (6 ft 2 in) in diameter and are 10.4 m (34 ft 3 in) high, approximately $5\frac{1}{2}$ times the diameter. The corner columns are slightly larger in diameter, with their spacing reduced to make it possible for the frieze to conform to the rule that it must terminate with a triglyph.

The Parthenon is the best example in Greek temple architecture of the practice of optical refinement. Apart from the entasis on the columns, the long, horizontal lines of such features as stylobates, architraves and cornices, which, if straight in reality, would have appeared to the Greek eye to sag or drop in the middle of their length, were formed with slightly convex outlines. In the Parthenon, the stylobate has an upward curvature towards its centre of 60 mm ($2\frac{3}{8}$ in) on the east and west ends, and of 110 mm ($4\frac{5}{16}$ in) on the sides. Vertical features were also inclined inwards towards the top to correct the appearance of falling outwards; thus the axes of the corner columns lean inwards 60 mm ($2\frac{3}{8}$ in) and the

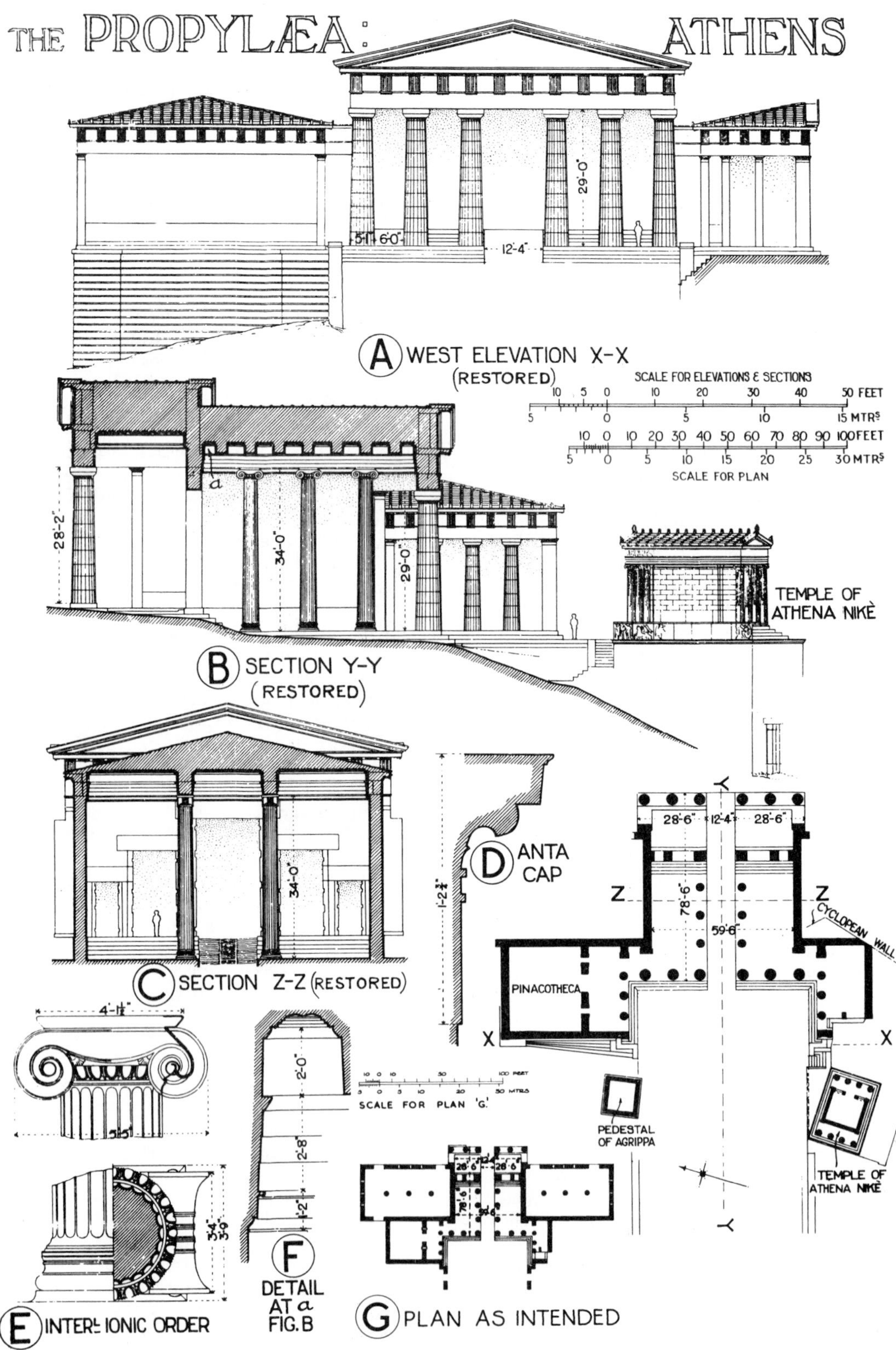
THE PROPYLÆA: ATHENS
29'-0"
5'11" 6'0"
12'-4"
A WEST ELEVATION X-X (RESTORED)
SCALE FOR ELEVATIONS & SECTIONS
10 5 0 10 20 30 40 50 FEET
5 0 5 10 15 MTRS
10 0 10 20 30 40 50 60 70 80 90 100 FEET
5 0 5 10 15 20 25 30 MTRS
SCALE FOR PLAN
28'-2"
34'-0"
29'-0"
TEMPLE OF ATHENA NIKÈ
B SECTION Y-Y (RESTORED)
D ANTA CAP
1'-2¾"
28'-6" 12'-4" 28'-6"
Z Z
78'-6"
59'-6"
CYCLOPEAN WALL
PINACOTHECA
X X
Y Y
C SECTION Z-Z (RESTORED)
4'-1½"
2'-0"
2'-8"
1'-2"
SCALE FOR PLAN 'G'
PEDESTAL OF AGRIPPA
TEMPLE OF ATHENA NIKÈ
E INTERR IONIC ORDER
F DETAIL AT a FIG. B
G PLAN AS INTENDED

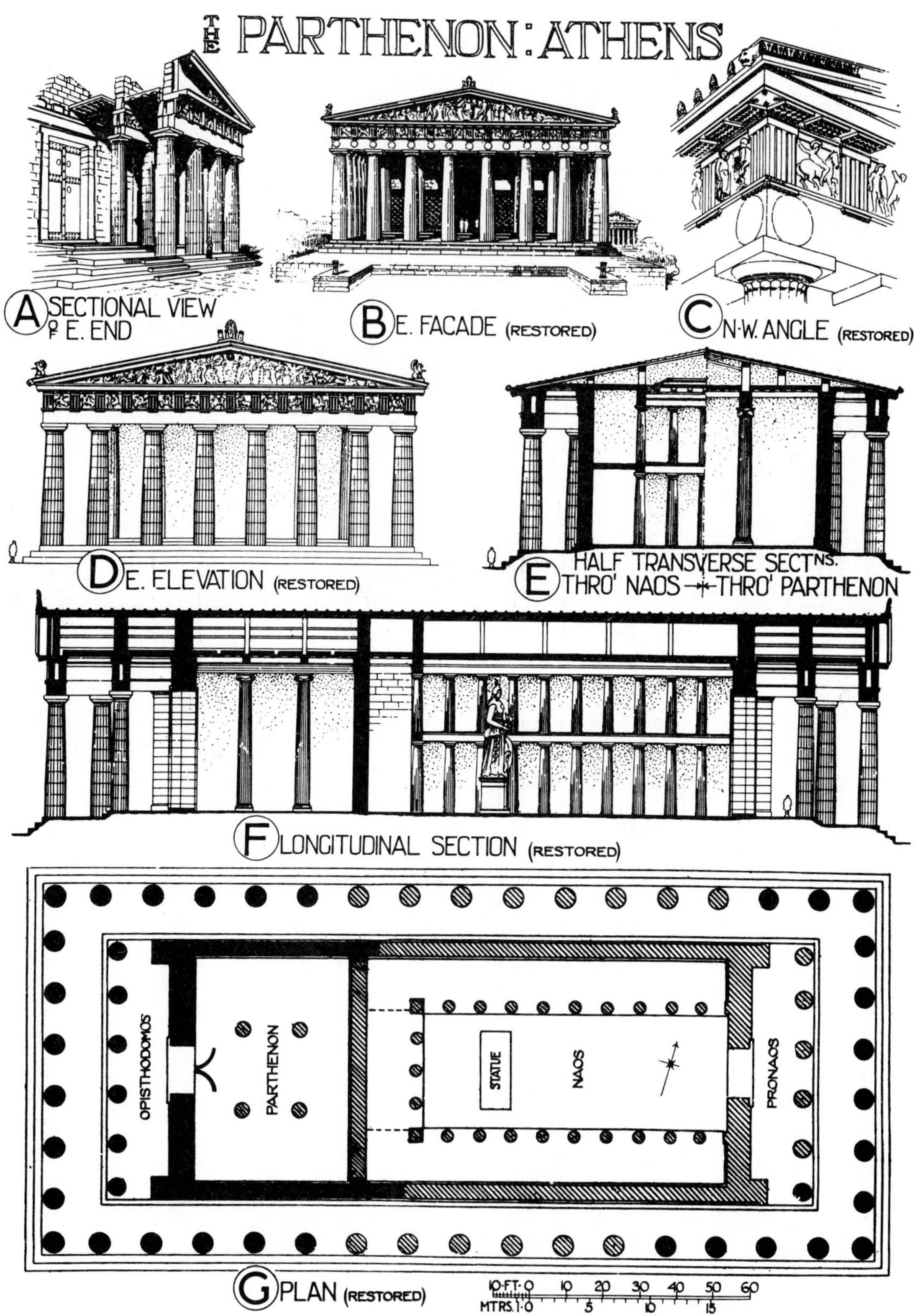
THE PARTHENON: ATHENS
A SECTIONAL VIEW OF E. END
B E. FACADE (RESTORED)
C N·W. ANGLE (RESTORED)
D E. ELEVATION (RESTORED)
E HALF TRANSVERSE SECTNS. THRO' NAOS — THRO' PARTHENON
F LONGITUDINAL SECTION (RESTORED)
OPISTHODOMOS
PARTHENON
STATUE
NAOS
PRONAOS
G PLAN (RESTORED)
10·FT·0 10 20 30 40 50 60
MTRS. 1·0 5 10 15

A. Parthenon, Athens (447–436 BC). See p.123

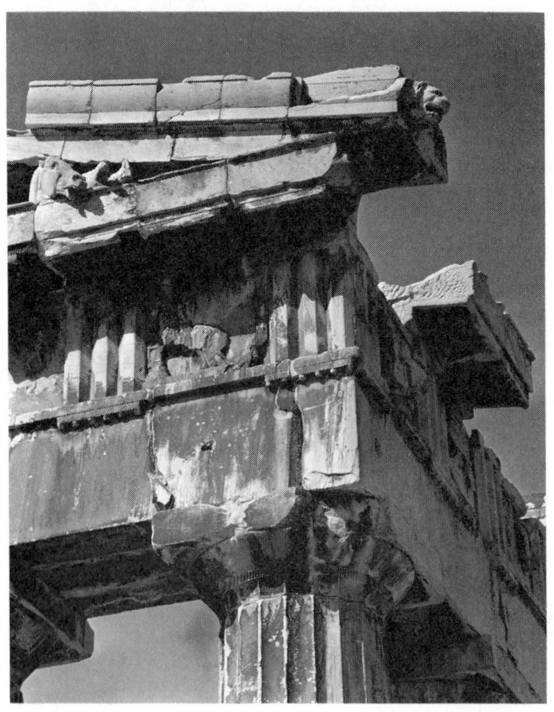

B. Parthenon: view of angle

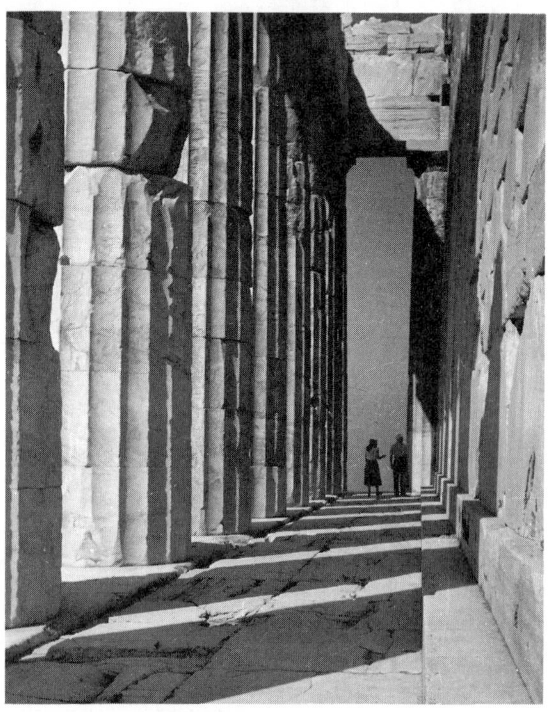

C. Parthenon: south peristyle

axes of the columns, if extended upwards, would meet at a distance of 2.4 km (1½ miles) above the stylobate. The joints of the marble roof tiles above the cornice were marked by carved antefixae, which formed an ornamental cresting along the sides of the building. There were no gutters except over the pediments, with short returns along each side decorated with false (unpierced) lion's head spouts. Below the colonnades, the coffered ceilings, of marble, were supported on marble beams. The pediments had large floral acroteria at the apex and lower angles. The sculptural decoration of the eastern pediment represented the birth of Athena, that of the western one the contest of Athena and Poseidon for the patronage of Athens. The carved decoration was exceptionally lavish. All the metopes, totalling ninety-two, were decorated in deep relief, depicting scenes of combat: there were gods and giants on the east facade, Greeks and Amazons on the west, Centaurs on the south, and battles of the Trojan war on the north. All symbolise allegorically the successful struggle of the Greeks against the Persians. Though the porch architraves had the regulae and guttae which normally occur under a Doric frieze, the frieze was in fact continuous in the Ionic style, in low relief. It is a masterpiece of design and execution and depicts a procession, with the gods seated in their home on Mount Olympus.

In the late sixth century the Parthenon was converted into a Christian church, dedicated to Divine Wisdom, thus perpetuating an attribute of Athena. An apse was formed at the eastern end, damaging the sculpture. From about 1204, under the Frankish Dukes of Athens, it served as a Latin church, until in 1458 it was converted by the Turkish conquerors into a mosque. During the siege of Athens by the Venetians in 1687 a powder store exploded causing considerable damage; fortunately drawings had been made of the sculpture which survived before the explosion. The north colonnade was restored in 1921–9, but the use of steel reinforcements, which have rusted, and the general atmospheric pollution of modern Athens, have necessitated a new and massive programme of conservation.

The other temples on the Acropolis are Ionic. The **Temple of Athena Nikè** (Nikè Apteros) (pp. 121, 124, 146A) stands on the bastion outside the Propylaea. It is tetrastyle amphiprostyle, with a continuous frieze and no dentils, and measures only 8.2 m × 5.4 m (27 ft × 17 ft 9 in). There is no conventional porch: the front of the cella has two rectangular piers between the antae which are closed by grilles instead of a wall with a door. More space for a conventional porch could have been obtained by omitting the rear colonnade; but this end, facing west, is the one that was visible on approaching the Acropolis. The temple replaces a simpler rectangular shrine which had been built shortly after 450, when Kallikrates was commissioned by the Athenian assembly to carry out improvements. The Ionic temple was built at the end of the first phase of the war between Athens and Sparta, about 421 BC. Subsequently, the temple was surrounded by a balustrade on the north, west and south sides of the bastion.

The second temple, the **Erechtheion** (pp. 121, 128, 129, 130A,B), was the replacement for the 'old' temple, and housed that temple's venerable wooden cult statue of Athena, which had been evacuated to Salamis at the time of the Persian invasion. There are three possible reasons why the new temple was not placed on the foundations of the old, but moved to an adjacent site immediately to the north: first, that it was not considered proper to rebuild a dedicated temple destroyed by the barbarians; second, that moving the temple to the north gave a better balance with the larger and wider Parthenon to the south; or third, that it was desired to incorporate under the protection of the new structure a number of monuments and sacred places. These included the salt pool (which had appeared at the spot where Poseidon had struck the acropolis with his trident) and the shrine of Erechtheus, the legendary king of Athens which was to give the new temple its 'popular' name. The resulting building is unusual and irregular in plan, but shows the same principles as those employed in the layout of the Propylaea, namely the gathering together of several elements into a complex but united arrangement. It is more likely that this was done deliberately, on the inspiration of the Propylaea, rather than that an original plan, similar to the 'old' temple, was gradually modified. The original architect is not known (inscriptions record only later building supervisors) and if he were not Mnesicles himself, he certainly had learned from Mnesicles. The temple was begun perhaps in 421 BC, and completed in 406 BC.

The site is not flat, but because of the sacred places there it was impossible to level it up by terracing. The cella is built on two levels, the eastern part at the higher, the western part at the lower. As in the old temple, the western contained an anteroom and two inner rooms placed side by side. The east porch, at the higher level, is hexastyle prostyle with columns 6.586 m (21 ft 7 in) high. The entablature, which has a continuous frieze in dark limestone with attached marble figures, extends along the sides of the cella, and across the west end. This ensured that the west columns were similar in size to the east, and they therefore form a screen above a section of wall which descends to the lower level and not a ground level porch.

The eastern cella is entered through a door, flanked, by windows, at a lower level than those of the Parthenon. The divisions of the western cella do not seem to have risen above the level of the wall on which the screen stands, and all parts of it were illuminated therefore by the light admitted through the openings between the columns. At the west end of the south side a low porch projected at the higher

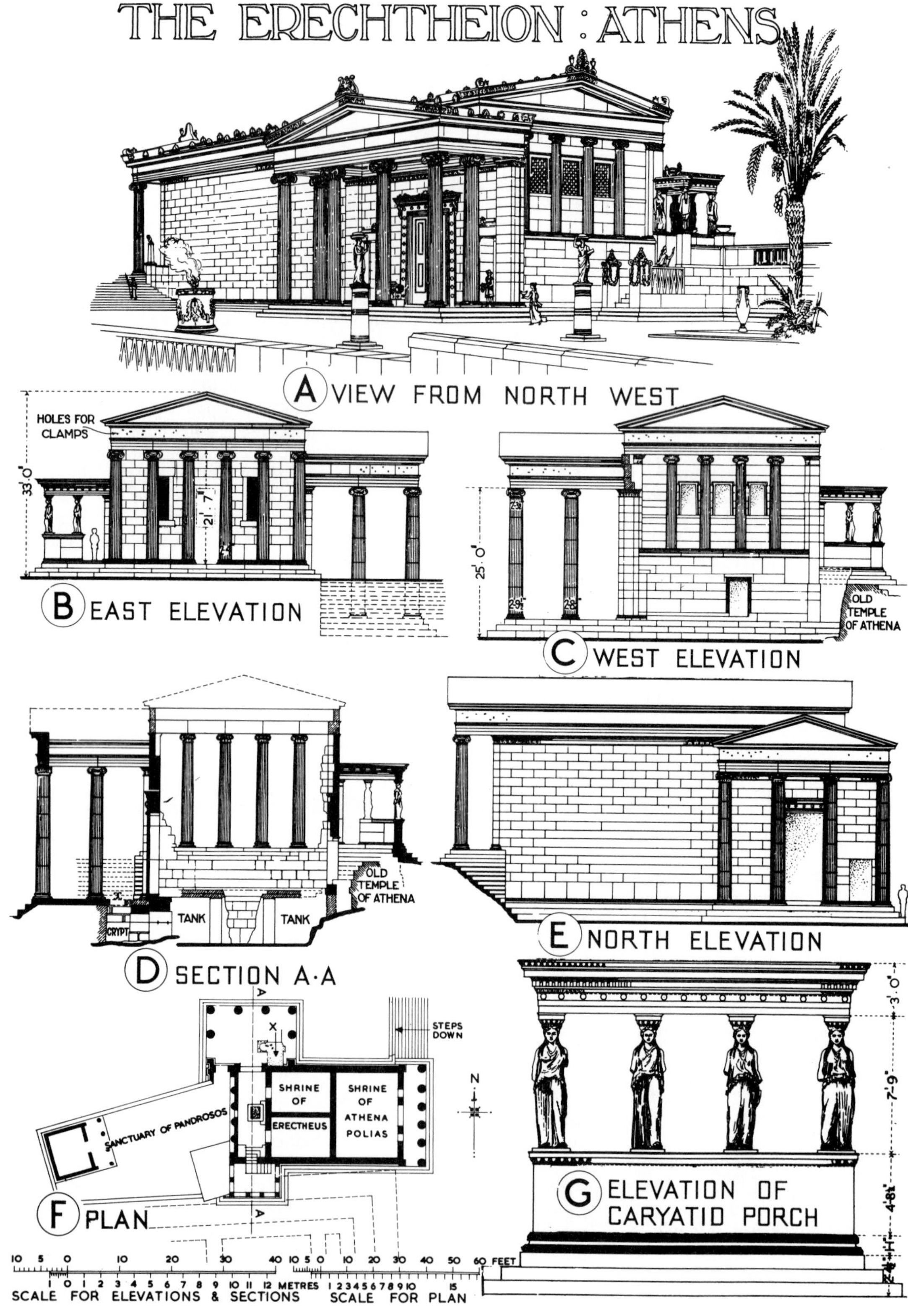
THE ERECHTHEION : ATHENS
A VIEW FROM NORTH WEST
HOLES FOR CLAMPS
33'-0"
21'-7"
B EAST ELEVATION
25'-0"
OLD TEMPLE OF ATHENA
C WEST ELEVATION
OLD TEMPLE OF ATHENA
TANK
TANK
CRYPT
D SECTION A·A
E NORTH ELEVATION
STEPS DOWN
SHRINE OF ERECHTHEUS
SHRINE OF ATHENA POLIAS
SANCTUARY OF PANDROSOS
N
F PLAN
3'-0"
7'-9"
4'-8½"
G ELEVATION OF CARYATID PORCH
SCALE FOR ELEVATIONS & SECTIONS
SCALE FOR PLAN
FEET
METRES

A. Erechtheion: Athens (*c.* 421–406 BC). See p.127

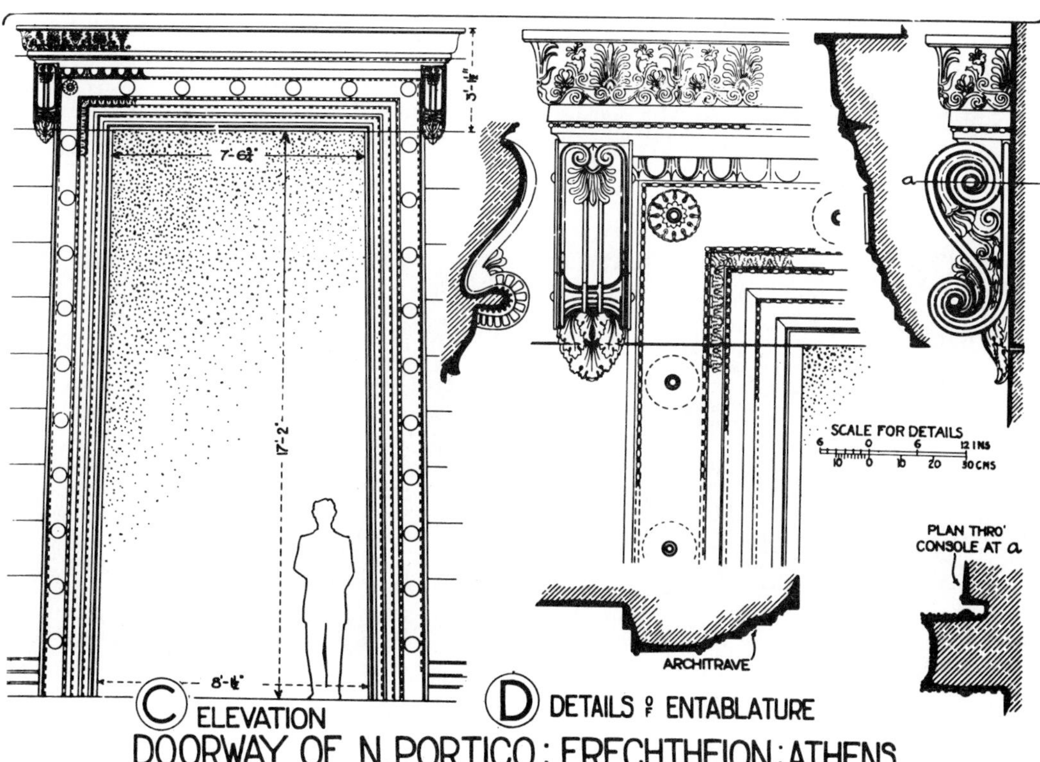

A. Erechtheion, Athens: Caryatid Porch (photograph taken before reconstruction *c.* 1990). See p.127

B. Erechtheion: Athens (from south-east)

C. 'Theseion', Athens (begun 449 BC). See p.142

ground level, the only part of the new temple to rest on foundations of the old. This consisted not of columns but of statues of young girls, the Maidens, of which there are four in front and another behind each of the corner figures. The term Caryatid, often used for the figures, should not properly be applied to it. The maidens stand on a low wall, with an opening between the eastern rear figure and the main cella wall, through which an angled stair led to the anteroom. The entablature incongruously resting on the maidens' heads is Ionic but has a dentil frieze, and supports a roof of flat slabs. Opposite is the great north porch at the lower ground level, similar in plan but with Ionic columns 7.6 m (25 ft) high; the west side of it, unlike the south porch, is not aligned with the west wall, but is placed still further to the west. This makes it possible for the porch to have two doors, a main central door, with elaborate Ionic details to its jambs and lintel, and a smaller door to the west which leads to the sanctuary of Pandrosus; this extended in front of the west end of the Erechtheion, at the lower level, and contained the sacred olive tree given by Athena to the Athenians during her contest with Poseidon; it was destroyed by the Persians but miraculously sprang to life again on their departure. This extension of the porch abuts very awkwardly against the decorated capital of the north-west anta to the main cella block. The north porch, like the main building, had a continuous frieze of dark limestone with attached white figures. Under the floor of the north porch are the marks where Poseidon's trident struck the rock, and above them an opening in the roof, presumably to avoid damaging the building should Poseidon choose to repeat the performance. Another awkwardness was caused by the tomb of Kekrops, a hero-king of Athens, under the south-west corner, which made it impossible to build either foundations or the lower part of the wall. But the design difficulties cannot detract from the superlative effects of delightful decoration and exquisite workmanship.

The temple suffered a severe fire in the first century BC, but was repaired. After the usual vicissitudes, the remains were cleared during the nineteenth century, and reconstructed. These reconstructions have proved unstable, and the Erechtheion has been largely dismantled and reassembled. The maidens (except one taken by Elgin) have suffered grievously in the pollution and acid rain of the modern city, and have been removed and replaced on the monument itself by casts. The northern column of the east facade, also taken by Elgin, has been replaced by a cast.

Other buildings on the Acropolis are less well preserved. They include, near the Propylaea, the separate **Sanctuary of Artemis**, an offshoot of her rural cult at Brauron. Between this and the Parthenon was the **Chalkotheke**, or armoury, consisting of a forecourt and a Doric stoa with a very large single room behind. Here were deposited the suits of bronze armour required from Athens' subject allies (theoretically its colonies) as offerings to Athena at its festival. Other buildings were less significant: they included, on the north side of the Acropolis, the room where the maiden priestesses of Athena, the Arrephoroi, dwelt during their period of office.

Besides **Olympia** (p. 132), **Delphi** (p. 133) and **Epidaurus**, which have already been mentioned, other important sanctuaries on the mainland include those of **Hera at Argos**, and the remote oracular sanctuary of **Zeus at Dodona** in north-west Greece. In the eastern Greek area are the great Ionic sanctuaries of **Hera on Samos, Artemis at Ephesus**, and **Apollo at Didyma** in the territory of Miletus.

Two rather different sanctuaries are those of **Demeter and Kore at Eleusis**, near Athens, and that of the **Kabeiroi** (originally Thracian deities) on the island of Samothrace in the north Aegean. At Eleusis there was a large roofed hall, the Telesterion, in which a secret ritual could be conducted away from profane eyes. These are the only buildings in Greek sanctuaries which are congregational in character.

Other Doric Temples

The principal Doric temples were in Greece, Sicily and southern Italy. Except for the Parthenon, which has been described already, they are listed below:

DORIC TEMPLES IN GREECE

c. 590 BC	The Heraion, Olympia (pp. 132, 137C,F)
c. 540 BC	Temple of Apollo, Corinth
c. 510 BC	Temple of Apollo, Delphi (p. 133)
c. 500 BC	Temple of Aphaia, Aegina (pp. 135,136)
c. 460 BC	Temple of Zeus, Olympia (pp. 132,147A)
begun 449 BC	Temple of Hephaestus ('Theseion'), Athens (pp. 130C, 139)
444–440 BC	Temple of Poseidon, Sounion
435–432 BC	Temple of Nemesis, Rhamnus
426 BC	The Athenian Temple to Apollo, Delos (p. 114G)
c. 425 BC onwards	Temple of Apollo Epicurius, Bassae (p. 140)

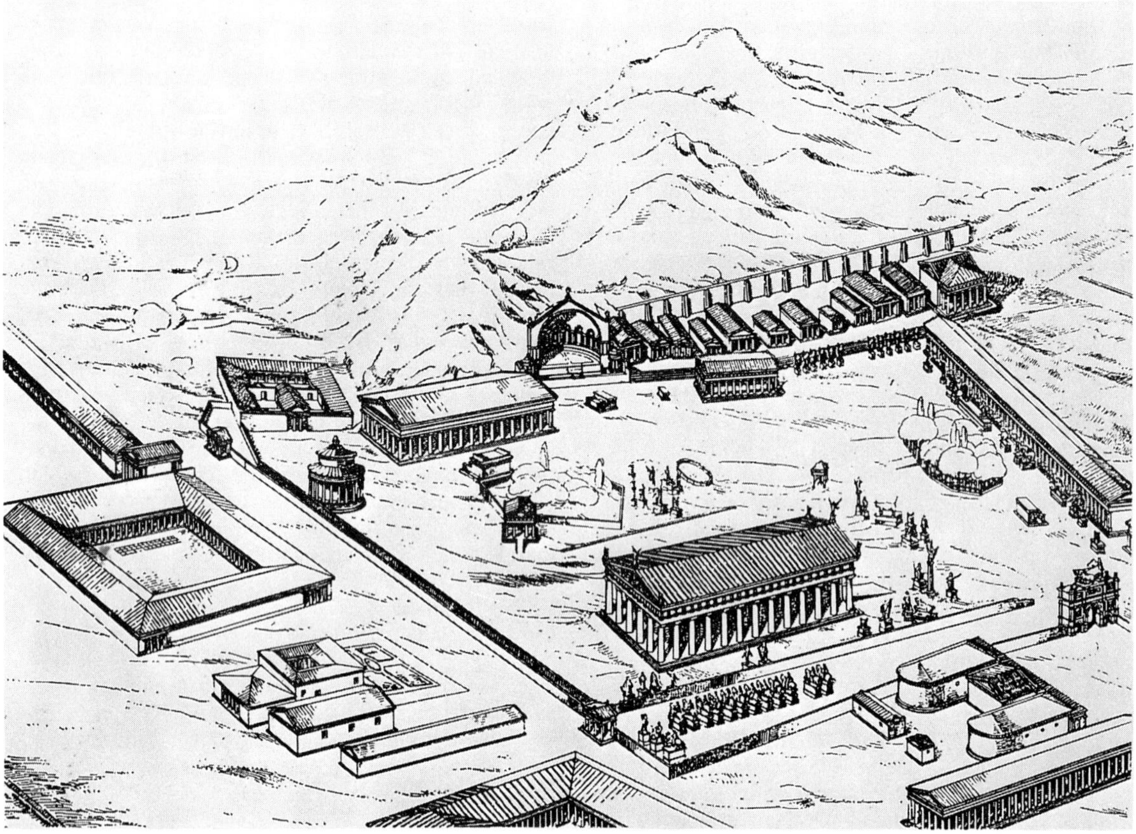

A. Altis, Olympia (restored). See p.131

1. Leonidaion
2. Pheidias' workshop
3. Palaistra
4. Prytaneion
5. Philippeion
6. Temple of Hera
7. Pelopion
8. Temple of Zeus
9. Treasuries
10. Metroön (Temple of Meter)
11. Stadium
12. Stoa of Echo
13. Bouleuterion
14. South Stoa
15. Gymnasium

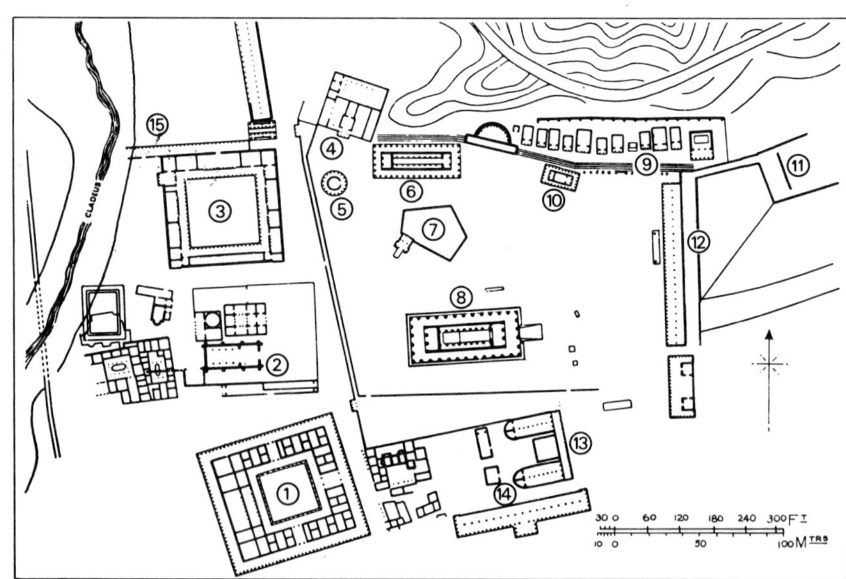

B. Olympia: plan of temenos (second century AD)

A. Delphi, Athenian stoa. Behind it, the polygonal wall and temple of Apollo VI (*c.* 510 BC). See p.131

B. Delphi: plan of temenos (*c.* 150 BC) (reconstruction by P. de la Coste-Messelière)

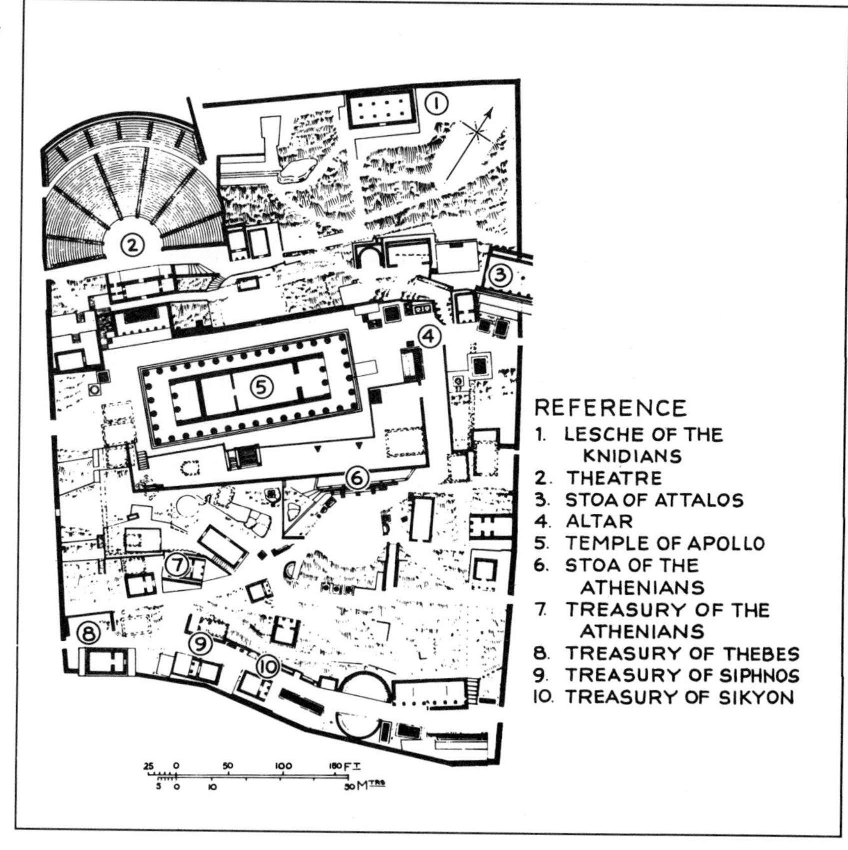

c. 370 BC	Temple of Asklepios, Epidaurus
after 350 BC	Temple of Athena Alea, Tegea
c. 336 BC	Temple of Zeus, Nemea

DORIC TEMPLES IN SICILY AND SOUTHERN ITALY

c. 565 BC	Temple of Apollo, Syracuse
c. 550–530 BC	Temple 'C', Selinus
c. 530 BC	The 'Basilica', Paestum (pp. 137E,H,141K)
c. 520–450 BC	The Great Temple of Apollo (G.T.), Selinus (p. 141L)
c. 510 BC	Temple of 'Ceres', Paestum (p. 114B)
c. 510–409 BC	Temple of Zeus Olympius, Agrigentum (p. 137J,K,L)
480 BC	Temple of Athena, Syracuse
c. 460 BC	Temple of 'Neptune', Paestum (pp. 114C, 137A,B,D,G,138)
c. 424–416 BC	Temple at Segesta, Sicily

The **Heraion, Olympia** (pp. 132, 137C,F), dedicated to Hera, illustrates the process of transition from timber construction to stone. It stands on a platform of two steps, measuring 51.2m × 19.6m (168 ft × 64 ft 6 in). As usual with early temples, it is long in proportion to its width. The thick naos walls are of ashlar stone to a height of 1.1 m (3ft 6in), but all the upper parts of the walls were of sun-dried brick, strengthened with wooden framing. Both internal and external columns were originally of wood, but were replaced with stone from time to time over a period of centuries. Thus they vary very much in their details and are either monolithic or built-up in a varying number of courses or 'drums'. The entablature remained always of timber, and the antae and the door casings were also of wood.

The **'Basilica', Paestum** (*c.* 530 BC) (pp. 141K, 137E,H), in reality a temple of Argive Hera, is unusual in being enneastyle, the central line of eight columns in the naos dividing the width of the temple into four parts and providing support for the roof timbers. For this reason too, the ambulatory is wide at the sides and the temple consequently almost pseudo-dipteral. The columns have a pronounced diminution and entasis, and the capitals are heavy and wide-spreading. A peculiarity of this temple and the neighbouring **Temple of 'Ceres'** (in fact, Athena) (*c.* 510 BC) is the decorative treatment of the trachelion, which shows Ionic influence.

The **Temple of Zeus Olympius, Agrigentum** (*c.* 510–409 BC) (p. 137J,K,L), also is of unique and freakish design, with a heptastyle, pseudo-peripteral arrangement and a plan with a central naos and two slightly narrower flanking apartments. At the west a portion of the naos was cut off to form a sanctuary. The temple is now a ruin. That there were pediments over the ends of the building is clear from an ancient description and from surviving fragments. The enormous attached, external columns, 4 m (13 ft 3 in) in diameter and over 17 m (56 ft) high, show traces of Ionic influence with mouldings across the base. In the upper portion of the screen wall, between the outer columns, were giant 'Atlantes', sculptured figures 7.6 m (25 ft) high, giving intermediate support to the massive entablature. The coarse stone was finished with a thin coating of fine marble stucco.

The **Temple of Aphaia, Aegina** (*c.* 500 BC) (pp. 135, 136), on an island about 40 km (25 miles) from Athens, is one of a group of temples in the area of the Saronic gulf – namely the 'old temple' of Athena at Athens (final version, *c.* 525 BC), Apollo at the town of Aegina (*c.* 510 BC), Poseidon at Calauria, on the island of Poros, and Poseidon at Hermione – which have proportions, width to length, of about 1:2 only. The Temple of Aphaia is hexastyle, but has only twelve flanking columns with a double range of interior columns separated simply by an architrave. All exterior columns had monolithic shafts, except three adjacent ones on the north side, which were built up in drums after the naos had been completed. The pediment sculptures, the elaborately carved acroteria, the antefixae, and the roof slabs over the pediments and eaves were in Parian marble; the rest of the roof tiles were of terracotta. The pediments contained remarkable sculptures which are clearly of different dates, the western pediment *c.* 500 BC, the eastern some 20 years or so later (though replacing an earlier group which was finally placed at ground level in the sanctuary). Most of the temple was of local limestone, usually treated with a coat of marble stucco.

The **Temple of Zeus, Olympia** (*c.* 470 BC) (pp. 132, 147A), designed by Libon of Elis, belongs to the phase of the developed, mainland temples of the fifth century BC. Continuity of pattern and formal organisation were achieved in what is arguably the finest manifestation of the Doric temple. It was orthodox in arrangement but grand in its dimensions – 27.7 m × 62.3 m (90 ft 9 in × 204 ft 4 in) over the stylobate – as befitted the supremacy of the god and the location. Its ratios – column height to spacing 2:1 – are simpler than those of the Parthenon, and in comparison the order is very heavy. Again it was built mostly of coarse limestone, faced with marble stucco, but the sculptured pediments were of Parian marble, as were the carved metopes over the inner porches,

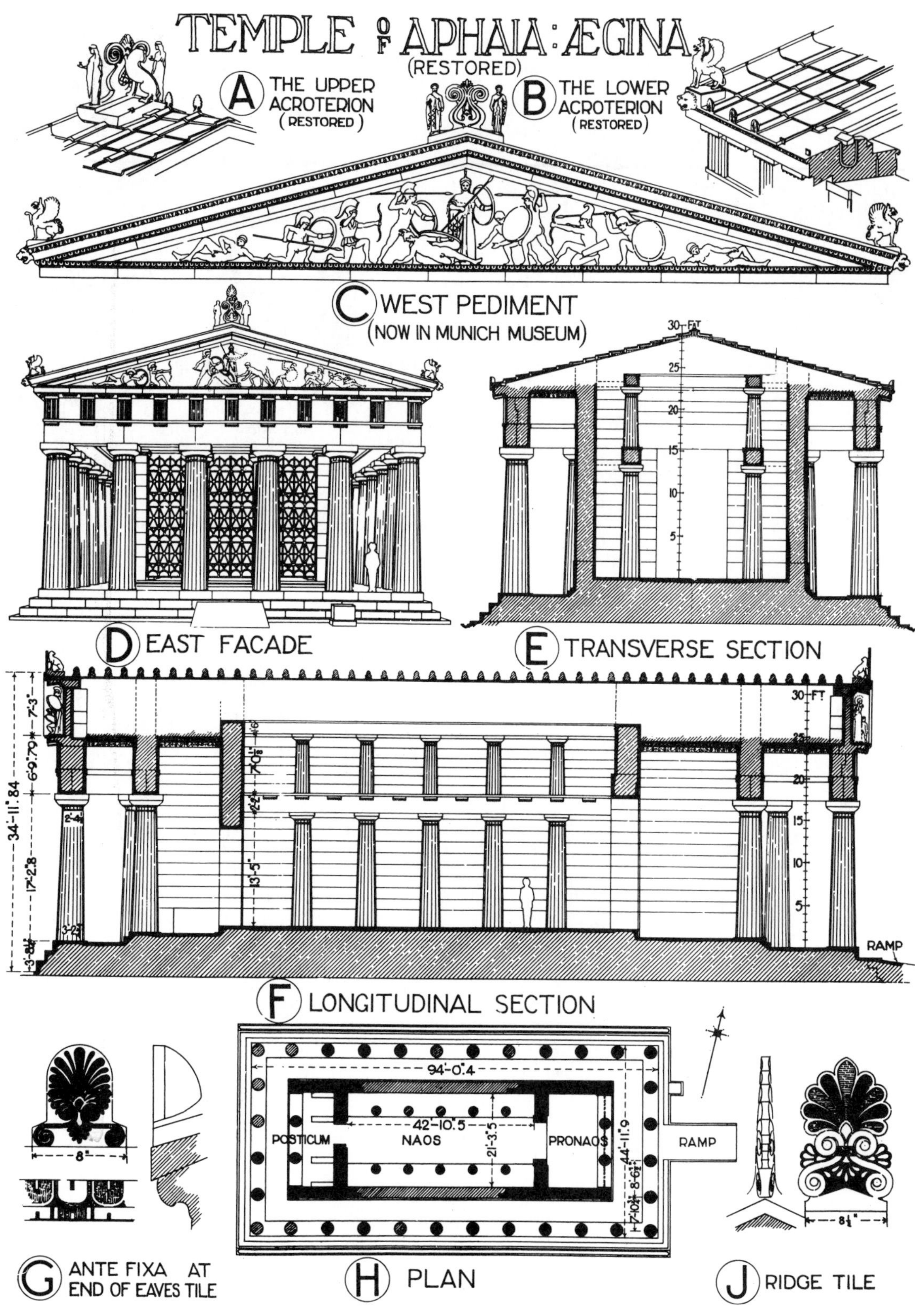
TEMPLE OF APHAIA : ÆGINA
(RESTORED)
A THE UPPER ACROTERION (RESTORED)
B THE LOWER ACROTERION (RESTORED)
C WEST PEDIMENT (NOW IN MUNICH MUSEUM)
D EAST FACADE
E TRANSVERSE SECTION
F LONGITUDINAL SECTION
RAMP
94'-0.4
42'-10.5
21'-3.5
44'-11.9
POSTICUM
NAOS
PRONAOS
RAMP
G ANTE FIXA AT END OF EAVES TILE
H PLAN
J RIDGE TILE

A. Temple of Aphaia, Aegina (*c.* 500 BC). See p.134

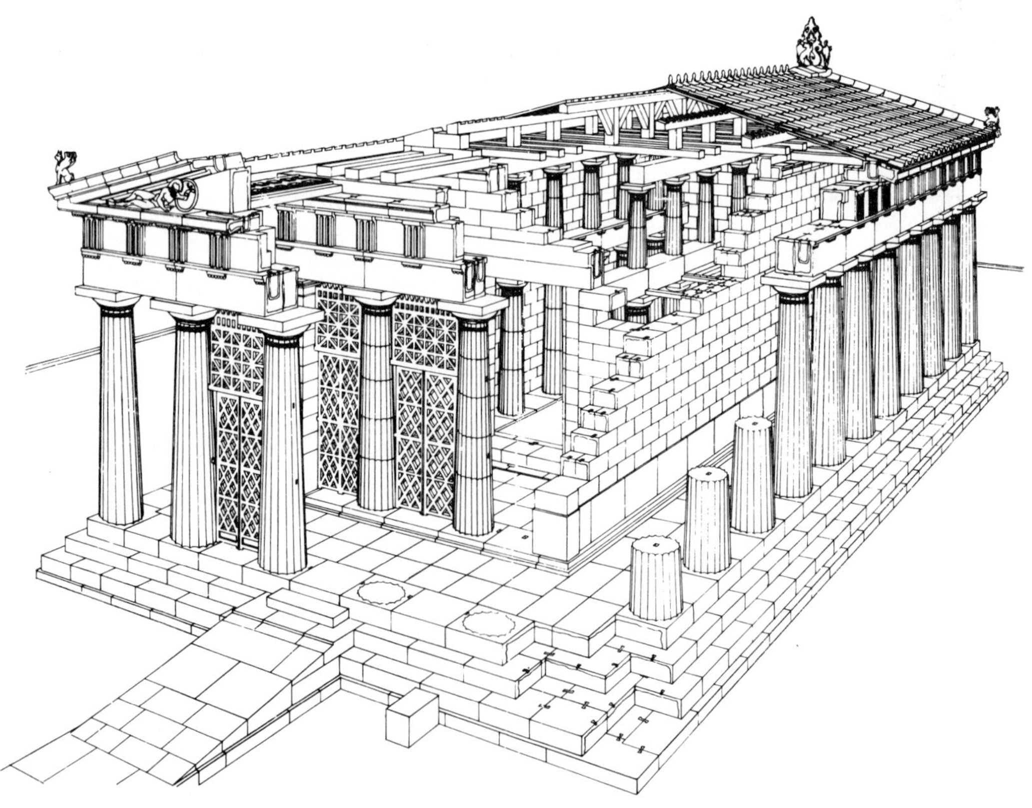

B. Temple of Aphaia, Aegina; sectional view, restored

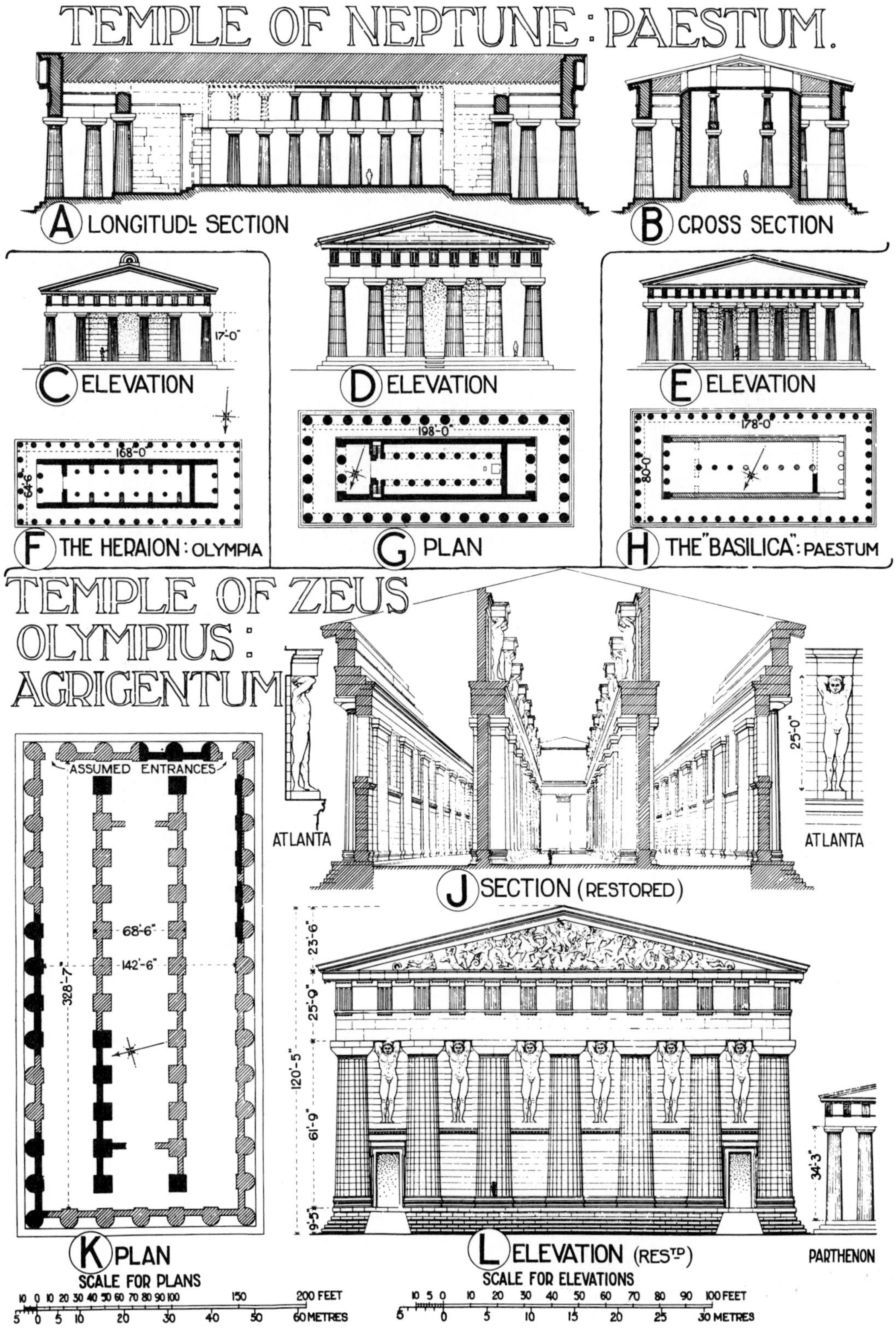
TEMPLE OF NEPTUNE : PAESTUM.
A LONGITUDL SECTION
B CROSS SECTION
C ELEVATION
17'-0"
D ELEVATION
E ELEVATION
168'-0"
64'-6"
198'-0"
178'-0"
80'-0"
F THE HERAION : OLYMPIA
G PLAN
H THE "BASILICA" : PAESTUM
TEMPLE OF ZEUS OLYMPIUS : AGRIGENTUM
ATLANTA
25'-0"
ATLANTA
J SECTION (RESTORED)
ASSUMED ENTRANCES
68'-6"
142'-6"
328'-7"
23'-6"
25'-9"
120'-5"
61'-9"
9'-5"
34'-3"
K PLAN
L ELEVATION (RESTD)
PARTHENON
SCALE FOR PLANS
10 0 10 20 30 40 50 60 70 80 90 100 150 200 FEET
5 0 5 10 20 30 40 50 60 METRES
SCALE FOR ELEVATIONS
10 5 0 10 20 30 40 50 60 70 80 90 100 FEET
5 0 5 10 15 20 25 30 METRES

A. Temple of 'Neptune', Paestum (*c.* 460 BC). See p.142

B., Temple of 'Neptune', showing superimposed columns

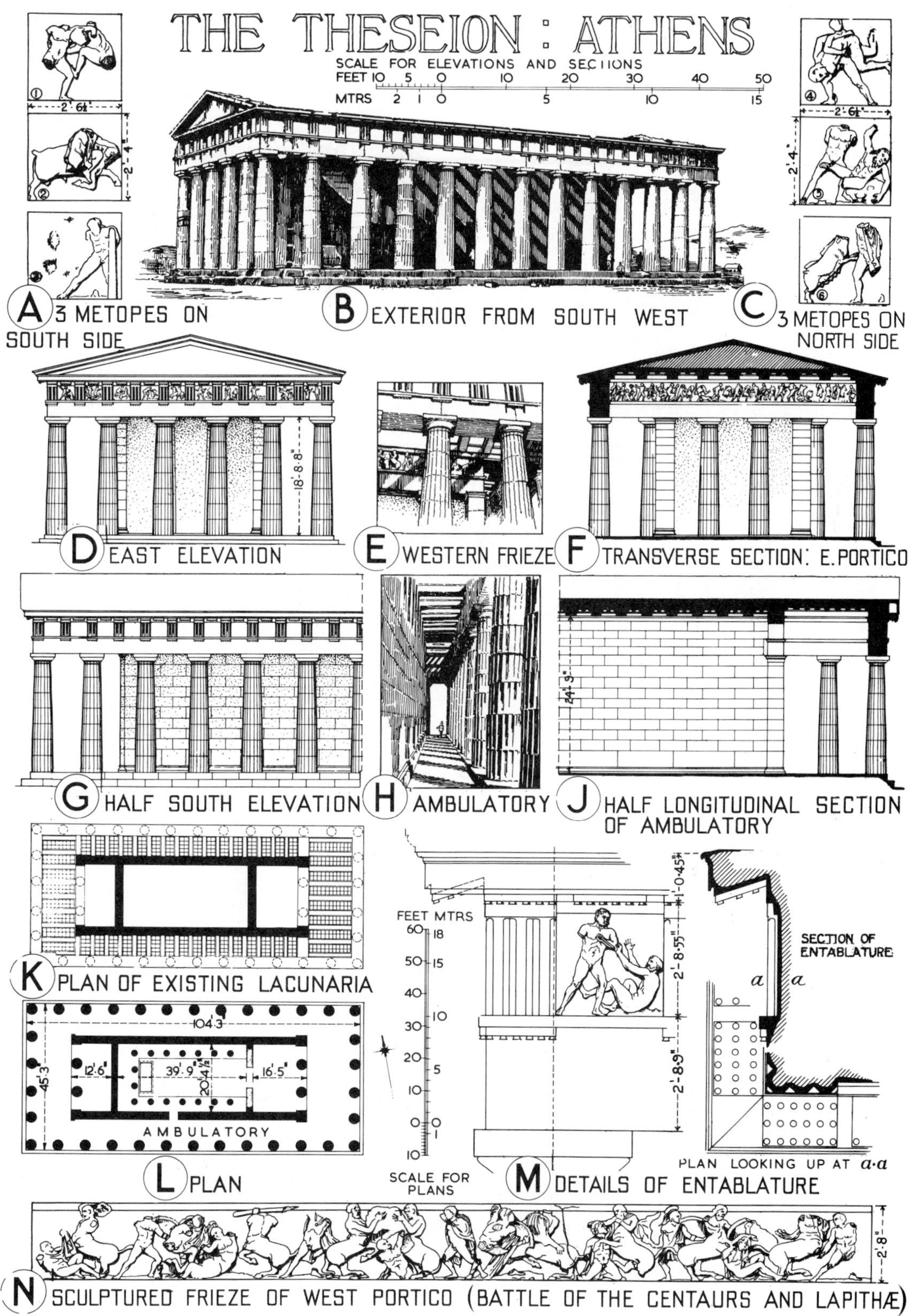
THE THESEION : ATHENS
SCALE FOR ELEVATIONS AND SECTIONS
FEET 10 5 0 10 20 30 40 50
MTRS 2 1 0 5 10 15
A 3 METOPES ON SOUTH SIDE
B EXTERIOR FROM SOUTH WEST
C 3 METOPES ON NORTH SIDE
D EAST ELEVATION
E WESTERN FRIEZE
F TRANSVERSE SECTION: E. PORTICO
G HALF SOUTH ELEVATION
H AMBULATORY
J HALF LONGITUDINAL SECTION OF AMBULATORY
K PLAN OF EXISTING LACUNARIA
L PLAN
AMBULATORY
SCALE FOR PLANS
FEET MTRS
SECTION OF ENTABLATURE
PLAN LOOKING UP AT a·a
M DETAILS OF ENTABLATURE
N SCULPTURED FRIEZE OF WEST PORTICO (BATTLE OF THE CENTAURS AND LAPITHÆ)

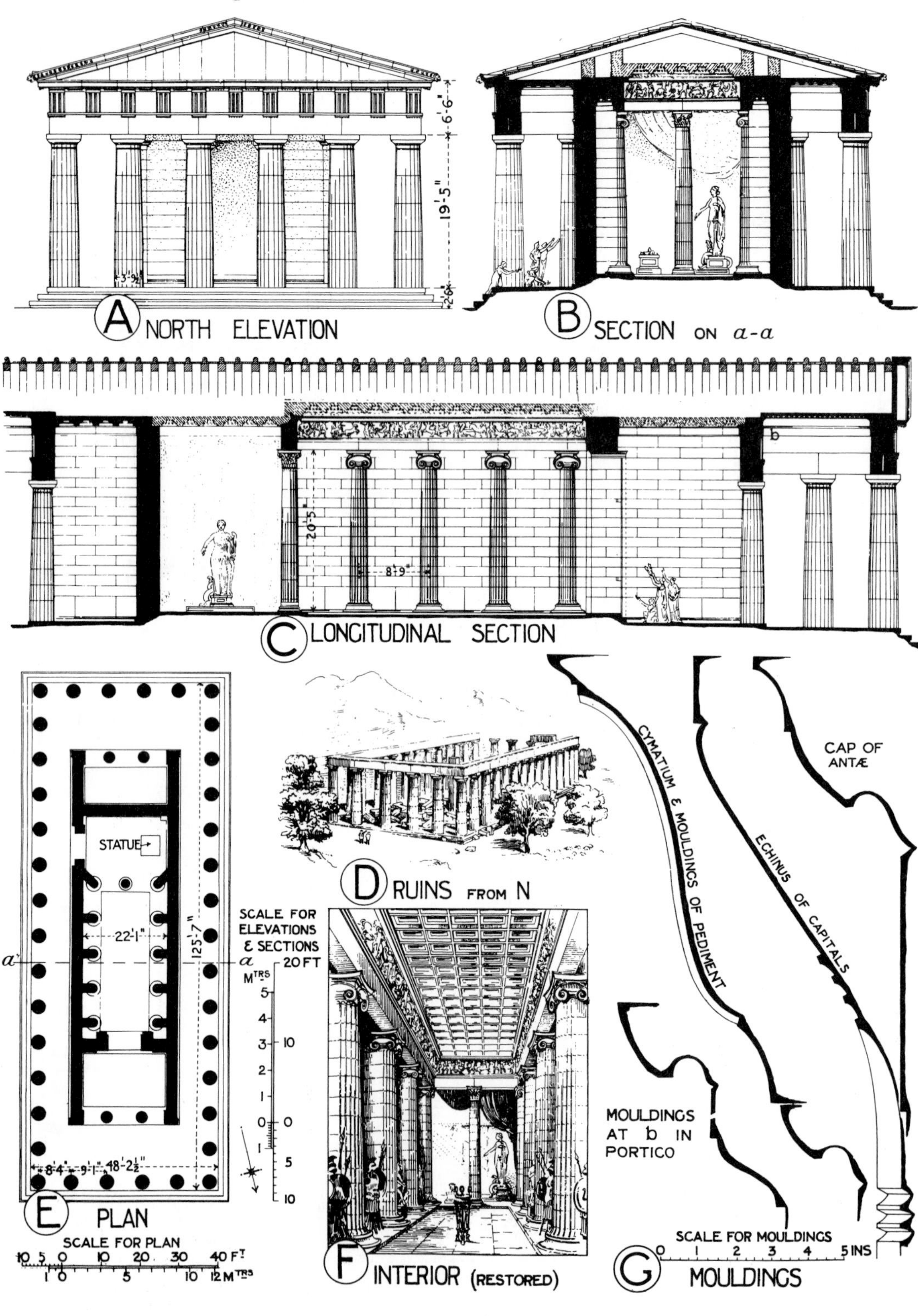
TEMPLE OF APOLLO EPICURIUS : BASSÆ
6'-6"
19'-5"
3'-9½"
2'-6"
A NORTH ELEVATION
B SECTION ON a-a
20'-5"
8'-9"
b
C LONGITUDINAL SECTION
STATUE
22'-1"
125'-7"
a
a
8'-4" 9'-1" 48'-2½"
E PLAN
SCALE FOR PLAN
10 5 0 10 20 30 40 FT
1 0 5 10 12 MTRS
D RUINS FROM N
SCALE FOR ELEVATIONS & SECTIONS
20 FT
MTRS
5
4
3 10
2
1
0 0
1
5
10
F INTERIOR (RESTORED)
CYMATIUM & MOULDINGS OF PEDIMENT
ECHINUS OF CAPITALS
CAP OF ANTÆ
MOULDINGS AT b IN PORTICO
SCALE FOR MOULDINGS
0 1 2 3 4 5 INS
G MOULDINGS

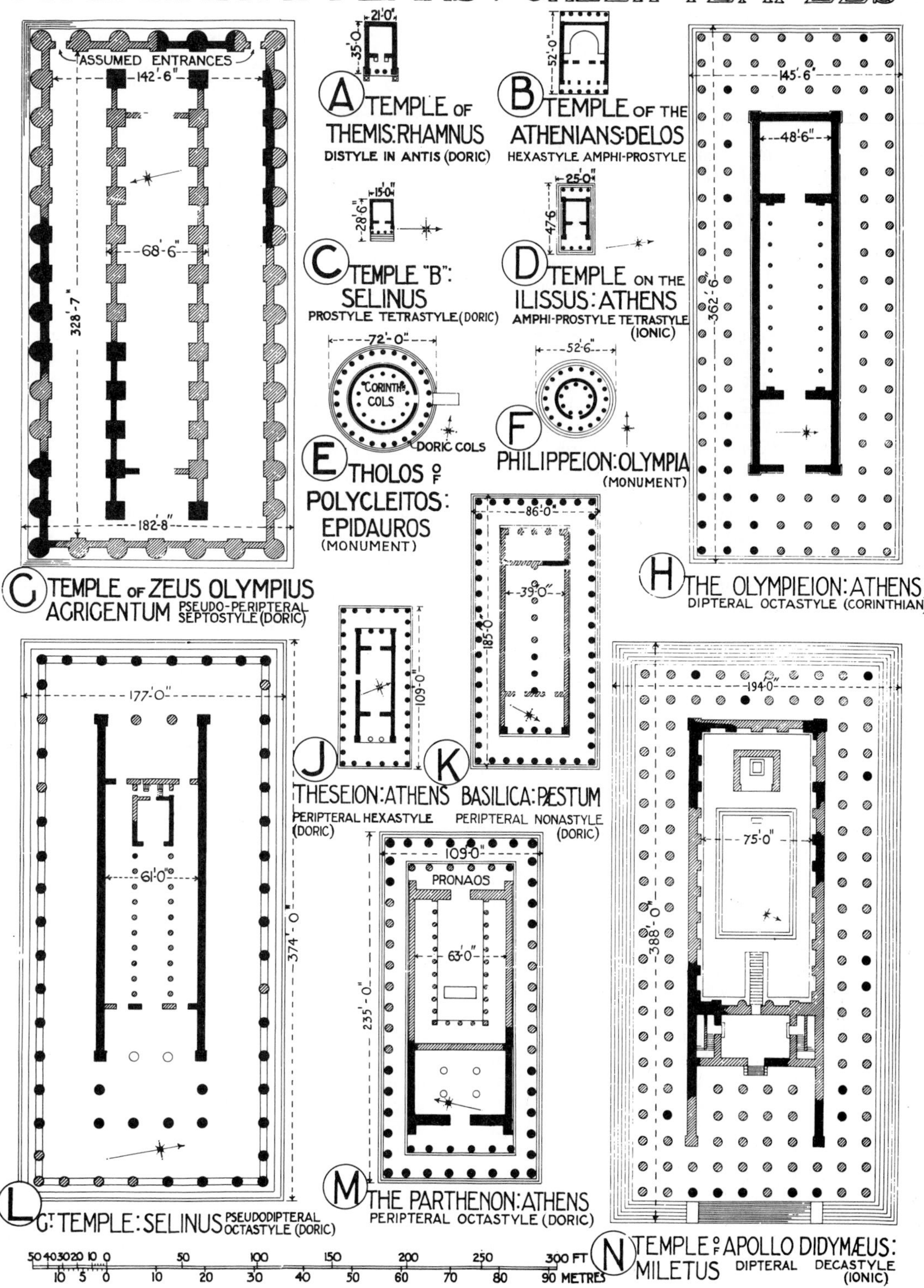
COMPARATIVE PLANS OF GREEK TEMPLES
ASSUMED ENTRANCES
142'-6"
68'-6"
328'-7"
182'-8"
G TEMPLE OF ZEUS OLYMPIUS AGRIGENTUM PSEUDO-PERIPTERAL SEPTOSTYLE (DORIC)
21'-0"
35'-0"
A TEMPLE OF THEMIS: RHAMNUS
DISTYLE IN ANTIS (DORIC)
52'-0"
B TEMPLE OF THE ATHENIANS: DELOS
HEXASTYLE AMPHI-PROSTYLE
15'-0"
28'-6"
C TEMPLE "B": SELINUS
PROSTYLE TETRASTYLE (DORIC)
25'-0"
47'-6"
D TEMPLE ON THE ILISSUS: ATHENS
AMPHI-PROSTYLE TETRASTYLE (IONIC)
72'-0"
CORINTH. COLS
DORIC COLS
E THOLOS OF POLYCLEITOS: EPIDAUROS
(MONUMENT)
52'-6"
F PHILIPPEION: OLYMPIA
(MONUMENT)
145'-6"
48'-6"
362'-6"
H THE OLYMPIEION: ATHENS
DIPTERAL OCTASTYLE (CORINTHIAN)
86'-0"
39'-0"
185'-0"
109'-0"
J THESEION: ATHENS
PERIPTERAL HEXASTYLE (DORIC)
K BASILICA: PÆSTUM
PERIPTERAL NONASTYLE (DORIC)
177'-0"
61'-0"
374'-0"
L GT TEMPLE: SELINUS PSEUDODIPTERAL OCTASTYLE (DORIC)
109'-0"
PRONAOS
63'-0"
235'-0"
M THE PARTHENON: ATHENS
PERIPTERAL OCTASTYLE (DORIC)
194'-0"
75'-0"
388'-0"
N TEMPLE OF APOLLO DIDYMÆUS: MILETUS
DIPTERAL DECASTYLE (IONIC)
50 40 30 20 10 0 50 100 150 200 250 300 FT
10 5 0 10 20 30 40 50 60 70 80 90 METRES

the sima and all the roof slabs. The sculpture of the pediment achieved a serenity and composure of supreme monumental quality. The external metopes, however, were not carved. About 431 BC the temple received the colossal gold-and-ivory statue by Phidias, who had been exiled from Athens. Inside the naos, once again, were superimposed colonnades. Fragments of large marble tiles, with elliptical holes through which light was admitted to the roof space, have been found on the site. During the fifth century AD the building was wrecked by an earthquake.

The **Temple of 'Neptune', Paestum** (actually dedicated to Hera) (*c.* 460 BC) (p. 114C, 137A,B,D,G, 138), is one of the best preserved of all Greek temples. Though more mature than the three last-named temples from Doric western territory – the two at Paestum, and that at Agrigentum – the plan is still rather long and the order heavy. The columns are about 8.8 m (29 ft) high and thus 4.3 times their lower diameter of 2 m (6 ft 9 in). The temple is peripteral hexastyle, with fourteen columns on the flanks, and has the normal crepidoma of three steps, pronaos, naos and opisthodomos. Near the entrance, steps led to the roof space. The columns in the naos, preserved almost intact, are in a double tier, the upper separated as usual from the lower by a stone architrave rather than a full entablature.

The **Temple of Hephaestus ('Theseion'), Athens** (pp. 130C, 139), begun 449 BC, is very well preserved externally. It was converted into a church by the Byzantine Greeks who, however, gutted the naos, constructed an apse at the east end and gave the temple its present concrete vault. The plan has a distinctive arrangement, the east porch being aligned with the third columns on the flanks. As in the Parthenon, over the porch the Doric frieze is replaced by a continuous Ionic frieze. The architrave, more suitably, has a continuous moulding at the top, rather than regulae and guttae. The building is almost wholly of Pentelic marble, except the lowest of the three steps, which is limestone. The east facade metopes and the first on each flank were carved with scenes depicting the deeds of Theseus (whence the erroneous popular name for the temple, the Theseion). The plan was altered during construction: the rear wall of the cella was moved, and a decorative inner colonnade was added. There was a large base for two cult statues of Hephaestus and Athena.

The **Temples of Poseidon at Sounion** and **Nemesis at Rhamnus** (along with the **Temple of Ares** originally in the 'deme' (village) of Acharnai north of Athens but moved to the agora of Athens in the first century BC) have design features which are similar to those of the Temple of Hephaestus. All four have connections with the war with Persia. If they are not by a single architect, they certainly fall within a single tradition. They may have been built in sequence or contemporaneously: they belong to the period between 449 BC and the outbreak of the Peloponnesian War. The temples of Poseidon and Ares are similar in size to that of Hephaestus and have 6 × 13 columns. The temple of Nemesis is smaller, 21.4 m × 10 m (70 ft × 33 ft), and has 6 × 12 columns. There are no internal colonnades. All are marble, but Poseidon and Nemesis took their stone from local quarries, not Pentelikos, and in both cases it is inferior in quality, with dark discolorations. Perhaps as a result of using inferior marble, the columns of Poseidon have no entasis, and only sixteen flutes.

The Athenian **Temple to Apollo** on the island of Delos (p. 114G) was built in 426 BC after the Athenians had 'purified' the island (by removing old burials) in expiation for the plague which had raged in their city in the early years of the Peloponnesian War. It lies between an earlier temple of the sixth century BC, and another begun after the Persian War, but abandoned when the headquarters of the Delian league was transferred to Athens in 454 BC. It was completed in the early third century BC. Space was restricted, so the temple was hexastyle amphiprostyle rather than peripteral. There is an interesting series of engaged pilasters, corresponding to the rear columns, along the back wall. It contained an abnormal horseshoe-shaped base for the cult statues. On this stood no fewer than seven statues. To enable all the statutes to get a decent view of the sanctuary outside, windows were provided on either side of the door. There was no horizontal ceiling; the underside of the ridged roof was visible from inside the cella, perhaps to give greater height for a large statue of Apollo on the centre of the base.

The **Temple of Apollo Epicurius at Bassae**, in Arcadia (p. 140), was begun in the fifth century BC but probably not completed till the fourth. Ictinus is named by Pausanias as the architect, but this must be regarded as dubious. A remarkable feature of this temple is the use of all three Greek Orders – Doric outside and Ionic and Corinthian within. The plan is hexastyle peripteral, with fifteen columns on the flanks, all built up in drums. Most of the building is of a hard, fine-grained grey limestone, but marble was used for the sculptures and the more decorative parts, including the ceilings over the pronaos, the opisthodomos, and the short sides of the ambulatory. The temple has other peculiarities. It faces north, instead of east (as did its predecessor) and the statue of Apollo was placed in an adyton, or inner sanctuary, partially screened off from the naos proper and lighted from a large door in the eastern wall. On both sides of the naos are Ionic half-columns, attached to spur walls, the recesses thus formed with the main naos wall having a stone, coffered ceiling. Between the adyton and the naos was a single, free-standing column, with a Corinthian capital (p. 120). The entablature was Ionic and continuous with that over the four Ionic half-columns on each side. The capitals of the latter were of unique design, with diagonal volutes, and they had high wide-flaring bases. The celebrated sculptured marble frieze over the half-columns, now in the British Museum, must have been poorly illuminated: it is 611 mm (24 in) high and 30.5 m (100 ft) long and represents battles of Centaurs and Lapiths, and Greeks and Amazons.

The **Temple of Asklepios at Epidaurus** was paid for by subscriptions collected throughout Greece for a cult which only developed in the fifth century BC, and then gained rapid and intense popularity. It was completed about 370 BC, and is interesting for the complete preservation, on an inscription, of the building contract. Externally it was conventional and rather dull, had 6 × 11 columns, and was built of limestone. There was no rear porch. None of the superstructure is standing.

The design of the **Temple of Athena Alea at Tegea** (*c.* 350 BC) is attributed to the fourth-century sculptor Scopas. It is built of marble, and its proportions recall those of its predecessor, destroyed in 384 BC.

The **Temple of Zeus at Nemea** was built some ten years later and also replaces an earlier building. It has 6 × 12 columns, six and three-eighths diameters in height, with very small capitals. It is built of poros limestone, and has free-standing internal Corinthian colonnades.

Other Ionic Temples

The principal examples of the Ionic Order were in Asia Minor and on the Greek mainland. Except for those already described they are listed below.

IONIC TEMPLES IN ASIA MINOR

c. 575 BC	Temple of Hera, Samos
c. 560 BC	Archaic Temple of Artemis, Ephesus (pp. 118A, 144)
c. 356 BC	Later Temple of Artemis, Ephesus (p. 144)
c. 334 BC	Temple of Athena Polias, Priene (p. 118F)

IONIC TEMPLES IN GREECE

c. 449 BC	Temple on the Ilissus, Athens (Temple of Artemis Agrotera) (p. 146A-F)

The **Temple of Hera, Samos**, an early peristyle temple, was first established at Samos in the seventh century BC, if not earlier, but was replaced by the sixth-century temple by the architect Rhoikos. It was dipteral octastyle, though the rear facade contained ten columns and had a deep portico. Scarcely finished, the building was destroyed by fire and replaced (*c.* 525 BC) by another, larger building measuring 54.6 m × 112.2 m (179 ft × 368 ft). The portico was octastyle, the rear facade had nine columns (enneastyle), and the double peristyle rows of twenty-four columns. The end colonnades were built with a third row of columns, making them tripteral. The colossal building was never completed.

The later **Temple of Artemis, Ephesus** (p. 144), was the fifth in succession to stand upon this famous site. The earliest had been relatively small; the immediate predecessor, the 'Archaic' temple (*c.* 560 BC), was burnt down in 356 BC and built anew in still more magnificent style, but on the same foundations and to an identical plan. The only substantial differences between the old and the new were in the details and the fact that the later temple stood on a platform of steps, about 2.7 m (9 ft) high, instead of a two-step crepidoma, as formerly. Yet owing to the scanty remains there are uncertainties about the arrangement of the plan, and several somewhat different restorations have been proposed. The temple was dipteral, octastyle at the front but perhaps enneastyle at the rear as at Samos. The object of an extra rear column would be to evade the serious difficulties of spanning the exceptionally wide central intercolumniation which, although preferred and traditional at the front, was not essential at the rear. The column spacings on the main front were progressively less wide from the centre outwards to the corners. The central span was more than 8.5 m (28 ft) and needed a marble architrave beam about 1.2 m (4 ft) deep. The temple was grand in its dimensions, though not the largest in Ionia. The entablature was relatively shallow, being of the usual Asiatic type, comprising architrave and dentilled cornice but no frieze. Equally characteristic are the deep pronaos with several pairs of columns within it, and the shallow opisthodomos which was probably absent in the archaic temple. It has been argued plausibly that the cella in both old and new temples was not roofed. About the internal arrangements of this temple, nothing is definitely known. The orientation is unusual, as for traditional reasons on this site the temple faced west instead of east. There were 117 columns altogether (interpretations differ), thirty-six of which bore sculptures on their lower parts. The preceding temple had similar sculptures, and fragments from both periods, along with pieces of corresponding capitals and shafts, make it possible to compare the early and late work at Ephesus (p. 118A,E). The building of the later temple extended well into the Hellenistic period. Like its predecessor, it ranked as one of the seven wonders of the Ancient World. The original designers were Demetrius and Paeonius of Ephesus, and probably Deinocrates who was later responsible for layingout the town plan of Alexandria. Famous sculptors, particularly Scopas, were employed in its decoration.

THE TEMPLE OF ARTEMIS: EPHESUS

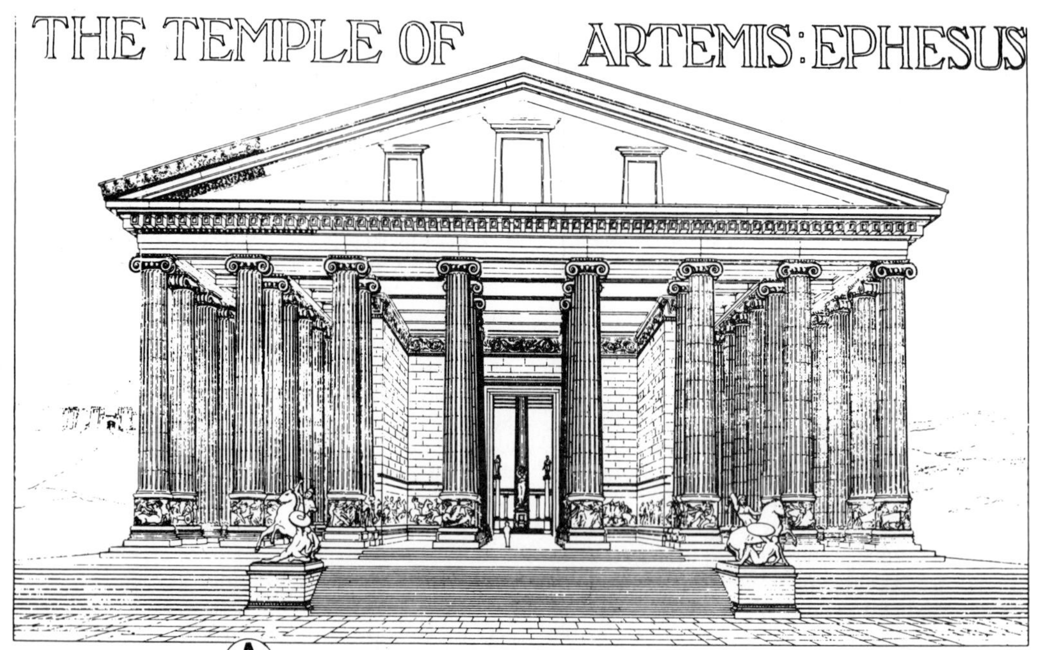

(A) RESTORED VIEW OF TEMPLE & TEMENOS: B.C. 356

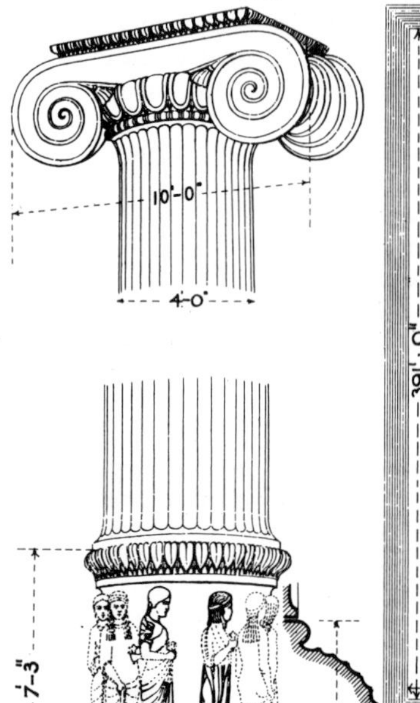

10'-0"
4'-0"
7'-3"
2'-9½"
BASE 2'-9½"

391'·0"
155'·0"
71'·0"
STATUE
NAOS
MOULDED BASES
SCULPTURED BASES
211'·0"

(B) PLAN

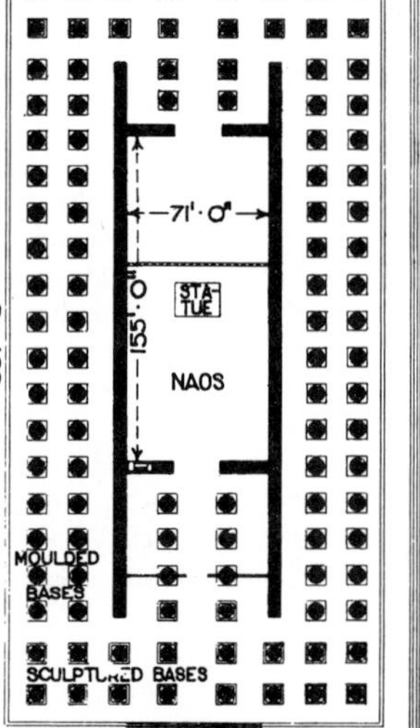

1'-8½"

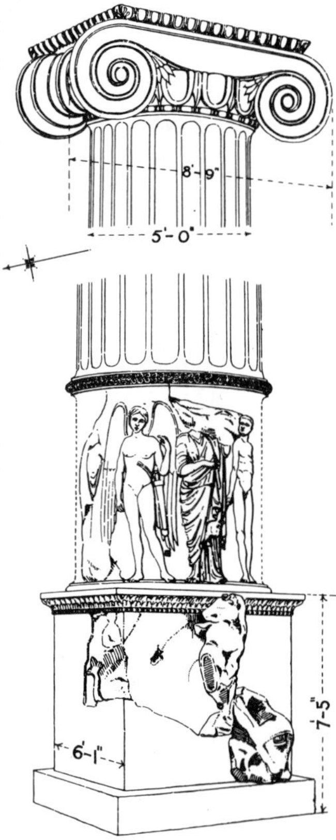

8'-9"
5'-0"
6'-1"
7'-5"

(C) COLUMN OF ARCHAIC TEMPLE : B.C. 550

(D) CARVING TO CYMATIUM.

(E) COLUMN OF LATER TEMPLE : B.C. 356.

The **Temple of Athena Polias, Priene** (p. 118F), is finely proportioned but more modest in plan and scale. Pythius, the architect, wrote a book about it. The plan is peripteral, 19.5 m × 37 m (64 ft × 122 ft) over the stylobate, with a hexastyle front and eleven columns on the sides, almost twice as long as it is broad. There is a broad pronaos and shallow opisthodomos, while the column bases have the now usual plinth. The two-part entablature still omitted the frieze. The colonnade was placed close to the cella walls, and the ceiling comprised a single row of large coffers carefully designed to take account of the foreshortened view from underneath.

The **Temple on the Ilissus, Athens** (p. 146), an amphiprostyle tetrastyle small temple, of Pentelic marble, measured about 6.1 m × 12.8 m (20 ft × 42 ft) 42 ft) over a three-step crepidoma. It was dedicated to Artemis Agrotera. It was similar to the temple of Athena Nikè on the Acropolis, but was built slightly earlier. It had a proper porch, however, with two columns in antis. It was converted into a church and was drawn and measured in the eighteenth century by Stuart and Revett, but was subsequently destroyed.

The **Temple of Apollo, Didyma**, near Miletus, was built in the late sixth century BC and destroyed by the Persians in 494 BC. Like Ephesus, its cella seems to have been unroofed. It was later rebuilt, to a similar plan, but enlarged somewhat and on a slightly different alignment: the later temple is described in Chapter 7.

Urban Architecture

Classical Greek cities were either the result of continuous growth, extending from prehistoric times through the Dark Age and Archaic periods, or created at a single moment, usually as the result of colonial settlement. The former had streets which followed lines of communication, curving and bending where necessary to avoid obstacles or to ease gradients; the latter generally had grid plans, with straight streets crossing at right angles, ignoring obstacles and becoming stairways where the gradients were too steep. Despite these differences, certain features and principles of arrangement are common to both.

Towns always had fixed boundaries. Already in the sixth century BC some were surrounded by fortifications, and these later became more frequent, but even where there were no walls the demarcation between interior and exterior was clear. There might be buildings such as temples outside, and, except for very privileged individuals, graves were always outside, often lining the roads that led away from the town. At times there were suburban houses, or rural farmhouses, but generally the Greeks preferred the safety and companionship of urban settlements, in villages if not in the principal cities.

In most Greek towns much of the available area was devoted to public rather than private use. The important gathering place was the agora, which was placed conveniently for communication, on flat ground and as easily accessible as possible from all directions. Coastal cities, such as Samos or Thasos, tended to place the agora by the harbour, for obvious reasons; otherwise it was sited in the centre.

The **Agora of Athens** (p. 147C) was situated on low-lying damp ground to the north of the Acropolis, which had been incorporated in the city in the early Archaic period. An essential stage in its development as the civic centre was the provision of effective drainage. The drain, built in superb polygonal masonry, runs near the western boundary of the agora. Civic and religious buildings were erected progressively around its perimeter. Most of those of the sixth century BC were architecturally nondescript, and were destroyed by the Persians in 479 BC. The sole survivor was the tiny **Stoa of the King** (stoa Basileia), a Doric building measuring 17.7 m × 7.2 m (58 ft × 23 ft 6 in) in which the Basileus (the king, elected annually in historical Athens) performed his official duties, which were religious and judicial.

Stoas proved useful buildings in the context of the agora. They provided shelter, and served many purposes, especially when they included rooms behind the colonnade. In addition, they were a way of embellishing the boundary of the agora, looking in towards the open space. Though early examples are separate, self-contained buildings, in time they came to give the agora the appearance of a colonnaded courtyard. More of them were built at Athens after the defeat of the Persians. On the north side the **Painted Stoa**, like the stoa of the King, was a simple colonnade between side walls, closed at the back, and with an inner colonnade to support the ridge. It housed a famous series of panel paintings depicting the victory of Marathon, and glorifying the role of Miltiades, father of the politician Cimon on whose behalf it was built in the 460s. Another Doric stoa, on the west side of the agora, the **Stoa of Zeus**, is a work of the later fifth century BC. This has two aisles, with projecting wings. The inner colonnade was Ionic. The aim seems to have been to echo the architecture and appearance of the temple of Hephaestus, standing on the nearby hill, the Kolonos Agoraios. Ionic columns were general for inner colonnades of stoas because they gave greater height, and supported, at much wider intervals, not a stone architrave, but the wooden ridge beam. Single-storey stoas did not normally have ceilings.

The third important stoa of the Classical agora at Athens, was placed on the southern boundary late in the fifth century BC. It measured 80.5 m × 14.9 m (264 ft × 49 ft), had a Doric colonnade, details of which are lost, and an inner colonnade, probably at double intervals and presumably Ionic. Behind the colonnades was a row of fifteen rooms each

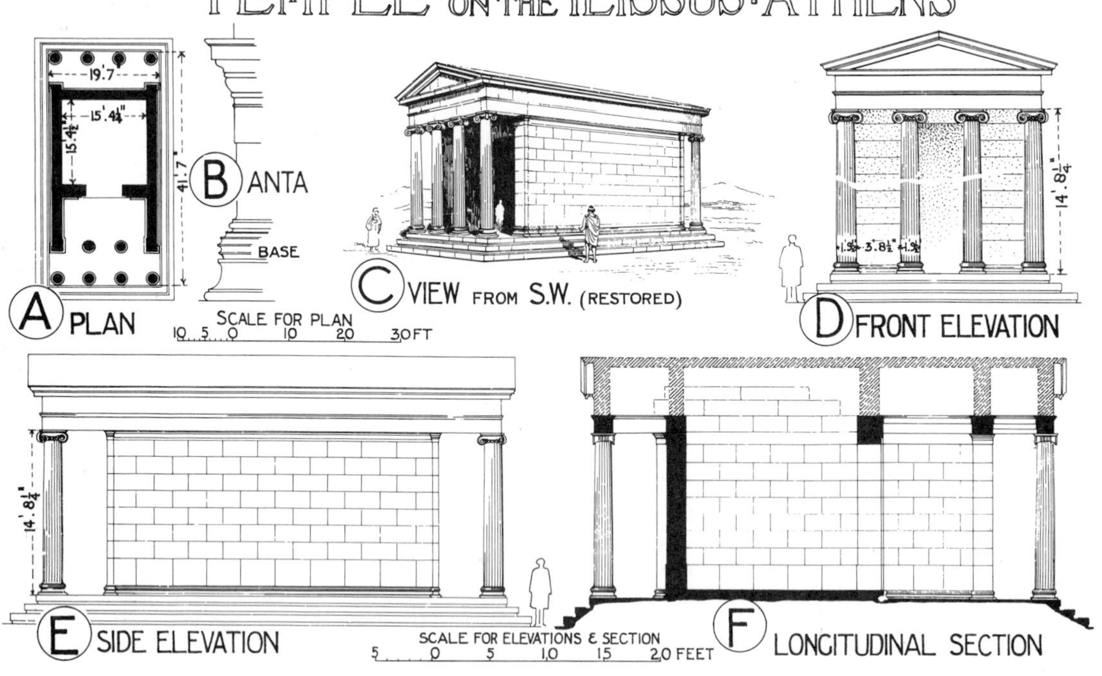

A. Temple of Athena Nikè (424 BC). See p.127

B. Athenian Treasury, Delphi (510 BC). See p.122

A. Temple of Zeus, Olympia (restored) (*c.* 470 BC). See p.134

B. Nereid Monument, Xanthos (*c.* 400 BC). See p.150

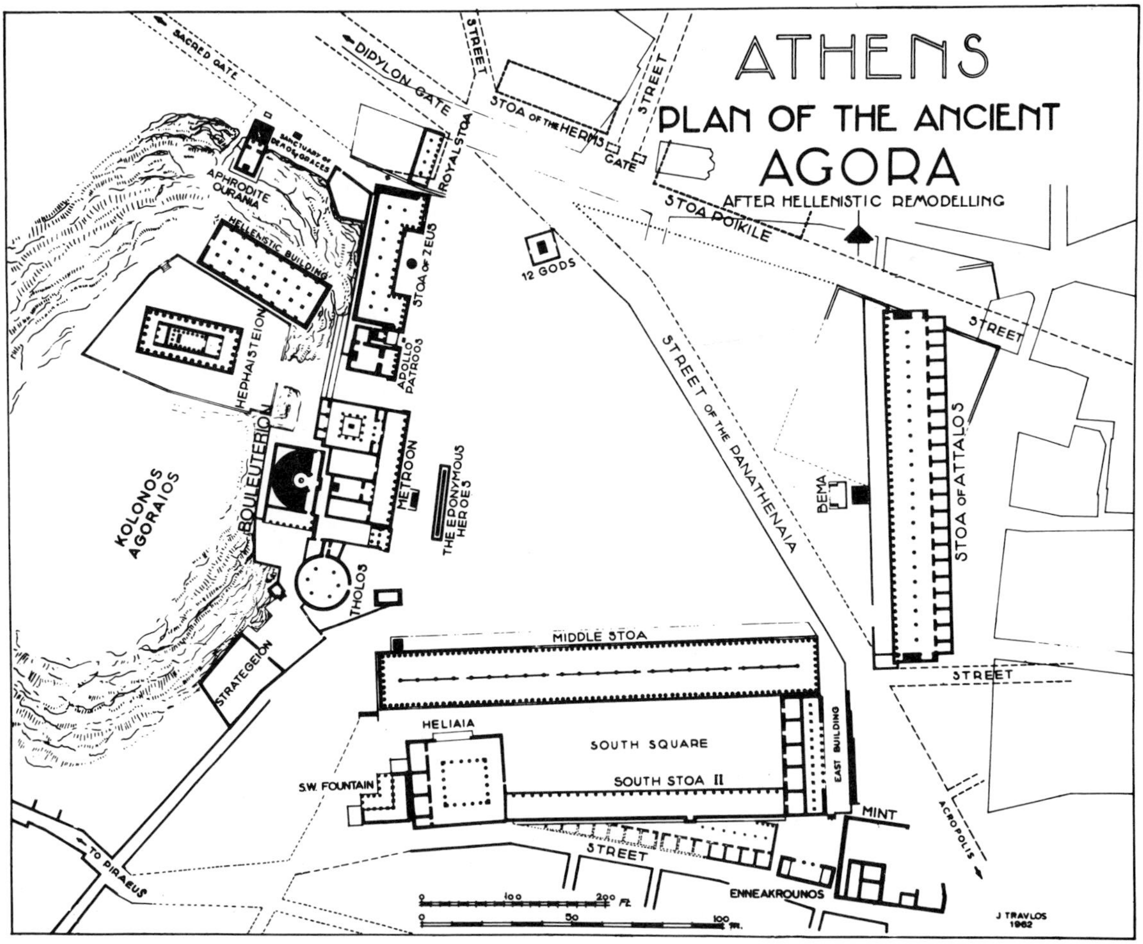

ATHENS
PLAN OF THE ANCIENT AGORA
AFTER HELLENISTIC REMODELLING

SACRED GATE
DIPYLON GATE
STREET
STOA OF THE HERMS
GATE
ROYAL STOA
SANCTUARY OF DEMOS & GRACES
APHRODITE OURANIA
HELLENISTIC BUILDING
STOA OF ZEUS
12 GODS
STOA POIKILE
STREET
HEPHAISTEION
APOLLO PATROOS
STREET OF THE PANATHENAIA
BOULEUTERION
METROON
THE EPONYMOUS HEROES
KOLONOS AGORAIOS
BEMA
STOA OF ATTALOS
THOLOS
STRATEGEION
MIDDLE STOA
STREET
HELIAIA
SOUTH SQUARE
SOUTH STOA II
EAST BUILDING
S.W. FOUNTAIN
MINT
STREET
TO PIRAEUS
ACROPOLIS
ENNEAKROUNOS
100 200 FT.
50 100 M.
J. TRAVLOS 1962

4.9 metres (16 ft) square, with off-centre doors and plinths round the walls to accommodate seven dining couches. The superstructure was of mud brick, the floors in rooms and colonnades were of beaten earth. Such cheaper forms of construction are frequently found in stoas and mean that they are rarely well preserved.

Other administrative buildings provided closed accommodation. On the west side were the **Bouleuterion** or council house and the **Tholos**. The council house held five hundred councillors who met in closed session. The original building was square, probably with windows set high in plain walls. The roof was pyramidal. The building was divided internally into an anteroom and an auditorium, which probably had straight rows of seats at its side and across the back. The Bouleuterion was built immediately after the expulsion of the Persians from Athens and was replaced at the end of the century by a rectangular building with a ridged roof, in which the auditorium had seats arranged in a nearly circular plan. Nothing but foundations of these buildings remains.

The Tholos was, as its name implies, a circular building. Though an official structure, its walls were of unbaked mud brick. The standing committee of the council, the prytaneis, when in office dined in this building at state expense. It is difficult to see how 50 dining couches could be readily accommodated to the plan, and it is possible that the prytaneis instead sat on chairs round the walls in the older (Homeric) manner. The roof supports (which were of wood) were arranged not, as might be expected, in a circle, but in an ellipse. The roof itself was conical, with scale-like tiles. It was built about 465 BC.

Two courtyard structures by the agora were the **Heliaea** (the meeting place of the jury court) on the south side, and, to the east, the **Shrine of Theseus**, a walled enclosure where Cimon buried the alleged bones of the legendary founder of Athens which he had unearthed on the island of Skyros in 472 BC. It must have been partly roofed (probably a peristyle court) for it contained famous wall paintings which would need to be sheltered.

Other colonnaded structures on the south side of the agora were the **fountain houses**, where a portico protected people drawing water, and kept the water cool. There were also other shrines (of Apollo Patroos and Hekate, for instance) and public buildings, such as the mint.

Generally speaking, the central area of the agora was free of buildings, but a long monument to the heroes who gave their names to the new tribes which formed the basis of the new democratic constitution introduced by Kleisthenes was placed near the great drain facing the old Bouleuterion; and there was, towards the north, a precinct fence (rather than a wall) surrounding an altar dedicated to the twelve Olympian gods. The agora of Athens is the most thoroughly excavated and so best known from the Classical period, and it is likely to be typical of those found in unplanned cities. That at Argos included a stoa with three wings, facing outwards to the north, east and west, and probably dating from the early fourth century BC.

Other public buildings in Classical Greek cities included gymnasia and stadia, and places for watching dramatic and related performances, which were generally part of religious ritual and, as we have seen, normally attached to sanctuaries. In the Classical period these were rarely monumental, though they began to develop in the fourth century BC; a discussion of them can be found in Chapter 7.

Private houses became more substantial in the Classical period, and were normally of the courtyard type. Literary sources refer to stone colonnades in the houses of the well-to-do, but wood was the normal material. Walls were of masonry or mud brick. The arrangement of rooms was generally asymmetrical. Two storeys were common, both in town houses and the few known rural houses. Typical Athenian examples are the houses excavated in the area immediately south of the agora; they vary surprisingly in plan, and are obviously responding to the often irregular shapes of their sites. More regular, because it was built at an unrestricted site, is the rural **Dema house** of about 420 BC, a farm building where the courtyard was essentially a forecourt with a high outer wall: the principal rooms were arranged in two storeys along the opposite side. Ground-floor rooms included formal dining rooms (andrones). Entrance to all these houses was, wherever possible, indirect, so that it was not possible to see into the courtyard from outside.

The most extensive series of houses of the Classical period are those excavated at the north Aegean town of **Olynthus**, which developed considerably in the late fifth and early fourth centuries BC; a new area was laid out in a regular grid plan. Here each house was allotted a regular square building plot, within which the owner could build as he pleased, so that no two plans are alike, though all include courtyards and have the principal rooms on the north side, facing south (for shelter against the cold Balkan winds of winter). Otherwise, there is no distinction here from the arrangements at Athens, or from the courtyard houses which have been discovered at the west Greek cities, such as Himera in Sicily.

Classical tombs were not usually monumental. Those at Athens are often grouped in family precincts (periboloi), which may include walled banks, rectangular or, in rare instances, circular, into which the ashes of the dead were deposited. On these mounds were erected markers, which in the fifth century BC were narrow upright slabs, perhaps surmounted by an acroterion, while those of the fourth century BC became wider, were decorated with sculpture (a

LION TOMB AT CNIDUS
(RESTORED)
18'-0"
13'-10"
5'-6"
39'-5"
26'-3"
17'-3"
A SIDE ELEVATION
B SECTION
C FRONT ELEVATION
WALL
101'-0"
5 0 10 20 30 FT
1 0 1 2 3 4 5 6 7 8 MTRS
SCALE FOR PLANS
5 0 5 10 FT
1 0 1 2 3 MTRS
SCALE FOR ELEVATIONS
D PLAN OF BASE
E KEY PLAN
F PLAN OF PERISTYLE
LID RAISED ON PROPS
ABT 7'-0"
LID
5'-6"
10'-4"
G H
THE "ALEXANDER" SARCOPHAGUS: SIDON
ABT 5'-6"
ABT 9'-5"
J TOMB AT CNIDUS
K TOMB OF THE WEEPERS: SIDON

tradition which descended from the Parthenon workshops) and were surrounded with a quasi-architectural frame.

Monumental tombs belonged to foreign dynasts, such as the rulers of the Lycian cities in southern Asia Minor or (the most famous of all) Mausolus, Ruler of Caria, a non-Greek region in the vicinity of Miletus. By the fourth century BC the proximity of important Greek cities had led to the gradual Hellenisation of the adjacent non-Greek communities. Mausolus became powerful in the second quarter of the fourth century BC, dominating the neighbouring Greek cities. He made Halicarnassus his capital and replanned it. When he died in 353 BC his tomb, the **Mausoleum**, was constructed in the city itself by his widow Artemisia. It stood in an open precinct on the slopes above the centre of the town, and was built from white marble. It consisted of a high rectangular podium, containing the burial chamber, surmounted by a colonnade carrying a stepped pyramidal roof which supported the statue of a four-horse chariot. It derives from an Asian tradition of monumental tomb-building, typified earlier by the vast chambered tumuli of the Phrygian and Lydian kings, and the tombs on high podia of the Lycian dynasts, such as the slightly earlier **Nereid Monument at Xanthos** (p. 147B). There is also a possible influence from the Tomb of Cyrus the Great, founder of the Persian Empire – Mausolus was nominally a local governor (satrap) under the jurisdiction of the Persian king. The Mausoleum was destroyed in 1402 by the Knights of St John to provide building material for their castle at Halicarnassus (Budrum). Recent studies have shown that the podium measured 38.4 m × 32 m (120 ft × 100 ft), decreasing in three 'steps' to a stylobate of 32 m × 26 m (105 ft × 85 ft 4 in) and decorated with sculpture at each step, including a frieze under the stylobate. The columns were Ionic, with a typical eastern Greek entablature with dentils rather than a continuous frieze. The roof decreased by twenty-four steps to the base of the enormous chariot group which crowned the monument. This probably contained statues, representing either Mausolus and Artemisia, or Apollo. The statues in the British Museum, often described as Mausolus and Artemisia, come from a series of statues, possibly representing the ancestors of the dynasty, which stood between the Ionic columns. This device was taken from the Nereid monument and repeated later in a sarcophagus in the royal cemetery at Sidon: decorated in the form of a roofed Ionic building, the **'Sarcophagus of the Mourning Women'** (p. 149K) also has a frieze beneath the colonnade. The architect of the Mausoleum was Pythius, in collaboration with Satyros. Pythius later became the architect of the temple of Athena Polias at Priene. The sculptural decorations were the work of fourth-century sculptors Scopas, Bryaxis, Timotheus and Leochares.

The Mausoleum not only became the generic term for monumental tombs, but inspired later imitators and derivatives. In the regions adjacent to Halicarnassus are two important Hellenistic examples, the **Lion Tomb at Cnidus** (p. 149A–F), perhaps of the second century BC, and the third-century **Mausoleum at Belevi**, in the territory of Ephesus. There is an early Roman example, smaller in scale but still monumental, at Mylasa, the original capital of Caria.

Another series of tombs which may have been inspired by the Mausoleum are very different in appearance. These are the tombs constructed for the members of the Argead dynasty which ruled Macedonia and are located at the old Macedonian centre of Aegeae, the modern Vergina. In the Mausoleum the burial chamber was situated deep in the podium; the form of the roof is uncertain, but it was probably a corbel vault which also seems to have been used in the Lion Tomb. In Macedon, earlier burials had been in pits, lined with stone or timber, covered with branches and with a small mound heaped on top. In these, of course, the woodwork soon decayed but in the first half of the fourth century BC the philosopher Democritus had described the principle of the keystone vault which was adopted by the Macedonian kings to give a durable roof to their burial pits. It was combined with the forms of conventional Greek trabeated architecture by the addition to the chamber of a facade, in the form of an engaged order with half-columns and entablature. An early example is the unplundered tomb found by Professor Andronikos in 1978, which is beyond reasonable doubt the **Tomb of Philip II**. This has two chambers, whose vaults, though continuous in line, were constructed separately. In front of them, the facade has two engaged Doric half-columns in antis with full entablature, but supporting a rectangular screen in the form of a painted frieze, rather than a pediment, in front of the vault. Somewhat illogically, later tombs combine the pediment screen with the vaulted roof. This tomb and the considerable series of later Macedonian tombs which derive from the royal burials demonstrate the competence of Macedonian architects in vaulted and arched construction. Being buried, the tombs preserve in almost perfect condition, and with the original tones, the painted decoration applied habitually to the Greek orders.

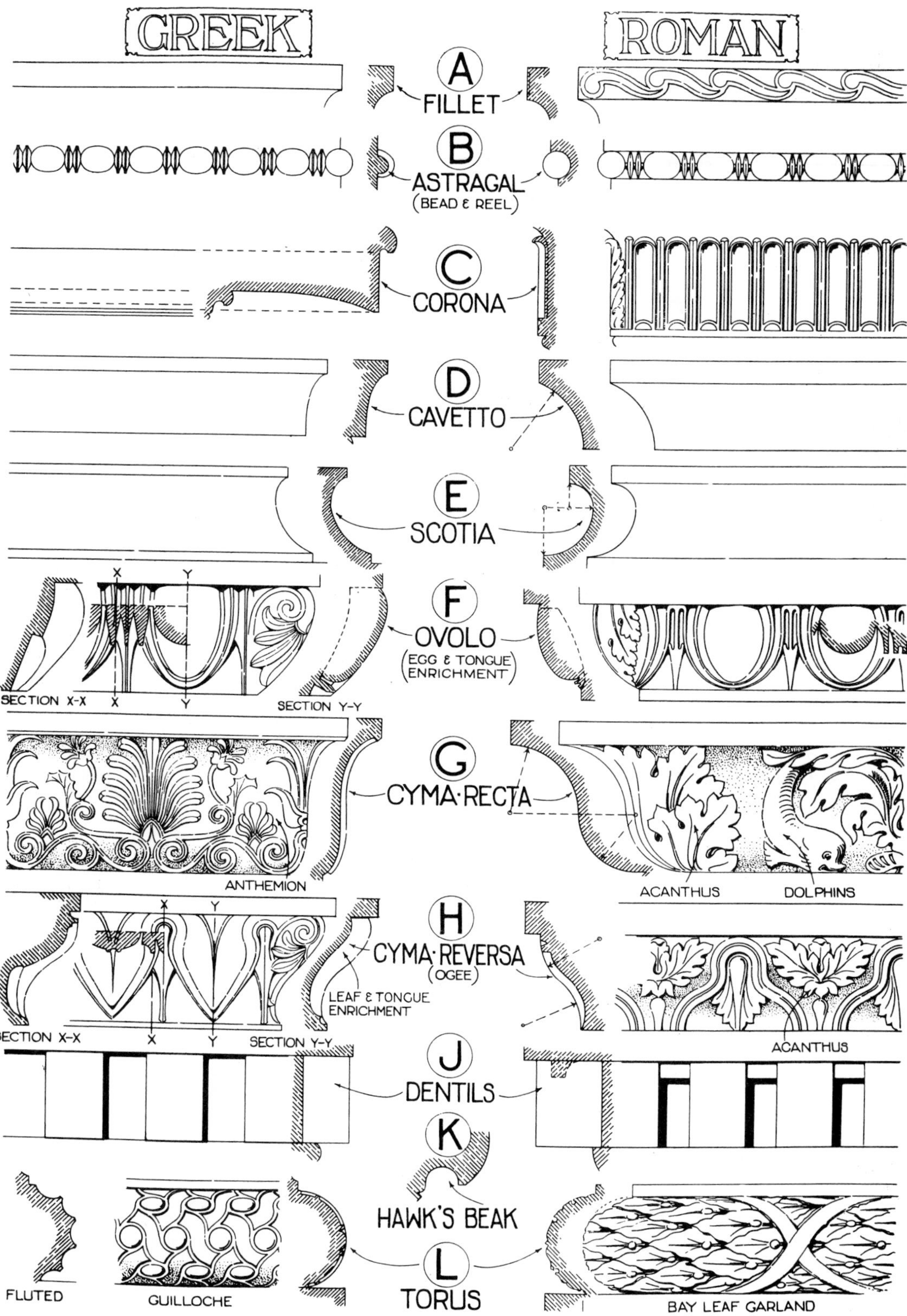
GREEK
ROMAN
A
FILLET
B
ASTRAGAL
(BEAD & REEL)
C
CORONA
D
CAVETTO
E
SCOTIA
X
Y
F
OVOLO
(EGG & TONGUE ENRICHMENT)
SECTION X-X
SECTION Y-Y
G
CYMA·RECTA
ANTHEMION
ACANTHUS
DOLPHINS
H
CYMA·REVERSA
(OGEE)
LEAF & TONGUE ENRICHMENT
SECTION X-X
SECTION Y-Y
ACANTHUS
J
DENTILS
K
HAWK'S BEAK
L
TORUS
FLUTED
GUILLOCHE
BAY LEAF GARLAND

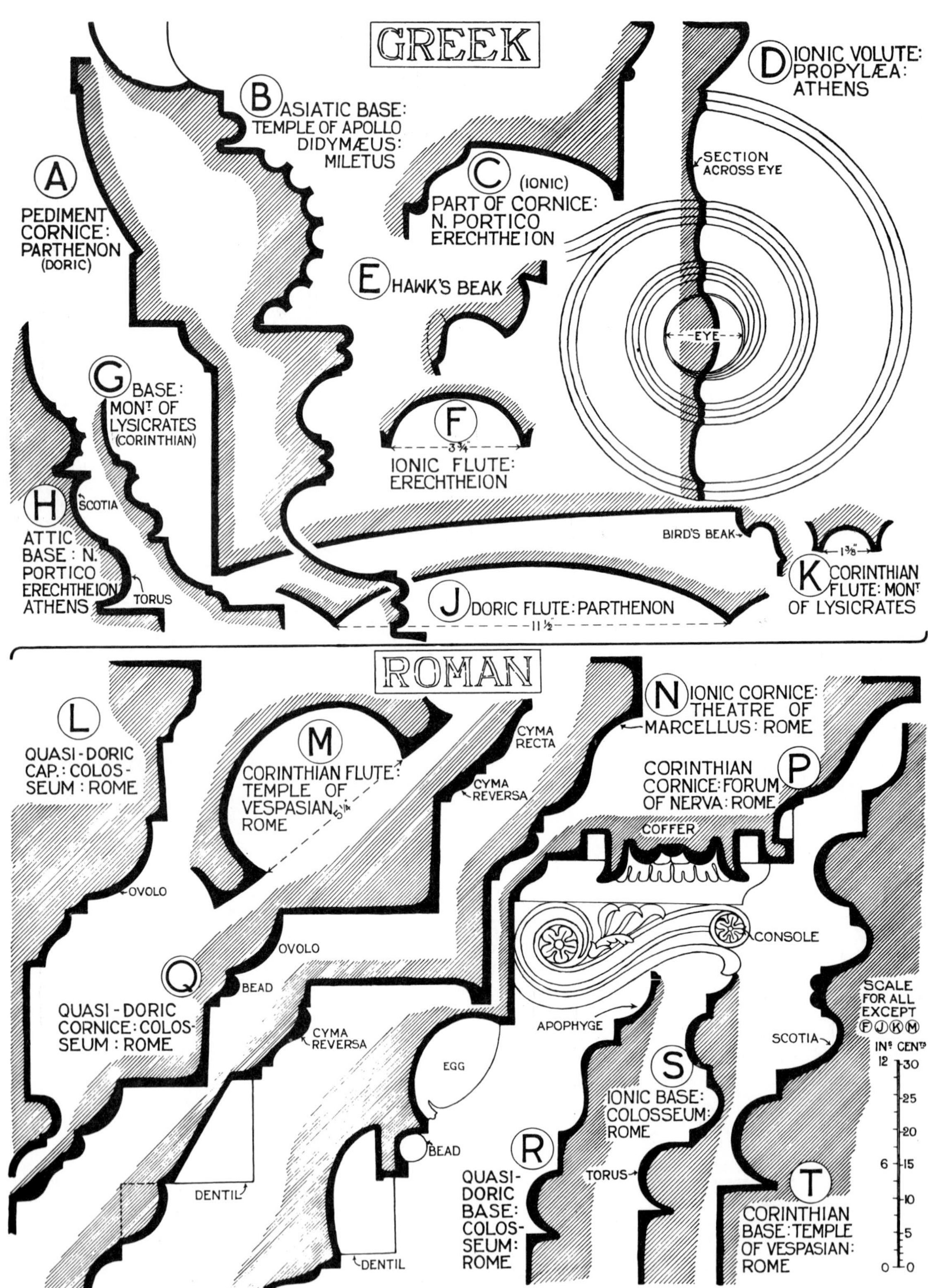

GREEK
A
PEDIMENT CORNICE: PARTHENON (DORIC)
B
ASIATIC BASE: TEMPLE OF APOLLO DIDYMÆUS: MILETUS
C
(IONIC)
PART OF CORNICE: N. PORTICO ERECHTHEION
D
IONIC VOLUTE: PROPYLÆA: ATHENS
SECTION ACROSS EYE
EYE
E
HAWK'S BEAK
F
3¾"
IONIC FLUTE: ERECHTHEION
G
BASE: MONT OF LYSICRATES (CORINTHIAN)
H
SCOTIA
ATTIC BASE: N. PORTICO ERECHTHEION ATHENS
TORUS
BIRD'S BEAK
1⅜"
K
CORINTHIAN FLUTE: MONT OF LYSICRATES
J
DORIC FLUTE: PARTHENON
11½"
ROMAN
L
QUASI-DORIC CAP.: COLOSSEUM: ROME
OVOLO
M
CORINTHIAN FLUTE: TEMPLE OF VESPASIAN, ROME
5¼
CYMA RECTA
CYMA REVERSA
N
IONIC CORNICE: THEATRE OF MARCELLUS: ROME
CORINTHIAN CORNICE: FORUM OF NERVA: ROME
P
COFFER
CONSOLE
OVOLO
Q
BEAD
QUASI-DORIC CORNICE: COLOSSEUM: ROME
CYMA REVERSA
APOPHYGE
EGG
BEAD
DENTIL
DENTIL
S
IONIC BASE: COLOSSEUM: ROME
TORUS
R
QUASI-DORIC BASE: COLOSSEUM: ROME
SCOTIA
T
CORINTHIAN BASE: TEMPLE OF VESPASIAN: ROME
SCALE FOR ALL EXCEPT F J K M
INS CENTS
12 30 25 20 6 15 10 5 0 0

Chapter 7
THE HELLENISTIC KINGDOMS

Architectural Character

Alexander's policies for controlling his empire included the foundation of Greek cities in strategically and economically important localities from Egypt to Bactria, a policy initiated by his father Philip in his subjugation of the Balkan peninsula, and continued by the Macedonian generals who carved kingdoms for themselves out of Alexander's empire after his death. Important examples are Antioch (Antiocheia) in Syria, Seleucia on the Tigris, and Apamea (named after the wife of Seleucus I) which are Seleucid foundations. The Ptolemies who ruled Egypt were more sparing in the use of dynastic titles and their only creation is Ptolemais in Upper Egypt; Ptolemais in Cyrenaica is an existing city, renamed. All these cities appear to have been given the institutions of Greek civic organisation, though they remained effectively under the control of the kings; the palace of the Ptolemies was in Alexandria, and the Seleucid kings ruled from Antioch. Architecturally also, they followed the model of the Classical Greek cities, but since they had royal connections, and served to enhance royal prestige, much more money was available for their embellishment, a process which spread by emulation to other, perhaps older, Greek cities which could afford such architectural indulgence, or could lay claim to the financial support of one or other of the kings.

In broad terms the Hellenistic age presents a cultural unity which transcends political borders, but there are nevertheless important differences between the various states and regions. The Greeks and Macedonians were always a minority, even if one includes with them peoples not Greek by origin who adopted the Greek language and way of life. Where the conquered country remained conscious of its identity, for example in Egypt or the Seleucid kingdom, the local vernacular styles continued. Other areas became more thoroughly Hellenised, especially regions adjacent to Greek cities founded before Alexander's conquests, or already subject to direct Greek influence. This is noticeable in Phoenicia, where the Kings of Sidon had already Hellenised, and above all in Asia Minor, following the earlier example of the Lycian and Carian dynasts. Thus there are different intensities of Greekness and so of Greek-styled architecture in the Hellenistic world, combined with different forms of local tradition and varying levels of wealth. An accidental difference, which limits knowledge of the period, is the widely varying degree of preservation (and discovery) of the buildings of the Hellenistic age. Important places such as Alexandria and Antioch were entirely ruined and much is lost. Other areas, particularly the coastal regions of Asia Minor, were far better preserved and have been most thoroughly explored. Allowance needs to be made for the distortions this causes, and generalisations based on inadequate evidence may be misleading.

Examples

Temples and Related Monuments

Though Alexander had attacked the Persian Empire as the champion of the Greeks and with Greek allies, the conquest was very much a Macedonian achievement. The successor kings were Macedonian, and Macedonian traditions were maintained at court. The architectural influence this created was essentially that of Macedon, which had been developed, at the end of the fifth century BC, by King Archelaos, and reinforced by Philip. It was part of the Greek mainland tradition and therefore emphasised the Doric order. There are some Ionic buildings at Samothrace, for example the so-called Temenos of 340 BC, and among the tombs. An important Macedonian Ionic building is the circular **Philippeion at Olympia** (p. 132), a marble building completed by Alexander in 336 BC, and consisting of a colonnade with eighteen Ionic columns supporting an entablature which combines a continuous frieze with a superimposed row of dentils, a form apparently used also in the Temenos at Samothrace, commissioned by Philip. At Olympia the continuous frieze has anthemion decoration and replaces the upper fascia of the architrave, coming above a low moulding. Later Hellenistic Ionic buildings normally combine the two forms of frieze while maintaining a full triple-fascia architrave. The columns of the Philippeion have only twenty flutes instead of the canonical twenty-four, a form found in Ionic orders from Peloponnesian (southern Greek) buildings. The Philippeion was a commemorative building for the Macedonian royal family, and housed statues of them. The distinctive form of its Ionic order was repeated for a Macedonian tomb at Aegeae, some time in the third century BC.

Nevertheless, Doric seems to have predominated in the Macedonian architecture of the newly conquered areas. Doric is found at Alexandria in tombs and the temple at Cape Zephyrion and at Seleucia on the Orontes, the harbour of Antioch. An early Hellenistic Doric temple (the date is disputed) was that dedicated to **Athena at Troy** by the successor King Lysimachus. Hexastyle with twelve columns along the flank, the capitals of this had the low straight-sided echinus which had evolved in the fourth century BC (the height and proportions of the columns are unknown), and which accord best with a date in Lysimachus' time, about 300 BC. The temple of **Athena Polias at Pergamum** in Asia Minor is another Doric building, possibly built for Lysimachus. It has 6 × 11 columns fully seven times their diameter in height and widely spaced so that there are three triglyphs and metopes for each intercolumniation. Another Doric temple at Pergamon was that probably dedicated to Asklepios, destroyed in the second century BC and rebuilt as Ionic (perhaps following the strictures of the important second-century architect Hermogenes, who proclaimed Doric to be unfit for temples. There is a small **Doric temple, to Demeter**, in the Ionian city of Priene. Doric temples were still built, of course, in the traditional Doric areas, such as the temple of Zeus at Stratos in north-west Greece. More spectacular seems to have been the imperfectly known, colossal Doric temple at **Lebadeia in Boeotia**, for which an interesting building inscription survives. It was dedicated to Zeus the King (Basileus) in about 175 BC, the gift of the Seleucid King Antiochus IV. The inscription suggests that the whole project is an example of a deliberate revival of earlier architecture.

Although the Ionic order seems to have become more important than Doric in the architecture of Hellenistic temples, this may result from our more extensive knowledge of the temples of Asia Minor, the traditional Ionic area.

The Ionic impetus had begun in the period before Alexander, with the reconstruction of the temple of Artemis at Ephesus which continued into the Hellenistic period, with the architecture of Mausolus and his successor Idrieus in the Carian sanctuary of Zeus at Labranda, and the temple of Athena at Priene, dedicated by Alexander the Great, who was allowed to put an inscription to that effect on the temple. This practice also relates to earlier Macedonian buildings at Samothrace and became common in the Hellenistic period. A most important Hellenistic revival is the **Temple of Apollo at Didyma** near Miletus (pp. 141N, 156J–P) on which work probably began before Alexander, but which was particularly supported by the successor king Seleucus, who restored the cult statue taken from the archaic temple to Persia by Darius when he destroyed it. This is an abnormal building, but the abnormalities appear to be copied from the sixth-century predecessor whose ruins were presumably still intelligible. It is very large, 51.1 m × 109.3 m (168 ft × 359 ft), and is the only Greek decastyle temple. There are twenty-one columns along the flanks and the arrangement is dipteral. They are 28.8 m (64 ft 8 in) high, and stand on a base with seven steps; the latter being too high for conventional use, they are doubled in number in front of the cella and set between projections which resemble the parotids of Roman temple bases. In plan the cella has the traditional Ionic form, with a deep porch and no false porch at the end; there is, however, an anteroom which appears on plan to be placed between the porch and the cella. This is misleading. Though the great front door opens into the anteroom it does not provide access to it, for its threshold is a full five feet above the level of the porch. Instead, two small doorways to either side lead to narrow, sloping vaulted passages which run direct to the cella, whose floor is at the original ground level, not, as is usual, at or a little above the level of the stylobate. The walls of the cella are decorated with a string course at stylobate level, with engaged piers above. The cella was not roofed, again a feature inherited from the earlier temple and probably shared with the temple of Artemis at Ephesus. The cult statue was placed in an inner shrine, a small tetrastyle prostyle Ionic temple within a temple. At the east end of the cella a splendid wide staircase leads up to the anteroom (the only possible means of approach) through doorways flanked by engaged Corinthian half columns. This peculiar arrangement may be connected with the oracular purpose of the shrine, and there must have been a religious necessity for it if, as seems likely, it is all repeated from the earlier temple. To either side of the anteroom are well-built and decorated staircases, now ruined but leading as high as the building is preserved; their purpose is uncertain: they may reflect Egyptian influence, since we know the Hellenistic kings of Egypt contributed to the building of this temple. Work on the temple was carried out in fits and starts, in the early third century BC, with later resumptions. Some of the construction belongs to the Roman period, and it was never completed.

Another large Ionic temple, also unfinished, is that of **Artemis at Lydian Sardis** whose cult goes back to the days of Lydian independence, when the rites were performed at an altar, rather than in a temple. The plan as first published was confused, but it is now clear it belongs to the third century BC, not earlier, as was once thought. Originally, about 281 BC, given a simple cella facing west, it was divided by an added cross-wall after 223 BC, and an extra door was cut in the formerly blank west end.

The **Temple of Artemis Leukophryene at Magnesia** on the Maeander was the masterpiece of Hermogenes, the most important architect of the Ionian revival during the Hellenistic period, who also wrote treatises on architecture known to Vitruvius and probably used by him for the Greek parts of his handbook. Hermogenes' date is a matter of some dispute, some authorities putting him at the beginning of the second century BC, though details at Magnesia suggest rather a date about 150 BC. This temple is pseudodipteral octastyle with widened central intercolumniation, which implies a revival, since this was not used in the temple at Priene, though of course it occurs in the rebuilt temple of Artemis at Ephesus. Vitruvius claims the arrangement was invented by Hermogenes, but it is rather, here, a revival of an earlier concept. There are fifteen columns on the flank and the overall dimensions are 58 m × 32 m (190 ft 6 in × 105 ft). The height of the column is unknown. More important than the details of the temple is its setting. It stands in a totally enclosed courtyard, whose alignment like that of the temple differs from that of the city grid plan. The entrance helps disguise this; it is made through a propylon contained within the surrounding colonnade of the agora, which lies in front – in this case, to the west. The temple dominates its enclosure (which may not have been completed), taking up a far greater proportion of the total area than in earlier Greek sanctuaries. The temple is placed not centrally, but towards the end of its precinct; in front of it is a monumental altar. A detail typical of Hermogenes' architecture is the double moulding at the top of the architrave – astragal surmounted by ovolo surmounted by cyma reversa. This moulding persisted in Roman architecture, both Ionic and Corinthian, but it is the concept of the temple in a relatively small colonnaded court which made the greatest impact on later architecture. It was repeated in appropriately modified form in the Imperial Fora at Rome and in the standard temple/forum arrangement of western Roman cities.

Equally important to later Roman architecture was the Hellenistic application of the Corinthian order to the external embellishment of temples. Corinthian was used for a **stoa at Miletus** in the third century BC, a building given to that city by the Seleucid queen Laodice, wife of Antiochus II. Its use for temples is first attested, however, in the second century BC, in two temples sponsored by Antiochus IV: that at Olba, Uzunçaburç in Cilicia, to Zeus Olbius, and the unfinished temple of Olympian Zeus at Athens, completed by Roman emperors Augustus and Hadrian. The **temple at Olba** is hexastyle 6 × 12 and measures approximately 22 m × 40 m (72 ft × 131 ft). The lower parts of the shafts have facets rather than flutes, which are used only on the upper part. The **temple at Athens** utilises the foundations of an earlier temple, attributable to the late sixth century BC and commissioned by the tyrant Hippias. It seems to have been intended as a Doric equivalent of the colossal archaic Ionic temples of Asia Minor, but the work was abandoned on the downfall of the tyrant. The new temple measured 41 m × 108 m (134 ft × 354 ft). It was dipteral (tripteral at the ends), 8 × 20. It had a deep porch, internal colonnades close to the walls, and an adyton at the west end. The architect, Vitruvius tells us, was a Roman citizen called Cossutius, but he was clearly working in a Hellenistic architectural tradition.

Another very important temple was that dedicated to **Serapis in Alexandria** by Ptolemy III in the second half of the third century, completely rebuilt in the Roman period, and stripped of its building material in the Middle Ages. It has been suggested that certain Roman coins of Alexandria depict the Hellenistic temple, and show it to have been Corinthian; if so, it would have been earlier than Antiochus IV's Corinthian temples, but the evidence is tantalisingly slight. However, in middle Egypt the temple at Hermopolis Magna, built during the reign of Ptolemy III, was definitely Corinthian, and there are numerous examples of its distinctive form of the Corinthian capital also in Alexandria.

It is likely that the use of Corinthian on the exterior of buildings, whether stoa or temple, is a reflection of local influence in the Seleucid kingdom and, probably, Egypt. For non-Greek taste, the Doric order, brought with them by the Macedonians, was too austere, while Ionic had evolved in a more formal way than its eastern prototypes. The tall Corinthian capital with its plant decoration reflected earlier Egyptian forms. It was, however, purely Greek in its developed form, and therefore acceptable to Greek taste. Less monumental, but showing much stronger Egyptian influence, are religious buildings put up in areas of Greek settlement, and not intended primarily for Egyptians. These are found in the Fayyum district, for example at **Soknopaiou Nesos**.

Urban Architecture

Urban architecture during the Hellenistic age became more substantial. It was dominated by the grid-plan cities created for Alexander and his successors. There were also grid-plan cities which were refoundations, either following earlier destruction or by a process (also seen in the Classical period) of merging together formerly scattered populations into new urban centres. These provide the most complete information, following the loss of

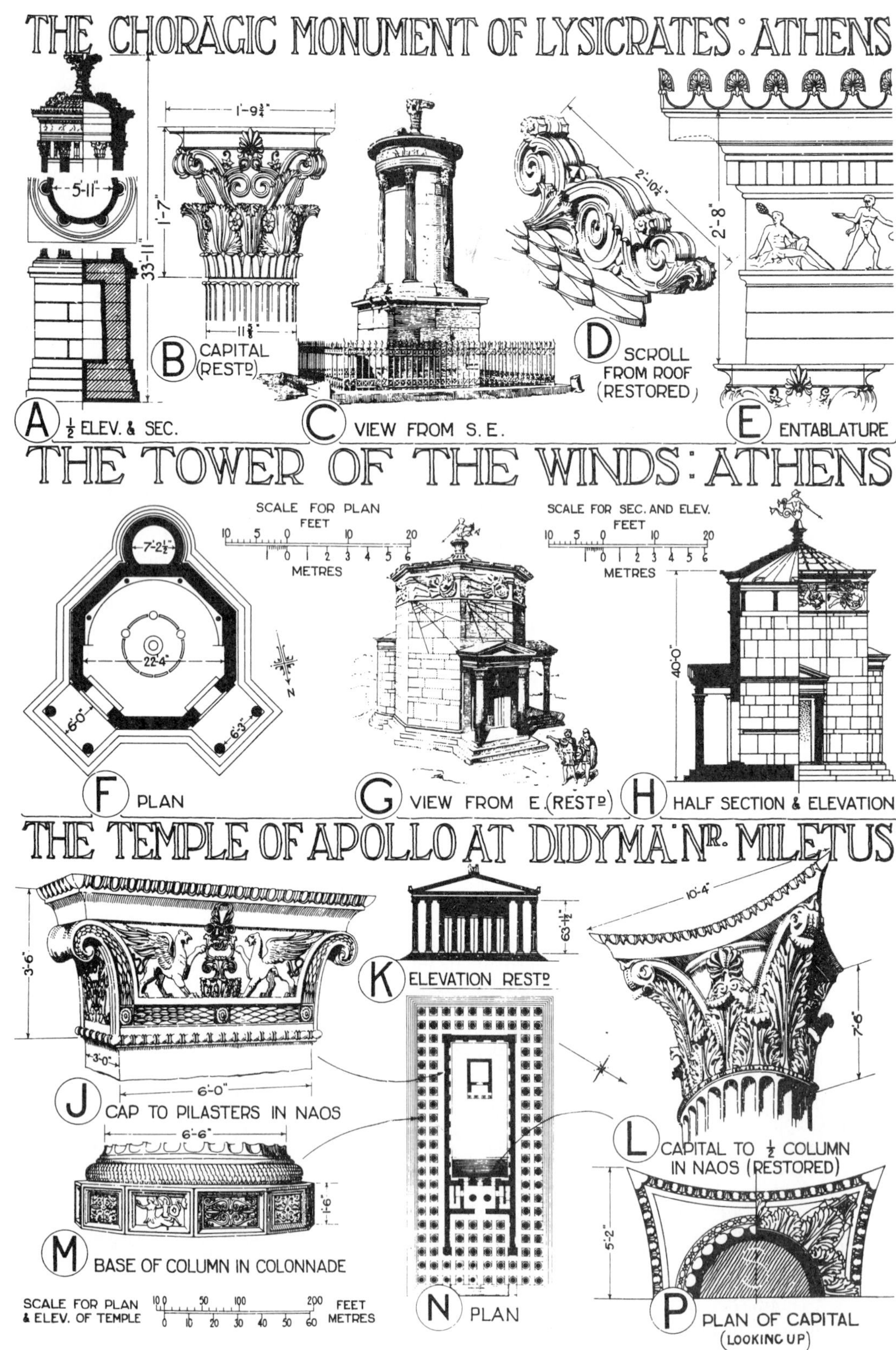
THE CHORAGIC MONUMENT OF LYSICRATES : ATHENS
1'-9¾"
1'-7"
5'-11"
33'-11"
11⅝"
2'-10¼"
2'-8"
A ½ ELEV. & SEC.
B CAPITAL (RESTD)
C VIEW FROM S. E.
D SCROLL FROM ROOF (RESTORED)
E ENTABLATURE
THE TOWER OF THE WINDS : ATHENS
SCALE FOR PLAN
FEET
METRES
SCALE FOR SEC. AND ELEV.
FEET
METRES
7'-2½"
22'-4"
6'-0"
6'-3"
40'-0"
N
F PLAN
G VIEW FROM E. (RESTD)
H HALF SECTION & ELEVATION
THE TEMPLE OF APOLLO AT DIDYMA NR. MILETUS
3'-6"
3'-0"
6'-0"
63'-1½"
10'-4"
7'-6"
6'-6"
1'-6"
5'-2"
J CAP TO PILASTERS IN NAOS
K ELEVATION RESTD
L CAPITAL TO ½ COLUMN IN NAOS (RESTORED)
M BASE OF COLUMN IN COLONNADE
N PLAN
P PLAN OF CAPITAL (LOOKING UP)
SCALE FOR PLAN & ELEV. OF TEMPLE
FEET
METRES

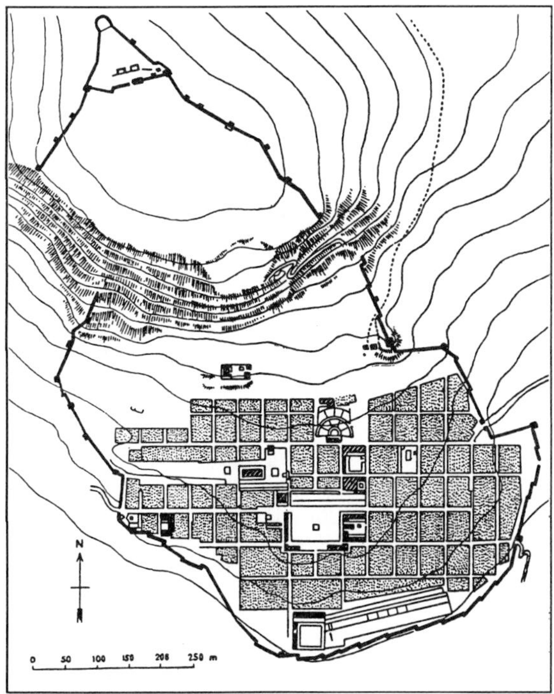

A. Town plan, Priene. See p.158

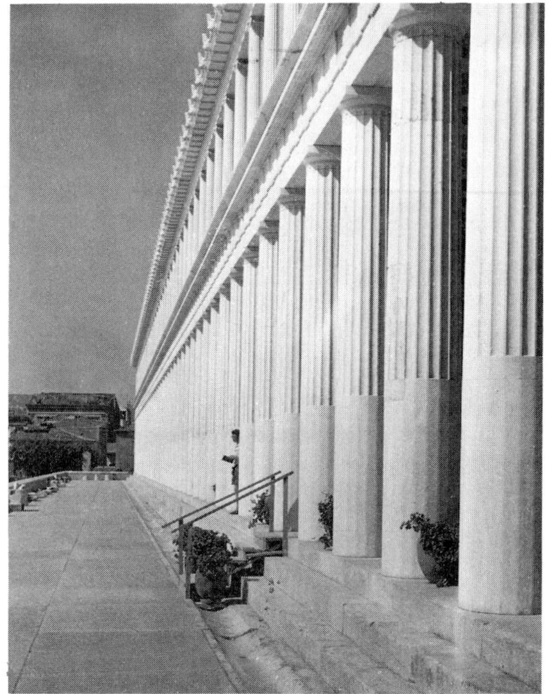

B. Stoa of Attalus, Athens (second century BC). See p.158

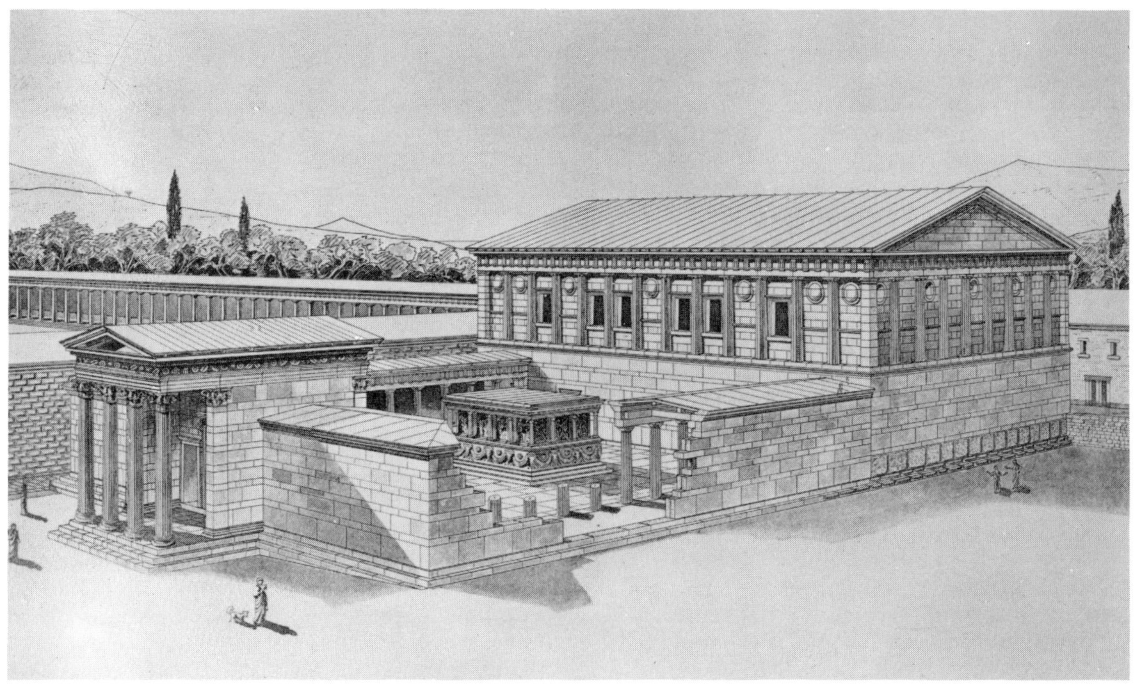

C. Bouleuterion (Council House), Miletus (*c.* 170 BC). See p.158

Hellenistic Antioch and Alexandria. The best known are the cities of Asia Minor, extensively excavated from the late nineteenth century: Priene, Miletus, Magnesia and Pergamum.

Priene (p. 157A) is the most completely explored of all Greek cities. It is disputed whether its refoundation was the work of Mausolus in the 350s, or of Alexander in the 330s, but its buildings belong essentially to the Hellenistic age. Not all the available area within the city walls was developed. The site is a sloping shelf below steeper mountain cliffs, on the top of which was a military stronghold. The town was limited to this shelf, and there was no building on the steeper slopes immediately below the cliff. At the centre of the grid plan was the **agora**, occupying two blocks of the grid, about one-fifteenth of the built-up area of the city. Some terracing was necessary on the south side to provide a sufficiently extensive flat area. The main street ran from the western gate of the city to the agora, and across its north side. (It is characteristic of the Greek agora, like the traditional Roman forum, that streets run through it. This can be seen at Athens, also.) The agora was completely bordered by **stoas**: one to the north of the road was an independent structure, while the one on the east, south and west sides was continuous, with the two outer north–south streets directed past the back of the stoas. They were built probably in the third century BC. As is usual with Hellenistic stoas, even in the Ionic area, they are built in the Doric order, with the wide spacing of the columns requiring three triglyphs and metopes to each intercolumniation. The north stoa probably had rooms behind it, as did the other on the west and south. The north stoa was destroyed, and replaced in the second century by a larger stoa, again Doric, with two aisles. This is extended along the width of the adjacent building block to the east, but has rooms only along the original length of the first two blocks. It measures 116.5 m × 16.8 m (382 ft × 55ft) including the rooms. The portico only is 11.8m (38 ft 9 in) deep. The outer colonnade is Doric, in the usual spacing, the taller inner columns Ionic. All these stoas are built of carefully worked limestone, though the detail tends to be mechanical and repetitive, and the floors are beaten earth. The **south agora at Miletus** is a much larger example, with a long stoa on the east side 189.2 m × 22.7 m (621 ft × 74 ft 6 in) with two sets of rooms, one accessible from the agora, the other from the street which passed outside to the east. There are two other L-shaped stoas on the north and south, with a gap between them (and between them and the east stoa). Here, as at Priene, the main road leads through the agora, but in late Hellenistic times it was shut off at both ends by gateways built between the east and the adjacent stoas.

Major improvements to the irregularly shaped traditional agora at Athens (q.v.) in the second century BC, with the support of the kings of Pergamum, were undoubtedly intended to convert it to a more regular form. Three stoas were built to achieve this; the **Stoa of Attalus** (p. 157B) on the east side is a two-storey building, 116 m × 19.4 m (381 ft × 63 ft 8 in), with a Doric colonnade on the ground floor, and an Ionic upper colonnade incorporating a balustrade. All the facade is in marble. The inner ground floor colonnades are equal in height to the exterior to support the floor above, but at double spacing they are Ionic. The inner colonnade of the upper floor has columns of palm-leaf design developed in Pergamum. There is a row of rooms behind the colonnades on both floors. The details are unsatisfactory, in comparison with the forms of Classical Athenian architecture. More important is the way the stoas are used to close off the agora to a regular plan. This is particularly noticeable in those which replace the original south stoa, that is, the **new south stoa**, 93.6 m × 8.5 m (307 ft × 28 ft), running at right angles to the stoa of Attalus, and the **middle stoa**, 146.6 m × 19.9 m (481 ft × 65 ft 6 in), which has colonnades to either side of a central longitudinal wall.

Stoas were employed at Pergamum and towns under Pergamene control not only to delimit open areas and courtyards, but to help create them. The same principle can be seen, earlier, in the south stoa of the agora at Priene, which is built over and along the terrace wall which helps create the flat area for the agora itself. Behind the **north stoa** at Priene is an **assembly building** (p. 159), substantially constructed with limestone walls, and with stone seats arranged in straight lines round three sides, to hold perhaps 640 people. It is for the restricted popular assembly of a small town rather than a council chamber, but the form is similar to the Classical council houses at Athens and at Miletus; the latter, like the Priene building, is second century BC in date. There is no architectural embellishment at Priene, except for the entrance doors and an arched opening in the south wall. It is structurally interesting; the original span of 14.5 m (47 ft 6 in) proved too great, and the roof collapsed. Subsequently the supports were moved in by two metres. The **Council House at Miletus** (p. 157C) was another gift of the Seleucid King, Antiochus IV, made in about 170 BC. It has seats arranged in a circular plan within a rectangular building, like the new Council House at Athens. The exterior was embellished with engaged Doric half-columns on the upper part of the wall, with echini carved in the Ionic manner in an ovolo pattern, supporting an Ionic entablature. This variation from Classical rules, and the use of a decorative pseudo-peripteral order, are distinctive aspects of later Hellenistic architectural taste.

During the Hellenistic period there were substantial improvements in buildings used for dramatic and athletic activities. **Greek theatres**, which were unroofed, consisted of three parts, the auditorium

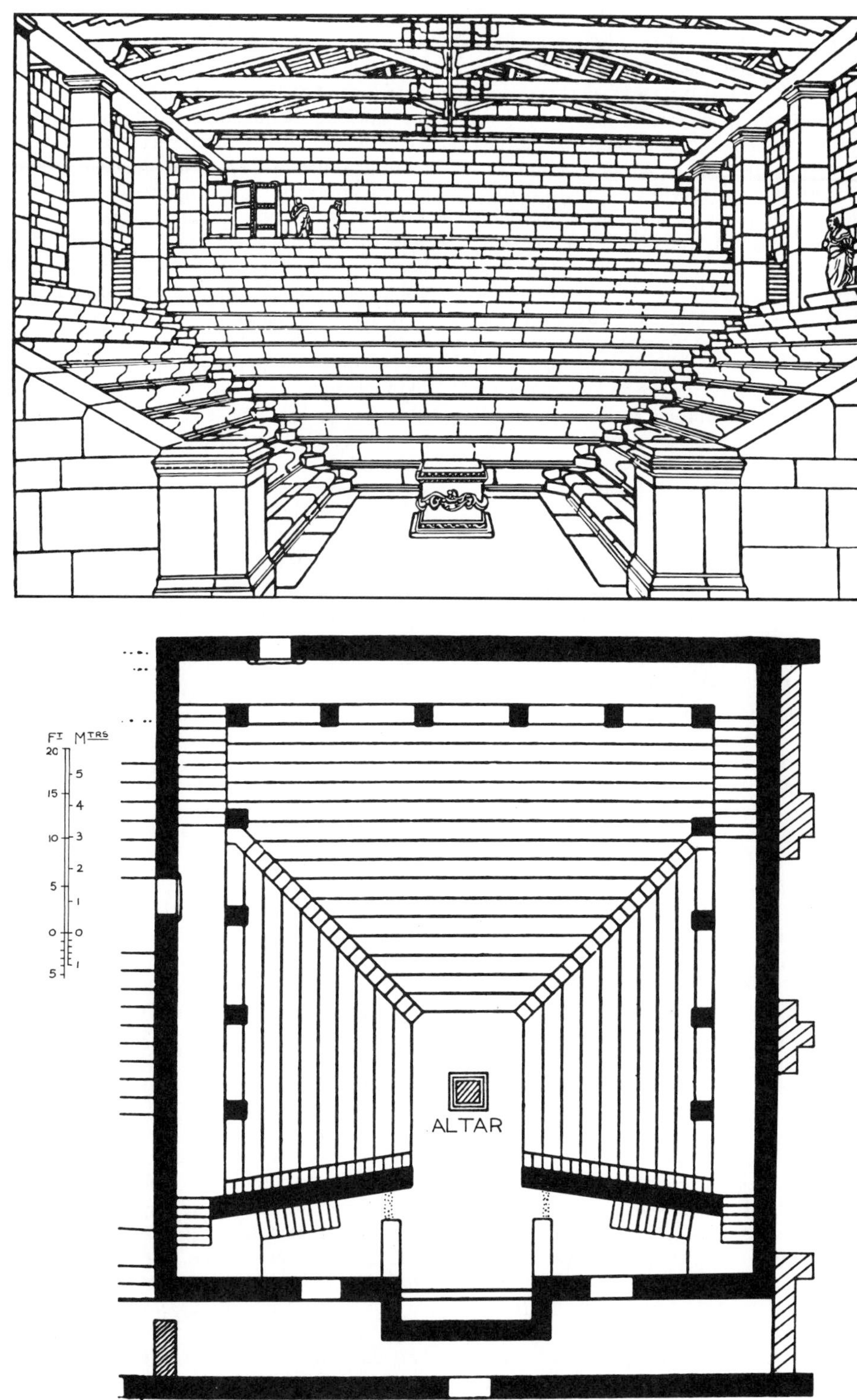

Ecclesiasterion (Assembly Hall), Priene (*c.* 200 BC): restored interior and plan. See p.158

(cavea or koilon), the orchestra or dancing floor, and the stage building or skene. The cavea provided seating for a mass audience, in most theatres numbered in thousands. The orchestra was the area where the chorus of each play danced and sang. This was an integral part of the drama in the fifth century BC. The actors were confined to an area behind the orchestra, possibly not yet raised in the form of a stage, but with some form of temporary structure behind (the stage building) which acted as a backcloth, and must have included the door openings which are seen to be necessary for the proper staging of the action in most plays that have survived. The stage building was separated from the cavea by a passage to either side, the parodos (plural, parodoi).

In the Hellenistic period, theatres were normally provided with permanent auditoria (caveas) in stone, and stage buildings. Stone seats of a rough and ready form had already appeared in the fifth century BC in the theatre at Thorikos in eastern Attica. This cavea was of irregular shape, having a straight central section of seating, which curved round at either end. The major **Athenian theatre** in the sanctuary of Dionysus on the south slopes of the Acropolis (p. 121C) had only wooden seating during the fifth and early part of the fourth century BC, and its exact arrangement is a matter of dispute. It was given stone seating in 346 BC. Here the cavea is placed round a circular orchestra (dancing floor), extending on either side beyond the diameter of a semicircle. The stage building was given durable form, though the arrangement of it at this date is again uncertain. The plan of the seating is not complete and symmetrical, because of adjacent structures.

The best-preserved cavea in Greece is that at the **Sanctuary of Asklepios at Epidaurus** (p. 161), built shortly after the middle of the fourth century BC, a date attested by epigraphic evidence. The seating, divided into segments by stairs, has a lower section with thirty-four rows of seats and an upper section with twenty-one, separated by a walkway or diazoma; the upper section does not extend as far as the lower. The orchestra has a diameter of 20.4 m (67 ft). The stage building is completely ruined, but had a raised stage, with higher rooms behind which were approached by ramps from the parodoi, which were later given entrance screens.

In Hellenistic theatres the circular orchestra was retained as an essential element in theatre design. Only in the theatres of the Roman period was it reduced to a semicircle, and used for seating. A good example of a Hellenistic theatre is that at **Priene** (p. 157A) situated on the hill slopes at the northern limits of the town. The cavea is relatively well preserved – recent excavations have revealed more of its upper seating – but the theatre is particularly important for its excellently preserved stage building. The stage is high, with a facade of Doric half-columns and an entablature. The stage building behind rose higher, and there is evidence for three doors or openings in it. There is epigraphic evidence for the existence of a theatre at Priene in the time of Alexander but the present cavea and stage building probably were constructed in the second century BC. This theatre was also used, as often in Greek cities, as a political meeting place in which the majority of the citizen population could gather.

During the late Hellenistic period the tendency appears to be for the building behind the stage to become higher and more ornately decorated with columnar facades, although that at Priene appears to have been of plain masonry only. Some auditoria hardly extended beyond the diameter of the semicircle (that at Miletus is a good instance), and it is likely that at least some of the well-preserved theatres in Asia Minor whose caveas are limited to the semicircle are late Hellenistic in date. There is thus a discernible tendency for the theatres of the Greek world to evolve towards the form employed for new theatres during the period of the Roman Empire.

The stadia for athletic contests were also improved during the Hellenistic age. The **stadium at Epidaurus** was placed in a natural elongated hollow, and this sufficed during the fourth century BC. In the third century it was given stone seating, with some artificial terracing to improve the layout. A stadion or stade is a unit of measurement (600 ft) and most athletic stadia conform to this. Recent excavations at the sanctuary of Zeus at **Nemea** have shown that a developed **stadium** with regular stone seating was constructed there about 325 BC. It had a tunnel-vaulted passage under the seating to give direct access from outside to the running track. Similar vaulted passages at Epidaurus and Olympia have usually been dated to the Roman period, but the evidence at Nemea is conclusive and they are better regarded as Hellenistic. The concept of the tunnel vault would seem to have been introduced into southern Greece from Macedonia, where it was already being employed for the royal tombs (q.v.). Similar vaulted passages were constructed through the cavea of the theatre at Sicyon, a building erected when that city was redeveloped by the Macedonian King Demetrius about 300 BC.

Other athletic activities took place in the gymnasium, which also assumed a more distinctly architectural character in the Hellenistic period. The gymnasium is another building type in which an open colonnaded court forms the major element. Some are very large, such as the **gymnasium at Olympia** (p. 132) though as this is in part eroded by the adjacent river Cladeus, its full extent cannot be measured. There are the remains of long Doric stoas on the north and east (the east stoa being double-aisled) and a separate propylon; south of this is a smaller building, conventionally termed the palaistra or wrestling ground, since its arrangement fits closely Vitruvius' description of this category of building. However,

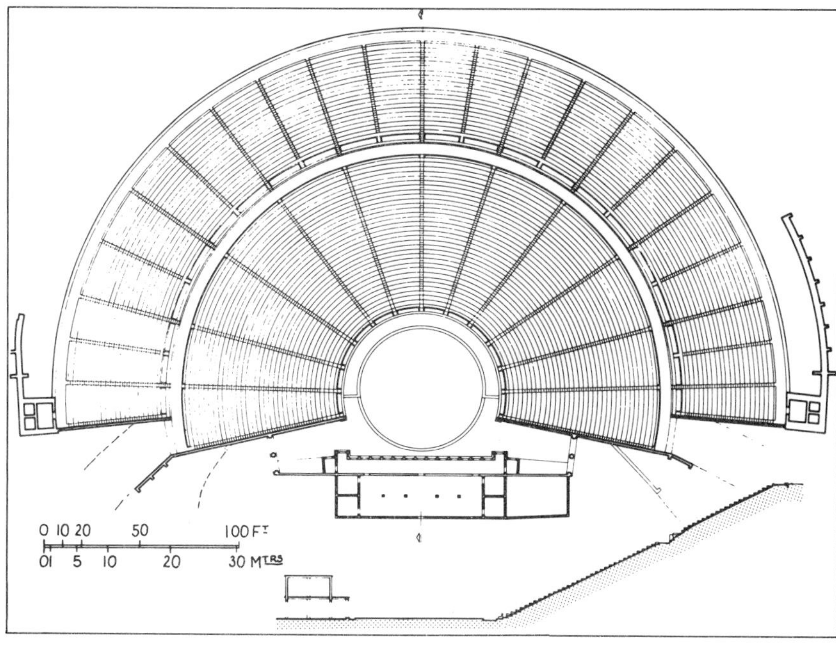

A (*above*)
Theatre, Epidaurus (*c.* 350 BC). See p.160

B. (*left*)
Theatre, Epidaurus: plan and section

both in size and form it is similar to a building by the stadium at Priene (p. 157A) which is known to have been the gymnasium. These are both totally enclosed Doric colonnaded courts, that at Olympia having a peristyle 41.5 m (136 ft) square with nineteen columns on each side, while that at Priene measures about 35 m (115 ft) square and has sixteen columns on each side. Both have rooms behind the colonnades. The **gymnasium at Priene**, unlike that at Olympia, functioned as a school. The open school hall on the north side has carved on its walls the names of school-boys who sat in it. There is also a well-preserved washroom, with stone basins round the wall, fed with cold water by lion's head spouts.

A similar 33 m (108 ft) square building at Epidaurus was thought also to be a gymnasium. The arrangement of the majority of rooms, however, indicates that this was clearly a building for feasting rather than athletic activity. Like other buildings at Epidaurus it was entered by a ramp rather than steps, probably to enable processions to make their way into the buildings with greater dignity.

The courtyard arrangement continues to be used for houses which in the Hellenistic period achieve a splendour and quality not readily found among their Classical predecessors. An example is the **Palace of the Macedonian Kings at Vergina (Aegeae)**, probably built at the end of the fourth century. It has a Doric peristyle court with sixteen columns on each side, about 42 m (138 ft) square. There are rooms on all four sides, many of them recognisably arranged to hold dining couches. Two on the south side with splendid mosaic floors were approached through a separate vestibule, and have marble thresholds. Others hold more couches, and were less splendidly decorated. The superstructure is mostly of unburnt brick.

Other royal buildings such as those of the Kings of Pergamum are less spectacular; they are modest houses, but with good quality decoration, and are well situated in an elevated position in the citadel town. Far more splendid must have been the royal quarter at Alexandria, now entirely lost and for knowledge of which we rely on written descriptions. Though conventionally called a palace it was a collection of buildings in a demarcated part of the city, of which it occupied a considerable proportion, perhaps as much as one-third. Apart from the royal apartments it included religious, administrative, reception and garrison buildings, as well as the museum and library arranged in a park. A particularly famous structure was a dining pavilion, a tent rather than a building in the proper sense, which held 100 couches and was most luxuriously equipped.

There are many ordinary **houses** of the Hellenistic period. Those at Priene (p. 157A) often include a megaron arrangement for their principal rooms, but this is unusual and is not found in the houses on the **Island of Delos** (p. 163). In both places the houses are provided with internal courtyards with indirect access, as in the earlier Classical buildings from which they evolved. Stone columns are frequent at Delos (where there is no timber) and some houses, to take advantage of a sloping site, have rooms at several levels, though two storeys are normal. The evidence for ordinary houses at Alexandria is scanty, but recent excavations have revealed that the multi-storey tenement houses of Roman date are rebuilt on Hellenistic foundations, showing that this type of dwelling already existed to house the very large population of the Hellenistic city.

Funerary architecture of the Hellenistic period is varied. Apart from the Mausoleum already described (Chapter 6), there are important series of rock-cut tombs, especially those at Cyrene, cut into cliffs or other vertical faces which are given regular architectural facades, leading either to burial chambers with recesses ('loculi') for sarcophagi, or with several openings in the facade leading directly to the loculi. Burial places at Alexandria include rock-cut chamber tombs, with stairway approach and chambers opening off a courtyard excavated into the flat rock surface. Those at Mustapha Pasha, to the east of the city, have Greek architectural forms, such as engaged Doric half-columns, and appear to date to the early second century BC. Others, such as those on the island of Pharos, are decorated with Egyptian motifs.

Another important part of Hellenistic architecture is the **circuit walls** which protected and defined the city. Even in the Classical period the lime-washed mud-brick fortifications had been considered an embellishment. Developments in the art of siege warfare, and the construction of more and more powerful siege engines, led to an improvement in the structure of walls. In the Hellenistic period these were normally faced in stone for their full height, with varying types of fill aimed at preventing the total collapse of the structure if part of the face should be breached. The masonry was normally heavily rusticated ashlar to give an impression of strength. In the later Hellenistic period there was a deliberate revival of the older polygonal masonry technique. The towers of fortifications were built higher to house defensive artillery. The rampart walks were protected, often by continuous parapets rather than battlements. Walls are generally best preserved in the remoter and less important cities: there are excellent examples at Herakleia near Miletus, where the masonry is rusticated ashlar, and, in a very well preserved state, at a site identified as the ancient Cydna, in Lycia, where revived polygonal masonry was used.

Late Hellenistic Architecture

Because the buildings so far described were largely in towns which were already Greek before Alexander's conquests, the element of continuity from Classical

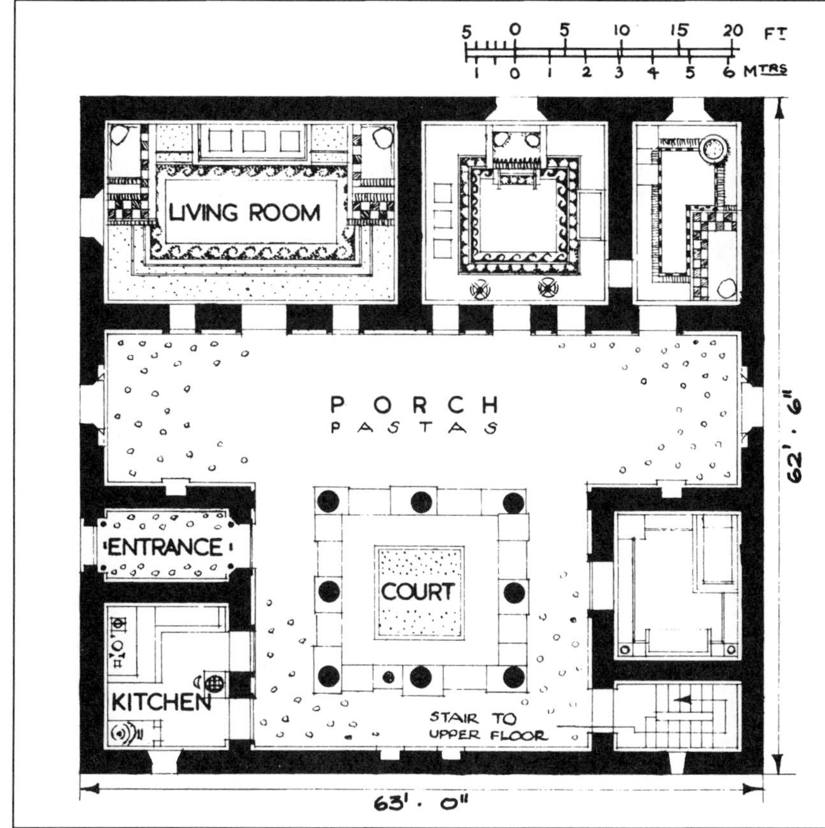

Maison de la Colline, Delos (second century BC): section and plan (restored). See p.162

times is clear. For the most part, they are improved versions of building types which existed in the fifth century BC. There are indications of different developments in other parts of the Hellenistic world. Excavations at **Ali Khanoum** in northern Afghanistan have revealed a **Hellenistic Greek city**, laid out on a grid plan. Buildings which have been investigated, such as the Propylaea, suggest a mixture of conventional Greek types with non-Greek elements, particularly in the methods of construction used, which suggest strong influences from the architecture of the Persian Empire. It seems likely that more florid architecture, involving the development of the Corinthian order, and increasing emphasis on decorative engaged orders, or columns used in non-structural screens placed against or close to walls, was particularly favoured in areas which were not traditionally Greek. Such architecture has been termed 'Baroque', though the use of a term which has a precise significance in later architecture is perhaps unfortunate. Nevertheless the term gives some indication of the flavour of these architectural forms.

The complete breakdown of the geographical distinctions between the principal Classical orders is a noticeable feature of the Hellenistic age. Ionian cities such as Priene and Miletus were as much dominated by their Doric colonnaded courts as by their major Ionic temples. The dynasts of Caria were already superposing Doric entablatures over Ionic columns in the fourth century BC, and this occurred again in the late Hellenistic period. The proportions of Ionic and Doric columns became similar, as Ionic grew slightly stockier, and Doric became distinctly more slender. During this late Hellenistic period the Corinthian entablature developed new forms. The ornate Corinthian columns were given entablatures in the full, Hellenistic Ionic form, with architraves divided into three fasciae, and dentils over continuous friezes with the appropriate carved mouldings; the number of mouldings increased – astragals (beads and reels) being added between the fasciae. Cornices were elaborated with modillions (consoles).

The late Hellenistic forms probably developed in the major kingdoms, Ptolemaic Egypt and Seleucid Syria; the best-preserved late Hellenistic city, however, is without any doubt **Pergamum**, which emerged (from very nondescript beginnings) in the third century BC as the capital of a dynasty which, with an increase in power and influence, elevated itself to royal status. It then had to catch up with the older royal capitals. The city occupies an impressive site, a hill overlooking the Caicus Valley, and was built on the slopes right up to the summit. On such a site no grid plan is possible and there are no flat areas on which to build; these have to be constructed by building massive terrace retaining walls. The terrace walls are visually of the greatest importance, and were often enhanced by additional fascia walls, supported perhaps with arcaded buttressing or colonnades. On such a site the details of the orders employed, so important to the character of Classical architecture, are less significant than the general effect. The resulting combination of details from the different orders, and the introduction of new elements such as volute-brackets or modillions under cornices typical of late Hellenistic architecture, were adopted and imitated by Roman architects.

As these forms developed, the Hellenistic world collapsed into political and economic ruin. The tradition, however, was firmly established, and was taken over (along with the architects and craftsmen) by the Roman conquerors. The final influence of the Hellenistic age can be clearly detected in some of the buildings of Augustan Rome, especially in monuments such as the Ara Pacis Augustae.

Part Two

THE ARCHITECTURE OF EUROPE AND THE MEDITERRANEAN TO THE RENAISSANCE

Chapter 8
BACKGROUND

Introduction

Archaeologists recognise five periods of European prehistory: the Paleolithic, or Old Stone Age; the Mesolithic, or Middle Stone Age, namely the time between the end of the most recent period of glaciation (*c.* 10,000 BC) and the beginnings of agriculture; the Neolithic, or New Stone Age (*c.* 6800–2500 BC), that is the period from the beginning of agriculture to the widespread use of metal tools; the Bronze Age (*c.* 2500–1250 BC); and the Iron Age (*c.* 1250 BC to AD 1). Each era produced significant developments in architecture which are dealt with chronologically under these headings (Chapter 9).

Towards the end of the Bronze Age and in the early part of the Iron Age – from *c.*1200 to 1100 BC – invaders from the north destroyed the Hellenic civilisation of Mycenae. By 1104 BC the conquest of western Greece and the Peloponnese by the Dorians was complete, and in the first century of the first millennium BC the Ionians had established settlements in the eastern Aegean and Anatolia.

Displaced peoples moved westwards, some of them to Italy, and formed new social groupings (of which the Etruscans were one) in new locations from the ninth and eighth centuries BC onwards, in the same period as the land- and trade-hungry Greek states were establishing their settlements along the northern seaboard of the Mediterranean, and in southern Italy and Sicily (Magna Graecia). In Italy the developing cultures of the displaced peoples culminated in the establishment of Rome, where, initially under the stylistic influence of Greece, a new architecture emerged which was to evolve into the Byzantine, Romanesque and Gothic styles.

The first Bulgar Empire was formed in the last quarter of the seventh century and so began a continuous evolution, especially of church architecture, which ran through the Slavic and Serbian ascendancies, Kievan Russia, the Novgorod federation and well into seventeenth-century Muscovy.

Physical Characteristics

Europe

The geography of Europe was profoundly different during the Paleolithic period, which coincides with the Pleistocene or 'most recent' geological period. The whole of Scandinavia and much of the British Isles, north Germany, Poland and north-west Russia were covered by vast ice-sheets, and sea levels were so much lower that Britain was still joined to the Continent, Sicily to Italy, while the Black Sea was a lake. Outside the glaciated zone, northern Europe was covered by a layer of permafrost, but in the Iberian peninsula and around the shores of the Mediterranean more temperate frost conditions prevailed.

This was a time of repeated ecological change. The expansion and contraction of the ice-sheets, the rise and fall of sea levels, and the shifts in the distribution of plants and animals in response to climatic change, combined periodically to alter the physical conditions to which early humans had to come to terms. This seems to have given impetus to technological and cultural development. The intense cold, particularly in eastern Europe where no natural shelter existed, stimulated the production of artificial shelter in the form of dwellings, amounting in some cases to significant architecture.

The Pleistocene period was succeeded by the Holocene (*c.* 12,000–10,000 BC), during which the more temperature climate produced the geography, topography, animal and plant life with which Europeans are now familiar. The contraction and disappearance of the ice-sheets affected human settlement by opening up new areas for occupation and replacing the arctic tundra with forest over most of northern Europe.

Throughout much of the Mesolithic period a climate which was warmer and wetter than that of today predominated. Food resources became more diverse and dependable, but more seasonal. As a result, seasonal movement became more important to

Mesolithic peoples than permanent shelter, particularly during the summer months. Mesolithic settlements were beside lakes and along rivers, on the sandy alluvial and flood plains, on river banks, or on terraces and high plateux overlooking rivers.

By contrast, archaeologists have emphasised the great climatic, geographical and ecological variability of the areas settled by Neolithic, Bronze and Iron Age peoples. Neolithic farming practices appear to have originated in the more favourable conditions of Greece and the Balkans (see Chapters 6 and 7) and spread to the coastal regions of the Mediterranean. This was followed by a major expansion of farming across central Europe, accompanied by more uniform cultural practices in house-forms and pottery. Modifications in the environmental conditions also brought about changes in the methods of construction of houses and led to the architectural developments which are the subjects of this part of the book.

Bronze Age peoples were efficient mixed farmers and increased the size and density of settlements, although not, on the whole, their architectural complexity. Settlements were on low-lying sites near water, except where natural defensive positions were exploited and incorporated into fortified settlements.

Throughout the Iron Age, farming efficiency increased still further and extensive field systems covered large areas of Europe. Iron Age settlements associated with them occupied defended sites. Fortified villages and townships predominated on the continent, while small, isolated palisaded hamlets and farmsteads were more typical of the British Isles.

Thus it was for climatic and topographical reasons, as well as for defensive and economic ones, that in the first millennium BC ethnic movements were southward and westward to the seaboard of Asia Minor, Greece, Italy and Sicily. In Italy the mineral wealth was concentrated in Etruria, and it was to the iron of the island of Elba and the copper and tin of the adjacent mainland that the rise of the Etruscan civilisation was due. These provided the means of economic exchange and were the principal materials of its manufactures, its crafts and its arts.

From being a vassal pastoral settlement under Etruscan domination, Rome established its power and had united most of Italy by the time of the first clash with Carthage in 264 BC, and at the end of another fifty or sixty years, and a series of three Punic wars, had acquired an overseas empire with footholds in Africa and Spain. The Roman empire was to grow to dominate the whole of Europe, and with the eventual formation of the eastern empire at the end of the fourth century, stretched from Dacia in the north-west to Egypt and Palestine in the south-east, and included the whole of Macedonia and Asia Minor to the shores of the Black Sea. The post-imperial decline and disintegration was followed by the development of Germanic and Frankish power; by the end of the tenth century western Christendom comprised about half of Spain, all modern France and Germany west of the Elbe, Austria, Italy and England.

The Romans had been masters rather than servants of topography, and aqueducts, bridges, roads and fortifications bear witness to a remarkable consistency of architectural as well as engineering achievement; an attitude which tended to ignore the physical characteristics of the terrain was perhaps essential in an empire so widely dispersed and so dependent upon its communications and its defences.

Nevertheless, the Byzantine buildings of the eastern empire, and the Romanesque buildings which emerged in western Europe, reflected the climates in which they evolved – from the sub-tropical sunshine and high temperatures of the east to the duller, colder conditions of the north and west. Typically, in the south, there were low-pitched and even flat roofs, with a few small windows, and thick walls to reduce the daytime effects of the sun; in the north, there were larger windows and more steeply pitched roofs to combat rain and snow. And it is to Romanesque architecture, evolved for the climate and topography of northern Europe, that the Gothic style owed its origins.

In spite of the Romans' ability to overcome local obstacles, the importance of topography to the evolution of European architecture can be clearly exemplified in France, for example, by the spread of ideas along the valleys of the Rhône, Saône, Seine and Garonne which connect the Mediterranean with the Atlantic Ocean and the English Channel. The different territories into which the country was divided, for instance in the Romanesque period, had strongly marked architectural characteristics, partly due to the difference in geographical position. Roman civilisation had spread along the Rhône valley, and the influence of the architecture of Rome itself is everywhere evident. Somewhat later, the trade route from the Mediterranean along the Garonne valley carried Venetian and eastern influence across the south-west of France to Périgueux, in Aquitaine, the centre of an area endowed with a large group of churches exhibiting eastern Mediterranean inspiration which can be traced specifically to Venice and Cyprus. The influence of the Norsemen who came by sea is apparent north of the River Loire, as well as that of the Franks who overran the country from the Rhine to Brittany.

It is generally agreed that the Gothic style was first fashioned in western France during the middle and later years of the twelfth century, whence it eventually spread, either by the movement of French architects or the imitation of French examples, into every part of mediaeval Europe. During the thirteenth and fourteenth centuries, it became an architectural lingua franca. In Italy it was progressively rejected during the fifteenth century, but elsewhere its predominance remained unquestioned until well into the sixteenth century; and there were places such as Bohemia and Oxford where it was never quite forgotten, even in the eighteenth century. From then on it was deliberately revived, most enthusiastically perhaps in England; and many of the best Gothic buildings were actually completed or even newly built in the nineteenth century.

The Balkans and Early Russia

The territory in which parallel developments in Christian architecture took place reach from present-day northern Greece, the former Yugoslavia, Bulgaria and Romania through the vast areas between the Black and Caspian Seas in the south, and the Baltic and the Gulf of Finland in the north. In terms of climate, Serbia, Bulgaria and Walachia were in roughly the same latitudes as central and southern Italy, Kievan Russia as the British Isles and northern Europe, while the Moscow principalities reached into the near-arctic conditions of north-western Russia.

The geography of Russia was one of the vital factors affecting the region's political history, and therefore the modes of architectural development. The extensively forested central and northern areas contrasted sharply with the open, treeless steppes over which wave after wave of invaders poured into Europe from eastern Asia. To avoid the Pechenegs who controlled the southern plains in the eighth century, for example, the southern Slavs moved northwards into what is now western central Russia, there to merge in due course with other interlopers from the north.

In the vast trackless steppes the easiest routes were by way of the great river systems of the region. It seems likely that by the eighth century Kiev was already a fortress and trading centre under the Khazars whose power in the early ninth century had already begun to wane, leaving Kiev in the control of the Polyane, the most powerful of the eastern Slavs. Thus the rise of Kiev as the key to the riverine trade routes, and the seizure of power by the Varangian Swedish Viking traders (also in the ninth century), indicate the vital part played by the topography of the territory. The subsequent patterns of historical and cultural development in the Balkans and in Russia relate directly to the scale and nature of the region, as do, for example, the Mongol incursions and the establishment of the Khanates which, while interrupting the normal evolution of architecture, also revitalised the occupying and indigenous populations, and helped to induce the extensive building activity of the Moscow principalities.

In the Balkan peninsular, the Mediterranean climate of the west Black Sea coastal plain was confined by the Carpathians, Transylvania and Hungary to the west and by the Byzantine empire (and subsequently the Ottoman empire) to the south. Here, similarly, there is no doubt that the geographical and ethnic bases of political evolution, which conspired, for example, to combine Romano-Dacian culture with Slav power under the architectural and artistic influence of Byzantium, helped to produce a characteristic and notably original architecture.

As in the case of Islamic architecture, geographical proximity and the availability of sea or river routes encouraged the importation of skilled craftsmen, particularly masons from Constantinople and elsewhere, and thus helped to imbue monumental architecture with a certain consistency of character. With the movement of the centres of power northwards, however, there was an increasing degree of isolation as a result of increasing distance from the more highly developed cultures. In Russia the culture remained fundamentally mediaeval for centuries after the Renaissance had transformed the cities of central and western Europe. The availability of materials, however, and especially the ample supplies of timber available in the north, had notable effects upon building form.

History

The Prehistoric Periods

The sophistication and complexity of societies in the Paleolithic period were reflected in the early evolution of large-scale, relatively permanent buildings with cache-pits and areas designated for specific activities. Hunting bands were known to have varied in size from as few as twenty to twenty-five people in western Europe to well over one hundred members in parts of eastern Europe. The composition of residential groups can only be guessed at. There was some regional exchange of raw materials and artefacts between culture groups. The many status items and objects of symbolic value found at some sites, and the specialised burial treatment of selected individuals, suggests that there may have been differentiated roles and statuses even at this early stage of development.

During the Mesolithic period, population densities increased throughout Europe, but the sizes of local groups contracted. As economies became more diversified, many adopted a semi-nomadic existence, seasonally exploiting the range of ecological conditions. Identifiable regional differences appeared in house-forms and the arrangements of settlements, in burial rites, and the associated artefacts. The exchange of goods and materials took place across considerable distances. Within local groups the differences between rich and poor became more pronounced.

Economic changes during the Neolithic period often involved the change from hunting and gathering to arable or pastoral farming, and this was accompanied by an increase in population and subsequent changes in the social structure. Archaeologists argue that large-scale monumental architecture is evidence of social inequality.

Long-distance trade, already well-established by this time, increased in scale and geographical range during the Bronze Age, and was reflected in the use of horses for riding and driving, the development of wheeled vehicles, and increased sophistication in boatbuilding and in the use of trackways. At the same time, regional cultural differences were strengthened, the diffusion or replacement of one form of society by another appears to have taken place at an increasing pace, and the gap between rich and poor widened. Characteristic of the later Bronze Age was the rise of fortified hilltop settlements and stockades. This began about 1000 BC, and generated the forms of fortification architecture which are linked with a less relaxed social atmosphere, although many fortifications may have been predominantly of strategic or symbolic significance.

During the Iron Age, highly stratified tribal societies appeared throughout Europe, with chiefly or princely rulers, warrior aristocracies, specialists in ritual and in the crafts. There were industrial areas, for example, smelting iron, working metal and producing salt, while in other locations centres of distribution were established. The pace of life quickened both through the internal developments described above and through contacts with the Mediterranean world, which lent technological and cultural impetus to the Iron Age societies of inland Europe. The societies of the Celtic world were technologically on a par with those of the Classical world in the later Iron Age, particularly in agriculture and the crafts, but by comparison were less unified politically.

The Etruscans

The antecedents of the Etruscans, who occupied west-central Italy in early times, are uncertain. According to Herodotus, writing in the fifth century BC, they were immigrants from Lydia in Asia Minor. Whatever their origins, they had begun to establish a recognisable urban civilisation by the eighth century BC, initially in the coastal regions. In the following century this civilisation spread to other centres further inland, and Etruscan sea power grew (as much by piracy as anything else) to challenge that of Greece in the western Mediterranean.

The zenith of Etruscan power was reached in the sixth century BC, when a loose federation of cities under Etruscan rule extended from the Po valley in the north of Italy to beyond the bay of Naples in the south; the rest of the country was occupied by a variety of other races including Ligurians to the north, Picenes to the east, Samnites and Latins in the southern-central regions, and Greek colonists around the coast in the south and in Sicily. At this time, Rome (founded according to legend in *c.* 753 BC) was still little more than a minor town in the southern part of Etruria, ruled by Etruscan kings aided by a form of popular assembly. But before the end of the century, Etruscan supremacy began to decline.

In 510 BC the Romans revolted against their king and established an independent city-republic which, by controlling the crossing of the Tiber, separated Etruria from its southern domains. Control in the northern plain was lost to the Gauls from further north, and Etruscan sea power was broken by the Syracusans, allies of Cumae, the oldest of the Greek colonies in the south. Further decline was accompanied by the rising influence and increasing dominance of Rome, and was marked particularly by the fall of the important city of Veii to the Romans in 397 BC; by about 250 BC the decline was virtually complete.

The Rise of Republican Rome

After the expulsion of its Etruscan kings, Rome had gradually assumed the leadership of a league of Latin settlements banded together for mutual defence against the tribes in the hills further inland which gave way to Roman dominance when internal dissensions led to the league being dissolved in 348 BC. Part of the Roman genius was then to incorporate other communities as almost equal associates, and to give them rights as well as duties. This, coupled with an expansionist outlook and their qualities as thrifty, patient farmer-soldiers, enabled them to become effective masters of the whole of central and south Italy by about 273 BC.

The expansion of Roman influence generated friction with Carthage, and led to the first Punic War (264–241 BC) which ended with the annexation of Sicily as the first overseas Roman province. The second Punic War (218–201 BC) became a bitter struggle for survival. Hannibal, the great Carthaginian general, entered Italy from the north via Spain and the Alps to circumvent Roman sea power, which had now taken the place of that of the Etruscans. He defeated Roman armies and ravaged Italy for years until recalled to meet a Roman counter-attack, under Scipio, on Carthage itself. Scipio's victory at Zama (202 BC) broke Carthaginian power, but a subsequent revival caused the Romans to seek its final destruction, which they accomplished by the third Punic War (149–146 BC), and Carthage, with its territory, became a Roman province in Africa.

Conquest of Macedonia (168 BC) and Greece (146 BC) added two more provinces to a growing empire and served as stepping stones to the assimilation of the Hellenistic kingdoms of Asia Minor and the rest of the eastern Mediterranean world, the major part incorporated in the Roman province of Asia by 133 BC. The remainder was gradually incorporated over the ensuing century and a half. With the conquest of Spain and later Syria in 64 BC, Roman rule extended from the Atlantic in the west to the Euphrates in the east.

These prolonged and often desperate wars, and the resulting conquests, had their adverse effects. The earlier farming economy in Europe was badly disrupted by the drain of manpower, the damage wrought by Hannibal, and the import of corn from Africa. Refugees, slaves and the dispossessed flooded into the capital, and the resultant social unbalance was increased by the newly won wealth of those who had profited from the situation. These troubles were further aggravated by the need to maintain large standing armies far from home. For this purpose a citizen soldiery had to be transformed into professional armies, the effective control of which first exasperated and eventually defeated the old republican government.

A series of civil wars led to a succession of military dictatorships, of which that of Julius Caesar (49–44 BC) was the most successful. His brilliant campaigns in Gaul (58–49 BC) had established new northern frontiers along the Rhine and the English Channel. But his attempt to reorganise the system of government was cut short by his assassination. A further period of confusion and civil war ensued. A triumvirate, consisting of Marcus Antonius, Caius Octavius (Caesar's nominated heir) and Marcus Aemilius Lepidus, defeated attempts to revive republican government. After they had fought for supremacy for some time, Caius Octavius defeated Marcus Antonius at Actium in 31 BC and proceeded to add Egypt to the empire.

Imperial Rome

It was Octavius who then re-established order and carried through the reorganisation that was necessary for the efficient running of the empire. He assumed the titles of Imperator and Augustus, and it is by the last that he is now best known. His long reign (27 BC–AD 14) – the Augustan Age – might be compared with the Periclean Age in ancient Greece. It was marked by a revitalisation of national life expressed in vast new building works and by the establishment of internal peace known as the Pax Romana.

Augustus, despite his effective personal assumption of all authority, never formally established dynastic rule. But, for the next half-century, he was succeeded by men who could make some family claim to what now became the imperial throne – Tiberius (AD 14–37), Caligula (37–41), Claudius (41–54), and Nero (54–68). However scandalous the abuses of power in their courts, the foundations laid by Augustus enabled development in the provinces to continue, so that these came to play an increasing role in the state. The only significant extension of the frontier was the inclusion of Britain, whose conquest was begun under Claudius. An event of more than usual architectural significance during Nero's reign was the great fire of AD 64 which, over nine days, destroyed a large part of the city of Rome.

Nero's suicide, without any obvious successor, led to a year of civil war during which the throne changed hands three times. An army commander, Vespasian, eventually restored order and founded the Flavian dynasty. During his reign (69–79) and those of his sons Titus (79–81) and Domitian (81–96), the frontiers were extended a little further in Britain and Illyricum (roughly what was recently Yugosalvia). A Jewish revolt was also finally crushed with the sacking of Jerusalem in AD 70. It was nine years later that Pompeii and Herculaneum were destroyed by an eruption of Vesuvius.

The murder of Domitian brought dynastic rule to an end. Subsequent emperors were adopted by the senate (though sometimes it was merely an endorsement of the reigning emperor's choice) from those considered to be most suitable, even if not of Roman origin. The reigns of Nerva (96–98), Trajan (98–117), Hadrian (117–38), Antoninus Pius (138–61) and Marcus Aurelius (161–80), collectively known as the Antonine Age, thus brought in new blood and gave increased importance to the provinces. Trajan, a Spaniard, was the first non-Italian, Hadrian was another Spaniard, while Antoninus Pius was descended from immigrants from Nîmes in Provence. Trajan and Hadrian were possibly the greatest emperors after Augustus. Under Trajan the empire reached its greatest extent with the conquest of Dacia and Parthia, and under Hadrian (p. 175A), although there was some withdrawal on the eastern frontier, much was done to weld the provinces together in a fruitful partnership. The resultant stability permitted a great new burst of building activity. The closing years of the reign of Marcus Aurelius were marred, however, by plague, and by the first barbarian inroads on the Danube frontier. With the accession and subsequent murder of his unworthy son and successor, Commodus (180–92), this era came to an end.

The Decline of the Western Roman Empire and Foundation of Constantinople

The third century was one of political confusion, civil wars, barbarian inroads on the frontiers, and economic instability brought about partly by the costs of maintaining large armies. After another rapid sequence of emperors, relative stability was restored by the North African Septimius Severus (193–211) and his son Caracalla (211–17), but this did not last after Caracalla's murder. From *c.* 230 the pressures on the frontiers so dominated the affairs of government that a long succession of soldier-emperors followed who were proclaimed in the field by their armies. Most ruled for a few years only, while the economy continued to decline and social life was increasingly disrupted. This decline was stemmed by the drastic reforms of the Illyrian, Diocletian (283–305), at the cost of his assumption of dictatorial power which he administered through a ruthless new bureaucracy. The reforms included a considerable measure of decentralisation, which greatly weakened the power of Rome by setting up new capitals in Nicomedia, Sirmium, Salonika, Milan and Trier. Diocletian himself ruled the eastern half of the empire from Nicomedia, there was a western co-emperor in Milan, and there were assistants (presumptive heirs, known as caesars) in Sirmium or Salonika and in Trier.

The Tetrarchy, as this system was called, did not, however, outlive Diocletian. Rivalries between his successors led to further civil wars from which Constantine finally emerged victorious – in the West by defeating Maxentius in 312, and then in the East by defeating Licinius in 324. Thus from 324 to his death in 337 there was again a single emperor, but now one who took all power into his own hands, and, exercising it in a manner that was more eastern than western or traditionally Roman, established a new dynasty.

Constantine's administrative system took over the principle of decentralisation introduced by Diocletian, with the empire divided into four prefectures. And he took two other decisions which were, in due course, to prove more momentous. First, in 313, he recognised Christianity as a religion equal to all others and himself began to favour it. Second, in 324 he chose to rule primarily from the East and chose as his capital not Nicomedia, but nearby Byzantium, and it was formally inaugurated in 330 as New Rome or Constantinople – City of Constantine.

Again the system did not long survive intact after the death of its founder. Inroads on the frontiers presented ever-increasing problems, particularly in the West, and effective control by a single emperor proved impracticable. The first formal partition of the empire occurred in 364 when Valentian became emperor in the West and his brother Valens in the East. Theodosius the Great (379–95) made one last attempt to rule the whole empire alone. But, after his death, the West was increasingly cut off from the now much richer and more populous East. In 407 the Rhine frontier was breached and barbarians occupied Gaul, severing the lines of communication with Britain. In 408 the Roman army withdrew from Britain and in 410 the Goths, under Alaric, invaded Italy and sacked Rome in spite of the protection of a strong new defensive wall, the construction of which had been started by Aurelian in 271 when the threat of invasion was first recognised. In the following decades the western provinces (including North Africa) were successively overrun and lost. Rome was sacked again in 455, and in 476 the last Roman emperor in the West, Romulus Augustulus, was deposed by the Goth Odoacer.

Thus, formally, the western empire might be said to have come to an end. Certainly it no longer existed as a single unit. But the break in Italy itself was not as dramatic and complete – or as significant for normal life – as this might suggest. Both Odoacer and his greater successor, the Ostrogoth Theodoric (490–526), saw themselves as continuing the imperial line; this was reinforced by their previous adoption of the Christian faith, which Theodosius had made the sole religion of the empire in 391. Indeed, Theodoric had ousted Odoacer with the encouragement and support of Zeno, the emperor in the East, and even their choice of Ravenna as the administrative capital was no break with the past, as it had already largely taken the place of both Rome and Milan in 404, when Honorius had made it his capital, leaving Rome as little more than a symbolic centre.

The final acts will be referred to in more detail below. There was first the attempt by Justinian to reunify the empire from his eastern base in Constantinople. Then, much later and after a more significant break during which much of Italy was ruled by Lombard conquerors, there was a nominal revival by Charlemagne under the name of the Holy Roman Empire – a revival marked by his coronation in Rome by Pope Leo III in 800. Symbolised by this last act, and central to the continued importance of Rome once it ceased to be an imperial administrative centre, was the growing prestige of the See of S. Peter in the Christian West – a prestige confirmed by its growing wealth and temporal power as it stepped into the vacuum left by the collapse of other authority.

The Eastern Empire from Theodosius to Justinian

The growth in importance of the new Rome in the East – Constantinople – and its eventual, almost complete, supplanting of Rome itself can hardly have been foreseen by Constantine. For much of the fourth century, its ultimate status remained uncertain, but it became clearer with the final partition of the empire in 395 and was fully confirmed in the course of the century which followed. From very small beginnings the city grew by the beginning of the sixth century to house perhaps half a million inhabitants, far outstripping the 200,000 or so to which the population of Rome must by that time have contracted from its peak several centuries earlier of around a million.

The eastern empire after the partition is now generally known as the Byzantine empire from the earlier Greek name of the city, Byzantium. However, the name should not be allowed to obscure the very real continuity with the eastern empire of Rome which had come into being many centuries earlier and had already assimilated much from the Hellenistic kingdoms it absorbed.

That eastern empire was more fortunate than the western in being less subject to the pressures of land-hungry barbarian tribes from the north. Some pressure of this kind was felt in the Balkans, but the chief threat was posed by the Persian empire to the east, despite the existence of the semi-independent Christian state of Armenia as a buffer on the northern part of the frontier. Intermittent warfare with Persia was punctuated by uneasy truces. In the early sixth century the greatest of Byzantine emperors, Justinian (527–65), nevertheless felt himself strong enough to attempt the reunification of the whole empire by the reconquest of the West. He came near to success, winning back the whole of North Africa, southern Spain and Italy. But the cost was high, especially that of the prolonged fighting in Italy as a result of which the whole economy suffered. Further damage was done in the latter part of his reign by serious outbreaks of bubonic plague which caused great loss of life.

The Byzantine Empire after Justinian

Justinian's successors had to concentrate increasingly on defending the eastern and Balkan frontiers, with the result that northern and central Italy (with the exception of an area around Ravenna), southern Spain, and much of North Africa were soon lost again to Lombards, Visigoths, and Berbers. Heraclius (610–41), after ejecting the ineffectual usurper Phocas, carried through reforms to meet the new situation. These included setting up an army based on local manpower rather than on mercenaries and the removal of the sharp division between civil and military authority retained since the time of Diocletian. He succeeded in defeating the Sassanian empire in Persia, only to be forced by Arab attacks to relinquish direct control of much of the Balkans. The Arab attacks developed so rapidly in the few years after the death of Mohammed (632) that Damascus fell in 635, and the whole of Syria was lost soon afterwards, as was Jerusalem. To the north Armenia fell and all of Egypt in the south. Arab raiders even penetrated deep into Asia Minor (see Chapter 15). Heraclius, therefore, looked out finally on an empire reduced to about half the size it had reached under Justinian.

Deprived of some of its richest and most populous provinces, the empire was never to return to anything like its earlier position. Its fortunes fluctuated. The Arabs, for instance, soon turned to easier conquests in North Africa and Spain. But cities declined, Ravenna was lost in 751, and there were further and more dangerous attacks on the Thracian frontier. Under Basil I (867–86) and the dynasty he established, there was a revival, reflected in new building activity, but this was followed by successive waves of Turkish infiltration from the east and by the depredations of crusaders in the thirteenth century.

Constantinople had become as central to the Byzantine empire as Rome had long been to the Roman empire, so that its loss in 1204 to Latin crusaders could well have been fatal. As it was, the imperial administration moved to Nicea and the city was retaken in 1261 by Michael Paleologus. There was a surprising last recovery, but not sufficient to stem Turkish advance. For much of the thirteenth century and the first half of the fourteenth, a powerful Ottoman sultanate held much of Asia Minor and was also closing in on Constantinople through Thrace. The city fell to the young Sultan Mohammed II in 1453.

This was the end of the Byzantine empire as a political entity. But it was not yet the end of the Orthodox church – that branch of the Christian church with which it had almost become synonymous. This survived through centuries of Turkish occupation in the Balkans and even in parts of Asia Minor. It also survived as a much more powerful force in Russia.

The Balkans and Early Russia

It was probably under pressure from other Far Eastern peoples including the Chinese, who by this time had been moving across the south Asian nomad corridor in successive waves for centuries, that the Huns turned southwards into what is now Iran, towards the end of the fourth century, to attack the Goths, and by displacement to initiate the series of invasions which overcame most of the Roman Empire. After what has been called 'the Hunnish storm' an ethnic intermingling took place and the races overlying the Slavs were pushed westwards. The Bulgars, some of whom settled along the middle Volga, also conquered the south-east Balkan Slavs and formed the first east European state outside Byzantium, namely the First Bulgar Empire (681–1018). In the course of the sixth and seventh centuries Constantinople had been forced to cede large parts of the Balkan peninsular to invading Slavic tribes. When subsequently the proto-Bulgarians, a tribe of Turkish origin from around the Caspian Sea and the Sea of Asov, arrived and took over the military leadership, a state was formed into which the old-established Thracians and part of the Greek population were assimilated.

Periods of peace with Byzantium alternated with periods of conflict. Exploiting the tensions between

Byzantium and the Carolingian Empire, Bulgaria grew into a third great power and extended its frontiers as far as the Adriatic and the Carpathians. Around the year 685, Khan Boris (852–889) introduced Orthodox Christianity under pressure from Constantinople, but adopted the Slavic written language for the liturgy to counteract Byzantine tutelage. It marked the end of the process of ethnic consolidation within the Slav state itself but not until the tenth century did it become possible to found an independent patriarchate. During this period basilican churches destroyed during the sixth and seventh centuries – before Christianisation – were restored or rebuilt, very largely with help from Byzantine masons.

This period drew to an end as, weakened by internal crises and attacks by Hungarians, Pechenegs and Russians, Bulgaria slowly fell back under Byzantine rule during the years 1018–1186. The residual Slavic state formed under Czar Samuel (987–1018) in the western parts of the Balkans, with its capital at Ohrid, was decisively defeated in 1014 by Emperor Basil II, the 'Bulgar-Killer'. It was over 150 years before Byzantine power again declined as a result of inner decay and the depredations of Seljuks and crusaders; during this period both new buildings and the restoration of old ones came under the direct control and influence of Constantinople. Towards the end of the twelfth century a rebellion broke out in the north Bulgarian town of Turnovo and spread across the Slav territories. This marked the beginning of the Second Bulgar Empire which was to last for over two centuries (1186–1396). Although cultural rebirth followed the establishment of an autocephalous patriarchate, internal consolidation was hindered by feudal dissension, peasant unrest and Tartar raids. As well as the improved ecclesiatical status, achieved by means of skilful manoeuvring between Rome and Constantinople, Czars Kaloyan (1167–1207) and Ivan Asen II (1218–1241) were also able to expand their territories well beyond the earlier boundaries of their empire. It was a period in which not only the character of the architecture changed but the scale of building as the lower nobility became increasingly involved in patronage.

In the long run, however, the Bulgar Czars failed to unite the southern Slavs in their midst and their interests collided with those of the Byzantine and Frankish emperors. By the end of the thirteenth century the Second Bulgar Empire was already beginning to break up into feudal principalities and by the end of the fourteenth century there began an almost 500-year period of Turkish domination.

The Serbs, who had accepted eastern Christianity and the old Slavic liturgy in the second half of the ninth century, repeatedly took advantage of these conflicts to advance their own independence. Nevertheless, they fell under Byzantine rule from the beginning of the eleventh century to the middle of the twelfth. The region had experienced changing tides of political and cultural influence from both wings of the Roman Empire from Early Christian times, so that when, under Stephen Nemanja (1159–1195), an independent Serbian kingdom, 'Ras', or Rascia, was formed, both influences tended to be combined in a new and vigorous school of building. The kingdom was extended under successive monarchs, and because Russia was preoccupied with the Mongol invasions and Byzantium with the crusaders in the early part of the thirteenth century, the Rascian school assumed major cultural importance.

To the north of the Danube, in what is now Romania, were the Dacians who had detached themselves from the Thracian tribal federation and who, as subjects of a Roman province, had assimilated Roman manners in language and culture. As a result of ethnic mingling two cultural areas took shape: Transylvania in the west, Walachia (Oltenia) and Moldavia in the east. Transylvania came under Hungarian control and despite the Orthodox beliefs of the majority of its population oriented itself under its Roman Catholic masters towards Romanesque and Gothic styles. Up to the fourteenth century the Romanesque tradition was stronger than Gothic innovation. Walachia and Moldavia were ruled by Orthodox princes who, in the fourteenth century, threw off Hungarian domination and appointed their own metroplitans under Constantinople. In spite of the efforts of Stephen the Great of Moldavia (1457–1504) the 'hospodars' (rulers) of both countries had become vassals of the Ottoman Empire soon after Stephen's death, although successive rulers enjoyed considerable privileges allowing them to develop their own cultures and to support the Constantinople patriarchate as well as the Mount Athos and Sinai monasteries well into the seventeenth century.

Kievan Rus, the early feudal state of the east Slavs, accepted eastern Christianity with the conversion of Grand Prince Vladimir (980–1015). On unifying the country he married the sister of the Byzantine Emperor Basil II and in the year 988 led the population of Kiev to be baptised in the Dnepr. The culture of the court was wholly oriented towards Constantinople and the influence of the Bulgarian patriarchate declined. The Kievan metropolis came directly under the jurisdiction of the patriarchate of Constantinople, and until the Mongol invasions it even became usual to appoint Greek hierarchs. Politically weak rulers had to pay as much attention to them as in the past they had done to the boyar council or the people's assembly. Building commissions, therefore, were often the result of complex balancing of interests, though the architectural influences of Byzantium were not in doubt. Vladimir was succeeded by his son Yaroslav (1016–54) who had begun his reign in Novgorod and extended Kievan power both east and west. His children intermarried with many of the European royal houses including

A. (*right*)
Hadrian's Wall. See p.171

B. (*below*) S. Gimignano: view of the towers (thirteenth–fourteenth century). See p.181

C. (*bottom*) Palais de Justice, Rouen (1493–1508). See p.181

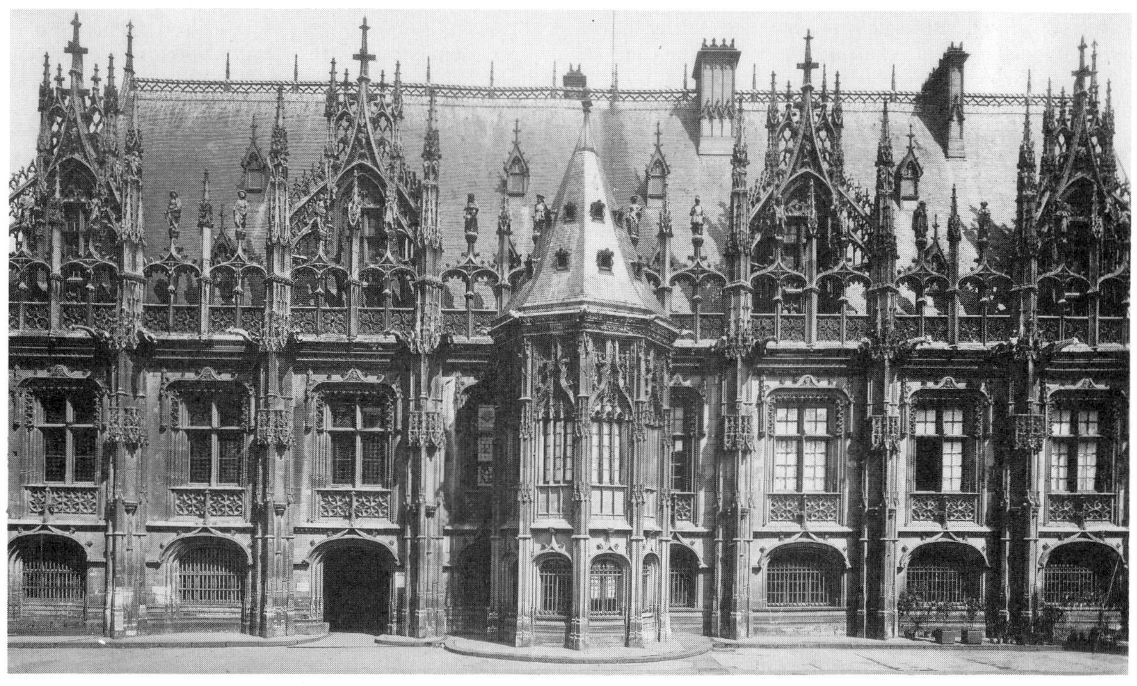

England and France. His death was followed by a troubled period in which the princes fought for power among themselves as well as waging foreign wars, and it was not until 1096 when the agreement of Lyubech was signed by all the princes of the house of Rurik that the secondary centres began to develop: at this time these were Chernigov, Pereyaslav, Novgorod, Polotsk, Volhynia and Galicia and a few other outlying principalities which acknowledged Kievan authority. Southern Russia suffered under attacks from the Cumans and hardly noticed the rise to power of Suzdal in the north-east until its prince, Andrei Bogoljubski, overthrew Kiev in 1169, reduced it to secondary status, declared himself Grand Prince, but remained in his northern capital of Vladimir thus transferring the centre of power from southern to central Russia.

But Suzdal did not achieve the position of undisputed power Kiev had enjoyed. Although Rostov rose to some prominence, the leading states of the twelfth and thirteenth centuries were Smolensk, Galicia and Novgorod. The last was beginning its period of expansion which culminated in the fourteenth and the early fifteenth centuries. It was a productive period in terms of development both civil and ecclesiastical, and more especially in the trading centres such as Novgorod. It was also the period of the first Mongol invasions, which imposed a new overlordship for two centuries from the 1230s. Novgorod seems to have suffered less than other powers at the hands of the Mongols, and apart from having to pay a poll tax to the Golden Horde continued to develop through the the thirteenth century in spite of trouble with the Lithuanians, whose power and influence had also risen during this period. One important result of the Mongol ascendancy was that, in view of the invaders' policy of non-interference in religious affairs, the church continued to increase its power even through the periods of greatest military, political and fiscal repression.

The consolidation of tax-collection duties by the Mongols under the prince of Vladimir invested that capital with the power to unify the Russian states, and through the son of Alexander Nevsky, the last great prince to reign from Vladimir, the power eventually passed to Moscow, until then an unimportant town in Suzdal. The yarlyk (the commission to collect taxes on behalf of the Golden Horde) remained thereafter, except for one short break, with the house of Moscow. All the achievements of the Moscow princes in the fourteenth and fifteenth centuries were as nothing, however, compared with those of Ivan III (1462–1505). From being a few hundred miles across when he succeeded to the title, the principality on his death had reached the arctic and the Urals, the upper Don and Desna and the middle course of the Dnepr. He took Novgorod, Vyazma, Chernigov and Seversk, strove to establish a centralised system of administration and justice, revoked the pledge of tribute to the Golden Horde, and finally assumed the title of Czar and Sole Ruler of all Russia. The proclamations by the 1448 and 1459 synods of the Moscow bishops of an autocephalous patriarchate and the downfall of Byzantium itself gave him theocratic authority within his own church and primacy in the Orthodox ecumene. He used his marriage to Sophia Paleologue, the niece of the last Byzantine emperor, to legitimate his claim to the succession in declaring Moscow the third Rome. This was the base for much building activity and for developing new styles, in spite of the declared aim of following the earlier church-building models. Later Czars, for example Vassily III (1505–33) and Ivan IV 'The Terrible', as well as expanding Muscovy still further, achieved a balance between political and social interests of the traditional and more recent aristocracy, the merchant classes and the church hierarchy.

The Early Mediaeval Period

In order to take up the historical strands related to the burgeoning influence of the western (Roman) Christian church and with it the development of the Romanesque style, it is necessary to move back in time from the period during which Byzantine political power was eclipsed to that of the decline of the western Roman empire which led to the rise of the independent states and nations of Europe.

The coronation of Charlemagne as Holy Roman Emperor in 800 (see below) marked the beginning of a new era with the establishment of a new central European state, politically ordered and bound by both ecclesiastical and political ties to Rome. The Carolingian Renaissance was based upon a Germanic culture allied with late Roman traditions. The great monastic foundations, supported by imperial patronage, proliferated and expanded, closely linked with economic revival, the fusion of Latin and Teutonic communities, and the absorption of Roman Law into the monastic rule. New architectural problems were posed in the building of religious houses and often the monastic tended to take the lead in changes of fashion and technique. Many of the nations of Europe by the tenth century had struggled into existence. By the end of the eleventh century stable Christian kingdoms were established in Scandinavia and Norman England, while the Crusaders set up states in the Holy Land with less durable prospects.

Italy

Central Italy. The Popes, although they had only small temporal domains, began to exercise influence in Italian politics. Pepin, king of the Franks, sided with Pope Stephen II against the Lombards, and restored to him Ravenna, the chief city of the

Exarchate. In 755 Central Italy became independent under the Pope, and so inaugurated the temporal power of the papacy. Then Charlemagne, invited by Pope Adrian I (772–95), advanced into Italy in 774, defeated the Lombards and entered Rome. He bestowed the dukedom of Spoleto on Pope Adrian, the wealth of the Church rapidly increased, and the papal connection with Constantinople was broken off.

Pisa, like Genoa in the north and Amalfi in the south, sent merchant fleets to Constantinople, the capital of the eastern empire, and Pisans were brought into contact with eastern art. At the beginning of the eleventh century Pisa was the rival of Venice and Genoa as a great commercial and naval power, and took the lead in the wars against the infidels, defeating the Muslims in 1025, 1030 and 1089. The Pisans captured Palermo in 1062, and this further contact with Islamic and Byzantine art probably accounts for the characteristic Pisan use of striped marbles. The Pisans were defeated by the Genoese in 1284, and this was the beginning of their decline. The rise of Florence dates from 1125, when the inhabitants of Fiesole moved there when their city was destroyed, and in the following century Florence rivalled Pisa in commerce. Lucca, another important city during this period, was rent by the feuds of the Guelphs, supporters of the Popes, and the Ghibellines, who sided with the Emperors.

North Italy. In spite of the intervening Alps, commercial and cultural contract between northern Italy and northern Europe was very lively. The inroads made by the Goths into the north Italian plains during the fifth and sixth centuries led to the gradual rise of Venice. The indigenous traders planted their new colony on the islands of the lagoon; there, safe from serious attacks, they settled on a republican form of government, which afterwards became an oligarchy under the Doge, who was invested with supreme authority. Commerce and art were the special concerns of the Venetians. Their close alliance with Constantinople greatly increased their commerce, so that by the end of the eleventh century it extended along the Dalmatian and Istrian coasts to the Black Sea as well as the western Mediterranean.

Southern Italy and Sicily. In 827 the Muslims landed and gradually overran Sicily, which had been part of the Byzantine empire. The latter part of the tenth century was the most prosperous part of the Islamic period, after which bloody religious struggles ended the Muslim dynasty. From 1061 to 1090 the Normans, under Robert and Roger Guiscard, were engaged in the conquest of the island, and in 1130 a descendant of the latter was crowned at Palermo. During the succeeding years Sicily was again prosperous, as may be judged by the number and beauty of the buildings of this period, and its fleet was powerful enough to defeat the Arabs and the Greeks.

France

France was part of the Carolingian Empire under Charlemagne (768–814) and Louis the Pious (814–40). Louis the Pious left it to his three sons, and the Treaty of Verdun (843) divided it into three kingdoms, with Charles the Bald as King of France. Subsequently, at the Treaty of Mersen (870), the Middle Kingdom was partitioned between France and Germany, the latter retaining the title of Roman Empire. That part of the Carolingian Empire which came to be known as France continued to be ruled by Carolingian kings until the death of Louis V, in 987. Hugh Capet was elected in his place, which broke the ties with the Empire and initiated the Capetian dynasty. The area bounded by Paris in the north and Orleans in the south (the 'Ile de France'), was the Royal Domain and the French kings' authority extended little beyond until the middle of the eleventh century, the greater part of France being held by the independent lords of Aquitaine, Auvergne, Provence, Anjou, Burgundy, Normandy and Brittany.

The eleventh century was marked by a widespread desire to withdraw from the world and embrace the monastic life; this resulted in the foundation of many religious houses (pp. 185–188), which gave an impulse to architecture and also fostered art and learning. Religious zeal was not, however, confined within monastic walls, but was allied with secular ambition to produce the Crusades, which began in 1096 and were continued under Louis VII (1147). The crusading King Louis (1137–80), aided by Abbot Suger of S. Denis, also displayed his religious zeal through church-building. On the other hand, he weakened his kingdom by divorcing Eleanor of Aquitaine (1152), who then married Henry of Anjou, Henry II of England, thus giving the English king dominion over more than half of France. The country rallied again under Philip Augustus (1180–1223), who was strong enough to subdue the feudal lords and attack Henry II, and it was in his reign that a number of the first Gothic cathedrals were begun (see pp. 423–443).

Central Europe

Under the influence of Rome, Christianity took root in southern Germany and in the Rhineland, while the rest of the region remained pagan. As early as the sixth century the bishops of Trier and Cologne were conspicuous in promoting church-building. Charlemagne ruled over central Germany and northern France, and established Frankish dominion over southern France and northern Italy as well as becoming the first Holy Roman Emperor. He restored civilisation in great measure to western Europe, and was a patron of architecture.

Charlemagne died in 814, and after the death of his son and successor, Louis the Pious, the division of the

Empire in 843 resulted in the establishment of an independent German kingdom. The German princes demanded the right to elect their own sovereign, and Conrad I (911–19) reigned as king of Germany. Henry the Fowler (919–36), the first member of the Ottonian dynasty to come to the throne, drove the Magyars out of Saxony and subjugated Bohemia and the tribes between the Elbe and the Oder to establish a united Germany. Otto the Great (936–73) was crowned king at Aachen. His wars, including his conquest of Lombardy (951), made him the greatest sovereign in Europe, and in 961 he received the Imperial crown at Rome.

When Conrad II became king of Germany in 1024, Denmark, under Cnut the Great, threatened his power in the north, and Poland and Hungary in the east, but he inaugurated the great Imperial age by restricting the power of both the secular and the ecclesiastical princes. Following wars between rival claimants, in 1138 Conard III became the first of the Hohenstaufen dynasty, and was succeeded by Frederick Barbarossa (1152–90), who was also crowned Emperor at Rome. He defeated Denmark and Poland, secured an alliance with Hungary and negotiated with France and England. But his interference in papal schisms brought disaster until Emperor and Pope were reconciled under Gregory VIII. The Imperial cause was again asserted in Europe by the brilliant Frederick II (1218–50), who united in himself the crowns of the Holy Roman Empire, Germany, Sicily, Lombardy, Burgundy and Jerusalem. The political connection of the Hohenstaufen (or Swabian) Emperors (1138–1254) with Lombardy is demonstrated by the similarity of the architecture of the two countries during the later part of the period.

Spain and Portugal

The Visigothic invasions of the fifth century across the Pyrenees displaced the northern tribes of Vandals and Suevi, and the Visigoths took nearly complete possession of the Iberian peninsula for three centuries until the Muslim conquest of all but Asturia in 711–18. The Muslim incursions in south-west Europe were checked by Charles Martel at Poitiers in 732, and subsequent Spanish mediaeval history is dominated by successive extensions of Christian influence and the regaining of territory until the very end of the fifteenth century.

Another outstanding feature of Spanish history during this period is the connection of Spain not only with France, its near neighbour, but also with England through royal marriages; with Italy through papal supervision and the quarrels with the Angevins in Naples and Sicily; and with the Moors from Africa. The Christian states of Castile, Léon, Navarre, Aragon and Portugal grew up simultaneously and gradually drove the Muslims into Andalusia. After many intermittent successes, the battle of Tolosa (1212) was the final turning-point in the decline of Muslim influence and also marks the introduction of Gothic architecture to Spain where it was most highly developed in Catalonia, immediately across the French frontier. James I (1213–76), King of Aragon, advanced in the east of Spain until the kingdom of Granada was the only portion left to the Muslims.

As to social conditions in Spain, only a small proportion of the population, including citizens of chartered towns, was free: under the system of land tenure the peasants were oppressed throughout the Middle Ages, a condition which produced the peasant's revolts of the fifteenth and sixteenth centuries. Society was dominated by the grandees and the clergy: churches and monasteries are the chief architectural monuments, while in domestic architecture there is little of importance except the houses of the nobility.

The British Isles

Christianity first made its way into Britain during the Roman occupation, but during the years of the Anglo-Saxon settlements, after the middle of the fifth century, church building was of historical importance only in Ireland. S. Alban, the first British martyr, died in 209. In 314 the bishops of York, London and Lincoln are recorded as attending the Council of Arles, but religious influences upon building in Britain were very small until S. Augustine landed in England in 597, converted the Kentish King Ethelbert and other kings of the Saxon Heptarchy, and introduced the Benedictine order to Britain. The Seven Kingdoms were based upon the migration of Jutes into Kent, Saxons into Sussex, Wessex and Essex, and of Angles into Mercia, East Anglia and Northumbria. The conversion to Christianity of the Anglo-Saxon kings and their people is evidenced by several surviving churches, towers and crosses of the seventh and eighth centuries.

The post-Heptarchy period, after the Danish invasions of the ninth century and the unification of the different kingdoms behind one leader, King Athelstan (927), until the Norman conquest, was characterised by Benedictine reform and by the monastic revival of the late tenth century. The principal supporters of this movement were King Edgar (959–75), S. Dunstan, who became Abbot of Glastonbury in 960, and Ethelwold, Bishop of Winchester in 963.

In 1042, Edward, son of the English King Ethelred, acceded to the throne. Norman by association and education, he consolidated the kingdom and, largely by the introduction of Norman favourites into the Court and the Church, ensured Norman influence on England before the Conquest. He appointed Robert, Abbot of Jumièges, as Archbishop of Canterbury in 1051, and meanwhile had begun about 1050 the construction of Westminster Abbey which had been planned in the current Norman fashion.

The Conquest of 1066 linked England to Europe and introduced a fully developed feudal system. Yet all land was held from the king, who established the most efficient and centralised government in Europe.

Just over a century later, William of Sens was rebuilding the choir at Canterbury and the transition from Romanesque to Gothic had begun in earnest.

The influx of religious orders from the Continent in the first half of the thirteenth century resulted in the building of many spacious new churches, while internal strife around the turn of the thirteenth and fourteenth centuries encouraged development of the architecture of fortifications and castles.

Scandinavia

Social history in Scandinavia in the early centuries of this era is obscure, but it is evident that kingdoms were established first in Denmark and Norway, and that by about the year 1000 Sweden was united to form part of the Svear Kingdom. The Viking expansion of the ninth century, which included the early Danish settlement in eastern England, the colonisation of Normandy and the establishment of Svear colonies in Latvia, all brought northern influences to bear upon European development.

The most distinctive building development of the period in Scandinavia followed the conversion of the northern races, which was started by the Frankish missionary Angar at Hedeby in Denmark in 826, but not completed until the end of the twelfth century. Some north German influences, encouraged by trade, can be traced, but the Norse Church itself was established from Britain, and Christianity was legally established in Norway, Greenland and Iceland by the end of the tenth century. In 980 the Danish King Harold made his people Christians, English bishops were introduced, and during the following century Cnut and his successors spread their empire to England. In 1030 the Norwegian Christian King Olav Haraldsson was killed in battle, and was later canonised. The cathedral at Trondheim was built as his reliquary. During the eleventh century Christian centres were established successively further north in Sweden, at Lund, Skara and Sigtuna, and in 1130 a diocese was established at Gamla (Old) Uppsala, after the destruction of the pagan temple there at the beginning of the century.

The pattern of mediaeval history in Scandinavia was largely determined by the continuing conflict between Denmark and Sweden. Danish solidarity was early reduced by revolt among the peasants and by conflicts between feudal landowners. By the middle of the thirteenth century the Hanseatic League of north German cities was able to intrude along the Baltic shores, and even on the Atlantic seaboard of Norway. In the southern Baltic the merchant interests of the Hansa were widespread, while the feudal administration of farming depended, particularly in Sweden, upon the alliance between the Crown and the feudal lords. The wars between the Danes against their neighbours and the League led to concessions of substantial land interests to German nobles. The resulting dispersion of aristocratic wealth reduced the opportunities for display in domestic or military architecture compared with other parts of northern Europe.

The Holy Land

The Latin Kingdom in the Holy Land was established as a direct consequence of the First Crusade undertaken by Christian Europe following the call by Pope Urban II in 1095. Earlier efforts had resulted in premature and ill-organised expeditions which met with great losses, but the response to Urban's call produced a force of 150,000 which forgathered in Constantinople in 1097. Later that year some of them passed through the Cilician Gates, the principal pass in the Taurus range, but when Jerusalem fell in 1099 the Crusader force probably numbered little more than one-tenth of those who had left Constantinople two years earlier. By about 1115, towards the end of the reign of Baldwin I, the Latin Kingdom was fully established, but, in spite of continuous reinforcement from Europe, it suffered from a persistent dearth of armed power, and the tendency everywhere was to replace soldiers with fortifications.

When Muslim forces were assembled under the united command of Zengi and Nur-ed-Din, the menace came not from the cities on the fringe of the eastern desert but from Mesopotamia. The loss of Edessa in 1144 was serious because it deprived the kingdom of both corn produce and auxiliary manpower drawn from the Armenian Christian community. The Second Crusade of 1148 was ineffective in compensating for this loss. Saladin's victory at Hattin in 1187 so drastically reduced the strength of the Crusaders in the Holy Land that it never recovered. Although Richard I took Jaffa, Acre and Ascalon in 1191 and 1192, and although Crusader defences were further strengthened and their fortunes varied throughout the ensuing century, the eventual outcome was inevitable: in 1292 the last of the Latins in the Holy Land sailed away from Chastel Pélérin to Cyprus.

The Gothic Period

The political and historical background in France, where the Gothic style originated in the Ile de France, is still significant. Capetian suzerainty of the great counties of France was strengthened and extended from time to time by marriage, as when Louis VIII married Eleanor, the heiress of Aquitaine; but equally, marriage alliances between the great vassals could bring dangerously threatening power blocks into being. The alliance of the houses of Blois and Champagne very nearly eclipsed the Capetians, but their greatest challenge emerged when Henry Plantagenet inherited Anjou from his father, Normandy from his mother, and married Eleanor of Aquitaine, recently divorced by Louis VIII, thus within a few years uniting the entire western seaboard of France, from the Channel to the Pyrenees, under one rule. Besides, Henry was also King of England, so that although the Capetians could claim suzerainty over his lands in France, they had no real advantage of rank.

The so-called Angevin Empire was too big to be really controllable, and liable to fragment into its constituent parts at any moment. But it was rich, and in those areas – England and Normandy – where Angevin control was tightest, administration and government had already, by the second half of the twelfth century, reached levels of efficiency far beyond the primitive and often ineffectual attempt to keep the peace that passed for government in the Capetian domains. Nevertheless, it was in effect the Plantagenet threat that galvanised the Capetians to set their own house in order, and to impose their own relatively centralised rule on the various French provinces.

A series of remarkable personalities guided the fortunes of the Capetians for the best part of a century. Philip Augustus (1180–1223), cautious, tenacious, very astute, was the real architect of Capetian success. He broke the Angevin stranglehold on western France, conquering Normandy and the English possessions apart from Aquitaine in 1204. In 1214, he defeated the Germans, English and Flemish at Bouvines, bringing the rich and well-organised county of Flanders under direct Capetian control. He allowed his son, the short-lived Louis VIII, to extend French royal power into the south of France – the very different Languedoc, with its separate language, troubadour culture and mores – on the pretext of a Crusade against the Albigensian religious sect, which had taken hold in the south, and had recently been declared heretic. At the same time, Philip ensured that French administration absorbed many of the advances of his Anglo-Norman rivals. His grandson, Louis IX, continued the trend toward more efficient and centralised government, but also acquired sufficient reputation as a good, just and pious king to be canonised in 1297.

Even by the twelfth century the Church had largely made good its claim to pre-eminence among the institutions of European society, and was prepared to call new tunes in matters of art and architecture. Essentially these were revised in the interest of ecclesiastical propaganda. Church architecture was progressively purified. A large part of the Church's finances was invested in new buildings, and this was augmented from secular sources in the form of benefactions and bequests. In addition to existing cathedrals and abbeys which were recurrently in need of repair and restoration, the spate of new foundations continued unabated until well into the thirteenth century, and although it subsequently slackened, it never really dried up until the end of the Middle Ages. The Cistercians, the regular Canons, and the orders of friars spread into the remote corners of the continent, and wherever they went they built abbeys, priories and convents. There was at least one parish church in every village and in the major towns sometimes ten or more. Every organisation, secular as well as ecclesiastical, had its own religious life which required a chapel, or access to some part of a church, for corporate worship. Every family of consequence had its private chapel, and from royalty down through the ranks of the nobility to the parvenus of commerce it was a recognised practice to found or to adopt religious institutions in the vicinity of their homes to safeguard the posthumous spiritual needs of generation after generation. The integration of religion into the ordinary conduct of everyday life was total, and the result was a constant flow of funds into ecclesiastical architecture of one kind or another.

At the end of the Middle Ages, Europe was probably more ostentatiously devout than ever before, and religion was certainly no less institutional in the sense that it expressed itself in buildings and the furnishing of buildings. But the central preoccupation of religious observance was increasingly personal and private. It sprang from the individual's concern over his or her own destiny in the world to come. The exponents of these devotions emerged at all levels of society, and most of them were laypersons rather then clerics.

At the highest political level secular rulers found it expedient to set good examples of proper Christian attitudes for their subjects. Already in the thirteenth century S. Louis of France had provided the model, and he also created fine displays of piety in the form of architecture. In the established monarchies of western Europe, royalty and the upper strata of the aristocracy founded chapels or added chapels to their palaces and castles. Rather belatedly the quality of Carthusian observance was recognised and it became fashionable for kings to found Charterhouses. On the eastern fringes of Europe, where enterprising rulers were in process of establishing new territorial and dynastic configurations, the Habsburgs in Vienna, Luxemburgers at Prague, and Casimir the Great of Poland provided their cities with great churches that could rival the cathedrals of the west.

In western Europe, the Hundred Years War (which ended in 1453) and the Black Death spanned a period of conflict and social change which left behind it the need for many kinds of new buildings, secular as well as ecclesiastical, as befitted a period of burgeoning urban expansion. Low down the social scale the burghers became acutely anxious about their spiritual prospects. Few were rich enough to found churches of their own, but collectively they invested heavily in their parish church and those of the mendicant orders, where they worshipped and in which they endowed chapels for soul-masses to be set against their sins in purgatory. Such churches are perhaps the most conspicuous surviving monuments of later Gothic.

They were built in proliferation in every city in Europe, from the Baltic to Tuscany, and from England and the Low Countries to the confines of Russia. Structurally they tended to be less ambitious than cathedrals, though on occasion in places as far apart as Venice, Lübeck and Barcelona (see, for example, S. Maria del Mar, Barcelona), they could rival or even exceed cathedrals in scale. What was really important about them was that they represented a continuous level of output which kept the architectural profession permanently at work.

But the churches, however, prominent, present only one side of the picture. Although they remained the principal focus of patronage, late Gothic was the period in which architecture diversified its attentions and detached itself from exclusive dependence on ecclesiastical patronage. Secular commissions, which earlier in the Middle Ages had been confined to palaces and castles, now extended to a wide range of gentry and vernacular houses in the country, and houses for domestic, commercial and industrial purposes in towns (p. 175C). Moreover, the public buildings of city centres, and amenities such as colleges or hospitals endowed by public-spirited citizens, made demands upon the resources of design every bit as great in their own way as the efforts lavished on purely religious works. Although hardly any of them now survive intact – Venice is perhaps the most notable exception – complete towns as such were perhaps the most important achievements of the later Gothic builders (p. 175B).

The wholesale process of secularising architecture no doubt prepared the way for the reception of the Renaissance; but the momentum was social rather than aesthetic. In the north especially it had proceeded a long way before there was any question of fundamental stylistic change. Nevertheless in adjusting themselves to the demands of urban and domestic building, Gothic architects were compelled to dissipate the original ecclesiastical character of the styles. There is not much about the merchant palaces of Venice or the burghers' houses of Rothenburg that deserves to be called Gothic, and to do so is not much more than a terminological convenience.

Culture

The Prehistoric Periods

Throughout Europe, Paleolithic art appears to have taken three principal forms: portable sculptures of women and animals, paintings on the walls and ceiling of caves, and the decoration of artefacts with geometric designs.

Mesolithic tools were made for a wide range of purposes and art continued to develop. Representational art depicted everyday events such as food collecting, hunting, building and warfare. More abstract, stylised representations were produced in large numbers and Mesolithic engravings have also been found.

The first pottery, as with querns and axes of ground stone, was a Neolithic innovation. Different Neolithic peoples evolved highly distinctive pottery and decorative modes. Stone-built tombs for collective burial, ritual structures and massive earthworks became uses for architectural and artistic elaboration.

The Bronze Age is characterised by the development of metallurgy, although artefacts were produced in a wide range of materials including pottery, glass, precious stones, bone, textiles and organic materials. New forms of burial resulting from the introduction of cremation lacked the elaborate architectural expression of the Neolithic age. The difference between rich and poor graves was marked by the extent to which the burial site was treated architecturally. Fewer elaborate ritual structures were built during this period; stone circles and standing stones were built in Atlantic Europe, and small temple-like buildings have been found throughout the remainder of the continent.

Late Iron Age societies developed a wide range of crafts. Pottery made on a wheel was produced professionally. Metalworking workshops of the kind used by the Etruscans, for example, evolved standard patterns throughout Europe. Carpentry, leatherworking, textile production and wheelwrighting were also highly evolved. Art, particularly in the La Tène period, was used to decorate status items and personal ornaments with stylised naturalistic designs, curvilinear forms and crisp geometric patterns. In some parts of Europe, sculpture in wood and stone was also produced. Burial practices and religion ceased to be the focus of architectural expression, although both were still socially significant. Grave goods continued to indicate differences in social status, while cult sites such as henges, ritual shafts, cemeteries and sanctuaries were still built throughout the Iron Age. Perhaps the greatest cultural difference between the Celtic world and the worlds developing around the Mediterranean seaboard was that the former conserved oral traditions while the latter were rapidly becoming literate.

The Etruscans

As Etruscan power grew, Etruscan society became more stratified and there was an expanding class of nobles. Their wealth depended more on the exploitation of deposits of copper, iron and silver than on animal husbandary and agriculture. With it, and under influence from Greece and further east, they embarked on the building of houses and temples of kinds not previously seen in Italy, as well as roads and other public works.

From primitive animist beginnings, their religion developed under Greek influence into belief in a broadly similar pantheon of gods. The feature which set it apart was a more fatalistic acceptance of the gods' will, which led to great emphasis on determining that will through divination (augury) and on placating it through sacrifices. The correct observance of ritual was held to be highly important, as was the correct following of prescriptions relating to the afterlife of the dead. The dead were buried in cemeteries well outside the cities, the more important in tombs which are now the main surviving monuments as well as the best evidence for the character of the houses of the living.

Republican Rome and the Early Empire

Archaeology helps to confirm the picture given by Virgil and other Latin authors of the simple ways of life of the early Romans. They were essentially farmers, with few of the comforts that contacts with Greece had introduced into Etruscan society. They do not seem to have been deeply religious, but rather to have adopted the practices of others with whom they came into contact, including the Etruscans to whom they probably owed their rituals of divination and sacrifice. As a result their early sanctuaries and temples closely resembled those of the Etruscans. Each house also had its shrine to the family gods.

Early Roman society was strictly patriarchal but balanced by the honour paid to Vesta, goddess of the hearth, and by a strong sense of duty and a dislike of anything sybaritic. Not until the middle of the first century BC were permanent places of entertainment admitted into the capital, though they had long existed in the Campagna to the south. The focus of the city was the forum, the chief place of public assembly, not only for business and political discussion, but also for such entertainments and spectacles as were provided.

This way of life was altered in a number of ways as Rome's power expanded. An early consequence of the Punic wars was a marked change in the pattern of settlement of the countryside outside the city. Small independent landowners were replaced by newly rich landlords whose big estates were run by hired labourers and slaves. In the capital itself the population was swollen by influxes of non-Romans including war captives, slaves, and dispossessed small farmers. To accommodate them, new forms of high-density housing and other major public works were called for. Their arrival and close contacts with numerous different cultures led also to other changes – from the import of new religious cults and practices to the adoption of many aspects of Hellenistic life and art. At the same time, the change in the pattern of government set in train by Augustus led to an unbridgable gulf between a minority of full citizens and a large urban proletariat with few, if any, rights. To keep this proletariat reasonably happy, a policy of providing free corn and free entertainments – bread and circuses – was adopted. Specifically Roman forms of entertainment were the chariot races that took place in the circus (see p. 243) and gladiatorial combats which had their origin in funeral rites involving human sacrifices for the future wellbeing of the dead. The profligate tastes of some of the successors to Augustus – himself a frugal man of simple tastes – and a new ostentatious display of the power of the empire, and the majesty of the emperor, completed the transformation. Linked with the last was the practice of deifying emperors after their deaths and erecting new temples in their honour.

The Later Roman Empire

Generalisation about the later empire is less easy because its territory was so widespread. The situation differed greatly between those provinces where the indigenous culture was less advanced than Rome's and those where it was initially at a higher level. As the new masters, Romans preferred to leave their subjects to conduct their affairs in their own way, subject only to certain obligations and to the oversight of a provincial governor. Thus, for instance, local religious practices were allowed to continue if they posed no apparent threat to Rome, and large new temples might even be erected to local gods. The same policy resulted in the import of new religions into Rome itself with the movements of armies, traders, captives, and slaves. Even the imperial throne was eventually occupied by non-Romans.

In so far as there was a consistent official attitude to religion, it was dualist in character. Something had survived of the fatalistic Etruscan belief that the future of the empire was ultimately in the hands of the gods and must be safeguarded by the proper observances which were in the hands of the priests, and successive emperors lavished money on building new temples to the gods of their choice. Personal wellbeing was the concern only of the individual so long as there was no conflict with the interest of the state. Thus the way was open for the spread and growth of other religions, notably those from the more monotheistic east. Of these, the worship of the sun became the most important in the third century, and was officially adopted by some emperors and paved the way for the later acceptance of Christianity by Constantine. Christianity spread chiefly among the underprivileged in those commercial centres visited by Jewish traders, but by the early second century its adherents were to be found in most strata of society, and by the third century they had become numerous enough to be regarded as a serious threat on several occasions. This led to ineffectual persecutions by Decius (249–51), Valerius (257–61), and Diocletian.

The significance of Constantine's conversion to Christianity stemmed from the fact that he saw the Christian god as a new protector of the state. Architecturally, this resulted in a vast new programme of church building, though pagan worship was not outlawed until 391.

A secular institution, the public baths, calls for some comment at this point. Its origins can be traced back to Republican times, and the first such bath in Rome itself had been built by Agrippa in the time of Augustus and was probably modelled on earlier baths built elsewhere, for example at Pompeii, Herculaneum and Baia. It is to the later empire, however, that the great surviving baths belong – usually known as thermae to distinguish them from the smaller earlier balneae. They were much more than the name now suggests. They embodied the Greek idea of the gymnasium, and were not only places for luxurious bathing but also for social intercourse and recreation in many different ways – intellectual as well as physical.

Constantinople and the Byzantine Empire

The continuity of the Byzantine empire with the earlier Roman empire in the east has already been stressed – as indeed it was by the Byzantines themselves. But the continuity did not preclude change in the pattern of life – nor even in the nature of the new official religion that lay at its heart – as the empire itself changed.

At least until the end of the sixth century, life in Constantinople and in the other cities of the Byzantine empire followed a similar pattern to that of Rome, with much the same institutions. The differences were differences of degree. The bloody contests associated with the amphitheatre had never been important in the East. The forum had become less a place of public assembly because the general public no longer played any part in government. The public baths were still important, and chariot races in the hippodrome became the chief public entertainment, with semi-official factions supporting the principal teams. In Constantinople the emperor presided over them, as he had done in Old Rome, and a dole of corn continued the earlier Roman practice.

A consuming interest in the finer points of religious doctrine probably stemmed partly from a more philosophical eastern approach aiming to define the indefinable, partly from a conviction that it was supremely important to get things right, and partly from the fact that religion provided an outlet for the expression of ideas that might have been expressed in more openly political terms in a freer society. Doctrinal differences had begun to arise as soon as the early Christian converts from the more intellectual strata of society sought to define their beliefs.

These differences mostly centred on the nature of Christ and his relation to God. In 325 Arianism, which had its source in Alexandria and which held Christ to be purely human, was condemned as a heresy by a Council summoned by Constantine in Nicea. Yet, in Italy, it was still a powerful counterforce to the accepted doctrine two centuries later, because of its adoption by the Gothic emperors who ruled in Ravenna. In the East, by this time, however, the chief difference was over the single or dual nature of Christ. Those who held the first view (the monophysites) were in the majority in Syria and Egypt, while the second view was the official orthodoxy in Constantinople. The difference led to persecutions of the monophysites fully comparable with the earlier persecutions of the Christian church by pagan emperors, and to alienation of the peoples in these regions that must have contributed substantially to the later rapid Arab conquests.

In the eighth century another heated controversy arose over the admission of representations (icons) of divine persons in church buildings. Leo III (717–41) forbade them, and this iconclastic view prevailed until 843, when the icons were restored – though the only representations allowed were those on a flat surface in paint or mosaic. They were never sculptural as their counterparts often were in the west.

There were parallel changes in practice which affected the detailed planning of churches. They are less important architecturally than the virtual end of church building in lands conquered by the Arabs, and less important also than the general decline in the fortunes of the empire from the early seventh century, which meant that virtually all later building was on a much reduced scale. Even the city as it had existed from Classical times was in sharp decline – a decline that was reversed only to a limited extent in the eleventh century. Too little secular building survives to indicate what architectural changes stemmed from Seljuk and Ottoman influence as a counterpart to changes in dress.

The Balkans and Early Russia

The Slavic monarchs derived their concept of the state, their ceremonial and their strategy of government from the Imperial court in Constantinople. Like the Byzantine emperors, they compared themselves to the apostles to vindicate their divine right, though – with the exception of the Russian czars after the downfall of Byzantium – they did not aspire to succeed Rome in world supremacy. The patriarchate of Constantinople enjoyed unchallenged precedence and conveyed canonical privileges which it used as the political situation required – from the formal confirmation of a spiritual leader nominated by a Slavic monarch to the appointment of a Greek hierarch to the metropolitan see. The monastic centre was Mount Athos, which adhered to the strict rule of the Studios Monastery in Constantinople. Slavic church worship was patterned on Byzantine worship and Old Slavic literature based itself on Greek models. However, S. Cyril and S. Methodius (see below) themselves had omitted the Imperial laws from their translation of the nomocanon, just as later Slavic translators always made their selections from the Greek texts.

The Byzantine heritage provided not only fixed models but, above all, a method. The revivals of Classical values stimulated the rediscovery of native tradition; furthermore, orthodoxy in religion and politics inculcated a particular 'style' of thought and perception – in a sense, a cultural 'code' in which analogy was of central importance. The Byzantine Empire was seen as an imitation of God's Empire in heaven, the church liturgy a repetition of the heavenly liturgy that Christ celebrates with the angels and apostles. The physical image, the icon, was held to mirror the spiritual image and the dome over the crossing was compared to heaven above earth, the domed church to the universe. Analogy was understood in the neo-Platonic sense as a 'dissimilar similarity'. The unchanging nature of the core of the liturgy, the iconographic fixity of pictorial types, the longevity of architectural norms are all connected with the cultural 'code', and because analogy did not necessarily demand total congruence of model and copy, it allowed some latitude. Standardisation was nevertheless inherent in it. Standards helped stabilise the religious, ideological and social system of the Christian Orthodox feudal state, and church-building served the same end.

It was in the second half of the ninth century that the conflict between the Carolingian and Byzantine empires for control of the Slavic east began. S. Cyril and S. Methodius were sent to Moravia by the patriarch of Constantinople to put an end to Frankish domination, but were subsequently enlisted by the Holy See. Their true intentions remain a mystery, but in addition to inventing the Old Slavic or Glagolitic alphabet one of their lasting achievements was a bible translation and a Church Slavic liturgy which helped bring the south and east Slavs towards Orthodox Christianity. The west Slavs joined the Roman Catholic Church with its Latin liturgy, and the deepening religious divide determined the development of church architecture. Bulgaria, Serbia, Macedonia, Walachia and Moldavia, which had mainly belonged to the east Roman Empire, and the Russian states from the Baltic to the lower course of the Dnepr all followed the example of Byzantium in architecture as in religion. Bohemia, Great Moravia, Poland, Hungary, Croatia and Transylvania opted for Rome and so for Romanesque and, later, Gothic architecture.

Mediaeval society outside Byzantium followed similar patterns to those in Byzantium itself. These included the alternation of strict, centralised monarchy and feudal fragmentation, the growing share in land ownership held by the churches and monasteries, the lack of social mobility and political independence in the towns, the Christian Orthodox state religion and strategy of government, the critical opposition movements with their heretical rejection of the liturgy and church worship as practised by such sects as the Bogomili and the Strigolniki. The Slavic monarchs were intent on preserving political and ecclesiastical independence but the cultural supremacy of Byzantium went unchallenged. They sought to equal, even to rival, the Byzantine emperor. The Bulgarian Czar Simeon and the Serbian king Stephen Dušan went so far as to claim in their titles dominion over the Greeks. The Russian Czar Ivan III proclaimed himself successor to the Imperial throne after the downfall of Byzantium. For all three, emulating the emperor also involved adopting the court ceremonial of Constantinople in which palace and church architecture played an important role. The symbolism of rank made building compulsory. It could be achieved either by striving for independence in art – as in politics and in religion – or by conforming to Byzantine norms. Either course recommended itself as a means of bridging the distance between the 'barbaric' upstart and Imperial Roman prestige. The choice was for each Slavic ruler to make individually and was determined by his circumstances: the need to involve other political forces, for example, the strength of native traditions, the existence of workshops in which the artistic and craft skills were available.

The rise of Kievan Rus under the east Slavs and the Varangian invasions led to a series of conflicts towards the end of the tenth century, and although Kiev had had a Christian church for a century before, it was the victory of Vladimir and his early conversion to Orthodox Christianity which was the turning point in Russian culture. In the early days of the new religion it was brought to the towns by Bulgarian priests who used the south Slav liturgy and the Cyrillic alphabet which led to the beginnings of Russian as a literary language. Under Yaroslav the fruits of the fusion of Slav with Byzantine culture were seen. New educational and legal institutions were founded – the Slav origins of the culture were stressed and Russian history was interpreted in terms of the Orthodox faith. The rise and fall of Vladimir, and the eventual movement of the power to the north – first Novgorod and then Moscow – as a result of Pecheneg dominance in the south, was another culturally vital stage in the transformation from Kievan Rus to Muscovy. But major political as well as cultural changes were on the way. The Seljuks were already converting Asia Minor to Islam, inflicting a devastating defeat on Byzantium at Manzikert in 1071, opening up the territory to the Turks. Shortly after this Slavonic Europe reached its apogee, and in less than another century the political and cultural scene was to change again with the fall of Constantinople to the crusaders in 1204, soon to be followed by the sack of Kiev by the Mongols. Even in the two and a half centuries which followed, before the eventual decline of Mongol power and the final triumph of the Ottomans over Byzantines, the decorative arts, much influenced by local skills, continued to be vigorous in the newly developing Russian towns, and this was to be supplemented by imported design and craft skills as early as the first half of the fifteenth century. But loyalty to Byzantine models influenced artistic development even after Constantinople had ceased to be the centre of ecclesiastical administration and power.

Early Mediaeval Culture

For hundreds of years after the collapse of the Roman empire, Europe to the west of the Elbe remained unimportant politically and culturally by comparison with the eastern empire of Byzantium. Architecture atrophied along with Europe's effective political unity and its basis of territorial power. Its eventual isolation, cut off from Constantinople by intervening Bulgars in the east and under threat from Islam to the south and south-west, meant that the foundations of a continental culture had to be laid in a context of confusion and conflict. When the cultural evolution restarted, it is not surprising, therefore, that there was, for example, evidence of Islamic influence in the mode of the further evolution of Italian Byzantine models. While the influence of the Byzantine church itself continued in parallel elsewhere (see Chapter 16), ensuring the extension of the style well past the middle of the second millennium, in Europe the Romanesque style, with its roots in the Roman basilica plan, was also evolving and would quickly be transformed into the Gothic of western and northern Europe.

Christianity and the influence of the religious orders, and with them education and culture, were spreading. The effects were secular as well as ecclesiastical, because often the erection of a church or monastery was the signal for the foundation of a town – further evidence, if such were needed, of the burgeoning power of the Church which rivalled or controlled such civil government as existed. By reason of their feudal possessions, bishops and abbots were also military chiefs who sometimes took the field in person. Everywhere the power and prestige of the Church increased. Religious enthusiasm and zeal found their material expression in the magnificent cathedral churches and monastic buildings, which were an even more significant outcome of this period than were the castles of feudal chiefs.

This same religious fervour led to the Crusades against Muslim occupation of Palestine and the Holy Places, and this intermittent warfare (1096–1291) between Christians of the west and Muslims of the east was not without its effect on western art. Monastic communities had existed since the fourth century, and by 800 the spread of Benedictine houses was being promoted by Charlemagne and other rulers. The eleventh century proved especially remarkable for the development of the monastic system, which encouraged new methods in agriculture and exercised its influence on architecture; indeed, until the end of the Middle Ages science, letters, art and culture were largely the monopoly of the religious orders. The schools attached to monasteries trained young men for the service of religion; monks and their pupils were often the designers of churches.

The principal religious orders were:

1. The Benedictine Order, founded early in the sixth century at Montecassino in southern Italy by S. Benedict of Nursia. Possessions were held in common, but the absence of particular vows of poverty facilitated charitable works and agrarian enterprise. Benedictine houses were commonly sited in towns, part of the church being devoted to offices for the laity.
2. The Cluniac Order, which also followed the rule of S. Benedict, founded by Abbot Odo in 910 at Cluny in Burgundy. By the twelfth century the abbey of Cluny was one of the most powerful institutions in Europe.
3. The Carthusian Order, founded by S. Bruno at the Grande Chartreuse near Grenoble in 1086, returned to eremitic and ascetic principles, which had elsewhere been relaxed. The order was recognised only in 1142. The Charterhouses, often remotely sited, provided separate cells for the monks, generally grouped around a cloister garth, and the community served a simply-planned church; Carthusian architecture is notably severe and unadorned.
4. The Cistercian Order ('White Monks'), founded in 1098 at Cîteaux, and shortly afterwards at Clairvaux. After 1134 all Cistercian churches were dedicated to the Virgin and had no separate Lady Chapel. The ascetic aims of the Cistercian Order produced an architecture which was at first simple and severe.

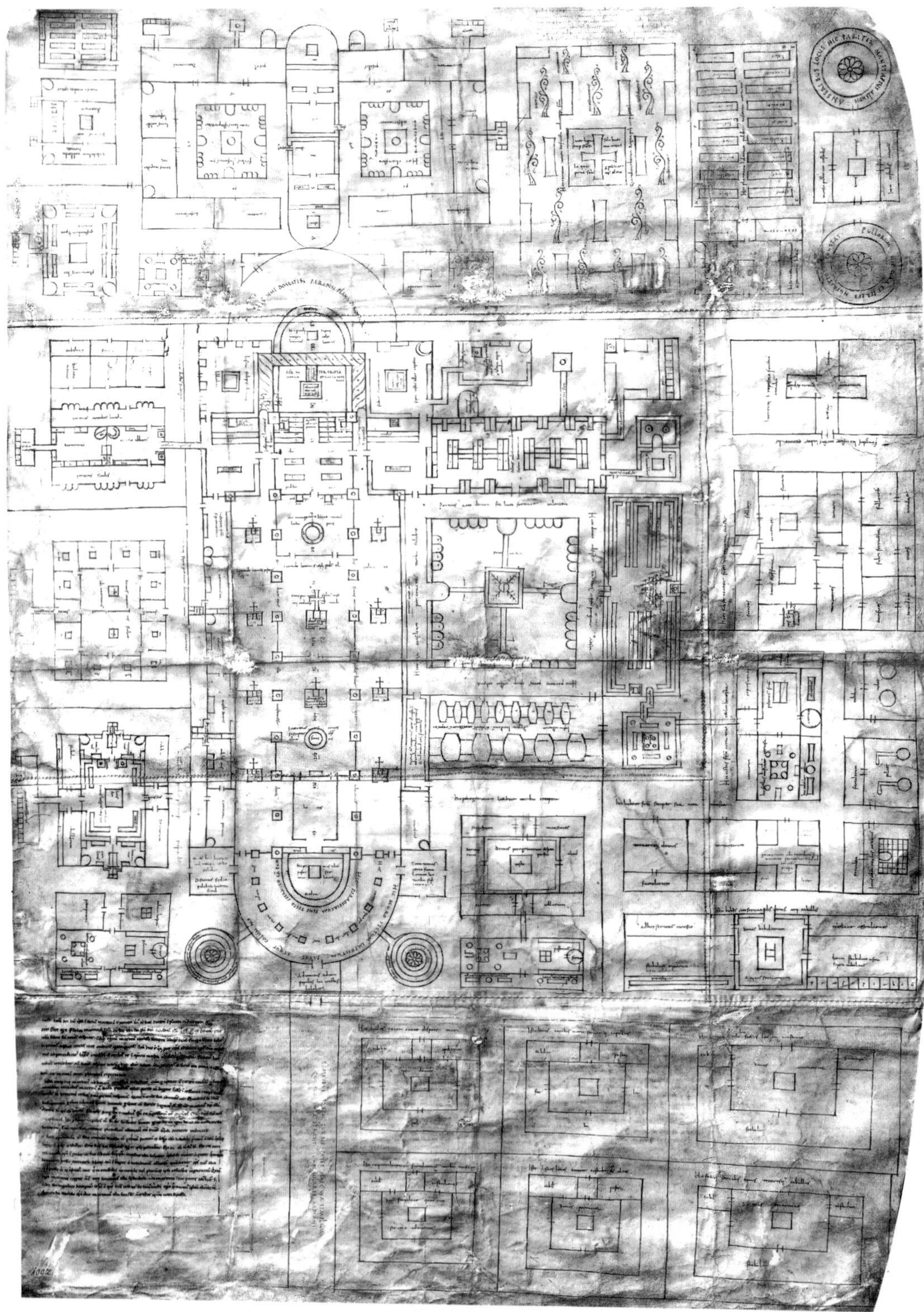

Monastery of S. Gallen (*c.* 820): original plan. See p.188 and opposite

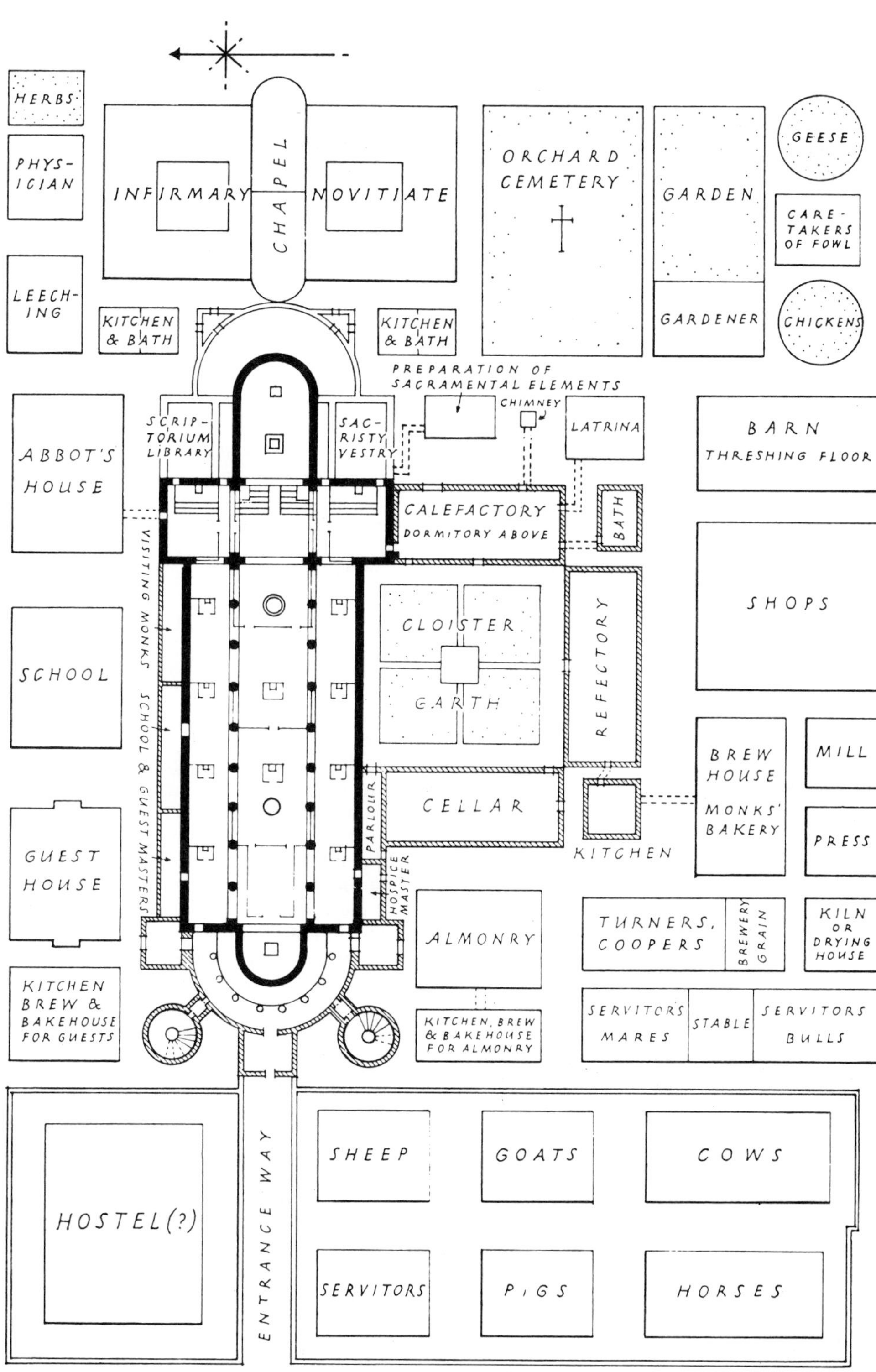

Monastery of S. Gallen: schematic diagram of plan opposite

5 Secular Canons, serving principally cathedral and collegiate churches. They lived according to the rule of S. Chrodegang of about 750.
6 Augustinian Canons ('Black Canons regular'), established in about 1050. They undertook both monastic and pastoral duties in houses often sited in towns, and planned similarly to those of the Benedictine Order.
7 Premonstratensian Canons ('White Canons regular'), founded in 1120 by S. Norbert at Prémontré in northern France.
8 Gilbertine Canons, an exclusively English order, founded in 1131 by S. Gilbert of Sempringham, which usually combined a house of canons under the Augustinian rule with another of nuns under the Cistercian rule, in conventual buildings attached to a common church divided axially by a wall.
9 The Knights Templar, founded in 1119 to protect the Holy Places in Palestine and to safeguard the pilgrim routes to Jerusalem. Templars' churches were modelled upon the Church of the Holy Sepulchre in Jerusalem.
10 The Knights Hospitallers, organised in about 1113 (the Knights of S. John of Jerusalem) under Augustinian rule. The order eventually held a great deal of property in Europe, but developed no characteristic architecture of its own.
11 The mendicant orders of friars, founded during the thirteenth century and headed by the Franciscans and the Dominicans. The functions of friary churches with an emphasis on preaching were sufficiently distinctive to demand planning of a characteristic kind, but they developed when Gothic architecture was already succeeding Romanesque throughout most of Europe. Their houses were usually sited in towns, where the friars preached and did charitable works among the common people. Some also played an important part in the rising universities throughout Europe.

Nothing is more expressive of the developing power of the holy orders and of culture in Romanesque Europe than the planning and building of monasteries. Typically, the developed monastery plan of the Middle Ages consisted of a square or rectangular cloister to the south of the abbey church, the projecting transept arm determining its eastern boundary. The cloister, open to the sky, had a covered walkway on each of its four sides supported on one side by arcades and on the other by the walls of the most important conventual buildings. To the east side of the cloister and to the south of the transept arm lay the chapter house where formal meetings were held to make decisions on the running of the community. Further south lay the dormitory at first floor level above an undercroft. To the south side of the cloister was the 'frater' or refectory and the kitchen. The frater often incorporated a pulpit from which readings were made during meal times. The west range contained the abbot's lodgings, guest rooms and a cellar for the storage of food. The other buildings of the monastery such as the infirmary, the brewhouse, the bakehouse, stables and farm buildings were arranged according to the limitation of the site. Fresh water was readily available with provision for washing in the cloister.

The abbey church itself was divided into two, the eastern parts reserved for the monks, the nave usually open to lay people. The partition or screen was normally situated two or three bays west of the crossing. It contained a pulpit and immediately to the west of it was placed the nave altar. The monks' stalls were immediately to the east and ran beneath the crossing. The high altar was situated in the main apse and there were various subsidiary chapels in the aisles, transepts and galleries. All the buildings of the monastery were contained within a walled precinct with gatehouses. Except for the absence of a chapter house, which became an essential element during the eleventh century, the ideal plan of S. Gallen (Switzerland) prepared early in the ninth century provided a model layout for the arrangement described above (pp. 186–187).

Not all monasteries adhered rigidly to this plan, however, and the particular requirements of some orders necessitated differences. This is especially important in the case of the Cistercian Order, which had to provide quarters for large numbers of lay brethren (*conversi*) who were required to run the monastic estates according to the Cistercian practice of direct management. They were housed in the west range with a separate frater and worshipped in the nave of the church separated from the monks' choir. In England, cathedrals were often run by Benedictine monasteries in conjunction with the bishop. In all other European countries, cathedrals were under the jurisdiction of the bishop and his own community of secular canons; monasteries were not under episcopal control and, indeed, were often critical of the bishop.

The Pilgrimage Churches

Pilgrimages were a much-practised form of religious devotion during the Middle Ages. Christian fervour inspired thousands to travel to the innumerable shrines and holy places throughout Europe and the Near East. The shrine of S. James (Santiago) at Compostela in the north-west of Spain was a principal centre of pilgrimage which attracted pilgrims from as far afield as Britain and Germany. Churches and monasteries en route were able to make considerable material gain from providing accommodation and facilities to worship. The wealth generated along the pilgrimage routes during the eleventh and twelfth centuries enabled religious communities to build vast new churches. Masons and sculptors were in constant demand and, understandably, frequented these routes and spread the new Romanesque style along the routes to Compostela from the 'Ile de France'.

The main pilgrimage churches are S. Martin at Tours (begun after 997, largely demolished at the time of the French Revolution), S. Foi at Conques (*c.* 1050–*c.* 1130), S. Sernin at Toulouse (1077–1119) and Santiago de Compostela (1078–1122). The churches share a mature Romanesque style, with ambulatories, compound piers and triforium galleries – all the principal Romanesque characteristics. A school of architectural sculpture covering south-west France and northern Spain evolved in connection with the design and construction of the pilgrimage churches.

Italy

Central Italy. The growth of an industrial population, the increase of commerce and the rise of powerful ruling families promoted the foundation of independent and fortified cities, such as Pisa, Lucca and Pistoia, all rivals in architectural achievements. The effects of internecine feuds between these city-states can be seen in architectural features such as the battlements of castles and fortifications. The artistic activity of Tuscany in the eleventh century showed itself chiefly in architecture, which in turn provided a setting for the arts of painting and sculpture.

North Italy. As a result of the alliance of Venice with Constantinople, precious freights were brought from the East to glorify Venetian buildings. Thus did the East triumph in the West through its influence on the buildings of the Queen of the Adriatic. The free cities of north Italy, such as Milan, Pavia, Verona and Genoa, vied with one another in the beauty of their public buildings, and this spirit of rivalry encouraged the most remarkable structural advances in all Italy.

Southern Italy and Sicily. Under Islamic rule in Sicily, even church facades were ornamented with geometrical patterns, because the Muslim religion forbade the representation of the human figure. The Muslim and earlier Byzantine influence persisted even after the Norman conquest of the region in 1061. The traditional use of mosaic in decoration was fostered by the Norman kings, who established a school of mosaic at Palermo. Southern Italy, which always maintained a close connection with Sicily, largely avoided Islamic influence, retaining close contact with the eastern empire.

France

Many of the major religious orders – for example, the Cluniacs, the Carthusians, and Cistercians – were founded in France (see p. 185). The French played a leading role in the Crusades and in the formation and government of the eastern Latin empire until its decline and final disappearance at the end of the thirteenth century. The culture of northern Europe was much influenced by the regional Romanesque art and architecture of France. The high reputation of the University of Paris, which originated in the cathedral schools, attracted influential teachers during the twelfth century and was widely recognised. Though intellectually distinguished, mediaeval France did not form a coherent cultural unit in any sense: different art forms, sculpture, and poetry, for example, as well as architecture, only gradually grew together under the Capetian kings to produce the French tradition as it is now understood. In literature as in architecture, the dominant themes were feudal loyalty and Christian faith, closely related as they were to the mystic ideal of the knight dedicated to the service of Christ.

The Romanesque style was developed to the point of near perfection in the structural articulation and architectural sculptures of Vézelay, Arles and Angoulême. The imposing recessed west doorways with sculptured tympana were the forerunners of the magnificent sculptured doorways of the Gothic period.

Spain and Portugal

Spain's many links with neighbouring countries, with England and with Italy, all affected in varying degrees the architecture of the Iberian peninsula. The evidence of Islamic influence appears in curious construction and exuberant detail and occurs quite often even in the Christian north, owing to the demand there for Muslim craftsmen with their superior ability. Muslim features were most evident in the churches of the Mozarabs – Christians who were tolerated in areas under Muslim control.

As a result of the exultation over the conquest of the Muslims at Tolosa in 1212, Christian art achieved a great impetus, aided by the plunder taken from the enemy.

Christianity reached the Iberian peninsula in the second century and flourished for most of the following two hundred years. The constant warfare, which was religious more than racial, gave a certain unity to the Christian states of the peninsula. Throughout the mediaeval period the Church was the strongest and most constant unifying force in the struggle against the Muslims, and as a result it obtained great temporal power and possessions. This fact, and the Spanish taste for dramatic ceremonial and ritual, determined the planning of the cathedrals and churches with their great sanctuaries and enormous chapels for the noble families. The Muslim religion forbade the human figure in sculpture and decorations, and encouraged geometrical ornament. The result of this ordinance is seen in the richness and intricacy of surface decoration even in Christian churches, on which craftsmen trained in Islamic traditions were often employed.

The British Isles

The main effects of monastic reform in the tenth century were to introduce the features of continental building, which had been briefly foreshadowed in Britain only in the northern work of the school of S. Wilfrid of York and in seventh-century Kent.

After the advent of William of Normandy, castles were built to strengthen the position of the conquerors. Towns, which grew up around abbeys and castles, became trading centres, and through their merchant guilds laid the foundations of urban government. Villages continued as mere collections of rudimentary dwellings. Settled government prompted the pursuit of learning, based in the twelfth and thirteenth centuries upon monastic schools and upon the two English universities. French was the language commonly used in court circles until the thirteenth century.

The First Crusade was preached in 1096 by Pope Urban II and Peter the Hermit. The later Crusades induced an exchange of ideas between East and West, and involved England in international movements. Richard I, son of Eleanor of Aquitaine and Henry II, after his experience of the Third Crusade, established a pattern of military architecture in his building of Château-Gaillard at Les Andelys in Normandy. The Crusades gave impetus to the progress of learning and in the foundation (1113–19) of the military orders which influenced some aspects of church-building later in the Middle Ages. In 1128 the Cistercians built their first English house at Waverley in Surrey, and in 1175 William of Sens began the rebuilding of Canterbury Cathedral choir in the new Gothic style.

Scandinavia

The monastic orders played an important part in reinforcing Scandinavian links with Europe. The Benedictine church architecture of Denmark and Norway followed very closely the custom of the order; several Cistercian abbeys were established in Denmark and Sweden, displaying the simple and robust characteristics of Burgundy, and plan forms derived from both Fontenay and Pontigny. Smaller churches in mediaeval Scandinavia, even as late as the fourteenth century, were built in simple Romanesque form. In more remote and secluded areas fashions in building were usually those of an earlier period. In Finland, for instance, the expansion of Swedish power in the eastern Baltic promoted church-building in stone after the beginning of the thirteenth century, but the stylistic characteristics which persisted were predominantly Romanesque.

The Holy Land

The Frankish fighting men were in a minority even in their own garrisons in the Holy Land, and some of the characteristics of the magnificent military architecture resulted as much from the need for security against internal revolt as against external threat. The continuation of the Holy War throughout the twelfth century produced buildings that were not only of immediate military value but were to have a wide influence upon later castle architecture in Europe.

It is worth emphasising that the building initiative of the Crusades was turned to the necessary religious functions, and in many cases these were combined: the Templars' hospice buildings in Palestine usually included a fortified church. No complete example remains, but there is a comparable late survivor at Luz (1260) in the French Pyrenees. The great inland castles almost invariably had a chapel, and Tortosa has a cathedral church. Churches were built, or more usually adapted from existing buildings, in many of the holy places. The centres of administration, however, and the communication network, were based upon the castles. Contemporary descriptions indicate clearly the importance of the castles as the secure centres of agrarian communities dependent upon the cultivation of the surrounding land, and owing allegiance of the feudal lord whose fief extended over the country commanded and protected by the castle.

Gothic Culture

While the Crusades of the thirteenth century atrophied and the Latin empire in the east dissolved, in northern Europe the energetic development of Frankish architecture produced buildings with pointed masonry arches and with vaults capable of covering the vast naves and transepts of the churches built on the plan forms evolved from Romanesque models.

It is essential to realise that Gothic was fundamentally an ecclesiastical style. This does not mean that Gothic architects did not build castles and houses. But the style was seldom at its best or fully realised in secular buildings. In every castle the chapel always looks more Gothic than the rest. It was eminently suited for vast vaulted halls, and not at all for small rooms, especially if they had to be placed on several floors. It was not impossible to construct one vaulted hall on top of another. It was done very effectively at the Albrechtsburg at Meissen and the Hradčany at Prague. But it was costly, inconvenient, and difficult to adapt. As soon as the conduct of affairs required uncluttered rooms, served by long corridors and imposing staircases, the days of Gothic were numbered. Conversely, the style attracted a lot of sympathetic attention in the nineteenth century when structural engineers were called upon to produce large sheds for railway stations.

There are no contemporary accounts which provide incontrovertible evidence that churches were thought to have specific meanings. On the other hand, imagery was rife, and the development of Gothic architecture went hand in hand with the development of Gothic sculpture, stained glass and painting, which provided the churches with a plentiful quota of permanent spiritual residents. Their presence leads naturally to notions of cathedrals as comprehensive symbols of the Heavenly Jerusalem or the Church Triumphant. In a strictly functional sense a cathedral was a collection of altars, each dedicated to its own saint whose title was represented by his relics, and for the sake of whose intercessions the endless, liturgical round was performed. By an easy extension the church itself could be regarded as a kind of monumental reliquary. Loosely, all these iconographical themes come together as research into shapes and spaces likely to induce attitudes of reverence and a lively sense of holiness.

It is not necessary to suppose that such ideas were indispensable, or that they were applied in rigid, literal ways. But whether they were taken seriously or not, they help to correct the impression put about by influential interpreters like Viollet-le-Duc to the effect that Gothic was nothing more than structural engineering. However important and distinctive the engineering it was always liable to be at the service of religious and aesthetic considerations. It was never an end in itself. Even at its most sensational, for example in the prodigy towns and spires of late Gothic, the aim was to project something visually exotic and obsessive on town and countryside for miles around. Nevertheless it remains indisputable that none of the brilliant effects of Gothic would have been possible without the high level of professional competence achieved by its craftsmen.

Resources

Prehistoric Periods

The advance and retreat of the ice-sheets throughout the Paleolithic period left little surviving evidence except in caves and rock-shelters. Moreover, the resources available to Paleolithic builders were limited. In western Europe, surface materials such as timber, brushwood, stones and the hides and bones of animals were collected and assembled into dwellings. A more abundant and spectacular architecture was found in the rigorous periglacial steppe regions of eastern Europe where, throughout the Paleolithic ice age, hunters systematically collected mammoth bones to build shelters.

Resources do not appear to have been systematically exploited during the Mesolithic period, but the Neolithic was notable for the development of mining. Igneous rocks and flint were actively exploited and raw materials were exchanged over long distances. Trees were felled and processed. Housing was mainly built from local materials, but the erection of monuments involved the use of non-local materials. A major resource during the Neolithic period was manpower. Major monuments are estimated to have taken many millions of man-hours of work and such practices appear to have continued into the Bronze Age, but with a steady increase in the availability of materials and products from distant locations.

In the Iron Age, a wide range of natural products was exploited. Ores were obtained by surface grubbing and deep shaft mining. Both iron-smelting and the construction of large-scale defences required the wholesale clearance of high-quality timber. Building materials were often transported over considerable distances.

Etruscan and Early Roman

Central Italy was less well endowed with the excellent readily available marbles that were exploited to such good effect by Greek architects. Local stone was used where strength and durability were important, as in some of the later defence walls and in temple platforms and tombs – though the latter were often cut directly out of the rock if it could be cut easily. There were, however, good brick earths. Until quite a late date, unfired mud brick or rammed earth was the usual alternative to wattle and daub for walls, fired terracotta being used only for roofing tiles and in other positions where durability was important or fine decorative detail was desired. Good timber was also readily available and was used for posts and beams and other roofing members.

Later Republican and Early Imperial Rome and Italy

The most significant changes in the materials accessible to the architect in later republican and early imperial Rome and Italy were the introduction of fired brick, great improvements in the quality of mortar brought about by adding natural pozzolanas (volcanic earths) to the lime and sand, and the import of foreign marbles coupled with the first large-scale exploitation of Carrara marble.

More extensive use was also made of locally available stones. In the neighbourhood of Rome these included tufa, a porous volcanic stone of varying degrees of hardness; travertine, a fine hard limestone from near Tivoli; and peperino, a stone of volcanic origin from the Alban Hills. None of these was of the quality and strength of Greek marbles. The bricks were, from the beginning, tile-shaped – those known as bipedales being about 40 mm (less than 2 inches) thick and having face dimensions of almost 600 mm (2 Roman feet) square. Their production was soon highly organised and standardised, as, at a somewhat later date, was that of marble columns and other marble elements.

Equally significant were the financial resources that came from the booty of foreign conquests. Victorious generals sponsored new public buildings and other public works, and Augustus himself set the pattern for later emperors by sponsoring new construction on an even larger scale. Wealthy individuals undertook both private and public commissions. Contacts with the Classical world of Greece and the Hellenistic east permitted the import of architectural skills, to which Vitruvius bears witness even while adopting a conservative pose and arguing for the maintenance of older native traditions. To undertake the vast building programmes, it is obvious that there were large bodies of both skilled and unskilled craftsmen. From the later first century AD we have some record of their organisation and their division into numerous specialised crafts, membership of which tended to become hereditary. It is also important to note that the almost universal adoption of brickfaced concrete by this time greatly reduced the need for skilled workers as compared with unskilled.

The Wider Roman Empire

In the provinces outside Italy there were, initially at least, great differences between one place and another. In those provinces where Rome took over long-established earlier Hellenistic kingdoms, the change in administration brought about no great change in the materials available. In much of the east and of North Africa, for instance, dressed stone continued to be the usual material for buildings of any importance. Fired brick was, however, introduced for walls and vaults where good stone was less plentiful and mud brick had been used previously. Mortars with similar properties to those made from natural Italian pozzolanas were made by adding crushed underfired brick to the mix. On the other hand, in the provinces north of the Alps where there was no comparable earlier tradition of building, new materials began to be used. Wherever possible these materials were of local origin in order to eliminate the high costs of transport. The most important from about the first century AD were those that could be employed to make variants of Roman brick-faced concrete.

The necessary skills in design and construction were already available in those provinces where well-developed building traditions existed and continued to evolve. If Roman rule made any difference here, it was probably in facilitating the movement of architects and the more highly skilled craftsmen from place to place, with a tendency for the best to be selected for imperial service – men like Trajan's principal architect, Apollodorus of Damascus. Elsewhere the necessary skills must initially have been imported; small cadres of skilled men were brought in to direct unskilled local labour.

Sponsorship followed a similar pattern to that already referred to in later republican and early imperial Rome, though on a varying scale according to local wealth and importance. Some major building programmes were undertaken in the home countries of non-Italian emperors like Septimius Severus; others, later, in places like Trier when they became imperial residences. One of the more surprising features of later imperial architecture is the scale of some of the works undertaken, especially in Rome, when the empire was already in decline and subject to severe economic problems. There are, however, indications of straitened circumstances in the growing reuse of materials – including highly worked masonry such as columns, capitals and decorated friezes – taken from earlier buildings.

The Early Christian Period and the Byzantine Empire

With the increasing Christianisation of the empire during the fourth century, patronage passed more and more to the Church, which soon acquired large holdings of land and other wealth by gifts.

Indications of straitened circumstances can nevertheless be seen in the even more widespread use of salvaged marble columns, for instance in the large number of new churches built soon after Constantine's adoption of Christianity, and in edicts of 334 and 337 seeking to made good shortages of skilled architects and craftsmen. Other evidence from this time emphasises again the mobility of such men and shows that plans for new buildings might be sent from one place to another when suitable local architects were not available. To set alongside Vitruvius's optimistic description of the ideal polymath architect in the first century BC, we have, on the other hand, a more factual description by Pappus of Alexandria of architectural training in the early fourth century. This stresses the necessity of a theoretical background in the then-known mechanical sciences for the leading practitioners, suggesting that there may have been a substantial increase in professional expertise at the highest level.

It was men with this background who were later chosen by Justinian for his major commission, the church of Hagia Sophia in Constantinople. It is clear from the magnitude of this undertaking, and from the scale of Justinian's other building works as recorded by the court historian Procopius, that, by the early sixth century, there was no longer any shortage of resources in the East, however much the position might then have deteriorated in the West. Some of the marble quarries that had supplied the earlier Roman Empire were no longer active, but many were still working and there was a large production of finished marble elements from the quarries of the Proconessian islands in the Marmara. There were ample supplies of fired brick, still of much the same type as had been introduced centuries earlier in Rome. And there was even an extensive use of iron – more extensive than at any earlier time.

It is equally clear that these conditions did not last. From the later sixth century onwards, all building works were on a much smaller scale. When, for instance, churches had to be rebuilt, they were almost invariably reduced in size – a change that cannot be wholly explained by the fact that it was no longer necessary to accommodate such large numbers of people. Nor were there any significant additions to the available materials in the later Byzantine Empire. On the contrary, choice was increasingly restricted. Even before this, long straight pieces of timber had already become scarce as a result of clearances of forested areas, and many earlier sources of marble were no longer accessible or the quarries were no longer worked, so that there was an increased dependence on what could be salvaged from earlier buildings.

The Balkans and Early Russia

The region's geographical location and physical characteristics have had a profound influence on the developmenent of its traditional architecture and on the spread and assimilation of foreign cultural influences. The northern boundary is formed by north Russia; an area of vast forests – mostly conifers and birch to the west but also oak and hornbeams, maple and lime. To the south of the forests are the great plains – the steppes, traversed by mighty rivers like the Volga along which merchandise, materials and cultural influences flowed into Russia from the south and, along the Dnepr from south-east Europe and, via the Vistula, from north-west Europe.

Good-quality building stone was in short supply within Russia although readily available in the Balkans. It was not until the conquest of the Baltic and Black Sea that Russia acquired a source for workable and durable stone. Brick, thin of form and usually painted or rendered and a legacy of Byzantine influence, was in common use by the sixteenth century for important public buildings, fortifications, monastries or mansions. But it was the use of timber – the only generally available and economic building resource – that came to characterise traditional Russian architecture.

As early as the first century BC Vitruvius recorded that the people of Colchis in the Pontus district bordering the Black Sea built houses of horizontally laid timbers with the gaps between logs filled with splinters of wood and clay. This system was to remain essentially the same for the next 2000 years for traditional timber construction around the Black Sea and in north Russia. Using mostly straight-logged coniferous trees such as pine and fir (but also oak), the carpenter worked using an axe but no saw or metal nails. Logs were laid hoizontally and interlocked at corners. Each log was hollowed slightly at the bottom to fit that below, with interstices being filled with moss or oakum. The timber was rarely seasoned, but laying the logs horizontally, one upon the other, meant that in the process of drying and shrinking the weight of the logs would tend to prevent individual timbers warping or splitting. The external face of the logs was usually left rounded (and sometimes covered with clay in exposed regions to increase the building's ability to exclude wind and water) but the interior face of the logs was usually axe-hewn flat and painted.

Indigenous building materials and technologies, along with the region's climate, had an immense influence on the architectural ideas imported into Russia and the Balkans. For example, the Byzantine forms, notably the half-spherical dome, developed in a warm Mediterranean climate, evolved in snowy Russia into the bulbous cupola.

Romanesque Period

The adoption in the Romanesque period, and more especially in the growing economic prosperity of the eleventh and twelfth centuries, of the basilican plan for abbeys and cathedrals laid emphasis, in terms of resources, upon the skills in design and execution of masons and the availability and accessibility of supplies of suitable stone for building. That is not to say that other skills and materials were unimportant. Brickmaking, for example, in north-west Italy, was also vital (S. Ambrogio, Milan, is a brick building), as were supplies of timber which continued to be used for roofing during this transitional period in the continuing development of stone vaulting into groined systems capable of spanning naves as well as aisles. Fire risks, both from accidental causes and under military attack, provided the primary motivation, but it was also necessary somehow to reduce the weight and complexity of both the centering system used in construction and the weight of such stone roofs as those of the Burgundy churches.

In some locations diverse skills and materials were combined in interesting transitional buildings. For example, S. Miniato, Florence, begun in the first quarter of the eleventh century, had a timber-framed roof over a marble-colonnaded nave, but was now divided into three compartments with transverse stiffening arches in place of the timber or metal ties used at Torcello and elsewhere.

Mosaics and wall painting continued to be executed, especially in those areas directly in touch with the Classical or Byzantine traditions, and such direct contacts, for example in south Italy and Sicily, still produced decorative bronze panels which were used to face pilasters, or to decorate wall panels.

There was little glass used in building before the ninth century, although for more than a century previously the demand for glass for churches had already begun to change the emphasis of glass production in the Seine–Rhine regions from domestic ware to window glass. Blown and spun so-called 'crown' or 'bullion' glass was produced by Syrian workers in the imperial Roman period; the Venetians learned the skill from them, and it was from Venice that the method passed across Europe to Normandy and to Britain. There is evidence that stained glass was used in Constantinople, but its development is associated with northern Europe and the earliest examples are in the later Romanesque churches.

The principal glory of Romanesque achievement, however, is in figurative and non-figurative sculpture, designed and integrated with structure and construction. Thus the availability of stone was of prime importance to the style but the availability of materials determined the constructional as well as decorative modes used in the countries and regions concerned.

Italy

Central Italy. Tuscany possessed great mineral wealth and an abundance of stone. Various building materials were used in Rome, including bricks, volcanic tufa or peperino, travertine stone from Tivoli, and marble from Carrara and from Paros and other Greek islands. Much material was also obtained from the ruins of Classical buildings.

North Italy. The low-lying plains of Lombardy supplied clay for making bricks, which, used with marble from the hills, gave a special character to the architecture. Venice imported marbles in its merchant vessels.

Southern Italy and Sicily. The mountains of south Italy and Sicily supplied calcareous and shelly limestone as well as many kinds of marble, while the sulphur mines, especially those of Sicily, largely contributed to that prosperity which was conducive to building enterprise.

France

France has an abundance of good stone, easily quarried and freely used for all types of buildings. In the north the fine-grained Caen stone was available throughout Normandy. In the volcanic district of Auvergne the coloured pumice and tufa were not only used for walls and inlaid decoration, but were so light in weight that they were also used in large blocks for the vaulted roofs peculiar to the district.

Central Europe

Stone from the mountains along the Rhine Valley was the material used for buildings in this district. Along the Baltic shores and in central and southern Germany there was an ample supply of timber. As there was no stone or timber in the plains of the north, brick was used almost exclusively in the district east of the Elbe, and the style consequently differs from that of other districts.

Spain and Portugal

The Iberian peninsula itself is a great rock massif, including the Sierras of Castile in the north, the mountains of Toledo in the centre, and the Sierra Morena in the south. Natural resources in building stone include granite in the north; limestone in the south and the Ebro basin; red sandstone in the Pyrenees and Andalusia, and both eruptive rock and semi-marbles distributed everywhere. Building generally relied upon the use of these stone sources. The eruptive rock served for rubble walling with brick bonding courses and quoins, which was used under Muslim influence with much success, as in the towers and gates of the city of Toledo; while in Valladolid bricks of Roman character are laid in thick mortar beds. There are few forests in Spain, and the conspicuous absence of timber suitable for building accentuates still further the predominance of stone in architecture.

The Holy Land

Here stone materials of eminent suitability for great castles and small churches were abundant, though timber was not as plentiful as in those parts of Europe from which the Crusader builders had come.

Britain

The varied geological formation of Britain was responsible for a wider variety of building materials, and in early times the survival of remains from the

Roman occupation provided ideas for variety in the methods of using them. In some instances, the Roman buildings provided opportunity for reuse of the materials themselves. The English hardwood forests, particularly in the north-western and south-eastern counties, provided roof-framing material for the more important buildings, and for lesser buildings which were entirely timber-framed. Most of the indigenous building stones were used in military and religious buildings. Local characteristics in masonry developed at an early stage, if only because of the difficulty of transport over long distances. Consequently, walling in flint is largely confined to East Anglia and the chalk hills in the south. Stone from Caen in Normandy was brought by means of sea and river transport for some building work under royal patronage. Except for isolated and mostly early instances of the reuse of Roman brick, it was not until Gothic had succeeded Romanesque that brickwork was redeveloped as a building material.

The Gothic Style

The introduction of the pointed arch and vault as a means of covering a rectangular shape on plan took place over a fairly long period in Europe; this makes it difficult, and in a sense unnecessary, to date the beginning of the Gothic period. But the flowering of the style and the refinement of its ethereal qualities depended largely upon the master masons of the time.

The foundation of their skills was an ability to cut and shape stone. There were Gothic carpenters of distinction, especially in England where the profusion of hardwoods in the deciduous forests sustained their efforts to rival the stonemasons; and right across northern Europe, from Belgium to Lithuania, brick was often used to great effect in place of stone. But the essence of the style was its stonework, and the best Gothic buildings depended on the plentiful supply of easily worked, fine-quality freestone.

Many of the best quarries were associated with the Jurassic limestone belt that lies diagonally across England from Yorkshire to the Dorset coast, and reappears across the Channel in the vicinity of Caen, whence it runs in a vast sweep, south via Le Mans and Angers to Poitiers, then eastwards, past Bourges, and north through Champagne. Of course, other stones could be used. In the west of England and up and down the Rhineland from Holland to Basle, local red sandstones were perfectly satisfactory. In chalk areas clunch was reckoned to be adequate for walls; and the art of knapping flints for use in building became something of a speciality in Kent and Norfolk, where they were plentiful. But material conditioned quality, and it is only necessary to compare what could be done with the granites of Brittany or the volcanic stones of the Auvergne, on the one hand, and the limestones to the east and north on the other, to realise the extent to which the Gothic style was a stonecutter's art.

The exploitation of local materials was an economic necessity. To move stone any distance was slow and expensive. Costs became prohibitive when it had to be moved overland. The only effective way of transporting quantities of stone over long distance was by water – even by sea, which explains why Caen stone found a market in England throughout the Middle Ages. As cathedrals and abbeys were the first large-scale users of stone, they had a vested interest in acquiring and working quarries, and the economics of church-building were for a long time handled by the ecclesiastical authorities themselves. This tended to put a limit on the scale and pace of operations. We can obtain a glimpse of the hand-to-mouth way in which work was carried out, even on an immense undertaking like the building of Dover Castle, from the building accounts of Henry III. It must have been apparent that stone would be needed in hundreds, even thousands of tons, yet it was ordered by the cartload, on a day-to-day basis. Quantity surveying, if it existed at all, was evidently at a rudimentary stage. But in the course of time, as the building industry diversified, it became expedient for masons to cope with all the problems of supply and to become in effect contractors. It was in this way that a mason like Henry Yevele in England could become prosperous enough to make his mark in the City of London.

Contracting was one of the ways in which masons made money; but the social status of the profession was bound up with the transformation of the stonemason into someone recognisable as the modern architect. There is an important sense in which the history of Gothic is reflected in the emergence of the architect as the designer of buildings. To imply that architects in previous periods did not prepare designs is perhaps an overstatement. No doubt Romanesque masons always had some idea of what they intended to do before they started to build; and no doubt most Gothic churches show signs of having been altered in the course of construction. It is a matter of degree and of complexity. The sense of a controlling overall design, even in such a relatively elaborate Romanesque building as Durham, is rudimentary, whereas at Laon and Bourges it is overwhelming, even though they took several generations to build, and more than one master was in charge of the work. They were thought out, right down to the level of quite small details, before a stone was laid. By comparison, Durham can almost be described as a happening.

Building Techniques and Processes

Prehistoric Periods

Throughout the Paleolithic period the basic forms of building were a teepee-like tent or oval hut of framed timber or bones. In some places additional protection was achieved by partially digging the dwelling into the ground.

Most of the houses built during the Mesolithic period were light wooden constructions of which little remains. The major developments appear to have occurred in finishes and forms of decoration, and in the adoption of different techniques for summer and winter dwellings.

Neolithic houses were detached, timber-framed with pitched and gabled roofs. They were built across much of Europe, although techniques and practices varied widely in accordance with plan forms and local materials. Mud and wattle were generally used as infill and reeds or thatch as a roofing material. Elsewhere, drystone dwellings were built. The Neolithic peoples were skilled in the working of stone, knew the precise properties of the parent rock and had highly developed methods of quarrying and dressing stone. The megalith builders used a range of drystone techniques including corbelling and coursed masonry walling. Copper smelting was practised in some parts of Europe.

Metalworking techniques were evolved throughout the Bronze Age, and included the sinking of deep mineshafts, and the smelting, casting and cold working of metals. Architectural development was almost entirely linked to the complex systems of ramparts and strongpoints in the landscape.

By the close of the Iron Age, building technology had become much more sophisticated. Increasingly complex carpentry and joinery were made possible by new tools such as the lathe, two-man saw and high-quality adzes. Improvements in timber technology, and the use of new materials like brickwork, were brought about by the need for stronger defensive systems. It has been argued that some of these new developments and techniques were imported from Greece and the ancient Near East.

Etruscan and Early Roman Period

The first Etruscan and Roman builders used the locally available materials in the simple ways that were characteristic of primitive building everywhere. By the seventh century BC, techniques that had long been common in Greece and elsewhere were introduced. Timber was used for free-standing columns, for spanning openings, and for the framing of walls and roofs. Where, in the more important structures, timber was exposed to the weather, it was given some protection by coverings of tiles and facings of terracotta. Unfired mud brick and undressed stone were used as infillings in timber-framed walls or were used as building materials in their own right. But as neither timber nor unfired brick was durable enough to last for long, even with some protection, first-hand knowledge of these techniques is largely limited to stone.

The way it was used varied with the nature of the stone. The soft volcanic tufa found chiefly in the neighbourhood of Rome could be cut easily into squared blocks and thus lent itself to construction in squared ashlar – which became known as 'opus quadratum' – from an early date. The harder limestones that were commoner elsewhere were less easily cut in this way. They were used initially, therefore, either as undressed rubble or, where maximum strength was required as in city defence walls, in a partially dressed polygonal form which allowed the blocks to be closely fitted together on the outside. No mortar was used in ashlar or closely fitted polygonal work, though the interstices behind the closely fitted joints would be packed with earth and smaller stones; when the wall was really a facing to a raised terrace or a podium, it would be completely filled in this way. Where rubble of smaller size was used a bonding mortar was necessary, however, and mortars composed simply of lime and sand seem to have been introduced from the Greek colonies in southern Italy by about the early third century BC.

Openings, even in masonry walls, would usually have been spanned by timber beams or lintels. In the earlier massive defence walls few gateways have survived to their full heights unchanged, and those that exist suggest that up to the third century BC the openings were always spanned by corbelling the masonry on each side to narrow or close the gap. It was thought that voussoir arches were constructed by the Etruscans much earlier than this and were used, for instance, in the Cloaca Maxima in Rome and the Porta all' Archo in Volterra in about the sixth century BC, but both the arched outlet of the former to the Tiber and the arch of the latter are much later reconstructions.

The earliest surviving voussoir-arched gates in central Italy date only from the later part of the third century – that is, from a time when Etruscan power had largely succumbed to Rome. Thus it seems almost certain that the stone voussoir arch was introduced to Italy from Greek colonies in the south, or from Greece itself – where it had made its appearance somewhat earlier, possibly inspired by the brick arches that had long been common in Egypt and Assyria. At about the same time it began to be used for road bridges and, in the form of the barrel vault, for roofing small underground tomb chambers, conduits, and the like.

Later Republican and Early Imperial Rome and Italy

The main development of the stone voussoir arch took place in the second and first centuries BC in situations where there was no surrounding masonry or earth to stabilise the arch against outward-spreading movement of the feet.

The really significant contribution of Roman builders to the early development of the arch – and then of the barrel vault – was to support it on freestanding piers. The full story cannot be traced without records of initial failures, but it is reasonable to surmise that the idea arose from the construction of bridges and aqueducts which called for several arched spans to be carried on quite low broad piers. The arch profile, it should be noted, was always semicircular (p. 248). This facilitated cutting of the voussoirs and construction of the timber centering on which the arch was erected. Bearing in mind that the arch ring was always substantial in relation to the span and that the haunches were always loaded by masonry placed above them, this profile was at least as efficient structurally as any other. In fact, the stability of any arch is far more dependent on the firmness of its supports than on its profile, which only becomes significant when the arch ring is shallow and there is no stiffening by masonry over the haunch.

There is, however, one partial exception to the universality of the semicircular profile to be noted. This is not an arch proper but another way of overcoming the lack of stone suitable, like Greek marble, for wide-spanning architraves. Single blocks of stone with sloping ends were set over the columns, and the gaps between them were then closed by dropping in further blocks with their ends cut to fit – a procedure that was to lead to the construction of flat lintel-like arches consisting of a larger number of voussoirs.

Alongside this development of the stone voussoir-arch in republican Rome, there were three other related developments in construction. The first was simply the more widespread use of cut stone where previously timber, rubble, or mud brick had been used – a parallel development to that which had taken place centuries earlier in Greece and Asia Minor, and even earlier in Egypt. As it occurred at the time when Roman expansion brought close contact with Greece and the Hellenistic world, it may have been inspired by this contact if not actually brought about by Greek architects. With it was associated the practice – also adopted earlier in the east – of fastening the blocks of stone together with bronze or iron cramps and dowels. The second and third developments, which eventually were largely to displace the first and to be of the greatest architectural importance, were the use of improved mortars to make a building material analogous to modern concrete and, linked with this, the introduction of fired brick of tile-like proportions in place of the earlier unfired brick.

Reference has already been made to the improved mortar incorporating natural pozzolana, known at the time as 'pit sand' to distinguish it from river and sea sand – for which it must have been regarded simply as a straight substitute until the superior quality of the mortar made with it was realised. Its use in place of the simple lime-sand mortar used previously in walls made of rubble stone could create an almost monolithic mass when it had fully hardened. Moreover it was capable of hardening without access to the air, and hence could do so both in the heart of large masses of masonry and under water. On account of this last property it is commonly referred to as a 'hydraulic' mortar.

To build a foundation or a wall, barrow-loads of stone and mortar were tipped in layers, one after the other. There was no premixing as today. But there was a need for some sort of containment of the fluid mass, especially as the practice developed of using quite small stones or pieces of broken brick – 'cementae' as they were called – and liberal amounts of mortar. Concrete for a foundation was usually confined between formwork made of timber boarding fixed to vertical studs. For walls above ground, however, facings of a more permanent character were preferred.

The earliest wall facings were of stone, much like the ashlar and polygonal masonry of earlier walls, but made from much smaller pieces of stone – a mere 100 mm (4 in) or so across. At first these were dressed only on the outside face if at all, giving the wall the appearance of rough small-scale polygonal work. The result was then known as 'opus incertum'. This led to the use of similarly sized pieces of soft tufa dressed square on the outer face, and cut pyramidally to tail back into the concrete behind so as to obtain a good key. These pieces were then set lozenge-fashion to create a net-like pattern on the surface, so that the resulting work became known as 'opus reticulatum'. In both these forms, larger blocks of square stone set in the normal manner were used to give greater strength to the vertical angles (p. 198).

Later, in 'opus testaceum' and 'opus mixtum', facings of fired brick were substituted for the reticulate tufa or combined with it, using brick at the corners in both cases in place of stone quoins. Most of the bricks were cut to a triangular form, tailing back into the concrete core to give a good key. But at intervals in the height of the wall, full bricks were laid across its whole thickness, presumably to bond the two facings together until the mortar hardened and to mark the end of a fresh 'lift', and to provide good seating for the short poles that were built in, as work proceeded, to support platforms for the workmen to stand on.

As these different manners of facing the concrete are such conspicuous features of surviving Roman

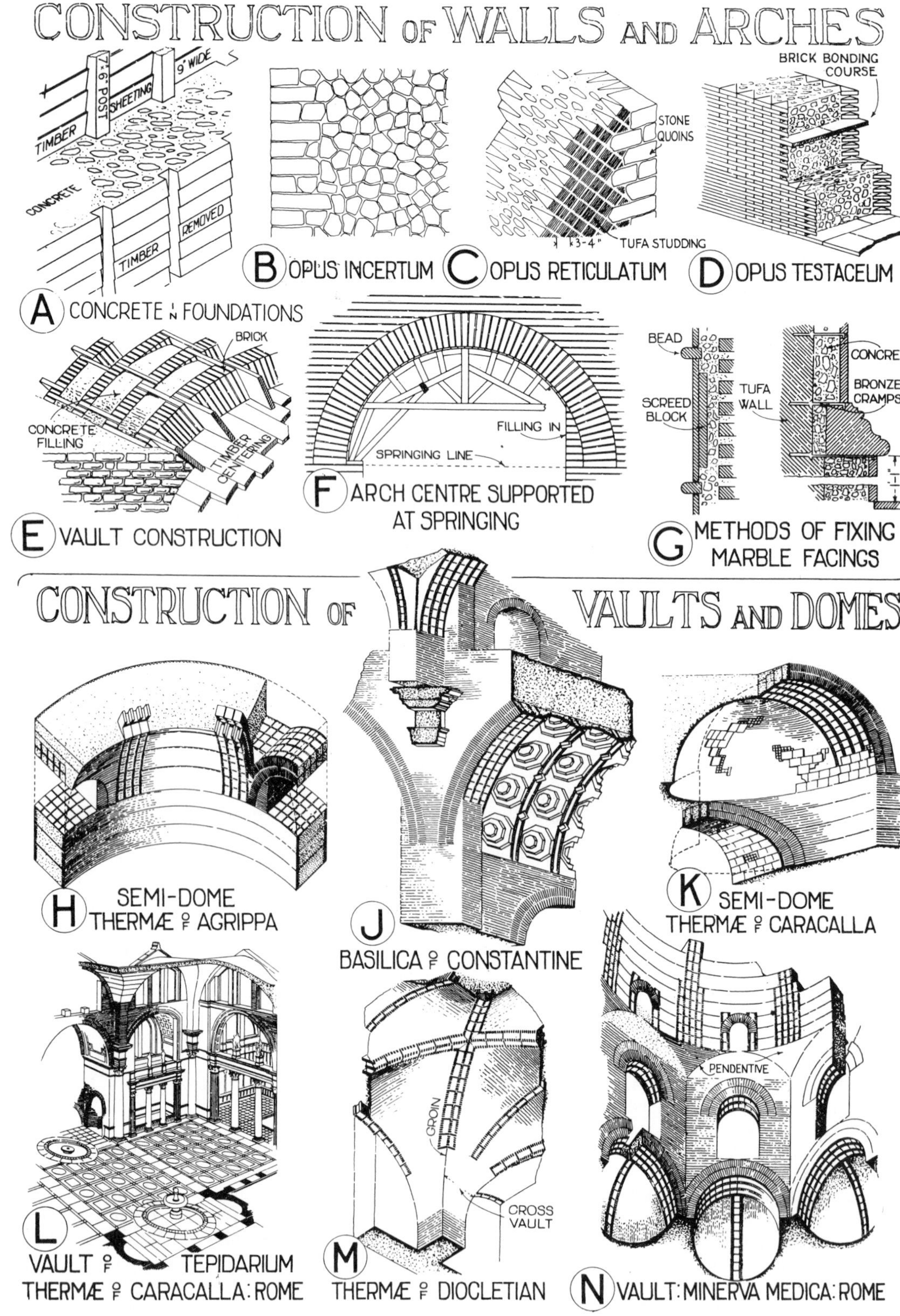
CONSTRUCTION OF WALLS AND ARCHES
7'-6" POST
9" WIDE
TIMBER
SHEETING
CONCRETE
TIMBER
REMOVED
STONE QUOINS
3-4"
TUFA STUDDING
BRICK BONDING COURSE
A CONCRETE IN FOUNDATIONS
B OPUS INCERTUM
C OPUS RETICULATUM
D OPUS TESTACEUM
BRICK
CONCRETE FILLING
TIMBER CENTERING
E VAULT CONSTRUCTION
FILLING IN
SPRINGING LINE
F ARCH CENTRE SUPPORTED AT SPRINGING
BEAD
SCREED BLOCK
TUFA WALL
CONCRETE
BRONZE CRAMPS
G METHODS OF FIXING MARBLE FACINGS
CONSTRUCTION OF VAULTS AND DOMES
H SEMI-DOME THERMÆ OF AGRIPPA
J BASILICA OF CONSTANTINE
K SEMI-DOME THERMÆ OF CARACALLA
L VAULT OF TEPIDARIUM THERMÆ OF CARACALLA: ROME
GROIN
CROSS VAULT
M THERMÆ OF DIOCLETIAN
PENDENTIVE
N VAULT: MINERVA MEDICA: ROME

monuments, and because they succeeded one another over a period of about two centuries in such a way as to serve as one indication of approximate date of construction, there has been a tendency in the past to exaggerate their importance. Architecturally, and even structurally, once the mortar was set, they are of little significance. It must first be emphasised that it was the concrete core on which the strength of the finished wall chiefly depended. Second, however well finished and decorative the facings were, they were rarely the final finish; they were usually covered by stucco or marble both inside and out.

The most important consequence of the introduction of concrete was the stimulus it gave to the development of all kinds of vault, which can be followed through from the early second century BC in the region around Naples, where natural pozzolana was first used, to almost the end of the imperial period (p. 198).

Like all arches, most vaults require temporary support while they are being built. This is true to much the same extent whether cut stone is used or concrete, but the more fluid the concrete is initially, the more need there is for continuous support over the whole inner surface. Timber formwork was mostly used for this purpose. Initially it was not fully realised that its presence, coupled with the initially almost monolithic character of the set concrete, obviated the need for a voussoir-like setting of the cementae. When this was realised, the cementae and mortar were simply tipped on the formwork in horizontal layers as they were when building a wall. As a result of this practice vaults were given a stepped external profile, or one that was simply vertical-sided up to a much flattened, almost conical top. The concrete of each layer could then be confined on the outside by means of vertical boarding or a permanent vertical-sided brick facing until the inward slope of the inner surface became flat enough for the remaining concrete to be finished externally to a similar slope without any containment. Successive layers were stepped back as the vault closed inwards and gave worthwhile saving of material and labour.

Even the simple groined vaults used in Hellenistic architecture had called for complicated dressing of the blocks of stone forming the groins. The use of concrete for vaulting was important because it did away with the need for this complicated stone-dressing and permitted a much freer choice of vault form. Because the concrete could take any form defined for it by the timber formwork and, whether it was then realised or not, because the practice of making the vaults vertical-sided at the foot resulted in such large relative thickness here that stability was scarcely affected by the geometry of the inner surface, this choice was now limited chiefly by the skill of the carpenter.

The dome was the simplest form of vault to build, as it always had been, and it continued to be the one with which the largest spans were achieved (p. 250). The difficulties of providing adequate temporary support did nevertheless increase, as for any other form, as the inside surface became more nearly horizontal. For this reason some of the earliest domes were more conical than hemispherical, and in later domes it was usual to evade the most difficult operation of closing the crown by leaving it open to the sky.

Less needs to be said about the arch. The introduction of fired brick led, of course, to the construction of arches that were the direct counterpart of the earlier mud-brick arches of Egypt and Mesopotamia, but in brick-faced 'opus testaceum' the arch was largely absorbed into the wall; only a few of its bricks were whole bricks penetrating through the full thickness of the wall. Once the mortar had hardened, the concrete largely took over. Semicircular profiles remained usual, although flatter segmental arches were used over smaller door and window openings, and even arches with completely flat soffits where, earlier, there would have been stone lintels or flat stone arches. The generally conservative and always empirical approach of the builders led, however, to the continuance of the practice previously adopted in ashlar 'opus quadratum' of placing a second full semicircular arch over the flat lintel-like one to relieve it of load if it later proved to be too weak by itself.

Finally, a fourth development of a different kind about which much less is known in detail was concerned with timber trusses to allow the construction of wider-spanning roofs carried on less massive walls than would be called for by concrete vaults. Precisely what forms the early roofs took is unknown because none survive and there are no adequate descriptions. Vitruvius, writing in the first century BC, suggests that at least the principle of tying together the feet of sloping rafters by means of horizontal timbers spanning between them was known in his day.

Later Developments in Imperial Rome

In major surviving monuments of the second half of the first century AD it is possible to see most of the types of construction described above except the timber roof-truss. By the early second century, brick-faced concrete was used almost universally for walls and for all but the most heavily loaded piers. It was faced with stucco or marble, frequently having nails driven into the mortar between the facing bricks to provide a better key or anchorage. Vaults were all constructed of concrete, sometimes with tiles laid flat on the timber formwork to provide an initial under-surface. Terracotta or lead flues, drains, water supply pipes and the like were buried in the concrete as construction proceeded.

Later there were gradual changes in the composition of the concrete, with a tendency to use more broken brick and less mortar. To lighten vaults, voids were deliberately created within the massive haunches by incorporating empty amphorae. And there was a progressive introduction of what look like embedded ribs of brick, associated with the use of lightweight cementae in the intervening concrete. They appeared not only where they might first be expected – along the groins of groined vaults – but also running transversely at intervals in simple barrel vaults and both radially and circumferentially in some late domes (pp. 198E,H–K,M,N). Though they have sometimes been likened to the ribs of much later Gothic vaults, and though they did sometimes survive when the surrounding concrete fell, there is little true likeness because they were built up integrally with the concrete rather than completed ahead of it, because they never projected below it, and because little care was taken over their precise form. They should also be distinguished from the rib-like surface patterns that resulted from forming coffers on the under-surfaces of vaults and domes. Such coffers were formed simply by suitable formwork, and the concrete of the rib-like projections was cast integrally with the remaining concrete without any distinction in its composition or the setting of the cementae.

The buildings of this period display vaults of almost all conceivable forms including, in particular, dome-like vaults whose inner surfaces are alternately concave and convex or consist of many similar lobed sections. At lower levels they often incorporate small triangular transition sections which enable them to spring from supporting walls or arches that are octagonal or decagonal in plan. Only very small domes were set over square bases; larger square or rectangular rooms or bays were normally covered by groined vaults.

However monolithic the concrete of a vault was initially, it was subjected to bursting stresses in the same way as any other material similarly used. It cracked, and then thrust outwards just as a masonry vault would have done. By what sequence of failures Roman builders learnt how much buttressing these thrusts required we do not fully know. Surviving structures show the fruits of experience: substantial systems of supports which buttressed the thrusts either by sheer bulk and weight or, with less bulk, by their form. In the latter category were outwardly curving walls crowned by semidomes. Piers that projected outwards from the line of support were commoner. Sometimes these were penetrated at floor level by arched openings to reduce the obstruction they created.

The building process had at least some of the characteristics of that process today in that it was highly standardised in many ways and must have been just as highly organised. There is ample evidence of mass production, not only of standard-sized bricks and similar small units but even of large marble columns. The use of concrete for most of the carcass meant that the need for highly skilled labour was greatly reduced. The most demanding tasks would have been the initial setting-out, construction of the timber centering that supported the formwork for large arches and vaults, and some of the finishing operations. In larger structures care often seems to have been taken to make possible the repetitive reuse of centering frames, which would have called for appropriate provisions for easing the frames away each time the concrete had set sufficiently.

The Wider Roman Empire

Outside Rome and its vicinity it was often necessary to adapt building techniques to local resources, except in those eastern and North African provinces where it was possible to continue to use earlier traditional methods with little change.

Adaptation of Roman techniques in the western provinces of Gaul and Britain included the development of another type of masonry rather like a multilayer cake. Layers of mortar-bound rubble of stone alternated with layers composed of several through-courses of flat bricks. These brick courses ensured the overall strength of the wall where the strength of the mortar-bound rubble concrete could not be relied upon. Elsewhere, where there was a suitable stone, construction in fine ashlar continued long after it had been superseded in Italy. Less commonly, notably in parts of the Balkans and Asia Minor, walls were built throughout of flat bricks of the usual Roman proportions.

The construction of vaults does not seem to have been attempted on the same scale as in Rome. Concrete was used much less. In its place there was a more widespread use of bricks and cut stone. Brick vaults, being constructed by a different process, were not given the exaggerated thicknesses at the foot that were characteristic of concrete vaults: they were much more uniform in thickness with weighting added around the foot at a later stage of construction. Sometimes ingenious patterns of bricklaying were adopted to reduce or even eliminate the need for centering. A further development with the same objective was the use of interlocking hollow tubes which could be laid in a continuous spiral that gradually closed in towards the crown. These differences in construction meant that there was much less freedom to depart from forms with simple cylindrical or part-spherical inside surfaces.

The Early Christian Period and the Byzantine Empire

As the early Christian period was one of straitened resources it was not notable for major developments in technique. For reasons that will be discussed later, the commonest new building type was a variant on the much older basilica – an aisled rectangular hall with, usually, a timber roof. With no recent precedent for the largest of these structures, there was probably further development of the trussed timber roof. Except in those regions where ashlar stonework remained the normal technique, walls were now more frequently constructed of brick throughout their thickness.

When, in the reign of Justinian, works were again attempted that bore comparison with the highest achievements of imperial Rome, some of the techniques seen in Roman monuments in Asia Minor, in places like Thessaloniki and in Rome itself were still sufficiently alive or understood to be used again. There was no more Roman concrete but, in its place, there was fine ashlar in heavily loaded piers, and elsewhere solid brickwork set in mortar which had an admixture of crushed brick to make good the lack of natural pozzolana – both of them finally sheathed, as before, in stucco, marble, or mosaic. Roman forms of pier, vault, and buttress were also used. There are, finally, the chief contributions of Byzantine architects to the repertoire of structural forms and their uses – the fully developed pendentive and the use of the semidome on a scale never before attempted, to buttress a thrust from above.

These innovations occurred in the construction of Hagia Sophia in Constantinople and are described more fully below. On a smaller scale, however, the pendentive became so characteristic of later Byzantine architecture that it must be given some attention here. It might be regarded either as a development of the small triangular infill regions by means of which earlier Roman domes were set above polygonal bases, or as an isolated triangular portion of a dome set directly over a square base and large enough to extend to the corners of the square. As each of a group of pendentives rises out of its corner, it gradually closes in towards the adjacent ones until all four meet in a complete circle. Byzantine pendentives were normally constructed of brick with some solid backing to resist the subsequent outward thrust. Above the final circle there was usually a cornice of stone, and on this the dome was constructed (p. 309B,C).

Byzantine domes and other vaults were also nearly always built of brick, which was often laid in such a manner as to eliminate or reduce the need for centering. Profiles of both arches and domes were usually semicircular, though ill-defined slightly pointed forms were used occasionally on a small scale and flatter segmental profiles on a larger scale when the rise of a full semicircle would have presented difficulties. Extensive use was made of visible ties of iron and of corresponding members of timber spanning between the springings of arches, though the latter would be equally if not more effective as struts and probably were introduced primarily to facilitate construction. Finally, probably in the ninth or tenth century there was the first use of a flying buttress of the type that was later to become so characteristic of Gothic architecture.

The Balkans and Early Russia

The monumental architecture of east Europe, like its pictorial art, 'sprang from a network of workshops whose activity, regardless of whether they were settled or not, was of very unequal duration and influence' (André Grabar, *Die Mittelalterliche Kunst Osteuropas*). Their workforce varied – Grand Prince Vladimir, for example, brought Byzantine masons to Kiev. They collaborated with Slavic builders who contributed their experience in wooden architecture. S. Sophia in Kiev uses 'opus mixtum' (a technique subsequently used in all Middle Byzantine architecture), the 'recessed brick' technique (which originated in Constantinople) and wooden pile foundations. The chronicles record that Grand Prince Bogoljubski invited craftsmen 'from all the lands' and 'from the Germans' as well, to Vladimir. Western and Caucasian masons worked alongside local craftsmen, who eventually took over from them completely. Opinions are divided as to the origin of the mixed brick and stone work and the associated articulation and sculptural enrichment of the facades, but there is general agreement that the technique was imported. The commissions of the Serbian king Stephen Nemanja at the end of the twelfth century, for example, were carried out by Greek and Dalmatian builders who brought with them from the Adriatic Romanesque techniques, forms and decoration. An earlier foundation by Stephen, S. Nicholas near Kursumlija, still used the recessed brick technique. In other examples built soon after, for example the Church of the Virgin at Studenica, ashlar masonry was used, and exterior walls were faced with marble slabs and brick. The portals, the windows of the apse and the corbel-table friezes are thought to be pure Romanesque in origin. Only the brick construction of the dome suggests the work of Byzantine craftsmen. And the latter is true to a very large extent of many major churches, where the plan and spatial design of the principal parts of the buildings stem from Byzantine models (see Chapter 11).

The marriages of Slavic monarchs to Byzantine princesses – those of Grand Prince Vladimir of Kiev, the Bulgarian Czar Peter and the Serbian King Milutin – opened the court to Byzantine customs and encouraged the influx of Byzantine masons, and on military excursions it was customary to bring from occupied territories builders and building techniques. Like numerous other east European motifs and forms, the 'Moldavian dome' is an indigenous invention; no-one knows who its inventors were, whether refugees from the Turks or masters of Gothic construction, whether foreign or native. Historical evidence of where the members of workshops came from is hard to come by. As a rule, local craftsmen gradually replaced foreigners, who came not only from Constantinople, northern Greece and the west European countries, but also – owing to the waves of emigration and the journeyman system – from the eastern provinces of Byzantium as well as Armenia and Georgia. Whether and to what extent they worked from pattern books, like the painters' workshops, is likewise unknown. For all east European countries Constantinople, and in a wider sense the Byzantine empire, was a constant source of inspiration, whereas the influence exerted in return was only slight except perhaps that of Serbia on Moldavia and Russia. The continuity of Byzantine influence is explained by the cultural aspirations of the Slavic rulers, without whose commissions no monumental structures could have been built.

Early Mediaeval and Romanesque

In the period running from *c.* 800 to the millennium, constructional techniques, like design, owed much, if not all, to Roman models. It was probably during this period also that the basilican plan proved its value in northern and central Europe, as it had done in Italy, as a building form for congregational or other lay worship. The constructional techniques were themselves well understood in areas settled by the Romans, although the skills may have atrophied during the period following the fall of Rome. They were to be taken up and developed again by the end of the tenth century – by the master masons of Como, for example, and other peripatetic groups of craftsmen and sculptors whose skills are evidenced in the pilgrimage churches of France. Regional skills had been developed under the direct influence of Rome, of traders from the Hellenistic east or, indirectly, of the Islamic masters of Spain. From the domed aisleless churches of the south-west to the great Romanesque churches of the Auvergne and Burgundy, there was little in the way of structural innovation, but there was notable evolution of plan articulation leading directly to the geometrical innovations of Gothic.

Many of the Roman and Byzantine decorative skills were also revived, including marble facing of rubble walls, the application of mosaic and wall-painting. The religiously inspired sculpture, whether in geometrical bands around recessed arches or corbel tables, or in architecturally related reliefs in tympana or on capitals, represents a new and exciting phase in the use of stones less elegant than marble, and was destined to evolve into the sculptural glories of high Gothic in northern Europe.

In the north, roofs were initially mainly timber-framed, and thus continued Roman practice. It may have been the desire to make these roofs more fire-resistant after the incursions of northern raiders that inspired the use of stone for roofing on slender walls, the development of the pointed arch and the beginnings of Gothic. The main Romanesque contribution to the development of vaulting was the invention of the rib vault, transitional though it was. This was a groin vault with projecting ribs supporting or reinforcing the groins. Because the diagonal of a square is longer than its sides, the diagonal arches or ribs have a larger span but the same height, and therefore assume a flatter segmented shape if the crown of the vault is to rise no higher than its side arches.

During the eleventh century the Lombards tried to overcome this by using a domical groin vault, as in the choir bays of S. Abbondio in Como, where the groins are semicircular and rise much higher than the sides of the vaults, thus resembling domes. Sometimes, as at S. Ambrogio, Milan, heavy ribs of rectangular section were used to reinforce the groins. The Lombard rib vault did not prove successful but was used, particularly in France, to vault single bays in towers rather than to cover several nave bays.

The level rib vault was achieved for the first time in Durham Cathedral (1093–1133). After a first attempt at the east end, where the main vaults collapsed and the surviving aisle vaults achieve their object only by using stilted side-arches and segmental ribs, a solution was found in the nave where, ironically, vaulting was not at first intended. A continuous, uninterrupted rib vault was successfully built due to two important innovations: the oblong bay and the pointed arch. By using an oblong bay, with the short sides contained in the nave walls, the difference of span between the diagonals and the long sides is considerably reduced; thus semicircular diagonals would rise only slightly higher than the semicircular sides. This slight difference was eliminated altogether at Durham through the introduction of the pointed transverse arch, which not only rises higher than its semicircular equivalent, but also reduces lateral thrust. The pointed arch was already well known in Europe; its use at Durham was innovatory in its context, not in its form. The further development of the rib vault belongs to the Gothic period.

The Byzantines solved the problem of placing a dome over a square plan with the pendentive. Romanesque domes on pendentives are found only in south-west France, possibly indicating strong cultural links with the eastern Roman empire, while the use of domes in the rest of Romanesque Europe depended on the technically inferior squinch – a little arch or vault spanning the re-entrant angle of a square bay. Four squinches reduce a square bay to an octagon, which is sufficient basis for a dome. For this reason domes were often octagonal rather than circular in plan. Domes were normally used over crossings, the churches of south-west France being an important exception.

The Gothic Period

As described above in the case of Durham Cathedral, the crux of the matter was the design of arches. The arch was the technological building unit of Gothic construction and before the Romanesque period it presented no problems. Romanesque solutions were somewhat *ad hoc* and it was the first great achievement of Gothic to impose system and order upon the design of arches. One might almost call it a theory.

The first Christian churches, the Roman basilicas, however large, were not unduly difficult to build. Provided there was a sufficient supply of columns for arcades, the only technical problem was how to build walls strong enough and stable enough. For this, what was required was a knowledge of how to lay foundations that would take the weight, and how to mix mortar of the right consistency to bind bricks or rubble into a rigid mass. The only arches were the triumphal arch at the end of the nave, the main arcades, and the frames for windows and doorways. These did not impinge upon one another, their size was a matter of elementary calculation, and they were invariably semicircular. The only aspects of the design that called for mathematical decisions were the dimensions of the space-frame (p. 206).

Similar observations apply to all pre-Romanesque churches except the rather specialised chapels and martyria in which centralised planning and vaults were used. It is clear that the impression of improvisation that is to be encountered in many of the larger Romanesque churches, especially the more ambitious ones, has much to do with the greater use of arches and the problems of fitting them together and making them stay up. Instead of large surfaces of continuous wall, Romanesque naves often present tier upon tier of arches in the manner of Roman aqueducts; and below the timber trusses of the roof-masonry vaults were sometimes introduced, again recalling Roman examples. The technology used by Romanesque architects may have been largely self-taught, and included a good deal of trial and error; but in so far as there was any considerable body of experience behind it, that experience was Roman, Byzantine, or occasionally Armenian.

There is no reason whatever to suppose that Gothic represented a sharp break with the past, or that it was in any sense a new beginning. What happened is that entire structures were conceived as frameworks of arches, and that arches were organised into coherent systems which reduced the structural functions of walls to a minimum (p. 204). (See also pp. 437, 438.) For this to be possible the sizes and shapes of arches had to be compatible, requiring far greater flexibility in the relation between the height and span of arches than the semicircular form allowed.

There is some evidence that Roman and Byzantine architects occasionally used arches that were not semicircular (p. 208). The hair-pin shape for gateways was as ancient as the Hittite Empire. The pointed arch had been known in the Middle East at least as far back as the beginning of the first millennium BC. Whether or not there was any direct transmission, it was taken up by the Muslims and it may have reached western Christendom from that source via North Africa. However, the Muslims in Spain preferred the horseshoe arch, which had essentially the same geometrical properties as the pointed arch, though a different visual form. The pointed arch could just as easily have found its way westward, along with other contributions, from the churches of Armenia. Either way, western architects' interest was aroused at precisely the moment when their own designs had reached a level of complexity sufficient to warrant its adoption.

The advantages of the pointed arch were almost certainly conceived and expressed in geometrical terms (p. 207). It was an arch with no fixed ratio between its height and its span. Within limits any suitable ratio could be used. Romanesque had been fumbling in this direction with stilted and segmental arches, and there were pointed as well as round arches at Cluny as well as Durham. Semicircular arches survived as a feature of Gothic ribbed vaults until well into the thirteenth century, for example at Bourges (q.v.). There was no sudden or complete conversion.

This suggests that what to us is the mechanical advantage of the pointed arch, its ability to carry heavy loads with greater efficiency, was not grasped for some time, and perhaps never really appreciated. If mediaeval architects had any insight into the mechanical behaviour of structures it was intuitive rather than theoretical. They certainly had lively imaginations and knew well enough that tall buildings crowned with heavy vaults were liable to be precarious. But the only quantitative means at their disposal for comparing the performance of one building with another was at the level of their dimensions.

Dimensions were never chosen at random but always formed themselves into mathematically related systems. Such systems were tested by experience. It is a truism that no two Gothic cathedrals are exactly the same size. What is more to the point, however, is that they tend to cluster around certain well-tried shapes and sections such as the square and the equilateral triangle; that the period of really radical experiment did not last much more than fifty years (*c.* 1190–*c.* 1250); and that when something unprecedented was attempted, architects did not creep forward cautiously into the unknown a little at a time,

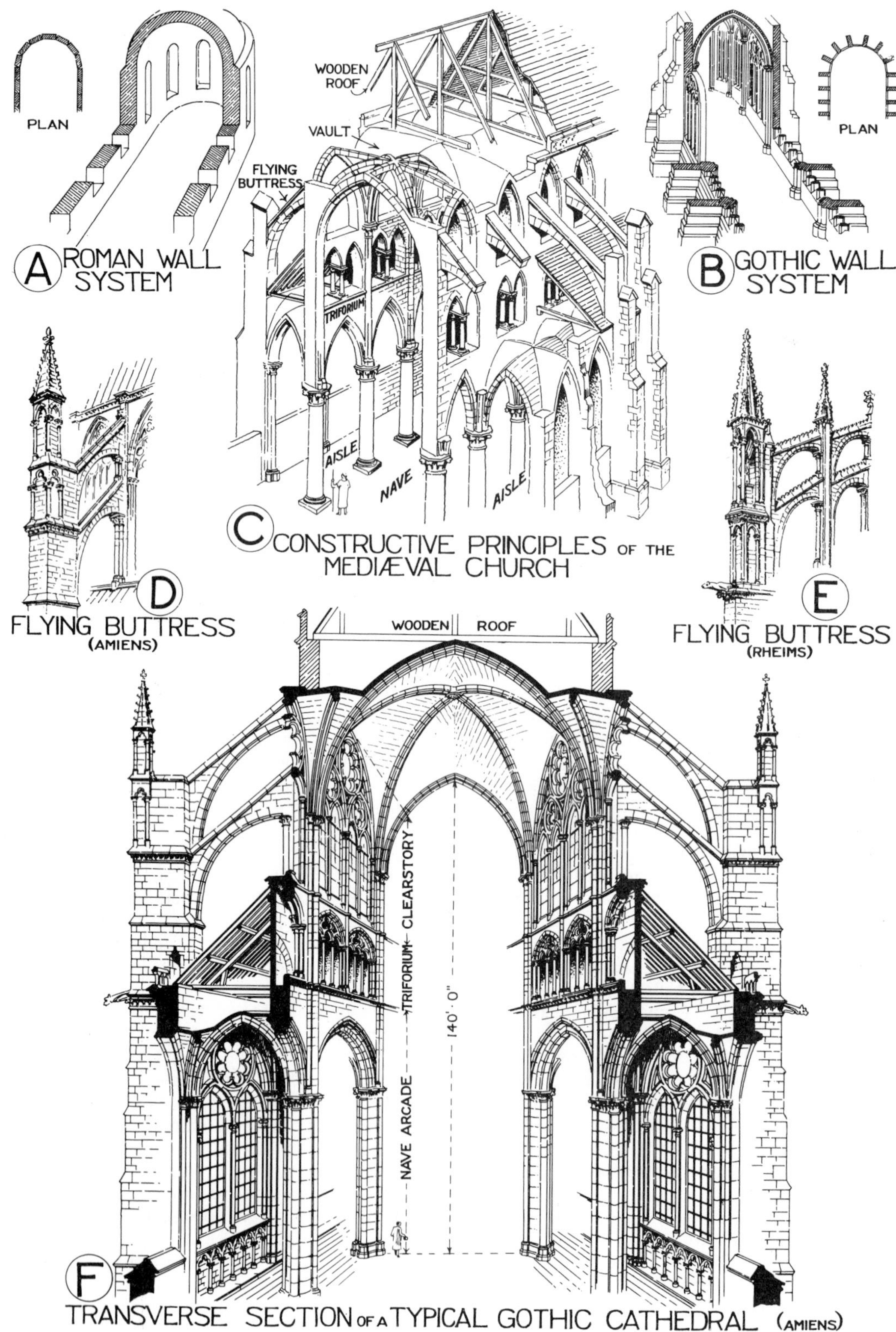
PLAN
A ROMAN WALL SYSTEM
WOODEN ROOF
VAULT
FLYING BUTTRESS
TRIFORIUM
AISLE
NAVE
AISLE
C CONSTRUCTIVE PRINCIPLES OF THE MEDIÆVAL CHURCH
PLAN
B GOTHIC WALL SYSTEM
D FLYING BUTTRESS (AMIENS)
E FLYING BUTTRESS (RHEIMS)
WOODEN ROOF
CLEARSTORY
TRIFORIUM
NAVE ARCADE
140' 0"
F TRANSVERSE SECTION OF A TYPICAL GOTHIC CATHEDRAL (AMIENS)

but took what seem to us great leaps from one set of controlling ratios to another.

If Gothic masons had a science it was geometry. This can be inferred from the few texts that have survived such as the notebook of Villard de Honnecourt (thirteenth century) and a series of little manuals on the technicalities of masoncraft written by a succession of German masons at the end of the fifteenth century and during the sixteenth. The tombstone of Hugues Libergier (1262), architect of S. Nicaise at Reims, shows him with the tools of his trade, which were a measuring rod, a square, and a pair of callipers. They are not tools for working stone. The inference to be drawn is that Master Hugues had attained the higher levels of his profession, and that it was largely concerned with a special kind of drawing, in which geometrical precision was all important.

The quality, character and extent of masonic mathematics should not be overrated. Essentially it was the residue of the rules of thumb used in antiquity to make quick and reliable calculations needed for practical purposes. It extended no further than a few favoured ratios (p. 209) and some of the regular polygons. The idea that there were unwritten, cabalistic secrets which have been lost, reflects the wishful thinking of a later age. Gothic architects shared the knowledge, such as it was, which had come down to them from the ancient world. They did not augment it, but merely used it in their own distinctive way. But the definition of structural forms was only part of the function of masonic geometry. There was no real structural theory. Throughout the Middle Ages architects made do with the barest minimum of guidelines, expressed in the form of simple ratios. This much can be gathered from the notebook of the sixteenth-century Spanish architect, Juan Gil de Hontañon, where the area (not the mass or volume) of buttresses is correlated with the linear span of vaults. Other similar mistakes are recorded in the late sixteenth-century debates at Milan, and if this represents the scale of mechanical know-how at the end of the Middle Ages, it is unlikely that earlier generations were better informed.

Design

The real purpose of Gothic drawing was to facilitate the design of complicated objects such as towers or spires, and complicated patterns such as vaults and window tracery. Such drawings were of two kinds. Some were full-size, for example templates for moulding profiles, or outlines of windows that were scratched on tracing floors of the kind that have survived at York and Wells. These would be of direct relevance to the execution of actual masonry. Others were drawn on paper or parchment much smaller than full-size. It is extremely doubtful whether the notion of scale played any part in their preparation. With very rare exceptions – all of them extremely late – there are no indications of scale on any of the surviving drawings. This makes it difficult to evaluate their precise significance. Few if any can be exactly matched with executed work, although many of them are close enough to be plausibly identified. The most likely explanations are that they were preliminary drafts, or else showpieces for patrons. In the nature of the case they were all two-dimensional, and where the subject was vaults they can have been no more than projections. Nevertheless it is evident that by the fifteenth century Gothic architects spent a good deal of their time producing drawings, and this is a fair indication of the direction in which the profession was moving.

It needs to be stressed, however, that so far as we can tell designs on paper stopped short of complete buildings. Plans were almost certainly worked out on the ground as the foundations were laid; and there were established rules for construing elevations from plans which German masons who subscribed to articles of their profession drawn up at Regensburg in 1459 promised not to divulge to the uninitiated. These were in effect definitions of space-frames; and it was this sort of thing the masons at Milan debated in the 1390s, when they wondered whether to build 'to the square' or 'to the triangle'. These were standard formulae, despite the need of an academic mathematician to show the Milanese how to implement their decision. They had probably been features of church architecture from the days of the early Christian basilicas. Like all the other formulae in use, they were norms of what was acceptable and possible. The question of whether they were desirable in any aesthetic sense was probably never discussed. It was left to Alberti and the architects of the Italian Renaissance to transform the practical rationale of the Middle Ages into theories of beauty and proportion.

EVOLUTION OF GOTHIC VAULTING

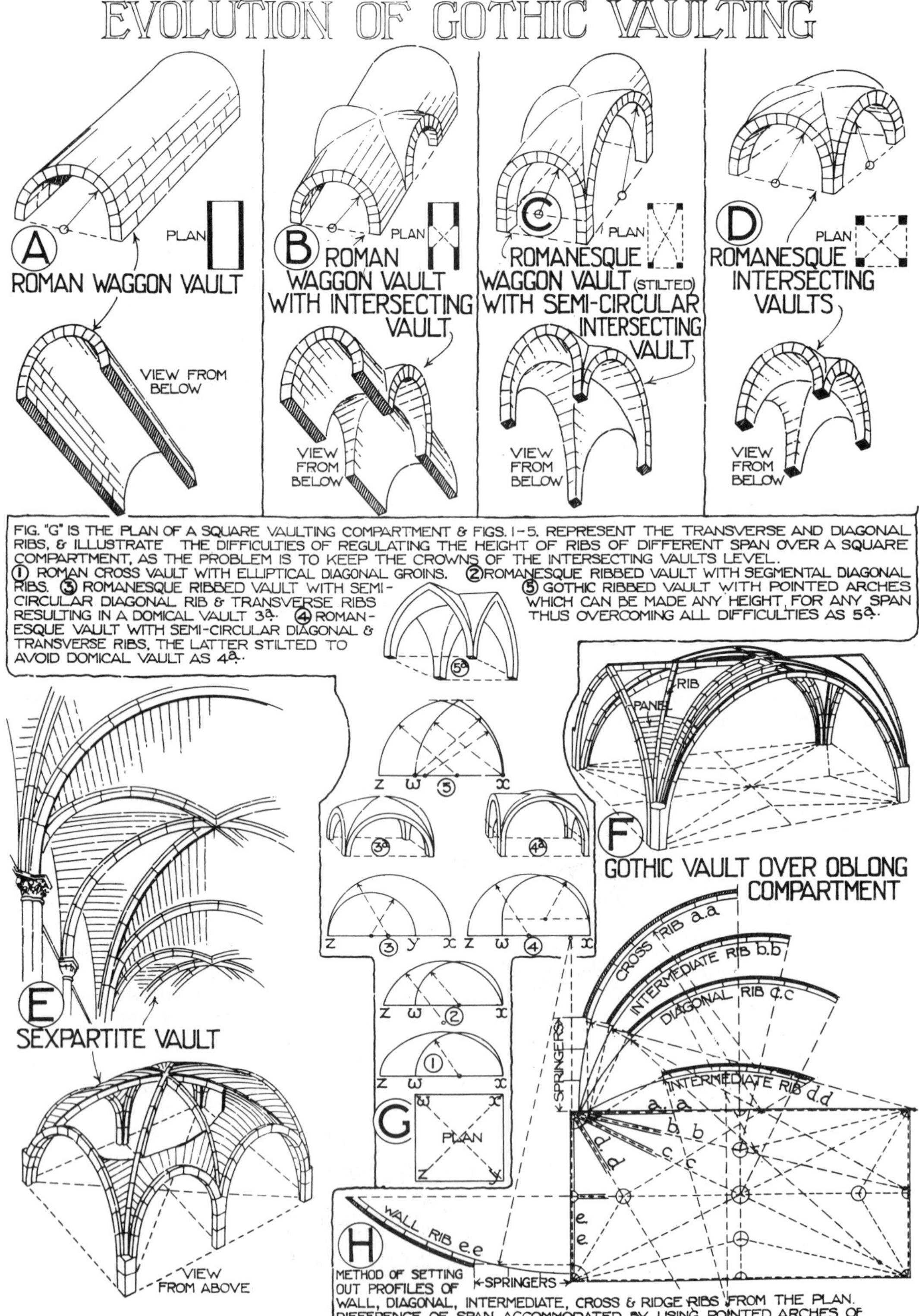

PLAN
A
ROMAN WAGGON VAULT
VIEW FROM BELOW
PLAN
B ROMAN WAGGON VAULT WITH INTERSECTING VAULT
VIEW FROM BELOW
C
PLAN
ROMANESQUE WAGGON VAULT (STILTED) WITH SEMI-CIRCULAR INTERSECTING VAULT
VIEW FROM BELOW
D
PLAN
ROMANESQUE INTERSECTING VAULTS
VIEW FROM BELOW
FIG. "G" IS THE PLAN OF A SQUARE VAULTING COMPARTMENT & FIGS. 1–5. REPRESENT THE TRANSVERSE AND DIAGONAL RIBS, & ILLUSTRATE THE DIFFICULTIES OF REGULATING THE HEIGHT OF RIBS OF DIFFERENT SPAN OVER A SQUARE COMPARTMENT, AS THE PROBLEM IS TO KEEP THE CROWNS OF THE INTERSECTING VAULTS LEVEL.
① ROMAN CROSS VAULT WITH ELLIPTICAL DIAGONAL GROINS. ② ROMANESQUE RIBBED VAULT WITH SEGMENTAL DIAGONAL RIBS. ③ ROMANESQUE RIBBED VAULT WITH SEMI-CIRCULAR DIAGONAL RIB & TRANSVERSE RIBS RESULTING IN A DOMICAL VAULT 3a. ④ ROMANESQUE VAULT WITH SEMI-CIRCULAR DIAGONAL & TRANSVERSE RIBS, THE LATTER STILTED TO AVOID DOMICAL VAULT AS 4a. ⑤ GOTHIC RIBBED VAULT WITH POINTED ARCHES WHICH CAN BE MADE ANY HEIGHT, FOR ANY SPAN THUS OVERCOMING ALL DIFFICULTIES AS 5a.
5a
RIB
PANEL
F
GOTHIC VAULT OVER OBLONG COMPARTMENT
Z ω ⑤ x
3a
4a
Z ③ y x Z ω ④ x
Z ω ② x
Z ω ① x
G
PLAN
E
SEXPARTITE VAULT
VIEW FROM ABOVE
CROSS RIB a.a
INTERMEDIATE RIB b.b
DIAGONAL RIB c.c
INTERMEDIATE RIB d.d
SPRINGERS
a. a
b. b
c. c
d. d
e. e
WALL RIB e.e
H
METHOD OF SETTING OUT PROFILES OF WALL, DIAGONAL, INTERMEDIATE, CROSS & RIDGE RIBS FROM THE PLAN. DIFFERENCE OF SPAN ACCOMMODATED BY USING POINTED ARCHES OF DIFFERENT RADII.
SPRINGERS

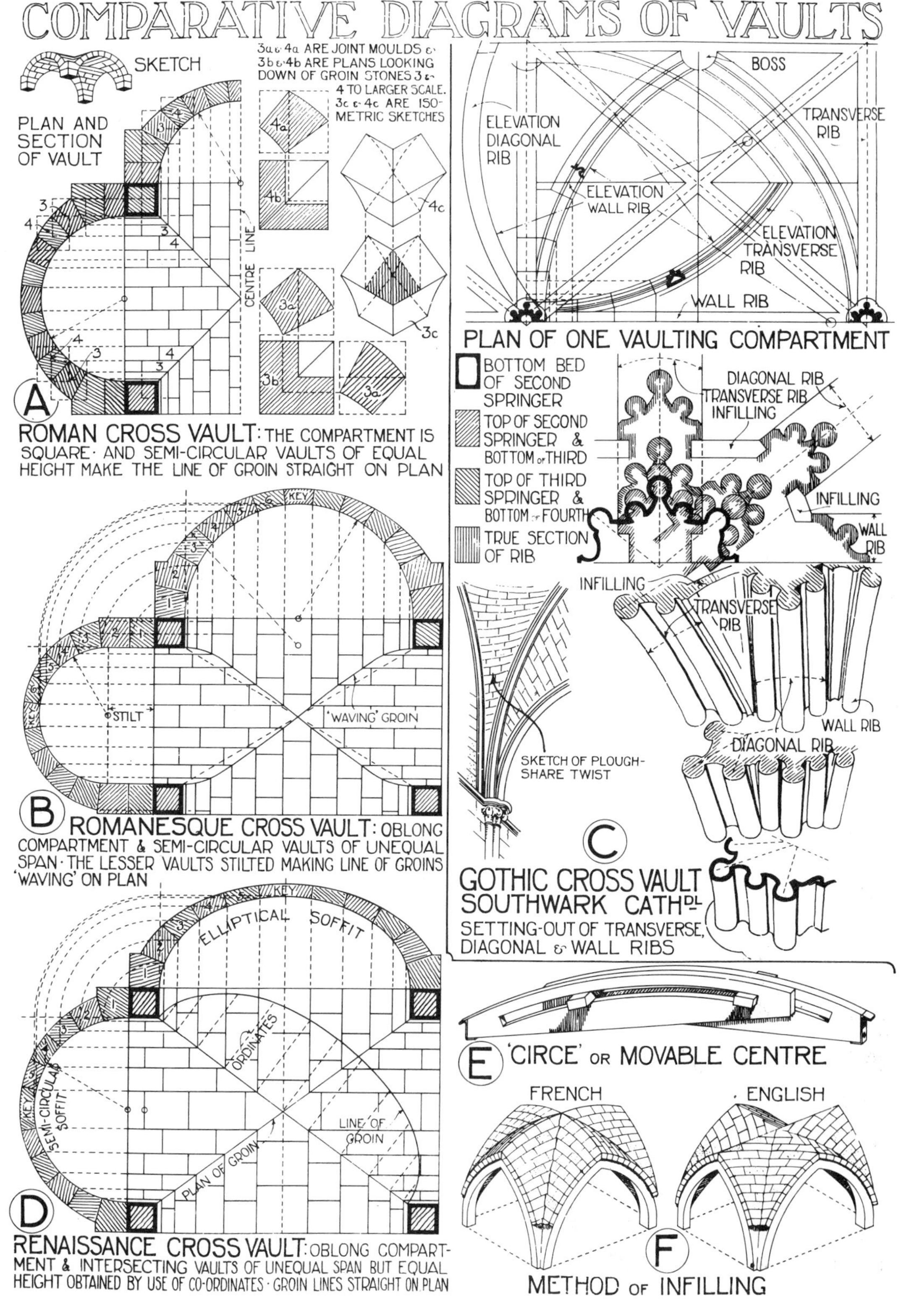
COMPARATIVE DIAGRAMS OF VAULTS
SKETCH
PLAN AND SECTION OF VAULT
3a & 4a ARE JOINT MOULDS & 3b & 4b ARE PLANS LOOKING DOWN OF GROIN STONES 3 & 4 TO LARGER SCALE. 3c & 4c ARE ISOMETRIC SKETCHES
CENTRE LINE
A
ROMAN CROSS VAULT: THE COMPARTMENT IS SQUARE. AND SEMI-CIRCULAR VAULTS OF EQUAL HEIGHT MAKE THE LINE OF GROIN STRAIGHT ON PLAN
KEY
STILT
'WAVING' GROIN
B
ROMANESQUE CROSS VAULT: OBLONG COMPARTMENT & SEMI-CIRCULAR VAULTS OF UNEQUAL SPAN. THE LESSER VAULTS STILTED MAKING LINE OF GROINS 'WAVING' ON PLAN
ELLIPTICAL SOFFIT
ORDINATES
SEMI-CIRCULAR SOFFIT
LINE OF GROIN
PLAN OF GROIN
D
RENAISSANCE CROSS VAULT: OBLONG COMPARTMENT & INTERSECTING VAULTS OF UNEQUAL SPAN BUT EQUAL HEIGHT OBTAINED BY USE OF CO-ORDINATES. GROIN LINES STRAIGHT ON PLAN
BOSS
ELEVATION DIAGONAL RIB
TRANSVERSE RIB
ELEVATION WALL RIB
ELEVATION TRANSVERSE RIB
WALL RIB
PLAN OF ONE VAULTING COMPARTMENT
BOTTOM BED OF SECOND SPRINGER
TOP OF SECOND SPRINGER & BOTTOM OF THIRD
TOP OF THIRD SPRINGER & BOTTOM OF FOURTH
TRUE SECTION OF RIB
DIAGONAL RIB
TRANSVERSE RIB
INFILLING
INFILLING
WALL RIB
INFILLING
TRANSVERSE RIB
WALL RIB
DIAGONAL RIB
SKETCH OF PLOUGH-SHARE TWIST
C
GOTHIC CROSS VAULT SOUTHWARK CATHDL
SETTING-OUT OF TRANSVERSE, DIAGONAL & WALL RIBS
E
'CIRCE' OR MOVABLE CENTRE
FRENCH
ENGLISH
F
METHOD OF INFILLING

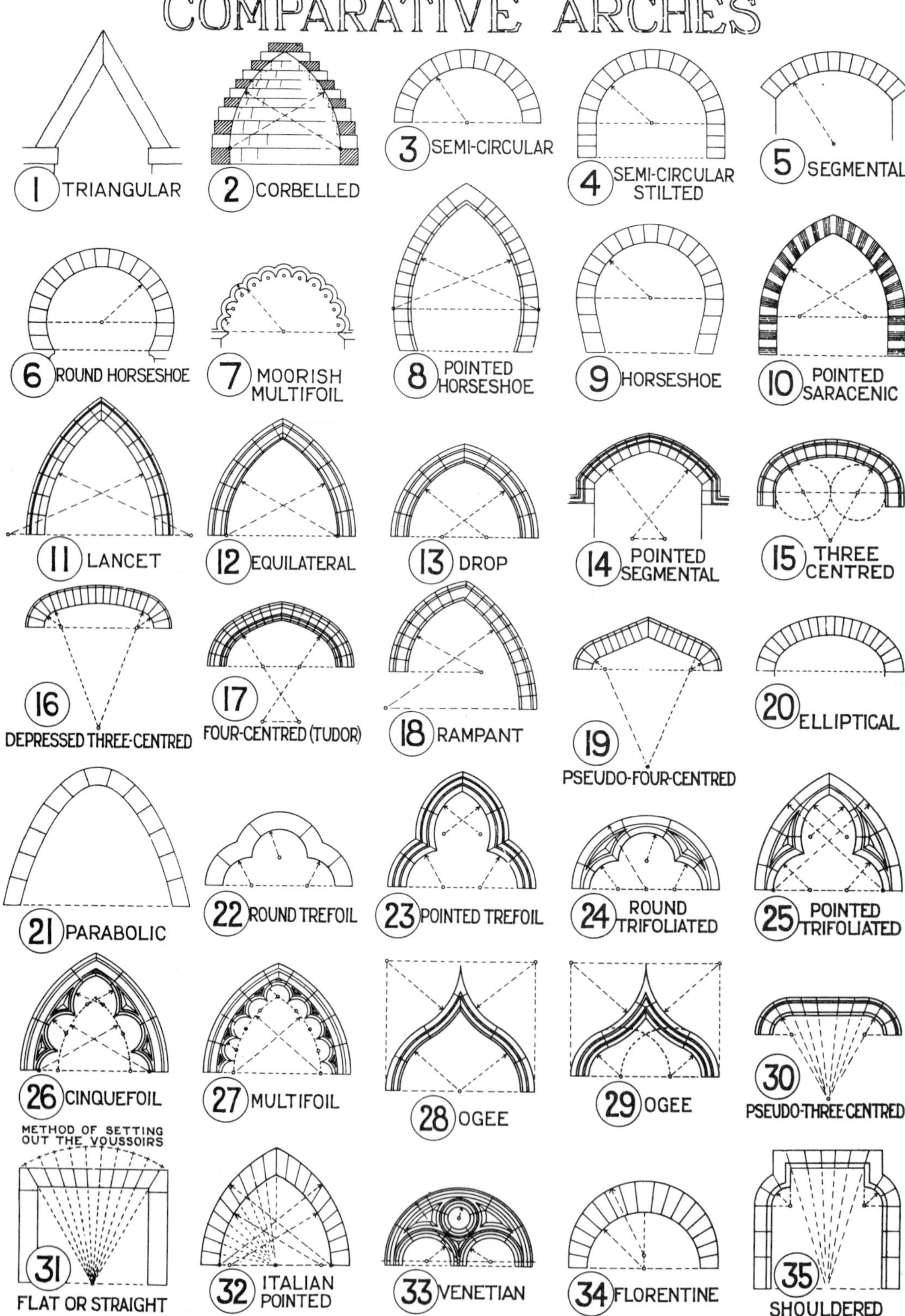

COMPARATIVE ARCHES
1 TRIANGULAR
2 CORBELLED
3 SEMI-CIRCULAR
4 SEMI-CIRCULAR STILTED
5 SEGMENTAL
6 ROUND HORSESHOE
7 MOORISH MULTIFOIL
8 POINTED HORSESHOE
9 HORSESHOE
10 POINTED SARACENIC
11 LANCET
12 EQUILATERAL
13 DROP
14 POINTED SEGMENTAL
15 THREE CENTRED
16 DEPRESSED THREE-CENTRED
17 FOUR-CENTRED (TUDOR)
18 RAMPANT
19 PSEUDO-FOUR-CENTRED
20 ELLIPTICAL
21 PARABOLIC
22 ROUND TREFOIL
23 POINTED TREFOIL
24 ROUND TRIFOLIATED
25 POINTED TRIFOLIATED
26 CINQUEFOIL
27 MULTIFOIL
28 OGEE
29 OGEE
30 PSEUDO-THREE-CENTRED
METHOD OF SETTING OUT THE VOUSSOIRS
31 FLAT OR STRAIGHT
32 ITALIAN POINTED
33 VENETIAN
34 FLORENTINE
35 SHOULDERED

PRINCIPLES OF PROPORTIONS
A
TETRASTYLE: 1 SQ.
B
HEXASTYLE: 1½ SQ. WITHOUT PEDIMENT
C
OCTASTYLE: 2 SQUARES WITHOUT PEDIMENT
ARCH OF TRAJAN BENEVENTUM
D
ARCH OF SEPTIMIUS SEVERUS ROME
E
F
BAPTISTERY: PISA
G
0
60°
8
16
MEDIÆVAL CATHEDRALS
H
HENRY VII'S CHAPEL WESTMINSTER
J
CHAPTER HOUSE: WELLS
S. GEORGE'S CHAPEL WINDSOR
K
S. GEORGE'S CHAPEL: WINDSOR
45'6"
L
KING'S COLLEGE CHAPEL

Chapter 9

PREHISTORIC

Architectural Character

Building technology began to develop early in the Paleolithic period. Early humans created structures in wood and stone, used fire, often in prepared hearths, and slept and worked in defined areas. No clear examples of special-purpose buildings of this period exist; they all appear to have been dwellings.

The best-documented examples from the Mesolithic period indicate that villages also were being arranged systematically; houses were aligned in rows, and were more regular in plan. The locations of artefacts within the dwelling were more regular.

The Neolithic period saw the first phase of agricultural expansion. Throughout Greece and the Balkans this was marked by the building of settlement mounds or tells made up of large numbers of small, detached, square or rectangular, single-roomed houses, using timber framing and wattle and daub infill. In the Mediterranean regions, by contrast, round or oval compounds were grouped together in large numbers and occasionally surrounded by deep ditches. The central European phase was characterised by the building of villages composed of rectangular or trapezoidal compartmented longhouses, in which heavy posts supported a framework of wattle walls daubed with clay. In these central and eastern European communities there do not appear to be any structures within the village that could be differentiated unambiguously from houses and storage buildings, and which, for example, might have been used as temples or communal shrines. However, in the final phase of agricultural expansion into north-west Europe, housing was grouped into small, isolated hamlets or clusters of dwellings, built of wood or stone, and it is here that the major development of collective tombs and sacred monuments took place.

The funerary architecture of the Neolithic period took the form of larger communal structures. The most important were megalithic passage graves, in which a clearly distinguishable passage led to a circular or polygonal inner chamber; megalithic gallery graves, where an elaborated entrance led to a large oblong chamber; earthen longbarrows, in which a large timber-framed communal mortuary house was covered with an earth mound; smaller, less elaborate structures such as dysse, or small, closed stone chambers; court cairns, which had trapeze-shaped mounds covering semicircular forecourts, and an internal gallery-like arrangement of separate burial compartments; wedge graves, in which a double skin of slabs filled with small stones defined a single chamber covered by a mound; and dolmens, which consisted of simple chambers of stone slabs covered with cap-stones.

Neolithic ritual structures of a non-funerary kind may be divided into temples and freestanding ceremonial sites. Of the latter, the most significant are cursus earthworks, or ritual enclosures, up to 150 m (490 ft) wide and 10 km (6 miles) long, defined by banks and ditches; enclosures with causeways, formed by single or concentric rings of banks and ditches crossed at intervals by causeways and enclosing a central circular or oval enclosure; and henges, in which banks and ditches contained stone or timber circles and standing stones. Megalithic monuments are found throughout north-west Europe, but freestanding earthworks and henges only in Britain.

On the whole, Bronze Age dwellings were smaller and more flimsy than their Neolithic counterparts. Throughout central and eastern Europe, houses of the megaron type appear to have been built of timber and clay, but they never developed into the monumental and stylised megarons as found in Greece. Bronze Age lakeside settlements of rectangular timber-framed houses have been excavated in eastern France, Switzerland and northern Italy. Drystone houses were built around the shores of the Mediterranean and in parts of the British Isles.

Early Bronze Age funerary architecture consisted of round barrows and tumuli containing individual graves, themselves occasionally placed in timber or stone mortuary houses. In the later Bronze Age bodies were cremated, and cinerary urns were placed within cemetery sites. Ritual architecture of a non-funerary kind was limited, throughout most of Europe, to small temple-like buildings, although in Britain henges continued in use well into the Bronze Age where, at sites like Stonehenge, they were augmented by stone settings.

Prehistoric Europe

By contrast, the architecture of fortifications began to develop in the late Neolithic and early Bronze Age. This was of two principal kinds: the earthworks and ramparts used to fortify settlements and farmsteads in Europe generally, and defensive towers, which were limited to Corsica, Sardinia and the Balearic Islands.

During the Iron Age, housing throughout the European continent took the form of rectangular or oval timber and stone-built houses collected within fortified sites. Layouts varied from small, irregular groupings of houses, to larger settlements like Citania (second to first century BC) in Guimareas, Portugal, Bibracte (first century BC) near Autun in France, and Manching (first century BC) in Bavaria. The latter had a layout of regular streets approximately 10 m (33 ft) wide, lined with timber-framed houses, barns and stores, with specialised streets containing workshops and 'bazaars'. By contrast, housing in Britain continued to perpetuate a tradition of isolated but architecturally more elaborate structures set within palisaded enclosures, as well as more conventional nucleated settlements within hill-forts.

Ritual and funerary architecture during the Iron Age was limited to cult sites – found throughout Europe, particularly during the later La Tène period – comprising ritual shafts, temples and sanctuaries. There are also Iron Age barrows, but the burials, particularly of high-status individuals, were frequently in waggons or chariots. Hillforts and ramparts were also built on a large scale in this period, but multivallate tended to replace earlier univallate forms and often had elaborate gateways. Fortified towers became common in northern Britain.

Examples

Paleolithic Period

Dwellings

Paleolithic dwellings can be divided into four constructional types: the hut, the lean-to, the tent and the pit house.

HUTS

The earliest known buildings in the archaeological record are on the Paleolithic period site, **Terra Amata** (300,000 BP) (p. 213A), in the southern French city of Nice. Excavation revealed traces of oval huts ranging from 8 m (26 ft) to 15 m (49 ft) in length and 4 m (13 ft) to nearly 6 m (19 ft) in width, built on sandy beaches close to what had been the shoreline. The hut walls were made of stakes about 75 mm (3 in) in diameter, set as a palisade in the sand and braced on the outside by a ring of stones. A line of stout posts, each about 300 mm (12 in) in diameter, was set up along the long axis of each hut, but evidence of the shape of the roof has not survived. The floor of each hut consisted of a thick bed of organic matter and ash. Each hut had a central hearth and these are among the oldest yet discovered anywhere in the world. The fireplaces were either pebble-paved surfaces or shallow pits between 300 mm (1 ft) and 600 mm (2 ft) in diameter, scraped out of the sand. Both types of hearth were protected from draughts by small pebble windscreens. Archaeologists have differentiated other areas within the huts as tool-manufacturing workshops. The huts are believed to have been rebuilt annually on the same sites by nomadic hunters who habitually visited Terra Amata in the spring.

Molodova I (44,000 BP) (p. 213B) was a much later and more sophisticated hut found near the village of Molodova on the Deniester River in the Ukraine. This measured about 8 m (26 ft) by 5 m (16 ft) internally. The shelter consisted of a wood framework covered with skins, held in place by a rough oval of mammoth bones, which also enclosed fifteen hearth areas.

In the mouth of the cave known as the **Grotte du Renne** (30,000 BP) at Arce-sur-Cure in the Yonne valley in France, post holes set in a rough oval about 2 m × 5 m (7 ft × 16 ft) enclosed hearths and occupational debris. The posts seem to have been mammoth tusks. Representations of similar huts were produced in later Paleolithic art.

The Moravian (Czech Republic) site of **Dolni Vestonice** (27,000 BP) comprised a number of huts surrounded by a palisade of mammoth bones and tusks set into the ground and apparently filled with brush-wood and turf: of these, the most important was a large structure of roughly oval shape, some 16 m × 10 m (52 ft × 33 ft), which contained five hearths, most of them with large blocks of limestone nearby. The walls of the structure were made of limestone blocks. Archaeologists suggest that this may have been a summer structure open to the sky. A second hut was circular, about 6 m (19 ft) in diameter, with a central hearth capped with an earthen dome used to manufacture ceramic figurines. This hut may have belonged to a shaman. It was estimated that at any one time five to six dwellings, each housing as many as twenty to twenty-five people, occupied the site, which appears to have been specifically a lodge for mammoth hunters.

In a particularly well-preserved example of a mammoth-bone hut at **Mezhirich** (22,000 BP) on the Dnepr, in the Ukraine, the foundation wall was built of mammoth jaws and long bones, capped by skulls, and roofed with tree-branches overlaid by tusks. A similar example from the same period has been discovered near Cracow, Poland.

LEAN-TOS

Le Lazaret (150,000 BP), Nice, France, was an early example of a lean-to, about 12 m × 4 m (39 ft × 13 ft), erected against one wall of a cave and defined at the base by rows of stones, and possibly post supports. A skin curtain and roof may have been draped over the posts, and the lean-to may have had two compartments separated by an internal partition, each with an entrance on the long side. The larger of the two compartments contained two hearths.

TENTS

Tents must have been extremely common in late glacial Europe. Teepee-like tent sites have been discovered as far apart as **Pavlov** (23,000 BP) in the Czech Republic, **Feldkirchen-Gonnersdorf** on the Rhine (13,000 BP) in Germany, and **Plateau-Parrain** (15,000 BP) (p. 213C) in the Dordogne region of France, where there was a tent with a floor area about 3 m × 3 m (10 ft × 10 ft). The skirts of the tent were weighed down with pebbles; inside was a small paved area, and outside a number of tool-manufacturing workshops. The tent-like structure at **Corbiac** (20,000 BP) in south-western France were unusual in that they had open-air hearths.

Molodova V (13,000 BP) in the Ukraine was a teepee-like structure measuring about 4 m × 5 m (13 ft × 16 ft), with wooden posts driven into the earth and

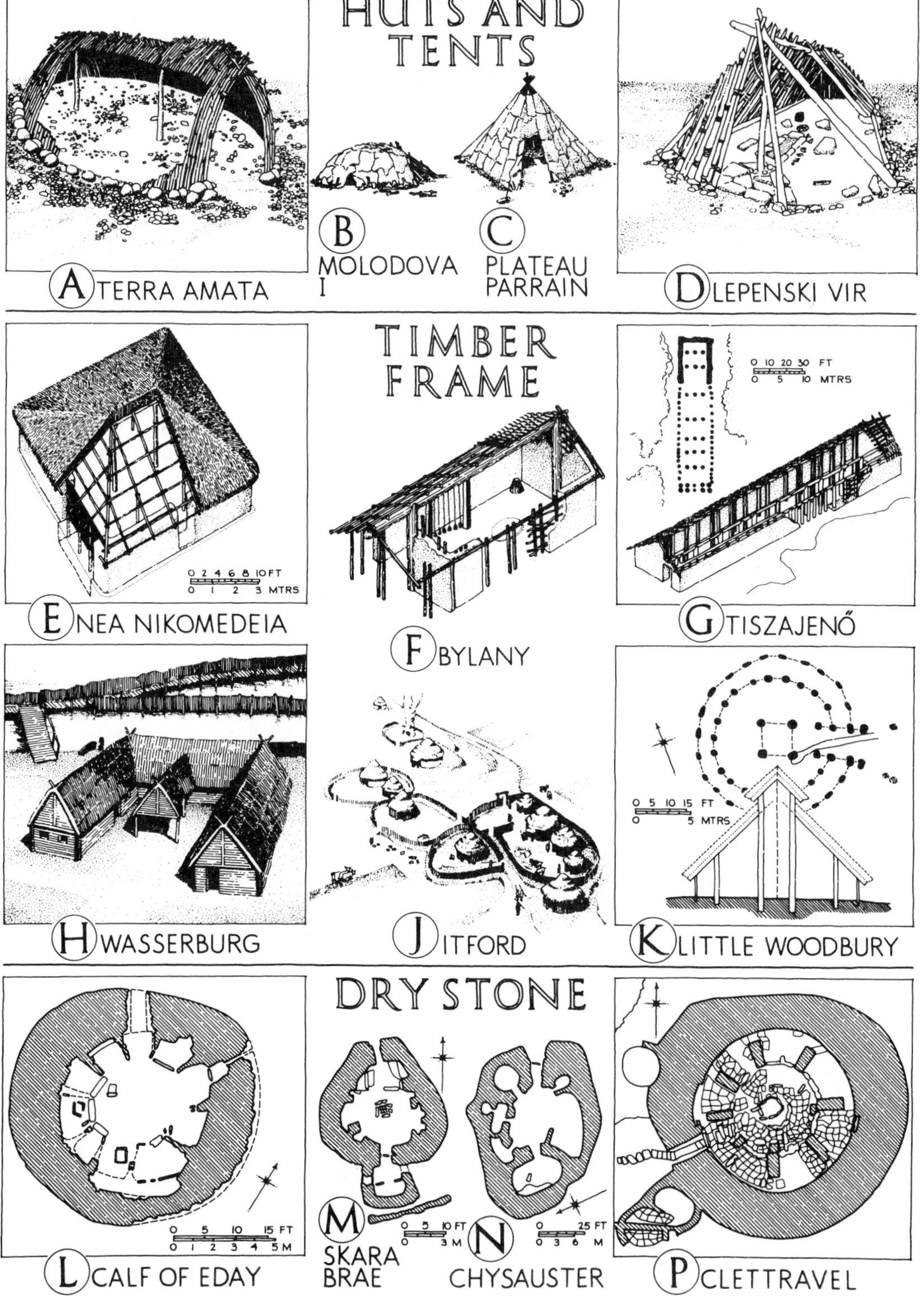
PREHISTORIC HOUSES
HUTS AND TENTS
A TERRA AMATA
B MOLODOVA I
C PLATEAU PARRAIN
D LEPENSKI VIR
TIMBER FRAME
0 2 4 6 8 10 FT
0 1 2 3 MTRS
E NEA NIKOMEDEIA
F BYLANY
0 10 20 30 FT
0 5 10 MTRS
G TISZAJENŐ
H WASSERBURG
J ITFORD
0 5 10 15 FT
0 5 MTRS
K LITTLE WOODBURY
DRY STONE
0 5 10 15 FT
0 1 2 3 4 5 M
L CALF OF EDAY
0 5 10 FT
0 3 M
M SKARA BRAE
0 25 FT
0 3 6 M
N CHYSAUSTER
P CLETTRAVEL

covered with skins secured with large wooden pegs, and enclosing a large single hearth. On the same site, in an even later circular example some 25 m (80 ft) square (12,000 BP) containing two hearths, the skins were secured by the antlers of reindeer. Similar sites have been found at **Mezin** (20,000 BP) in the Ukraine, and others, dating from the final glacial period, such as **Ahrensburg** (10,500 BP) near Hamburg in Germany.

PIT-HOUSES

Dwelling pits appear to have been more common in eastern Europe, where the climate was particularly severe. At **Barca** (37,000–30,000 BP) in the Czech Republic, oval, trapezoid and pear-shaped examples have been found, varying in size from 2.5 m to 3.5 m (8 ft to 11 ft) in width and 5 m to 18 m (16 ft to 59 ft) in length. Central post-holes indicated the existence of roofs. Later examples from the same site took more regular cross- and H-shaped forms, and different activities were assigned to different parts of the pits.

At **Kostienki** (22,000 BP) on the River Don in Russia, more ambitious houses were constructed by making shallow depressions in the ground and surrounding these with a ring of mammoth bones and tusks with hides draped over them. Some houses were relatively large; one example was 35 m × 15 m (110 ft × 49 ft) with nine hearths ranged down the long axis, suggesting that several families may have passed the winter together. It is unlikely that this was covered under a single roof. The Kostienki group produced a variety of decorative artefacts, including representations of women and chalk drawings of animals. At **Avdeevo** (20,000 BP) and **Pushkari** in Russia, mammoth-hunting communities were living, at least seasonally, in similar encampments or villages of pit-houses, each about 3 m × 5 m (10 ft × 16 ft) partially dug down into the sub-soil and roofed with hides stretched over a framework of mammoth bones or tusks.

Mesolithic Period

Dwellings

Traces of Mesolithic houses indicate that the range of dwelling-types was broadly similar to that of the Paleolithic period; those few which are well-preserved tend to be the more durable pit-houses and huts, built for occupation in winter.

HUTS

The most substantial Mesolithic dwellings have been found at the site of **Lepenski Vir** (5410–4610 BC) (p. 213D) on the Danube. The houses were built on terraces, in rows of about twenty. They were trapezoidal in plan, and ranged in size from about 5.5 m to 30 m (18 ft to 100 ft) square. All had uniform proportions and internal arrangements, and were oriented with the wide end containing the entrance facing the river. The floors were of hard limestone plaster covered by a thin red or white burnished surface, and were surrounded by posts reinforced with stones which supported a solid wooden superstructure. The long pit hearths were lined with limestone, often surrounded by a pattern of thin red sandstone. In nearly all the houses, a carved block of river-worn limestone was placed near the hearth opposite the entrance. The carvings are thought to represent humans or fish.

PIT-HOUSES

At **Soroki** (5500–5400 BC) in the Dniester valley in the Ukraine, shallow oval pits 6 m to 9 m (19 ft to 30 ft) long and 2 m to 5 m (7 ft to 16 ft) wide, possibly roofed with a light timber structure, contained hearths and stone-working areas. Similar examples have been found at **Tasovice**, Czech Republic, **Tannstock** and **Juhnsdorf-Autobahn**, Germany, **Schotz**, Switzerland, and **Farnham**, England.

Neolithic Period

Dwellings

During the Neolithic period more substantial dwellings of timber and stone were erected throughout Europe. Timber-framed houses were either small, square or rectangular single-family dwellings, or longhouses lived in by expanded or multiple families. Elsewhere, small, single or multi-cellular drystone family houses were built.

TIMBER-FRAMED HOUSES

Nea Nikomedeia (*c.* 6220 BC) (p. 213E) in Macedonia, northern Greece, was one of the oldest Neolithic settlements in Europe. It contained a number of square houses, about 7.5 m × 7.5 m (25 ft × 25 ft) in plan, with mud walls supported by a framework of oak saplings set into 1 m (3 ft) deep footings about 1 m (3 ft) apart and infilled with bundles of reeds set on end. These were plastered internally with a mixture of mud and chaff, and externally with white clay. The houses are thought to have had pitched and thatched roofs with overhanging eaves. The interiors had a raised plaster platform at one end into which was sunk a small hearth and storage bin. Other contemporary examples have been found at **Otzaki-Magula** and **Tsangli** in Thessaly, Greece.

Similar one-roomed dwellings, on average 8 m × 4 m (26 ft × 13 ft) in plan, have been excavated at **Azmak** and **Karanovo**, Bulgaria (5600–3800 BC) where the method of construction appears to have been to erect a framework of thin, closely-spaced wooden posts on which were built thick walls of clay and chaff. At Karanovo the houses were detached, but close-packed in rows, separated by a street which may have been covered by logs. Elsewhere, at **Tiszajenö**, Hungary (p. 213G), houses of a similar size were built by erecting a framework made from a few heavier upright posts, and facing these with plaited branches or wattles which were daubed with clay. In both types of houses, the walls were painted red and white, the floors were of beaten earth; most contained a round hearth which was frequently located opposite the entrance. Later houses from Azmak and Karanovo (3800–3000 BC) were similarly constructed, but the plan had evolved to include a small porch area or anteroom at one end. Pottery models indicated that these houses had roofs made of wood daubed with clay or covered in thatch, sometimes with an animal head over the entrance. Inside were square clay ovens built on solid foundations of stone or slate.

LONGHOUSES

Middle Neolithic houses (*c.* 4200 BC) from the settlement of **Bylany** (Czech Republic) (p. 213F) were of the longhouse type, grouped together and oriented in a north-west, south-east direction. They were rectangular in plan, with a constant width of about 6 m (20 ft) and lengths which varied from 8 m (26 ft) to 45 m (150 ft). Heavy oak posts supported a framework of wattle walls covered with clay. Three types of plan were found: a tripartite plan with an entrance section facing south-east, a central living bay, and a deeper storage area; a bipartite plan in which the entrance and living areas were combined; and a single-bay houses with a living area only. Similar houses have been excavated at **Elsloo**, Holland (*c.* 4500–4105 BC).

Longhouses of the Tripolye culture from **Vladimirovka** and **Kolomiishchina** in the Ukraine (3500–3000 BC) were smaller, with central interior rows of posts supporting gabled roofs. Additional structural support came from substantial internal partitions of wattle and daub. Models recovered from the site indicated that the gable walls were moulded, and the interior and exterior walls painted. The floors were made of a layer of clay on a base of logs.

DRYSTONE HOUSES

Some of the most striking evidence of drystone Neolithic dwellings has come from the settlement of **Skara Brae** (*c.* 2500–1700 BC) (p. 213M, 218A) in the Orkney Islands, off the north-east coast of Scotland. Here, the major group consisted of substantial stone-built houses with double-skin walls about 3 m (10 ft) thick overall. The inner and outer leaves were of drystone walling over a metre thick. The cavity was filled with domestic refuse. The houses were rectangular in plan, with rounded corners, and were up to 7 m (23 ft) in diameter. Access was by a tunnel-like passageway, enclosed by doors which could be locked in position with horizontal bars. The dwellings appear to have been roofed with turf or thatch, with a smoke-hole positioned over the central hearth which was about 1 m (3 ft) square and edged with low kerb-stones. The interiors were remarkable for their stone furniture. Similar examples have been excavated at **Rinyo** in the Orkneys and **Yoxie** in the Shetlands.

Collective Tombs

A striking architectural feature of Neolithic settlement patterns in western Europe was the widespread construction of collective tombs. There are between 40,000 and 50,000 large, elaborate megalithic tombs throughout the western Mediterranean, Iberia, France, Holland, northern Germany and Scandinavia. They fall into two classes, passage graves and gallery graves, but a great deal of regional variation has been found in the plans and in the methods of construction. The practice of building such tombs seems to have originated between 4500 and 1500 BC. The evidence is that these monuments related to the disposal of the dead, but it cannot be assumed that this was their primary purpose, nor that they all functioned in the same way. The distribution of megaliths in the landscape may have related to demographic variables, and linked the shape and layout of the tombs to the form of dwellings. Burials in timber mortuary chambers beneath earthen longbarrows were more particular to Britain in the megalithic period.

MEGALITHIC PASSAGE-GRAVES

At **Maes Howe, Orkney Islands**, a covering mound 38 m × 32 m (126 ft × 107 ft) (p. 216A) was surrounded by a wide space, beyond which was a wide ditch. An entrance passage 1 m (3 ft) in width and 1.5 m (5 ft) high, consisting first of coursed masonry and then of stone slabs, led to the burial chamber, which was about 15 m (49 ft) into the mound. The burial chamber was 5 m (16 ft) square, with buttressed corners. Inclined walls supported a stone corbelled vault originally some 5 m (16 ft) or so high. The walls were smooth, built with rectangular blocks with fine joints. Opening from three sides of the chamber were cells, raised about 1 m (3 ft) above the floor of the main chamber, and entered through window-like openings which could be sealed by stone slabs. A similar example with drystone walls and a corbelled roof has been found at **Los Millares**, Spain (p. 216C), and a simpler version with a round chamber, coursed

PREHISTORIC MONUMENTS

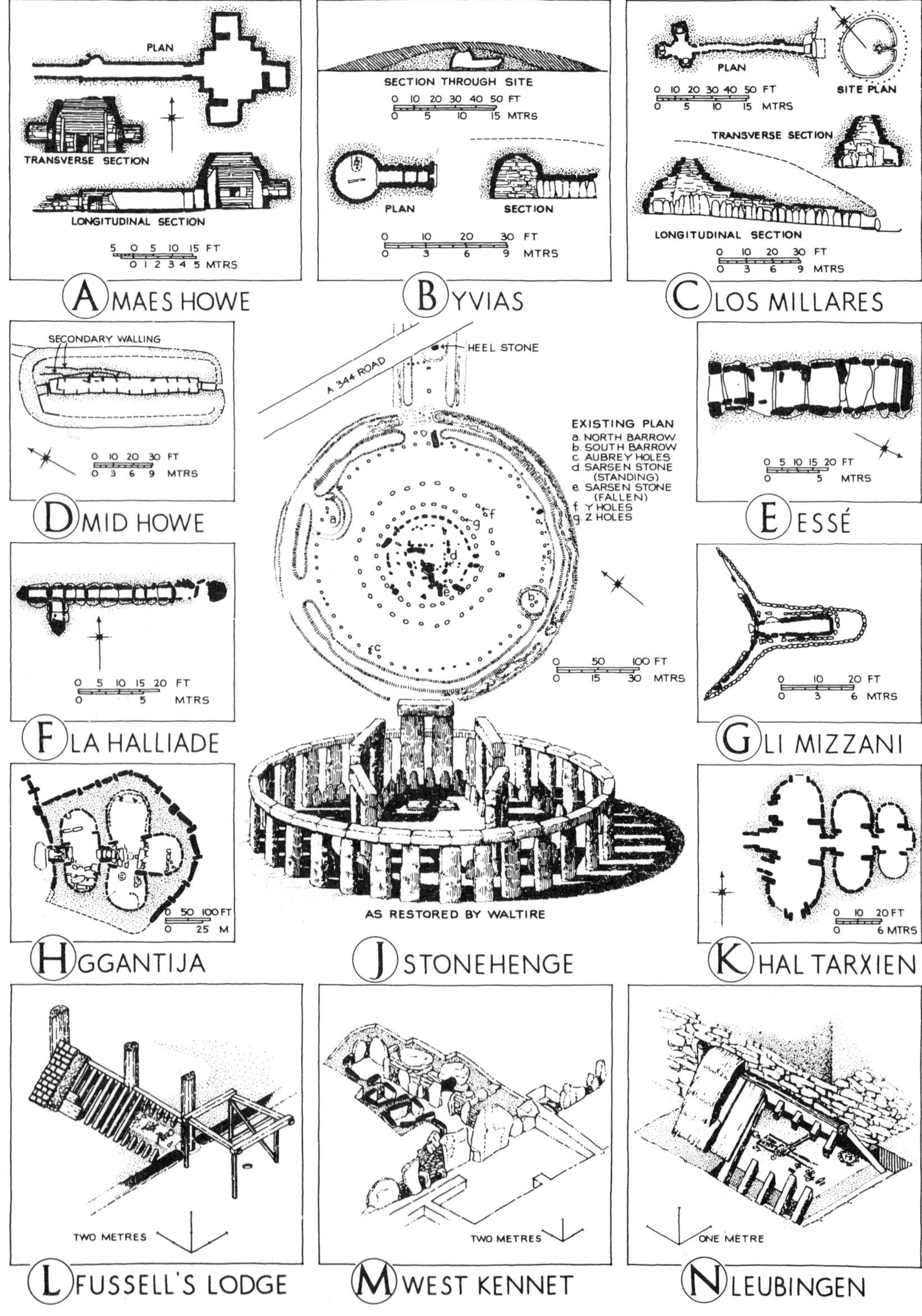

masonry walls and a corbelled roof at **Yvias, Brittany** (p. 216B). There are other fine passage-graves at **New Grange, Dowth** and **Knowth**, in Ireland (2500–1700 BC); these contained murals, which were produced by pecking, pounding and incising the surfaces of the stone to make geometric, curvilinear, zig-zag and lozenge patterns.

MEGALITHIC GALLERY-GRAVES

There is a fine gallery-grave at **Mid Howe, Shetland Islands** (p. 216D). It consisted of a stalled chamber with twelve sections some 23 m (76 ft) long overall, and was covered by a rectangular mound approximately 33 m × 13 m (110 ft × 43 ft) in plan. Fully compartmented gallery-graves have been excavated in France, as at **La Halliade** (p. 216F) in the southwest, where a covering mound some 21 m (69 ft) in length covered a grave just over 12 m (39 ft) long. The grave was entered at right-angles to the gallery, which was divided into eight separate compartments. A more typical example was found at **Essé, Brittany** (p. 216E), where the 6 m (19 ft) long grave was divided into an entrance porch, and a gallery with three transverse slabs as at Mid Howe.

The more complex gallery grave with a transept at **West Kennet** in south-west England (p. 216M) lay under a grass-covered chalk mound overlying a core of boulders; the 12.2 m (40 ft) long burial chamber was set into the eastern end, and was entered through a flat facade of large upright sarsen stones, in the centre of which was a blocking stone. Behind this was a semicircular forecourt onto which the burial chamber opened. The central gallery led to two pairs of chambers with transepts and a terminal chamber lined with megalithic slabs. The gaps between the slabs were filled with drystone walling, and the roofs of the chambers were roughly corbelled and closed with large capstones. It is estimated that this grave originally contained the bodies of about fifty people.

Li Mizzani (*c.* 1900 BC) (p. 216G), on the island of Sardinia, was a late instance of a small, elaborate gallery grave. It was entered through a central facade which framed a semi-circular forecourt. The 6.5 m × 1.5 m (21 ft × 5 ft) chamber was built of megaliths and roofed with slabs. The covering mound was extended to form two horns behind the wings of the facade at the entrance end.

EARTHEN LONGBARROWS

The longbarrow at **Fussell's Lodge** (3230 BC) in Wiltshire, England (p. 216L), was a trapezoid mound some 40 m (130 ft) long, and varying from 6 m (19 ft) wide to 12 m (39 ft) wide at the entrance end. This appears to have had an entrance porch supported by four posts. The earthen mound was surrounded by a bedding trench over 1 m (3 ft) deep and about 0.5 m (18 in) wide; it housed a substantial timber retaining wall about 2 m (7 ft) high. The mortuary house was located immediately behind the entrance and was constructed from three split tree-trunks about 600 mm (2 ft) in diameter, set 7 m (23 ft) apart, which supported a ridge post. Against this rested sloping timbers which formed a triangular framework about 1.5 m (5 ft) high and 2.4 m to 3 m (8 ft to 10 ft) wide at ground level. This appears to have been covered with planks, over which was placed a layer of flint nodules. The whole building was finished with a layer of turves. It is thought that over fifty people were buried here in four separate groups. Similar examples of longbarrows have been found in England at **Willerby Wold** and **East Heslerton, Yorkshire**, and **Giant's Hill, Lincolnshire**.

Temples and Ritual Structures

Although less numerous than tombs, temples have been found dating from the Neolithic period. They represent some of the earliest European buildings with a specific function.

TEMPLES

The trefoil-plan temples of **Ggantija** (2700 BC) (p. 216H) and **Hal Tarxien** (2000 BC) (p. 216K, 218) in Malta were constructed from megalithic elements backed by stone-faced earthen walls. The temples were formally planned, had concave monumental facades, trilithion entrance passages, and pairs of lateral and terminal chambers built of tooled orthostatic and meglithic blocks. The inner chambers could be closed off by doors. Successive courses were corbelled, allowing the roof-openings to be narrowed, before being closed with beams and thatch, the earliest known use of this method of construction; it has been suggested that contemporary teracotta models and engravings of facades were prepared in advance of buildings to show what was required. Some of the stones were decorated with spiral relief carvings, and the temples were probably plastered internally and then painted.

Apart from temples, two main classes of open-air ritual structure have been found in Neolithic Europe, one elongated, the other roughly circular. The former range from small rows of late Neolithic and Bronze Age upright stones like those found in the south-west of England, at **Merrivale** and **Stalldon Down** on Dartmoor to the large cursus monuments, such as the **Dorset Cursus**, or the multiple stone alignments of **Carnac, Brittany**. An equally wide range of circular arrangements has been found in England, varying from small circles, like **Scorhill** on Dartmoor, through the more complex configurations of **Stanton Drew, Somerset**, and **Long Meg and her Daughters, Cumbria**, to large enclosures

A. (*above*)
Drystone Houses, Skara Brae (*c.* 2500–1700 BC). See p.215

B. (*left*)
Neolithic temple, Hal Tarxien, Malta (2000 BC). See p.217

with causeways (3300–2500 BC) and henge monuments (2500–1500 BC) with central features, such as stone or timber circles, cairns, burials and pits, and outlying stone or timber posts. These were a purely British phenomenon.

ENCLOSURES WITH CAUSEWAYS

The enclosure with a causeway at **Windmill Hill** (2960–2570 BC) in Wiltshire is the largest of its type. The three rings were more or less evenly spaced, regular ovals. The inner oval measured some 84 m × 76 m (275 ft × 248 ft). The second enclosure was between 46 m (150 ft) and 96 m (315 ft) beyond it, and the outer enclosure, spaced at similar distance, measured some 400 m × 305 m (1300 ft × 1000 ft) overall. The ditches marking the rings were flat-bottomed, between 2 m (7 ft) and 3 m (10 ft) wide, but the height of the original banks cannot be estimated accurately. Other examples of enclosures of this kind have been found with a single ring, as at **Whitesheet Hill, Wiltshire**, with two rings, at **Robin Hood's Ball,** also in Wiltshire, and with four rings, at **Whitehawk, Sussex**.

HENGES

Avebury henge monument, **Wiltshire**, consisted of a circular area of approximately 11.5 ha (28.5 acres), enclosed by a ditch some 348 m (1140 ft) in internal diameter and an outer bank of 427 m (1400 ft) in diameter. Four causeways, approximately on the points of the compass, led to the central area. Within the central area were two inner circles, the southern circle over 50 m (164 ft) in diameter containing 29 stones, at the centre of which stood a pillar-stone about 6 m (19 ft) high. The northern inner circle was about 49 m (160 ft) in diameter and originally contained some 27 stones around an inner ring of twelve stones. At the centre of this circle stood three massive sarsen stones forming a three-sided enclosure. Stretching for just under 2.4 km (1.5 miles) from the southern entrance to the henge ran an avenue of a hundred pairs of 3 m (10 ft) high sarsen stones set in pairs about 15 m (49 ft) apart. The stones seem to have been paired by shape, tall and narrow alternating with short and diamond-shaped stones. There is an outstanding smaller stone henge-monument at **Arbor Low, Derbyshire**, England, and an even simpler one, apparently unbanked, with upright stones and no central features has been found in the Orkneys, at the **Ring of Brodgar**.

Timber henges also have been found with concentric rings of post-holes, perhaps used for roof supports. At **Woodhenge, Wiltshire**, the earthworks consisted of a ditch and outer bank of overall diameter more than 82 m (269 ft), with a single entrance facing north-east. Inside were the remains of six concentric rings or post-holes for wooden uprights, ranging in diameter from 44 m (144 ft) across the outer ring to 12 m (39 ft) at the innermost ring. The best-known reconstruction shows a circular roofed structure with a central space open to the sky, but it has also been suggested that it was a free-standing arrangement of concentric timber posts. Similar configurations have been found at **Durrington Walls** and Marden in Wiltshire and **Mount Pleasant in Dorset**.

Bronze Age

Dwellings

Many European Bronze Age dwellings were little more than rough shacks in which cooking and storage took place, but the overall form of the settlement was more significant, particularly where it was palisaded or ringed with earthworks. In parts of Britain, the latter types of enclosure are also found around individual timber-framed and drystone farmsteads.

TIMBER-FRAMED HOUSES

On the Federsee in southern Germany, there is a rare settlement containing substantial log-built houses, at **Wasserburg** (*c.* tenth-ninth century BC) (p. 213H), each with a central hall and lateral wings. The largest of these approached the size, proportions and layout of a small mediaeval hall-house, with six rooms, five of which contained hearths, and a main hall measuring 10 m × 5 m (33 ft × 16 ft). The logs were interlocked by means of notches cut near the extremities. Log-built houses have also been found at **Biskupin**, Poland (1660–500 BC) (p. 222C). They were remarkably similar in size and internal arrangements to those described above. They were square, 9 m × 9 m (30 ft × 30 ft), with an entrance porch extending the length of one side and facing the street, and with a living area and loft, the latter accessible by ladder. To the left of the entrance was a stone hearth and a family bed was located against the southern wall. The floors were made of wood and the roof was thatched. The houses were placed together in rows oriented roughly east and west. The remains of a chieftain's house near **Heuneburg**, Germany (600 BC), was rectangular in plan, with four rooms comprising a kitchen with hearth and oven a main central hall with two hearths, and two small unheated rooms which may have been used for sleeping.

Circular Bronze Age houses have been found also at **Itford Hill** in southern England (*c.* tenth century BC) (p. 213J). They were a linked group of earthwork enclosures and hut platforms, measuring 134 m × 55 m (440 ft × 180 ft) overall. The principal enclosure was surrounded by a timber fence, and contained four circular huts of which the largest was about 7 m (23 ft) in diameter, with a ring of 250 mm (19 in) timber uprights supporting a thatched roof, and beyond it an independent, light outer wall. The remains suggest that there may have been a small porch in front of the entrance. The other three huts ranged in size from 4.8 m (16 ft) to 6 m (19 ft) in diameter and were similarly constructed but without porches. The latter buildings, it has been suggested, were roofed shelters for livestock. The remaining three enclosures contained a further four huts, and there were an additional five huts outside the palisaded area. Only four of the huts appear to have been dwellings, while the remainder served as outbuildings. Smaller groups with similar arrangements have been found at **Thorny Down, Salisbury**, and **Plumpton Plain**, both in England.

Burial Mounds

The begining of the Bronze Age was marked by the first individual or single-grave burials beneath circular mounds, and there is great variety in their external form, interior arrangements and grouping. At their simplest, barrows consisted of only an earth or stone mound; in more complex examples, as well as mounds there were timber mortuary houses or stone cists to contain the corpse.

The barrow at **Leubingen, Germany** (*c.* 1500 BC) (p. 216N), was 34 m (112 ft) in diameter, and stood 8.5 m (28 ft) high. The central cairn was delimited by a ring-ditch some 20 m (66 ft) in diameter, and it covered a thatched oak burial-chamber built with eighteen posts arranged in a rectangle 3.9 m × 2.1 m (13 ft × 7 ft). The chamber was triangular in section, with the side-supports set at an angle and notched into a central timber ridge-post. The side-supports also were notched to receive the boarded timber floor. The mortuary house itself was made of oak planks and thatched. It contained a single grave. Another example of the same date at **Helmsdorf,** also in Germany, lay under a cairn of similar dimensions, but did not have a ridge-post. Stone revetments retained the side-supports to the burial chamber, which had a sandstone paved floor at the northern end and a reed floor at the southern end. The cairn was also contained within a stone wall.

Temples and Ritual Structures

The remains of Bronze Age temples are flimsy by comparision with the megalithic buildings of the Neolithic period. Small temple-like structures have been excavated at the sites of **Tustrup**, Denmark (mid-third millennium BC), and at **Salacea**, Russia, in the Carpathian Basin. The latter had three rooms, measured about 8.8 m × 5.2 m (29 ft × 17 ft) overall, and had a megaron-like porch which led to a room containing a hanging altar, and from there to a large squarish room with a plaster frieze and two fixed altars on raised clay platforms set against the side walls. Six post-holes in the floor may have held supports for the roof, which was of reed thatch. Similarly, remains from the site of **Bargeroosterveld**, Holland (*c.* 1050 BC) may indicate an open-air temple or shrine-like structure.

Henges and open-air ceremonial sites continued to be built in Britain during the Bronze Age. The best known of the British henge monuments, **Stonehenge in Wiltshire** (p. 216J), was unique rather than typical, although the sophistication of the original structure and the many refinements made later suggest that its designers were drawing on a well-established architectural tradition. The first, late Neolithic and Early Bronze Age, phase (*c.* 2600 BC) consisted of earthworks, a low bank 30.5 m (100 ft) outside the stones, an outer ditch, and a number of standing stones and timber structures of uncertain kinds. The second (Bronze Age) phase (*c.* 2100 BC), involved the erection of two concentric stone rings, 22.5 m (74 ft) and 26 m (85 ft) in diameter; there were 38 dolerite or bluestone blocks from Pembrokeshire in south Wales in each ring and all were set in radially arranged pairs. The final phase, dated to the middle and later Bronze Age, entailed the clearing of the central area and the erection of 82 completely new stones. Sarsen blocks, each averaging over 26,000 kg (57,300 lb), were brought from Marlborough Downs 32 km (20 miles) to the north and set upright in the circle and horseshoe arrangements which remain today. The lintel stones were dovetailed into each other, and morticed and tenoned into the uprights, which were themselves carefully shaped to counteract the effects of perspective. The inner and outer faces of the lintels were curved so that the completed ring formed an almost perfect circle. The stones of the horseshoe setting were erected in five groups of three trilithions. The axis of the sarsen setting pointed to the midsummer sunrise. In an intermediate phase, the dismantled bluestones were reset in an oval arrangement inside and outside the sarsen horseshoe, but in about 1800 BC the arrangement was given its final form, in which sixty of the bluestones were set in a circle between the sarsen horseshoe and the outer circle, while a horseshoe of nineteen bluestones was placed inside the trilithions in an arrangement which increased in height towards the centre of the setting.

Defensive Structures

One of the most remarkable types of structure in later Bronze Age Europe was the fort or stockade. These ranged from palisaded forts in low-lying areas, to hill-forts on low hills or knolls and spur forts on steep promontories. Those on steep slopes were usually restricted to the provision of ramparts at the most vulnerable points. In some cases these were multivallate. Defences on gentle slopes usually took the form of encircling ramparts. Low-lying forts had massive encircling ramparts enclosing a roughly circular or oval area. Rampart construction has been classified into four types. The most common was that in which two plank walls were erected 2 m to 3 m (7 ft to 10 ft) apart, with tie-beams between them; the space between the palisades was filled with earth and rubble. In the second type, usually found in upland areas, stone was substituted for timber. A third type, of earlier date, consisted of a timber grid; parallel rows of timbers were laid in consecutive layers at right angles to each other, the interstices were filled with wood chips, earth and stone, and the whole was capped with planks. A fourth and chronologically later type of rampart consisted of rubble-filled boxes.

The Bronze Age also saw the evolution of fortified buildings of some sophistication, namely the torre, nuraghi and tayalot towers of the Mediterranean islands.

FORTIFICATIONS

Early examples of late Neolithic and early Bronze Age fortifications have been found on the Iberian peninsula at **Los Millares**, Spain (*c.* 2340 BC), where the settlement was surrounded by a stone wall with semicircular bastions. Similar examples are to be found at **Villa Nova de Sao Pedro, near Lisbon**, Portugal, where a small chieftain's castle was defended by means of a bastioned wall, and at **Zambujal,** also in Portugal.

The fortified settlement of **Biskupin**, Poland (1660–500 BC) (p.222C) was a fine timber-palisaded fort; here the exterior was coated with clay to prevent burning, and the interior was supported by massive timber revetments. It is thought that the stockade was originally some 5 m to 6 m (16 ft to 19 ft) high, with crenellations and a protected high-level walkway. Biskupin was entered through a gate-tower and entrance causeway. Similar settlements have been discovered throughout the region of **Lausitz in Germany** (p. 222A).

STONE TOWERS

Torre have been found in Corsica dating from the early second millennium BC. These circular towers ranged from 10 m to 15 m (33 ft to 49 ft) in diameter, and were built in drystone walling. Some had an internal corridor, and were about 3 m (10 ft) high, while others, standing up to 7 m (23 ft) high, had a main chamber roofed by means of false corbelling. It has been suggested they served both defensive and ritual purposes. The most famous torre are at **Filitosa**, where standing stones in the shape of warriors were incorporated into the buildings, but those at **Foce** (p. 222D) and **Balestra** are more typical.

Nuraghi, or circular defensive stone towers, have been found in Sardinia dating from 1800 BC onwards. These ranged from single tower units to complex structures with curtain walling and extra towers for technologically related activities. Early towers contained a single chamber and later had up to three floors of accommodation with sleeping niches let into the walls. The nuraghi at **Murartu** and **Sa Coa Filigosa** (p. 222D) were typical of the period, but the tower at **Sant' Antine** (p. 222D) was a later, more developed example with a central tower and triple defensive corner towers linked by a wall. The whole was built to withstand siege equipment and battering rams.

There are square and round tayalot towers in the Balearic Islands dating from about 1400 BC. These were stone-built towers, about 10 m (33 ft) in diameter. Some of them were completely solid, while others contained rooms at ground level, or upper levels, the latter approached by external ramps or internal stairs. Typical towers were at **San Agusti Vell**, Minorca, **Cala Pi**, Lluchmayor (p. 222D), **Son Lluch**, Majorca, and **Plana d'Albarca**, Escura (p. 222D).

Iron Age

Dwellings

Iron Age houses continued to fall into the two constructional types found in the Bronze Age, namely timber-framed and drystone. Architecturally elaborate houses are rare in continental Europe, but domestic architecture continued to develop in Britain, where a tradition to detached farmsteads was maintained throughout the period.

TIMBER-FRAMED HOUSES

Perhaps the best-known housing from the prehistoric period is at **Little Woodbury, near Salisbury**, in the south-west of England (*c.* 300–100 BC) (p. 213K). The principal building was a circular timber house, over 15 m (49 ft) in diameter, set within an oval timber-palisaded enclosure 120 m × 90 m (394 ft × 295 ft) overall. The palisade consisted of upright stakes about 2 m (7 ft) high set edge to edge in a trench some 300 mm (1 ft) deep. The main house was defined by four groups of post-holes. Those in the outer rings held oval posts, each 450 mm × 300 mm (18 in × 12 in) in section, and these supported the outer wall. The main roof-support was probably provided by a second ring of posts, each 300 mm to 375 mm (12 in to 15 in) in diameter, and by the four central posts, each

PREHISTORIC DEFENCES

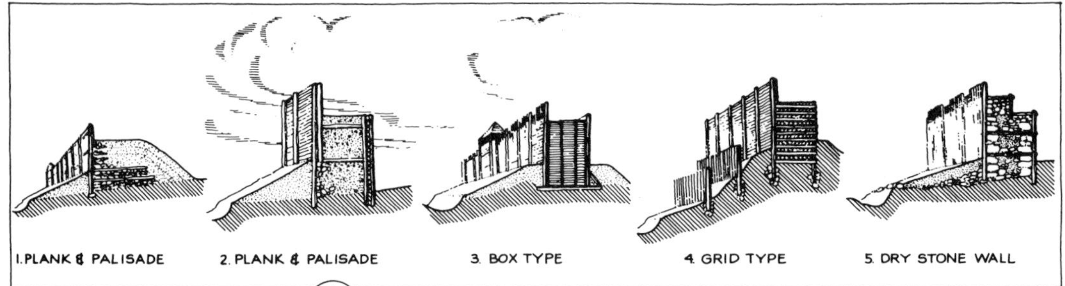

A LAUSITZ FORTIFICATIONS

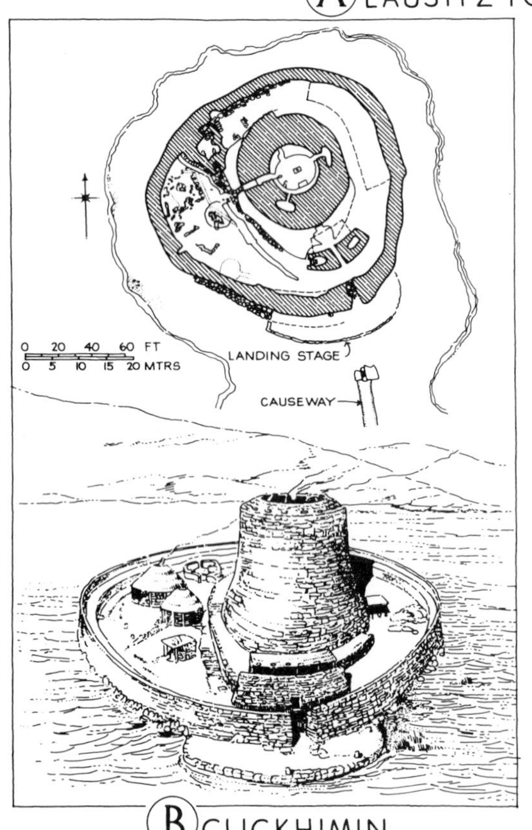

B CLICKHIMIN

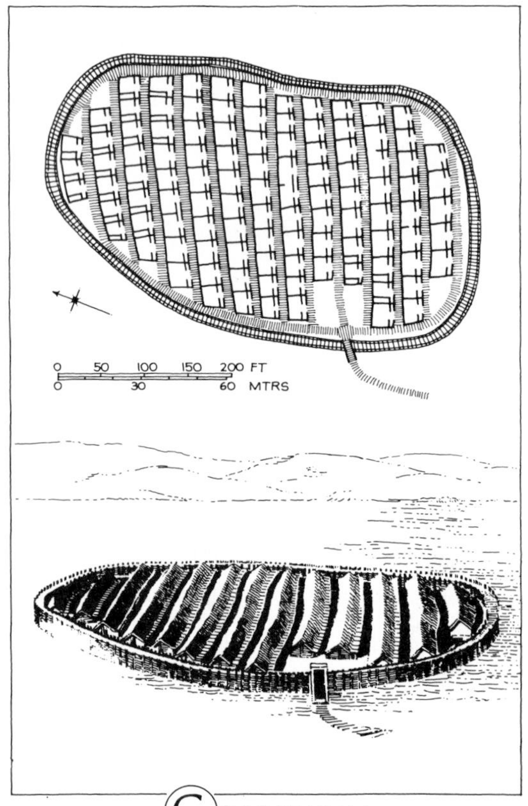

C BISKUPIN

0 10 20 30 FT
0 5 10 MTRS

SA COA FILIGOSA

FOCE

SANT'ANTINE

0 2 4 6 8 10 FT
0 1 2 3 MTRS

PLANA D'ALBARCA

CALA PI

D STONE TOWERS

600 mm (2 ft) in diameter. It is assumed that both sets of posts had continuous lintels on which sloping rafters rested. These were overlaid by lighter horizontal members to which the roof covering, probably thatch, was attached. It has been conjectured that the roof construction at the apex took the form of a raised canopy which would have allowed smoke to escape from the building. The final group of post-holes defined an elaborate porch or entrance passage some 5 m (16 ft) long and over 2 m (7 ft) wide, and it may be that the house had a central loft. A number of related ancillary buildings and storage pits were excavated within the palisaded enclosure. Similar dwellings have been found at **Longbridge Deverill, Wiltshire**, and at **Pimperne, Dorset**, both in south-west England, at **West Brandon, County Durham**, in northern England, and at **West Plean**, Scotland.

DRYSTONE HOUSES

Chysauster, in Cornwall in the extreme south-west of England (p. 213N), has yielded exceptionally wellpreserved and elaborate Iron Age drystone houses similar to those found in Scotland in the Neolithic period, but with open rather than roofed courtyards. The houses were strung out in two rows of four, set about 15 m (49 ft) apart. They were oval in plan and up to 27 m × 21 m (89 ft × 69 ft). Access was from the east into the courtyards, onto which three or more rooms opened. At the rear of each courtyard, opposite the entrance, was the main living room, usually paved, and anything up to 10 m (33 ft) in length. To the left of this was a roofed but open-fronted shelter, and to the right a long narrow room, possibly used for storage. Some of the houses had additional rooms; many had drains and external terraced areas which were probably garden plots.

In Scotland, drystone aisled-roundhouses and wheelhouses attained considerable internal complexity. The aisled-roundhouse at **Clettravel in the Outer Hebrides** (p. 213P) was circular, 8.5 m (28 ft) in diameter internally and 14 m (46ft) externally, and its walls had two leaves of drystone walling forming a cavity which was filled with turf and rubble. An upper gallery was supported on eight freestanding stone piers, which would have also supported a substantial roof. They also created an aisle around the circumference of the dwelling and extended it some 2 m (7 ft) from the side walls, leaving a double-height space at the centre. The wheelhouses at Jarlshof were circular in plan, 10 m to 12 m (33 ft to 39 ft) in diameter overall, with walls about 1 m (3 ft) thick. Internally they had radial walls tapering in plan towards the central space defining a number of compartments. These were roofed with stone slabs, the central area by means of corbelling. A similar house was found at **Clickhimin in the Shetland Isles** and at the **Calf of Eday, Orkney** (p. 213L).

Funerary Monuments

Funerary monuments and ritual structures ceased to be built during the Iron Age. Cult sites are of three kinds:

1 Artificial shafts, such as that found at **Holzhausen** in Bavaria dating from the first century BC, and other ritual wells, sunk to depths of between 12 m (39 ft) and 40 m (130 ft), and containing deposits of animals, human bones and votive offerings.
2 Small double-square temples, such as those excavated at **Heathrow**, England, and **Ecury-le-Repos and Fin D'Ecury in Marne**, France (*c.* 300–100 BC), in which ditch and earthwork enclosures, measuring about 10 m × 10 m (33 ft × 33 ft) in plan, surrounded post-holes for timber structures.
3 Long parallel-sided rectilinear or elongated oval 'sanctuary sites' enclosed by ditches and earthworks, as at **Aulnay-aux-Planches, Marne**, France (*c.* 1100–1000 BC), and **Libenice**, (Czech Republic) (*c.* 300 BC), containing standing stones, post-holes and hearths. All speak of a rapidly evolving European civilisation and a developing pattern of settlements over a wide area.

Defensive Structures

By contrast, fortifications, already well-established in central Europe during the Bronze Age, spread to north-west Europe to such an extent that from about 1000 BC onwards hill-forts became the commonest monument of the Celtic world, numbering at least 10,000 in Europe. Parapet construction varied from a simple sloping-fronted earthwork of triangular section with ditch and occasionally backed by stone revetting, as at Maiden Castle in south-west England (*c.* 100 BC), to a timber or drystone revetted form of construction, which presented a vertical face to the attacker. In more elaborate types of rampart, crenellations, breastworks, walkways and stepped sections were found. Common in Iron Age Europe were box ramparts and timber-laced ramparts, in which stone-built fortification walls were reinforced with timbers. They were occasionally fired to vitrify and fuse the stones. In northern and western Scotland hill-forts were rare, but fortified buildings known as duns (small, stone-built, circular forts) and brochs (stone-built, circular towers) were common.

HILL-FORTS

Maiden Castle (see above) illustrates a typical progression of building in the development of Iron Age hill-forts. The occupation of Maiden Castle took place in four phases. First, about 350 BC, the hill was ringed with a single rampart and ditch; this was faced with timbers and then built from chalk, quarried from an external ditch. At this stage it had gates at the east and west ends of the enclosure. About a century later, the eastern gate was elaborated by claw-like extensions which funnelled traffic into the entrance passages. At the same time, the fort was enlarged to take in areas to the west. In the third period (*c.* 150 BC) there was further enlargement of the ramparts, which were then reinforced with stone, and additional defences added at the entrances, which were further elaborated in the final phase (*c.* 100–75 BC).

FORTIFIED BUILDINGS

Both a broch and a dun have been found at **Clickhimin** (p. 222B) in the Shetland Isles, Scotland. The broch at Clickhimin was nearly 20 m (66 ft) across, with walls over 5 m (16 ft) thick at the base, enclosing a central court of about 10 m (33 ft) in diameter. The entrance passage was on the western side. From the central court, narrow doorways gave access to two oval intra-mural chambers with corbelled roofs. Timber-galleried accommodation was built against the inside wall, giving access to a staircase which spiralled upwards within the thickness of the block wall to a rampart walk at the top of the tower. This is estimated to have been between 10 m (33 ft) and 15 m (49 ft) high. Similar well-preserved fortified buildings are to be found at **Mousa in the Shetland Islands**, and **Gurness** and **Mid Howe in Orkney**. The dun was of similar size, with galleried accommodation built against the inner face, and doorways leading from the upper floor to a rampart wall. **Dun Kildalloig** and **Borgadel Water** on the Mull of Kintyre, Scotland, were comparable versions but had no galleries.

Chapter 10

ROME AND THE ROMAN EMPIRE

To the barbarian invasions

Architectural Character

Etruscan and Early Roman

Up to the seventh century BC there were no buildings of architectural significance in central Italy. Both the findings of archaeology and the surviving literary sources from a somewhat later period show that late Bronze Age and early Iron Age dwellings had not evolved beyond primitive huts (see Chapter 9), and that even temples were no more than sacred enclosures with simple open-air altars. Indeed the word 'templum' originally meant only a space on the ground or in the sky marked out for the purpose of taking omens. A rock-cut tomb at Cerveteri – the so-called Tomb of the Thatched Roof, probably of the early seventh century – represents a typical hut, with low walls, probably of wattle and daub, low benches of earth or rubble around them, and apparently, as the name indicates, a thatched roof.

In the sixth century, under the influence of Greek and other traders from the eastern Mediterranean, houses of the Greek megaron type seem to have appeared, to be followed by larger houses with internal courts or atria, off which opened the living rooms, for the richer members of the community. Still built largely of timber and mud brick, these houses cannot have had a long life but their forms have been preserved in other rock-cut tombs in the large cemeteries the Etruscans built outside their city walls. They had flat or sloping ceilings, sometimes coffered or elaborately carved, carved doorframes, and coloured dados around the walls. Roof and ceiling beams were given intermediate support in the larger tombs by columns which take a variety of forms, square, polygonal or circular in plan, sometimes fluted and with a variety of capitals including crudely cut Doric and Ionic. Some of the later tombs have atria with roofs sloping inward to a central opening to drain rain-water to a tank beneath.

Temples began to show Greek influence in having buildings within the enclosure to house the god or cult image. The original name for this structure was simply 'aedes' or building. The temple building bore a limited resemblance to the Greek temple: rectangular in plan, raised on a podium, and with a wider-spreading roof partly supported by outer columns. But there the resemblance to the contemporary Doric temple ended. There were several differences in plan arrangement and form:

1. The temple building was set at the back of the enclosure facing the entrance and had a blank rear wall. An open-air altar was retained on the axis between the front of the temple building and the entrance to the enclosure.
2. The axial arrangement was emphasised by raising the building on a podium considerably higher than the stylobate of the Greek temple and by providing entrance steps only at the front, facing the altar.
3. Usually, columns were employed only at the front of the building to assist in carrying the roof of the porch. Occasionally they were used at the sides also but were never carried round the whole periphery of the building.
4. The cella was a simple rectangular room, though it was not unusual for there to be three cellas side-by-side for a triad of gods. Where there was only one cella, there might be open wings at the sides, giving a very similar plan. The proportions were much shallower than in Greece, making the whole structure more nearly square in plan.

Other differences in character stemmed from the fact that everything but the podium was built of timber, mud brick and terracotta. The use of these materials in place of marble or other stone gave rise

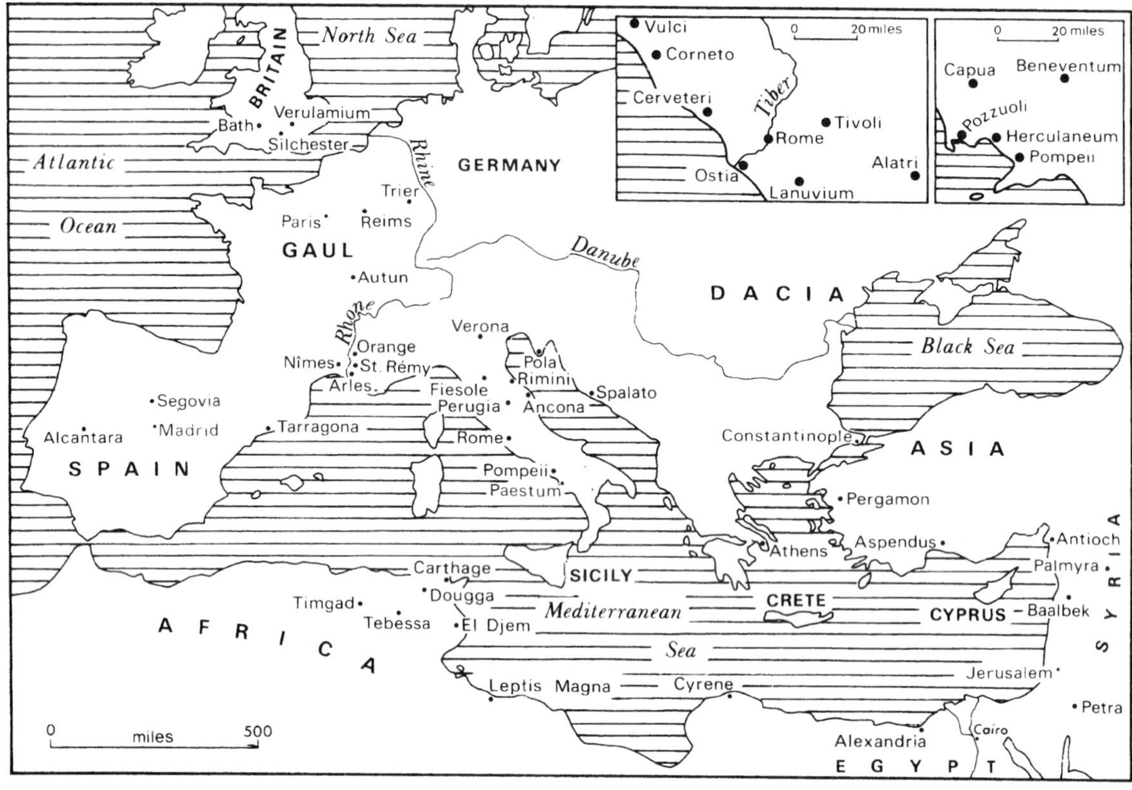

The Roman Empire

to differences in proportion and details. Wide roof overhangs were necessary to throw rain-water clear of mud-brick walls. Columns and architraves were more slender, even when protected by coverings of terracotta, and column spacings were wider. The type of detail to which terracotta lent itself was different from the finely cut detail of the Greek mason. In his subsequent attempt to codify what he saw as the ideal Etruscan form, Vitruvius described and specified a Tuscan order which bore some resemblance to the simplified Doric that tended to result. But the order was not really found as he described it until considerably later.

What is known of the earliest Etruscan towns shows that they were probably no more than products of natural growth. Evidence of conscious planning is first seen in temple layouts, but around 500 BC regular grid layouts appeared in new towns on fairly level sites. Cemeteries, to which even more care seems to have been devoted, display similar patterns, with regular layouts introduced rather later; reference has already been made to some of the tombs, of which large numbers survive. The earliest took the form of stone burial chambers concealed below conical tumuli. Most were simply cut into the rock and approached by descending stairs, unless it was possible to cut horizontally into a rock face, in which case they would be provided with a simple carved facade. As well as representing contemporary house forms, some of them were decorated with wall paintings of funeral rites and similar scenes.

In the larger towns, it appears that considerable attention was given to such matters as drainage, though the well-known principal sewer of Rome – the Cloaca Maxima – was for a long time merely an open drain over most of its length. The fine defensive walls of polygonal or ashlar masonry, which are now the principal remains of the early towns, date only from the period when Rome was gaining the ascendancy and good defence became increasingly necessary. Most of them are no earlier than the fourth century. Bridges at this time seems to have had simple timber spans, though the piers may sometimes have been of stone.

Late Republican and Early Imperial Roman

From the early second century BC, marked changes occurred. They were the result primarily of direct exposure to influences from the Hellenistic East and the already Hellenised Campagna, the exploitation of local travertine and tufa, and the import of foreign marbles. But in other directions the changes were stimulated and made possible by a growing mastery of the new concrete, and were evident not only in previously existing types of building – temples and dwelling houses – but also in the introduction of many new types such as public baths, basilicas, and places of public entertainment.

Architecturally, the changes might be summarised as the introduction of new proportions relating to the use of different materials; the adoption of the Classical Greek orders, particularly the Corinthian; the combination of these orders with an arched form of construction; and the widespread use of vaulted and domed forms.

The first two types of change are most evident in temple buildings, where conservatism usually resulted in the retention of earlier plan forms. Republican and early Imperial temples were still set on high podia, approached only from the front up flights of steps – which were now flanked by massive low walls, projecting forwards from the podia and serving as bases for statuary. Usually they still had simple rectangular cellas preceded by columned porticoes, and sometimes had columns or attached half-columns along the sides, but less frequently around the back. They were still roofed in timber, sometimes with suspended coffered ceilings. But the use of stone for the columns and architraves resulted in closer spacings of the columns, and its use also for the cella walls removed the need for such large roof overhangs. All three Greek orders were used in temples of the second and early first century BC, but the proportions of the Roman Doric are noticeably more slender than those of its Greek prototype. The only exception to the traditional Italian rectangular plan was the occasional adoption of the Greek circular plan, usually with little change from the prototype.

It was usual to site an important temple building in a commanding position in relation to the city forum, unless it was still isolated in its own precinct. In the former case, the altar was set immediately in front of the entrance steps or even set into them. The latter arrangement emphasised still further the axial planning of Roman temple buildings. The outstanding examples are the Temples of Fortuna Primigenia at Palestrina and of Hercules Victor at Tivoli, where the rectangular precincts are surrounded by colonnaded rows of shops and the temples are approached by semicircular flights of steps which served also as seating for theatrical performances.

The forum, corresponding to the Greek agora, was originally an irregularly shaped open space serving as market, general meeting place, and the setting for political discussions and demonstrations. Even in late Republican times it might still be a multi-purpose space, hemmed in by unplanned groups of dwellings, shops and workshops. But it was usually a more formal rectangle, closed at one end by a temple, whose extended temenos or sacred enclosure it effectively became. On other sides it would be largely surrounded by colonnades and public buildings, usually including markets and a basilica.

It is in some of these and other public buildings that the characteristically Roman combination of the orders with the arch made its appearance, though there is some evidence (notably a representation on a funerary urn of uncertain date from Chiusi) that tentative experiments may have been made a little earlier. The combination presumbaly came about because of the lack of suitable stone for wide-spanning lintels when stone replaced timber as the principal structural material. Openings, where needed, were made narrower, and were spanned by arches. Half-columns were then placed in front of the wall containing the openings, and the semblance of an entablature was constructed between them and above the arch by means of blocks of stone projecting forwards from the wall. The arched openings in the wall were framed by the columns and entablature, and the order became purely – or at least primarily – applied surface decoration.

The arch and vault had already been exploited more openly in a variety of more utilitarian buildings such as warehouses, and in various substructures. They appeared most frequently as a sequence of barrel-vaulted bays, set side-by-side as in the much earlier brick-vaulted storerooms of the Ramesseum at Thebes. Similar vaulted bays, slightly tapered in plan, served to support the seating of early theatres. To a more limited extent, the dome also was used, chiefly over the frigidaria of public baths.

The basilica was one of the first large-scale Roman building types in which the interior took precedence over the exterior. It was, in one sense, a small enclosed forum surrounded by its own colonnades or stoas. Its central space, usually rectangular like the forum, had a trussed timber roof and was open at the sides to lower aisles behind the colonnades. Light frequently came from clerestory windows above the colonnades, and there might be side galleries above the aisles. One of its more specialised uses was for the dispensing of justice, for which purpose there was often an apse opening off the centre of one side or off one end of the central rectangle. The best preserved early basilica is that in Pompeii, which may indicate that the form came to Rome from Campagna.

Be this as it may, there is no doubt that buildings like public baths and theatres first appeared in this coastal region around Naples that had not only been exposed to Greek influence for much longer but also, at Baia, possessed natural hot-water springs.

As compared with its Greek counterpart, the theatre differed chiefly in that it was usually constructed on level ground instead of having its seating set in a natural bowl. Seating was restricted to a semicircle, and a raised stage set in front of it was backed by a tall structure extending from one side of the auditorium to the other. The amphitheatre was similar in construction. But, as its name implies, it was theatre-in-the-round, with its seating completely encompassing the central arena. Because of their construction, both theatre and amphitheatre rose prominently from their surroundings. The baths had no direct Greek counterpart. They consisted originally of a series of rooms of very different forms reflecting their uses in the bathing sequence, which progressed from a cold plunge to a warm room and then a hot room. The rooms were compactly grouped together, seemingly without any attempt at first to produce an architecturally meaningful ensemble.

The self-indulgence manifest in these buildings was also first reflected in domestic architecture in the southern region, and the chance preservation of many examples by the eruption of Vesuvius in AD 79 has left an excellent picture of the new luxury of the houses of the more wealthy. The atrium was still entered through a passage in an otherwise blank street facade, unless the rooms to either side of it were let off as shops, but it was now sometimes two-storey instead of single-storey as before. Beyond it opened another court, always unroofed and used as a garden. This was surrounded by colonnades (for which reason it was called the peristyle), and by the more private living rooms. In the country and on sites facing the sea, where there was less need for privacy and a good view of the surrounding landscape, a more open plan was adopted – that of the so-called portico villa, portrayed in numerous wall paintings of the period. Here, the principal rooms were strung out in line to enjoy the view and were faced with colonnades or porticoes on one or two storeys.

It was in these houses and villas that the first extensive use seems to have been made of imported marbles for columns and other exposed structural items and, in sheets little more than 10 mm (nearly ½ in) thick, for wall facings and for paving. Marble column-shafts were usually unfluted monoliths, polished to show the veining to best advantage. The alternative treatment for walls was painted fresco decoration applied to several successive coats of stucco.

Different styles of painting succeeded one another over a period of some two centuries. The first simply imitated coloured marble. Architecturally the most interesting is the second, which dated from the early first century BC to a little after the middle of the same century. Paintings represented extensions of the interiors and dissolved the solid walls into open colonnades similar to those which surrounded the peristyle courts. Among the usual straight entablatures, arches carried directly on free-standing columns rather than piers also appear in the paintings. The earliest surviving built examples of this style, which was subsequently to become of great importance, are in a vestibule of the Suburban Baths of Herculaneum, built about a century later. But it was a structural arrangement whose early experimental uses are less likely than most to have survived to the present day. In the later styles of painting, architectural forms become more and more attenuated and increasingly fantastic. In these villas, there were also many pieces of classical sculpture imported from Greece.

The mass of population was, of course, very differently housed. In Rome itself there was already, in later Republican times, considerable congestion in the central district around the forum. People were packed in crowded tenements several storeys high and constructed with timber frames and mud-brick walls. Fire and structural collapse seem to have been common until the great fire of AD 64 led to rebuilding in a more substantial manner.

Finally it was during this period that the most extensive public works of another kind were undertaken or begun, namely the building of roads, bridges, aqueducts, defence walls for new towns in frontier areas, and other facilities needed by a large empire and large concentrations of people. Among these works bridges, elevated sections of aqueducts, and gateways are of architectural interest. The bridges and aqueducts included some of the major achievements of Roman engineers, who were quite familiar with the possibility of piping water down into a valley and then up again on the far side, but had difficulty in making and maintaining lead pipes able to withstand the pressures that were generated at the foot of a dip, and therefore preferred the aqueducts to be open channels with a consistent slight downward fall to the distribution reservoirs. Both the bridges and the elevated sections of aqueducts were now superbly built of cut stone in simple arched forms which were usually left to speak for themselves but were occasionally given a more decorative surface treatment.

Later Imperial Roman

The principal innovations of the next century – broadly from the reign of Nero to that of Hadrian (AD 54–138) – were in spatial planning, and were made possible by the complete mastery of concrete for vaulting.

It would be an exaggeration to say that an architecture of the interior began at this time. The domestic architecture just described was more concerned with interiors than with exteriors, and the architecture of the country villa even sought to establish new relationships between the interior and the landscape; indeed it was in the design of the villa that the innovations were first seen. The interior had already assumed primary importance in the basilica as it had done in such buildings as the Greek bouleuterion and the audience halls or throne rooms of Achaemenid palaces, which might be regarded as being among its ancestors. But the interior did now become more widely important in a way that is epitomised by a comparison of Hadrian's Pantheon with the Athenian Parthenon. Whereas nearly all attention was given in the Parthenon to the exterior, the exterior of the Pantheon counts for little in relation to its vast domed interior. And this was, above all, an interior of a new kind, no longer bounded by four walls and a roof.

In this change, a central role was played by the dome, which both dissolved the distinction between wall and roof and furnished a means of covering large spaces without intermediate supports. Initially its use did impose a severe restriction on planning, but by expanding the space immediately beneath it in various ways, more freedom was gained. Further freedom came from the parallel development of large-scale vaults of other kinds. There was a further exploration of the relationships between spaces – of the ways in which they could be made to lead from one to another in calculated sequences.

Though the change was pioneered in the design of imperial villas and palaces, most people would have experienced the new architecture chiefly in the large public baths built by successive emperors in the capital. The earliest that now survive in a fairly complete state are those of Caracalla, but substantial remains of the baths of Trajan, and drawings by Palladio of the baths of Titus, show that the form was well established by the end of the first century AD. The uncompromising axial symmetry of these buildings (achieved to a large extent by duplicating many of the rooms that lay off the central axis) meant that there was less surprise in changing axes than in some of the late villas. Nevertheless, the sequence of different spaces opening off one another – some with groined vaults, some domed, some almost as overwhelming individually as the Pantheon, and others smaller and more readily comprehensible to give a greater sense of scale – must have created a deep impression.

Today, however, it is difficult to visualise fully what this impression would have been. Mostly we see only a ruined carcase. Even in the Pantheon, which has the best preserved interior, much has changed. And there has been even more change in that part of the baths of Diocletian converted into the church of S. Maria degli Angeli. We must try to visualise them with the same opulence of surface as was typical of the richest villas of the early Imperial period, with walls largely sheathed in coloured marbles, and vaults or ceilings richly gilded or decorated with paint or mosaic. The wall surfaces were far from flat; they were broken up, not by painted colonnades, but by attached columns of coloured marbles and by niches filled with classical statuary. When they were in use, the bath halls would have been further enlivened by colourful crowds, and perpetual streams of running water, issuing, perhaps, from the mouths of lions carved in marble or cast in bronze, and falling into marble basins.

The exteriors are even less well preserved. The decorative use of the orders referred to above continued in some types of structure, but it became less usual on buildings where the interior was of primary importance. The exterior was usually relatively plain and unadorned apart from a facing of stucco or marble. The Pantheon, for example, presented externally a completely unbroken wall surface apart from the portico; and the baths did likewise except to the extent that some of their wall surfaces were broken by rows of window openings which served to create another rhythm. Exteriors did sometimes, however, acquire a new plastic interest when they directly mirored complex interior forms such as the projection of the circular space under a dome, or when they served as a direct communication between the interior and its landscape setting, as in the earlier portico villa.

In this architecture and its decorative detail it is also possible to detect what can best be described, by analogy with something very similar in the seventeenth century, as a Baroque trend. It resulted from the adoption of complex plan forms of continuously flowing curves and complex shapes of vault. A corresponding trend in decorative surface treatments had appeared already in Republican wall paintings, and it is seen a little later in actual construction in details such as broken pediments.

Alongside these developments, there were further changes in town planning and in housing. The beginning made by Augustus on the construction of a new forum in Rome was carried further, first by Nero and then, most notably, by Trajan, to give the related and unified sequence of large public spaces that extended almost from the Colosseum to the foot of the Capitol. As part of Trajan's contribution, Rome acquired both its largest basilica and its finest market complex. The Basilica Ulpia was, for its time, a fairly conventional structure in all but size. The adjacent market was not. It rose – and still rises – in numerous levels up the slope to the north of the forum, with several terraces and streets of shops, and two large and very different vaulted halls. The entire complex was conceived and built as a whole, using brick-faced concrete everywhere except in some heavily loaded piers.

The developments in mass housing were closely related to what is seen in the market, no doubt because the design and construction of the market were undertaken against the background of major changes in housing construction after the fire of AD 64. First, the opportunity was taken to replan large areas with straight broad streets, thereby creating rectangular blocks or insulae. In a further attempt to prevent similar fires in the future, the use of timber was virtually prohibited: principal walls and floors, at least, were made of concrete. Balconies or external porticoes were called for to facilitate fire-fighting. Today the resulting plan-form is best seen in the abandoned port town of Ostia, and an example will be described below. One feature which must be mentioned here, however, is the increasing use in these buildings of arcades in which the arches were carried on tall slender piers. In the courts of the houses of the more wealthy, arcades in which the arches were carried upon free-standing columns also made their appearance. Examples survive from *c.* 300 AD.

The final phases of architecture in the capital were marked by occasional revivals of earlier forms and introductions of others from the provinces, and by the construction of the last large basilica in the capital – the Basilica Nova, begun by Maxentius and completed by Constantine. This basilica was by far the most significant. It isolated as a completely self-sufficient structure the large rectangular groin-vaulted hall that had previously served as the central hall – the frigidarium – of the great bath complexes. It did so on an unprecedented scale. Its exterior owed virtually nothing to a top dressing of the orders. It derived almost all its interest from the pattern of fenestration, which reflected the interior to a greater extent than before. Though it was without direct issue, it is difficult not to see in it a foretaste of later achievements in the East.

Architecture in the Provinces

As might be expected, the character of architecture in the provinces differed from that in Rome and Italy, in ways that reflected local resources, local traditions, and the differing requirements of climate, culture and religion. The differences were also more marked at some times than others.

In the West, where there was little local tradition or culture to match that of the Romans themselves, Roman forms were imported virtually unchanged by the new masters. Except in a few favoured places, they were scaled down. Buildings like the Maison Carré and the amphitheatre in Nîmes, the theatre in Orange, and the Pont du Gard might just as well have been built at the same time in Rome or its vicinity. Where something new appeared, like a different temple form, it was in response to a different requirement. The chief lack in the western provinces up to the time of the tetrarchy is any real counterpart to the great Roman vaulted architecture.

In the East and in much of North Africa, there were long-established Hellenistic traditions which remained strong, and there was often no clearly discernible break with the architecture of pre-Roman times. Differences did nevertheless appear. One such difference is an increased emphasis on height in the temple. The great temples, such as the Temple of Jupiter at Baalbek, do not quite equal the largest Greek and Hellenistic temples in size, but they do exceed them in height. Again, where the requirements of local cults were different, there were forms not wholly inspired by Rome. There were a few counterparts, on a somewhat smaller scale, to the great vaulted architecture of the capital, but not outside the Balkans and Asia Minor. Climate here was possibly the principal reason. The chief monumental structures, after temples, were probably the theatres – always open to the sky apart from a projecting roof over the stage and an awning to give some further shade. The chief difference as compared with Rome in the later centuries was the long persistence of construction in cut stone, in much of Asia Minor, the whole of Syria, and most of North Africa. It was coupled with the persistence of related Hellenistic forms and a largely independent evolution of these towards something more Baroque in style.

Towards the end, in the time of the tetrarchy and afterwards, there was a trend towards greater uniformity throughout the empire, or at least as between the new provincial capitals where most new building was to be found. Today this is best seen in the architecture of Constantine's time in his capital, Trier, which differs in hardly anything but scale from that of Rome.

Examples

Etruscan and Early Roman

Sanctuaries and Temple Buildings

The **Etruscan Temple** as described by Vitruvius (Bk IV chap vii) has already been referred to. He does not describe any particular structure, but lays down the proportions that he considers to be correct, basing them, presumably, on what he has seen of such temples as they existed in the late first century BC. The model shows a possible interpretation of his description in the light of surviving terracotta details and early burial-urn models (p. 231A). Vitruvius specifies that the spaces alongside the central cella, each three-tenths of the total width, may be either secondary cellas or open wings. They are shown in the model as secondary cellas. A surprising feature is the extent of the projection of the pediment in front of the columns of the porch, but this is supported by some independent evidence.

Of the considerable number of temples that have now been excavated, the plans of some conform to his specifications, whereas others have substantially different plans. Indeed the specified cella widths could not have been generally applicable. Nor could the specified numbers of columns or the rule that the height of the column should be one-third of the width

A. Model of Temple of Juno Sospita, Lanuvium (fifth century BC). See p.230

B. Temple of Fortuna Virilis (second century BC) and Round Temple (first century BC), Forum Boarium, Rome. See p.236

of the temple. This is because the size and spanning limitations of timber columns and beams would have called for proportionately lower heights and narrower widths, and for more columns, as the overall plan dimensions increased.

The remains of the **'Ara della Regina' Temple, Tarquinia**, provide one example of a different plan. This temple had a single cella and side wings. But its length of 77.5 m (254 ft) was more than twice its width rather than only a fifth greater, and it must have differed also in other respects.

The plans of the **Portonaccio Temple, Veii**, and the **Belvedere Temple, Orvieto** (fifth century BC), were closer to the Vitruvian proportions. The second of these had a wall that extended laterally to each side of the porch, and then forwards, to enclose a rectangular area in front. A large temple at **Falerii** (fourth or third century BC) with three cellas was built against the rear wall of a similar enclosure, the rear wall now serving also as the rear wall of the cellas.

The **Capitoline Temple, Rome** (end of the sixth century BC), dedicated to Jupiter, Juno and Minerva, and also called the **Temple of Jupiter Optimus Maximus**, was the largest Etruscan temple now known. There were three cellas dedicated to the three gods, a real wall that projected beyond them, side colonnades enclosing wings alongside the outer cellas, and three rows of six columns each to support the roof of a porch equal in depth to the cellas. The podium, constructed of cut stone (and still surviving in part), was about 4 m (13 ft) high and 62 m long × 53 m wide (204 ft × 175 ft), close to Vitruvian proportion and rivalling in width the largest Greek temples. Though the temple was burnt in 83 BC, such was the importance attached to it that it was apparently rebuilt to virtually the same plan. According to Pliny, however, it was rebuilt with marble columns brought from the Olympeion in Athens, not timber columns. On the basis of those still remaining, the columns would have been almost 17 m (56 ft) high, which is higher than seems likely in the original temple. The fact that this height is equally close to the Vitruvian proportion suggests that this reconstructed temple may have been his chief model – though, having in mind the usual construction of temples of more modest size, he specified fewer columns, ignored the colonnaded wings, and called for greater eaves overhangs than would have been practicable on this scale.

Cemeteries and Tombs

The earliest tombs were partly cut into the rock and then roofed by means of oversailing courses of flat-bedded stone, as in many other examples of early stone construction, from the galleries of the Mycenean fortress at Tiryns to the porticoes and internal stairs at Mayan sites like Tikal (q.v.). The **Regolini Galassi tomb, Cerveteri** (*c.* 650 BC), has two long rectangular chambers roofed in this manner. A tomb from **Casal Marittimo** (now rebuilt in the Archaeological Museum, Florence) and others at **Quinto Fiorentino** (all *c.* 600 BC) have circular chambers similarly roofed. They are on a much smaller scale than the great Mycenean tholos tombs, having diameters not exceeding 5 m (16 ft); even so, they have central piers to help support the crown of the vault. Also, the insides of the blocks of stone were not cut away to give a smooth continuous surface as they were at Mycenae.

The biggest concentration of rock-cut tombs, whose interiors resemble the interiors of the larger houses of the time, is to be found in the **Banditaccia Cemetery, Cerveteri**, many of them in groups surmounted by large conical tumuli of earth retained by low outer walls of stone (p. 233A). Among them are the **Tomb of the Cornice** (fifth century BC) (p. 234A) and the **Tomb of the Reliefs** (fourth century BC) (p. 234B). The latter is so named because the walls and pillars are decorated with carved reliefs of household utensils, furniture, weapons, and other personal possessions associated with daily life.

The extensive necropolis at **Tarquinia** is chiefly notable for the large number of rock-cut tombs which retain on their walls paintings of daily life and of funeral rites and banquets. These tombs are mostly simple rectangular chambers of limited architectural interest. But one later tomb, the **Mercareccia Tomb** (possibly third century BC), has an outer chamber with a timber roof sloping to a central opening which reproduces the atrium of a house of the time as described by Vitruvius. Around the walls are friezes of carved reliefs, now in a relatively poor state of preservation.

Houses

The **House of the Surgeon, Pompeii** (fourth to third century BC) must have been one of the larger houses of its time in this southern region, and was more solidly built than the houses of Etruria. An almost square atrium stands in the middle and was entered by a relatively narrow passageway from the street which was subsequently flanked by shops. Off the atrium, and facing the entrance, were the principal reception rooms, and other rooms opened off each side. In the centre of the atrium, beneath an opening in the roof, there was a pool.

Bridges

The **Pons Sublicius, Rome**, was the first recorded crossing of the Tiber, and has been attributed to the Etruscan king Ancus Marcius. As its name indicates,

A. Banditaccia Cemetery, Cerveteri: tumulus tomb (*c.* 500 BC). See p.232

B. Porta all'Archo, Volterra (first century BC). See p.236

C. Temple of Hercules, Cori (late second century BC). See p.236

A. Banditaccia Cemetery, Cerveteri: Tomb of the Cornice (fifth century BC). See p.232

B. Banditaccia Cemetery, Cerveteri: Tomb of the Reliefs (fourth century BC). See p.232

A. Porta Saracena, Segni (fourth century BC). See p.236

B. Porta di Giove, Falerii Novi (third century BC). See p.236

it was a timber-piled structure, perhaps like that which Caesar later described as having been built over the Rhine during one of his campaigns. Though several times rebuilt, nothing remains of it.

Defence Walls and Gateways

The **Wall** and so-called **Porta Saracena, Segni** (probably fourth century BC) (p. 235A), are fine early examples of the fortifications constructed during the period when Rome was challenging seriously Etruscan power. Segni is in the limestone region to the south-east of Rome, so the wall is of fine large-scale polygonal masonry, and the gateway, with an opening at the foot of about 3 m (10 ft), has typical inward-sloping sides to reduce the gap at the top to one that could be spanned by a single stone lintel. Similar walls survive also at other Etruscan sites such as **Fiesole** (third century BC).

Surviving stretches of the final Etruscan **Defence Wall, Volterra** (fourth century BC), are constructed of roughly squared local stone. At one of the principal entrances are the original piers forming the two sides of the present **Porta all' Archo** (p. 233B). The arch, as noted above, is clearly a later reconstruction, probably dating only from the first century BC. It has voussoirs of a different stone. But it incorporates badly weathered carved heads which seem to be Etruscan and may have come from an earlier arch. The **Porta Marzia** and the **Arch of Augustus, Perugia**, are also of post-Etruscan date in their present form.

The **Defence Wall, Falerii Novi** (latter part of the third century BC), was constructed when the previous Faliscan city of Falerii was destroyed by the Romans in 241 BC and a new one was built to replace it on level ground some distance away. The wall is built of blocks of squared tufa, and is chiefly notable for the fine arched **Porta di Giove** (p. 235B) of the same date. This is probably the earliest extant stone voussoir arch in Italy. The unusually deep voussoirs are cut from tufa from a source different from that used for the wall. They rest on an impost moulding, and there is a similar moulding running around their outer curve, with a small head of Jupiter projecting from it above the keystone.

Late Republican and Early Imperial Roman

Sanctuaries, Forums and Temple Buildings

It has been seen that some Roman temple buildings were set in their own sanctuary precincts and others at the head of a forum. The distinction between these settings is not a sharp one because the sanctuary precinct was no more reserved solely for religious ceremonial than was the forum, though the non-religious uses did differ. It is therefore convenient to consider temple buildings in both settings together.

The **Sanctuary and Temple of Fortuna Primigenia, Palestrina** (perhaps late second century BC, but probably *c.* 80 BC), is the finest Republican example of this form. In an earlier example at **Gabii** (between Palestrina and Rome) the temple was set in a large rectangular precinct on fairly level ground. This precinct was flanked on both sides by rows of shops and had a theatre stage and stepped seating facing the centrally placed temple; in a later example at **Tivoli** (*c.* 50 BC) there was a similar arrangement in which the whole precinct was a large level platform raised on vaulted substructures on a hillside. At **Palestrina**, however, the sanctuary is constructed on several terraces that rise up a steeper hillside above the basilica and curia, though without any direct interconnection with them. There are seven terraces in all, most of them connected by steep flights of steps, but the third and fourth by long ramps that climb from each side to meet in the centre. The fifth and sixth terraces are faced by porticoes which once contained shops, and the sixth terrace – much deeper than the narrow ones below it – had porticoes at both sides as well as at the rear. In the centre of the rear porticoes, a flight of steps leads to the small semicircular top terrace. This served as the orchestra for the theatre, and was surrounded by stepped seating, much as in a Greek theatre. Finally, at the top of the seating, a semicircular, double portico framed a round temple, which was the climax of the whole grand composition.

The so-called **Temple of Hercules, Cori** (late second century BC) (p. 233C), also standing on a commanding hillside site, is an example of early Republican Doric. There is a single cella preceded by a deep porch with four columns at the front and two additional columns at each side – a fairly normal plan for an Etruscan or early Roman temple smaller in scale than those Vitruvius had in mind. Though the order has been Hellenised, the elongated proportions, reminiscent of timber construction, could never be mistaken for the native Greek Doric. The steps in front of the podium have disappeared.

The so-called **Temple of Fortuna Virilis, Rome** (late second century BC) (p. 231B), is a corresponding and much better preserved example of Hellenised re-interpretation of a similar earlier form, adopting the Ionic in place of the Doric. Here, attached half-columns continue the order around the sides of the cella.

The **Maison Carrée, Nîmes** (AD 1–10) (p. 237A–C), perhaps the best preserved of all Roman temples, is a third and later example, now using the Corinthian order. Technically, it is a pseudo-peripteral pro-style hexastyle, meaning that it is like the so-called temple of Fortuna Virilis in having attached half-columns

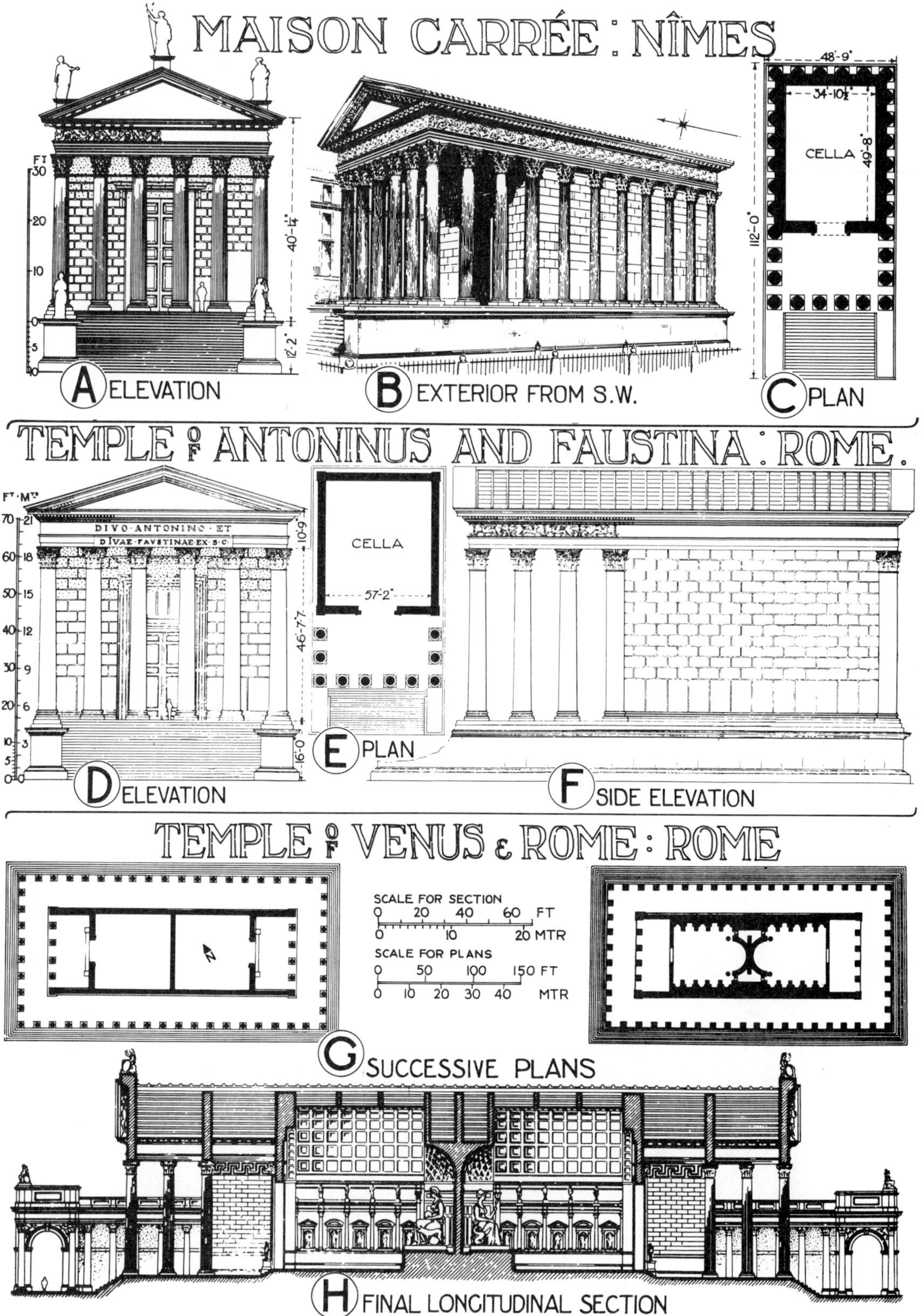
MAISON CARRÉE : NÎMES
FT
30
20
10
0
5
0
40'-1¼"
12'-2"
A ELEVATION
B EXTERIOR FROM S.W.
48'-9"
34'-10½"
CELLA
49'-8"
112'-0"
C PLAN
TEMPLE OF ANTONINUS AND FAUSTINA : ROME.
FT·MTS
DIVO·ANTONINO·ET
DIVAE·FAVSTINAE·EX·S·C·
10'-9"
46'-7.7"
16'-0"
D ELEVATION
CELLA
57'-2"
E PLAN
F SIDE ELEVATION
TEMPLE OF VENUS & ROME : ROME
SCALE FOR SECTION
0 20 40 60 FT
0 10 20 MTR
SCALE FOR PLANS
0 50 100 150 FT
0 10 20 30 40 MTR
G SUCCESSIVE PLANS
H FINAL LONGITUDINAL SECTION

IMPERIAL FORA: ROME

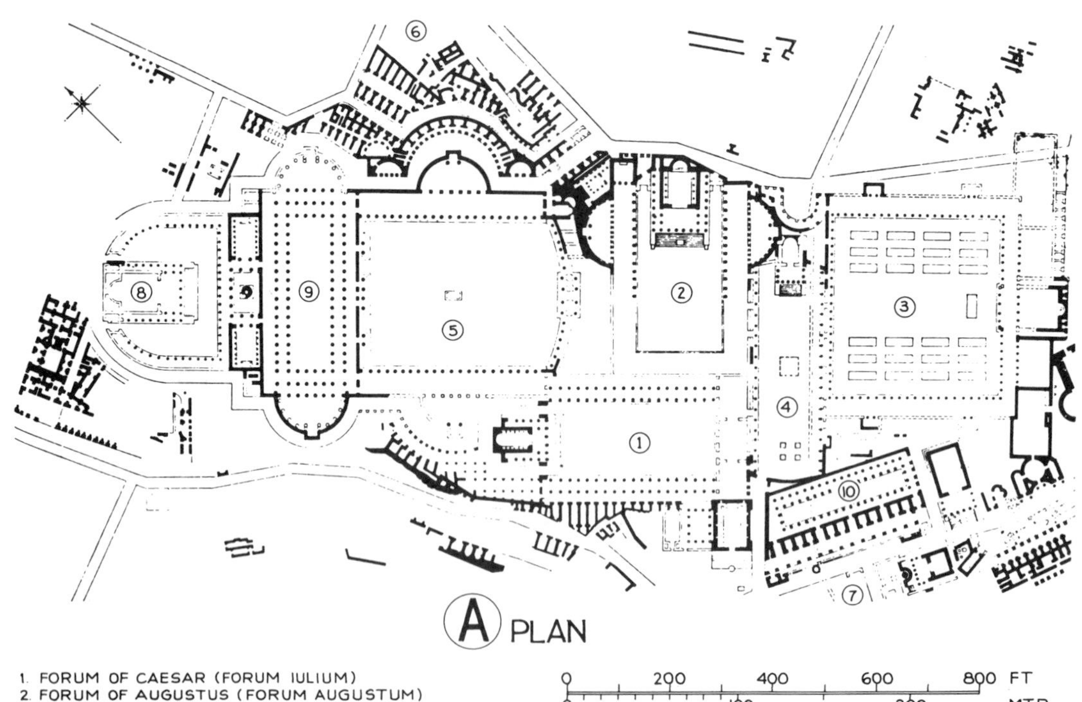

(A) PLAN

1. FORUM OF CAESAR (FORUM IULIUM)
2. FORUM OF AUGUSTUS (FORUM AUGUSTUM)
3. TEMPLUM PACIS
4. FORUM TRANSITORIUM
5. FORUM OF TRAJAN
6. MARKETS OF TRAJAN
7. N.E. CORNER OF THE FORUM ROMANUM
8. TEMPLE OF TRAJAN
9. BASILICA ULPIA
10. BASILICA AEMILIA

(B) FORUM OF AUGUSTUS (RESTORED)

A. Temple of Mars Ultor, Rome (first century AD). See p.240

B. Theatre of Marcellus, Rome (23–13 BC). See p.242

C. Arch of Tiberius, Orange (late first century BC). See p.243

around the cella. But it has six columns across the front of the porch, whereas the latter had only four. The details, which include a rich entablature and an early instance of a cornice with modillions, bear a close resemblance to those of the Temple of Mars Ultor (referred to below) and suggest that the construction was undertaken partly by craftsmen sent from Rome. Originally the temple stood on its podium within a forum surrounded by porticoes.

The round **Temple of Vesta, Tivoli** (early first century BC), on the other hand, was a pure Greek import except for its podium, the fact that it has steps leading up to the cella only on the axis of the entrance, and the manner of construction. The walls of the cella were constructed largely of opus incertum. There were eighteen Corinthian columns 7 m (23 ft) high and, above them, a frieze decorated with ox heads linked by festoons. The capitals have, unusually, a large six-petalled flower on each face and the leaves are derived from a crinkly variety of the 'acanthus mollis'.

The **Round Temple on the Forum Boarium, Rome** (first century BC) (p. 231B), is generally similar, slightly larger, and more complete, though it underwent repairs in later Imperial times and has lost its entablature. It is constructed of Parian marble, including the cella walls, and has twenty Corinthian columns 10.5 m (34 ft) high. The cutting of the capitals suggests Greek workmanship. As at Tivoli, there is no evidence for the original roofing: it was probably of timber like that of contemporary rectangular temples.

The **Forum of Caesar and the Temple of Venus Genatrix, Rome** (commenced 51 BC, dedicated 46 BC and finally completed under Augustus) (p. 238A), were part of the first attempt to give the heart of Rome a more formal and worthy character. The long rectangular forum was flanked by double colonnades with shops behind them and had the temple (dedicated to Caesar's divine ancestress) at its head.

The **Rostra Augusti, Rome**, was the speakers' platform on the old forum, rebuilt by Caesar in 44 BC and completed by Augustus. It was used as a place for displaying the prows of captured ships, and it was from these that it took its name. Some of the prows were on the wall below the platform and others were mounted on commemorative columns. There were further columns supporting statues.

The **Forum of Augustus and the Temple of Mars Ultor, Rome** (late first century BC to early first century AD – dedicated but incomplete in AD 2) (pp.238B, 239A), continued the remodelling of the central area begun by Caesar. The forum was laid out at right angles to that of Caesar, with the temple again at its head but now on a somewhat larger scale. The site was not quite symmetrical, apparently because of difficulties in land acquisition. But the plan has a very strong axial emphasis, and the lack of symmetry was so skilfully disguised that it would never have been apparent except on close inspection of the side porticoes. (A Greek architect would have been more likely to have turned the lack of symmetry to account in his plan rather than hide it.) The colonnaded porticoes had entablatures borne by caryatids, and from each portico a large, almost semicircular courtyard was placed in line with the broad flight of steps leading up to the temple. Near the foot of the steps (but not shown in the reconstruction drawing) was the centrally placed altar. The temple itself (p. 239A) had a single, almost square, cella with an apsidal recess at its far end – an early instance of this feature in a building of this type – and internal columns and pilasters to reduce the roof span. The cella was flanked by relatively narrow wings that were formed by continuing the outermost lines of columns of the deep porch along its sides. The porch itself was octastyle. Construction of the walls of the cella and the outer walls of the forum was of peperino stone, faced with thin slabs of Luna marble which were tied back at intervals in the height by solid marble bonding courses. The podium was faced with thicker slabs of marble and the Corinthian columns, 17.5 m (58 ft) high, were also of marble.

The temple was dedicated to Mars the Avenger, having been vowed at the battle of Philippi in 42 BC which avenged Caesar's murder. But it is clear, from what is known of the statuary which originally adorned both temple and forum, that the whole project was also a public assertion of the achievements of Rome and of Augustus himself and his house. Today this is doubly difficult to appreciate. Not only has the statuary gone, but almost half the forum is now buried beneath the broad Via dei Fori Imperiali; of the rest, only the rear wall, parts of the curving walls of the semicircular courtyards, the podium and steps of the temple, and a few of the columns remain. In its day it was one of the chief bases for the claim of Augustus to have 'found Rome a city of brick and left it a city of marble'.

Basilicas and Related Structures

The **Basilica, Pompeii** (second century BC), stands towards the opposite end of the forum to the temple. But whereas the temple looked down the length of the forum, as did the last two Roman temples just described, the basilica was aligned at right angles to one of the longer sides. The structure was damaged in the earthquake of AD 62 and had not yet been restored when Vesuvius erupted 18 years later. It is, therefore, a very early example of the basilica form. It is a rectangular hall about 62 m (205 ft) long and 25 m (80 ft) wide, without any apse but with a projecting tribune at the far end. A single order of tall Ionic columns (here made of brick) ran round all sides internally, presumably to carry a timber roof. It is not

THEATRES AND CIRCUSES: ROME

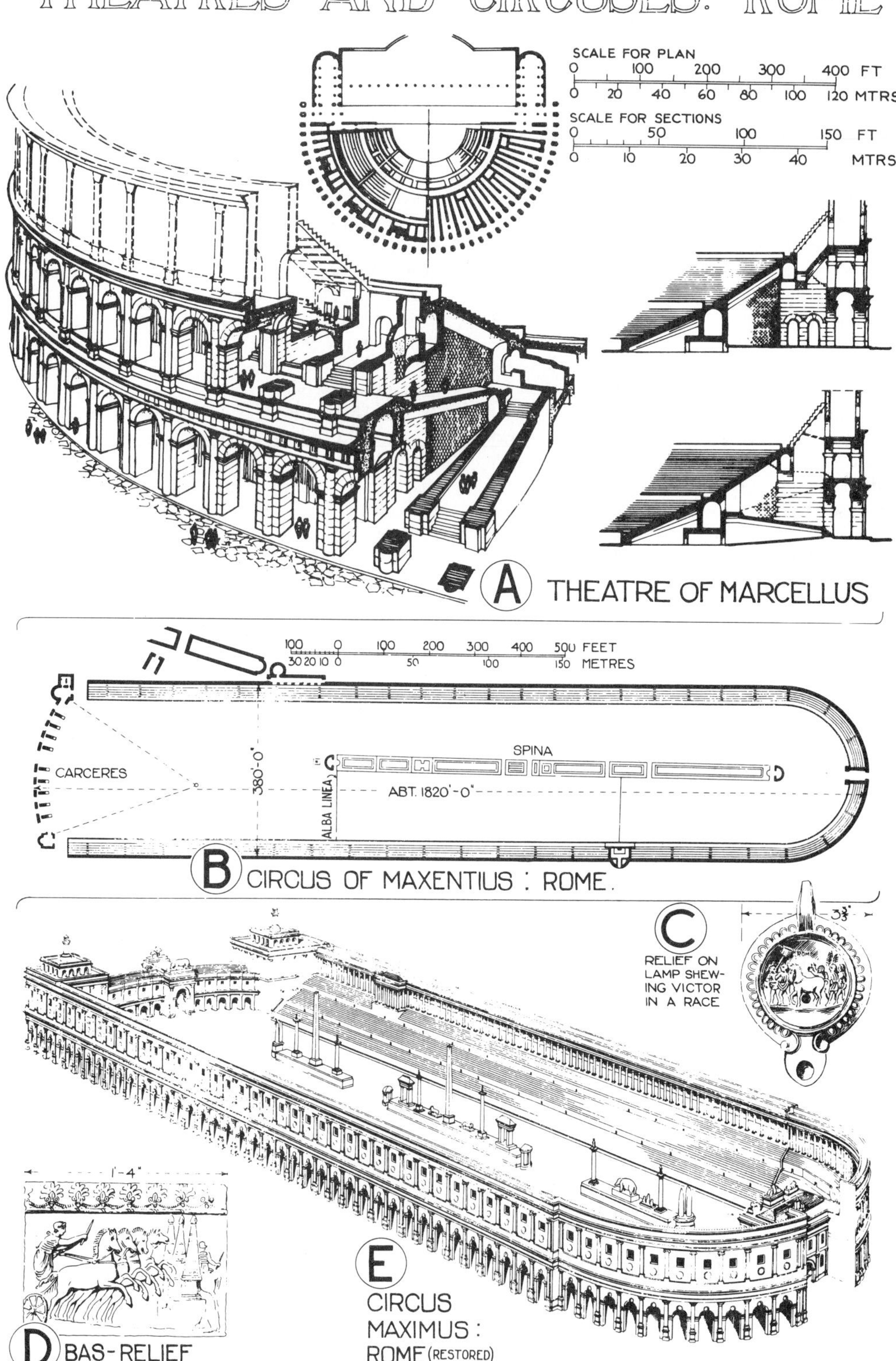
SCALE FOR PLAN
0 100 200 300 400 FT
0 20 40 60 80 100 120 MTRS
SCALE FOR SECTIONS
0 50 100 150 FT
0 10 20 30 40 MTRS
A THEATRE OF MARCELLUS
100 0 100 200 300 400 500 FEET
30 20 10 0 50 100 150 METRES
CARCERES
380'-0"
SPINA
ALBA LINEA
ABT. 1820'-0"
B CIRCUS OF MAXENTIUS : ROME.
C
RELIEF ON LAMP SHEWING VICTOR IN A RACE
1'-4"
D BAS-RELIEF
E
CIRCUS MAXIMUS : ROME (RESTORED)

clear whether there were galleries above the aisles. There was an open colonnade at the end adjacent to the forum, so that the interior communicated directly with it.

The **Basilica Aemilia** and **Basilica Julia, Rome**, were corresponding early Roman examples. The Basilica Aemilia was the earlier of the two, but little remains of the original structure erected in *c.* 179 BC. It was restored in 78 BC and then rebuilt in 55–34 BC. A coin issued before this rebuilding shows a two-storey colonnaded elevation, the upper storey being of less height than the ground storey. The structure was again a rectangular hall some 90 m long × 27 m wide (300 ft × 90 ft). The Basilica Julia, begun by Julius Caesar, damaged by fire in *c.* 12 BC, rebuilt and rededicated by Augustus in AD 12, and twice again restored in 305 and 416, was substantially larger, being 105 m long × 45 m wide (345 ft × 150 ft). Structurally it consisted of three ranges of two-storey arcades carried on rectangular piers around both short sides and one of the longer sides, and of two such ranges on the remaining long side, behind which was a row of shops. The other long side was open to the adjacent forum and the two short sides were also open. The double aisles thus formed on all sides were vaulted, while the relatively narrow central space had the usual timber roof. As in Pompeii, there was no apse in either structure. It appears that, in the Basilica Julia, parts of the central space were curtained-off as required for court use.

The Basilica Julia shows one early instance of the characteristically Roman combination of the arch with an applied decorative use of the orders, and the nearby **Tabularium, Rome** (78 BC), is the first example of the combination to have survived. It was built as the public record office, and its facade towards the Roman Forum still forms part of the front of the present Palazzo Senatorio on the Capitol.

The **Market, Leptis Magna** (*c.* 8 BC and AD 31–7), is an early example of a common form. A large rectangular court is surrounded by porticoes. In the centre are two arcaded circular pavilions surrounded by octagonal colonnades with flat entablatures. Some later examples, for instance at Pompeii and Pozzuoli, have only a single pavilion.

Balneae and Thermae

The **Stabian Baths** (second century BC, partly remodelled early first century BC) and **Forum Baths** (*c.* 80 BC), **Pompeii**, are the earliest public baths which combine the bath proper with an exercise yard or palaestra. Both consisted of separate baths for men and women, with separate entrances. In each of these a vestibule led first into a changing room (apodyterium). Opening off this were the cold bath (frigidarium) and the warm room (tepidarium). Finally, the warm room led to the hot room (caldarium). The rooms varied in shape and size, both according to function and between one group of users and another. Those for the men were architecturally more distinguished; their frigidaria were circular in plan, with small niches around the circumference, and were roofed with the first known examples of concrete domes. In addition to these rooms there were small private baths, latrines, and so on. In the final development of the Stabian Baths, there was a natatio or swimming pool directly open to the palestra.

The overall planning seems to have aimed only at making the fullest use of the available area consistent with convenience and servicing. The men's and women's caldaria were placed, for instance, on opposite sides of a single central furnace – though heating in the Stabian Baths was originally by brazier, and not by the underfloor hot-air system that was introduced early in the first century BC. Apart from the fact that in both establishments all the principal rooms were arranged around the palestra and were surrounded externally by corridors or shops, there was little in common between the two plans. As the street frontages were largely given over to shops, there was little to indicate externally the function of the establishments.

All the rooms of these baths were of quite modest size, with widths or diameters not much more than 5 m (17 ft) and lengths not more than 20 m (68 ft). In the **Baths at Baia**, drawing on natural hot water springs like those at Bath in England, several much larger domed halls were built. The earliest of these, the so-called **Temple of Mercury**, is the best preserved. It has an internal diameter of 21.5 m (71 ft), almost half that of the Pantheon, and appears to date from the latter part of the first century BC.

The **Baths of Agrippa, Rome** (late first century BC), were the first in the capital. They were destroyed in a great fire in AD 80, but it is clear that they were on a considerable scale and, like those at Baia, more openly planned than the early baths in Pompeii, being set among gardens with porticoes and an artificial lake.

Theatres

The **Large Theatre, Pompeii** (second century BC, enlarged subsequently), is the oldest theatre of Roman construction in Italy. It has a form intermediate between that of the Greek theatre and that of later Roman theatres, with the seating set partly in a natural bowl in the ground and surrounding the horseshoe-shaped orchestra.

The **Theatre of Marcellus, Rome** (23–13 BC) (p. 239B, 241A), was the first permanent one in the capital. It was built on level ground near the Tiber, with all the seating raised on arcaded and vaulted substructures which ingeniously incorporated radially aligned ramps and circumferential corridors to provide access to it. The tiers of seating were now semicircular, and the stage ran from side to side in front of it, backed by a tall enclosing wall. Externally the remaining lower two storeys of the facade have the same combination of arcade and superimposed orders noted above at the Tabularium and the Basilica Julia. Here the lower order is Doric, the next Ionic.

Amphitheatres and Circuses

The **Amphitheatre, Pompeii** (*c.* 80 BC with later modifications and additions), also preceded by a long interval any similar building in the capital. It is oval in plan, measuring 150 m × 105 m (500 ft × 350 ft) on its long and short axes. Again it represents a transition between the most comparable Greek form – that of the stadium – and the later Roman form. The seating (originally probably timber benches only) was supported on earthen banks and not on vaulted substructures, and there were no substructures beneath the arena – the sanded area on which the combats took place. To retain the earthen banks, there was, on the outside, a massive concrete wall buttressed by closely spaced piers carrying an arcade. Access to most of the seats was by means of external ramps which led to a terrace around the top.

The **Circus Maximus, Rome** (p. 241C–E), was the oldest in the city and underwent a long series of enlargements, modifications and embellishments. It lies in the valley between the Palatine and Aventine hills and probably consisted originally of little more than a marked track, a low central wall (spina) around which the chariots were raced, and the starting gates (carceres). Later, a few rows of wooden seats were provided, and there were cone-shaped columns at the ends of the spina to mark the turning points. By the late first century BC, the plan of the Circus seems to have been essentially as it subsequently remained, some 600 m long × 200 m wide (2000 ft × 650 ft), though later emperors added fresh embellishments; it is the possible appearance in the fourth century AD which is shown in the restoration drawing. There were then three tiers of seats and twelve carceres, in spite of the fact that not more than four chariots seem to have raced together. Each race was of seven laps, equal to a distance of about 3.6 km (2.2 miles). The bas-relief gives a good idea of a racing quadriga, and the relief on a lamp shows the victor of a race.

Triumphal Arches

Monumental triumphal arches, which seem to have been built first during this period, are perhaps large-scale sculpture rather than architecture. But their basic form is the particularly Roman architectural unit of the arch carried on isolated piers and decorated with superimposed orders, now further embellished with bas-reliefs and statuary commemorating a victorious campaign.

The so-called **Arch of Tiberius, Orange** (late first century BC) (p. 239C), originally commemorated the achievements of the second legion in the conquest of Gaul, but later its inscription was changed to honour the emperor Tiberius. It is triple-arched with Corinthian three-quarter columns between the arches, on the two end faces, and on the outer corners. There are two attic storeys, filled, like the wall surfaces below, with a profusion of military motifs and trophies. Remarkably, for this early date, the entablature above the columns on each end face is broken between the central pair to allow an arched recess to rise into a pediment similar to that over the central arch.

Town Gates

The gate known, in its partly restored present form, as the **Porte S. André, Autun** (p. 260H), illustrates a fairly typical pattern which will be seen, with minor variations, in later gates. It has lost the usual rectangular inner court and the two flanking towers.

Tombs

As Roman law forbade burial within the city confines, cemeteries lined the roads outside the gates. Both burial and cremation were practised, but it made little difference to the type of tomb structure whether it was built to take a sarcophagus for the body or an urn for the ashes. Designs for the more monumental tombs initially tended to be conservative, drawing on Hellenistic or other earlier models.

The **Tomb of the Julii, S. Rémy** (*c.* 40 BC) (p. 262H), in Provence, is a cenotaph that rises in three stages. There is first a base ornamented with reliefs. On this stands a pedestal penetrated by arched openings flanked, on the four corners, by engaged corinthian columns. At the top is a circular storey with smaller Corinthian columns and entablature, crowned with a conical stone roof. The motifs of the reliefs are mythological Greek scenes, though the Julii appear to have been rich Gauls who had acquired Roman citizenship.

Several **Tombs near Uzuncaburg** (p. 244A), the ancient Olba, subsequently called Diocaesaria, also show strong Hellenistic influence despite their essentially Roman, and sometimes two-storeyed, temple-like forms.

The **Mausoleum of Augustus, Rome** (28–23 BC), built by Augustus as his own family tomb, looks back to the Etruscan tumulus for its basic form, though it broke the long-standing rule forbidding burial inside the city. Like the later Mausoleum of Hadrian, it had as its base a huge cylinder, 88 m (290 ft) in diameter.

A. Tombs near Uzuncaburg. See p.243

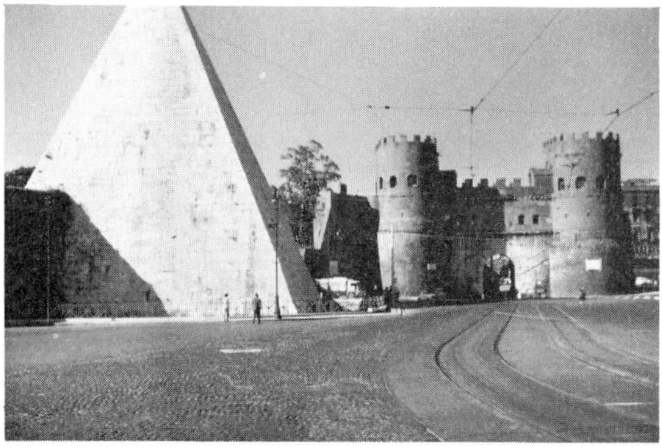

B. Pyramid of Cestius and Porta Ostiensis in the Aurelianic walls, Rome. See p.246

C. Tomb of Caecilia Metella, Rome (*c.* 20 BC). See p.246

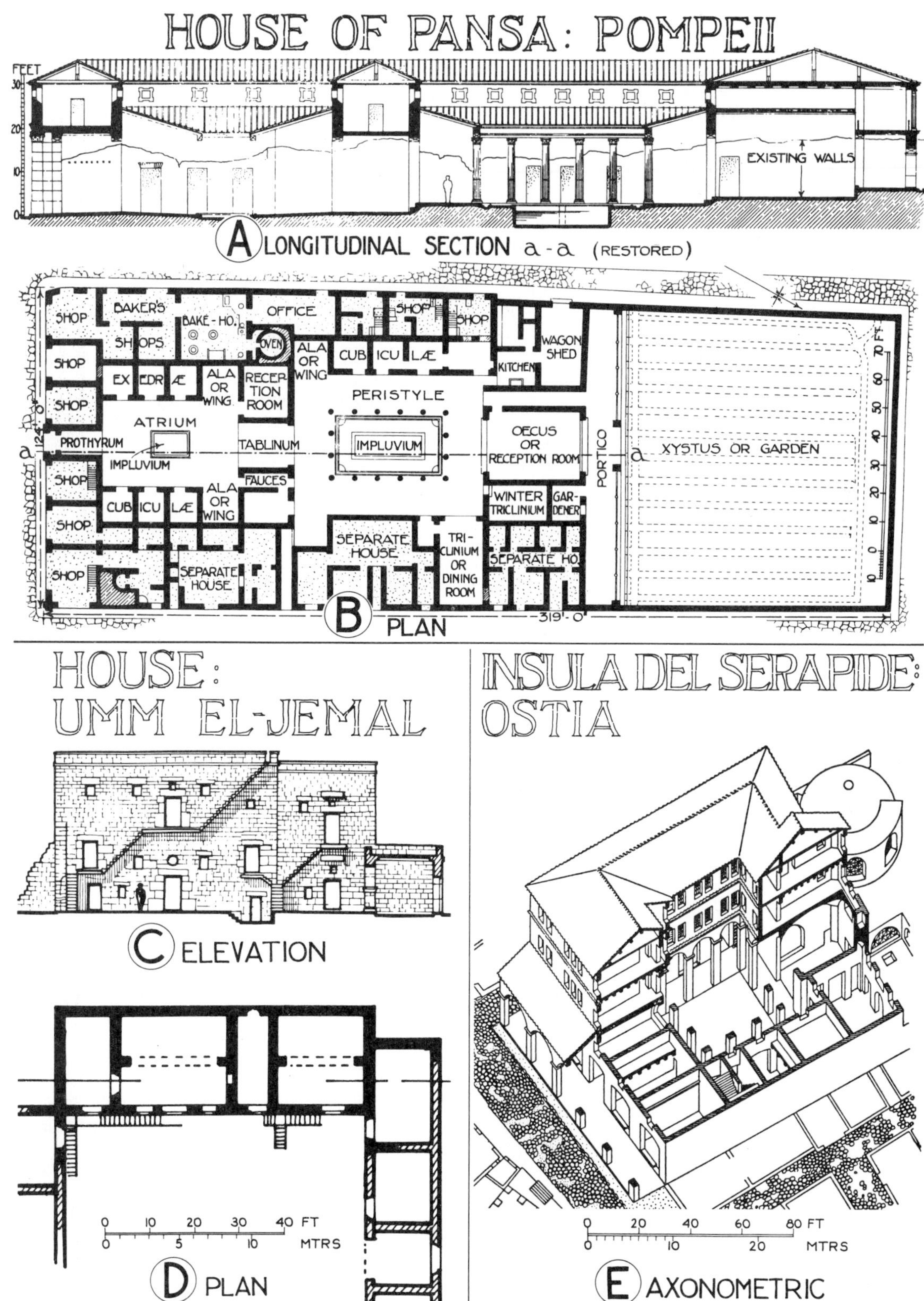
HOUSE OF PANSA: POMPEII
FEET
30
20
10
0
EXISTING WALLS
A LONGITUDINAL SECTION a-a (RESTORED)
SHOP
BAKER'S SHOPS
BAKE-HO.
OVEN
OFFICE
SHOP
SHOP
ALA OR WING
CUBICULÆ
WAGON SHED
KITCHEN
SHOP
EXEDRÆ
ALA OR WING
RECEPTION ROOM
PERISTYLE
SHOP
ATRIUM
PROTHYRUM
IMPLUVIUM
TABLINUM
IMPLUVIUM
OECUS OR RECEPTION ROOM
PORTICO
XYSTUS OR GARDEN
FAUCES
SHOP
CUBICULÆ
ALA OR WING
WINTER TRICLINIUM
GAR-DENER
SHOP
SEPARATE HOUSE
TRICLINIUM OR DINING ROOM
SEPARATE HO.
SHOP
SEPARATE HOUSE
124'-0"
319'-0"
B PLAN
HOUSE: UMM EL-JEMAL
C ELEVATION
0 10 20 30 40 FT
0 5 10 MTRS
D PLAN
INSULA DEL SERAPIDE: OSTIA
0 20 40 60 80 FT
0 10 20 MTRS
E AXONOMETRIC

The outer wall was constructed of concrete, faced with travertine opus quadratum. Behind this, a complex system of four circumferential and numerous radial walls, similarly constructed of concrete but now mostly faced with opus reticulatum, divided the interior into concentric compartments, though, apart from the sepulchral chamber and the passages leading to it, these compartments were simply filled with earth. They supported a final mound of earth planted with evergreen trees at a height of 44 m (145 ft) above the ground, and the central core was surmounted by a bronze effigy of Augustus. The surroundings were landscaped with further trees. The first burial was in 23 BC and the last – that of the emperor Nerva – in AD 98. The structure was converted to a fortress in the twelfth century and more recently served a variety of other uses, including that of a concert hall. It is now an empty shell.

The **Tomb of Caecilia Metella, Rome** (*c.* 20 BC) (p. 244C), on the Via Appia, is a smaller building of the same type. It has a podium 30 m (100 ft) square, above which rises the main cylindrical structure (only slightly smaller in diameter), in the centre of which was the tomb chamber – the sarcophagus from which is now in the Palazzo Farnese. The exterior was again faced with travertine and carried an entablature with a frieze decorated with ox skulls and festoons.

The **Pyramid of Cestius, Rome** (*c.* 12 BC) (p. 244B), on the Via Ostiensis, revived a much older form. It is constructed of concrete faced with white marble. Inside the pyramid the vault and walls of the tomb chamber were decorated with figure paintings.

Houses and Villas

The **House of Pansa, Pompeii** (second century BC) (p. 245A,B), represents the large fully developed family mansion which occupied with its garden a whole city block or insula. It comprises two main portions: the atrium at the front, which served for formal occasions as well as normal use; and the peristyle at the rear, which was for more private activities. Earlier, as in the House of the Surgeon, the atrium constituted the entire house; the addition of a colonnaded peristyle became common from the second century onwards.

A measure of privacy was ensured even in the atrium portion of the house, since nearly all the rooms faced inwards – being lit, in the absence of window glass, through tall doorways which were closed either by curtains or by doors with metal grilles. The atrium itself contained the shrine of the family gods, and near to the impluvium (the water tank beneath the opening in the roof) stood a marble table, a traditional survival of the ancient banqueting board. An open living room or tablinium was curtained off between the atrium and the peristyle, and was flanked on one side by a passageway. The peristyle, with sixteen marble Ionic columns supporting the inner margins of its roof, was laid out with flower beds and graced with statuary, fountains and water basins. Bedrooms or cubicula, dining rooms or triclinia (so-called from the three couches provided against the walls for the host and his guests) with different aspects for summer and winter, a reception room or oecus, and wings for informal conversation, surrounded it. The rooms had mosaic floors, and the walls were covered with fresco paintings. Furthest from the entrance, but with convenient access from the side street, were a kitchen and pantry. There were smaller upper rooms around both atrium and peristyle. Most of the separate houses and shops shown on the two long sides resulted from modifications by a later owner.

The **House of the Faun, Pompeii** (also second century BC), was an even more splendid house of similar character, from which came not only the delightful bronze of a dancing faun from which the present name derives but also the superb floor mosaic of the Battle of Alexander against the Persians, now in the National Museum, Naples. The house includes a further innovation of this time, namely the introduction of four columns in the atrium to support the margins of the opening in the centre of the roof.

The **House of Livia**, on the Palatine in Rome (mid-first century BC), was probably occupied by Augustus after he became emperor, and might thus be regarded as the first imperial palace. As far as it has yet been excavated, it is a modest structure compared with the two earlier Pompeian houses just described – more like the even earlier House of the Surgeon, with its atrium with the reception rooms opening off it. The walls were frescoed in contemporary styles.

Aqueducts and Bridges

Numerous aqueducts were built to supply Rome with water from the late fourth century BC onwards, but neither before nor after the period under review did the elevated sections of any of them approach in magnificence the **Pont du Gard**, near **Nîmes** (late first century BC or early first century AD). The aqueduct was constructed to bring water from near Uzès to Nîmes, and it was carried almost 50 m (160 ft) above the deep valley of the river Gard on three tiers of arches. The lower two tiers correspond closely to one another, with the widest span of 24 m (80 ft) in the centre over the water. The arches are 6 m (20 ft) wide, and were constructed in three identical parallel rings from large blocks of stone pre-cut to fit exactly. Projecting blocks on the piers served to support the temporary timber centering. The top tier carrying the water channel itself is narrower and is composed of thirty-five arches of little more than 4 m (14 ft) span. The whole structure is completely unadorned. In the seventeenth century, the piers of the second tier were partly cut away to make room for a roadway. Then, in 1747, a new bridge was built alongside the aqueduct.

The **Pons Fabricius, Rome** (62 BC, restored AD 19) (p. 248A), is the oldest surviving bridge in the capital and remains virtually unchanged except for a new roadway and parapets and an enlargement of the starlings that protect the piers from scour. Inscriptions running across the faces of the arches record the building and restoration of the bridge. Despite the sometimes reviled duality which results from its having a single central pier, it is a superb design, with a smaller arch placed over the pier to increase the waterway in time of flood. An engraving by Piranesi shows similar small arches at each end where the present river embankments now form the abutments. The continuation of the main arches below the water to make complete circles of masonry also shown in the engraving, however, has no known factual basis. The bridge crosses only one branch of the Tiber. A second bridge, the **Pons Cestius**, was built at the same time on the other side of the island to complete the crossing, but this bridge was completely rebuilt late in the nineteenth century.

The **Bridge of Augustus, Rimini** (early first century AD) (p. 248B), makes the easier crossing of the Marecchia with five similar arches varying in span from 5.1 m (17 ft) in the centre to 4.2 m (14 ft) at the extremities, the piers here being almost as wide as the arches in the direction of the span. The fine decorative detailing, still reasonably well preserved, was noted by Palladio and, through him, served as an inspiration for numerous later bridge designs.

Imperial Roman from Tiberius to Hadrian

Temples

The examples which follow illustrate the remarkable variety of shapes adopted for temple buildings and related structures during this period, including forms which had their origins in the Hellenistic East and another which was indigenous to Gaul.

The **Temple of Jupiter, Baalbek** (probably mostly mid-first century AD) (p. 253G,H), was one of the largest Roman temples, though its dimensions of 88 m × 48 m (287 ft × 157 ft) fell considerably short of those of the largest Greek temples. It was the first part to be completed of the Roman remodelling of an earlier sanctuary. With its high podium, and with columns 20 m (66 ft) high and a height from the base of the podium to the top of the pediment of nearly 40 m (130 ft), it gave a Roman character to a building with an essentially Greek peripteral plan. The podium was constructed of huge blocks of a hard limestone, and the masonry of the superstructure, including the unfluted column shafts, was almost as cyclopean in scale. There were two rows of nineteen columns along each side, and the deep porch was ten columns wide and three deep.

The **Temple of Trajan, Rome** (completed by Hadrian *c.* AD 118), no longer exists, but it seems to have been virtually a copy of that of Mars Ultor on a larger scale. It stood at the furthest end of the Forum of Trajan, which is described below. Its scale is indicated by the remains of one of its columns which is almost 18 m (60 ft) high.

The **Temple of Hadrian, Ephesus** (dedicated *c.* AD 118) (p. 256A), is a small street-side structure and not, therefore, designed to impress chiefly on a distant axial approach. Its porch is notable for the square corner piers, and for the combination of flat architrave and central arch.

The **Pantheon, Rome** (AD 118–*c.* 128) (p. 250,251,252A) was by far the most important temple, if importance may be measured by technical achievement and influence. Though Justinian's Hagia Sophia, Constantinople, surpassed it in a number of ways, its most notable feature – its great dome, with a span of 43.2 m (142 ft) – was unchallenged until 1420–36, when Brunelleschi vaulted the crossing of Florence Cathedral with a dome of slightly greater maximum diameter.

In several ways the form is a puzzling one. It combines a huge portico with an even larger rotunda, crowned by the dome. The portico leads into the rotunda but there is little other relationship between them, certainly not the sort of relationship that there was between porch and cella in earlier temples. An inscription on the porch attributing the construction to Agrippa, and the fact that there was a temple built by Agrippa (burnt in AD 80) on the same site, led to a belief that the porch was a survival from this earlier temple and that the rotunda only was new. It has been conclusively shown, however, that everything belongs to Hadrian's rebuilding. Presumably a porch of the traditional kind was still considered necessary to relate the temple to its surroundings, which were considerably different from those of today. Originally it stood at the head of a colonnaded square, whose ground level was substantially below that of the present piazza, and whose end walls, together with the colonnades, would have framed the porch in much the same way as the side colonnades and rear wall of the Forum of Augustus framed the porch of the Temple of Mars Ultor.

It is more difficult to say why a huge, domed circular cella was substituted for the traditional rectangular one, usually no larger than the porch itself. There were precedents, as we have seen, for a circular plan. The most relevant in Rome would probably have been the Temple of Vesta near the old forum, which was many times rebuilt and will be referred to later. This did not have quite the same function as the normal temple, and possibly the Pantheon did not do so either. It has been suggested

A. Pons Fabricius, Rome (62 BC, restored AD 19). See p.247

B. Bridge of Augustus, Rimini (early first century). See p.247

that the intentions behind its construction may have been as much political and personal as religious, just as Augustus' intentions seem to have been partially personal in the case of the Temple of Mars Ultor. We know nothing of the temple ritual. We know merely that the building was adorned with numerous statues, including two in the portico of Augustus and Agrippa, and others inside of Julius Caesar, Mars and Venus. Certainly also the resemblance of the dome to the vault of heaven was recognised fairly soon, but this does not necessarily mean that it was intended from the start.

The porch is eight columns wide and three deep, and the unfluted monolithic columns of Egyptian granite are 14 m (46 ft) high, reducing in diameter from 1.5 m (5 ft) at the base to 1.3 m (4.3 ft) at the top, and have Corinthian capitals of white Pentelic marble (p. 251A). They support an entablature which carries the inscription already referred to and a pediment which may originally have had a bronze eagle relief affixed to it (as suggested by the pattern of the fixing holes that remain). On its rear wall, on either side of the entrance to the rotunda, are two deep niches which held the statues of Augustus and Agrippa. The roof is no longer the original one. But sixteenth-century drawings and descriptions of it show its trussed framing to have been fabricated partly of timber and partly from riveted plates of bronze. The walls of the rotunda rise through three storeys constructed of brick-faced concrete separated by stone cornices, each storey now disclosing, in the brick facing, a ring of brick relieving arches. Originally, all this brickwork would have been faced with marble and stucco, but there was never any decorative use of applied orders as in most theatres and amphitheatres. The dome, seen fully only in more distant views, has the shallow stepped profile referred to as characteristically Roman in Chapter 8.

Once inside, the exterior is soon forgotten (p. 252A). Geometrically, it is essentially a large sphere with its lower half expanded outwards to cylindrical form, and whereas the exterior cylinder was divided into three storeys, the corresponding part of the interior is lower and is divided into only two. As the section shows, this is because it corresponds to only the lower two external storeys, the uppermost external storey being above the springing level of the dome. Internally, the taller bottom storey has eight recesses around the circumference, alternately square-ended and rounded, and divided from the space directly beneath the dome by pairs of monolithic columns of differently coloured marbles, the shafts of which are reeded in their lower portions and fluted above. Corinthian capitals carry the entablature which marks the division between the two storeys. Above the next storey is the dome, with a large, central unglazed eye which is the only source of light when the bronze entrance doors are closed. On its surface are five rows of square coffers of diminishing size – surprisingly twenty-eight to a row, a number which does not correspond to the eight-fold division of the circumference below. They are designed so as to appear to diminish equally on all sides at each recession when seen from a central position at floor level.

Not all of the interior looks as it originally did, though it is the best preserved of all large Roman interior spaces (p. 251B). The coffers were probably covered with stucco with moulded edges, and they had large gilded bronze rosettes in their centres. Most of the marble facings to the walls and floor are comparatively recent. The upper (or attic) storey was, for instance, refaced to a different design in 1747. But a section of it has been restored to the earlier design, and six capitals of the original marble pilasters may now be seen in the British Museum (p. 251C). Their shallow relief carving, partly done with a drill, is remarkably close to some later Byzantine work (p. 304A).

If, finally, one turns to the construction, it soon becomes apparent that the basic simplicity of the form belies a far more complex structural organism. It would be out of place here to describe it in detail, but it may be noted first that the 6 m (20 ft) thick cylindrical drum on which the dome stands has many more voids than the recesses already noted. These voids rise into the second storey behind the attic, and there are also hidden voids both above them and between them. In fact it would be truer to regard the whole drum as consisting of three continuous arcades corresponding to the three tiers of relieving arches visible on the outside of the building. The piers stand on a massive circular foundation, 4.5 m (15 ft) deep. Above the level of the highest external cornice, the dome is of solid concrete construction, reducing finally to about 1.2 m (4 ft) thick at the open eye. But a refinement here is a progressive variation in the nature of the cementae for the purpose of reducing the density of the concrete towards the top. Horizontal layers of travertine and tufa at the foot give way first to layers of tufa and brick, and at the top, to tufa and pumice.

The **Temple of Asklepios Soter, Pergamon** (*c.* AD 130 onwards), was an early smaller-scale copy of the Pantheon, centrally situated on one side of the large court of the sanctuary of Asklepios. It has an internal diameter of about 21 m (70 ft) and had a brick dome. Now only the beautifully constructed ashlar base of the drum remains.

In the **Temple of Venus and Rome, Rome** (consecrated AD 135) (p. 237G,H), seemingly designed by Hadrian himself, the Hellenistic version of the Classical Greek temple was brought to Rome. In place of the traditional Roman cella, fronted by a deep porch and looking out in one direction only from its high podium, there were two cellas, back-to-back, dedicated respectively to Venus, mythical ancestress

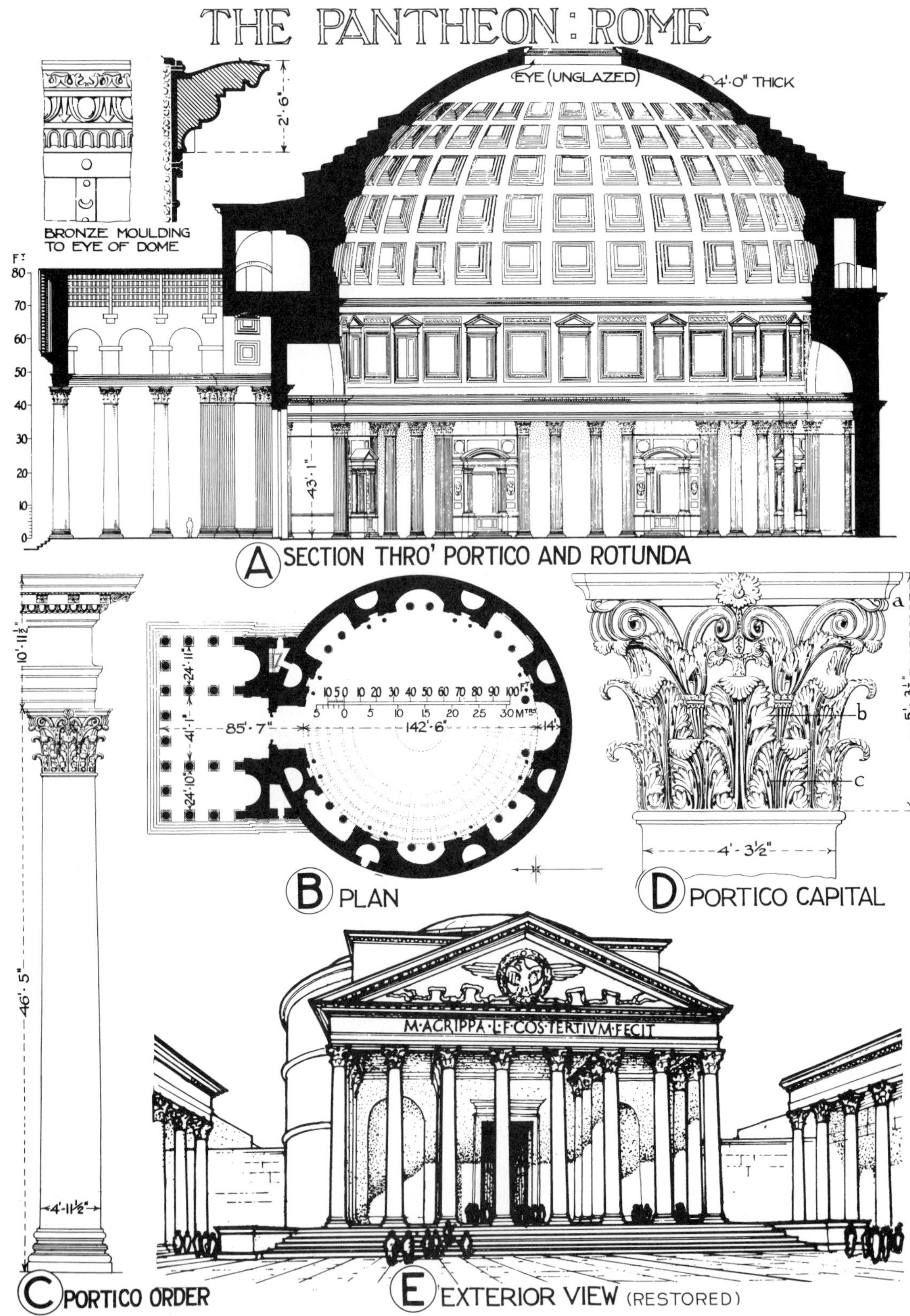
THE PANTHEON : ROME
EYE (UNGLAZED)
4'·0" THICK
2'·6"
BRONZE MOULDING TO EYE OF DOME
FT
80
70
60
50
40
30
20
10
0
43'·1"
A SECTION THRO' PORTICO AND ROTUNDA
10'·11½"
24'·11"
41'·1"
24'·10"
85'·7"
142'·6"
14'
10 5 0 10 20 30 40 50 60 70 80 90 100 FT
5 0 5 10 15 20 25 30 MTRS
a
b
c
5'·3½"
4'·3½"
B PLAN
D PORTICO CAPITAL
46'·5"
4'·11½"
M·AGRIPPA·L·F·COS·TERTIVM·FECIT
C PORTICO ORDER
E EXTERIOR VIEW (RESTORED)

A. Pantheon, Rome (118–*c.* 128). See p.247

B. Pantheon: interior from entrance

C. Pantheon: interior showing restored attic

A. Pantheon: drawing of interior by Piranesi. See p.249

B. Temple of Janus, Autun. See p.254

C. Library of Celsus, Ephesus (117–120). See p.254

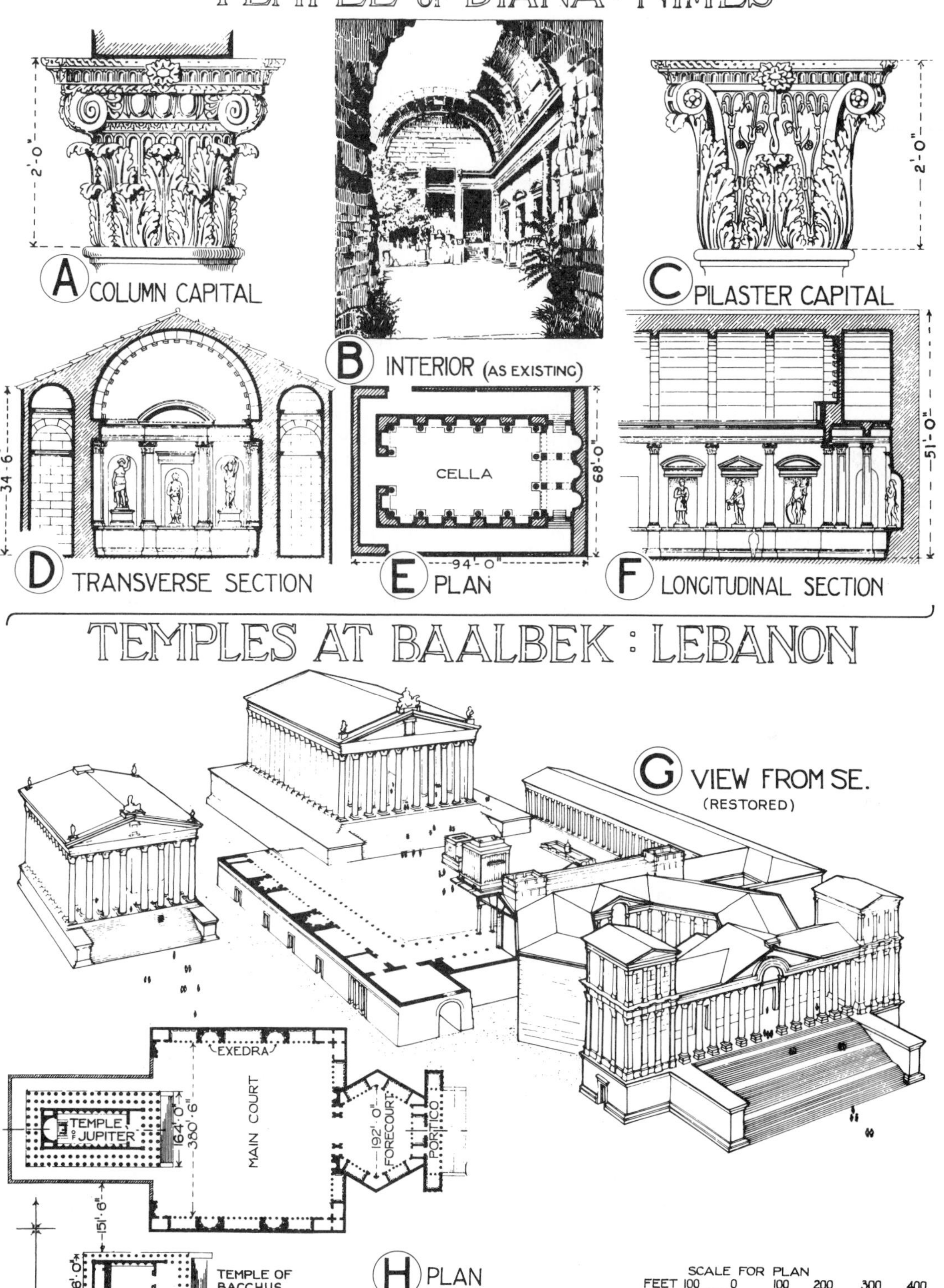
TEMPLE OF DIANA : NÎMES
2'-0"
A COLUMN CAPITAL
B INTERIOR (AS EXISTING)
C PILASTER CAPITAL
34'-6"
D TRANSVERSE SECTION
CELLA
68'-0"
94'-0"
E PLAN
51'-0"
F LONGITUDINAL SECTION
TEMPLES AT BAALBEK : LEBANON
G VIEW FROM SE.
(RESTORED)
EXEDRA
TEMPLE OF JUPITER
164'-0"
380'-6"
MAIN COURT
192'-0"
FORECOURT
PORTICO
151'-6"
116'-0"
TEMPLE OF BACCHUS
H PLAN
SCALE FOR PLAN
FEET 100 0 100 200 300 400
METRES 10 0 50 100

of the Roman people, and to Rome itself. In place of just a columnar porch – or two such porches – there was now a colonnade that surrounded the double cellas on all sides, with ten columns across each front and twenty along each side. And, in place of the high podium, the whole temple was set on a low platform surrounded by steps. Next to this, and a little distance from it, were further colonnades on the two long sides. A fire destroyed the timber roof in 283, and a major rebuilding followed, as will be described later.

The so-called **Temple of Diana, Nîmes** (*c.* AD 130) (p. 253A–F), was a pavilion, the precise function of which has not been determined, in the sanctuary of the local water god Nemausus, after whom the town is named. It is constructed wholly of fine ashlar, and is architecturally important as the best surviving example of a type of structure that reappeared, with virtually no change, in the Romanesque buildings of this region of France. The central barrel-vault, semicircular in profile, was stiffened at regular intervals by ribs projecting downwards, and its thrusts were partly carried over to the outer walls of side passageways.

At Nîmes, the temple itself has disappeared. The so-called **Temple of Janus, Autun** (p. 252B), is less well preserved, but it serves to illustrate one of the types built to meet the needs of conquered peoples. The setting did not differ greatly in overall character from that of the earlier sanctuaries already described. The temple itself usually had a tall cella – square, circular, or octagonal – and, around this, a portico with a sloping lean-to roof on all sides. At Autun, only the square cella remains.

Forums, Basilicas, and Related Structures

The **Forum, Basilica, and Market of Trajan, Rome** (*c.* AD 100–112) (p. 238A), designed by Apollodorus of Damascus, were among the principal monuments of this age. The more conventional basilica was possibly the most highly esteemed of all Roman buildings in the following centuries, and the market showed off admirably the new concrete architecture then coming to the fore and contrasting sharply with the earlier type of market described above.

There were very close similarities with the nearby **Forum of Augustus**, to which Trajan's Forum was also related spatially. Its equally dominant central axis was set exactly at right angles to that of the earlier forum. As before, the forum had colonnaded porticoes on each side, beyond which opened semicircular courts, and even their architectural detail was similar. The chief differences were at the far end where, instead of the forum leading directly to the temple, the basilica was interposed; behind this, there was a monumental column (described below) flanked by two identical library blocks. The market rose up the slope of the Quirinal hill to the north, though this would hardly have been seen from the forum, as it would have been shut off by the northern boundary wall. To create the level area needed for forum, basilica, libraries, and temple, vast quantities of earth were cut away from the slope of the hill.

The basilica, known as the **Basilica Ulpia** (p. 255A, 256B), was set transversely over the full 120 m (400 ft) width of the forum, and consisted of a huge rectangular nave, 25 m (80 ft) wide, surrounded on all sides by double colonnades, and extended beyond the end colonnades by two semicircular apses with attached orders for internal decoration.

There were probably galleries over one or both of the aisles created by the colonnades, and there must have been a trussed timber roof over the central nave; its span was almost identical with that of the fourth century basilica of S. Peter's, so that it could have served as the model for that roof. The ceiling is known to have been sheathed with gilded bronze, while the walls were covered with multi-coloured marbles.

The **Market** (p. 256C,D,E) consisted largely of many shops of the standard form, which was little more than a vaulted rectangular room, open to the front, and tall enough to take a timber mezzanine floor. The shops were disposed along straight and curved streets on different levels which followed, at the foot, the curve of the northern boundary wall of the forum and at higher levels were adapted to the contours of the hill. But at the highest level there was a large tall hall with a series of groined vaults, structurally rather like the tepidaria of the Imperial baths (p. 256C). Other shops opened off this, and it presented a four-storey facade – with balconies at an intermediate level – to the street which ran, lower down, past its western side (p. 256E).

Though little remains of the libraries behind the basilica, the **Library of Celsus, Ephesus** (AD 117–120) (p. 252C), is much better preserved and its facade has recently been reconstructed. It is a rectangular building, wider than deep and measuring approximately 17 m × 11 m (55 ft × 36 ft). Internally there were shallow square-backed recesses for the books or scrolls at three levels and narrow galleries carried on closely spaced columns for access to them. A further feature was that the walls containing these recesses were not the outer walls. There were other walls separated by a narrow ambulatory to accommodate the stairs to the galleries and to give added protection – almost an early example of cavity construction. The facade was embellished with two storeys of columned aedicules, pairs of columns carrying flat entablatures in the first storey, and different pairs carrying alternately curved and triangular pediments in the top storey.

A INTERIOR (RESTORED)

BASILICA OF CONSTANTINE, ROME.

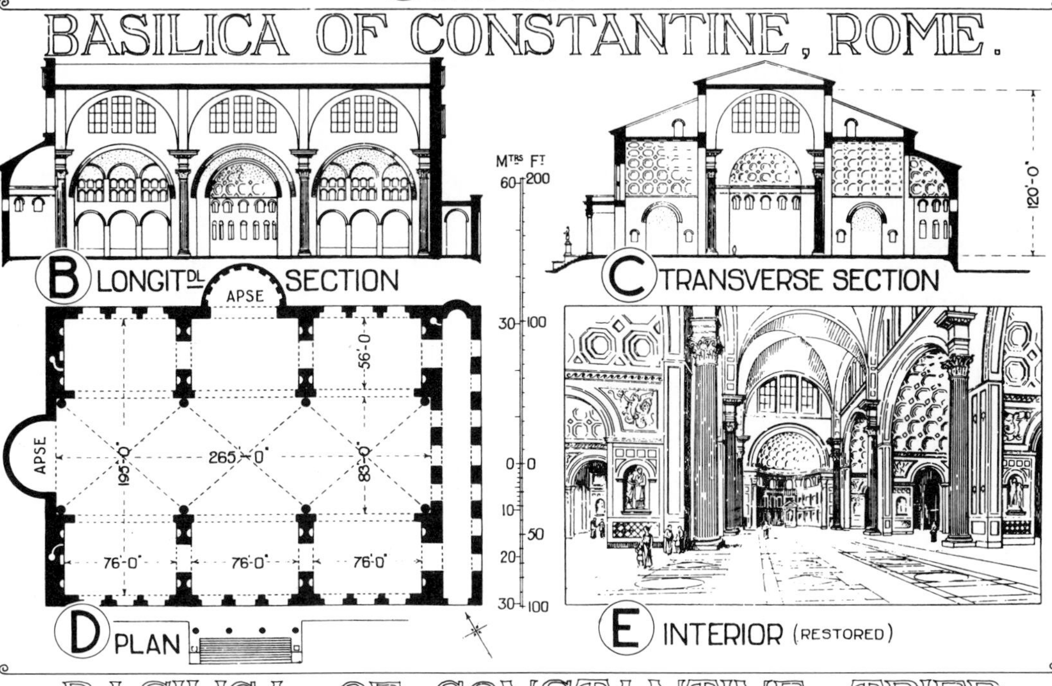

B LONGITDL SECTION

C TRANSVERSE SECTION

D PLAN

E INTERIOR (RESTORED)

BASILICA OF CONSTANTINE: TRIER

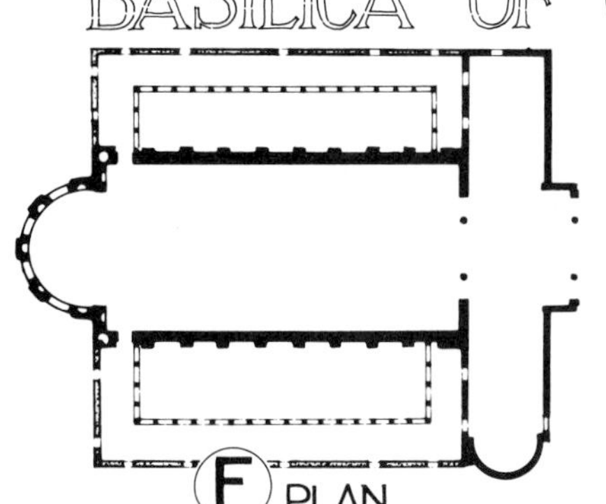

F PLAN

G EXTERIOR VIEW

A. Temple of Hadrian, Ephesus (dedicated *c.* 118). See p.247

B. Forum of Trajan, Rome, looking across the colonnades of the Basilica Ulpia towards Trajan's column. See pp.254, 261

C. Trajan's market: the main hall. See p.254

D. Forum of Trajan, Rome, looking across the northern semicircular court to the hemicycle of the market

E. Trajan's market: west side of main hall

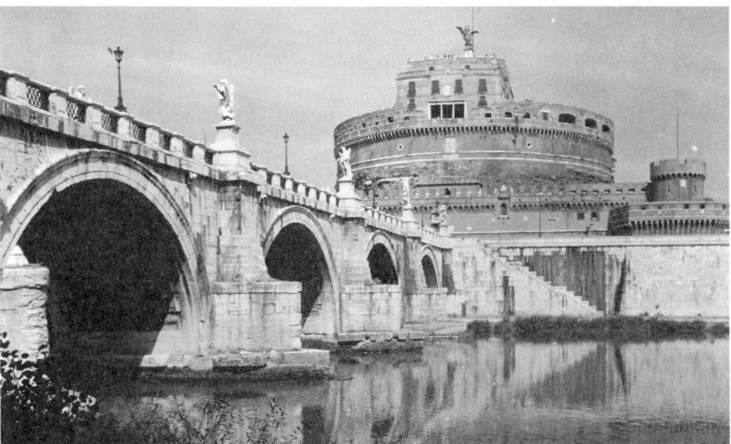

F. Pons Aelius, leading to the Mausoleum of Hadrian, Rome (135–139). See pp.261, 266

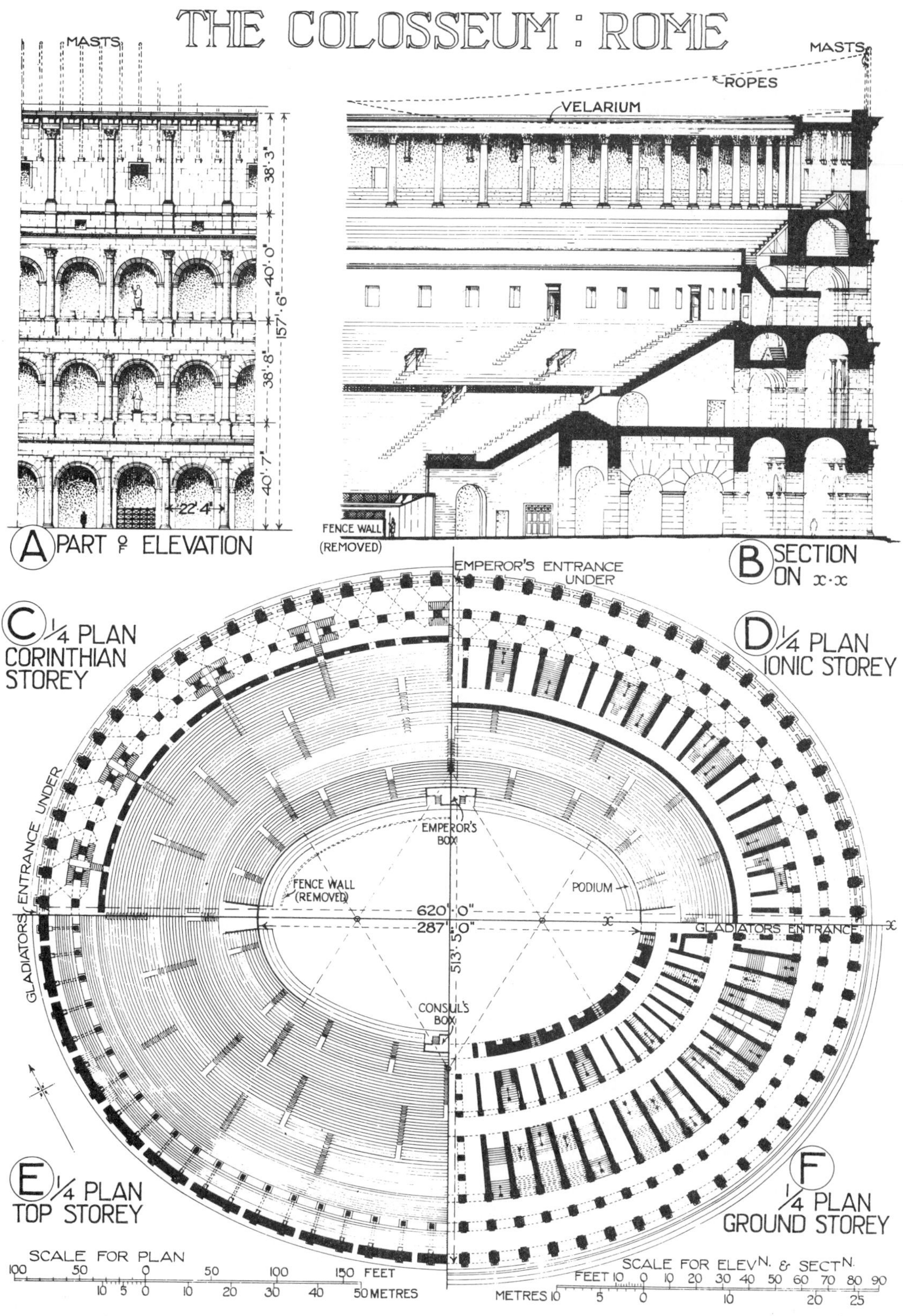
THE COLOSSEUM : ROME
MASTS
MASTS
ROPES
VELARIUM
38'·3"
40'·0"
157'·6"
38'·8"
40'·7"
22'·4"
FENCE WALL (REMOVED)
A PART OF ELEVATION
B SECTION ON x·x
EMPEROR'S ENTRANCE UNDER
C 1/4 PLAN CORINTHIAN STOREY
D 1/4 PLAN IONIC STOREY
ENTRANCE UNDER
GLADIATORS
EMPEROR'S BOX
FENCE WALL (REMOVED)
PODIUM
620'·0"
287'·0"
513'·5"
GLADIATORS ENTRANCE
CONSUL'S BOX
E 1/4 PLAN TOP STOREY
F 1/4 PLAN GROUND STOREY
SCALE FOR PLAN
100 50 0 50 100 150 FEET
10 5 0 10 20 30 40 50 METRES
SCALE FOR ELEVN. & SECTN.
FEET 10 0 10 20 30 40 50 60 70 80 90
METRES 10 5 0 10 20 25

Thermae

According to drawings by Palladio, the **Baths of Titus, Rome** (AD 80), of which nothing now remains, were the first to have many of the features of the layout that then became characteristic of later Imperial baths.

More remains of the considerably larger **Baths of Trajan, Rome**, built above part of Nero's Domus Aurea after it had been burnt in AD 104. The baths were dedicated in AD 109. They include the characteristic later feature of a spacious outer precinct with meeting rooms, lecture halls, and other accommodation for a wide variety of social activities – features which will be referred to in more detail in the description below of the Baths of Caracalla.

Theatres

The **Theatre, Orange** (*c.* AD 50), is a good early example of a theatre in a western province. Built against a hillside, it has its seating largely set against the natural slope. It is notable for the good state of preservation of the wall behind the stage, which is almost 100 m (325 ft) long and 35 m (116 ft) high.

Amphitheatres

The **Colosseum** or **Flavian Amphitheatre, Rome** (pp. 257,259A,B), was commenced by Vespasian in AD 70 and inaugurated by Titus in AD 80, though not completed until a little later by Domitian. It is in the valley between the Esquiline and Caelian Hills where, not long previously, an artificial lake had been created as part of Nero's great landscaped Domus Aurea. As the first permanent amphitheatre in the capital, it was designed to take some 50,000 spectators, and a major concern in design must have been the practical problems of access and crowd control. The system devised was essentially that already adopted on a much smaller scale in the Theatre of Marcellus, a system of radial ramps and stairs giving access to circumferential passageways. Vaults spanning between radial and circumferential dividing walls supported the many tiers of seating as well as the ramps and some of the passageways.

The plan is a vast ellipse, measuring externally 188 m × 156 m (615 ft × 510 ft). There are eighty radial walls, and almost as many separate entrances around the circumference. Corresponding to these walls there are three tiers of outer arcades, tripled at the first two levels, and all carrying circumferential vaults to create double ambulatories at all three levels. From them there is direct access to the first two tiers of seating for those of equestrian rank and for other Roman citizens, while flights of stairs from the top ambulatories gave access to a third tier, which was separated from the others by a high encircling wall that took the place of the innermost arcade at this level. Beneath the arena, there is a further complex system of passageways, together with the dens for wild beasts and other provisions for staging the often gruesome spectacles for which the structure was built.

The floor of the arena has been lost, as has the original marble seating and the timber seating above. But much of the exterior is well preserved, despite the losses from the use of the structure as a quarry over many centuries. The three superimposed arcades are faced, in the manner already noted on earlier monuments, by three-quarter columns and entablatures. These are Doric in the first storey, Ionic in the second, and Corinthian in the third. Above them is a deep attic storey with shallow Corinthian pilasters and small square window openings in alternate bays to light the uppermost tier of seating, which seems to have been set within a continuous portico. In the other bays there were large bronze shields in place of the windows. At the top there are brackets and sockets to carry the masts from which a canopy, known as a velarium, was hung to give shade.

The feat of planning and organisation entailed in carrying out such an enterprise is a good index of Roman abilities. It was made possible partly by a careful combination of different types of construction: mass concrete for the 12 m (40 ft) deep foundations, a cautious use of travertine opus quadratum for the piers and arcades, tufa infillings of these piers to create the radial walls at the two lower levels, and brick-faced concrete for the similar infillings at higher levels and for most of the vaults.

The **Amphitheatres of Nîmes** and **Arles** (probably late first century) are just two of the many later ones which followed essentially the same plan as the Colosseum on a smaller scale. They differ in being built almost entirely of ashlar and in the detailing of the exterior. In the Colosseum, the horizontals were emphasised by the way in which the entablatures swept unbroken around the whole circumference. In these structures, the vertical continuity of the columns was equally stressed by stepping forward and returning the entablatures above each column.

Triumphal Arches and Columns

The **Arch of Titus, Rome** (after AD 81) (p. 260A–C), was erected after the emperor's death, to commemorate chiefly the capture of Jerusalem. It has a single opening flanked on each outer face by attached columns with early examples of the Composite capital. On the coffered soffit of the arch and the wall faces below it are reliefs of the emperor and the spoils from the Temple in Jerusalem. The outside faces of the piers are exemplary nineteenth-century restorations undertaken as far back as 1821 after demolition

A. The Colosseum, Rome (70–82). See p.258

B. The Colosseum, Rome: arena and auditorium

C. Arch of Trajan, Beneventum (*c.* 115). See p.261

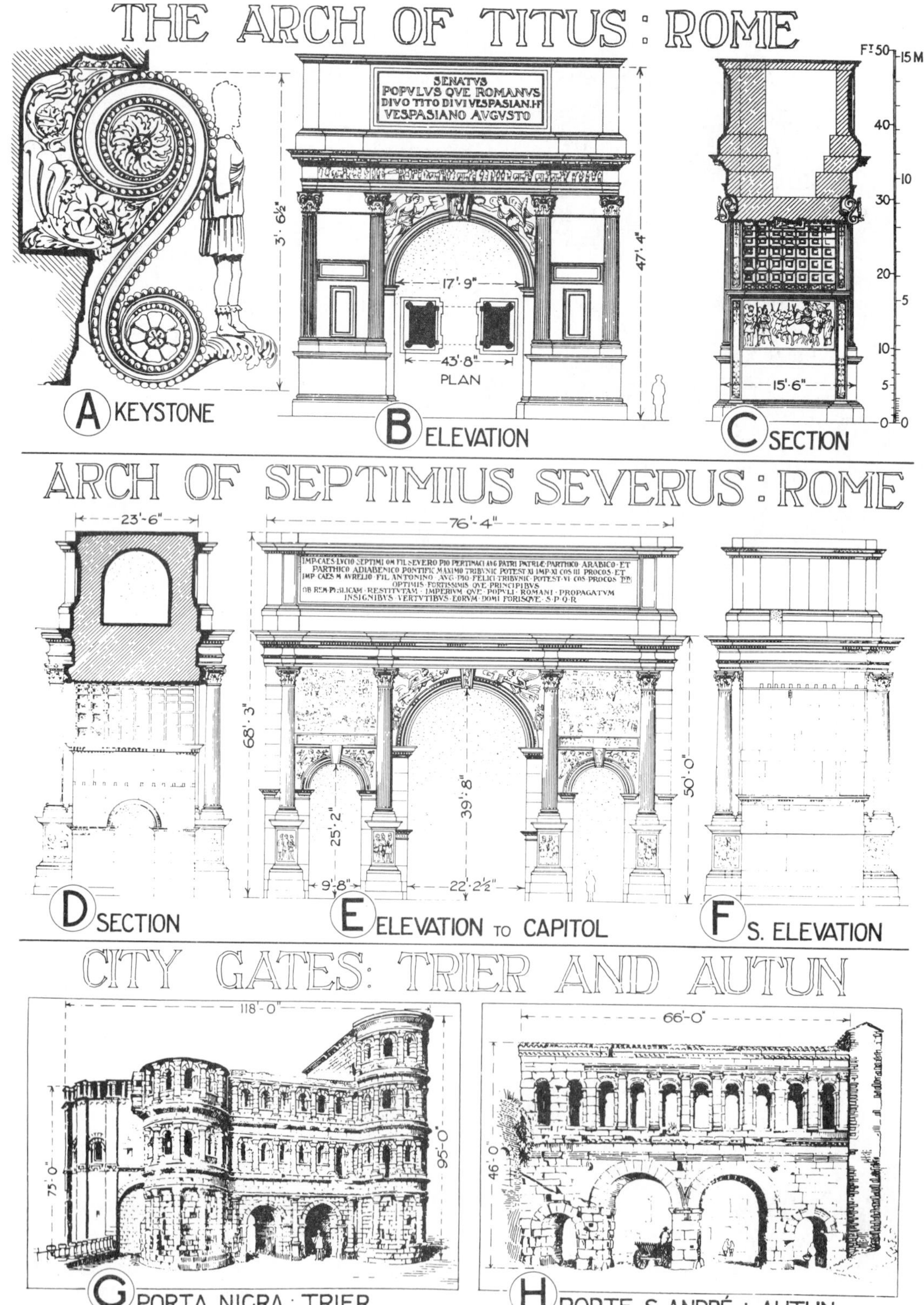
THE ARCH OF TITUS : ROME
SENATVS
POPVLVS QVE ROMANVS
DIVO TITO DIVI VESPASIANI F
VESPASIANO AVGVSTO
3'. 6½"
17'. 9"
43'. 8"
PLAN
47'. 4"
15'. 6"
A KEYSTONE
B ELEVATION
C SECTION
ARCH OF SEPTIMIUS SEVERUS : ROME
23'-6"
76'-4"
68'. 3"
25'. 2"
39'. 8"
50'. 0"
9'. 8"
22'. 2½"
D SECTION
E ELEVATION TO CAPITOL
F S. ELEVATION
CITY GATES: TRIER AND AUTUN
118'. 0"
95'. 0"
75'. 0"
66'-0"
46'. 0"
G PORTA NIGRA : TRIER
H PORTE S. ANDRÉ : AUTUN

of the fortification in which the arch had been incorporated in the Middle Ages. They make good what had been destroyed, without any attempt at deceit.

The **Arch of Trajan, Beneventum** (*c.* AD 115) (p. 259C), still in a fine state of preservation, is of similar type but with almost an excess of relief decoration.

Trajan's Column, Rome (*c.* AD 112) (p. 262A–G,256B), whose setting has already been mentioned in the description of the Forum, served a similar commemorative function to the arches and became the model for several later columns such as that of **Marcus Aurelius** (AD 174). In form it was closest to the Doric order. But its height of 35 m (115 ft), its decoration with a continuous spiral frieze narrating Trajan's Dacian wars, the bronze eagle, and a statue of the emperor (which originally stood where there is now a statue of S. Peter) were its more telling features. Even from the buildings which originally flanked it, it can never have been easy to see all the incidents portrayed; they are more visible today in a full-size cast in the Victoria and Albert Museum, London.

Town Gates

The **Porta Palatina, Turin**, and **Porta dei Borsari, Verona** (both first century), are slightly later examples of the type of gate, part ceremonial and part defensive, already seen in Autun. Here the road arches are surmounted by two galleries, whose smaller arched openings were framed by applied orders, entablatures, and even pediments.

Tombs

There is doubt whether the **Khasneh (Treasury)** (p. 262J) and the similar but even larger **Deir (Monastery), Petra** (both possibly late first century), were tombs or temples. Their size, and the location of the second, make the latter seem possible. But the Khasneh was included in previous editions of this book as a tomb, so they are both included here under that heading. They come within a much older eastern-Mediterranean tradition of rock-cut tomb and temple architecture, in which all emphasis was on the facade which usually made use of features taken from contemporary built architecture. At Petra, the Khasneh is the more classical of the two, but the difference in style between them is not large. The upper storeys are more three-dimensional than the lower ones. They call to mind some of the motifs of Pompeian wall painting, but are almost certainly direct developments of the local Hellenistic architecture. The scale exceeds even that of the temples at Abu-Simbel (see Chapter 3). The facade of the Khasneh is 27 m wide × 39 m high (92 ft × 130 ft) and that of the Deir 45 m wide × 40 m high (154 ft × 132 ft), but the simple rectangular chambers behind the facades are of less interest than the Egyptian temple interiors.

The **Mausoleum of Hadrian, Rome** (AD 135–139) (pp.256F,262L), obviously modelled on the Mausoleum of Augustus which it closely resembles in shape and size, in the Middle Ages became the Papal Castel S. Angelo. It was originally faced with Parian marble and decorated with statues around the drum, and was crowned by a cylindrical tower on which was a large sculptured quadriga. Internally there was a system of radial and circumferential walls, within which a corridor climbed to the central barrel-vaulted tomb-chamber containing the porphyry sarcophagus.

Villas and Palaces

The **Domus Aurea (Golden House), Rome** (AD 64–68 and possibly later), was built or begun by Nero after the great fire in AD 64. It was less a palace than a series of pavilions and a long wing comprising living and reception rooms, all set in a vast landscaped park with an artificial lake in its centre where the Colosseum now stands. Most of it has largely disappeared. The main architectural interest lies in the wing just referred to, known as the Esquiline wing, which stood a little to the north of the lake and was subsequently built over to form part of the enclosure of the Baths of Trajan. It most resembled the country and seaside portico villas of Campagna, and was open to the views of and beyond the lake. The more westerly part, which was certainly of Nero's time, also had a peristyle behind the facade. In the centre, the facade was set back, following three sides and two half-sides of an octagon. To the right of this was the less conventionally planned eastern part, which contained the feature of greatest importance and originality (pp. 263C, 264A). This was an octagonal hall roofed by a concrete dome, 14.7 m (50 ft) across the corners, and open on all sides to the garden or to surrounding smaller rooms – as far as is known the first appearance in a building of this kind of a new concept of interior space which was to come increasingly to the fore over the next half-century. It is possible that it was never completed. But it is said that the decoration of those parts of the palace that were completed was unusually lavish. Some of the painted stucco survives, and when it was discovered in the Renaissance it provided the inspiration for some of Raphael's decorations in the Vatican.

The **Flavian Palace (Domus Augustana), Rome** (inaugurated AD 92 and with later additions) (pp. 263A,B,D,264B), occupied much of the top of the Palatine Hill, but was more compactly planned. To obtain more space, substantial parts were built over deep vaulted substructures. The parts of chief interest are the official or state rooms grouped around

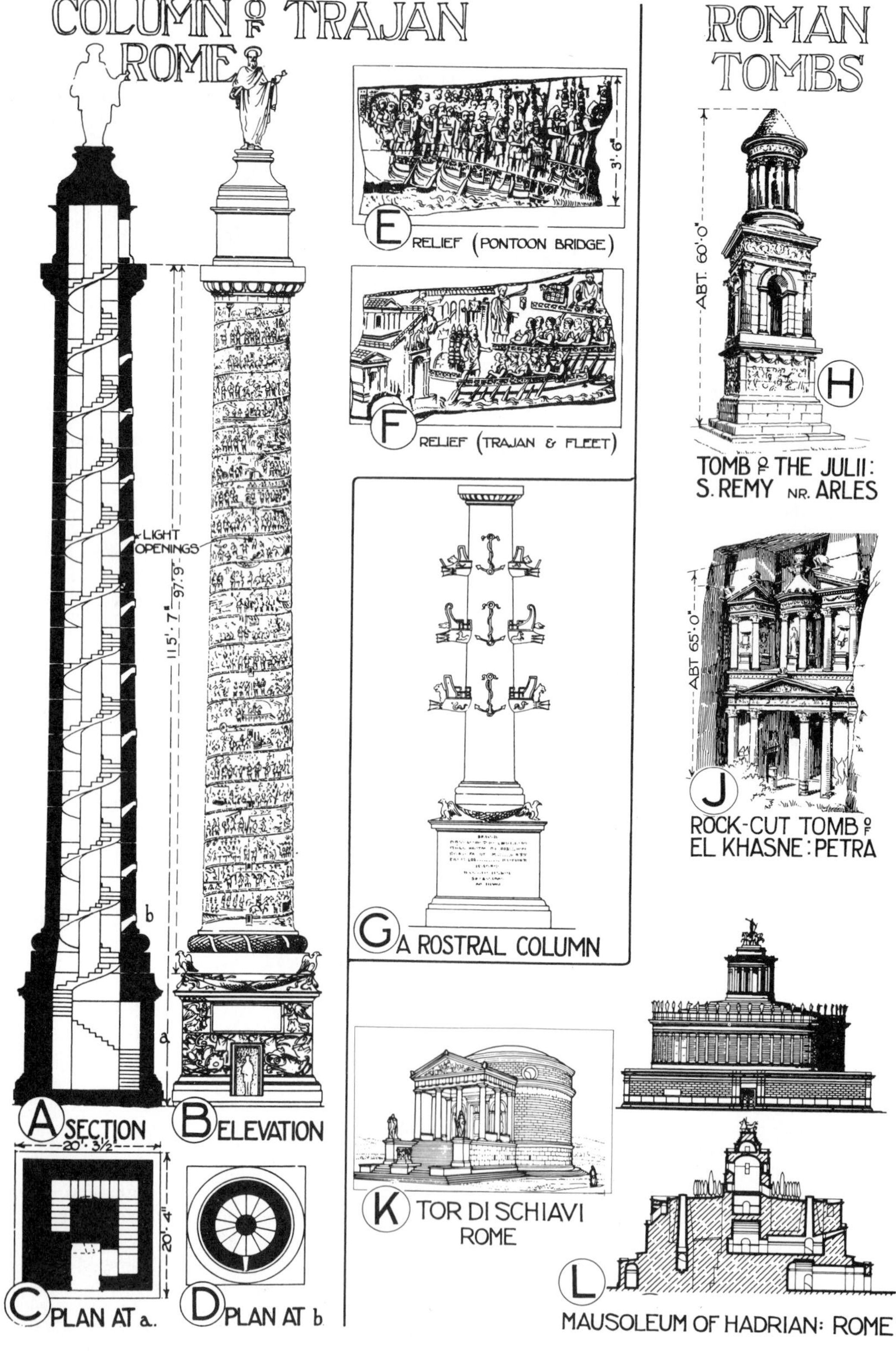
COLUMN OF TRAJAN
ROME
LIGHT OPENINGS
115'. 7"
97'. 9"
b
a
A SECTION
B ELEVATION
20'. 3½
20'. 4"
C PLAN AT a.
D PLAN AT b
3'. 6"
E RELIEF (PONTOON BRIDGE)
F RELIEF (TRAJAN & FLEET)
G A ROSTRAL COLUMN
ROMAN TOMBS
ABT. 60'.0"
H
TOMB OF THE JULII: S. REMY NR. ARLES
ABT 65'.0"
J
ROCK-CUT TOMB OF EL KHASNE: PETRA
K TOR DI SCHIAVI ROME
L
MAUSOLEUM OF HADRIAN: ROME

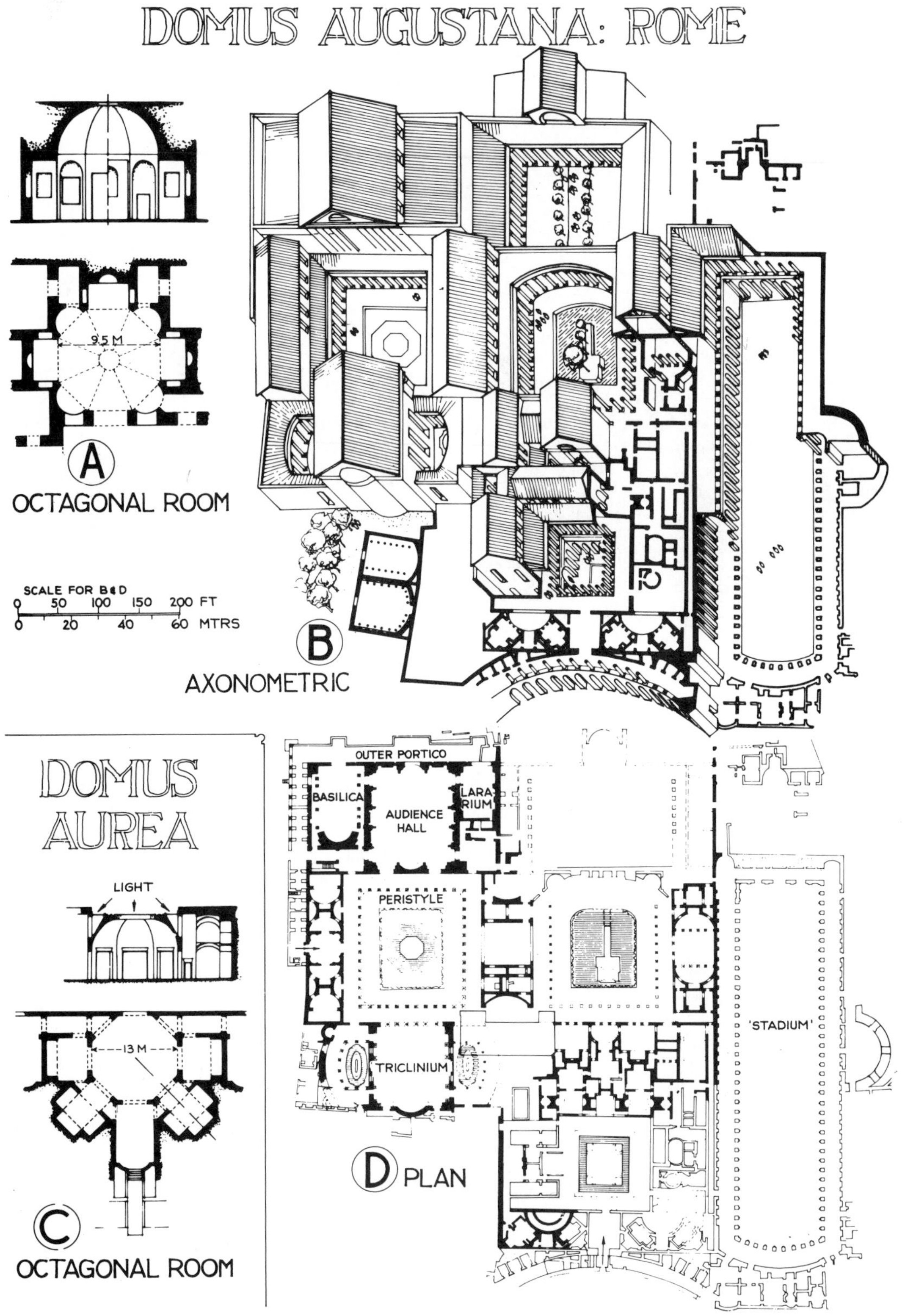
DOMUS AUGUSTANA: ROME
9.5 M
A
OCTAGONAL ROOM
SCALE FOR B & D
0 50 100 150 200 FT
0 20 40 60 MTRS
B
AXONOMETRIC
DOMUS AUREA
LIGHT
13 M
C
OCTAGONAL ROOM
OUTER PORTICO
BASILICA
AUDIENCE HALL
LARARIUM
PERISTYLE
TRICLINIUM
'STADIUM'
D PLAN

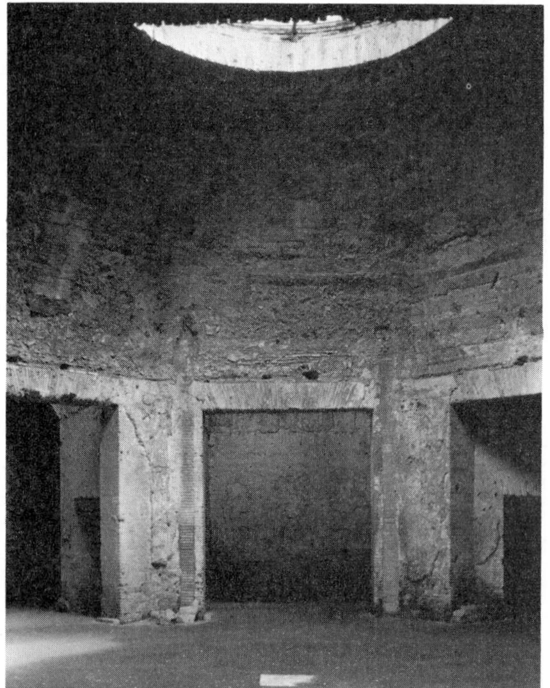

A. The octagon, Domus Aurea, Rome. See p.261

B. Garden court in the private wing. Domus Augustana, Rome. See p.261

C. Hadrian's Villa, Tivoli: the Canopus. See p.266

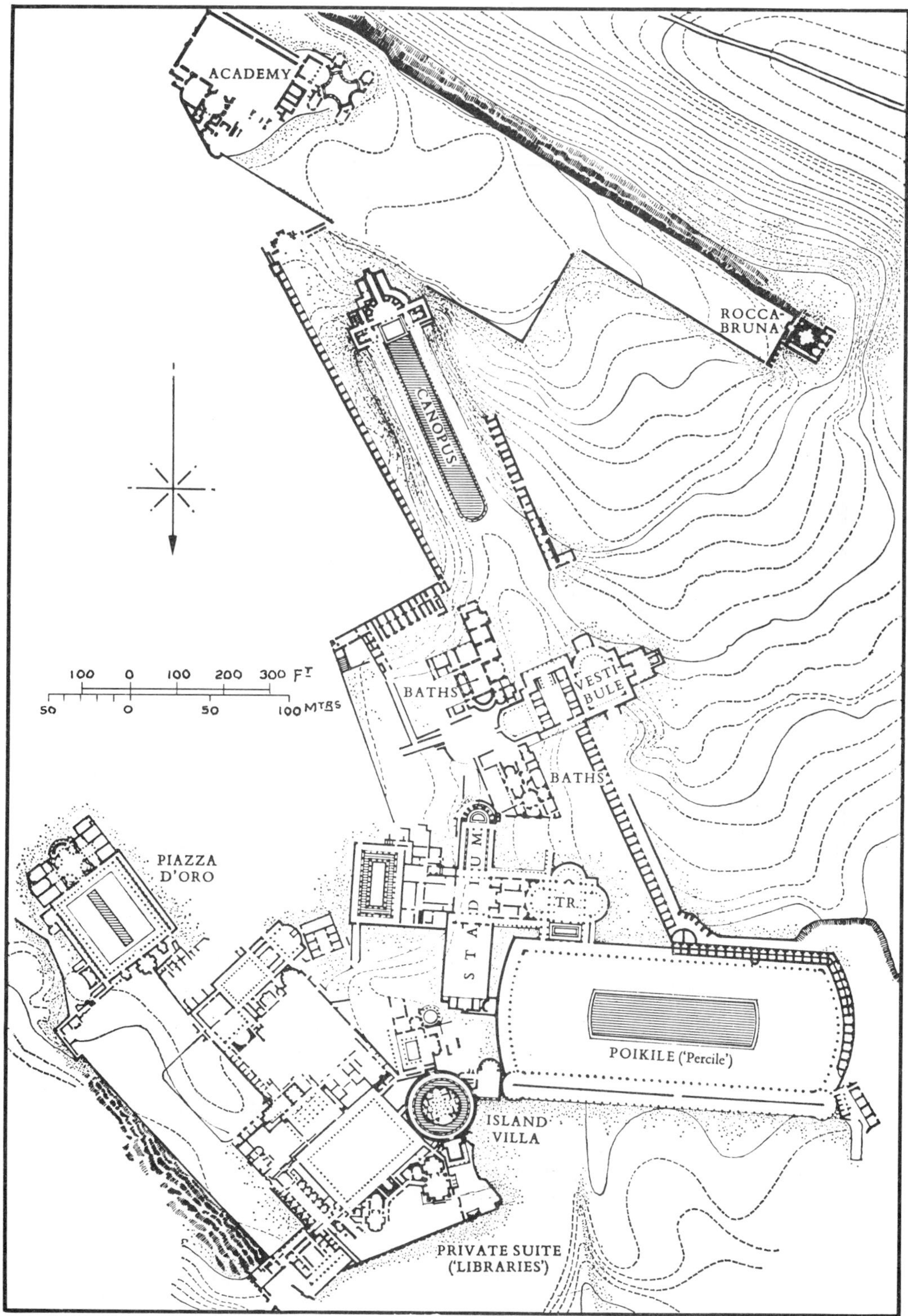

Hadrian's Villa, Tivoli (*c.* 118–134). See p.266

a peristyle on one side of the palace, and a pair of rooms that open off a smaller court in the private wing set between the official wing and a long sunken garden in the form of a stadium on the opposite side.

The uses of the principal state rooms are not precisely known. The one named on the plan as the basilica may have been vaulted, in much the same way as was the so-called Temple of Diana at Nîmes, but now in concrete. However, this is much less likely in the case of the audience hall, despite previous restorations showing it with a wide barrel vault. The private wing is notable for the strict axial symmetry of its planning. The pair of rooms referred to were mirror images of one another opening off the north wall of the court (p. 264B centre left and right). They were vaulted like the octagonal room of the Domus Aurea, but the plan below was different, being now a square the corners of which were filled with diagonally set apses. Half-domes over these apses turned the square into an octagon, just as the squinch did in later architecture (p. 263A).

Hadrian's Villa, Tivoli (*c.* AD 118–134) (pp. 264C, 265, 267), is a later counterpart of the Domus Aurea, though built as a retreat in the country rather than being set in the city. Walking around it today, it is still possible to experience something of the variety of architectural forms and settings, and the skilful way in which Hadrian and his architect have contrived the meetings of the axes, the surprises that await the turning of a corner, and the vistas that open to view. It was possible here to experiment with new forms and new types of spatial composition, and some of the results are seen in the Island Villa, the vestibules at the ends of the Piazza d'Oro, the Small Baths, and the Canopus. The most characteristic feature is a constant play upon curves and counter-curves in place of the rectilinear shapes used in most earlier planning. Within a circular outer wall, the Island Villa (p. 267B) contains a colonnade and moat, and a bewildering arrangement of apsidal, convex, and concave rooms focused on a central fountain court. The domed northern vestibule of the Piazza d'Oro has a form related to that of the two rooms in the Domus Augustana just described. But here there are apses opening off most sides of the octagon, and the apses project externally to create a new volumetric expression of the interior (p. 267A). The central room to the south has a more complex plan, with apses alternating with inwardly projecting curved columnar screens. This room can hardly have been vaulted (or, if it was, the vault would not have stood for long) but there is a vestibule in the Small Baths where the walls are similar in plan, and which is vaulted over a similarly undulating surface internally. And at the head of the Canopus there was a pavilion of equally complex plan, open at the front and with water cascading into it at the rear (p. 264C).

Aqueducts and Bridges

The **Aqua Claudia, Rome** (AD 38–52 with numerous later repairs and restorations) (p. 268A), was one of the principal channels of water supply to the capital at the time of its completion, bringing water, originally, from a source 66 km (41 miles) away. For long distances outside Rome, the channel was carried at heights of almost 20 m (68 ft) above the original ground level on lofty arches constructed partly of opus quadratum and partly of concrete.

Trajan's Danube Bridge, Turnu Severin (AD 104–105), perhaps designed by Apollodorus of Damascus, architect of Trajan's Forum, is known only from remains of the pier foundations, from descriptions, and from a relief on Trajan's column. It is included here as a later example of timber construction. Framed timber arches were carried on twenty masonry piers over a total length of 1100 m (almost ¾ mile) with individual spans of between 35 m (115 ft) and 38 m (130 ft).

Trajan's Bridge, Alcantara (AD 105–106) (p. 268B), is the most impressive survivor of the type of Roman bridge, with tall piers and wide-spanning arches, that was built over deep valleys. The central arches are 27.3 m and 28.5 m in span and carry the roadway 48 m above the River Tagus. A commemorative arch stands over the central pier and an inscription records the name of the architect: C. Julius Lacer. There have been several restorations of some of the arches.

The **Pons Aelius, Rome** (now the Ponte S. Angelo, completed AD 134) (p. 256F), was built to give access to Hadrian's Mausoleum. The central three arches are Hadrian's, though the decorative treatment is largely of the sixteenth and seventeenth centuries, including the statues of angels by Bernini. Pairs of smaller arches at each end were rebuilt as single arches in the nineteenth century to give a level roadway from end to end when the present Tiber embankments were constructed.

Imperial Roman from Antoninus Pius to Constantine

The **Temple of Antoninus and Faustina, Rome** (begun AD 141) (p. 237D–F), was built by Antoninus in honour of his deceased wife. It was of simple traditional Roman form, raised on a podium, and with a deep porch leading to a spacious cella of the same width.

Construction of the **Sanctuary of Jupiter Heliopolitanus, Baalbek** (pp. 253G,H, 271A), already referred to in the description of the temple, continued until the mid-third century. Its other chief features were the main court, in which were set two tall altars, a hexagonal forecourt and, in front of this, a

A. (*above*)
Hadrian's Villa. Tivoli; vestibule in the Piazza d'Oro. See p.266

B. (*left*)
Hadrian's Villa, Tivoli, Island Villa: colonnade

A. The Aqua Claudia, Rome (38–52). See p.266

B. Trajan's Bridge, Alcantara (105–106). See p.266

magnificent propylaeum or porch with towers at each end. There were colonnaded porticoes along both sides of the main court, and, behind these, alternating rectangular and semicircular exedrae which were partly screened by further columns of red and grey granite (p. 271A). The forecourt and propylaeum are less well preserved, so that the details are conjectural. But note the arch which again interrupts the flat architrave on the front of the propylaeum.

The **Temple of Bacchus, Baalbek** (mid-second century) (pp. 253G,H,270), stands a little to the left of the sanctuary. It is on a scale not much less than that of the Temple of Jupiter, and has a large cella at the far end of which is another smaller temple-like structure: the adyton or holy-of-holies (p. 270A). The fact that this second temple was built so close to the Temple of Jupiter suggests that it was to accommodate adherents of one of the newer mystical religions. The architectural detail of the temple is rich (p. 270B) and includes two-storey aedicules which break up the wall surfaces behind the interior columns. Equally rich detail is found on the soffits of the ceiling slabs which span between the cella walls and the outer colonnades.

The much smaller **Temple of Venus, Baalbek** (third century) (pp. 271B, 272D–F), also stands nearby, looking towards the entrance of the main sanctuary. It combines a circular cella with a square-fronted porch wide enough for the lines of the outer columns to be continued unbroken round the outside of the cella. Here, the bases and capitals of the columns are five-sided, and both the podium and the entablature curve inwards between each pair of columns in a Baroque manner.

The **Serapeum, Pergamon** (third century), has a more frankly Eastern arrangement. The central structure here was a large brick-built rectangular building with nave, aisles and galleries, and an apse at the far end, whose massive outer walls and equally massive foundations for the nave colonnades are still largely preserved. It stood in a huge rectangular precinct, where it was flanked by two symmetrical colonnaded courts, each with a pool for ritual bathing and a tall domed rotunda at its far end.

The **Temple of Vesta on the Forum Romanum, Rome** (an early third century rebuilding of a much more ancient structure) (p. 272A–C), retained the simple circular plan seen already in several other temples. Here it may have derived directly from the primitive round hut. The temple differed in function from most other temples in Rome in being the place where a sacred fire was kept burning, tended by the Vestal Virgins who lived close by. The present partial reconstruction of the temple is based on excavations and representations on reliefs and coins.

The **Temple of the Sun, Rome** (AD 275–280), built by Aurelian, brought to Rome a largely Eastern form: essentially that which is seen, for instance, in the Sanctuary of Bel at Palmyra, but with some features more reminiscent of the sanctuary at Baalbek. It is known chiefly from drawings by Palladio which show a circular, central temple building set in a large rectangular court approached through a smaller rectangular court with half-circular ends.

The **Temple of Venus and Rome, Rome** (pp.237G,H,271C), as restored by Maxentius between AD 307 and 312, had new cellas built within what had survived of the walls of the timber-roofed Hadrianic cellas. The thicker new walls, decorated with columnar aedicules and faced with marble, supported coffered vaults. A further innovation was the replacement of the earlier square ends by back-to-back apses with concrete semi-domes, whose surfaces were enlivened by lozenge-shaped coffers that diminished in size towards the top (p. 271C).

Basilicas

The plan of the **Basilica, Leptis Magna** (dedicated AD 216), is remarkably similar to that of the central building of the Serapeum, Pergamon, except for the fact that it has two identical apses, one at each end. The walls were constructed of stone throughout, with the two-storey colonnades that separated the aisles and galleries from the nave continued, as attached columns, around the walls of the apses.

The **Basilica, Trier** (early fourth century) (p. 255F,G), was an aisle-less rectangular hall with an apse at one end only. Unusually for this area, its walls were constructed of brick throughout their thickness. The elevations were given a simple grandeur by double ranges of round-headed windows, set, on the outside, within taller blind arcades – a foretaste of the wall treatment of later Christian basilicas such as S. Sabina, Rome. Less typical of these later basilicas were subtle variations in the size of the apse windows to make the apse appear larger and deeper than it really was.

The **Basilica of Constantine, Rome** (AD 307–312 and later) (pp.255B–E,273A), also known as the **Basilica Nova,** was begun by Maxentius and completed and partly remodelled by Constantine. Its design derived from the central halls of the later Imperial baths. But it is larger in scale than any of these and has been isolated from the other rooms that surrounded the bath halls. The central nave, 80 m long and 25 m wide (260 ft × 80 ft), was roofed by three coffered concrete groined vaults rising 35 m (115 ft) above the floor. To reduce slightly their spans, they sprang, like the similar vaults in the bath halls, from short lengths of entablature carried by monolithic columns – here of Proconnesian marble. To each side of the nave were three lower transverse bays separated by massive piers and spanned by coffered barrel vaults. Little now remains standing, apart from three bays on the north side. Nevertheless, they give some idea of the scale of the interior, if not

A. (*above*)
Temple of Bacchus, Baalbek: interior of cella (restored). See p.269

B. (*right*)
Temple of Bacchus, Baalbek: interior detail

A. Exedra in the great Court, Sanctuary of Jupiter Heliopolitanus, Baalbek. See p.266

B. Temple of Venus, Baalbek (third century). See p.269

C. Temple of Venus and Rome, Rome: apse (as restored by Maxentius, 307–312). See p.269

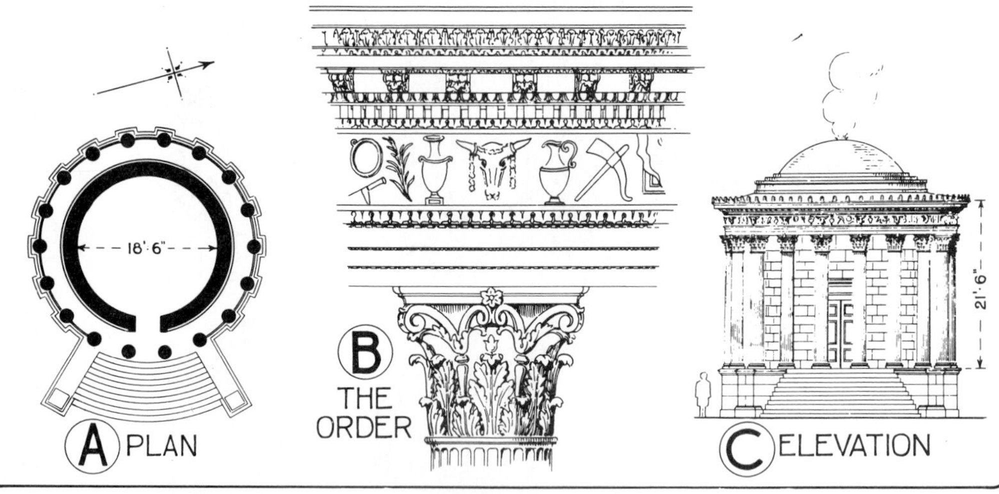
TEMPLE OF VESTA: ROME (RESTORED)
18'·6"
21'·6"
A PLAN
B THE ORDER
C ELEVATION

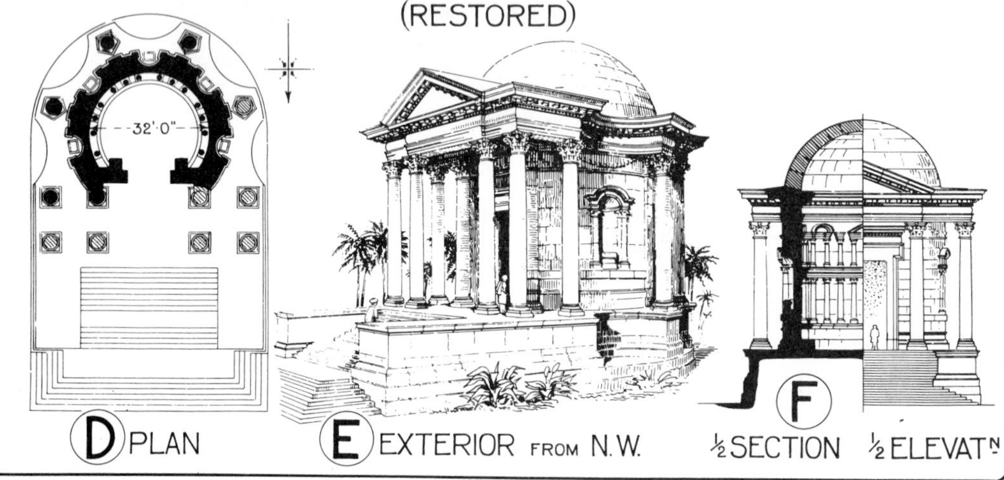
TEMPLE OF VENUS: BAALBEK (RESTORED)
32'·0"
D PLAN
E EXTERIOR FROM N.W.
F ½ SECTION ½ ELEVATN.

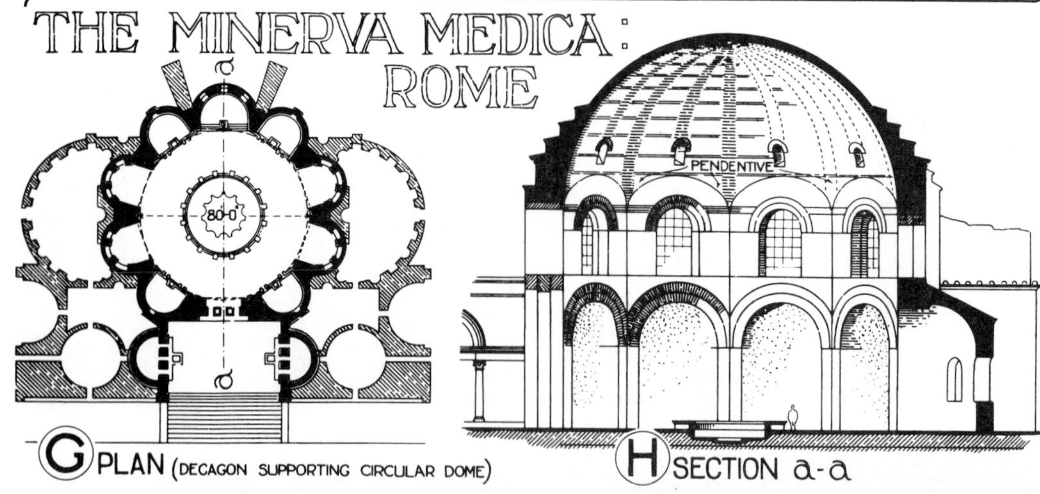
THE MINERVA MEDICA: ROME
a
80'-0"
a
PENDENTIVE
G PLAN (DECAGON SUPPORTING CIRCULAR DOME)
H SECTION a-a

A. Basilica of Constantine, Rome (307–312 and later): reconstructed interior. See p.269

B. Facade of the Baths seen from the Gymnasium, Sardis. See p.274

of the opulence of its marble finishes. There were two apses, a narthex-like porch at one end, and a central porch on the south side. The narthex and end apse are part of the original design. The chief modification for which Constantine was responsible was a shifting of the major axis by the addition of the northern apse and the southern porch. The manner of buttressing the thrusts of the high vaults of the nave is similar to that adopted later in the transverse direction in Justinian's Hagia Sophia, and, in principle, to that seen in some Romanesque and most Gothic churches.

Thermae

The **Baths and Gymnasium, Sardis** (second century and beginning of the third century) (p. 273B), represent the final fusion, in the Eastern empire, of the Roman thermae with the Greek gymnasium. The baths block stands at the end of the large porticoed square of the gymnasium, itself fronted by a colonnaded court of typically Eastern character looking out over the gymnasium.

The **Baths (Thermae) of Caracalla, Rome** (AD 212–216) (p. 275), today give the best idea of the layout of the fully-developed Imperial bath, being, though partly ruined, unencumbered anywhere by later structures. The completely symmetrical planning about the principal axis, the compact arrangement of all the parts of the baths proper in a single block, and the setting of this block in a much larger landscaped park surrounded by shops, services, and pavilions for other uses, will be apparent from the plan. Even the main block measured 225 m × 115 m (750 ft × 380 ft) without the projecting mass of the caldarium. Arranged in sequence on the main axis of this block were the open swimming bath or natatio, the central hall or frigidarium (both of these with their longer axes running transversely), the smaller tepidarium, and finally the domed circular caldarium. This last was lit by large windows in its drum, while the central hall was lit chiefly by windows in the clerestory, just below the vaults. Other rooms opened off to each side, duplicating one another exactly, with the two exercise yards or palaestrae towards the two extremities. All but the south side presented, on the exterior, large expanses of wall with relatively small window openings. But the rooms to each side of the caldarium on the south had much larger areas of window, looking over the gardens.

The **Baths of Diocletian, Rome** (*c.* AD 298–306), were built on an even vaster scale, and again large parts are well preserved. The general arrangement was similar to that of the Baths of Caracalla, but the planning of the main block was somewhat tighter, and the circular-domed caldarium was replaced by a form that was a smaller-scale version of the central hall with the addition of apses in the centres of all four sides. As already mentioned, the central hall is now the church of S. Maria degli Angeli, the initial conversion having been carried out to the designs of Michelangelo with modifications by Vanvitelli.

The **Imperial Baths, Trier** (early fourth century), show a variation on this plan on the somewhat smaller scale appropriate to a provincial capital of the tetrarchy. Here, the rectangular porticoed palaestra is the largest unit, and as at Sardis the baths proper close its fourth side. As originally planned, the principal rooms were not only symmetrically disposed about the main axis, but were almost equally symmetrical about the transverse axis, with the circular tepidarium as the central hub and no natatio.

Theatres, Amphitheatres and Circuses

The **Theatre at Aspendos** (AD 161–180) (p. 276A) shows no significant change in general design from the earlier theatres of the imperial period. But the stage buildings remain intact, except for the loss of the columns of the two-storey aedicules facing the cavea, and of the statuary which they must have contained, so that the structure gives a better impression of the original appearance of a Roman theatre than most of them now do.

The **Amphitheatres, Verona** and **El Djem** (early third century), are similar to the Colosseum, but smaller and with less emphasis on the decorative external orders, so that the arcades are the dominant features.

The **Circus of Maxentius, Rome** (early fourth century), (pp. 241B, 277A), was similar to the Circus Maximus, but was built on level ground alongside Maxentius' Palace on the Via Appia. The tiers of marble seats were therefore supported, as in most amphitheatres, on raking concrete vaults and surrounded by a wall. There are tall towers at each end of the carceres.

Triumphal Arches, Columns and Colonnades

The **Column of Marcus Aurelius, Rome** (AD 174), is very similar to Trajan's Column, and, like it, formerly stood in front of a temple dedicated to the emperor. The statue of the emperor has now been replaced by a statue of S. Paul.

The **Arch of Septimius Severus, Rome** (AD 203) (p. 260D–F), commemorating the emperor's Parthian campaigns, was built of white marble in traditional triple-arched form, but shows a new freedom in the style of its relief decorations.

The **Arch of Constantine, Rome** (*c.* AD 312–315) (p. 276B), was the last of these arches in Rome. Again it follows the traditional form. Though it is finely proportioned, close inspection shows that much of the relief decoration was taken from earlier monuments and reused.

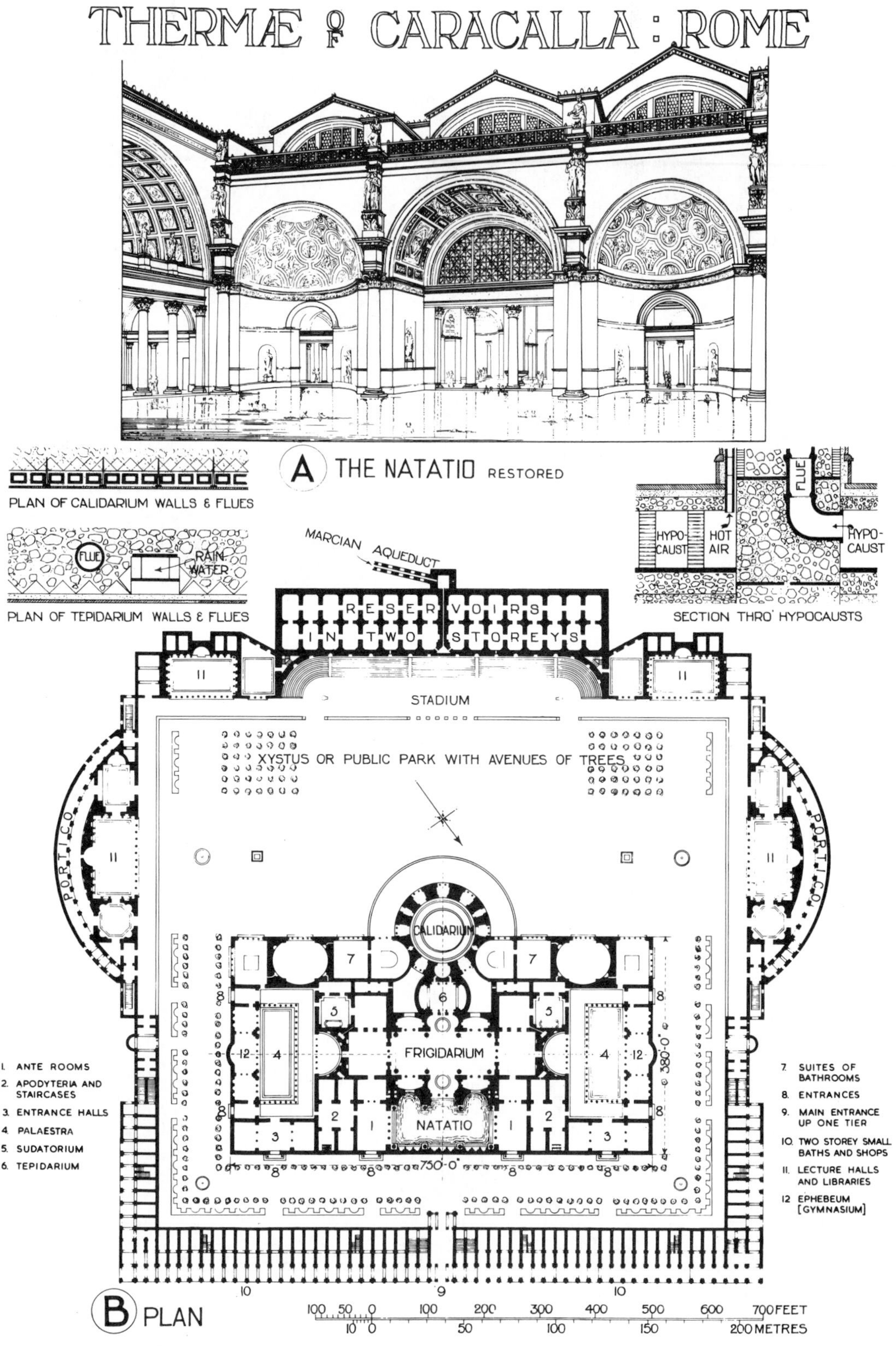
THERMÆ OF CARACALLA : ROME
A THE NATATIO RESTORED
PLAN OF CALIDARIUM WALLS & FLUES
PLAN OF TEPIDARIUM WALLS & FLUES
FLUE
RAIN WATER
MARCIAN AQUEDUCT
SECTION THRO' HYPOCAUSTS
HYPO-CAUST
HOT AIR
HYPO-CAUST
RESERVOIRS IN TWO STOREYS
STADIUM
XYSTUS OR PUBLIC PARK WITH AVENUES OF TREES
PORTICO
CALIDARIUM
FRIGIDARIUM
NATATIO
380'-0"
750'-0"
B PLAN
1. ANTE ROOMS
2. APODYTERIA AND STAIRCASES
3. ENTRANCE HALLS
4. PALAESTRA
5. SUDATORIUM
6. TEPIDARIUM
7. SUITES OF BATHROOMS
8. ENTRANCES
9. MAIN ENTRANCE UP ONE TIER
10. TWO STOREY SMALL BATHS AND SHOPS
11. LECTURE HALLS AND LIBRARIES
12. EPHEBEUM [GYMNASIUM]
100 50 0 100 200 300 400 500 600 700 FEET
10 0 50 100 150 200 METRES

A. Theatre, Aspendos (161–180). See p.274

B. Arch of Constantine, Rome (*c.* 312–315). See p.274

A. Circus of Maxentius. Rome: the carceres and end towers. See p.274

B. Temple of Minerva Medica, Rome (mid-third century), as seen in *c.* 1790. See p.278

Similar arches were also erected during this period in the provinces. But it is of more interest now to note a commoner type of monumental arch in use in the East, especially in the provinces of Syria and Arabia. This was more like some of the city gates described above, but stood at a focal point of the city's main thoroughfares. There are good examples still standing in cities like **Jerash** and **Palmyra**. With them was associated another characteristically Eastern form – the colonnaded street, which was to develop soon into another type of market.

Tombs

The family tombs of the **Vatican Cemetery, Rome** (disclosed by excavation beneath the present S. Peter's and mostly second century), those of the **Isola Sacra Cemetery, Ostia** (second to fourth century), and those along the **Via Appia** and **Via Latina, Rome**, are counterparts of the tombs in Etruscan cemeteries described above. Like them, they reproduce contemporary domestic architecture, though now in a more abbreviated form and in brick-faced concrete. The **Tomb of the Caetennii, Vatican Cemetery** (mid-second century), is one of the more splendid examples. The heads of the entrance door and windows on the facade are ornamented in stucco. Inside, there is a single square room, with columned and pedimented niches and other aedicules around the walls with low recesses for sarcophagi below them.

The **Mausoleum of Maxentius, Rome** (*c.* AD 310), and the better preserved **Tor de'Schiavi, Rome** (*c.* AD 300) (p. 262K), were virtually smaller copies of the Pantheon. There were differences of proportion and detail, including a closer relationship between porch and rotunda and the presence of windows in the attic storey of the rotunda – which was again, internally, the base of the dome. They differed also in being raised on a podium and free-standing.

Rotundas which were probably intended as their mausolea in the palaces of Diocletian at **Spalato** and of Galerius at **Salonika** were further examples of this form of about the same date, though the shape of the latter was more akin to that of the caldarium of the Baths of Caracalla. These two later became, respectively, the cathedral and the church of S. George.

Palaces, Villas and Garden Pavilions

The so-called **Temple of Minerva Medica, Rome** (mid-third century) (pp. 272G,H,277B), was really a pavilion in the villa of the emperor Gallienus. It is a building in which the possibilities opened up by some of the pavilions in Hadrian's Villa at Tivoli were developed further, and it led on towards some of the early centralised church plans of the next century. A central decagon was expanded by apses on all sides except that of the entrance. Four of these apses were bounded originally by open colonnades instead of solid walls. Above them, in the decagonal drum, there were large windows and, above this, a dome with rib-like circumferential and radial bands of brick embedded in the concrete. However, the initial design appears to have been too daring, and two large flanking hemicycles and two projecting buttresses were added later on the outside.

The **Palace of Diocletian, Spalato** (*c.* AD 300–306) (pp. 279B,280A,D), was built on the eastern shore of the Adriatic as a place of retirement. It was planned to be self-sufficient in a way that a palace situated within a city did not need to be, and it has the aspect of an Eastern frontier town with its basic grid plan and defensive perimeter wall. The extensive use of ashlar as well as concrete, the colonnaded streets, and much of the architectural detail, strongly suggest that the architect came from Syria or Arabia.

Today, much of the site is still occupied by the town (now called Split) that grew up later within the walls. But the plan of the palace is reasonably clear, with the imperial apartments concentrated on the side that faces the sea. There was a domed circular vestibule to these apartments on the central axis of the whole plan, just behind the portico. To each side of the peristyle (p. 280A,D) there were courts containing, on one side, a small temple with barrel-vaulted cella and two smaller rotundas, and, on the other side, the probable mausoleum rotunda, now the cathedral, referred to above. Around the remaining sides of the complex were many smaller rooms, presumably providing accommodation for soldiers and for the emperor's domestic establishment. There were three monumental entrance gates, each guarded by a pair of octagonal towers, and there were other square towers between them around the perimeter. Blind arcading, echoing the arcades of the peristyle, formed the chief decoration of the gates and perimeter wall.

The large so-called **Imperial Villa, Piazza Armerina** (early to mid-fourth century) (p. 279A), provides a sharp contrast to Diocletian's Palace, being comparatively undefended in its remote Sicilian valley. It consisted of groups of single-storey buildings and courts set, apparently informally, in the landscape. It is much more like Hadrian's Villa at Tivoli, and was originally thought (partly on the basis of the great expanses of mosaic flooring) to have been a country retreat of Diocletian's co-emperor Maximian. Comparison with Hadrian's villa shows, however, a much greater compactness and a marked inward-looking quality. As at Tivoli, the buildings at Piazza Armerina fall into clearly defined and axially planned groups for different uses: public rooms, private apartments and baths. But there is little space between the groups, so that the changes of axis are more abrupt. There are also forms that did not appear in Hadrian's Villa, but were introduced only at this time or during the previous century or so, and were to have

PALACE OF MAXIMIAN: PIAZZA ARMERINA

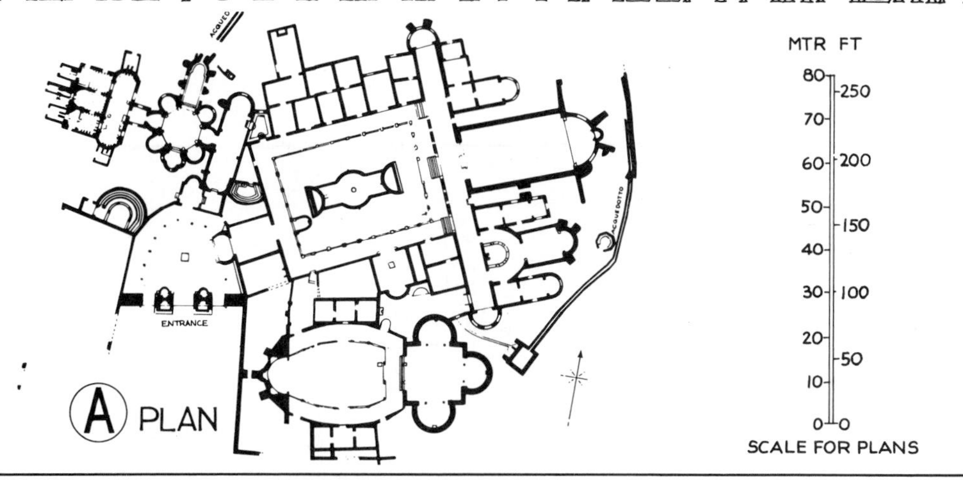

PALACE OF DIOCLETIAN: SPALATO

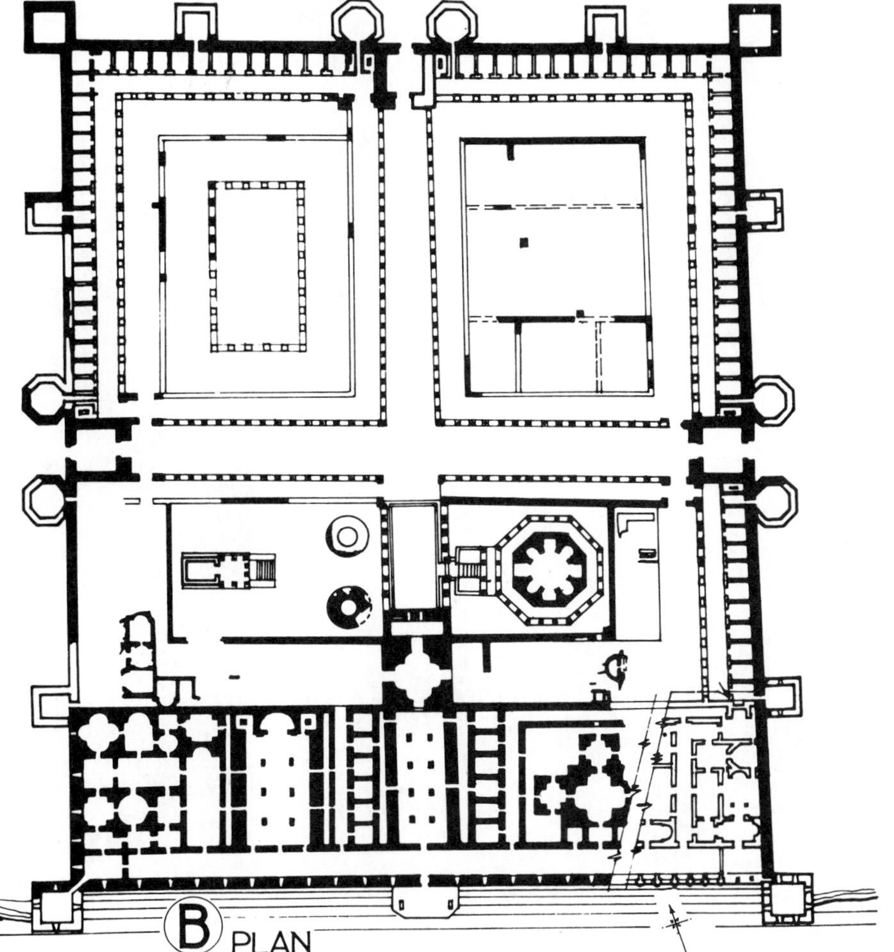

A. Peristyle, Diocletian's Palace, Spalato (*c.* 300–306). See p.278

D. Detail of the peristyle arcade, looking towards the mausoleum rotunda, Diocletian's Palace, Spalato

B. House of Diana, Ostia (on the left). See p.281

E. Arcades in the House of Cupid and Psyche, Ostia (*c.* 300). See p.281

C. Facade of the Horea Epagathiana, Ostia (*c.* 145–150). See p.281

considerable importance in later architecture. One of these, the multilobed rotunda, has been seen already on a larger scale in the so-called Temple of Minerva Medica. The others are a triple-apsed reception hall or triconch, and curved porticoes or sigmas giving access to such rooms – so named from the resemblance of the plans to the capital form of the Greek letter sigma, which was written at the time as the Latin capital C.

Domestic Architecture

The later evolution of domestic architecture in Italy can best be followed in Rome's original port of **Ostia**. The town was fairly densely built up from the early second century onwards, with the commonest type of development being a multi-storey block for multiple occupation built around one or more internal courts. Four storeys were usual, with brick-faced concrete walls carrying concrete vaults for the alternate floors, and with intermediate floors of timber.

The **House of Diana at Ostia** (mid-second century) (p. 280B) has a typical street frontage. Shops occupied the rooms opening to the street, and the small windows just below the balconies provided daylight to the timber-floored mezzanines which were reached by internal timber stairs. Concrete stairs gave access at two points to the higher floors. The **Horea Epagathiana** (*c.* AD 145–150) (p. 280C), a large warehouse and store with living accommodation above, in the centre of the town, has a more elaborate entrance front. The **House of the Serapide** (late second century) (p. 245E), adjacent to a public bath building, shows typical internal planning.

Perhaps because of their durable concrete construction and consequent long life, blocks such as these established a tradition of tenement design that lasted virtually unbroken in Italy and some neighbouring countries until the beginning of the present century.

The importance of Ostia declined, however, with the result that later construction there was usually on a smaller scale, as seen in the **House of Cupid and Psyche** (*c.* AD 300) (p. 280E) where, around a fountain court, there were columnar arcades similar to those of grander scale in Diocletian's Palace.

Domestic architecture in those provinces where construction techniques and climate were not greatly dissimilar seems broadly to have followed the pattern seen in Ostia. In Syria and Arabia, different construction techniques and a substantially different climate did, however, lead to different forms. A house block at **Umm el-Jemal** (third or fourth century) (p. 245C,D) is an Arabian (now Jordanian) counterpart of the larger blocks in Ostia. Here, windows are smaller, and construction including floors is entirely in cut stone. Where rooms were too wide to be spanned by single blocks, the spans were reduced by corbelling or throwing arches across them at intermediate points. Flat roofs were provided for outdoor sleeping.

Aqueducts and Bridges

The design of aqueducts and bridges did not change much during this period. But, to reduce the necessary height of its piers and arches, the **Aqueduct, Aspendos** (third century), was constructed with pressure pipework over the long elevated section that crossed the valley near the town. Towers were then provided near each end at which the water was allowed to find its natural level and thereby control the pressure in the pipes.

Defence Walls and Town Gates

The **Porta Nigra, Trier** (probably early fourth century) (p. 260G), was a later counterpart of the gates like the Porta Palatina, Turin, with double entrance arches, two-storey arcaded galleries with superimposed decorative orders, and round-fronted towers at each side. Here, though, the gallery arcades were carried around the towers also, only one of which seems to have been completed to its full intended height.

The **Aurelianic Walls, Rome** (*c.* AD 270–280), were the principal defence work of the period, with a total length of about 19 km (over 12 miles), some 380 projecting square towers 100 Roman feet (or two arrow shots) apart, and fourteen principal gates. Of these, the **Porta Ostiensis** (now Porta S. Paolo) (p. 244B) still has virtually its original form, with a round-fronted tower at each side of the entrance archway and a gallery above it for the portcullis. Some gateways had two entrance archways, but none seems to have had the embellishment seen in Turin and Trier.

Chapter 11
THE BYZANTINE EMPIRE

Architectural Character

Early Christian

Early Christian architecture was an integral part of the architecture of the later Roman Empire. Architecture in the service of the Christian church did not begin with Constantine's formal recognition of Christianity. Nor did large-scale secular building end with it. In Rome, for instance, Constantine was responsible not only for the first large new churches but also for the completion of the Basilica Nova begun by Maxentius, for the last large Imperial baths, and for several other projects of the kind undertaken by previous emperors, such as the construction of two monumental arches. In Constantinople, he undertook further secular buildings, as did his successors. But it was in new buildings for the church – places of worship, memorial structures and baptisteries – that the only new forms were created. It was chiefly these forms that continued to evolve in the following centuries, and it is in these that the chief interest of the period after Constantine lies.

The first Christians already had the synagogue as their place of worship, and, believing in an imminent end to this world, felt no need of anything more. When that expectation receded and they grew in numbers and largely severed their Jewish ties, they met for prayer and for their central act of worship – which gradually developed into the formalised liturgy of the eucharist – in whatever rooms could be made available to them by members of the group. They buried their dead, just as most of their pagan contemporaries did, and, like them also, met for commemorative meals at the cemeteries. In Rome, and in a few other places, these cemeteries were mostly underground catacombs. But there was no special significance in that: it was essentially a consequence of the high price of land and the favourable circumstance that there was an easily tunnelled rock just below the surface which permitted burials one above another down to considerable depths. Simple structures were built nearby to accommodate those sharing the meals.

By the third century, purpose-built churches or adaptations of existing buildings were being commissioned. But they were too small and architecturally insignificant – deliberately so in order not to challenge too blatantly the official state religion – to serve as a model for Constantine's architects. Nor could the pagan temple serve as a model: something distinctively different was needed to serve a different kind of use. When large numbers of people participated in the ceremonies associated with the temple they did so in the open air, but the eucharist called for a different sort of participation. It was one to which only initiates were admitted and was performed inside, where enough room had to be provided for all those taking part. Baptism also had its special requirements, as it was performed at this time by immersion. Only the tomb and the other provisions at the cemetery made no new demands.

Completely new types of building do not, however, come into existence overnight. Certainly they could not do so when it was even more necessary than it is today to rely on experience in all practical matters of design and construction. Constantine wished to make an immediate impact with his new church commissions, and so did churchmen who wished to take advantage of the new official recognition of Christianity. For the church building itself, therefore, the form chosen was that which was suitable with virtually no major modification, had few undesirable connotations arising from its previous uses and could be built rapidly at relatively low cost. This was the basilica as it was generally known, until it was reinterpreted by Maxentius in the Basilica Nova – a timber-roofed rectangular hall with a colonnaded central space with aisles and perhaps galleries above them. The main space, built higher than the aisle galleries, had clerestory lighting, and one or more apses in which legal business was transacted. It could easily be varied in size and precise form, and had already appeared in many such variations. The only real limitation was on the width of the central space, which had to be within the spanning capacity of known forms of timber roof. Seating could be provided in the apse for the clergy, as it had been for the magistrate and his assessors, and a Christian altar

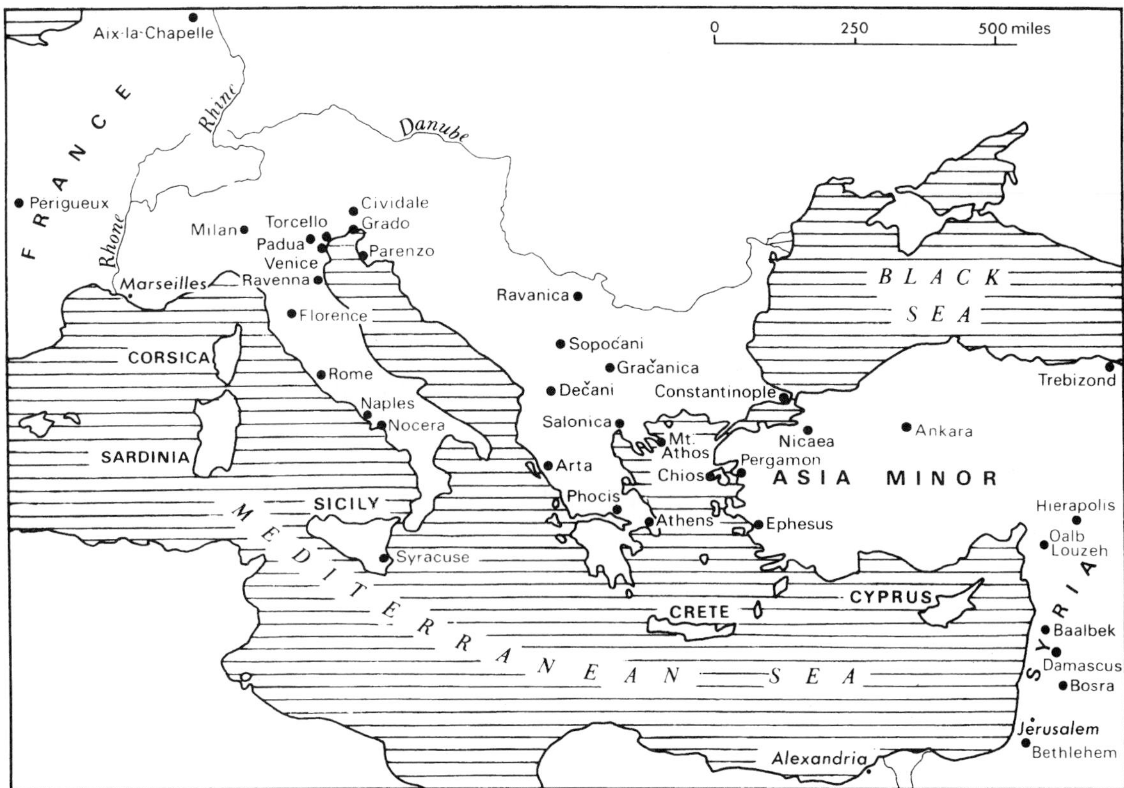

The Byzantine Empire

could be placed in front where, previously, there had been a small altar for libations.

Thus the commonest form of the early church (and also of contemporary synagogues as seen, for instance, at Sardis) was rectangular hall, timber-roofed, usually with one or two aisles to each side of the central nave, and with an apse at one end facing the principal entrances at the other. Corresponding roughly to the sacred enclosure in front of the temple, and to the atrium of a typical early Roman house, was a courtyard which was also referred to as an atrium and frequently had a fountain in the centre. One or more semicircular rows of seats were set against the wall of the apse for the clergy, with a raised throne in the centre for the bishop. An open screen in front of them marked off a sanctuary from the rest of the nave, and within this area was set the altar. To give it greater emphasis and dignity, it was usually surrounded by four or more columns and surmounted by a canopy, known as a baldachino or ciborium.

The impression given by the interior of one of these churches today, in comparison with surviving but less well preserved Roman buildings, is of great richness. Looking down the length of the nave, one sees long rows of marble columns, sometimes carrying flat entablatures, and sometimes rows of arches. Above these, and between the clerestory windows, the walls may be faced with marble, or sometimes with mosaics made up from small tesserae of coloured glass. There may be further iridescent mosaics on the 'triumphal arch' which terminates the nave proper, and on the semidome of the apse which opens into it. These mosaics, if surviving from the early period, will mostly be either narrative scenes from the Bible or single figures seen against stylised landscapes or plain gold grounds. There is likely to be a coffered and richly gilded ceiling to the nave, while on the floor there will be a pavement of grey-white and black marble, inlaid with geometric patterns of coloured marbles.

But it should be remembered that much of what is seen is often the result of later changes. The ceiling, for instance, is likely to be a Baroque refurbishment and the marble paving from the eleventh or twelfth century. Much of the facing of the walls will probably be comparatively recent. There are few surviving original furnishings. Yet the impression of richness, if the effort is made to discount any Baroque heaviness, is not wholly misleading. There is evidence that gilt, coffered ceilings already hid the roof trusses of some churches in Constantine's time. In place of the marble floor there would have been mosaic, such as those recently uncovered at Aquileia and Jerash. Marble, painted stucco, and mosaic would have covered much of the wall surfaces. And the furnishings, such as the altar and its ciborium and the screen around the sanctuary, would doubtless have been richly gilded and even studded with jewels.

In fact, it is quite clear that, from the start, Constantine wanted his new churches to be just as magnificent as any other existing buildings: to have made them less so would not have proclaimed the new faith as he wished. The chief way in which they did fall short of earlier Roman buildings was that the columns, capitals and similar features were frequently reused from earlier buildings, with little regard for close matching, but paradoxically such idiosyncrasies imparted a greater liveliness to interiors than they might otherwise have possessed. In the new churches there was much more frequent use of the arch to span between the columns of a colonnade. Although the flat entablature was not deliberately abandoned and seems to have remained the preferred form, a shortage of readily available architrave blocks of the necessary sizes encouraged the use of the arch.

Variations in character reflected different local resources and traditions of construction. In Syria, where there was still a fine live tradition of cutting stone, there was, for instance, more emphasis on carved decoration and on the exterior – which, elsewhere, counted for little at this time. In central Anatolia and Armenia there was probably an early use of stone vaulting in place of timber roofing. Variations also developed in those detailed aspects of planning that catered for the specific needs of a liturgy which evolved differently throughout the empire. They involved such matters as the provision of entrances, internal barriers, and secondary spaces.

The rectangular basilica was not, however, the only form adopted for the church. More centralised plans, focused on a central vertical axis rather than a longitudinal horizontal one, were also adopted occasionally. The reasons for this are still debated, and probably there was more than one. There were two possible Roman prototypes: the circular temple (such as the Pantheon) and the centralised audience hall or garden pavilion (such as the so-called temple of Minerva Medica) which became typical of later Roman palaces. The second seems the more likely, since its connotations of 'House of the Lord' would not have been inappropriate to the House of God or *Domus Ecclesia*, and there was at least one early example (in Salonika) of the conversion of such a pavilion to church use. The centralised church plans varied from the completely circular to more complex lobed (usually tetraconch or four-lobed) forms set within an overall octagon or square.

Only one major example of a newly built church of completely circular plan has survived: S. Stephano Rotondo in Rome. In detailed design this church resembled normal contemporary basilicas. But its effective use must have presented considerable problems, and the lack of any follow-up suggests that it was acknowledged to have been a mistaken experiment. There were more examples of the tetraconch plan and variants, probably beginning with the Golden Octagon in Antioch and including S. Lorenzo in Milan a little later. Here the principal central space was expanded, not just by a continuous ambulatory, but also by semicircular exedrae. There was a secondary longitudinal axis running from the entrance to the altar. To these variants on the rectangular basilica must be added a few examples of basilicas dating from the late fifth and early sixth centuries in which a square bay of the nave just in front of the apse was accentuated by allowing it to rise into a low tower, thus giving a central vertical emphasis of a different kind.

The requirements for the baptistery were simple: a central font into which those to be baptised could descend, and sufficient space around it for officiating clergy. For this purpose a simple circular, octagonal, or other centralised plan was the obvious and almost universal choice. If the structure was large enough to warrant it, there was an ambulatory around the central space. There was usually a central dome, which might be decorated with a representation in mosaic of Christ's baptism.

Individual tombs followed earlier Roman patterns, and were distinguishable chiefly by the subject matter of their decoration, although even this was sometimes sufficiently ambiguous to make it possible to question whether the building (for instance, the mausoleum of Constantine's daughter Constantia, now the church of S. Costanza) had been a Christian or a pagan one from the start. The covered cemetery was, on the other hand, another new form, albeit a short-lived one and largely confined to Rome if surviving examples are a valid guide. In most respects its usual plan might be regarded as a simplification of the basilican church layout. It was a long apsidal-ended rectangle consisting of a nave flanked by single aisles, but with the aisles continued around the apse without any interruption to serve as an ambulatory. Little is known of the usual decoration. In due course the floor would have been covered with burials, and it became usual to add free-standing mausolea around the sides for the more important burials.

A related group of new buildings might be referred to generally as memorial structures. Many, but not all, were martyria in the strict sense of structures built over martyrs' tombs. One of the earliest and most important was the Constantinian church of S. Peter's in Rome, built over what was believed to be the saint's tomb. The other important Constantinian foundations of this kind were the memorial structures erected on the principal sites in the Holy Land associated with Christ's birth, ministry, death, and resurrection. An important later example was the church of S. Simeon Stylites built around his column at Kalat Siman. The forms of these buildings were widely varied because, apart from their purely commemorative role, they usually served also some of the functions of the normal community church in providing for throngs of pilgrims and in serving as covered cemeteries for those who wished to be buried alongside the saints they commemorated. Indeed it must have been through this that the practice developed of interring relics of saints beneath the altars of normal churches. In addition to the forms already noted, the cross-shaped plan with four long arms was also used and was probably adopted as much because it allowed larger congregations or different activities to focus on a central shrine or other memorial as for its Christian symbolism.

Sixth-century Changes

Christian architecture in the sixth century is dominated by one building, Justinian's church of Hagia Sophia, or Divine Wisdom, in Constantinople. Indeed so great was its impact that all subsequent Byzantine church architecture was profoundly affected by it, and its influence spread also to the new Russian state in the tenth century.

Hagia Sophia was the greatest vaulted space without intermediate supports that had ever been built, and it remained so throughout the history of the Byzantine empire. All who entered it were overwhelmed by a central dome that hovered high above them – seemingly 'suspended by a golden chain from heaven', in the words borrowed by the court historian Procopius from Homer – and the use of the dome became almost obligatory in later Byzantine architecture. With it, of course, came a centralising emphasis on its vertical axis. Hagia Sophia also showed how this emphasis could be combined with an equally important longitudinal one. But the manner in which the basilican plan was fused with the earlier tetraconch plans was less easy to emulate satisfactorily on a smaller scale, and the designers of later Byzantine churches were content to allow the central axis to predominate over the longitudinal one, as it had done in the contemporary church of SS. Sergius and Bacchus.

Partly because of the great impression that Hagia Sophia made on the Turkish conquerors in the fifteenth century, it was spared the fate meted out to some churches, and has come down to the present day in a state which, though much changed, does make it possible to visualise the impression it created in the sixth century. To anyone susceptible to the effects of enclosed spaces, its unique spatial quality would have coloured all else.

Not only were the emphases on the two axes perfectly brought together, but this was done in a way that left the spatial boundaries elusive. Furthermore, the enfolding surfaces took away all sense of the massiveness of the piers which sustained the dome and other vaults. Walls and piers were sheathed in marble in a manner which reflected Early Christian adaptations of Roman techniques, and they were interrupted by two-storey open colonnades which – unclassically – had different column spacings at the two levels. Gold mosaic using purely non-figural motifs originally covered all the vault surfaces, and probably also the wall spaces between the windows at the highest levels. Large windows – considerably larger than today – flooded the whole interior with light which caused the marble and mosaic to glow with a seemingly internal radiance. Still more refulgent colour was contributed by the silver and gold that covered altar, ciborium, screens and other furnishings long since lost. Finally, there was a new vocabulary of carved ornament. Up to the late fifth century classical forms, though changed in their precise interpretation and execution, had continued in use. Now, for example, there were capitals with integral impost blocks all the surfaces of which were decorated with shallowly cut and undercut leaves, basket work, and other motifs – although they were more restrained in Hagia Sophia than in some other contemporary work.

Hagia Sophia, however, was by no means Justinian's only church commission. Procopius enumerates more than thirty other churches for which Justinian was responsible in Constantinople alone, the most important being his rebuilding of the church of the Holy Apostles. For this, and for the rebuilding of the large basilica of S. John at Ephesus, a cross-shaped plan was adopted, with nave, transepts, and eastern arm divided into square bays each vaulted with its own dome. As in Hagia Sophia, these had pendentives to carry the domes over the four arches that bounded each bay. Elsewhere, with other patrons, other variants of the domed basilica were tried, not always successfully, and there were further examples of the tetraconch arrangement, notably in S. Vitale in Ravenna where, in contrast to Hagia Sophia, the mosaic portrayed human figures.

Later Byzantine Churches

It is impossible not to see the subsequent history of Byzantine architecture as an anticlimax. Invention did not cease, but the later churches lack the power and majesty and vigour of Hagia Sophia and its nearest contemporaries and successors. The reduced vigour and scale of new construction reflected a contraction of Byzantine power, a lowering of the sights, and a preference for satisfying the modest needs of monastic communities rather than for making great public statements.

The almost universal use of the dome and the associated adoption of centralised plans has already been referred to. Certain earlier plan forms were retained for a time, notably circular and tetraconch plans which are to be found on the eastern fringe of the empire, particularly in Armenia. The trend, however, was to contain the church within a square, with a dome over its centre, and usually four cross-like arms which might be either square-ended or apsidal-ended.

Plans initially differed chiefly in the way in which the left-over spaces in the corners of the enclosing square were filled and the relationships between them and the main central space. Usually, only the main apse containing the altar was allowed to project beyond the square, though smaller projections might be allowed in the two flanking corner spaces which contained secondary areas, known as pastophoria, used by the clergy. But there was less emphasis on the enclosing square in those more easterly regions which had remained Christian after the Arab conquests. In Armenia and Georgia, more frankly cross-shaped plans were also adopted. Finally, in Greece and Constantinople, the piers that supported the dome were reduced to single columns, and all the side thrust previously resisted by the piers was passed over to the outer walls. This unified the corner spaces with the central one and with the arms of the cross. But at about the same time it became the usual practice to enclose the sanctuary area in the eastern apse, and the two pastophoria, behind a much more substantial screen, the iconostasis; this change, which reflected changes in the performance of the liturgy, introduced a new spatial division.

In partial compensation for the contraction of the dimensions of the plan, heights were, in proportion, increased. This was done partly by raising the central dome on a high drum which, from inside, created a wholly different impression from that created by the wide-spreading dome of Hagia Sophia. A further change, perhaps partly responsible for this emphasis on height and certainly related to it, was an increased emphasis on the exterior. This was seen also in the grouped massing of other vaults around the central dome, and in decorative surface treatment of the brickwork or masonry of the walls.

Hagia Sophia, through the very nature of its internal space, its marble facings and its resplendent non-figurative golden mosaic, must have seemed to be almost a heaven-on-earth, and to have no real need of figurative decoration. None of the interiors of these later churches could have created anything like the same impression by architectural means alone. But their walls, and more particularly the curved surfaces of their vaults and domes, did provide suitable grounds for the creation of an iconic heaven in fresco or mosaic.

Monastic churches of the ninth and tenth centuries show how perfectly the possibilities were exploited, once the period when all human representation was forbidden came to an end in 843. With a kind of realism that is totally different from that of the illusionistic decorations of the seventeenth and eighteenth centuries, Christ and the Virgin were represented in the central dome and the conch of the apse, sometimes in scenes like the Ascension and sometimes majestically alone against a golden background. On the curved surfaces of the pendentives and other high vaults, the principal events in Christ's life, such as the Annunciation, Baptism and Transfiguration, were presented as if actually taking place in the spaces enfolded by these sufaces. On the walls lower down, closer to those present below, were figures of those of their predecessors who were now among the saints.

In churches built or decorated during the last centuries of the Byzantine empire, this rigorously hierarchic scheme tends to be abandoned in favour of an all-over decoration which is of a more narrative character and more like that of contemporary churches in the West, though in place of the boldness and otherworldliness of the earlier mosaics there was a new refinement and humanity which has parallels in Western painting of this period.

A final characteristic of later church building is the frequency with which new churches or chapels were added to existing ones, possibly to economise in the numbers of clergy needed to serve them. This trend is particularly noticeable in Constantinople, where groups of two or three churches, often separated in date by several centuries, together create external combinations of form very different from the strictly organised massing of the single-dome church.

Later Church Building in the West

The architecture considered so far has been essentially that of the undivided empire from the time of Constantine onwards, and that of the eastern or Byzantine empire from the time of Justinian. In the West, during the latter period, there were three types of church architecture which were closely related, either to the architecture of the early Christian phase itself or to later architecture in the East.

The first is the church architecture of Rome right up to the thirteenth century. Perhaps partly on account of limited resources, this displayed an almost unparallelled conservatism and led to its being classed simply as 'Early Christian'. Because of this conservatism, it is unnecessary here to consider the differences further, but they will be referred to again below in looking at representative examples.

The second is the church architecture of the western outposts of the Byzantine empire and places which maintained close ties with it, notably Ravenna and Venice, southern Italy and Sicily. In Ravenna and Venice, in churches like S. Vitale and S. Mark's, there are close reflections of the architecture of Constantinople, which even assist in visualising what has been lost in Constantinople itself. In southern Italy and Sicily the characteristics of the architecture of Constantinople were more subject to influences from elsewhere – Norman, Lombard, even Western Islamic – and were sometimes so modified by them that little remained of the style beyond the use of mosaic and certain details of decoration.

The third is Western church architecture influenced either directly or indirectly by that of Constantinople. This is considered in later chapters.

Secular Architecture

The secular building undertaken by Constantine, both in Rome and Constantinople, almost certainly was more extensive than his new church building. Similarly, Justinian embarked upon more secular than church work. A large proportion of it was for defence. With the general decline of city life after the sixth century the amount of non-ecclesiastical work must have diminished greatly, possibly more than did the building of new churches. But it did not end. For instance, new palaces and many new monasteries were built.

Since, even in Justinian's time, there appears to have been little significant development compared with the late Roman period, little needs to be added here, apart from observing that certain forms fell out of favour and that the resemblances between church architecture and the types of secular architecture on which it had been modelled remained close, except for the obvious differences in furnishing.

It has already been noted that the Byzantine empire had little use for the theatre and still less for the amphitheatre. The chief place for public entertainment was the hippodrome, virtually identical with the Roman circus. This also became the chief place of public assembly and the place where, in the capital, the emperor confronted the people in his special box. Baths continued to be built in much the same manner as before, and in fact the new baths erected much later by the Turkish conquerors still followed the Roman pattern. Works of civil engineering, such as aqueducts and reservoirs, also reflected Roman precedent, though Constantinople was provided with more underground cisterns than any previous city, and a characteristic form was developed for these with brick groin-vaulted roofs carried on long parallel rows of columns.

Byzantine domestic architecture has been studied far less than that of Rome and its provinces, but if it was significantly different from the latter it was almost certainly because of a regression in the standards of accommodation and construction. There are no Byzantine examples to compare with the insulae and separate houses of Rome, Ostia, Herculaneum and Pompeii, and this cannot be attributed to more widespread destruction. The older monasteries show that the living quarters had to be rebuilt periodically or were at least extensively restored, so that little remains of the early construction. The more soundly constructed, later palace-architecture, although in ruins, shows considerable Western influence.

Examples

Early Christian Religious Architecture

Though the examples under this sub-heading are chiefly those defined earlier as Early Christian, it is convenient to include with them a few examples of the continued use of similar forms in the time of Justinian and later. As the categories of church, commemorative structure or martyrium and covered cemetery overlap they are grouped together, leaving only mausolea and baptisteries for separate consideration.

Churches, Commemorative Structures and Covered Cemeteries

The **Lateran Basilica (S. Giovanni in Laterano) Rome** (*c.* 313–20) (p. 289B), was Constantine's first church commission in Rome. Erected on the eastern outskirts of the city on the site of a former military barracks, it was built as the cathedral of the Bishop of Rome. It was later remodelled several times, notably by Borromini in the seventeenth century, and again in the nineteenth century. Enough of the fourth-century church has survived at foundation level and in the form of earlier records to permit a precise reconstruction. It was a basilica with a wide central nave terminating in an apse, double aisles at each side (of which the inner were taller than the outer), and shallowly projecting wings which cut short the ends of the outer aisles and probably served a purpose similar to that of modern sacristies. The tall nave colonnades carried horizontal entablatures and those of the lower aisles carried arcades. There were no galleries. Early records speak of gilt roofs or ceilings, silver altars, and silver and gold candlesticks as well as coloured marble columns and wall-facings – all contrasting strongly with what must have been a very plain exterior.

Closely contemporary with the Lateran Basilica were a number of new cathedral churches elsewhere which are known only from excavations or descriptions. Among these, the **Cathedral of Tyre** (consecrated 316 or 317) shows that, even outside the part of the empire then under Constantine's jurisdiction, a very similar basilican form could be adopted. According to Eusebius, this church had only two aisles, but his description refers also to an atrium with a fountain in its centre, approached from the street through a monumental propylaeum.

If the emphasis placed upon it by Eusebius may be taken as a guide, the **Church of the Holy Sepulchre, Jerusalem** (p. 289E), was Constantine's most important church foundation in the East. Its present form is the result of several major reconstructions and adaptations, most notably in the twelfth century by the Crusaders who built the Gothic choir and the tall entrance facade on one side. Recent excavations have done much to clarify its original form, which was not fully achieved until near the end of the fourth century. It consisted of several related structures: the **Anastasis Rotunda** rising over the tomb; a porticoed court embracing, in one corner, the Rock of Calvary; the **Memorial** or **Martyrium Basilica**, serving also as the cathedral; and an outer atrium. This last – irregular in shape because of the nature of the site and the pre-existing structures on it – was approached from the street, as in Tyre, through a propylaeum. The basilica was shorter in relation to its width and had galleries as well as double aisles on each side. The precise form at the altar end is not yet fully established. In his description, Eusebius refers to its being 'encircled by twelve columns', and it is possible that they were set rather tightly against the curved wall of the apse, like those in the apses of the basilica at Leptis Magna. Another possibility is that they belonged to the altar ciborium.

Somewhat similar, but simpler because there was only a single holy site to be enclosed, was the parallel Constantinian foundation of the **Church of the Nativity, Bethlehem** (p. 289D). This was rebuilt in the latter part of the sixth century, and the present basilica dates essentially from that rebuilding. It terminates in a large triconch arrangement, comprising a central apse and two similar apsidal transept arms, below which is the Grotto of the Nativity. The nave and aisles of the original basilica probably did not differ greatly from the present ones, but, in place of the triconch termination, they opened into a large octagon, probably with a conical roof, over the grotto.

Back in Rome, Constantine undertook the construction of his largest work of this kind, to commemorate the principal apostle and honour his tomb. This was the **Basilica of S. Peter** (*c.* 320–330) (p. 289A). Again the church that is seen today is a rebuilding, in this case to a totally different design and on a substantially enlarged scale. The original church survived without much change until towards the end of the fifteenth century, however, and the nave for almost another century, and there are ample remains of its foundations below the present floor as well as numerous sixteenth-century drawings to give a full picture of its form (p. 291A). Only the details of the atrium are not certain.

The church was constructed over a cemetery which extended along one side of an earlier circus; since there was a considerable slope, one side was constructed above the tombs of the cemetery and the other side cut into the hill. A ciborium-like canopy, whose barley-sugar twisted columns are now set into the great piers that carry Michelangelo's dome, was erected over the tomb believed to be that of S. Peter. A broad raised platform, or bema, extended to each side of this, and an apse projected behind it (westwards, on account of the topography of the site). In front stretched the basilica, some 64 m (210 ft) wide with its double aisles on each side, and some 90 m (295 ft) long, not counting the bema and apse. Twenty-two huge antique columns, varying in size and colour and with equally varied capitals, supported the nave walls on a horizontal entablature as in the Lateran Basilica, while similar numbers of shorter columns carrying arcades divided aisle from aisle.

S. Peter's seems to have differed from the churches considered hitherto in having had, originally, no permanent altar. The reason for this is that a second function of the church, and probably the chief justification for its size, was to serve as a covered cemetery. Bema, as well as nave and aisles, would normally have been given over to pilgrims and to those coming to commemorate their own dead. The floor was carpeted with graves, and records refer to funeral banquets being held over them as late as 400. The funerary character of the structure is also attested by the large mausolea attached to one side.

The covered cemetery of **S. Agnese, Rome** (*c.* 340 onwards) (p. 289C), is one of several more normal representatives of this type of architecture. Part of it survives, situated between the sixth-century church of the same name and the mausoleum of **S. Costanza**, and the plan – of the typical form already referred to – has been more fully disclosed by excavation. Of the other similar structures, that of **S. Sebastiano** (probably begun *c.* 313) seems to have been the first, and is the one whose exterior is most crowded by separate mausolea. These structures were built over catacombs containing the tomb that gave the site its special significance, but not directly over the tomb itself, to which there was separate access. When it became desirable to improve this access and provide more accommodation for pilgrims, the tomb was exposed by excavation and another basilica built over it. Where the nave was below ground level, it was provided with a gallery, as in the later church of S. Agnese (625–38) and at S. Lorenzo (579–90) (p. 291B).

EARLY BASILICAS: ROME AND THE HOLY LAND

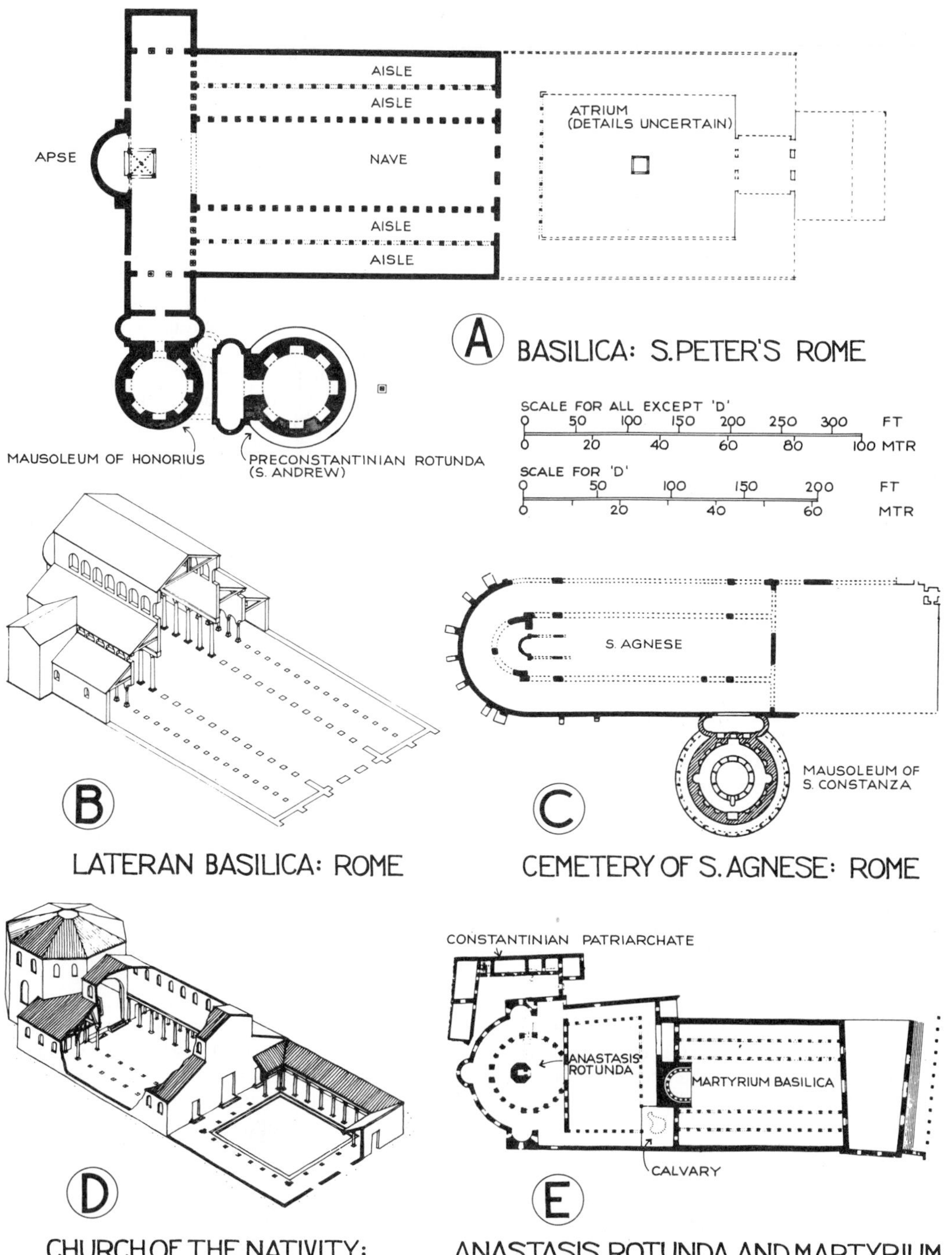

(A) BASILICA: S.PETER'S ROME

(B) LATERAN BASILICA: ROME

(C) CEMETERY OF S.AGNESE: ROME

(D) CHURCH OF THE NATIVITY: BETHLEHEM

(E) ANASTASIS ROTUNDA AND MARTYRIUM BASILICA: JERUSALEM

Two other Constantinian foundations are known only from descriptions and from later structures modelled on them. The **Church of the Holy Apostles, Constantinople** (*c.* 335), seems to have been built partly as Constantine's own mausoleum but also to provide his new capital with its own martyrium as a counterpart to those of Rome and the Holy Land. It was cross-shaped in plan, with the four arms focused on a crossing space in which symbolic stele were erected to represent the apostles. Round it was a large court. The **Golden Octagon, Antioch** (*c.* 330), was the cathedral of the city which, after Jerusalem, was the principal Christian centre in this part of the empire. Apart from its octagonal plan, it is known to have had both a continuous two-storey ambulatory and exedrae, though it is not clear whether the exedrae opened directly off the central octagon, which probably had a pyramidal timber roof, gilt inside and perhaps outside as the name indicates.

S. Stefano Rotondo, Rome (468–83) (pp. 293E,294A), was the only subsequent major church in the old capital to depart from the rectangular basilican form. It has already been briefly described. There was probably a light conical roof over the central space: the columns below could not have carried a heavy dome, and some stabilisation was necessary later, when the transverse arcade was added. Though the interior is now largely bare, there are indications of rich marble revetments on the walls.

Other fifth-century churches in Rome, while keeping to the rectangular basilican plan, introduced a new and more classical refinement into the design as may be seen today, despite some remodellings and the loss of much original wall decoration, in the churches of **S. Sabina** (422–32) (p. 292) on the Aventine and, more particularly, **S. Maria Maggiore** (*c.* 432–40) (p. 296A). The columns and capitals are now closely matched – Corinthian in S. Sabina and Ionic in S. Maria Maggiore, the latter carrying a straight entablature. Above this entablature there remains a fine series of original mosaic panels depicting scenes from the Old Testament, complemented by others of the childhood of Christ above the arch of the apse. Their narrative manner is reminiscent of that of the sculptured friezes on earlier triumphal arches and columns. The apse itself, the ciborium over the altar, the nave ceiling, and the whole exterior are of considerably later date. But the exterior of S. Sabina does largely retain its original character, reminiscent of the plain brickwork, relieved by little more than the rhythmic pattern of the windows, of Constantine's basilica in Trier.

S. Lorenzo, Milan (*c.* 378) (p. 293F), may perhaps be regarded as the first Western counterpart – in what was at the time the effective capital in the West – of Constantine's Golden Octagon in Antioch. It is basically square in plan, opened out by exedrae and surrounded by a two-storey ambulatory. Sufficient exists of the original structure beneath remodellings in the twelfth and sixteenth centuries to show that there were always towers over the four corners of the outer square, suggesting that the central square may originally have been roofed by a groined vault. In front of the original narthex was an atrium, approached through a colonnade which still survives. Grouped around the church are several subsidiary octagonal structures which, alone, retain their original marble and mosaic decorations.

S. Nazaro, Milan, was originally built as the **Church of the Holy Apostles** (*c.* 382) (p. 293G) in deliberate emulation of Constantine's church of the same name at Constantinople. It differs in that the cross consisted here of a long aisle-less nave from which two arms projected and were partly cut off by colonnades. The altar-shrine was in the centre of the cross, so each arm of the cross again focused on it.

This cross plan reappeared, for similar reasons and with local variations, in the original **S. Croce, Ravenna** (*c.* 425), in the first church of **S. John, Ephesus** (*c.* 450), and in the great **Martyrium of S. Simeon Stylites, Kalat Siman** (*c.* 480–90) (p. 293J), though this has an octagonal rather than a square core whose diagonal sides are expanded in a manner not unlike that seen in S. Lorenzo, Milan. In the very centre was the saint's column, and it seems likely that this was left open to the sky as it had previously been. Each arm of the cross was now given greater width by means of aisles, and there are triple apses at the end of the eastern arm. A large group of buildings surrounded the martyrium itself for such purposes as the reception of pilgrims and for baptisms. Construction is in the fine ashlar typical of this eastern Mediterranean region, and the carved decoration, which emphasises the structural lines of arch, doorway, column or pilaster, is as evident on the exterior as on the interior.

This is also true of the many simple basilican churches of the region, a good representative of which is that of **Qalb Lozeh** (late fifth century). Whereas aisled basilicas in other parts of the empire always had their aisles separated from the nave by colonnades, here the division is achieved by more substantial arcades carried on widely spaced piers, three to each side.

The **Martyrium of S. Philip, Hierapolis** (modern Pamukkale, early fifth century) (p. 294B), was an earlier example, on a similarly large scale, of a building with an octagonal core, though here all eight sides of the octagon were opened out in the same manner to form radiating arms. The resulting star form was then enclosed within a larger square containing the rooms for the reception of pilgrims, and there were secondary triangular spaces with lobed corners, probably used as chapels, in the left-over spaces between the radiating arms.

The **Cathedral, Bosra** (512) (p. 293H), was one of a number of early sixth-century, fully centralised

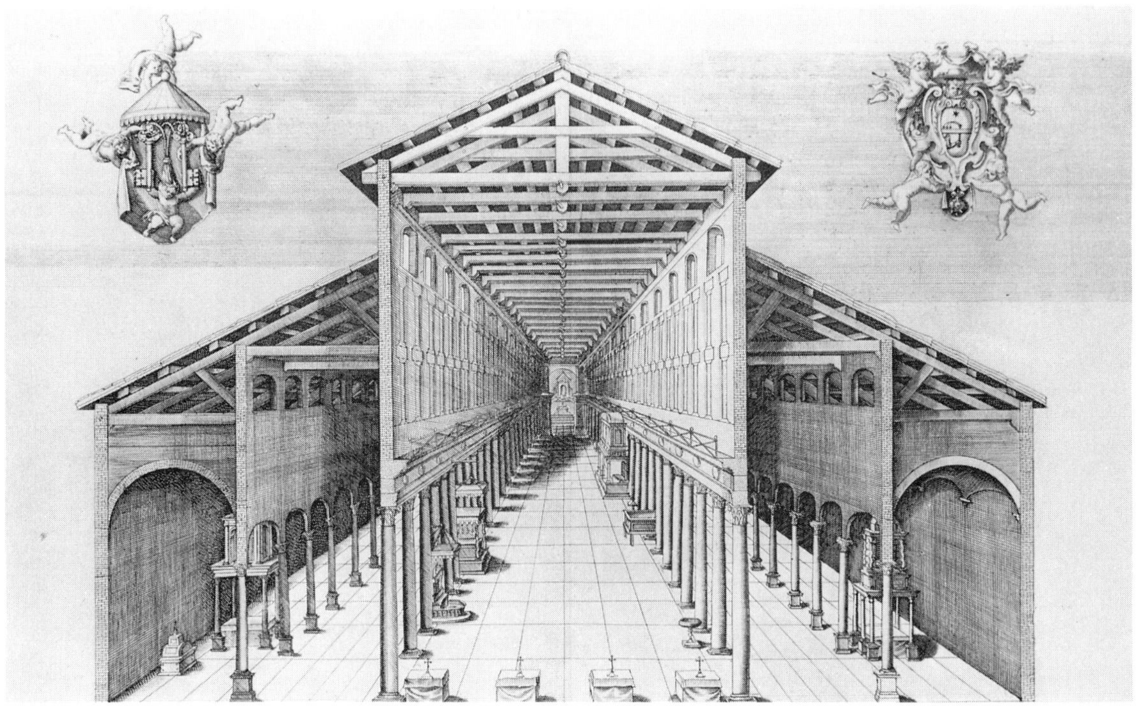

A. S. Peter's, Rome, in the sixteenth century. See p.288

B. S. Lorenzo fuori le Mura, Rome, looking from the thirteenth-century nave towards the sixth-century church over the saint's tomb. See pp.288, 295

A. The basilican church of S. Sabina, Rome (422–32). See p.290

B. S. Sabina, Rome: interior

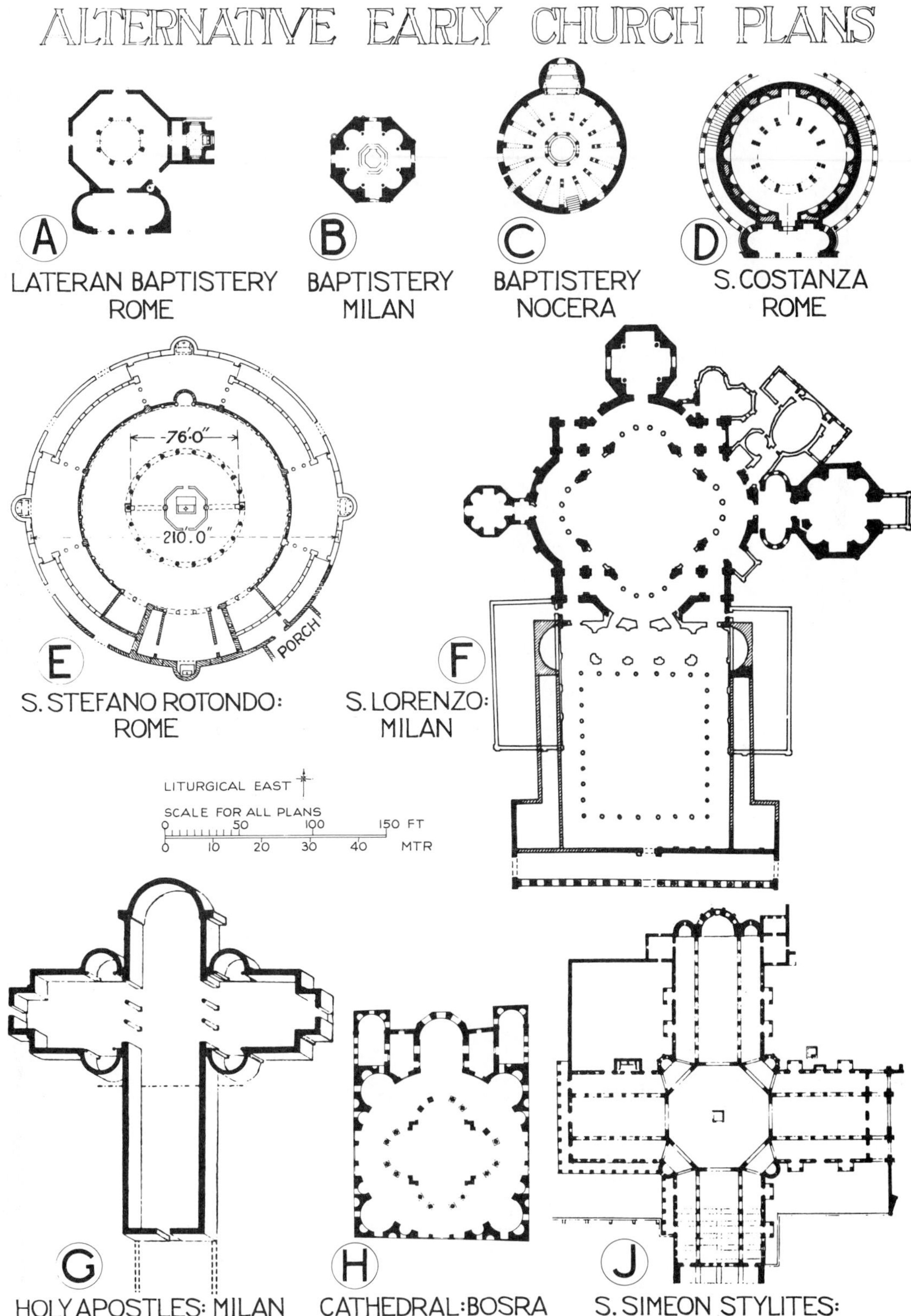
ALTERNATIVE EARLY CHURCH PLANS
A
LATERAN BAPTISTERY
ROME
B
BAPTISTERY
MILAN
C
BAPTISTERY
NOCERA
D
S. COSTANZA
ROME
76'0"
210.0"
PORCH
E
S. STEFANO ROTONDO:
ROME
F
S. LORENZO:
MILAN
LITURGICAL EAST
SCALE FOR ALL PLANS
0 50 100 150 FT
0 10 20 30 40 MTR
G
HOLY APOSTLES: MILAN
H
CATHEDRAL: BOSRA
J
S. SIMEON STYLITES:

A. S. Stefano Rotondo, Rome (468–83): interior. See p.290

C. East church, Alahan Manastir (late fifth century). See p.295

B. Martyrium of S., Philip, Hierapolis (early fifth century). See p.290

D. The basilican church of S. Apollinare in Classe, Ravenna (*c.* 534–49). See p.295

E. Monastery of S. Simeon, Aswan (fourth century onwards). See p.295

cathedrals and martyria in Arabia, Syria and Mesopotamia which, like S. Lorenzo in Milan, had a central square expanded by exedrae and surrounded by an ambulatory. The cathedral at Bosra differed from others in having further exedra-like projections from the ambulatory, the whole being enclosed in a square outer wall, interrupted only by three projecting apses at the east. There does not appear to have been a gallery, and the original method of roofing the central space is uncertain.

The **East church, Alahan Manastir** (late fifth century) (p. 294C), is the best preserved of a number of Cilician basilican churches in which a special emphasis was given to a square bay at the east of the nave, just in front of the apse. This bay rose as a low tower above the main roof level. Corner squinches at this level at Alahan suggest there was a timber roof of octagonal pyramidal form. More significant than the precise shape, however, is the combination of a longitudinal plan with an almost central tower which was placed above some of the principal action of the liturgy, thus creating a strong vertical secondary axis.

S. Demetrius, Salonika (original construction late fifth century), **S.Apollinare Nuovo, Ravenna** (late fifth century), and **S. Apollinare in Classe, Ravenna** (*c.* 534–49) (pp. 294D,296B), are contemporary and slightly later examples of the simple basilican form. The first was a martyrium church built over part of a Roman bath which was incorporated as a crypt beneath the transept-like east end. Apart from this it probably differed little, except in size and architectural detail, from the double-aisled and galleried Martyrium Basilica in Jerusalem. Some of the capitals of the nave arcades (which have survived two rebuildings after serious fires, the most recent in 1917) are early examples of the wind-blown acanthus type. A few mosaics also still exist, but these are later than the original church. The Ravenna churches are of the single-aisled type without galleries which was more usual in Italy, and they are particularly notable for their early mosaics. In S. Apollinare Nuovo, processions of male and female saints and martyrs advance along the two nave walls above the arcades towards figures of an enthroned Christ and the Virgin and Child next to the apse, emphasising the strong longitudinal axis. Above them, and between the windows, are set narrative panels of the life of Christ. The interior of S. Apollinare in Classe is particularly spacious and well proportioned, though it has been somewhat changed from the original by the raising of the floor of the apse to create a crypt. There are fine mosaics also in the apse and on the arch in front of it, and externally there is a fine detached campanile, with graduated numbers of window openings in the successive storeys.

Many further examples were to be found throughout the empire. In the more remote areas, local traditions were understandably more in evidence, even where there was imperial sponsorship as at the **Church of the Virgin, S. Catherine's Monastery, Mount Sinai** (*c.* 540 onwards) (p. 298A). This church, set within what is really a fortress, is of the simplest stone construction, though it has the oldest extant timber trussed roof, which must have been fabricated elsewhere. It contains, perfectly preserved, the finest apse mosaic of the period, portraying the Trans-figuration and clearly made by craftsmen despatched from Constantinople. Much further south, the **Monastery of S. Simeon, Aswan** (fourth century onwards) (p. 294E), also virtually a fortress with its enclosing wall, is largely built of mud brick with vaulting almost identical with that seen in some Egyptian structures thousands of years before.

Before passing from these truly Early Christian structures to later instances of the basilican form, it should also be noted that, from the early fifth century onwards, there were increasingly numerous conversions or adaptations of earlier structures built for other uses. Initially these were buildings other than temples, but they did include temples after pagan worship had been prohibited. With a building like the **Pantheon, Rome**, converted in 610 to the church of **S. Maria ad Martyres**, no structural change was called for. In the early fifth-century conversion of a rotunda of the **Palace of Galerius, Salonika**, into what later became known as the church of S. George, an apse was broken through at the east, an encircling ambulatory and narthex were added, and the dome was decorated with mosaics of martyrs set within architectural frames. The cellas of temples of the usual rectangular plan could be adapted as readily as the Pantheon. Sometimes a smaller new structure was built within the cella, or the outer columns of the peristyle were filled in to make new outer walls, and the existing walls of the cella were broken through, thereby creating a larger aisled interior. This was done in 640 at the **Temple of Athena, Syracuse**, to create the present Cathedral.

S. Clemente, Rome (early twelfth century) (p. 297), is the most interesting of many examples of the continued Roman use of the early basilican plan until well into the Romanesque period. In its present form it dates from a rebuilding undertaken in *c.* 1110–30. This largely follows the plan of the earlier church (*c.* 380), a substantial proportion of which still exists below its floor, though the width was reduced in the rebuilding. Most of the details, including the fine marble floor and the mosaics, cannot, of course, be described as Early Christian, but the furnishings from the early church, remarkably complete and well preserved, were reused. They give one of the best present-day impressions of the original character of such furnishings.

The late sixth-century church of **S. Lorenzo, Rome** (p. 291B), erected over the saint's tomb, was, on the other hand, extended rather than rebuilt at the beginning of the thirteenth century. This was done by

A. The basilican church of S. Maria Maggiore, Rome (432, with later alterations). See p.290

B. S. Apollinare in Classe, Ravenna: nave looking east. See p.295

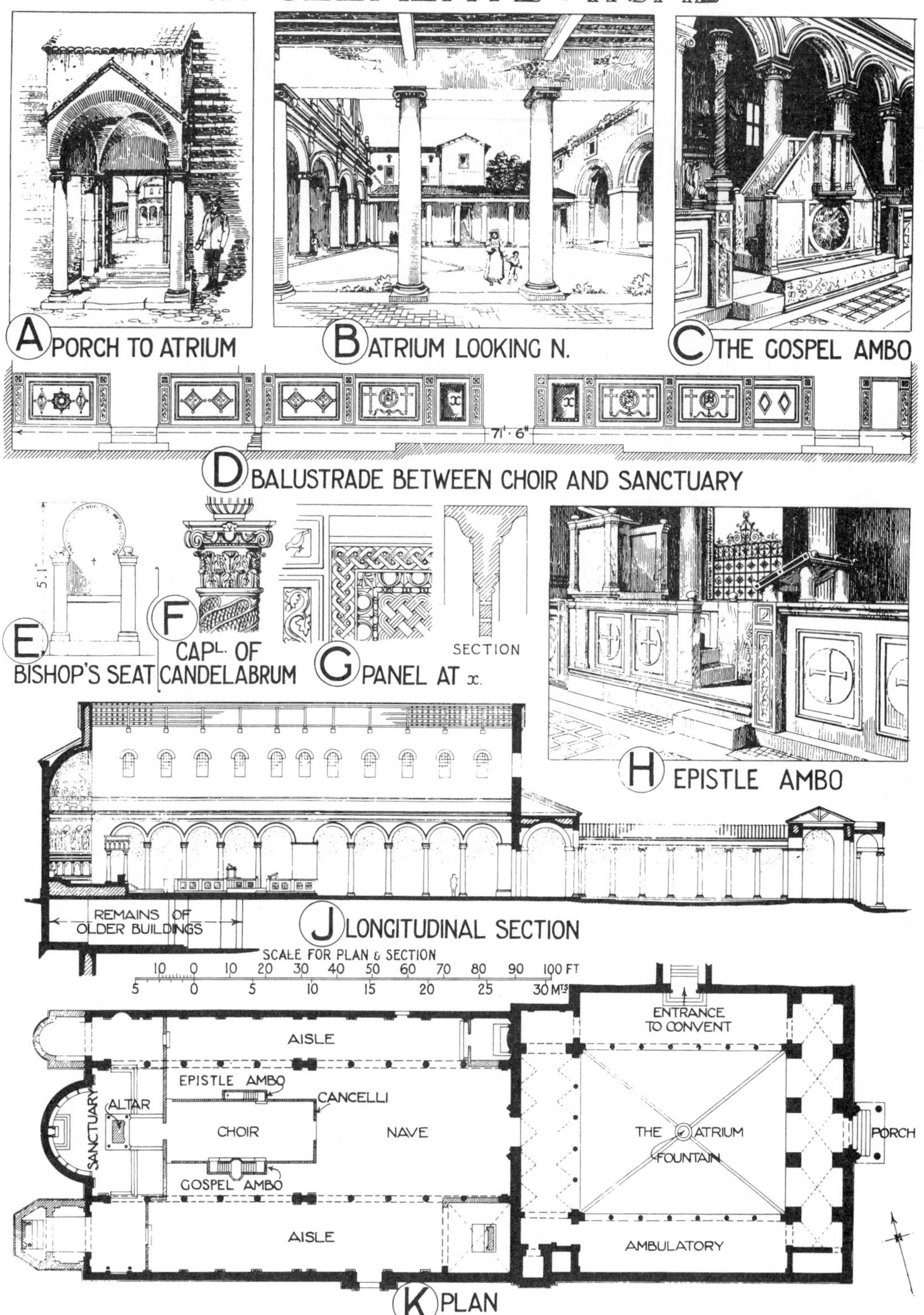
S. CLEMENTE : ROME
A PORCH TO ATRIUM
B ATRIUM LOOKING N.
C THE GOSPEL AMBO
71'·6"
D BALUSTRADE BETWEEN CHOIR AND SANCTUARY
5'·1"
E. BISHOP'S SEAT
F CAPL. OF CANDELABRUM
SECTION
G PANEL AT x.
H EPISTLE AMBO
REMAINS OF OLDER BUILDINGS
J LONGITUDINAL SECTION
SCALE FOR PLAN & SECTION
10 0 10 20 30 40 50 60 70 80 90 100 FT
5 0 5 10 15 20 25 30 MTS
ENTRANCE TO CONVENT
AISLE
EPISTLE AMBO
CANCELLI
ALTAR
SANCTUARY
CHOIR
NAVE
THE ATRIUM
FOUNTAIN
PORCH
GOSPEL AMBO
AISLE
AMBULATORY
K PLAN

A. S. Catherine's Monastery, Mount Sinai (mid-sixth century). See p.295

B. S. Sergius, Old Cairo, showing the Coptic Good Friday Service. See p.299

C. Columns from S. Polyeuktos, Constantinople, now outside S. Mark's, Venice. See p.299

demolishing its apse and adding a new basilican-plan nave in its place. The earlier church then became the chancel, with a new raised floor over what had been its nave to make good the difference in floor levels and to house a crypt below it. The galleries were allowed to remain, though they had lost their *raison d'être*.

The **Cathedral, Torcello** (largely *c.* 1008, but *c.* 1259 in its final form) (p. 316B), shows the survival of a basilican plan through several enlargements. Its interior has a superb spatial quality achieved by very simple means, given scale by a fine marble screen across the chancel, and even by the tie beams that run across both nave and aisles. It is further enhanced by colour and the play of light which enters as much through the windows of the aisles as through the clerestory. The apse holds the bishop's raised throne and is lined with mosaics of a standing Virgin and Child above rows of apostles, and the whole west wall is filled by a huge mosaic of the Last Judgement.

S. Sergius, Old Cairo (crypt probably fifth or sixth century, present church probably largely reconstructed in the eleventh century on an earlier plan) (p. 298B) shows the continued use of the basilican plan in a country long under Muslim rule. The church is a normal single-aisled basilica with narthex and gallery over this. But it has the added interests of showing considerable Islamic influence in its decoration and having the later form of a tall solid screen – or iconostasis – running across both nave and aisles and separating completely the area open to the congregation from the sanctuary and pastophoria. Beyond this screen can be seen the dome of the altar ciborium. After the Muslim conquest, churches in Upper Egypt were frequently multidomed like contempoary mosques.

Mausolea

S. Costanza, Rome (*c.* 350) (pp. 293D, 301A), subsequently converted to a church, was built as the mausoleum of Constantine's daughter Constantia. It is of the common earlier circular form, except that the central domed circular space is completely surrounded by an ambulatory with an annular barrel vault. The dome is carried by an arched colonnade of coupled columns with separate Corinthian capitals linked by deep common impost blocks. The whole aisle vault still has its original mosaic decoration, largely of geometric motifs and intertwined vines. More specifically Christian subjects originally appeared in the recess next to the sarcophagus and in the dome. Elsewhere there was the usual multicoloured marble revetment.

The small **Tomb of Galla Placidia, Ravenna** (*c.* 425), was attached to one end of the narthex of the original church of S. Croce referred to above. Like the church, it is cross-shaped in plan. Over the crossing rises a low square tower, terminating in a dome with merging pendentives (p. 309A). The whole of the vault surfaces are covered in mosaic and the walls below in marble. Sarcophagi still stand in the three shorter arms of the cross.

The **Tomb of Theodoric, Ravenna** (*c.* 526), is a two-storey structure of which the lower (externally decagonal) storey is, in effect, a crypt with a cruciform vault of fine ashlar. The principal storey is circular inside and is roofed by a unique single slab of stone, its under-surface cut in the shape of a shallow dome with the vestiges of a mosaic cross.

Baptisteries

The present **Lateran Baptistery, Rome** (*c.* 432–40) (p. 293A), is a remodelling of the original building alongside the Constantinian basilica, and has itself been subject to further change in the sixteenth and seventeenth centuries. The octagonal plan of the original baptistery has been preserved. The font filled the central space between the columns, which probably supported a timber roof. The original **Cathedral Baptistery, Milan** (*c.* 350 or 380) (p. 293B), was also octagonal, but with niches corresponding to the eight sides and the whole interior open to the central font.

The **Orthodox Baptistery, Ravenna** (*c.* 400 and *c.* 450), is a smaller structure in which the dome (constructed of hollow tubes) springs directly from the octagonal outer walls, leaving an unobstructed space around the font. It is particularly notable for the preservation of nearly all its internal decoration of marble, painted stucco, and mosaic.

The **Baptistery of S. Maria Maggiore, Nocera** (probably sixth century) (p. 293C), also has the font in the centre, but otherwise is much closer to the mausoleum of S. Costanza in form, especially in its ring of coupled columns supporting the central dome.

Byzantine Religious Architecture of the time of Justinian

These examples illustrate the use of the dome in the early formative stage of Byzantine architecture, sometimes over an octagonal bay as previously, but more significantly over a square bay.

S. Polyeuktos, Constantinople (524–7), may have been the first large-scale example of a church with a domed nave, perhaps broadly resembling the East church, Alahan Manastir, in having a similar emphasis on a square eastern bay. Unfortunately the recent excavations of the platform on which it stood provided no grounds for a firm reconstruction of the superstructure. They showed merely that it was an aisled basilica whose plan was a square with 52 m (170 ft) sides, and that it was preceded by a narthex approached up a broad flight of steps from the direction of the palace of its founder, Anicia Juliana. The rich diversity of decorative motifs on the surviving marble columns (p. 298C), cornices and so on has already been mentioned above.

SS. Sergius and Bacchus, Constantinople (possibly begun *c.* 527, completed before 536) (p. 308E), was a much more modest structure, but has survived largely intact, though its dome can hardly be the original one. Its plan is a development of the tetraconch form with surrounding ambulatory which had been seen at places as far apart as Milan and Bosra, and may have had a precursor in Constantine's Golden Octagon. An octagonal core is expanded on the four diagonal sides by exedrae, and the east and west sides are open, respectively, to the chancel and towards a narthex. There is a gallery over the ambulatory. The church was commissioned by Justinian to stand alongside the palace he occupied before becoming emperor, and there is a strong likelihood that it served, in part, as one model for the design of Hagia Sophia. There is a remarkable lack of geometric precision in its setting out, though this may have resulted partly from the nature of the site and the prior existence of other buildings to which the church was joined. Inside, beneath Turkish whitewash, the fine carved detail of capitals and frieze is still visible. The building is now a mosque and the furnishings are those appropriate to this use.

Hagia Sophia, Constantinople (532–7) with later partial reconstructions and additions) (pp. 301B–305), was Justinian's principal commission. The dedication to Hagia Sophia (Divine Wisdom) was really a dedication to Christ, and the church was also known simply as Megale Ecclesia (Great Church). It stood on the site of two earlier churches at one end of the ancient acropolis, alongside the principal square of the city – the Augusteion – and only a short distance from the imperial palace. The first church, founded by Constantius, was dedicated in 360 and burnt in 404. It was rebuilt under Theodosius II, rededicated in 415, and burnt in the Nika riot of January 532. Both these churches, were, almost certainly, basilicas with double aisles and galleries like the Martyrium Basilica in Jerusalem and S. Demetrius in Salonika, though larger than either. The second church, at least, was preceded by an atrium that was entered through a monumental propylaeum. As Constantinople increased in importance and its bishop became the patriarch of a large part of the Eastern Church, Hagia Sophia became not only the cathedral but also the patriarchal church.

Justinian's church was designed by Anthemius of Tralles and Isidorous of Miletus – men with a deep knowledge of the mechanical science of the day who are referred to, not as architects, but as *mechanicoi* or *mechanopoioi*. That science was, however, more akin to the geometry of today than to the science of the modern engineer, and it is the masterly geometric ordering of the space and the vaults that cover it that is most apparent from a detailed study of the design. Statically, the design was not completely successful, because the dome partly collapsed barely 30 years after completion and had to be rebuilt to a modified design. But that collapse was at least partly attributable to the great speed of erection, far exceeding that of any comparable later structure, and to an unusual sequence of earthquakes in the intervening years. It is also necessary to bear in mind that the design went far beyond previously proven practice.

The main body of the church is enclosed within a rectangle almost 70 m (230 ft) wide and 75 m (245 ft) long, with a projecting apse at the east end and double narthexes preceded by an atrium at the west end. In the centre of this is a square whose sides measure exactly 100 Byzantine feet (31.2 m). Over it sits the dome, carried on pendentives which bridge between great semicircular arches carried on piers standing just outside the square. Other piers face these piers across the aisles to help resist the outward thrusts of the dome to north and south. To the east and west the arrangement is different, and was even more novel than the use of pendentives to convert the central square to a circle. Here, butting against the transverse arches that carry the dome, are two semidomes equal in diameter to the dome itself and carried partly by further piers set against the outer east and west walls. These piers finally take the thrusts to east and west, but at a lower level where they are potentially less damaging. Below the semidomes are great hemicycles that double the east–west extent of the nave. Between the main piers and the secondary piers just referred to, these hemicycles open into smaller semicircular exedrae similar to those in earlier tetraconch churches. Single aisles run from end to end at each side (p. 305), narrowed somewhat by the main masses of the piers and narrowed further by pairs of inward projections from the piers that have been shown to be additions to the original design made at a late stage of construction when the horizontal forces generated above had begun to push the piers aside in an alarming way. Because of the presence of the great hemicycles and the exedrae at the east and west, their inner boundaries are very different in their different bays. They communicate at the west with the inner narthex. Above them and above the inner narthex are similarly shaped galleries.

Partly to carry the aisle and gallery vaults, arched colonnades run between the piers around the nave, and further columns stand within the aisles and galleries. All have monolithic shafts, encircled at top and bottom by bronze collars where, in classical columns, there would have been integral projecting neckings. The shafts within the aisles and galleries are of white Proconnesian marble; those around the

A. S. Costanza, Rome (Piranesi) (*c.* 350). See p.299

B. S. Sophia, Constantinople, from SW (532–7). The minarets are a Turkish addition. See pp.300, 306

S. Sophia, Constantinople: interior looking towards apse. See pp.300, 306

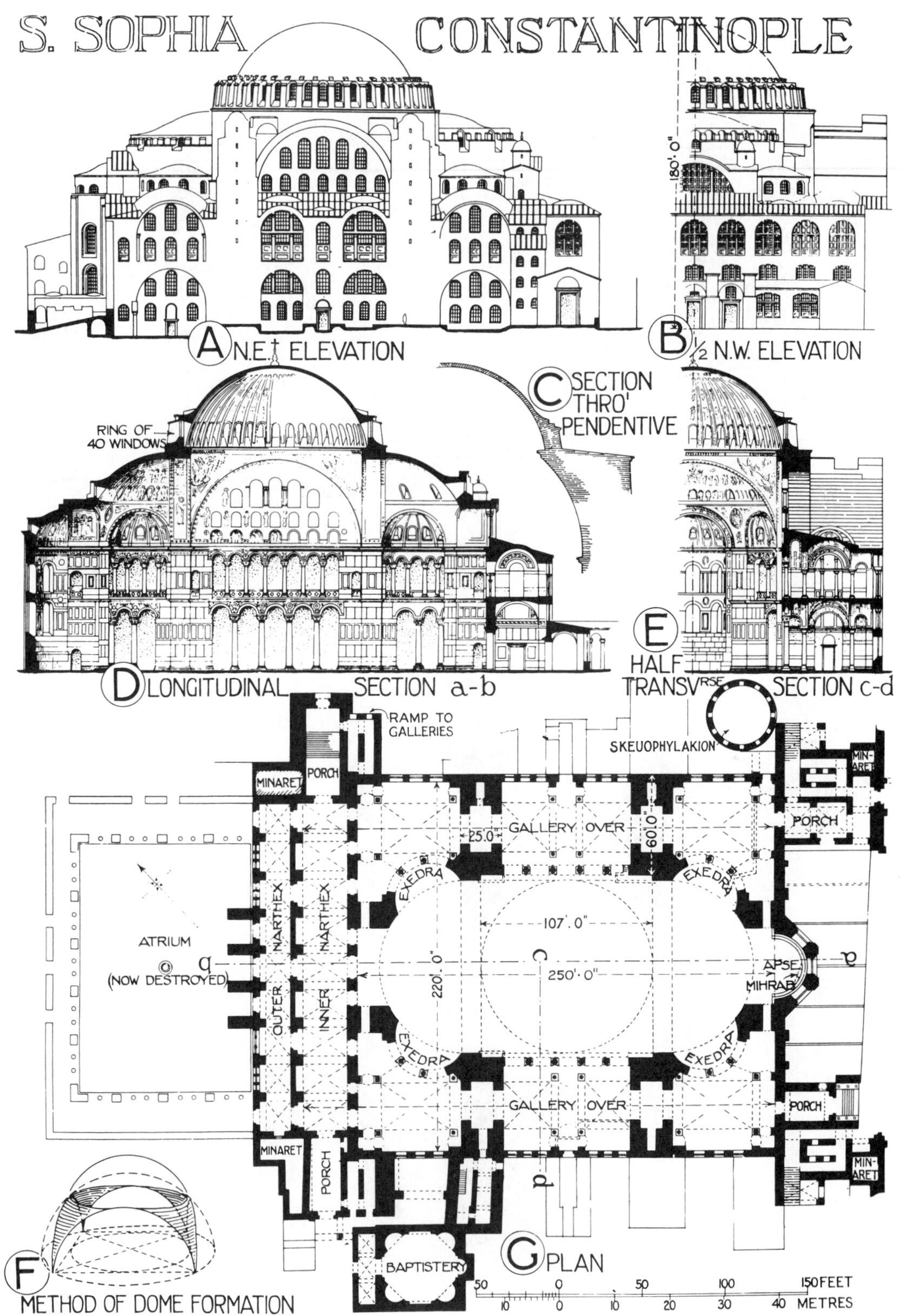
S. SOPHIA CONSTANTINOPLE
A N.E. ELEVATION
B ½ N.W. ELEVATION
180'. 0"
C SECTION THRO' PENDENTIVE
RING OF 40 WINDOWS
D LONGITUDINAL SECTION a-b
E HALF TRANSVRSE SECTION c-d
RAMP TO GALLERIES
SKEUOPHYLAKION
MINARET
PORCH
MIN-ARET
GALLERY OVER
25.0"
60.0"
EXEDRA
107'. 0"
ATRIUM
(NOW DESTROYED)
OUTER NARTHEX
INNER NARTHEX
220'. 0"
250'. 0"
APSE
MIHRAB
BAPTISTERY
G PLAN
F METHOD OF DOME FORMATION
50 0 50 100 150 FEET
10 0 10 20 30 40 METRES

A. S. Sophia, Constantinople: column capital, pilaster capital and soffit decoration. See pp.300, 306

B. S. Sophia: north side of nave

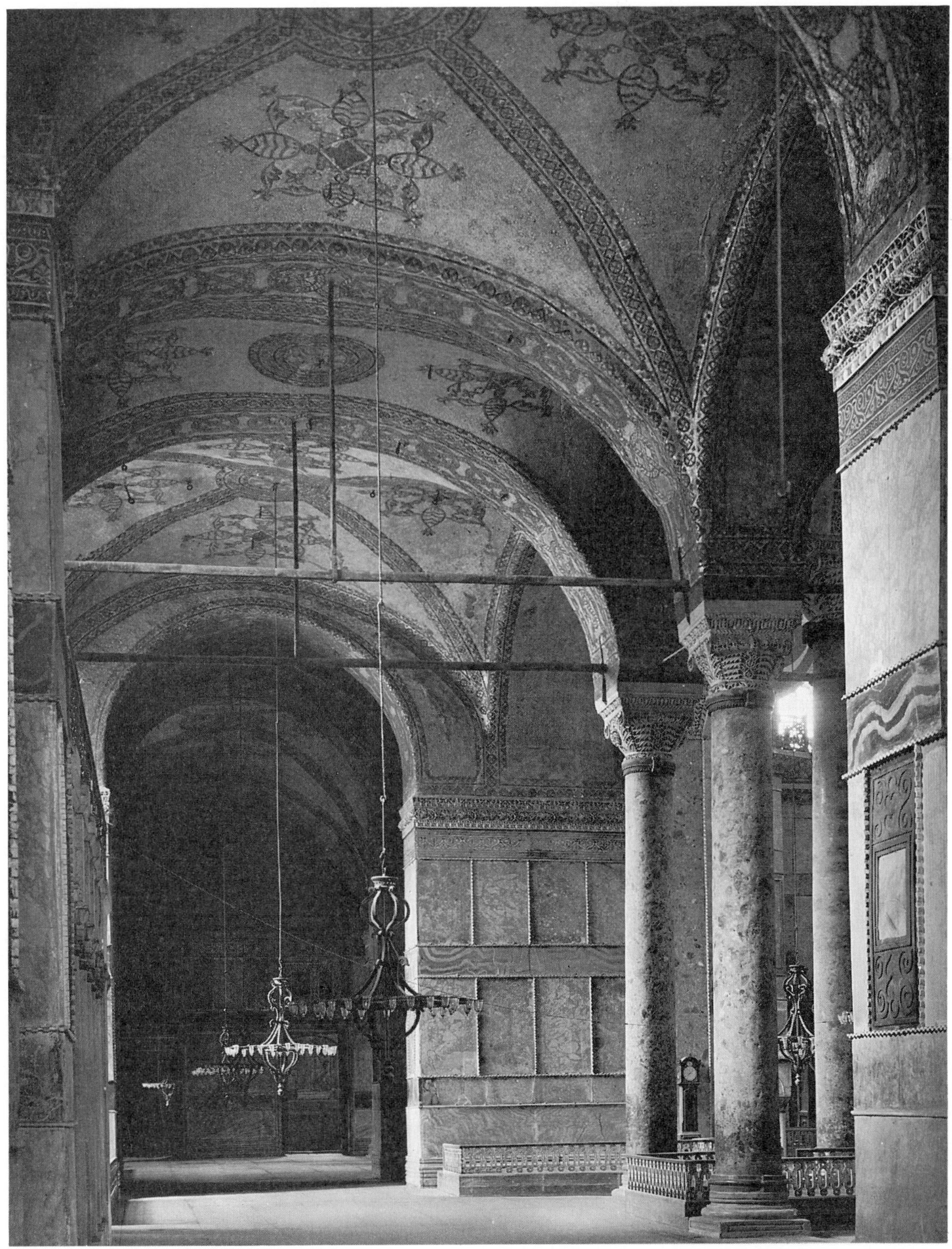

S. Sophia, Constantinople: north aisle, looking east. See pp.300, 306

nave are of green Thessalian marble or red porphyry, the latter only in the exedrae at ground level. They carry superb capitals of several different designs, all of which incorporate integral impost blocks. These capitals, as well as the carved cornices and similar features, were clearly cut for the purpose. So were most of the shafts, despite significant variations in size and the legends of provenance from earlier temples. But the porphyry shafts vary more in size than the others and do seem to have been reused. The arrangements are similar at the two levels, except that the colonnades that run around the nave at gallery level – both the straight central colonnades and the curved ones around the exedrae – are not only lower than those below, as might be expected, but have more columns and closer column spacings.

Above the second cornice, which runs unbroken around the entire church, are the springings of the main semidomes, smaller semidomes over the exedrae, and the arches that carry the dome. The semidomes were all originally quarter spheres, though the western main one now has a flattened crown and rises more steeply up to it. All originally had five window openings, some of which are now blocked. Below the main arches at north and south are window-filled walls known as tympana. These have been reconstructed, the window area originally having been greater – with a large single window in the upper part. Forty windows originally lit the dome, four of which are now blocked.

The main structure was partly built of large well-fitted blocks of limestone and a local granite, and partly of brick, of the usual Roman flat tile-like proportions. Ashlar was used for the lower parts of the piers, but it gave way to brick at the higher levels and for all vaults even at ground level. A notable characteristic of the brickwork is that the mortar joints were almost as thick as the bricks. This must have contributed greatly to the early large deformations and the subsequent partial collapse of the dome.

The plan is most notable for the way in which the longitudinal emphasis of a basilica is combined with the centralising emphasis of the dome. Detailed study of the setting out shows how the two were brought together. Not everything in the design was as deliberate, however. The unpremeditated addition of stiffening projections from the piers has already been referred to. There is evidence of improvisation in the vaulting of the aisles and galleries, particularly of the irregular spaces next to the nave. Most revealingly, it appears highly likely that the lack of correspondence between the colonnades at ground and gallery levels around the nave was also not originally intended.

Entering the church today (now a museum after more than nine centuries as the principal church of the Byzantine empire, and almost five centuries as a mosque) there is much that must be discounted and much that has gone that must be borne in mind (p. 302). Multi-coloured marble facings remain largely undisturbed on most of the surfaces of the piers visible from the nave and much of the original gold mosaic on the aisle and narthex vaults. At the higher levels, however, one is mostly confronted with badly discoloured nineteenth-century painted plaster. Much of the natural light that would have originally flooded the interior has been blocked by the filling-in of windows and the construction of bulky buttresses against the outer walls. All the original fittings for lighting Hagia Sophia after dark disappeared long ago, as did all the original furnishings clad in gold and silver and studded with precious stones.

Within the nave, the overall impression is of a single surface which envelops walls, colonnades and vaults – a surface that is divided into horizontal bands by the colonnades and cornices, sometimes disappears from sight, and is far from impenetrable, but barely hints at the great mass of the piers that actually sustain the dome (p. 304). Within the aisles there is an even more lively complexity resulting from the varied bay shapes, the juxtapositions of columns of varying types, colours and heights, the changing glimpses of the nave as one moves about, and the contrasts in light. What is most difficult to envisage is the focus that would previously have been provided by the canopied altar rising behind a chancel screen projecting well forward between the eastern exedrae, the great ambo set further forward under the dome and connected to the chancel by a screened passageway, and the colour, movement, singing and incense of the sacred liturgy – a liturgy in which the emperor himself took a formal part on great feasts. In partial compensation, there are now, over the south door of the inner narthex, over its central door into the nave, in the apse semidome, and in various positions on the walls of the galleries and above, fine figurative mosaics added after the end of iconoclasm in the ninth century.

Outside there is much more to be discounted to arrive at the original form with its large areas of glazing and marble facings on at least some of the walls (p. 301B). Originally, the dome was lower than at present, and the square base on which it stands did not rise up quite as high. Both main semidomes were reconstructed in later centuries (the western in the tenth century and the eastern in the fourteenth), and the form of the western one was changed in the manner already noted.

Most notably, there have been many additions to the exterior, initially to provide additional buttressing to the dome and other high vaults, then in the sixteenth century and later to make fuller provision for use as a mosque. Among the first additions were buildings of the patriarchal palace situated against the south-west corner of the church and along its south side, and of flying buttresses set against the wall of the outer narthex and spanning over its roof to abut the wall of the west gallery. Their date has not been precisely established, but they were probably added in the ninth or tenth century, well before the use of similar forms in Gothic architecture in the West. When the church was first completed, the upward continuations of the piers to the north and south of the dome as great buttressing arms above the gallery roofs would have been even more conspicuous than they are today.

Apart from the additions, there have been major losses. Most of the atrium has disappeared, for instance, replaced now by a museum garden. Once inside the outer narthex, one can nevertheless still experience, much as before, the thrill of moving into the much taller inner narthex and then through one of its great doors into the nave – noting that most of the doors do not, and never did, line up with one another.

Finally, it is worth noting that there were no pastophoria within the church. Previous attempts to identify areas adjacent to the apse as the prothesis and diaconicon – or sacristy and vestry – have been shown to be mistaken. Though such provisions were made at the time inside some churches, they were not called for here. Priests robed before they led a mass entry of the congregation into the church from the atrium and narthexes. The elements for consecration in the service were prepared in a separate structure, the skeuophylakion, which is situated a little to the north, and which is the principal survival from the church of Theodosius II.

S. Vitale, Ravenna (built *c.* 540–48) (p. 308D), was commissioned at some time between 521 and 532, during the period when Italy was ruled by the Ostrogoths, but cannot have proceeded far until a decade later when the city had fallen to Justinian. Even before that, there was close contact with Constantinople, so that a strong Byzantine character is not unexpected. The resemblance to SS. Sergius and Bacchus is obvious, though the impressions created by the two interiors are dissimilar, chiefly as a result of the different relationships between height and width; there is a similar contrast between S. Vitale and the later, and proportionately even taller, derivative church built by Charlemagne at Aachen, now Aachen Cathedral (q.v.).

Like SS. Sergius and Bacchus, S. Vitale has a domed octagonal core surrounded by a ground-level ambulatory with a gallery above it. The diameter of the core is greater, but by less than a metre. Yet the crown of the dome is some 6 m (20 ft) higher, and the impression of height is reinforced by an emphasis on the verticality of the piers, which contrasts with the emphasis on horizontal continuity created by the deep cornice which runs unbroken across the faces of the piers at gallery level in SS. Sergius and Bacchus. As in the latter, there are exedrae opening off the central space, but now there is one between each pair of piers, except at the east end, where again there is a deeper opening terminating in an externally projecting apse. The outer wall of the ambulatory is octagonal, presumably because this was more logical and because there was no constraint, as there was at SS. Sergius and Bacchus, arising from the proximity of existing buildings.

Other contrasts between the two buildings are in construction and decoration. The chief constructional difference is that the dome of S. Vitale is formed of hollow tubes, like the Orthodox Baptistery already referred to. Over it is a tiled timber roof, whereas the normal practice in Constantinople was to cover vaults and domes with lead laid almost directly on the brickwork, so that their forms were clearly expressed externally; it was only by raising the dome on a drum that it could be given greater height. Internally, the fact that S. Vitale has always been a church has allowed it to retain most of the original mosaic that covered the upper parts of the walls and the vaults of the chancel. Here are life-size representations of Justinian and his equally remarkable consort, Theodora – the first shown as if entering the church with the bishop and other clergy and his own entourage for its consecration, and the second with the ladies of her court standing in the atrium as if about to enter.

Hagia Irene, Constantinople (begun 532 or shortly after, but extensively reconstructed after 740), replaced a church which was the cathedral before the first Hagia Sophia was built, and which was badly damaged by fire in 532. It stands not far from Hagia Sophia and was served by the same clergy. Now, only the lower parts of the walls belong to Justinian's rebuilding: the galleries and vaults were reconstructed after earthquake damage in 740, and there have been further subsequent changes. It seems most likely that, in Justinian's church, there was a single dome over the main square bay of the nave in front of the apse, and that there were barrel vaults spanning from side to side further west. Thus the form would have been a vaulted equivalent of that at Alahan Manastir, though on a larger scale and with the addition of galleries. Part of the present interest of the church lies in the iconoclastic mosaic in the semidome of the apse, and in the well-preserved synthronon – the stepped seats for the clergy – below. After a long period as an armoury, the church has now had most of its interior stripped bare.

The **Holy Apostles, Constantinople** (*c.* 536–65), was Justinian's rebuilding of Constantine's church. After several later partial rebuildings and remodellings, it was swept away after the Ottoman conquest to make room for the first Fatih Mosque. Nothing is known of it other than from descriptions, representations in illuminated manuscripts, and later copies. Apparently it was cross-shaped in plan, like its Constantinian predecessor, but with a dome over each arm of the cross and a taller dome over the crossing. S. Mark's, Venice, is possibly the closest copy.

S. John, Ephesus (before 548–65) (p. 309E), was Justinian's other major church rebuilding. The earlier church was enlarged and, like the Holy Apostles,

FULLY CENTRALISED STRUCTURES COMPARED

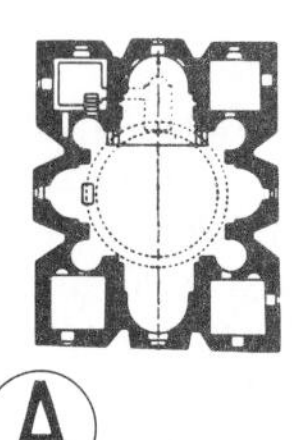

(A) S. HRIP'SIME: VAGHARSHAPAT

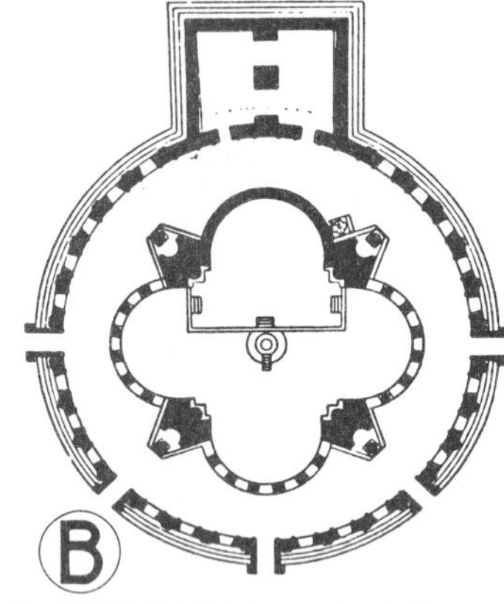

(B) S. GREGORY: ZVART'NOTS

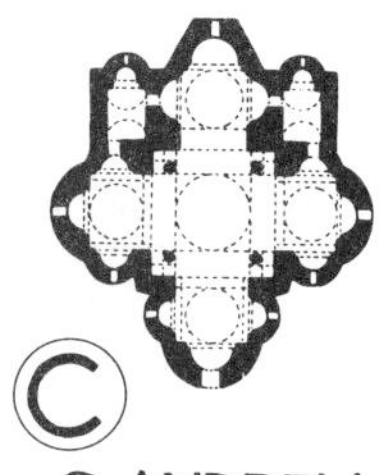

(C) S. ANDREW: PERISTERAI

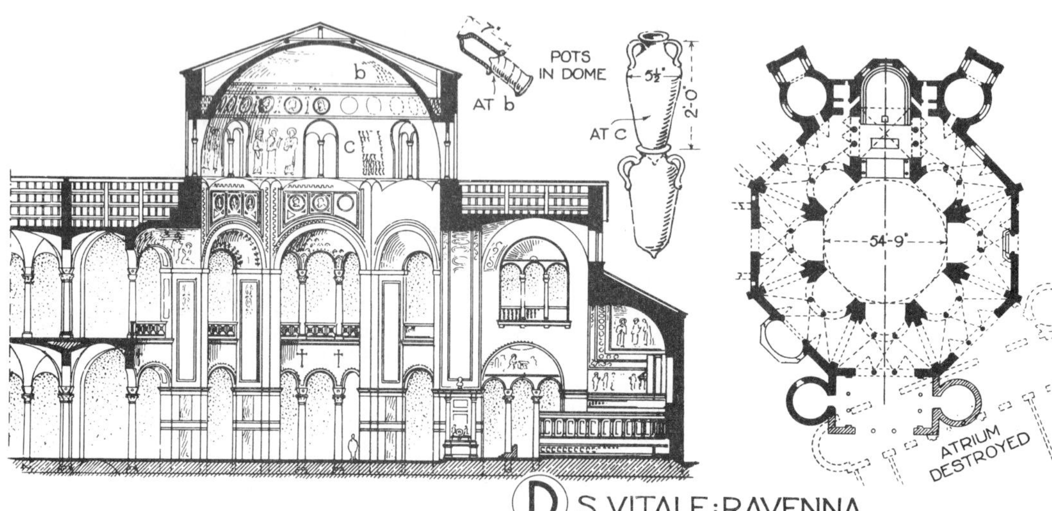

(D) S. VITALE: RAVENNA

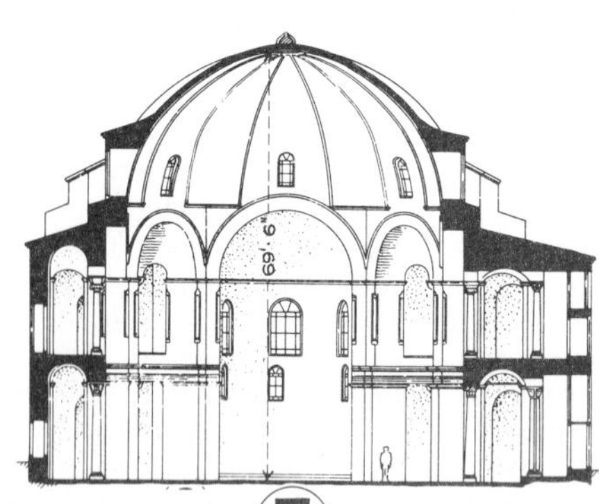

SCALE FOR PLANS
0 50 100 FT
0 10 20 30 MTR

SCALE FOR SECTIONS
0 10 20 30 40 50 FT
0 5 10 15 MTR

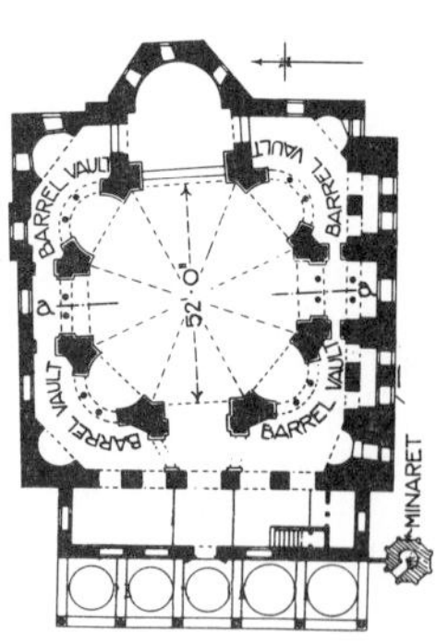

(E) SS. SERGIUS AND BACCHUS: CONSTANTINOPLE

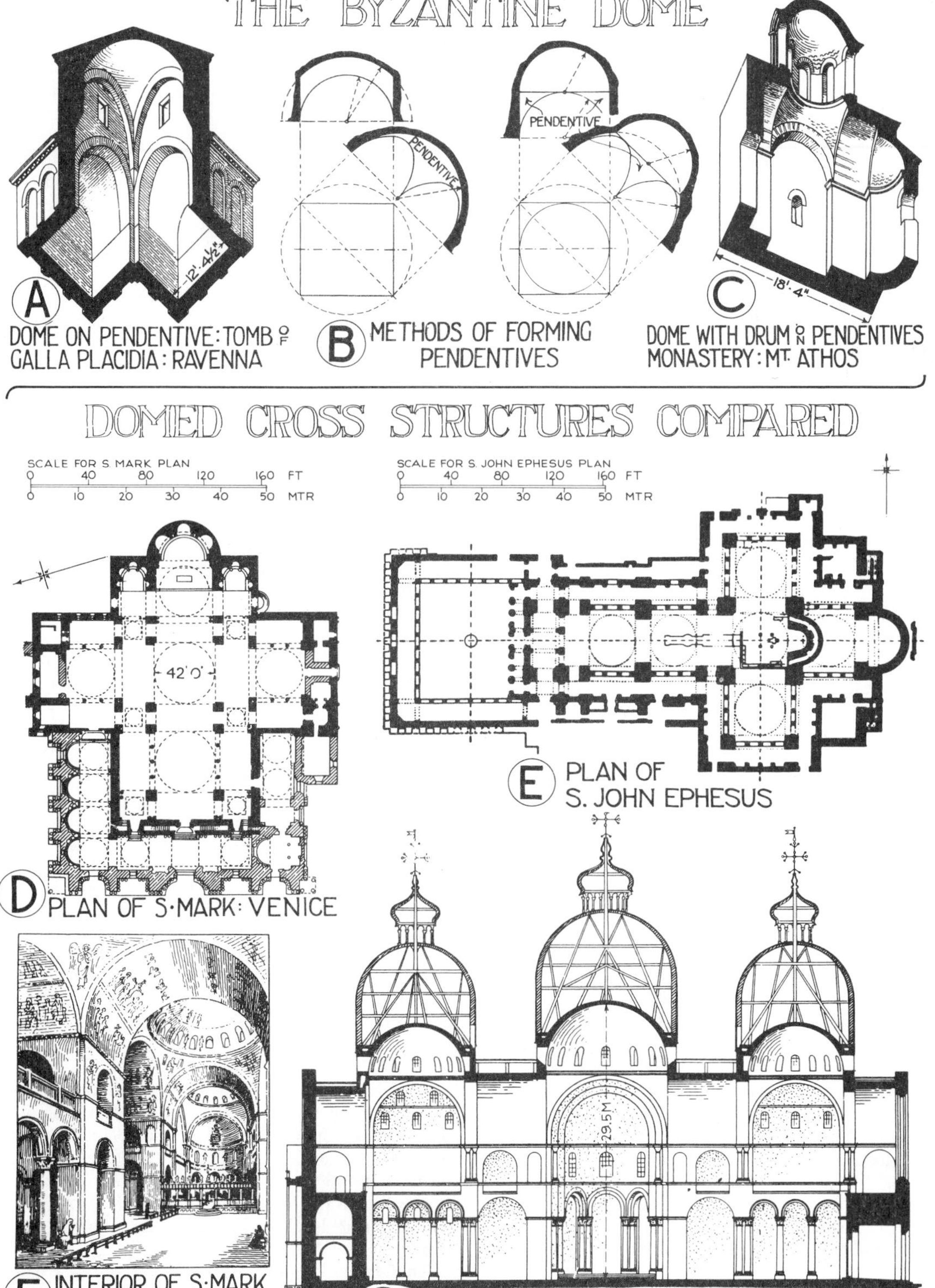
THE BYZANTINE DOME
PENDENTIVE
PENDENTIVE
12'-4½"
18'-4"
A
DOME ON PENDENTIVE: TOMB OF GALLA PLACIDIA: RAVENNA
B
METHODS OF FORMING PENDENTIVES
C
DOME WITH DRUM ON PENDENTIVES MONASTERY: MT. ATHOS
DOMED CROSS STRUCTURES COMPARED
SCALE FOR S. MARK PLAN
0 40 80 120 160 FT
0 10 20 30 40 50 MTR
SCALE FOR S. JOHN EPHESUS PLAN
0 40 80 120 160 FT
0 10 20 30 40 50 MTR
42'0"
D
PLAN OF S·MARK: VENICE
E
PLAN OF S. JOHN EPHESUS
29.5 M
F
INTERIOR OF S·MARK LOOKING E.
G
TRANSVERSE SECTION OF S·MARK

vaulted throughout with a series of domes – the chief difference here being that the west arm was longer than the others and called for two domes. The excavated (and now partly reconstructed) remains show that the manner of construction closely resembled that used in Hagia Sophia, with fine ashlar piers and brick arches and vaults.

Basilica B, Philippi (*c.* 540) (p. 311B), is a counterpart to the last three examples, in which an attempt was made to vault a more complicated plan incorporating a broad transept-like arm running across the eastern end of the nave. Again a dome was set over the square bay at the east, where nave and transepts met. The remainder was covered by barrel and groin vaults. Despite very careful construction like that of Hagia Sophia and S. John, the eastern piers proved inadequate to resist the thrusts of the dome. This collapsed and thereafter the structure seems to have been abandoned due to lack of resources. The two western piers still stand to their full heights.

Byzantine Religious Architecture after Justinian

The following choice of examples from the long period after the formative decades of Justinian's reign is, necessarily, more selective, and it is convenient to group them under regional headings that reflect rather different lines of development in, and on the edges of, an increasingly fragmented empire. Russian examples are described elsewhere.

Constantinople and Greece

Hagia Titos, Gortyna (possibly late sixth century, but perhaps later) (pp. 311A,312A), provides one link with the uses of the dome just described. There are similarities with Basilica B at Philippi, in particular. The deeper chancel makes the transept into more of a cross arm, and the two apses in which it terminates, plus the eastern apse, recall the Roman triconch and tend further to centre the composition on the dome. What now remains is constructed of fine ashlar throughout. The present church of **Hagia Sophia, Salonika** (probably early seventh century) (p. 311C), replaced a much larger early basilica, and shows a further move in the same direction. Massive square piers, each tunnelled through on both axes, support the central dome and simultaneously define the short arms of a cross. Aisles and a narthex surround this central cross on three sides, while the chancel and two flanking pastophoria complete the fourth side. Despite much loss, there are still fine mosaics in the apse and dome.

S. Andrew, Peristerai (*c.* 870) (p. 308C), is a much smaller structure with later additions at the west end. Here the domed cross form was used without any filling-in of the angles, except for the side chapels at the east end.

The north church of the **Monastery of Constantine Lips (Fenari Isa Cami), Constantinople** (dedicated in 908) (p. 311E), was an early example of the cross-in-square plan that resulted when the piers carrying the central dome were contracted to single columns and the corner bays of the square that enclosed the cross were brought into the main space. The south church, and shortly afterwards the narthex and the parekklesion on the south side, were added early in the fourteenth century.

The **Theotokos, Hosios Lukas** (tenth century) (p. 311D), is a better-preserved Greek example of the same form. The adjacent **Katholikon** (early eleventh century), built on a larger scale, has a more complex plan in which eight piers carry the dome, and squinch-like arches span between them to bridge the diagonals of the central square. There are galleries over the narthex and over the bays that surround the central square. This church is particularly notable for the fine preservation of the marble facings of the walls and piers, the marble window grilles, and the complete scheme (somewhat restored) of mosaic decoration of the vaults, so that it gives the best impression available anywhere today of the character of a church interior in the first few centuries after the end of iconoclasm.

The **Katholikon, Great Lavra, Mount Athos** (end of the tenth or early eleventh century) (p. 312B), the earliest of the surviving Athonite churches and the model for others, is another cross-in-square example, but with the addition of projecting apses to the two side arms of the cross as at Hagia Titos, and of side chapels flanking the western narthex. The **Church of the Koimisis, Daphni** (*c.* 1080) (p. 313A), resembles the Katholikon, Hosios Lukas, but for the absence of galleries. Though less well preserved than the latter, it also retains many of its mosaics, including a superb Christ Pantocrator in the dome.

Elmali Kilise, Goreme, Cappadocia (possibly eleventh century) (p. 313B), is one of many rock-cut churches in a region of central Anatolia where the soft volcanic rock lent itself readily to the excavation of cave-like churches and dwellings. Its cross-in-square plan illustrates the strong hold that this arrangement then had.

The **Holy Apostles, Salonika** (1310–14), is a later example of the cross-in-square plan, showing the later preference for constructing smaller domes over the corner bays and for raising all the domes on high drums to obtain a more impressive exterior. It also illustrates a contemporary liking for decorative exterior brickwork. Again, there are mosaics inside.

The **Parekklesion and outer narthex, Chora Monastery (Kariye Cami), Constantinople** (*c.* 1303–20), were additions to an earlier simple domed

LATER BYZANTINE CHURCHES

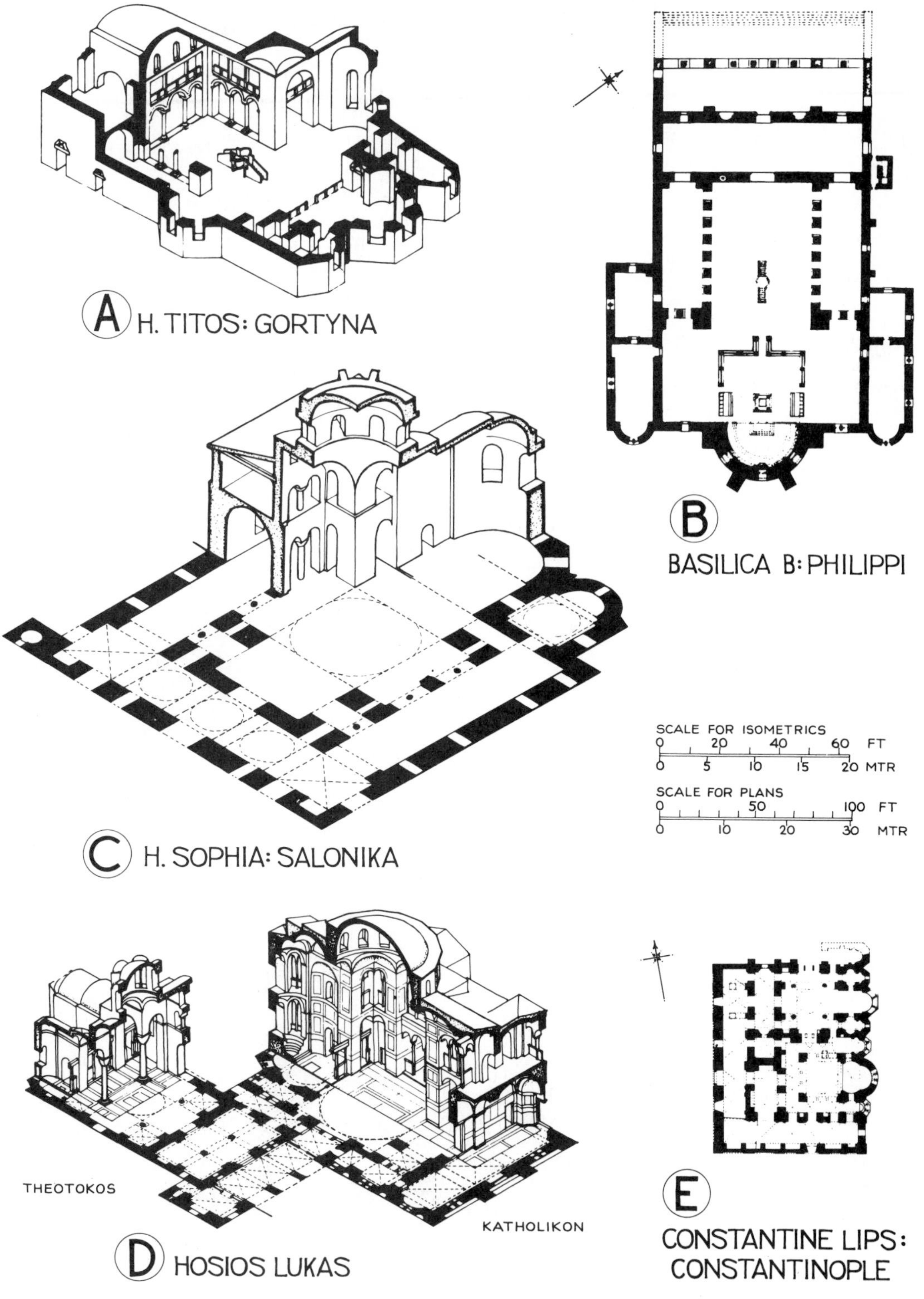

(A) H. TITOS: GORTYNA

(B) BASILICA B: PHILIPPI

(C) H. SOPHIA: SALONIKA

(D) HOSIOS LUKAS

(E) CONSTANTINE LIPS: CONSTANTINOPLE

A. Hagia Titos, Gortyna (possibly late sixth century). See p.310

B. Katholikon, Great Lavra, Mount Athos, from NE (end tenth or early eleventh century). See p.310

A. Pantocrator mosaic, dome of the Church of the Koimis, Daphni (*c.* 1080). See p.310

B. Elmali Kilise, Goreme, Cappadocia (possibly eleventh century). See p.310

C. Gračanica Church from SE (early fourteenth century). See p.310

cross church and are of little more interest architecturally than the similar extensions to the monastery church of Constantine Lips. They are notable, however, on account of the perfectly preserved decorative schemes – of mosaic in both inner and outer narthexes and of fresco in the parekklesion. The mosaics are like those in the narthex of S. Mark's, Venice: the frescos cover the entire surface of walls and vaults in the same way as, for instance, Giotto's frescos in the Arena Chapel, Padua, and constitute the finest extant examples of late Byzantine painting.

Serbia and Macedonia

The church at **Gračanica** (early fourteenth century) (p. 313C) is one of several in these regions that have affinities with the later churches in Greece. The plan is essentially a cross-in-square but the central space is relatively small, and there are grouped piers in place of the single columns at its corners. As in the Holy Apostles, Salonika, there are domes over the four small corner bays as well as in the centre, and all the domes are raised on high drums. But there is a more powerful piling-up of forms towards the crescendo of the central dome, achieved partly by the repetition of arched hoods over the barrel vaults that roof the interior around the domes.

Armenia and Georgia

It has been claimed in the past that Armenia, which became officially Christian before the Roman empire proper, was the cradle of the domed centralised church and certain types of vault. There are no early examples to substantiate this claim, and the circumstantial evidence that has been adduced will more readily admit of other interpretations. The examples presented here are best regarded as the outcome of local developments that drew, as would be expected, on the earlier and parallel developments elsewhere which have already been described.

The **Palace church, Zvart'nots** (641-*c.* 652) (p. 308B), though not the earliest example to be considered, is mentioned first because it illustrates the long survival in Armenia of the tetraconch plan. It is the combination with an overall circular plan that is new. The exedrae of the tetraconch project into an outwardly circular ambulatory. No more than the bases of columns and a few metres of the piers and outer walls remain above ground, so it is difficult to establish the appearance of the elevation. Later circular churches in this region suggest that it might have been proportionately taller than SS. Sergius and Bacchus and S. Vitale.

S. Hrip'sime, Vagharshapat (*c.* 618) (pp. 308A,316A), is the earliest well-preserved example of what was the more usual form: a fully centralised structure with four apse-ended arms opening off a central square, with smaller niche-like spaces opening off it between them, and with separate rooms in the corners of an enclosing rectangle. Externally there is more suggestion of a cross-in-square than there is inside. This results from arching over the re-entrants beside the apses to form flat-faced gables at roof level. Internally, one is chiefly conscious of the central domed space and the four main arms opening off it. The narrow niche-like spaces between these arms are too small to do much more than break up the surfaces of the piers, and the corner rooms barely communicate with the main body of the interior. As in other Armenian churches, the construction is of fine ashlar. The west porch is a later addition.

The **Church of the Holy Cross, Aght'amar** (915–21) (p. 315A), is a much later example of essentially the same type, except that the almost independent corner rooms that fill out the plan to an overall rectangle have been omitted to give a more clearly expressed cross form: the relative height has been increased, much as it was elsewhere in later centuries. Similarly, a greater emphasis on the exterior is apparent, now expressed through relief ornament on friezes and around the walls; the carving is sometimes delightfully naïve in character. The interior is frescoed, but the paintings are now poorly preserved.

The church at **Samtavisi** (*c.* 1030) (p. 315C) illustrates a Georgian interpretation of the cross-in-square form. Though the ancestry is clear from a comparison with S. Hrip'sime, the increase in the height of the cross element and the playing down of the external niches by the blind arcading that covers the entire external walls create, on the outside, an effect closer to that of some Romanesque architecture in the West. The bold cross motif and other such motifs which enliven the wall surfaces have no parallel, however, and nor do the tall drum of the dome and the conical roof over it. The interior was again frescoed, and there is less similarity to western Romanesque.

The main church, **Gelati Monastery** (early twelfth century) (p. 315D), is a further Georgian example, which differs somewhat in having flanking chapels on the north and south and a narthex on the west side. The north chapel is of later date, but the south chapel and narthex seem to result from an original intention to have a continuous ambulatory on all sides but the east. In the semidome of the apse there is a fine mosaic of the Virgin and Child, resembling that in Hagia Sophia, Constantinople, and there are also well-preserved frescoes.

Italy and Sicily

S. Mark's, Venice (*c.* 1063–73 and later) (p. 309D,F,G), was an enlarged reconstruction of at least one earlier church, perhaps also cross-shaped in

A. Church of the Holy Cross, Aghtamar (915–21). See p.314

B. Cathedral, Monreale (*c.* 1174–82). See p.317

C. Church at Samtavisi (*c.* 1030). See p.314

D. Main church, Gelati Monastery (early twelfth century). See p.314

A. S. Hrip'sime, Vagharshapat (*c.* 618). See p.314

B. S. Fosca, Torcello (*c.* 1100): the basilican cathedral and campanile on the left. See pp.299, 317

plan and built *c.* 830 to receive the relics of the apostle Mark, brought from Alexandria. Already the model was, presumably and quite reasonably, Justinian's church of the Holy Apostles in Constantinople. By 1063, Justinian's church had, itself, been partly remodelled, and it was this that served as the basis for the reconstruction in Venice.

There are five domes, each carried on a group of four piers. Originally, as shown on a mosaic at gallery level in the south arm of the cross, they seem to have had a simple covering of lead as weather protection, as was usual in Constantinople. But, by about the mid-thirteenth century, as shown by another mosaic over one of the western doors, they had been given a more impressive external profile by the addition of outer timber-framed domes. At dates not yet established, the narthex was extended around each side of the nave, with a baptistery on the south side. Perhaps because this made the aisles too dark, the galleries that had previously existed above them were reduced to mere walkways over the side colonnades.

The interior of the church now gives the best impression, on a larger scale than the Katholikon at Hosios Lukas, of the richness of surface and furnishing that was previously typical of the more important Byzantine churches. But the decoration is far from homogeneous in character. The mosaics which cover the arches, vaults and domes range in date from the twelfth to the sixteenth century. Whereas the earlier mosaics perfectly complement the architecture, the style of the latest seems far from appropriate, either to the building interior or to the medium. Much less typical of other Byzantine churches is the equal richness of the exterior, which owes much to additions made from the early thirteenth century onwards, beginning with some of the spoils brought back from Constantinople after the sack in 1204. These included the four antique bronze horses in front of the large central window of the western gallery, which also appear in the mosaic over the northernmost of the porches below. There are also large numbers of columns of different coloured marbles, clustered beside the porches and set against the walls elsewhere with an abandon that often makes little pretence to structural logic. Reflecting the fact that Venice was as much a part of the West as an outpost of the Byzantine East, there is a profusion of late-Gothic canopied niches, ogee arches, crocketed pinnacles, and sculptured figures of saints and angels.

S. Fosca, Torcello (*c.* 1100) (p. 316B), is a variant on the single-domed cross type. It is unusual in that the arms of the cross, except for the eastern one, are very short, so that the dome itself dominates the interior and exterior – or would do so if it still existed and had not been replaced by a timber roof. Only its lower part survives, consisting of two ranges of shallow squinches that span the corners of the irregular octagon framed by the eight supporting columns. Except at the east, the church is surrounded by an octagonal portico.

The **Cathedral, Monreale** (*c.* 1174–82) (p. 315B), is one of several churches in Sicily that displays a different and more complex mix of Byzantine characteristics with other influences ranging from western Romanesque to Islamic. The simple basilican form is more western than Byzantine, but much of the detail is Byzantine and was possibly executed by Byzantine craftsmen – in particular the mosaic decoration of the nave walls and the sanctuary, which includes a wholly Byzantine Christ Pantocrator looking down the church from the semidome of the apse with as much authority as the similar figure in the dome of the church of the Koimisis at Daphni.

Ethiopia

The **rock-cut churches of Tigre Province** (most probably eleventh to fifteenth century) also illustrate the widespread influence of the architecture of Constantinople in a region which was not part of the empire proper – which had, indeed, been politically isolated by the Arab conquests in North Africa in the seventh century. As in Cappadocia, some of the churches have early basilican plans. A few have cross plans, but the most numerous are variations on the cross-in-square. They differ from the Cappadocian examples in that the ceiling more often represents local traditional timber roofs than brick or masonry domes, and in that there is often a more equal emphasis on all the bays, which may indicate an influence from the multibay mosque.

Secular Architecture

What is known of Byzantine secular architecture in Constantinople serves to emphasise its continuity with, and similarity to, the architecture of the later Roman empire.

The outline of the **Hippodrome** (begun *c.* 200, extended *c.* 326–30 and again *c.* 379–95, and with later additions), is largely preserved in the present elongated square in front of the Mosque of Sultan Ahmet, though the only remains now visible are the brick barrel-vaulted substructures – up to 20 m (65 ft) high – that sustained its curved south-western end where it projected beyond the natural ridge, and some of the features that adorned the spina. These include an Egyptian obelisk and a bronze tripod of intertwined serpents which came from Delphi. The design was similar in most respects to that of the Circus Maximus in Rome. At the starting gates were four bronze horses but it cannot now be established whether it was these horses, or another group said to have been harnessed to a chariot of the sun, that were later taken to Venice and placed on S. Mark's. There

A. Palace of Porphyrogenitus (Tekfur Saray), Constantinople (probably late thirteenth century). See p.319

B. Basilica Cistern (Yerebatan Saray), Constantinople (*c.* 532). See p.319

was an arcaded colonnade around the top of the outer wall above the banked seats.

The Imperial box, which is represented in reliefs on the base of the obelisk, was in the centre of the south-eastern side and could be entered directly from the palace, which was located immediately behind it.

Of the **Great Palace** itself (fourth to tenth century) very little is now visible, and much of its site is occupied by the Mosque of Sultan Ahmet and its dependencies. What is known of it, largely from surviving descriptions of court ceremonial, indicates that it was not a single structure but a group of many different ones – like the earlier palaces at Rome, Tivoli and Piazza Armerina, and such later palaces as the Alhambra at Granada and the Ottoman Topkapu Saray. State and private apartments, churches, chapels and colonnaded porticoes were grouped around courtyards, pools, and fountains within a large walled enclosure. The principal dining hall, known as the Hall of Nineteen Couches, may be envisaged as a long hall with an apse at one end for the emperor and nine niches along each side for the couches of his guests. Another ceremonial hall, the Golden Hall, was a domed octagon. The records speak of the same rich decorations of marble and mosaic as were found in the large churches. Part of the mosaic pavement of one portico of a large courtyard to the south of the Golden Hall (now incorporated in the Mosaic Museum) has been uncovered and calls to mind some of the floors at the Piazza Armerina, though the modelling is finer.

More is known of the plans of the **Palaces of Lausos** and **Antiochus** (early fifth century), thanks to recent excavations. In both there was a semicircular colonnaded portico, or sigma, off which opened the reception rooms. In the Palace of Lausos, the principal room was round, with eight niches between facing doorways. It must have resembled the so-called Temple of Minerva Medica, though on a smaller scale. The further door led to a long hall similar to the Hall of Nineteen Couches in the Great Palace, but with only three niches on each long side. In the Palace of Antiochus, the principal room was hexagonal, with its sides opened into larger niches. This room was later converted to the church of S. Euphemia. It was flanked by smaller circular rooms.

It is only in the last centuries of Byzantine rule that a significantly different form is seen. The so-called **Palace of Porphyrogenitus (Tekfur Saray)** (probably late thirteenth century) (p. 318A) is a three-storey building of simple rectangular plan, narrow enough to have required no intermediate supports for the vaults that carry the first floor or the timber beams that carried the second floor. Like the roughly contemporary **Palace at Mistra**, it is more Western in character, apart from the decorative polychrome treatment of the facades which were mostly constructed in fine ashlar. Surprisingly, it was built on the line of the Theodosian city wall, as was the nearby and slightly earlier **Blachernai Palace**, which was the principal Imperial residence after the Latin occupation.

The **Theodosian Walls** (408–13 and 447) did, after the addition of an outer wall in the latter year, mark a considerable advance on the Aurelianic walls of Rome. They consisted of a main wall with ninety-six two-storey towers along its length, an outer wall, with a similar number of towers, and, in front of these, a moat which could be flooded in time of seige. The construction was in alternating bands of brick and ashlar-faced concrete.

The **Forum Tauri** or **Forum of Theodosius** (remodelled 393) was the largest forum and owed its first name to a bronze statue of a bull which stood there. As well as a commemorative column it contained the **Arch of Theodosius** (393), a triumphal arch differing somewhat from those previously described. It had three archways, the central one wider and taller than the others. They were supported on four groups of four columns each, all with Corinthian capitals but with shafts of an unusual kind: their surfaces were cut in a manner resembling streams of teardrops or the trunk of a cypress tree. A broad colonnaded street lined with shops, the **Mese**, linked the forum to other areas of the city.

The **Basilica Cistern (Yerebatan Saray)** (possibly *c.* 532 but perhaps earlier) (p. 318B) is so named because it was constructed beneath the Stoa Basilica, a porticoed public square. It was the largest of the covered cisterns, all of which were supplied by aqueducts from open reservoirs in the forests to the north of the city. A rectangular area was roofed by means of more than 400 shallow brick domical vaults carried by columns set in twelve rows of twenty-eight columns each. Some have fifth-century acanthus-leaf capitals which were probably the surplus stock of a marble yard, others have plain cushion capitals which seem to have been made for the purpose. Though never intended to be seen, the interior, with its boundaries barely visible in a dim light, is as impressive as the multi-bayed interiors of the covered prayer halls of some of the larger early mosques in places like Cairo, Cordoba and Isfahan, or the early nineteenth-century Skin Floor of London's Tobacco Dock.

Chapter 12
EARLY RUSSIA

Architectural Character

Khan Boris, who introduced Orthodox Christianity to the first Bulgar empire (681–1018) in the mid-ninth century, commissioned a new residence and seven episcopal cathedrals including the archiepiscopal basilica (870–80), in Pliska. Bulgarian scholars believe the revival on a large scale of the Early Christian, three-aisled basilica is to be interpreted as an assertion of independence *vis-à-vis* Constantinople, but the form is found up to the tenth century in some Byzantine regions such as Kastoria and Sparta. In the reign of Czar Simeon, who moved the capital to Preslav, the disciples of Cyril and Methodius were given considerable scope for their activities. In a 'Golden Age' of Old Slavic literature they produced not only new translations from the Greek, but also original works of their own.

At the beginning of the tenth century the so-called 'Bulgarian Renaissance' reached church architecture. The 'Golden' or Round Church of Preslav revived the Early Christian domed rotunda with enveloping niches and ambulatory, its ornament – cyma, palmette, and acanthus – taken mainly from Hellenistic models. The variety of buildings at this time, some sophisticated, others primitive in form, is typical of the Balkan region: local traditions and middle Byzantine influences were intermingled. Thus, as well as three-aisled basilicas with wooden roof trusses or barrel vaults, for example Hagia Achilleos on Achilleos Island in Lake Prespa, at Ohrid and at Nessebâr, and hall churches, there are cross-in-square churches, mainly in the area around Preslav and Pliska, and complex, domed, central-plan structures such as those at Viniza and Ohrid. Simeon's education in Constantinople and the marriage of his successor, Czar Peter, to a Byzantine princess may have favoured the assimilation of middle Byzantine culture as exemplified in the Avradak Monastery. The squared-stone masonry that is the distinguishing feature of the double fortifications of both capitals (Pliska and Preslav) and of the palaces and important churches can be traced back to either regional and Hellenistic or proto-Bulgarian building techniques. Middle Byzantine 'opus mixtum' is also found and, in simple parish churches, rubble masonry with clay mortar. The architecture of the First Bulgar Empire survives only in ruins.

There are conflicting views on how the early Christian-early Byzantine tradition came to be assimilated, ranging from the suggestion that because the South Slavs and proto-Bulgarians were 'barbarian nomads' they had no tradition of monumental buildings; through explanations based on the need, after two hundred years of inactivity, to bring in masons (from Constantinople and the eastern provinces of Byzantium) to reproduce indigenous models; or the assertion that proto-Bulgarians on the lower reaches of the Volga had schooled themselves in the architecture of Armenia, Sassanid Persia and the Hellenised Orient; to the theory that early Byzantine tradition had been kept alive in Romanised and Hellenised towns in the coastal region, to be passed on to the newly-settled Slavic and proto-Bulgarian population.

As Bulgarian power waned and the region returned to Byzantine rule, from the beginning of the eleventh century onwards, a Greek archbishop replaced the Bulgarian patriarch, and S. Sophia in Ohrid, Czar Samuel's capital, was turned from a basilica into a cross-domed church. Most bishoprics and abbacies were filled by Greeks, Greek was made the official and liturgical language, and large estates were made over to Mount Athos monasteries. Buildings were repaired in middle Byzantine style under contracts issued by the new hierarchy and Byzantine officials resident in the country. Two types of building were especially favoured: the cross-in-square plan type with five domes and either two or four crossing-piers as at Kaloša, Nerezi (1164), and the aisleless domed church whose transept arms are either let into the wall as in the church at Bojana, or projecting as tetraconches at Veljusa (1080), where the dome rests on corner pilasters. Gregorios Pakourianos – a Georgian or Armenian by birth – founded the Backovo Monastery in the Rhodope Mountains in 1083 where the aisleless mortuary chapel is still standing.

The second Bulgar Empire (1186–1396), formed as Constantinople's power declined, set up a new capital at Turnovo and obtained for its archbishopric

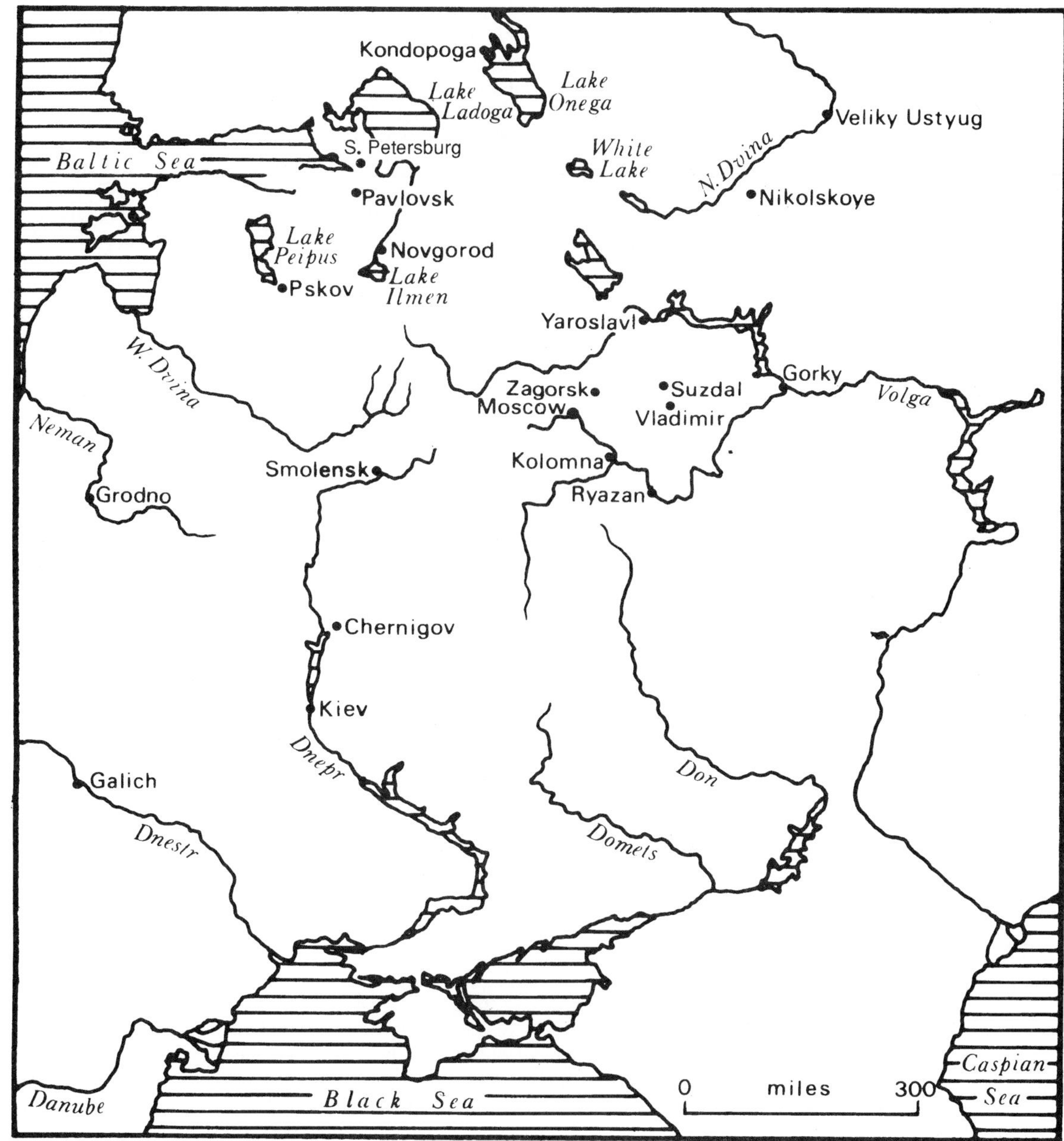

Early Russia

the status of an autocephalous patriarchate. A cultural renaissance followed, though it was largely confined to the new capital. The so-called 'Greater Turnovo School' produced polychrome facades replete with carved ceramic decoration (dishes, discs, flowers) as early as the twelfth century. The style of the frescos changed from linear to picturesque, and in the thirteenth century ceramic incrustation grew more elaborate and was used on facades in horizontal bands alternating with zones of recessed blind arches and bands of richly varied ornamental brickwork. Similar trends are found in other regions influenced by the 'Paleologan Renaissance', especially in the Hellenised South as exemplified in the buildings of Nessebâr. In the 'opus mixtum', bands of bricks run parallel to layers of well-cut limestone and tufa blocks.

The growing involvement of the lower nobility and middle classes in patronage was responsible not only for the density of new church building – there are over forty crowded onto the tiny peninsula of Nessebâr – but also for their reduced dimensions and for the intimacy of their interiors. The most widespread types were the domed or barrel-vaulted hall-church (S. Demetrius in Turnovo (1180), Assenovgrad, Nessebâr) and the domed church with projecting transept arms (Bobashevo, Turnovo). The cross-in-square plan type with four free-standing piers continued to be used (Church of SS. Peter and Paul at Turnovo, Church of the Pantocrator and S. John Aleiturgetos at Nessebâr) (p. 324A). In monastic architecture a variant of the Athonite plan (see Chapter 11) gained importance. An example is the Church of the Archangel at Tran, where the transept arms terminate in semicircular conches for the singers (hence the description 'triconch') and the inner narthex (liti) becomes a spacious chamber for the monks' midnight service. Increasingly, a bell-tower appears over the narthex – a borrowing from Western architecture. Wherever national symbolism carried on the traditions of the First Bulgar Empire, spoils and imitations of Early Christian sculpture and low-relief are to be seen. After his victory at Klokotniza, Ivan Asen II built the Katholikon in the form of a three-aisled basilica in his court monastery of the 'Forty Martyrs'.

The independent Serbian kingdom established in the second half of the twelfth century inherited a synthesis of the Byzantine and Romanesque styles. The single, square room with corner pilasters supporting a drum and dome, pendentives, transverse arches and dividing arches – a building type dating from Comnene times – was combined with the plan of a barrel-vaulted, Romanesque hall church. To the west they placed the narthex, often with a bell-tower, and to north and south of the naos square side-chambers with tribunes. The foundations of Stephen Nemanja mark the beginning of the so-called Rascian school. S. Nicholas at Kuršumlija (*c.* 1168) was followed by the Church of the Virgin at Studenica (*c.* 1190) which served as a tomb for the royal family and to which, at the beginning of the thirteenth century, King Radoslav added an exonarthex with lateral conches in the manner of Constantinople. Later, Greek masons probably worked increasingly with Dalmatian craftsmen in the same workshop. Exteriors and sculptural decoration show growing Romanesque influence but the ground-plan was not altered. From 1270 onwards there was a trend towards taller, slimmer proportions as in the Church of the Trinity, Sopočani (*c.* 1290). In the first half of the thirteenth century, the Rascian school became the artistic centre for all of eastern Christendom as Byzantium and Russia were both hindered in their cultural development by the crusades and the Tartar invasions respectively.

In the first half of the fourteenth century two kings, Milutin (1282–1321) and Stephen Dušan (1331–55), extended the Serbian Empire as far as Macedonia. Cultural influence, however, operated in the reverse direction: a new architectural school emulating Byzantine examples discovered the cross-in-square plan. The Ljeviska Church at Prizren (1306–7) and the Church of S. George at Staro Nagoričino (1312–13), with five domes, free-standing crossing piers and three apses, were commissioned by Milutin. Their ground-plans were adaptions of earlier basilican buildings, of which the broad gables of the transept arms and drum bases rise high above the square body of the church, and here the masonry points to the involvement of Greek craftsmen.

Milutin's last foundation, on the other hand, the Church of the Virgin at Gračanica (*c.* 1320) (p. 313C), is the work of South Slavic masons who gave the building its dynamic and vertical character. The semicircular gables of the transverse arms, chancel, nave and corner bays, recessed against each other, rise towards the tall drum and dome of the centre bay. Double pairs of slim columns unify the interior. The centre bays are surmounted by four subsidiary domes. The decorative masonry, consisting of sandstone blocks framed by bricks and inlaid work, is characteristic of the region (see also Chapter 11). The monastery church of Dečani (1327–35), built as a tomb for Stephen Dušan and his father Uros, presents a unique solution. The architect, a Dalmatian Franciscan, enlarged a five-aisled, cross-domed church by adding a three-aisled narthex, clad the facades with marble slabs in two different colours, added rich, late Romanesque sculpture in the Tuscan style (including columned portals, friezes and windows), and yet chose to use early Gothic ribbed vaulting. The Katholikon of the Chilandar Monastery on Mount Athos (1303), which has the Athonite, triconch ground-plan, was also one of the Milutin's foundations.

In the second half of the fourteenth century the Serbian kingdom split into several principalities which became vassals of the victorious Turks. Only the Morava valley region retained its independence into the middle of the fifteenth century. The Morava school took up the heritage of the two earlier Serbian schools. On the one hand, it adopted the Athonite triconch plan, developed around a quincunx core with four free-standing piers, and gave it five domes. Examples of this arrangement are the churches at Ravanica (1377), Ljubostina (1387), and Manasija (*c.* 1410). On the other hand, the three semicircular conches were transferred to the Rascian-domed hall-church, as at Kruševac (1377–8) and at Kalenić (*c.* 1415). The spacious Athonite esonarthex was usually reduced in size and topped with a bell-tower. The elegance of exteriors increased: to the 'opus mixtum', blind arcading and ornamental bands of brickwork and ceramic incrustation were added rose windows, low-relief sculpture on the portals, archivolts, and sculptured ornament around the windows. The motifs included guilloche, foliage and mythical creatures. Paintwork heightened the decorative effect. The impact of the Morava school is particularly apparent in the architecture of Walachia and Moldavia, in spite of their having developed their own distinct schools of 'design' towards the middle of the fourteenth century. They also shared a common heritage, namely the impact of the 'Paleologan Renaissance'. At this time the Serbian-Byzantine Morava school had greater prestige than that of Constantinople, but the Byzantine and South Slavic refugees brought their own experience with them.

A Serbian monk from Mount Athos, Nicodemus, for example, in his numerous monastic foundations is believed to have introduced the triconch plan. Masons who had fled from the Turks introduced 'opus mixtum' and ornamental facades, and artists introduced exterior paintwork and late Byzantine iconography. On the other hand, military architects from Transylvania, Hungary, Bohemia and Poland were brought in to build fortresses. The Romanesque and Gothic styles and the construction techniques they used exerted an influence on church architecture.

The first type of church to appear in Walachia was of the cross-in-square kind with four free-standing piers, for example, S. Nicholas at Curtea de Argeş (*c.* 1340). Soon this gave way to the domed hall-church developed on the Athonite triconch plan, following the example of the Morava school, at Clozia Monastery (1386), where a separate, square room formed the narthex and in other additions at the end of the fifteenth century the tendency towards verticality and the emphasis upon exterior ornament grew more pronounced. Two domes on tall drums and square bases were placed over the corners of the narthex. A prominent cornice divides the facade into two zones with blind arcades and decorative window surrounds. The motifs betray Caucasian and Islamic influence, for example in Dealu Monastery (1502), the episcopal monastery church at Curtea de Argeş (1517) and the Tirgovischte Monastery (1517).

The domed triconch hall-church underwent further modifications in the work of the Moldavian school of architects, which had close links with the local tradition of wooden architecture as well as western European culture. Closed bays with thick dividing walls and narrow passageways are built one above another, like building houses with logs. The interior walls and transverse arches between the bays are often supported by flying buttresses to east and west. The ground-plan was usually elongated by inserting a bay before the apse and adding a burial chamber between narthex and naos. The domical vault over the naos either disappears beneath the steep, Gothic saddleback roof with projecting eaves as at Siret (*c.* 1380) and Arbore (1502), or sometimes it interrupts the roof and rises on a slim drum with a cupola as at Putna (*c.* 1467), Neamţ (1497), and Voroneţ (1488) (p. 325A). Originally, roofs were more strongly articulated than later restoration work suggests.

Both the naos and the other bays have so-called Moldavian vaulting, a synthesis of Byzantine and Gothic styles and principles of construction in which the usual corner pilasters are omitted. The transverse arches and the arches between nave and aisles span from wall to wall, and pendentives provide the base-line for the dome. A second tier of arches and pendentives, developed diagonally – over the apex of the lower ones – forms a pyramidal structure and narrows still further the circular base-line. The blind calotte may be placed directly on this base or a drum may be interpolated between them (p. 324B). This particular form of vault is an original solution developed in Romania in the fifteenth century. Attempts have shown that no genuine comparisons can be drawn with anything from the Caucasus or from Islamic architecture.

The Moldavian school took shape during the reign of Stephen the Great (1466–81). As well as numerous fortresses – for example, Putna, Moldovita – he also built twenty-four churches and monasteries and building activity increased yet again in the sixteenth century. Figurative fresco-painting on the exterior walls became characteristic: there are examples at Suceava (*c.* 1530), Humor (1530), Moldovita (1537), Arbore (1541) and at Voroneţ (*c.* 1547) (p. 325A). The iconography is similar in nearly all the churches, with motifs relating to the two great cycles – the theophany in the east and the Last Judgement in the west. Although figurative exterior painting was not new in Byzantine art, in no other region is it found in such iconographic richness and quality. Inside and out, the church is turned into an iconostasis of the Orthodox faith.

Before the conversion to Christianity of Vladimir I in 989, Kievan Rus had mainly wooden architecture, and even in the later Middle Ages wood churches outnumbered those built in stone. The social and technical-aesthetic assumptions implicit in log building methods prompted a continuous process of development from simple to more complex groupings of the same forms. The real change of style took place in monumental architecture. Vladimir at first replaced the ruined pagan shrines with wooden churches, but soon dispatched a mission to Byzantium to recruit masons: to maintain his feudal prestige, he was obliged to build a monumental court church and a stone palace.

The masons brought with them the middle Byzantine cross-in-square constructed in 'opus mixtum' and 'recessed brickwork', and the new stone is best preserved in the Cathedral of S. Sophia in Kiev (see below). Of Vladimir's court church of the Assumption, also known as Desyatinna Church (989–96), only the foundations survive.

A. S. John Aleitourgetos, Nessebâr, Bulgaria (fourteenth century). See p.322

B. Moldavian dome, S. George, Suceava, Romania (1514–22). See p.323

A. Monastery Church, Voronet, Rumania (1488, exterior painted *c.* 1547). See p.323

B. Church of the Intercession, Bogolyubovo (1165). See p.329

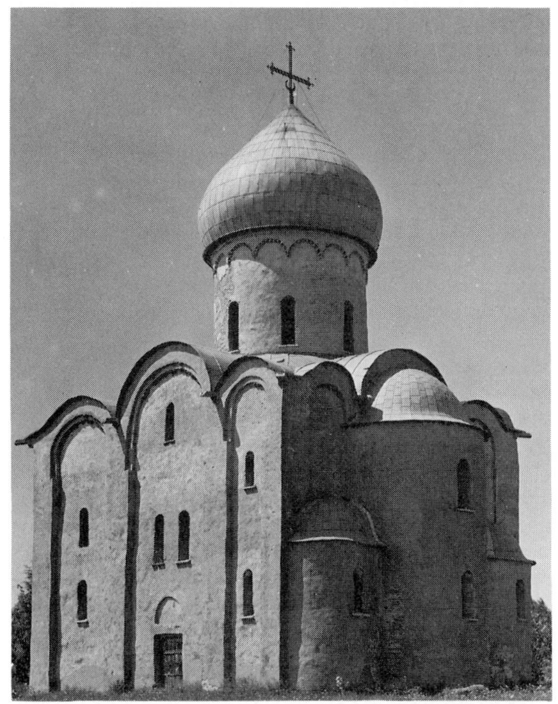

C. Church of the Saviour, Nereditsa, Novgorod (1198). See p.329

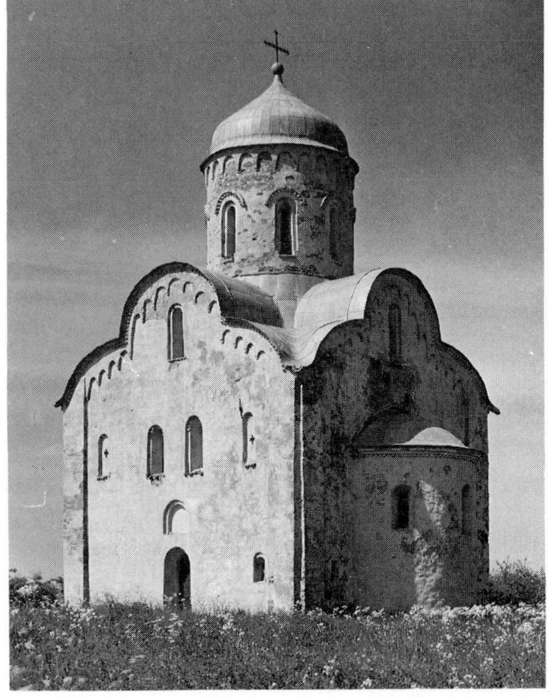

D. Church of S. Nicholas, Lipna, Novgorod (1292). See p.329

Emulating the Byzantine emperor, Justinian, Grand Prince Yaroslav the Wise (1019–1054) took over the politically significant dedication and grand proportions of Hagia Sophia, in commissioning a major church, the Cathedral of S. Sophia in Kiev (pp. 327B, 328,333F). The cross-in-square plan, usually adopted for small parish churches, was expanded to include five naves with wide surrounding galleries and an imposing three-sided tribune. However, Yaroslav favoured the simple variant: the eastern crossing piers are engaged with the dividing walls of the apses. The central groin vault forms a single, lofty and well-lit space, while around the periphery of the ground floor are low, gloomy, domical-vaulted side-chambers. This was where the congregation sat while the ruler and his court occupied the tribune, which was also used for acts of sovereignty. The external appearance is distinguished by its thirteen domes on elongated drums and curved gable-ends, grouped pyramidally, and by two domed staircase-towers at the western entrance. The pyramidal silhouette has been attributed to the function of the church as a mass assembly place and the associated wish to allow more light to penetrate to the royal tribune, or more simply to the influence of indigenous forms of log building. It is not known whether Yaroslav still had at his service the Byzantine masons recruited by his father Vladimir, nor to what extent he employed Russian masons. The style is new, but not 'un-Byzantine'. The Greek inscription in a side apse indicates that Byzantine masons and artists may have been involved. The 'recessed-brick' technique used in the masonry, the decorative niches and some of the motifs point to Constantinople; other features suggest influences from the eastern Byzantine provinces, the Caucasus and west European Romanesque architecture. The iconography is middle Byzantine in character and consists of fresco and mosaic work; it is ascribed to a mixed workshop but such extensive building activity would not have been possible without Russian masons. Yaroslav extended Kiev, his capital, to six times its previous size as well as commissioning the 'Golden Gate' and further churches in imitation of Constantinopolitan models.

The cathedrals of S. Sophia in Novgorod and Polotsk (both *c.* 1050) have the same five-naved ground-plan as their Kievan model of the same name, but the structure is simplified and the number of domes reduced. The Transfiguration Cathedral at Chernigov (1036), on the other hand, was planned with three naves and four free-standing crossing piers. A curtain wall, pierced by arcades, separates the naves at either side of the crossing. Four subsidiary domes allow light into the corner bays. Unlike the three Kievan S. Sophias, the narthex is closed off from the naos to form a separate transverse compartment. The same segregation of the western narthex is to be seen in the Dormition Cathedral of the Monastery of the Caves at Kiev (1037–78), the builders of which came specially from Constantinople. It was commissioned by Prince Svjatoslav and Abbot Feodosi as a single-domed, three-naved cross-in-square plan with two free-standing crossing piers. Flat engaged pillars articulated the facade into four panels and connected with the pilasters of the 'zakomari' which formed a curved roof line.

The Monastery of the Caves, along with its Katholikon, set a new architectural standard. The decline of the monasteries had coincided with the process of feudal fragmentation after Yaroslav's death, and building on the grand scale as in the first half of the century became impossible. There were local variations on the model of the Kievan monastery cathedral, of course – a staircase-tower, side-chambers, the number of domes, or the style of decor. The segregation of the narthex, however, remained an isolated episode. The transverse compartment was sometimes turned into a basilican extension of the naos and usually housed a gallery supported by two piers as in S. Anthony and Yur'yev Monasteries in Novgorod, the Cathedral of SS. Boris and Gleb in Chernigov, the first Dormition Cathedral in Vladimir and the Dormition Cathedral in Vladimir-Volynsk (all twelfth century). An ambulatory often took over the function of the narthex.

The formation of independent principalities in the regions of Rostov-Vladimir-Suzdal, Vladimir-Volynsk (Volhynia), Smolensk and Galič (Galicia) was associated with the foundation of separate bishoprics and schools of architects. Independently of local styles, however, a second type of roofline (as well as 'zakomari') became popular, namely the trefoil roof with halved barrel vaults, and gable-ends in the form of quadrants over the corner bays as in the Cathedral of the Archangel Michael at Smolensk (1191–4). Both variants were common after the middle of the twelfth century when the basilican western section of churches was eliminated in a further process of simplification. The cross-in-square was reduced to the eight bays surrounding the central dome, and the western pair of piers is either truly free-standing or supports the gallery. The facades are articulated into three round-headed bays by means of pilasters, while arched gables and blind arcading emphasise the skeleton of supports without diminishing the impression of massive walls.

In early Russian architecture, solid mass was frequently used to counteract thrust. The simplified, single-domed form also made its first appearance in Kievan monastic architecture, but it soon came to be adopted in towns and princely residences as increasing fragmentation of feudal territories reduced space requirements. The linear variant with zakomari (wavy line) roof is found both in the magnificent, courtly style of Vladimir-Suzdal and in the plain, bourgeois style of Novgorod. A pyramidal variant with trefoil curved roof appears at the beginning of the thirteenth century in South Russia, for example in the Pjatnica

A. Faceted Palace (Granovitya Palata), Kremlin, Moscow (1487–91). See p.332

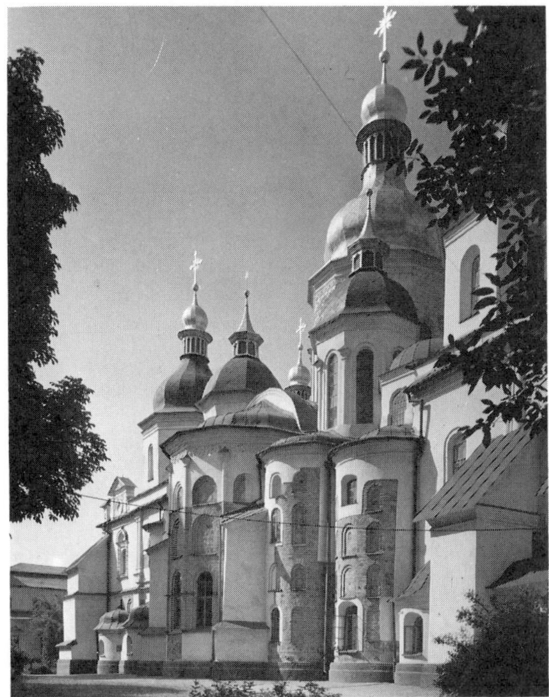

B. Cathedral of S. Sophia, Kiev (1037–61): east aspect showing original masonry. See pp.326, 334

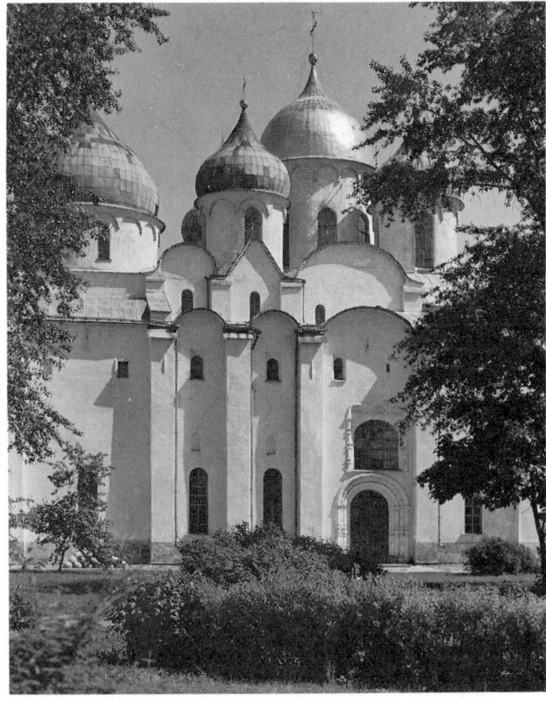

C. Cathedral of S. Sophia in the Kremlin, Novgood (1045–52). See p.334

Cathedral of S. Sophia, Kiev: north transept, showing two-storey triple arcade. See pp.326, 334

Church at Chernigov, at Novgorod, Kovaljevo, and Volotovo, and more notably, later at Moscow. This form also varies with region and period. Characteristically Russian features are the merging of the eastern crossing piers with the walls of the apse, the regrouping of the western bays, and the construction of the vaults.

The north-eastern principality of Vladimir-Suzdal began to flourish in the middle of the twelfth century when Prince Andrei Bogoljubski (1157–74) attacked and defeated Kiev in 1169. The architecture of Vladimir-Suzdal differed in style from that of other Russian regions in its use of stone-faced rubble masonry. Small, whitish-grey limestone blocks were laid in courses on very thin mortar joints. The space between the facing walls was filled with mortar and rubble. This technique gave rise to a new system of articulation and encouraged the use of sculptural decoration.

Prince Andrei Bogoljubski remained in the north and modelled his new capital, Vladimir, on Kiev. He attached particular importance to the 'Golden Gate' (1164) (p. 330B) with its symbolic carvings, but his efforts to create a second Russian metropolitan see were unsuccessful. The Dormition Cathedral, intended for the metropolitan bishop, was designed along the lines of the cathedral of the Monastery of the Caves and was given the miraculous icon of Our Lady of Vladimir which had been stolen from the court at Kiev. The two staircase-towers on the west side were similar to those of Prince Andrei's residence, Bogoljubovo, built outside the capital in 1158–64. The palace-church conformed to the linear variant of the simple cross-in-square plan with two free-standing piers and no basilican western section. It was nonetheless richly decorated, a combination that was to become an architectural hallmark of the Vladimir-Suzdal ascendancy largely attributable to Romanesque influence. Bands of blind arcading on ornamental colonnettes articulated each storey: there are deeply recessed portals with columns, pilasters with projecting half-columns, Corinthianesque foliated capitals, moulded window surrounds, and figurative sculpture on the facade and corbels. Neither Caucasian nor Romanesque architecture has anything comparable to the exterior ornament of Vladimir-Suzdal. Not far from Bogoljubovo on the River Neri stands the Church of the Intercession (*c.* 1165) (p. 325B), a dedication Prince Andrei adopted in opposition to Byzantium. It is similar in execution to the palace church and has a royal gallery.

The Cathedral of S. Demetrius at Vladimir was commissioned by Prince Vsevolod (1176–1212) (pp. 326,333E). Here, the slim, elegant proportions of the Church of the Intercession gave way to monumental solemnity. After the fire of 1185 in Suzdal, he also had the Dormition Cathedral rebuilt on a larger scale, with four subsidiary domes over the corner bays. Two buildings have survived from the time of the decline of the Vladimir-Suzdal Rus at the beginning of the thirteenth century: the six-piered, five-domed Rozhdestvensky Cathedral in Suzdal itself and the four-piered, single-domed Cathedral of S. George at Yur'yev-Pol'sky (p. 330A). The three square, outer porches are a distinctive feature that had appeared shortly before in Kiev, Smolensk and Novgorod under South Slavic or Georgian influence.

The regional style of Novgorod began to emerge after a city revolt deposed the princes in 1136 and the Republic of the 'Veche' was instituted. Land ownership, trading capital and political privilege were concentrated in the hands of a patrician class. Although they had occasionally to strike a compromise with the people's assembly, they nevertheless sent representatives to the boyar council and had the final say in the appointment of the archbishop, who acted as head of state. The system of municipal self-government was supplemented by the creation of colonial districts in North Russia and of towns such as Pskov, Old-Ladoga and Isborsk. The change in society is apparent in the modest design of the last royal foundation, the Church of the Saviour on the Nereditsa Hill, Novgorod (1198) (p. 325C), a simple, one-dome cross-in-square plan with two free-standing piers and a curving roof. It is small in scale and dispenses with decorative niches and sculptural ornament. It does, however, contain a feature peculiar to Novgorod architecture: the eastern bay of the longitudinal facades is narrower than the western bay, while the three apses billow outward. The western section contains a tribune with enclosed side-chapels. Other patrician and merchant patrons favoured the same type of construction, for example, Mirozhsky Monastery in Pskov (1156), and the church at Arkazh (1179). The local workshops used 'opus mixtum' with various combinations of brick, ashlar and rubble.

Dimensions, roof construction and the treatment of facades were continuously revised. At the beginning of the thirteenth century the trefoil curved roof-line superseded the 'zakomari' roof as in the Pjatnica and Rozhdestvensky Churches. The Mongol invasion of 1238 initially led to a decline in building activity, but in the fourteenth century the economic prosperity, stemming from the flourishing Baltic trade, gave rise to a 'Golden Age' of architecture and pictorial art in Novgorod. The ethos of the middle classes with their urge for self-portrayal and the impact of the so-called Paleologan Renaissance and of South Slavic adaptations of Byzantine design were the chief sources of greater dynamism and richer ornament. At first the mass of the bourgeois-patrician church with its triple-curve roofline retained an appearance of simplicity and solidity, for example, at S. Nicholas on the Lipna (1292) (p. 325D), but later the proportions accentuated height, the walls were inclined inwards, drums became taller, apertures narrower and geometrical

A. Cathedral of S. George, Yur'yev Monastery, Novgorod (1119–90). See p.335

B. Golden Gate, Vladimir (1164): east side; above the gate the Church of the Miracle of the Veil (fifteenth to nineteenth century). See p.335

C. Church of S. Theodore Stratelates, Novgorod (1360–1): view from SW, bell tower and extension (seventeenth century). See p.335

ornament more lavish. The local 'begunet' (bricks laid diagonally to form triangular openings) enliven the appearance, while arched and dog-tooth friezes and stone crosses are inlaid in the facade. There is only a single apse, however, and pastophoria follow the eastern pattern. The enclosed side-chambers of the tribune were used as private chapels or even as trading offices, as for example in the Church of S. Theodore Stratelates (*c.* 1360) (p. 330C) and the Church of the Transfiguration (*c.* 1375).

The bourgeois-patrician church continued to be built, both in the more ostentatious style of SS. Peter and Paul in Kozhevniky (1406) and in a plainer style as in Vlassi Church (1407) or in the form of a so-called 'warehouse church' of which S. Demetrius (1381) is an example. In the latter, a cellar, distinguishable from outside the building by the small window openings, served as a storeroom. A gable-and-valley roof with four triangular gables replaced the trefoil shape. In the middle of the fifteenth century, under pressure from Moscow, the patricians had many of the Novgorod churches, which date from its rise to power in the twelfth century, either rebuilt or remodelled, as in the case of S. John on the Rock. Numerous tiny private chapels were also created in traditional form and style, such as the Church of the Apostles in the Ravine.

The Novgorod tradition was taken up in Pskov. This town had withdrawn from the Novgorod federation in 1348 and here political power lay in the hands of craftsmen and merchants. The walls of the buildings are thicker, the proportions more compact, the ornament more modest. The cross-in-square church with two free-standing piers is enveloped – as a rule asymmetrically – by a deep western porch, side-chapels, ambulatories and storerooms. Cellars were also provided for storage. A bell-gable, as in the Church of the Epiphany at Pskov (p. 341A), or a bell-wall was usually placed above the western entrance. The patrons dispensed with a tribune, but lateral apses, omitted in Novgorod, were reintroduced. At first, the cross-arms were given saddleback roofs and the corner bays lean-to roofs, but later gable-and-valley roofs were used to cover the entire building. In the 'opus mixtum' the local workshops took to using the Permian slabs quarried locally and even the 'begunet' was cut in stone.

The vaulting system they adopted was that of a pyramid of stepped arches, as in the Church of the Dormition at Meljotovo (1462). First in the Parreklesion, S. Basil on the Hill (1413) and later in small churches such as S. Nicholas by the Stone Wall (*c.* fifteenth century), they dispensed with piers altogether: a series of arches springing directly from the walls on both axes rise in steps towards the centre, forming a square base which, via pendentives, supports a miniature drum and dome. The master-builders of Pskov earned fame all over Russia with this original construction technique and in the fifteenth and sixteenth centuries were repeatedly summoned to Moscow by the czars.

When, a half a century or so after the first Mongol invasions (1237–40), the Golden Horde began to experience difficulties, the principality of Moscow began its rise to power, supported by the Orthodox Church. The Metropolitan sanctioned its claim to the dynastic succession, and in 1325 transferred his see to the Moscow Kremlin. This complex of citadels, princely residences and administrative headquarters was fortified during the fourteenth century with walls and towers built of limestone blocks and was provided with churches in the Vladimir-Suzdal style. The fortifications were soon imitated in other regions. As a result, when Dmitri Donskoi (1362–89) called on the princes to join forces in a campaign against the Mongols, troops were able to muster in safety. A first victory was won with terrible losses on the Kulikovo-Pole in 1380, but without achieving complete liberation. However the fear was lifted, and building activity resumed.

The subsequent 'gathering of the Russias', as it has been called, gave birth to a new, central Russian style. Moscow became a melting-pot of diverse influences from other regions and yet succeeded in imposing on them its own composite forms and motifs. Old and new factors came together: they included the development of the pre-Mongol heritage and in particular that of Vladimir-Suzdal, the impact of Byzantine architecture of the Paleologan period with that of Serbia and Bulgaria, the emergence of a unified Russian language and literature, the anchoritic movement which was bound up with the colonisation of the north, the revival of the symbiosis of church and state, and the founding of large monastic communities, some of them fortified. The resulting developments heralded, on the one hand, the end of the regional schools and, on the other, the historicism of the future czarist empire.

This transitional style left its mark on, among others, the Cathedral of the Dormition on the Citadel at Zvenigorod (1399), the Trinity Cathedral of S. Sergius Monastery in Sergejevsk (1422) (pp. 333H, 337A), and the Cathedral of the Saviour in the Andronikov Monastery in Moscow (beginning of the fifteenth century) (p. 337B). Comparisons with the Church of the Intercession and S. Demetrius in Vladimir (p. 336), the Pjatnica Church in Chernigov and the Church of the Virgin in Gračanica, Serbia, suggest themselves. The courtly, single-domed form from Vladimir appears in a simplified version with stone-faced rubble masonry. At the same time a pyramidal form began to be expressed through the use of high podiums and the layering of vaults and gables. As pointed arches replaced round arches the roof of artichoke form evolved. Connected with this transitional style was the emergence of the Russian form of iconostasis.

Ivan III (1462–1505) was responsible for the eventual unification of Russia under Moscow, having subdued Novgorod, striven to establish a centralised system of administration and discontinued payment of tribute to the Golden Horde. He used his marriage to Sophia Paleologus, the niece of the last emperor, to legitimate his claims to the succession, which later culminated in the ideology of 'Moscow, the third Rome'. Court ceremonial was assimilated to late Byzantine norms but for his architectural ideas Ivan III turned towards the Italian Renaissance. Beginning in the 1470s, he had architects brought in from north Italy and south-east Europe. The Russians called them 'Frjasi', or Franconians, as they did all foreigners. Together with the 'Frjasi', local master-builders (Jermolin) set about building in cheaper and more robust brick masonry, a new style, in the Moscow Kremlin.

Court architecture was characterised by the diversity of individual designs, although historicism provides a stylistic link between them. The five-domed construction of the main cathedral, the Cathedral of the Assumption in the Moscow Kremlin (1475–9) (pp. 333J,337D), used for the coronation of the czars and for the enthronement and interment of the metropolitans, provides a characteristic example. Even contemporary chroniclers were full of enthusiasm for the fine simplicity, proportion and airiness of the interior of this building, designed by the Bolognese architect Aristotele Fioravanti. The Cathedral of the Archangel Michael (1505–8) (p. 340C), by another Italian architect, Alovisio Novo, has the Classical articulation of a Renaissance palace, but as the mausoleum of the reigning dynasty its interior conforms entirely to the traditional cross-in-square form. The Italians Marco Bono and Petrok Maly designed, respectively, the octagonal 'Ivan the Great' Bell Tower (1505–8) and the monumental bell-wall on the north side (1532) around a type of bell-cage that had come into use in the region of Novgorod and Pskov in the second half of the fourteenth century. Marco Ruffo and Pietro Antonio Solaro built the so-called Faceted Palace, Granovitaya Palata (1487–91) (p. 327A), in Renaissance style using diamond-shaped limestone blocks. Yet they modelled the 'Holy Hall', the throne-room on the first floor, on reception rooms common in wooden architecture. The court church of the Annunciation, originally three-domed but subjected to extensive alterations, was built in brick by Pskov masters and imitates the early Muscovite monastery churches. The emerging style of the Kremlin was taken further with the restoration in authentic style of S. George's Cathedral at Yur'yev-Pol'sky (1471) (p. 330A) and the Golden Gate at Vladimir (1469) (p. 330B) at the order of Ivan III.

Moscow's main cathedral, dedicated to the Feast of the Assumption, became the model for many important town and monastery cathedrals built to government commissions: they included Novodevichy Convent in Moscow and the Trinity Monastery of S. Sergius. In some cases, the five-domed configuration was transferred to the simpler version of the cross-in-square form without a basilican western section, for example at Novgorod and Mozhaisk. A three-domed version with subsidiary domes placed over the pastophoria also came into use in monastic architecture at Suzdal, Volokamsk and Jaroslav.

By far the greater number of simple parish and monastery churches built in the fifteenth and sixteenth centuries, however, particularly those in the new suburbs and north Russian filiations of the great central Russian monasteries, are variations on the simple type with a single dome. Brickwork predominates, though limestone was preferred for the decoration. In the interiors, stepped vaults rise towards drum and dome, while the corner bays have barrel vaults and groin vaults; examples are Therapontos Monastery, Kyrill-Belosersk Monastery and Rozhdestvensky in Moscow. The 'kreshcaty' vault dispenses with interior piers: there are flat barrel vaults or stepped arches over the cross-arms and lunettes over the corner bays, as in the Church of S. Anne, Church of S. Triphon, and the Old Cathedral in the Donskoy Monastery, all in Moscow. Roofs take the form of either a trefoil curve, a pyramid of ornamental gables or a gable-and-valley roof. The facades are articulated to correspond to the interior pillars or vaults by means of pilasters or pilaster strips, a string course and roof cornice. The decor was a combination of Novgorod-Pskov ornament and Renaissance motifs. The foundation storey, terraces, ambulatories and side-chapels lent these buildings an air of intimacy and homeliness; since they were financed mainly by municipal parishes, the term 'possad (sub-urban) architecture' came to be used. Regional styles are scarcely distinguishable. Novgorod 'warehouse churches', built by wealthy Moscow merchants in the first half of the sixteenth century, for instance, use a vocabulary that is quite untypical of the region, for example the Church of the Women carrying Anointing Oil and Prokopius Church (p. 341B).

An official, imperial style began to dominate architecture throughout the country. The building workshops played a part in this development and from 1583 onwards state contracts were supervised by the Inspectorate of Stone Buildings.

Moscow's spire- and tent-churches are often regarded as the most original and impressive achievement of early Russian architecture. They have become a national phenomenon, inconceivable without the rebirth and centralisation of the state, without the influence of military architecture and without the vocabulary of wooden architecture. In these structures the cross-in-square plan is swallowed up in striving for pyramidality and centrality. In the development of architecture, however, they remain a historical episode. With the Vozhnesensky Church in

COMPARATIVE CHURCH PLANS

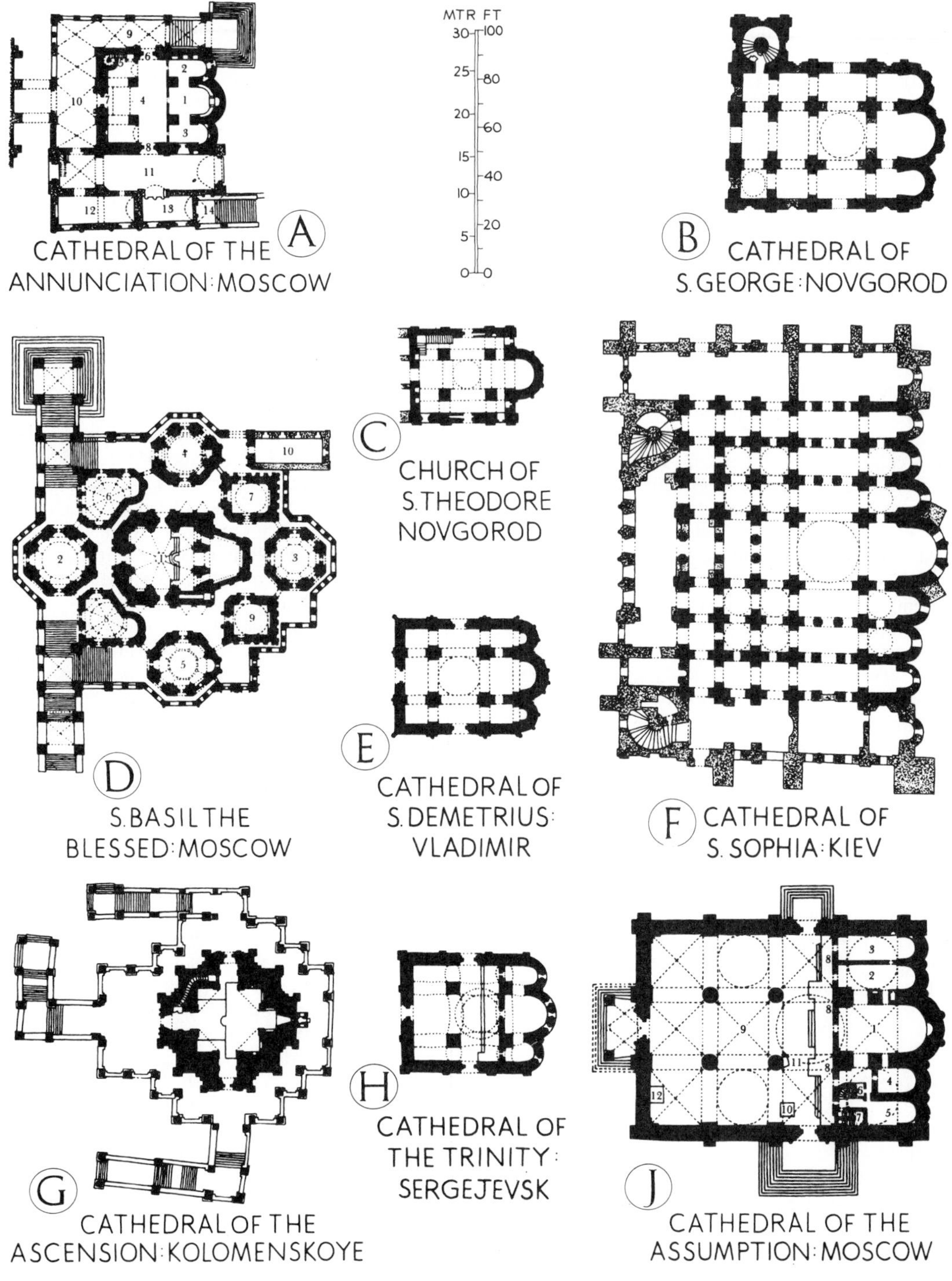
MTR FT
30 100
25 80
20 60
15 40
10 20
5
0 0
A
CATHEDRAL OF THE ANNUNCIATION: MOSCOW
B
CATHEDRAL OF S. GEORGE: NOVGOROD
C
CHURCH OF S. THEODORE NOVGOROD
D
S. BASIL THE BLESSED: MOSCOW
E
CATHEDRAL OF S. DEMETRIUS: VLADIMIR
F
CATHEDRAL OF S. SOPHIA: KIEV
G
CATHEDRAL OF THE ASCENSION: KOLOMENSKOYE
H
CATHEDRAL OF THE TRINITY: SERGEJEVSK
J
CATHEDRAL OF THE ASSUMPTION: MOSCOW

Kolomenskoye (1530–2), the Church of S. John the Baptist in D'yakovo (1547), the Church of the Intercession on Red Square (1555–60) (p. 342C) and a few later buildings at Ostrov, Alexandrov, Pereslavl-Zalesskiy and Krasnoje, the new style had already virtually exhausted itself. It was then relegated to its original function: bell-tower and refectory churches in the large monasteries.

Churches of this type have certain features in common: the purpose for which they were built, namely to commemorate important national events, the eight-pitched tent-roof on an octagonal base, the small area and uniformity of the pillarless, vertical interior, the reduction of the bema, the high podium with ambulatories, and the combination of traditional Russian ornament with new motifs derived from Italian Renaissance architecture. The Cathedral of the Intercession has been compared to designs by Filarete and Leonardo. But the architectural revolution had no lasting consequences. Old Russian historicism, which, as an element of the dominant culture, was also felt in painting, literature and theology, tied the development of architectural styles to early mediaeval tradition until the seventeenth century. This did not by any means result in stagnation or a decline in artistic quality, but it was, nonetheless, a cul-de-sac.

Each east European state outside Byzantium followed its own path in art and culture as in politics and society. The Middle Ages dragged on into the seventeenth and eighteenth centuries. In the Balkan states Ottoman rulers placed the originally national churches back under the jurisdiction of the patriarchate of Constantinople, and so fostered the development of a post-Byzantine style. In Russia, whose czars claimed the imperial succession and had the support of the church in their role as political leaders of the Orthodox ecumene (religious primacy remained with the patriarch of Constantinople), a complete break was made with Byzantine tradition. In both regions the encounter with western European Gothic, Renaissance and Baroque architecture led to important changes. But a theology based on the image as a method of thought and perception – a theology which bears also on church architecture – ensured that loyalty to conventional standards was maintained in all Christian Orthodox countries.

Examples

The **Cathedral of S. Sophia, Kiev** (1037–61) (pp. 327B,328,333F), was founded by Jaroslav as the 'mother of Russian churches'. The core is an example of the cross-in-square plan with five naves, twelve cruciform piers, five apses and thirteen domes. The main nave, at 7.5 m (25 ft), is twice as wide as the side naves. The dome reaches a height of 25 m (80 ft) at its apex. The core is surrounded on three sides by an ambulatory (originally open) which had an additional storey added at the end of the eleventh century to help transfer the thrust from the vault to the ground; a second, wider aisle was built, first in the south-west then in the north-west, with two staircase-towers. The gallery frames the three sides, the cross-arms of which terminate in two-storey triple arcades (p. 328). The aisles and inner galleries mainly have domical vaults, and the ambulatories cloister vaults. The external appearance is determined by the stepped roofline of the ambulatories and naves, each rising successively higher towards the main dome set on a drum above the crossing. Four domes on drums, supported on clustered pillars, surmount each of the two western halves of the gallery and the eastern pastophoria. Today the structure is heavily overlaid with Ukrainian Baroque accretions. The facades were originally stuccoed and whitewashed, or picturesque in effect with their 'opus mixtum', 'recessed' brickwork, rows of blind niches and Byzantine friezes (p. 327B). The mosaics (about 250 m^2) and the frescoes (about 2000 m^2) of the inner rooms are iconographic and are representative examples of mediaeval Byzantine decoration of the period.

The **Cathedral of S. Sophia, Novgorod** (1045–52) (p. 327C), was founded by Vladimir, Jaroslav's son, and based on S. Sophia, Kiev; it is constructed in polygonal masonry with only piers, vaults, sculptural decoration, door and window surrounds in brick. There are three apses, five domes on drums (a subsidiary dome over each of the corner bays) and a staircase-tower in the south-west corner. As in Kiev, the gallery surrounds the cross arms on three sides. The square pedestals of the domes on drums over the pastophoria rise flush with the east wall. The eastern bays of the side naves, without apses, have halved barrel vaults so that their gables take the form of quadrants. The pilasters of the facades correspond to those of the interior, and semicircular gables alternate with triangular ones. The ambulatories to north and south are shifted asymmetrically to the west in relation to the core. The cornices of the drums have Romanesque arcading with dogtooth ornament, a feature that became a characteristic of the local school.

The **Cathedral of S. George in the Yur'yev Monastery, Novgorod** (1119–90) (pp. 330A,333B), was built by Master Peter on the plan of the Dormition Cathedral of the Monastery of the Caves in Kiev. Constructed in 'opus mixtum', it is a three-naved basilican cross plan with three domes, three apses and six cruciform piers. The eastern crossing piers merge with the apsidal walls and the free-standing western piers carry the main dome. The third pair supports the gallery which extends only along the transverse western compartment and is sumounted at the southern end by a subsidiary dome. The latter is a companion to the dome over the staircase-tower, rising asymmetrically in the north-west corner. Pilasters divide the longitudinal facades into four and the western facade into three panels and were originally continuous with the bands on the curved gable-ends. Decoration is limited to windows and double-tiered niches, the narrow arches of which emphasise the verticality of the composition. The corbel-table frieze on the dome bases is similarly tiered.

Paraskeva-Pjatnica Church in the Market, Chernigov (twelfth century), rebuilt by P. D. Baranovski, was originally a convent katholikon and was constructed in brickwork. It is a cross-in-square plan with one dome, with three apses and four cruciform piers, the eastern pair of which merged with the apsidal walls. As the four arches of the crossing are built higher than the barrel vaults of the cross-arms and the latter higher than the semicircular gables of the facade, the roof rises in steps towards the tall central drum and dome. This construction was to be influential in Moscow and Pskov in the fourteenth and fifteenth centuries. The triple curved roofline corresponds with the vault segments over the corner bays. The facades are divided into three panels by pilasters with projecting responds. The 'picturesque' ornament consists of archivolts, recessed panels, both round-headed and pointed niches, astragals, brick lattice-work, and various friezes (arched, dog-tooth, 'begunet' and meander).

The **Cathedral of S. Demetrius, Vladimir** (1194–7) (pp. 333E,336), was founded by Vsevolod as a court church in the Kremlin. It was built in stone-faced rubble masonry and is a single-domed cross-in-square with western tribune, high corner bays, three apses and four cruciform piers, the eastern pair of which merge with the apsidal walls. The ground-plan is elongated in the longitudinal axis; without apses it was 14.9 m × 16.2 m (49 ft × 53 ft). Three Romanesque recessed portals with columns but without tympana led into the interior. The facade is articulated by wall pillars with superimposed half-columns and by a belt of dog-tooth friezes, blind arcades and ornamental colonettes. There is a row of semicircular gable-ends, the middle of the three being slightly higher than the others. The upper facade and arcading are entirely covered with low-relief sculpture which follows the joints of the limestone blocks. The iconography, consisting of anthropomorphic, animal and vegetable carvings, is dominated by courtly, cosmic and paradisal motifs. King David appears in all three middle pediments as a preacher with his scroll. The Corinthian capitals on the facades and the lion-head capitals in the interior are also symbolic of royal prestige. The lower part of the facade is not ornamented, probably because it was originally surrounded by an ambulatory.

The **Golden Gate, Vladimir** (1164) (p. 330B), the only surviving city gate of this period, is in stone-faced rubble masonry, but has suffered extensive alterations. The gate-chapel, restored in the fifteenth and eighteenth centuries, originally had a gilded roof. The clear height is 14 m (46 ft), and pier arches are continued over the main barrel vault, forming the entrance way. There was a wooden siege platform beneath the transverse arch and barrel vault, and a second platform with a parapet around the chapel.

The **Church of S. Theodore Stratelates, Novgorod** (1360–1) (pp. 330C,333C), was founded by the mayor Semjon Andrejevitch and is a classic example of the local bourgeois style. It is a single-domed cross-in-square, with one apse and four piers, the eastern pair of which form the inner walls of the small pastophoria. The eastern bays are about half the breadth of the western bays containing the tribune, which is in three sections and completely closed off from the naos. The trefoil curve of the roof corresponds with the vault-segments over the corner bays. Pilasters articulate the facades into three panels, wider in the centre than either side, narrower to the east than to the west.

Ornament is concentrated around the apse and drums. Externally, there are decorative arched and dog-tooth friezes, archivolts, 'begunet', moulded responds, blind arcading and stone crossings. The simple recessed portals have ogee arches.

The **Trinity Cathedral at the S. Sergius Monastery, Sergejevsk** (1422) (pp. 337A,333H), was commissioned by Abbot Nikon as a burial place for his canonised predecessor and founder of the monastery, Sergius of Radonezh, and built with royal funds. Moscow's grand dukes were baptised here in the fifteenth and sixteenth centuries. It is a cross-in-square church with one dome, three apses and four free-standing piers, the whole standing on a podium reached by a flight of steps. The eastern bays are shortened so that the dome is shifted perceptibly to the east. The transept arms have stepped vaults. On the south side is a columned recessed portal with ogee archivolts and annulets. Pilaster strips and wide ogee arches divide the facades into three sections which do not correspond with the interior supports and vaults. 'Kokoshniki' (ornamental ogee gables) are set diagonally at the four corners of the square pedestal of the dome. Built in stone-faced rubble masonry, the facades are articulated horizontally by a broad band consisting of three low-relief friezes carved in limestone and depicting crosses entwined in foliage. A similar band appears as a roof cornice. Between 1411 and 1422 Andrei Rublyov, a monk of the Sergius Monastery, created the famous 'Trinity' icon and, between 1425 and 1427, the wall-paintings and iconostasis.

The **Cathedral of the Saviour at the Andronikov Monastery, Moscow** (between 1410 and 1427) (p. 337B), was built with funds provided by the Yermolin family of merchants on the plan and in the transitional style of early Muscovite monastery churches. The traditional cubic shape of the core is completely dissolved by the stepped construction of

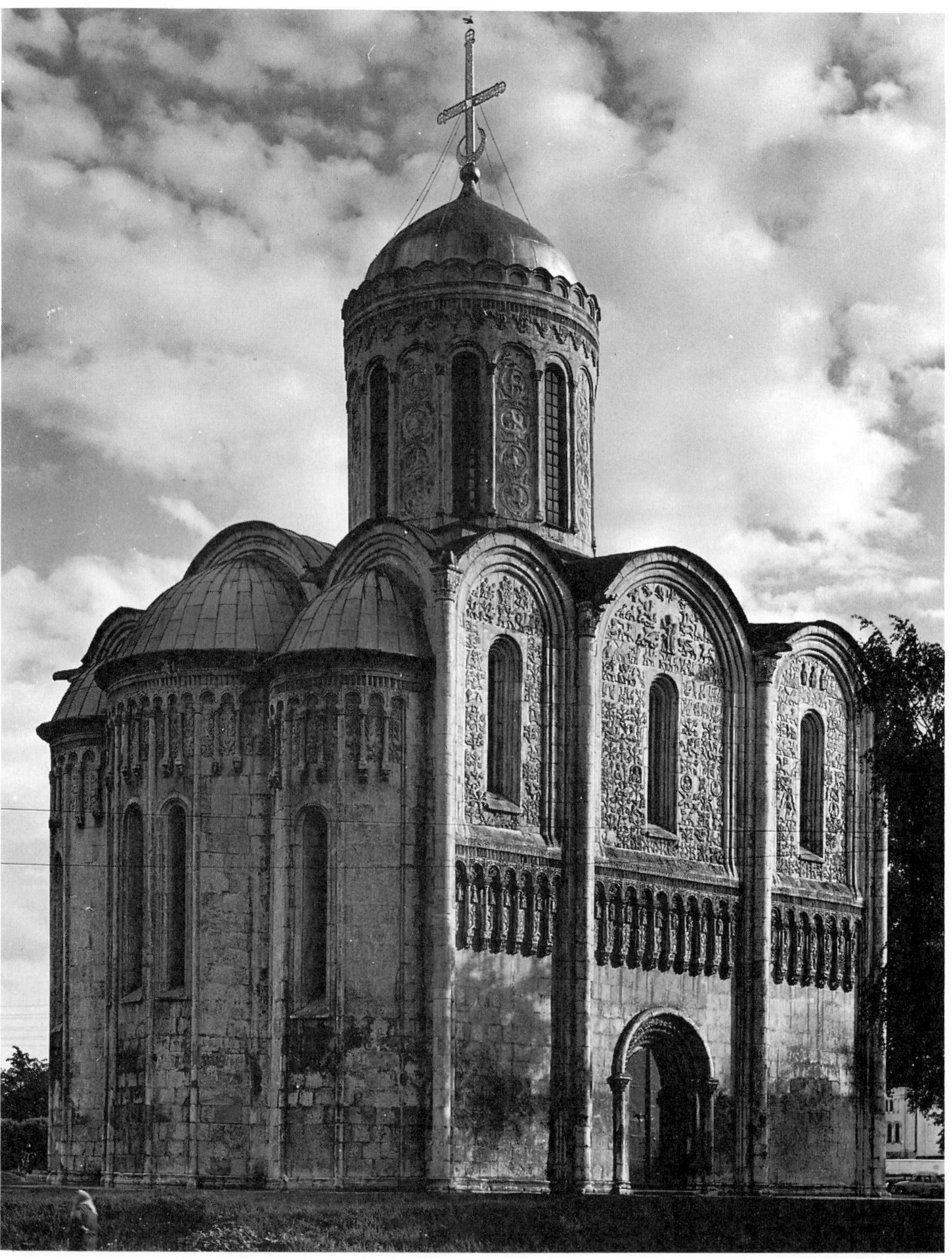

Cathedral of S. Demetrius, Vladimir (1194–7). See p.335

A. Cathedral of the Trinity, Monastery of the Holy Trinity and S. Sergius, Sergejevsk (1422). See p.335

B. Cathedral of the Saviour, Andronikov Monastery of the Saviour, Moscow (1410–27). See p.335

C. Church of the Holy Spirit, Monastery of the Holy Trinity, Moscow (1476). See p.338

D. Cathedral of the Assumption, Kremlin, Moscow (1475–9): south front from Cathedral Square. See p.338

the corner bays, cross-arms and crossing. The drum and dome are raised on a tall pedestal and the ogee forms convey an impression of dynamic movement. Founded in the second half of the fourteenth century as a filial monastery to the Trinity Monastery of S. Sergius, today it houses the Rublyov Museum for Old Russian art, as the painter-monk Rublyov is believed to have painted the cathedral and to be buried there.

The **Church of the Holy Spirit at the Trinity Sergius Monastery, Moscow** (1476) (p. 337C), was built by Pskov architects in the form of a belfry-church. It is built in brick masonry, with a podium and recessed portals of limestone. A tall, slim structure on the cross-in-square plan with four piers and three apses, the belfry with its arcading rose from the crossing and is surmounted by a dome on a tall drum. Picturesque ceramic tiles are used in the exterior decoration of this church for the first time in Russia.

Ivan III commissioned the Bolognese architect Rudolfo (known as Aristotele) Fioravanti to design the **Cathedral of the Assumption (Dormition) in the Moscow Kremlin** (1475–9) (pp. 333J,337D), after the model of the Vladimir Dormition. It was intended for the most important state ceremonies. Planned as a five-domed cross-in-square, it has a ground-plan divided by six piers into three naves and twelve equal square bays. The interior is lofty and of uniform height, has five flat apses but no gallery. The new church, originally begun by Moscow builders in 1472, had collapsed during an earthquake in 1474; through the mediation of his ambassador in Venice, Ivan III engaged an experienced architect who ordered the total demolition of the ruin. He had the foundations dug 4 m (13 ft) deep ('as he thought fit and not after the manner of Moscow builders') and a brickworks was set up to make hard-fired bricks; he used mortar of specially thick consistency and inserted tie-rods between the brick-built piers and the pilasters. The design of the interior was new: four slim, free-standing columns in the naos, flat groin vaults of equal height over the cross-arms and western section of the nave, two piers in the east merged with the walls of the main apse and the stone altar breast. The side naves form two narrow chapels in the chancel area. As the internal bays are all square and equal, the five drums should have been equal in diameter. Traditionally, however, the drum of the central dome was supposed to be larger. So Fioravanti had it placed on a round pedestal, thus allowing its diameter to be increased. Although the proportions of the exterior are based on the Golden Section, the forms are mainly borrowed from Vladimir-Suzdal. The building is faced in limestone blocks, articulated by 'zakomari' pilasters and blind arcading on ornamental colonnettes, and has recessed portals with columns. The buildings stands on a podium that was originally 3.2 m (11 ft) high in relation to ground-level and required long flights of steps to reach the entrances in the west, south and north. The south facade on the Cathedral Square was decorated as a showpiece. Later extensions and alterations scarcely detract from the original appearance of the cathedral. At the beginning of the seventeenth century, when cracks appeared in the vaults, the weak spots were secured with additional iron ties, in the process of which the Corinthian capitals were knocked off. The earliest frescos date from the end of the fifteenth century and are to be found on the stone altar breast and in the side chapels. They have been ascribed to Dionissi and his workshop and to pupils of Rublyov. The paintings were renewed in the middle of the seventeenth century without altering the iconography.

The court church of Ivan III, the **Annunciation Cathedral in the Moscow Kremlin** (1484–9) (pp. 333A,338A,B), was erected on the foundations of two earlier fourteenth- and fifteenth-century buildings, in brick masonry by Pskov builders. Originally a three-domed cross-in-square, it has three apses whose walls merge with the eastern pair of piers. The western piers support the gallery which is connected to the palace by a passageway. There are subsidiary domes over the pastophoria and stepped arches in the cross-arms. The facades were originally articulated by pilaster strips and blind arcading. A row of 'kokoshniki' masks the vaults, and there is a second tier on the octagonal pedestal of the central drum. The surrounding terraces were turned into ambulatories, perhaps as early as the sixteenth century. In 1562–6, at the order of Ivan IV 'the Terrible', some alterations were carried out: two blind domes were added on the west side to balance the pair in the east, though since the western corner bays are larger they have a greater diameter. A terrace roof was built over the vaults of the ambulatories, linking four small, single-domed chapels which had been added symmetrically at gallery-level at the four corners. Further false gables and the division of the facades into coffer-like panels, as in the Archangel Cathedral, supplemented the decoration. The ogee was the dominant motif: even the traditional helmet domes were replaced with onion domes. The iconostasis, containing work by Theophanes the Greek and Andrei Rublyov, was taken from the earlier building. Ivan IV had an elaborate Renaissance portal built in each of the north and west ambulatories and the floor surfaced with jasper slabs.

The **Cathedral of the Archangel Michael in the Moscow Kremlin** (1505–8) (p. 340C), built by Alovisio Novo, was commissioned by Ivan III. It was to serve as the mausoleum of the reigning dynasty in place of the old sepulchre church (1333). It is a five-domed cross-in-square with six piers, the eastern pair of which are merged with the apsidal walls. The interior is of uniform height, but the cross-arms are wide and barrel-vaulted in the traditional manner. The high pedestals of the piers and the pilasters and arches linking them combine to reduce the width of the side naves. For the women of the ruling house, Alovisio added a raised gallery in a separate antechurch. As a result, the core was shifted to the east and the chancel area reduced; the dimensions of the subsidiary domes were determined by the smaller eastern pastophoria and the larger western bays. This change could have destroyed the symmetry of the structure had it not been compensated by articulation of the facades and drums. The traditional system of articulation was abandoned. The spirit of the Renaissance is apparent in the adoption of a Classical order, using Corinthian capitals with acanthus, volutes and flowers (varying individually in execution), a cornice dividing the facades horizontally, with blind arcading below and recessed rectangular panels above, and a heavy entablature supporting the 'zakomari', in this case formed by semicircular pediments, each of which consists of a sculptured scallop-shell. The roof over the barrel vaults undulated, following the lines of the curved gables, which originally had Ionic acroteria. The building was also surrounded on three sides by an ambulatory; during state ceremonies on Cathedral Square the north ambulatory would be occupied by guests of honour. It is thought the facades were not stuccoed. The masonry consists of special red (so-called 'Alovisio') bricks, which contrasted with the limestone podium and stone sculptural ornament. The west entrance zone is distinguished by a Renaissance portal in the open porch and the round windows in the centre gable. The decor was widely imitated in Russia. The building was later subjected to many alternations. The paintings in the interior date from the middle of the seventeenth century: only a few fragments of the frescos in the diaconicon have been dated earlier.

The **'Ivan the Great' Bell Tower in the Moscow Kremlin** (1505–8) (p. 340D) was commissioned by Ivan III and built by Marco Bono (Bon Fryazin) on the model of an earlier structure which it replaced, namely the Church of S. John Klimakos (1329), in which the base of the drum had been adapted as a bellcote with open arcading. The new belfry began as a two-storey octagonal tower, the upper storey narrower than the lower, with a chapel on the ground floor. In 1600, under Czar Boris Godunov, it was raised by a further storey, drum and dome to a total height of 81 m (265 ft). The foundations, which are 10 m (33 ft) deep, the podium and exterior decoration are of limestone, the walls and vaults of brick. The walls on the ground floor are about 5 m (16 ft) thick, on the first floor 2.5 m (8 ft) thick, and on the second floor 0.9 m (3 ft). The staircase is built into the thickness of the walls on the ground floor, there is a central spiral on the first floor, and a spiral stair around the inside of the walls of the second floor. Scholars disagree about whether the monumental bell-wall built on the north is by Petrok Maly (1532–43) or was only built in the seventeenth century after a Pskov model on the foundations of the latter's Church of the Resurrection. In 1624 Patriarch Filarete had a further bell-wall erected on the north side. The 'Ivan the Great' Bell Tower has twenty-one bells, the largest weighing 66 tonnes.

The **Church of the Conception of S. Anne 'in the Corner', Moscow** (1478–83) (p. 342A), was commissioned by a suburban parish community and is typical of many so commissioned at this time. S. Anne's, 'in the Corner' of the town wall at Kitai-gorod, has walls of limestone blocks, a pillarless, brick 'kreshcaty' vault, barrel vaults or stepped arches over the cross-arms, and dome segments over the corner bays. There is a stone altar rail in front of the low semicircular apse and a square naos with a triple-curved roof corresponding to the vaults. The facades are articulated vertically into three panels by pilaster strips, and horizontally by cornices halfway up the walls and under the roof. There is a cellar.

The **Church of the Epiphany, Pskov** (1496) (p. 341A), also founded by the parishioners of an 'end' (an area or locality), was a single-domed cross-in-square with three apses and four piers, and a gable-and-valley roof. There have been numerous extensions, including the four-arched bell-wall in the north-west corner. The thickness of the pillars and the distance between the arches was determined by the size and weight of the bells.

The **Church of the Women carrying Anointing Oil, Novgorod** (1510) (p. 341B), founded by the Moscow merchant J. Syrkov, is a single-domed building with a cross-in-square plan and with three apses constructed in brickwork. It is a 'warehouse church', extended to three storeys: in the cellar below ground level and on the ground floor were the storerooms, and the upper storey served as a private or parish church. The corner bays are the same height as the barrel-vaulted cross-arms, while the crossing arches rise a step higher. The chancel area and the corresponding eastern sections of the longitudinal walls were not shortened as was normally the practice in Novgorod. The narthex is separated off and subdivided into two storeys. The decor combines forms derived from regional tradition (niches) and from Moscow (ogee arches). A two-arched bell-gable towers above the centre bay of the west facade.

The earliest of the new type of tower-and tent-roof churches which for a short while ousted the cross-in-square plan was the **Church of the Ascension at Kolomenskoye** (1530–3) (pp. 333G,342B). Commissioned by Czar Vassily III, it was built near the wooden summer palace at Kolomenskoye on the raised bank of the Moscow River to celebrate the birth of the heir, the future Ivan IV. The building is in brickwork with white stone trimming and detail. The date 1533 inscribed on a capital in arabic numerals and using a chronology that was not in use in Russia at that time points to the involvement of western European masons. A Russian chronicler notes that the church is built 'in the wooden manner'. The pillarless

A. Cathedral of the Annunciation, Kremlin, Moscow (1484–9): interior of main dome and corbelled arches in main apse. See p.338

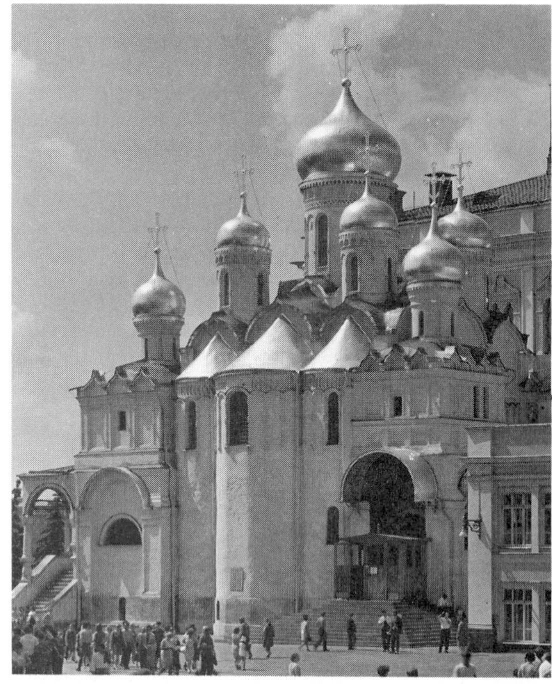

B. Cathedral of the Annunciation, Kremlin, Moscow: view from NE

C. Cathedral of the Archangel Michael, Kremlin, Moscow (1505–8). See p.338

D. 'Ivan the Great' bell tower, Kremlin, Moscow (1505–1624). See p.339

A. Church of the Epiphany, Zapskovye, Pskov (1496). See p.339

B. Court of Yaroslav, Novgorod: view from east showing Church of S. Prokopius (left) (1529), and Church of the Women Carrying Anointing Oil (right) (1510). See p.339

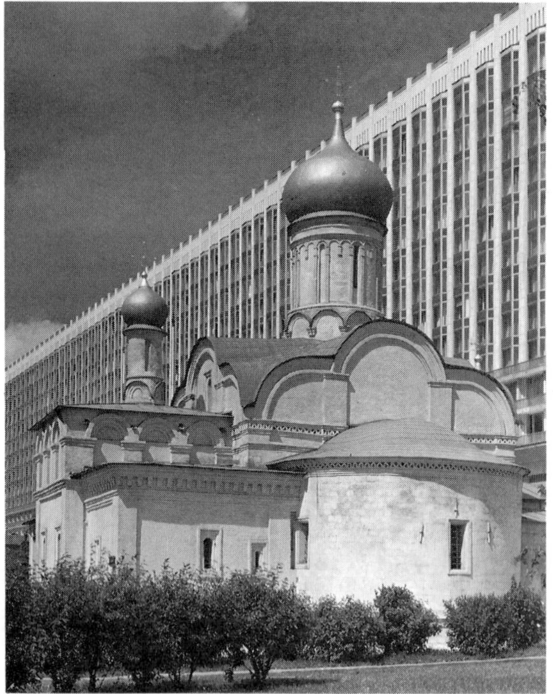

A. Church of the Conception of S. Anne 'in the Corner', Moscow (1478–83). See p.339

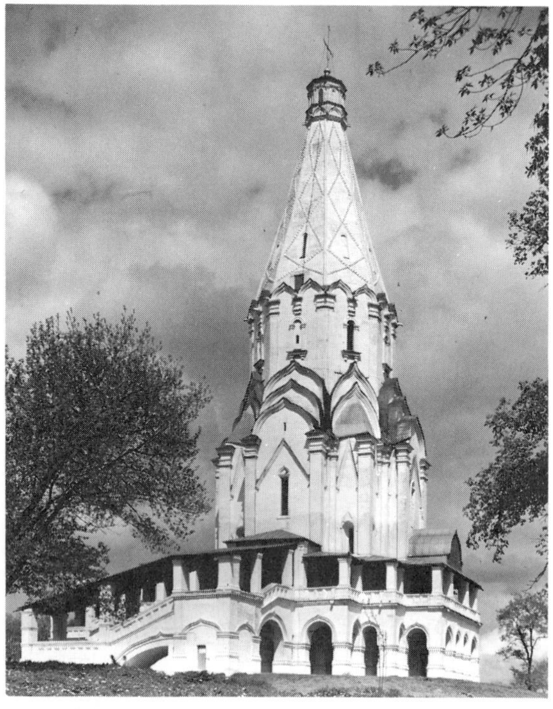

B. Church of the Ascension, Kolomenskoye, Moscow (1530–3). See p.339

C. Cathedral of the Virgin of the Intercession 'by the Moat' (Basil the Blessed), Moscow (1555–61). See p.343

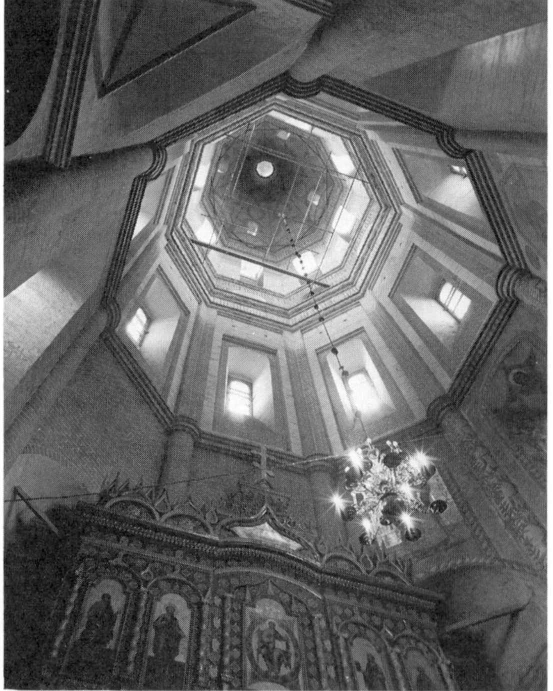

D. Cathedral of the Virgin of the Intercession 'by the Moat': interior of tent roof and dome of central tower-church

interior has an area of some 64 m^2 (690 ft^2), a third of the total area with walls up to 3 m (10 ft) thick. The core is a square with small, rectangular cross-arms projecting from it, the eastern-most taking the place of the apse. Pilasters on pedestals support cornices, and the arches and vaults they support lead to an octagon held together by a ring of iron ties. In constructing the tent roof each successive course of bricks was corbelled over the one below; the ribs are structural. The windows, which continue up into the tent roof, produce a pyramid of light. A vault with eight segments closes the spire two-thirds of the way up, 41 m (135 ft) above the floor. From the exterior the building has four zones: the podium, enveloped by extensive terraces and later roofed to form ambulatories, branching out in various directions, a massive base storey with projecting bays, a compact octagon, and above that a 28 m (92 ft) tent roof, topped by a small drum and dome which earlier housed a lookout. The twenty corner pilasters with triple-tiered capitals, the ornamental 'darts' over the narrow windows, the three tiers of massive ogee gables which carry the lateral thrust and conceal the base octagon, the rhomboid network of ribs on the tent roof – all emphasise the pyramidality which fits organically into the landscape of the riverbank. Native and – after the model of the Archangel Cathedral – Italian Renaissance motifs make up the decor. On the terrace, with its back to the east side of the church and beneath an ogee barrel-roof, stands the 'Czar's Throne', carved in limestone, from which the ruler could survey the surrounding countryside.

The **Cathedral of the Intercession 'by the Moat' (Basil the Blessed)** on Red Square, Moscow (1555–61) (pp. 333D,342C,D), was commissioned by Ivan IV 'the Terrible' and built by Pskov architects, Barma and Posnik, as the capital's main parish church. It is a tower- and tent-church, enveloped by eight domed tower-chapels, constructed in brick with stone dressings. The buildings were consecrated following the celebrations to mark the important battles for Kazan, one of the last Mongol strongholds. Basil the Blessed, who later gave the church its name, is buried in a chapel annexed to the north-east of the building in 1588. The ground-plan is an eight-pointed star, at the centre of which is a rectangular chamber and a trapezoid apse; there are octagonal bays on the main axes and heart-shaped bays in the four corners. They are connected by an inner and (originally open) outer ring of small corridors and 'spaces'. The structure is set on a high podium reached on the west side by two symmetrical flights of stairs. Whereas the octagon is the dominant form in the ground-plan, in the silhouette and in the form generally, extensive use is made in the decoration of motifs from native and Renaissance architecture. The bizarre, fairytale excesses, however – the ribbed and faceted onion domes, the picturesque roofing of ambulatories and staircases, the polychrome paintwork of the facades – are seventeenth-century accretions. Written sources indicate that the octagon is a reference to the new Jerusalem, the Russian Empire and liturgy.

Chapter 13

EARLY MEDIAEVAL AND ROMANESQUE

Introduction

For the purpose of this introduction it is convenient to deal separately with the two centuries before the year 1000 (here referred to as pre-Romanesque) as distinct from the two centuries immediately following it.

Pre-Romanesque

The areas of Europe where buildings were constructed during this period have little in common other than their sources of inspiration. The most significant regions are the Carolingian homelands (northern France and the Rhineland), the Asturias in northern Spain, northern Italy and Anglo-Saxon England. The first of these was the most ambitious and the most influential on the emerging Romanesque style. Charlemagne, intent on re-creating the Roman Empire, based his architecture on Roman models. His palace chapel at Aachen (pp. 364K, 375A) owes much to S. Vitale at Ravenna (p. 308D), a product of the Eastern Roman Empire, and Fulda Abbey was intended to be a literal reproduction of Emperor Constantine's church of S. Peter in Rome (p. 289A). The basilican plan, as at Fulda, proved to be the most practical for abbey and cathedral churches; the Carolingians adapted it to their particular liturgical and monumental requirements by introducing the westwork, a multi-storey massif attached to, yet functionally and aesthetically separate from, the nave of the church as at Corvey-on-the-Weser. The eastern tower as at S. Riquier, which was a precursor of the crossing tower, was also introduced, and a type of crypt in the form of a lean-to passageway, as at Brixworth (pp. 397C, 399A), around the eastern sanctuary of the church to facilitate the circulation of processions past the principal reliquary of the church beneath the main altar. This form of crypt derives from the internal ring crypt added to the church of S. Peter by Pope Gregory during the seventh century.

For the rest, basilican churches followed the Early Christian model. They were aisled with arcades on columns or on piers of rectangular section as at Steinbach, had timber-framed roofs and large areas of smooth, unarticulated wall surface above the arcades, undisturbed except by simple arched windows and colourful painted decoration. The best surviving illustration of this is in the Early Christian church of S. Apollinare in Classe at Ravenna (pp. 294D, 296B). The transept, first employed at S. Peter's again, was copied in several Carolingian buildings, for example at Fulda and S. Denis.

Romanesque

Romanesque architecture is characterised by the desire to articulate, to stress or underline every structural division in order to produce unified compositions. The smooth surfaces and undifferentiated colonnades of Early Christian and Carolingian interiors are mostly rejected in favour of articulating bay divisions in a variety of ways. The separate parts of the Carolingian church – the westwork, the transept and the outer crypt – are gradually incorporated into a single harmonious composition by the transformation of the westwork into a towered facade, by absorbing the transept into the design through the creation of the crossing, and by making the outer crypt simply an extension of the aisles carried round the sanctuary to form the ambulatory.

The first signs of this new movement in architecture appeared in different parts of Europe at roughly the same time – around the year 1000 – and the desire to articulate structure manifested itself in different ways according to the area. The most important innovations were the development of pier forms, the introduction of the triforium gallery, the regular crossing, the inclusion of wall passages, ambulatories with radiating chapels, the evolution of new concepts in external massing, and an increasing mastery of architectural sculpture.

The greater complexity of piers proved to be an effective way of stressing bay divisions and thus articulating the interior elevations. It started with simple elements of a pier being allowed to project beyond the wall plane and from there being taken up the full height of the interior elevation. This occurs in its simplest form at S. Martin du Canigou (p. 385A), where a pair of cruciform piers carry pilasters which become transverse arches reinforcing the barrel vaults. Soon every pier is treated in this manner and the number of pier elements or orders is multiplied as at Cardona (p. 385B). After this the most important development was the introduction of half-columns, as at Santiago de Compostela (pp. 382A, 386A,B), and later nook shafts or small columns which carry the outer orders of the main arches, as at S. Etienne, Caen (p. 370A,E). In Germany, the Early Christian colonnade remained popular. However, concessions were made to the new desire for articulation with the use of alternating columns and piers. The church of S. Michael at Hildesheim (p. 375C) stresses bay divisions with piers of plain square section which contrast strongly with the columns and divide the nave into three compartments.

The triforium gallery (an upper aisle) was first used in western Europe in the church of S. Cyriakus at Gernrode (pp. 374H, 375B). It did not become popular in Germany and was developed instead mainly in France. It gradually acquired more importance in the elevation, growing from small twin arches at Bernay Abbey into an arcade in its own right echoing the dimensions of the main arcade below at S. Etienne in Caen (pp. 370, 371D). The arcade was often subdivided as at Peterborough Cathedral (p. 404). The triforium gallery played an essential role in the Romanesque preoccupation with breaking up the smooth wall surfaces and transforming them into articulate architectural units.

Transepts during the Early Christian and Carolingian periods were either rooms (porticus) to the north and south sides of the choir as at Steinbach, or a virtually separate building laid across the eastern end of the nave (the continuous transept) as at S. Peter's in Rome (p. 289A), Fulda and S. Denis, Paris (p. 371E). The Romanesque period incorporated the transept into a unified design by creating the regular crossing: a square or nearly square bay bordered on each side with an arch of equal size corresponding to the four arms of the church as at S. Michael at Hildesheim (p. 375C). The crossing was normally surmounted by a tower.

Wall passages contained within the thickness of walls were common in Germany, Italy, Britain and Normandy. The primary purpose was, again, to articulate the wall surface by forming, on one side of a passage, small architectural compositions of columns and arches. They were usually confined to the uppermost sections of walls where the loss of mass is not detrimental to stability. In Germany and Italy they opened outwards and decorated the exterior wall-faces as at Speyer Cathedral (p. 375E), while in Britain and Normandy they opened inwards, passing in front of the clerestory windows as at Peterborough Abbey (pp. 404, 462D).

An ambulatory is the extension of the aisles around an apsidal sanctuary so that they join, creating a continuous curved passageway. Usually a number of chapels are attached as at Santiago de Compostela (pp. 282A, 386A,B) and Conques Abbey. This is a Romanesque innovation illustrating admirably the desire to incorporate a variety of interdependent forms into a single harmonious composition.

Exterior massing during the Romanesque period is also characterised by the desire to achieve legibility through stressing the elements which make up an architectural composition. Thus the nave, aisles, transepts, crossing, subsidiary chapels and even stair turrets can be immediately identified from a cursory examination of the exterior. The Church of the Apostles at Cologne (p. 376), for example, can be seen to have a trefoil east end, an aisled nave, a western transept and a western tower. Towers also mark the eastern crossing, the stair turrets flanking the sanctuary and the west end.

Architectural sculpture developed dramatically during the Romanesque period. Styles of carving vary greatly with the region, but one constant emerges, and this is the primarily architectural role of sculpture. Sculptural decoration and carved mouldings are used to emphasise certain architectural features and epitomise the Romanesque preoccupation with articulation. Therefore sculpture is normally confined to capitals, doorways, windows and arcades. The angle roll (p. 370A,E), first used at S. Etienne at Caen during the 1060s, is commonly found on arches, and serves to create continuity between the shafted pier and the arch. Doorways often receive lavish decoration, sometimes with carved tympana (pp. 362, 364, 367, 374, 386B). Capitals most commonly derive from the antique Corinthian capital (pp. 362, 364), interpreted in many different ways with varying degrees of detail. The cushion capital, a purely geometric form consisting of a cube and sphere combined, is Germanic in origin, its popularity spreading to Britain and Normandy at the time of the Norman Conquest (p. 404J).

While it is convenient to describe the contributions of the Romanesque period to architectural development in terms of ecclesiastical buildings in an age whose ethos is dominated by the church, this does not imply that there was no other building work carried out. Surviving manor houses, town houses and farmhouses are few, but military architecture in the form of castle and keep is more common because more substantially constructed. Brief notes on their forms are given in the relevant sections on Architectural Character in this chapter and a substantial number of them appear among the examples.

Italy: Architectural Character

Central Italy

The basilican type of church was closely adhered to during this period. The Italians were slow to adopt a new system of construction and preferred to concentrate on beauty and delicacy of ornamental detail, while retaining an architectural character much governed by Classical traditions. The most pronounced features of facades were the ornamental wall passages which rose one above the other, sometimes even into the gables (pp. 350A, 353A). The use of marble-faced walls distinguishes Romanesque architecture in Italy from that of the rest of western Europe. Churches had, for the most part, simple open timber roofs ornamented with bright colouring. Quite commonly naves were divided from aisles by antique columns (p. 350C).

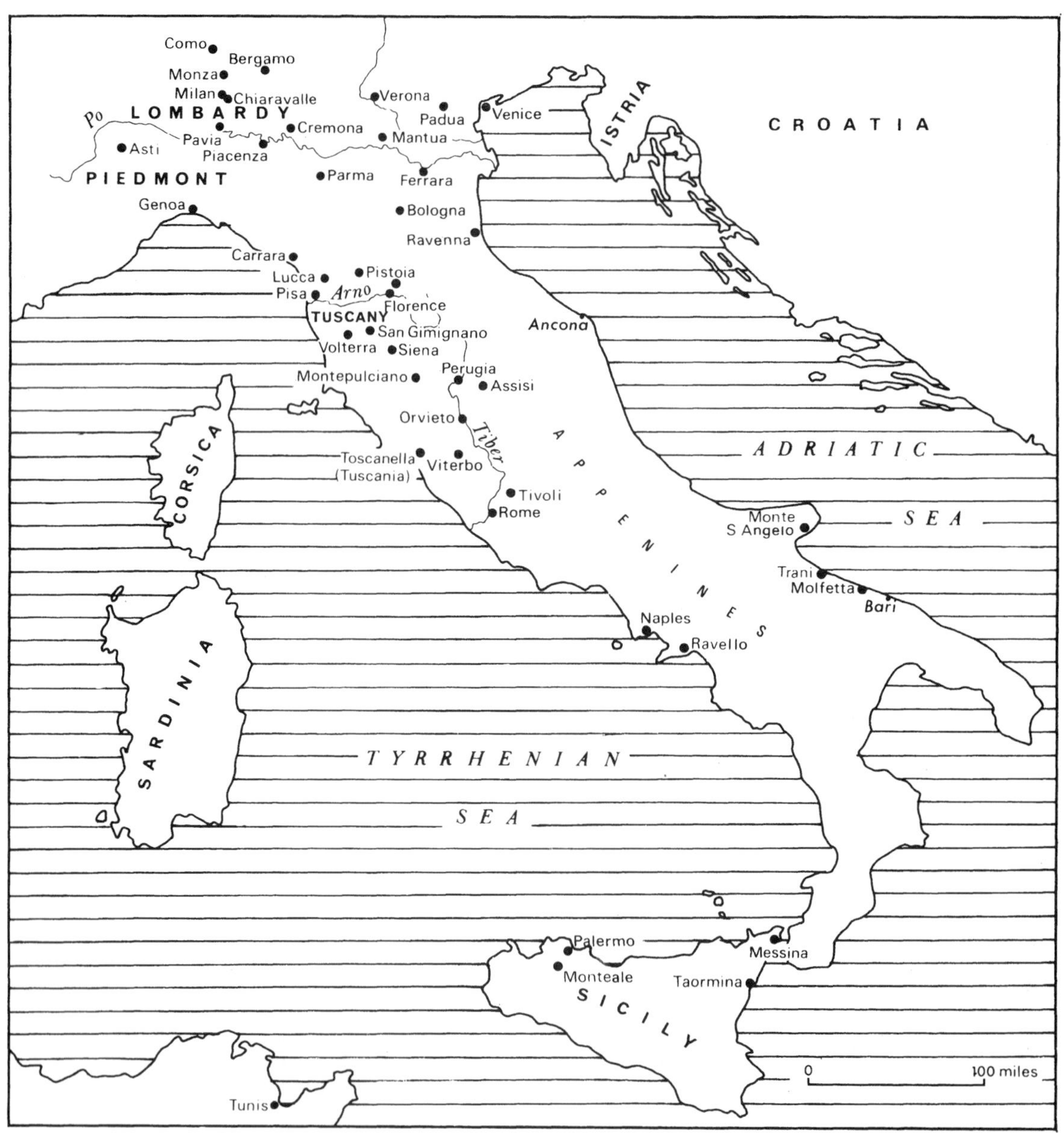

Italy in the Middle Ages

B DETAILS OF DOORWAY: S. CRISTOFORO: LUCCA

C DOORWAY: S. CRISTOFORO: LUCCA

D RINGHIERA: BROLETTO: MONZA

E APSE: S. MARIA MAGGIORE: BERGAMO

F E. END: S. ABBONDIO: COMO

G APSE: S. FEDELE: COMO

H CLOISTERS: S. PAOLO: ROME

J PORCH: S. ZENO MAGGIORE: VERONA

K DOORWAY: BAPTISTERY: PISA

A BISHOP'S THRONE: S. MICHELE: MONTE S. ANGELO

B PULPIT: S. AMBROGIO: MILAN

C HIGH ALTAR: S. MARIA MAGGIORE: TUSCANIA

D BRONZE PILASTER DOOR OF TRANI CATHEDRAL

E F COUPLED CAPITALS CLOISTERS: MONREALE

G BRONZE PILASTER DOOR OF RAVELLO CATHL.

H CORBEL TABLES: S. AMBROGIO: MILAN

J DOOR LINTEL: S. GIUSTO: LUCCA

K MOSAIC PAVING S. PIETRO: TUSCANIA

L FONT: BAPTISTERY: PARMA

The choir was occasionally raised above a crypt reached by steps from the nave.

In consequence of the brilliant climate, while arcades are universal, doors and windows are small and unimportant, with 'jambs' in rectangular recesses or 'orders' filled in with small shafts, crowned with semicircular arches (p. 347B,C) in contrast to the Classical architrave. Window tracery was at no time employed to any great extent in Italy, and even wheel-windows are only rudimentary in pattern. Timber roofs over naves are of the simple, open basilican type with rafters and tie-beams often effectively decorated in colour (p. 354A); while aisles occasionally have groin vaults of small span, divided into compartments by transverse arches.

A vast number of columns from ancient Roman temples were used in the new churches, and this retarded the development of the novel types of column which were introduced in districts more remote from Rome (pp. 350C, 354A). The finely carved and slender twisted columns in the cloisters of S. Giovanni in Laterano and S. Paolo fuori le Mura, Rome, are delicate variations of the Classical type (p. 347H). There are rough imitations of old Classical mouldings, but elaborate variations of a more pronounced Romanesque type in recessed planes were used in doorways and windows (p. 347B-E).

Classical precedent in ornament was followed so as to suit the old fragments incorporated in the new buildings, and rough variations of the Roman acanthus scroll are frequent (p. 348D,J). The rows of Apostles on doorway lintels, as at Pistoia, are similar in style to Byzantine ivories. In all parts of Italy Christian symbolism now entered into decorative carving and mosaics. The monogram of Christ, the emblems of evangelists and saints, and the whole system of symbolism, represented by trees, birds, fishes and animals, are all worked into the decorative scheme. At Tuscania, the high altar in S. Maria Maggiore and the mosaic paving in S. Pietro (p. 348C,K) are characteristic of the region and of their period. Byzantine influence was strong in Ravenna and Pisa, which developed their own individual styles. Campanili or bell-towers, which seem to have originated in the sixth century, henceforward gave a special character to ecclesiastical architecture (pp. 350A, 351A–D).

Northern Italy

It was in Lombardy that the most important advances took place. The principal innovations were the development of the rib vault, the exterior wall passage and the arched corbel table. The Lombard rib vault was short-lived but exterior wall passages (no more than niches in the first instance) and arched corbel tables, introduced in simple forms during the tenth century, spread quickly to northern Spain, central Italy, Burgundy and the German Empire. Arched corbel tables are an eaves decoration consisting of corbels interconnected with arches (p. 348H).

The northern Italian churches are basilican in type, but naves as well as side aisles are vaulted and have external wooden roofs. Aisles are often two storeys in height, while thick walls between the side chapels act as buttresses to resist the pressure of the vaults. The flat, severe entrance facades stretch across the whole church, thus making externally the division of nave and aisles. There is often a central projecting porch, with columns standing on the backs of crouching beasts and a wheel window above to light the nave. The gable is characteristically outlined with arched corbel tables and there are also arcades round the apse under the eaves. The general character becomes less refined, as stone and brick are used instead of marble, and ornament shows a departure from Classical precedent. The Comacene masters, a privileged guild of architects and sculptors originating in Como, built churches with characteristic decoration during the eleventh century, not only in the north, but also in other parts of Italy.

There were many baptisteries, usually octagonal or circular, such as the one at Novara, which is connected to the Cathedral by an atrium similar to the more famous one at S. Ambrogio, Milan. Wall passages round such features as apses and octagonal lanterns give great charm to the buildings externally (p. 347E,G). Towers are straight shafts, often detached, as at Verona (p. 357A), without buttresses or spires (pp. 347F, 353C, 354C). The composition of facades usually relies upon simple pilaster strip decoration, running from the ground and ending in arched corbel tables, as at S. Abbondio, Como (p. 347F). Internally, sturdy piers faced with attached half-columns took the place of the Classical column, to provide support for the heavy stone vaulting (p. 355B,D). The half-columns on the side towards the nave were carried up as vaulting shafts, and this was the beginning of a system which was destined in the Gothic period to transform the shape of piers.

As decoration there are roughly carved grotesques of men and beasts and vigorous hunting scenes and incidents of daily life. Crouching beasts supporting columns of projecting porches and interior furnishings such as bishops' thrones (p. 348A) and fonts (p. 348L) and corbel tables (p. 348H) are typical.

Southern Italy and Sicily

The changing architectural character can be traced through Byzantine, Muslim and Norman rule, and each successive period carried with it something from the past. Byzantine influence is evident in the mosaic decoration of interiors and predominates in the plans of such buildings as the church of Martorana at

PISA CATHEDRAL
CAMPANILE
CATHEDRAL
BAPTISTERY
A THE PISAN GROUP FROM S.W.
NAVE
x
x
B PLAN
SCALE FOR PLAN
FEET 100 50 0 50 100 150
METRES 10 0 10 20 30 40
C INTERIOR LOOKING E.
D BIRD'S-EYE VIEW FROM CAMPANILE
100 FT
90
80
70
60
50
40
30
20
10
0
162'-0"
NAVE
APSE
E TRANSVERSE SECTION x·x
F LONGITUDINAL SECTION

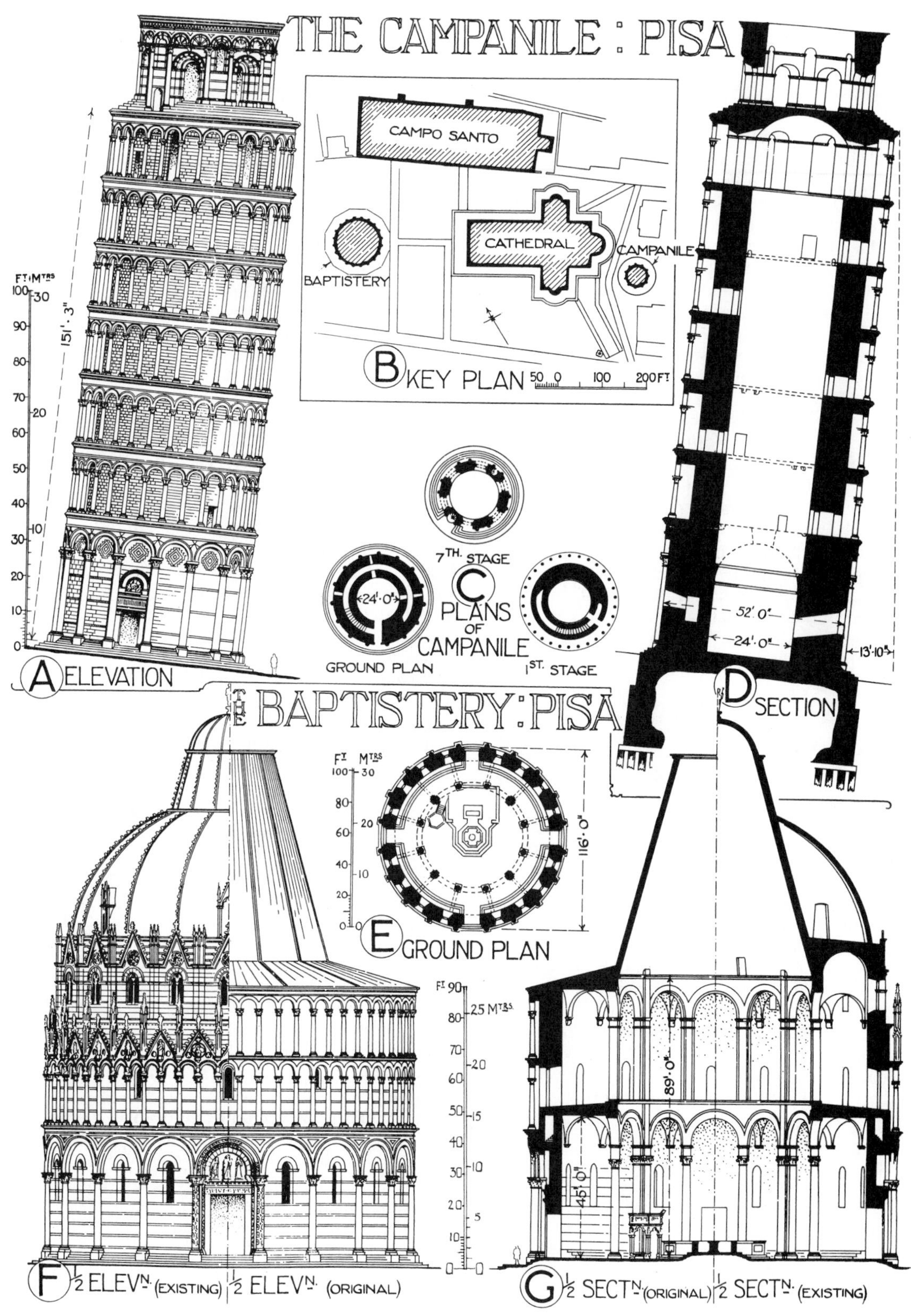
THE CAMPANILE : PISA
CAMPO SANTO
CATHEDRAL
BAPTISTERY
CAMPANILE
B KEY PLAN 50 0 100 200 FT
7TH. STAGE
C PLANS OF CAMPANILE
GROUND PLAN
1ST. STAGE
24'. 0"
FT MTRS
151'. 3"
A ELEVATION
52'. 0"
24'. 0"
13'. 10"
D SECTION
THE BAPTISTERY: PISA
116'. 0"
E GROUND PLAN
89'. 0"
45'. 0"
F ½ ELEVN. (EXISTING) ½ ELEVN. (ORIGINAL)
G ½ SECTN. (ORIGINAL) ½ SECTN. (EXISTING)

Palermo, where the dome, supported on four columns, covers the square central space. Muslim influence is apparent in the application of coloured marbles in striped patterns and in the use of stilted pointed arches. Norman influence is displayed for example in the planning and construction of the cathedral of Monreale: it has a cruciform plan although it is decorated with mosaics and has a nave arcade of stilted pointed arches. In southern Italy domes rather than vaults were adopted, but in Sicily under Muslim influence timber roofs were the rule and had stalactite ceilings, rich in design and colour.

Lateral walls were occasionally decorated with flat pilaster strips connected horizontally by arched corbel tables. Wheel windows, as in the churches of Palermo, are often made of elaborately pierced sheets of marble. There was greater variety in columns and capitals, because of the successive introduction of Byzantine, Muslim and Norman influence. This is evident in the nave arcade and the coupled columns in the cloisters at Monreale (pp.348E,F, 358A).

In southern Italy elaborately modelled bronze outer doors are characteristic. Coloured mosaics add to the beauty of the interiors of Palermo churches and indeed colour, used in geometric designs, was predominant in the internal decoration of southern Italian and more especially of Sicilian churches, while bronze pilasters (p. 348D,G) indicate a lingering reflection of the Classical tradition.

Italy: Examples

Central Italy

Pisa Cathedral (1063–1118 and 1261–72) (pp. 350, 351) with Baptistery, Campanile and Campo Santo, together form one of the most famous building groups of the world. The cathedral is one of the finest of the Romanesque period and has a strongly marked individuality. It resembles other early basilican churches in plan, with long rows of columns connected by arches, double aisles, and a nave which has the usual timber roof. The exterior has bands of red and white marble, and the ground storey is faced with wall arcading, while the entrance facade is thrown into relief by tiers of wall passages which rise one above another right into the gable. The transepts, each with an apse at the end, were an advance on the simple basilican plan. The elliptical dome over the crossing is of later date. The building depends for its interest on its general proportions and on the delicacy of its ornamental features, rather than on any new structural development, such as may be seen in northern Italy.

The **Campanile, Pisa** (1174–1271) (pp. 350, 351), is a circular tower, 16 m (52 ft) in diameter, rising in eight storeys of encircling arcades. This world-famous leaning tower, which is the most arresting feature of the group, has been the subject of much discussion, but there is little doubt that its inclination is due to subsidence in the foundations. The upper part of the tower now overhangs its base more than 4.2 m (13 ft 9 in), and it thus has a very unstable appearance. The bell stage was not added until 1350.

The **Baptistery, Pisa** (1153–1265) (pp. 350, 351), was designed by Dioti Salvi, on a circular plan, with a central space or nave, 18.3 m (60 ft) in diameter, separated by four piers and eight columns from the surrounding two-storey aisle, which makes the building nearly 39.3 m (129 ft) in diameter. Externally it is surrounded on the lower storey by half-columns, connected by semicircular arches, under one of which is the door (p. 347K), with, above, an open arcade of small detached shafts. This arcade is surmounted by Gothic additions of the fourteenth century, which disguise the original design. The structure is crowned by an outer hemispherical roof, through which penetrates a truncated cone capped by a small dome, covering the central space (p. 351F,G).

S. Martino, Lucca (facade 1204) and **S. Michele, Lucca** (1143 and later) – with a facade (1288) of which the gables are mere screens – are very similar in style to the buildings of the Pisan group, because at the time of their erection Lucca had fallen under the power of Pisa.

Pistoia Cathedral (thirteenth century) (p. 353A) was also built under the influence of the Pisan school, and with its porch and arcaded facade in black and white marble followed the style of other churches in the city, including **S. Andrea** and **S. Giovanni fuor Civitas** (late twelfth century).

The **Cloisters of S. Giovanni in Laterano, Rome** (1234) and of **S. Paolo fuori le Mura, Rome** (*c.* 1200) (p. 347H) are of special interest because, so persistent was the Classical tradition, they are among the few instances of Romanesque art in Rome which are progressive in character. The use of Roman architectural fragments still gave the churches a basilican character. Delicate twin twisted columns, inlaid with patterned glass mosaics, are the special feature of these cloisters, and are a triumph of craftsmanship. The coupled columns carry semicircular arches in groups of five or more openings between the recurrent piers, and form an arcade round the four sides of the cloister.

S. Miniato al Monte, Florence (1018–62) (p. 354A), shows some innovations: the length of the church is divided by piers of quatrefoil section and transverse diaphragm arches into three main compartments, of which the raised eastern portion has a crypt open to the nave and containing the tomb of the saint. In between the compound piers the nave arcade is carried on pairs of columns. This division seems a prelude to the idea of vaulting in compartments, and

A. Pistoia Cathedral (thirteenth century). See p.352

B. S. Pietro Agliate (early eleventh century). See p.356

C. S. Ambrogio, Milan, showing atrium (*c.* 1080–1128). See p.356

A. S. Miniato al Monte, Florence (1018–62): nave looking east. See p.352

B. Baptistery, Cremona (1167). See p.356

C. Torre Asinelli (1100) (right) and Torre Garisenda (1100), Bologna, See p.361

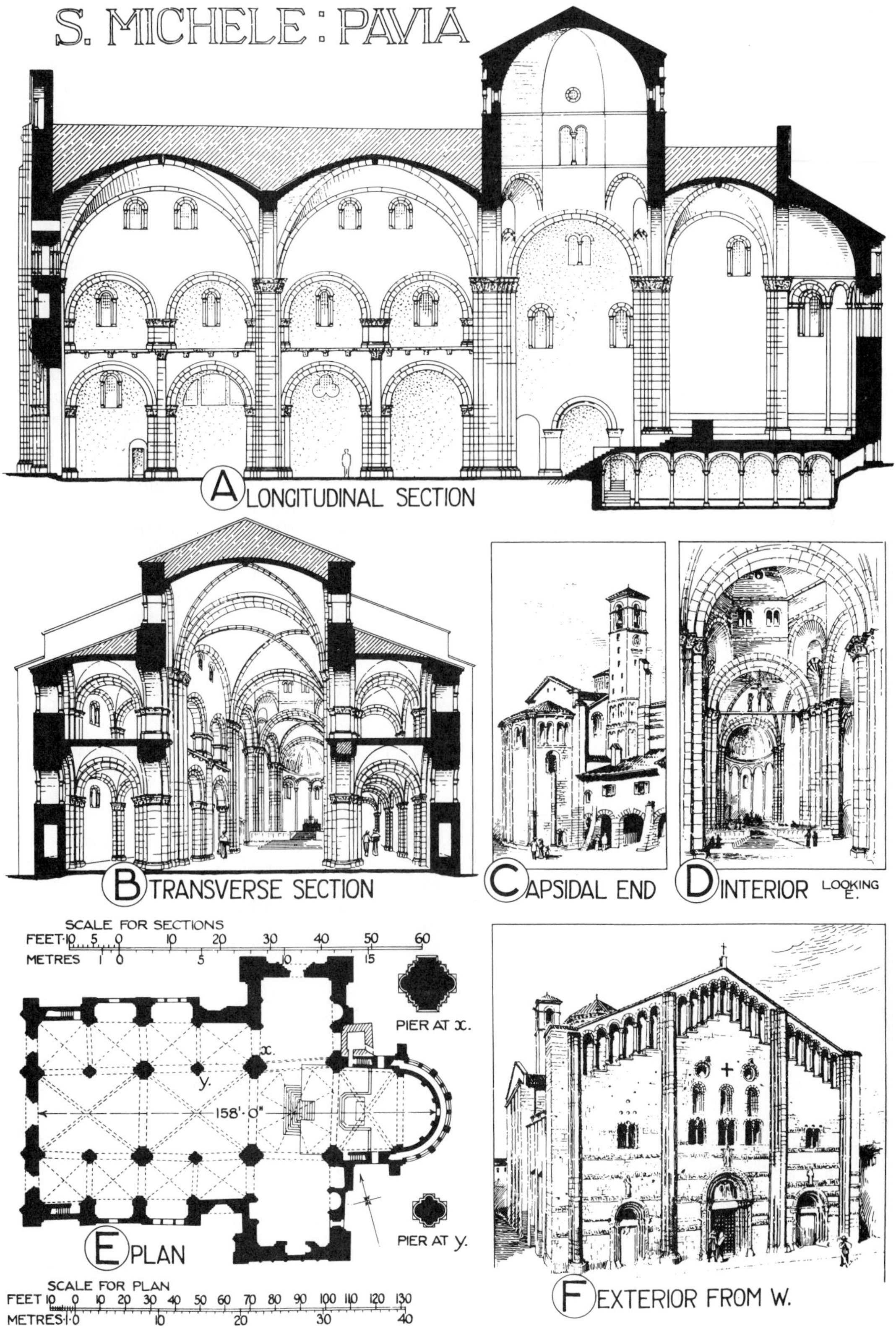
S. MICHELE : PAVIA
A LONGITUDINAL SECTION
B TRANSVERSE SECTION
C APSIDAL END
D INTERIOR LOOKING E.
SCALE FOR SECTIONS
FEET 10 5 0 10 20 30 40 50 60
METRES 1 0 5 10 15
PIER AT x.
x.
y.
158'-0"
PIER AT y.
E PLAN
SCALE FOR PLAN
FEET 10 0 10 20 30 40 50 60 70 80 90 100 110 120 130
METRES 1 0 10 20 30 40
F EXTERIOR FROM W.

is a departure from the basilican type of long, unbroken ranges of columns and arches. The novel panelling and banding in black and white marble of both exterior and interior surfaces were carried further in the Gothic period in Italy. Instead of glass, the sanctuary has translucent marble in the window openings. The open timber roof is decorated with bright colours.

Northern Italy

S. Pietro, Agliate (early eleventh century) (p. 353B), is an early Lombard church. It is built of coursed rubble, the exterior simply articulated with pilaster strips. The main apse is decorated at eaves level with a series of niches hollowed out above the vault. This was a form of decoration which would develop into arcaded wall passages.

S. Ambrogio, Milan (*c.* 1080–1128) (p. 353C), founded by the great S. Ambrose in the fourth century, raised on its present plan (*c.* 850) and partly rebuilt with vault and dome in the twelfth century, has a proud history, and provided a model for Lombard churches, as did its founder for Lombard ritual, which included the metrical chanting of the Mass. Here S. Augustine was baptised, the Emperor Theodosius was excommunicated, and Lombard kings and Germanic emperors were crowned. The church is built of brick. The plan includes the only existing atrium among Lombard churches, a narthex flanked by towers, vaulted nave and aisles with an octagon over the crossing, triforium gallery, raised choir over the crypt, and an apse. The interior is severely plain and impressive. The pulpit, which is built over a sixth-century sarcophagus, consists of an arcade with characteristic Lombard ornamentation of carved birds and animals.

S. Michele, Pavia (twelfth century) (p. 355), is a version in stone of the structural system of S. Ambrogio, which itself is an advance on the divisions, marked only by piers, in S. Miniato; for here not only is the nave divided into square bays by transverse arches but the dividing piers are of a clustered character, shaped to receive the vaulting ribs. The nave vaults themselves have been rebuilt. This church is cruciform in plan with well-defined transepts and a raised choir, under which is a vaulted crypt. The side aisles, which are two storeys in height, are also vaulted in square compartments, two of which correspond to one vaulting bay of the nave. The flat facade shows little play of light and shade, with its three simple recessed portals and four vertical pilaster strips from ground to gable, almost akin to buttresses. The wide-spreading gable stretches across nave and aisles and is emphasised by a characteristic raking arcaded wall passage – the only prominent feature of this simple design.

S. Zeno Maggiore, Verona (*c.* 1123 and later) (p. 357A), has a facade which is stern in its simplicity. The fine projecting porch has two free-standing columns, which rest on the backs of crouching beasts and support a semicircular vault, over which is a gabled roof. Above is the great wheel window to light the nave, one of the earliest in Italy, and the whole facade is relieved by pilaster strips connected by corbel tables under the slopes of the centre gable and side roofs. The interior has a nave arcade of compound piers with uncarved capitals, and the nave shaft is carried up as if to support a vault. Intermediate columns with carved capitals support semicircular arches, surmounted by a wall banded in red brick and stone. There is no triforium, but a clerestory, and above this is a wooden ceiling of trefoil form. The choir, 2.1 m (7 ft) above the nave floor, has a high pointed fourteenth-century vault and an apse, beneath which is the crypt, in seven aisles, and containing the shrine of S. Zeno. This is a development of the traditional arrangement of high choir over crypt in pilgrimage churches which can be traced back through S. Ambrogio (p. 353C), S. Pietro at Agliate (*c.* 1000) (p. 353B), S. Apollinare in Classe at Ravenna (pp. 294D, 296B) and the seventh-century adaptations of the east end of Old S. Peter's in Rome. The campanile is detached, as is usual in Italy, has no buttresses, and is of alternate courses of marble and brick, terminating in open arcades to the bell-chamber, angle pinnacles and a high-pitched roof. The sturdy tower formerly belonged to a residence of the mediaeval German emperors and is finished with Ghibelline battlements.

Baptisteries are a special feature of Italian architecture and represent a period of Christianity when the baptismal rite was of special ceremonial importance and therefore required a large and separate building. The **Baptistery, Cremona** (1167) (p. 354B), is octagonal, and has a projecting porch and the usual pilaster strips, corbel tables and arcading. The **Baptistery, Asti** (1060), and the **Baptistery, Parma** (1196–1270), are octagonal, modelled on that of Constantine, Rome (p. 293).

The campanili or bell-towers are a product of the period, and, unlike the church towers of England, France and Germany, generally stand alone, though they were sometimes connected by cloisters to the church. In northern Italian towns campanili are often civic monuments rather than integral parts of churches, and, like the civic towers of Belgium (p. 514), were symbols of power and served also as watch towers. They are square in plan, without the projecting buttresses which are usual north of the Alps, and their design is generally simple, broken only by windows which light the internal staircase or sloping way. The window openings increase in number with the height of the tower and at the top often form an open loggia, through which may be seen the swinging of the bells, and the whole is often surmounted by a

A. S. Zeno Maggiore, Verona (*c.* 1123 and later). See p.356

B. Fondaco dei Turchi, Venice (twelfth century but largely rebuilt). See p.361

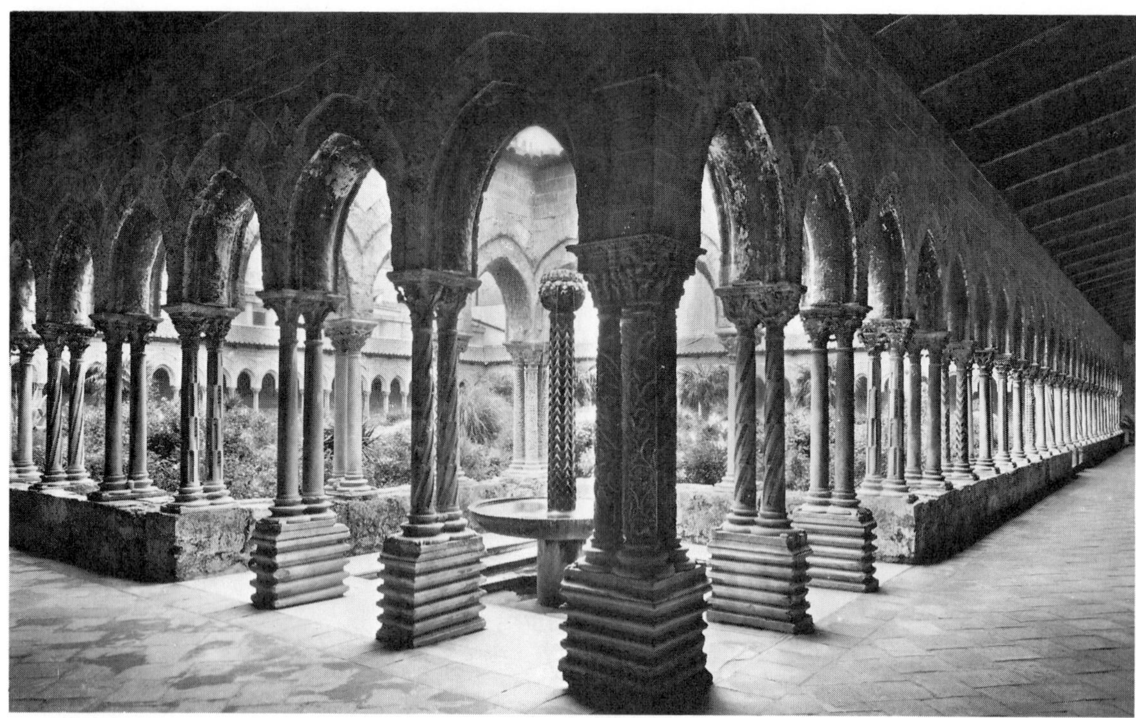

A. Monreale Cathedral: the cloisters (1172–89). See p.361

B. Cappella Palatina, Palermo: interior (1129–43). See p.361

C. La Zisa, Palermo (1154–66). See p.361

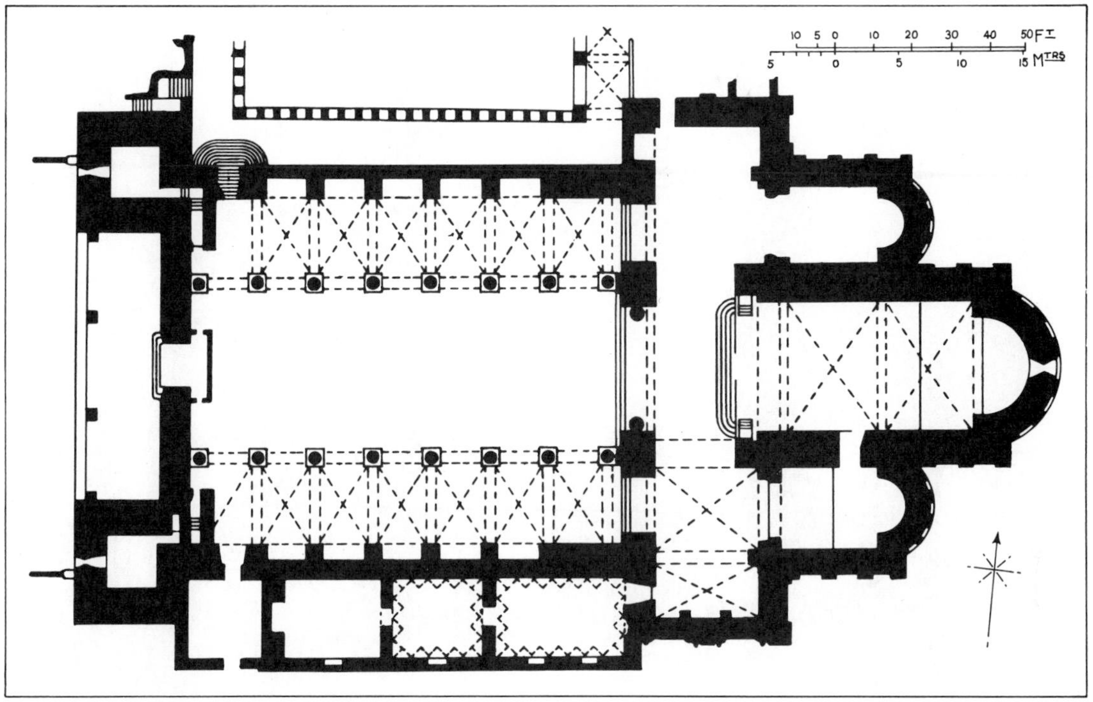

A. S. Nicola, Bari: plan (*c.* 1058–1132). See p.361

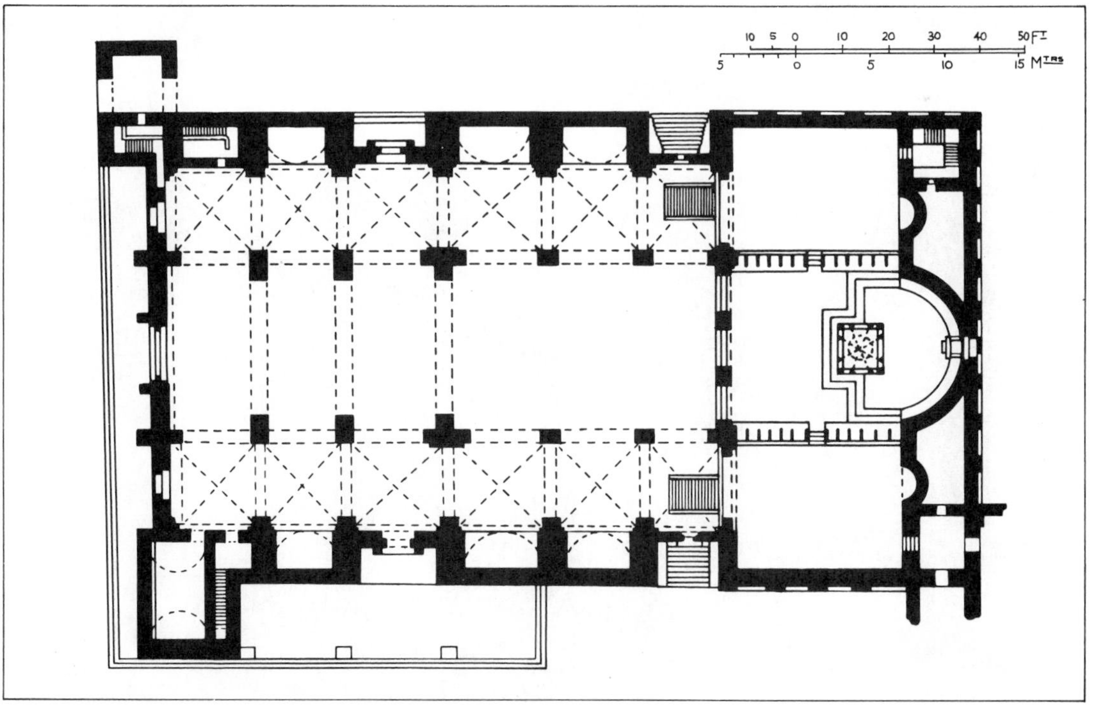

B. Cefalù Cathedral: plan (1131–1240). See p.361

A. S. Nicola, Bari: interior (*c.* 1085–1132). See p.361

B. Cefalù Cathedral: from SE (1131–1240). See p.361

pyramid roof, as in the rebuilt campanile of S. Mark, Venice, originally built in 888, and also in that of **S. Zeno Maggiore**, Verona (p. 357A), which dates originally from 1172.

The **Torre Asinelli, Bologna** (1109) (p. 361C), 69 m (225 ft) high, and the **Torre Garisenda, Bologna** (1100), 40 m (130 ft) high, date from the time when the town was prominent in the struggles of the period, and are the leaning towers referred to by Dante.

The **Fondaco dei Turchi, Venice** (p. 357B), a twelfth-century mercantile palace (since rebuilt) on the Grand Canal, demonstrates the high level of quality domestic architecture achieved in Venice as one of the outcomes of its prosperous trade with the East. The **Palazzo Farsetti** and the **Palazzo Loredan** (twelfth century) are in the same style, with cubiform capitals carrying semicircular arches, some of which are stilted.

Southern Italy and Sicily

S. Nicola, Bari (*c.* 1085–1132) (pp. 359A, 360A), a Benedictine church, was the prototype of the Romanesque of the late eleventh and twelfth centuries in Apulia. It has an aisled western arm, transepts, three eastern apses and two western towers. The most distinctive and influential feature is the structural organisation of the nave, with its main arcade on piers and grouped columns, triforium and clerestory generously proportioned. The nave has added diaphragm arches and a flat timber ceiling; the groined aisle vaults support a gallery. This church shares fine masonry details, including projecting porches, wheel windows, a refined carved decoration in the Greek tradition, with other Apulian churches (mostly cathedrals) modelled upon it. They include **Bari** itself (*c.* 1160 and later), **Trani** (*c.* 1139 and later), a pilgrimage church with basilican nave, a large crypt and some Lombard detail, **Bitetto** (early twelfth century), **Ruvo** (twelfth century), and **Bitonto** (1175–1200).

Cefalù Cathedral (1131–1240) (pp. 359B, 360B), founded by Count Roger (King Roger II of Sicily) as a royal pantheon, was served by Augustinian canons. Externally it is the most distinctly Romanesque church in Sicily, and has a basilican nave with groined aisle vaults, columnar arcades, a high transept and a triapsidal east end with later ribbed vaulting over the presbytery and south transept. The two western towers, of minaret proportions, enclose a columned porch.

Monreale Cathedral (1174–82) (pp. 315B, 358A) stands on the heights south-west of Palermo, and is the most splendid of all the monuments erected under Norman rule in Sicily. The plan is basilican in its western part though more Byzantine in its eastern part, with a choir raised above the nave and with eastern apses. The nave columns have capitals of Byzantine form with 'dosseret-blocks' encrusted with mosaic, to support pointed arches, which are not in recessed planes as in northern Romanesque buildings, and in the aisles there are pointed windows. (This building is also included in Chapter 11, where the Byzantine characteristics are outlined.) The open timber roofs, intricate in design, are brightly painted in the Muslim style. The interior is solemn and grand, an effect produced by the severity of the design, enhanced by the coloured decoration. The low, oblong central lantern and the antique bronze doors add to the beauty and distinction of this famous church. The cloisters (1172–89) (p. 358A), the only remaining portion of the Benedictine monastery, are the finest of the style. They consist of coupled columns, in some cases inlaid with glass mosaics, supporting pointed arches, and have beautiful Corinthianesque capitals (p. 348E,F), one of which represents William I of Sicily offering the Church to the Virgin.

The **Capella Palatina, Palermo** (1129–43) (p. 358B), the chapel in the Royal Palace, is decorated with gilt and coloured mosaics, and has a dome of Byzantine origin, 5.5 m (18 ft) in diameter, while the stalactite ceiling, pulpit, candelabra and organ gallery are the work of Muslim craftsmen.

S. Giovanni degli Eremiti, Palermo (1148), **La Martorana, Palermo** (1143–51) (S. Maria del Ammiraglio), and **S. Cataldo, Palermo** (1161) are other churches which, in the arrangement of domes and the character of ornamentation, also blend Islamic with Byzantine influence.

La Zisa, Palermo (Arabic, El Aziza, the Palace of Delights) (1154–66) (p. 358C), is a three-storey Norman castle with a battlemented parapet, much influenced by Islamic art. The vestibule is rich in marble columns and coloured tiles, while the stalactite vaults over the alcoves recall the glories of the Alhambra, Granada (q.v.).

France: Architectural Character

In the south, churches were usually cruciform in plan and frequently had naves covered with barrel vaults. Cloisters are treated with the utmost elaboration, as at S. Trophîme, Arles (p. 362F), and are special features in the plans of many churches of the period. Circular churches are rare, but the development of the semicircular east end as an ambulatory, with radiating chapels, is common in both northern and southern France.

The south is remarkable for richly decorated church facades and graceful cloisters, and for the use of old Roman architectural features which seem to have acquired a fresh significance. Roman buildings at Arles, Nîmes, Orange and other places in

A S. ESTEPHE
B FIREPLACE & CHIMNEY: ABBEY OF SENANQUE: S. GILLES
C WEST FAÇADE: ECHILLAIS
D MONASTIC KITCHEN: FONTEVRAULT
F CLOISTERS: S. TROPHÎME: ARLES
G APSE: S. PIERRE: AULNAY
H NAVE PIERS: LESSAY
JAMB
9'-10"
5'-5½"
J DOORWAY: SERQUIGNY
K PORCH: S. TROPHÎME: ARLES
L DOORWAY: FONTGOMBAULT
M
EARLY NAVE PIER
5'-6"
N
CERISY-LA-FORET
7'-3½"
P
S. GILLES
5'-2½"
Q
ABBAYE AUX DAMES CAEN
4'-9"
R
BERNIERES-SUR-MER
NAVE PIERS

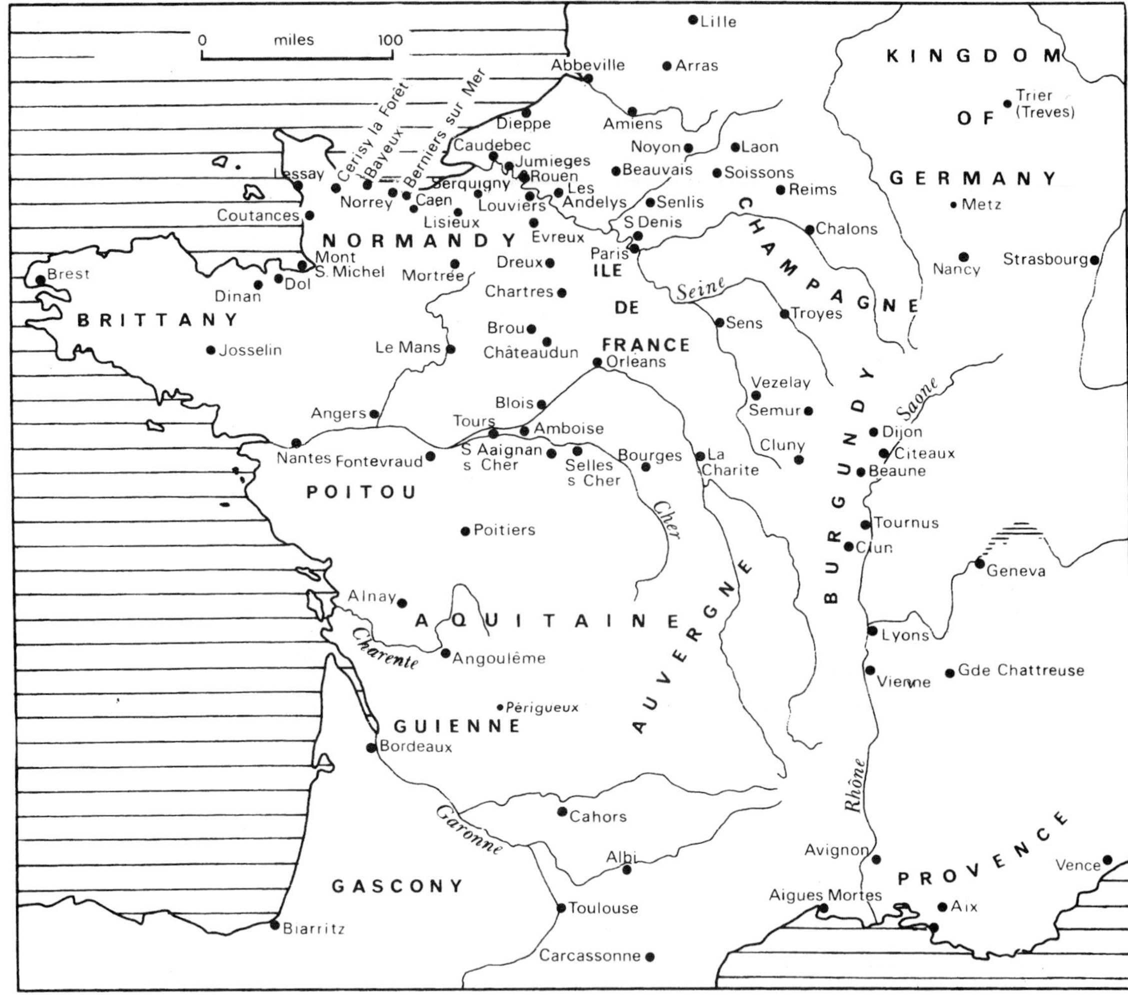

France in the Middle Ages

the Rhône valley naturally exerted considerable influence throughout Provence. Vaulting, supported only by the massive walls of the recessed chapels, recalls the great halls of Roman thermae. The development of vaulting (see Chapter 8, pp. 198 to 207) progressed, and naves were often covered with barrel vaults, whose thrust was resisted by half-barrel vaults over two-storey aisles, thus suppressing the clerestory, as at Notre Dame du Port, Clermont-Ferrand. Aisleless churches often have blind nave wall arcades (p. 369A,B,F), while cloister arcades are elaborated with coupled columns in the depth of the walls, and with carved capitals which support the semicircular arches of the narrow bays, which were left unglazed as in Italy (p. 362F). The western portals of such churches as S. Trophîme, Arles (p. 362K), and S. Gilles (p. 367A) recall the columns and horizontal entablatures of the Romans, but in other cases doorways have recessed jambs as usual in this period (p. 362J,L). Narrow windows with semicircular heads and wide splays internally suffice to admit light, especially in the south (p. 362G).

In the north, where Roman remains were less abundant, there seems to have been greater freedom to develop a new style, and western facades of churches, especially in Normandy, are distinguished by the introduction of two flanking towers. Plain, massive side-walls with flat buttresses emphasise the richness of the facades. Naves usually had wooden ceilings until the introduction of the rib vault in the early twelfth century. The compound pier comprising four attached half-columns around a square core (p. 362P) was also evolved in northern

A CAPITAL: FLEAC
B TYMPANUM: LA CHARITÉ-SR-LOIRE
C CAPITAL: S. AIGNAN-SR-CHER
D TWIN CAPITALS: S. SERNIN: TOULOUSE
E APSIDAL END: SELLES-SUR-CHER
F CARVING: VENCE
G TWIN CAPS CLOISTER S. TROPHÎME: ARLES
H BASES: AIX CATHL
J SCULPD FRIEZE: ANGOULÊME CATHL
K PIER AND COLUMNS: CLOISTER: AIX CATHL
L DOORWAY: S. GILLES
M SCULPD SPANDREL. BAYEUX CATHEDRAL

France, and introduced at Auxerre Cathedral after the fire of 1023. Variations of this type of pier were common throughout France by the end of the eleventh century.

France: Examples

Ecclesiastical Architecture

Southern France includes Aquitaine, Auvergne, Provence, Anjou and Burgundy, each with its special architectural peculiarities.

S. Philibert, Tournus (*c.* 950–*c.* 1120) (p. 366A), is an early Romanesque abbey church embellished later with vaults, a transept and towers. The east end has one of the first ambulatories with radiating chapels (the crypt was dedicated in 979). It also has a three-bay westwork or narthex of two storeys with arched corbel tables externally. The nave vaults are extraordinary, consisting of transverse barrel vaults supported on diaphragm arches.

S. Sernin, Toulouse (1077–1119 and later) (p. 366C), in Aquitaine, is cruciform with nave, double aisles and transepts. The nave has a semicircular barrel vault, with plain square transverse arches, and the high triforium chamber has external windows which provide light to the nave, in the absence of a clerestory. The central octagonal tower (1250) with a spire (1478), 66 m (215 ft) high, belongs to the Gothic period (q.v.). Santiago de Compostela, Spain, is similar in many respects: both buildings were principal pilgrimage churches. **Angoulême Cathedral** (*c.* 1105–28 and later) (p. 369), in Aquitaine, has a long aisleless nave, 15.2 m (50 ft) wide, transepts with lateral chapels, and an apsidal choir with four chapels, forming a Latin cross on plan. The nave is covered with three stone domes on pendentives and a double dome over the crossing, raised on a drum with sixteen windows and crowned by a finial. Both transepts originally had towers, but the southern one was destroyed in 1568. The western facade (p. 369D) is rich with tiers of arcades divided into five bays by lofty shafts. Over the entrance is a high window, framed in sculpture, and there are two flanking western towers.

Notre Dame du Port, Clermont-Ferrand, S. Austremoine, Issoire, and **Le Puy Cathedral**, all in Auvergne and of the twelfth century, have local character imparted to them by the lightweight vaults and multicoloured inlaid decoration, all executed in the lavas of the Puy de Dôme district.

Notre Dame, Avignon (*c.* 1100), is one of the numerous Provençal churches of the eleventh and twelfth centuries in which pointed barrel vaults were used, and which show Classical influence.

S. Trophîme, Arles (1150), has beautiful cloisters with coupled carved capitals (p. 362F) and a fine porch (p. 362K), based on a Roman triumphal arch, but with modifications, such as deeply recessed jambs and columns resting on lions, behind which are sculptured saints; the entablature carries a row of figures and the sculptures in the tympanum represent Christ as Judge of the World.

The **Church of S. Gilles-du-Gard** (*c.* 1135–95), near Arles, has probably the most elaborate sculptured facade in southern France (pp. 364L, 367A), with three porches connected by colonnades perhaps suggesting the facade of S. Mark, Venice (q.v.).

Notre Dame la Grande, Poitiers (*c.* 1130–45) (p. 367C), in Anjou, has a fine sculptured west front and an imposing conical dome over the crossing, while the interior has neither triforium nor clerestory, but is covered by a barrel vault with prominent unmoulded transverse arches.

Fontevraud Abbey (*c.*, 1100–19 and later) (p. 371A), also in Anjou, resembles Angoulême Cathedral in its nave and general arrangement but its east end has a typical ambulatory with radiating chapels.

Cluny Abbey (1088–1130) was one of the most important monastic establishments in Europe. The church, of which only one transept arm survives, was the longest in Europe. It had double aisles, double transepts, an ambulatory with radiating chapels and a barrel-vaulted nave. The pointed arch was used for the nave arcades and probably also for the vault as became customary in Burgundy and Provence.

Autun Cathedral (*c.* 1120–32 and later) (p. 366B), another Burgundian church, has a nave covered with a pointed barrel vault on transverse arches. The nave elevation probably derives from Cluny and consists of three storeys including a clerestory and a blind triforium. The building has sculpture of high quality.

S. Madeleine, Vézelay (*c.* 1104–32 and later) (pp. 367B, 368), in Burgundy, has a most remarkable narthex (*c.* 1132) with nave and aisles. This leads into the church, which also has nave and aisles. The transepts, choir and chevet were completed about 1170. The nave has no triforium, but a clerestory with small windows. The nave is groin-vaulted, unusual for a main space, and is divided by polychrome transverse arches. The central portal (p. 368), with two square-headed doorways separated by a Corinthianesque column, is spanned by a large semicircular arch containing a relief of the Last Judgement. Left and right are side portals, and in the upper part of the facade is a large five-light window richly sculptured and flanked by towers, that on the left rising only to the height of the nave.

Northern France includes Normandy, the Ile de France, Brittany and the Champagne. (For S. Riquier Abbey, see Central Europe; for S. Martin du Canigou, see Spain.)

A. S. Philibert, Tournus (*c.* 950–*c.* 1120): nave. See p.365

B. Autun Cathedral: interior looking towards sanctuary (*c.* 1120–32). See p.365

C. S. Sernin, Toulouse, from SW (1077–1119 and later). See p.365

A. S. Gilles-du-Gard, near Arles: west facade (*c.* 1135–95). See p.365

B. S. Madeleine, Vézelay: narthex (*c.* 1132). See p.365

C. Notre Dame La Grande, Poitiers (*c.* 1130–45). See p.365

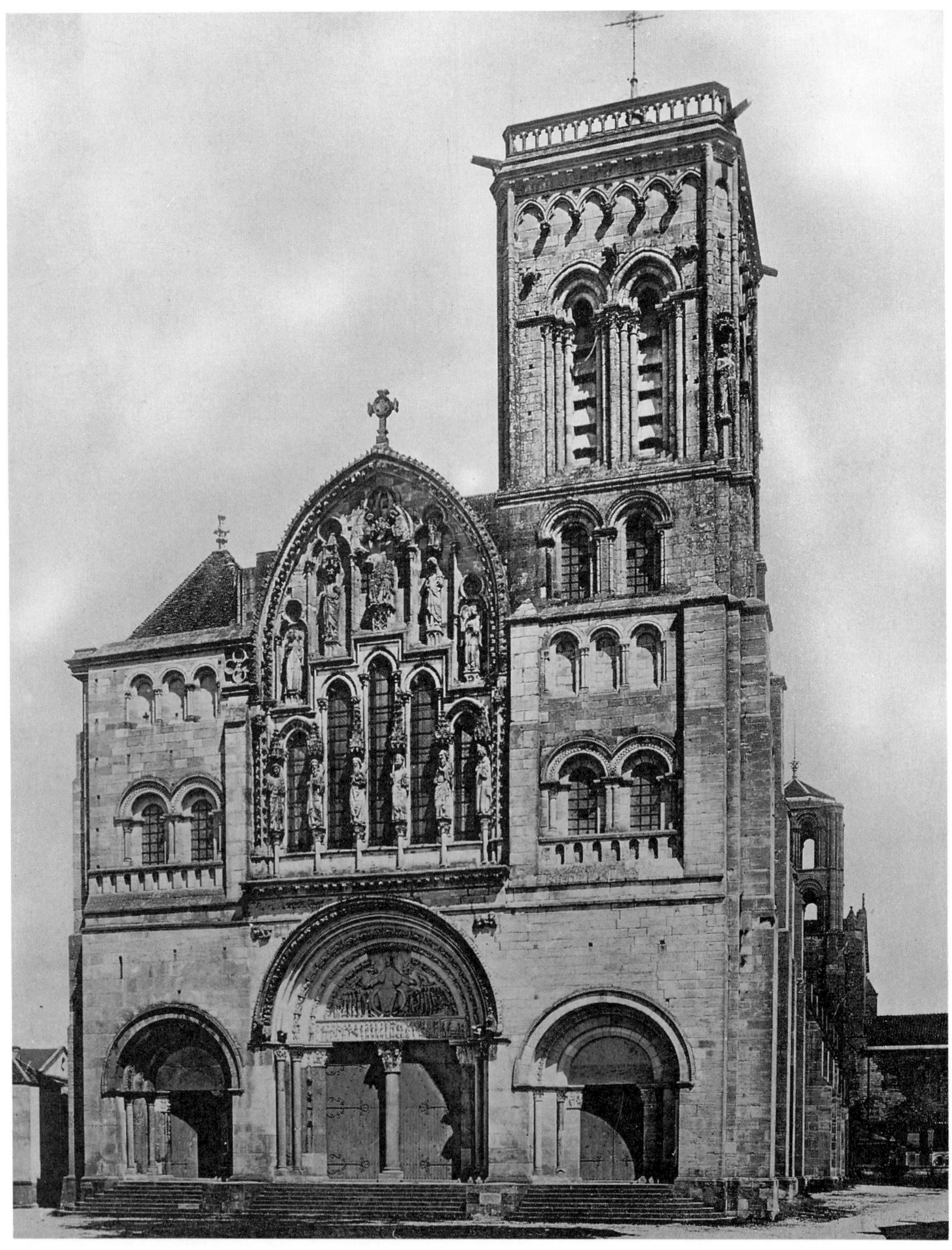

S. Madeleine, Vézelay: facade. See p.365

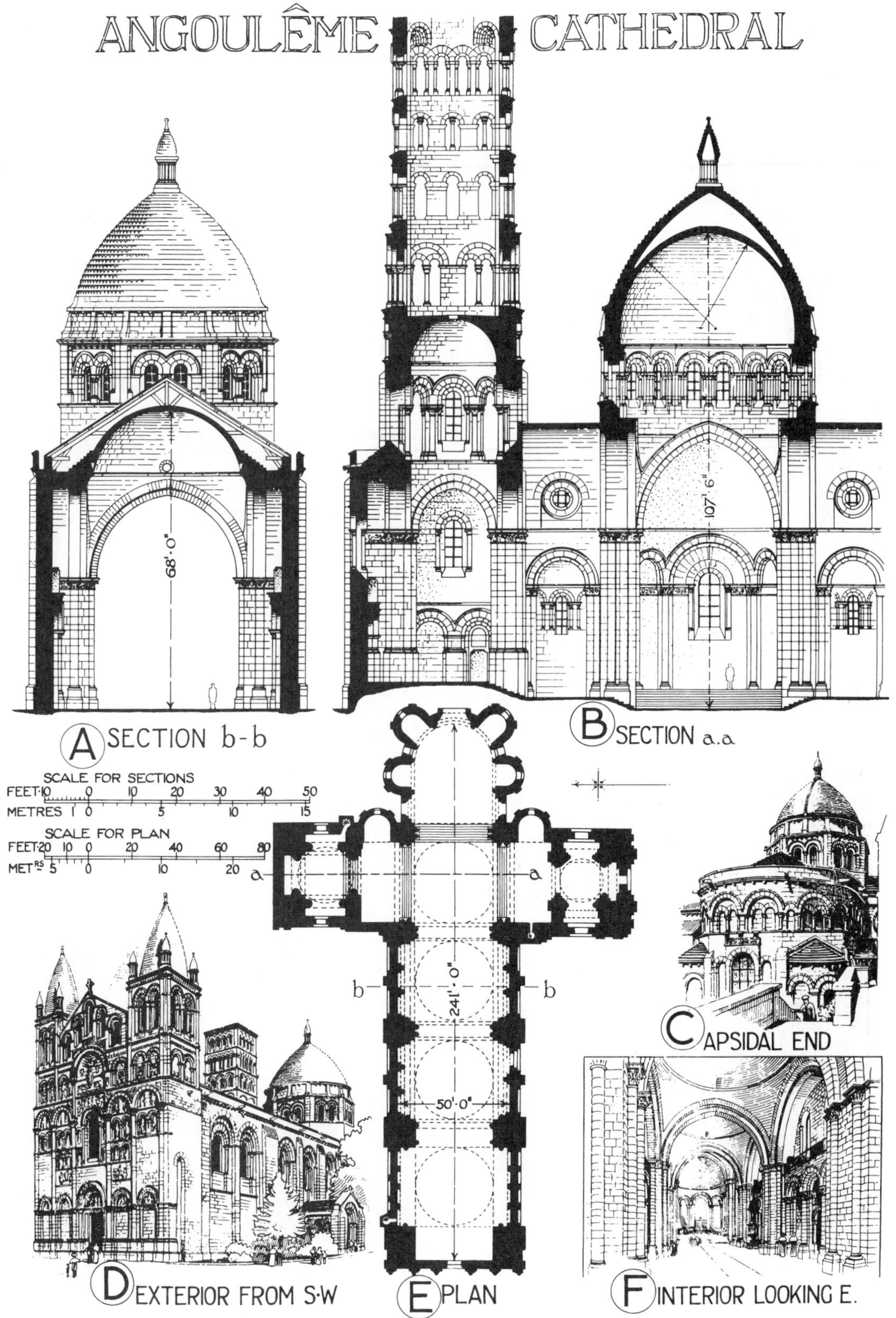

A SECTION b-b

B SECTION a.a

C APSIDAL END

D EXTERIOR FROM S·W

E PLAN

F INTERIOR LOOKING E.

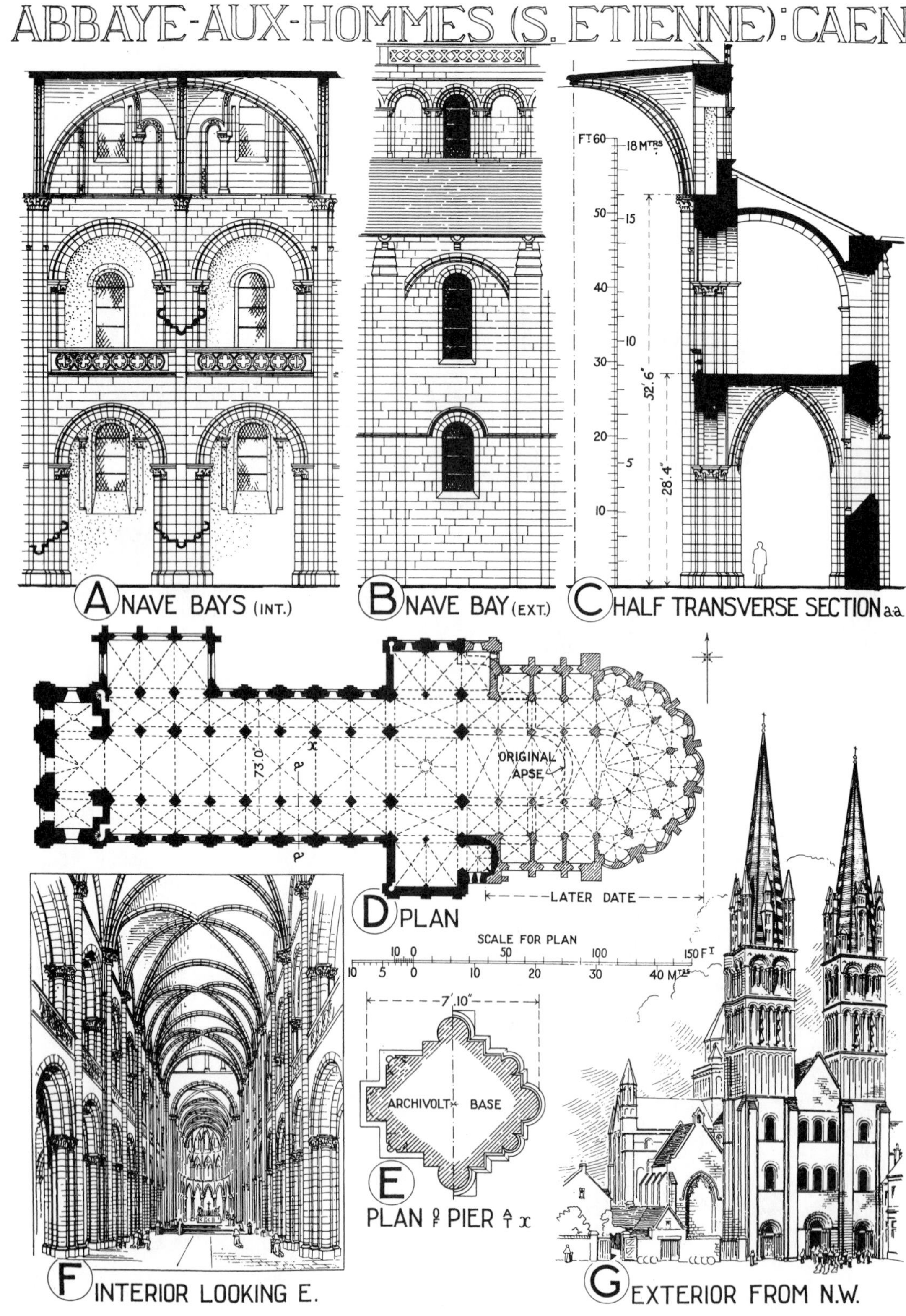
ABBAYE-AUX-HOMMES (S. ETIENNE): CAEN
A NAVE BAYS (INT.)
B NAVE BAY (EXT.)
C HALF TRANSVERSE SECTION a.a
FT 60
18 MTRS
50
15
40
10
30
52'.6"
20
5
28'.4"
10
73'.0"
ORIGINAL APSE
LATER DATE
D PLAN
SCALE FOR PLAN
10 0 50 100 150 FT
10 5 0 10 20 30 40 MTRS
7'.10"
ARCHIVOLT BASE
E PLAN OF PIER AT x
F INTERIOR LOOKING E.
G EXTERIOR FROM N.W.

A. Fontevraud, from NE (*c.* 1100–19 and later). See p.365

B. Jumièges Abbey (*c.* 1040–67). View of nave showing alternation of clustered piers and columns. See p.372

C. Abbaye-aux-Dames, Caen (1062–*c.* 1130). See p.372

D. Abbaye-aux-Hommes (S. Etienne), Caen (*c.* 1060–81: west front. See p.372

E. S. Denis, near Paris: SW bay of narthex (*c.* 1135–44). See p.372

The **Abbey of Bernay** (first half of the eleventh century) was probably the first important Norman church. It had a nave of seven bays – of which five are still intact – divided into arcade, triforium and clerestory. The choir and side-aisles terminate in rebuilt apses, and there are transepts and a regular crossing.

Jumièges Abbey (*c.* 1040–67) (p. 371B) in Normandy has a nave arcade supported alternately on plain circular piers or columns and simple compound piers with attached half-columns, a system which was to develop in England after the Conquest. The transepts have internal wall passages.

The **Abbaye-aux-Hommes, Caen** (*c.* 1060–81) (pp. 370, 371D), known as S. Etienne, is one of the many fine churches in Normandy of this period which were the product of the prosperity and power of the Norman dukes. It was begun by William the Conqueror, and contains several innovatory features which influenced subsequent architectural development. The western facade, flanked by two square towers crowned by octagonal spires which, with angle pinnacles, were added in the thirteenth century, was the prototype of later Gothic facades. The nave vaults are later insertions replacing the original wooden ceiling. The wall passage in front of the clerestory windows is original, however, and is an early example of this feature. There is a fully developed triforium gallery with half-barrel vaults, and angle rolls were used for the first time on the main arches.

The **Abbaye-aux-Dames ('La Trinité'), Caen** (1062–*c.* 1130) (p. 371C), founded by Mathilda, wife of William the Conqueror, has a fine western facade with two square towers in arcaded stages, strengthened at the angles by flat buttresses and formerly crowned by spires. The massive walls of nave and aisles with slightly projecting buttresses and the square tower over the crossing complete this homogeneous design. The interior, which has been very heavily restored, has a remarkable intersecting pseudo-sexpartite ribbed vault, in which two bays are included in each vaulting compartment, with semicircular diagonal and transverse ribs and intermediate ribs which support a diaphragm wall.

The **Abbey of S. Denis** (*c.* 1135–44) (p. 371E), near Paris, in the Ile de France, was built by the Abbé Suger. The Abbey Church is of great interest as the burial-place of French kings. The eastern end, though still retaining many Romanesque features, is probably the earliest truly Gothic structure (see Chapter 14).

Secular Architecture

Secular buildings have not been well preserved, because they were not sacred against attack, because they were often built for military purposes and so were liable to destruction, and because they were liable to destruction by fire or adaptation to changed requirements. **Fortified towns** like **Carcassonne** which dates from Roman times; **bridges** like the **Pont d' Avignon** (1177–85), built by the *frères-pontifes* or sacred guild of bridge builders; **castles** such as the **Château de Châteaudun** and the fortified **Abbey of Mont S. Michel** (p. 446C), and the stone **houses** of the twelfth century still found at **Cluny** and elsewhere, are types of buildings which were begun in the Romanesque style, but much altered or extended in the Gothic period (q.v.). The **Monastic Kitchen, Fontevraud** (*c.* 1115) (p. 362D), with its fine roof, and the fireplace and chimney from **S. Gilles** (p. 362B), are remnants which illustrate secular work of this period.

Central Europe: Architectural Character

Romanesque architecture in Central Europe exhibits a continuous combination of Carolingian tradition and Lombard influence. In later and larger examples, the resulting composition in external mass and formal arrangement is as distinguished as in any of the great Romanesque achievements in other European regions. The significant structural developments in the High Romanesque of Burgundy, Normandy and Lombardy were followed in Germany with reluctance, however, and pointed arcades and ribbed vaults made only a late appearance.

In monastic churches particularly, the principal features of Carolingian planning survived strongly. They include a choir at the west end, often accommodated in a western apse (pp. 375D, 377A,J), but occasionally provided in a square west end with either transept or tribune (p. 376D). This western choir was commonly built over a crypt in the manner of the Lombardic high choir. In France this arrangement appeared rarely. The westwork in the German examples sometimes was supplemented by the traditional narthex (p. 375D), and both transepts are frequently furnished with crossing towers (originally timber-built in diminishing stages) and cylindrical staircase towers (p. 377F). A distinctive characteristic of the architecture of the lower Rhineland, and of the valleys of the Moselle and Main, during the later eleventh and twelfth centuries, is a three-apse plan of trefoil form (p. 376D). Nave arcades are frequently unmoulded and the semicircular arches spring from piers (p. 377B) or cylinders, while alternate piers are sometimes used. Cloisters often have small columns supporting arches in groups of three (p. 374P). Arcaded exterior wall passages to apses, towers and

Central Europe in the Middle Ages

aisles are very common and are clearly derived from Lombardy (p. 347E). They are sometimes carried entirely round the body of the church, as at Speyer Cathedral (p. 375E).

Naves were usually roofed in timber, as at Gernrode (p. 375B). Square towers, divided into storeys by moulded courses, frequently terminate in four gables with hipped rafters rising from the apex of each, and the roofing planes intersect at these rafters and thus form a pyramidal or 'helm' roof with four diamond-shaped sides meeting at the apex (p. 374K). Polygonal towers have similar roofs, but with valleys between the gables (p. 376).

Plain wall surfaces are relieved by pilaster strips connected horizontally at different stages by ranges of arches on corbels which, owing to the smallness of scale, have the appearance of moulded string courses (pp. 374K, 376C, 377F). Doorways are frequently in the side aisles instead of in the west front or transepts, and have recesses with nook shafts (p. 374R–T). Windows are usually single, but occasionally grouped (p. 374M), and sometimes have a mid-wall shaft (p. 374H,Q). The cushion capital was the most common type and in the later period was often elaborately carved.

Internally the flat wall surfaces were painted originally, but the general effect today is one of bareness. Characteristic carved bands were used (p. 374G), and in the north, lines of coloured bricks appeared externally. The sculpture is often well executed (p. 374N), and the craftsmanship of this period is seen in the bronze doors of Hildesheim Cathedral (1015), which are wrought in wonderful detail to represent the Creation, the Fall and the Redemption.

Central Europe: Examples

Aix-la-Chapelle (Aachen) Cathedral (792–805) (p. 375A), built by the Emperor Charlemagne as his tomb-house, resembles S. Vitale, Ravenna (p. 308D). The entrance, flanked by staircase turrets, leads into a polygon of sixteen sides, 32 m (105 ft) in diameter. Every two angles of this polygon converge on one pier, and thus form an internal octagon, the eight piers of which support a dome 14.5 m (47 ft 6 in) in diameter, rising above the two-storey surrounding aisles. The building has been much altered since the

A
B
CAPITALS
ABBEY-CHURCH, CONRADSBURG.
C
D
CAPITALS
ILSENBURG : CONRADSBURG.
E CAPITALS: LIMBURG
F
G ORNAMENT: LIMBURG.
H
WINDOW: GERNRODE.
J
COLUMN
HECKLINGEN
K
W. TOWERS: LIMBURG CATH.
L COLUMN
ILSENBURG.
M WINDOW: LAACH.
N PORTAL: BÂLE.
P
CLOISTERS: ASCHAFFENBURG.
Q
TOWER: S. COLUMBA, COLOGNE.
JAMB
5'.8"
11'.3"
R DOORWAY
S. MARTIN, WORMS.
S DOORWAY: STRASSBURG CATH.
T
N.E. PORTAL: BAMBERG.

A. Aachen Cathedral (792–805). See p.373

B. Gernrode Abbey (begun 959–63). See p.379

C. S. Michael, Hildesheim (1010–33). See p.379

D. Maria Laach Abbey Church: exterior from NW (1093–1156). See p.379

E. Speyer Cathedral (1030–61 and later): exterior from NE. See p.379

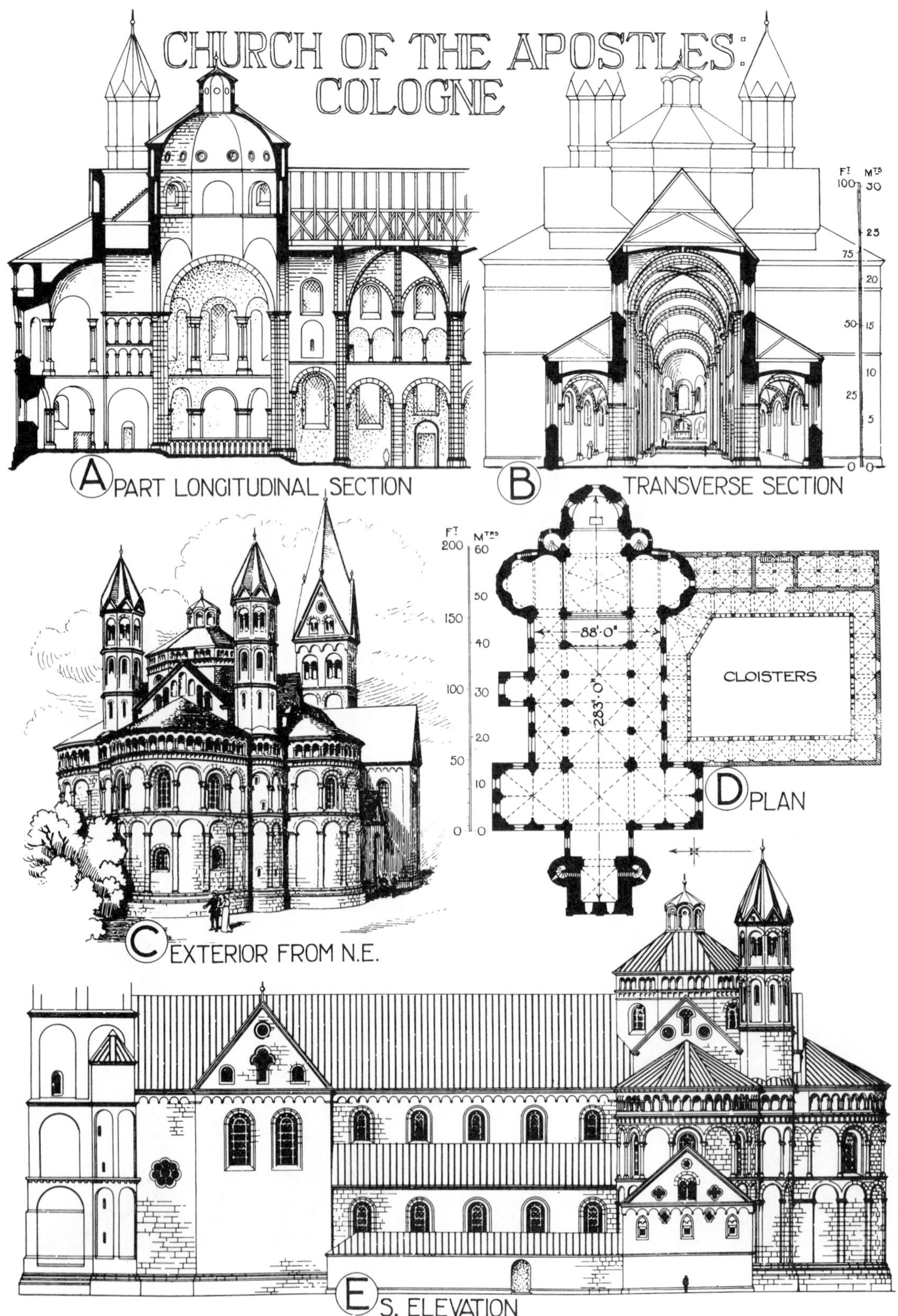
CHURCH OF THE APOSTLES: COLOGNE
A PART LONGITUDINAL SECTION
B TRANSVERSE SECTION
FT MTS
100 30
25
75
20
50 15
10
25
5
0 0
FT MTS
200 60
50
150
40
100 30
20
50
10
0 0
88'-0"
283'-0"
CLOISTERS
C EXTERIOR FROM N.E.
D PLAN
E S. ELEVATION

WORMS CATHEDRAL
SCALE FOR SECTIONS &c.
5 0 25 50 75 FT
1·0 5 10 15 20 MTRS
88'·0"
A WESTERN APSE
B NAVE BAY (INT.)
C TRANSVERSE SECTION x·x
D CORNICE (EXT.)
G EXTERNAL ANGLE OF CHOIR
ELEVATION
E NAVE PIER
F EXTERIOR FROM N.E.
PLAN
6'·5"
WESTERN APSE
84'·0"
353'·0"
EASTERN APSE
ELEVATION
PLAN
H JAMB OF N. DOORWAY
SCALE FOR PLAN
50 0 50 100 150 FT
10 0 10 20 30 40 MTRS
J PLAN

A. S. Martin, Cologne: nave (1185 and later). See p.379

B. Mainz Cathedral from SW (1009, 1181 and later). See p.379

C. Trier Cathedral (1016–47) and Liebfrauenkirche (1242–53), from W. See p.379

time of Charlemagne; the Gothic choir was added (1353–1413), the gables date from the thirteenth century and the lofty outer roof of the octagon from the seventeenth century. The surrounding chapels are of the fourteenth and fifteenth centuries and the western steeple has been added in recent years. The building is of historic interest as the prototype of other similar churches in Germany, but especially as the coronation place of the Holy Roman Emperors.

Corvey-on-the-Weser Abbey (873–85). The westwork is the only surviving part of the Carolingian church. It consists of a vaulted ground floor nearly square in plan supported on columns with carved capitals and piers. The first and second floor levels are uninterrupted, surrounded by storeys of aisles with arcades. The towers and the transverse gallery are twelfth-century additions.

S. Riquier Abbey (*c.* 790–9) was reconstructed by Abbot Angilbert, an important member of Charlemagne's court. Only a seventeenth-century engraving of this important church survives. In combination with the documentary evidence it shows us that there was a westwork with a timber tower rising from it, an aisled nave and a timber eastern tower flanked by two-or three-storey buildings beneath lean-to roofs (similar to the westwork arms). The main sanctuary was contained within an apse around which an outer crypt was added, probably during the tenth century.

The **Ideal Plan of S. Gallen** (*c.* 820) (pp. 186–7) is a copy of a plan prepared at the council of Inden in 816 and is associated with Einhard, an adviser to Charlemagne. It shows an ideal monastic layout, arranged in a rectilinear manner, with provision for every activity, both agricultural and religious. The principal building is the church with cloisters to the south, around which the main conventual buildings are arranged in a manner which was to become standard throughout Europe.

Gernrode Abbey (begun between 959 and 963) (p. 375B) was the first building in western Europe in which the triforium gallery was used and has the earliest surviving instance of alternating supports.

S. Michael, Hildesheim (1010–33) (p. 375C), is an early example of a truly Romanesque building. It has a pair of regular crossings surmounted by towers. The nave has alternating paired columns and square piers, which divide the nave into three square compartments.

Speyer Cathedral (*c.* 1030–61) (p. 375E) is a major Imperial church. The inner faces of the piers of the main arcade have half-columns rising to carry the arches over the clerestory windows – an early example of the compound pier. In the later eleventh century groin vaults replaced the wooden roof and every alternate pier was widened to carry the transverse arches. The exterior of the building has a remarkable arrangement of towers, and wall passages surround the entire building.

The **Church of the Apostles, Cologne** (*c.* 1190 and later) (p. 376), is one of the series of trefoil churches in that city. The church has a broad nave, aisles half its width, western transepts, and a triapsidal choir, and over the crossing a low octagonal tower gives dignity to the external grouping. The entrance is by a northern porch; there is no great western portal as in France, the west end being occupied by a tower flanked by stair turrets, crowned with a typical Rhenish roof, consisting of a steep gable on each face from which rise the ridges of a helm roof. The trefoil end has wall arcading in two storeys crowned with the characteristic wall passage, and on the south side are the cloisters.

S. Maria im Capitol (*c.* 1040–65) and **S. Martin** (1185 and later) (p. 378A) are also trefoil-plan churches in Cologne, and there are other examples at **Neuss, Roermond** and **Bonn**.

Worms Cathedral (mainly later eleventh and twelfth centuries) (p. 377) and **Mainz Cathedral** (after 1009, 1181 and later) (p. 378B) are representative of the greater churches of the period. The plan of Worms is apsidal at both ends, with eastern and western octagons, and a rib-vaulted bay of the nave corresponds with two of the bays of the aisles (p. 377B,J). Twin circular towers containing stairs flank the eastern and western apses, and the crossing of the nave and transept is covered with a low octagonal tower with a pointed roof. The entrances are in the aisles, a position favoured in both Germany and England. The lateral facades have round-arched windows, between characteristic flat pilasters.

Maria Laach Abbey (1093–1156) (p. 375D), south of Cologne, is a Benedictine church. The plan differs from most others because on either side of the western apse, which is used as a tomb-house, are entrances from the cloistered atrium which still exists. There are also three eastern apses. The vaulting bays of nave and aisles are of the same width – an advance towards the Gothic system. The church is built chiefly of local lava and is a fine grouping of six towers, double transepts, and east and west apses.

Trier Cathedral (1016–47 and later) (p. 378C) is reminiscent of the importance of this ancient city which, in the fourth century, was one of the residences of the Roman Emperors. The cathedral replaced a basilican church destroyed by Franks and Normans.

Spain: Architectural Character

The consequences of the migration of Germanic tribes at the fall of the Western Roman Empire included the establishment in Spain of the Visigothic Kingdom which lasted for three hundred years, until the Islamic invasion of the early years of the eighth century. The tangible remains are scarce, but are

Spain and Portugal in the Middle Ages

sufficient to show that Visigothic art provided a link between eastern and western Mediterranean cultures long before the Moorish influences were introduced. Some features of church design of this period anticipated the distinctive characteristics of mature Spanish Romanesque architecture. The most important of these was the horseshoe arch. Church planning, as shown in the few authenticated examples of this time, was varied, and includes instances of both basilican and Greek-cross forms. Decorative devices include cable mouldings and other motifs (rosettes, circumscribed stars) rather crudely executed in low relief. Some of the details suggest occasional reuse of antique Roman material.

Following the Muslim invasion in 711, Christian Spain was reduced by 718 to the Visigothic Kingdom of Asturia, to which Galicia was added by reconquest early in the reign of Alfonso the Catholic. By about 780, a national school of church architecture, painting and sculpture had developed; in the ninth and tenth centuries it achieved a stature, largely independently, quite comparable with that of contemporary Lombardy or Saxon England. The most typical plan form for these Asturian churches is basilican, with lateral chapel projections providing a kind of transept. The east end incorporated sanctuary and square flanking chapels; the apse was unknown. In earlier examples, round arches in brick occur, springing from piers instead of from Visigothic columns, and decorative sculpture was confined to the sanctuary. In later examples, carved decoration is more elaborate, but the quality of its execution is inferior to that of contemporary Islamic work.

Churches built for Christian communities under tolerant Moorish control were based principally upon mosque-building traditions. Together with the churches built for refugees from the later persecutions of Abd ar-Rahman II and of Mohammed I during the middle years of the ninth century, these Mozarabic churches stand apart from the contribution to the Romanesque style made by the Asturian and Galician churches. Although varied, they have in common a return to the Visigothic form of horseshoe arch, the reuse of ancient materials, and decorative, often exquisitely carved though debased, Classical or Byzantine forms.

In Andorra and Catalonia, on both sides of the Pyrenees, Mozarabic architecture was succeeded after the middle years of the tenth century by a truly Continental Romanesque style initiated in Lombardy soon after 900. This was imported into Catalan monastic church building by both land and sea as Mediterranean and Oriental trade developed, following the expulsion of the Moors late in the eighth century from this part of Spain. In all the earliest examples, nave and aisles were covered with continuous barrel vaults, and it is significant that these occurred in a region neighbouring that which had already produced vaulted churches based on Roman provincial models. The mass needed to support vaults brought about the use of massive rectangular piers instead of columns in aisled churches, and from the beginning of the eleventh century transverse arches were introduced. Planning was usually on the basilican pattern, frequently with some form of transept projection.

The abbey church at Ripoll (*c.* 1020–32) is the outstanding example of early Catalan Romanesque, and is on a grander scale than anything which preceded it in Spain. It has been largely restored but it represents many of the characteristics of its place and period, and the influence of the early Romanesque of Lombardy is clearly evident. These features include eastern apses (seven at Ripoll), with arcaded wall passages below the eaves and blind arcading and pilasters on the wall-faces of apse and aisles. Most of the monastic examples have massive square-plan bell-towers, reproducing the character of Lombardic and Piedmontese towers down to the finest detail.

Early Catalan churches were frequently roofed in stone laid directly on the vault. Some eleventh-century examples of cruciform plan have a crossing dome supported on squinch arches, and groined aisle vaults with transverse arches supported on cruciform piers. There was little sculpture or decorative carving in the earliest of Catalan Romanesque work, but it developed to a high degree towards the end of the twelfth century. Where columns were used in arcades, Corinthianesque capitals often simulate the standards set by Mozarabic predecessors. Carved architectural detail and free sculpture in cloisters are particularly fine, and many of the motifs betray Islamic inspiration.

The early Romanesque, largely Lombardic, traditions survived in Catalonia until they were overtaken by Gothic fashions, but in north-western and central Spain after about 1050, French ideas were introduced and led to the development of a mature Franco-Spanish Romanesque style which displaced the native architecture as effectively as did that of Normandy in England. These French ideas were carried across the Pyrenees by pilgrims to Santiago de Compostela, by Cluniac monks (who became very influential in northern Spain), and by itinerant French craftsmen.

An incidental but significant phase of Romanesque evolution in Spain came about through church building in parts of Castile and Aragon newly recovered to Christian rule. The craftsmanship and design traditions of the north were adopted both by Christian masons of Mozarabic descent and by Muslims living in these regions. Most of the products of this Mudéjar movement are simple churches without aisles, with only sanctuaries barrel-vaulted – timber ceilings elsewhere – and some form of eastern apse, usually polygonal in plan. Because the Mudéjars had inherited all the craft skills of their forebears, these small parochial churches were built both economically and skilfully, mostly in brick. Much of the later Mudéjar work in Castile comprises brick-built versions of the earlier Lombard models used in Catalonia, with their basilican plans, eastern apses and external blind horseshoe arcading, set in Moorish panels. After the beginning of the thirteenth century, arcades became pointed and cusped, though the architecture is still predominantly Romanesque in character. In Aragon the Mudéjar style developed continuously through the mediaeval period, and even as late as the fourteenth century it referred back to its Romanesque origins.

The first appearance of mature vaulted Romanesque Spanish church architecture was in León shortly after the middle of the eleventh century, and it evolved principally in churches marking the stages of the pilgrimage route to Santiago de Compostela. The French influences can be traced back through the routes in France from the Loire – in Touraine and Poitou – from Anjou, Burgundy and Languedoc. Few of the smaller pilgrimage churches survive unaltered, but their general form was aisled, with barrel-vaulted nave, barrel- or groin-vaulted aisles, and either no clerestory or a very low one. Occasionally bold barrel-vaulted transepts occur, and parallel eastern apses were usual.

Spain is well endowed with mediaeval military architecture, and grand castles are particularly numerous in Castile. Most of the remaining examples are those of the feudal nobility of the fourteenth and fifteenth centuries; fortifications of Romanesque date and character are few but impressive. The earliest castles and town walls occur in Andalusia and are related to Moorish work in Morocco. Christian work of early date is very similar, except that stonework was in rubble, which presented difficulty with quoins. Curtain walls were therefore furnished with circular towers, and battlements were usually of Islamic form, having a single block surmounting each merlon weathered to a pyramid form. The finest of Romanesque castles in Spain is at Loarre in Aragon (p. 387A); it incorporates an important Augustinian church. The city walls of Avila (1088–91) (p. 387B), in central Castile, are of granite, are splendidly preserved, and constitute one of the more distinguished works of military architecture in Europe. They were built by

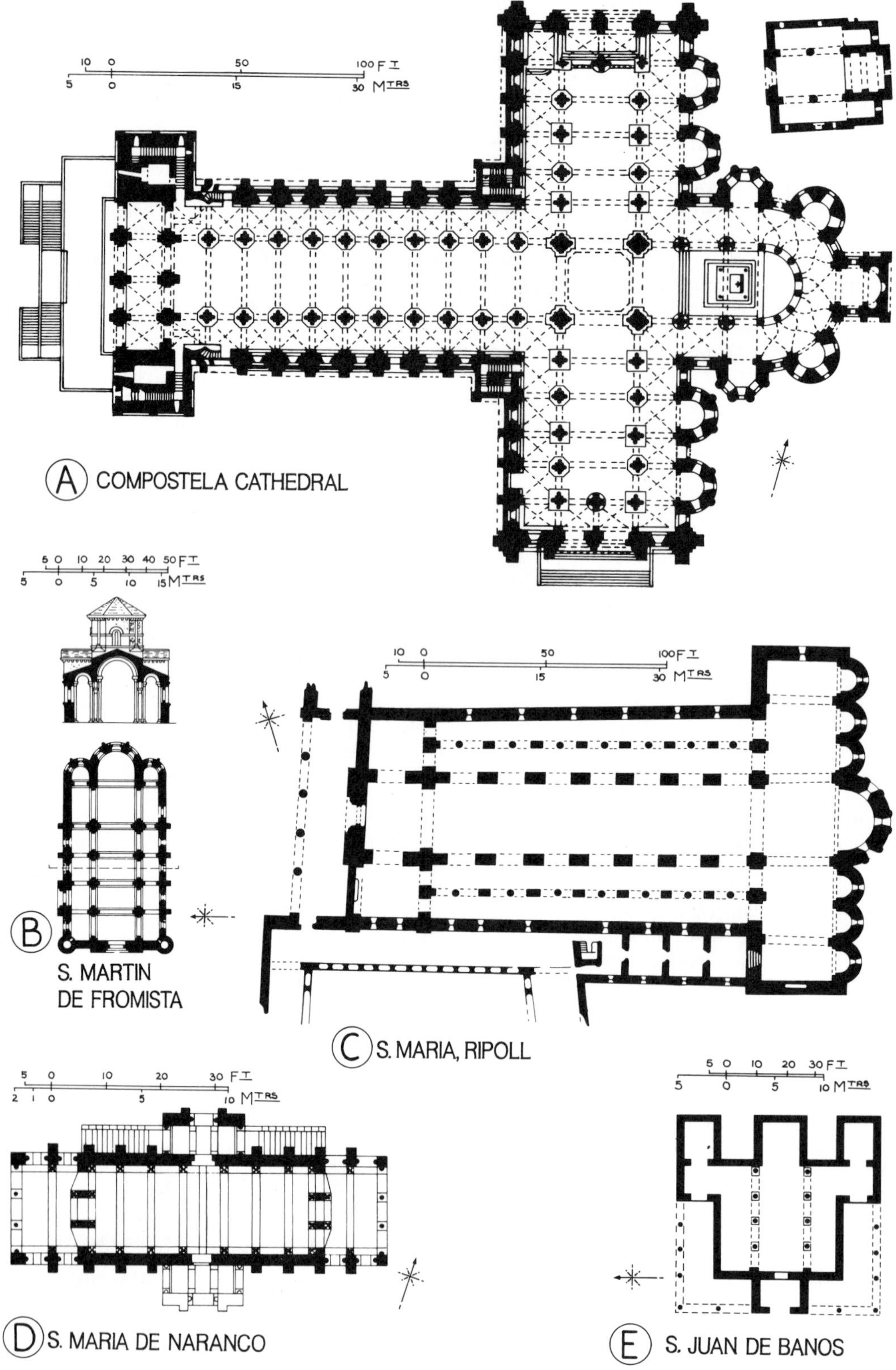

10 0 50 100 FT
5 0 15 30 MTRS
(A) COMPOSTELA CATHEDRAL
5 0 10 20 30 40 50 FT
5 0 5 10 15 MTRS
(B) S. MARTIN DE FROMISTA
10 0 50 100 FT
5 0 15 30 MTRS
(C) S. MARIA, RIPOLL
5 0 10 20 30 FT
2 1 0 5 10 MTRS
(D) S. MARIA DE NARANCO
5 0 10 20 30 FT
5 0 5 10 MTRS
(E) S. JUAN DE BANOS

Raymond of Burgundy, using Burgundian craftsmen, though the designer was a Roman. There are eighty-six identical semicircular towers and ten gates. The fortified eastern apse of the cathedral was later incorporated.

Spain: Examples

Religious Buildings

S. Juan de Baños de Cerrato (661) (pp. 382E, 384A), of royal foundation, is the finest surviving Visigothic church, planned as a three-aisle basilica with a four-bay nave, originally with a transept with eastern chapels at the outer ends. Outside the nave aisles was a colonnade connected to a western narthex, in a manner similar to that current in Syria and Armenia, which probably inspired the introduction of the lateral portico common in later Spanish Romanesque churches. The nave arcade has horseshoe arches springing from a variety of Corinthian columns, and the arched window openings are small, with horseshoe heads.

S. Julián de los Prados (Santullano), near Oviedo (*c.* 830), is among the best preserved of the early Asturian churches, and was somewhat restored not long before the Spanish Civil War. It has a typical basilican form, with a wide transverse bay forming a kind of transept, outer lateral chapels, a square sanctuary with flanking chapels and a western narthex. Only the eastern chapels are vaulted, and the timber ceiling include some original decorated beams.

S. Maria de Naranco (848) (pp. 382D, 384B), was built by Ramiro I next to his palace near Oviedo, and ably represents the structural advances in church architecture of the Visigothic kingdom of Asturia. It has a long rectangular nave with open tribunes at both ends, over a crypt. Both stages and the tribunes are barrel-vaulted with transverse arches and external buttresses. The arch corbels are vigorously carved and the same sort of decoration occurs in the capitals of columns in the tribunes. The building is likely to have been intended principally to provide for sacred royal ceremonial. There is no indication of its having had any kind of sanctuary.

S. Cristina de Lena (*c.* 905) represents a development of the completely vaulted form of Naranco. The nave and square sanctuary have barrel vaults with transverse arches which are carried down below the supporting corbels in decorative bands, and the vault form is repeated in two lateral chapels abutting the nave. The narrow western porch is vaulted too, but without arches. The walls are stiffened with external piers and the entire masonry construction is roughly coursed, except for the geometrical transennae and a remarkably decorated three-arch iconostasis on smooth Corinthianesque columns.

S. Miguel de la Escalada, near León (913) (p. 384C), is the finest and largest of the Mozarabic churches. It was founded by Córdoban refugees and relies upon some of the craft traditions of the Mosque of Córdoba. It has a basilican plan, with a nave of five bays, and fine horseshoe arches on antique columns (probably from a late Roman or Visigothic church on the same site) which are returned across the nave as an iconostasis screen. The three eastern apses are of horseshoe form, in plan, with lobed domical vaults, the whole enclosed within a single masonry mass. The high timber ceiling is later in date and decorated in the Mudéjar manner. There is a shallow clerestory with small horseshoe-headed openings, and a southern portico of about 930 with twelve arched bays similar to those of the nave arcades.

Other Leónese Mozarabic churches of importance include **Santiago de Peñalba** (919), which has a nave of two bays, with a lobed dome over the eastern one, lobed vaults over both eastern and western apses, and barrel-vaulted transepts; **S. Maria de Lebeña, near Santander** (924), which has some of the Asturian character of its locality, but the arcades are of horseshoe shape and the detail is in the Córdoban tradition; and **S. Maria de Melque, near Toledo**, a small cruciform church with arches, window heads, and apse plan all of horseshoe shape, but with no evidence of any decorative scheme. The church may have been built before the Christian refugees left Córdoba and dates from about 900.

The **Monastery of S. Martin du Canigou** (1007–26) (p. 385A), in French Catalonia (Roussillon), has a church of 'hall' form with both aisles and nave barrel-vaulted over a vaulted crypt. The arcades are wide-spaced on simple columns, with compound piers at the centre. There is no clerestory. The only natural lighting comes from the ends of the church.

S. Maria, Ripoll (*c.* 1020–32) (pp. 382C, 385C), despite heavy restoration, is the finest of the eleventh-century early Romanesque churches. It has a double-aisled basilican nave of seven bays, and the outer arcades alternate to produce double bays in the outer aisles, in the Lombardic manner. The bold transept has seven eastern apses. Externally, the church portrays many of the Lombardic features which accompany its formal derivation from Italian models. These include arcaded wall passages, blind wall arcading and pilaster strips, and gable wall passages on the west front.

S. Vincente de Cardona (1019–40) (p. 385B) incorporates many Lombard devices, but the nave has a high clerestory, the aisles have groin vaults, and the transverse arches bear upon pilasters engaged to arcade piers. At the crossing is a cupola carried on squinches. The transepts are of shallow projection, and there are three eastern apses, the central stilted to form a deep barrel-vaulted bay.

A. S. Juan de Baños de Cerrato (661): sanctuary. See p.383

B. S. Maria de Naranco (848). See p.383

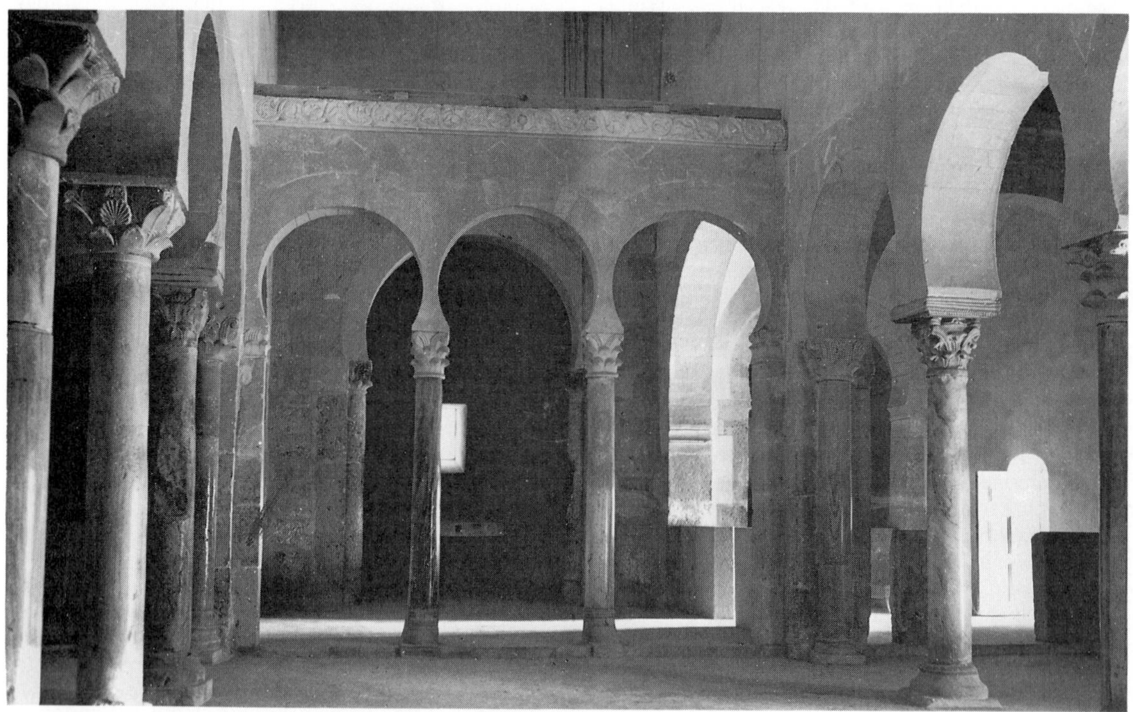

C. S. Miguel de la Escalada, near León (913): crossing and sanctuary. See p.383

A. Monastery of S. Martin du Canigou (1007–26). See p.383

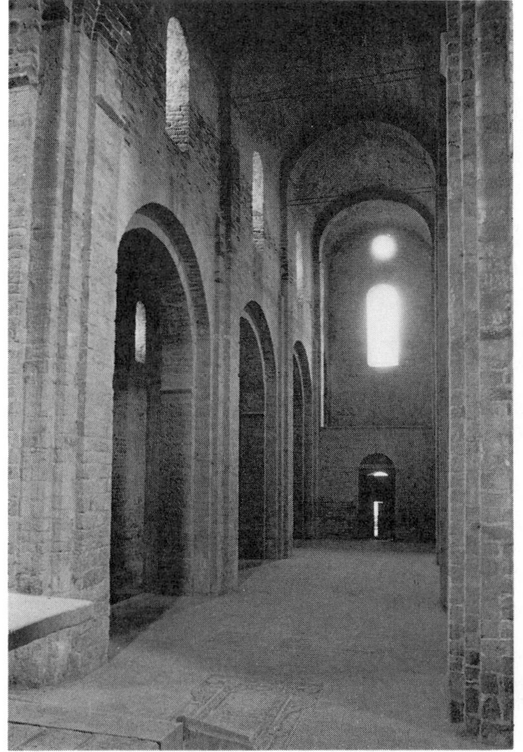

B. S. Vincente de Cardona (1019–40). See p.382

C. S. Maria, Ripoll (*c.* 1020–32). See p.383

D. S. Martín de Frómista (*c.* 1066). See p.388

E. Collegiate Church, Toro (1162–1240). See p.388

A. Santiago de Compostela: (1078–1122 or 1124, with later addition): nave. See p.388

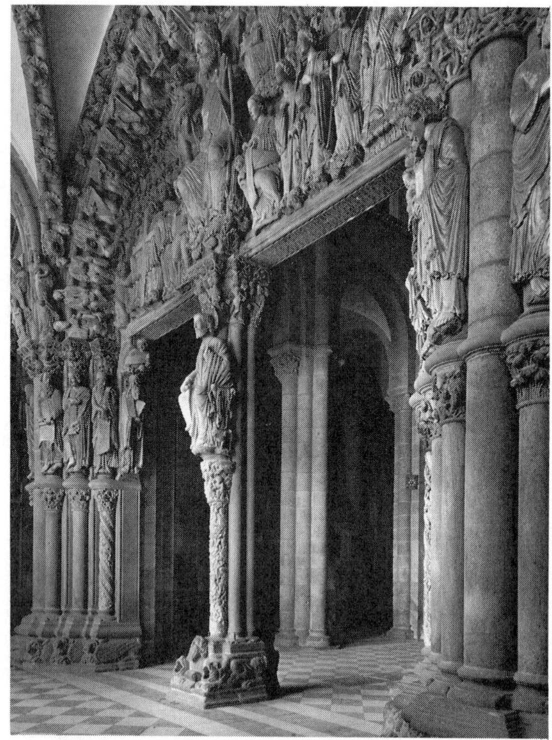

B. Santiago de Compostela: Portico de la Gloria (1168–88)

C. La Lugareja, Arévalo (thirteenth century). See p.388

D. S. Vicente, Avila: principal doorway (thirteenth century). See p.388

A. Loarre: castle exterior (*c.* 1070 and *c.* 1095). See p.388

B. Avila, Castile, showing town walls (1088–91). See p.388

S. Tirso, Sahagún (*c.* 1145), one of the earliest brick Mudéjar churches, has much of the eleventh-century character of Catalan Romanesque, though with Moorish overtones, such as the horseshoe-headed blind apse arcading, set in rectangular panels.

La Lugareja, Arévalo (thirteenth century) (p. 386C), is the finest example of Mudéjar building in brickwork. A Cistercian church, it has many Lombardic devices, and a bold central tower enclosing a lantern cupola on pendentives.

S. Martín de Frómista (*c.* 1066) (pp. 382B, 385D) is the only complete example of the Spanish 'pilgrimage' style, with a four-bay nave, shallow transept, and three parallel apses. It has barrel vaults on fully articulated cruciform piers throughtout but, like Canigou, it approaches 'hall church' form. The aisle vault springs nearly at the same level as that of the high vault, so that there is no clerestory. There is a tall octagonal lantern at the crossing. It has been heavily restored.

S. Isidoro, León (1054–67 and 1101), built by Ferdinand I of Castile and his wife Sancha, now includes only the western narthex of the original construction, the 'Panteón de los Reyes', adjoined on two sides by the 'Portico'. The burial porch is composed of six columned compartments covered by domed groin vaults. It is French in style and the carvings of capitals and the painted fresco decoration of about 1175 are among the most impressive of early Spanish Romanesque work. The body of this church was rebuilt progressively by French architects and now has a barrel-vaulted nave and transepts, groin-vaulted aisles, and a triapsidal east end, which has been replaced. At the crossing the transept arches are cusped, and rise through the height of a generous clerestory.

The **Cathedral of Santiago de Compostela** (1078–1122 or 1124) (pp. 382A, 386A), at the end of the pilgrims' route, was unequalled in magnificence and maturity in Spain in its time. The tomb of S. James, son of Zebedee, was recognized in 813. By the middle of the ninth century, a Benedictine monastery had been established at Compostela, and before its end the international pilgrimage had become established. The plan is cruciform, aisled, with galleries which run continuously around the building; when designed, it was the only church in Spain with ambulatory and radiating chapels; the barrel-vaulted nave has transverse arches, the aisle vaults are groined. The galleries are covered with a half-barrel opposing the high vault, and the bays at this level are separated by diaphragm arches. The structural technique is advanced and assured, and is matched by the quality of decoration, particularly in relief sculpture. The interior survives largely unaltered, except for the loss of the twelfth-century 'coro' at the east end of the nave, and the introduction of Baroque furnishings and fittings in the choir. Externally, the east end is largely concealed, and the only original facade is that of the south transept of 1103, the 'Puerta de las Platerias', and even that was altered after a fire in 1116. The 'Portico de la Gloria' at the west front (p. 386B) was added (1168–88) within the vestibule. Modelled upon the inner portal of the narthex of La Madeleine at Vézelay (p. 367B), it is one of the finest works of mediaeval Christendom.

The Gloria at Santiago de Compostela was imitated in the thirteenth-century portico of **Orense Cathedral** (the 'Paraíso') and in other minor derivatives such as those in the churches of **S. Jerónimo, Compostela; S. Julián de Moraime, Carboerio; Evora** in Portugal, and **S. Martin de Noya**, as late as the fifteenth century in date. The main features of the structure and planning of Santiago de Compostela were also quoted in other great churches of the region: **Orense Cathedral** (1132–94) has triforium galleries and much of the Burgundian quality; **Tuy Cathedral** (1150–80), in Pontevedra, has galleries, including those of the transepts, but the triforium stage is blind; **Lugo Cathedral** (1129) has barrel vaults to the galleries instead of half-barrels with diaphragm arches; the **Old Cathedral of Coimbra** (Sé Velha) (1162), in Portugal, is another variant without a clerestory, and with three parallel eastern apses, but the Cluniac chevet was adopted again in S. Julián, Carboerio, and in **S. Maria de Cambre, La Coruña**.

The Salamantine group of twelfth-century churches includes **Zamora Cathedral** (1152–74), the **Collegiate Church at Toro** (1162–1240) (p. 385E), the **Old Cathedral, Salamanca** (1160) (pp. 526B), **Ciudad Rodrigo Cathedral** (1165–1230), and the abbey church of **S. Martín de Castaneda**. All of these, except S. Martín, have a lantern crossing dome on pendentives (at Salamanca and Toro pierced for double tiers of lights), and domical ribbed vaults on the Angevin pattern, pointed arcades, pointed high barrel vaults (in the cases of Toro and the Zamora transepts), traditional Romanesque basilican triapsidal planning and massive stone ashlar construction with distinctly Islamic overtones in decoration. **S. Vicente, Avila** (1109 and later), has a characteristic plan of the same sort, groin-vaulted aisles and a ribbed high cross-vault, with a square crossing tower, and a distinctive western portal (p. 386D) which appears to owe much to both Burgundy and Poitou.

Military Buildings

The finest Romanesque castle in Spain is at **Loarre** (*c.* 1070 and *c.* 1095) (p. 387A), a complex of circular towers and curtain walls incorporating a church of Augustinian canons, sited on a spur overlooking the Gállego valley. The town defences at **Avila, in Castile** (1088–91) (p. 387B), include a curtain wall 2.5 km (1½ miles) long, with eighty-six identical circular towers, built in granite by Raymond of Burgundy, largely using French masonry techniques. There are ten gates, each formed by an arched opening between two adjoining towers. There is little of Islamic influence in this work, and because of their remarkable state of preservation these ramparts present one of the most extensive and impressive examples of mediaeval military architecture. At **Berlanga de Duero, Soria**, there are extensive remains of curtain walls with circular towers, and at **Almonacid** in Castile there are double ramparts with similar towers but without loopholes and crudely constructed.

The Holy Land: Architectural Character

Military Buildings

The castles of the Crusaders were of three kinds, each having a specific function, which depended on geographical location.

Pilgrim forts. Sited and designed to secure the routes from coastal ports to Jerusalem, principally by way of Joppa (Tel-Aviv) and Ascalon, they were generally designed on a Byzantine pattern derived from the ancient Roman 'castrum' or legionary fort. The installations included a thin curtain wall with rectangular corner towers of small projection, a large fosse or ditch, and an outer earth rampart. In some cases there was a central citadel. These forts were of no very great strength, and relied upon relatively plentiful manpower. After 1128 the Templars took charge of and developed the forts on the pilgrimage roads.

Coastal fortifications. The Levantine coastal ports were fortified to secure the sea links with the West. They include Ascalon, Joppa, Tyre, Sidon, Beirut and Tortosa. They took the form either of a 'bastide town' – a civil settlement under the protection of a castle (which had contact directly with the countryside, as at Giblet (Gibail), or with only the sea, as at Sidon (Saida), which could be isolated by cutting a sea-dyke) – or of a coastal castle with no dependent township, like Chastel Pélérin, which had very limited access across the narrow peninsula neck.

Strategic inland castles. The principal functions of these great castles were to protect the coast road, as in the case of Margat, above Baniyas in Syria; to safeguard the mountain passes, such as Safita and the Krak des Chevaliers, which commanded the Homs Gap; to secure the river valley routes, as in the case of Beaufort, overlooking the gorge of the Litani; and to provide visual command of the approach routes across the eastern frontier, as Subeibe, on the slopes of Mount Hermon, overlooked the routes from Damascus to Tyre and Galilee, and as Baldwin's Montreal in Idumaea controlled both the caravan route between Damascus and Egypt and the ancient spice route out of Arabia by way of Wadi Araba. The latter was also within striking distance of the pilgrim road of the Haj to Medina and Mecca.

A large part of the strategic strength of the Crusader castles lay in the elaborate system of communication between them by means of carrier pigeon and visual signalling. Both techniques were probably of eastern origin and were borrowed from Arab and Byzantine practice.

The general form of the large castles makes it possible to divide them into two main types. The first kind are those of the twelfth century, up to about the time of Hattin (1187), when the main strategic process was one of hopeful expansion, and the purpose of the fortifications was primarily offensive. New works were usually relatively simple in form and mostly comprised strongpoints from which to effect the capture of the ports still under Islamic control, and castles on remote eastern sites, beyond the Jordan, intended to support attacks upon the inland trade routes. Other building work of this period was incorporated in existing castles and fortified towns wrested by both Franks and Armenians by force of arms from Byzantine and Arab control.

The common characteristic of most of the new work of this kind was the tower keep. It was not in itself capable of providing more than a readily defensible base and refuge for armoured knights, and was imported into the Holy Land principally from Normandy, where it had not then reached a high state of development. At the time of the First Crusade, there were only a few Norman castles of this type, for example, at London (p. 408) and Colchester. The early twelfth-century keep in Crusader work was therefore derived from relatively simple models, and it was adapted to its Syrian setting, usually having a single entrance at ground level (instead of at the first stage with a forebuilding) and commonly only two storeys. The upper floor was supported on vaulting in place of the timber beams of the higher stages of western European castle keeps of the time, for heavy timbers were not generally available.

The keep was usually sited at the most vulnerable part of the castle, where its mass would be most effective, but in some castles on level sites on the coastal plain it was built centrally in order to afford cover to all parts of the bailey and its surrounding defences. These included a curtain wall corbelled out to carry a wall-walk or 'alure', and punctuated with towers of limited salient which became progressively more numerous and more boldly projecting. The curtain towers in early examples tend to be square in plan, rather than rounded, though practice in this respect was variable. Where the topography provided a single obvious approach for attack, a fosse was cut;

The Holy Land of the Crusaders

in some cases this became so essential an element of the defences as to involve excavations, sometimes in rock, on a dramatic scale.

The second type of castle belongs mostly to the period of nearly one hundred years after Hattin, and shows the need for increasing defensive strength in place of depleted manpower. Only four important new castles were built (Chastel Pélérin, Montfort, Margat and Saphet) and two of these are on old sites. The design of these four examples, and the reconstruction of several others, illustrate the most important and influential features of the military architecture of the Crusades. Several were carefully planned in concentric form, with double rampart systems, probably inspired by Byzantine and Arab town-defence systems. This was combined with the use of round towers of bold salient, grouped at gates or placed so as to provide an inner refuge or donjon for security from a disaffected mercenary garrison.

Both curtain towers and the ramparts were often provided with a 'talus' in the form of the classical glacis, a bold sloping addition to thickness at the foot of walls and towers as a deterrent to mining and to deflect missiles. Another device developed with considerable ingenuity is the 'bent entrance', which compelled investing forces to follow a devious and confined route while exposed to lateral fire and the hazards of retaliation by way of meurtrières in the vaults over gatehouses and passages through curtain walls; in some cases the planning of a bent entrance limited the use of a battering ram. This was almost certainly an idea borrowed from Saracen town defences such as the Great Gate at Aleppo, or the Damascus Gate (Bab-al-Ahmood) in the Walls of Suleyman at Jerusalem.

After the end of the twelfth century, as passive defensive devices became more important, archery played an increasing part, particularly as flanking fire-power was augmented by the greater projection of towers, and less of the fighting was conducted from the crenellations of the top of curtain walls. The arrow-slits in the Norman keep were relatively few, but the later castles were equipped with carefully designed long loopholes and large inner embrasures which allowed a wider field of fire.

The general shortage of timber caused difficulties in providing the tops of walls and towers with the projecting brattices and palisades common in European fortification. Instead, later Crusader work includes stone machicolations developed from those of box form found in Saracen town walls. Among the most effective of siege weapons were water shortage and famine, and the capacity of underground storage chambers and cisterns in some of the larger castles was immense. Margat was customarily provisioned for a thousand men to withstand siege for as long as five years; one vaulted cistern at Saone held over thirteen million litres (three million gallons), while the Krak had a windmill, enormous granary spaces, oil presses, an aqueduct and a well.

Religious Buildings

The Church of the Holy Sepulchre in Jerusalem (p. 289), by its origin and function, is the most sacred in Christendom, and its holy places were the final objective of the Crusades. As is to be expected, it represents the finest and most ambitious of Crusader church architecture, the sources of which can be traced to Provence, Poitou, Burgundy, Languedoc and the art of the Santiago pilgrim routes, all overlaid with native Levantine characteristics.

Lesser churches in the Latin Kingdom in several cases are well preserved, largely because of sound construction in fine masonry. High vaults are usually of barrel form, with transverse stabilising arches, though groin vaults to aisles are not uncommon. A triapsidal east end occurs in Beirut Cathedral, but Tortosa has pastophoria of Byzantine form. Apses quite frequently are enclosed in rectangular masonry masses. The Crusaders left evidence of their art in many buildings which they adapted to church purposes, and were responsible, for instance, for the ornamental iron balustrades in the Dome of the Rock (q.v.) which, with the Al-Aqsa mosque in the Haram at Jerusalem, was a Christian church under the control of the Templars. Decoration of the chapels in castles under the care of the military Orders was often exuberant, and included fine examples of the crafts of mosaic, patterned tiles and carved stonework.

The Holy Land: Examples

Military Buildings

The **Château de Mer, Sidon**, in the Lebanon (1228) (p. 392A), is the best surviving example of a coastal Crusader castle, separated from its dependent township by a sea-dyke crossed only by a later causeway. It was capable of independent defence after the town had been invested, particularly if support could be maintained for the castle alone by sea. It still possesses substantial remains of a two-storey keep, an imposing land gate with decoratively carved box machicolations, large storage and domestic buildings within the ward, and clear evidence of the use of ancient column shafts as binders through the curtain-wall masonry. Sidon remained a Frankish stronghold almost to the end of the Crusader period of territorial control in the Holy Land.

Giblet, on the site of the Phoenician port of Byblos, was extensively refortified during the twelfth century. The ancient defences were rebuilt as a new curtain wall with square towers, and a substantial two-storey keep.

Chastel Pélérin (Pilgrims' Castle), Atlit, was built in 1218 by the Templars with the help of the Teutonic Knights and of the many pilgrims from whom it derives its name. The castle is now largely in ruins, but its plan is clearly discernible. It stands upon a peninsula commanding the approach to one of the principal passes between the coast and the Palestinian interior. The main defences are on the landward side, and include a stone glacis, a moat which could be opened to the sea, and a double range of ramparts crossing the whole width of the promontory, both furnished with square towers, covering alternating fields of fire. The defences on the sea fronts were provided by a massive curtain of which little now remains. The buildings within it included a church probably planned on the customary Templar pattern. This was the only castle, apart from Tortosa, never taken by siege.

Margat Castle commands a narrow neck of the coastal plain at Baniyas, south of Latakia, on the seaward side of the Gebel Alawi, the northern extension of the Lebanon mountains. It supported the

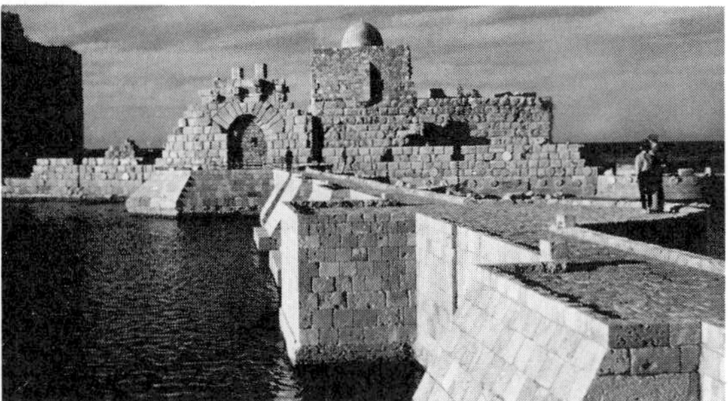

A. Château de Mer, Sidon (1288): east curtain wall and gateway. See p.391

B. Saone: the east curtain wall. See p.393

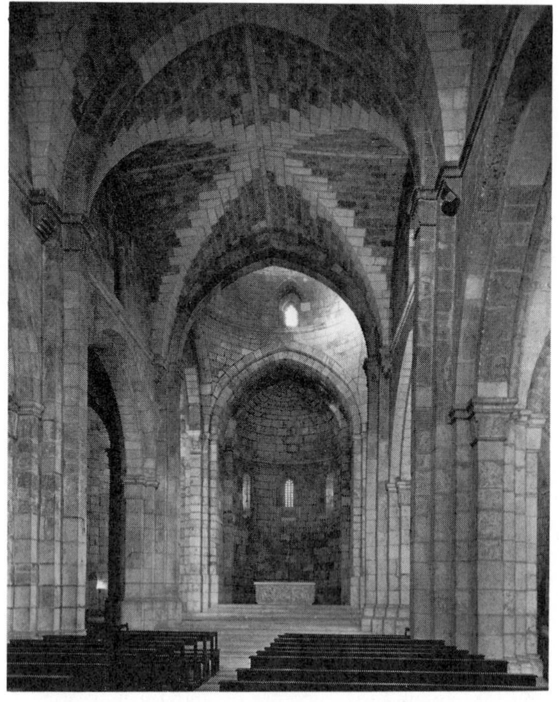

C. S. Anne, Jerusalem (1142): interior. See p.394

D. Krak des Chevaliers (mainly *c.* 1200): aerial view. See p.393

Assassin (Ismaili) strongholds of Kadmus and Masiaf. It was acquired from the Midi family of Mazoir by the Hospitallers in 1186, and while under their control Margat became the largest of all the Crusaders' castles. The double concentric fortifications enclose an enormous area, and incorporate a narrow outer bailey on the western side, with a large circular tower-keep above a bold circular outer tower in the lower curtain, furnished with a tall double talus and box machicolations. The castle was attacked in 1288 by the Sultan Qala'un, and the outer defences were successfully mined. The keep resisted assault until, after it had been seriously mined, the Hospitallers withdrew to Acre.

Beaufort guards a pass through the Lebanon mountains. It stands at the head of the gorge of the river Litani on a site readily accessible only from an adjoining plateau, from which it was divided by a shallow rock-cut moat. The square keep is built into the curtain, and a natural glacis is reinforced on the western flank with a built escarpment.

Kerak, in Moab, was part of the eastern line of defensive strongholds, standing on a mountain spur at the junction of two wadis in the high plateau east of the Dead Sea. The castle covers its dependent village from attack based on higher ground to the north, and is isolated from both by a rock-cut fosse in the Byzantine tradition, similar to that at Beaufort, with which it also shares the device of a strong keep in the curtain commanding the most likely approach route.

Saone (p. 392B), at the north end of the Gebel Alawi, was built on a site previously fortified by the Greeks in Byzantine fashion, with a thin outer curtain wall punctuated with shallow rectangular towers, and a keep commanding the most vulnerable part of the curtain. It was taken during the passage southward of the First Crusade, and became a dependency of the Princes of Antioch. The main Crusader work was carried out soon after 1120, and represents one of the best examples of the earlier phases of castle building in the Latin Kingdom. It stands upon a triangular spur, the ground falling sharply on two sides. On the third side, separating the castle from its outworks, which extend nearly half a mile, is an enormous rock-cut ravine, 20 m (65 ft) wide where it abuts the postern gatehouse towers, and involving the excavation of 173,300 tonnes (170,000 tons) of bed-rock. Since it was not possible to span this fosse with a single drawbridge, a pinnacle was left in the excavation to provide a central support. Above the fosse stands a square two-storey keep with a single narrow doorway and three round towers, of which two are possibly the earliest of all Crusader towers of this form. The postern gatehouse on the face of the great fosse is formed of two circular towers. Elsewhere in the curtain the towers are square and of small salient, without loops, but with an alure at the top, as was customary at their early twelfth-century date. The main gatehouse on the south side has an entrance in its flank, with a direct approach from the inner face to the ward, which probably represents the first Latin use in the eastern Mediterranean of the 'bent entrance'.

The **Krak des Chevaliers** (mainly *c.* 1200) (p. 392D), described by T. E. Lawrence as 'the best preserved and most wholly admirable castle in the world', is the easternmost of a chain of five castles sited so as to secure the Homs Gap; the Krak was in visual signal communication with Akkar, at the north end of the Litani valley (La Bocquée), and with Safita, Chastel Rouge and Arima, nearer the coast. The castle stands upon a southern spur of the Gebel Alawi, on the site of an earlier Islamic 'Castle of the Kurds'. In 1142 it was given by Raymond, Count of Tripoli, into the care of the Knights Hospitallers, and it was they who, during the ensuing fifty years, remodelled and developed it as the most distinguished work of military architecture of its time.

The Krak has two concentric lines of defence, the inner ramparts lying close to the outer and continuously dominating them. The single ward of the original twelfth-century castle covered about the same area as the later inner enclosure, and some of the remains of the early work on the crest of the spur are incorporated in the existing building. The outer curtain is furnished on the north and west sides with eight round towers, of which one is later than the Crusader occupation, and of which two form the north barbican, also extended at a later date. The curtain towers are generously provided with carefully disposed loops, and the whole outer wall-walk has loops and merlons above box-machicolations, some of which are recent restorations. The main gateway is on the east flank, and gives access to a long ramped and vaulted 'bent entrance', defensible at the gatehouse by moat and drawbridge; machicolations over the external wall, four gates and at least one portcullis; the vaulted ramp itself has meurtrière holes in the roof, and is exposed at three points to flanking assault from the outer ward. The greater part of the inner defences dates from the late twelfth and early thirteenth centuries, though the inner gatehouse, the inner north-west postern tower, and the chapel (of which the apse forms a tower above the outer ward) belong to the Latin occupation before the time of the hospital. The most remarkable single feature of the inner castle is the colossal glacis on the west and south sides, which the Arabs call 'the Mountain', rising formidably above the great cistern and the outer ward, more than 25 m (80 ft) thick at the base. At the south end of the inner structure is a stronghold formed of three great round towers, linked by a sentry-walk on two tiers of vaults, and containing what was clearly the finest set of apartments, serving as a refuge as much from the hostility of a disaffected mercenary garrison as from that of invading forces. The vaulted loggia in the upper court is a fine mature early Gothic addition.

The Krak was attacked unsuccessfully on twelve separate occasions, but eventually, in March of 1271, the Sultan Baybars (the 'Panther') laid siege to the castle, and the knights were brought to surrender, in April, by means of forged instructions. Except for a brief period during the First World War this magnificent castle has been in Arab hands ever since.

Religious Buildings

Crusader church architecture generally followed Cistercian and Burgundian fashion and many examples possess transitional half-Gothic features, though traditional Romanesque planning was customary. **Tortosa Cathedral**, built within the fortified precinct which became the headquarters of the Templars, has a characteristically Burgundian barrel-vaulted nave, groined aisle vaults, and compound piers with foliated capitals, but the sanctuary planning is Byzantine, with pastophory chapels. **Beirut Cathedral**, now a mosque, has a similar structural composition, though with a clerestory, and the east end has three apses. Crusader churches at **Tyre, Sebastieh** and **Caesarea** have cruciform plans, and square apses occur at **Nazareth** and **Ramleh**. One of the best preserved of the smaller churches of the Crusaders is **S. Anne, Jerusalem** (1142) (p. 392C), which commemorates the site held to be that of the home of the parents of the Virgin, and consequently her birth-place. The church was built by the queen of Baldwin I as that of a Benedictine nunnery, and was beautifully restored after 1878 by the White Fathers, to whom it now belongs. It has a typical Benedictine plan; it is aisled with a groin-vaulted nave, shallow transepts, three eastern apses, and, unusually, a dome on pendentives at the crossing of exactly the Périgord kind. The arches are generally pointed, and the central west door is a finely proportioned near-Gothic feature (p. 392C) embellished with moulding enrichments which anticipate the thirteenth-century dog-tooth. The Crusader work on the Church of the Holy Sepulchre, Jerusalem, is described in Chapter 11.

The British Isles: Architectural Character

Roman period. The architecture of the Romans in Britain was of the same character as in other parts of Europe, and much still survives, in remains such as those of Hadrian's Wall and of urban building in Silchester, Bath, Chester, Corstopitum (Corbridge), Viroconium (Wroxeter) and Verulamium (near S. Albans). Fora, basilicas, baths, a theatre (at Verulamium), temples in Aquae Sulis (Bath) and Londinium (the city of London), villas (at Verulamium), and a palace (at Fishbourne) have been uncovered. Examples of mosaic flooring, pottery and sculptures indicate the care which the Romans bestowed on dwelling houses and public buildings. The characteristics of Roman architecture were so virile that they inevitably influenced subsequent Anglo-Saxon and Romanesque architecture in Britain.

The form of the Christian church in Britain before the end of the Roman occupation is exemplified at Silchester. This was a small church, with a basilican plan, probably built early in the fourth century. It had a western apse, for the ritual at this time required that the celebrant face east from beyond the altar. It had transeptal projections in the form of Byzantine pastophoria (a diaconicon accessible from the sanctuary as a sacristy, and a prothesis accessible from the nave as an offertory); and a triumphal arch derived directly from Roman precedent as a sanctuary screen.

Anglo-Saxon period. The two principal schools of church building during the Heptarchy were Kentish and Northumbrian in provenance. The southern examples derived from fifth- and sixth-century Ravenate churches. They can be represented by the church at Reculver in Kent (p. 397B), founded in 669, and having a broad rectangular plan, with eastern apse, two pastophoria, porticos on north and south as burial chapels, a western porch and narthex, and a three-arch iconostasis. The Northumbrian school showed the influence of Roman techniques and Germanic design and is represented by the church at Escomb, of the late seventh century (p. 397A). The Northumbrian monasteries of Monkwearmouth (673) and Jarrow (684/5), of which only parts survive and others have been excavated, are important. Jarrow was the home of the Venerable Bede. The Mercian monastic church of Brixworth also belongs to the pre-Danish period (probably early ninth century). Its basilican plan with a series of porticus rather than aisles, the separated choir space and the outer crypt have parallels in Carolingian architecture.

Late Anglo-Saxon architecture (tenth and eleventh centuries) is characterised by the use of western and central towers and by distinctive decorative and constructional techniques such as long-and-short quoining (p. 396C,P), stripwork (narrow pilasters sometimes forming decorative patterns as at Earls Barton) (p. 396C), twin openings, sometimes with triangular heads, supported on mid-wall shafts (p. 396C,H,J,P), and bold mouldings either of simple rectangular section (p. 396H) or of a bulbous and more complex form (p. 396F). Double-splayed windows (p. 396Q) and megalithic construction are also characteristic. Before the Norman Conquest certain Romanesque elements such as the regular crossing

England and Wales in the Middle Ages

with tower (for example, Stow, Lincolnshire, *c.* 1034–55) were being used. The most mature pre-Conquest Romanesque building was Edward the Confessor's Westminster Abbey which was an aisled cruciform church with alternating supports similar to Jumièges Abbey. Of equal sophistication if small dimensions is the church of Great Paxton in Cambridgeshire (pp. 397G, 399B), the only substantially surviving pre-Conquest building in mature Romanesque style. It is an aisled cruciform church with a crossing but no tower and alternating compound piers supporting arches of two orders.

Norman period. The Normans imported a type of architecture, ecclesiastical as well as military, destined to symbolise the new order. Their first (1070) major project was to replace the two Canterbury foundations, probably the most venerated sites in England, initiated by S. Augustine himself, with vast new churches directly over their razed predecessors. Sheer size was an important factor; Winchester Cathedral reached an astonishing total internal length of 157 m (515 ft), equalling Cluny Abbey as one of the longest buildings in Europe. While the starting point for the new architecture was clearly in Normandy, it developed quickly and soon eclipsed the grandest buildings in the duchy. The major innovations were the development of the compound pier, with the number of half-columns and nook shafts multiplying and rising up to articulate the whole elevation (pp. 362R, 400, 404H); the tripartite

ANGLO-SAXON STYLE
RESTORED
15'.0"
A PLAN AT BELFRY STAGE
B EARLS BARTON: TOWER WINDOW
C EARLS BARTON: TOWER
D SOMPTING: TOWER ARCH
E SOMPTING: TOWER
F S. BENET: CAMBRIDGE: IMPOST
G S. MARY THE YOUNGER: YORK: TOWER WINDOW
4'.11"
GLASS
GLASS
PLAN
H WINDOW: WORTH CH. SUSSEX
J DEERHURST: GLO'STERSHIRE: TOWER WINDOW
K BOARHUNT CH: HANTS
L WORTH CHURCH: SUSSEX
M BRADFORD-ON-AVON CH: WILTS
59'.6"
18'.6"
N PLAN
P S. BENET: CAMBRGE. TOWER
PORCH
14'.0"
42'.0"
Q PLAN

ANGLO-SAXON CHURCH PLANS

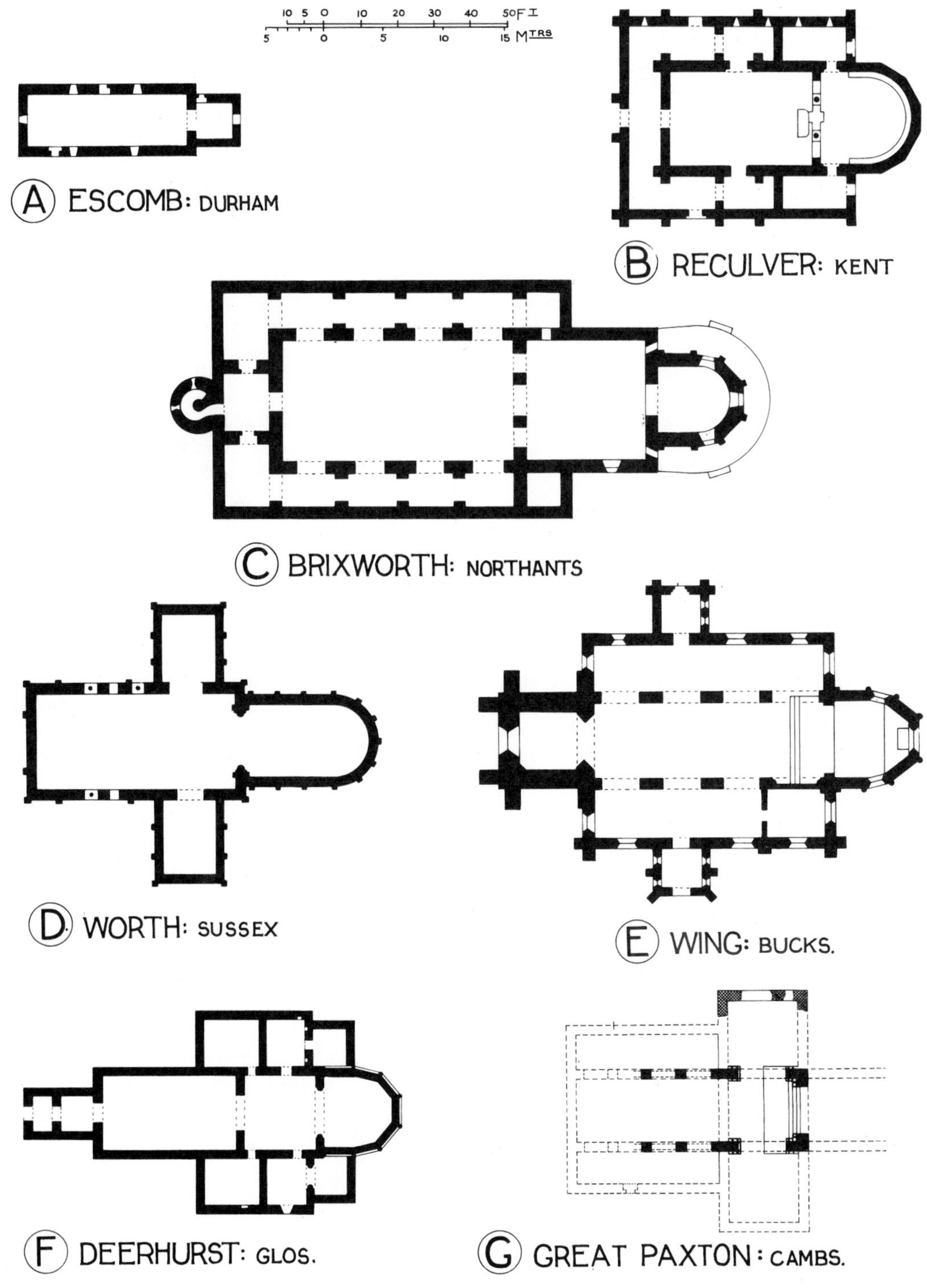

clerestory bay, first used at Winchester, with the internal face, in front of the wall passage, transformed into a three-arch composition supported on columns (p. 404E,F); the introduction of the cushion capital, which was unknown in Normandy before the Conquest; the introduction of architectural sculpture – by about 1100 high quality carving began to be used for capitals and portals, the work usually being attributed to Anglo-Saxon sculptors, and new ornamental motifs such as chevron and beak-head appeared (pp. 399C, 400); and the introduction of the rib vault (Chapter 8).

The British Isles: Examples

Anglo-Saxon

Bradwell-next-the-Sea, Essex (after 669), is the best preserved church of the Kentish school. The nave remains to its full height with plain buttresses and splayed windows. Originally it had an apse to the east separated from the nave by a triple arcade and flanked by a pair of porticus.

Reculver, Kent (669) (p. 397B). Only the lowest courses of walling survive, most of the building having been demolished during the last century. The reused Roman columns of the three-arch screen are now in the crypt of Canterbury cathedral.

Escomb, County Durham (late seventh century) (p. 397A), preserves its long, narrow and lofty nave with a square chancel. It is constructed of reused Roman masonry and the chancel arch jambs are constructed in the long-and-short manner. The arch itself may be Roman. Porticus have been excavated to the west and to the north of the chancel.

At **Monkwearmouth, County Durham** (674), there remains a simple rectangular church with a western tower of which the lower storeys, also probably seventh century, form a porch. Of the monastic buildings excavated the most interesting is a long passageway running due south from the church.

Jarrow, County Durham (684), the home of the Venerable Bede, was the sister monastery of Monkwearmouth. Of the original two churches one still stands, forming the chancel of a later church. The large conventual buildings were excavated to the south of the church.

Brixworth, Northamptonshire (early ninth century) (pp. 397C,399A), is a basilican church of large dimensions with a four-bay nave of arches turned in reused Roman brick and supported on big rectangular piers. Instead of aisles there was a series of porticus which have been demolished. The western tower was originally of only two storeys with a tribune. There is a rectangular choir space which was separated from the nave by a screen, a reconstructed apse and an outer crypt.

Wing, Buckinghamshire (early ninth century) (p. 397E), is similar to Brixworth in that it has a basilican plan. The original polygonal apse survives only at crypt level, the rest having been rebuilt with stripwork during the eleventh century. The crypt is vaulted with irregular supports. The western tower and the reconstructed aisles are late mediaeval.

Deerhurst, Gloucestershire (eighth-eleventh century) (p. 397F), is a complex building with a fragment of an eleventh-century polygonal apse and a chancel arch, attached to an earlier building with flanking porticus. The east wall of the tower has a doorway at first floor level suggesting the existence of a platform. In the same wall is a highly elaborate twin opening with triangular arches supported on a fluted rectangular shaft and similarly fluted responds (p. 396J).

Bradford-on-Avon, Wiltshire (early eleventh century) (p. 396M,Q), is a small church constructed in finely jointed ashlar. The tall rectangular nave has a chancel to the east and only one of the former pair of side porches. The exterior is decorated with pilaster strips and blind arcading of a Romanesque type. The doorways are surrounded by pilaster strips and they have simple square-sectioned imposts. It is an early Romanesque building articulated by surface decoration and perfectly proportioned.

Earls Barton, Northamptonshire (early eleventh century) (p. 396A–C), consisted originally only of a tower with a chancel attached to its east side – a rare type of church plan. The tower is extravagantly decorated with stripwork, the most extreme example of the technique in the country. The arched bell openings are supported on typical bulbous shafts; the doorway is surrounded by stripwork and has square-sectioned imposts with slightly recessed decorative arcading.

Boarhunt, Hampshire (eleventh century) (p. 396K,N). The only sign of Anglo-Saxon workmanship on the exterior is the stripwork on the chancel gable. There is also a blocked double-splayed window on the north side of the chancel. The interior has a fine chancel arch surrounded by stripwork and with multi-roll-moulded imposts. The western part of the nave was originally separated by a wall to form a western compartment.

Worth, Sussex (mid-eleventh century) (p. 397D), has a cruciform plan formed by porticus and by a stilted apse which was rebuilt in 1871. The exterior has decorative vertical pilaster strips and three remarkable original, arched twin windows supported on bulbous mid-wall shafts. The three principal arches inside the church are surrounded by stripwork and the porticus arches have large stripped imposts of square section. The chancel arch is particularly impressive, supported on massive half-columns with roughly shaped capitals.

A. Brixworth Church, Northamptonshire (early ninth century). See p.398

B. Great Paxton, Camridgeshire (mid-eleventh century): interior. See p.402

C. Canterbury Cathedral: Norman tower, SE transept (*c.* 1096–1125). See p.402

Durham Cathedral: nave (1110–33) looking E. See p.402

FOUNTAINS ABBEY: YORKSHIRE

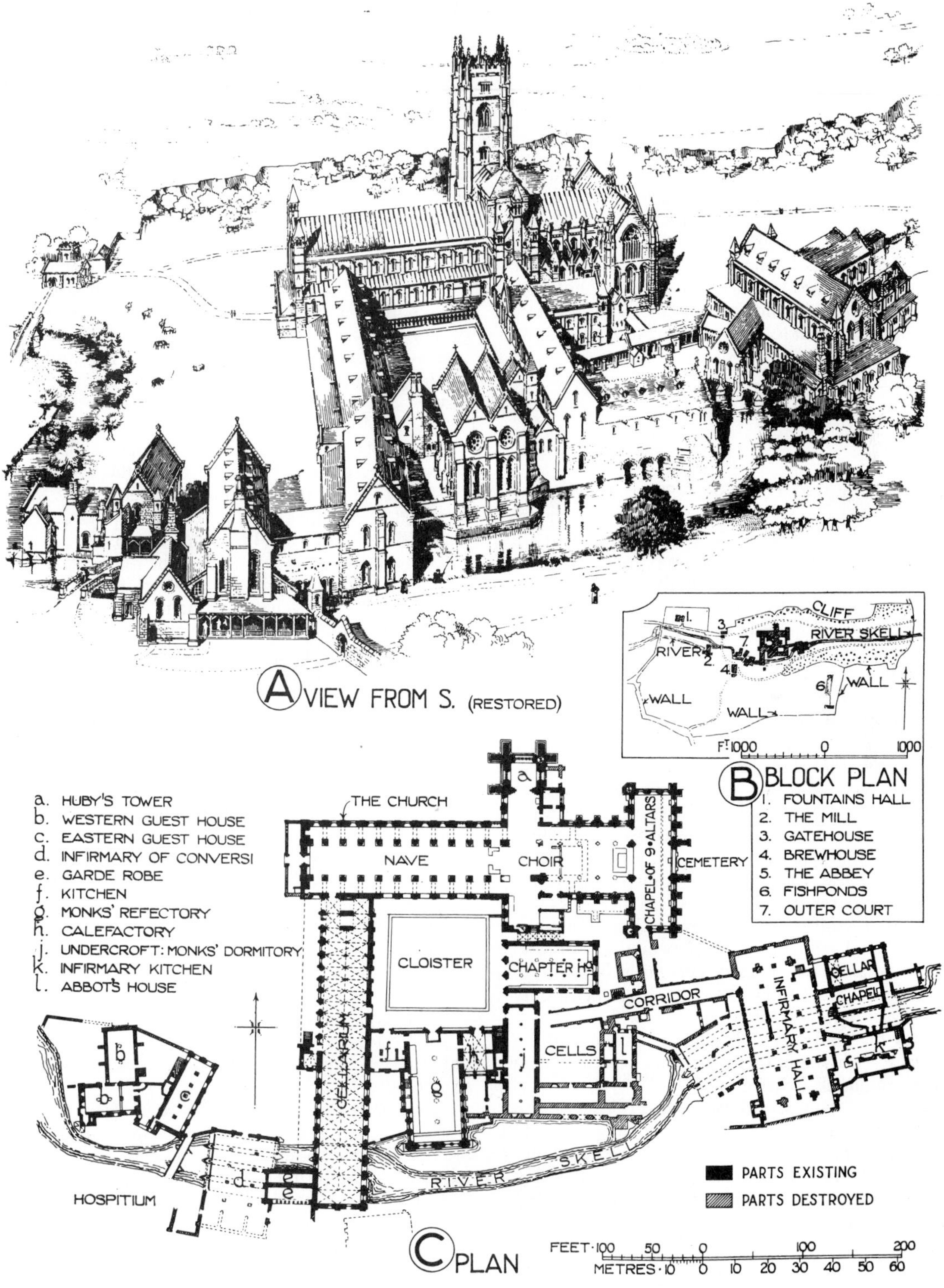

Ⓐ VIEW FROM S. (RESTORED)
CLIFF
RIVER SKELL
RIVER
WALL
WALL
WALL
1.
2.
3.
4.
6.
7.
FT 1000 0 1000
Ⓑ BLOCK PLAN
1. FOUNTAINS HALL
2. THE MILL
3. GATEHOUSE
4. BREWHOUSE
5. THE ABBEY
6. FISHPONDS
7. OUTER COURT
a. HUBY'S TOWER
b. WESTERN GUEST HOUSE
c. EASTERN GUEST HOUSE
d. INFIRMARY OF CONVERSI
e. GARDE ROBE
f. KITCHEN
g. MONKS' REFECTORY
h. CALEFACTORY
j. UNDERCROFT: MONKS' DORMITORY
k. INFIRMARY KITCHEN
l. ABBOT'S HOUSE
THE CHURCH
NAVE
CHOIR
CHAPEL OF 9 ALTARS
CEMETERY
CLOISTER
CHAPTER Ho
CORRIDOR
CELLARIUM
CELLS
INFIRMARY HALL
CELLAR
CHAPEL
HOSPITIUM
RIVER SKELL
PARTS EXISTING
PARTS DESTROYED
Ⓒ PLAN
FEET 100 50 0 100 200
METRES 10 0 10 20 30 40 50 60

Sompting, Sussex (late eleventh century) (p. 396E), is particularly important for its surviving helm roof. It also has a fine tower arch with half-columns columns supporting a soffit-roll and with carved capitals.

Great Paxton, Cambridgeshire (mid-eleventh century) (pp. 397G,399B). The church has two surviving bays of an aisled nave which originally had four bays. Each pier consists of half-columns arranged around a square core set diagonally. The alternation is effected by rounding-off the protruding angles of the square core on the easternmost pair of piers. The eastern crossing piers are L-shaped and the western ones were originally cruciform, their north and south elements having been cut back. The faces of the piers are decorated with rippling half-columns and the masonry is laid in long-and-short fashion. Some original double-splayed clerestory windows survive.

Norman

Canterbury (pp. 402C, 463B, 468A). Benedictine cathedral priory. Archbishop Lanfranc's church (1070–77) in imitation of S. Etienne, Caen (q.v.); choir replaced and enlarged, incorporating an extensive crypt (1096–1126); choir rebuilt on remains after fire and extended eastwards 1174–85 by William of Sens and his English successor on a plan contracted in width to preserve radiating chapels.

Carlisle (founded *c.* 1102) (p. 465B). Augustinian monastery. Two Norman bays remain.

Chichester (1091–1184) (p. 464G). Norman nave, transitional retro-choir.

Durham (1093–1133) (pp.400, 427E). Benedictine cathedral priory. Norman work in choir transepts and western towers among the finest in England; the vaults of the eastern arm are probably the earliest essays in ribbed vaulting outside Italy, and those of the nave the earliest to incorporate pointed transverse arches. Alternating compound and circular piers, the circular piers with impressive grooved decoration.

Ely (1083–1179) (p. 462A). Benedictine cathedral priory. Norman nave and transepts with timber roof, lower parts of west front (beyond the Galilee), only the southern part remaining.

Exeter (*c.* 1090) (p. 464E). The disposition of the two transept towers, the only surviving Norman work, is unique in Britain.

Fountains Abbey, Yorkshire (1137–*c.* 1200) (p. 401) is a representative example of mature, largely Romanesque monastic architecture. The community was founded (1132) soon after Rievaulx, the first Cistercian establishment in that county (1131), and before Kirkstall (1152). It is thought to have been named from the springs in the valley of the Skell. Because of the care with which the abbey ruins have been uncovered, it is easy here to make a mental picture of a great monastery. The gatehouse led into the outer court; south of this were the guest house and the infirmary of the 'conversi', or lay brethren, and east of it was the cellarium, no less than 90 m (300 ft) long, comprising storehouses and refectory for the conversi on the lower floor, with their dormitory above. Opposite the gatehouse is the conventual church, of which the nave and transepts belong to the first phase of building, but the choir was enlarged between 1203 and 1247, and at the same time the 'Chapel of the Nine Altars' was built. The tower, by Abbot Huby (1495–1526), is still the dominating feature in this beautiful valley. The door in the south-east angle of the nave leads into the cloister court, round which were ranged the chapter house, the monks' dormitory and its undercroft, the calefactory or warming house, the monks' refectory, the kitchen with two great fireplaces, and alongside the kitchen a washing lavatory, part of which still remains. Still farther east were the cells for refractory monks and the abbot's lodge, north of which a corridor led to the infirmary hall, with adjacent chapel, cellar and kitchen. The chapter house, of which the vaulting is now destroyed, was rectangular, and against the walls were stone benches rising one above another on which the monks sat. The complete monastic establishment must have existed till the time of Abbot William Thirsk (1526–36), after which the estate was sold (1540) to Sir Richard Gresham, whose successor pulled down the infirmary and the stone wall, and built Fountains Hall (p. 401B) on the site in 1611.

Gloucester (1089–*c.* 1130). Benedictine abbey. Norman choir cased early fourteenth century.

Hereford (*c.* 1090). Extensive Norman remains internally visible in nave, choir and south transept.

Norwich (1096–1145) (p. 463D). Benedictine cathedral priory. Long Norman nave, aisleless transepts, choir with ambulatory and radiating chapels.

Oxford (1158–80). Augustinian priory. Norman nave and choir with a giant-order main arcade and suspended triforium gallery.

Peterborough (1118–44) (pp. 404, 462D, 471C). Benedictine abbey. Fine Norman interior; original nave timber ceiling; choir apse enclosed by late fifteenth-century work. Western transept, in Transitional style, not originally intended.

Rochester (*c.* 1080–1124) (p. 464H). Benedictine monastery. Crypt, nave and west door of Norman church survive.

S. Albans (1077–88) (p. 464F). Benedictine abbey. Norman nave, transepts, choir and central tower built of reused Roman brick and very little ashlar, resulting in the rather plain interior.

Southwell (1108–50) (p. 464K). Norman nave, transepts and towers. The west front is the best illustration in the country of the Romanesque twin-tower facade.

Winchester (1079–93) (p. 462C). Benedictine cathedral priory. Norman transepts and extensive crypt. Some of the original nave piers survive, though cut back during the later Middle Ages.

Worcester (1084–*c.* 1095) (p. 463A). Benedictine cathedral priory. An extensive crypt and the transept arms survive from the Norman church. Chapter house on distinctive circular plan.

Ireland

Cormac's Chapel, Cashél (1127–34) (p. 405A–F,H), illustrates the influence of the Anglo-Norman style combined with traditional Irish techniques. The blind arcading, the ornament and the rib-vaulted chancel are clearly Anglo-Norman; the pointed, corbelled vaults of the upper storey can be traced back to monastic cells such as the **Oratory of Gallerus, Dingle, County Kerry** (probably eighth century) (p. 406A).

The round towers of **Devonish** and **Kilree** (tenth to twelfth century) (p. 405G,J) are representative of over one hundred such towers existing in Ireland. They are constructed of finely cut ashlar and served as refuges as well as bell towers. The doorways are situated high above ground level for reasons of defence, and the uppermost storeys have bell openings.

Castles

Of some 1500 castles in England, more than 1200 were founded during the eleventh and twelfth centuries. Only a few of the most important had stone keeps from the outset; the majority began as 'motte and bailey'earthworks. The motte or mound usually was partly natural, partly artificial, its sides steepened by a ditch dug around its base. The flat-topped crest sometimes was broad enough to accommodate a timber dwelling. In other cases it probably served solely as a citadel, carrying a wooden defence tower, raised on angle posts. The dwelling and ancillary buildings then were sited in the bailey, this being a zone which looped from the foot of the motte, defined by ditches and earthen ramparts, and which was spacious enough also to provide refuge for dependants, peasantry and stock in times of need. The fringe of the motte crest and the summits of the earth ramparts were lined by palisades of close-set timber baulks, or occasionally by rough stone walls.

Thetford, Norfolk, affords a fine instance, 24.4 m (80 ft) high, of the hundreds of surviving mottes.

The motte and bailey of **Dromore Castle, N. Ireland** (*c.* 1180) (p. 406B), are in almost pristine condition, and the castle is a relic of the Norman overlordship of Ireland after 1171.

Stone 'curtain' walls soon began to replace the perishable timber palisades, and in the twelfth century, particularly the latter half, mottes assumed that form known as the 'shell-keep', because of the empty-looking crowning ring of high walls. The bailey stone walls rose up the mound to join those of the shell-keep. **Windsor Castle** (p. 407A) has a shell-keep of about 1170 (the upper half and the windows are nineteenth century), with an elongated bailey on each side. Other twelfth-century examples are **Carisbrooke, Isle of Wight** (*c.* 1140–50) (p. 407C); **Launceston**, within which a round keep was built about 1240; **Restormel** (p. 406C); and **Trematon**. The last three are in Cornwall.

The greatest castles of the period had stone keeps. The **Tower of London** (*c.* 1086–97) (p. 408) assumed its form as a 'concentric' castle, with successive lines of fortification, only after several reigns. Here, the rectangular keep of three storeys – the topmost was divided into two, later on – 28 m (92 ft) in height, stands in the centre of an inner bailey, surrounded by a wall with thirteen towers (*c.* 1250), which is, in its turn, enclosed by an outer bailey and wall with eight towers and an encircling moat (*c.* 1280). Other examples, numbering about fifty, include **Colchester** (*c.* 1090), **Corfe, Dorset** (*c.* 1125), **Castle Rising, Norfolk** (*c.* 1140), **Rochester** (1126–39), and **Hedingham, Essex** (*c.* 1140) (p. 406D). **Chilham, Kent** (*c.* 1160), **Orford, Suffolk** (1166–72) (p. 406E) and **Conisborough, Yorkshire** (1185–90) (p. 407B), with octagonal or circular plans, are later developments of the keep. Keeps tended to become less magnificent as the strength of the outer defences was increased.

Manor Houses

Such few examples as remain are mostly in the south-east. They have suffered various drastic modifications. In the majority, stone-built, the domestic accommodation is raised on a first floor, over an 'undercroft' or storage 'cellar', this type probably reflecting contemporary castle-keep arrangements. **Boothby Pagnell, Lincolnshire** (p. 409C), **S. Mary's Guild, Lincoln** (p. 409B), and the **Norman House, Christchurch, Dorset** (p. 409A), are instances. On the first floor there might be little more than the one room, the hall, or additionally a smaller private chamber or 'solar', at the opposite end to the entrance. Cooking was probably done outdoors, and supplementary accommodation provided in frail shelters elsewhere in the enclosure. The second type, often wholly in timber, was a 'nave-and-aisles' single-storey structure, like a very simple church, all ancillary needs being provided for separately, as before. Roofs in general were of the 'trussed-rafter' kind typical in the south-east, lacking a ridge-piece; in the north-west, there normally were principals spaced down the length of the building, carrying purlins and a heavy ridge.

PETERBOROUGH CATHEDRAL
10'·0"
A ROSE WINDOW: CENTRE GABLE: W. FRONT
B EXTERIOR FROM N.E.
10'·0"
C ROSE WINDOW: SIDE GABLES: W. FRONT
20'·0"
84'·0"
CLEARSTORY
PASSAGE
TRIFORIUM
56'·0"
78'·0"
52'·0"
CHOIR ARCADE
31'·0"
82'·3"
20'·0"
78'·0"
FEET 10 0 10 20 30 40 50
METRES 1 0 5 10 15
D EXTERNAL BAY
E TRANSVERSE SECTION THRO' CHOIR
F INTERNAL BAY
G W. FRONT
H INTERIOR LOOKING E.
J S. TRANSEPT LOOKG. S.E.

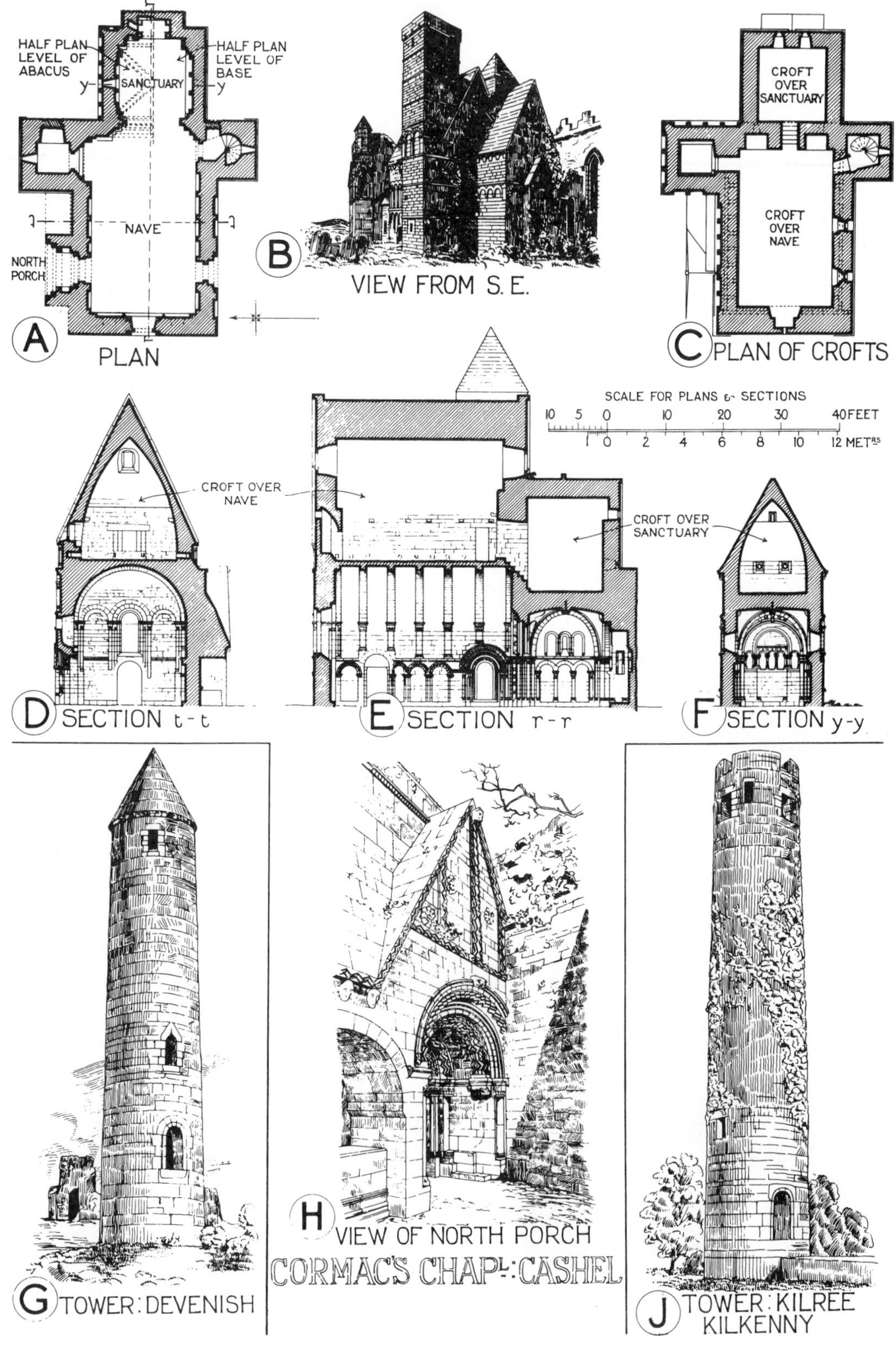
HALF PLAN LEVEL OF ABACUS
HALF PLAN LEVEL OF BASE
SANCTUARY
NAVE
NORTH PORCH
A PLAN
B VIEW FROM S.E.
CROFT OVER SANCTUARY
CROFT OVER NAVE
C PLAN OF CROFTS
SCALE FOR PLANS & SECTIONS
10 5 0 10 20 30 40 FEET
1 0 2 4 6 8 10 12 METRES
CROFT OVER NAVE
CROFT OVER SANCTUARY
D SECTION t-t
E SECTION r-r
F SECTION y-y
G TOWER: DEVENISH
H VIEW OF NORTH PORCH
CORMAC'S CHAPL.: CASHEL
J TOWER: KILREE KILKENNY

A. Oratory of Gallerus, Dingle County Kerry (probably eighth century). See p.403

B. Dromore Castle, N. Ireland (*c.* 1180). See p.403

C. Restormel Castle, Cornwall (twelfth century and later). See p.403

D. Castle Hedingham, Essex: the keep (*c.* 1140). See p.403

E. Orford Castle, Suffolk: the keep (1166–72). See p.406

A. Windsor Castle: aerial view from W. See p.403

B. Conisborough Castle, Yorkshire (1185–90): the keep. See p.403

C. Carisbroke Castle, Isle of Wight (*c.* 1140–50): aerial view. See p.403

THE TOWER OF LONDON

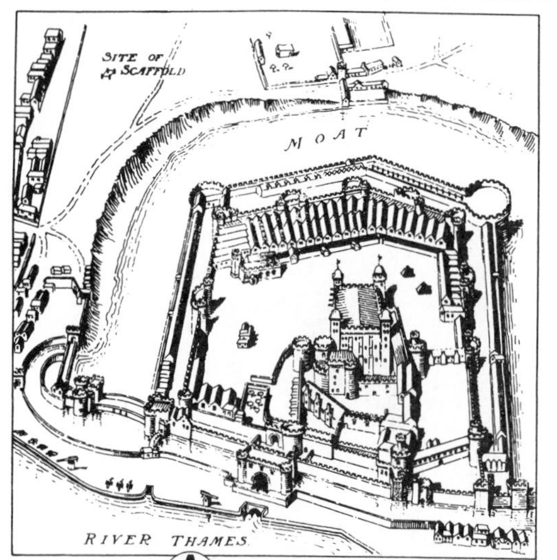

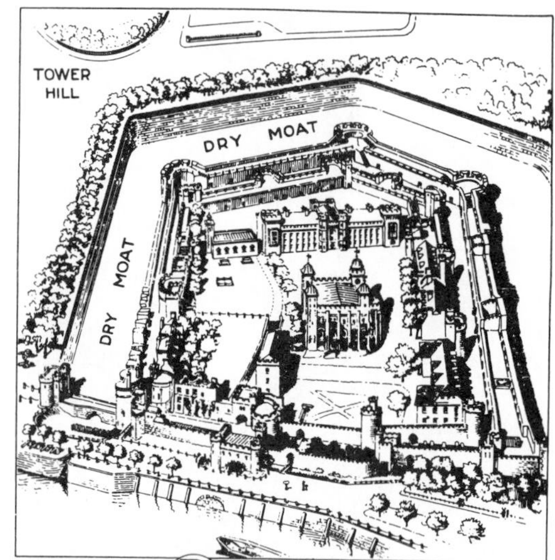

(A) A·D 1597 BIRD'S EYE VIEWS (B) A·D 1918.

(C) INTERIOR OF S. JOHN'S CHAPEL LOOKING E.

(D) WHITE TOWER FROM S.E.

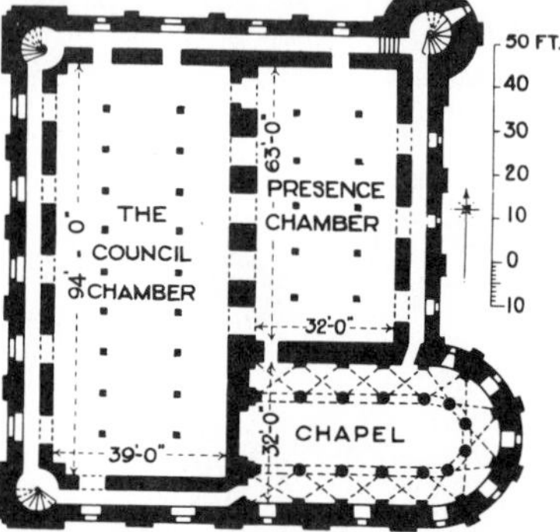

(E) PLAN OF WHITE TOWER AT THIRD FLOOR LEVEL

(F) INTERIOR OF BYWARD TOWER

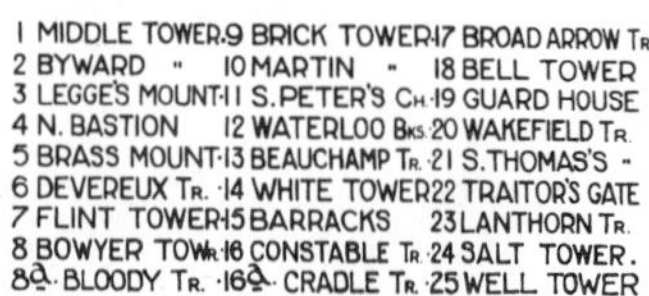

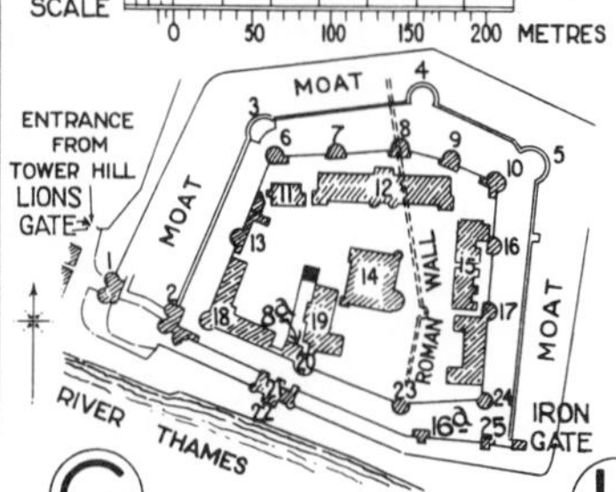

(G) BLOCK PLAN

(H) BLOODY TOWER GATEWAY TRAITOR'S GATE BEYOND

MEDIÆVAL MANOR HOUSES

HOUSE AT CHRISTCHURCH (NORMAN) (A)

S. MARY'S GUILD, LINCOLN (NORMAN) (B)

BOOTHBY PAGNELL (NORMAN) (C)

CHARNEY-BASSET : BERKS (EARLY ENGLISH)

(E) THE SOLAR

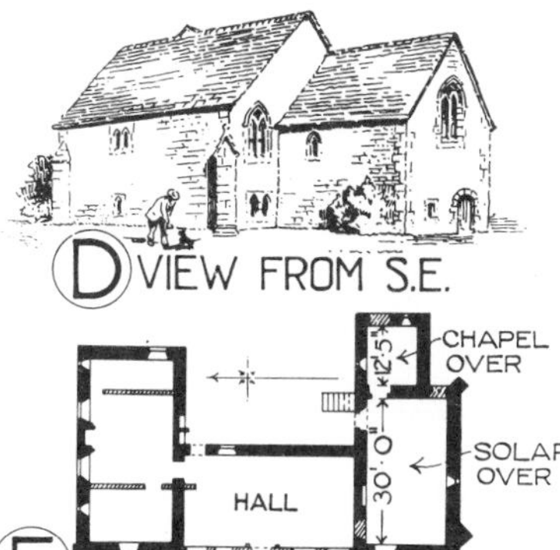

(D) VIEW FROM S.E.

(F) GROUND PLAN

(G) THE CHAPEL

LITTLE WENHAM HALL : SUFFOLK (EARLY ENGLISH)

HALL (H) WINDOWS CHAPEL

(J) VIEW FROM N.W.

(K) THE HALL

(L) ENTRANCE TO CHAPEL

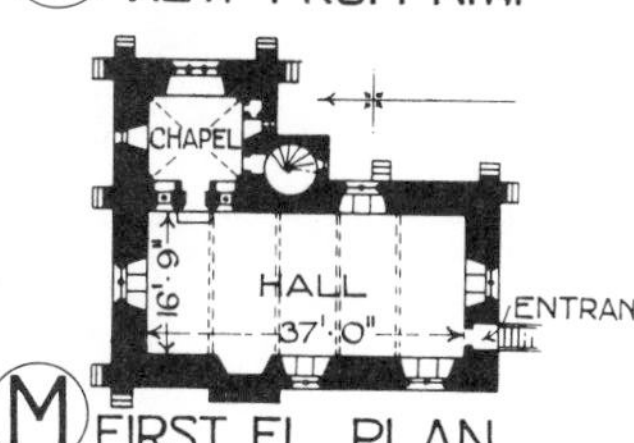

(M) FIRST FL. PLAN

(N) CHAPEL & TOWER STAIRS

Scandinavia: Architectural Character

Truly Romanesque characteristics did not appear in the architecture of Scandinavia until both British and Continental European influences upon church building in stone became effective towards the middle of the eleventh century. In Norway, the early timber techniques were particularly persistent, and significant masonry building was sparse until the early years of the twelfth century. The traditions of building in timber (of earlier date than the tenth century) supported the development of a distinctive native architecture of which there is ample early evidence, and which, in its finest fully mature form, is represented by a number of surviving examples. The most highly developed form of stave church has an inner timber colonnade which contributes to a basilican section with a (blind) clerestory, and a steep scissor-trussed roof.

Masonry techniques in church building suggest an early dependence particularly upon English and Norman models. Churches at Husaby (p. 412B) and at Sigtuna (p. 414B) have axial towers and eastern apses, with either continuous or crossing vaults. A series of round churches on Bornholm represent an incident in Danish progress towards a mature Romanesque architecture. They may reflect the ideas generated by King Sigurd's pilgrimage to Jerusalem in the years 1107–11. The Bornholm examples are all of the twelfth century, and have central vault piers, apsidal projections and bold plain buttresses (p. 413A).

Twelfth-century cathedral churches in Scandinavia show a progressively more mature Romanesque character, incorporating the effects of Norman and German development in masonry techniques and structural design aimed at fully-vaulted composition. Early precedents at Roskilde in Denmark were based upon a simple aisled nave, with an aisleless choir and a square west end projecting between two towers. Lund Cathedral (1103) displays a marked Rhine-Lombardic character, emphasised by the western addition of later date. The Norwegian examples at Stavanger (1130) and Kirkwall in the Orkneys are modest interpretations of the northern Anglo-Norman formula. Cluniac

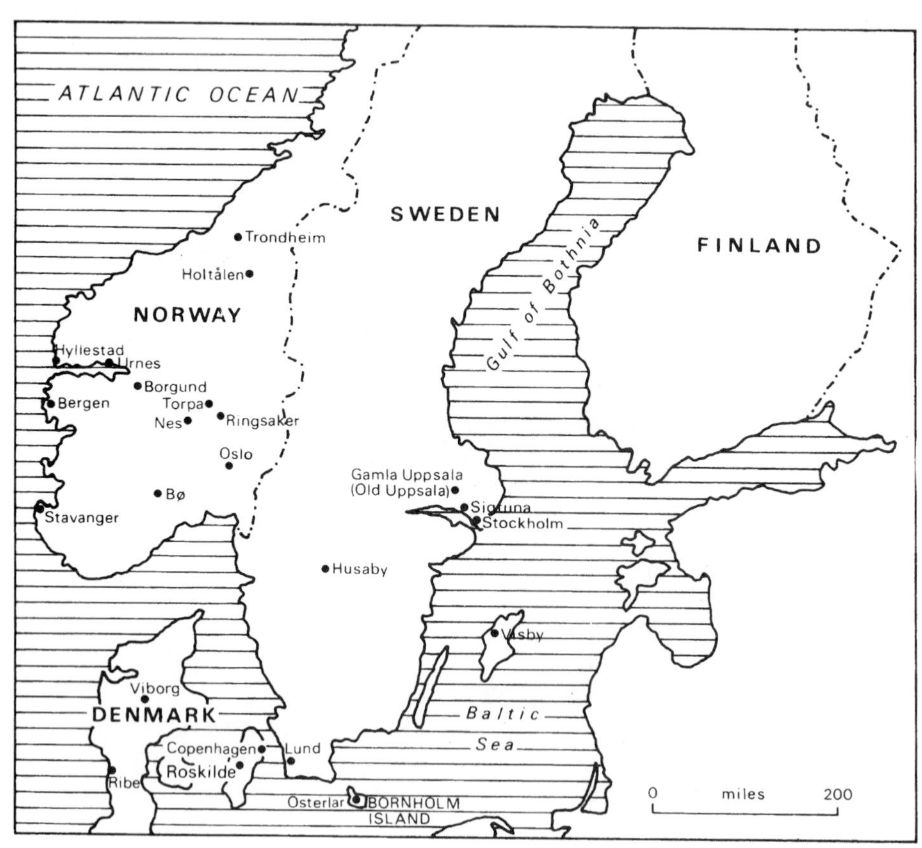

Scandinavia in the Middle Ages

influences, operating through Germany and Denmark, were most marked in south and east Norway, and were best represented in Oslo and Hamar, now ruined. They are still evident at Ringsaker, which belongs mostly to the period 1113–30, and has a barrel-vaulted nave, half-barrel aisle vaults, long narrow transepts and a bold crossing tower. In Jutland, the cathedrals of Ribe and Viborg illustrate the continuing German influences upon mature Scandinavian Romanesque churches. Carved decoration of considerable richness, as in Lund Cathedral, is not uncommon in the mature Scandinavian greater church.

Scandinavia: Examples

Religious Buildings

The stave churches represent a most distinctive indigenous architectural phenomenon of the early Middle Ages in Scandinavia. They were probably most common in Norway, but there are important examples in Sweden and Denmark.

Sancta Maria Minor, Lund (*c.* 1020) in Sweden, revealed by excavation, is probably the earliest example of the timber stave churches. Of the simplest type, it is nearly basilican in plan, having two cells, with the outer palisade walls constructed of halved and splined logs very similar to those at Greenstead in Essex.

The **Hoaltålen** stave church from Gauldal, now preserved in the Folk Museum at Trondheim, is the most typical of the numerous and persistent type of small church. Of later eleventh-century date, it has a two-cell plan and stout timber columns at the corners framed into sills, with head beams and laterally-trussed steeply pitched roof. In this case the palisade walls are tongued and grooved.

Later examples, exemplified by the group of churches at **Sogne, near Bergen**, have an internal timber colonnade and basilican section. The most celebrated of these is that at **Borgund** (*c.* 1150) (pp. 412A, 414C), which illustrates the full development of the structural design of the stave church. The chancel has an eastern apse of later date, and the upper gables are embellished with carved dragons' heads, reminiscent of the figureheads of pagan times. Internal decoration is limited to carved heads as capitals to the main columns and foliated carvings on the bracing timbers above the level of the aisled walls. Another of this group, at **Urnes** at the head of the Sogne Fjord (p. 412C), exemplifies the vigorous character of carved decoration most usually applied in wood carving of the west front, and particularly the west entrance doorway. The carving belongs to an earlier church of *c.* 1060 on the same site and is reused in its surviving twelfth-century successor. Urnes gives its name to a style of Viking ornament of which there are many surviving examples, mainly in metalwork. A later example from **Hyllestad Church in Setesdalen** (p. 412D), of about 1200, involves both vine coils and human figures in an allegorical composition of pagan origin, and while much of the detail is archaic, the vigour of the craft tradition was clearly maintained.

Stone-built church architecture in Scandinavia, particularly after the middle of the twelfth century, was most profoundly influenced by Norman and Anglo-Norman Benedictine fashion. Some examples, however, such as **Husaby in Skaraborg** (*c.* 1150) (p. 412B), reflect German characteristics such as the axial western tower flanked by stair turrets, and midwall shafts in window openings.

S. Peter at Sigtuna, on Lake Mälar (p. 414B), probably dating from the end of the eleventh century, although largely ruined, has windows with mid-wall shafts; its plan reveals a design based upon axial towers at both crossing and the west end, a two-aisled nave formed by a central colonnade, and abbreviated, but purely Norman, eastern and transept apses.

Some of the earliest twelfth-century examples are those comprising the group on Bornholm island, of which that at **Österlar** (p. 413A) is representative. They have much in common with the central planning of the Templars' churches, though usually with a central vault column instead of a ring arcade, and probably derive from the same Jerusalem prototype.

Lund Cathedral (pp. 413B, 414A), then in Denmark, now in Sweden, was built after 1103 to an enlarged design by Donatus, probably a Lombard architect. The plan is organised on a double-bay system, and incorporates a western tribune and towers begun about 1150 but completed in Lombardic style in a much more recent restoration. The arcaded eastern apse with wall passage is strongly Lombardic. Richly decorated capitals, arches and tympana reflect a continuing Nordic tradition increasingly responsive to southern inspiration, sometimes of Classical origin.

The **Cathedral of S. Swithin at Stavanger**, in Norway (*c.* 1130), has massive cylindrical piers in the nave like those of Durham, but is without a vault and has small clerestory windows in the wall over the arcade piers instead of in the crowns of the bold arches themselves.

The **Cathedral of S. Magnus, Kirkwall**, in the Orkneys, a little later than Stavanger, is part of the Norwegian Romanesque succession, but with a full triforium over an arcade in both nave and choir supported again by cylindrical piers, and with square chapels on the eastern side of the transept.

A. Borgund Church, Sogne Fjord, Norway (*c.* 1150). See p.411

B. Husaby Church, Skaraborg, Sweden (twelfth century). See p.411

C. Urnes Church, Sogne Fjord, Norway (early twelfth century): detail of doorway. See p.411

D. Hyllestad Church, Setesdalen, Norway (*c.* 1200): detail of doorway. See p.411

A. Östelar Church, Bornholm island, Denmark (twelfth century). See p.411

B. Lund Cathedral, Sweden (begun *c.* 1103): west front. See p.411

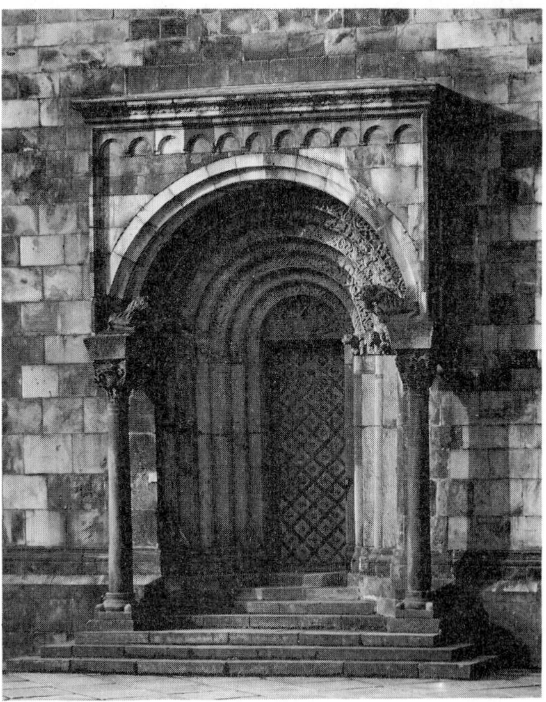

C. Lund Cathedral, Sweden: detail of doorway

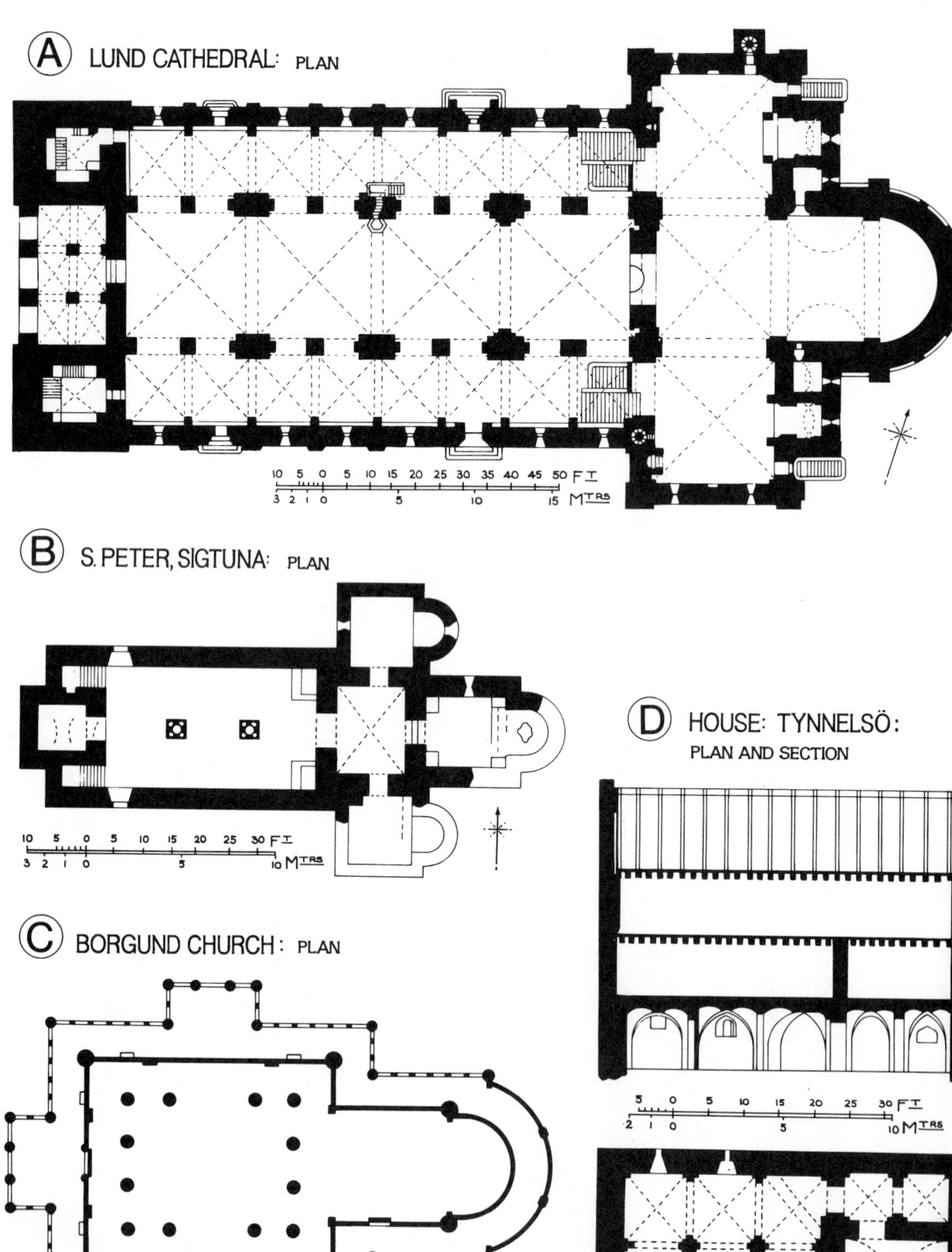

(A) LUND CATHEDRAL: PLAN
10 5 0 5 10 15 20 25 30 35 40 45 50 FT
3 2 1 0 5 10 15 MTRS
(B) S. PETER, SIGTUNA: PLAN
10 5 0 5 10 15 20 25 30 FT
3 2 1 0 5 10 MTRS
(C) BORGUND CHURCH: PLAN
(D) HOUSE: TYNNELSÖ: PLAN AND SECTION
5 0 5 10 15 20 25 30 FT
2 1 0 5 10 MTRS

Secular Buildings

Early mediaeval minor domestic architecture in Scandinavia generally conformed to the strong tradition of the timber construction, and little original work survives. The traditional forms themselves are fairly readily discerned, and the construction techniques were apparently similar in many respects. Stone-built dwellings followed the continental custom, and must have had much in common with the Norman manor house in England. An example at **Tynnelsö** (p. 414D) may be compared with those at Lincoln and Boothby Pagnell (p. 409B,C). The lower storey is a groin-vaulted undercroft probably used for storage and occasional accommodation of livestock, with a hall and chamber at first-floor level. In Sweden this form of dwelling was more ambitious than in the English examples; at Tynnelsö a ceremonial hall was superimposed at second-floor level. In another case, at **Torpa in Västergötland**, the house has two upper floors and a base storey, and begins to assume the scale and form of a tower keep.

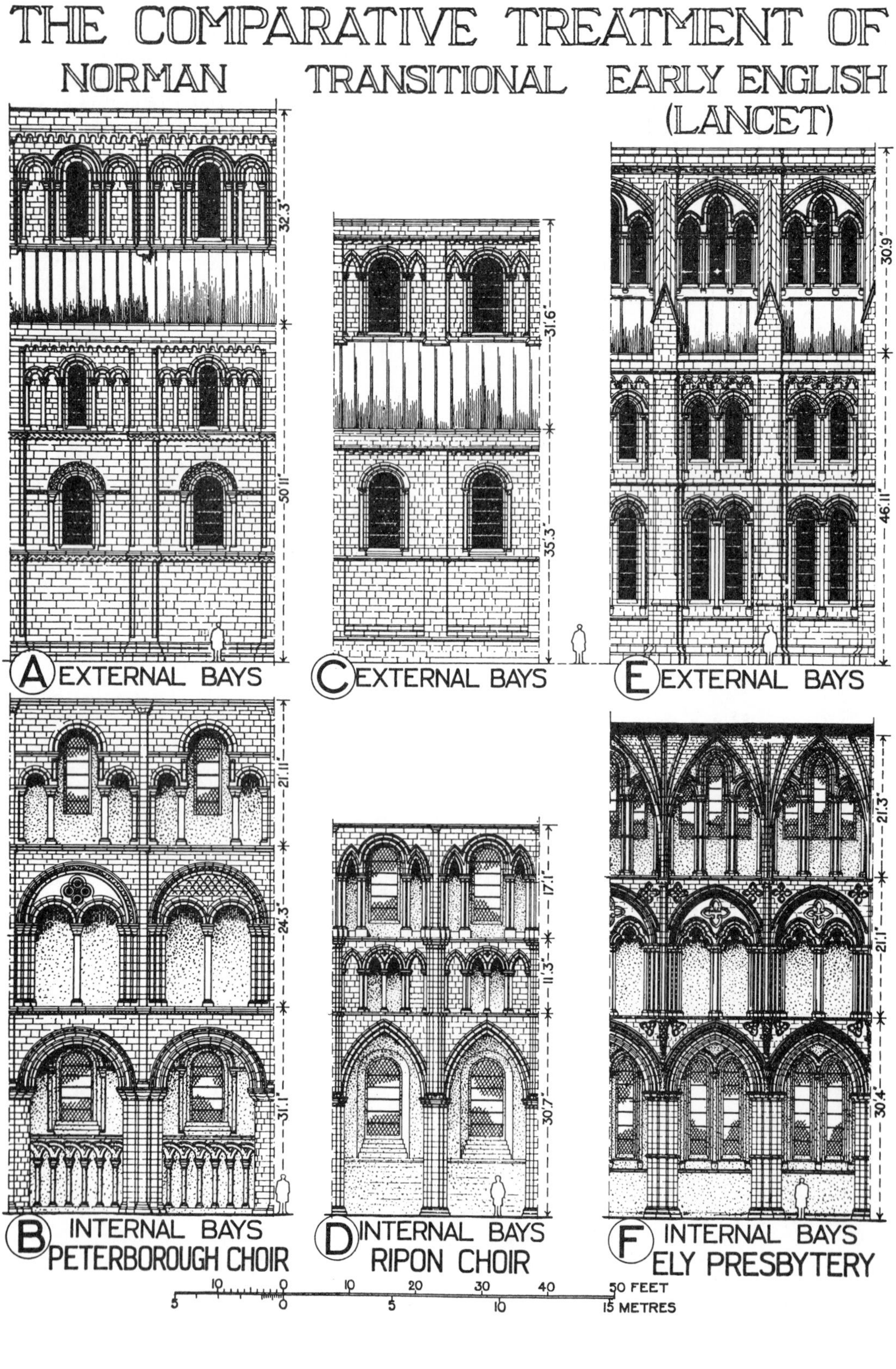

THE COMPARATIVE TREATMENT OF

NORMAN TRANSITIONAL EARLY ENGLISH (LANCET)

32′3″ 50′11″ 31′6″ 35′3″ 30′9″ 46′11″

A EXTERNAL BAYS

C EXTERNAL BAYS

E EXTERNAL BAYS

21′11″ 24′3″ 31′1″ 17′1″ 11′3″ 30′7″ 21′3″ 21′1″ 30′4″

B INTERNAL BAYS PETERBOROUGH CHOIR

D INTERNAL BAYS RIPON CHOIR

F INTERNAL BAYS ELY PRESBYTERY

10 0 10 20 30 40 50 FEET

5 0 5 10 15 METRES

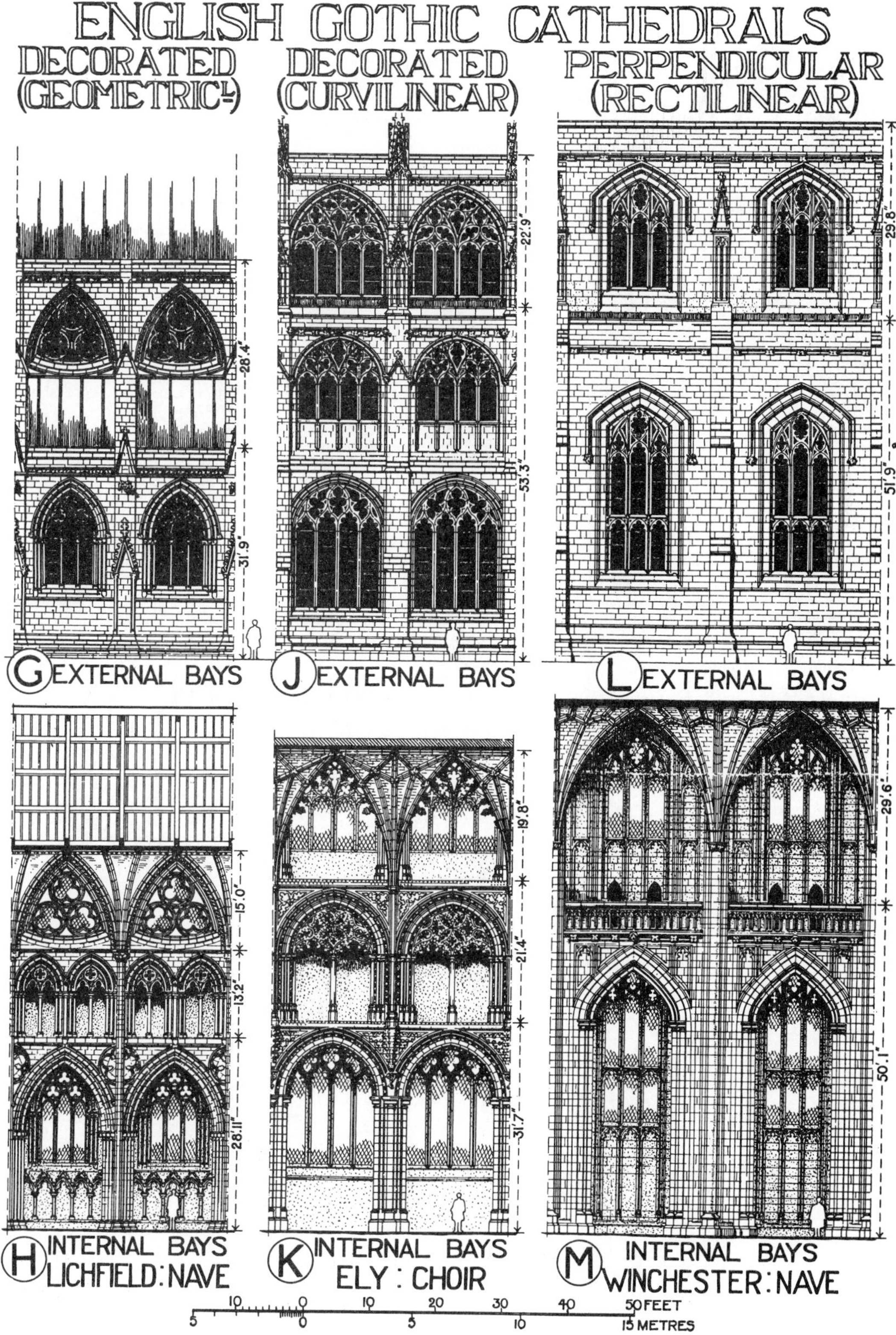
ENGLISH GOTHIC CATHEDRALS
DECORATED (GEOMETRICL)
DECORATED (CURVILINEAR)
PERPENDICULAR (RECTILINEAR)
28'4"
31'9"
22'9"
53'3"
29'8"
51'9"
G EXTERNAL BAYS
J EXTERNAL BAYS
L EXTERNAL BAYS
15'0"
13'2"
28'11"
19'8"
21'4"
31'7"
29'6"
50'1"
H INTERNAL BAYS LICHFIELD: NAVE
K INTERNAL BAYS ELY : CHOIR
M INTERNAL BAYS WINCHESTER: NAVE
10 0 10 20 30 40 50 FEET
5 0 5 10 15 METRES

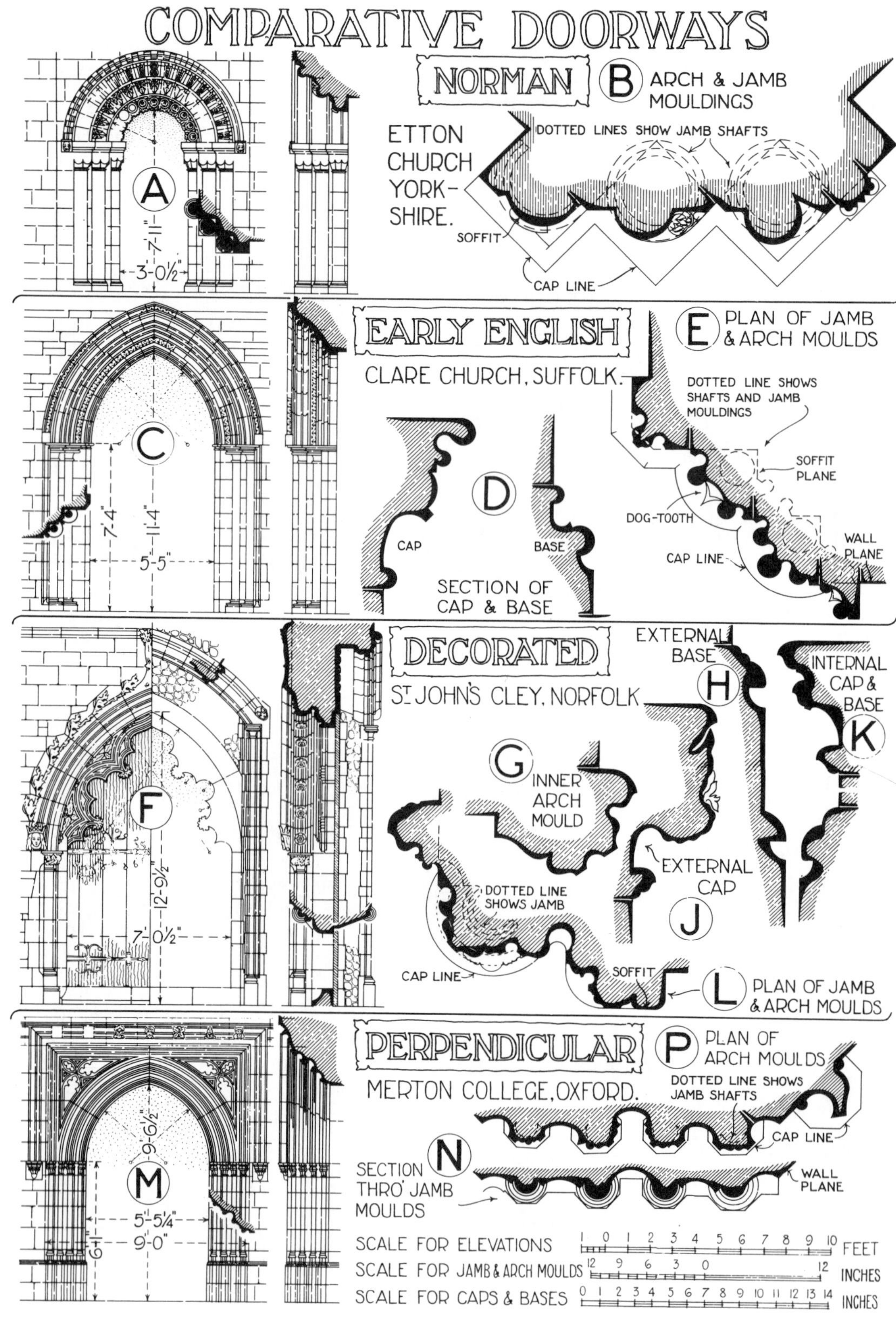
COMPARATIVE DOORWAYS
NORMAN
B ARCH & JAMB MOULDINGS
ETTON CHURCH YORKSHIRE.
DOTTED LINES SHOW JAMB SHAFTS
SOFFIT
CAP LINE
A
7'-11"
3'-0½"
EARLY ENGLISH
CLARE CHURCH, SUFFOLK.
E PLAN OF JAMB & ARCH MOULDS
DOTTED LINE SHOWS SHAFTS AND JAMB MOULDINGS
SOFFIT PLANE
DOG-TOOTH
WALL PLANE
CAP LINE
C
7'-4"
11'-4"
5'-5"
D
CAP
BASE
SECTION OF CAP & BASE
DECORATED
ST JOHN'S CLEY, NORFOLK
EXTERNAL BASE
H
INTERNAL CAP & BASE
K
G INNER ARCH MOULD
EXTERNAL CAP
J
DOTTED LINE SHOWS JAMB
CAP LINE
SOFFIT
L PLAN OF JAMB & ARCH MOULDS
F
12'-9½"
7'-0½"
PERPENDICULAR
MERTON COLLEGE, OXFORD.
P PLAN OF ARCH MOULDS
DOTTED LINE SHOWS JAMB SHAFTS
CAP LINE
N
SECTION THRO' JAMB MOULDS
WALL PLANE
M
9'-6½"
5'-5¼"
9'-0"
6'-1"
SCALE FOR ELEVATIONS 1 0 1 2 3 4 5 6 7 8 9 10 FEET
SCALE FOR JAMB & ARCH MOULDS 12 9 6 3 0 12 INCHES
SCALE FOR CAPS & BASES 0 1 2 3 4 5 6 7 8 9 10 11 12 13 14 INCHES

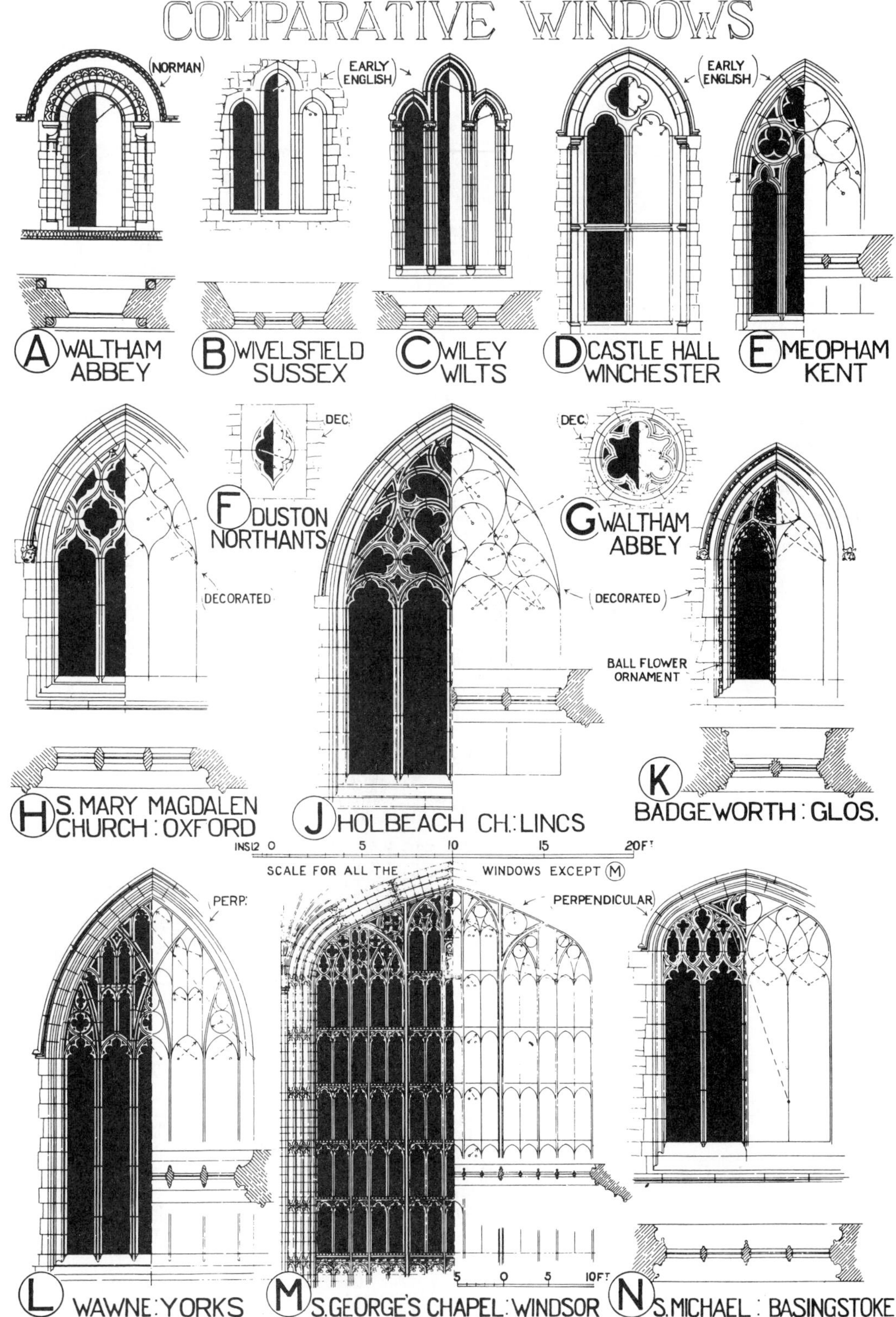
COMPARATIVE WINDOWS
(NORMAN)
(EARLY ENGLISH)
(EARLY ENGLISH)
A WALTHAM ABBEY
B WIVELSFIELD SUSSEX
C WILEY WILTS
D CASTLE HALL WINCHESTER
E MEOPHAM KENT
DEC.
DEC.
F DUSTON NORTHANTS
G WALTHAM ABBEY
DECORATED
(DECORATED)
BALL FLOWER ORNAMENT
H S. MARY MAGDALEN CHURCH : OXFORD
J HOLBEACH CH.: LINCS
K BADGEWORTH : GLOS.
INS 12 0 5 10 15 20 FT
SCALE FOR ALL THE WINDOWS EXCEPT M
PERP.
PERPENDICULAR
5 0 5 10 FT
L WAWNE: YORKS
M S. GEORGE'S CHAPEL: WINDSOR
N S. MICHAEL : BASINGSTOKE

COMPARATIVE CARVED CAPITALS

NORMAN

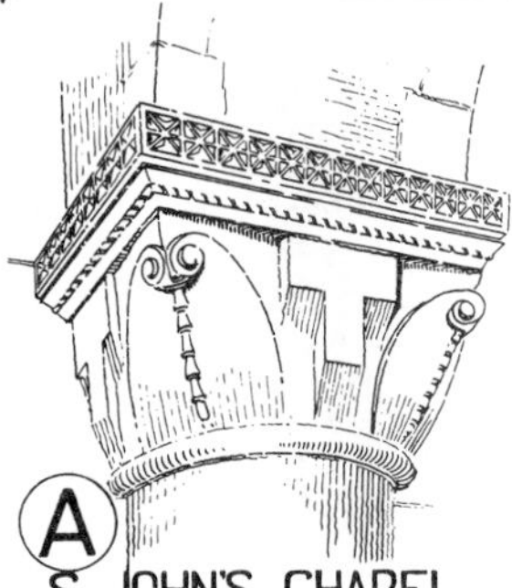

A S. JOHN'S CHAPEL TOWER of LONDON

B S. PETER: NORTHAMPTON

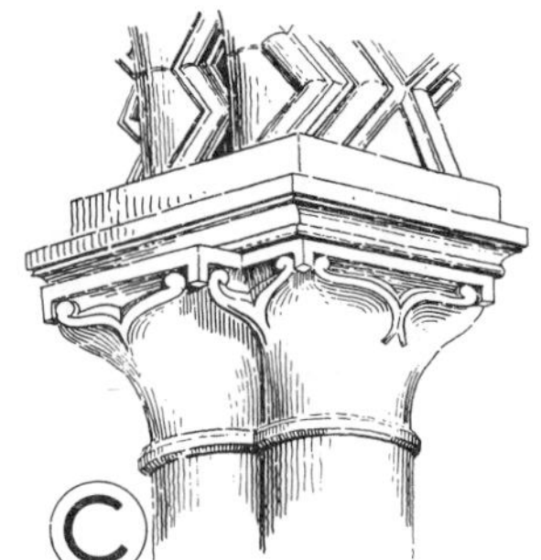

C GALILEE: DURHAM CATH.

EARLY ENGLISH

D GALILEE PORCH ELY CATHEDRAL

E BRIDLINGTON PRIORY: YORKS

F CHAPTER HOUSE SALISBURY CATH^L

G BEVERLEY MINSTER: YORKS

H CHAPTER HOUSE SOUTHWELL MINSTER

J LADY CHAPEL ELY CATHEDRAL

PERPENDICULAR

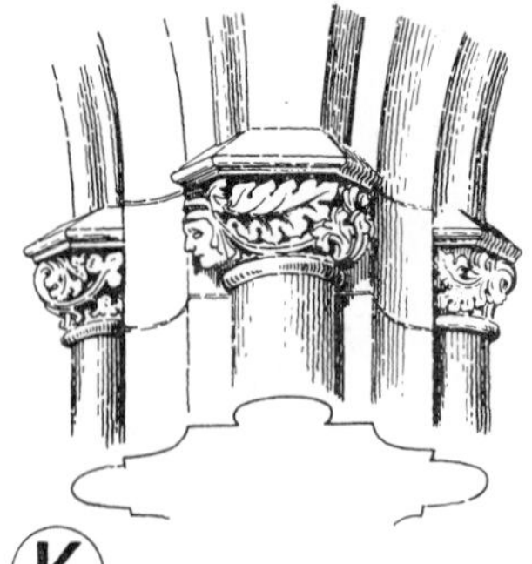

K PIDDLETON: DORSET

L WOLBOROUGH: DEVON

M KENTON: DEVON

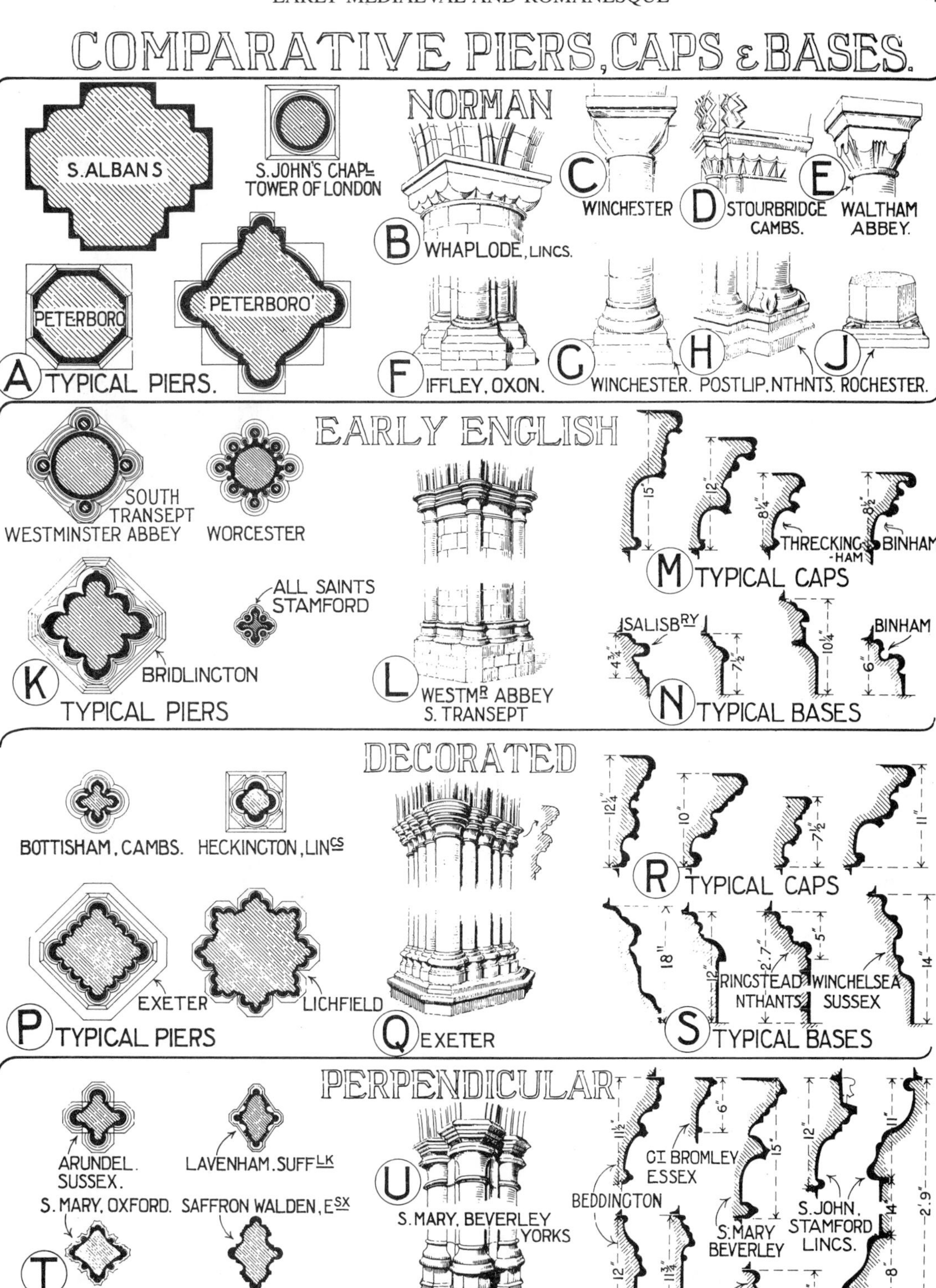
COMPARATIVE PIERS, CAPS & BASES.
NORMAN
S. ALBANS
S. JOHN'S CHAPL TOWER OF LONDON
PETERBORO
PETERBORO'
A TYPICAL PIERS.
B WHAPLODE, LINCS.
C WINCHESTER
D STOURBRIDGE CAMBS.
E WALTHAM ABBEY.
F IFFLEY, OXON.
G WINCHESTER.
H POSTLIP, NTHNTS.
J ROCHESTER.
EARLY ENGLISH
SOUTH TRANSEPT WESTMINSTER ABBEY
WORCESTER
ALL SAINTS STAMFORD
BRIDLINGTON
K TYPICAL PIERS
L WESTMR ABBEY S. TRANSEPT
THRECKINGHAM
BINHAM
M TYPICAL CAPS
SALISBRY
BINHAM
N TYPICAL BASES
DECORATED
BOTTISHAM, CAMBS.
HECKINGTON, LINCS
EXETER
LICHFIELD
P TYPICAL PIERS
Q EXETER
R TYPICAL CAPS
RINGSTEAD NTHANTS
WINCHELSEA SUSSEX
S TYPICAL BASES
PERPENDICULAR
ARUNDEL. SUSSEX.
LAVENHAM. SUFFLK
S. MARY, OXFORD.
SAFFRON WALDEN, ESX
T TYPICAL PIERS
SCALE FOR PLANS
10 FEET
3 METRES
U S. MARY, BEVERLEY YORKS
CT BROMLEY ESSEX
BEDDINGTON
S. MARY BEVERLEY
S. JOHN, STAMFORD LINCS.
HERNE KENT
V TYPICAL BASES & CAPS

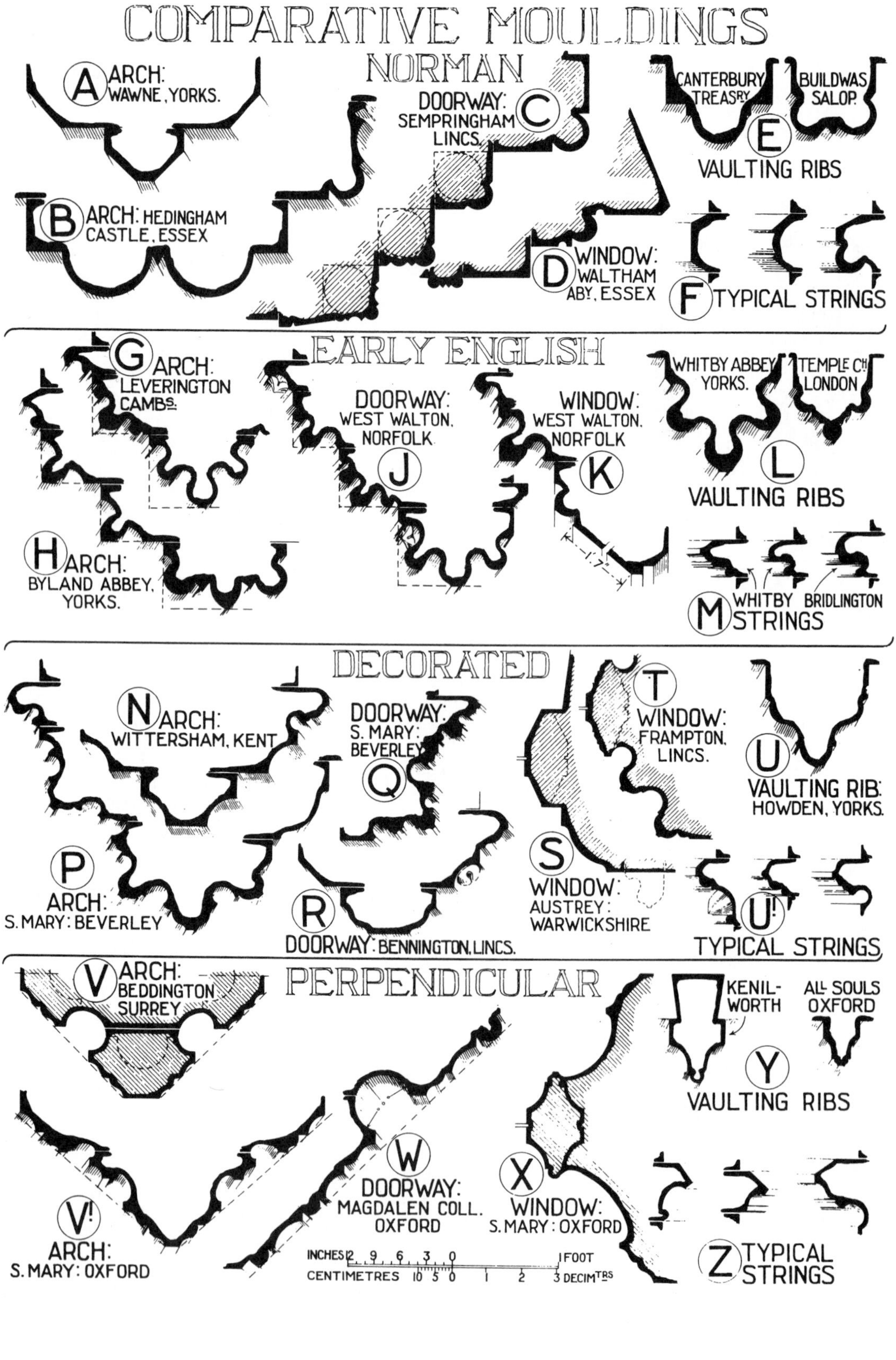

COMPARATIVE MOULDINGS

NORMAN

A ARCH: WAWNE, YORKS.

B ARCH: HEDINGHAM CASTLE, ESSEX

C DOORWAY: SEMPRINGHAM LINCS.

D WINDOW: WALTHAM ABY. ESSEX

CANTERBURY TREASRY. BUILDWAS SALOP.

E VAULTING RIBS

F TYPICAL STRINGS

EARLY ENGLISH

G ARCH: LEVERINGTON CAMBS.

H ARCH: BYLAND ABBEY, YORKS.

J DOORWAY: WEST WALTON, NORFOLK.

K WINDOW: WEST WALTON, NORFOLK

1'.7"

WHITBY ABBEY YORKS. TEMPLE CH. LONDON

L VAULTING RIBS

WHITBY BRIDLINGTON

M STRINGS

DECORATED

N ARCH: WITTERSHAM, KENT

P ARCH: S. MARY: BEVERLEY

Q DOORWAY: S. MARY: BEVERLEY

R DOORWAY: BENNINGTON, LINCS.

S WINDOW: AUSTREY: WARWICKSHIRE

T WINDOW: FRAMPTON, LINCS.

U VAULTING RIB: HOWDEN, YORKS.

U1 TYPICAL STRINGS

PERPENDICULAR

V ARCH: BEDDINGTON SURREY

V1 ARCH: S. MARY: OXFORD

W DOORWAY: MAGDALEN COLL. OXFORD

X WINDOW: S. MARY: OXFORD

KENIL-WORTH ALL SOULS OXFORD

Y VAULTING RIBS

Z TYPICAL STRINGS

INCHES 12 9 6 3 0 1 FOOT

CENTIMETRES 10 5 0 1 2 3 DECIMTRS

Chapter 14
GOTHIC

Introduction

Gothic took many forms and no single definition is adequate to cover them all; but a common stock of building types and building methods constitutes a loose yet easily recognisable tradition. So far as can be ascertained, Gothic was never articulated into a fully fledged theory of architecture. Even so, the rules which governed the practice of those for whom it was the only kind of architecture known were meticulous in both aesthetic and technological senses. It was the style of professional craftsmen who relied upon the accumulated experience of generations, handed down from masters to apprentices, often within the same families.

Gothic is remarkable because it appears to represent a complete break with the architectural inheritance of Greece and Rome. When it was consciously revived in the nineteenth century it was regarded as the antithesis of everything the Classical tradition stood for; and it took its place in the repertory of styles as a legitimate alternative to all the versions of Classical architecture currently or recently in vogue, whether Baroque, Rococo, Palladian, or strict Greek. Historically, however, it is extremely doubtful whether any such comprehensive repudiation was ever in the minds of the men who invented Gothic. It is much more likely that they saw themselves as taking liberties with what they had received from the past for strictly contemporary purposes, much as the musical innovators of the twelfth-century School of Notre Dame thought they were manipulating the Classical modes.

The prime movers were almost certainly not the architects themselves, but their patrons, the higher clergy. Gothic was the outcome of intense and incessant brooding on the theme of the great church: what was the right form for such churches? The succession of experiments with novel forms of construction and decoration was inspired as much by the need to impress and edify the pious congregations of Christendom as by technical progress or changes of taste. Patronage remained an essential ingredient throughout the evolution of Gothic, although the centre of gravity shifted somewhat from ecclesiastics to laymen who were themselves increasingly preoccupied with religion.

The techniques and skills of Gothic masons evolved without interruption over a period of 400 years. The building in which the style achieved its first magisterial expression was the abbey church of S. Denis outside Paris (q.v.) which was partly rebuilt by its abbot, Suger, in the decade before 1144. Suger's personal contribution is difficult to isolate, but he certainly represents the decisive intervention of ecclesiastical patronage. Whatever he may have specified, the new choir at S. Denis was visually quite unlike the heavy, monumental Romanesque of the adjacent regions of France: extremely light and open in structure, making use of fine materials akin to antique marble, with two rows of prominent, virtually contiguous stained-glass windows in ambulatory chapels and clerestory, forming a luminous back-drop to the sumptuous altar that was its liturgical centrepiece. Masonry was reduced to a skeletal minimum. It provided a frame for the windows and defined the spatial components without disrupting their essential unity.

S. Denis was not a very big church, but most of the ingredients of the High Gothic cathedrals were already anticipated. Chartres was S. Denis writ large. Before Chartres, however, a long series of experiments was needed, of which Sens, Senlis, Noyon, Laon and Notre Dame, Paris, survive. The fundamental problem was how to apply the S. Denis style to the grander scale and somewhat different ecclesiastical purposes of cathedral churches. Here height mattered as much as if not more than light and colour, and this raised in acute form the problem of buttressing the high vaults. The first solution was essentially an adaptation of the Romanesque idea of using galleries above the side aisles as the basis for the necessary supports. The result was the four-storey elevation which enjoyed a considerable vogue in northern France during the second half of the twelfth century.

Galleries, however, created their own problems. If they were left unglazed there was a broad dark band between the two rows of windows; if they were glazed, the windows could not be seen. The great creative moment in the evolution of Gothic came at the end of the twelfth century when it was decided to dispense with galleries, and at the same time vastly to increase the overall size of cathedrals. This was made possible by the imaginative use of flying buttresses, which provided the same structural support as galleries but without walls or roofs. This device opened the way to two far-reaching developments. The disappearance of the gallery as such allowed the organisation of interior spaces to be greatly simplified and the possibility of further spatial unification to be explored. On the other hand, flying buttresses made it feasible to greatly enlarge the clerestory windows.

The two innovatory monuments were Chartres and Bourges (q.v.). At Bourges a high degree of spatial integration was achieved which pointed in the direction of future hall churches. At Chartres the first truly monumental clerestory prepared the way for the soaring heights of Amiens, Beauvais and Cologne, which are to all intents and purposes glass caskets mounted on what are themselves lofty spacious halls. Both formulas were widely repeated and refined, mainly in France, although for the most part the French, after the realisation of these prodigious compositions, were content to explore the decorative potential of bar-tracery. High Gothic was imperceptibly transformed into Rayonnant (see French Gothic below).

Insofar as the great French prototypes were ever surpassed, it was only on rare and special occasions in other countries: for example, Cologne in Germany, Milan in Italy, or Barcelona and Seville in Spain.

As pure architecture the High Gothic cathedrals were spectacular achievements. The architects responsible for them enjoyed much social prestige. It was not possible to regard such men as humble manual workers, even if they had not enjoyed the benefit of a liberal education at the universities. It is perhaps no coincidence that from the thirteenth century onwards their arms are preserved in increasing numbers. Yet the two greatest of them all, the men responsible for Chartres and Bourges, remain anonymous. The fact that they are unidentified, whereas the name is known of practically every mason who built the Perpendicular parish churches of fifteenth-century England, is a sad reminder of how fickle history can be.

Although Gothic spread across the rest of Europe from its birthplace in northern France, it did so in fits and starts, and often without due deference to French prototypes. This is nowhere more true than in England. Gothic reached Canterbury while still in its formative stages, and until the second half of the thirteenth century it pursued an idiosyncratic, insular development which suggests that few Frenchmen came to England and fewer Englishmen went abroad; yet those who stayed at home were not short of ideas of their own as to what great churches should look like. English clergymen never really saw the point of excessive height, nor were they disposed to countenance the spatial unity which left French cathedral chapters virtually cheek by jowl with the laity under a single vaulted canopy. They invariably preferred to be exclusive and to shut themselves away in the long eastern limbs of their cathedrals, at a safe distance from their social inferiors in the naves. Although they were not averse to displays of stained glass, they never encouraged it on the scale of Chartres where everything else was secondary. Their ecclesiastical predilections produced a very different kind of Gothic: long, low vistas which showed off to advantage rich encrustations of costly materials, and where an exuberant sense of pattern was seldom inhibited by any structural restraint. It was a style which combined happily with the cult pattern which had evolved in English cathedral worship. Instead of having centrally planned apses which focused upon the high altar, English cathedrals tended to distinguish between the high altar and the retrochoir, where local cults were accommodated. They also showed a great respect for the orientation of altars.

These tendencies consolidated themselves in the aftermath of the martyrdom of S. Thomas at Canterbury in 1170, and did much to determine the special character of early English Gothic. It was only after Westminster Abbey and the nave of York Minster (q.v.) had so to speak reintroduced High Gothic and Rayonnant ideas into England that English architects made a determined effort to come to terms with what the French had been doing with bar-tracery, and brought themselves into line with prevailing Continental fashions. The result was a series of rather precocious exercises involving tracery, vaults and polygons – the so-called Decorated Style.

In one sense English Decorated is symptomatic of the triumphant spread of the French conception of Gothic into the rest of Europe, but it also marks the point at which the initiative in stylistic invention passed out of French hands. Splendid and beautiful Gothic buildings continued to be built in France right into the sixteenth century. But the exploration of the further architectural possibilities of Gothic was henceforth conducted outside the region of its origin, for a while in England and Catalonia, here and there in Italy, but most consistently and fruitfully in the German-dominated lands of Central Europe.

The various shifts of emphasis which allow late Gothic to be distinguished from its earlier manifestations are partly stylistic. Late Gothic is a collective term for a variety of styles: English Perpendicular, German Sondergotik, French Flamboyant. These are quite distinct, and the national flavour is by no means unimportant. But late Gothic can also be presented in terms of changes in the incidence of patronage, and the efforts of the architectural profession to meet new and growing demands on its capacity.

France: Architectural Character

The France in which the first experiments of Gothic architecture were made, around 1140, was a geographical rather than a political entity. The Capetian ruling family, with their domains centred on Paris, had only recently established a precarious control of the local baronage and it was to take them nearly a century to establish the power and prestige which culminated in the canonisation of Louis IX in 1297 (see also Chapters 8 and 13).

This event had real political significance. It welded France into a single state, as neither Philip Augustus's nor Louis VIII's conquests could do, and allowed Louis, and thus by implication France, to be accepted as arbiter of Europe in the disputes between the Empire and Papacy. France's central position within western Europe became an asset, not a liability. Paris was now more than ever the administrative and cultural centre of France, and an education at the University of Paris became *de rigueur* for anyone wishing to attain high position in either church or state. In effect, Paris became the cultural cynosure for the whole of western Europe.

This early consolidation of the French state took place against the most rapid economic growth of the Middle Ages. Population expanded, inflation spiralled, towns and trade grew, particularly from *c.* 1180, though by around 1230 the rate of growth was levelling off.

Thus the great age of Gothic architectural experiment coincided with this century of France's political and economic expansion. The earliest development occurred in the Ile de France in the 1130s, as architects tried to vault the thin walls that were traditional in the area, and culminated in Suger's choir at S. Denis, which achieved a new luminosity and spaciousness. The Capetian Ile de France, backward architecturally as well as politically, had never experienced the Romanesque flowering that had already animated most of the other French regions, so that early Gothic is to an extent the Romanesque of the Ile de France. Certainly it drew heavily on the fertile Romanesque experiments of the French provinces, such as the technical advances of Normandy and Burgundy, and the decorative exuberance of the south-west.

S. Denis and Sens seem to have been the earliest large-scale architectural programmes of undoubtedly 'Gothic' nature. S. Denis was small and elegant, as were most of the buildings, such as Senlis, Noyon, or S. Germain des Prés, which attempted to follow its lead. Sens, however, with its considerable width and height, established scale as a vital element in Gothic design, and prepared the way for the next generation of buildings – buildings which in grandeur of conception surely earn the soubriquet of High Gothic – notably Laon in the Aisne Valley and Notre Dame in Paris. The third member of this trio, all begun around 1160, was the cathedral of Arras, now destroyed and known only through drawings. The entire north-east of France – Flanders, Champagne, and, above all, the Aisne Valley between these two areas – proved between 1180 and 1200 outstandingly fertile for architectural ideas, especially the introduction of a variety of wall-passage arrangements.

The last years of the twelfth century brought an increase in the scale of buildings – the cathedral of Bourges drawing largely on Parisian traditions, and Chartres drawing on the Aisne Valley. Bourges is perhaps the grandest of all mediaeval churches, but Chartres proved the more popular design, providing the model for big cathedrals and followed almost slavishly on ever-increasing scale at Reims and Amiens. The Bourges tradition, however, gave rise to its own group of ambitious buildings, notably Le Mans and Coutances, whereas the cathedral of Beauvais was a conflation of both traditions.

Beauvais was also the last of the monumental High Gothic churches. Taste was changing subtly but surely towards what is generally known as the Rayonnant style. Buildings such as S. Denis, S. Urbain at Troyes and S. Chapelle were less gigantic in scale, more intimate in design, and covered with tracery and rich details intended to be appreciated at close quarters. The Rayonnant evolved in Paris, and spread rapidly to the provinces with all the prestige of a metropolitan style, and one that was also to some extent associated with S. Louis and his court, obliterating the flourishing regional Gothic of Burgundy and Normandy, as High Gothic, which was suitable only for the very largest buildings, had never done. The new style became established even in the south, in the wake of the Albigensian Crusade.

The change of taste coincided with, and was undoubtedly connected with, two historical trends. Around 1230, the enormous economic expansion of the twelfth century began to fade. The situation did not become serious until the beginning of the fourteenth century, but the massive High Gothic cathedral became too expensive, as Beauvais, which was some sixty years in the building, showed. At the same time, a shift in patronage is discernible. Most of the great Romanesque architectural undertakings had been monastic. But the great churches of the early Gothic period are typically cathedrals, built by the towns themselves. These were flourishing as never before, becoming established as communes with rights protected by royal charter, and organised into professional guilds. At Chartres, for example, the various guilds paid for their own windows, each representing the patron saint of its craft.

Although gifts from royalty and magnates, both secular and ecclesiastical, remained vital, the great cathedrals were, in a quite new way, the expression of local communal pride, and the result of corporate patronage. As the thirteenth century wore on, however, a new shift in patronage became apparent. Partly on account of economic stagnation, partly because most wealthy towns now possessed splendid new cathedrals, the typical patron of the Rayonnant era was private, and the archetypal Rayonnant building was a palace chapel, like the S. Chapelle or S. Germain-en-Laye, or a personal collegiate foundation which could be as lavish as Pope Urban IV's S. Urbain at Troyes. At the very lowest end of the scale were the many small private chapels which began to proliferate, from the late twelfth century, along the flanks of all the great cathedrals and abbey churches.

When the Capetian line failed in 1328 the Valois succession was disputed by the English king Edward III, who began what became known as the Hundred Years War in 1337 – a conflict not finally settled until 1453, though there was a substantial period of peace, established by the cultured and immensely able Charles V, between 1380 and 1415. This period was one of great social dislocation in France, with disastrous harvests, an ailing economy, and the Black Death in 1348. Not surprisingly, in the period of peace from 1380 to 1415, and again when the war was finally over, a vast amount of building was necessary to replace damaged or destroyed churches, especially in the north and east. The later sixteenth century was hardly more stable, as the impact of Protestantism led to virtual civil war and again destruction meant more rebuilding.

The new Flamboyant style that emerged owed its richly decorative repertory of tracery patterns, somewhat ironically, to English Decorated and Perpendicular styles. In many ways, Flamboyant had a regional quality reminiscent of Romanesque or early Gothic. In this it seems to have reflected the political situation: France had, after the Paris-centred government of the thirteenth century, once more disintegrated into great principalities. Paris did not play the major role in the generation of Flamboyant that it had played in the Rayonnant.

In spite of all the unrest and depredations, France remained fundamentally the best endowed of all European countries, and by the end of the fifteenth century it was possible to build once again on a scale reminiscent of High Gothic, with an emphasis on such grand architectural effects as spacious plans and giant orders, culminating at S. Eustache in Paris. But throughout the sixteenth century Classicising details drifted across the Alps from Renaissance Italy, heralding the end of the Gothic era. S. Eustache, indeed, represents the point at which the Renaissance was still an infiltration and not quite yet a new style: architecturally S. Eustache may be in the grandest of Gothic traditions, but every detail is Classical.

France: Examples

Around 1135, the energetic abbot, Suger, began to rebuild the venerable but outmoded Carolingian basilica, the **Abbey of S. Denis, near Paris** (pp. 371E, 427A), in the Gothic manner. He began with the west end, adding a narthex with tribunes, and a twin-towered west facade. The west front seems to have been the first to have incorporated a triple portal with column figures. The choir was finished and consecrated in 1144, and although the main elevation and upper parts of the choir were rebuilt in the thirteenth century (see below, Rayonnant) the earlier ambulatories and chapels are still intact. There are two ambulatories, with a continuous ring of shallow radiating chapels. The outer arcade piers are very slender, and cannot have supported a tribune above them; the radiating chapels are lit by enormous stained glass windows. S. Denis is an eclectic building, as Suger had been impressed by, and wished to emulate, Early Christian basilicas in Italy. The result, however, was something completely new. S. Denis was, in effect, the cradle of the Gothic style. Both west front and choir were highly influential.

The **Cathedral of Sens** (p. 427B) was virtually contemporary with S. Denis. The choir was begun around 1140, and construction progressed westwards. The west front and the west portals date from around 1200. The plan comprised single aisles and ambulatory, with three spaced chapels, but originally no transepts.

The span of the nave is unusually large. The piers alternate between composite and double-column designs, and correspond with the sexpartite high vault spanning double bays. The elevation consists of the alternating arcade, surmounted by decorative openings into the aisle roofspaces with clerestory above. Flying buttresses were present in the original design, though the present ones date from the thirteenth century, when the clerestory windows were much enlarged. Sens seems to have been the first Gothic building to adopt the Norman Romanesque sexpartite vault, in all likelihood on account of the great width of the nave. Sexpartite vaulting, pier alternation and the double column support proved very popular in the next generation of Gothic buildings.

The **Cathedral of Notre Dame in Paris** (pp. 434C,E,F, 427C, 428) was begun by Bishop Maurice de Sully around 1163; the west towers were the last to be completed in 1250. The original plan comprised double aisles and ambulatories and was on a bent axial line. The transepts, as so often in the Paris region, did not project beyond the aisle wall. The interior elevation was originally of four levels, with an arcade of columnar piers; a tribune, originally covered with transverse barrel vaults, and lit by round windows; decorative oculi opening into the tribune roofspaces; and small clerestory windows. The high vault is sexpartite, covering double bays. The vault is very high – just over 30 m (100 ft) – and the wall which supports it very thin and articulated by very slender 'en délit' (face-bedded) shafts. Double-span flying buttresses support the nave. These are often

A. Abbey of S. Denis, near Paris (*c.* 1135–44). See p.426

B. Sens Cathedral (*c.* 1140). See p.426

C. Cathedral of Notre Dame, Paris (*c.* 1163–1250). See p.426

NOTRE DAME : PARIS
A ANGLE OF CHOIR & S. TRANSEPT
B EXTERIOR FROM S.E.
C BUTTRESSES & PINNACLES: CHEVET
SCALE FOR ELEVNS. & SECTNS.
FEET
METRES
90
80
70
60
50
40
30
20
10
0
25
20
15
10
5
0
79' 0"
36' 6"
TRIFORIUM
D NAVE BAYS (EXT.)
E HALF TRANSVERSE SECTION
F NAVE BAYS (INT.)
NAVE
154' 0"
CHOIR
25 0 25 50 75 100 FEET
G PLAN
METRES 10 0 10 20 30

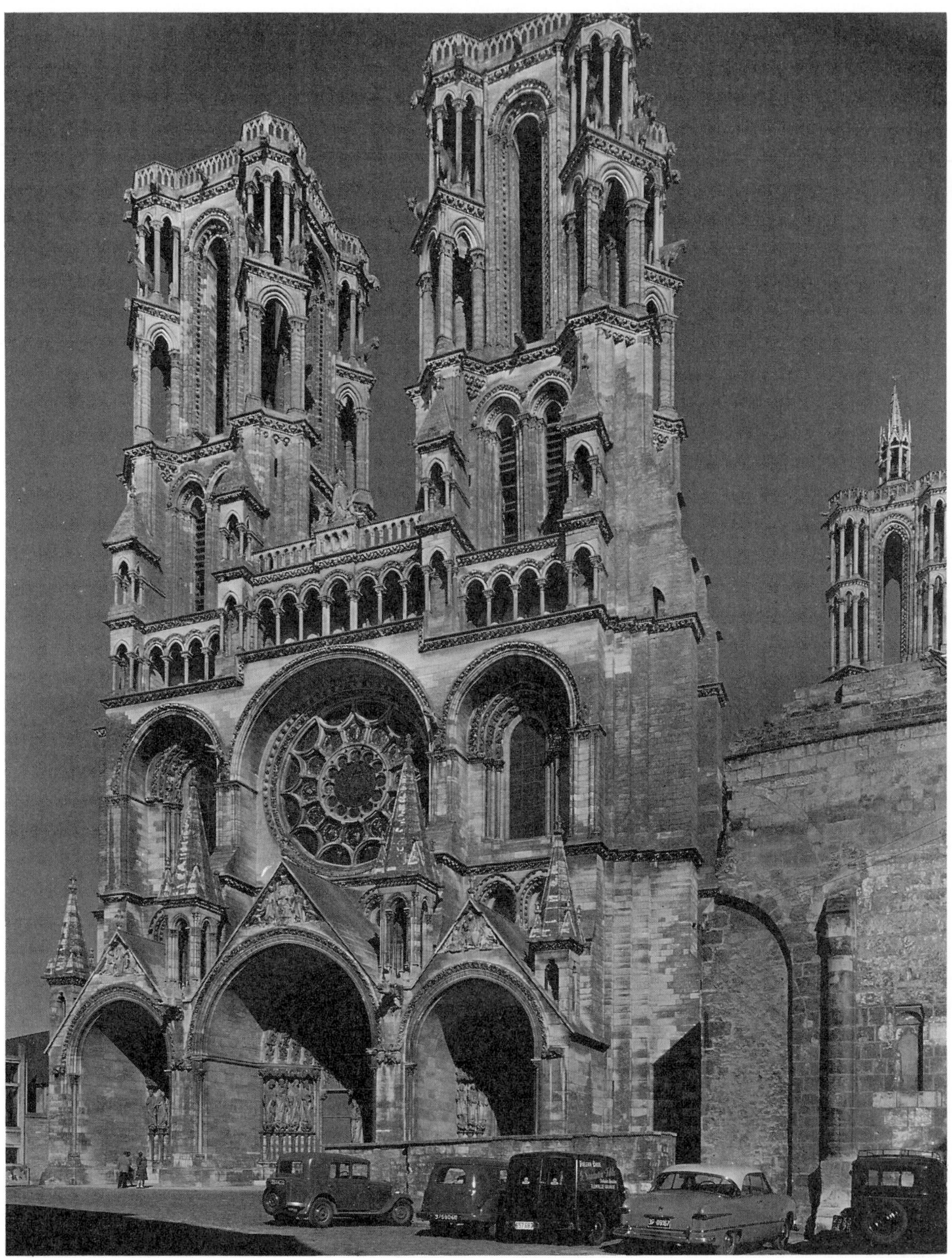

Laon Cathedral: west front (*c.* 1160–*c.* 1230). See p.430

said to be the earliest flying buttresses, though it is now clear that earlier buildings, for example Sens, also had them. In the thirteenth century attempts were made to lighten the interior by expanding the clerestory windows downwards, swallowing the decorative oculi of the third storey: the tribunes were rebuilt with larger windows and ordinary quadripartite vaults.

Laon Cathedral (pp. 429, 434G) was begun around 1160. The original choir and transepts were completed by *c.* 1180, the nave by *c.* 1200. The choir was rebuilt in 1205 and extended eastwards by a full eight bays, and the west and transept towers were completed by *c.* 1230. The original 1160 choir was apsidal, but the enormous extension is rectangular, which is very unusual in France in a large, non-Cistercian building. There are massive projecting transepts, three bays deep and aisled on all sides. The interior elevation has four levels and the high vault is sexpartite. Most of the shafting is 'en délit', with heavy ring mouldings. The upper levels are supported both by 'mur boutant' (buttress walls) behind the triforium walls, and by flying buttresses. The building contains three splendid rose windows. The north transept window, dating from *c.* 1190, is of heavy plate tracery type, with window patterns cut out of a skin of wall. The west and east windows, of *c.* 1210, are large areas of glass supported by spokes and arches of stone. The exterior was designed with no less than seven towers, two on each transept (of which not all were completed), two on the west front and a crossing tower. The west and transept towers are of a striking open, octagonal design, decorated with figures of oxen. The west front has a splendid triple portal, under boldly projecting, and originally open, porches, topped with gables and turrets.

The Cathedral of Laon was extremely influential. It undoubtedly supplied the architect of (and hence the basic design for) Chartres and also had considerable influence in eastern France, at Reims, and in Germany, for instance at Bamberg and Limburg an der Lahn.

The choir of the **Abbey Church of S. Rémi at Reims** (p. 431A) was built *c.* 1170–90. The main internal elevation was fairly standard: four levels, with an arcade of double columns, a vaulted tribune, and a triforium passage. The vaults were quadripartite, and supported by massive double-span flying buttresses. The outstanding feature of the building is the ambulatory chapels: they are unusually deep, and a wall passage runs in front of their windows, marking the first appearance of the so-called Rémois or Champenois passage. The entrances to the chapels are screened from the ambulatory by two additional slender shafts. Both the Rémois passage and the additional shafts screening the chapel entrances were influential, the former being particularly favoured in Champagne, Burgundy and Normandy, and the chapel entrance shafts reappearing at Auxerre (both in the cathedral and the church of S. Germain) and S. Quentin, Mainz.

The earliest part of **Soissons Cathedral** (p. 431B) is the south transept, which was finished by *c.* 1190. The rest of the cathedral, built to a very different design, was completed *c.* 1300. The difference between the south transept and the rest of the church is striking, and shows the speed with which architecture was developing at the end of the twelfth century. The south transept is apsidal, like the transepts of some other north-eastern buildings, such as the Cathedrals of Noyon, Tournai and Cambrai. The transept is aisled, with a tribune and two-level east chapel. The elevation has four levels, with a band triforium above the tribune. The design is sophisticated, with most arches and windows arranged in groups of three, and complex piers of clustered 'en délit' shafts at the entrance to the east chapel. The elevations of the choir, nave and north transept, on the other hand, are of three levels, with a columnar arcade surmounted by a band triforium, and then by a clerestory of enormous windows descending below the vault capitals. The windows have plate tracery with large oculi above twin lancets. The whole cathedral is very closely related to Chartres, with which it is almost contemporary.

Chartres Cathedral (pp. 431C, 432E, 433A) was rebuilt after a fire in 1194 and completed *c.* 1220, incorporating substantial remains of the previous church. The extensive crypt (ninth–twelfth century) was left intact, but slightly extended to support the new choir above it. The western nave bay, two west towers, and much of the west front, of early Gothic date (*c.* 1135–60), were also undamaged, and retained in the present building. Resources came from the pilgrims who flocked to visit the Robe of the Virgin, the cathedral's most treasured possession.

Chartres was designed as a pilgrimage church, with broad aisles, doubled in the choir, for easy circulation, and enormous aisled transepts with triple portals and porches to rival the west front. The aisles are of equal height, not stepped like Bourges. All vaults are quadripartite, that of the nave some 37 m (120 ft) high. An arcade of alternately round and octagonal cored 'piliers cantonnés' (piers flanked by four attached shafts) supports a band triforium and a clerestory with windows reaching down below the vault springings, and almost as tall as the arcade itself. The windows are of plate tracery, with a rosette set above twin lancets. Indeed, Chartres was almost designed around its windows. Vast rose windows decorate the west front and the two transept facades. The stained glass which fills the windows of Chartres is among the finest produced in the Middle Ages. The exterior, as originally designed, would have had seven towers, including a crossing tower (p. 434B). To support the enormous areas of window, Chartres is very sturdily built, with substantial flying buttresses, decorated with spokes (p. 435B), like sections of rose

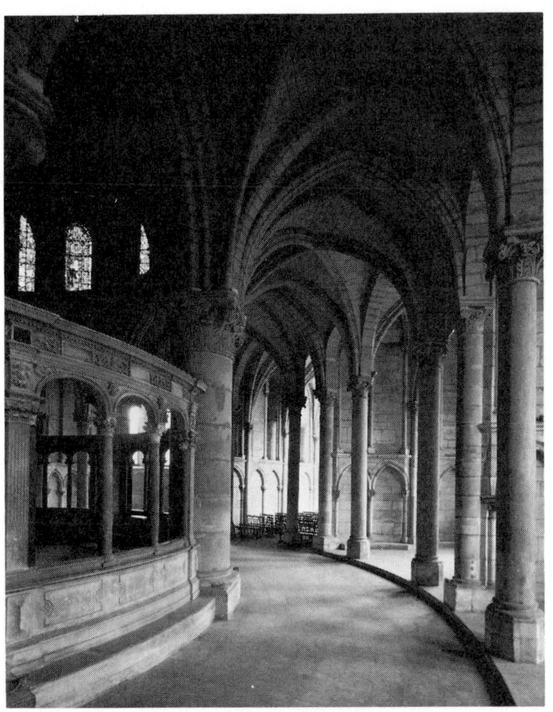

A. Abbey Church of S. Remi, Reims (*c.* 1170–90) See p.430

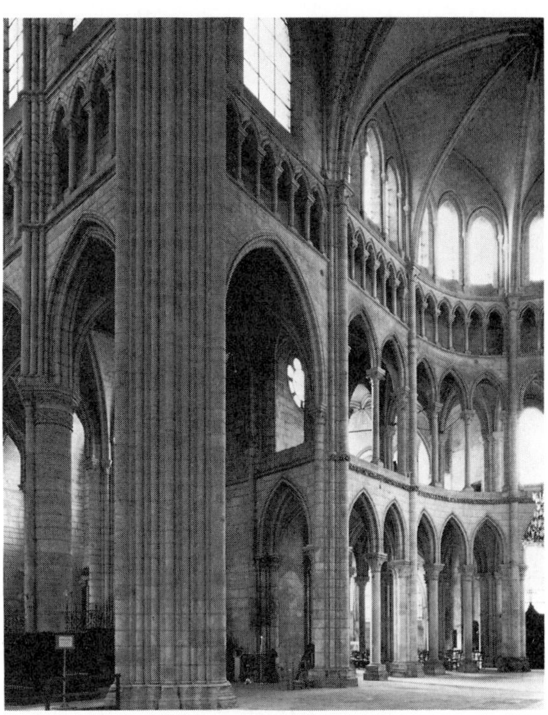

B. Soissons Cathedral (*c.* 1300). See p.430

C. Chartres Cathedral: interior looking west. See p.430

D. Bourges Cathedral (*c.* 1190–1275): interior looking east. See p.436

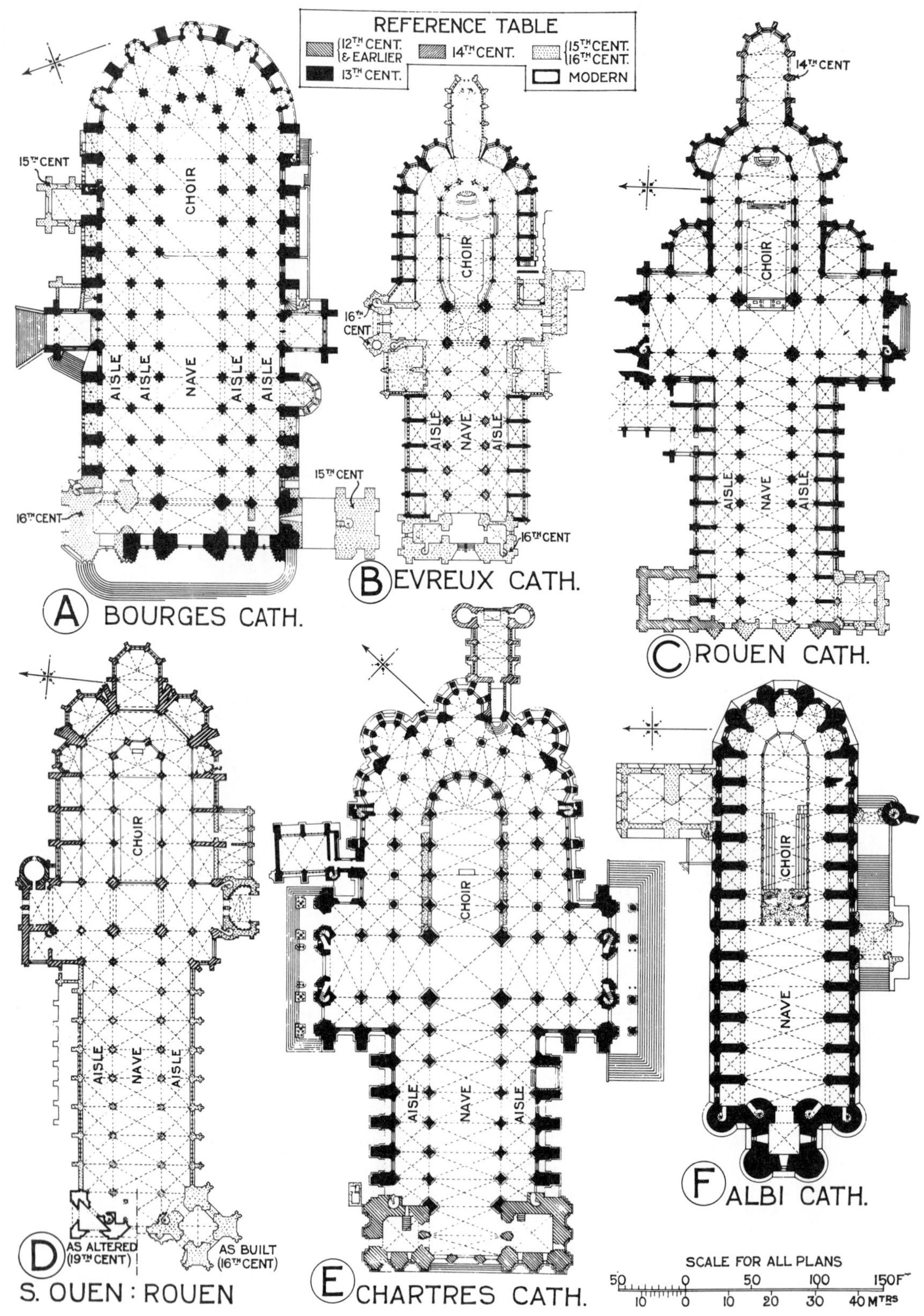
REFERENCE TABLE
12TH CENT. & EARLIER
14TH CENT.
15TH CENT. 16TH CENT.
13TH CENT.
MODERN
15TH CENT
CHOIR
AISLE
AISLE
NAVE
AISLE
AISLE
16TH CENT
A BOURGES CATH.
16TH CENT
CHOIR
AISLE
NAVE
AISLE
15TH CENT
16TH CENT
B EVREUX CATH.
14TH CENT
CHOIR
AISLE
NAVE
AISLE
C ROUEN CATH.
CHOIR
AISLE
NAVE
AISLE
AS ALTERED (19TH CENT)
AS BUILT (16TH CENT)
D S. OUEN : ROUEN
CHOIR
AISLE
NAVE
AISLE
E CHARTRES CATH.
CHOIR
NAVE
F ALBI CATH.
SCALE FOR ALL PLANS
50 0 50 100 150FT
10 0 10 20 30 40 MTRS

A. Chartres Cathedral (1194–*c.* 1220): view from NW. See p.436

B. Le Mans Cathedral from SE (nave twelfth century; south transept fourteenth century; choir 1217–54). See p.443

C. Bourges Cathedral: west facade. See p.436

A S. W. TOWER
AMIENS CATHL
B S.W. SPIRE: CHARTRES
C N. W. TOWER
NOTRE DAME: PARIS
D WINDOW
S. MARY: DINAN
41'6"
E ROSE WINDOW
NOTRE DAME: PARIS
2'2"
15'10"
F STONE PULPIT STAIR
NOTRE DAME: PARIS
G CHAPEL: LAON CATHL
32'6"
H ROSE WINDOW: S. OUEN: ROUEN
J CHOIR CHAPEL: NORREY

A FLYING BUTTRESSES NOTRE DAME: LOUVIERS

B FLYING BUTTRESSES CHARTRES CATHEDRAL

C AMIENS CATHEDRAL FROM S.W. SHOWING POSITION OF FLECHE

D ½ PLAN: LADY CHAPEL CAUDEBEC CHURCH

E PORCH: S. URBAIN: TROYES

F PORCH: S. VINCENT: ROUEN

G PIERS: NORTHERN FRANCE

H FLECHE: AMIENS CATH.

J PIERS: SOUTHERN FRANCE

windows. The influence of the Aisne valley, particularly the Cathedral of Laon, is everywhere apparent. Chartres itself had enormous influence, providing a simplified but highly effective design for a big, impressive cathedral, such as Reims or Amiens.

The rebuilding of the Romanesque **Cathedral of Bourges** (pp. 431D, 432A, 433C) was begun by bishop Henri de Sully around 1190, and progressed from east to west. Two Romanesque portals were retained from the previous church, one on the north, the other on the south side of the nave. A large, double-aisled crypt supports the apse. This was necessary because the ground falls away steeply to the east of the cathedral. The upper church is also double-aisled in plan, with five small radiating chapels opening off the outer ambulatory. The main space is continuous, with no transepts. The main elevation is of three storeys, with an immensely high arcade, a triforium under transverse arches, and a long clerestory with plate-tracery windows crowned by a sexpartite nave vault 38 m (125 ft) high. The aisles are of unequal height, and the inner aisle is high enough to enjoy its own three-storey elevation, which echoes that of the nave. Both internal elevations are articulated by a giant order which swells out beyond the wall plane, and runs uninterrupted from base to vault. The upper levels are supported by a double range of double-span, steeply angled flying buttresses. Bourges owes much, including plan, proportions, and many details, to Notre Dame in Paris and was itself influential in varying degrees at **S. Martin at Tours**, the Cathedrals at Le Mans (q.v.) and Coutances (q.v.) in France, and the Cathedrals of Burgos, Toledo and Palma in Spain, and of Milan in Italy.

Reims Cathedral (pp. 438, 439) was begun in 1211, and construction and embellishment continued throughout most of the thirteenth century. The building history is complex, and still the subject of controversy, but construction proceeded from east to west, reaching the west front around 1260. The overall design is derived from Chartres, but the aisles of the western arm are broadened for the eastern arm (completed 1241) into a nave and double aisles so as to include the transepts, thus providing space for coronations. The deep radiating chapels, however, have the Rémois passage derived from S. Rémi at Reims. The windows at all levels are enormous. Bar-tracery, where the windows are divided by spokes, piers and arches of masonry, rather than sections of wall, seems to have been invented in the radiating chapels at Reims, and was used throughout the building. The west front and the north and south transept facades are all dominated by large rose windows, which also occupy the portal tympana on the west front. The cathedral is unusually rich in sculpture both inside and out, as befitted its royal status. The arcade piers have magnificent, often naturalistic, foliage capitals, figure sculpture extends the full height of the west front, there are richly decorated portals to both transept facades and the west portals are covered with figure sculpture.

Amiens Cathedral (pp. 434A, 435C,H, 440B, 441A,B) was begun, somewhat unusually, from the west end in 1220. The nave was complete by 1236, the choir and transepts by 1270. The names of all the architects are known: the architect of the nave was Robert de Luzarches; the choir was begun by Thomas de Cormont, and finished by his son, Regnault. The upper parts of the west front, including the two west towers and the Flamboyant west rose window, were not completed until at least a century later than the main volumes. At the same time, a series of richly decorated chapels were added to the south nave aisle. Amiens is very tall – the vault is 42 m (140 ft) high – and very expansive, with double aisles in the choir, aisled transepts, and a ring of seven radiating chapels. The internal elevation throughout is on three levels, with a tall arcade of 'piliers cantonnés', a triforium passage, and a vast traceried clerestory. The quadripartite vaults are supported by a splendid range of flying buttresses. The choir and nave are structurally identical and the change of architect is apparent only in the development of details, particularly tracery forms. In both architecture and sculpture Amiens, like Reims, belongs to the tradition established at Chartres but tracery forms are much more developed, Amiens having played an important role in the evolution of the Rayonnant style. The lower parts of the choir are so close to the S. Chapelle, Paris (q.v.), as to suggest that the same architect was responsible for both, while the more spiky upper levels of the choir relate closely to Cologne Cathedral in Germany.

The choir of **Beauvais Cathedral** (p. 437) was begun around 1220. It was enormous both in width and height – 48 m (157 ft) to the vault – and was very slow in the building. By 1240, only the ambulatory and chapels were finished. In 1284 some of the newly built choir vault collapsed, and the choir was reconstructed and consolidated with additional piers. The transepts were erected in the sixteenth century, but in 1573 the 150 m (500 ft) crossing spire collapsed. The nave was never built, and the gigantic east end is still attached to the old tenth-century nave known as the 'Basse Oeuvre'. The choir has double aisles of stepped design, with a full elevation in the inner aisle, and a ring of seven radiating chapels (p. 437G). The main internal elevation is of three levels, consisting of an arcade of enormous 'piliers cantonnés', and a glazed triforium surmounted by immense traceried windows (p. 437E,F). In many ways the design for the cathedral unites the grand traditions of Chartres and Bourges, and at the same time, in the glazed triforium and the tracery of the upper levels, introduces new Rayonnant elements. It was intended to

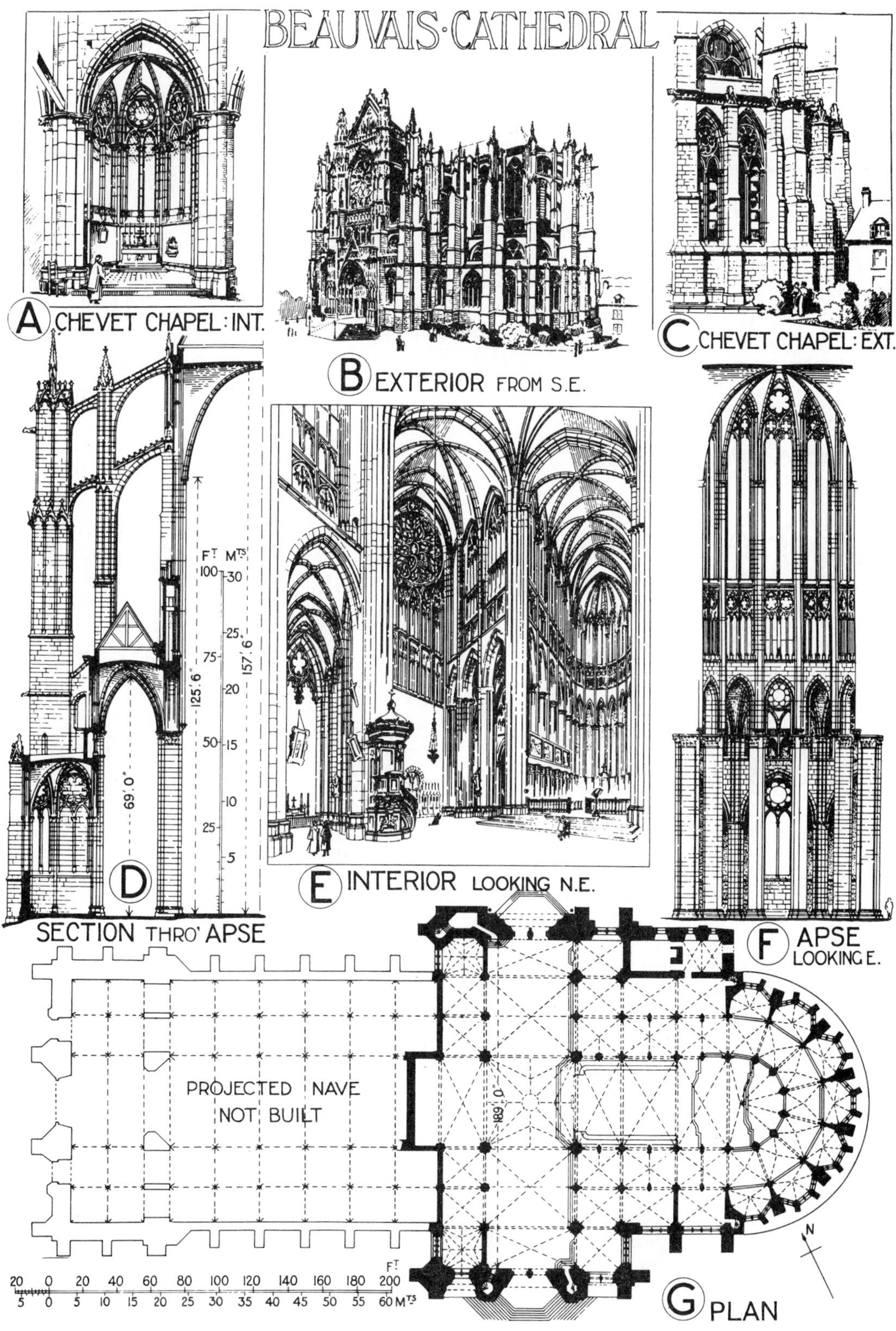
BEAUVAIS·CATHEDRAL
A CHEVET CHAPEL: INT.
B EXTERIOR FROM S.E.
C CHEVET CHAPEL: EXT.
D SECTION THRO' APSE
FT MTS
100 30
25
75
157'6"
125'6"
20
50 15
69'0"
10
25
5
E INTERIOR LOOKING N.E.
F APSE LOOKING E.
PROJECTED NAVE NOT BUILT
189'0"
N
20 0 20 40 60 80 100 120 140 160 180 200 FT
5 0 5 10 15 20 25 30 35 40 45 50 55 60 MTS
G PLAN

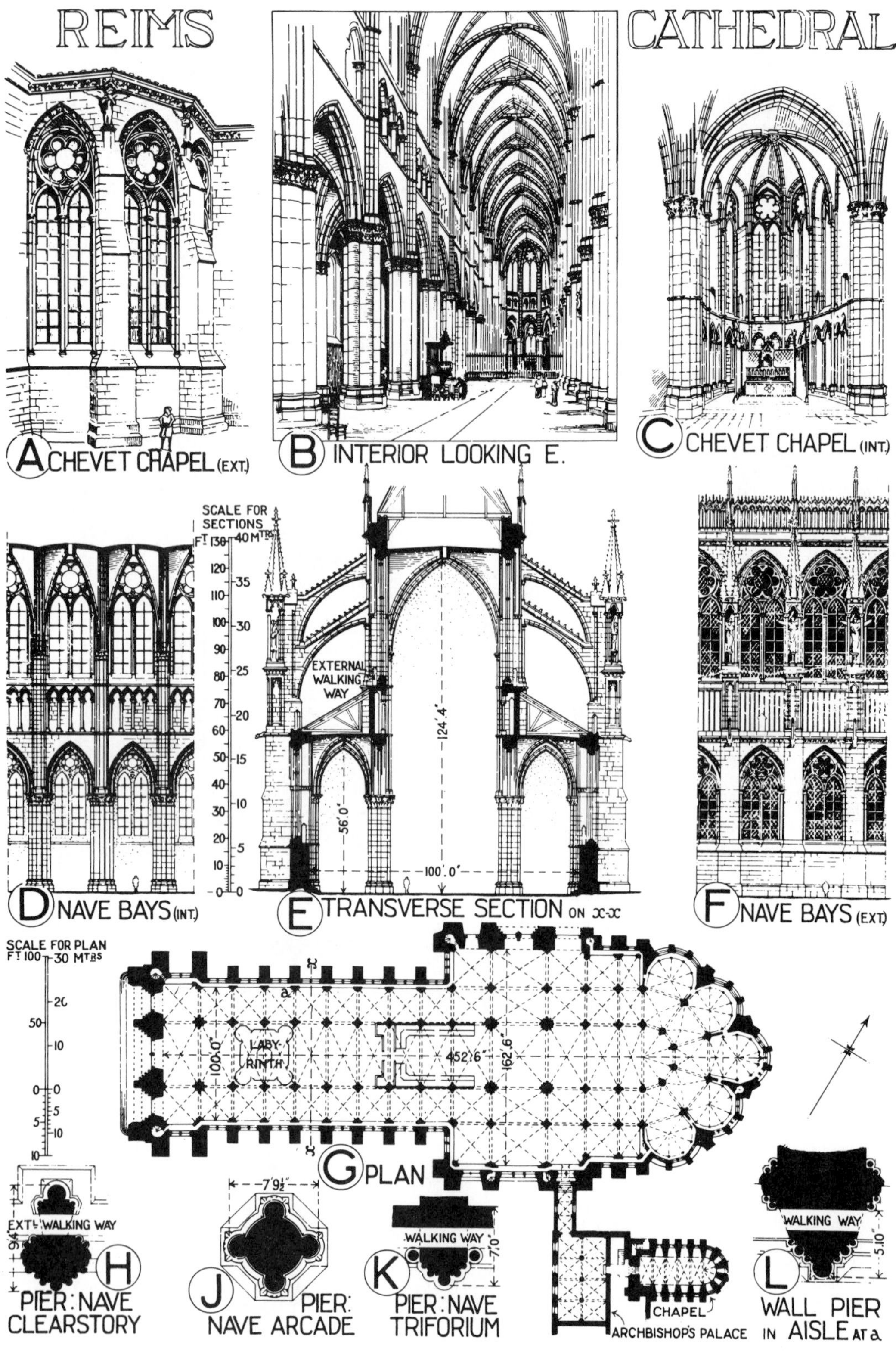
REIMS CATHEDRAL
A CHEVET CHAPEL (EXT.)
B INTERIOR LOOKING E.
C CHEVET CHAPEL (INT.)
SCALE FOR SECTIONS
D NAVE BAYS (INT.)
EXTERNAL WALKING WAY
124'4"
56'0"
100'0"
E TRANSVERSE SECTION ON x-x
F NAVE BAYS (EXT.)
SCALE FOR PLAN
LABYRINTH
100'0"
452'6"
162'6"
G PLAN
EXT^L WALKING WAY
H PIER: NAVE CLEARSTORY
7'9½"
J PIER: NAVE ARCADE
WALKING WAY
7'0"
K PIER: NAVE TRIFORIUM
CHAPEL
ARCHBISHOP'S PALACE
WALKING WAY
5'10"
L WALL PIER IN AISLE AT a

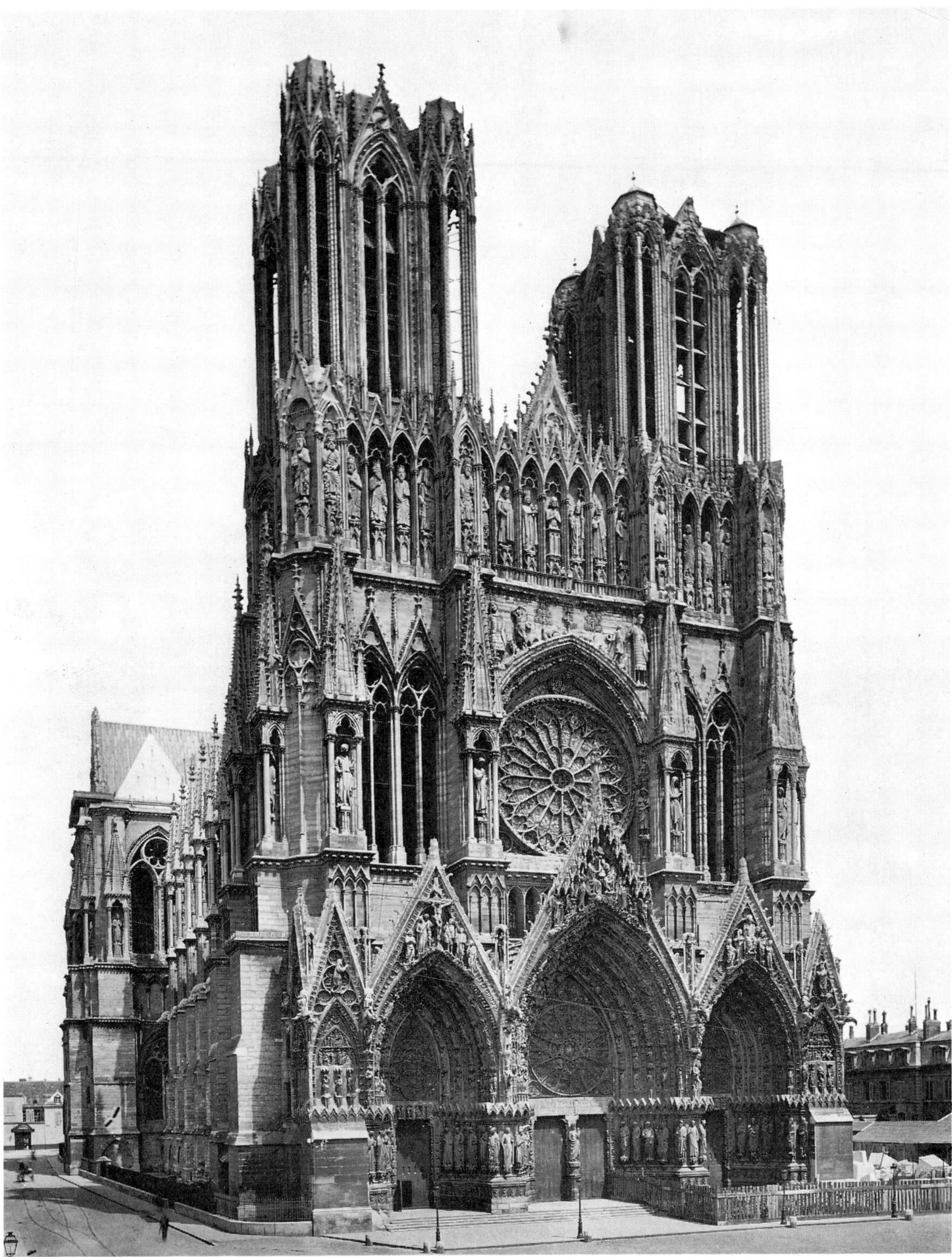

Reims Cathedral from west (1211–end thirteenth century). See p.436

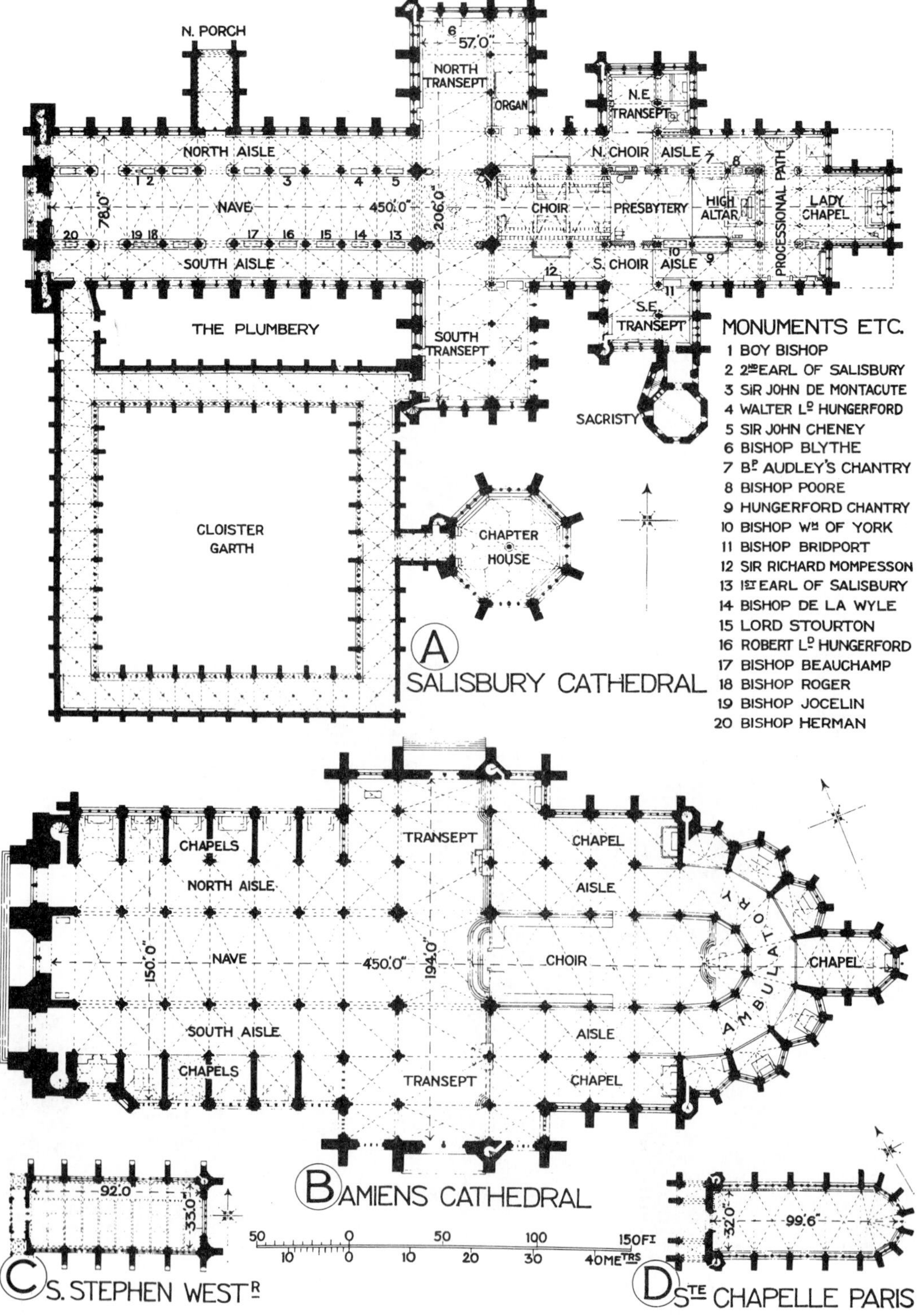
TYPICAL ENGLISH & FRENCH GOTHIC PLANS
N. PORCH
NORTH TRANSEPT
57'0"
ORGAN
N.E. TRANSEPT
NORTH AISLE
N. CHOIR AISLE
NAVE
450'0"
78'0"
206'0"
CHOIR
PRESBYTERY
HIGH ALTAR
PROCESSIONAL PATH
LADY CHAPEL
SOUTH AISLE
S. CHOIR AISLE
S.E. TRANSEPT
THE PLUMBERY
SOUTH TRANSEPT
SACRISTY
CLOISTER GARTH
CHAPTER HOUSE
A SALISBURY CATHEDRAL
MONUMENTS ETC.
1 BOY BISHOP
2 2ND EARL OF SALISBURY
3 SIR JOHN DE MONTACUTE
4 WALTER LD HUNGERFORD
5 SIR JOHN CHENEY
6 BISHOP BLYTHE
7 BP AUDLEY'S CHANTRY
8 BISHOP POORE
9 HUNGERFORD CHANTRY
10 BISHOP WM OF YORK
11 BISHOP BRIDPORT
12 SIR RICHARD MOMPESSON
13 1ST EARL OF SALISBURY
14 BISHOP DE LA WYLE
15 LORD STOURTON
16 ROBERT LD HUNGERFORD
17 BISHOP BEAUCHAMP
18 BISHOP ROGER
19 BISHOP JOCELIN
20 BISHOP HERMAN
CHAPELS
TRANSEPT
CHAPEL
NORTH AISLE
AISLE
NAVE
150'0"
450'0"
194'0"
CHOIR
AMBULATORY
CHAPEL
SOUTH AISLE
AISLE
CHAPELS
TRANSEPT
CHAPEL
B AMIENS CATHEDRAL
92'0
33'0
C S. STEPHEN WESTR
50 0 50 100 150FT
10 0 10 20 30 40METRS
32'0
99'6
D STE CHAPELLE PARIS

A. Amiens Cathedral (1220–70): exterior from SE. See p.436

B. Amiens Cathedral: interior – crossing looking NE

C. Abbey Church of Fécamp (1168–1218): choir. See p.443

D. Bayeux Cathedral choir (*c.* 1230–40): north elevation. See p.443

A. Coutances Cathedral (*c.* 1220–91): west facade. See p.443

B. Troyes Cathedral (1208–1429): west facade. See p.443

C. Notre Dame, Semur-en-Auxois (*c.* 1230). See p.443

D. Angers Cathedral (*c.* 1160–1220): nave looking east. See p.443

be the grandest, and was, in the end, the last, of the great French High Gothic cathedrals.

The choir of **Le Mans Cathedral** (pp. 433G, 435B) was rebuilt between 1217 and 1254. The design derives from Bourges, with double ambulatories with thirteen chapels of unusual projection and stepped elevations and a complex system of flying buttresses. But the building is unusual in that it bears the imprint of three completely different architects. The outer aisle and chapels are the work of a master trained in the Aisne valley; the inner aisle and the main arcade are by a Norman master who made lavish use of the rich mouldings and foliate ornament typical of the duchy. The clerestory, however, with its great bartraceried windows, is by a Paris-trained Rayonnant master.

Normandy

Early Gothic architecture in Normandy was very conservative, with heavy composite piers supporting thick walls with clerestory passages, three-level elevations with tribunes, all crowned by quadripartite vaulting. The **Abbey Church of Fécamp** (1168–1218) (p. 441C) epitomises this architectural style. A handful of buildings, notably the nave of **Lisieux Cathedral** (*c.* 1166–80), showed greater awareness of contemporaries, such as Laon and Notre Dame in Paris, in the Ile de France. The nave of **Rouen Cathedral** (*c.* 1200–30) (p. 432C), with its three beautiful towers, varied the Fécamp type by adopting a four-level nave elevation, with unusual floorless tribunes, inspired by the High Gothic cathedrals of the Ile de France.

The choir of **S. Etienne (Abbaye aux Hommes) at Caen** (*c.* 1190–1200) (pp. 370, 371D) introduced a new, more imaginative approach with rippling, shadowed forms for the composite piers and rib mouldings, more elegant passages within the thick walls, and spacious, intercommunicating radiating chapels. All available wall surfaces were encrusted with geometrical or foliate oculi or paterae. This formula proved effective and popular, and was taken up again at **Bayeux Cathedral** choir (*c.* 1230–40) (p. 441D) and **Coutances Cathedral** choir (*c.* 1220–40) (p. 442A). Coutances, at the same time, belongs to the tradition of Bourges and Le Mans, with double aisles of stepped external elevations, and boasts a high octagonal crossing tower, one of the most splendid in France.

Normandy is renowned for its many mediaeval churches: other well-known examples are the **Cathedrals of Noyon** (1145–1228), **Troyes** (1208–1429) (p. 442B) and **Dôle** (1204 to the sixteenth century), the last a massive building with a square east end; and the churches of **S. Urbain, Troyes** (1262) (p. 435E), with its triple porches, **S. Pierre, Caen** (1308–1521), and **S. Pierre, Lisieux** (1170–1235).

Burgundy

In the twelfth century in Burgundy architectural coherence is provided by the large number of important Cistercian abbeys in the area. Their character is elegant, but structurally conservative and small in volume, and with two-level elevations, such as those at **Pontigny Abbey** (nave *c.* 1160; choir 1180–1200). A similar structural conservatism, though with richly sculpted detail, informs the **Cathedral of Langres** (*c.* 1160). The choir of **S. Madeleine at Vézelay** (*c.* 1180–1200) (pp. 367B, 368, 435J) was more in tune with Gothic developments in the Ile de France, with spacious intercommunicating chapels, based, like the three-level elevation, on S. Denis.

Auxerre Cathedral (*c.* 1215–33) continues this awareness of French developments, deriving its Rémois passages from Reims, and its three-level elevation with band triforium, great traceried clerestory and double-span flying buttresses from Chartres. A new openness produces an elegant result and a new formula for the nave of **Lyon Cathedral** (*c.* 1230) and at other Burgundian churches such as **Notre Dame at Dijon** (*c.* 1220) and at **Semur-en-Auxois** (*c.* 1230) (p. 442C) which, in the nave, reintroduced as a fashionable design the two-level elevation.

Western France

Gothic architecture in western France inherited from its Romanesque forbears an emphasis on width rather than height, and a predilection for the hall church, for example **Poitiers Cathedral** (*c.* 1160–1200), or the 'nef unique' (nave only) church, as at **Angers Cathedral** (*c.* 1160–1220) (p. 442D). In the south-west, the 'nef unique' was favoured at both **Toulouse** and **Bordeaux Cathedrals**. In both types the outer walls tended to have windows set rather high with wall passages running inside them. In the south, a tradition of small rectangular chapels opening off the grand central space along the length of the building developed, such as that in the friars' church, **Les Jacobins at Toulouse** (p. 445A). The Romanesque tradition of square bays and square quadripartite vaults continued, particularly in Anjou and Poitou, and developed into the domed, so-called Angevin vault, with elegant and multiple ribs, often supported on extremely slender columns, for example, **S. Serge at Angers** (*c.* 1215–20).

Albi Cathedral (1282–1390) (pp. 432F, 445C), an impressive fortress-like hall church built in brick, 18 m (60 ft) wide – the widest vaulted space in France – has an apsidal east end with a series of flanking chapels separated by internal buttresses.

Rayonnant

From about 1230, there was a reaction against the enormous scale of the great High Gothic cathedrals. Structural approaches changed little, and the roots of the most striking feature of Rayonnant architecture, the complex window tracery, can be traced to High Gothic Reims and Amiens. But the smaller scale brought a new intimacy and increasing complexity of detail.

The new style seems to have emerged in the rebuilding of S. Denis, begun in 1231. The three-level section with triforium was derived from High Gothic building, but the clerestory was filled with interlocking bar tracery, and the back wall of the triforium was lit to create the effect of a great sheet of glass in the upper levels. Clerestory and triforium were linked more closely still by shared mullions, and the whole internal elevation was tied together with composite piers and uninterrupted vault shafting. Similar designs were used at **Troyes Cathedral** (*c.* 1240) (p. 442B); **Strasbourg Cathedral** (*c.* 1245–75) (pp. 445B,D), in conjunction with a splendid Rayonnant west front, veiled by screens of descending mullions and the later recessed portal with tracery in two planes; and in the choir of **Amiens** (*c.* 1236–69) (q.v.). The two-level section was taken to its logical conclusion at **S. Urbain at Troyes** (*c.* 1262–70). The decorative nature of the style made it ideal for smaller buildings, especially palace chapels, of which the most spectacular example is the **S. Chapelle in Paris** (p. 446A), built between 1242 and 1248 by S. Louis to house the relic of the Crown of Thorns. In their rich decoration of elaborate pinnacles and gables, these buildings themselves resemble metalwork reliquaries.

In the latter half of the thirteenth century, the style, which had developed in the Ile de France and Champagne, spread to Normandy, with **Evreux Cathedral** (*c.* 1250–1350) (p. 432B) and the choir of **Sées Cathedral** (*c.* 1270) (p. 447A), and to the south at **Clermont-Ferrand Cathedral** (*c.* 1250–86), **Narbonne Cathedral** begun 1272, and the church of **S. Nazaire at Carcassonne** (*c.* 1270–1325). The Rayonnant style spread right across France, in a way that High Gothic design had never done, ousting the regional Gothic styles that had flourished in the earlier part of the century.

Flamboyant

The amount of rebuilding necessary after the Hundred Years War, especially in the north, gave a fresh impetus to architectural developments, though the Flamboyant style had been emerging through the fourteenth century, for instance at **S. Ouen at Rouen** (pp. 432D, 434H, 447B), begun in 1318. The net of tracery patterns now stretches across all available surfaces, including the vault, which is patterned with complex star designs by the addition of small subsidiary 'tierceron' and 'lierne' ribs, as for example at **S. Nicholas du Port** (*c.* 1495–1574). The effects were enhanced by the suppression of capitals, and the use of continuous mouldings, as in the church of **Brou at Bourg-en-Bresse** (1506–32) or the choir of **Mont Saint-Michel** (p. 446C), begun in 1446.

Tracery patterns seem to have developed in two contradictory directions: on the one hand, influenced by English Decorated architecture, towards rich, flame-like forms, for instance the west front of **La Trinité, Vendôme** (*c.* 1450–1500), or **S. Wulfram at Abbeville** (1488) (p. 446B); on the other, influenced by English Perpendicular design, towards a panelled severity as in the **Cathedral of Orléans** (end of the fifteenth century) (p. 447C). The spikiness of Rayonnant was increased by an emphasis on prismatic mouldings and high prismatic bases, as for instance on the transept facades at Sens Cathedral (*c.* 1494), or Beauvais (*c.* 1499) (q.v.), or the west front of Troyes Cathedral (*c.* 1506) (q.v.), all by Martin Chambiges.

Indeed, exterior design became richer than ever, as the entire south flank of **Notre Dame at Louviers** (late fifteenth century) (p. 447D) culminating in the filigree encrustations of the south porch, bears witness. Apse and porch plans, which had been stable since the end of the twelfth century, reflected the new interest in triangular forms: see, for example, the apse of **Caudebec-en-Caux** (*c.* 1426) (p. 435D), and the west porch of **S. Maclou at Rouen** (*c.* 1436–1520), probably the richest of all Flamboyant buildings. There was renewed interest in the giant order, for instance at S. Nicholas du Port, and at **S. Etienne du Mont in Paris** (1452–1540). Finally the magnificent **S. Eustache in Paris** (1532–1640) (p. 432B), although almost entirely Renaissance in detail, returns to the great double-aisled and stepped elevation that had preoccupied the architect of Bourges.

The cloisters at Cistercian **Fontenay** (p. 448A), with elegant 'en délit' shafting and waterleaf capitals, form an outstanding and virtually complete example of monastery buildings from the mid-twelfth century. And those of the Merveille of the Benedictine **Abbey of Le Mont Saint-Michel** (*c.* 1215–28), on a particularly spectacular site, contain two splendid vaulted halls, which must have rivalled contemporary palaces, as well as a richly sculptured cloister.

Secular Buildings

Château Gaillard (now in ruins), built between 1196 and 1198 by Richard I of England to protect Normandy from the Capetians, was probably the finest castle in France, designed with great subtlety to avoid areas of dead ground around a massive keep. Most of the major French castles of the next century, built to house garrisons, were rectangular enclosures

A. Church of the Jacobins, Toulouse: interior, looking east. See p.443

B. Strasbourg Cathedral (*c.* 1245–75): nave looking east. See p.444

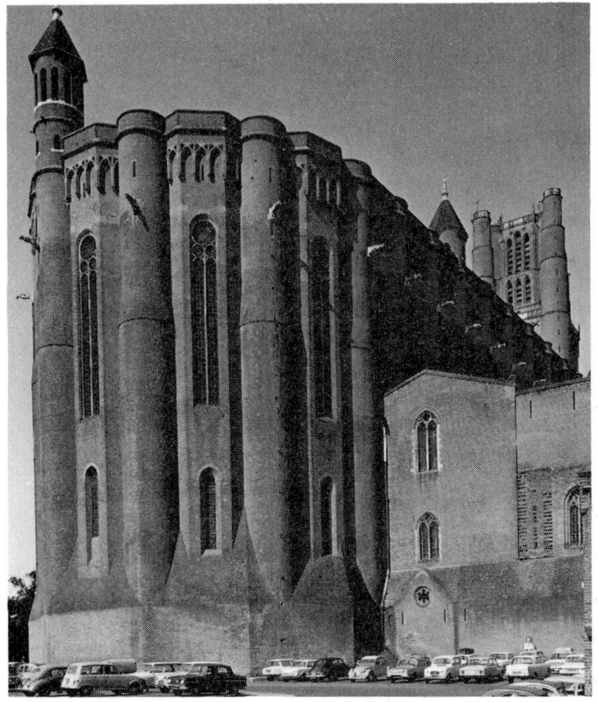

C. Albi Cathedral (1282–1390): exterior from east. See p.443

D. Strasbourg Cathedral: west facade

A. S. Chapelle, Paris (1242–8): exterior from NE. See p.444

B. S. Wulfram, Abbeville (1488): west front. See p.444

C. Mont Saint-Michel from the south. (Church; Romanesque nave 1122–35; Gothic choir 1446–). See p.444

A. Sées Cathedral (*c.* 1270): choir. See p.444

B. S. Ouen, Rouen (1318–), from SE. See p.444

C. Orléans Cathedral (end fifteenth century): interior. See p.444

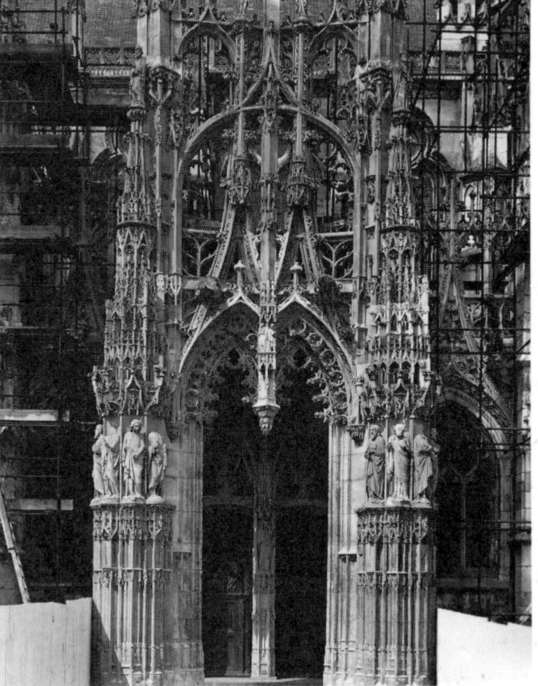

D. Notre Dame, Louviers (late fifteenth century): south portal. See p.444

A. Cistercian Abbey, Fontenay (mid-twelfth century). See p.444

B. Château de Vincennes (1365–73): keep. See p.452

C. Hôtel de Jacques Coeur, Bourges (1442–53): the courtyard. See p.452

D. Avignon: aerial view from south, showing Palais des Papes (1316–64). See p.452

A. Carcassonne: entrance to château with bridge over moat (1240–85). See p.452

B. Château de Josselin, Brittany (rebuilt early sixteenth century). See p.452

A LE CHATEAU D'O MORTREE

B PALAIS DE JUSTICE: ROUEN

C HOTEL DE VILLE: BOURGES

D TIMBER HOUSE CAEN

E LOUIS XII STAIR: CHAT. DE BLOIS

F STONE CHIMNEY-PIECE HOTEL DE VILLE: BOURGES

G TIMBER HOUSE: BEAUVAIS

H HOTEL DE CLUNY: PARIS

J HALF-TIMBER HOUSE: S.LO

A. Hôtel de Ville, Arras (1510). See p.452

B. Hôtel de Ville. Compiègne (early fifteenth century). See p.452

C. Hôtel de Ville, Dreux (1502–37). See p.452

D. Hôtel de Cluny, Paris (1485–98). See p.452

with corner towers. Increasing emphasis was placed on fortified gates which could be effectively defended without prejudicing ease of movement, such as the **Castle at Carcassonne** (1240–85) (p. 449A). The **Château d'Amboise** (begun in 1434) is another example, but much altered in Renaissance style. The same principle was extended to protect entire towns, for instance at **Carcassonne** and **Aigues-Mortes** (1271–1300). In the horrors of the Hundred Years War, however, the castle often was, as at the **Palais des Papes at Avignon** (1316–64) (p. 448D), in effect, a heavily defended palace. There was a renewed emphasis on the keep, which was usually rectangular with four corner towers, as, for instance, at **Vincennes** (1364–73) (p. 448B).

There were few Hôtels de Ville as there was little municipal life under the feudal system. The **Hôtel de Ville, Arras** (1510) (p. 451A), has a fine arcade at street level and a giant, 76 m (250 ft) high belfry, but like the **Hôtel de Ville at Compiègne** (early fifteenth century) (p. 451B) was damaged in the 1914–18 war and has been restored. The **Hôtel de Ville, Bourges** (fifteenth century) (p. 450C,F), has a Flamboyant tower and that at **Dreux** (1502–37) (p. 451C) has pinnacled corner towers and a high pyramidal roof.

Country Houses

On the introduction of gunpowder, and with the development of the new social order in the fifteenth century, country houses took the place of fortified castles, though they were still called 'châteaux'. The **Château d'O, Mortrée** (p. 450A), and the **Châteaux de Châteaudun** (rebuilt 1441) are both stately mansions rather than castles. The **Château de Blois** (east wing) (1498–1504) (p. 450E) has a thirteenth-century Salle des Etats and gateway to the court, around which later buildings were added. The Gothic spiral staircase of Louis XII was probably the model for the marvellous staircase of Francis I of the early Renaissance period. The **Château de Josselin, Brittany** (p. 449B), although dating from the twelfth century, was rebuilt in the early sixteenth century; with its circular towers, ogee door-heads, mullioned windows, traceried parapet, and steep roof with dormer windows, it is typical of many others scattered throughout France.

Town Houses

The 'maisons nobles' began to rise in the fifteenth century when French nobles ceased to be feudal lords in fortified castles, and erected houses, known to this day as 'hôtels', planned, as in the country, round a court and with an elaborate facade to the street. The **Hôtel de Jacques Coeur, Bourges** (1442–53) (p. 448C), is undoubtedly among the finest mediaeval town residences in France. It was built by a merchant prince, partly on the town ramparts, round a central court and has seven turret stairs. The **Hôtel de Bourgtheroulde, Rouen** (*c.* 1475), is a good example of this type of house, with its enclosed court surrounded by facades somewhat resembling the Palais de Justice in the same city. Juxtaposed in the court is an early Renaissance building of 1501–37, on which the lower bas-relief panels depict the meeting of François I and Henry VIII of England on the 'Field of the Cloth of Gold' in 1520. The facades were severely damaged in 1944. The **Hôtel Chambellan, Dijon** (fifteenth century), was one of the great town houses of this period. The central court contains an angle turret stair with newel branching into a richly carved head, while the street facade has some fine figures carved in wood. The **Hôtel de Cluny, Paris** (1485–98) (p. 451D) – now a museum – retains its mediaeval character, and is a fine specimen of late Gothic. The chapel stands above an arcade which supports on its central pier an oriel window of pleasing proportions with Flamboyant tracery, crockets and finials. In the **Hôtel de Sens, Paris** (1485), the outside walls are pierced with large, symmetrically-placed windows, indicating a marked change in architectural manners and, perhaps, anticipating a more stable urban society.

Smaller domestic buildings still exist, as in Cluny, where doors and windows are of the later Romanesque type; while in S. Lô (p. 450J), Lisieux, Caen (p. 450D), Chartres, Beauvais (p. 450G), and Rouen there are timber houses with carved barge-boards and overhanging storeys; but a large number have succumbed to the ravages of time and fire. They are not generally earlier than the fifteenth century.

The British Isles: Architectural Character

Gothic had a longer and perhaps more varied history in England than anywhere else in Europe outside France. For a number of reasons English attitudes toward French models were ambivalent, casual, even critical. At no stage did they put themselves *in statu pupillari* to the French as the Germans did. In this independence and lack of respect, English Gothic architects resembled the Italians far more than the Germans. Yet they made Gothic their own in a way the Italians failed to do. John Harvey may have been carried away by enthusiasm when he called Perpendicular the national style of England, but there is no other serious contender for the title.

Gothic reached England before the experimental phase in France was over. Already in the 1160s architects in the north of England were showing interest in what was happening to church designs in

France. The Cistercians, as elsewhere in Europe, may have given the lead but the choir of York Minster (later replaced) was probably the key monument from which a whole school of northern Gothic was descended. Similarly precocious but equally superficial experiments took place in the west country slightly later, with Wells and Glastonbury as the outstanding achievements. This early Gothic of the north and west was cosmetic rather than structural. That is, a Gothic veneer was applied to walls which in every important respect remained much as they had been in Anglo-Norman times. A preoccupation with appearances was to remain a constant feature of English Gothic to the end; and the attempt to graft Gothic details and ornament on to space-frames that no Frenchman would accept as Gothic was certainly the result of a critical examination of alternatives and a genuine expression of preference.

However, this attitude was not uniform and there were important exceptions. The new choir at Canterbury (1174), as might be expected from the fact that its architect was French, and despite the plan which was inherited from the previous building, was Gothic in both the structural and visual senses. The same was true of Lincoln (1192), even though from the start Lincoln displayed a predilection for eccentricities which probably owed nothing to any precedent. These were the English equivalents of early French Gothic. A generation or so later, Salisbury (1220), though with qualifications, and Westminster Abbey (1245) stood in somewhat similar relation to French High Gothic.

If Lincoln be allowed for purposes of argument to belong to the south-east, this can be regarded as a third region of Gothic enterprise in England, closer in every way to France and open to Continental ideas and fashions to an extent that did not often apply elsewhere. Even so the result was an aesthetic programme quite unlike anything developed in France. Instead of soaring spaces and tall stained-glass windows, the English preferred rich mouldings and plentiful encrustations of polished shafts such as Purbeck marble. They made no particular fetish of vaults, although they were used for the grandest buildings. But they only began to take an interest in vaults when they saw the possibilities of making patterns out of them; and for precisely the same reason, timber roofs excited their attention as nowhere else in Europe.

The fact that the Gothic of the south and east was relatively more advanced than that of the rest of the country no doubt played a part in subsequent events, when the decisive factor was the emergence of London as the national capital. Gothic in London began modestly enough at Southwark and the Temple, but it became pre-eminent among the architectural centres of England during the second half of thirteenth century. The seminal buildings were Westminster Abbey and S. Paul's.

Westminster has received critical attention out of all proportion to its merits. The accident that it happens to be unusually well-documented has probably had the effect of exaggerating its historical importance. It was not the first great church to enjoy royal patronage; but the half-hearted effort which it represents to transplant High Gothic into England has been hailed as a turning point in the history of English architecture, while its association with the crown has qualified it to pose as the fountainhead of something called the Court style. The idea that the court in England or anywhere else was actively engaged in the creation of a style is a misconception. Styles were invented not by patrons but by architects trying to please patrons.

For 'Court' we should read 'London'. The thirteenth century witnessed a notable expansion both in the number of architectural commissions and in their scope and diversity. In 1200, so far as we can tell, it was still normal for a skilled mason to work on one job at a time and to spend most of his working life on the payroll of a single ecclesiastical employer. By 1300 architects could find themselves handling several jobs at once. They supplied designs for details and acted as consultants. By 1400 some of them were in the contracting business as well. There were few places in the country big enough to provide continuous employment on this scale. Bristol, York and Norwich may have qualified; but London far outstripped them all. The best patrons, including the court, tended to foregather there; it was where they would expect to find architectural talent when they had need of it; and it was where any aspiring provincial mason who had made good in his local quarry would go, like Dick Whittington, to seek his fortune. William Ramsey came from East Anglia; Henry Yevele probably from Derbyshire.

The essence of the matter was that up to about 1250 architects in England were left to themselves and could develop their own ideas about Gothic. They were under no pressure to conform to French stylistic norms. Most of them were probably unaware of what was going on in France. During the next hundred years, however, things changed. The better-informed patrons were familiar with France. It was fashionable to affect French tastes. The consequences for architecture were not so much to bring English Gothic into line with French, as to lift it out of the condition of being a provincial backwater and launch it into the forefront of invention. If late Gothic is a set of variations on themes proposed by French Rayonnant, for a time the English led the way. The transformation was brought about partly by direct acquaintance with details from abroad, but far more by the intelligent mastery of the fundamental methods of Gothic design and the realisation that they could be extended into aspects of architecture which the French had not yet explored. The most remarkable of these English achievements involved the manipulation of surface patterns in three dimensions. For example, tracery patterns were composed with an eye to the spaces in which windows were to be seen, and polygonal planning was exploited to heighten their impact. Likewise patterns of ribs were no longer tied to the shapes of vaults. This notional separation of ribs and shells had far-reaching consequences in every sense of the word (see Germany).

In their different ways the aisles of Bristol, the retro-choir at Wells, and the octagon at Ely are among the most sophisticated architectural conceptions of any period, and because they are exceptional they figure prominently in history books. It is therefore important to realise that the period of creative experiment did not last long and that the number of remarkable designs was not large. Yet when the excitement subsided and something like unanimity was restored on matters of style, nothing was ever the same again.

There ensued two hundred years in which English Gothic was almost as insular as it had been at the outset; but now the best designs were conceived almost entirely in terms of thin, linear mouldings, and grids of panelled tracery (p. 470B). Even vaults tended to turn into tracery, for example fan vaults. There was an evident desire to impose an all-over uniformity on interior spaces. It was an ideal better suited for single-chamber chapels than for aisled churches, although of course it could be adapted to their special needs. It was most perfectly realised on the grand scale in the Chapel of King's College, Cambridge; and otherwise more or less in miniature, in the countless chantry chapels which private patrons endowed for the celebration of soul-masses on their own behalf.

The broad divisions of Gothic set out in the three preceding paragraphs correspond roughly to the traditional classification into Early English, Decorated and Perpendicular. They are illustrated alongside English Romanesque (Norman) examples for purposes of comparison in terms of external and internal elevations, doorways, windows, column capitals and bases, and mouldings (pp. 416 to 422). However, it would be a mistake to suppose that the characteristics of Early English, Decorated or Perpendicular that are set out in the pages of Rickman or other nineteenth-century manuals (see the Bibliography) adequately define the styles they purport to identify. They may suffice to date buildings approximately in default of documents, and perhaps to group buildings into workshops. But they tend to bring everything down to the same level. In fact they work better for parish churches than for cathedrals and abbeys precisely because parish churches, as architecture, tend to be simpler than cathedrals. But in the later Middle Ages even the parish church could rise to the status of an art form in its own right, and it would be an insult to regard some of them merely as collections of detail (pp. 455, 456).

Thomas Rickman, to whom we owe the familiar names and periods of English Gothic, based his divisions on the evidence most readily available to him, namely the ecclesiastical buildings which were still in daily use. Most of them are still in use today. Although these churches represent the best efforts of the architectural profession, they were only a tiny fragment of what was actually built. Almost all the rest have disappeared, fallen into ruin, or been transformed out of recognition. The odds in favour of the survival of ecclesiastical monuments and against everything else, no doubt reinforces the historical fact that Gothic was invented to serve the needs of the Church, but it also disguises the extent to which mediaeval architecture ceased to be Gothic in any meaningful sense where buildings other than churches are concerned. The one large sample of mediaeval buildings other than churches about which it is possible to form an adequate impression is castles. These have seldom survived intact; but even in their ruined or restored state it is easy enough to see that there were few opportunities for castle-builders to indulge in the stylistic fancies that abound in churches, and when they do occur they are most conspicuous in chapels, for example Beaumaris. The logic of a castle was essentially military, and if further thought was given to the design it was to the provision of domestic amenities for those who had to live in them. As a result their Gothic seldom extended beyond a few pointed arches.

Serious castle-building was virtually a royal monopoly, and it was this, far more than church building, which brought the crown into contact with the building industry. On rare occasions when emergency measures were required, for instance in the case of Edward I's castle in Wales, the king could conscript every available mason.

The thought that went into castle-building was of a different order from that which produced cathedrals – intelligence rated higher than imagination. The north Welsh castles were in this sense more impressive perhaps than anything outside the Holy Land. Beaumaris was a fortified bridgehead that controlled Anglesey; Harlech was a police-station; Conway (and Caernarvon) were royal residences as well as castles; and between them they cornered Snowdonia, the ultimate redoubt of any Welsh resistance. But the value of the exercise was as much psychological as practical. They were clusters of towers which formed forbidding silhouettes. As images of power they would be every bit as eloquent as great churches.

There was always a potential conflict between the military and the domestic functions of castles. Accommodation was inevitably restricted in the interest of defence, and given the growing confidence in the rule of law, not to mention methods of warfare which rendered castles obsolescent, there was a steady tendency for those who could to abandon

A. Tilty Church, Essex (thirteenth and fourteenth centuries). See p.454

B. S. Thomas of Canterbury, Salisbury, Wiltshire (early sixteenth century): the Doom painting over chancel arch. See p.454

A. Southease Church, Sussex (fifteenth century). See p.454

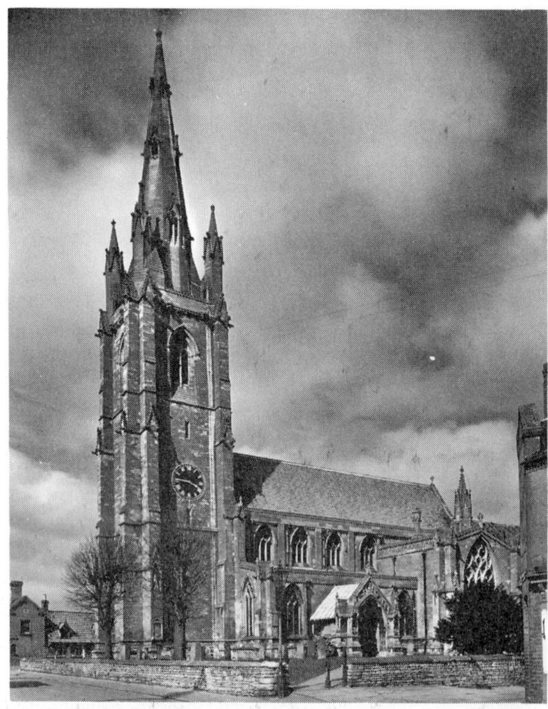

B. S. Andrew, Heckington, from SW (fourteenth century). See p.454

C. Holy Trinity Church, Blythburgh, Suffolk: nave looking east. See p.454

D. Dennington Church, Suffolk: rood loft. See p.454

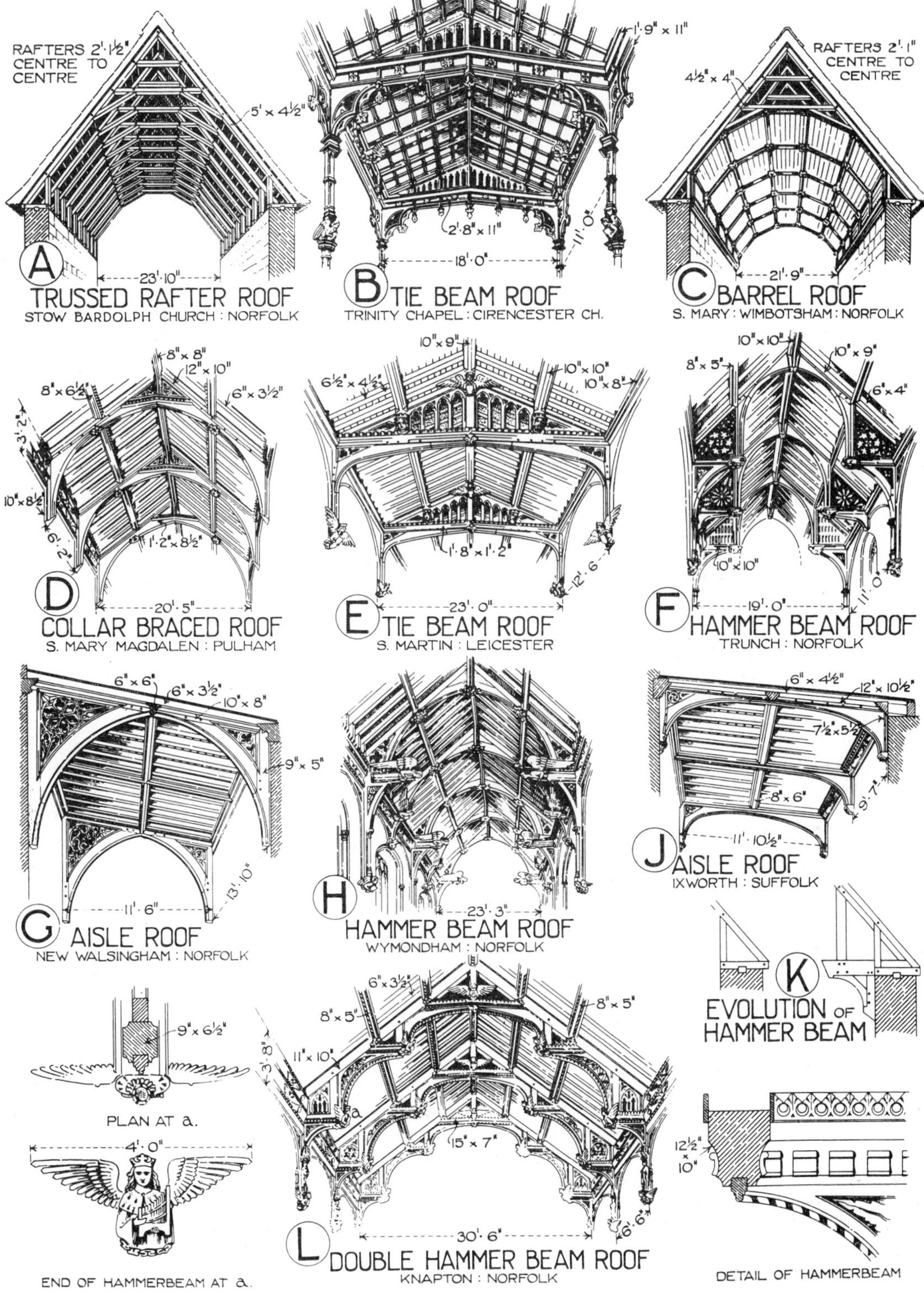
TYPES OF TIMBER CHURCH ROOFS
RAFTERS 2'·1½" CENTRE TO CENTRE
5' x 4½"
23'·10"
A
TRUSSED RAFTER ROOF
STOW BARDOLPH CHURCH : NORFOLK
1'·9" x 11"
2'·8" x 11"
18'·0"
11'·0"
B
TIE BEAM ROOF
TRINITY CHAPEL : CIRENCESTER CH.
RAFTERS 2'·1" CENTRE TO CENTRE
4½" x 4"
21'·9"
C
BARREL ROOF
S. MARY : WIMBOTSHAM : NORFOLK
8" x 8"
12" x 10"
8" x 6½"
6" x 3½"
3'·2"
10" x 8½"
6'·2"
1'·2" x 8½"
20'·5"
D
COLLAR BRACED ROOF
S. MARY MAGDALEN : PULHAM
10" x 9"
6½" x 4½"
10" x 10"
10" x 8"
1'·8" x 1'·2"
12'·6"
23'·0"
E
TIE BEAM ROOF
S. MARTIN : LEICESTER
10" x 10"
8" x 5"
10" x 9"
6" x 4"
10" x 10"
19'·0"
11'·0"
F
HAMMER BEAM ROOF
TRUNCH : NORFOLK
6" x 6"
6" x 3½"
10" x 8"
9" x 5"
11'·6"
13'·10"
G
AISLE ROOF
NEW WALSINGHAM : NORFOLK
23'·3"
H
HAMMER BEAM ROOF
WYMONDHAM : NORFOLK
6" x 4½"
12" x 10½"
7½" x 5½"
8" x 6"
9'·7"
11'·10½"
J
AISLE ROOF
IXWORTH : SUFFOLK
K
EVOLUTION OF HAMMER BEAM
9" x 6½"
PLAN AT a.
4'·0"
END OF HAMMERBEAM AT a.
6" x 3½"
8" x 5"
8" x 5"
3'·8"
11" x 10"
a
15" x 7"
30'·6"
6'·6"
L
DOUBLE HAMMER BEAM ROOF
KNAPTON : NORFOLK
12½" x 10"
DETAIL OF HAMMERBEAM

castles in favour of houses purpose-built for the pursuit of a peaceful, private life.

Unlike the great churches and a sizable proportion of the castles, the great houses of the Middle Ages have mostly disappeared, overtaken by unforeseen changes in life-styles for which they were not suited. But a few were refurbished rather than rebuilt, and some actually managed to survive intact, at least in part, either because their owners were too impoverished to rebuild, or because in certain social circles it came to be considered a status symbol to have a mediaeval house in the post-mediaeval world.

The immense social changes that took place in England between the Conquest and the Reformation were no doubt accurately reflected in domestic architecture. At the beginning of the period only the relatively well-to-do had anything that could be called a house. It would be the physical centrepiece of each manorial unit. The lord of the manor lived his life almost entirely in public, at the centre of a circle of dependants, and for this the indispensable domestic setting was a hall. Private life was represented by the minimum attachment of a single chamber. Development proceeded in two directions: outwards and upwards. Rooms for special purposes such as chapels, cooking, storage and so on could either be built alongside the hall, as, for instance, in some of the more spacious bishops' palaces; or they could be compacted into tower blocks with rooms on several floors. Architecturally the latter was the more ambitious and in the long run perhaps the more fruitful exercise. Tower houses needed stairs for them to function properly, and considerable ingenuity was often needed to make particular stairs serve particular rooms.

Planning also manifested itself in the setting-out of houses on the ground. The grouping of apartments into ranges and the grouping of ranges around courtyards, with imposing gatehouses as the centrepieces of facades, was a mediaeval not a Renaissance invention. This aspect of mediaeval architecture in England is now best represented by colleges at the older universities. But although the best of them are to be seen at Oxford or Cambridge, colleges were by no means confined to academic institutions. They were the architectural expression of an ideal of corporate life which spread from the monasteries which provided the basic model, to a whole range of social organisations, most of them financed by deeds of charity, in which the beneficiaries were expected to eat together and worship together, regularly and with due ceremony. As a result the most conspicuous features of such establishments were always a hall and a chapel (pp. 459A, 460A). Even so, there was no clear-cut distinction between a large house such as Hampton Court and a large college like S. John's at Cambridge.

Hampton Court (begun *c.* 1520) (pp. 459B, 486) was exceptional by any standards. By the time it was built brick was already well established as a suitable substitute for stone, if not for churches at least for large houses. But by far the greater part of all domestic architecture made use of timber frames. This must have always been the case, and it continued to be the case long after the conventional end of the Middle Ages.

The earliest forms of timber construction are shrouded in obscurity, represented if at all in rows of post-holes brought to light by archaeological spades. It is only from the thirteenth century that datable standing structures survive. From then on timber-framed houses can be seen evolving into a succession of vernacular formulas which, though they varied from region to region and overlapped one another chronologically, were all designed to cater for the changing needs of emerging social groups. Insofar as parvenus aspire to ape their betters, there were echoes of established upper-class patterns. The nucleus was always in some sense of the word a hall with service areas and chambers attached; development conformed to a fairly rigid sequence and took such forms as adding rooms upstairs and enclosing open fires in fireplaces with chimneys. But the modest scale of middle-class life made it impossible for its mediaeval exponents to effect anything more than a distant and imperfect reflection of well-to-do houses.

Vernacular architecture developed its own impetus, and the logic of vernacular designs was strictly geared to the practicalities of daily life. It was also conditioned by the technicalities of timber construction. The strength of a timber frame was measured by its joints and the efficiency of its load-bearing members. The expertise involved was so peculiar to timber work that there is hardly any point in associating it with Gothic masoncraft. There was equally little scope for imagery in timber construction, and decoration was either extraneous and ephemeral, or else achieved in ways that owed nothing whatever to ecclesiastical architecture. The two skills were quite independent of one another.

This does not mean that there was no interaction at all between masons and carpenters. The extent to which they may have influenced one another is difficult to determine, partly because the surviving evidence has polarised into what one may suspect to be unrepresentative extremes, and partly because students have themselves tended to be specialists in one field or the other with the result that few on either side are in a position to ask the right questions. That there were occasions for collaboration is not in dispute. All churches had wooden roofs, whether or not they had vaults as well (p. 457). Some, like York Minster, had vaults of wood made to look like masonry. It is not out of the question that the crucks of vernacular building were inspired by the curved ribs of such timber vaults. Conversely the hammer-beam roof of Westminster Hall (1399) (p. 479A) is pure timber construction

A. Eton College (1440): aerial view. See p.458. 1. Entrance; 2. Chapel; 3. College Hall; 4. Upper School; 5. Weston's Yard; 6. Provost's Lodge; 7. Headmaster's House

B. Hampton Court: the West Gatehouse (*c.* 1520). See p.458

A. Cambridge: aerial view from south. See p.461. 1. Senate House; 2. S. Mary; 3. King's College; 4. Clare College; 5. Trinity Hall; 6. Trinity College; 7. Gonville and Caius College; 8. S. John's College; 9. Magdalene College

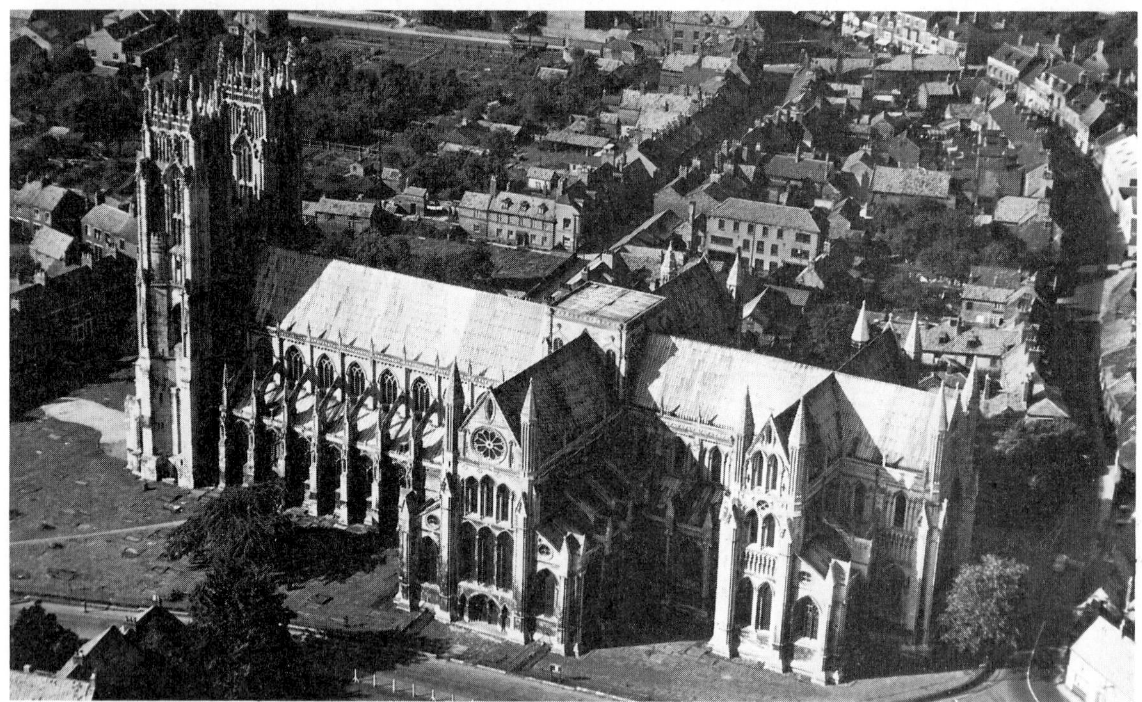

B. Beverley Minster (thirteenth, fourteenth and fifteenth centuries): aerial view. See p.461

raised to the level of art-work with nothing more than superficial allusions to stone tracery in the ornament. Fancy roofs of this kind go a long way to explain the paucity of masonry vaults in English Late Gothic. There were master carpenters who could produce in wood canopy work every bit as intricate as stone tombs or metal shrines and monstrances (for example, the choir stalls at Chester Cathedral), which implies that some of them had access to the pattern books or working methods of specialists in Gothic art who worked in other materials. This traffic in ideas need not have been all in one direction. But the important question is whether the designers of timber-framed houses (q.v.) used the same geometrical procedures as the designers of churches; if so, whether they had always done so, or when they began; and if not, what they used instead. No definite answers are yet forthcoming.

But even without answers, one thing is certain. Whereas at the outset of the Gothic period the centre of gravity of the building industry lay entirely with masons in the realm of great churches, at the end it had passed to the secular end of the spectrum, and this meant to some extent the integration of timber-work and masonry. The shift was not just a matter of statistics, although the sheer number of secular buildings was impressive enough. Even more decisive was the simple fact that ecclesiastical Gothic was too specialised, too closely wedded to one particular type of design to meet the growing variety of demands made on the industry by a society moving towards a higher level of complexity and sophistication. Late Gothic met these demands by becoming less and less Gothic.

It may be wrong to lay too much stress on the antithesis between ecclesiastical and secular, but it conveniently matches the historical circumstances of the fifteenth century. When the Reformation effectively put an end to church building and all the attendant forms of religious patronage, the architectural profession found itself compelled to shed the last traces of a tradition which had shaped its evolution over four centuries. The search for an alternative set of stylistic conventions became virtually obligatory.

The British Isles: Examples

Churches

Descriptions of greater and lesser churches are given first, as representing the development of the Gothic style in Britain, and by the historical accident of location England in particular. Many of them can be referred to in a series of comparative plans (pp. 462–465) and in the other comparative drawings of elevations and details (pp. 416–422). Both categories of church are placed in alphabetical order for ease of reference; C, A, P and CC indicate the original status of the Church or Cathedral, Abbey, Priory or Collegiate Church.

Beverley, CC (p. 460B). Begun first quarter of thirteenth century. Choir and both pairs of transepts complete by mid-thirteenth century. The general design is derived from Lincoln while much of the detailing closely resembles the contemporary choir at Fountains Abbey (q.v.). The fourteenth-century nave continues basic design of eastern parts but with updated detailing. West front (*c.* 1380–*c.* 1430) is modelled on earlier west front at York Minster.

Bristol, A (p. 465K). Augustinian chapter house (*c.* 1150). Complex intersecting arcades on walls relate to earlier chapter house at Worcester. Elder Lady Chapel (*c.* 1218–34) may be by a master mason from Wells, Adam Locke. Hall choir (1298–1332) (p. 470A), nave by Street (nineteenth century) to match east end. The hall-church formula occurs only rarely in England (see London, Temple Church). Many details suggest some awareness of continental ideas.

Cambridge, King's College Chapel, CC (pp. 460A, 466). Built in three phases (1446–61, 1477–85 and 1508–15), the last being the construction of fan vaults by John Wastell (see Peterborough). Free-standing, tall rectangular chapel 24.4 m × 12.2 m (80 ft × 40 ft), lit by giant Perpendicular windows. Aisleless but with a continuous row of low chapels on north and south sides. Panelling applied equally to all surfaces including vaults, the logical conclusion of the first Perpendicular experiments at Gloucester.

Canterbury, AC (pp. 463B, 468A). First Norman Archbishop, Lanfranc, began reconstruction in 1070. Part of original crypt remains, identifiable by Corinthianesque capitals. Area of crypt with elaborately carved cubic capitals dates from time when choir was replaced and enlarged after 1096 (dedicated 1130). Remainder of crypt belongs to 1175–84). East end rebuilt after fire of 1174 (completed 1184). The master masons were William of Sens and William the Englishman. Building intended as shrine for Thomas à Becket. East end is first example of whole Gothic system in England. The three-storey internal elevation follows changes to similar formula in northern France in the 1170s. Canterbury belongs to this milieu. Lower parts of previous choir retained, thus determining the pier forms. Earliest example of double transepts in England, an idea which was to enjoy great popularity. Nave rebuilt (1379–1405) by Henry Yevele, chief royal architect who died in 1400. Early example of main volume wholly in Perpendicular style. Upper storeys are unified but the small glazed area at high level darkens vaults and enhances the mystic effect by contrast with well-lit main arcade.

Carlisle, AC (p. 465B). Choir rebuilt after 1292 fire, still in progress in 1322. Elaborate display of latest curvilinear Decorated tracery.

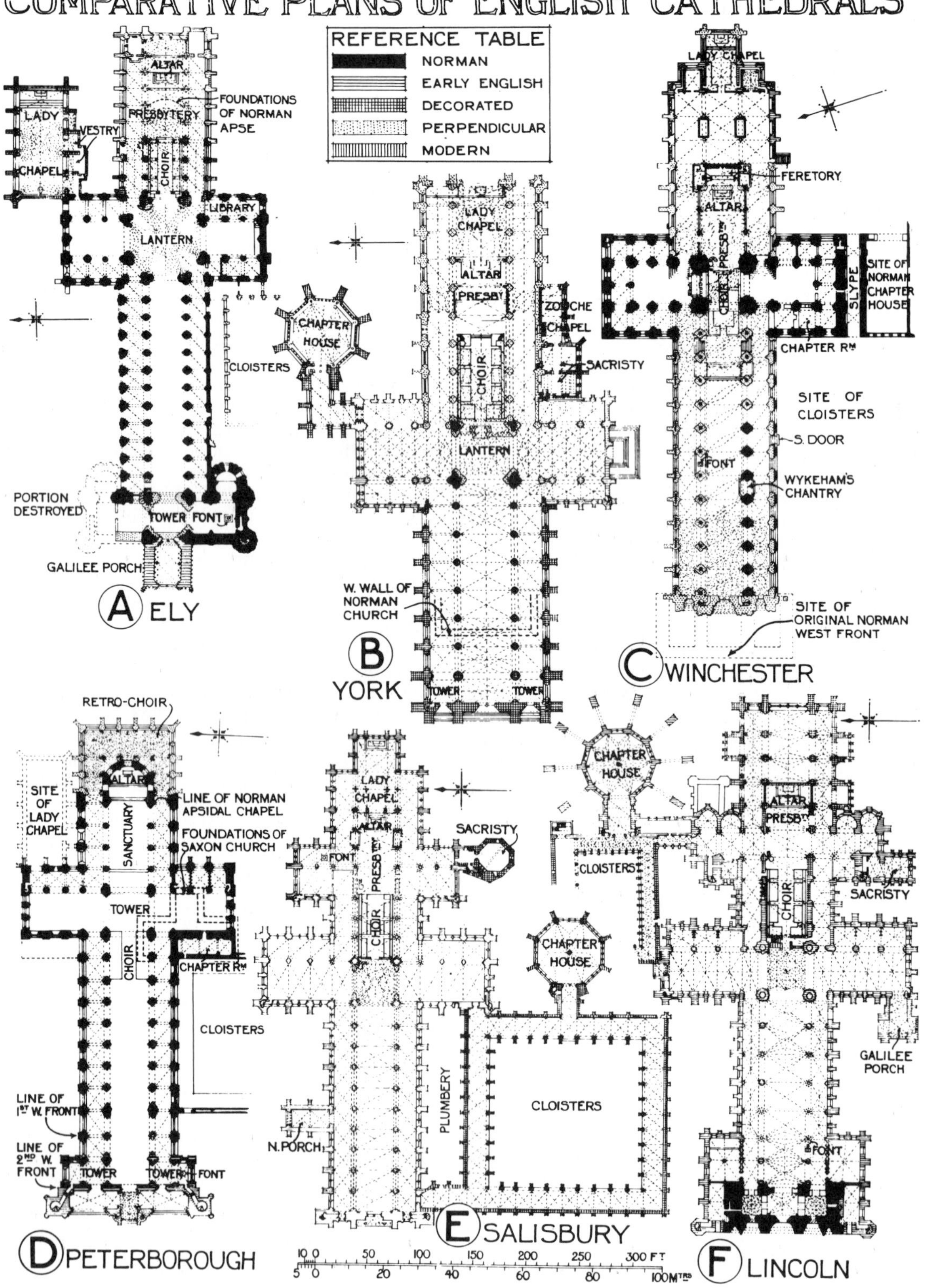
COMPARATIVE PLANS OF ENGLISH CATHEDRALS
REFERENCE TABLE
NORMAN
EARLY ENGLISH
DECORATED
PERPENDICULAR
MODERN
ALTAR
FOUNDATIONS OF NORMAN APSE
LADY CHAPEL
VESTRY
PRESBYTERY
CHOIR
LIBRARY
LANTERN
CLOISTERS
PORTION DESTROYED
TOWER
FONT
GALILEE PORCH
A ELY
LADY CHAPEL
ALTAR
PRESBY
ZOUCHE CHAPEL
CHAPTER HOUSE
CHOIR
SACRISTY
LANTERN
W. WALL OF NORMAN CHURCH
TOWER
TOWER
B YORK
LADY CHAPEL
FERETORY
ALTAR
PRESBY
CHOIR
SLYPE
SITE OF NORMAN CHAPTER HOUSE
CHAPTER RM
SITE OF CLOISTERS
S. DOOR
FONT
WYKEHAM'S CHANTRY
SITE OF ORIGINAL NORMAN WEST FRONT
C WINCHESTER
RETRO-CHOIR
ALTAR
SITE OF LADY CHAPEL
LINE OF NORMAN APSIDAL CHAPEL
SANCTUARY
FOUNDATIONS OF SAXON CHURCH
TOWER
CHOIR
CHAPTER RM
CLOISTERS
LINE OF 1ST W. FRONT
LINE OF 2ND W. FRONT
TOWER
TOWER
FONT
D PETERBOROUGH
LADY CHAPEL
ALTAR
FONT
PRESBY
SACRISTY
CHOIR
CHAPTER HOUSE
PLUMBERY
CLOISTERS
N. PORCH
E SALISBURY
CHAPTER HOUSE
CLOISTERS
ALTAR
PRESBY
CHOIR
SACRISTY
GALILEE PORCH
FONT
F LINCOLN
10 0 50 100 150 200 250 300 FT
5 0 20 40 60 80 100 MTRS

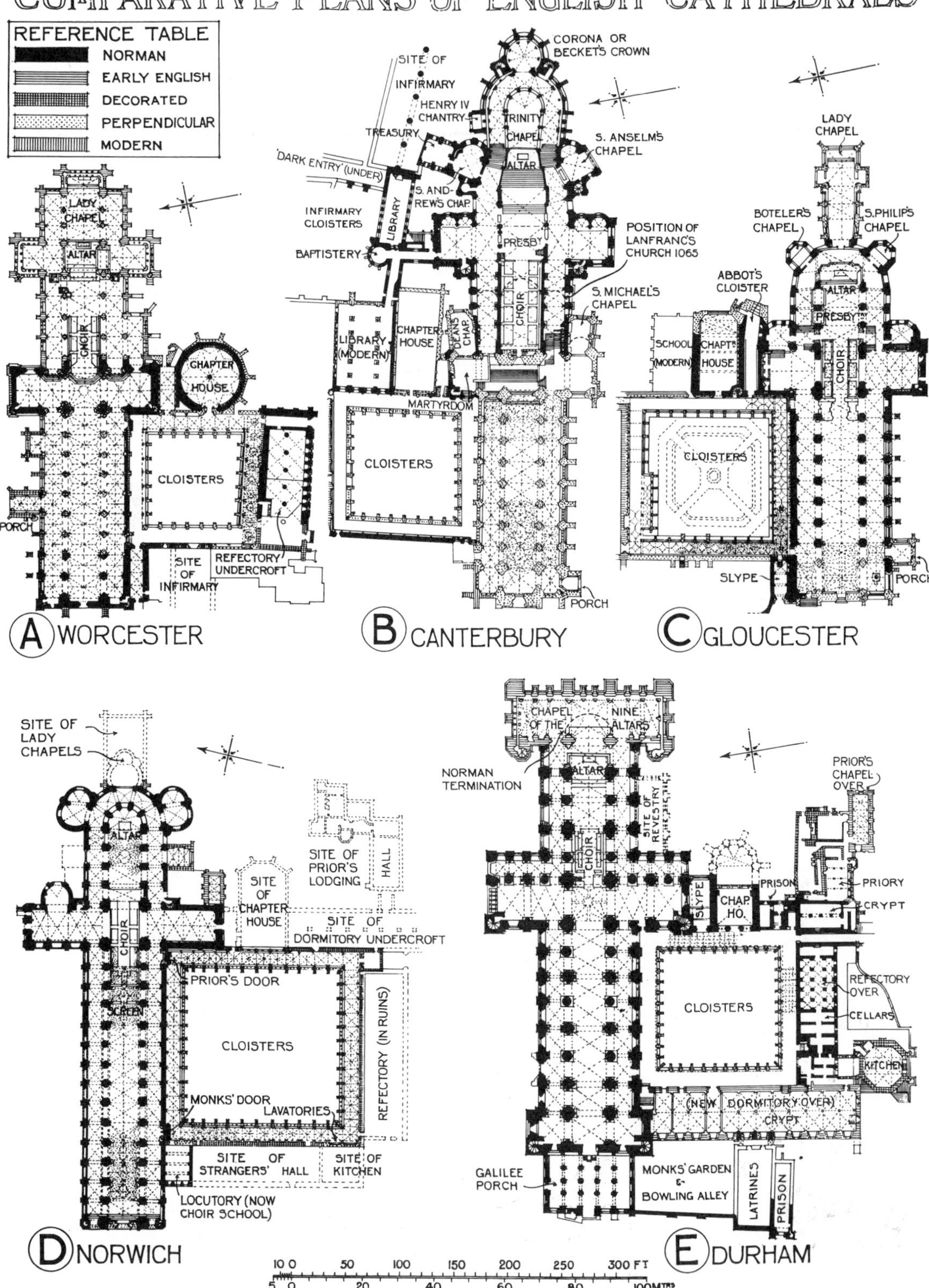
COMPARATIVE PLANS OF ENGLISH CATHEDRALS
REFERENCE TABLE
NORMAN
EARLY ENGLISH
DECORATED
PERPENDICULAR
MODERN
LADY CHAPEL
ALTAR
CHOIR
CHAPTER HOUSE
CLOISTERS
PORCH
SITE OF INFIRMARY
REFECTORY UNDERCROFT
A WORCESTER
CORONA OR BECKET'S CROWN
SITE OF INFIRMARY
HENRY IV CHANTRY
TRINITY CHAPEL
TREASURY
S. ANSELM'S CHAPEL
'DARK ENTRY' (UNDER)
ALTAR
S. ANDREWS CHAP.
INFIRMARY CLOISTERS
LIBRARY
PRESBY
POSITION OF LANFRANC'S CHURCH 1065
BAPTISTERY
S. MICHAEL'S CHAPEL
LIBRARY (MODERN)
CHAPTER HOUSE
DEANS CHAP.
CHOIR
MARTYRDOM
CLOISTERS
PORCH
B CANTERBURY
LADY CHAPEL
BOTELER'S CHAPEL
S. PHILIP'S CHAPEL
ABBOT'S CLOISTER
ALTAR
PRESBY
SCHOOL (MODERN)
CHAPT'R HOUSE
CHOIR
CLOISTERS
SLYPE
PORCH
C GLOUCESTER
SITE OF LADY CHAPELS
ALTAR
SITE OF PRIOR'S LODGING
HALL
SITE OF CHAPTER HOUSE
SITE OF DORMITORY UNDERCROFT
CHOIR
PRIOR'S DOOR
SCREEN
CLOISTERS
REFECTORY (IN RUINS)
MONKS' DOOR
LAVATORIES
SITE OF STRANGERS' HALL
SITE OF KITCHEN
LOCUTORY (NOW CHOIR SCHOOL)
D NORWICH
CHAPEL OF THE NINE ALTARS
NORMAN TERMINATION
ALTAR
SITE OF REVESTRY
PRIOR'S CHAPEL OVER
CHOIR
SLYPE
CHAP. HO.
PRISON
PRIORY
CRYPT
CLOISTERS
REFECTORY OVER
CELLARS
KITCHEN
(NEW DORMITORY OVER) CRYPT
GALILEE PORCH
MONKS' GARDEN & BOWLING ALLEY
LATRINES
PRISON
E DURHAM
10 0 50 100 150 200 250 300 FT
5 0 20 40 60 80 100 MTRS

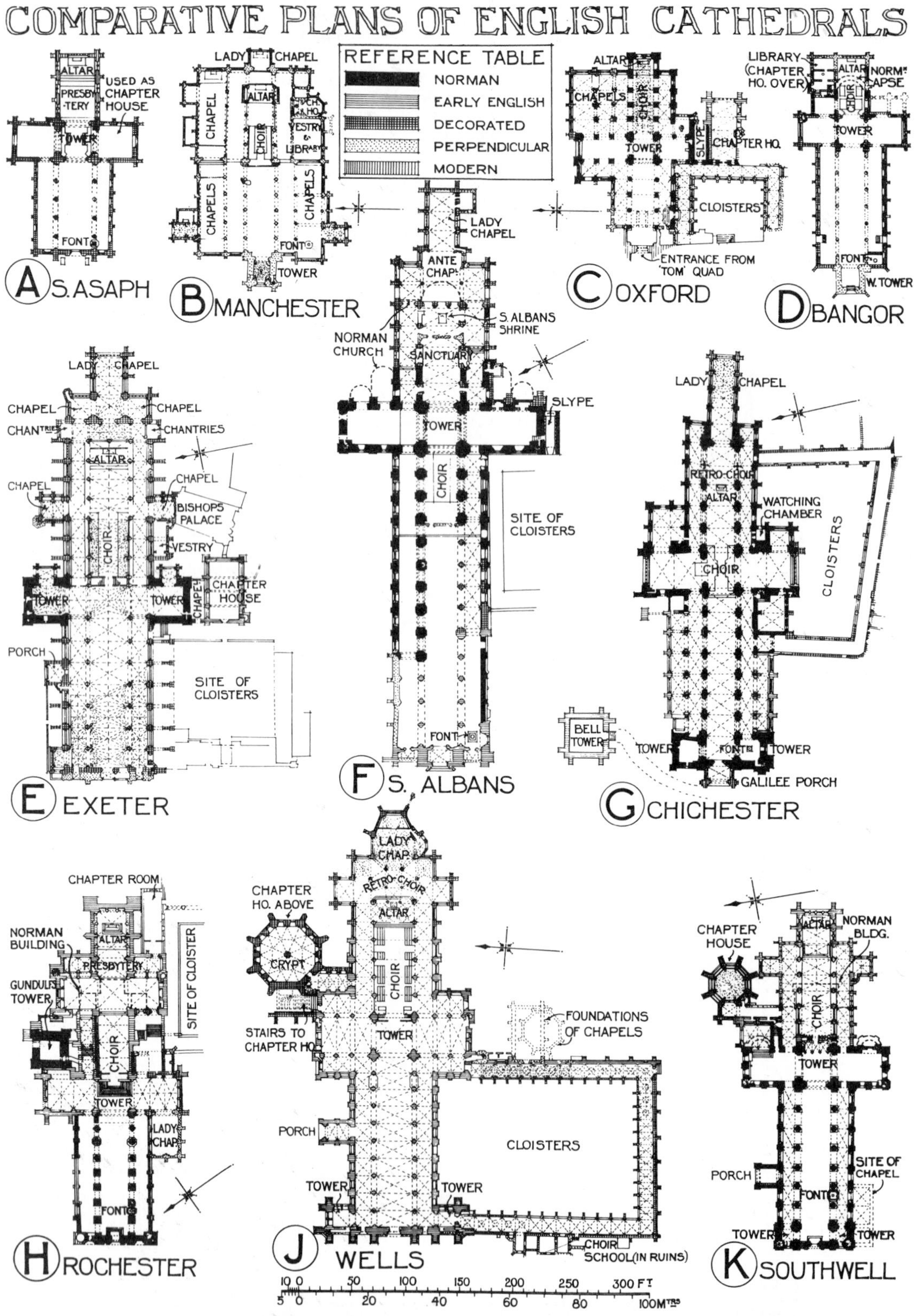

COMPARATIVE PLANS OF ENGLISH CATHEDRALS

REFERENCE TABLE
NORMAN
EARLY ENGLISH
DECORATED
PERPENDICULAR
MODERN

(A) S. ASAPH — ALTAR; PRESBYTERY USED AS CHAPTER HOUSE; TOWER; FONT

(B) MANCHESTER — LADY CHAPEL; CHAPEL; ALTAR; CHOIR; CH. HO.; VESTRY & LIBRARY; CHAPELS; FONT; TOWER

(C) OXFORD — ALTAR; CHAPELS; CHOIR; TOWER; SLYPE; CHAPTER HO.; CLOISTERS; ENTRANCE FROM 'TOM' QUAD

(D) BANGOR — LIBRARY (CHAPTER HO. OVER); ALTAR; NORMN APSE; CHOIR; TOWER; FONT; W. TOWER

(E) EXETER — LADY CHAPEL; CHAPEL; CHAPEL; CHANTRIES; CHANTRIES; ALTAR; CHAPEL; CHAPEL; BISHOPS PALACE; CHOIR; VESTRY; TOWER; TOWER; CHAPEL; CHAPTER HOUSE; PORCH; SITE OF CLOISTERS

(F) S. ALBANS — LADY CHAPEL; ANTE CHAP.; S. ALBANS SHRINE; NORMAN CHURCH; SANCTUARY; SLYPE; TOWER; CHOIR; SITE OF CLOISTERS; FONT

(G) CHICHESTER — LADY CHAPEL; RETRO-CHOIR; ALTAR; WATCHING CHAMBER; CLOISTERS; CHOIR; BELL TOWER; TOWER; FONT; TOWER; GALILEE PORCH

(H) ROCHESTER — CHAPTER ROOM; NORMAN BUILDING; ALTAR; PRESBYTERY; GUNDULFS TOWER; SITE OF CLOISTER; CHOIR; TOWER; LADY CHAP.; FONT

(J) WELLS — LADY CHAP.; RETRO-CHOIR; ALTAR; CHAPTER HO. ABOVE; CRYPT; CHOIR; STAIRS TO CHAPTER HO.; TOWER; FOUNDATIONS OF CHAPELS; PORCH; CLOISTERS; TOWER; TOWER; CHOIR SCHOOL (IN RUINS)

(K) SOUTHWELL — ALTAR; NORMAN BLDG.; CHAPTER HOUSE; CHOIR; TOWER; PORCH; SITE OF CHAPEL; FONT; TOWER; TOWER

10 0 50 100 150 200 250 300 FT
5 0 20 40 60 80 100 MTRS

COMPARATIVE PLANS OF ENGLISH CATHEDRALS

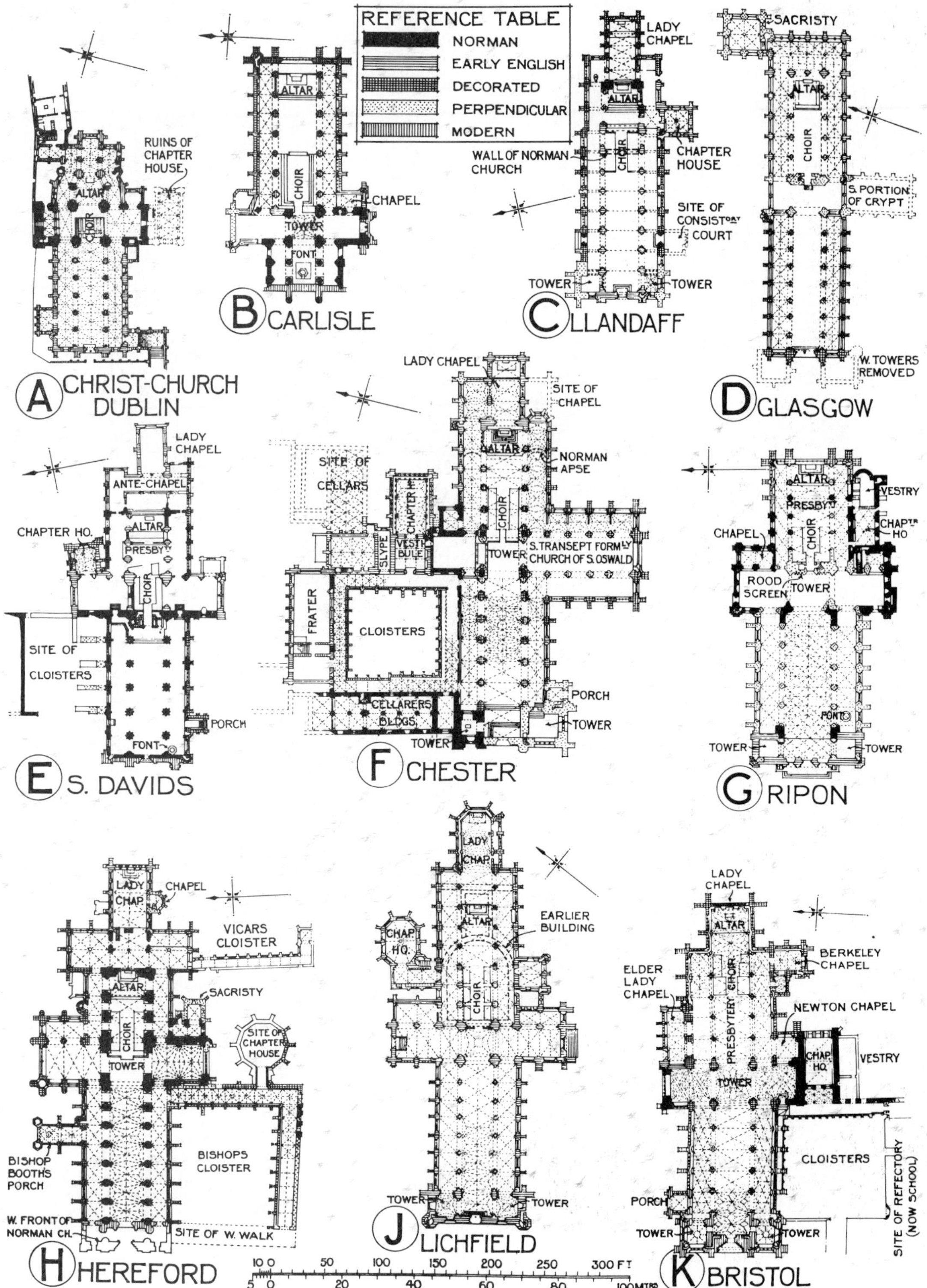

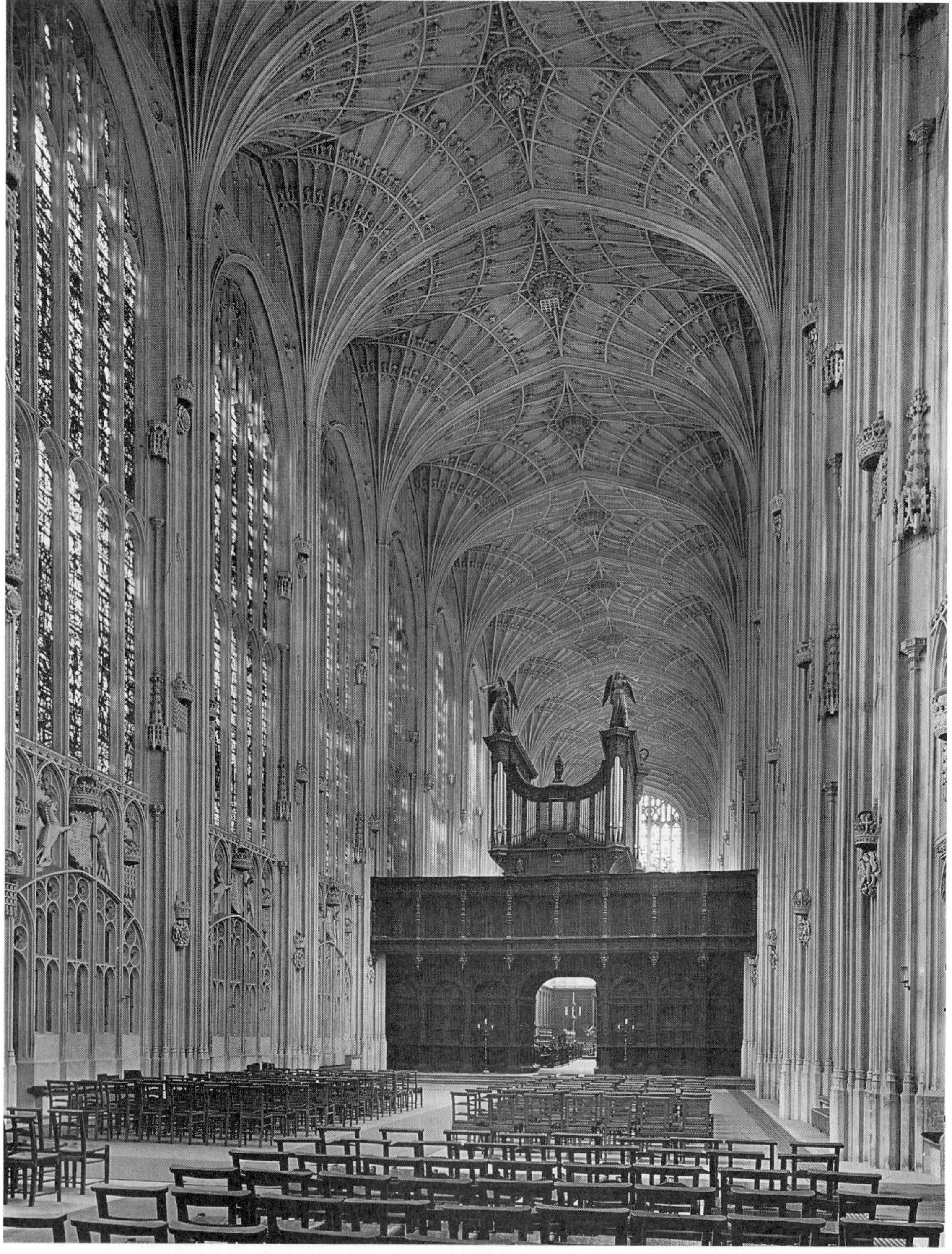

King's College Chapel, Cambridge (1446–1515): nave. See p.461

Chester, A (p. 465F). Choir begun before 1283, completed by 1315, probably by Richard Lenginour. French influence apparent in the elevation, perhaps through the Savoyards and Gascons employed by the King to construct the castle.

Chichester, C (p. 464G). Choir (*c.* 1091) probably complete when consecrated in 1108. Nave completed by *c.* 1140. Norman apse squared off after fire in 1187: chapel added in style derived from newly completed Canterbury. Earliest example of this type of retro-choir which was further developed at Winchester, Salisbury, Exeter and Wells (q.v.).

Durham, AC (pp. 400, 463E). Choir 1093–1104; transepts *c.* 1100–10; nave *c.* 1110–28, vaulted 1128–33. Rib-vaulted throughout. Originally only choir was to be vaulted. Present choir vaults thirteenth century; original vaults were first in Europe to be built over the main volume of a church. Very influential in Normandy and northern France where the system formed a central feature of the newly developing Gothic style. Vaulting enjoyed little immediate success in England but native masons rapidly adopted the new decorative forms pioneered at Durham (for example, chevron-decorated piers, moulded arches). Galilee chapel at west end (*c.* 1175) built in highly ornate local transitional style. Chapel of Nine Altars, an eastern transept (*c.* 1242–90). Plan derived from Fountains Abbey.

Ely, A (pp. 416E,F, 417J,K, 462A, 468B, 470B). Norman church (begun 1080s) by Simeon, brother of Bishop Wakelin of Winchester. Transepts *c.* 1080–1110. Nave *c.* 1100–50. Elevation of three equally tall storeys derived from slightly earlier work at Winchester. Ely influential on Norwich and Peterborough, and is central to a definite East Anglian Romanesque style. Western transept completed *c.* 1170–1230; choir extended eastwards *c.* 1235–52 by adding a square-ended presbytery which is an ornate derivative of the nave at Lincoln, from where the tierceron vaults were also adopted. Lady Chapel begun 1321, unfinished in 1349, vault possibly fifteenth century. Interior perhaps most elaborate example of the fantastic in the work of some architects of the Decorated period. Central tower collapsed 1322 and replaced by an octagonal timber lantern.

Exeter, C (pp. 464E, 470C). The only substantial remains of the Norman cathedral are the towers over the transepts, dating from the first half of the twelfth century. Reconstruction in Decorated mode began at east end *c.* 1270. Choir and transepts complete by 1311. East bays of choir begun with two-storey elevation, the deep upper storey containing a passage on a formula comparable to Tintern and Netley. Later a false triforium was inserted to harmonise with the rest of the interior. Elaborate choir furnishings built *c.* 1311–25. Nave (*c.* 1328–48) continues choir design. West front *c.* 1340–70.

Glastonbury, A. On 25 May 1184 fire destroyed earlier church. Lady Chapel completed in 1186: structurally and decoratively less advanced than Wells but important example of local western style in its detailing. Church begun after fire. Remains of east wall of south transept (late twelfth or early thirteenth century), important work using west country vocabulary. Rare example of internal elevation constructed around a giant order.

Gloucester, A (pp. 463C, 469A, 470D). Choir (1089–1100) may have had four-storey elevation and a stone vault. Lower two storeys retained when choir reworked in fourteenth century. Nave *c.* 1100–50. Tribune eliminated to create a giant main arcade when nave constructed (*c.* 1100–50). Vault *c.* 1245. In south transept (*c.* 1331–7) existing Norman structure was recased in an elaborate net of tracery; similarly choir in *c.* 1337–77. Earliest surviving work in the Perpendicular style. North transept 1368–74. Four walks of cloister (1351–1412) continue Perpendicular experiments and contain early fan vaults.

Hereford, C (p. 465H). Choir dates from last quarter of eleventh century. East transept added (1186–99) in a style related to the latest west country developments. North transept (*c.* 1250–70) was first example of new French ideas spreading into the provinces by way of Westminster. Destroyed chapter house (*c.* 1350–70) may have had first large-scale fan vaults.

Lichfield, C (p. 465J). Built from east to west (after *c.* 1195). Nave (second half of thirteenth century) related to north transept at Hereford. Presbytery rebuilt (*c.* 1337–49) perhaps by William Ramsey, pioneering architect of early Perpendicular period.

Lincoln, C (pp. 462F, 469B). Norman building begun *c.* 1073: lower parts of west front are the only remains of this building. Three portals and frieze (1140s) by sculptors familiar with S. Denis, Paris. Reconstructed after earthquake (1185). S. Hugh's choir, east transept and original polygonal apse completed by *c.* 1200, west transept *c.* 1200–20, nave *c.* 1120–40. Many themes and motifs from Canterbury (for example piers, Purbeck marble, the elevation, vault types and double transepts) are adapted and enriched. Experiments in vaulting led to the perfected tierceron vault of the nave. As first truly English Gothic building it became an important source for subsequent building at Worcester, Ely, York, Beverley and elsewhere. Angel Choir (1256-*c.* 1280) designed as a shrine for S. Hugh of Lincoln. Elevation is greatly enriched, particularly by the use of tracery, the latest French import received here from Westminster.

Llandaff, C (p. 465C). Begun 1120. Elaborate arch into Norman choir survives between the present choir and Lady Chapel. Reconstruction (*c.* 1190) in style indicating close contacts with Wells.

Norwich, AC (pp. 463D, 471A). Norman cathedral begun 1096. Choir, transept and east bays of nave complete by 1119, west bays of nave *c.* 1120–50. Internal elevation follows the model of Ely in having three nearly equally tall storeys and in its detailing.

A. Canterbury Cathedral from SW. See p.461

B. Ely Cathedral: aerial view from SW. See p.467

A. Gloucester Cathedral from SE. See p.467

B. Lincoln Cathedral (eleventh to thirteenth centuries). See p.467

A. Bristol Cathedral: choir (1298–1332), looking east. See p.461

B. Ely Cathedral: Bishop West's Chantry (1533). See p.467

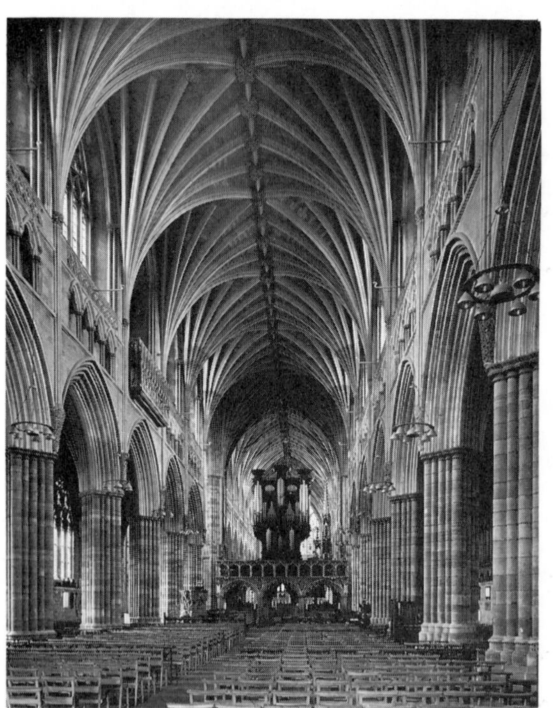

C. Exeter Cathedral: nave looking east (*c.* 1328–48). See p.467

D. Gloucester Cathedral: Lady Chapel looking west. See p.467

A. Norwich Cathedral: presbytery and apse (eleventh to fourteenth centuries). See p.467

B. Oxford Cathedral (Christ Church): interior looking east (*c.* 1160–80). See p.472

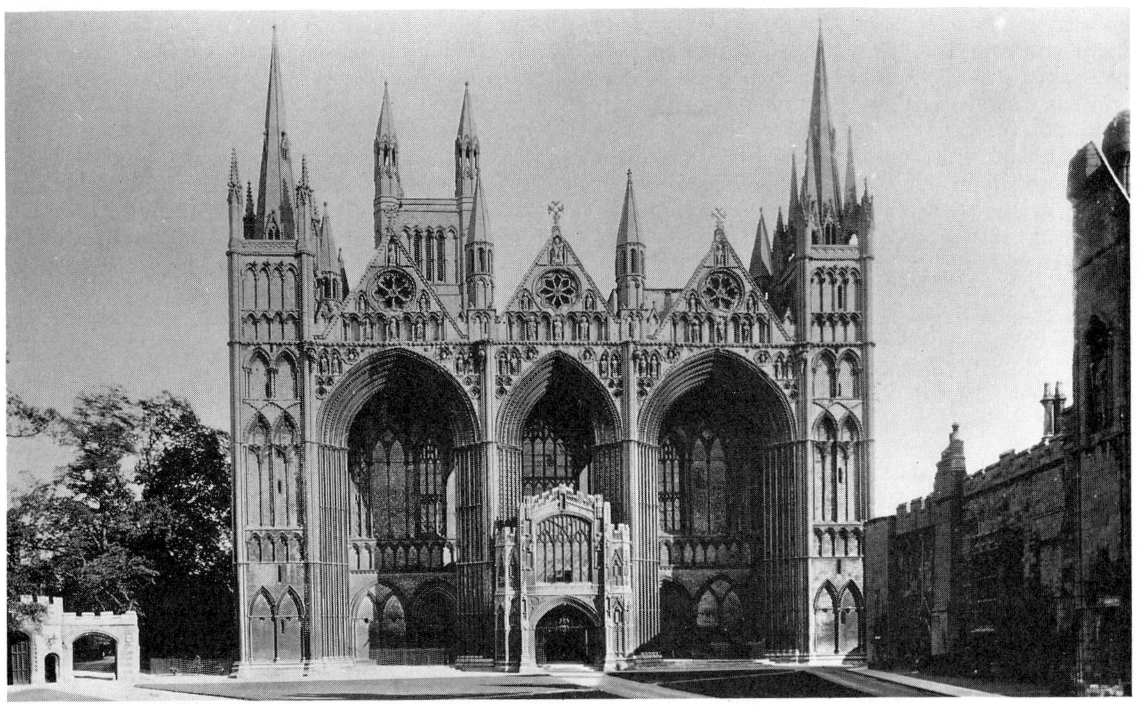

C. Peterborough Cathedral: west facade (late twelfth and early thirteenth centuries). See p.472

Ramsey family responsible for east and south walks of cloister (1299–1325) and for the Carnary Chapel (1310–25). William Ramsey later worked at Old S. Paul's and perhaps Lichfield and Gloucester.

Oxford, P (pp. 464C, 471B). Choir begun *c.* 1150–60, consecrated 1180. Work on the nave continued into the thirteenth century. Main arcade and reduced triforium united beneath a giant arch with a clerestory above. Similar arrangements at Glastonbury, Dunstable, Romsey and Jedburgh.

Peterborough, A (pp. 416A,B, 462D, 471C). Begun 1117. Choir, transept and six east bays of nave complete by *c.* 1175. Interior completed *c.* 1195. Up to end of twelfth century internal elevation is a developed version of the one invented at Ely in 1080s. West front, late twelfth and early thirteenth century. Giant arches derived from Norman facade at Lincoln. East chapels begun mid-fifteenth century and completed first quarter of sixteenth by John Wastell.

Ripon, CC (pp. 416C,D, 465G, 474A). Vestiges of nave built while Roger of Pont L'Evêque was Archbishop of York (1154–81): probably related to his choir at York. West front, second quarter of thirteenth century. Choir begun *c.* 1286–8, completed *c.* 1330. Tracery betrays close contacts with York.

Rochester, AC (p. 464H). Nave built in second and third quarters of twelfth century. Unusual floorless arrangement in tribune gallery. West front *c.* 1165–75. Sculpture relates to contemporary Kentish and northern French work. Choir reworked and north transept rebuilt *c.* 1179–1200. East transept and presbytery *c.* 1217–27. Early adoption of double-transept plan of Canterbury. North transept refaced *c.* 1240–50.

S. Albans, A (p. 464F). Begun 1077, may have been complete by 1115. Bold, unarticulated interior largely due to extensive reuse of bricks from nearby Roman city of Verulamium. West front and west bays of nave begun *c.* 1195, completed *c.* 1235. Eastern extension to choir (*c.* 1260–1326) relates to contemporary work at Westminster and Old S. Paul's.

S. David's, C (p. 465E). Begun *c.* 1180 at west end of nave: church completed by mid-thirteenth century. Nave design relates to Wells and Worcester in general form and detail. Elaborate ceiling over nave built 1472–0009.

Salisbury, C (pp. 440A, 462E, 473). Begun 1220, completed by 1266. Rare example of an English Gothic church built entirely to one basic design. Internal storeys clearly separated into strong horizontal bands: extensive use of Purbeck marble to create a strongly coloured scheme. Chapter house and cloister 1263–84, the former closely modelled on the slightly earlier one at Westminster.

Selby, A (p. 477A). Choir built *c.* 1280–1350. Early examples of curvilinear tracery culminating in elaborate east window. Important centre of Decorated architecture.

Southwark (S. Saviour, or S. Mary Overie), A (p. 207C). Choir 1213–38. Proportions may reflect elevation of Norman church, while details suggest some awareness of contemporary French developments. Transepts, late thirteenth century: nave rebuilt in nineteenth century.

Southwell, CC (p. 464K). Nave, transept and three towers of twelfth century. Nave elevation of three unlinked storeys in a composition suggesting Roman aqueducts. Choir *c.* 1230–40. Polygonal chapter house without central column (1290s) may have been the model for York. It retains its rich display of naturalistic carving.

Wells, C (pp. 464J, 476A,C). Begun *c.* 1175–80. Choir and east side of transept complete by *c.* 1190. Rest of transept and eastern half of nave *c.* 1190–1206. West bays of nave and west front *c.* 1215–39. Although roughly contemporary with Canterbury, Wells reveals little awareness of the new French ideas arriving in Kent. Mostly derivative of earlier local forms but creates a rich, plastic interior without parallel. The west front is a screen which is wider than the nave and elaborately covered with sculpture. It is the prototype for later screen facades, none of which rival it in scale or complexity. Chapter house *c.* 1300–20. Pattern and details suggest that a mason from Exeter was responsible. Extension of choir began *c.* 1310. Three-bay early Gothic choir was opened eastwards and reworked to harmonise with the extension. Elongated octagonal Lady Chapel with elaborate net vault *c.* 1310–19. The master was conversant with contemporary work at Exeter and may have been Thomas of Witney himself. Choir *c.* 1330–40: scissors arches in crossing built in 1338. Other examples of this buttressing technique at Salisbury and originally perhaps at Glastonbury.

Westminster, A (pp. 474B,C, 475). Norman abbey church (*c.* 1045–65), probably the earliest example of Norman influence in English building, even predating 1066 as Edward the Confessor was surrounded by Norman advisers. Excavations suggest a design based on Jumièges. Henry III laid foundation stone of new Lady Chapel in 1220, took over responsibility for funding of church building in 1245: choir, transepts, chapter-house and east bays of nave were completed by 1269 by three master masons, Henry de Reyns (1245–53), John of Gloucester (1253–61) and Robert of Beverley (1261–84). Henry III aimed to create a shrine for the Royal Saint, Edward the Confessor. The architect appointed, Henry de Reyns, was English, not from Reims, although he was certainly well versed in French developments of the previous three decades. The workshops at Amiens, Reims and Soissons, in addition to Paris (Notre Dame, S. Chapelle, S. Denis), were the origin of much of the detailing as well as the plan and the tall, relatively narrow interior. Some details (for example the two-skin triforium, the extensive use of Purbeck marble) show the designer's English origins. Henry VII's

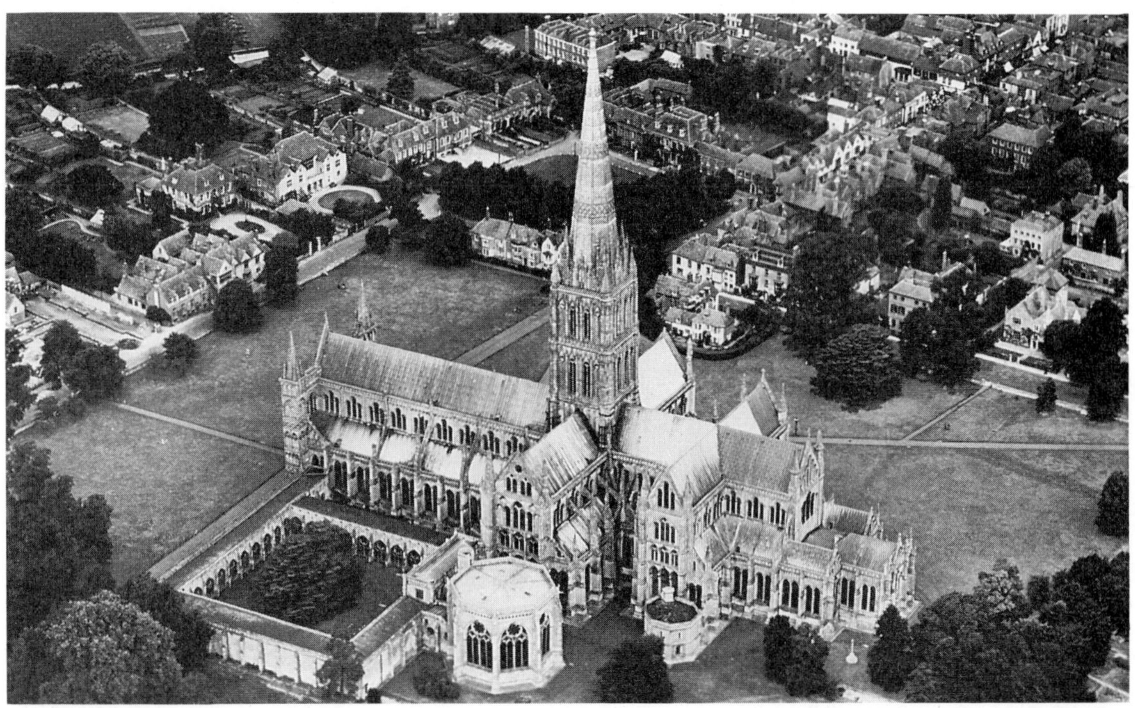

A. Salisbury Cathedral (1220–66): aerial view from SE. See p.472

B. Salisbury Cathedral: nave looking east

C. Salisbury Cathedral: chapter house (1263–84)

A. Ripon Minster: west facade (*c.* 1233). See p.472

B. Westminster Abbey: nave looking east

C. Westminster Abbey from SE: Henry VII's Chapel (1503–19) on right. See p.472

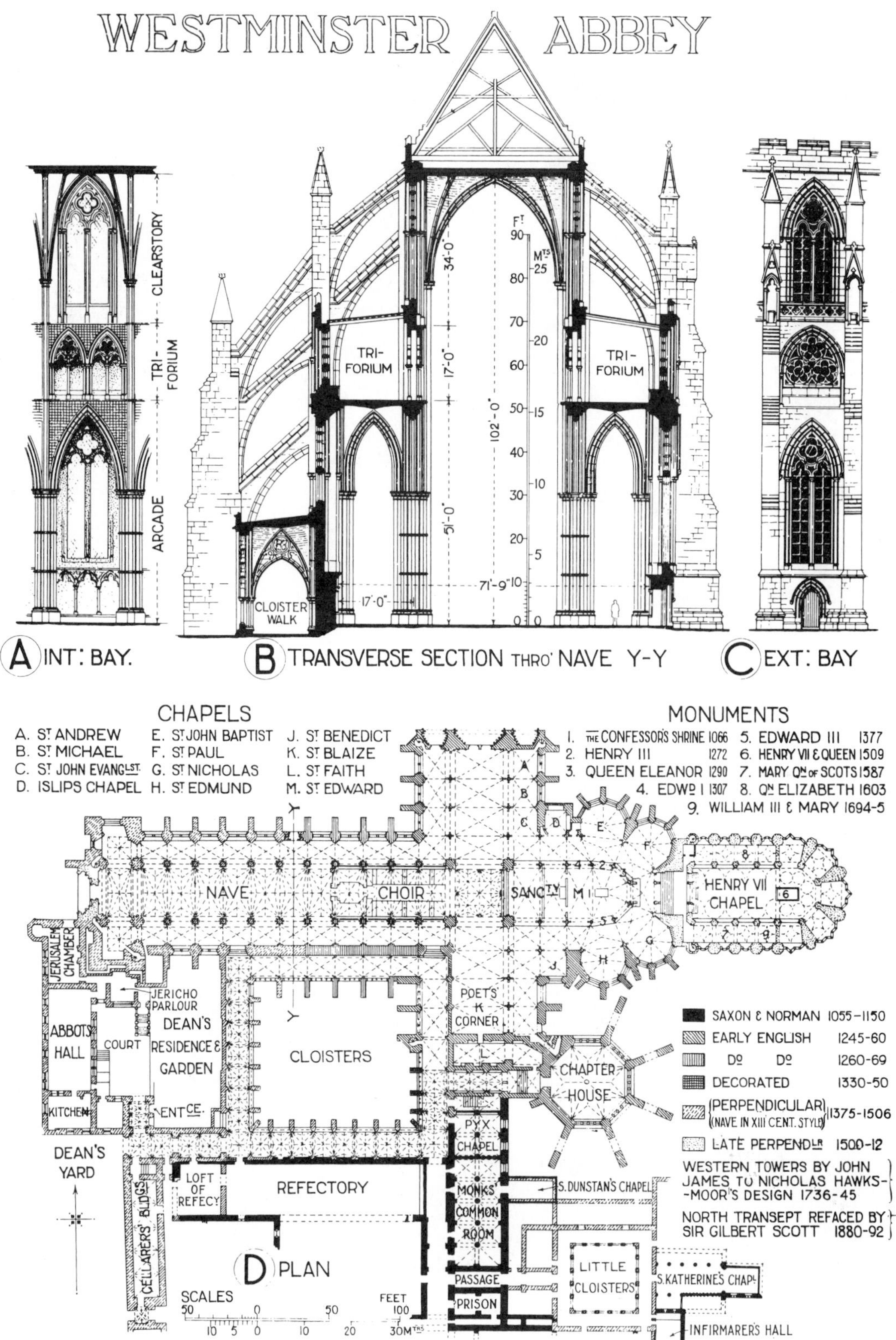
WESTMINSTER ABBEY
CLEARSTORY
TRI-FORIUM
ARCADE
TRI-FORIUM
CLOISTER WALK
A INT: BAY.
B TRANSVERSE SECTION THRO' NAVE Y-Y
C EXT: BAY
CHAPELS
A. St ANDREW
B. St MICHAEL
C. St JOHN EVANGLST.
D. ISLIPS CHAPEL
E. St JOHN BAPTIST
F. St PAUL
G. St NICHOLAS
H. St EDMUND
J. St BENEDICT
K. St BLAIZE
L. St FAITH
M. St EDWARD
MONUMENTS
1. THE CONFESSOR'S SHRINE 1066
2. HENRY III 1272
3. QUEEN ELEANOR 1290
4. EDWD I 1307
5. EDWARD III 1377
6. HENRY VII & QUEEN 1509
7. MARY QN OF SCOTS 1587
8. QN ELIZABETH 1603
9. WILLIAM III & MARY 1694-5
NAVE
CHOIR
SANCTY
HENRY VII CHAPEL
JERUSALEM CHAMBER
JERICHO PARLOUR
ABBOTS HALL
COURT
DEAN'S RESIDENCE & GARDEN
KITCHEN
ENTCE.
CLOISTERS
POETS' CORNER
CHAPTER HOUSE
PYX CHAPEL
DEAN'S YARD
LOFT OF REFECY
REFECTORY
MONKS' COMMON ROOM
S. DUNSTAN'S CHAPEL
CELLARERS' BLDGS
LITTLE CLOISTERS
S. KATHERINE'S CHAPL.
PASSAGE
PRISON
INFIRMARERS HALL
D PLAN
SCALES
FEET
SAXON & NORMAN 1055-1150
EARLY ENGLISH 1245-60
Do Do 1260-69
DECORATED 1330-50
(PERPENDICULAR) (NAVE IN XIII CENT. STYLE) 1375-1506
LATE PERPENDLR 1500-12
WESTERN TOWERS BY JOHN JAMES TO NICHOLAS HAWKSMOOR'S DESIGN 1736-45
NORTH TRANSEPT REFACED BY SIR GILBERT SCOTT 1880-92

A. Wells Cathedral: nave looking east with fourteenth-century strainer arches under central tower. See p.472

B. Winchester Cathedral. See p.478

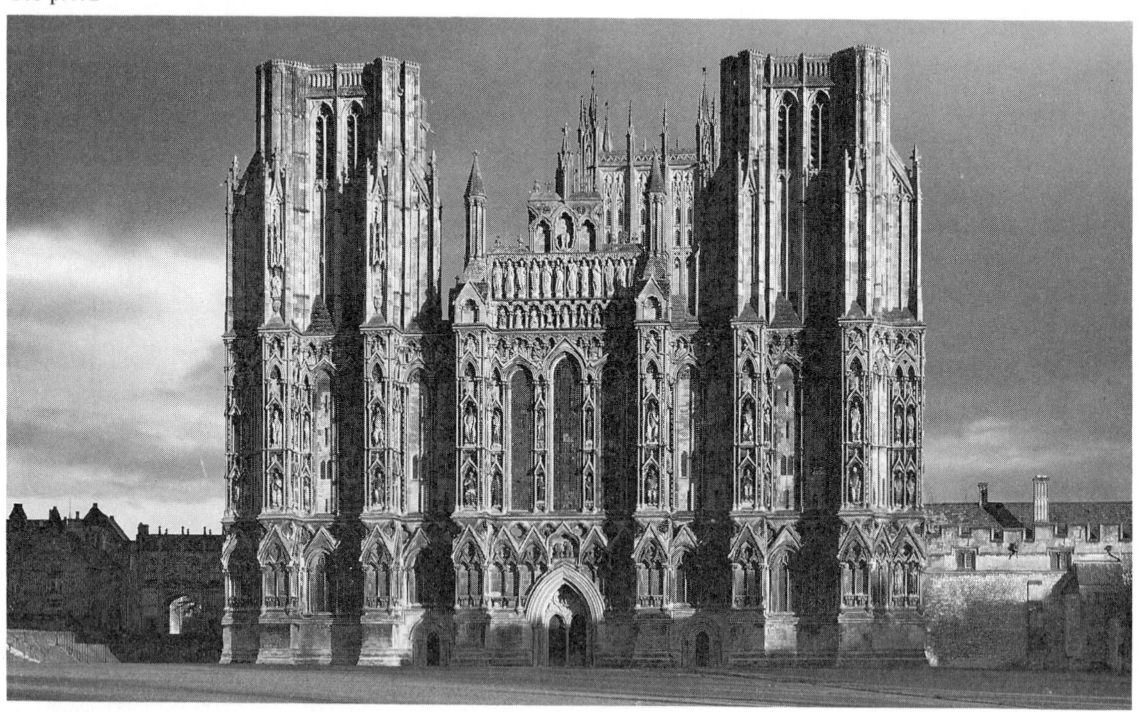

C. Wells Cathedral; west facade (*c.* 1215–39)

A. Selby Abbey: choir from NE (1280–1350). See p.472

B. York Minster (twelfth to fifteenth centuries) from south. See p.478

Chapel 1503–19, the richest Perpendicular interior. Decorative devices cover every surface, inside and out, of this chapel built for the King's private use.

In the adjoining Palace of Westminster two major mediaeval buildings were preserved in the nineteenth-century reconstruction. Westminster Hall (1394–1400) (p. 479A) has the most impressive surviving example of a hammer-beam roof, devised by the King's carpenter Hugh Hurland. The other survivor is the undercroft of S. Stephen's Chapel (1292–7). The upper chapel (1292–1348), destroyed, seems to have transmitted in England those French ideas which led to the formation of the Perpendicular style.

Winchester, AC (pp. 417L,M, 462C, 476B). Begun 1079, consecrated in 1093 by which time crypt and choir may have been complete. Transepts nearing completion when crossing-tower collapsed in 1107. Nave built in twelfth century – fragments still visible near east end of nave. It is the surviving English building closest in design to its Norman predecessors and even has Anglo-Norman architecture (for example Ely, Old S. Paul's). Retro-choir (*c.* 1200–30), built as a shrine for relics of S. Swithin, subtly echoes the eastern extension at Canterbury in purpose and plan. It is one of the earliest examples of a mature English Gothic style. Most of the work on present nave 1394– *c.* 1410: Norman structure retained, cut back and covered with a skin of Perpendicular panelling, thus explaining the mass and plasticity of the nave.

Windsor, S. George's Chapel, CC (p. 209). Begun 1474, built east to west, completed by mid-sixteenth century, to honour S. George and the Yorkist dynasty. In this, the most completely Perpendicular interior since Gloucester choir, the proportions of individual panels echo the form of the whole elevation, taking the notion of total effect to a logical conclusion. The architect employs a vault that is neither a true lierne nor a genuine fan vault.

Worcester, AC (p. 463A). Begun 1084, crypt and choir perhaps complete by 1092. Apsidal east end derived from Winchester. Arches between choir aisles and west transept survive. Circular chapter house *c.* 1130–50, earliest example of centrally planned chapter house which was to become standard form in England. West bays of nave *c.* 1165–75 as completion of, or extension to, Norman nave. Central tower collapsed in 1175 necessitating the reconstruction and redecoration of the west transepts. Earliest Gothic work in western England, revealing contacts with northern French building in addition to perpetuating characteristics earlier found in the chapter house. Retro-choir built after 1202 fire, dedicated 1218–*c.* 1240. The influence of Lincoln is clear.

York, C (pp. 462B, 477B). Crypt (1154–81) is the sole visible remains of the choir built by Roger of Pont L'Evêque. It was probably the central work of the later twelfth century in northern England. Main transept *c.* 1220–50, of which low clerestory and tall triforium probably reflect the disposition of the twelfth-century choir. Vault intended but never constructed. Chapter house *c.* 1280–1307. Signs of contacts between York and the latest developments in Paris and London became apparent in the nave, begun in 1291. Unique stained glass: west window glazed in 1338. East end extended from 1361 onwards. Presbytery complete by *c.* 1375. Choir *c.* 1380–1400. East window glazed 1405–8. Last great eastern extension to an English cathedral: general disposition of nave elevation was adopted but given updated detailing.

Other important churches include the following.

Abbey Dore, Herefordshire, A. Cistercian. Founded 26 April 1147. Transept (*c.* 1175) shows evidence of contact with contemporary northern French Cistercian architecture. Choir (*c.* 1200) is similar in places to Morimond, the French house from which Abbey Dore was founded.

Boxgrove, Sussex, P. The choir (*c.* 1220–30) is a rare example of double main arcades in each bay. Some details relate to contemporary work in Normandy.

Bristol, S. Mary Redcliffe, Avon, PC (p. 479B). Hexagonal porch at north-west corner of nave (*c.* 1325). Elaborately foliated, ogee-arched portal and highly ornate interior of porch demonstrate the strong fantastic element apparent in some Decorated work. Most of church dates from the fifteenth century and has tall, thin Perpendicular interior covered with net vaults, a local type of vault.

Byland, Yorkshire, A (p. 422H). Cistercian. Founded 1134, monks moved to present site in 1177 by which time part of church was complete. More developed three-storey internal elevation than Roche, built in style close to local contemporary work. Vaulting of main volume was rejected in favour of a lighter structure.

Great Malvern, Worcestershire, P. Norman church begun *c.* 1084. Nave with later clerestory survives. Partial reconstruction *c.* 1450–80, derivative of Gloucester.

Hexham, Northumberland, A. Augustinian. Choir *c.* 1180–1210. Transepts *c.* 1215–30. A central work of a group of churches in northern England and Scotland which are the first fully developed Gothic buildings in this area. Others are at Jedburgh, Arbroath and Brinkburn.

Howden, Yorkshire, CC. Late thirteenth-century nave shows impact of continental Mendicant church design deep in England in the use of tall, widely spaced main arcades with short upper storey. Two-arch clerestory with passage is an English feature. Chapter house (*c.* 1380–1400) is highly ornate example of local Perpendicular style.

London, S. Etheldreda's Holborn. Built probably in 1280s. Interior design reminiscent of exterior of

A. Westminster Hall (1399). See p.478

B. S. Mary Redcliffe, Bristol: nave looking east. See p.478

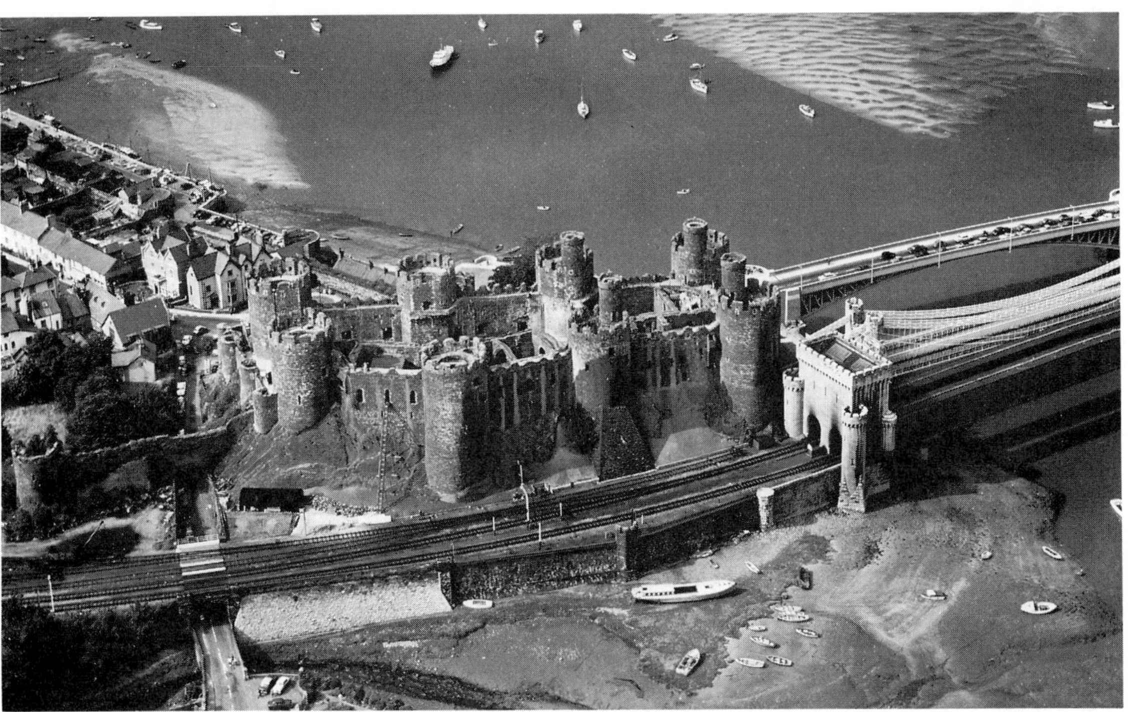

C. Conway Castle, Caernarvonshire (1283–9). See p.483

choir chapels at Notre Dame de Paris. Tracery patterns adopt the latest French ideas and develop them along peculiarly English lines (for example, Y-tracery, odd numbers of lights).

London, Temple Church (p. 422E). Round nave begun *c.* 1175, dedicated 1185: rebuilt early nineteenth century and after 1945. Elevation and details relate to contemporary buildings in northern France. Hall choir *c.* 1240, rare example in England of this spatial formula (cf. Bristol) although comparable ideas were explored in cathedral retro-choirs (for example, Salisbury).

Ottery S. Mary, Devon, CC. Nave and choir (*c.* 1337–60) exhibit close contacts with latest developments at Wells and Bristol, particularly in the use of net vaulting.

Rievaulx, Yorkshire, A. Cistercian, founded 1132. Fragments of transepts and nave are the earliest remains of Cistercian architecture in England. Choir rebuilt *c.* 1225–49 in local style (cf. Whitby, York transepts). Little remains of a distinct architecture particular to the Cistercian order as in the twelfth century.

Roche, Yorkshire, A. Cistercian, founded 1147. The design of the church probably dates from 1160s. First English Cistercian church to introduce a triforium and to be vaulted throughout. Important example of French Gothic ideas entering England before Canterbury.

Sherborne, Dorset, A. Nave fan vaults belong to last quarter of fifteenth century and are perhaps the earliest examples of this fragile and structurally inefficient type of vault over the main volume of a church.

Tewkesbury, Gloucestershire, A. Benedictine. Norman choir completed 1102. Remodelled in second quarter of fourteenth century and provided with an elaborate lierne vault. There is evidence in the south transept for four-storey internal elevation which would predate Tournai nave and the related northern French Gothic group. Giant columnar piers replaced low main arcades and tribunes of eastern parts in the nave, built in the first half of twelfth century, and influenced nave of Gloucester.

Tintern, Monmouthshire, A. Cistercian, founded 1131. Total reconstruction of church begun 1269. Presbytery, south transept and two nave bays finished by 1288. Rest of nave and north transept finished by mid-fourteenth century. Early example of two-storey internal elevation with tall clerestory (cf. Netley, Exeter choir east bays originally). Part of important shift from the orthodoxy of constructing large churches with three-storey elevations.

Winchester, S. Cross, Hampshire. Begun *c.* 1160. Choir finished *c.* 1175–85. Transept *c.* 1185–1200. Despite heavy Romanesque structure many of the details indicate early contacts with advanced northern French building.

York, S. Mary's, A. Benedictine. Proportions and general form of elevation are derived from the transepts in the Minster. Much updated by the incorporation of more recent London and French tracery developments.

Castles

The main strength of Norman motte and bailey castles had been either in the shell keep, or in the 'donjon' within the bailey. From the early thirteenth century, however, the outer encircling walls were strengthened, made thicker and higher, to bind together the whole castle as one defensive unit. Occasionally an old keep was retained, as at **Goodrich, Herefordshire**, embedded in later walls, or at **Helmsley, Yorkshire**, where it became one among a whole series of mural towers. At **Framlingham, Suffolk** (*c.* 1200) the wall towers are rectangular, but like the later keeps at **Orford, Suffolk** (1166–72) (p. 406E) or **Conisborough, Yorkshire** (*c.* 1190) (p. 407B), they were usually made polygonal or circular, so as to resist the dangers of mining more effectively.

The castle-building programme of Edward I in Wales began in 1277 and was largely directed by the royal mason, Master James of S. George, who imported the latest techniques in fortification from the Continent. Since the main strength of a curtain wall system was the outer wall itself, the gatehouse and entrance arrangements were of crucial importance; a pair of towers built close together would have several doors, drawbridges, pits and barbicans. There are particularly elaborate gatehouses at **Denbigh, Chepstow** and **Pembroke**, so massive that they are the equivalent of the old keeps. Where possible, some principal apartments were contrived in the towers, but the courtyard within was normally disposed with the larger residential rooms, great hall and stables leaning against the outer walls in such a way that there was access above along the whole length of the ramparts.

Three defensive principles affected the design of the great enclosure. First, by means of battered walls and spurs, where possible with ditches and water defences, attackers were kept away from the base of the curtain. Second, maximum command of the intervening walls was secured by the generous projection of the mural towers and the construction of overhanging crenellations, although at first these might be wooden hoardings on galleries, and later machicolations of stone. Third, it was desirable that each tower and sector of wall should be individually defensible. A tower would be accessible by stairs, having doors at each level to isolate one or more floors or section of rampart. Occasionally small surmounting turrets were placed on towers (already higher than the walls) to give extra command of the

A. Harlech Castle (1283–90). See p.483

B. Beaumaris Castle, Anglesey (1283–1323). See p.483

C. Raglan Castle (*c.* 1430–60). See p.483

A. Stokesay Castle, Shropshire (1285–1305). See p.483

B. Bramall Hall, Cheshire (fifteenth century and onwards): courtyard. From a nineteenth-century lithograph by Joseph Nash. See p.484

rooftops. This principle of limited internal defence was frequently extended, so that the bailey or ward was subdivided into parts defensible to some extent on their own, with a strong gate between them.

Conway (1283–9) (p. 479C) and **Caernarvon** (1283–1323) are the most sophisticated examples of this type. A ring of eight towers in all, projecting well away from the walls, surrounds the natural crag on which Conway castle stands. The four towers nearest to the river are grouped closer together (with an upper turret apiece) and were approached by a further barbican and gatehouse from the waterside. The outer subsidiary towers and those of the town wall are backless, i.e. semicircular in plan, to prevent their use inwards by attackers who managed to gain the ramparts. Caernarvon has the added strength of several superimposed mural galleries between its polygonal towers, which allowed concentrated fire to be directed from the south face of the enclosure. At both places the courtyards were originally divided into two self-contained parts, and whilst their strength and grandeur are exceptional, at a host of other castles old walls were surrounded and strengthened by the construction of subsidiary outer lines of defence.

By this means the 'concentric' principle was developed which, at **Caerphilly** (1267–77), **Harlech** (1283–90) (p. 481A) and **Beaumaris** (1283–1323) (p. 481B), takes on a more systematic and symmetrical form. At Beaumaris a pair of large gatehouses (each composed of four towers, two large and two small) are centrally sited at the opposite ends of an enclosure linking six other major towers detached for three-quarters of their circumference. Outside this there is a narrow surrounding courtyard within a further wall lower than the first. A wide moat, originally linked to the sea by a channel, is crossed by an elaborate gatehouse itself associated with a strong town wall.

Settlement within a planned township, adjoining a castle, was frequently encouraged by the granting of chartered rights and privileges. Perfect examples of these 'bastides' are **Flint, Conway, Caernarvon, Beaumaris, Ludlow** and **Chepstow**, in which the original grid pattern of streets is apparent in spite of later encroachments. Later in the Middle Ages other towns, especially the wealthy merchant cities of York, Chester, Norwich and Southampton, enlarged their walls for self-defence. At **Chester** the walls right round the town are in good order to a height of about 3.7 m (12 ft), but all the old gates have gone. Two and a half miles of wall survive on both sides of the river Ouse at **York**, dating mainly from the mid-fourteenth century. There are numerous towers, and of the three remaining gateways, **Bootham Bar, Micklegate Bar** and **Walmgate**, the last retains substantial parts of its elaborate barbican.

By the end of the fourteenth century the military importance of the castle had declined as the character of warfare changed. A more polite society demanded higher standards of comfort, and fortified manors became popular alternatives to the old castles. Some great fortresses were rebuilt or substantially modified. **Kenilworth Castle, Warwickshire**, is an example representing many periods of construction. To a Norman keep (1160–80) a large outer bailey was added (1200–60) surrounded by extensive water defences. In 1571 the Earl of Leicester added a new gatehouse and a range of modern apartments. In its weakened state it withstood a seige in the Civil War like the even more splendid **Raglan Castle, Monmouthshire** (*c.* 1430–60) (p. 481C), where the old defences consisted of a moated tower linked to a curtain wall enclosure. In the sixteenth century new apartments were made, windows enlarged, a new decorative gatehouse built and the moat spanned by a two-storey bridge. In its restored state Raglan perfectly illustrates the outlook of the later Middle Ages, when there was a curious revival of interest in feudal chivalry – a movement which found its most bizarre expression in the mock mediaeval keep at **Bolsover Castle, Derbyshire** (1612–21).

After 1400, obsolete castles rapidly fell into ruins, but as late as the sixteenth century there were a few new constructions, notably a series of artillery forts along the south coast. Two examples are **Deal** and **Walmer**, both in Kent and started after 1540, which have spacious gun platforms and ammunition stores; gun ports replaced arrow-slits. Sometimes a castle was brought up to date by the reduction and filling of the old towers as a solid base for ordnance. Walled earth banks, their ends shaped like the more ambitious Continental fortification schemes, can be seen at **Carisbrooke, Isle of Wight**, and elsewhere. They surrounded an older conventional curtain wall, part of a concentric system, pivoting about an ancient motte and shell keep. Five centuries of history are thus shown.

There is a group of buildings which, while not castles in the full sense, possess defensive features beyond those of a normal domestic manor house, which might be securely planned round a courtyard with nothing more than a strong gatehouse. **Stokesay Castle, Shropshire** (1285–1305) (p. 482A), is such an instance. Its plan is essentially domestic, with a great hall of a kind rapidly becoming typical, and the modest protection afforded by a crenellated polygonal tower, a moated curtain wall and a gatehouse (the latter rebuilt *c.* 1620–5). A northern tower erected in the thirteenth century has a jettied half-timbered storey of the period 1285–1305. **Maxstoke, Warwickshire** (1346), and **Wingfield, Derbyshire** (1441–55), are other good examples. **Tattershall Castle, Lincolnshire** (1436–46), is a five-storey tower house about 34 m (112 ft) high, built of excellent brickwork, rectangular in plan with angle turrets. Its rooms are compressed into this single block, reminiscent of an old keep, standing on the edge of the moated inner bailey of a thirteenth-century castle.

Until well into the sixteenth century a dominant tower, astride a gateway, was a quasi-military feature common in domestic and collegiate buildings, for example at **Layer Marney Towers, Essex** (1520), **S. John's College, Cambridge** (1511) and **S. James's Palace, London**.

Manor Houses

At the beginning of the thirteenth century it was still necessary to retain some defensive character, and many licenses to 'crenellate' or fortify manor houses were granted by Henry III. They include **Little Wenham Hall, Suffolk** (*c.* 1270–80) (p. 409), one of the best-preserved of the period, **Charney Basset Manor House, Berkshire** (*c.* 1280) (p. 409), and **Penshurst Place, Kent** (1341–8) (p. 485).

The fifteenth century witnessed much improvement in social conditions and commercial prosperity, and manor houses became more comfortable – windows were larger and internal planning was concerned with privacy and amenity. Among these are **Haddon Hall, Derbyshire** (p. 485), **Bramall Hall, Cheshire** (fifteenth century) (p. 482B), **Hever Castle, Kent** (rebuilt 1462), still with its moat and drawbridge, **Compton Wynyates, Warwickshire** (1520), one of the finest of all Tudor mansions, but **Hampton Court Palace**, built for Cardinal Wolsey (1472–1530) (pp. 459B, 486) to the designs of Henry Redman, is the greatest house of the period.

Lesser Domestic Architecture

There was presumably a manorial hall at the centre of the holdings listed in Domesday Book. Such halls run into thousands. What they were like, how they varied from place to place, and how they evolved over time as the economy expanded and the social patterns became more sophisticated, remain matters of conjecture. As for the dwellings of the peasantry, these were probably too primitive to merit consideration under the heading of architecture. But it must have been otherwise in towns, where merchants and craftsmen gradually assumed the character of a class outside the prevailing rural hierarchy; that is, they were men with money but without social status (p. 487C). The same would be true of yeoman farmers when they appeared on the scene. Such men wanted houses to match their social ambitions as well as their wealth. The trend was always upward. As soon as they were in a position to do so, the lesser gentry aspired to build with stone in the manner, if not on the scale, of the nobility. When stone was beyond their means they resorted to superior sorts of timberwork. Later they took to brick. In their wake came the merchants and yeomen, adapting to their own special needs as well as conforming. On the one hand there was the intense conservatism which expressed itself in the retention of the hall as the fundamental domestic apartment. On the other, as domestic life became more private, and specialised activities required separate accommodation, there was a growing need for many smaller rooms. In this context there is a sense in which the Middle Ages did not come to an end until the last vestiges of the hall had been eliminated. In some parts of the country that was not until the seventeenth century.

It is clear that alongside the practitioners of fine architecture who produced the churches and palaces, there was a building industry which catered for the everyday, practical needs of secular society. Although they can have had little use for each other's skills, the two groups did not operate entirely in isolation. The problems of roofing were common to both; and as soon as the design of house passed beyond the consideration of primitive economic necessities, elements of artistry were liable to creep into the execution of details. Aesthetic criteria were not confined to one branch of the profession.

However, the divergences are far more conspicuous than the similarities. They start with basic materials. The principal difference between an aisled hall used as a church and an aisled hall that was lived in was not so much the matter of size as the fact that the former was likely to be made of stone, much of it ashlar, whereas the latter was nearly always made of timber. Ashlar was hardly ever used for domestic building. Between the castles of the great and the hovels of the peasantry, the whole middle range of houses was characterised by various forms of timber-framing in which the beams were combined with whatever sort of infilling came most readily to hand. The tradition of timber construction extended back without a break for many centuries, as witnessed by the post-holes of preconquest archaeological sites, for example. In some form or other it was older than building in stone.

The nature of the material recommends that timber structure should be of the post-and-lintel type. It is this that sets carpentry apart from masonry (p. 487A). But mediaeval timber work had its counterparts to the arches of the masons. These were crucks, pairs of curved timbers used as primary supports for the walls and roofs of houses or barns (p. 487B). Their origins are shrouded in obscurity and have been the subject of much speculation, a lot of it fanciful. There are none extant from before the thirteenth century. By then cathedral architects in England had been known to use timber ribs to simulate masonry vaults, and these must have resembled crucks; but whether there was any connection, and if so which influenced which, it is impossible to say. Crucks were an English speciality. While not entirely unknown across the Channel,

PENSHURST PLACE, KENT.

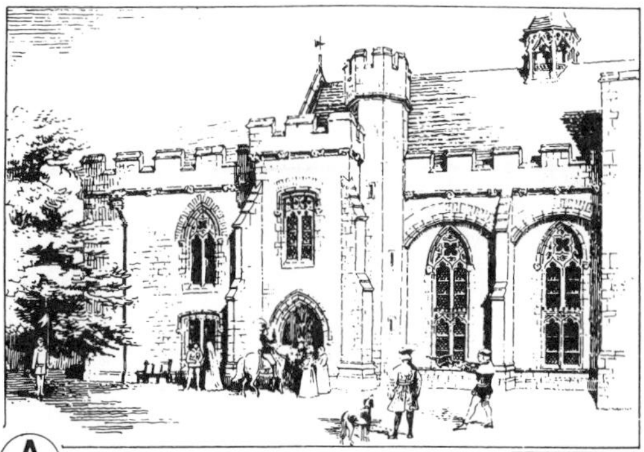

A NORTH FRONT

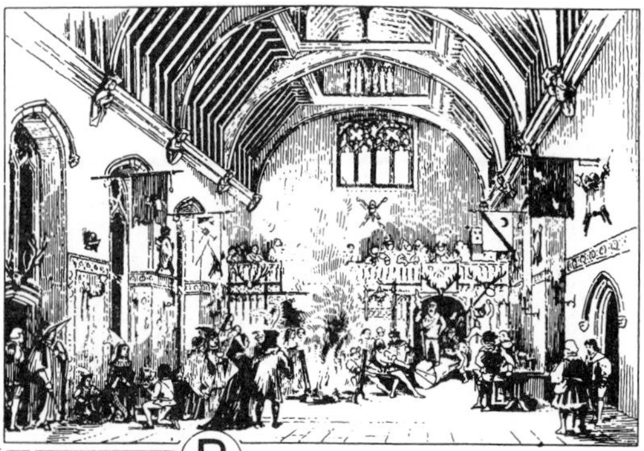

B INTERIOR OF GREAT HALL

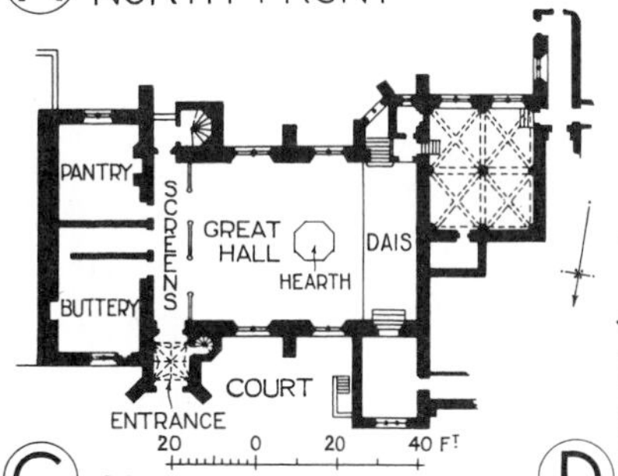

PANTRY
SCREENS
GREAT HALL
HEARTH
DAIS
BUTTERY
COURT
ENTRANCE
20 0 20 40 FT

C GROUND PLAN

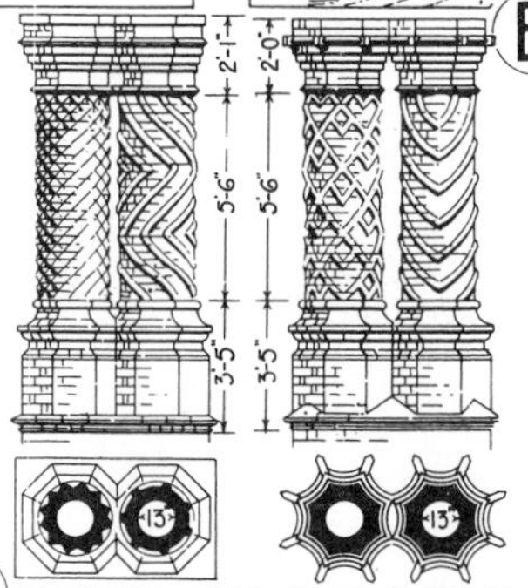

2'-1"
2'-0"
5'-6"
5'-6"
3'-5"
3'-5"
13"
13"

D DETAIL OF CHIMNEYS

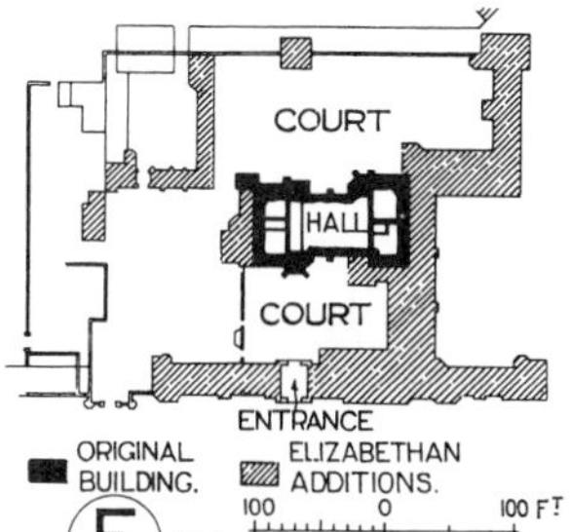

COURT
HALL
COURT
ENTRANCE
ORIGINAL BUILDING.
ELIZABETHAN ADDITIONS.
100 0 100 FT

E BLOCK PLAN

HADDON HALL, DERBYSHIRE.

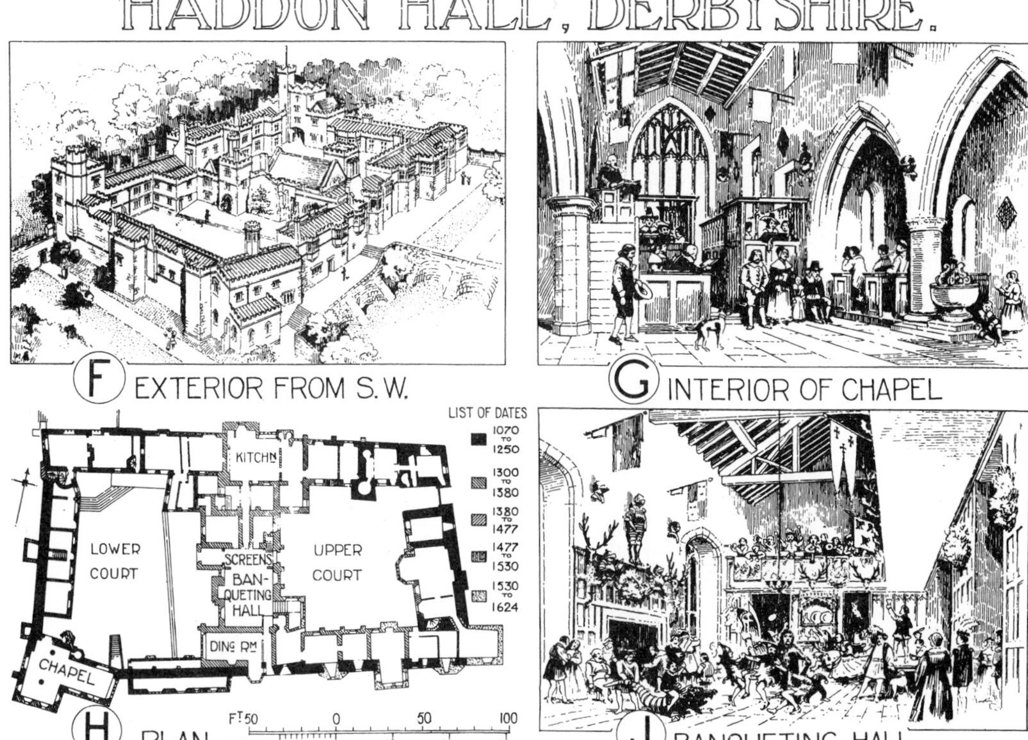

F EXTERIOR FROM S.W.

G INTERIOR OF CHAPEL

LIST OF DATES
1070 TO 1250
1300 TO 1380
1380 TO 1477
1477 TO 1530
1530 TO 1624
KITCHN
LOWER COURT
UPPER COURT
SCREENS
BANQUETING HALL
DINg RM
CHAPEL
FT 50 0 50 100
METRES 10 5 0 10 20 30

H PLAN

J BANQUETING HALL

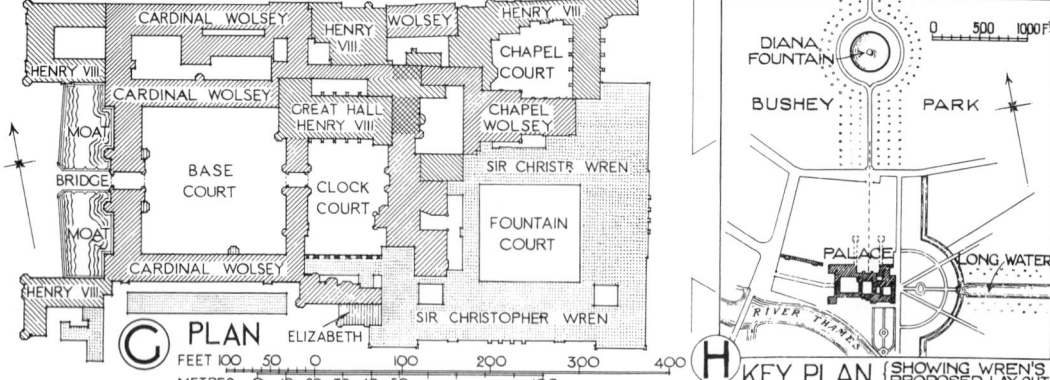

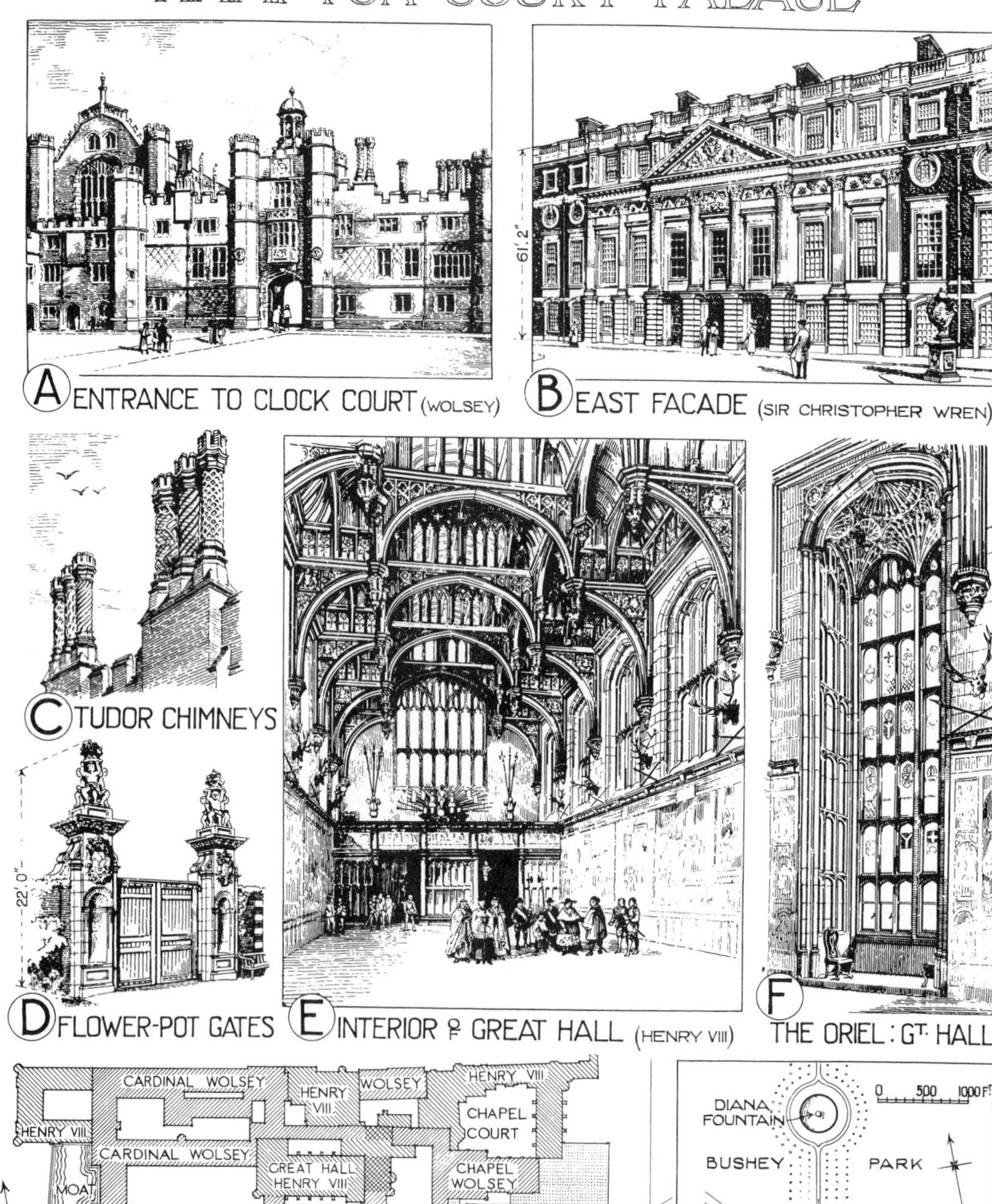
HAMPTON COURT PALACE
A ENTRANCE TO CLOCK COURT (WOLSEY)
B EAST FACADE (SIR CHRISTOPHER WREN)
61' 2"
C TUDOR CHIMNEYS
D FLOWER-POT GATES
22' 0"
E INTERIOR OF GREAT HALL (HENRY VIII)
F THE ORIEL: GT. HALL
CARDINAL WOLSEY
HENRY VIII
WOLSEY
HENRY VIII
CHAPEL COURT
HENRY VIII
CARDINAL WOLSEY
GREAT HALL HENRY VIII
CHAPEL WOLSEY
MOAT
BRIDGE
BASE COURT
CLOCK COURT
SIR CHRISTR WREN
FOUNTAIN COURT
MOAT
CARDINAL WOLSEY
HENRY VIII
SIR CHRISTOPHER WREN
ELIZABETH
G PLAN
FEET 100 50 0 100 200 300 400
METRES 0 10 20 30 40 50 100
0 500 1000 FT
DIANA FOUNTAIN
BUSHEY PARK
PALACE
LONG WATER
RIVER THAMES
H KEY PLAN (SHOWING WREN'S PROPOSED LAY-OUT

A. Farm at Abbey Dore, Herefordshire (fourteenth century and later). See p.484

B. Small house with crucks, Putley, Herefordshire. See p.484

C. Late mediaeval houses in High Street, Lewes. See p.484

they are sufficiently rare for it to be certain that they did not originate there. To make crucks trees were needed with branches of the right thickness, growing from the trunk at a certain height and suitable angle. These were only to be found in the deciduous forests of western Europe, and were particularly plentiful in England. But the concentration of crucks in the highland zone of the western parts of the country probably owes as much to historical as to geographical causes.

The number of mediaeval timber-framed houses that have survived is much greater than was at one time realised. Many of them were never pulled down, but merely brought up to date, the frames disappearing behind post-mediaeval cladding. Single-storey halls were turned into two-storey houses by the expedient of inserting an intermediate floor. But roofs were not as a rule tampered with. They were either replaced outright or left alone. So roofs are by far the most useful clue to the age and history of a house. If there is mediaeval woodwork in a roof, the house is mediaeval in origin. Fortunately it is not difficult to recognise the better sort of mediaeval roof, and the survivors tend to be of this kind. The arrangements of the timbers and the joints which articulate them reveal technical skills of a very high order. Church roofs are the show-pieces, but they are only the tip of the iceberg. The majority of timber structures are to be found in barns and above all houses. There are still thousands of them, and they deserve to be acknowledged among the highest achievements of mediaeval English craftsmanship.

Germany and Central Europe: Architectural Character

The battle of Bouvines in 1213, in which Philip August of France defeated King John of England and his German ally the Guelf Emperor Otto IV, had far-reaching consequences for Germany. The immediate result was the establishment of the Hohenstaufen Frederick II as emperor in place of Otto. But the price of Frederick's acceptance was virtual autonomy for the territorial princes who actually ruled Germany. The fragmentation of the country was not reversed until the nineteenth century. The decline of German political power and the corresponding ascendancy of France coincided with the appearance of High Gothic at Chartres and Bourges. In these circumstances the cautious assimilation of Gothic by German architects is apt to look like cultural colonisation.

However, although the process was slow it was not due to reluctance. The Germans themselves took the initiative and their response took two forms. On the one hand, at Cologne and Strasbourg they deliberately set out to match every aspect and every detail of French procedure – in effect to build French cathedrals on German soil. It was in these lodges that a generation of German masons served their apprenticeships, and from which they dispersed across the country, taking the new style with them. On the other hand they were often content to dabble with the superficial appearances of Gothic. They worked out a simplified version of the style suitable for the plainer tastes of the Cistercians and Premonstratensians. In due course this was taken up by the Mendicant orders, and it proved equally adaptable to the exigencies of brick, which was the ubiquitous building material of the north German plain. Above all, they made the form of the hall-church their own.

Patronage in Germany evolved its own distinctive pattern. Imperial architecture as such was non-existent. Insofar as the emperors were responsible for great building projects, for example the Luxemburger Charles at Prague or the Habsburgs at Vienna, they did so as promoters of their own local dynastic interests. Such as it was, real power and therefore effective patronage was in the hands of the electors and the free cities. The electors fell into two groups. In the west were three long-established ecclesiastical provinces – the archbishoprics of Cologne, Mainz and Trier. It was here, naturally enough, that French influence was strongest. Counterbalancing these in the east were the three secular electors, Brandenburg, Bohemia and Austria. These were frontier territories, growing in power, and open to bolder, less fastidious tastes than were fashionable along the Rhine. Bavaria alone of the ancient duchies survived into this world. Lesser rulers, like the Wettiner margraves of Meissen, tried to ape the examples of their larger brethren. The whole order of princes formed a closely knit social group.

The free cities of the Empire enjoyed privileges which made them virtually autonomous. Though small in size and politically weak, they were often by the standards of their time extremely wealthy.

Some of the trading cities organised themselves into loose federations such as the Hanseatic League centred on Lübeck, with depots throughout the Baltic, across Scandinavia, and as far west as London. To what extent commercial activities had any direct bearing on the spread of Gothic is problematic. Gothic was simply the style of the times; and the wealth, language and culture of the Hansa towns provided generous incentives for its dissemination. During the fourteenth century when the Teutonic Knights, a crusading order, were at the height of their power, they were responsible for several architectural innovations which bore exotic fruit in the adjacent regions. And after the initial probationary period of the thirteenth century German Gothic developed along two distinct lines, which eventually converged from opposite directions.

Rayonnant Gothic, which the Germans called 'opus francigenum', established itself firmly on the Rhine at Cologne and Strasbourg. But while the choir of the former and the nave of the latter were content to be copies of French models, their respective facades departed boldly from French precedents. Ever since Goethe it has been conventional to recognise the west front of Strasbourg as marking the point at which German genius emancipated itself from French tutelage. All the late Gothic towers and spires, such as Freiburg and Ulm, were descended from Strasbourg and Cologne.

It was the work of masons trained at these two centres to transform the simplified Gothic which had sufficed east of the Rhine during the thirteenth century. Southern Germany was a land of superb building stone, and from the middle of the fourteenth century dynasties of craftsmen emerged to impose crisp mouldings and virtuoso tracery patterns on churches of every shape and kind.

The other line of advance was from the east and was largely to do with vaulting. French Rayonnant was not particularly interested in the unnecessary elaboration of vaults. There were parts of France, however, such as Anjou, where this was not the case; and in England almost from the start, eccentric arrangements of ribs had been considered quite in order, for example at Lincoln Cathedral. The primary distinction was between ribs which were conceived as arches, and which defined and took precedence over the component shells or webs of the vault, and ribs which in effect were patterns applied to the surfaces of the shells and whose geometrical definition was quite independent of, and prior to, any rib pattern. Mainstream Gothic in France never really got beyond the first of these positions. The second had become an established feature of vaulting in England by 1300; and whether or not the Germans derived their inspiration from a knowledge of English Decorated, the English attitude was soon taken up with enthusiasm in various centres on the eastern fringes of the German world, in Pomerania, East Prussia, Poland, Silesia, Bohemia and Austria.

During the two hundred years that followed, vaulting became something of a German speciality. It evolved in ways that were unknown in western Europe or which, if known, were never taken up there: net vaults composed of intersecting sets of parallel ribs; cell vaults in which the surfaces between the ribs of a net vault were recessed into pyramids; jagged or jumping ribs; undulating, doubled-curved ribs forming monstrous flower patterns; and ribs superimposed over other ribs, or standing free in evocative congestions. The preoccupation eventually spread to all parts of the country; but statistically at least the evidence suggests that the taste for fancy vaults was always more at home in the east than the west.

These two trends came together in the work of Peter Parler in Prague in the 1350s. Parler was the precocious son of a mason from Cologne who moved to Schwäbisch-Gmund where he was responsible for the choir of the Heiligenkrenzkirche. This background represents the Rayonnant side of his pedigree. It has been much debated whether Parler travelled to England or was acquainted with English designs such as York or Wells. What is not in question is that he produced the first true net-vault for the choir of Prague cathedral, or that he was regarded by later German masons as in some sense the founding father of their craft. His personal prestige was sufficient to secure for other members of his family some of the best commissions of the time. There were Parlers everywhere – in South Germany, Switzerland, even at Milan – during the second half of the fourteenth century.

The Parler clan was emulated by a succession of other masters, all of them less gifted in the art of designing masonry. As architects their great achievements were the splendid town churches which proliferated across the country, from Rostock, Stargard and Danzig in the Baltic coastlands, to Breslau (Wroclaw) in Silesia, Kutna Hora in Bohemia, Nüremberg, Ingolstadt, Landshut and Salzburg in the south. In their hands the hall church became an art form in its own right: tall piers or columns rising sheer into the vaults whose ribs diverge in all directions; walls pierced by windows extending the full height of the building, and fringed with family chapels, once endowed with carved altar-pieces that have mostly failed to survive. The carefully contrived distribution of zones or focal points of visual emphasis against bare surfaces or spatial voids gives these buildings their own distinctive character, quite different from that of the French High Gothic cathedrals, and no less impressive. For the German late Gothic is *Deutsche Sondergotik*, and the national flavour is as authentic as English Perpendicular or French Flamboyant.

German late Gothic makes a further claim upon the attention of historians of architecture. It so happens that nearly all the evidence for the working methods of mediaeval masons comes from Germany. No doubt there is a large element of caprice about the way in which things that managed to survive in one country were destroyed in others. But German masons were more highly organised than their French or English counterparts. They were attached to four more or less permanent lodges, and these remained undisturbed long after the Middle Ages came to an end. Even when they were eventually wound up, quantities of working drawings were preserved, many of them finding their way into the imperial collections at Vienna. Apart from a few showpieces which include the complete elevations of towers, they are almost all of details such as patterns for vaults and window tracery. There are no signs that they were drawn to scale and this considerably limits their practical value. The one thing that can be said about them is

A OLD HOUSE: BRUNSWICK

B KLINGENTOR ROTHENBURG

C THE KAISERWORTH: GOSLAR

D OLD HOUSES: NUREMBERG

E THE CUSTOM HOUSE: NUREMBERG

F WINDOW: FURSTENBURG PALACE: INNSBRUCK

G RATHHAUS REGENSBURG

H CHAPEL OLD RATHHAUS: PRAGUE

that they were drawn in the same way as everything else that masons drew, that is to say they provide insight into the basic processes of designing buildings.

At the very end of the Middle Ages a few German masons also took to print and in a limited way their manuals shed considerable light on the drawings and need to be read in conjunction with them. They leave us with a clear impression of how the profession of architecture was conducted at the end of the Middle Ages. It was in the hands of a closely knit group of men, somewhat akin to Wagner's Mastersingers. They were proud of their craftsmanship and the theoretical knowledge on which it was based, perhaps even given to secrecy about it. How to take an elevation from a ground-plan was something that some of them promised not to disclose to anyone who was uninitiated into the mysteries of their craft. To us their science seems very meagre.

A few practical rules of calculation and geometrical construction were evidently sustained by a vast accumulation of unwritten but well-remembered experience. The two fundamental talents on which their achievements were based were the ability to reduce masonry to components conceived in terms of abstract geometrical shapes, however complicated; and the technical ability to execute such masonry, piece by piece, to the required standards of precision. The rest was a problem of assembly. With these means they managed to realise some of the most remarkable feats of human imagination and engineering.

This needs to be said because in the debate with the Renaissance which brought mediaeval architecture to an end, the Gothic point of view was remarkably inarticulate, and the theoretical element in it is apt to seem negligible. In fact, such as it was, the masonic geometry of late Gothic Germany can be traced to other countries and back to earlier periods. In its essentials it was inherited by the Middle Ages from Classical antiquity. It is therefore appropriate that it may have had some bearing on Central European Baroque.

Germany and Central Europe: Examples

The town of **Rothenburg** presents an almost perfect example of the pattern of urban development in mediaeval Germany. The starting point was the **Castle of the Counts of Rothenburg, Hohenlohe**, which occupies a narrow spur, surrounded on three sides by a loop of the River Tauber. Outside the gate of the castle on the landward side and under its protection, a settlement formed. The earliest church was actually inside the castle, but the townsfolk soon acquired their own **Parish Church of S. James**, and with the help of the Hohenstaufen emperors, emancipated themselves from the irksome feudal jurisdiction of the castle. This process culminated in 1274 when Rothenburg became an imperial free city. In 1204 a defensive wall with towers was built (p. 490B). At the centre was a market square with the **Rathaus** on one side (1240) (p. 493A). The parish church was close by. It was rebuilt as a spacious hall church between 1373 and 1471, and it remains the outstanding monument of the town. By the fourteenth century Rothenburg had spread beyond the original wall, and a second wall was built further out. More churches belonging to the various religious orders were founded, some even outside the second wall. One of these, **the Spitalkirche**, with its attendant amenities and the residential area around it, formed a veritable suburb, the **Kappenzipfel**, which was joined to the main town by a separate wall (1380). The population must have reached its peak at the time of the Black Death (1348). In spite of much rebuilding in the vernacular the town has never lost its mediaeval character.

The **Cathedral of Regensburg** (p. 493C,D) is the largest Gothic church in Bavaria but it has been somewhat overshadowed by more distant rivals and by churches in other categories. It was started in 1273 nearly a generation after Cologne and the nave of Strasbourg, although the dependence on French models is still evident. The most interesting feature of the design is the apse, which dispenses with ambulatory and chapels in favour of the largest possible displays of stained glass and tracery. The contemporary chronicler Burchard von Hall called such architecture 'opus francigenum'. The nave in which the triforium is barely distinguished from the clerestory has the same French antecedents as the nave of York Minster, with which it is contemporary. Work on the west front had started by 1340 and as executed by three successive generations of the Roriczer family through the fifteenth century it emerged as an orthodox two-towered facade, relieved by a small but interesting triangular porch. The upper parts of the towers were only completed between 1859 and 1869, very much under the influences of Cologne.

Immediately to the east of the cathedral, and an integral part of the complex, is the **Parish Church of S. Ulrich** (p. 493B). This has a curious vaulted gallery at the west end of an otherwise unvaulted nave. Another important early Gothic work in Regensburg is the **Church of the Dominicans**, started in 1246.

The **Cathedral of S. Severus, Erfurt** (p. 492G,J), is an imposing group of ecclesiastical buildings which stand on a terrace below the Petersberg, the site of the fortress which was the origin and nucleus of the city. The cathedral had a complicated building history. A Romanesque choir (1154) was followed by a Gothic nave (mid-thirteenth century). The old east end was replaced by the present elegant chapel and choir in the fourteenth century – the site precluding

20'3"
SKETCH·PLAN
A
½-TIMBER HOUSE: ERFURT.
B
STONE SCREEN: OBERWESEL.
C
HOUSE: HILDESHEIM.
D
HOLY WELL
RATISBON CATHEDRAL.
E
CHOIR: HALBERSTADT CATHEDRAL.
F
SOUTH PORCH
S. LAWRENCE, NUREMBERG.
G
PORCH: ERFURT CATH.
H
W. PORTAL: S. ELIZABETH, MARBURG.
J
CHOIR: ERFURT CATH.

A. Rathaus, Rothenburg (1240). See p.491

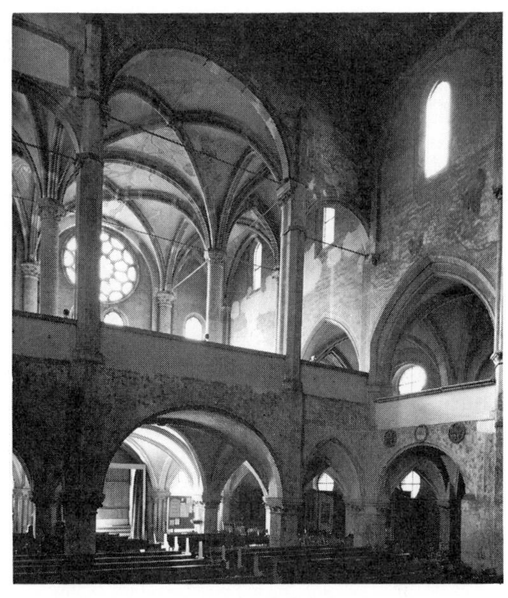

B. S. Ulrich, Regensburg. See p.491

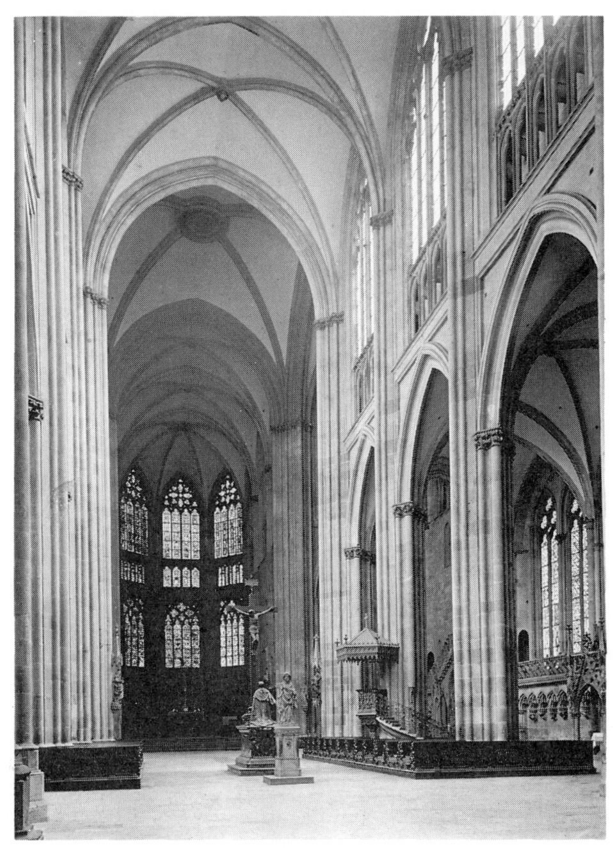

C. Regensburg Cathedral (1273 to fifteenth century): nave. See p.491

D. Regensburg Cathedral

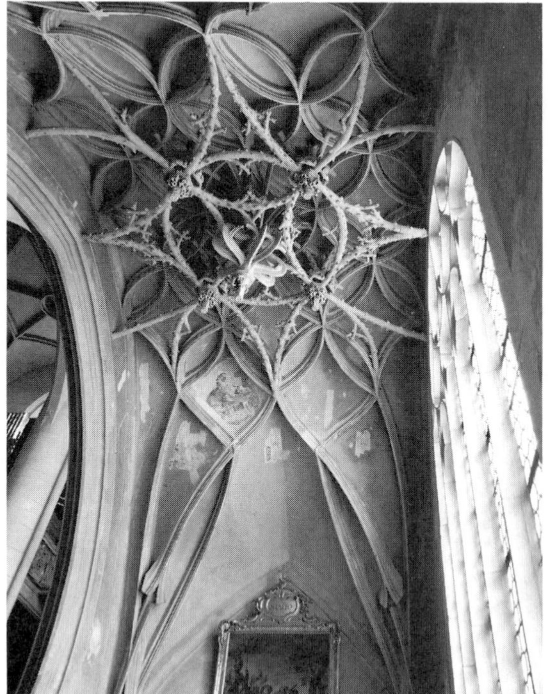

A. Frauenkirche, Ingolstadt: chapel vault (1520s). See p.495

B. S. Martin's, Landshut (fifteenth century). See p.495

C. Church at Neuötting. See p.495

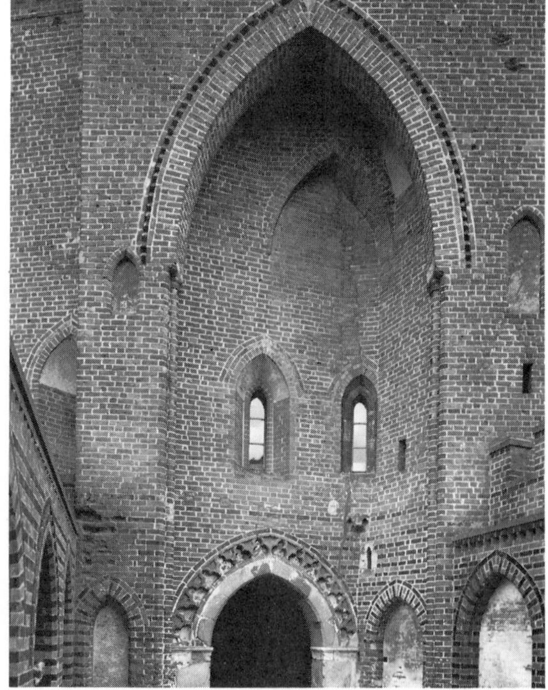

D. Marienburg Castle, Poland (fourteenth century). See p.495

anything more extensive. The nave was transformed into a hall after a collapse in 1452.

The rebuilding of S. Severus began *c.* 1278. It is a five-aisled hall church, a rare type but one which gets the maximum effect out of the hall form. There is another example in the **Marienkirche at Muhlhausen** (*c.* 1318) not far from Erfurt. Erfurt also retains its two thirteenth-century friars' churches: **Barfusser** (Franciscan) and **Prediger** (Dominican), which were features of many important mediaeval towns in Germany.

The **Frauenkirche at Ingolstadt** (p. 494A) is a late Gothic church built of brick, the general design of which calls for no particular comment except perhaps to note the oblique placing of the west towers which may be symptomatic of a widespread predilection among the last generation of mediaeval architects for twisting forms out of their normal alignments (compare the west front intended for S. Ouen at Rouen). But the nave is flanked by a series of chapels covered by the most extraordinary vaults ever erected. They are no longer structural features but expressionistic works of art in their own right, evoking images of the crown of thorns, monstrous insects or malign plants. They date from the 1520s, the excited years of the Reformation and the Peasants' War. The architect has been named as Ulrich Heidenreich.

Hans von Burghausen began the new choir of the **Franciscan Church in Salzburg, Austria**, in 1408. It was finished by 1452. The contrast between the two components of the church as it now stands is spectacular but fortuitous. The nave is an undistinguished late Romanesque work, low, dark and heavy. The choir soars, and its ample space is flooded with light. In certain respects the choir is the most radical of all German hall churches. The outer wall of the apse has severe sides. The internal colonnade, if it can be called that, makes the turn in two. No rib or arch goes directly from column to column or column to respond. All sense of bay definition has gone. Instead, each of the five columns stands at the centre of a spreading canopy of ribs which join to form an all-over pattern. The pursuit of spatial unity could hardly have been taken further except by the total removal of all internal support.

The town of **Annaberg** owes its existence to the discovery nearby of rich deposits of silver in 1492. It was founded by the Elector of Saxony in 1496. The **Church of Annaberg** (begun 1499) is one of a group of magnificent late Gothic hall churches along the southern border of electoral Saxony – others are at **Zwickan, Pirna,** and **Freiberg in Sachsen**. But the vaults of Annaberg have tell-tale flower patterns which point to the Bohemian side of the Erzebirge. They were actually constructed by local craftsmen, but the consultant was a close colleague and follower of Benedict Ried, Jacob Heilmann of Schweinfurt, who was responsible for the very similar vault in the **church at Most (Brux) in Bohemia**.

An epitaph in the wall of **S. Martin's Church at Landshut**, Germany (p. 494B), names Hans von Burghausen as the architect. It also assigns to him the **Spitalkirche in Landshut**, and **churches at Salzburg, Neuötting** (p. 494C), **Straubing** and **Wassenburg**. They all survive, some much altered, but apart from the fact that they are all hall churches, no two are much alike, and without the explicit testimony of the inscription it is unlikely that they would have been attributed to the same man. Burghausen died at Landshut in 1432 before the church was finished. His design combined exceedingly tall, exceedingly plain piers, leading up to a simple net vault, a formula which echoes the elements of the window tracery. The effect is stunning and largely depends on the interaction of height and recession. The tower, 133 m (436 ft) high, was not finished until 1498.

The Spitalkirche at Landshut, which was under construction at exactly the same time as S. Martin's, differs in plan, pier form, vault pattern and proportions, but is equally effective. Straubing and Neuötting are less distinguished. The vaults of Wasserburg belong to a later period.

In 1309 the Grand Master of the Order of Teutonic Knights transferred his residence from Vienna to **Marienburg Castle, Marienburg (Malbork)**, Poland (p. 494D). The building was part castle, part monastery. The Knights formed an exclusive aristocratic community; their principal apartments were designed for communal activities, and consisted of a chapel, a chapter house, and refectories for different seasons of the year. These were built piecemeal in the course of the fourteenth century, but they were united by common features, notably their vaults which make great play with cones of ribs and triradials. The cones are reminiscent of English chapter houses or the retro-choir at Wells.

The **Heiligenkrenzkirche, Schwäbisch-Gmund**, Germany (p. 498A), was the principal parish church of the town which became an imperial free city during the thirteenth century. First the nave was built, then the choir. Both are halls. None of the vaults are fourteenth-century. The church (begun 1351) owes its fame to the fact that Heinrich Parler, master builder, founder of the Parler dynasty, was architect of the choir when he moved south from Cologne where work had stopped in *c.* 1330. Strenuous efforts have been made to demonstrate that German late Gothic began with the Heiligenkrenzkirche, but without the name Parler is would be difficult to see why. The prestige which subsequently got the commission at Prague for Peter Parler when he was not much more than twenty, must have been Heinrich's. But it is intriguing to note that Peter's work at Prague included far more novelties than Heinrich's work at Schwäbisch-Gmund.

Nuremberg (p. 490D,E) began like many mediaeval towns as a market under the protection of a castle. The **Castle** still dominates the city, a carefully preserved monument much of which dates from the time of the emperor Frederick Barbarossa. It became a free city of the Empire in 1219, and the principal churches belong to the three centuries which followed. The city is divided by the river Peguitz into two halves, named after the two largest **churches: S. Sebald** and **S. Lawrence** (p. 492F). Both naves date from the thirteenth century. S. Sebald has a three-storey elevation; S. Lorenz two. Both choirs were replaced. That of S. Sebald dates from 1361 to 1379. Internally it is a hall church after the manner of the Wiesenkirche at Soest, less elegant and more robust. Externally it looks like an enlarged version of S. Chapelle, Paris. This impression was almost certainly deliberate. The choir was designed to house the reliquary shrine of S. Sebald, although this was not made until the sixteenth century. The choir of S. Lawrence (1439–77) is also a hall, but it follows a different model. The windows are in two rows like the Parler church at Schwäbisch-Gmund. The vaults have the wayward intricacy of late Gothic designs totally lacking at S. Sebald.

A third important church, the **Frauenkirche** (pp. 498B,C), in the marketplace, was built as an imperial chapel by the Emperor Charles IV, somewhat on the lines of the Hohenstaufen chapel in the castle. Started before 1352 and substantially finished by 1358, it was the first Gothic hall church in the region and an early work of the Parlers.

The importance of **Vienna** dates from the arrival of the Habsburgs in 1276 and the victory of the Marchfeld in 1278 which put them in control of the duchy of Austria. **S. Stephen's Church** (p. 497) had recently been rebuilt in a late Romanesque style. The west front of that church with its richly sculptured portal, the Riescutor, was incorporated into the present building, presumably because the cost of replacing it was considered too great. The towers normally found on west fronts stand in lieu of transepts at Vienna. Work on the Gothic building began in 1304. There was a consecration in 1340, which implies that the choir was by then ready for use. In 1359 Rudolf IV laid a foundation stone which marks the extension of operations to the nave and may have included the south tower as well. The south tower has a chapel which includes a pendant vault similar to the one in Peter Parler's sacristy at Prague.

Like Ulm, Vienna was lifted out of the ordinary by its towers. They are remarkable not just for their position. The south tower was up by 1433, that is before Strasbourg, though it is not so high. A corresponding north tower was started in 1450, but it was abandoned half-finished in the sixteenth century. The designer was Hanns Puchspaum, the man who had vaulted the nave by 1446. The decision to have towers flanking the nave instead of at the west front enabled Vienna to avoid the problem which led to the heightening of the nave at Ulm. The nave remains relatively low – slightly higher than the aisles but without a clerestory. Such a nave was compatible with the old west front. It also required a timber roof of enormous dimensions which made the external silhouette bulky enough to hold its own with the towers without affecting the hall-like interior. From a distance S. Stephen's is all roof, and it has remained the distinctive feature of the city skyline ever since it was built. It is a curious way of making what is really an overgrown parish church seem bigger than it actually is. Although emperors lived at Vienna, the city lacked the prestige and above all the wealth of the imperial free cities. This is reflected in its one great mediaeval church.

Until 1377 the parish church of **Ulm**, Germany, lay outside the city walls. Parts of the old building were actually brought into the city to be incorporated into the new **Ulm Cathedral** (p. 498D). The first three architects were all members of the Parler clan. They planned a hall church with aisles and nave of equal width, like Vienna, but with a chapel choir. Only the choir was built to this design. By 1391 Ulrich von Ensinger had taken over. His speciality was colossal towers, and he designed one for Ulm on the model of the single west tower at Freiburg, but higher even than the towers of Cologne. With such a tower the Parler hall church would have been ridiculous, so Ulrich redesigned the nave as a basilica 41 m (136 ft) high. For most of the fifteenth century work proceeded according to this programme under three successive generations of the Ensinger family. Subsequently Matthäus Böblinger redrew the upper stages of the tower and Burkhard Eugelberg turned the church into a five-aisled basilica. By 1543 only the great tower remained unfinished. Nothing much was done between then and 1844, when the prospect of the completion of Cologne stung Ulm into action. By 1890 the octagon and spire were built according to Böblinger's drawing which had been preserved. The height is 160 m (530 ft), which rather belatedly made Ulm the tallest mediaeval building in Europe.

Until it became French in 1681, **Strasbourg** had been a free city of the German empire, a privilege which it acquired in 1262. Before that the exercise of authority had been a matter of dispute between the bishop and the citizens' guilds. **Strasbourg Cathedral** (pp. 445B,D) took over 250 years to build and falls into four clearly defined phases. First, the east end is all that was finished of a late Romanesque reconstruction, started between 1176 and 1190. Second, the transepts were added during the second quarter of the thirteenth century. The north transept is earlier than the south (*c.* 1290), and the style became progressively more French and more Gothic. Third, the nave was pure French Rayonnant and entirely up to date. It belongs to the third quarter of the thirteenth century, though built on the foundations of its predecessor which affected the proportions. Fourth, the west front was started in 1277, after Strasbourg became a free city, and it was very much a monument

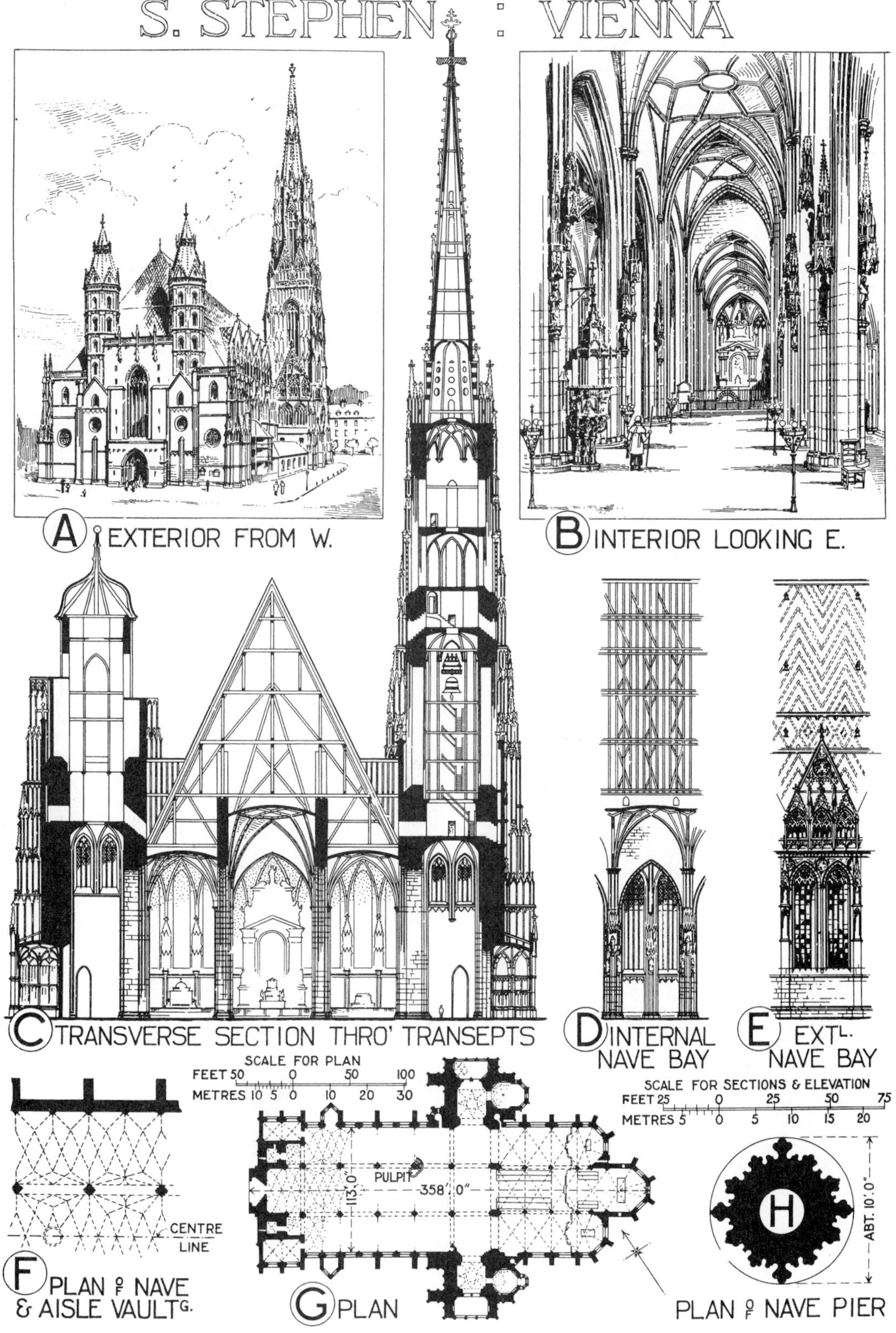
S. STEPHEN : VIENNA
A EXTERIOR FROM W.
B INTERIOR LOOKING E.
C TRANSVERSE SECTION THRO' TRANSEPTS
D INTERNAL NAVE BAY
E EXTL. NAVE BAY
SCALE FOR PLAN
FEET 50 0 50 100
METRES 10 5 0 10 20 30
SCALE FOR SECTIONS & ELEVATION
FEET 25 0 25 50 75
METRES 5 0 5 10 15 20
CENTRE LINE
F PLAN OF NAVE & AISLE VAULTG.
PULPIT
113'0"
358'0"
G PLAN
H
ABT. 10'0"
PLAN OF NAVE PIER

A. Heiligenkrenzkirche, Schwäbisch-Gmund (begun 1351). See p.495

B. Frauenkirche, Nuremberg (mid-fourteenth century). See p.496

C. Frauenkirche, Nuremberg: interior looking east

D. Ulm Cathedral (fourteenth to sixteenth century, octagon and spire nineteenth century). See p.496

to the pride of the citizens. Between 1383 and 1388 the two towers were joined by a belfry, forming a solid block out of all proportion to the rest of the cathedral. Then in 1399 Ulrich von Ensinger, who had already conceived the colossal west tower for Ulm, began the much enlarged octagon for the single north tower. Johannes Hültz of Cologne finished the spire in 1439. It is 140 m (465 ft) high. Plans were prepared for a corresponding south tower but these never got beyond the drawing stage.

Strasbourg offers a splendid case study of the reception and assimilation of Gothic outside France: tentative beginnings (the transepts) followed by a thoroughgoing exercise (the nave) in which the apprentices graduated to the ranks of masters. Finally in the west front the Germans did things with Gothic hardly contemplated in France. But the fortunes of the west front also illustrate the way in which architectural decorum could be distorted by the affectation of patronage. The escalation was almost certainly touched off by the desire to compete with Cologne, and the rivalry, once launched, was taken up elsewhere. Strasbourg was not the only sky-scraper to be completed during the Middle Ages, but it was the highest, and for long was regarded as one of the wonders of the world.

The collegiate church of **S. George, Limburg an der Lahn**, Germany (p. 374E–G,K), was attached to the castle and forms an extremely picturesque group above the river which somewhat offsets its lack of architectural distinction. The present building dates from *c.* 1220. It is a not entirely felicitous essay in early Gothic by architects whose instincts were still thoroughly Romanesque. It has a four-storey elevation, vaguely reminiscent of Noyon, but heavy and clumsy where the French model is already light and delicate. Similar observations could be applied to the west front: a two-towered facade with a rose window based on Laon, but quite devoid of any feeling for Gothic. In every sense of the word it is a transitional building, like many of the Rhenish churches to which it is affiliated, for example **Bonn, Neuss, S. George at Cologne**.

The **Albrechtsburg, Meissen**, Germany, the castle which occupies the same eminence above the Elbe as the cathedral, was rebuilt between 1471 and 1485 to a design by Arnold of Westphalia, an architect otherwise unknown. It was an ambitious attempt to combine fortification with late mediaeval notions of gracious living. The apartments are on four floors, and access to the upper storeys is by means of a magnificent spiral staircase projecting into the courtyard, an updated version of Raymond de Temple's fourteenth-century prototype at the Louvre in Paris. The principal rooms on the main floors, though relatively low, are completely dominated by vaults. The ribs spring from a level not much above the floor, and the panels between the ribs are recessed. This must have been the first occasion when cell vaults were used to full effect. They became immensely popular everywhere in eastern Europe from Bohemia to the Baltic. Occasionally they turn up as far south as Austria, for example the **Castle of Greinberg** on the Danube (1488–93), where the effect produced is startlingly modern, by contrast with Meissen.

An inscription in the choir of the **Wiesenkirche, Soest**, Germany, gives the name of the architect as Johannes Scheudeler and a date which can be construed as either 1314 or 1331. The latter is the more likely. Scheudeler is otherwise unknown. In the history of hall-church designs, the Wiesenkirche marks the point where the form was translated into Rayonnant elegance. There is an interest in verticality not evident in the thirteenth century; and the unity of the interior is emphasised by the way windows and piers rise unbroken the full height of the building. There are no capitals. The arches of the vaults simply merge into the pier profiles. It was a step toward the conception of the supports as centres of cones of ribs as opposed to the corners of rectangular bays, although the arches that frame the bays of the Wiesenkirche are still more prominent than the diagonal ribs.

The church of **S. Barbara, at Kutna Hora**, Czech Republic (p. 504A), was started by Peter Parler in 1388. It was conceived on the lines of a cathedral with an ambulatory and ring of chapels. Work stopped in 1401 before much had been done, and little work was added until the end of the fifteenth century, when a succession of local Bohemian masters were active. The choir was vaulted by 1499. In 1512 Benedikt Ried was appointed consultant architect and work proceeded briskly for the next twenty years. He died in 1534 but was responsible for turning the nave into a hall, and he designed the high vaults. With aisles as though for a Peter Parler basilica and Ried's high galleries over the inner aisles the result was unique in mediaeval church architecture. The vaults are centred on two rows of cones, from which the ribs spiral off to form the petal-patterns which are Ried's stylistic signature, while at the springers they deliberately overshoot the tas-de-change in mock untidiness.

The residential buildings of **Prague Castle (Hradčany)**, Czech Republic, the **Wladislav Hall** (1493–1502), occupy a sloping site between the cathedral choir (to which they are connected) and the south wall of the fortress. The hall formed the third and top storey. It was the work of Benedikt Ried, who also modernised the fortifications. The hall is fantasy architecture on the grand scale. It was used for jousting, and was approached by a stepped ramp, suitable for horses to negotiate. It is over 16 m (52 ft) wide, the greatest span to be vaulted in a mediaeval secular building. The vault is a conflation of cones and shallow domes, over which is spread a writhing skein of sinuous ribs. In plan the ribs are a series of simple arcs all drawn to the same radius and formed into flower patterns, Ried's favourite motif. But as executed in their dimensions, they appear double-curved. Benedikt Ried was one of the first architects in northern Europe to use Italian Renaissance details. He handled them in the same cavalier spirit as his Gothic forms. Pilasters, consoles and entablatures alternate with purely Gothic buttresses. Sometimes the pilasters are inclined at 45 degrees to the surfaces in which they are set; and there is a door in the hall where the flanking pilasters are actually twisted through 90 degrees as they rise. This was more than twenty years before Mannerism was invented in Italy.

Until the fourteenth century Bohemia formed part of the archdiocese of Mainz. In 1344 the King of Bohemia, later the Emperor Charles IV, persuaded the pope to separate them, and Prague was elevated into an independent archbishopric. It was the first step in a direction which led to the Hussite movement and the remarkable outburst of Czech nationalism associated with it. **Prague Cathedral** (p. 504B) was at once started on a scale worthy of its new dignity. The apse and chapels were laid out by a Frenchman, Matthias of Arras, whose experience had been acquired in the cathedrals of southern France, notably Narbonne. But Matthias died in 1352 before work had advanced very far. He was succeeded by a young, relatively untried German, Peter Parler from Schwäbisch-Gmund. Parler completed the choir, which was consecrated in 1385, and much of the south transept before he died in 1397. Work was halted during the Hussite disturbances of the fifteenth century. The whole of the nave and the west front belong to the nineteenth century. Parler's choir was an epoch-making work. It introduced into the cathedral architecture of central Europe many novelties such as pendant vaults, net vaults with parallel ribs, and triradials. The sources of these motives are uncertain but there were Parlers everywhere in south Germany in the last decades of the fourteenth century and between them the family influence was profound for they did much to establish the stylistic character of late Gothic in that part of the world.

The more exotic aspects of Prague cathedral, such as the mosaic decorations of the Wenceslas chapel and the south facade, probably reflect the emperor's personal taste in trying to outdo the church of its rival Habsburg dynasty at Vienna.

Lübeck, Germany, was refounded on a new site in 1143, and the event marked the beginning of a new phase in the German colonisation of the Baltic coastlands. The bishopric of Oldenburg was moved there in 1163 by Duke Henry the Lion, who also gave the town its charter. It became the model for subsequent settlements further east and eventually became the headquarters of the Hanseatic League. Until it was virtually destroyed during World War II, it retained many of its mediaeval buildings, notably the rathaus, the hospital, two city gates, many houses and five major churches. Of these the **Cathedral** has a transitional hall nave of the Westphalian type and a later choir (started 1266), modelled on the choir of **S. Mary's Church**, which although only a parish church is the great church of the city – a reversal of the normal order of precedence characteristic of the free cities of the Empire, and of the Baltic cities in particular. S. Mary's is a brick church which gradually acquired the scale and form of a cathedral. In its final form it is over 36 m (120 ft) high. It was started early in the thirteenth century as a modest basilica with a huge west tower of which the nave was converted into a hall church (*c.* 1251). Then between 1260 and 1280 the 'cathedral' choir was added. In the late fourteenth century the hall nave and the old west front were replaced by a nave to match the choir, and a two-towered facade.

The other interesting church is **S. Peter's**, which is one of the rare instances of a five-aisled hall church. The churches of Lübeck, and especially S. Mary's, were imitated with varying degrees of fidelity at Schwerin, Wismar, Rostock and Stralsunet; and the general influence of Lübeck 'backsteingotik' was felt throughout the area of German colonisation.

Elizabeth of Hungary, the widow of one of the landgraves of Thuringia, died at Marburg in 1231. She was canonised in 1235. The cult was both popular and fashionable. The foundation stone of the **Church of S. Elizabeth, Marburg**, Germany (p. 501), was laid the same year, and the Emperor Frederick II himself attended the translation of her relics the following year. The church was ready for consecration in 1283. It falls into two parts: a centrally planned east end, designed as a martyrium for the shrine, one area of which became the burial chapel for the landgraves of Thuringia and Hesse; and a hall nave. The plan of the east end has connections with the contemporary Liebfrauenkirche at Trier, as does the two-storey elevation. Most of the hall churches of the second half of the thirteenth century in Germany were variations on the theme of Marburg.

Minden Cathedral, Germany, is the most impressive though not the earliest of a group of Westphalian hall churches (nave 1267–90). The ultimate French source seems to have been Poitiers cathedral with several German intermediaries, notably Paderborn Cathedral (1225–60), though Paderborn is hardly yet Gothic. The group represents the first considerable manifestation of German interest in the hall-church form, a type which became exceedingly popular during the late Gothic period, especially for churches below cathedral rank.

The **Parish Church of Freiburg im Breisgau**, Germany, was begun *c.* 1200 as a burial church for the Dukes of Zahringen in the Romanesque styles of the Upper Rhineland. After the death of the last duke in 1218 the task of completing the church was taken over by the town. Although in effect no more than a parish church, the architecture became progressively

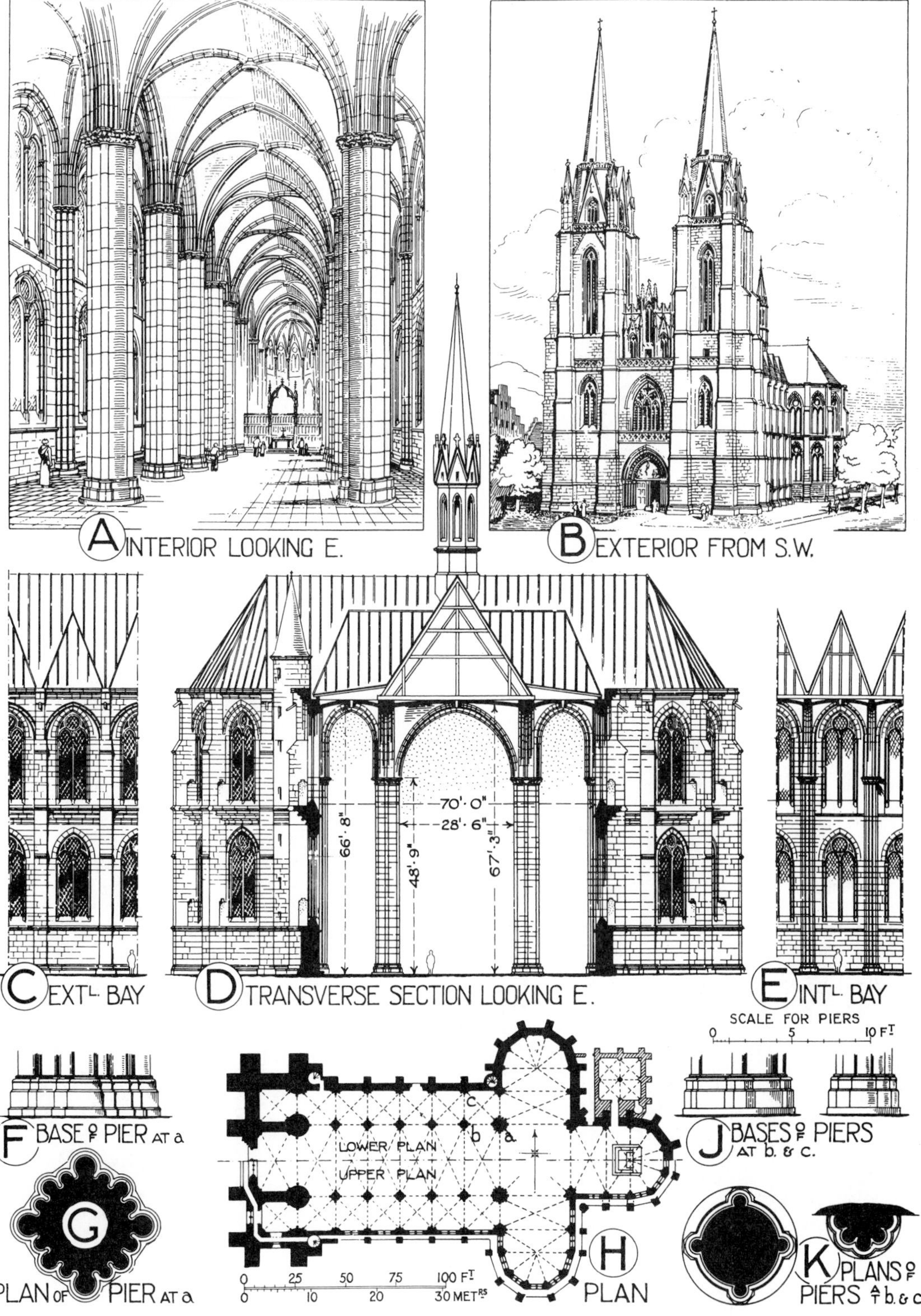
S. ELIZABETH : MARBURG
A INTERIOR LOOKING E.
B EXTERIOR FROM S.W.
70'·0"
28'·6"
66'·8"
48'·9"
67'·3"
C EXTL. BAY
D TRANSVERSE SECTION LOOKING E.
E INTL. BAY
SCALE FOR PIERS
0 5 10 FT
F BASE OF PIER AT a
J BASES OF PIERS AT b. & C.
c
b
a
LOWER PLAN
UPPER PLAN
G
PLAN OF PIER AT a
0 25 50 75 100 FT
0 10 20 30 METRS
H PLAN
K PLANS OF PIERS AT b. & c.

Cologne Cathedral (begun 1284; completed 1842–80). See p.505

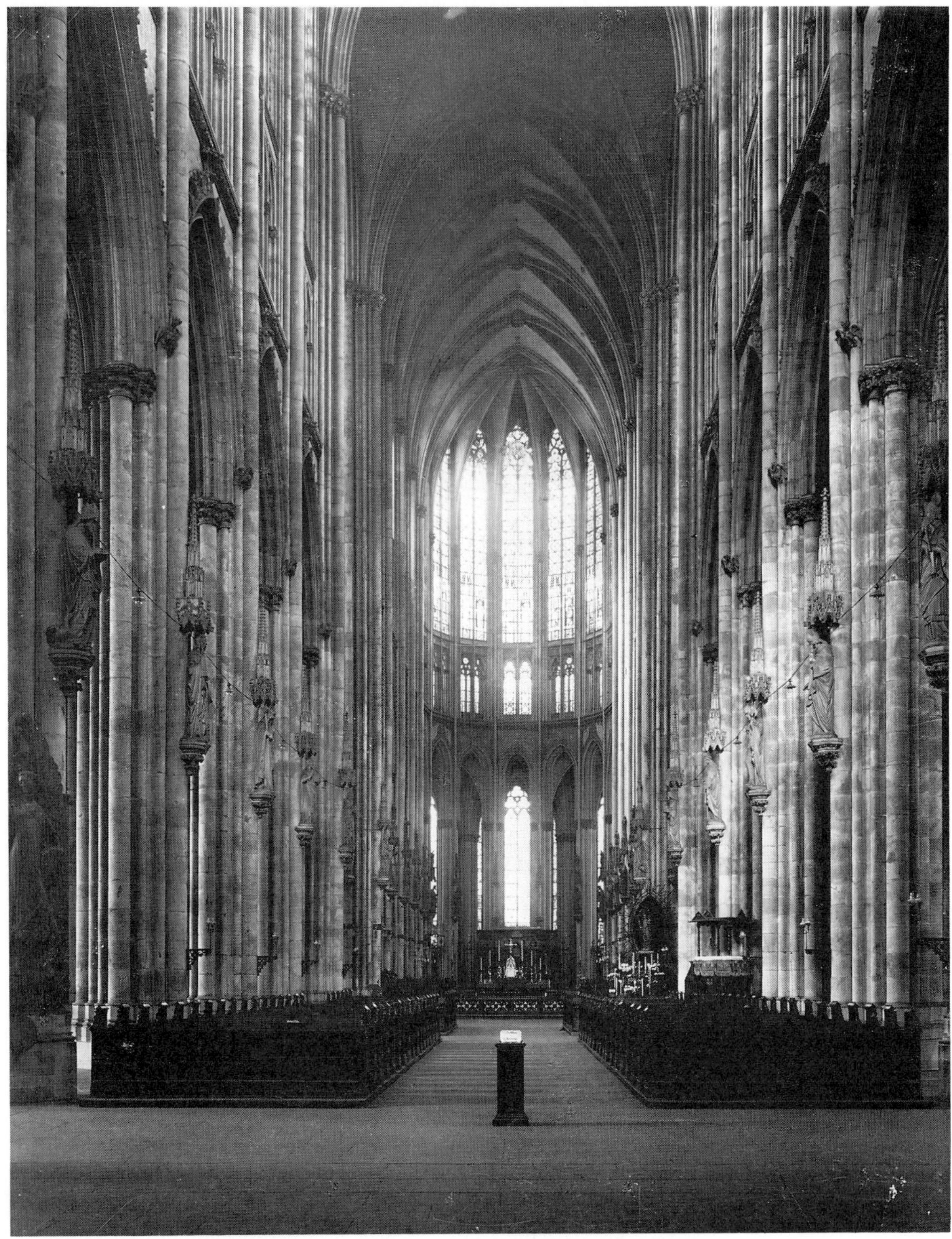

Cologne Cathedral: nave. See p.505

A. S. Barbara, Kutna Hora (1388–1534). See p.499

B. Prague Cathedral (fourteenth to fifteenth centuries: nave, nineteenth century). See p.500

C. Liebfrauenkirche, Trier (1235–60). See p.505

D. Liebfrauenkirche, Trier: interior

more ambitious. The nave is a simplified version of Strasbourg, but the octagon and spire which crown the single tower/porch at the west end were developments rather than derivates of their Strasbourg models. Started *c.* 1300 they were the first of their kind to be completed in Germany, and their perfection was never equalled. They were used as models for Cologne, and in a less direct way their influence can be detected throughout German late Gothic, and even as far afield as Italy.

The emperor Charlemagne, who died in 814, was canonised in 1165. His shrine, **Aachen Cathedral**, Germany (p. 375A), was finished when Frederick II was crowned in 1215; but it was left to Charles IV to provide the royal saint with a suitable reliquary chapel. It was built between 1355 and 1414 and is now the cathedral choir. It was clearly based on the S. Chapelle in Paris, but is taller and the east end is more obviously centrally planned.

Although there was a flourishing local school of transitional Gothic in the lower Rhineland at the time, the archbishop of Cologne wanted something quite different for the new **Cathedral of Cologne**, Germany (pp. 502, 503) that was started in 1284. The designer was Master Gerhard who, though no doubt German, was thoroughly conversant with contemporary French Gothic, in particular the works of Thomas de Cormont at Amiens and the S. Chapelle. The cathedral was consecrated in 1322, by which time designs for the west front had already been prepared. But work ground to a halt *c.* 1330, and thereafter proceeded intermittently and slowly until 1560, when it was abandoned in a half-finished state. The fragment narrowly escaped destruction in the time of Napoleon but was eventually completed to the mediaeval design in a fit of nationalistic euphoria between 1842 and 1880.

The design falls into two distinct parts. The choir, and by implication the nave as well, was a painstaking exercise in French High Gothic and Rayonnant. It provided the experience in which two and more generations of German masons mastered the secrets of the art.

In the fourteenth century masons from Cologne carried the style into the remoter parts of the German world, and in due course began to develop Gothic in directions quite different from those taken by the French. The west front is a case in point. Instead of the sham facade of Amiens, they accepted the challenge of matching real towers and spires to the height of the interior. It entailed spires over 500 feet high. The model was Freiburg, and to a lesser extent Strasbourg. Although Cologne remained unfinished during the Middle Ages, it inspired a whole new category of prodigy towers and spires throughout Germany and the Low Countries.

The Constantinian cathedral of **Trier**, Germany, had two churches which stood side by side. The northern component, much altered and augmented, survives as the present cathedral. The southern church, the **Liebfrauenkirche** (pp. 504C,D), had to be replaced in the thirteenth century. It had become especially associated with the cult of the Virgin and served as a kind of superior Lady Chapel. Work on the new church began *c.* 1235 and was finished by 1260. The plan is centralised as though for a martyrium, like the Elizabeth church at Marburg, but without a nave. Its most celebrated features are the pairs of chapels, inclined at 45 degrees to the main axes, set over against each of the four piers of the crossing. The ultimate source of this idea was S. Yved at Braisne, but there are Burgundian features at Trier which suggest that a more immediate inspiration was the S. Chapelle at Dijon. Despite its somewhat remorseless logic, the Liebfrauenkirche is one of the first churches in Germany to display real insight into the possibilities of the Gothic style.

Low Countries: Architectural Character

The position of the Low Countries, to the north of the parts of France where Gothic began, and to the west of Germany where its most extragavant later flourishes are to be found, tends to colour impressions of their architectural history during the Middle Ages. They are seen as taking their character first from one, then the other of their greater neighbours. While this interpretation is not entirely untrue, it is somewhat misleading. The historical picture has been seriously distorted by the destruction of several outstanding monuments such as S. Donatianus at Bruges, S. Pierre at Ghent, the cathedral of S. Lambert at Liège, and the west front of Louvain. If they had survived it would be clear that Flanders was almost as deeply involved as northern France in the formative stages of Gothic, and that in its later days it owed nothing to the Germans in respect of prodigies and fantasies.

Patterns of architectural development do not necessarily coincide exactly with the incidence of wealth, but lavish and ostentatious patronage has always been a *sine qua non* for experiment, and the mere fact that during the Middle Ages the Low Countries were the only part of Europe which came anywhere near to having an industrial economy should remind us that at the very least the financing of great buildings was never a problem there. Another inducement was the intense local patriotism and rivalry between the cities. It actually mattered at Louvain that the great church of the town should have the tallest spire for miles around, and vast sums were spent on this not particularly pious project.

Prodigy towers were something of a speciality in the Low Countries, but history has not been kind to them. The most ambitious either came to grief, or else

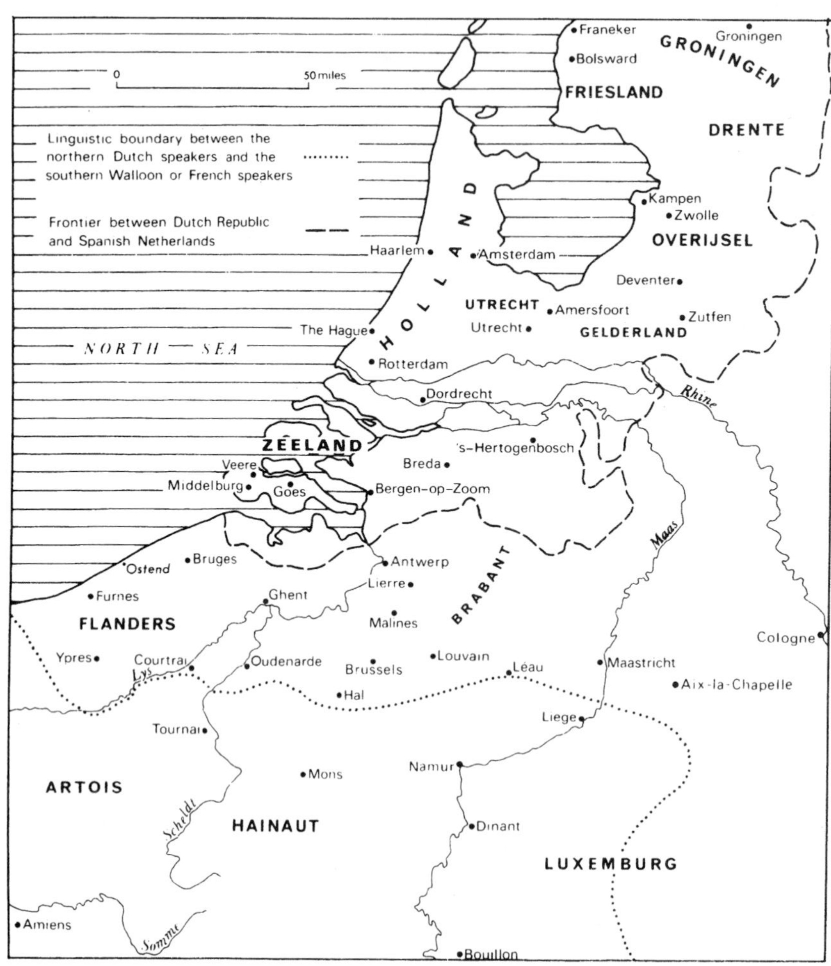

The Low Countries in the sixteenth century

were never finished. There is a seventeenth-century drawing of the free-standing tower at S. Lievans, Zierikzee in Zeeland, Holland, with an octagon in the style of Rombout Keldermans, which it has been reckoned would have been over 200 m (660 ft) high. This was probably regarded as a kind of lighthouse; but there is no evidence that it was ever more than a speculative drawing.

A further manifestation of civic pride in architecture was the series of fine public buildings such as the cloth-hall at Ypres and the town halls at Brussels and Louvain. In this respect the Low Countries resembled nothing so much as northern Italy.

In Romanesque times the art for which the Low Countries were chiefly celebrated was metalwork. The craftsmanship on which this fame was based did not disappear. The Gothic shrine-makers of the Meuse valley became adept at what might be called 'toy' architecture – metal structures which reproduced on a miniature scale the forms and features of real churches. The Shrine of S. Gertrude at Nivelles (1272) was in effect a tiny Rayonnant cathedral, complete with rose window and sculptured portal. (It was destroyed in 1940). Because there were no structural problems, these designs could assume a delicacy and a degree of fantastic elaboration far beyond the scope of real masonry. However, the examples of metalwork were a spur to the ingenuity of the architects, and much of the virtuoso masonry to be seen in the towers and spires of late Gothic was inspired by conscious rivalry.

The extent to which Gothic churches were actually meant to be understood as reliquary shrines has been much argued; but there can be no doubt that masons and metalworkers shared the same methods of design. There is documentary proof of this from Germany at the end of the fifteenth century. However, there is every likelihood that the affinities between the two arts emerged in the Low Countries before they appeared in Germany, France or Italy. It may even be suggested that this represents the principal contribution of the Low Countries to the history of Gothic architecture. In this connection it may be noted that curvilinear tracery, which is not something that would readily occur to a stonemason, might easily recommend itself to someone working strip-metal. In stone, curvilinear tracery turned up in England during the first half of the fourteenth century. A century later it became the defining characteristic of French Flamboyant. How it got from one to the other has always been something of a puzzle. English soldiers at large in France during the Hundred Years War are not likely to provide a solution. There is a distinct possibility that the agents of transmission may have come from the Low Countries.

All the relevant buildings have disappeared. It is impossible to say whether there was a distinctive kind of Gothic peculiar to the Low Countries. On the evidence of Tournai, Antwerp and s'Hertogenbosch, their cathedrals were as ambitious as any in Europe. But it is the town churches that we would wish to know more about.

In spite of their considerable autonomy the towns of the Low Countries were never far removed from the wider stage of mediaeval politics. The cloth industry depended largely on the wool trade with England. Their manufactured goods found outlets southward through the fairs of Champagne, and eastward to the Rhineland. Dynastic links with their powerful neighbours shaped their history. One notable marriage in the fourteenth century joined Flanders to French Burgundy; another in the late fifteenth century turned them into a possession of the House of Habsburg. A somewhat unexpected consequence of this last connection was that large numbers of Flemish masons and craftsmen found employment in Spain at a time when large sums were being invested in art and architecture. Quite a lot of the best Flemish work of the early sixteenth century is to be found in Spain, for example Astorga. On the other hand there is a distinctly Spanish opulence about the latest of the late Gothic churches of the Low Countries, S Jacques at Liège.

Low Countries: Examples

The **Basilica of Notre Dame, Tongres** (p. 510A), was started during the thirteenth century in a style which reflects a mixture of Rayonnant and provincial Burgundian. The apse was replaced in the fourteenth century with tall chapel-choir windows, and the nave was completed in the fifteenth century. The single west tower never received the projected spire which would have put it into the prodigy class, but it has a polygonal porch by way of compensation.

Tournai Cathedral (p. 508B) was rebuilt after the diocese was split in 1112 (the other half was Noyon). It falls into two parts. The four-storey nave was followed by apsidal-ended transepts with a distinctive cluster of five towers, one over the crossing and two on each transept (compare Laon). The transepts are later than the nave but both were fundamentally Romanesque. The choir (started *c.* 1247) is on a totally different scale. It was derived from Cambrai (destroyed) and like Cambrai owed much to Amiens. Together they mark the arrival of High Gothic from France, but at the same time they illustrate the transition from High Gothic to Rayonnant, for example the appearance of glazed triforia and of gables over clerestory windows.

S. Gudule, Brussels (p. 509). Together with **S. Martin at Ypres** and Notre Dame de la Pamele at Oudenarde it represents the earliest surviving Gothic in Belgium (choir stated 1226). Although rustic and out of date for its time by French standards, it took a long time to complete and reflects many changes of style. The two-towered west front was only completed in the sixteenth century.

Cathedral of S. Rombout, Malines (p. 510C). A fourteenth-century church with a late Gothic west tower. The tower rises over 90 m (300 ft).

The Collegiate Church of S. Peter, Louvain (p. 510B), started in 1425 had perhaps the finest of all the prodigy facades to be built: a three-towered design, of which the central one reached a height of over 150 m (500 ft). It was destroyed in a storm in 1606.

Collegiate Church of S. Waudru, Mons (p. 510D). This late Gothic church was started in 1450, and work was abandoned in 1621. Built on the scale of a cathedral it was intended to have the most prodigious of all the prodigy towers – it would have been over 180 m (600 ft) high. Only the foundations were built.

Collegiate Church of Notre Dame, Huy (p. 512A). A fourteenth-century church with a chapel choir, which is to say it had no ambulatory and tall windows ran the full height of the building. The choir was flanked by a pair of towers – a Romanesque feature, although all the details are Gothic. The entrance to the canons' cloister has one of the rare surviving examples of portal sculpture – the so-called Bethlehem (late fourteenth century).

The Cathedral of Notre Dame, Antwerp (p. 511), was started in 1352 and is the largest Gothic church in Belgium. It was unusual in having no less than three aisles on either side of the nave, the outer rows being in effect chapels. Its outstanding feature is the west front, in particular the north-west tower, which is over 120 m (400 ft) high. It was built in conscious emulation of Strasbourg, but is quite different in detail, being far more ornate. It was the first of a series of prodigy towers and spires to be projected in Belgium and the only one to have survived.

The Romanesque **Cathedral of S. Martin, Utrecht** (pp. 512B,C), was burnt in 1253 and the present church started the following year. The nave

A WINDOWS TOWN HALL: LOUVAIN

B S. APSE: TOURNAI

C ARCHWAY S. JACQUES: LIEGE

D CHIMNEY-PIECE: TOWN HALL: COURTRAI

E CHIMNEY-PIECE: TOWN HALL: OUDENARDE

F ARCADE & VAULTING: THE BOURSE: ANTWERP

G SCREEN: AERSCHOT

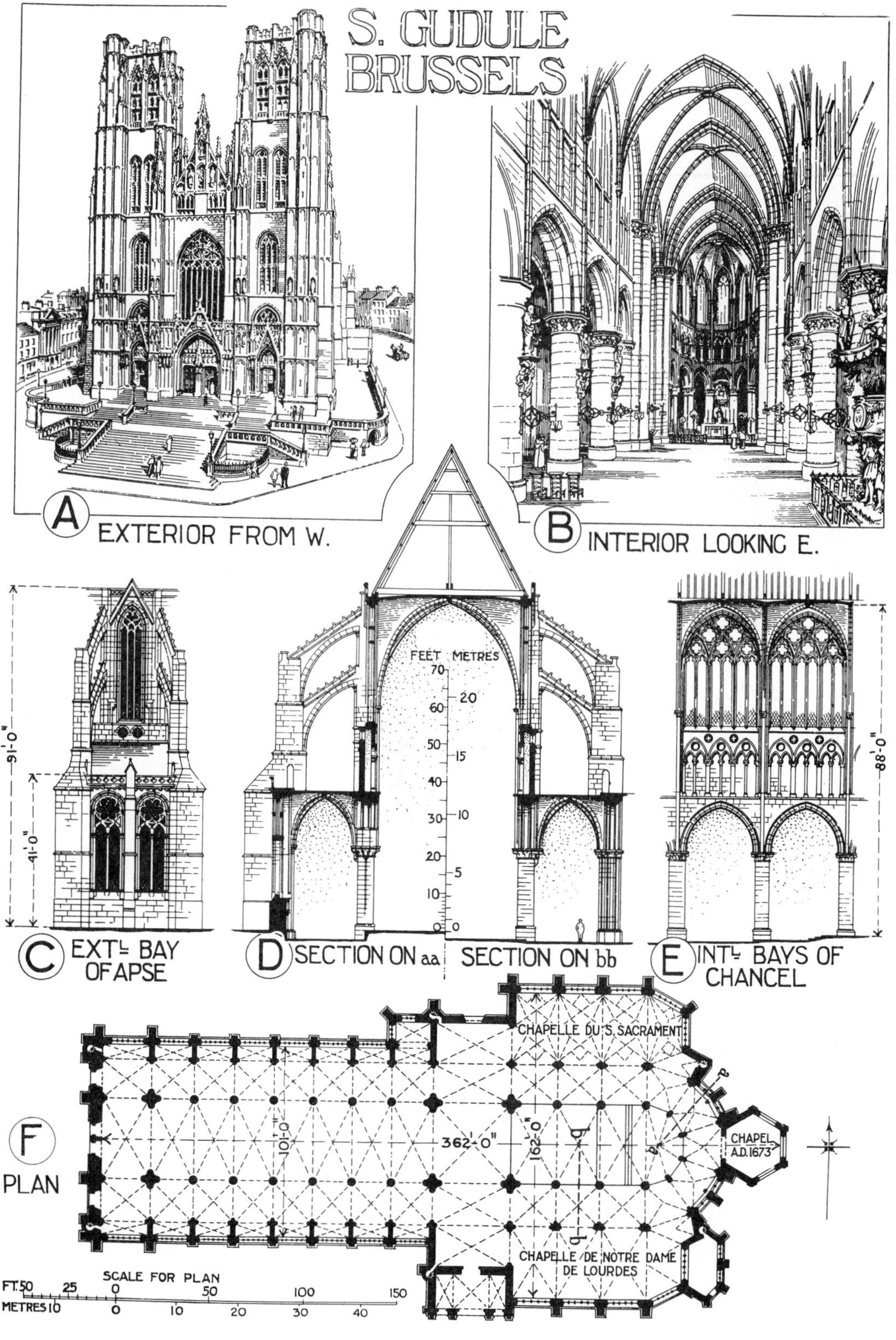
S. GUDULE
BRUSSELS
A EXTERIOR FROM W.
B INTERIOR LOOKING E.
91'-0"
41'-0"
FEET METRES
70
60
20
50
15
40
30
10
20
5
10
0
0
88'-0"
C EXTL BAY OF APSE
D SECTION ON aa SECTION ON bb
E INTL BAYS OF CHANCEL
CHAPELLE DU S. SACRAMENT
101'-0"
362'-0"
162'-0"
CHAPEL A.D. 1673
CHAPELLE DE NOTRE DAME DE LOURDES
F PLAN
SCALE FOR PLAN
FT. 50 25 0 50 100 150
METRES 10 0 10 20 30 40

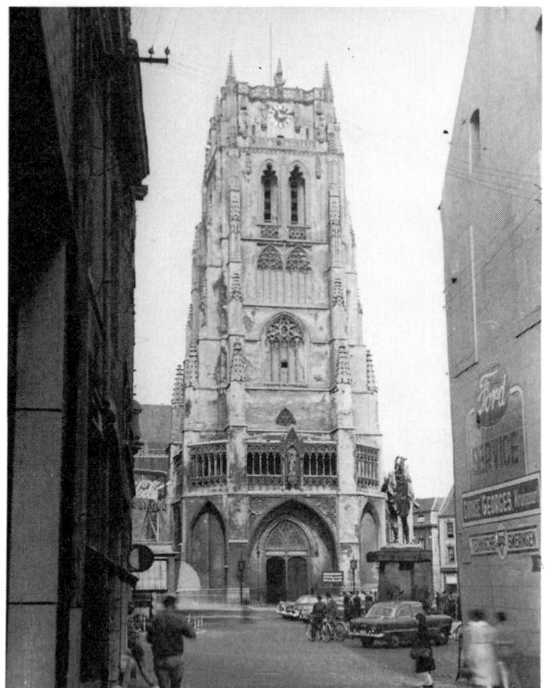

A. Notre Dame, Tongres (thirteenth to fourteenth centuries). See p.507

B. S. Peter, Louvain (1425–, facade destroyed 1606). See p.507

C. Cathedral of S. Rombout, Malines (fourteenth century). See p.507

D. S. Waudru, Mons (1450–1621). See p.507

E. Great Church, Dordrecht (1339–sixteenth century). See p.516

ANTWERP CATHEDRAL

a — a
AISLES — NAVE — AISLES
388'0"
172'0"
TOWER

(A) PLAN

(B) INTERIOR LOOKING E.

92'0"

(C) SECTION a-a

50 0 50 100 150 FT
10 0 10 20 30 40 MTS

(D) EXTERIOR FROM N. W.

A. Notre Dame, Huy (fourteenth century). See p.507

B. Utrecht Cathedral: choir (1254–67). See p.507

C. Utrecht Cathedral: detached west tower

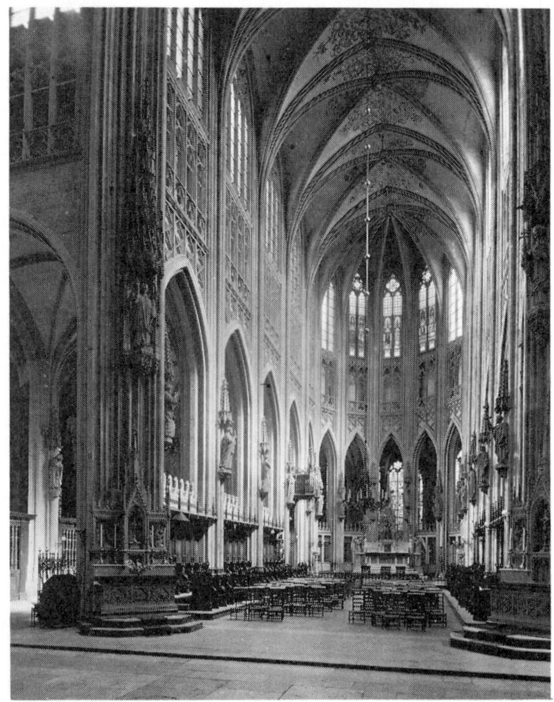

D. S. Janskerk, s'Hertogenbosch: choir (1370–1415). See p.516

A. Goes: Church and Town Hall. See p.516

B. Rabot Fort, Ghent (1488). See p.516

C. Town Hall, Ghent (1515–28 and later). See p.516

A
TOWN HALL: OUDENARDE
B THE SKIPPER'S HO. GHENT
C CLOTH HALL & BELFRY: BRUGES
D OLD HOUSES MALINES
E TOWN HALL: BRUSSELS
F TOWN HALL: BRUGES
G TOWN HALL: LOUVAIN

A. Castle of Muiden, near Amsterdam (thirteenth century). See p.516

B. Cloth Hall, Ypres (rebuilt since World War I). See p.516

collapsed in 1674, separating the single west tower from the choir and transept. The choir is a simplification of Cologne – the dominant influence in the lower Rhineland when Utrecht was being built. The fourteenth-century tower has the open-work octagon which first appeared at Freiburg in Breisgau (*c.* 1300), and was itself the source for the west-front towers of Cologne. The tower of Utrecht, which is 115 m (384 ft) high, was celebrated throughout the Low Countries. It can be recognised in the Van Eyck painting, the Holy Lamb, at Ghent.

S. Janskerk, s'Hertogenbosch (Bois-le-Duc) (p. 512D). The most important church in north Brabant. Originally a parish church, it became collegiate in 1366, and a cathedral in 1559. Rebuilding started in the late fourteenth century and continued throughout the following century. Although not on the largest scale, it is extremely ornate – not the least of its embellishments being a particularly fine set of choir stalls.

S. Nicholas, Kampen. A mainly fourteenth-century church, reflecting the prosperity of a port – which silted up in the fifteenth century. Its principal interest is the net vault over the choir, which was clearly derived from German models. The architect, Rutza of Kampen, was working in Prague during the 1370s under Peter Parler, and his daughter married Peter Parler's nephew.

S. Jacques, Liège (p. 508C). Built between 1513 and 1538, it is the latest and also perhaps the most ornate of all Belgian churches. It has by far the most complicated vault – a pattern of liernes which resembles many late Gothic vaults in Spain. Although it was fundamentally Gothic in design, much of its decoration is already Renaissance in character, especially the glass.

Notre Dame de la Pamele, Oudenarde (1234 and after), made of blue-black Tournai limestone, is by Arnould de Binche, partly in the local Scheldt Gothic style which soon afterwards established itself in Zeeland.

Notre Dame, Bruges (1239–97), with its tall plain tower, and **S. Bavon, Ghent** (choir, 1274–1300), are characteristic of early Flemish Gothic adapting itself to brickwork.

The Great Churches of **Dordrecht** (1339–sixteenth century) (p. 510E) and **Haarlem** (1400–90) are more typically Dutch, being of brick and stone, spacious and plain. Both are simplified Brabantine, with Haarlem belonging to the local style of Aerschot, called Demer Gothic. Dordrecht has brick vaulting, but that of Haarlem nave is timber. In Zeeland the churches of **Middelburg, Goes** (p. 513A), **Hulst, Veere** and others followed the Scheldt and coastal Flemish-Brabantine traditions. **S. Michael, Zwolle** (*c.* 1350–1450), is a hall church deriving from Germany; these are common in east and central Holland but rare in Belgium – **Damme**, in west Flanders, is an exception.

The ruined **Abbey Church of Villers** (Belgian Luxembourg) (1216–67) and the **Dominican Church, Maastricht** (after 1260), represent early Maas (Meuse) Gothic with blind triforium arcades and typical leaf capitals, while **Meersen** (fourteenth century) is later and richer. This Mass style includes tall, narrow apse windows reaching to within a couple of metres of the ground.

In the north-east of Holland at **Bolsward, Franeker** and **Groningen** there are churches in provincial variants of the main styles. Here the parish churches in villages are of brick and very simple, with high domed vaults and much wall arcading – very different from those of other parts; examples are **Stedum** and **Zuidbroek**.

Secular Architecture

At **Kampen**, three fifteenth-century gateways, white and capped by steep conical roofs, give an idea of a Dutch mediaeval walled town; at **Ghent**, the **Rabot Fort** (1488) (p. 513B) remains of the fortifications together with the **Château des Comtes** (twelfth century); while at **Bouillon** is a castle more typical of the countryside. In Holland the **Castle of Muiden** (thirteenth century) (p. 515A), near Amsterdam, relied largely on water for its defence, and the **Binnenhof**, seat of the Counts of Holland at The Hague, has a knights' hall of 1250 with a typical large arch-braced roof.

The **Hospital**, the **Byloke, Ghent** (thirteenth century and later), and the **Béguinage** there, are examples of precinct planning and grouping. A Béguinage (Dutch Begijnhof) is an open order for women, founded in Brabant in the thirteenth century, and peculiar to the Netherlands; the work of the Sisters is among the poor, and they live in houses grouped around a court containing a chapel. The establishments at **Bruges, Courtrai** and **Breda** are still in use, but not that at **Amsterdam** – few have much mediaeval building left.

Belgium, and to a lesser extent Holland, is rich in mediaeval town halls symptomatic of the wealth of its cities. **Bruges** (1376–) (p. 514F), **Louvain** (1448–63) (p. 514G) by Mathieu de Layens, **Ghent** (1515–28 and later) (p. 513C) by D. van Waghemakere, **Oudenarde** (1525–30) (p. 514A) by Jan van Pede and **Brussels** (1402–) (p. 514E) by Jakob van Thienen, with a tower (1448–63) by Jan van Ruysbroeck (1448–63), are magnificent and ornate; simpler is **Damme** (sixteenth century), near Bruges. Dutch examples in the Flemish-Brabantine style are **Middelburg** (1412–1599), by the Keldermans of Malines (rebuilt after 1945), and **Veere** (1474–1599). Weighhouses are also typical of Holland; the one at **Deventer**, of brick and stone, is late Gothic.

The greatest of the Cloth Halls was at **Ypres** (1202–1304) (p. 515B), outstanding not only because of its size, 134 m (440 ft) long, but also because of its majestic simplicity. It was destroyed in 1915, and the present one is a replica. That at **Bruges** (p. 514C) has a tower 80 m (260 ft) high (1282 with later lantern), and is typical of Flemish brick and stone civic architecture. The Guild Houses in the Grand' Place, **Antwerp** (p. 1002C), though sixteenth-century, have only a little Classical ornament, but those of **Brussels** (p. 1003A) belong to the early Renaissance. The **Maison des Francs Bateliers** ('Skipper's House'), **Ghent** (1531) (p. 514B), and the **Vieille Boucherie, Antwerp** (1501), are further examples of Guild Houses.

The **Maison Havart, Liège** (1594), and **S. Peter's House, Middelburg** (sixteenth century), are among the few surviving timber-framed houses; patricians' and merchants' houses in stone, such as some at **Malines** (p. 514D), and others in brick are more numerous. The **Zoudenbalch House, Utrecht** (1467), and **Het Lammetje, Veere** (House of the Scottish Merchants) (mid-sixteenth century), are stone houses of very different types. Typical brick houses are found at **Furnes** and **Goes** in the Flemish style, and in eastern Holland at **Zutfen**.

Spain: Architectural Character

Early Gothic

The Cistercian Order introduced a primitive brand of Gothic architecture into the peninsula. It is characterised by standardised plans, restricted decoration, the replacement of barrel vaults by rib vaults and the solid, Romanesque, wall. Moreruela (Zamora), their first abbey (founded 1131), is in picturesque ruins but one of their grandest foundations, Alcobaca (Portugal), survives.

Fully fledged Gothic architecture arrived in the late twelfth and thirteen the centuries from northern France. It is recognised by its sophisticated plans, foliate capitals and the exploitation of the rib vault. This resulted in an increased size and better interior illumination. At first only its influence was felt but soon an entire cathedral was built. This was Avila and is quite close in time to the first Gothic structure, the Abbey of S. Denis, Paris (1140s).

Early Gothic architecture remained aloof from both Romanesque and Islamic Spain. Indeed, it was imported by such kings as Alfonso VIII of Castile (1158–1214) and Prelates like Archbishop Rodrigo of Toledo (died 1247) in protest against them. The trilobed triforium of the inner ambulatory at Toledo Cathedral – derived from the Mudéjar synagogue of S. Maria La Blanca, Toledo – is an aberration. León, like Pamplona, is emphatically French. When a synthesis did occur, as at the College of San Miguel, Aguilar de Campós (1346), the imported style, that of Burgos, was combined with the simple plan and enormous scale of the traditional great church.

Late Gothic

Late Gothic began like early Gothic architecture with the importation of northern architects. In 1442 Alonso de Cartegena, Bishop of Burgos, brought to Spain the Rhinelander, Hans of Cologne (Juan de Colonia), to refurbish his cathedral. However, while the great achievements of early Gothic are largely French those of late Gothic are essentially Spanish.

It consists of two styles. Isabelline architecture is that of the Catholic monarchs, Ferdinand and Isabella (1474–1516). It is propaganda in stone. Plans are traditional but the love of display is new. The Portuguese equivalent is Manueline architecture. Plateresque architecture, as the word indicates, is 'silversmith-like'. This analogy was first used by Cristobal de Villalon in 1539 in a description of León Cathedral. Contemporaries, however, characterised it as being *a la romano*, that is, like that of the ancient Romans. The facade of the University, Salamanca, is appropriately described in terms of metalwork but the contemporary phrase does more justice to Granada Cathedral. These styles are distinct – Isabelline has Gothic, Plateresque has Renaissance detailing – but not antithetic. For example, the most remarkable invention – that of the retable-like facade – made by Isabelline architects to satisfy the desire for advertisement was exploited by Plateresque designers. This suggests that late Gothic architecture can be treated as a whole.

It is from this perspective that its Spanish character is revealed. For instance, Islamic art was revived. This took place in Burgos as well as Toledo. It gave to even such an impecably Gothic structure as La Capilla del Condestable, Burgos, an exotic feeling. Apparently, the northern architects found the Islamic love of hanging, patterned ornaments congenial, and patrons seem to have accepted a new definition of a Christian building. Furthermore, the great late-mediaeval cathedrals depend upon Iberian precedents, especially Toledo Cathedral which was only completed in 1429. Gothic or Plateresque, they employ indigenous structures; thus a building type imported to underline the Reconquista was still used, thanks to New World riches, at Granada. It gives Spain's Gothic experience a unique coherence.

Catalan Gothic

This is a late Gothic, national style: its formation mirrors the history of Aragon-Catalonia. Just as the dynastic union of Aragon-Catalonia (1137) was turned into a Mediterranean power by Jaime I (1213–76) and his successors, in competition with the

A. Tarragona Cathedral (1117–1331). See p.519

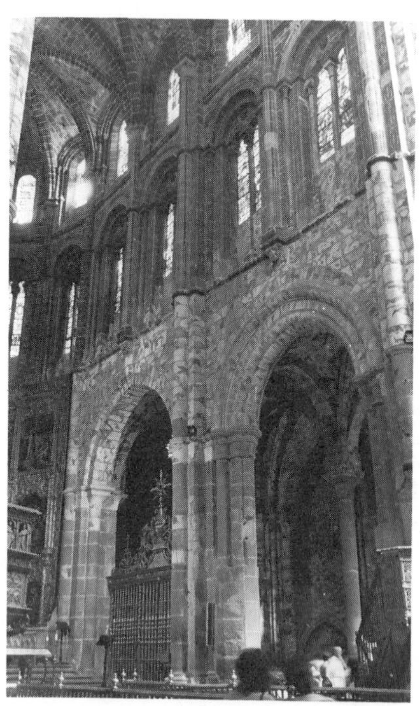

B. Avila Cathedral (begun *c.* 1180). See p.519

C. Toledo Cathedral from SW (1227–1493). See p.521

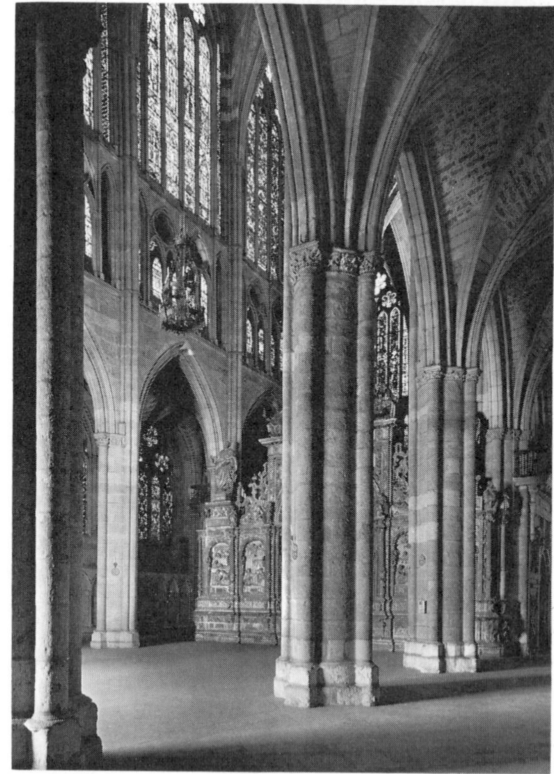

D. León Cathedral: interior (1255–1303). See p.521

Capetians, so Catalan Gothic was created by rivalry – through emulation – with French Gothic architecture. Furthermore, as Catalan influence spread so did its architecture; for example, the Abbey Church of La Chaise-Dieu (Haute-Loire) is related to Manresa Cathedral.

The style is characterised by exploitation of the internal buttress, a distinctive taste and the determined pursuit of ambiguity. The internal buttress as first found in the chevet of Barcelona Cathedral derives from southern French Gothic architecture. However, it had been used widely in Catalonia before this time to support both wooden roofs (Liria) and ribbed vaults (Catarina, Barcelona). The success and development of the style in large-scale Catalan architecture is explicable only in terms of the impact of an indigenous tradition. For example, the passageway between the tribunes of the nave of Barcelona Cathedral is foreshadowed by that between the lateral chapels of Barcelona's Dominican convent (1245–75), and the same tradition formed the taste embodied on a grand scale in, say, S. Maria del Mar, Barcelona. While the internal buttresses of a primitive structure like S. Felix, Jativa, cut across the spectator's view and dominated the space with their plain masonry, the buttresses of a triple-vasselled church like S. Maria del Mar are less prominent. The triumph of the wall over the skeletal structure of French Gothic architecture is clear. In Catalonia space was contained and cut up, not illuminated and etched out.

The ambiguity of conception of Catalan churches can be considered together with their obsession with size – a French legacy. After all, Narbonne Cathedral on which the chevets of Gerona and Barcelona Cathedrals are based had stepped elevations – halfway between being a basilican and a hall church. But Catalan architects, in seizing upon this idea, rejected the balanced pose of their French exemplar. Moreover, ambiguity was pursued at a time when French architects favoured basilicas. It is almost as if Catalan architects were picking their way between rejecting the French solution and so becoming outcasts and accepting it and so becoming French. Thus one finds structures like S. Maria del Mar, Barcelona, and the nave of Barcelona Cathedral which threaten to dissolve the basilican format, or a building like Manresa which seeks to reintroduce it. Gerona Cathedral gives up the attempt at reconciliation and opts for erecting the largest hall; the Cathedral of Palma de Majorca seeks the best of both worlds.

Spain: Examples

Early Gothic

Tarragona Cathedral (p. 518A) was the epitome of the Spanish great church before the introduction of Gothic architecture and was built in two stages as the metropolitan Cathedral of Tarragona (1171–1331). At first, it was conceived as a massive and relatively dark structure – the main structure is 14 m (46 ft) wide and barrel-vaulted. The aim was to honour and emulate the city's Roman past and antique remains: the site is that of a Temple of Jupiter. To do so, ideas were borrowed from Romanesque France. Double attached columns with flanking colonnettes were planned to support the tranverse arches. These responds must be derived from such a building as S. Etienne de la Cité, Perigueux, but they do have a Roman bulkiness. Similarly, the Benedictine plan was adopted but modified – by the addition of chapels projecting from the transepts – to achieve an antique scale.

In about 1180, another idea had become available: the rib vault and its associated, proper, clerestory. As a result, in the east end the responds were heightened to create room for the windows, and the role of flanking colonnettes changed to that of rib supports. What resulted was a lighter but no less massive structure. Indeed, its size was enhanced as the nave now rose to a height of 26 m (85 ft). It is this cathedral, cavernous and muscular, which was imitated and elaborated upon throughout north-east Spain, though Tudela (consecrated 1204) has more light, Matallana (begun 1228) more complicated piers.

Avila Cathedral (p. 518B), its choir begun *c.* 1180 by Fruchel, is one of the first Gothic structures in Spain. Only its site seems characteristically Spanish, as if it were the chapel of a castle like that of the Archbishop Rodrigo at Briheuga (Guadalajara); its exterior wall comprises part of Avila's town walls (largely built 1091–*c.* 1135). However, the battlemented exterior hides a luminous, spacious chevet without precedent in the peninsula.

The plan is derived from that of S. Denis: there is the same double ambulatory and ring of shallow chapels. The elevation, including the choir's curious rib arrangement, is based on that of Vézelay (begun 1185–90). However, the details show the influences of the Burgundian, Romanesque scuptural tradition which was so strong in late twelfth-century north-west Spain. Cistercian influence is apparent. The use of ribs with pointed ends and moulded capitals in the inner ambulatory testifies to this. The technical means employed were French but eclectic. This separation of the source of the plans and the features used in a building, and the eclectic nature of these features, is a characteristic of other Spanish cathedrals. Happily, at Avila the mixture works: although the choir is tall – 28 m (92 ft) – as befits a French design, the ambulatory is intimate and the whole is warm and not unduly austere.

Founded in 884 as an outpost on the Christian frontier, by the late twelfth century Burgos had become the unofficial capital of Castile and had a

BURGOS
CATHL.
A CAPILLA DEL CONDESTABLE
B TRANSEPTS & CIMBORIO
C EXTERIOR FROM S.E.
CAPILLA
DEL CONDES-
TABLE
CHOIR
172'.0"
350'.0"
CLOISTERS
FOUNTAIN
ARCHBISHOP'S PALACE
D PLAN
FT 50 0 50 100
MTRS 10 0 10 20 30
E EXTERIOR FROM W.

Romanesque Cathedral. It must have seemed inappropriately dingy to the participants in the marriage of Fernando III which took place there in 1219. At any rate between 1221 and 1260 **Burgos Cathedral** (p. 520B–E) was built in the French manner. It consists of three separate brands of Gothic architecture. Inside, the impact of Bourges is most obvious, although Norman Gothic architecture influenced the clerestory and vaults. Outside, the dominant tone is that of Reims. The same elevation was used for the transept and nave, which were constructed thirteen years later, as for the chevet – even though when building resumed it was under the direction of an architect called Henri (died 1277) trained at Reims Cathedral, a building with a more advanced elevation.

The plan is derived from that of Cistercian Pontigny and the whole ensemble fits into that early thirteenth-century group of three-storey elevations with tribune-like triforia of the Ile de France. However, the effect of the original structure is now difficult to recapture. The cimborio (1539–68) caused a dramatic transformation of the interior.

When Islamic power in the peninsula was finally overcome at Las Navas de Tolosa (1212), Islamic art lost its prestige. Christian art was preferred to proclaim the Reconquista. Thus, when in 1227 Fernando III and Archbishop Rodrigo commissioned **Toledo Cathedral** (pp. 518C, 522D, 523B) they initiated a project to be based on French models and one which symbolically was to swallow up the site of the Great Mosque. An architect, Martin, is mentioned in 1227 and 1234: his workmen had been trained at Bourges (begun 1195).

Toledo has a particular flavour. The proportions of the stepped elevation differ from those of Bourges and the towering height of Bourges's inner ambulatory was abandoned. Instead, the ambulatories were stretched so that the chevet at Toledo measures 55 m (180 ft) across to Bourges's 40 m (130 ft). In short, the vertical expansion of space was replaced by a horizontal one. It seems as if the architect thought of his chevet as being centrally planned, the choir revealed by peeling back the inner ambulatory, a pioneering achievement with distinctive qualities.

Begun in 1255 by Bishop Martin Fernandez, **León Cathedral** (p. 518D) is the first and most impressive Rayonnant building in Spain. It was promoted by Alfonso X (1252–84) for political reasons in much the same way as Westminster Abbey by Henry III. In this case, the rebuilding of the cathedral of Spain's imperial city, León, in the style associated with the prestigious Capetian monarchy, was intended to advertise Alfonso's suitability as a candidate for the imperial crown.

The structure demonstrates a striving for modernity, so the plan is a reduction by a third on that of Reims. This is not surprising as Henri of Burgos was made responsible for León as well. His commission demanded up-to-date features from the architecture of S. Louis's capital. Thus, the interior passageway of the nave aisles was modelled on that of S. Germain en Laye, Paris (*c.* 1238), and the tracery of the straight bay of the hemicycle was based on Parisian designs of the 1240s such as that of the S. Chapelle, Paris (1242–8).

The cathedral is famous for its stained glass – the finest collection of late thirteenth- and fourteenth-century windows in Spain – and for the extensive thirteenth-century sculpture of its portals. Unlike the architecture the latter belongs to the end, not the beginning, of a style. For example, the arrangement of the three portals of the west facade was developed from that of the transepts at Chartres (1205–15); that on the trumeau of its central portal was derived from Amiens (begun 1220). However, the cathedral remains a unity, its sculptural embellishement an essential aspect of that French cathedral Alfonso X and Henri wished to construct.

Pamplona Cathedral is in the capital of Navarre, the traveller's first stop after the Roncesvalles Pass which from 1234 was ruled by the Counts of Champagne. The city boasted a number of examples of up-to-date French architecture of the day, the most notable example of which is the cathedral. Begun in 1397 by Charles III (1387–1425), it was completed in about 1525. In 1439 Jean de Lomme from Tournai became the cathedral architect. It is an advanced, Flamboyant structure. The choir is related to Norman fifteenth-century churches like Caudebec, while combining ambulatory and chapels under one set of vaults is derived from Soissons Cathedral. Pamplona is a good example of a refined, late mediaeval French cathedral only explicable in terms of its francophile patron.

Other **cathedrals** showing French influence include **Valencia** (*c.* 1262–1356) and **Lerida** (1203–78) (p. 522E), the latter an impressive early building with an octagonal cimborio, its roof slabs carried directly on the vaults. There are interesting smaller **churches** at **Valladolid** (1276–1492), **S. Pablo** (p. 525C), and at **Barcelona, SS. Justo y Pastor** (1345) and **S. Maria del Pino** (1453).

Late Gothic

La Capilla del Condestable, Burgos Cathedral (pp. 520A, 525D) – an octagonal, sepulchral chapel built by Simón de Colonia in 1482–94 for Pedro Fernandez de Velasco, Constable of Castile (died 1492) – belongs to a well-defined, late mediaeval, Spanish building type. The chapel is prized for its late Gothic portal and heraldic displays: the Constable's escutcheon appears to be held by wild men in front of the balustrades of the tribune and suspended diagonally from the walls below. But above all, there is the vault. Its ribs describe an eight-pointed star as in La

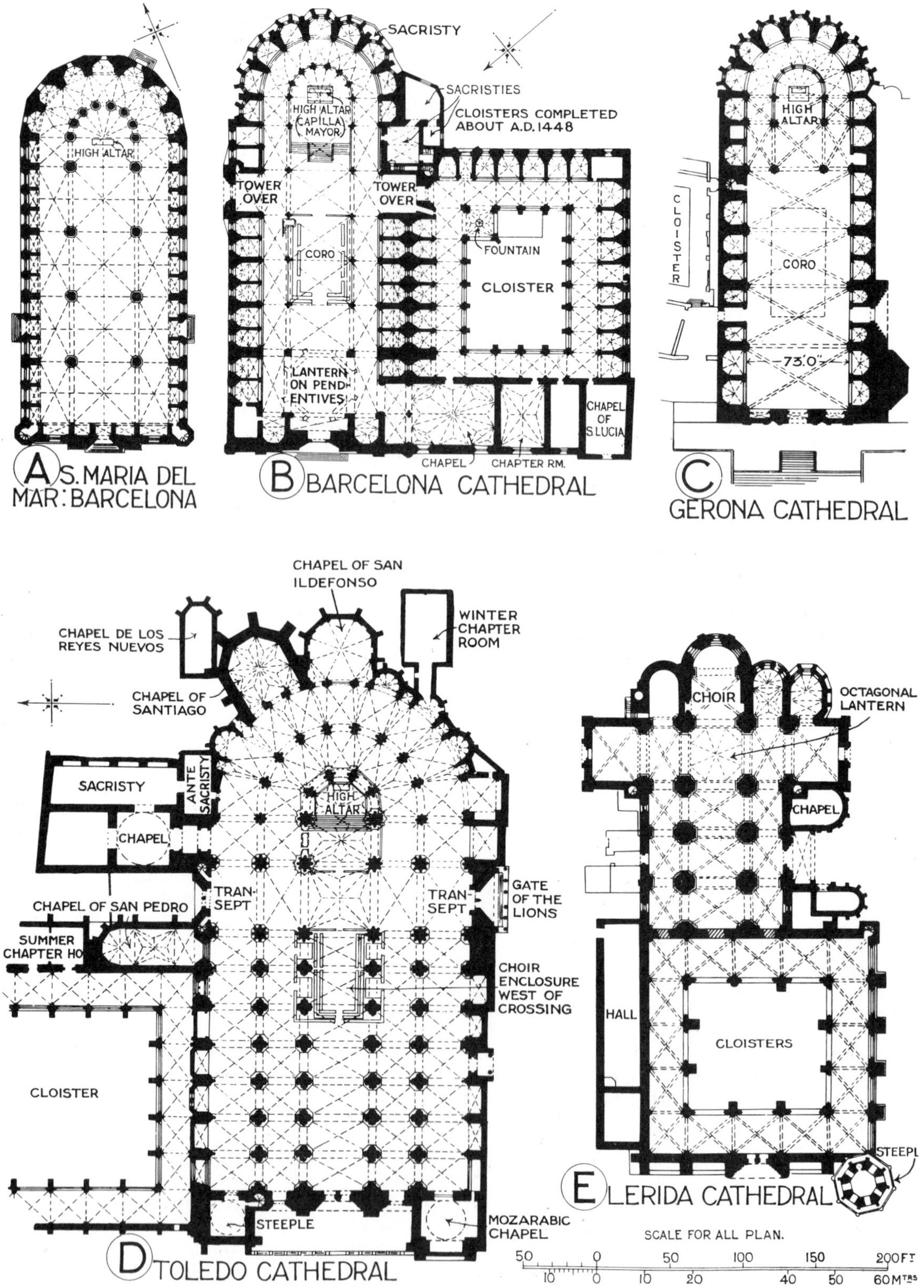

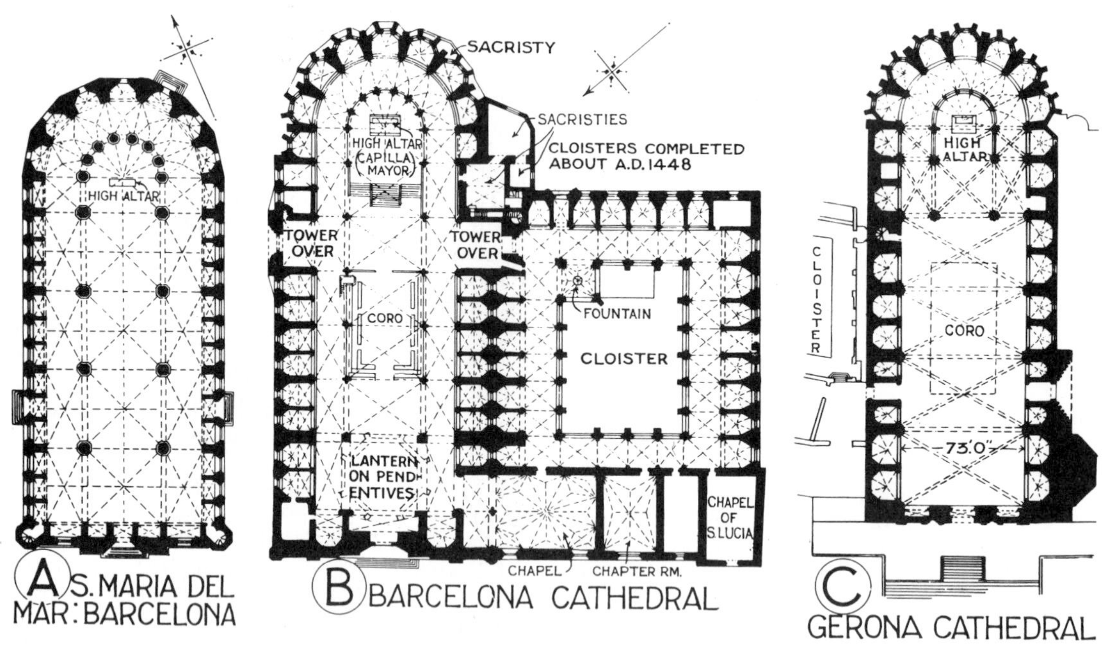

SACRISTY
SACRISTIES
CLOISTERS COMPLETED ABOUT A.D. 1448
HIGH ALTAR
HIGH ALTAR (CAPILLA MAYOR)
TOWER OVER
TOWER OVER
CORO
FOUNTAIN
CLOISTER
LANTERN ON PENDENTIVES
CHAPEL OF S.LUCIA
CHAPEL
CHAPTER RM.
CLOISTER
HIGH ALTAR
CORO
73'0"
A S.MARIA DEL MAR: BARCELONA
B BARCELONA CATHEDRAL
C GERONA CATHEDRAL
CHAPEL OF SAN ILDEFONSO
CHAPEL DE LOS REYES NUEVOS
WINTER CHAPTER ROOM
CHAPEL OF SANTIAGO
SACRISTY
ANTE SACRISTY
HIGH ALTAR
CHAPEL
CHAPEL OF SAN PEDRO
SUMMER CHAPTER HO
TRANSEPT
TRANSEPT
GATE OF THE LIONS
CHOIR ENCLOSURE WEST OF CROSSING
CLOISTER
STEEPLE
MOZARABIC CHAPEL
D TOLEDO CATHEDRAL
CHOIR
OCTAGONAL LANTERN
CHAPEL
HALL
CLOISTERS
STEEPL
E LERIDA CATHEDRAL
SCALE FOR ALL PLAN.
50 0 50 100 150 200FT
10 0 10 20 40 50 60MTRS

A HIGH ALTAR: SARAGOSSA CATHEDRAL

B CHAPEL OF SANTIAGO: TOLEDO.

C CLOISTER: S. JUAN DE LOS REYES: TOLEDO

D DOORWAY TO CAPILLA DE LOS REYES: GRANADA CATHEDRAL

Capilla de Catalina (1316–54), but so as to leave an empty field of the same shape in the centre. The open vault is an Islamic idea but Simón de Colonia treated it in his own way: the tracery infilling recalls the western towers of Burgos Cathedral built by his father, Juan de Colonia, between 1442–57.

San Juan de los Reyes, Toledo (pp. 523C, 525A), a Franciscan convent, was funded in 1477 by the Catholic monarchs in thanksgiving for the victory of Toro (1476) over Alfonso V of Portugal. It is the best example of Isabelline style and is the masterpiece of Juan Guas (died 1496), the most exciting late mediaeval Spanish architect.

The church consists of a single volume with internal buttresses and lateral chapels. The choir is polygonal, and although the transepts do not project sideways there is an unmistakable crossing emphasised by the lantern tower. This ensemble has a long tradition in central Spain – Vilamuriel de Cerrato (Palencia) is a thirteenth-century example. Thus, this unambitious structure demonstrates how wide-ranging were the Spanish roots of Isabelline art. The political nature of the style is more fully developed elsewhere. The exterior walls of the transepts are hung with the shackles of Christians liberated by the Catholic monarchs when they recaptured Malaga in 1487, and saints punctuate an heraldic celebration of the monarchy. No device was ignored which might glorify Ferdinand and Isabella.

The ribs of the lantern vault are arranged according to an Islamic design first found in the ruler's enclosure of the Great Mosque, Córdoba (961–5). The present church has a nave elevation like that of Brou, Bourg en Bresse (Ain), built between 1506 and 1532, with a tall clerestory and balustraded interior passageway. Guas explored the Gothic idiom as well as Islamic practices to produce a luxuriant hybrid – a building in which the universal pretensions of the Catholic monarchs were encapsulated.

The **Facade of the College of San Gregorio, Valladolid** (p. 525B). Facades in late fifteenth-century and early sixteenth-century Spain were treated as if they were retables: they were characterised by complex architectural structures within which heraldry or scenes were placed. The stone facades, like the wooden retables, were partly painted. The facade of this college, founded in 1480 by Fray Alonso de Burgos, the Confessor of Isabella of Castile, is the best Isabelline example.

The arboreal forms of the structure are striking. For example, the outer arch of the portal is conceived of as a root and culminates in a tree with putti playing in its branches. Similar forms are used by Gil de Siloe on his retable for **La Cartuja de Miraflores** (1496–9), suggesting that he also designed this facade.

The meaning of this facade has been much debated. Perhaps the placing of the royal escutcheon, held by the eagle of S. John and flanked by two lions, above the tree, symbolising Granada, is meant to proclaim the city's reconquest, the greatest triumph of the Catholic monarchs.

The dimensions of **Seville Cathedral** (1402–1519) (p. 526A) are prodigious. Its nave might not be the highest at 40 m (130 ft) or the widest at 13.9 m (46 ft), but with four aisles and surrounding chapels the whole rectangular ground-plan at 11,020 m^2 makes it the largest of all mediaeval cathedrals.

It has both Spanish and foreign features. The plan and size were determined by the symbolic necessity of covering the site of the Almohad mosque. The lateral chapels with internal buttresses came from Catalonia and the original choir was modelled on that of San Francisco, Seville. Its five volumes were laid out using the method employed at Toledo Cathedral. However, more modern Gothic features are present and Seville Cathedral, because of its detailing as well as its size, transformed the architectural scene of central Spain.

Salamanca New Cathedral (p. 526B). By the sixteenth century an increased population and the university's prestige had made Salamanca's cathedral too small. So in 1510 Anton Egas of Toledo and Alfonso Rodriguez of Seville were ordered to draw up plans for a new one. However, the chapter appointed as architect Juan Gil de Hontañon in 1512. The first stone was laid on 12 May 1513. Toledo contributed the stepped elevation and non-projecting transept, Seville the lateral chapels and balustraded interior clerestory passageway. The most important development was the increased use of Classical forms. At first, only the Italianate balustrades and spandrel medallions are obvious, but at the crossing is the Baroque cimborio of Joaquín de Churriguera (1714–25). It is the colourful, light and animated ambience thus created which so distinguishes this cathedral.

The architectural masterpiece of Diego de Siloe (*c.* 1495–1563) is **Granada Cathedral** (begun in 1523) (pp. 523D, 965A,B); it nevertheless bears the imprint of its first designer. Enrique Egas, the architect of Toledo Cathedral. Indeed, it is best understood as a transformation of the latter Gothic structure. Both buildings have ambulatories divided into alternately rectilinear and triangular bays, and both have a nave and four aisles. Moreover, unlike other buildings with such features, they both have non-projecting transepts. However, Diego de Siloe, who was appointed architect in 1528, radically altered the choir. The pentagonal plan of Toledo became a decagonal one at Granada, and the inner ambulatory was reduced to a passage through enormous radiating piers upon which was erected a dome. In short, the expansive Gothic chevet became a rotunda and the outer aisles of the nave were built to the same height At Granada Diego de Siloe added lower lateral chapels so the stepped elevation remains.

Diego de Siloe wanted to build *a la romano* so the choir is influenced by those late fifteenth- and

A. San Juan de los Reyes, Toledo: cloister. See p.524

B. College of San Gregorio, Valladolid: facade (1480). See p.524

C. S. Pablo, Valladolid: principal doorway (1486–92). See p.521

D. La Capilla del Condestable, Burgos Cathedral (1482–94). See p.521

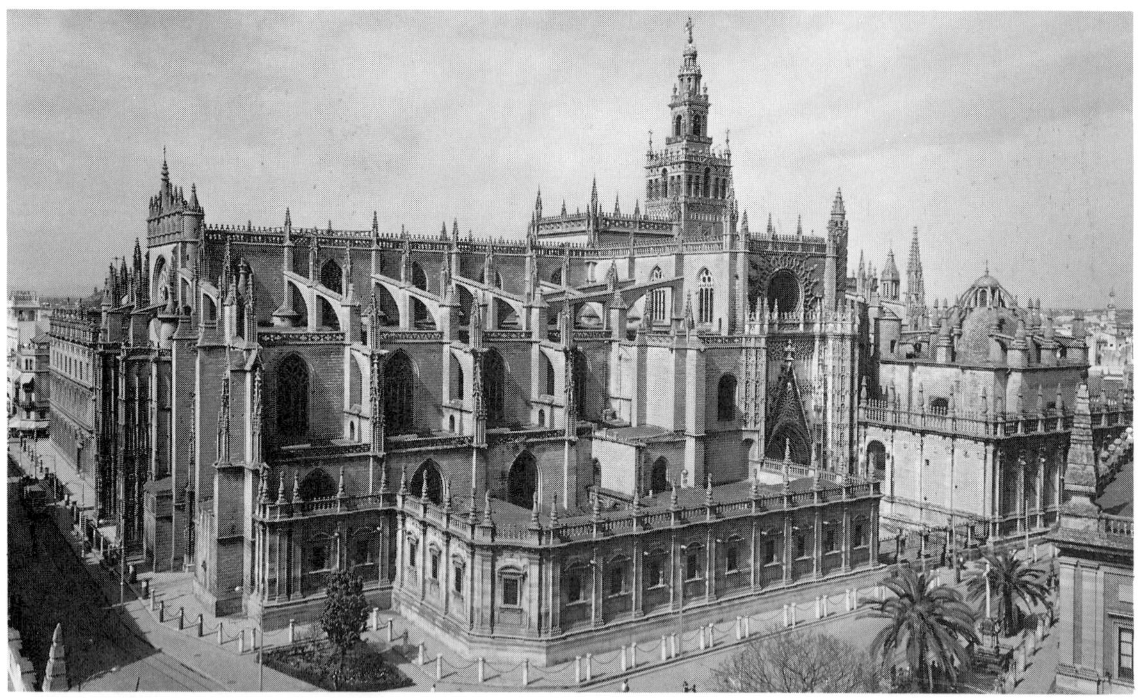

A. Seville Cathedral from SW (1402–1519). See p.524

B. Salamanca: the Old Cathedral (1120–78), backed by the New Cathedral (1513–). See p.524

sixteenth-century churches of Lombardy with tall rotundas capped by domes such as Bramante's baptistery for S. Maria presso S. Satiro, Milan (begun shortly after 1486); these in turn were based on buildings like S. Costanza, Rome. But regardless of his motive, Diego de Siloe built the greatest and most typical Plateresque Cathedral – one in which the ghost of Gothic architecture stalks, so that even the nave piers, assuredly based on Renaissance illustrations of Roman buildings, appear possessed of the soaring, composite nature of Gothic piers. (See Chapter 30.)

Catalan Gothic

Of all the major Catalan structures the chevet (*c.* 1312–47) of **Gerona Cathedral** (p. 522C) is the closest to French High Gothic models. Its plan is that of Narbonne Cathedral (begun 1272). Its elevation should be compared to that of the Norman Cistercian church of Hambye. Both are stepped, and the clerestories of the ambulatory and choir are given equal weight. In both cases the choir's middle storey consists of a succession of dark holes unconnected by a passageway. Furthermore, there are French features: for instance, the windows (which do not occupy the whole of the available space) are derived from those southern French cathedrals such as Clermont-Ferrand (begun 1248) attributed to Jean Deschamps. Enrique and his successor from 1321, Jacques Favran from Narbonne Cathedral, designed a small, well-lit church. The nave (1417–1598) has the widest Gothic vault in Europe: 22 m (74 ft). Internal buttresses, 6 m (20 ft) deep, rise the full height of the structure to counteract its thrust.

Barcelona Cathedral (pp. 522B, 528A), its chevet (1298–1329) and nave (finished in 1420) derived from the Gothic architecture of southern France, is remarkably fine. The plan of the chevet is also like Narbonne, and the triforium runs behind rather than through the piers as at Limoges. In the nave the lateral chapels are divided into rectangular and pentagonal bays as at Clermont-Ferrand. The whole is reminiscent of Albi, but the character of Barcelona Cathedral is very different from that of its sources and springs from the ambiguity of its conception. It seems to hover between a basilican and hall church. The balanced stepped elevation used for the chevet of Gerona Cathedral was rejected in favour of one approximating more closely to a hall church. The choir is lit from the ambulatory, and so seems united to it, because in the main elevation there is only room for oculi in the vault lunettes. These oculi, set above a tall, dark triforium as in the inner ambulatory of Toledo Cathedral, alone recall a basilica. The vaults were erected over almost square nave and oblong aisle bays. This means there is only one pier every 14 m (46 ft) in comparison with, for example, 8 m (26 ft) at Reims. The cloisters were completed *c.* 1448 and contain twenty-two chapels.

S. Maria del Mar, Barcelona (p. 522A), its plan and elevation based on the chevet of Barcelona Cathedral, is a parish church (1329–83) containing a number of far-reaching innovations. The outer walls of the chapels were moved out to the extremity of the internal buttresses so as to form one continuous wall, and the non-projecting transepts and triforium were abandoned. In other words, the essential structure was uncovered. Then the number of piers was reduced, creating enormous square nave bays flanked by oblong aisle bays, and the number of chapels increased, even placing four of them on the inside of the west facade. The result was the perfect urban church, a vast unencumbered space for crowds, complete with chapels for private prayer. Thus, larger than the cathedral and more austere – the supports are plain octagonal shafts, not composite piers – S. Maria del Mar seems magnificently suited to the proud, personal religion of the rich merchants for whom it was built.

The designer of **Manresa Cathedral** (p. 528B), Berenger de Montaigut, based the Cathedral (1328–1596) on a single-volume church like S. Catalina, Barcelona. He enlarged his model – the nave is 23 m (76 ft) wide – and extended its square lateral chapels around the choir to make it suitably commodious. But then he transformed it in the light of French ideas and preoccupations. First, the internal buttresses between the chapels were pierced to form an aisle. Its vault remains that of the chapels. In the nave, this results in a structure similar to the lateral chapels of the choir of Narbonne Cathedral whose upper glazed structure is also repeated here, using superimposed flying buttresses in the same way.

Manresa, however, does not look like a French cathedral. The amount of uncompromising wall – the internal buttresses and octagonal piers – and the ambiguity of conception locate it firmly.

The **Cathedral of Palma de Majorca** (p. 528C) is in fact three buildings: the funerary chapel of Jaime I of Majorca to the east (commissioned in 1306), the choir (1314–27) and the nave (begun in the second quarter of the fourteenth century). Coherence is achieved by the use of false pendentives – derived from the palatine chapel of Perpignan (finished in 1309) – in both the choir and lateral chapels, and by placing rose windows above the entrances to the chevet as at Gerona.

The nave is the largest in Catalan Gothic architecture. It measures 121 m × 15 m (394 ft × 49 ft). The height of the nave is 44 m (144 ft) and that of the aisles 30 m (100 ft). The nave is unusually well-lit for a major Catalan church: there are tall windows in the chapels, aisles and nave. In addition to the internal buttresses, flying buttresses had to be used because of the nave's clerestory. So the viewer from the harbour

A. Barcelona Cathedral (1298–*c.* 1448). See p.527

B. Manresa Cathedral (1328–1596). See p.527

C. Cathedral of Palma de Majorca (1314–). See p.527

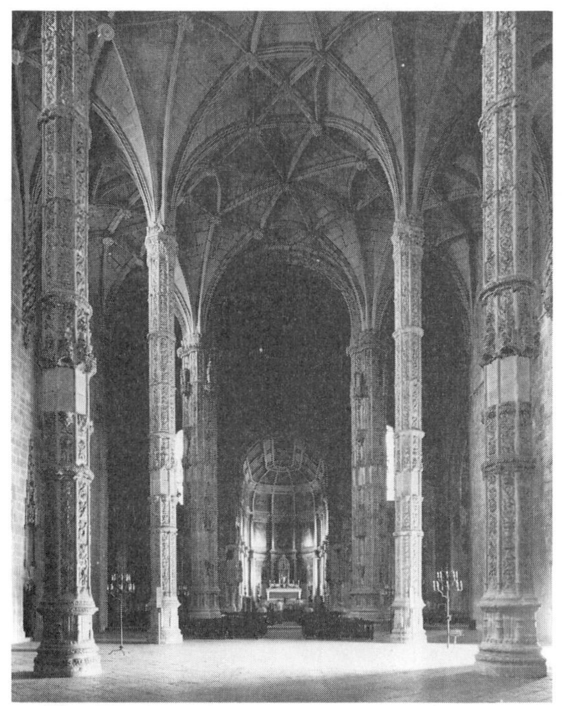

A. S. Maria de Belém, Lisbon (1502–). See p.531

B. Church of Military Order of Christ, Tomar (rebuilt 1510–14). See p.531

C. Capillas Imperfectas, Batalha (1434–). See p.531

D. Lonja del Mar, Palma de Majorca (1426–*c.* 1451). See p.533

A. Casa de las Conchas, Salamanca (1475–83). See p.531

B. Castillo de la Mota, Medina del Campo (1440–79). See p.534

C. The Alcázar, Segovia (fifteenth century, restored 1882). See p.534

below sees the spectacular sight of the chapels' wall buttresses dwarfed by enormous internal buttresses from which flying buttresses arise.

Portugal

The Iberian peninsula contains some of the most impressive and extensive remains of mediaeval **Cistercian monasteries**. For example, that at **Alcobaça**, Portugal (founded in 1153), contains a church (1178–1252), cloister, chapter house, dormitory, refectory, kitchen and lavatorium.

The church is especially interesting. It was begun according to the plan of Clairvaux II (begun 1135), its mother house. In 1195 the monastery was sacked by the Almohads and the present church was then built using part of the original foundations but according to the plan of Clairvaux III (begun 1153). This meant that the flat chevet was replaced by one with an ambulatory and radiating chapels, and the transept and nave enlarged.

It is a hall church with the aisle-windows providing the only direct light. That is, the nave and aisle vaults – rising 20.1 m (66 ft) and 18.7 m (62 ft) respectively – spring from the same height. The narrow aisles and massive piers contribute to its lofty grandeur, reminiscent of Poitiers Cathedral (1162–1350).

S. Maria, Belém (p. 529A), a monastic church, was begun in 1502 by Dom Manuel I (1495–1521) to commemorate the journey of Vasco da Gama to India in 1497 which brought to Portugal the wealth upon which the Manueline style was founded. Diogo Boytac (active 1490–1525) constructed it up to the cornice-level; João de Castilho (active 1515–52) erected the nave piers and the vaults of the nave and transept (after 1519).

The plan is like that of Selubal (1494–8), also by Boytac, and recalls San Juan de Los Reyes, Toledo. The vaults relate to the fifteenth-century family of late hall churches (Seo, Saragossa) and civic edifices (La Lonja del Mar, Palma de Majorca). In the nave the vaults rise 75 m (250 ft) over the three aisles while in the transept, where the piers have been suppressed, they reach 80 m (260 ft). The whole structure and not just Boytac's decoration seems to refer to the Portuguese voyages of discovery.

The **Church of the Military Order of Christ, Tomar** (p. 529B), was rebuilt by Diogo de Arruda (active 1508–31) for Dom Manuel I between 1510 and 1514. The work consisted of adding a single volume containing the nave, chapter house and coroalto to the old octagonal church of the Templars which was itself refurbished to become the apse. The church was the headquarters of the Military Order of Christ, established in 1320 by Dom Diniz (1279–1325), to provide a home in Portugal for the disbanded Templars. As the order played a considerable role as conquerors and administrators in the Portuguese Empire the detailing proclaims with unparalleled ingenuity and imagination the triumphs of the order and of its Master and patron, Dom Manuel I. In stone he articulated Manueline self-esteem.

The **Capillas Imperfectas, Batalha** (p. 529C) – the Unfinished Chapels of the Dominican monastery of S. Maria da Vitoria at Batalha – form the climax of the Manueline style. Designed by Ouguete in 1434 for Dom Durate (1433–8), this octagonal mortuary chapel with seven radiating chapels lies beyond the church's choir. It was abandoned unfinished upon its founder's death, only to be taken up again by Manuel I. Sadly, it was never vaulted.

It is considered the most prodigious centrally planned building in Europe, apart from the Karlshofkirche, Prague (1371–77), while its portal (1509) is held up as a marvel of Manueline art. The way the archivolts' decoration runs, almost without interruption, on to the jambs and the numerous orders of ogee arches resembles the portal of the north porch of S. Mary Redcliffe, Bristol – not an unlikely connection given the dynastic and trading links between the two countries. But the decoration is purely Portuguese and was carved by Mateus Fernandes (active at Batalha *c.* 1490–1515).

Secular Architecture

El Palacio del Infantado, Guadalajara, was built by Juan Guas for the second Duque del Infantado. It was sacked in 1809 and suffered in a fire in 1936. Fortunately, though, its facade (1480) and patio (1483) survive to demonstrate the exuberant originality of its design.

The facade consists of a tall wall covered by alternating rows of projecting, faceted stones pierced by a portal, set to one side, surmounted by the Mendoza escutcheon carried by two wild men. An open gallery runs along the top interrupted by seven semicircular balconies. Originally, the escutcheon was lower. Its displacement took place when a row of windows was inserted by the fifth Duque del Infantado. In this design, Juan Guas was as involved in Islamic art as he was at San Juan de los Reyes, Toledo. The only Gothic feature is the tracery of the portal's tympanum.

The patio relates more directly to other Isabelline buildings. The arches-framed-by-pinnacles motif of the upper storey is found in the upper storey of the cloister of San Juan de los Reyes itself (p. 525A). Above all, as at San Gregorio, Valladolid, the patio is conceived of as a field for heraldic display. But it is the abundance of carving, its constantly shifting depth and texture, which is so characteristic and so exhilarating.

'La Casa de las Conchas', Salamanca (p. 530A). Talavera Maldonado, Professor of the University of

A COURT: DUCAL PALACE GUADALAJARA

B COURT: THE AUDIENCIA BARCELONA

C DOORWAY: FOUNDLING HOSPITAL: CORDOVA

D LA LONJA: VALENCIA

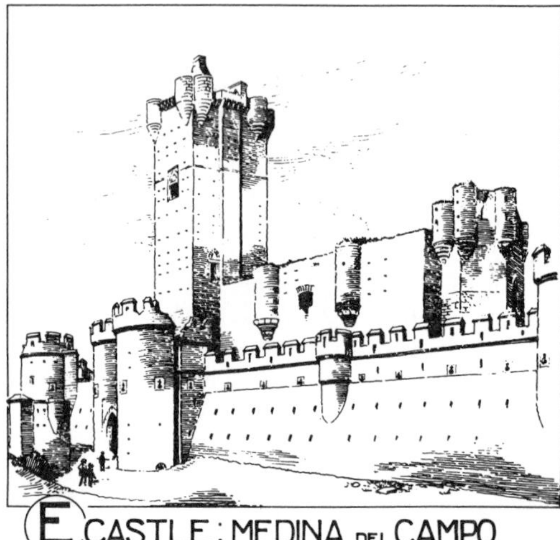

E CASTLE: MEDINA DEL CAMPO

F PUERTA DE SERRANOS VALENCIA

G WINDOW IN BISHOP'S PALACE: ALCALA

H PUERTA DEL SOL: TOLEDO

Salamanca, Master of the Military Order of Santiago and Ambassador to France and Portugal, had his house rebuilt between 1475 and 1483. It is both one of the best-preserved late mediaeval Castilian town palaces and a fine piece of Isabelline architecture.

The name of the palace refers to the alternating rows of shells covering the exterior walls of the Order of Santiago and relates to the owner's membership, the badge of which was a shell. The pattern was taken from a Mudéjar structure. The shells, by enlivening the wall and breaking up the sunlight, attract and refresh the eye which elsewhere is assailed by brilliant light on bare masonry.

The Isabelline love of display pervades the palace. The facade, characterised by four two-light windows, has a portal with an escutcheon, with fleur-de-lys supported by two lions, carved on it. The patio, which is on two levels linked by a staircase, accords with traditional practice in being the centre of life in the palace. The rooms are arranged around it. The mezzanine floor contains a kitchen pantry, cellar and servants quarters and the main floor consists of apartments and sitting rooms.

Catherine of Lancaster, wife of Enrique III (1390–1406), King of Castile, founded the **University, Salamanca** (p. 962A) in 1413. It was erected between 1415 and 1433. The layout is typical. A central patio gives access to a lecture room (west side), the chapel (east side) and via a staircase to the library (south side). The streets are reached by two portals. A battlemented wall surrounds the group of buildings.

The staircase and the gateway in the Plaza de las Escuelas are notable features. The staircase (sixteenth century) has railings decorated with hunting scenes and bullfights. The gateway (begun before 1516; completed in 1529) – a Plateresque masterpiece – has the same screen-like appearance as the facade of San Gregorio, Valladolid. The carving is of such high quality that it seems as if the facade is of cast metal.

El Castillo del Bellver, Majorca, is strategically situated on a hill overlooking the road from Palma to the port of Porto-Pi and enjoys remarkable views across the central plain. Bellver was begun by Jaime I of Majorca in 1300 and was sufficiently complete for his son, Sancho I (1311–24), to take up residence there in 1314.

The plan – like the site – reflects the fact that it was intended as both a stronghold and country retreat. A circular tower of five storeys stands apart from the main structure, which consists of a circular patio surrounded by rooms whose circular outer wall is punctuated by three towers and four bartizan turrets. A ditch surrounds both buildings, and the towers and outer wall were originally crenellated. Thus the complex is well fortified but the garrison in the isolated tower was kept apart from the royal quarters centred on the patio, a plan derived from fortifications in southern France such as La Tour de Constance, Aigues-Mortes (begun 1241). The sophistication of the plan suggests Bellver was designed by an architect of experience, even though the buildings were constructed by local craftsmen.

Begun on 6 April 1392, by Pedro Belaguer, **La Puerta de Serranos, Valencia** (p. 532F), the city gate, is a beautiful and imposing example of late mediaeval Catalan town fortification. Originally, it stood behind a ditch and was connected to the wall. It consists of two polygonal towers astride a gateway above which stretch blind arcades as at La Puerta del Sol, Toledo. Its most notable feature is the fact that the towers and gateway have open galleries looking out through wide-span arches on the town-side of the gateway. This is also found at Madrigal de las Altas Torres (Zamora), *c.* 1300, and was meant to prevent the gate fortifications, if ever occupied, being used against the city.

The **Lonja del Mar, Palma de Majorca** (p. 529D), is perhaps the most beautiful civic building in Spain. It is an Exchange and was begun in 1426 by Guillem Sagrera. Arnau Piris completed it about 1451.

It belongs to the standard type of mediaeval hall (compare, for example, the **Lonja de la Seda, Valencia** (p. 532D)), consisting of a rectangular, three-aisled box measuring 24 m × 30 m (78 ft × 100 ft). However, the vaults unwind from six spiral columns without the interruption of capitals. Similarly, the ribs merge into the walls. Thus, the box is transformed: it seems filled with sheltering trees. Spiral columns had long been used decoratively but Sagrera was the first to use them for a large, vaulted area and combine them with octagonal buttresses as corner turrets and wall buttresses.

Castles

Gothic Spain was created by the Reconquista, but despite such marvels as the **Muslim castle of Gormaz (Soria)** and the **walls of Avila** it was during the internecine Castilian feuding of the fifteenth century that the most impressive and characteristic Spanish castles were built. However the technology used was conservative. The shift from keep and courtyard to the fortified gatehouse type did not take place in Spain.

The main development in fifteenth-century castle-building was the emergence of the castle-palace. Patrons began to demand luxurious apartments and impressive rather than impregnable fortifications. Artists, often Mudéjar craftsmen, rather than engineers, were employed. Thus, Penafiel (Valladolid) rebuilt by Don Pedro Giron, Master of the Order of Calatrava, in the mid-fifteenth century, as a stronghold was succeeded by La Calahorra (Granada), erected by Don Rodrigo de Vivar y Mendoza in

1509–12, where immense and visually impressive walls shelter the exquisite Italianate palace of Michele Carlone of Genoa.

The **Alcázar, Segovia** (p. 530C) (the Arab word denotes a fortified palace), belongs to the class of 'Castillos roqueros' – castles built on inaccessible hills so that nature could contribute to their impregnability. Its site at the western extremity of the ridge upon which the town stands, high over the confluence of the rivers Eresma and Clamores, combines with the fairy-tale pointed slate roofs of its turrets – added by Philip II – to create an unforgettable impression. Juan II (1406–54) gave the palace the appearance it has today and built the tower which bears his name, with its decorative stonework, canopied windows, bartizan turrets and crenellations. It was gutted by fire in 1862 and restoration began in 1882.

Fifteenth-century records show that originally there were two alabaster patios and that La Sala de los Reyes – begun by Alfonso X – contained thirty-four golden statues of seated Castilian kings.

The **Castillo de La Mota, Medina del Campo, Valladolid** (p. 530B), is set high above the town so as to defend the eastern approach of this important trade centre. La Mota's fortifications date from two periods. The southern, eastern and western walls of the inner ward are probably thirteenth-century: the walls are partly of mamposteria (pebbles and cement) and the square corner towers have narrow arrow-slits. The northern wall and torre del homenaje (keep) are attributed to Fernando de Carreno who began the reconstruction of the castle in about 1440 for Juan II. Alonso Nieto completed the castle in about 1479 for the Catholic monarchs who had received La Mota in 1475 as a coronation gift. The material used, brick, indicates that Mudéjar craftsmen were employed but none of the military engineering shows Islamic influence.

The best example of Mudéjar castle-building and the most remarkable fifteenth-century castle-palace, **Coca (Segovia)**, was built by the fabulously wealthy Don Alonso de Fonseca, Archbishop of Seville, as much for show as for strength. Coca is built of brick, some of it decorative – the work of Mudéjar craftsmen told to embellish as well as to build the walls. The crenellated parapets were picked out by using a dark red brick and a brickwork pattern which resembles basket-work. The walls were erected in alternate layers of different shades of lighter red brick. All in all it is evident that Coca was designed to give pleasure as well as security.

There are other notable Catalan secular buildings in Barcelona and elsewhere. The **Palacio de la Audiencia, Barcelona** (p. 532B), is built around an extraordinary courtyard with a picturesque external staircase, and only marginally less distinctive in the same city is the **Casa del Ayuntamiento** (1373–). **The Puerta del Sol** (p. 532H) and the remarkable **Puente de Alcantara** (1258), both at **Toledo**, the **Torre del Clavero, Salamanca** (1480), and the **Gateway of S. Maria at Burgos** are all worthy of mention.

Italy: Architectural Character

Gothic came late to Italy, and although the style was practised for more than two hundred years it never took root there in quite the way it did everywhere else in northern Europe. Not only did Gothic have to contend with a flourishing Romanesque tradition and even entrenched memories of an early Christian past, but it came to be identified as something essentially alien or at any rate not quite Italian. One way of regarding the Renaissance was as an effort to achieve a genuinely Italian style of architecture. Educated Italians were acutely aware that Classical antiquity was Italian antiquity. In purging their architecture of what they affected to regard as the solecisms of the barbarous Gothic north, they concocted a view of architectural history and an attendant set of architectural values which have never ceased to command devoted adherents, even though few historians would now endorse them with quite the original conviction.

The Renaissance tends to obscure the fact that there was a period between 1200 and 1400 when Gothic was accepted without question in Italy simply because it was the architecture which commanded the general approval of the Church. A version of the style was introduced at the end of the twelfth century by the Cistercians, who for a while seem to have been regarded as the arbiters of what was or was not Gothic. It is often possible to recognise Cistercian influences in the plain, often very large and simple Gothic churches built for the Franciscans and Dominicans as soon as they were in a position to exercise patronage on a grand scale, that is by the middle of the twelfth century.

The great Mendicant churches loomed large in Italian urban life, and for most Italians they would convey whatever was meant by Gothic. The great rebuilding of Italian cathedrals took place in Romanesque rather than Gothic times, and although there are several enormous and spectacular Gothic cathedrals to be seen in Italy, they were exceptions to the general rule. Although they form a special category of Gothic, they confirm and augment the general impression that Gothic in Italy was closely bound up with and reflects the vitality of the cities.

From the point of view of patronage mediaeval Italy falls into two parts, north and south. Rather conveniently the line of demarcation coincides with the Papal states, which extended diagonally across the peninsula from Rome to Ravenna. To the north the country was divided into communes and city states, or principalities ruled from cities. The cities were turbulent, ambitious and contentious. Some of them were extremely rich and four emerged into special prominence: Venice, Florence, Siena and Milan. Each produced its local version of Gothic.

The position of Rome itself was curiously ambivalent. As the religious capital of western Christendom and until 1307 the centre of Papal government, it might have been expected at least to have participated in an architectural movement which was primarily ecclesiastical. Yet Rome has only one modest Gothic church. The explanation is that Rome had no need of churches. The early Christian city acquired more than enough to cater for its needs, and in any case mediaeval Rome was only a fragment of what it had once been. If Papal Rome recognised an architectural style, it was that of the early Christian basilicas. Moreover, when the popes removed themselves to Avigon the principal source of patronage dried up.

The south was quite different. After the Norman conquest it became the single kingdom of Sicily. This had cultural links with several parts of northern Europe, and these are reflected in the Romanesque architecture of Apulia. Otherwise its architectural inheritance was Mediterranean, with Byzantine and Arab influences in construction. The substitution of the German Hohenstaufen dynasty for the indigenous Normans in 1195 brought in its wake certain repercussions of taste. Frederick II (1196–1250) owed his German throne to French arms, and he shared something of the contemporary vogue for everything French. His Apulian castles have many Gothic features as well as their more publicised Classical details. But it was only when the Frenchman Charles of Anjou was called in by the Pope to eliminate the last vestiges of the Hohenstaufen (1264) that genuine French Rayonnant can be said to have reached Naples. Even so it never penetrated into Sicily. After the Sicilian Vespers (1282) Sicily became separated from the mainland kingdom and was gradually absorbed into the orbit of Aragon. Rather belatedly Sicily in the fifteenth century acquired a scattering of Spanish Gothic buildings.

It was typical of Frederick II, though not typical of his generation of rulers, that he should have many castles and no churches to his credit. This apparent bias has made him seem a portent of the secular princes of the Renaissance. In another sense, however, this preoccupation with what were in effect police stations was no more than a reflection of architecture in the service of government. Another aspect of the same concern was the lavish expenditure of all the Italian city-states on imposing municipal buildings. The town hall is as much a feature of Gothic Italy as the great church. Great town houses were probably equally conspicuous, although only in Venice have they survived in sufficient numbers to give any idea of what the mediaeval city may have been like.

Although Italian masons must have shared the common theoretical knowledge and practical expertise of their profession, they seem to have differed in certain respects from their northern brethren. The discussions which took place at Milan during the 1390s, and of which records were kept, reveal that when Lombard masons encountered Frenchmen or Germans they did not always see eye to eye with one another or perhaps even fully understand one another. Some of the entrenched attitudes voiced by the Italians seem wilfully perverse. The great size of Milan may have made it a special case; but Milan apart, Italian tastes in masonry predisposed them to stand apart from mainstream northern Gothic. They were prepared to indulge in florid ornamental sculptures, and they loved the smooth surfaces and chromatic effects that could be achieved with marble. But they had no liking for the fussy encrustations that enliven the more expensive Gothic churches of France, Germany or England. Most of their masonry is plain to the point of austerity, and this was often deliberately done in order for it to be painted.

In the pecking order of prestige, masons probably came below painters, and certainly well below sculptors. There were occasions when painters and sculptors such as Giotto and Arnolfo di Cambio were put in charge of major projects. Giotto almost certainly had a hand in designing the Arena Chapel at Padua, which is nothing more than a frame for his frescoes. Whereas beyond the Alps designers *par excellence* were metalworkers who shared the same formal repertory and procedural methods as masons, in Italy the emphasis could fall the other way. Ability to design was identified with artistic genius, with the result that architecture seems to have been practised by men who were in some sense amateurs. Exactly what happened in given cases the records seldom disclose. When Brunelleschi undertook to build the dome of Florence cathedral, the sculptor Ghiberti was given a watching brief – one amateur being set to keep an eye on another. But in principle it was this state of affairs which allowed men like Brunelleschi and Alberti, not professional masons in the mediaeval sense at all, to question and reject the presuppositions of the professional architects of their day.

It needs to be emphasised, however, that Brunelleschi and Alberti, like most revolutionaries, represented a minority opinion in their own times. Gothic did not disappear instantly everywhere. Great projects like Milan Cathedral or San Petronio at Bologna kept it alive until the sixteenth and seventeenth centuries; and it may be argued that certain Gothic sympathies found belated, transfigured expression in the forms of Baroque. After all, Borromini began his career in the mason's yard at Milan.

Italy: Examples

Milan Cathedral (pp. 536, 537, 538A). The decision to replace the ancient double cathedral by a single

A EXTERIOR FROM S.W.

B INTERIOR LOOKING E.

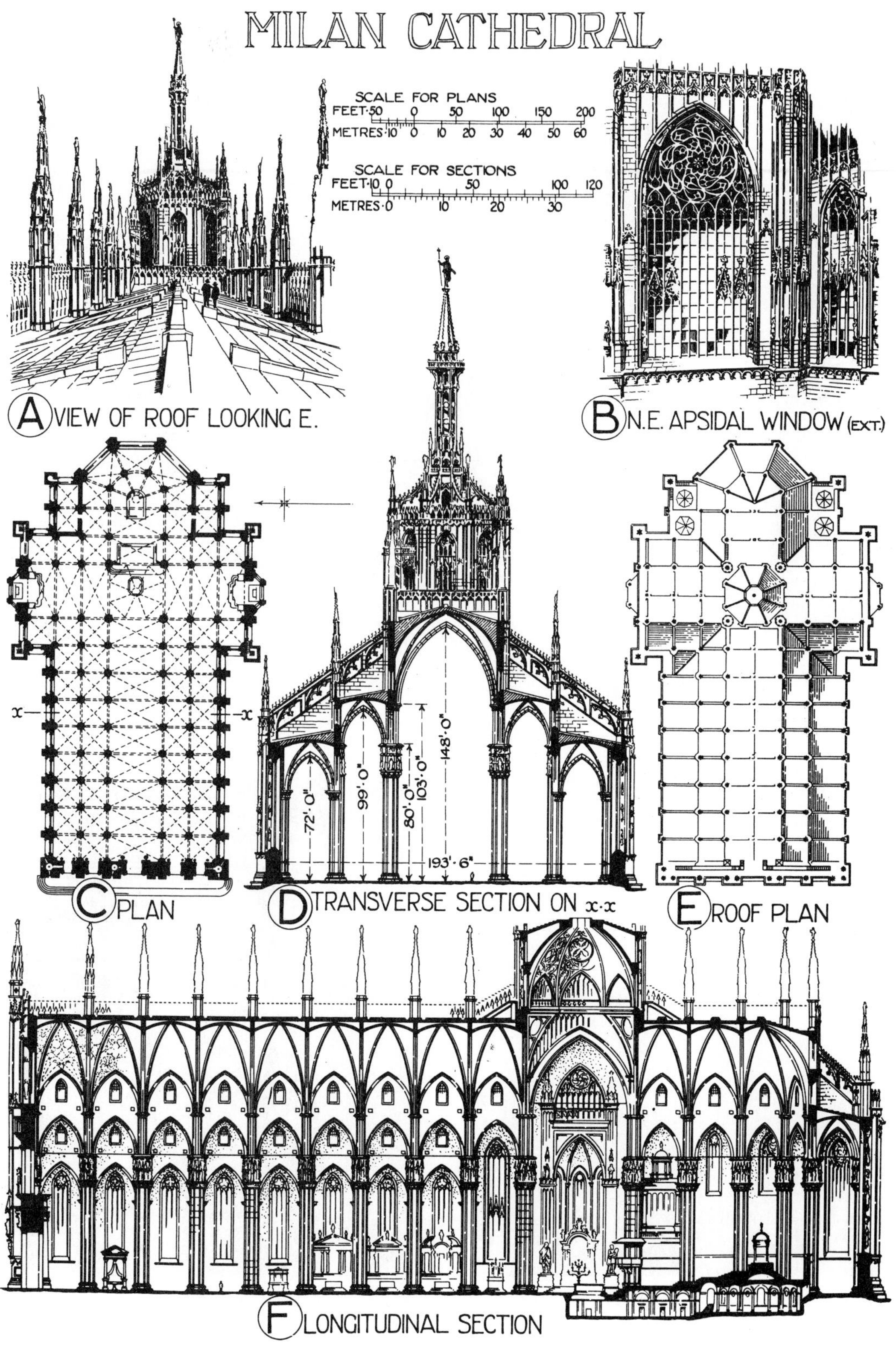

(A) VIEW OF ROOF LOOKING E.

(B) N.E. APSIDAL WINDOW (EXT.)

(C) PLAN

(D) TRANSVERSE SECTION ON x-x

(E) ROOF PLAN

(F) LONGITUDINAL SECTION

A. Milan Cathedral from NW (*c.* 1385–1485). See p.535

B. Arezzo Cathedral (*c.* 1277–). See p.539

C. S. Francesco, Assisi: upper church. See p.539

building of great size was taken some time before 1386, when the duchy of Milan was at the height of its power. From the outset the undertaking was far beyond the experience of the local architects and masons involved in its construction. This led to a succession of difficulties and the original design had to be modified on more than one occasion. The debates that took place during the formation period between the various contracted parties were duly minuted, and their records have survived to shed some fitful and often perplexing light upon the working methods of a mediaeval masons' lodge.

The earliest evidence for the design is a drawing by Antonio di Vicenzo, the architect of San Petronio at Bologna, who *c.* 1390 drew the plan and sections. It is only a sketch but unless it is wildly inaccurate it implies that the height of the main vault at that time was going to be something in the vicinity of 116 Milanese braccie (67 m). Nothing remotely as high had ever been seriously contemplated before, let alone successfully accomplished. By 1393, there were evidently doubts as to the feasibility of such a project. Foreign experts were called in and suggestions of a more realistic nature put forward. In 1392 it was argued whether to build 'to the square' or 'to the triangle', that is, whether the height should equal the width (96 braccie) or whether the section should be defined by an equilateral triangle. They opted for the triangle. This brought the height down to 84 braccie, about 48 m (160 ft). Later it was reduced again to 76 braccie, about 43 m (145 ft).

In spite of the contractions in height, the basic conception remained unchanged. There were always to be five aisles in echelon, an early Christian arrangement very possibly represented in the previous cathedrals of S. Tecla. Among earlier Gothic cathedrals, Bourges in France would have provided the most appropriate model, especially if the section was to be defined by an equilateral triangle. But the scale of Milan is so enormous that even the staggered spatial effects of Bourges fail to register. To all intents and purposes it is a vast pillared hall of uncertain and uneven height, the uncertainty being enhanced or aggravated by indifferent lighting. In such a church ordinary capitals would be lost, and heroic efforts were made to retrieve the orthodox impression expected of capitals by turning them into friezes of niches inhabited by full-scale statues around each column. The principal decorative effects were, however, reserved for the exterior, which was covered with the only extensive display of Gothic architectural ornament to be found in Italy. Much of it is post-mediaeval, but it gives Milan a cosmopolitan or at least a northern quality which is not entirely out of place in view of the international experience consulted during its inception.

The exterior is a gleaming mass of white marble with lofty traceried windows, panelled buttresses, flying buttresses and pinnacles crowned with statues (p. 538A), the whole wrought into a soaring design of lace-like intricacy. The three magnificent traceried windows of the apse, 20.7 m × 8.5 m (68 ft × 28 ft), are the finest of their type in Italy (p. 537B). The flat-pitched roofs are constructed of massive marble slabs laid on the vaulting (p. 537A), and over the crossing is a domical vault, 65.5 m (215 ft) above the ground. The later facade (p. 536A), which has the wide-spreading gable lines of Romanesque churches, was only completed at the beginning of the nineteenth century.

Arezzo Cathedral (begun *c.* 1277) (p. 538B) was influenced by the nave of S. Maria Novella at Florence, of which it is a contemporary variant, though less elegant or spacious. In northern Europe such a design would not have been considered suitable for a cathedral. This illustrates the prestige which friars' churches enjoyed in Italy, but also perhaps the modest circumstances of the cathedral chapter at Arezzo. Its most distinguished feature is the three tall windows of the polygonal apse, which run the full height of the building and emphasise the hall-like unity of the interiors.

The **Certosa, Pavia** (1396–1497) (p. 549D–F), a famous Carthusian monastery, was commenced by Giovanni Galeazzo Visconti, and forms a splendid memorial of the Milan dynasties. In plan it is a Latin cross and similar to many German churches in the triapsidal terminations to sanctuary and transepts, but the nave is in square and the aisles in oblong bays, in the Italian manner. On the south are the two cloisters, richly wrought in terracotta. The exterior is a fascinating instance of Lombard transitional Gothic-Renaissance style with arcading and terracotta ornament, while the monumental facade (1473–*c.* 1540) is wholly of Renaissance character (p. 857C).

S. Antonio, Padua (1232–1307) (p. 541B), is a seven-domed pilgrimage church resembling S. Mark, Venice, in general conception. The nave is in square bays covered with domes on pendentives, which are also placed over the crossing, transepts and choir, beyond which is an apse and chevet with nine radiating chapels similar to contemporary churches in France. The exterior has an arcade of pointed arches and an upper arcaded gallery, like the Romanesque churches of Lombardy.

S. Francesco, Assisi (pp. 504C, 538C). S. Francis died in 1226 and was canonised in 1228. Despite the difficulties of the site where he had been interred a pilgrimage church was at once started. Most of it was finished by 1239, the remainder by 1253. The church belongs to no general type, and was not copied by other major churches of the Franciscan order. Essentially it is two aisleless churches one above the other. The contrast between them was carefully contrived. The lower church is dark, cavern-like with heavy ribbed vaults, the upper church high, spacious and well-lit. Many of the architectural details were the very latest thing from France. Whether or not it was

A. S. Anastasia, Verona (1261–). See p.542

B. Fossanova Church (*c.* 1170). See p.542

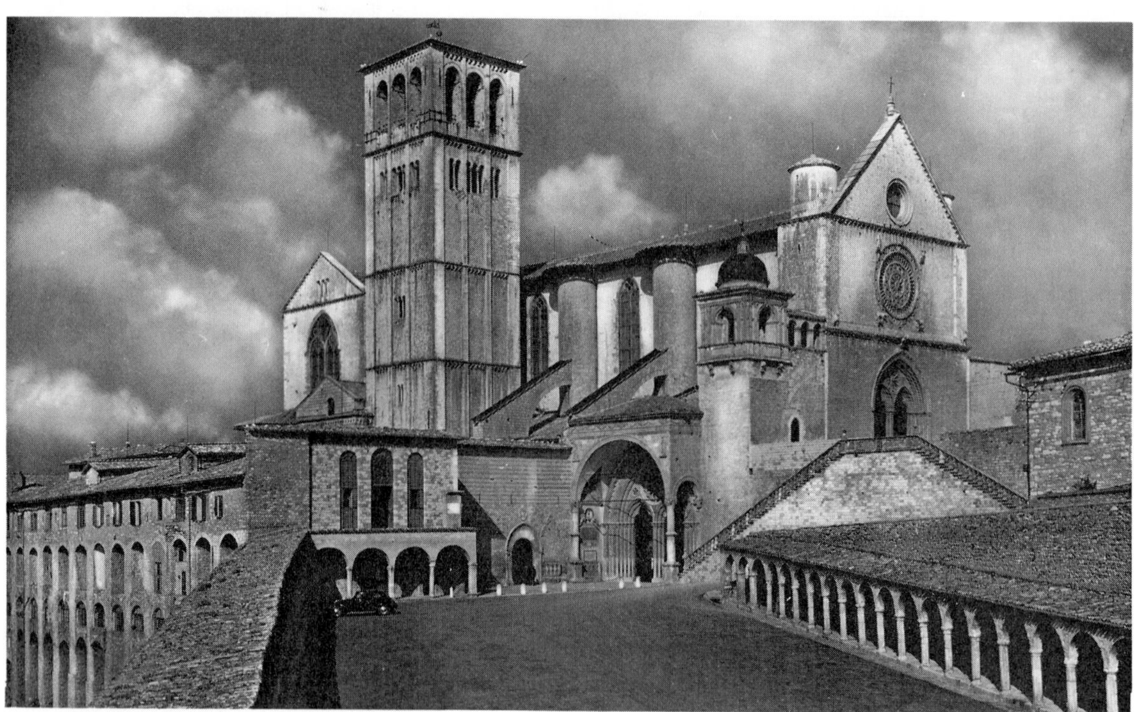

C. S. Francesco, Assisi (1226–53). See p.539

A. S. Petronio, Bologna (1390–1659). See p.542

B. S. Antonio, Padua, from NW (1232–1307; domes heightened 1424). See p.539

designed for the purpose, the church at both levels was admirably suited for large-scale painted decoration. This was mainly executed at the end of thirteenth century or later; but even so San Francesco stands at the head of a long and distinguished line of Italian frescoed churches and chapels.

The **Cistercian Church at Fossanova (South Lazio)** (begun *c.* 1170) (p. 540B). The first and best preserved of a series of Cistercian churches which introduced into Italy the proto-Gothic favoured by the order in Burgundy. It has few Gothic details and makes no use of advanced Gothic structural ideas. But the interior is entirely shaped by pointed arches and groined vaults, and these are sufficient to distinguish it from any species of Italian Romanesque. Other churches of the type are **San Galgano near Siena** (begun 1224), now a ruin, and at **Casamari (South Lazio)** (begun 1203).

SS. Giovanni e Paolo, Venice (1260–1385) (p. 543A), a Dominican church of imposing proportions and historic importance, contains the tombs of the Doges. The Latin cross of the plan is elaborated by pronounced transepts with eastern chapels, and by a polygonal apse to the choir. The interior is essentially Italian in the wide spacing of piers, the square bays of the nave vaulting, and the oblong bays of the aisles, and internal wooden ties take the place of external flying buttresses. The exterior is of beautiful brickwork with pointed windows and moulded cornices, and the clerestory is loftier than usual in Italy, while a dome of later date crowns the crossing.

S. Maria Gloriosa dei Frari, Venice (1250–1338) (p. 544E–G), is a Franciscan church, designed by Niccolo Pisano, in which there are six eastern transept chapels. The interior has lofty stone cylindrical piers tied together by wooden beams, supporting an arcade of pointed arches and brick vaulting in square bays with massive ribs resting on shafts rising from the pier capitals. The exterior is in fine coloured brickwork. The square campanile has vertical panels and a belfry of open arches, and is crowned with an octagonal lantern. The apse, with its double tiers of pointed tracery windows, flanked by the eastern transept chapels, is the great glory of the church.

S. Anastasia, Verona (1261–) (p. 540A), with its delightful portal and brick campanile, is a beautiful expression of Italian Gothic. **S. Andrea, Vercelli**, founded in 1219 by a cosmopolitan cardinal for a community of Victorine canons from Paris, has a number of features which derive from French Gothic sources; for example, the east end is a copy of the east end of Laon. However, the design as a whole shows little understanding of and less sympathy for Gothic construction as such. There are neither galleries nor a triforium; windows remain small and the overriding impression is of vast areas of unbroken wall surface. Outside the solid towers, the external galleries at roof level and even the rudimentary flying buttresses are more Romanesque than Gothic.

S. Petronio, Bologna (p. 541A), was started in 1390 and abandoned with only the nave completed in 1659. S. Petronio if finished would have been over 180 m (600 ft) long and 135 m (450 ft) across the transepts. The architect was Antonio di Vicenzo, and his brief was to outstrip or at any rate rival the contemporary cathedrals of Milan and Florence. He went to Milan where he drew the plan and section by way of preparations for his own work. That he was familiar with the churches of Florence is clear from San Petronio itself. The cross-section is roughly that of Milan, the elevation is an enlargement of S. Maria Novella, and many of the details were taken from Florence Cathedral. However, the proportions of San Petronio give it an individuality which deserves a place among the greatest churches of the Middle Ages, and especially among the brick churches of Italy.

The **Doge's Palace, Venice** (p. 546), has facades which date from 1309–1424, designed by Giovanni and Bartolomeo Buon. The palace, started in the ninth century, several times rebuilt, and completed in the Renaissance period, forms part of that great scheme of town-planning which was carried out through successive centuries. The facades, with a total length of nearly 152 m (500 ft), have open arcades in the two lower storeys, and the third storey was rebuilt after a fire in the sixteenth century, so as to extend over the arcades. This upper storey is faced with white and rose-coloured marble, resembling patterned brickwork, pierced by a few large and ornate windows and finished with a lace-like parapet of oriental cresting. The arcade columns, which originally stood on a stylobate of three steps, now rise from the ground without bases, and the sturdy continuous tracery of the second tier of arcades lends an appearance of strength to the open arches. The capitals of the columns, particularly the angle capital which was eulogised by Ruskin in *The Stones of Venice*, are celebrated for the delicate carving in low relief, which was made possible by the use of finegrained marble. The whole scheme of columned and pointed arcades, with its combination of carved capitals and long horizontal lines of open tracery, is of that unique design which can only be termed Venetian Gothic.

The **Palazzo Pubblico, Cremona** (1206–45), the **Palazzo Pubblico, Piacenza** (1281–), and the **Mercanzia, Bologna** (1382–4) (p. 545G), are similar with pointed arcades and an upper storey, often with a projecting *ringhiera* or tribune, and the familiar forked battlements.

The **Ca d'Oro, Venice** (1424–36) (p. 555C), is another fine design by the architects of the Doge's Palace. The windows are grouped together in the usual Venetian manner to form a centre for the facade, which in this instance seems to lack one wing. The arcaded entrance of five arches, lighting the deep

A. SS. Giovanni e Paolo, Venice (1260–1385). See p.542

B. Ponte di Castel Vecchio, Verona (1335). See p.547

A WHEEL WINDOW: CARRARA CATH.

B WINDOW: DOGES' PALACE: VENICE

C ORVIETO CATHEDRAL INTERIOR LOOKING E.

D CAMPANILE: PAL. DEL COMUNE: VERONA

E S. M. GLORIOSA DEI FRARI VENICE: THE APSE

F INTERIOR LOOKING E. S. M. GLORIOSA DEI FRARI: VENICE G EXTERIOR FROM W.

A THE FONTE GATTESCHI VITERBO

B A TOMB OF THE SCALIGERS VERONA

C ANGLE WINDOW VENICE

D LA CERTOSA: CHIARAVALLE

E PORCH: S.M. MAGGIORE BERGAMO

F PORCH: THE DUOMO FERRARA

G LOGGIA DEI MERCANTI BOLOGNA

H FACADE: S. AGOSTINO BERGAMO

DOGE'S PALACE : VENICE

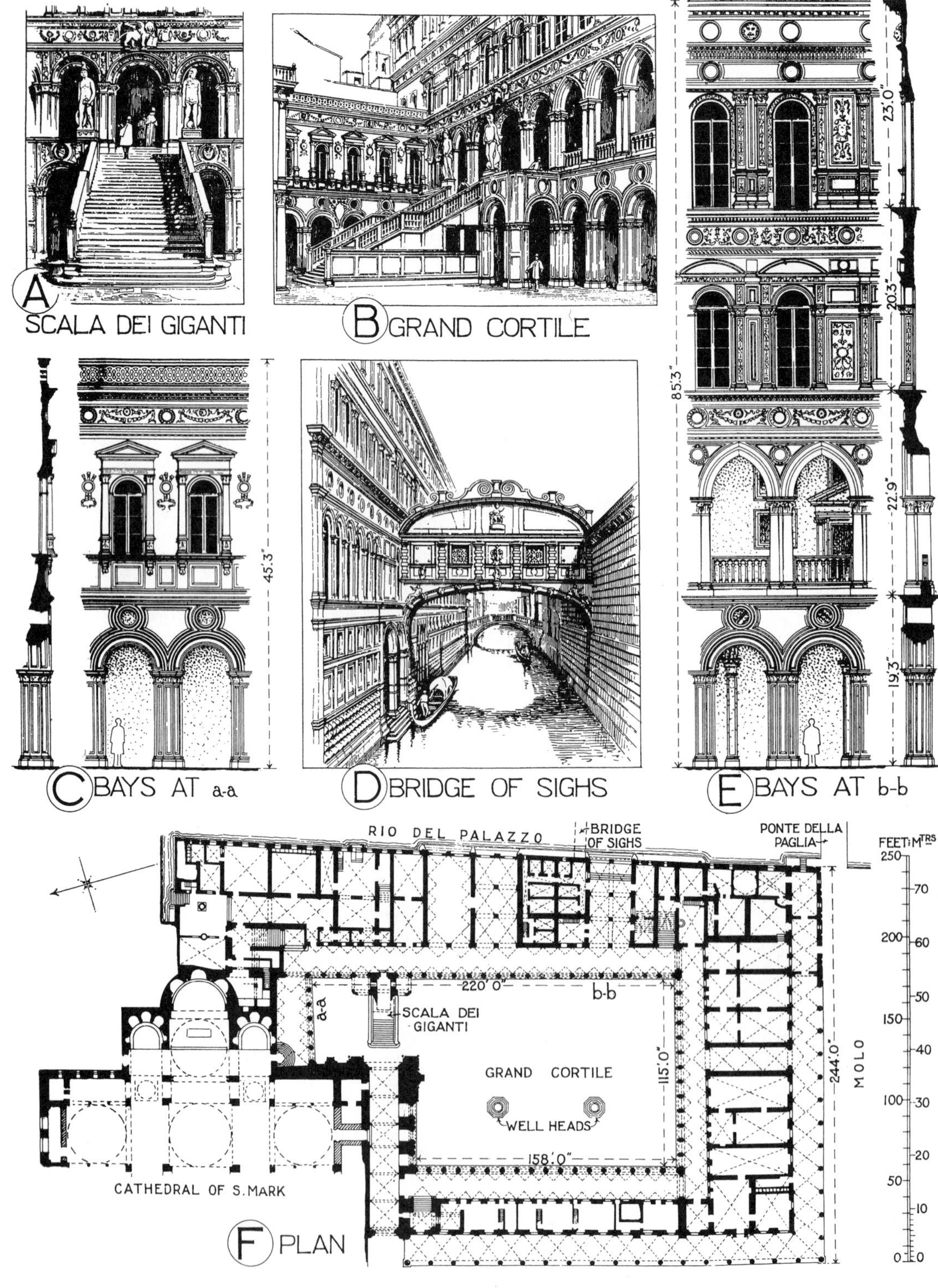

central hall, is surmounted by an arcade divided into six openings, filled with characteristically Venetian tracery.

The **Palazzi Foscari** (fifteenth century), **Contarini-Fasan** (fourteenth century), **Cavalli** (fifteenth century) and **Pisani** (fifteenth century) (p. 555B) are all on the Grand Canal. They have centrally placed traceried openings to light the hall and solid unbroken wings.

The **Ponte di Castel Vecchio** or **Scaligero, Verona** (1335) (p. 543B), wholly destroyed in World War II, was one of many bridges which were of such importance as a means of intercommunication that they were considered sacred. It was a fortified bridge across the Adige, with a tower on either bank, and had segmental arches, a low octagonal tower at every pier, and forked Ghibelline battlements along its whole length.

The **Torre Del Comune, Verona** (1172) (p. 544D), is one of those communal towers which served as bell towers to summon the citizens and as watch towers against fire and enemies. The square shaft of striped stone and brickwork has a belfry of three lights on each face. The octagonal turret which rises to a height of 83 m (272 ft) was added after 1404, when the city lost its independence of Venice.

Two other notable towers of the period are the **Torrazzo, Cremona** (1261–84), which at 122 m (nearly 400 ft), was the highest in Italy, and the celebrated **Campanile of S. Mark, Venice**, rebuilt since its collapse in 1902.

Florence Cathedral (S. Maria del Fiore) (pp. 548, 550A,B). Thanks to Brunelleschi's dome, the cathedral has come to be regarded as the monument *par excellence* of the incipient Renaissance. It needs to be remembered that the specification for the dome was already fixed by 1360, even if no-one was clear how it was to be built; and something of the kind was almost certainly a feature of the first design for a new cathedral, which goes back to *c.* 1294 and is associated with the name of Arnolfo di Cambio. At the end of the thirteenth century the architectural connotation of a vast, centrally planned east end would have been an Early Christian martyrium. What is not so certain is whether the 1294 design envisaged a vaulted nave. The other work in Florence ascribed to Arnolfo, S. Croce (q.v.), has wide arcades, slender walls and a wooden roof, all of which are to be found in one or other of the two rival cathedral designs of the time, namely Orvieto and the unfinished project at Siena (q.v.). The inference to be drawn is perhaps that the cathedral which Arnolfo projected was essentially a conflation of two early Christian types: the basilica and the martyrium. Oddly enough, the first unmistakable sign of interest in genuine Gothic was the octagon intended for the top of Giotto's campanile, for which there is a drawing, but which was never built. In the form we have it, the actual Gothic nave with its sturdy piers and heavy ribbed vaults, which looks like a blend of S. Maria Novella and S. Croce, was the conception of Francesco Talenti, who was in charge of the work between 1350 and 1366. There is a picture of this cathedral somewhat as he intended it to be, in the Spanish chapel at S. Maria Novella (*c.* 1365).

The **Campanile, Florence** (1334–59) (pp. 548A, 550A), on the site of an earlier tower (888), is 14 m (45 ft) square and 84 m (275 ft) high. The design by Giotto, who lived to complete the lowest stage, was twice changed as it proceeded, first by Andrea Pisano and finally by Francesco Talenti. It rises sheer from the pavement without supporting buttresses, and all its four sides are panelled in coloured marble and embellished with sculptured friezes and marble inlay. It is divided into four principal stages, of which the topmost is the belfry instead of Giotto's intended octagon.

The **Baptistery, Florence**, thought to have started as a fifth-century church, converted into a baptistry in the middle of the eleventh century, received various minor adornments during the thirteenth century. The octagon, 27 m (90 ft) in diameter, is covered with an internal dome, 31 m (103 ft) high, probably modelled on that of the Pantheon. The facades are in three stages of dark green and white marble, crowned with a pitched roof and lantern. The Baptistery is noted for the workmanship of its bronze doors, which were added in the fourteenth (1330–6) and fifteenth (1403–24 and 1425–52) centuries by Andrea Pisano and Lorenzo Ghiberti. In 1514, in view of threatened collapse, Michelangelo introduced an iron chain around the base of the dome.

Siena Cathedral (pp. 549A–C, 550C). The fact that Cistercian monks from San Galgano were actively involved in the construction of the thirteenth-century cathedral might suggest that it was already a proto-Gothic design. But other evidence seems to indicate that it was more like a Romanesque hall church with barrel vaults and no proper clerestory. The nave was finished by 1260, and the dome over the crossing soon after. The facade, for which Giovanni Pisano carved the sculptured figures, was started in the 1280s.

The interest of the building lies in what happened to it during the fourteenth century. In 1316, presumably as a riposte to the newly started and enormously high cathedrals of Orvieto and Florence, a new nave was begun to the south of the existing church, on a north–south axis. The facade and arcades of this structure can still be seen: vast, fragile and spacious. Unlike Orvieto, it was to be vaulted throughout, although the stability of the high vaults must have been questionable. If it had been completed, the earlier building would have formed the lower part of the transept of a much enlarged cathedral. By 1322, however, the project had run into difficulties. A commission of enquiry was appointed, led by Lorenzo Maitani, and the report survives – one

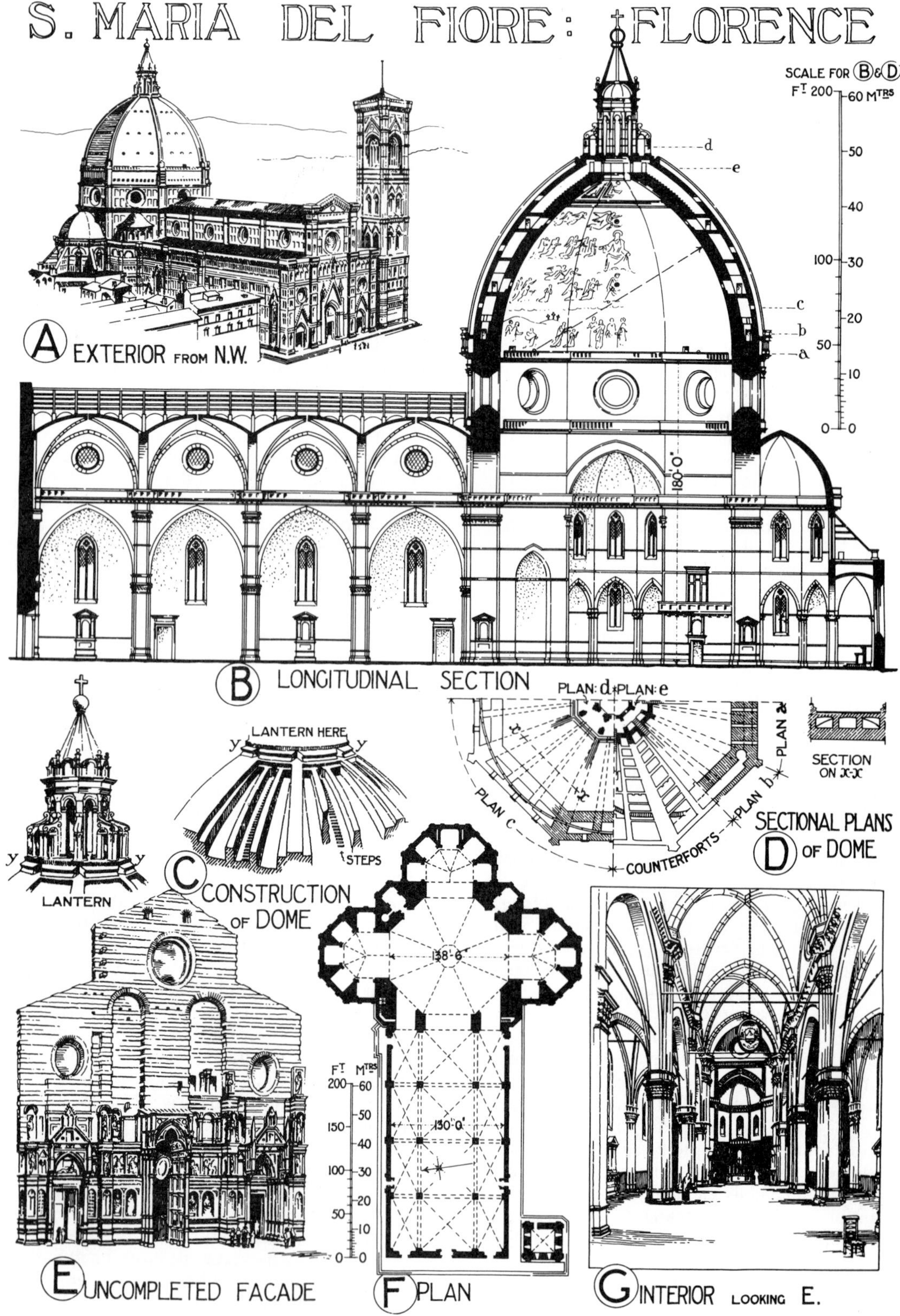
S. MARIA DEL FIORE: FLORENCE
SCALE FOR B & D
FT 200 60 MTRS
50
40
100 30
20
50 10
0 0
d
e
c
b
a
180'-0"
A EXTERIOR FROM N.W.
B LONGITUDINAL SECTION
PLAN: d PLAN: e
PLAN a
SECTION ON x-x
PLAN c
PLAN b
COUNTERFORTS
SECTIONAL PLANS
D OF DOME
LANTERN HERE
y y
STEPS
LANTERN
C CONSTRUCTION OF DOME
138'-6"
130'-0"
FT MTRS
200 60
150 50
100 40
50 30
0 0
E UNCOMPLETED FACADE
F PLAN
G INTERIOR LOOKING E.

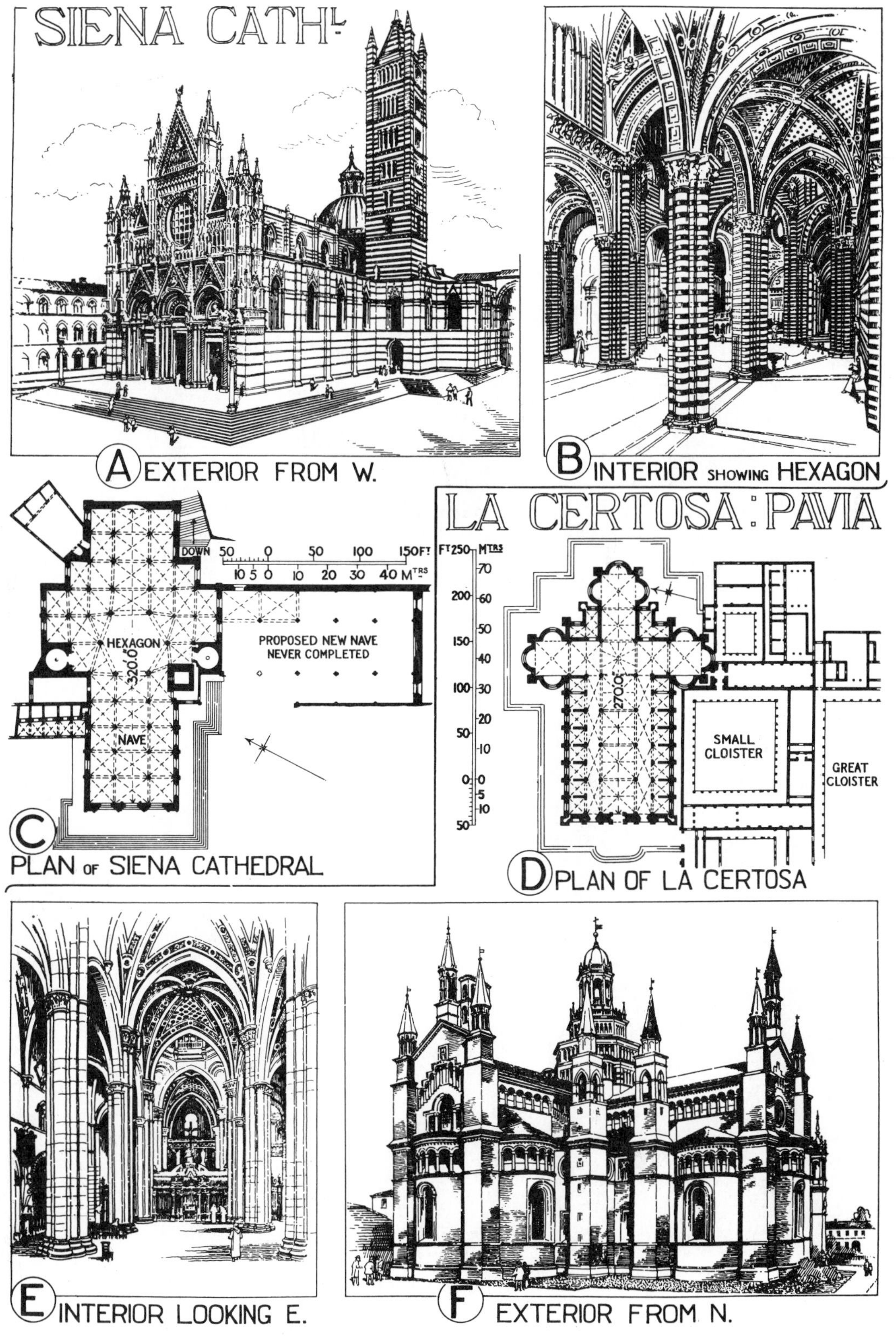
SIENA CATHL.
A EXTERIOR FROM W.
B INTERIOR SHOWING HEXAGON
DOWN
50 0 50 100 150FT
10 5 0 10 20 30 40 MTRS
HEXAGON
320.0
NAVE
PROPOSED NEW NAVE
NEVER COMPLETED
C
PLAN OF SIENA CATHEDRAL
LA CERTOSA : PAVIA
FT 250 MTRS
70
200 60
50
150 40
100 30
20
50 10
0 0
5
10
50
270.0
SMALL
CLOISTER
GREAT
CLOISTER
D PLAN OF LA CERTOSA
E INTERIOR LOOKING E.
F EXTERIOR FROM N.

A. Florence Cathedral from SE (1296–1462, campanile 1334–59). See p.547

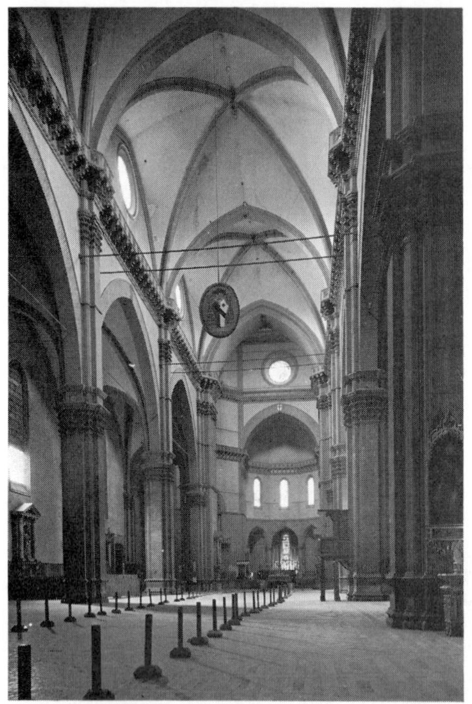

B. Florence Cathedral: nave looking east

C. Siena Cathedral: exterior (*c.* 1260–*c.* 1360). See p.547

A. S. Maria sopra Minerva, Rome (*c.* 1280, restored 1847). See p.553

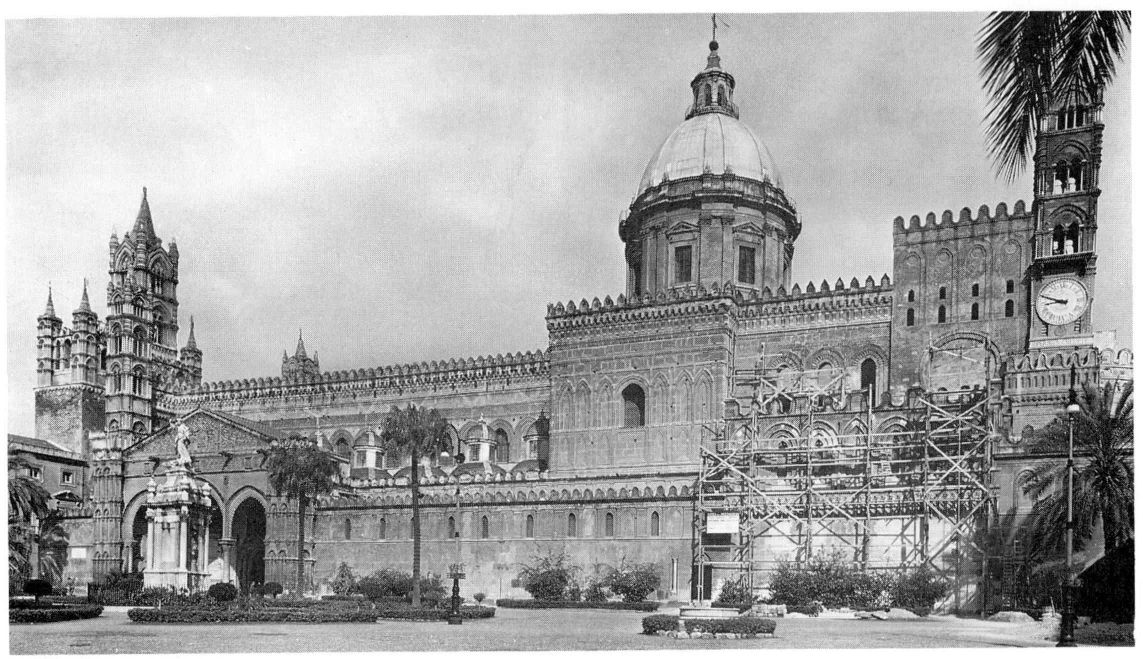

B. Palermo Cathedral from south (1170–85; dome 1781–1801). See p.553

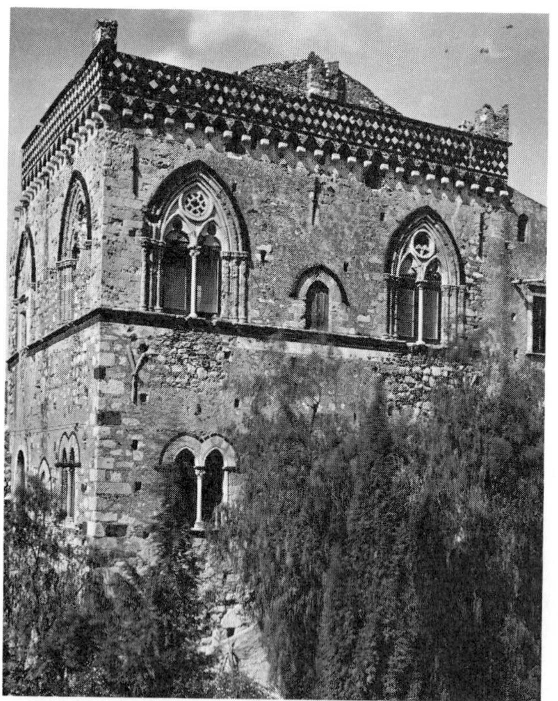

A. Palazzo S. Stefano, Taormina (1330). See p.553

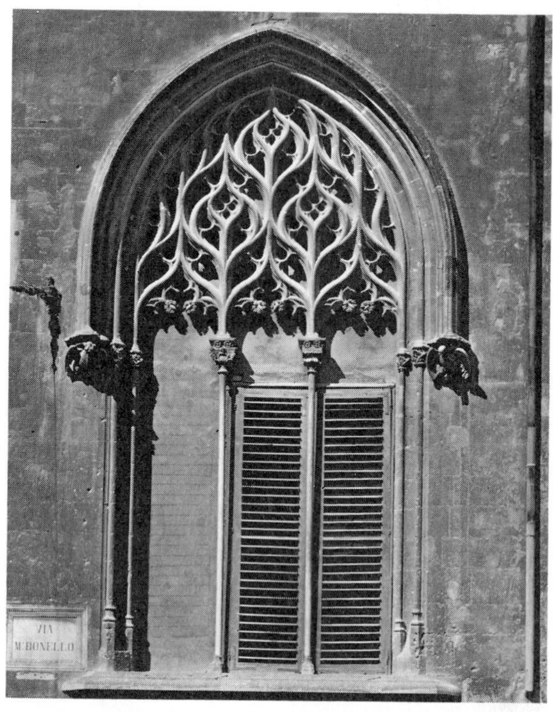

B. Window in Palazzo Arcivescovile, Palermo (fifteenth century). See p.553

C. S. Croce, Florence: nave (1294–1442). See p.553

of a small number of contemporary documents that shed light on mediaeval architectural thinking. It recommended that work should cease. Despite the warning, work continued until the middle of the century. It was finally abandoned after the Black Death. In the event, the thirteenth-century cathedral was given a clerestory and the centre of the existing facade heightened to bring it into line. This was completed *c.* 1360.

In its final form the cathedral of Siena is celebrated for its sumptuous decoration, both chromatic and carved. But the unfinished fragment deserves to be remembered as an exercise on a colossal scale – more daring than Orvieto and a precursor of Milan and San Petronio at Bologna. Inside and out, the walls are zebra-striped in marble, as is the shaft-like campanile (thirteenth century) with its six stages of windows which increase in both height and number as they rise up the building.

Orvieto Cathedral (begun 1290) (p. 544C) was a direct consequence of the miracles at Bolsena and the formal inception of the feast of Corpus Christi in 1264. More than any other Italian church of its time it conveys the reluctance of Italian architects and/or their ecclesiastical patrons to accept Gothic conventions, which were in effect confined to the facade. The interior, with its round arcade arches and open timber-trussed roof, seems far closer to Early Christian basilicas. It is supposed to have been based on S. Maria Maggiore in Rome. The principal decorative feature – alternating horizontal stripes – was achieved by using two kinds of stone. Another oddity is the flanking chapels, which are eccentric to the main arcades. On the other hand the facade (*c.* 1310–30) can only be described as Gothic. Drawings survive in the Opera del Duomo. It is an imposing screen, designed to dominate the main piazza of the town, and with hardly any relation to the interior. But although the conception is undeniably Gothic, it depends heavily on coloured marbles and mosaic; and the famous sculptured reliefs, done partly by and under the supervision of Lorenzo Maitani of Siena, are pictorial rather than architectural.

S. Maria sopra Minerva, Rome (p. 551A), was under construction by 1280. Like Arezzo Cathedral, it follows the general design of S. Maria Novella at Florence, and has been attributed to the same Dominican architects. It is the only Gothic church in Rome and, like many such mediaeval monuments in southern Italy, during the seventeenth and eighteenth centuries it was disguised beneath a veneer of Baroque plaster. It was restored to its original appearance in 1847.

One consequence of the Papal feud with the Hohestaufen, which ended with the elimination of the dynasty by the French Charles I of Anjou in 1266, was that Naples became the permanent capital of the kingdom of Sicily. There are documents to show that French masons found their way to **Naples**, and French details can be seen in the choir of the church of **San Lorenzo** (*c.* 1270–84). Given the French connection it might have been expected that Naples would have become the centre of Rayonnant Gothic in Italy; but only one church, **S. Maria Donna Regina** (1307), really looks at all French. Within a generation the profession had reverted into the hands of local masons who had little enthusiasm for what they regarded as an alien style. Already at **S. Chiara** (1310) the idiom had become completely Italian. The **Castello Nuovo** was built by Charles I in the last quarter of the thirteenth century with machicolated towers and curtain walls, later pierced with Renaissance windows.

Palermo Cathedral (1170–85) (p. 551B), repeatedly altered, built on the site of an earlier Muslim mosque, is basilican in plan and was commenced by King William the Good of Sicily. The open porch (*c.* 1480), with slender columns supporting stilted pointed arches, is reminiscent of the Alhambra, Granada; the roof battlements recall those of the Doge's Palace. At the west end the cathedral is connected by two pointed arches to the tower of the Archbishop's Palace. Two slender minaret towers on either side resemble those at the east end, and the skyline of the whole group suggests northern Gothic. The dome is an addition of 1781–1801.

The **Palazzo S. Stefano, Taormina** (1330) (p. 552A) – one of many palaces in that ancient precipice-city which have pointed two-light windows with trefoil heads and crowning machicolated cornices – and the **Palazzo Arcivescovile, Palermo** (p. 552B), designed with Flamboyant tracery windows (fifteenth century), are typical secular buildings of the mediaeval period.

S. Croce, Florence (p. 552C). The Franciscans had a church in Florence by 1225. The present building dates from 1294, and has been attributed, like the Duomo, to Arnolfo di Cambio. The task of combining the simplicity required by the order with the prestige and influence it had acquired in Florence, not to mention Florentine expectations that all art and architecture should be worthy of the city, was not easily fulfilled. By the end of the thirteenth century S. Croce had become one of the principal focal points for private devotions, and no less than ten chapels had to be provided along the transept for the benefit of influential lay patrons. These, together with the altar chapel on this axis, were vaulted, and were eventually entirely covered with fresco cycles by the leading Florentine painters of the day. The rest of the church was left unvaulted. The absence of any serious structural problems allowed masonry to be reduced to a minimum, and the interior is high, bright and spacious. In form it is basilican, and the detail, such as it is, is all Gothic. It thus contrives to suggest that it was a thoroughly modern building, yet at the same time it was faithful to the mainstream Florentine tradition (compare S. Miniato), and indeed positively

A. S. Maria Novella, Florence (1278–1350; facade 1456–70). See p.557

B. Palazzo Vecchio (1298–1314) and Piazza della Signoria, Florence, with the Loggia dei Lanzi (right) (1376–82). See p.557

A THE BIGALLO: FLORENCE
B PALAZZO PISANI: VENICE
← PROJECTED EXTENSION →
C PALAZZO CA D'ORO: VENICE
D PALAZZO PUBBLICO: SIENA
E BALCONY: VENICE
F PAL. DEI PRIORI: VOLTERRA
G MEDIÆVAL Hº: VITERBO
H PAL° PUBBLICO: MONTEPULCIANO

A. Castle, Volterra (1343). See p.557

B. Ponte Vecchio, Florence (1345). See p.557

C. Castel del Monte, Apulia (*c.* 1240). See p.557

old-fashioned in its evocations of Early Christian purity which in time would satisfy the standards of all but the most exigent of Franciscan Spirituals.

S. Maria Novella, Florence (p. 554A). The church of the Dominican Order in Florence. A convent of friars was already established by 1221, and there was a church in use in 1246. But the present building was only under construction shortly before 1279. In conception the east end is pure 'plan Bernardin', and shows the extent to which the Dominicans were indebted to the Cistercians for their ideas about church design, even through the chapels on the transepts were put to different use. The nave was less derivative and more influential. It is neither a true basilica nor a true hall church, but a blend of both. The arcades are wide and high, no doubt to facilitate preaching. The clerestory has been reduced to a series of oculi set in bare walls. It was a formula repeated on several occasions, both in Florence and beyond, but never with the same unerring good taste. The effect owes much to this quality of the materials and the restraint with which the visual patterns were formed. It clearly left a deep impression on Brunelleschi. But in the last resort the aesthetic merit of the nave depends on the perfection of its proportions, which were not just a matter of mathematical ratios, and which eluded all who tried to emulate it. Alberti's Renaissance facade has no organic or stylistic connection with the Gothic building behind it; but as it is a pure frontispiece this hardly matters. In this respect S. Maria Novella stands in direct line of descent from Orvieto.

The **Palazzo del Podesta** or **Bargello, Florence** (1255–), the **Palazzo Vecchio, Florence** (1298–1314) (p. 554B), the **Palazzo Pubblico, Siena** (1289–1309) (p. 555D), the **Palazzo del Municipio, Perugia** (1281–), and the **Palazzo Pubblico, Montepulciano** (late fourteenth century) (p. 555H), represent the municipal life and enterprise of these mediaeval cities, and stand, grave and severe, with their lofty watch towers and fortified facades.

The **Palazzo dei Priori, Volterra** (1208–57) (p. 555F), is in four storeys with two-light windows, now irregularly placed. It is crowned with heavy battlements, and the square tower rising above the front wall is capped with a belfry.

The **Bigallo, Florence** (1352–58) (p. 555A), is a delicately arcaded little loggia, designed to shelter foundlings.

The **Loggia dei Lanzi, Florence** (1376–82) (p. 554B), with its bold semicircular arches and compound piers, forms part of a scheme embracing the Piazza della Signoria but never completed.

The **Mediaeval House, Viterbo** (p. 555G), with its arcaded ground storey and traceried windows, exemplifies smaller urban dwellings of the period.

The **Castle, Volterra** (1343) (p. 556A), high on its rocky site, is a typical mediaeval stronghold of imposing outline with massive walls, small windows, central circular keep, round towers and machicolations.

San Gimignano (p. 175B) on its hill-top still retains thirteen towers built by rival local families – adherents of the Ghibellines and Guelphs – mainly in the tenth and eleventh centuries. They still impart a strangely mediaeval aspect to this picturesque hill-city.

The **Ponte Vecchio, Florence** (1345) (p. 556B), by Taddeo Gaddi, the oldest bridge in Florence, has three segmental arches springing boldly from massive piers to withstand the waters of the Arno when swollen with the melting snows of the Apennines, while along both sides of its roadway are the small shops of the goldsmiths' quarter.

Castel del Monte, Apulia (p. 556C). Most of the castles of Frederick II were military installations to which residential facilities were optional additions. Castel del Monte differs from the rest in so far as it was conceived as a private residence for the Emperor's leisure time, a hunting lodge on the Murge of Apulia, well away from the busy coastal plain. The isolation was deliberate. It dates from *c.* 1240. Its fame rests on a few Classical features which are supposed to reflect Frederick's imperial tastes, and his proto-Renaissance spirit. In fact Castel del Monte is far more Gothic than Classical, and the important thing is that in Italy at least, there was evidently nothing incompatible about mixing styles of widely different origins.

The castle is symmetrical to the point of monotony: an octagonal perimeter around an octagonal courtyard with octagonal towers at the corners and eight virtually identical trapezoid rooms on each of the two floors. All the rooms are small, dark and ribbed-vaulted. Nevertheless a great deal of thought was given to how the building was to be used. Only certain rooms have fireplaces or gard-robes; very few have both. Some rooms have direct access to staircases; others form extended suites. Some doors could be opened inwards, others outwards, and locked and barred accordingly. There is one discreet escape stair.

Part Three

THE ARCHITECTURE OF ISLAM

Chapter 15
BACKGROUND

Islam and its Predecessors

This part is concerned with an architectural continuity that ran parallel with the history of western architecture from the second century BC. The eastern movement of Greek and then Roman classical architecture merged with locally generated styles – Achaemenid, Parthian, Sassanian, and peripheral eastern variants of localised Hellenistic styles – to provide the basis for a thousand years of architectural creativity extending across Asia and Africa and spreading into Europe.

No architectural style, other than Muslim, is designated by concordance with a religion. This is for the special reason that Islam has created a coherence of lifestyle over wide geographical areas. This focuses on the requirements of the religion, the behaviour that derives from it and a living language, Arabic, which is understood throughout the Muslim world. The consequence is a centrality created by, among other things, the annual pilgrimage to Mecca in the Hejaz in western Saudi Arabia. Within Islam, however, the variation in styles is distinctive: so much so that to many Muslim scholars the common pattern is blurred to the extent that they deny that there is any such thing as Islamic architecture. These varied styles have evolved around tribal or dynastic foci by which they are known.

Muslim architecture may be seen as the one great product of two streams of development, one in the Mediterranean and the other in south central Asia. The coalescence took place over a period from about 300 BC to 800 AD with a melding of influences spread over a very much longer period. Initially there were two very different traditions. In the Mediterranean, Greek architecture rose in Periclean Athens to a level of extraordinary perfection, to be echoed and repeated in the west down the ages. In the east the Achamaenid traditions culminating in the great royal palace at Persepolis demonstrate a powerful and separate evolutionary pattern of trabeated building. Their intermingling began with the injection into the east of Greek culture carried in the wake of the thrusts of Alexander, a Macedonian prince who by 332 BC had overcome the rulers of this wide region, founding separate cities in the Greek administrative mould wherever he passed. His loosely arranged empire fell to his generals, collectively known as the Seleucids and Ptolemies, who controlled or ruled an area approximating to that now known as the Middle East. The fusion of Greek culture was as inevitable as it was deliberate but the sheer weight of local populations determined the ultimate subfusion and integration of the cities of Seleucid and Ptolemaic foundation in the burgeoning of later empires.

Among their greatest cities were Alexandria on the western edge of the Nile Delta and Seleucia on the Tigris, close to modern Baghdad; of these and many others not a trace of the original buildings remains as a standing structure. The most impressive architectural monument of this injection of classical design into the East is the palatial core of a desert city at Hatra, now in Iraq (see Chapter 16), but the passing and the influence of these extreme eastward penetrations of Greek culture are still to be found in inscriptions, and works of art, such as the classically modelled statues of the Buddhist kingdoms at Gandhara in northern India.

The incursions of the Seleucids halted an evolution of native styles for some hundreds of years and it is not until the time of Christ that strong local traditions re-emerged on and about the Iranian plateau. There the Parthian dynasty focused a nationalism which allowed the East again to confront the West militarily with thrust and counterthrust across Asia Minor succeeded by Roman incursions into Mesopotamia and Persia. Some lasting works were built by Roman prisoners who brought their skills of masonry and engineering to the bridges and perhaps to the early domes of their Parthian captors. These long conflicts left a trail of detritus across the region in terms of peoples and influences. Captive Romans were set to work in Persia – Persian forts were thrown up in Egypt. Byzantine architects built towns on the Euphrates and bridges on the Orontes. Trade routes traversed the regions carrying men with skills between opposing Empires and an important channel of influence arose in a new and pervasive religion – Christianity. Initially the Apostles proselytised most successfully south and eastwards. Until the fourth

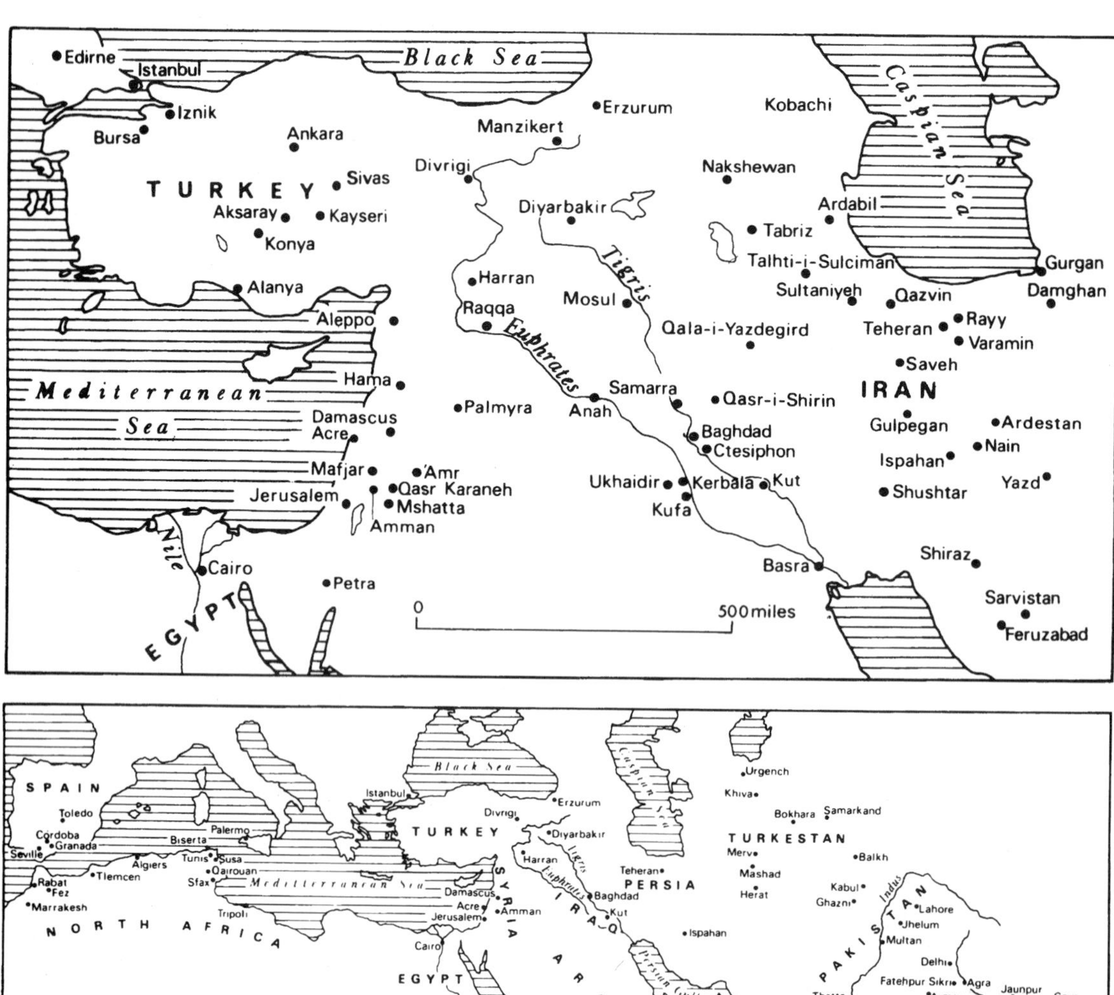

The Islamic World

century their incursions into the Roman heartland were resisted. They were seen as a threat to established power. The extent to which the eastward traffic carried with it the classical style well established in Palestine has yet to be fully evaluated but in the design of churches it is to be seen clearly in the movement of the religion southwards and in the early churches of the monotheistic versions of the faith in the Nile valley where the Copts, inheritors of the religion of the Pharoahs, found no difficulty in absorbing the concepts of the afterlife and the faith of the one God. The early churches stylistically took over the forms of Greek and Roman temples or basilicas and a gentle tide of influence moved eastwards with the adherents of the religion.

Contemporary Parthian royal building has survived sufficiently to be reconstructable. The great royal palaces of Sarvistan and Firuzabad demonstrate an architectural evolution which was to provide a basis for much that followed in the architecture of Islam – in particular the dome and iwan. The resolution of a square sub-structure to a ring by squinches is apparent by the third century AD and the evolution of the iwan – an open-fronted barrel vault – had by then also reached monumental proportions. Both had a determinant effect upon plan forms.

The predominant eastern dynasty until the coming of Islam arose in Fars – southern Persia – ruling from the fourth until the seventh centuries when an enfeebled king, Yazdegerd II, fled before the invading Muslims and was slain by one of his followers.

The Sassanian dynasty built its winter capital, Ctesiphon, within a mile of the flourishing Seleucid city, Seleucia-on-the-Tigris, on the opposite bank of the river. Few Sassanian buildings have survived in recognisable state although a number of their palatial complexes are sufficiently complete to allow adequate reconstruction and at Ctesiphon itself there survives the iwan and one wing of the greatest royal palace of all, known from its traditional attribution to Chosroes II as the Tak-i-Chisra. It was under this ruler that the Persian empire expanded finally, and to its greatest extent in antiquity. Pressures from the west restrained the Byzantine emperors such as Justinian I on their eastern frontiers, with the result that Chosroes and his successors were able to establish and maintain their hold on territories as far west as Syria, Palestine and Lower Egypt. These areas had long been Roman provinces and architecturally were replete with a distinctive classical style. Moreover, the fabric of Christianity lay across the region and although fire worship was the religion of the royal families of the Sassanian era eastern Christianity was widespread and influential in both Orthodox and Nestorian forms.

In its eastern and southern provinces the Byzantine Empire produced local patterns of architecture in which the occasional work of architects from the Metropolis stands out distinctly. Destruction in these lands of the eastern Byzantine Empire has been so continuous that their architectural significance in the early Christian era is shrouded. War, pillage and the agricultural changes that followed misgovernment and exploitation have left much of these lands desolate and their buildings robbed. In northern Syria the great ruin fields of the 'Dead Cities' testify to once-rich populations with a highly developed architectural style and the story is repeated throughout the Mediterranean littoral into Sinai and Egypt. In Cairo, at a few desert sites and in ruined Coptic towns in the Nile valley some understanding of these rich and extensive cultures can be gained but where the great cities survive, Alexandria being an extreme case, the basilicas, the baths, the library, the port have all been so completely effaced that they are only to be understood from inference and literary record. These eastern marchlands of the Roman Empire had an architectural heritage which was intrinsically Graeco-Roman in background but distinctively local in its interpretation and since very little of the work was associated with major dynastic achievements much of it has escaped historical attention. The church, however, was a major influence in these pre-Muslim centuries, modelling and remodelling forms of Roman temples and meeting halls and adapting to new rituals structural forms and designs which had served purposes as diverse as fire temples and the rites of Isis.

These eastern frontier lands in the first centuries of our era were architecturally inventive and beneath the broad mantles of Persian and Roman suzereignty contained many local groupings, vassal states or provinces where architecture evolved distinctively. In north-east Asia Minor Georgia and Armenia gave rise to developing forms of centralised church building echoed on the Euphrates in that earliest of Christian states, the Kingdom of Edessa (present-day Urfa). Likewise, the early church flourished in northern Mesopotamia. On the steppe lands on both sides of the Arabian desert Christian Arabs, the Lakhimids, and Ghassanids continued the Roman traditions that had left forts and towns scattered across the region. The deserted city of Resafa in northern Syria is one of the better-known surviving examples. Towards the coast a rich architectural heritage was developed in northern Syria focusing on Antioch and Damascus, leaving a legacy today in scores of ruined and deserted townships. Here in the region between Aleppo and the coast and in southern Syria near Bosra in the Hauran there emerged an inventive, tradition of sophisticated and magnificently executed stone buildings indicative of high levels of social organisation where great domed churches, such as Kalat Semaan, immense basilicas and fine houses were wrapped in wreathing string courses and adorned with sumptuous carving in a manner unparalleled elsewhere. This group of cities, known as the Decapolis, of which Jerash is the most prominent survivor, adhered to the classical tradition on a monumental scale but in powerfully and distinctively remodelled forms. These influences are to be traced southwards through the Nabatean kingdoms where the baroque exuberance of Petra still carries its astonishing message of classical design in cliffs carved from red and yellow sandstone, and down to cities such as Sana'a where the Syrian tradition of domed churches faced in mosaic was to be found in the long-destroyed cathedral church.

The Monophysite doctrine was strong across this region and nowhere more than in the Nile valley where the Copts had readily taken to Christianity following the arrival of the Apostle Mark. The ancient churches here are of the basilican form with a wide transverse space before the triple-apsed east end and some of the very early churches in Egypt may be the earliest of all survivors of Christian building. It was in Egypt also that the monastic traditions began in the fourth and fifth centuries, being carried westwards through the Roman Empire after its formal acceptance of Christianity. Under Diocletian imperial authority had persecuted the native churches so ferociously that the reign of that emperor is still used by the Copts to mark the beginning of their era. By the sixth century Byzantine churches were being introduced at the exhortation of the Emperor Justinian while his Empress Theodora supported the Monophysite cause and the Coptic Church. Where they survive, as in ancient Cairo (Deir Bablun) they are architecturally a different breed. The native church can still be found here and in the monasteries, now deserted, of the Upper Nile or those still extant on the Red Sea and in the Wadi Natrun. From this southern part of the region to northern Mesopotamia and even to Central Asia the eastern form of church with triple isolated sanctuaries facing a broad transverse nave can be found coupled sometimes with a basilican form.

At the beginning of the seventh century the Persian emperors controlled the land from the Caucasus to the Nile Delta and they were restored again to the Byzantine Empire by the heroic exploits of Heraclius who defeated the Sassanian armies in their heartland at Ctesiphon and recovered Jerusalem in 628. His tremendous exertions in the military and political fields were simultaneously and more lastingly paralleled by the Prophet Mohammed, pursuing his theological enquiries with Christian monks as he traversed the caravan routes from Mecca into Palestine and then in his later years receiving revelations and leading the first adherents of the new monotheism. Heraclius, enthroned in Constantinople, failed to recognise the significance of these events and made no effort to check or respond to this new expression of the worship of the one God.

Islam means literally submission, and Muslims are those who submit to the expression of the will of God by the Prophet Mohammed. Emnities have clouded the inherent relationship between Christianity, and its predecessor Judaism, with Islam. The fact of the emergence of Islam from Christian theology has important parallels with the emergence of Christianity from Judaism and it is intrinsic to Islam that the peoples adhering to these earlier religions were treated with sympathy and given protection as being 'peoples of the book'. The architectural consequence of this keystone of Muslim philosophy was the natural acceptance of buildings appropriate to the circumstances of the new religion. Although from a twentieth-century viewpoint the emergence of Islam seems revolutionary it was in fact an evolution in theological, philosophical and architectural terms.

In his maturity Mohammed received revelations which Muslims accept as the Word of God. These were revolutionary in terms of Mohammed's status as a member of one of the leading cities of Mecca in the Hejaz – the western region of Arabia – where idolatry was the literal stock-in-trade of the city which depended even then on pilgrim traffic. Hence the Muslim retreat to Yathrib – the Hegira – and the beginning of the Muslim era.

Mesopotamia and Persia

Both brick and rubble masonry were the prime building elements in the Seleucid East, Parthia and the Sassanian Empires. These materials are generally not used for roofing and it must be recognised that much roof construction was of timber, probably laid as pole joisting with brushwood and palm frond covering finished with mud. In more monumental buildings vaulting and arching were used and dome construction is apparent for the first time in the Orient. Fired brick therefore came to be used in the vaults, squinches, arches and domes and some distinctive techniques of construction were evolved. To take advantage of the effects of quick setting of gypsum mortars (the set of plaster of Paris) flat fired bricks were laid radially as voussoirs but with their long axis on the line of the arch being formed. The effect was to give a large area of adhesion so that the voussoir would stay fixed in position without the support of centring within minutes of its application. In such vaults and occasionally in arches the initial courses would be corbelled in for up to one fifth of the height to be succeeded by arches of 'ring-arch' construction. Over openings such as windows and doors a flat light timber lintel would be set at the springing line and on top of it temporary centring would be formed in mud brick, perhaps to the full width of the lintel, forming a wider arch than the opening below and producing on removal of the mud brick the distinctively Parthian and Sassanian keyhole arch. Arch forms in this period varied from the predominant half-round to the vertical semi-ellipse and broken segments giving arches with quite sharply pointed profiles. The barrel vault was the predominant structural device throughout the region and this is true also of Upper Egypt. To avoid the use of timber centring arches were built inclined against an end wall, the work on the lower voussoirs of the advancing vault being several rings ahead of the completion of the upper segments.

In this period the squinch (arch or small vault across a corner) first makes its appearance. Larger domes rose over the great halls of palaces in Parthian and Sassanian Iran. Here also appeared the talar and iwan – open-fronted spaces serving ceremonial and living functions. The emergence of these spaces can be traced archaeologically as sheltered recesses fronting unroofed areas in homes and ceremonial buildings. They came to form an important part of the architectural vocabulary in the Middle East, appearing as rationalised cave-like openings, arched or supported by columns, sometimes being a high or large central unit flanked by two similar smaller openings and also appearing as two or four opposed openings facing each other.

A large vocabulary of decorative elements is associated with this period. Facades were regularly enlivened with blind arcading, frequently carried on coupled colonettes or sometimes even triple colonettes. Applied stucco decoration was widely used for dados, friezes, linings and framings to openings, roundels in spandrels, string courses and crestings. The Classical orders were entirely absent except where Greek influence persisted in and after the Seleucid period. Distinctive crenellations were adopted, each being stepped three or four times giving a sawtoothed profile and crenellations of this style became used as a frieze. Stucco was regularly incised and modelled with patterning and was enriched with paint. Large clay sculptures were created in addition to the stone carvings. Strong pigments were regularly used to heighten patterns and sculptures.

In urban planning there was a marked contrast between the formal concepts introduced by the Greeks where reticulate straight-line layout contrasts with the native form of city development which is entirely organic and tends to produce a near-circular perimeter as at Takht-i-Suleiman.

Syria and Egypt

Classical influences pervaded the Mediterranean coastline reaching inland to Western Asia Minor, to the Syrian steppes inhabited by the Ghassinid Arabs, to the Nabataean Arab Kingdoms and into the Nile Valley beyond the Delta. Traditions of finely worked trabeated masonry predominated in monumental building and the Corinthian Order was predominant, giving rise to variations such as wind-blown acanthus and basket capitals. Architecturally this was an inventive land sufficiently beyond the 'Pale' to develop its own idiosyncratic versions of Classical orders and their handling. From Jerusalem to Diyarbakir, in the Decapolis and around Antioch the extant remains of monumental buildings in finely worked masonry carry complex and elaborate ornament of powerful and fluid design matched nowhere else. Elaborate string courses wreath around windows ropelike and in the finest work heavy torus moulds are deeply undercut with fretted detail. Much of the architecture was entirely lithic with door leaves and window shutters in stone and floors and roofs formed with long stone planks. Timber was extensively employed and surviving masonry clearly indicates the seating for large timber domes. In contrast to lands further east arching was almost invariably round although with occasional slight accentuation to a central point. Plate tracery in stone was in regular use and vaults were buttressed by contraforts. Occasionally these were detached as primitive flying buttresses. Burned brick was rarely used, and where it is found the origins may be traced to metropolitan influences.

Further south, Nabataean building developed with an exuberance that can only be called baroque, broken pediments and stylised urns on steeples featuring prominently. Although nothing is left of coastal Egypt in this period much Coptic church building survives in the Upper Nile and at the head of the Delta. Churches supply our principal evidence for a basilican form terminating in a broad cross-choir fronted by three haikals (chapels). The aisles and nave are divided by colonnades of Corinthian columns carrying a massive timber entablature while the roofs are invariably of timber.

Sites identified and excavated have tended to be those which ceased to be cities. Where they continued in use, such as at Alexandria in Egypt, evidence of this early period lies deeply buried or destroyed in redevelopment.

The transition from Seleucid to Parthian rule came with the ascendancy of the native population over the incursive Greeks. Henceforward Rome, and thenceforward Byzantium, was to be the natural enemy.

History of Islam

At the end of the sixth century, when the prophet Mohammed was a young man (his date of birth is not known), Sassanid Persia stretched from the Mediterranean to the Indus, and from the Aral Sea to the Indian Ocean. In the first twenty years of the seventh century the last great monarch, Chosroes II, moved to revenge the death of his one-time ally Maurice, the Byzantine Emperor, at the hands of a usurper. He overran Syria, took Jerusalem in 615, and in the next few years invaded Egypt. His armies even approached Constantinople itself. This Persian threat to the heart of the Byzantine empire coincided almost precisely (in 616) with the final overthrow of the Romans in Spain by the Visigoths. Byzantium was rescued by Heraclius, who as soldier–emperor made incursions deep into the Sassanian empire, sacking Ctesiphon in 628 to rescue the True Cross, with which he returned in triumph to Jerusalem.

Two other factors complicate the background of Islam at the beginning – one religious, the other secular. Although for a time officially tolerated Orthodox Christianity was largely eschewed in Zoroastrian Persia whereas Manichaeism (which united Jewish and Christian beliefs, with Persian mysticism) and Nestorian Christianity were both accepted, the latter because it had been banned by Rome. Incursions from eastern and central Asia continued as successive tribes were displaced in the westward movements that had begun over a thousand years earlier. They reduced the settled oasis cities – Samarkand, Bokhara, Merv and Khiva – and moved westwards, allying themselves expediently with the great powers. In the first quarter of the seventh century the Huns were succeeded first by the Avars and then by Turkic tribes (Khazars, and others) whose provinces ran from the Pamirs to the Oxus.

In Arabia the provinces of Rome had indeterminate boundaries eastward. The struggles in Palestine by which the Jews had been subjugated or expelled were not reflected in the marchlands of the Empire, where Nabataean and other groupings were peripheral to the dictats of the Caesars. Along the trade routes of Romanised Arabia culture and architectural styles reached beyond the writ of Roman and Byzantine law although the cultural influences extended further.

The Prophet Mohammed, to whom Islam owes its existence, was born into an important family (the Kureish) in the mountain city of Mecca in western Arabia in the late sixth century. He travelled as a merchant into the Arabian provinces of the Roman empire, then vibrant with Christianity. He is believed to have debated intensively with philosophers and clerics, contrasting the long religious traditions and multiplicity of forms of worship in the area with theorising upon monotheism under Christian leadership.

In his maturity Mohammed received revelations which, to Muslims, represent the Word of God. The threat this posed to established religious practices in Mecca caused the Prophet, with a small band of his followers, to be driven from the city in 622. He took refuge in Yathrib, a town to the north, which thereafter became the City of the Prophet or, simply al-Medina – 'The City'. The flight from Mecca – the Hegira – marks the beginning of the Muslim era. The faithful became a coherent body and adopted the practice of praying towards Jerusalem, but on reconciliation with Mecca turned towards that city in their prostrations. The Prophet remained in Medina until his death in 632, establishing the framework of the religion and the beginnings of a military organisation charged with spreading the Faith.

The explosive expansion of Islam carried the faith north-east into Mesopotamia, west into Egypt and beyond and into the fertile lands of the Mediterranean littoral (present-day Israel, Lebanon, Jordan and Syria). One prime objective was the defeat and conversion of the Byzantine emperor. In Constantinople the Emperor, Heraclius, was astonishingly supine in the face of a threat he underestimated. The Arab armies aimed first at Jerusalem, then at Damascus and finally, but unsuccessfully, at Constantinople. Their northward advance was deflected eastwards as it entered the southern foothills of the mountains of Asia Minor and then it petered out.

The parallel attack carried another Muslim army north-eastwards into the Tigris and Euphrates basin, the heartland of the Sassanian empire. Defeated in the first encounter at Qadisiyeh the Sassanians crumbled finally at Nihavand in 641, but in the west Jerusalem gave way only after long resistance. The Byzantine empire established an erratic frontier with Islam in the mountains of Asia Minor, and despite an audacious direct seaborne attempt on Constantinople the Arabs were held at bay.

Blocked by Byzantium in the north-west and stretched perilously far in the north-east, the Arabs opened new fields of conquest by turning westwards along the coast of Africa. In 640 they conquered Egypt, and within 30 years had gained control of the whole of the Mediterranean coast of North Africa. By 711 they were established in southern Spain, and 50 years later had conquered almost all the peninsula, striking deep into southern France before being halted in 732 by a major defeat at Poitiers at the hands of Charles Martell, hence called the 'Saviour of Europe'. Poitiers marked the limit of Arab expansion into western Europe.

Settled in Palestine, the Umayyad Caliphate was, to a considerable degree, Hellenised, by contrast with the overtly Persian influence on their forces penetrating the Iranian plateau into Central Asia and beyond even into China. Rivalry developed into a rift under the banner of the Abbasids.

The first century of Islam is imbued with Byzantine overtones, and its architecture owes much to the vigorous Hellenism of Syria, Palestine and Lower Egypt. In 750 the Abbasids swept this influence aside. They eliminated almost the whole of the Umayyad clan and for two centuries or more Palestine became a cultural vacuum. Syrian administrators and courtiers made their way westwards to the new Umayyad capital at Cordoba to perpetuate in Spain (where they posed no threat to Abbasid power) the values and characteristics brought from Syria.

The Caliphate itself was moved first to a briefly inhabited site in northern Mesopotamia and then in 762 to the City of Peace (now Kadhimain near Baghdad) and then in 832 to Samarra. There for sixty years, the Abbasids ruled as autocrats. They were immensely powerful and, in volume, their material achievements far outstripped those of their Umayyad predecessors. They returned to Baghdad towards the end of the ninth century to rule a diminishing Empire. While retaining pre-eminence as leaders of the Faithful the Abbasid Caliphs were never again to rule on their earlier scale and the government of the region from Afghanistan to Syria lay with the interrelated Seljuk and Zengid dynasties whose architectural achievements were both diverse and inventive. As the Abbasid Caliphs became weaker their authority was usurped in central Asia, Afghanistan and in Asia Minor, Syria and Egypt, where the Tulunid and Fatimid dynasties were dominant.

By the twelfth century much of Palestine had become the focus of incursion from the west. The Crusades brought to Asia Minor, Palestine and, in the thirteenth century, to Egypt new and more fearsome antagonists than the armies of Byzantium. Latin kingdoms were established in Syria, Palestine and on the upper Euphrates, but the Asian provinces of Byzantium fell piecemeal to Turkish invaders, who reached the Meditarranean on the Ionian coast. Far to the east the Ghorids, a Muslim dynasty of Turkish origin, established Islam in northern India at the beginning of the eleventh century. Meanwhile the Muslim kingdoms in Spain were pressed increasingly hard by Christian forces from the north and the Crusaders' footholds in the Holy Land became more and more precarious although the Christian kingdoms of Edessa, Outremer and Jerusalem survived into the thirteenth century. In 1291 Acre (Akka) fell and the power of the Frankish knights was broken (see also Chapter 13).

In Egypt the Tulunids were succeeded eventually in the eleventh century by the the Fatimids, whose Mamluks (slaves from Asia Minor and Russia) in turn succeeded them. The Mamluks ejected the Crusaders from the Holy Land. Subsequently they met and successfully resisted the Mongol challenge in Syria to consolidate what was to be a long-sustained political dominance. Ultimately they were defeated by the Ottomans in 1517. Henceforth Egypt was to lie within Turkish sovereignty.

From the Scythian incursions of the middle centuries of the first millennium BC (Scyths overran the post-Seleucid Bactrian kingdoms as late as 141 BC) through invasions by the Hsing-Nu (Huns) and the Juan-Juan (Avars) to the later movements of Turkish tribes from Mongolia, the corridor across southern central Asia had continued to attract the eastern barbarian peoples to the settled oasis towns of central Asia and then across northern Persia into Asia Minor. This flow became a raging torrent in the early thirteenth century under Genghis Khan and his successors. His grandson, Hulagu, swept from central Asia into Persia, Syria and Asia Minor, and with terrifying rapacity flooded westwards into Europe itself. In 1258 Baghdad was sacked by Mongol armies whose declared aim was the utter destruction of everything and everyone daring to resist them. A century later under Timur (Tamurlane, a khan of combined Turkish–Mongol origin) there ensued a further period of destruction. Timur made Samarkand his capital in 1370, invaded Persia ten years later and was in Asia Minor inside a decade. He took Sultaniyeh, captured Baghdad in 1393, and Damascus a few years later. Timur was never defeated in battle and at the turn of the century ruled from central Asia to the Nile, and from northern India virtually to the Bosphorus, having reduced Delhi in 1399. He embraced Islam, and proclaimed the faith across his territories. Under his rule Samarkand became the focus of architectural development and its influences spread widely across the lands in Timurid rule. His defeat of the rapidly rising Ottomans in 1400 gave a brief respite to the Byzantine emperors before their eclipse half a century later.

Timur himself commissioned buildings across the Levant and from the Aral Sea to Delhi. Unfortunately the Timurid architecture of the region – in Herat, Merv, Tashkent, Bokhara and, above all, Samarkand – survives only in badly shattered form but its influence is to be seen in Moghul India and Safavid Persia.

The Timurids were active patrons who gathered together the inventive skills of Seljuk architects. Some of their own work survives, despite losses in the cities of Afghanistan and Turkestan. In this period, the Timurids created and perfected the formal paradise garden which later became so essential a feature of Persian and Indian architecture, and developed the art and techniques of tilework and three-dimensional surface decoration.

Mongol dynasties in Persia and northern India also began to create where once they had destroyed. The creative energies of the Timurids persisted through the fourteenth and fifteenth centuries producing in their capital, Samarkand, an architecture of power and influence. But as Timurid rule in central Asia diminished minor dynasties were established around cities such as Merv, Kiva, Kokand and Bokhara. In Afghanistan and northern India a series of independent princedoms emerged, their capitals being at Jodhpur, Ahmadabad, Gaur, Gulbarga, Golkonda and Bijapur.

On the south-west fringe of Europe the Ottomans captured Constantinople in 1453, and had mastered the whole of western Islam within a hundred years. They extended their power from the gates of Vienna to the Barbary Coast, from Egypt and the Hejaz to the Crimea, while in the east they reached out into Mesopotamia and to Baghdad by the early sixteenth century. Their distinctive style with steepled minarets, leaded domes and clear ashlar walling is to be found in Egypt, the Balkans, Turkey and Syria. Overwhelmingly, Thrace, Istanbul and western Asia Minor are its homeland, where the requirements of the greatest of the Ottoman Sultans and their viziers produced architecture of impeccable quality.

The sixteenth and seventeenth centuries were the great period of imperial achievement. In addition to the Ottomans, two great dynasties arose to dominate their minor neighbours. In Persia the Safavids united the country and extended their rule across the highlands to reach intermittently into southern Russia. By the end of the sixteenth century the Moghul empire covered much of northern and north-western India. Their courts were at Delhi, Agra, Fatehpur Sikri and Lahore. Here Islamic forms were developed using red sandstone, trimmed and embellished with carved marble. As wealth and confidence increased, sandstone was replaced by marble. The finer stone was used in ever more elaborately carved forms, such as pierced screens and lightly framed structures. Inlay techniques were used in which semi-precious and even precious stones were embedded in marble in an extension of the pietra dura technique.

These three great powers of later Islam – Ottoman, Safavid and Moghul – rose and flourished in parallel, and each faded gently into insignificance. The history of the westernmost sultanates of Islam in the

Mahgreb is less dramatic but runs a similar course. The relative stability of each of the local powers was reflected in the considerable architectural achievements of Tunisia, Algeria and Morocco in the face of European expansion and colonialism. In microcosm the city of Fez, which continued an astonishingly even tenor of creative architecture, exemplifies the persistence of the mature Muslim style into modern times.

Although there has been a tendency in Islamic architecture to make use of the resources of the locality, a series of common characteristics evolved which called for similar craft skills without regard to location. Nevertheless a great variety of local and regional influences, including climate, produced significant effects upon building form and construction. Some areas produced styles entirely specific to small regions such as the mountainous terrain of the Yemen, the oasis towns of the Nejd (northern Saudi Arabia) and further-flung Muslim communities in the Himalayas, Indonesia, north central China, East Africa down to Zanzibar and West Africa below the deserts down to Timbuctoo.

In modern (but necessarily approximate) terms, the following countries have been governed by Muslim rulers and substantially populated by Muslim peoples.

- European Turkey, Bulgaria, Greece, southern Yugoslavia: fifteenth and sixteenth centuries
- Sicily: eighth to eleventh centuries
- Southern and central Spain: eighth to sixteenth centuries
- Cyprus: sixteenth to twentieth centuries
- North Africa: fifteenth century onwards
- Turkey in Asia: eleventh and twelfth centuries onwards
- Syria, Palestine, the Gulf States, Iraq, Iran, Afghanistan and south-central Russia: eighth century onwards
- Northern India: twelfth century onwards
- East Africa: fourteenth century onwards
- Indonesia: seventeenth century onwards.

Other important Muslim communities were established in isolation outside these areas in places such as Zanzibar, Madagascar and western China, and twentieth-century mobility has brought Islam to outposts throughout the world, with architectural consequences in places as far apart as Sydney and South Shields.

Islamic building types developed originally in the hot dry climate of the Middle East, where the impact of solar radiation produced the need for shaded courtyards and cool spaces darkened against the sun by day; and for heavy construction to retain and reradiate heat internally by night. As Islam spread across the world it embraced an ever-increasing variety of climates, but the forms evolved for the hot, arid areas of the Middle East and western Asia were retained; in some cases (for example, the monsoon areas of India) concessions were made to encourage the better flow of air so essential to comfort in humid conditions. Nevertheless many of the traditional forms to be found in temperate climates are more related to ritual than to function. Combinations of Islamic features with the local vernacular were inevitable. As might be expected, therefore, in places such as the islands of Indonesia or the jungles of central Africa, variants have arisen which run counter to otherwise fair generalisations.

Philosophy and Lifestyle

Islam is the third great monotheistic religion to have sprung from the Semitic peoples. By its adherents it is regarded as the natural successor to Judaism and Christianity and, like them, it looks back to the Prophets and Patriarchs which it shares with the preceding faiths. Its foundation was, in essence, an attempt to purify the established pattern of worship, rejecting paganism and providing a fundamental base for monotheism free from idolatry.

'Islam' is the description for the religion itself, 'Muslim' is the word for one who professes the Faith which took its authority from revelations vouchsafed to the Prophet Mohammed in the years 610–622, during which times its articles were codified and its essential characteristics established. The precepts governing the lives of Muslims imply requirements for buildings peculiar to believers. The annual pilgrimage, or Haj, brings the faithful from all parts of the Muslim world to Mecca. This imparted a degree of unity which justifies a separate category for Islamic architecture to encompass a group of styles spread widely across Asia and Africa in many different climates and kingdoms, and in time over more than a millennium. It includes all those buildings previously termed Saracenic, Moorish and Mohammedan.

Muslim thought is codified in three works. Of these, the Koran is regarded as a revelation through the medium of the Prophet Mohammed; the Hadith is a collection of his sayings or injunctions, and is of lesser weight; while the Law is extracted from the Prophet's instruction, from tradition and example. On these basic compilations rests the whole philosophical structure of the Islamic world. The faith produced in successive generations of its followers a way of life and a set of attitudes which had great influence on their architecture. These may be summarised as an acceptance of the dominance of Islam and the immutability of its revelations and an abhorrence of image-worship. The effects of these beliefs on Islamic architecture can be seen in the following characteristics: there is no essential differentiation in techniques between buildings with a directly religious connotation and other buildings; important architectural endeavour is normally expended on buildings having a direct social or community purpose, including that of worship; decorations tend towards the abstract, using geometric, calligraphic and plant motifs, with a preference for a uniform field of decoration rather than a focal element; decorated surfaces are controlled by framing and an inherent conservatism discourages innovations and favours established forms.

The Islamic system of thought was partly produced by the use of Arabic as a common language and as the only language of the Koran. This cultural concentricity did much to unify the philosophies of the Islamic peoples, to govern their way of life, and to unify their architecture. The synthesis of the styles of many conquered peoples under the impact of one philosophy and one religion in the many different circumstances of the first four centuries of Islam was a cultural achievement of which only one facet is an architecture fundamentally centred upon worship. At its heart is the mosque, an inward-looking building whose prime purpose is contemplation and prayer. Its prayer space is removed from the immediate impact of worldly affairs, although it is not designed to be emotionally uplifting nor to produce a sense of exultation. There is no positive object of adoration. It is entirely a place of congregation for the faithful and for appropriate communal activities. Although it is not set apart, it does become an exemplar, embodying architectural styles and fashions which, even though they may have evolved elsewhere, are codified and stabilised in the mosque and its associated monumental buildings.

Above all things, the mosque is democratic. In the mosque all have equal rights, and the building may serve many functions other than prayer. It is still commonly used as a school, business transactions may be made there and treasures may be stored. Proclamations are made there and consultations held. Under the complex pressures of modern society, however, some of the historically important functions of the mosque have been transferred elsewhere. Although the mosque may retain its libraries these too have been superseded, and travellers reaching a town no longer go first to the mosque and its ancilliary buildings, where shelter and hospitality once were provided to the newly arrived traveller and to the poor.

Nevertheless, although it is now less possible for the community to bathe, eat, sleep, debate and be schooled there, the mosque complex remains the focus of Muslim life – something between a forum and a prayer-house. Historically the mosque was of such central importance to the life of the community that it became the dominant building, and this form is echoed in structures built for other purposes. It is always planned on an axis directed towards Mecca. With the exception of the earliest instances, this axis was always terminated on the inner face of the mosque by the mihrab, usually a niche, where the leader of the congregation makes his prayers. This act, which involves prostration, must be observed from other parts of the prayer chamber, and lateral vision is therefore important. The congregation assembles in lines traversing the main axis and takes its cue from the leader or those in the centre of the line in a position to observe him. A multi-columned hall with transverse aisles makes an acceptable space. Ideally there should be no columns, hence the popularity of the dome. Since there is nothing sacrosanct about the mihrab, secondary mihrabs are often placed in other positions of convenience for the use of smaller congregations or individuals. The prayer space is furnished only with the mimber, from which formal pronouncements can be made, although a part of the prayer space may be railed-off or fitted with a balcony for special uses – those of a dignitary or ruler, or of muezzins or women. There may also be a fixed reading desk or preaching stool.

Apart from the buildings, with their numerous subtleties of form and their range of decorative techniques, Islamic culture produced many other requisite artefacts such as carpets and ceramics. It is held, however, that Islam's greatest cultural medium is the spoken and written word, and although little survives from very early Islam, this is to be set beside the vast quantity of literature, much of it scientific, which has survived – often unknown to Western scholars: indeed a proportion of the manuscripts remains unread.

Arabic as the lingua franca has made possible the essential synthesis of Islamic cultural achievement. Through it Greek philosophy and science became available and to it Hellenistic, Christian, Jewish, Zoroastrian and Hindu ideas brought further intellectual vigour, leading in mediaeval times to profound achievements in science, mathematics, history and geography.

Arabic numeration provides a significant example of the inventive mode which had been systemised and applied in a practical context ideas derived from elsewhere – in this case from India. Medicine, astronomy and commerce are among other areas which owe major debts to Muslim scholarship and enterprise.

Architectural Character

The countries into which Islam first expanded were already rich in building tradition, and the important techniques of exploitation of natural resources for building work and trade in building materials had long been established. Brick-making and walling in mud brick and pisé were almost universal in the

A. Islamic dome construction: combined squinch and pendentive. See p.571

B. Islamic muqarnas construction. See p.571

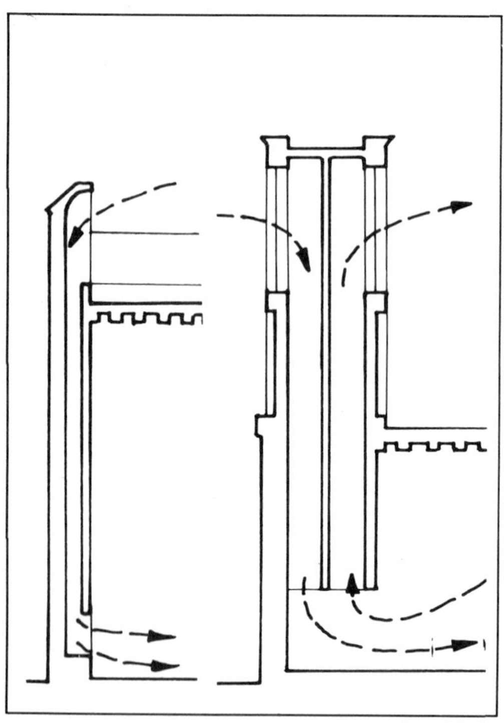

C. Wind-scoops. See p.571

D. Wind-scoop: exterior

alluvial plains: in the stone-bearing areas the arts of selecting and quarrying stone were well established. Marble was generally available as an article of trade if not native to the locality. Lime and gypsum for mortars and plasters were usually readily procurable. A rich variety of building stones is found in areas reaching from Asia Minor and Egypt to northern India, and the techniques of working them and building in masonry had been highly developed before the advent of Islam. Cyclopean masonry had survived from antiquity, and Roman quarries such as those at Baalbek still yielded massive stones. The buildings in such areas commonly had suspended floors and roofs of stone planks, stone window shutters, stone leaves to doors and even interlocking stone rings used structurally to tie in the haunches of stone domes. Decorative marble slabs and grilles, plate tracery and mosaics were commonplace. Most masonry structures of importance were in arched, vaulted or domed forms (p. 570A), however, continuing the Roman and Byzantine building traditions. True voussoirs were used in the curved shapes, and interlocking voussoirs guarded against earthquakes. Glass manufacture was sufficiently advanced to provide window glass, and there was a long history of ceramic production. Cements, plasters and stucco were used for bas-relief carving, and the highly decorative muqarnas techniques employed in domes, vaults and arches (p. 570B). Coloured external surfaces were achieved first with mosaic but the developing skills of mediaeval potters solved the problems of producing brilliant colour in glazed earthenware, which was used first in small areas as inlay. In the earlier periods complex patterning was achieved by making or cutting to the necessary shapes tiles of a single colour.

Timurid architects employed tiles fired at temperatures to suit each individual colour. In the fifteenth century a method of firing was developed which enabled tiles of regular size to be produced bearing the painted pattern. This change allowed much larger surfaces to be covered and the intricacies of pattern-making became the purview of the potter rather than the tile cutter and mosaicist.

Lead-working, bronze-casting and the use of iron were well-established techniques. Domes, roofs and steeples were often weathered in lead and iron was widely used in tie-bars, grilles and cramps.

The skills and techniques for wood-working and timber engineering were used from the earliest period for roof construction including early domes. Timber components such as doors, windows, fittings and furniture were built in interlocking geometric assemblies of rare timbers, mother-of-pearl, metals, ivory and various stones. At a simpler humbler level flat timber roofs were extremely common and timber-framing was used extensively in walling and the construction of upper floors. Timber structures were inevitable in forested areas such as Indonesia and Malaya but it also played an important structural role from the Balkans through Asia Minor, the Caucasus and the mountains of Iran, to the Himalayas and northern India.

No history of Muslim building can overlook the extensive use of unbaked brick and other forms of earth construction. Lime and gypsum were sometimes used to stabilise earth-bricks. Fired-brick was sometimes used in conjunction with earths to achieve ribbed and groined domes and vaulting. By far the greatest volume of building in Islamic lands has been achieved with earth walling.

Taken as a whole, the architecture of Islam must be seen primarily as a matter of arcuated masonry construction in which its artisans achieved the highest levels of finish and invention. The prevalence of earthquakes across much of the centre of the Muslim world gave particular importance to the inventive skills of masons and resulted in the employment of specialised structural techniques.

It remains only to add that the construction techniques used to meet climatic conditions, while usually simple, contributed significantly to the character of the buildings. From the use of small window openings in thick walls to the sophisticated wind-scoops (p. 570C) used to carry air into the interiors, the technical mastery of climate in the hot and arid Middle East, was a notable achievement in constructional terms.

The essence of any style is the specific handling of forms, spaces and massing; the combination of features, the decoration and the inflections of individual elements in the vocabulary. While Muslim architecture shares with other styles many individual features having borrowed some and donated others, it is only by collective description that it can be identified satisfactorily.

Among the notable outwardly characteristic features of Muslim architecture are the pointed arch, and the horsehoe arch in which the lower segment is carried below the normal springing point. The origins of both may be traced back to the pre-Muslim era in the eastern territories of Byzantium, and to the Sassanian Empire. The pointed arch itself appears in the earliest significant Muslim monuments, and both were carried to the western Mediterranean by Muslims in the eighth century. Thereafter, the pointed arch is as typical of Islamic architecture as it is of Gothic. Although in the West the horseshoe shape is frequently round-headed, in the East the round arch virtually disappeared after the ninth century, when the four-centred arch was evolved.

Less crucial was the use of cusping and of guarding colonnettes or nook-shafts. Cusping has a pre-Muslim history in church buildings in Syria in the sixth century, but it was first used regularly in decorative frets to arches in late eighth-century Iraq. Nook-shafts are found in Coptic and Hellenistic Christian architecture of the fifth and sixth centuries. Intermittently

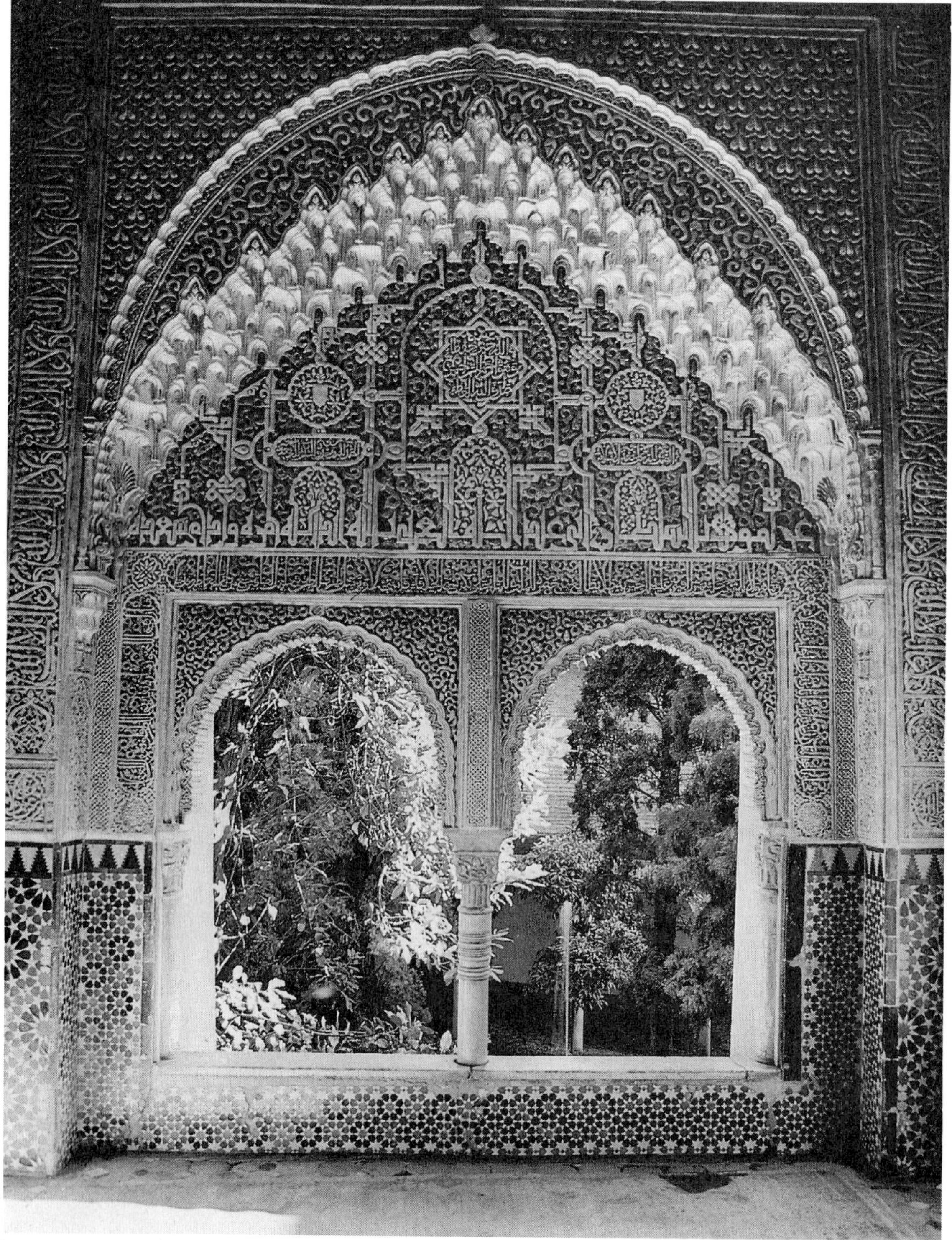

Muqarnas arch over window: the Alhambra. See p.573

they have appeared at all periods but their regular use in Muslim architecture can be firmly dated to the ninth century, after which they were used widely for entrance openings of significance.

By the eleventh century other important decorative elements had also become established, among them the peculiarly Islamic muqarnas or stalactite corbel. Muqarnas are superimposed corbels, angled so that the quoin of the lower corbel is coincident with the groin of two superimposed corbels above. From the tenth to the fifteenth centuries they were developed into a range of astonishingly varied, intricate and imaginative patterns of crystalline brilliance to become one of the most distinctive features of Muslim architecture (p. 572). Initially colour was achieved by the use of mosaics, and sometimes quartered marble panels, but mosaic eventually gave way to coloured glazed earthenware.

The absence of figurative design in Islamic imagery has given rise to much misunderstanding and not a little debate. The prohibitions do not arise directly from the injunctions of the Prophet, but from comments based on the impropriety of man attempting to usurp the function of God in creating representations of living creatures. Early Islam was in rivalry with the established Christian churches when iconoclasm was at its height, and the teachings of the church affected the attitudes of early converts to Islam. Consequently, calligraphy and pattern-making took the place of figures.

The most comprehensive range of features, however, does not make a coherent architecture. This arises only from the methods of handling form and space. It is typical of Islamic building that there is no attempt to collect numerous spaces and volumes within one great envelope whose facades then describe a single mass. Each component stands identified in its own right, and is expressed as part of a sequence of linked structures. The coordination and articulation of the individual components together supply the prime discipline. Dome, iwan, cloister or portal may be emphasised or diminished as required within its proper station, and each contains elements which display the essential structural form.

Some fundamental aspects of building derive from use and lifestyle. The actual form of the mosque is unique to the faith. So are its madrassas (medreses) or schools and colleges. The emphasis upon privacy and public segregation of the sexes leads to specific handling of the house, the entrance, the sheltered window and the street facade. The uniform height of many settlements derives from the requirement for privacy of rooms used for sleeping. The intricate street structure gives privacy of access. The great mosque may be all but invisible from within the city because the urban matrix engulfs it completely. The external facade is unusual and the formal urban space is equally rare.

Chapter 16

SELEUCID, PARTHIAN AND SASSANIAN

Of all the settlements and colonies established by Alexander and his Seleucid successors none survive visibly, although excavation has provided evidence that many of them were substantial cities laid out and built on Greek colonial lines. Far flung, they were the more impressive for that. In Central Asia on the Oxus the city now known as **Ai Khanum** was probably a foundation of Alexander himself – **Alexandria Oxiana**. There the administrative quarter stood around a colonnaded courtyard 137 m × 108 m where porticos face each other across the minor axes. If the attribution is correct its date is *c.* 328 BC. The principal streets were straight, dividing the city into quarters. Public buildings included a temple, gymnasium, baths, palaces and cemetries with mausolea. The great halls were hypostyle with Corinthian columns, decorated with painted plaster internally.

The Seleucid city, once **Merv**, now Mari, on the same latitude but further west was likewise laid out with a reticulate plan with straight streets and a rectangular city wall. It was built for Alexander's successor Antiochus I. It contained a theatre, agora, temples and buildings for administrative purposes.

Another great capital city stood on the Tigris a little below present-day Baghdad at **Seleucia**. This also had a grid-iron form and like other Greek cities was defended by substantial fortifications having the same pattern of civic buildings which betoken life in the Greek pattern. At **Babylon** not far south-west on the Euphrates the Greek city has yielded to the excavator's spade a substantial theatre and gymnasium while near Ispahan at **Khurha** stand the remaining columns of a Greek temple of the Ionic Order, an isolated fragment of a once-substantial city.

Poised between east and west on the upper Euphrates stands the substantially excavated site of **Dura Europos**. The city was fortified and its streets were laid out on a grid plan. Aspects of the domestic life revealed in the city include an early synagogue and early Christian buildings. The most architecturally impressive surviving monument to this fusion of Classical design with eastern traditions is **Hatra, Iraq** (p. 576A).

The Seleucids gave way to the Parthians and the arrival of this dynasty marks a shift in emphasis towards native traditions. The earliest Parthian settlement known (second century BC) is near Askabad at **Nysa**. The city appears to have been a capital with a palatial complex at its heart and to have been built for Mithridates I. In the palace three rooms are important – a square chamber with quadrilobate columns carrying the roof in the Achaemenid tradition, a 17 m diameter room formed in a mass of masonry externally square in plan but internally circular, demonstrating that masons had not yet mastered the techniques of using squinches to build a dome over a square, and finally an open-fronted iwan with four columns carrying its roof. At a contemporary site at **Saksanakhyr** a similar iwan appears, again with columns in the manner of the later talar. These structures are the beginning of the history of the open-fronted iwan, ultimately so important in Muslim architecture. At Nysa the interiors were painted, plastered and finished with decorative terracotta friezes. It seems that at this stage hypostyle construction remained the norm, domed construction was tentative and the iwan was making an appearance in primitive form.

In the late third century BC the Parthians made a capital at **Hecatompylos** the present **Shahir-i-Qumis, Damghan**. The city was extensive and parts of its buildings survive up to the second storey. For the first time the pointed arch appears in consistent although not exclusive use.

By the end of this first Parthian period wars with Rome had ensued, beginning in 92 BC and peaking with the defeat of Crassus in 54 BC, when 10,000 Roman prisoners were taken to Merv in central Asia. By 40 BC the Parthians controlled Palestine and Asia Minor. We may perhaps attribute a new phase of Parthian building to the arrival of the technically experienced Roman soldiery. The city of **Labbaneh – (Assur)** stood on the Tigris south of Nineveh and flourished during the first and second centuries AD. Although sacked by the Romans it survived until the Sassanian conquest. For the first time massive vaulted brick iwans are to be seen, behind rich facades in brick with blind arcading and decorative friezes dividing the storeys. The distinctive Parthian vertical brickwork occurs here with horizontal lay between vertical coursing – two courses broken bond horizontally, two superimposed courses cross-laid vertically. Vaulting had been developed to the point where a square room containing four columns could be roofed with barrel vaults rather than timber. The Hellenistic influence apparent earlier is supplemented in this second Parthian period by Roman structure and detailing, although always subordinate to the native plan. The combination is found at Hatra in the thinly grassed steppes west of the Tigris where the capital of an Arab vassal state was surrounded by a near-circular wall, buttressed with square towers which withstood the sieges of Trajan in AD 116 and Septimus Severus in AD 198. Within the walls lay a complex filigree of courtyard houses. At its centre a great square court faces a triple-iwan of fine ashlar. Behind this stood a palace. The iwan itself was framed in a frieze with egg and dart moulding in its cornice. Four giant attached Corinthian columns dominated the facade which may have carried a pediment. Human busts were built into the decoration in a manner reminiscent of Palmyra, the equivalent trading city on the western side of the desert.

The late Parthian period offers the first evidence of a dome on a cubic structure and adapted to the circular profile by means of squinches. A particularly powerful example of the vault on square structure with distinctive Parthian vertical brick lay is found at **Qala-i-Zohak, Mianeh**. In the mountains where the Mesopotamian plain rises to the Persian plateau, at **Qala-i-Yazdegird** a hill-top fortress town of the early second century AD has yielded rich evidence of the sculptural techniques of the period which are strongly eastern in character. There is a spirit of rugged independence about these final Parthian buildings with their winged dogs, swastikas and rosette borders suddenly overtaken by the rise of the Sassanian vassal dynasty which seized power in AD 224. Ardeshir, the conqueror from Fars in southern Persia, was an ambitious builder creating a capital city **Ardeshir Ghurra**, later abbreviated to **Gur** and now **Firuzabad** (p. 576C). His palace, 104 m × 55 m in plan consisted of the three successive elements in the Parthian tradition, the public zone, the reception zone and the private areas brought together into one great structure. Fronting a circular lake stood a high barrel-vaulted iwan in a facade decorated with blind arcading. Barrel-vaulted chambers were ranged on each side of the iwan and behind it across the axis were ranged three great domes. The structure was stepped up a rising hillside surrounded by luxuriant gardens. Behind the domed reception rooms a great court, itself fronted by two iwans, gave on to the private courtyards. The external relief of plain facades with attached columns and blind arcades was matched internally by carved plaster. The accompanying city was laid out to a geometrically circular plan and set nearby in the plain.

Civil works of this period include building major roads, cisterns and resting places. The defeat of the Roman emperor, Philip the Arab, brought prisoners of technical skill to the Sassanian domains and two bridges over the river Karun (which flows into the Shatt-al-Arab) are attributed to them, on stylistic evidence; one at **Shushtar** and the other at **Ghir**, each with some 40 great piers and arches. Possibly also from this period, although probably later, is a high-arched bridge spanning 20 m and rising to the same height over the Little Zab much further north on the route which provided an important link to the northern territories. Most Sassanian building, however, was in the southern provinces. The city of **Bishapur**, west of Shiraz was built *c.* AD 260 under Shapur I. It was still inhabited in the tenth century, having enjoyed a longer life than many such artificially conceived foundations. Its wall was rectangular and the ruler's palace at its core contained a 7 m square courtyard, fronted by four iwans, which archaeologists speculate carried a high parabolic dome. Mosaic floors in Roman design and frontal heads in the Palmyrene fashion built into the walls clearly indicate the source of the decorative craftsmanship. Its two main streets crossed at right angles, and in AD 266 the local governor erected in honour of his sovereign a monumental tri-pylon with Corinthian columns. Shapur II rebuilt the **Iwan-i-Kherkha, Susa**, following his sack of the city after a Christian revolt in AD 350. As rebuilt the town measured 5 kilometres by 1.2 kilometres. A building of uncertain function has a central bay covered with a dome on squinches astride which lateral wings are roofed with barrel-vaults whose open ends light the interior. This is the first appearance of an ingenious structure found immediately subsequently in the **Palace, Sarvestan** (p. 577A), one of the best preserved of all Sassanian buildings of the middle period. It is uncertainly dated to the fourth century but later dates – even an Abbasid attribution – have been postulated, the building having been in use well into the Islamic era. Originally it was faced internally in carved stucco. Its structural importance lies in the squinches carrying the central dome and the coupled columns detached from the wall which support cross-arching in the lateral chambers. The arches then carry transverse vaults in the manner of the lateral wings at the Iwan i-Kherkha near Susa.

Similar coupled columns ranked along the length of a vault were to be found in the **Martyrium of Mar Tamazgerd, Kirkuk.** This important building recorded before it was destroyed by an explosion in 1916 was one of the most important survivors of the Christian buildings of the region, dated by implication to the early fifth century. The martyrdom of a Magi turned Christian took place in AD 446. The

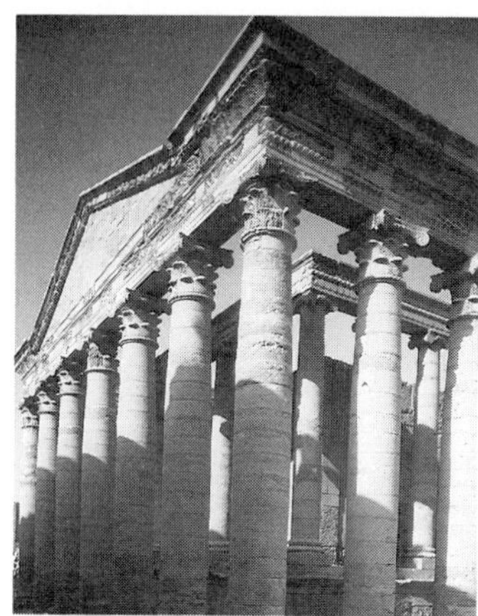

A (*left*). Hatra, temple complex. See p.574

B (*right*) Qasr at Amman, Jordan (early seventh century). See p.578

C (*below*). The palace of Ardeshir, Firuzabad. See p.575

A. Sassanian palace, Sarvestan. See p.575

B. Qasr Karaneh, Jordan (early seventh century). See p.578

C. El-Deir, Petra. See p.579

martyrium was built soon after the event. Also in Kirkuk and of similar date the church of **Al Adra (The Virgin)** demonstrates the essentially basilical form adopted by the eastern sects in the Sassanian era.

In north-west Persia the **City of Shiz**, known as Takht-i-Sulaiman, was built around a circular lake of volcanic origin, surrounded in turn by a circular wall with half-round towers. The masonry of the walls is in part of squared ashlar in which long and short stones alternate in the Parthian manner. The temple complex is axially sited and terminates in a great iwan which faces the lake. The approach leads into the square fire temple with a secondary court beyond. The site has been occupied from Seleucid times and the whole complex was refurbished in the sixth or seventh century by Khusrau II (Parviz). This immensely powerful monarch also built on the western slopes of the Zagros mountains in the north a great palace known as **Qasr-i-Shirin** on a raised platform some 9 m in height and nearly 300 m × 100 m in plan. Double flights of stairs gave access to a great parade ground dominated by a triple iwan structure leading to a domed reception hall with two lateral wings. Behind this, in the established pattern, a range of axial courtyards was flanked by domestic courts, each fronted by its own east-facing iwan. Nearby the monarch built one of the greatest fire temples, all of which were domes on arch-sided cubic bases with squinches.

Whether it was Chosroes II (ruled 591–628) or an earlier ruler, perhaps Chosroes I (531–578), who built the great palace at Ctesiphon remains an open question but the scale of this huge parabolic brick vault standing just south of Baghdad, suggests that it was a work of the very late Sassanian period when their territories reached out into Palestine and Egypt (conquered 619), and the Empire was at a peak of wealth and experience. The great structure survived intact until early this century when floodwaters brought down the northern wing. A giant brick buttress has been built against the south facade to guard against its toppling and the north facade is being rebuilt with the salvaged brickwork. The great vault spans 25 m, is virtually 34 m in height, parabolic in profile and almost 50 m front to back. A giant cusped frieze embraces the great arch and the flanking wings rise through five ranges of blind arcading. The wall probably rose through a further two diminished ranges. The arch is the largest vault of unreinforced brickwork known.

Two other buildings standing on the caravan road across the desert, linking Ctesiphon and Jerusalem appear to date from the first quarter of the seventh century before the Palestinian provinces were recovered for Byzantium by the Emperor, Heraclius, in 628. At **Amman** on the citadel the Persians found a Roman palace which apparently they fronted with an iwan structure now known as the **Qasr** (p. 576B). A high central court, probably never roofed (although a dome has been proposed), was faced with opposing iwans on both axes. The telltale detail of blind arching, dog-toothed friezes, coupled columns and vertical parabolae carved on the pendentives strongly suggests Iranian origins. No mosque has been found and the plan arrangement in which the reception hall fronts a parade ground with an axial street lying behind it giving access to private courtyards is designed for Persian ceremonial.

Going eastwards from Amman at the end of the first desert stage towards the wells of Azraq stands the fortified courtyard building, known as **Qasr Karaneh** (p. 577B). Its lack of a mosque and strongly Persian detailing with multiple coupled columns and parabolic arching makes this building too a prime candidate for the short-lived ascendancy of the Sassanian monarchs over the Mediterranean littoral. In both buildings there is strong evidence of the employment by Persian overlords of a local workforce.

Elsewhere in Syria and Palestine contemporary building shows only the influences of Rome. In the late Roman and early Hellenistic periods Palestine and Syria were prosperous and wealthy provinces where Hellenistic design was dominant and inventive to the point where highly localised styles were developed. While cities such as **Palmyra** and **Jerash** retained strong Classical characteristics with colonnaded streets and Classical details they developed also characteristic designs such as the tower tombs of Palmyra and the great oval forum in Jerash. The tower tombs were three and four storeys high, each containing ranks of stone coffins with the individual likenesses carved upon them. Tower tombs of this sort were found in other cities along the desert fringe particularly in the basaltic area of the Hauran where in towns such as **Kanawat, Shabha**, and **Ezra'a** an entirely lithic architecture was evolved in which basalt plank first floors and roofs were complemented by solid basalt doors on pintols and similar window shutters. Windows were closed with stone grilles and inventive structural systems included joggled arches with over-sailing relieving lintels and even with interlocking stone rings to resist the outward thrust of domes, as in the **Church of S. George, Ezra'a**, where a high central dome restrained by vertically interlocking stones forming a ring in the central drum was surrounded by an octagonal ambulatory roofed with tapering basalt planks. This church survives largely complete apart from the dome, illustrating the powerfully inventive structural forms found in the sixth century in a region on the fringe of the Byzantine Empire and one of the earliest to be absorbed by the Muslims. A circular plan form was also adopted for the now-destroyed **Cathedral, Bosra**, whose structure appears to have echoed S. George at Ezra'a on a larger scale. Even under Roman suzereignty these provinces of Arabia Deserta had a quasi-independence deriving from their earlier free status under the Nabataean kings.

The Nabatean trading city of **Petra** built into a bowl in the southern hills of Jordan, ringed by cliffs and bisected by the Wadi Musa, has perpetuated the ideosyncratic styles of the region because much of its monumental structure was carved out of solid rock rather than having been built. Its architecture is based on the Classical orders and most of the monuments now to be seen are civic or funerary, the original township with its colonnaded Roman street and amphitheatre having largely disappeared. This architecture is baroque in its wilful handling of established patterns. A device several times repeated has a portico of columns, entablature and pediment, surmounted by a further giant broken pediment carried on attached columns centred on a circular edicule surmounted by a conical roof, above which rises an urn. Two of the most impressive of the monuments of this type are the fancifully named **Khazneh Fara'un** (Treasury of the Pharaohs), which is some 34 m in height, and the giant **El-Deir** standing in an upper valley above Petra, a rock-cut reception hall, which is 45 m high and 50 m wide (probably late third century AD) (see p. 577C and Chapter 10). Its entrance door is 8 m in height. These and the bulk of the other finely worked surviving structures may be dated to the floruit of this trading city in the third or fourth centuries.

Another identifiably separate people were the Copts of the Nile Valley. Descendants of the races of Pharaonic Egypt, they took readily to Christianity in the first century and their Monophysite church quickly became a powerful force despite Roman attempts, particularly of Diocletian, to suppress it. Studies of their most ancient churches demonstrate that the type adopted was a combination of native and Roman influences with possibly some derivative influence from the eastern churches. Among monastic churches, **S. Anthony** and the first **Churches of the Wadi Natrun – Deir Abu Makar (S. Makarios), Deir Baramus** and **Anb Bishoi** are the earliest. The most significant ancient churches in Cairo are **Abu S'fein, Al Adra in the Harat Zuweila** and **the churches Sitt Barbara, Abu Sarga** and **Al Muallaka** in Deir Bablun, the original walled city. In all these churches the east end containing the sanctuary was massively constructed, consisting of a large central terminal bay, flanked by two separated chapels (haikkals) fronting a transverse congregational space. This transept ran effectively across the entire church and was joined on its western side by an aisled nave derived from the Roman basilica. The nave was divided from the aisles by a colonnade of Corinthian columns carrying a flat timber beam on which an arcade was placed. In the later churches or rebuildings, the Corinthian columns were replaced by stumpy piers of masonry. The roofs were of timber.

The domed Byzantine church found no place in this vocabulary and it is clear from the decorative arts of the Copts that theirs was a separate stream of development. When the Arab armies under Ibn al As entered Egypt in 642 the native architecture they encountered, except in the Greek cities of the coast, was a Romanised version of a vigorous native culture.

Chapter 17

ARCHITECTURE OF THE UMAYYAD AND ABBASID CALIPHATES

At **Mecca** stands the **Kaaba**, a cubic structure containing a black stone of fundamental importance to believers. Although pre-Muslim the cloth-shrouded cubic masonry aedicule towering over a processional space has been constantly repaired. Its mystical importance is in inverse ratio to its significance as an architectural prototype, for it is never copied.

The Prophet and his first followers did not seek a building in which to pray but made their prayers five times a day wherever they were. This example is still followed and the Muslim world has many outdoor praying places. At Medina the Prophet first prayed facing towards Jerusalem, but spontaneously at a small mosque on the outskirts of al-Medina he faced towards Mecca. Thereafter this was the rule. The heavily rebuilt mosque is still known as **Quiblatain – The Mosque of the Two Directions**.

The House of the Prophet was the congregational mosque of the first community. It was simply a courtyard with a covered arcade for prayers at the end nearest to Jerusalem and then, after remodelling, to Mecca and with domestic appurtenances on the other sides. The call to prayer was made from the walls of the house. The simplicity of this building is reflected in the mosques which immediately followed. There was no other model and as yet there were no architectural objectives, so the Prophet's house provided an adequate example.

Casual influences determined some of the characteristics of the mosque as a building type. The form of the earliest mosques in Mesopotamia, for example, followed the precedent of the country's first mosque at Kufa. Built shortly after the Islamic conquest of the country its size was determined by successive arrow-casts in four directions. In Syria, converted Christian churches were used, and Muslims were obliged to pray facing across the axis of the nave and aisles, Mecca being to the south. This set a precedent in favour of cross-arcading, which is to be found in many congregational mosques on the western side of the Arabian desert.

The early custom of building the governor's residence and treasury against the kibla wall of the mosque followed a burglary. The Caliph gave instructions that the two should be joined so that the users of the mosque would constitute a 'watch by day and night'.

The use of pre-Muslim buildings in Persia caused some of the first mosques to be adaptations of hypostyle halls – at **Isakhr** (Persepolis) and **Qasvin** – if literary references are any guide.

There is no evidence that in the seventh century the Arabs of Mecca and Medina possessed either architectural knowledge or tradition beyond the vernacular. The only literary references available refer to the Kaaba at Mecca – a very simple structure. To meet religious and administrative needs in lands they had conquered, and to establish their dominant political position therefore, the Arabs made use of local craftsmen. They did not impose a style, having none to impose, and consequently local traditions and techniques were continued. They did, however, establish new settlements.

The new town of Kufa was founded within a few years of the death of Mohammed, on the desert fringe of the cultivated lands of the Tigris and Euphrates. Its mosque and palace were short-lived, but important in establishing a type and in demonstrating the acceptance of local influences. Initially the **Great Mosque, Kufa** (638), was a primitive building whose courtyard was marked only by a ditch. On its southern or kibla side, a covered colonnade extended across the full width. There was no mihrab. The attached **Dayr al-Imara**, or governor's palace, consisted of a courtyard structure buttressed by half-round attached towers which reflected the square plan of the frontier forts of the Roman Empire. The central court terminated in an aisled hall which led to the domed chamber. Thus even at the earliest period, the dome was used as a focus. **The Mosque and Palace of al-Walid, Kut** (703) were similar.

The **al-Aqsa Mosque** on the **Temple Mount in Jerusalem** was rebuilt about the year 711 under the Caliph al-Walid, with the first variation on the courtyard plan. It contained a large prayer hall whose dominant feature was a high arcaded central nave aligned on the kibla axis. Its distinctive features may have been due in part to the employment in its construction of Palestinian and Coptic Christians. The present building is predominantly of later construction (including the Crusader period) but contained some of the original arcades until recent times. Significantly rebuilt after earthquake damage by the Abbasid Caliph al Mahdi, by the Fatimid Caliph al-Zahir and remodelled by the Mamluks under Saladin it has subsequently merely been repaired, if somewhat heavily. Only very recently (1988) it was most thoroughly and painstakingly overhauled. The Umayyad work is therefore only fragmentary but its importance lies in its evidence of the form of a very early plan and arcade structure which was influential far afield, as being the prime mosque of the then capital.

A building central and crucial to the whole history of the architecture of Islam stands in the centre of the Temple Mount. It is the **Dome of the Rock, Jerusalem** (p. 582), begun in 688 and with the Prophet's Mosque and the Kaaba is among the most important Muslim shrines. With its contemporary and similar satellite, the **Dome of the Chain**, it covers the summit of Mount Moriah the 'Furthest Sanctuary' from which the Prophet is believed to have been carried on a night-ride to heaven to receive fundamental revelations. Its high timber dome was carried on a stone arcade of pointed arches on Corinthian columns alternating with marble-faced piers. Surrounding arcaded aisles are set out on an octagonal plan. From the outset the interior was richly finished in glass mosaic and quartered marble. Pierced marble and ceramic lunettes fill the window openings, which once had iron tracery. The entire outer surface was coated in a glittering mosaic which, if it followed the surviving mosaics internally, was a rich Hellenistic composition of swirling patterns with vegetal motifs and a liberal admixture of gold tesserae among the predominantly green colouring. In the sixteenth century, under Ottoman rule, the external mosaics were replaced with patterned tiles from Iznik or Damascus, recently renewed.

The dome was a double-shelled timber structure apparently very similar to that on or intended for the church of S. Simeon Stylites in northern Syria. Repaired at various stages in its history the dome survived until 1967 when it was replaced by a lightweight construction sheathed in anodised aluminium, now itself renewed in traditional materials. The building was a focus for pilgrimage centred on a cave containing a mihrab on a flat marble slab worked in bas-relief with colonnettes and a pointed arch. Its detailing shows a combination of Hellenistic and Sassanian influences. It may be the earliest extant mihrab in Islam.

The introduction of the concave mihrab came only a few years later when, under the orders of the Caliph al-Walid I, the **Mosque of the Prophet, Medina**, was greatly enlarged and reconstructed, (707). Literary evidence records the presence there of Coptic workmen and this could account for the introduction of a central niche terminating the main axis – a universal feature in Coptic churches. One minaret may have been introduced in the Prophet's Mosque, as it was in the repairs and extensions to the Mosque of 'Amr in Cairo carried out on the instructions of the same Caliph. The first known minarets in Islam, however, were probably the extant towers of the Great Temple which became the **Great Mosque of Damascus** (706–15) (p. 583A).

It was traditional and symbolic in the early years of Islam that the principal church of a city which had resisted the Muslims should be taken over as the congregational mosque. Damascus was partly conquered and partly offered to the Muslims; and the principal church was left to the Christians. Part of the compound was set aside for Muslim worship. In 705 the Christians were displaced, and in adapting the great compound of the temple to Muslim purposes, al-Walid's architects made a number of decisions which were to become fundamental in Umayyad Islam. The entire southern side of the compound was converted into the prayer chamber of the mosque, with arcades set against the outer walls. The southern entrances were blocked and a mihrab was built in the place of one of them. A further minaret was introduced centrally on the northern side and there was a high nave with lateral aisles of double-tiered arcading at right-angles to it. In this, the Great Mosque of Damascus set a precedent, and its transverse aisles, cut through by a central nave, became the hallmark of Damascene, and hence of Umayyad, influence in other city mosques. The upper surfaces of the walls were sheathed in enormous fields of rich mosaic, and from them it is clear that by this period figurative designs were already eschewed in religious buildings.

The Umayyad dynasty and its court was composed very largely of men long bred to the traditions of the desert. As a complement to and perhaps as a release from an irksome urban life, they built a series of 'retreats' on the desert fringes of the lands they had conquered. The form of these desert palaces derived from Roman forts which had defended the eastern frontiers of Arabia Deserta. Although some Umayyad palaces were actually built into the ruins of these forts, the resemblance ended at the outer wall. Internally, a regular tripartite subdivision was common, and a court or system of courts dominated the plan.

Dome of the Rock, Jerusalem (688–). See p.581

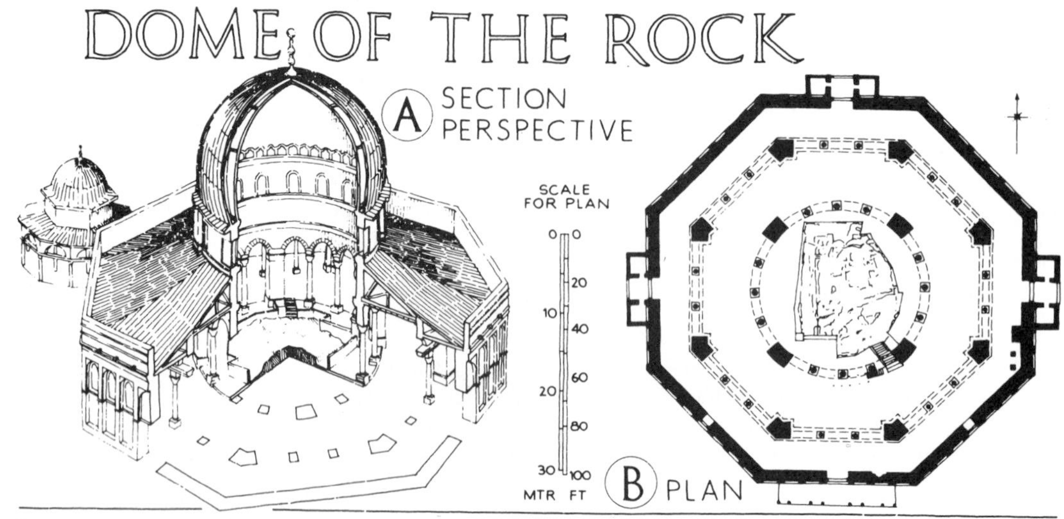

A. The Great Mosque, Damascus: interior of prayer-hall looking east (706–15). See p.581

B. The Alhambra, Granada. See p.599

The bath-house known as **Hammam as-Sarakh** (probably 720–30) is perhaps the most elegant of the surviving bath-houses of the Umayyads. It is built in the superb masonry of the Palestinian coastlands, and the original dome over the calidarium was handsomely formed with segmental ribs carried on spherical triangle-pendentives rising over the calidarium. This dome, buttressed by two adroitly built half-domes, reflected in miniature the roofing system of Hagia Sophia in Constantinople. Its entrance hall, which served as a gathering room, was roofed by three parallel barrel vaults supported at their junctions by pointed arches of long span, and the whole building was decorated in painted plasterwork with a wide-ranging selection of figurative motifs.

On the hill above Hammam as-Sarakh stand the remains of a Roman frontier fort converted to an Umayyad princely settlement, **Qasr al-Hallabat** (thought to be *c.* 725). From the tumbled remains archaeologists have made out a mosque whose prayer chamber was constructed of triple parallel barrel vaults carried on two intermediate pointed arches, in much the same way as in the baths. A strikingly similar building is to be found to the south-east, in a shallow wadi. The **Baths of Qasr ‘Amr** have the same plan form without such elegance of execution, as the building was constructed of massive rough rubble. But here the paintings survive, and from one of them it may be inferred that the building dates from approximately 712–15. The paintings throw light on the life of Umayyad princes and their use of the steppes, particularly in the spring pasturage. Its massive construction and comparative isolation have contributed to its preservation; its domes and vaults have survived almost intact. The paintings, in the Hellenistic tradition, were carried out by Greek craftsmen and are the most extensive Umayyad paintings in existence. They are largely figurative, and portray scenes of daily life, wild animals, the hunt, dancing girls and the zodiac, in addition to portrayal of the defeated enemies of the Caliphs.

The buildings of the **Palace, al-Minya** (eighth century), cover about half a hectare focusing on a central courtyard. Like Qasr Karaneh, the palace was two-storeyed and it was entered through a divided half-round tower covered by a dome. Its mosque was in the traditional position, close to the main entrance, for the convenience of those coming in only for prayers. The direct entrance faced the great hall across the courtyard and was entered transversely. The outer wall was crenellated in Sassanian style.

In Syria two estates have survived in a form which allows some reconstruction of Umayyad lifestyles: **Qasr al-Hair al-Sharki** (728–9) and **Qasr al-Hair al-Garbi** (early eighth century). Al-Gharbi is famous for its great entrance portal, richly decorated with stucco carvings in a geometric pattern. Reconstruction has demonstrated Sassanian and Hellenistic motifs. The caravanserai of al-Sharki with its high, rounded towers stands in the thin grassland stretching north-east from Palmyra. Machicolations over the gateways continue a tradition well established in Syria, as do the joggled voussoirs of the flat arches. These are possibly the first examples in Islam of a feature which was to become important as a decorative motif.

The most elaborate palace of the period is at **Khirbat al-Mafjar**, in the state of Palestine (probably 743–8) (p. 585A,B). Its history of expansion is evident from the plan, which suggests that an initial rectangular compound wall was enlarged to provide an outer court, enlarged subsequently to provide a palatial baths hall. Its builder was probably the Caliph al-Walid II, one of the most libertine of the Umayyad caliphs, whose statue, in Sassanian robes, stood in a niche above the entrance to the baths. The structural form and detailing shows a remarkable integration of Sassanian and Syrian skills.

The mosques of Syria and Palestine followed the example of the Caliph's Great Mosque at Damascus, with its square, high minarets, axial central nave and triple transverse aisles. The mosques at Aleppo, Amman, Hama, Maraat en-Numan, Dera'a, Diyarbakir and Bosra were of this type, and the design was influential in the west at Qairouan in Tunisia and Cordoba in Spain, as it was in Anatolia and in northern Persia. The least altered of these early examples are the mosques at Dera'a and Bosra, and of these the mosque at Dera'a (*c.* 720) follows the Damascus precedent so closely that it may have been the work of the same building teams.

Two important, although small, single-chambered examples of the Umayyad period survive at Bosra in Syria, in the **al-Khidr** and **al-Fatma Mosques** (eighth century). These small mosques have tall, square tapering towers terminating in double-headed windows, following the pattern of the sixth century churches and monasteries of the region. The **Umar Mosque, Bosra**, is of the same period but modelled on the Great Mosque in Damascus.

The final phase of Umayyad building follows Mesopotamian models more closely. This is evident in the palaces of **Qasr M'Shatta** and **Qasr al-Tuba, Jordan** (eighth century), which represent a significant step forward in the genesis of a true architecture of Islam. The outer compound wall of the former was heavily decorated with deep friezes of intricate carved stonework, embodying Hellenistic and Sassanian motifs, most of which was removed to Berlin in the Ottoman period. Minor examples are still to be seen on-site. A giant outer compound wall, buttressed by half-round towers, is subdivided by a processional axis. The mosque lies adjacent to the main entrance gate on the east. The caliphal audience hall is a tri-conch structure in which the approach axis passes under a triumphal arch, to provide an unusual focus on the person of the Caliph. The building was not completed.

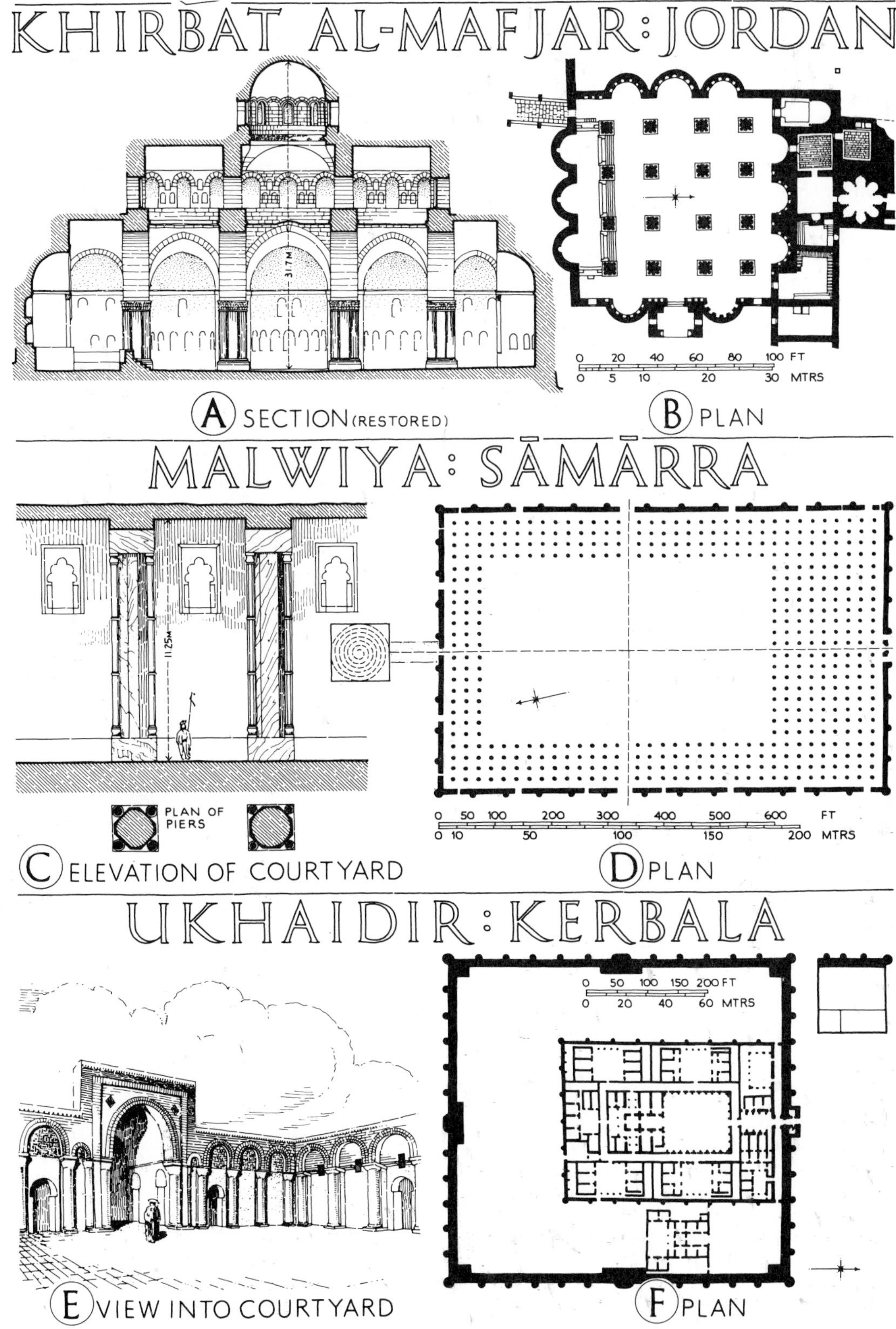
KHIRBAT AL-MAFJAR: JORDAN
31.7M
0 20 40 60 80 100 FT
0 5 10 20 30 MTRS
A SECTION (RESTORED)
B PLAN
MALWIYA: SĀMĀRRA
11.25M
PLAN OF PIERS
0 50 100 200 300 400 500 600 FT
0 10 50 100 150 200 MTRS
C ELEVATION OF COURTYARD
D PLAN
UKHAIDIR: KERBALA
0 50 100 150 200 FT
0 20 40 60 MTRS
E VIEW INTO COURTYARD
F PLAN

The last Umayyad Caliph, Marwan II, built a mosque at Harran on the Euphrates in northern Syria, of which little remains although the plan reveals that right to the end Damascus remained the model. The eclipse of the Umayyads in 750 terminated Hellenistic influence in Islamic architecture except in the western Mediterranean. Elsewhere Mesopotamian and Persian traditions dominated and the architects of Islam combined fresh repertoires with their earlier traditions, to produce a new architecture. It was fashioned in rough rubble and mud-brick masonry (occasionally fired bricks) and faced with carved or moulded stucco.

The Abbasids moved the centre of gravity of Islam from Syria and Palestine to Iraq. Perso-Arab influence permeated their society, and with these changes came the fundamental rift that since then has run through Islam giving rise to important buildings. The Shi'a persuasion differs from orthodox Islamic beliefs by reverence for the Imams, whose lineal succession from the Prophet is held to entitle them to leadership.

The Abbasid Caliph, al-Mansur, established his new **City of Baghdad** (767 onwards) a few miles north of the decaying Sassanian city of Ctesiphon. Although called the Abode of Peace, his new capital became known as the Round City. It was nearly 2750 m (9000 ft) in diameter, had entrances on the four principal axes, and was surrounded by a massive mud-brick towered fortification 18 m (59 ft) high, consisting of several walls and a moat. An outer ring of living quarters surrounded a circular open space, in the middle of which stood the Caliph's and other palaces and a congregational mosque. The high, copper-covered dome of the palace came to symbolise the capital. The inhabitants were the ruler's entourage with supporting troops and households, while the populace lived outside the walls. Not a trace of the city remains above ground.

Ukhaidir in modern Iraq (possibly *c.* 780) (pp. 585E,F, 587A) has been variously described as a palace and a fortress: it is something of both. The remarkable ruin stands near a small wadi on the eastern fringe of the Arabian Desert and appears to be associated with two other isolated ruins of similar character.

One is a tower known as **Minar Mujdeh**, the other is a brick-built caravanserai, **Khan at'Shan**. These two buildings stood on the route which followed the Euphrates to the city of Kufa, and their relationship is an important indicator of the origins of Ukhaidir, which consists of a buttressed rectangular enceinte over 165 m (540 ft) square, standing within a low-walled compound (p. 587A). A courtyard-palace stands within the outer wall: its axial approach runs through a large hall into a reception court, whence a circulation route leads to individual suites of rooms (bayts). A mosque stands adjacent to the entrance. The entire structure is of rough rubble with elliptical and pointed vaults, and is enriched with vigorous decoration of bars, diagonal ribbing, dogtoothing and interlocking geometric forms. Sassanian motifs recur repeatedly in the dogtoothing, in roundels and sunken eyes, and in the coupled pilasters which lack both capitals and bases. Cusping in the arcading of the mosque is the first evidence of this feature in Muslim building.

The City of Samarra, Iraq (836 onwards), was founded by the Caliph al'Mu'tasim. It was large, informally planned and lay on the east bank of the river Tigris. After three phases of expansion it was abandoned when the Abbasid court returned to Baghdad in 892. A small mediaeval walled town now stands in the middle of the site. The ruins of Samarra are of major importance in tracing the evolution of Muslim architecture from the tenth century onwards. In its remaining buildings the evolution of the four-centred arch can be discerned. The deeply cut stucco decoration of the early period is closely related to stucco work of the early Muslim period in Ctesiphon. A second, transitional stage is notable for its flowing lines and softer contours, and in the third period had evolved abstract moulded forms which took the place of the earlier naturalism. This new form eventually produced the sinuous arabesque patterns so important to the character of later Islamic architecture. It was at Samarra also that the first Muslim tomb was built.

In effect the administrative core of the new town was the immense **Bulkwara Palace**. Its residential and administrative sections, surrounded by courtyards and gardens, were planned on intersecting axes. Built largely of mud-brick, little remains except a gaunt ruin of triple iwans built in fired brick, standing on a cliff edge facing the river Tigris. This was the ceremonial chamber overlooking open meydans or parade grounds. The Bulkwara Palace itself is important for its marble and stucco dados and the traces of painted plasterwork which survived in the areas protected by debris.

The Great Mosque or Malwiya, Samarra (848 onwards) (pp. 585C,D, 588B), now disaffected, was the largest mosque ever built. Although probably started by his predecessor, it is generally regarded as the work of the Caliph Al-Mutawakkil, who also built the nearby mosque of Abu Dulaf (see below). The Malwiya consisted of an immense walled courtyard planned on a ratio of three to two, 155 m × 238 m (510 ft × 780 ft), surrounded by four aisles except on the south side where nine aisles form the prayer chamber. The internal structure of mud-brick piers and timber pole-joisted roofs has long since disappeared, but the massive brick outer walls remain, buttressed at intervals of 16 m (52 ft) by half-round towers. The dramatic and evocative feature of this building is the enormous helicoidal minaret at the northern end, isolated from the mosque, but on the main axis. Although a number of Mesopotamian ziggurats had survived until this time, this form of helical ramp around a massive core seems to have been original in

A. Fortress-palace, Ukhaidir, Iraq (780). See p.586

B. The Great Mosque, Samarra, Iraq (848–). See p.588

C. Mosque of Abu Dulaf, Samarra, Iraq (860–1). See p.588

its own terms, although there may have been precedents in Baghdad. The buttressed wall of the compound was capped by a frieze of large dished panels, and was itself surrounded by an outer compound wall. A large rectangular mihrab, now reconstructed, was guarded by marble shafts.

The form of the minaret of the Malwiya was repeated in another similar building, the **Mosque of Abu Dulaf, Samarra** (860–1) (p. 587C). Only remnants of the inner arcades, built of fired brick, still stand. Although many of the arches have fallen, their forms can be reconstructed sufficiently accurately to indicate that architects from Samarra repeated them in Cairo in the Mosque of Ahmed ibn Tulun (see below), which has survived in a restored condition. On the evidence of the mosque of ibn Tulun, it can be presumed that both the Great Mosques of Samarra carried fretted crenellations around the whole of their outer walls.

The first known mausoleum of Muslim history, the **Kubat as-Sulaibiya** (863) at Samarra, consists of a domed chamber, square on plan, surrounded by an octagonal ambulatory. Neither the original dome nor the roof of the ambulatory survived, but the building has been reconstructed recently. The importance of the Kubat is that it provides a precedent. The notion was carried into Egypt, Persia and southern central Asia and so into India, and from this little building springs the long history of the domed mausolea of Islam. The Kubat crowns a small hill on the infertile western bank of the river. To the north there stands the castle-like **Qasr al-Ashik**, whose high rectangular podium, perched on a bare ridge, was surrounded by massive buttressed brick walls and guarded by a complex arrangement of covered ramps which formed the entrance at its northern end. The substructures have survived relatively intact, but the whole of the superstructure was destroyed, with the exception of a part of the curtain wall at the north-west corner. The outer arches spanning between buttresses, comparable with those at Ukhaidir, have here been translated into cusped decorative arching with a four-centred profile. It was shortly after the building of al-Ashik that Samarra was abandoned. The surviving ruins of the city provide crucial examples of early Muslim domestic architecture. The houses have courtyards and the plan proportion of 3:2 recurs frequently. The street wall of each house was blank and the principal chamber was a talar or open verandah at the end furthest from the entrance. The houses were built of mud-brick with pole-joisted flat roofs surfaced with compacted mud on palm leaves. In the more important houses, decorated wall plaster has been found and on the floors there were polychrome patterns to simulate mosaics or carpets.

The second city of Bagdad was built on the opposite (east) bank of the river and further downstream. Of the Abbasid fortifications one important gate, the **Bab al-Wasitani** (twelfth century), survives as a fortified bridge over the moat and an outer chamber for the guard. It was built in burned brick with four-centred arches and decorated with recessed panels and inscribed friezes.

Two riverside courtyard buildings survive to demonstrate the techniques of the period. In both of them, intricate muqarnas decoration is combined with elaborate carved brickwork of astonishing geometric intricacy. Of the **'Abbasid Palace'** (*c.* 1180–1230), the entrance portico and two sides of the courtyard have survived intact. The structure is of two storeys. Arcades with opposed iwans face the courtyard at both levels. The **Mustansiriyeh** (1233) (p. 589A), a madrassa or college, has no arcades, but it has iwans on the cross-axis, and the entrance faces a prayer chamber on the kibla axis. Both these buildings are renowned for the intricate detail of their decorative brickwork, cut *in-situ* in the soft yellow bricks of Baghdad. They demonstrate a sophisticated style established by the time the Abbasid Empire faced the Mongol incursions.

At Raqqa in Syria on the Euphrates stands part of the outer face of another gate, the **Baghdad Gate** (tenth or eleventh century). It is a part of the outworks of the main walls and stands below a large rounded bastion, acting as a reception and guard chamber on the road to the capital. Cusped four-centred arching forms a blind frieze across the top of the structure. A few fragments of a contemporary palace also survive with richly modelled internal decorations.

During the late Abbasid period semi-autonomous Seljuk princes and their Zengid underlings in northern Syria were developing a style distinctly their own. It was essentially a masonry style of building, and now offers the first dated range of muqarnas corbelling, which by the eleventh century was in widespread use and had reached the level of maturity that indicates a considerable period of prior development. One important building seems to link this Seljuk work to the Abbasids, the **Mosque and Tomb of the Imam Dur, Samarra** (Muslim ibn Kureish) (1085). An earlier mosque (now destroyed) formed the forecourt to the tomb, which consists of a high, square, brick chamber with battered walls, surmounted by a complex steeple made up of a series of reducing zones incorporating offset squinches or muqarnas. This structure is expressed externally and modulated internally by a series of linear patterns. Some later examples of this form of construction were given conical steeples, for example the **Tomb of Imam Yahya, Mosul** (1229).

Many other Seljuk tombs are to be found in Persia, Turkey and Iraq (q.v.). In Baghdad itself, the Tomb of the Imam Dur had a direct successor in the famous **Tomb of Sitt Zubeida** (*c.* 1180). External expression of the muqarnas, however, was shortlived, and the importance of Seljuk and Zengid architecture is better expressed in the logic and clarity of the building forms and the precision of their detailing. New

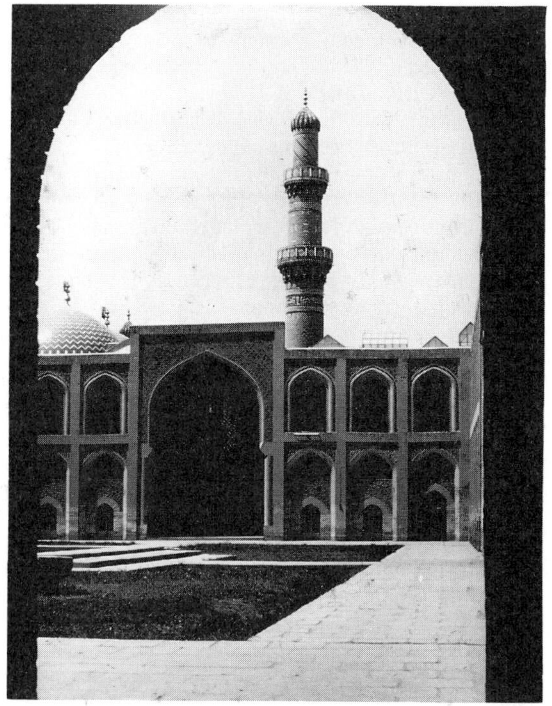

A. Mustansiriyeh Madrassa, Baghdad (1233). See p.588

B. The Great Mosque, Qairouan: interior

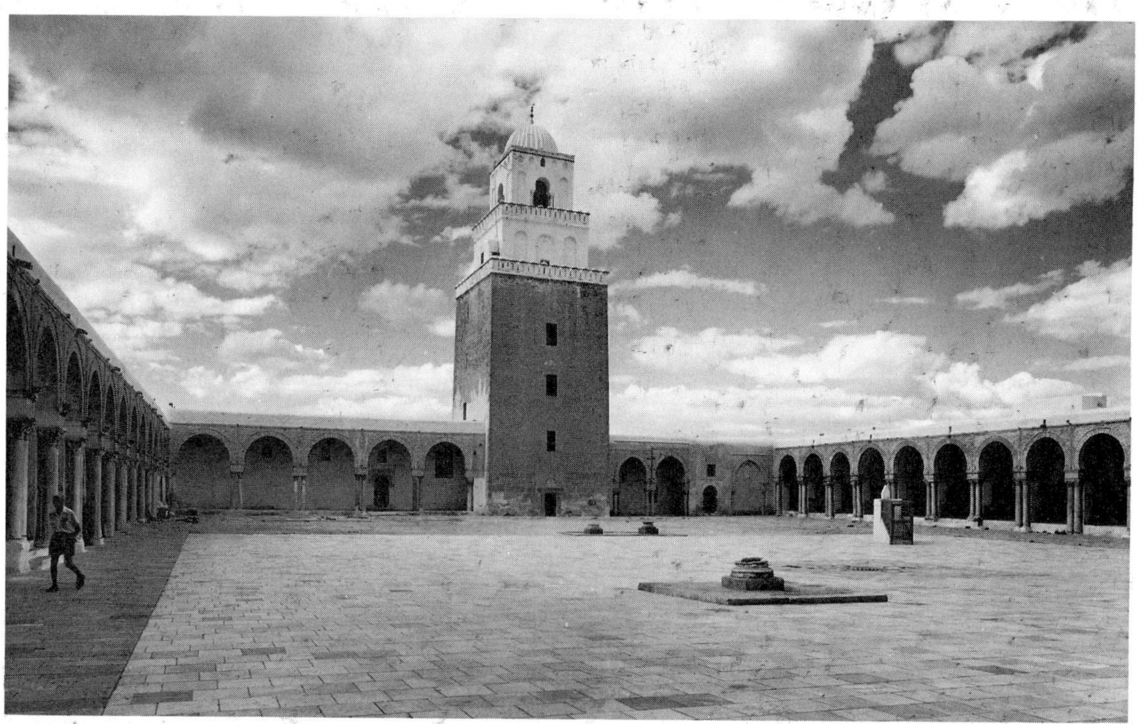

C. The Great Mosque, Qairouan, Tunisia (836–): courtyard looking north-east. See p.590

building types began to evolve, in particular the college or madrassa, which was to become a regular element of Muslim building. The **Madrassa al-Nuriya al-Kubra, Damascus**, to which the tomb of its patron Nur al-Din is attached, is an important early example of the development which led to such perfectly formed madrassas as that of **al-Firdaus** (1235–6) at Aleppo. Zengid architecture of northern Syria is nowhere better expressed, however, than in the great square-shafted minaret built for the congregational mosque at **Aleppo** (*c.* 1090). A series of cusped, blind-arch patterns on the stages of the tower terminate in a muqarnas balcony surmounted by a dome. The mosque itself is of the Damascus type now rebuilt as a vaulted structure, retaining the plan of the prototype.

Egypt, Eastern and Central North Africa

The Muslim conquest of the lower Nile and the seaboard of North Africa was followed by slow penetration southwards. Understandably, almost all the early monuments of importance lie close to the Mediterranean. Cairo became by far the liveliest centre of architectural development, and its immense legacy of mediaeval buildings puts it high on the list of cities of outstanding historic importance. Standing at the head of the Nile delta, the city had a long tradition of building in stone although at the time of the Muslim invasion it consisted of little more than the heavily walled Byzantine fortress of Babylon, which looked out from the lee of the Mukattam hills across the river to the giant pyramids of Gizeh (q.v.). A little to the north and east of this fortress city, in the middle of the seventh century, the Arab commander Amr Bin al-As set up the encampment which was to become the first Muslim city of Egypt.

Although there was a tradition that the principal Christian church of a city which had resisted the Muslims should become the great mosque , at Cairo it was the mosque of the camp of besiegers, rather than any of the existing churches, which became the congregational mosque – probably for the simple reason that the churches were too small. Consequently, the Mosque of ‘Amr at Fustat, Cairo (643–), is entirely uninfluenced by ecclesiastical architecture and in all probability derives from an early state of the Prophet’s Mosque in Medina. Very little survives, but it is clear that in the original building the arcades ran parallel to the kibla wall in the Syrian manner although they now run at right-angles to it. The first rebuilding was undertaken on the instructions of Al-Walid at the beginning of the eighth century, when minarets were added. They were among the first purpose-built minarets in Islam. That which survives is largely thirteenth-, fourteenth- and eighteenth-century work, recently extensively and thoroughly reconstructed.

Fustat (early Cairo) was burned in the face of Fatimid armies and the Fatimids built their new city to the north. It has been possible, therefore, to use the site of Fustat to provide information on urban life in the early Muslim period. The houses are of the courtyard type with iwans arranged informally. There is no evidence of systematic urban design; the streets were narrow winding lanes between houses built in a dense matrix of mixed single- and two-storey constructions in mud brick, usually around courtyards.

As the Arabs moved westwards, they left the marks of conquest upon the Mediterranean coastline of Africa in a series of small forts at Biserta, Sfax, Tripoli, Monastir and Susa in Tunisia. The **Ribat of Susa** (*c.* 810–21) is preserved in a restored form complete with its tower standing on a square bastion at the south-east corner of a square fortress buttressed by half-round towers.

The **Great Mosque, Qairouan, Tunisia** (from 836 – rebuilt under Yazid bin Hakim, governor) (p. 589B,C) is the principal building of the Aghlabids and has an important relationship to the mosques of the Umayyad and Abbasid capitals. Its square minaret stands on the centre line of the building. The original structure of the early eighth century was swallowed up in the reconstruction of the ninth century. More bays were added to the courtyard face of the prayer-hall, and a central dome (since rebuilt) was constructed over it. Also at this stage a mihrab was constructed – faced with lustre tiles, the earliest example of its kind in Islamic architecture, probably imported from Iraq or Syria. The building has slightly pointed horseshoe arches carried on capitals of Corinthian derivation. The gored dome is carried on cusped squinches. An important precedent was set in the prayer-chamber which has a T-shaped plan where a central nave intersects the transverse aisle against the kibla wall. The giant, square tapering minaret with its recessed stages as well as the incorrect southward orientation of the building itself reflect eighth-century Syrian origins. It was the model for the **Zaytuna Mosque, Tunis** (*c.* 860), among many others. Here again are the T-shaped plan, the dome on the central aisle and the single square minaret on the centre line of the building.

The **Great Mosque, Sfax** (849), was similar although on a smaller scale. In its original form, the square minaret was central also and the prayer-hall was six aisles deep. Some of the decoration on the balcony of the minaret has survived, including pierced crenellations, angled corbelling, Kufic inscriptions and a frieze of roundels. The **Mosque of Three Doors, Quairouan** (866), is an important example of the small urban mosque, equivalent to the Syrian single-room type. The important surviving section of this example is the triple-arched portico with its slightly pointed, slightly horseshoe arches, above which are four fields of Kufic inscriptions surmounted by a bracketed cornice.

In Cairo, the Abbasid Caliphate maintained a somewhat distant tenure, but of this period only one significant monument remains, the unique **Nilometer** (861) (p. 592A) at the southern tip of Rhoda Island in the Nile. It was constructed for the Caliph al-Mutawakkil and consists of a measuring shaft set in a deep, square, stone-built well which can be descended by a winding staircase. Tunnels connected to the river terminate on the inner face in pointed two-centred arches with colonettes and moulded hoods. Despite a distinctly Gothic appearance, these examples of pointed arches pre-date almost every European example by nearly three centuries.

The **Mosque of Ibn Tulun** (876–9) (pp. 592C, 594A,B) in the new City built by Ahmed ibn Tulun was modelled on precedents in Samarra, whence he came. The mosque retains its original character despite several restorations. It is built in brick but is faced with stucco in which friezes are incised. The mixture of several forms of ornamental detailing found separately at Samarra suggests not only that the Mosque of Ibn Tulun was essentially an Iraqi building, but that it was built by craftsmen from the Abbasid capital who had arrived in Egypt only a relatively short time before.

The **Aqueduct, Basatin** (*c.* 880), is the only secular work of Ahmed ibn Tulun to survive in its original form. It carried water from a source above Cairo to the new capital. Two-centred arches built in fired brick indicate Mesopotamian rather than Egyptian craftsmanship.

In the middle of the tenth century the Fatimid dynasty invaded Egypt from Tunisia and renamed the capital Al-Kahira ('The Victory'), a name which was later Latinised to 'Cairo'. The builders again moved into open land to the north to found what was to become the famous mediaeval metropolis under their Ayyubid and Mamluk successors. Only the core of the first Fatimid congregational mosque remains, concealed by many later accretions and partial rebuildings. This, the **al-Azhar Mosque** (970–1131 and later), has for long been a prime centre of Muslim learning and is the home of the oldest extant theological university. It contained a hypostyle prayer-hall, the transverse arcades of which were broken by a central nave terminating in a dome before the mihrab. Two further domes were placed at the termination of the transverse arcade in the kibla wall. On either side of the main courtyard there were widened riwaqs, serving as additional teaching spaces. The roof was carried on arcades of two-centred arches on a Corinthian order.

The **Mosque of al-Hakim, Cairo** (1013), followed the same general plan as the al-Azhar. Its flat-roofed prayer-hall was filled with the massive system of piers deriving from the Mosque of Ibn Tulun, and the courtyard also was enclosed by an arcade on all sides. The minarets stand on salient bastions. It is defunct.

The slightly later **al-Guyushi Mosque, Cairo** (1085), was not intended to serve the general populace and its much smaller prayer-hall was domed. Its muqarnas pendentives and its minaret, rising through a series of square stages to a domed termination, are the earliest surviving Fatimid examples of these features in the city. They provide important precedents for later buildings.

The late eleventh century **Fortifications of Fatimid Cairo** (together with the city wall of Diyarbakir in Turkey) are the most important military architecture of the period. They are closely related. The builders of the walls of Cairo were Armenians or Syrians who came from Asia Minor. The first stages of the work were carried out between 1087 and 1092 by the Vizier, al-Jamali. The bonding and vaulting used in the gates of **Bab Futuh, Bab an Nasr, Bab Zuwelya** (p. 592D) and the gate of the citadel were important exemplars for future buildings. The Fatimid caliphs, particularly al-Mustansir, also rebuilt much of the existing mud and rubble walling of the city in superbly dressed stone.

From the late Fatimid period two important mosques survive: the **al-Aqmar** (1225) and that of **as-Salih Talai** (1160). Both exhibit the mature Fatimid style, with keel-arching, stalactite pendentives, fluted domes and gored roundels. The facade of the al-Aqmar is the first of many examples in which the street orientation is adapted to the kibla direction by a wedge-shaped adjustment to the plan. Its frontage was also the first to be designed as a fully decorated street facade and was originally symmetrical, with blind arches repeated on each side of the entrance block. Both mosques had multi-pillared prayer-halls and wide uninterrupted transepts along the kibla wall. The mosque of as-Salih Talai was located outside the Bab Zuwelya and its facade incorporated a deep portico behind a Corinthian arcade of Fatimid arches.

In 1171 the Fatimids gave way to Saladin – the first of the Ayyubid dynasty. In response to the threats of the Crusades the dynasty extended its hold over Palestine and Syria carrying Egyptian influence into Jerusalem, Damascus and **Aleppo** where the complex and magnificently finished **Barbican to the Citadel**, built by the Sultan al-Zahir Ghazi (1209-10), employs the most up-to-date defensive techniques. Of the palace the Sultan built in the citadel itself little survives beyond foundations and a portal in ablaq technique.

In 1250 the Ayyubids were succeeded by the Mamluks. Sultan Baybars established the status of the dynasty by moving the city boundaries of Cairo northwards yet again and by building another great courtyard mosque, the size of which is comparable to those of 'Amr, Ibn Tulun and Hakim. The **Mosque of Baybars** (begun *c.* 1260) was a hypostyle mosque in a

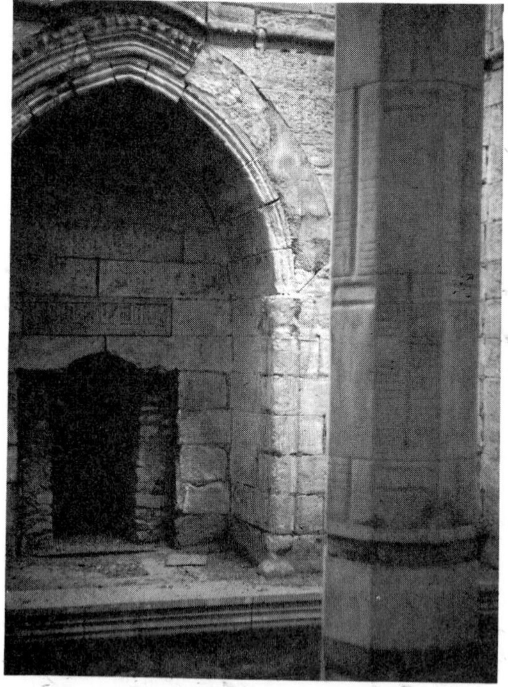

A. Nilometer (861). See p.591

B. Madrassa of Sultan Qalun, Cairo (1283–5). See p.593

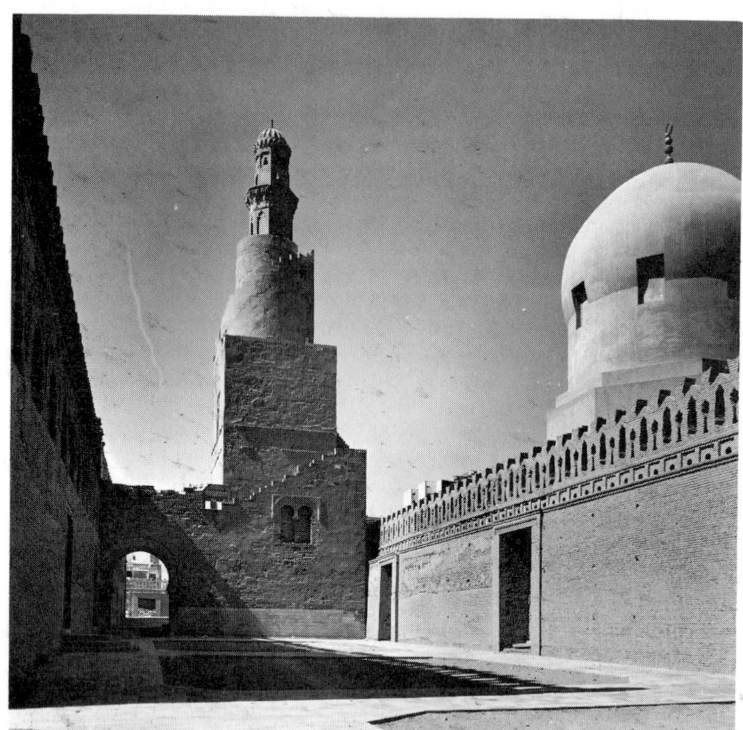

C. Mosque of Ibn Tulun, Cairo (876–9). See p.591

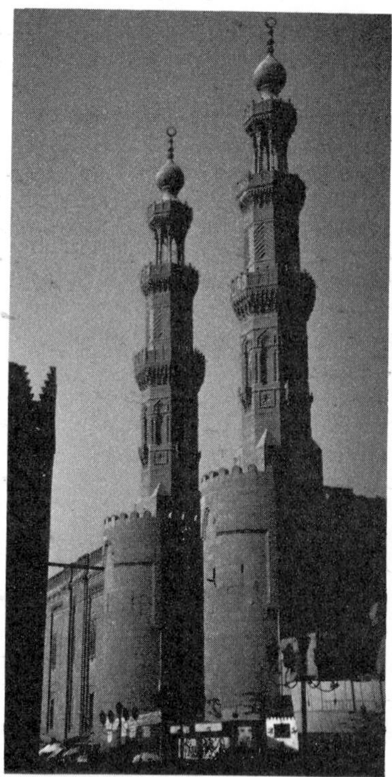

D. Bab Zuwelya, Cairo. See p.591

rectangular enclosure. Its prayer-hall and surrounding arcades were carried on piers and Corinthian columns, and the axial gates projected forward in salients as in the mosque of Hakim. The dome before the mihrab was enlarged to become visually dominant.

In a remarkably short period the immensely powerful Sultan Qalun built a complex of buildings containing a madrassa sufficiently large to contain a congregational mosque, a hospital (maristan), a very large domed tomb-chamber and a massive minaret. The whole is known as the **Tomb and Madrassa of Sultan Qalun, Cairo** (1283–5) (p. 592B). The maristan has been almost entirely destroyed but the remainder survives intact. The prayer-iwan was substantially enlarged by the creation of a central nave with side aisles, so that it became virtually a mosque in itself, with a deep reciprocal iwan facing it across the court. The plan of the tomb chamber is square. An octagon set within it carries a dome, originally constructed of wood. The whole interior is lavishly and brilliantly detailed with geometric inlays, rich stucco work, and embossed and gilded friezes surmounted by inlay within the dome. It is richly finished and evocative.

Immediately adjacent to the madrassa of Qalun stands the **Madrassa of an-Nasir Mohammed**, begun by Sultan Ketbuga in 1295 and completed in 1303. The entrance portal, brought from a Crusader church at Acre in Palestine, provides a crucial illustration of the compatibility of the styles. Intricate stucco work remains in the kibla iwan and the minaret. Elaborately enriched it continues the tradition of a square shaft rising to an octagonal-domed upper stage. In the citadel there is also the austere **Mosque of an-Nasir Mohammed** (1318–34), where dome and multi-pillared hall are combined as in the Mosque of Baybars. The minarets are faced in tile mosaic suggesting a foreign influence.

Almost immediately afterwards (1303–4) an important double mausoleum was built which marks the full evolution of the minaret. **The tomb of Emirs Salar and Sanjar al-Jawali** is a twin-domed structure, with a square- shafted minaret which rises high above the domes. The core is reduced to an elegant octagon in plan and is pierced with windows above the balcony; it then rises through a further stage to a domed cap. The domes, built on high drums, have serrated ribs, and they set the pattern for funerary architecture in the city.

Alternative plan-forms were adopted for larger mosques in Cairo at the height of its maturity: the first was the hypostyle prayer-hall with a large dome before the mihrab fronting a rectangular arcaded court which had direct access to the street; the second was the madrassa-mosque with an elaborate street frontage giving on to an oblique approach to a courtyard with confronting iwans and a prayer-chamber which was itself usually an iwan expanded laterally, sometimes by the addition of arcades.

One of the greatest mosques of this latter type was built between 1356 and 1363 – the **Mosque and Madrassa of Sultan Hassan** (p. 594C,D) which has survived largely intact, although its domed ablutions fountain and minaret have been reconstructed and its main doors taken elsewhere. An immense portal with an elaborate muqarnas-headed opening gives access to a majestic, domed entrance hall from which a tortuous approach leads obliquely into the central court. The massive iwans, standing within walls some 30 m (100 ft) high, produce a powerful sense of seclusion which justifies the scale. The tomb of the founder stands on the axis of the building, behind the mihrab, and in the centre of the court an elaborate domed fountain with wide eaves suggests the hand of Syrians and other northern artisans who were brought in at this time. Around the courtyard the skyline is fretted with a fleur-de-lys crenellation which henceforward in Cairo replaced the stepped motif of Sassanian inspiration.

With the Burji Mamluk sultans, Cairo reached the height of prosperity as a great mercantile metropolis. *Intra mures* Sultan Barkuk built a madrassa and mosque (1386), enriched with geometric marble inlays. On a far greater scale and carrying his father's name, Barkuk's son, Sultan Faraj, built a double-domed mausoleum in the northern cemeteries. It is known as the **Khanaqah and Tomb of Barkuk** (1399–1411) and forms a giant square at two corners of which identical domed mausolea are opposed to two slender and finely formed minarets at the other corners. The prayer-hall introduces into Cairo the Persian practice of covering large areas with multiple domes.

One further large congregational mosque was built in Cairo, and that was the **Muaddiye Mosque** (1415–21) by Sultan Mu'ayyad Sheikh. Having been imprisoned beside the Bab Zuwelya, the Sultan had vowed to build a mosque on the site of his incarceration. He placed twin minarets on the bastions and brought to his building the great doors of the Mosque of Sultan Hassan. The high, ribbed dome of his mausoleum, carried on elegant stalactites, lies immediately beside the wide prayer-hall of the mosque itself, whose giant court is now a garden. The hypostyle prayer-hall without a dome brings together features of the earlier congregational and madrassa-tomb mosques in one building, and fittingly marks the conclusion of the series of great congregational mosques in the mediaeval capital.

The later Mamluks were prolific builders, and high standards were maintained in a city which had developed rich craft traditions. The great formal cemeteries were extended northwards. Among many others, **Sultan Inal**, who acceded in 1453, built a **tomb, convent** and **madrassa** with a widened prayer-chamber. It has an elegant minaret with chevron ribbing, muqarnas corbelling to all the balconies and transitional zones of blind arcading and patterned

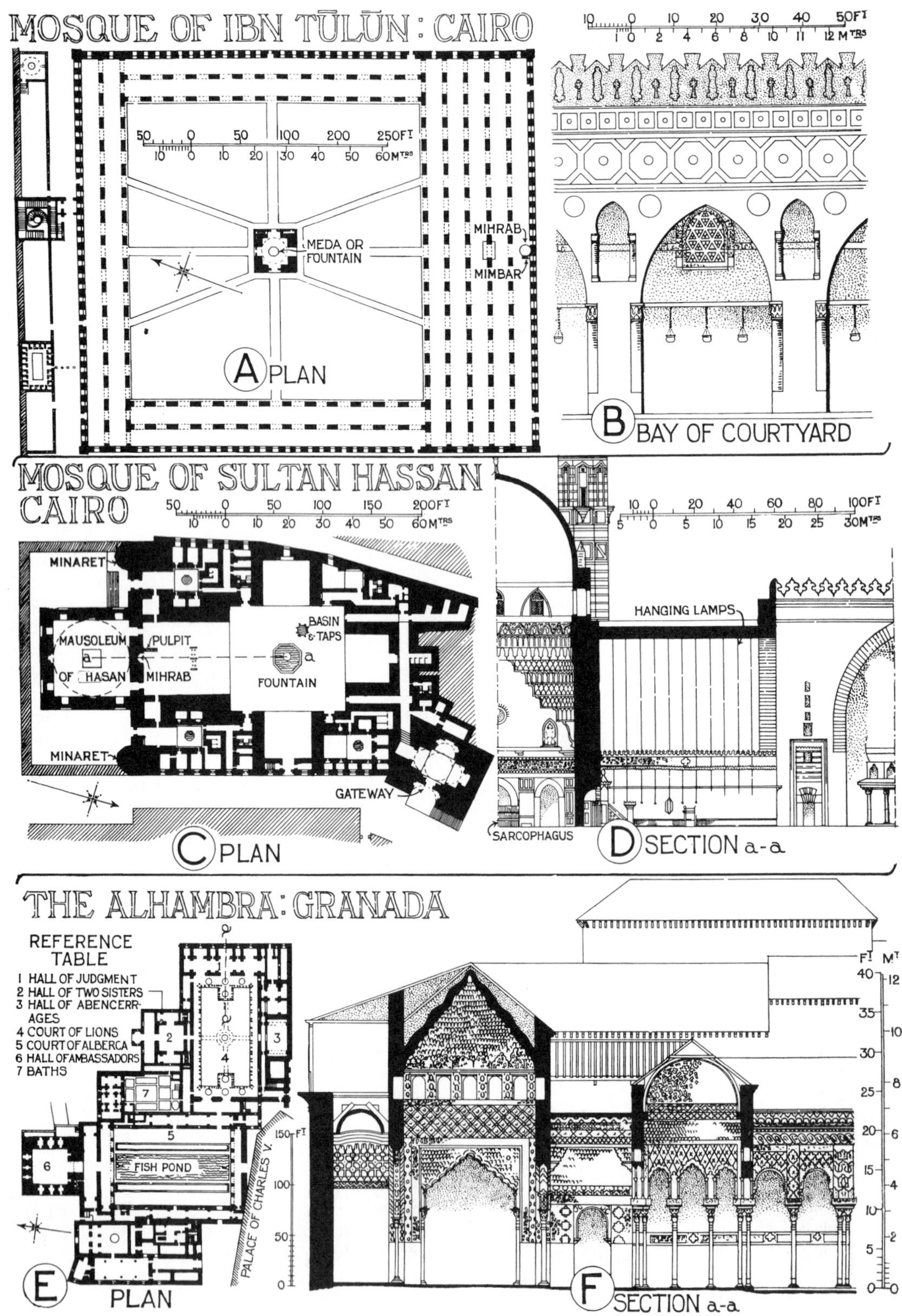
MOSQUE OF IBN TŪLŪN: CAIRO
MEDA OR FOUNTAIN
MIHRAB
MIMBAR
A PLAN
B BAY OF COURTYARD
MOSQUE OF SULTAN HASSAN CAIRO
MINARET
MAUSOLEUM OF HASAN
PULPIT
MIHRAB
BASIN & TAPS
FOUNTAIN
GATEWAY
C PLAN
HANGING LAMPS
SARCOPHAGUS
D SECTION a-a
THE ALHAMBRA: GRANADA
REFERENCE TABLE
1 HALL OF JUDGMENT
2 HALL OF TWO SISTERS
3 HALL OF ABENCERRAGES
4 COURT OF LIONS
5 COURT OF ALBERCA
6 HALL OF AMBASSADORS
7 BATHS
FISH POND
PALACE OF CHARLES V.
E PLAN
F SECTION a-a

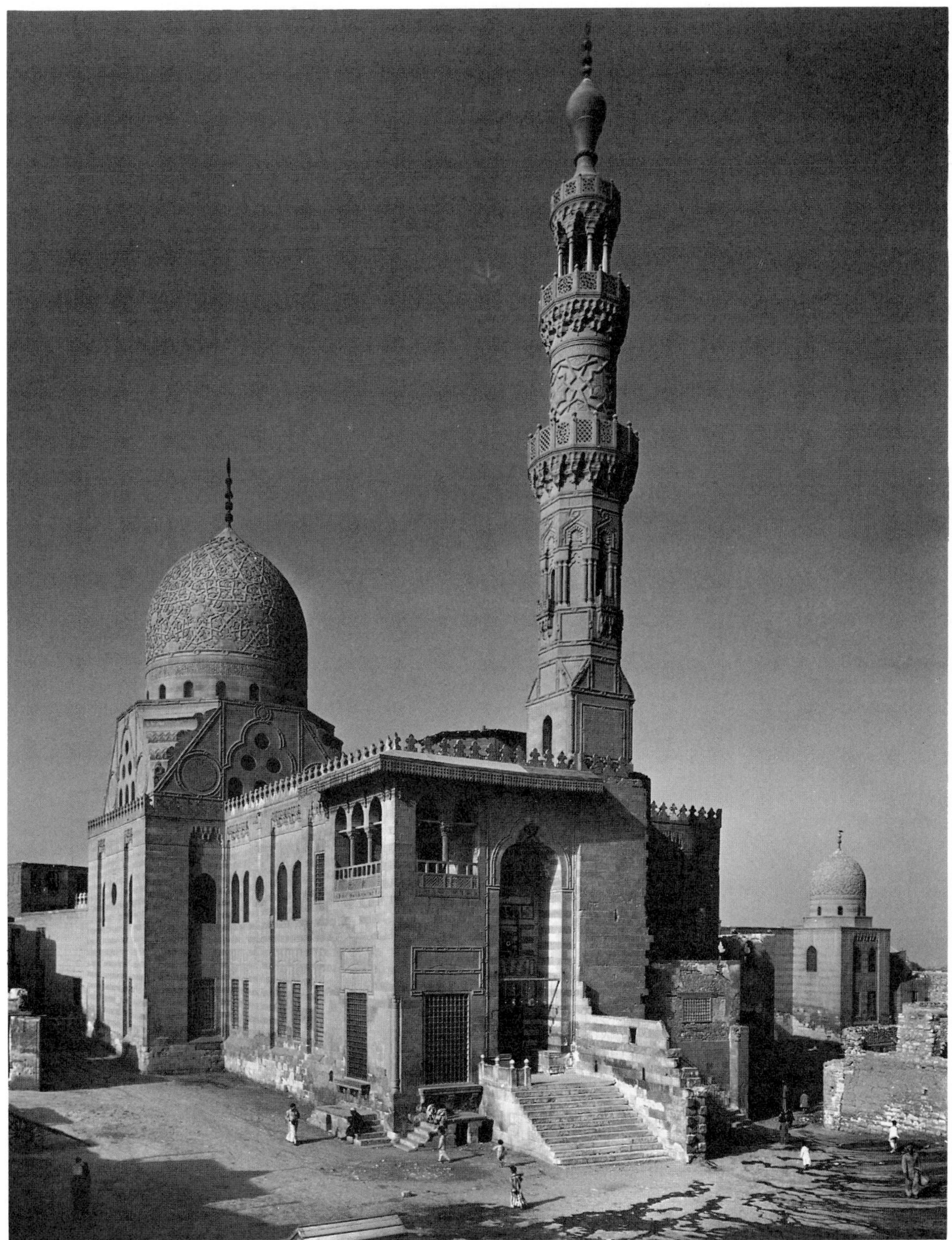

Madrassa of Qaitbay, Cairo (1472–4). See p.596

panels. The dome is haunched with chevron patterning, a form established in the mausoleum of Barkuk, and repeated immediately in the dervish convent and mausoleum built in 1506. In these and other buildings of the period, the use of courses of masonry of contrasting colours (ablaq) was increasingly common. Even higher standards of masonry are apparent and the external faces of walls and domes were modelled and contoured for decorative purposes.

Cairo owes much of its finest building to Sultan Qaitbay, one of the longest-reigning Mamluk monarchs. There are two surviving caravanserais in his name, one at **al-Ahzar** (1477) and the other near **Bab an-Nasr** (1481). His congregational mosque was built in 1475 and is remarkable for its exquisite complexity, which is also characteristic of his mausoleum. Both the buildings incorporate madrassas; the more famous of the two, the **Madrassa of Qaitbay** (1472–4) (pp. 595, 597A), is the ultimate achievement of architectural development in Cairo. It survives complete, and has been fully restored. A slender minaret reduces from the square to the octagon and then to the circle and an open colonnade on which stands the high-shouldered dome, the form of which is echoed by the dome over the tomb itself. The picturesque aspect of the asymmetric exterior is heightened by the striated facing, whose colours are picked up in the elaborately banded inlaid decoration of arches, friezes and cresting. The external surface of the dome is deeply carved with bars intertwined with floral arabesques.

While the interior of the tomb is calm, with simple ashlar surfaces rising through elaborate muqarnas to the dome, the interior of the mosque itself, with four iwans fronting the covered court is, like the facade, intricately inlaid and carved. By this period Cairo, unlike most Muslim cities, had developed the street facade as an important feature of its principal routes.

One of the most distinguished urban buildings of the late Mamluk period is the **Mosque of Quijmas al-Ishaqi** (1480–1) who was Master of the Horse to Sultan Qaitbay. It stands on an island site and is joined by a bridge to its school on the opposite side of the street. The interior of the mosque is rich with inlaid marble floors and walls, above which stucco window grilles carry stained glass.

At a principal junction in the centre of the mediaeval city stands the **Mosque and Tomb of Sultan Qansuh al-Ghuari** (1505–15), the last of the Mamluk sultans to enjoy a substantial reign. The waqla or khan is one of the most important and unusual of this series of buildings. It rises through six storeys and is built around a courtyard. The lower two floors are incorporated into an arcade and the upper levels have handsome oriel windows with intricate mushrabiye (the brise-soleil screens common throughout the Muslim world). The adjacent madrassa, on a four-iwan plan, demonstrates the final evolution of the prayer-chamber into a congregational mosque. Here it has been widened until its total width is nearly three times that of the courtyard. It is a richly detailed and impressive piece of urban architecture. On the opposite side of the street stands the immense tomb chamber, the ill-fated dome of which has fallen three times. It is now roofless, and beside it there stands another madrassa prayer-hall with one deep iwan facing a mihrab wall. An enclosed fountain of particular charm, with wide eaves and windows, projects into the street.

Mamluk architecture did not suffer complete eclipse with the death of the last Mamluk Sultan at the hands of the Ottoman executioner in 1517, but thereafter the prosperous mercantile city owed tribute to Istanbul, and its trade declined as Europeans found new routes to the East. Egyptian talent was attracted elsewhere and its great patrons were no more.

Spain and Western North Africa – the Mahgreb

In the middle of the eighth century Abd ar-Rahman, the sole Umayyad prince to escape death at the hands of the Abbasids, fled from Syria, first to Tunisia and thence to Spain. He was accompanied by numbers of his Syrian court. Their arrival in the west transformed what had been a distant and relatively unimportant province into a centre of intellectual and creative energy which was to proclaim its own Caliphate. Tunisia, however, fell within Abbasid authority in the closing years of the eighth century and Abbasid colonisation reached beyond Tunis and Biserta while the remainder of western North Africa and Spain were left to the Umayyads.

The earliest significant building of Umayyad Spain is the **Mosque of Cordoba** (785) (p. 597B,C). The first stage of the mosque, still encapsulated within the later structure, displays a vigorous architectural style that sets the pattern for the three major additions of 848 (Abd ar-Rahman II), 961 and 968 (al-Hakim) and 987 (al-Mansur). These additions made the mosque comparable in size with the Malwiya (p. 585C,D) and Abu Dulaf mosques in Samarra, and its covered prayer-space was larger than either. The architectural style of the first mosque is simple but distinctive. A massive, buttressed stone wall forms a compound, of which a half, at the kibla (southern) end, forms the covered prayer-hall which has arcades parallel to the main axis. The incorrect southward orientation, as at Qairouan, is evidence that the architect was Syrian. The lower arches in the arcades are of horseshoe-form with voussoirs of alternating colour outlining the lower profile of the stilted voids of the upper arches. Precedent for the use of alternating brick and stone bands and for the horseshoe forms can be found

A. Madrassa of Qaitbay, interior. See p.596

B. Mosque, Cordoba (785): Capilla de Villaviciosa. See p.596

C. Mosque, Cordoba: arcades

D. The Alhambra, Granada (1338–90): Court of Lions. See p.599

both in northern Syria before and during the Umayyad period, and in Spain itself. Three domes cover the maksura and another the mihrab itself, creating for the first time in a mosque a form of sanctuary at the focus of prayer. Part of the west wall and the internal arcades remain intact, and, apart from the insertion of a Gothic chapel into its core, the mosque survives very much as it was in the tenth century.

The Cordoba mosque was repeated in miniature in a palace commissioned by Abd ar-Rahman III, and called **Medinat al-Zahra** (936–45). There the mosque had a buttressed outer wall with arcades parallel to the main axis and a square minaret adjacent to the axial main entrance. The palace itself, at present being restored, has horseshoe round-headed arcades carried on wide dosseret blocks supported by a Corinthian order. Its extent gives an indication of the wealth and power of western Islam two centuries after the defeat of the Umayyads in Syria. The large rectangular compound stood on a sloping site through which ran a water course, producing an informal arrangement of courts and pavilions on descending terraces. Work ceased when the city was sacked and the court was moved back to Cordoba.

In the western Mahgreb, the focus of Muslim activity was the mountain-ringed city of Fez. The **Qarawiyn Mosque** (859, 956,1136 and later) was the congregational mosque of the city and, like the al-Azhar in Cairo, was the centre of a theological university. Its history of additions and enlargements considerably extended the original building, in which a hypostyle prayer-hall was bisected by a central nave with a roof which rose above the adjoining structures.

S. Cristo de la Luz, or more properly, the **Mosque of Bab Mardun, Toledo, central Spain** (*c.* 960), consists simply of a square chamber with four isolated columns carrying a system of arches and nine domes, under a pitched, tiled roof. Projecting on one side is a substantial chamber forming the mihrab in much the same way as at Cordoba. It is a brick building with exterior arcades of cusped pointed arches, interlinked horseshoe arches, cusped openings and geometric friezes. Stylistically, the building is something of an enigma. Its proportions and decoration suggest eastern precedents.

In 1031 Umayyad power in Spain had declined and ultimately the peninsula was dominated by a separate dynasty – the Almoravids. Under their overlordship a local dynasty – the Hudids – built a palace, the **al-Jaferiya, Zaragoza, Toledo** (1050). It is contained within a rectangular compound, approximately 86 m × 73 m (280 ft × 240 ft), buttressed by half-round towers and divided into thirds as in the Umayyad buildings of Syria. There is a coupled Corinthian order carrying lobate arches, sometimes interlaced and cross-braced as at Cordoba. This localised style continued until the fall of Cordoba to Christian forces in 1118.

The Almoravid dynasty, moving up from the south in the eleventh century, set up capitals at Marrakesh soon after 1060, at Tlemcen 20 years later, and Algiers shortly afterwards. In each city they built large congregational mosques. The mosque at **Tlemcen** has a square minaret on the central axis and an arcading system which survives from the original construction. In this it follows the prototype at Qairouan but without the transverse aisle next to the kibla wall. Round horseshoe arches predominate, with heavy cusping in the dominant central zones. Flat timber roofs are used in all the larger of these North African mosques. In a dome before the mihrab an inner shell of stucco forms a filigree of arabesques between interlaced ribs. Supporting squinches are cusped and hung with filigree patterns in which motifs derived from sources as diverse as Hellenistic Syria and Sasanian Iraq are mingled. At **Algiers**, the mosque was completed by the end of the eleventh century. Its structure is much the same as the mosque at Tlemcen.

An architecture of originality, incorporating complex pattern-making and decoration in its components combined with high levels of craftsmanship, flourished across Andalusia and North Africa under the Almoravids. It is exemplified in the congregational mosque at **Tinmal** (1153), the contemporary Qarawiyn Mosque, Fez and the **Quttubiyya Mosque, Marrakesh** (1147). The last boasts a stone-built minaret – a giant, square tower with cusped, framed openings, horseshoe-headed, round windows and interlaced arching, surmounted by stepped crenellations and a small cupola. It is a precursor of the great brick minaret built by Yusef I as part of the **Great Mosque, Seville** (1172–82). Only its courtyard and the great tower, the Giralda, survive. The enormous prayer-chamber was swept away by Christian workmen in building the most extensive of all Gothic cathedrals. The minaret is now disguised by Renaissance additions but the geometric complexities of its richly worked panelling survive unscathed.

The vast mosque of **Sultan Hassan, Rabat** (started 1191, left unfinished 1199), had a magnificent and massive tower which rose to two-thirds of its planned height before being abandoned. The tower was axial, standing at the entrance to a prayer-hall almost 137 m (450 ft) square, behind the courtyard and surrounded by wide riwaqs. This was the largest mosque attempted in North Africa and introduced two novel features – courtyards within the prayer-hall itself and triple lateral aisles against the kibla wall.

In the **Great Mosque of the Almohads, Fez**, and in the **Great Mosque of Fez, as-Jedid** (1276–1307), the filigree dome of the earlier (late eleventh century) mosque at Tlemcen was repeated with even greater intricacy, as it was at Tlemcen itself in the **Mosque of Mansura** (1303–6 and 1336). Here an axial minaret and axial entrance were combined, and if the building had been finished it might have proved to be the supreme achievement of the period. It was proportioned with skill and certainty, and embodied the distinctive features which the dynasties of the Mahgreb made their own.

Tomb building in the Mahgreb was reserved for holy men rather than potentates, so funerary buildings of the type found in Cairo were relatively unknown. Even the madrassa, as a building type, was unusual, although in the fourteenth century a considerable number were built. Of these, the madrassa known as the **Bou Inaniya, Fez** (1350–5), was undoubtedly the most elaborate and handsomely decorated. Its attenuated shafts and pilasters are panelled with intricate patterns running through friezes, spandrels, blind arching and frames, extending to muqarnas pendentives and multi-lobed arches.

The **Alcazar, Seville** (1364), rebuilt for the Christian monarch Pedro I, is a relatively modest, two-storeyed palace planned around a central courtyard. Every detail is Islamic, even to the Arabic inscriptions in the friezes. The upper walls, richly modelled in stucco, are complemented by the lower sections of ceramic mosaic. Although Seville had become Christian, one minor Muslim dynasty – the Nasrids – survived in Spain until 1492 and was responsible for the **Alhambra, Granada** (principally 1338-90) (pp. 594E,F, 597D), one of the most elaborate and richly decorated of Muslim palaces. It is set on a steep-sided spur, projecting into a fertile valley. Richly planted terraces sparkling with watercourses and set about with jewel-like pavilions, were used to convert the fortress palace of the eleventh century into a 'paradise'. Its most important part dates from the second half of the fourteenth century, and consists of a series of interlocked pavilions set on a terrace on the northern side of the ridge, above a cliff that falls dramatically into a ravine. Two great courts at right-angles dominate the composition: the Court of the Lions (p. 597D) is surrounded by an arcade in which slender columns carry arches pierced and interlaced with the greatest virtuosity to give the impression of fine filigree. The vertical surfaces are covered with endless fields of interwoven arabesques in carved stucco, given additional emphasis by an elaborate display of miniature columns, blind arching, arabesque interlacements and calligraphic friezes.

Channels of water, enlivened by small fountains, provide a shimmering core to the arrangement and are carried in turn to the lower levels to sparkle through basins and tumble into further pools. In the Court of the Myrtles a more urbane quality comes with the wide central pool which reflects the tall arcades and the battlemented Tower of Komares, containing the Hall of Ambassadors. From this almost cubic chamber, crowned by a polygonal dome, triple doors lead through profusely decorated walls to viewing balconies high above the city.

Chapter 18

LOCAL DYNASTIES OF CENTRAL ISLAM AND PRE-MOGHUL INDIA

The oldest surviving Muslim building in Persia is the **Tarik-Han Mosque** (early eighth century) at Damghan in northern Persia near the south-east extremity of the Caspian Sea. The courtyard plan is essentially Arabian, The prayer-hall originally had a vaulted roof (now replaced by low domes) carried on arcades running parallel to the main axis. Massive circular columns of radial brickwork repeat the building technique used in Sassanian palaces. The prayer-hall originally had a wide central aisle with arcades parallel to the kibla axis – a plan indicative of the influence of the al-Aqsa Mosque. Its probable lack of a mihrab at the time of its building also suggests a very early date.

Originally conquered by the Umayyads in 710, Bokhara, beyond the Oxus, flourished in the ninth and tenth centuries under the Samanid dynasty. The **Tomb (supposedly) of Ismael the Samanid, Bokhara** (*c.* 905–10) (p. 601A) is a relatively small domed mausoleum, constructed in elaborately decorated brickwork within and without. Shaped and cut bricks are used in relief to form complex patterns. The building is an almost perfect cube, battered back externally, on which is superimposed a hemispherical masonry dome. It represents an architecture which has largely disappeared because of the impermanence of mud brick and the losses due to Mongol depradations. Even this tomb escaped only by having been buried. Ismael's tomb was built at a time when fired brick was coming into use and is a precursor of the age of monumental tomb building in south-west Asia.

A series of tomb towers was built in the early eleventh century in northern Persia. The most impressive is that built by Qabus Ibn Bashmigir – the **Gunbad i Qabus, Gurgan** (1006–7) (p. 601B) on the shores of the Caspian Sea just north of Damghan. It stands some 50 m (170 ft) high and is a cone-topped, tapering cylinder constructed entirely of brick with ribs in a stellar pattern. It is without ornament other than bands of Kufic inscription. Among other similar tombs were those of **Pir-i-Alander** (1021) and **Chihilpuktaran** (1058), both near Damghan. The tombs of **Allah a-Din, Varamin** (1287), **Beyazit, Bistam** (1313), the **Gunbad Abdullah, Damavend** (twelfth century), and the tomb of **Doghrul, Rayy** (1139), all came later and are in the same region to the south of the Caspian; none is so tall and stark as the Gunbad i-Qabus.

Echoes of these powerful forms are to be found in Seljuk architecture in the West. The **Doner Kumbet, Kayseri** (*c.* 1276), in Anatolia is the most famous of these less monumental but often elegant tombs in Asia Minor. Its dodecagonal shaft has a blind arcade on each face and the motif is repeated on the conical cap. A shallow muqarnas cornice divides the two, and the plinth is chamfered with Turkish triangles at the corners, to give a comfortable transition from the multi-faceted drum to the square base. A series of rich friezes, bas-reliefs, patterns in the panels, muqarnas-headed doors and Armenian-inspired bas-relief carvings make this little building the outstanding culmination of a series which includes the **Mahperi Khatun Tomb, Kayseri** (1237), and the similar but earlier **Sitte Melik Gunbad, Divrigi** (1196).

A number of mosques were built in a multi-domed Persian style from the **Mashad Mosque Anah** in the west to Balkh in the east. In Balkh, the **No Gunbad Mosque** (late ninth century) has only recently been identified. Mud brick and rubble in mud mortar were commonly used in this period and most such mosques were rebuilt during the Seljuk and Mongol periods. Very few survive in the original material or form, common though they once were. One such, the **Friday Mosque, Faraj**, near Yazd (ninth or tenth century) consists of a simple mud-brick arcade around a court, with a two-bay prayer-hall and a very early cylindrical minaret. Its survival at Faraj on the

A. Tomb of Ismael the Samanid, Bokhara (*c.* 905–10). See p.600

B. Tomb of Gunbad i-Qabus, Gurgan (1006–7). See p.600

C. Stellar Minaret: Mosque of Bahramshah, Ghazni (mid-twelfth century). See p.602

D. Chifte Minare Madrassa, Sivas (1271–2). See p.605

southern fringes of the desert allows comparison with the **Masjid-i-Jami, Nain** (probably no later than *c.* 960), a mosque in a more urban location. The latter has an early minaret, important because it illustrates the transition from the square and massive Syrian precedent to the slender-shafted Persian form. The mihrab section of the mosque has a rich and evocative series of arabesques in stucco which, in their uninhibited richness and rustic irregularity, display some of the forms evolved at Samarra.

The important surviving mosques of the Seljuk period are to be found in Persia at **Zavareh** (1135–6), **Ardestan** (eleventh-twelfth centuries), and especially the **Great Mosque, Ispahan** (eleventh century). Like others this building was a pre-Muslim shrine and has been a mosque since the seventh century. The congregational mosque of the period evolved on the four-iwan plan traditional in Persia, with a domed prayer-chamber placed behind the prayer-iwan. This development of the prayer-hall into a further domed chamber appears to have taken place in the eleventh century and on the Iranian plateau. The advantage of a closed chamber for winter prayers needs no emphasis. At Ispahan the form is fully developed. The mosque as it stands today is an accretion of several different periods, but the work of the Seljuk masons stands out, and reaches its peak of achievement in the **Gunbad-i-Kharka**, a domed chamber built apparently as a reception hall for the monarch. It has no mihrab and can be dated to 1088–9. The interior is enriched with brickwork laid in multiple patterns and highlighted with carved plaster inserts. Cusped squinches achieve the transition from the square chamber to the drum, where a ring of groined squinches finally transposes the octagon to the circle. A complex pattern of linear ribs reduces to a five-pointed stellar form in the dome. The muqarnas-filled iwans fronting the courtyard are linked by two-storey arcades, and the iwan of the prayer-hall opens into a domed prayer-chamber before the mihrab. In its Seljuk form, multi-pillared halls completely filled the spaces between the iwans and the rectangular outer compound wall. The mosque was extended northwards at a later date, and an important chamber was made on the western side containing the mihrab of Oljeitu, with fine bas-relief stucco arabesques. The whole of the building, consisting of vaults, cross-vaults and domed chambers, covers an area 120 m × 90 m (400ft × 300 ft) and dates largely from the eleventh and twelfth centuries; it is built entirely of brick and demonstrates the Seljuk mastery of two- and four-centred arch construction, structural muqarnas, squinches, domes and groined vaults. The elegant prayer-chamber of the **Friday Mosque, Gulpegan** (1105–18), has similar features and may be taken as typical of the type.

One of the many isolated Seljuk caravanserais in Asia survives. It is the **Ribat-i-Sharaf** (1114 and 1155) on the route into central Asia from northern Persia. The main courtyard had four iwans and the building was richly decorated with stucco and carved brickwork. The entrance portal is massively framed with a rich geometric field enclosed by a powerful Kufic frieze.

The Ghaznavid palace at **Lashkari Bazar** in southern Afghanistan (twelfth and thirteenth centuries) may be seen in the same context. In its original form a heavily buttressed wall contained a central courtyard which was bisected axially and terminated in external and internal iwans. Two storeys of blind arcading surrounded the courtyard, and the audience hall echoed the forms of the great Seljuk mosques with the dome behind the iwan.

The Seljuks built a remarkable series of towers in many places across Asia. A minaret, stellar in plan of the middle of the twelfth century survives from the **mosque of Bahramshah, Ghazni** (p. 601C); although its upper sections have been destroyed, the rippled surfaces of the lower stage of the tower display a brilliant complexity of geometric decoration. The **Ghurid Minaret, Jam** (p. 603A) (1191–8) is isolated but well preserved in a rocky valley in central Afghanistan. It is nearly 60 m (200 ft) in height and consists of a tapering cylindrical shaft on an octagonal base which is still partly buried. The decoration on the trunk of the minaret consists of calligraphic relief in brickwork, alternating with geometric patterning. At Bokhara, the later **Kalyan Mosque** (1514) retains the minaret of the same name, dated 1127 (p. 603B). This is a decorated tapering tower, almost 46 m (150 ft) high, and has survived in a good state of preservation, the only substantial structure to have been left intact by the Mongols. The tower of the **Friday Mosque, Saveh** (1110), although only a stump remains, is closely comparable with the latter minaret, but the bands of brick ornament are perhaps more refined. The minaret of the **Khalifiye, Baghdad**, is also comparable (1289). The mosques once served by these minarets have disappeared. There is also an important minaret (1170–2) which now belongs to the modern **Nur-ed-Din Mosque, Mosul**. The circular brick shaft, which leans but has been reinforced recently, is richly banded and ornamented with brick patterning.

Under Sultan Sanjar (1118-57) eastern Seljuk power focused upon Merv (Mari), and it was there the Sultan built for himself the **Tomb of Sultan Sanjar, Merv** (1157), of which the tomb alone survives, lacking the upper part of its dome. The massive brick base was capped with an arcade of deep recesses with pointed-arched heads. The dome was 37 m (120 ft) high and was surfaced externally with turquoise blue tiles. Internally there are zones of carved brick and incised stucco, and some of the latter was worked to represent brick inlay.

One of the few surviving early madrassas of Persia is the **Haydariya at Qazvin** (twelfth century). Its high oratory extends dramatically forward of the

A. Ghurid Minaret, Jam (1191–8). See p.602

B. Minaret, Kalyan Mosque, Bokhara (1127). See p.602

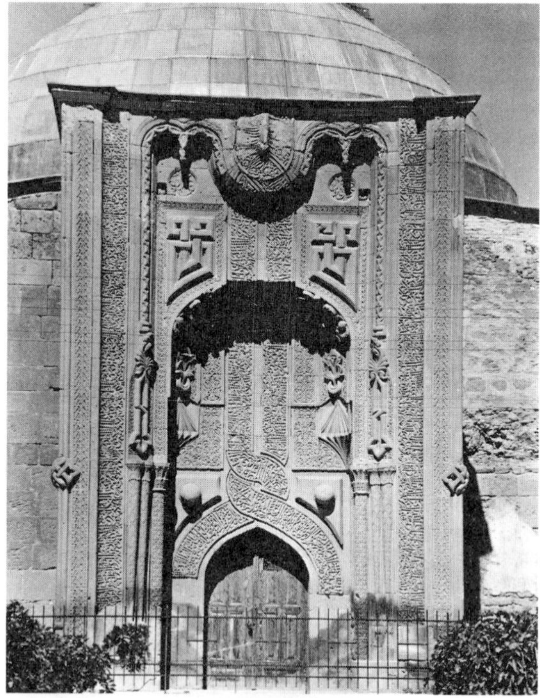

A. Inje Minare Madrassa, Konya (*c*. 1260–5). See p.605

B. Mosque of Qawat-al-Islam, Delhi (1197–1225). See p.605

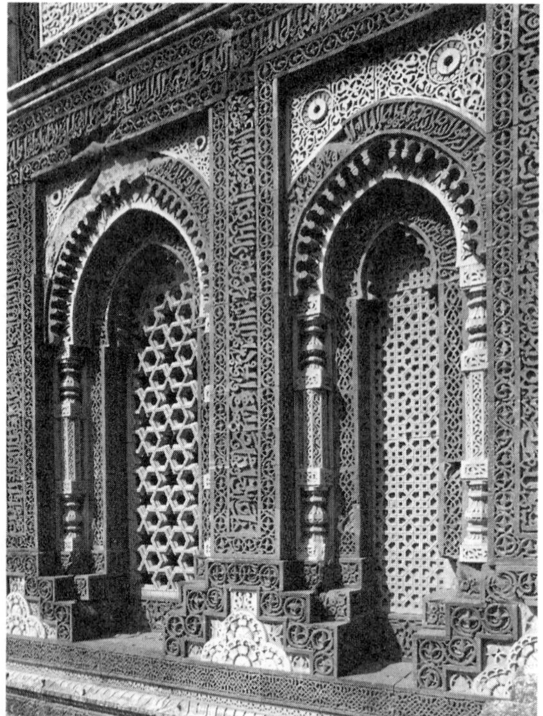

C. Ala i-Darwaza (1305), Tomb of Iltutmish, Delhi. See p.606

D. Rukn-i-Alam, Multan (1320–4). See p.606

surrounding cells, to dominate the courtyard which has a responding iwan on the axis and lateral entrances.

In Asia Minor, however, a rich heritage of Seljuk buildings includes madrassas, caravanserais, mosques, and tombs as well as civil works. On the south coast, at Alanya, under the walls of the fortress there survive vaulted shipyards (1226) built by an architect from Aleppo, and on the caravan routes are to be found major caravanserais such as that at **Sultanhan** (1232–6) and **Agzigharahan**. The latter have stalactite decorated portals, and prayer-chambers set as pavilions in central courtyards surrounded by cavernous vaulted accommodation for people and animals. The many lesser caravanserais on the trade routes often contained refined and elegantly decorated prayer-houses and were approached through high and richly decorated portals. The arched iwan of Sassanian origin by this time has been formalised into the high-fronted structure which framed the entrance to a building, and by its scale and decoration gave dignity and status to all that lay within. In Asia Minor, in the Seljuk period, the portal was combined with the dual minaret arrangement which was later to be associated with Persia. At **Sivas**, the **Gök Madrassa** (1271) had two such minarets astride a great muqarnas-headed doorway. The entire portal was heavily framed with friezes and mouldings, and the form was emphasised by strongly modelled interlacing patterns. The **Chifte Minare Madrassa** (1271–6) (p. 601D) and the **Gök Madrassa**, both at Sivas and both built in 1271, were similar, and buildings expressing this tradition were repeated elsewhere, in particular the **Chifte Minare Madrassa, Erzerum** (1273). At the **Inje Minare Madrassa, Konya** (*c.* 1260–5) (p. 604A) the very tall, richly patterned minaret (now largely destroyed) served the adjacent mosque. Here the madrassa was made more compact and the open courtyard was reduced to a size which could be covered by a dome. This building is famous for the extraordinarily impressive decorations on the entrance portal; the knotted mouldings and swirling shapes are idiosyncratic expressions of the originality of the architects of Seljuk Asia Minor. Little of their civic buildings survives, but the combined mosque and hospital at **Divrigi** (1229–) is an exception. A single compound wall contains mosque and hospital side by side. The wild exuberance of the bas-relief on the portals exceeds anything known, even in this region of extravagant modelling, and is atypical of the control normal to Muslim building. The mosque is entirely roofed. Twenty-five domes or vaults are carried on the sixteen columns of the prayer-hall. Behind the mihrab wall, a small court repeats the opposed iwan plan, and in the intervening spaces there are cells for inmates. A utilitarian work of monumental scale is the bridge over the **Batman Su** built in 1147; a giant arch rises 18 m (60 ft) to span nearly 30 m (100 ft). The original appurtenances included guard-houses and caravanserais.

In the period of Seljuk dominance lasting incursions were being made into northern India. Although there had been Arab invasions into north-west Sind (now southern Pakistan) as early as the first half of the eighth century, the Ghaznavid dynasty held sway (albeit under Abbasid sovereignty) as far east as Lahore, in Pakistan, for nearly two hundred years from the end of the tenth century. All Muslim invasions of India have come from Persia by way of Afghanistan. Having devastated the Hindu kingdoms of North West India the Ghaznavids did little creatively in the Princedoms they established. Mahmood al Ghori, a rebel against Ghaznavid rule, crushed the Rajput princes by the end of the twelfth century and established himself as Sultan in Delhi in 1206. This was just over a decade before the first Mongol incursions into central and south-west Asia (Genghis Khan conquered Samarkand and Bokhara in 1219). Islam was well established in the north and west by this time, and continued to evolve over the next two centuries before Mongol power was felt extensively in the region. Timur's incursions and the consequent Hindu massacre, although devastating, were comparatively short-lived, and over a century passed before Babur marched south-east from Afghanistan to establish the Moghul dynasty. Its adherence to Islam was to affect the history of architecture across much of the subcontinent from the middle of the sixteenth century onwards.

Mahmood's Tomb, Delhi (*c.* 1231), is one of the few buildings of the pre-Mongol period to survive, standing like a small fortress in the plain of Delhi, its corner turrets accentuating a square podium. Its walls are arcaded internally. The dominant figure in Mahmood's conquests was his general, Kutub ad-Din, who rebuilt a Hindu temple near Delhi as the **Qawat al-Islam Mosque** (1197–1225) (p. 604B). Although the upper stages of its minaret were reconstructed in 1396 the Ghaznavid origins are clear from its stellar plan, while evidence of imported craftsmanship can be seen in the muqarnas balconies of its four stages. Calligraphic bands in Arabic alternate with geometric and floral patterning. The minaret stood outside the compound of the rectangular mosque, whose relatively modest prayer-hall was covered with low domes. Within 25 years the entire mosque was encircled by a further arcaded courtyard formed, like the first, from components of previous buildings The second stage of construction includes the **Tomb of Iltutmish** (*c.* 1235). Its builder, Shams ad-Din Iltutmish, added to the greatly enlarged mosque a square tomb within which attached arches carried a corbelled dome. Its importance lies in the richly worked interior where Hindu motifs and Muslim designs are linked into combined patterns. The enlargement of the mosque continued in the

Khalji period. A minaret of even greater size than the first was begun, but the only significant work completed was the gateway, the **Ala i-Darwaza** (1305) (p. 604C), which demonstrates the increasingly powerful impact of Muslims from Persia or Afghanistan upon northern India.

Tughluq I was of mixed Turkish and Mongol descent. He rose to power as governor in the lower Punjab. There he built a tomb now known as the **Rukn-i-Alam, Multan** (1320–4) (p. 604D). On his accession he left Multan to govern from Delhi and made over the building to his tutor in spiritual matters, Rukn-i-Alam. The tall octagonal structure rises through two stages and is surmounted by a high hemispherical dome. On the lower stage the slightly battered walls are accentuated by the tapering, rounded corner-buttresses, and the verticality of the second stage heightens the predominantly blue tile-work with elaborate friezes and crestings that contrast with carved and plain yellow brickwork. Persian influence can be seen in this and other tombs of the period in Multan and elsewhere in the Indus basin.

In 1321, Ghias ad-Din Tughluq founded at Delhi a new capital whose walls, now largely in ruins, stand outside the present city. The buildings, used as a quarry for centuries, had qualities of simplicity, and their precise adherence to arcuated structural principles indicates central Asian origins. The only significant structure to survive intact lies outside the city on a rocky eminence in what was once a lake. It is reached by a causeway which now crosses fields to the polygonal fortification containing the **tomb of Ghias ad-Din Tughluq** (1325). The square base with sharply battered sides directly supports a low octagon carrying the pointed dome. Red sandstone inlaid with white marble in an upper string course rises to frame each door opening – a combination of materials which was to be used in monumental buildings in central India for centuries to come.

The **Beganpuri Mosque, Delhi** (*c.* 1370), is of the same period, and is raised on a massive podium and approached through three axial gateways. Within the courtyard a large iwan forms the entrance on each face, and the largest leads into the domed prayer-hall. The dome itself is concealed by the central iwan producing a conflict between the predominant iwan and the triple-arched prayer-hall.

The **Khirki Mosque, Delhi** (*c.* 1374), by contrast, has a square enclosure raised high on a podium, likewise approached axially from three directions. The corners are accentuated by turrets, but the interior is divided symmetrically, so that the whole area is roofed over apart from four open courtyards. A cluster of domes in front of the mihrab gives special emphasis to the focal point of the prayer-chamber.

Timur sacked Delhi in 1398 before he turned his army north and west to move against the Ottomans. His dominance of the region strengthened the influence of his capital and Persian architecture upon India. Meanwhile Islam had penetrated into the Himalayas where the **Great Mosque of Sirinager** (1398–1400) combines the timber architecture native to the region with the courtyard plan traditional to Islam. The original building, including the external walls, was probably entirely in timber. The arcades on all sides of the courtyard were virtually equal in depth, but the main prayer chamber was partially covered by a local form of dome, with a pitched pagoda-like roof.

In **The Great Mosque, Gulbarga** (1367), the entire prayer space, capable of holding 5000 worshippers, is roofed with small domes carried on pointed masonry arches. An outer aisle is spanned by pointed barrel vaults. A major dome before the mihrab occupies nine small bays, and there are smaller domes at the corners. The design was unique in India and seems attributable to Persian influence.

The Great Mosque, Cambay (1325), in Gujerat, on the western coast of India, established the important Indian tradition in which the prayer-chamber is a great triple-arched pavilion rising above, and set forward from, the surrounding arcading. Direct sea-borne contact with the rest of the Muslim world may account for the Arabian influences evident in the Gujerati style, particularly in the capital, Ahmadabad, which was founded in 1411. The **Mosque of Sayd Alam** at **Ahmadabad** (1412) repeats the Cambay design, while a decade later the Friday **Mosque of Ahmad Shah** (1423) has a three-bay portico leading into a triple-aisled structure in which the central aisle is higher, the whole reminiscent of a triumphal arch. This building established the influential form of a Gujerati prayer-hall.

In the **Atala Mosque, Jaunpur** (1408), the emphasis on the central arch of the prayer-chamber, developed in Gujerat and Gaur, was taken further. A massive arched portal, 23 m (76 ft) high, had twin tapering towers, between which a large iwan concealed the entrance to the main, domed prayer-chamber. The central emphasis may have been an attempt to combine the Tughluqid influence of Delhi in the west with the style developed in the east at Gaur. Evidence of the new adherence to orthodox Muslim forms can be seen in the **Friday Mosque** at **Mandu** (1440–54), the mountain capital founded by Alp Khan in 1398. The arcades around the courtyard were covered by small domes, and higher, stilted domes were used over the entrance porch which projects forward and over the prayer-hall before the mihrab. The remarkable **Fortifications of Mandu** also reflect Timurid precedents and influence. By the end of the fifteenth century, the Lodi dynasty had succeeded the Timurids, and left in Delhi an important but modest mosque known as the **Mothki Masjid** (1505). It has the triple-domed prayer-chamber which was to become the common arrangement for Indian mosques. Each dome has its own mihrab, and the central bay is emphasised only by modest enlargement of the dome. Although not free of local influence, the calligraphic friezes, muqarnas pendentives, glazed tiles and carved stucco are redolent of central Islam, and there was a return to the use of red sandstone with white marble inlay which had been used extensively for the finer buildings of the early fourteenth century.

If the creative heartland of Islam may be said to have been in Syria in the eighth and Mesopotamia from the ninth to the twelfth centuries it then moved to Asia Minor and Persia with the Seljuks and then south-central Asia with the Timurids. The influences of Egypt with Syria and Spain with Morocco were localised whereas the development of the Islamic style focused, after the Mongol period, on Persia and the Timurid Empire. Samarkand took the place of Abbasid Baghdad as the magnet and focus of development.

Despite horrific destruction at the hands of the Mongols, Mesopotamia recovered. An impressive survival is the **Khan Mirjan, Baghdad** (1357–60). The khan was a wakf supporting a madrassa whose minaret and portal still exist. The courtyard here is covered by giant brick arches and transverse vaults. It is a unique structure whose stepped transverse vaulting allows light to penetrate into the depths of the hall. The entrance areas and passageways are richly decorated with carved brickwork incised with a linear geometric pattern, and the balcony is carried on a powerful muqarnas which runs uniformly round the interior.

The increasing use of glazed ceramics to decorate the internal and external surfaces of buildings had been evident from the twelfth century, and in **Sanjar's Mausoleum, Merv** (1157–60), in western Asia (Turkestan), south-west of Samarkand, the surface of the dome was completely tiled.

An extraordinary palimpsest of the architectural styles of Central Asia survives in the burial ground, **Shah-i-Zindeh, Samarkand** (thirteenth to fifteenth centuries) (p. 608A). A cousin of the Prophet had been buried there on a low hilltop and a shrine at his tomb may have survived Genghis Khan's destruction in 1220. Restorations date from the late thirteenth and mid-fourteenth centuries. The area, which by that time had become a necropolis, was enhanced continuously by the internment of Timurid nobles from the late fourteenth to the mid-fifteenth centuries, at which point Sultan Ulughbeg built a gateway effectively sealing it off. The necropolis was crowded with tombs, of which over twenty major monuments survive with many variations of the contour and finish. Tall, ribbed domes on high drums, ceramic mosaic facings and the bold use of patterned brickwork – all find their place in this architectural proving ground. The typical dome on cube mausoleum has a shallow iwan as its portal. Turquoise, cobalt and green tilework predominates and in later buildings these colours are augmented with yellow and black.

In western Persia the **Tomb of Oljeitu, Sultaniyeh** (*c.* 1300–7) (p. 609), is the sole monumental remnant of a new town intended to be the Mongol capital. Its turquoise-tiled, pointed double dome stood over 50 m (165 ft) high on an octagonal base pierced with arcades. Painted, carved stucco enlivened the interior and eight minarets, surviving only as stumps, rose from the corners of the high brick octagon. Conservation and some restoration have halted the decay of this structure of prime importance in Seljuk building.

At the end of the fourteenth century, Timur embarked on a gigantic building operation, despoiling the territories of northern Islam to enrich his capital, Samarkand. He commissioned the immense **Bibi-Kanum Mosque, Samarkand** (1399–1404). Its internal courtyard was approximately 87 m × 63 m (285 ft × 205 ft) and the main portal is nearly 40 m (130 ft) in height. Multi-domed roofs carried by 480 columns surrounded the courtyard, and it was intended that there should be eight minarets. Ceramic-faced brick was used to provide panel upon panel of elaborate patterning, much of which survives and serves to guide present-day restorers. The building was unfinished when Timur died, to be buried in the tomb which dominates the funerary complex known as the **Gur-i-Amir, Samarkand** (1404) (p. 608B). The group includes a tomb, a madrassa and a caravanserai. An abnormally high drum is surmounted by a high-rising, bulbous dome said to have been rebuilt to satisfy an emperor with a passion for impressive height. The wall surfaces faced in ceramics and marbles and the vault itself in gold and blue patterned inlay are magical and complete. The exterior shorn of its upper structure is gaunt and awkwardly proportioned. Originally the dome rose from within a high and complex mass of lower structures, their parapets topped by crow-stepped merlons.

Timur's successors did not inherit his megalomaniac urge to build, but nevertheless their buildings were impressive and varied. In the early fifteenth century the **Observatory of Ulughbeg, Samarkand,** was constructed. Its circular arcaded structure contained a huge masonry sextant with supporting instruments and elaborate representations of celestial events. In the centre of the city, the **Madrassa of Ulughbeg** (1417–20) dominates the central square (the Registan) each iwan being framed in an impressive high arch. Slender minarets rise from each corner as though from buttresses.

A little earlier, the same patron built a smaller madrassa at **Bokhara,** and in both the conventional courtyard plan is amplified by cruciform corner chambers. Almost isolated in time is the college and tomb of Ayub, known as **Cheshme Ayub** (1380) because it contains an important water source. Its steepled mausoleum terminates an axial composition of domed compartments lighted by a central lantern.

A. Shah-i-Zindeh (thirteenth to fifteenth centuries). See p.607

B. Tomb of Gur-i-Amir, Samarkand (1404). See p.607

Tomb of Oljeitu, Sultaniyeh (*c.* 1300–7). The dome of the tomb is a double shell. See p.607

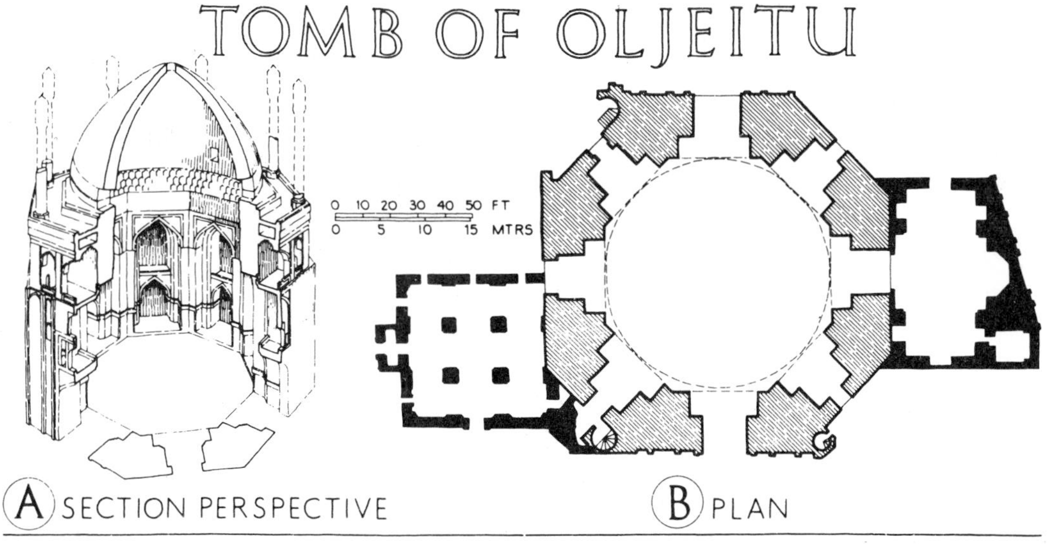

It is the only building of the Seljuk period in this area. Bokhara remains one of the most richly endowed cities of the Mongol period in Central Asia with the great Kalyan Mosque and Mir Arab Madrassa adjoining the earlier Kalyan minaret (q.v.), the present structures of both being of the early sixteenth century. Bokhara is rich too in other civic buildings, including baths and markets such as the sixteenth-century multi-cellular, **Taqi-Zargaran**, whose high central dome rises over a street crossing and the vaulted multi-angular **Taqi-Tilpak Furnshan**. Outside the city stands a complete entity, the **Char Bakr**, built between 1560 and 1566 with a college, tomb, mosque, library, baths, monastic group and residential complex on a palatial scale behind a monumental entrance. Its founder was Abd Allah Khan.

Khiva, a city containing the Ichen Kala (i.e. fortress within) was founded in the late sixteenth century on the models of Bokhara and Samarkand with the **Madrassas of Islam Khawaja** and **Sher Gaza Khan**, a great mosque with a minaret modelled on the Kalyan and the high-domed **Mausoleum of Pahlavan Mahmud**, with its baths and markets.

The fourteenth-century tomb of **Tugtabeg Khanum, Urgench** (*c.* 1330, possibly earlier), built for the Sufi dynasty, is essentially hexagonal, but modelled externally into a dodecagon with deeply inset muqarnas-headed framed openings in each face. Although the high conical steepled dome has lost much of its blue tilework externally the interior still contains some of the most remarkable geometrical tile mosaic of the period.

South of the Iranian desert, the **Friday Mosque, Yazd,** begun in 1375, was intermittently under construction until well into the fifteenth century. The earliest part is the mihrab and dome-chamber which lie behind a great iwan, facing a long arcaded court whose lateral entrances are placed close to the prayer-iwan. No other openings intrude upon the prayer-chamber which is high and sparsely decorated with carved brick plugs set into the face of the brickwork. There is a lofty entrance-portal and two extremely tall and slender minarets; the entire mosque is surfaced in ceramic mosaic with inset moulded terracotta.

When the political power of Samarkand waned, its place was taken by **Herat,** now in Afghanistan. Few buildings here have survived later depradations. The **Madrassa of Gawhar Shad** (1417–32), however, is one of them. A high drum carried a sharply haunched, pointed dome, now exposed more than was originally intended. Only one minaret remains. The decoration survives in substantial areas, and is distinguished by having white marble separations to the panels in sharp counterpoint to the deep blues and purples of the tiling. The internal muqarnas is elaborated into a complex interwoven ribbing with gored and radiating panels, and the wall surfaces themselves scintillate with networks of ceramic mosaic. The outer shell of the dome has rounded ceramic-faced ribs which terminate in muqarnas corbels much as in the tomb of Timur. Recent fighting has further damaged this building.

Among the later Timurid monuments the **Abu Nasr Parsa Shrine, Balkh** (*c.* 1461), a domed building of uncertain function, is of mature and powerful design. Paired minarets support the portal, which is framed by immense spiral colonnettes. Powerful rounded ribbing on the dome terminates in tiled muqarnas corbelling above the inscribed frieze on the drum.

Chapter 19

SAFAVID PERSIA, THE OTTOMAN EMPIRE AND MOGHUL INDIA

In the late sixteenth century the whole weight of Persian intellectual and artistic activity focused on the Safavid capital at Ispahan where a new town arose to the south of the mediaeval city. It centred on the famous **meydan,** one of the few formal external spaces of Islamic monarchs to survive in unaltered form. The meydan was created as a polo ground rather than as a place of gathering for the citizenry. The long axis terminates on the main street of the suq and, at the opposite end, on the portal of the Royal mosque. The entire new town was laid out with axial formality incorporating ranges of centralised gardens.

The pavilion known as the **Ali Kapu, Ispahan** (1598), overlooks the meydan and was superimposed on an earlier structure. Its high, pillared balcony conceals a complex eight-storeyed building with a high central hall. The carefully restored, incised and painted stucco ceilings and the shell muqarnas vaults represent a high peak of achievement in this peculiarly Persian detailing. Opposite the pavilion, the small **Mosque of Sheikh Lutfullah** (1601–17), its low dome covered in ceramic arabesques, lies behind the recessed tiled facade which is part of the double-height arcades of the meydan interrupted by its portal with a rich ceramic muqarnas. The original tile mosaic survives internally.

The new palace consists of a number of isolated pavilions within formally arranged gardens, one of which, the **Chehel Situn** (*c.* 1645), is a tall, airy building, penetrated by long pillared halls which catch the summer breeze. A wide and high verandah, carried on twenty slender columns, spans a pool cooling the surrounding sitting spaces in the gentle airs of summer.

The terminal feature of the meydan at Ispahan is the **Masjid-i-Shah** (1612–38) (p. 612A), the Royal Mosque, ingeniously adapted to the change in axis. Its portal is flanked by minarets 33 m (110 ft) high, forming a giant gateway preceded by a deep bay through which the visitor passes into cavernous low-domed chambers and emerges on the kibla axis. The tilework is predominantly blue, heightened with spiralling mouldings of turquoise. The large, pointed dome is set off by the coupled minarets astride the iwan.

The brilliance and richness of these royal foundations are echoed across both Iran and Iraq, but those in the most important sanctuaries can be extremely difficult of access even in periods of political ease. The buildings of the **Shrine of Imam Resa, Meshed** (ninth century onwards), include caravanserais, oratories, libraries, hostels, madrassas, mosques and many ancillary buildings. Mysticism and colour permeate the architecture, which is inventive and vital. Competition between the shrines produced local variations further west in Qum, Najaf, Kerbala, Kadhimain and Samarra. Despite local invention there is an important unity of character which became symbolic of the Shi'a persuasion and Persian taste. The **Shrine of Kadhimain, Baghdad** (ninth century, sixteenth century and later), has a double-domed mausoleum coupled with a low-domed prayer chamber dominated by twin minarets reminiscent of Safavid Persia.

It was the Safavids who also developed bridge structures which could be used in a remarkable combination of ways. The **Pul-i-Khaj, Ispahan** (*c.* 1650), for example, arcaded above and with a stepped terrace below, served as a bridge to carry traffic across the river, as a galleried arcade, as a dam and as a waterside promenade. An octagonal central pavilion was complemented by half-octagons at the ends of the bridge, and the whole structure was an intricate two-level combination of vaults, arcades, cut-waters and buttresses, with decorated spandrels and soffits. The earlier **Bridge of Allah Verdi Khan** (*c.* 1600) also at **Ispahan,** was similar in form.

A. Masjid-i-Shah, Ispahan (1612–38). See p.611

B. Madrassa Madar-i-Shah, Ispahan (1706–14). See p.613

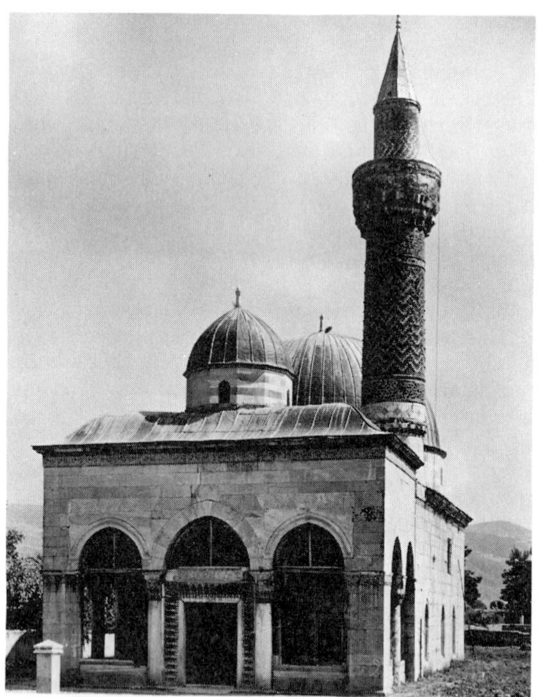

C. Yeshil Mosque, Iznik (1378–92). See p.613

D. Uch Sherefeli Mosque, Edirne (1438–47). See p.613

The **Madrassa Madar-i-Shah, Ispahan** (1706–14) (p. 612B), is a late example of the tradition of the four-iwan madrassa, combining the shapes of the high-pointed domes of Shah Abbas with deep, two-storey arcading around a broad garden crossed by axial canals – the classical paradise garden.

The Ottoman Period

From the thirteenth century the Turkish tribesmen pressing westwards across Asia Minor in the face of Byzantine resistance developed an architecture that took much from the milieu in which they settled. Within 200 years they developed a distinctive style which stabilised and has persisted into the modern era. The emerging style is seen shortly thereafter in the **Yeshil Mosque, Iznik** (1378–92) (p. 612C), typical of the simple mosques initially erected by the Ottomans on their Anatolian frontiers. The entrance porch rises to the full height of the body of the prayer chamber which is square in plan and domed. Green glazed bricks are used as a facing to the minaret, the surface of which is modelled to create a simple rhythmic pattern. Each structural element carries a single dome. Prototypical, robustly proportioned and demonstrating a sturdy independence from Byzantine influence the Yeshil mosque is the first Ottoman building whose architect is known, Haji-bin-Musa. Although the multi-domed prayer hall is rare in Ottoman building it is found in the **Ulu Mosque, Bursa** (1395–9). Twenty domes, ranged in four ranks of five, cover the great prayer space. Yet another form is to be found in the **Yeshil Mosque, Bursa** (1421), derived from the madrassa with opposed iwans, but here the courtyard has been covered by one large dome. A fountain under the central dome recalls the origins of the form and a marble-fretted balcony-rail divides off the south-western iwan as a separate prayer space. Mosques at Bursa of somewhat earlier dates but of a similar architectural character are those of **Murad** (1366), **Yilderim Beyazit** (1391), and at **Amasya, the Mosque of Beyazit Pasha** (1414–20).

It was in Europe, however, that a typical Ottoman style of architecture emerged. In their campaigns against the Byzantine empire, the Ottoman sultans moved into European Turkey. Before the fall of Constantinople they made their capital at Adrianopolis (now Edirne) in Thrace. The **Uch Sherefeli Mosque, Edirne** (1438–47) (p. 612D), is the first great building there in Ottoman style although retaining characteristics of the preceding Beylik period. Interlocking voussoirs of alternating colours, repetitive use of two-centred arches, stalactite capitals and doorheads, and the gently swelling lead-covered domes are all found here in precise and developed forms. There are four minarets, one of which is dominant, rising to 67 m (220 ft), far above its neighbours, and is graced with three balconies which give the mosque its name; it has the distinctive Ottoman pencil shape. The entire central space is spanned by a hexagonal dome 20 m (66 ft) high. The lateral extensions of the prayer-space are each covered by two domes.

Just before the fall of Istanbul, the Ottoman Sultan built a great fortress on the shores of the Bosphorus, **Rumeli Hisar, Istanbul** (1451–2). Like most other Ottoman fortifications, it consists simply of a giant crenellated outer wall buttressed by round towers, some of which are enlarged to serve as redoubts. There are three towers in Rumeli Hisar, linked by a curtain wall that straggles along the waterside and climbs to link the upper towers to the lower. Originally these towers had conical roofs such as that which still covers the earlier Genoese tower at Galata in the northern suburb of Constantinople.

The **Fatih Mosque, Istanbul** (1463–71), replacing the Apostoleion, was the first mosque built by the Conqueror, and was begun within ten years of the capture of Constantinople by Mehmed Fatih. It was replaced in turn by a building of different design after earthquake damage in the eighteenth century. The mosque was surrounded by a series of colleges and charitable institutions to form the largest group of civic buildings in early Ottoman architecture. The original structure is important because its domed prayer-space, buttressed by a half-dome over the mihrab, is an early Ottoman example of the structural arrangement of dome and half-dome which later was widely used by Turkish architects and stemmed from the great church of Hagia Sophia which had been converted to a mosque immediately after the conquest.

The unusual **Chinli Kiosk, Istanbul** (1472) (p. 614A), has a plan much influenced by Persian pavilions. The cruciform central space is surmounted by a low dome, and the chambers forming the arms of the cross terminate in tile-encrusted, colonnaded verandahs and balconies. The spaces between them complete the square, and provide self-contained suites of rooms. Its centralised form is later found in other royal pavilions and in many a waterside house or Yali on the Bosphorus, Marmara and Black Sea.

The elegant group of buildings (Kulliye) of **Beyazit II, Edirne** (1486-8), backs on to the river Tunca and consists of interlinked courtyards used for public and charitable purposes. The low grey domes of a medrese, a hospital, a kitchen to serve the poor, and a refectory are dominated by the dome and twin minarets of a mosque. The medrese, which was essentially a medical college, had space for eighteen students in the cells ranged round its courtyard, and the hospital has a cloistered arrangement of cells and a domed hexagonal building to house the living

A. Chinli Kiosk, Istanbul (1472). See p.613

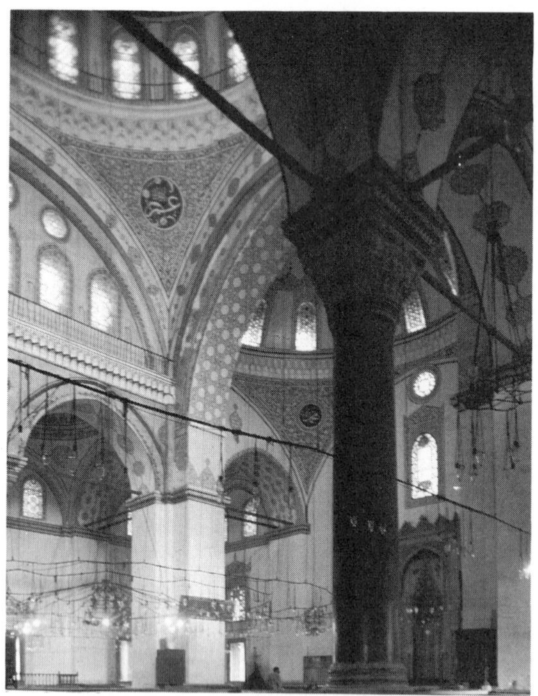

B. Mosque of Beyazit, Istanbul (1501–8). See p.616

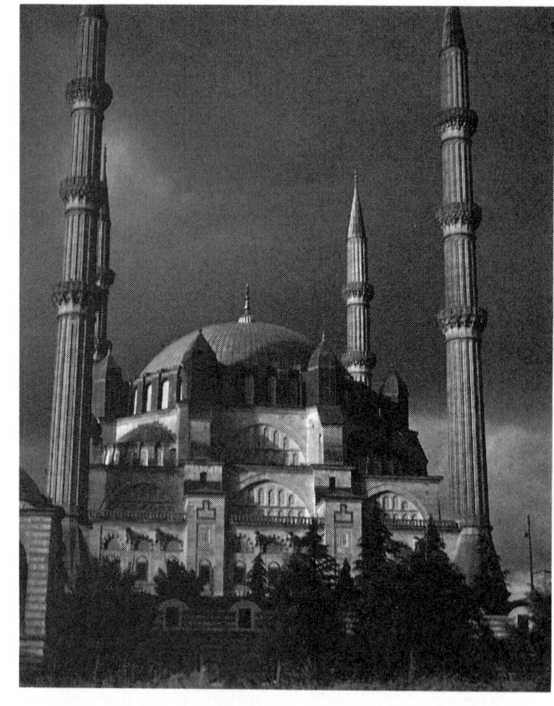

C. Selimiye Mosque, Edirne (1569–74). See p.617

A. Suleymaniye Mosque, Istanbul (1551–8). See p.616

B. Sokullu Mehmet Pasha Mosque (1560–5). See p.617

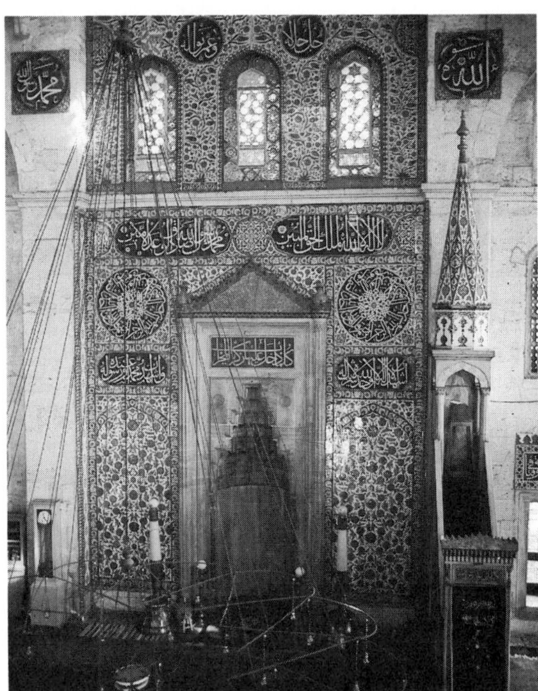

C. Sokullu Mehmet Pasha Mosque: interior

quarters. It is in this building, standing in Europe in lands taken from the Byzantine Empire that Ottoman architecture can first be seen in its mature and classical form.

The **Mosque of Beyazit, Istanbul** (1501–8) (p. 614B), is the earliest surviving imperial mosque of the capital. Four large piers carry the major dome, which is buttressed by two opposed half-domes on the long axis. The side aisles are roofed with secondary domes and are closely integrated with the main prayer-space. The ablutions-court has the normal domed arcade on all sides, but the latecomers' space in the front of the mosque itself is extended into two remarkable lateral wings which terminate in wide-spaced towers carrying tall and slender minarets. The wings may have been intended to provide reception rooms or lodgings.

The **Shezade Mosque, Istanbul** (1544–8), built for Sultan Suleyman the Magnificent by the architect, Sinan, exhibits to perfection the classical relationship between the component parts of the Ottoman mosque. A rectangular courtyard for ablutions, surrounded by a domed arcade and cloister, is complemented by a domed prayer-chamber from the western corners of which rise two slender uniquely ribbed and decorated minarets. Beyond the prayer-chamber, almost in the centre of a garden stands the **tomb of Prince Shezade**, the heir apparent to Sultan Suleyman. An octagonal tower, unusually faced with decorative stone inlay, is capped with a ribbed dome, which reflects central Asian traditions. The Shezade Mosque is noteworthy for the symmetry of the prayer-chamber, in which half-domes buttress the central dome on all four sides, while four subsidiary domes complete the square internal plan.

Like other imperial foundations, the **Suleymaniye Mosque, Istanbul** (1551–8) (pp. 615A, 618D,E), is the centre of a group of civic buildings. Around it stand baths, schools, colleges, a hospital, shops, library, public restaurants, cemeteries, and living quarters with houses for officers and holders of civic and religious posts. The whole series, designed by the architect Sinan, was built in less than a decade, including the initial construction of a large level platform for the mosque which now dominates the sloping site. In it Sinan reverted to the structural precedents of the nearby Beyazit mosque and the church of Haghia Sophia. The two minarets on the west face of the prayer chamber are supplemented by a further pair of lesser height at the extreme western end of the ablutions-courtyard. The Suleymaniye is a large building – its dome has a diameter of 26 m (85 ft) and a height of 52 m (170 ft) The lead-faced domes, softly contoured but of powerful shape, are terminated in outward-surging eaves which contrast markedly with the lean elegance of the minarets. Internally, the ceramic panels are sparse but perfect. White calligraphic inscriptions on blue grounds are surrounded by intricate borders, and the great, glowing windows of coloured glass are carried in grilles of carved stucco typical of Ottoman work.

Sultan Suleyman and his wife Roxelana are buried in modest octagonal domed mausolea whose internal surfaces are rich with dazzling displays of Iznik tilework: exuberant white stylised blossoms on a blue ground for the consort and rich but more sober carpets of patterning for the monarch. A uniform system of construction and decoration is applied to all the buildings in the complex rising to occasional crescendo in features such as the marble pool and fountains in the courtyard of the principal college.

A typical provincial group surrounds the **Sokullu Mehmet Pasha Mosque, Luleburgaz** (probably 1560–5) (p. 615B,C), laid out on an axial plan with a domed library at its axial termination at the south-eastern end and a cross-vaulted, covered bazaar on the north-west. The mosque itself is characteristic of the larger wayside groups of buldings, with a dome just over 12 m (39 ft) in diameter. Typically, the college and ablutions-courtyard are merged so that the cells of the students surround the court in front of the mosque.

A particularly fine balance is achieved in the **Tekke Mosque, Damascus** (*c.* 1560), commissioned by Sultan Suleyman himself. It stood on the caravan route to Mecca and was the place of assembly for the great northern caravan of the Haj. Having been used by a Dervish community it is known as a Tekke, and was sited in green meadows on the banks of the Barada river some distance outside the walls of the city. The cells and ancillary buildings are set around a central court with a pool instead of the usual tanked ablutions-fountain. Being an imperial foundation the mosque has two minarets and is built in masonry with courses in alternating colours. This was the 'ablaq' technique derived from Egypt and found rarely in Turkey. The caravan mosque at **Gebze** (1528–) is similarly finished.

Buildings such as reservoirs, warehouses, dams, quays, aqueducts and bridges were numerous in the burgeoning Ottoman Empire of the sixteenth century. Among them the elegantly arched **Bridge of Alpulu, Edirne,** survives, now isolated from the river it once spanned. Its central arch spans over 20 m (66 ft) and is 10 m (33 ft) in height. A series of lesser arches carry the highway in long ramps to ground level. The cut-waters are pierced with round-headed arches, and a corbelled balcony projects from the crest of the central arch. At **Buyuk Chekmeje** between Edirne and Istanbul a series of multiple-arched bridges carry the western arterial highway between islands across an estuary. They were completed by 1567.

Closer to Istanbul, the now part-submerged **Maglova Aqueduct** (1564) had a double range of arches rising elegantly to about 20 m (66 ft) and carrying a watercourse across a valley for nearly

300 m (1000 ft). It has the power and scale of a Roman aqueduct, which reputedly it replaces. It is only one of a series (some a great deal longer) which were served by a high barrage at Ayvad (1565), supplying water to the capital.

In improvements to the Sultan's palace, the **Topkapu Serai, Istanbul** (*c.* 1550), the architect Sinan rebuilt a great range of identical kitchens; each of the large square chambers carried a conical, lead-faced stone roof which is crowned by a central vent and cap. Another of Sinan's sumptuous contributions to the palace was the suite for Sultan Murad III, completed in 1578. Close to Haghia Sophia, the Sultan's consort endowed the **Hasseki Hurrem Baths, Istanbul** (1556), one of the finest of many public baths in the city, with four domes aligned on a single axis. Like the following four mosques it was designed by Sinan.

Among the many vizieral mosques of the capital, that of **Rustem Pasha, Istanbul** (1560), is notable for the wealth of its tilework. It stands with its dependencies in one of the busiest bazaar quarters of the city. Ingeniously, the mosque is built at first-floor level above the shops and warehouses, and its dome rises above the commercial buildings. Its internal proportions lose nothing by this elevation, for the dome is carried high over the prayer-chamber and the internal wall surfaces are richly sheathed in patterned tilework.

The **Mosque of Mihrimar, Topkapi, Istanbul** (*c.* 1562), is a secondary royal mosque, in which the single dome is carried directly onto the four outer walls of the prayer-chamber, each wall being a windowed infill beneath a giant masonry arch. The large number of windows produces an extraordinarily light interior, comparable with that achieved in the **Mosque** of the vizier **Zal Mahmut Pasha, Eyup, Istanbul** (*c.* 1580).

On a steeply sloping site near the Hippodrome, Sinan ingeniously resolved site constraints to build a **mosque and medrese for Suleyman's Grand Vizier,** Sokullu Mehmet Pasha (1570–4) (p. 615B,C). The building is approached axially under the oratory of the medrese by stairs rising into the courtyard. The domed ablutions fountain is placed centrally, the dome, with its slender minaret, rising in vertical perspective beyond. The building combines richness and restraint. The mihrab wall alone is sheathed in tiles in a lyrical arabesque pattern set off by the more simple treatment of the surrounding elements. The mosque contains some of the most handsome stained glass windows of the period outside the Suleymaniye.

The Ottomans' and the architect Sinan's greatest achievement is the **Selimiye Mosque, Edirne** (1569–74) (pp. 614C, 618F,G). It crowns a hilltop, standing supreme on its terrace. Two low medresess complete the compound and a large vaulted bazaar runs below it on one side. Eight massive piers carry the largest dome in the Ottoman Empire, 31 m (100 ft) in diameter, rising to a height of 42 m (138 ft), and the rectangular envelope thrown around it has, at each corner, a slender minaret over 82.9 m (275 ft) high and reducing to less than 4 m in diameter. The shafts of the minarets are boldly panelled and their balconies rise from elegant and complex muqarnas. The three balconies of each minaret are reached by separate stairs spiralling within each other. The mihrab is set within a separate rectangular bay roofed with its own half-dome.

The **Mosque of Sultan Ahmed, Istanbul** (1610–16) (p. 619A), has six multi-balconied minarets; its structural system resembles that of the Shezade Mosque (q.v.), in which four subsidiary half-domes buttress the central dome, and the roofing of the square prayer hall is completed by a dome in each corner. The four main unduly heavy piers are capped with minor domes, and the buttressing system which runs out from each pier cascades downward in a series of leaded roofs and domes. The external profile produces what is probably the most successful pyramidal composition of all the great Ottoman mosques.

The four-iwan madrassa was rejected for the typical Ottoman medrese which centres on a single prayer-room in a symmetrical cloistered courtyard of domed chambers. This form served other functions such as hospitals and is found from the works of Beyazit I to the great series of dependencies of the foundations of Suleyman I across the Empire.

In the eighteenth century the Ottoman Court was influenced by European taste to a greater extent than the courts of other Muslim powers. Contact with the Austro-Hungarian Empire and with Italy and Paris introduced Baroque classical ideas which melded with traditional forms into a true hybrid architecture. The **Nuru-osmaniye Mosque, Istanbul** (1748–55), stood behind a rounded ablutions court and the rounded plan was introduced into the mihrab bay. The detailing verges on the rococo but the giant arches carrying the prayer chamber retain the power and form of Sinan's Mihrimah Mosque (q.v.).

Other royal mosques in Istanbul continued the style. The **Laleli Mosque** (1759–64) followed almost immediately. Here the distortion of traditional plan forms is less overt. The robust rectilinear forms are fundamentally Ottoman and the elements of Baroque are restricted to the curvilinear classical detailing. At this point a bulbous top replaces the slender steeple on the minaret – a clear signal of the Ottoman Baroque which produced in 1825 the **Kuchuk Effendi Mosque** with a transverse elliptical plan, and in 1826 the **Nusretiye Complex,** where undulating eaves and waving string courses follow rounded plan forms in the lower structures through which rises strong rectilinear massing.

SULEYMANIYE: ISTANBUL

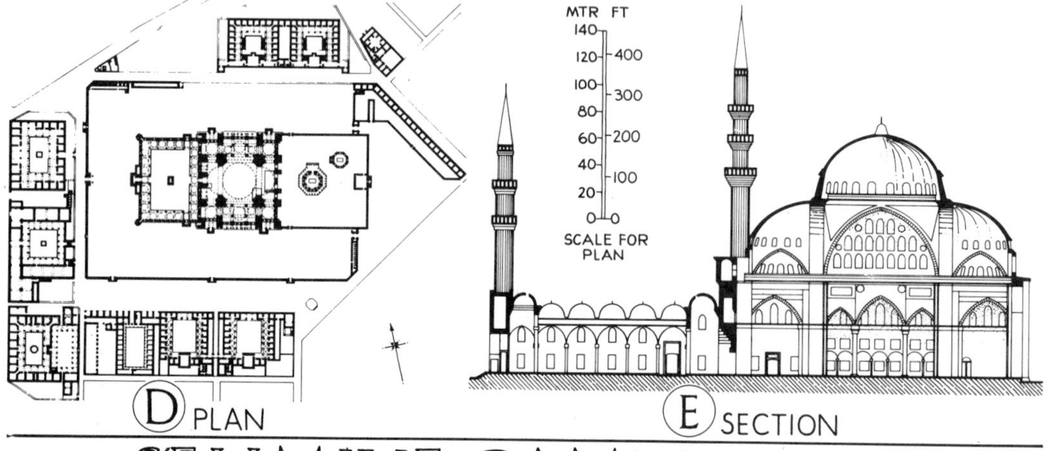

SELIMIYE CAMI: EDIRNE

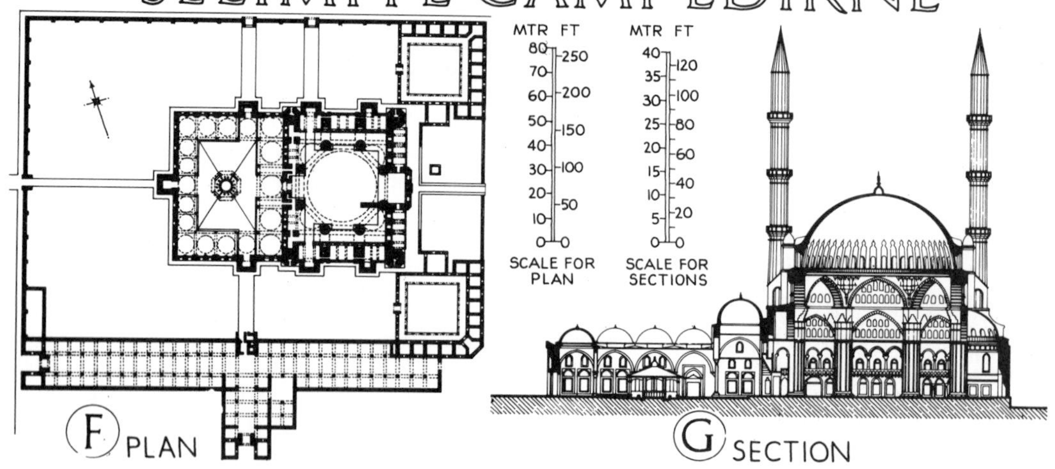

A. Mosque of Sultan Ahmed, Istanbul (1610–16). See p.617

B. Tomb of Humayun, Delhi (1556–66). See p.620

The Moghuls in India

In 1526, Babur Shah, a descendant of Timur, advanced through the Punjab, defeating Ibrahim, Sultan of Delhi, to open the way to the domination of the greater part of India by the Moghul dynasty. His son Humayun was the first of the line to build substantially, although most of his work has disappeared. It is to his usurper, Sultan Shershah, therefore, that the surviving works of this period are due. Shershah, of the Sur dynasty, seized the throne of Delhi and excluded Babur's family for fifteen years. Humayun himself took refuge in Persia. Shershah's first act on seizing power in 1540 was to refortify the old citadel, Puranakila, as the focus of a new capital. Part of the walls, two gates and a mosque are all that remain. **The Great Gate,** or **Bara Dawaza, Delhi** (*c.* 1542), is a robust, red sandstone building with inlays of white marble. The **Kila-i-Kuhna Masjid** (1544) is a crucial indicator of the genesis of the Moghul style. It was a private mosque, and therefore relatively small and without a minaret. Its multi-domed prayer-chamber, standing behind a simple entrance court, extends over five bays with a simple low dome in the centre. Each bay contains a shallow iwan.

To consolidate his domains, Shershah ordered the construction of forts around his territories. Near Jhelum in the Punjab, he built the **Fort of Rohtas** (*c.* 1545) whose twelve gateways are set in walls over 10 m (33 ft) thick. As in the capital, the gateway and its surrounding mass is conceived as a feature of the architecture. It is handsome in design and execution and large in scale. The most complete example, the Sohal gate, is some 22 m (73 ft) in height.

The most famous of the Sultan's works was completed by his son. The **Tomb of Shershah, Sasaram** (1540–5), stands on an island in an artificial lake. Originally it was richly coloured and still retains panels of tilework, although the areas of painted primary colours are no longer visible. The main body of the tomb and its surrounding arcades are complemented by a series of small pavilions. This is the first example of the complex fretted appearance given by the juxtaposition of tiny kiosks with the main mass, a characteristic of later Moghul architecture.

The great period of Moghul building, however, followed the accession of Akbar, son of Humayun. Indian craftsmen under Persian masters built the **Tomb of Humayun, Delhi** (1556–66) (p. 619B), set in a formal garden intersected by a grid of canals and paths and entered through monumental gateways on each axis. The tomb itself stands on a massive red sandstone podium and is powerfully arcaded with deep blind iwans. The sequence of arches is framed with an inlay of white marble which also outlines piers, spandrels and openings and forms a high frieze with a series of cartouches. From the podium rises the domed tomb itself, consisting of four octagonal towers containing a central space, above which rises a white, marble double-shelled dome with a more elongated external profile than its predecessors. It stands on a high drum and is reminiscent of the domes of Central Asia. With its great height, positive massing and delineation of the facade, the tomb did much to establish the early Moghul style. The mausoleum itself is set in gardens whose axes project those of the building into the landscape, and carry into grand effect the Persian ideal of a paradise garden.

Akbar the Great moved his capital southwards from Delhi, the city his father had lost and recovered. Early in his reign he began the task of rebuilding the **Red Fort, Agra** (1564–80) on the banks of the Jumna. Its enclosing wall of red sandstone, 20 m (66 ft) high on the river side and facing a 10 m (33 ft) moat, is over a mile long. Two sophisticated multiple gates provide access and, although palatial internally, it remains a fortress. The main buildings of the palace are set on the eastern flank overlooking the river Jumna. Polygonal towers are decorated with inlaid panels, string courses and domed pavilions, and are topped with massive and carefully aligned crenellations.

Akbar's Fort at Lahore carries panels of ceramic mosaic on its outer walls. At Delhi the sandstone walls of the **Red Fort** are inlaid with white marble. Within the Red Fort at Agra, the **Jehangir Mahal**, built by the emperor for his son, survives in good condition. The palace focuses upon a large court and its principal apartments, which include an exquisitely decorated library, are poised on the cliff-like river face.

The peak of Akbar's building activity was the creation of a new town, **Fatehpur Sikri** (1569–*c.* 1580). It has survived almost as built, having been deserted by the court as a result of the problems of supplying water to a large population on a hilltop site. It was built on an angular rocky peninsula that projected into the plain, which at that time was either swamp or lake. At the foot of the hill a substantial township flourished. The crest was irregularly laid out with the buildings of Akbar's city which, like its predecessors, was really a palace and cantonment coupled with a congregational mosque. It survives as a remarkable monument to Moghul architecture in a virtually unaltered state, and displays techniques of construction which may be described as 'stone joinery'. The new town had supplies of sandstone and marble which could be sawn into slabs, planks, beams and columns and jointed together dry or with a minimum of cement. Skilled labour was available to form every possible profile and to cut elaborate stone grilles as windows or screens. These techniques gave the builders the opportunity to produce stone structures of unparalleled lightness. The palace buildings are pavilions with wide-eaved lower storeys, and the upper floors are mere platforms carried on slender columns surmounted by further platforms and ultimately by domed roofs, also with wide eaves.

The **Panch Mahal** (p. 622A) rises through five airy storeys, each diminishing in size while the isolated **Diwan-i-Khas** (p. 622B) is a unique, cubic throne-room in which the first floor consists of an isolated central platform carried on a stone pier. Bridges on the diagonal axes connect the platform and a peripheral gallery which is reached by spiral stairs in the corner turrets. It is a unique architectural invention. Ornamental pools and courtyards are grouped informally to link guest houses, baths, guard's quarters, stables, treasuries, the harem, public and private reception rooms, and the mosque.

The **Great Mosque, Fatehpur Sikri** (1571–96) follows the regular Moghul plan with a central pavilion boasting triple domes. Its rectangular arcade is interrupted by entrances, a teaching chamber and, on the western side, the multi-columned prayer-hall. The tall central iwan masks the primary dome, and each secondary dome is carried on a masonry structure which cuts through the system of arcading. The courtyard of the mosque, measuring approximately 110 m × 130 m (360 ft × 430 ft), is surrounded by arcaded cloisters surmounted by a continuous frieze of chattris. The great iwan of the mosque is faced in white marble, leaving visible only narrow bands of the sandstone base. The formal axis is by the southern gate rebuilt by Akbar as a triumphal monument, known as the **Buland Darwaza** (1596) (p. 622C). It is very much higher than any other part of the mosque or any other building in the vicinity. Its giant iwan stands at the head of a monumental pyramid of steps, below which streets run steeply down to the town. An entrance iwan opens through half an octagon into a high rectangular hall which faces the courtyard of the mosque itself. Marble inlay transforms the exterior of the mosque into linear designs of red upon white, but internally red sandstone predominates.

The focal point of the composition, however, is a tomb which, in defiance of normal practice, stands within the courtyard itself. This exceptional position was given to Akbar's spiritual tutor, but the extraordinary building to be seen today was rebuilt by Akbar's grandson, Shah Jehan. In its present form, the **Tomb of Sheikh Salim Chisti** (*c.* 1580 and *c.* 1610) (pp. 623A, 625E,F) is refined in detail, square in plan, and surmounted by a simple dome. Its external walls are composed of pierced marble panels of the utmost delicacy, set between marble posts. The sepulchral chamber is surrounded by an ambulatory, entirely enclosed within the marble grille. Marble eaves are carried on unique serpentine brackets.

The decoration at Fatehpur Sikri is largely of Muslim origin but has become highly stylised. Wide eaves, fretted and carved balustrades and panelled walls predominate. Some buildings, such as the **Diwan-i-Am** (the hall of public audience) are severely simple, while in others, such as the **House of Rajah Burpal,** the **House of the Turkish Consort,** and the **Hall of Private Audience,** the stone surfaces are overlaid with bas-relief of great complexity and delicacy. In the mihrab chamber of the mosque the inlaid patterns executed in carved marble already suggest the ingenuity to be achieved a few years later in the tomb of the Emperor himself.

The **Tomb of Akbar the Great, Sikandra, Agra** (1604–12) (p. 623B,C), stands in a garden intersected by watercourses. The approach is through a monumental gateway crowned by four minarets, richly encrusted with floral and geometric inlays of marble and semi-precious stones. This is the elaborate, if conventional, prelude to a unique building for which the terraced pavilions of Fatehpur Sikri were a precedent. Four superimposed terraces in diminishing sequence form a flat-topped pyramid with an upper stage entirely in fretted marble. The lower stages are made of sandstone and the whole stands on a high, arcaded podium. A spectacular effect is gained by piling layer upon layer of stone pavilions on slender columns and crowning the whole with finely-worked chattris. The range of decorative techniques includes ceramic mosaic in addition to marble and stone inlay; within the tomb, bas-relief carving in stone and stucco is painted and inlaid with designs which are distinctly Persian. The highest terrace of white marble is open to the sky and is surrounded by a cloistered walk where every external panel consists of a delicate marble filigree.

The **Itimad ud-Daula, Agra** (1628), was erected by Akbar's son Jehangir. He built little but, having completed his father's tomb, commmissioned this mausoleum to the father of his consort in a garden on the banks of the river Jumna. The square plan with cruciform internal arrangements and minarets at each corner was a rehearsal for his own mausoleum. The tomb chamber rises from the centre of the building to a low dome with wide eaves.

The transition from red sandstone to white marble facings for monumental and court buildings came in the early seventeenth century, by which time the practice in inlaying in pietra dura (semi-precious stones) was so consistently and superbly used that the technique, while probably of European inspiration, came to be thought of as Moghul in origin. At **Bijapur** (1626–1660) **the congregational mosque** was the initial monument of an immense building campaign by the virtually independent Adil Shahi dynasty (p. 625G,H). It combined the domed and multi-columnar traditions in a powerful but restrained style. Its builder Ali Shah I was succeeded by ever more ambitious scions. The **Gol Gumbaz** (The Tomb of Sultan Muhammed Adil Shah, 1627–57) was one of the largest single-domed tombs ever built and was itself the focus of an immense urban complex.

A. Panch Mahal, Fatehpur Sikri. See p.621

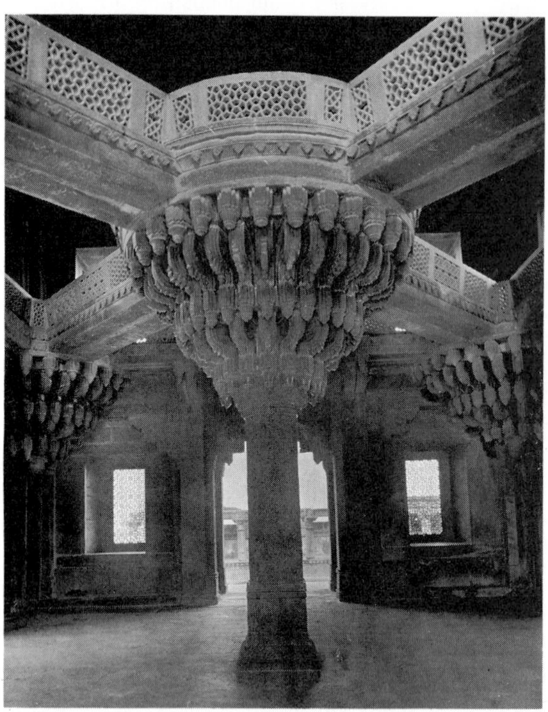

B. Diwan-i-Khas, Fatehpur Sikri. See p.621

C. Buland Darwaza, Fatehpur Sikri (1596). See p.621

A. Tomb of Salim Chisti, Fatehpur Sikri (*c.* 1580 and *c.* 1610). See p.621

B. Tomb of Akbar, Sikandra

C. Gateway to the tomb of Akbar, Sikandra (1604–12). See p.621

The **Tomb of Jehangir, Lahore** (1627–30) brings to the banks of the Ravi in the Punjab the concept of the paradise garden, secure within its walled compound and focusing upon a pavilion tomb. Here a wide, low, single-storey building is deemed sufficient for the mausoleum, and the minarets are placed at the corners of the tomb itself. The minaret had in fact played little part in the architecture of India and there had been no evolution of this feature comparable with Cairo, Istanbul and Ispahan. After the inception in the subcontinent Indian minarets were inconsistent and often clumsy, and it was only with the building of the mausolea of Akbar and Jehangir that a consistent evolution can be seen. Therefore the relatively slender, banded towers of Jehangir's tomb, capped with small domes on an octagon of columns, assume a greater significance than their simple appearance would otherwise suggest. The mausoleum itself was set in formal gardens with watercourses and axial paths, each vista closed by a gateway.

Humayun is said to have brought with him from Persia a love for the formal garden, which seems to have been adopted in receptive Indian minds. In the **Shalimar Gardens, Lahore** (1633–45), three separate terraces are each divided into quarters by watercourses. The long axis of the middle terrace is set transversely to the main axis of the entire garden, and emphasises the play upon geometry which runs through every aspect of the design. Pavilions stand at focal points and terminate the axes, marble walkways are carried across fountain-filled pools to stone islands, and the visual effects of intricate fretted marble are enhanced by reflection (see also Chapter 20).

The **Fort at Lahore** (sixteenth and seventeenth centuries) is a Moghul fortified enclosure built over earlier structures. On the upper terraces the Sultan Shah Jehan continuing his father's work created a series of reception pavilions and a throne room in the public section of the buildings, as well as a number of exquisite pavilions and courts in the private areas. A small triple-domed palace mosque in white marble graces one court, and in another the deep sweeping eaves of the Bengal roof, for which the fashion had penetrated thus far west, seem to rest on fretted marble screens which enclose space but allow light and breezes to pass through them. Part of the outer wall of the fort has panels of tile mosaic set into framed brickwork. White, yellow, orange, green, turquoise, deep blue and purple-black were the principal colours employed, and the work is to be found on such modest buildings as the **Tomb of the nurse to Shah Jehan** (*c.* 1640) and in almost undamaged richness on the contemporary mosques of the city.

The **Wazir Khan Mosque, Lahore** (completed 1634), is sumptuously coated in tile mosaic with geometric patterns, floral arabesques and calligraphy. The work is carefully articulated in relation to structural forms. There are four minarets of somewhat stumpy proportions, disposed near the extremities of the courtyard building. The entrance is through a domed vestibule which is preceded by a large iwan containing the portal. A covered bazaar, the revenues of which support the building runs transversely through the vestibule, and may have contributed significantly to its survival. Five domes of modest size cover the prayer-chamber, which opens through an arcade of five arches into the courtyard. There is much here which seems closer to Timurid Asia than to the Moghul India of Shah Jehan whose regime was described as a 'reign of marble'.

The **Red Fort and Palace, Delhi** (1639–48 and later), display the dazzling techniques and immense building energies of the empire under Shah Jehan. The palace within the fort occupies an area about 490 m × 980 m (1600 ft × 3200 ft), although the enceinte following the line of Akbar's canal is substantially greater. The two gates, each contained within a salient of the immense red sandstone walls, are high structures stiffened by tapering octagonal towers to form a barbican. At the lower level within the walls, vaulted bazaars lead into a reception square, from which the platform of the public reception areas may be reached. The throne hall, **Diwan-i-Am,** for public reception is centred on the main axis, and under its multiple arcades there is an ornate balcony on which the Emperor would appear. Higher formal terraces extend to the river wall of the fort, along which a marble channel carried water to each successive pavilion. The refined grace and delicacy of these achievements reached its peak in the **Rang Mahal,** where the water rises in a fountain into an inlaid marble lotus-basin. There is a continual interplay of cusped arches and lace-like pierced screens with wide eaves reflected in water, and domed chattris poised on slender columns. The effect was enhanced by bulbous dome, lotus-finials, inlaid pavings, and coffered ceilings with encrustations of semi-precious (and sometimes precious) stones.

The **Great Mosque (Jami Masjid), Delhi** (1644–58), also was built by the Emperor Shah Jehan, on the edge of the bazaar quarter, to serve the populace at large. In stands on a high podium approached by three pyramids of steps. Because of its height, the outer wall at courtyard level is nothing more than an open arcade from which it is possible to look out and down into the city. Two slender, multi-faceted minarets are set at the forward corners of the prayer-chamber, the main entrance of which is strongly emphasised by an iwan which virtually conceals the high bulbous central dome. The **Moti Masjid, Agra** (1646–54), was built in marble within the palace of the Red Fort. An elegant, triple-domed building, it faces on to a court 45 m (150 ft) square. The prayer-hall of the mosque is preceded by an arcade of cusped, pointed arches similar to those in the fort at Delhi. The three domes

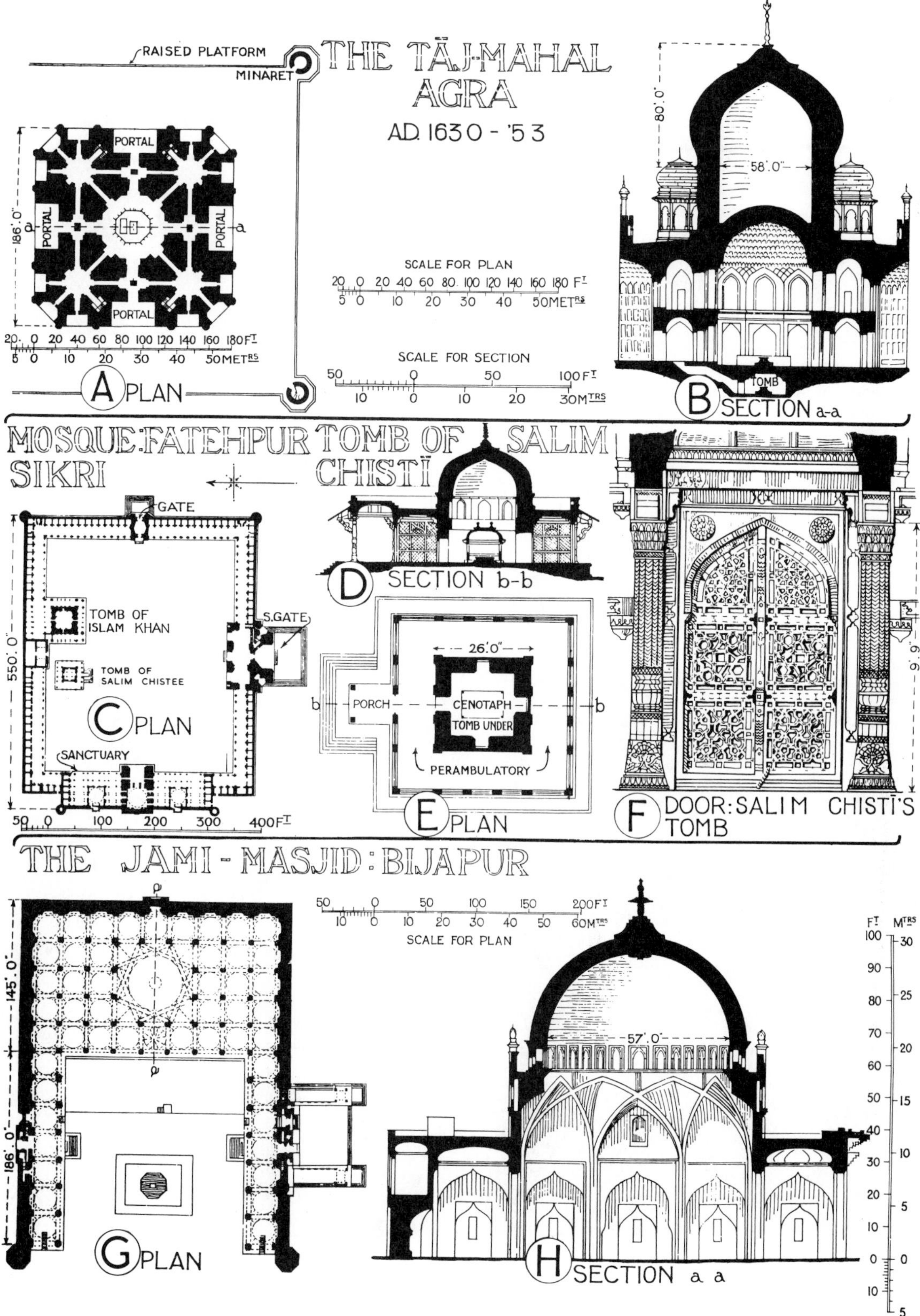
THE TĀJ-MAHAL AGRA
AD. 1630 - '53
RAISED PLATFORM
MINARET
PORTAL
186'.0"
SCALE FOR PLAN
SCALE FOR SECTION
A PLAN
80'.0"
58'.0"
TOMB
B SECTION a-a
MOSQUE: FATEHPUR SIKRI
GATE
TOMB OF ISLAM KHAN
S.GATE
TOMB OF SALIM CHISTEE
550'.0"
C PLAN
SANCTUARY
TOMB OF SALIM CHISTĪ
D SECTION b-b
26'.0"
PORCH
CENOTAPH
TOMB UNDER
PERAMBULATORY
E PLAN
9'.6"
F DOOR: SALIM CHISTĪ'S TOMB
THE JAMI - MASJID: BIJAPUR
145'.0"
186'.0"
SCALE FOR PLAN
G PLAN
57'.0"
H SECTION a a

A. Diwan-i-Am, Agra Fort (1628–58). See p.628

B. Taj Mahal, Agra: gateway. See p.628

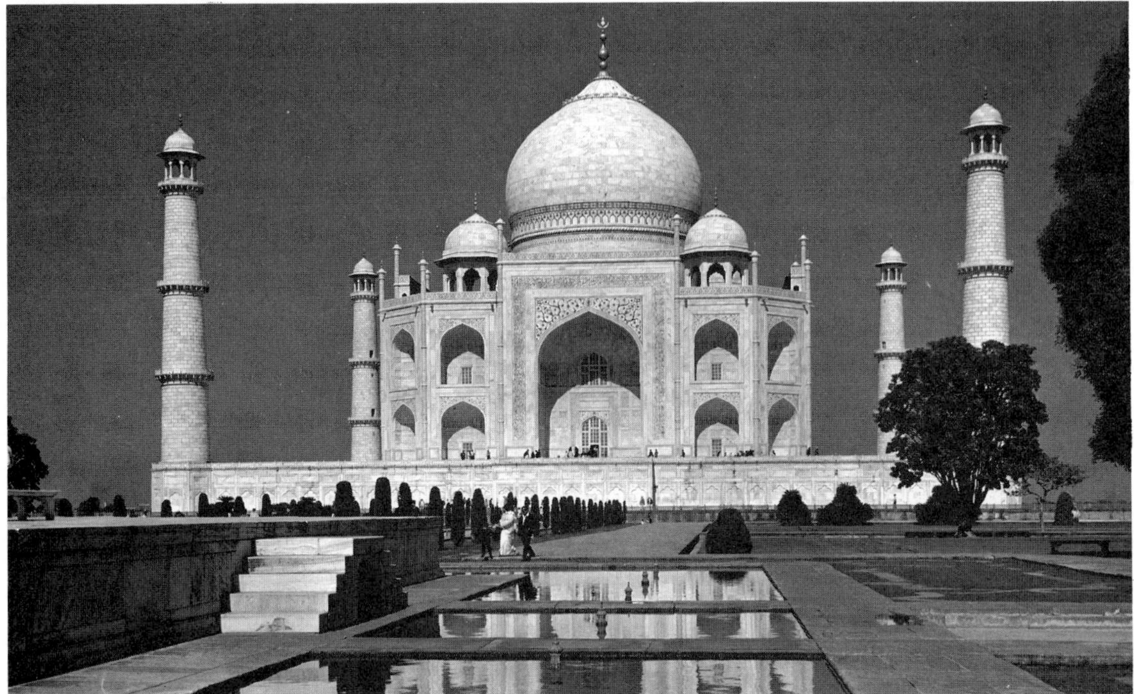

A. Taj Mahal, Agra (1630–53). See p.628

B. Taj Mahal, Agra: marble screens. See p.628

of the prayer-chamber have bulbous profiles, and a series of chattris enlivens the frontage to the court. Although finely finished, it is less exuberantly detailed than many of the Emperor's palatial works. The **Diwan-i-Am** (p. 626A), a multi-pillared audience-hall measuring 63 m × 23 m (210 ft × 77 ft), is stylistically similar, although it has no domes. Shah Jehan also added a masjid in the harem and a private audience hall known as the **Diwan-i-Khas** (1637).

The mausoleum **Taj Mahal, Agra** (1630–53) (pp. 625A,B, 626B, 627A), stands in a formally laid-out walled garden entered through a pavilion on the main axis. The tomb, raised on a terrace and first seen reflected in the central canal, is entirely sheathed in marble, but the mosque and counter-mosque on the transverse axis are built in red sandstone. The four minarets, set symmetrically about the tomb, are scaled down to heighten the effect of the dominant, slightly bulbous dome. The mosques, built only to balance the composition, are set sufficiently far away to do no more than frame the mausoleum. In essence, the whole riverside platform is a mosque courtyard with a tomb at its centre. The great entrance gate with its domed central chamber (p. 626B), set at the end of the long watercourse, would in any other setting be monumental in its own right.

The mausoleum is 57 m (190 ft) square in plan and the building reflects the scheme of the tomb of Humayun, but with proportions and massing brought to perfection. Four complex but basically octagonal towers are linked to carry a great dome spanning the void between them. Smaller domed pavilions cap each tower, and the circular tapering minarets are placed at the corners of the podium. The central inner dome is 24.5 m (81 ft) high and 17.7 m (58 ft) in diameter, but is surmounted by an outer shell nearly 61 m (200 ft) in height. Centrally under the dome, the cenotaphs are enclosed by marble screens of incredible elaboration and delicacy (p. 627B), inlaid with precious stones in controlled profusion. The interior of the building is dimly lit through pierced marble lattices and contains a virtuoso display of carved marble. Externally the building gains an ethereal quality from its marble facings, which respond with extraordinary subtlety to changing light and weather.

The **Badshai Mosque, Lahore** (finished 1674), is a very large congregational mosque, simple in concept and severe in detail. Like the Friday Mosque in Delhi, it is raised on a podium. The triple-domed prayer-hall stands forward into the courtyard. A massive entrance portal frames the view of the prayer-hall, over which rise three white, slightly bulbous marble-faced domes. The tall, multi-faceted, tapering minarets at the extreme western corners of the courtyard have replaced four earlier minarets which once stood at each corner. This building, erected by the Master of Ordnance to the Emperor Aurangzeb, has a powerful dignity and mature robustness which contrasts markedly with the effeminacy of the tiny mosque which the Emperor commissioned as a private oratory in the palace in the Red Fort at Delhi. This triple-domed and elegantly finished **Moti Masjid** (1659) displays exaggerated curvilinear detailing which preceded a long period of decline.

Chapter 20

VERNACULAR BUILDING AND THE PARADISE GARDEN

The complex urban groupings typical of Muslim vernacular building reflect the closely knit society and the climate of the regions in which they have evolved. These settlements typically have narrow and irregular streets bounded by high walls, behind which lie densely packed courtyard dwellings. Important commercial streets were roofed to form shopping arcades (bazaars or souks). Urban districts tended to focus upon the mosque, school and baths, around which enlarged courtyards accommodate workshops and markets.

In the mediaeval period there was no great difference in structure between the cities of Europe and those of the Islamic world, but while Europe was overtaken by the principles of Renaissance planning in the formation of public spaces and the presentation of external facades, no such philosophy permeated Islam. Show and pretention were not absent from the Muslim world but its philosophies of equality and humility subordinated them in the common man. The ruler's palace and the great man's tomb were exceptions reserved for those in authority not to be emulated by lesser members of society. With the stability of Muslim communities a conservatism emerged which contributed to the retention of established forms.

The agglomeration of tightly packed dwellings seen in the many isolated townships (Kasrs) such as **Amzruh** in the valley of Draa in southern Morocco is found in larger urban structures – **Tunis, Aleppo, Fez, Kadimain, Shiraz, Ispahan, Bokhara and Lahore** among them. The advantages of the tight-knit cohesion offered by close-packed courtyard houses were a combination of short walking distances particularly for the supply of clean water (usually carried), of maximisation of population within a defensible perimeter and the improved microclimate achieved by intercepting the sun's rays at roof level across the whole community. For these advantages the population was prepared to pay the price of living at high density. In consequence it had to create codes and rules to protect individual privacy. These could be complex and their effects may be seen in the conglomerate form of the fully developed city. In areas where it was common to sleep on the roof no house would be higher than its neighbour and the roofscape, therefore, took on a uniform upper profile. Privacy within the family was important. Consequently outer and inner parts of the house were reserved as public and private spaces, women often being restricted in their movements both within the house and within the community. Entrances to houses were placed on minor culs-de-sac and were not opposed. A group of houses on one such street would form a nodular community; perhaps a dozen such communities would focus on a local mosque. The mosque itself usually provided a school, baths and often the local water supply. Larger foundations, perhaps serving several smaller communities or even a whole town could provide lodgings, library, hospital, college and charitable kitchens in addition. Trade would congregate along the busier streets and these might be sometimes covered over to form closed bazaars which themselves would perhaps be grouped with the mosque and in many long-established communities the revenues of the commercial establishment would be returned to the mosque and its associated facilities through the medium of trusts known as wakf. Houses would abut each other, the city walls and the mosque itself so that the whole urban structure became one single coherent mass. The repair or replacement of any one unit would tend to be sequential, each renewal being isolated. Therefore, the city structure remained constant in plan. The courtyard house in particular provided immense opportunities for the creation of elaborate decorative spaces bright with gardens, fountains, tilework, mirrors, paint, plasterwork, timber-latticed screens and sophisticated joinery. Of the many examples conserved the wealthy **merchant's house of Haqiqi, Ispahan** (eighteenth century) may be cited as a formal upper-class example where the courtyard is a generous garden facing a principal iwan with two secondary iwans looking out across it. On the Gulf

A. Kasbah: Ait Ben Haddon, Morocco. See p.632

B. Shibam, southern Arabia. See p.632

A. 'Beehive' village near Aleppo, Syria. See p.632

B. Shalimar Gardens, Lahore (1633–45). See p.632

the shoreside meeting houses for the merchant families adapted the house form to the special function of business gatherings. One such, combining residential and business functions survives in the **Bayt al-Ghanim, Kuwait** (nineteenth century). It has a formal two-storeyed courtyard opening towards the beach with a secondary court behind. Distinctive architectural forms have emerged. including the fortress-like **kasbahs of Algeria and Morocco** (p. 630A), towered cities such as **Shibam in southern Arabia** (p. 630B), the cantilevered structures of the Balkans and Kashmir, and the domed villages of northern Syria (p.631A).

Of the many other types the towered structures of the Yemen express in their height the problems of compression and internal circulation found in cities such as Jeddha, Makka and coastal towns on the Red Sea. Here an important nineteenth-century port lies abandoned at **Suakin** where **Sherrifa Miriam's house** typifies the constricted three-storey dwelling. On a larger scale and more typical of the architecture of Arabia generally is the **Bayt al-Basha, Suakin,** with a courtyard on to which faced a verandah and private rooms while the formal accommodation opened off a small covered entrance court.

Even when it was possible to look outward the house typical of the Islamic world tended to contain its garden rather than be contained within it, reflecting the concept of the garden as a space made by man.

The Paradise Garden

The ideal of the enclosed garden isolated from outside, watered, planted, and controlled has long suffused the literature and arts of the Muslim world. Woven into rugs, painted on tiles and extolled by the poet, the idyll of the earthly paradise is as much a statement of place as is a room in a building. Its geometric formality and the peace of its enclosure detach it from the harsh reality of the outer world.

Out of the rubble and wreckage of the Palatine city of **Medinat al-Zahra** near **Cordoba**, Spain, the ancient gardens are being recovered. The city begun by Abd ar Rahman III in 936 was built on a site chosen without constraint where springs from the mountains flowed over esplanades and terraces as they fell to the plain. The whole formal composition of pavilions and canals flanked by greenery was secured within a compound wall creating a paradise. The city was despoiled by a Berber army in 1010.

Another great Iberian garden has had a longer life. The **castle of Granada** stands on a foreland jutting from a mountainside and long before the Nasrid dynasty created its exotic splendours the inhabitants of the castle disported themselves on the adjacent terraces where the soil was fertile and copious water flowed. The palace had its own gardens so the **Generalife** separated from the palace by a ravine, later bridged, was something of a country estate. Its formal garden focuses on a long watercourse on the principal terrace, terminating in a pavilion with immense views framing the palace below. Although its occupation has been continuous the Nasrid gardens have changed significantly under the impact of Western taste.

Literary references and the accounts of Moghul visitors make it clear that the formal garden of Persia had been developed well before the Safavid era and some of these gardens survive. Undoubtedly Safavid are the gardens of rectilinear layout forming the new city lying between the mediaeval Ispahan and the river. Common to all these gardens is the pattern of crossing axes defined by stone-bordered canals, terminating in pavilions.

In its maturity the Islamic garden adopted a tripartite arrangement with an upper terrace, a transverse intermediate terrace and a lower terrace forming a single elongated garden with a pavilion or principal building at its termination and perhaps at the centre. This design was carried into Moghul India and is to be seen in Lahore at the **Shalimar** (p. 631B). The reign of Jehangir saw the creation of gardens at **Verinag, Achabal, Nishat** and **Shalimar** in Kashmir where the rush of ample waters and the fertility of the verdant landscape set these gardens in a different context. But the pattern remained; parterres, terraces, stone canals and marble basins, waters flowing through pavilions, cascading into pools and fountains playing in serried ranks while control of vegetation and rich floral display were of the essence. The great ceremonial palaces in the forts at Agra, Delhi and Lahore and the great tombs were all embellished by similar paradise gardens made more deferential and controlled in the curtilages of great buildings. The garden of the **Taj Mahal** is a square sub-divided into quarters and quartered again with crossing double canals on the axes. Here the predominance of the gate and the great mausoleum itself remove any need for emphasis of the principal axis.

In more recent times the Persians have continued to create the formal enclosed paradise. At **Mahan** near Kerman the nineteenth-century **Qajar Shazdeh Gardens** are filled with the sounds of rushing water which tumbles and cascades down the central axis filtering into lateral gardens. The terraces are tree-filled. From the porticoed entrance the fountain-filled central canal lifts the eye beyond the terminal pavilion to snow-capped peaks from which the waters surge down through that most Persian of devices – the quanat, a tunnel driven into the water table of the hills.

Part Four

THE ARCHITECTURE OF THE PRE-COLONIAL CULTURES OUTSIDE EUROPE

Chapter 21
BACKGROUND

Introduction

Parts 1 and 2 have described the evolution of architecture in the Mediterranean basin (including Egypt and the Nile valley), the ancient Near East and Europe (including the emergent Russia) and Part 3 has covered the world of Islam. Architecture in these regions seems to have developed autonomously, by imposition in the wake of military subjection or as a result of the proselytising zeal of Christian or Muslim devotees. Here in Part 4 the architecture of the early non-European cultures is brought to a point of development similar to that at which European architects began to resort to deliberate revival of Roman and Greek models – the Renaissance – and related innovations in science and engineering encouraged them to carry these models abroad and establish them in new and often creative ways, first in trading ports and later in ever-expanding European settlements around the world.

The clearly discernible cross-cultural influences responsible for many unexpected architectural events are, of course, as evident in India, Sri Lanka, the countries of the Malaysian peninsula, China and Japan as in western Asia, Africa and Europe. Architecture evolved in ways similar to those described above except that Brahmanism, Hinduism, Jainism and Buddhism, Shintoism and other religions must be added to those of Egypt, the Near East and Europe. Buddhism spread throughout the Far East, South and South-east Asia, but lost ground eventually to Hinduism in the Indian peninsula itself, to which Islam came in force comparatively late. Perhaps only the Central and South American civilisations were free from contemporary external cultural influences until the advent of the Spanish in the early sixteenth century.

Extended Description

Africa

It was in Africa that the first tool-producing hominids appeared some 3 million years ago. Virtually all remains from this period are from East Africa where, at sites like Olduvai Gorge in northern Tanzania, tools and living floors have been found. Remains of early humans have also been discovered in the limestone caves of southern Africa. Throughout the Paleolithic and Mesolithic periods, Africans subsisted by hunting and gathering. Artificial shelters have been found from 50,000 years ago at Orangia, in the northern Cape Province, where six semicircular settings of stones defined huts 2–3 m (7–10 ft) across, all opening to the west. But for the most part habitation was in caves or rock shelters, even after the beginning of the transition to agriculture, along a line from West Africa to the Horn in the fourth millennium BC. North Africa was brought into the Mediterranean world around 3000 years later with the arrival of first the Phoenicians and then the Romans. From this point, its history diverges from that of sub-Saharan Africa.

There was no distinct Bronze or Copper Age: in most of Africa south of the Sahara, food-producing and iron-working took place together around 200 BC with the central Nigerian Nok culture. About the same time, the independent kingdoms of Meroe in ancient Nubia (*c.* 750 BC–AD 300) and Axum in Ethiopia (*c.* AD 200–600) were producing monumental architecture and tombs. In the seventh century, North Africa was incorporated into the Islamic world (see Part 3). Traders established routes across the Sahara to West Africa where small, urbanised kingdoms arose.

For its last thousand years, pre-colonial Africa was shaped by the development of long-distance trade. In West Africa this was accompanied by a proliferation of kingdoms and city-states, the most important of which were ancient Ghana (*c.* AD 1200–1300), Mali (*c.* 1300–1400) and Songhay (*c.* 1400–1600). By the sixteenth century, the focus of trans-Saharan trade had shifted eastwards to the Hausa states and Bornu, leaving a residue of small independent kingdoms in its wake. From about the tenth century Arab traders visited East Africa, building up a chain of coastal trading towns. From the thirteenth century southern Africa was dominated by the Shona kingdom, with Great Zimbabwe and its monumental drystone buildings at its centre. Christian Ethiopia (900–1400) was isolated but built churches inspired by its Axumite heritage, evidence of which remains in the form of carved stone stelae. The power vacuum in West Africa was filled in the eighteenth century by the kingdoms of the Yoruba and Ashanti.

The Americas

The early indigenous peoples of North and South America erected a wide variety of buildings ranging from casually built temporary shelters, and ingenious portable dwellings to large, permanent megastructures that housed whole communities. Impressive as many of these were, the transition from a craft-based vernacular tradition to one of conscious, symbolically conceived architecture occurred only in a few areas. In North America, a vigorous monumental architecture evolved in the region known as the Eastern Woodlands, which followed the great Mississippi and Missouri river basins from Florida to the Great Lakes and into southern Ontario, Canada. The zone which is richest in pre-colonial architecture and urbanism in the Americas, however, is that known as Mesoamerica; it comprises areas of the mainland running from north of present-day Mexico City through southern Mexico, the Yucatan, Guatemala and El Salvador, a second area in the northern part of Honduras, Nicaragua and Costa Rica, and a third major area in South America, located in modern Peru, Bolivia, and part of Ecuador.

China

House-building in China dates from the second millennium BC and the Xia dynasty. An architectural style based on wooden structures gradually took shape and was used to produce a number of building forms related to social needs. The style was capable of adaptation to various geological and climatic conditions as well as building functions. Historically the techniques had been widely applied in the construction of palaces, temples and other religious structures as well as residences and gardens. The early evolution of a unique Chinese style influenced the architecture of South and South-east Asian countries and, when better contacts were established with Europe, architecture generally.

As early as the first and second centuries AD, an integrated system of architecture was established and continued to develop under the influence of foreign cultures from the third to the fifth century. In the later years of the sixth century Chinese architecture entered a period of maturity during which high artistic levels were attained. Chapter 24 deals with these periods and through to the fourteenth century, when still greater diversity of building types was created with the application of the traditional wooden structure to houses and gardens. This period ended with the stagnation of Chinese architectural development in the nineteenth century and the introduction of Western architecture and building techniques.

Korea

It is necessary to have an appreciation of Korean architecture as a complement to the evolution of Japanese work in the earlier periods. This is dealt with separately under each heading, immediately prior to Japan.

Japan

Chapter 25 covers Japanese architecture from prehistoric times through to the early historical period and the beginning of Chinese influences introduced by way of Korea, to its decline in the ninth and its resurgence with the introduction of Zen Buddhism in the thirteenth century, and onward through the mediaeval vicissitudes of the shogunates and the conflicts of the pre-modern daimyo. The first Tokugawa shogun relocated the capital in Edo (Tokyo) in the early seventeenth century. The feudal period continued until the restoration of the emperor in 1867 and this is also included in Part 4.

South Asia: Afghanistan, Bangladesh, India, Nepal, Pakistan, Sri Lanka

The Indus civilisations (Harappa and Mohenjodaro) having been dealt with in Chapter 5, along with prehistoric Chinese cultures, Chapter 26 examines the enormously diverse range of religious architecture that evolved to serve the southward spread of Brahmanism, Buddhism and Hinduism following the decline of Vedic culture and the birth of Gautama. Here again, however, the continuity of development was interrupted and diverted but also enriched by the superimposition of Muslim ideals and the application of Islamic architecture in both religious and secular buildings.

Over so widespread a region, the introduction of European influences *per se* was limited to the north-west, where the might of Alexander the Great's early fourth-century BC incursions brought Graeco-Bactrian artefacts south-east across the Indus and ensured that Greek architectural and technological knowledge was put to the service of early Buddhism. Certain northern and north-western influences also entered in the thirteenth and fourteenth centuries with Timur's armies, but until the European colonial period began in the late fifteenth and early sixteenth centuries, the indigenous craftsmen produced their unique buildings from the Indus to Nepal and from the Ganges to Kerala, Anuradhapura and Polonnaruwa, continuing into the eighteenth and nineteenth centuries, even in the face of successive colonisations by the Portuguese, Dutch and British.

South-east Asia: Burma, Cambodia, Indonesia and Thailand

Early architectural history in this region is also closely related to the spread of Buddhism and Hinduism. As on the Indian subcontinent, few buildings other than those designed to serve these religions have survived from the long period from the last century in pre-Pagan Burma through to the second half of the nineteenth century in the same country and to the beginnings of the French protectorate in Cambodia (Indo-China) a little earlier. Indonesia, and especially Java, is a little more complex owing to Muslim influence and eventual political control in the fifteenth century, before the beginnings of early European colonial incursions.

Physical Characteristics

Africa

For much of its history, sub-Saharan Africa has been protected from contact with North Africa, the Near East and the Mediterranean world by the Sahara Desert, particularly after the desiccation of the Sahara shortly after 3000 BC. East Africa is dominated by a series of mountain ranges from the Ethiopian highlands in the north, through the Kenya highlands to the Drakensberg Mountains in the southern Cape. Small mountain ranges run along the southern fringe of the Sahara, piercing through the Sahel Corridor, a belt of savannah and tropical grasslands which, historically, has facilitated the east–west movement of peoples. To the south, around the Zaire basin, lies tropical rain forest, and yet further south is the equally inhospitable Kalahari Desert. Rainfall varies from over 4000 mm (13 ft) of rain annually in the rain forests to under 100 mm (4 in) per annum in the arid semi-desert regions. In the forest areas, temperatures are high but stable, while the semi-deserts and highlands suffer from extremes of temperature on a daily and annual basis. The great rivers are only nevigable over short distances. Even in the more humid of the sub-Saharan regions, the dense vegetation, poor soils and unpredictable rainfall have made settlement above the village level difficult. The extremes of humidity and rainfall, varying from a persistent drizzle in some areas to monsoon conditions in others, and of temperature, requiring shade by day and warmth at night, coupled to the perishable nature of many building materials, have imposed severe technical constraints on African architecture.

The Americas

The eastern United States has extensive river systems, large areas of deciduous forests (now greatly reduced), rolling hills and well-sheltered valleys. Climate throughout the area varies from humid subtropical or humid continental to relatively cold subarctic conditions in the northern third.

In Central America there are two distinct zones: the spring-like climates, with reliable rainfall, in the upland plateau of present-day Mexico City, the Oaxaca valley and the Guatemalan highlands, and the humid tropical lowlands of Yucatan and northern Guatemala, the central region of Mayan civilisation, where the brief dry season in April and May critically affects agricultural success. The raised pyramidal platform as a device to elevate living surfaces above the forest floor seems clearly understandable as a response to conditions of high humidity and vigorous plant growth in the lowland areas. Extensive paved surfaces were used not only for the staging of ceremonies but also as a run-off surface for the collection of rainwater. The paved platforms produced a microclimatic effect that reduced the humidity in and around buildings.

The Andean coastal regions experience the most striking climatic contrasts, changing very abruptly from extreme desert conditions to lush, well-watered river valleys. Low rainfall made adobe construction feasible throughout the coastal zone. The highlands of Peru, on the other hand, offer only complex mountainous terrain, the elevated grassland plateaux of which defy habitation. Only the upland valleys with their fertile and productive (though thin) soils were found suitable for settlements in ancient times as they are today.

China

China is 9.6 million km^2 (3.7 million square miles) in area. Thirty-three per cent of the country is covered by mountains, mainly in the west, including the Tibet-Qinghai Plateau which averages 4000 m (13,000 ft) above sea-level. Loess plateaux in the north-west give way to hills which cover the greater part of central southern China to coastal plains in the east. There are more than 5000 islands along the eastern and southern coasts, the largest of which are Taiwan and Hainan.

Numerous rivers run through China – more than 1500 of them with catchment areas of over 1000 km^2 (386 square miles). The Changjiang (Yangtze) River and Huanghe (Yellow) River basins are the largest and formed the cradle of China's ancient civilisation. The 1794 km (1114 miles) Grand Canal, built in the seventh century, connects the five major water systems, including the Changjiang and Huanghe rivers, and played a major role in the economic development of ancient China as well as directly affecting the location of ancient capitals.

The greater part of China has a monsoon climate. From September or October to March or April northerly winter monsoon winds from Siberia and the Mongolian Plateau cross China, becoming weaker as they move southward. As a result the weather in winter is cold and dry. Temperatures in China are 5°–18°C (9°–32°F) lower than in other countries which span the same latitudes. The south-east monsoon brings humid air from over the ocean between April and September, and weather in the central, eastern, south-eastern and south-western parts of China is hot and the precipitation high. The northernmost Heilongjiang province, on the other hand, is near-subarctic and has little summer, and in Tibet Qinghai mountain is perpetually covered with snow, while the Yunnan-Guizhou Plateau enjoys continuous springlike weather and Hainan Island semitropical summer all year long. The hinterland in the north-west has a typical continental climate, the influences of which can be seen in Chinese architecture. For instance, in the north, buildings are oriented southward to the sun; in the south they are designed for shade and to encourage natural air movement as is common in tropical monsoon climates.

Korea

Korea is a peninsula on the north-east seaboard of Asia between 33° and 43° north latitude and 124° and 132° east longitude. It borders Manchuria and the Soviet Union to the north along the Yalu and Tumen rivers, China to the west across the Yellow Sea, and Japan to the east and south across the East China Sea and Korea Straits.

Because of its geographical location, Korea has always been of great strategic importance. It had frequent cultural exchanges with China by both land and sea routes, and when routes were opened from Korea to the Tsushima and Kyushu regions of Japan they served as a cultural channel between China and Japan. Japan thus received Chinese culture by way of Korea.

About two-thirds of Korea is mountainous and mainly granitic. The southern region is alluvial and provides fertile lands for agriculture. The mountains are rugged and the rivers are clear. The climate is temperate, but tends towards continental characteristics. There are four distinct seasons, of which summer and winter are the longest, the former a monsoon-induced rainy season. There is a considerable difference in temperature between the seasons.

It is thought that the Korean peninsula was inhabited from the early Paleolithic period. Between 3000 and 2000 BC, the population began to build subterranean pit-dwellings and, later, dwellings made of logs and others with raised floors. 'Ondol' heating, a method of heating by means of flues under the floor, was developed.

Tribal states were formed from the first century BC, and by the end of the fourth century AD three kingdoms – Koguryo, Paekche and Shilla – existed in the Korean peninsula. Koguryo began to build Chinese-influenced palace buildings and accepted Buddhism, which had been introduced by way of China. An architecture was evolved which incorporated timber, granite and clay. Pagodas, stupas, Buddhist figures, grottoes and stelae were constructed in granite, and tombs of brick were used in an individual style.

Japan

Japan is composed of a chain of islands considerably further from the east coast of Asia than is Britain from the European mainland. At the extreme points Japan stretches in latitude from 45° north to 20° north and in longitude from 153° east to 123° east. The four main islands of Hokkaido, Honshu, Shikoku and Kyushu run from north-east to south-west in that order and innumerable tiny islands add variety to their coastlines. The much smaller southernmost Ryukyu islands include Okinawa. The Sea of Okhotsk is to the north-east, and then, moving counterclockwise, the Sea of Japan and the East China Sea and the Pacific Ocean. The Tsushima and Korea Straits between the Sea of Japan and the East China Sea form a relatively narrow channel with islands like stepping stones linking northern Kyushu and South Korea. Japan's total area of 378,000 km^2 (146,000 square miles) is about one twenty-fifth of the area of mainland United States.

The Japanese archipelago lies between the continental shelf that terminates the eastern edge of Asia proper and the oceanic crust of the Pacific Ocean. Geologically, Japan is divided latitudinally by the Itoigawa–Shizuoka fault into two major areas, north-east and south-west. Another great fault, the Median Tectonic Line, runs longitudinally through south-western Japan from the Ina mountains to Oita prefecture. Volcanic eruptions and moderate to severe seismic disturbances are common in Japan, and relate to the continuing crustal instability. The rugged mountainous terrain which accounts for over two-thirds of the land mass contains many deep gorges cut by swiftly flowing rivers. Narrow plains along the river bank accommodate rich paddies, and terraced hillsides nurture various other crops. There are a few broad plains such as those of the Kanto and Niigata regions.

Climatic conditions vary widely from the subarctic north to the subtropical south, but the largest area of the country is in the temperate zone. The islands are subject to strongly marked seasonal changes governed by cold air from the Asian continent in winter and warm air from the South Pacific in summer. In winter the high mountain ranges running north to south protect the Pacific side of Japan from the frigid cold and heavy snows of the western seaboard (Sea of Japan). The Black Current brings warmth to the Pacific coastal regions. Abundant rainfall combined with hot humid summers have produced lush vegetation, including vast quantities of excellent timber. The forms of traditional architecture suggest the conscious effort made to provide protection from the heavy rains and gale-force winds.

Indian Subcontinent

India and Pakistan together with Afghanistan, Nepal, Tibet, Bangladesh, Sri Lanka and the Maldives constitute the geographical area called the Indian subcontinent in this book. To the north the region is bounded by high mountains stretching from the Hindu Kush in the west, through the Pamir, Karakoram and the Himalayas to the mountains of Sichuan in China to the north-east. On the east, south and west it is bounded by the sea (the Arabian Sea to the west and the Bay of Bengal to the east). From the earliest times land communication was through the passes of the north-west and north-east, notably from Persia and western Asia (Graeco-Roman), via Afghanistan. Sea communication developed gradually, but by the first century AD there was a thriving maritime trade with the Roman Empire. The great rivers in the north, the Indus and the Ganges, and their tributaries provided water transport and many important cities were founded along them.

Climate and conditions vary from those of equatorial coral reefs to those of snow-capped mountain regions in the Himalayas. Much of the area lies south of the Tropic of Cancer, which crosses the Indian subcontinent between the Indus and Ganges deltas. In the coastal belt of the Bay of Bengal there is little variation of temperature between summer and winter, a heavy monsoon season (May to August) and moderate rainfall throughout the year; the climate is warm and humid, but not excessively hot. In most of the peninsula, the temperature is fairly equable throughout the year, but the distinctions between dry and wet seasons are more clearly marked. In the plains of the north temperatures rise high in the summer months (May to July) and drop markedly in the winter. The rainy season is generally late and is of shorter duration. The climate on the whole is dry but with a cool winter. In the north-west, the hot and cold seasons are of equal duration. In the hot season temperatures rise to about 50°C (120°F); the winter often brings night frost and sleet. Both high-angle sun over much of the area and intense and continuous rain in the monsoon regions have affected architectural forms.

From a historical point of view, it seems that major climatic changes have taken place in parts of south Asia. Excavations at Mohenjodaro have indicated that the Lower Indus Valley, now largely semidesert, once supported rich agricultural settlements of the kind associated with tropical jungles. This may explain, in part, the replacement of wood by stone as a building material in later periods.

South-east Asia

Burma, bounded on the north-west by the Indo-Pakistan subcontinent and in the south-east and east by China, Laos and Thailand, lies between latitudes 28° and 15° north, with a narrow tongue of land extending south to 10° north. Its early history (*c.* first century BC–first century AD) is confined to the river valleys of central Burma: those of the Irrawaddy, navigable for over 1450 km (900 miles), Salween, Sittang and Chindwin, which divide the hills in Upper Burma ranging from 150 m to nearly 2000 m (550 ft to 6000 ft) and form a delta in the south, opening into the Bay of Bengal and the Indian Ocean, whence Indian culture and Buddhism entered the country. There was also a land route from India to China which passed through Upper Burma and was certainly used by immigrants. The climate is tropical, with south-west monsoon rains in summer.

Cambodia covers the areas of the Mekong river delta and the China Sea to the south, and the midwestern Mekong region around the latitudes 10° to 15° north, bordering the Gulf of Siam in the west and separated on the east from the ancient Vietnam by the eastern Moi highlands, and, in the north, by the mountains of central Laos. The early history (Funanese period, third–seventh centuries AD) centred around the deltaic region, but subsequently the focus of events shifted further inland to the middle reaches of the Mekong, as far as Bassak and the Roi-Et highlands (during the Khmer period, seventh–fourteenth centuries). Both these episodes must have contributed to the development of the sophisticated hydraulic works constructed during the later years of the Khmer empire. The cooling rain and wind of the south-west monsoon provide the only relief from tropical humid conditions.

Thailand is bordered on the north and west by Burma, and on the north-east and east by Laos and Cambodia. It extends from latitude 20° north to the Malay Peninsula, some 1600 m (1000 miles) to the south, 5° north of the Equator. To the north there are hills in central Thailand, a vast alluvial plain which is flooded in the wet season (June to October). In the north-east is a basin-shaped sandstone plateau and in the south a peninsula, shared with Burma on the west side and Malaysia in the south. This is of the tropical monsoon type but, because it is further south, has less temperature variation between seasons than Burma.

The Malay peninsula is bounded by southern Thailand in the north, and on the west and south by the Straits of Malacca which separate it from Sumatra, which in turn is separated from Java on the south-east by the narrow Sunda Straits. Java is the first of a chain of islands, extending eastward – Bali, Lombok, Sumbawa, Flores, Sumba and Timor, whence a host of smaller islands leads almost to New Guinea. Another group of islands lies to the east of Sumatra and north of Java across the Java sea. The largest in this archipelago is Borneo, separated by the Straits of Macassar on the east from Celebes. To the north of Borneo and Celebes lie the Philippines. Much of this vast heterogeneous region is mountainous. A long curving band of active and extinct volcanoes passes through Sumatra, Java and Bali.

Indonesia bestrides the Equator, with a tropical climate and no great seasonal variation in temperature. The climate is also generally humid and under the influence of both monsoons.

History

Africa

The major forces shaping pre-colonial African societies were the impact of iron-working and trade contact with more advanced societies. Iron-working was established in Africa with the Phoenicians (*c.* 814 BC), and the ancient Egyptians were aware of techniques of iron-working, but it was not widely used until after Egypt was incorporated into the Assyrian empire in 662 BC, when it spread to the Sudan; there it became an important component of the Meroitic economy and gave the kingdom such economic and military advantages over its neighbours that it was able to sustain an affluent royal court, to sponsor towns and to commission monumental temples and funerary buildings. After about AD 200 Meroe's supremacy was challenged by the ceremonial centre at Axum, a major trading kingdom whose power derived from the control of trade between the Red Sea and the Nile valley. Iron-working spread across the savannah to the Nok culture and from there it was carried eastwards and southwards by Bantu-speaking people over the next seven centuries. As a result the Stone Age pygmies and bushmen were pushed into the more marginal rain forests and southern Africa. Outside those areas settled by Iron Age farmers, stone-tool technology continued right up to recent times. After about AD 500 metal-working in iron was supplemented by the use of precious metals, the most important of which was gold. Early iron-using communities lived in open villages of round huts with a population of twenty to thirty households. Villagers practised swidden cultivation, regularly revisiting the same sites.

From about AD 600 the long-distance trade in metals – particularly gold – brought about contacts between West Africa and the North African coast. The wealth derived from this trade resulted in the growth of state-like societies along the southern fringe of the Sahara and seems to have been responsible for cultural development in Senegal and the Gambia where, about AD 750, megalithic builders were active. Considerable craft specialisation and the concentration of wealth and power can be deduced from the size and contents of burial mounds. The kingdom of Ghana, in the upper Niger and Senegal river valleys, dated from around AD 500, and by 1000 was a powerful state with its capital at Kumbi. This ancient capital was divided into two areas: one surrounded the royal residence and was in local African style with round houses built of mud, the other was inhabited by Muslim traders and immigrants from the north, was stonebuilt and included mosques. This division reflected the deep economic, religious and social conflicts between the diverse cultural groups.

The succeeding centuries saw rapid urbanisation in West Africa, and the conversion of many primitive states to Islam. Mosques became common in West African cities. In the thirteenth century Mali rose to power through control of the gold trade, to be succeeded in the fifteenth century by Songhay. The power of the former eventually spread over much of sub-Saharan West Africa, with power and wealth concentrated in great cities like Timbuktu and Jenne. Songhay, a state based on the town of Gao on the River Niger, began to expand about 1340. It was intensely militaristic, extending into lands previously under the control of Mali until it too collapsed under the Berber invasions of 1591. By the sixteenth century the focus of long-distance trade had shifted eastwards to the Hausa states and Bornu. Over the next three centuries a chain of small kingdoms was built up along the line of the Sahel Corridor and interacted with Fulani and Shuwa Yoruba pastoralists. On the Nigerian coast, about 1700, the highly centralised Yoruba kingdom took over from its smaller, ceremonially organised neighbours as the major intermediary in the exchange of European goods for slaves. Finally the Ashanti empire, based on Kumasi, took control of trade between Africa and Europe, and this royal house maintained control locally through a system of paramount chiefs.

Between the eleventh and fifteenth centuries, Arab traders established trading townships along the coasts of East Africa. Gold mined in Zimbabwe was marketed through the Arab town at Kilwa in Tanzania. This trade with the Shona kingdom brought about some of the most imposing architecture of the Iron Age in Africa at, for example, Great Zimbabwe, where large numbers of artefacts from Persia, China and the Near East have been found. Trading was supplemented by a cattle-rearing economy, the latter an important factor in the tribal economies of southern Africa, where it gave rise to a variety of 'kraal' forms.

The Americas

The date of the first migrations to the Americas remains the subject of research and debate, but as early as *c.* 11,500 BC small groups of nomadic, big-game hunters had spread throughout both continents. In North America larger communities evolved based on a varied economy of hunting, fishing and collecting, and after *c.* 8000 BC they developed social structures and craft specialisations fundamental to building. The shift to agriculture, after *c.* 5000 BC, established a settled way of life that permitted a greater investment in permanent building, and by *c.* 2000 BC monumental, ceremonial architecture began to appear. For Mesoamerica, the history of cultural artefacts is usually divided into three major stages: the Pre-Classic, 2000 BC–AD 200; the Classic, AD 200–900; and the Post-Classic, AD 900–1500. The Classic period, in which the traditions of monumental architecture and urbanism reached maturity, is sub-divided into the Early Classic, AD 200–600, and the Late Classic – the period of the greatest Mayan developments from AD 600 to 900. Artefacts with Pre-Classic characteristics were widely distributed throughout Mesoamerica, but it is not clear whether this indicates political unification or cultural diffusion. During the Early Classic period, a major power-centre emerged at Teotihuacan in the Valley of Mexico and its influence was felt over the whole of Mesoamerica. Following the collapse of the Classic Maya cities, Mixtec and Toltec states emerged in the highlands of Mexico and these had fallen under Aztec dominance about a century before Europeans arrived to terminate pre-colonial history.

Agriculture started earlier, *c.* 8000 BC in South America. Monumental construction appeared as early as 3000 BC but settlements were small and widely separated. Cities developed after *c.* 200 BC in the Early Intermediate Period, and from these centres emerged the expansionist states of Tiahuanaco and Huari (*c.* AD 600–900), after which local kingdoms, such as the Chimu, flourished until 1476, when the Inca empire came to power, only to be cut off in its turn by the Spanish in 1532.

China

Tribes led by Emperor Huangdi (the half-legendary ancestor of the Chinese people) and Emperor Yandi are said to have inhabited the Huanghe River valley before the beginning of the historical period of Chinese history. Begun in the twenty-first century BC, slave society lasted in China through the dynasties of the Xia, Shang, Zhou and the Spring and Autumn periods. Written records date from the later years of the Shang dynasty (1600–1028 BC) and played an important role in the development of architecture.

Feudal society began in 457 BC and lasted to the end of the Qing dynasty in 1911. (See Chronological Tables in the Introduction.)

The first stage of the Chinese feudal period was between 475 BC and 220 AD. In 221 BC Emperor Qin Shi Huang unified the country and founded a centralised feudal empire for the first time in China's history. By the Han dynasty (206 BC–AD 220), China had become an unprecedentedly powerful nation which sent envoys to central Asia and opened up trade routes along the old silk road between China and Europe.

The second stage was between AD 220 and 581, when different local powers existed alongside each other in China. Central China was ravaged by war and in consequence its economy developed slowly. The founding of the Sui dynasty in 581 brought to an end the conflicts between the southern and northern regions.

During the third stage (581–907) Chinese feudal society reached its apogee, especially after the founding of the Tang dynasty in 618. Political rule became stable, and the economy and culture flourished as never before. As a powerful and influential nation China established diplomatic relations, conducted trade and made cultural exchanges with Persia, the eastern Roman Empire, Japan and Korea. In the later years of the Tang dynasty, however, China was again subject to internecine wars between rival regimes.

The fourth stage, approximately to the mediaeval period in Europe, lasted from 907 to 1368. The Song dynasty, founded 960, unified central China and areas south of the Changjiang River and was contemporary with the regimes of Liao, Jin, Western Xia and Yuan in northern China. China was finally unified by the Mongols, who founded the Yuan dynasty (1279–1368). In Song-ruled areas, production techniques were advanced, the economy developed rapidly and the urban economy, in particular, enjoyed a period of great prosperity. New maritime trade routes were opened up and a number of ports were built. Trade in hand-crafted goods flourished. Science and technology reached high levels of achievement. The compass, gunpowder and printing techniques, sometimes referred to as China's three greatest inventions, were introduced to Europe through central Asia, and made important contributions to development in the fields of navigation, warfare and the dissemination of knowledge among others. The oppressive Yuan dynasty was overthrown in 1368.

The founding of the Ming dynasty (1368–1644) marked the beginning of the fifth and final stage of Chinese feudal society. The decadent feudal system declined during this time and embryonic capitalism took shape in China. After 1840 China was reduced to a semi-colonial and semi-feudal society with the incursions of imperialist powers. In 1911, the Qing dynasty was overthrown.

The small-scale peasant economy occupied an extremely important place throughout feudal society and was conducive to the development of timber construction. Small houses were self-sufficient in materials, and much less manpower was needed than in stone. As a result, this kind of building became traditional and remained in use for a very long time. On the other hand, centralised feudal power enabled the state to mobilise manpower and building materials on a nationwide scale and to engage in large-scale construction projects. One example is the Great Wall, but there were also many palaces and other major buildings in capital cities which had to be rebuilt after sacking by the new rulers. Examples of this were Xianyang, capital of the Qin dynasty, Daxing, capital of the Sui dynasty, and Dadu, capital of the Yuan dynasty. The so-called 'block system' adopted in feudal capitals embodied the feudal rulers' thinking on centralised control. That used in Daxing, capital of the Sui dynasty (its name was changed to Chang'an in the Tang dynasty), was typical; walls were built around each site on blocks along the edges of the streets. After curfew the populace had to retreat behind the walls or risk being arrested by soldiers on patrol. Professional officials appointed by the government were assigned to take charge of design and engineering work. Workshops for construction crafts were set up, and to guarantee the quality of construction and facilitate the management of the workshops the officials laid down norms of quantity and quotas for the consumption of building materials. *Yingzaofashi (The Method of Architecture)*, compiled by Engineering Supervisor Li Jie for the Song dynasty, and *Gong Cheng Zuo Fa (Convention of Engineering Construction)*, compiled by Qing engineering and construction officials, were typical works of their kind which arose from this system of control. The official development of building trades promoted standardisation of the forms of Chinese architecture.

Korea

Traditionally, Korea was founded by Kija, the leader of a group of refugees from China towards the end of the twelfth century BC. He called it Choson, and his descendants are said to have exercised a beneficent authority in Korea for a thousand years thereafter. Towards the end of this period, tradition has it that, in preference to subjugation by China, the state was incorporated into the Han empire as a colony known as Nangnang. In the first three centuries or so of the Christian era, Nangnang achieved a culture of great sophistication, unrivalled even by the most splendid achievements elsewhere in the Han empire. It succumbed in the fourth century to invaders from the north who, in time, consolidated in the same area the kingdom known as Koguryo.

In the south-east of the peninsula at an earlier date the kingdom of Shilla was formed and in the west the kingdom of Paekche. Thus began the Three Kingdoms Period which lasted until 668 when, with the rise of the Tang dynasty, the country south of the Taedon River was unified by the Shilla, and held subject to an unexacting Chinese suzerainty. Tang culture flourished, but in the early tenth century a decadent Shilla was overthrown by a rebel general and a new kingdom, Koryo, was set up.

Buddhism had been brought to Korea by Indian monks in 384. It was in the ascendancy in Korea by the tenth century, and as Chinese political and cultural influence waned, the Buddhist priesthood grew in power and influence. Internal conflicts between Buddhism, Confucianism and the militaristic nobles, as well as the introduction of slavery on a massive scale, left the kingdom of Koryo with little ability to resist the cycles of foreign invasion which ensued in the first half of the thirteenth century, and by 1260 it was reduced to the status of a Mongol province. Kublai Khan enforced the alliance later in the century in support of his abortive expeditions against Japan, and this, together with continuous Japanese raiding along the coasts, eventually brought to an end the insecure kingdom of Koryo when Yi Song-gye defeated both Mongols and Japanese and in 1392 declared himself ruler of a new kingdom, Choson, with its capital at Hanyany (modern Seoul).

The fifteenth and sixteenth centuries, immediately following those events, are regarded as Korea's golden age, which coincided with the introduction of a native (Ming) dynasty in China and a benevolent overlordship that encouraged cultural and artistic developments. They ended with the invasion of the Japanese under Hideyoshi in 1592 and many years of incursion by Manchu tribes from the north. Two hundred years of complete isolation from external contacts followed.

Japan

Although recent excavations have produced definite proof that the Japanese islands were inhabited between 30,000 and 20,000 BC, findings suggest it was only from 10,000 to 300 BC (Jomon period) that a hunting–gathering people populated large areas of the islands. Communal centres, where numerous sites of pit-dwellings have been unearthed, contain extensive middens but no evidence of an agrarian society.

Migrants of Mongoloid stock between 400 and 300 BC brought wet rice culture, iron and bronze with them and settled down in communities with pit dwellings and raised-floor storehouses. The most famous site is at Toro (Shizuoko prefecture) where superstructures have been restored as shown in the low reliefs of four buildings which decorate the reverse side of a bronze mirror, in an engraving on a bronze bell, and in an incised drawing on a pottery sherd. The advent of the Mongoloids began a new era called the Yayoi period (300 BC–AD 300).

The period between AD 300 and 538/552 is a protohistorical age during which contacts with the Asian mainland increased and society became more rigidly structured. Both the *Kojiki* (712) and *Nihon-shoki* (720) record events of this time, but their contents were strongly influenced by an effort to emulate Chinese dynastic histories, and therefore must be viewed to a great extent as more legendary than factual. The myth that the emperor descended from the Sun Goddess gave credence to his divinity and underlies the fact that he was never deposed. Legend revolves around three principal areas of Japan: Izumo, northern Kyushu and Yamato (Nara Area). The last became the centre of Japanese development in the early historical periods. Society was theocratic and founded on worship of the Sun Goddess and innumerable lesser deities, with the emperor as chief priest.

When emperors died, they were deified and elaborate tombs were built to house their remains. It is because of these tombs that the historical era is also called the Tumulus (Kofun) period. Clay models of buildings in a variety of styles found in these tombs tell us much about the architecture of the period; the large group of models unearthed at the Chausuyama, Akabori site in Gumma prefecture even allow some speculation regarding building techniques and uses.

The historical period began with the introduction of Buddhism from Korea in the mid-sixth century. With it came the Chinese language, a bureaucratic form of government and new methods and styles of building. The new religion, though first strongly resisted by the conservative supporters of the indigenous Shinto religion, soon became firmly established. Buildings were needed for housing images, chanting sutras and accommodating the ever-increasing numbers of priests and nuns, and totally new structural techniques had to be acquired to meet the demands.

In spite of the ardent support of Buddhism by the Prince Regent, Shotoku, and his prodigious effort to raise the level of Japanese civilisation, civil strife was rampant after his demise in 622 and Japan was not strongly unified. In 645, the Taika reforms, based on the Chinese system of government, included a proposal to establish a permanent capital. Although there had been many previous 'capitals', according to Shinto belief, they were defiled by the death of the emperor, thus requiring a new capital to be established at a different site. As a result, royal residences and official edifices were not constructed with permanence in mind.

It was not until 710 that the court moved to Heijo (Nara) where the new capital was laid out on a grid plan based on the capital of the Tang dynasty at Chang-an. It included an imperial palace and seven great temples. Although Chinese influence reached its height in the eighth century, the Japanese had made astonishing progress in every facet of culture and achieved such perfection in building that this century is often considered to be the classical age of Japanese architecture. Nevertheless, economic presures, Ainu uprisings, an unsuccessful expedition against Korea and the excessive power of the Buddhist priests led to the capital at Heijo being abandoned and a move to Nagaoka near Kyoto in 784. One misfortune followed another, and in 794 the capital was again moved, this time to the Heian capital, Kyoto.

After the beginning of the Heian period (794–1185) contacts with China decreased until they ceased altogether. A new era of Japanisation began. It was characterised by concentrated efforts to assimilate the knowledge and skills acquired during the previous two and a half centuries. The Japanese became selective, integrating only those elements of Chinese culture which they found useful and to their taste. The earlier bureaucratic form of government was replaced by an aristocratic regency held by the Fujiwara family which supplied the empresses to the throne. The early retirement of emperors to specially appointed temples became common, thus ensuring the continuance of the political power of the Fujiwaras behind the throne. The Heian period was – at least in Kyoto – an aristocratic age when emphemeral beauty and aesthetic inspiration took precedence over all else. The shinden-style palaces of the nobility, although no longer extant, can be reconstructed to some extent from contemporary paintings and from descriptive passages in the astonishing literature of the age. But the world of the vast majority of the population – the common people – was remote from that of the aristocracy and representations of genre scenes are limited to a few picture-scrolls of the late twelfth and thirteenth centuries. These illustrate street scenes with the humblest type of dwellings.

In the ninth century two new sects of Buddhism, Shingon and Tendai, were brought from China by Japanese priests. These esoteric types of Buddhism required additional buildings for special rites. The rugged terrain of the remote mountain sites preferred by these sects necessitated radical changes in the arrangement of structures within the temple compounds. During this period a certain amalgamation between Buddhism and Shinto occurred. It is not uncommon to find a small shrine attached to a temple, or Shinto buildings which closely resemble the style of those associated with Buddhism.

While the aristocracy in Kyoto was absorbed in the cult of beauty and the arts, provincial lands to which they held title were left in the hands of executors who, in many cases, were distant relations who were hardened by frontier life and by skirmishes with the marauding Ainu or by battles with rival families. At the same time, Buddhist monks accrued enough power to force the elite in Kyoto to meet their demands.

By the end of the twelfth century, the provincial warrior Minamoto-no-Yoritomo, who had seized power from Taira-no-Kiyomori in Kyoto, set up a military government in Kamakura (1185–1333), far from the debilitating influences in Kyoto, and forced the emperor to confer the title of shogun upon him. Thus began the feudal age of the samurai with its code of Bushido, 'the way of the warrior'. A second wave of Chinese influence introduced Zen Buddhism, new styles of architecture, and tea, the last to be used as the centre of ritual in the tea ceremony for which a uniquely Japanese building in the sukiya style was evolved.

The long feudal age, lasting until 1868, can be divided into the mediaeval (1185–1568) and premodern (1568–1868) eras. As a result of successive civil wars, successive powerful families obtained the shogunate. While the dominion of the Minamoto and Hojo (Kamakura period) and the Ashikaga shogunates (Muromachi period) prevailed, the daimyo (lords) of outlying provinces exercised considerable control over their own domains.

In 1392, the Ashikaga shoguns returned the political capital to Kyoto where they became renowned as patrons of architecture, the arts and the entire Zen establishment. Intercourse between Japan and China was expanded, and Chinese influence is clearly aparent in every facet of the Ashikaga cultural renaissance. However, deep preoccupation with the arts diverted attention from political prerequisites indispensable for maintaining a strong central government. Kyoto was finally devastated by internecine war, and the landed daimyo became virtually independent.

The gradual waning of the centralised power of the Ashikaga shogunate came to an end in Kyoto with the Onin civil war (1467–77) caused by the rivalry between two noble families closely related to the house of Ashikaga. The shogunate was so weakened that it could not control the rival factions or prevent the war, which decimated the population of Kyoto and caused the destruction of innumerable age-old monuments. With the end of the Onin war in 1477 began Japan's 'Hundred Years' War' in which warfare among the daimyo was endemic. It was a century of feudalism without any central authority. Even the old imperial system which had maintained some administrative jurisdiction over outlying regions became defunct.

Authority rested entirely with each daimyo and was exercised over those within his domains. It might be expected that such turbulent conditions would militate against economic growth. On the contrary, however, the daimyo in each feudal domain encouraged the development of agriculture and the fashioning of goods for daily use by the villagers. Eventually, production exceeded local demand and this resulted in the creation of new markets where surplus commodities could be exchanged or sold. New centres were initiated in ports like Osaka (Sakai) and Hakata and gave rise to a merchant class which grew wealthy by acquisition of merchandise rather than land. By the middle of the sixteenth century Japanese goods were being exported in Japanese ships, and it was at this time that the Japanese made their first contacts with Europeans, when Portuguese ships reached southern Kyushu. Christian missionaries who had already established themselves on the Asian mainland followed in the wake of the traders. The Japanese displayed their characteristic interest in new things and quickly recognised the advantages and profit to be gained in trading with them.

The century since the end of the Onin war, with its paradoxes of continual strife and rapid economic growth, finally came to an end around 1568/76 and brought to an end the mediaeval era.

Even the briefest résumé of Japanese history cannot omit the names of three outstanding rulers: Oda Nobunaga (1534–82), who laid the groundwork for better control of the daimyo by the shogunate; Toyotomi Hideyoshi (1536–98), who rose to power from the peasantry, brought the age of civil wars to an end and patronised architecture and the arts; Tokugawa Ieyasu (1542–1616), who, although supportive of Hideyoshi while he lived, quickly fought a decisive battle against the daimyo remaining loyal to Hideyoshi after his death in 1598. By 1616, Osaka Castle was destroyed and with it Hideyoshi's son and heir. Ieyasu became the first Tokugawa shogun and established Edo (Tokyo) as the political capital.

A man of genius, Ieyasu laid plans for total control over his subject lords. He established a hierarchial stratification of society, then composed of noblemen and their retainers, peasants, artisans and merchants, and governed by rigid codes of personal behaviour, dress and dwelling-type. Strict laws were enacted prohibiting the building of new castles, and funds for repairs to old ones were very scarce. Each provincial lord was required to maintain an Edo domicile, where his family remained as virtual hostages when he himself, followed by an elaborate retinue of attendants, returned to oversee his rural domains. This system secured the Tokugawa hegemony until the Meiji Restoration in 1868.

By 1638 Japan was closed to foreign intercourse and Christianity was eliminated for fear that a European invasion was imminent. Only the Dutch and Chinese, confined to the man-made island of Dejima in Nagasaki harbour, were permitted to carry on a very limited trade. In spite of the policy of seclusion, however, Japan did not stagnate. More than two hundred years of peace unencumbered by external problems enabled the Japanese to evolve their own social and political systems and to develop distinctive economic and cultural patterns. But the internal and external pressures which had begun in the early nineteenth century undermined the power of the central government until the last Tokugawa shogun resigned in 1867. After a brief civil war the emperor was restored and centuries of feudalism came to an end.

Indian Subcontinent

The Indus civilisation (see Chapter 5) was eventually superseded by tribes of nomadic Aryans from western and central Asia over a period of centuries which began about 1500 BC. These incursions of Aryan settlers took place in what has been called the Vedic Age, the name derived from the Vedas, the ancient sacred literature of Hinduism which they founded (see also Culture). They moved eastwards to the Ganges basin and in due course intermarried with and absorbed the customs of an indigenous people, dasyus, and over this period initiated the social system based on caste. The dasyus may have been connected with the Dravidians, who had also entered India from the north-west at an earlier date and many of whom were driven south by the Aryan invasions. It was from this union that the Hindu peoples eventually emerged and in this period that the burgeoning civilisation moved eastwards and the Ganges became their sacred river. By the sixth century BC, Hinduism had become a complex of estoric rituals known only to the Brahmans (the highest caste), and this precipitated the 'protestant' movements of Buddhism and Jainism. Buddha was born about 563 BC and in his forty-five years of preaching throughout northern India, before his death in 483 BC, he laid the foundation for the second great religion of Asia.

Darius the Great made the Punjab the twentieth satrapy of the Persian Empire in 516 BC. It was not overthrown for nearly two hundred years when, in 327 BC, Alexander the Great set out to complete his conquest of Persia by annexing it to his empire. He crossed the Indus in February 326 BC and entered Taxila, established a naval base near the mouth of the Indus and returned to Susa by way of the Makran in March 324 BC.

The Mauryan Empire

When Alexander died at Babylon little more than a year later, the Greeks were expelled from the Punjab by Chandragupta Maurya of Pataliputra (called Sandrocottus by the Greek historians of Alexander), who also deposed the satrap and made himself ruler in his stead. He founded the Mauryan Empire, which by the end of the fourth century BC reached across India from coast to coast. Under his grandson Ashoka (*c.* 274–232 BC), who was converted to Buddhism, the empire was extended to bring Buddhism into temporary predominance across the whole of his empire, which by the middle of the third century BC covered all the peninsula except the southernmost regions (Kerala and Carnatic). He sent Buddhist envoys to many other neighbouring countries. His conversion to Buddhism was an act of the utmost importance in that it transformed Buddhism from an obscure religious sect to the official religion of a great empire whose envoys carried it abroad (including Egypt and Syria) and helped to establish it also in many Eastern and South-east Asian countries. In his later years Ashoka extended his empire through spiritual persuasion. Sri Lanka was an outstanding example: King Devanampiyatissa was converted to Buddhism by Ashoka's son, who planned and constructed a monastery for 3000 monks at Anuradhapura, and the Sacred Bo-Tree was brought from Bodh Gaya by Ashoka's daughter, a Buddhist nun. When Ashoka died in 232 BC, the Mauryan empire declined and the Mauryan emperor was murdered by his commander-in-chief, Pushiyamitra Sunga, in 185 BC. The way was open for further invasions from the north-west and for a series of transitory dynasties which seized power in central and southern India.

The Bactrian Kingdoms of the North-west

The Bactrian Greeks and Parthians who left the Seleucid empire in the middle of the third century BC were driven southward across the Hindu Kush by the Sakas (Scythians) from beyond the Oxus. Menander of Sagala, a Greek prince who led the invaders and established a kingdom in the Punjab (Gandhara was to the north-east in the low foothills of Kashmir), was converted to Buddhism and was killed in battle with the Scythians in 160 BC, before he could make a planned attack on the Mauryan capital. The *Milindapantra (Questions of Menander)*, a contemporary text, refers to and describes cities of the period – with moats and ramparts, market places and squares, shops, parks and lakes. Mithridates I of Parthia took the kingdom of Taxila about 138 BC and Scythian satrapies were set up in the Gujerat and as far south as Nasik. In Sri Lanka King Pandukabhaya set apart an area at the west gate of Anuradhapura as early as the fourth century BC for the Yavanas – the traders from the north-west – also called Yonas and perhaps none other than the Ionians of Greek history. It was in this period in the north-west that the fascinating amalgam of Greek and Indian culture was formed: it is best seen in the excavated remains of cosmopolitan Taxila of the second century BC (q.v.).

The Kushan Empire

The north-western states were absorbed by a later wave of invaders from central Asia, the Kushans, whose greatest king Kanishka (120–162 AD) made his capital at Peshawar. The Kushan empire included Gandhara, Kashmir and the Indus and Ganges basins, its provinces ruled by viceroys. Like Ashoka, Kanishka was converted to Buddhism, and Kushan emperors maintained and developed trade and cultural relationships with Rome, Palmyra and Alexandria in the west, Sassanian Persia and central Asia to the north, and China to the east. It was through Kushan influence that Buddhism first reached China. Important centres of art such as those at Mathura (near Delhi) produced the first Buddha images and rock-cut shrine-rooms at a later date. There are excavated remains at Sirkap (Taxila) and representations of other shrines at Bamiyan and in other Greek remains, for example at Ai Khanoum on the River Oxus (see Chapter 7), both the latter in northern Afghanistan. Fa-hsien, the Chinese pilgrim, described a relic tower built by Kanishka at Peshawar. It had three stages: a basement stage, 45 m (150 ft) high, a timber superstructure of thirteen storeys, and a finial consisting of twenty-five gilt 'umbrellas', perhaps some 120 m (400 ft) in all.

The Gupta Empire

Chandragupta (not to be confused with Chandragupta Maurya who founded an earlier empire) became ruler of a new group of territories and was crowned with full orthodox Brahmanical rites in 320 AD, following conquests in the Ganges-Jumna plain. He was succeeded by his son Samundragupta, who soon extended the Gupta empire across most of northern India to include the smaller states that had formed as the Kushan empire broke up, and the remaining Saka (Scythian) satrapies of the west. Although Guptas were themselves Hindu they liberally patronised Buddhists and Jains as well as other sects in their territories. They extended their influence by alliances as well as conquests. As with other Indian rulers since the inception of the Anuradhapura period in the fourth century BC, Sri Lanka formed religious and cultural ties with the Gupta empire and shared in the cultural and artistic renaissance of the period.

It was in this period that the Hindu temple began to take shape. While the older rock-cut apsidal temples persisted in ever more elaborate forms as at Ajanta, free-standing buildings began to appear at Sanchi and Cherzala in the fifth century: these were simple square temples with columniated porches, or slightly more elaborate somewhat later ones with a second level as in the burga temple at Aihole. Stupa building continued both on the mainland, for example at Mirpur Khas in the Sindh (fourth century) and the Dhamekha stupa at Sarnath (sixth century), as well as in Sri Lanka with the Jetavana stupa at Anuradhapura (fourth century).

The Gupta empire was overthrown by the White Huns in the last quarter of the fifth century. Except for a brief period in which Harsha of Thanesar reigned over a state in the Ganges valley north of Delhi, eventually moving his capital to Kanauj near Lucknow, a period of confusion followed the Hun incursions, and when the country emerged from it in the ninth century it was radically changed. Buddhism was fast disappearing except in Bengal, giving way to orthodox Hinduism and Jainism, and the Rajput clans had formed in the Punjab and were assuming their role as the 'sword arm of Hindustan'. They fought constantly among themselves and supported and patronised different sects, although the power of the Brahman priesthood grew, and many of the orthodox Hindu practices were instituted. This was the position when they were swept aside by the Muslim invasions of the eleventh century. They built many fine buildings, among which were the Siva temples at Khajuraho and the Dilwarra (Jain) temples on Mount Abu (q.v.).

The Satavahana Dynasty

The Sungas brought the Mauryan empire to an end about 185 BC and ruled in west central India for over a century. They were superseded in 70 BC by the Andhras, who had been a powerful force in the Deccan since about 230 BC and who continued to hold sway there until well into the third century AD. The Andhra kings belonged to the Satavahana dynasty, whose capital was at Nasik, and their domains extended from sea to sea between the Kistna and Godavari Rivers. Ashoka had sent his missionaries to them, and although both Sungas and Andhras were orthodox Hindus their attitudes were tolerant, to judge by the development of Buddhist and Jain monuments of this period up to the fourth century. From this time also date the caves at Barabar, Nasik and Ajanta and the chaitya at Karli, near Poona, the elaborate railing and thoranas at Sanchi, Barhut and Bodk Gaya and the decorated third-century stupa at Amaravati. The west coast ports of Sopara, Thana and Kalyan were in Andhra territory; following the discovery of the regularity of the monsoon winds, commerce with the west and with Alexandria in particular was much stimulated.

The Hindu Kingdoms of Southern India

Among the many kingdoms of the Deccan which succeeded the demise of the Satavahana dynasty the Chalukyas should be mentioned: their capital was Badami (now in the Bijapur region of Mysore). They were succeeded by the Rashtrakutas, of which dynasty Krishna I commissioned the Kailasa temple at Ellora, and other monarchs of the same line built the Jain and Brahmanical temples at that site. Another dynasty of the period, the Hoysalas of Mysore, built the elaborately carved temples at Halebid, and the Somavi and Ganga kings of Orissa the splendid temples with curvilinear sikhara roofs, for example at Bhuwaneshwar. The Pallavas of Kanchi, who held their power from the sixth to ninth centuries, were hereditary enemies of the Chalukyas. Towards the end of the seventh century Narsimhavarman I built the monolithic ratha temples (seven 'pagodas') of Mamallapuram (Mahabalipuram), near Madras, and his successor of the same name the great Kailasantha shrine at Kanchipuram. The Dravidian (largely Tamil) south of India differed widely from the Aryan north in language, literature and art, though influenced by Jain and Brahman missionaries. Its prosperity was based on spices and precious stones which were exported in quantity from Malabar (a name given to the west coast of the Indian peninsula) to the coasts around the Red Sea and the Persian Gulf from early times; these commodities were in great demand, for example in Rome from the first century AD onwards. The region was divided into three kingdoms held by the Cheras in the east. Muziris, modern Changanore, was the principal port and attracted a Roman colony which boasted a temple of Augustus. Strabo tells us that an Indian ruler, Pandion (Pandya), sent an ambassador to Augustus in 25 BC, offering him an alliance.

The early Pandyan Kingdom seems to have its capital at Kolkai near the port of Kayal (a visit to which is recorded by Marco Polo in the late thirteenth century), but at the same stage the seat of government was removed to Madura at least from the twelfth century onwards up to the eventual absorption of the state in the eighteenth century. There were long periods in between when the Pandyas were under attack from or dominated by their powerful Chola neighbours of Trichinopoly.

From the tenth century to the thirteenth, the Cholas ruled the greater part of Madras province, the northern part of Sri Lanka and a part of the Maldive Islands. The Pandyas allied themselves with the Sri Lankans in the tenth century and defeated the Cholas at Madura. The Cholas were fanatical Hindus, persecuted the Jains and built great temples and enclosures with gigantic gopurams at Tanjore, Rameswaram, the thirteenth-century east gopuram at Chidambaram and many others. Rajaraja I built Shiva and Vishnu Shrines in Sri Lanka, for example the Shiva Devale No. 2 at Polonnaruwa (*c.* 988) (p. 648A).

The greatest of the Pandyan rulers was Jatavarman Sundara Pandya I, whose territory in the thirteenth century extended from Travancore to Kanchipuram, just south of modern Madras. He was responsible for parts of the great temples at Chidambaram and Srirangam. There was a later (seventeenth and eighteenth century) Pandyan Nayak dynasty at Madura, whose members built a number of buildings including a palace at Madura much influenced by Islamic architecture in both planning and detail.

Vijayanagar was founded on the Tungabhadira River in central Mysore in 1336 by five brothers, who it is said may have fled from the Hoysala kingdom when it was attacked by the Muslims. Harihara I expanded the kingdom southward to Trichinopoly and northward to the Godavari later in the fourteenth century. It reached the peak of its splendour and influence under Krishnadeva Raya (1509–25) who encouraged all travellers of whatever race or creed to the capital. Domigo Paes, a Portuguese traveller of the early sixteenth century, gave a striking picture of the city, whose perimeter was 97 km (60 miles) long and its central road 13 km (8 miles) from end to end. The palace, which showed some Muslim influence, was said to be exquisitely decorated, the walls lined with carved ivory. The rulers of Vijayanagar saw themselves as the natural enemies of the Muslim Bahmani sultans and their successors at Bijapur, and in spite of efforts to patch up an alliance the sultans united to defeat the Hindus in a desperate battle late in 1564 at Talikota on the Kistna. Three days later the Muslims entered the city itself and systematically sacked it, leaving scarely one stone upon another, if contemporary records are to be believed.

In Sri Lanka the Anuradhapura period lasted from the fourth century BC until the tenth century AD, during which the foundations were laid for political, social and artistic traditions which were to continue almost intact for many centuries. Among the several Sinhalese kings of this era noted for their great building works one stands out above the rest, Kassapa I (sixth century AD), who left Anuradhapura to create a unique city constructed on and around an immense rock-hill, Sigiriya. In the latter part of the first

A. Shiva Devale No. 2, Polonnaruwa (*c.* 988). See p.647

B. Buddhist monastery, Wutai Mountains. See p.653

millennium AD Ceylon's development and affluence was such that it was able to withstand many invasions and even to counter-invade south India.

The Polonnaruwa period (eleventh to thirteenth centuries) began when, after years of invasions and occupations from Cholan, south India, and the sacking of Anuradhapura, the capital was removed to Polonnaruwa, no doubt because it commanded the main roads and trade routes. The building of this city was the principal architectural undertaking of King Parakrama Bahu 'The Great' (twelfth century), who had re-established sovereignty over the whole country. The glory of Polonnaruwa, with its palaces, monasteries, temples, parks, lakes and irrigation works, lasted only to the thirteenth century, by which time it had been reduced to ruins from constant attacks by foreign invaders. The court moved again, to a series of impermanent settlements, Yapahuwa, Dambadeniya and Kotte (thirteenth to fifteenth centuries).

The Kandyan period (fifteenth to ninteenth centuries) saw the division of the country into several kingdoms, with the capital of the most considerable at Kandy (a corruption of Kandenuwara, hill city), in an area initially undisturbed by foreign interference. The adjacent maritime provinces, however, were occupied by the Portuguese in the sixteenth century, by the Dutch in the seventeenth and, last, by the British who succeeded in annexing the Kandyan kingdom in 1815.

The Muslims in India

The Muslim incursions into India, Timur's expedition and the Delhi massacre are dealt with in Part 3. It should be noted that although the Muslims had been content to remain in the more northerly parts of India up to the end of the thirteenth century, Ala-ud-Din (1296–1316) holder of the Delhi Sultanate decided to move southwards: a raid was made in 1310 by Malik Kafur, a general who had once been a Hindu slave. He moved right through the Tamil south and wiped out the last stronghold of Hindu rule in India.

The Moghuls in India

The Moghul period and its culmination under Akbar is also dealt with in Part 3. The decline of the Moghuls had already begun, however, with the succession of Jehangir in 1605. The Portuguese established the colony of Goa under Albuquerque's governorship in 1510. The first Englishmen, Ralph Fitch and Thomas Newberry, brought letters from Queen Elizabeth I in 1585, and the first East India Company ship, *Hector*, with William Hawkins bearing a letter to Jehangir from James I asking for trading rights, reached India in 1608. The European colonial period began and continued in parallel with the gradual decline of the Moghuls. When Aurungzeb, the last of the great Moghul leaders, was demoralised and defeated in a running encounter with the Marathas, whom he had overcome twenty years earlier before subduing the Deccan, the way was opened for the eighteenth-century period of Maratha dominance. When the Marathas were eventually overcome by the Muslim Ahmad Shah at Panipat in 1761, it heralded the beginning of British rule in India.

Afghanistan

In the fourth century BC Afghanistan was part of the Achaemenid empire of Darius. It was next occupied by Alexander the Great's armies (356–323 BC) followed by Bactrian Greek colonists who created a colonial Greek city-state in Balkh (northern Afghanistan). There was continual cultural contact with Greece through Asian Greek settlements, with Persia and, by the first century BC, with India. Subsequent Scythian invasions (Kushan dynasties: see above) left an enduring impression. The city of Kapisa (now Begram), the capital of the Kushans, was a famous Mahayana Buddhist site and cosmopolitan meeting place on the great trade route from the Far East. In the fourth and fifth centuries AD the Kushan empire gave place to the Sassanian occupation, which had a profound cultural influence throughout the East, spreading even to China. The Chinese pilgrims Fa-hsien (fifth century) and Hsuan Tsang (seventh century) have described the Afghanistan of those days, with its magnificent palaces and monasteries.

Successive Muslim invasions followed after 650, the best-known by Mahmood of Ghazni (993–1030), and throughout the Mongol period of the thirteenth and fourteenth centuries the country was ruled by Mongol, Arab and Turk or Hindu princes. Babur made Kabul his capital before moving southward to found the Moghul empire in India in 1525; Afghanistan remained a part of the empire until the middle of eighteenth century when it was again overrun by Persians under Nadir Shah in 1741. In 1747 Nadir's bodyguard assassinated him and declared himself king of Afghanistan with his capital at Kandahar.

Nepal

The bulk of the population are Newars and Gurkhas (of Tibetan–Mongol stock), who settled in Nepal in very early times and established an indigenous style in art and architecture, which successive migrations and invasions from India have never materially modified. The arts flourished especially during the reign of the Mulla Rajas (thirteenth to eighteenth centuries), and, more particularly, in the fourteenth, fifteenth and early eighteenth centuries. In 1768 a Gurkha Raja seized the kingdom and a Gurkha dynasty, Hindu by adoption and intermarriage, calling itself Rajput, has since ruled the country. Real power, however, lay for more than a century in the hands of hereditary prime ministers.

South-east Asia

Burma

Four main periods are recognised in Burmese history, the first of which is known as pre-Pagan (first century BC to eight century AD). The earliest inhabitants appear to have been the Pyu, of Tibeto–Burman stock, who settled in Upper Burma. The Mon-Talaing, of Khmer origin, with a highly developed culture, settled in Lower Burma around Thaton and further south in Dvaravati (later part of Thailand); in the eighth century AD they conquered the Pyu and established a capital at Pagan, in central Burma, on the Irrawaddy. Indian settlements were also established.

The Pagan period (ninth to thirteenth centuries) did not produce anything approaching a unified society until the reigns of King Anawrahta (1044–77) and his successors, during which a Burmese state was created which ushered in the classical phase in art and architecture All this was to end in the thirteenth century with the invasion of Burma by Chinese Mongols under Kublai Khan.

The post-Pagan period (fourteenth to seventeenth centuries) offers a confused picture of internecine power struggles between Shans, Mons, Thais, Laotians, Chinese and Khmers. During these years several new capitals saw the light, including the Shan-Burmese city of Ava and a splendid city at Pegu (sixteenth century), built during an interlude of restored prestige under the powerful King Dayinnaung. Thereafter the process of disintegration continued, again briefly halted under King Alaungpaya, who built the port of Rangoon in 1755 (sacked by the Chinese in 1773). By this time British colonisation was under way, culminating in the annexation of Burma, which became a province of the Indian Empire in 1886. One of the last Burmese kings, Mindon (1852–78), built his capital city at Mandalay, which constituted a final manifestation of the Rangoon-Mandalay period (eighteenth to nineteenth centuries).

Cambodia

Funanese period (third-sixth centuries AD). Early Indo-China consisted of many small states which ultimately took shape as Cambodia, Laos and Vietnam. The oldest of the trio was Cambodia, corresponding approximately to Funan and founded, according to Chinese tradition, about the second century AD by a king Chandan or Kaudinya, who may have been a Kushana of Indo-Scythian stock (their royal title was Chandan), which would account for the marked evidence of Scythian–Persian influences. At its height at the end of the sixth century, the empire of Funan included much of Chenla, Indo-China and parts of Malaya. Chinese records mention the close relations which existed between Funan and India and China, and the high cultural standards, economic strength and impressive social organisation of the country.

Later Funanese and Early Khmer period (seventh-eighth centuries). This period was characterised by political confusion and war. The neighbouring state of Chenla gained suzerainty over Funan and, for the first time, reference is made to the authority exercised by the Khmer kings and people, whose capitals (of Chenla-Funan) near Kampong Thom at Sambor and Prei Kuk survive in an impressive group of pre-Angkor ruins. The dominant power in South-east Asia, however, was exercised by the Srivijaya and Sailendra dynasties of Java and Malaya.

Early Classical Khmer period (ninth century). The primordial role of architecture in Khmer society becomes apparent in this period. King Jayavarman II (800–50) released Cambodia from Javanese thraldom and founded a unified Angkor kingdom, building the first city of Angkor at Phnom Kulen. Among his successors, Indravarman I (877–99) built the Bakong, the first stone temple in the grand style, and introduced the elaborate system of irrigation which became not only an integral part of subsequent architectural schemes but also a vital element in the economic and social life of the nation. The disintegration of the system caused the final abandonment of the city of Angkor in the sixteenth century. Indravarman's son, Yasovarman I, founded the second city of Angkor and initiated a period of splendour in which Khmer civilisation took the form of an aristocratic and intellectual oligarchy under a god-king, with a middle class of artist-craftsmen, and a menial working class.

Transitional Classical Khmer period (tenth-eleventh centuries). This saw an interlude of dynastic quarrels and the creation of other capital cities. But King Rajendravarman (944–68), who was a cultivated man and an indefatigable builder, returned to Angkor, extending and consolidating Khmer power throughout the region. In the reign of his son and successor, Jayavarman V, the Brahman royal tutor Yajnavaraha built one of the most beautiful of Khmer temples, the Banteay Srei ('Citadel of Women'), a remarkable exercise in the eclecticism of earlier styles. Suryavarman I (1002–50), who followed, completed the Ta Keo, the first temple to be built of sandstone. Despite the unsettled conditions of the next decades, the magnificent gilded

Baphuon Temple-Mountain dates from the reign of his heir, Udayadityavarman II.

Classical Khmer period (twelfth-thirteenth centuries). This represented a hundred years of pomp and glory before the gradual decline. Suryavarman II (1112–52), most powerful of Cambodian kings, skilled in diplomacy and successful in war, is chiefly remembered for the building of the great Temple-City of Angkor Wat, the supreme achievement of Khmer genius and an architectural expression of god-king ideal. He also built Angkor Thom, which was almost immediately destroyed in 1177 by marauding Chams, and rebuilt by Jayavarman VII (1180–1218) in a programme unparaleled in the immensity, extravagance and speed of construction, entailing armies of masons, sculptors, decorators and labourers. The king's activities, although he was a mystic and Mahayana Buddhist, were not confined to the building of temples and palaces. He extended his empire by military prowess into Annam, Vientiane, Burma and southern Malaya. Indeed, by the end of his reign the country was exhausted by wars and grandiose architectural schemes, and was ready to welcome Theravada Buddhism, which had no need of magnificent architecture and elaborate ritual, preached the virtues of simplicity and rejected the god–king image. This change in religious and philosophical attitudes marked the end of the Classical Khmer period and was a prelude to the decay of the empire and the eventual conquest of Cambodia by Thailand. Angkor was captured by the Thais in 1437, and the destruction of the reservoirs and hydraulic works had made life in Angkor impossible by the end of the sixteenth century, by which time most of the country had passed into Siamese (Thai) hands. A Cambodian enclave survived in the south, and its capital Phnom-Penh, on the Mekong river, remained the principal city of Cambodia when much of Indo-China became a French protectorate in the nineteenth century.

Thailand

In the sixth century it appears that the Mon people (Buddhists) from Lower Burma imposed their authority over what is now central Thailand and founded the kingdom of Dvaravati. Early in the eleventh century the Khmers annexed Dvaravati and their influence became paramount in central Thailand, although Dvaravati's prestige as the centre of Buddhist orthodoxy remained largely unimpaired. In the north, where Thai–Syam migrants from south-west China established a semi-independent state with its capital at Chiengsen (modern Chiengmai), a gradual fusion of Mons and Thais led to infiltrations southwards and, in the thirteenth century, to the expulsion of the Khmers and the creation and consolidation of the kingdom of Sukhothai. The centre of gravity, however, continued to move south. In the fourteenth century Ayudhya became the capital, with direct access to the sea and the Cambodian trade routes, a city destined to be renowned throughout the Indo-Chinese world for wealth and luxury, destroyed by the Burmese in 1767 and now a desolate ruin. This was not the first incursion by Burma into Siam. In 1555 Ayudhya had fallen briefly into Burmese hands, but foreign domination has always been short-lived and, apart from the Japanese occupation during World War II, Thailand remains unique among the countries of South-east Asia in having maintained a considerable measure of independence throughout its national history. Despite Portuguese, Dutch, French and British commercial intrusion from the sixteenth century onwards, Thailand was always suspicious of European intentions, and managed to evade colonialist occupation. The present capital, Bangkok, was founded in 1782 to take the place of Ayudhya, which lies a short distance to the north.

Indonesia

In the civilisation which developed in Sumatra and Java under Indian cultural and religious influence and example, society was divided between court and peasantry. Literature, sculpture and architecture were the prerogative of the 'Kraton', or court. The peasants formed an agricultural community whose rituals, customs and origins dated back to Neolithic times and whose lives were almost untouched by the court culture. The first important Indonesian kingdom, and expression of this form of civilisation, seems to have been that of the Srivijaya Dynasty (seventh to thirteenth centuries). Srivijaya emerged as a major power with hegemony over the Malayan peninsula, Borneo and western Java, and with mercantile connections extending as far as Persia. Unhappily no architectural records survive. Concurrently with the early years of Srivijaya leadership in Sumatra, two principal dynasties ruled in Java; the Hindu Sanjaya in the central provinces (mid-seventh to tenth centuries) and the Buddhist Sailendra a little further east. Both have left impressive architectural evidence. It is surmised that the Sailendra line ended with the marriage of a daughter to a Sanjaya king, Rakryan Pikatan, in about the year 840. Thereafter the history of the Srivijaya kingdom in Sumatra is concerned with wars for supremacy over Java, the declining strength of the Sanjaya, and ultimately with defeat (*c.* 1220) at the hands of the east Javanese dynasties of Singasari and Majapahit, with the former first in the ascendant and the latter inspiring a final renaissance of Javanese art and architecture in the fourteenth century. In the meantime Muslim influence had been gaining ground throughout Indonesia and, by the end of the fifteenth century, Islamic ruler Balen Pata, himself a

Javanese, had assumed control of the whole of Java, including the state of Majapahit. The subsequent evolution of Indonesia is interwoven with the activities of European colonial powers: the Portuguese, the British and, for three and a half centuries, the Dutch. In 1945 the independent Republic of Indonesia came into being, and in 1954 the last tenuous threads which held the Netherlands–Indonesian Union together were severed.

Culture

Africa

For most of its history, Africa was populated by craft-based societies with predominantly oral traditions. There was specialisation of labour in the urban centres, but little in the villages other than by age and gender. This applied to building, and because reconstruction was frequent most people had direct experience of the process.

The earliest African art was rock painting and engraving, but it later became three-dimensional. Portable art was not restricted to ritual objects like masks and figures carved in local hardwoods or modelled in terracotta, but was found in objects of everyday use such as baskets and bowls. Many of the larger scale artefacts were designed to be viewed in association with buildings – from the life-size sculptures and reliefs of Meroe and Axum to the carved doors and houseposts of the Yoruba. Decoration was frequently applied to buildings particularly to thesholds and doorways, and on the interior of walls and roofs. Household shrines, granaries and women's rooms were often preferred locations for decoration, as were significant buildings such as the dwellings of chiefs and sacred buildings. From about AD 650, the doctrine of Islam gained a foothold in north-east Africa, and spread gradually eastwards and southwards, until by about 1400 it was established among all the peoples north of the Sahel Corridor, with the exception of Ethiopia where groups of Christian churches were hewn out of the solid rock. Islam also took root on the east coast of Africa but here, in contrast to West Africa, the mosques lacked minarets, and animist rituals continued to flourish alongside Muslim observances. Further south indigenous religions were practised but did not produce much large-scale architecture, though sacred sites were established, and shrines and temples were built in some areas. Funerary architecture was uncommon in pre-colonial Africa other than at Meroe and Axum, but in some parts of North and West Africa and on the eastern seaboard megalithic burials, barrow graves and pillar tombs have been found.

The Americas

The high civilisations of Mesoamerica and South America consisted of peasant farmers ruled by hereditary elites whose basis of power was the belief that they had been created to govern and had access to the gods. Only the elite could petition the gods on behalf of the peasants, and favours would be granted only if duties had been faithfully performed. They believed the gods controlled natural phenomena as well as human ventures and that their cooperation was essential in any undertaking; thus religious observance was regarded as a kind of commerce, in which a favourable prognostication for any project could be obtained only by paying the necessary price – offerings, sacrifice, and the performance of ritual. Under this system, secular and religious establishments were closely interconnected. The temples were used as much for political as for religious purposes and the iconography was as much dynastic as sacred. North American societies were less stratified but held similar beliefs about the intercession of supernatural powers in human and earthly affairs, and it was these beliefs that caused pre-colonial American societies to make massive investments in ceremonial architecture.

One aspect of the culture that had a powerful influence on architecture was the belief that supernatural powers were literally present in certain places – thus determining the siting of ceremonial buildings. The gods were then believed to reside within the fabric of the structure. For this reason, enclosed spaces were of little significance in pre-colonial temples; the gods dwelt in the masonry, not in the rooms. This explains also why the people were willing to undertake such enormous building projects and why they constructed later temples over partially demolished or even wholly intact earlier ones. A new temple provided a new fabric to house the deity, but had to be built in the same place as the old one where the god was known to be present.

China

China's culture has a long history of continuous development and a strikingly individual character. The sage and philosopher Confucius (551–479 BC) emphasised 'ren' (benevolence) and 'li' (moral concepts). Confucianism, which occupied a leading position in China, included a set of ethical concepts and moral standards in human relationships to encourage mutual respect between elders and young people, and between upper and lower classes. The architectural layout of the courtyards of Chinese residences, for example, embody this kind of feudal etiquette. The practice of honouring ancestors and family clans took shape and, as a result, temples to house sacrificial rites and tributes to ancestors played an extremely important part in the layout of cities, for example the capital of the Zhou dynasty (1027–770 BC) and in Beijing, capital of the Ming dynasty (1368–1644).

Early Daoist thinking is embodied in two books, one dealing with the 'way', the other with its 'virtue', by Lao Ze and Zhuang Ze, both of whom may be legendary figures whose names may be confused with the names of the books. Daoism developed in the four or five centuries immediately before the Christian era, was suppressed in the Han dynasty under a government which supported Confucianism, but arose again in the Wei (220–265) and Jin (265–420) dynasties. The Daoists were quietists who believed in an underlying unity affecting the whole of the phenomenal world: to be in tune with the fundamental laws of nature was one of the first steps in Daoist discipline. This produced an important turning point in China's culture. Landscape poems and paintings extolled nature and led to the development of Chinese garden architecture. The ideal of gardening was the pursuit of natural effects through man-made intervention – to mimic hills and forests, rivers, creeks and lakes as found in nature. Even the rockery in Taihu Lake, for example, was designed in imitation of natural forms. A unique gardening system began to evolve and culminated in a theoretical work, *On the Construction of Gardens*, published in the early seventeenth century.

Buddhism was introduced from India and was first received favourably about AD 68 by the Eastern Han Dynasty, but after periods of official hostility was not firmly established until an edict of the Jin Dynasty permitted monasticism (355). It spread to Korea a few years later. The introduction of Buddhism brought new building types to Chinese architecture, but their forms were developed on the basis of the traditional wooden structure, assimilating the new culture but retaining Chinese cultural independence in the evolution of architecture.

The simultaneous practice of and cross-fertilisation between Buddhism, Daoism and Confucianism also affected the development of architecture. Halls for Buddhist worship were to be found in more and more residences and the difference between Daoist and Buddhist buildings grew less and less, except for ornamental themes which tended to retain their own distinctive features. Daoist attention to nature also affected Buddhist temples. Both chose scenic locations for their sacred buildings. The Wutai (p. 648B), Emei, Jiuhua and Putuo mountains are examples of Buddhist siting, while Daoist temples girded the Taishan, Huashan, Hengshan, Wudang and Qingcheng mountains.

Members of the Yin-Yang school (originated about 305 BC) held that dynasties reigned by virtue of one of the five elements, fire, water, earth, metal and wood. Their 'Book of Changes' expounds the symbolism of yin and yang (originally the dark and the bright), which came to imply that all things in the universe could be divided into two aspects which were opposed to each other but interdependent – for example, heaven and earth, sun and moon, cold and warm, man and woman, and odd and even numbers. Hence heaven, sun, warm, man, and odd numbers were classified under the category of yang, and their opposites as yin. In groups of palace buildings, for example, open courts in which audiences were held were in the yang category – halls occurred in odd numbers; the halls themselves, however, were in the yin category as internal spaces. In the 'five elements' theory, on the other hand, many natural phenomena and things were placed under the five categories. Given below are some items relevant to architecture:

Five Elements – Wood, Fire, Earth, Metal, Water
Position – East, South, Middle, West, North
Weather – Windy, Hot, Humid, Dry, Cold
Colour – Green, Red, Yellow, White, Black
Evolution of Living Things – Birth, Growing Up, Changing, Weakening, Hiding
Symbolic Significance – Prosperity, Riches and Honour, Power, Desolation, Death

It is clear that there was some difficulty in fitting the symbolism to architectural design. During the Tang (618–907) and the Ming-Qing (1368–1911) periods, the palace-hall for the crown prince was located in the east to represent new birth, while the building to house the empress dowager was in the west to symbolise the feeble nature of old age. Buildings used by the emperor were roofed with yellow-glazed tiles to symbolise authority. Those used by the crown prince had green-glazed tiles to indicate new birth and prosperity.

Korea

Koreans are descendants of several Mongolian tribal groups which migrated from Manchuria in prehistoric times and were early fused into a separate, homogeneous race. Anthropologically the Korean people are Mongoloid and their language stems from the Altaic family of languages. The origins of religion in the country are obscure but were probably similar to the animistic beliefs held elsewhere in Siberia. Historically, however, Korean architecture was influenced by Chinese beliefs – Confucianism, Daoism, yin and yang, the five elements, and geomancy and astronomy.

Buddhism was brought to Korea in the late fourth century and reached its zenith in the seventh century during Shilla, the kingdom which unified the Korean peninsula in 668. In the process, many Buddhist architectural and sculptural masterpieces were created. However, in Koryo (918–1392), the new kingdom which replaced Shilla in the tenth century, Buddhism gradually declined in influence. It was suppressed by the Confucian-oriented court of Choson (1392–1910), the kingdom that superseded Koryo in 1392 and was ruled by the Yi Dynasty.

Given its strategic location between north Asia and the outside world, Korea has experienced numerous invasions by foreign powers. The Mongolian invasion in the thirteenth century and the Japanese invasion in the sixteenth century were most devastating, and resulted in the destruction of almost all of the wooden structures dating from the Three Kingdoms period to early Choson. It is, therefore, difficult to classify Korean architecture of that period chronologically.

Traditional Korean architecture never regained the aesthetic and artistic sensibility that characterised it before the sixteenth-century Japanese invasions. The seventeenth and the eighteenth centuries saw Korea's first introduction to Western culture and the emergence of the School of Practical Learning (Shirhak), a group of scholars dedicated to practical learning and the promotion of welfare for all people.

Japan

The close links between Japanese political and social history and culture will be apparent from the section on History above. In the proto-historical period preceding the introduction of Buddhism from China through Korea (middle of the sixth century) the theocratic society was founded upon a main deity, the sun-goddess, and a polytheistic animism with many lesser deities. Though without a well-defined moral code, Shintoism laid great stress upon ancestor and nature worship. Elaborate images or temples were unnecessary to its tenets. Religious practices gradually grew to combine belief in 'nature-spirits' with one or other sect of Buddhism. This integration of the religions began as early as the ninth and tenth centuries when Shingon and Tendai Buddhism was introduced from China, and in reaction to the aestheticism of the Heian period in Kyoto.

A further significant event was the introduction in the twelfth century of Zen Buddhism – contemporarily with the formation of the Kamakura military government. Introduced from China at the end of the twelfth century, Zen stresses the contemplative aspects of Buddhism and significantly influenced Japanese culture because it appealed to the putative feudal knighthood, the samurai. It provided a method of achieving enlightenment through secular pursuits such as archery, the tea ceremony and flower-arrangement. It appealed also because of its anti-intellectualism and the belief that enlightenment might spread spontaneously from everyday events. The Shin and Nicheren sects also took root in Japan. The domestic rituals with which Buddhism and Shinto beliefs were combined, though not conducive to a formal or subtle theology, concentrated attention upon informal (often domestic) religious exercises and inculcated a veneration for the ideal of pilgrimage to holy shrines.

The mystic symbolism of Buddhism inspired the artistic Japanese temperament to produce countless images of every size and fantastic form. The priesthood contributed greatly to the development of the country even in the construction of roads and bridges, thus encouraging the unification of the country by improving communications between its often-isolated regions.

Christianity was introduced in 1549 by S. Francis Xavier, but this missionary effort led to many conflicts. Envoys from Japan visited Europe in 1582. Korea was invaded by the Japanese in 1592. Despite these tentative contacts with the outer world. Japan reverted to isolationism and in 1614 all foreign priests were expelled. The Spaniards were driven out in 1624, and the Portuguese in 1638. Christianity was finally interdicted on the departure of the Portuguese, and then for a period of almost two hundred years Japan was closed to the outside world.

Indian Subcontinent

The religions of the Indian subcontinent have been given some prominence both in the section in this chapter on History and in Chapter 26, because, perhaps more than in other areas, the development of architecture is so closely linked with the building of sacred edifices – usually the only permanent structures to have survived. Brahmanism and Hinduism originated in the period during which Aryan invaders imposed their rule upon the indigenous Dravidians. This was the Vedic Age (*c.* 1500–*c.* 500 BC) named after the four great Sanskrit books – the Vedas – to which were added the Brahmanas (commentary on the Vedas) and a little later (*c.* 600 BC) the Upanishads, philosophical commentaries which contain the basic laws of Hinduism. The Dravidian cult of 'bhakti' (devotion to an incarnation) seems to have been combined with the Aryan dedication to abstract principles to produce the basis of Hinduism out of Brahmanism, the highly complex system of ritual and religious observance of the mid-sixth century BC, based upon the Brahmanas and the Upanishads. By the beginning of the Christian era, the early pantheism of the Vedic age had given way to the Hindu theology, sometimes explained in terms of a trinity with Brahman or Brahma as the creator of the universe, Shiva the destroyer and Vishnu (of whom Krisha and Rama are incarnations) the preserver of the universe; both Shiva and Vishnu were the centres of major Hindu cults and many temples were dedicated to their worship. For the Hindu, the natural law,

Karma, determines the individual's station in life, which is considered to be the result of actions in the previous incarnation; it is essential to follow the duties of the present life (Dharma) and through dedication and a continuing series of reincarnations to achieve 'moksha' – losing the individual consciousness to reach universal open existence. Religious belief thus reinforced the caste system which was, and remains, the basis of the society.

Many concepts, animals and individuals were related to the worship of Shiva and Vishnu, sometimes as a result of writings, for example that of the Sanskrit poet Kalidasa in the sixth century, who advocated Shivaism by priestly persuasion or through the growing popularity of new secular concepts.

Buddhism sprang from the teaching of Siddartha Gautama (*c.* 563–483 BC), who was born of the princely Kshatriya sect and while no doubt rebelling against the growing influence of the Brahman (priestly) caste, also began what became a reform movement to simplify and clarify the increased complexity and prolixity of Brahmanism. He was vouchsafed a vision after six years of contemplation, and thereafter was called the 'enlightened one', the Buddha: he preached throughout northern India for 45 years until his death. Buddhism accepts reincarnation but rejects the caste system, and has no god in the Western sense of the word; Buddhist monks demonstrate by example the meditative way of life. Buddhism divided into two major sects, Mahayana (the Major Vehicle) and Hinayana (the Minor Vehicle). The Mahayana was the larger of the two.

Although the doctrine of early Theravada was deeply abstract and the laity was allowed little participation, after the Third Council under King Asoka in the third century BC texts such as the Mahaparinibbanasutta were widely released. They encouraged the erection of stupas over relic deposits as places of worship, ritual and flower offerings by the laity. Visits were suggested to the four places sanctified by the Buddha's birth, attainment of enlightenment, his first sermon and his death. Such visits would convey merit and benefit the pilgrim in afterlife. All members of the laity were thought to be capable of attaining Buddhahood and should work towards this end.

Also to satisfy the cravings of the laity, at first Buddhist symbols, and later the Buddha image itself, were allowed by the Mahayana in the first century AD. This set off a major construction programme of image houses across the length and breadth of the Buddhist world. Other forms of worship associated with Buddhist religious buildings included those conducted at or around the stupas and the Bo-tree shrines. This took the form of making offerings at each shrine and circumambulation of the stupa in a meditative attitude. Preaching halls also were built for the purpose of public participation. In them the monks met the laity and communicated to the public the spiritual experiences of meditation.

Buddhism declined in India after the seventh century but continued in Sri Lanka, South-east Asia and the Far East.

Jainism was traditionally founded by Mahavira (roughly contemporary with Buddha) who was himself a Brahman. The twenty-four Tirthakavras, 'fordmakers across the stream of existence', also preached the Jainist doctrines to the people, and as the religion retained the Hindu attachment to icons from its inception, with Mahavira they provided the pantheon of images with which Jain temples are decorated. Some of the earliest figure sculptures of the Indian subcontinent are of Jainist origin and date from the Mauryan and Sunga periods. Jainism spread from its early origins in northern India into the Deccan where the Chalukyan court became its centre and stronghold. The goal of the religion, like Hinduism, is salvation through successive rebirth, the ideal vehicles being rigid asceticism, the preservation of every living creature and the cultivation of natural as opposed to artificial objects and values. Some of their buildings, perhaps paradoxically, are distinguished by an extraordinary richness and complexity of sculptural ornament.

Afghanistan has passed through many religious phases – Achaemenid and Parthian, Sassanian (Zoroastrian), Indian Buddhist, Greek Hellenist (with Alexander the Great), and Scythian. The impact of Mahayana Buddhism, however, became the predominant influence, superseding the earlier Buddhist faith, until in the eighth century the Muslim religion penetrated the country and, under a Turkish Ghazni dynasty and after, Afghanistan became a Muslim kingdom.

Ashoka brought Buddhism to the valley of Nepal and built many stupas to commemorate his mission. We know also that in the fifth century AD, and again in the seventh century, both Buddhist and Hindu settlements were formed, conversions made and monasteries founded. Since then, Hinduism and Buddhism, with Tibetan Tantric influences, have existed side by side. Tibetan influence is also apparent in the mysticism and symbolism inspired by the great mountains and the lonely grandeur of the country.

South-east Asia

Burma

In Burma art and architecture are a reflection of Buddhist devotion. According to the Mawavamsa, the Emperor Ashoka (*c.* third century BC) sent two monks from India to preach the faith, and by the fifth century AD Buddhism was widely established. Later immigrants brought Nat worship (a pantheon of water and tree spirits, and 'nagas' – snakes), but they were ultimately converted to Buddhism, although Nat superstitions were still widespread.

Cambodia

In the pre-Khmer era the indigenous animistic beliefs of the people in the sacred mountain, the Naga princess (water spirit) and ancestor worship were fused with the Indian religious beliefs of the king, the court and the scholars. Hinduism predominated, with Mahayana Buddhism as a subordinate religion. The worship of Harihara (Shiva and Vishnu in a single body, whose image has four faces, and sometimes eight arms) was a particular characteristic. From the ninth century of the Khmer period the cult of the Deva-Raja, the God-King, worshipped in the form of Shiva, began to develop, influencing the style of the great pyramid temple-cities of the Angkor region. A great change took place in the thirteenth century, when the process of conversion to Theravada Buddhism assumed the momentum of a popular movement. This particular doctrine involved no elaborate ceremonial, and its missionaries preached self-denial and the simple life.

Thailand

Buddhism came early to this region, via Sri Lanka and Burma, superimposed upon the indigenous animism, and for 1500 years has remained the prevailing influence on art and architecture.

Indonesia and the Malay Archipelago

Two interacting movements have moulded the character of Indonesian art and architecture: the ancient indigenous peasant culture of animistic myth and ancestor worship, and the Hindu–Buddhist beliefs brought to the region, and to Java in particular, from the fourth century AD by Indian immigrants who, by the seventh century, had made both Sumatra and Java centres of religious learning and pilgrimage. Many years later Islam came to north Sumatra and Malaya, also from India, and by the fifteenth century had spread throughout Java, ousting the Hindu–Buddhist and ancestral spirit cults, which found a lasting haven in Bali.

The impact of Islam upon India and other south and South-east Asian cultures is dealt with in Part 3. On the Indian peninsula itself it was responsible for the southward movement of Buddhism and Hinduism and the related changes in social and political structures implied in the outlines given in the History section of this chapter.

Resources

Africa

Resources used in the construction of buildings in the ancient civilisations in the Nile valley, in the Greek and Roman settlements along the north coast of Africa and in Islamic buildings from the seventh and eighth centuries onwards have been described in the background chapters of Parts 1, 2 and 3 (Chapters 1, 8 and 15).

In sub-Saharan Africa the principal building materials were clay, vegetable materials and stone. Sun-dried bricks were used in the Sudan and Hausaland, and burnt bricks were found along the line of the Sahel Corridor. In forest areas brick-clay was uncommon, and mud was used as a plastic medium. Reeds, grasses, bamboo and palm fronds were widely available, and produced elegant roofs in a wide variety of distinctive, usually steeply pitched, shapes. Stone buildings were widespread, particularly in mountain areas, but most buildings were of a temporary nature, using local materials and cooperative, voluntary manpower. With regular attention, buildings in mud and timber lasted many generations.

The Americas

Earth and timber were the most usable natural resources available for building in the eastern woodlands of North America. In Mesoamerica, although timber was widely used, and elaborately carved wood fittings embellished major buildings, stone and clay were of greater importance. Mortars and plasters of clay, lime and mud were developed and were often of durable quality. Lime plasters of remarkable hardness sealed the exterior surfaces of lowland Maya buildings against the rain, fungus, plant growth, and animal and insect attack that must be thwarted in the tropics. In Central America, mineral-based pigments were widely used to paint buildings – usually in red (specular hematite), occasionally dark blue-grey, or in polychrome on sculptures and interior mural painting. The limestone which is available over the whole of the Maya lowlands proved to be ideally workable with the commonly used flint, chert and jadeite cutting tools. Many of these limestones were relatively soft when quarried, and hardened on exposure. The soft white marls of Yucatan, chemically very pure, made excellent mortar. The Andean regions relied more on pure clays for use as mortars or on the accuracy of stone-cutting to achieve stability through closeness of fit. Here copper tools were available for working the harder stones. Massive human resources needed to produce the buildings were provided by the highly coercive social systems.

In the case of the Maya, superior organisation of labour, rather than the invention of new tools or techniques, made possible the great volume of construction accomplished during the Late Classic period as compared with the earlier periods during which only a few very large buildings were sequentially completed.

China

Ancient China was well forested and in most places timber was more easily available than stone. The Greater and Lesser Hinggan mountains and the Changbai mountains in the north-east, the Tianshan and Altay mountains in the north-west and the hilly areas in the south-west and south-east were all important forest areas. Pines and China firs were the main building materials. Some rare species like nanmu, red sandalwood and rosewood were used exclusively for palace buildings.

Very early (late second millennium BC) buildings along the middle reaches of the Huanghe River were erected on rammed loess platforms supporting timber columns on boulder bases: cave and semi-cave dwellings also developed into beamed wooden structures. In marshland areas along the lower reaches of the Changjiang River, nest-dwellings made of reeds evolved into thatched forms supported on raised platform floors. Woven bamboo was used for roofs and walls, and houses were made entirely from it in some areas south of the river.

Tiles were first produced in the early Zhou dynasty (770–265 BC). During the Warring States period (475–221 BC) figured bricks and large hollow clay blocks began to make their appearance, and by the Han dynasty (206 BC–AD 220) some tomb chambers were being built of bricks. It was not until the Yuan period (1271–1368), however, that bricks were used to any extent for buildings above the ground. Only in the seventeenth century, following the Ming dynasty (1368–1644), were bricks produced in large quantities.

Glazed tiles and bricks were regarded as high-grade building materials. Glazed tiles were first used for palace buildings in the Northern Wei period (386–534). In the Song dynasty (960–1279), the techniques for making coloured glazes were upgraded and thereafter some pagodas were surfaced all over with glazed bricks. The Ming-Qing period (1368–1911) produced greater varieties of glazed products, some with multi-coloured designs which were laid together to form mosaic-like patterns.

In most cases stone was used for the foundations of wooden structures. Only a few types of structure, such as bridges, tombs and pagodas, were built entirely of stone blocks. Stone houses were built occasionally in mountainous areas of the country.

After the Song dynasty (960–1279) the doors and windows of wooden structures were made with increasingly fine workmanship. Apart from paper, screens of silk or cotton, thin mica sheets and shells were used as translucent materials.

Metals were widely used for ornamental items such as gate nails and knockers and for the spires of pagodas. Cast-iron components were also used to reinforce stone or wooden buildings.

Korea

Korea had mixed deciduous and coniferous temperate forests, a substantial proportion of which were destroyed by the 'hwaijon' method of agriculture in which new areas for cultivation were prepared by firing the existing, wild vegetation. Nevertheless, historical architectural development in Korea, as in China, was based largely upon timber-framed buildings.

Japan

Considering the volcanic activity, Japan might be expected to have large quantities of stone suitable for construction purposes. But in spite of an abundance of metamorphic rock, it is generally badly fractured owing to incessant seismic activity. Although granite, gneiss and porphyry deposits exist, they lack the quality needed for purposes other than ramparts and veneers. Sandstone and tuff are plentiful but are too soft for use in any sizable building. Furthermore, the frequency of earthquakes would have discouraged stone construction even if high-quality stone had been available.

As has been described, Japan has abundant rainfall, and produced great quantities of excellent timber. This encouraged the development of meticulous timber constructional techniques, examples of which are described in Chapter 25; a brief explanation may be found in the section on Building Techniques and Processes in this chapter. The hazard of earthquakes also militated against the use of heavy materials; only column bases and plinths are formed from the granites, porphyries and volcanic rocks which abound. Metal castings and burnt clay tiles were also available.

Labour became specialised, and artisans with particular skills organised themselves into guilds with closely guarded rights of membership, often hereditary. Those concerned with architecture included guilds of stonemasons, sawyers, carpenters, tile makers, plasterers, and metalworkers. They received patronage from noble families, shrines and temples, and were held in high esteem

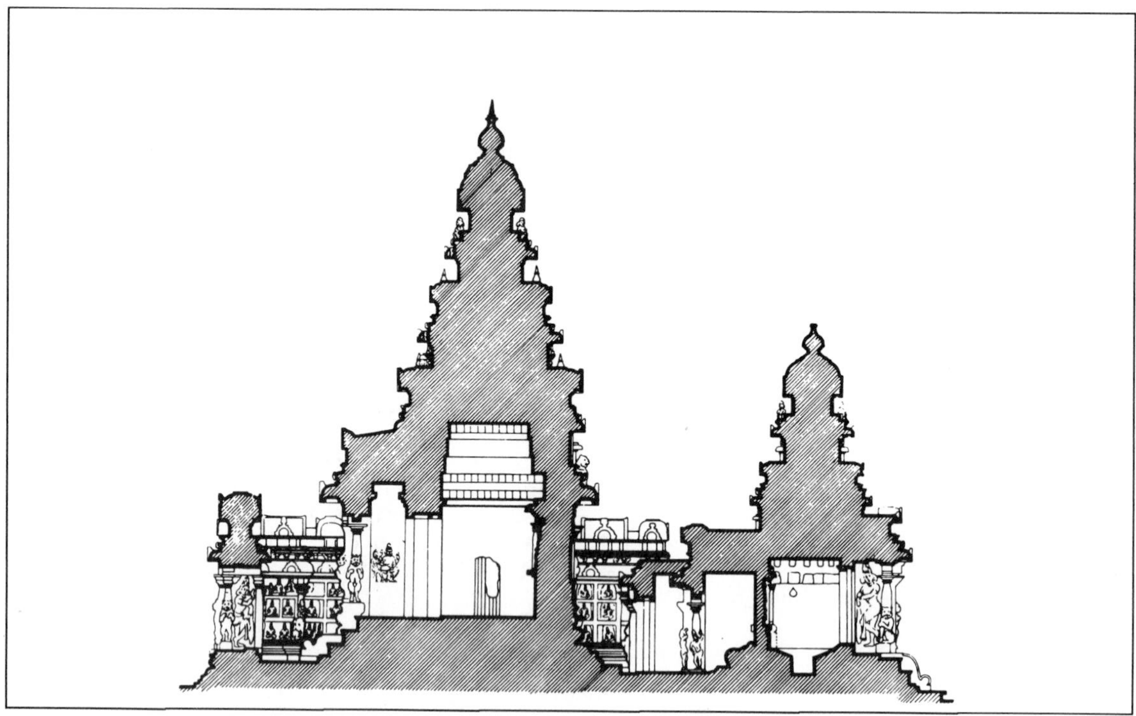

A. Shore Temple, Mamallapuram: section. See p.664

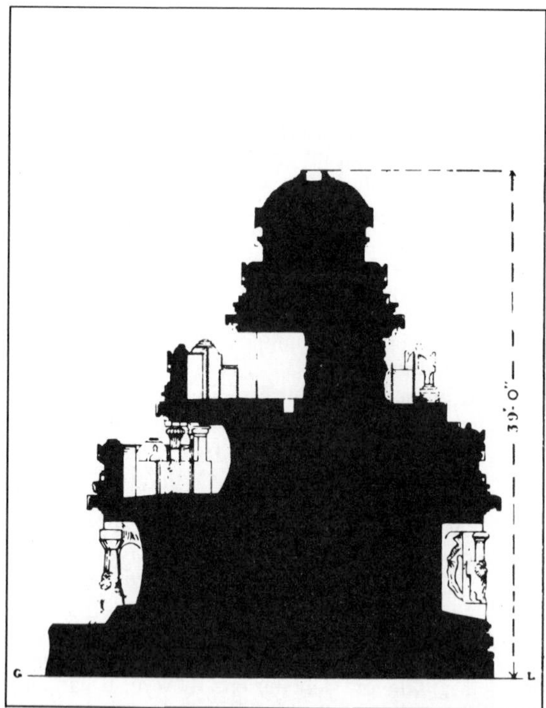

B. Dharmaraja ratha, Mamallapuram (600–900): section. See p.664

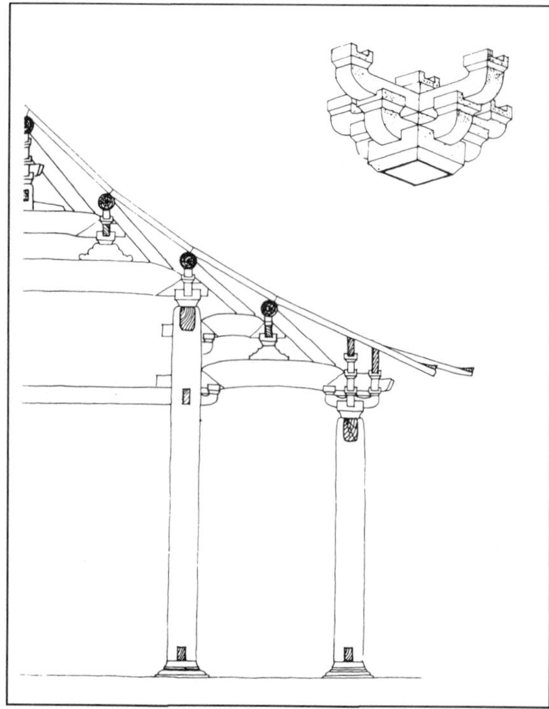

C. Chinese timber construction: typical part section and details of bracket-set. See p.661

despite their low rank, especially during the ebullient and creative early Edo period. Famous painters and craftsmen who were capable of producing ornamentation in relief, lacquerwork and metal casting, together with master carpenters, united to accomplish the magnificence at Nikko.

Indian Subcontinent

The lack of building stone along the Indus and Ganges valleys, and the easily available timber which was floated down the rivers from the mountains, influenced architecture in the area from the earliest times. Masonry traditions derived their architectural vocabulary from carpentry techniques. There is good white marble in Rajasthan, widely used in buildings, and fine red and cream sandstone from the neighbourhood of Agra; generally speaking, however, these are used mainly as facing materials for rubble walling behind. In the centre and south, the 'trap' and granite of the Deccan and the chloritic schist of southern Karnataka made their own contributions to the development of regional characteristics. In the Western Ghats, the horizontal rock strata which rise in perpendicular cliffs made possible the rock-cut sanctuaries of Karli (p. 751B), Ajanta (p. 753B) and Elephanta. At Mamallapuram and Ellora (p. 753C). The rock-cut temples of Mamallapura in the south were hewn out of granite. As far as timber is concerned, hard teak is found in Burma and in the eastern and western coastal mountains. An excellent softwood, deodar, is found abundantly in the northern mountain ranges; shisham, a hardwood somewhat inferior to teak, grows everywhere in the river valleys of the north. In the riverine plains of Bengal, Uttar Pradesh and the Punjab, the alluvial soil makes good bricks which were, and are, used extensively in these areas. Terracotta has been used from the earliest times; the ease with which the plastic clay can be pressed into moulds or carved, before firing, may be responsible (together with the traditions of woodcarving) for the exuberance of decoration in subsequent periods. Lime for building was obtained by burning limestone, shells and kankar, a nodular form of impure lime found in the river valleys.

In Sri Lanka, granite, limestone, laterite and sandstone were used – often, as in many buildings at Anuradhapura and Polonnaruwa, for the lowest storey on which higher timber structures were erected. Here, too, stone was often used in timber-like sizes. Clay for bricks, tiles and pottery was available and fired bricks were widely used. But Sri Lanka has much of its land area covered in tropical forest and jungle, and both soft and hard timbers can be grown rapidly as can bamboo and grasses for thatch and mats. Coconut palm trunks were used for posts and roof timbers, their leaves for thatch and woven wall-panels.

The availability of materials is nowhere more influential upon the character of buildings than in Afghanistan and Nepal. In Afghanistan the techniques of stone building were developed early at Bamiyan where, apart from the rock-cut cliff face, cupola roofs span the square chamber angles with arched squinches, lantern roof and coffered dome. Nepal on the other hand has a brick and timber architecture – brickwork facing the stupa mounds and forming the raised processional plinths, and timber used as the principal framing material in most domestic architecture.

South-east Asia

Burma is rich in timber, ores and precious stones, while teak and brick are much used in buildings. The climate is tropical, with south-west monsoon rains in summer. Burmese bricks measure about 305 mm × 203 mm × 76 mm (12 in × 8 in × 3 in), and are set in mud or glue mortar. The true arch was much used in Burma – it was never exploited in India – with radiating voussoirs to form semi-pointed barrel vaults (compare the great arches of the porticoes of the Ananda Temple).

In Cambodia timber was the principal building material in the delta area, together with laterite, sandstone and a terracotta brick in the hinterland.

Thailand is immensely rich in durable and decorative timbers, including teak and ebony, suitable for all types of construction work. The other principal building material is brick; stone was little used, except for foundations and during the years of Khmer influence.

Volcanic rock (solidified lava) has been extensively used for construction work in Indonesia. Eruptions have brought down buildings, but it has sometimes been possible to reconstruct important architectural monuments with the original undamaged stones. This is certainly true in part of the ninth-century masterpiece of Barabudur in Java. Timber is abundant and varied and has always been used for most building types, especially for houses. The traditional dwelling is a 'long house', generally raised on stilts, and often sheltering an entire clan. It is seen at its architectural best in the Menangkabau homes of south-central Sumatra, which are carried on carved and decorated wooden pillars, the facades adorned with colour patterns of intertwined flowers in white, black and red, and inward-sloping ridge ('saddleback') roofs with high gables at each end ornamented with buffalo horns.

Building Techniques and Processes

Africa

Building techniques varied widely with the availability of materials in the locality and the development of skills in relation to them (see under Resources).

In many parts of sub-Saharan Africa, where superstructures were comparatively flimsy, foundations were made of stone to resist insect attack. Walls were roughly framed in timber with infill matting woven in cleft wood, grasses and other vegetable matter. Elsewhere walls were constructed in mud or stones, planked in a variety of patterns, coursed in mud or bricks, or built of stone which was either roughly dressed and embedded in mud mortar or carefully dressed and dry set. Some stone walls had rubble cores or were reinforced with timbers. Roofs were lightweight, beehive or tent-like forms made from poles, brushwood, bamboos or bundles of grass or reeds embedded in the ground at the perimeter or supported on timber posts or, in some cases, on loadbearing walls. More substantial flat roofs were constructed of mud over a framework of timbers and matting, and in a few places vaulted and domed roofs were built in mud and stone. The weathering surfaces of roofs varied from reed and leaf thatch to skins or mats.

The Americas

Throughout North America, many constructional techniques evolved: the laced-plank communal lodges of the Canadian north-west; the bent-sapling Iroquois long-houses; earth lodges partly excavated and roofed with timbers; and in the American south-west, rubble masonry multi-storey pueblos, with timber floors and roofs. But the most impressive structures in North America, the earth-platform temples of the Eastern Woodlands, were accomplished with the most rudimentary means, the simple piling-up of basket-loads of earth.

In Central America, the Maya vault presents the most highly evolved of all American pre-colonial constructional devices, and it is also the most widely misunderstood. Although generally referred to as the corbelled vault, few Early Classic vaults were corbelled (see, for example, the Five Storey Pyramid, Edzna, p. 682A). The best-known Late Classic vaults depended for stability upon the adhesive properties of mortar and acted monolithically. The boot-shaped vault stones of northern Yucatan (see for example the Nunnery Complex, Uxmal, p. 687A) reveal the structural intention most clearly. These stones had their ends cut away so that the mortar of the core of the vault came as near as possible to the inner surface, where tensile stresses were concentrated. The stones at the surface provided a facing that could be dressed and shaped, and during construction acted as permanent shuttering, but they did not contribute significantly to the ultimate structural strength of the vault. The Late Classic vaults at Tikal (for example, Maler's Palace, p. 686A) are known to have been built in separate halves that did not lean against each other for support; the capstones merely covered the narrow slot between the two self-supporting halves. The Maya followed a structural concept quite different from that behind the voussoir arch and vault.

The massive structural elements of Maya buildings were independently stable; the cores or hearting of pyramidal substructures were built up so that the exterior facings were merely skins to shed the rain or to give meaningful forms but were not needed as retaining walls. The absence of bonding patterns in stonework suggests the Maya realised that the masonry facings did not keep the hearting material in place.

Andean constructions share some of these ideas but only to a limited degree. Most Inca and pre-Inca construction did not have distinct hearting masonry comparable to that of Maya structures. In South America the same kind of masonry and mortar was used for both inner and outer parts. The pitched roof on purlins and rafters received much greater attention in South America than it ever did farther north, where it hardly existed at all. True corbels were used extensively in Andean work to support floor and roof timbers. The famous Inca polygonal masonry (see, for example, Saqsaywaman, p. 690D), laid without mortar and very closely fitted, is unique among pre-colonial methods of construction, although the technique of cutting each stone to fit in one specific place was very widespread. The Late Classic masonry of the Maya was nearly all of this sort. Exceptions are the stones cut for mask elements in the Puuc (Codz-Poop, Kabah, p. 684B), in the Toltec-Maya work of northern Yucatan, and in the intricate stone mosaic surfacing on the palaces of Mitla (p. 689A), in the Oaxaca valley.

China

The historical evolution of the architectural style associated with ancient China is closely associated with timber-framed structure. Typically it was made up of three parts: foundation, columns and roof. The foundation, usually very shallow, was a layer of rammed earth. Columns stood on carved stone blocks on brick or stone bases. Floors were made of rammed earth and paved with bricks. Timber columns (usually of circular section) were notched to take the main lintels which ran parallel with the elevations of the building. Then a system of brackets was constructed over the top of each column (p. 658C). These bracket-sets, as they are sometimes called, consisted of superimposed sets of four bow-shaped or cranked arms at right angles to each other and known as 'gong', each higher set of increased length supported on the lower one by means of a notched block or 'dou'. The uppermost brackets supported eaves purlins directly through a series of fascias where necessary, and provided the bracketed support for transverse roof beams, which also reduced in length to provide the essential points of support for purlins placed in the concave configurations needed for such roofs. Bracket-sets were also carried at mid-span or elsewhere on both lintels and transverse beams in order to carry shorter beams above or to support purlins directly, in this case via a chamfered and stepped block notched to carry the lowest brackets. The purlins supported rafters which were boarded and covered with tiles fixed in mud. Ridge-tiles were added where the two sloping surfaces met, and edge tiles were fastened to appropriate timber members by nailing. The nails used for this purpose were covered with the decorative carved animal motifs of various sizes which characterise the roofs of many Chinese buildings.

Buildings of different forms and scales were roofed in different ways – with hipped roofs (see Chapter 24), hipped and gabled roofs, overhanging gable roofs (p. 663A), parapet-gable roofs (p. 663B), and double-hipped roofs (p. 663D). The various categories were combined in many ways, some of which can be seen from the illustrations.

Korea

Two forms of timber construction were introduced to Korea from China, each involving a method of relating the column to the superimposed framing of floors and roofs. The first is column-head bracketing in which the capitals and bearing blocks on top of the columns are reinforced with a kind of cornice, the undersides of the bracket arms are cut in undulating waves, short struts are fitted along the beams between the pillars, and no brackets are extended into the framework of the ceiling. The second type is multi-cluster bracketing in which there must be a thick, sturdy architrave beam on the tie-beam to provide space for clusters of intercolumnar brackets, which gain height by repeating the basic unit of transverse and longitudinal arms two, three or four times to grip the next bearing blocks on both sides of the wall until they are worked into the framework of the ceiling. Bracket arms are usually finished in arcs.

In addition to these two systems introduced from China and adapted to Korean architecture, a style with wing-like brackets was developed by simplifying the column-head bracketing system, and it was used in many public and monumental buildings.

In time, all three styles underwent gradual modifications. Ornamental elements of the column-head brackets were accentuated as cornices disappeared, the undulating curves under the bracket arms became more pronounced, and the ends of the arms, which had been bluntly vertical, were slanted. As for multi-cluster bracketing, the transverse arms, which had protruded from the wall in a stubby downward slant, became longer and curved upward, while those protruding into the building formed a harmonious cluster embellished by cloud-shaped carvings.

Column-head bracketing is most frequently found in the main halls of early Choson temples. It gradually disappeared from use around the mid-Choson period. The Korean predilection for multi-cluster bracketing is apparent from its use in important palatial structures, public monuments, and the main halls of a few early temples and most of those built after the mid-Choson period. Simple wing-like bracketing was used in minor palatial structures, government offices, and educational buildings such as Confucian academies, as befitted the austere Confucian ideas of the time.

Influenced by Shirhak (see Culture), Korean architects began to take an interest in Western technology. Such modern devices as cranes and pulleys were used in building the walls of the Suwon Fortress, constructed in the early nineteenth century, and meticulous building records were kept during its construction. Construction materials and wages were standardised and bricks were used for the first time.

Japan

The constructional techniques used in historical Japanese temple buildings are explained below, with reference to constructional drawings presented in Chapter 25.

Traditional Japanese architecture is of timber construction and uses only the post-and-lintel system. The basic plan consists of a central core (moya) with a one-bay deep aisle-like addition (hisashi) placed on one, two, three or four sides. Sometimes a second similar aisle-like addition (magobisashi) is constructed across the front of the building. To increase interior space further, another one-bay area with a separate pent roof (mokoshi) is either added to the hisashi, or, omitting the hisashi, placed around the moya. The timber structures are erected on podia made of hard-packed earth covered with dressed stone slabs, or of natural stones or wooden flooring set over a plaster-covered mound. Rows of pillars set on base-stones mark the exterior frame, separate the moya and hisashi or mokoshi, and define the number of longitudinal and transverse bays (p. 730C).

Bracket complexes (tokyo; kumimono), ranging from a single boat-shaped bracket arm to six stepped complexes, are usually set on top of the pillars to carry bracket-tie beams and eaves purlins and to receive the ends of transverse beams and tail rafters (odaruki). The most common complex is composed of a large bearing block (daito), carrying a bracket arm (hijiki) topped by three small bearing blocks (masu) (p. 730B). Frog-leg struts (kaerumata), bearing-block-capped struts (kentozuka) or additional bracket complexes may be placed between those on the pillars.

There are two methods of roof framing: first, corbelled transverse rainbow-beams (koryo) with frog-leg struts (struts placed at the centre of the upper rainbow-beam carry a bracket arm with bearing blocks to support the ridge); second, single transverse beams supporting central struts strengthened by diagonal braces (sasu) (single bearing blocks are placed at the peak to support the ridge) (p. 730A).

The hidden roof (noyane), an ingenious system using two sets of rafters, came into universal use in the early Heian period. The exposed base rafters conceal a secondary cantilevered framework which supports a set of hidden rafters (nodaruki) above (p. 734B). This enables the hidden rafters to be set at an appropriate pitch to facilitate the flow of rainwater or the removal of snow while the exposed rafters (keshodaruki) are given a more gentle incline allowing maximum infiltration of daylight. With the development of the hidden roof, ceilings over the moya became common. Ceiling types ranged from plank or board and batten methods to the most intricate forms of coffering. Exposed rafters over the hisashi needed no additional ceiling (p. 733B).

Eaves are either single (composed of a single row of base rafters upon which is placed a long horizontal support for the eaves, kayaoi), or double (relatively short rafters called flying rafters are added to the base rafters and held by a flying rafter support, kioi) (p. 730A). Because the flying rafters extend from the interior to the exterior, they increase the overhang of the eaves. A support for the eaves is positioned, therefore, across the ends of the flying rafters to support the eaves; because it is given a slight upward lift at the corners, it counteracts the downward thrust.

Rafters (taruki) are usually set in parallel rows and continue in shortened lengths when attached to the hip rafters at the corners of hip-and-gable roofs. From the mediaeval period, rafters were often set so that they radiated toward the corners. These are called fan rafters (ogidaruki).

Under the eaves there are shallow latticed ceilings, latticed ceilings with curved ribs (shirin), a line of curved ribs in parallel arrangement, or the last plus another crossed set of curved ribs, forming a lozenge pattern. On the interior the ribs are coved.

The four roof types are gabled (kirizuma-yane), hipped (yosemune-yane) (p. 733A), pyramidal (hogyo-yane), and hip and gable combined (irimoya-yane) (p. 740A). The last is the most common. Roofing materials include tile (kawarabuki), cypress bark (hiwadabuki) (p. 739B), multi-layered, thinly cut wood shingles (kokerabuki) and, recently, copper sheeting over a timber base (dobanbuki). Except for metal spikes driven through the rafters to secure them to the purlins, all other members were assembled by various jointing techniques including the use of dowels.

South and South-east Asia

For the historical cultural reasons described earlier in this chapter, the surviving architecture of these regions in this period, mainly associated with the principal religions, is more remarkable for its symbolism and form than for its technological innovation by comparison with contemporary structures elsewhere. Not that it lacked virtuosity – often of the most remarkable kind – ranging from the delicate lace-like marbles of Islamic palaces and mausolea to the great Buddhist stupas of Sri Lanka, Cambodia, Thailand and Burma and the soaring sculptured gopura of southern India.

Though Buddhist meeting halls and stupas were intended for participation on the part of large congregations, they are nevertheless structurally and constructionally comparatively simple, but where they are gigantic in scale they are remarkable achievements in any terms. In some of the early rock-cut halls (chaityas) the forms of timber prototypes are preserved and though no timber example has survived, paintings at Ajanta and the descriptions left by early Chinese travellers show they had steeply pitched roofs covered with thatch, similar in form to pyramidal stone roofs on square buildings still surviving in Kashmir which are also thought to be masonry reproductions of timber originals. Other rock-cut examples such as those in Afghanistan seem to be less influenced by earlier models and develop logical rock-cut forms – battered jambs and walls carrying roughly semicircular arches and vaults.

At Anuradhapura and Polonnaruwa in Sri Lanka only the closely spaced stone columns of the huge ground-floor halls remain. They represent a remarkable level of sophistication in structural framing (upper floors and roofs were in timber to reduce superimposed loading) on a par with the virtuosity of the performance of the stone carvers in producing the rock-cut halls.

The stupas, gigantic symbols of the Buddhist world, were, in effect, monumental tumuli encased in more or less permanent veneers of stone or brick, often stuccoed or whitened. The podia formed the essential lower retaining walls for the mounds which were set back to provide the processional way at high level for ritual use. Although there is a considerable variety in stupa shapes, the ring construction with

A. Overhanging gable roof. See p.661

D. Double-hipped roof. See p.661

B. Parapet-gable roofs. See p.661

C. Graeco-Bactrian masonry. Acropolis, Sirkap. See p.664

E. Graeco-Bactrian masonry detail, Sirkap. See p.664

earth core support presents little technical difficulty other than that to do with sheer size. The brick or stone veneers are often bracketed at intermediate levels and the whole structure surmounted by 'umbrella' or other terminals, usually with characteristic regional profiles related to the traditional uses of local materials.

Early influence from the Mediterranean civilisations is evident in the north-west of the Indian subcontinent. Sophisticated examples of stone walling (p. 663C,E) show the influence of Hellenistic techniques and their use in reminiscent, though degraded, Classical forms, again usually in buildings in which structure is unproblematic, such as those at Sirkap (Taxila).

Some early Jain temples, like Buddhist chaityas, were in rock-cut caves, exact copies in rock of wood and thatch structures, their walls polished to a mirror finish. Later Jain temples (after about 1000), like contemporary Hindu structures, were roofed with flat domes, the stonework so elaborately carved as to completely conceal the construction technique, which consisted of successively diminishing courses of stone. To form the flat domes, the stone courses were corbelled (with stones laid either diagonally or in the more usual concentric rings), the final opening covered with a single capstone, sometimes developed as a carved pendant.

Hindu temples are sculptural in character rather than architectonic as compared with much Western architecture (but see the description of the carving of Greek temples after construction in Chapter 2). Even internal and external galleries, where they exist above ground level, are carved out of the stone, whether actually from the solid or from coursed masonry. At Mamallapuram, the Dharmaraja ratha (*c.* 650) (p. 658B), exemplifies the technique of carving from solid rock; the Shore Temple is a coursed example of similar scale (p. 658A), and the same character is also typical of the great seventeenth-century gopurams in which the minimal enclosed space is insignificant by comparison with the sculptural symbolism of the external forms.

Other less common forms of construction, such as the cupola roofs at Bamiyan, Afghanistan, are to be found in the region. Arched squinches are used across the angles of the chambers (anticipating Sassanian fire-temples), and there is an idiosyncratic lantern roof, a coffered dome and an elaborate system of hexagons and triangles to a central octagon.

Timber construction varied in complexity from the simple framed and strutted techniques used for domestic buildings in conjunction with brick, wattle or timber-lattice panels, to the complex Chinese methods described earlier in this chapter. Examples of the latter can be seen in the temple and palace roofs of Nepal and Thailand. The simpler timber buildings in such areas as the Mekong delta, Cambodia, must have contrasted strangely with the massively coursed stone buildings of Angkor and Phimeanakas.

Building techniques used in the Muslim buildings of the region are covered in Chapter 15.

Chapter 22
AFRICA

Architectural Character

Today Africa is inhabited by over a thousand different peoples, each with a unique material culture. For many traditional societies, architecture was one of the principal means to cultural identity, not only in the way in which buildings were laid out, constructed and decorated, but also in the way in which they were grouped together. In many communities more than one type of house was built to indicate a difference in gender or status. In addition, three types of special-purpose building have been found: palaces or the dwellings of chiefs; religious buildings, such as shrines, temples, mosques and churches; and funerary and other monuments.

Meroitic architecture drew upon Egyptian building forms. Axial planning was common in important buildings, and rooms were organised in sequences or smaller rooms were arranged within larger ones. Many buildings were decorated with inscriptions or reliefs depicting Meroitic victories over neighbouring peoples. At Axum planning was formal, with recursive groups of rooms around courtyards. There were many multi-storey structures with plain, articulated stone walls. On the East African coast Muslim influences are apparent, and layouts here were also based on rooms in sequence, with reception spaces for guests leading to private suites of rooms further from the street. Door and window openings as well as decoration drew upon and adapted Islamic themes. The palaces of West Africa were planned and constructed in a similar way to the houses of commoners, but the basic building block comprising a single dwelling was repeated where a large building was required. Frequently palaces were arranged around open courtyards. The conversion of West African monarchs to Islam influenced architectural styles in the region, but in the absence of stone or large timbers, a local mud-brick and timber style reminiscent of termite hills evolved. While it is difficult to generalise about the character of African pre-colonial architecture it is clear that African buildings were never direct copies of those of other cultures. The layout, methods of construction and forms of decoration were unique to Africa.

Examples

Domestic buildings

Because of the perishable nature of the materials with which most traditional dwellings were built, extant examples of pre-colonial houses are rare.

Examples of brick-built **Meroitic houses** have been found on the island of **Gaminarti** in ancient Nubia. Meroitic houses had two rooms – a larger living and sleeping room about 3 m × 5 m (10 ft × 16 ft) in plan, containing cooking pots and a hearth, led to a smaller, squarish interior room, used as a store. The two-roomed units were arranged to form a larger complex which is thought to have housed a small community or a large, extended family.

Axumite houses in Ethiopia consisted of only one rectangular or circular room and were stone-built. A clay model recovered near Axum represents a house dating from about 400. Two-storey round-houses were also built from sandstone and had basalt foundations. Both types were reinforced with timbers. Similar houses are found today in Tigre.

Houses from the ancient kingdom of Ghana have been found **at El Ghaba**, where the king and royal court resided. The town consisted of a fortress and domed huts of acacia wood, enclosed by a wall. Some six miles to the north lay the town of **Kumbi Saleh**, where the Muslim traders lived in substantial, stone-built houses dating from the eleventh century. The room adjacent to the street contained the stairs to the upper floor, and from it led a sequence of narrow rooms which filled the entire width of the house. Each room was about 1.5 m (5 ft) deep and up to 10 m (33 ft) wide. The house walls abutting the street contained alcoves within the thickness of the wall, and there were smaller niches in many of the interior rooms which were plastered and painted.

A spatial progression from the street can also be seen in **Swahili houses** from the town of **Gedi** in Kenya (*c*. 1300). They were clustered in small groups. A large door led to a private courtyard and thence to a sequence of narrow rooms of similar proportions to those at Kumbi Saleh. The front court

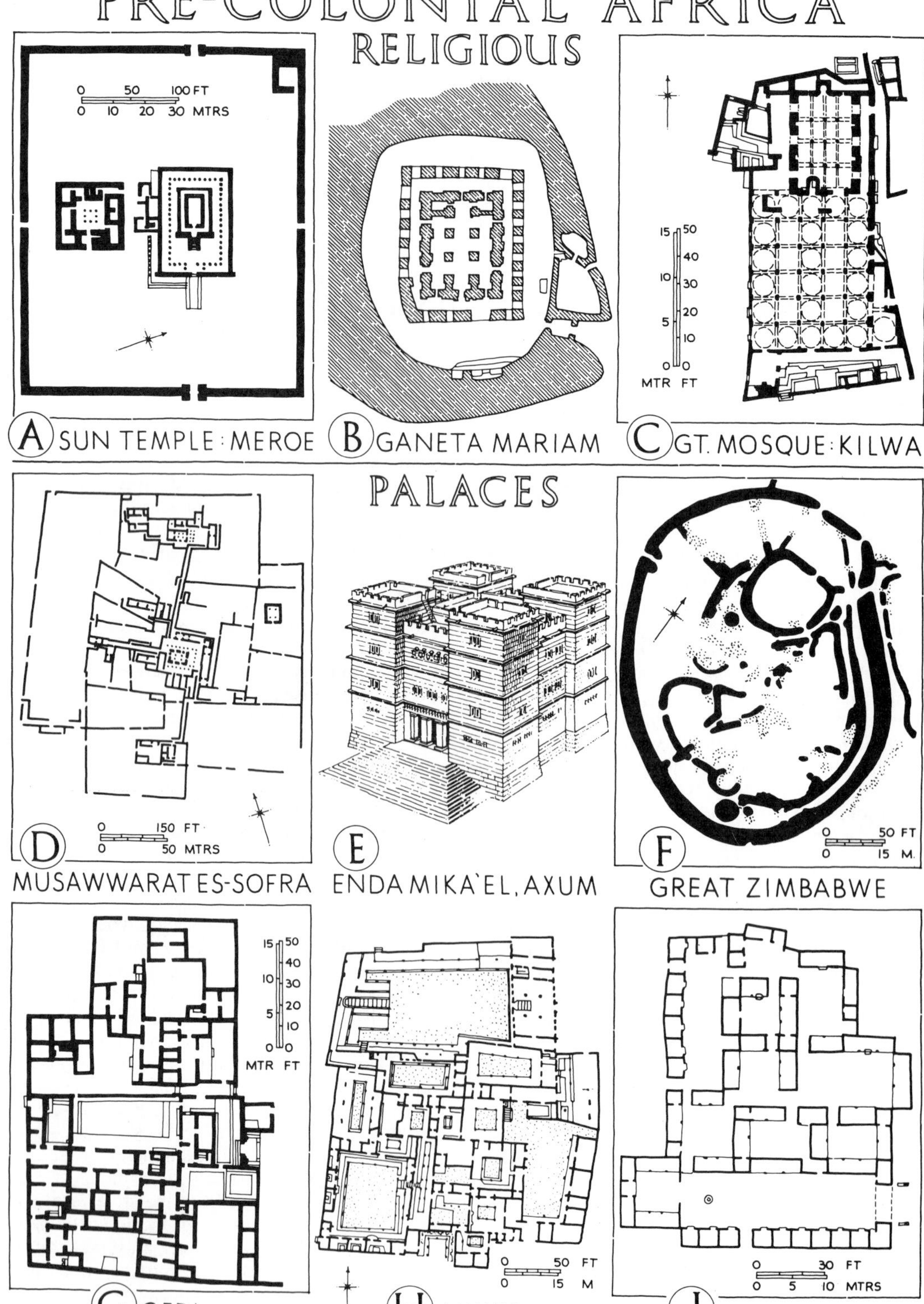

(A) SUN TEMPLE: MEROE (B) GANETA MARIAM (C) GT. MOSQUE: KILWA

(D) MUSAWWARAT ES-SOFRA (E) ENDA MIKA'EL, AXUM (F) GREAT ZIMBABWE

(G) GEDI (H) AKURE (J) KUMASI

usually had a sunken central area with seating around three sides. The larger houses were built of coral ragstone, mortared and plastered with burnt coral lime. Typically, doorways had a wide pointed arch set in a recessed rectangular field, with small niches on either side containing oil lamps. These houses were originally single-storey, although many had upper floors added in the fifteenth and sixteenth centuries. The lower floor was windowless, but the upper floor had windows overlooking the courtyard. Access to the upper floor appears to have been by timber ladders. The House of the Cowries had a small entry leading to a long narrow court which gave access to the room in which visitors were received. The house had a flat roof carried on mangrove poles. The outer room had a tiled ceiling, while those to the rear had roofs of stamped red earth. Similar **Swahili houses** dating from the fifteenth century were found at **Songo Mnara**, Tanzania.

Sixteenth-century **houses at Mvuleni**, Zanzibar, were detached and set within walled compounds. A central block of long, narrow rooms similar to those at Gedi was surrounded by verandahs and heavily buttressed external walls which carried an upper storey or flat roof.

Monumental Architecture

Palaces and Chiefs' Dwellings

The **Meroitic Western Palace, Faras**, in Nubia (*c.* 100) was a squarish building of sun-dried brick, approximately 40 m × 45 m (130 ft × 150 ft). It comprised a pillared courtyard surrounded by a series of small rooms, which enclosed a central building.

The Axumite royal residence of **Ta'akha Mariam, Axum** in modern Ethiopia, was a multi-storey, monumental group of stone buildings forming a closed rectangle, 120 m × 80 m (400 ft × 260 ft). It had two large interior courts and several small courts at different levels, many hundreds of rooms and dozens of staircases. In the centre was an eight-storey structure with towers at the corners: this is thought to have been the royal residence. It was square in plan, 24 m × 25 m (78 ft × 82 ft), and was approached by a flight of stone steps leading to a portico. A similar tower has been excavated at **Enda Mika'el, Axum** (p. 666E), and at **Dongur** where an irregular square palace complex covering 3000 m^2 (32,280 ft^2) and dating to about 600 has been discovered. Here the main building was at the centre of a closed ring of large and small buildings which formed a multi-roomed complex with four interior courts. The rooms were grouped into four principal blocks and there were a further four courts between the main building and those surrounding it. Axumite palaces combined the character of a castle with the luxury of a villa. Timber beams and framing combined with monolithic stone panels, columns, slabs and large-scale polished stone blocks in a form of mixed construction known as 'monkey head'. The arch was unknown to Axumite builders. Palaces were decorated with carved wooden friezes, and had floors inlaid with basalt, granite, marble, and limestone.

The Iron Age ruins at **Great Zimbabwe** in Zimbabwe (*c.* 1000–1500 BC) (p. 666F) are some of the most impressive in Africa. They form three main groups. The **Great Enclosure** comprises a massive, free-standing outer wall enclosing a second, incomplete smaller wall at the southern end of which stands a solid conical tower. This was probably a chief's residence. The outer wall was about 10 m (33 ft) high, and about 3 m (10 ft) thick, enclosing an ellipse measuring roughly 90 m × 65 m (300 ft × 210 ft). Circular houses were built within the Enclosure: they were constructed of poles, wattle and daub with thatched conical roofs and rammed earth floors. The enclosure also contained audience platforms and monoliths. To the north lies the **Acropolis**, a fortified granite kopje of drystone walls and terraces. Between the two lie the **Valley Ruins**, a labyrinth of walling, cattle kraals and small stone enclosures. The building stone was local granite, roughly dressed and securely packed. Foundations were rough, often non-existent. The walls of the Acropolis were skilfully built to incorporate naturally occurring rounded boulders. The walls of the Great Enclosure were curvilinear and the entrance openings were of curved shape. Some were decorated in chevron, chequer, dogtooth and herringbone patterns, and inset with courses of dolorite blocks. Most remains date from the fifteenth century BC and later. Many other similar but smaller ruins have been found in the region at **Khami**, near Bulawayo, where there were platforms decorated with chequer patterns, battered walls infilled with stones, and the remains of seven pole and daga huts with thatched roofs, at **Dhlo-Dhlo**, at **Mapungubwe**, and at **Inyanga** where the remains of terraces and enclosures for cattle have been found.

On a headland west of Kilwa, on the Tanzanian East Coast, lies the **Palace of Husuni Kubwa** built by the Sultans of Kilwa about 1245. It measures 150 m × 75 m (500 ft × 250 ft) and contains over a hundred rooms. It is built of coral ragstone set in lime mortar, with dressed stone door openings and vaults. Sandstone slabs were used for steps and seats. Ceilings were over 3 m (10 ft) high, and as there were no windows interiors were dark. Roofs were of rectangular coral blocks carried on closely spaced timbers; floors of white plaster were laid directly onto the subsoil but courtyards were unpaved. The buildings were axially planned, around two large courtyards. Other rooms surrounded the principal suites, but were simpler in character. The main approach was from the seashore up a flight of steps cut into the cliffs to mark a reception courtyard with rooms at the northern end. These were roofed with barrel vaults and ornamented with decorative stonework. To the west lay an octagonal open-air bathing pool, surrounded by an ambulatory, and to the north a court used for assemblies. The court was flanked by high walls and at its eastern end was a bank of nine seats, 14 m (46 ft) wide. Opposite these were two chambers in sequence, each with three entrances. A short distance to the east of Husuni Kubwa lay a fort-like enclosure known as **Husuni Nnogo**.

The fifteenth-century **Swahili palace at Gedi**, Kenya (p. 666G), covered 18 ha (44 acres) and was approached from the town square. The main entrance was through a portal with pointed arches. Beyond was a sunken reception court with benches down the long sides; this led to an audience court. The ruler's quarters, which faced the audience court, comprised an outer room and inner private rooms which were divided to form two suites. One of the innermost spaces had a strongroom, entered by a trapdoor in the wall. Separated from the palace by a narrow alley was an annexe comprising four small suites each with an outer room, inner room, lavatory and courtyard. In the alley between the two buildings there were several tombs, including a hexagonal pillar tomb. The reception rooms were decorated with niches, and there were recesses for oil lamps and pegs for wall hangings and carpets.

The **Swahili palace at Kilwa**, Tanzania, was a two-storey building on three sides of a large rectangular courtyard measuring approximately 20 m × 30 m (66 ft × 100 ft). A series of double rooms in sequence adjoined the courtyard to the north and south. At the south-west corner was a rectangular tower with battered walls which was approached by a passage leading directly from the main courtyard. The palace was set in a walled enclosure about 2 ha (5 acres) in extent and containing a mosque. The building is of more than one period, but none of it is older than the eighteenth century.

The West African palaces of the Yoruba, the Ashanti and the Edo of Benin cannot be dated precisely. Many of the examples recorded by travellers in the nineteenth century appear to date from precolonial times. In Yorubaland, palaces were built of puddled mud mixed with palm-oil, and had roofs which were thatched with palm-leaf mats. They were surrounded by high mud walls, enclosing the buildings, and by large tracts of forest. **Yoruba palaces** were collections of individual courtyard buildings, in which four rectangular rooms with verandahs surrounded central open courts. The roofs of the verandahs were supported on iroko pillars. Each building had an impluvium to catch and store rainwater, and drains were provided to conduct the water away. Some of these palaces had over a hundred courtyards, some small and shaded, and others large enough to accommodate gatherings of people: each was dedicated to a different function. The roof-posts and doors were elaborately carved from solid wood, and the roofs of palace buildings had raised, projecting gables. Some of the courtyards were paved with quartz pebbles and potsherds. The **palace at Akure** (p. 666H) is one of the best-preserved extant examples.

Benin city was destroyed by fire in 1879 after its capture by the British. Travellers' accounts from the sixteenth century onwards describe the palace as a large complex of ordinary Benin houses built in coursed mud. Unlike Yoruba houses, these were rectangular and based on a sequence, with an entrance court containing an altar, a reception court with impluvium, and private rooms and other courts with impluvia behind. Rooms were narrow, and ran the entire width of the house, but how the individual units were laid out is not clear. The buildings had hipped roofs covered with shingles or palm leaves, and some of them had towers clad with shingles and decorated with bronze birds. The palace was of greater height than the houses of commoners.

The **Ashanti palace at Kumasi** (p. 666J) was also destroyed by the British in the late nineteenth century but was subsequently rebuilt to the traditional plan. The palace was built around several courtyards. The walls were decorated with curvilinear reliefs modelled in mud plaster and painted in a variety of earth colours.

Religious Buildings

Indigenous religions did not produce much monumental architecture. Most rituals took place at sacred open-air sites, and although some peoples built shrines, often their significance lay in the act of building rather than in their regular use. Permanent shrines and temples seem to have been built only where ritual specialists had emerged. Temples featured prominently in the religious life of the kingdoms of Meroe and Axum. Mosques accompanied Islamic traders, and wood and stone and rock-cut churches on a basilican or cross-in-square plan were built by the Coptic Christians of Ethiopia.

SHRINES

The **Ashanti shrine at Bawjwiasi**, Ghana, was probably built in the late nineteenth or early twentieth century, but the plan form is much older. It comprised four distinct rectangular rooms built from wattle and daub on a timber frame, each measuring about 5 m × 3 m (16 ft × 10 ft) and arranged around an open courtyard. The rooms were joined by walls to form a closed square. The external walls were decorated with animal motifs and the roofs were thatched with palm leaves cut into a distinctive tiered shape. Inside, three of the rooms were open to the courtyard while the fourth, the shrine room, was shielded from view by a richly decorated openwork screen.

TEMPLES

Meroitic temples have survived from a number of sites including that at **Kawa** near the modern town of Dongola, in the Sudan. Most remains date to New Kingdom times but the **Eastern Palace** was purely Meroitic and dedicated to the Lion God, Apedemek. It was a rectangular brick building of the first century BC with a stone entrance flanked by recumbent lions in red sandstone.

The **Temple of Amun at Meroe** in ancient Nubia was about 150 m (500 ft) long and was approached through a small kiosk or shrine. The route from the kiosk to the temple itself was flanked by four stone rams. The temple was of fired brick with dressed sandstone facings, doorways, pylons and columns. The plan of the temple comprised an outer peristyle hall, in the middle of which was a stone shrine, while to the west there was a stone dais or pulpit with steps. Beyond the main hall lay a series of smaller ones culminating in the sanctuary, in which stood an altar decorated with religious scenes. To the west was a Hall of Columns, painted predominantly blue on a background of white stucco. The purpose of this room is unknown.

The **Sun Temple at Meroe** (p. 666A) was surrounded by a red-brick wall with stone-faced gateways, inside which a ramp led to a colonnade enclosing the sanctuary with two nested rooms. The external walls were decorated with reliefs depicting Meroitic conquests, and floor and walls were covered internally with blue glazed tiles. This temple is thought to have been built about 600 BC, and to have been restored in the first century. Other important temples at **Meroe** include the **Lion Temple**, the **Temple of Isis** and the **Shrine of Apsis**. The site of Jebel Barkal contained important temples and pyramids, begun in the New Kingdom and restored by Meroitic rulers. There were a number of temples at Naqa including a **Lion Temple** dedicated to Apedemek.

The **Great Enclosure at Musawwarat es-Sofra** (p. 666D), also in ancient Nubia (*c.* 100), comprised buildings and walled enclosures covering an area of 40,000 m^2 (430,400 ft^2) surrounding a temple similar in design to the Sun Temple at Meroe. From the temple, a colonnade gave access to a series of passages and ramps connecting the various parts of the group of buildings. Its function is obscure, but it may have been used for the training of war elephants. These animals featured prominently in the reliefs decorating the walls.

The **pre-Axumite temple at Yeha**, in Ethiopia, was a square multi-storey tower with blank exterior walls, on the scale and proportions of Axumite royal residences. The entrance was by way of a flight of steps leading to a portico.

MOSQUES

The **Great Mosque at Kilwa**, in Tanzania (p. 666C), dating from the twelfth century, was divided into square bays, each of which was roofed with a dome supported by square capitals on octagonal pillars of dressed coral. The mihrab was of dressed coral, and the walls were of coral rubble and lime cement. The original mosque was considerably enlarged in the fifteenth century; four rows of columns were added, making it one of the largest mosques in East Africa.

The **Sanskore Mosque at Timbuktu** in ancient Mali was built of mud on a permanent scaffolding of timber to permit regular maintenance. It is the earliest extant example of its type, dating to the early fourteenth century. A similar pisé and timber **mosque** was built at **Jenne** with buttresses and pinnacles. It was set on a mud-brick platform, and entered by way of a flight of steps. The original mosque was destroyed about 1830, but was rebuilt in a similar style.

The **Swahili mosque at Gedi**, Kenya, dates from the mid-fifteenth century. It was a rectangular, congregational mosque with a mihrab in the north wall and a minabar with three steps to the right. The flat roof was supported on three rows of six rectangular pillars. The three rear bays were screened by a wall, possibly to demarcate the women's area. Around the walls were pilasters with square niches to carry oil lamps. The mihrab had a pointed and stilted arch set in a square frame which was decorated with porcelain bowls. Each of the long walls had three doors. To the west lay an anteroom, subsequently coverted into an open platform, to the east were a verandah and a court containing a well, conduit, cistern and lavatory, while at the north end there was a store and a flight of steps leading to the roof from which the faithful were called to prayer. The mosque was roofed in coral tiles, set in lime mortar.

CHURCHES

Lalibela, the ancient Zagwe capital in Ethiopia, has eleven churches in three groups of six, four and one, all hewn out of solid rock during the twelfth and thirteenth centuries. Many have features which can be traced back to Axumite buildings. One of the most elegant of the monolithic churches is the isolated **Biet Giorgis**. It is approached through a narrow, winding trench cut into the rock. The church is a 12 m cube, cut into the form of a cross, with a flat roof into which is cut a triple cross. It stands on a plinth, and is approached by a short flight of steps. The main door has a monumental triple frame and the ground floor has nine blind windows. At a higher level there are twelve ogival windows ornamented with leaves carved in low relief. The stone beams supporting the upper windows are carved to imitate wood and are decorated with acanthus leaves. The interior of the church has four three-sided pillars and the roof of the sanctury is cut into the shape of a dome.

Ganeta Mariam (p. 666B), several miles from Lalibela, was also chiselled out of the solid rock. It is thought to date from about a century later than the groups of churches mentioned above. A single entrance leads to a hewn-out courtyard and thence to the square, freestanding block from which the church was cut. Ganeta Mariam has a pitched roof and stands on a high plinth with a colonnade around the exterior. It has two aisles and a nave cut from the solid rock and separated by pillars. The nave has a barrel-vaulted ceiling and the interior is decorated with painted friezes depicting biblical scenes. There are similar, but less elaborate, rock-cut churches in Tigre.

FUNERARY AND OTHER MONUMENTS

The **Royal Cemetery at Meroe** in Nubia contains the pyramid burials of many of the dynastic rulers of ancient Meroe. Meroitic pyramids, small and sharply pointed, were built of dressed sandstone blocks on a rubble core. A chapel with pylons at the entrance was built against the east face. The chapel walls were covered with reliefs and inscriptions. The burial chamber was dug into the rock beneath the chapel, and was approached by a stairway located to the east of the chapel. Meroitic **pyramids** have also been discovered at **Nuri, Jebel Barkal** and **El Kurru**.

Axumite burials have been found at **Nefas Mawcha, Axum**, in Ethiopia, where a giant granite slab was supported on a substructure of smaller slabs which together formed a central chamber and a number of surrounding rooms. The **Tomb of the False Door** was an Axumite subterranean mortuary of dressed granite slabs connected to a surface structure which simulated a temple or palace building. The mortuary chamber contained a stone sarcophagus. At **Axum**, giant pillars or **stellae** up to 33 m (110 ft) high and hewn from single pieces of rock were erected in the burial area at the perimeter of the town. Some of these stellae were carved into stylised representations of multi-storey buildings.

At **Igbo-Ukwu**, in Nigeria, a tomb has been discovered dating to 900–1100. It was subterranean, and was lined with wooden planks jointed with iron clamps and nails. Matting had been placed on the floor. The corpse was buried sitting on a stool propped in a corner, with his arms supported by copper brackets. The tomb had a wooden roof, above which lay the bodies of slaves. Two nearby cache pits contained grave goods.

A number of tall, tapering pillar tombs were built during the fifteenth century in East Africa, at a number of locations along the coast. Some of the finest are at **Kaole** in Tanzania, and at **Malindi** and **Mnarani** on the Kenyan coast. Early pillars were built of coral rubble and later examples were in stone. The tall pillars usually rose from one end of a low, panelled stone grave. Those at **Mambrui** in Kenya are later – from the sixteenth century – and are more squat in shape.

The **Cross River Monoliths** in West Africa are standing stones, 1 m (3 ft) to 1.5 m (5 ft) high, decorated with human and geometric designs. They date from the sixteenth century. Some appear to have had phallic significance. Standing stones have also been found in Mali at **Tondidaro**, and they are widespread in Senegal and Ethiopia. Occasionally standing stones are associated with burials. Some standing stones are decorated with specifically African designs, mainly daggers, bands and circles, and human figures.

Chapter 23
THE AMERICAS

Architectural Character

The history of pre-colonial architecture in the Americas extends over thousands of years and includes uncountable numbers of buildings (see Chapter 21). Here the focus is on temples and palaces, building types which predominated in the areas of high civilisation and served as vehicles for the most significant developments in architecture.

Temples were vertical and pyramidal in form with nearly square plans and restricted interiors, usually consisting of a few narrow, dark rooms. A number of quite large temples contained no interior spaces. Examples of these are Cahokia, La Venta, The Cuidadela (Teotihuacan), and the Temple of the Sun (Moche). Palaces, on the other hand, enclosed large areas in proportion to the size of their substructures, usually made up of groups of long, narrow rooms adjacent to each other, as for example in Maler's Palace, Tikal.

North America

Pre-colonial monumental architecture can be found throughout the eastern United States in the form of truncated earthen pyramids, often grouped around ceremonial plazas or clustered in precincts. The pyramids did not have facing materials and assumed large, simple forms with little terracing or surface articulation. Rectangular and square plan-shapes predominated, but a few temples were circular, and other were shaped like serpents or totemic figures. Volumes ranged from a few hundred to almost a million cubic metres (35 million cubic feet) as at Cahokia; only a handful are known to have had pole and thatch buildings as part of them. Today the remains of these temples are barely recognisable as human artefacts, and the great majority of them have been destroyed within the last few decades.

In the south-west United States, impressive communal structures were built by the Anazasi and Pueblo cultures at Pueblo Bonito, Mesa Verde, the Chaco canyon and other sites. These buildings incorporated the functions of temples and palaces in their rectangular systems of rooms, which were used for various purposes and were punctuated by circular kivas used as ceremonial spaces. In these structures the geometry of ritual architecture was hidden, accessible only to initiates, quite the opposite to the high cultures in Mesoamerica, where the ceremonial features were made as conspicuous as possible.

Mesoamerica

In contrast to the disparate architectural forms in North America, monumental ceremonial architecture of the Mesoamerican high civilisations (Olmec, Maya, Zapotec, Toltec and Aztec) generally conformed to a single model that varied only in detail with location and period. This was based on a clear distinction between superstructure and substructure (p. 673). It is a method of composition still practised among the rural Maya. Typical vernacular Maya houses built today have a raised floor pad of crude masonry to carry walls and roofs of wattle, pole or thatch.

Lowland Maya builders vaulted the temple buildings (p. 673) and expressed the vaulting on the exterior by means of a horizontal band known as the upper zone, on which were highly conspicuous symbolic images in painted relief. The vault may have had symbolic significance based on its earlier use in tombs.

Substructure platforms were also symbolic. In fully developed Maya temples of southern Mexico and Guatemala elaborate substructures were formed as additive assemblies of distinct, three-dimensionally recognisable 'bodies', and to some extent were standardised. A description of Temple I at Tikal, in Guatemala (p. 684A), for example, with its six component types – basal-platform, pyramid, supplementary-platform, building-platform, building, and roof-comb – is equally applicable to more than a hundred temples built over more than 800 years. Ceremonial architecture may have been less disciplined in other places, but similar groups of elements can be clearly identified even though they may not be always the same set found at Tikal.

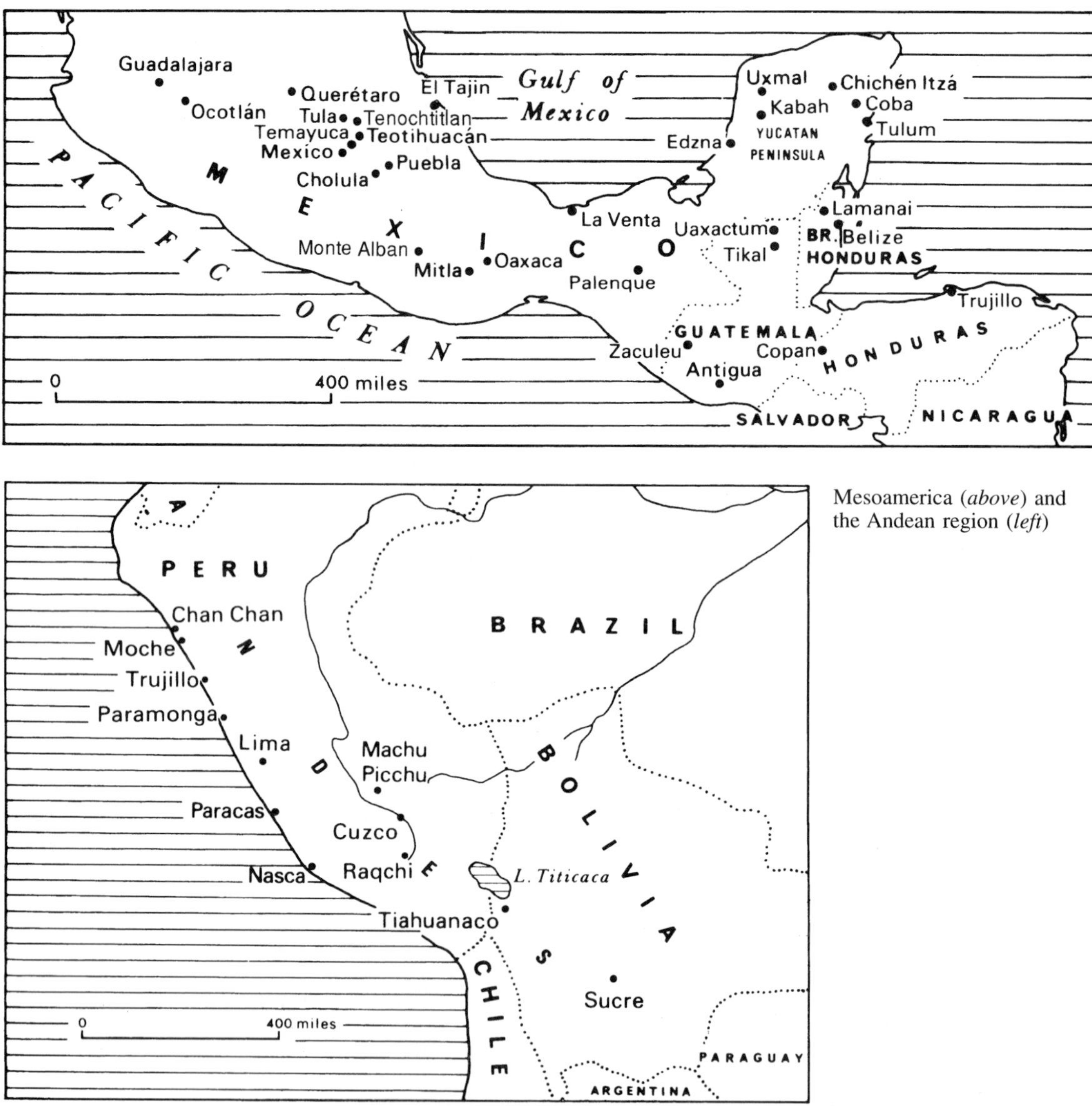

Mesoamerica (*above*) and the Andean region (*left*)

Terraces, stairs, insets, outsets, and sculptural panels articulated the surfaces of the elements of the temples. In the lowlands of the Maya regions of northern Guatemala, in Belize and southern Yucatan, the apron profile (p. 673) predominated as a device to emphasise the surface of the terrace. A quite different profile known as the tablero-talude (p. 673) was used in the highlands and appeared only rarely in the lowlands. Insets and outsets were applied as facets to substructure surfaces beside stairs, at the corners, on the sides, and centrally at the rear. In some cases the outset profiles repeated the terrace profiles, for instance in Structure 5D–22, 1st, at Tikal (p. 675), and in others staircases were given distinct profiles of their own, as for example the stair-side outsets of Structure B–4, 2nd A, Altun Ha (p. 682B).

Substructures constituted a 'landform' language that acted as an architectural extension of the natural topography and connected the temple to the earth in both a literal and figurative way. As originally built, in Central America and the Andean region, the masonry construction was concealed with plaster and painted red, or, more frequently, left unpainted and burnished white. A similar plaster finish was used to pave the open spaces in front of temples,

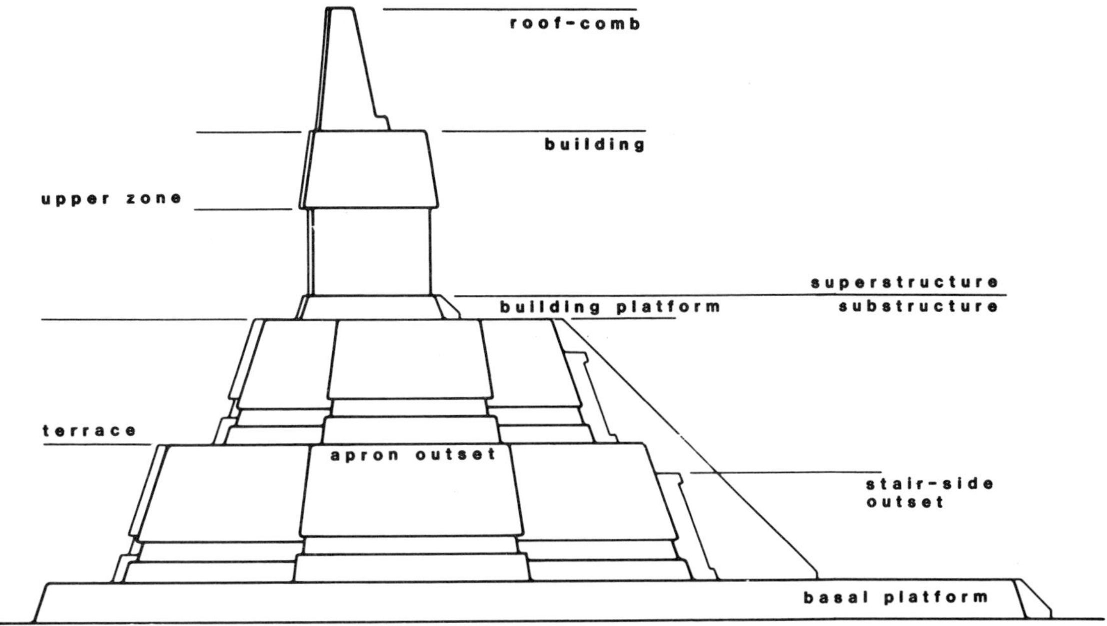

MAYA TEMPLE SCHEMATIC

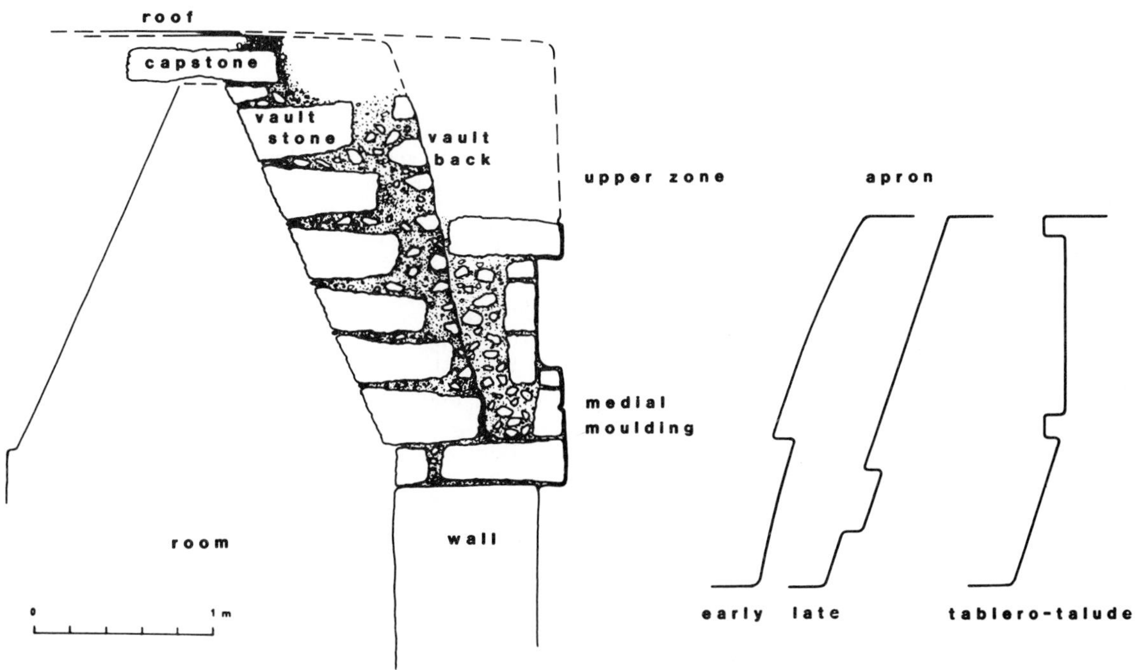

MAYA VAULT

MAYA TERRACE PROFILES

thus providing a continuity of surface treatment to the whole precinct. A continuous plaster finish of this kind has not been attempted in modern restorations, but would drastically change the architectural character from that we know today. We see the temples as powerful elements within park-like settings, but if the plaza surfaces were plastered as they were originally, the precinct would appear as an integral part of a landscape with individual shapes rising out of a monolithic topography. The effect of strong sun on polished, reflective surfaces, together with the smoke of incense and the stench of blood sacrifices, would make the temple precincts into places of overwhelming ritualistic power and influence.

Numbers have mystical significance in the design of pre-colonial temples and palaces. In Maya cosmology, nine was the number of major lords of the underworld, thirteen the number of gods in the sky and of the names of the days. The number four was associated with the sun god and the universe had four sides. Five was associated with 'Imix', the earth deity, and three with the stones of the hearth. All the numbers from one to thirteen and multiples of twenty were accorded some mystical significance, often greatly complicated by number combinations. The meanings attached to numbers have deep significance in ceremonial architecture, for example in the number of terraces, of rooms, of doorways in front facades, and of major elements in temple form.

The essential elements of ceremonial architecture in Central America were established in temples of the Pre-Classic period (200 BC to AD 200). The huge substructures of Cuicuilco and Teotihuacan (p. 678C) dwarfed the comparatively insubstantial buildings they supported. Even in Structure N10–43 at Lamanai (p. 677A), which had four separate buildings at its upper levels, the substructure was the dominant element. Its extensive surfaces display all the details of apron profiles, outsets, inset corners, stairs, stairside outsets and sculptural features. Subsequent developments throughout the Classic period (200–900) were little more than refinements of the early maturity evolved at Lamanai.

A new kind of temple giving more emphasis to the superstructure which now was commonly vaulted (not necessarily corbelled vaulting), and with a smaller but more elaborate substructure, emerged in the Early Classic period (200–600). The best-known examples of Early Classic Maya temples are those on the North Acropolis at Tikal, Structure 5D–22, 1st (p. 675), and at the nearby site of Uaxactun in northern Guatemala. The composite forms of these temples were made up of elements that had been more separated in earlier periods. They had distinct front and rear parts in both substructure and superstructure: the rear parts were higher and supported roofcombs encrusted with emblematic and hieratic symbols. In the southern lowlands, at Tikal for example, the sculpture of the upper zone was confined to the front part of the building. Substructure masks appeared only at the front. Strict bilateral symmetry was combined with equally emphatic front-to-rear asymmetry.

The terracing of substructures of the Early Classic period had convex apron profiles and double-height apron outsets spanning two or more terraces, as for example in Structure 5D–22, 1st, Tikal (p. 681B). The masonry of the substructures, in Early Classic work, was usually of well-cut, squared blocks, smoothly finished and giving a sharp contrast with the smaller, crudely shaped stones of the vaulted superstructures. This difference in the character of the masonry may have reflected intrinsically different significance ascribed to the substructure, as distinct from that attaching to the building it carried.

In the case of the Maya there was a third major evolution of temple form in the Late Classic period (600–900). The change, best exemplified by Temple I, Tikal (p. 684A), related to the development of large ceremonial plazas and causeways for processional rituals involving large numbers of people and public spectacle. The substructures became very high while the vaulted building became even smaller in size.

Several architectural attributes were transformed in the Late Classic period. Masonry became more precise and stones were dressed after walling to produce straight-line profiles. Plaster thickness decreased dramatically and interior surfaces (even inaccessible chambers in roof-combs) were finished to the same standards as the exteriors, although distinctions between substructure and superstructure parts still remained. Apron profiles changed to narrow, horizontal shadow bands recessed in the terrace face, the depth of all projections and mouldings tended to decrease, and stairs were fully outset. Although vaulting techniques improved in the Late Classic period, they had surprisingly little effect on the dimensions of rooms in temples. Late Classic temples frequently had thicker walls, higher vaults and narrower rooms than their Early Classic counterparts.

Although the Late Classic is most important architecturally in the lowland Maya area, a few structures in other parts of Mesoamerica, such as El Tajin on the gulf coast of Mexico, and Xochicalco on the western slopes of the central plateau of Mexico, introduced distinctive architectural features at the end of the period. Temples in both places merged highland and lowland forms, and blurred the distinction between substructure and superstructure.

In Post-Classic temples at Mayapan, Chichen Itza (p. 690A), Tulum, Coba, and other sites in northern Yucatan, Classic period features such as the masonry vault and the three-element moulding, like those in the Governor's Palace, Uxmal (p. 687B), continued in use, though somewhat transformed and of poorer

Tikal: North Acropolis perspective. See p.674

workmanship. Other features, like the apron profile, the carved upper zone and the roof-comb, fell into general disuse. Throughout both highlands and lowlands, the terracing of substructures in the Post-Classic period had shallower projections, fewer mouldings and steeper, nearly vertical profiles. Stairs became broader and less steep, and were flanked by wide stair-side ramps known in Spanish as 'alfardas'. Free-standing columns and beam-and-mortar roofs came into much wider use and appeared in a number of temples, such as that at Tula (p. 689B).

The Aztecs, in the late Post-Classic period, built double temples, such as those at Tenayuca and Tenochtitlan. Twin superstructures dedicated to different deities were supported on common substructures, each one served by two stairways. Drawings and descriptions of Aztec temples found in documents from the period of the conquest indicate that the Post-Classic trends were continued. The landform morphology was maintained even though the buildings were not vaulted and their upper elements and roof extensions, designed to display hieratic symbols, were constructed in timber.

The palace architecture of Mesoamerica is known almost exclusively in terms of buildings of the Late Classic and Post-Classic periods, although it existed earlier. Maler's Palace, Tikal (p. 686A), is often regarded as the archetype of Maya palace architecture. Palaces were built most frequently as groups of buildings around courtyards or quadrangles, as for example the Nunnery, Uxmal (p. 687A). In this case a number of separate blocks were combined to form a multi-chambered complex around a plaza. The separateness of each palace was maintained as strictly as the identity of each temple within the whole ceremonial arrangement of buildings. This is true of almost all Maya palaces where the buildings were vaulted. The palace at Palenque is an exception in that a number of rooms were arranged collectively around the quadrangle, although even here some individual buildings retained their separate identity. At Teotihuacan and Yagul in Mexico, flat beam and mortar roofs were used to cover contiguous multiroomed buildings around interior courtyards. The palace at Mitla (p. 689A) seems to have combined both of the arrangements described above.

South America

Earlier than *c.* 900 BC, architectural ideas remained confined to their original localities, but subsequently a series of regional styles spread more widely through the Andean area. Rubble and field stone as well as cut stone were used in the Chavin temples. Carved stone and modelled stucco were used for decoration. The period following the spread of Chavin (*c.* 200 BC to AD 600) is notable for the construction of large adobe platform-temples such as the Sun and Moon pyramids at Moche and in many southern and central coastal locations, not always associated with settlements. From 600 to 1000, new empires emerged with capitals at the cities of Tiahuanaco and Huari, characterised by very rigid, formal architecture on a gridiron plan. Chan Chan near Trujillo, and Viracochapampa near Huamachuco in the highlands, both exemplify this monumental pre-Incaic architecture which combined civic with religious patterns of use.

The Inca empire perpetuated bureaucratic, institutionalised forms of architecture even more emphatically than the older polities. The Incas used a variety of constructional techniques ranging from rubble masonry in clay mortar to polygonal dry stonework of impressive scale, precision and finish, as for example at Saqsaywaman (p. 690D).

Examples

North America

Monks Mound at Cahokia (900–1200), with a base 270 m × 210 m (886 ft × 689 ft) and 30 m (98 ft) high, was the largest single ceremonial building of precolonial North America. Its massive platform, of truncated pyramidal form, has four asymmetrical levels built up entirely of earth, and dominated a palisaded ceremonial precinct. The site, of which Monks Mound is a part, is in a particularly fertile part of the Mississippi valley; it covered 13 km^2 and included some 120 pyramidal mounds of various sizes.

Central America

Pre-Classic

La Venta (*c.* 800 BC), an Olmec ceremonial centre on an island in the Tonala river delta at the edge of the Gulf of Mexico, is one of the earliest ceremonial centres of the region. The sacred precinct, entirely paved with clay, contained a number of symbolic stone heads and buried mosaic pavements as well as truncated pyramidal platforms. All were organised symmetrically about a north–south axis. The major temple, now a lobate conoid 130 m (426 ft) across at the base, and 30 m (98 ft) high, does not incorporate a building of any kind. Its shape is thought to represent a mountain. This interpretation has never been tested by excavation, and as significant erosion must be assumed in this region of heavy rainfall, it seems unlikely that the present shape is anything like its appearance in Pre-Classic times.

A. Lamanai: Structure N10–43 (*c.* 200 BC). See p.679

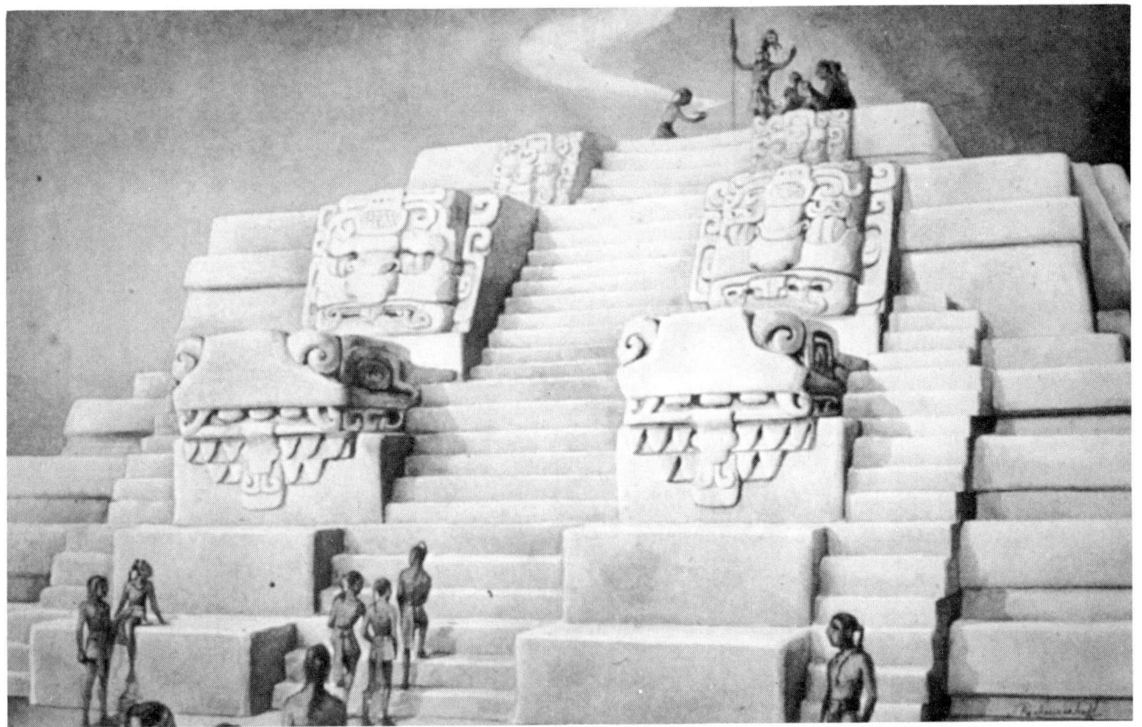

B. Uaxactun: E-VII sub (*c.* 200 BC). See p.679

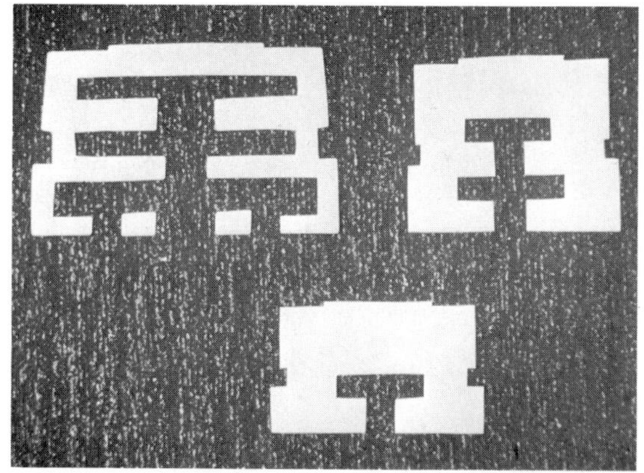

A. Maya Temple Building Plans: Tikal, Structures 5D–95, 5D-96, 5D–22

B. Dzibilchaltun: Temple of the Seven Dolls (*c.* 500). See p.679

C. Teotihuacan: the Pyramid of the Sun (*c.* 50). See p.679

D. Teotihuacan: the Ciudadela (*c.* 200). See p.679

The Temple Pyramid of Cuicuilco (*c.* 400 BC), which was 150 m (492 ft) in diameter and about 20 m (66 ft) high, now stands in a park in the suburbs of Mexico City. It was buried about 200 BC in a volcanic deposit. Initially a circular truncated pyramid, the temple had two west-facing terraces, on the upper one of which were a number of open-air altars. A later addition reversed the orientation and increased the number of terraces to four, which then supported a perishable building at the top. Construction was of adobe with boulders included to define the amount to be built at any one time. The facings to outer terraces have disappeared but the pumice casing to some inner units of adobe hearting can still be seen.

The structure known as **Structure E-VII sub, Uaxactun** (*c.* 200 BC) (p. 677B), with a base 25 m (82 ft) square and 7 m (23 ft) high, not counting thatched building, was until quite recently the only well-known later Pre-Classic Maya temple. Its substructure has three bi-axially symmetrical lower elements with stairs on all four sides between modelled stucco mask-panels. The undecorated upper platform, which originally supported a timber building, has three levels, foreshadowing the three-room pattern characteristic of later, Classic-period temple buildings. The thick stucco finish and rounded corners to the terraces are attributes typical of Pre-Classic and Early Classic work.

Structure N10–43, Lamanai (*c.* 200 BC) (p. 677A), was 50 m × 55 m (164 ft × 180 ft) at its base, and 30 m (98 ft) high. It is the most architecturally advanced late Pre-Classic Maya work known at present, and the earliest known example of the 'Lamanai Temple' such as Structure B–4, 2nd A, Altun Ha (p. 682B), and N10–9 at Lamanai (p. 681A). The temple had three main parts to its substructure, with three stairways rising the full height at the front. At the top, two buildings faced towards the central axis and subsequently two more were added. Large, but very poorly preserved, masks flanked the stairs. Terraces of the upper element of the substructure had apron mouldings and double-height apron outsets constructed in large, squared blocks of soft, white limestone which became seriously eroded during the time the temple was in use. The surfaces were coated in thick grey plaster and painted monochrome red. About seven centuries after its construction the temple was completely encased within a new structure of significantly different form.

The Pyramid of the Sun, Teotihuacan (*c.* 50) (p. 678C), marks the first (Tzacualli) phase of urbanisation. It was positioned just to the east of the Street of the Dead, the main axis, and was aligned to the ceremonial orientation which controlled all subsequent development throughout the great city, namely 15 degrees 30 minutes east of north. The pyramid we now see was an enormous substructure with five elements which once supported a building on a sixth platform now largely destroyed. The pyramid is 217 m (712 ft) square at the base and survives to a height of 57 m (187 ft). Terraces were of unequal heights and without mouldings. The slight stair projection typifies Pre-Classic work. Abutting the base on the west (front) is a small platform, the 'plataforma abosado', which had tablero-talude terraces. It was made of adobe, or puddled mud, laid up by the basket-load and surfaced with stone (pumice) which in turn was coated with thick, concrete-like stucco. The pyramid covered a pre-existing structure which overlaid a still earlier one.

Early Classic

The Ciudadela, Teotihuacan (*c.* 200) (p. 678D), some 375 m (1230 ft) square with an average height of about 6 m (20 ft) in area, was the largest pre-colonial temple of both North and South America. It included a monumental sunken courtyard 195 m × 265 m (640 ft × 869 ft), to accommodate large numbers of people. The complex of buildings was located at the precise centre of Teotihuacan, where the two major north–south and east–west axes intersected. Within its courtyard was the temple of Quetzalcoatl, a major architectural work in itself. It had six terraces with tablero-talude profiles, the recesses of which contained sculptured images of feathered serpents and various marine creatures. It was later encased within a larger pyramidal temple with plain tablero-talude profiles.

The **Temple of the Seven Dolls, Dzibilchaltun** (*c.* 500) (p. 678B), an Early or Middle Classic Maya temple in northern Yucatan, about 29 m (95 ft) square at the base and about 15 m (49 ft) high, is diminutive in size compared with major Pre-Classic temples. Rough stone masonry and thick stucco relief typify Early Classic work, but the bi-axially symmetrical plan, the arrangement of the substructure terraces, and its ample windows and centred roof construction are quite unusual.

Structure N10–9, Lamanai (*c.* 500) (p. 681A), 20 m (66 ft) high and 54 m (177 ft) square at the base, exemplifies the Lamanai type of temple in which a vaulted building was placed part of the way up the front (north) side of the substructure instead of at the top of the pyramid. This arrangement persisted at Lamanai throughout the Classic period and was used in the Late Classic period at Altun Ha, for example in Structure B–4, 2nd A (p. 682B). Here the truncated pyramid cannot be considered as a substructure but must be interpreted as a feature significant in itself. The terraces, which are without mouldings, had rounded inset corners, while superior and basal mouldings adorned outsets at the sides of stairways. Jaguar masks, in Olmecoid style, appeared on the basal platform, and the whole of the pyramidal temple was painted monochrome red. Structure N10–9 is of poor workmanship: terrace facings were uneven, and the masonry of the core consisted of boulders set in friable soil and black mud. Built on top of an earlier demolished structure, the north facade was much altered in the Late Classic and Post-Classic periods.

The dominant temple on the North Acropolis at **Tikal** is **Structure 5D–22, 1st** (*c.* 550) (p. 681B). It is 23 m × 25 m (75 ft × 82 ft) at the base and 23 m (74 ft) high: the stair projects 7 m (23 ft). It was one of the most important ceremonial buildings at this major site in the lowland Peten district of northern Guatemala and is regarded as the definitive version of the Early Classic Maya temple. The building had three narrow, crudely vaulted rooms, each of different size, accessible through three doorways on the south side of the building. Aprons on the substructure terraces had convex, curved profiles, large outset aprons extended from top to bottom at the centre of the sides and rear, deity masks flanked the front stairway, and a roof-comb, now almost totally collapsed, rose above the upper zone. The entire exterior was painted monochrome red. The design of the temple took the form of two 'houses', each on its own base and placed one in front of the other. This composition persisted in major temples at Tikal throughout the Late Classic, see for example **Temple I** (p. 684A), and is the hallmark of the 'Tikal Temple'. The wide front stairway has been reconstructed recently; the western side of the substructure surfaces remains as excavated and reveals parts of several earlier superimposed temples, and the east side is still unexcavated.

Late Classic

The **Five-Storey Temple, Edzna** (*c.* 600) (p. 682A), 53 m (175 ft) square at the base and 32 m (104 ft) high, known locally as the 'templo major', dominated the ceremonial centre of an extensive Maya settlement of the Classic period in Campeche, Mexico. Its pyramidal form was composed of vaulted buildings on each of four levels of terracing. An unusual five-roomed, double-fronted building with a high, openwork roof-comb crowned the whole ensemble. Here the two building types, Temple and Palace, that make up most Maya ceremonial centres are combined. But the temple was not conceived as a single work; some parts of it were added or modified at a later date. The vaults of the upper building are typical of Early Classic corbelled work, while others on the lower terraces are of the more advanced Late Classic non-corbelled form (see Chapter 21). Some of the wall-facings also originated in the later period. The west (front) face of the structure has been cleared and restored, but the other three faces remain collapsed and shrouded in debris.

Structure B–4, 2nd A, Altun Ha (*c.* 600) (p. 682B), is 17 m (56 ft) high and 44 m (144 ft) square at the base, including the frontal platform. It illustrates the architectural form characteristic of Lamanai temples such as Structure N10–9 (p. 681A) and Structure N10–43 (p. 677A), but differs in that the vaulted building stood on its own separate platform in front of the pyramid. The vaulting was unusual here because the two long rooms were spanned vaults joined at the ends whereas it was common practice to vault each room separately. The building had nine doorways and is more typical of palace than temple in its plan arrangement. This suggests the two building types were functionally compatible and not mutually exclusive. Although the terrace profiles and masonry characteristics suggest the Late Classic period, upper-zone sculpture was executed in a thick stucco technique typical of the Early Classic period. Inset corners are absent from the pyramid, which is typical of Maya work in Belize, and it is clear that inset corners on the platform supporting the building had special symbolic significance in this location.

Structure 1, Xuphil (*c.* 600) (p. 683A), 43 m × 16 m (141 ft × 52 ft), had a low substructure supporting twelve vaulted rooms between three vertical towers which were shaped to resemble pyramidal temples with shallow, unusable stairs, niches for doorways, 'buildings' without interior spaces, and roof-combs. The incorporation of pseudo-temples into a building of this type suggests a symbolic purpose that may have been more widely applicable to this architectural type, though perhaps rarely displayed so obviously elsewhere.

The most outstanding of the great temples of the Maya Late Classic period is **Temple I (the Temple of the Giant Jaguar), Tikal** (730) (p. 684A). It is 44 m (145 ft) high and 36 m × 32 m (118 ft × 105 ft) at the base, and demonstrates the evolution that had taken place from the mid-sixth century buildings such as the Early Classic Tikal Temple, Structure 5D–22, 1st (q.v.). The earlier design was systematically transformed to achieve the great scale and height to be seen in Temple I in the Late Classic period. The terrace profiles were now made in straight lines with apron mouldings which were reduced to narrow, horizontal shadow-lines; terraces followed a systematic inset pattern identical at all corners and on all nine levels; sculptural treatment was confined to the frontal upper zones and to the roof-comb, which depicts a throned figure flanked by serpent motifs. This imposing structure was erected on the site of an earlier temple and on top of the elaborate vaulted tomb of a ruler. Secondary stairs on the south and north sides, rising up to the sixth terrace level, suggest that the exterior substructure as well as the vaulted rooms of the building were regularly used. The masonry of the pyramid was extensively restored in the early 1960s, but the building itself and the roof-comb are largely in original condition.

The Temple of the Inscriptions, Palenque (700–800) (p. 683B), 56 × 40 m (184 × 131 ft) at the

A. Lamanai: Structure N10–9 (*c.* 500). See p.679

B. Tikal: Structure 5D–22, 1st (*c.* 550) (background); Structure 5D–21 (foreground). See p.680

A. Edzna: Five-Storey Temple (*c.* 600). See p.680

B.Altun Ha: Structure B-4, 2nd A (*c.* 600). See p.680

A. Xuphil: Structure 1 (*c.* 600). See p.680

B. Palenque: Temple of the Inscriptions (700–800). See p.680

A. Tikal: Temple (730). See p.680

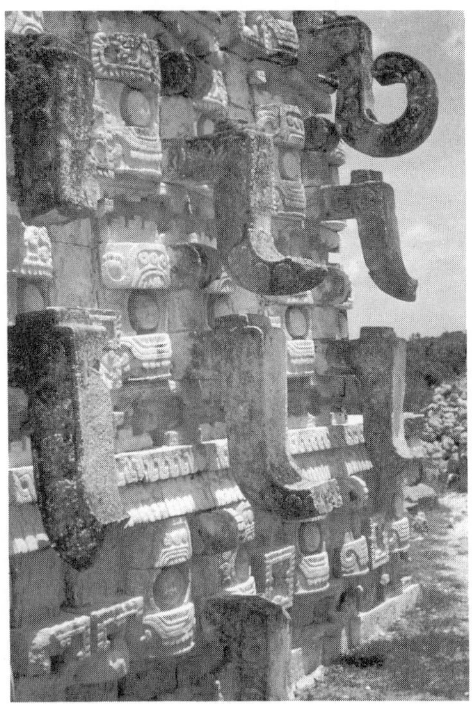

B. Kabah: Codz-Poop (*c.* 850). See p.685

C. Zaculeu: Temple I (*c.* 900–1200). See p.685

base and 35 m (115 ft) high, contains a tomb chamber vaulted in the Late Classic, monolithic fashion, which is accessible by means of a stair tunnel and which leads down from the rear room of the building. As originally built the pyramid was a simple rectangle; terrace outsets were added later to produce the distinctive inset corners so typical of Late Classic Maya temples. In this and other buildings at Palenque, vaulting reached an unusual degree of sophistication made possible through the use of the excellent building stone available at the site. There are large stone panels with carved inscriptions giving dates and dynastic histories on the walls of the first room. The terracing of the pyramid has been extensively restored.

One of the most impressive buildings of the Late Classic period in the Central Acropolis at **Tikal** is **Maler's Palace** (*c.* 750) (p. 686A). Some 35 m (115 ft) long by 10 m (33 ft) wide, it was originally built as a single storey of nine rooms facing north. A second storey, facing south, was added later. The lower storey is so well preserved that its carved wooden vault beams and uncarved lintels are still intact. An elaborately sculptured upper zone extended around the lower storey, but its equivalent at the upper level and the upper-storey vaults have collapsed.

The Ball Court, Copan (*c.* 775) (p. 686B), which is 30 m × 7 m (98 ft × 23 ft) in the playing alley, may be considered as a temple. Ball courts appear frequently within ceremonial centres, where they served a ritual purpose relating to divination based on the outcome of the game. The court at Copan, preserved beneath later construction, occupies a prominent site at one end of the Great Plaza and at the foot of the Acropolis. Above the open-ended playing alley stand two blocks of vaulted buildings.

Codz-Poop, Kabah (*c.* 850) (p. 684B), 80 m (262 ft) square at the base of the platform, was a Late Classic palace building in quadrangular plan. An unusual and startling effect was produced by completely covering the west facade with masks representing the rain god. The masks were repetitive stone elements which projected about half a metre from the surface of the wall. Those entering the building first passed through the space occupied by the deities represented in deep relief on the wall. Although this building clearly belongs to the palace category, the powerful evocation of the deities suggests its function was not entirely secular.

The Nunnery, Uxmal (*c.* 900) (p. 687A), shows the sophistication attainable by the pre-colonial architect in the Americas. This complex of buildings, one of the world's great urban spaces, surely must reflect some individual native architectural genius. The level of precision achieved here in every aspect, from the manipulation of space to the cutting and jointing of stone, is not excelled in any other surviving work of pre-colonial architecture in the Americas. In the Nunnery, which is a name applied fancifully in historic times, decoration in modelled stone mosaic in intricate iconographic patterns was carried around the four facades of the courtyard, starting with the east building and culminating with the higher and more elaborate north block.

The Governor's Palace, Uxmal (*c.* 900) (p. 687B), is another impressive Late Classic palace. It stands on a broad substructure (not visible in the illustration) which supported smaller buildings around its edges and a ceremonial platform at the centre. It was 180 m × 150 m (590 ft × 492 ft) at the perimeter of the basal platform, and 96 m (315 ft) long by 11 m (36 ft) wide at the levels of the building. High upper zones, defined by mouldings with three elements, were filled with elaborate sculptural relief in carved stone mosaics in which a series of motifs undulate and interweave from end to end of the building. The east front facade, divided into three parts by steep vaulted arches, was an elaborately organised composition based on the arrangement of doorways. Vaulting was of the Late Classic monolithic or non-corbelled type (see Chapter 21). The facade has been extensively restored, but details were used which had survived intact up to the beginning of the twentieth century.

Post-Classic

Temple I, Zaculeu (*c.* 900–1200) (p. 684C), 40 m × 32 m (131 ft × 105 ft) at the base and about 15 m (49 ft) high, was the principal structure of a defensive group of buildings in the Guatemalan highlands, which was used by the Maya as a religious centre, a dynastic centre and a refuge, from Classic-period times to the conquest. There have been at least seven buildings on this site, of which Temple I is the Early Post-Classic temple. This is visible today, with its unvaulted rooms and vertical terraces which were extensively restored in the 1940s. Zaculeu is the only site at which restoration has included replastering so that the effects of continuity of surface can to some extent be recaptured.

The Palace of the Columns, Mitla (*c.* 1000) (p. 689A) – base 55 m × 45 m (180 ft × 148 ft), height 8 m (26 ft) – was a dynastic and religious centre of the Mixtec–Zapotec peoples in the Valley of Oaxaca up to the time of the conquest. It was the principal building in one of several groups built around open spaces. It consisted of single-storey unvaulted rooms arranged around a courtyard and raised on a platform 2.5 m (8 ft) high. All the platform and wall surfaces, interior and exterior, were covered with elaborate geometric patterns based on repetitive stone units cut with impressive dimensional precision

A. Tikal: Maler's Palace (*c.* 750). See p.685

B. Copan: the Ball Court (*c.* 775). See p.685

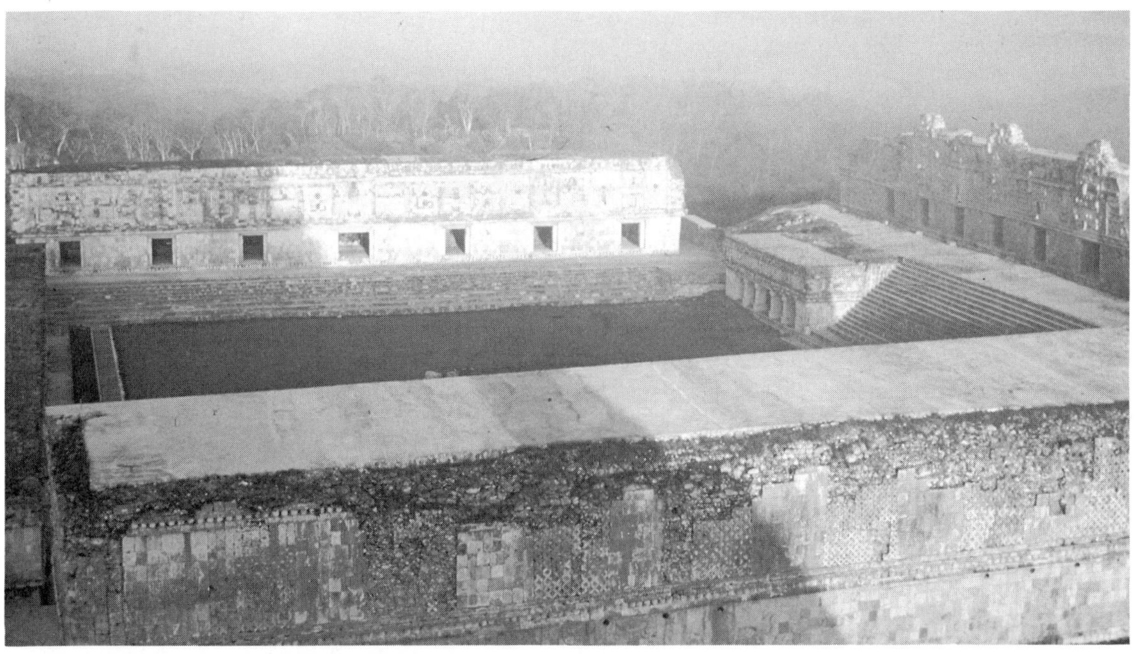

A. Uxmal: the Nunnery (*c.* 900). See p.685

B. Uxmal: the Governor's Palace (*c.* 900). See p.685

from soft limestone. The lintels in the Mitla palaces were the largest single blocks of stone of any used in pre-colonial work.

The Temple of the Warriors, Chichen Itza (*c.* 1000–1100) (p. 690A), had a substructure 42 m (138 ft) square and 11 m (36 ft) high. Its estimated total height, including vaults which have now fallen, was 23 m (75 ft). The temple occupied the east side of the central plaza, just south of the celebrated Well of Sacrifice. Its square building, renowned for the serpent columns in the west doorways, had two large rooms with masonry vaults on wooden beams, themselves carried on masonry columns. Failure of the wood precipitated total collapse including the upper zones of the building. Substructure terraces were of the tablero-talude kind (p. 673) usually associated with the highlands of Guatemala and Mexico. Although, in the Maya lowlands, the Post-Classic period is generally considered to represent social and technical decline, this structure retained Classic-period qualities. The substructure was superimposed over an earlier version of a similar building.

The Temple of Tlahuizcalpantecuhtli, Tula (1000–1100) (p. 689B), is the definitive Toltec temple. It is 43 m (141 ft) square at the base, and has a substructure 9 m (30 ft) high. Its five terraces depicted jaguars, coyotes, eagles eating human hearts, and the planet Venus (Tlahuizcalpantecuhtli) on tablero-talude panels. The building contained one large room roofed with wood beams resting on stone columns shaped to represent Toltec warriors. The structure was violently destroyed in the twelfth century by invaders from the north who were known as Chichimec.

The Temple of Xiuhcoatl, Tenayuca (1200–1500) – 67 m × 75 m (220 ft × 246 ft) at the base, with a substructure 19 m (62 ft) high – was an Aztec temple. A substructure with twin stairways supported twin buildings dedicated to two major deities. During the three centuries 1200–1500, eight nearly identical temples were built here, each superimposed on its predecessors. It is thought that the rebuilding of each temple coincided with a 52-year cycle in the sacred calendar, but this cannot be definitely established.

The Castillo (*c.* 1400) (p. 691A) was the principal temple at **Tulum**, a major Post-Classic Maya site on the east coast of northern Yucatan. The base is 28 m × 16 m (92 ft × 52 ft) with stair projections of 5 m (16 ft). Its two vaulted rooms were built over an earlier building with beam and mortar roof. The Castillo contained a number of architectural features which distinguish the Post-Classic from the Classic period: the whole structure was relatively small, the upper zones were non-existent, and the masonry was crude and rough. The buildings at Tulum were still in use at the time of the conquest and have required only minimal restoration.

South America

The Temple of the Sun, Moche (*c.* 200–600), with a base 136 m × 228 m (446 ft × 748 ft) and 41 m (135 ft) high, consists of a square lower platform of five terraces supporting an offset pyramidal platform of seven terraces. The whole was built in adobe and none of the facing has survived. Because of erosion, the original form can hardly be recognised, even though this was one of the largest single ceremonial structures in South America.

The city of **Chan Chan** (*c.* 1200–1470) covered some 21 km^2 (4942 acres) and included a ceremonial centre of 6 km^2. It was the capital of the Kingdom of Chimor until subdued by the Incas. The town was organised within nine large, rectangular enclosures, some of them containing hundreds of identical small rooms; some of the rooms were empty, and others dominated by pyramidal platforms. The construction is of adobe brick and many of the surfaces are finished with decorative patterns carved in high relief. The site has been much destroyed by looting.

The Fortress, Paramonga (*c.* 1200–1400) (p. 690B), is an impressive example of adobe brick construction and demonstrates a remarkable grasp of the principles of fortification. Upper-level terraces and walls were arranged to give protection to the lower stages, while projecting corner bastions provided cover to the main walls. A major outpost of the Chimor empire, the complex was as much temple as fortress.

The Gate of the Sun, Tiahuanaco (*c.* 600–1000) (p. 690C), 3 m (10 ft) high by 3.8 m (12 ft 6 in) wide, is the most ornate of a series of stone portals found in the ceremonial centre of the city of Tiahuanaco. Such portals of adobe walls gave access to major buildings which have since all but disappeared, leaving the gateways as isolated monuments.

Saqsaywaman (completed *c.* 1520) (p. 690D), usually referred to as a fortress, was closely associated with the Inca capital of Cuzco. It covered an area of some 400 m × 250 m (1312 ft × 820 ft) astride a natural ridge overlooking a wide levelled open space of irregular shape. The building is now thought to have been used for dynastic and religious purposes. The gigantic stones of the lower ramparts, quarried nearby, were cut with great precision.

Machu Picchu (*c.* 1500) (p. 691B) is a late Inca town dramatically sited on the saddle between two mountains, overlooking the Urubamba River, which winds 900 m (3000 ft) below it. Its buildings, all constructed of local stone, use various types of walling, from coursed ashlar to roughly dressed rubble, and incorporate characteristic trapezoidal doorways. Some of the walls have rectangular niches formed on the inner side. Masonry gables still stand and some buildings have trapezoidal

A. Mitla: the Palace of the Columns (*c.* 1000). See p.685

B. Tula: Temple of Tlahuizcalpantecuhtli (1000–1100). See p.688

A. Chichen Itza: Temple of the Warriors (*c.* 1000–1100). See p.688

B. Paramonga; the Fortress (*c.* 1200–1400). See p.688

C.Tiahuanco: the Gate of the Sun (*c.* 600–1000). See p.688

D. Saqsaywaman: the fortress (completed *c.* 1520) See p.688

A. Tulum: the Castillo (*c.* 1400). See p.688

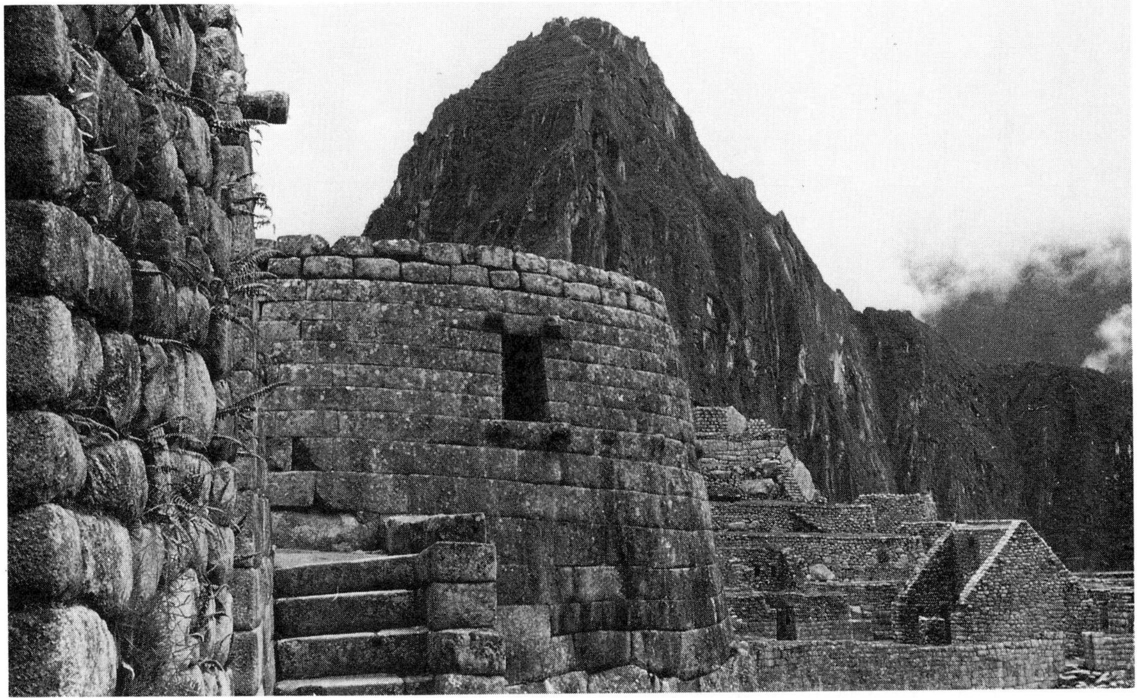

B. Machu Picchu (l*c.* 1500). See p.688

window openings. The steep slopes of the site are terraced with masonry retaining walls to hold soil for the gardens, and the various levels of the town are linked by stone stairways.

The Temple of Wiraqocha, Raqchi (*c.* 1400–1500) was a major Inca temple in a small, remote settlement; 92 m (302 ft) long by 25 m (82 ft) wide and with a roofed area of 2323 m^2 (24,996 ft^2), its form was that of the Inca Kallanka or multi-purpose civic hall. Inside, a spine wall ran the length of the building directly under the ridge of the roof, dividing it into two long, narrow rooms, each of which was divided again by a row of eleven columns of rubble stone up to a height of 2 m (7 ft) and adobe to a height of 12 m (39 ft). The double-pitched roof was thatched.

Chapter 24
CHINA

Architectural Character

Dougong, the system of brackets inserted between the top of a column and a crossbeam (each bracket being formed of a double bow-shaped arm called 'gong' which supports a block of wood called 'dou', on each side) had just appeared during the Western Zhou dynasty (1027–770 BC), and was widely used in buildings constructed in the 'beam-in-tiers' technique. But concave roofs, which characterise China's wooden buildings, were seldom seen at this early date. The building style of the period was rough, simple and unadorned.

China began to evolve its own distinct architectural character in the Eastern Han dynasty (25–220). By that time commonly used structural techniques included, 'beam-in-tiers' and 'column-and-tie-beam' methods, either of which could be combined with ground floors supported on substantial plinths or raised on stilts. Simpler, 'log-cabin' methods were, of course, still used in forest regions.

It was from the period of the Three Kingdoms to that of the Northern and Southern dynasties (220–589), however, that China's architecture first developed noticeably. As a result of the growth of Buddhism, pagodas and grottoes appeared in many parts of China and the styles of India, Persia and Greece were introduced.

The Tang and Song dynasties (618–1279) saw China's building methods maturing rapidly. Examples of the architectural skill of the period are the Linde Hall, the main building of the Daminggong Palace, which has 188 pillars and was built in the Tang dynasty, and the 67 m (220 ft) high wooden Sakyamuni pagoda in the Fogongsi Temple built in the Liao dynasty in Yingxian province. From the Song dynasty, the architectural use of colour and decoration became more and more exquisite.

In the later periods of the Ming and Qing dynasties (1368–1911), high levels of skill were developed in the arrangement and layout of groups of buildings.

The five main characteristics of Chinese architecture which emerged in these periods were:

Unity of structure with architectural art. This was achieved by beautifying the structural components themselves instead of applying additional ornament. For example, a pillar might be shuttle-shaped and a beam formed as an arc so that, when used with a concave roof, they achieved harmony of design with construction.

Good anti-seismic function. The structural components of a wooden building were connected by mortises and tenons and were thus able to move under earthquake conditions without causing the buildings to collapse. Similar techniques were applied to the connection of columns to plinths. Chinese wooden buildings have no deep foundations for columns, so that columns can shift when an earthquake occurs, and many ancient structures still stand even after exposure to many earthquakes.

A high degree of standardisation. A building is composed of a group of beams carried on columns with curved corbel-brackets forming a kind of roof truss, or is supported on a series of vertical frames serving the same purpose. The space between two such beams is called jian (a bay). These two constructional techniques were used in most buildings with rectilinear plan shapes. The dimensions of structural components are based on standard modules. For example, buildings of the Song dynasty took 'cai' as the basic module. This was the vertical section of the gong part of 'dougong', or of 'fang', a piece of wood which had a height:width ratio of three:two. *Yingzaofashi* (The Method of Architecture) describes in detail the meaning and measurements of cai, of which there are eight permissible sizes. The module used in the Qing dynasty is 'doukou' – the width of gong – and the supplementary module is the diameter of a pillar. Doukou has eleven sizes, enough to control the measurements of each single building in a group in such a way as to set off the main building.

Bright colours. The practice of painting wooden buildings to prevent weathering and insect infestation and to achieve decorative effects began in the Early Spring and Autumn period (722–481 BC). Gradually

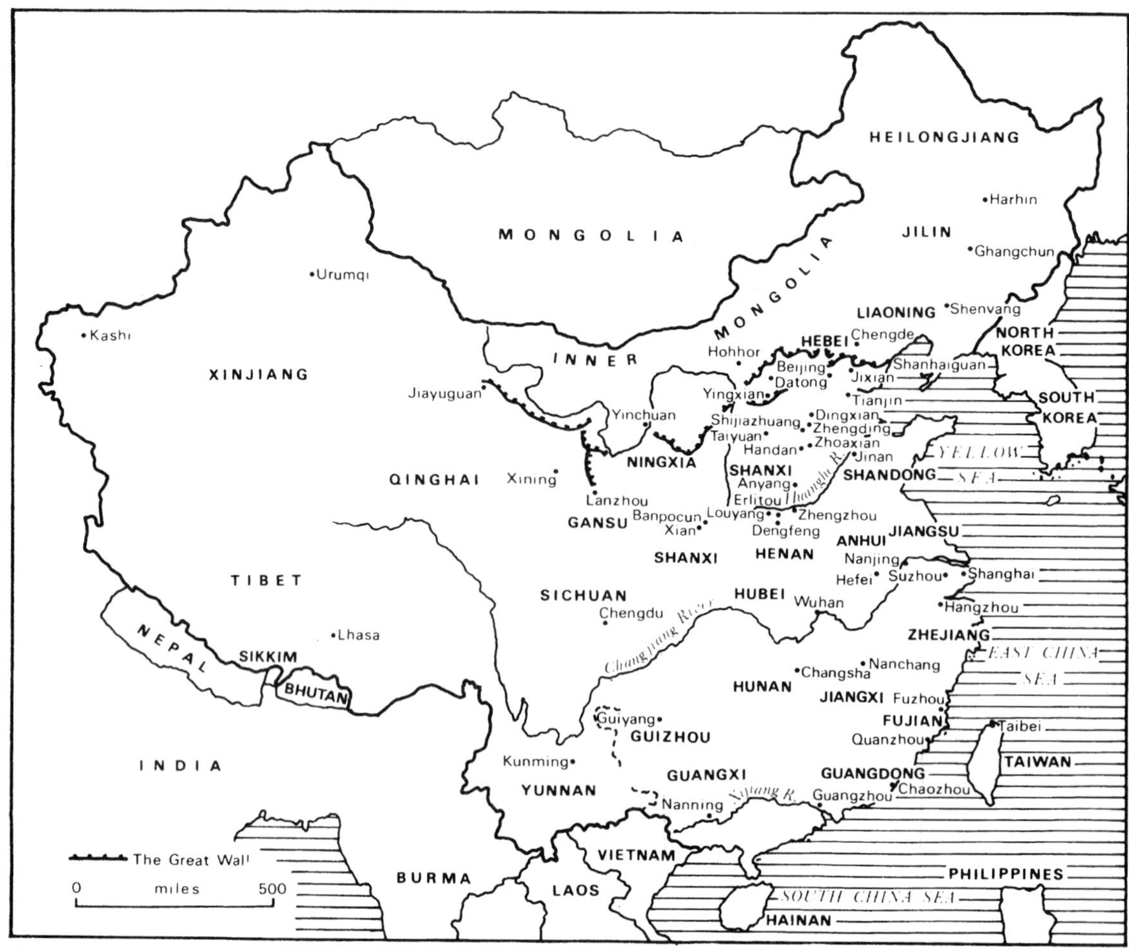

China

the Chinese learned to employ colours appropriate to the nature of the building, or the element on which it was used. For example, in palaces or temples, walls, pillars, doors and window frames were painted red, while the roof was yellow. Cool colours, often blue and green, were applied under the eaves.

The systematic grouping of buildings. The traditional Chinese method of arrangement was to plan a single building around a courtyard and then to use courtyards as basic units to form groups of buildings. On a large scale, these consisted of many courtyards arranged along parallel or other subsidiary axes. There may be free-standing halls within courtyards or linked to surrounding buildings with galleries or side rooms. Complex planning of this kind is found in palaces, shrines, temples, mausolea and monasteries. Less formal though still axial arrangements were used for buildings, such as the pavilions in parks and for gardens.

Examples

Palaces and Villas

Most of the luxurious palaces of the emperors of China were destroyed when the dynasties fell. Only the **Forbidden City** in **Beijing** (pp. 695, 701A), built in the Ming and Qing dynasties, is preserved intact. Construction began in 1406. The battlemented perimeter wall extends 760 m (2500 ft) from east to west and 960 m (3150 ft) from north to south and encloses an area of 73 ha (180 acres).

The **Royal Palace** was divided into an outer court and an inner court. Around the outer court were the Taihedian (the Hall of Supreme Harmony), the Zhonghedian (the Hall of Central Harmony), the Baohedian (the Hall of Preserved Harmony), the Wenhuadian (the Hall of Literary

A. The Forbidden City, Beijing (1406–). See p.694

B. The Forbidden City: Tiananmen, main gate to the Imperial City (1406–). See p.699

C. The Forbidden City: the Wumen or Meridian Gate (1406–). See p.699

D. The Forbidden City: Hall of the Taihedian (1406–20). See p.699

A. (*left*)
The Forbidden City: Hall of the Taihedian, timber ceiling (1406–20). See p.699

B. (*below*)
The Summer Palace, Beijing (1750, 1888, 1903). See p.699

A. The Summer Palace: typical building. See p.699

B. The Summer Palace: the Foxiangge Tower and the Paiyundian Hall

C. The Summer Palace: the long gallery

D. The Summer Palace: lakes and Xiti (West Embankment)

A. Tiantan Shrine: the Huanqiutan (Min and Qing dynasties). See p.700

B. Tiantan Shrine: the Qiniandian Hall of Prayer (Ming and Qing dynasties)

Glory) and the Wuyingdian (the Hall of Martial Valour). The Wenhuadian served as a study for the crown prince and the Wuyingdian as a place for the emperor to receive his ministers. The other halls were used for receptions, the administration of the empire and the celebration of important festivals. In the inner court were the Qianqinggong (the Palace of Celestial Purity), the Kunninggong (the Palace of Terrestrial Union), containing the emperor's and empress's bedchambers, as well as the Dongliugong (the Six Eastern Courtyards) and the Xiliugong (the Six Western Courtyards), both the latter inhabited by concubines and maids. There were also bedrooms for the crown prince and dowager empress as well as small stages, gardens and halls for the worship of Buddha.

The buildings of the Forbidden City are arranged in two rows on either side of a north-south axis which stretches for 8 km (5 miles) and divides Beijing into its eastern and western halves (p. 695A). The axis, known as the meridian line, passes through thirteen buildings and inside the walls of the palace they are symmetrically arranged on either side of it. Also on the axis are courtyards of various sizes: the first on the south end is known as Daqingmen and is the gateway to the inner city of Beijing, behind which is a T-shaped square which stretches into the front of the **Tiananmen** (p. 695B), the main gate to the Imperial City, which virtually surrounds the Forbidden City. Behind the gate is a square courtyard; north of the courtyard is the Duanmen, the Gate of Correct Demeanour, and another rectangular square. The **Wumen or Meridian Gate** (p. 695C), the main entrance to the Forbidden City itself, is immediately north of this square.

Inside the Forbidden City on the meridian line there are eight courtyards, of which the second, known as Taihedian, is the largest (about 4 ha in area).

The **Hall of the Taihedian**, the main hall of the Forbidden City (p. 695D), is 27 m (90 ft) high, 64 m (210 ft) wide and 37 m (120 ft) deep. It has a roof with double eaves and is decorated with carved dragons and phoenixes (p. 696A), most of which are gilded. The building is raised on a three-tiered terrace, 8 m (26 ft) high, enclosed by marble balustrades, while those around the same courtyard were kept lower so as to set off the magnificence of the hall.

The red walls, pillars and yellow glazed roof-tiles, and the dougong and beams decorated with dark-green designs of dragons, phoenixes and geometric figures, are conspicuous against the grey background of Beijing. Begun in 1406, the fourth year of the reign of Yongle (Ming dynasty), the City was completed fourteen years later; partial reconstruction took place during the period of the Qing dynasty. Twenty-four emperors lived in and ruled China from the Forbidden City over nearly 500 years.

The emperors also built country villas and set them in landscaped parks. Most of those existing today were created in the Qing dynasty; the most famous is the **Summer Palace** on the north-western outskirts of **Beijing** (pp. 696B, 697, 701D). Begun in 1750 and restored in 1888 and 1903, the park's main features are Wanshoushan (Longevity Hill), and Kunminghu (Kunming Lake), and it covers an area of 2900 ha (7166 acres), three-quarters of which is water.

The Summer Palace itself is divided into four parts, the first of which is that nearest the Donggongmen (East Palace Gate) where the emperor and empress lived and affairs of state were conducted. The groups of courtyards in this part of the palace are symmetrical. Although roofs were not glazed, the section through the building is characteristic of an imperial palace (p. 697A). The second part is on the southern slope of Wanshoushan, looking down on Kunming Lake, and contains the **Foxiangge (the Tower of Buddhist Incense)**, an octagonal building, 37 m (120 ft) high, set on a platform. The Foxiangge is the symbol of the park, and in front of it is the **Paiyundian (the Cloud Dispelling Hall)** (p. 697B) where the court held its celebrations. Both stand at the middle of the southern slope of Wanshoushan and form an axis which is flanked by more than ten groups of smaller buildings. A gallery, 760 m (2500 ft) long, (p. 697C) runs east and west from the Paiyundian and links together all the scattered buildings to make this section the most beautiful in the park.

The northern slope of Wanshoushan, together with a stream, is the site of the third part. All the buildings here, except for a religious group, stand in the centre of the area, hidden in a landscape modelled on the private gardens of south China.

The fourth part of the park consists of Kunming Lake, South Lake, West Lake and its island. The water surface is 1700 m (5575 ft) from west to east and 2000 m (6560 ft) from north to south. The lakes are separated by embankments, the longest of which is Xiti (the West Embankment), modelled upon Suti of Hangzhou city in Zhejiang province, south China. Six bridges of different types stand on Xiti, linking the Summer Palace with the outside world. From the east bank of Kunming Lake, Xiti links the inside and outside views of the Summer Palace, and hills and pagodas can be seen in the distance (p. 697D). The scene looks like a traditional Chinese mountain-and-water painting.

Shrines

Shrines were used in ancient China for making sacrifices to ancestors and famous historical personages, as well as to the gods. The most famous is the group of buildings known as **Tiantan Shrine** in the southern district of **Beijing**. It extends over an area of 280 ha (690 acres) and was built for emperors of the Ming and Qing dynasties. There are two groups of buildings, the **Huanqiutan** for the worship of heaven, and the **Qiniandian** for prayers for good harvest. There is also a group named **Zhaigong (the Fasting Palace)**.

The buildings of the Huanqiutan also include the **Huangqiongyu (Imperial Vault of Heaven)**, which houses a sacred tablet. The Huanqiutan itself is a three-tiered circular, marble terrace (p. 698A), the uppermost tier of which is 26 m (86 ft) and the lowest tier 55 m (180 ft) in diameter. The height of the three terraces is 5 m (16 ft). Marble balustrades enclose each tier. The paving stones and the balusters are arranged in multiples of nine, symbolishing the Ninth Heaven where, it is said, the god of heaven lives. The Huanqiutan is enclosed by two walls, the outer one being square on plan and the inner one circular. The walls are pierced by four sets of doors; that in the north faces the Huangqiongyu, a single-roofed circular structure about 20 m (66 ft) high and 16 m (52 ft) in diameter set in a circular courtyard.

A brick pavement, 400 m (1300 ft) long and 30 m (100 ft) wide, to the north of the **Huanqiutan** (p. 698A), leads to the Qiniandian, the main feature of which is a circular, wooden Hall of Prayer, 32 m (106 ft) high and 24 m (78 ft) in diameter (p. 698B). It has a triple, conical roof of deep-blue glazed tiles topped with a large gold-plated ball, and red columns, door and window frames, dark green dougong and beams. It stands on a three-tiered circular terrace 7 m (23 ft) high and maximum 90 m (300 ft) diameter. The terraces have white marble balustrades.

Heaven was said to be circular and the earth square. Thus square courtyards were used to locate heaven on earth, while high platforms for the buildings, placed behind comparatively low surrounding walls, gave an impression that the buildings were close to the sky. Road surfaces on either side of the approach-paths were built to slope from south to north and planted with pines and cypress to extend the perspective, so that as the road surface continued to rise buildings such as Qinandian seemed to be built in heaven.

Though Tiantan Shrine was completed in the Ming dynasty, it was subsequently rebuilt many times. Today's Huanqiutan, for example, was reconstructed in 1749 and the Qiniandian in 1890.

Mausolea

Elaborate funerals and lavish tombs were provided for the rulers of ancient China. The imperial tombs are of two kinds – above ground and below. Those underground are usually only chambers to house emperors' coffins, and at first were wood-framed structures, but after the Eastern Han dynasty (25–220) were built of stone or brick. Later tombs are either built above ground or combine underground chambers with commemorative buildings above the ground.

The **Shisanling Tombs in Changping** county, north of Beijing at the foot of Mount Tianshou, were used for the burial of thirteen Ming emperors and empresses. A stone pailou proclaims the entrance (p. 703A) and beyond it the road is lined by giant statues of officials, warriors, horses and camels. The designs and layouts of the thirteen tombs vary only slightly, but the Changling Mausoleum is perhaps the most imposing. It is the tomb of the Emperor Cheng Zu of the Ming dynasty, built in 1424. The buildings above ground consist of a memorial hall, the Fengcheng Minglou and the Treasured Crown. The **Lingen Memorial Hall** is one of the largest ancient timber-framed buildings existing in China today (p. 703B). Inside the hall are thirty-two 'nanmu' wood pillars, the four largest 1.17 m (3 ft 19 in) in diameter and 23 m (76 ft) high (p. 704A). Behind the sacrificial hall is a burial mound encircled by a massive brick wall – the Treasured Crown. Beneath the mound is the huge burial chamber, known as the Underground Palace. The Fengcheng Minglou (literally the square city and bright tower) is a pavilion housing a sacred stone tablet.

The **Underground Palace of the Ding-ling Mausoleum** (the tomb of Ming Emperor, Shengzong), another of the Ming imperial tombs, is the only one that has been fully excavated (p. 701C). It has three chambers and a long passage leads to the main burial chamber. The palace was built in the late sixteenth century and is constructed entirely of arched stonework.

Ancient architectural remains in China, however, are mostly associated with religion. They include Buddhist temples, monasteries and grottoes, Islamic mosques and Daoist monasteries.

Buddhist Temples

There were two types of Buddhist temple: the first combined a tall, symbolic feature (a stupa or pagoda) with a temple-hall; the second and later type consisted of buildings arranged around courtyards. The earliest examples of the first type were temples with stupas which had been introduced from India at the time of the Eastern Han dynasty (first century). The stupas, which usually stood in the centre of the group of temple buildings, were said to contain Buddha's remains and were objects of homage for his disciples. By the time of the Northern Wei dynasty, temple-halls were combined with pagodas. This kind of temple was built from the fourth to sixth centuries and later was passed to Japan through Korea (q.v.).

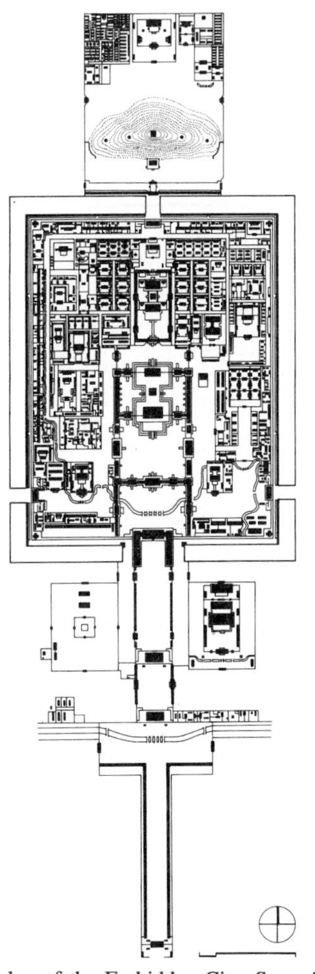

A. Master plan of the Forbidden City. See p.707

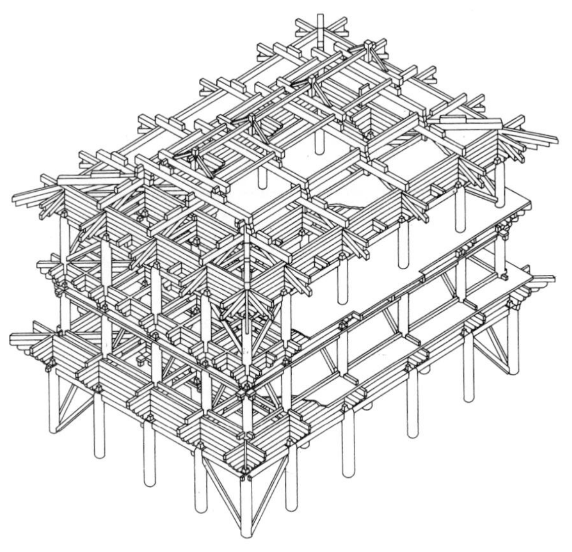

B. Construction illustration of Gua-yin Pavilion in Du-le Monastery. See p.708

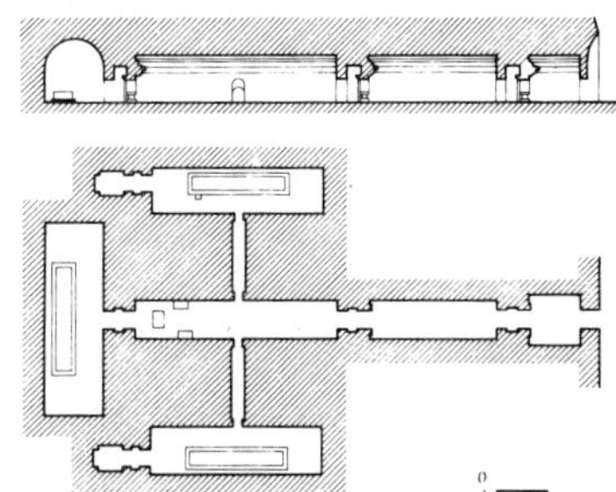

C. Underground floor plan and section of Ding-ling Mausoleum. See p.700

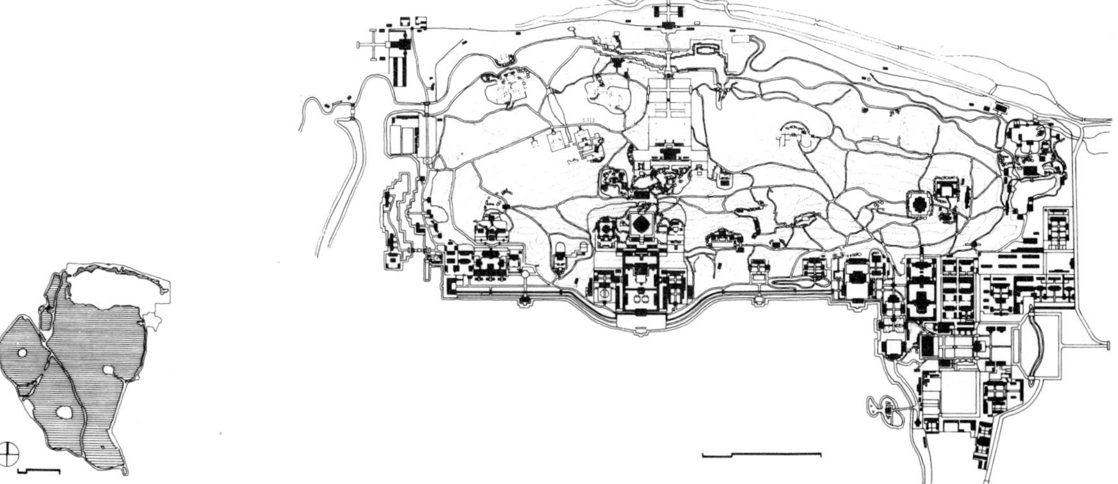

D. Master plan of Summer Palace and the site plan of the buildings on Wan-shou Mountain. See p. 699

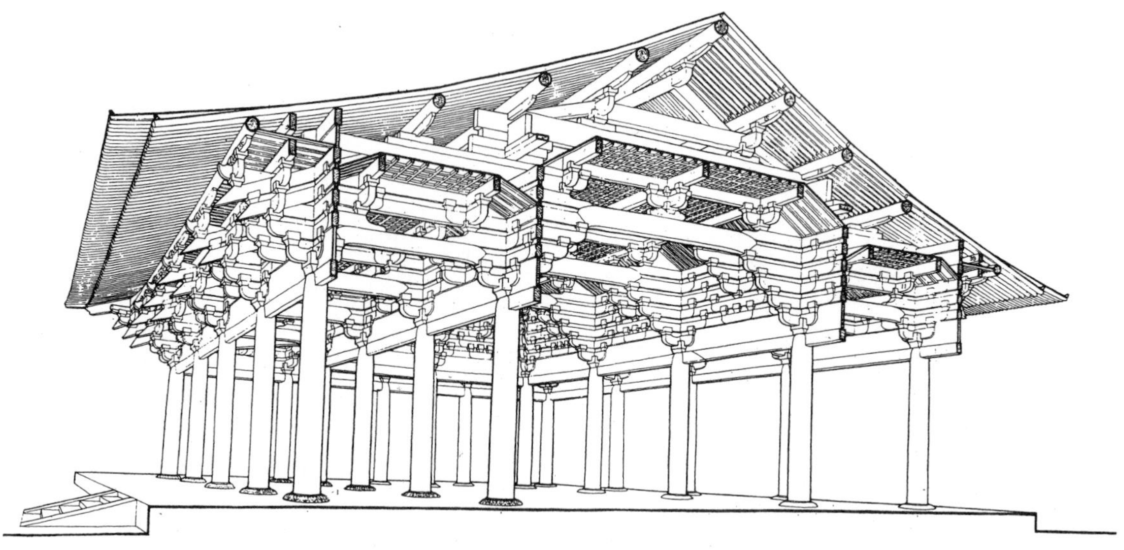

A. Construction illustration of the Grand Hall in Foguang Temple. See p.707

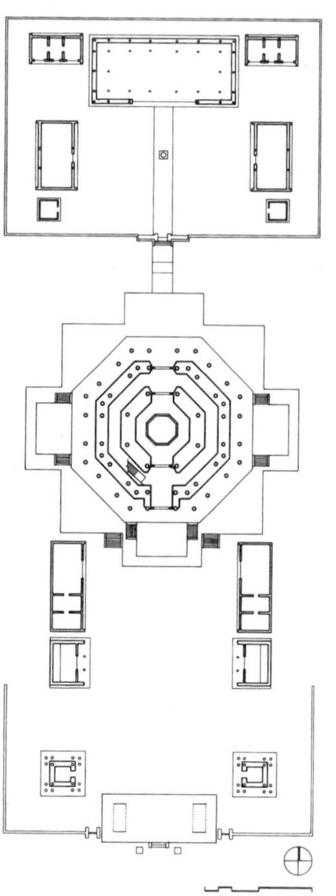

B. The master plan of Foguang Temple. See p.707

C. The section of Shijia Pagoda in Foguang Temple. See p.707

A. The Shisanling, Changping, near Beijing: the pailou. See p.700

B. The Changling Mausoleum: Lingen Memorial Hall (1424). See p.700

A. The Changling Mausoleum, Lingen Memorial Hall: interior. See p.700

B. Lesser Wild Goose Pagoda, Xi'an, Shanxi province (Tang dynasty). See p.707

C. Songyue Temple, Henan province (520). See p.707

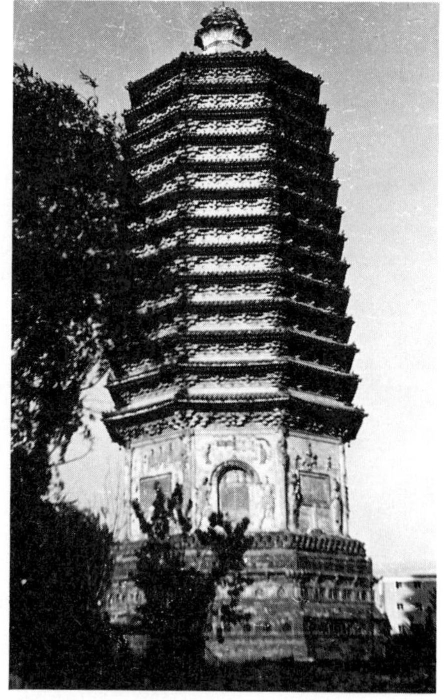

D. Tianning Temple Pagoda, Beijing (Liao dynasty). See p.707

A. Kaiyuan Temple Pagoda, Quanzhou (1241–52). See p.707

B. Kaiyuan Temple Pagoda, Dingxian, Hebei province (thirteenth century). See p.707

C. Bao'en Temple Pagoda, Suzhou (1131–62). See p.707

D. The White Pagoda, Temple of Miaoying, Beijing (1271). See p.707

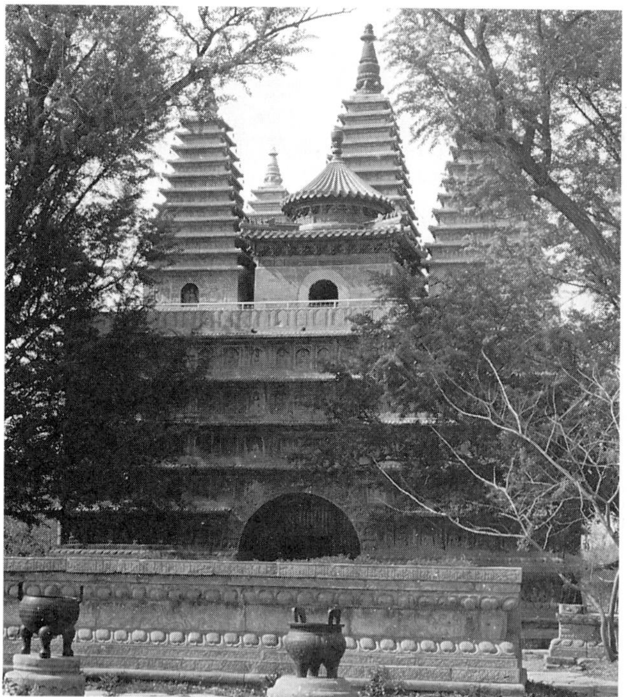

A. Zin Gang Bao Zuo Pagoda at Zheng-jue Temple, Beijing province. See p.707

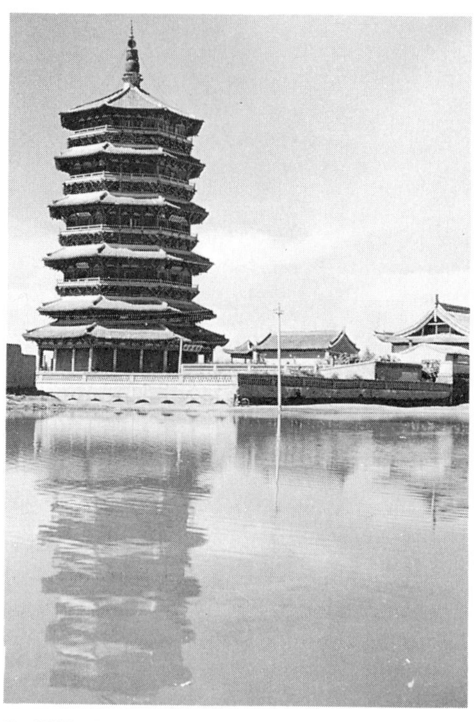

B. Shijia Pagoda, Shanxi province (1056). See p.707

C. Guan-yin Pavilion, Du-le Monastery, Jixian, Hebei province (984). See p.708

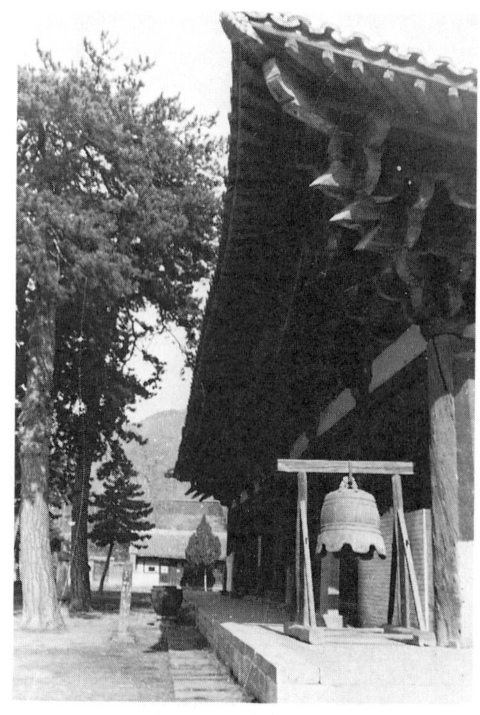

D. Foguang Monastery, Shanxi province: Main Hall (857). See p.707

In the south of China under the Eastern Jin dynasty (317–420) a style evolved in which two pagodas were placed symmetrically in the courtyard of the temple. During the Tang dynasty (618–907) there were independent courtyards for pagodas; from the Song dynasty (960–1279) onwards, pagodas were placed behind the temples, but they were built only rarely in the Ming and Qing periods.

The second type of temple without either stupa or pagoda evolved in many parts of China between the first and sixth centuries. Bureaucrats, nobles and emperors donated their palaces and grand residences for use as temples, and as these buildings usually had a number of courtyards, similar plan arrangements came to be used for new buildings. The large temples of the Tang period (618–907) had scores of courtyards, and later, after the Yuan (1271–1368), Buddhist temples were planned symmetrically along a main axis. There were traditional locations for the Hall of the King of Heaven, the Grand Hall of the Buddha and the Buddhist Classics Repository; each temple had a Bell and Drum Tower.

It is the pagoda which characterises the Buddhist temple in China. Most of those still existing are of brick and stone, and there are more than two thousand of them. Only one wood-framed pagoda has survived. Pagodas can be classified into six types.

Pagodas with closely layered eaves, of which the earliest remaining example is the oldest pagoda of the **Songyue Temple** built in 520 at **Mount Songshan**, in Henan province (p. 704C). Externally it is twelve-sided, but its interior is octagonal. The temple was 41 m (131 ft) high, its diameter at the base about 14 m (46 ft), and its foundation wall 2.5 m (8 ft) thick. Its long, slender body had four doors and eight imitation windows. There are fifteen eaves in the upper part, and the total outside contour forms a longer parabola shape. Its top was a brick spire and it contained an internal staircase. However, it is now in ruins.

During the Tang dynasty, the eaves pagoda became very popular and a square plan shape was evolved. The **Lesser Wild Goose Pagoda at Xi'an** in Shanxi province is an example of the square pagoda (p. 704B). In the Liao dynasty the octagonal plan was preferred and the eaves were no longer parabolashaped. The **Pagoda of Tianning (Haven of Peace)** temple in **Beijing** (p. 704D) is of this kind and is built to imitate timber-framed building style.

The storeyed pagoda. The Chinese storeyed building combined the pagoda form with that of the Indian stupa. The earliest existing storeyed pagodas were built in the Tang dynasty and were square in plan (an example is the **Greater Wild Goose Pagoda in Xi'an**) but the more popular form, from the tenth to thirteenth centuries, is octagonal. Some of them, such as the stone pagoda in the **Temple of Kaiyuan in Quanzhou** built between 1241 and 1252 (p. 705A), resembled earlier wood-framed pagodas. Others, such as the **Kaiyuan Temple Pagoda**, which is 82 m (269 ft) high, in **Dingxian** county, Hebei province (p. 705B), have less decoration. Some brick pagodas have an outer wooden gallery. The **Bao'en Temple Pagoda in Suzhou**, built in 1131–1162 (p. 705C), is of this kind. The brick pagoda has various structural forms. Some are constructed on a single brick tube, others on twin tubes or bricks packed together with space inside for only a flight of spiral steps. This kind of pagoda was popular for more than 1000 years.

Vase-shaped pagodas evolved directly from stupas: they were first built in the late Tang dynasty, but became popular only after the Yuan dynasty in the temples of Lamaism. The **White Pagoda in the Temple of Miaoying (Divine Retribution) in Beijing** (p. 705D) was built in 1271 with the guidance of a Nepalese craftsman. It is 56 m (184 ft) high. These pagodas were usually built in groups, sometimes five or more in a line or arranged symmetrically around a major building. The surface of the pagodas are faced in glazed brickwork.

Groups of pagodas honouring Buddha's warrior attendants, popular in the Ming and Qing periods, were built in imitation of the Buddh Gaya relic-house complex in India (see Chapter 26). Five pagodas were usually placed along the diagonals of a square terrace decorated with carved statues. Each was a closely-layered eaves pagoda and pyramidal in shape, for example the **Zin Gang Bao Zuo Pagoda in the Zheng-jue Temple, Beijing** (p. 706A).

Single-storey pagodas were built as tombs for monks and nuns. They may be square, octagonal, circular or hexagonal. They are often found in groups or lines adjacent to temples. There are collections of pagodas at the **Shaolin Temple, Henan** province, and at the **Lingyan Temple, Shandong** province (p. 706A).

Wooden tower pagodas were built from the third century onwards, but the **Shijia Pagoda** in the Buddhist Palace Temple, **Shanxi** province, built in *c.* 1056 (p. 706B), is the only surviving building of this kind in China. It is 67 m (221 ft) in height, and 26 m (86 ft) in diameter at its base. Between each of the five outside storeys there is a hidden interior storey. The storeys diminish in height between the layers from top to bottom. The outside of the pagoda is timber-framed, and the hidden storeys are trussed. Spiral stairways are arranged along the edges of the pagoda. It has survived some 900 years despite seven earthquakes, as well as bombardments (p. 702C).

Halls, Pavilions and Monasteries

The **Main Hall of Foguang Monastery, Wutai Mountain**, Shanxi province (857) is one of China's earliest extant wooden structures (p. 706D). Its facade, divided into seven bays, is 34 m (112 ft) long, 17.3 m (57 ft) deep and 13.6 m (44 ft) in height. There are framed windows at both ends and in the rear wall. There are five wooden doors in the front side but none elsewhere. The columns of the hall are short, about 5 m (16 ft) high, but there is a large cluster of brackets at the top of each column supporting the eaves. The cantilever length of the brackets is half the length of the columns. The hall is in the Tang style, and sculptures, paintings and murals of that period are displayed in the building (p. 702A).

The **Guan-yin Pavilion of Du-le Monastery** (984) **in Jixian**, Hebei province, is one of China's earliest surviving pavilions (pp. 701B, 706C). The building has five bays and is 20 m (66 ft) long, 14 m (47 ft) deep and 22 m (73 ft) high. The roof has a single eaves and has both hipped and gabled elements. A 16 m (52 ft) high Liao dynasty Guan-yin statue is enshrined in the pavilion. The construction is earthquake resistant and the pavilion has survived twenty-eight earthquakes without damage.

Longxing Monastery in Zhengding, Hebei province, is an important existing example of a Buddhist monastery of the Song dynasty (960–1127). It has an obvious axis, along which lie the main halls, pavilions and courtyards. There is a rich variety of shapes in the halls and pavilions. The living quarters of the monks are located on the eastern side, as are the stables. The Mo-ni Hall, Ci Shi Pavilion and Zhuan-Lun-Zang Hill (repository for Buddhist scriptures) are the principal remaining buildings. The **Mo-ni Hall** dates from 1052 and has a cruciform plan shape (p.709A). The roof is a sophisticated structure, light in form and ingeniously constructed.

Built in 1645–95, the **Potala Palace in Lhasa, Tibet**, is a large-scale Lama Monastery (p. 709B). It comprises the White Palace and the Red Palaces, and rises 200 m (660 ft) against the slope of a hill. Inside the palace are nine storeys in wood and stone. A part of the Red Palaces with three wooden-framed roofs inlaid with golden tiles has been called the Golden Palace and stands beside five vase-shaped towers covered in gold leaf. Against the red and white stone walls, they form a colourful and splendid scene.

A group of buildings with both Han and Tibetan architectural features is **Puning Monastery, Chengde**, Hebei province. It is divided into two sections, one in the Han style, set around a group of courtyards, the other constructed according to the doctrine of Lamaism on a platform 9 m (29 ft) high. The centre of the group is the **Dacheng Pavilion** (p. 710A), a T-shaped, five-storey building 24 m (80 ft) long and 20 m (66 ft) deep. The space in the centre of the hall is 24 m (78 ft) high, and enshrines a 23 m (75 ft) high Guanryin statue. The hall has five separate roofs covered with glazed yellow tiles and a golden baoding on the top of each pinnacle. Around the main hall are several smaller halls, colourful vase-like towers and red and white platforms.

Grottoes

The Buddhist grottoes were introduced to China from India. They are shrines carved into cliff faces and inside the caves. The earliest in China are the **Mingshashan Grottoes in Dunhuang**, Gansu province (353), and the **Heseer Grottoes in Xinjiang**, also cut in the fourth century. The practice reached the height of its popularity in the Northern and Southern, Sui and Tang dynasties between the middle of the fifth century and the beginning of the tenth century. The sixth-century examples had giant columns at their entrances, and ceilings were often carved to resemble wooden structures. Among the best-known grottoes are the **Mogao Grottoes in Dunhuang**, Gansu province, the **Yungang Grottoes in Datong**, Shanxi province (pp. 710B,C), and the **Longmen Grottoes in Luoyang**, Henan province.

The development of grottoes in China is an example of the historical merging of Chinese and foreign cultural ideas. The rock caves of the Yungang Grottoes cut during the Northern Wei dynasty (386–534) vary with date. Grottoes carved on natural cliffs are large and without decoration: they belong to the first stage. The appearance and clothing of the giant Buddhas reveal the influence of India and Central Asia. The second stage is distinguished by square caves with central columns. Niches for statues of the Buddha were carved on some of the central columns, while others were shaped into Buddhist pagodas. The grottoes at this time had many designs taken from India, Persia and Greece, for example flamboyant lions, twin-headed beasts back to back and Ionic capitals.

Islamic Architecture

Most of the existing Islamic buildings in China were constructed after the end of the fourteenth century. They are of two kinds, the first developed from the Islamic styles in Central Asia. This category includes the **Arbahejama in Kashi**, Xinjiang province, which consists of a mosque, prayer halls, and mausolea of the imams. The style combined and developed traditional Chinese architectural styles with Islamic ideas. The **Niu-jie Mosque, Beijing**, is one of these and contains a chanting hall, a ritual bath, imams' rooms and a prayer-hall. It was constructed in 994 and renovated in 1442. It has a courtyard on an east–west axis. The structure of the mosque is mainly in the Chinese (Han) style, although the decoration in the prayer-hall incorporates central Asian features – tendril patterns, pointed arches and inscriptions in Arabic lettering (p. 711A).

A. The Mo-ni Hall, Longxing Monastery, Zhengding, Hebei province (1052). See p.708

B. Potala Palace, Lhasa, Tibet (1645–95). See p.708

A. Puning Monastery, Chengde, Hebei province: Dacheng Pavilion. See p.708

B. Pagoda in Yungang Grotto

C. Yungang Grotto, Datong, Shanxi province (sixth to tenth centuries). See p.708

A. Nin-jie Mosque, Beijing: interior (renovated 1442). See p.708

B. Tianshidong Daoist Temple, Gụanxian, Sichuan province: See p.714

C. Siheyuan, courtyard houses, Beijing (Qing dynasty). See p.714

A. Houses at Anhui, south of the Changjang River. See p.714

B. Houses in Sichuan mountaineous region, south of the Changjang River. See p.714

C. Adobe houses at Fujian. See p.714

A. Anji Bridge, Zhaoxian, Hebei province (605–17). See p.714

B. The Wangshi Garden, Suzhou (Ming and Qing dynasties). See p.714

C. Arch Bridge, Summer Palace, Beijing. See p.714

D. Great Wall (seventh to fifth centuries BC). See p.714

Daoist Temples and Palaces

A few ancient Daoist temples and palaces survive. The earliest is the **Yongle Palace** built in 1262 **in Yongji** county, Shanxi province. Its main buildings are three halls and a large gate, aligned on an axis. Each of the buildings is similar, in traditional Buddhist architectural style. In the 1950s the palace was moved to Ruicheng county to make way for a reservoir.

Most of the existing Daoist buildings are of the Ming and Qing dynasties. They were built mainly in beautiful mountain areas and are in a free architectural style. The **Daoist Temple** in the Qingcheng Mountains in **Guanxian** county, Sichuan province, is in the vernacular style of the locality (p. 711B).

Houses and Private Gardens

Due to diverse economic, geographic and climatic conditions and living habits in different parts of the country, houses in China vary greatly in style, and each of the styles has a long history. Only a few houses remain from the Ming period, but most of the oldest remaining houses are of the Qing period. They vary from the formal to the vernacular and are of the following kinds: Beijing's 'siheyuan' (compounds with houses around courtyards) (p. 711C), houses or compounds south of the Changjiang (Yangtze) River (p. 712A), houses of the mountainous regions south of the Changjiang River (p. 712B), cave dwellings, yurts, Tibetan block houses, houses on stilts or bamboo houses in Yunnan and Guizhou provinces, adobe multi-storeyed houses in Fujian (p. 712C), flat-roofed houses in Xinjiang.

Residences of high officials and rich merchants in Beijing and south of the Changjiang River were constructed with the finest building materials. They reflect the rigid patriarchal society of ancient China. The 'siheyuan' had a south–north axis and rooms were strictly laid out on either side of it. The principal rooms, facing south on the axis, were for the head of the family, those in the wings were for his brothers and children. Some siheyuan had an outer compound for entertaining guests and another for the private use of the family.

In the Ming and Qing dynasties officials and rich merchants in south China built magnificent residences. Some of them had two or three axes and a dozen courtyards, and some had more than two storeys. Small courtyards were used to provide shade and ventilation to counteract south China's tropical climate.

Many private gardens were provided in south China and in the north, mainly in Beijing. Private gardens **in Suzhou** are typical of the south – **Zhuozhengyuan (The Humble Administrator's Garden), Liuyuan (Garden to Linger In), Shizilin (Lion Grove), Wangshi (Fishermen's Garden)** (p. 713B) and **Canglangting (Pavilion of the Surging Waves)** were among the most famous.

Bridges

China has a long history of bridge building, and tens of thousands of bridges still exist. They assume many different forms and structural systems: wooden bridges of various kinds, arched stone bridges, beam bridges (including those with wooden beams carried on stone pillars), and bamboo, rattan and steel cable bridges. Most of the surviving ancient bridges are made of stone and demonstrate a high level of bridge-building skill (p. 713C).

Anji Bridge in Zhaoxian county, Hebei province (p. 713A), built during the Sui dynasty (605–17), is the world's oldest arched bridge with open spandrels: it was constructed 700 years earlier than the first example of this type in Europe. Its span is 37 m (121 ft), the height of the arch 7 m (23 ft) and the total length 51 m (167 ft). The two ends of the bridge are wider than the middle section, tapering from 9.6 m (31 ft 6 in) to 9 m (29 ft 6 in). The bridge has twenty-eight stone arches.

Wanan Bridge in Quanzhou, Fujian province, built at the end of the eleventh century, is a stone beam bridge of forty-eight arches, 540 m (1770 ft) long. It spans the Luoyang River, which is deep with swift currents. It is said the builders bred oysters to help stick together the stone blocks of the bridge foundations, which for this bridge are similar to raft foundations in modern bridge design, constructed some 800 years before the establishment of the theory.

Guangji Bridge in Chaozhou, Guangdou province, built during the Song dynasty (960–1279), is the world's earliest bascule bridge. It is 5 m (16 ft) wide and 518 m (1700 ft) long, divided into three sections. The middle section, a 93 m (310 ft) long floating bridge, consists of many wooden boats linked by cables to a stone bridge at each end.

The Great Wall, 6000 km (3726 miles) long, was built between the seventh and fifth centuries BC. In the fourth century BC, the states of Yan, Zhao and Qin built separate sections to resist the incursions of nomadic peoples from the north. It was the Qin empire (late third century BC), however, which unified the country, connected the walls together and expanded them into the present Great Wall (p. 713D).

The wall was continuously strengthened and extended right up to the Ming period, when the eastern section was refaced with stone blocks and bricks. Generally the wall was 7 m to 8 m (23 ft to 26 ft) high, but at strategic points it was 14 m (46 ft) high. At its base the wall was between 6 m (20 ft) and 7 m (23 ft) thick and at the top 5 m (16 ft). Guard houses and armouries were built on the wall and there were beacon-towers for communication purposes. Garrison towns, such as Jiayuguan Pass, Pingxingguan Pass and Juyongguan Pass, were constructed to house the troops manning the wall and their weapons. The scale of the Great Wall is unparalleled in the history of the architecture of fortifications.

Chapter 25
JAPAN AND KOREA

The architectural character of Japanese architecture of the early period, like its other artefacts, is similar to that of Korea; most of the earliest Chinese influences reached Japan from Korea. Many of the formal qualities are related to structure and a rigorous conformity with traditional models.

While the architectural evolution of Japan and Korea were parallel, and both much indebted to the Chinese and the Mongols, Korea is dealt with first in this chapter. The consonant nature of the developments in both countries will be apparent. The main classification for Korean architecture is by building type; within each category, architectural character is dealt with by period.

Korean Architecture from the Three Kingdoms Period to the End of the Choson Period

An outline of Korean architecture is essential to an understanding of the development of Japanese architecture. It is the link between the classical traditions of Chinese building form and the unique transformations thereof in Japan.

The Three Kingdoms Period (57 BC–668)

No wooden structures survive from the period when Korea was divided into three kingdoms (Koguryo, Paekche and Shilla), only a few stone buildings, including two pagodas of Paekche and one of Shilla construction; also from the latter kingdom is the Ch'omsongdae, an astronomical observatory.

Timber Buildings

Building during the Koguryo Kingdom (57 BC–668) may be envisaged from the murals depicting fortress walls in the Samshilch'ong, Yodongsongch'ong and Yaksuri tombs and in houses in the Ssang-yongch'ong (p. 718A), Anak No. 1 and T'onggu No. 12 tombs. Painted pillars and beams in the murals at the corners of the burial chambers of Muyongch'ong, Kwigapch'ong and Anak No. 1 tombs provide insight into the building techniques of the times. It can be deduced from these sources that Koguryo structures often had round pillars with entasis, supporting simply executed brackets. Short struts with bearing blocks or inverted V-shaped trusses were fitted on beams and purlins to sustain the framework of hipped or gabled roofs. Most of the houses depicted in the murals have tiled roofs. In all probability the architecture of Koguryo was influenced by that of the later Han (25–219) and of the Northern Wei (386–534) dynasties of China.

The founders of the Paekche Kingdom (18 BC–660) were blood relations of the rulers of Koguryo and their architecture was probably similar. The Paekche Kingdom expanded over the south-western part of the peninsula, however, and its architecture was no doubt influenced by that of the southern part of China. Without examples of architecture of that period, it can only be guessed that it resembled Japan's Horyuji Temple (q.v.), the construction of which was strongly influenced by the architecture of Paekche.

Little is known about the wooden architecture of the Shilla Kingdom (57 BC–935), but the excavation of the **Hwangnyongsa Temple in Kyongju**, the capital of Shilla, suggests Koguryo influence.

Stone Buildings

Two pagodas remain from the Paekche period. One is at **Iksan**, Chollanam-do Province on the site of **Miruksa**, a temple believed to date from the reign of King Mu-wang (600–641), and the other is a five-storey structure on the site of the **Chongnimsa Temple in Puyo**, Ch'ungch'ongnam-do Province (p. 718B). The Miruksa Pagoda, the earliest known example in stone, is believed to have had seven or nine storeys though only parts of six now remain. Each component was hewn from a separate stone and

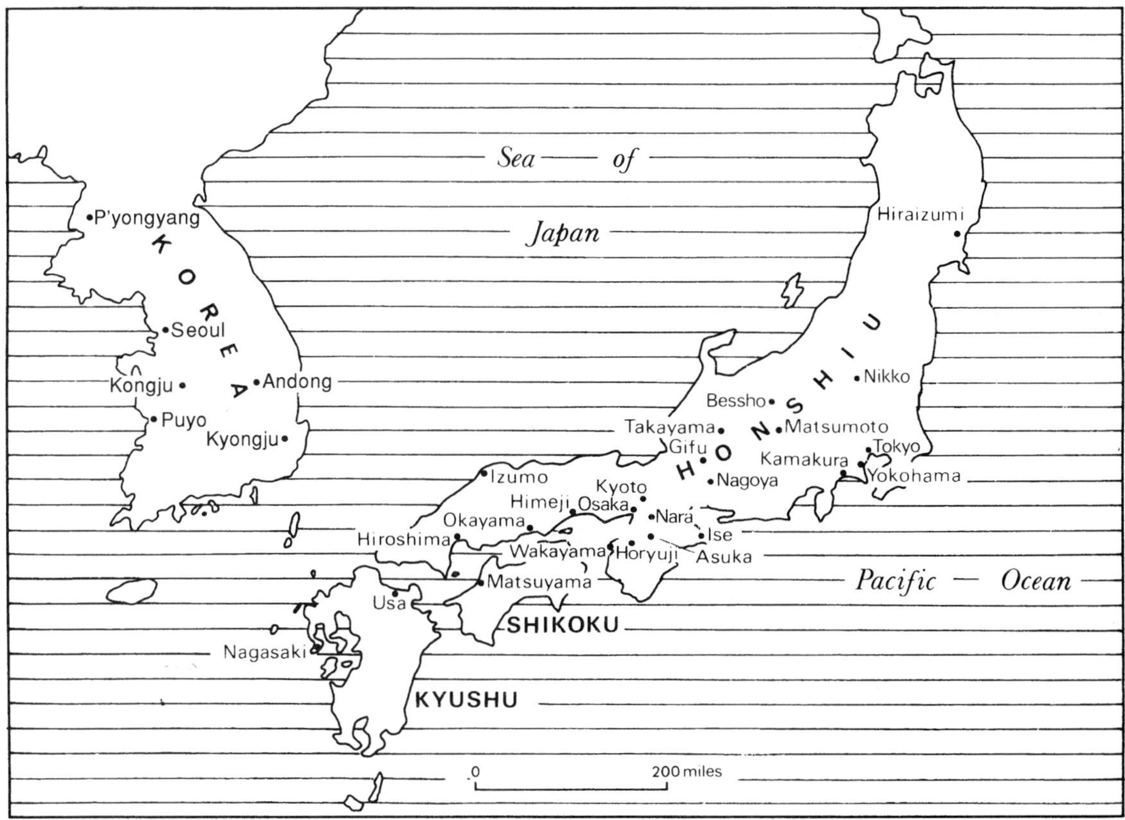

Japan and Korea

fitted as though made of timber. The pagoda of Chongnimsa emerged in the process of improving the constructional technique of the Miruksa Pagoda which had proved unsatisfactory. It became the prototype for the future Paekche pagodas with its ideal combination of a simple two-tiered foundation and an elegant five-storey main body.

There are two major stone buildings in Kyongju constructed before the Shilla defeated the Paekche and Koguryo to unify the peninsula. One of them, the **Ch'omsongdae Observatory** (p. 718C), is preserved almost intact. The cylindrical monument, slightly convex in outline, rises in meticulous courses and has square windows at high level.

Dating from the same period is a pagoda on the site of **Punhwangsa Temple**. It is made of stones cut to the size and shape of bricks and resembles a brick pagoda; only three of the original nine storeys now remain. Stone beasts are stationed at the four corners of its foundation and stone images of Vajradhara, guardian deities of the temple, at either side of the niches of the body of the pagoda.

The Unified Shilla Period (668–935)

Timber Buildings

There are no extant wooden structures from this period, though a few wooden pieces believed to be construction materials were found during the excavation of Anapchi Pond in Kyongju. Many of the stone structures of the period, however, imitate wooden construction and give an insight into the contemporary wooden structures. Another source of information is the *Samguk sagi (The History of the Three Kingdoms)* written in the twelfth century. It makes possible speculation on some aspects of the construction of the time. It can be deduced that houses for the upper class had tiled roofs, the eaves of which were dressed with end tiles, and that each end of the ridge had an ornamental tile shaped like a bird's tail, while the ends of the hip-ridges were finished with grotesque masks. The gables were decorated with hanging ornaments resembling fish, the eaves were double tiered and supported by brackets on top of the pillars, and the

A. Koguryo wall painting from the Ssang-yongch'ong tomb, showing a house (fifth–sixth century). See p.716

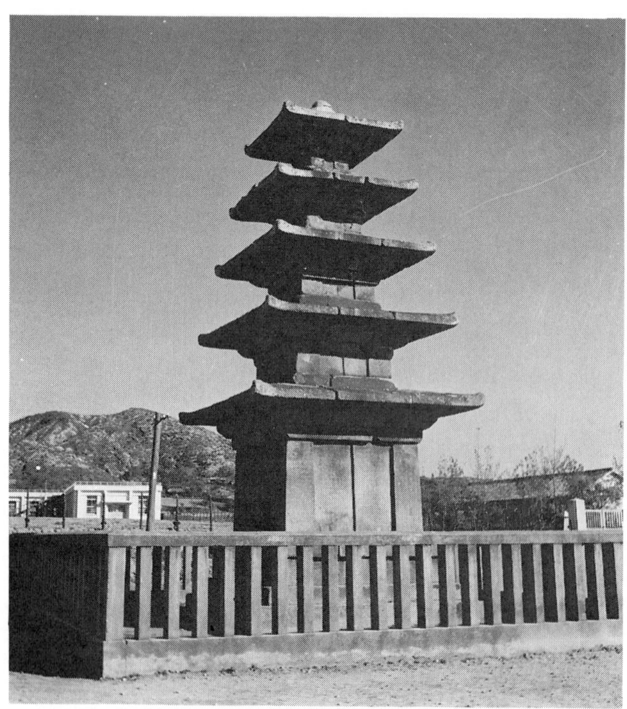

B. Chongnimsa Pagoda (Paekche, sixth–seventh century). See p.716

C. Ch'omsongdae Observatory (Shilla, seventh century). See p.717

A. Pulguksa, Sokkat'ap Pagoda (Shilla, eighth century). See p.721

B. Pulguksa, Tabot'ap Pagoda (Shilla, eighth century). See p.721

C. Pusoksa Muryangsujon (Koryo, thirteenth century). See p.721

A. Ssangbongsa Ch'olgam Stupa (Shilla, ninth century). See p.721

B. Wolchongsa Pagoda (Koryo, eleventh century). See p.721

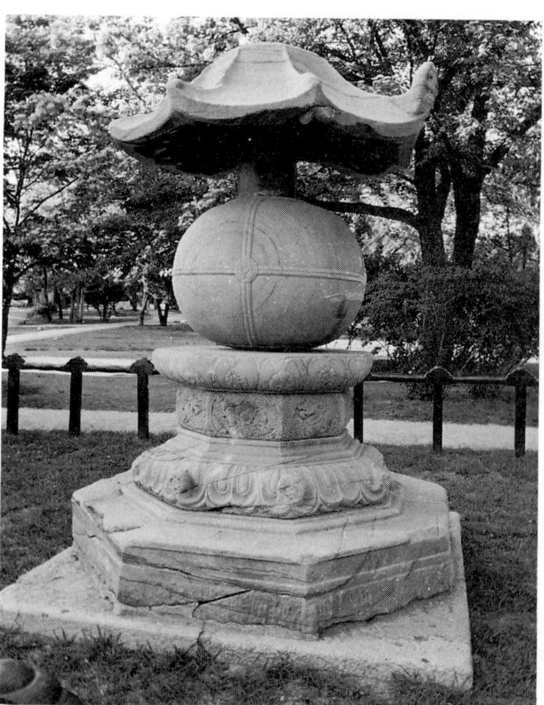

C. Pulguska, Hongbop Stupa (Koryo, eleventh century). See p.723

D. Pongjongsa taeungjon (bracketed eaves) (Choson, thirteenth–fourteenth century). See p.723

wooden part of the structure was coloured and covered richly with gold and silver ornament. The architecture is believed to have been influenced by that of Tang China with which Shilla had close diplomatic and cultural relationships.

Stone Buildings

The major stone edifice of Shilla construction is **Sokkuram**, a man-made grotto built in the middle of the eighth century. It comprises a rectangular antechamber and an arched rotunda, at the centre of which is a seated Buddha. The walls are covered with reliefs of Bodhisattvas and Buddhist guardians.

The development of Shilla pagodas through experiments based on the Miruksa Pagoda has been mentioned above. Most Shilla pagodas are three-storey, the earliest being the twin pagodas on the site of **Kamunsa Temple in Wolsong**, Kyongsangbuk-do Province, but perhaps the finest is a three-storey pagoda called **Sokkat'ap at Pulguksa Temple in Kyongju** (p. 719A), which is supported on a square pedestal with pillars carved upon it. Each storey and each roof is carved from a single stone.

There were also some interesting variations from the three-storey prototype, such as the **Tabot'ap Pagoda in Pulguksa** (p. 719B) and the thirteen-storey stone pagoda of **Chonghyesa Temple in Wolsong**. The pagoda in **Hwaomsa Temple in Kurye**, Chollanam-do Province, also deserves special note for its pedestal which consists of four carved figures of crouching lions. There are several five-storey brick pagodas dating from the Unified Shilla period in the Andong region of Kyongsangbuk-do Province.

Stupas to house the sarira (the remains of very holy persons) and relics of high-ranking monks were an important part of Buddhist architecture. They are classified by shape in Chapter 26.

Most Shilla stupas are octagonal in shape, the oldest being that built for the High Priest, Yomgohwasang, in about 844. The body of the stupa is decorated with reliefs of lions, apsaras (heavenly beings) and four Buddhist guardian kings. The roof-stone is carved to simulate the tiled roof of a wooden building with the tiles, rafters and other details faithfully rendered. Its decorative richness is surpassed only by the stupa of Zen Master Ch'olgam, erected around 868, at the **Ssangbongsa Temple of Hwasun**, Chollanam-do (p. 720A).

The Koryo Period (918–1392)

Timber Buildings

Wooden buildings preserved from the Koryo period include the **Kungnakchon** (Nirvana Hall) **of Pongjongsa Temple in Andong**, and the **Muryangsujon** (Amita Hall) **of Pusoksa Temple in Yongju** (p. 719C), both of which date from the thirteenth century, and the **Taeungjon** (Sakyamuni Hall) **of Sudoksa Temple in Yesan**, built towards the end of the fourteenth century. Rather than a continuation of Shilla architecture, with the exception of the Kungnakchon, these buildings indicate that a new style was emerging from a wave of Chinese influences during the middle and late Koryo periods. A southern Chinese construction style using brackets on top of the columns and with curved bracket arms was introduced to Korea through frequent contacts with the Southern Sung (1127–1279). In Korea a new style of column-head bracketing was evolved and was quite different from its Chinese model. This new style had crystallised by the time the Muryangsujon was built at Pusoksa Temple; although undergoing minor changes in the Taeungjon of Sudoksa and the **Ungjinjon** (Arhans Hall) **of Songbulsa Temple** in North Korea, it continued to flourish through the rest of the Koryo and into the Choson period.

In the fourteenth century a style introduced to northern China under the Yuan (Mongol) dynasty also found its way to Korea. This style, with clusters of brackets on the column-heads and on the horizontal beams between them, was much heavier than that previously introduced from China. Multi-cluster bracketing was soon widely adopted. Some of the best examples of it are the **Pogwangjon** (Vairocana Hall) **of Shimwonsa** and the **Ungjinjon of Sogwangsa**, both in North Korea. The style became even more popular in the Choson period.

Stone Buildings

The pagoda style developed in the Unified Shilla period was continued in the Koryo period. The three-storey pagoda of **Yon-goksa Temple in Kurye**, Chollanam-do, is typical of Koryo pagodas built in the Shilla tradition. The use of Bodhisattvas as decorative reliefs which had begun in the Shilla period is also continued, for example on the three-storey pagoda at **Chunghung Sansong Fortress in Kwang-yang**, Chollanam-do.

Some of the Paekche style also survived in the region that had been Paekche territory. The three-storey pagoda in **Changha-ri, Puyo**, though built during the Koryo period, is identical in style and construction to the Chongnimsa Pagoda, which is of Paekche construction.

Chinese influence from the Song and Liao dynasties (960–1279) is evident in polygonal pagodas such as that at **Kumsansa Temple in Kimche**, Chollabuk-do, which is hexagonal, and in the octagonal, nine-storey pagoda of **Wolchongsa Temple in P'yongch'ang**, Kang-won-do (p. 720B). The ten-storey pagoda of **Kyongch'onsa**, which is now in Seoul, is

A. Sujongsa Pagoda (Choson, fifteenth century). See p.723

B. Ch'anggyonggung Myongjongjon Hall (Choson, fifteenth century). See p.723

C. Namdaemun (South Gate) (Choson, fifteenth century). See p.723

a meticulously sculptured stone replica of a wooden structure and shows a strong Yuan (1271–1368) influence.

With the flourishing of Buddhism during the Koryo period, a great number of elaborate stupas were built. The predominant type was octagonal, but bell-shaped stupas began to appear towards the end of the period, rich sculptural embellishment appeared on the body of octagonal stupas, and the size of the roofstone was reduced. The stupa that enshrines the remains of High Priest Chongjin in **Pongamsa Temple, Mun-gyong**, Kyongsangbuk-do, is one of this type. A stupa on the site of **Kodalsa Temple in Yoju,** Kyonggi-do, is noted for the bold carving of a dragon and tortoise motif on its pedestal.

Two unique stupas are the lamp-shaped stupa of Royal Preceptor Hongbop at **Pulguksa Temple** (p. 720C) and the palanquin-like stupa of Royal Preceptor Chigwang at **Popch'onsa Temple**. The body of the former is topped with a roofstone shaped like a lotus leaf, and the latter is covered with elaborate carvings.

The Choson Period (1392–1910)

Timber Buildings

The **Kungnakchon of Muwisa Temple in Kangjin**, Chollanam-do, **Taeungbojon**, the main hall of **Chongsusa Temple in Kanghwa**, Kyonggi-do, and the **Kuksajon** (National Preceptor's Hall) **in Songgwangsa Temple in Sungju**, Chollanam-do, are some examples of fifteenth-century structures with column-head brackets. The Sakyamuni halls (taeungjon) of **Pongjongsa Temple in Andong** (p. 720D), **Kwallyongsa Temple in Ch'angnyong** and **Kaeshimsa Temple in Sosan** are of an early Choson style with multi-cluster bracketing, while those of **Naesosa Temple in Puan** and **Sonunsa in Koch'ang**, Chollanam-do, are in a mid-Choson style. Multi-cluster bracketed temples built in the late Choson period abound all over the country.

The **Namdaemun (South Gate)** (p. 722C) and the **Tongdaemun (East Gate)**, the ancient entrances to the city of Seoul, have two-storey roof structures of similar size built in the multi-cluster bracketed style. The roof structure of the Namdaemun was built in 1448 in the early Choson period and that of Tongdaemun in 1869.

There are four ancient palaces in Seoul: **Kyongbokkung, Ch'anggyonggung, Ch'angdokkung** and **Toksugung**, and all four are reasonably well preserved. **Myongjongjon**, the main audience hall of **Ch'anggyonggung** (p. 722B), and the gate in front of it are the oldest extant palace structures, having been constructed in the fifteenth century. The buildings in **Kyongbokkung**, including its audience hall **Kunjongjon**, were built in the nineteenth century.

Stone Buildings

Due to the suppression of Buddhism in favour of Confucianism in the Choson period, the number and quality of stone pagodas and stupas greatly declined. Rather than develop a style of their own, most Choson artisans continued to build pagodas in the ancient tradition. However, although there are a number of changes in the seven-storey stone pagoda at **Naksansa Temple in Yang-yang**, Kang-won-do, it is a typical Shilla design. Variations from the traditional styles are found in the octagonal, five-storey pagoda of **Sujongsa Temple in Yangju**, Kyonggi-do (p. 722A), and the ten-storey pagoda of **Won-gaksa Temple in Seoul**, which is a faithful imitation of the Kyongch'onsa pagoda of the Koryo period. Perhaps the most characteristic Choson example is the multi-storey pagoda of **Shilluksa Temple in Yoju**, Kyonggi-do.

Bell-shaped stupas continued during the Choson period. Most Choson stupas, with the exception of that on the site of **Hoeamsa Temple** near Seoul, are devoid of notable sculptured ornament. The Hoeamsa stupa has a stone railing at its base, lotus, arabesque and floral patterns ornately sculptured on its pedestal, and a dragon and cloud pattern on its bell-shaped main body.

Other than pagodas and stupas, underground ice stores were the most frequently built stone structures of the period, though they have survived only in the Kyongsang-do region including Kyongju, Andong, Ch'ongdo, Ch'angnyong and Yongsan. Rectangular stones were used to form a number of arches, between which weight-supporting stones were fitted to uphold the frame of the cylindrical storage chamber. Ice cut from the rivers in winter was stored for use through the summer.

Japanese Architecture from the Asuka Period to the End of the Edo Period (552–1868)

Shinto Architecture

Shinto shrines are, more than any other architecture, the crystallisation of the Japanese homage to tradition. They contribute to the landscape as opposed to architecture in the normal sense, and reflect the worship of the spirits of the environment whose vagaries, it was believed, determined the quality and quantity of the crops.

The introduction of agriculture to Japan, from about the third century BC, encouraged the establishment of permanent villages in which festivals were held at certain times of the year, to express thanks for good crops and to pray for rain and good harvests in the future. At first the sacred site was probably distinguished by a simple surrounding fence (tamagaki) and an entrance gate (torii) – the first architectural elements to be employed. As the festivals developed, the deities symbolising natural forces were given physical form, such as a wooden column at the centre of the festival place.

It was at a considerably more advanced stage that such symbols took an architectural form. Shrines were built to welcome the gods, who descended temporarily to the earth, and were housed in temporary buildings, used only once, for the god's sojourn on the earth.

Shrines only achieved the status of monuments comparable with those of Buddhist temples when the deity of the Ise Shrine came to be worshipped as the ancestral goddess of the imperial family and as the national god. The Ise Shrine has continued to be the principal Japanese shrine from the seventh century until the present day, thus influencing the forms of other shrine buildings. The first remarkable architectural feature of the Ise Shrine is that it attained its distinction by refining its archetype, a storehouse with an elevated floor. At Ise, all the shrine buildings have columns embedded in the earth instead of being set on stone bases as was the general practice elsewhere. The traditional method of handing down the form of shrines, known as shikinen-sengu (the transfer to new shrines in certain ceremonial years), was established. It became customary to rebuild all shrine buildings every twenty years: a pair of adjacent sites of the same shape and size was required for each set of shrines. By creating such a custom, it became possible to repeat the same building activity once in each generation, to transmit faithfully the ancient religious ceremonies as well as the architectural forms to posterity. The present shrine buildings at Ise were rebuilt in 1973, and they are little different from those first constructed in the seventh century.

The 'torii' is the entrance gate of a shrine precinct, and consists primarily of two pillars and two horizontal beams. Both of the pillars are usually embedded directly in the earth. Shimmei torii (those of the Ise Shrine, for example) are the simplest form (p. 725A), and the Myojin torii (for example, those of the Kamo Shrine) has double lintels curved to resemble the eaves of temple architecture (p. 725B).

By the beginning of the eighth century, festivals were arranged nationally. As a result the **Ise Shrine** (p. 727A) came to possess vast lands and Ise became the generic name for a group consisting of numerous shrines in that area. These were divided into two sets of shrines: the Inner Shrine (naiku), which enshrines the ancestral god of the imperial family, and the Outer Shrine (geku) dedicated to the local god. In addition, there are more than 120 small shrines in and around the city, owing loyalty to one or other of the main shrines. The custom of reconstructing the buildings every twenty years began at the end of the seventh century and has been continued ever since in both sets of shrines.

The Inner Shrine is constructed in Japanese cypress and is 10.9 m (36 ft) wide and 5.5 m (18 ft) deep. Pillars are set directly in the ground; the floor is elevated and verandahs surround the building. A staircase leads to the entrance and, except for the central doorway, there are no other openings in the plank walls. On the ridge of the thick reed-thatched roof are ten ridge billets (katsuogi), and the bargeboards project upward through the roof to form two pairs of forked finials (chigi) at the ends of the ridge. A free-standing pillar supporting the ridge (munamochi-bashira) on each side is another characteristic of the Ise Shrine.

The characteristics of the Ise Shrine are consistent with having been derived from existing building methods before the introduction of Buddhist architecture into Japan. The katsuogi, chigi and munamochi-bashira are stylised forms of the primitive elements of the storehouse, and the elevated floor and closed interior also suggest that the archetype of the shrine is more likely to be a storehouse than a dwelling.

Local cultural characteristics are still frequently discernible in their architecture. But all have gabled roofs, are reed-thatched or covered with cypress bark, raised floors and plank walls. Although the architectural forms of shrines were established between the seventh and the ninth centuries, when Buddhist temples were being built throughout Japan, the shrines derive from earlier models and it would be reasonable to assume that the elements of Buddhist architecture were rejected in their favour. In fact, each shrine was intent upon preserving its unique character through periodic rebuildings, and tried to transmit the unchanged form to posterity.

Shrines as old as the Ise Shrine, worshipped by powerful local clans, usually have particular forms of their own, for example the Izumo Shrine in Shimane prefecture, the Sumiyoshi Shrine in Osaka, the Usa Shrine in Kyushu, the two Kamo Shrines in Kyoto, and the Kasuga shrine in Nara. The last two examples still retain the ancient form of movable shrines.

Many localities came gradually to acquire the structural and ornamental elements from Buddhist architecture. Among them were the adoption of column-base stones, brackets, roof curves, and painted surfaces. A transition gradually took place from preserving the old forms by periodic reconstructions to erecting permanent buildings. Among the shrines founded in the mediaeval period are some unique examples of design, such as the Itsukushima Shrine

SHRINES

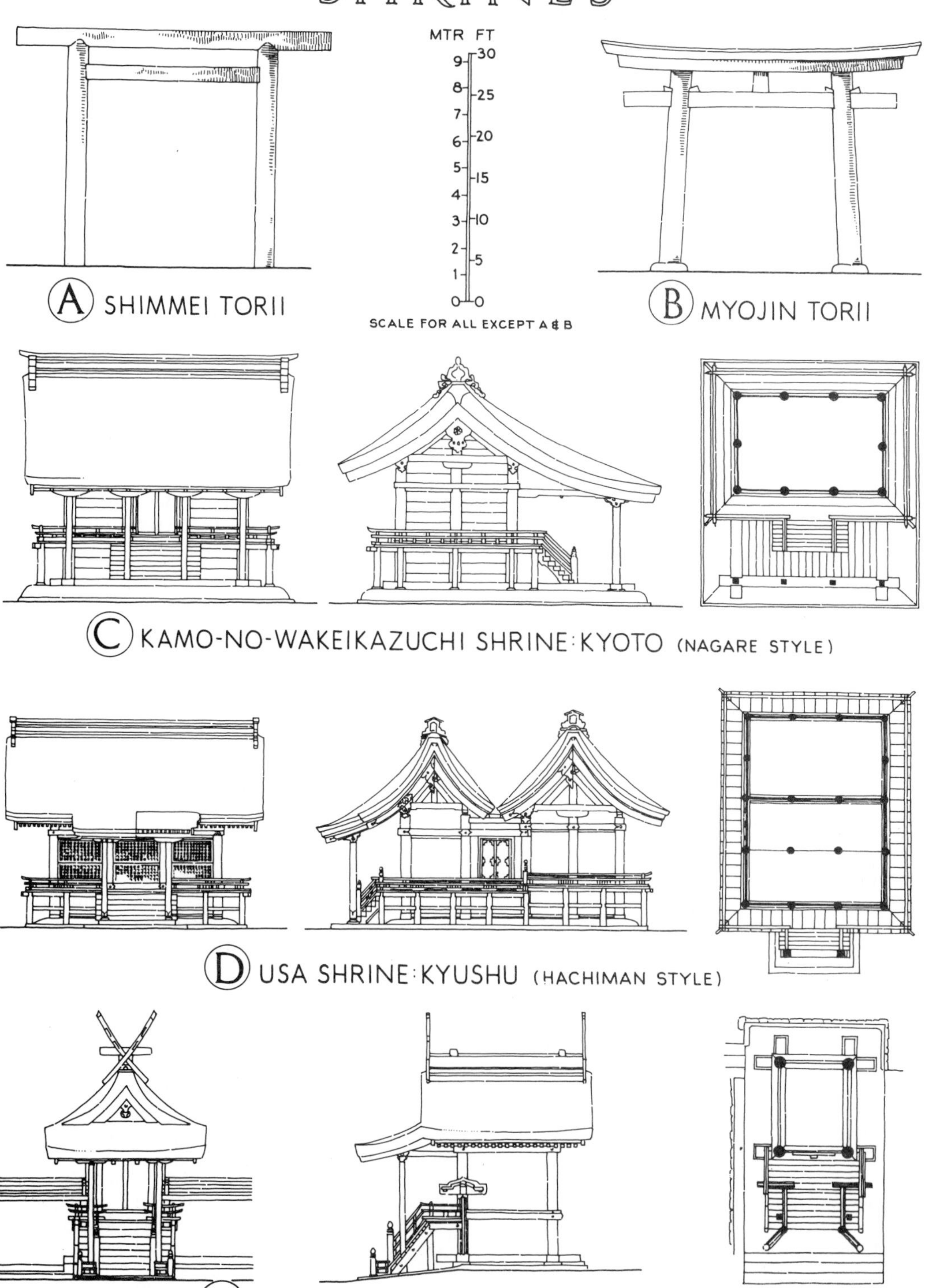
MTR FT
9 8 7 6 5 4 3 2 1 0
30 25 20 15 10 5 0
SCALE FOR ALL EXCEPT A & B
A SHIMMEI TORII
B MYOJIN TORII
C KAMO-NO-WAKEIKAZUCHI SHRINE: KYOTO (NAGARE STYLE)
D USA SHRINE: KYUSHU (HACHIMAN STYLE)
E KASUGA SHRINE: NARA (KASUGA STYLE)

which stands at the edge of the sea on Miyajima Island or the Kibitsu Shrine, Okayama prefecture, with its magnificent main building, as monumental as Buddhist architecture.

A number of mausolea are also regarded as shrines. The first of these is the **Kitano Shrine**, built in the Gongen style in Kyoto. It was founded in the tenth century to enshrine Sugawara Michizane (845–903), a distinguished statesman. After the civil wars at the end of the sixteenth century Toyotomi Hideyoshi built for himself a shrine of similar style (Hokoku-byo, later demolished). The Tokugawa Shogunate followed the same custom, and built a number of mausolea-shrines for the Tokugawa family, including the famous Toshogu at Nikko which enshrines the founder Ieyasu.

The **Izumo Shrine** (p. 727B). The Izumo clan was a powerful one and the Izumo Shrine was famous from ancient times for its grandeur. It is reported that in the eleventh and twelfth centuries the shrine collapsed frequently, probably because the structure was unable to support its great height which in the earliest period was 48 m (160 ft). The present building is a smaller version rebuilt in 1744, 24 m (80 ft) in height from the ground to the top of the forked finials. It is 10.9 m (36 ft) square in plan and each side is divided into two bays. The gabled roof, covered with cypress bark, has a slight curve, two separate forked finials at each end, and three ridge billets.

The **Main Shrines at Sumiyoshi** (p. 728A). There are four of these facing west where once existed a beautiful seashore to the south of Osaka. To enshrine four gods, four separate buildings of the same shape and size were erected. Three of them stand in a line, one behind the other, and the fourth to one side, in an L-shape layout. Each shrine is two bays wide measuring 4.8 m (16 ft) in total, and four bays deep measuring a total of 8 m (26 ft), and the interior is divided into two rooms. Although the exteriors are brightly painted, the interiors are natural wood. Furthermore, there is no curve in the roof. The present buildings were last reconstructed in 1810, but have a long history of periodic reconstruction between the eighth and fifteenth centuries.

The **Kasuga Shrine** (p. 725E) is at the foot of Mount Mikasa on the eastern boundary of the city of Nara. The four main buildings, each 1.83 m × 2.64 m (6 ft × 9 ft), are adjacent to each other, their corner pillars set on a grid frame placed on the ground. The roofs are covered with cypress bark and have two ridge billets. The present buildings were last reconstructed in 1863, but the style was established in the Heian Period (794–1192) as can be ascertained from the shape of the forked finials and the subtle curve connecting the pent roof over the front steps with the main roof. These buildings are archetypal in that they are diminutive in size and are constructed on a grid frame.

The Main Shrine at **Kamo-no-Wakeikazuchi** (p. 725C) was last reconstructed in 1864. It is located on the Kamo River in Kyoto and is redolent of mysterious legends and esoteric ceremonies. The innermost precinct contains adjacent twin buildings facing south: the east building is the main shrine, the west building a temporary shrine used when the main shrine is under reconstruction or repair and the associated rituals at such times have important significance. The buildings are constructed on a grid frame like those at Kasuga, but are 5.9 m × 7.2 m (19 ft × 23 ft), hence much larger.

The **Usa Shrine, Kyushu** (p. 725D), rebuilt 1855 to 1861, is unusual in form. Each of the three main buildings consists of two gable-roofed structures placed one in front of the other with a large gutter in the valley between them. The interiors are continuous spaces, however, divided into two rooms, both having seats for the god. Thus, it cannot be presumed that the front space served as a worship hall, as occurs in Buddhist temples. Although distant from Nara and Kyoto, the shrine was revered by the imperial court as early as the eighth century, and may have been established under Buddhist influence.

The shrine buildings of **Itsukushima** are constructed on the shore of an island in the Inland Sea, and at high tide seem to float above the sea with the island as a background; indeed a grand torii stands in the sea at some distance from the other buildings. The group comprises two central shrines located at right angles to each other, various attached buildings, other small shrines and open corridors connecting them. The buildings were first constructed in 1168 and after two fires was wholly reconstructed in 1241 in approximately the same form as can be seen today.

The main structure of the **Kibitsu Shrine** (1425) (p. 728B) is the largest of all Japanese shrine buildings: 14.5 m (48 ft) wide by 17.9 m (59 ft) deep. It comprises some unusual elements, such as a large roof with a pair of gables on both sides, deeply projecting eaves, and a high podium. The building's unique plan called for an unprecedented size. At the centre of the building is the main sanctuary, encircled by aisles and with floor and ceiling levels becoming higher from the outer to the inner spaces.

Toshogu at Nikko, reconstructed in 1636 as a mausoleum for Ieyasu, founder of the Tokugawa Shogunate, is a complex assembly of numerous buildings, each of which is richly adorned. The principal buildings include a main hall and a worship hall in the Gongen style, approached through the karamon (Chinese gate) and the famous **Yomei Gate** (p. 729A) dividing the front court and the holy precinct. Sculpture, lacquer work, painting and metalcraft all play a part in the decoration: the structural timbers and the walls are sculptured, and black lacquer, rich red and green coatings are picked out by the gold of metal fittings.

A. Ise Inner Shrine, Main Shrine, Ujiyamada City (rebuilt 1973). See p.724

B. Izumo Shrine, Main Shrine, Shimane Prefecture (rebuilt 1744). See p.726

A. Sumiyoshi Shrine, Osaka (rebuilt 1810): rear gables of Second Main Shrine and Fourth Main Shrine (left). See p.726

B. Kibitsu Shrine, Okayama Prefecture (1425): Main Shrine and Worship Hall (right). See p.726

A. Toshogu, Yomei Gate, Nikko City (1636). See p.726

B. Yakushiji three-storeyed pagoda (early eighth century). See p.731

C. Horyuji kondo (late seventh century). See p.731

TEMPLES

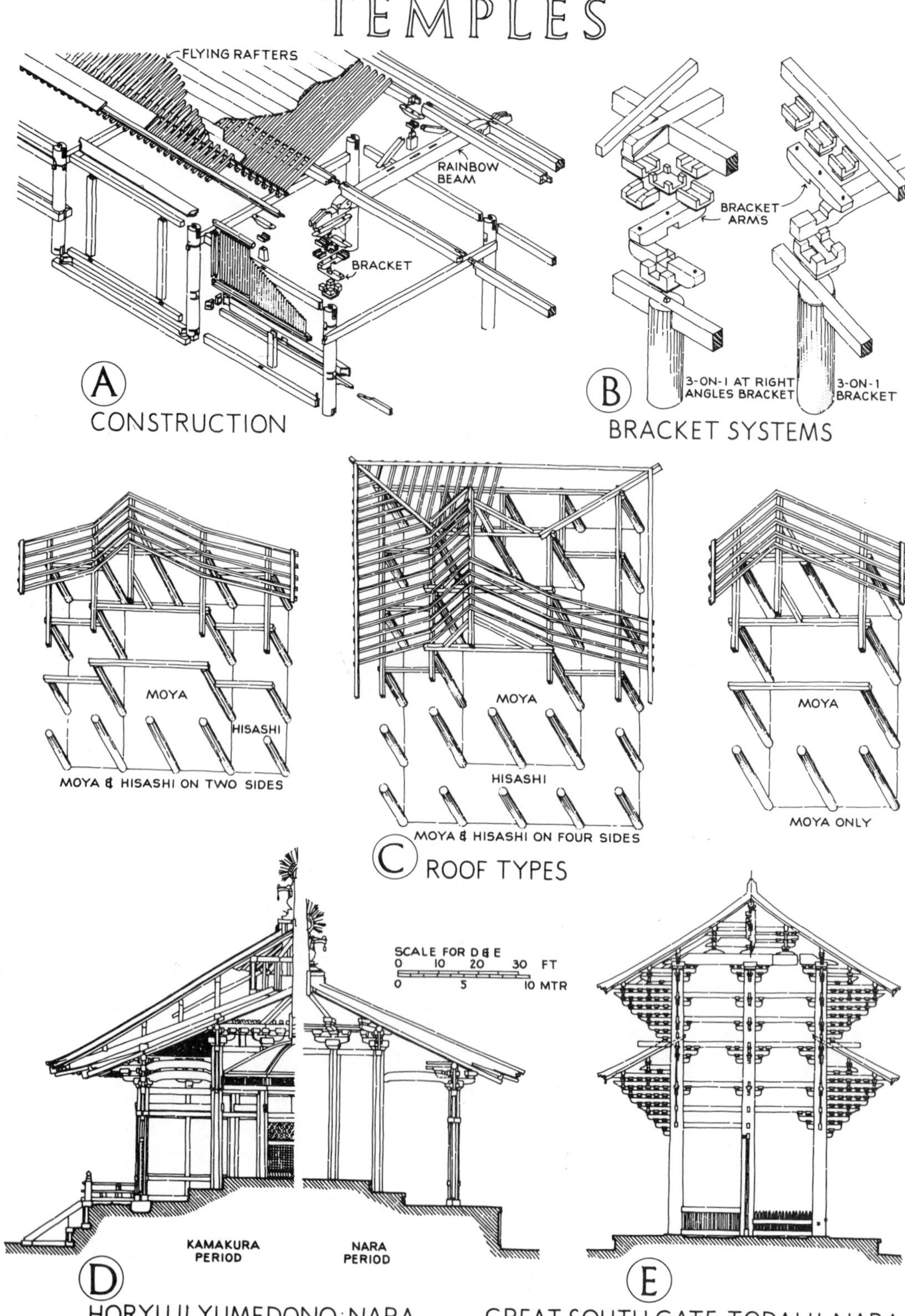
FLYING RAFTERS
RAINBOW BEAM
BRACKET
A
CONSTRUCTION
BRACKET ARMS
3-ON-1 AT RIGHT ANGLES BRACKET
3-ON-1 BRACKET
B
BRACKET SYSTEMS
MOYA
HISASHI
MOYA & HISASHI ON TWO SIDES
MOYA
HISASHI
MOYA & HISASHI ON FOUR SIDES
MOYA
MOYA ONLY
C
ROOF TYPES
SCALE FOR D & E
0 10 20 30 FT
0 5 10 MTR
KAMAKURA PERIOD
NARA PERIOD
D
HORYUJI YUMEDONO: NARA
E
GREAT SOUTH GATE, TODAIJI: NARA

Temple Architecture

Early Historic (sixth to twelfth centuries)

ASUKA AND EARLY NARA (HAKUHO) PERIODS (552–710)

Little more than a generation after the advent of Buddhism, when opposition to the foreign religion had been crushed, Soga Umako, a Chief Minister to Emperor Sujun, an ardent devotee of Buddhism, was responsible for the construction of the Hokoji (Asuka-dera) temple in Nara in 588. Other temples, such as Shitennoji (Osaka), Yamadadera, Kawaradera and Horyuji in Nara, followed in the seventh century.

In the ancient period, the layout of Buddhist monasteries was strictly prescribed. The main gate faced south and behind, at some distance, was the middle gate (chumon) to which was attached the semi-enclosed roofed corridor (kairo) surrounding the most sacred area where a reliquary for sacred objects (a pagoda) led to an image hall (kondo). Eventually, two pagodas occupied the sacred enclosure. A lecture hall (kodo) was either attached at the rear of the corridor or placed behind it, outside the sacred precinct. The belfry and sutra repository were placed near the lecture hall. The refectory, priests' and monks' quarters and bathhouse completed the basic requirements.

Of the seventh-century temples only Horyuji now remains, but excavations of other temple compounds reveal considerable variations in the configurations of building groups. The temple at Hokoji closely resembles those excavated at Ch'ongam'sa in the Koguryo kingdom of northern Korea, while the arrangement at Shitennoji and Yamadadera is clearly of Paekche lineage (q.v.). Some temples, like Kawaradera and Horyuji, placed the kondo and the pagoda on a lateral axis, but no corresponding sites have yet been discovered in either China or Korea.

In excavations carried out at Yamadadera in 1983 and 1984 remarkably preserved timber sections of the semi-enclosed corridors of a temple dated 643 were unearthed. The discovery of structural members, particularly those of an exterior wall containing vertically mullioned windows, allowed comparisons with the semi-enclosed corridor at Horyuji. The ample differences suggest that the most ancient buildings of the Horyuji temple are not representative of the pure Asuka style.

The kondo and pagoda at **Horyuji**, the world's oldest extant wooden buildings, were constructed after the original Horyuji temple was destroyed by fire in 670 (p. 729C). The present kondo, 9 bays long and 7 bays wide, 18.5 m × 15.2 m (61 ft × 50 ft) including mokoshi, was completed by 693 in time for the nationwide rites celebrating the promulgation of the Prajnaparamita sutra; the pagoda was finished about a decade later. Characteristic of the kondo, pagoda, middle gate and miniature Tamamushi shrine at Horyuji, as well as of the pagodas at nearby Horinji (burned 1944, rebuilt during the 1970s) and Hokiji (all built between the later seventh and early eighth centuries), are the cloud-shaped bracket complexes (kumo-tokyo) which support the eaves. No known prototype has been found on the continent. Also characteristic of these buildings is a marked entasis on the pillars. And between the tops of the columns and the large bearing blocks there are plate blocks (sarato). Railings, supported by struts resembling inverted Vs alternating with simple bracket complexes, are enhanced by decorative frets. 'Mokoshi' surround both the lower storeys of the kondo and the pagoda. Their pent roofs are made of heavy planks. All other roofs are covered with alternating convex and concave tiles decorated at the edges of the eaves with lotus and arabesque patterns.

The five-storeyed pagoda (in the same style as the kondo) is crowned by a spire. Excluding the mokoshi surrounding the first storey, it is 3 × 3 bays and including the mokoshi it is 9 × 9 bays, 10.85 m (35 ft) square. A central pillar, set deeply below ground level, rises far above the roof and forms the core of the spire upon which the metal covers and symbolic ornaments are placed. Even in later periods, when the central pillar is set on ground level or above the ceiling of the first storey, the same conventionalised spire (sorin) can be seen.

With the establishment of the capital at Heijo (710) in Nara, the first permanent capital, **Yakushiji** was rebuilt (730), like the original one constructed at the Fujiwara capital (694–710). Now, however, the kondo was set upon the central axis and two pagodas were positioned close to the south-east and south-west corners. This change in plan points to new stylistic influences from Tang China, probably brought from Korea where such influences had already been absorbed, as revealed by excavations at the Sa'ch'on-wang'sa in Kyongju.

The three-storey **Yakushiji** east pagoda (p. 729B) is the only building surviving from the early eighth century. Its dimensions, 5 × 5 bays, 10.85 m (36 ft) square, including mokoshi, are close to those of the five-storeyed pagoda at Horyuji, but in style and structural method it is quite different. Mokoshi surrounded by shallow verandahs with simple balustrades were added below the main roofs of each storey. The small latticed ceiling installed under the eaves and two three-stepped bracket complexes with tail rafters supporting them are indications of transition to the more mature style of the mid-eighth century. However, the old style of round base rafters and square flying rafters is retained.

LATE NARA (TEMPYO) PERIOD (710–785)

One-storey octagonal buildings were constructed primarily as memorial halls at some of the ancient temples. The most famous is the **Yumedono**, located in the centre of the east precinct at **Horyuji** (p. 730D). Each bay is 4.17 m (14 ft) wide. When the pyramidal roof was rebuilt in the Kamakura period, an extra bracket in each complex allowed for a greater eaves overhang, and additional cantilevers (hanegi) and hidden rafters gave the framework a steeper pitch.

The kondo at **Toshodaiji** (p. 733A), still close to its original form, is the only extant example from the middle of the eighth century, and is a good example of the classical age of Japanese architecture. Founded by the Chinese priest, Chien-chen (Ganjin), it was a small unofficial temple built with the support of aristocratic families.

The single-storey building, 7 × 4 bays, 27.9 m × 14.6 m (92 ft × 48 ft), has an open colonnaded porch spanning the breadth of the building. The three-stepped bracket system with intermediate bearing-block-capped struts (kentozuka), the circular base rafters, square flying rafters, and tail rafters are used in much the same way as they were on the Yakushiji three-storey pagoda. There are, however, some differences: the bracket complexes are structurally more advanced and the bracket arms have no concavity on their upper surfaces, but the rafters have a gentle upward curve. A shallow latticed ceiling is retained between the wall purlin and the second-stepped bracket, but, unlike Yakushiji, curved ribs form a transition to the eaves purlin.

The 'moya' (inner core) is covered by a finely latticed ceiling with coved ribs which extend from the ceiling joists to the purlins, and are supported by bracket complexes above the pillars. Edo period repairs structurally altered and raised the roof some 2.5 m (8 ft). The roof is tiled and decorated with an acroterion on each end of the ridge.

The storehouse is an important early building type with none of the stylistic characteristics previously described. The most famous example is the **Shoso'in at Todaiji**, Nara, which houses the collection of treasures left by the Emperor Shomu (724–49). The building is 108.4 m × 30.5 m (356 ft × 100 ft) raised high above the ground on stout posts and divided into three parts. The two end sections are constructed in the 'azekura' style of logs, notched and fitted together in such a way that their ends cross each other and project beyond the corners. The central section was enclosed with heavy planks and all three parts have board doors centrally placed. The roof was originally framed with a triple beam system separated by struts, but this has now been replaced by a Western-style truss. The whole is covered by a tiled hipped roof.

HEIAN PERIOD (785–1185)

When the main lecture hall (daikodo) was rebuilt at **Horyuji** (p. 733B) in 990, the semi-enclosed roofed corridor was extended and included in the sacred precinct with the sutra repository and belfry. It is 9 bays long and 4 bays wide, 33.8 m × 16.5 m (111 ft × 54 ft), and continues the classical eighth-century style externally, while the interior contains revolutionary changes in the method of roof framing. It is the oldest extant building with the hidden roof system, in this case limited to the 'hisashi' (outer galleries) where the base rafters are exposed. A relatively low, latticed ceiling placed over the moya hides the usual roof framework. The tiled roof is of the hip-and-gable kind with structural elements visible in the gable ends.

From the late tenth century, certain priests, primarily of the Tendai sect, taught a greatly simplified doctrine of salvation ensured through the veneration of Amida Buddha (Amitabha) who rules over the Western Paradise, a Pure Land accessible to all. By the end of the twelfth century, the sect was firmly established, and nobles erected temples intended to recreate the Western Paradise with Amida Buddha as the focal point: they are known as Pure Land (Jodo) Amida Halls.

One of the most celebrated of these temples is the **Phoenix Hall at Byodo'in** in Uji, near Kyoto (p. 734A). Originally a villa, it was remodelled as a temple of which only the Phoenix Hall (1053) remains. It faces a large pond, a characteristic of Heian gardens and a foretaste of the envisioned paradise.

The central hall (chudo) enshrines a large gilded statue of Amida seated upon a lotus throne beneath a magnificent baldachino made of wood carved to filigree fineness and finished in gold-leaf. The upper areas of the walls are filled with carvings and every timber surface is richly decorated.

The 5 × 4 bay central hall is 14.2 m × 11.8 m (46 ft × 39 ft). It consists of the moya and open mokoshi along the front and sides. The high, finely latticed ceiling is of two levels connected by coved ribs.

The structural method is that of the middle of the eighth century, but the manner of interlocking the corner bracket complexes had been gradually improved in successive buildings until perfected in the Phoenix Hall. A hidden roof framework supports the hip-and-gable roof of the central hall. The L-shaped wings extending from each side of the central hall are purely decorative.

A type of temple hall built to enshrine the nine statues of Amida (also called Kutaiji) was very popular during the late Heian Period. The only extant example is the tiled hipped-roofed hondo (main hall) at **Joruriji**, in the Kyoto prefecture (1107). It is 11 bays long and 4 bays wide, 33.8 m × 16.5 m (111 ft × 54 ft) with a moya two bays deep and nine long surrounded by a one-bay deep hisashi. The nine bays of the moya house a stepped dais with a figure of Amida in each bay. To accommodate a larger central figure, the middle bay was widened and covered with a high gable-shaped ceiling with exposed base rafters.

The elevation is low with simple boat-shaped bracket complexes confined to the corners. Both base

A. Toshodaiji kondo (mid-eighth century). See p.732

B. Horyuji daikodo (990) See p.732

A. Byodo'in Phoenix Hall (1053). See p.732

B. Kongorinji hondo, model cross-section. See p.735

and flying rafters are square in section. Each corner bay facing the front has the old type of vertically mullioned windows while the remaining nine bays have board-backed latticed doors (shitomido).

The worship of Amida flourished from the late Heian period and has remained popular to the present day, but the esoteric sects also were well entrenched and continued to exert influence and to build temples.

An example of the architecture of the esoteric sects from the Heian period is the hondo (Mandarado), at **Taimadera** in Nara prefecture. It is 7 bays long and 6 bays wide, 21 m × 18 m (69 ft × 59 ft). It took its present form in 1161 when rebuilt for the third time. Within the 'naijin' (inner sanctuary) there is a very large mandala, representing the myriad realms sacred to esoteric Buddhism. This building is the oldest extant deep hall accommodated under a single roof. Separate gable roofs were placed over the naijin and the 'gejin' (outer area); ridges were extended from peak to peak and finally a hidden roof was constructed over the entire building.

Mediaeval (twelfth to sixteenth centuries)

KAMAKURA PERIOD (1185–1333)

The Wayo style. The standard style and method of temple building up to the end of the Heian period came to be called Wayo or 'Japanese' style, after the beginning of the Mediaeval Age, to distinguish it from new styles introduced in the Kamakura period. The term Wayo is never used for architecture constructed before the Kamakura period. Wayo architecture, of course, originally derived from the mainland, but by the late Heian period had become Japanised. It continued in use throughout the history of traditional architecture, especially at esoteric Buddhist temples, occasionally absorbing elements from the newer styles. These temples were usually established on a mountainside or hilltop near a village. Scenic views and natural surroundings were important; rocks or waterfalls within the temple grounds were often sanctified.

The hondo was the focal point of the esoteric temple, with a three- or five-storey pagoda or tahoto, a unique structure enshrining a statue of the Dainichi Buddha or the Lotus Sutra itself, placed to one side. A gate was erected at the main approach to symbolise separation of the mundane from the sacred. It was free-standing, unattached to any kind of fencing.

In mediaeval temples the interior of the hondo became more important than the exterior because the building was no longer merely an image hall: the pious now entered the building to pray.

Hondo are five, seven or nine bays wide and almost the same number of bays deep. The interiors are divided into outer areas (gejin) for worshippers, and inner sanctuaries (naijin) which are dimly lit, mysterious and remote, behind latticed sliding partitions. Sanctuaries, accessible only to priests, house many images and ritualistic paraphernalia. Above the sliding partitions are transoms filled with lozenge-patterned lattices. In the most ancient halls, the naijin had earthen floors but were later floored in timber.

Although these halls retain the basic plan of the moya with surrounding hisashi, a variety of complicated arrangements of space could be accomplished through the use of the hidden roof constructed over the entire building. Some pillars could be omitted or moved off the traditional axes, to open up areas where space was needed.

Exposed rafters serve as ceilings in hisashi, while a variety of ceiling types were used over gejin and naijin. Frequently, the ceiling is low in the former area and higher in the latter to accommodate statues larger than life size.

The 'tahoto' at **Ishiyamadera** in Shiga prefecture (1194), is the oldest extant example of the Wayo style. It is approximately 6 m (20 ft) square, with 3 bays in each direction, and is built on a raised timber platform with a shallow verandah surrounding the mokoshi walls. A raised Buddhist altar occupies the square sanctuary, which is defined by four corner pillars. The ceiling is coved, coffered and finely latticed. A white plastered drum above the pent roofs of the mokoshi is protected by a pyramidal roof supported by four-stepped bracket complexes.

The three-storey pagoda at **Saimyoji**, also in Shiga, built in the middle of the Kamakura period, reflects the pure Wayo style. It is 4.2 m (14 ft) square, three by three bays, constructed on a raised wooden platform. The plan and interior of the first storey closely resemble those of the Ishiyamadera tahoto, but at Saimyoji the lintels, boarded walls, pillars and ceilings are painted with designs and Buddhist themes.

Bracket complexes have three steps with bearing block-capped struts set between on the first and second storeys and each storey has curved struts, base and flying rafters covered with cypress bark. All the roofs contain hidden rafters and the main roof is much steeper than the others.

Kongorinji hondo in Shiga (p. 734B) is large in scale, seven bays in each direction, 21 m × 20.7 m (69 ft × 68 ft) and dated from 1288. The gejin is clearly distinguished from the surrounding one-bay hisashi by a row of heavy pillars – a new tendency in the late thirteenth century. Sliding lattice screens separate the gejin from the naijin, and also divide the side hisashi on the same lateral axis. Ceilings are of various types including exposed rafters, board-and-batten and open beam in gable shape. By this time hidden roof construction had become commonplace and cantilevers were inserted between the exposed and hidden rafters.

The roof is hipped and gabled, covered with cypress bark, and all seven front bays are filled with

A. Todaiji, Great South Gate, detail (1199). See p.737

B. Kakurinji hondo, front view (1397). See p.738

C. Enkakuji Shariden (fifteenth century), interior detail. See p.738

boarded doors, faced with lattice and divided horizontally (shitomido). The upper section opens upwards and out and is hooked under the eaves. If necessary the lower section can be lifted out.

The **Taisanji hondo** (1305), in Ehime prefecture, is the largest esoteric Buddhist hall, seven bays by nine, 16.4 m × 21 m (54 ft × 69 ft). Decorative open-frame frog-leg struts fill the interstices between the simple bracket complexes across the front facade, while on the sides and rear they are replaced by struts with bearing-block caps. The tiled roof is hipped and gabled. When it was repaired in the nineteenth century, the huge gable pediments were filled with double rainbow beams, frog-leg struts (nijukoryo-kaerumata) and bottle struts (taiheizuka, the latter an intrusion from a new style).

Daibutsu Style. The victory in 1185 of the Minamoto clan over the Taira ended the Heian period. During the struggle for power, many temples were destroyed. One was Todaiji, the most prestigious of eighth-century Nara. The priest, Chogen (1121–1206), who visited south China three times, supervised the rebuilding at Todaiji. His choice of style, based on one popular in south China during the Sung dynasty (960–1279), was the antithesis of the conservative Wayo style. Only two of his original buildings in the new Daibutsu style (Tenjikuyo) exist today. The older is the Jododo (Amida Hall) (1192) at Jodoji, in Hyogo prefecture, followed by the Great South Gate (1199) at Todaiji; these buildings display. the characteristics common to the Daibutsu style.

The **Jododo (Amida Hall) at Jodoji** is a square building, three bays in each direction, 18 m (59 ft) wide, with a pyramidal roof. Simple panelled doors swing on pole hinges set in projecting sockets attached top and bottom to penetrating tie-beams.

Most prominent are massive timbers including rainbow beams with curved ends, separated by bottle struts instead of frog-leg struts. The inner ends of the struts are inserted directly into the pillars of the moya and their outer ends are corbelled, to produce the roof slope.

Without ceilings, the structural elements are clearly visible. Bracket arms are also inserted into the pillars, and some of them carry purlins. Penetrating tie-beams (nuki) provide greater stability than the non-penetrating ties (nageshi) common in the Wayo style. Single eaves are finished with fascia boards covering the ends of the rafters, which generally are laid parallel but in a fan pattern at the corners.

Seen from outside, the building looks comparatively small (the walls are low and the roof has no curve), but the interior is overwhelmingly large in appearance due to its height and the size of the constructional members.

The two-storey, five by two bay **Great South Gate (Nandaimon) at Todaiji** (pp. 730E, 736A) is of immense proportions, 29 m × 11 m (95 ft × 36 ft). The pillars rise about 20 m to support rainbow beams, and the eaves of the main roofs and the pent roofs are supported by six-stepped bracket complexes. A comparison of the bracket complexes with those of the Jododo reveals, however, an almost perfect regularity in the arrangement and stacking of the small bearing blocks reminiscent of the Wayo style.

Zen style. The Zen style (Karayo) favoured by the Zen sects was the other important new style introduced at the very beginning of the thirteenth century. Its characteristics can be understood best by examining the belfry at Todaiji, the kaisando at Eihoji and the Shariden at Enkakuji.

The **Todaiji Belfry** (p. 740A), a large-scale single-bay, 7.6 m (25 ft) square open structure, can be viewed as a transition from the Daibutsu to the Zen style. Built between 1207 and 1211 it has a typical Daibutsu-style framework, but the four-stepped bracket complexes placed directly on the pillars, the pronounced curve of the long eaves and the ample sag in the roof line all point towards the Zen style.

Since Eisai (1141–1215), the successor of Chogen at Todaiji led the way in establishing Zen beliefs in Japan, it is not surprising to discover certain elements of the Zen style already appearing in the belfry. Successive Japanese priests studied Zen in China and returned to found Zen temples which were built in the new style. Unfortunately, the buildings erected during the thirteenth century have disappeared, but the oldest extant ground plan (1331) of **Kenchoji in Kamakura** shows the buildings to have been arranged along a central axis for the purposes of the new sect of Buddhism. But one immediately noticeable omission is the lack of a pagoda and even in later Zen temples, if pagodas were included, they were relegated to remote parts of the compounds.

NAMBOKUCHO PERIOD (1333–1392)

The **Eihoji kaisando**, the Founder's Hall (1352), in the Gifu prefecture, consists of a gejin, a broad connecting passage (ai-no-ma) and a naijin with mokoshi on three sides. While this plan is not typical of Zen buildings, which are usually square, the construction itself is characteristic of the Zen style.

The **Shariden at Enkakuji** in Kamakura is perhaps the most representative hall in the Zen style. Although burned in 1563, the present building is in the Zen style of more than a century earlier, and documentation suggesting that the Shariden was moved to Enkakuji from another temple may be true.

Buildings in the Zen style had earthen floors with slender pillars rounded top and bottom, set on stone or wooden plinths resting on base-stones. The nosing (kibana) of the wall-plates and head-penetrating tiebeams (kashira-nuki) were extended beyond the corner pillars and were finished with moulded and incised designs.

Although bracket-complexes of the Shariden have three steps, they appear to be clustered, because the bracket arms are extended to accommodate five small bearing-blocks on the uppermost brackets, and one or two intercolumnar bracket-complexes are positioned on the wall-plates between the pillars. Double tail rafters with curved outer ends are visible inside amidst a maze of beams, bracket-complexes and rafters: rainbow beams (koryo) are supported by bottle struts. Over the moya is a smooth boarded ceiling (p. 736C).

Mokoshi are common to Zen-style buildings, and lobster tie-beams (ebikoryo) within the mokoshi have an exaggerated curve. The rafters over the mokoshi are always set in parallel positions, in contrast to the fan raftering used on the main roof. Pent roofs are subtly curved in comparison with the pronounced curves of the main roofs, which are usually covered with multi-layered thin wooden shingles. Doors are panelled, with pole hinges placed in decorative projecting sockets. Windows are cusped.

MUROMACHI PERIOD (1392–1568)

The **Kakurinji hondo** (1397), in Hyogo, is a superb example of the Conglomerate (Setchuyo) Style – mainly Wayo in character, but with easily recognisable elements of the Zen and Daibutsu styles. It is 7 × 6 bays, 17 m × 15.2 m (56 ft × 50 ft) with simple, Wayo-style two-stepped bracket complexes, between which are placed a Zen-style arrangement of small frog-leg struts with bearing blocks supporting a further bracket arm which in turn carries twin bearing blocks. The tiled roof is hipped and gabled, with Wayo-style rainbow beams and bottle struts (the latter characteristic of both the Zen and Daibutsu styles) visible in the gable. There are Zen-style panelled doors in all seven front bays (p. 736B), in five bays on each side and four in the rear. Horizontally planked walls enclose the rear corner bays.

Curved ends to the tail rafters, decorative nosings on head-penetrating tie-beams and mouldings on the ends of members extending from interior to exterior show strong Zen influence, as do the lobster beams used in the front hisashi. In the Daibutsu style huge, almost circular rainbow beams span both gejin and naijin and bracket arms are inserted directly into the pillars. The arrangement of the sliding lattice screens dividing the interior, however, is in the esoteric Buddhist Wayo style.

Pre-modern (sixteenth to nineteenth centuries)

MOMOYAMA AND EDO PERIODS (1568–1867)

Temple architecture had reached its apogee by the end of the Mediaeval Age. Structural methods had been perfected and building types conventionalised. A tendency toward the use of a modular system (kiwari) had begun but did not become customary until the Pre-modern period. Although efficiency and speed of construction were accomplished, the modular system had a stultifying effect. Only the addition of elaborate sculptural detail, the occasional use of the undulating gable (karahafu) and impressive size saved the early pre-modern Buddhist buildings from the monotony of a conventional mould.

A number of new carpenter's tools appeared, among which were several types of planes that permitted considerable advances in creating a great variety of new, highly refined types of joinery. Unfortunately, the complex joints are seldom visible except when a building undergoes extensive repair.

An excellent example of the magnificence displayed in Momoyama architecture is the gate attached to the **Kannondo at Hogonji** (p. 739A), in the Shiga prefecture. The gate was perhaps moved from Hideyoshi Toyotomi's mausoleum in 1603 to provide an elegant entrance to the Kannondo. It is a shallow single-bay gate 3.3 m × 6.1 m (11 ft × 20 ft), with an undulating gable. Sculptured and openwork decoration fills the space between the lintel and the rainbow beam, and the side panels and doors are elaborately ornamented with peony and arabesque patterns. The frog-leg strut not only frames carved floral reliefs but is completely surrounded with carved birds and flowers. Metal decoration also abounds.

The **Kiyomizudera hondo** (1633) (p. 739B) expresses the grandiose taste of the Edo period. Constructed on a mountainside east of Kyoto, it is 11 × 8 bays, 33.5 m × 32.2 m (110 ft × 106 ft) and is the culmination of esoteric Buddhist building design, in this case dedicated to the Kannon Bodhisattva who was associated traditionally with steep rocky areas. The Wayo style is evident in the use of simple bracket-complexes with bearing block-capped struts between, double parallel rafters and a cypress-bark hipped roof. A mokoshi skirts the east, west and part of the north side, and hipped and gabled roofs project forward from the huge main roof to cover the wings on either side of the open stage. The wings and stage are suspended over a steep slope, supported by an enormous structure of posts and tie-beams.

The **kondo (Daibutsuden) at Todaiji** is one of the largest wooden buildings in the world. It was originally built in the middle of the eighth century but destroyed at the end of the Heian period. The building as restored by Chogen at the end of the twelfth century was burned in 1565 and not reconstructed until 1709. Today it is 7 × 7 bays, 57 m × 50 m (187 ft × 164 ft), smaller than either of the earlier structures, but retains the same height, 47.5 m (156 ft). Although there are elements of the Daibutsu style, there are considerable modifications, for example the use of the undulating gable over the break in the mokoshi roof at the front entrance, and the row of bracket complexes under the main roof recall the Zen style. There are coffered finely latticed ceilings reminiscent of the Wayo style.

A. Hogonji Kannondo entrance (late sixteenth century). See p.738

B. Kiyomizudera hondo (1633). See p.738

A. Todaiji Belfry (1207–11). See p.737

B. Shishinden, Imperial Palace, Kyoto (rebuilt 1855). See p.741

Dwellings, Urban Areas and Castles

Early Historic (sixth to twelfth centuries)

ASUKA AND NARA PERIODS (552–785)

Chinese techniques of construction and methods of city planning had an important influence on the Japanese way of life and on the design of Japanese dwellings. From the middle of the seventh century to the end of the eighth a system of planning was developed in which the imperial palace formed the focal point and streets were planned on grid patterns. The method was modelled on Ch'ang-an, the capital of Tang China, and was applied to the Japanese ancient capital of Naniwa in 652, Fujiwara in 694, Heijo (Nara) in 710, and Heian (Kyoto) in 794. They were much smaller, and were not enclosed by city walls.

Excavations of the ancient Nara capital, Heijo, show that buildings, other than Buddhist temples, in which Chinese methods were used were confined to one quarter of the palace enclosure only, including the Daigokuden, Chodoin and main gates, all of which had foundation stones and tiled roofs. Other buildings, including the emperor's residence and government offices, were structures with pillars set directly into the ground and roofed with cypress bark, wood shingles or thatch.

The Chinese method of arranging buildings symmetrically along a central north-south axis had considerable influence in Japan; aristocratic residences, as well as imperial palaces and government offices, were planned in this way when groups of buildings were required.

HEIAN PERIOD 785–1185)

The **Heian capital (Kyoto)**, established in 794, was the last of Japan's ancient cities to be based on Ch'angan. It measured 5.3 km (3.3 miles) from north to south and 4.5 km (2.8 miles) from east to west. The imperial palace stood in the middle of the north side, and the city was divided into a left or west segment and a right or east segment by an exceptionally broad avenue, Suzaku-Oji, 84 m (275 ft) wide, forming the north–south axis. It terminated at the Rajo gate in the south wall. The Heian capital had a city wall only on the south side, suggesting that it was thought to emphasise the majesty of the emperor rather than to provide a fortification.

The city was divided into 120 m (390 ft) square lots by a grid of streets, 24 m (78 ft) or 12 m (39 ft) wide, running north–south and east–west. Two temples (Toji and Saiji) as well as two markets were arranged symmetrically to the east and west of Suzaku-Oji.

Shinden Style. The shinden style of aristocratic residences reached maturity in the Heian capital during the eleventh and twelfth centuries. The shinden is in the centre with corridors connecting it to the east and west annexes, and a 'chumonro' extends south from one or both of the annexes. This complex of buildings defined a south garden, containing a pond and a stream flowing from north to south. The shinden and its annexes had no fixed interior partitions; instead, movable furnishings such as various kinds of screens, curtains, mattresses, straw mats and shelved cabinets sufficed to define interior spaces and to fulfil the ordinary or ceremonial needs of daily life. Externally, removable hinged and suspended latticed screens, placed in the bays between pillars, permitted a continuous flow of space from outside to inside, and produced a unity between the interior and the garden.

The **Tosanjo Palace** was one of the most famous residences belonging to the noble Fujiwara family and was a centre for many important ceremonies. The scale of the complex, which existed from 1043 to 1166, measured 120 m (400 ft) from east to west and 240 m (800 ft) from north to south. At the heart of the palace were two large buildings, the central shinden and the east annex, surrounded by corridors (watadono) two bays 6 m (20 ft) wide, and also narrower corridors one bay wide. The broad corridors were used as habitable spaces, while the narrow corridors were simply passages defining adjacent external spaces, such as the south garden. The positions of individual buildings show less adherence to symmetrical planning.

After the Imperial palace in Kyoto was burnt down in 1227, the emperor's private quarters, or dairi, were moved into aristocratic residences or imperial villas. A permanent site was established in 1331. The building styles changed from period to period, of course, and at the end of the eighteenth century an effort was made to rebuild the Shishinden and Seiryoden in the style of the Heian period, but the present buildings date from 1855.

The **Shishinden** (p. 740B) now consists of an inner core or moya, nine bays long and three bays wide, surrounded by outer galleries or hisashi, on all four sides. The imperial throne is placed on a high raised floor in the centre of the moya. Because the Chodo'in, an administrative and ceremonial centre, was not rebuilt after the 1227 fire, the Shishinden has since served as a place for ceremonies including the coronation. The **Seiryoden**, a residential area, contains various kinds of movable partitions, allowing subdivision of space as needed.

The **Chodo'in**, 230 m × 160 m (750 ft × 520 ft), contained the main government offices and was located in the centre of the Imperial Palace facing Suzaku-Oji. The Chodo'in was never rebuilt after the fire in 1227. The architectural style had been established at a very early date. Buildings were erected on foundation stones, timbers were lacquered in vermilion, and roofs were tiled. It was composed of three parts: encircling galleries surrounding all buildings; the Daigokuden, a hall for the emperor, at the inner end; and in the centre, twelve buildings juxtaposed, with two subsidiary structures enclosed at the south end.

Mediaeval (twelfth to sixteenth centuries)

As the rituals which had been closely connected with aristocratic daily life gradually declined owing to wars and political disturbances, some changes began to appear in the composition of residential buildings. The symmetrical arrangement and the spatial composition surrounding the south garden lost their significance, and in their place a greater stress on convenience tended to become the leading factor. Between the thirteenth and fifteenth centuries, the single large open space of the shinden was divided up into small rooms with 'fusuma' screens, and floors were covered with 'tatami'; sliding wooden or translucent paper screens (shoji) replaced the hinged and suspended latticed screens (shitomi) previously used in the bays between posts around the exterior of buildings. The span between posts was made to conform to the length of the tatami, the dimensions of which gradually became the standard units of length and area. The length of one bay was fixed at 1.97 m (6 ft 6 in) to equal the length of one tatami. By the late fifteenth century the floors of living rooms were already covered with tatami, regardless of the social status of the occupants. No dwellings survive from either the Kamakura (1185–1333) or the Nambokucho (1333–92) periods.

MUROMACHI PERIOD (1392–1568)

It became fashionable in dwellings of the fifteenth century to place Chinese imported scrolls, pottery and porcelain in carefully chosen positions for decorative purposes.

In the late fifteenth century, Ashikaga Yoshimasa ordered the construction of a villa, **Higashiyama-dono**. It comprised a residence (tsune-no-gosho), a reception hall (kaisho), the Ginkaku pavilion, the Togudo (a private Buddha sanctuary), and many subsidiary buildings. The reception hall was used for private meetings and social intercourse, and was completed in 1487. All the rooms had tatami on the floors. Pictorial documentation suggests that the reception hall was furnished with a built-in, shallow boarded recess (oshi-ita), a recess with staggered ornamental shelves (chigaidana), and an attached study alcove (tsuke-shoin). These elements provided a frame for the display of ornaments arranged according to certain aesthetic rules. Now a temple, Jisshoji, contains only the Ginkaku pavilion, the Togudo and the garden.

The **Daisen'in Hojo** (1513) (p. 743A) is representative of an abbot's private residence, and is also a subsidiary temple belonging to the Daitokuji of the Zen sect. The layout of these private residences (hojo) is similar to the reception buildings in warriors' residences. The two central rooms enshrined statues or mortuary tablets of the founder and patrons, while two tatami rooms to the east served as the abbot's private quarters, and the two to the west were for patrons. Common features in this class of dwelling during the Muromachi period were straw-matted floors, boarded ceilings, sliding fusuma screens on which pictures were drawn, and narrow bands of plastered wall or pierced transom between the lintels and the ceiling. A small, finely designed garden adjacent to the north-east side could be viewed from the drawing room in the north-east corner of the dwelling.

The architecture of the tea ceremony, which later influenced the design of Japanese dwellings, came to maturity during the sixteenth century. Rooms ranged in size from two to four and a half tatami. In this intimate space, the host and guests sat together, enjoying discussion, the taste of tea, and the harmony of ceremonial tea utensils. Behind the architectural forms of the rooms used for the tea ceremony lay the special philosophy and aesthetic attitudes associated with the Zen sect, which themselves characterised the tea ceremony, 'cha-no-yu', and appealed especially to warriors, aristocrats and wealthy merchants. The aesthetic qualities found in tea ceremony rooms derive largely from the sensitive use of natural materials, avoidance of undue emphasis on any particular element and the creation of an overall harmony. The **Myokian tea ceremony room** (p. 743B), dated about 1582, is believed to have been designed by Sen-Rikyu, a famous tea master. It consists of a two-mat floor space 2 m × 2 m (7 ft × 7 ft) and 'toko-no-ma'. Guests enter through an opening called 'nijiriguchi', 788 mm (2 ft 7 in) high and 715 mm (2 ft 5 in) wide, placed opposite the toko-no-ma. Three kinds of ceilings, varied in height or style, and windows of different sizes placed at different heights created a unique illusion of space.

One of the very few extant examples of mediaeval farmhouses is the **Furui house** (*c.* sixteenth century) in the Hyogo prefecture. It is characterised by low eaves, exterior walls with few openings, and slender posts and beams. Light partitions define the three rooms with board and bamboo floors, and half the total area contains an earthen floor. This house illustrates that the division of space was made according to the functional needs of a farmer. The roof-supporting posts are free-standing, set in from the exterior walls. The rooms are divided by sliding, solid plank screens and boarded partition walls extending only to lintel height. No attempt was made to enclose the space between lintel and ceiling.

Pre-modern (sixteenth to nineteenth centuries)

MOMOYAMA AND EDO PERIODS (1568–1867)

After the reunification of Japan by Nobunaga and Hideyoshi, castle-towns (jokamachi) arose and retainers, artisans and merchants established themselves at

A. Daisen'in Hojo, interior (1513). See p.742

B. Myokian tea ceremony room, Kyoto, interior (*c.* 1582). See p.742

C. Himeji Castle, Donjon, Himeji City (1608–9). See p.746

A. Nijo Castle: Ni-no-maru residence, Kyoto (1603). See p.746

B. Katsura Detached Palace, Shoin Building, Kyoto (early and mid-seventeenth century). See p.746

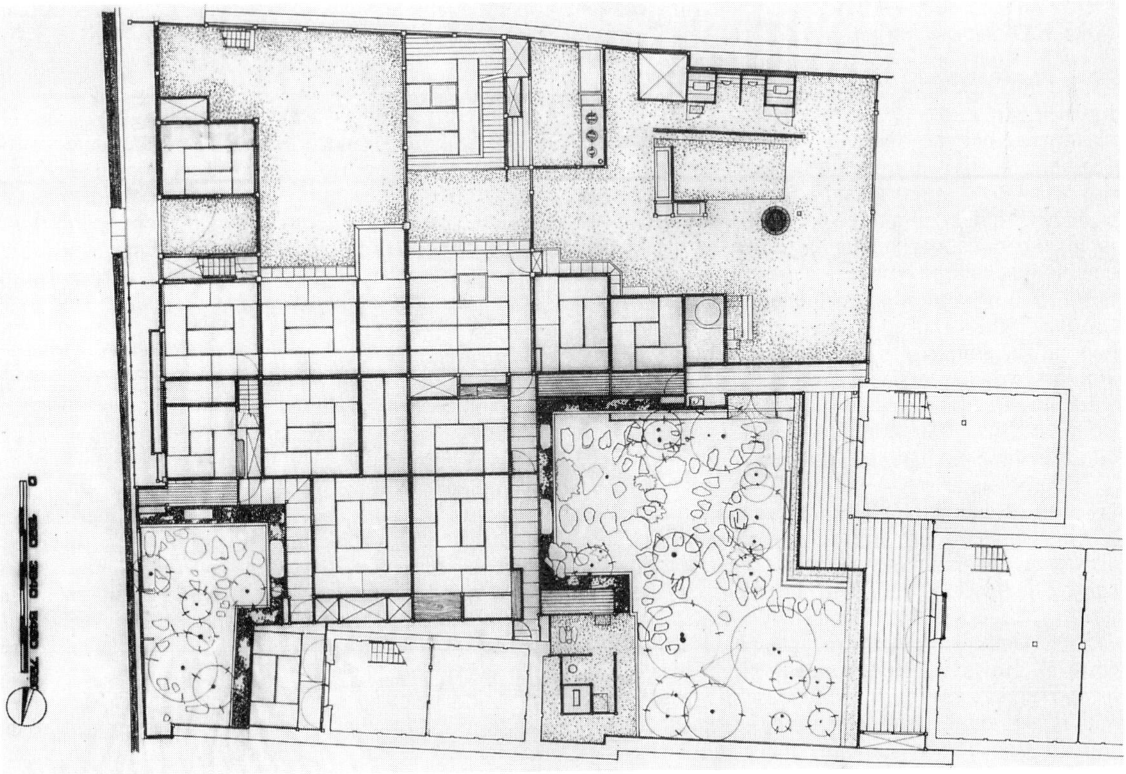

A. Yoshijima House, Takayama City, plan (1907). See p.746

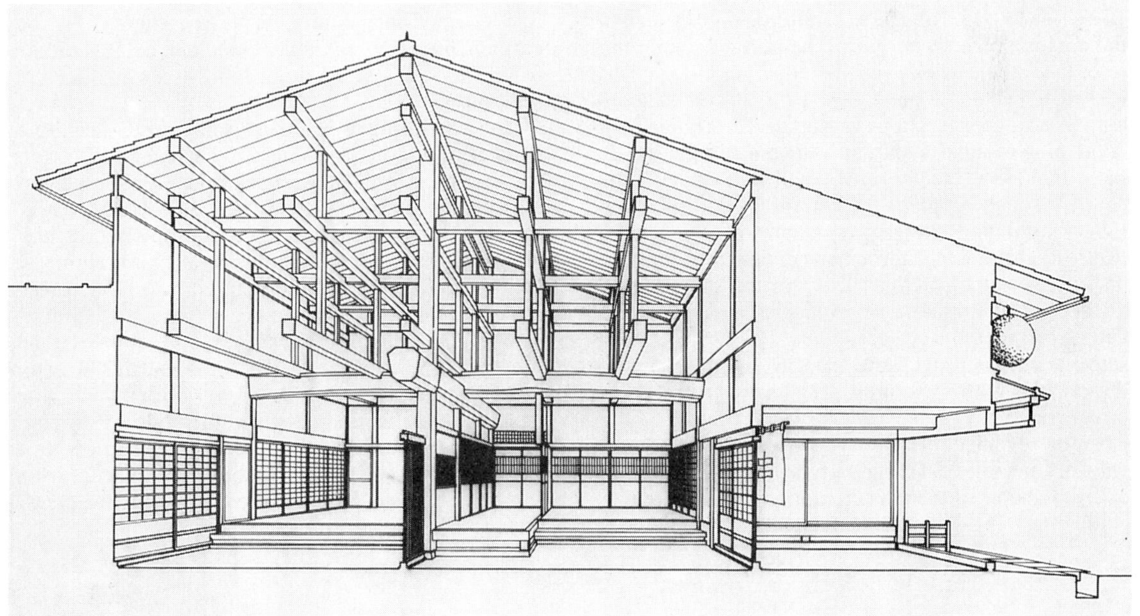

B. Yoshijima House, cross-section

the foot of the castle. A good example is the **castle-town of Okayama**. Based on a grid pattern of streets, zones for each class were established with the higher-ranked retainers closer to the castles, which were fortified with moats and ramparts. Many castles were constructed between the end of the sixteenth and the beginning of the seventeenth century, and construction techniques improved rapidly. The interior of the castle was divided into three parts. At the centre of the main compound was the donjon and keep; the second compound contained the residence of the lord and his family, while in the third compound were dwellings for the highest-ranked retainers as well as storehouses. The donjon was usually a five-storey building with its wooden members wholly coated in thick white plaster. It served as a landmark in the city. Loopholes were provided for shooting arrows and guns, and machicolations for dropping stones.

Himeji Castle (p. 743C), built between 1601 and 1614, represents the highest achievement in Japanese castle architecture. It is the sole example in which almost all the buildings other than the donjon still survive today. In addition to the usual compounds, turrets (yagura), turret-gates (yagura-mon) and earthen walls were constructed within the castle complex. However, the donjon was higher than usual; it had six storeys with a series of pent roofs, undulating gables and decorative dormers. Three small donjons (ko-tenshu) are connected by corridors linking the turrets. For defence purposes, gates were complicated by maze-like spaces to confuse the enemy.

The **Nijo Castle** (Kyoto) (p. 744A) was built in 1603, for Ieyasu Tokugawa when paying respects to the emperor. The ni-no-maru (the second compound) residence was partially reconstructed on a large scale in 1624. Facing a pond, the residence is actually composed of six sections in staggered arrangement, containing rooms for shogun warriors and guests; the most important are the grand hall (ohiroma) in the centre of the complex, the unofficial audience hall (Kuroshoin) and the private abode of the shogun (Shiroshoin). Each of these halls contains a jodan-no-ma, a raised floor area reserved for the shogun, with an alcove (tokonama), staggered shelves (chigaidana) and a writing alcove (tsukeshoin). The walls, fusuma screens and ceiling were coated with gold leaf, decorated with pictures, patterns and metal ornaments.

In the seventeenth century aristocrats and cultured warriors in Kyoto developed a type of villa, containing many elements of the tea ceremony room, where they could relax. The **Katsura Detached Palace** (p. 744B) is an example of such a residence in staggered plan, containing tea ceremony houses and gardens with bridges, stone lanterns, ponds, streams and artificial hills. The palace design has an informality contrary to the rigidly arranged warriors' dwellings.

Townhouses (machiya) for merchants and craftsmen were generally constructed on limited sites with narrow frontages but with considerable depth. The fronts, open to the street, served as shops. Earth floors ran along one long side of the buildings, serving as passageways from the street to rear yards. Rooms were also aligned along the passages, and small inner courts brought fresh air and light to the rear of the main rooms.

After the seventeenth century the scale of farmhouses as well as townhouses increased, and construction became more sophisticated in regions where the local economy had improved. Structures were completely coated with a type of stucco to protect them from fire, and the use of tatami in reception rooms became common. Even in folk dwellings (minka) characteristic forms were originated and developed particularly in the structural members visible in the space above the earthen floor. The structure was made up of hand-hewn beams supported by stout struts.

Takayama City, originally a castle town, developed into an industrial and commercial city after the eighteenth century. The **Yoshijima** family prospered in the nineteenth century, and descendants rebuilt the family house (p.745A,B) in 1907 after a big fire in 1905. It retains the cultural traditions of earlier times. The main house, built on a plot 27 m × 66 m (89 ft × 216 ft), faces the street. Within it there is a long earthen passageway, along which there is a double row of ten rooms, the inner rooms of which have no separate access.

The **Yoshimura House** is a rural farmhouse situated south of Osaka City. It was one of the largest in the region in the sixteenth century. From the early eighteenth century, the Yoshimuras served as headmen over eighteen villages. An old drawing depicts a large village residence which includes a main house, an entrance gate, plastered storehouses (dozo), and other subsidiary buildings set in spacious grounds. The original main house was burnt down in 1615 and was reconstructed in the 1620s. The later structure had a large earthen floor and several rooms, to which were added reception rooms in the style of warriors' residences. Most characteristic is the earthen floor with huge transverse beams above it. Adjacent to the earthen floor is a small planked area which served as an entrance to the rooms.

Chapter 26
INDIAN SUBCONTINENT

Buddhist Religious Architecture

When the Buddha was born in 563 BC, Brahmanism (the name given to early forms of Hinduism) had been evolving for perhaps a thousand years. Yet the earliest surviving architecture in the Indian subcontinent, apart from the ancient remains of the Indus Valley civilisation, is Buddhist. Vedic sacrificial ritual, and even less so the mysticism of the Upanishadic sages, did not lead to the erection of durable monuments. The Mauryan ruler Ashoka (*c.* 269–32 BC), who made Buddhism an official religion of his large and, by Indian standards, remarkably centralised empire, gave the initial great impetus to Buddhist monumental architecture. However, it should be remembered that in South Asia stone structures were always vastly outnumbered by buildings made of perishable materials – wood, bamboo, thatch and brick.

After the Buddha's death, places of pilgrimage grew up, initially around objects associated with the Buddha, and relics of him and his disciples. Pilgrimage sites often lay along trade routes, and merchants played an important part as pilgrims and patrons. The same sites became the centres of Buddhist monasticism. Some monastic centres became universities, the most famous being at **Nalanda, Bihar**, which attracted scholars from all over Asia.

Eastern India being a last stronghold of Buddhism in India itself, Nalanda survived until the thirteenth century. Elsewhere, even by the seventh century, Buddhism had largely been absorbed into Hinduism. By this time, Buddhism was well established in the Far East. Within the Indian subcontinent it continued to flourish in Sri Lanka and the Himalayan valleys.

Stupas

The supreme sacred monument of Buddhism is the stupa, of which the basic form is a solid domical mound crowned by a parasol. Its origins are at least twofold. First, it relates to burial mounds, and early stupas contained relics of the Buddha himself, of his disciples or of saints. Ashoka is said to have distributed relics of the Buddha to numerous sites, and to have built brick stupas to house them; several of these survive at the core of later stupas. Second, the stupa form, with its vertical axis representing the *axis mundi* or world axis, has cosmic implications. There is evidence that many early stupas actually contained wooden pillars running through their full height, emerging in the parasol at the summit.

The honorific parasol, often depicted in paintings or narrative reliefs as shading the Buddha or a sacred object associated with him, is one of the kingly symbols associated with the Buddha, who had renounced his early life as a prince. One symbolic implication of the stupa is the reference to the dharmachakravartin, or emperor as upholder of the cosmic law.

Whether as containers of actual relics, aids to meditation, or as symbols of enlightenment, stupas became the principal object of veneration for the Buddhists. Holy sites filled up with innumerable small votive stupas.

The more monumental stupas were surrounded by a railing (vedika), probably recalling the railing around a vedic altar, with gateways (toranas) at the cardinal points. Railings and gateways now in the Indian Museum, Calcutta, survive from **Bharhut, Madhya Pradesh**, datable to the second century BC. The richly ornamented railings, a little over 2 m (7 ft) high, are the earliest surviving example of the typical form: though massive and of stone their forms reproduce timber construction, with horizontal bars of lenticular section mortised into the uprights.

Another Central Indian example, the **Great Stupa** (Stupa 1), **Sanchi**, though dismantled for excavation by the British and subsequently re-erected, gives the most complete view of these early monumental stupas (p. 749A). Datable mainly to the Satavahana period (first century AD), its core is one of the brick stupas built by Ashoka in the third century BC. The hemispherical dome (anda) is raised on a circular platform (medhi) about 40 m (130 ft) in diameter, reached by two stairways (sopanas). Railings around the platform and at ground level define an upper and a lower passageway for the rite of circumambulation (pradakshina). At the summit, railings enclose a

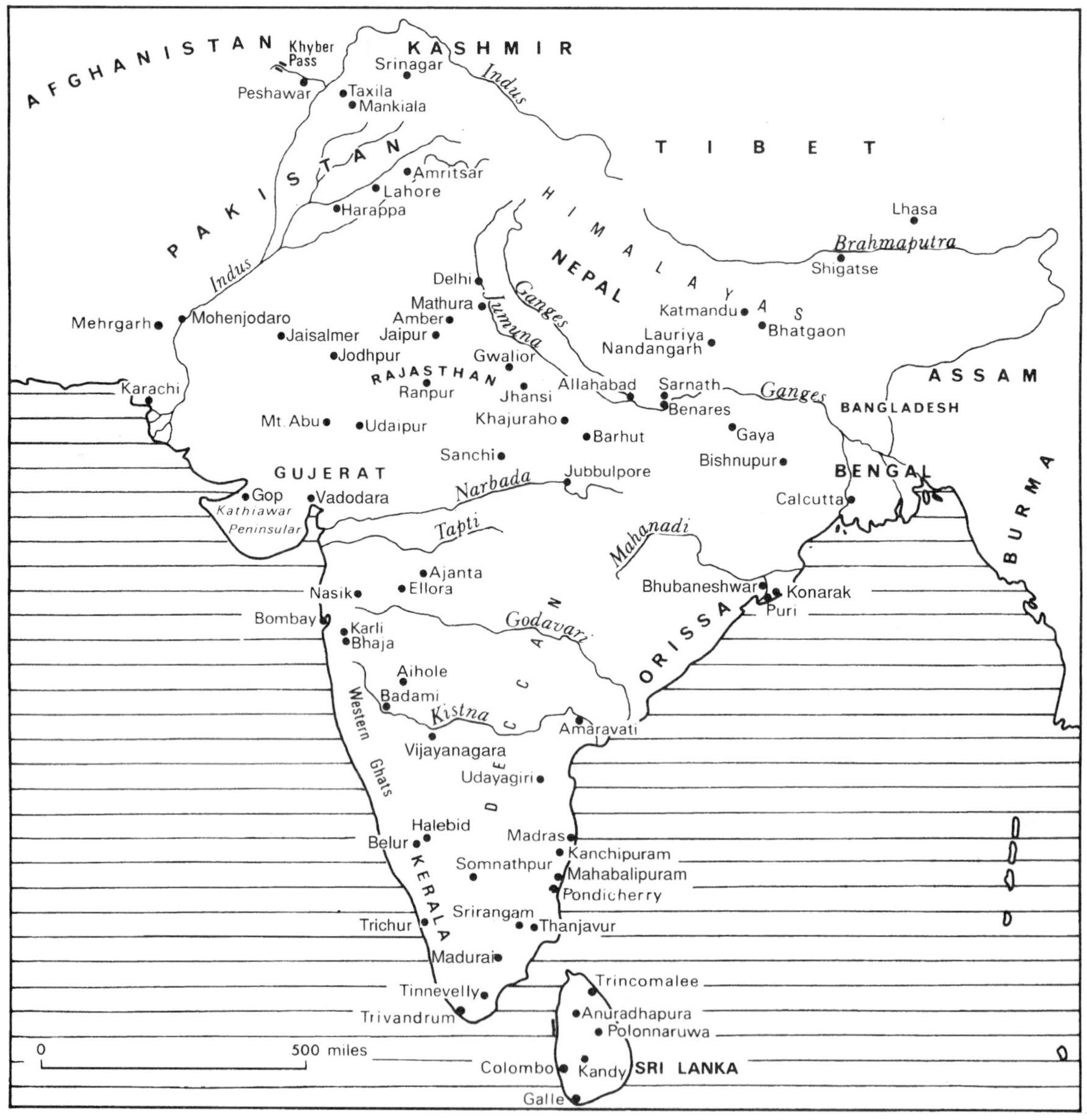

Indian subcontinent

square platform (harmika) containing the triple umbrella on its axial mast (yashti). At the cardinal points are magnificent gateways, 8.5 m (27.5 ft) high, teeming with sensuous relief carving (p. 749B), in contrast to the austere power of the unadorned railings and the stupa itself.

Ashoka is known to have built stupas as far south as Andhra, and monumental stupas continued to be built there, under the Satavahanas and Ikshvakus, up to the fourth century AD. The most important stupa in that region was at **Amaravati** (*c.* second century). Although the stupa itself does not survive, much of its sculpture, including some of the greatest and liveliest narrative reliefs of ancient India, is preserved at the Government Museum, Madras, and in the British Museum, London.

A. Great Stupa (Stupa No. 1), Sanchi (*c*. first century BC). See p.747

B. Relief from gateway of Great Stupa, Sanchi. See pp. 748, 755

C. Swayambhu Stupa, Kathmandu. See p.750

Remains of large stupas in **Gandhara**, as at **Guldara** (second to fourth centuries AD), have multi-tiered bases, often with pilasters of Corinthian derivation. (It should be remembered that this was the region invaded by Alexander the Great in 326 BC, and which maintained its contacts with the Graeco-Roman world.) Smaller stupas of that region show a transformation of the domical stupa 'mound' from a hemisphere to a bulbous form. With this development, here and elsewhere in South Asia, the stupa form becomes taller in proportion. This tendency is emphasised by a multiplication of the base platforms (later superseded by the adoption of base mouldings) on which the stupa sits, and of parasol canopies.

Nepal has remained a stronghold of Buddhism, and its oldest stupas, many times restored and none securely dated, are of brick and follow the low 'Ashokan' dome form, supporting large, solid harmikas, onto which eyes are painted. The most important is the **Swayambhu stupa, Kathmandu** (p. 749C). Typically of the Kathmandu valley, its crowning parasol is in metalwork.

Colossal brick stupas survive at **Anuradhapura, Sri Lanka**, the **Ruwanveliseya stupa**, originally of the second century BC, though much restored, is 90 m (292 ft) high, and the **Jetavana stupa** (*c.* fourth century) rises to 120 m (390 ft). A form of circular shrine housing a stupa within is unique to Sri Lanka, the finest example being the twelfth-century **Watadage, Polonnaruwa** (p. 751A). When this was complete, a central conical roof and descending subsidiary roofs, with clerestory lighting in between, were supported on rings of stone pillars. Four stairways are entered via semi-circular 'moonstone' thresholds. Their monster balustrades and flanking guardian figures are related to similar features in contemporary Hindu temples in south India.

Buddhist Shrines and Rock-cut Images

Apart from stupas, various other kinds of sacred constructions or shrines are depicted in relief carvings from the great stupas, including altars and hypaethral (open-air) shrines, and timber and thatch structures. A relief from **Ghantasala** (*c.* 200 AD), now in the Musée Guimet, Paris, showing a circular, three-storey shrine, is particularly interesting for the way in which it prefigures the stepped pyramid form of Hindu temples in South India. From the Bharhut stupa (early first century BC) survives a relief showing a multi-storey enclosure enshrining the bodhi tree of **Bodh Gaya**, under which the Buddha attained enlightenment. This perhaps represents the temple erected at that holy site by Ashoka, and the precursor of the present Mahabodi temple. The latter, a large, brick structure, relates loosely to the Hindu temples of North India, but its present appearance is mainly due to nineteenth-century work, the most recent of many restorations.

In Nepal there are timber-built shrines of two or more diminishing storeys, known as 'pagoda temples'. Most surviving examples date from the eighteenth and nineteenth centuries. Each storey has a pitched roof, supported by carved, angled struts.

Colossal Buddha figures are associated with some monastic complexes. The complex at **Bamiyan, Afghanistan** (fifth century), where Persian and Central Asian influences are apparent, includes two huge figures. These provided prototypes for the colossal image cults of China and Japan. The images were rough hewn, the features and draperies modelled in mud mixed with straw and finished in lime plaster painted and gilded. One Buddha is 54 m (175 ft) high. The Gal Vihara group near **Plonnaruwa, Sri Lanka**, includes a 14 m (45 ft) recumbent figure, probably the best-known representation of the dying Buddha about to enter Nirvana.

Chaitya Halls

As early as the Mauryan period, 'cave temples', of various simple forms, were being excavated out of the living rock of cliffs and hillsides. These were mainly for the Buddhists, but in the **Nagarjuni Hills, Bihar**, are caves carved out to shelter ascetics of the Ajivka cult during the monsoon. The **Lomas Rishi cave** in the **Barabar Hills, Bihar**, consists of a rectangular chamber with a circular chamber protruding into it at one end, probably intended to house a small stupa or some other cult object. Both chambers have rounded ceilings, roughly hewn out. Unusually, by later norms, the cave runs parallel to the cliff, and is thus entered laterally. Its small entrance facade represents the end of a wagon-roofed, thatched timber structure, with projecting ends of joists (p. 752A). These support a gable which is virtually semi-circular, but actually ogival by virtue of a small point at the apex, carrying a finial. Such a translation into stone of the carpentry forms is typical of Indian rock-cut architecture.

The Lomas Rishi can probably be considered an early example of a 'chaitya hall'. 'Chaitya' means a sacred place or object, and the term 'chaitya hall' has come to refer to a form of rock-cut sanctuary housing a stupa within a space for congregational worship. These spaces may be rectangular with a flat ceiling, occasionally circular and domed (as at **Guntapalli, Andhra**). But the typical form is apsidal at the rear, with pillars defining a barrel vaulted nave and narrow, half barrel-vaulted side aisles. The stupa sits in the apse of the nave, the aisles running round behind as an ambulatory.

This apsidal form is derived from a once-widespread type of thatched timber structure, used for various functions, secular as well as sacred. Many

A. Stupa shrine, Watadage, Polonnaruwa (twelfth century). See p.750

B. Indoor stupa: chaitya hall at Karli (first century BC). See pp. 754, 757

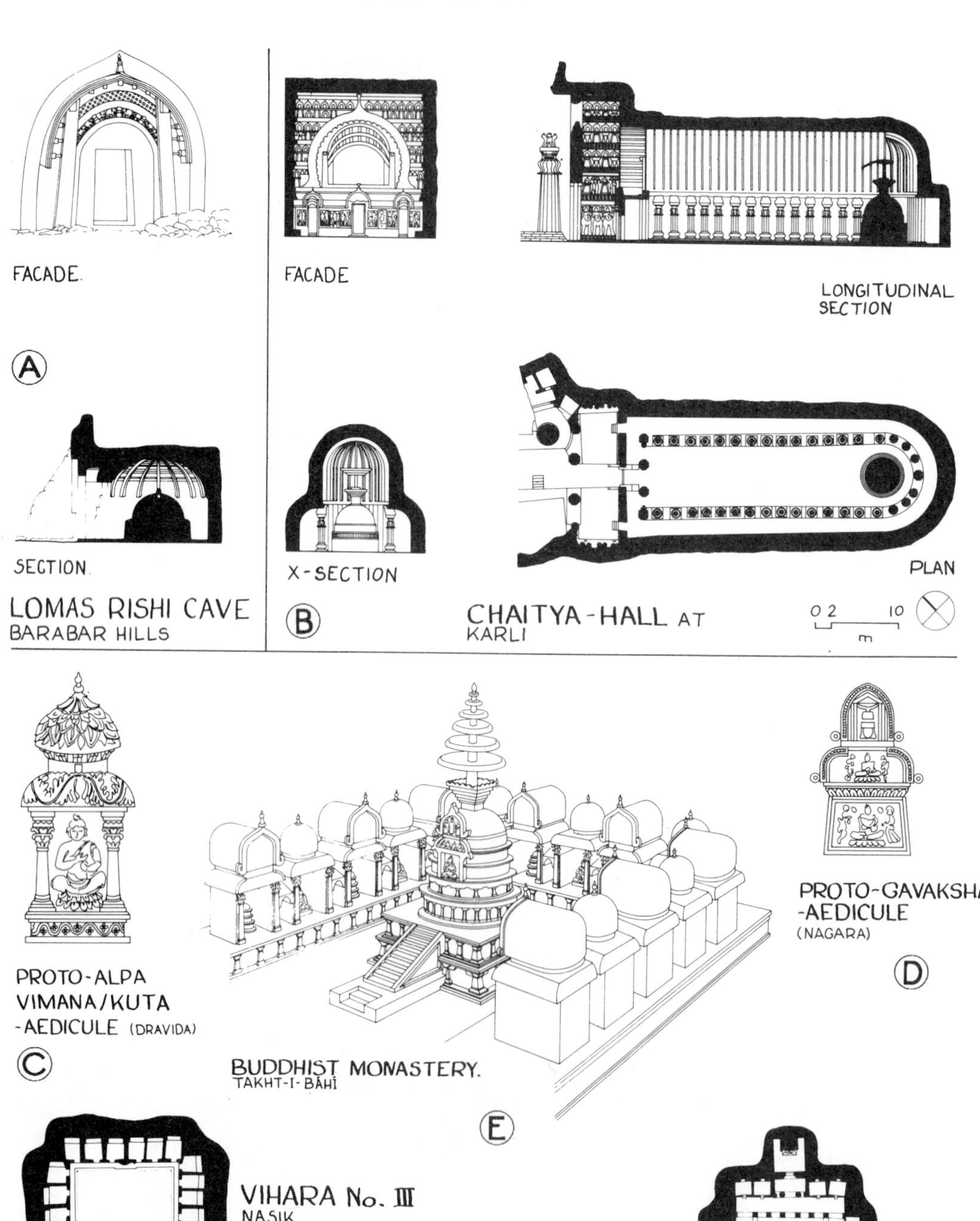
FACADE.
FACADE
LONGITUDINAL SECTION
A
SECTION.
X-SECTION
PLAN
LOMAS RISHI CAVE
BARABAR HILLS
B
CHAITYA-HALL AT KARLI
0 2 10
m
PROTO-ALPA VIMANA/KUTA -AEDICULE (DRAVIDA)
C
PROTO-GAVAKSHA -AEDICULE (NAGARA)
D
BUDDHIST MONASTERY.
TAKHT-I-BĀHĪ
E
VIHARA No. III
NASIK
0 5 10 30 FT
F
PLAN OF AJANTA-
CAVE 1
G
0 10 20 50 FT

A. Chaitya Hall, Cave 18, 'Pandulenya' (first century BC) and vihara, Cave 20 (*c.* second century), Nasik. See pp. 754, 755

B. Chaitya hall, Cave 19, Ajanta, façade (late fifth century). See p.754

C. Vishvakarma chaitya hall (Cave 10), Ellora, façade (seventh century). See p.754

images of such buildings, with or without aisles, appear in the early narrative reliefs and depictions of holy sites. Foundations of brick chaitya halls remain, as at **Sanchi**, and in the late third- to early fourth-century monastery at **Nagarjunakonda, Andhra**, where a pair of such structures, without aisles, faced one another, one containing a stupa, the other a Buddha image.

By far the greatest number of rock-cut chaitya halls is found in present-day Maharashtra, especially from the period from the second century BC to the second century AD, belonging to the 'Hinayana' phase. These were generally associated with monastic complexes and sited on trade routes. Fine early examples are at **Bhaja, Pitalkhora** (Cave 3), and **Kondane**. Support holes indicate that these had timber screen walls at the front rather than the rock facades that became the norm. On the ceiling of a typical chaitya hall are great hoop-like curved beams, carved in the rock, with carved purlins running longitudinally and emerging out into the giant horseshoe-gable sun window which opens in the façade, either directly on the cliff-face or preceded by a verandah (p. 753A,B). This horseshoe-arch-gable form, prefigured by the Lomas Rishi cave, becomes an almost ubiquitous motif in the sacred architecture of India. The curved beams in the barrel-roofed ceiling were sometimes actually of timber, as can still be seen in the magnificent chaitya hall at **Karli, Maharashtra** (*c.* AD 50–70), where the open timber screen in the sun window also survives (p. 751B).

The **'Vishvakarma'** (Cave 10), **Ellora, Maharashtra**, the latest of India's rock-cut chaitya halls, belongs to around the mid seventh century (p. 753C). Its colonnaded forecourt has an upper storey connected to a musicians' gallery at the front of the hall.

Monasteries

It is in Gandhara that the most extensive remains of early Buddhist monasteries survive, such as the **Dharmarajika monastery, Taxila, Pakistan**, and the monastery at **Kalawan**. These complexes, built of brick, included major and minor stupas, and viharas, the residential quarters consisting of monks' cells lined up around courtyards.

At **Takht-i-Bahi** (*c.* second to fourth centuries AD) a vihara court is formally related to the 'court of the stupa' (p. 752E). Here the courtyard, surrounding the stupa platform, is composed of interconnected shrines, probably once housing alternately Buddha images and miniature stupas, and joined by smaller, intermediate chambers. Enough survives of these shrines for their forms to be deduced. Each one consisted of a square cell, opening into the courtyard, with a curved, overhanging brick canopy, or roll cornice, at ceiling level, supporting an upper pavilion. The upper pavilions were of two kinds: a circular 'hut' with a domical roof, and a wagon-roofed pavilion, apsidal at the rear. Below the latter type, the brick canopy was not carried across the front of the shrine. Instead, on the front elevation, its appearance as two half-gable-ends was emphasised, along with the arched gable of the wagon roof, thus creating an analogy with the cross-section of a chaitya hall. These shrine types are prototypes of two perennial forms in Indian temple architecture, and are masonry versions of ideas originally conceived in timber and thatch.

In addition to structural viharas were those carved out as 'caves'. The rock-cut monasteries of **Udayagiri, Madhya Pradesh**, and **Khandagiri** and **Udayagiri**, in **Orissa** of the early first century AD, were probably Jain rather than Buddhist. Best preserved at these sites is the **Rani Gumpha, Udayagiri**, consisting of a large open court on two storeys. The second-century **Gautamiputra** (Cave 3), **Nasik, Maharashtra**, shows the typical arrangement for rock-cut viharas (p. 752F): a square hall (equivalent to the central courtyard found in structural examples) with cells opening along the sides and rear, and usually with a verandah across the front. On the rear wall of the Gautamiputra a stupa is carved in relief. Already by this date, viharas were more like monastic temples than everyday living quarters, used for worship as much by the lay community as by the monks.

After the second century, rock-cut architecture was hardly patronised until the later part of the fifth, when an incomparable series of Buddhist caves, both viharas and chaitya halls, was excavated under the Vakataka rulers at **Ajanta, Maharashtra**. Five caves of the early centuries AD had already been carved in the side of this dramatic, horseshoe-shaped ravine. In the vihara plan that is typical at Ajanta a square of pillars has been introduced into the centre of the hall, and a Buddha shrine, often with an antechamber, is placed centrally at the rear (p. 752G). The longitudinal axis between entrance and shrine progresses from fierce sunlight towards a dimly lit Buddha figure in the dark depths, through layers defined by steps, thresholds, doorways and lines of pillars. In central positions on the flat ceilings are painted lotus-centred, mandala-like patterns, prefiguring the carved and often corbelled lotus-ceilings of many Hindu temples.

Ajanta is best known for its beautiful narrative murals, but painting is not limited to these. Where it survives, painting decorates both carved and plain surfaces. Architecture, sculpture and painting create one integral, almost hypnotic experience, which once would have been accompanied by ritual and reverberating chants.

At **Aurangabad, Maharashtra**, 100 km south-west of Ajanta, is a lavish series of Buddhist caves where some of the Ajanta ideas are developed. In the sixth-century Caves 6 and 7, the Buddha shrine is placed at the centre of the hall, allowing circumambulation – a concept echoed in the contemporary Hindu caves of the region. At nearby **Ellora**, variations on the vihara plan were carried out between the late sixth and early eighth centuries, including two- and three-storeyed versions (Caves 11 and 12, the 'Don Thal' and 'Tin Thal').

Architectural Language

An essential aspect of Indian sacred architecture, in its monumental, masonry forms, is its representational character. A formal and symbolic language in brick or stone is composed of imagery derived from buildings made of wood and thatch. While early stupa railings and early chaitya hall interiors followed timber prototypes closely, a formalised language, as opposed to literal copying, began to develop at an early date.

Relief carvings on stupa gateways and railings show the kind of timber architecture that has since, for centuries, been referred to in masonry. The relief showing the dream of Maya, the Buddha's mother, from the (west) gateway of the **Great Stupa, Sanchi** is typical, with its busy townscape of multi-storeyed palaces or 'harmyas' (p. 749B). Though perhaps idealised, evoking the poetic visions of sky-scraping palaces recounted in the Indian epics, the construction of these harmyas is clear. Typically, their thatched roofs, lined with finials, are (like chaitya halls) 'barrel-vaulted', with horseshoe gables at the ends and over projecting dormers. Timber balconies surround the upper storeys, with the familiar hefty railings, and with bracket-headed posts. These often support rounded, thatched canopies, which are the origin of the stone roll cornice (kapota) and other eave-like mouldings.

Bound up with the representational nature of Indian architecture is the importance of aedicules – images of small buildings – as elements of composition. This is particularly the case in Hindu temple architecture, but the roots of this characteristic are found in Buddhist monuments. The two shrine types already noted in the monastery of **Takht-i-Bahi** (p. 752E) are the basis of later shrine and aedicule types, explained below. Both are depicted in Gandharan reliefs. One type is shown, for example, enshrining the Buddha, in a relief of about the second century AD now in the British Museum, London (p. 752C). Corinthianesque pillars support the canopy and upper pavilion, both of which are thatched with leaves. In later centuries, this form would reappear as the Dravida alpa vimana and kuta-aedicule (pp. 756B, 766A, 767G), while the type crowned by a chaitya hall cross-section (p. 752D) would become the Valabhi temple mode and its corresponding niche type (pp. 763E, 767B, 783C).

Gandharan stupa bases sometimes contain niches of the latter kind. The base of the stupa known as the **'Shrine of the Double-headed Eagle', Sirkap, Taxila, Pakistan** (*c.* first century BC to first century AD), reflecting the eclecticism of this region, has aedicular niches of three types: with pointed 'chaitya arches', in the form of toranas (gateways) like those of Sanchi, and with triangular, European pediments.

Comparison of earlier and later chaitya hall façades (p. 753A,B) shows a transformation of the horseshoe-arch form, with increasing emphasis of its curvaceous outline, leaving behind its structural origins. Minor versions of the motif ornament the facades and verandah walls of early chaitya halls, along with strips of railing pattern and stepped parasol patterns. Sometimes a storeyed palace architecture is evoked, but already not literally portrayed: even at the **Pandulenya, Nasik** (p. 753A), where a whole blind colonnade is carved, the railing strips have no functional logic and are cut through by gables and stupas.

While it is arguable whether of not there was an 'aniconic' phase in Buddhism, it is clear that during the Gupta era, corresponding to the blossoming of Mahayana Buddhism, images of Buddhas, past and future, proliferate, along with those of boddhisattvas (saints). Thus, in the fifth-century chaitya halls at **Ajanta** (Caves 19 and 26), large Buddha figures are framed on the front of the elaborate stupas, with smaller images sitting along the 'gallery' between nave colonnade and barrel-vaulted ceiling, as well as all over the rock facade. The architecture develops accordingly. These facades consist of carved reliefs representing storeyed palaces, regularised and repetitive to provide a framework for enshrining the numerous images. An interlinked row of Buddha-housing barrel-roofed pavilions (shalas), foreshadowing the language of temple architecture shortly to develop in south India, runs along the top of the Cave 19 facade, and another over the verandah colonnade of the vihara Cave 1. In Hindu as well as Buddhist architecture, the idea of a chain (hara) of pavilions became widespread, over cave facades (p. 756C), over doorways, and as a kind of blind clerestory.

Pillars

Widespread fragments of free-standing stone pillars or 'laths' survive, the earliest dating from around the time of Ashoka (third century BC), and some inscribed with his edicts. Whatever their origin – often thought to be Persian – such pillars became associated with Buddhist sites. Up to about 14 m (45 ft) high, these had plain, monolithic shafts, crowned by animal figures (lions, bulls, elephants) standing on a polished capital consisting of an abacus over a tassel-like inverted bell shape. The **Lion Capital** from **Sarnath, Uttar Pradesh** used as the emblem of the Republic of India, is the best known.

A. Ravana-ki-khai cave (Cave 14), Ellora (early seventh century). See p. 758

B. Arjuna's Penance relief, Mahabalipurum (mid-seventh century). See pp. 755, 770

C. Cave, Mahabalipurum (late seventh century). See pp. 755, 761

The **Lion Column, Lauriya Nandangarh, Bihar**, stands intact (p. 784B).

A related pillar type came to be used in rock-cut chaitya halls and viharas of the Hinayana phase (pp. 751B, 753A). This can be seen at the chaitya hall **Karli, Maharashtra** (p. 751B), in front of which stands a monolithic, free-standing version of the type. The inverted bell/tassel had become assimilated into a form full of symbolic potential, the pot or vase, hereafter related to various architectural mouldings as well as to pillar components. Even more explicit jar forms were often placed at the foot of a pillar. In place of the abacus of the 'Ashokan' order, there appeared the ribbed cushion form, the amalaka, often framed in an open-sided box, surmounted by an inverted stepped pyramid, like the upper portion of the harmika over a stupa.

An unprecedented richness and variety of pillar and pilaster designs arose in the Gupta period, and can be seen in the fifth-century caves at **Ajanta, Maharashtra**. One type, with mirrored roundels, relates back to early stupa railings with their lotus medallions. Types with a brimming vase (purnaghata) capital, usually surmounted by a plain abacus and brackets, have countless descendants in north Indian temple building traditions; while types with a cushion capital (a ghata, or 'pot', often treated here as a ribbed amalaka), often surmounted by a cyma or lotus moulding, are the basis for the form which becomes a standard in Dravida or southern temples. In fact the slender pilaster universal in Dravida temple exteriors is found, fully formed, in the facade of Cave 19 at Ajanta.

Hindu Temple Architecture

During the first millennium BC, the broad spectrum of religious modes known as 'Brahmanism' or 'Hinduism' almost certainly included the worship of gods in the form of images. The early shelters for such images must have been made of perishable materials, like the humble shrines still built today all over the Indian countryside. As image worship came to predominate in organised religion, monumental masonry temples began to be built, remains of brick structures surviving from the early centuries AD. The earliest substantial remains are from around the fifth century, products of the cultural milieu of the Gupta empire, and the first rock-cut Hindu cave sanctuaries also date from this period. A huge growth and flowering of temple building took place between the seventh and thirteenth centuries. From this time Muslim invasions disrupted many of the regional traditions, but the Vijayanagara empire between the fourteenth and sixteenth centuries, and Nayaka rulers for a further two centuries, patronised vast temple complexes in south India. Survivals and revivals have also occurred at various times in other regions, and temples are still being built today in the traditional way.

The temple architecture of the Jains (who consider themselves Hindus, in a broad sense), in a given period and region, is not fundamentally different from Hindu temple architecture, often being the work of the same architects and craftsmen, and even patronised by the same rulers. Differences are a matter of iconography rather than form and style. The same is true of the different cults of Hinduism, of which the main division is between those worshipping Shiva as supreme divinity, and those for whom Vishnu holds this place. Sikh temples (gurudwaras) also need to be mentioned here. Following the founding of the Sikh religion in the seventeenth century, temples were built for that faith, principally in the Punjab.

The master architect (sthapati), well versed in the canonical treatises (shastras), headed all the various grades of craftsmen. Patronage of temples brought religious merit. Many of the more important temples were founded by kings or queens, but other important or wealthy people were also patrons, and sometimes guilds of merchants or craftsmen. Once founded a temple would attract pious gifts and grants, including grants of land, and could achieve a powerful role in social and economic life. It might perform educational and charitable functions, and have hundreds of employees, from priests and administrators to masons, dancers, cooks and potters.

Most important architecturally, symbolically and ritually is the shrine itself, the sanctuary with its outer walls and superstructure. The sanctuary is a dark cuboid cell, called the garbhagriha, meaning 'womb-chamber', housing the principal image (murti) of the deity. As a house for the god the function of the shrine is not just to offer shelter but also to manifest the presence within, to be a concrete realisation, a coming into the world of the deity. Symbolically the shrine is the body of the god, as well as the house, and many Sanskrit terms for architectural elements reflect this. The embodied divinity, its power radiating from within, is revealed in the exterior, where architectural expression chiefly resides. At the same time a cosmic symbolism is evident in the axial organisation of the shrine. Emphasis is given to the cardinal axes, and from their point of intersection rises a vertical axis (world axis) linking the heart of the sanctuary with the point on the finial of the superstructure. Reinforcing this cosmic symbolism, a mandala, or cosmic diagram, known as the vastupurushamandala, is ritually traced on the ground where a new temple is to be built.

A theological hierarchy is ascribed to the gridded squares of the vastupurushamandala, but this is not the same as the hierarchy of sculpted deities which may be enshrined in the temple walls. Principal images of the main deity appear on the cardinal axes of the shrine. A proliferation of images leads, in some mediaeval temples, to seething masses of mythological figures, divine, semi-divine, human and animal. In some traditions, voluptuous heavenly nymphs are prominent, and sometimes celestial loving couples. Among mortals depicted, kings and sages are usual, though not in the most important positions. Elements such as plinths may contain narrative friezes, often relating the epics or the life of Krishna.

Quite apart from these sculpted images, the whole character of Indian temple architecture, in its main varieties, is sculptural. This character, stemming from the early practice of cutting shrines from the living rock, is appropriate to the constructional techniques used in masonry temples, based on beams, corbelling, and the piling up of horizontal courses. The same principles applied where the material was brick, which was carved *in situ* and, once rendered and painted, would have been indistinguishable from stonework finished, as it generally was, in the same way. Means of construction are not in any way 'expressed', and it is equally meaningless to focus too closely on the logic of load and support in the imagery of timber and thatch buildings which is created in stone or brick. It is the imagery, the representation, that is essential: stone or brick structures are composed of images of wooden buildings, translated into a language of masonry. The depiction is formal and symbolic rather than literal or 'tectonic', and is increasingly abstracted from its wooden prototypes.

The nature of this representation is aedicular – the whole is composed of aedicules or shrine-images, whose interrelation is the basis of the formal (as opposed to physical) structure. While, except in the simplest works, the sanctum and its tower evoke the idea of a many-storeyed heavenly palace, this divine abode has many mansions. The great house for the god is made up of a collection of little houses, of various kinds and sizes, reflecting belief in one god with many forms or manifestations. Just as each sculpted divinity in the temple walls displays an aspect of the unity whose supreme embodiment is enshrined at the centre, so every shrine-image reflects the totality of the god's house of which it is part.

It is important to understand that the aedicular elements of composition are not 'surface decoration'. Not only are they formally and symbolically significant, but they are conceived three-dimensionally, embedded in and emerging from their background or one another. Various traditions develop in such a way that, increasingly, the whole shrine is imbued with an expression of growth and dynamism. Interpenetrating forms are made to appear to emerge and expand centrifugally. The temple can thus be understood as a vivid symbol of divine manifestation as a continuous process, by which unity appears in multiplicity as the Absolute pours out into the world.

By the beginning of the seventh century temple architecture in India was becoming differentiated into two main branches, classified in the texts as Nagara and Dravida. The former is associated with northern parts of India, the latter with the south, though neither is entirely confined to its respective region. A Nagara shrine is most immediately recognisable by its curved spire or shikhara, a Dravida one by its tiered pyramid form. Nagara and Dravida are often referred to as the northern and southern 'styles', though architectural 'languages' is perhaps a more appropriate term. Each provides a vocabulary, a range of elements, and certain rules for putting these together. Principally, the languages are characterised by their aedicule types and the ways in which these are combined. It is aedicules not columns that could be seen as the essential elements of architectural 'orders': particular pillar types do become associated with either Nagara and Dravida, but not exclusively, and never becoming the key to the whole composition.

Rock-cut Temples

The fifth-century Gupta caves at **Udayagiri, Madhya Pradesh**, are more important for their carved mythological scenes than for their architecture. The flowering of Hindu rock-cut architecture began in the next century, in the north-west Deccan and the adjacent coastal region of the Konkan, inheriting the tradition which had developed in the Buddhist caves of Ajanta and Aurangabad.

Intrinsic to the experience of this architecture is the overwhelming presence of sculpture, not only in the sanctum itself but also in complex mythological panels filling whole bays along the walls as in the **Ravana-ki-khai cave, Ellora** (p. 756A). Powerful sculpture panels are found in the great Shaiva cave at **Elephanta** (first half of sixth century), **Bombay**. In the vast multi-pillared hall beams emphasise the east–west orientation and the longitudinal axis running towards the free-standing, four-faced sanctum. A transverse axis runs towards the Maheshvara image in the south wall.

The plan of the **'Rameshvara'** (Cave 21), **Ellora** (p. 759B), belonging to the second half the the sixth century, is characteristic of the first phase of Hindu caves at this site. Of a similar date, and stylistically related, are the beautiful Hindu and Jain cave temples of the Early Chalukyas at their capital **Badami, Karnataka** and at nearby **Aihole**. The **Ravalaphadi cave, Aihole** (p. 759C), is located beneath a rocky outcrop, in order, like the tower of a structural temple over its cave-like sanctum, to evoke the idea of a mountain of the gods.

Around the end of the sixth century, traditions of carving cave temples were established in Andhra Pradesh and Tamil Nadu. These closely related traditions draw on the legacy of Buddhist architecture and narrative carving in Andhra, and both display

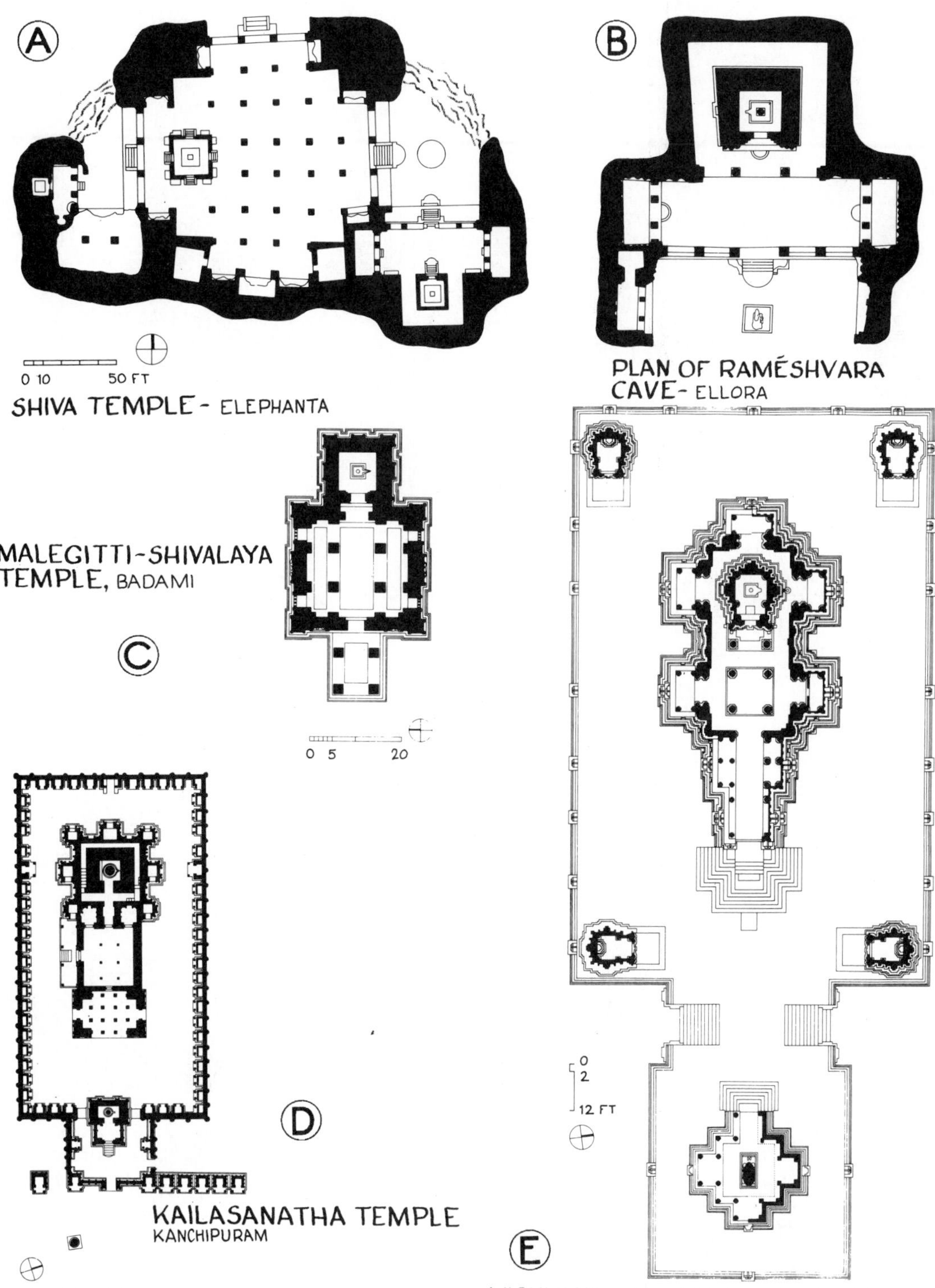
A
0 10 50 FT
SHIVA TEMPLE - ELEPHANTA
B
PLAN OF RAMÉSHVARA
CAVE - ELLORA
MALEGITTI-SHIVALAYA
TEMPLE, BADAMI
C
0 5 20
D
KAILASANATHA TEMPLE
KANCHIPURAM
0 10 50 FT
E
0
2
12 FT
VISHVANATHA AND NANDI TEMPLES
KHAJURAHO

Adinatha (Vimala Vasahi), temple, Dilwara, Mount Abu: mandapa interior (twelfth century). See p. 761

details which prefigure the structural temple architecture of those regions. For example, pavilion-chains (haras) sitting on roll-cornices (kapotas), further conventionalised versions of those met with at Ajanta, appear over the facade of a three-storey rock-cut complex at **Undavalli, Andhra Pradesh**, and over the later (seventh to eighth century) rock-cut caves of the Pallava dynasty at **Mahabalipuram** (or Mamallapuram), **Tamil Nadu** (p. 756C). The monolithic 'rathas' at this coastal site will be discussed in relation to Dravida temple architecture. A granite mound over the Varaha cave at Mahabalipuram is another 'natural tower'. Over the **Akkanna-Madanna caves, Vijayawada, Andhra Predesh**, parts of rock-cut proto-Dravida ('proto-southern') superstructures survive.

Ellora witnessed a second phase of rock-cut architecture under the Rashtrakutas in the eighth century, when the plans of cave temples often follow closely those of structural versions. Many Dravida characteristics appear, through contacts with southern temple-building traditions, as in the two-storeyed Jain cave the **'Indrasabha'** (Cave 32) of which the forecourt contains a free-standing rock-cut vimana of a boldly experimental Dravida form, as well as a free-standing monolithic pillar and a monolithic elephant.

The monolithic pillar standing in front of the Indrasabha is a feature also found in the most famous complex at Ellora, completed a few decades earlier. This centres around the greatest of India's monolithic temples, the **Kailasa**, named after the mountain abode of the god Shiva (p. 773C). The temple is carved in a great excavated pit, about 40 m (130 ft) wide and extending some 80 m (260 ft) into the hillside, with colonnades and cave shrines around its sides. Raised on an 8 m (26 ft) high platform, which includes life-sized caryatid elephants, the temple itself, its tower rising to 33 m (107 ft) above the courtyard, is a development from the great Dravida works at **Pattadakal, Karnataka** (cf. p. 772B).

Temple Layouts

Sanctuary and superstructure, constituting the shrine proper, are together called the vimana in the Dravida context (from the Sanskrit root ma, to measure) and mulaprasada for the Nagara (meaning the main prasada or main temple, prasada implying a seat or palace). Sometimes an interior pradakshinapatha (circumambulatory passage) runs around the sanctum.

Individual devotees visit the shrine for darshana, 'seeing' of the god, and make offerings before the image in the sanctuary, with the assistance of a priest. Since Hindu worship is not fundamentally of a congregational nature, the only essential part of a temple is the shrine proper, with its symbol-laden threshold and doorway, normally facing east. However, in all but the most basic temples other elements are present, at least a porch, and often an antechamber (antarala) and a hall (mandapa).

Mandapas may be flat roofed or, particularly in northern traditions, have pyramidal superstructures, sometimes of a composition as complex as that of the mulaprasada. Mandapa ceilings began with beam and slab construction, which continued to be the basic method. Triangular slabs came to be used to bridge across corners, successively, creating a diminishing pattern of nested squares. Many ceiling designs may be seen as mandalas or yantras – meditational cosmic diagrams. Most impressive are the lotus domes developed in mediaeval times, in which concentric rings of corbelled masonry rise to a capping stone in the form of a stamen-like pendant. The twelfth-century, white marble Jain temples at **Dilwara, Mount Abu, Rajasthan**, take this idea to extremes of lacy intricacy (p. 760).

During the mediaeval period there arose the need for additional structures for performances of sacred music and dance, sermons and recitals of mythological stories. An open pillared hall might be placed, either as a substitute for, or axially in front of, an enclosed mandapa, often with a parapet-backed seat (kaksasana) around the perimeter (p. 775A). In central India, notably at **Khajuraho, Madhya Pradesh** (p. 759E), the main mandapa could be fronted by two successive porches, enhancing the stepped progression inwards from light to dark, profane to sacred. The porch superstructures, with that of the mandapa, descend in a diminishing series from the mountain peak of the shrine itself (p. 768B). Subsidiary vimanas or prasadas could be integrated in various ways into a temple design. Many temples, particularly Nagara ones, in addition to the moulded base or plinth on which all temples stand, are raised on a circumambulatory platform (jagati), sometimes with small subsidiary shrines at the corners. The five-shrine (panchayatana) arrangement so formed is found already in the sixth-century Gupta temple of **Dashavatara, Deogarh, Madya Pradesh**. Temples dedicated to Shiva may be preceded by a free-standing pavilion sheltering an image of the bull Nandi, Shiva's vehicle.

An important temple can be set in a walled enclosure, called a prakara, occasionally lined with minor shrines, as in the great **Kailasanatha** (or Rajasimheshvara) **Temple, Kanchipuram, Tamil Nadu** (p. 759D), built by Pallava king Rajasimha in the first quarter of the eighth century. In northern regions, the most significant temple enclosures are those of Jain temples in western India, beginning in the eleventh-and twelfth-century groups at **Kumbharia, Gujarat** and **Dilwara, Rajasthan**, and culminating in the **Adinatha Temple, Ranakpur, Rajasthan**. Whereas the earlier compounds are rectangular, the latter is square, edged with eighty-four towered minor shrines, and entered on all four sides through three-storeyed entrance halls, on the cardinal axes of the main, central shrine. The western entrance hall is more important, marking the predominant west–east axis. Four subsidiary shrines within the enclosure give the temple a pancyatana pattern. The white marble, pillared mandapas are lit from open upper storeys, with sixteen main domes.

A temple can be preceded by an archway (torana), as at the **Mukteshvara Temple, Bhubaneshwar, Orissa**. Toranas are usually free-standing, rather than incorporated into enclosure walls. In south India a temple enclosure is generally entered through a towered gateway (gopura). The design of gopuras will be dealt with below, in relation to Dravida temples.

The later 'temple cities' of the south are the most extensive complexes. Their successively built, concentric prakaras enclose tanks, numerous shrines, 'thousand-pillared halls', educational facilities, residential quarters, dining halls, granaries and storehouses. With each additional prakara, the gopura or gopuras had to be taller than the previous ones, the centrifugal expansion expressing the same radiation of divine power that is sensed in an individual shrine. The **Nataraja Temple, Chidamabaram, Tamil Nadu**, is the earliest of these great complexes (mainly twelfth and thirteenth centuries), later examples including the largely sixteenth-century **Ekambareshvara Temple, Kanchipuram, Tamil Nadu** (p. 778A), and the **Great Temple**, (Minakshi Temple) **Madurai, Tamil Nadu**, chiefly of the seventeenth and eighteenth centuries (p. 780A). The Pudu mandapa in the Madurai complex is one of the splendid seventeenth-century pillared structures in Tamil Nadu, others being the great Chokkattam corridor at **Rameshwaram, Tamil Nandu**, and the seventeenth-century 'Horse mandapa' – with large rearing horses on the pillars – at the **Ranganatha Temple, Srirangam, Tamil Nadu**. The Srirangam complex, near Tiruchirapalli, covers 63 ha (156 acres), and has the full, canonical complement of seven prakaras. The south gopura to the outermost prakara, the tallest in the world, was completed only recently.

Tanks and Step Wells

It has always been important for temples to be associated with water, and perhaps the most impressive of all subsidiary structures are tanks or reservoirs. Their sides are generally stepped, and sometimes lined with small shrines, as in the great tank in front of the eleventh-century **Surya Temple, Modhera, Gujarat**.

Separate from temples, but nevertheless of sacred as well as utilitarian significance, are the magnificent mediaeval step wells built in Gujarat, and to a lesser extent in Rajasthan, created under both Hindu and Muslim rulers. The wells are reached by flights of steps descending through open structures of columns and beams. Most monumental among these wells is the recently excavated, late eleventh-century **Rani Vav** (Queen's Well) **Patan, Gujarat**, sculpted and ornamented as richly as any temple.

This conception of water-source as inside-out temple is very clearly represented by the early eleventh-century tank at **Sudi, Karnataka**.

Nagara Temples

The Gupta milieu in Central India gave rise to proto-Nagara monuments such as the fifth-century brick temple at **Bhitargaon, Uttar Pradesh**. Once the family of forms defining the Nagara 'language' had been established, there arose, in addition to the early Latina type with its simple sikhara (tower), various ways of arranging these forms, various modes of organisation, notably the Valabhi, the Shekhari and the Bhumija. These are explained below.

While a common architectural language is shared, hugely varied stylistic characters arose. Contemporary temples in, for example, Gujarat and Orissa might be similar in composition, yet totally different in feeling, because of different proportions, different moulding shapes, different decorative encrustations, different 'handwriting' in the way of carving. Very broadly speaking, general stylistic zones of Nagara architecture can be seen to emerge from around the seventh century: most importantly western India and, closely related, central India; eastern India (principally Orissa); the Deccan (Maharashtra, Karnataka, Andhra Pradesh).

The types and sequential stratification of horizontal mouldings are largely common to the different modes and different stylistic zones of Nagara temple architecture. Generally, each of the mouldings corresponds to a course of masonry, and has a symbolic meaning as well as an architectural function. The smaller **Shiva Temple, Kiradu, Rajasthan**, has mouldings from ground level to the base of the tower (p. 763F). This developed, eleventh-century shrine has almost the full complement of mouldings available at its time. Less elaborate temples would be without the moulded sub-base (pitha), but from an early date the elements of the base proper (vedibandha) were universal (pp. 764C, 768A, 771B): kapotali (representing an overhanging roof), often a separate antarapatra (recess), kalasha ('vase', a cushioning element), kumbha ('pot'), khura ('tortoise', a toe to the kumbha, with which it is often combined in a single unit). In the example illustrated, the wall-zone (jangha, 'thigh') is moulded to represent a frieze of pillars.

In pillar design there is no single Nagara 'order', but many types have capitals in the form of the purnaghata ('brimming vase').

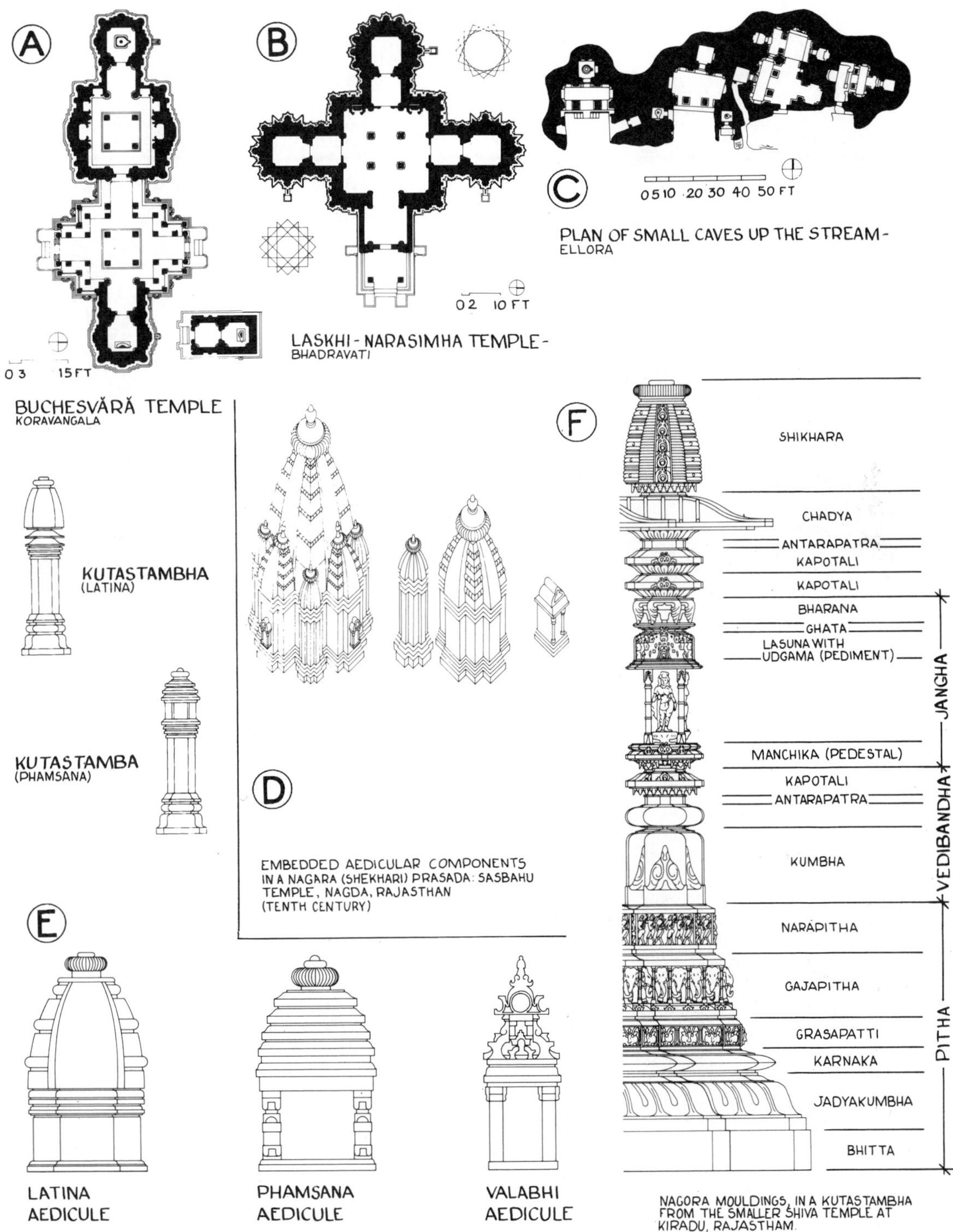
A
B
C
0 5 10 20 30 40 50 FT
PLAN OF SMALL CAVES UP THE STREAM-
ELLORA
0 2 10 FT
LASKHI-NARASIMHA TEMPLE-
BHADRAVATI
0 3 15 FT
BUCHESVĂRĂ TEMPLE
KORAVANGALA
KUTASTAMBHA
(LATINA)
KUTASTAMBA
(PHAMSANA)
D
EMBEDDED AEDICULAR COMPONENTS
IN A NAGARA (SHEKHARI) PRASADA: SASBAHU
TEMPLE, NAGDA, RAJASTHAN
(TENTH CENTURY)
E
LATINA
AEDICULE
PHAMSANA
AEDICULE
VALABHI
AEDICULE
NAGARA AEDICULAR COMPONENTS
F
SHIKHARA
CHADYA
ANTARAPATRA
KAPOTALI
KAPOTALI
BHARANA
GHATA
LASUNA WITH
UDGAMA (PEDIMENT)
JANGHA
MANCHIKA (PEDESTAL)
KAPOTALI
ANTARAPATRA
VEDIBANDHA
KUMBHA
NARAPITHA
GAJAPITHA
GRASAPATTI
KARNAKA
PITHA
JADYAKUMBHA
BHITTA
NAGORA MOULDINGS, IN A KUTASTAMBHA
FROM THE SMALLER SHIVA TEMPLE AT
KIRADU, RAJASTHAM.

A. Lakshmana temple, Sirpur (*c.* early seventh century). See p. 765

B. Galaganatha temple, Pattadakal, shikara (mid-eighth century). See p.765

C. Ghateshvara temple, Badoli (tenth century). See p.765

The Latina mode

The Latina (p. 767A) is unitary, not composite: its form, unlike the other modes, is not essentially an aggregation of aedicules. The sides of the unitary shikhara (spire) are made up of horizontal mouldings, representing the overhanging thatched eaves of a storeyed divine palace, and sometimes, in earlier examples, sheltering blind colonnades. On the summit platform (skandha, 'shoulder'), a cylindrical shaft (griva, 'neck'), marking the vertical axis, supports the 'cogged wheel' or amalaka ('myrobolan fruit'). Over this, the kalasha (vase-finial) marks the top of the vertical axis.

In the corner segments of the shikhara, the eaves-like strata are punctuated, every few courses, by amalaka forms. The presence of these crowning elements in these positions is a survival from an earlier stage, before a process of fusion had taken place – a 'proto-Latina' form which was multi-aedicular as in the **Lakshmana Temple, Sirpur, Madhya Pradesh** (p. 764A).

Latina temples erected at **Aihole, Karnataka**, and elsewhere in the Deccan during the seventh and eighth centuries by the Early Chalukyas, alongside Dravida and other kinds of temple, are among the earliest fully evolved examples of the mode. In western India the Latina had its heyday between the eighth and tenth centuries, at centres such as **Roda, Gujarat** and **Osian, Rajasthan**. The tenth-century Ghateshvara temple at **Badoli** (or Baroli), **Rajasthan**, is a lavish example (p. 764C). Soon after this, the Latina began to be seen in that region as inferior to the Shekhari, which would be used for temples of any pretension.

The Orissan masons, however, remained loyal to the Latina. Development can be traced from the robust **Parasurameshvara temple** (*c.* 600) to the exquisite **Mukteshvara** (ninth/tenth century), both at **Bhubaneshwar**. Later Orissan works include the three most monumental examples of the Latina: the **Lingaraja temple, Bhubaneshwar** (late eleventh century), **Jagannatha temple, Puri** (twelfth century), and the lavishly sculpted **Sun Temple** (or temple of Surya, the sun god), **Konarak** (thirteenth century). The shikhara at Konarak is no longer standing; those of the Lingaraja and Jagannatha are respectively about 37 m (120 ft) and 57 m (185 ft) high.

The more evolved forms of Latina prasada have wall-projections (with or without recesses in between) numbering three, five or even seven one each side, running up into the shikhara segments, and increasingly bulging out along the cardinal axes (p. 764C). Although the shrine as a whole is unitary, secondary aedicules may appear in the wall projections – most importantly the central ones, enshrining, the principal cult images of the exterior – and in the recesses of the shikhara.

An essential role in the formal dynamics of this kind of temple is played by the horseshoe arch motif, called, in this context, the gavaksha ('cow eye'). This appears as dormers in the layered eaves of the shikhara, in the pediments of the minor aedicules (p. 763E), and in the sukhanasa ('parrot's beak') projection which emerges from the front of the tower, over the antarala (antechamber). With its window, solar, and lotus associations, the motif carries a powerful symbolism of transition between the inner and outer worlds, reinforced by the patterns into which it is woven. A widely used configuration, consisting of a complete gavaksha resting on two half-gavakshas, has been noted earlier. It has been seen, in relation to Cave 10 at Ellora, how the idea of gavakshas splitting apart expresses a process of sequential emergence. This concept is developed in a particularly sculptural way in Latina works of the Early Chalukyas at **Alampur, Andhra Pradesh**, and **Pattadakal, Karnataka** (p. 764B).

The Valabhi mode

Within the Nagara language, the Valabhi (p. 767B) is the earliest alternative mode to the Latina, and the only one not to include the Latina shikhara as an essential component. Instead, it is made up of aedicular components crowned by gavaksha patterns.

One way of developing the whole-and-two-halves gavaksha configuration, already described, is to show enshrined within it a smaller version of the same arrangement, perhaps with a yet smaller repetition inside that. Such a concept is the basis of a Valabhi shrine. This is rectangular on plan, with a barrel-roofed superstructure running at right-angles to the direction of entry to the sanctuary. It is the two ends of the rectangle which lend themselves to an elevational treatment based on a diminishing series of gavaksha patterns, inscribed one in another, projecting progressively further forward, giving the impression of an outward de-telescoping at the same time as a lateral drifting apart of the split elements.

Examples of this kind of temple belong mainly to the eighth century, including the best known, the **Telika Mandir, Gwalior, Madhya Pradesh**, and the **Vaital Deul, Bhubaneshwar, Orissa**. Simple versions are found at **Jageshvara**, in the Himalayan foothills (p. 783C). Here the form can also be seen in the sukhanasas of Latina temples and, unusually boldly, as emergent shrine-images on the remaining three sides of Latina shikharas.

The Shekhari mode

The Shekhari mode of Nagara appeared during the tenth century in western and central India, where for

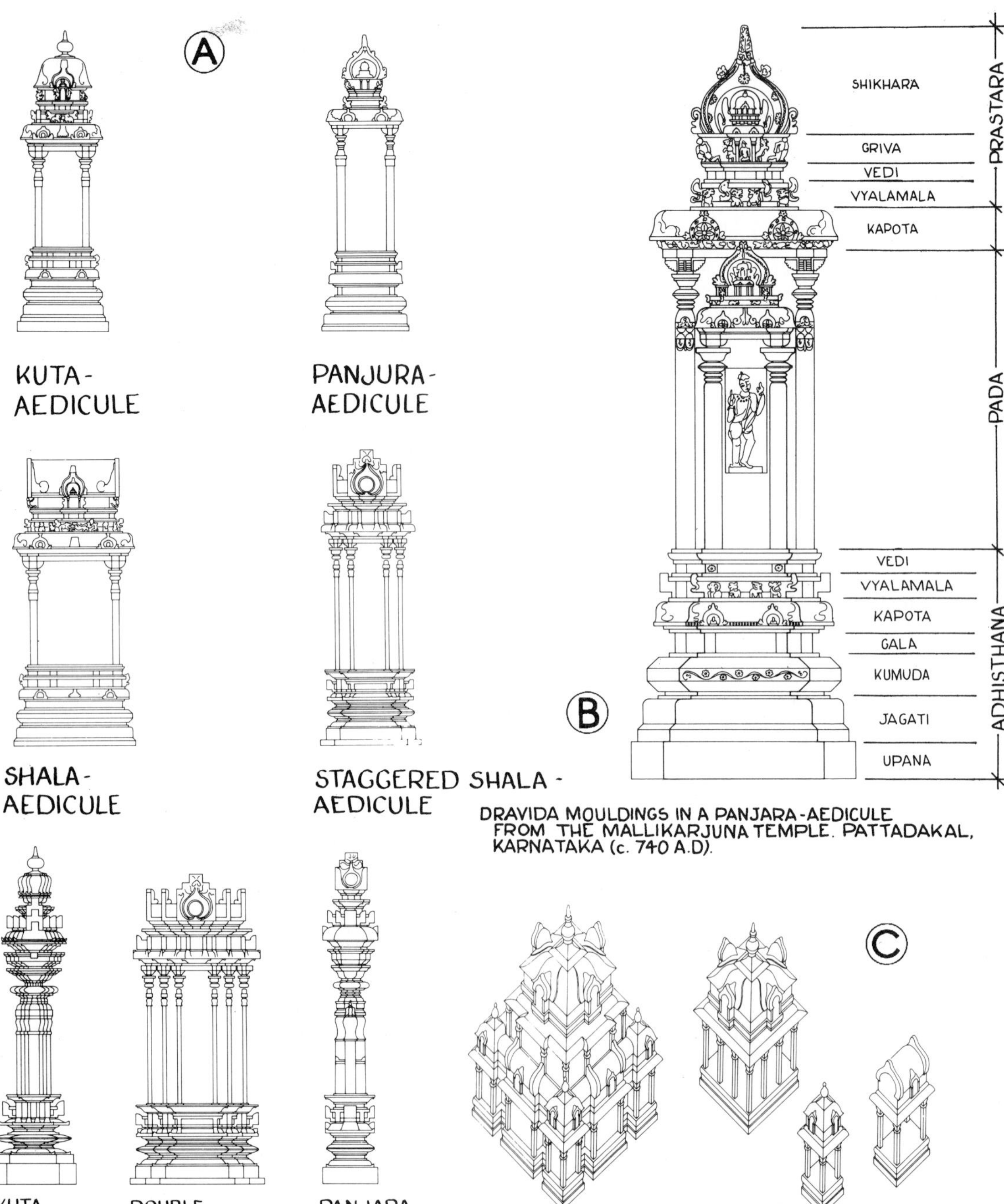

DRAVIDA AEDICULAR COMPONENTS

DRAVIDA MOULDINGS IN A PANJARA-AEDICULE FROM THE MALLIKARJUNA TEMPLE. PATTADAKAL, KARNATAKA (c. 740 A.D).

EMBEDDED AEDICULAR COMPONENTS IN A DRAVIDA VIMANANA: THE BHUJANGESHVARA TEMPLE, BHAVANASI SANGAM, ANDHRA PRADESH (9th CENTURY).

NAGARA TYPES

LATINA-
KRAKOTAKESHVARA TEMPLE, NARESAR, MADHYA PRADESH. (8th CENTURY)

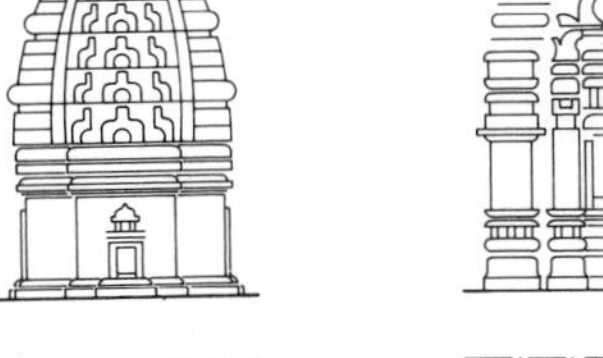

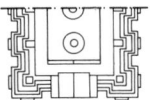

VALABHI-
VAITAL DEUL, BHUVANESRARA, ORISSA. (8th CENTURY)

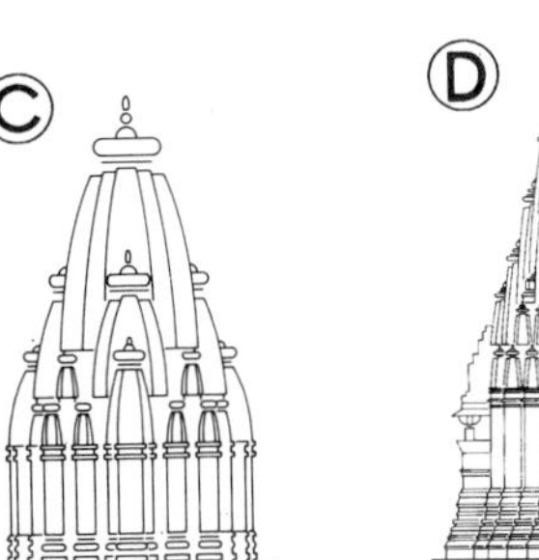

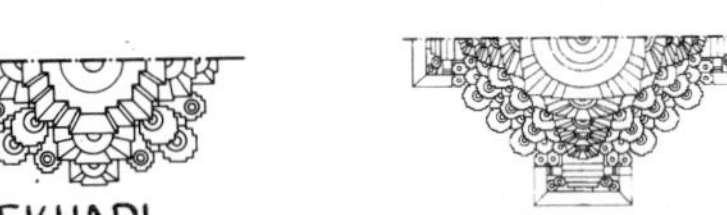

SHEKHARI-
(EXPANDING SQUARE PLAN) BAIJANATHA MAHADEVA TEMPLE. BADNAVAR, MADHYA PRADESH (C. 1100)

SHEKHARI-
(STEPPED DIAMOND PLAN) KANDARIYA MAHADERA TEMPLE, KHAJURAHO, MADHYA PRADESH (11th CENTURY)

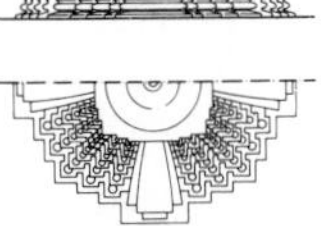

BHUMIJA-
(EXPANDING SQUARE PLAN) GONDESHVARA TEMPLE, SINNAR. MAHARASHTRA (12th CENTURY)

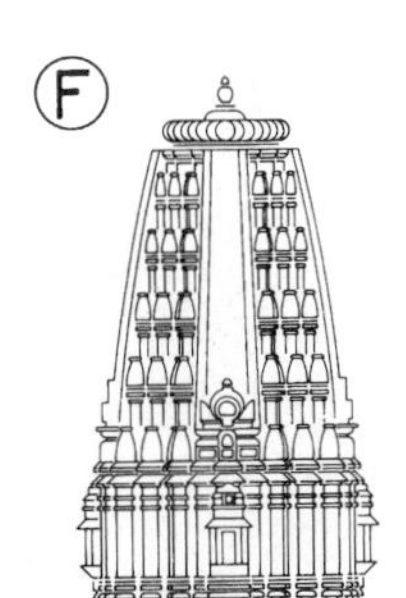
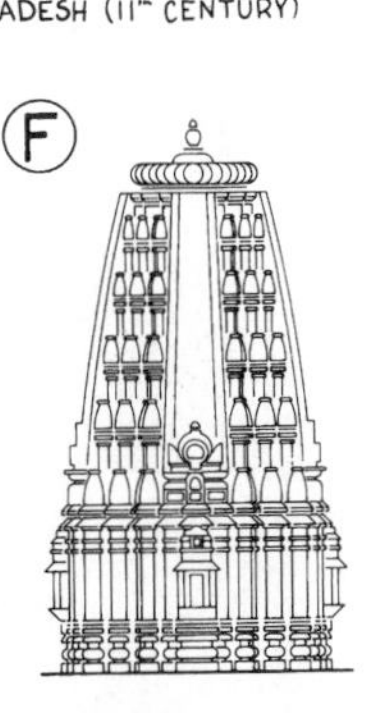

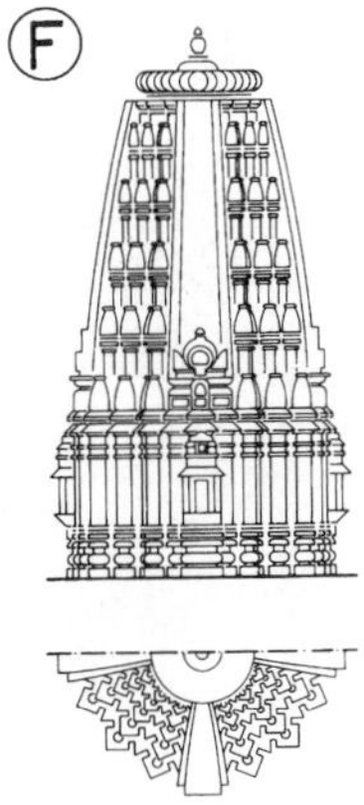

BHUMIJA- (STELLATE PLAN) MAHAKALESHVARA TEMPLE No. 2. UN, MADHYA, PRADESH. (11th CENTURY)

DRAVIDA TYPES

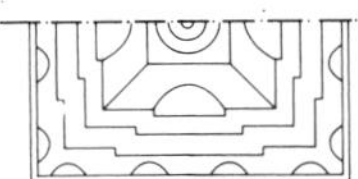

ALPA VIMANA
SHIVA TEMPLE, ENADI. TAMIL NADU. (10th CENTURY)

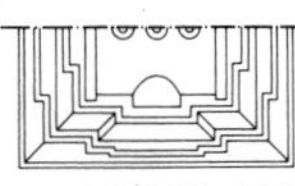

SHALA-TOPPED SADVARGA ALPA VIMANA
SUBSIDIARY SHRINE AT THE KAILASA TEMPLE, ELLORA, MAHARASHTRA. (8th CENTURY)

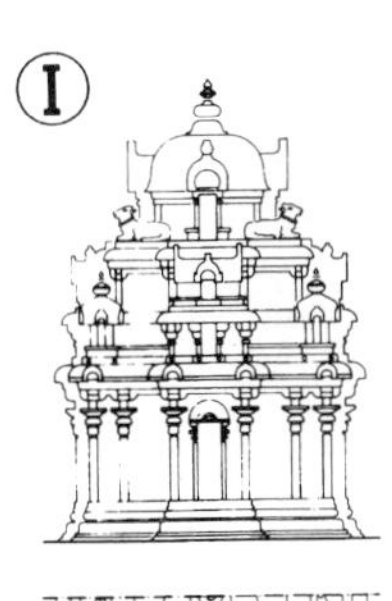

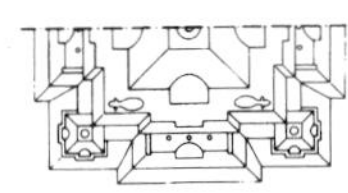

A DRAVIDA TWO-TIER TYPE
AGASTISHVARA TEMPLE, KILAIYUR, TAMIL NADU. (9th CENTURY)

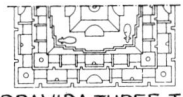

A DRAVIDA THREE-TIER TYPE
BHOGANDISHRARA TEMPLE, NANDI, KARNATAKA. (9th CENTURY)

LATE KARNATA DRAVIDA
(EXPANDING SQUARE PLAN) MAHADEVA TEMPLE, ITTAGI, KARNATAKA. (12th CENTURY)

LATE KARNATA DRAVIDA
(STELLATE PLAN) KESHAVA TEMPLE, SOMNATHPUR, KARNATAKA, (13th CENTURY)

A. Ambamatha temple, Jagat (960). See p. 769

B. Vishvanatha temple, Khajuraho (1002). See p.769

C. Jasmalnath Mahadeva temple, Asoda (twelfth century). See p.769

D. Kandariya Mahadeva temple, Khajuraho (mid-eleventh century). See p.769

centuries it remained the predominant type among the grander temples. In Orissa the Latina remained the principal type of shrine, but the Shekhari was not unknown (**Rajarani temple, Bhubaneshwar**, of the eleventh century).

In the simplest form of Shekhari prasada (p. 763D) based on a staggered square plan with three projections, a central Latina prasada form is buttressed centrally on each of its free sides (the three sides not facing the mandapa) by half a smaller Latina prasada form. Conceptually, these half-prasadas are whole ones, half-embedded, emerging along the cardinal axes of the shrine. At the corners, quarter-embedded, are kuta-stambhas, pillar forms crowned by Latina shikharas.

The exquisite little **Ambamatha temple, Jagat, Rajasthan** (p. 768A), dedicated in 960, is basically of the simple Shekhari form, with the addition of three secondary aedicular components fronting each central projection, in the form of two slender kuta-stambhas flanking a projection crowned by a miniature mandapa (hall).

Characteristically, evolution of the mode takes the form of a centrifugal unfurling, where the simplest type to composition becomes the upper portion of the superstructure – the whole, as it were, proliferating downwards. This is is illustrated in the mulaprasadas of the **Lakshmana** and **Vishvanatha temples, Khajuraho, Madhya Pradesh** (dated respectively 954 and 1002) (p. 768B). In both cases the simple Shekhari form sits over a bottom tier of five projections, the corner and intermediate projections being kuta-stambhas, while the central ones – pushing past and overlapping the kuta-stambhas on either side – are balconied porches, with gavaksha pediments, admitting light into the ambulatory around the sanctum.

Essentially the same composition, on a small scale, can be seen in the subsidiary shrines of the **Jasmalnath Mahadeva temple, Asoda, Gujarat** (p. 768C). Here the main shrine, still with the simple Shekhari form as its upper portion, shows further degrees of complexity: additional embedded shikharas emerging sequentially from each face, and quarter-shikharas nestling beside the half-shikharas. Conceptually these belong to three-quarters-embedded prasada forms, and imply that the pattern of the whole, of a form reproducing itself along its cardinal axes, repeats itself within the parts.

The eleventh-century **Kandariya Mahadeva, Khajuraho** (pp. 767F, 768D), has a central series of four emergent shikharas on each axis (thus five shikharas forms, including the central shikhara), in addition to quarter-shikharas and the shikharas crowning kutastambhas. The latter are based on overlapping squares, since the plan has developed to the extent that the centre has pushed far forward, the corners falling back into line with the other projections. Thus the plan is a kind of stepped diamond.

The Bhumija mode

Less widespread than the Shekhari, the Bhumija mode originated in Central India during the eleventh century. Like the Shekhari, the Bhumija can be seen as a development of the Latina (pp. 767E,F, 771A,B). The central spine of the shikhara is left intact, while intermediate and corner segments, together with the corresponding wall-projections, are replaced by vertical chains of kuta-stambhas. The central projection, though too wide to be pillar-like, continues the stambha-mouldings of the other projections, and is crowned, at the base of the spine, by a giant gavaksha.

A staggered square plan (sometimes of the stepped diamond type) can have five or seven projections, and accordingly there will be three or five vertical chains of kuta-stambhas between the central projections of two adjacent sides. The mode lends itself perfectly to the stellate plan, with the kuta-stambhas located on the principle of the rotated square (p. 763B), but retaining orthogonal central projections with corresponding spines in the shikhara.

Ancient Malwa (eastern Madhya Pradesh) and Seunadesha (western Maharashtra) were the true homeland of the Bhumija, the earliest dated example, and the most magnificent, being the **Udayeshvara temple, Udayapur, Madhya Pradesh**, built between 1059 and 1080 and based on a stellate plan of thirty-two points (p. 771A). Twelfth-century orthogonal examples in Maharashtra are the **Gondeshvara temple, Sinnar**, and the **Mahadeva temple, Jhodga** (p. 771B). Some significant Bhumija works are found in Rajasthan, such as the **Mahanaleshvara temple, Menal** (late eleventh century) and a few variants appear as far south as Karnataka and Andhra Pradesh. The **Chennakeshava temple, Belur, Karnataka** (1117), is a Bhumija composition, though this is no longer immediately obvious because there is no surviving superstructure.

Dravida Temples

The emergence of South Indian or Dravida temple architecture from earlier, pan-Indian traditions can be traced from Ajanta and the Buddhist traditions of Andhra Pradesh to sixth-century rock-cut architecture in the south. Through the seventh and early eighth centuries, the full development of a Dravida 'language' for structural temples can be observed in the area around Badami in northern Karnataka, capital of the Early Chalukyas, followed by related developments in Andhra. In parallel, with much interaction, the Tamil version of the Dravida came to fruition under the Pallavas.

Dravida temple architecture also spread to Kerala, and, under the Cholas, the predominant dynasty in Tamil Nadu between the ninth and thirteenth centuries, to Sri Lanka. The Tamil Dravida tradition, while attaining unprecedented degrees of scale and teeming complexity in the planning of its temple complexes, is conservative in architectural form and detail.

In Karnataka, however, the same kind of evolution takes place as in northern traditions. By the beginning of the eleventh century, the Dravida forms had been transformed to the extent that they are no longer immediately recognisable as Dravida. Scholars have therefore suggested that the later Karnata-Dravida may be the Vesara, the elusive third main category cited in the canonical texts, along with Nagara and Dravida. The later Karnata-Dravida tradition spread to Andhra Pradesh, and was known in Maharashtra. By the early fourteenth century, following Muslim invasions, it died out. From 1336 the Vijayanagara empire re-established Hindu rule in South India for 200 years. Rather than reviving the regional Karnata idiom, which for its later intricacies had found the perfect medium in a fine-grained schist, Vijayanagara turned mainly to the Tamil tradition which worked, more massively, in granite.

The simplest form of Dravida temple is the alpa vimana ('minor shrine'), with roots traceable back to one of the shrine types of Buddhist Gandhara (p. 767G, cf. 752C). Derived from wood-and-thatch prototypes, this type when rendered in masonry has a moulded base, walls – usually with pilasters – enclosing the square sanctum, an overhanging canopy or roll cornice (kapota), and a crowning domed pavilion (kuta), usually square. Alternative alpa vimana forms are rectangular, crowned by a barrel-roofed pavilion (shala), and apsidal (gajapristha, 'elephant-backed'), crowned by an apsidal shala.

An early example of a kuta-topped alpa vimana (p. 772A), built around the beginning of the seventh century, is a small, sandstone shrine, fronted by a porch, south of the Ravana Phadi cave temple at **Aihole, Karnataka**. The depiction of timber and thatch forms is already brought about through a language essentially of masonry, with an established sequence of superimposed mouldings. Aedicules carved in relief either side of the cave temple represent the same form. An alpa vimana crowned by a circular kuta is shown on p. 775B. Examples of the apsidal form of alpa vimana, possibly considerably older than the Aihole shrine, but with the same moulding sequence in the superstructure, are found at **Ter, Maharashtra**, and **Cherzala, Andhra Pradesh**. Both are brick buildings and probably originally Buddhist.

The basic alpa vimana types become the superstructures, the 'upper temples', of more elaborate shrines. Most simply, the alpa vimana, rather compressed, sits directly over the roll cornice (kapota) of the ground storey, the whole remaining uni-aedicular in concept. Shala-topped vimanas of this kind, respectively early and mid/late eighth century, are the **Mahendravarmeshvara shrine** at the **Kailasanatha temple, Kanchipuram** and the axial subsidiary shrines of the **Kailasa, Ellora** (pp. 767H, 773C). In more complex conceptions, the alpa vimana remains the usual form for the uppermost storey. Thus, the top storeys of the vimanas of the **Shore Temple, Mahabalipuram, Tamil Nadu** (early eighth century) (p. 773A), or of the **Muvarkovil, Kodumbalur, Tamil Nadu** (ninth century), correspond to kuta-topped alpa vimanas, with octagonal and square domes respectively. An entirely circular alpa vimana forms the third and crowning tier of the ninth-century **Vijaya Cholishvara temple, Narttamalai** (p. 775B).

Sculpted figures – bulls or dwarves – sit in the 'neck' (griva) of the last three examples. Often this position is occupied by a parapet, in the form of a hara, a chain of kuta and shala pavilions. The 'Five Rathas' at **Mahabalipuram**, carved from solid granite around the middle of the seventh century, are like a catalogue of different shrine forms. In the apsidal Nakula-Sahadeva ratha the 'upper temple' is an apsidal alpa vimana, with a hara necklace. Arjuna's ratha is a square, two-storey vimana, the upper part being a square alpa vimana, with hara, and an octagonal dome. The lower storey (apart from the porch on the west side) has projections in the wall corresponding to the kutas and shalas of the parapet, as in the upper two stages of the Dharmaraja ratha, a square, three-storey vimana.

This correspondence of wall projections with parapet pavilions is, in fact, the norm among Dravida temples, and needs to be recognised in order to understand their multi-aedicular concept and composition. A projection, with pilasters at the corners, crowned by a kuta or a shala, is an image of a slender alpa vimana. Alpa vimanas of these proportions, descended from the Gandharan shrine (p. 752C) are often depicted in narrative relief carvings, where they are meant to represent wooden shrines, with a decorated post at each corner to support a thatched canopy and an upper pavilion. A shrine of this form, housing an image of Vishnu, is seen in the **Arjuna's Penance relief**, carved on a huge boulder at **Mahabalipuram** (mid-seventh century) (p. 756B). Here the timber detailing has already become abstracted into mouldings, following conventions established by this time in masonry temples, where the wooden corner posts are represented by narrow pilasters. (The universal Dravida pilaster mirrors, in the shapes and sequence of its moulded parts, the pillar type used most widely in Dravida temples (p. 756C). The earliest types of shrine-image or aedicule to be used as compositional units correspond to kuta- and shala-topped alpa vimanas. They may be referred to respectively as 'kuta-aedicules' and 'shala-aedicules' (p. 766A). A little later to appear are the 'panjara-aedicules'. These compositional units, interlinked into 'cloisters' around the storeys (talas) of pyramidal

A. Udayeshvara temple, Udayapur (1059–80). See p.769

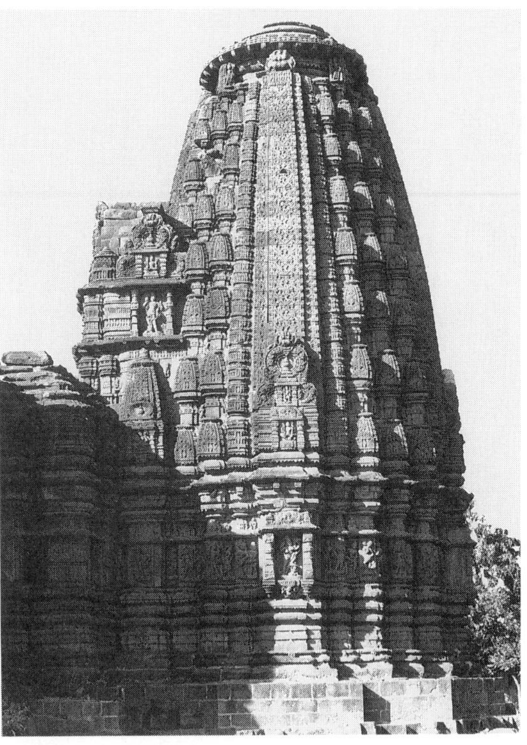

B. Mahadeva temple, Jhodga (twelfth century). See p.769

C. Surya temple, Ranakpur (fifteenth century). See p. 779

A. Ravalaphadi cave, Aihole (late sixth century), with a small Dravida shrine (early seventh century) in the foreground. See p.770

B. Virupaksha temple, Pattadakal (*c.* 740). See pp. 761, 774

A. Shore temple, Mahabalipuram (eighth century). See pp. 770, 774

B. Airavateshvara temple, Darasuram (twelfth century). See p. 774

C. Kailasa temple, Ellora (mid to late eighth century). See pp. 761, 770

Dravida shrines, are conceived three-dimensionally, as if embedded in the wall (p. 766C). It should not be difficult, with the aid of pages 766 and 767, to understand the aedicular compositions of the temples illustrated. Occasionally the pavilions of a parapet, without taking account of the wall below, are the full aedicule forms (pp. 773A,B). The parapet is called 'sadvarga' ('of seven divisions').

Within the primary aedicules of a Dravida temple, emerge secondary aedicules, in the wall zone, often enshrining sculpted deity niches. A monument such as the great eighth-century **Virupaksha temple, Pattadakal, Karnataka** (p. 772B), contains a whole family of different aedicular forms at different scales. The moulding sequence that had become established is shown on page 766B: in the parapet, the shikhara moulding represents a thatched roof, the griva ('neck') the habitable verandah, the vedi a railing, the vyalamala (band of mythical vyalas and makaras) the ends of joists over the kapota, a thatched eaves. The sequence shown in the moulded plinth became the norm in Karnataka (pp. 772B, 775A, 777B), while in Tamil Nadu this element was of various types.

The Chola monarchs built the biggest vimanas, including the **Brihadeshvara** temples **of Tanjore** (or Thanjavur), **Tamil Nadu** (*c.* 1010) (p. 776B), **Gangaicondacholapuram, Tamil Nadu** (mid-eleventh century), and the **Airavateshvara temple, Darasuram,** (mid-twelfth century) (p. 773B). The Tanjore vimana is about 66 m high. It was as entrances to this temple precinct, aligned on its eastward axis, that the first two monumental gopuras (gopuram in Tamil) were erected (pp. 778A, 780B). The gopura form has its origin in early Indian barrel-roofed gateways, depicted in reliefs such as those at Sanchi, and in South India takes on a form that is essentially that of a shala-topped shrine, with a passageway in the middle of the long side. A simple gopura such as the late tenth century one at **Laddigam** (p. 778E) corresponds to a shala-topped alpa vimana, which becomes the uppermost tier of multi-storeyed compositions.

In the Dravida tradition of Karnataka, and in the temples which this influenced in Andhra Pradesh, tendencies already apparent in the early Chalukya works at Pattadakal continued, over the ensuing three centuries, to transform Dravida shrine forms into the form sometimes labelled 'Vesara'. 'Vesara' means 'mule', and late Karnata Dravida temples do exhibit some Nagara-seeming characteristics – but this is because they evolve in the same way, their axial projections pushing further and further out, their components proliferating and fragmenting. The underlying tiered pyramid, and the aedicule and moulding types, remain Dravida, however much transformed.

Increasingly stepped forward walls are accompanied by a proliferation of offsets within individual components. In particular, the staggered shala-aedicule developed around the ninth century is further transformed into a double-staggered form (pp. 775A, 777B). Positioned centrally, this element is essential to the complex, dynamic character of late Karnata Dravida vimanas. Conceptually it is a configuration of five aedicules – a panjara-aedicule (that is, an end-on shala-aedicule) at the centre, with two shala-aedicules emerging one from the other on either side. This 'double-staggered shala-aedicule', used already by the turn of the eleventh century, was the first and most widespread of many ingenious composite, interpenetrating forms.

One other type of aedicular component should be mentioned here: the Dravida kutastambha (p. 766C, left). Consisting of a kuta crowning a stambha, or pillar form, it is used principally for intermediate projections, as in the west vimana of the **Kedareshvara temple, Belgave** (p. 775A, left) and the **Mahadeva temple, Ittagi, Karnataka** (p. 767K). Here, in four identical storeys, the kutastambhas are between corner kuta-aedicules and central double-staggered shala-aedicules. In the latter, a looped torana (archway) pouring out from each central nasi (horseshoe dormer) creates a cascade down the face of the superstructure.

From the early twelfth century, the complexity of Karnata Dravida temples was supplemented under the Hoysala dynasty in southern Karnataka by an ornateness, chiselled in chloritic schist or 'soapstone'. The Hoysalas developed varieties of stellate vimana, on the principle of the rotated square (pp. 763B, 777A,B). The most usual form is seen in the three vimanas of the thirteenth-century **Keshava temple, Somnathpur, Karnataka**, each based on a sixteen-pointed star, with four storeys, and with kuta-aedicules used throughout (p. 777A). The twin vimanas of the great **Hoysaleshvara Temple, Halebid** (begun 1121), are also stellate, but with orthogonal projections on the cardinal axes. The superstructures have not survived.

Even in this region, well south of the Deccan, Nagara forms were known, and sometimes built full size. The **Keshava Temple, Belur**, as already noted (p. 769), is actually Bhumija, and miniature versions of this mode appear in the shrines which line the steps leading to its mandapa (p. 776A). Other Nagara experiments in miniature appear, along with Dravida and other modes, in the increasingly complex shrine 'models' used as niche canopies, or secondary aedicules, within the walls of Karnata Dravida temples (pp. 775A, 777B).

Other Modes, Hybrids and Regional Types

Beginning in the seventh century, the Early Chalukyas and their successors erected a number of massively built 'hall temples' at **Aihole, Karnataka**, as well as Nagara and Dravida shrines. The sanctum

A. Kedareshvara temple, Belgave (*c.* early twelfth century). See p.774

B. Vijaya Cholishvara temple, Narttamalai (ninth century). See p. 770

A. Keshava temple, Belur, steps to mandapa (twelfth century). See p.774

B. Brihadeshvara temple,Thanjavur (eleventh century). See p.774

A. Keshava temple, Somnathpur (thirteenth century). See p.774

B. Bucheshvara temple, Koravangala (1173). See p.774

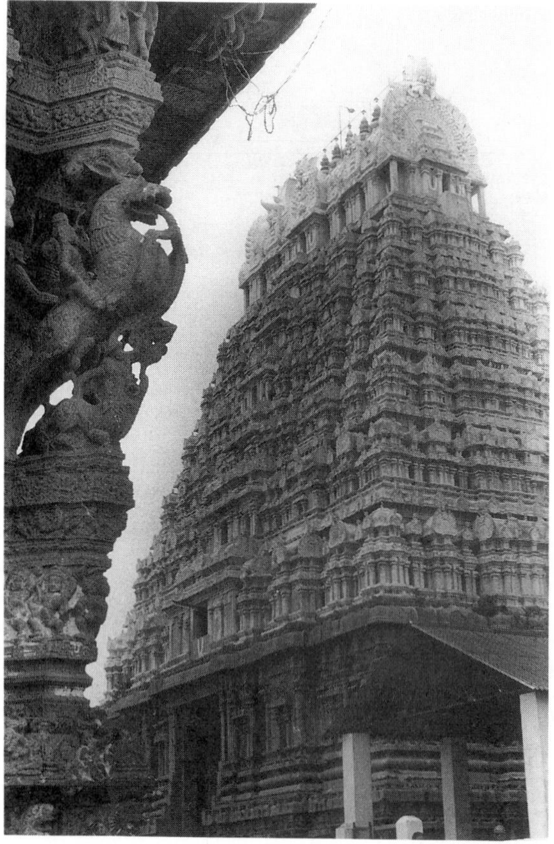

A. Ekambareshvara temple, Kanchipuram: south gopura (1509). See pp. 762, 774

B. Chergaon temple, Chamba. See p.779

C. The old temple at Visavada (seventh century). See p.779

D. Golden Temple, Amritsar (1766). See p.781

E. East gopura, Nilakanteshvara temple, Laddigam (tenth century). See p.774

was set within a rectangular pillared hall. Best known of these is the **Lad Khan temple**. Apsidal shrines were also built at and around this site, notably the **Durga temple, Aihole** (*c.* 700), with its external ambulatory verandah in addition to an interior pradakshinapatha.

With its Nagara tower, and mixture throughout of Nagara and Dravida elements, this is an early example of deliberate hybridity. Various experiments in mixture and synthesis were made in the Deccan in the ensuing centuries, most subtly, perhaps, in the twelfth-century **Someshvara temple, Lakshmeshvara**, which, without using a single Nagara detail, arranges Karnata-Dravida elements in a Nagara (Shekhari) manner. Within northern traditions, different modes of Nagara may be mixed, as in the Shekhari-Bhumija combinations found in the Surya temples of **Jhalrapatan** (late eleventh century) and **Ranakpur** (fifteenth century), both in **Rajasthan**. Both have the radiating kuta-stambha chains of the Bhumija, with the 'half shikharas' of the Shekhari on the principal projections. The **Ranakpur shrine** has, conceptually, eight principal projections instead of the usual four, occurring on the diagonal as well as the cardinal axes (p. 771C).

A widespread alternative mode is the Phamsana, with a pyramidal superstructure made up of eaves-mouldings. Rock-cut representations testify to its early origins. Found from the Deccan northwards to the Himalayas (p. 778C), and from Gujarat to Orissa, Phamsana shrines have Nagara or Dravida traits depending on region and date. The mode was predominant in the Saurashtra region of Gujarat between the sixth and eighth centuries; examples are temples at **Gop** and **Visavada** (p. 778C). The Jain **Anantanatha temple, Lakshmeshvara** (*c.* 1200), illustrates how, in the Deccan, the Phamsana became a modest alternative to the Dravida; its dome, central spine, pilasters and plinth are Karnata Dravida, but note the Nagara wall-shrine. Even more than as a shrine, the pyramidal Phamsana shape is familiar through its adoption in northern traditions as the usual shape for a mandapa (hall), either unitary, or as a constellation of Phamsana aedicules or kuta-stambhas (pp. 764C, 768B).

A shrine form not unrelated to the Phamsana developed in Kashmir between the seventh and tenth centuries, flavoured by a legacy of contact with Western classical architecture. The **Surya temple, Martand, Jammu and Kashmir** (*c.* 725–750) is a monumental early example, the **Shiva temple, Pandrethan**, in the middle of a small tank, being a well preserved shrine of two centuries later (p. 783A). An aedicule type with a steep-pitched gable containing a cusped trefoil – the ancient 'Gandharan chaitya hall cross section' (p. 752D) – gives these Kashmiri monuments an uncannily Gothic feeling.

In Orissa there appeared a mode that could be classified as the regional version of Dravida, rectangular, organised in talas (storeys) in the southern way, with its own forms of kutastambha, panjarastambha and shalastambha, and a shala-like crowning dome. A fine example is the late tenth-century **Varahi temple, Chaurasi, Orissa** (p. 783B). The central projections in the mulaprasada of the **Mukteshvara temple, Bhubaneshwar**, represent the emergent ends of Chaurasi-type shrines.

Temples with steep, tiled roofs developed in areas of high rainfall and plentiful timber. In Kerala and coastal Karnataka, Dravida-related stone structures were given wooden roofs, often in several tiers. Examples from Kerala include circular temples with conical roofs, such as the **Niramankara temple, Nemam** (*c.* 1050–1100), and two shrines within the **Vadakkunnatha temple, Trichur, Kerala** (twelfth century and later). Wooden temples with tiered roofs are also characteristic of the Himalayan regions. Here the highest roof, over the sanctum, is often conical, as in the **Chergaon temple, Chamba, Himachal Pradesh** (p. 778B), and the **Mahadeva temple, Behna, Himachal Pradesh** (sixteenth to seventeenth century). These temples relate in general type to the 'pagoda temples' of Nepal, already mentioned – a type used for Hindu as well as Buddhist shrines.

In the sixteenth century, a revival of Hinduism in Bengal, following two centuries of Muslim rule, led to a new and varied temple types, built in brick with terracotta ornament. Examples are the **Shyama Rama temple, Bishnupur, West Bengal** (1643), and the **Vasudeva temple, Bansberia, West Bengal** (1679). These buildings combined the Islamic structural techniques – arches, vaults, domes – with shapes derived from the thatched roofs of the local domestic vernacular, most conspicuously a form in which ridge and eaves follow an arched curve.

While indigenous craftsmen left their stamp on the varieties of Indo-Islamic architecture, it was by no means only in Bengal that Islamic influences affected Hindu temple architecture, especially during Moghul rule. Domes and pointed arches were the most conspicuous borrowing, whether 'true' (with radiating voussoirs), corbelled or, in the case of arches, pierced in a solid slab. Cusped arches became, by the eighteenth century, a form constantly repeated in all kinds of monumental architecture. This form had a long ancestry in India, stemming from 'chaitya hall cross-section' imagery, passing through lobed torana (archway) motifs, and readily assimilated to the 'Islamic' pointed arch. Cusped pointed arches are seen in the Govindadeva temple, and the other late-sixteenth-century red sandstone temples of Vrindavan, Uttar Pradesh.

Through contact with Islamic traditions, new forms of aedicule entered the Indian repertory. Domed kiosks, with slender stone posts and overhanging chajjas (canopies of slabs), already cluster round domes on the tombs of the Delhi Sultanate (thirteenth and fourteenth centuries). The Moghuls and Rajputs,

A. Great Temple, Madurai (*c.* mid seventeenth century). See p.774

B. Brihadeshvara Temple, Thanjavur (eleventh century with later plasterwork on superstructure): inner gopura. See p. 774

in their palace architecture, began to add arch shapes, pierced in slabs, between the posts. Through contact with Persia, domes became bulbous. Another aedicule type was derived from the curved Bengali roof, the 'bangaldar' roof. Understanding aedicules, Hindu temple builders readily incorporated these novelties into their work.

A monument closely related to late Moghul and Rajput architecture is the **Golden Temple** at **Amritsar, Punjab** (late eighteenth century and later), the principal shrine of the Sikhs (p. 778D).

Secular Architecture

City planning

In the traditional Indian theory of city planning there is no clear distinction between secular and sacred uses and forms. The shastras, the ancient theoretical treatises, prescribe various types of mandala, or gridded, centralised diagram, as the basis for city planning, as for temples. A social hierarchy, with castes or professions occupying allotted areas, is overlaid on the cosmological-theological hierarchy. As with temples, the model seems to have been more metaphoric than literal, but cardinal axes marked by roads are characteristic, along with temples and royal palaces occupying central locations, and areas inhabited by particular professions.

However, little survives, to compare practice with theory, earlier than the remains of the great city of **Vijayanagara**, spread across a spectacular landscape of hills and granite boulders, around the present-day village of Hampi, Karnataka. The empire of Vijayanagara ('City of Victory') was established at the end of the fourteenth century. The cosmopolitan character of the capital is reflected in the combination of Hindu and Islamic forms in the surviving monuments, which include an impressive range of elephant stables. A Portuguese visitor in the 1520s concluded that the capital was the 'best provided city in the world', but in 1565, following a disastrous battle against an alliance of Muslim forces, the city was sacked, and the empire swiftly declined.

Excavations in recent years have shown how the planning of Vijayanagara is conceived as a mandala, without following a strictly geometrical form. At the heart of the city, beyond a number of lines of fortification, was a walled urban core containing a separate sacred centre, with several important temples, and walled royal centre. Central to the whole scheme, in the middle of the royal centre on a north-south axial route, was the Ramachandra temple. It was to Rama, hero of the Ramayana epic, that the kings most often compared themselves, as upholders of cosmic law and guarantors of prosperity. A mythical geography pervaded the city and its landscape, relating places and natural features to the Ramayana story and other mythologies.

The place often seen as the archetypal Indian city is **Jaipur, Rajasthan**. In fact, as a city planned and built at one go, it is unique; the only comparably planned settlements surviving are a few villages built for Brahmins on gridded mandala plans. Rajput King Jai Singh of Amber (1699–1743) moved his capital from nearby Amber in 1727. In conscious reinterpretation of shastric injunctions, a nine-square mandala is defined by a grid of principal streets, each square constituting a ward, and subdivided by a grid of lesser streets. The central square is occupied by the royal palace. For reasons of topography and defence, the 'perfect' mandala, shown on drawings before building had begun, was modified: the square at the north-west corner was omitted, an additional square being substituted to the south-east. The rich, almost theatrical architecture of Jaipur was given stylistic uniformity, partly through the operation of planning codes. State controls over shops ensured their conformity, along with the provision of shady colonnades, the roofs of which served as public viewing terraces for royal processions. A sense of unity is enhanced by the uniform material: rendered rubble painted pink in imitation of sandstone – though originally the colour may have been cream, like the palace at nearby Amber. Quarters are inhabited, in the traditional way, by single jatis or occupations, so that, even today, the shops in a given area sell the same goods.

Jaipur functions, no doubt, because its planned form fitted cultural patterns already long established. A richly layered spatial hierarchy, making social hierarchies concrete, is apparent in many cities of north India and Pakistan that, in contrast to Jaipur, have grown in a gradual and organic fashion. **Ahmadabad, Gujarat**, for centuries a thriving centre of the textile trade, is a perfect example. Though this state capital is a modern metropolis, its old walled city, housing a complex fabric of Hindu, Jain and Muslim communities, is still a living social reality, not the shell of a dead culture. While the main monuments of the city, including Friday mosque and fort, were erected by Muslim rulers in the fifteenth century, the ancient Hindu scheme is followed with the four cardinal main streets, and districts apportioned according to caste and profession. A hierarchical street pattern descends from the four main bazaar streets to lesser bazaar streets, residential streets and, finally, the labyrinthine enclaves known as pols or mohallas.

Each Ahmadabad pol, traditionally inhabited by people of the same jati or occupation, is entered through a single defensive gateway. This leads to a tree-like hierarchy of lanes branching into alleys and passageways, all shaded by high wooden houses with overhanging upper floors. Larger pols contain sub-pols, sometimes with their own, secondary gateways. Small squares or chowks within the pols contain local community buildings, including shrines and dovecotes. Domestic life spills out onto raised plinth verandahs (otlas), a further transition towards the privacy of the individual family homes. The central courtyards of the houses can be glimpsed through carved doorways.

Palaces and forts

Palace architecture had a prominent place in ancient Indian literature. Idealised representations of palaces are seen in Buddhist narrative carvings and the murals of Ajanta. Indian palaces were eulogistically described by foreign visitors, as was Ashoka's palace at Pataliputra (third century BC) by the Greek envoy Megasthenes. Palatial imagery was incorporated into the architecture of temples, conceived as divine abodes. Yet very little survives of early palaces, partly because they were predominantly of perishable materials, and partly because, unlike temples, they were considered inherently part of the transient order, and not worthy of preservation.

Some of the earliest palace remains are in Sri Lanka. The fifth-century fortress-palace at **Sigiriya**, known for its graceful wall paintings (stylistically related to those at Ajanta), was built in brick on top of a 120 m (390 ft) high granite outcrop. Access was via a stairway between gigantic lion paws of brick and stucco, and from there on by ladders up the cliff face. Below the defensive eyrie on the rock, terraced pleasure gardens, pools and cascades were laid out, all within a fortified enclosure. A later Sri Lankan mountain fort is the thirteenth- to fourteenth-century rock-fortress of **Yapahuwa** (p. 784A). Its well-preserved, dramatic stairway and entrance are a rare survival of the Dravida architectural language used for a 'secular' purpose. Of the palace at **Kandy** (sixteenth to nineteenth centuries) the most interesting survival is the Audience Hall, a richly carved wooden structure of nave-and-aisles cross section.

Palace architecture in south India includes the Nayaka palaces at **Madurai** and **Tanjore**, both in **Tamil Nadu** (seventeenth and eighteenth centuries). The Royal Palace at **Padmanabhapuram, Kerala** (mainly eighteenth century) is a magnificent complex, built of timber, with steeply pitched roofs (p. 784C).

The Indian palace architecture that is most memorable is that built for the Moghul emperors (see Chapter 19) and Rajput kings between the fifteenth and eighteenth centuries. There was constant interaction between the architectural traditions of the Moghuls and the Rajputs, the same craftsmen sometimes working for both. But their palaces are distinct in character. Moghul palaces, such as the **Red Forts** at **Delhi** and **Agra, Uttar Pradesh**, consist of separate buildings on level ground within a fortified enclosure, whereas the garh palaces (fort-palaces) of the Rajputs tend to be continuous masses of combined fortification and palace, raised on a hill. Typically, they are asymmetrical and dramatically irregular, often partly because their growth was gradual, but also because of a desire for complexity, ambiguity and a sense of mystery.

Like the Moghul palaces, those of the Rajputs are divided into men's and women's quarters (mardana and zenana), and include halls for public and private audience (diwan-i-am and diwan-i-khas). Most rooms do not, however, have specific functions; instead a range of multi-functional spaces is provided, of various sizes and degrees of enclosure, from interior rooms, to an open hypostyle hall, colonnades and kiosks, to courtyards open to the sky.

Architectural language in Rajput palaces makes great use, like Hindu temple architecture, of repetition and variation of aedicule designs, informally and picturesquely disposed. Domes and curved bangaldar roofs are typical, often sitting over chajjas. Open kiosks – not the solid aedicules of temples – spike the skyline in parapets or crowning turrets. Some are miniature, others full size, habitable pavilions, at roof level, or free standing on the ground. Wall surfaces are peppered with diverse jarookhas, projecting aedicular balconies, sometimes superimposed to form oriels running through several storeys, terminating at roof-level pavilions. Particularly in the zenana (women's quarters), jarookhas and colonnades are filled with jalis (pierced screens). Forms derived from the temple tradition of beams, brackets and corbelling, are gradually replaced by arcuated construction and imagery, with multi-cusped arches ubiquitous by the eighteenth century. The Islamic arch-in-rectangle motif becomes widespread, for windows, doors, niches and wall-surface articulation.

The earliest Rajput fort-palaces, built before the Moghul accession in 1526, include the **palace of Rana Kumbha, Chittor, Andhra Pradesh** (1433–68), the **palace of Raja Kirtti Singh, Gwalior, Madhya Pradesh** (1454–79) and the largest of four Gwalior palaces, the palace of Man Singh Tomar, known as the **Man Mandir** (1486–1516) (p. 785A). The latter, with its impressive, cliff-like south wall with kiosk-topped circular turrets, has unique coloured ceramic decoration. Later palaces, built between the later sixteenth and the eighteenth centuries, and all in Rajasthan include those of **Udaipur, Rajasthan** (p. 785B), **Amber** (p. 785C), **Jaisalmer, Bikaner, Jodhpur, Bundi, Kota** and **Jaipur**. Part of the Jaipur palace is the so-called Hawa Mahal, or Palace of the Winds (begun 1799). Its eastern front, acting as a purdah screen to the zenana behind, has storeys mounting up in receding planes, and crowded, interpenetrating jarookhas, making it – albeit with Rajput/Moghul aedicule forms – like a Hindu temple that has been unfolded and flattened out into a façade.

At **Orchha** and **Datia**, near **Jhansi, Madhya Pradesh** a series of palaces were built by the Bundela

A. Shiva temple, Pandrethan, Kashmir (tenth century). See p.779

B. Varahi temple, Chaurasi (late tenth century). See p.779

C. Jageshvara temple complex (*c.* eighth century). See pp. 755, 765

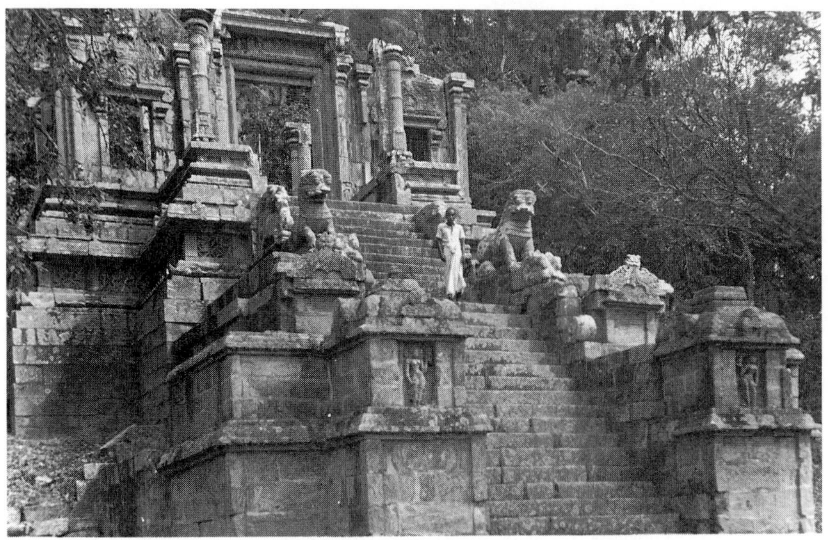

A. Yapahuwa rock-fortress, stairway and entrance (fourteenth century). See p.782

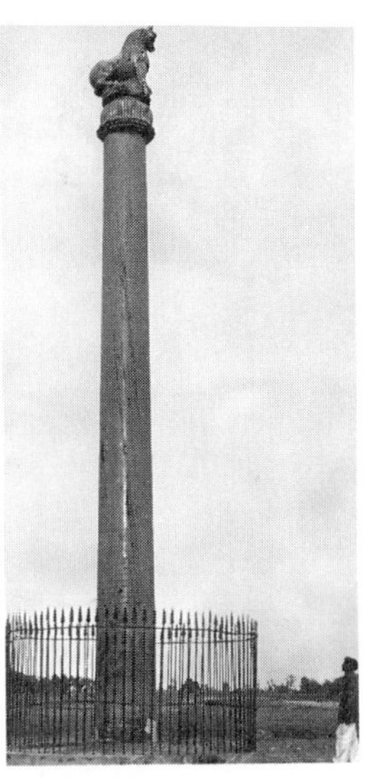

B. The Lath (Lion Column), Lauriya Nandangarh (243 BC). See p. 757

C. Royal Palace, Padmanabhapuram, Kerala, women's quarters (mainly eighteenth century). See p.782

A. The Man Mandir: south front (1486–1516). See p.782

B. Udaipur, the City Palace (1567–72 and later). See p.782

C. Audience hall and gate of the Shish Mahal, Amber. See p. 782

rulers between about 1530 and 1605. Unlike other Rajput works, these were built at one go, as centralised, symmetrical compositions. As in the case of the Jaipur city plan, the creators of these building seem to have been reinterpreting ancient shastric ideas about mandalas.

Apart from their major fort-palaces, the Rajput rulers built small pleasure palaces, such as the **Mohan Mandir** (1628–2) and **Jag Niwas** (1734–51), now a hotel, both on islands in the lake at **Udaipur, Rajasthan**. The small palace of **Man Singh, Benares, Uttar Pradesh**, with its fine balcony, was probably used mainly as a religious retreat.

Domestic architecture

Courtyard houses existed in **Mohenjodharo, Pakistan**, and **Harappa, Pakistan**, and are found, built one against another, or separated by narrow lanes, in those regions of the subcontinent that are predominantly hot and dry. The courtyard houses of northern India and Pakistan, particularly the larger town houses, are known as havelis. Traditionally a haveli has been inhabited by a joint family, though the inherent flexibility of the type nowadays allows subdivision to accommodate several nuclear families. As in Rajput palaces, spaces are not intended for single activities, but are multifunctional. The central courtyard or chowk, heart of the home, may be used for sitting, sleeping, washing and drying clothes, or keeping cattle. Hindu havelis contain puja (worship) rooms. On the street frontage there may be a shop or workshop. In regions where flat roofs are usual, the rooftops of havelis, in common with those of more humble forms of house, become additional living spaces, often used for sleeping.

In general terms, Hindu havelis are taller, with a more well-like courtyard, than Muslim havelis, and with the women's areas on lower floors, rather than at the rear. Courtyard houses in **Maharashtra**, built by wealthy Marathas during the eighteenth and early nineteenth centuries, are known as 'wadas', and containing from two to as many as fourteen successive courtyards in their deep plans.

Because surviving havelis date back scarcely beyond the seventeenth century, they tend to relate stylistically to Moghul and Rajput architecture, often with multi-cusped arches and jarookhas (aedicular balconies) with jali screens. There are many regional variations. Perhaps the most monumental are the stone houses built by rich merchants in the desert city of **Jaisalmer, Rajasthan**, notably the early nineteenth-century Patua haveli complex. Gujarat had a tradition of timber-framed havelis, found in such cities as **Ahmadabad, Baroda** (Vadodara), and **Broach** (Bharuch), decorated with very richly carved teak, imported from as far away as the Malabar coast or even Burma.

Within the subcontinent, Gujarati carved woodwork is equalled only by that of the **Kathmandu valley, Nepal**, mainly of the eighteenth century and later, but displaying centuries-old patterns and iconography. Temples (the 'pagoda temples' mentioned earlier), monasteries, palaces and houses share a common style. Built of brick, their ornate doorways and windows, with their pierced screens, are in timber. Lintols and cills project laterally far beyond the jambs, and wing-like side panels, often with figure carving, curve up to meet the lintols.

While the domestic architecture so far discussed might be described as vernacular, it is largely urban and built by specialist craftsmen. Only the briefest mention can be made here of the extraordinarily varied rural vernacular traditions of the Indian subcontinent – traditions of building and embellishment by people for themselves, whether tribal or non-triabal, nomadic or settled. Though endangered in varying degrees, many such building traditions are alive today, together with the associated crafts of use and adornment.

Chapter 27
SOUTH-EAST ASIA

Architectural Character

Burma

The development of Burmese architecture follows the four historical periods (see Chapter 21, p. 650). Few significant buildings survive from the early centuries. The majority of Burma's important architectural monuments date from the Pagan period (ninth to thirteenth centuries) and almost all buildings of distinction are religious. The stupa (also known in Burma as zedi), as in India and Sri Lanka, was a massive brick construction of domical external form, built upon a plinth of three or five diminishing terraces; the temple was usually square in plan with brick walls enclosing narrow vaulted corridors embracing a solid masonary core, which had centrally-placed niches on each side to accommodate statues of Buddha; walls were decorated with frescos or sculptured bas-reliefs. The central core rose in a series of receding storeys, and was crowned with a tapering shikhara-shaped finial. Both kinds of religious building were also referred to as pagodas (paya).

The monasteries (kyaung) and ordination halls (thein) for monks were derived from wood prototypes, and libraries (pitakat-taik), housing the sacred Buddhist texts, resembled the simpler temple designs.

In the Pagan period there are said to have been 5000 stupas and temples within the boundaries of the capital (p. 791A). In the post-Pagan era Burma declined architecturally, as well as politically. Chinese influence contributed to the emergence of the 'Pagoda' style, which characterised the architecture of the seventeenth to nineteenth centuries. No matter what their particular functions might be, all buildings were treated, constructionally and aesthetically, in a similar manner. Typical of the Burmese feeling for rich and intricate artistry, this architecture of carved wood, lacquer and gilt is essentially a folk art, expressing the imagination, vitality and craft skills of the people.

Cambodia

The earliest recorded capital of Cambodia (*c.* fifth century AD) was Vyadhapura (Angkor Borei) on the lower reaches of the Mekong River, 200 km (120 miles) from the sea and the port of Oc Eo. It was an agglomeration of wooden houses on piles, connected by little canals linked to larger waterways capable of taking sea-going ships. Later Funanese and early Khmer architectural development (seventh and eighth centuries) was centred upon Sambor and Prei Kuk, in the forests near Kampong Thom, on the road from Saigon to Angkor, not far from the later Angkor capitals. Wooden buildings gave way to more substantial brick and stone imitations of timber prototypes, which show a mixture of Indian forms grafted on to indigenous elements, and rich decorative sculpture derived from wood carving (harbinger of the exuberant Angkor ornamental art). Examples of temples and shrines still exist, if in a ruined state, at Tat Panom (Sambor) on the Mekong and Phnom Bayang.

At the beginning of the Early Classical Khmer period three important architectural events occurred, indicating the transitional stages between the pre-Angkor and early Angkor styles. The first was the creation of a city and temple-mountain in 800 AD on the hill of Phnom Kulen, near Angkor and the lake of Tonle-Sap. The second (chronologically the third) was the building of another capital (893) on the hill and round the temple mountain of Phnom Bakeng, close to Phnom Kulen, terraced into the hill as a five-levelled pyramid, with isolated towers on the topmost tier and smaller towers at the lower levels. Both cities presaged the typical Khmer town plan: a walled rectangle, the temple at the central intersection of the principal avenues radiating towards gates in the four sides of the moated enclosure, the main gate facing east. The third event, the second in date, was the construction at Roluos, Angkor, of the archetypal Khmer urban irrigation system. An immense artificial lake, 'Baray' Lolei about 3 km (2 miles) long and 800 m (half a mile) wide was formed by earthen dykes to store water from the Stung Roluos river

South-east Asia

flowing into a network of moats and waterways. The lake provided for the needs of the whole community, its final purpose being to irrigate the paddy fields. Such systems could only be realised under a highly centralised authority exemplified, in this context, by the god-king and universal ruler.

In the transitional Classical Khmer period (tenth and eleventh centuries) the evolution of the temple-mountain mountain was continued in Baksei Chamkrong, Angkor (*c.* 911), the first to be built-up in stone (laterite) in pyramidal terraces from flat ground, and Koh Ker (921), 64 km (40 miles) north-east of Angkor, constructed on an artificial lake by damming a stream, the normal east-west axis of the city altered to align with it – proof perhaps that the practical needs of the irrigation system were considered more important than a symbolic gesture to religion. As a rule, however, the symbolic axis was respected. A further stage in the evolutionary process came in the Ta Keo (completed *c.* 1010), in which the classical five terraces and five colossal towers were introduced, and still another in the Baphuon (*c.* 1050), in which the style and scale of the temple mountains became formalised. The culmination of Khmer building art was now in sight.

The Classical Khmer period (twelfth and early thirteenth centuries) was dominated by two majestic architectural achievements: the creation of Angkor Wat, the temple city of Suryavarman II (1113–50), and of Angkor Thom, the remodelled capital of Jayavarman VII (1180–1218), the latter a fantastic, baroque manifestation of a declining civilisation. Khmer architecture, as expressed in these works, is characterised by grandeur of conception, brilliant landscaping, unsurpassed town-planning in a strictly formal sense, and exuberant sculptural decoration on a grandiose scale, but of exquisite refinement. Building techniques, however, remained unsophisticated. Stone was used like wood, and stone walls were often reinforced with concealed timber beams, inserted in the hollowed-out centres; when the wood rotted, the stone blocks fell. The corbelled vaulting was never modified and permitted only the spanning of small spaces; hence the confined nature of each 'room' and the grouping together of many such units, and their interconnection by galleries to create an impression of size. To express the verticality of the invariable mountain theme, these galleried groups were placed round and above the central pyramid (compare the Ta Keo, an early example of 889). No mortar was used; the stone masonry was stabilised by the sheer mass of the construction, and the fine joints of the roofs fitted so perfectly that they remain watertight after several hundred years of neglect. Everywhere sculptural ornament breaks through the architectural lines, often spreading over the whole wall surface. At Angkor Thom this domination of the architecture by sculpture is even more marked than at Angkor Wat.

Thailand

Architecture in Thailand reflects the influences of the Buddhist countries and of the various groups with which it has mingled and associated for two millennia. The resultant complex picture may be divided into four periods.

The Dvaravati period, central Thailand (sixth-tenth centuries), is characterised by Burmese Buddhist forms surviving only in buildings which, strictly speaking, postdate the Dvaravati era, for example Lampun and Haripunjaya. There are no other architectural remains, except for fragments of foundations which give some idea of the plans, but not the style, of buildings at Nakhon Pathom (later Lopburi), the earliest known capital. Constructed of brick and stone, these plinths, with mouldings similar to those of Buddhist structures from Sri Lanka to north India of the first millennium, have granite bases with mortise holes for pillars which must have supported timber superstructures.

The Khmer-Lopburi (or Mon-Khmer) period, central and eastern Thailand (tenth–thirteenth centuries), has been described as a provincial manifestation of the Khmer-Angkor style of architecture, but it also mirrored earlier building traditions of the Mons and Talaings of southern Burma, who brought with them architectural echoes of Pagan. Most of the buildings are in a ruined condition, but well-preserved survivals can be seen at Lopburi and in Sukhothai. The Khmers introduced the use of stone, in place of the traditional brick or rubble bonded with vegetable glue.

The Thai period (thirteenth–seventeenth centuries) is sometimes subdivided into (1) Sukhothai style, (2) Ayudhya style, and (3) Northern Chiengmai style, although more for convenience than clear differentiation. Sukhothai art and architecture were not inventive, but harmoniously eclectic, employing Indian, Mon-Dravidian, Mon-Pagan, Sinhalese and Khmer motifs. Out of this diversity certain distinctively Thai features emerged, apparent in the typical Buddhist temple complex (wat), normally erected on a terrace. These had a central sanctuary, which sheltered a colossal Buddha statue screened by a high wall. The latter had a narrow arched aperture through which the image was viewed and worshipped. Over the sanctuary (reached through a pillared hall) rose a tapering tower, not unlike a minaret. The usually rectangular surrounding stupas carried similar elongated finials, but in the Ayudhya style the stupa was generally circular in plan, ring-based and bell-shaped, as in Sri Lanka. In the Chiengmai manner of the north cosmopolitan influences were less conspicuous, although here too the custom of copying venerated monuments from abroad as 'reminders' of the need for religious observance was the origin of some of the finest architecture (for example, Wat Jet Yot). In all phases of Thai building the part played by sculpture and, in interiors, by mural painting is important.

The Bangkok style was created in the late eighteenth and nineteenth centuries. The new capital was designed to emulate the destroyed city of Ayudhya. Many religious buildings and palaces were erected in which the traditional forms were overlaid with ornamentation of Chinese character, introduced to Thailand by refugees. Surfaces were often finished with porcelain tiles. Sometimes the walls are white stuccoed brick, which contrasts with the brightly coloured glazed tiles of the multi-levelled overlapping timber roofs. Gables and bargeboards are decorated with Angkor-Hindu iconography: 'nagas', Vishnu on a 'garuda' (a mythical bird), Shiva on a bull, and so on. Doors and window shutters are of carved wood, lacquered in black and gold, or painted or inlaid with mother-of-pearl depicting themes of guardian divinities, enchanted forests, ferns, flowers and still life.

Indonesia and the Malay Archipelago

It has already been noted (Chapter 21) that there are no significant architectural remains in Sumatra, Malaya or Borneo surviving from the Srivijaya empire; but from the contemporary Sanjaya and Sailendra dynasties in middle Java a number of buildings of extraordinary distinction still exist on the high table-lands – the Dieng Plateau and the Kedu plain – dating mainly from the eighth and ninth centuries and exemplifying a synthesis of Hindu-Indonesian and Buddhist-Indonesian features. It would appear that this architecture of solid stone walls and corbelled arches, and with no load-bearing columns, which reached its consummation with the stupa of Barabudur and the temple complex of Prambanam, was always associated with isolated religious communities and never with large centres of population. The apparent influence of Gupta (Indian) fifth- and sixth-century styles and of the Sanchi and Barhut stupa reliefs suggests that there was at this period a wide-ranging movement in Buddhist art from India to the China seas.

A new development, characterised by a lessening of Indian influence and increased evidence of the native Indonesian tradition, began with the shift of power to eastern Java in the eleventh century. It was reflected in the sculpture which foreshadowed the folk art of the Javanese 'Wayang' puppet drama. This tendency was even more marked in the Majapahit period (compare the temple group at Panataram, q.v.). The coming of Islam ended the Hindu-Buddhist architectural tradition in Indonesia, except in Bali, where it lingered on as a folk art, while the arrival of the Dutch introduced European elements.

Examples

Burma

There were stupas dating from the pre-Pagan period, perhaps as early as the third century, at **Bir-Paya, near Pagan**, and in the seventh and eighth centuries at **Prome**, the **Banbangyi, Payagyi** and **Payama pagodas**. All had convex, domical outlines, a shape displaced in the great Burmese building period which began in the eleventh century by what is now regarded as the characteristic, concave bell-shaped stupas of the region.

The **Mingalazedi Stupa, Pagan** (1274), comprises a high square plinth of three stepped terraces, with stairways in the centre of each side leading to the platform, from which the circular bell-shaped main structure rises. At each angle of the square stands a small replica of the stupa. The design has Javanese precedents (for example, the Stupa at Barabudur, q.v.).

The **Shwe Dagon Pagoda (stupa), Rangoon** (sixteenth and seventeenth centuries) (p. 791B), built over older foundations and added to many times, reflects Burma's cultural connections with India and China, while expressing the exuberance typical of later phases of Burmese art. In form, the traditional rounded tumulus of the stupa had now evolved into a tall attenuated structure, rising in this case by repeated additions to a height of 113 m (370 ft) above the processional platform. The supporting plinth is multiplaned, its many angles bearing miniature pagodas, the processional platform crowded with carved, gilded and lacquered shrines and spirelets.

The other characteristic religious building was the square temple, of which there were many examples in various parts of the country. The brick voussoir arch and vault were used in buildings throughout Burma and had an important influence upon their visual character (see also Chapter 21, p. 659). The plan of the temples consisted of a massive solid masonry core – the base of the stupa which crowned each building – surrounded by narrow, vaulted passageways and quite small chambers or vestibules, usually symmetrically arranged and located to give views of one or more Buddha figures. These square centrally planned temples represent the classical period of Burmese architecture. There is a comparatively small and simple square temple at **Abhayadana, south of Pagan**, probably begun in the eleventh century (p. 791C): the entrance to the vestibule is through an arch with a single ring of voussoirs. The brick building is coated in stucco and pilasters reinforce its corners; windows are characteristic with plastered jambs, decorative pediments and regularly perforated stone or brick plate filling to the opening. The shallow ogival roof is typical of the square temples. Windows of the **Nan-Paya Temple, also south of Pagan**, boast a somewhat different sculptured form of pediment and pilasters (p. 793A), indicating Chinese or Cambodian influence.

The Nan-Paya Temple is considered to be one of those which provided prototypes for the **Ananda Temple, Pagan** (twelfth century) (p. 792A,B), the supreme attainment of Burmese classical architecture. It is a massive white brick building, with finely graduated tiered roofs and, projecting on each side, elaborately decorated portico entrances which give the temple the plan-form of a Greek cross. A golden tapering spire rises over the central stupa, which also carries smaller gilded spires. Inside are two concentric ambulatories, the inner one passing before four Buddha statues, 9 m (30 ft) high, recessed into each side of the masonry core.

The **Thatpyinnyu** and **Tsulamani Temples**, also at **Pagan** (p. 793B) and of similar date, have upper storeys with a central image-house cell and ambulatory.

The influence upon the character of Burmese buildings of the use of voussoir arches is perhaps most clearly shown in the **Kyaukku Temple to the north of Pagan** (eleventh century) (p. 793C). The ground-floor arches with wide pilasters rising to a continous frieze made an unusual base to the upper levels, which rose successively to the central mass of the stupa. The **Thitsawada Temple**, also **near Pagan**, and possibly of earlier (eleventh century) date (p. 795A), was smaller; except for its main (arched) entrances it presented impermeable pilastered walls at ground-floor level somewhat reminiscent of Dravidian temples of the same period in southern India. But the smaller dimensions and steeper terracing of the upper levels produced an outline reminiscent of European centralised churches of much later date.

Apart from the **sacred library at Pagan** (eleventh century), which had a high ground storey with

A. Ruins of stupas and temples, Pagan, Burma. See p.790

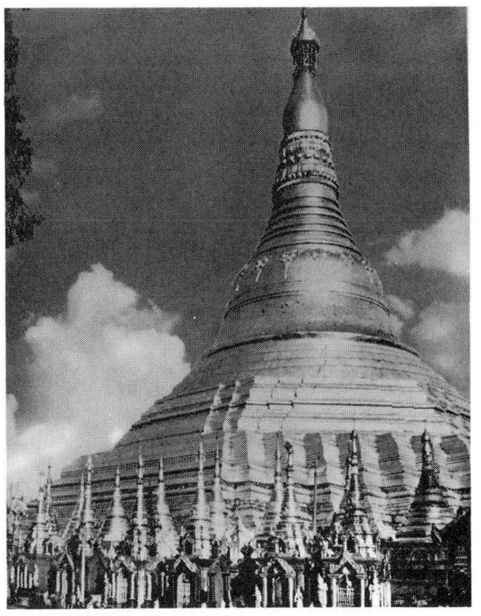

B. Shwe Dagon Pagoda, Rangoon, Burma (sixteenth and seventeenth centuries). See p.790

C. Abhayadana Temple, south of Pagan (*c.* eleventh century). See p.790

A. Ananda Temple, Pagan, Burma (twelfth century). See p.790

B. Ananda Temple, Pagan

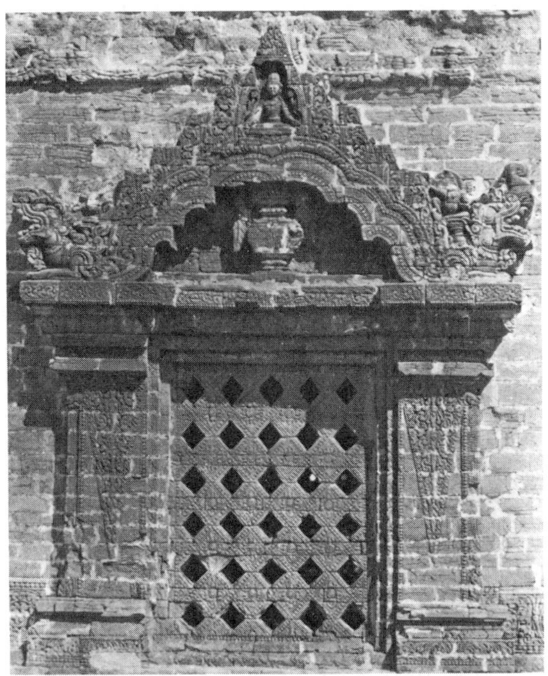

A. Window of the Nan-Paya Temple, south of Pagan, Burma. See p.790

B. Tsulamani Temple, Pagan: upper porch (twelfth century). See p.790

C. Kyaukku Temple, Pagan (eleventh century). See p.790

windows and five levels above, equally stepped back with ogee roofs, all other buildings were of timber construction, including monasteries. Most of them were of the pagoda-roofed kind, with various numbers of storeys, highly decorated with carving and finials.

King Mindon's capital, **Mandalay**, dates only from 1857, but its plan embodied many of the features of Kublai Khan's Peking of the thirteenth century. The layout consisted of concentric square enclosures, each with its perimeter wall. The palace occupied the central square, and comprised a large number of single-storey wooden buildings on a brick platform nearly 1.8 m (6 ft) high, supported on immense wood pillars and extending some 300 m (1000 ft) on its longest side. All the buildings were profusely decorated with gilding, carving and lacquer, providing a fanciful panorama of roofs, gables, parapets and slender pagoda spires. Mandalay suffered immeasurable destruction during World War II.

Cambodia

A number of temples and shrines survive from the Late Funanese era, including a Buddhist building of the sixth or seventh century at **Tat Panom** (Sambor), in terracotta brick of marked Indian character; another brick structure, the **Temple of Shiva, Phnom Bayang** (early seventh century), rectangular and of three receding storeys with a keel-shaped roof; and a small sandstone shrine at **Prei Kuk**.

The **Preah Ko Temple** (894) (p. 795B) is one of two important temples built by Indravarman I. Situated in the city-water complex, for which the king was also responsible, it is a single-terrace construction (that is, not yet a temple-mountain) with six towers and lavish carving showing strong Javanese influence.

The **Bakong Temple, Roluos** (Angkor) (881) (p. 795C), the second important temple built by Indravarman I, typifies the emergence of the Khmer temple-mountain concept. An architecturally simple stone pyramid, it comprises five superimposed terraces, decreasing in size from an almost square base with sides of 70 m (230 ft) to one with 21 m (69 ft) sides at the top, which is 14 m (47 ft) from the ground. The resemblance to Barabudur (Java) (q.v.) is conspicuous.

Other temples of the Early Classical Khmer period exemplifying the pyramidal superstructure are the **Lolei** (893), set in the Roluos lake, near **Angkor**, and the **Bakheng, Angkor**, of the same date, which largely follows the pattern of Bakong.

Pre-Rup, a red and pale pink three-stepped pyramid with five towers at the summit, came some seventy years later and, like the relatively small, delicate, graceful and subtly proportioned **Banteay Srei** (967), built 20 km (12 miles) from Angkor, belongs to the Transitional period. A few years after Pre-Rup and Banteay Srei the temple mountain of **Phimeanakas** (p. 796A) was completed, probably in 978, at the centre of the Angkor of Jayavarman V. It differs from the former in that the long stone chambers of the third terrace have become a continuous covered gallery.

The **Ta Keo Temple** (970–1010) is of more fundamental significance, in that it may be said to epitomise the results of two hundred years of development of the Khmer temple-mountain. Very large, 103 m × 122 m (339 ft × 402 ft) at the base and 48 m (156 ft) at the top, it has five terraces, the highest being 40 m (129 ft) from the ground, and carrying five colossal stone towers (compare Pre-Rup).

The **Baphuon Temple-mountain** (*c.* 1050) is on the scale of Angkor Wat, and was in many respects a prelude to it. Vaulted stone galleries now enclose the first and second terraces, as well as the third.

The **Neak Pean shrine** (twelfth century) (p. 796B) symbolised paradise floating upon the primeval seas, and fits into no precise category. The circular plinth rises out of a square basin, from which the water flowed through gargoyle fountains, with lion, horse, elephant and human heads, into four symmetrically sited pools (now dried up), and thence through canals to the river, an enchanting conception.

The **City of Angkor Wat** (twelfth century) (p. 797A,B), together with that of Angkor Thom, is one of the prodigious monuments of the last phase of the Khmer civilisation at its Classical period. It was built by Suryavarman II (1112–52) as a temple to the god-king image, as a monument to himself, and as his own sepulchre. In plan it is a vast rectangle contained by a moat 4 km (2½ miles) long, and in form it is the familiar stepped pyramid, a third and final level supporting the inner sanctuary and crowned by an immense central conical tower, with four smaller towers of similar design at the corners of the great galleried platform. The Angkor Wat temple-mountain is approached by a paved causeway and entered by a monumental portico leading to a colonnaded and arcaded gallery, which embraces the first terrace. Nearly 800 m (2500 ft) of the walls of this gallery are decorated with bas-reliefs depicting allegorical tales and legendary events from the Indian epics, the Mahabharata and the Ramayana.

Angkor Thom, the rebuilt capital of Cambodia, laid out by Jayavarman VII (1180–1218), lies a little to the north of Angkor Wat. Planned as an almost square rectangle, with each of its sides over 3 km (2 miles) long and protected by a moat 90 m (300 ft) wide and a laterite stone wall nearly 6.7 m (22 ft) high, it incorporates the two earlier temple-mountains of Baphuon and Phimeanakas. Bridging the moat and leading to five towered gateways were five stone causeways with parapet-balustrades on either side, composed of rows of stone giants holding 'nagas' (symbolic serpents). At the centre of the city the king

A. Thitsawada Temple, Pagan (eleventh century). See p.790

B. Preah Ko Temple, Cambodia (894). See p.794

C. Bakong Temple, Roluos (Angkor), Cambodia (881). See p.794

A. Royal Palace, Phimeanakas, Cambodia (*c.* 978). See p.794

B. Neak Pean shrine, Angkor, Cambodia (twelfth century). See p.794

A. Temple of Angkor Wat, Cambodia (twelfth century). See p.794

B. Central tower, Temple of Angkor Wat

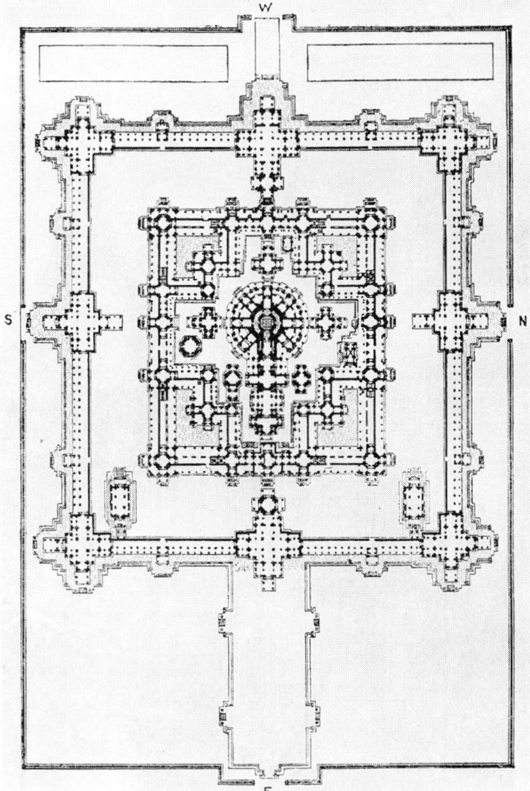

C. The Bayon, Angkor Thom: plan. See p.799

A. The Bayon, Angkor Thom, Cambodia (early thirteenth century). See p.799

B. Throne Room, Royal Palace, Bangkok, Thailand. See p.799

built his own temple-mountain, the Bayon (q.v.). His palace, close to the Phimeanakas, has completely vanished.

The **Bayon, Angkor Thom** (early thirteenth century) (pp. 797C, 798A), symbolising the god-king cult, originally consisted of a system of vaulted galleries and small pavilions disposed in a cruciform plan. Later similar galleries were added at the corners to form a rectangle, which was then enclosed by outer galleries linked to the inner complex by sixteen chapels, subsequently destroyed. A podium at the centre carried the shrine, which had an image of the Buddha under a naga hood identified with Jayavarman, the Deva-Raja. This motif was reflected on fifty-four towers, each bearing four Buddha heads carved on each side, which crowned the chapels and pavilions.

Thailand

Wat Kukut Temple, Lampun (early twelfth century, rebuilt 1218 after an earthquake) represents (and post-dates) the last phase of the Dvaravati style. From a high square platform, with 23 m (75 ft) sides, rises a slender brick pyramid of five diminishing storeys of 28 m (92 ft). On each face of each storey are three terracotta Buddha images, making sixty in all.

Wat Mahadhatu Temple, Lopburi (*c.* twelfth century), restored in the fifteenth century, is a building of the Khmer-Angkor type. It stands in a walled court, and comprises a sanctuary tower (sikhara) and attached portico (mandapa) raised on a high moulded plinth. Especially noteworthy are the heavy arched tympana above the openings, recalling Angkor.

Wat Jet Yot Temple, near Chiengmai (*c.* 1455), apparently built to record the 2000th anniversary of the Buddha's death, is a smaller version of the Maha Bodi Temple (relic house), Bodh Gaya, India (see Chapter 26), but with added stucco reliefs of celestial beings paying homage. Other examples of the 'copy' type are the **Cetiya Si Liem** (the 'Four-square Reminder', **Chiengmai** (*c.* 1300), and **Wat Mahathat** (Great Relic Monastery), **Sukhothai** (fourteenth century).

Among the ruins of **Ayudhya** it is possible to gain some impression of the evolution of the Thai 'bell' stupa or 'prachedi', normally surrounded by miniature stupas or shrines of similar form. By Buddhist tradition, such structures housed the relics of holy men but at Ayudhya they were no doubt erected as funeral monuments to the kings. Inside the stupas were secret chambers decorated with frescos and filled with votive objects. Examples include the **Wat Phra Ram** (*c.* 1369); **Wat Phra Mahathat** (*c.* 1374); **Wat Rat Burana** (*c.* 1424); and the most complete and impressive **Wat Phra Sri Sarapet** (*c.* 1500) (p. 800A).

Typical of the Bangkok 'pagoda' manner of later years, a form applied to palaces as well as religious buildings, is the Throne Room of the **Royal Palace, Bangkok** (p. 798B), in which the two main roofs intersect at right angles (that is, in cruciform plan), with a spire rising at the intersection. The style is used for other building types, even for comparatively recent religious buildings such as the **Wat Phra Keo**, with its elongated columns and surrounding prachedi.

Indonesia and the Malay Archipelago

The **Tjandi Bhima, Dieng** (*c.* 700) (p. 800B), is one of a number of small Hindu temples and 'Tjandi' (sepulchral monuments) to survive in central Java from the early years of the Sanjay-Sailendra dynasties. It comprises a simple, single-cella shrine, square in plan, beneath a pyramid tower, entered by a prominent porch. Each level of the tower has niches which hold figures of the Buddha. The plinth mouldings of cella and porch run through at the same level, but the lower cornice of the porch is awkwardly joined to the cella below cornice level. The plinth moulding is interrupted by the entrance doorway.

Another, somewhat later example, **Tjandi Arjuna** (p. 800D), carried the classical analogy a little further. The entrance doorway is raised by a short flight of stairs to the plinth level and the roof of the porch sits a little more comfortably under the archway of the main cornice.

At **Kalasan**, a little further south, there is a Buddhist shrine temple (*c.* 770) built to hold the ashes of the consort of a Sailendra prince, and planned in the shape of a Greek cross, with projecting wings forming side chapels, each entered through a portico with elaborate pediment surmounted by a 'Kirtimukha', the grotesque mask later so typical of Javanese sculpture (p. 800C). While clearly a development of Tjandi Bhima, Kalasan shows a maturity in execution which presages an Indonesian style. Here the cornice, some 10 m (33 ft) above ground, ran at the same level around the porches and the central square building; there were three stepped-back levels above it, giving a total height of about 21 m (69 ft).

Tjandi Sewa (ninth century), in the same district, is another Buddhist shrine, but in a far more ruinous condition. In conception the shrine resembles that at Kalasan, but surrounded by four rows of smaller shrines (some 249 in all), it must once have had something of the grandeur of Barabudur and Angkor. **Tjandi Medhut** (p. 801A) of the same date, general plan and structure as the last two monuments, is noteworthy for the well-preserved sculpture, including a renowned Buddha trinity which graces the interior.

The **Stupa of Barabudur** (eighth to ninth centuries) (p. 801B,D), theatrically sited on the Java plains against a background of smoking volcanoes, is the supreme expression of Indonesian art, and an

A. Wat Phra Sri Sarapet, Ayudhya, Thailand (*c.* 1500). See p.799

B. Tjandi Bhima, Dieng, Java (*c.* 700). See p.799

C. Buddhist temple, Kalasan, Java (*c.* 770): portico to one of the side chapels. See p.799

D. Tjandi Arjuna (late eighth century). See p.799

A. Tjandi Medhut, Java (ninth century). See p.799

B. The Stupa, Barabudur, Java (eighth to ninth centuries): aerial view. See p.799

C. The Stupa, Barabudur: low-relief sculpture from the galleries. See p.802

D. The Stupa, Barabudur

E. Shiva Temple, Prambanam, Java (*c.* 900). See p.802

architectural masterpiece of the Sailendra dynasty. In the form of a shallow stone-clad hill, this extraordinary building symbolises the world mountain ('Meru') of Indian cosmology and the Mahayana Buddhist cosmic system through the nine stages – there are nine storeys of terraces – which lead to nirvana. Square in plan, each 150 m (500 ft) side with five slightly stepped faces (diminishing to three at the higher levels), Barabudur rises through five rectangular closed galleries and three circular open terraces (the latter carrying seventy-two bell-like stupas) to the crowning central stupa. The galleries display some 1300 panels of sculpture (p. 801C) depicting the life of the Buddha and legends from the sacred Buddhist texts. Every detail in the design and conception of Barabudur is dictated by religious rather than architectural principles, but the result is spectacular architecture.

At **Prambanam** there is a remarkable complex of one hundred and fifty shrines arranged about a vast two-tier terrace, which reflects the decline in Mahayana Buddhism in the ninth and tenth centuries, and a return to the Hindu gods. Most of the shrines are in ruins, but the **Shiva Temple of Loro Djongrang** (*c.* 900) (p. 801E), the main feature of Prambanam, has been considerably restored. Cruciform in plan, on a square base, with four broad formal staircases and a central cella, the temple has much fine sculpture, including a gallery containing forty-two bas-reliefs illustrating the 'Ramayana' epic.

The **Temple group at Panataram** (*c.* 1370) is a final manifestation of continuing Hindu culture (Majapahit dynasty) in eastern Java. The Siva 'Tjandi' is particularly interesting and well preserved: the traditional form of the single cube-like cella and surmounting pyramid is retained, but the treatment is now entirely Javanese. Especially characteristic are the large Kirtimukha masks over the doorways, which anticipate a technique used centuries after in the Wayang puppet plays.

Part Five

THE ARCHITECTURE OF THE RENAISSANCE AND POST-RENAISSANCE IN EUROPE AND RUSSIA

Chapter 28
BACKGROUND

Introduction

The broad term 'Renaissance', which is used in the heading of this part of the book to cover European and Russian architecture from *c.* 1420 (in Italy) to 1830, has been retained although in current terminology the Renaissance style is said to have yielded to the Baroque by *c.* 1630 or even to Mannerism by *c.* 1520. The value of the wider term (which implies a conscious revival of the Graeco-Roman style) is that it makes continuous acknowledgement of antiquity as the stylistic norm and paragon. This allegiance, occasionally ruffled by the Gothic tendencies of certain Baroque architects, was not seriously threatened until the eclecticism of the later eighteenth century brought about a revival of non-European styles and of the Middle Ages; positive opposition to Roman models is rarely found until the time of A. W. N. Pugin (1812–52). Thus a certain cohesiveness can be claimed for this very long and variegated sequence of buildings dispersed over all the countries of Europe. (Renaissance buildings outside Europe are covered in Part 6.) In Russia the introduction of Renaissance forms overlaps the much-extended Byzantine period (see Part 2, Chapter 12).

At the beginning of the period Roman architecture was the predominant influence, and it was not until the eighteenth century that ancient Greek buildings were seriously studied, producing the neo-Classical belief in the superiority of Greek architecture. By the early nineteenth century the word 'Classical' began to take on one of its modern meanings in that it conveyed the Greek qualities of harmony, proportion, rationality and balance. By an unfortunate extension it has come to be applied to all manifestations of the Graeco-Roman world, however irrational or bizarre. In this part of the book, therefore, the word 'Classical' is not used to designate a historical period. The more neutral term 'antique' is used to denote Greek, Hellenistic and Roman models. Where the word 'Classical' is used, it implies, however loosely, an adherence to certain architectural values, initially found in the treatise of Vitruvius, and much re-studied later in the forms of Greek architecture. Many Roman buildings were not 'Classical' in this sense, but exercised equal influence on Renaissance architects.

Within the period as a whole, separate stylistic phases can be discerned, although they occur at different times in different regions, and the transitions between them are seldom abrupt.

The terms used here are Early Renaissance, High Renaissance and Mannerism, Baroque and Rococo, and neo-Classical.

The stylistic application of these terms is more fully considered under 'Architectural Character' in each chapter. Only Early Renaissance and neo-Classical can be described as self-conscious movements in reaction to previous styles; the others represent evolutionary developments of style and were branded with the derogatory labels 'Mannerist', 'Baroque' and 'Rococo' by critics of various periods with Classicising tendencies.

The Renaissance of the arts began in Italy as part of a more general revival of Graeco-Roman culture. Early Renaissance architectural styles spread from Florence (*c.* 1420) to other major cities in Italy in the middle of the fifteenth century, and won rapid acceptance throughout the peninsula. Outside Italy, only Russia and Hungary have notable fifteenth-century Renaissance buildings.

By the early sixteenth century, however, Renaissance forms had reached all the countries of Europe. Whereas in Italy this 'High Renaissance' period is marked by greater understanding of the principles and physical remains of ancient architecture, elsewhere the Renaissance more often meant the adoption of Italianate motifs (pp. 806–808) that became ever more bizarre in the process of copying and transmission. Thus, while in Italy in the 1520s architects like Raphael, Giulio Romano and Peruzzi were expanding their range of sources, their vocabulary and, above all, the less Roman-based inventions of Michelangelo could in the hands of Spanish, French or Flemish masters (p. 809) seem very remote from ancient forms. The engravings of the School of Fontainebleau played a particular role in the spread of such

A' FRIEZE : PAL. VECCHIO : FLORENCE
HIC EST PANIS VIVUS QI DE CELO DESCENDIT
A TABERNACLE S. CROCE : FLORENCE
B CANTORIA (SINGING GALLERY) MUSEUM OF S. MARIA DEL FIORE FLORENCE
C HOLY WATER STOUP SIENA CATHEDRAL
QUESTA·OPA·AFACTA·FARE·LACONPAGNIA·DICASTELSAGIO·VANNI·PELANIMA DEBENEFATORI·EOPERATORI·DIDETTA·CONPANGNIA
D 'LAVABO' S. M. NOVELLA FLORENCE
E ALTAR-PIECE : S. CROCE : FLORENCE
F PULPIT : S. M. NOVELLA FLORENCE
G BRACKET TO PULPIT S. CROCE : FLORENCE
H RELIQUARY S. SALVADORE D' OGNISSANTI : FLORENCE.
J BALUSTRADE TO PULPIT SIENA CATHEDRAL

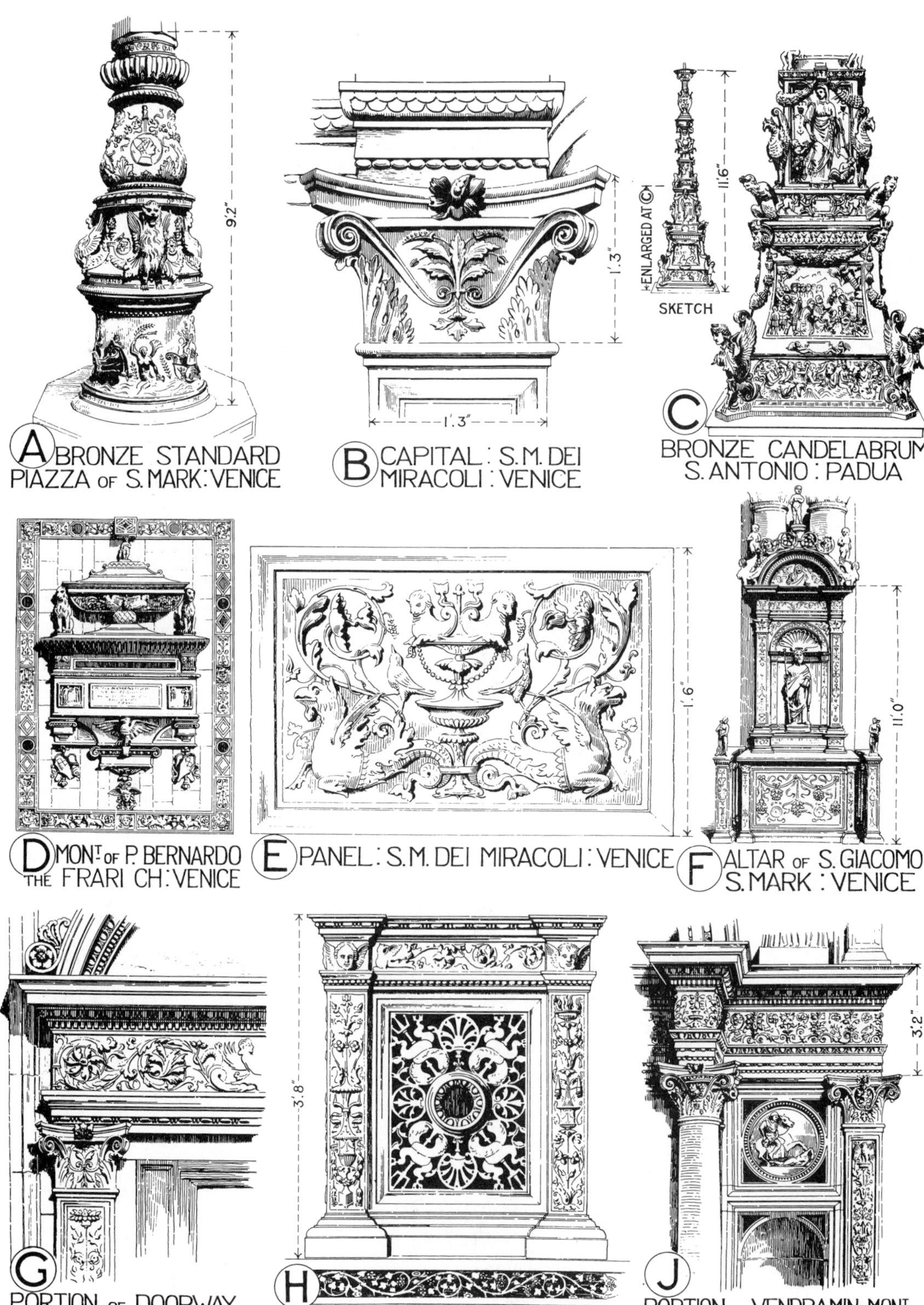

A BRONZE STANDARD PIAZZA OF S. MARK: VENICE

B CAPITAL: S.M. DEI MIRACOLI: VENICE

C BRONZE CANDELABRUM S. ANTONIO: PADUA

D MONT. OF P. BERNARDO THE FRARI CH: VENICE

E PANEL: S.M. DEI MIRACOLI: VENICE

F ALTAR OF S. GIACOMO S. MARK: VENICE

G PORTION OF DOORWAY ORFANI AI GESUATI: VENICE

H BALUSTRADE: S.M. DEI MIRACOLI: VENICE

J PORTION OF VENDRAMIN MONT. SS. GIOVANNI E PAOLO: VENICE

ANGLE OF CORNICE AT a
A
B
PLAN LOOKING UP AT y-y
C
ANGLE OF CORNICE AT b
y
y
a
b
D
DOORWAY: PAL. GAMBARO GENOA
E
DOORWAY: PAL. CAREGA: GENOA
SECTION THRO' COFFERS
F
LAVABO OLD CONVENT GENOA
G
COFFERED CEILING: VILLA CAMBIASO IN ALBARO
H
TYPICAL CAP.
5'. 5"
J
DOORWAY GENOA
K
PILASTER VILLA CAMBIASO
6'. 4"
GROUND LINE
L
DOORWAY VERONA

A B BENCH-ENDS: DORDRECHT

C GABLE END WITH IRON TIES

D DOOR THE MUSEE PLANTIN ANTWERP

E DOORWAY: ANTWERP

F FROM CHIMNY PIECE: MUSEUM: BRUSSELS

G CAPITAL FROM THE MONUMENT OF GUILLAUME DE CROY, L'EGLISE DES CAPUCINS: ENGHIEN

H STAIRCASE: MUSEE PLANTIN: ANTWERP

J ORNAMENT TO COLUMN L'EGLISE DE CAPUCINS: ENGHIEN

K FIGURES FROM CHIMNEY PIECE IN THE PALAIS DE JUSTICE AT ZALT BOMMEL

'grotesques' and were reinforced by the pattern-books of Hans Vredeman de Vries and Wendel Dietterlin to create a kind of international 'Mannerist' style in the later sixteenth century.

In the seventeenth and early eighteenth centuries stylistic currents in the different European countries were markedly out of phase, and labels such as the 'Age of the Baroque' are particularly misleading. The characteristics of the Roman and Piedmontese Baroque – illusionism, curvilinear movement, spatial experiment and bizarre detail – were whole-heartedly adopted only in Austria, Bohemia and southern Germany. Protestant England and Holland went through a 'Palladian' revival which produced much plainer, simpler forms, even when Baroque influences were felt at the end of the century. France developed a distinctive national manner based on rational geometries, columnar facades and a crisp handling of stone, together known as French Classicism.

Similarly, early eighteenth-century Rococo, which is essentially a late flowering of Baroque – even more curvilinear in tendency and incorporating asymmetrical surface decoration – had a very different degree of penetration in different countries. In France it was essentially a style of domestic interiors, leaving exteriors and ecclesiastical architecture unaffected. In Austria and southern Germany it was both more pervasive and more extreme, continuing the tendencies of the Baroque in those areas. Meanwhile in England the anti-Baroque Palladian revival, originating in the second decade of the eighteenth century, nipped Rococo in the bud, except as far as interiors and furniture were concerned. The mid-eighteenth-century neo-Classical movements in France, Italy and Germany were programmatically anti-Rococo.

Neo-Classicism was more than a revival of Greek and other more exotic antique styles. Architecturally it was connected with a return to rational structural principles and their expression in building. In this respect neo-Classicism could favour Gothic solutions over Roman, and it was no accident that architects such as Karl Friedrich Schinkel and Jacques Soufflot admired Gothic architecture – not for its tracery or ornament but for its structural achievement.

The social changes that culminated in the French Revolution and the transitory international suzerainty imposed by Napoleon were the principal factors in the breakaway from the formal disciplines of neo-Classicism. The title 'post-Renaissance' has been given to this period, and it has been included in this part of the book to bring the evolution of European architecture to approximately the end of the nineteenth century before dealing with the architecture of European colonialism, in the later phases of which nineteenth-century eclecticism played an important part, as did the technological developments of the period. The continuing rapid growth of population and the quickening pace of industrialisation and urbanisation were all conducive to the removal of the symbolic authority of antique forms and motifs no matter how removed from Greece and Rome.

In this chapter the emphasis has been placed upon the political, social and cultural history of the Renaissance and post-Renaissance periods in the countries of Europe and Russia. It is important to stress, however, that the division by 'country' is a convenience only. In the formative centuries of the Renaissance styles, each of the 'countries' of central and southern Europe in particular was divided into many independent or near-independent city-states, dukedoms etc., and political alignments changed frequently. Political and economic status affected the invention and evolution of building types and helped to provide Renaissance architects with the extensive range and number of commissions which ensured the continuity of development which in due course took Renaissance forms to every part of the known world (see Part 6). The great variety of the post-Renaissance period in Europe is covered in Chapter 34; in this background chapter each of the sections on History and Resources and Building Techniques concludes with a section on the post-Renaissance period in Europe as a whole.

Geographical and climatic conditions across Europe helped in this worldwide diffusion of the styles, models for which had already been tried in Europe in similar, if not identical, conditions. In Europe itself the physical considerations significantly affected the form and appearance of buildings. From the soft reds of low-pitched tiled roofs and pastel-coloured piazzas of Italy and the French Mediterranean seaboard to the angular elegance of the high blue-grey roofs and the more severe lines of northern France, Britain and Scandinavia, the architects of the Renaissance period adapted their models to local materials and climate. The stylistic battles of the nineteenth century and the developing architecture of industry, communications, public health and housing continued this dissemination process throughout the post-Renaissance period and indeed well into the twentieth century.

History

Changes in architectural style and building types are closely bound up with historical shifts during the period. New styles were diffused through connections between powerful patrons, by war and conquest, by the invention of printing, by the movement of architects in search of employment, and, more generally, by the appropriation on the part of rulers and the ruling class of an architectural language to reinforce their political and social positions. The built-in discipline of the Classical language of the orders provided a powerful visual metaphor for social hierarchies, and to this may be attributed much of its success.

STAIRCASE: ASHBURNHAM HOUSE: LOND.

CHIMNEY PIECE: STOKE HALL: DERBYSHIRE

C DINING ROOM: BELTON HOUSE: GRANTHAM: LINCS.

In the fifteenth century the new Italian architectural language was spread above all by patronage connections. For example, the Italianising tendencies of the court of Matthias Corvinus, King of Hungary, reinforced by his marriage with Beatrice d' Aragona of Naples, brought the early appearance of Renaissance forms in Budapest. Particular dynastic connections continued to be as important as larger historical forces in the diffusion of architectural ideas.

The Italian wars (1494–1530) reinforced a taste for Italian architecture in the French kings and the Habsburg emperors, and, as in ancient Greece, the Italian states gained cultural hegemony by losing their independence. Only in the second half of the seventeenth century did the France of Louis XIV displace Italy as the major source of architectural models, which were seen to be more appropriate to an age of absolutist monarchy than were those of the petty Italian courts. The seventeenth- and eighteenth-century European wars had more localised architectural implications (see the sections dealing with the history of individual countries below), but in this period it was Napoleon's European campaigns that left the most enduring imprint on the political and cultural institutions of Europe.

The revival of Classical learning that began with Dante (1265–1321) and Petrarch (1314–74) led naturally to an interest in the visual remains of antiquity, and it was fostered by the fifteenth-century Italian humanists and archaeologists. The text of Vitruvius's treatise on architecture, known but only partially understood in the Middle Ages, was compared with Roman buildings by Alberti (q.v.) and edited by scholar archaeologists. The fifteenth-century inventions of woodcut and copperplate engraving and of printing with movable type were important for the transmission of architectural theory and visual models all over Europe; the printed editions of Alberti (1485) and Vitruvius (1486), and especially the illustrated works of Serlio (1537–), Vignola (1562) and Palladio (1570), made it possible to build in the new style without visiting Italy. Architectural publications are surveyed for each country below.

The religious transformations in western Christendom that resulted from the Reformation movement led by Martin Luther (1483–1546) had important implications for church architecture, resulting in plain forms and uncluttered interiors without subsidiary altars. The internal movement of Catholic reform known as the Counter-Reformation was spearheaded by the new religious orders, especially the Jesuits, whose proselytising missions took Roman sixteenth-century church forms all over Europe. There is no single Counter-Reformation church plan, but aisleless single-nave churches with side chapels and the choir placed behind the altar were particularly favoured for monastic and collegiate churches. Centralised plans based on the circle or the Greek cross, which had been popular for votive and commemorative churches from the 1470s, continued to be so used in the Catholic world throughout the period. They also proved suitable for Protestant churches, which did not require a single focus on the main altar.

The Italian urban palace and country villa (p. 813A,B) were adapted to the different political, social and economic conditions of the rest of Europe. It took more than a century, however, for monarchical and aristocratic patrons to abandon the outward signs of power such as towers and crenellations, and to adopt the more subtle language of dominance implied by the Classical orders. It was left to France and Austria to devise an architectural setting for the exercise of absolute power, as at Versailles and Schönbrunn. Secular public buildings such as town halls, guild halls, hospitals and buildings for charitable foundations were characteristic of independent city-states. Seventeenth- and eighteenth-century royal initiatives were often connected with military training or rewards for military service, like the Invalides in Paris, and the Greenwich and Chelsea hospitals in England. Eighteenth-century movements for social reform in Europe brought a renewed emphasis on public buildings, and the late eighteenth and early nineteenth centuries are notable for the construction of hospitals, prisons and institutions of public education, such as museums, or of entertainment, such as theatres and opera houses.

The use of gunpowder artillery and the metal cannon ball rendered obsolete the late mediaeval defences, which had been based on high walls and towers. In late fifteenth-century Italy new defensive systems were pioneered which involved low walls punctuated by arrow-shaped bastions, to provide both offensive capability and defensive coverage of the curtain wall by flanking fire. Italian military engineers and treatises on defensive systems spread these ideas all over Europe in the sixteenth century, and they influenced the design of city defences until the eighteenth century.

Linked with military needs were Renaissance ideas of city planning based on radial street systems and centralised plans. They were most commonly put into practice in founding new fortress citadels, such as the Venetian town of Palmanova (1593), or new capitals such as Karlsruhe (1715). Within existing cities, streets were widened, straightened or newly planned on geometrical principles to focus on important monuments, fountains or obelisks. The successive interventions of Renaissance and Baroque popes in expanding and rationalising Rome itself provided a model for many Baroque princes all over Europe. The need for military control and the increase in the use of carriages and coaches made wider streets desirable. City planning provided the opportunities for uniform architectural developments such as terraced housing and with them the beginnings of speculative building.

A. Boboli Gardens, Florence (sixteenth century). See p.812

B. Villa Gamberaia, Settigano (*c.* 1550). See p.812

Italy

The religious and intellectual unity of Christendom had begun to crumble in the fourteenth century, when Marsiglio of Padua (d. 1342), John Wycliffe (d. 1348) and John Huss (d. 1415) all attacked the temporal power and wealth of the Church. The papacy, held captive at Avignon since 1309 by the French kings, returned to Rome in 1377, only to be disputed for over half a century between two and sometimes three rival popes, each supported by a group of nations. The Conciliar Movement, aimed at reforming the Church and controlling the popes through a series of General Councils, collapsed in 1449, leaving the papacy to recover its independent power. The career of Julius II (1503–13) placed the papacy in control of a relatively strong state stretching across central Italy. On the other hand, its moral authority throughout Europe sank to new depths under the vicious Alexander VI, the warlike Julius II and the aesthete Leo X (d. 1521).

The political history of fifteenth-century Italy is marked by shifting alliances and petty wars between the numerous city-states which made up a wholly disunited country. Attempts by the French to assert dynastic claims in Naples led to the French invasion of 1494; this was followed by the Italian wars, during which the peninsula became the battleground between France and the Habsburg emperors. During their campaigns the northern rulers acquired a taste for Italian art, and the Sack of Rome in 1527 by the emperor Charles V and his Lutheran troops accelerated the dispersal of High Renaissance architects to other centres.

By the 1530s a power structure was established that was to endure until the Napoleonic wars. The Spanish Habsburgs now directly ruled Milan, Naples and Sicily, and Genoa, and exercised much influence over the Medici Grand Duchy of Tuscany and the Dukes of Savoy in Turin. Venice remained an independent republic; though its maritime empire had dwindled, it retained the territories of the terra firma (Padua, Vicenza, Verona, as far west as Bergamo and east to Trieste). Rome had consolidated its grip on the Papal States from Fossanova to Rimini, Bologna and Modena. The great families held almost regal court in their palaces, vying one with the other in cultivated extravagance. The popes, avaricious of their revenues outside the city, spent them prodigally within, and even ran up enormous debts. Before they were brought under effective papal authority in the time of Julius II or later, certain of the more northerly of the States of the Church held their own petty but brilliant courts of the leaders of the families which governed them, such as the Malatesta family of Rimini, the Montefeltri of Urbino or the Este of Ferrara; thus, for a while, architecture in these centres was more responsive to local factors than to developments in Rome. During the seventeenth century the Grand Dukes of Tuscany passed through varying fortunes and the Venetians were intermittently at war with the Turks.

Architecture had a great part to play in the policy of active propaganda that followed the Counter-Reformation. Bourbon claims to the Spanish empire, involving the Spanish possessions in Italy, met with opposition from Austria, England and Holland, and the Treaty of Utrecht (1713) gave Milan and Naples to the Austrians, while the Dukedom of Savoy became a kingdom. In 1718 Venice lost its Adriatic possessions, and by 1737 the House of Medici became extinct and the Duchy passed to Austria.

The Napoleonic invasions (1796–7, 1800), though marking the end of the Venetian republic, meant partial liberation from the Austrian yoke, and an unprecedented unification of the north, from Piedmont to the Adriatic. At the Congress of Vienna (1814–15), the peninsula was repartitioned into eight states and remained under Austrian domination until the 1848 revolution.

The economic prosperity of late mediaeval Italy depended on early urbanisation, precocious development of banking and the textile industries (especially in Lombardy and Tuscany), maritime trade (Genoa and Venice) and the revenues of the church (Rome). South of Rome economic development was backward: huge agricultural estates supported an absentee aristocracy. However, the central and northern Italian city-states had already begun to lose their economic pre-eminence in Europe as early as the later fifteenth and sixteenth centuries, and there was a gradual return to the land by the urban ruling class. This, together with the dependence on foreign courts, made for an aristocracy based on the merchant classes.

The humanist revival of ancient literature pioneered by Petrarch in the fourteenth century produced a growing interest in the physical remains of antiquity and by 1420 this interest had spread to architecture. Florence pioneered the revival, along with the transformation of the Tuscan dialect into a literary language, but the papal court and Venice, with its access to Greek culture, were equally important centres of new learning. The enlightened despots of the smaller city-states also gave employment to artists and scholars at their courts. The arrival of printing from Germany in the middle of the fifteenth century meant that treatises could be published, and architects were pioneers in conveying information through engraved and woodblock plates.

The challenge of Protestantism in the north, and the Counter-Reformation put in train by the Council of Trent (1545 and reconvened several times in the middle years of the sixteenth century), gradually eroded the supremacy of humanist culture, a change typified by the desire of Sixtus V (1585–90) to turn the Colosseum into a wool factory. This did not, however, mean a reaction against the language of Classical architecture: Baroque architects continued to draw their inspiration from Roman buildings. Italy continued to be a magnet for artists and writers from north of the Alps; as examples, Goethe's visits and Winckelmann's prolonged residence were crucial for the neo-Classical movement.

The planning of churches was influenced by symbolism, liturgical change, reforming movements and the new religious orders as well as by the aesthetic preferences of architect and patron. 'Decorum' was a fundamental rule of Renaissance culture, and the function of a church was crucial to its plan. Centralised plans based on circle, square and Greek cross were praised for their symbolic perfection but often acknowledged to be unsuitable for cathedral or monastic churches. In practice, commemorative structures associated with miracles, plague deliverance or martyrdom provided opportunities for central plans with domes, exploiting the precedent of the Church of the Holy Sepulchre, Jerusalem, associated with the tomb of Christ. A composite plan, attaching a longitudinal nave to a domed centralised crossing, was an acceptable compromise, where processional functions and traditional Latin-cross symbolism were important. Later, an oval plan provided a directional axis in a basically centralised plan.

Monastic churches in mediaeval Italy had substantial rood screens across the nave, separating the laity from the monks' choir and presbytery. This practice died out in new churches of the fifteenth century, and the choir was removed to a chapel behind the high altar. After the Council of Trent screens were systematically taken out to accord with the emphasis on preaching and participation in the mass. The new religious orders of the second half of the sixteenth century, the Jesuits, Barnabites and Oratorians, tended to adopt single-nave plans, often with interconnecting side chapels, abbreviated transepts and clear division of the parts.

The large urban dwellings ('palazzi') of the urban patriciate exhibit considerable regional variation in their plans, although by the 1530s they tended to use a common language of decoration. Shared features are the rectangular block of three storeys, the central colonnaded courtyard, and the placing of the main apartments on the first floor (the 'piano nobile'), facing on to the street; the vaulted ground floor may house shops, summer apartments and, by the sixteenth century, stables, while children's and servants' rooms are on the second floor, wine, oil and fuel storage in the basement. Apartments consisted of suites of interconnecting rooms of diminishing size, from the great 'salone' to the small 'camera'. Corridors were rare and the functions of rooms flexible, depending on their size rather than their furnishings. The number of rooms was relatively small in mercantile palaces of the fifteenth century; only high ecclesiastics and petty princes retained large households. By the seventeenth century the number of domestic staff greatly increased and the use of carriages necessitated large service areas and stables with wide entrances. Symmetrical planning was common from the early fifteenth century but the Baroque period saw an increasing emphasis on multiple axes, spectacular staircases and interconnecting courtyards.

In Florence ground-floor shops, common in the fourteenth century, tended to disappear from palace facades, which nonetheless retained an embattled air with rusticated stonework. A continuous stone bench for public use around the base of a palace was a characteristic Florentine feature. In the sixteenth century the use of rustication was often restricted to quoins and voussoirs, and large pedimented windows supported on volutes ('kneeling windows') appeared on the ground floor. In 1581 Montaigne was shocked to find oiled linen or paper used in the windows instead of glass, but glass was rare until the seventeenth century.

In Rome cardinals' palaces were larger, initially more loosely planned, and had loggias at upper levels for maximum shade and air. Corner towers and cross-mullioned ('Guelph') windows were common until the end of the sixteenth century, when the Cancelleria introduced planning and decoration reminiscent of the Ducal Palace at Urbino. The Palazzo Farnese was the sixteenth-century model of a large palace, with its colonnaded vestibule, monumental courtyard, and axial relationship with the garden. A smaller-scale palace was evolved for members of the enlarged papal bureaucracy: grandeur of facade, staircase and courtyard was given precedence over size. These palaces seemed inconveniently small in the seventeenth century.

The distinctive planning of Venetian palaces was related to their waterside setting and conservative mercantile occupants. Openings concentrated at the centre of tripartite facades corresponded to long transverse entrance halls for unloading merchandise and to 'through' salons above. Sites were longer and narrower, and courtyards smaller, than in central Italy, and palaces were sometimes divided vertically between different members of the family. In the mainland towns of the Veneto such as Vicenza and Verona, something of the same tripartite planning is found, and courtyards are often replaced by gardens. Palladio introduced self-consciously Vitruvian elements, such as tetrastyle atria, into Vicentine palace design.

The villa as a distinctive architectural type re-emerges in the Renaissance after its disappearance in late antiquity. Villas vary so enormously according to function (agricultural centre, hunting lodge, suburban retreat), region, patron and architect that only a few common features, such as external loggias, can be discerned. Land reclamation, agricultural improvement and consolidation of estates preceded villa construction in Tuscany and the Veneto. Palladio drew

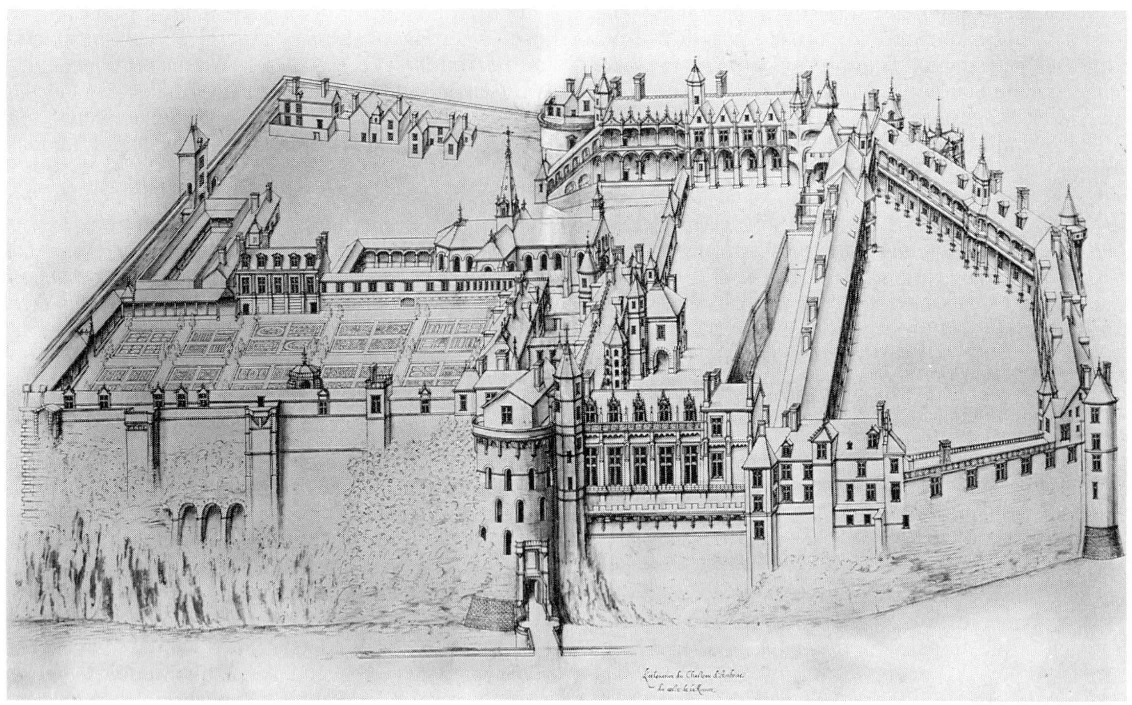

A. Château d'Amboise from north (1434 and later). Drawing by J. A. du Cerceau in sixteenth century. See p.817

B. The Escorial, near Madrid (1562–82): south front. See p.818

on the traditions of the Veneto to evolve a particularly functional and flexible series of villas for agricultural proprietors. They incorporated barns, storage loggias and granaries into hierarchically unified groups of buildings, dominated by the pedimented fronts. In Rome the suburban villa modelled on literary descriptions of ancient villas was popular with members of the pleasure-loving papal court. Vistas giving long perspectives, staircase ramps, niched exedrae and grottoes, influenced by Bramante's Cortile del Belvedere (1503–13) and Raphael's Villa Madama (begun 1516), became features of garden planning in the sixteenth century; water played an increasing part, feeding fountains, cooling dining tables, and powering elaborate automata.

France

After the end of the Hundred Years War and the expulsion of the English in 1453, France was less a feudal kingdom and more a modern monarchy with a powerful tendency toward centralisation and absolute rule. The Valois kings came to power in 1515 and ruled until Henry III was assassinated in 1589, having previously recognised Henry of Navarre, and thus ushered in the Bourbon dynasty which was to remain in power until the revolution two centuries later. During these periods the kingdom was enlarged to include Brittany, and extended eastwards to the Rhine; the frontier with Flanders was also pushed back.

The advance of centralised royal power under François I (1515–47) and Henri II (1547–59) was seriously shaken by the wars of religion of the 1570s and 1580s. Henri IV of Navarre (1589–1610) entered Paris in 1593 and embarked on a campaign of national recovery and political centralisation which was later continued by Louis XIII (1610–43) and Louis XIV. When the latter took over the reins of government when Mazarin died in 1661, France was already the most populous, the richest and probably the best organised country in Europe. Louis XIV ruled with absolute power for over half a century. His military might ensured French hegemony, and was only checked by a coalition of European powers in the ruinous war of the Spanish succession (1704–13). Louis's brilliant minister Jean Baptiste Colbert, who worked ceaselessly to improve France's commerce and industry, had little influence on policy, and the Bourbon successors, Louis XV (1715–74) and Louis XVI (1774–93), soon found that the costly wars in Europe, North America and India, and the general inflationary trends of the eighteenth century, made it essential to raise additional revenues. By 1789 the country was near to bankruptcy, and growing discontent led to a meeting of the Estates General and to the revolution, which was to simplify and rationalise the processes of government, decentralising control to eighty-three departments – its financial problems to be solved by the nationalisation and sale of church property. Napoleon emerged as the new ruler of France (Emperor 1804–14) and for fifteen years dominated the continent by force of arms until his defeat at Waterloo.

Many fine Roman buildings had survived in Provence, but it was not until the French invasions of Italy in 1494 and 1508 that French architects were constrained by Italian example to pay heed to the lessons of antiquity. Charles VIII returned from Italy to the Château d'Amboise on the Loire (p. 816A), the first royal residence in France, built originally almost entirely in the fifteenth century. He brought Italian artists and craftsmen home with him and initiated the early period of château-building on the Loire, most examples dating from the first quarter of the sixteenth century. It was in these châteaux that a Franco-Italian style flourished. They were in hunting country accessible to the King, and the importance of hunting as a means of attracting royal visits (and the resultant preferments) ensured that the château remained a prime building type until the court was finally centralised in Versailles in the 1660s.

From the end of the sixteenth century a growing proportion of royal and state business was conducted in Paris, and the king came increasingly to rely on his appointed civil servants to run his affairs rather than on the hereditary aristrocracy. As a result, between 1600 and 1660, Paris saw the construction of a large number of rich private residences – 'hôtels' – which became a characteristic building type exercising influence on domestic planning throughout the whole of Europe. In both châteaux and hôtels the adoption of a certain kind of Italian manners made fashionable by the Marquise de Rambouillet (1588–1665) led to a considerable refinement of plan. Moving away from the unitary feudal household, where much of life was conducted in the great hall, French fashion sought to create a number of small rooms for private social activities. These were usually grouped in threes or fours: an 'antichambre'; a 'chambre', in which formal receiving normally took place, with the host reclining on the bed; a more intimate 'cabinet', where special friends would be received and where objects of particular value were often displayed; and, if space permitted, a 'garderobe'.

With the refinement of social life went a desire to conceal the coarser elements of the household. Stables were, if possible, banished to a separate service court; servants' quarters communicated with the principal apartments by hidden passages and stairs. At the Château de Maisons, near Paris (1542–6), a tunnel was constructed so that food, wood and other necessities might be brought in unseen.

As patrons' demands became more complex, so the number of sites available for development in Paris became fewer and more restricted. Architects were obliged to show great ingenuity in fitting the necessary rooms into confined and irregular spaces. The most striking example in the seventeenth century was Antoine Le Pautre's Hôtel de Beauvais, Rue François Miron, Paris (1656). Although the construction of both châteaux and hôtels slowed down after the court moved to Versailles, these trends in domestic planning were continued in Parisian private houses of the eighteenth century after the Regent returned to Paris in 1715.

In church building, the Reformation made little impact. Although officially tolerated between the Edict of Nantes in 1598 and its revocation by Louis XIV in 1685, apart from Salomon de Brosse's Temple at Charenton, the Huguenots commissioned few important buildings. The new Counter-Reformation had an important impact on Roman Catholic church buildings, especially in the first half of the seventeenth century. As elsewhere in Europe, the later sixteenth-century Roman church types with aisleless nave and two- or three-storey facades were initially predominant, but in the later seventeenth and eighteenth centuries there was a return to the basilican plan, with a preference for a nave colonnade which continued around the apse as a semicircular screen. The Napoleonic era saw a brief preference for the antique temple form, as in the Madeleine, Paris (begun 1806).

The unparalleled centralisation of royal power produced in Versailles a building which, if it remained unique in France, set a pattern which was imitated throughout Europe. The long sequence of magnificently decorated state reception rooms set a new standard for state expenditure on such projects, and the inordinate length of the facade created a new kind of architectural scale or – more precisely – demonstrated the impact to be achieved by abandoning notions of scale altogether. And when the court tired of such grandiose living and moved to the Trianons, they too set a fashion for intimate comfort which was widely followed in continental Europe. Versailles is also the supreme example of the garden as an adjunct to the house – laid out on its axes, continuing its lines across large areas of the surrounding country. The garden, as devised by André Le Nôtre, is an integral part of the architectural conception.

From the royal plans for Paris in the mid-sixteenth century to Ledoux's revolutionary designs two hundred years later, the organisation of urban space was a constant preoccupation of French architects. Henry IV's great schemes, the Place Dauphine and the Place des Vosges, which were imitated in Covent Garden, London, and elsewhere, began a tradition of grand public squares which reaches to Dijon, Bordeaux, Nancy and many other towns.

The second half of the eighteenth century saw the emergence of new types of public building: for instance, markets, which often provided opportunities for novel structural techniques; and theatres, U-shaped auditoria with portico-fronts, which begin to appear in many provincial towns from the 1770s onwards. Napoleon initiated a major programme of public buildings, such as the Paris Bourse, General Post Office, and Ministry of Foreign Affairs, and this continued under the Restoration and Second Empire.

Spain and Portugal

In the fifteenth century the Iberian peninsula was divided into several small states with different languages and creeds. In the south the last Islamic foothold on western European soil was the Kingdom of Granada. It was surrounded by the Christian kingdoms of Portugal, Castile and Aragon: the small kingdom of Navarre bordered on France. Unification took place in the latter part of the fifteenth century with the marriage between Isabel I of Castile (d. 1504) and Fernando V of Aragon (d. 1516). Together they then led a crusade against Granda, which fell in 1492, and annexed Navarre in 1512 to give Spain and Portugal their present borders.

Turkish domination of the eastern Mediterranean trade routes encouraged in Spain and Portugal the spirit of more broadly based maritime enterprise, which is powerfully reflected in the architectural symbolism of the buildings of the Convent of Christ at Tomar (see Chapter 14). Spain's search for alternative routes led to the discovery of the Cape of Good Hope (1487) by Diaz and of the Americas by Columbus (1492). Portugal too extended its influence; Vasco da Gama took trade to the East Indies (1497) while Brazil became its largest overseas colony. Territorial expansion heralded the dissemination of Spanish and Portuguese architectural styles in the New World.

In 1520 the Habsburg king Charles I of Aragon and Castile was crowned Charles V of the Holy Roman Empire. This event thrust Spain for the first time to the forefront of European politics and brought its dominion over the Netherlands, Sardinia, Sicily, Naples, Milan and Germany. To this European empire, greater than any since Charlemagne, Charles added by conquest Mexico, Peru, Chile and Central America before he abdicated in 1556.

Philip II (1556–98), during whose reign the Escorial (p. 816B), one of Europe's greatest palaces, was built, inherited the problems of this vast empire. The first was rivalry with France, a burgeoning power in European politics. The second was discontent in the Netherlands, which was fuelled by England and led ultimately to the ill-conceived and catastrophic Armada. This contributed to the gradual depletion of the Spanish purse, and was offset only by Philip's successful claim in 1580 to the Portuguese throne, which remained in Spanish hands until 1640. The monarchy's desire for the purity of the Catholic faith resulted in a policy of religious intolerance. Its instrument, the Spanish Inquisition, had been established by 1487, and by 1502 Muslims and Jews on Spanish soil had been either converted or expelled. Even the converted Muslims, the Moriscos, were deported in 1609. The result was the loss of many fine architectural craftsmen.

Spain's involvement in the Thirty Years War was a drain on resources and its hold over Italy was weakened. Trade and industry continued to languish and by 1700 Spain had become a protégé of Louis XIV, who upon the death of the last Habsburg king placed his own grandson on the Spanish throne as Philip V. This event led to the War of the Spanish Succession (1701–13) and the loss of Naples, Sardinia and Milan to Austria. The relative peace and prosperity of the late eighteenth century, a period during which architecture and the arts were fostered, was shattered by Napoleon's invasion at the beginning of the nineteenth century. With powerful help from the British armies under Wellington, the French were finally driven out of Spain in 1813. From the period of the Peninsular War the American colonies revolted, contributing to the further decline of Spain and Portugal, and eventually won their independence.

Austria, Germany and Central Europe

The area considered here is present-day Germany, Austria, Switzerland and the Czech Republic, with parts of Poland and Hungary. In the period 1450–1830 it was divided into many independent and dependent states and cities with shifting political allegiances.

Renaissance culture had its first real flowering outside Italy at the enlightened humanist court of Matthias Corvinus of Hungary (1458–90). Close contacts with Italy had been a feature of Hungarian culture since the fourteenth century, and Matthias's reforming reign, which raised Hungary to the status of the greatest power in central Europe, saw an influx of Italian artists. Thereafter, power shifted to the Jagellonian Kings of Bohemia who, for a brief period, controlled an empire which included Hungary and Poland, and Renaissance influences spread to Prague and Cracow. Hungary's Renaissance was brought to a close by the Turkish invasions (1526) and the subsequent division of the country: the Jagellonian period in Poland ended in 1572.

The dominions of Spain, Burgundy and the Netherlands were added to those of the old Holy Roman Empire under Charles V (Charles I of Spain) in 1520. The first religious wars following the Reformation were brought to an end by the Peace of Augsburg, under which each ruler was allowed to determine the religion of his territory. Broadly, southern Germany, Austria (after Protestant beginnings) and the Rhineland remained Catholic, while northern Germany adopted Lutheranism. The Habsburg territories were divided between Spain, on the one hand, and the old empire, centred on Austria and Bohemia, on the other. Political and religious fragmentation meant that the importation of Renaissance forms was sporadic and localised in the sixteenth century, but a lead was given by the free cities of Nuremberg and Augsburg, and by the proselytising Jesuits in Austria and Southern Germany. The struggle with the Turks was a constant preoccupation.

The Thirty Years War (1610–48) between Catholic and Protestant princes brought a halt to building, and recovery was slow, even after the Peace of Westphalia. The influence of the Austrian empire in Germany declined in the second half of the seventeenth century, and the principalities built up their sovereignty. Prussia began to gain power in the north; Frederick I became King of Prussia in 1701.

Austro-Prussian rivalry came to a head in the eighteenth century with the War of the Spanish Succession (1740–48) and the Seven Years War (1756–63). Frederick II (the Great) (1740–86) raised Prussia to a position of pre-eminence among the German states; he embellished his capital of Berlin with palaces and public buildings. In Austria Joseph I's reign (1705–11), marked by creative architectural patronage, was followed by the reforming period of Maria Theresa (1722–80), while her son Joseph II (1780–90) attempted to impose the ideas of the Enlightenment.

Napoleon's campaigns brought the Holy Roman Empire to an end, eliminating dozens of free cities and ecclesiastical territories. As elsewhere in Europe, Napoleon both aroused liberal expectations and united his new subjects in feelings of nationalistic opposition. At the Congress of Vienna (1815) the map of central Europe was redrawn. The three hundred or so margravates, palatinates, electorates, duchies, ecclesiastical states and imperial cities of Renaissance Germany, under the suzerainty of the reigning houses of Habsburg, Hohenzollern, Wittelsbach and Wettin, were reduced to thirty-nine states subject only to Austria.

The Protestant liturgy introduced by the Lutheran reformation, with its rejection of imagery and the cult of the saints, favoured extreme simplicity in church design. Such few Protestant churches as were built had plain hall-like interiors and galleries to accommodate larger congregations; sometimes communion table and pulpit were aligned on the central axis. The Jesuits, who began to combat Protestantism in the second half of the sixteenth century, favoured churches deliberately modelled on Roman examples (for example, Michaelskirche, Munich, 1583). The Baroque and Rococo in Germany and Austria were the popular styles for hundreds of Catholic churches and rural monasteries built by wealthy abbeys and powerful bishops between 1680 and 1780. Often erected on spectacular hill-top sites, many of them were places of pilgrimage.

This period saw the decline of feudalism, and in the conduct of warfare mercenaries replaced the feudal troops. There were also internal influences at work, such as the power of the great trading towns of the Hanseatic league, the position of the guilds in civic government, and the attempts of the peasants to secure their freedom. A major factor was the growing influence of the universities, notably of Heidelberg, the main seat of the humanist movement. This was strengthened by the invention of printing and the publication of literary works which aroused interest in the art and architecture of ancient Greece.

The growing importance of civic government led to the commissioning of an increasing number of public buildings. Early examples were in the free cities of Nuremberg and Augsburg where mercantile governments built town halls and civic structures. In the later seventeenth and eighteenth centuries the countless smaller rulers in Germany asserted their territorial pretensions with costly palace buildings in emulation of the French and Austrian courts, as well as patronising music and theatre. Prussian ambitions were expressed in a range of public buildings in Berlin, where neo-Classical ideas appeared early and continued to pervade city gates, prisons, theatres, academies and museums and other buildings of the early nineteenth century.

The Low Countries

During the fifteenth century the rule of the Duchy of Burgundy, established first in Flanders in 1384, was extended over most of the Low Countries, and passed to the Habsburg emperors by the marriage (1482) of Maximilian of Austria to Mary of Burgundy. On the abdication of Charles V (1556), the Low Countries came under the rigid rule of Philip II of Spain (1556–98). A long and bitter revolt, led by William the Silent, Duke of Orange, and involving both religious and political dissent, was ruthlessly opposed by Cardinal Granvelle and the Duke of Alva, and by 1590 Spain had reconquered the ten southern provinces, corresponding roughly to modern Belgium. The seven northern provinces won their independence, and became the Dutch Republic in 1581. Calvinist Protestantism became the basis of the Dutch Reformed Church, while the Belgian provinces remained Catholic.

The Thirty Years War ended with the Peace of Westphalia in 1648, the independence of the north was recognised and the port of Antwerp was closed to commerce. The result was catastrophic for Belgium's trade, and war with France further reduced its fortunes. The stagnation of architecture in the later seventeenth century reflects this decline.

By contrast, the Dutch Republic, though equally plagued with wars, became a great naval power and maritime trading nation, acquiring overseas colonies in its 'golden age', the seventeenth century. Although the Princes of Orange maintained a court at The Hague, economic power lay with the burghers of the great trading cities of Holland and Zeeland, who constructed richly decorated and furnished houses, creating an unprecedented demand for paintings 'off the peg'.

In 1688 William of Orange and his wife Mary became King and Queen of England, reinforcing the already strong influence of Dutch architecture in that country. The prosperity of the United Provinces survived the major European wars of the eighteenth century, and a middle-class revolt in the 1790s.

Belgium had a period of French rule in the early eighteenth century (1700–6), and under the Treaty of Utrecht (1713) passed to Austria. In 1789 there was an internal revolt, and occupation by the French revolutionary forces (1794) was a prelude to Belgium's absorption, along with Holland, into Napoleon's empire. The Congress of Vienna briefly united the two countries into a Kingdom of the Netherlands (1815), which survived only until 1830 when Luxembourg as well as Belgium became independent.

The beliefs of Luther and Calvin were received early in the Low Countries, but their adherents were bitterly persecuted by their Spanish rulers. The final division between Catholic Belgium in the south and the Protestant United Provinces in the north resulted in strongly differing traditions of church building in the seventeenth century. The Dutch Reformed and Lutheran churches in Holland follow the Lutheran pattern early established in Germany (austere in character, the interior focused on a dominant pulpit), but Dutch churches make less use of galleries and give a prominent role to the baptismal font. Without the need for a strong axis, there was much experimentation with central plans. Architectural evidence of the religious tolerance in Amsterdam is found in the Portuguese-Israeli Synagogue (1671), an interesting structure with a pilastered exterior and three equal barrel-vaulted spaces internally.

The many new churches in seventeenth-century Belgium were mostly built by the religious orders and societies, especially the Jesuits, but also included several pilgrimage churches with centralised plans, and the characteristically Belgian béguinages, charitable communities of lay women.

The town halls, guild houses and merchants' residences of the Low Countries testify to a prosperous and competitive urban culture. From 1613, the city of Amsterdam was extended in a huge semicircle around the old centre with a web of radial and circumferential canals, along the banks of which the merchants built their houses. The Palladian style of Jacob Van Campen (1595–1657) (which became for later architects a symbol of

Dutchness) is appropriate to The Hague or Amsterdam not only because building poses structural difficulties similar to those found in Venice, but also because Venice provided a model for a mercantile republican régime. The semi-monarchical Court of the Princes of Orange, unlike Holland as a whole, looked to France for inspiration.

Belgian secular architecture is not noted for its grandiose palaces or châteaux, but French and Austrian influences were nonetheless predominant from the early eighteenth century onwards. The proximity of France, its foreign policy and its linguistic ties with the south-eastern half of Belgium were important factors. The Place Royale in Brussels was rebuilt in 1775 to designs by French architects, and is almost a replica of the Place Royale at Reims (q.v.).

Britain

The direct and indirect influence of the monarchy on architectural development varied greatly during the Tudor, Stuart and Hanoverian dynasties. Henry VIII's secure hold of the throne (1502–47) facilitated early contacts with European monarchs, the most famous being the meeting with François I on the Field of the Cloth of Gold in 1520. Henry's deliberate importation of Italian, French and Flemish craftsmen for work on the royal palaces largely brought about the introduction of the Renaissance style. The architectural effects of the break with Rome and the adoption of Protestantism (1534) were less important in church planning (see below) than in the transfer of the monastic estates into private hands, thus fostering the building of country houses. Under Edward VI (1547–53) the Latin mass was replaced by the Book of Common Prayer, though the reign of Mary (1553–8), who married Philip II of Spain, was marked by a brief return to Catholicism. The accession of her sister Elizabeth I (1558–1603), however, brought a new Act of Supremacy (1559) restoring the Anglican Church with the monarch as its Supreme Governor. The defeat of the Spanish Armada confirmed the independent position of England, facilitated trade and exploration overseas, and promoted an atmosphere of confidence at home. Elizabeth was too economical to be a great builder but she encouraged the construction of country houses by her courtiers as an indirect expression of sovereignty. In Scotland, still an independent nation until the Act of Union of 1707, the 'auld alliance' meant strongly French architectural characteristics in castle building which, owing to unstable political conditions, were still functionally necessary.

The Stuart kings were drawn to the absolutist notions of monarchy prevailing on the continent, and architecture was used to express them. The patronage of James I (1603–25) enabled Inigo Jones to introduce Palladian architecture into England and to design the elaborate court masques favoured by the early Stuarts. During the reigns of James I and his son, English colonising enterprise led to the expansion of trade and a consequent accession of numbers to the wealthy classes, who built country houses in emulation of the King. Charles I's disastrous foreign and domestic policies were accompanied by a highly sophisticated taste in the arts. He amassed an unrivalled collection of pictures and continued to favour Inigo Jones, who with John Webb designed grandiose schemes for a palace at Whitehall which was never realised. The Civil War (1642–9) and the period of the Commonwealth under Cromwell (1649–60) meant a near-halt to building.

The restoration (1660) of Charles II, who had lived at the court of Louis XIV, brought renewed emphasis on architecture as an expression of centralised monarchical power in the French style. The Great Fire of London (1666) gave Sir Christopher Wren an unparalleled opportunity for church building, which had been almost at a standstill since the later Middle Ages, although his plans for rebuilding the City on rational lines were not adopted. James II's reign (1685–8) was speedily brought to a close by his unpopular religious policies. The 'Glorious Revolution' of William of Orange and his wife Mary, daughter of James II, reinforced the Dutch influences already present in English architecture. Queen Anne's reign (1702–14) saw the Fifty New Churches Act (1711), which resulted in some of the finest buildings of the English Baroque. In this restoration period many fine characteristic smaller buildings, both urban and rural, were built (pp. 822–4).

The monarchy ceased to be the pace-setter in architecture after the accession of George I (1714–27), although George IV (1820–30), especially during his Regency (1811 onwards), was an active patron of building. The landed aristocracy, many of whose members were amateur architects, promoted both Palladianism and neo-Classicism in country-house architecture, and developed their London estates with building leases. Prosperity, based on naval supremacy, expansion of the colonies, home and overseas trade, and agricultural reform, produced a still greater demand for houses, and a ready market for speculative buildings. The manufacture of goods for the home market became increasingly important to British prosperity. Between 1750 and 1800 the population of the British Isles rose by some 6 million to a total of 16 million, compared with an average rise of one million for each of the previous five half-century periods. This and the introduction of new materials and techniques in the Industrial Revolution, together with improved communications, brought increased urbanisation and unprecedented increases in building activity. At the end of the eighteenth century London had a population of almost a million, far exceeding any other in size and political influence.

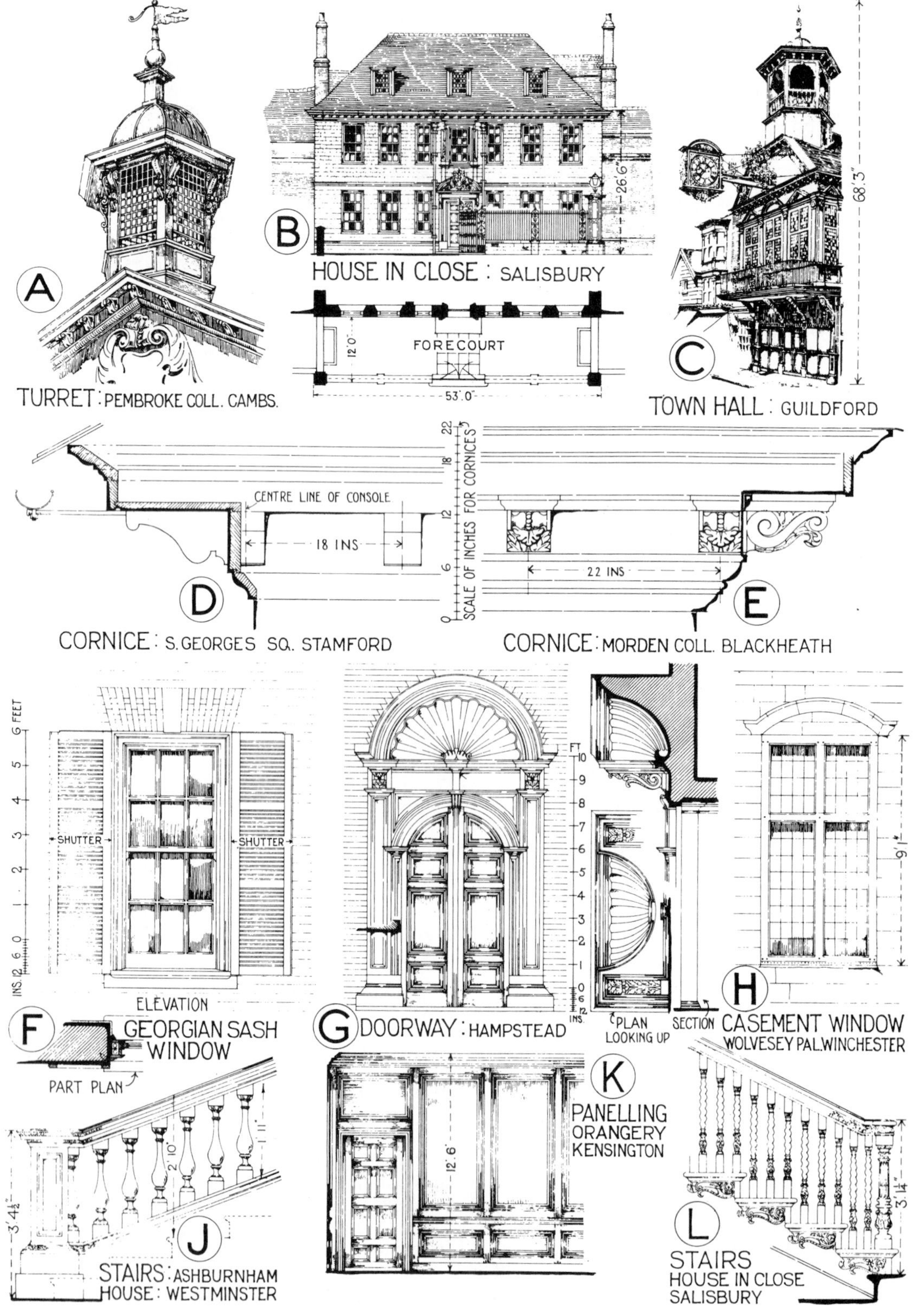
A
TURRET: PEMBROKE COLL. CAMBS.
B
HOUSE IN CLOSE : SALISBURY
FORECOURT
12'0"
53'0"
26'6"
C
TOWN HALL : GUILDFORD
68'3"
CENTRE LINE OF CONSOLE
18 INS
SCALE OF INCHES FOR CORNICES
0
6
12
18
22
22 INS
D
CORNICE : S. GEORGES SQ. STAMFORD
E
CORNICE : MORDEN COLL. BLACKHEATH
6 FEET
5
4
3
2
1
0
6
12
INS.
SHUTTER
SHUTTER
ELEVATION
F
GEORGIAN SASH WINDOW
PART PLAN
FT
10
9
8
7
6
5
4
3
2
1
0
6
12
INS.
G
DOORWAY : HAMPSTEAD
PLAN LOOKING UP
SECTION
H
CASEMENT WINDOW
WOLVESEY PAL. WINCHESTER
9'1"
J
STAIRS : ASHBURNHAM HOUSE : WESTMINSTER
3'4½"
2'10"
1'1"
K
PANELLING
ORANGERY
KENSINGTON
12'6"
L
STAIRS
HOUSE IN CLOSE
SALISBURY
3'1¼"

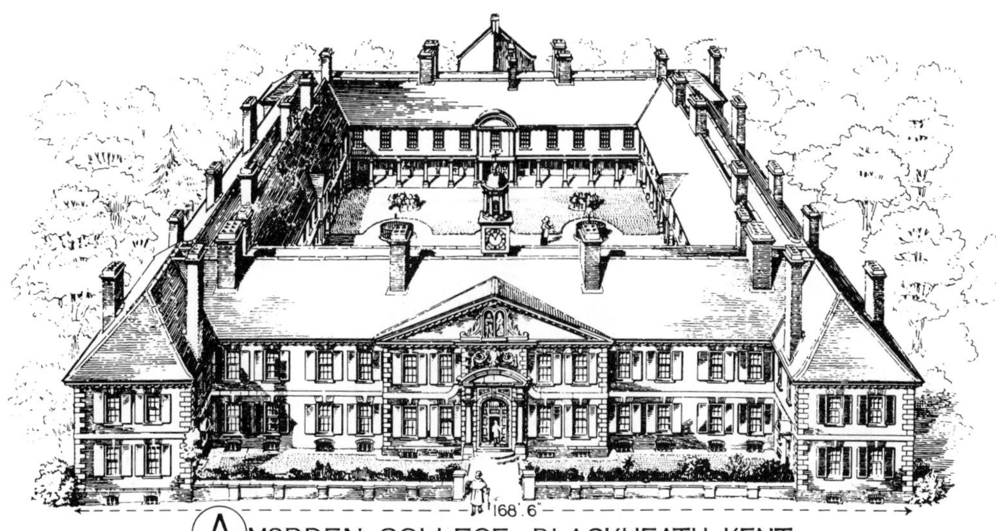

A MORDEN COLLEGE : BLACKHEATH : KENT

B BUTTER MARKET
BARNARD CASTLE : DURHAM

C GARDEN HOUSE
POUNDISFORD PARK : SOM.

D BUTTER MARKET
BUNGAY : SUFFOLK

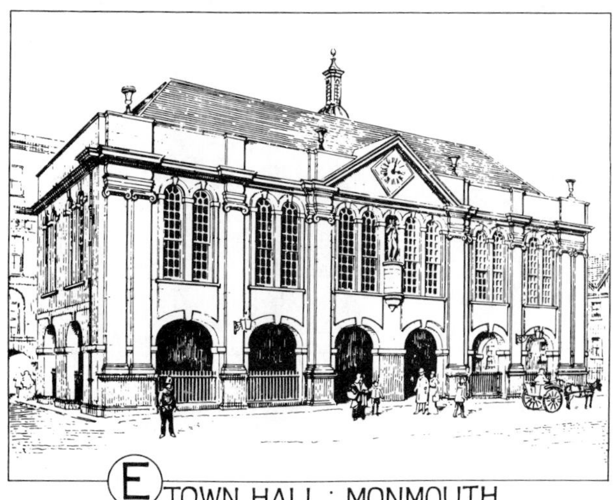

E TOWN HALL : MONMOUTH

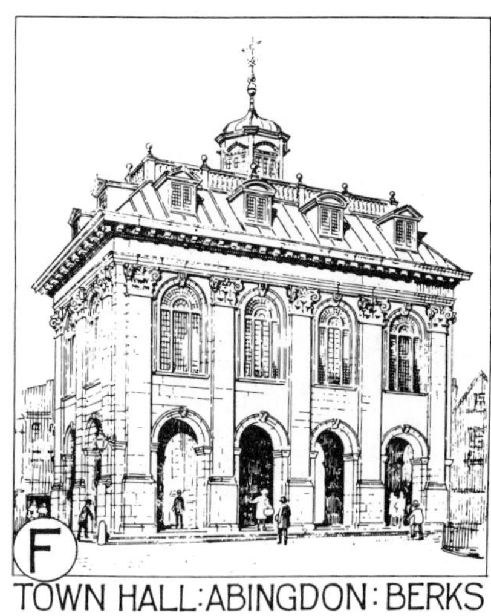

F TOWN HALL : ABINGDON : BERKS

A SWAN HOUSE: CHICHESTER

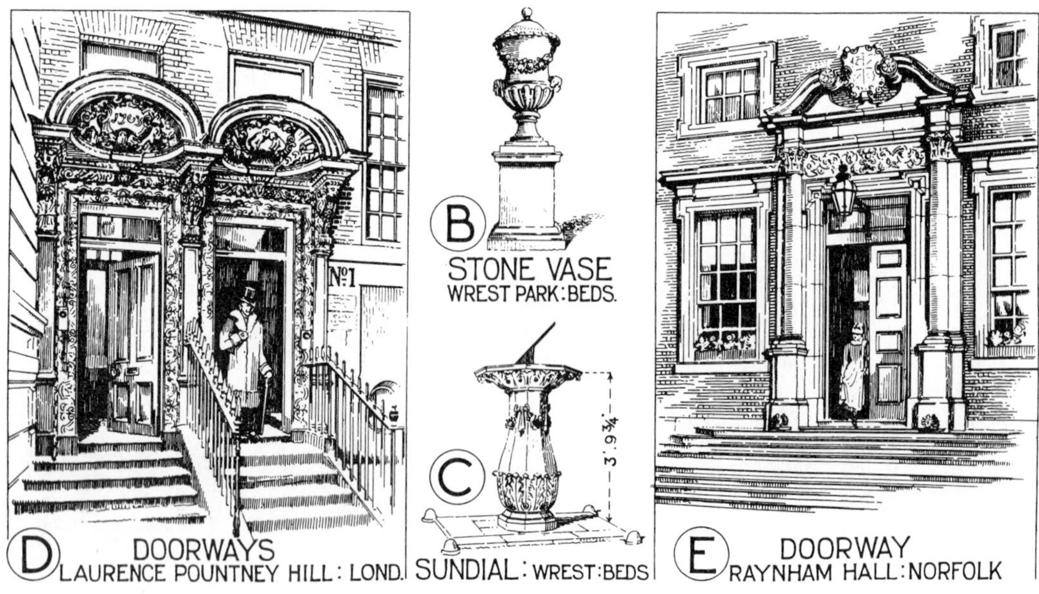

B STONE VASE WREST PARK: BEDS.

C SUNDIAL: WREST: BEDS

D DOORWAYS LAURENCE POUNTNEY HILL: LOND.

E DOORWAY RAYNHAM HALL: NORFOLK

Norwich with its weaving and banking and Bristol with its West Indies trade were next in importance to the capital.

Changes in country-house planning between 1500 and 1830 reflect changes in household structure and organisation as well as those in response to foreign models. Whereas England followed France and Italy in formal planning for much of the period, in the middle of the eighteenth century English country houses pioneered the informality that marked a new sensibility.

Sixteenth-century plans incorporated some enduring features from a past when the great lord's house was a centre of feudal power and the seat of an enormous household. The great hall with a ceremonial staircase leading to the great chamber took centuries to become a vestibule in the continental manner, but increasing emphasis on privacy removed all eating functions from the hall. The symmetrical facades of Elizabethan houses frequently mask an internal asymmetry where the great hall is set off to one side. Galleries (covered interior walks with large windows) became important features of Elizabethan houses, and began to be used to display paintings and sculpture as in France and Italy. Some staircases began to be made of wood, rather than stone.

The influence of Palladio's centralised house plans and their diffusion over Europe brought a greater formality to planning in the seventeenth and early eighteenth centuries. The hall and parlour were placed centrally on the ground floor and the 'saloon' replaced the great chamber on the floor above. Symmetrical groups of rooms of diminishing size – with-drawing chamber, chamber, closet-cabinet – opened off the central rooms.

The Palladian revival of the eighteenth century took over this type of planning, relegated the service areas to the 'rustic' basement and elevated the main entrance into the hall by external staircases. The apartments could be strung out as wings on either side of the central block. In the second half of the eighteenth century the apartment system was broken up for the first time, and the reception rooms were arranged around a central staircase. Private apartments could then be removed to the other side of the house or to the upper storeys. More time was spent in the common areas of the house, and the private apartments shrank in size. By the late eighteenth century a desire for informality and greater rapport between house and countryside brought about looser plan arrangements. The servants were moved to the wings, while the main rooms were placed asymmetrically at ground level to obtain views of landscape features or better sunlight penetration. The picturesque sensibility had conquered Palladian formality.

With isolated exceptions, church building in England during the period resulted from a series of state interventions: the rebuilding of the City churches after the Fire of London (1666), the Fifty New Churches Act of 1711 and the Church Building Act of 1818. Both pieces of legislation were in response to government fears of increasing popular support for the Nonconformist churches in areas of expanding population.

The moderate character of English Protestantism meant relatively few changes in Anglican church design after the Reformation. Screens were not destroyed, though images sometimes were, especially in the Cromwellian period, and stone altars were replaced by wooden tables. Emphasis in the Prayer Book on corporate worship, preaching, and reading the gospel, brought the lectern and the pulpit into the nave and made good acoustics a prime requirement. The Laudian revival of high-church transcendentalism brought a brief mediaevalism to church architecture in the 1630s and 1640s, and the communion rail was introduced to protect the altar. Galleries for extra seating, a Lutheran invention much used in Holland, first appeared in the seventeenth century and, though unpopular with architects, became a lasting feature of church design until the Gothic revival. Wren's experiments with central planning in the City churches were dictated more by site restrictions and continental influences than by liturgical requirements. The Fifty New Churches Act of 1711 aimed to combine dominating size and splendour of materials with commodious interiors giving good visibility and acoustics. Hawksmoor shared with some contemporary theologians an interest in reviving primitive Christian arrangements. Eighteenth-century church interiors had high box pews, multi-level pulpits and Classical screens, almost all of which were removed and lost during the Gothic Revival. The 'Commissioners' churches' which followed the 1818 Act were not innovative in design (see Chapter 34).

Russia

The growing power of Moscow in the fourteenth and fifteenth centuries (see Chapter 8) culminated in the unification of Russia under Ivan the Great (1462–1505). His imperial ambitions led to outward-looking cultural policies and the employment of Italian architects. Ivan IV 'the Terrible' (1533–84) pushed Muscovite frontiers well into Siberia, and established a ruthlessly autocratic government in Moscow. A more introverted period of architectural development pursuing more traditional (Byzantine) cultural goals followed. After a prolonged period of civil strife, Mikhail Romanov, founder of the Romanov dynasty, was elected Tsar in 1613, and his grandson Peter the Great (1682–1725) brought about profound changes in Russian society. Following the Great Northern War with Sweden (1700–21), he determined to remedy Russia's isolation by founding a new, more accessible, capital at S. Petersburg. The now 'Imperial' court was moved to it, and Italian architects were imported to design its buildings. Under Peter's daughter Elizabeth (1741–61) and Catherine II 'the Great' (1762–96), the city became one of the great cultural centres of Europe. Russia suffered military defeats at Austerlitz (1805) and Friedland (1807) and during the reign of Alexander I (1801–25) Moscow fell to the French when Napoleon invaded in 1812, but Russia rapidly recovered its position in the forefront of European affairs.

As the Russian Orthodox Church had originated as a branch of Greek Orthodoxy, church planning followed Byzantine models (see Chapters 8 and 12). Patriarch Nikon (elected 1652) became so committed to the restoration of 'primitive orthodox' practice that he even condemned native Russian architectural elements such as the tent roof, an attitude reflected both in the simplicity of the Church of the Twelve Apostles, Moscow, and in the use of the Holy Sepulchre Church as a model for the Monastery of the New Jerusalem, Istra. Votive churches with octagonal towers crowned by tent roofs appeared from the sixteenth century onwards.

It was under Peter the Great that civil architecture looked to the west. Not only Paris and Rome but also nearby Stockholm provided models for S. Petersburg, the first modern capital built to a predetermined plan. Court life took on the aspect of Versailles, the clear source for his daughter Empress Elizabeth's royal palaces.

Scandinavia

Scandinavian history in the Renaissance period is dominated by the Kingdoms of Denmark and Sweden. Through the Union of Kalmar (1397) the three Nordic Kingdoms (Denmark, Sweden and Norway) were united under Danish supremacy. In Denmark, Copenhagen was established as the capital in 1416; the accession of Christian I in 1448 marked the foundation of the Oldenburg dynasty, which still continues on the throne today. Danish history of the sixteenth and seventeenth centuries is punctuated by wars with Sweden (1513–23, 1563–70, 1613–15, 1643–5, 1675–1720). The turbulence of the period, which included the Reformation and a war with Germany (1625–9), did not prevent the initiation of large public works programmes under Christian IV (1588–1648), and they were renewed in the more peaceful years from 1720–1801. Between 1801 and 1814 Denmark was involved in the Napoleonic Wars against England, after which Norway was ceded to Sweden.

Sweden broke away from Danish dominance under Gustavus Vasa (1523–60), who established a hereditary monarchy and introduced Protestantism to Sweden (1527). The increasing power of the Crown in the seventeenth century coincided with a period during which grandiose buildings were constructed, particularly in Stockholm. Throughout the period, and especially during the reign of Queen Christina (1632–54), Sweden became a European power of some importance. However, wars at the end of the century against both Denmark and Russia caused Swedish prestige and the influence of the monarchy to be reduced at home. After the Congress of Vienna (1814) Sweden gained Norway, but lost Finland, which had been a Swedish province since the fourteenth century. It had been repeatedly devastated in the eighteenth century during the wars between Sweden and Russia, and in 1809 was incorporated into the Russian empire as a semi-autonomous Grand duchy. Such wealth as Norway and Finland had was based on the supply of raw materials, especially iron and timber.

Gradually country houses replaced the castle-like dwellings which were the favoured expression of wealth and authority among the Danish and Swedish nobility and royalty. Many country houses were built in the seventeenth and eighteenth centuries, often on forested estates, constructed of wood.

The cityscapes of Copenhagen and Stockholm reflect the increasing centralisation of court life in the seventeenth century, and the rivalry between the two capitals. Copenhagen was modernised under Christian IV, while Stockholm took on much of its present-day character later in the seventeenth century.

The Lutheran reformation in Scandinavia greatly affected church design in Denmark, Sweden and Norway. Here, as with much domestic building, Scandinavia was inspired by Protestant Holland. Emblematic steeples remained characteristic features of Scandinavian religious (and secular) buildings, while centralised plans were often favoured for churches.

During the eighteenth century the two capitals were gradually eclipsed by the new S. Petersburg. Copenhagen, which had been ravaged by fire in 1721, embarked on a phase of urban renewal inspired by early neo-Classicism in Paris. After 1800, the architects of the Finnish capital, Helsinki, looked to S. Petersburg and to Napoleonic Paris for inspiration, while Oslo (then called Christiania and by that time Swedish) turned for inspiration to Schinkel's Berlin.

Scandinavia has a rich history of urban planning: an early example of a new town is Kristianstaad (Denmark), designed on a grid layout under Christian IV; Oslo (1624) and Stockholm (*c.* 1625) also have extensive gridded street plans.

Further major fires in Copenhagen (1794 and 1795) necessitated the rebuilding of large parts of the city, which, as a result, has an astonishingly unified neo-Classical character. Many public buildings were rebuilt and reflect the enlightened Danish attitude to reform.

The capital of Finland was moved from Turku, the centre of the Swedish-speaking intelligentsia, to the fishing village of Helsinki in 1812. Like his colleague C. H. Grosch in Christiania (later Oslo), C. L. Engel in Helsinki was given commissions for a wide range of building types needed to serve a government administrative centre.

Post-Renaissance Europe

Europe was indelibly affected by the French Revolution of 1789 and the Napoleonic Empire. At its zenith in 1810 the Empire comprised the whole of France, Belgium and the Netherlands, and parts of Germany, Italy and the Dalmatian coast. However, Napoleon's influence extended beyond this to encompass most of mainland Europe, and the only areas which were neither under his control nor allied to him were on the periphery: Portugal, Britain, Sweden, Russia, the Ottoman Empire, Sardinia and Sicily. Almost inevitably, therefore, the influence of France on European life was considerable, a factor of especial consequence being the Code Napoléon which laid the foundations of modern law in many European countries.

On the fall of Napoleon the Congress of Vienna (1814–15) tried to impose on Europe its earlier political structure and restore its royal rulers without regard for the new feelings of nationalism (stimulated, at least in part, by the internationalist system enforced by Napoleon), while memories of 1789, with its intoxicating ideals of liberty, fraternity and equality, were impossible to erase. The leading figure at the Congress of Vienna was the future Austrian Chancellor, Prince Klemens Metternich (1773–1859), who sought to suppress political reform in Europe, but in 1830 there were revolutionary eruptions from Portugal to Poland. In France the restored monarchy tottered, but found brief uneasy survival under the more liberal Louis-Philippe. Belgium achieved national identity and independence from Holland. Greece, for centuries part of the Ottoman Empire, regained its freedom in 1829. Unrest in Britain prompted the passing of the first parliamentary reform Act in 1832. In the years that followed there was a good deal of public building activity, as various European governments – whether restored or reformed – asserted their authority.

Although for the most part outwardly at peace after 1830, thanks in large measure to the political dexterity of Metternich, by 1848 Europe was once again in the throes of revolution. The outcome was a strengthening of constitutional liberty in Denmark, Holland, Belgium and Switzerland, emancipation of the peasants in the Austrian Empire and German states, and universal (male) suffrage in France, where the Second Republic was inaugurated. The same year saw the publication of the 'Communist Manifesto' of Karl Marx (1818–83) and Friedrich Engels (1820–95). The French Second Republic lasted only until 1852, when it was succeeded by the initially repressive Second Empire of Napoleon III. In Austria Franz Josef succeeded to the throne in 1848, and his long reign, marked by reactionary conservatism, lasted until 1916.

After 1848 the seeds of nationalism which had been sown in the Napoleonic era (and in some cases earlier) grew to maturity in several countries. The unification of Italy, championed by the romantic patriot Giuseppe Garibaldi (1807–82), was gradually achieved between 1859 and 1870, and the German states were formed into a cohesive whole between 1866 and 1870 under the high-minded opportunism of the Prussian chief minister Otto von Bismarck (1815–98). At the same time there were widespread moves for independence on the part of national groups within the larger political units. Hungary achieved partial autonomy in 1867 when the Austrian Empire was transformed into a dual monarchy; Serbia and Bulgaria gained full independence from Turkey in 1878; and Norway broke away from Sweden in 1905. Not all nationalist movements fared so well, however: a Polish uprising was suppressed by Russia in 1863, and successive British governments failed to implement Irish home rule.

It can be said that between 1830 and 1870 Europe was imbued with liberal and national movements, while after 1870 it was increasingly dominated by power politics, based largely on the economic rivalry of France and Germany. The brief and ill-starred Franco-Prussian War of 1870 ended the Second Empire in France, and marked the beginning of the Third Republic, which survived until World War II. In 1871 the German Empire (the 'Second Reich') was created: dominated by Prussia, it endured until the dissolution of Imperial Germany in 1918. Franco-Prussian rivalry was, however, only part of a complex pattern of growing distrust in Europe and it was eventually Austria's annexation of Serbia which led to World War I, in which Austria was allied with Germany against Russia on the Eastern Front and France, Belgium, Britain and Italy on the Western Front.

The conflict between the aggrandisement of the major European powers and the desire of the lesser nations for autonomy is reflected in the public buildings of the later nineteenth century. Rome and Berlin joined Paris and London as cities of imperial ambition, the building programme in Vienna continued undiminished, and spending on public buildings in Prague increased enormously as Bohemia gained some autonomy within the Austria Empire. In the major cities of the smaller independent nations, such as those of Scandinavia, public building was promoted as a sign of national vitality.

International rivalry in Europe was given an added edge during the nineteenth century by the Industrial Revolution. Major inventions in metallurgy, cotton manufacture and the development of steam-power in the latter half of the eighteenth century laid the foundations of more rapid changes in the nineteenth century. Britain, as the 'workshop of the world', dominated these changes, and as early as 1826 the German architect Schinkel on a visit to Britain had marvelled at the number of warehouses and factories, some as large as the Royal Palace in Berlin, and the thousands of factory chimneys belching smoke. By the early 1840s Britain was annually producing 40 million tons of coal and 1.3 million tons of iron, and was exporting 734 million yards of cotton per annum. By the middle of the nineteenth century, Belgium, France and Germany were developing apace, and over the following years pockets of industry were established in parts of Poland, Austria, Scandinavia, Spain and Italy.

During the second half of the nineteenth century output grew significantly, and as continental Europe began to flourish industrially Britain turned to its empire to provide outlets for its manufactured goods and for capital investment. In this way Britain maintained its leading position, and by the early 1900s was exporting over 5000 million yards of cotton and producing 200 million tons of coal each year. Steel, whose manufacture first became cheaper in 1856 with the process invented by Henry Bessemer (1813–98), gradually superseded cast iron as the desirable material for most machinery, railways and steamships because it was less brittle. Britain's lead in iron and steel production was maintained until the 1890s, by which time it was overtaken not only by the USA but also by Germany.

The industrial changes of the nineteenth century were reflected in the growth of communications. The rivers of Europe, the traditional arteries of trade, remained of vital importance, and carried increasing quantities of goods as, from the 1830s, steamboats facilitated the transport of large cargoes upstream as well as downstream. As the Industrial Revolution gathered pace the rivers were supplemented by canals, and during the later eighteenth century in Britain a network of canals was constructed, linking the midlands with the industrial north and with London. During the nineteenth century the chief river systems of mainland Europe began to be connected, for instance the Rhine–Marne canal of 1838–53.

The spread of canals was constrained, however, by the rise of railways, in which Britain again took the lead, building almost 11,000 km (6635 miles) by 1850. Initially, the railways linked neighbouring cities such as Manchester and Liverpool (1830) or Brussels and Antwerp (1836), but national and international routes were created quite quickly, and during the second half of the century the Alps were conquered, connecting Italy with Austria (through the Brenner Pass, 1864–7), France (the Mont Cenis Tunnel, 1857–71) and Germany (the S. Gotthard Tunnel, 1872–82). The provision of railway stations, from small buildings on branchlines to metropolitan termini, was one of the most pervasive signs of the nineteenth-century revolution in communications.

An increased birth rate and reduction in infant mortality contributed to a steady rise in population during the nineteenth century. The figures for Europe as a whole increased from about 180 million in 1800 to 274 million in 1850 and 400 million in 1900. In the most industrially advanced countries the growth was proportionately greater: in England and Wales the population rose from over 9 million in 1801 to about 18 million in 1851 and 33 million in 1901; and between 1851 and 1901 Germany's population grew from 34 million to 56 million. In Britain the increase was preponderantly urban: by 1851 only half the population could be defined as rural, and by 1901 only a quarter. Elsewhere the balance changed more slowly, and Germany was the only other major country to become predominantly urban by 1900. Nonetheless, the growth of cities was a striking phenomenon in most parts of Europe. The two major centres of population were London and Paris, which grew respectively from less than one million to about five million, and from half a million to about three million during the nineteenth century. But many other cities expanded prodigiously; among those whose population increased tenfold between 1800 and 1900 were Berlin, Warsaw and Glasgow.

The cities of Europe were not ideally equipped to cope with the hugely augmented numbers. Outside the city gates of Berlin, for instance, people lived in makeshift huts or barns, and in almost every city there were districts with densely built tenements (or more usually in England, terraced houses) which were grossly overcrowded. They were speculatively built, generally close to places of work, and with poor ventilation, light and sanitation. Outbreaks of cholera in the 1830s and 1840s focused attention on the need for reform, and it became common for public authorities to establish systems for the inspection of housing and to insist on basic standards of hygiene. In Britain, for instance, the Public Health Act of 1848 made local government responsible for sewerage, refuse collection and water supplies. There were also improvements to ancient street systems, sometimes ensuring a degree of social control, as in the case of Haussmann's (1809–91) Paris or the Ringstrasse in Vienna. The development of urban transport was fostered and was to culminate around 1909 in the appearance of motor buses, electric trams and underground electric railways. At the same time there were more radical approaches to town planning, most notably the garden city ideal promoted by Ebenezer Howard (1850–1928) in 1898 and the industrial city scheme exhibited in 1904 by Tony Garnier (1869–1948).

If the growth of the urban working classes was one of the most notable features of nineteenth-century life, hardly less important was the rise of the urban bourgeoisie, sustained as much by the needs of trade, banking, the law and government (both local and national) as by industry itself. Shops, offices and public buildings were the conspicuous signs of prosperity, growing more elaborate as the century progressed, and there was concomitant development of affluent residential districts. Between the wealthiest of the middle classes and the traditional aristocracy there was a blurring of distinctions. The relative decline of agricultural wealth gradually weakened the old power base – although some of the aristocratic landowners profited by the presence of coal or other resources on their estates – but for many of the newly rich the building or acquisition of a country seat remained the symbol of success.

In religious matters the nineteenth century was generally marked by tolerance. In western Europe particularly there was a gradual removal of civil disabilities from religious minorities, affecting not only Christian groups such as the Huguenots in France or the Catholic and Protestant Nonconformists in Britain but also the Jews. This toleration was accompanied by a slackening in the institutional power of the established churches, and the success of the Gothic Revival in church-building may be partly understood as a search for an ecclesiastical architectural language, distinct from the predominantly Classical forms of other public buildings. Distinctions between religious groups also became important, and the common adoption of a Romanesque style for synagogues or the revival of mediaeval liturgical forms in the Catholic churches designed by Pugin reflect a desire for denominational definition amid the religious pluralism of the nineteenth century.

In the first half of the century there was a proliferation of proselytising sects, especially among the new urban communities in Britain and other parts of western Europe, but after about 1850 there were fewer such initiatives. David Strauss's controversial *Life of Christ* (1835–6) and Charles Darwin's *Origin of Species* (1859) challenged many religious assumptions, and Protestants increasingly fell into two groups – the fundamentalists who accepted the Bible as literal truth in spite of modern scholarship, and others who attempted to adapt Christian beliefs to the views of contemporary science. In the Catholic church authority became more and more centred on Rome, and at the Vatican Council of 1870 the dogma of papal infallibility was proclaimed, the same year marking the end of the temporal power of the papacy with the final unification of Italy. The building of large cathedrals, like that at Westminster of 1895–1903, can thus be seen as an affirmation of religious identity in the face of rapidly growing secularism.

If the progress of religion during the nineteenth century was somewhat halting, the quest for knowledge knew no bounds. The great national libraries, such as that in Paris (1859–67), were like banks in which all human knowledge was stored, their huge reading rooms the halls for borrowers and depositors. Museums – of both science and the arts – were another characteristic feature of the nineteenth century, more extensive and more accessible than the generally private collections of previous centuries. The broadening of scientific and technical knowledge was reflected in the widespread creation of new education institutions, starting with the French Ecole Polytechnique (1794) which inspired similar polytechnic schools in Prague, Vienna, Stockholm, Zurich and many German cities. As the industrial and commercial basis of European life became more sophisticated it became increasingly desirable to extend education provision to all classes. Universal primary education was to be found in most countries of western and central Europe by the 1800s, and there were various supplementary facilities including public libraries and adult education centres.

The nineteenth century displayed an appetite not only for 'useful knowledge' but also for the arts, and almost every significant European city had its cultural powerhouses. These great concert halls, opera houses, theatres and art galleries catered for an increasingly large middle-class audience and were sometimes built with a splendour that might in previous times have been reserved for cathedrals and palaces.

Resources and Building Techniques

The period saw a transformation in the training, role and social position of the architect, and this is discussed below in relation to each country. Again Italy, where the designer-architect was already the norm in the fifteenth century, and where the architectural treatise was pioneered by Alberti, provided the initial model. The foundation of academies from the second half of the sixteenth century onwards further enhanced the intellectual standing of architects, but the later French architectural academy (founded 1671) for many years remained unusual in providing a systematic education in design. The economic position of architects improved with increasing specialisation, and many made fortunes in the seventeenth and eighteenth centuries from speculative contracting. Despite growing professionalism during this period, however, the dilettante gentleman architect continued to be influential.

Renaissance architecture is not notable for structural innovation. Probably the most spectacular structural achievements of the period were the great domes – Florence Cathedral, S. Peter's in Rome and S. Paul's in London. All are multi-shell constructions. Brunelleschi's famous achievement of building the Florentine dome (S. Maria del Fiore) (p. 548) without centering was based on techniques closer to Islamic domes (brickwork with spiralling courses) than to ancient Roman models. The dome of S. Peter's (p. 869–71) applies the same techniques to hemispherical shells, while Wren's dome of S. Paul's (p. 1031) is a complex mixture of stone inner dome, brick intermediate cone and timber roof, and was influenced by French examples such as Les Invalides in Paris (p. 949).

Italian Renaissance architects experimented with the revival of the masonry techniques of ancient Rome, but Roman concrete construction was little emulated. Stucco was reintroduced using Roman recipes, and was widely taken up all over Europe both for decorative interiors and to simulate stonework externally.

The processes of building and the economic structure of the building industry remained comparatively unaltered over the period. However, the increasing refinement and systematisation of architectural drawing (described more fully below) resulted in a greater degree of separation of the architect from the building site.

Italy

South of the Alps, the Po valley creates a vast northern plain stretching from Turin to Padua, embracing many of the cities of Lombardy and the Veneto: here Milan is the centre of an area of brick building, where Renaissance forms are expressed in brick and stucco or clothed with moulded terracotta. Venice, sited in its lagoon, imported wood from the mainland forests, red marble from nearby Verona, and stone from Istria, part of its empire. Easily worked Istrian stone hardens on exposure to the air and lends itself well to fine sculptural detail (p. 845).

Florence had abundant if coarse arenaceous limestone (pietra forte) in quarries to the south of the city, while the grey sandstone (pietra serena) of Fiesole and Settignano could be used in monolithic columns as well as carved in the fine detail required by the new architecture. White marble was quarried at Carrara and Seravezza, where the Medici opened new quarries and searched out also the coloured marbles so highly prized in the later sixteenth century. Siena, to the south of Florence, built much in brick, but, like other Tuscan hill towns, had access to tufa and travertine.

Rome had retreated from its seven hills in the Middle Ages to the low-lying areas beside the Tiber. Reinhabiting the hills – the policy of successive popes – required the rehabilitation and use of the ancient aqueducts. The characteristic materials of Roman Renaissance architecture are fine brick and travertine from the quarries around Tivoli, but volcanic peperino and tufa were also used, the latter providing a light vaulting material. White and coloured marbles were still pillaged from the ancient ruins.

Southern Italy and Sicily were less developed than the northern and central parts of the peninsula. Naples was, however, an important centre. Neapolitan stone is all volcanic, from the yellow tufa used for walling to the grey-black peperino employed for cut stone detail. Sicily, which enjoyed an architectural flowering in the Baroque period, is well endowed with calcareous tufas and soft limestones.

The varied climate of the Italian regions had its effects on building types. The cooler and wetter towns of the north often have arcaded streets. The drainage of the Po valley meant an increasing demand for villas in the Veneto. Restricted sites and lack of gardens and courtyards in Venice produced taller palaces with belvederes, balconies and clustered windows. In the hotter, drier climate of Rome, palaces had large courtyards with loggias, and water played a fundamental role in villa design. All over Italy windows were smaller than in northern Europe, and open arcades were provided to give shade. With little rain roofs could be gently pitched, lending themselves to cornices and balustrades.

In the fifteenth and sixteenth centuries Italian architects came from a wide variety of design-allied backgrounds: painting, sculpture and goldsmithing as well as carpentry and stoneworking. Antonio da Sangallo the Younger (1484–1546), Michele Sanmicheli (1484–1559) and Andrea Palladio (1508–80) were among the few architects of the High Renaissance to be brought up in the building trades. Knowledgeable patrons with access to the treatises could have as decisive an influence on the design as an architect in the fifteenth century. Architects shared in the improvement in the status of artists as the traditional trade guilds declined in importance, and joined painters and sculptors in the 'three arts of design' upon which the Florentine artists' academy was founded in 1563. The Academy of S. Luke was also founded in Rome, but there was as yet no formal system of training. Architectural dynasties and workshops such as that at S. Peter's, Rome, provided continuity of design and building knowledge.

In Baroque Rome routes into architecture now included literature, law and the church as well as the traditional path of the Lombard mason; carpentry was seen as a source of inventive detail and variety, and the new craft of stucco-working also produced practising architects. The study of geometry was particularly important for the complex spatial inventions of the Baroque. In the eighteenth century there was a move towards the standardisation of architectural training, such as that established in France in 1671. An architectural scholarship was established at the Roman Academy of S. Luke in 1702, and a chair of civil architecture was founded in Padua.

In the fifteenth century no architect could survive merely by supplying designs. Continued activity in another art, an official post in a board of works or a court, or a supervisory role on a building site was essential to an architect's livelihood. Florence, with few salaried positions and no court until 1530, became a net exporter of architects to other centres. In city republics and at royal or ducal courts architects were expected to turn their hands to civil engineering and to the design and construction of fortifications.

Financial rewards improved in the sixteenth and seventeenth centuries and architects' pretensions are mirrored in their portraits and private houses. Competition for their services from foreign princes enhanced their market value at home, as witnessed by the career of Bernini. At the papal court leading architects could now expect knighthoods and valuable *ex gratia* gifts in addition to their regular salaries. The design of fortifications became an increasingly specialised activity, entrusted to military engineers.

The techniques of architectural drawing were greatly advanced during the Renaissance. Brunelleschi's invention of linear perspective enabled architects to make convincing renderings of their own designs and of the antique buildings they studied; Francesco di Giorgio and Leonardo brought refinement to bird's-eye views and perspectival sections. Drawing in perspective was, however, little help in the building process, as Alberti had already observed in his *De Re Aedificatoria* (1452), in which he stressed the need for plans, elevations and sections. Raphael reiterated the demand in his *Letter to Leo X* of *c.* 1519, and it is in his workshop at S. Peter's that we first find evidence of a three-fold system of orthogonal drawings to the same scale. The standardisation of drawing practice freed the architect from the site, though many preferred to maintain day-to-day supervision.

Peruzzi continued to explore the possibilities of perspective, producing remarkable sections and perspectival axonometrics. Michelangelo's use of heavily worked-over drawings in chalk with multiple corrections was contemporary with Palladio's exquisite precision in pen and ink. The Michelangelesque tradition was continued by Buontalenti, Bernini and Borromini in the new medium of graphite. Borromini's drawings show evidence of complex constructional geometry.

The use of wooden models is attested by documents from the Middle Ages onwards. In the Renaissance they served to explain the architect's ideas to patrons unfamiliar with drawing, and to provide a more enduring record than the drawings, which were frequently consumed in models. The model by Sangallo the Younger for S. Peter's was strongly criticised by Michelangelo. While models of entire projects frequently lacked details, full-scale wooden maquettes of capitals were often made; Michelangelo tested out his design for the Palazzo Farnese cornice in a full-scale wooden model, and also used clay models for complex forms such as the Laurentian Library staircase. Metal templates for profiles were standard practice.

The organisation of the building trades remained relatively static over the period, and was not marked by great technological advances, although there was some tendency towards large-scale contracting. In the fifteenth century task-rate salaries and day-labour were the norm, and contracting 'in great' for an entire building was rare. Separate contracts were issued for each artisan, and accounts kept by the purveyor or patron. In Venice, where guild boundaries remained rigid, contracting for more than one trade was forbidden by law. On a large site stonecutters, wallers, plasterers and carpenters all had separate foremen ('capomaestri'): to be the capomaestro of the stonemasons, who supplied cut-stone detail, was often tantamount to being the architect, whereas the waller's job, frequently the best paid, involved little design skill, and such men rarely became architects.

The dictatorial ducal regimes of the sixteenth century saw the further dissolution of guild boundaries, greater centralised supervision and even the use of commandeered labour for ducal buildings. In papal Rome, too, architects more frequently acted as contractors, and there was some speculative building when the city was expanded.

France

The large windows, high-pitched roofs and tall chimneys, developed in France in response to climate, posed problems for the assimilation of an Italian architectural vocabulary. The proportion of window to wall remained greater in France than in Italy, and until *c.* 1650 the plan elements of a building were always roofed as discrete units, usually with slates. Chimneys were incorporated into a Classical design only with difficulty and frequently attracted eccentric decoration.

France is rich in building stone and slate which could be transported by river. Stone was the traditional material for monumental or grand urban buildings, though brick remained popular, even with aristocratic patrons, until the 1630s. The use of wood and plaster was widespread in vernacular architecture, but few buildings constructed in these materials have survived.

France's prolonged prosperity led to the construction of major buildings throughout the country, from Rennes to Besançon and Bordeaux to Aix-en-Provence, in the seventeenth and eighteenth centuries. If perhaps less influential than those in the Paris region, they are often no less distinguished.

Although Giuliano da Sangallo, Fra Giocondo, Leonardo da Vinci, Primaticcio, Vignola, Serlio and Bernini all visited France, it was a long time before the French architect was able to enjoy the status of his Italian counterpart. At the beginning of the sixteenth century, the architect was most likely to be a mason and a contractor, and it is clear that one of the mechanisms of social advancement was the publication of treatises, such as that by Philibert de l'Orme or Jean Bullant. Both of these also had the advantage of having travelled in Italy – an important help to the acquisition of status.

Although neither François Mansart nor Louis Le Vau wrote a treatise, nor, as far as is known, went to Italy, it is clear that they achieved a social level quite different from that of the sixteenth-century architect. At Vaux-le-Vicomte, for example, Le Vau was provided with rooms in the main body of the house while construction was in progress. This improvement in standing was confirmed by the establishment in 1671 of the Royal Academy of Architecture, which moved architects firmly out of the artisan class and conferred on them the status of artists and intellectuals. Architects continued, however, to make money through contracting, and Hardouin Mansart, Boffrand and Gabriel all prospered from the speculative development of Paris in the eighteenth century. Fees were fixed by law only after the Revolution, but a 5 per cent charge had become the norm under Louis XV. Napoleon's Ecole Polytechnique, founded in 1794, where architecture was taught by Jean-Nicolas-Louis Durand (1760–1834), within a curriculum of science and technology, marks a further crucial change in attitudes to architectural education.

Far from dying completely during the period, Gothic survived until nearly 1700 as a living form, and soon after was consciously revived. From an early date, the geometrical complexity of Gothic stone-cutting attracted attention, and several manuals of stereotomy were published, perhaps the most important being Derand's *Architecture des voûtes* of 1643. And although building in wood and plaster also seemed old-fashioned by 1600, Le Muet in his *Manière de bien bastir* of 1623 includes prolonged discussion of timber building.

Spain and Portugal

Despite the Iberian peninsula's varied climate (wet and temperate in the north, extremes of heat and cold on the central plains and subtropical in the south), its architecture generally seems to be best suited to hot climes. Low-pitched roofs and small windows predominate, as do open-air staircases and courtyards ('patios') for internal circulation.

As in earlier periods, granite was the principal building material particularly in the northern half of the peninsula. Its dark colour, grey in Spain and grey-green in Portugal, sometimes produced severe exteriors but its frequent combination with white stucco created some lively effects. Further south, below the Tagus and Mondego rivers, limestones and sandstones were more common. Here the use of building materials was influenced by the persistence of Islamic Mudéjar building traditions. Brick, the main building material of the Muslims, was often combined with intricate stucco decoration and, particularly in Portugal, glazed tiles ('azulejos'). Throughout Spain the rich iron ore deposits were exploited for the popular 'rejas', decorative iron grilles. Wood was relatively scarce but nevertheless became popular for the extravagant architectural sculpture of chapel decoration during the seventeenth and eighteenth centuries.

Roman Catholic fervour and the economic power bestowed by exploration and conquest in the New World in the sixteenth and seventeenth centuries provided the vital background to both religious and secular architecture until the Thirty Years War and the beginning of French dominance.

Austria, Germany and Central Europe

The northern part of Germany is a uniform alluvial plain, where moulded brickwork continued to be used in great variety. The plateaux of Bavaria, other mountain regions and the low plains of the Rhineland all yield building stone. From the old Austrian territories which form one of the most mountainous areas of Europe, traversed by the Danube which divides the Alpine region from Bohemia and Moravia to the German lowlands, the climate is highly varied, but there is a tendency to high rainfall; thus, as in France and England, large windows, steep roofs and prominent chimneys came to be incorporated in the architecture.

Despite the decline of the guilds, craft traditions in building persisted. In the earlier period architects emerged most commonly from the building trades or from sculpture, though the painter-architect was not unknown. In the Baroque period stucco-workers came to the fore, and the late Baroque period is characterised by family teams, often of brothers, working together to produce a church complete with its decoration: examples were the Asam brothers, Cosmas Damian (1686–1739) and Egid Quirin (1692–1750), gifted fresco painters as well as architects, and the Zimmermanns, Dominikus and Johann Baptist (the latter 1680–1758) and their sons Franz Dominikus and Joseph. Fischer von Erlach's (1656–1723) knighthood, awarded to him by the Emperor Joseph I, marks a distinct advance in the status of architects. Characteristic of central Europe is the military origin of several of the leading architects, including J. L. von Hildebrandt, Georg Wenzeslaus von Knobelsdorff, and Balthasar Neumann.

Aristocratic patronage was extremely important for the development of style: a liberal education was held to include the study of architecture, and the travels of patrons are as important as those of architects for the introduction of new ideas. Academies were founded in the later seventeenth century, and visits to Italy or France became part of the education of a young architect. An official position as court architect was the major route to advancement, and by the neo-Classical period offered a vast range of responsibilities, as exemplified in Schinkel's career as head of the Public Works Department in Berlin.

The Low Countries

Holland is the lowest part of the low-lying region around the mouths of the Rhine, Maas and Scheldt. Sinking land and rising waters have meant that much of the country is below sea level. The work of drainage and reclamation, enclosing land (polders) in networks of dykes and canals, was greatly accelerated in the seventeenth century, helped by the introduction in the previous century of the rotating turret windmill to operate water pumps. Shifting foundations made lightweight open structures advisable, and in the canal city of Amsterdam architectural solutions comparable with those of Venice were devised. Lack of building stone led to the early development of expertise with brickwork. The 'Flemish bond' method of brick-coursing is well known. Wood construction continued to play an important part in vernacular building, church towers and vaults, and windmills.

In Belgium, the flat lands of Flanders are balanced by the forested plateaux of the Ardennes to the East, from which came freestone, limestone and slate, as well as timber. The cool rainy climate all over the Low Countries, as in other countries of northern Europe, led to such characteristic features as steep roofs and large windows.

The diverse origins of Italian architects in sixteenth-century Netherlands, for example Tommaso Vincidor, a painter, and Alessandro Pasqualini, a goldsmith, were echoed in the emerging native tradition in which painters and amateurs were as important as stonemasons. Although Cornelis Floris, Lieven de Key and Hendrik de Keyser all worked with stone, Jacob van Campen, Wenceslas Coberger (*c.* 1560–) and Jacob Francart (1583–1651) were all trained as painters, and the last had spent many years in Italy. In seventeenth-century Belgium, amateur architects abounded, especially Jesuit intellectuals like Pieter Huyssens (1577–1637) and Wilhelm Hesius; and a nun, Aldegonde Desmoulins, designed the Benedictine church in Liège in 1666. Rubens's interest in architecture set an important example. In Holland, too, a key promoter of the Palladian movement was the intellectual statesman and connoisseur Constantijn Huygens, who described van Campen as the man 'who vanquished Gothic folly'.

Britain

The geographical isolation of the British Isles from the continent meant that England came late under the influence of the Renaissance, which was received by way of France and the Netherlands. Foreign travel for architects and patrons was, however, considered increasingly desirable from the early seventeenth century onwards, with a brief intermission during the Napoleonic Wars. Improved internal communications during the eighteenth and early nineteenth centuries, together with good road-making and canal construction, facilitated the transport of building materials. The result was that at the end of this period regional variations due to materials were lessened, without disappearing altogether.

Timber gradually fell into disuse as a major building material, because stone and brick provided more stable, weather-proof and prestigious structures, which were more resistant to fire in crowded towns. Exposed timber frames were still the norm in the sixteenth century, however, and persisted under surface cladding such as plaster or tile-hanging in vernacular country buildings where stone was not readily available. Stone became more usual in the seventeenth century for clothing prestigious domestic as well as religious buildings. Portland stone, a close-grained oolitic limestone of dazzling whiteness, was first employed by Inigo Jones in his London buildings, and continued in use thereafter for important churches and public buildings. Many other types of stone were or became available – red and grey granites, freestones and slates as well as a number of varieties of limestone. Exposed brick became popular for domestic buildings: 'Flemish bond' replaced 'English bond' after the mid-seventeenth century. Stucco over brickwork was used as an economical substitute for stone, for example at Chiswick House (p. 1045B), and became popular for town housing in the second half of the eighteenth century. Coade stone, a patent terracotta manufactured by the Coade family from 1769 to *c.* 1840, was a successful substitute for stone used for decorative detailing. Thin slates for roofing were used increasingly after the middle of the eighteenth century. Cast iron as a structural material – an early product of the Industrial Revolution – appeared well before 1800.

As in France and the Netherlands, the cool wet English climate meant some modification of the Italian Renaissance style in terms of windows and pitched roofs, though a more rigorous Palladianism was conducive to smaller window openings. The more general use of coal as a fuel in the reign of Charles I made possible more comfortable interiors and brought fireplaces in every room, and the design problems associated with chimneys.

Architecture as a professional activity entirely separate from the building trades, with its own professional body, system of education and structure of fees, cannot be said to have existed until the very end of this period. During the three centuries under consideration, the position of the architect gradually evolved from that of a mediaeval master mason to that of a professional designer. In the sixteenth century the design of buildings, for example the great Elizabethan houses, was often carried out piecemeal and might be entrusted to a diversity of individuals. Architectural drawing was primitive, and foreign sources were copied at second hand. Even outstanding designers like Robert Smythson attained no international reputation. Inigo Jones was perhaps the first recognised designer-architect in England: trained as a painter, with first-hand knowledge of Italian buildings, he brought a new intellectual authority to English architecture, and artistic distinction to the Surveyorship of the King's Works.

Respect for Jones's example and for Italian practice, and the passion for architecture among the gentry, spread the demand for architectural design outside court circles in the seventeenth century, despite the disruptions of the Civil War. Although mason-architects were still the norm, routes into architecture from other levels became more common and various, for example from military engineering (William Winde) and the natural sciences (Christopher Wren and Robert Hooke). Amateur involvement in architecture ranged from active participation (Sir Roger Pratt) to a theoretical interest expressed in writing (Roger North, John Evelyn, Henry Wotton). Of the major figures, only John Webb, Jones's nephew, could be described as an architect by training.

The Office of the King's Works was of enormous importance to the development of the profession in the seventeenth and eighteenth centuries, providing the only real opportunity for training at the highest level. Nicholas Hawksmoor was perhaps the greatest English architect to receive his education there, without the advantages of foreign travel. But the continued importance of the amateur, whatever the prevailing architectural style, is demonstrated by those very different figures Sir John Vanbrugh and Lord Burlington.

By the second half of the eighteenth century apprenticeship to a successful architect became a possibility. Robert Taylor and James Paine both took on pupils, whose apprenticeship lasted five or six years, and this system remained in force well into the twentieth century. The foundation of the Royal Academy (1768) brought academic recognition to a select few, but the lectures in architecture held in the Academy Schools provided merely an educational frill for young architects training in London. Travel to Italy continued to be a seminal phase in architectural education, and in the second half of the eighteenth century architects went further afield in search of Greek remains. Despite repeated attempts from the 1790s onwards to found an association of architects, it was not until 1835 that the Institute of Architects came into being; it was incorporated by Royal Charter in 1837.

Few architects made a living exclusively by designing and supervising buildings until the nineteenth century, and professionals had to supplement their income in a variety of ways. In addition to contracting for their own buildings (a practice frowned on in Nash's day), and measuring the work as it was built (hence the term 'surveyor'), architects often made money through speculative development (for example, John Wood of Bath). Regular salaries could be earned in institutional appointments, from the surveyorships and clerkships in the Royal Office of Works down to posts with charities or corporations. In 1792 the Architects' club agreed to charge 2½ per cent for measuring in addition to the usual 5 per cent for design and supervision.

Mediaeval distinctions between craftsmen associated with building (masons, bricklayers, carpenters, joiners and plasterers) remained, and separate contracts between the patron or surveyor and each of the trades were usual until large-scale entrepreneurial contracting, under which the builder undertook to supply all the necessary tradesmen, became common right at the end of this period in the early nineteenth century (for example, as operated by the Cubitt family in London). Entrepreneurial contracting may be seen as a natural development from speculative building, which was a common means of providing town housing from the time of Nicholas Barbon in the late seventeenth century in London.

The exact relationship between architect and craftsman is hard to pinpoint where architectural drawings do not survive. In the sixteenth century, John Thorpe's and Robert Smythson's surviving 'sketchbooks' are more in the nature of model-books than working drawings. Smythson's drawings reveal originality of planning without the Classical precision of draughtsmanship introduced into English architecture by Inigo Jones with the help of his collection of drawings by Palladio (now the nucleus of the RIBA Drawings Collection). This tradition was carried on by Jones's nephew Webb, and from the time of Wren and Hawksmoor abundant drawings survive to testify to the architect's control over detail as well as general form, though it is generally believed that the 'English Baroque' allowed greater latitude to the invention of the individual craftsman than the Palladians, with their insistence on 'correct' minutiae. Wooden models were used as a way of presenting and preserving designs and ensuring their durability from the time of Jones to that of Hawksmoor and Gibbs. The fate of Wren's Great Model of S. Paul's illustrates the dangers of working out a model too completely. This period in England, as elsewhere in Europe, was not one of great innovations in structural method: Wren's dome of St Paul's is perhaps the greatest structural feat of the time, and

Wren looked mainly to France for inspiration. By the end of the period the Industrial Revolution had created the demand for works of structural engineering *per se*, and this was to be intensified by the advent of the railway. The Society of Civil Engineers was founded in 1793.

Russia

There are few mountains, and little building stone was available to architects of the Renaissance in Russia. Land communications were exceptionally difficult, while navigable inland waterways were scarce, often frozen for much of the year. An abundance of trees in northern Russia, therefore, produced a mediaeval architecture almost wholly dependent on wood. As late as the eighteenth century, timber was used for monumental buildings; and such a continuously occurring feature as the tent roof, even when constructed in masonry, betrayed its timber origins. In southern Russia brick remained the predominant building material, and despite the increasing desirability of stone, even buildings erected in the eighteenth and nineteenth centuries in S. Petersburg are usually made of brick coated with stucco.

The progress of the native architectural profession in Russia was slow, as the Czars, with architectural pretensions, usually commissioned foreign practitioners, particularly from Italy and France. Russian architects were expected to be well versed in Western developments, and the Academy of Fine Arts in S. Petersburg (1757) was conceived with this in mind. Neither native nor immigrant architects involved themselves to any degree in self-generated theory or the writing of treatises before the reign of Alexander I, which saw only a Russian edition of Vignola and two collections of engravings by Thomas de Thomon.

Timber construction, or indeed the translation into stone of traditional Russian forms, involved craftsmanship or technical expertise of remarkable ingenuity. By contrast, where foreign styles were imported much structural interest was sacrificed, and replaced by a more superficial attitude to design. Despite its sheer size, Russian architecture can be structurally disappointing, although this is compensated for in the early nineteenth century by a new inventiveness in design and planning.

Scandinavia

Norway and Sweden lie to west and east of a great ridge which divides the peninsula, its coastline broken by countless rivers and fjords. Southern Sweden, Finland and Denmark are flat and low-lying, with numerous watercourses and lakes. Sweden has very important deposits of iron and copper, both more significant to its economic well-being than to its building crafts. The country also has granite, marble and, in the south, suitable clay for bricks. The Danish earth-crust, like that of Skåne and north Germany, is predominantly boulder clay, and it is not surprising that in all these regions brick is the principal building material. Norway, Sweden and Finland have vast tracts of forest, and wood is the basis of vernacular architecture in the three countries. In 1666 Norway supplied the timber for the rebuilding of London after the Great Fire.

Owing to the proximity of the sea throughout Scandinavia, and to the influence of the Gulf Stream and the effects of the prevailing west and south-west winds, the climate almost everywhere is less harsh than in countries further east of similar latitude, although the winters are habitually long and severe. The wide availability of timber, with its effective insulation and weather-resistant properties, and the early development of ingenious wood-construction techniques counteracted to some extent the rigours of domestic life in the protracted cold season.

A purely Swedish development, which spread to other parts of Scandinavia, was the 'säteri' (manor-house or Italian) roof. This is basically two roofs, with a small break or clerestory between, the lower part being usually curved in section. It first appears on a major building in the Riddarhus, Stockholm.

Post-Renaissance Europe

It was only in the course of the nineteenth century that architecture can be said to have become a profession. Although articled pupillage remained the training ground for many, it was increasingly common also to follow a more formal course of education. The tradition of technical education and civil engineering was perhaps strongest in France, where it was rooted in the eighteenth-century Ecole des Ponts et Chaussées and continued in the Ecole Polytechnique, the first school of general engineering. The Ecole served as a model for polytechnic schools throughout central Europe at a time when universities had a much more limited curriculum. From 1819 architectural training of an academic nature was provided by the Ecole des Beaux-Arts in Paris, and in due course there were similar facilities in the Academies of Fine Arts in Copenhagen and Vienna, at the Architectural Academy in Berlin, and elsewhere. In Britain the approach was more pragmatic: although university courses in architecture were offered in London from 1841, it was the Royal Institute of British Architects which became guardian of professional status and in due course gave way statutorily to the Architects Registration Council of the United Kingdom. Not until 1882 was admission to Associateship of the RIBA subject to examination.

Between the late eighteenth century and World War I the development of building materials and technologies progressed at an unprecedented pace. The possibilities of iron construction were most dramatically illustrated in 1779 by the Iron Bridge at Coalbrookdale, Shropshire, created by the iron-founder Abraham Darby III (1750–91) and probably based on a design by the architect Thomas Farnolls Pritchard (1723–77). Cast iron was soon adopted on a growing scale for structural purposes and in the 1790s William Strutt (1756–1830) erected several cotton mills at Belper, Derbyshire, partly supported internally by cast-iron columns. The first known building with a consistent internal cast-iron column and beam system (previously mill floors had been supported on heavy timber beams) is the Benyon, Bage and Marshall flax mill at Shrewsbury (1796–7). The advantages of such a system were considerable, since the structure required little floor area, allowed greater flexibility in design through the bay system, permitted a larger number of storeys than was practicable with masonry alone, and could be made more fire-resistant by constructing the floors on shallow brick arches ('jack arches') spanning between the floor beams. Mills of this type, constructed eight or nine storeys high, and with outer walls of conventional brick or masonry, were not uncommon in the English textile towns by the 1830s. An example of great modernity, the Phillips, Wood and Lee mill at Salford, Lancashire, built in 1799–1801, was powered by a Boulton and Watt steam engine and heated by steam transmitted through the hollow cast-iron columns. Gas lighting was added in 1805.

Through the early years of the nineteenth century iron became quite widely used for columns, roof supports and staircases, and occasionally for entire buildings such as the conservatory at Carlton House, London (1811–12). The combination of glass and iron, successfully employed in Fontaine's Galerie d'Orléans in Paris (1829–31), was an attractive one where plenty of natural light was required, and became the usual choice for some of the most notable new types of building: shopping arcades, conservatories, markets, exhibition halls and railway stations. The use of large panels of sheet glass – thinner and cheaper than plate glass – which was pioneered in the conservatory at Chatsworth, Derbyshire (1836–40), was an important advance, and the availability of relatively cheap wrought iron after about 1820 was significant because its tensile properties were ideal for ties, bolts and trusses, where cast iron was too brittle. The new materials were sometimes deftly combined with the more monumental effects of conventional masonry, as at the Library of S. Geneviève, Paris (1839–50), or the University Museum, Oxford (1854–60), but the new structural possibilities were unequivocally displayed in buildings such as the Crystal Palace, London (1850–1), or the Halles Centrales, Paris (1853). Iron and glass structures could be erected speedily from components carried to a site by modern transport systems, and they embodied advanced technology in a way that was appropriate for railway stations or the many international exhibitions which followed that held in the Crystal Palace in 1851. Prefabricated iron buildings were also manufactured for export to all parts of the world.

The 1880s mark the next phase in the development of structural iron. For the 1889 international exhibition in Paris, Gustave Eiffel (1832–1923) created the famous 300 m (985 ft) high tower which bears his name and was the tallest structure in the world, while the Galerie des Machines spanned an unprecedented 114 m (375 ft) with almost miraculous ease. By this time rolled steel beams were being produced in quantity and superseded wrought iron in the construction of wide-span buildings, leading ultimately to fully steel-framed structures, masonry-clad as a fire precaution, as at Kodak House, London (1910–11). In the meantime, the more fluent characteristics of iron and glass were being expressively exploited in Art Nouveau works, for instance the Maison du Peuple, Brussels (1896–8) or the Paris Métro stations (1900).

The advent of reinforced concrete in the years around 1909 introduced a material capable of withstanding great compressive and tensile loads, as steel could do, but with the further important advantage of a high degree of fire resistance. Concrete – that is, a mixture of cement and rubble or gravel with water – had become a reliable material with the introduction and development of durable 'Portland' cement during the nineteenth century, and was quite widely used for foundations and floors, where its strength under compression was most required. Before concrete could be safely employed for more complex structures, however, some form of reinforcement was necessary to counteract its weakness under tension, and many methods were tried. Fançois Coignet (1814–88) patented a system of iron tension rods in 1856, and in 1877 Joseph Monier (1823–1906) took out a patent for cement and iron beams, which was developed by the German firm of Wayss who published the important theoretical work *Das System Monier* in 1887. Crucial work was undertaken by a Belgian, François Hennebique (1842–1921), who substituted steel for iron and devised hooked connections for the reinforcing bars (1892). One of the most prominent early demonstrations of Hennebique's system was in staircases at the Petit Palais, Paris (1897–1900).

The profound advances which occurred in building materials and technologies during the nineteenth century was summed up in the Post Office Savings Bank, Vienna, of 1904–6. Here steel stanchions, a suspended glass ceiling, reinforced concrete, glass floor slabs, central heating and aluminium details contribute to an air of confident modernity. Yet even in the materials of more ordinary buildings the nineteenth century saw many changes. Hand-made bricks were gradually superseded by more regular wire-cut or machine-pressed bricks, often efficiently burnt in continuous kilns such as that designed by Friedrich Hoffmann in 1858. The availability of cheap sheet-glass from mid-century meant that large-paned windows could be afforded for buildings of relatively modest size. Where decoration was desired an enormous range of panels, lintels and sculpture was available, mass-produced in brick or terracotta. Cast-iron balconies, railings and roof finials were also common. As transport systems improved and the same kinds of materials – whether natural or manufactured – became available in most parts of Europe, vernacular traditions were increasingly threatened.

Although structural advances produced the most dramatic changes in building technology, the provision of services was also of great consequence for nineteenth-century architecture. Gas lighting was sufficiently refined to be introduced into houses by the 1840s, and continued to be improved until, by the turn of the century, it began to be superseded by electricity. In 1880 electric lights were installed at Cragside, Northumberland, by the English pioneer Joseph Swan, and by 1900 mains electricity was provided in most major cities. Great improvements in urban life also occurred through advances in drainage and sanitation. The introduction of the water-closet (especially the washout closet of about 1870), effective main drainage, and the provision of pure water were not only civilising factors in domestic design, but also prerequisites for the development of large commercial buildings. The problems of heating and ventilation in large buildings were the object of much experimentation, often involving hot-water radiators or hot-air ducts. An alternative was the 'Plenum' system, filling a building with warm (or cool) air under slight pressure, as employed at Glasgow School of Art (1897–1909). The advent of the telephone by the 1880s was a further factor in the development of major commercial buildings.

Architectural Publications

Italy

The writing of treatises was pioneered in Renaissance Italy, first through manuscripts and then through printed books. Leon Battista Alberti's *De Re Aedificatoria* (written 1452, printed 1485/6), the first architectural book since antiquity, gave, though unillustrated, a rich theoretical basis to Renaissance architecture. Antonio Filarete's utopian *Libro* (1465) and Francesco di Giorgio's two *Trattati* (1470s, 1490s) circulated in manuscript. The latter were particularly influential for their fortification designs and marginal illustrations.

The text of Vitruvius was seriously studied in this period, the first printed edition appearing in 1486. Illustrated scholarly editions (Fra Giocondo, 1511) followed, and Italian translations with commentaries (Cesarino, 1523), the best being Daniele Barbaro's version with Palladio's illustrations (1556).

Illustrated handbooks of the 'rules' of the Classical orders were pioneered by Sebastiano Serlio (Book IV, 1537) and Giacomo Barozzi da Vignola (1562). Andrea Palladio was the first to publish some systematic rules, antiquities, and examples of his own buildings in his hugely influential *Quattro Libri* (1570). Vincenzo Scamozzi's encyclopaedic *Idea* (1615) was particularly successful in Holland and England, especially through his Book VI on the orders. In the Baroque period Francesco Borromini's *Opus architectonicum* (1725) is a posthumous publication of his designs for the Oratory, while Guarino Guarini (*Architettura civile*, 1737) and Bernardo Vittone (1760–6) combined their own work with general instruction. Carlo Lodoli's functionalist ideas, so important for neo-Classicism, were transmitted in Francesco Algarotti's *Saggio* (1756) and Andrea Memmo's *Elementi* (1786). Francesco Milizia's *Principi* espoused a more empirical neo-Classicism, while his architectural biographies follow in the important tradition of Giorgio Vasari (1550, 1568) and Francesco Baldiniucci.

Sketchbooks of antiquities, advocated by Alberti, were fundamental for the diffusion of the Renaissance style. The first published repertories are by Serlio (Book IV, 1540) and Antonio Labacco (Libro, 1552 etc.). G. B. Montano's fantastic reconstructions of ancient buildings (1624 etc.) were influential on the Roman Baroque, while Giovanni Battista Piranesi's engravings and polemical treatises (1761, 1765, etc.) were even more formative for neo-Classical conceptions of antiquity.

France

France has perhaps the richest and certainly the most strongly theoretical tradition of architectural writing, to which it is impossible to do justice in a brief survey.

Vitruvius was edited by the architect Guillaume Philandrier (Philander; 1544, 1550) and translated in 1547 by Jean Martin, who also prepared editions of Alberti and Serlio. After his move to France, Serlio published his Books I, II and III in Paris (1545, 1547) and his *Libro Straordinario* in Lyons (1551). His Book VI on domestic architecture remained unpublished until recently, but influenced J.-A. du Cerceau the Elder's three *Livres d'Architecture* (1559–72). His *Plus excellents bâtiments* of 1576–9 gives a precious record of the great sixteenth-century châteaux, and begins a long tradition of publishing French buildings.

French theoretical treatise-writing begins with Jean Bullant's *Reigle générale d'architecture* of 1568, based on his antiquarian studies in Rome. Philibert de l'Orme's *Premier tome de l'Architecture* (1567) is of great importance for its discussion of stereotomy, as well as its enthusiastic nationalism, evident in the introduction of a 'French' order. His mastery of practical geometry also comes out in his *Nouvelles Inventions de bien bastir* (1561). The grotesque strain in later sixteenth-century French architecture is exemplified by Hugues Sambin's *Oeuvre de la diversité des Termes* (1572). Relatively modest designs for town houses are presented in Le Muet's *Manière de bien bastir* of 1623.

French obsession with the orders reached its apogee in the seventeenth century. While Fréart de Chambray's *Parallèle de l'architecture antique et de la moderne* (1650) insisted on the supremacy of the original three antique orders, belief in absolute canons of proportion for the orders was challenged by Claude Perrault, who asserted a customary rather than a rational basis for architectural beauty. Perrault's translation of Vitruvius (1673) became the standard edition, while his *Ordonnance des cinq espèces de colonnes* (1683) was equally influential.

The teaching at the Royal Academy of Architecture produced a new kind of publication, the *Cours d'architecture*, but the initial emphasis, as in François Blondel's *Cours* (1675, 1683), was still firmly on the orders. Daviler's *Cours* (1691) was more heterogeneous, and included discussions of Vignola and Michelangelo and a dictionary of terms. The more practical everyday side of architecture was dealt with in such books as L. Sarot's *Architecture françoise* (1642) and P. Bullet's *L'Architecture pratique* (1691), while the tradition of self-publication in the du Cerceau mould was continued by Antoine Le Pautre's *Desseins de plusieurs palais* (1652–53). Jean Marot's collections known as *Le Grand Marot* (*c.* 1665) and *Le Petit Marot* (*c.* 1655–60) made designs of contemporary buildings widely available.

The rationalist tendencies that were to lead both to neo-Classicism and to the Gothic Revival are early stated in the Abbé de Cordemoy's *Nouveau Traité* of 1706, espousing an architecture of right-angles based on structural honesty. The Abbé Laugier restated these ideas in the *Essai sur l'architecture* of 1755, with its celebrated statement of the architectural primacy of the primitive hut. The most widely read general handbook of the eighteenth century was Jacques François Blondel's *Cours d'architecture* (1771–7), a broad-minded and comprehensive work. Germain Boffrand's *Livre d'architecture* (1754) is a series of essays with many plates of his own work, espousing an aesthetic of *bon goût*. Like Blondel, Boffrand believed every building type should have an appropriate 'caractère', derived not so much from the orders as from its overall composition. These ideas were developed by Le Camus de Mezières (*Le Génie de l'architecture*, 1780). 'Caractère' assumes a heavily symbolical aspect in Claude Nicolas Ledoux's *L'architecture* (1804), where the buildings of the utopian community of Chaux are described.

The commodious planning of interiors, in which the French excelled, was expounded in numerous handbooks on domestic building, such as J. F. Blondel's *La distribution de maisons de plaisance* (1737) and C. E. Briseux's *L'art de bâtir des maisons de campagne* (1743).

Etienne-Louis Boullée's *Essai sur l'art*, with its ideal geometrical projects, remained unpublished until this century. His pupil Jean-Nicolas-Louis Durand produced the most influential architectural book of the neo-Classical movement: his *Précis des leçons d'architecture* (1802–5). Here buildings are dealt with in terms of structural elements ('vertical combinations') and functional types, and the huge array of exemplars, especially of public buildings, furnished models for the next generation of architects all over Europe.

The Low Countries

The first translation of Serlio's Book IV was published in 1539 in Antwerp, a major centre for sixteenth-century architectural books. Pieter Coeck's prints of triumphal arches (1549), Cornelis Floris's collections of ornament (1556, 1557) and, especially, the works of Hans Vredeman de Vries were widely disseminated in Europe, as well as influencing architecture at home. Vredeman's *Architectura* (1577–81) popularised the strap-work and grotesque characteristic of the northern Renaissance; his *Variae Architecturae Formae* is a collection of fantastic cityscapes. Rubens's *Palazzi di Genova* (1622), a collection of engraved drawings of Genoese palaces, was intended to inspire emulation among urban patrons.

The true nature of 'Dutch Palladianism' is revealed by the absence of seventeenth-century Dutch translations of Palladio, whereas twenty-two editions of Scamozzi's treatise appeared between 1640 and 1715. These included abbreviated handbooks of the Orders such as those of Simon Bosboom. A knowledge of de Keyser's work in Amsterdam was diffused via Salomon de Bray's *Architectura Moderna* (1631) and Philip Vingboons's engravings of his own work published in 1648.

Britain

Architectural treatises and pattern books imported from Italy, France and the Low Countries were a fount of inspiration for Renaissance architecture in

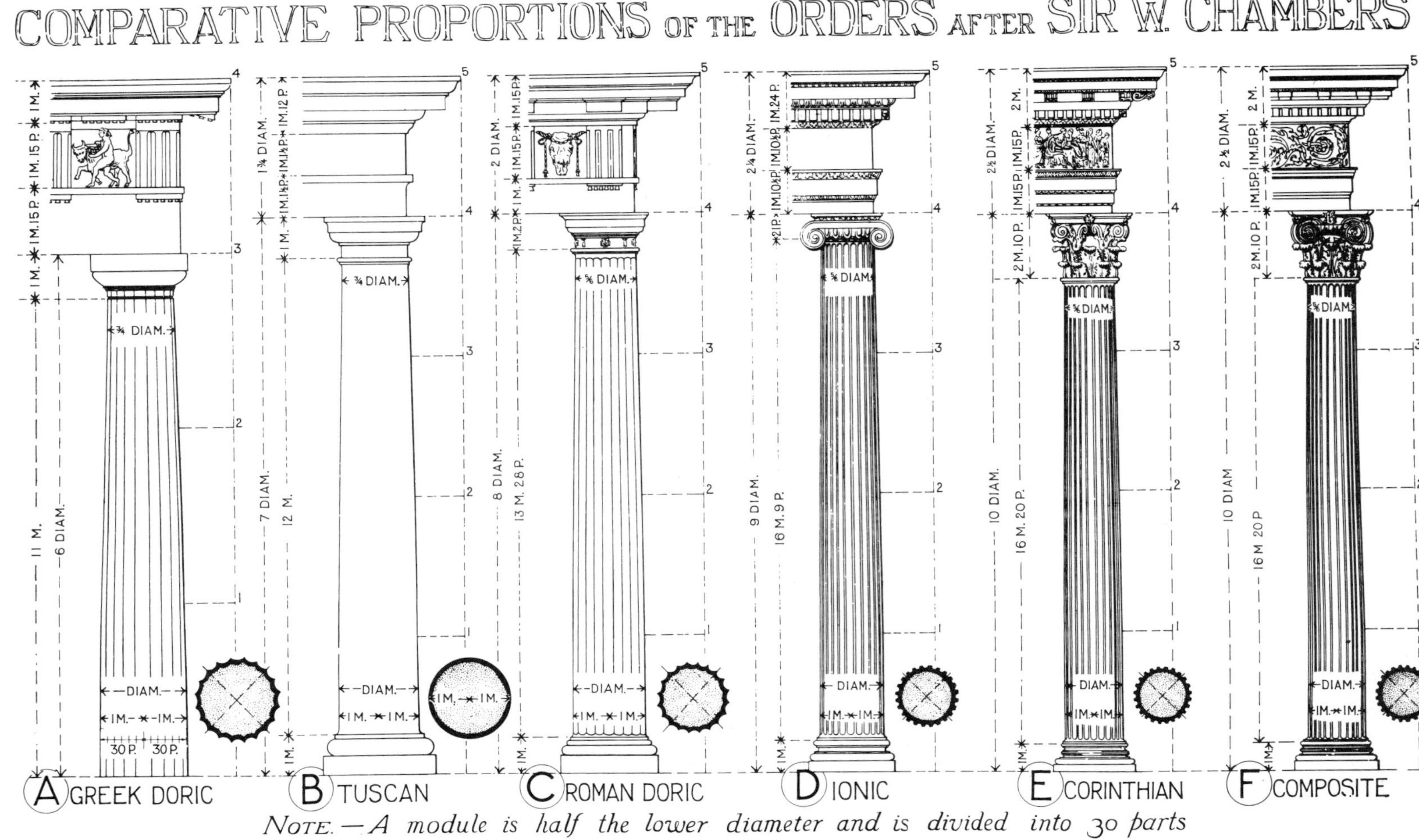

Note.—A module is half the lower diameter and is divided into 30 parts

Britain from the early sixteenth century. The first native architectural publication was John Shute's *First and Chief Groundes of Architecture* (1563), closely based on Serlio's account of the orders. Sir Henry Wotton's unillustrated *Elements of Architecture* is a wide-ranging essay, drawing on Alberti and Philibert de l'Orme as well as Vitruvius and incorporating personal observations of architectural practice in the Veneto. Another amateur production was John Evelyn's translation of Fréart's *Parallèle* (1665).

The later seventeenth and eighteenth centuries were the great period of Classically-oriented English architectural publications of the most diverse kinds: translations of foreign treatises, measured surveys of ancient and modern buildings, and British architects' publication of their own works. The English distrust of intellectualising theory and the absence of an architectural academy meant a lack of systematic rationalising treatises such as those of Perrault, Blondel and Durand.

Translations of Serlio (1611), Alberti (1723, Leoni), Palladio (1716, Leoni; 1738, Ware) and Vignola (1659 and 1702 by Joseph Moxon) became available. Although a satisfactory translation of Vitruvius appeared only in 1771, acknowledgements of his and other writers' contributions (for example, Scamozzi) on the Orders were common. The publication of *Vitruvius Britannicus* (1715–25), where Colen Campbell included his own designs and those of Inigo Jones, had an enormous influence on the Palladian revival. Lord Burlington published Palladio's drawings of the Roman baths (1730), and later publications of antiquities such as Wood's *Palmyra* (1753) and *Balbec* (1757), Stuart and Revett's *Antiquities of Athens* (1762) and Robert Adam's *Spalato* (1764) gave an important impetus to neo-Classical architecture.

James Gibbs's *Book of Architecture* (1728) was primarily a compilation of his own designs and was widely used as a pattern book. Sir William Chambers's *Treatise on Civil Architecture* (1759, 1768, 1791) is perhaps the most ambitious and comprehensive of the English treatises (p. 839). The publications which diffused the Classical style most widely through the ranks of ordinary builders were the handbooks such as Batty Langley's *Builder's Compleat Assistant* (1738), *The Builder's Jewel* (1757) and Isaac Ware's *Complete Body of Architecture* of 1756, which enabled the simplest terraces to be built to a high standard of design.

Specialised model books for farmhouses, cottages and villas were a feature of the growing taste for the Picturesque, and exotic styles became known through books such as Langley's *Gothic Architecture Restored and Improved* (1741) and Chambers's *Chinese Buildings* (1757). After 1800 Gothic architecture began to be studied more seriously in antiquarian works, the most important of which is the *Attempt to Discriminate the Styles of English Architecture* (1817) by Thomas Rickman, who invented the enduring labels Early English, Decorated and Perpendicular.

Scandinavia

Suecia Antiqua et Hodierna (1693–1714), a series of engravings after drawings by the architect Eric Dahlberg (1625–1703), illustrates the great wealth of country houses built in Sweden in the seventeenth century. Lauritz de Thurah's sumptuous, two-volume *Danske (Danish) Vitruvius* (1746–9), although it included illustrations of his own work, must really be considered a graceful tribute to the wealth and supposed good taste of the Oldenburgs. Not until the publication of C. F. Hansen's *Samling af forskjellige offentlige og private Bygninger* (1847) do we find a Scandinavian architect publishing his own work in the way pioneered by the Adam brothers in Britain. Hansen was probably influenced, however, by the appearance of Karl Friedrich Schinkel's *Sammlung* (1825–).

Chapter 29

ITALY

Architectural Character

The architecture produced in Italy between 1400 and 1830 may be broadly divided into four main periods:

Early Renaissance – fifteenth century
High Renaissance and Mannerism – sixteenth century
Baroque and Rococo – seventeenth and early eighteenth centuries
Neo-Classical – mid-eighteenth to early nineteenth centuries

Early Renaissance

The Renaissance revival of ancient architectural principles began in Florence with the work of Filippo Brunelleschi (1377–1446), who set an enduring stamp on the Early Renaissance style. His architecture is based on simple modular proportions, clarity of design, and a standardised vocabulary of monolithic grey stone columns and pilasters set against white plaster walls. In detail, his forms depend less on ancient Roman buildings than on the Tuscan Romanesque, especially the Florentine baptistery which was believed to be an antique structure. His use of arches supported on columns is the norm in such Romanesque churches as SS. Apostoli, and his favourite pendentive vaults owe little to Roman buildings. By contrast, the approach to antiquity of Leon Battista Alberti (1404–72) was far more archaeological: comparing Roman buildings with Vitruvius's text, he introduced specific ancient features such as the triumphal arch and the temple front into his churches. He understood but was not hidebound by Vitruvius's account of the orders, and took care to combine arch with pier, and column with straight entablature, in the Roman manner. Alberti's career was peripatetic, and enthusiasm for the new architecture spread to patrons in Rome, Ferrara, Mantua, Rimini and Urbino. In the later fifteenth century architects like Giuliano da Sangallo and Francesco di Giorgio compiled extensive sketchbooks of ancient buildings, often reconstructing the monuments in a recognisably Early Renaissance manner.

High Renaissance and Mannerism

Bramante's work in Rome (*c.* 1500–14) marks the beginning of the High Renaissance style. The aim was monumentality, even on a small scale, emulation of the massive spatial effects of Imperial Roman architecture, and a more Vitruvian use of the language of the orders. Raphael (1483–1520), who criticised the bareness of Bramante's buildings, came closest of all Renaissance architects to realising the decorative richness and variety of ancient architecture, and was followed by Peruzzi (1481–1536) and Giulio Romano (*c.* 1499–1546) in his imaginative and undogmatic approach to the Classical vocabulary; Antonio da Sangallo the Younger, by contrast, tended to seek out the Vitruvian elements amid the confusing variety of antique remains. Thus the stage was set for the emergence of two main themes in sixteenth-century architectural style: on the one hand, a tendency to 'correctness' and the formulation of rules (Sangallo, Vignola); on the other, an inventiveness verging on eccentricity (Michelangelo, Ligorio, Alessi). The latter is often called 'Mannerist', but it is important to realise that, while often breaking the Classical 'rules', it did not imply rejection of ancient example.

The movement of patrons and architects from Rome to other centres, and the publication of architectural books and engravings, resulted in the rapid diffusion of High Renaissance forms throughout Italy and all over Europe. Sansovino (1486–1570) and Sanmicheli (1484–1559) took the new language to the Veneto, while Giulio Romano pursued more fanciful goals in Mantua. The two most influential architects of the mid century, Michelangelo (1475–1564) and Palladio (1508–80), seem to stand at opposite ends of the sixteenth-century spectrum. Michelangelo's plastic approach to the wall mass, his spatial innovations and fantastic sculptural detail, pave the way for the Baroque; Palladio's clear, harmonious proportions, masterly deployment of

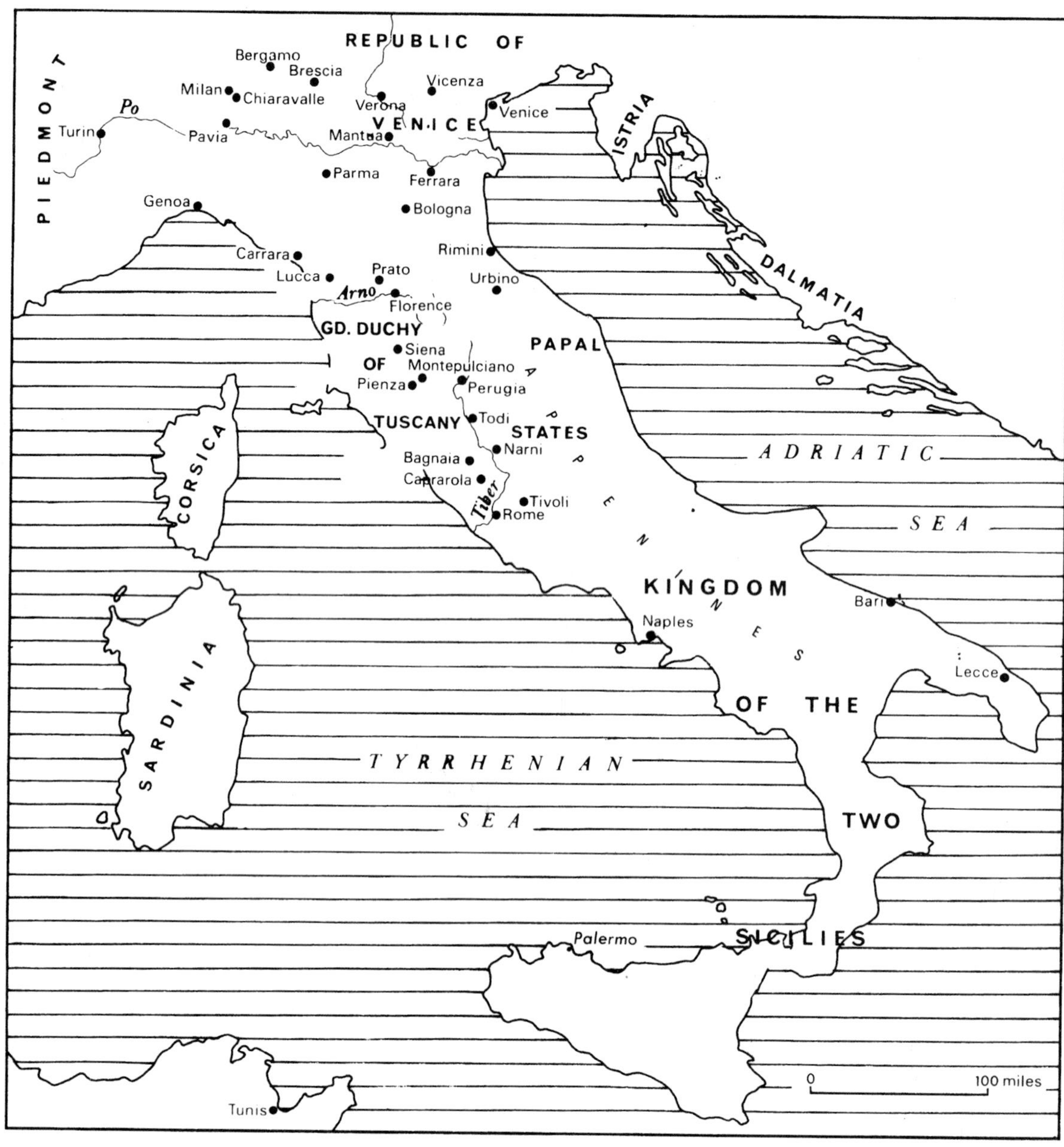

Italy in the sixteenth century

select, almost standardised antique forms, and commitment to systematic formulations of rules, made his buildings a model for Classicising architects all over Europe. Yet Michelangelo adhered firmly to a clear structural framework and the principles of symmetry, while Palladio, especially in his later buildings, permitted himself odd juxtapositions and the use of bizarre detail.

Baroque and Rococo

The movement, spatial invention, drama and freedom of detail associated with the Baroque are in some ways a delayed response to Michelangelo's achievement. Bernini (1598–1680) represents the theatrical, entrepreneurial side of the Roman Baroque, welding the arts of painting, sculpture and architecture into

A
CAPITAL IN CORTILE
PAL. GONDI : FLORENCE
B
CAPITAL AND BRACKETS
THE BADIA DI FIESOLE : Nr FLORENCE
C
PILASTER CAPITAL
S. SPIRITO : FLORENCE
11' 4"
D
WINDOW IN CORTILE
PAL. QUARATESI : FLORENCE
E
NICHE : NATL. MUS : FLORENCE
27' 4"
F
WINDOW AND FOUNTAIN
PALAZZO PITTI : FLORENCE
17' 8"
5' 10"
G
DOORWAY
S. CROCE : FLORENCE
H
CHIMNEY PIECE
NATIONAL MUS : FLORENCE
J
PORCH
S. ALESSANDRO : LUCCA

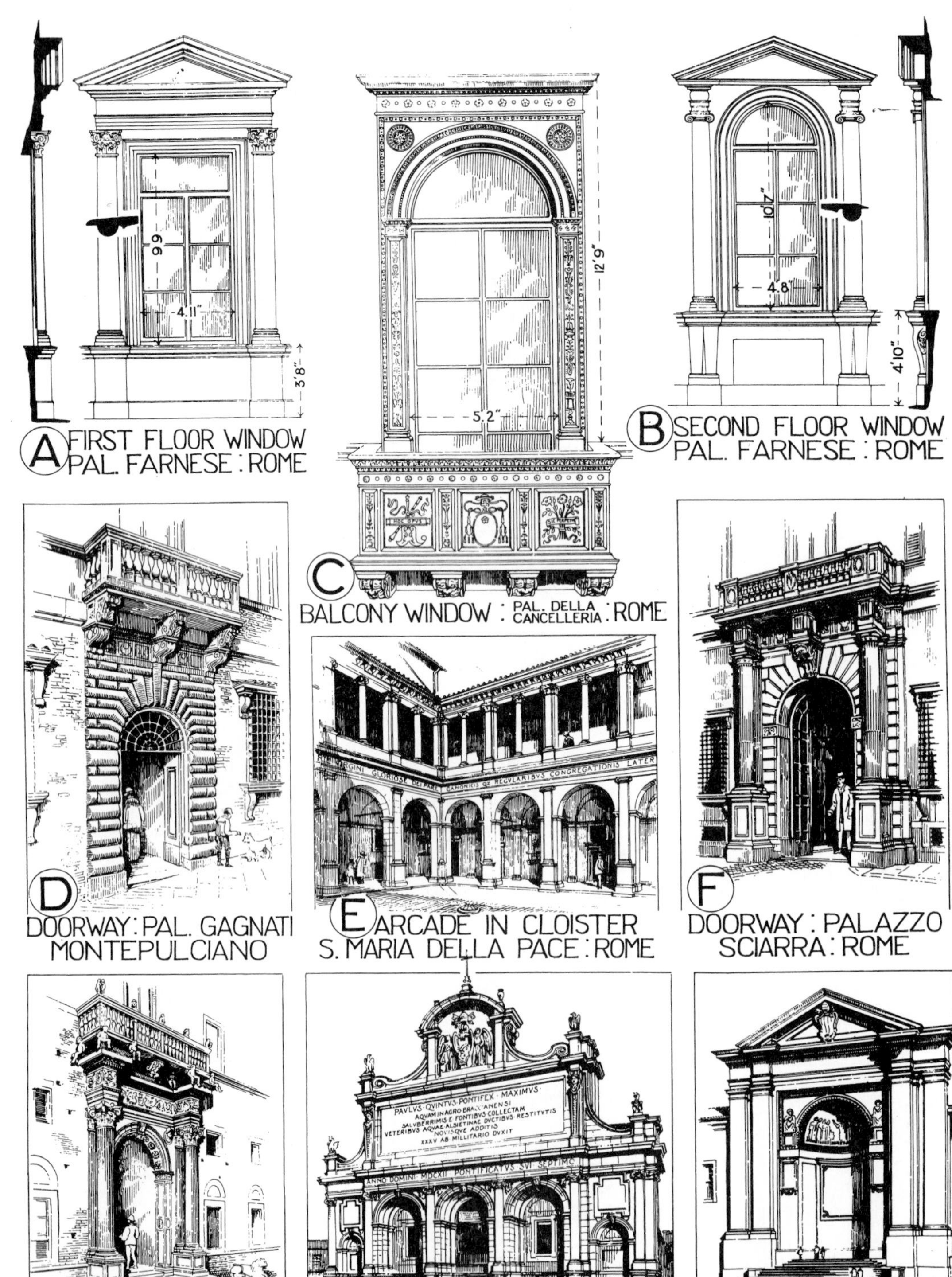

A FIRST FLOOR WINDOW PAL. FARNESE : ROME

B SECOND FLOOR WINDOW PAL. FARNESE : ROME

C BALCONY WINDOW : PAL. DELLA CANCELLERIA : ROME

D DOORWAY : PAL. GAGNATI MONTEPULCIANO

E ARCADE IN CLOISTER S. MARIA DELLA PACE : ROME

F DOORWAY : PALAZZO SCIARRA : ROME

G DOORWAY PAL. SACRATI : FERRARA

H FONTANA PAOLA : ROME

J TRICLINIUM OF LEO III : ROME

(A) DOORWAY S. ZACCARIA : VENICE

(B) BALCONY : PALAZZO FRANCHINI : VERONA

(C) DOORWAY : SCUOLA DI S. ROCCO : VENICE

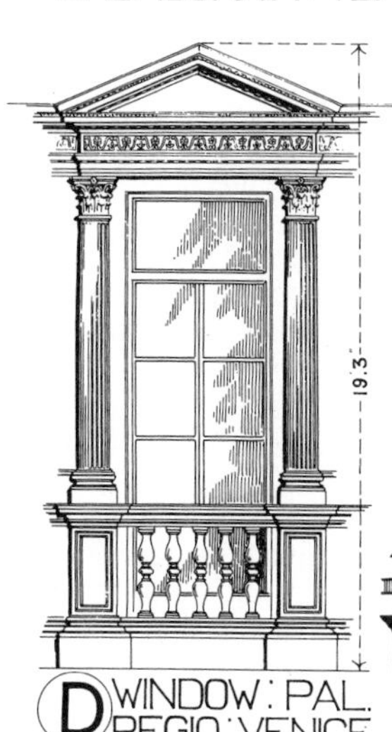

(D) WINDOW : PAL. REGIO : VENICE

(E) THE RIALTO BRIDGE VENICE

(F) STATUE-NICHE : PAL. CORNARO : VENICE

(G) MONUMENT TO GEN COLLEONI : VENICE

(H) THE LOGGETTA : VENICE

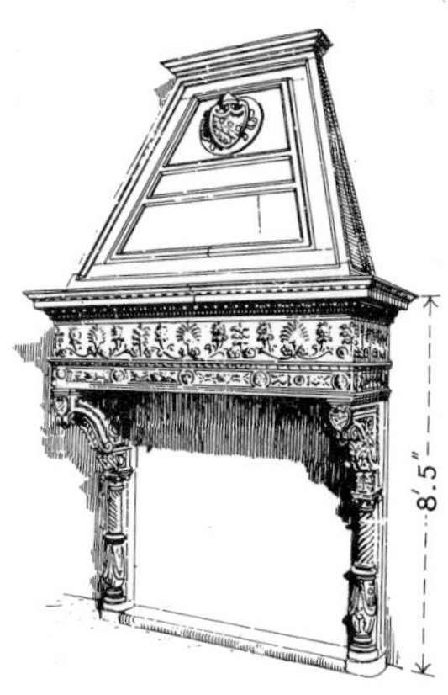

(J) CHIMNEY-PIECE DUCAL PALACE VENICE

spectacular unified effects. Pietro da Cortona (1596–1669) was a very powerful designer, moving towards a strongly columnar architecture, marked by dramatic chiaroscuro.

The most revolutionary exponent of the Roman trio was Francesco Borromini (1599–1667), however, who attained heights of spatial complexity and of audacious curving surfaces equalled only by Guarino Guarini (1624–83) and Filippo Juvarra (1678–1736) in Piedmont, where Baroque had its late Italian flowering. In early eighteenth-century Rome some architectural and urban designs, such as the Spanish Steps (p. 917A), possess a curvilinear elegance and sprightliness which may be called Rococo, but a vein of severe monumentality in the work of architects such as Ferdinando Fuga (1699–1782) and Alessandro Galilei (1691–1737) prepared the way for neo-Classical tendencies.

Neo-Classical

A Palladian-Scamozzian kind of Classicism had never entirely disappeared from the Veneto and was explicitly revived in the early eighteenth-century Venetian works of Andrea Tirali (1657–1737), G. A. Scalfarotto (1690–1764) and Giorgio Massari (1687–1766). The Venetian Franciscan theorist Carlo Lodoli (1690–1761), whose lectures were published in 1786, was a pioneer of the rationalising functionalist strand of neo-Classical thought. The Greek Revival, however, took little hold in Italy, for obvious reasons, Piranesi being the passionate champion of the Roman side in contemporary debates on the nature of Classicism. The megalomaniac vision of Roman architecture, expressed in Piranesi's engravings of ancient buildings and his 'carceri' series, was an enormoulsy influential counterweight to Rococo frivolity. By the 1780s a more rigorous Classical style was firmly established in Italy, and the Napoleonic period brought a flurry of French-inspired neo-Classical public buildings, as well as grandiose town-planning schemes in Milan and elsewhere. Italian neo-Classicism, however, tended to be somewhat feeble and derivative; for the first time Italy was importing taste rather than generating the stylistic impetus for the rest of Europe.

Examples

Early Renaissance

Florence

Filippo Brunelleschi (1377–1446), credited in his own time with the reintroduction of the 'ancient manner of building', transformed the appearance of architecture in Florence and all over Italy, even though many of his works were incomplete at his death.

The **Dome of Florence Cathedral** (1420–34) (pp. 548, 550A), which Brunelleschi constructed without the use of centering supported by scaffolding, is his most famous achievement. The octagonal drum, pointed profile and double shell were settled before Brunelleschi won the competition, but he devised the spiralling courses of herringbone brickwork, sloping masonry beds and hoisting machines which made its construction possible. Although both shells are octagonal, their constructional geometry is circular, and the corner and intermediate ribs serve to join the shells, not to provide the main support as in a Gothic structure. Stone and timber chains were also used. Brunelleschi added (1438–) the semicircular exedrae with paired half-columns and niches at the base of the drum, and the elegant marble lantern with its double volute brackets, completed by Michelozzo and Bernardo Rossellino (1436–67). Herringbone brickwork continued to be used for Florentine domes, and the two-shell construction influenced S. Peter's, Rome (q.v.), and many subsequent domes in Europe.

The **Foundling Hospital, Florence** (1419–) (p. 852A), Brunelleschi's first building, already embodies his rational and systematic principles of design. The loggia (originally nine bays) is based on repeated modular elements, with sail vaults supported on monolithic grey stone columns and semicircular arches. The vocabulary, while probably aiming at an 'antique' effect, is close to the Tuscan Romanesque of such buildings as S. Miniato (p. 354A), SS. Apostoli, and especially the baptistery, then thought to be a Roman building. The ground-plan of the hospital behind, with two cloisters, church and dormitories, is governed by modular and mathematical proportions and is roughly centralised, without being symmetrical. The main hospital and the side bays of the facade were not executed by Brunelleschi.

S. Lorenzo, Florence (1421–) (p. 847G–L), has a complicated design and building history, as much influenced by the prior, the parishioners and the Medici family as by Brunelleschi. The west (liturgical east) end was started first, with square sail-vaulted chapels and a sacristy grouped around the domed crossing and transepts. The Old Sacristy, which doubled as a Medici funerary chapel, is essentially a cube, with a hemispherical umbrella dome supported on pendentives, and a smaller domed altar chapel with concave niches.

Donatello added pedimented doors leading to the service rooms and completed the sculptural decoration in a plastic, polychrome style which blurred the clear grey on white articulation of Brunelleschi's design. The main body of the church (1442–), mostly built after Brunelleschi's death, is basilican in form, its central arcaded flat-ceilinged space flanked by sail-vaulted side aisles, and shallow dark side-chapels

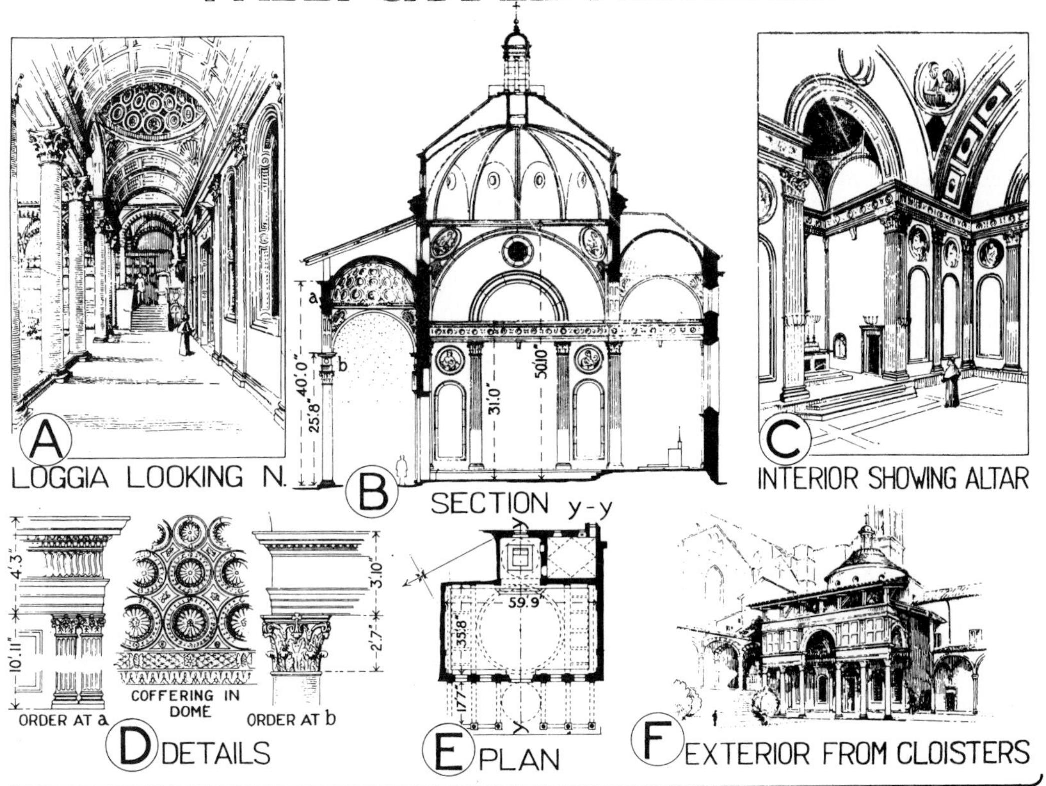
PAZZI CHAPEL: FLORENCE
A LOGGIA LOOKING N.
B SECTION y-y
C INTERIOR SHOWING ALTAR
40'0"
25'8"
50'0"
31'0"
4'3"
10'11"
3'10"
2'7"
59.9
35.8
17.7
COFFERING IN DOME
ORDER AT a
ORDER AT b
D DETAILS
E PLAN
F EXTERIOR FROM CLOISTERS

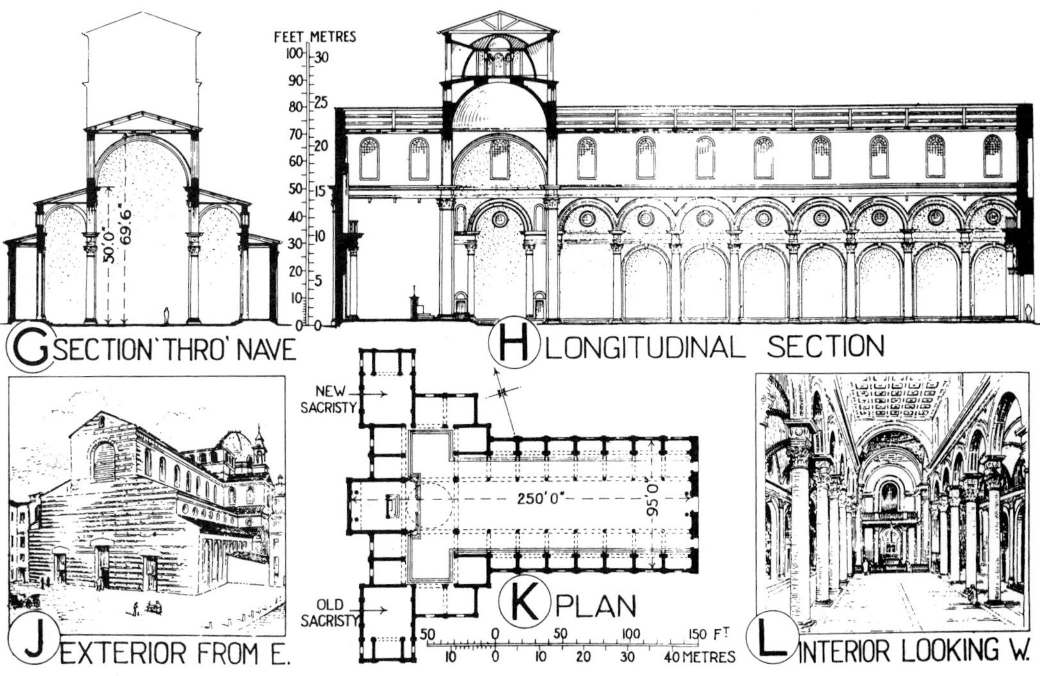
S. LORENZO: FLORENCE
FEET METRES
50'0"
69'6"
G SECTION THRO' NAVE
H LONGITUDINAL SECTION
NEW SACRISTY
OLD SACRISTY
250'0"
95'0"
J EXTERIOR FROM E.
K PLAN
L INTERIOR LOOKING W.
150 FT
40 METRES

added after 1463. The nave is brightly lit from clerestory windows and oculi in the aisles, and has Brunelleschi's characteristic restraint of detail. (For Michelangelo's New Sacristy and library in the cloister, see p. 888.)

A comparison with his other basilican church, **S. Spirito, Florence** (1436–) (p. 849A–E), shows the maturing of Brunelleschi's style in a plan which he himself described as 'fulfilling his intentions'. Here the square sail-vaulted aisle-bays and the semicircular side-chapels continue right round the centralised crossing, giving the plan a modular unity not found at S. Lorenzo. The exterior–interior correspondence is marred by later decisions to wall in the side-chapels, originally curved on the exterior, and to replace Brunelleschi's four doors with a more conventional three-doored facade. (For the sacristy, see p. 853.)

The **Pazzi Chapel, S. Croce, Florence** (1429–61) (p. 847A–F), is in many ways the perfect Brunelleschian building, though much of it was constructed after his death. The plan extends the square of the Old Sacristy by two barrel-vaulted bays to meet the requirements of a chapter house. The grey and white articulation of the interior, each element clearly distinct, and the glazed terracotta roundels (by Luca della Robbia and others) are in keeping with Brunelleschi's aesthetic. It is not clear whether the delicate colonnaded porch with its central arch and panelled upper storey in any way reflects a Brunelleschi design.

The **Oratory of S. Maria degli Angeli, Florence** (1434–7) is one of Brunelleschi's most influential buildings, despite its truncated state. An octagonal interior is ringed by interconnecting square chapels with apsidal ends, resulting in a sixteen-sided exterior eaten away by niches. The more plastic approach to the wall mass suggests a renewed influence of ancient Roman architecture, though connections with the fourteenth-century crossing arms of Florence Cathedral have been pointed out. The unfinished structure was brutally restored in the 1930s.

The great hall of the **Palazzo di Parte Guelfa, Florence** (*c.* 1430–), is Brunelleschi's only surviving wholly secular building, and is also incomplete. It is notable for the use of pilasters on the interior.

Michelozzo di Bartolommeo (1396–1472), the favourite architect of Cosimo de'Medici (1389–1464), though younger than Brunelleschi, continued to mix Gothic and antique elements in an architectural style that has been characterised as one of 'allusive contrast'; he used polygonal piers and groin vaults along with capitals and moulding more consciously based on Roman examples than those of Brunelleschi. He worked in Ragusa (Dubrovnik) after being dismissed from the cathedral works. At **S. Marco, Florence** (1437–), Michelozzo redesigned much of the church and convent for the Observant Dominicans, at the request of Cosimo de'Medici. The church (transformed in the eighteenth century) was a simple aisle-less hall with a polygonal groin-vaulted altar-chapel and half the interior was screened off as a monks' choir. The most remarkable element of the monastery building, largely executed in a simplified Brunelleschian style, is the Library (1457–) with its airy Ionic arcades, narrow barrel-vaulted central space, and groin-vaulted side aisles for the desks.

The **Medici Palace (Palazzo Riccardi), Florence** (1444–), by Michelozzo (p. 851), set the pattern for fifteenth-century Tuscan palace design. The plan, while not fully symmetrical, is organised around a central arcaded courtyard of modified Brunelleschain style with a garden at the back. An internal staircase leading off the courtyard rises to the main living quarters on the first floor, which are organised in suites of apartments containing interconnecting rooms of diminshing size. The second and attic storeys were used for children, services, and so on. The exterior is faced with stone, graduating from heavy rustication on the ground floor to smooth ashlar on the second floor, and is crowned with the first 'all'antica' cornice found in a domestic building. The two-light windows divided by columns are Renaissance versions of those on the Palazzo della Signoria (q.v.). The ground floor 'kneeling' windows in the filled-in loggia are by Michelangelo (1516–17), and greatly influenced later Tuscan window design. The palace was extended in 1680 by the Riccardi family, who added six window bays to the original eleven.

Michelozzo also adapted country buildings into **villas** for the Medici at **Trebbio, Careggi** and **Caffagiolo**. These all retain some mediaeval elements such as towers, machicolations and octagonal piers, though Careggi opens out to the countryside at the back, with arcaded loggias in the Renaissance manner. The **Villa Medici at Fiesole** (1458–61, much transformed) was influential in the history of villas for its exploitation of the hillside site with front-and-back loggias and terracing.

The circular tribune (a monks' choir ringed by chapels) at **S. Annuziata, Florence** (1444–), Michelozzo's most antique-influenced design, can be compared to the so-called Temple of Minerva Medica in Rome (Orti Liciniani). It was completed in altered form under the supervision of Alberti.

Leon Battista Alberti (1404–72), a polymath and scholar turned architect, wrote (by 1452) the first full-length architectural treatise since Vitruvius (printed 1485–6). He based the activity of the architect firmly in a social and political context, provided a wealth of practical information, and, above all, introduced an architectural aesthetic based on order and proportion, extending Pythagorean whole-number musical ratios to the visual arts. He was the first to understand the Vitruvian orders, adding to them the Italic (Composite) from his own observations of ancient buildings.

In his first building, **S. Francesco, Rimini** (*c.* 1450–) (p. 856A), often called the Tempio Malatestiano, Alberti himself designed only the outer shell,

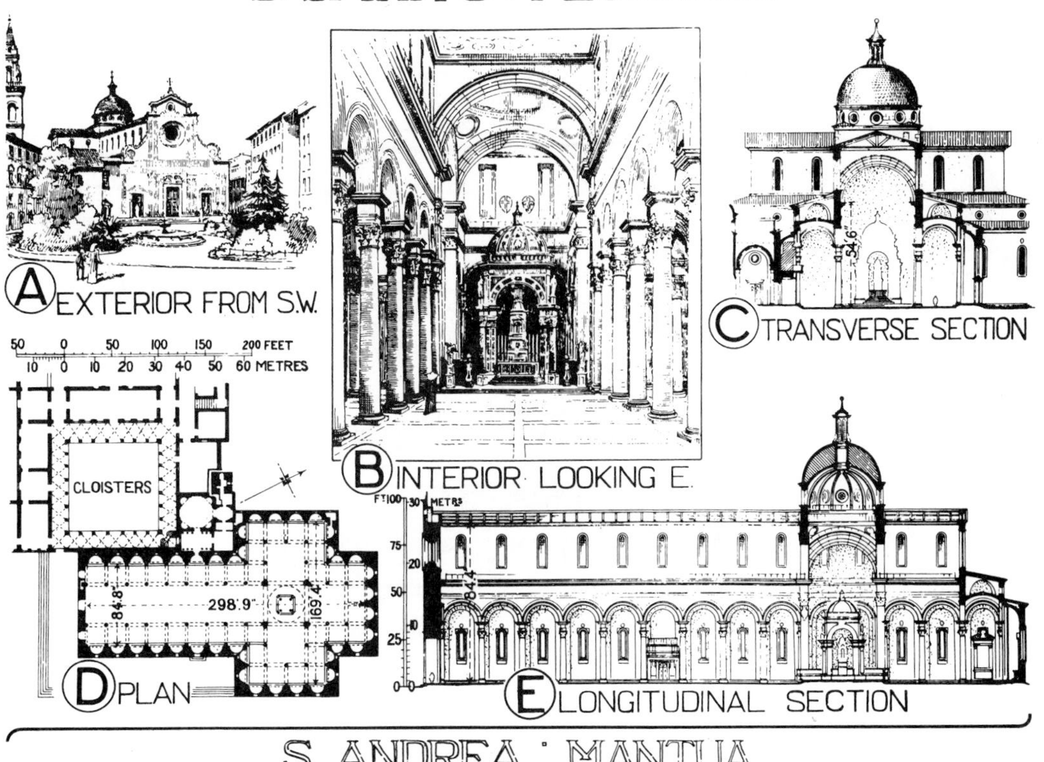
S. SPIRITO : FLORENCE
A EXTERIOR FROM S.W.
B INTERIOR LOOKING E.
C TRANSVERSE SECTION
54'6"
50 0 50 100 150 200 FEET
10 0 10 20 30 40 50 60 METRES
CLOISTERS
84'8"
298'9"
169'4"
D PLAN
FT 100 30 METRES
75 20
50
25 10
0 0
84'4"
E LONGITUDINAL SECTION

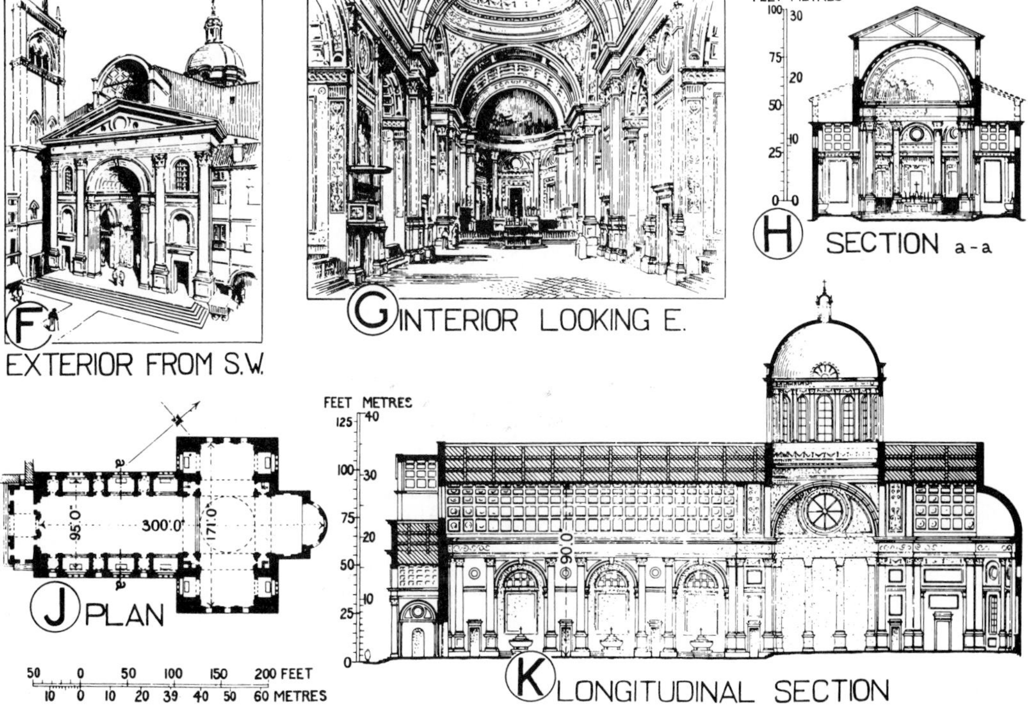
S. ANDREA : MANTUA
F EXTERIOR FROM S.W.
G INTERIOR LOOKING E.
FEET METRES
100 30
75 20
50
25 10
0 0
H SECTION a-a
a
95'0"
300'0"
171'0"
a
J PLAN
50 0 50 100 150 200 FEET
10 0 10 20 39 40 50 60 METRES
FEET METRES
125 40
100 30
75 20
50
25 10
0
90'0"
K LONGITUDINAL SECTION

PALAZZO PITTI: FLORENCE

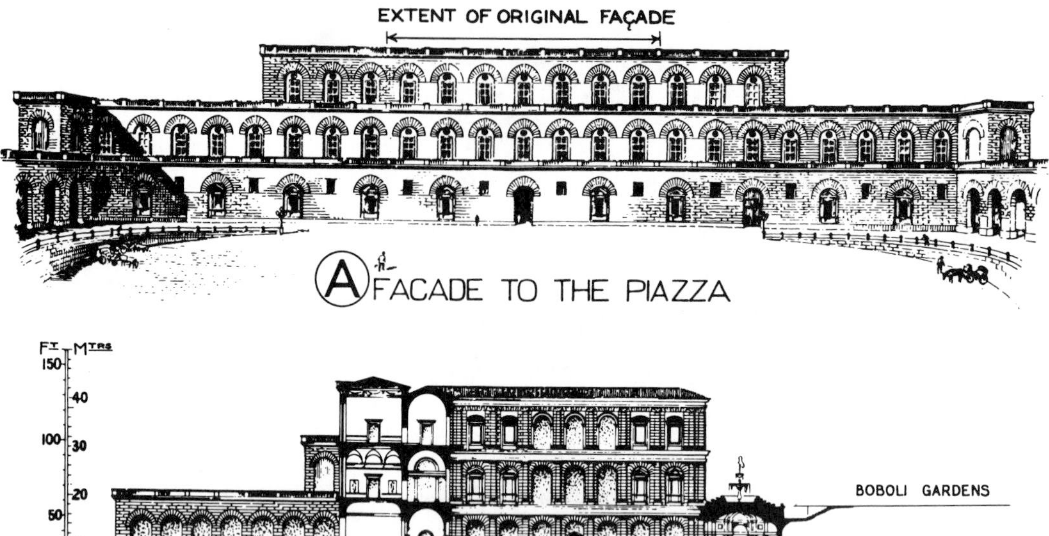

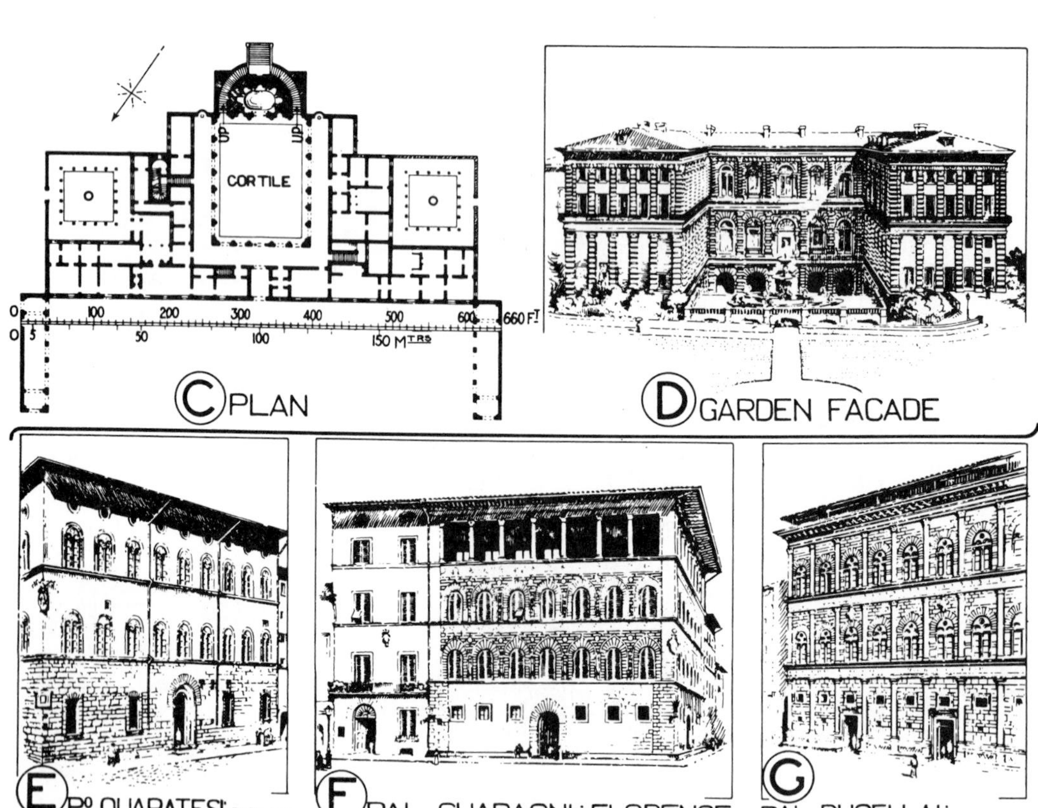

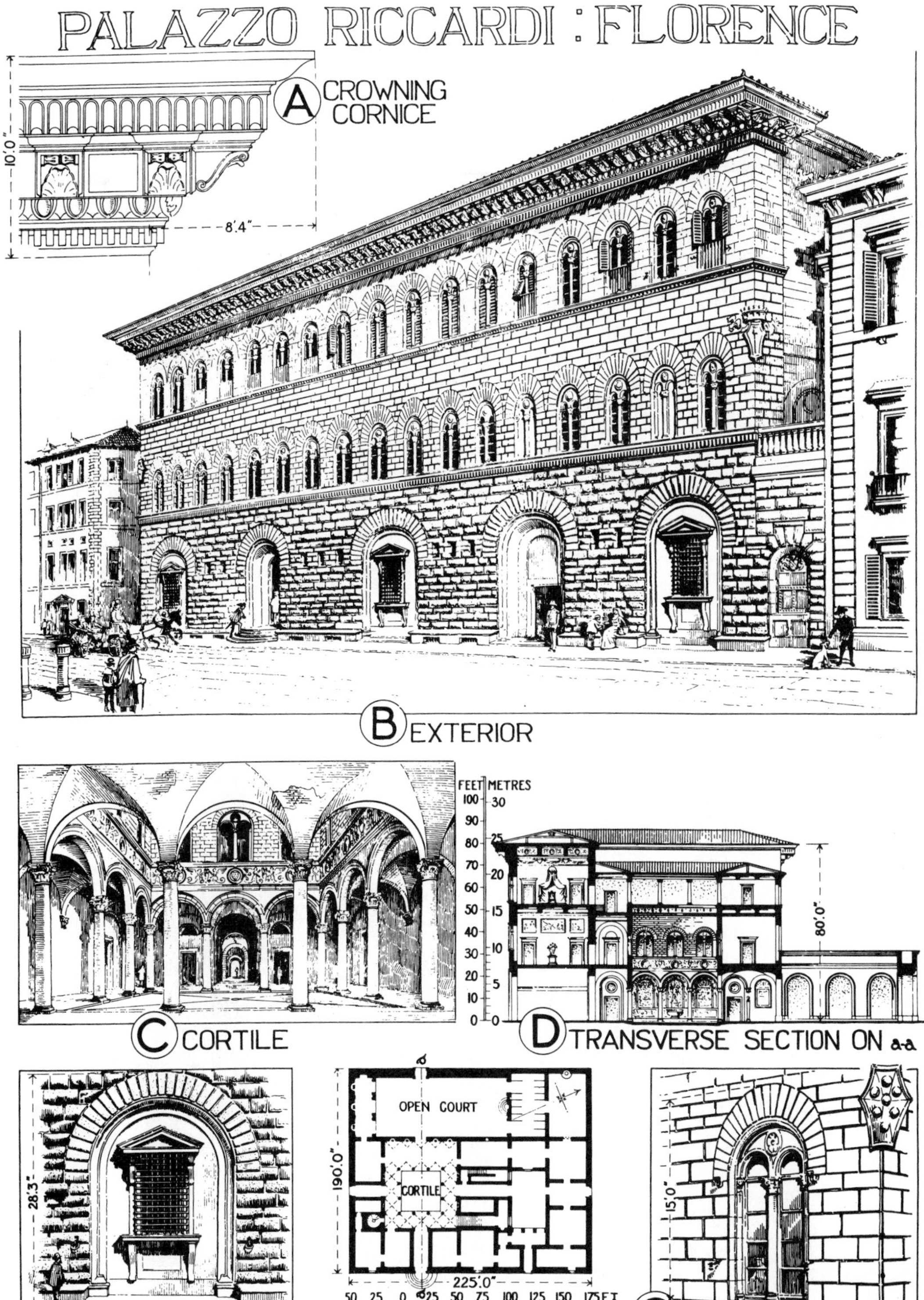
PALAZZO RICCARDI : FLORENCE
A CROWNING CORNICE
10'0"
8'4"
B EXTERIOR
C CORTILE
FEET
METRES
D TRANSVERSE SECTION ON a-a
80'0"
E GRD FLOOR WINDOW
28'3"
OPEN COURT
CORTILE
190'0"
225'0"
F PLAN
G FIRST FLOOR WINDOW
15'0"

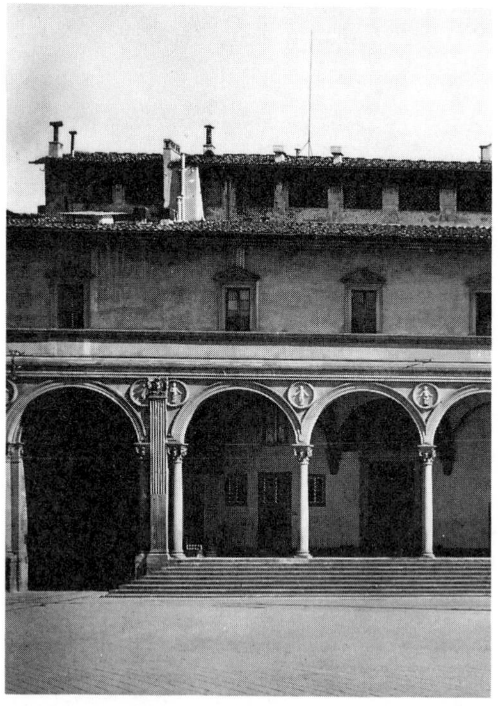

A. Foundling Hospital, Florence: loggia (1419–). See p.846

B. Palazzo Ducale, Urbino (1450–, 1465–): cortile. See p.854

C. S. Maria di Calcinaio, Cortona (1484–). See p.859

D. S. Maria delle Carceri, Prato (1485–): facade. See p.853

the interior being simultaneously transformed from its Gothic appearance by his site architect, Matteo de'Pasti. The incomplete facade is inspired by the Arch of Augustus at Rimini, and the side arcades supported on piers are also strongly Roman in form. Alberti intended there to be a Pantheon-type dome, but construction was abandoned before the death of the patron, Sigismondo Malatesta, who had brought the remains of the neo-Platonic Greek philosopher, Gemistos Plethon, to be entombed in the side recesses along with other figures from the court.

In his native city, Florence, Alberti designed the facade of the **Palazzo Rucellai** (*c.* 1453–) (p. 850G), the first domestic building articulated with Classical orders – Doric for the ground floor and two varieties of Corinthian for the upper storeys. Originally five bays, the palace was extended as the patron acquired more property, and left incomplete. The delicate and refined network of pilaster orders over drafted masonry, with the patron's emblems inserted in the friezes, does not correspond with the actual blocks of masonry; thus the use of the orders is purely ornamental. The executant architect was probably Bernardo Rossellino, and Alberti did not contribute to the plan or interior design.

For the same patron, Giovanni Rucellai, Alberti completed the polychrome marble **facade of S. Maria Novella, Florence** (1456–70) (p. 554A), incorporating the pre-existing mediaeval elements into his design. Here the volutes planned at S. Francesco, Rimini, are used for the first time to mask the aisle roofs – a highly influential solution. (For Alberti's Mantuan churches, see p. 854.)

The **Palazzo Pitti, Florence** (1458–66) (p. 850A–D), was designed for Luca Pitti, a rival of Cosimo de'Medici, by several architects including Luca Fanelli and prob ably Brunelleschi, although construction begun after his death. The original seven-bay structure is notable for its massive rustication and regular placing of windows and doors, each storey recessed behind a continuous balustrade. A large private piazza was cleared in front of the palace. Purchased by the Medici in 1549, the building was enlarged by Ammannati (1558–70), who added the courtyard, continuing the robust mood with the rusticated orders made fashionable by Giulio Romano and Serlio. Ammannati's interior planning was a response to the much more complex needs of the Ducal household, the increasing size of which necessitated further enlargements by G. and A. Parigi (1620–40), the outer wings being added by F. Ruggieri (1764–83). The Boboli Gardens behind were also successively elaborated by the Medici, with grottoes (the work of Buontalenti), fountains, statuary and a grassy amphitheatre.

The **Badia Fiesolana**, outside Florence, is one of the most intriguing buildings of the mid-century. Traditionally attributed to Brunelleschi, the church (1461–) is closer in general plan to Alberti's S. Andrea, Mantua (q.v.), with its unlit aisleless barrel-vaulted nave and dark side chapels, the light being concentrated at the crossing and east end; the ornament, however, is sparse but Brunelleschian. The abbey itself was closely supervised by the patron, Cosimo de'Medici; the architect is again unknown.

Giuliano da Maiano (1432–90) was one of several woodworker-architects in Renaissance Florence. The **Palazzo Pazzi-Quaratesi** (*c.* 1460–9) (p. 850E) combines influences from Brunelleschi (attic oculi) and the Palazzo Pitti with refined decorative detail reminiscent of the Palazzo Ducale at Urbino (q.v.); it has an imaginative courtyard with closed back wall and hanging garden.

Giuliano da Maiano also designed the **Palazzo Spannocchi in Siena** (1473–), taking the biforate windows and 'all'antica' cornice of the Medici palace and the smooth channelled masonry of the Rucellai palace to the rival Tuscan centre. His **Cathedral at Faenza** (1474–) is an excessively horizontal and unwieldy structure with wide side-aisles and side-chapels, the nave a series of huge square sail-vaulted bays. (For Maiano's work in Naples, see p. 866.)

Giuliano da Sangallo (1443–1516) was the most gifted Florentine architect of the second half of the fifteenth century. Also trained as a woodworker, he specialised with his brother Antonio (q.v.) in architectural models; they also worked together on fortifications. Sangallo was taken up by Lorenzo de' Medici (1449–92) to give built form to the 'Magnifico's' exceptional architectural interests. On Lorenzo's recommendation he gained the contract for **S. Maria delle Carceri, Prato** (1485–) (p. 852D), a new church built to house a miraculous image. Like other such churches in the Renaissance, it is domed and centralised; the Greek-cross plan is adapted from Alberti's S. Sebastiano. The interior pilaster capitals are characteristically bizarre and ornate. Similar capitals, based on antique figurated types drawn by Sangallo in Rome, are found at the **Sacristy of S. Spirito, Florence** (1489–), avowedly based on the baptistery, but in plan closer to the so-called 'Baths of Viterbo', a favourite antique building of Giuliano's. The stone barrel-vaulted columnar vestibule laid transversely recalls early Christian narthexes, but is far more monumental in conception.

At **S. Maria Maddalena dei Pazzi, Florence** (1488–) (p. 856D), Sangallo showed his awareness of Albertian principles by using the column and lintel system for the cloister (1491–), supporting the corners and entrance arches on piers. The droopy Ionic capitals are based on extant Roman examples in Fiesole.

For Lorenzo's private use Sangallo designed the **Medici Villa at Poggio a Caiano** (1485–), the first attempt to apply Vitruvian and Albertain principles to villa design. The plan is square and perfectly symmetrical, with four corner apartments, the front and back wings joined by a two-storey barrel-vaulted salone (the arrangement was to influence Inigo Jones's Queen's House, Greenwich; q.v.). The whole building is raised on an arcaded podium, and the entrance vestibule, originally reached by a straight double-ramp staircase (the present curving stairs were built in the nineteenth century), carries an embedded triangular pediment like a temple-front, the first appearance of this motif in domestic architecture. Sangallo experimented here, as at his own house in Florence (**Palazzo Panciatichi-Ximenes**, 1490–) and the **Palazzetto Scala** (1472–80), with cast stucco vaults of Romanising design.

The **Palazzo Gondi, Florence** (1490–1501) (p. 843A), has a particularly sophisticated form of smooth rustication on the facade, the voussoirs subtly keyed into the surrounding blocks. The ornament is of high quality, and the staircase is, unusually for Florence, built into the arcade of the courtyard. The palace was enlarged in the nineteenth century by Giovanni Poggi.

Sangallo made the wooden model for the **Palazzo Strozzi, Florence** (1489–) (p. 855), still kept in the building today. The most ambitious of all fifteenth-century Florentine palaces, it has a completely symmetrical plan, the two halves being intended for different brothers. The palace is taller in reality than in the model, with vaulted upper rooms. The building was supervised by the stonemason-architect Cronaca (Simone del Pollaiuolo, 1457–1508), who designed the splendid courtyard and the crowning cornice, based on a Roman example from Trajan's Forum. The facade is somewhat monotonous, but relieved by Caparra's elegant ironwork.

Cronaca's **Palazzo Guadagni** (1504–6) (p. 850F) set the pattern for the simpler palaces of the sixteenth century in Florence, its stonework confined to the rusticated voussoirs and quoins. The crowning loggia for shade and air is also characteristic.

Mantua

Alberti's churches in Mantua, designed for Marquis Ludovico Gonzaga, are reinterpretations of ecclesiastical architecture in antique terms. **S. Sebastiano** (1460–) is a Greek-cross votive church raised over a high crypt packed with piers. The facade (the steps are modern) is a flattened temple front articulated with four pilasters, the central window breaking into the pediment. It is a puzzling structure, never completed, and marred by twentieth-century restorations.

S. Andrea, Mantua (1470–) (p. 849F–K), described by Alberti as his 'Etruscan temple' fulfils many of his ideas about sacred architecture, though it was largely constructed after his death. The executant architect, as at S. Sebastiano, was the Florentine Luca Fancelli, court architect to Ludovico Gonzaga. The deep entrance portico, which mirrors the nave articulation but does not mask the whole facade, is a combined triumphal arch and temple front, articulated with pilasters. The magnificent barrel-vaulted nave is supported by very thick side walls pierced by large barrel-vaulted side chapels alternating with chambered piers, a more massively Roman effect than any yet seen in Renaissance architecture. It is unclear whether the eighteenth-century transepts and choir in any way reflect Alberti's conception; the dome is by Juvarra (completed 1763).

Bernardo Rossellino (1407/9–63), a Florentine sculptor by origin, and designer of the strongly architectural **Bruni Tomb** (1445) in **S. Croce, Florence**, was apparently Alberti's executant architect at the Palazzo Rucellai, Florence (q.v.). He worked for Pope Nicholas V, the dedicatee of Alberti's architectural treatise, on the new crossing area planned for S. Peter's, Rome (1450–).

At **Pienza**, where Pope Pius II transformed the centre of his native village into a miniature Renaissance city, Rossellino rebuilt the **Cathedral** (1459–) as an Italian version of the German hall-churches admired by Pius in his travels. The facade has an ingenious if uncanonical use of superimposed columns flanking wide buttress-like piers. The facade of **Palazzo Piccolomini** (p. 856B) is a coarse version of the Palazzo Rucellai, with the rustication carried over the lower pilasters. The interior planning, however, is more interesting, and superimposed loggias on the garden facade overlook the valley and Monte Amiata. Together with Rossellino's redesigned **Palazzo Communale**, and reworked **Palazzo Vescovile**, both buildings face on to a harmonious city square.

Strongly influenced by the Palazzo Piccolomini was the second phase of the **Palazzo Ducale at Urbino** (first phase 1450–; second phase 1465–) (pp. 852B, 856E), the outstanding building of the third quarter of the century. With Luciano Laurana (1420/5–79) as his architect, Federigo da Montefeltro united his scattered residences in a loosely composed group, unified by the harmonious and majestic central courtyard, Brunelleschian in its inspiration, but turning the corners with clustered piers. The public face of the palace on the city square was to be grandly articulated with a stone facade, while the intimate apartments on the valley side, including the marquetry-lined studiolo, are turned to enjoy the view; here elegant superimposed loggias are flanked by romantically mediaeval round towers. The interior plan, with its grand staircase and suites of interconnecting rooms forming apartments, became the inspiration for such Roman palaces as the Cancelleria (q.v.), but the stone ornament of window and door frames, fireplaces and vaults, here reaches an unsurpassed pitch of refinement.

Francesco di Giorgio (1439–1501), a Sienese painter and bronze sculptor, became the most seminal fifteenth-century designer and theorist of fortifications, and a highly influential architect working in

PALAZZO STROZZI: FLORENCE

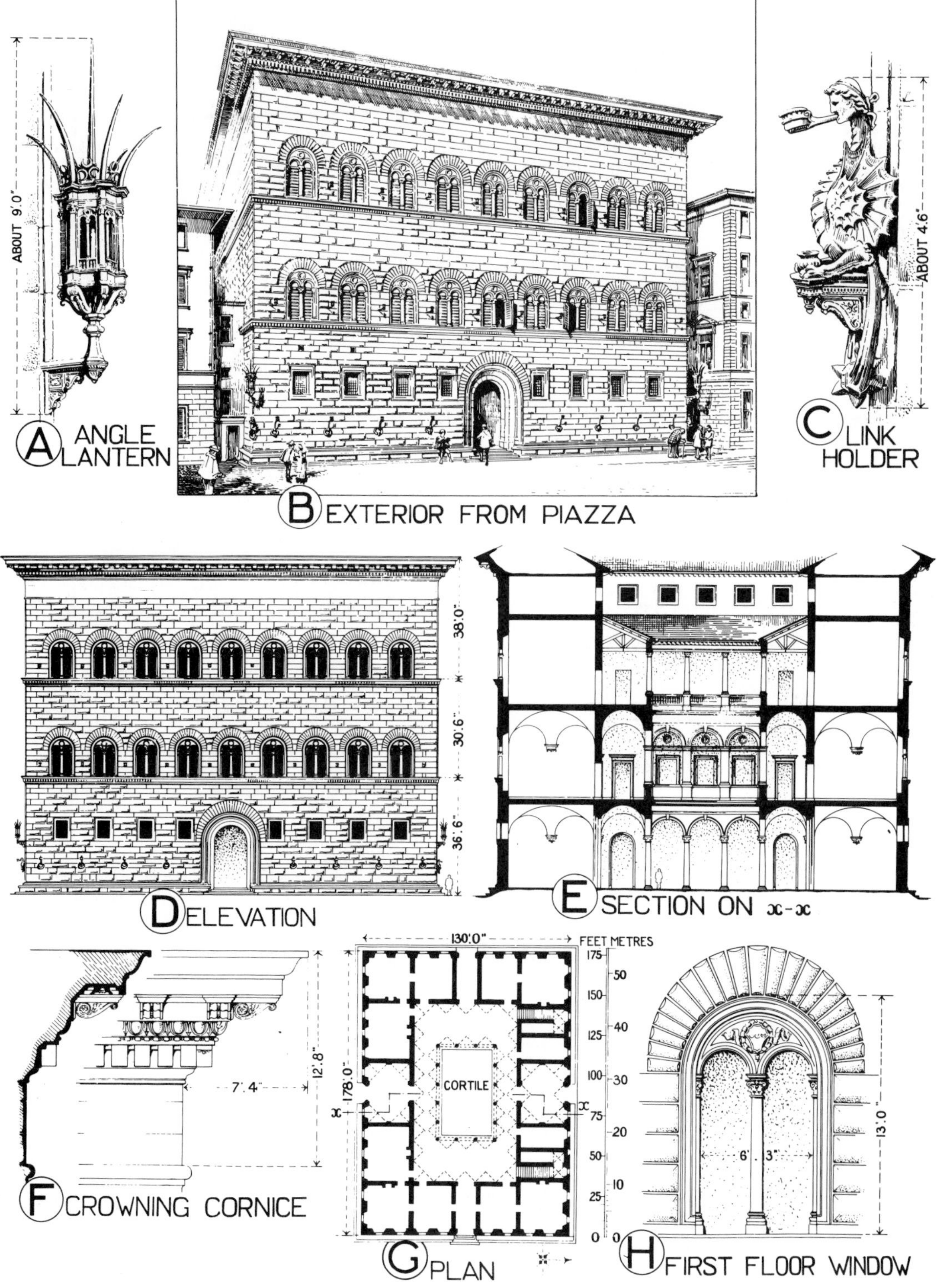

A. S. Francesco, Rimini (*c.* 1450). See p.848

B. Palazzo Piccolomini, Pienza (*c.* 1460). See p.854

C. Palazzo Venezia, Rome (1455–). See p.860

D. S. Maria Maddalena dei Pazzi, Florence: cloister (1488–). See p.853

E. Panel (possibly by Piero della Francesca) in the Ducal Palace, Urbino. See p.854

A. Fortress, S. Leo (late fifteenth century). See p.859

B. S. Maria della Pace: cloister (1478–83). See p.860

C. Certosa di Pavia, from NW (1396–; west facade 1491–). See p.860

S. MARIA DELLE GRAZIE: MILAN

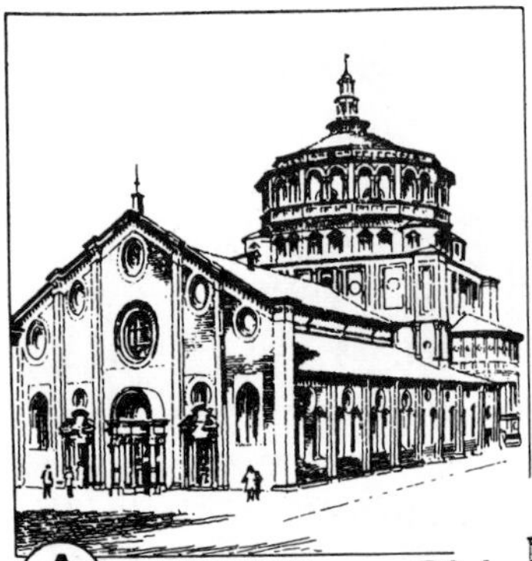

A EXTERIOR FROM S.W.

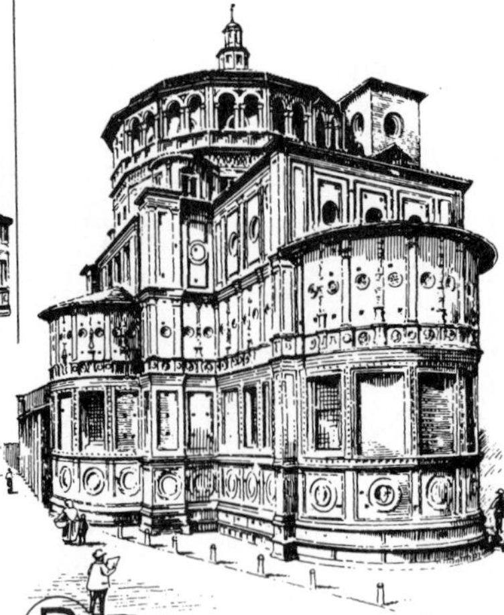

B EXTERIOR FROM S.E.

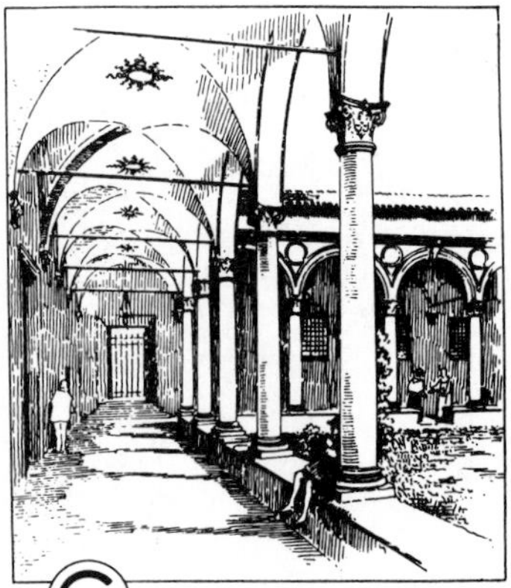

C THE CLOISTERS

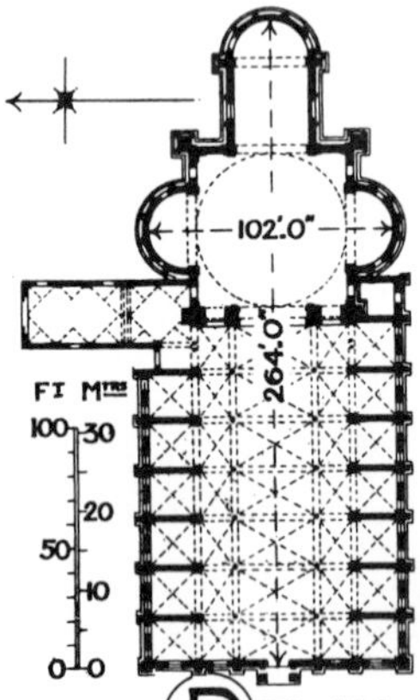

102'.0"
264'.0"
FT MTRS
100 30
20
50
10
0 0

D PLAN

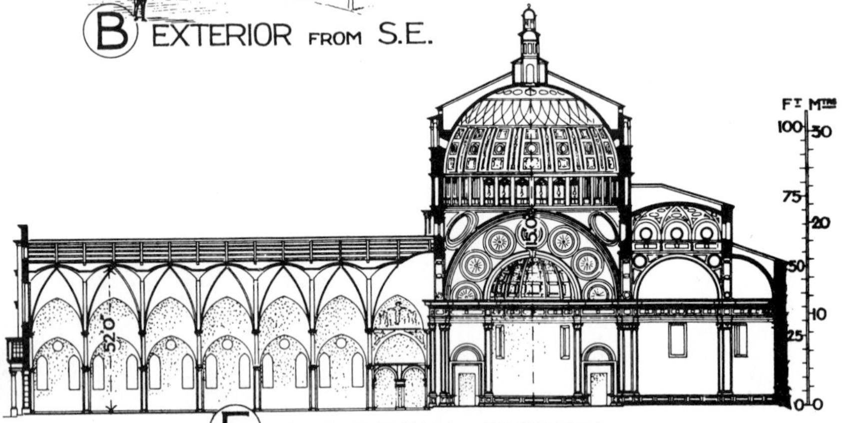

52'.0"
FT MTRS
100 30
75
20
50
10
25
0 0

E LONGITUDINAL SECTION

THE OSPEDALE MAGGIORE: MILAN

935'.0"
GRAND CORTILE
395'.0"
VIA DELL' OSPEDALE

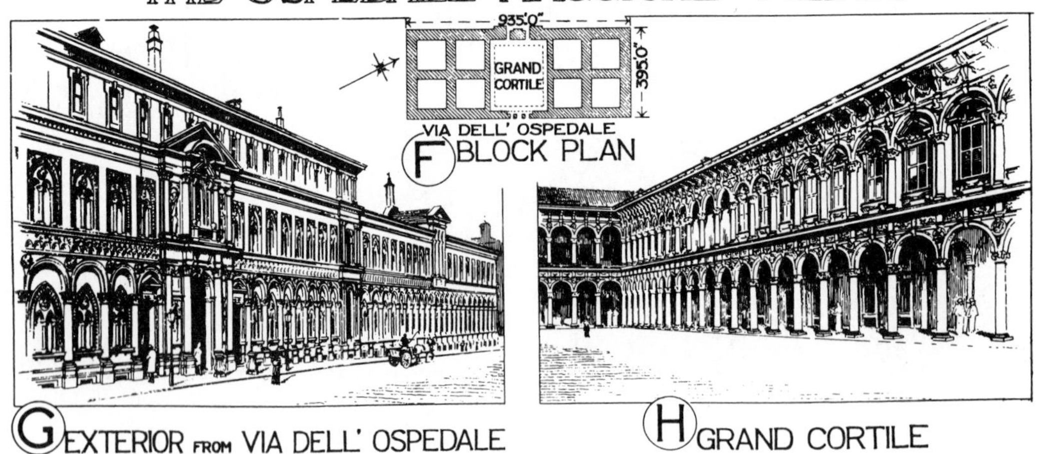

F BLOCK PLAN

G EXTERIOR FROM VIA DELL' OSPEDALE

H GRAND CORTILE

Urbino and Naples as well as his native Siena. He wrote two versions of an illustrated treastise on architecture and fortifications and left many drawings of ancient buildings.

In Urbino, Francesco continued work at the Ducal Palace, being responsible for the city facade as well as completing the courtyard and adding stables and a spiral ramp staircase. His design for the Duomo is now concealed by Valadier's alterations. The church of **S. Bernardino** (1482–) is Francesco's most complete surviving building in Urbino. Built as a mausoleum for Federigo da Montefeltro, it has a single barrel-vaulted nave leading to a square domed crossing where four free-standing columns support the pendentives. Originally all three arms of the crossing were apsidal; the altar chapel has since been extended. A characteristically Urbinate inscription in Roman capitals runs round the frieze of the interior – one of the most lucidly articulated spaces of the fifteenth century in Italy.

S. Maria di Calcinaio, Cortona (1484–) (p. 852C), built to commemorate a miracle, is a simple aisleless Latin cross with octagonal dome over squinches and a barrel-vaulted nave. The walls are massive, to support the vault, and have semicircular side-chapels carved out of their thickness. A very sparing use of continuous mouldings running round the interior gives it a strong sense of cohesion.

The same characteristics are found in Francesco's fortresses for Federigo da Montefeltro (such as **S. Leo** (p. 857A), **Sassocorvaro**), which combine a pioneering approach to defence against artillery with a foreboding but elegant robustness of design.

Milan

Florentine architectural forms reached Milan in the second half of the fifteenth century. The **Portinari Chapel, S. Eustorgio** (1460s), is essentially based on Brunelleschi's Old Sacristy, San Lorenzo, Florence (q.v.), but decorated with exuberant illusionistic paintings and reliefs, and on the exterior with pepper-pot turrets and an elongated lantern.

Antonio Averlino, called Filarete (*c.* 1400–69), received his early training as a goldsmith and sculptor in his native Florence, under Lorenzo Ghiberti (1378–1455). His most important sculptural work, the bronze door of S. Peter's in Rome, was completed in 1445. By 1451 he was resident in Milan, where in addition to being employed on the architectural projects of Duke Francesco Sforza (1401–66) he composed a curiously original *Treatise on Architecture* (*c.* 1460–64) which describes the building of the imaginary city of Sforzinda.

The **Ospedale Maggiore in Milan** (p. 858F,G,H), begun in 1456 but not completed unitl the eighteenth century, is Filarete's greatest achievement and one he describes in his *Treatise* (Bk XI, fol. 79r ff.). Perhaps influenced by the Spedale di Santa Maria Nuova in Florence, which the patron, Francesco Sforza, sent him to see, Filarete designed two large cruciform wards separated by a huge central cloister. Under the domed crossing of each ward there was an altar, so that all patients could see the mass. Cloisters between the ward arms gave access to light and air, and also gave the building its sense of thorough integration between the parts.

Donato Bramante (1444–1514), later to be the founder of the High Renaissance architectural style in Rome, worked as architect for the Sforza Dukes of Milan for twenty years (*c.* 1477–99). Born near Urbino, and trained as a painter, his early specialism in illusionistic perspective informed his whole architectural career.

S. Maria presso S. Satiro, Milan (1476–), founded to commemorate a miraculous image in the adjacent ninth-century Greek-cross oratory, S. Satiro, is built on a restricted site exploited by Bramante for perspective effect. A short barrel-vaulted aisled nave, of deceptively grand appearance for its size, is attached to a long domed transept, like an elongation of Brunelleschi's Pazzi Chapel; this leads into S. Satiro, which was reworked in fifteenth-century idiom. The apparently barrel-vaulted altar-chapel is entirely illusionistic. The ornament throughout is in terracotta, as was customary in Milan. The sacristy (1488), close in plan to the sacristy of S. Spirito in Florence (q.v.), has upper galleries and is richly ornamented in terracotta by Agostino di Fonduti.

At **S. Maria delle Grazie, Milan** (p. 858A–E), Bramante added a 'tribune' (domed crossing and choir, 1493–) to the nave built by Guiniforte Solari in a largely Gothic idiom (1463–). Intended as a mausoleum for the Sforza dukes, the interior of the square crossing is like a vastly expanded version of the altar chapel in Brunelleschi's Old Sacristy, with the side walls opening into semicircular arms crowned by half-domes. The drum recalls the attic of the Pantheon, but the flat illusionistic decoration is very quattrocento in character. The choir arm, covered by an umbrella vault, is lit through circular windows over the half-domed apse. In this building the limits of Brunelleschian spatial effects have been reached. On the exterior (attributed to Amadeo) the drum is built up into a galleried sixteen-sided structure, and the dome is concealed, in Lombard fashion, behind a conical roof, the whole encrusted with Lombard terracotta work.

Bramante projected an even grander design (largely unrealised) for **Pavia Cathedral** (1488–), an enlarged version of Brunelleschi's S. Spirito, Florence (q.v.), bodly conceived in terms of assembled masses. At **S. Ambrogio, Milan**, Bramante added the Doric and Ionic cloisters in the 1490s, showing a new awareness of Vitruvian considerations, while in the Canonica he uses playful tree-trunk columns alluding to the origins of the orders. The triumphal arch motif found here also appears at **S. Maria at Abbiategrasso** (1497), and at the **Piazza Ducale at Vigevano** (mid-1490s), a huge city square laid out by Bramante with continuous arcades covered with illusionistic painting.

S. Maria della Croce, near Crema (1493–), by G. Battagio, is one of several interesting centralised churches in Lombardy. A simple, but large, round domed church, it has four subsidiary arms arranged like a Greek cross. Superimposed galleries pierce the outer drum, which bears imaginative terracotta decoration.

The **Certosa di Pavia** (1396–) (p. 857C) was begun in Gothic style, following a Lombardo-Romanesque plan, reorganised with more systematic geometric proportions. The galleried cupola over the crossing is a reworking in early Renaissance vocabulary of the Gothic lantern at Milan cathedral. The west front (1491–), designed by Amadeo (1447–1502), is the most elaborate marble facade of the fifteenth century, remarkable more for its exquisite sculptural detail than for its overall conception.

The **Colleoni Chapel, Bergamo** (1470–3) (p. 861), an early building by Amadeo, is the burial chapel of Bartolommeo Colleoni, the famous mercenary general. The fusion of Milanese and Venetian decorative work and the accumulation of festive polychrome decoration on the exterior obscures rather than articulates the architectural form, but the sheer range of the ornamental vocabulary is remarkable.

Rome

Early Renaissance architecture was launched in Rome by Nicholas V (Pope 1446–55), whose plans for the city included restoration of the ancient churches, rebuilding the choir of S. Peter's, restoring the aqueducts and extending the habitable areas within the Aurelian walls. This sketchy blueprint for the city's development was filled in by successive popes, culminating in the work of Sixtus V.

The **Palazzo Venezia, Rome** (1455–) (p. 856C), and the titular church of **S. Marco** it incorporates (*c.* 1460–50), were, with the old **Benediction Loggia** at S. Peter's (1461–), the first notable examples of Renaissance building in Rome. The corner tower, L-shaped plan and cross-mullioned windows of the Palazzo Venezia, characteristic of fifteenth-century cardinals' places, seem conservative. However, the unfinished courtyard and the facade of S. Marco have the ancient Roman combination of arches on piers with trabeated half-columns (as in the Colosseum or the Theatre of Marcellus, Chapter 10). A delightful walled garden which was originally attached to the corner of the building was moved to the side of the piazza in the 1930s. The executant architect here and at the Benediction Loggia was Francesco del Borgo.

Unlike Brunelleschi's basilicas in Florence, Roman fifteenth-century churches generally have groin-vaulted naves. The most impressive is **S. Maria del Popolo** (1472–), built by Sixtus IV (Pope 1471–89), which gives a Roman vocabulary to the Gothic basilican form. Massive piers with squat attached half-columns support the nave arcade, delightfully embellished by Bernini in the seventeenth century. The square chapel and apsidal choir behind the altar were added by Bramante (1507–), giving some idea of his intended apse for the choir of S. Peter's (q.v.).

The **Ospedale di S. Spirito, Rome** (1474–82), is a well-balanced design commissioned from an unidentified architect by Sixtus IV. The wards extend either side of a central chapel; the additional ward extending at the rear, although not built until later, was probably part of the original scheme, and indicates the derivation from Lombard and Tuscan cross-plan hospitals, such as S. Maria Nuova in Florence. The exterior, fronted by a long loggia, treated with simplicity and restraint, combines Renaissance forms with such Gothic forms as octagonal piers and cusped window tracery.

S. Agostino, Rome (1479–83), built by Jacopo da Pietrasanta, has a very high nave with large clerestory windows; every second pier is articulated, with a half-column and minor order above supporting the groin vault. The semicircular side-chapels were originally expressed on the exterior. On the facade giant flowery volutes join nave to side aisles.

S. Maria della Pace, Rome (1478–83) (p. 857B), a pilgrimage church built under Sixtus IV's patronage, has a short two-bay aisleless nave with side chapels leading to an octagonal domed 'tribune' ringed with chapels moulded, as in the nave, out of the thickness of the massive walls. The semicircular porch, facade and approach road are by Pietro da Cortona (q.v.), and the Ionic and Corinthian square cloister is one of Bramante's early Roman works (1501–4).

The most influential palace of the later fifteenth century in Rome was the **Cancelleria** (*c.* 1485–) (p. 862), architect unknown, perhaps by Baccio Pontelli (1450–92/4), a Florentine who had worked in Urbino and designed fortifications in Rome in these years (his major work is the fortress at Ostia). The large wedge-shaped site incorporates the church of **S. Lorenzo in Damaso**, also completely rebuilt by the patron, Raffaelle Riario. Shops line a subsidiary facade, and the traditional Roman corner towers have become slight projections. The cladding is delicate drafted travertine, articulated on the upper storeys with a triumphal-arch rhythm of Corinthian pilasters, and labelled with a long Latin inscription. The doorways are later, that on the left by Domenico Fontana (1589). The large rectangular courtyard has two airy arcades in ornamented Doric, with piers at the corners, and a closed, Urbino-like upper storey, while the planning of apartment suites on the piano

Colleoni Chapel, Bergamo (1470–3). See p.860

PAL. DELLA CANCELLERIA : ROME

Ⓐ FACADE TO THE PIAZZA

Ⓑ THE CORTILE FROM UPPER STOREY

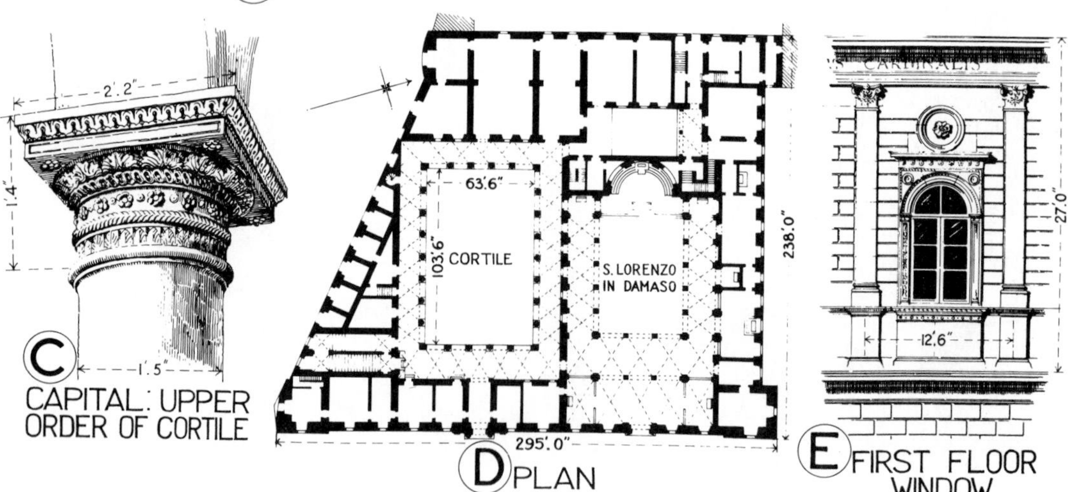

Ⓒ CAPITAL: UPPER ORDER OF CORTILE

Ⓓ PLAN

Ⓔ FIRST FLOOR WINDOW

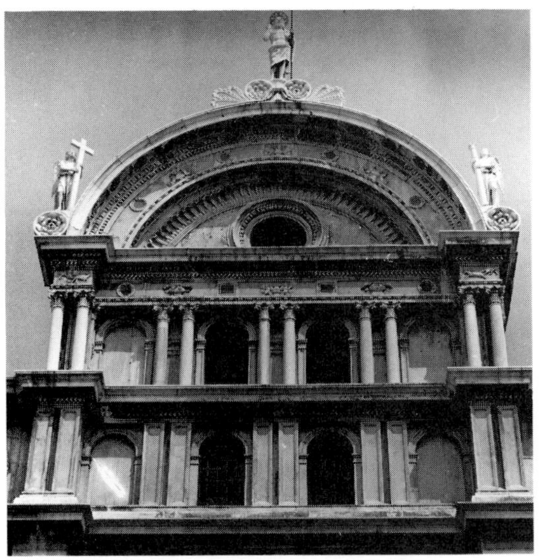

A. S. Zaccaria, Venice (1444–83). See p.865

B. Palazzo della Loggia, Brescia (1492–). See p.866

C. Scuola di San Marco, Venice, from south (1488–95). See p.865

S. MARIA DEI MIRACOLI : VENICE
A EXTERIOR FROM S.W.
B PLAN
CANAL
FEET METRES
106'0"
32'7"
C INTERIOR LOOKING INTO SANCTUARY
D TRANS. SECTION
37'5"
E LONGITUDINAL SECTION
46'3"
S. GIORGIO DEI GRECI VENICE
F EXTERIOR FROM N.W.
G PLAN
36'0"
102'0"
H LONGITUDINAL SECTION
86'6"
52'0"

nobile and the connection with the church also recall Urbino. The quality of detail is exceptionally refined.

Venice

Gothic modes of building survived in Venice to the middle of the fifteenth century. The first structure modelled on antiquity is the **Porta dell' Arsenale** (1460), based on the Roman arch at Pola (q.v.).

The unfinished **Ca' del Duca** (1445–61), probably by Bartolomeo Buon (q.v.), begun for the Duke of Milan, is, with its diamond-faceted rustication and corner columns, an explicit attempt to introduce 'modern' forms into Venice.

The **Chancel Chapel of S. Giobbe**, added in the 1460s to this new Franciscan church (1450–), imports Brunelleschian spatial effects.

The greatest Venetian architect of the fifteenth century was Mauro Coducci (*c.* 1440–1504), who combined technical brilliance and a knowledge of Alberti's work with a respect for Veneto-Byzantine forms.

S. Zaccaria, Venice (p. 863A), where Coducci completed (1483–) a church (largely by A. Gambello) begun in 1444, has a curious nave colonnade raised on high polygonal bases, and an ambulatory around the Gothic choir. The top half of the facade, marked by much more confident and structural handling of the orders, is Coducci's contribution to the exterior. The clustering of windows at the centre is borrowed from Venetian palace facades, and the emphatic projections and strong effects of light and shade were to continue to characterise Venetian architecture in the sixteenth century.

S. Michele in Isola (completed 1478), a monastic church with choir gallery at the west end, has a flat, brilliant white Istrian stone facade with channelled masonry continuing across the gaint pilasters. The crowning semicircular pediment with volutes is echoed (as at S. Zaccaria) by segmental gables hiding the aisle roof. The enchanting hexagonal chapel to the left was built in 1527–43 by Guglielmo dei Grigi.

Coducci's other churches are reworkings of the Byzantine quincunx plan (central dome with four corner domes) found at S. Marco, domed spaces being a hallmark of the Venetian Renaissance. **S. Maria Formosa, Venice**, rebuilt by Coducci (1492–1504), partially follows the traditional plan of the eleventh-century church, but transforms it into a shortened Latin cross with domed crossing and trilobed apse. The interior is a loosely connected sequence of individually vaulted spaces, now brightly lit from (later) oculi.

S. Giovanni Crisostomo, Venice (1497–1504), a small parish church on a crowded site, is a more compact version of the quincunx plan, with three additional eastern chapels. The piers are oddly divided into vertical sections, the subsidiary domes springing from the upper imposts.

Giorgio Spavento's magnificent and airy **S. Salvatore, Venice** (1506–), is composed of three quincunx units, with three identical domes, fused to form a longitudinal church with nave and side aisles. The ingenuity of the plan is matched by the controlled logic of the interior articulation.

S. Maria dei Miracoli, Venice (p. 864A–E), by Pietro Lombardo (1481–9), combines the functions of a nunnery church with the celebration of a miraculous image. It has a timber barrel-vaulted nave without side aisles and a raised choir with a pendentive dome. Both interior and exterior are clad in panels of richly-coloured marbles. Similarly decorative marble work is seen at the **Ca Dario** (*c.* 1488), dedicated by its inscription to the genius of the city (*genio urbis*). Serpentine columns and roundels sliced from antique porphyry embellish the facade, where the clustered windows lighting the salone are pushed asymmetrically to one side.

The facade of the **Scuola di S. Marco, Venice** (1488–95; built as a confraternity hall, now a hospital) (p. 863C), was successively designed by Giovanni Antonio Buora, Pietro Lombardo, and Coducci (who added the effervescent crowning storey). The effect is of a pictorial composition in coloured marbles, heightened by the perspectival scenes flanking the two portals. At the **Scuola di S. Giovanni Evangelista**, Coducci built the most spectacular surviving staircase of the fifteenth century (1498), with its smoothly barrel-vaulted flights and domed landing supported on free-standing corner columns.

The **Palazzo Corner Spinelli, Venice** (*c.* 1485–90), attributed to Coducci, is the most attractive and consistently designed of Venetian quattrocento palaces. The ground floor is faced with drafted masonry punctuated by contrapuntally-placed narrow windows; the upper storeys use biforate windows paired in the centre and single at the sides to light the salone and bedrooms. The building is unified vertically by the superimposed corner pilasters and horizontally by continuing the balustrade and balconies as wide string courses. A particularly elegant touch is the trilobed curve of the side balconies on the piano nobile.

The **Palazzo Vendramin-Calergi** (*c.* 1500–8) is also attributed to Coducci and is the culmination of his career, achieving a High Renaissance clarity of design with a quattrocento vocabulary. The colossal and very sculptural facade is a tripartite grid with clustered openings in the centre and paired Corinthian half-columns articulating the side bays. The triumphal-arch effect is emphasised by the garlands linking the capitals on the piano nobile, while the heavy crowning entablature is punctuated with sculptured reliefs which carry up the line of the columns.

Venetian quattrocento skill at large-scale pictorial effects is summed up in Bartolomeo Buon's

Procuratie Vecchie (1514–), giving a uniform facing to the left side of Piazza S. Marco, and by the **Torre dell'Orologio** (1496–9, perhaps by Coducci) which closes the vista of the Piazzetta S. Marco in a picturesque manner.

The **Palazzo del Consiglio, Verona** (1476–92) (p. 880H), architect unknown, is the most notable fifteenth-century building in that city. The eight-bay colonnaded loggia is symmetrical around a centrally placed pilaster, with further pilasters placed at the corners (on the left an additional arch gives the effect of a triumphal entrance in the manner advocated by Alberti). The closed upper storey has four wide biforate windows flanked by pilasters, two of them supported by bracket capitals in the spandrels of the ground floor arcade. The highly consistent but unorthodox design is reminiscent of Coducci's work in Venice.

The **Palazzo della Loggia, Brescia** (begun 1492) (p. 863B), is one of the outstanding public buildings of Renaissance Italy, only equalled in the sixteenth century by Palladio's Basilica in Vicenza. The balloon-like wooden roof (reconstructed) is modelled on the fourteenth-century Palazzo della Ragione at Padua. The massive lower storey combines a confidence in handling the Roman Colosseum-style arcading with an exquisite attention to detail. The upper floor, modified after a fire (1550–60), with its majestic trabeated windows (by Palladio), pilasters with candelabra decoration and crowning statuary, continues this refined idiom.

The **Palazzo Bevilacqua, Bologna** (*c.* 1480–), is chiefly notable for its diamond-faceted rustication and for the fluted columns in the courtyard. The **Palazzo del Podesta, Bologna** (1485–1500), has even more unusual rose-petalled rustication on the piers of its arcade, and rusticated windows divided by pilasters on the upper storey.

Ferrara was twice expanded in the fifteenth century with additional quarters created in the west by Duke Borso d'Este (1413–71) and the whole northern part of the city added (1492) under Duke Ercole (1471–1505).

Biagio Rossetti (1447–1516) was the ducal architect, planning a whole series of buildings from monastic and parish churches to terrace housing. His churches, such as **S. Francesco** (p. 868A), **S. Benedetto** and **S. Cristoforo** are clearly planned and soberly eclectic with much use of domes and domical vaults. The most interesting palace in the Addizione is the **Palazzo dei Diamanti, Ferrara** (1493–), on a corner site with a scarped base, highly decorated corner pilasters with balcony, and two facades covered in diamond-point rustication. (For a late sixteenth-century derivative, see the **Palazzo dei Diamanti, Verona** (1580), p. 880G.) Rossetti's own house, the **Casa Rossetti, Ferrara**, is an enlarged version of a single Emilian row house with terracotta trim.

Naples

Naples under its fifteenth-century Aragonese rulers was an important centre of humanist culture.

The **Aragonese Arch at the Castel Nuovo** (1452) celebrates the entry of King Alfonso I and is the first Renaissance monument in Naples. Superimposed triumphal arches alternate vertically with zones of sculpture showing Alfonso in triumph and the virtues of his rule. A later gate, the **Porta Capuana** (1485, by Giuliano da Maiano), is also antique in inspiration.

Most of the fifteenth-century buildings in Naples are lost, including the highly influential **Villa of Poggio Reale**, designed by Giuliano da Maiano (1487-) with advice from Lorenzo de'Medici. This had a four-towered main block with a colonnaded sunken courtyard surrounded by theatre-like stepped seating giving on to terraced gardens overlooking fishponds and incorporating antique-style baths. A version of the building was published by Serlio, and its layout of terracing and gardens influenced the Villa Madama, Rome (q.v.).

High Renaissance and Mannerism

Rome, 1500–1540

The High Renaissance begins with the work of Bramante in Rome.

Bramante's **Tempietto** in the cloister of **S. Pietro in Montorio, Rome** (1502) (p. 867A–C), is a tiny but impressive building with a severity and antiquarianism new to Renaissance architecture. The circular domed chapel commemorates the traditional site of the martyrdom of S. Peter, visible in the crypt below (remodelled 1628) through a hole in the floor. A stern Doric colonnade with a consciously correct Doric entablature encircles the exterior, which resembles a Roman peripteral temple, although the projecting drum and semicircular dome befit an important Christian shrine. Restrained in ornament, wall surfaces are sculpturally treated 'all'antica' with arrangements of pilasters and shell niches. The Tempietto rapidly achieved the status of a modern classic. S. Pietro in Montorio itself (*c.* 1490), attributed to Baccio Pontelli, is an important aisleless church with an extended east end.

The **Cortile del Belvedere, Vatican, Rome** (begun 1505, much altered by subsequent architects), was designed by Bramante for Pope Julius II. It is a gigantic enclosure over 300 m (1000 ft) in length connecting the fifteenth-century papal palace with the Belvedere of Innocent VIII (1485–7) and Julius II's sculpture court, to which it ascends in three terraces now sadly partitioned into separate courtyards. From the large lower terrace (where semicircular steps were later palced to provide seating for spectators) the upper terraces and gardens were approached by a

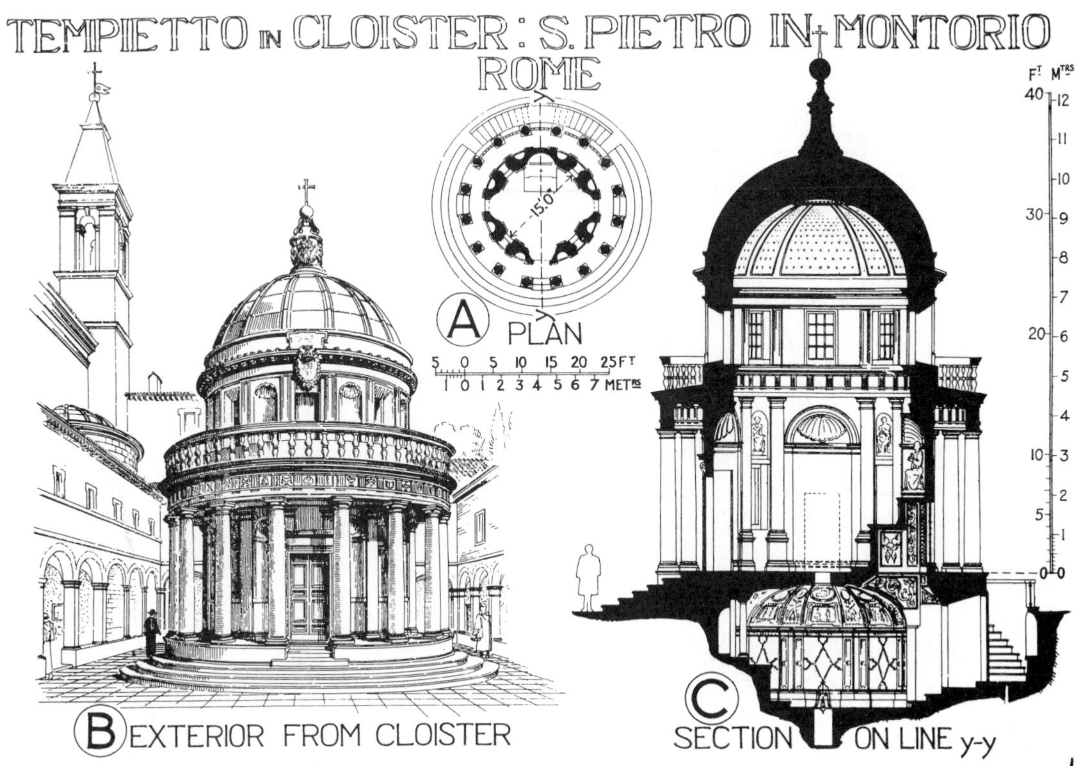
TEMPIETTO IN CLOISTER: S. PIETRO IN MONTORIO ROME
A PLAN
15'0"
5 0 5 10 15 20 25 FT
1 0 1 2 3 4 5 6 7 METRS
B EXTERIOR FROM CLOISTER
C SECTION ON LINE y-y
FT MTRS

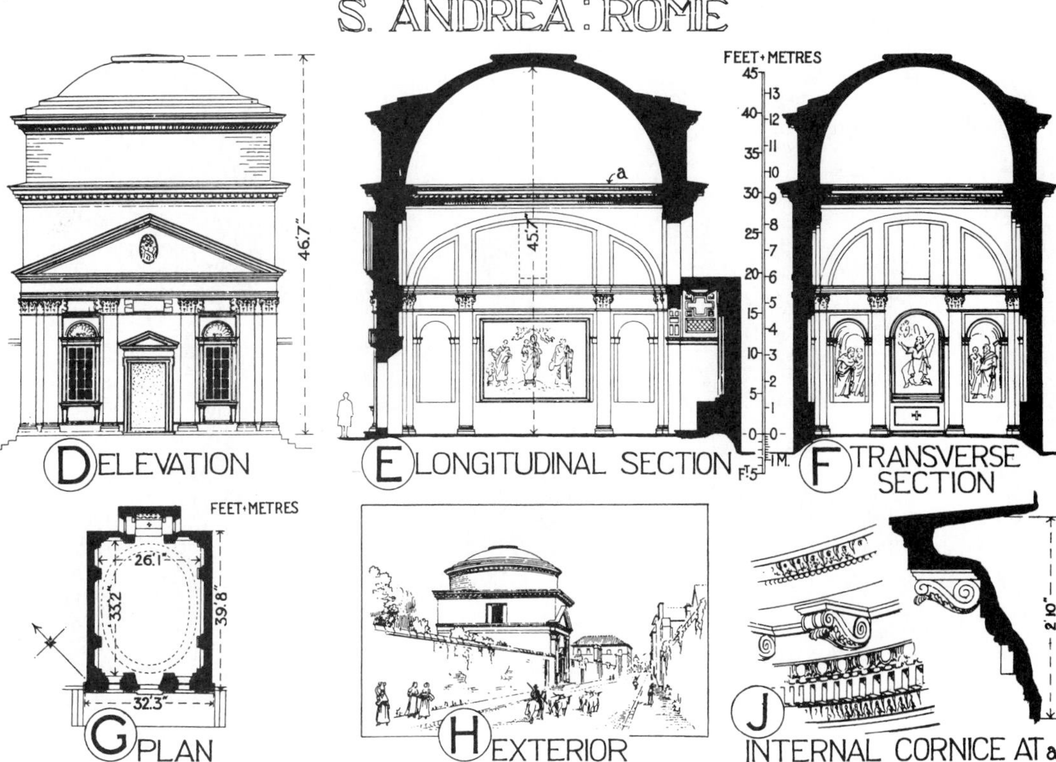
S. ANDREA: ROME
46'7"
45'7"
a
FEET + METRES
D ELEVATION
E LONGITUDINAL SECTION
F TRANSVERSE SECTION
FEET + METRES
26'1"
33'2"
39'8"
32'3"
2'10"
G PLAN
H EXTERIOR
J INTERNAL CORNICE AT a

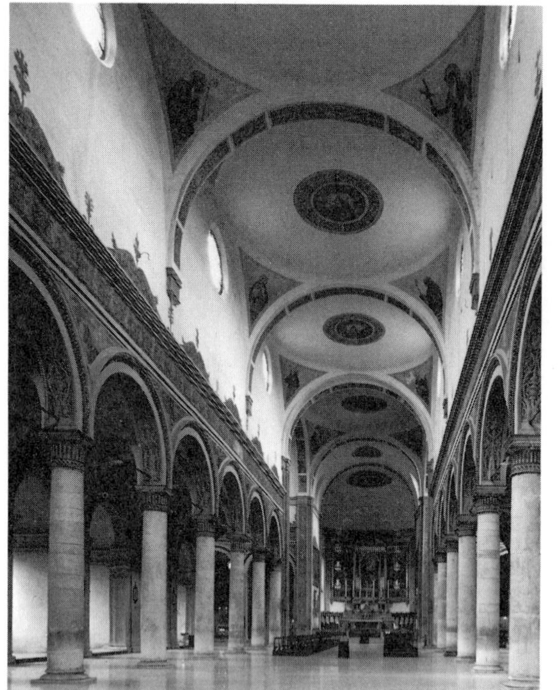

A. S. Francesco, Ferrara (late fifteenth century). See p.866

B. Madonna di S. Biagio, Montepulciano (1518–64). See p.872

C. S. Peter, Rome (1506–1626): drawing of interior by Piranesi. See p.869

broad flight of steps and by zigzag ramps flanking a nymphaeum. At the far end a semicircular exedra was once reached by an ingenious concave and convex staircase. This was the culmination of a view from the papal apartments reminiscent of such Roman complexes as the Sanctuary of Fortuna, Palestrina. The covered walkways flanking the Cortile (today the Vatican Museums), decrease from three storeys to one at the far end (later increased under Pirro Ligorio, 1561–), thereby producing a constant roofline. The brick and stucco facades were variously articulated: the triumphal-arch rhythm of the upper court, recalling the Cancelleria, was to be enormously influential, while in the lower court the pilasters ascend from Doric to Corinthian for the first time since antiquity. Columns follow the same sequence in Bramante's spiral staircase, built for direct access to the sculpture court.

Bramante's revolutionary **Palazzo Caprini, Rome** (1501–2), had the most influential palace facade of the sixteenth century, although it had disappeared by 1600. Above an arcaded rusticated basement housing shops, paired Doric half-columns flank the pedimented windows of the piano nobile, which has a full Doric frieze. A cluster of three half-columns provides an elegant solution to the corner, particularly prominent in the street leading up to the Vatican palace. The expressive differentiation between rusticated base and Classically 'ordered' first floor was to be adopted in domestic architecture all over Europe.

S. Peter's, Rome (begun 1506, consecrated 1626) (pp. 868C, 870, 871, 902C, 905), the largest and most important building of the Renaissance, owes the nucleus of its design to Bramante, although many other architects were to work on it. It was Julius II's whim to install a colossal tomb for himself in the choir (begun by Nicholas V, *c.* 1450) that precipitated the decision to rebuild the ancient basilica completely. Bramante made several variant designs for the new building, but all envisaged that directly above the tomb of S. Peter would rise an enormous dome of roughly the same size as the Pantheon's, supported upon four massive crossing piers. The so-called 'Parchment Plan' (Uffizi, Florence) and the foundation medal of 1506 show a Greek-cross plan within a square, with four subsidiary domes, towers at the corners, and half-domes terminating each of the four arms. Such a design is the realisation of the theoretical preference for centralised planning, but also derives from such esteemed funerary churches as S. Mark's, Venice, as well as ancient mausolea. Despite its size, however, the Greek-cross plan would not have covered the site of the old basilica, nor would it have suited congregational or processional needs: ultimately a Latin cross with an extended eastern arm was preferred (p. 871G).

Bramante's building would have had a relatively severe exterior, depending for its effect on the hierarchical massing of geometric forms (rather like his earlier project for Pavia Cathedral). The dome, known both from the medal and from a woodcut in Serlio's treatise, was to be a single-shelled hemisphere, presumably made of concrete and with a stepped profile derived from the Pantheon; it would have been raised up on a colonnaded drum and surmounted by a lantern (p. 870B). For the interior of the building Bramante intended to use paired Corinthian pilasters supported on tall pedestals (the floor level was later raised by Sangallo). His highly original and influential chamfered crossing piers, although later much enlarged, still survive in the completed building, enabling the nave and transepts to widen at the crossing and giving a smooth transition between pier and pendentive. In general, Bramante's sculptural approach to piers and wall mass, inspired by Roman architecture, represents a new spatial conception of great importance.

After the death of Julius (1513), Leo X appointed Fra Giocondo and the ageing Giuliano da Sangallo as co-architects, but on Bramante's own demise (1514) it was Raphael who became architect-in-chief.

At this period numerous proposals were made for the continuation of the building. Raphael's own design was a Latin cross retaining many of Bramante's ideas including the dome, although the crossing piers were enlarged. Raphael proposed the addition of ambulatories around the ends of the three short arms of the cross, and intended the building to have a monumental porticoed facade, with a giant order interlocking with smaller orders, between elaborate towers. At Raphael's death (1520), Antonio da Sangallo the younger was elevated to architect-in-chief, assisted by Peruzzi. Peruzzi proposed many designs, including a return to the Greek-cross idea, but Sangallo's final model, commissioned in 1539, is essentially a revision and expansion of Raphael's design. The Sangallo scheme (p. 870D,G) has been much abused following Michelangelo's condemnation of its 'German' qualities and lack of light. The apparent lack of unity in the model would have been offset in execution by the very scale of the building, complemented by the massing of so many parts. The western region of the model (liturgical east end) is a Greek cross with three ambulatories, but the plan becomes a Latin cross by the addition of a subsidiary domed link connecting with the facade block. Between the towers the close-packed articulation of the two-storey facade projects at the main portal with an unprecedented plasticity.

When Michelangelo was appointed as Sangallo's successor in 1546 he embarked on a radically new project involving the demolition of the Raphael/Sangallo southern ambulatory. By Michelangelo's death (1564), his project was all but realised, and his designs for the dome were essentially followed afterwards. Michelangelo's S. Peter's, claimed to be a restoration of Bramante's, is in fact a reduced and simplified Greek cross (p. 870F) ingeniously formed

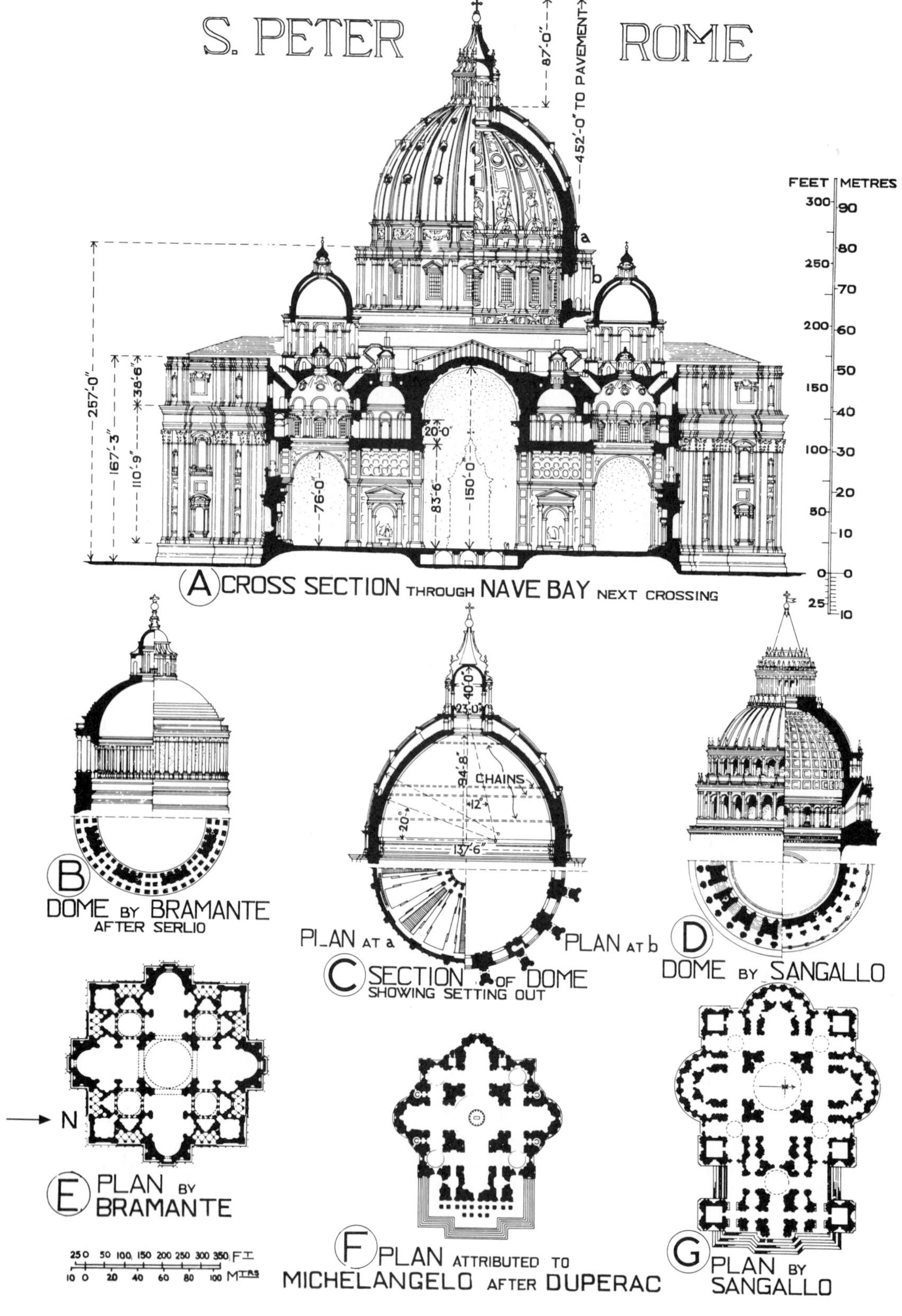

S. PETER ROME
87'-0"
452'-0" TO PAVEMENT
FEET METRES
300 90
80
250
70
200 60
50
150
40
100 30
20
50
10
0 0
25 10
257'-0"
167'-3"
110'-9"
38'-6"
20'-0"
76'-0"
83'-6"
150'-0"
a
b
A CROSS SECTION THROUGH NAVE BAY NEXT CROSSING
B DOME BY BRAMANTE AFTER SERLIO
40'0"
23'-0"
94'-8"
CHAINS
12
20
137'-6"
PLAN AT a
PLAN AT b
C SECTION OF DOME SHOWING SETTING OUT
D DOME BY SANGALLO
N
E PLAN BY BRAMANTE
F PLAN ATTRIBUTED TO MICHELANGELO AFTER DUPERAC
G PLAN BY SANGALLO
25 0 50 100 150 200 250 300 350 FT
10 0 20 40 60 80 100 MTRS

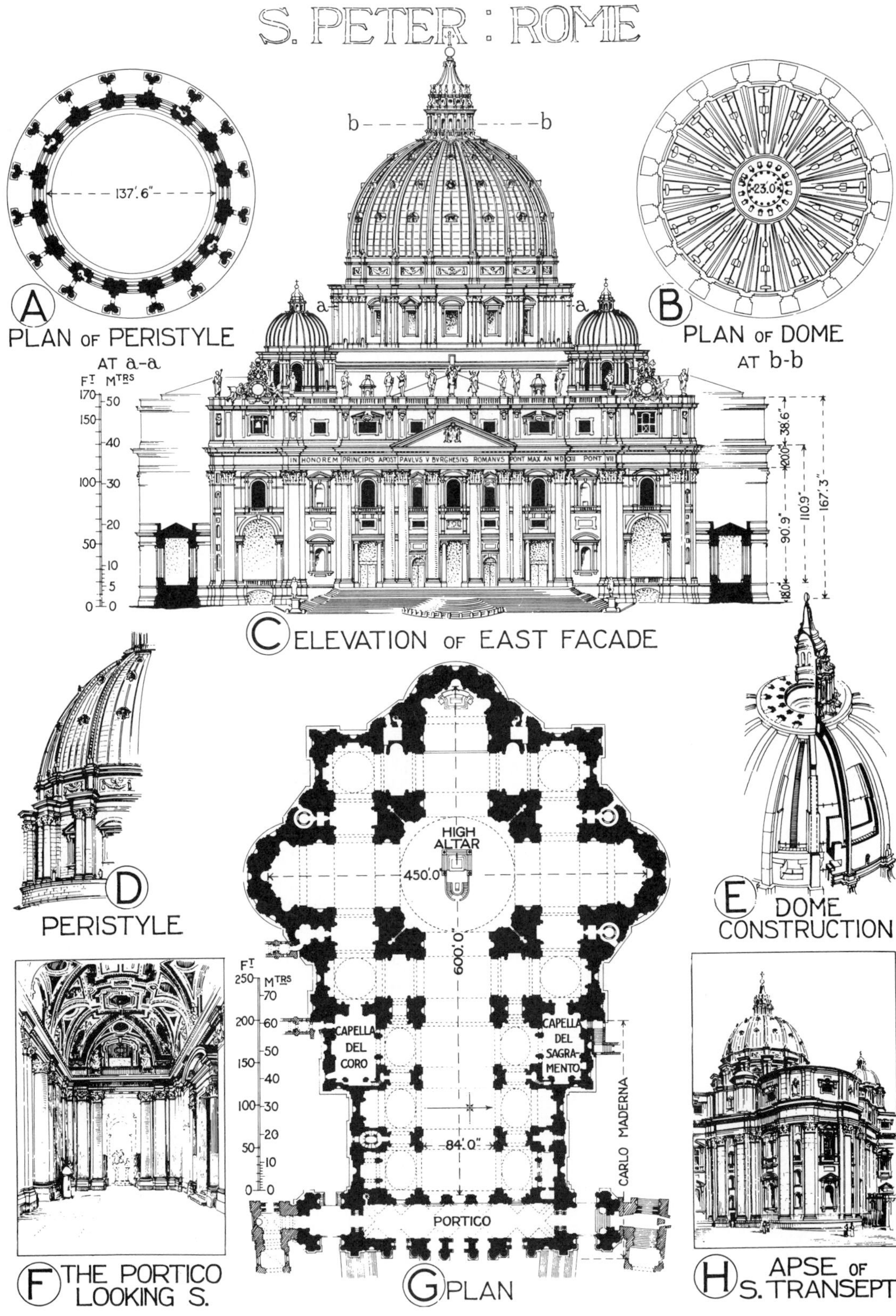
S. PETER : ROME
137'.6"
A PLAN OF PERISTYLE AT a-a
b b
a a
23.0
B PLAN OF DOME AT b-b
FT MTRS
170 50
150 40
100 30
20
50
10
5
0 0
IN HONOREM PRINCIPIS APOST PAVLVS V BVRGHESIVS ROMANVS PONT MAX AN MDCXII PONT VII
38'.6"
20.0"
90'.9"
110'.9"
167'.3"
18.0"
C ELEVATION OF EAST FACADE
D PERISTYLE
E DOME CONSTRUCTION
HIGH ALTAR
450'.0"
600'.0"
FT MTRS
250 70
200 60
50
150 40
100 30
20
50 10
0 0
CAPELLA DEL CORO
CAPELLA DEL SAGRAMENTO
CARLO MADERNA
84'.0"
PORTICO
F THE PORTICO LOOKING S.
G PLAN
H APSE OF S. TRANSEPT

from the nucleus inherited from Sangallo. The abolition of the ambulatories created a much better lit and more unified interior at greatly reduced cost. The external walls are articulated with rhythmically spaced giant Corinthian pilasters, laid over unmoulded vertical strips. By splaying the re-entrant angles the pilaster wall skirts the building like a giant curtain. Above an attic, concealing much of the vaulting, rises Michelangelo's majestic dome (built by Giacomo della Porta, 1588–91), which has a drum buttressed by paired attached columns, continuing up into external ribs on the dome surface, and further paired columns in the lantern. The pointed profile of the dome (although rather steeper than Michelangelo intended) recalls Florence Cathedral, as does its double-shelled method of brick construction. This allows the outer shell to rise much higher than the inner, forming with the four subsidiary domes a pyramidal composition the unity of which is enhanced by the verticality of all the external articulation. With its crown-like lantern the building rises to 137.5 m (451 ft). Thus, despite the reduction in scale, Michelangelo's building is still enormous – the dome is 42 m (138 ft) in diameter, only 1.5 m less than the Pantheon.

Michelangelo's design was continued by Vignola (appointed 1564), Ligorio (1565), Giacomo della Porta (1572) and Domenico Fontana (1585). Carlo Maderno lengthened the nave, converting the church into a Latin cross (building length 194 m, 636 ft) (p. 871G) and designing his own facade (1606–12), which, although continuing Michelangelo's giant order, looks back to the designs of Raphael and Sangallo. Maderno's extension unavoidably conceals much of Michelangelo's dome even from Bernini's piazza (q.v.).

The sumptuous internal decoration was largely carried out in the seventeenth century under Bernini, who succeeded Maderno as architect-in-chief in 1629. Also by Bernini is the famous bronze baldacchino (1624–33) over S. Peter's tomb, and the spectacular Cathedra Petri (1656–65), filling the western apse and housing the supposed throne of the apostle.

S. Maria della Consolazione, Todi (1508–1607) (p. 894A–C), begun under the supervision of Cola da Caprarola, is a pilgrimage church of unclear authorship; it seems to be related to Bramante's S. Peter's, begun two years before, and also recalls Leonardo's 'ideal' church designs. The geometrically composed centrally-planned building is perhaps the most perfect and uncompromising example of its theoretically desirable type. A square crossing surmounted by a dome is abutted by four semi-domed apses, the one containing the altar being semicircular, the other three polygonal. The interior unusually combines double storeys of pilasters with a giant order at the crossing.

The **Madonna di S. Biagio, Montepulciano** (1518–64) (p. 868B), was designed by Antonio da Sangallo the Elder (1455–1534), brother of Giuliano (q.v.). Like the Todi church, it is a pilgrimage centre just outside the town, and it also has connections with S. Peter's. Here the plan is a conventional Greek cross, a domed crossing and barrel-vaulted arms, but with an extension at the rear (to provide a sacristy), and a pair of towers at either side of the front facade (of which only one was completed). The mostly stone interior is much more sculptural, employing Doric half-columns and projecting pilasters, and with arched alcoves housing subsidiary altars.

Piazza S. Annunziata, Florence, was continued by Antonio da Sangallo the Elder and Baccio d'Agnolo, with the construction of a second loggia (begun 1517) facing Brunelleschi's Ospedale degli Innocenti and replicating its forms almost exactly. This established a bilaterally symmetrical piazza around the axis from the Via dei Servi to the entrance of S. Annunziata, which was given a similar loggia in the early seventeenth century.

Raphael (Raffaello Sanzio) (1483–1520) came as a young painter to Rome in 1508 to work for Julius II. In 1514 Leo X appointed him architect-in-chief of S. Peter's and thereafter he supervised most of the major architectural enterprises in Rome. As suggested in his important letter to Leo X (1519), Raphael sought to revive the sumptuousness of Roman architecture, lavish interior decoration inspired by such monuments as the Golden House of Nero being for him an essential aspect of design. He was commissioned to make a survey of ancient Rome and was at the forefront of a more far-reaching and open-minded interest in antiquity, strongly reflected in his own buildings.

The **Chigi Chapel, S. Maria del Popolo, Rome** (*c.* 1513–), is a significant departure from the architecture of Bramante, although the bevelled niches of the corners are clearly inspired by the crossing piers of S. Peter's. The intention here, however, is to provide a self-enclosed space set apart from the church, with an undulating wall surface. Two pyramidal tomb monuments under blind arches occupy the side walls of the chapel, which is well lit from windows in the drum, and encrusted with polychrome decoration: statues in the niches, bronze reliefs, coloured marbles, paintings and mosaics give it a richness of effect suited to the wealth of the patron (Agostino Chigi, papal banker) and to Raphael's ambition to equal the splendour of Roman architecture. Left unfinished in the sixteenth century, the chapel was completed with some modifications by Bernini.

The **Villa Madama, Rome** (*c.* 1516–) (p. 893J), although never completed, is one of the most innovative and influential works of the sixteenth century. It was designed for Cardinal Giulio de'Medici (later Clement VII) and his cousin Leo X as a papal retreat on the slopes of Monte Mario just outside the city. A large circular courtyard was to separate two wings terraced against the hillside (only half the courtyard and the rear wing were built). Behind the courtyard a semicircular 'all'antica' theatre would have cut into the hill. The rear (summer) wing leads onto a terraced garden built up over a fish pond below, while the front (winter) wing would have been approached by steps from an enclosed forecourt flanked by round towers. The terracing, not unlike Bramante's Cortile del Belvedere, was suggested to Raphael by ancient Roman villas, as were the fish pond and subterranean nymphaea below the garden. Also particularly Roman in inspiration is the vaulted three-bay loggia leading out to the garden, with its variety of vaults, its hollowed-out wall surfaces and brilliantly painted and moulded stucco decoration. The exterior of the constructed block is articulated with a giant order of Ionic pilasters, a novelty at this date.

Palazzo Branconio dell'Aquila, Rome (1518–20; destroyed), one of the most festive palace facades of the Renaissance, lay on the main thoroughfare to S. Peter's. The lowest storey, a blind arcade with Tuscan Doric half-columns, provided space for shops. The tall piano nobile had an unprecedented complexity: between tabernacle windows with alternating triangular and segmental pediments were niches for statuary, both denying and affirming continuity with the order below; above this, mezzanine windows alternated with painted stucco medallions and swags. The more restrained third storey was finally crowned with a projecting cornice and delicate roof-top balustrade.

Antonio da Sangallo the Younger (1484–1546), nephew to both Giuliano and Antonio the Elder (q.v.), is the most maligned and misunderstood architect of the sixteenth century. Born in Florence, he began his career as a carpenter making formwork for Bramante's S. Peter's, but in 1516 he was appointed assistant there to Raphael, and from 1520 until his death he was architect-in-chief. A dedicated and scrupulous archaeologist, he supervised as papal architect most of Rome's major buildings as well as the fortifications of the Papal State. His numerous works include the elegant **Palazzo Baldassini, Rome** (1516–25), the **Papal Mint (Zecca), Rome** (1525–7), and the influential **S. Spirito in Sassia, Rome** (1538–90). Much of the town of **Castro**, of which very little survives, was planned by Antonio for Pier Luigi Farnese.

Palazzo Farnese, Rome (begun 1517 to the designs of Antonio da Sangallo the Younger, redesigned 1534 and 1541, modified under Michelangelo from 1546, and completed 1589) (pp. 844A,B, 874), is the most imposing Italian palace of the sixteenth century. The 56 m (185 ft) facade (1541–), occupying the longer side of a spacious piazza, is three storeys tall (recalling Florentine palaces) and thirteen bays wide. It is built of brick with strong stone quoins and has a heavily rusticated portal. Each storey has different window frames (alternating pediments for the piano nobile) placed in dense rows against the flat neutral wall surface, which enhances the sense of scale. The crowning cornice was substantially enlarged by Michelangelo (who also designed the window over the portal) and casts a heavier shadow onto the facade than that envisaged by Sangallo. Sangallo's spectacular three-aisled vestibule (*c.* 1520–), inspired, for example, by Roman nymphaea, with its central barrel vault supported on Doric columns, is notable for the sculptural quality of surface. The internal rooms, which are not symmetrically disposed, are arranged around the five-bay square courtyard, of three storeys, which, like the Colosseum, ascend from Doric to Ionic to Corinthian. The two sharply detailed lower storeys with their attached half-columns are Sangallo's; the lofty, almost weightless, pilastered upper storey, with its bizarre windows, is Michelangelo's. Beautiful though it is, it is not wholly in sympathy with Sangallo's design. The block at the rear was not completed until 1589.

Porta S. Spirito, Rome (1543–4, incomplete), provides access through sixteenth-century fortifications to the Vatican area. Its facade is inspired by the Arch of Constantine, but most unusually is gently concave (as is Sangallo's Zecca). The detailing of the all-stone facade is a good example of Sangallo's expertise in this field.

Baldassare Peruzzi (1481–1536) was born in Siena and trained as a painter before settling in Rome, *c.* 1505. Much of his career was spent in the shadow of Bramante and Raphael, only becoming assistant to Sangallo for S. Peter's. Following the Sack of Rome (1527), most of Peruzzi's later years were spent in Siena and northern Italy. His best buildings and his many surviving project drawings reveal an imaginative and flexible mind less inclined to dogma than many of his contemporaries. His ideas influenced Serlio's books on architecture.

The **Villa Farnesina, Rome** (1505–) (p. 893H), is a very early suburban villa designed for Peruzzi's fellow Sienese Agostino Chigi. The U-shaped plan incorporates two vaulted ground floor loggias frescoed by Peruzzi, Raphael and others, one between the projecting entrance wings and the other facing towards the Tiber; upstairs the imposing salone is decorated with *trompe l'oeil* vistas through fictive columns. The four brick facades, once brilliantly painted, all have two storeys of Doric pilasters framing large rectangular windows or loggia arches. The splendid terracotta frieze of the crowning entablature, incorporating the attic windows, is enlivened by candelabra, putti and festoons.

Peruzzi's **Palazzo Massimi 'alle Colonne', Rome** (1532–) (p. 875), is a most ingenious and innovative variant of the High Renaissance palace. The planning of a difficult site is remarkably economical, with interrelated symmetrical parts rather than overall symmetry. The daringly convex exterior follows the

PALAZZO FARNESE: ROME

PALAZZO PIETRO MASSIMI : ROME

A ENTRANCE CORRIDOR

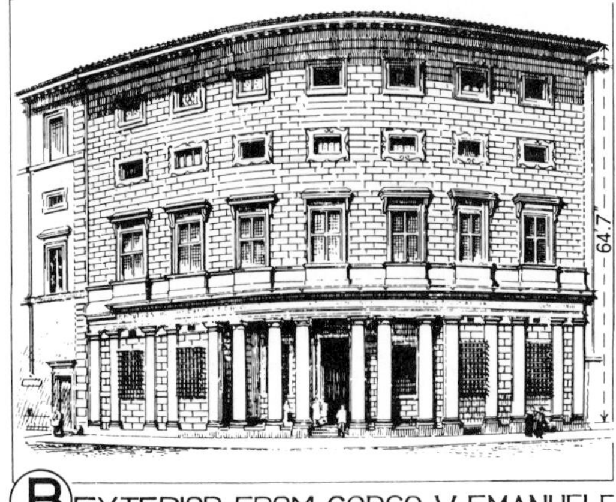

B EXTERIOR FROM CORSO V. EMANUELE

C VESTIBULE

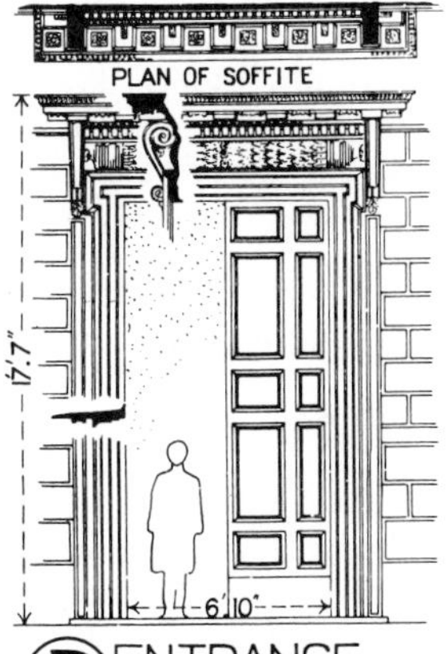

D ENTRANCE DOORWAY

E INTERIOR OF GRAND SALON PIANO NOBILE

F UPPER LOGGIA

G CORTILE

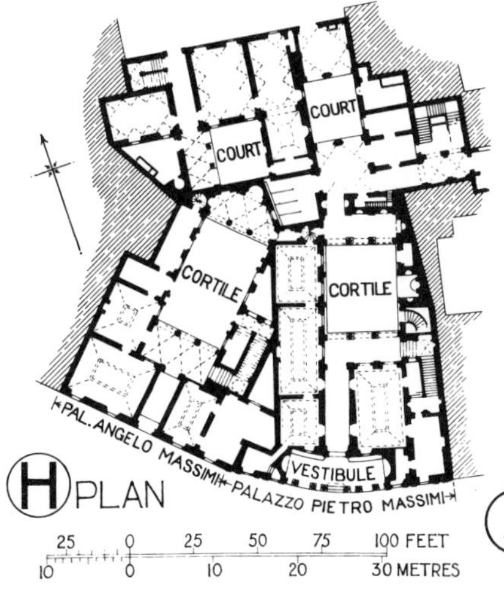

H PLAN

J PORTICO TO CORTILE

curve of the street and uses space from the adjoining palace to extend the facade to the left, thereby allowing an axial approach from a street opposite. The paired Doric columns of the central vestibule develop as pilasters at either side, the central intercolumnation being perceptibly the widest. Above, piercing an expanse of smoothly rusticated astylar wall, the trabeated windows of the piano nobile are followed by two storeys of smaller but elegant mezzanine and attic windows, each type of different proportions. The deliberate varying of the facades of the courtyard recalls Raphael's lost Palazzo Branconio dell'Aquila (q.v.).

Northern Italy, 1520–1600

Giulio Romano (*c.* 1499–1546) began his career in Raphael's workshop and became his leading assistant. Following Raphael's death (1520), Giulio worked as both painter and architect in Rome before being invited in 1524 to become court artist to the Gonzagas in Mantua, where he remained in charge of all artistic production until his death. His buildings there are constructed of local materials, especially brick and stucco, but have a grandeur rivalling contemporary Rome, and an inventiveness bordering on quirkiness. Many of his buildings have fared badly in restoration or have vanished altogether, but **Mantua Cathedral** (1545–7) and the nearby abbey church of **S. Benedetto Po** (1539–) are excellent surviving examples, as is his own stucco-fronted **house in Mantua** (1538–46) (p. 877A) with its bizarre gabled portal breaking into the rusticated arched piano nobile above.

The **Palazzo del Te, Mantua** (1525–), is Giulio's surviving masterpiece. Located just outside the city walls on what was originally an island, it formed a villa retreat for the Gonzaga duke and was constructed in distinct phases. Four one-storey wings are arranged around a large open court. The rusticated northern wing, which faces the city, incorporates an earlier structure; this partially accounts for the unusual spacing of the apertures and of the Doric pilaster articulation which has an increased rhythm at each end of the facade. The fantastic four-columned atrium of the western block is based on the Palazzo Farnese vestibule, but has curious Doric columns encased in stucco 'rustication'. The courtyard facades are even more sculptural but even less conventional than the exterior, broken pediments combining with voussoirs over the windows. Some triglyphs in the east and west facades appear to have 'dropped' from their accustomed positions in the frieze. The exterior facade of the eastern wing, the last to be built, plays variations on the Serliana motif, with complex groupings of pilasters, columns and arches, culminating in a central three-arched loggia. In front of this facade is a moat-like fish pond crossed by a bridge leading into a long enclosed ornamental garden. The sumptuous exterior architecture (originally painted) is complemented by spectacular decorations inside by Giulio's workshop.

The **Villa Imperiale, Pesaro** (1530–), is one of the many magnificent villas of this period. Designed by the painter-architect Girolamo Genga (1476–1551) for the exiled Duke of Urbino, Francesco Maria della Rovere, it incorporates a fifteenth-century residential area to which is attached a series of courts and terraced gardens inspired by Raphael's Villa Madama. The monumental brick forecourt facade is closely modelled on the ruins of the Basilica of Maxentius, while the imposing courtyard behind with its seemingly many-layered surface has a tall Ionic pilaster order with a continuously varying rhythm.

Giovanni Maria Falconetto (1468–1535) came to architecture late in life, often working in collaboration with his friend and patron Alvise Cornaro. Born in Verona, he studied the antiquities there and in Rome, and was one of the pioneers of a more Classicising style in the Veneto.

The **Loggia and Odeo Cornaro, Padua**, were designed for the garden of Alvise Cornaro's palace. The Loggia (1524–), a work of striking Classicism, formed the backdrop for theatrical performances. Above a Doric arcade, Ionic pilasters frame windows with alternating pediments, recalling recent buildings in Rome. The Odeo (*c.* 1553–), a pavilion, has a central octagonal vaulted sala reminiscent of ancient Roman halls, while the general arrangement of the rooms seems closely related to a building then thought to be the villa of Varro.

The **Villa dei Vescovi, Luvigliano, near Padua** (1530s), designed for the bishops of Padua, is a square one-storey building on a dramatic hill-top site. The two arcaded facades with their delicate Doric pilaster order are approached by zigzag staircases (inspired by the Cortile del Belvedere) which ascend heavily rusticated platformed substructures.

Jacopo Sansovino (1486–1570), born in Florence, worked as a sculptor there and in Rome where he won the architectural competition for S. Giovanni dei Fiorentini. In 1527, following the Sack of Rome, he moved to Venice where he effectively became official architect to the city. Sansovino was largely responsible for introducing High Renaissance architecture to Venice; though greatly influenced by his contemporaries, his best buildings are as inventive as they are beautiful.

The **Library of S. Mark's, Venice** (1537–) (p. 878), the city's most magnificent Classical building, was begun as accommodation for Venetian officials but was almost immediately designated the Library. A white stone facade of three bays overlooks the lagoon (completed by Scamozzi, 1583–8), while a twenty-one-bay facade runs along the Piazzetta, facing the Doge's Palace, embellishing the appearance of this important ceremonial space. A full Doric order of half-columns is applied to the ground floor

A. Giulio Romano's house, Mantua (1538–46). See p.876

B. Porta Palio, Verona (*c.* 1545–). See p.881

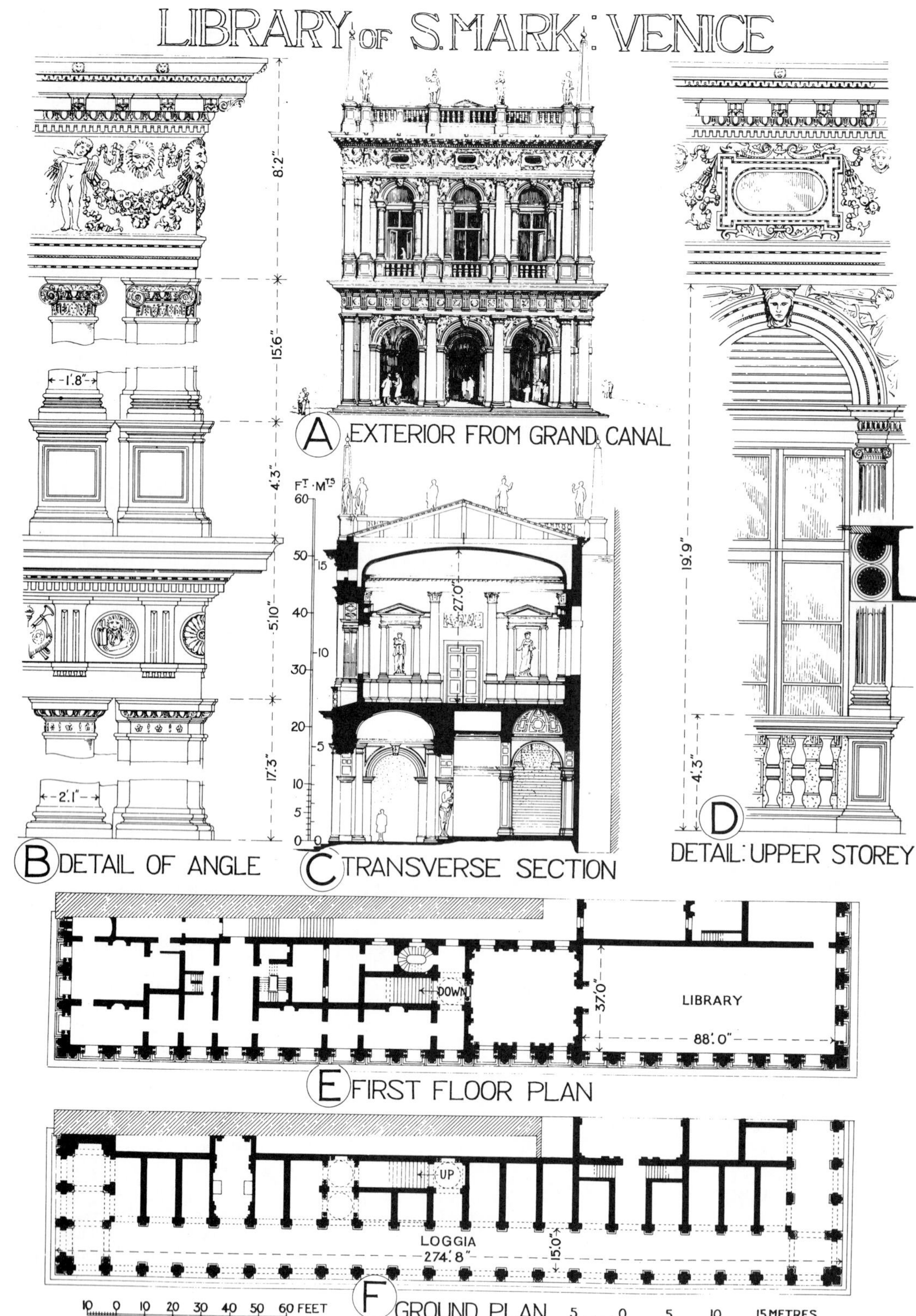
LIBRARY OF S. MARK: VENICE
8'2"
15'6"
1'8"
4'3"
5'10"
17'3"
2'1"
A EXTERIOR FROM GRAND CANAL
FT · MTS
60
50
40
30
20
10
5
0
15
10
5
0
27'0"
19'9"
4'3"
B DETAIL OF ANGLE
C TRANSVERSE SECTION
D DETAIL: UPPER STOREY
DOWN
37'0"
LIBRARY
88'0"
E FIRST FLOOR PLAN
UP
LOGGIA
274'8"
15'0"
10 0 10 20 30 40 50 60 FEET
F GROUND PLAN
5 0 5 10 15 METRES

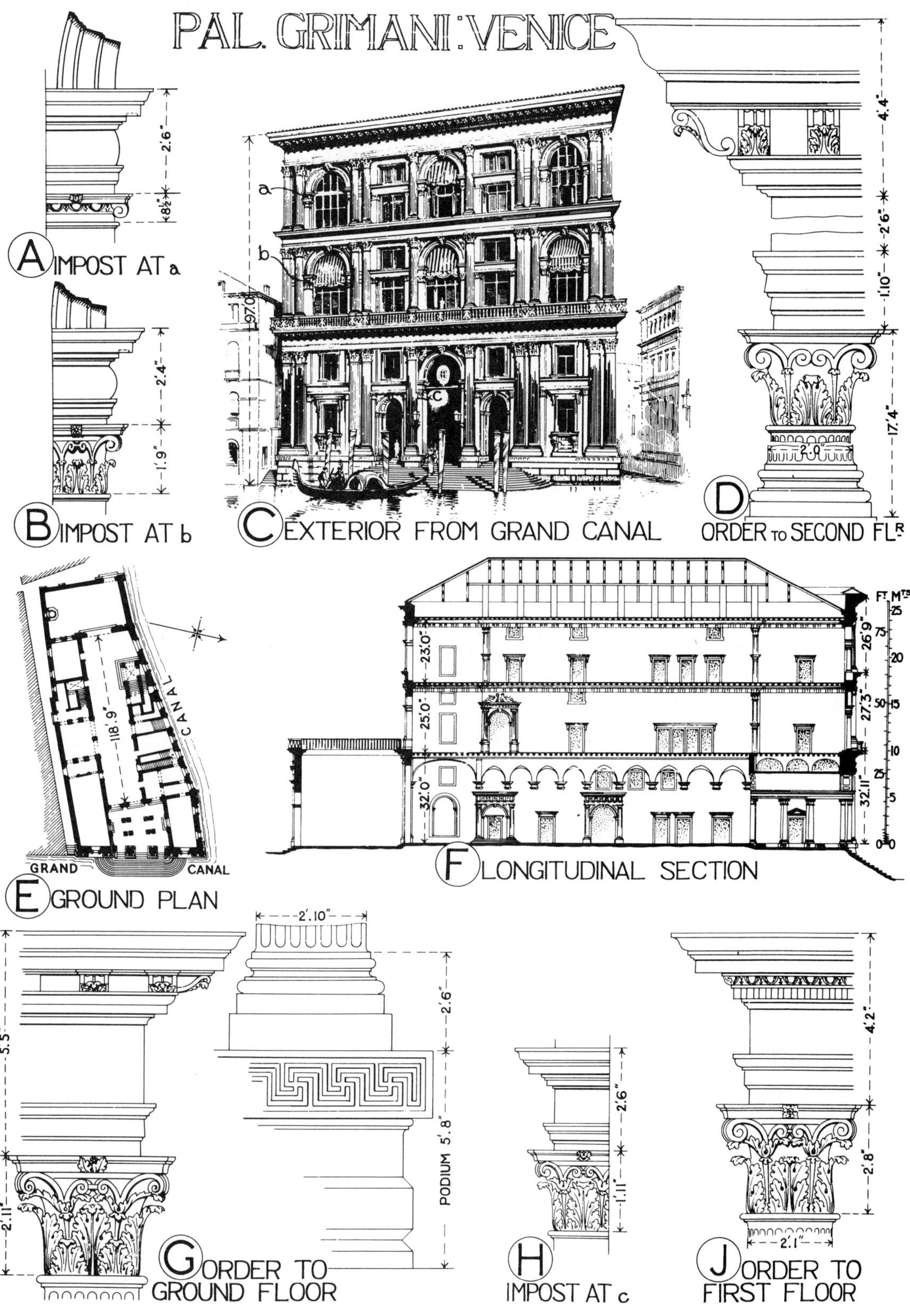
PAL. GRIMANI: VENICE
A IMPOST AT a
B IMPOST AT b
C EXTERIOR FROM GRAND CANAL
D ORDER TO SECOND FLR
E GROUND PLAN
GRAND
CANAL
F LONGITUDINAL SECTION
G ORDER TO GROUND FLOOR
H IMPOST AT c
J ORDER TO FIRST FLOOR
PODIUM 5'.8"
FT. MTS

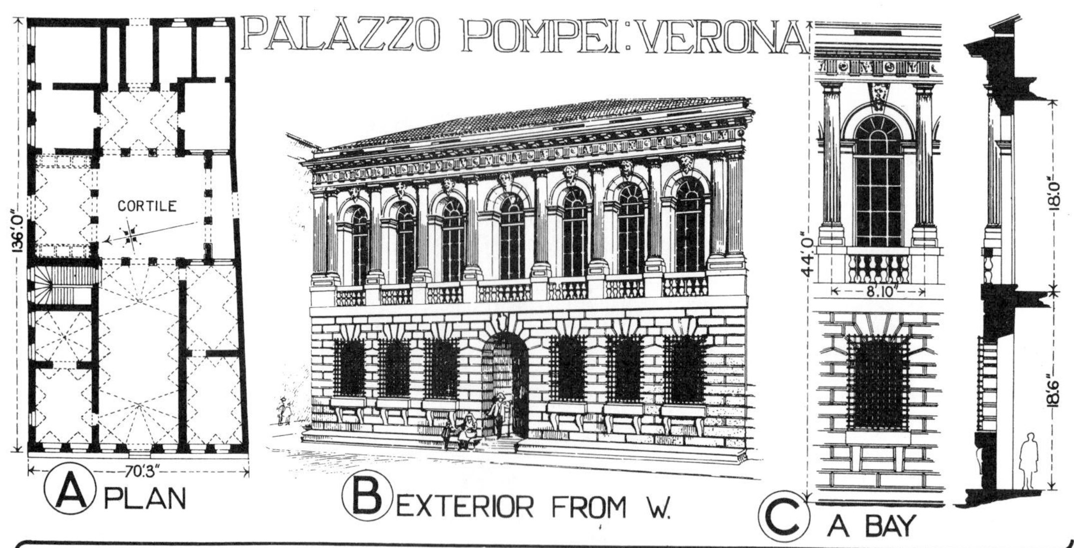
PALAZZO POMPEI: VERONA
CORTILE
136'0"
70'3"
44'0"
8'10"
18'0"
18'6"
A PLAN
B EXTERIOR FROM W.
C A BAY

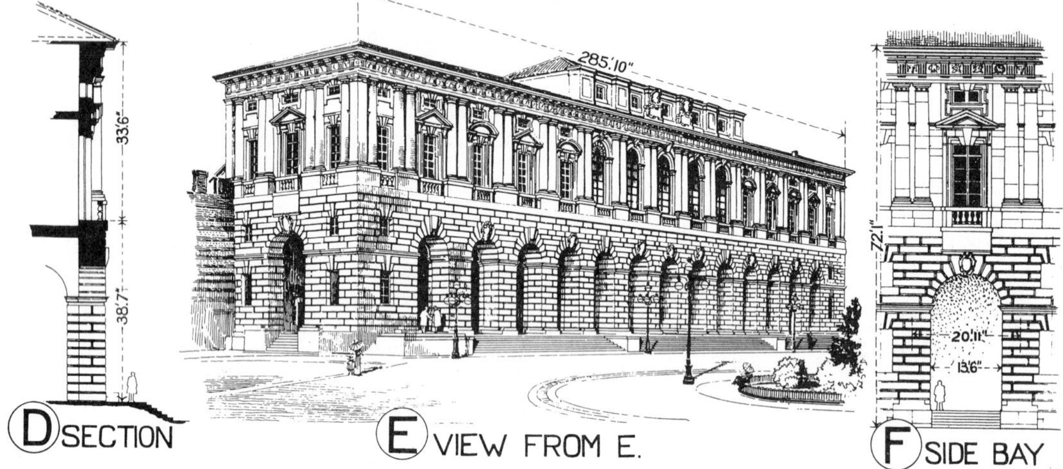
GRAN GUARDIA VECCHIA: VERONA
33'6"
38'7"
285'10"
72'1"
20'11"
13'6"
D SECTION
E VIEW FROM E.
F SIDE BAY

OTHER PALACES AT VERONA
G PAL. DEI DIAMANTI
H PALAZZO DEL CONSIGLIO
J PAL. BEVILACQUA

arcade; here Sansovino allowed for the half metope at the corners advised by Vitruvius by pairing the final half-column with a pilaster overlaying a pier. The Ionic order above frames round-arched windows springing from free-standing Ionic colonnettes, a kind of compressed Serlian motif. In the spandrels are carved victories above and sea-gods below. The rich broad frieze is pierced with oval windows, and the crowning balustrade topped by statues and obelisks. Sansovino's Library was part of a more comprehensive scheme to rebuild the south side of Piazza S. Marco, continued by Scamozzi with the Procuratie Nuove (1586–). The realignment of the Piazza established by the Library had the important effect of opening up the view of S. Mark's, creating a spectacular and more balanced effect.

The **Zecca (Mint), Venice** (1536–), has a severe appearance in keeping with its function. Above the rusticated basement are banded Doric half-columns, the windows between having heavy projecting entablatures supported on corbel blocks. The facade abuts the contrasting lagoon elevation of the Library, although the various cornices do not align. The late addition of a third storey (*c.* 1560) did not enhance Sansovino's design.

The **Loggetta, Venice** (1537–) (p. 845H), positioned at the base of the Campanile opposite the main entrance to the Doge's Palace, was intended as a meeting place for nobles. The facade is a triple triumphal arch, with free-standing Composite columns, inspired by the Arch of Severus. Polychrome facing marbles, statuary in the niches, and relief sculpture in attic and spandrels, make this little building the most ornate and festive in Venice.

Palazzo Cornaro, Venice (1545–) (p. 845F), is one of the most imposing palaces on the Grand Canal. Above a high rusticated basement are two living floors with paired Ionic and Corinthian half-columns. The tight grouping of the three central bays marking the salone follows Venetian tradition in creating a tripartite facade. The arrangement is emphasised by the severe three-arched portal below. Flanking this are bizarre windows with banded Doric columns and squashed pediments, while elongated Michelangelesque volutes frame the mezzanine openings above. The strongly sculptural effect is enhanced by trophies in the spandrels.

Michele Sanmicheli (1484–1559), a native of Verona, went as a young stonemason to Rome where he came into contact with the circle of Bramante. From 1509 to the early 1520s he was chief architect of Orvieto Cathedral, and in 1526 inspected the fortifications of the Papal States with Sangallo the Younger. Moving back to the Veneto, he became architect-in-chief of Venice's defences from before 1530 until his death, but most of his non-military works were for the local aristocracy in his native Verona. He excelled in particular in the masterly detailing of stone facades.

Palazzo Bevilacqua, Verona (*c.* 1530) (p. 880J), has a seven-bay stone facade intended to be continued to one side. Alternating bay widths and a great variety of detail create an exceedingly complex rhythm. The major bays of the piano nobile are defined by Corinthian half-columns with alternately vertical and spiral fluting; river gods and victories adorn the spandrels, and segmental and triangular pediments alternate over the windows of the minor bays. The long balcony separating the storeys is carried on volutes which replace the triglyphs of the Doric order below, where emperor-bust keystones and lion window-ledge supports enliven the severity of the rustication.

Palazzo Pompei, Verona (*c.* 1550) (p. 880A–C), inspired by Bramante's Palazzo Caprini, has an order of fluted Doric half-columns over a rusticated basement. There are a number of subtleties: the widened central bay, the additional pilasters at the corners giving added visual strength, and the simplification of the rusticated supports and cill of the windows below.

Palazzo Grimani, Venice (*c.* 1556–) (p. 879), is the most magnificent palace on the Grand Canal. Although the use of Corinthian columns over pilasters and the pairing of the order in the side bays recall the Palazzo Vendramin-Calergi (q.v.), the Palazzo Grimani facade is even more grid-like in character with strongly emphatic horizontal cornices. The three storeys diminish in height, and the Venetian grouping of the bays allows great variety within the unified structural grid. The tripartite columnar vestibule is based on the Palazzo Farnese, Rome (q.v.).

Porta Palio, Verona (*c.* 1545–) (p. 877B), is one of Sanmicheli's three gates for the city. The external three-bay facade is Doric, using paired half-columns with pilasters at the corners. The stonework design is here very elaborate, especially the patterning of the rustication and the huge projecting keystones. The three entrances are set back into rectangular recesses, very likely the outcome of Sanmicheli's study of the Roman theatre in Verona, while rusticated Doric is both appropriate to a fortified gateway and also characteristic of Roman monuments in the city.

The **Madonna di Campagna, Verona** (1559–), a pilgrimage church a little way outside the mediaeval city, is one of the most ambitious centrally planned churches of the sixteenth century. It comprises an enormous domed rotunda with a smaller domed space housing the altar behind. A peripteral Tuscan-Doric colonnade runs around the rotunda exterior, while the octagonal interior has two Composite stories.

Sanmicheli's other influential religious building is the **Cappella Pellegrini, S. Bernardino, Verona** (*c.* 1527–), with its beautiful two-storey interior inspired by the Pantheon and Raphael's Chigi Chapel. The rhythmic complexity of the articulation and delicate extravagance of the ornamental detailing relate the Chapel to the Palazzo Bevilacqua.

The very large **Palazzo della Gran Guardia, Verona** (1610–14, completed 1819–53) (p. 880D–F), by Sanmicheli's pupil Domenico Curtoni, is the best example of subsequent Sanmichelian style in Verona which persisted until the nineteenth century.

Andrea Palladio (1508–80) is perhaps the most celebrated architect of the Renaissance. Born in Padua of humble parentage, he trained as a stonemason, moving to Vicenza in 1524. Here, encouraged by the intellectual Gian Giorgio Trissino, and making frequent visits to Rome to study the ancient monuments, he learned the profession of architecture. His first works are mainly palaces and villas for Vicentine patrons, but from *c.* 1555 he worked increasingly for Venetians. His penetrating studies of ancient buildings and his systematic approach to design led to a Classical style of great adaptability yet sympathetic with local materials and traditions, capable of providing grandeur on a limited budget. His enormous influence derives largely from his exemplary publication of his own designs in the *Quattro Libri* (1570), which became a handbook of good design.

In 1549, Palladio's scheme to replace the Gothic arcades of the council chamber, now known as the **Basilica, Vicenza** (p. 883), was accepted in preference to designs by other notable architects. The new stone facades run around three sides of the building (four in the *Quattro Libri* plan) and are of two storeys, Doric below and Ionic above. Serliana openings (the so-called Palladian motif) are framed by half-columns which are doubled at the corner. This brilliantly flexible solution allows for site constrictions and irregular bay widths due to the Gothic core behind, since the side openings of the Serliana can be expanded or contracted at will. A balustrade punctuated by sculpture crowns this soberly magnificent structure.

The **Palazzo Thiene, Vicenza** (1542–) (p. 885A), is an early palace in a rusticated idiom very much indebted to Giulio Romano. Above a rusticated brick basement, the Corinthian pilasters of the piano nobile, paired in the corner bays, frame window tabernacles with alternating triangular and segmental pediments supported by Ionic colonnettes encased in a series of blocks. Deriving from the lost house of Giulio Romano in Rome, these were to have a long history in English Palladian architecture.

The **Palazzo Chiericati, Vicenza** (1551–), responds to its awkward shallow and broad site with a highly unusual solution. Of its eleven-bay facade (only the left four bays executed by Palladio; the remainder completed in the late seventeenth century) all but the central five bays of the piano nobile are open in the form of a two-storey trabeated portico, built out over the piazza. The closed bays contain the windows of the great salone.

The **Palazzo Valmarana, Vicenza** (1565–) (p. 884D), is a late palace in which Palladio uses an order of giant Composite pilasters for the central five bays of the seven-bay facade. A smaller Corinthian order frames the windows of the lower storey. In the outer bays the giant order is replaced by a bizarre two-storey solution of Corinthian pilasters below and lone warriors in carved relief above, supporting the extremities of the main entablature. This highly individual facade, notable for the variety of its stucco decoration, achieves the effect of a superimposition of several layers. At the very sculptural and decorative **Palazzo Barbarano, Vicenza** (1570–5), Palladio superimposes Ionic and Corinthian half-columns. Yet another variation of the High Renaissance palace facade is the unfinished **Palazzo Porto Breganze (Casa del Diavolo), Vicenza** (1570s) (p. 884G), which, with its giant Composite half-columns, would if completed have been seven bays wide.

The **Loggia del Capitaniato, Vicenza** (1571–2), a meeting place in front of the residence of one of the main Venetian officials, has a three-bay facade on the piazza with a giant order of Composite half-columns. The tall windows of the assembly room above the arched loggia break through the architrave, and are supported below by strange Michelangelesque blocks.

The **Teatro Olimpico, Vicenza** (1580–) (p. 889B), was the first permanent theatre to be built since antiquity. Inspired by ancient theatres, the seating area is actually half an oval so as to fit into an earlier structure, while the elaborate (wooden) background to the stage resembles the 'scenae frons'. The perspective vistas behind, with their street facades of diminishing scale, were added by Scamozzi (1584–5).

Villa Poiana, Poiana Maggiore (*c.* 1549), is typical of Palladio's early villa farmhouses, other good examples being **Villa Pisani, Bagnolo** (1541–4), and **Villa Saraceno, Finale di Agugliaro** (finished 1545). All have two apartments of three differently-sized rooms flanking a loggia and rectangular salone, a plan which remained Palladio's preferred scheme for villas. The components of Villa Poiana's single-storey facades are unusually simplified, especially the Serliana entrance. The attic above, a produce store, is gabled over the entrance to form a pediment.

The **Rotonda (Villa Almerico-Capra), near Vicenza** (finished by 1569) (p. 884A–C), was not a villa-farm but a palatial retreat from the city. The round form of the central domed salone gives the villa its name. Like most of Palladio's later villas, it uses the pedimented temple-front motif, but this building is distinguished by its centralised square plan with four identical projecting porticoes overlooking spectacular views. This unusual design was especially popular in eighteenth-century England (see Chapter 32).

The **Villa Barbaro, Maser** (mid-1550s), unites the country house with farm buildings to form a monumental composition of great influence. The linking barns terminate emphatically with pedimented dovecotes. The attached temple-front facade occupying the full width of the main block is an interesting

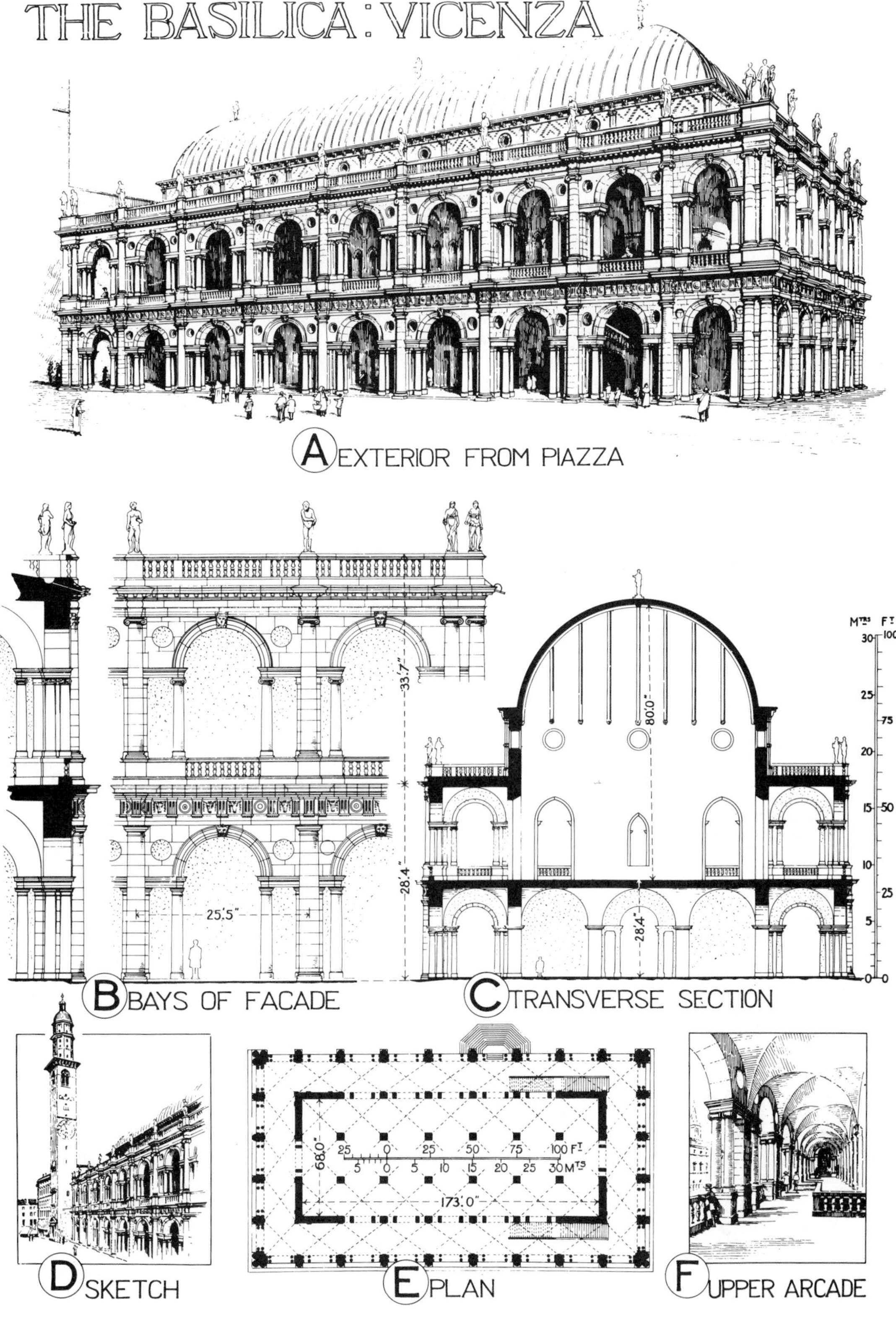

(A) EXTERIOR FROM PIAZZA

(B) BAYS OF FACADE

(C) TRANSVERSE SECTION

(D) SKETCH

(E) PLAN

(F) UPPER ARCADE

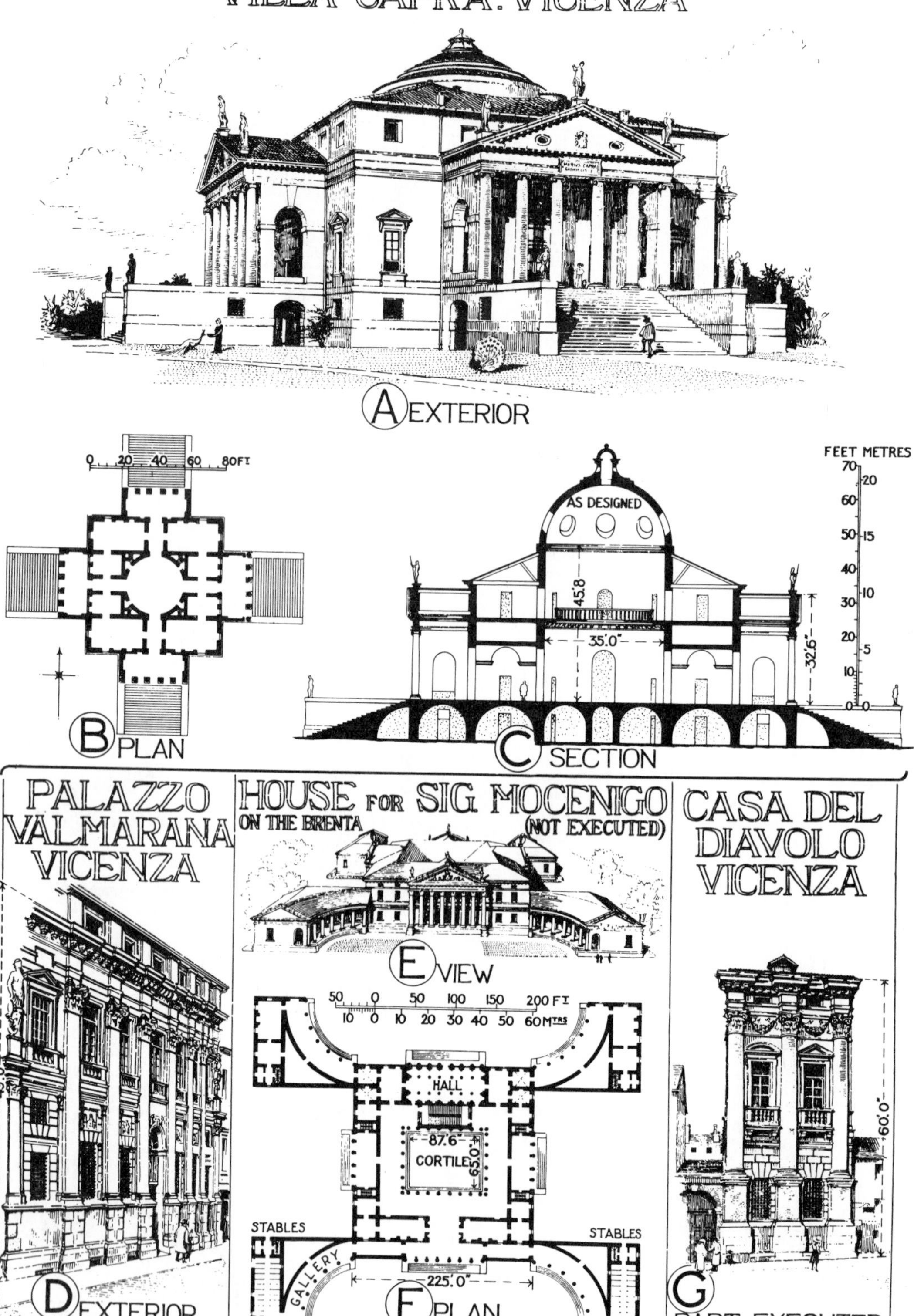
VILLA CAPRA: VICENZA
A EXTERIOR
0 20 40 60 80 FT
B PLAN
FEET METRES
70 60 50 40 30 20 10 0
20 15 10 5 0
AS DESIGNED
45.8
35'.0"
32'.6"
C SECTION
PALAZZO VALMARANA VICENZA
49'.0"
D EXTERIOR
HOUSE FOR SIG MOCENIGO ON THE BRENTA (NOT EXECUTED)
E VIEW
50 0 50 100 150 200 FT
10 0 10 20 30 40 50 60 MTRS
HALL
87.6
CORTILE
65.0
STABLES
STABLES
GALLERY
225'.0"
F PLAN
CASA DEL DIAVOLO VICENZA
60'.0"
G
PART EXECUTED

A. Palazzo Thiene, Vicenza (1542–). See p.882

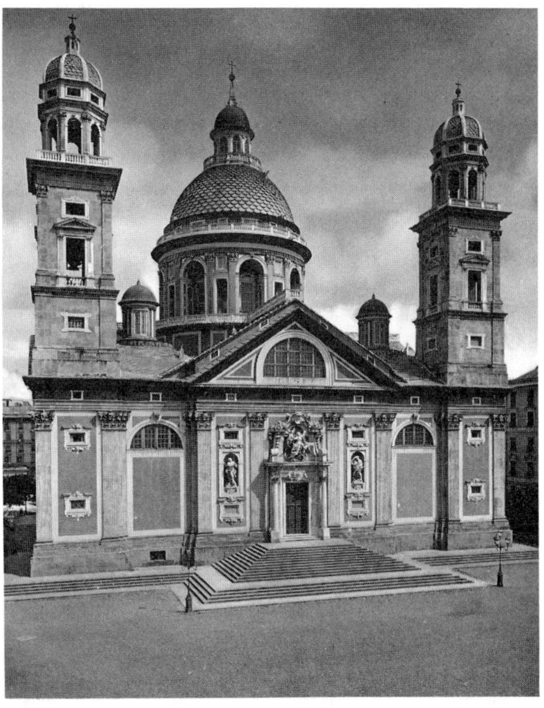

B. S. Maria di Carignano, Genoa (1549–1603). See p.887

C. S. Giorgio Maggiore, Venice (165–). See p.887

S. GIORGIO MAGGIORE : VENICE

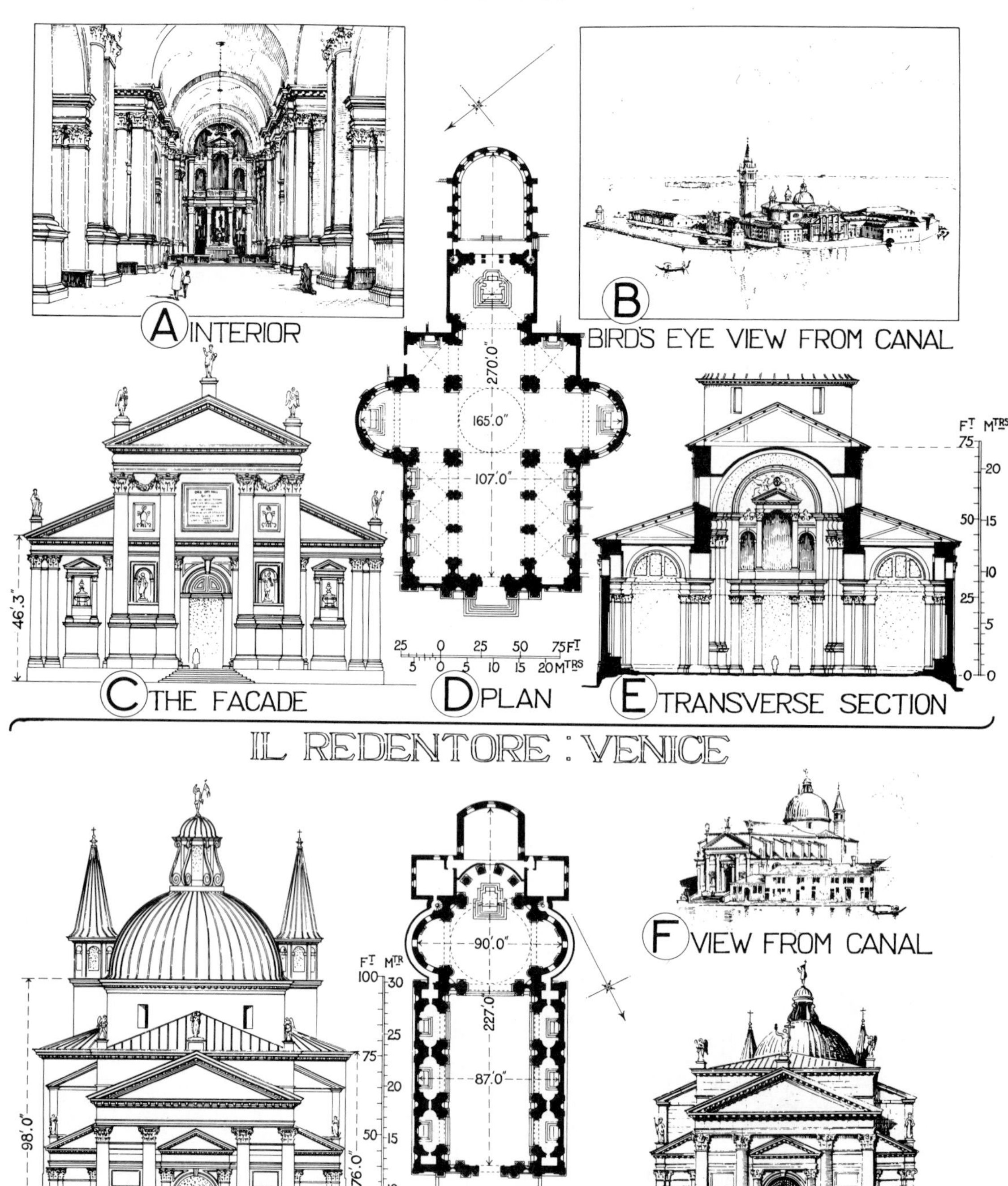

A INTERIOR

B BIRD'S EYE VIEW FROM CANAL

C THE FACADE

D PLAN

E TRANSVERSE SECTION

IL REDENTORE : VENICE

F VIEW FROM CANAL

G THE FACADE

H PLAN

J PERSPECTIVE VIEW

alternative to Palladio's more usual format. **Villa Pisani, Montagnana** (1552), and **Villa Cornaro, Piombino Dese** (1552–3), with their two-storey attached porticoes, provide further variants, while the **Villa Foscari, Malcontenta** (before 1560), has an additional gabled attic. Among Palladio's most ambitious designs is the unexecuted **Villa Mocenigo, on the Brenta** (designed before 1570) (p. 884E,F), where four curved colonnaded wings radiate from a pedimented block with central courtyard. The simpler **Villa Badoer, Fratta Polesine** (1556), provides a built example with curved wings.

S. Giorgio Maggiore, Venice (1565–) (pp. 885C, 886A–E), has a Latin-cross plan, with a short nave and domed crossing. As a major Benedictine church it caters for monastic requirements, having side aisles, deep apsidal transepts, and a retrochoir (common in sixteenth-century Venice). Grouped Corinthian pilasters articulate the aisles, and the nave is lined with giant Composite half-columns on pedestals grouped with pilasters at the crossing. The white stone and plaster interior, well lit at clerestory level by huge thermae windows in the vault, has the pristine clarity thought appropriate by Palladio for churches. The facade treatment is a departure from earlier half-columns and Corinthian pilasters reflect the internal disposition. The four half-columns of the central section are raised on high bases, and crowned by a temple-front pediment; the smaller order effectively continues the whole width of the facade, carrying half-pediments at each side.

The **Church of the Redentore, Venice** (1577–) (p. 886F–J), Palladio's finest church, was built by the Venetian government to mark the end of a severe plague. The single-naved plan has a trilobed crossing, a curved columnar screen behind the altar leading to the simple monks' choir. Interconnected side chapels flank the vaulted nave lit by thermae windows. As at nearby S. Giorgio, the facade is composed of major and minor orders, rising this time from the same level. Seen from across the water, the dome, turrets and projecting buttresses unite with the facade to form a complex but strongly unified composition.

The **Rocca Pisani, Lonigo** (1576), is the name given to a gem-like villa designed by Vincenzo Scamozzi (1552–1616). Scamozzi was Palladio's principal follower and published a very influential treatise, his *Idea* (1615). The villa, which stands alone on a large hill, is a compact single-porticoed version of Palladio's Rotonda with an octagonal rather than circular salone. Relatively small windows are brilliantly placed within expansive white walls, giving a serene geometric effect.

Galeazzo Alessi (1512–72), born of a noble family and trained in Rome, first worked in his native Perugia before moving to Genoa (1548) and then Milan (1557). Much indebted to his contemporaries, his numerous works are nevertheless very individual. In particular he had a deep feeling for unorthodox 'all'antica' detailing and stucco decoration. Several of his domestic buildings in Genoa embody novel variations of level, exploiting the difficult topography of the hilly city.

S. Maria di Carignano, Genoa (1549–72; completed 1603) (p. 885B), built on the summit of a hill, has a plan which closely follows Bramante's S. Peter's: a Greek cross within a square with a central dome and four smaller domes on the diagonals. The somewhat squat pedimented facade is flanked by two corner towers (a matching pair was intended) rising from the cornice of the pilaster order. The plainness of the exterior walls contrasts with often very elaborate architectural elements, in particular the small rectangular windows.

Villa Cambiaso, Genoa (1548–), on high ground above the city, has a simple nearly-square plan not unlike a Palladian villa but with a hall at the centre of the building behind the entrance loggia. The facade recalls Peruzzi's Villa Farnesina, Rome (q.v.), although the sculptural handling and intricacy of the architectural members are very different. This provides a foretaste of the astonishing decoration of the upper loggia, encrusted with lavish ornament.

The **Strada Nuova, Genoa** (1550–), was almost certainly planned by Alessi to accommodate new palaces for the Genoese nobility. The palaces on the north side of the street are shelved into the steep hillside behind, Alessi's **Palazzo Cambiaso** (1558–60) on the initial corner having a typically ornamental facade. The best palace, **Palazzo Doria-Tursi**, was supervised by Alessi's associate Rocco Lurago. From a vestibule, a monumental flight of steps leads up to the imposing courtyard (on a level with the terraces on either side of the palazzo). At the rear, another staircase leads to a grotto, and further flights ascend to the upper level. A similarly ambitious series of levels appeared in Alessi's **Villa Sauli, Genoa** (*c.* 1550, little remaining).

Palazzo Marino, Milan (1558–*c.* 1570) (p. 890B), was designed by Alessi for a Genoese, T. Marino, who had bought himself the title, Duke of Terranuova. The building is fittingly megalomaniac, standing on a huge island site. The main facade, three storeys high and eleven bays wide (the east side has fifteen bays), is densely decorated in a repetitive yet bizarre manner, using motifs derived from Michelangelo and Giulio Romano. The courtyard is more modestly scaled but exceptionally lavish: above the Doric Serlian elements of the lower storey, attached herms, niches and elaborate panels smother the upper arcades.

Pellegrino Tibaldi (or Pellegrini) (1527–96) – a painter-architect from Bologna – was brought by the reforming Cardinal S. Carlo Borromeo to Milan, where he succeeded Alessi as chief architect. His buildings often have a dynamic austerity, particularly the **Collegio Borromeo, Pavia** (1564–), with its powerfully effective fenestration arrangements. Very impressive also is his modernisation of the **Sanctuary at Saronno** and his round votive church of **S. Sebastiano, Milan** (1577–). The Jesuit church of **S. Fedele, Milan** (1569–, east end altered) resembles Alessi's earlier **SS. Paolo e Barnaba, Milan** (1561–7), in its compact form. The nave consists of two square bays, the domical vaults supported on free-standing columns. Beyond a domed crossing is an apse, while the transept is actually less wide than the nave. The bright interior is unadorned with paintings.

S. Maria (Madonna di Vico), Vicoforte di Mondovi (1596–), is the masterpiece of Ascanio Vitozzi (*c.* 1539–1615), an architect from Orvieto who worked around Turin. Oval in plan, it is the largest centralised building of the sixteenth century. With the miraculous image at the centre, the main entrance and high altar are on the main axis, and there are two lateral entrance vestibules, four diagonal chapels (for Ducal tombs), and four corner towers which recall Alessi's S. Maria di Carignano. The church's Ducal and votive character is underlined by the lavish stucco decoration of the interior.

Florence and Rome, 1540–1600

Michelangelo Buonarroti (1475–1564) became an architect in mid-career, although his architectonic bias is apparent in his early painted masterpiece, the Sistine Chapel ceiling (1508–12). By far the most individual of Renaissance architects, he was profoundly influential not only in the later sixteenth century but also in the Baroque period. He combined a firm sense of the visual unity of a building, often using giant orders and strong horizontal cornices to bind the design together, with a wilfully unorthodox, often bizarre approach to sculptural detail. Both qualities are seen at S. Peter's, Rome (q.v.), a fitting climax to his long architectural career.

The **New Sacristy, Florence** (1519–) (p. 889A), was commissioned by Cardinal Giulio de'Medici, later Clement VII, as a second family mausoleum in the church of S. Lorenzo. In plan it mirrors Brunelleschi's Old Sacristy opposite, and the grey stone and white plaster interior is also very similar, but with the addition of an attic zone (recalling Giuliano da Sangallo's S. Spirito sacristy). In strong contrast to this sober grey *pietra serena* articulation are the bizarre tomb monuments in the centre of the side walls, made of highly polished white Carrara marble. In the corner bays are marble doors with slab-like cornices doubling as the cills for oversize niches above, their recesses capriciously breaking upwards and outwards into their crowning segmental pediments. Beneath the coffered dome, the Sacristy is illuminated by four extra windows with exaggeratedly tapering frames.

The **Laurentian Library, Florence** (1524–) (p. 890A), is located in the cloister of S. Lorenzo. The library itself is a long room with reading desks, well lit by rows of windows between pilasters which correspond to the beams of the ceiling (completed 1550s). This reposeful and clearly articulated space is preceded by a much taller monumental vestibule of square plan, almost entirely filled by an extraordinary staircase (executed by Ammanati, 1559–), spilling from the library door and multiplying into three flights of stairs, of which the outer two are hardly usable. The vestibule walls are particularly unorthodox: paired columns rising from insubstantial volutes are recessed behind the white plaster wall surface from which project tabernacle niches with pilasters perversely widening towards their capitals.

The **Capitoline Palaces, Rome** (*c.* 1539–) (p. 891), form the most coherently planned group of buildings of the sixteenth century and provide an appropriate setting for the traditional heart of the city. The three palaces are symmetrically disposed around a trapezoidal piazza which widens towards the **Palazzo del Senatore** (completed 1600). This palace and the **Palazzo dei Conservatori** (1561–84), on the right-hand side, were refaced, and a new building, the **Palazzo Nuovo** (Capitoline Museum) (1603–54), with a matching facade was built to complete the trio. The piazza is entered by a monumental flight of steps ascending the steep slope, and the parapet at the top is surmounted by redeployed Roman sculptures. The piazza itself is dominated by the Roman bronze equestrian statue of Marcus Aurelius (p. 891C), standing on an oblong pedestal at the centre of a large oval mound. Additions have been made to the piazza following Dupérac's engraving of Michelangelo's scheme (1569), the last being the interlaced twelve-pointed paving (1946). Of the Palazzo del Senatore facade only the double-ramped staircase was built by Michelangelo, the remainder being completed by Martino Longhi with a rather disappointing stucco articulation. The Palazzo dei Conservatori, by contrast, was faced in stone with only minor modifications to Michelangelo's proposals, and is one of his most successful designs (the Palazzo Nuovo follows it almost exactly). Giant Corinthian pilasters laid over piers support a massive cornice crowned by a balustrade and punctuated with statuary. The lower storey is a trabeated loggia with daringly wide voussoir lintels supported by columns placed close to the piers. Despite the overall sense of restraint and structural order, the sculptural detailing is characteristically inventive. The larger central openings are by Giacomo della Porta.

The **Porta Pia, Rome** (1561–4, completed later with modifications), is the culmination of a new street built by Pope Pius IV and replaces a Roman gateway. Its portal is one of Michelangelo's most characteristically unorthodox inventions. Particularly notable are the angular arch, the entablature segments reminiscent of giant triglyphs, the curving form between, inspired by a thermal window, and the portions of a

A. New Sacristy, Medici Chapel, S. Lorenzo, Florence (1519–). See p.888

B. Teatro Olimpico, Vicenza: interior (1580–). See p.882

C. Uffizi, Florence (*c.* 1560–*c.* 1580). See p.892

A. Laurentian Library, Florence; entrance (1524–; staircase, 1559). See p.888

B. Palazzo Marino, Milan: cortile (1558–*c.* 1570). See p.887

C. Casino of Pius IV, Rome (1558–61): garden pavilion. See p.895

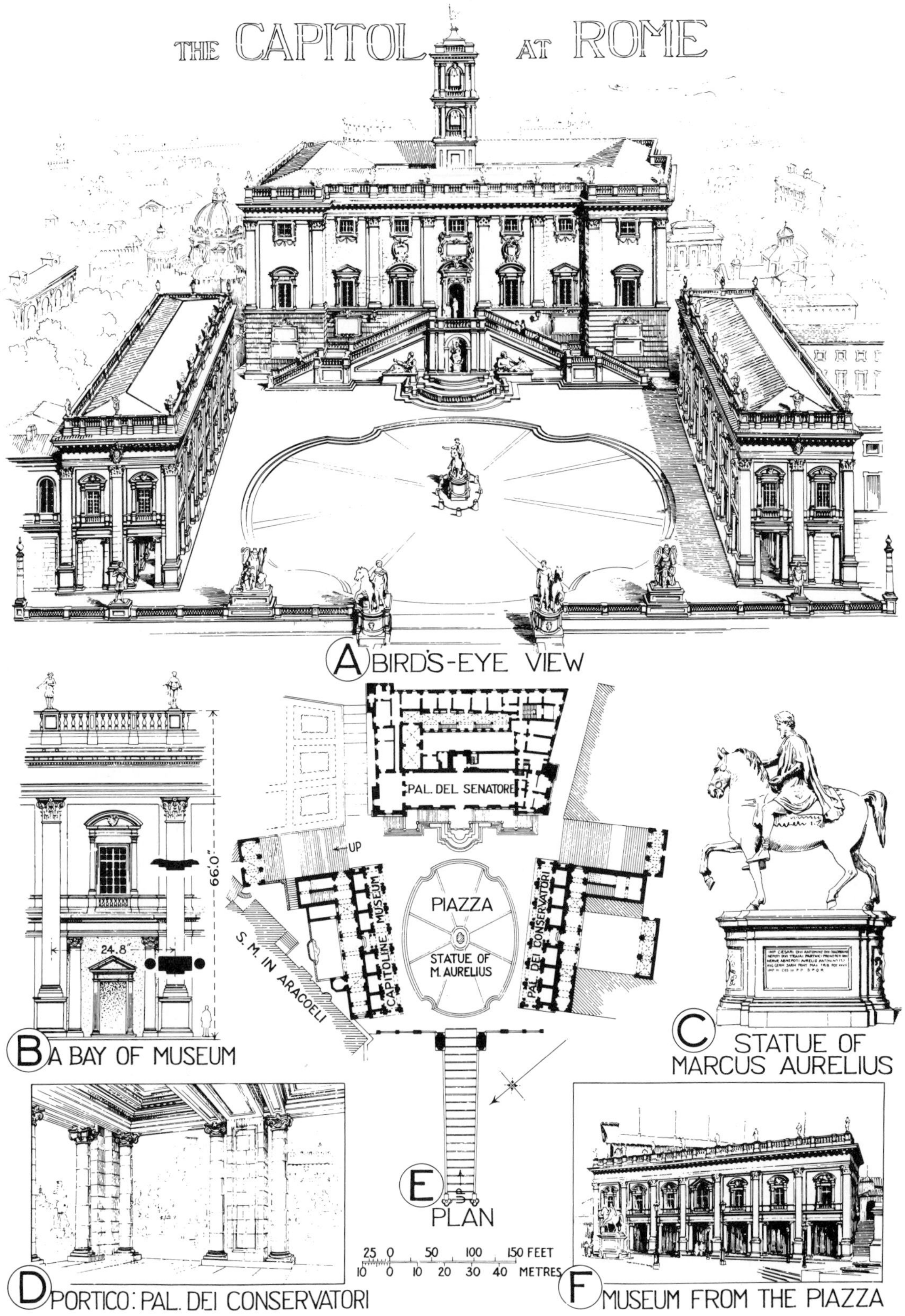
THE CAPITOL AT ROME
A BIRD'S-EYE VIEW
B A BAY OF MUSEUM
66.0"
24.8"
PAL. DEL SENATORE
UP
PIAZZA
STATUE OF M. AURELIUS
CAPITOLINE MUSEUM
PAL. DEI CONSERVATORI
S. M. IN ARACOELI
E PLAN
25 0 50 100 150 FEET
10 0 10 20 30 40 METRES
C STATUE OF MARCUS AURELIUS
D PORTICO: PAL. DEI CONSERVATORI
F MUSEUM FROM THE PIAZZA

broken segmental pediment above, which ends in tight volutes supporting a hanging garland.

The **Cappella Sforza, S. Maria Maggiore, Rome** (1560–73), is a work almost prophetic of Borromini and the seventeenth century. The central area is marked by four detached columns centred at 45°, with an altar area projecting beyond; but to either side are substantial recesses with gently curving rear walls, and in the vaults above are extraordinary tapering windows.

Michelangelo's other religious projects are just as unconventional. For **S. Maria degli Angeli, Rome** (1561–), he converted the tepidarium of the Baths of Diocletian into a church, but established the main axis about the width of the hall. His final design (1560) for **S. Giovanni dei Fiorentini, Rome** (project designs submitted by leading architects from 1518, ultimately built as a conventional Latin-cross church by Giacomo della Porta and completed by Maderno, 1620, facade by Galilei, 1734) proposed a circular domed space with eight alternating rectangular and oval vestibules and chapels.

Giorgio Vasari (1511–74), famous for his biographies of the artists, was also a prolific painter and talented architect working mostly in Florence for the Medici Duke Cosimo I, and in his native Arezzo.

The **Uffizi, Florence** (begun *c.* 1560, completed by Alfonso Parigi and Bernardo Buontalenti soon after 1580) (p. 889C), was built primarily to house thirteen Florentine magistracies and guilds in one place, and forms a long U-shape between the Palazzo Vecchio and the River Arno, which the short side overlooks. Around the enclosed piazza, 140 m (459 ft) in length, are loggias with a mezzanine, one major storey and an attic above. The long loggias, with repeated pairs of columns between piers containing statue-filled niches, culminate in the narrow end elevation with its open Serlianas, forming a spectacular vista from the Piazza della Signoria. A notable feature added by Buontalenti is the renowned **Porta delle Suppliche** (after 1574) with its divided and reversed segmental pediment. The Uffizi also incorporates a section of Vasari's **Corridoio**, a covered passageway for the duke connecting the Palazzo Vecchio with the Palazzo Pitti (q.v.) across the Arno. In 1581 Buontalenti began converting the upper storey of the Uffizi into ducal galleries (hence today's museum), constructing there the famous **Tribuna** (1584–), an exceptionally opulent octagonal room which housed the core of the collection.

Bartolomeo Ammanati (1511–92) and Bernardo Buontalenti (1531–1608) were leading Florentine architects of the second half of the century. Buontalenti built several **villas** for the Medici outside Florence, notably at **Pratolino** (1569–, destroyed) and at **Artimino** (1594), which is an expanded version of Poggio a Caiano (q.v.). He was also renowned for his theatre spectaculars, and his garden designs and ornamental features such as the surviving stalactite encrusted grottoes in the **Boboli Gardens, Florence** (1583–8). Ammanati's best work in Florence is the heavily detailed rusticated rear facade of Palazzo Pitti (q.v.), but he also worked extensively in Padua, Lucca, Rome and elsewhere. Ammanati's **Collegio Romano** (1581–5), one of the earliest theological colleges to be built in Rome, is of a scale anticipating the following century. The imposing brick facade is divided into three parts, and the arrangement of windows and doors of very different sizes in varying groups creates an interesting compositional effect.

The **City Walls, Lucca** (1504–1645), the work of local architects, constitute the most substantial surviving city defences of the sixteenth century. Their low battered profile is well suited to the realities of contemporary warfare, and their multi-angular course with frequent bastions caters well for defensive cross-fire.

Giacomo Barozzi da Vignola (1507–73), born near Bologna and trained as a painter, came to prominence as one of Rome's leading architects largely through the patronage of Paul III and the Farnese family. In 1562 he published his *Regola*, a series of engraved plates on the five orders with explanatory captions; this first systematic treatment of the subject was to have a great impact, particularly in France. His built works include the imposing **Portico dei Banchi** (*c.* 1561–) along the side of the main square in **Bologna**, as well as the unfinished gargantuan **Palazzo Farnese, Piacenza**.

The **Villa Giulia, Rome** (1551–) (p. 893A–G), was built for Pope Julius III just outside the city walls. Vignola's exterior two-storey facade is severe, with rusticated quoins and portal, the voussoirs characteristically overlapping the entablature. Immediately beyond, however, a semicircular courtyard loggia with large and small orders leads into a delightful enclosed garden, much of which was actually designed by Ammanati. Beyond a pavilion at the end of the first garden court, steps curl down to a lower level, from which a nymphaeum with caryatid figures can be seen still further below; here emerge the waters of the Aqua Vergine restored by Julius. The effect is to create a series of very different and surprising spaces which are essentially inward rather than outward looking.

The **Gesù, Rome** (1568–) (p. 894D–H), the mother church of the Jesuits, was financed by Cardinal Alessandro Farnese and is Vignola's best-known building. The simple plan, deriving from Alberti's S. Andrea, Mantua, and Raphael's S. Peter's, has a wide aisleless barrel-vaulted nave, with chapels between paired pilasters and a domed crossing with barely projecting transepts. The well-lit interior allows an unobstructed view of the altar, now placed in the eastern arm of the church. The magnificent painted decorations date from the following century (nave, 1672–85; Andrea Pozzo's famous

VILLA OF POPE JULIUS: ROME

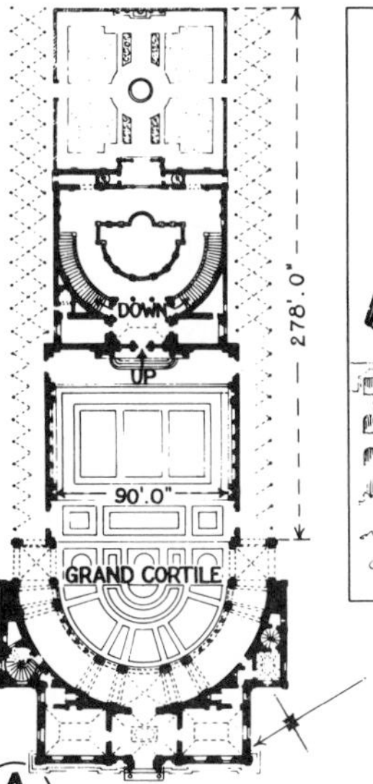

278'.0"
DOWN
UP
90'.0"
GRAND CORTILE

(A) GROUND PLAN

b
a
55'.0"

(B) ENTRANCE FACADE

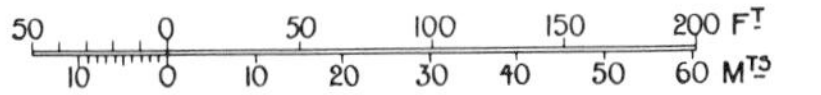

4'-0"
20'-2"
5'-10"

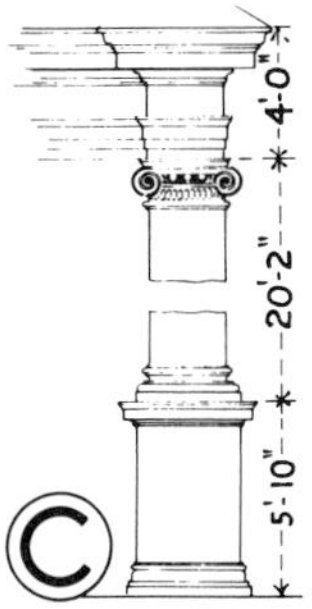

(C) LOWER ORDER GRAND CORTILE

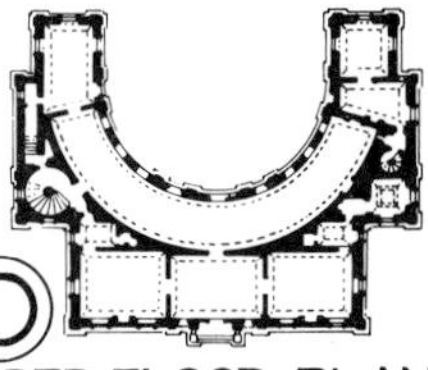

(D) UPPER FLOOR PLAN

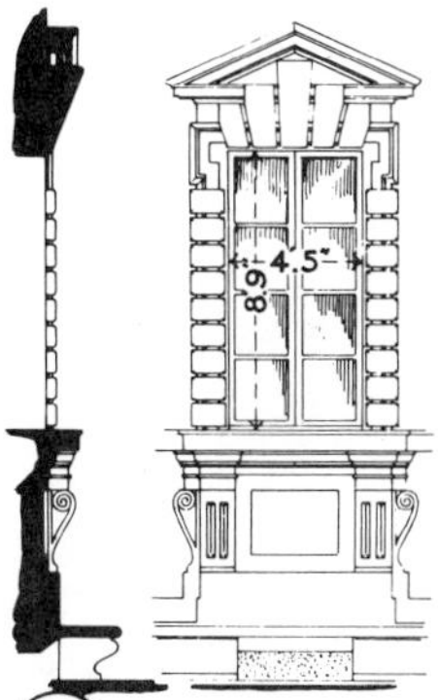

50 0 50 100 150 200 FT.
10 0 10 20 30 40 50 60 MTS

8'.9" 4'.5"

(E) WINDOW AT a

(F) GRAND CORTILE

8'.10" 4'.4"

(G) WINDOW AT b

(H) VILLA FARNESINA: ROME

(J) VILLA MADAMA: ROME

S. MARIA DELLA CONSOLAZIONE : TODI

125'0"
AT a-a
AT b-b

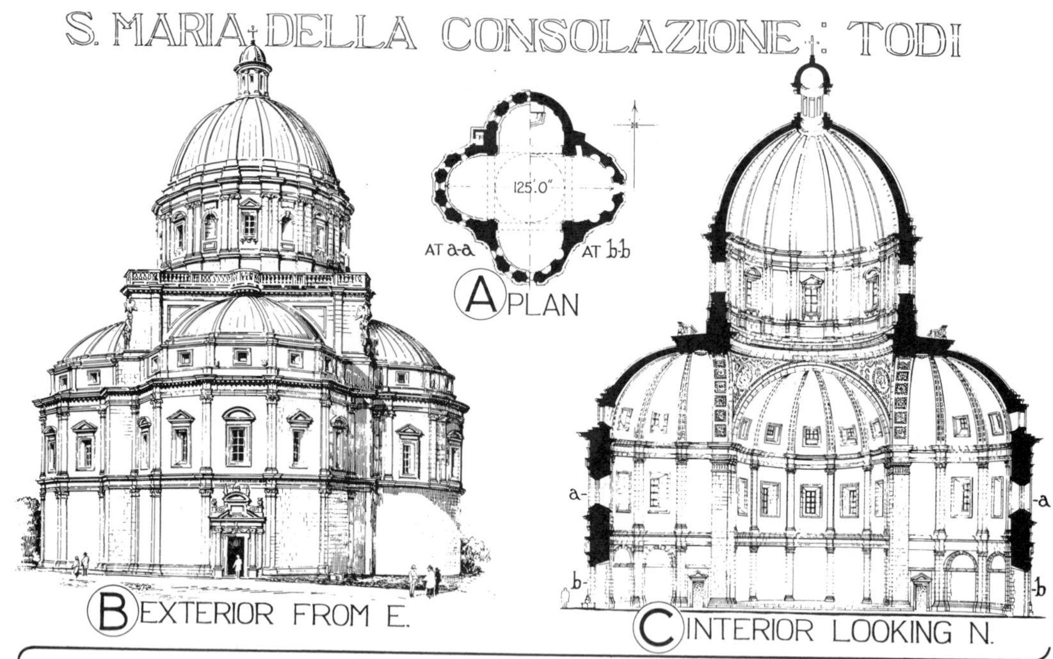

A PLAN

B EXTERIOR FROM E.

a-
-a
b-
-b

C INTERIOR LOOKING N.

IL GESU : ROME

E EXTERIOR FROM W.

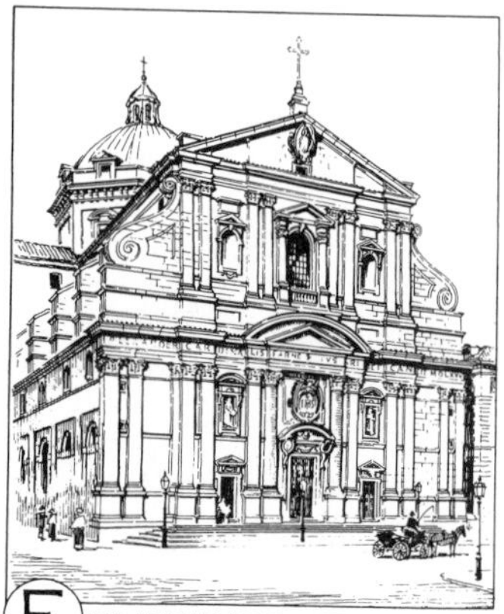

115'0"
225'0"
55'0"

D PLAN

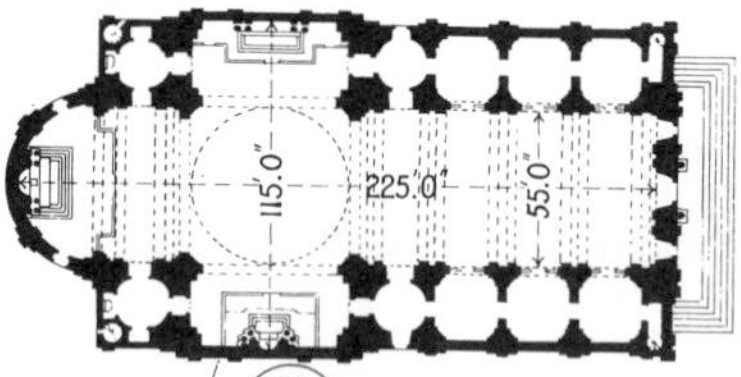

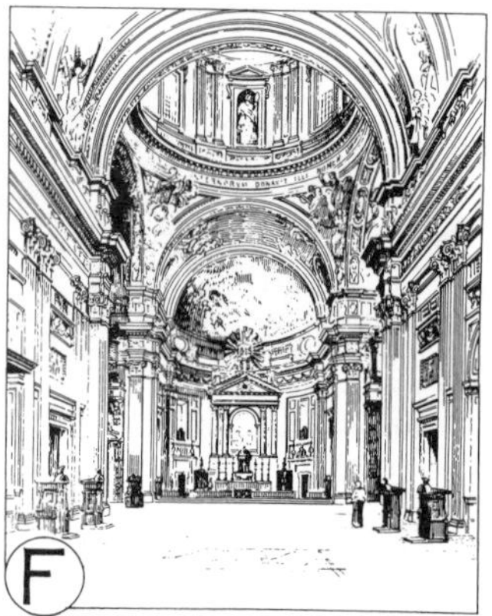

F INTERIOR LOOKING E.

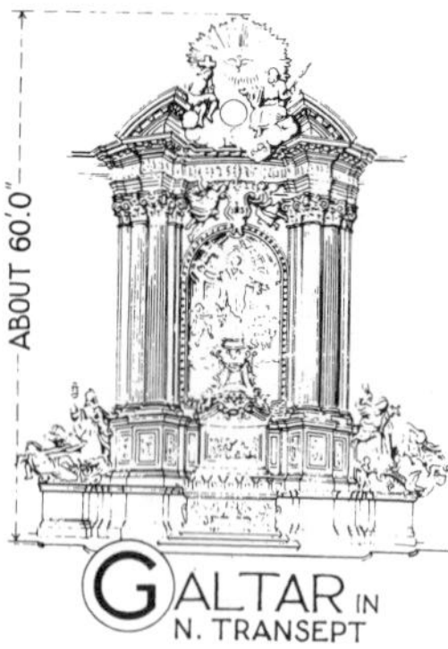

ABOUT 60'0"

G ALTAR IN N. TRANSEPT

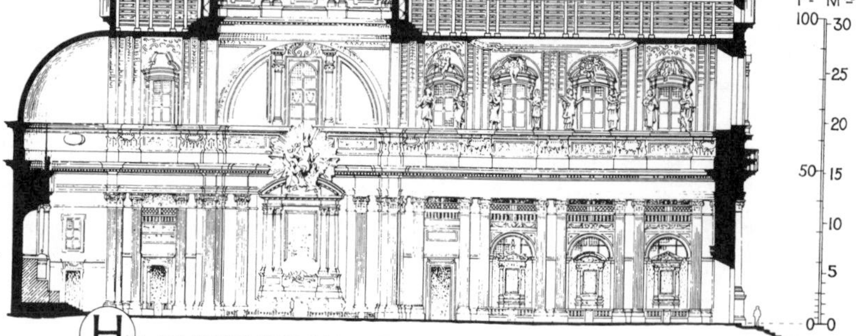

FT MTS
100
30
25
20
50
15
10
5
0
0

H LONGITUDINAL SECTION LOOKING S.

altar in the north transept, 1696–1700), but Vignola may not have intended the interior to be left bare. Giacomo della Porta's slightly more unified facade (1571–), which places a new emphasis on the portal, was eventually preferred to Vignola's.

S. Andrea, Via Flaminia, Rome (1550–*c.* 1553) by Vignola (p. 867D–J), a church of simple design, has a facade distantly inspired by the Pantheon. The rectangular interior is of interest for its oval dome carried on oval arches.

In **S. Anna dei Palafrenieri, Rome** (1565–), these ideas are developed further. Although the outer shell of the church is still rectangular, the interior is an oval with four rectangular additions to the main axes, service rooms taking up the remaining space. The facades on two adjacent sides correspond to two main altars inside, but the oval plan provides unambiguously major and minor axes. **S. Giacomo degli Incurabili** (1592–), begun by Francesco da Volterra and completed by Maderno, is another very important late sixteenth-century church in Rome with an oval interior.

The **Palazzo Farnese, Caprarola** (1559–) (p. 896), which dominates this village north of Rome, is a massive palatial villa transformed by Vignola from a fortress designed by Sangallo the Younger. The pentagonal building rises in two storeys from a rusticated basement which projects as bastions at the corners, echoed above by the blank end bays of the upper storeys. The state apartments, notably the Gran Sala with its cave-like encrusted decoration, are grouped around a circular courtyard articulated with a two-storey Serlian motif. The palace is approached up the steep rise by a truly spectacular series of monumental ramps and terraces, commensurate with the huge scale of the building above.

Villa Lante, Bagnaia, near Viterbo (1566–), attributed to Vignola, is most notable for its splendidly preserved gardens. Two casinos overlook a formal parterre with a pool and central fountain reached by bridges. From between the casinos rises an axial series of steps, ramps and terraces with fountains, water chains and water-cooled dining tables. A second less formal garden (bosco) has an itinerary punctuated by fountains and sculptural ensembles.

The **Sacro Bosco, Bomarzo, near Viterbo**, is less convincingly associated with Vignola. This garden is laid out on very different principles: rocky outcrops scattered in woodland are carved into fantastic and exotic beings and creatures. The entrance to a cave takes on the form of a grotesque face, and a tower is designed as a leaning ruin. Yet at the centre of these scattered delights a tempietto with portico and dome provides a serious, even solemn culmination.

Pirro Ligorio (*c.* 1510–83) began his career as a painter before turning to architecture, briefly becoming architect to S. Peter's (1564–5). During his later life he was employed by the D'Este family in Rome, then in Ferrara. He was the most dedicated of all sixteenth-century archaeologists, and many of his illustrated notebooks survive.

The **Casino of Pius IV, Rome** (1558–61) (p. 890C), actually begun for Paul IV, stands in the Vatican gardens. Two portals and two loggias (one in front of the Casino proper) are grouped around an oval enclosure reminiscent of Ligorio's reconstructions of naumachias. The extremely elaborate encrusted stucco decoration is also inspired by antiquity, especially Roman tomb interiors.

The **Villa d'Este, Tivoli** (*c.* 1565–72) (p. 897A,B), has perhaps the most ambitious garden of the sixteenth century. It is laid out over a series of terraces on the hillside below the villa itself, previously a Benedictine monastery. One main axis leads down from the south-west facade, and is crossed by several subsidiary axes usually terminating with fountains or other architectural features, such as the marvellous organ fountain (p. 897A) (once housing a hydraulic organ) with its orders of rusticated herms and caryatids, and the Rometta, which traces the course of the Tiber through a miniature reconstruction of ancient Rome. Yet it is the sheer quantity of waterjets, fountains, pools and channels that gives this villa its unique quality.

The **Villa Medici, Rome** (1564–) (p. 897C), designed by Annibale Lippi, and continued by Ammanati (1576–), has a massive stern facade overlooking the city but an exceptionally ornate garden front modelled on the Casino of Pius IV, which incorporates pieces of antique sculpture.

Giacomo della Porta (1533–1602) was the most talented of the architects working in Rome towards the end of the sixteenth century. He completed the Gesù at Vignola's death (1573) and became chief architect at S. Peter's, constructing Michelangelo's dome (q.v.). Deeply indebted to Vignola, and especially to Michelangelo, his works have a unity of design foreshadowing the following century.

S. Andrea della Valle, Rome (begun 1591, continued by Maderno, 1608–25; facade by Rainaldi, 1655–65), the mother church of the Theatines, is inspired by the Gesù, although the nave has grouped pilasters which continue as well-defined ribs across the barrel vault, giving the expansive interior a strong cohesion.

Villa Aldobrandini, Frascati (1598–1602, completed 1604 by Maderno and G. Fontana), has a large astylar multi-storey facade standing on a high terrace. Two barely projecting wings support the sides of a colossal broken pediment, the raking angles of which align with the much smaller pediment over the taller central attic. The rear gardens are terraced into the hillside behind and include a semicircular area with an elaborately articulated rear wall incorporating statues and fountains; marking the vista at the head of a flight of steps behind is a pair of large and ornate free-standing helical columns.

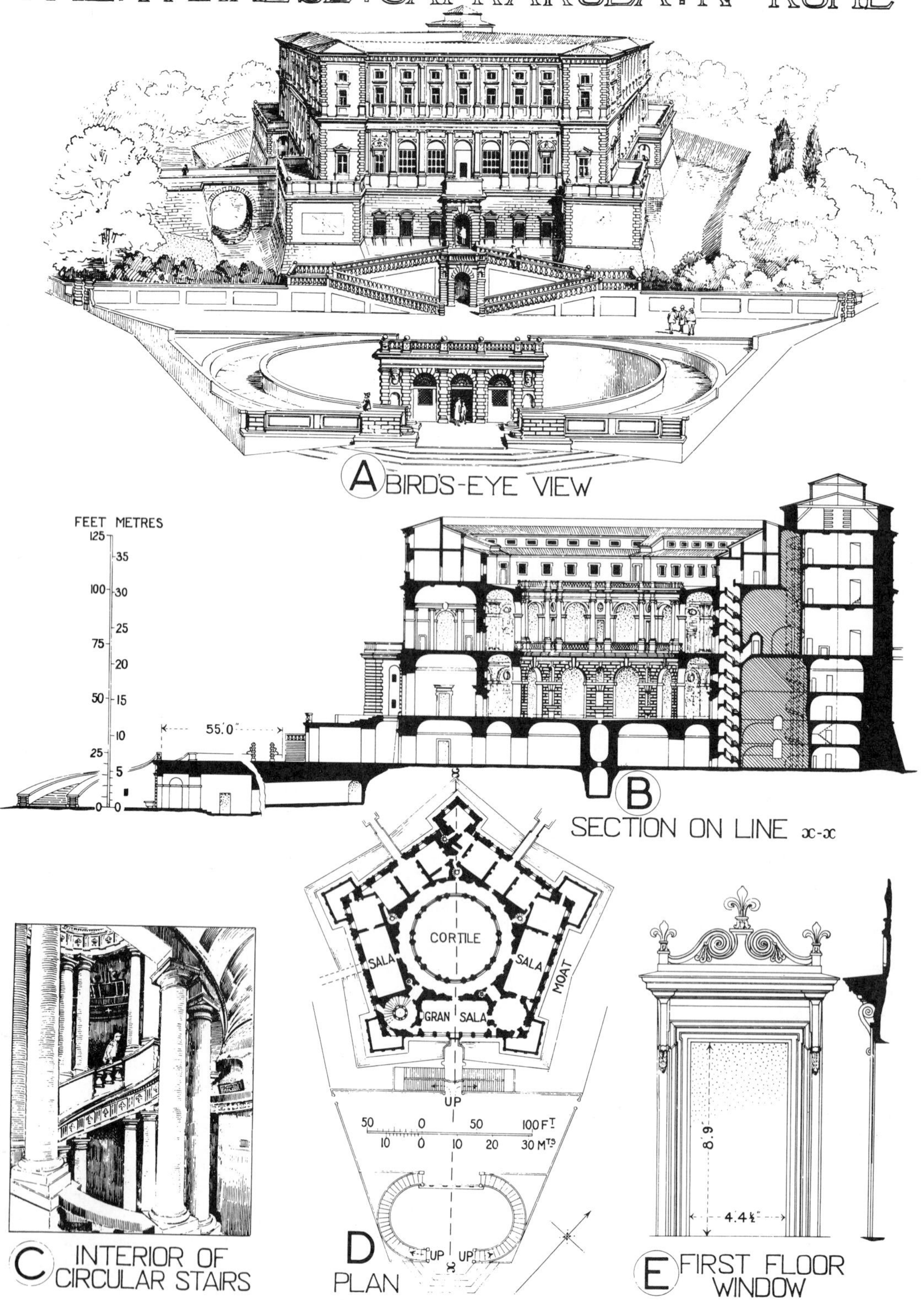
PAL. FARNESE: CAPRAROLA: Nr ROME
A BIRD'S-EYE VIEW
FEET METRES
125
35
100
30
25
75
20
50
15
10
25
5
0
0
55.0"
B
SECTION ON LINE x-x
CORTILE
SALA
SALA
MOAT
GRAN SALA
UP
50 0 50 100 FT
10 0 10 20 30 MTS
UP UP
8.9"
4.4½"
C INTERIOR OF CIRCULAR STAIRS
D PLAN
E FIRST FLOOR WINDOW

A. Villa d'Este, Tivoli (*c.* 1565–72): Organ Fountain. See p.895

B. Villa d'Este, Tivoli

C. Villa Medici, Rome (1564–). See p.895

Palazzo Zuccari, Rome (*c.* 1590), the palace which the painter Federigo Zuccari designed for himself, has a garden facade with a portal and windows conceived as giant masks reminiscent of the cave at Bomarzo. The horrible faces would form a contrast with the sophisticated delights of the garden behind.

Domenico Fontana (1543–1607), from Lugano, achieved distinction as architect to Sixtus V. Although very typical of their period, his buildings can be very dull, for example, his elephantine **Lateran Palace, Rome** (1586–), a watered-down version of the Palazzo Farnese. He was particularly influential in the field of town planning.

Capella Sistina, S. Maria Maggiore, Rome (1585–), designed for Sixtus V, has an unremarkable cruciform plan, but its sumptuous interior is the first of many to be veneered with polychrome marble.

The new streets centring on S. Maria Maggiore (*c.* 1587) are among several laid out by Fontana for Sixtus to link the principal pilgrimage churches. Four here converge at the church, one sighted on an obelisk moved from the Mausoleum of Augustus. Obelisks were erected for similar effect elsewhere – at the Piazza del Popolo, the Lateran, and in front of S. Peter's.

Baroque and Rococo

Carlo Maderno (1556–1629), a nephew of Domenico Fontana, introduced a vigorous, sculptural approach to architectural design in the first decade of the seventeenth century. Apart from his additions to the basilica of S. Peter, Rome (p. 872) his designs include the **Palazzo Mattei, Rome** (1598–1616), and the dome of S. Andrea della Valle, Rome (q.v.).

The mediaeval church of **S. Susanna, Rome** (1597–1603) (p. 899A), was radically transformed by Maderno who redecorated the interior, inserted a crypt, added convent buildings and, most importantly, designed its impressive facade. Conceived as a dramatic frontispiece, the facade relates to the piazza rather than the very small church it screens. Symmetrical three-bay convent buildings flanking the facade are differentiated from the church by the use of brick rather than stone, but are visually unified by horizontal alignments and by the crowning balustrade which is inventively extended over the church's pediment. The facade has a five-bay lower storey with three bays above. The bays become emphatically wider towards the middle, breaking progressively forward, while the applied ornament becomes more sculptural.

Constructed for the Barberini family of Pope Urban VIII, the **Palazzo Barberini, Rome** (1628–33) (p. 900A,B) became the most significant domestic building in early seventeenth-century Rome. All leading architects of the Roman Baroque contributed to its design. It was begun by the aged Maderno, with contributions in detailing from his nephew, Borromini. At Maderno's death in 1629, the precocious Bernini was appointed architect while Pietro da Cortona furnished the design of the theatre. The building differs from town palaces in its surrounding gardens and its unusual H-shaped plan, which together with the open, arcaded facade give a villa-like effect. The seven-bay central block has three Classical superimposed orders rising above the adjoining wings. An attic over the central three bays corresponds to the top of the huge first-floor sala adorned with Cortona's impressive ceiling fresco. Novel features of the plan are the square, open-well staircase, the stoa-like ground-floor atrium, and the now destroyed transverse oval sala, which was later to appear in Bernini's architecture.

Few buildings by Francesco Maria Ricchino (1583–1658) have survived, and perhaps as a result history has dealt roughly with him. The **Collegio Elvetico (Swiss Seminary), Milan** (1627), has one of the most remarkable facades of its time; while its component parts owe much to Michelangelo (for example the window frames) and to sixteenth-century Florentine palace architecture (for example the quoins), its most notable feature is the concave plan. The Vignolesque balconied doorway is emphasised by the convex balustrade which contrasts with the curve of the facade, a practice which heralds the architecture of the great trio of seventeenth-century Rome, Borromini, Bernini and Cortona.

The plan of Ricchino's **S. Giuseppe, Milan** (1607–30) (p. 899B), is of a type going back to the sixteenth-century churches of Antonio da Sangallo the Younger and Sanmicheli. Of the two adjoining centrally planned spaces, both Greek cross in form, one is intended to house the altar, the other the congregation. The larger of the two has shallow arms little deeper than the width of the columns that frame them. Both spaces differ in interior elevation, most significantly in their upper zones. Pendentives support a dome in the larger space, while a simple cross vault crowns the chancel. In contrast to many Renaissance centrally planned churches a significant directional emphasis is given to the building by its ornamental facade, in which one pedimented tabernacle is set within another, concentrating attention on the facade's centre. This type of 'aedicule facade' became one of the most popular during the Baroque era.

Giovanni Battista Aleotti (1546–1636) was the leading architect in early seventeenth-century Emilia. His **Teatro Farnese, Parma** (1618–28) (p. 899C), is modelled on those of Palladio in Vicenza (q.v.) and of Scamozzi. The deep U-shaped auditorium is closer to that of Scamozzi's theatre in Sabbioneta, as is the treatment of the proscenium arch, but the novel two-tier arcade looks back to Palladio's Basilica, Vicenza (q.v.).

A. S. Susanna, Rome: facade (1597–1603). See p.898

B. S. Giuseppe, Milan: facade (1607–30). See p.898

C. Teatro Farnese, Parma: auditorium (1618–28). See p.898

A. Palazzo Barberini, Rome (1628–33): general view, west side. See p.898

B. Palazzo Barberini, Rome: entrance block, west side

C. Oratory of S. Philip Neri, Rome (1637–50). See p.901

The imposing **Palazzo dell'Università, Genoa** (1630) (p. 902A,B), built as a Jesuit college, was designed by Bartolommeo Bianco (*c.* 1590–1657), Genoa's leading Baroque architect. Bianco here capitalised on the potential of the steep sloping site, characteristic of the city. The differing levels allow for spatial experiments with staircases, now becoming a more fundamental aspect of architecture than ever before. The arcades with paired columns look back to Alessi's work in Genoa and Milan. The inspiration for the vista from vestibule through courtyard to staircase can be found in Rocco Lurago's Palazzo Doria-Tursi, Genoa (q.v.).

The **Villa Borghese, Rome** (1613–15), built for Scipione Borghese by the Flemish architect Giovanni Vansanzio, stands in gardens immediately outside the Aurelian walls. It fits into the tradition of the 'villa suburbana', an antique building type revived in the sixteenth century from ancient literary descriptions. The core of the structure is a rectangular block to which are attached four tower-like wings, a vestige of castle design. Those at the front are lower than the central block while those behind are taller. This gives the villa a predominant axis as well as a principal viewpoint. It is entered through the once open arcade which led into a small courtyard. By contrast with its most important model, the Villa Medici, Rome (q.v.), it is the main facade rather than the garden front which is studded with niches and roundels containing fragments of ancient sculpture.

The ancient church of **S. Sebastiano fuori le Mura, Rome** (1609–13), was renovated by Flaminio Ponzio for Scipione Borghese and completed by Vansanzio, the builder of the Villa Borghese. The monochrome architecture adopted here contrasts strongly with Ponzio's contemporary multi-coloured **Cappella Paolina, S. Maria Maggiore, Rome** (1605–11), as does the restrained Classicism of the design. The paired columns used on the facade were a popular motif at this time, as witnessed by the Palazzo dell' Università, Genoa (q.v.).

Francesco Borromini (1599–1667), whose use of curvilinear forms to create vital spatial effects was to revolutionise architecture, came to Rome from Lombardy as an itinerant mason. His links with the Fontana and Maderno families made initial entry into the Roman artistic scene relatively easy, but an antipathy for the pre-eminent Bernini was not to help his career. His first independent commission was from the Trinitarian order to design **S. Carlo alle Quattro Fontane, Rome** (1634–82) (p. 903A), one of the masterpieces of Roman Baroque architecture. Complexity characterises both plan, combining elements of oval and Greek cross, and interior wall treatment, which can be read in two ways. Overlapping three-bay units focus attention now on the altars, now on the subsidiary chapel openings. Thus the eye moves constantly around a structure which has no strong visual caesuras. The oval dome with its elaborate 'all'antica' coffering is set directly on pendentives without a drum and is crowned by an oval lantern. The exterior profile of the dome is enclosed, following Lombard rather than Roman models. The undulating facade symbolically heralds the interior by taking up its triadic bay system. The upper level was completed after Borromini's death by his nephew and probably does not follow his design. The buildings also include a convent, an elaborate crypt and a courtyard, all ingeniously laid out and highly unconventional in plan and detailing.

The **Palazzo Falconieri, Rome** (1646–49), though much altered, is still Borromini's most significant essay in domestic architecture. He remodelled earlier buildings on the site, endowing them with such hallmarks of his style as the punning falcon-headed capitals of the facade, and the curvilinear concave ends of the sculptural belvedere.

The **Collegio di Propaganda Fide, Rome** (1662) (p. 903B), was built as a training centre for missionaries, Borromini providing two courtyards and a chapel. The giant pilasters of the facade, at once uncanonical and severe, flank impressive concave window embrasures with alternating segmental and triangular crowning motifs. In the central entrance bay, emphasised by its concavity, the triangular window now becomes convex. The chapel which the facade masks is remarkable for its attempt to create a coherent, visually unified space; the skeletal structure of pilasters continues up through the entablature and across the vault in a unifying stucco network.

Perhaps Borromini's most prestigious commission was to renovate the venerable basilica of **S. Giovanni in Laterano, Rome** (1646–69) (p. 903C). The alterations included encasing much of the early Christian nave and four aisles in stucco-covered brick. The piers were decorated with marble tabernacles whose convex pediments front oval canopies combining ideas of pediment and crown. The pomegranates carved in the nave capitals allude to the biblical descriptions of the Temple of Solomon.

The **Oratory of S. Philip Neri, Rome** (1637–50) (p. 900C), is the central house of the Oratorians, a Counter-Reformation order founded by S. Philip Neri. Granted the church of S. Maria in Vallicella, the order began the adjacent conventual buildings in the early seventeenth century to the designs of Paolo Maruscelli. Borromini, elected to replace Maruscelli, was in large part limited by his predecessor's plan. The most impressive feature is the facade. Built in brick so as not to rival the adjacent church front by Fausto Rughese (1605), it is one of the earliest monumental concave facades. It is unconventional in much of its detail – for example the crowning pediment which fuses triangular and segmental types.

S. Ivo della Sapienza, Rome (1642–50) (p. 903D), is the chapel attached to the university begun in the mid-sixteenth century by Pirro Ligorio and continued

A. Palazzo dell'Università, Genoa (1630): vestibule. See p.901

B. Palazzo dell'Università, Genoa: cortile

C. S. Peter, Rome: aerial view from east, showing Vatican on right, with covered approach from Castle of S. Angelo (1506–1626; piazza 1656–). See pp.869, 904

A. S. Carlo alle Quattro Fontane, Rome (1634–82). See p.901

B. Collegio di Propaganda Fide, Rome (1662). See p.901

C. S. Giovanni in Laterano (1646–69): nave looking west. See p.901

D. S. Ivo della Sapienza, Rome: from cortile (1642–50). See p.901

under Giacomo della Porta. The chapel's unusual plan is composed of two interlocking triangles forming a six-pointed star whose ends are alternately convex and concave curves. The form chosen was certainly symbolic, referring to the star of wisdom (sapienza) and possibly to the bee found in the coat of arms of the patron, Urban VIII. The most remarkable feature of the structure is the way in which the star-shaped plan is retained in the dome, gradually transforming itself into the circular oculus on which the lantern stands. As at S. Carlo alle Quattro Fontane the dome is encased in a drum and is surmounted by a spiral lantern which has been variously interpreted as the Tower of Babel, the lighthouse of Alexandria, the biblical pillar of fire, and even the papal tiara.

S. Agnese, Rome (1652–) (p. 906A), built as part of a redevelopment of Piazza Navona by the Pamphili pope Innocent X, was integrated into the large palace which occupies the west side of the square. It was begun by Gerolamo and Carlo Rainaldi, altered first by Borromini and then again by Carlo Rainaldi. Borromini's concave facade has the effect of making the dome very prominent and fully visible. The device of towers framing a dome was to become especially popular in eighteenth-century Austria.

The sculptor-architect Giovanni Lorenzo Bernini (1598–1680), born in Naples, was the pre-eminent artist of the Roman Baroque. He introduced a new virtuosity into sculpture with his ability to create many textural effects in stone, and exploited the arts of painting and architecture to control the spectator's experience and to vitalise and dramatise his sculptural settings. However, his approach to architecture was largely Classical and he could never come to terms with the licence of Borromini's inventions.

S. Andrea al Quirinale, Rome (1658–70) (p. 906B), was begun as the chapel of a Jesuit seminary. Having initially suggested a pentagonal plan, Bernini ultimately chose one of his favourite forms, the transverse oval, with entry on the short axis. Ten openings leading to portals and chapels set into the thickness of the wall do not detract from this simple conception. In contrast to Borromini's monochrome architecture, Bernini, here as in his sculpture, used voluptuous multi-coloured marbles. The design is so manipulated that the three arts of painting, sculpture and architecture relate the story of S. Andrew. Crucified in the painting on the high altar, he then, transformed into sculpture, rises to heaven through the broken pediment of the columnar screen, while putti in the oculus of the dome descend to show him the route. The use of colour is also symbolic, pink for the terrestrial domain and gold for the dome of heaven. The dome combines two previously alternative vaulting types, coffering and ribs. The high altar is visually linked and physically separated from the main congregational space by a columnar screen. This is heralded by the springy oval porch which is the focal point of the concave forecourt.

At the **Cappella Cornaro, S. Maria della Vittoria, Rome** (1645–52) (p. 906C), Bernini successfully employed painting, sculpture and architecture to create one of his most spectacular effects. Encased in an oval shrine, invitingly thrust forward by the architecture, S. Teresa is seen in the ecstatic throes of a vision. Raking light from a hidden source dramatises the scene and also symbolises the mysterious hand of God. Her vision is watched by members of the Cornaro family, sculpturally portrayed in balconies at the chapel's sides. The visitor becomes a participant in the visionary scene, an effect emphasised by the virtuosity of sculptural technique. Such resources became standard elements in Baroque chapel design.

The **Piazza of S. Peter's, Rome** (1656–) (pp. 902C, 905), is a forecourt impressive enough to match the most important church in Roman Catholic Christendom. Bernini designed a vast oval piazza surrounded by Doric colonnades. Although the area is open towards the east, Bernini's original intention was to close most of this gap, leaving two symmetrically placed entrances either side of the main axis. In the seventeenth century the piazza was reached from the narrow streets of the Borgo (the present Via della Conciliazione was widened in the 1930s), and the contrast between confinement and open space would originally have been much greater. In designing the piazza, Bernini had to take into account the functions of Benediction from both S. Peter's and the Vatican palace. A relatively low colonnade permitting wide visibility for pilgrims was the result. However, four columns deep from many viewpoints, the colonnades give the spectacular impression of a forest of verticals.

At the bottom of Bernini's **Scala Regia, Vatican, Rome** (1663–66) (p. 906D), the arms of Alexander VII break the curve of the arch and are celebrated by trumpeting angels. Bernini brilliantly overcame site restrictions in designing this new ceremonial stair. The converging walls gave him the chance for perspective illusion. The columns, vault and steps all diminish in size and give the impression of greater length and monumentality. A shaft of light breaks the visual ascent, creating the chiaroscuro of stage lighting.

S. Maria Assunta, Ariccia (1662–64) (p. 908A), a domed, cylindrical structure preceded by a portico, is closely modelled upon the Pantheon, a building which Bernini had renovated in the previous decade. Ariccia differs mainly in the adoption of an arcaded portico. This is well suited to the design as blind arches decorate the exterior of the rotunda and also frame the interior chapels. A vast embracing structure emphasises the centralised nature of the design. As at S. Andrea al Quirinale, the iconography of the dedicatory saint adorns the interior.

The **Palazzo Chigi-Odescalchi, Rome** (begun 1664) (p. 909B), though substantially altered in the

S. PETER : ROME

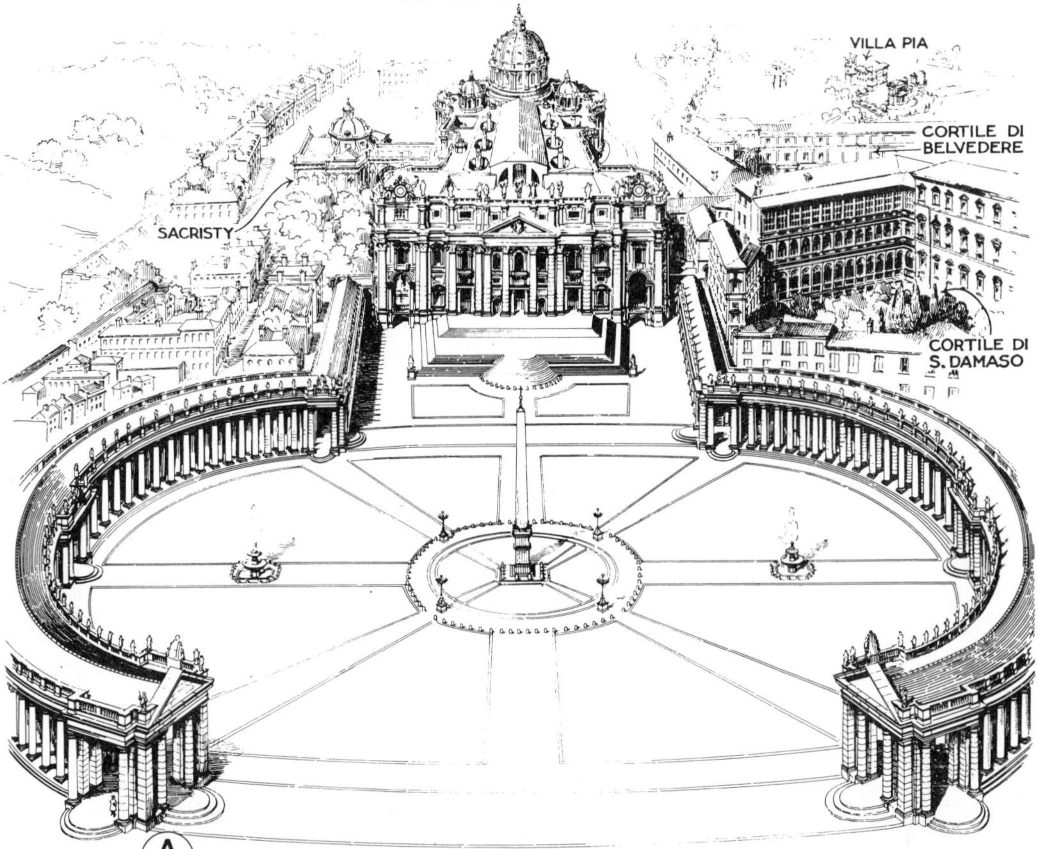

VILLA PIA
CORTILE DI BELVEDERE
SACRISTY
CORTILE DI S. DAMASO

(A) BIRD'S-EYE VIEW OF S. PETER AND THE VATICAN

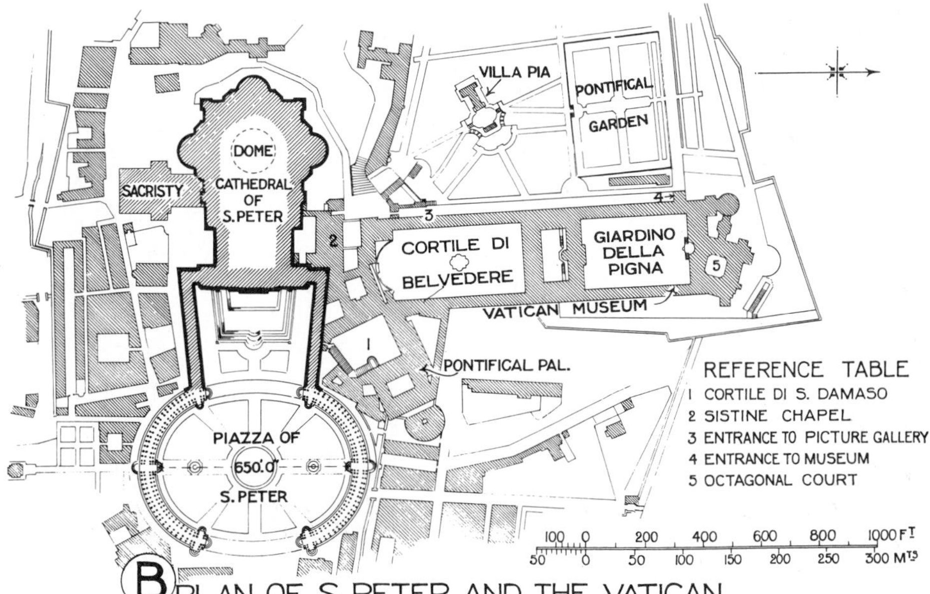

(B) PLAN OF S. PETER AND THE VATICAN

A. Fountain (1647–52) and S. Agnese (1652–), Rome. See p.904

B. S. Andrea al Quirinale, Rome (1658–70). See p.904

C. Cappella Cornaro, S. Maria della Vittoria, Rome (1645–52). See p.904

D. Scala Regia, Vatican, Rome (1663–6). See p.904

eighteenth century, holds an important position in the development of Roman palace facades. In place of the traditional astylar type of Sangallo and Fontana, here is a pilastered facade which looks back to Bramante's Palazzo Caprini (q.v.). Eight bays divided by Corinthian pilasters stand above a basement with a single Doric portal. The tripartite facade originally had a central stylar section framed by two recessed three-bay wings.

The **Palazzo Ludovisi** (now **Palazzo di Montecitorio), Rome** (1650), was built for the family of Innocent X, and completed late in the seventeenth century by Carlo Fontana. The vast facade is composed of five sections, each symmetrical about its own centre. The bay sequence 3–6–7–6–3 stresses the centre and portal, as does the angling of the five sections which, though individually straight, give the appearance of a curved front, an idea perhaps suggested by the Palazzo Massimi alle Colonne.

Pietro da Cortona (1596–1669) repeatedly claimed to be a painter rather than an architect but operated as both with equal success. His experiments in the spatial unification of piazzas and the modulation of wall surfaces were remarkably influential.

SS. Martina e Luca, Rome (1635–50) (p. 908B), was built on the site of a church used by the Academy of S. Luke, founded in 1593, one of the earliest academies of art. During excavation for Pietro da Cortona's tomb a body was unearthed and generally taken to be that of S. Martina. Francesco Barberini, Cortona's patron, immediately undertook to construct the church *de novo*. Cortona's Greek-cross plan, a traditional form for memorial architecture, seems at first glance entirely symmetrical, but the length of the main axis is exaggerated: the bays and apses are deeper than those of the transept arms. It is surprising that Cortona allowed so little space in the church for what was after all his main profession – painting. This perhaps reflects a belief that one art form should not be compromised by another, an attitude altogether different from that of Bernini. The two-storey facade squeezed between embracing piers is the earliest of the Baroque to adopt a curving plan. Cortona has dissolved the wall surface, constantly varying the plane with inserted columns and applied pilasters, thereby subtly creating a dramatic climax at the centre.

The **Vigna del Pigneto, Rome** (before 1630), once sited near the Vatican, is Cortona's earliest architectural work. Fountains and ponds mark the dominant axis with Baroque theatricality. Terraced into the hillside, the villa is approached by a series of ramps, two of which are functionless, contributing solely to the splendour of the ensemble. While the villa looks back to Palladio in its curved wings and to Bramante for its apsidal focus, the composition as a whole is novel.

Cortona's facade for **S. Maria in Via Lata, Rome** (1658–62), is a two-storeyed portico rather than a veneer. The progressive widening of intercolumniations toward the centre emphasises the entrance, as does the arcuated lintel above – a motif found in Renaissance architecture, but ultimately deriving from such antique models as Diocletian's Palace at Split.

Cortona modernised the facade of **S. Maria della Pace, Rome** (1656–57) (p. 912A), and entirely reorganised the small forecourt in front. The design marks a new departure in the planning of piazzas. All the sides of the square have been designed to set off the facade, while two of the three streets leading into the square have been masked to produce a greater cohesion. The concave wings flanking the facade on the first storey give an illusion of greater space, and contrast effectively with the convex facade. Above the semi-oval portico the facade recalls that of S. Martina and Luca but uses a different system to produce a central climax. Here there is a sculptural build-up from flat panel, to pilaster, to column.

Carlo Rainaldi (1611–91) and his father Girolamo formed one of the leading family practices of seventeenth-century Rome. They worked largely as a team, but Carlo produced his best buildings after his father's death. His design for **S. Maria in Campitelli, Rome** (1663–7) (p. 911C), has a barrel-vaulted nave followed by a domed presbytery full of light. The strong columnar impression of the interior is carefully gauged to emphasise the chapels. The sculptural facade, of the 'aedicule' type, presents a complexity in the treatment of planes that owes much to Cortona.

The **Piazza del Popolo, Rome** (1662–79), immediately inside the northernmost gateway into the city, gave most travellers their first impression of Rome. Alexander VII entrusted the task of monumentalising the square to Carlo Rainaldi. Three streets converged at this point, forming two wedge-shaped sites facing the gate. Rainaldi planned two churches with large domes, **S. Maria di Monte Santo** and **S. Maria dei Miracoli** (p. 909A), as pavilions on either side of the central street. The different shapes of the seemingly identical domes (one being oval, the other circular) are the result of the differently shaped sites.

SS. Vincenzo ed Anastasio, Rome (1646–50), was planned by Martino Longhi the Younger (1602–60), a member of a large dynasty of Roman architects. The facade facing the Piazza di Trevi is his major work. Two groups of three boldly conceived columns flank the main door, and the motif is repeated in the upper storey. The columns break progressively forward and each pair is joined by a pediment, giving the impression of three superimposed aedicules. On careful reading the systems of the two tiers differ in conception but this does not detract from the powerful effect.

Carlo Fontana (1638–1714) ran the most influential architectural practice in late seventeenth-century Rome. He had worked as a draughtsman for many of the masters of the previous generation – Bernini, Cortona and Rainaldi – and was to pass their ideas on

A. (*above*)
S. Maria Assunta, Ariccia (1662–4). See p.904

B. (*left*)
SS Martina e Luca (1635–50): interior (central dome). See p.907

A. (*right*)
S. Maria di Monte Santo and S. Maria dei Miracoli, Rome (1662–79). See p.907

B. (*below*)
Palazzo Chigi-Odescalchi, Rome (1664–). See p.904

to the international scene through his pupils, for example Juvarra, Pöppelmann and Gibbs (q.v.). His facade of **S. Marcello al Corso, Rome** (1682–3) (p. 911D), by contrast with those of Borromini and Cortona, is easy to read, looking back to the relative simplicity of Carlo Maderno's S. Susanna (q.v.). His buildings are representative of a Classical trend in Roman late Baroque.

Venice

Baldassare Longhena (1598–1682), Bernini's almost exact contemporary, was the most distinguished Venetian architect of the seventeenth century. His church **S. Maria della Salute, Venice** (begun 1631) (p. 911A,B), was, like Palladio's Redentore (q.v.), commissioned by the Venetian state to mark the end of a plague. The building is composed of two domed, centrally planned spaces: an octagonal congregational area with an ambulatory and a square chancel with two flanking apses. The chapels, linked by hidden corridors, protrude from the exterior of the octagon. As in earlier Venetian churches the interior is strictly monochrome. The apsidal transepts of the plan look back to Palladio's Redentore, and in overall configuration the layout resembles Sanmicheli's Madonna di Campagna, Verona (q.v.), both votive churches. The exterior has an entrance portico in the form of a triumphal arch, and the drum is visually united with the lower storey by giant highly sprung scrolls topped with statuary.

Longhena's **Palazzo Pesaro, Venice** (1652–1710), is heavily indebted to the palace type established by Sansovino. The strongly sculptural seven-bay facade wraps around the corner, a traditional Venetian feature. The rusticated bottom storey has two entrances, as was popular in palaces owned by brothers. The rhythmic single and paired column articulation of the upper storeys produces the characteristically Venetian tripartite effect.

Turin

Guarino Guarini (1624–83), a Theatine priest, was an intellectual fascinated by three-dimensional geometry, and his architecture is characterised by spatial experimentation. He was more open-minded than his contemporaries about Gothic architecture and included Gothic forms among the orders in his posthumously published treatise, *Architettura Civile*, of 1737. Although he worked predominantly in Turin, buildings by him were erected as far afield as Lisbon (S. Maria da Divina Providencia, q.v.) and Paris (S. Anne la Royale, 1662–).

Guarini's **Cappella della S. Sindone, Turin** (1667–90) (pp. 912B, 913), is attached to the east end of the cathedral. This intriguing circular structure was built to house the Turin Shroud, owned at that time by the Royal House of Savoy. The wall is divided into nine equal bays and, above, an unusual triangular pendentive system converts the large circle of the ground plan into the smaller circle of the drum. This theme is echoed in microcosmic form in the entrance vestibules. Two elaborate types of coffering differentiate apse from pendentive, one of Guarini's favourite effects. The high arches of the drum break into the vault where the circle is turned into a hexagon. By a succession of open ribs acting as squinches, the vault converges on a suspended twelve-pointed star. On the exterior, the typical Lombard drum enclosing the dome is stepped and crowned with a helix not unlike Borromini's S. Ivo, Rome (q.v.).

At **S. Lorenzo, Turin** (1668–87) (p. 914), the rectangular block-like exterior, with its rectangular altar chapel at the back and portico at the front, gives little idea of the extraordinary interior. Inside, Guarini converted a square into an octagon with curved sides bulging into the main congregational area. The sense of spatial complexity is increased by the curvilinear entablatures inside the chapels. Ingeniously, the octagon is converted into a Greek cross at pendentive level and then into a circle at the base of the drum. The interlacing open ribs restate the octagonal theme and create a rich diaphanous effect.

The **Palazzo Carignano, Turin** (1679), is the best-known of Guarini's domestic buildings. The undulating central section encloses paired grand staircases and a large oval hall. The facades are built of unstuccoed terracotta, moulded to form extravagant window frames and idiosyncratic rustication.

Filippo Juvarra (1678–1736) was born in Messina and grew up with Guarini buildings on his doorstep but trained with Carlo Fontana in Rome. It was only after Vittorio Amedeo II of Savoy had been made the King of Sicily and requested his services in Turin that Juvarra emerged as a prominent architect. He also worked extensively in the applied arts and theatre design.

Vittorio Amedeo II, commissioning the **Palazzina di Stupinigi, near Turin** (1729–33), enabled Juvarra to create one of the most extravagant villas of the late Italian Baroque. Juvarra abandoned the bi-axial rectangular plans of earlier villas and introduced a theme based upon the tri-axial hexagon. An entrance court leads to a magnificent enclosed hexagonal piazza with openings into and through the palace at all the corners. Dominating the piazza is the oval domed block housing a huge access hall, the focal point of the plan through which all the axes pass. This block is differentiated from the rest of the complex by its curvilinear form, apparent in both its plan and its arched windows. The stag crowning the dome indicates the palace's function – a hunting lodge.

Founded as a hilltop sanctuary, the **Superga, near Turin** (1717–31) (p. 912C), combines church and monastery into a single unit. The church is in front of

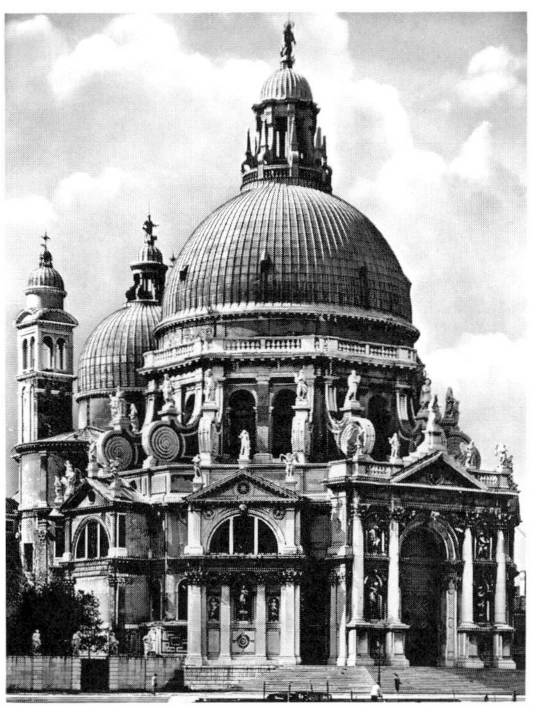

A. S. Maria della Salute, Venice (1631–). See p.910

B. S. Maria della Salute, Venice: interior

C. S. Maria in Campitelli, Rome (1663–7). See p.907

D. S. Marcello al Corso, Rome (1682–3): facade. See p.910

A. S. Maria della Pace, Rome: facade (1656–7). See p.907

B. Capella della S. Sindone, Turin: dome (1667–90). See p.910

C. Superga, near Turin (1717–31). See p.910

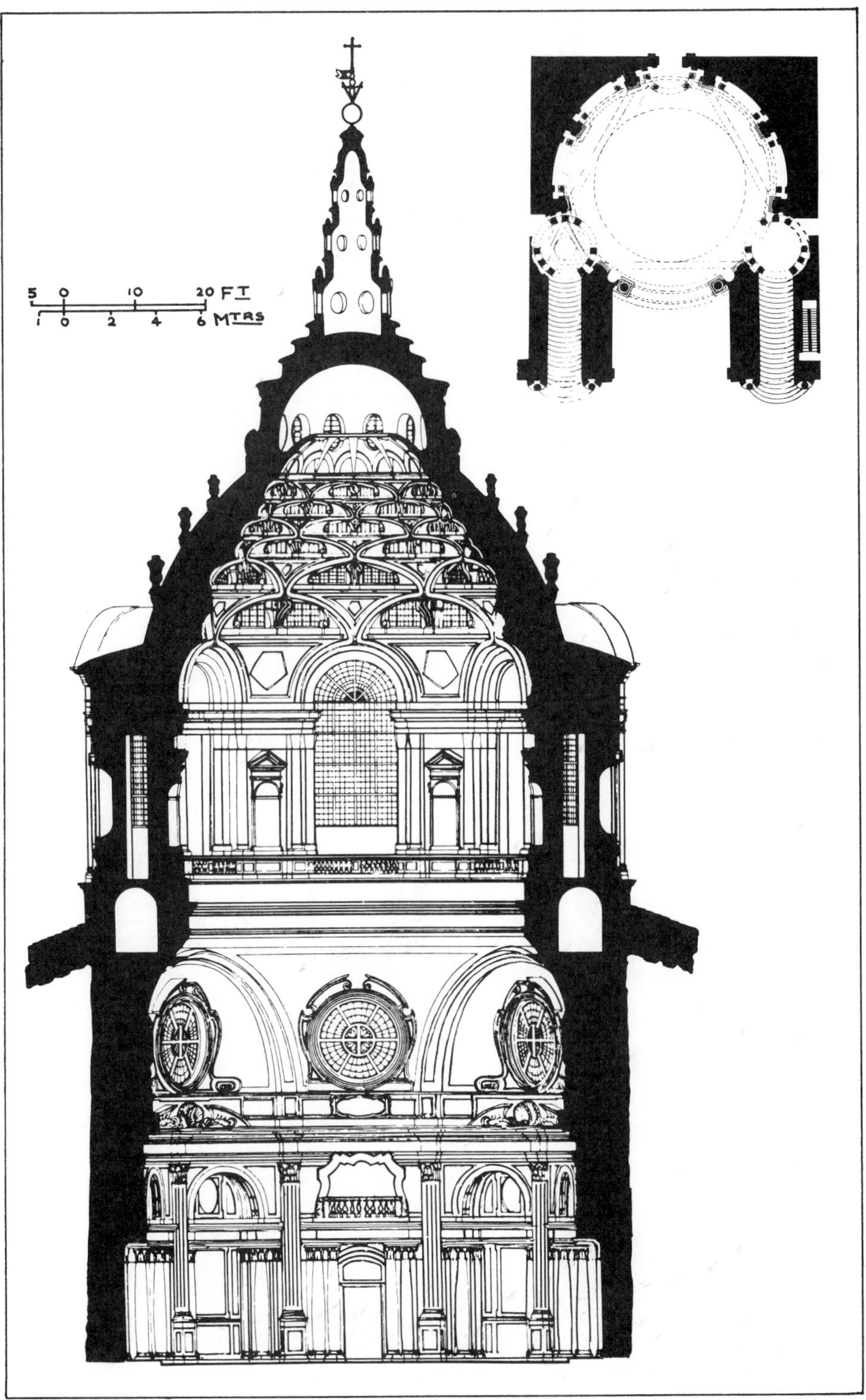

Capella della S. Sindone, Turin (1667–90): plan and section. See p.910

S. Lorenzo, Turin (1668–87): plan and section. See p.910

a rectangular cloister and dominates the conventual buildings, from which it is distinguished by scale and materials. The church is preceded by a projecting square portico which invites entry on each of three sides. Inside, Juvarra confronts the visitor with a single tall cylinder which has windows in both dome and drum, and chapel openings at the lower level. In its simplicity it contrasts strongly with the churches of Guarini erected less than fifty years earlier.

Juvarra's **Palazzo Madama, Turin** (1718–21), built for Vittorio Amedeo II of Savoy, reflects the strong connections between French and Piedmontese architecture. The nine-bay facade, with its central projecting portion articulated with columns rather than pilasters, resembles in its general lines the garden front of Versailles (q.v.). Almost the whole width of the facade is taken up on the interior by a grand staircase hall.

Bernardo Vittone (1702–70), who worked mainly in Piedmont, assimilated the styles of both Guarini and Juvarra. The exterior of the **Sanctuary, Vallinotto, near Turin** (1738–39), consists of four diminishing superimposed tiers similar in vein to Guarini's reinterpretation of the northern Italian tradition of enclosed domes. The plan is hexagonal, each side housing a semicircular chapel. Alternate chapels have convex balconies. As at Guarini's S. Lorenzo there is a semicircular ambulatory behind the high altar. Particularly fascinating is the spatial experimentation in the dome. Six interlocking open ribs permit a view through to three successive vaulted levels – two frescoed domes with diminishing oculi, crowned by the lantern. In contrast to Guarini's methods of changing plan at every level, Vittone retains the hexagonal form throughout and attempts to unite horizontal zones visually.

The **Church of S. Croce, Lecce** (1606–46), has a Baroque exuberance which owes much to Sicily and Naples but also incorporates Romanesque ideas, such as the console figures supporting the balcony and the foliate rings halfway up the column shafts. Plain surfaces are contrasted with zones of intense low-relief decoration.

Rococo

The **Palazzo Stanga, Cremona** (early eighteenth century) (p. 916B), has a tripartite nine-bay facade of which the central three bays are set off by pilasters, paired either side of the portal. The fanciful curving frames of the arches and windows are characteristic features of Rococo architecture.

Designed by Carlo Francesco Dotti (1670–1759), the Marian sanctuary of the **Madonna di S. Luca, Bologna** (1723–57) (p. 916A), stands on a hill outside the city walls. Elaborate arcades line the pilgrimage route to the shrine. An undulating facade fronts the oval exterior of this curvilinear Greek-cross church.

Francesco de Sanctis (1693–1740) turned the grassy slope linking the Piazza di Spagna, Rome, with the church of the Trinità de'Monti into a dramatic staircase known as the **Spanish Steps** (1723–5) (p. 917A). At the base the broad steps are divided into three flights; as at Michelangelo's Laurentian library (q.v.) the central flight billows out into the square. Ascending the hill, the flights narrow and fuse, part and expand onto a broad landing, and diverge again into two curving ramps leading to the upper piazza.

In **Piazza S. Ignazio, Rome** (1727–8), Filippo Raguzzini (*c.* 1680–1771) reworked a theme established by Cortona at S. Maria della Pace (q.v.), using the elevations of several different buildings to form a unified space – here composed of three connecting ovals. The design decision here concerned the shape of the space rather than the buildings – a departure from Renaissance ideas on urban planning.

The **Trevi Fountain, Rome** (1732–7) (p. 917B), was designed by Niccolo Salvi (1696–1751) who developed Cortona's idea of fusing a palace facade with a fountain. This fountain marks the end of the ancient aqueduct (the Aqua Virginis) and replaced a fifteenth-century structure. The use of the triumphal arch motif in this context was probably borrowed from the nearby fountain erected by Sixtus V to decorate the end of the Acqua Felice. The fountain does not simply stand in front of the palace but is fused with it; the man-made rock formations from which the water gushes climb high up the basement level.

The facade of **S. Giovanni in Laterano, Rome** (1733–6), was designed by Alessandro Galilei (1691–1737). In essence this example of late Baroque Classicism was modelled upon Maderno's facade for S. Peter's, Rome (q.v.). There is, however, a greater emphasis on verticality achieved through the closer spacing of the giant columns, and also on chiaroscuro attained by means of opening up much more of the facade to create contrast. The vocabulary used takes its lead from Bernini rather than Borromini.

The **Palazzo Sanfelice, Naples** (1728), was designed by the most gifted and prolific early eighteenth-century Neapolitan architect Ferdinando Sanfelice (1675–1750), unsurpassed master of staircase design. Here the stairs fill an entire side of the courtyard and are open on both sides so that the function of ascent is expressed on the courtyard elevation.

The facade of **S. Gregorio, Messina** (tower 1717, facade 1743), illustrates the exuberant imagination of Sicilian eighteenth-century architecture. Though heavily indebted to Borromini's S. Ivo (q.v.), the helical spire is by no means a copy. It is embraced by miniature versions of itself, and at its summit sit a papal tiara and keys proclaiming the importance of the succession of S. Peter. The facade transforms the pediment into a vital surging crown. Its acute apex

A. Madonna di S. Luca, Bologna (1723–57). See p.915

B. Palazzo Stanga, Cremona (early eighteenth century). See p.915

A. Scala di Spagna (Spanish Steps), Rome (1723–5). See p.915

B. Trevi Fountain, Rome (1732–7). See p.915

C. SS. Simeone e Giuda, Venice (1718–38). See p.919

A. Royal Palace, Caserta (1752–). See p.919

B. La Scala, Milan (1776–8). See p.920

and appended crockets resemble Gothic gables. A window bursts into the entablature, producing an interesting essay in flamboyant arcuation.

S. Giorgio, Ragusa Ibla (1746–75), was designed by Rosario Gagliardi. This facade type, typical of eighteenth-century Sicily, has several diminishing tiers and fuses the notions of church facade and bell tower. The triple break forward is marked by free-standing columns recalling SS. Vincenzo ed Anastasio in Rome (q.v.), while the gently curving central bay augments the tower-like impression. Further extravagant examples of this type are **S. Giorgio, Modica** (eighteenth century), and **S. Placido, Catania** (finished 1769).

Villa Valguarnera, Bagheria (1709–39), by Tommaso Napoli, is one of several exciting eighteenth-century villas surrounding the town. An elaborate double-ramp staircase undulates in the deep concave facade and opens into the convex entrance porch which dominates the centre. Other nearby villas are **Villa Palagonia** (1705) and **Villa Larderia** (*c.* 1752).

Neo-Classical

Giovanni Battista Piranesi (1720–78), best known for his dramatic architectural etchings and for championing Roman architecture at the expense of Greek, produced at **S. Maria del Priorato, Rome**, his most important essay in built architecture. Designed for the Knights of Malta, the church is situated in an elaborate five-sided piazza. Much of the decoration has symbolic significance, the Knights' emblems being freely interpreted in the facade capitals. The obelisks punctuating the piazza reflect Piranesi's fascination with ancient Egypt.

Designed by Giovanni Antonio Scalfarotto (1690–1764), **SS. Simeone e Giuda, Venice** (1718–38) (p. 917C), departs from the exuberant forms of Longhena's S. Maria della Salute (q.v.) and moves toward a more rigid Classicism, inspired by the Pantheon. A pedimented portico gives on to a rotunda through an intermediary block, and inside there are projecting tabernacles and columnar screens. The dome is of the stilted Byzantine type traditional to Venice.

The facade of **S. Nicolò da Tolentino, Venice** (1706–14), marks a change in direction in the work of Andrea Tirali (1657–1737). While his earlier work, such as the chapel of S. Domenico in SS. Giovanni e Paolo, is in a High Baroque tradition, S. Nicolò is more Classical in vein. A pedimented hexastyle portico of a type projected by Palladio, but new in Venice, is all that was built. The Corinthian columns respond to the pilasters of the inner facade. It is the extravagant oval in the pediment that distinguishes it from its Palladian ancestors and its neo-Classical descendants.

Luigi Vanvitelli (1700–73), the son of a Dutch landscape painter, was commissioned by Charles III of Naples to build the **Royal Palace, Caserta** (1752–) (p. 918A), situated twenty miles north of Naples. The vast palace, with its 1200 rooms, includes four courtyards arranged in a grid-like pattern reminiscent of the Escorial, Madrid (q.v.), or Inigo Jones's designs for Whitehall Palace. A love of symmetrical exactitude is revealed in the reiteration of the central octagonal vestibule in the two other entrance halls on the same axis. These open octagonal spaces provide a variety of vistas, often in several directions at once. Although the scenographic effects look back to Baroque interests, the austere plan and facades look towards the neo-Classical future.

Vanvitelli's design for the **Piazza Dante, Naples** (1755–67), transformed the concave sweep of seventeenth-century church and palace facades into a crescent. It is dominated at the centre by a clock tower set on a triumphal arch which in turn leads onto a street; this idea is not dissimilar to the gateways of French châteaux, but the vocabulary comes from Bernini's Piazza of S. Peter's (q.v.).

The **Tempietti, Villa Albani, Rome** (*c.* 1760), were designed for Cardinal Albani by Carlo Marchionni (1702–86) as garden pavilions for his new villa (begun 1746). Albani had as artistic adviser the most important theoretician of the age, J. J. Winckelmann. While the villa is late Baroque in style these tempietti take a fresh look at Classical antiquity. Similar in conception to eighteenth-century English follies, the Tempietto Diruto is built from spoils of ancient buildings. It was conceived not as a reconstruction of antiquity but as a ruinous symbol of transience.

While Michaelangelo Simonetti (1724–81) was the architect of the **Museo Pio Clementino, Vatican, Rome** (begun 1771), it was Pope Clement XIV who conceived the idea of transforming the northern end of the **Cortile del Belvedere** (q.v.) into a permanent museum. The sixteenth-century sculpture court of the Belvedere was transformed by the insertion of an octagonal colonnade. More impressive is the **Sala Rotonda** (1776–), a domed, cylindrical structure consisting of a ring of identical niches framed by an order of Composite pilasters. In the attic, thermae windows repeat the curve of the niches below and provide strong light for the exhibits. Echoes of Renaissance architecture are stronger in the **Sala a Croce Greca** (begun 1776) which, with its bevelled corners at the crossing, resembles Bramante's church designs. As at the Villa Albani Tempietti (q.v.), antique materials were employed in the construction; ancient granite columns and figures are used as supports while Roman mosaics are set into the floor.

The renovation by Giacomo Quarenghi (1744–1817) of the church of **S. Scolastica, Subiaco** (1774–77), was to provide a model for many subsequent neo-Classical church interiors. A simple barrel-vaulted nave is flanked by apsidal chapels. The vault is raised and widened at the chancel and the altar is set in an apse whose half-dome is supported by Ionic columns, creating a screen similar to that in Palladio's Redentore (q.v.). Apart from occasional garlands the wall surface is unadorned.

La Scala, Milan (1776–8) (p. 918B), by Giuseppe Piermarini (1734–1808) is one of many theatres built in the late eighteenth century. The seven-bay facade has an arcaded ground floor with flat banded rustication, while the upper level is articulated with an order of paired Composite columns. The attic is crowned by an historiated pediment characteristic of the late settecento. The flamboyant curvilinear approach to design and the surface decoration which typified the earlier part of the century have been replaced by a sobriety that looks back to French architecture.

The **Palazzo Serbelloni, Milan** (1780–94), by Simone Cantoni, is more impressive than his **Palazzo Ducale, Genoa**. In the former, a long fifteen-bay facade has a pedimented three-bay central section. Relief is created not by projections but by recession of the wall plane, necessitating full columns to support the entablature. Thus the column is conceived not as an ornament but as a functional support. The sense of depth in this shallow space is intensified by the inclusion of a balustrade, and by the continuous relief running behind the order. The lunette window in the pediment is inventively treated as a balustraded loggia.

Leopold Pollack (1751–1806), a Viennese architect, who had worked under Piermarini, designed the **Villa Reale Belgioioso, Milan** (1790–3). French influence can be detected in the plan: the courtyard is entered through a screen wall and two low wings flank a *corps de logis*. Apart from the Doric entrance and Ionic frontispiece the courtyard is astylar, in strong contrast to the elaborate garden facade.

The late eighteenth and early nineteenth centuries saw the erection of many city gateways in Milan. The **Porta Ticinese, Milan** (1801–14), designed by Luigi Cagnola (1762–1833), has the appearance more of a tempietto than a gate. Isolated from its attendant custom houses it is a symbolic rather than functional structure, modelled on the Roman Portico of Octavia; two pedimented temple fronts are set back to back with arches set into the sides. Other impressive Milanese gates of this period include Rodolfo Vantini's **Porta Venezia** (1827–33), Giuseppe Zanoia's **Porta Nuova** and Giacomo Moraglia's **Porta Carnasina**.

Il Ginnasio, Orto Botanico, Palermo (1789–92), is the work of Leon Dufourny (1754–1818), a French architect working at the Sicilian court. His studies with the archaeologist Le Roy are strongly reflected in its design. The cuboid block has a Doric order which is deliberately archaic in its detail. The exaggerated entasis of the Doric shafts, the heavy entablature and the encircling steps are all characteristics of the temple architecture of ancient Magna Graecia, especially Paestum (q.v.).

The **Palazzina Cinese, Villa della Favorita, Palermo** (1799–1802), sometimes ascribed to Giuseppe Marvuglia and sometimes to Giuseppe Patricola, was born of a similar orientalism to that which created the Brighton Pavilion (q.v.). A light airy effect is achieved through the use of a supporting skeletal structure. The desire to remove the wall surface is especially apparent in the open minaret-like staircase. The curved eaves of the portico mimicked by the gate posts are Chinese in inspiration, but Islamic and Pompeian art forms also make their appearance. Such delight in combining varieties of exoticism can also be found in G. D. Tiepolo's frescos in the Villa Valmarana ai Nani, near Vicenza.

The work of Giuseppe Valadier (1762–1839) reflects a familiarity with current trends in French architecture. His **Arch on the Ponte Milvio, Rome** (1805), was the successor to both antique and Renaissance arches on the same site. Valadier abandoned the time-honoured triumphal arch for a design with a more military character. Any reference to the orders has been omitted in the two superimposed cuboid blocks. Fortification is implied by the battering of the basement and the use of flat banded rustication. The massive voussoirs of the arch break forward from the receding wall plane, lending a sense of weight to the structure.

In less sombre vein is Valadier's redevelopment of the **Giardino del Pincio, Rome** (1806–14). An impressive three-bay loggia housing an equestrian monument was set against the vertical terrace wall. Above he created a casino enjoying wonderful views towards S. Peter's. A semicircular Ionic portico decorates the entrance to the building and the Ionic character is continued at the sides, where free-standing columns frivolously bear urns.

The most famous work by Giuseppe Japelli (1783–1852) is the Caffè Pedrocchi, Padua (1816–42) (q.v.). This widely travelled and knowledgeable architect created one of the most splendid examples of this new building type. Run as a gentleman's club, it included dining and billiard rooms as well as libraries and a ballroom. The facade has two projecting Doric porches which frame a huge recessed Corinthian loggia on the first storey. Elements from both Greek and Roman Revivals are evident: a Roman-inspired frieze appears above baseless Greek Doric columns in the porches. (See Chapter 34.)

The **Tempio Canova, Possagno** (1819–33), was designed in collaboration by Giovanni Antonio Selva (1753–1819) and the great neo-Classical sculptor Antonio Canova (1757–1822). The building dominates Canova's birthplace and houses his tomb.

It was inspired by the Pantheon, one of the architectural preoccupations of the age; but as in other contemporary derivatives, such as the cemetery temples of Brescia and Verona, the model has been Hellenised. The Corinthian order of the original is replaced by Greek Doric, and the surface decoration has been minimised so as not to obscure the fundamental geometric forms.

The impressive **Cisternone, Livorno** (1829–42), designed by Pasquale Poccianti (1774–1858), has a facade reminiscent of the drawings of Etienne Boullée (q.v.). The wall is unadorned except for the window openings, some appropriately thermal, while the centre is marked by a severely Doric portico and crowned by a vast niche resembling a cross-section of the Pantheon.

Chapter 30

FRANCE, SPAIN AND PORTUGAL

Architectural Character

France

French architectural development from 1494 to 1830 may for convenience be divided into three stylistic periods:

1 The French Renaissance (1494–1610), the period from the Italian wars to the death of Henry IV, the reigns of Charles VIII (1483–98), Louis XII (1498–1515), François I (1515–47), Henri II (1547–59), François II (1559–60), Charles IX (1560–74), Henri III (1574–89), Henri IV (1589–1610)
2 The Classical period (1610–1715), the reigns of Louis XIII (1610–43) and XIV (1643–1715)
3 Rococo and neo-Classical (1715–1830)

The French Renaissance

The Italian campaigns of Charles VIII and Louis XII encouraged the introduction of a new architectural style that was influenced by antiquity only at second hand, through imported Italian craftsmen and architectural books. Initially Renaissance detail was merely grafted on to traditional building types – towered châteaux and churches with Gothic vaults, buttresses and pinnacles. In château architecture the orders were used to link window-frames and frontispieces into vertical sections, and to embellish fantastically ornamented dormers and chimneys. In church architecture, too, Gothic ideas of proportions and stone-cutting remained, despite a veneer of Renaissance vocabulary. Under François I, Rosso and Primaticcio initiated the Fontainebleau style of decoration, with its reliance on strap-work, grotesques, and etiolated stucco figures; through engravings this manner became widely diffused elsewhere in Europe.

The arrival in France (1540) of Sebastiano Serlio (1475–1555) and the visits to Italy of Philibert de l'Orme (*c.* 1510–70) and Jean Bullant (*c.* 1520/5–78) encouraged a more confident use of the orders as articulation rather than surface trim. The Louvre facade of Pierre Lescot (1500–78) is comparable with the earliest buildings of Palladio in its masterly handling of Renaissance pilaster orders and sculptural detail. Philibert's vocabulary is more massive and columnar, but far from rule-bound: he proposed a 'French order' with banded decoration to conceal the joints. Bullant introduced giant orders and syncopated rhythms in château architecture, while Jacques Androuet du Cerceau the Elder (*c.* 1520–84) favoured fantastic and wilful surface decoration. The late sixteenth century brought a fondness for verticality and rustication: highly characteristic of the period 1580–1620 is the use of rusticated quoins, chaînes and window-surrounds alternating with vertical bands of brickwork, a formula that continues into the early work of Jean Androuet du Cerceau (*c.* 1585–1649) and of François Mansart (1598–1666).

The Classical Period

The use of the word 'Classical' to characterise seventeenth-century French architecture is not intended to imply a direct imitation of antique models, but rather to indicate a preference in that period for qualities of logic, balance and clarity. Two highly individual figures mark a transitional phase at the beginning of the period: Pierre Le Muet (1591–1669), whose Hôtel d'Assy, Paris, has an impressive courtyard with giant pilasters, and Salomon de Brosse (1571–1626), whose massive architecture is marked by a powerful sense of three dimensions.

The greatest architects of the Classical period are Jacques Lemercier (1585–1654), François Mansart (1598–1666) and Louis Le Vau (1612–70). Lemercier introduced into French architecture the sober but rhythmical language of the later sixteenth century in Rome; his two-storey church facades are strongly influenced by Giacomo della Porta (q.v.). Mansart's mature work is similarly majestic and restrained, with much use of paired superimposed orders, simple pediments and, of course, the double-pitched roof that

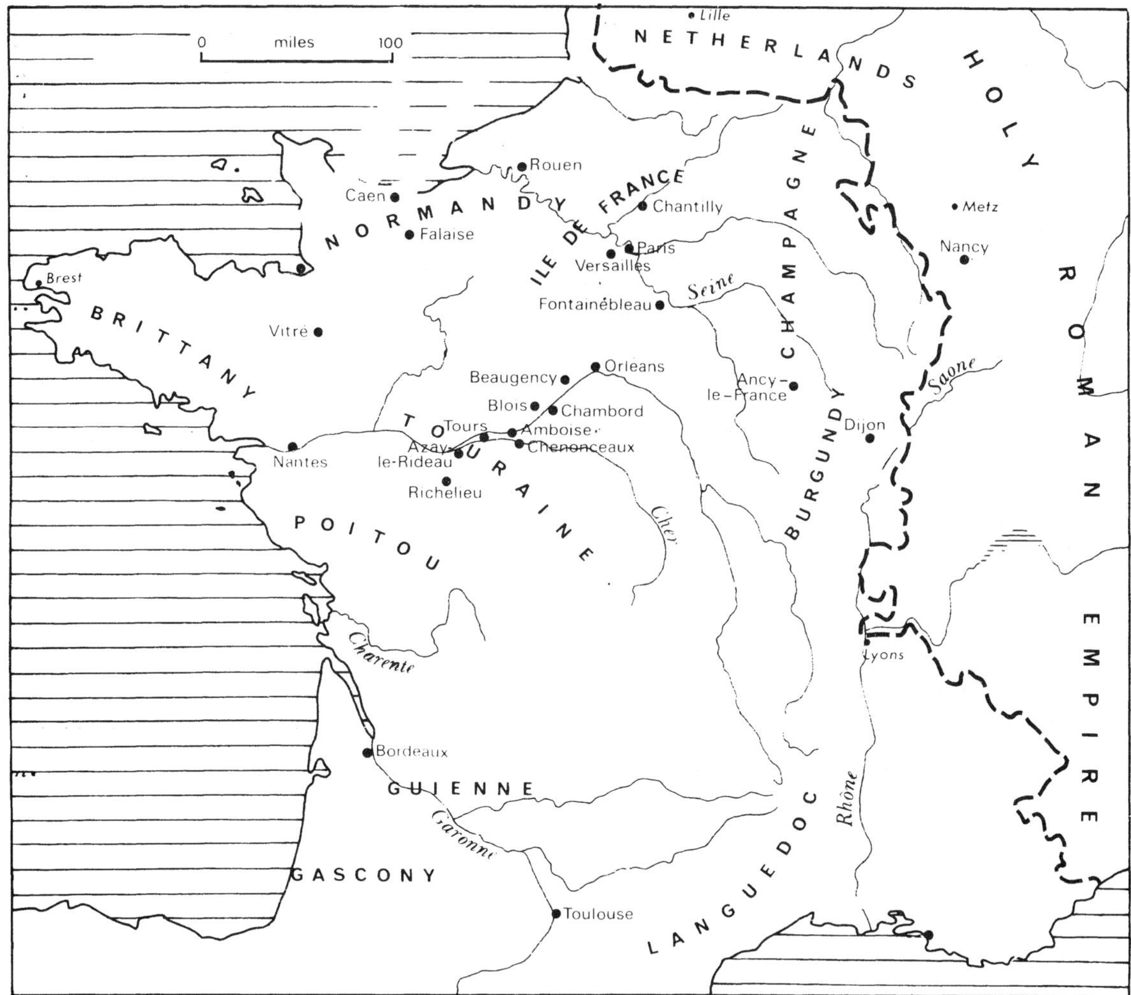

France in the sixteenth century

bears his name. On the whole, seventeenth-century France resisted the Baroque, and Bernini's designs for the Louvre found no favour. Louis Le Vau (1612–70) comes the closest to the dramatic build-ups and theatrical effects of the Baroque in his facade for the Collège des Quatre Nations (q.v.). An enduring motif of French architecture is the screen of free-standing paired columns against a closed wall, first found in the east front of the Louvre (1667–), and perhaps due to Claude Perrault (1613–88).

J. H. Mansart (1646–1708) and Germain Boffrand (1667–1754) are the most interesting architects of the later seventeenth and early eighteenth centuries, both notable for their ingenious use of variously shaped rooms in château planning and for a highly sculptural approach to facades. Interior decoration grew ever more brilliantly diffuse during the period, with the use of scrolls, nymphs, wreaths and shells in stucco and papier-mâché. Boffrand's later interiors were very influential on the Rococo in Germany (for example, the Residenz, Würzburg).

Rococo and Neo-Classical

French Rococo was essentially a style of interiors, and no stylistic break is evident in the design of facades, which become, if anything, simpler and less reliant on the orders, often using vertical pilaster *chaînes*. This is an architecture of intimate comfortable residences, with greater separation of private and public apartments, and much use of rounded corners and sinuous curves. Rococo decoration, particularly associated with J. A. Meissonier (1695–1750), is characterised by asymmetrical arabesques, the use of 'C' and 'S' curves, and the scalloped shellwork known as 'rocaille'. For reasons of decorum, Rococo had little part in the design of French churches.

The neo-Classical movement in France drew on the long traditions of Classically based teaching in the Academy of Architecture in Paris, as well as the new, more archaeological ideas emanating from Legeay and the French Academy in Rome. Initially, as is evident in the work of Ange-Jacques Gabriel (1698–1782), it was as much a return to the Italian sixteenth century and the French seventeenth century as to antiquity itself. The Abbé Laugier's *Essai sur l'architecture* (1753), with its emphasis on the structural logic of the orders, was echoed in Soufflot's S. Geneviève (Panthéon, 1757–), combining the ancient orders with a Gothic structural lightness. Claude Ledoux (1736–1806) moved gradually towards the simplified primitive vocabulary of block-like shapes and robust Doric forms associated with revolutionary neo-Classicism, although his works in this style date to the last years of the Ancien Régime. A further reduction is found in Etienne-Louis Boullée's utopian designs, which speak in a symbolic rather than a functional language of megalomaniac pyramids, spheres and cylinders. The rational, functionalist side of neo-Classicism was given theoretical expression in the enormously influential writings of J. N. L. Durand (1760–1834), delivered as lectures at the new Ecole Polytechnique. The Napoleonic period, despite the popularity of Greek and Egyptian styles in furniture and interior design, saw a return to ancient Roman models in the architecture of Charles Percier (1764–1838) and Pierre François Léonard Fontaine (1762–1853), J.-F. -T. Chalgrin (1739–1811) and Pierre Vignon (1762–1828).

Examples

France 1500–1600

The **Château de Gaillon** (1502–10) was built partly using Italian craftsmen by Cardinal Georges d'Amboise, Archbishop of Rouen, who was chief minister of Louis XII, Viceroy of Milan, and a pioneering patron of Renaissance art in France. The main entrance, though in the traditional form of a fortified gate tower, uses Italianate pilasters to unite the mullioned windows into vertically continuous panels.

The original appearance of the **Cháteau de Bury** (1511–24) (p. 925G,H), now ruined, is known from a drawing by du Cerceau. Built for Florimond Robertet, a former courtier of Louis XII, it set the pattern for sixteenth-century château design. A square four-towered main court is entered by a fortified gateway, with a long gallery to the right and minor rooms and entrance to a service court on the left. The main apartments (*corps de logis*), one room deep, were placed between the main court and the garden. Apart from the colonnade on the entrance wing, Renaissance detail was confined to window panels and dormers, while the elevations were bound together horizontally by continuous string courses.

The first part of the **Château de Chenonceaux** (1515–23) (pp. 926G,927A) was the simple rectangular four-towered block with steeply pitched roof standing on piles in the River Cher. An Italianate straight staircase with landings opens off the long central corridor that bisects the building. The five-arched bridge was added by Philibert de l'Orme (q.v.) for Diane de Poitiers (1556–9); the gallery above, with its 'mannerist' windows, is due to Jean Bullant (q.v.) (1576).

The **Château d'Azay le Rideau** (1518–27) (p. 927B), built by Gilles Berthelot, has a compact, towered L-shaped plan, surrounded by a moat. The horizontal and vertical panelling of windows and string courses is interrupted by the fantastic entrance pavilion where the arbitrarily proportioned orders are interspersed with Gothic niches and sculptural panels.

Building in the Loire was promoted by François I who brought the court there for much of the year. At **Blois** (1515–24) (p. 925A–F,928A) he added a wing to the existing mediaeval château. The court facade (much restored) has panelled mullions and vertically linked pilaster strips, crowned by a complex would be Classical cornice; it is dominated by the projecting polygonal open-work staircase enriched with the emblems of François I. The facade over the town has superimposed loggias surmounted by an open colonnade terrace under the roof, the whole arrangement recalling the Vatican loggias of Bramante and Raphael. The château was completed (1635–8) by François Mansart (q.v.) for Gaston d'Orléans, and the other courtyard facades are his.

The second of Francois's buildings, the **Château de Chambord** (1519–47) (pp. 926C,F,H,928B,929), is the most exciting of the Loire châteaux in plan and structure. The original wooden model was by an Italian, Domenico da Cortona, but was much altered in execution. Leonardo da Vinci, who designed a palace for François at Romorantin, may have been involved. At first sight mediaeval in plan, with a four-towered square 'donjon' inside a rectangular four-towered enceinte, Chambord has a Renaissance vigour of design. Four rectangular vaulted halls on each floor form a cross-shape, meeting in the centre with the spectacular double-helix open-work staircase, where people can ascend and descend simultaneously without meeting. This and the subsidiary staircases are crowned with lanterns. In the corners of the cross and in the towers are separate apartments composed of hall, bedchamber and 'cabinet'. The base of the steep roofs, which are punctuated with fantastic dormers and chimneys of varied heights, is a

CHATEAU DE BLOIS

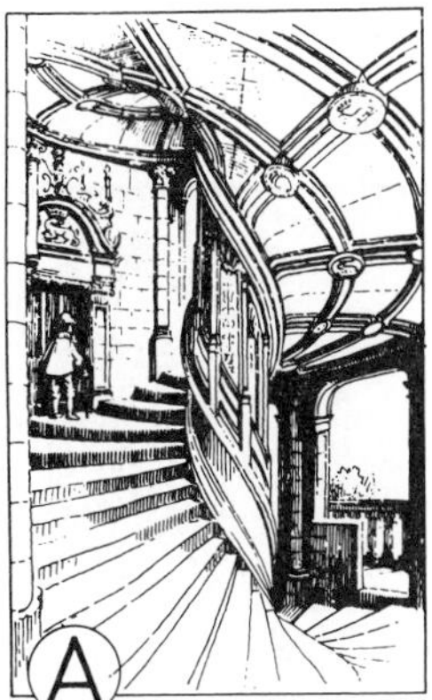

A STAIRCASE TOWER (FRANCIS I)

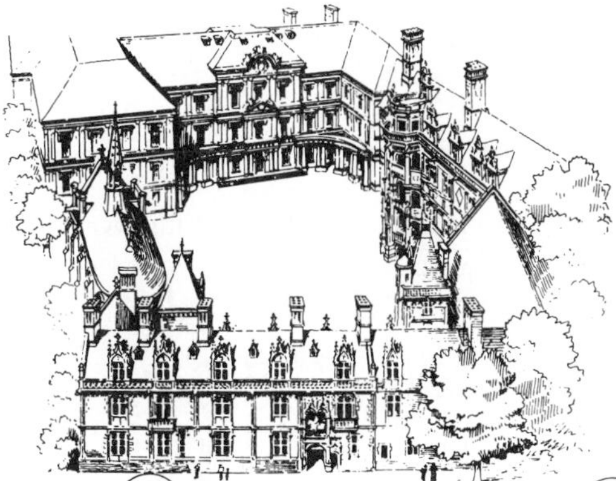

B BIRD'S-EYE VIEW

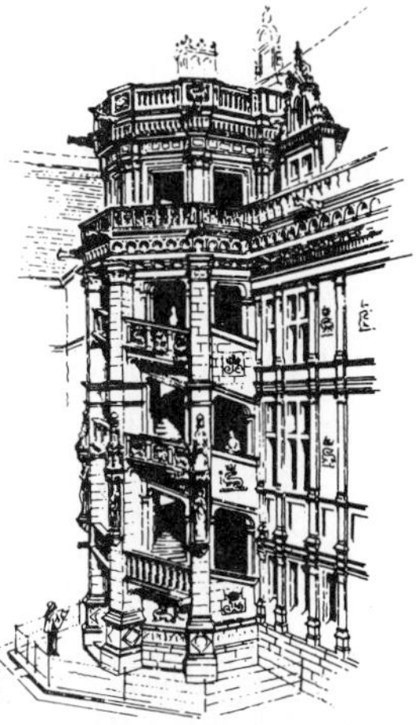

C STAIRCASE TOWER (FRANCIS I) AT X

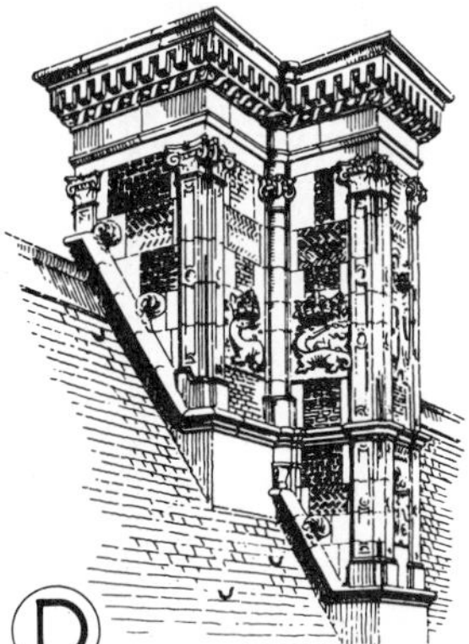

D CHIMNEY STACK (FRANCIS I)

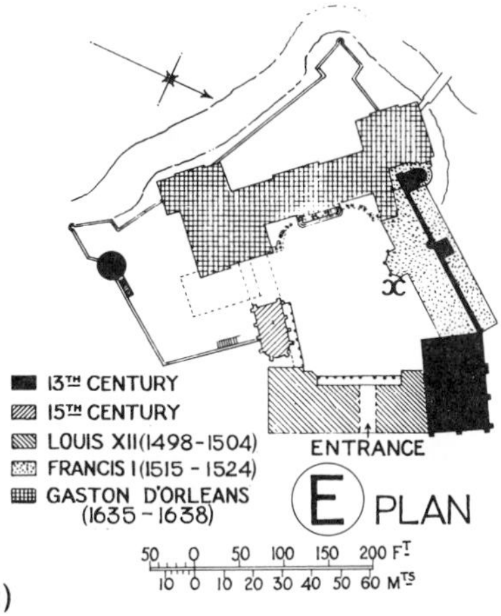

X
13TH CENTURY
15TH CENTURY
LOUIS XII (1498-1504)
FRANCIS I (1515-1524)
GASTON D'ORLEANS (1635-1638)
ENTRANCE
50 0 50 100 150 200 FT
10 0 10 20 30 40 50 60 MTS

E PLAN

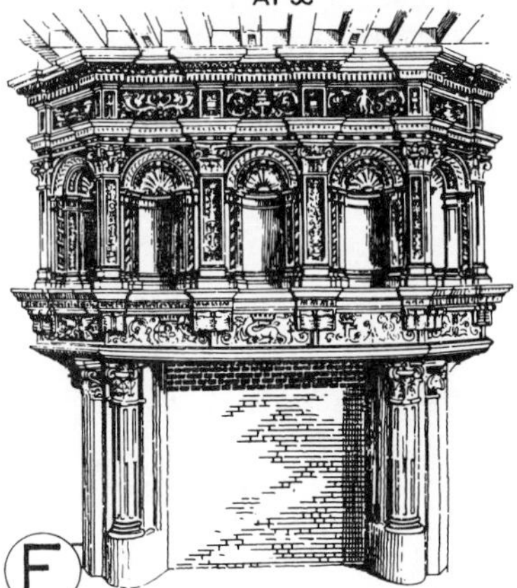

F CHIMNEY-PIECE (FRANCIS I)

CHATEAU DE BURY

MOAT
CHAPEL
GARDEN
GARDEN
160.0
MOAT
50 0 50 100 FT
10 0 10 20 30 MTS
COURT
MOAT
MOAT
ENTRANCE

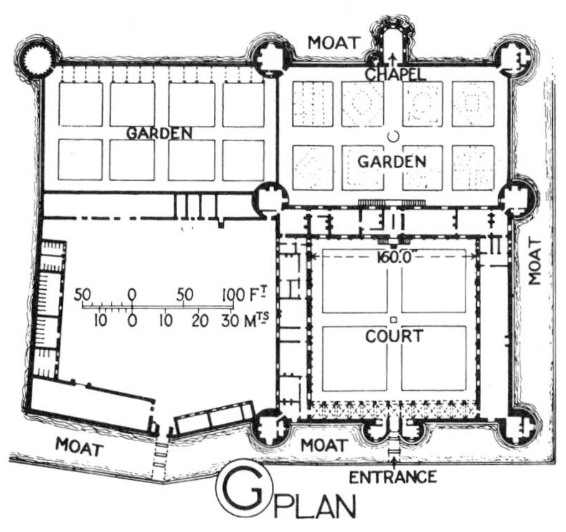

G PLAN

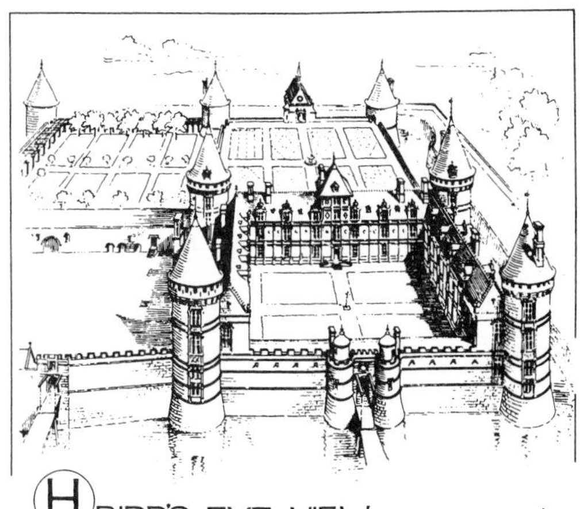

H BIRD'S-EYE VIEW (RESTORED)

A FRONT VIEW
B SIDE VIEW
CAP. PALAIS DE FONTAINEBLEAU
1533
C CAP. CHATEAU DE CHAMBORD
D PANEL: PALAIS DE FONTAINEBLEAU
E PANEL: PALAIS DE FONTAINEBLEAU
F CAP. CHATEAU DE CHAMBORD
PLAN OF NICHE
ROOF
SECTION
ELEVATION
PLAN
G DOORWAY CHATEAU DE CHENONCEAUX
ELEVATION
PLAN
H DORMER WINDOW: CHATEAU DE CHAMBORD

A. Château de Chenonceaux (1515–23). See p. 924

B. Château d'Azay le Rideau (1518–27). See p. 924

A. Château de Blois (1515–24). See p. 924

B. Château de Chambord (1519–47). See p. 924

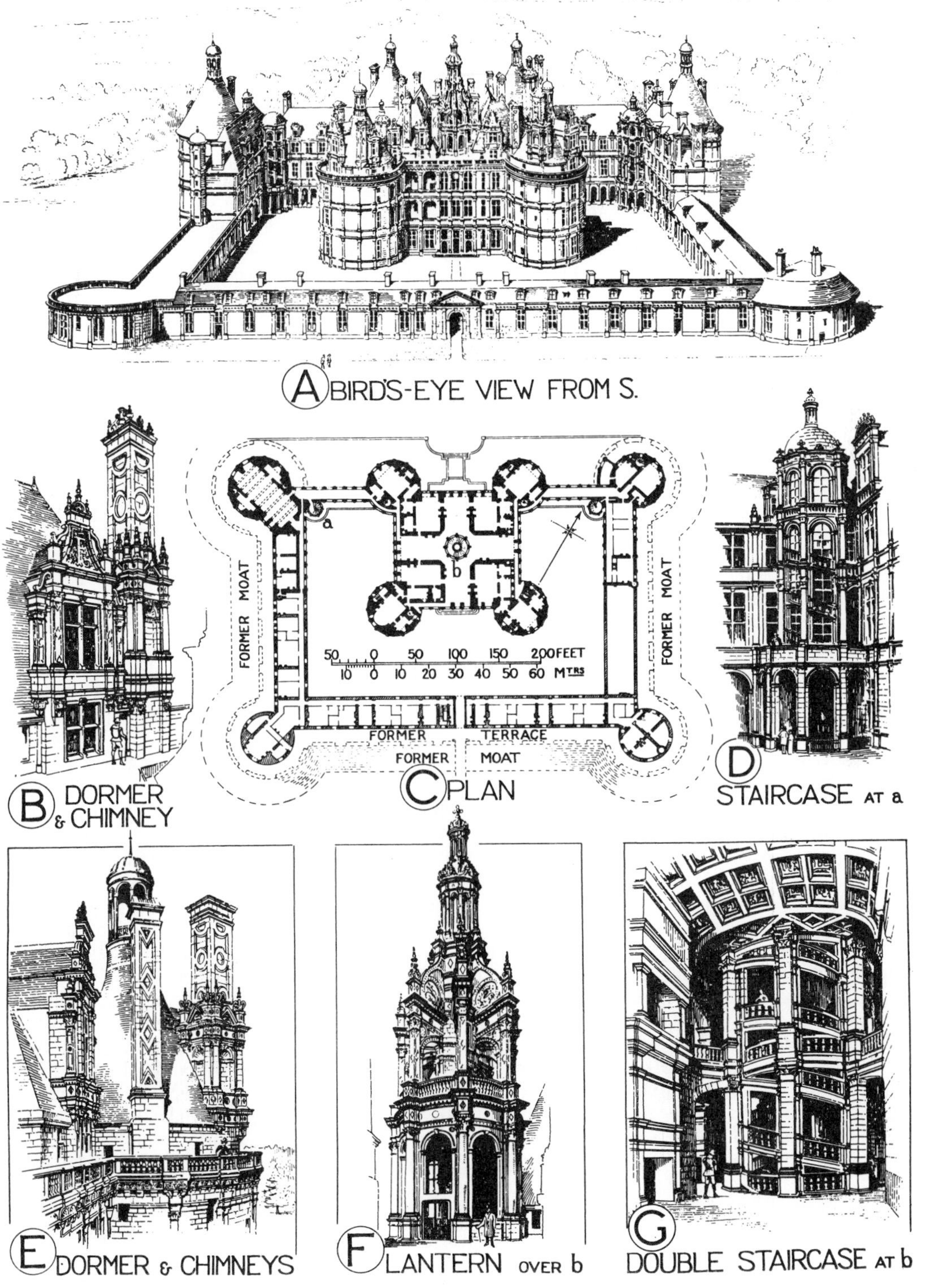
CHATEAU DE CHAMBORD
A BIRD'S-EYE VIEW FROM S.
B DORMER & CHIMNEY
C PLAN
FORMER MOAT
FORMER TERRACE
FORMER MOAT
a
b
50 0 50 100 150 200 FEET
10 0 10 20 30 40 50 60 MTRS
D STAIRCASE AT a
E DORMER & CHIMNEYS
F LANTERN OVER b
G DOUBLE STAIRCASE AT b

flat terrace which both repeats the cross-plan and continues with a balustrade all around the exterior of the donjon. The detailed carving shows the individual hands of many masons, both French and German.

The **Château de Madrid, Paris** (1528–, destroyed) marked François I's decision to base himself in Paris. The plan was of two square blocks of apartments linked by a recessed wing containing the main *salles*. Superimposed loggias between towers articulated the exterior, and coloured terracotta work by Girolamo della Robbia was found both inside and out. The **Château de S. Germain** and **La Muette de Saint-Germain** were built at the same period by Pierre Chambiges and his successors.

The portions of the **Palais de Fontainebleau** (pp. 926A,B,D,E,931B) constructed under François I were built by Gilles le Breton (died 1553). François added to an older structure the Porte Dorée, with its superimposed arches flanked by pilastered towers punctuated with vertically connected tabernacle windows; the effect is somewhat like the Ducal Palace at Urbino (q.v.). The Cour du Cheval Blanc is soberly articulated with brick or stone pilasters against white plaster, but is now chiefly notable for Jean du Cerceau's flamboyant double-curved staircase. The most remarkable of François' additions to Fontainebleau was the gallery (p. 931A), with painted and stucco decoration by the Italian painter Rosso (1494–1540) which set the pattern for the 'School of Fontainebleau'. The other important Italian painter at Fontainebleau, Francesco Primaticcio (1504/5–70), became the architect of the building in the 1540s, designing the Grotte des Pins (*c.* 1543) in the manner of Giulio Romano (atlas figures are applied to a rusticated facade) and the Aile de la Belle Cheminée (1568) which recalls the more frigid 'correctness' of Vignola; this is a long wing with pavilions at the corners and superimposed triumphal-arch motifs in the centre. From the main door, exterior ramped staircases rise to the pavilions at either side.

Church building of the first fifty years of the century is marked by the grafting of Renaissance detail on to Gothic structures. **S. Etienne du Mont, Paris** (1517–) (p. 932A), has a curious nave system with superimposed arcades and a gallery between; the famous rood screen (jubé) with its cantilevered spiral staircase (*c.* 1545) has been attributed to Philibert de l'Orme but is rather crude in execution. The centre of the facade, added 1610–25, has a triangular pedimented triumphal arch supported by ribbed Corinthian half-columns, continued up into a segmental broken pediment surrounding the rose window.

S. Eustache, Paris (1532–1640) (p. 932B), has a Notre Dame-like Gothic plan but Renaissance detail; on the interior the orders are stretched like ribbons, compressed like telescopes and arbitrarily superimposed to fit the pier clusters. The general effect remains Gothic, with an impressively majestic sense of space. The sober superimposed temple-front facade (1754–) is by Jean Hardouin Mansart de Jouy.

At **S. Michel, Dijon** (1537–), the effect of round arches and superimposed orders in a two-towered facade is curiously akin to Romanesque.

Sebastiano Serlio (1475–1555) arrived in France from Italy in 1540, after publishing the enormously influential Books IV and III of his architectural treatise in Venice (1537 and 1540). He continued to publish in France, and is more important as a writer than as a practising architect. Of his buildings, the **Château d'Ancy le Franc** in Burgundy (*c.* 1546–), built for Antoine de Clerment-Tonnerre, is the most complete. Variant projects appear in his Book VI on domestic building. It is a four-towered structure, with a square central courtyard. The pilaster articulation is entirely Doric on the exterior and Corinthian in the courtyard, where the triumphal-arch rhythm is derived from Bramante's Cortile del Belvedere (q.v.) The decoration of the interior, by Primaticcio, Niccolo dell'Abbate, Philippe Quantin and others, is impressively complete.

Serlio's house, **Le Grand Ferrare, Fontainebleau** (1544–6), for the papal nuncio, Cardinal Ippolito d'Este (builder of the Villa d'Este, Tivoli (q.v.)), though now lost, had a great influence on French hôtel design. Serlio's drawings show three wings one room deep around a courtyard, closed off from the street by a screen wall with rusticated entrance doorway (still extant). The *corps de logis* at the back of the courtyard had a suite of rooms lit from both court and garden. To the left was a long gallery and chapel, to the right service rooms and a stable court.

François I initiated the rebuilding of the mediaeval palace of the **Louvre, Paris** (1546–) (pp. 933B,934). Pierre Lescot (1500–78) redesigned the first wing of the Cour Carrée, revealing an ability to use the Italian language of the orders to entirely French ends. The nine-bay facade (to the left of the later Pavillon d'Horloge) is punctuated by three triumphal-arch-like frontispieces, the whole festively arrayed in Composite over Corinthian with superb relief sculpture by Goujon in the attic zone. Catherine de Médicis continued Lescot's design round the south side of the court and conceived the idea of connecting the Louvre and the **Palais des Tuileries** (p. 933A), begun for her by Philibert de l'Orme, with a gallery along the Seine, a scheme not fully realised for some 300 years.

Lescot's **Hôtel Carnavalet, Paris** (1550–), is in plan a smaller version of Serlio's Grand Ferrare. The rusticated entrance (somewhat in the manner of Giulio Romano's house in Mantua, q.v.) was originally a screen between two high pavilions. This and the courtyard were completed by Mansart and 'restored' in the nineteenth century. The rear courtyard facade of the *corps de logis* is Lescot's up to the second cornice, using wide relief panels of the seasons (sculpted in the manner of Goujon) instead of

A. Palais de Fontainebleau: Galerie de François I. See p. 930

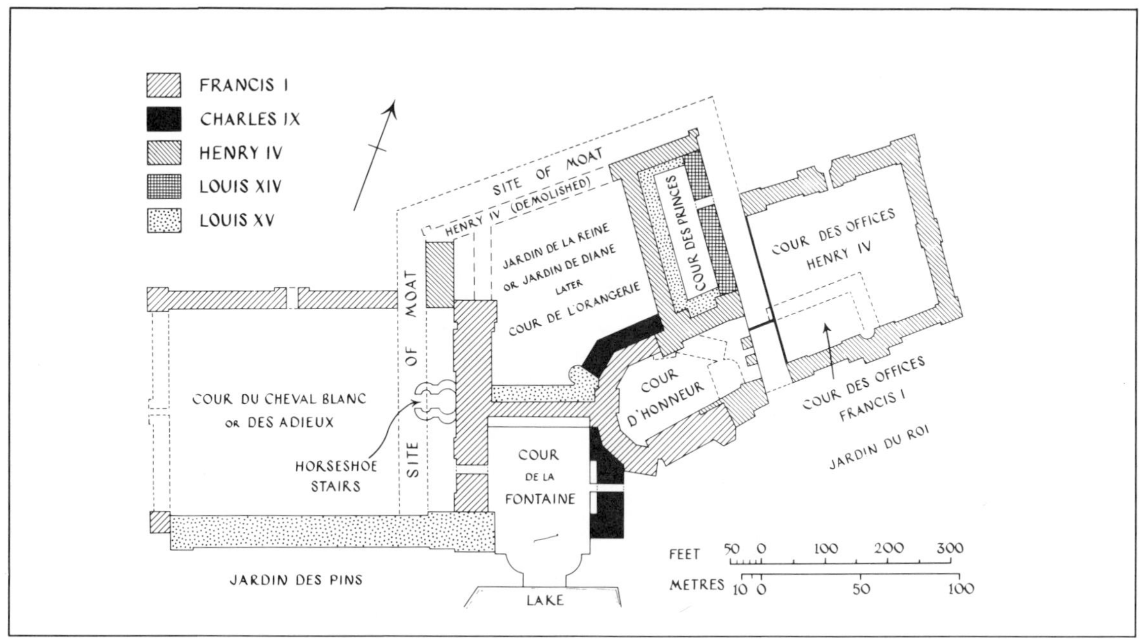

B. Palais de Fontainebleau: plan showing dates of erection

A. (*above*)
S. Etienne du Mont, Paris (1517–): showing jubé (*c.* 1545; screens across aisles 1606). See p. 930

B. (*left*)
S. Eustache, Paris (1532–1640). See p. 930

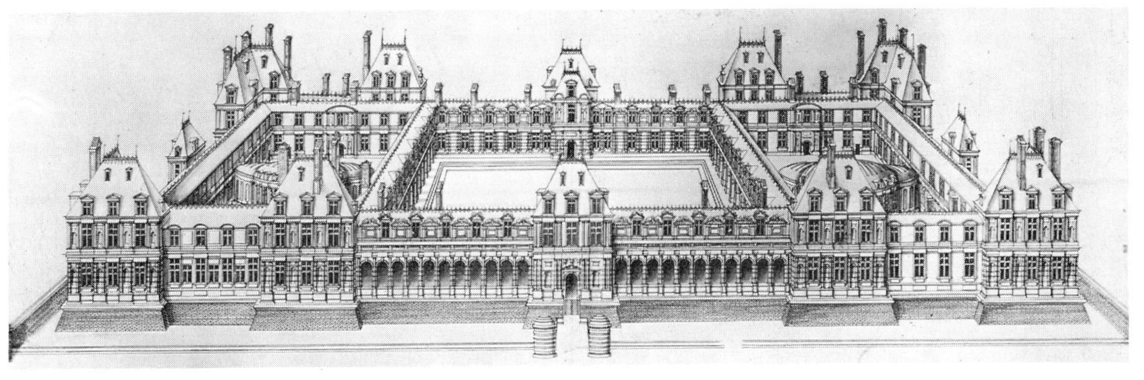

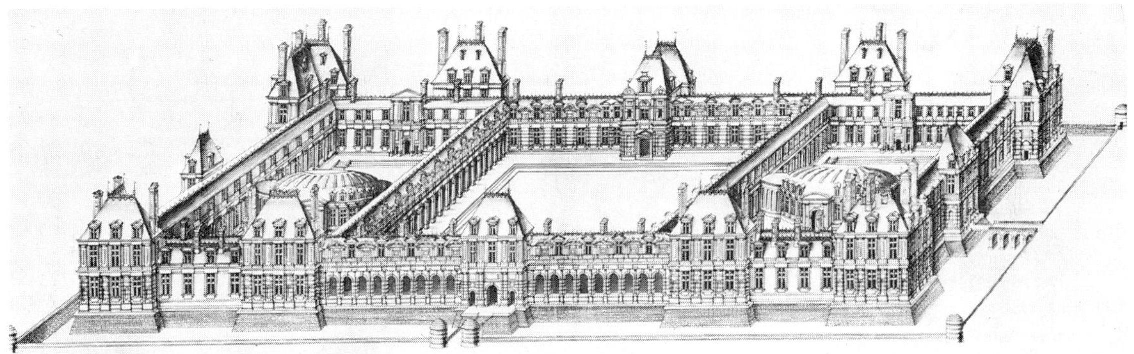

A. Palais des Tuileries, Paris (destroyed); drawings by J. A. du Cerceau I made in 1579. (*Above*) view from west, (*below*) view from east. See p. 930

B. (*right*) Palais du Louvre, Paris: Galerie d'Apollon (decorated by Lebrun 1662). See p. 930

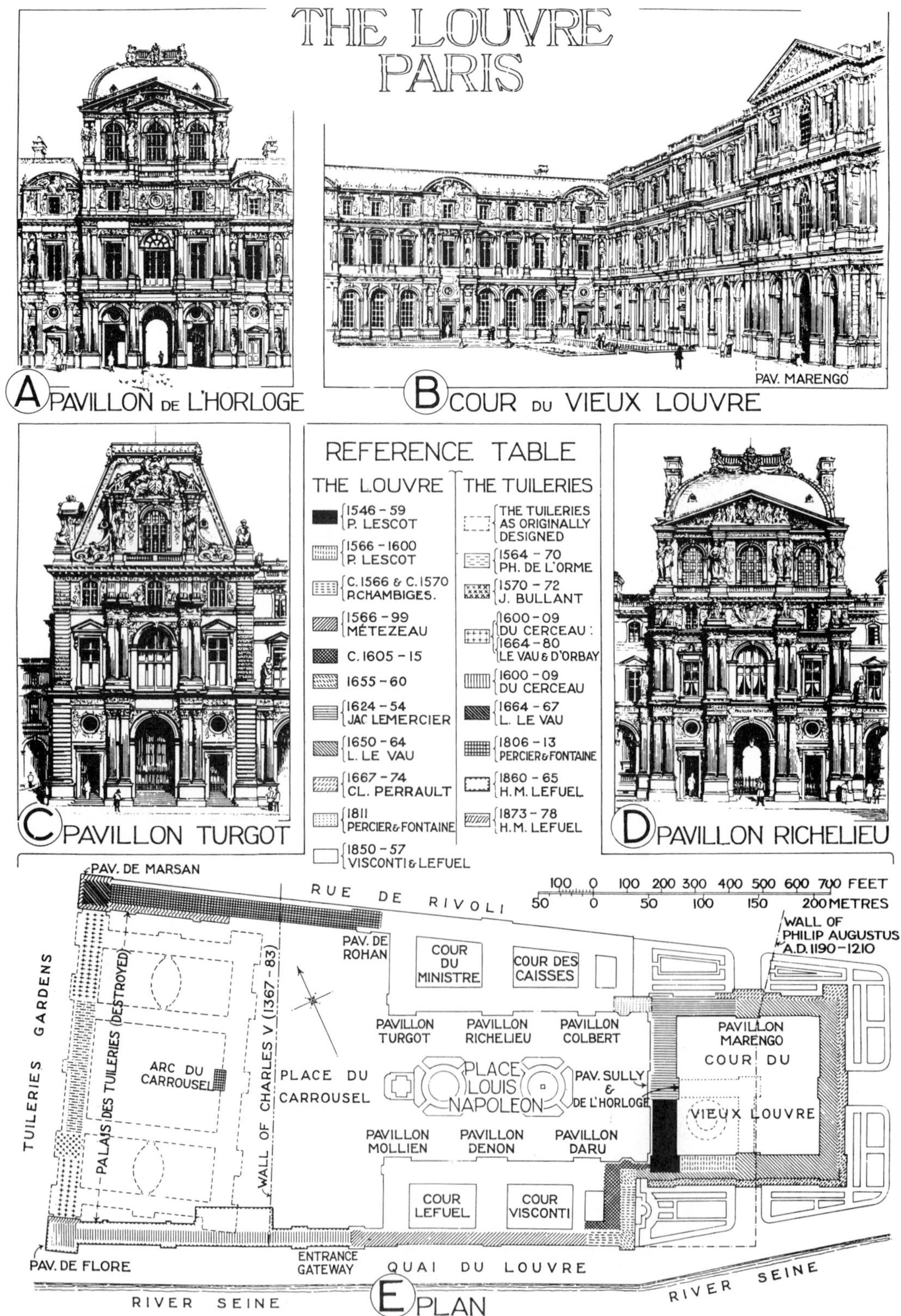
THE LOUVRE
PARIS
A PAVILLON DE L'HORLOGE
B COUR DU VIEUX LOUVRE
PAV. MARENGO
C PAVILLON TURGOT
D PAVILLON RICHELIEU
REFERENCE TABLE
THE LOUVRE
1546 - 59 P. LESCOT
1566 - 1600 P. LESCOT
C. 1566 & C. 1570 P. CHAMBIGES.
1566 - 99 MÉTEZEAU
C. 1605 - 15
1655 - 60
1624 - 54 JAC LEMERCIER
1650 - 64 L. LE VAU
1667 - 74 CL. PERRAULT
1811 PERCIER & FONTAINE
1850 - 57 VISCONTI & LEFUEL
THE TUILERIES
THE TUILERIES AS ORIGINALLY DESIGNED
1564 - 70 PH. DE L'ORME
1570 - 72 J. BULLANT
1600 - 09 DU CERCEAU : 1664 - 80 LE VAU & D'ORBAY
1600 - 09 DU CERCEAU
1664 - 67 L. LE VAU
1806 - 13 PERCIER & FONTAINE
1860 - 65 H. M. LEFUEL
1873 - 78 H. M. LEFUEL
PAV. DE MARSAN
RUE DE RIVOLI
100 0 100 200 300 400 500 600 700 FEET
50 0 50 100 150 200 METRES
WALL OF PHILIP AUGUSTUS A.D. 1190 - 1210
PAV. DE ROHAN
COUR DU MINISTRE
COUR DES CAISSES
TUILERIES GARDENS
PALAIS DES TUILERIES (DESTROYED)
WALL OF CHARLES V (1367 - 83)
ARC DU CARROUSEL
PLACE DU CARROUSEL
PAVILLON TURGOT
PAVILLON RICHELIEU
PAVILLON COLBERT
PAVILLON MARENGO
COUR DU VIEUX LOUVRE
PLACE LOUIS NAPOLEON
PAV. SULLY & DE L'HORLOGE
PAVILLON MOLLIEN
PAVILLON DENON
PAVILLON DARU
COUR LEFUEL
COUR VISCONTI
PAV. DE FLORE
ENTRANCE GATEWAY
QUAI DU LOUVRE
RIVER SEINE
E PLAN
RIVER SEINE

an order. Despite its transformations, the Carnavalet is the best-preserved example of a mid-sixteenth-century hôtel.

Philibert de l'Orme (*c.* 1510–70) is the best-known French architect of the sixteenth century, partly because of his two architectural treatises (1561 and 1567). He combined knowledge of Italy and ancient Rome (spending three years in Rome 1533–6) with mastery of French engineering in stone (stereotomy).

For Henry II's mistress, Diane de Poitiers, Philibert designed the **Château d'Anet** in Normandy (1541–63) (p. 936B), of which only the chapel and entrance gate survive *in situ*, while the frontispiece from the courtyard, with its superimposed orders, is now in the Ecole des Beaux-Arts, Paris. Compared with Lescot's Cour Carrée (q.v.), Philibert's frontispiece is bolder, more three-dimensional and less refined, with its free-standing columns and polychrome detail. The chapel is circular in plan, and directly derived from the antique. The gateway is an eccentric pile of disparately shaped elements.

Jean Bullant (*c.* 1520–78) was a gifted architect and writer of two treatises (1563 and 1564), little of whose built work survives. He introduced the giant order into French architecture in the pavilion added (*c.* 1560) to the **Château d'Ecouen** (1538–55), north of Paris, where the lateral niches were intended to house Michelangelo's *Dying and Rebellious Slaves*. Ecouen follows the square four-towered pattern of earlier châteaux but is notable for its frontispieces, elaborate dormers and the clarity of its internal planning, with much original decoration of fireplaces and friezes.

Bullant's originality may be seen at the **Petit Château, Chantilly** (*c.* 1560–) (p. 936A), designed for the same patron as at Ecouen, the Constable of France, Anne de Montmorency. It stands in a lake setting around three sides of a courtyard adjoining the old château (rebuilt in the nineteenth century). This is a building full of surprises, where every facade is different from, but entirely consistent with, the next. Most original is the use of an order which spans the storeys but is in turn broken through by the bizarre upper windows which continue as dormers. The rhythm is syncopated but ingeniously controlled.

Jacques Androuet du Cerceau the Elder (1520–84), founder of a dynasty of architects, is best known for his books of architecture (1559–) with engravings of contemporary buildings and projects (see Chapter 28). He also designed two important châteaux, **Verneuil** (1568) and **Charleval** (1570–) for Charles IX, both lost. The facades as published by du Cerceau contain a wealth of extravagant detail.

The **Hôtel Lamoignan, Paris** (1584–), by Louis Métezeau, built for Diane de France, natural daughter of Henri II, is the most sophisticated Parisian hôtel of the later sixteenth century. The giant Corinthian pilasters of the courtyard, with their segments of pulvinated frieze interrupted by dormer windows, show a thorough knowledge of both Michelangelo and late Palladio.

In the provinces outside the circle of the court, French sixteenth-century architecture reflects the diversity of local traditions, influences and building materials. At the beginning of the century, the **Town Halls** at **Compiègne** (1502–10) and **Orléans** (1503–13) and **Beaugency** (1526) are built on similarly Franco-Flemish plans, with belfries, but at Orléans pilasters are used to continue vertically the line of the window frames.

Northern France continued to be susceptible to Flemish influence and maintained a tradition of building in wood. Town houses in cities like Rouen show the introduction of the orders into wooden architecture.

In the south-west and Provence, Classical influences were derived directly from antiquities *in situ*. Guillaume Philandrier (Philander), translator of Serlio and commentator on Vitruvius, added a complete Roman church facade in miniature as a gable to the **Cathedral of Rodez** (*c.* 1562). The **Château de Bournazel, Aveyron**, has a screen composed of a massive superimposed triumphal-arch motif with free-standing columns.

Nicholas Bachelier built a number of fine Renaissance buildings in Toulouse in a strongly sculptural style. The doorway of the **Hôtel de Bagis** (1538) is supported by expressively carved herm figures; the courtyard of the **Hôtel d'Assézat** (1552–62), perhaps by a different architect, is a highly three-dimensional application of Bramante's continuous triumphal-arch motif, popularised by Serlio.

The triumphal arch at **La Tour d'Aigues, near Aixen-Provence** (1571), shows a very direct use of local antiquities.

Several fine sixteenth-century houses survive at **Dijon**, of which the most flamboyant is the **Maison Milsand** by Hugues Sambin (*c.* 1561), encrusted with coarse swags, human and animal heads and curlicues. The effect, as with much northern provincial architecture, is more Flemish than Italian.

France 1600–1750

The **Château de Grosbois, Seine-et-Marne** (*c.* 1600) (p. 937A), is built in an inventive version of the mixed brick and stone manner characteristic of the turn of the sixteenth century in France: brick *chaînes* and stone quoins enliven the white stucco surface. A U-shaped plan is formed by two low wings preceding the main residential block and two paired pavilions. The noteworthy concave curve of the facade was perhaps inspired by the stable block at Fontaine-bleau.

The **Place des Vosges** (formerly Place Royale), **Paris** (1605) (p. 937B), was developed by Henry IV

A. Petit Château, Chantilly (*c.* 1560–). See p. 935

B. Château d'Anet (1541–63): frontispiece (now in Ecole des Beaux-Arts, Paris). See p. 935

C. S. Gervais, Paris (1616–21). See p. 938

A. Château de Grosbois, Seine-et-Marne (*c.* 1600). See p. 935

B. Place des Vosges, Paris (1605). See p. 935

on the site of the old Palais de Tournelles, taking up an idea of Catherine de Médicis. The centrally placed equestrian monument recalled Michelangelo's Capitol (q.v.) but the notion of encircling a space with uniform private housing rather than civic buildings is new. While the arcading is continuous and uniform, the houses, of four bays each, have individual roofs and an added emphasis in the system of *chaînes*. The two larger axial pavilions were reserved for the King and Queen.

Although little of the **Place de France, Paris** (1610–) (p. 939A), was executed, the scheme survives in an engraving by one of the architects, Claude Chastillon. Just inside the city wall, it was semicircular and formed the focus for eight radial streets with an encircling ring road. The streets were to be named after French provinces, and the whole was to be a monument to national unity.

Jean Androuet du Cerceau (*c.* 1585–1649), a member of the large family of architects, was particularly important as a designer of hôtels. More significant than his **Hôtel de Bretonvilliers, Paris** (1637–43), is his **Hôtel de Sully, Paris** (1624–9) (p. 939B). Named after its second owner, the first minister of France, the Duc de Sully, it was originally built for the wealthy banker Mesme Gallet. The plan follows the standard sixteenth-century hôtel type: at the back of a court is the residential block flanked by two wings, while facing the road is an entrance and two pavilions. The court has a lower storey of segmentally pedimented windows with doors laid over the central window on each side. Above, windows with triangular pediments set between *chaînes* are flanked on the main axes by statues in niches. The capriciously detailed dormer windows take up the theme of the fan over the central door.

Salomon de Brosse (1571–1626), related to the du Cerceau family, was the most inventive architect of his age. The most prestigious of his commissions was the **Palais du Luxembourg, Paris** (1615–24) (p. 943E,F), erected for Marie de Médicis. It is traditional in plan with a court enclosed by two wings, a rear *corps de logis* and an open screen facade. Symmetrical about two axes, the residential block has a pavilion at each corner, providing complete apartments on every floor. New in de Brosse's work is a sculptural quality and a more economical use of the orders, particularly evident in the delightful centrally planned entrance gate, with its dome and rusticated columns. The overall use of rustication is a clear reference to Ammanati's Pitti Palace courtyard, Florence (q.v.).

At the now-destroyed **Château de Blérancourt** (1614–19), Salomon de Brosse adopted the scheme used at the Palais de Luxemboug but with significant modifications. The wings of the courtyard were eliminated, producing a free-standing building more closely resembling Italian villas. The low-pitched roof is also Italianate, as is the attempt to disguise the dormer windows by setting them into an attic. The severe Doric and Ionic orders were not limited to the frontispiece as in many earlier structures but applied to the whole building.

Commonly attributed to Salomon de Brosse, **S. Gervais, Paris** (1616–21) (p. 936C), marks an important point in the development of French ecclesiastical architecture in its use of three strongly Classical orders, Doric, Ionic and Corinthian superimposed in their correct sequence to order the facade. The most significant difference from Italian models is the adoption of three rather than two storeys, which was determined by the height of the Gothic nave behind. The paired, free-standing columns have the dual role of framing both outer and central bays. Italian architecture also informs Salomon de Brosse's **Palais de Justice, Rennes** (1618) (p. 941A). Although the typically French tall pitched roof has been retained, the articulation of the facade below looks back to Bramante's Palazzo Caprini (q.v.). A tall rusticated basement has windows framed by projecting piers which carry paired Doric pilasters at the upper level. The pilasters become full columns at the main entrance and support a small pedimented attic. The corner pavilions differ from the central block in adopting smaller basement windows and pedimented rather than arched windows on the first storey.

Jacques Lemercier (*c.* 1580/5–1654) was one of the leading architects of seventeenth-century French Classicism. The son of a master mason, he spent much of his twenties in Rome, an experience he was to put to good effect on his return. Although Louis XIII commissioned him to design extensions for the Louvre, his main patron was Cardinal Richelieu, for whom he built the **Church of the Sorbonne, Paris** (1635–42) (p. 941B). The design of the principal facade is of a Roman two-storey type with Composite pilasters standing over Corinthian columns. Being a university church, it had to include two entrances, one from the street and another from the college. The main axes of the church are focused on these portals and the result is a church plan symmetrical both longitudinally and transversally. A barrel-vaulted nave is interrupted in the middle by a dome and two shallow transepts. Either side of the dome paired arches open onto spacious chapels.

Little remains of Lemercier's three châteaux, Ruel, Liancourt and Richelieu. Of them the **Château de Richelieu, Richelieu** (1631–7) (p. 942A), was the most magnificent and the largest in scale. The house, designed along familiar lines, was only the centrepiece of a much grander complex which included a huge forecourt surrounded by office buildings, a semicircular gateway, and a newly-planned township. The château itself is retrogressive in its design, the square domes looking back to Salomon de Brosse and the dormer windows to sixteenth-century models.

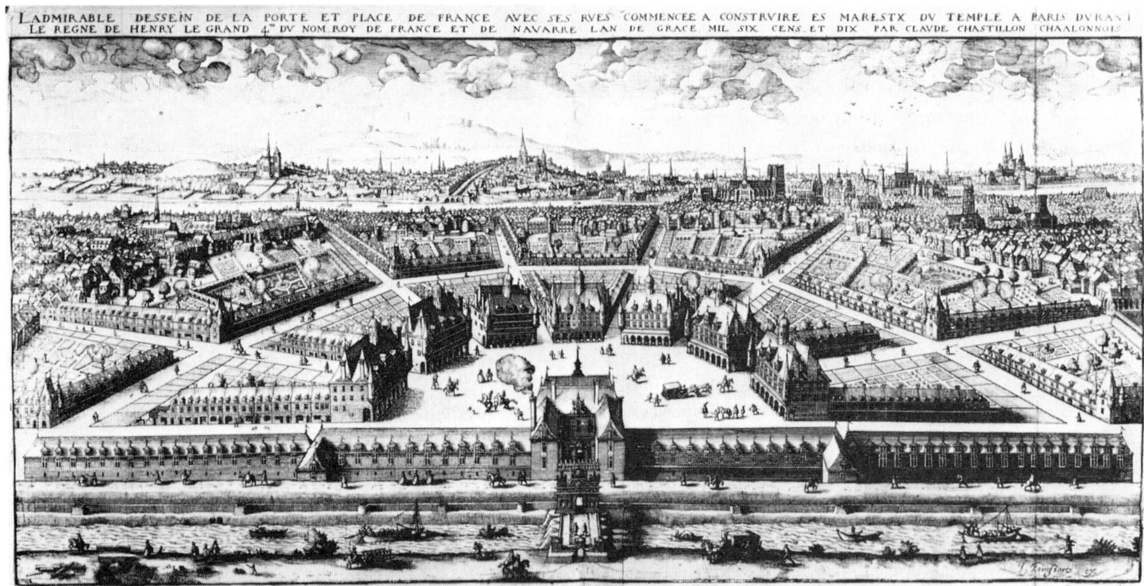

A. Place de France, Paris (1610–) (engraving by Claude Chastillon). See p. 938

B. Hôtel de Sully, Paris (1625–9). See p. 938

François Mansart (1598–1667), the leading figure in French seventeenth-century Classical architecture, probably began his career working under Salomon de Brosse at Coulommiers. Although he never visited Italy his profound understanding of Italian Classicism was in part due to this early contact. His career was troubled by his temperamental nature, his tendency to change his ideas frequently and an inability to compromise with patrons. Working mainly for the bourgeoisie, he introduced significant changes into hôtel planning as in the **Hôtel du Jars, Paris** (1648) and the Hôtel Carnavalet, Paris (1655) (q.v.), where the living quarters were spread around the court and not limited to the *corps de logis*. Mansart's **Château de Balleroy, near Bayeux, Calvados** (*c.* 1626) (p. 942B), still in the astylar brick and *chaîne* style of Henry IV's time, reworks a theme already established in his **Château de Berny, Seine** (before 1624). A tall three-bay central block is flanked by lower, individually-roofed side blocks, beyond which one-storey additions continue along the transverse axis. Mansart has abandoned the traditional formula of an enclosed court, omitting even the entrance screen. A further novelty is the dramatic focus achieved by increasing the heights of the blocks progressively toward the centre. With the exception of the semicircular steps leading to the main door, derived from Bramante's Belvedere courtyard (q.v.), Mansart's vocabulary is almost entirely French.

Mansart's small centrally planned church of **S. Marie de la Visitation, Paris** (1632–4), has a domed circular congregational area off which open oval chapels. The scheme recalls Philibert de l'Orme's designs for Anet (q.v.) as well as some of Michelangelo's schemes for S. Giovanni dei Fiorentini, Rome.

Gaston, Duc d'Orleans, commissioned Mansart to renovate the old **Château de Blois, Blois** (1635–8) (p. 925B,E), which had originally been built by François I. It was to rival the Luxembourg (q.v.) in size and grandeur by including extensive gardens and a forecourt as well as a *cour d'honneur*. Only the central block was built and this shows Mansart at his most Classical. Three superimposed orders are used consistently throughout. The ground-floor Doric pilasters spring into full relief in the Palladio-inspired quadrant screens. The central three bays of the facade project forward and upward and the middle bay is given the greatest relief. Like Brosse, Mansart rejects the dormer window and introduces the broken roofline, later known as the mansard roof.

The **Church of the Val-de-Grâce, Paris** (1645–67) (p. 941C), was commissioned by Anne of Austria in fulfilment of a vow. Mansart began the building but was replaced after only one year by Lemercier. By this time the plan had been established and the zone up to the first entablature built; above this the design was modified by Lemercier. A nave flanked by raised chapels and adorned with Corinthian pilasters culminates in a wide crossing surmounted by a dome. The baldacchino above the main altar is closely based upon S. Peter's, Rome (q.v.), as is the crossing itself. Four wide diagonal piers create the impression of an octagon, a space larger and more magnificent than the adjoining nave. The shallow apses that complete the crossing were used again for the **Chapel at the Château of Fresnes** (date unknown).

The **Château de Maisons, Maisons** (1642–6) (p. 943A–D), was designed by Mansart for René de Longueil. The U-shaped plan consists of a *corps de logis* and two small wings, vestiges of the old-fashioned, enclosed court type. The design reflects a maturing of the ideas found in Balleroy (q.v.). Like the latter it is still conceived in terms of an agglomeration of units, distinguished by breaks in the roofline. There is also an emphasis on height at the centre: at the sides, two single-storey oval vestibules front the tall wings and the central block of the *crops de logis* rises high above the rest of the building. In addition, the central bay, stressed by projection and widely spaced pilasters, forms a frontispiece which breaks through the roofline and culminates in a domed lantern. As elsewhere, Mansart uses strictly Classical superimposed orders for the exterior but allows himself greater licence for the interior, which survives in its entirety. The Classical design is not compromised by the use of polychromy. Particularly impressive is the domed staircase which has an unusual balustrade composed of complex interlacing curved supports.

Louis Le Vau (1612–70), more adaptable if not as brilliant as his contemporary Mansart, was the most successful architect of his age. Like his Italian counterpart, Bernini, he ran a huge workshop of painters, sculptors and stucco-workers. Like Mansart, he worked initially for the bourgeoisie but from 1661 on, through his connections with Fouquet and Colbert, increasingly for the crown. Many of the unusual features of Le Vau's **Hôtel Lambert, Paris** (1640–) (p. 950A), are the result of site restrictions; the garden, overlooked by a long gallery, is situated to the right and not behind the *corps de logis*. As in earlier hôtels, the staircase takes pride of place at the centre of the residential block. More complex than those of Mansart, it constantly surprises the visitor with interesting vistas, in particular that from the top of the stairs, through the oval vestibule, to the long gallery. Externally, the rectangular courtyard has curved corners at one end focusing attention on the two superimposed loggias which provide light and access to the main stair. This curvilinear feature has a precedent at Blois (q.v.) but perhaps reflects knowledge of Borromini's Oratory of S. Philip Neri, Rome (q.v.). The Ionic and Doric orders of the court are replaced by a giant order on the garden facade, a notion that would have been foreign to the more strictly Classical architecture of Mansart.

A. Palais de Justice, Rennes (1618). See p. 938

B. Church of the Sorbonne, Paris (1635–42). See p. 938

C. Church of the Val-de-Grâce, Paris (1645–67). See p. 940

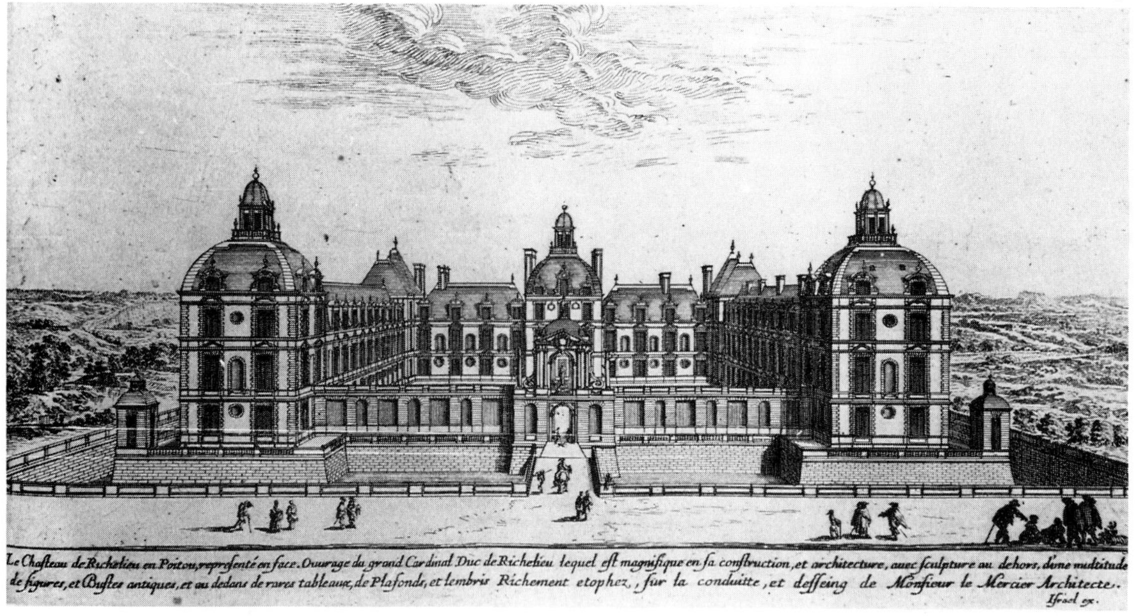

Le Chasteau de Richelieu en Poitou, representé en face. Ouurage du grand Cardinal Duc de Richelieu lequel est magnifique en sa construction, et architecture, auec sculpture au dehors, d'une multitude
de figures, et Bustes antiques, et au dedans de rares tableaux, de Plafonds, et lembris Richement etophez, sur la conduitte, et desseing de Monsieur le Mercier Architecte.
Israel ex.

A. Château de Richelieu, Richelieu (1631–7). See p. 938

B. Château de Balleroy (*c.* 1626). See p. 940

CHATEAU DE MAISONS: NEAR PARIS

A ENTRANCE FACADE

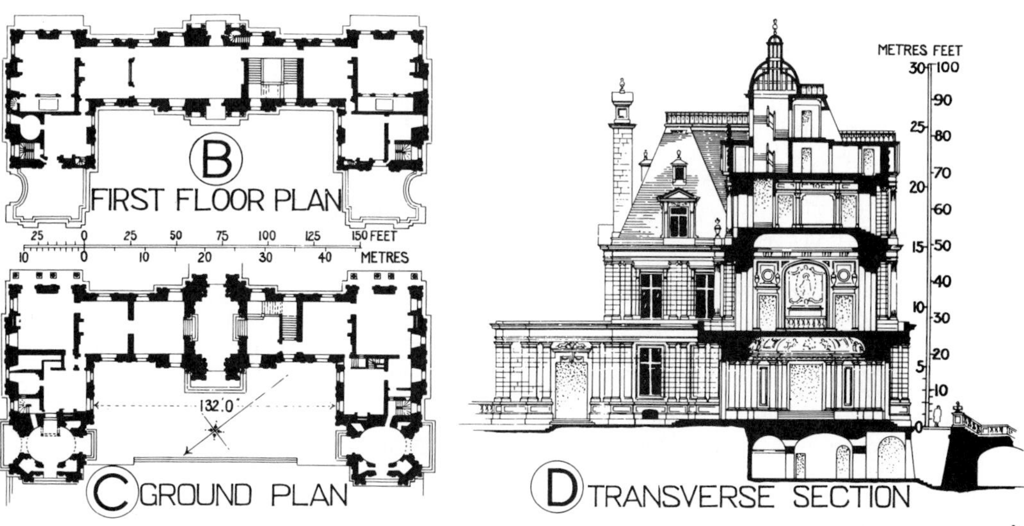

D TRANSVERSE SECTION

PALAIS DU LUXEMBOURG: PARIS

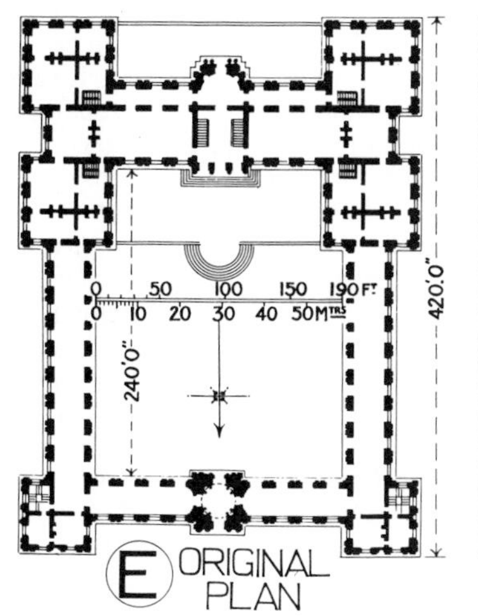

E ORIGINAL PLAN

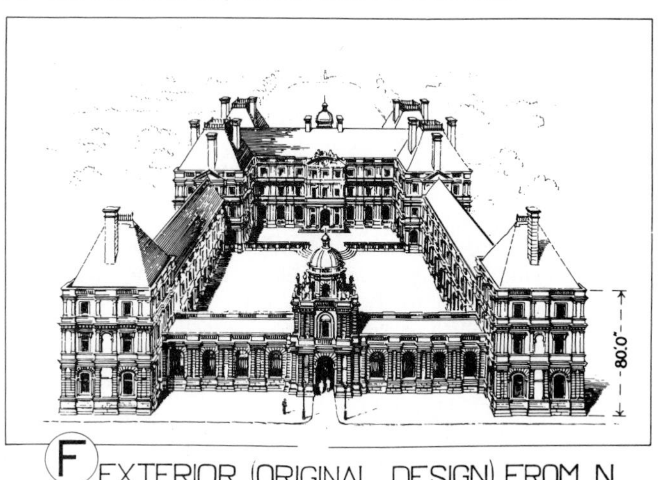

F EXTERIOR (ORIGINAL DESIGN) FROM N.

Before the east facade of the Louvre was completed Louis XIV decided to move his court out of Paris to **Versailles** (pp. 945A,B,946A). The château had been built in 1624 by Louis' father as a hunting lodge. It followed the usual format of châteaux with *corps de logis*, wings and entrance screen. Three major redevelopments, all initiated by Louis XIV, were to alter the building radically and create one of the largest and grandest palaces in Europe. In 1661 Le Vau added two service wings while André Le Nôtre (1613–1700) laid out a formal garden on a magnificent scale with geometrically arranged avenues, woods and canals. The decision to move the court (1668) engendered a more radical transformation. Resisting Colbert's desire to demolish and start afresh, the King asked Le Vau to produce a design incorporating the existing buildings as much as possible. The forecourt of the early château was retained as the 'Cour de Marbre' but enveloped by the new complex. The conception was on a new scale appropriate to absolute monarchy. A twenty-five bay facade was set at the top of a series of ascending terraces. An arcaded basement with banded rustication ran right across this facade forming a platform. Upon this three ranges looked onto a central terrace open towards the garden. Internally Le Vau's most impressive contribution is the 'Escalier des Ambassadeurs' (1671) in which two ramps diverge from a few centrally placed steps, an idea perhaps borrowed from Primaticcio at the Aile de la Belle Cheminée, Fontainebleau (q.v.).

The coherence and scale of Le Vau's design was destroyed in the enlargements which began in 1678 under the direction of Jules Hardouin Mansart. Le Vau's terrace was screened with a long gallery known as the 'Galerie des Glaces' (p. 946A). Mansart added wings to the north and south to accommodate the swelling number of courtiers, bringing the total length of the facade to almost half a kilometre. Le Vau's 'Trianon de Porcelaine' and 'Orangerie' were replaced by larger structures according to Mansart's design and a huge stable block was added. Internally the Galerie des Glaces, while repeating elements found elsewhere at Versailles, also breaks new ground. The extravagant decoration and use of mirrors to heighten the lighting look forward to Rococo. The beautiful chapel repeats the articulation of the exterior with its arcaded basement and colonnaded gallery. Like the palace itself, the chapel was to be much imitated, as at Luneville (q.v.).

In 1742, a scheme by Ange-Jacques Gabriel to reconstruct the palace totally for Louis XV came to nothing and his transformations were limited to the 'Salle d'Opéra' and the 'Petit Trianon' (q.v.).

The **Château of Vaux-le-Vicomte** (1657–61) was built by Le Vau for the Surintendant des Finances, Nicholas Fouquet. It follows, for the most part, the plan of the earlier **Château Le Raincy** (1645), especially in its adoption of a large oval salon, a prelude to Bernini's design for the Louvre. Like Blérancourt and Maisons, the château is a free-standing block without court or wings and it mimics the former in having four corner pavilions. A leitmotif of Le Vau's style is the triple opening found throughout this structure. It is at this château that Le Nôtre appears for the first time as a garden designer, creating a garden that anticipates Versailles.

Le Vau's initial designs for the **east facade of the Palais du Louvre, Paris** (1667) (p. 946B), were obstructed by Colbert, newly appointed as Surintendant des Bâtiments. Subsequently Mansart was asked to provide a design, and opinions were requested from all architects working in Paris. Unable to find a design to his liking, Colbert looked to Rome; Bernini, Rainaldi and Cortona all submitted designs, none of which found approval. The final design seems to have been a collaborative effort by Le Vau, the doctor and amateur architect Claude Perrault, and the painter Charles Le Brun. It abandoned all Bernini's suggestions and resembles most closely Le Vau's first scheme of 1664 without its attic storey. Above an austere basement stands an order of paired Corinthian columns with a continuous entablature that lends an emphatic horizontality to the structure. While the corner pavilions are adorned with pilasters, the order is separated from the facade wall in the intervening zone and the free-standing columns create a tall but shallow loggia. The novel motif of wide intercolumniations between paired columns was to have resonance for more than a century in French architecture.

The **Collège des Quatre Nations, Paris** (begun 1662), was designed by Le Vau as a pendant to the Louvre on the opposite bank of the Seine. Money had been left for the project in Cardinal Mazarin's will. The conception of a palace embracing a domed church with a concave forecourt goes back to Borromini's design for S. Agnese in Piazza Navona, Rome (q.v.). The side pavilions sport a giant order which balances that of the church facade while the concave college facade has two superimposed orders. The church facade, with its narrowly spaced columns and pilasters, makes use of ideas formulated by Pietro da Cortona. Part of Le Vau's original conception was to build a bridge joining the college and the Louvre but it was executed, in altered form, only in the nineteenth century.

After Mansart and Le Vau the most inventive architect of the seventeenth century in France was Antoine Le Pautre (1621–81). He is remembered primarily for his **Hôtel de Beauvais, Paris** (1652–5) (p. 947A), a tour-de-force of imaginative planning. Two adjoining sites of extremely irregular shape were developed to produce a coherent design. On the predominant axis, behind the ground floor shops of the facade, is the *corps de logis* with the main staircase and principal rooms on the first floor. Variety and invention are found in the spatial effects of the courtyard and in the staircase designs which

A. Palais de Versailles: park facade (1678–88). See p. 944

B. Palais de Versailles: aerial view from the park (1661–1756)

A. Palais de Versailles: Galerie des Glaces (1678–84). See p. 944

B. Palais du Louvre, Paris: east facade (1667). See p. 944

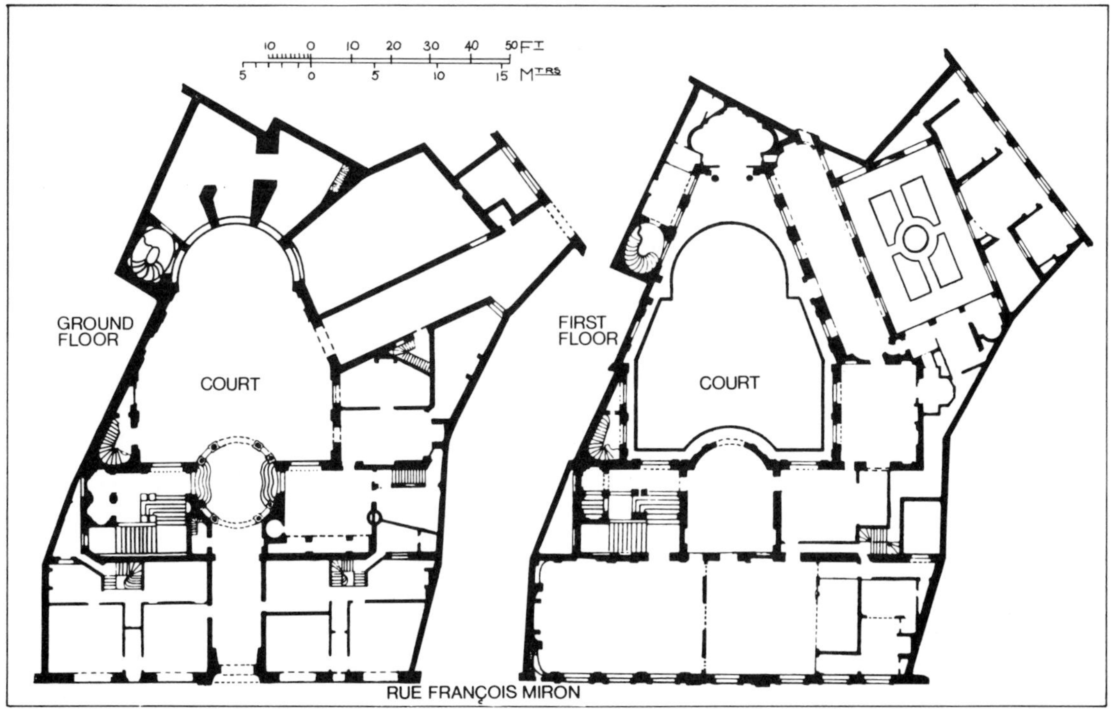

A. Hôtel de Beauvais, Paris (1652–): plans. See p. 944

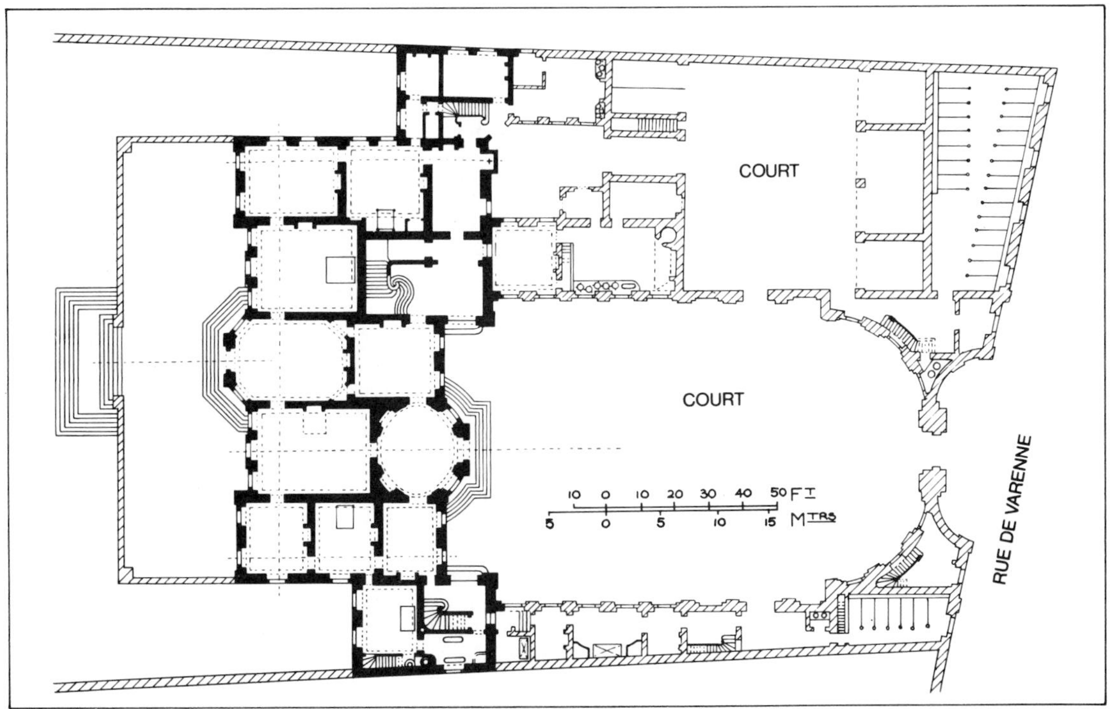

B. Hôtel de Matignon, Paris (1722–4): plan. See p. 951

include oval, triangular and even more complex types. Floor plans are also varied, the first floor facing the Rue de Jony bearing little resemblance to the lower. Walls are not set on walls, and the gallery looks onto a terraced garden and grotto suspended above the stables.

Jules Hardouin Mansart (1646–1708), the most Baroque of French seventeenth-century architects, was the great-nephew by marriage of François Mansart. Possessed of a precocious talent, he designed both the **Hôtel de Noailles, S. Germain**, and the **Hôtel de Lorge, Paris**, before he was twenty-four. In addition to being a skilled designer he managed a vast workshop which provided many architects of the next generation like de Cotte with a solid training. His work on Versailles and popularity in royal circles earned him a barony.

The **Château du Val, S. Germain** (1674), was designed for Louis XIV only one year after Hardouin began work in a minor capacity at Versailles. The single-storey elevation has the horizontal stress that was to become typical in the early eighteenth century. The plan, reminiscent of the Château de Madrid (q.v.), has two suites of rooms flanking a central salon used for dining after the hunt. One suite has four rooms of different shape, all heated by the same fire, anticipating the ingenious planning of Boffrand (q.v.).

Les Invalides, Paris (1670–1708) (p. 958B,C), was initially designed by Libéral Bruant (1635–97) as a hospital for disabled army veterans and completed by 1677. However, even before the completion Louis XIV was planning a second chapel on a grander scale. In 1680 J. H. Mansart produced the final design for the Dôme des Invalides (p. 949A–C), a Greek cross inscribed in a square with an attached circular presbytery. It differs from its model, S. Peter's in Rome (q.v.), in its adoption of a circular crossing with vast free-standing columns and diagonal passages to the corner chapels. Externally, a towering effect is achieved by the pointed profile of the dome, the steeple-like lantern and the unusual insertion of a tall attic above the drum. Of the three shells of the dome two are visible internally. A coffered dome with a very wide oculus opens onto a further frescoed skin, an idea which was later developed by Vittone at Vallinotto (q.v.).

J. H. Mansart's ability in town planning is best exemplified by the **Place Vendôme, Paris** (1698–) (p. 950C). Louis XIV's original intention (1685) was to create a cultural enclave housing the royal library and academies. This scheme was dropped for lack of funds, and private houses were built behind Mansart's unified facade of giant pilasters over a rusticated basement. At the centre and chamfered corners, half-columns replace pilasters and form frontispieces. The square has the monumentality of the Roman Baroque, but tempered with French Classicism.

François Blondel (1618–86), after an early career as a military engineer and extensive travel, became the first Director of the Royal Academy of Architecture and 'ingénieur du roi'. His *Cours d'Architecture* became an important textbook for young architects. Of his few works the most important is the **Porte S. Denis, Paris** (1671). It was the biggest triumphal arch built up to that time, surpassed later only by the Arc de Triomphe. It is also notable for its novel decoration. The piers framing the central arch are faced with obelisks bearing trophies.

Germain Boffrand (1667–1754), playwright, engineer and architect, was a pupil of J. H. Mansart. His style is marked by a love of the giant order and sculptural mass combined with restrained detailing. Most representative of his work is the vast **Château de Luneville, Luneville** (1702–6 and 1720–23), built for the Duc de Lorraine. The spreading low ranges are modelled on Versailles. At the centre of the main facade a pediment supported by giant free-standing Composite columns crowns three arches with views of the gardens beyond. A fire in 1719 destroyed part of the complex, for which Boffrand supplied a new design. The most notable introduction was the chapel, a less opulent version of that at Versailles. Two orders of free-standing columns with continuous entablatures support the barrel-vaulted ceiling and provide the building with an impressive gallery.

For another foreign patron, the Elector Max Emmanuel of Bavaria, Boffrand planned the **Hunting Pavilion, Bouchefort** (1705), a centrally planned structure in the middle of a circular place, surrounded by woodland and radiating roads framing regularly-placed ancillary buildings. The pedimented porticoes placed on four of the eight sides recall Palladio's Villa Rotonda (q.v.), while the idea of centrally planned villas on such a scale originated with Serlio's extravagant designs.

Boffrand's **Hôtel Amelot, Paris** (1712) (p. 950B), was built on a speculative basis without patronage restrictions and embodies better than any other building his ideas on planning. Spatial variety is a primary interest. An oval courtyard leads to a square vestibule with rounded corners and then to a pentagonal staircase. A rounded rectangle, projecting out over the garden, forms the main salon but access to it was purposely restricted. Boffrand forced the visitor through a sequence of rooms in order to reach it, placing spatial experience before functional ease.

Perhaps designed by Boffrand, **S. Jacques, Luneville** (1730–47), abandons the Italian facade type of S. Maria Novella, Florence (q.v.), and looks to the twin-tower facades of mediaeval France. The immediate inspiration could have come from J. H. Mansart's **Church of the Primatiale, Nancy** (1699–1736). Also noteworthy is the Rococo decoration of the towers (especially the clock), becoming increasingly extravagant as it moves up the building.

The **Hôtel de Soubise, Paris** (1705–9), was designed by the generally conservative architect

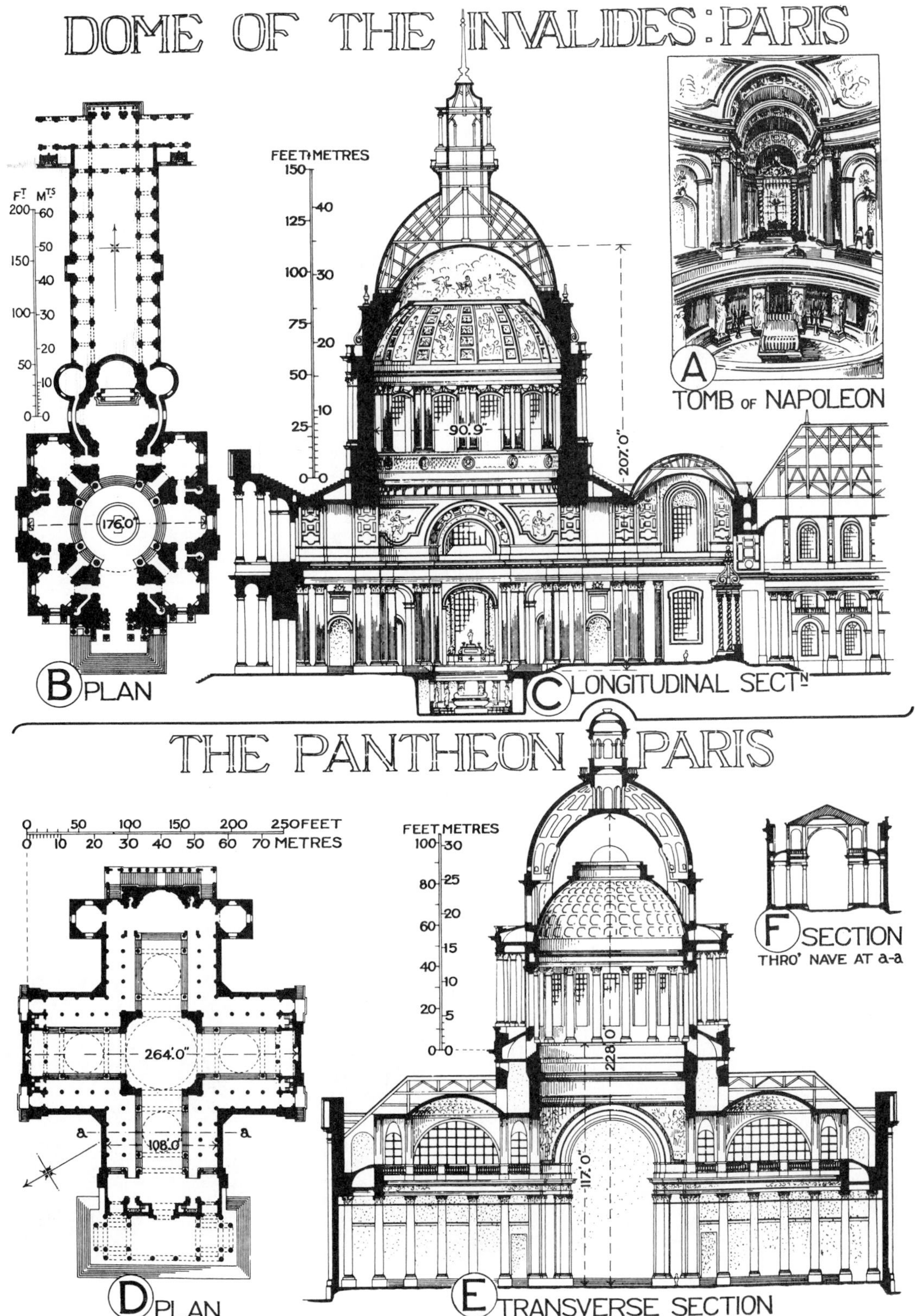
DOME OF THE INVALIDES: PARIS
FEET METRES
150
125
100
75
50
25
0
40
30
20
10
0
FT MTS
200
150
100
50
0
60
50
40
30
20
10
0
176'0"
90'9"
207'0"
A
TOMB OF NAPOLEON
B PLAN
C LONGITUDINAL SECTN
THE PANTHEON PARIS
0 50 100 150 200 250 FEET
0 10 20 30 40 50 60 70 METRES
264'0"
108'0"
a
a
D PLAN
FEET METRES
100
80
60
40
20
0
30
25
20
15
10
5
0
228'0"
117'0"
E TRANSVERSE SECTION
F SECTION
THRO' NAVE AT a-a

A. Hôtel Lambert, Paris (1640–): court. See p. 940

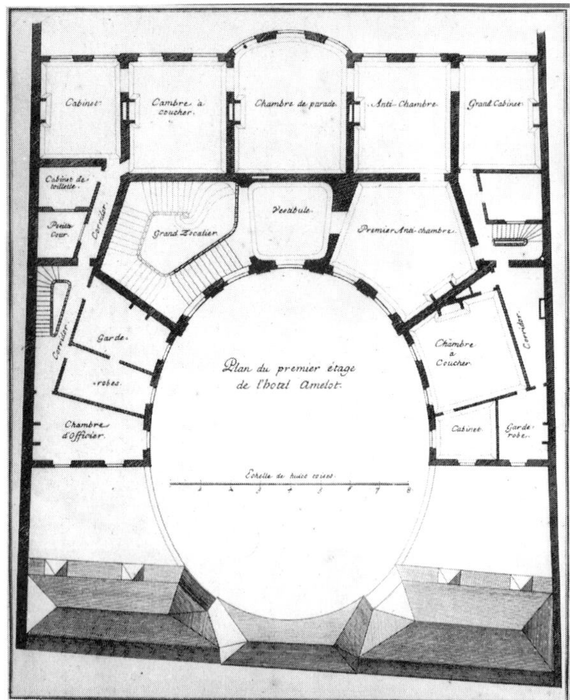

B. Hôtel Amelot, Paris (1712). See p. 948

C. Place Vendôme, Paris (1698–). See p. 948

Pierre-Alexis Delamair. Its paired free-standing columns and balustrade abutting the pediment are features recognisably modelled upon the east facade of the Louvre (q.v.). The order of paired columns continue around the *cour d'honneur*, forming an open colonnade. Also based on the Louvre (Le Vau's first project) are the statues which enliven the plain wall of the upper storey.

Primarily a theoretician and academy professor, Jean Courtonne (1671–1739) is remembered largely for his **Hôtel de Matignon, Paris** (1722–4) (p. 947B). A desire to include a *cour d'honneur* and a second stable court made it possible to align the small court and large garden facades. The solution was to abandon any attempt at symmetry of planning and to use the form of displacement already adopted in the seventeenth-century Hôtel de Bretonvilliers or at the Hôtel du Jars.

Boffrand's most important contemporary was Robert de Cotte (1656–1735), famous for his châteaux. His largest schemes, such as the châteaux at **Schleissheim** and **Bonn** designed for the electors of Bavaria and Cologne, remained incomplete. Without ever leaving France he ran a workshop which built as far afield as Portugal and Turkey. For the Prince-Bishop of Strasbourg he built the Château de Rohan, Strasbourg (1731–42). A columnar screen provides an entrance to a court with a *corps de logis* behind, a traditional formula. His main contribution to planning was to create lighter, airy buildings with improved interior accessibility and privacy. This was achieved through the extensive use of corridors instead of Italianate *en suite* apartments.

Begun in the seventeenth century by Lemercier, the **Church of S. Roche, Paris** (1719–36), was completed by Robert de Cotte with the facade added by his son Jules Robert following his father's design. Although dependent upon a format reminiscent of S. Susanna, Rome (q.v.), and the Val de Grâce, Paris (q.v.), the facade is much more severe than its prototypes and almost devoid of surface decoration.

The facade of **S. Sulpice, Paris** (1736) (p. 952A), made Jean Nicolas Servandoni (1695–1766), painter and stage designer, famous as an architect. Although much altered, it has, like S. Jacques, Luneville, a two-tower facade. The outer bays form bell-towers while the five central bays are opened up on both storeys to form loggias. The effect achieved is not unlike Wren's facade for S. Paul's Cathedral, London (q.v.).

Jacques Gabriel was a colleague of de Cotte and succeeded him as Surintendant des Bâtiments. He directed the reconstruction of Bordeaux and Rennes which had been destroyed by fire. His most interesting design is the **Town Hall and Law Courts, Rennes** (1736–44). Two five-bay corner pavilions frame a concave forecourt with a fountain placed in an impressive clock-tower. The scheme is similar to Le Vau's Collège des Quatre Nations (q.v.) and Vanvitelli's Piazza Dante, Naples (q.v.).

Place Royale, Bordeaux (1735–55), was designed by Jacques Gabriel and realised by a local architect André Portier. With its focal statue of the King, it is the first of the great squares to celebrate the French monarchy, and its position, open to the adjacent River Garonne, provided a model for A.-J. Gabriel's Place Royale (de la Concorde) in Paris. Two streets converge at the centre of the rear side of a broad rectangle. The two rear angles are cut off diagonally to give greater emphasis to the statue at the other side of the square overlooking the river.

Built by Jacques Hardouin Mansart de Sagonne, **S. Louis, Versailles** (1743–54), is a late example of full French Baroque. The expensive sculptural facade with its carefully gauged climax and free-standing columns combines the Italian two-storey and French twin-tower facade types.

France 1750–1830

Ange-Jacques Gabriel (1698–1782), the most consistent and refined of French eighteenth-century architects, trained under his father Jacques in Paris, worked with him on the royal commissions and succeeded him as Premier Architecte du Roi. For the most part he abandoned the Rococo and decorative styles of his predecessors, preferring a more sober, severe and very French Classicism. The scale of many of his works prepared the way for the neo-Classically orientated younger generation.

The **Gros Pavillon, Fontainebleau** (1750–4), actually a wing of the royal palace, looks back to Le Vau's rear facade at Versailles. The facades have central projections, and Doric colonnaded balconies without pediments supported on rusticated arcades. Despite their height, they have a new strong horizontal emphasis characteristic of A. J. Gabriel's work.

Place de la Concorde (originally Place Louis XV), **Paris** (1753–75) (p. 953A), continues the great French tradition of city squares, although no work of this kind had been initiated in Paris since the time of Louis XIV. It is situated on the north bank of the Seine, the river forming its southern perimeter (not unlike Place Royale, Bordeaux), and was laid out on land made available by the King west of the Louvre. To preserve the royal vista through to the Champs Elysées, the buildings are restricted to the northern side, two identical ranges separated by the Rue Royale running northwards towards the Madeleine. This forms the main axis, originally focusing on a statue of Louis XV at the square's centre. Each of the two ranges is symmetrical, a long colonnaded facade with no central emphasis but with pedimented end pavilions, and together with the Madeleine (the present church not built until 1804–49) would have formed a monumental composition. The architecture itself looks back to Le Vau and Perrault's Louvre facade but is even more plastic and unified.

A. S. Sulpice, Paris (1736). See p. 951

B. The Mint, Paris (1768–75). See p. 955

C. Saint-Vaast, Arras (*c.* 1755–). See p. 955

D. S. Philippe du Roule, Paris (1774–84). See p. 956

A. Palaces, Place de la Concorde, Paris (1753–75): angle pavilions. See p. 951

B. Place de la Carrière, Nancy (1750–7). See p. 955

A. Ecole Militaire, Paris (1751–73). See p. 955

B. S. Geneviève (Panthéon), Paris (1757–90). See p. 955

The **Ecole Militaire, Paris** (1751–73) (p. 954A), is conservative in many ways with its typically French dome over the centre of the facade. It is, however, also characterised by a new Italianate, even Palladian, Classicism, notable in the projecting temple-front portico, the expansive smooth wall surface and the alternation of window pediments in the central portion.

The **Petit Trianon, Versailles** (1762–68) (p. 958A), was built as a garden retreat for Mme de Pompadour in the palace gardens, and is a gem of domestic architecture. Square in plan with tripartite facades, it presents many similarities with English Palladian villas which may have been influential. Nevertheless, Gabriel's own tendencies towards rectilinear forms (for example avoiding pediments), clearly defined shapes, and restrained decoration, are the predominant determining factors of the design – as well as the deliberate allusion to the architecture of Louis XIV. In French terms, the interiors are also restrained, in spite of the extensive panelling and use of mirrors.

Place Stanislas (formerly Royale), and the surrounding vicinity, **Nancy** (1752–5), laid out by Emmanuel Héré, an Austrian, for the dethroned King Stanislas of Poland (father-in-law of Louis XV), is a masterpiece of town planning. The project entailed mass demolition in order to link Place Stanislas by a bridge over a moat, via a triumphal arch (based on that of Severus) to more squares in the old town, the **Place de la Carrière** (p. 953B) and the Hémicycle. All the squares are organised along one giant vista. The layout incorporates various buildings by Boffrand as well as new buildings designed in similar style. The long Place de la Carrière is lined with avenues of trees, while the transverse hemicycle is flanked by decorative exedra-screens, all of which contributed to a new town centre of considerable splendour.

The **Mint, Paris** (1768–75) (p. 952B), the masterpiece of Jacques-Denis Antoine (1733–1801), who after Gabriel was the leading architect of the period, is the most impressive French public building of the eighteenth century. It is close in spirit to Gabriel's work: a very long facade with a projecting central colonnade over a rusticated arcade, and in place of a pediment a row of statues fronting a low attic. Otherwise there is very little decoration, even such elements as window frames being much simplified, adding to the rectangularity of the composition.

The **Peyrou Terraces, Montpellier** (1767–), laid out by A. and E. Giral, mark the end of an aqueduct supplying the city, itself reminiscent of the Roman Pont du Gard with its two tiers of arches. From the city the terraces are approached from an archway (1689) on the main axis, while on the upper terrace at the termination of the aqueduct is the so-called Château d'Eau, a restrained triumphal-arch-like structure, almost square in plan with a slightly concave front; its selective Classical detailing and decoration provide the equivalent of an ancient nymphaeum.

Saint-Vaast, Arras (begun *c.* 1755) (p. 952C), by Pierre Contant d'Ivry (1698–1777), is an important early neo-Classical church, even though in general terms it resembles many Gothic buildings in Flanders. Colonnades with sumptuous Corinthian capitals divide aisles from nave, and with their flat entablatures give the interior a strongly Roman flavour. Grouped columns mark the domed crossing, also emphasised by supported urns, while emphatic paired columns divide off the east end.

Jacques-Germain Soufflot (1713–80), the son of a Burgundian lawyer, was one of the most influential figures of the eighteenth century. In 1731, he went to Rome to study ancient architecture for seven years. After designing the Hôtel-Dieu, Lyon, he returned to Italy for a further two years accompanying the brother of Mme de Pompadour. His masterpiece, S. Geneviève, which occupied his later life, became a cornerstone of European neo-Classicism.

The **Hôtel-Dieu** (formerly the Exchange), **Lyon** (1740–8), anticipates even the works of A.-J. Gabriel, marking a decisive break with Rococo. The facade has no corner pavilions, but rather an emphatic central section of three slightly projecting bays, topped by a domed attic rather than a pediment. Despite Soufflot's studies in Rome, the architecture looks not to antiquity, but rather to Le Vau, in its strong sense of mass and form and in the handling of the stone detailing.

S. Geneviève (called the **Panthéon** after the Revolution), **Paris** (1757–90) (pp. 949D–F, 954B), is the great masterpiece of early neo-Classicism, fulfilling the theoretical ideal of fusing Classical style with the structural lightness of Gothic architecture. Although the building was very much altered and modified, the plan resembles S. Mark's, Venice: a Greek cross with a central dome and four subsidiary domes between pairs of barrel vaults, here coved to reduce weight. The supporting members are very slight; apart from the four bevelled crossing piers, which were enlarged, all the other interior supports are elegantly fluted Corinthian columns. The exterior, its windows now sadly filled in, achieves a dynamic appearance through the sheering off of the re-entrant angles of the cross (compare S. Peter's Rome) and the fullness of the projecting drum, dome and lantern (the subsidiary domes being hidden). The dome, very like Wren's S. Paul's, has three shells (as has the Invalides) although a lower two-shelled dome had originally been intended; also like S. Paul's is the concealment of the Gothic buttress system. Yet apart from its size and restraint, its most Classical feature is the main facade, a Corinthian temple-front with a sculpture-filled pediment approached from a tall flight of steps.

Etienne-Louis Boullée (1728–99) built little but had much influence through his widely publicised theories and designs. Often wholly impractical, they convey an ideal grandeur through their scale, geometric purity and bare Classicism. Boullée's extraordinary design of 1784 for the **Tomb of Newton** goes beyond a reconstruction of the Mausoleum of Augustus (or Hadrian): a sphere emerging from the second drum (symbolising the heavens) is visually completed by a shelving recess in the lower drum; the vast dark spherical interior was to contain Newton's sarcophagus. Equally awe-inspiring are many of Boullée's starkly Classical interiors, often for buildings, like his **Library Hall**, of modern function.

Claude-Nicolas Ledoux (1736–1806) began his career in the genteel employment of Mme du Barry, but became Europe's most extreme practical exponent of neo-Classicism. He trained under Blondel, never visited Italy, and from 1733 was Architecte du Roi; yet despite all this he abandoned all vestige of conservatism in his buildings. In a more theoretical vein, he also planned an 'ideal' city of **Chaux**, individual buildings for which are almost as fantastic as Boullée's, but compose one of the grandest conceptions of the period. Imprisoned at the Revolution, he narrowly avoided execution, eventually emerging to publish his designs in a treatise (*L'architecture Considérée* ...) in 1804.

The **Hôtel de Montmorency, Paris** (1769–70), an early work by Ledoux, has two adjacent facades which in character recall A.-J. Gabriel. Yet the absence of window frames, diminished basements and the giant orders produce an effect of greater starkness. The plan is quite unusual: the main entrance is placed at the angled corner, while the various rooms are organised symmetrically about the diagonal, the main saloon placed above the entrance.

The **Royal Saltworks, Arc-et-Senans** (1774–9), despite its utilitarian function, is Ledoux's most ambitious executed work. Conceived as a circular complex at the heart of Ledoux's proposed visionary city of Chaux, only one hall of the Saltworks was built. The overall effect of the giant compound is of simple geometric masses, the sparing use of architectural forms increasing their impact. Entry is through a hefty pedimented propylaeum, with stubby unfluted Greek Doric columns, fronting a massive rusticated voussoir arch: the low walls on either side are blank except for seemingly huge embedded jars pouring forth water which take the place of windows. The cave-like tunnel beyond the propylaeum is a chunky simplification of an Italianate grotto. The facing Director's residence has an (aptly) uncompromising Doric portico, the columns of which are rusticated with smooth blocks.

The **Barrière de la Villette, Paris** (1785–9), is one of four surviving toll houses out of forty that once ringed the city, the others torn down in the Revolution. Intended to convey the power and grandeur of Paris, all were composed from simple, but different, geometric forms and incorporated extremely reduced if often bizarre Classical ornament. Here a rotunda rises from a square platform preceded by a squat octastyle portico. The tapering square-sectioned columns have rudimentary Doric capitals, while the entablature above is reduced to a lintel and coping.

S. Philippe du Roule, Paris (1774–84) (p. 952D), by J.-F.-T. Chalgrin (1739–1811), a pupil of Boullée, is an exceptionally fine neo-Classical church. Fluted Ionic columns run along the nave and around the east end; the nave is covered by a coffered barrel vault, designed to provide clerestory windows, giving a vertical counterweight to the pervading horizontality.

The **Bagatelle, Paris** (1777), a work of F.-J. Belanger (1744–1818), is a pavilion built for Louis XVI's brother (in a remarkable sixty-four days to win a bet), and is an exquisitely detailed building of great refinement. Neo-Classical in much of its decoration, it has a simplicity and geometric purity typical of the period, although in other respects, for example the pilaster strip articulation, it is somewhat reminiscent of buildings fifty years earlier.

Hôtel de Gallifet, Paris (1775–96), by J.-G. Legrand, has a remarkable courtyard where a central octastyle colonnade, two storeys in height, appears quite detached from the three-storey facade behind.

Similar effects are found at the facade of the **Odéon** (originally Théâtre Français), **Paris** (1778–82, rebuilt after a fire in 1807), the work of M.-J. Peyre. Here a Doric colonnade is attached to a plain expanse of rustication, that of the attic storey differing but slightly in type. The high pyramidal roof covering the horseshoe-shaped auditorium (the first in Paris) adds to the strong geometric quality of the building.

At **Château Moncley, Franche-Comté** (*c.* 1778) (p. 957A), by C. A. Bertrand, open screens connect the main block with circular mediaeval towers. The concave facade might be old-fashioned, but the projecting Ionic portico is here particularly Palladian.

Château Saverne (1779–89), designed by N. Salins for the Bishop of Strasbourg, has an impressively wide facade with a giant order anachronistically terminating with corner pavilions, but with a more contemporary octastyle central emphasis.

Hôtel de Salm, Paris (1784, destroyed by fire 1871, rebuilt 1878) by A. Rousseau, has a garden facade with a semi-projecting rotunda articulated with Corinthian half-columns. The treatment is here typically neo-Classical with architectural elements set against a rusticated wall surface, even if it is more decorative and less brutal than many other buildings of the period.

The **Madeleine, Paris** (1804–49) (p. 957C), is the masterpiece of the French Empire. It is the work of Pierre Vignon (1762–1828), who had trained under Ledoux and who in 1793 became Inspecteur Général des Bâtiments de la République. The building replaced an incomplete structure, designed by P. Contant d'Ivry, which related to A.-J. Gabriel's Place

A. Château Moncley, Franche-Comté (*c.* 1778). See p. 956

B. Arc de Triomphe de l'Etoile, Paris (1808–). See p. 959

C. The Madeleine, Paris (1804–49). See p.956

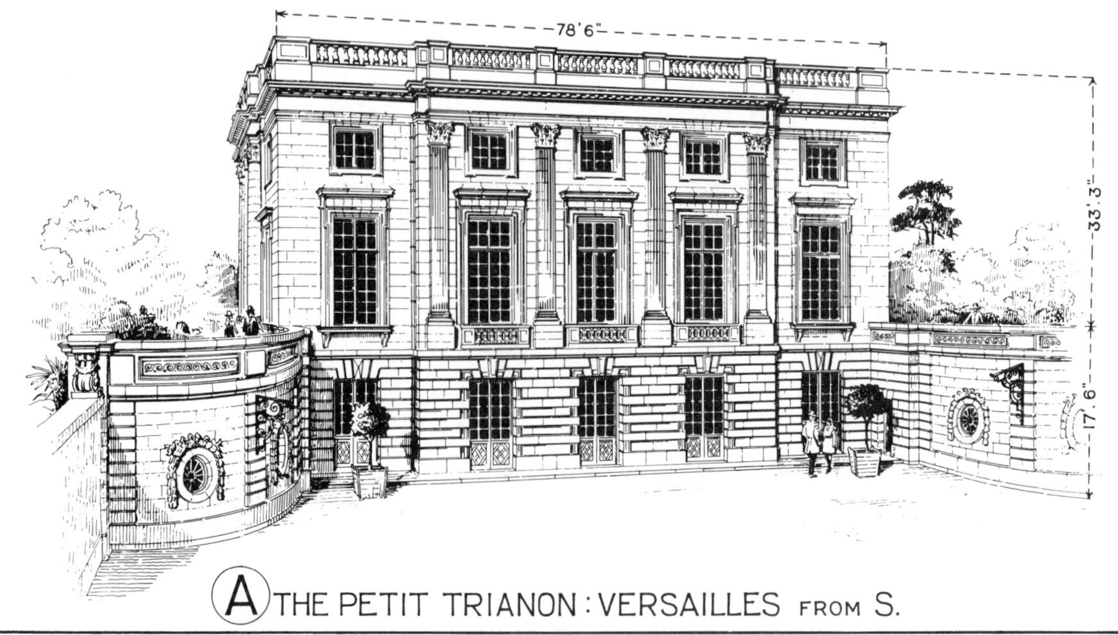

(A) THE PETIT TRIANON : VERSAILLES FROM S.

(B) LUCARNE (DORMER WINDOW) HOTEL DES INVALIDES PARIS

(C) LUCARNE (DORMER WINDOW) HOTEL DES INVALIDES PARIS

(D) MARBLE VASE VERSAILLES

(E) HOTEL: RUE DU CHERCHE-MIDI: PARIS

(F) MARBLE VASE VERSAILLES

de la Concorde to the south. In 1806 Napoleon decided the new building should be a Temple of Glory rather than a church – a decision reversed in 1813. Nevertheless, the external design deliberately sets out to imitate a Roman temple – Corinthian, octastyle and peripteral (like the Temple of Castor) – and has exceptionally elaborate sculpture in the pediment. The height of the podium (7 m, 23 ft), the isolated site and the rising approach all add to the impact of the building. The interior is also impressive: the nave, divided into three bays, with saucer domes on pendentives supported by Corinthian columns and lit by oculi, terminates at an apse with a semi-dome.

The **Bourse, Paris** (1806–15), by A.-T. Brogniart, is a not dissimilar building. Standing on a square podium it is enclosed by four thirteen-bay Corinthian colonnades, which largely mask the pyramidal roof.

The **Chambre des Députés, Paris** (1807), by B. Poyet, stands across the Seine facing Place de la Concorde, and has a massive dodecastyle portico preceded by a huge flight of steps flanked by statues. The portico here projects forward from rusticated wings articulated with isolated corner pilasters and ornamental panels.

The **Arc de Triomphe de l'Etoile, Paris** (p. 957B), is another work by J.-F.-T. Chalgrin (architect of S. Philippe du Roule). It dominates the eastern vista from Place de la Concorde formed by the Avenue des Champs Elysées, standing about 3 kilometres (2 miles) distant. The astylar design (compare Porte S. Denis) and vast dimensions of the arch recall no specific antique prototype, although size and geometric simplicity are themselves neo-Classical qualities. However the arch is richly embellished with antique-style trophies, victories and relief decoration, which soften its severity.

Pierre François Léonard Fontaine (1762–1853) was, together with Charles Percier (1764–1838), Napoleon's favourite architect and chief creator of the Empire style of decoration. He and Percier were extensively employed by Napoleon in the remodelling of a succession of consular and imperial residences. **Rue de Rivoli, Paris** (1802–55), laid out by Percier and Fontaine, faces the Tuileries Gardens and forms part of a larger planning scheme initiated in the area by Napoleon. The uniform street frontages with their ground-level arcades are reminiscent of Place des Vosges. The repetitive but simple Classical facades above are unified horizontally by elegant iron balconies.

The **Chapelle Expiatoire, Paris** (1816–24), was designed by Fontaine for Louis XVIII in memory of his executed brother Louis XVI, and Marie Antoinette. A funerary rotunda, it recalls Raphael's Chigi Chapel (q.v.) in its organisation, although the articulation and decoration are grandly, and coldly, neo-Classical.

Notre Dame de Lorette, Paris (1823–36), is the work of L.-H. Lebas, and has a basilican plan reminiscent of S. Philippe du Roule but modelled much more closely on Early Christian churches. It has four side aisles with Ionic colonnades, a flat ceiling, and an apse containing a baldacchino beyond a domed chancel; the interior is richly decorated with murals. The facade, however (unlike an Early Christian basilica), has a tall temple-front portico.

Architectural Character

Spain

The transition from Gothic to Renaissance architecture in Spain took place during the latter years of the fifteenth century and the first quarter of the sixteenth. The period is dominated by a style known as the Plateresque – a pejorative term coined in the seventeenth century and meaning 'silversmith-like'. It is descriptive of a taste for ornamental surface decoration which is liberally applied in low relief and which bears no relation to the underlying structure.

Far from fitting into a neat stylistic category, this taste embraced both Gothic and Renaissance ornament and is usually divided into two chronological periods: the Gothic Plateresque (*c.* 1480–*c.* 1504), sometimes called Isabelline, and Renaissance Plateresque (1504–56). Buildings frequently combine elements from Gothic, Renaissance and Mudéjar architecture like the Infantado Palace, Guadalajara, but gradually a Renaissance decoration with candelabra, baluster columns and grotesques borrowed from the north Italian Lombard tradition begins to predominate. Although the early sixteenth century saw the pre-eminence of the Renaissance Plateresque it was not a universal style. It co-existed with both Gothic, as exemplified by Segovia Cathedral (1529–91), and Gothic Plateresque. The work of many architects reflects this diversity. Diego de Riaño, for example, could build in both Gothic and Renaissance Plateresque styles.

The Classical period (1556–1650) saw the development of purist styles in which the principles of Italian Renaissance architecture were fully assimilated. Newly professional architects, such as Pedro Machuca, did much to enhance the status of architects in Spain. Indeed, Juan Bautista de Toledo, who had been an assistant to Michelangelo at S. Peter's in Rome, was appointed official architect to Philip II, becoming the first man in Spain to gain such a title. At the Escorial he initiated a project of a scale and complexity that demanded the kind of professionalism that had developed at the 'fabbrica' of S. Peter's. Toledo's severe Classical style was developed in a more subtle and proportionally harmonious way by his successor, Juan de Herrera (*c.* 1530–97), who had travelled in Flanders as well as in Italy.

Spain and Portugal in the seventeenth century

Between 1650 and 1750 the Baroque and Rococo flourished so vigorously and variously in Spain that it seems almost a reaction against the formalism of Herrera and his followers. While the Italian Baroque was a powerful influence, a fantastically extravagant version developed during the late seventeenth century, called 'Churrigueresque', after the Churriguera family of architects, who were its leading though not its most extreme exponents. Essentially a style of architectural ornament, Churrigueresque emerged first in interior decoration such as stucco work and church reredoses. This long-lived style (*c.* 1680–1780) went through three distinct phases. The first (1680–1720) is characterised by the use of the 'Salomonica', a twisted barley-sugar column. The second (*c.* 1720–60) popularised the 'estipite' (an inverted obelisk or cone), while the third (*c.* 1760–80) fuses these elements with an appreciation of the emerging neo-Classical style. One of the most imposing monuments of the Churrigueresque is the west facade of the Cathedral of Santiago de Compostela (1738–49) by Fernando de Casas y Nuova.

As in central and western Europe generally, architecture during the neo-Classical period (1750–1830) in Spain turned more and more towards ancient models, fine examples being the facade of Pamplona Cathedral (1783) by Ventura Rodríguez (1717–85) and the Prado, Madrid (1785–87) by Juan de Villanueva (1739–1811). This new style, promoted by the recently founded academies in Madrid (1752) and Valencia (1768), finally ousted the Churrigueresque toward the end of the eighteenth century.

Portugal

The Manueline style, a peculiarly Portuguese phenomenon, was contemporary with the period of Renaissance Plateresque in Spain. Taking its name from King Manuel I, who reigned from 1495 to 1521, it is decorative rather than structural in character and, because it was generally superimposed upon Gothic forms – the great monasteries of Belem and Batalha are notable examples – it is often classified as mediaeval. Manueline drew its exuberant inspiration from the voyages of the discoverers, exploiting in fantastic patterns the symbols of the armillary sphere, ropes, corals and the Cross of the Order of Christ, which Vasco da Gama and his fellow navigators bore on the sails of their ships. It is seen at its most bewildering in the group of buildings of the Convent of Christ at Tomar.

Apart from the Manueline, Portuguese architecture showed few distinctive characteristics during the Renaissance period until the splendid phases of Baroque and Rococo in the first half of the eighteenth century, when sudden wealth, deriving from the discovery of gold and diamonds in Brazil, led to a spate of building. The exquisitely beautiful interior of the University Library of Coimbra, a poem of chinoiserie, is of this date. In 1755 occurred the appalling disaster of the Lisbon earthquake, and from the rubble of destruction emerged some fine, if rather monotonous, town planning, exemplified at its best by the formal splendour of the Praca do Comercio, one of Europe's most impressive squares.

The style of the rehabilitated capital, in particular of the important quarter of the Baixa, with the regular grid of the street plan, and the plain, nearly uniform facades and standardised building elements, is sometimes called Pombaline, after the Marquis of Pombal, the ruthlessly efficient minister who directed the reconstruction programme with the able assistance of the engineers and architects Manuel de Maia, Carlos Mardel and Eugenio dos Santos. Their sober work here was in marked contrast to the contemporary High Rococo of Queluz and the imposing Roman Baroque of the vast convent-palace of Mafra (begun in 1717 by J. F. Ludovice), which reflect the royal manner of the Joanine period (so called after the king Dom João V).

But, if the explanation of the sobriety of rebuilt Lisbon lay partly in the need for economy, a dichotomy has generally been apparent in Portuguese architecture between an instinct for simple elegance in the form of buildings and a love of sumptuous embellishment. In the north the local granite proved an appropriate vehicle for the rich flamboyant Baroque of Niccolo Nasoni, a Tuscan architect, painter and sculptor, who worked in Malta before emigrating to Oporto, where in thirty years of the mid-eighteenth century he transformed the face of the city. Nasoni's death in 1773 was followed by a revived interest in Palladianism, to which the British colony of vintners certainly contributed, notably in the spacious hospital of S. Antonio, built to the designs of John Carr of York (1723–1807).

Examples

Spain

The **Royal Hospital, at Santiago de Compostela** (1501–11), built for pilgrims, is representative of the new wave of functional civic buildings constructed during the Isabelline period. Designed by Enrique Egas (died 1534), it has wards arranged in the form of a large cross with a vaulted crossing at the centre, a scheme derived from Italian quattrocento hospitals such as the Ospedale Maggiore in Milan (q.v.). The richly decorated main portal, Gothic in its overall form, was begun in 1518 by French sculptors.

The **University facade, Salamanca** (1514–29) (p. 962A), is a masterpiece of Plateresque design of admirable craftsmanship and embodying, within a Gothic frame, a number of Italianate motifs such as putti, panelled pilasters infilled with arabesques, portrait roundels and candelabra as well as the arms of Ferdinand and Isabella and of Charles V, all embedded in a wealth of surface ornament of Moorish inspiration.

S. Esteban, Salamanca (1524–1610), was designed by Juan de Alava (active 1505–37) in a hybrid style that interprets Gothic structure in terms of Classical form. The buttresses, apparently eminently Gothic with their crocketed finials, are faced with Classicising pilaster strips, and all are set against plain and simple, though massive, wall surfaces. With a sense of contrast typical of the mixed style, the church has a rich Plateresque west facade.

The **Casa de Ayuntamiento** (Town Hall) **at Seville** (1527–64) (p. 962B) is the only major work of Diego de Riaño (active 1517–34). It has a symmetrical front fully articulated with single and paired pilasters, and on the upper storeys by attached columns treated as candelabra. The design in reminiscent of Italian Lombard architecture of the late fifteenth century, but has the excessive elaboration of the Plateresque.

The **University facade, Alcalá de Henares** (1537–53) (p. 962C), by Rodrigo Gil de Hontañón (1500/10–77) is a taut and balanced design that reflects Gil's interest in geometry. The ornate central bay, so characteristic of Spanish architecture, receives its proportions from a system of overlapping squares, as do the divisions between the storeys at each side. Within this rational grid, which focuses on the centre and on the piano nobile, the windows with their side scrolls, fulsome pediments and iron grilles give a lively sense of sparkle and intensity.

The **Palace of Charles V at Granada** (1527–68) (p. 963A) was designed by Pedro Machuca (active 1517–50) and continued after his death by his son Luis, but was never completed for occupation. Deeply influenced by the Roman palaces and villas of Bramante (1444–1514) and Raphael (1483–1520), Machuca enclosed a majestic circular patio, 30.5 m (100 ft) in diameter and composed of superimposed Doric and Ionic colonnades, within a square palace block. The external facades have rusticated Doric pilasters on the ground level, except for the centre bays where paired and fluted half-columns stand on high pedestals. The pairing of the order is continued at the upper level with Ionic half-columns, while on both storeys the windows are

A. University, Salamanca (facade 1514–29). See p. 961

B. Casa de Ayuntamiento, Seville (1527–64). See p. 961

C. University, Alacalá de Ḥenares (facade 1537–53). See p. 961

A. Palace of Charles V, Granada: central court (1527–68). See p. 961

B. Afuera Hospital of San Juan Bautista, Toledo (1542–78): facade. See p. 964

surmounted by roundels. Both patio and facades work well in isolation, but their interaction is awkward and allows only confined stair and room spaces.

The **Afuera Hospital of San Juan Bautista at Toledo** (1542–78) (p. 963B) was designed by Bartolome de Bustamante (1499/1501–70), priest and secretary to the patron Cardinal Tavera. Italianate in conception, both facade and patio reveal knowledge of the published designs of Sebastiano Serlio (1475–1554). The severe facade of the rectangular block has smooth rustication over the first two levels, which contrasts strongly with the vigorously protruding rusticated quoins at the second level and the voussoirs around the windows. The central portal, however, is typically Spanish in the way it is developed upwards through all three storeys. The double patio within (1547–8), with its graceful superimposed Doric and Ionic arcades, most fully reflects the Italianate taste of courtly patrons.

Granada Cathedral (1528–63) (p. 965A,B), designed by Diego de Siloe (*c.* 1495–1563), is one of the grandest Renaissance churches in southern Spain and a remarkable example of the Plateresque style. The broad nave leads to a semicircular chevet, with ambulatory and radiating chapels designed to facilitate the adoration of the eucharist displayed on the high altar. Charles V considered Siloe's Italianate work out of keeping with the already constructed Gothic **Capilla Real** (1504–21), which, entered through a magnificent wrought-iron *creja*, was built to contain the tombs of Ferdinand and Isabella. The huge recessed bays of the facade were based on Siloe's plan, but brilliantly articulated and decorated in the Baroque period to the design of Alonso Cano (1601–67).

Jaén Cathedral (begun 1546) (p. 965C) was designed by Andrés Vandelvira (1509–75), a pupil and assistant of Diego de Siloe. A hall church like Granada Cathedral, Jaén is smaller and also simpler in that it has a rectangular east end, based on that of Seville Cathedral. As at Barcelona Cathedral, there are two side chapels to each bay of the nave. The imposing Baroque facade (1667–86), which, with side towers and recessed upper level, echoes the west front of S. Peter's in Rome, was designed by Eufrasio Lopez de Rojas.

The **Alcázar at Toledo** (1537–53) (p. 966A), a mediaeval castle of mixed Moorish and Gothic character, was remodelled by Alonso Covarrubias (1488–1570) for Charles V. It was Alonso's most important work, but was largely destroyed during the Civil War (1936–9). For the sake of striking decorative effect, the top storey was rusticated and crowned by a roof balustrade, while the tabernacle windows on the lower levels were set off against a plain wall, inverting the normal Classical scheme. The central entrance, flanked by Ionic columns and surmounted by an overdoor bearing the arms of Charles V, leads to a spacious patio of superimposed Corinthian columns.

The **Escorial** (1562–82) (pp. 967,969A), near **Madrid**, was begun for Philip II by Juan Bautista de Toledo (died 1567), who was responsible for the overall plan. The enormous task was completed by Juan de Herrera (*c.* 1530–97), who took charge in 1572. This austere group of buildings on a lonely site consists of monastery, college, church (dedicated to S. Lawrence) and palace. The grand entrance in the centre of the west front opens into the **Patio de los Reyes**, which forms the atrium of the church. To the right is the monastery with its four arcaded courts, beyond which lies the **Patio de los Evangelistas**. To the left of the atrium is the college, also with four courts, and beyond this the great court of the palace is connected to the state apartments, which project behind the church to make the plan into the form of a gridiron. The western part of the plan is similar to Italian hospital designs (1456). The domed church (1574–82), designed by Herrera, is similar in type to S. Maria di Carignano at Genoa (q.v.), but its Spanish character is seen in the position of the choir over a vaulted vestibule at the west end, which shortens the nave so that the main building is Greek cross in plan. The simple facade has noble Doric columns surmounted by granite figures of the Kings of Judah, which stand before the slightly recessed upper level. The windows between the statues light the raised choir within. The interior, although cold, is impressive in its simplicity. The granite walls contrast strongly with the frescoed vaults, while the magnificent reredos with its quiet blending of colour further emphasises the subdued effect. The Escorial owes much of its character to the yellowish-grey granite of which it is built, a material which imposed restraint upon the architect and may indeed have accorded with the ascetic taste of Philip II. The external facades, made of great blocks of granite and with monolithic door architraves 3 m (10 ft) high, show no attempt at window grouping, as on the Alcázar facade, and the openings generally are devoid of ornament.

Valladolid Cathedral (p. 965D) was designed *c.* 1585 by Herrera as a large rectangle with corner towers and a domed crossing at the centre. Although never completed as planned, Herrera's scheme was very influential in Spain and Spanish America. It was finished at a much reduced size between 1729 and 1733, the upper register of the west facade being by Alberto Churriguera (1676–1750), who adopted a vigorous Baroque style to enliven the severity of Herrera's lower register, sensitively avoiding the intricacy associated with the Churriguera family.

The **Casa Lonja, Seville** (1583–98), from designs by Juan de Herrera, shows in its patio of Ionic-over-Doric arcades, in which the attached orders enframe the arches in the Roman manner, the cold academic character widespread at the time.

A. Granada Cathedral (1528–63): interior looking west. See p. 964

B. Granada Cathedral: facade (1667–1703)

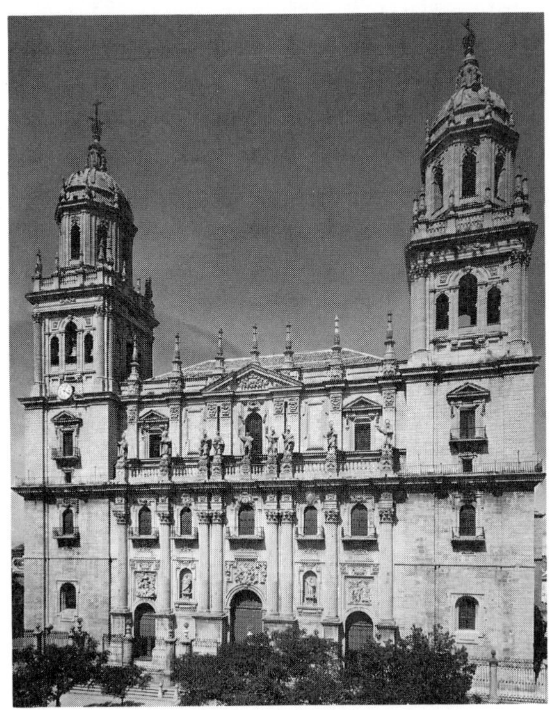

C. Jaén Cathedral: facade (1667–86). See p. 964

D. Valladolid Cathedral: facade (lower part *c.* 1585–; upper part 1729–33). See p. 964

CAR·VRO. IMP. HISP. REX MDLI
FT. MTRS
A CENTRAL PORTION OF N. FACADE: THE ALCAZAR: TOLEDO.
B PATIO: THE CASA POLENTINA: AVILA

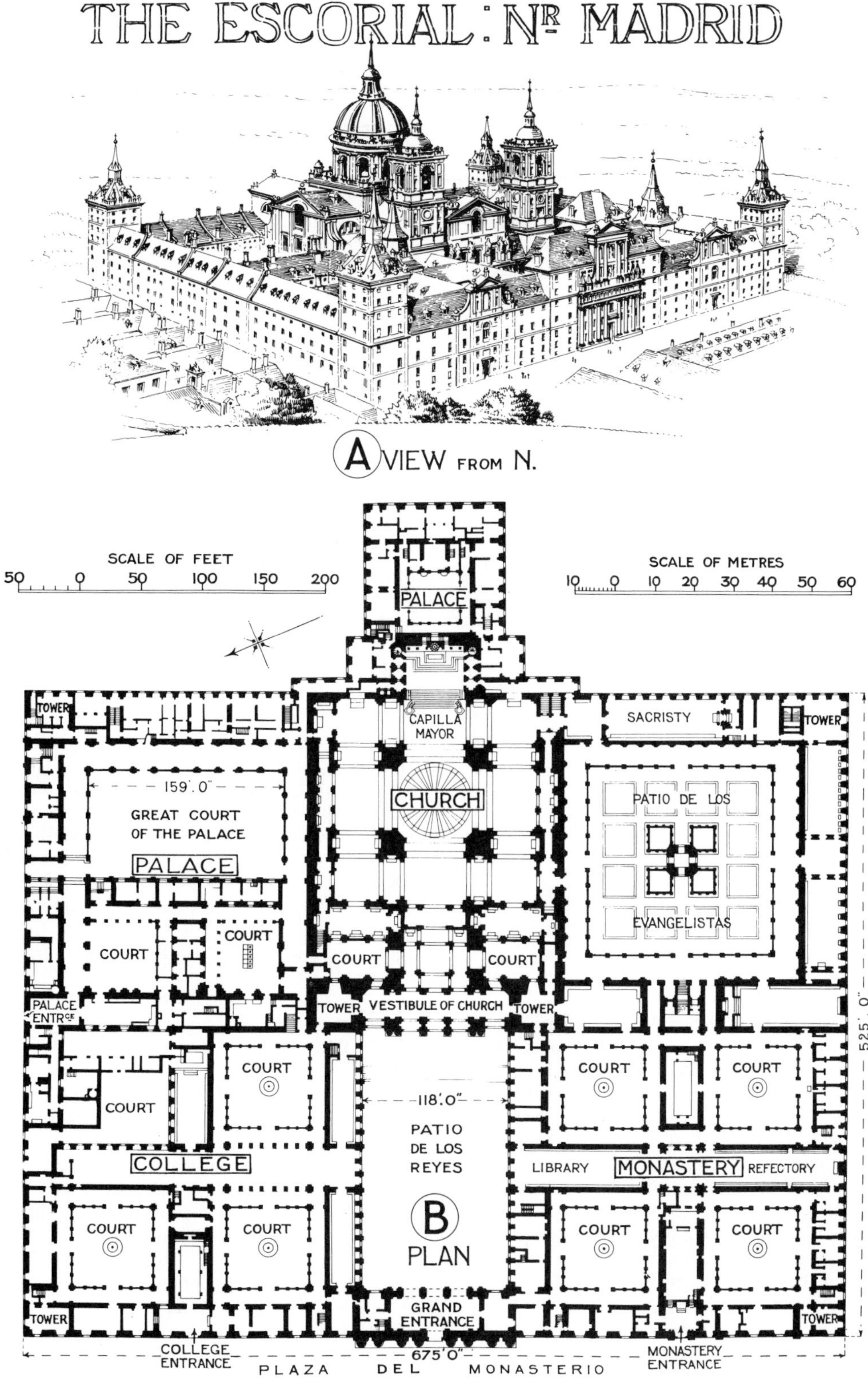
THE ESCORIAL: Nr MADRID
A VIEW FROM N.
SCALE OF FEET
50 0 50 100 150 200
SCALE OF METRES
10 0 10 20 30 40 50 60
PALACE
TOWER
CAPILLA MAYOR
SACRISTY
TOWER
159'.0"
GREAT COURT OF THE PALACE
PALACE
CHURCH
PATIO DE LOS EVANGELISTAS
COURT
COURT
COURT
COURT
PALACE ENTRCE
TOWER
VESTIBULE OF CHURCH
TOWER
525'.0"
COURT
COURT
COURT
COURT
118'.0"
PATIO DE LOS REYES
COLLEGE
LIBRARY
MONASTERY
REFECTORY
COURT
COURT
COURT
COURT
B PLAN
TOWER
GRAND ENTRANCE
TOWER
COLLEGE ENTRANCE
675'0"
MONASTERY ENTRANCE
PLAZA DEL MONASTERIO

The **Casa de los Guzmanes, Léon** (*c.* 1560), is a representative building of the Classical period, the architectural elements being used with discretion and restraint. The special Spanish note is struck by the angle pavilions – normal to domestic architecture, the columned doorway flanked by statues, small windows protected by iron grilles, and continuous arcaded upper storey in the deep shadow of wide-spreading eaves.

The **Sacristy of La Cartuja** (Charterhouse), **Granada** (1713–47) (p. 969B), is a truly extravagant example of Churrigueresque architecture, probably begun by Francisco Hurtado (1669–1725) but with an interior decorative scheme designed by a later generation. The windows are set at a high level and leave the walls free for the bizarre fretted plasterwork, executed during the 1740s, which encloses picture panels, inlaid doors and cupboards, and covers the pilasters.

The **University facade, Valladolid** (p. 970A), begun in 1715 by Narciso Tomé, has a powerful central portal, articulated by a paired giant order and filled with sculptural detail, which is part of the Plateresque revival of the early eighteenth century.

The **S. Fernando Hospital, Madrid** (1722–), designed by Pedro Ribera (*c.* 1683–1742), also has a main portal of great and intricate elaboration, rising upwards with sudden spurts of movement till it breaks through the main cornice at the top. This remarkable concentration of French-inspired sculptural detail, which includes hanging draperies, swags and putti, stresses the overriding predominance given to principal doorways, frequently on buildings that were otherwise treated with simplicity.

The **Palace of the Marqués de Dos Aguas, Valencia** (1740–4) (p. 969C), was designed by the painter Hipólito Rovira Bocandel in a French-inspired Rococo style of great efflorescence. The outstanding feature of the building is the alabaster door frame, executed by Ignacio Vergara, which has a pair of Michelangelesque figures, personifications of the two rivers of Valencia, set amid a wealth of plant and animal life.

The **Royal Palace, La Granja**, near Segovia (1719–39) (p. 970B), was begun by Teodoro Ardemans and extended by the Italians Andrea Procaccini (1671–1734) and Sempronion Subisati (*c.* 1680–1758), who designed the north and south courts. The centre of the garden facade, which has a giant Corinthian order, was built by G. B. Sacchetti to the design of Filippo Juvarra (1678–1736). The splendid gardens, designed by René Carlier and laid out between 1727 and 1743, give a French ambience to this powerful Italianate building.

The **Royal Palace, Madrid** (1738–64) (p. 971A), was initially commissioned by Philip V in 1735 from Juvarra, who planned a three-court complex. After Juvarra's death, his successor, Sacchetti, constructed the single-court block, using Bernini's design for the Louvre as a model. The result is wholly Italian Baroque in style, but with a new Classical spirit.

Ventura Rodríguez (1717–85) was a Spanish-born architect of neo-Classical tendencies whose greatest design, that of 1761 for **S. Francisco el Grande, Madrid**, was never carried out. Similar to S. Peter's in Rome, his project set a pedimented portico between tall corner towers, while above the whole was to rise a high Michelangelesque dome. Something of the scheme was realised in the facade of **Pamplona Cathedral**, which Rodŕiguez designed in 1783. Based on Classical Roman as well as High Renaissance models, it is a severe work which achieves remarkable grandeur by the massing of its monumental tetrastyle Corinthian portico, and also a romantic and evocative sense of the contrast between the broad columnar forms and the deep shadows between.

El Pilar Cathedral, Saragossa (p. 969D), was first designed *c.* 1675 by Filepe Sánchez, whose symmetrical scheme was developed in 1680 by Francisco de Herrera the younger (1622–83). The plan as a rectangular aisled basilica with corner towers follows Juan de Herrera's Valladolid project of *c.* 1585, but the work was incomplete when Francisco died in 1685 and his ideas suffered by later changes, particularly to the interior disposition, which was remodelled by Ventura Rodŕiguez in 1750. The striking domed elevation is also wholly the work of later architects.

The Prado, Madrid (1785–87) was designed by the second of the great eighteenth-century Spanish architects, Juan de Villanueva (1739–1811). His extravagant first project combined both a museum of Natural History and a Temple of Science intended to house learned societies and dropped in the more modest final design. The central block is attached to two vast pavilions by extended wings. The structure is characterised by a restraint in the use of ornament and by the adoption of columnar and arcaded screens. Under Ferdinand VII the Prado was turned into a picture gallery.

Portugal

The **Great Cloister of the Convent of Christ Tomar** (begun 1557) (p. 971B) was designed by Diego de Torralva (1500–66), most impressive of Portugal's sixteenth-century Classicists. Entirely in tune with developments in Italy, it has sculpturally conceived columns arranged in a syncopated rhythm of small and large bays reminiscent of Bramante's Cortile del Belvedere, Rome (q.v.). The Serlianas of the upper storey reflect an acquaintance with either Palladio's design for the Basilica in Vicenza (q.v.) or, more probably, Serlio's treatise on architecture (1537–).

The **Church of the Serra do Pilar, Vila Nova de Gaia** (1576–83), by João Lopes and Jeronimo Luis, is

A. Escorial, near Madrid: facade of church (1574–82). See p. 964

B. Sacristy of La Cartuja, Granada (1713–47). See p. 968

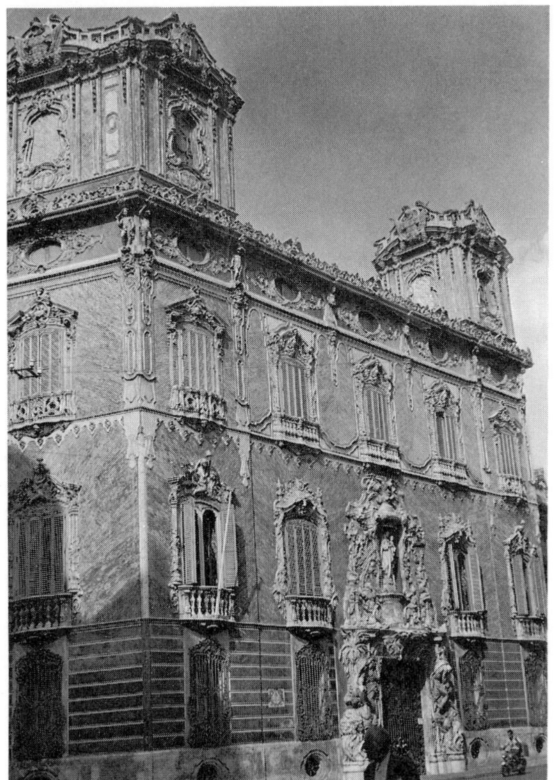

C. Palace of the Marqués de Dos Aguas, Valencia (1740–4). See p. 968

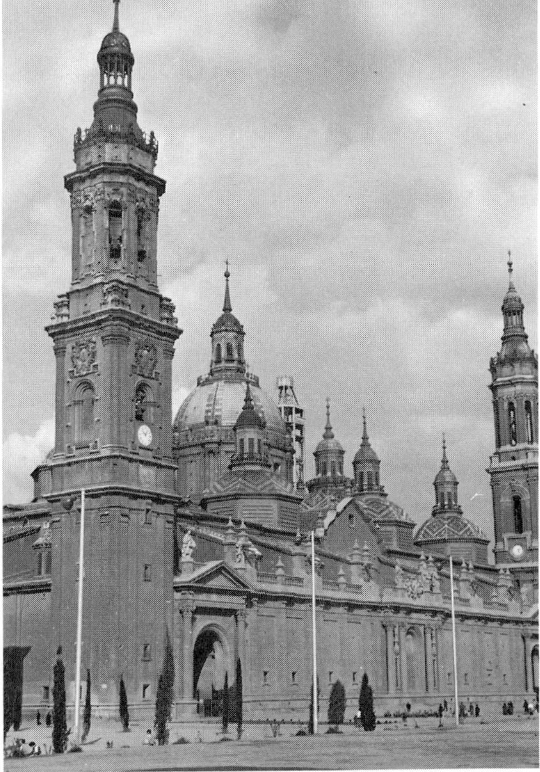

D. El Pilar Cathedral, Saragossa (*c.* 1675–1766). See p. 968

A. University, Valladolid: facade (1715–). See p. 968

B. Royal Palace, La Granja: garden facade (1735–9). See p. 968

A. Royal Palace, Madrid: facade (1738–64). See p. 968

B. Great Cloister, Convent of Christ Tomar (1557–). See p. 968

C. Basilica and Palácio Nacional, Mafra (1717–30). See p. 974

Church of S. Francisco, Oporto. See p. 974

A. Church of S. Pedro dos Clérigos, Oporto (1732–50). See p. 974

B. Palácio Nacional, Queluz (1747–60). See p. 974

C. Bom Jesus do Monte, near Braga (rebuilt 1784–). See p. 974

unusual in combining a circular church with a circular cloister. The latter, with its trabeated Ionic colonnade, was probably modelled upon the courtyard built by Pedro Machuca for Charles V at Granada.

S. Maria da Divina Providencia, Lisbon (mid-seventeenth century; destroyed 1755), was designed by the Italian architect Guarino Guarini. Longitudinal in plan, the design is made up entirely of interlocking oval spaces which herald the work of the Dientzenhofers and Neumann in central Europe. Guarini also makes use of what he called the 'supreme' order: Composite columns and pilasters with barley-sugar shafts, surmounted by an entablature which perpetuates the undulating theme. This order was to be influential upon the Baroque styles of the eighteenth century in Spain and Portugal.

The Basilica and Palácio Nacional, Mafra (1717–30) (p. 971C), designed by the German-born architect João Frederico Ludovice (1670–1752), was begun by King João V in thanksgiving for the birth of an heir. The enormous complex resembles the Escorial (q.v.) in plan and in function: a palace fused with a convent and church. The facade, dominated by its centrally placed church, resembles S. Agnese in Piazza Navona (q.v.), while the corner pavilions are of German inspiration. The complex is characterised by an architectural restraint which contrasts strongly with the work of Nasoni.

The **Church of S. Francisco, Oporto** (p. 972), a late mediaeval church remarkable for its grotto-like interior, is completely faced with extravagant eighteenth-century carved and gilded woodwork. Such treatment of surfaces, which is known as 'talha', is typical of Portuguese architectural ornament.

The **Church of S. Pedro dos Clérigos, Oporto** (1732–50) (p. 973A), by Niccolo Nasoni (died 1773), a Tuscan architect who had worked in Rome and southern Italy, is a skilful pastiche of seventeenth-century Italian Baroque. The plan, curiously attenuated owing to the exigencies of the site, incorporates an elliptical nave, entered at the sides and not through the monumental doorway of the richly decorated facade, which is blind. The surging tower, rising to 76 m (250 ft), is a *tour de force* of Baroque design. The concentration of surface modulation at the rounded corners endows the structure with a powerful verticality.

The **Palácio de Mateus, Vila Real** (mid-eighteenth century) was designed by N. Nasoni, who introduced to Portugal the Italian idea of a villa designed on several terraces. Two long wings flank a five-bay main facade with a raised doorway reached by a double ramped stair. The severe wings are intentionally contrasted with the explosion of ornament and curvilinear forms of the main facade. Here architraves bulge to make room for shells, and the repercussion is felt in the roof-top balustrade.

The **Palácio Nacional, Queluz**, near Lisbon (1747–60) (p. 973B), begun by the Portuguese Mateus Vicente de Oliviera (1710–68) and completed by the Frenchman J. B. Robillion (died 1768), is an exquisite Rococo country house, a typical if elaborate example of the 'quinta'. The superb gardens, also designed by Robillion, include a canal lined with panels of 'azulejos', the traditional coloured tiles and a decorative feature of Portuguese architecture, though of Moorish origin.

The Pilgrimage Church of **Bom Jesus do Monte, near Braga** (p. 973C), was rebuilt from 1784 in a neo-Palladian manner by Carlos Luis Ferreira da Cruz Amarante (born 1748). Set in superb gardens, it stands at the head of a steeply rising ceremonial granite staircase (1723), adorned with fountains and sculptured figures which appear to anticipate the statues of the prophets at Congonhas do Campo, carved by Aleijadinho in colonial Brazil.

Chapter 31

AUSTRIA, GERMANY AND CENTRAL EUROPE

Architectural Character

The heterogeneous development of architectural style in central Europe may be divided into the following approximate periods:

Renaissance (*c.* 1470–*c.* 1610)
Proto-Baroque (*c.* 1610–*c.* 1680)
High Baroque (*c.* 1680–*c.* 1750)
Neo-Classical (*c.* 1750–*c.* 1830)

The Renaissance style first appeared in Hungary at the court of Matthias Corvinus (1458–90), who employed the Bolognese Aristotele Fioravanti (q.v.) to design fortifications, and the Florentine Chimenti Camicia to build his castle at Buda (1480–), of which only fragments survive. A strong Early Renaissance Florentine flavour is characteristic also of the early sixteenth-century buildings of the Jagellonian court in Prague and Cracow, designed respectively by Benedikt Ried (1454–1534) and the imported Italian architects who continued to dominate court and aristocratic building in Poland, Bohemia and Moravia in the sixteenth century. Brunelleschian domed chapels with pendentives, four-towered castles with superimposed courtyard arcades, and rectangular mullioned windows without transoms are recurring features in this period, while crested parapets and gables spread to vernacular architecture.

In Germany and Austria, Renaissance elements were introduced by native architects around 1519 into largely Gothic buildings, while contacts with Italian trading centres, particularly Venice, inspired such examples as the Fuggerkapelle at Augsburg (1510–12). In Prague, the Austrian Habsburgs continued the tradition of importing Italian architects for a remarkable villa, the Belvedere (1534–63): it was designed by Paolo della Stella and continued by Bonifaz Wohlmut (died *c.* 1579), a truly High Renaissance architect with an easy mastery of the orders. Italian craftsmen were also brought in by Duke Ludwig X of Bavaria to Landshut to build the Stadtresidenz (1537–43), and the Bolognese Alessandro Pasqualini designed the Residenz at Jülich (1548–*c.* 1571). Outside the Renaissance courts, by contrast, and especially in the northern plains, from Brunswick to Gdansk, influences in the sixteenth and early seventeenth centuries tended to be predominantly Netherlandish, with Flemish pattern-book decoration applied to high stepped gables. The Jesuit church of S. Michael, Munich (1583–97), is among the first large-scale ecclesiastical buildings to reflect contemporary Roman models.

At the beginning of the seventeenth century in Augsburg, Elias Holl (1573–1646) pioneered a more rigorous Renaissance style, using a vocabulary distilled from late sixteenth-century Rome. The Cathedral at Salzburg (1614) was also in this more Classicising tendency, which fell victim to the upheavals of the Thirty Years' War (1648). During the long period of recovery, the most significant buildings were by Italian and French architects in Vienna and Prague.

The period 1680–1729 saw the flowering of central European Baroque, with the works of J. B. Fischer von Erlach (1656–1723), Jakob Prandtauer (1660–1726) and J. L. von Hildebrandt (1663–1745) in Austria, and of the Dientzenhofer family in Bohemia and Franconia. Von Erlach brought back from his years in Rome a taste not only for ancient and contemporary architecture, but also for the new techniques of illusionistic painting. His own architecture is highly eclectic, and somewhat lacking in unity. The work of Guarino Guarini (q.v.), who stayed in Prague in 1679, had a fundamental influence on the complex spatial effects and undulating surfaces of the mature Baroque in central Europe, as is evident in the works of J. L. von Hildebrandt, who had worked in Piedmont as a military engineer. The Dientzenhofer brothers spread their ideas to Franconia and northern Bavaria, while M. D. Pöpplemann (1662–1736) brought to the court of Augustus the Strong, Elector

Central Europe in the Renaissance period

of Saxony, the fruit of his studies in Vienna and Prague as well as in Paris and Italy. There were also attempts to fuse Baroque classicism with the idiosyncratic Central European Gothic tradition, as expressed in the work of Johann Blasius Santini Aichel (1667–1723). A Bohemian of Italian extraction born in Prague, Aichel worked in a Baroque manner inspired by Borromini and Guarini but, in his most memorable works, combined complex Baroque plans with Gothic forms and details.

Rococo decoration and ornament derived from France began to lighten the effect of late Baroque architecture from *c.* 1720. The major architects of the period were Balthasar Neumann (1687–1753), the architect of the Würzburg Residenz and of Vierzehnheiligen in Franconia, Johann Michael Fischer (1692–1766), and the Asam brothers, Cosmas Damian (1686–1739) and Egid Quirin (1692–1750). South German Rococo church interiors reach riotous heights of exuberance found nowhere else in Europe, aided by the spectacular *trompe l'oeil* effects of painters such as Johann Baptist Zimmermann, Johann and Januarius Zick, and Franz Anton Maulbertsch.

Early stirrings of neo-Classicism are to be found in the eclectic buildings constructed for Frederick the Great in Prussia, in Poland under Stanislas Augustus and, to a lesser extent, in the Austria of Maria Teresa. C. G. Langhans's Brandenburg Gate, Berlin, ushered in the Greek Revival element of neo-Classicism, which was to be particularly important in the work of Friedrich Gilly (1772–1800), Karl Friedrich Schinkel (1781–1841) and Leo von Klenze (1784–1864). Friedrich Gilly's magniloquent projects, such as that for the monument to Frederick the Great, were enormously influential both in Germany and elsewhere. His pupil Schinkel was the most important German architect of the nineteenth century, drawing on neo-Greek, 'Rundbogenstil' (a round-arched Romanesque cum Early Renaissance style), and Gothic, to give appropriate forms to the different types of building he was called on to design. Profoundly influenced by Durand, he was also impressed during his visit to Britain (1826) both by the picturesque qualities of English and Scottish architecture, and by the iron structures of the industrial revolution, which influenced his 'functionalist' use of metal frames. These eclectic yet highly rigorous tendencies were shared by and continued in the work of Klenze, who also pioneered the Renaissance revival.

Examples

Renaissance

The great late Gothic architect Benedikt Ried was instructed to import into **Hradshin Castle, Prague** (1493–1510), the Florentine forms of Hungarian royal architects as seen in Matthias Corvinus's lost castle at Buda. The result is a fascinating hybrid in which Ried's spectacular vaulting systems are combined with inventive, sometimes satirical, variations on Italianate door and window frames.

At **Wawel Castle, Cracow** (1502–50), a series of architects including two Florentines added new wings to the old royal castle, unified around the interior courtyard by superimposed Renaissance arcades – the earliest example of the type outside Italy. The two lower storeys, with columns supporting semi-circular arches, are authentically Florentine in flavour, but the elongated shafts of the upper columns, interrupted by fretted rings, are very curious.

The **Bakócz Chapel, Esztęrgom** (1506–, later reconstructed), is the first of a large series of domed cubical chapels based on Italian models to be built in eastern Europe. The architect of this very Florentine structure, with its red marble decoration, is unknown, but the altar (1519) is by Andrea Ferrucci of Fiesole.

The **Sigismund Chapel, Wawel Cathedral, Cracow** (1517–38), is the tomb chapel of Sigismund I of Poland. Designed by the Florentine Bartolommeo Berrecci, it is an updated version of Brunelleschi's Old Sacristy (q.v.), encrusted in red and white marble ornament and sculpture of very high quality. The chapel was imitated in less magnificent form all over Poland.

The **Fuggerkapelle** (1510–1512) in the Gothic Carmelite church of **S. Anna, Augsburg**, is the earliest building in Germany to display Italian Renaissance influence. It was commissioned in 1509 as a family burial chapel by Jakob Fugger (1459–1525) and his older brother Ulrich (1441–1510). Although the architect is not documented, he was probably the sculptor Sebastian Loscher (d. 1548), whose initials 'S. L.' appear on a surviving drawing, perhaps the original design approved by the Fuggers in 1509. Added to the west end of the church, the chapel consists of a square central space flanked by side aisles. The square entrance piers are faced with coloured marble pilaster strips, and above spring the round arches that open to the side aisles. Pilasters rise to the main entablature on the upper level, which supports the high entrance arch. Consistent use of round arches and features like the large oculus in the end wall give the chapel its Renaissance character. Yet the vaulting is covered with a net of Gothic ribs, creating an uneasy contrast. The entrance balustrade, with its little Tuscan columns, has been related to similar balustrades on the facade of the Fondaco dei Tedeschi at Venice, a Fugger establishment which may have been an important channel for Italian ideas entering Germany.

Loscher may also have been involved in the building of Jakob Fugger's palace, the **Fuggerhäuser** (1512–15) in the Weinmarkt at Augsburg. The severely horizontal facade was originally enlivened by painted decoration and by turrets that rose from the eaves. The entrance hall to the **Damenhof** has squat Ionic columns supporting round arches and cross-vaulting, the latter without ribs. But most Italianate is the Damenhof itself, which, although irregular in plan, has a fine round-arched arcade carried on slender, well-proportioned Tuscan columns.

The **Neupfarrkirche** (1519–40) at Regensburg was designed by Hans Hieber of Augsburg (d. 1522) as a pilgrimage church with the dedication 'Zur schönen Maria', a title abandoned when it was made over to the Lutherans in 1549. Although it was not finally completed until 1860, its major elements correspond to Hieber's wooden model of 1519–20, the earliest of its kind to survive in Germany. It is unusual because the whole church is raised on a podium, the plan consisting of a hexagonal nave joined to a rectangular choir with an apse at the east end. While the orderly handling of the forms is Renaissance in flavour, Gothic elements like the pinnacled buttresses and planned series of rose windows make it a transitional work.

The **Johann-Friedrichs-Bau** (1533–6) at **Schloss Hartenfels, Torgau**, was built for the Elector of Saxony, Johann Friedrich, by Konrad Krebs (1492–1540), an architect born in Hesse. The court facade of the rectangular block is dominated by a magnificent central open stair-tower, of horseshoe plan, rising from a square base to culminate in a convex gable high above. Four cross-gables that once flanked and balanced the stair gable have, unfortunately, been lost. Continuous mouldings around the arches combine with rich arabesque decoration to give the stair-tower fluidity and lightness, while rows of curtain-topped windows and a long balcony at second floor level counteract its verticality. The **Wächterturm** (1535) at the left of the facade has particularly delicate open galleries on two levels.

The **Rathaus, Heilbronn** (1535–96, severely damaged) (p. 978A), is an attractive building of essentially Gothic character. Its arcade of stumpy columns encloses a market, while steps at the sides lead up to the piano nobile. A central panel bears the signs of the zodiac and, above the level of the eaves, there is a clock with figures and a bell. The steep roof has three stages of small dormer windows and an open turret at the top.

At **Poznan Town Hall** (1550–60), Giovanni Battista Quadro, from Lake Lugano, reclothed the

A. Rathaus, Heilbronn (1535–96). See p. 977

B. Stadtresidenz, Landshut (1537–43). See p. 980

C. Pellerhaus, Nuremberg (1602–7). See p. 981

HEIDELBERG CASTLE

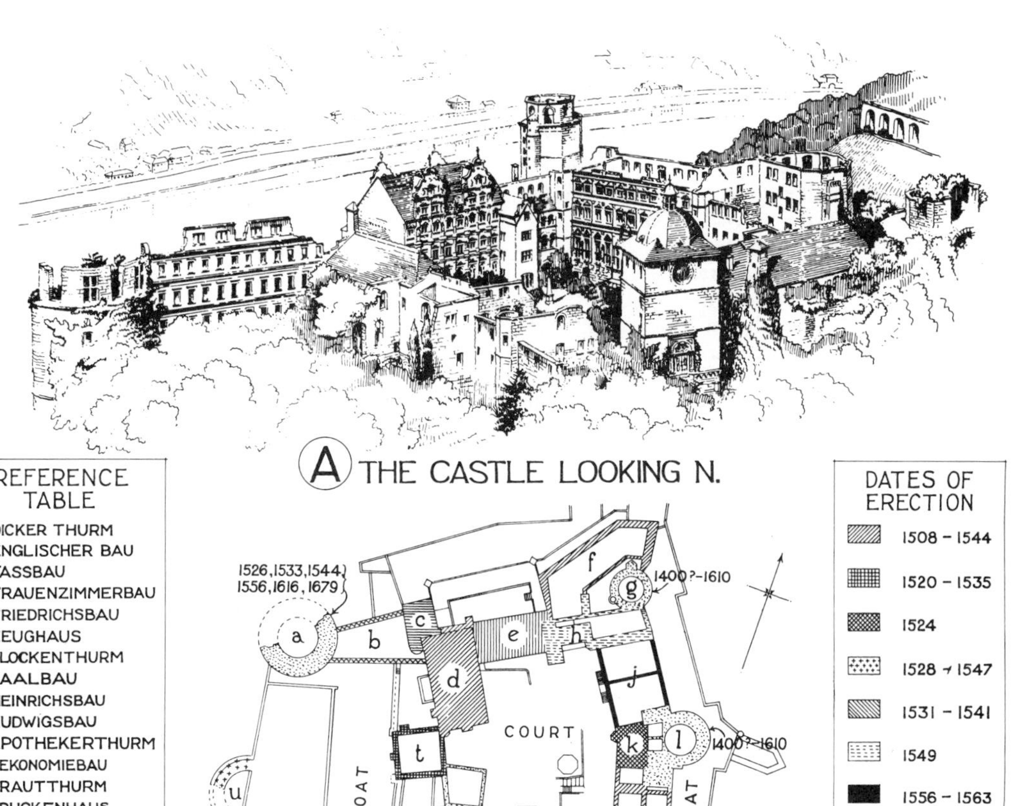

A THE CASTLE LOOKING N.

REFERENCE TABLE

- a DICKER THURM
- b ENGLISCHER BAU
- c FASSBAU
- d FRAUENZIMMERBAU
- e FRIEDRICHSBAU
- f ZEUGHAUS
- g GLOCKENTHURM
- h SAALBAU
- j HEINRICHSBAU
- k LUDWIGSBAU
- l APOTHEKERTHURM
- m OEKONOMIEBAU
- n KRAUTTHURM
- p BRUCKENHAUS
- q THORTHURM
- r RUPPRECHTSBAU
- s SELTENLEER
- t BIBLIOTEKBAU
- u RONDELL

DATES OF ERECTION

- 1508 – 1544
- 1520 – 1535
- 1524
- 1528 – 1547
- 1531 – 1541
- 1549
- 1556 – 1563
- 1583 – 1592
- 1601 – 1607
- 1612
- VARIOUS DATES

50 0 100 200 300 FEET
10 0 20 40 60 80 100 METRES

B PLAN

C HEINRICHSBAU

D FRIEDRICHSBAU

Gothic building in three storeys of trabeated arcades with a high parapet, turrets and clock tower above. The line of the corner turrets is continued down through the closed bays at either end of the facade. The doubled rhythm of smaller arcades on the third storey derives from Serlio's plate of a lost Roman building, the 'Crypta Balbi', and the semicircular steps no doubt stem from the same printed source.

The **Stadtresidenz at Landshut** (1537–43) (p. 978B) owes much to the Palazzo del Te at Mantua (q.v.), which had impressed the patron, Duke Ludwig X of Bavaria, when he visited the Gonzaga in 1536. Ludwig enlisted a band of Mantuan craftsmen, and they, while avoiding the irregularities and quirks of Giulio Romano's work, gave his new palace its fully Italian courtyard and principal rear facade. The court arcade of Roman Doric columns supporting rusticated arches has narrow end bays containing simple niches, reminiscent of the narrow bays of both the court and exterior elevations of Palazzo del Te. There is, however, no rustication on the upper level, where Corinthian pilasters frame windows that have alternating triangular and segmental pediments.

The **Belvedere, Prague** (1534–63), was designed for Ferdinand, King of Bohemia, by an Italian, Paolo della Stella (d. 1552) of Genoa. The form of the building, a simple two-storey rectangle with high curved roof and continuous ground floor arcades, is that of north Italian town halls, such as those at Padua and Brescia (q.v.). The graceful loggia has arches borne on columns, while a more academic tone, perhaps derived from Serlio, is struck by the door and window surrounds. The upper level and the copper roof are the work of Bonifaz Wohlmut, who had taken over in 1558. A terraced garden with fountains in the Italian style adjoins the hill-top villa.

Bonifaz Wohlmut (died *c.* 1579) came to Prague from Vienna in 1554. His architecture shows a confident restraint in the use of the orders most unusual for his time and place. The **Royal Ball-Court, Prague** (1567–9), is a long low pavilion with a five-bay central arcade on heavy piers and deep niches above arches at either end. The monumental Ionic order with pulvinated frieze, and the entablature broken over the half-columns, gives a robustly Palladian feeling to the whole.

Archduke Ferdinand of the Tirol collaborated with two Italian architects, Giovanni Maria del Pambio and Giovanni Lucchese, to design a remarkable star-shaped hunting lodge outside **Prague, Hrezda Castle** (1555–6). A sequence of diamond-shaped rooms surrounds a dodecagonal central hall with monochrome stucco decoration. Surrounded by its low fortification system designed by Bonifaz Wohlmut, the villa, with its austere fenestration, looks almost like a neo-Classical fantasy by Boullée (q.v.).

A series of four-towered castles with superimposed courtyard loggias on the model of the Wawel Castle in Cracow were built in Bohemia and Moravia in the second half of the sixteenth century. Interesting examples are **Bucovice** (1567–82), by Pietro Terrabosco and Pietro Gabri, with its magnificent stuccoed interiors, and **Litomysl** (1568–73), by the Aostalli brothers, Giovanni Battista and Ulrico, which has repeated gables forming a parapet – a very popular motif of the time. All these architects worked at the Court of Rudolf II in Prague.

The **Zitadelle at Jülich** (1548–*c.* 1571) suffered severe damage during World War II, but enough remains of the rectangular Ducal Residence at the centre, and particularly of the **Schlosskapelle** (1552–3), to reveal a degree of sophistication in the treatment of High Renaissance forms previously unknown in Germany. The architect was an Italian, Alessandro Pasqualini (1485–1558), who had earlier worked in Holland, and was called to Jülich in 1548 by the patron Duke Wilhelm V of Kleve. Certainly familiar with the work of Bramante and his followers, Pasqualini gave the chapel exterior a firm base with a Doric order bearing rusticated bands, allowing the Ionic order above to rise with both lightness and strength. Within, an Ionic order of paired half-columns brilliantly articulates the interaction between the curve of the apse and its window openings, creating remarkable sculptural richness.

The **Residenz, Munich**, once a mediaeval Wittelsbach castle, was rebuilt as a Renaissance palace from the 1560s on by the Dukes of Bavaria. Of special interest is the **Antiquarium**, a long barrel-vaulted crypt intended to contain Albrecht V's collection of antiquities. It was begun in 1569 by Wilhelm Egckl (died 1588) to designs supplied by the Milanese architect and art dealer Jacopo della Strada (died 1588), and despite modifications by Fredrick Sustris (1524–99) during the 1580s, when the floor level was lowered and the lavish decoration added, the origins of the design in vaulted subterranean Roman chambers (cryptoportici) is still apparent. The adjoining **Grottenhof** (1580–88), which is enlivened by statue-filled niches, was also constructed by Sustris.

Heidelberg Castle (1531–1615) (pp. 979,982A–C) was developed and expanded during the Renaissance by successive Electors Palatine, whose home it was. The **Gläserner Saalbau** (1549), overshadowed by the octagonal **Glockenthurm** (1531–41) of Ludwig V (1508–44), was built in a restrained style for Friedrich II (died 1556). Its court facade, the work of the mason Conrad Förster, has round-arched arcading on three levels, with heavy proportions and stumpy columns lacking Italianate sophistication. The **Ottheinrichsbau** (1556–59) suffered severe damage during successive wars and stands now a hollow shell. The elaborate court facade, however, remains intact except for the loss of the gables. Exploratory in its sometimes ungrammatical use of classical forms, the facade reflects the more developed architectural interest of the patron, Ottheinrich (died 1559), who owned copies of Vitruvius and Serlio. Superimposed

Ionic and Corinthian pilasters, and Composite half-columns on the upper level, divide the facade into five double bays, each containing a pair of ornate two-light windows and a central statue-filled niche. The symbolic statues are by the Netherlandish sculptor Alexander Colin (*c.* 1528–1612), who was also responsible for the central portal (1558–59). The **Friedrichsbau** (1601–7), designed for Friedrich V by Johannes Schoch (died 1651), is a successful counterpart to the Ottheinrichsbau. Based on the same scheme, it is a more satisfactorily controlled and proportioned composition, particularly in the way the storeys and the niches are graded in height. The Gothic idiom is harmoniously introduced on the lower level, where the round-arched windows are filled with fine tracery, a decorous way of indicating the chapel within. The **Englischer Bau** (1613–15), built for Friedrich V by an unknown architect, survives only as a skeletal structure. The south facade has even rows of rectangular windows, without pediments or excess ornament, which strike a refined Palladian note reminiscent of the early works of Inigo Jones.

The **Rathaus Portico (Doxal), Cologne** (1567–71), an open two-storey arcaded porch added to the mediaeval building, was executed by Wilhelm Vernukken (died 1607), who used as models a pair of still surviving perspective drawings which are signed 'C. F'. (Cornelis Floris) and dated 1557. Five bays wide and two deep, the round arches of the ground level have Corinthian columns in front, while the upper storey has a Composite Order and slightly pointed arches, indicating some Gothic traits in this exquisite Renaissance structure.

The **Julius Universität at Würzburg** (1582–92), together with its church, the **Neubaukirche** (1583–91), were designed by Georg Robin for Prince Bishop Julius Echter, first of the Würzburg 'building bishops'. Representative of the eclectic *Juliusstil*, the court facades are severe and have little variety apart from the rusticated blind arcading in the ground level and the graceful late Gothic tracery of the church windows. Sculptural decoration appears only on the main portal (*c.* 1592) in the north facade, which is crowned by a relief of the Pentecost.

The **Church of S. Michael, Munich** (1583–97) (p. 982J), was designed for the Jesuits by Fredrick Sustris (1524–99), although the financial patron was a layman, Duke Wilhelm V of Bavaria. The first great Jesuit church in northern Europe, it has similarities with Vignola's Gesù in Rome (begun 1568), the model for Counter-Reformation churches everywhere. But there are differences, such as the tribune storey over the side chapels, derived from northern Protestant models like the **Chapel of Augustusburg Schloss** (1569–73). The facade by Hans Krumpper (*c.* 1570–1634) has a central niche flanked by two side portals of red marble, the latter designed by Sustris.

The **Gewandhaus, Brunswick (Braunschweig)**, the body of which is Gothic, has an eastern facade (1592) illustrating typical north German Renaissance characteristics, introduced via the Low Countries. The ground-level arcade is surmounted by three storeys of Ionic, Corinthian and Composite three-quarter columns, while above rises an immense gable of four storeys of herms, framed by the customary side-scrolls of the stepped gables.

The **Arsenal at Gdansk** (1602–5), by Antonius van Opbergen, the architect of the castle at Helsingør (q.v.), is one of several magnificent civic buildings erected in this city in a Netherlandish Renaissance style. The repertory of ornate gables, strapwork cartouches, obelisks, and banded orders is familiar from Belgian buildings of the period, as are the use of brick and the mullioned and transomed windows.

The new town of **Zamosć** (1587–1605) was built by the eminent Polish dignitary Jan Zamoyski in the centre of his estates. The Venetian architect Bernardo Morando combined castle and town in an up-to-date polygonal bastioned enceinte with a large arcaded square in the centre of a grid plan of streets. The result is in accord with Italian Renaissance treatises on town planning and fortifications.

Baroque and Rococo (1600–1750)

The **Pellerhaus, Nuremberg** (1602–7) (p. 978C), was designed by Jakob Wolff the Elder and Peter Carl for the Peller family. The patrons' desire for an Italianate design led to a fusion of two traditions: Venetian details were grafted onto a German substructure. The three-storey facade is crowned with a gable of three diminishing tiers similar in effect to Netherlandish architecture. The rustication, arched windows, crowning obelisks, sequence of Doric, Ionic and Corinthian orders, all give the facade an Italian character which becomes specifically Venetian in the blind balustrades running across the facade and in the notion of fusing a scallop-shell and segmental pediment.

Luder Von Bentheim modernised the **Town Hall, Bremen** (1608–13), while retaining the Gothic core and old-fashioned high-pitched roof. The architect transformed the pointed into semicircular arches, added a crowning balustrade and symmetrically arranged gables, and topped the windows with alternating triangular and segmental pediments. The profusion of carved ornament looks back to an indigenous tradition.

The **Cathedral, Salzburg** (1614–28), was rebuilt by the Italian architect Santino Solari for a great-nephew of Pope Pius IV. Vincenzo Scamozzi (q.v.) had contributed a design but it was not adopted. The two-storey, twin-tower facade would not seem out of place on Italian soil. Three superimposed orders as well as Michelangelesque relief decoration, such as pedimented panels with garlands, emphasise this effect.

A WINDOWS & NICHE WITH DIANA: HEINRICHSBAU, HEIDELBERG CASTLE
B CHARLES THE GREAT: FRIEDRICHSBAU, HEIDELBERG CASTLE
C WINDOWS & NICHE WITH SATURN: HEINRICHSBAU, HEIDELBERG CASTLE
D CAPITAL: FOUNTAIN OF S.JEAN: FREIBURG SWITZ^D
E GABLE: HEILBRONN
F CAPITAL: FOUNTAIN OF THE SAMARITAN: FREIBURG: SWITZ^D
G WINDOW: ERFURT
H CARTOUCHE: HEILBRONN
J DOORWAY S.MICHAEL: MUNICH

Only the stilted domes crowning the towers seem locally inspired. Together with the Jesuit churches at **Dillingen** (1610–17), **Mindelheim** (1625–6), **Vienna** (1627–31), and **Innsbruck** (1627–40), it was among the first churches north of the Alps to be treated wholly in a Renaissance manner.

Jean Baptiste Mathey (*c.* 1630–95), born in Dijon, worked in Prague from 1675–94. His design for the **Troja Palace, Prague** (1679–96) (p. 986A), combines French notions about château planning with Italianate detailing. A central *corps de logis* is flanked by two wings to form three sides of a courtyard. An elaborate double ramp stair with a profusion of statuary focuses attention on the main portal and the grotto set immediately below.

Carlo Antonio Carlone (died 1708), the most distinguished member of an expatriate Italian family of artists, designed the **Abbey Church of S. Florian** (1686–1708). Here he introduced to Austria the 'Platzgewolbe', a type of flat domical vault which was to become the most popular vehicle for the elaborate unifying ceiling frescos so common in later buildings.

Jakob Prandtauer (1660–1726) trained as a master mason and sculptor, and paid extremely careful attention to the construction of his buildings throughout a career devoted primarily to church architecture. His masterpiece is the **Benedictine Monastery, Melk** (1702–14) (p. 984A,C), sited on a rocky ledge overlooking the Danube. Prandtauer made the most of its elevated position, continuing the upward surge of the rock in his design. Thus the building rises in gradual stages from the undulating atrium screen to the taller wings housing the library and the marble hall, reaching a climax in the multi-tiered bell-towers and dome.

Johann Bernhard Fischer von Erlach (1656–1723) was the dominant figure in central European architecture towards the end of the seventeenth century. Trained in his father's profession of sculpture, he spent formative years in Italy, where the buildings of Bernini and Borromini made an immense impression on him. It was he who introduced such ideas as the unification of the arts to Austria. Though famous primarily as an architect, he also holds an important position as an early historian of architecture, publishing his *Entwurf einer historischen Architektur* in 1721.

The **Castle, Vranov** (1690–4), is an early work in which Fischer's predilection for the oval form is evident throughout; the great oval hall, perhaps based on French models such as Vaux-le-Vicomte (q.v.), has large oval windows piercing the low dome and is preceded by an oval vestibule. The vault has a unifying scheme of fresco decoration owing much to the innovations of Carlone at S. Florian (q.v.).

Designed for the Prince-Bishop Ernst Count Thun-Hohenstein, Fischer's **Church of the Holy Trinity, Salzburg** (1694), is a reworking of Borromini's scheme for S. Agnese in the Piazza Navona (q.v.). The domed church is the centrepiece of a much larger group. While church and palace are united at basement level, the orders above differ in scale, giving the church extra emphasis. The concave church facade culminates in twin towers and a dome. As at Vramov, the transverse oval entrance heralds a longitudinal oval interior, in this case fused with a Greek cross.

The **Karlskirche, Vienna** (begun 1716) (p. 984B), was built by Fischer for the Emperor Joseph I, in fulfilment of a vow made to S. Charles Borromeo. The plan develops an idea – the fusion of oval and Greek cross – found in his earlier Church of the Holy Trinity. In this case the oval chapels have replaced niches on the diagonal axes. The main congregational space is articulated with pilasters while the columns are restricted to the chapels. Dividing chancel from choir behind the main altar is a semicircular columnar screen unashamedly borrowed from Palladio's Redentore (q.v.). The most novel feature of the design is the facade, almost twice as wide as the building it screens. As in Maderno's facade for S. Peter's, Rome (q.v.), arches through twin towers give access both into the church and through it, but the two huge columns modelled on those of Trajan and Marcus Aurelius in Rome which dominate the facade and frame the dome are an oddly historicist introduction. Adorned with spiral reliefs, they symbolise the triumph of faith over the disease which had threatened the patron. The facade curves gently around these columns, unifying the scheme, and the pedimented portico is thrust out between them.

The **Abbey Church, Einsiedeln** (begun 1703), designed by Hans Georg Kuen and completed by his pupil Caspar Mosbrugger (1656–1723), has an unusual plan related to its second function as pilgrimage site. Immediately upon entry the visitor is confronted by an older structure, the venerated Chapel of S. Meinrad. Above this stands the huge octagonal vault, the largest of the church, while beyond, three centralised spaces diminish towards (and focus attention on) the high altar.

The **Imperial Library, Vienna** (begun 1722), reflects the growing austerity (for example the banded rustication of the battered basement and *porte-en-niche*) and susceptibility to French influence found in Fischer's work. The central pavilion with its three-tier roof and vertical oval windows – a characteristic feature of Fischer's vocabulary – houses the main hall, which in plan fuses a rectangle and a transverse ellipse.

Fischer's **Palace of the Hungarian Guard, Vienna** (1710–12) (p. 986B), consists of a rectangular block with a projecting pedimented frontispiece. The basement with its banded rustication curves almost imperceptibly forward at the Doric portal, and the frontispiece is adorned with exaggeratedly high paired pilasters. Although astylar, the

A. Benedictine Monastery, Melk (1702–14). See p. 983

B. Karlskirche, Vienna (1716–). See p. 983

C. Benedictine Monastery, Melk: interior of church

main body of the palace has windows so narrowly spaced that it gives the impression of having an order, an illusion emphasised by the capital-like scrolls at the top.

Johann Lukas von Hildebrandt (1663–1745) was born in Genoa, the son of a German soldier. Having studied with Carlo Fontana in Rome, he was prized as a military engineer, and succeeded Fischer von Erlach as Surveyor General of Imperial Buildings. His name is associated with a style which emerged in the first decade of the eighteenth century. Heavy garlands and acanthus decoration began to give way to more lively and less naturalistic forms of decoration. Although he was obviously impressed by the works of Borromini, his true architectural preferences were for the north Italian Guarini and his followers. Guarini's influence is evident at **S. Laurence, Jablonne v Podjestedi** (1699). Similar in plan to S. Lorenzo, Turin (q.v.), it is more spatially complex than anything Fischer von Erlach had produced. The rectangular exterior belies the complexity of the interior, where the ovals of the entrance vestibule and altar chapel generate the concave lines of the central space. These curves interlock with those of the niches marking the diagonal axes and create a sensation of overlapping, intersecting spaces.

The **Upper Belvedere, Vienna** (1721–2) (p. 987A), was laid out by Hildebrandt for Prince Eugene as a garden pendant to the recently completed **Lower Belvedere** (1715). The centre of the facade is dominated by a tall, projecting pavilion with a three-tier roof. A two-tier roof distinguishes the lower flanking ranges, while beyond, yet lower astylar wings with single-tier roofs adjoin octagonal corner pavilions. The notion of multi-tiered roofs is traditional in central Europe; here they are used to create a Baroque crescendo. In many respects the design is similar to the almost contemporaneous Imperial Library.

The **Daun Kinsky Palace, Vienna** (1713–16) (p. 986C), is characteristic of Hildebrandt's style. Above an ashlar basement rise two storeys, unified by giant narrowly-spaced pilasters. The central three bays of the seven break forward and are further subtly distinguished by increased applied decoration, a crowning balustrade, differing fenestration and decorative flat pilasters. The concave portal framed by supporting caryatids was probably taken from French models, even though German precedents can be found (for example at Heidelberg Castle).

The **Cernin Palace, Prague** (1668), designed by Francesco Caratti, has an extensive Italianate facade. The giant order uniting the upper storeys stands on a basement decorated with diamond-faceted rustication, into which are inserted two bulging portals.

Georg Dientzenhofer (1643–89) settled in Prague and, together with his brothers, created the distinctive style of Bohemian Baroque, a style Georg subsequently introduced in Franconia with his **Pilgrimage Church, Waldsassen** (1685–89). The plan of the structure is generated by a triangle to which three vast apses were attached, forming a triconch. Chapels are set into the thickness of the wall, the staircase towers are built into bulges which mark the junctures between the three apses, and the whole is surrounded by a continuous arcade. This geometrically conceived plan points to an interest in the work of Borromini and Guarini.

Christoph Dientzenhofer (1655–1722), a contemporary of Fischer von Erlach, was the most distinguished architect working in Bohemia. His fascination with the work of Guarini, who had visited Prague, was to transform Bohemian Baroque.

For the Jesuits, Christoph built the nave of **S. Nicholas on the Lesser Side, Prague** (1703–11) (pp. 987B,988). The two-storey exterior becomes three-storeyed on the main facade, and the flatness of the sides gives way to a play of concave and convex rhythms. Inside, curves again predominate. Three ovals flow into one another, emphasized by the projecting angular piers with their curving pilasters. The use of strong verticals concetrates attention on the elaborate ceiling decoration. Inspired by Guarini, this design seems to be based, in particular, on the church of S. Maria di Divina Providencia, Lisbon (q.v.).

S. Margaret, Brevnov, near Prague (1708–21) (p. 990A), built by Christoph Dientzenhofer for the Benedictines, has an interior similar in conception to that of S. Nicholas. Two pilasters meeting at acute angles form the piers which support the four interlocking oval vaults. On the exterior, by contrast, Dientzenhofer gives the impression of a centrally planned church, by folding the main facade around the corner and applying almost identical gables to front and side.

Johann Dientzenhofer (1663–1726) was the youngest of the Dientzenhofer brothers. He designed the **Schloss, Pommersfelden** (1711–18), in collaboration with Hildebrandt, whom the patron, Elector Lothar Franz von Schonborn, had asked for advice. The exterior, characteristic of Johann's strongly sculptural style, has a vast central pavilion with rounded corners. The giant order is set on tall pedestals flanking arches, an idea perhaps borrowed from the Cernin Palace, Prague (q.v.). As the order moves from the sides to the centre, single pilasters become paired, then clustered and emerge as free-standing columns at the portal. A similar system is seen in the marble saloon, where an arcuated cornice rises over oval windows similar to those used by Fischer von Erlach. Of Johann Dientzenhofer's other designs the most remarkable are the **Abbey Church, Banz** (1710–18), and the **Neumunster Striftskirche, Würzburg** (facade 1710–19).

Johann Blasius Santini Aichel (1667–1723) made a very individual contribution to central European architecture in the early eighteenth century with his

A. Troja Palace, Prague: garden front (1679–96). See p. 983

B. Palace of the Hungarian Guard, Vienna (1710–12). See p. 983

C. Daun Kinsky Palace, Vienna (1713–16). See p. 985

A. Upper Belvedere, Vienna (1721–2). See p. 985

B. S. Nicholas on the Lesser Side, Prague (1703–52): entrance front. See p. 985

C. Frauenkirche, Dresden (1725–42). See p. 989

S. Nicholas on the Lesser Side, Prague: interior (1703–11). See p. 985

inventive mix of idiosyncratic Baroque and late Gothic. Most characteristic are his buildings at **Zdar, Moravia**, including additions to a Cistercian monastry, now known as **Castle Kinsky** (1706–23), a **plague cemetery** (1709) and the **pilgrimage chapel of S. Johannes Nepomuk** (1719–23). Aichel's works to Castle Kinsky include the polygonal former monks' refectory which appears externally as a strange blister rising above the roofscape. Internally the room is decorated with a giant order of pilasters and a richly frescoed ceiling. The plague cemetery comprises three oval chapels representing the Trinity (a fourth was added later) linked by curved walls which, in plan, form the outline of a human skull. Aichel's masterpiece is the pilgrimage chapel which has a plan derived from a star and a tongue, the symbols of S. Johannes Nepomuk, set within a star-plan cloister. The elevations and many of the details of the chapel are in an abstract, almost cubist, Gothic idiom of Aichel's own invention.

In the **Abbey Church, Grüssau (Kerzeźow)** (1728–55), Anton Jentsch produced the most important building of the Silesian Baroque. The curvilinear surfaces of the twin-towered facade exceed even Christoph Dientzenhofer's S. Nicholas in complexity, by introducing wave-like elements to the horizontals to augment the dynamic verticality. Charles XII of Sweden obtained from the emperor permission for the Silesian Protestants to build six churches. Following the Swedish model of S. Catherine, Stockholm (q.v.), they favoured centrally-planned structures designed as auditoria for sermons. Restrained in detail and avoiding Baroque opulence, a church like the **Gnadenkirche, Hirschberg** (1709–18), by Martin Frantz contrasts strongly with the Abbey Church, Grüssau.

Mathaes Daniel Pöppelmann (1662–1736), a contemporary of Fischer von Erlach, was the most successful and inventive architect of his age in Upper Saxony. Visits to Rome and Vienna in 1710 dramatically influenced his style, as is evident in his most famous building, the **Zwinger, Dresden** (1709–) (p. 990B). Built into a bastion, it was to serve as an orangery as well as a grandstand for court festivities. The Zwinger has two main foci, the **Kronentov** (1713) and the **Wallpavillon** (1716). Both are conceived as pavilions, rising above the single-storey, omega-shaped enclosure. In contrast to the more sober treatment of the orangery, their dynamic clustering of vertical elements, whether herms or columns, produces an almost Gothic effect.

Another architect with a successful practice in Dresden was George Bahr (1666–1738). Trained as a carpenter, he went on to design such impressive buildings as the **Frauenkirche, Dresden** (1725–42) (p. 987C); destroyed February 1945. A Protestant church, it was essentially a Greek cross set in a square, surmounted by an elongated dome that obviated the need for a drum. The facade system of tall pedimented tabernacles framing long windows was repeated in the projecting corner turrets, giving an almost octagonal character to the exterior. The interior had a skeletal structure which rivalled those of Balthasar Neumann in its daring restriction of supports.

Andreas Schlüter (1659?–1714), sculptor and architect, began his career in Warsaw but worked predominantly in Prussia. His architectural style is characterised by the importance he accorded to the role of sculpture. Latterly he fell into disgrace because of technical and structural faults in his buildings. For Ernst Bogislav von Kamecke he built the **Kamecke House, Berlin** (1711–12). This charming villa has two lateral wings whose lower cornices overlap the central pavilion. The undulating three-bay facade of the latter is articulated with abstracted vertical pilaster strips culminating in the silhouetted figures of Classical deities arrayed on the roofline. While the scheme resembles the Zwinger in Dresden, here the architectural ornament is starkly reduced in order to show off the sculpture.

Cosmas Damian Asam (1686–1739) and his brother Egid Quirin Asam (1692–1750) were Bavarian by birth. Cosmas had trained as a painter in Rome, and Egid as a sculptor in Munich. Following Bernini's lead, they fused the arts to produce effects of spectacular illusionism, creating a style which spread rapidly in central Europe. It was Egid himself who paid for the construction of **S. Johannes Nepomuk, Munich** (1733–46) (p. 991A). Emerging from a rock bed rather like the Trevi Fountain, Rome (q.v.), a gaint order of slightly concave pilasters supports a writhing pediment. Within this frame are two equally extravagant superimposed aedicules crowned by ecstatic sculptural groups. In order to create as light an interior as possible, much of the facade, including the portal, is given over to glass. The undulating interior, with its barley-sugar columns, has been partially marred by the removal of the figure of S. John over the high altar, and by the blocking of the hidden light source.

Balthasar Neumann (1687–1753) brought Baroque architecture in Franconia to its climax. Born into a family of clothiers, and trained as a bell-founder, he emerged first as a military architect. He later taught architecture at Würzburg University but never gave up his military status.

The **Residenz, Würzburg** (begun 1719) (p. 991C), was designed largely by Neumann with advice from Hildebrandt, von Welsch, Boffrand and de Cotte. A vast U-shaped plan encompasses four enclosed courts as well as the *cour d'honneur.* The triple–arched frontispiece is similar to that of Hildebrandt in the Upper Belvedere, Vienna (q.v.), as is the pavilion of the garden facade; the pilasters on the upper tier taper towards the bottom and frame windows curved symmetrically at top and bottom. From the French architects came the pavilion character of the side wings and changes to the staircase design. Instead of

A. S. Margaret, Brevnov, near Prague (1708–21). See p. 985

B. Zwinger, Dresden (1709–). See p. 989

A. S. Johannes Nepomuk, Munich (1733–46). See p. 989

B. Abbey Church of S. Gall (rebuilt 1748–70): library. See p. 992

C. Residenz, Würzburg (1719–). See p. 989

flights either side of the vestibule, a single grand stair was proposed, filling the whole zone between the vestibule and one of the inner courts. The result, with its gentle incline, its gradually unfolding spatial effects and its lively ceiling painted by G. B. Tiepolo is the most monumental of German Baroque staircases. The chapel (1730) was also built to Neumann's design, although Hildebrandt devised the decoration. Its highly complex plan owes much to Guarini and the Dientzenhofers. A series of interlocking transverse and longitudinal ovals fuse to create a vital interior, in which an inventive system of wall decoration responds to the columnar screens supporting galleries.

The **Schloss, Bruchsal** (1731–2, now destroyed), was designed for Damian Hugo von Schonborn, Prince of Speyer. A series of architects was rapidly dismissed between 1720 and 1728. One of these, Franz Freiherr von Ritter, included in his design for the main residential block a transverse oval staircase situated between two internal courts. This was transformed by Neumann, who connected the state rooms on the entrance and garden facades by a new enlarged oval landing. The result brought Neumann international renown.

The **Pilgrimage Church, Vierzehnheiligen** (1743–72) (p. 994A,C), was again the product of more than one mind. While Neumann's rivals had suggested centrally planned designs with the alter, dedicated to the 'fourteen saints', at the centre, his Latin-cross project won initial approval. The executive architect departed from this plan, and Neumann was asked to redesign the building incorporating the already constructed chancel. The final design was made up of a series of three longitudinally placed ovals, along the main axis of which the central one, housing the altar, is the largest. Two circles form the transepts while two small ovals are inserted into the side aisles. The use of large windows, white walls and gilded stucco produce a light, glittering Rococo effect.

A strong contrast to Vierzehnheiligen can be found in Neumann's slightly earlier **Parish Church, Etwashausen** (1741–5). The design elements are familiar: a skeletal structure, columnar screens and interlocking ovals produce a complex vaulting system. However, the Rococo overlay is missing. An austere Doric replaces fanciful Corinthian and there is a total absence of arabesque stucco work and lavish light-hued frescos. Neumann and Hildebrandt collaborated again in the design of the **Schloss, Werneck** (1734–45), where the chapel was designed entirely by the former. The circular plan was given a decagonal character by the insertion of giant concave niches, counterbalanced by gently curving convex galleries above, similar to those designed by Vittone at Vallinotto (q.v.). Strong vertical emphasis is achieved by the constant breaks in the entablature at every opportunity and by the Rococo stucco decoration, which halts the horizontal flow of the arches.

Johann Michael Fischer (1692–1766) was the leading exponent of Rococo architecture in Bavaria. In general, his buildings are less spatially complex than contemporary Bohemain designs, a tendency which becomes gradually more apparent in his later work. His Benedictine **Abbey Church, Ottobeuren** (begun 1737), similar in plan to the earlier abbey at Weingarten, has a domed vestibule followed by three nave bays, the central one of which acts as the crossing while interconnecting chapels form aisles. The spatial simplicity is counterbalanced by the ubiquitous decoration which blurs and fuses zone with zone.

Fischer's **Abbey Church, Rott am Inn** (1759–63), less extravagant in its decoration, takes up one of his favourite themes: the octagon with unequal sides. This shapes the crossing of a church not unlike Ottobeuren in plan. Here, however, the centralised character is more marked and the interior elevation has continuous galleries.

The **Pilgrimage Church, Steinhausen** (1728–31), was designed by Dominikus Zimmermann (1685–1766), a predominantly ecclesiastical architect who had trained as a plasterer and master mason. This is the first Bavarian Rococo church, light and white in effect, instead of dark and mystical. Spatially the design is simple: the large longitudinal oval body has a transverse oval presbytery, while the internal arcade supports the dome and creates a continuous ambulatory. His later church at Steinhausen, the **Wieskirche** (1745–54) (p. 994B), though larger, adopts a similar plan.

The final rebuilding of the **Abbey Church, S. Gall** (1748–70) (p. 991B), was undertaken by Peter Thumb (1681–1766) and Giovanni Gaspare Bagnato. Its double-apsed design was taken over from the mediaeval structure it replaced. In the monastic library Thumb used low domical vaulting to brilliant effect. The internal balcony undulating around the piers is characteristically cantilevered out, as in his earlier **Pilgrimage Church, Birnau** (1746–58).

Neo-Classicism

Georg Wenzeslaus von Knobelsdorff (1699–1753), a Prussian aristocrat, had a career in the army, and worked as a painter before turning to architecture. With an eye to developments abroad, and financed by Frederick the Great to travel to Italy, Vienna and Paris, he introduced a more sober style of architecture which had much in common with Palladianism in England.

The remodelled **Stadtschloss, Potsdam** (1744–51, now destroyed), despite its spectacular Rococo interior, had a remarkably subdued exterior which, if anything, shows a return to the solemn grandeur of seventeenth-century Baroque. The court elevation was articulated with a paired gaint order, pilasters in the wings and half-columns in the unpedimented central section, relieved only by three arched windows with perspectival frames.

The **Opera House, Berlin** (1741–3), very much a royal building, was in part designed by the King himself. Here the model for the temple-front over a high basement is clearly the English Palladianism of Burlington and Kent, for example Chiswick House (q.v.). Particularly English are the expansive smooth wall surface and relative smallness of the window openings.

Sanssouci, Potsdam (1745–), was also designed in collaboration with King Frederick, and quarrels over it ended Knobelsdorff's career. The gymnastic herms supporting the cornice recall the Dresden Zwinger (q.v.), but beneath the Rococo decoration the basic design has a great simplicity.

The **Observatory, Benedictine Academy for Young Noblemen, Kransmunster** (1748–60), is an unusually eloquent example of a similar change of architectural emphasis in Austria. The tall panelled facade, almost stripped of any ornament, has a strong sense of structure and a clarity almost worthy of Schinkel.

The **Schloss, Karlsruhe** (1749–71) (p. 995A), by A. F. von Kesslau, has a fan-shaped plan echoing the arrangment of the town, laid out from 1715 as a radial pattern of thirty-two streets. The result of several designs, including three by Neumann, the main facade is nevertheless characterised by sober repetition.

The **Neues Palais, Potsdam** (1755–66), was designed for Frederick II by J. G. Buring and H. L. Manger, and seems to have been inspired by Vanbrugh's Castle Howard. However, the huge facade with its central dome has a flatness and abstracted geometrical simplicity more akin to neo-Classicism.

The **Town Hall, Potsdam** (1753), by J. Boumann of Amsterdam (1706–76), is a building of remarkably purified Classicism. From a rectangular facade, articulated with eight half-columns and virtually lacking a central emphasis, rises a cylindrical drum and a stepped dome above.

At the **Old University** (now Academy of Sciences), **Vienna** (1753), by J. N. Jadot de Ville Issey (1710–61), Austrian Rococo is replaced by a French style which has much in common with A.-J. Gabriel (q.v.). The pedimented wings and unaccentuated centre in particular recall his hôtels in Place de la Concorde, Paris.

The **Palace, Lubostron** (1797–1806), is the work of S. Zawadzki. Towards the end of the eighteenth century, Poland in particular turned to Palladianism, and this impressive example is a single-porticoed version of the Villa Rotonda, Vicenza (q.v.).

The **Teppet Palace, Warsaw** (*c.* 1780), the work of S. B. Zug, is a more antiquarian interpretation of the same theme. At the forefront of neo-Classicism, Zug also designed the charming **Temple of Diana, Arkadia** (1783), one of the great romantic pleasure gardens outside England.

The remarkable **Cathedral, Vac** (1763–77), Hungary, was designed by Isadore Canevale. The aisleless domed building has a severe towered facade visually unrelieved by ornament, save for a projecting Corinthian portico without pediment.

Friedrich Gilly (1772–1800), the son of an architect of French descent was, with Boullée, Ledoux and Soane, one of the great visionary architects of the period. His masterpiece is his unexecuted project for a national **Monument to Frederick the Great** (1797), where antiquarian ideas are powerfully combined with simple geometric forms: a Greek Doric temple stands on a massive podium; the temple precinct is entered through an equally severe block-like astylar propylaeum, but adorned with a quadriga.

The **Brandenburg Gate, Berlin** (1789–93) (p. 995B), by C. G. Langhans (1733–1808), is the first of the great Doric ceremonial gateways, based upon the Propylaea of the Acropolis, Athens.

The **Marktplatz, Karlsruhe** (1804–24), was laid out by Friedrich Weinbrenner (1766–1826). The temple-fronted Evangelical Church faces the City Hall across the square, the two buildings balanced but not identical. The block-like quality of all the buildings, anticipating von Klenze's work in Munich, is complemented by a plain pyramidal monument in the centre.

Leo von Klenze (1784–1864) trained with Gilly before studying in Paris under Durand, and Percier and Fontaine. His two great monumental works realised the Greek Revivalist dreams of Gilly, but many of his buildings are designed in a variety of Italian Renaissance styles, a taste he was largely responsible for introducing.

The **Glyptothek, Munich** (1816–30), was built for the superb collection of Greek and Roman sculpture it still houses. The long, austere facade, which is interrupted by an Ionic portico, formed a deliberate contrast with the sumptuous polychrome interiors (destroyed in the 1940s) where the heavy vaults of the exhibition rooms were enlivened with delicate antiquarian decoration. The square plan of the museum with its central courtyard owes more to sixteenth-century Italy (for example Giulio Romano's Palazzo del Te) than to antiquity. The **Propylaea, Munich** (1846–60), provides an entrance into Königsplatz, the square in front of Klenze's earlier Glyptothek. Despite the Greek Doric portico, the towered facade owes much to the propylaea of the Roman Temple of Jupiter, Baalbek, or an Egyptian pylon, and has an uncompromising austerity enhanced by the deep recesses of the portals and upper galleries which lend it an almost military aspect.

The **Walhalla, near Regensburg** (1829–42), a monument to the German spirit, was the brainchild of Crown-Prince Ludwig of Bavaria. The German defeats of Napoleon and of Augustus's legions are represented in the pediments of this re-creation of a Greek Doric temple, recalling Gilly's projected

A. Pilgrimage Church, Vierzehnheiligen (1743–72): west front. See p. 992

B. Wieskirche, Steinhausen (1745–54): interior. See p. 992

C. Pilgrimage Church, Vierzhnheiligen: interior

A. Schloss, Karlsruhe (1749–71). See p. 993

B. Brandenburg Gate, Berlin (1780–93). See p. 993

C.Altes Museum, Berlin (1823–30). See p. 997

A. Schauspielhaus, Berlin (1819–21). See p. 997

B. Court Gardener's House, Charlottenhof, Potsdam (1829–31). See p. 997

monument to Frederick the Great. The interior, however, with its busts of German worthies in coloured marble, aims at sumptuous effect rather than Classical purity. The hill-top siting of the building – like an ancient temple – is truly spectacular. The ascending ramps and terraces are themselves ancient in inspiration even though symptomatic of early nineteenth-century romanticism.

The **Befreiungshalle, near Kelheim** (1842), commemorating the wars of 1813–15 against Napoleon, is a brutally severe interpretation of an ancient heroum, or mausoleum, a stone rotunda carrying high up a peripteral Doric colonnade. In the extraordinary polychrome interior, statues of angels linking hands provide a counterpoint to the pilasters of the lower storey. The **Konigsbau Residenz, Munich** (1826), is built to resemble to the Palazzo Pitti, Florence (q.v.), although the pilaster articulation of the upper storeys comes from Palazzo Rucellai (q.v.). The fifteenth-century Florentine style was actually suggested by Crown Prince Ludwig as fitting for the renovation of the city during this period.

Karl Friedrich Schinkel (1781–1841) was the greatest German architect of the neo-Classical period. A pupil of Gilly, in 1810 he joined the Prussian state public works office which he was to head from 1830. In this capacity he supervised many of the major building works in and near Berlin which established the city more fittingly as a major European capital. Although Classicism remained his main source of expression, he also worked in many other styles, and, following the theories of Durand, in various functional modes, where style has a secondary importance. Schinkel's work has a breadth which that of his contemporaries outside England lacked, but also a formal sensitivity and clarity of expression which transcends the growing eclecticism of the period.

The **Neue Wache** (New Guard House), **Berlin** (1816–18), has a Greek Doric portico projecting from the windowless block behind. The tall projecting wings at either side emphasise the grid-like composition, as do the victories in the frieze placed directly above the columns.

The **Schauspielhaus, Berlin** (1819–21) (p. 996A), a powerful work in Greek Revival style, is marked by the strong, geometric control of its boldly articulated masses. The entablature of the pedimented hexastyle Ionic portico continues around the building, binding together its rectangular forms. A high, pedimented attic, expressing the central auditorium, dominates the building. On each of its faces, openings are grouped together as continuous bands, divided by pilaster-like mullions. The building was extensively damaged during World War II.

For the facade of the **Altes Museum, Berlin** (1823–30) (p. 995C), Schinkel designed an Ionic stoa, with eagles on the roofline above the columns. The imposing staircase and a recessed attic provide the only emphasis to the central five bays. A contrast to this severe exterior is provided by a colourful mural under the portico designed by Schinkel himself, and then by the exotic interior. The attic in fact hides an enormous two-storey domed rotunda, recalling that in the Vatican Museum, but here with a colonnade below and plain wall above. More particularly, the planning follows Durand's principles, with the two-storey periphral galleries laid out on a modular system.

The **Non-Commissioned Officers' School, Potsdam** (1826–8), is one of the most 'functional' of Schinkel's designs. Here the Classical vocabulary is almost wholly reduced to an organisation of horizontals and verticals. The central five-bay block of the three-storey facade is distinguished by the simplified pilasters and entablatures of the upper two floors, and by a rudimentary attic. The long wings with their under-stated flat rustication have rows of large three-light windows of only distant Classical ancestry.

Almost as sparse is the **Pavilion of Friedrich Wilhelm III, Charlottenburg, Berlin** (1824–25), which is not unlike the Petit Trianon, Versailles (q.v.), but has its ornamental detail kept to a minimum. Emphasis is placed on the pristine geometry of the building, and the contrast between the flat walls and the deep recesses of the loggias.

The **Court Gardener's House, Charlottenhof, Potsdam** (1829–31) (p. 996B), is a remodelling of an existing building in a manner inspired by the English Picturesque houses of Nash. Together with Schinkel's **Tea House** and **Roman Bath** (1833–4) it forms a compact but asymmetrical group, and is cast in an Italian vernacular style with low pitched roofs, overhanging eaves, and a belvedere. Charlottenhof itself, remodelled 1826 onwards for the Crown Prince, is a Classical mansion with a Greek Doric portico – here following the authority of, for example, the Erechtheion, Athens.

The **Kavalierhaus on the Pfaueninsel, near Berlin** (1824), is a Gothic building with an asymmetrical facade which recalls Gothic-style houses in England. The formal handling is particularly masterly, the smooth wall surface providing a foil to the delicate detailing, while the larger of the two towers daringly accommodates exceptionally large windows.

The **Church at Maseritz (Miedzyrzecz)** in Poland (1828–33), is one of many buildings of the period designed in the Romanesque-Renaissance style often referred to as Rundbogenstil (round-arched style) which was widely used in this period. But, with its simple bold cornices, Schinkel gives to the facade a distinctive geometric clarity.

The **Academy of Architecture, Berlin** (1831–6), is a huge block-like four-storey edifice of brick. Massive pilaster strips running the height of the building articulate the facades and express the structural framework. However, the Renaissance-styled window detailing is exquisitely handled and provides a contrast typical of Schinkel.

The **Women's Prison, Würzburg** (1809–10), the work of Peter Speeth (1772–1831), exploits the same contrast of scale between the portal and the largely unarticulated expansive facade as is characteristic of the projects of Boullée.

The **Theseus Temple, Vienna** (1820–3), by P. von Nobile, is a conspicuous example of Greek Revival architecture in Austria. Built to house Canova's Theseus Group, it is closely based on the Temple of Hephaistos ('Theseus'), Athens.

Wilno Cathedral in Poland (1777–1801), by W. Gucewicz, very much anticipates the work of Hamilton and Playfair in Edinburgh (q.v.). Attached to the huge Doric temple-like building are long side colonnades, which with other constituent elements combine to form an imposing composition.

Esztergom Cathedral (Hungary) (1822–*c.* 1850), by J. S. Pack and J. Hud, is another impressive neo-Classical composition. The church itself, with imposing Corinthian octastyle portico, colonnaded drum and semicircular dome, is connected by means of arches to flanking campanili.

Chapter 32

THE LOW COUNTRIES AND BRITAIN

Architectural Character

The Low Countries

After following a similar pattern in the early Renaissance, the architectural paths of Belgium and Holland diverged widely in the seventeenth century, but returned to parallel, if separate, routes in the period 1700–1830.

Netherlandish Renaissance (c. 1515–1600)

Renaissance decorative motifs began to appear in the Netherlands from about 1515, but the first major buildings in the style date from the 1530s. Breda Castle (1536–), by the painter Tommaso Vincidor who had worked in Raphael's studio in Rome, shows the influence of the Vatican Palace in its planning, while the Italian architect Alessandro Pasqualini introduced the vertical sequence of orders into his church tower at IJsselstein (*c.* 1532). The Antwerp Town Hall of Cornelis Floris is undoubtedly the greatest creation of Netherlandish sixteenth-century architecture, and also the most knowledgeable in its handling of Renaissance vocabulary. Secular buildings lent themselves to the use of orders, which could be deployed to separate the huge rectangular windows that crowd the facades of town houses: the result is a grid-like framework somewhat reminiscent of Venetian architecture. But utterly characteristic of the Low Countries are the highly decorated multi-storey gables where Italianate decorative vocabulary easily replaces late Gothic Flamboyant detail in a tradition which continues in Belgian civic architecture until the eighteenth century (for example, the Grand' Place, Brussels). This Netherlandish Renaissance style was successfully exported to Scandinavia, Germany and Poland, both through the emigration of Netherlandish architects and via the pattern books of Vredeman de Vries (q.v.), which popularised a vocabulary of herms, obelisks, strapwork and banded orders ultimately derived from Fontainebleau. At the end of the century Lieven de Key's Leiden Town Hall (1597) and highly individual Meat Hall, Haarlem, are still in this tradition.

Dutch Palladianism (c. 1600–1700)

In the newly independent northern provinces Hendrik de Keyser (1565–1621) eliminated pattern-book fancies from his plainer Dutch manner, characterised by the use of arches and Tuscan or Doric columns, with the full entablature placed above the arcade. Jacob van Campen (1595–1657) initiated the so-called 'Dutch Palladian' style, in fact much influenced by Scamozzi, and similar in character to the contemporary English aesthetic of Inigo Jones (q.v.). The secular facades of van Campen and Pieter Post (1608–69) have central pediments over pilasters, often used in giant orders, and are discreetly embellished with occasional Classical swags. De Keyser's and van Campen's simple but spatially inventive church interiors and elegantly exuberant steeples were highly influential on Wren's London churches. The remarkable buildings of Steven Vennecool (1657–1719) mark a change of direction: dispensing with the orders, he relied on central projections and a well-judged deployment of recessed sash windows to achieve an austerely geometrical effect.

Seventeenth-century Belgium

During the first half of the seventeenth century church building predominated, with a heavy reliance on well-known Italian models. Even in Belgium, however, true Baroque style made no profound impression, and it is only in the rear portion of Rubens's house that the spirit of Italian Baroque comes through. Elsewhere secular building continued to elaborate on sixteenth-century pattern-book themes.

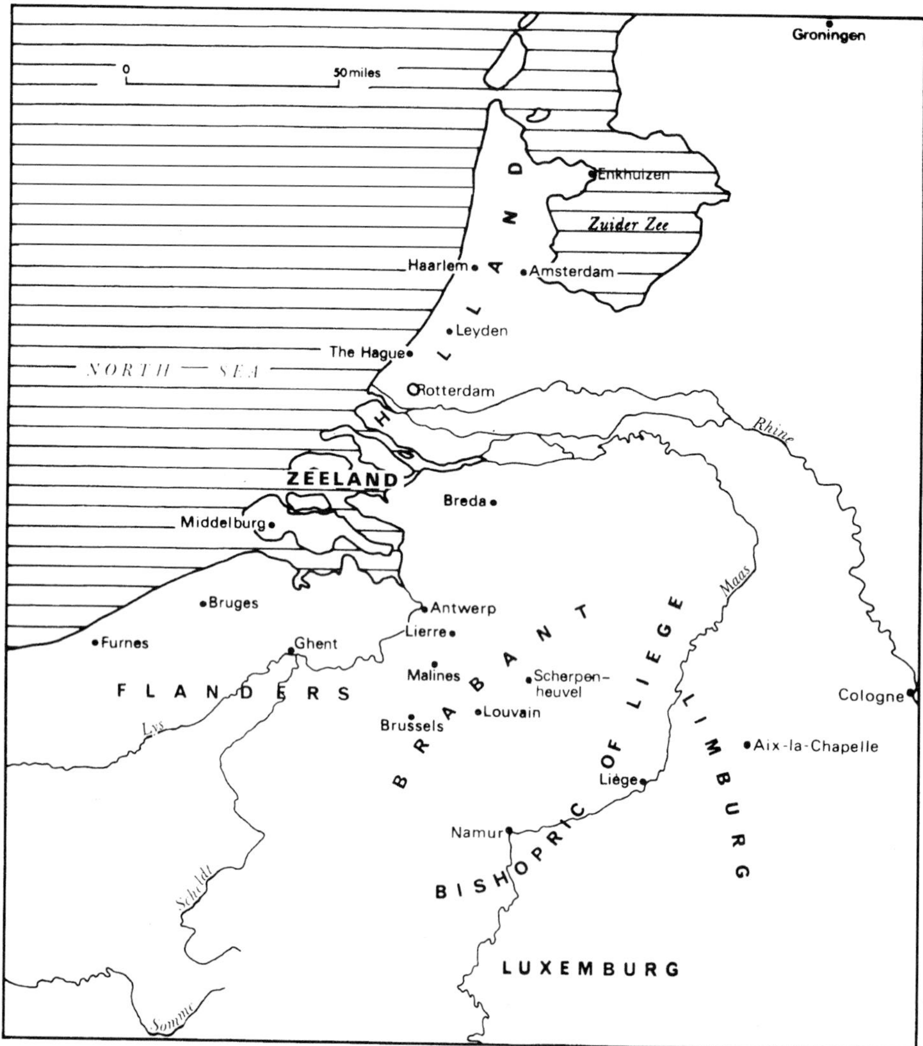

The Low Countries in the seventeenth century

Rococo and Neo-Classicism (1700–1830)

The arrival in Holland of Daniel Marot (1661–1752), a Huguenot refugee from France, in 1685, brought a more French-oriented style to the courtly circle, and this was continued in the work of Pieter de Swart (1709–72). Links between Holland and Belgium at this period are exemplified by the Antwerp buildings of J. P. van Baurscheit the Younger (1699–1768), who had worked for Marot in the Royal Library at The Hague. Minor and provincial architecture in Holland retained a more emphatically Dutch character, and the neo-Classical period saw a conscious revival of van Campen style, as well as a renewed Palladianism.

Examples

The Low Countries

Belgium

An early but spectacular example of Renaissance vocabulary is provided by the courtyard of the former **Bishop's Palace, Liège** (1526), where large, almost grotesque, balusters take the place of columns in the lower loggias below a more sober arcaded piano nobile.

The **Old Chancellery, Bruges** (1535) (p. 1002A), has a two-storey facade with large cross-mullioned windows divided by Doric half-columns supporting a frieze without architrave or cornice. The three gables above them, with their curving side-scrolls, relief decoration and statuary, appear Baroque in flavour; in fact they represent a perpetuation of Flamboyant Gothic.

S. Jacques, Liège (1558–60), preserves an interesting facade by Lambert Lombard. So Classical a design is highly unusual in the Low Countries at this date, but its decorative, predominantly Venetian character would already have been thoroughly outmoded in Italy.

The **Town Hall, Antwerp** (1561–6) (p. 1002C), was designed by Cornelis Floris (1514–75), the most distinguished sculptor and architect of the century in the Low countries. It is a magnificent building, of great width, with an assured grasp of the Classical orders. Above an arched, rusticated basement are two storeys with pilasters, then an open gallery under the projecting eaves. The centre is dominated by the decorative but imposing three-storey frontispiece (Doric, Ionic, Corinthian) with attached half-columns in a continuous triumphal-arch motif, while above, a further two storeys make up a pseudo-gable (there is no roof behind). The building represents the culmination of a tentative assimilation of the Classical style, imported from such sources as Serlio into Flemish and Netherlandish tradition. Also facing onto the Grand' Place are many-storeyed facades, built in a variety of late Gothic and Classical styles.

The **Guild Houses, Grand' Place, Brussels** (p. 1003A), were all built within a relatively short period beginning in the 1690s. Here a variety of Baroque decorative detail is applied to the traditionally multi-storey gabled facades. With much use of statuary orders and relief ornament, each attempts to be different from its neighbour, yet a surprisingly unified effect is created.

The domed octagonal pilgrimage church **Onze Lieve Vrouwekerk, Scherpenheuvel** (1609–) (p. 1002B), near Louvain, by Wenceslas Coberger, was built to house a miraculous image. It is reminiscent of Antonio da Sangallo the Younger's design for S. Giovanni dei Fiorentini, Rome, especially the volutes over the angle buttresses. The earliest dome of the Low Countries is very similar in its pointed profile to S. Peter's, Rome; the two-storey pilastered arcade also is Italianate but dwarfed in scale by the vast domed structure behind it.

S. Pieter, Ghent (1629–), presents a far more coherent prospect. The plan is very unusual – a square frontal portion with a dome rising from four piers, followed by an enormous east-end extension with nave and aisles – but the effect recreates the solemnity of the great sixteenth-century churches in Rome. The facade is closely modelled on Vignola's design for the Gesù, making the attribution to Jesuit Pieter Huyssens (1577–1637), documented as working there, a likely one. Certainly **S. Carolus Borromeus, Antwerp** (1615–25), was the work of Huyssens but it was mostly rebuilt following a fire in 1718. Despite the (originally wooden) barrel vault, and the galleries above the aisles, the columned interior here is much more simple (but was once flamboyantly painted by Rubens). The facade, however, is strongly Italianate, apparently modelled on a project for Florence Cathedral by Buontalenti, which had particularly inventive niche surrounds and window frames. It is flanked by a pair of extremely ornamental towers where late sixteenth-century Italian forms are assembled into highly individual compositions.

The **Church of the Trinity, Brussels,** was given the facade formerly belonging to the **Augustinian Church** (by J. Francart, 1642) which is clearly Baroque in spirit. The central section is tightly clasped by pairs of half-columns carrying quarter pediments, while the upper storey is braced by steeply rising scrolls.

S. Michael, Louvain (1650–70) (p. 1005A), is the work of Wilhelm Hesius (Hees) and others. The interior here is essentially mediaeval, despite the half-hearted use of Classical motifs. The remarkable facade (not by Hesius), however, is truly up to date: a tall, ornate, tightly knit and genuinely Baroque design, in which the two-storey composition, clustered half-columns and especially the sculpture-encrusted attic storey serve to emphasise the centre.

The **Groot Begijnhof (Grand Béguinage), Louvain** (fourteenth to eighteenth centuries), is one of many such establishments to survive in Belgian towns. They housed small communities of lay-sisters, centring on a church, and incorporated such facilities as infirmaries. At Louvain houses for around two hundred nuns were organised about a tight network of streets adjacent to the church and infirmary.

Rubens's House, Antwerp (1610–17, extensively restored) is a magnificent example of a patrician mansion. The house, designed by the artist for himself, has a remarkably subdued exterior, but the courtyard is one of the most florid architectural creations of the period. The rear facade and projecting wings are laden with sculptural decoration, as are a screen and pavilion conceived as a triumphal arch which completes the courtyard and provides access to a delightful garden beyond. The architecture is inspired by the most extravagant and ornamental examples from sixteenth-century Italy, combined with such northern forms as cross-mullioned windows and steeply-pitched roofs to form an original synthesis, free of mere imitation.

The **Jacob Jordens House, Antwerp** (1641–), the mansion of Rubens's pupil, is nearly as inventive. The compact rusticated facade is interrupted by an extremely elaborate portal bay, complete with a broken pediment, and incorporating flowing combinations of curving and serpentine broken pediments, arches and volutes.

A. Old Chancellery, Bruges (1535). See p. 1000

B. Onze Lieve Vrouwekerke, Scherpenheuvel (1609–). See p. 1001

C. Town Hall, Antwerp (1561–6). See p. 1001

A. Guild Houses, Grand' Place Brussels (1690s–). See p. 1001

B. Town Hall, Lier (1740). See p. 1004

C. Mauritshuis, The Hague (*c.* 1633). See p. 1008

Château Modare, near Dinant (1649), is a much sterner building inspired by French models, with a steeply pitched roof and projecting wings. The facade is articulated with giant pilasters carrying a broken pediment over the central bay.

Maison de la Bellone, Brussels (1697), by Jean Cosyn, has a pedimented facade articulated by giant Ionic pilasters, the bays almost fully occupied by large rectangular windows. Even so, the quantity of decoration might be compared with the similarly designed but stern mansions of this period in Holland.

The **Town Hall, Lier** (1740) (p. 1003B), by J. P. van Baurscheit the Younger (1699–1768), is a restrained but typical example of French-influenced Rococo architecture in Belgium. The flat, almost papery, facade with its delicate window frames is given a subtle articulation with rusticated pilaster strips or gently recessed panels of the same shape.

The former **Benedictine Abbey, Gembloux** (1762–79), is the work of Laurent Benoit Dewez (1731–1812) who introduced to Belgium a sober Classicism like the contemporary style of A. -J. Gabriel in Paris. Projecting from the centre of the long repetitive facade is a bold rhetorical Ionic portico.

The **Château, Seneffe** (*c.* 1760), was also designed by Dewez. The wide facade, with its end-bays and pedimented central section articulated with pilasters, connects with long quadrant colonnades terminating with domed pavilions which enclose an expansive forecourt. The scale of the conception and formal disposition of the masses can be compared with French projects of this period.

It is the **Place Royale, Brussels** (1775–) (p. 1005C), which most particularly looks to France. The square was planned by Parisian N. Barre and is closely modelled on the Place Royale, Reims (1756–60), a layout itself close in spirit to A.-J. Gabriel's Place de la Concorde (q.v.). The square is bordered on three sides by sober blocks, each articulated with giant pilaster strips over a rusticated arched basement. On the fourth side, a Corinthian portico serves as the entrance to the church of **S. Jacques sur Coudenberg** (1766–87, largely designed by the square's executive architect, B. Guimard; lantern added 1849).

Château de Duras, Saint-Trod (1789), is a neo-Classical building of exceptional beauty. To the centre of a particularly understated facade with projecting wings is applied a semicircular colonnade with projecting drum and dome, essentially an elegant version of Bramante's Tempietto.

Holland

The **Church Tower, IJsselstein**, near Utrecht (*c.* 1532), was designed by Alessandro Pasqualini, an Italian working in the Netherlands. This remarkable building brings to the north an unprecedented and isolated Classicism. Three pilaster storeys (Doric, Ionic, Corinthian) constitute the tower itself, which supports an octagonal drum. The building has decorative qualities typical of the north, for example the alternating brick and stone courses for such features as the surrounds to the niches.

The **Steeple, Oude Kerk, Amsterdam** (1565–6), by Joost Jansz, has an exuberance more typical of the Netherlands at this period. It consists of many diminishing stages making free use of Renaissance forms and characterised by their diversity of shape, material and structure, open elements alternating with solids.

The **'House of Charles V', Zwolle** (1571), is a typical Dutch town house from the late sixteenth century. Rusticated Doric pilasters are applied to two storeys. A third articulated attic storey extends into the gable, characteristically framed with superimposed scrolls. Here, as so often, the problem of applying an order to an attic is not satisfactorily resolved – particularly in the way the scrolls support the entablature.

The **facade of the Town Hall, Leiden** (1597) (p. 1006D,G), is a very decorative work by Lieven de Key from Antwerp (*c.* 1560–1627). An impressive central emphasis is achieved by the use of a double-ramped triangular staircase (compare the Capitoline Hill, Rome) and the concentration of sculptural detail around the central bay. The repertory of ornament – strapwork, fretwork and banded orders – is derived from such books as those by Vredeman de Vries. The multi-tiered spire, beginning with obelisks and culminating in a pierced bulb-shape, is particularly fine.

Hendrik de Keyser (1565–1621) was a stonemason and sculptor before becoming the leading architect in Amsterdam. His works, engraved and published by Salomon de Bray, introduced a sobriety into Dutch architecture heralding a new era.

The **Zuiderkerk, Amsterdam** (1606–14), is one of the earliest Protestant churches in Holland. De Keyser provided a plan with nave and aisles, and non-projecting transepts, reminiscent of a mediaeval church but clothed in a superficially Classical vocabulary: while piers are replaced by Doric columns, there is still tracery in the windows. The spire recalls that of Leiden Town Hall; although extravagant in detail, the constituent elements are assembled with some restraint.

The **Westerkerk, Amsterdam** (1620–31), has an impressive two-storey Classical interior (despite rib-vaults and tracery). The simple plan is rectangular, incorporating two pairs of transepts, while the bunched Doric columns forming the nave piers are slender enough to allow a pervading sense of space. The tower is more sober than in earlier examples and the steeple is made up of three block-like elements of diminishing size.

Jacob van Campen (1595–1657), also a painter, was the greatest of all Dutch architects. He probably

A. S. Michael, Louvain (1650–70). See p. 1001

B. Niewe Kerk, The Hague (1649–56). See p. 1008

C. Place Royale, Brussels (1775–). See p. 1004

D. Royal Palace, Amsterdam (1648–65). See p. 1008

E. Nieuwe Kerk, Haarlem (1645–9). See p. 1008

A PINNACLE HAARLEM
B FINIAL HAARLEM
C GABLE ANTWERP
D SPIRE TOWN HALL LEYDEN
SPIRE NEW CHURCH HAARLEM E
WOOD
STONE
PILASTER UTRECHT F CATHL
PILASTER UTRECHT H CATHL
1549
G TOWN HALL: LEYDEN

A. Trippenhuis, Amsterdam (1662). See p. 1008

B. Town Hall, Enkhuizen (1686). See p. 1008

C. Royal Library, The Hague (1734). See p. 1008

studied in Italy where he may have known Scamozzi, as his works have a strong affinity with Palladio's leading follower. Working principally in Amsterdam he was able to adapt Palladian Classicism to Dutch tradition, producing some exceptionally beautiful buildings.

The **Mauritshuis, The Hague** (*c.* 1633) (p. 1003C), was built for Johan Maurits van Nassau, by then a successful general. The almost square plan is derived from the villas of Palladio and Scamozzi – two central reception rooms with private suites of three rooms at either side. Over a low basement, the facades are unified by a giant order of Ionic pilasters framing large windows with elegant surrounds, while above rises a typically Dutch steep roof, once dominated by tall chimneys. The pedimented central section is given very little emphasis. The harmonious exteriors are embellished with a restrained decoration of swags and relief sculpture.

The **Royal Palace** (formerly the Town Hall), **Amsterdam** (1648–65) (p. 1005D), is a much more ambitious work. The monumental scale of the building has no equal in Palladio's built architecture, and even surpasses the designs in Scamozzi's *Idea*. The vast rectangular layout, incorporating two courtyards separated by a gigantic double-storey central hall, has a number of oddities: there is no proper access into the courtyards, which function simply as lightwells, there is no monumental entrance into the building whatever, while access into the main hall is through a series of very narrow passages. The facade has two storeys of repetitive pilaster articulation. The pedimented central portion projects forward more strongly than the corner pavilions, and is marked by a domed lantern. This feature, probably derived from one of the smaller domes of S. Peter's, Rome, replaces the tall central gables, or bell towers, of earlier town halls.

The **Nieuwe Kerk, Haarlem** (1645–9) (pp. 1005E,1006E), is in plan a Greek cross inscribed within a square with slight projections for the altar and entrance. Square Ionic crossing piers and subsidiary Ionic columns (absent along the longitudinal axis) support coffered ceilings at the corners, while the central space is covered by a groin vault. The church is not unlike those by de Keyser, except that the detailing is more purely Classical. The earlier tower (1613), the work of de Key, is marvellously complicated, providing a foil to the almost excessively austere exterior of the church, with its Doric entablature and curious tapering buttresses.

The **Nieuwe Kerk, The Hague** (1649–56) (p. 1005B), by Pieter Noorwits and van Bassen, is still somewhat Gothic in character (tracery and a very steep roof) but very unusual in plan. Essentially it is a rectangle with six polygonal apses, one at each end and two at the sides, while the focal pulpit and baptismal screens are perversely placed against the walls between the side apses.

The **Nieuwe Lutherse Kerk, Amsterdam** (1668), designed by Adrian Dortsman (died 1682), is a remarkable building with a domed rotunda ringed for only half its circumference by a congregational ambulatory. Almost as bold is the exterior with its Doric pilasters rising from a rusticated plinth, its copper-clad dome and its daringly glazed lantern.

The **Portuguese Synagogue, Amsterdam** (1671–5), a gaunt but imposing building by Elias Bouman, is one of several synagogues built as a result of the religious freedom in seventeenth-century Holland. As was noted at the time, Dutch synagogue design is reminiscent of the Protestant churches of the period. Here the interior is divided by rows of Ionic columns into three equal barrel-vaulted aisles, with galleries attached to the side walls; while the plain exterior has a giant order of pilaster strips. Similar in design but more imposing than the other contemporary Amsterdam synagogues, this particular example stands within a large precinct.

The **Poppenhuis, Amsterdam** (1642), the work of Philip Vingboons, is one of many buildings deeply indebted to van Campen. With its giant order and pedimented central section, the facade is of great elegance. The **Trippenhuis, Amsterdam** (1662) (p. 1007A), was built for two brothers Trip by Justus Vingboons, brother of Philip. The pilaster order here rises two and a half storeys, the entablature breaking out over the central pedimented section and the end bays. From the roof ridge rise chimneys disguised as gun barrels, referring to the occupation of the owners.

The **Huis den Bos, The Hague** (1645–), was designed by Pieter Post (1608–69), previously an associate of van Campen. A suburban residence, it is a centrally planned building ultimately dependent on Palladio's much smaller Villa Rotonda. The cruciform central hall (decorated under the direction of van Campen himself), with its domical vaulting, occupies the full height of the building, and is crowned by an octagonal cupola projecting above the roof line.

The **Town Hall, Enkhuizen** (1686) (p. 1007B), by Steven Vennecool (1657–1719), is a compact block with central projection and crowning lantern. The essentially astylar facade is enlivened at the corners by rusticated quoins and in the centre by a clustering of variously-shaped openings. The result is an interesting and harmonious composition. The **Manor House, Maddachten** (1695), also by Vennecool, is similar in conception although here much more is made of the recessed wings, the battered basement descending into the moat, the curving forms of the approach bridge, and the much more prominent central projection, the cornice of which expressively arches upwards at the centre.

The **Royal Library** (originally Hôtel Huguetan), **The Hague** (1734, wings added 1761) (p. 1007C), was designed by Daniel Marot in a style which is clearly French. The side wings have an all-over rusticated surface, while the recessed bays of the central section are divided by immensely tall rusticated *chaînes*; an ornamental cartouche replaces the pediment above.

The **Royal Theatre** (originally Nassau Weilberg Palace), **The Hague** (*c.* 1765), is by Pieter de Swart who had studied in Paris. The concave facade, with its hefty side-pavilions, illustrates the continual French influence throughout the eighteenth century.

The **Town Hall, Groningen** (1777–1810), the work of J. Otten Husby, with its giant columns and pilasters, is undoubtedly a neo-Classical work, although it also forcibly recalls van Campen's era.

Villa Brockhuizen, Leersum (1794, enlarged 1810), by J. Berkman and B. W. H. Ziezenis, is a building with a far more generally Palladian manner, being in effect an enlarged and adapted version of Palladio's Villa Foscari, while the **Oud Raadhuis, Rotterdam** (1825–), by A. Munro is typical of European neo-Classicism at this period. A porch projects from the long facade, but above rises a tall lantern, Classical in form but unmistakably Dutch in character.

Architectural Character

Britain

Architecture in England from 1500 to 1830 did not pass through a neatly chronological sequence of styles, Renaissance, Baroque, Rococo and neo-Classicism, as found in continental Europe. The initial delay in the arrival of the Renaissance, the eclecticism of the seventeenth century, the neo-Palladian movement of the early eighteenth century, which was out of phase

England in the Renaissance period

with continental developments, and the precociousness of the Gothic Revival all make it hard to identify architectural style with specific periods. For these reasons, several divisions based on the successive dynasties of the royal family have been retained here, although major stylistic changes overlap them: Tudor, Elizabethan and Jacobean (1505–1625); Stuart, Commonwealth and Restoration (1625–1702); Georgian (1702–1830), including Baroque, Palladian, neo-Classical and Picturesque.

Tudor, Elizabethan and Jacobean

Henry VIII (1509–47) attempted to introduce Italian and French modes into the buildings of the court, but Renaissance elements tended to be used as decorative details grafted on to a late Gothic stock.

The architecture of Elizabeth I's reign (1558–1603) saw the introduction of large-scale Renaissance motifs somewhat indiscriminately taken over from French, Italian and Flemish books on architecture. The orders were used to articulate window bays and as frontispieces in the French manner. The most important printed sources were Serlio, du Cerceau and Philibert de l'Orme, and later Wendel Dietterlin (q.v.) Strapwork and grotesques derived from Fontainebleau through Flemish pattern books were influential on both exteriors and interiors. However, Robert Smythson (1536–1614) was capable of rising above the amiable but chaotic eclecticism of his contemporaries to produce well-structured plans which display an overall control of design. Generally, the external silhouette of Elizabethan buildings displays a varied skyline of towers, gables, parapets, balustrades and chimney stacks: facades are enlivened by large mullioned oriel and bay windows. The effect is similar to French sixteenth-century architecture, but the grouping is less rigid and more picturesque.

In Jacobean architecture German and Flemish decorative elements, brought by immigrant craftsmen rather than copied from books, tended to predominate over the French and Italian. Jacobean country houses unify the diverse elements of Elizabethan architecture into a more identifiable style, often using brick with stone dressings, capped turrets and Flemish gables, the orders being confined to frontispieces.

The great revolution brought about in English architecture by Inigo Jones (1573–1652) begins in the later years of James I (1603–25), but is more conveniently treated in the next section.

Stuart, Commonwealth and Restoration

Jones's buildings for James and Charles I (1625–49) and their consorts introduced into English architecture a throughgoing Classical style based on pure geometrical shapes, interrelated proportions and a Vitruvian use of the 'correct' forms and symbolic language of the orders. Jones's sources, derived from two visits to Italy and an extensive collection of drawings and architectural books, were above all Palladio and Scamozzi: he abjured the licentious use of 'composed ornaments' made fashionable by Michelangelo, except for interiors, where French influences were also allowed.

Jones's work was restricted to court circles, and his style was adopted in full only by his nephew and pupil John Webb (1611–72). Webb's King Charles's building at Greenwich shows a remarkable mastery in pulling together a very long (24-bay) facade. The deployment of centre and corner pavilions to punctuate the facade is partially French, but the language is Palladian. During the Protectorate, Roger Pratt (1620–84) was a masterly designer of houses in a lucidly symmetrical but practical manner. He introduced the 'double-pile' at Coleshill (parallel rows of apartments separated by a spine-corridor), and built the very influential Clarendon House. His plain astylar facades with large simple windows, pedimented dormers and chunky chimneys, set a new standard in unostentatious Classicism.

The majority of buildings of the period 1620–1660, however, showed little response to the innovations of Jones and his contemporaries. Outside court circles, an 'artisan style' prevailed in domestic building, characterised by Dutch gables with curved volutes and pedimented tops, heavy cornices and hipped roofs. The use of brick and wooden-framed windows was also taken over from Holland.

The Restoration saw the emergence of one of the greatest figures in English architecture, Sir Christopher Wren (1632–1723). Wren's instincts were rationalising and geometrical, and were thus in sympathy with the tradition of Jones and Webb, but he was also influenced by the relativist aesthetics of Hobbes and Perrault. He was much impressed by the French architecture he saw on a trip to Paris in 1665 and his later architecture shows the increasing influence of the Baroque. Wren's early buildings are close to the plain Dutch style of Hugh May (1622–84), with the use of giant pilasters and arches to articulate a facade. The ravages of the Great Fire of London offered Wren hitherto unprecedented opportunities in ecclesiastical architecture in the rebuilding of S. Paul's and the City churches. For the latter he devised a great variety of plan types, using the Greek cross, polygons, simple rectangles and galleried basilicas. The vaulting was also varied, most brilliantly complex at S. Stephen Walbrook, where the S. Paul's solution is adumbrated. It seems probable that Wren's city churches were influenced by de Keyser's and van Campen's church architecture in Amsterdam. The later stages of S. Paul's and the spires of the city churches show a greater experimentation with perspectival effects and complex curves which brings Wren closer to the Baroque. However, he never

13.10"
9.9"
6.0"
A ORIEL WINDOW
BRAMSHILL HOUSE: HANTS
B TOWER IN COURT
BURGHLEY HO. NORTHANTS
ANNO DOMINI 1602
C BAY WINDOW
HINCHINGBROOKE HALL
3.3"
D BALUSTRADE
BRAMSHILL HOUSE: HANTS
WB
1628
E RAIN WATER HEAD
CLAVERTON MANOR
3.5"
F BALUSTRADE
KINGSTON HOUSE: BRADFORD ON AVON
18.6"
8.0"
G ENTRANCE
BLICKLING HALL: NORFOLK
H PORCH: ST CATHERINE'S
COURT: SOMERSET
16.6"
9.2"
J ARCADE: BRAMSHILL: HANTS

showed much relish for the curved facades and fantastic detail of the continental Baroque, remaining rational and empiricist to the last.

The 'Wren' style was diffused in the country not only by his circle, such as his trusted assistant and colleague in the Royal Society, Robert Hooke (1635–1703), but also by a multitude of contracting masons and carpenters who perpetuated the robust red brick and stone-quoined Dutch manner associated with the Restoration.

Georgian

This long and heterogeneous period is most conveniently divided into English Baroque (1702–25), Palladianism (*c.* 1715–50) and neo-Classicism (1750–1830). The Gothic Revival grew up alongside the neo-Classical and in its pre-Pugin phase was practised by the same architects.

Hawksmoor, Archer, Gibbs and Vanbrugh are the architects associated with the English Baroque. Of these only Archer and Gibbs knew Italian Baroque at first hand, the latter having studied with Carlo Fontana in Rome. Sir John Vanbrugh (1664–1726) was a courtier, soldier and dramatist as well as an architect, becoming Controller of the Royal Works through the influence of his patron at Castle Howard, the Earl of Carlisle. Vanbrugh's great country houses at Blenheim and Castle Howard were executed with the aid of Nicholas Hawksmoor (1661–1736), and their relative contributions are hard to disentangle; Hawksmoor was the profounder, more original designer, Vanbrugh was the more flamboyant personality. The style they developed is marked by a feeling for mass, rhythm and drama of composition. The giant order is deployed rhythmically to break up great areas of rusticated stonework, keystones project from arches, and the skyline is punctuated by fantastically shaped projections. The planning and general effect are certainly more French than Italian, but the language is entirely individual. Hawksmoor's own particularly idiosyncratic manner is best seen in his London churches, which have a massive sculptural geometry composed of powerful block-like elements that are welded together by a rigorous consistency. The ornament is austere and pared-down, but at the same time bizarre, triglyphs and Roman altars cropping up in unexpected contexts. Thomas Archer (1668–1743) reveals a first-hand knowledge of Bernini and Borromini in his small group of churches and houses, while the early buildings of James Gibbs (1682–1754) also betray Roman influences, notably S. Mary le Strand, London, with its powerful use of giant tabernacles to articulate the side facades.

The publication of *Vitruvius Britannicus* (1715, 1717, 1725) by Colen Campbell (died 1729) marked the Palladian reaction against the short-lived English Baroque. The search for a 'national' style in reaction against prevailing continental models was political as well as aesthetic, the Baroque being identified with absolutist monarchy and the Catholic church. Lord Burlington retraced Inigo Jones's footsteps to Vicenza in 1719, bringing back Palladio's drawing of the Roman baths to add to those Jones had collected. English Palladianism was as much a revival of Jones as of Palladio, and Burlington, Kent and Campbell also avoided Palladio's later, less orthodox designs. The result is inevitably a rather dry and pedantic Classical style, but one that lent itself to efficient and acceptable reproduction at all levels of domestic architecture, perhaps especially in town houses. Architects like William Kent (1685–1748) and James Gibbs in his later career did not submit completely to the tyranny of Palladianism. Kent's less restrained side is seen in his furniture designs, in his occasional forays into the Gothic, and, above all, in his pioneering informality in landscape gardening taken up by Capability Brown and Humphrey Repton. This picturesque strain had rightly been seen as an abiding *leitmotif* of English architecture. Gibbs's later buildings continue to exhibit a full-blooded sculptural quality and a powerful sense of rhythm that distinguish them from the Palladian movement.

Palladianism was in a sense a neo-Classical style, and many of its principles were carried over into the more archaeological neo-Classicism of the later eighteenth and early nineteenth centuries. At this period, however, neo-Classical tendencies in England coincided with those in France, Italy and Germany, and were especially influenced by Piranesi and Laugier. Robert Wood's *Ruins of Palmyra* (1753), Stuart and Revett's *Antiquities of Athens* (1762) and Robert Adam's *Ruins of the Palace of Diocletian at Spalato in Dalmatia* (1764) extended the available range of ancient architectural models, while the excavations at Pompeii and Herculaneum gave a more complete picture of the decoration of ancient Roman interiors.

For Robert Adam (1728–92) the study of the ancient baths and of Raphael's revival of Imperial Roman ornament was as important as the more exotic sources, and the Adam style of painted stucco interior decoration is essentially a rather refined and 'tasteful' version of Raphael's interiors. His use of curves and niches in his interior planning also looks to Raphael and to Burlington as well as their common source, the Roman baths. His exteriors give fresh deployment to hackneyed antique elements such as the temple front and the triumphal arch and show an appreciation of picturesque silhouette which is easily reclothed in Gothic forms. James Wyatt (1746–1813) practised a Classical style similar to that of Adam but without the latter's charm. William Chambers (1723–96), however, abhorred Adam's light style. After extensive travels as a merchant seaman he trained in Paris under Blondel and Soufflot (q.v.) and practised a robust and unaffected Classicism which was open to sixteenth-century Italian and English Baroque influences. His *Designs of Chinese Buildings,* based on his early voyages, influenced the taste for chinoiserie. The work of James Gandon (1743–1823), a pupil of Chambers who had a successful practice in Dublin, is particularly impressive and made use of elements from Wren.

The best works of George Dance the Younger (1741–1825), which unfortunately have been destroyed, embody the grandly simplifying strand of neo-Classicism espoused by Laugier. Dance's Newgate Prison was especially important, with its Renaissance modes of rustication to give a suitably repellent aspect to the facade. Henry Holland (1745–1806), like Gandon, introduced consciously Greek orders into his buildings.

At the turn of the century two styles existed amicably side by side, and were often practised by the same architects. The Picturesque, which became a theoretical term in the writings of Payne Knight and Uvedale Price, encouraged mediaevalising tendencies in architecture as well as giving a rationale to Humphrey Repton's garden 'improvements'. The neo-Classical brand of antiquarianism blended into a thorough Greek Revival, while picturesque mediaevalism was to become in the next generation a more ideological Gothic Revival. Architects like Nash, Wilkins and Smirke practised in both of these styles as well as others, although the most original architect of the period, John Soane, avoided the Gothic.

Sir John Soane (1753–1837) evolved a highly personal style which combined a slightly mannered preciosity with a stripped-down abstract geometry. The closest parallels are perhaps Vanbrugh and Hawksmoor, whom he greatly admired. The vaulting of his interiors is particularly ingenious. John Nash (1752–1835), a figure of outstanding entrepreneurial energy, was able through royal favour to lay out Regent's Park and to join it with a new north–south street to the West End of London. He was an innovator in the informal mode of country-house planning and introduced the Italianate villa, based on the paintings of Claude (1600–82).

The dominant practioners of the Greek Revival were Smirke and Wilkins, although the Inwoods' S. Pancras Church, inspired by the Erechtheion, is one of its most delightful productions. William Wilkins (1778–1839), designer of University College, London, and of the National Gallery, built Downing College, Cambridge, in a programmatically Greek Doric style. Sir Robert Smirke (1780–1867) used the giant Greek Ionic to impressive effect at the British Museum. Thomas Hamilton's High School in Edinburgh is perhaps the most successful Greek Revival composition of this period. Scottish architects carried on the tradition of the Greek Revival after its expiry in England, notably W. H. Playfair (1790–1857) in Edinburgh and Alexander 'Greek' Thomson (1817–75) in Glasgow. The strong criticisms levelled at the feebleness of the 'Commissioner' churches, built in Greek and Gothic style as a result of the Church Building Act of 1818, paved the way for the ecclesiological phase of the Gothic Revival.

Examples

Britain

Tudor, Elizabethan and Jacobean (1505–1625)

The Renaissance style first manifested itself in England, as in France, in the design of decorative detail. The most impressive examples from the first half of the sixteenth century may be associated with the patronage of Henry VIII. The **Tomb of Henry VII** (1509) (p. 1014A) in **Westminster Abbey**, by the Florentine Pietro Torrigiani, is an early and exquisite example; the angle pilasters, putti and detailed carving of the black marble mark it out as a Renaissance work. The screen and stalls of King's College, Cambridge (1533–6), donated by Henry VIII, are in up-to-date continental Renaissance style, with grotesques.

Henry VIII's lost **Palace of Nonsuch, Surrey** (1538, destroyed 1687), was built around two courts, of which the inner had octagonal corner towers and fantastic pinnacles. The whole structure, wood over a stone base, was faced with a slate skeleton enclosing stucco panels in the manner of Fontainebleau; some fragments survive. Other examples of this style are at Lacock Abbey, Wiltshire.

Another lost building of great importance is **Old Somerset House, London** (1547–52), built for the Protector Somerset and supervised by Somerset's steward John Thynne (died 1580). Thynne's drawing of the Strand front shows centre and corner pavilions in the French manner; the central 'frontispiece' recalls Ecouen (q.v.) and in addition the vertical linking of windows with superimposed pilaster strips is also influenced by France, though horizontal divisions are here also emphasised.

Longleat House, Wiltshire (1568–) (pp. 1014C, 1015D), designed by John Thynne, for himself with Robert Smythson (?1536–1614), is skilfully arranged around two inner courts where staircases, chimneys and services are disposed; the entirely symmetrical exterior breaks forward at intervals with two-bay projections articulated with superimposed pilasters in the manner of Old Somerset House. Though the recessed bays are astylar, the entablatures run all around the house. It is an entirely coherent design.

A. Tomb of Henry VII (1509) and his Queen (1503), Westminster Abbey. See p. 1013

B. Kirby Hall, Northamptonshire (1570–5): south front of north range. See p. 1017

C. Longleat House, Wiltshire (1568–). See p. 1013

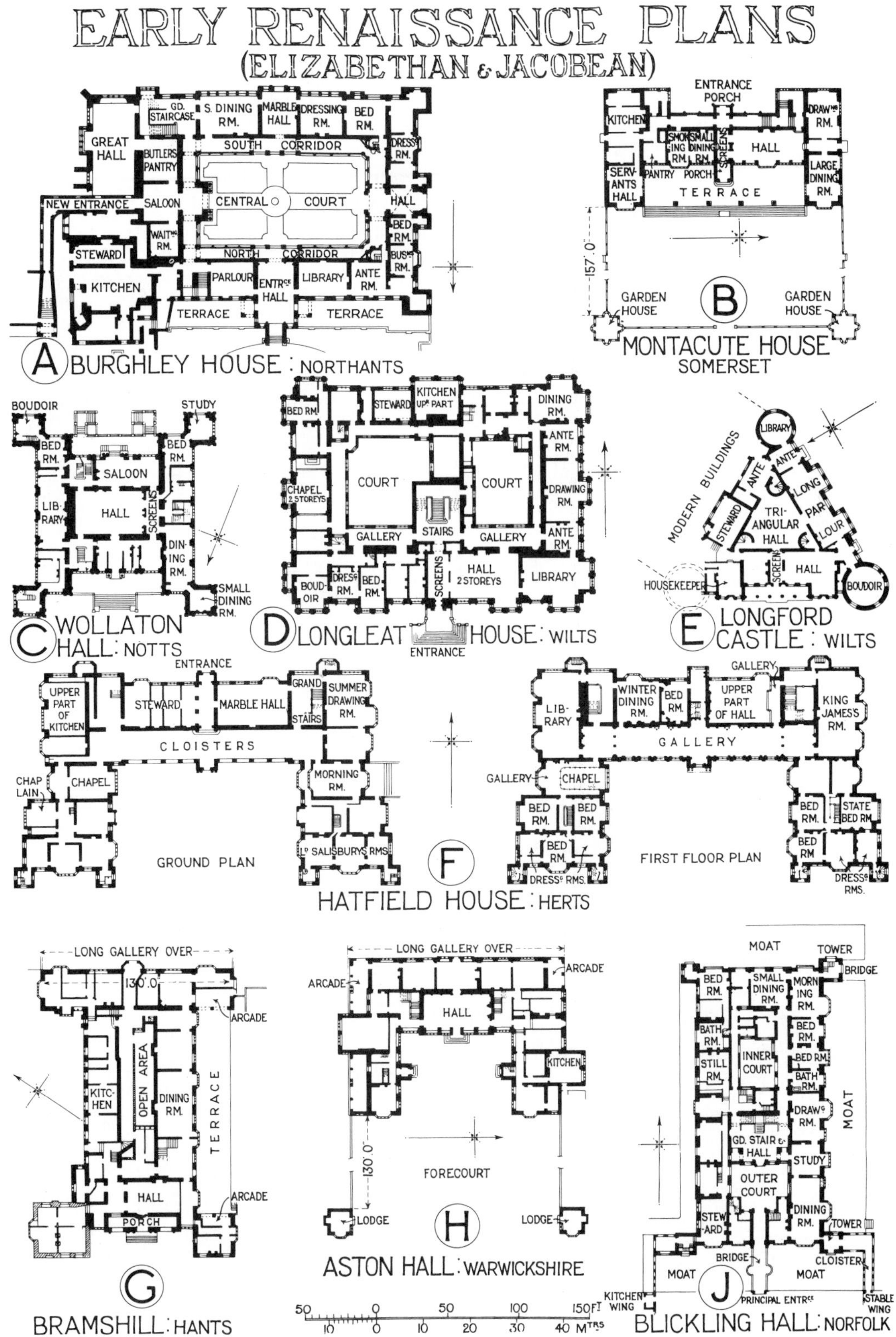
EARLY RENAISSANCE PLANS
(ELIZABETHAN & JACOBEAN)
A BURGHLEY HOUSE: NORTHANTS
B MONTACUTE HOUSE SOMERSET
C WOLLATON HALL: NOTTS
D LONGLEAT HOUSE: WILTS
E LONGFORD CASTLE: WILTS
F HATFIELD HOUSE: HERTS
GROUND PLAN
FIRST FLOOR PLAN
G BRAMSHILL: HANTS
H ASTON HALL: WARWICKSHIRE
J BLICKLING HALL: NORFOLK

A. Woolaton Hall, Nottingham (1580–5). See p. 1017

B. Burghley House, Northamptonshire (1552–87). See p. 1017

Wollaton Hall, Nottingham (1580–5) (pp. 1015C, 1016A), by Smythson, has a four-towered plan derived from Serlio's variant on Poggio Reale (q.v.) The centrally placed hall rises up to a clerestory and has a turreted banqueting room above it, giving a castle-like effect. The exterior facades are entirely articulated with superimposed paired pilasters, bunched at the centre and separated by niches at the extremities. The detail is much more Flemish than at Longleat, with banded pilaster shafts and strapwork gables.

Kirby Hall, Northamptonshire (1570–5) (p. 1014B), is a highly personal and eclectic building, combining French, Flemish and Italian sources taken from books. The arrangement of giant pilasters and arches (the pedimented windows breaking the entablature are later) is close to Jacques Androuet du Cerceau's Château de Charleval (q.v.) while other details, for example the horse capitals, come from Serlio. This bizarre building, never completed, may be by John Thorpe's father, Thomas Thorpe.

William Cecil, Queen Elizabeth's principal minister, built mansions at **Theobalds** (destroyed 1650) and **Burghley House, Northamptonshire** (1552–87) (pp. 1011B, 1015A, 1016B). The exterior of Burghley reflects Tudor models, with its turreted entrance and corner towers. The clock-tower in the courtyard, dated 1585, is somewhat in the manner of Philibert de l'Orme's frontispieces at Anet with its free-standing superimposed columns and heraldic beasts, but the (later) obelisk motif is an original, if funereal, fancy.

Montacute House, Somerset (finished 1599) (pp. 1015B, 1018A), is built on the H-shape plan first found at Wimbledon House (1588–, destroyed eighteenth century). The elevations are plain and regular with restrained Flemish gables capping the projections.

Hardwick Hall, Derbyshire (1590–7) (p. 1019A,B), designed by Robert Smythson for the redoubtable and much-married Bess of Hardwick (whose initials appear on the parapet), has an oblong plan with projections, the long gallery spanning the east facade at second-floor level. The extravagant fenestration gave rise to the saying 'Hardwick Hall, more glass than wall'. The interiors are very well preserved, with overmantles and stucco work reminiscent of those at Fontainebleau, and original tapestries and embroideries.

Some late Elizabethan houses incorporated symbolism into their plans, one such example being **Longford Castle, Wiltshire** (1580) (p. 1015E), based on the diagram of the Trinity. **Castle Ashby, Northamptonshire** (1572–) (p. 1019C–E), has an U-shaped Elizabethan plan, made square by the addition of a gallery wing in the style of Inigo Jones (*c.* 1635). Biblical inscriptions (Psalm 127) are built into the parapet.

The mansions built under James I show less variety and individuality than the Elizabethan examples.

Audley End, Essex (1603–16) (p. 1018B), by Bernard Janssen, was originally designed around two courtyards, of which only the inner one remains. The turrets, projection and varying height of the parts make for a picturesque effect, despite the insistent symmetry.

Hatfield House, Hertfordshire (1607–11) (pp. 1015F,1020A), built for Robert Cecil, first Earl of Salisbury, is the most spectacular surviving Jacobean mansion. Built at the instigation of James I, it is an ungainly sprawling variant on the H-plan incorporating separate apartments for the King and Queen in the two wings. The facades are of plain brickwork with stone quoins and window mullions, except for the central wing which is faced on the south side with pilasters and carries a three-storey columned frontispiece, the work of Robert Lyming. The two-storey hall with mullioned windows, minstrels' gallery and modelled plaster ceiling is a Jacobean version of the traditional mediaeval hall, but there is an unusual connecting gallery at the east end.

Bramshill House, Hampshire (1605–12) (p. 1015G), was designed for Lord Zouche. Its unusual plan, partly due to an older building, is an H-type, with entrance on the short side and a curious narrow internal open area. The arcaded terrace (p. 1011J) and oriel window over the porch (p. 1011A) (by Gerard Christmas) relieve the plain brick facades. **Charlton House, Greenwich** (1607) (p. 1020B), is a regular H-plan with the hall running front-to-back from the central entrance, richly carved in the Dietterlin manner.

Bolsover Castle, Derbyshire (1612–21), is a precocious (or late) exercise in mock mediaevalism, designed by John Smythson (died 1634), son of Robert, with additions by John's son, Huntingdon. It incorporates some details crudely copied from Inigo Jones.

ELIZABETHAN AND JACOBEAN COLLEGES

Oxford and Cambridge contain some of the most interesting exercises in the Renaissance style outside the court and country-house circles. The tiny **Gate of Honour, Gonville and Caius College, Cambridge** (1572–3) (p. 1021A), is one of two allegorical gateways based on Serlio and built by the College's founder, John Caius, who had studied in Padua. Thomas Bodley applied all the five orders to the new **Schools Building (Bodleian Tower), Oxford** (1613–) (p. 1021B), itself built in plain college Gothic style under the control of the masons John Bentley and John Akroyd. Superimposed orders appear also at **Merton** (1610) (p. 1021C) and **Wadham** (1610–13) **Colleges,**

A. Montacute House, Somerset (1580–99). See p. 1017

B. Audley End, Essex (1603–16). See p. 1017

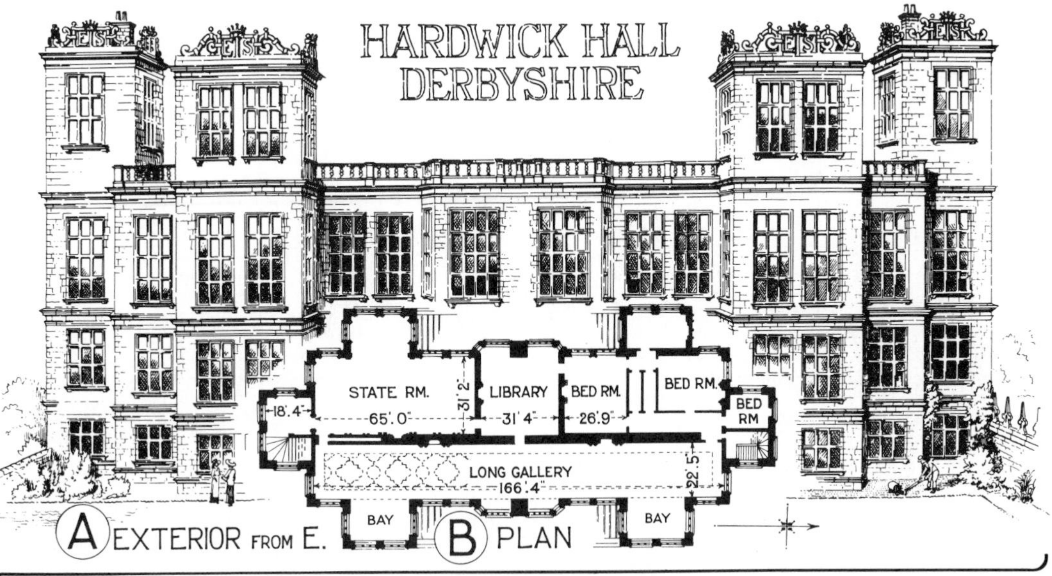

(A) EXTERIOR FROM E. (B) PLAN

CASTLE ASHBY : NORTHANTS

NI SI DO MI NVS
NI VANVM
DOMINVS CVSTODIAT
INTROITVM
45' 0"
30' 0"

(C) EXTERIOR FROM S.

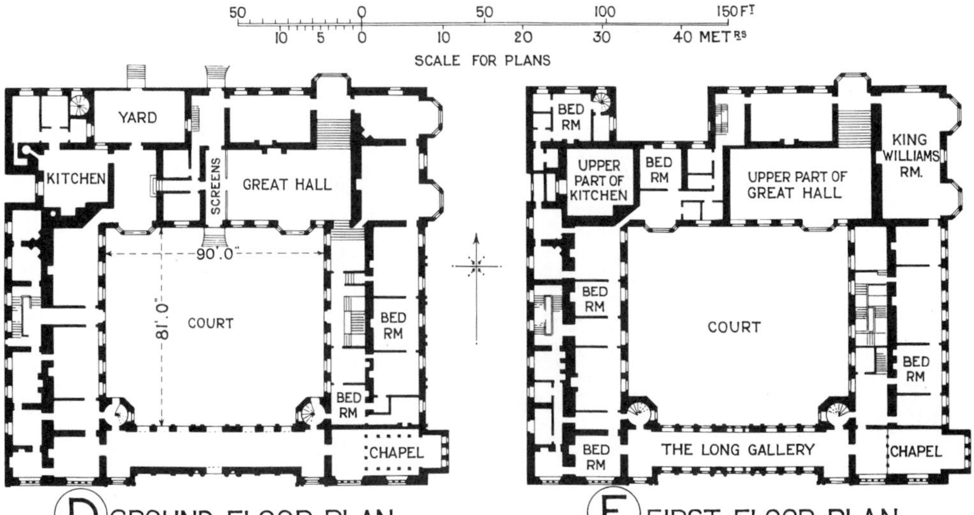

50 0 50 100 150 FT
10 5 0 10 20 30 40 METRS
SCALE FOR PLANS

YARD
KITCHEN
SCREENS
GREAT HALL
90' 0"
81' 0"
COURT
BED RM
BED RM
CHAPEL

(D) GROUND FLOOR PLAN

BED RM
UPPER PART OF KITCHEN
BED RM
UPPER PART OF GREAT HALL
KING WILLIAMS RM.
BED RM
COURT
BED RM
BED RM
THE LONG GALLERY
CHAPEL

(E) FIRST FLOOR PLAN

A. Hatfield House, Hertfordshire (1607–11). See p. 1017

B. Charlton House, Greenwich (1607). See p. 1017

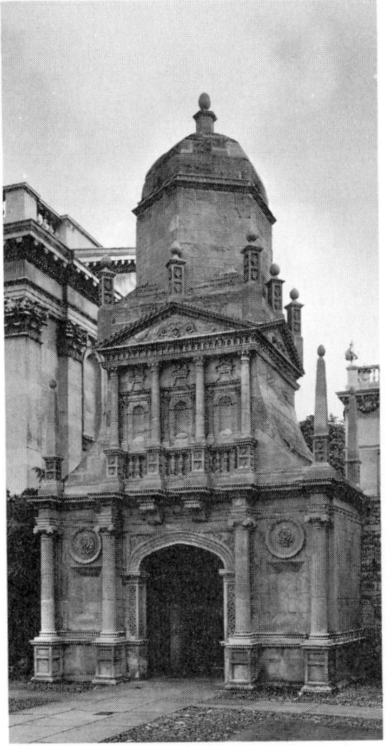

A. Gate of Honour, Gonville and Caius College, Cambridge (1572–3). See p. 1017

B. Bodleian Tower, Schools Building, Oxford (1613–). See p. 1017

C. Merton College, Oxford, entrance (1610). See p. 1017

D. Wadham College, Oxford: hall (1610–13). See p. 1022

E. Middle Temple Hall, London (1562–70). See p. 1022

Oxford. Nevile's Court at Trinity College, Cambridge (1593–1615) is built with light arcades on columns. The hall at Wadham (p. 1021D) has a fine beamed roof, an interesting comparison with the **Middle Temple Hall, London** (1562–70) (p. 1021E), with its double hammer-beams and magnificent screen.

TOWN HOUSES

Elizabethan and Jacobean timber-framed town houses built by the prosperous merchant class tend to be double- or triple-fronted, with projecting upper stories or 'jetties' supported on consoles. The gables are lower and much simpler than their equivalents in northern Europe. Fine examples may be found in Shrewsbury and especially Chester, which also has an exceptionally interesting system of first-floor pedestrian galleries, known as the 'Rows', along its principal streets.

The most impressive timber-framed country houses in the 'black and white' Elizabethan style are found in Cheshire and Lancashire. **Little Moreton Hall, Cheshire** (1559), has a multi-gabled and jettied facade with abundant oriel windows, the beams forming diamond and quatrefoil patterns on the exterior. **Speke Hall**, near **Liverpool** (1490–1626), is in a similar style.

The early Renaissance in Scotland has a distinctly French flavour, reinforced by James V's marriages first to the daughter of François I, and then to Mary of Guise. James's **Falkland Palace, Fife** (1539–42), is an early but unheeded attempt to introduce the orders. The courtyard facade has a regular pattern of five bays, with columns over piers applied to projecting buttresses. Roundels with portrait busts punctuate the facade, as at Hampton Court. The effect is usually described as French, but the modular approach to the bays is Italian in spirit.

Crichton Castle (*c.* 1590), built by the fifth Earl of Bothwell, who had travelled on the continent, has diamond-faceted rustication in the manner of Italian examples such as the Palazzo dei Diamanti, Ferrara (q.v.).

Sixteenth-century Scottish castles, built on redistributed monastic lands, have a highly characteristic and individual style, combining French influences with the native tradition of the peel tower. Round towers placed at the corners help to make up 'L', 'T' or 'Z' plans. Exterior walls sheer from the ground with few and small openings, all the ornament being concentrated at roof level where the buildings break out into conically-roofed turrets and decorated dormers. Also very French are the corbelled-out stair-turrets placed in angles. The finest example of this 'Scottish Baronial' style is perhaps **Fyvie Castle, Aberdeenshire** (*c.* 1600–3), where the extremely spare detailing gives the building an almost abstract quality.

Stuart, Commonwealth and Restoration (1625–1700)

Inigo Jones (1573–1652) introduced the Classical canons of Italian Renaissance architecture to England. During two trips to Italy he immersed himself in contemporary as well as ancient architecture, buying many of Palladio's drawings which were to be a constant source of ideas. He began his career as designer of court masques but soon emerged as England's foremost architect, becoming Surveyor of the King's Works (1615). His influence extends into the eighteenth century, as his buildings were formative for the Palladian revival.

The **Queen's House, Greenwich** (1616–35) (pp. 1023A, 1024C,E), was built by Jones for Anne of Denmark, wife of James I, in the grounds of Greenwich Palace. Conceived as a hunting lodge, it also fulfilled the secondary function of a bridge over the public road to Deptford, which divided the park in two. Jones placed two blocks either side of the road and joined them at first-floor level by means of a bridge. This H-shaped plan, perhaps modelled on the Medici villa at Poggio a Caiano (q.v.), was later filled in by Webb's addition of two further bridges on the side elevations. A two-storey cubic hall facing the river gives access to the bridge and then to a loggia overlooking the park. Either side of this axis are two suites of rooms. Typically Palladian, the facades are tripartite with a central projecting portion. Plain walls are set upon a rusticated ground floor and crowned by a balustrade. Curving steps lead up to the main entrance, while the internal circular staircase is of a type recommended by Palladio.

Jones's **Banqueting House, Whitehall, London**, (1619–22) (p. 1025C,D), if not the first truly Classical building begun in seventeenth-century England, was certainly the first to be completed. An addition to the mediaeval palace of Whitehall, it was built as a setting for masques and court festivities. For the plan Jones adapted the ancient three-aisled basilica, pushing the aisle columns to the sides so as not to obstruct the centre of the room. Transformed into half-columns, they symbolically support the cantilevered balcony that runs around the double-cube room. Originally a large apse completed the scheme, underlining the basilican origins of the design. In true Classical fashion the Ionic and Composite orders correspond on interior and exterior. The seven-bay facade has a central section which breaks forward. Here, the order changes from pilaster to half-column and window panels become balconies. There was no entrance in the facade, and perhaps for this reason Jones abandoned an early pedimented scheme.

Jones's first ecclesiastical building, the **Queen's Chapel, S. James's Palace, London** (1623–7), was designed as a Roman Catholic chapel, and used by Henrietta Maria, wife of Charles I. The simple exterior avoids reference to Catholic ecclesiastical

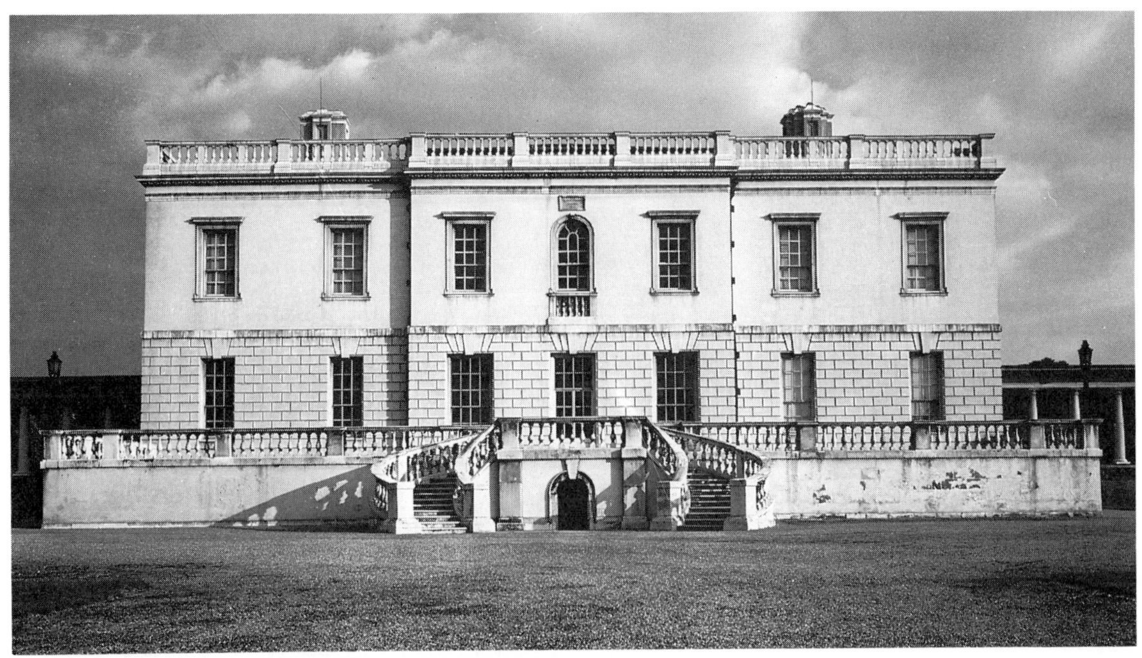

A. Queen's House, Greenwich (1616–35). See p. 1022

B. Coleshill House, Berkshire (*c.* 1650; destroyed by fire 1952). See p. 1027

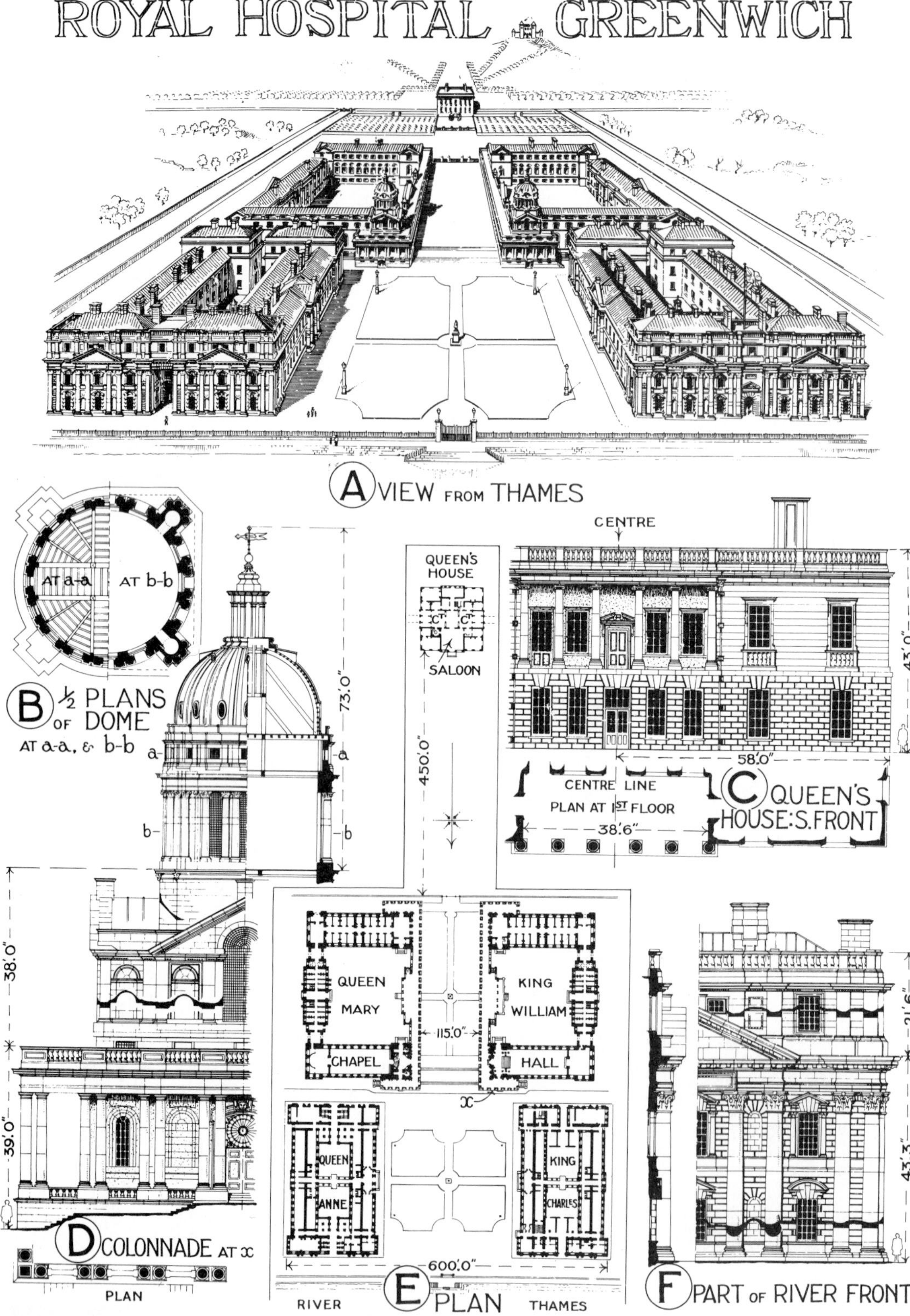
ROYAL HOSPITAL GREENWICH
A VIEW FROM THAMES
AT a-a
AT b-b
B ½ PLANS OF DOME AT a-a, & b-b
73'0"
a
b
CENTRE
QUEEN'S HOUSE
SALOON
450'0"
43'0"
58'0"
CENTRE LINE
PLAN AT 1ST FLOOR
38'6"
C QUEEN'S HOUSE: S. FRONT
38'0"
39'0"
D COLONNADE AT x
PLAN
QUEEN MARY
CHAPEL
KING WILLIAM
HALL
115'0"
x
QUEEN ANNE
KING CHARLES
600'0"
RIVER
E PLAN
THAMES
21'6"
43'3"
F PART OF RIVER FRONT

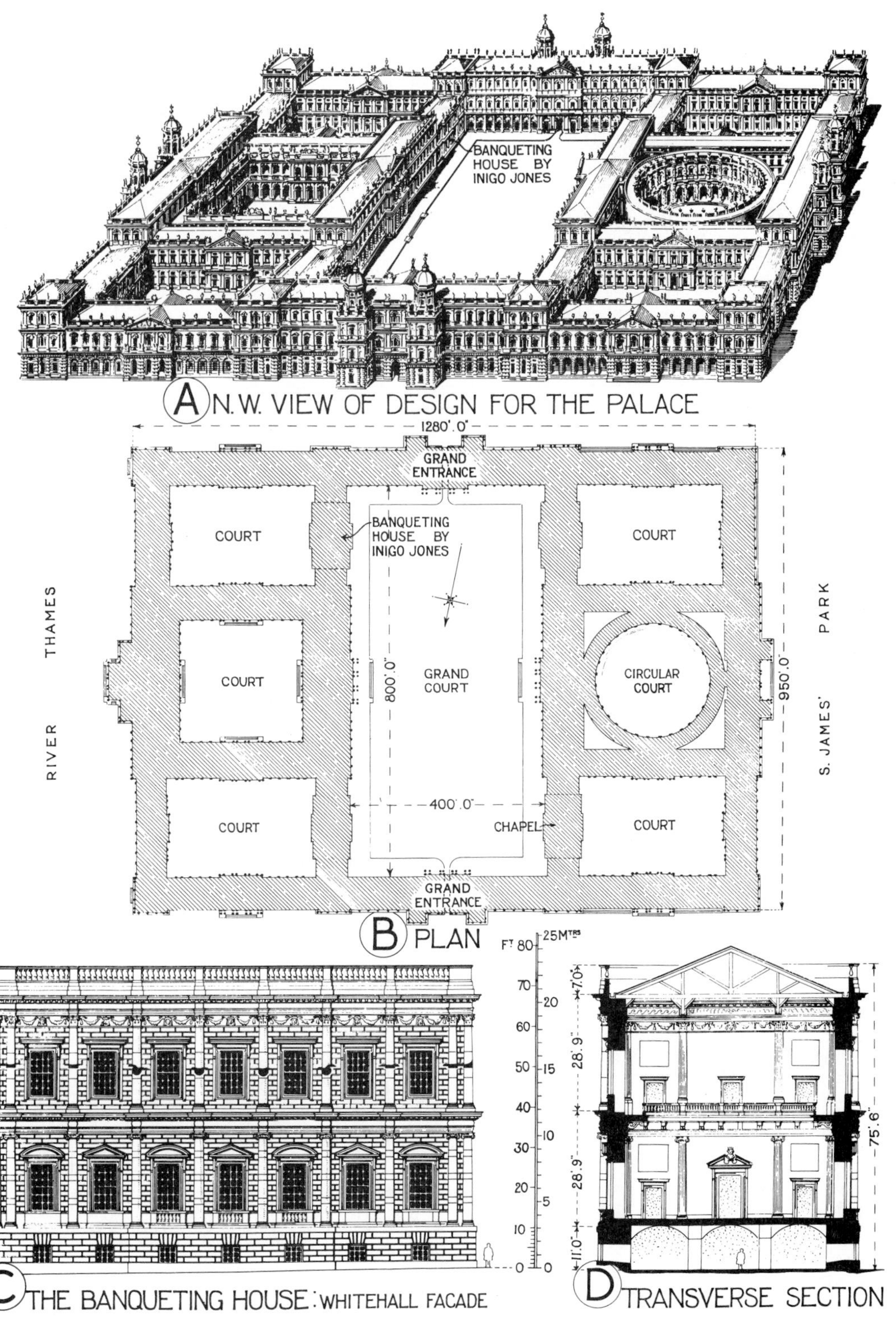

(A) N.W. VIEW OF DESIGN FOR THE PALACE

(B) PLAN

(C) THE BANQUETING HOUSE: WHITEHALL FACADE

(D) TRANSVERSE SECTION

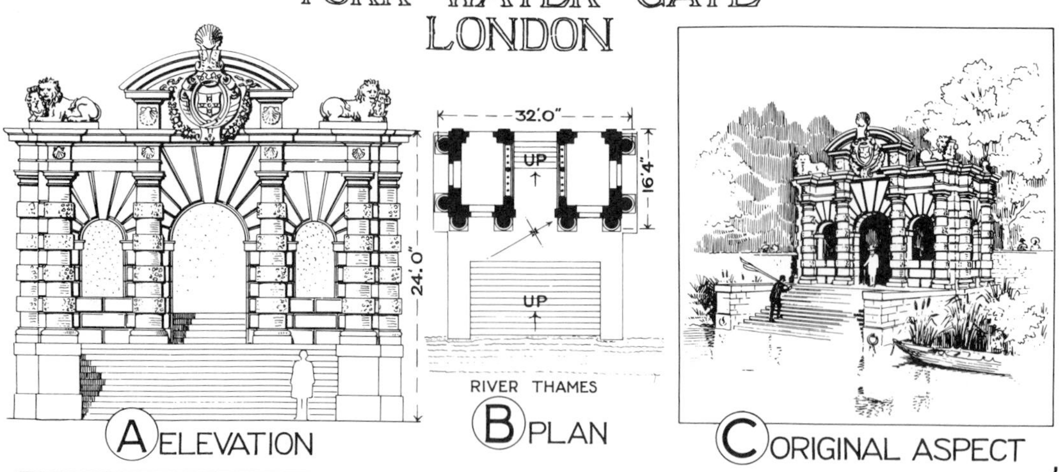

A ELEVATION B PLAN C ORIGINAL ASPECT

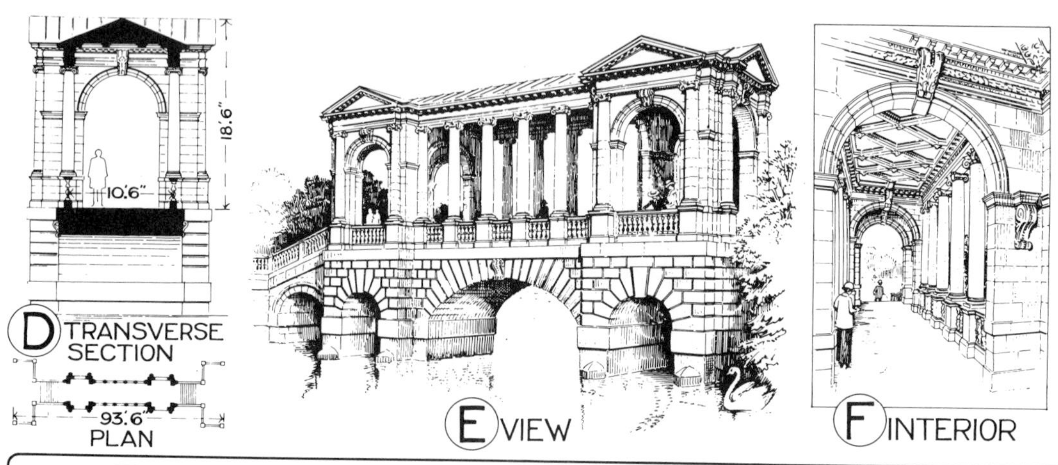

D TRANSVERSE SECTION PLAN E VIEW F INTERIOR

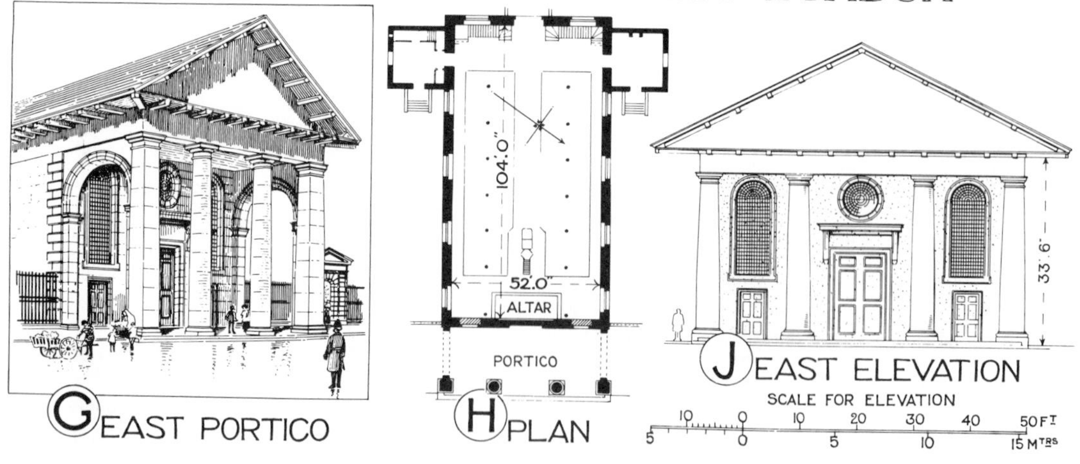

G EAST PORTICO H PLAN J EAST ELEVATION

types. The windows, doors and quoins point to domestic architecture and resemble Jones's drawings for the Prince's Lodging at Newmarket. The sole ecclesiastical reference can be found in the pedimented gable. The contrastingly lavish interior has a Serlian window above the altar (a type which was to become popular in later seventeenth-century architecture), and an elaborate semi-oval coffered vault.

S. Paul's, Covent Garden, London (begun 1630) (p. 1026G–J), was designed for the fourth Earl of Bedford as part of the first geometrically planned urban development of seventeenth-century England. Perhaps inspired by similar layouts in Livorno and the Place des Vosges, Paris (q.v.), rows of Classically severe houses with ground floor arcades fronted two sides of the square, the earl's residence and the church making up the other two. Designing a church suitable for Protestant services in the new Classical manner, Jones makes plain the fundamental character of the new religion, as well as following his patron's desire for economy. A simple rectangular box, it once contained galleries to allow more people to hear the scriptures clearly. The adoption of the Tuscan order is a deliberately austere choice, producing what Jones described as 'the handsomest barn in England'. The Tuscan tetrastyle portico with its large eaves is strictly Vitruvian in its use of detail.

Heriot's Hospital, Edinburgh (begun 1621), was founded by George Heriot to provide an education for orphaned young boys. Designed by William Wallace (died 1631), the square plan with a large internal court and corner towers is based on a design in Serlio's treatise. The towers with their corner turrets look back to traditional Scottish castle types like Fyvie (q.v.) while the central clock tower recalls the frontispieces of English country houses such as Hatfield (q.v.).

John Webb (1611–72), pupil of Inigo Jones, designed a vast palace for Charles II on a U-shaped plan, of which only one wing, the **King Charles Block, Greenwich** (1662–9) (p. 1024E,F), was built. A five-bay river front with a pedimented three-bay central section was to be surmounted by a vast dome, a new combination in English architecture and important for such later buildings as Castle Howard and the National Gallery, London; the source is Palladio's designs for the Villa Trissino at Meledo. The executed block is wholly rusticated, and is monumentalised at the centre and ends by the application of a giant order.

Roger Pratt (1620–84) had a wealthy and educated background and travelled in France, Italy and the Netherlands (1643–9). He built five large houses and then retired to the country seat he had designed at Ryston. His most remarkable building was **Coleshill House, Berkshire** (*c.* 1650, destroyed 1952) (p. 1023B). At the centre of the double square plan were the main show rooms, the Great Parlour and the magnificent hall with its encircling double-ramped stairs. These were flanked by the main living rooms connected by a long corridor which formed the spine of the house. The exterior, with its unevenly spaced windows, had a disguised tripartite character reminiscent of Palladio and Jones. The dormer windows, rooftop balustrade and lantern looked back to French architecture, in particular to Mansart's Balleroy (q.v.).

At **Eltham Lodge, Kent** (1664) (p. 1028A), Hugh May (1622–84) introduced to England a style based on Dutch seventeenth-century Classicism characterised by the use of red brick with white stone detailing and almost obligatory pilaster strips. The plan, unlike the elevations, is similar to Pratt's 'double pile' house, Coleshill (q.v.). Of May's other works, such as **Cassiobury, Hertfordshire** (begun 1674), and Windsor Castle interiors, little survives.

Sir Christopher Wren (1632–1723) came to architecture late, having already made a name for himself as a 'natural philosopher' at Oxford, where he was Gresham Professor of Astronomy. He never went to Italy and left England only once to visit Paris in 1665. Through his vast output and that of his pupils he created a style which became the basis of the English Baroque.

The **Sheldonian Theatre, Oxford** (1664–9) (p. 1028C), was designed by Wren as a hall for university ceremonies, and was modelled on the theatres of antiquity. Rusticated arches on the lower storey together with the rounded rear end hark back to such sources. Internally, semicircular tiers of seats are the focus of the spectator's attention, thus reversing the antique relationship between the seating and 'frons scenae'. The English climate necessitated a roof, but Robert Streeter's ceiling painting suggests open-air Classical models by its allegorical figures set against an open sky. Lacking an appropriate facade model for such a building, Wren combined arches with a pedimented two-storey elevation reminiscent of Italian Renaissance churches.

Pembroke College Chapel, Cambridge (1663–5), is traditionally attributed to Wren and was designed for his uncle, Matthew Wren. It has an austere pedimented and pilastered facade, derived very directly from a design published by Serlio.

At **Emmanuel College, Cambridge** (1667–73), Wren designed a chapel set into a courtyard. Its facade is distinguished from the flanking arcaded screen by a giant Corinthian order, pediment and lantern. The central bay can be read independently as a steeple.

Wren's **Library, Trinity College, Cambridge** (1676–84) (p. 1032A), was originally designed as a free-standing square block at one end of an open court. He ultimately preferred the more conventional enclosed court scheme. Facing the court two superimposed Classical arcades mask the interior arrangement, the first-floor level being at the springing line of the ground-floor arches. This allows the windows

A. Eltham Lodge, Kent (1664). See p. 1027

B. S. Paul's Cathedral, London (1675–1710): the crossing. See p. 1033

C. Sheldonian Theatre, Oxford (1662–3) (seventeenth-century engraving). See p. 1027

S. PAUL : LONDON

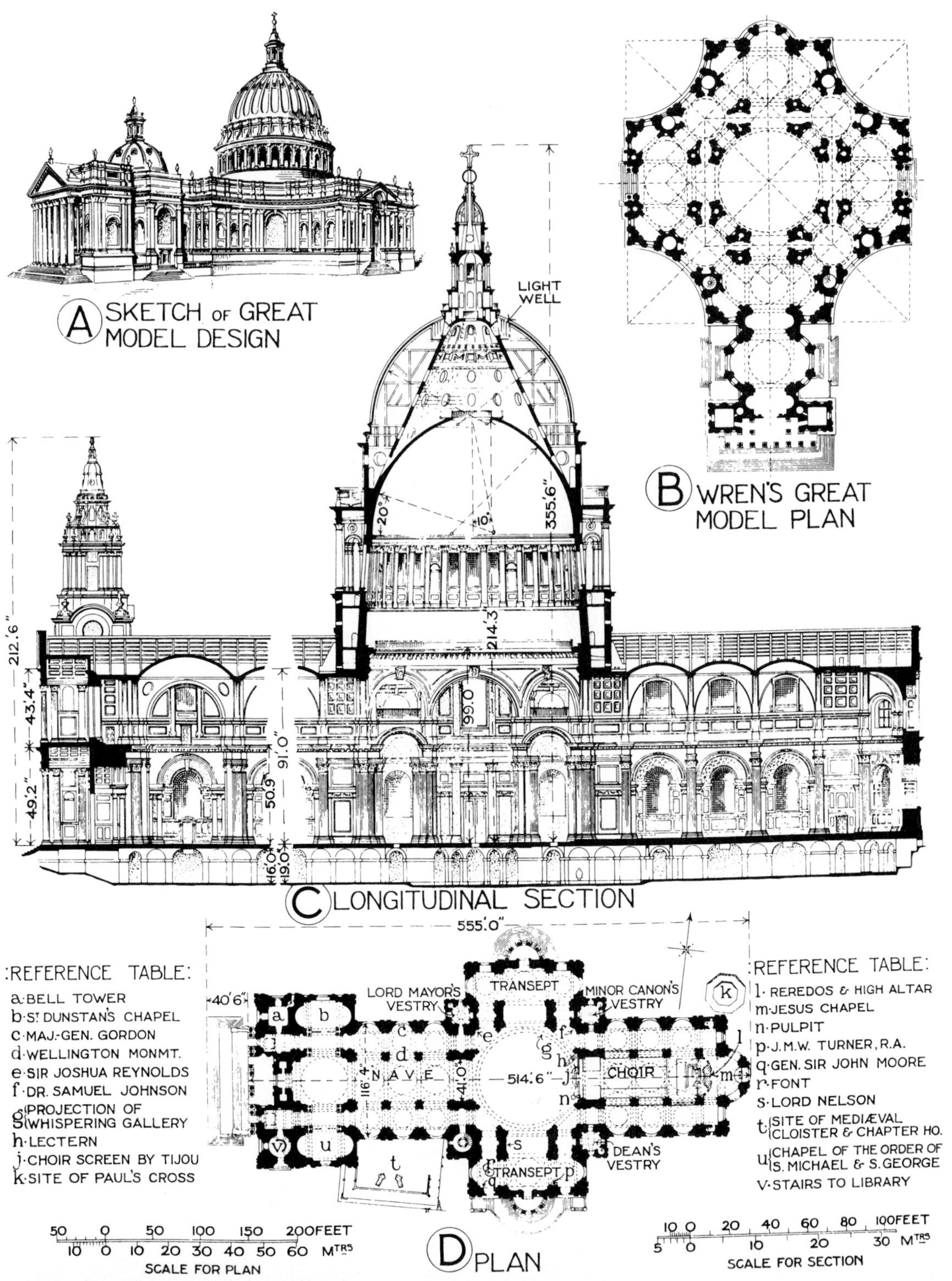

A SKETCH OF GREAT MODEL DESIGN

B WREN'S GREAT MODEL PLAN

C LONGITUDINAL SECTION

D PLAN

REFERENCE TABLE:
a·BELL TOWER
b·ST DUNSTAN'S CHAPEL
c·MAJ.-GEN. GORDON
d·WELLINGTON MONMT.
e·SIR JOSHUA REYNOLDS
f·DR. SAMUEL JOHNSON
g·PROJECTION OF WHISPERING GALLERY
h·LECTERN
j·CHOIR SCREEN BY TIJOU
k·SITE OF PAUL'S CROSS

REFERENCE TABLE:
l·REREDOS & HIGH ALTAR
m·JESUS CHAPEL
n·PULPIT
p·J.M.W. TURNER, R.A.
q·GEN. SIR JOHN MOORE
r·FONT
s·LORD NELSON
t·SITE OF MEDIÆVAL CLOISTER & CHAPTER HO.
u·CHAPEL OF THE ORDER OF S. MICHAEL & S. GEORGE
v·STAIRS TO LIBRARY

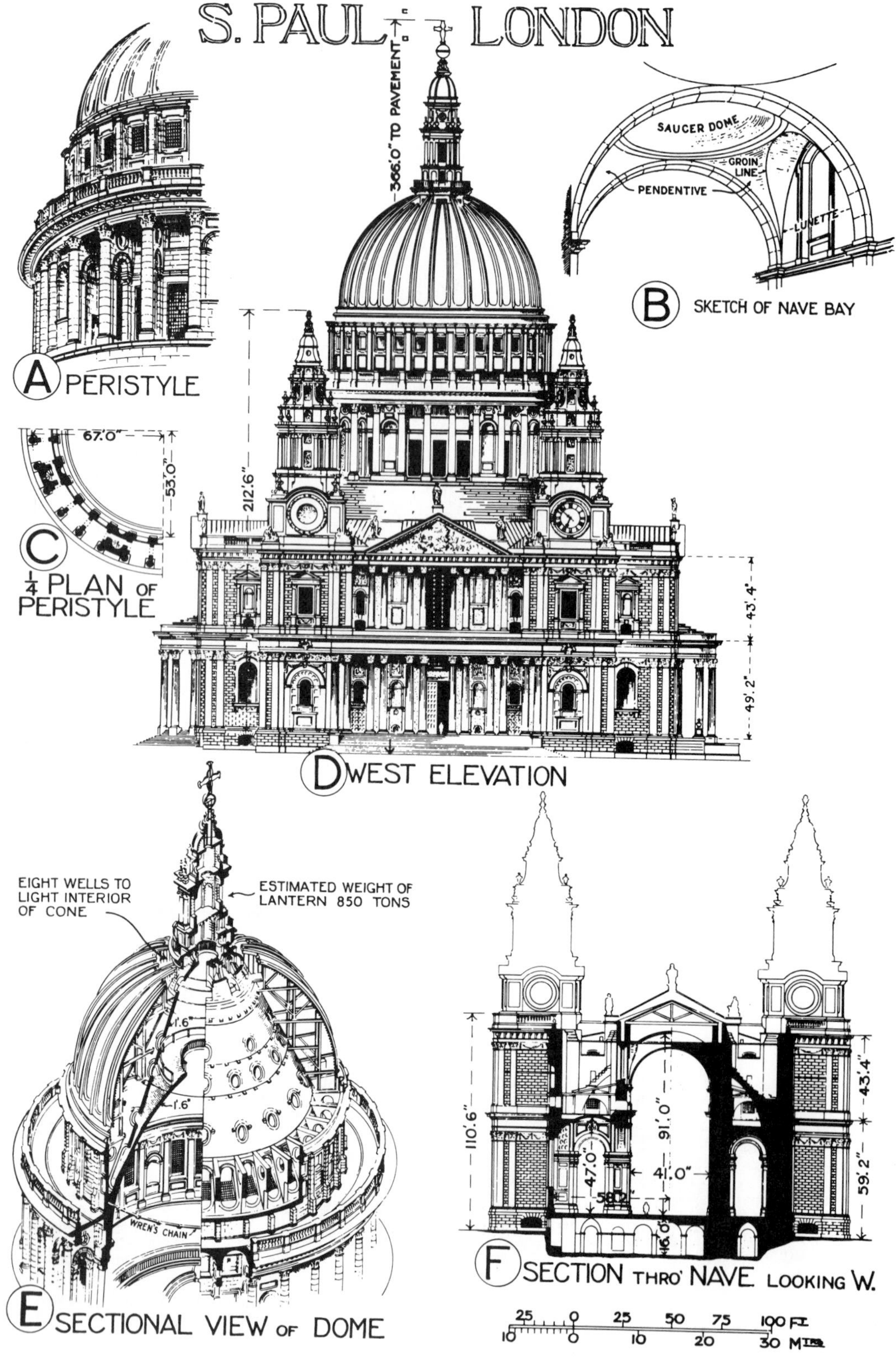
S. PAUL : LONDON
366'.0" TO PAVEMENT
SAUCER DOME
GROIN LINE
PENDENTIVE
LUNETTE
B SKETCH OF NAVE BAY
A PERISTYLE
67.0"
53.0"
C
¼ PLAN OF PERISTYLE
212'.6"
43'.4"
49'.2"
D WEST ELEVATION
EIGHT WELLS TO LIGHT INTERIOR OF CONE
ESTIMATED WEIGHT OF LANTERN 850 TONS
1.6"
1.6"
WREN'S CHAIN
E SECTIONAL VIEW OF DOME
110'.6"
91'.0"
47'.0"
41'.0"
58'.2"
16'.0"
43'.4"
59'.2"
F SECTION THRO' NAVE LOOKING W.
25 0 25 50 75 100 FT
10 0 10 20 30 MTRS

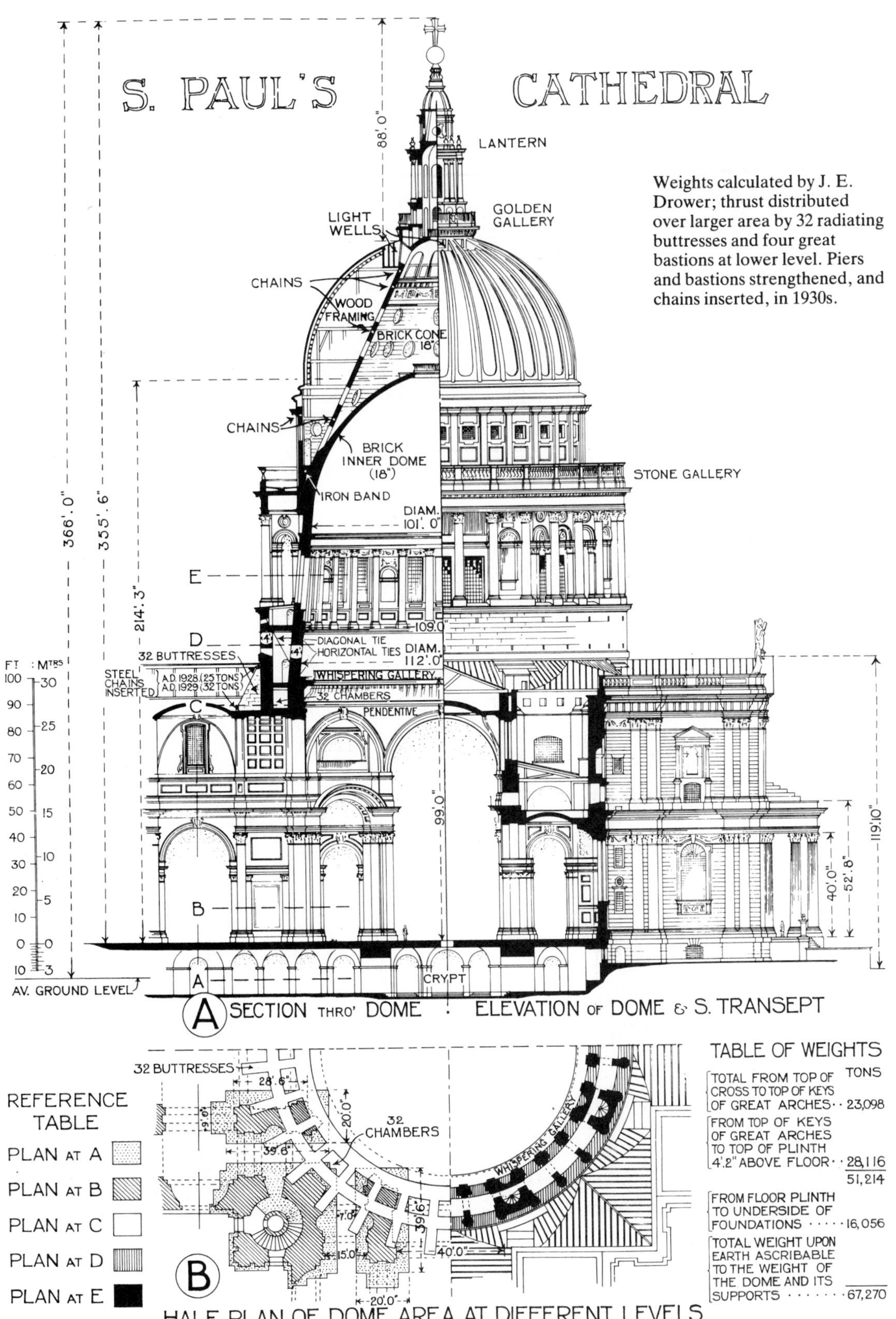

Weights calculated by J. E. Drower; thrust distributed over larger area by 32 radiating buttresses and four great bastions at lower level. Piers and bastions strengthened, and chains inserted, in 1930s.

A. Trinity College, Cambridge: Nevile's Court (1593–1615), looking towards library (1676–84). See p. 1027

B. Hampton Court Palace: south facade (1689–94). See p. 1033

to be placed high above the interior book stacks, giving maximum light. On the river facade the columns of the upper arcade are replaced by pilaster strips with recessed windows, and the closed ground floor has three handsome Doric portals.

The destruction of the Gothic **S. Paul's Cathedral, London**, in the Great Fire of 1666 was not total. Following in Jones's footsteps, Wren began a partial rebuilding but it became clear by 1668 that a complete reconstruction (1675–1710) (pp. 1028B, 1029, 1030, 1031) was necessary. Five stages in the design history can be quickly outlined. A modest project with domed vestibule was discarded in favour of a Greek-cross design (1672). This was extended to form the 'Great Model' design (1673–74) (p. 1029A,B). This had a large domed crossing and a smaller dome over the vestibule, while the four arms were linked by concave quadrants. The cathedral chapter reacted unfavourably to Wren's favourite design, perhaps because it seemed too different from normal English cathedrals and too similar to the popish S. Peter's (q.v.). The 'warrant design' (1675) saw a return to the Latin cross and the final design is a development from it.

To east and west of the domed octagonal crossing are three saucer-domed bays flanked by side aisles, forming presbytery and nave, the latter fronted by a deep vestibule. Much of the two-storey exterior is sham, the upper level screening the aisle roof and vault buttresses from view. Wren has attempted to give the whole a consistent external appearance by using two storeys of drafted masonry with applied orders, resembling Jones's Banqueting House (q.v.); at the transept ends this system is fused with a convex portico reminiscent of Cortona's S. Maria della Pace, Rome (q.v.). The facade continues the paired pilaster articulation in column form between twin towers.

The dome is like an enormous version of Bramante's Tempietto (q.v.). Here, however, the colonnade is given a rhythm by blocking one in four of the intercolumniations as buttresses, a syncopation imitated in the facade lanterns. The dome, like Hardouin Mansart's Invalides (q.v.), has three shells: the inner brick dome, a near hemisphere, has an open oculus looking through to the tall brick cone which supports the lantern; the outer hemisphere is a light timber framework covered with lead. On the interior, the base of the drum appears to rest on eight equal arches; in reality the octagon, reminiscent of that at Ely Cathedral, has alternating wide and narrow bays, and much of the thrust is carried out to the corner buttresses.

The building of S. Paul's spanned Wren's entire career as an architect and shows the development of his ideas from French-influenced Classicism to a greater openness to the Baroque.

Following the Great Fire of London in 1666, Wren was placed in charge of reconstructing the destroyed churches (p. 1034), fifty-one of which were to be rebuilt. For the sake of economy, he often made use of old foundations, ingeniously adapting the elevations to create interesting and varied effects. He also Classicised the typical English steeple, giving each church an individual character visible from afar and endowing London with a distinctive skyline. Designed to meet the requirements of Protestant worship they included galleries following Jones's lead at S. Paul's, Covent Garden.

S. Stephen Walbrook, London (1672–87) (p. 1035), has one of Wren's most exciting interiors. Though rectangular in plan, it is treated as an essay in centralised planning. The sixteen Corinthian columns of the interior are disposed in grid-like fashion and the entablature they carry forms an elaborate Greek cross. Above this, arches cut across the corners, forming an octagon which, in turn, supports a hemispherical dome. The light wood and plaster structure permits windows to be inserted easily, creating a luminous interior.

Wren considered his **S. James's Piccadilly, London** (1676–84; reconstructed after World War II bomb damage) (p. 1036A–D), to be a model city church. The rectangular interior is covered by a wooden barrel vault and abutted by the transverse vaults of the galleries, which are treated as integral parts of the design. They stand on Doric piers and act as a pedestal level for the Corinthian order above. Behind the altar Wren adopted the Serlian motif used earlier by Jones at the Queen's Chapel (q.v.).

At **S. Mary-le-Bow, Cheapside, London** (1670–77) (pp. 1034G, 1037A,B,E), Wren created his first great Classical steeple. As with earlier Gothic examples, this was an adjunct to the main body of the church and housed a French-inspired portal in a concave niche. The belfry, adorned with pilasters, supports a circular columnar tempietto. A second smaller tempietto is reached by flying buttresses and the whole is crowned by an obelisk.

S. Bride's, Fleet Street, London (1671–8) (pp. 1036E–H, 1037C,D,F), gutted in 1940, was on a simpler rectangular plan with stepped galleries supported on eight columns.

Wren's late steeple of **S. Vedast's, London** (1694–7), is very different in conception. The sculptural massing of elements and the alternation between concave and convex tiers looks back to the architecture of Borromini, in particular the church of S. Ivo (q.v.). The hand of Hawksmoor has sometimes been suspected in the design.

For King William and Queen Mary, Wren designed additions to the sixteenth-century palace of **Hampton Court** (1689–94) (pp. 486B,G, 1032B), which were intended to rival Louis XIV's palace at Versailles (q.v.). The use of red brick allows Wren's park fronts to harmonise with the rest of the palace; dressed stone is used to emphasise the central features of the elevations. The circular windows are unusual and probably derived from French sources.

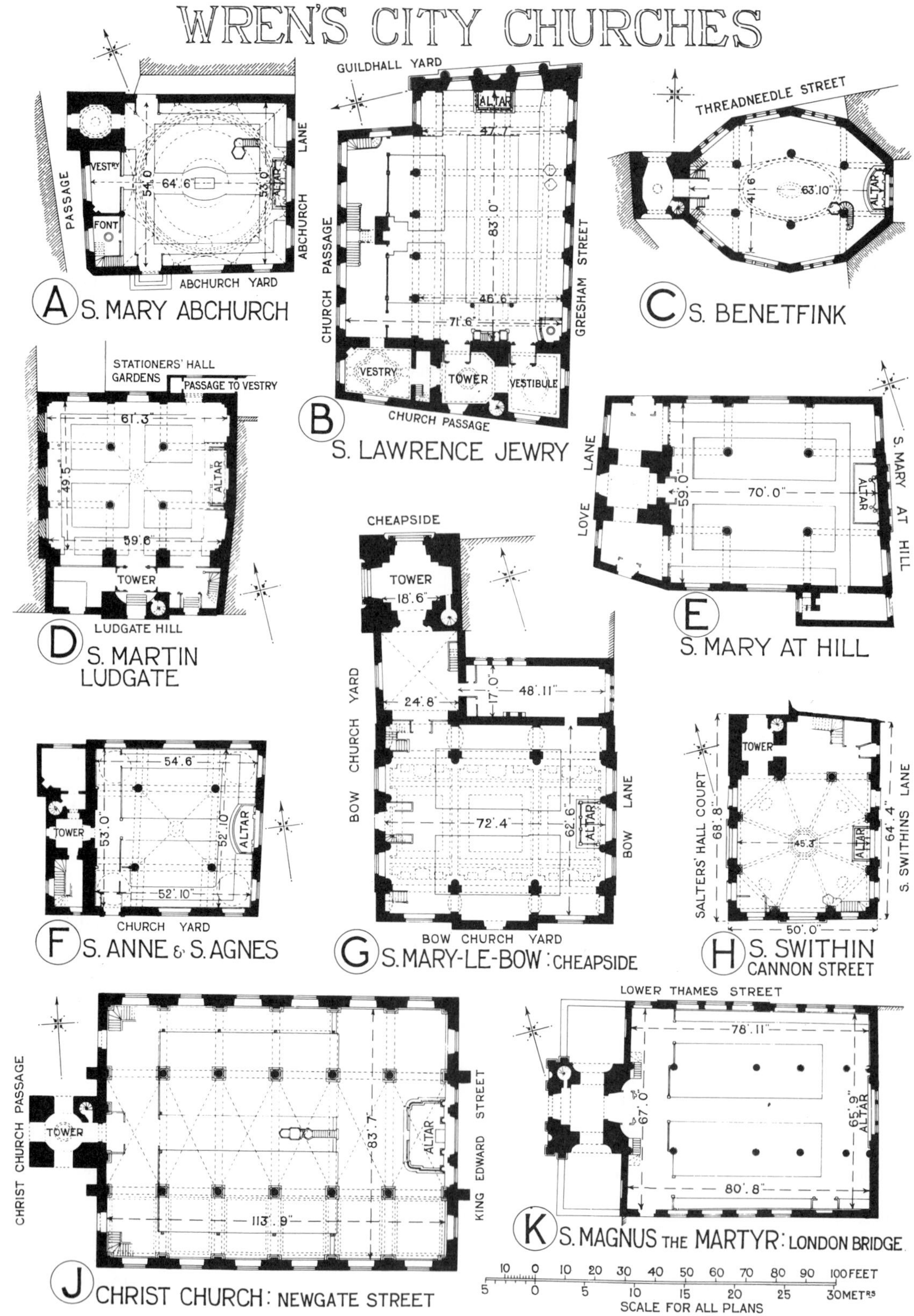
WREN'S CITY CHURCHES
GUILDHALL YARD
ALTAR
47'.7"
PASSAGE
VESTRY
FONT
64'.6"
54'.0"
53'.0"
ALTAR
ABCHURCH LANE
ABCHURCH YARD
A S. MARY ABCHURCH
CHURCH PASSAGE
83'.0"
46'.6"
71'.6"
GRESHAM STREET
VESTRY
TOWER
VESTIBULE
CHURCH PASSAGE
B S. LAWRENCE JEWRY
THREADNEEDLE STREET
41'.6"
63'.10"
ALTAR
C S. BENETFINK
STATIONERS' HALL GARDENS
PASSAGE TO VESTRY
61'.3"
49'.5"
ALTAR
59'.6"
TOWER
LUDGATE HILL
D S. MARTIN LUDGATE
LOVE LANE
59'.0"
70'.0"
ALTAR
S. MARY AT HILL
E S. MARY AT HILL
CHEAPSIDE
TOWER
18'.6"
BOW CHURCH YARD
24'.8"
17'.0"
48'.11"
72'.4"
62'.6"
ALTAR
BOW LANE
BOW CHURCH YARD
G S. MARY-LE-BOW: CHEAPSIDE
54'.6"
TOWER
53'.0"
52'.10"
ALTAR
52'.10"
CHURCH YARD
F S. ANNE & S. AGNES
TOWER
SALTERS' HALL COURT
68'.8"
45'.3"
ALTAR
64'.4"
S. SWITHINS LANE
50'.0"
H S. SWITHIN CANNON STREET
CHRIST CHURCH PASSAGE
TOWER
ALTAR
83'.7"
113'.9"
KING EDWARD STREET
J CHRIST CHURCH: NEWGATE STREET
LOWER THAMES STREET
78'.11"
67'.0"
65'.9"
ALTAR
80'.8"
K S. MAGNUS THE MARTYR: LONDON BRIDGE
10 0 10 20 30 40 50 60 70 80 90 100 FEET
5 0 5 10 15 20 25 30 METRS
SCALE FOR ALL PLANS

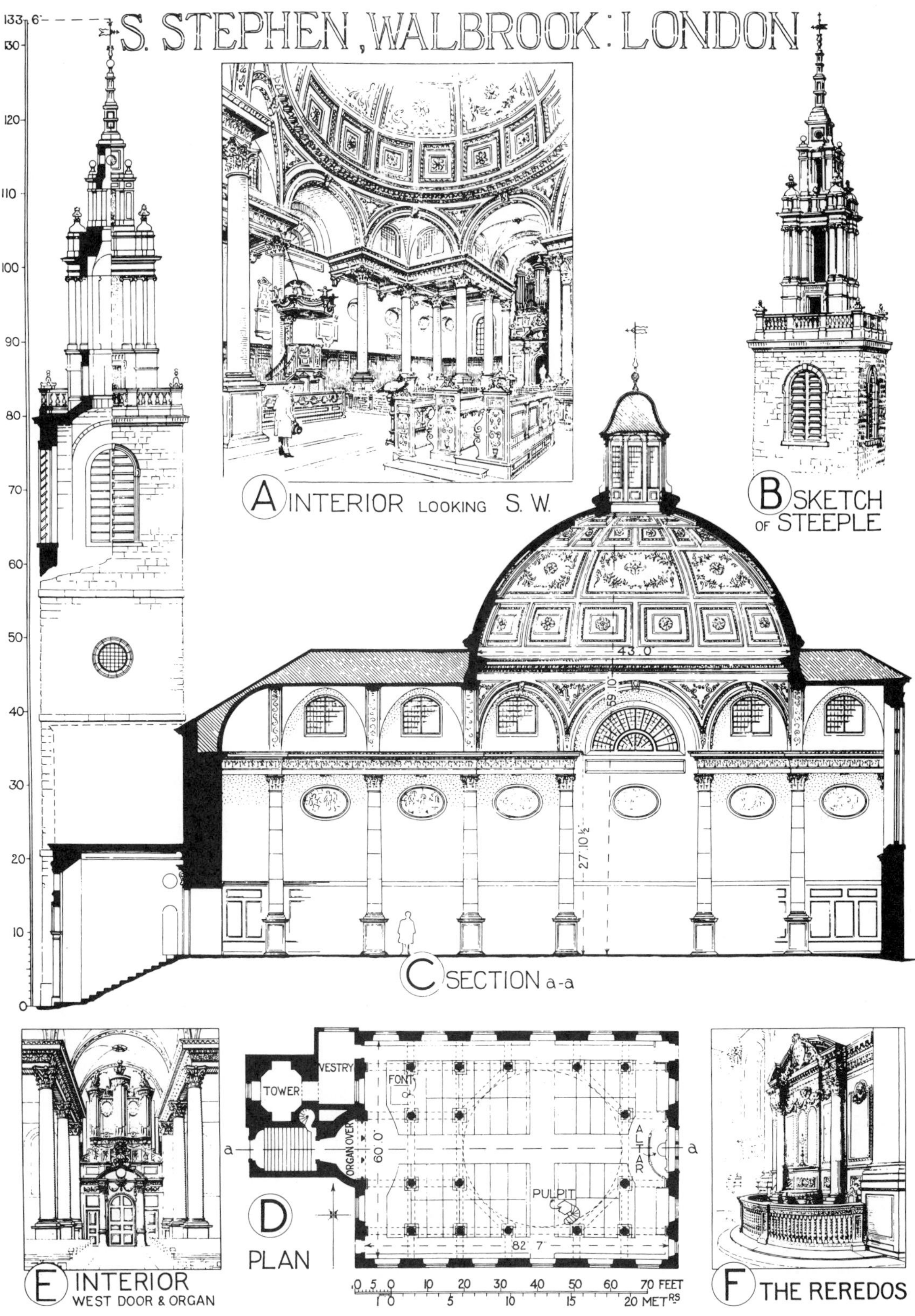
S. STEPHEN, WALBROOK: LONDON
A INTERIOR LOOKING S.W.
B SKETCH OF STEEPLE
C SECTION a-a
43'0"
59'10"
27'10½"
D PLAN
TOWER
VESTRY
FONT
ORGAN OVER
60'0"
ALTAR
PULPIT
82'7"
a
a
0 5 0 10 20 30 40 50 60 70 FEET
1 0 5 10 15 20 METRS
E INTERIOR WEST DOOR & ORGAN
F THE REREDOS

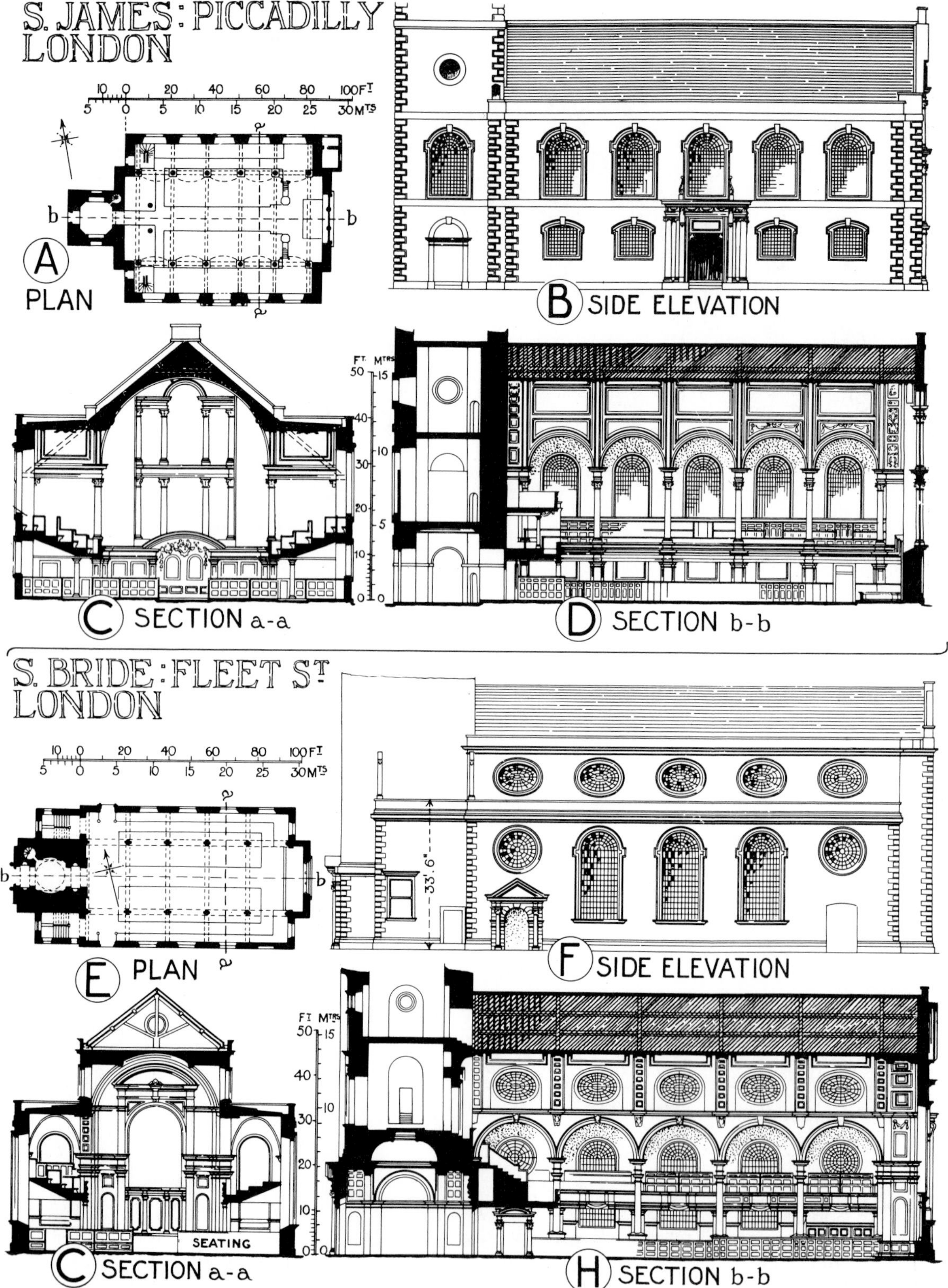
S. JAMES: PICCADILLY LONDON
10 0 20 40 60 80 100 FT
5 0 5 10 15 20 25 30 MTS
a
b
b
a
A PLAN
B SIDE ELEVATION
FT MTRS
50 15
40
10
30
20
5
10
0 0
C SECTION a-a
D SECTION b-b
S. BRIDE: FLEET ST LONDON
10 0 20 40 60 80 100 FT
5 0 5 10 15 20 25 30 MTS
a
b
b
a
33' 6"
E PLAN
F SIDE ELEVATION
FT MTRS
50 15
40
10
30
20
5
10
0 0
SEATING
C SECTION a-a
H SECTION b-b

S. MARY LE BOW LONDON
S. BRIDE LONDON
PLAN AT a
PLAN AT b
PLAN AT g
PLAN AT h
WEIGHT & THRUST OF UPPER PORTION TAKEN BY INVERTED TRUSSES
CORBEL OR PENDNTVE
CORBELS OR PENDENTIVES
STAIRS
33'.10"
17'.9"
19'.0"
104'.6"
111'.7"
103'.8"
226'.11"
25'.9"
18'.3"
20'.10"
16'.0"
FT MTRS
A SECTION
B ELEVATION
C ELEVATION
D SECTION
½ PLAN AT C
½ PLAN AT d
½ PLAN AT e
½ PLAN AT j
½ PLAN AT k
½ PLAN AT l
20'.6"
19'.1"
E PLAN AT f
F PLAN AT m

When designing **Tom Tower, Christ Church, Oxford** (1681–82), Wren 'resolved it ought to be Gothick to agree with the Founder's work. Yet I have not continued so busy as he began'. This suggests that the style of the tower springs not from a conscious revival of Gothic architecture but from a desire to complete an earlier building in an appropriate manner. Above the square base rises an octagon with a silhouette of pinnacles and ogee arches.

The **Royal Hospital, Chelsea, London** (1682–9) (p. 1039A), was conceived as a home and hospital for veteran soldiers, an idea derived from the slightly earlier institution in Paris, Les Invalides (q.v.). The artistic model, however, was Webb's plan for a palace at Greenwich (q.v.). A court open towards the river has a pedimented portico with a giant order and is topped by a domed lantern. The building's austere barrack-like quality is emphasised by the use of the Doric order. The central entrance portico is bolder than flanking features either side, which are abstracted and flattened, and the resulting change in fenestration has unusual results. The entablature cuts two windows in half while the central window breaks through it. The contrast between the tall order and the small windows monumentalises the facades.

English Baroque (1702–25)

Thomas Archer (1668–1743), more than any other English architect of the time, was fascinated by the Roman Baroque, which he knew at first hand. References to Bernini and Borromini abound in his work, as at **S. Philip, Birmingham** (1709–15) (p. 1039B), which is notable chiefly for its Borrominesque steeple. Its concave sides are transformed into a polygonal dome and even the windows are flagrantly borrowed from S. Ivo (q.v.).

Archer designed two of the fifty new churches projected for the City of London in 1711. The first was **S. Paul's, Deptford** (1712–30), which, though rectangular, was conceived as being centrally planned internally with a strong transverse axis. The front is dominated by a powerful semicircular portico surmounted by a spire, providing a model for Nash's All Souls, Langham Place (q.v.). The elevated church is approached by elaborate stairs, rectilinear at the sides and curving at the front. At **S. John's, Smith Square, London** (1714–28, rebuilt after being gutted in 1941), the main entrances are now on transverse axes. The single spire has been replaced by four corner towers developing the staircase corner spaces found at S. Paul's, Deptford.

William Talman (1650–1719) designed his most famous work for the first Duke of Devonshire – **Chatsworth House, Derbyshire** (begun 1686) (p. 1039C). The uninteresting internal planning is compensated for by the impressive south front, sometimes described as the earliest true Baroque facade in England. The tripartite design is unusual in having twelve bays, and thus placing the central accent on a wall rather than an opening. This effect is minimised by the (later) double-ramped stairs, which treat the two central bays as equal, and by the emphasis placed on the ends of the facade. Here, the use of a fluted Ionic giant order creates the central section, with stags' heads decorating the keystones.

Nicholas Hawksmoor (1661–1736) was Wren's most talented pupil and his role in the workshop grew increasingly important. To distinguish their respective hands in projects is often impossible. Hawksmoor's style is characterised by an abstract geometry and a massive severity in the design of detail. He was further fascinated by the lesser-known buildings of antiquity and was sympathetic to Gothic forms.

S. George-in-the-East, London (1714–34), had a rectangular plan with a centralised interior prior to its gutting in World War II. The main longitudinal axis was crossed by three subsidiary axes, the central one of which was marked by the main cross vault. In the largely astylar exterior Hawksmoor experiments with scale, using openings of three distinct sizes in the nave, staircase towers and steeple, and placing disproportionately large keystones above the doors. The octagonal steeple, which takes up a theme already stated on a different scale in the staircase towers, is inspired by Gothic architecture.

The plan of **Christ Church, Spitalfields, London** (1714–29) (p. 1040A), is similar in theme to that of S. George, a rectangle given a centralised character internally. In this case a strong cross axis leads to side doorways. The most impressive part of the church is the west steeple. A tetrastyle portico has an arched barrel-vaulted central bay, a motif taken up again in abstracted and flattened form in the next storey. The central arch is reduced and repeated a number of times to the top of the spire.

S. Mary Woolnoth, London (1716–27) (p. 1040B), was the least conventional of all Hawksmoor's churches. A basement, with both window and portal designed *en niche* has banded rustication extending round the two extremely tall Doric columns. Above this a free-standing Corinthian order encircles the belfry and supports twin turrets.

Easton Neston, Northamptonshire (1696/7–1702) (p. 1040C), is the only major country house built by Hawksmoor alone. A strikingly monumental effect is achieved by the use of extremely tall windows squeezed between closely-spaced giant pilasters. The facade breaks forward twice, the second time more emphatically: two huge Composite columns frame the main doorway and create an unusual one-bay portico. The facade masks the internal disposition of the house, which in certain portions has up to four storeys.

Like Wren, Hawksmoor employed his own brand of Gothic, most notably at **All Souls College, Oxford** (1716–34). Ultimately he was to design the whole

A. Royal Hospital, Chelsea, London (1682–9). See p. 1038

B. S. Philip, Birmingham (1709–15). See p. 1038

C. Chatsworth House, Derbyshire (1686–). See p. 1038

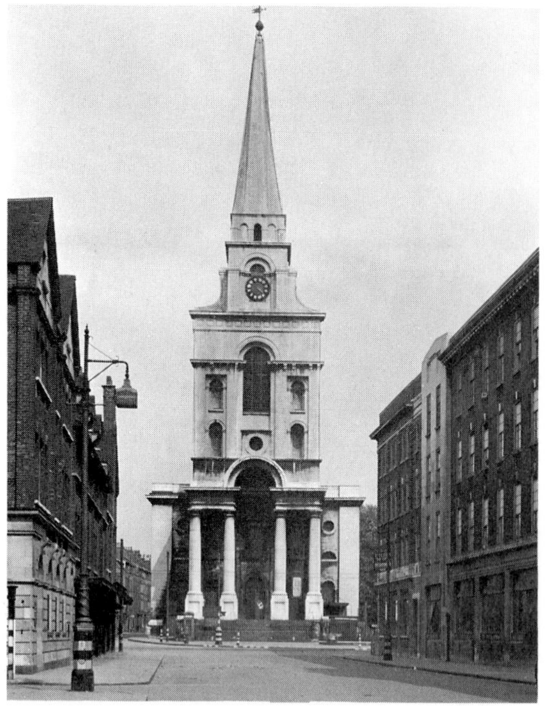

A. Christ Church, Spitalfields, London (1714–29). See p. 1038

B. S. Mary Woolnoth, London (1716–27). See p. 1038

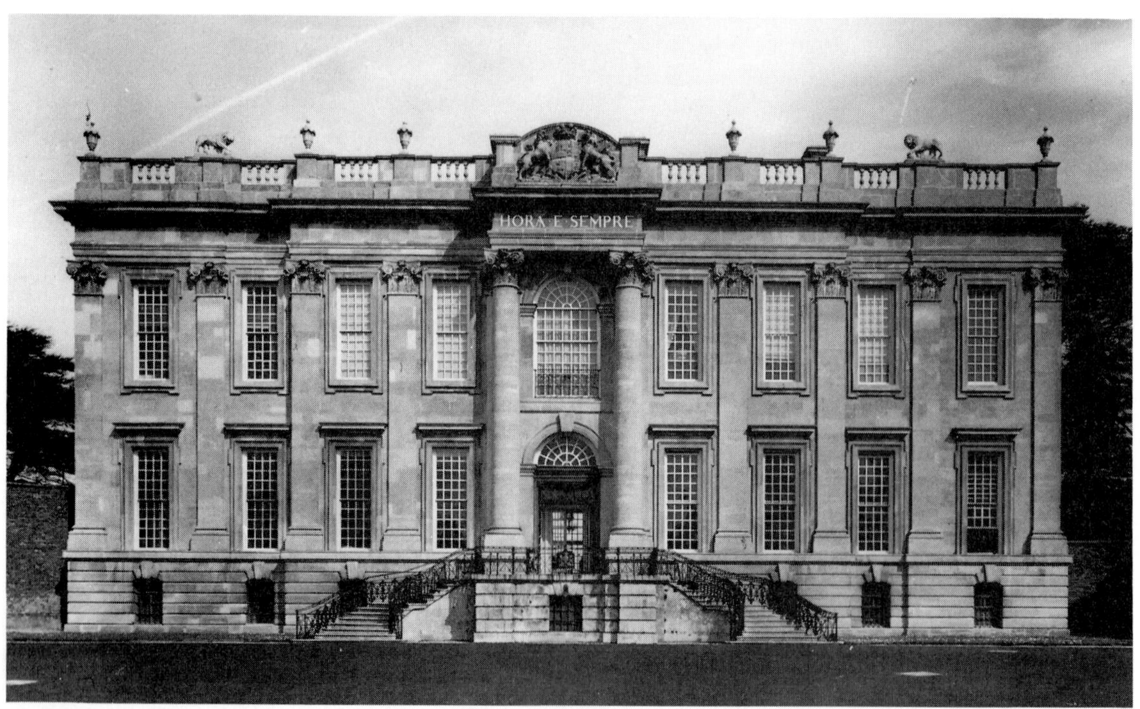

C. Easton Neston, Northamptonshire (1696/7–1702). See p. 1038

CASTLE HOWARD : YORKSHIRE

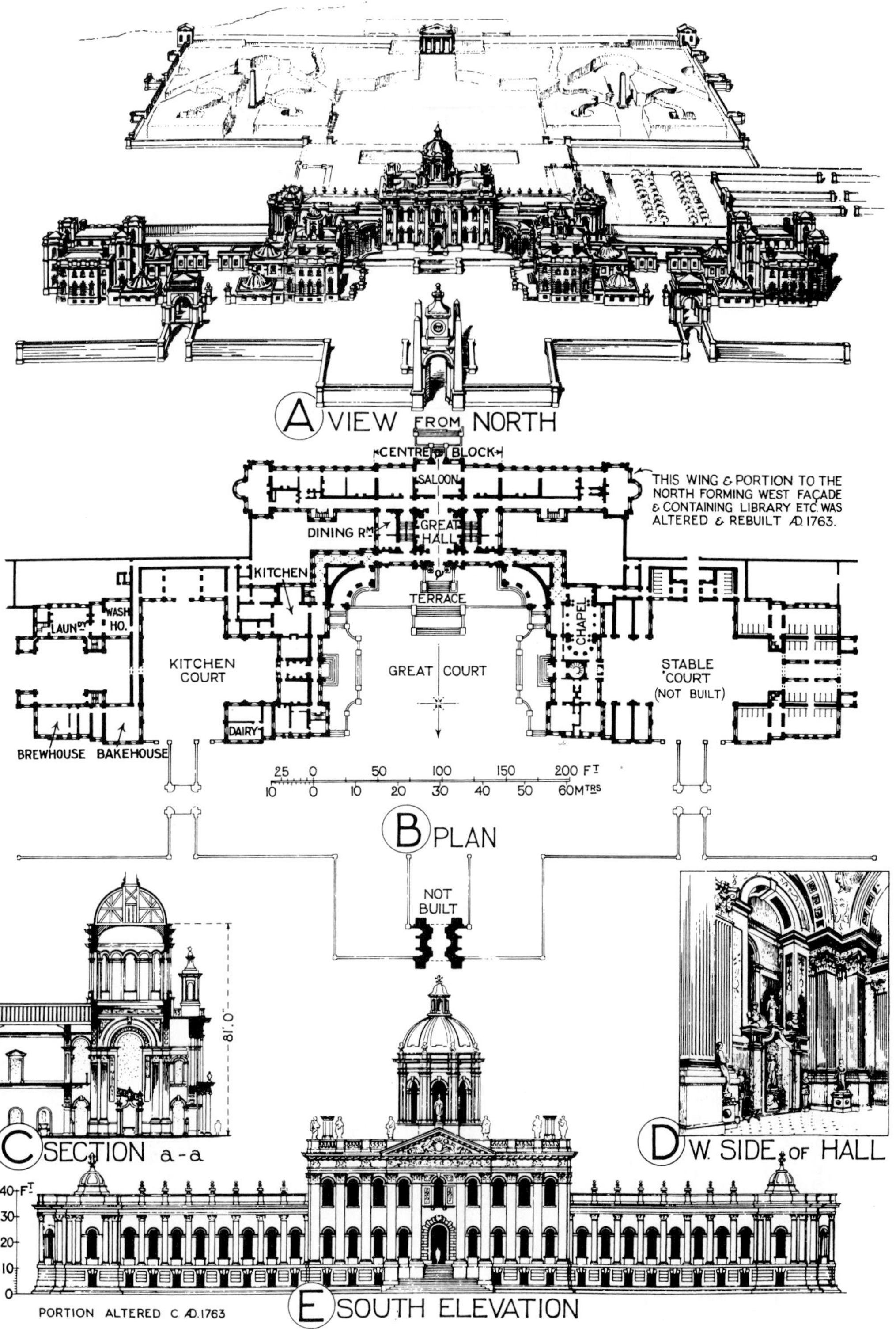
A VIEW FROM NORTH
CENTRE BLOCK
SALOON
THIS WING & PORTION TO THE NORTH FORMING WEST FAÇADE & CONTAINING LIBRARY ETC WAS ALTERED & REBUILT A.D. 1763.
DINING RM
GREAT HALL
KITCHEN
TERRACE
CHAPEL
LAUNDY
WASH HO.
KITCHEN COURT
GREAT COURT
STABLE COURT (NOT BUILT)
DAIRY
BREWHOUSE
BAKEHOUSE
25 0 50 100 150 200 FT
10 0 10 20 30 40 50 60MTRS
B PLAN
NOT BUILT
81'0"
C SECTION a-a
D W. SIDE OF HALL
40 FT
30
20
10
0
E SOUTH ELEVATION
PORTION ALTERED C. A.D. 1763

BLENHEIM PALACE: OXON

A EXTERIOR FROM N.

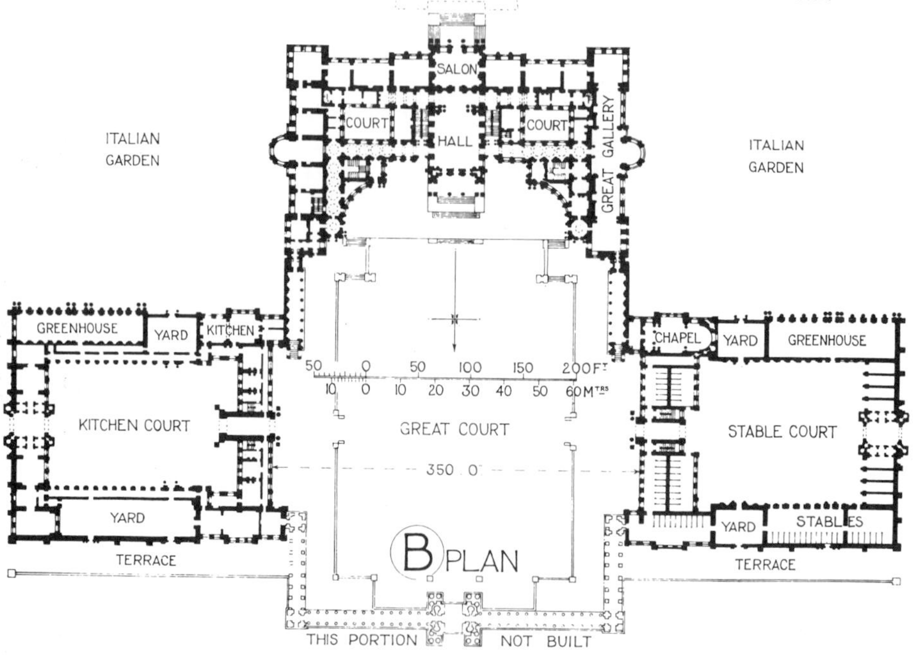

B PLAN

C GREAT HALL

D EXTERIOR FROM S.E.

exterior of the north quadrangle to harmonise with the earlier buildings on the site. The main facade is strictly symmetrical, with two towers framing the central entrance. Gothic two-centred and ogee arches abound.

John Vanbrugh (1664–1726), after an early career in the army, became not only one of Britain's greatest architects but also a renowned playwright. In his more complex and larger commissions he collaborated with Nicholas Hawksmoor, a thorough professional who complemented his own untrained flair for architecture.

Castle Howard, Yorkshire (1699–1712) (p. 1041), Vanbrugh's first country house, was built largely in collaboration with Hawksmoor. The impressive facade of the 'great' court screens an extended transverse range housing the principal apartments. Two service courts either side contain kitchens and stables. This vast complex resembles Wren's early project of 1695 for Greenwich Hospital. The low astylar wings of the 'great' court have French banded rustication and the corner arcades curve in towards the central block in the manner of Palladio's Villa Badoer (q.v.). The additional storey of the central block surges high above the wings and is overlaid with giant Doric pilasters in a syncopated rhythm. A dome set high on a drum rises above the main entrance hall. Such a feature had never been so forcefully used in English domestic architecture. The less severe garden front uses similar techniques to those at Easton Neston in order to achieve monumentality; elongated, closely spaced pilasters frame tightly packed windows. Also noteworthy are Vanbrugh's **Temple of the Winds** and Hawksmoor's **Mausoleum** which decorate the extensive grounds.

Blenheim Palace, Oxfordshire (1705–24) (pp. 1042, 1044A), was built by Vanbrugh and Hawksmoor for the Duke of Marlborough as a commemorative monument to the victory over the French at Blenheim. The palace is an enlarged variation on the theme of Castle Howard. A 'great' court is flanked by stable and kitchen courts, and the main show rooms are similarly placed on the main axis. However, Vanbrugh has turned the long range with principal apartments into a block forming two small internal courts. Two cleverly intertwined orders articulate the facade. The low Doric of the flanking colonnades is interrupted by the rusticated towers and emerges in a different form in the curving quadrants. Continuing across the main block, it is now overlaid with a giant Corinthian order, breaking forward at the centre to form a portico. The use of detail is sculptural, large in scale and unorthodox throughout, as for example in the interpretation of pilasters as obelisks.

Seaton Delaval, Northumberland (1720–8) (p. 1045A), is more intensely dramatic. The rusticated entrance on the north front is framed by ringed Doric columns. Its centre was gutted by fire in 1822.

Vanbrugh Castle, Greenwich (*c.* 1717), was one of three houses that Vanbrugh built for himself. Constructed almost entirely of brick, it has the stripped character of fortifications. It is enlivened in fortress fashion by the variation in square and round towers with flat and pointed roofs and also by crenellation and machicolations.

James Gibbs (1682–1754) was a Scottish Roman Catholic who studied under Carlo Fontana in Rome and brought back a knowledge of Italian architecture rivalled at the time only by Archer. Through Gibbs the Baroque enjoyed a late flourish at a time when the Palladian revival was already under way.

S. Martin-in-the-Fields, London (1721–6) (p. 1044B), was to become the most influential of Gibbs's designs. His original scheme, also much imitated, for a circular church was rejected on economic grounds. The final rectangular building owes much to Wren, particularly in the arrangement of the internal galleries and vaulting system. The sculptural exterior with its characteristic window surrounds has recessed columns marking the side entrances and a pedimented portico protecting the main portal. The steeple emerges through the roof from behind the portico, a feature much criticised and much copied.

Gibbs's library, known as the **Radcliffe Camera, Oxford** (1739–49) (p. 1044C), was developed from an earlier design of 1715 by Hawksmoor. Both were free-standing and circular in form with a rusticated base supporting a Corinthian order. The syncopated rhythms of this design are novel. Alternating projections and recessions characterise the polygonal base. Above this, paired Corinthian columns frame alternately wide and narrow bays and the rhythm is continued through to the balustrade. At this point the pattern changes, the curving buttresses of the dome falling in the centre of each bay below. This contradiction of the Classical rules of architecture is adopted for dramatic effect.

Palladianism (c. 1715–50)

Colen Campbell (died 1729), author of *Vitruvius Britannicus* (1715, 1717, 1725), was one of the founders of the Palladian style in England. Son of a Scottish laird, he began his career as a lawyer, and came to architectural prominence through the publication of *Vitruvius Britannicus*. **Wanstead House, London** (1714; destroyed 1824) was the first self-consciously Palladian country house. The main floor was raised over a 'rustic' basement, and the higher central portion had a hexastyle temple-front portico. Campbell also planned corner towers with Serliana windows, never built.

Houghton Hall, Norfolk (1722–6), built by Campbell for Sir Robert Walpole, Prime Minister of England, is a four-towered block, originally without wings, the apartments in symmetrical arrangement flanking the central saloon and the cubic hall,

A. Blenheim Palace, Oxfordshire: north front (1705–24). See p. 1043

B. S. Martin-in-the-Fields, London (1721–6). See p. 1043

C. Radcliffe Camera, Oxford (1739–49). See p. 1043

A. Seaton Delaval, Northumberland (1720–8). See p. 1043

B. Chiswick House, Chiswick, London (1725). See p. 1046

C. Mereworth Castle, Kent (1723). See p. 1046

modelled on Jones's Queen's House. The exterior has an attached tetrastyle portico of half-columns on the park front and Venetian windows in the domed towers. The entrance front has rusticated windows of the type of Palladio's Palazzo Thiene, Vicenza.

Campbell's **Mereworth Castle, Kent** (1722–5) (p. 1045C), is a close imitation of Palladio's Rotonda (q.v.), and the finest of several such Palladian 'villas' in England.

Lord Burlington (1694–1753), the other central figure in the Palladian movement, had a more intellectual approach to Palladian principles. Not only a distinguished amateur architect and important patron, he became the acknowledged arbiter of taste in Palladian England. At Chiswick he added to his Jacobean mansion (destroyed) a smaller version of the Rotonda, **Chiswick House** (1723–9) (p. 1045B), which also takes ideas from Scamozzi's Rocca Pisani (q.v.). The plan has two suites of apartments around an octagonal domed saloon. The sequence of variously shaped rooms, round, octagonal and apsidal-ended, reappears at Holkham Hall, Norfolk, and influenced Robert Adam. On the exterior, tastefully selected openings punctuate the neutral wall surface. The recessed Venetian windows of the rear facade were to have a long history in Palladian building. The interiors and furniture were by Burlington's protégé William Kent (1685–1748), brought back from Italy in 1719 to become the designer of Palladian interiors. From the 1730s Kent became a successful architect, introducing Palladianism to public building, through his post as Deputy Surveyor to the Board of Works.

At the **Assembly Rooms, York** (1730) (p. 1047A), Burlington used Palladio's colonnaded Egyptian Hall for the ball-room, which was flanked on front and side by rooms of varying shapes incorporating niches and apses like those in Roman baths. The original facade had a curved portico pierced by colonnaded screens with thermal windows above.

Holkham Hall, Norfolk (1734–65) (p. 1048A), built for Thomas Coke, Earl of Leicester, and executed by Matthew Brettingham (1699–1769), embodies Burlington's ideas very clearly, almost certainly through designs by Kent. The plan has four wings containing chapel, kitchen, library and guest rooms at each corner of the four-towered central block. The clear demarcation and separate roofing of each element gives the exterior a varied but strongly hierarchical character which is truly Palladian, although it lacks the organic quality of Palladio's architecture. The gallery derives from Chiswick, while the magnificently dramatic columned hall incorporates the main staircase.

The plan and facade of **Wentworth Woodhouse, Yorkshire** (1735–*c.* 1770) (p. 1047B), by Henry Flitcroft, known as 'Burlington Harry' (1696–1769), constitute a long-drawn-out version of Houghton Hall; this is one of many substantial Palladian mansions built by the followers of Burlington and Campbell. The mansions' interiors are magnificent.

The Palladian movement also spawned many villa-like smaller houses, of which Roger Morris's **Marble Hill, Twickenham** (1724–9), is an influential early example, using a pedimented and pilastered frontispiece over a rustic zone to give focus to the building. Morris (1695–1749) rose through the building trades to become a successful speculative architect; his relative Robert Morris (*c.* 1702–54) wrote an influential series of architectural publications, giving an aesthetic base to the Palladian movement.

The **Horse Guards, Whitehall** (1750–8) (p. 1048B), by John Vardy (died 1765) after designs by Kent, extends the Palladian country-house facade to a public building: the clearly delineated massing, varied roof line and recessed Venetian windows owe much to Burlington, and the all-over rustication comes from Burlington's house for General Wade, itself based on a drawing by Palladio.

Isaac Ware (died 1766), the best English translator of Palladio and author of *A Complete Body of Architecture* (1756), designed a group of country houses of which the best is **Wrotham Park, South Mimms, Middlesex** (1754); its long facade has a central villa-like block flanked by wings and a domed octagonal pavilion.

James Paine (1717–89) was the most successful country-house architect of the mid-century, a staunch defender of Palladianism against the growing interest in 'inconsistent antiquated modes'. **Wardour Castle, Wiltshire** (1770–6), introduces some variety into the bulky Palladian facade by its use of paired pilasters at the corners and a more complex rhythm of attached columns in the portico. The staircase is particularly fine, rising into a Pantheon-like circular temple.

In Scotland, William Adam (1689–1748) continued a restrained version of the English Baroque tradition, with a few Palladian elements. The magnificent but eclectic **Hopetoun House** (1723–48) (p. 1048C) has a giant pilaster order and balustraded parapet reminiscent of Chatsworth (q.v.), concave curves and linked arched windows recalling Vanbrugh, but beyond, a Palladian colonnaded quadrant.

Sir Edward Lovett Pearce (1699–1733) was a highly original Palladian, and an important figure in the history of Irish architecture. The **Parliament House, Dublin** (1728–39), is fronted by an E-shaped Ionic colonnade incorporating the entrance portico. The domed House of Commons (destroyed in 1914) had a sophisticated columned gallery, the columns paired at the corners of the octagon.

TOWN HOUSES

English Palladian town houses adopt the formula of a rusticated base and applied (or implied) upper orders culminating in a balustrade or parapet. Georgian London is characterised by more-or-less uniform rows of such houses built along streets or around the private

A. Assembly Rooms, York (1730). See p. 1046

B. Wentworth Woodhouse, Yorkshire (1735). See p. 1046

C. Bath, Avon: aerial showing Circus and Royal Crescent (1754–75). See p. 1049

A. Holkham Hall, Norfolk (1734–65). See p. 1046

B. Horse Guards, Whitehall, London; west facade (1750–8). See p. 1046

C. Hopetoun House, West Lothian, Scotland (1723–48). See p. 1046

squares developed by speculative builders on the estates of aristocratic landlords. The idea of unifying separate houses on a square with pedimented centre-pieces, found in Mansart's Place Vendôme, Paris (q.v.), is ingeniously applied at **Grosvenor Square, London** (1725–35), and more convincingly at **Queen Square, Bath** (1729–36), to give the impression of a single symmetrical facade. This becomes an enduring British urban solution. The most spectacular examples of eighteenth-century urban development are at Bath (p. 1047C), where John Wood (1705–54) and his son John Wood II (1728–81) laid out Queen Square, the **Circus** (1754) and the **Royal Crescent** (1767–75), together with the streets connecting them. References to the Roman past of Bath are evident in the Circus, with its three storeys of paired half-columns, and in the Royal Crescent, unified by a giant order of engaged-columns.

The urban ideal of the square formed by four uniform palace-fronted terraces was finally achieved in eighteenth-century London with the construction of **Bedford Square** (1776–86), with elevations probably designed by the Bedford Estate surveyor Robert Palmer (perhaps with Thomas Leverton) and executed under the control of the speculative builders William Scott and Robert Grew.

The fullest expression of the rational Classical city, formed by an orthogonal grid encompassing streets of varied scale and importance and incoporating squares of uniform palatial design, was achieved at **Edinburgh New Town** (begun 1766), designed by James Craig. The second and third New Towns, built during the early years of the nineteenth century, extended the orthogonal first New Town in picturesque manner by the construction of sublimely sited circuses, crescents and uniform terraces of prodigious length; for example, **Great King Street** (1812–20) built under the control of Robert Reid; **Royal Circus** (1820) and the **Royal Terrace** (begun 1821) both by James Playfair and **Moray Place** (1822–30) by James Gillespie Graham.

FOLLIES

A characteristically British building type of the period is the folly. Follies are structures of unconventional design, their primary purpose being visual delight. They usually stand on private estates but outside the confines of the garden. A good example is **Arnos Castle, Bristol** (1750), a mock castle with a keep, turrets, castellations and pinnacles. It is built almost entirely from black copper slag and was christened the 'Devil's Cathedral' by Horace Walpole.

Neo-Classicism (1750–1830)

Robert Adam (1728–92), one of the most inventive of all British architects, was the son of leading Scottish architect, William Adam. Following a tour of Italy (1754–8) he settled in London, and rose to prominence with his transformations of older mansions. His works are particularly notable for their comprehensively designed interiors with their 'embroidered' ornamental surfaces of arabesques, grotesques and painted and stuccoed medallions, adding up to the characteristic 'Adam style'. His room shapes and decorative detail, inspired by his antiquarian studies, fundamentally contributed to the development of British neo-Classicism.

Kedleston Hall, Derbyshire (begun by James Paine, 1757–9; completed, including the south front, by R. and J. Adam, 1759–70) (p. 1050), represents a distinct break with Palladianism. Paine's plan is similar to but more extravagant than Holkham, with corner pavilions linked by quadrants, and the north facade is likewise in the grand Palladian manner. However, Adam's south facade replaces the pedimented temple-front formula with an antiquarian, sculpturally ornate, triumphal arch modelled on the Arch of Constantine. The interior is very imposing; Paine's hall and saloon were modified by Adam, the saloon resembling an ancient rotunda (as at Spalato), with a stepped Pantheon-like dome.

Osterley Park (1763–80) and **Syon House** (1762–9), both in west London, are remodellings of earlier buildings. Osterley, an Elizabethan court and mansion, was gutted and redecorated in various antiquarian styles. A pedimented entrance portico was inserted into one wing, its form inspired by the Portico of Octavia in Rome, though in detail the slender Ionic columns are Greek.

At Syon, originally a Jacobean building, Adam had intended to insert a massive rotunda into the central courtyard. The remodelled interiors are particularly fine, containing characteristic sequences of variously shaped rooms, with niches, alcoves, and engaged and detached columns to give richly sculptural spatial effects.

Culzean Castle, Ayrshire (1777–92) (p. 1051A), the most extravagant of Adam's castle-houses, was built for the Earls of Cassilis and incorporates a mediaeval keep. Turrets and battlements give an overall castellated impression but the window details and interiors are wholly Classical.

Charlotte Square, Edinburgh (1791–1807), is one of several terraces of houses designed by Adam. One whole side of the square is given a unified architectural treatment, with central portico and prominent end pavilions. Although in many respects it recalls earlier terraces, the detailing and decoration are characteristically Adam. Also by Adam are similar terraces of **Fitzroy Square, London** (1790–4), and his first venture of this kind, **the Adelphi, London** (1768–72, largely demolished 1937), with terraces overlooking the Thames, perched upon arched openings at the quayside.

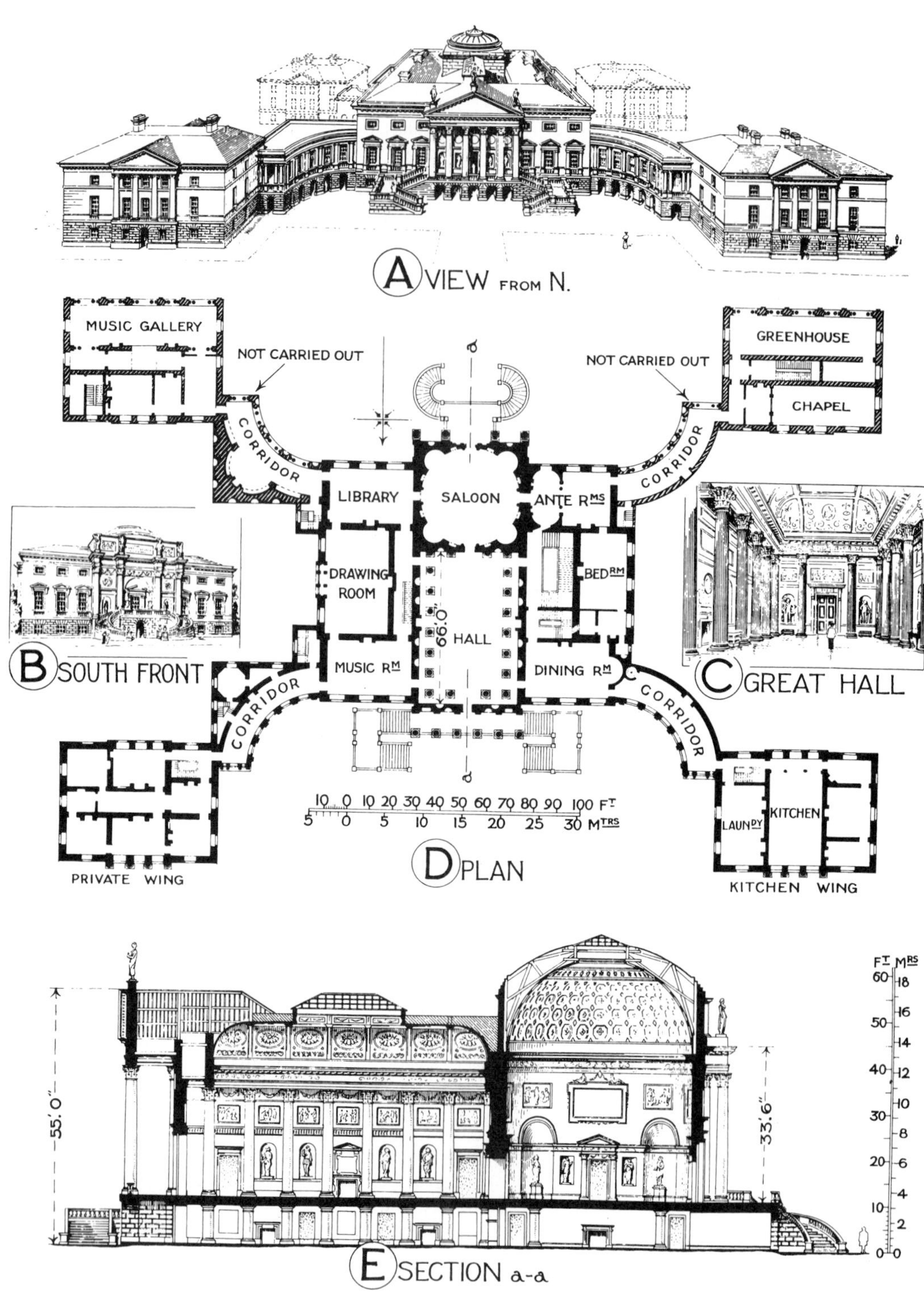
KEDLESTON HALL: DERBYSHIRE
A VIEW FROM N.
MUSIC GALLERY
NOT CARRIED OUT
GREENHOUSE
NOT CARRIED OUT
CHAPEL
CORRIDOR
LIBRARY
SALOON
ANTE RMS
CORRIDOR
DRAWING ROOM
BED RM
HALL
66.0
MUSIC RM
DINING RM
B SOUTH FRONT
C GREAT HALL
CORRIDOR
CORRIDOR
10 0 10 20 30 40 50 60 70 80 90 100 FT
5 0 5 10 15 20 25 30 MTRS
LAUNDY
KITCHEN
PRIVATE WING
D PLAN
KITCHEN WING
55'0"
33'6"
FT MRS
E SECTION a-a

A. Culzean Castle, Ayrshire (1777–92). See p. 1049

B. No. 20, Portman Square, London (1773–6). See p. 1052

No. 20, Portman Square, London (1773–6) (p. 1051B), and **No. 20, S. James's Square, London** (1771–4), are the best of Adam's surviving London town houses. They are notable not only for their spectacular neo-Classic decoration but also for their ingenious planning on tight sites. In neither case could the entrance be centrally placed, yet Adam still contrived to integrate whole suites of sculpturally shaped rooms.

At **Stowe House, Buckinghamshire**, Adam designed the south front (1771–9) as part of the extensive modernisations carried out by the owners Viscount Cobham and Lord Temple. The grounds had been landscaped by Bridgeman, Kent and others, and they constitute one of the major surviving gardens of this period. The variety of the landscape is complemented by a wide assortment of impressive garden buildings designed by Vanbrugh, Gibbs, Kent and others, in various styles.

Sir William Chambers (1723–96) was trained as an architect in Paris (1749–50) and Italy (1750–55). Only a year after his settling in London (1755), he was appointed architect and tutor to the Prince of Wales, and thence became the leading royal and official architect of the period. Although influenced by the neo-Classicism of Soufflot, his works are notably wide-ranging in style.

Somerset House, London (1776–86, east and west extensions completed 1835 and 1856) (p. 1053A), was built to house government offices and fills a huge site between the Strand and River Thames. The Strand facade is a modest nine bays in width, with an order (half-columns) above an arched rusticated basement in the manner of a sixteenth-century Italian palace. Beyond the facade opens a vast court twice its width. The long side and end elevations with their central unpedimented projections call to mind A.-J. Gabriel's Petit Trianon, for example, as well as buildings by Vanbrugh; despite their size they are relatively subdued. The dignified river facade, despite nineteenth-century modifications, still closely reflects Chambers's intentions. It is very long, nearly 200 m (600 ft), symmetrical, but broken into several subsidiary sections rather like Versailles. The outer sections have connecting water gates resembling Palladian bridges. The central inset colonnade with its pedimented attic above and dome behind provides a discreet central emphasis.

The **Casina, Marino, near Dublin** (designed before 1759; not begun until 1769) (p. 1055E), built for Lord Charlemont, is a work of very different scale. It is a Greek cross in plan and recalls Vanbrugh's Temple at Castle Howard, although Chambers's building is studiously Doric and in other elements carefully Classical. The breaking-out of the order and the resulting voids at the corners give this little building an unusual sculptural quality.

Kew Gardens, London, the gardens attached to the royal residence, Kew House, were supervised by Chambers from 1757 till 1763. They are particularly notable for the variety of styles of the garden buildings. Even before Chambers's time a building in a Moorish style (the 'Alhambra') had been built. Chambers himself added some temples, the Roman Arch and the famous Chinese Pagoda which still survives; a Turkish 'mosque' and Gothic 'cathedral' were also included.

Nuneham Courtenay, Oxfordshire (1773), a village of nineteen semi-detached cottages, was planned by Chambers and is an early example of such a venture. The low cottages with their dormer windows are pleasantly simple, if unremarkable in design. Such 'model' villages became increasingly common during this period, especially in northern England.

The **Custom House, Dublin** (1781–91) (p. 1053B), and the **Four Courts, Dublin** (1786–1802) (p. 1054A), are works of James Gandon (1743–1823), an associate of Chambers. The Custom House has references to Wren's Chelsea Barracks and Greenwich Hospital, but is clearly related to Somerset House. Likewise, the Four Courts is closely dependent on Wren's S. Paul's except that the characteristic dome and lantern have been replaced by a saucer shape creating a simplified silhouette reminiscent of Ledoux.

At **Shugborough, Staffordshire**, there are notable garden buildings (*c.* 1760–71) designed by James 'Athenian' Stuart (1713–88), publisher with Nicholas Revett of the *Antiquities of Athens*. In the grounds are reproduced replicas of Athenian monuments – the Arch of Hadrian, the Tower of the Winds and the Monument to Lysicrates.

Strawberry Hill, Twickenham, Middlesex (1748–77) (p. 1056A,B), was created by Horace Walpole (1717–97) as his own retreat with architectural contributions from John Chute, Richard Bentley, Robert Adam, James Wyatt and James Essex. The earlier phases reflect the mid-eighteenth-century approaches to Gothic architecture, in their simple substitution of fanciful Gothic for Classical detailing, but as work progressed the building became truly innovative. Apart from the range and quantity of such 'Gothic' elements as towers, turrets, gables, battlements, chimneys, and pointed windows, overall symmetry both of the whole and many of the parts was avoided; the effect is of a haphazardly enlarged mediaeval mansion.

James Wyatt (1746–1813) was the most prolific architect of the period. After spending six years in Venice (1762–8), he established his reputation with his Pantheon, and much of his huge body of work was very consciously neo-Classical. Towards the end of his career he favoured the Gothic manner.

The **Pantheon, London** (1769–72), burned down 1792, finally demolished 1937), was a famous suite of assembly rooms on Oxford Street. The largest room (to which the name refers), used for masquerades, was actually a neo-Classical interpretation of

A. Somerset House, London (1776–86): waterfront. See p. 1052

B. Custom House, Dublin (1781–91). See p. 1052

A. Four Courts, Dublin (1786–1802). See p. 1052

B. Stratton Park, Hampshire (1803–4) (demolished except for portico). See p. 1057

A PEDIMENTED GATEWAY
B DOORWAY
STILT
C VENETIAN WINDOW
13 MODULES
18 MODULES
9 MODULES
D DOORWAY OR PORTION OF IONIC ARCADE: COLS WITHOUT PEDESTALS
HALF PLAN OF CELLAR
E CASINO AT MARINO NEAR DUBLIN
HALF PLAN OF PRINCIPAL FLOOR
5 MDS
16 MODULES
20 MODULES
24½ MODULES
11½ MODULES
6 MDS
F DOORWAY OR PORTION OF CORINTHIAN ARCADE COLS WITH PEDESTALS
NOTE: A MODULE IS ½ A DIAMETER AND IS DIVIDED INTO 30 PARTS
4½ M
20 MODULES
6 M. 12 P.
7 MOD. 18 P.
8 MOD. 24 P.
18 MODULES
6 MOD.
7 MOD.
G
H
3⅜ M
23 MODULES
15 MODS. 18 P.
11 MODS. 3 P.
13 MODULES
9 MODULES
1⅓
J SUPER-IMPOSED ORDERS
4 MDS
20 MOD. 25 P.
18 MODULES
9 MODS. 20 P.
11 MODULES 22 P.
16¼ MODULES
15 MODULES
9 MODULES
10 MODULES 25 P.
1½
K SUPER-IMPOSED ORDERS WITH PALLADIAN ARCADES & PEDESTALS
SUPERIMPOSED ORDERS WITHOUT PEDESTALS

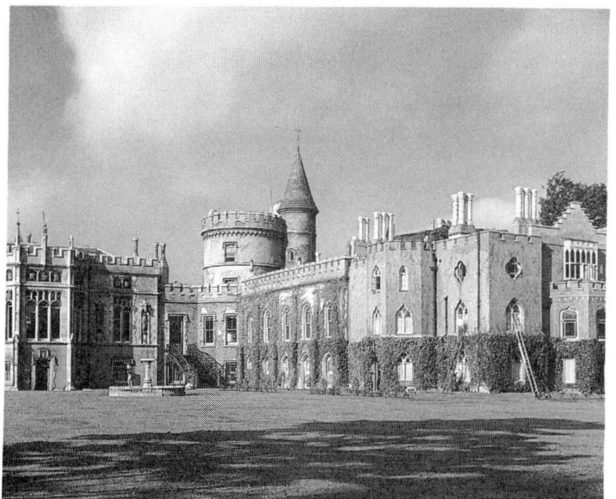

A. Strawberry Hill, Twickenham, Middlesex (1748–77). See p. 1052

B. Strawberry Hill, Twickenham, Middlesex: gallery

C. Dodington, Gloucestershire (1798–1808). See p. 1057

D. Radcliffe Observatory, Oxford (1773–). See p. 1057

E. Ashridge Park, Hertfordshire (1808–13). See p. 1057

Hagia Sophia, Istanbul, with a (wooden) coffered dome and oculus, and flattened supporting arches. Of Wyatt's neo-Classic country houses, **Dodington, Gloucestershire** (1798–1808) (p. 1056C), is particularly splendid with its Greek portico, the unpedimented rear facade recalling Chambers.

The facade of Wyatt's neo-Classical **Radcliffe Observatory, Oxford** (1773–) (p. 1056D), is a bold composition of geometric forms including as its top storey a variant of the Tower of the Winds, Athens.

Fonthill Abbey, Wiltshire (1796–1812, tower collapsed 1825, demolished), was an extraordinary Gothic residence planned as four disparate elongated wings, with an octagon at the crossing resembling Ely cathedral. Fonthill must have achieved its effect not only through the enormous height of the tower but also through a series of stunning vistas through cavernous interiors. Something of this can be appreciated in Wyatt's final work, **Ashridge Park, Hertfordshire** (1808–13) (p. 1056E), with its awesome central hall occupying the entire height of a tower. **Taymouth Castle, Tayside** (1806–10), by A. and J. Elliot, is very much inspired by Wyatt and also has a spectacular towering hall.

George Dance the Younger (1741–1825), son of Dance the Elder (architect of the Mansion House, London) went as a youth of seventeen to Italy for seven years, where he probably acquired the knowledge of continental neo-Classicism later displayed in his works. He exercised a great influence over his celebrated pupil, Sir John Soane.

Newgate Prison, London (1769–80, demolished 1902) (p. 1058A), had a forbidding rusticated facade thoroughly befitting its function, similar in mood to Piranesi's *Carceri* etchings. Three enclosures lay behind the facade, the central element of which was closely modelled on Florentine palaces such as the Palazzo Pitti, and was strangely out of scale with the blind window recesses in the side projections of the wings.

Stratton Park, Hampshire (1803–4, portico only survives) (p. 1054B), is a house of uncompromising severity close in spirit to Ledoux. The portico projected from an almost flat facade, and had unfluted Greek Doric columns with a shallow Doric frieze.

Henry Holland (1745–1806), the son of a builder, worked under Capability Brown and married his daughter. His largest work, **Carlton House, London** (1783–95, demolished 1826), which he enlarged for the Prince of Wales, initially formed the focal point of Nash's Regent Street development. Receptive to many ideas, particularly from France, his works have a new simplicity. With George Dance the Younger, he was one of the masters of John Soane.

The new **facade of Dover House**, overlooking Whitehall, **London** (1787), masks the earlier house behind. It consists of a rusticated wall to which is attached a projecting Ionic portico, with free-standing columns at either side, the entablature breaking out above each and supporting an urn. Behind the portico is a circular Doric vestibule, with curving staircases leading to the house behind.

Sir John Soane (1753–1837) studied under George Dance the Younger and Henry Holland before spending three years in Italy (1778–80). In 1788 he was appointed surveyor to the Bank of England. Although much influenced by continental buildings, he was ultimately the most individual of the later eighteenth-century architects and one of the least prone to pastiche; he is rightly placed among the greatest of British architects.

The **Bank of England, London** (1788–1823, mostly demolished 1927, present interiors by Sir Herbert Baker, 1930–40 but Bank Stock Office of 1792, reconstructed in 1990) (p. 1058B), was Soane's masterpiece. The site is bordered by rusticated windowless screen walls which largely still survive, incorporating the famous 'Tivoli Corner', closely adapted from the Roman round temple at Tivoli. The cavernous interior halls recall engraved interiors of Roman buildings by Piranesi. Especially impressive was the Rotunda, added to the Bank Stock Office. Articulation was here confined to niches, windows and doors, and to simple bands of decoration, the wall surface continuing up into the dome almost without interruption. Most of the interior effect was achieved by the interplay of curves, and by the spectacular lighting, both from the base of the dome and from a lantern above (supported on barely perceptible caryatids) casting shadows of great variety. The more delicate Old Dividend Office also dispensed with a lower order; here the arches supporting the dome above converged without interruption on exceptionally slender piers. Most of the crucial interior lighting was again from above, the dome now incorporating more bulky paired caryatids, but largely consisting of daring expanses of glass.

No. 13, Lincoln's Inn Fields, London (1812–13) (p. 1058C), now the Soane Museum, was the architect's own town house. The facade, with its planar three-bay arcaded projection, is rather eccentric; the interior, which widens towards the rear, opens out into a myriad of interconnecting rooms packed, then as now, with its varied collections. Soane employed his typical curving vaults, and experimented further with lighting, making conspicuous use of mirrors: a variety of spatial experiences are created, from the airy to the claustrophobic.

Tyringham Hall, Buckinghamshire (1793–*c.* 1800, dome added 1909), is one of a number of country houses designed by Soane. Its refinement is enhanced by variations in the spacing of the tall slender pilasters and columns.

Dulwich Art Gallery, London (1811–14) (p. 1059A), was built with a limited budget bequeathed by Sir Francis Bourgeois; attached to one side is his mausoleum. The brick exterior is almost stripped of decoration, the design expressed by subtle changes

A. Newgate Prison, London (1769–80, demolished 1902). See p. 1057

B. Bank of England, London (1788–1823, mostly demolished 1927): Old Dividend Office – NE angle showing doorway to Rotunda. See p. 1057

C. Soane Museum, No. 13, Lincoln's Inn Fields, London (1812–13). See p. 1057

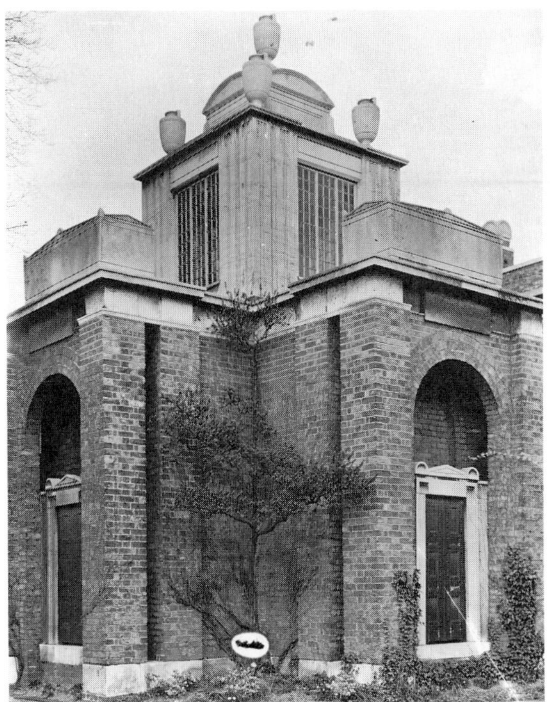

A. Dulwich Art Gallery, London (1811–14). See p. 1057

B. Park Crescent, London (1812–). See p. 1061

C. Cronkhill, Shropshire (*c.* 1802). See p. 1061

D. Royal Pavilion, Brighton (1815–21). See p. 1061

E. Sezincote, Gloucestershire (*c.* 1805). See p. 1061

A. Cumberland Terrace, Regent's Park, London (1812–13). See p. 1061

B. University College, London (1825–7). See p. 1061

C. British Museum, London (1823–46). See p. 1064

of surface. The central mausoleum (which has a coloured Doric interior) apparently projects as a Greek cross, the three arms and crossing tower surmounted by sarcophagi and urns. The primitive quality of the architecture is enhanced by the archaic Greek surrounds to the blind doors of the mausoleum, located in the virtually detached, arched extremities of the arms.

S. Peter's, Walworth, London (1823–4) is a typical Soane church. Above an unpedimented Ionic portico rises an attenuated, elegant if stark, block-like steeple.

John Nash (1752–1835) began his career as a speculative builder turning-out stucco-fronted houses in London before bankruptcy in 1783. After 1795 he began a new and successful career as a country-house architect, at first in partnership with Repton, working in a plethora of styles. Although commissioned in 1825 by George IV to build Buckingham Palace, he was soon suspected of sharp practice, his design was not successful and on the death of the King in 1830 he was replaced by Edward Blore.

Luscombe Castle, Devon (1800–4), and **Cronkhill, Shropshire** (*c.* 1802) (p. 1059C), are two of Nash's early country house designs. Luscombe is conceived as a Gothic castle with an asymmetrical plan centring on an octagonal tower. Cronkhill is loosely based upon Italian vernacular farm architecture of the type that might be admired in a Claude painting.

Blaise Hamlet, Gloucestershire (1811), is a remarkable village built for the owner of a nearby mansion in a vernacular English style. Each cottage differs, making use of such features as porches, gables, tall chimneys and even thatched roofs.

The **Royal Pavilion, Brighton** (remodelled by Nash, 1815–21) (p. 1059D), is in an Orientalising style, dominated on the exterior by lattice-work, onion domes, and minarets. The interior is equally exuberant; the splendid banqueting room is close in form to Soane's Bank halls, although the dense, exotic and vividly coloured decoration is worlds removed.

Regent Street, Regent's Park (p. 1060A) and surroundings, **London**, occupied Nash from 1811 until 1830. Apart from the Regent Street facades, much of the work still survives, especially that to the north around Regent's Park. This huge, coherent urban project was largely formed from farmland reverting to the Crown in 1811. Out of it was formed a landscaped area (Regent's Park), with its lake and groves of trees surrounded by imposing terraces and comfortable villas. Southwards from the park a new street (Portland Place and Regent Street) wound down to terminate at Carlton House, the residence of the Prince Regent, to provide a Royal Mile. Apart from various formal features along the route (such as Oxford Circus), most of the lining buildings were notably *ad hoc* in character, which, with the changing axis of the street, would have added to the intended variety of the royal route. Ultimately, Nash's plans for the southern zone were greatly expanded to embrace Buckingham palace with the Mall to the west and Trafalgar Square and the Strand to the east. Of the surviving buildings, the semicircular **Park Crescent** (1812–) (p. 1059B), at the entrance to Regent's Park, has a typical white stucco exterior (hiding cheap brickwork) typical of Nash. With its sweeping arc of doubled Ionic columns it is one of the finest and most dramatic of Nash's terraces, although not nearly as ornate and flamboyant as many others, notably Cumberland Terrace (1827–) overlooking the park. **All Souls, Langham Place** (1823–4), has a cylindrical entrance tower almost detached from the main body of the church and is positioned to align with Regent Street. Geometric clarity is also applied to the steeple above: the conical spire breaks through the colonnaded drum. Another imposing vestige of Nash's scheme is the **Marble Arch** (1828), closely modelled on the Arch of Constantine, Rome. It once stood in front of Buckingham Palace at the far end of the Mall, but was moved to the present position in 1850–1.

Sezincote, Gloucestershire (*c.* 1805) (p. 1059E), built by S. P. Cockerell (1753–1827), is probably the earliest 'Indian' building in Britain (although the interiors are Classical). The details were chosen by Repton from drawings made in India by Thomas Daniell. Cockerell also designed the remarkable, centrally planned, **S. Mary's, Banbury, Oxfordshire** (1792–7).

William Wilkins (1778–1839), son of an architect, travelled extensively in Italy, Greece and Turkey before beginning a career in which he became a champion of the Greek Revival.

Dalmeny House, Lothian (1814–17), is a very early example of a period-conscious Tudor Gothic style, this despite Wilkins's usual preference for Greek.

Downing College, Cambridge (1807–20), is notable not only for its Greek style but for its remarkable conception: a series of separate structures organised around a large central grassed area. Individual buildings are rather bland (despite detail scrupulously derived from the Erechtheion) but the ensemble achieves an appropriately scholarly dignity.

Of **University College, London** (formerly London University) (1825–7) (p. 1060B), only the central range of buildings at the back of the quadrangle is by Wilkins. Much less antiquarian, its huge portico and open area in front make it very imposing; it was followed in many similar public buildings. Wilkins's **National Gallery, London** (1833–8), is not dissimilar, although the extended facade here owes something to Chambers's Somerset House.

The **Scottish Academy** (originally Royal Institution), **Edinburgh** (1822–35), was designed by W. H. Playfair (1790–1857), who, along with Robert Adam,

A. High School, Edinburgh (1825–). See p. 1064

B. Old Town Hall, Manchester (1822–4). See p. 1064

A. S. Chad, Shrewsbury (1790–2). See p. 1064

B. S. Pancras, London (1819–22). See p. 1064

C. Tetbury Church, Gloucestershire (rebuilt 1777–81). See p. 1064

D. S. Luke, Chelsea, London (1820–4). See p. 1064

Thomas Hamilton and others was substantially responsible for the redevelopment of Edinburgh in the years around 1800. It has a projecting Greek-Doric portico, and the long Doric side colonnades resemble Greek stoas but project at each end, where paired sphinxes enliven the roofline.

The **High School, Edinburgh** (1825–) (p. 1062A), designed by Thomas Hamilton (1785–1858), is one of the most spectacular neo-Classical buildings in Britain. A central hall in the form of a Greek Doric temple is one of many block-like elements linked together and placed at varying levels to form a monumental, dramatic composition.

The **British Museum, London** (1823–46) (p. 1060C), designed by Sir Robert Smirke (1780–1867), is more successful than Wilkins's large-scale public buildings. It is designed in the Greek Revival manner on a scale comparable with similar public buildings in Germany. The Ionic octastyle portico with its splendid pediment sculpture projects from a massive colonnade running right around the winged facade.

Smirke's **County Buildings, Perth** (1815–19), also include a portico projecting from a colonnade, but this time the order is a much more severe Greek Doric.

The **Old Town Hall, Manchester** (1822–4, demolished 1912, partly rebuilt in Heaton Park, near Manchester) (p. 1062B), is a block-like Greek Revival building designed by F. Goodwin with exceptionally elegant detailing.

The **Town Hall, Birmingham** (1832–4), by J. Hanson and E. Welch, places an auditorium inside a reconstruction of the Temple of Castor, Rome, raised on an arched rusticated basement.

The **Athenaeum, London** (1829–30, attic added later) a club founded for academics, was designed by Decimus Burton (1800–81). The plain exterior has a rusticated lower storey with a projecting portico of paired Doric columns. Below the crowning cornice, the wonderful Classical bas-relief (a cast of the Parthenon frieze) contrasts with the plainness of the wall below.

Engineers began increasingly, to design industrial buildings during this period: notable examples are Telford's warehouses at **S. Katharine's Dock, London** (1827–9), and the remarkable **Cotton Mill, Manchester** (1801), by James Watt and Matthew Boulton, with its iron-frame construction.

S. James, Great Packington, West Midlands (1789–90), designed by J. Bonomi (1739–1808), who came to England from Italy in 1767, has a severe brick exterior and a remarkable interior with a crossing supported on stubby Greek Doric columns, and extensive use of simplified Classical detailing formed from carefully cut stonework.

S. Chad, Shrewsbury (1790–2) (p. 1063A), the masterpiece of George Steuart (*c.* 1730–1806), has a huge circular nave with a three-storey tower preceded by a pedimented Doric portico, an arrangement inspired by one of Gibbs's designs for S. Martin-in-the-Fields.

S. Pancras, London (1819–22) (p. 1063B), by W. and H. W. Inwood, is perhaps the most impressive Greek Revival church in Britain. Flanking the east end are two caryatid porches, closely modelled on the Erechtheion, while the steeple over the entrance is inspired by the Tower of the Winds, Athens, treated as two superimposed lanterns.

Caledonia Road Free Church, Glasgow (1856–7), a late neo-Classical church by Alexander 'Greek' Thomson (1817–75), owes much to Schinkel in its picturesque composition of inventively positioned Classical elements.

Tetbury Church, Gloucestershire (rebuilt 1777–81, except steeple), (p. 1063C), by Francis Hiorne (1744–89) is one of the earliest Gothic Revival churches. The interior is most impressive: tall slender compound piers (made of wood) support a simple rib vault (wood and plaster). It is well lit and creates a good impression of a late mediaeval church.

S. Luke, Chelsea (1820–4) (p. 1063D), by James Savage (1779–1852), is the earliest and one of the finest Commissioner churches in London in the Gothic Revival style. The emphatically vertical tower fronting the nave rises visually from the ground and incorporates the principal portal of the entrance porch. Unusual in having a structural stone vaulted nave and flying buttresses over the aisles, the building strives to convey the monumentality of a larger (Perpendicular) mediaeval Gothic church, with a keener historical exactitude increasingly typical of the period.

Chapter 33
RUSSIA AND SCANDINAVIA

Architectural Character

Russia

Although three phases can readily be detected in Russian architecture between 1475 and 1830 – Renaissance (1475–*c.* 1690), Baroque (*c.* 1690–*c.* 1760), and neo-Classical (*c.* 1760–) – this schema is complicated by periods of Russian revivalism and by prodigious eclecticism. Under Ivan III (1462–1505) the first wave of Italian architects arrived, the Bolognese Aristotele Fioravanti, P. A. Solari and Marco Friasin, architects at the Kremlin, and Alevisio Novi, perhaps from Montagnana, near Padua. Some buildings of this first Renaissance flowering, notably the Cathedral of S. Michael, Moscow, consist of a traditional Byzantine core with an Italianate (in this case Venetian) veneer, while others, even Fioravanti's Cathedral of the Dormition, Moscow (see Chapter 12), have no Italianate detailing, the Bolognese architect's expertise being directed there towards engineering problems. From the time of Ivan the Terrible until the later seventeenth century, architects might make use of Italianate motifs while pursuing essentially indigenous effects: chaotic skylines, vividly coloured surfaces, and piled-up conglomerations culminating in billowing onion domes (for example the Cathedral of S. Basil, Moscow (p. 342C,D). Even a building as apparently pure in aim as the Cathedral of the Twelve Apostles, Moscow, gives an equally Russian impression. The Baroque idioms that began to filter into Russia following its union with the Ukraine were initially applied as surface decoration on traditional buildings.

When Western influences again became important under Peter the Great (1682–1725), Baroque styles, introduced by Italian, German and French architects, became dominant. However, Peter's own architect Domenico Tressini (1670–1734) produced different styles for different occasions. The same is true of the Empress Elizabeth's architect Bartolomeo Rastrelli (1700–71), who, although inspired by Versailles for the Royal palaces around S. Petersburg, was fully aware of more recent Western developments, and was also concerned to give his facades a pleasingly Russian polychromy.

In the flowering of Russian architecture under Catherine the Great, eclecticism picks from a range of overwhelmingly Classicising sources. The Academy of Fine Arts, S. Petersburg (1765–82), is as whole-heartedly French as Quarenghi's villas and palaces are Palladian, and neo-Classicism had already made a profound impact on Russia well before Napoleon's invasion. Charles Cameron (1746–1812) introduced the luxuriant Roman Classicism of Robert Adam and Clérisseau, while Ivan Yegorovich Starov (1744–1808) added neo-Greek to an original and inventive mix. After Napoleon's retreat from Russia the increasingly Imperial Roman-flavoured French neo-Classicism of Napoleonic Paris provided the model for Russian state architecture. A. D. Zakharov (1761–1811) imbued it with an indomitable Russian spirit, and later, in the work of Karl Ivanovitch Rossi (1775–1849), the style achieved a grandeur which surpassed its French equivalent.

Examples

Russia

The **Church of the Decapitation of S. John the Baptist, Dyakovo** (1555), like the Church of the Ascension, Kolomenskoye (p. 342B), is a centralised brick votive church. It originally consisted of a central octagon flanked by four smaller octagonal chapels. Many of the forms employed in this exotic building such as the lunettes and gables, have a fifteenth-century Italian ancestry, here interpreted in a very free manner.

The **Old Cathedral, Monastery of the Virgin of the Don, Moscow** (1593), by contrast is far more restrained. Above a central block three receding tiers of Italian lunettes form a transition to the tall lantern and onion dome.

The **Kremlin, Rostov** (*c.* 1670–83), is an outstanding example of this type of complex (see Chapter 12). Palaces and fortified churches are arranged within the walls with no regard for symmetry, and the buildings here bear little trace of Italian influence. The impressive towers and gateways achieve their effect through massive military forms and exaggerated silhouettes.

The **Kremlin, Pskov**, of about the same period, is partly of wood and much more utilitarian in character, giving rise to a very different architectural quality.

The **Church of the Trinity and of the Georgian Virgin, Moscow** (1628–53), by G. Nikitnikov, is a building very reminiscent of the Old Cathedral in the Monastery of the Virgin of the Don, exhibiting the now conventional combination of Byzantine and Classical motifs, but with a greater use of colour. The asymmetrical massing is partly determined by the site, but is also typical of the period.

S. John the Baptist, Zagorsk (1693–99), reveals a renewed interest in Classical forms. A simple square structure with a recessed upper storey, it is sparsely articulated with half-columns, and apart from the characteristically enlivened profile, decoration is relatively limited.

The remarkable **Monastery of the New Jerusalem, Istra** (1658–85; roof rebuilt by Rastrelli, 1747–60), was intended by Patriarch Nikon to embody his proposed reforms in church architecture. In plan it is closely based on the church of the Holy Sepulchre, Jerusalem (which one of his monks was sent to study), and even houses a replica of the Sepulchre itself in a rotunda under the western conical roof. The architectural forms employed are far purer, plainer and geometric than is usual in the seventeenth century, although after the Patriarch's deposition (1666) the church was completed in a more exuberant manner.

The **Church of the Intercession of the Virgin, Fili, Moscow**, (1690–3) (p. 1067A), by Prince Lev Kirillovich Naryshkin, uncle of Peter the Great, is the earliest genuinely Baroque church in Russia. In silhouette this four-apsed building is no stranger to the Russian tradition of centrally planned churches, but the counterpoint of curving forms and the delicacy of their treatment is much more akin to, for example, the buildings of Guarini.

The similarly planned **Church of the Virgin of the Sign, Dubrovitsy** (1690–1704), built for Prince B. A. Golitsyn, Peter's tutor (possibly by a foreign architect), is much more massive, but no less Baroque in detail and ornament, even if much of the treatment of the curving facade is ultimately derived from Sansovino's Palazzo Cornaro.

The **Church of the Archangel Gabriel, Moscow** (1701–7; partly rebuilt after 1773), designed for Prince Alexander Danilovich Menshikov by I. P. Zarudny, is conceived as a tower. Here the influences are Dutch and English, the building treated as a sober massing of simple block-like forms.

Domenico Tressini (1670–1734), a Swiss-Italian, was working in Copenhagen when he was invited to Russia by Peter the Great's ambassador there. He was put in charge of construction work at the newly founded city of S. Petersburg where he designed several important buildings.

S. Petersburg's first church, the **Cathedral of SS. Peter and Paul in the Fortress** (1712–33; partly rebuilt after 1756), stands within the Peter and Paul fortress. Its curious angularity may reflect the taste predominant at the time of its rebuilding: it is closely dependent on the Baroque Lutheran architecture of northern Europe with which Tressini was familiar. The dome and particularly the spire, 120 m (400 ft) high, mark a decisive break with the domes defining the skylines of older Russian cities.

Count Bartolomeo Francesco Rastrelli (1700–71) was the greatest architect of the period. Arriving in Russia when only fifteen his aptitude for architecture was stimulated by two lengthy study trips in the 1720s. He was court architect to the Empress Elizabeth until *c.* 1760 when his marvellously fluent but essentially Baroque style became outdated.

The **Imperial Palace, Peterhof**, was originally designed (1716–17) for Peter the Great by French architect J. B. A. Le Blond to resemble Versailles. From 1747 to 1752 it was doubled in length by Rastrelli, who added an extra storey and connected two pavilions to the main block by low screens. In the pavilions Rastrelli modified the restrained Classicism of the central range by adding extravagantly bulbous domes, a revival of a traditional Russian feature, in keeping with Elizabeth's interest in the native vernacular.

Smolny Cathedral, S. Petersburg (1748–57, completed 1835), stands at the centre of Elizabeth's huge convent complex which, like the cathedral itself, is laid out as a Greek cross, with domed pavilions at the inner angles. Despite its traditional ground-plan and characteristic towered and domed silhouette, the blue and white cathedral is a compact Baroque design of great power, its facade conceived as a number of superimposed elements and the towers angled at 45 degrees.

The **Catherine (or Great Palace, Tsarskoe Selo** (1749–52) (p. 1067C), was remodelled for Elizabeth by adding side wings to an already substantial core: the resulting facade is 298 m (978 ft) wide. The walls were originally yellow (now blue), the articulation white, and decorative elements like caryatids gilded, so that the effect of the exterior with its rusticated basement and order above is like a highly decorated Rococo version of Versailles.

The **Cathedral of S. Andrew, Kiev** (1747–67) (p. 1067B), also designed by Rastrelli, is a perfect fusion of Russian elements with the western European Baroque. The domed Greek-cross church, two arms slightly extended, has four diagonal buttresses

A. Church of the Intercession of the Virgin, Fili, Moscow (1690–3). See p. 1066

B. Cathedral of S. Andrew, Kiev (1747–67). See p. 1066

Catherine Palace, Tsarkoe Selo (1749–52). See p. 1066

carrying subsidiary onion-domed turrets, creating a silhouette in harmony with both traditions.

The **Winter Palace** (now Hermitage Museum) **S. Petersburg** (1754–62) (p. 1069A), also for Elizabeth, is again quite gigantic, with a fifty-bay facade overlooking the Palace Square. Painted blue, these facades are, however, inspired by Italian rather than French models, and have a more sculptural if less decorative appearance. A three-storey arrangement of two ranges of half-columns (the upper order is giant) on the Square facade breaks forward in a series of steps, and added variety is provided by the grouping of the orders, the variation of window frames and the pediments, balustrades and statuary of the roofline.

The **Imperial Palace, Kiev**, an imposing building designed by Rastrelli in a French style, was originally built in wood, but in 1819 following a fire was reconstructed in stone to the original design.

The **Academy of Fine Arts, S. Petersburg** (1765–82) (p. 1069B), is the work of A. F. Kokorinov and J.-B. M. Vallin de la Mothe (Vallen Delamot, 1729–1800). Related to J.-F. Blondel's proposal for an academy in Moscow, the work represents a decisive break with Rastrelli's Baroque. Of square plan with a large circular central court and four subsidiary rectangular courts, the imposing facade has three projecting portions with half-columns over a rusticated basement in the French manner. However, its stressed horizontality and Pantheon-like dome behind the central pedimented portions reflect the new neo-Classicism of western Europe.

The **Monastery of the Holy Trinity, Zagorsk** (see Chapter 12), has an imposing Baroque towered entrance (added 1741–70); although the forms are Western, their piled effect is clearly Russian.

The **Church of the Trinity, Nenoska** (1727), is one of many wooden churches still being built in the eighteenth century. The central octagon with four rectangular projections is typical of the type. Each part has an octagonal attic, conical tent roof and onion pinnacle, all traditional features, the only concession being the modern shapes of the windows.

The **Marble Palace, S. Petersburg** (1768–85) (p. 1070A), is by an Italian, Antonio Rinaldi (*c.* 1710–94), who had studied with Vanvitelli. It is so named because of its innovative granite and marble facing. Despite this unprecedented richness of material, the conventional facade (basement and giant pilaster order) is remarkably restrained. The central section, with its arched window opening and projecting attic, reflects a growing preoccupation with such ancient monuments as the Arch of Constantine.

A blue and white pavilion with a curious hat-like dome is all that survives of Rinaldi's **Sliding Hill, Oranienbaum** (1760–8), a type of helter-skelter. A complex arrangement of circular hall with three square wings, it is nevertheless given a Classical treatment which emphasises the block-like geometry.

The **Pashkov Palace, Moscow** (1784–6) (p. 1071A), attributed to V. I. Bazhenov and M. F. Kazakov, is a particularly bold neo-Classical design. A central, almost cubic, block with a tall drum and dome and a projecting arcade is linked to what are in effect two small prostyle Ionic temples.

The **Petrovsky Palace, near Moscow** (1775–82, restored 1840) (p. 1071B), is the work of M. F. Kazakov (1738–1813), one of the leading architects of the period. It is built in the Russian revival (neo-Gothic) style promoted by Catherine II, partly out of a genuine interest in architectural history, partly as an element in a very broadly based attempt to consolidate her position as a foreigner in a notoriously xenophobic country. Pointed arches, bi-lobed windows, swollen, baluster-like columns and complex skylines signified the first period of Russian imperial greatness on the front of a building which followed a perfectly regular plan. The Petrovsky Palace was in fact built to commemorate Catherine's victory over the Turks.

Ivan Yegorovich Starov (1744–1808), who trained in Paris, is one of Russia's most important native neo-Classical architects. The **Church and Belfry, Nikolskoye** (1773–6, belfry destroyed), formed a majestic group. The domed church has a severe Doric temple front, while the free-standing belfry with its four tabernacle porticoes is reminiscent of the Temple of the Winds, Athens. The contrasts in scale, the use of the Doric and the windowless rusticated rotunda make the building comparable with the projects of Boullée and Ledoux.

Tauride Palace, S. Petersburg (1783–9, remodelled early nineteenth century and after 1905) (p. 1070C), designed for Catherine's lover Grigory Potemkin, is one of the most impressive town mansions of the period in the world. The exterior, with its Doric portico, is almost spartan in its lack of ornament. The spectacular interior has a central domed rotunda resembling the Pantheon, and reaches its climax with the gigantic transverse (Catherine) hall at the rear, its apsidal ends projecting beyond the side walls of the building, and its two long walls articulated with eighteen pairs of 5 m (18 ft) tall Greek Ionic columns.

Giacomo Quarenghi (1744–1817) arrived in Russia in 1780, after working with the painter Mengs in Rome; under Catherine the Great he reached the height of imperial favour and received many commissions. The **English Palace, Peterhof** (1781–9, destroyed), was a Palladian building with a simple rectangular plan and attached Corinthian portico, but on a vast scale, incorporating a Pantheon-like rotunda as an entrance-hall. Equally grand and Palladian is the **Academy of Sciences, S. Petersburg** (1783–7) (p. 1071C), its severe facade broken by an octastyle Ionic portico.

The **Hermitage Theatre, S. Petersburg** (1783–7) (p. 1070B), has an unpedimented facade and barely projecting, unarticulated ressauts. The semicircle of

A. Winter Palace, S. Petersburg (1754–62). See p. 1068

B. Academy of Fine Arts, S. Petersburg (1765–82). See p. 1068

A. Marble Palace, S. Petersburg (1768–85). See p. 1068

B. Hermitage Theatre, S. Petersburg (1783–7). See p. 1068

C. Tauride Palace, S. Petersburg (1783–9). See p. 1068

A. Pashkov Palace, Moscow (1784–6). See p. 1068

B. Petrovsky Palace, near Moscow (1775–82). See p. 1068

C. Academy of Sciences, S. Petersburg (1783–7). See p. 1068

A. Palace, Pavlovsk (1782–6): the Grecian Hall. See p. 1073

B. New Admiralty, S. Petersburg (1806–23). See p. 1073

C. General Staff Headquarters, S. Petersburg (1819–29). See p. 1073

the auditorium pushes out the external shape of the building.

The **Palace, Pavlovsk** (1782–6) (p. 1072A), is the work of the mysterious British architect Charles Cameron (1746–1812), summoned by Catherine in 1779 to Russia, where he remodelled the interiors of the imperial palaces at Tsarskoe Selo, especially the exquisite colonnaded **Cameron Gallery** added to the Catherine Palace, and here in an Adamesque style. Facing onto an expansive oval forecourt, Cameron's squarish rebuilt palace is dominated by a low colonnetted drum with a Pantheon-like saucer-dome above.

The **Cathedral of the Virgin of Kazan, S. Petersburg** (1801–11), was designed by A. N. Voronikhin (1760–1814), born a serf, who was first sent by his master to S. Peter's Academy and then on a lengthy stay to Paris and Rome. Inspired by various buildings, not least S. Peter's in Rome, Palladio's Villa Badoer, and Soufflot's S. Geneviève in Paris, the church has a semicircle of Corinthian columns embracing the porticoed entrance of the north transept – two other projected colonnades remained unbuilt. Despite a mixture of styles, the building conveys a cold grandeur typical of Paris at this period, the white stone exterior contrasting with a heavy polychromy inside.

The far more neo-Classical **Academy of Mines, S. Petersburg** (1806–11), also by Voronikhin, has a huge twelve-column Greek Doric portico projecting from blank wings, in a manner here reminiscent of contemporary public buildings in Paris.

With a broad knowledge of Western architecture gleaned in his years in Paris and Italy, Adrian Dmitrievitch Zakharov (1761–1811) adapted the revivalist forms of late neo-Classicism to a more Russian mode of expression. In his masterpiece, the **New Admiralty, S. Petersburg** (1806–23) (p. 1072B), he succeeded where so many of his predecessors had faltered, in handling a gigantic building without succumbing to monotony. The plan was determined by the previous Admiralty, a double row of buildings separated by a narrow court. The main facade, some 408 m (1340 ft) in length, is treated as a series of large, simple but contrasting pavilions terminating in twelve-columned Doric temple-fronts. Piled up above the entrance arch is a bewildering succession of forms including the Mausoleum of Halicarnassus, a Baroque dome and lantern and a Gothic spire, while the gateway below combines a Russian extravagance of detail with a scale, geometry and application of symbolic sculpture worthy of Boullée.

The **Exchange, S. Petersburg** (now Museum of Naval History) (1804–16), was the work of the French architect Thomas de Thomon, who like Cameron had built nothing before his arrival in Russia. It is bounded by a Doric Peripteral colonnade predating that of the Bourse in Paris. Above the colonnade the building rises to a gable with a large thermae window within a voussoired arch, reminiscent of projects by Boullée and Ledoux: Ledoux (the first volume of *L'Architecture* was dedicated to Alexander I) indeed considered the exchange to be the spiritual centre of a city.

Karl Ivanovich Rossi (1775–1849), a half-Italian who visited Italy only once (1804–6), was largely responsible for introducing a richer and more fluid Classical style and rejecting the revivalist or French-oriented styles of previous architects. His works have something in common with those of Rastrelli, not least in their scale. Rossi redesigned whole districts of S. Petersburg after his move there from Moscow in 1816. A notable example is **Ulitsa Zodchevo Rossi**, a sublimely monumental street of *c.* 1820, with Doric column-clad elevations which frame a vista to the neo-Classic Pushkin Theatre.

The **General Staff Headquarters, S. Petersburg** (1819–29) (p. 1072C), faces Rastrelli's Winter Palace across the square. It is a colossal triangular building with a curved concave facade occupying the square's entire south side. The rather sober facade with its rusticated basement is interrupted at the centre by a massive barrel-vaulted arch surmounted by a quadriga. At the centre of the square, R. de Montferrand installed in 1834 a huge monolithic red granite column (the Alexander Column) supporting an angel.

The **Senate and Synod** (now Russian State Archives), **S. Petersburg** (1829–34), are two buildings with central colonnades and end pavilions linked together by a triumphal arch crossing an intervening street. This central feature, topped by a squat stepped pyramid, combines a new complexity of composition with richness of material and copious sculptural decoration.

The **Bell Tower, Gruzino**, near Novgorod (1822), is the work of V. P. Stasov, and although Classically purer, is conceived in the same additive manner as the entry to Zakharov's New Admiralty. The tempietto and obelisk which form it are of stark neo-Classical design individually but together make a delicate and graceful composition.

The **Cathedral of S. Isaac of Dalmatia, S. Petersburg** (1818–58), designed by R. de Montferrand (1786–1858), is a Greek-cross building which, despite its towers, is not unlike Soufflot's S. Geneviève. Overpoweringly large, and with red granite portico columns and a gilded dome, it suffers somewhat from lack of coherence.

Architectural Character

Scandinavia

The Renaissance appears first in the castles of Sweden and Norway in the form of occasional Classical motifs or interiors in the Fontainebleau manner (for example Kalmar Castle). The characteristic brick gables, multi-tiered steeples and ornamental skylines of Danish architecture in particular are strongly Netherlandish in character. Hans van Steenwinckel and Antonius van Opbergen, both from Flanders, worked on the royal palace at Elsinore.

Dutch influence remained important to the mid-seventeenth century, but now in the 'Palladian' mode. Church designs reveal an acquaintance with the protestant aesthetic of de Keyser and van Campen, while Vingboons's Riddarhus (1653) introduced the Dutch mansion style to Stockholm. By the end of the century a first-hand acquaintance with the architecture of France and Italy was evident in Sweden in the works of Simon de la Vallée (*c.* 1590–1642), his son Jean and Nicodemus Tessin the Elder. The last's son, Tessin the Younger (1654–1728), succeeded in the Royal Palace, Stockholm, in creating an original synthesis of mainstream Baroque ideas. Inspired by Bernini, he also prepared designs for the Louvre and for a proposed new palace in Copenhagen.

Before the twentieth century, Scandinavia's most impressive architectural achievements were perhaps in the neo-Classical period. The work of C. F. Harsdorff (1735–99) in Copenhagen reveals his familiarity with the avant-garde led by Soufflot and Ledoux in Paris. His pupil C. F. Hansen (1756–1845) was one of the most distinguished and imaginative early nineteenth-century exponents of neo-Classicism. In the new capitals of Oslo and Helsinki Schinkel's influence was paramount: C. L. Engel (1778–1840), who designed many public buildings in Helsinki, had been a fellow-student of Schinkel in Germany, while C. H. Grosch (1801–65) enlisted the aid of the great Berlin architect for his University buildings in Oslo.

Alongside the mainstream development of Classicising architecture in the capitals there persisted a vernacular tradition of building in wood. Wooden barn-like churches with painted interiors and free-standing bell-towers are characteristic of the northern villages of Norway, Sweden and Finland. In Finland, they were built by architects of Engel's stature in the most advanced neo-Classicism well into the nineteenth century. Externally, Classical details – pilasters, pediments, quoins and even channelled rustication – were reproduced in wood in both religious and domestic structures.

Examples

Renaissance (to 1630)

Denmark

Rosenholm Castle, Jutland, begun around 1560 and completed forty years later, appears in modified form in du Cerceau's *Verneuil*. The gatehouse facade is dominated by a central tower with dome and spire, and connected by low wings to two-storey gabled pavilions. Ornament is simple but Classical: a loggia in the trapezoidal courtyard soon showed itself to be unsuitable in the Danish climate and was bricked in.

Kronborg Castle, Helsingør (Elsinore) (p. 1075A), is a vast fortified palace begun for Frederick II in 1574 by the Flemish architect Hans van Paeschen and completed two decades later by the latter's fellow countryman Antonius van Opbergen who arrived in 1577 (q.v.). Enclosing a mediaeval castle, it has four wings with corner towers disposed around a square courtyard. The elaborate gables and typically Flemish towers are all slightly different, enriching the lively skyline and contrasting with the severity of the outer walls. The peripheral bastions, moved well away from the castle, were designed in the Italian manner in accordance with the new demands of artillery warfare. The castle was rebuilt after a fire (1629–) by Hans van Steenwinckel, but retains much of its original appearance.

The **Royal Castle, Frederiksborg** (1602–, restored after 1859) (p. 1075B) was rebuilt for Christian IV by the Dutch architects Hans and Louvens van Steenwinckel. The huge complex stands on three islands, the main building a severe four-storey block with corner towers. By contrast, the three steeples and many gables and pinnacles reflect contemporary Netherlandish architecture at its most extravagant, and the sculptural decoration is also lush enough for the palace of the 'King of the North'.

The **Exchange, Copenhagen** (1619–40; spire 1624–5) (p. 1077A), is one of several Copenhagen buildings instigated by Christian IV and built under the leadership of Hans van Steenwinckel the younger. The long repetitive two-storey facades with their exceptionally large windows and ornamental dormers are enlivened by the extraordinary central lantern tower (by Ludwig Heidriffer), where dragons' tails form a twisting upward spiral.

The **Round Tower, Copenhagen** (1637–42), one of the strangest buildings of the period, is a huge 34 m (110 ft) cylinder, intended to serve as both church tower and observatory. Inside, a spiral ramp facilitated the movement of equipment, as in earlier Swedish gun towers. The external treatment, almost entirely mediaeval, includes the cipher and astrologically symbolic iron railings, which are evidence of the building's original hermetic secrets.

Sweden

Kalmar Castle is a heavily fortified castle with an outer circle of bastions. As with Danish castles of the period, however, severity ends at the extravagant skyline.

Vadstena Castle (begun 1545; upper parts modified late sixteenth century) was designed for King Gustavus Vasa by the military architect Joachim

A. Kronborg Castle, Helsingør (1574–, rebuilt 1629). See p. 1074

B. Royal Castle, Frederiksborg (1602–). See p. 1074

Bulgerin. The large symmetrical facade is flanked by low cannon towers. Ornament is spare but Classical, and three decorative towers enliven the facade.

Baroque and Rococo (1630–1760)

Sweden

Axel Oxenstierna's City Palace, Stockholm (*c.* 1650–4) (p. 1078A), built for Queen Christina's first minister by the French engineer Jean de la Vallée, the son of Simon, the Royal Architect, is the first townhouse in Sweden designed in the Roman manner, with rusticated ground floor and elaborate tabernacle windows and aedicules above. In fact the clear dependence on the Renaissance palazzi of Raphael and Peruzzi (for example Palazzo Branconio and Palazzo Massimi, Rome) is most unusual for the period.

The **Riddarhus, Stockholm** (*c.* 1641–74) (p. 1077B), the nobles' assembly building, was begun by Simon de la Vallée and completed by the Dutch architect, Joost Vingboons (q.v.), and Jean de la Vallée. Vingboons's facade, with its giant order and central pediment, reflects contemporary Dutch Palladianism, although the architectural treatment is particularly dense. The characteristic Swedish 'Säteri' roof, with clerestory halfway up, appears here for the first time in a monumental building.

Hedvig Eleonora Church, Stockholm (begun 1669), designed by Jean de la Vallée, and completed 1724–37, is an octagonal church with central cupola (built 1865–8) of great refinement. A smooth pedimented entrance interrupts the restrained banded rustication of the exterior. The vocabulary of the energetic cupola is distinctly French.

Nicodemus Tessin the Elder (1615–81), the leading Scandinavian architect of the day, became Stockholm's City Architect in 1661. Born in Flanders, he had toured Europe and was particularly aware of developments in France, which enabled him to develop a suitable royal style for Sweden.

Drottningholm Palace, near Stockholm (1662–) (p. 1079A), was built by the elder Tessin for Dowager Queen Hedvig Eleanora. The exceedingly long garden facade recalls Versailles, although the architecture is far simpler. Very unusual are the giant tabernacles attached to each end of the wing blocks. In the grounds is the **Kina Slott** (Chinese Pavilion) begun in 1763 by Carl Fredrik Adelcrantz and Carl Cronstedt in a Rococo/Chinese style prophetic of the Oriental interests of the Swedish-born Sir William Chambers (q.v.).

The **Villa** of the Royal Chancellor Magnus Gabriel de la Gardie, **Mariedal, Västergötland** (1666) was designed by Jean de la Vallée. Palladian in spirit, it has an exceptionally tall central temple-front interrupting the low pilaster articulation of the facade.

The **Caroline Mausoleum, Riddarholms Church, Stockholm** (1671; dome redesigned 1740s), was designed by Tessin the Elder to house the royal tombs. Greek-cross in plan, it has a simple volumetric exterior solemnly articulated with free-standing Doric columns, and a sculptural compactness comparable with French architecture of the period.

The **Cathedral, Kalmar** (1681–) has a plan based on an elongated Greek cross. The main facade with its flanking towers draws on a number of twin-towered Italian models, but the skyline achieves a northern delicacy.

Nicodemus Tessin the Younger (1654–1728) trained under his father Tessin the Elder before travelling extensively in England, France and Italy (1673–80). He gained a thorough knowledge of Baroque architecture and even submitted designs for the Louvre. His works in Stockholm establish him as Sweden's finest architect.

The **Royal Palace, Stockholm** (*c.* 1690–1708, 1721–54) (p. 1079B), is above all the work of Tessin the Younger, with the collaboration of other architects, notably Hårleman. Four low wings jut out from a massive rectangular block with a central courtyard. The four main facades are all rather different, since designing continued as work progressed, but all receive an equally severe Classical treatment. The most dynamic is the south facade, where six colossal Corinthian half-columns are applied to the central portion, the entablature breaking separately over each one. The balustraded parapet and concealed roof add to the block-like monumentality of the exterior.

The **Tessin Palace, Stockholm** (1694–1700), is the younger Tessin's own house which faces the Royal Palace. Here an irregular trapezoidal site is wonderfully exploited to accommodate a series of courts and gardens. The diverging walls of the main gardens widen towards an end elevation of remarkable spatial boldness: behind a fountain are two free-standing concave quadrant screens providing a foil to the sober basement of the end wall, which carries an upper loggia of great depth.

The **East India Company Building, Gothenburg** (1740) (p. 1078C), by C. Hårleman, is an austere astylar building with a pedimented projecting central section and segmental pediments over the slightly projecting central bays of the wings.

The **Exchange, Stockholm** (1773–78) (p. 1078B), by E. Palmstedt, is a commercial building in a similarly restrained Classical style, with here a rather more severe projecting two-storey arcaded portico and a lantern behind.

Habo Church, Västergötland (1720) (pp. 1080A, 1081), one of many timber churches in Sweden, is the only example with aisles and galleries. The exterior is shingled and boarded, and there is a free-standing belfry. Inside, every inch is painted, the structural members being marbled, while the altar and pulpit are richly carved in a Baroque repertory of barley-sugar columns, swags and putti.

A. Exchange, Copenhagen (1619–40; spire 1624–5). See p. 1074

B. Riddarhus, Stockholm (*c.* 1641–74). See p. 1076

A. Axel Oxenstierna's City Palace, Stockholm (*c.* 150–4). See p. 1076

B. Exchange, Stockholm (1773–8). See p. 1076

C. East India Company Building, Gothenburg (1740). See p. 1076

A. Drottingholm Palace, near Stockholm (1662–). See p. 1076

B. Royal Palace, Stockholm (*c.* 1690–1708, 1721–54). See p. 1076

A. Habo Church, Västergötland (1720). See p. 1076

B. Church of Our Saviour, Copenhagen (1682–96; tower and spire added 1750). See p. 1082

C. Amalienborg Palace, Copenhagen (1750–4). See p. 1082

Habo Church, Västergötland: interior. See p. 1076

Denmark

Charlottenburg Palace, Copenhagen (1672–83), has been attributed to the Dutchman, Ewert Janssen (who was the contractor) or another, unknown Dutch architect. Its restrained Classicism is typical of the period in Holland, but is innovatory enough in Denmark, where this building is considered to herald the 'Danish Baroque'. Understated pilasters provide a slight central emphasis on the brick facades.

Amalienborg Palace (Place Royale), **Copenhagen** (1750–4), designed by N. Eigtved as part of a coherently planned city district, was conceived as four smaller palaces (p. 1080C) placed across the angles of an octagonal piazza. The main axis is aligned with Frederikskirke. Originally designed as town mansions for the four greatest nobles of the country, they were bought by the royal family in 1794, and today in succession serve as the royal palaces. With its equestrian statue of Frederick V in the centre, and the restrained Classicism of its facades, particularly with the two storeys of arches in the central ressaut, the square recalls French prototypes. They are among the most important early neo-Classical interiors in Europe.

The **Hermitage, Dyrehaven** (1734), by L. de Thurah, is an exquisite royal hunting and dining-lodge which still serves its original function. Very French in design, it has projecting wings, a banded rusticated lower storey, an elegant upper storey, and a steep hipped roof.

The **Church of Our Saviour** (Vor Frelsers Kirke), **Copenhagen** (1682–96; tower and spire added 1750) (p. 1080B), is the work of Lambert van Haven, who had studied in Italy and Holland. The cross-shaped structure with the filled-in corners is built up on a module with four central supports. The simple interior is akin to the Churches of de Keyser in Amsterdam (q.v.). The helical spire added by Lauritz de Thurah (1749–50) is a rarefied and elongated interpretation of Borromini's S. Ivo (q.v.).

The French architect Gabriel was among those who made designs for the **Marble Church** (Frederikskirke), **Copenhagen** (1756–late nineteenth century). N.-H. Jardin's design of 1756, which combines a domed interior with a temple-front portico, was accepted, construction was interrupted and the ruinous building lay as Copenhagen's forum until the dome was completed in 1894.

Norway

Austråt, Orland, Trøondelag (1654) (p. 1083A), a most unusual house, has open wooden galleries embracing a courtyard. The ground floor has simple supports, but at the upper level strange caryatid figures standing on baluster plinths support the roof.

The **Church of Our Saviour, Oslo** (1697; rebuilt 1848), preserves much of its original Dutch apperance. The cruciform plan remained the standard form for Norwegian ecclesiastical architecture through the eighteenth century. The exterior of this church is dominated by a massive squat tower from which rises the ornamental spire.

The **Church at Kongsberg** (1740–61) (p. 1083B) by J. A. Stuckenbrock is a beautifully composed arrangement of restrained block-like forms. Apart from the lantern, the simple shapes of the openings and clock faces constitute the only exterior features. The timber Baroque interior has two storeys of galleries which can seat 3000 people, facing an altar/organ loft/pulpit combination of unusual Baroque exuberance.

Stiftsgården, Trondheim (1774–8) (p. 1083C), one of the great wooden palaces of the period, probably designed by General Friedrich von Krogh, is a huge nineteen-bay structure articulated with pilaster strips and a central pediment. The detailing is Rococo, but a curious feature is the paired alternation of triangular and segmental window pediments. The plan is surprisingly *retardataire*.

The Neo-Classical Period

Denmark

The **house** of C. F. Harsdorff (1735–99), in **Kongens Nytorv, Copenhagen** (p. 1085A), marks the beginning of neo-Classicism in Scandinavia. Harsdorff was the first Danish architect to get a regular civil training at the new Copenhagen Academy (founded 1754), and subsequently in Paris and Rome. The house, with its Ionic pilastered temple front, was designed as an example to students and Copenhagen residents alike, but curiously the volutes of the capitals are placed side-on to the facade.

Harsdorff's **Frederik V Chapel, Roskilde Cathedral** (begun 1774, completed early 1800s) (p. 1086A), is a jewel of early neo-Classicism. Entrance to the Greek-cross interior is through a columnar screen while fluted pilasters panel the walls. The shallow arms have coffered barrel vaults and the crossing is covered by a semi-elliptical gored dome of rather Byzantine character.

The **Hercules Pavilion, Copenhagen** (1773), also designed by Harsdorff, closes a vista in the King's Garden. The miniature mock-shrine is entered through two Doric columns 'in antis'.

C. F. Hansen (1756–1845), Harsdorff's student, was the foremost Scandinavian exponent of neo-Classicism. After his studies at the Academy he went to Rome, then worked for twenty years in Schleswig and Holstein (now part of Germany) before returning to design a remarkable series of buildings in Denmark.

A. Austeråt, Orland, Trøndelag (1654). See p. 1082

B. Church at Kongsberg (1740–61). See p. 1082

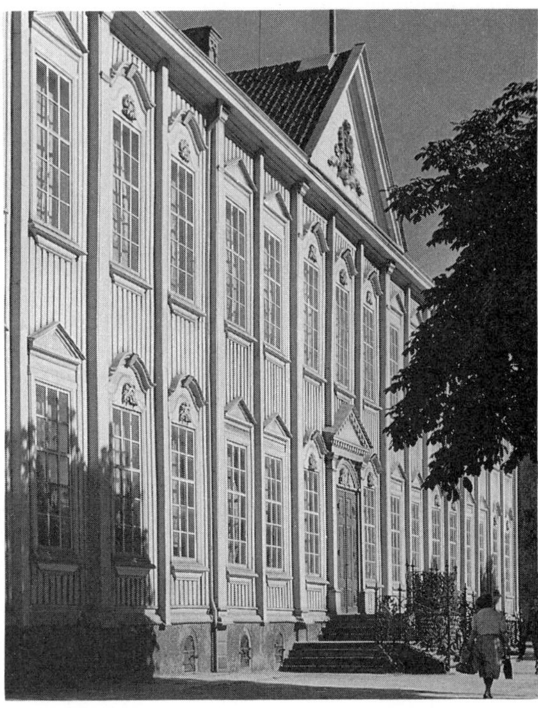

C. Stiftsgården, Trondheim (1774–8). See p. 1082

Vor Frue Kirke (Church of Our Lady), **Copenhagen** (1810–29) (p. 1086B), has a Greek-Doric facade portico projecting from an absolutely blank wall. Above rises a three-stage tower with tiny openings (reminiscent of Boullée). The magnificent barrel-vaulted interior with its colonnades above plain pier arcades is like Mansart's Chapel at Versailles (q.v.) – an example of an eighteenth-century architect reinterpreting the basilican form, archaeologically and theogically suitable for Catholic and Lutheran alike.

The **Surgical Auditorium, Copenhagen** (Museum of Medical History) (1786), is the work of Peter Meyn. Like Condour's Paris Academy (q.v.), which Meyn saw under construction, it is semicircular in plan like an ancient theatre. It is covered by a flattened coffered dome incorporating an oculus.

Sweden

The **Botanicum, Uppsala** (1788) (p. 1085B), by L. J. Deprez, has an interesting early neo-Classical portico. The eight Greek-Doric columns are unusually squat, giving this little building an extraordinary monumentality, which reflects its visual importance as the termination of a vista from the castle, and the prestige which botanical studies had already acquired in this, the birthplace of Linnaeus.

Skeppsholmskyrkan, Stockholm (1824–42), by Fredrik Blom, is a centrally-planned church with octagonal exterior and circular interior, where the central area is separated from the surrounding aisle by an arcade of eight pairs of Classical columns. The external arrangement of neo-Classical motifs placed against plain stuccoed walls recalls Hansen's work in Copenhagen (q.v.).

Norway

Damsgård, Bergen (rebuilt 1770–95) (p. 1086C), is a charming Rococo villa, largely designed by its owner, J. S. C. Geelmayden. The delicate facade has a central gable and tower flanked by delightful dormer windows and compact curvilinear pavilions.

Sør-Fron Church, Gudbrandsal (1786–92), by Svend Aspaas, is a very simple octagonal church with projecting lanterns. Externally, Doric pilasters are applied to the corners; inside, four slender wooden Corinthian columns support the roof beams while a gallery incorporating pulpits runs around the periphery.

The **Exchange, Oslo** (1826–52, enlarged 1910) (p. 1087A), was designed by the City Architect, C. H. Grosch, whose influence is apparent in the broad low look of the portico with its widely-spaced tapering Doric columns, and in the simplified entablature with heavy mutule blocks.

The **Norwegian Bank, Oslo** (1828) (p. 1087B), also by Grosch, has a more tightly compact Greek-Doric portico whose compression was suitable to the building's serious intent.

The **University, Oslo** (after 1838), Norway's first, was built by Grosch after designs by Schinkel and has a most imposing Ionic portico 'in antis'. The use of Norwegian granite represents its first monumental application since the Middle Ages.

Finland

The **Church of Hämeenlinna** (1798; enlarged 1892), by the French architect L. J. Deprez, is the earliest Classicising church in Finland and remains one of the most severely neo-Classical anywhere. The circular building (the altar was originally in the centre) had rectangular blocks at front and back containing apse and vestibule. Its severe stucco facade has squat recessed Doric half-columns with lobed 'echini' flanking the splayed door-frame.

C. L. Engel (1778–1840) was a German-born architect who spent some years in S. Petersburg and Tallinn before working from 1815 in Finland, providing monumental public buildings in the new capital (after 1812) of Helsinki.

The **Old Church, Helsinki** (1826–) (p. 1087C), is a cruciform wooden building standing isolated in a city park. Four identical Doric porticoes project from the central block articulated with Doric pilasters. Above is a pedimented square tempietto carrying a dome. The simply-conceived church lacks the pomposity of much of Engel's later work.

The **Lutheran Cathedral** (S. Nicolai), **Helsinki** (1830–40) (p. 1088A,B), is the focal point of the city centre, standing at the top of an immense flight of steps almost the full width of Senate Square. The Greek-cross building has a tall narrow central drum and cupola, four subsidiary towers and four identical hexastyle Corinthian porticoes. On the interior the four massive supporting piers of the crossing contrast dramatically with the colonnaded ambulatories inside the apsed arms; the inspiration is from early sixteenth-century designs for S. Peter's, Rome (q.v.).

The **Senate Square, Helsinki**, in front of the Lutheran Cathedral, was planned by J. A. Ehrenström and is bordered by several other buildings designed by Engel. The **Senate House** (1818–22), occupying the entire east side, has a rather academic three-storey facade with a central Corinthian portico. On the facing side is the **University** (1828–32), restored after bomb damage in 1944, with its impressive three-storey staircase of, from bottom to top, Doric, Ionic and Corinthian columns. To the north of this is the **University Library** (1836–45) (p. 1089A,B); here a Corinthian order runs the entire width of the seventeen-bay building,

A. House of C. F. Harsdorff, Kongens Nytorv, Copenhagen. See p. 1082

B. Botanicum, Uppsala (1788). See p. 1084

A. Frederik V Chapel, Roskilde Cathedral (1774–). See p. 1082

B. Vor Frue Kirke, Copenhagen (1810–29). See p. 1084

C. Damsgård, Bergen (rebuilt 1770–95). See p. 1084

A. Exchange, Oslo (1826–52). See p. 1084

B. Norwegian Bank, Oslo (1828). See p. 1084

C. Old Church, Helsinki (1826–). See p. 1084

A. Lutheran Cathedral, Helsinki (1830–40). See p. 1084

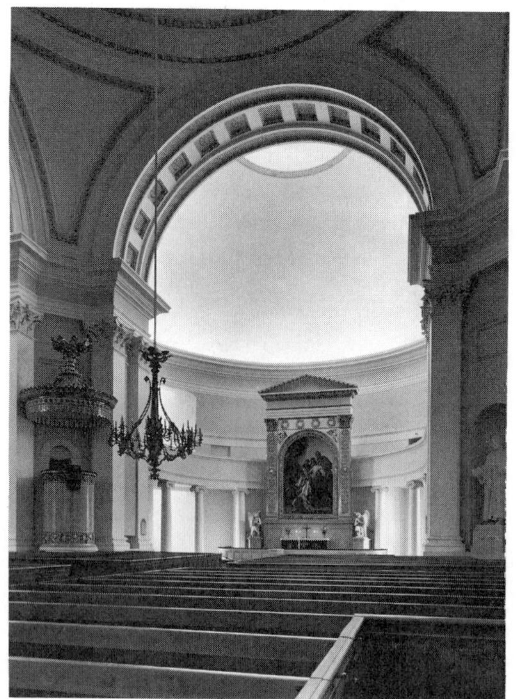

B. Lutheran Cathedral, Helsinki: interior

C. Old Academy, Turku (1802–15). See p. 1090

A. University Library, Helsinki (1836–45). See p. 1084

B. University Library, Helsinki: interior

with half-columns for the unpedimented central projecting and deep pilasters at the sides. Inside are three reading rooms with galleries supported on giant Corinthian colonnades. The central room has a coffered dome; the other two are barrel-vaulted.

The **Old Academy, Turku** (1802–15) (p. 1088C), is the work of the Stockholm City architect C. Gjörwell and C. F. Bassi. The austere facade with its very large pediment is unmistakably neo-Classical, particularly in the employment of such simplified elements as the upper window frames.

The **New Academy, Turku** (1832–3), by Bassi (designed as a house), makes use of similar window frames. Here the facade is dominated by a projecting portico of Doric columns standing on a rusticated basement and topped by a stepped attic.

Chapter 34

POST-RENAISSANCE EUROPE

Introduction

The most conspicuous characteristic of nineteenth-century European architecture is its diverse use of historic styles. It differs from earlier periods not because architects had previously avoided reviving historic forms, but because of the broad range of styles from which the nineteenth-century architects could choose. The Picturesque movement had stimulated interest in a great variety of architecture, both Western and exotic, and during the nineteenth century architecture became increasingly comprehensive, so that architects were better informed than ever about the architecture of the past. However, there was no consensus as to the most desirable style for architects to follow: for instance, one town hall might be modelled on a Classical temple, evoking the noble aspects of Greek civilisation, while another might be based on a Flemish cloth-hall, suggesting parallels with the industrial and mercantile prosperity of the late Middle Ages. But the implicit comparison between nineteenth-century life and the standards of previous ages was not always a flattering one, as Pugin concluded (see below). As the century progressed many architects turned to eclecticism, combining features from different sources in an endeavour to achieve original effects. Only at the end of the century was there a successful attempt to create a 'new' style, as peculiar to the modern world as the Gothic cathedral was to the mediaeval.

Despite a dependence on the past, the buildings of nineteenth-century Europe are not replicas of historic monuments, and in their planning, use of materials and decorative detail they are products of their age. There were many new types of building – for instance, railway stations, factories and department stores – all requiring designs for which there were no ancient precedents. But traditional types of building were now also likely to be designed in a more complex way: parliament buildings, town halls and schools, for example, became more elaborate as well as larger in response to the needs of an industrial society. Houses and flats, too, tended to become more ambitious, with more differentiated rooms. Even in the case of churches, where there was some attempt to revive ancient usage, 'inventive imitation' was accepted.

The development of new materials and forms of construction is a major feature of nineteenth-century European architecture, but orthodox materials remained prevalent for much of the period. Externally stone and brick were the most common of these, while timber construction persisted in remoter parts of Europe. Towards the end of the century faience became a common facing material in cities, partly as an answer to severe atmospheric pollution, but vernacular materials enjoyed a revival in rural and suburban locations. As it remained usual until about 1900 for external walls to be load-bearing, conventional arrangements of windows were followed, but windows tended to be larger and have fewer glazing bars from the 1840s onwards as sheet glass was introduced. The combination of structural ironwork and large sheets of glass permitted great display windows to be introduced into shop fronts, and led to the amazing trainsheds, market halls and exhibition buildings which are so distinctive a part of the nineteenth-century century city. The cast-iron frame, often used only internally, facilitated the development of taller buildings and led to more open interior spaces. Steel-framed framed buildings were not developed in Europe as early or as spectacularly as in America, but became usual in large cities after 1900, generally rising to eight or nine storeys. Reinforced concrete was the other innovation of these years to challenge the supremacy of the load-bearing wall.

The pattern of European architecture in the years between 1830 and 1900 is a complicated one, and it is convenient to study it in three phases: 1830–50, 1850–70, 1870–1900.

Architectural Character

1830–50

The period 1830–50 coincides approximately with the Early Victorian phase of architecture in Britain, and the era which in the German-speaking world is known as 'Biedermeier'.

In spite of widening eclecticism, the Classical tradition showed astonishing resilience, and a Classical design was the natural choice for most public buildings throughout this period. The Greek Revival, although culminating in the period around 1830, remained a potent influence for many years after, as the Hansens' work in Athens and Vienna demonstrates. The planning and spatial organisation of such buildings was often affected by the rationalist theories of Jean-Nicolas-Louis Durand (1760–1834), whose *Précis des leçons d'architecture* (1802–5) demonstrated a system of design based on symmetry and formal geometry. Durand's influence was especially strong in Germany, and is well illustrated by the Altes Museum, Berlin (1823–30) (p. 995C), by Karl Friedrich Schinkel (1781–1841). In Britain the purity of the Greek Revival was superseded in the 1840s by a Graeco-Roman phase of great magnificence, used for public buildings such as S. George's Hall, Liverpool (1840–54), by Harvey Lonsdale Elmes (1814–47), a design of much greater spatial complexity than those recommended by Durand.

For domestic and commercial buildings, less rhetorical forms of Classicism, of Renaissance derivation, were often preferred. In London the Italian 'palazzo' model was adopted for the Travellers' Club (1829–31) and the Reform Club (1837–41), both by Sir Charles Barry (1795–1860), while in Paris the conventions of French Renaissance architecture were apparent in schemes such as the Rue de Rivoli (west) (1811–35) by Charles Percier (1764–1838) and Pierre François Léonard Fontaine (1762–1853) (see Chapter 30). The Library of S. Geneviève, Paris (1839–50), by Pierre-François-Henri Labrouste (1801–75), represents a more radical development of Renaissance formulae, and is a triumph of rational eclecticism. In Germany, under the influence of Durand, there was a preference for more sharply articulated buildings, often characterised by round-arched forms which might suggest Renaissance, Romanesque, Byzantine or Roman precedents. The Friedenskirche, Potsdam (1845–8), by Ludwig Persius (1803–45), is an Early Christian example of this 'Rundbogenstil'.

In northern Europe the taste for Gothic, which was part of the legacy of the eighteenth century, had strong national associations, and during the nineteenth century knowledge of mediaeval architecture steadily improved through the publication of such studies as *An Attempt to Discriminate the Styles of English Architecture from the Conquest to the Reformation* (1817) by Thomas Rickman (1776–1841). In France the writer Prosper Mérimée (1803–70) was appointed Inspector General of National Monuments and Historical Antiquities in 1834, and his protégé, Eugène-Emmanuel Viollet-le-Duc (1814–79) was responsible for an enormous amount of restoration and reconstruction work on mediaeval monuments, including the S. Chapelle (1840) and Notre Dame, Paris (1845–56). In Germany a concern with the mediaeval past is seen in the completion of Cologne Cathedral as a national monument: restoration work began in 1824, and construction continued from 1833 under E. F. Zwirner (1802–61) until its completion in 1880 by R. Voigtel (1829–1902).

The British contribution to the Gothic Revival was in many ways the most significant and included the New Palace of Westminster or Houses of Parliament (1836–68) by Sir Charles Barry, a magnificent national symbol which was the outcome of a competition in which 'Gothic or Elizabethan' styles were stipulated. Barry's Classical inclination can be seen in the general arrangement of the building, but the details were largely the work of A. W. N. Pugin (1812–52), a passionate Gothicist, whose book *Contrasts* (1836) devastatingly compared the meagre designs of the day – both Classical and Gothic – with the richness of late mediaeval buildings. Pugin brought a new moral fervour to nineteenth-century architecture, asserting that Gothic was the only truly Christian form of architecture, and condemning Classical styles as pagan. His desire for a return to the ritual of mediaeval worship led to the creation of churches with separate chancels and processional aisles – as, for example, at S. Wilfrid, Hulme (1839–42). Such features became axiomatic for the influential Ecclesiological Society. Pugin's attitude to architecture was both romantic and rational, combining a liking for irregularity with the desire for a consistent expression of structure, and a natural outcome of this was the 'Picturesque utility' of buildings such as the Vicarage, Coalpitheath (1844–5), by William Butterfield (1814–1900).

The predominant architectural tone of the period after about 1830 was one of earnestness. The town halls and museums of the Greek Revival were redolent of nobility and Classical learning, while the application of monumental Greek, Roman or Egyptian forms to railway stations, bridges and factories suggested a desire to compare nineteenth-century technological achievements with the greatest civilisations of the past. The Gothic Revival was dedicated to different ideals, but was no less serious, and implicitly challenged the utilitarian elements of the age by a reassertion of Christian and national values. Only in domestic building of the period is a more indulgent attitude likely to be apparent as, for instance, in the mixture of Elizabethan and Baroque at Harlaxton Hall (1834–55), or the lavish eclecticism of Hluboká (1840–71).

In all this, almost regardless of style, there was a tendency to emphasise solidity of structure. The concern for structure had been encouraged by Jean-Baptiste Rondelet (1734–1829), whose five-volume *Traité théorique et pratique de l'art de bâtir* (1802–3). emphasised the scientific basis of architecture, and A. W. N. Pugin, whose *True Principles of*

Pointed or Christian Architecture (1841) insisted that if ornament were introduced it 'should consist of enrichment of the essential construction of the building.' Increasingly, brickwork was left exposed rather than rendered, and the flimsy Gothic of the eighteenth century was rejected. Even in iron there was a shift from the more decorative treatment – for instance, of the Conservatory, Carlton House (1811–12) – to one which emphasised the distinctive structural properties of the material – as at the Crystal Palace of 1850–1.

1850–70

The period 1850–70 coincides roughly with the French Second Empire and the High Victorian phase of British architecture. Although neo-Classical buildings continued to be built at this time, for instance by Alexander 'Greek' Thomson (1817–75), in Glasgow, it was the Renaissance Revival which was predominant. The new richness which this mode signalled was largely French in inspiration, and the characteristic features were pavilions, high mansard roofs, and opulent decoration of fifteenth- or sixteenth-century origin. The fashion can be attributed at least in part to the building of the New Louvre (1852–7), while the Paris Opéra (1861–74) by Jean-Louis-Charles Garnier (1825–98) marked a step towards further richness that was almost neo-Baroque. Equivalent developments in other countries are indicated by Leeds Town Hall (1853–9) – the work of Cuthbert Brodrick (1822–1905) – and Národní Divadlo, Prague (1868–83), by Josef Zítek (1832–1909). One strength of the Renaissance revival was its versatility: it supplied a suitable hierarchy of ornament for large blocks such as Theophil Hansen's Heinrichshof, Vienna (1861–3; destroyed 1945), and could also be employed in situations as various as the Galleria Vittorio Emanuele, Milan (1865–77), by Giuseppe Mengoni (1827–77), or the asymmetrical Foreign Office, London (1861–3), by Sir George Gilbert Scott.

In almost all European countries there was an increase in the number of Gothic churches as the Gothic Revival gathered pace after 1850. In some cases the new churches embodied the same attitudes as the earlier generation of neo-Gothic designs: the Votivkirche in Vienna (1856–79) by Heinrich von Ferstel (1828–83) is a good example of such conservatism. But in Britain, particularly, the revival developed a new character as the dependence on native Gothic forms was superseded by a strong interest in the mediaeval architecture of Italy (and subsequently France and other countries), stimulated by such publications as *The Stones of Venice* (1851–3), by John Ruskin (1819–1900) and *Brick and Marble of the Middle Ages* (1855) by George Edmund Street (1824–81).

An immediate sign of this new spirit was the use of 'constructional polychromy', bands of different coloured brick or stone emulating the decorative effect of different marbles in the North Italian churches admired by Ruskin. An early example was All Saints, Margaret Street, London (1849–59), by William Butterfield, but almost equally striking was Street's S. James-the-Less, Vauxhall Bridge Road, London (1859–61), which has a detached campanile of Italian inspiration.

Gothic was increasingly used for secular purposes, and the Oxford Museum (1855–9) by Deane and Woodward also reflects Ruskin's influence, while in later examples, such as Manchester Assize Courts (1859–64) by Alfred Waterhouse (1830–1905) or Sir George Gilbert Scott's S. Pancras Hotel, London, (1865–71), the Gothic ingredients include more disparate influences. French Gothic was an important source for William Burges (1827–81), whose recreation of Castell Coch, near Cardiff (1875–91), compares favourably with the restoration of Carcassonne (1855–79), and Pierrefonds (1859–70), by Viollet-le-Duc. Indeed, Viollet-le-Duc's own designs (such as S. Denys-de-l'Estrée, S. Denis, of 1864–7), are rarely more than worthy, although his interpretation of Gothic in terms of structural rationalism was extremely influential through the publication of his *Dictionnaire raisonné de l'architecture française du XIme au XVIme siècle* (1854–68), and his *Entretiens sur l'architecture* (1863–72) seems to suggest more daring architectural forms.

In many ways the architecture of the 1850s and 1860s was less restrictive than that of the preceding decades. Unlike the stricter Greek Revival, the Renaissance Revival was essentially permissive and provided a range of motifs which could be used on buildings of all shapes and sizes; the Gothicists, relieved of narrow nationalism, were able to take a more eclectic attitude to mediaeval sources. There was a reaction against the purer forms and monotonous surfaces of neo-Classicism, leading to generally livelier and more plastic effects, and in the Gothic Revival surface interest was supplied by new combinations of colours and textures.

Another aspect of the more liberal spirit of this period is the shift away from a preoccupation with temples and cathedrals as it became increasingly common to admire domestic buildings of the past, be it the Louvre of François I or the Ca d'Oro in Venice. Indeed, one new development of these years sprang directly from an interest in relatively humble houses. The 'Old English' manner adopted by Richard Norman Shaw (1831–1912) arose from an interest in vernacular materials and motifs, which he employed in country houses of irregular plan and outline to achieve highly picturesque effects.

Shaw's 'Old English' style is one aspect of the reaction against urban and industrial development, and it was in the period after 1850 that many European cities experienced radical changes.

Paris was virtually replanned by Baron Eugène Georges Haussmann (1809–91), who cut ruthlessly through the old city with enormous avenues and provided impressive settings for prestigious buildings such as the Opéra (q.v.), without neglecting practical facilities such as the markets of the Halles Centrales (begun 1853). The intention was to create a capital worthy of the Second Empire and, with memories of the 1848 revolution still fresh, to ensure that it could be adequately controlled by police and troops.

A similar desire for imperial prestige and civil order was apparent in Vienna where the young Emperor Franz Josef I ordered the building of the Ringstrasse (begun 1858) on the site of the old city walls. The new road, designed by Christian Friedrich Ludwig von Förster (1797–1863), was gradually embellished with buildings in a panoply of styles, including the neo-Renaissance Heinrichshof (1861–3; destroyed 1945) by Theophil Hansen, the polychromatic Army Museum (1856–77), by Förster and Hansen in a style reminiscent of Byzantine, and the enormous red-brick neo-Gothic Rathaus (1872–83) by Friedrich von Schmidt (1825–91).

Among other cities which were much enriched at this time was Budapest, the second capital of the Austro-Hungarian Empire, while in 1859 the expansion of Barcelona was planned by Ildefons Cerdà (1815–76), with an ambitious scheme of grid form, intersected by two diagonal avenues.

1870–1900

The period from 1870 to 1900 covers the early period of the German Second Reich and the Late Victorian phase of British architecture. It is marked by a steady increase in the pace of architectural change, a broadening of the range of structural and stylistic possibilities, and the swan-song of historicism, trends which continue to develop after 1900.

A Baroque richness and imperial scale was often maintained for major buildings such as the Berlin Reichstag (1884–94), by Paul Wallot (1841–1912), or Ludwig II's Herrenchiemsee (begun 1878) by Georg von Dollmann (1830–95). In many places the Baroque tradition continued until the early twentieth century, and in Britain especially it gained a new vigour by an infusion of Picturesque influences, as in the case of Colchester Town Hall (1898–1902) by John Belcher (1841–1913). Quite counter to this was the tendency to turn to antique Classicism, as signalled by the Victor Emmanuel II Monument, Rome (1885–1911) and the rise of a more ordered Beaux-Arts spirit in buildings such as the Petit Palais, Paris (1897–1900), by Charles Girault (1851–1932). The British architect Sir John James Burnet (1857–1938), who had trained at the Ecole des Beaux-Arts in Paris, is characteristic of a number of architects at this time who developed a sort of 'stripped Classical' manner which was readily compatible with steel-framed structures, for instance in his Kodak House, London (1910–11). In a similar way the Austrian architect Otto Wagner (1841–1918) distilled from the Classical tradition an essentially non-historicist manner, as exemplified in the banking hall of the Post Office Savings Bank, Vienna (1904–6). (For detailed descriptions of buildings after 1900 see Chapter 44.)

The Gothic Revival was by no means a spent force after 1870, and provided the basis of much church architecture until well into the twentieth century. The air of scholarly refinement, as in the churches of John Loughborough Pearson (1817–97) – for instance, Truro Cathedral (1879–1910) – was gradually superseded by a more licentious Gothic, such as in Holy Trinity, Chelsea (1888–91), by John Dando Sedding (1838–91), or the Rylands Library, Manchester (1890–9), by Basil Champneys (1842–1935). Elsewhere the more rationalist influence of Viollet-le-Duc was apparent, and new effects were achieved through a reinterpretation of the structural principles of Gothic architecture. At S. Jean-de-Montmartre, Paris, designed in 1894 by Joseph-Eugène-Anatole de Baudot (1834–1915), the flat profiles of the piers and ribs express the use of reinforced concrete and bricks, while at S. Andrew, Roker (1905–7), by Edward Schroeder Prior (1852–1932), concrete was used in conjunction with irregular masonry to create a more rudimentary kind of Gothic. Most radical of all, perhaps, was Gaudí's Sagrada Familia, Barcelona (begun 1882), in which the structural rationalism of Viollet-le-Duc was only the starting point for an almost organic architecture, as richly suggestive as any monument of the Middle Ages.

It is in some ways surprising that European architecture of the late nineteenth century was not more affected by the increasing knowledge of architecture from distant parts of the world. In fact European countries tended to export architectural taste to their imperial outposts, and examples of importation at this time (such as the Indian-style Durbar Room added to Osborne House in 1890–1 for Queen Victoria) were exceptional. There was an undercurrent of Japanese influence in the aestheticism of the White House, Chelsea (1877–9) by E. W. Godwin, and in church-building there was a certain interest in Byzantine architecture, ranging from the Sacré Coeur, Paris (begun 1875), by Paul Abadie (1812–84), to Westminster Cathedral (1895–1903), by John Francis Bentley (1839–1902).

What commanded more attention, however, were the native traditions of the various parts of Europe, and especially those outside the well-known categories of mainstream Classicism, Gothic, or Italian Renaissance. The vernacular revival in Britain was an early instance of this phenomenon, providing a range of relatively informal motifs for houses not only in the 'Old English' spirit (see above) but also in the so-called 'Queen Anne' style, as at Kinmel Park (1868–74), by William Eden Nesfield (1835–88). Similarly, in many other countries a range of styles was developed which avoided the Classical/Gothic dichotomy of earlier decades, and enabled architects to give a predominantly local character to buildings while not excluding features from other sources. The Rijksmuseum in Amsterdam (1877–85), by P.J. H. Cuijpers (1827–1921), with its strong flavour of the Dutch Renaissance, is a clear illustration of that tendency, and the former Prague Waterworks of 1883 by Antonin Wiehl (1835–1907) is another.

The turning towards native architectural traditions was often associated with a wider desire for national or regional identity. Gaudí's work in Barcelona, for instance, can be seen as part of a renewed consciousness of Catalan culture, while the revival of simple timber architecture by Dušan Jurkovič (1868–1947) was part of a Slavonic regionalism. The movement for cultural independence in Scandinavia was called National Romanticism, and it found varied architectural expression, ranging from the relatively eclectic design for Copenhagen Town Hall (1892–1902), by Martin Nyrop (1849–1921), to the simpler motifs of the Grundtvig Church, Copenhagen (designed 1913), by Peder Vilhelm Jensen Klint (1853–1930). There was a revival of rustic Scandinavian vernacular forms and of emphatically rugged masonry – as, for instance, in Tampere Cathedral (1899–1907), by Lars Sonck (1870–1956). Paradoxically, much of this regionalist architecture may have been inspired by the American 'Shingle Style', by the more massive quasi-Romanesque work of H. H. Richardson, and by the English Arts and Crafts movement which inherited from Ruskin and Pugin a concern for the 'honest' use of building materials, and added to this a feeling for vernacular traditions. E. S. Prior's The Barn, Exmouth, (1896–7), is an important example of this development.

It is possible to see the vernacular revivals of the late nineteenth century as a late flowering of the Picturesque movement, but it is also true that there grew from them more ordered kinds of architecture. For instance, the dour masonry of Glasgow School of Art (1897–1909), by Charles Rennie Mackintosh (1868–1928), is strongly suggestive of traditional Scottish building, and similarly the unashamed use of brick in the Amsterdam Stock Exchange (1898–1903), by Hendrik Petrus Berlage (1856–1934), declares the architect's sympathy for indigenous materials. But both buildings eschew the primitivistic tendency of the Arts and Crafts movement, and boldly incorporate iron and glass in structures whose rationalism is an equivalent of Otto Wagner's in the Post Office Savings Bank in Vienna. A similar movement away from the Picturesque can be observed in smaller buildings such as the Eagle Insurance Building, Birmingham (1899–1900), by William Richard Lethaby (1857–1931), and Upmeads, Stafford (1908) (see Chapter 44), by Edgar Wood (1860–1935).

The most distinctive architectural development of the 1890s was Art Nouveau, a style not based on any architecture of the past, but characterised by irregular, organic curves and generally tendril-or flame-like lines. The name 'Art Nouveau' was derived from a shop which Samuel Bing opened in Paris in 1895, selling craftware and works of art, and it is mainly to the fine and applied arts that one has to look for the origins of the style.

In architecture it was pioneered by the Brussels architect Victor Horta (1861–1947), who combined swirling Art Nouveau decoration with structural ironwork to create buildings of dynamic form and unfettered interiors, such as the Hôtel Tassel (1892–3) and the Maison du Peuple (1896–8). Horta's counterpart in France was Hector Guimard (1867–1942), who employed the flowing lines of Art Nouveau for the prefabricated ironwork of the Paris Métro stations (1900–1), while in Barcelona Antoni Gaudí (1852–1926) created buildings of biomorphic plasticity, including the Casa Batlló (1904–6), and the Casa Milá (1905–10). Elsewhere the widespread influence of Art Nouveau was to be found in interior design, such as Mackintosh's Willow Tea-Rooms, Glasgow (1902–4), and in the use of sinuous surface ornament such as embellished the Elvira photographic studio, Munich (1897–8), by August Endell (1871–1925). In a more general way Art Nouveau was associated with a preference for curved outline, as in the Rotunda of the 1902 Turin exhibition by Raimondo d'Aronco (1857–1932).

In the thirty years which preceded World War I the problems of urban expansion affected Europe more acutely than ever before. In Britain a number of progressive industrialists created model villages, such as Port Sunlight (begun 1888), Bournville (from 1895), and New Earswick (begun 1902), with houses of generally Tudor spirit picturesquely arranged in green surroundings. This tradition came to be linked with the theories of Ebenezer Howard (1850–1928), whose *Tomorrow: a Peaceful Path to Real Reform* (1898) advocated the creation of 'garden cities' of limited size, combining the virtues of urban and rural life. Letchworth, begun in 1903, was the only true garden city (with a variety of industries) to be built before 1914, but the movement was more widely influential, especially in the creation of what were in effect garden suburbs as at Hampstead, near London (from 1906), or Hellerau, near Dresden (begun 1906). Although such developments were clearly designed in contrast to the regular terraced streets of British cities and the blocks of flats common in continental Europe, their picturesqueness was often modified in execution by the return to more formal architectural values. Thus, for instance, the centre of Hampstead Garden Suburb was laid out with neo-Georgian symmetry by Edwin Lutyens (1869–1944), while at

Hellerau Heinrich Tessenow (1876–1950) introduced a new regularity into his designs for the public hall and some of the houses.

Examples

1830–50

The **Biblioteka Raczyńskich, Poznań** (1822–9) (p. 1097A), with its calculated rhythm and reduced number of architectural motifs, is in the tradition of 'simple' Rational Classicism, generally held to have begun with the east facade of the Louvre of the late seventeenth century. It is also an example of the patronage of a Polish nobleman, Edward Raczyński, in a town which had recently been acquired by Prussia, as well as demonstrating the efforts of private patrons to provide educational facilities for a wide public.

The **Palais de Justice, Lyon** (1835–42) by Louis-Pierre Baltard (1764–1846), exemplifies the kind of Rational Classicism which was promoted at the Ecole des Beaux-Arts in Paris, where Baltard taught. Its giant colonnade of twenty-four Corinthian columns is punctuated only by the slightly wider central inter-columniation. The concourse is equally imposing but offers variety with its sequence of domed spaces.

Thorwaldsen Museum, Copenhagen (1839–48), (p. 1097B), by M. G. B. Bindesbøll (1800–56), a pupil of the neo-Classicist Christian Frederik Hansen (1756–1845), was built to house the work and collections of the Danish sculptor Bertil (Alberto) Thorwaldsen (1770–1844). Greek Revival in spirit, the bold severity of its astylar forms recalls the work of Schinkel, and to some extent Egyptian architecture, especially in the internal courtyards. The barrel-vaulted ceilings of the galleries are decorated in the Pompeian style, while on the external walls murals by Jøorgen Sonne (1801–90), depict the transportation of the contents of the museum from Rome.

The **Old Palace, Athens**, (1837–41), (p. 1098A), by Friedrich von Gärtner (1792–1847), now used as the Parliament building, was designed for Otto von Wittelsbach on his accession to the Greek throne. The three-storey building achieves a forceful effect by the use of a simple incisive fenestration pattern, and on the principal facade a three-bay pedimented central element with a sturdy unpedimented single-storey Greek Doric decastyle portico, flanked by seven-bay wings.

The **University, Athens** (1839–49), by Hans Christian Hansen (1803–83), is a carefully designed neo-Classical building with a facade of Schinkelesque inspiration and an impressive Ionic-columned hall. It was later flanked by the Ionic buildings of the **Academy** (1859–87) and the Doric **National Library** (1859, 1888–91), which were designed by Theophil Hansen (1813–1891), to create one of the most remarkable set-pieces of the Greek Revival.

S. George's Hall, Liverpool (1840–54), (p. 1097C), by Harvey Lonsdale Elmes, is one of the most magnificent neo-Classical monuments in Britain. Elmes succeeded in winning two separate competitions for a concert hall and for assize courts for Liverpool in 1839 and 1840. Subsequently the accommodation was combined in this one design. The planning is strongly axial, but satisfies the complex requirements ingeniously, and the different elements are freely expressed externally. The exterior reveals Elmes's knowledge of Schinkel's work, while the great hall takes its inspiration from the Baths of Caracalla in Rome. After Elmes's death in 1847 the building was completed by the engineer Sir Robert Rawlinson (1810–98) and by Charles Robert Cockerell (1788–1863), who was responsible for the sumptuous decoration of the circular concert room.

The **Fitzwilliam Museum, Cambridge** (1837–47) (p.1099A), is by George Basevi (1794–1845). Its giant Corinthian portico is extended by short colonnades with rich corner pavilions which give an almost Baroque sense of display to the facade, in marked contrast to the plain side elevations. The interior was completed by C. R. Cockerell after Basevi's death, and Edward Middleton Barry (1830–80) further enriched the staircase hall in 1870–75.

The **Ashmolean Museum (University Galleries)** and **Taylorian Institution, Oxford** (1841–5), by C. R. Cockerell, is a building which combines Classical features of different periods in a most original manner. The central block has a portico of Ionic columns with capitals derived from those at the Temple of Apollo Epicurius, Bassae (q.v.), which Cockerell had been one of the first to study. The high wings break forward to the street and culminate on the east side with a composition of detached columns carrying statues, as on a Roman triumphal arch. The whole composition, which is made more varied by the use of yellowish stone with white stone dressings, is tied together with a bold entablature.

The **New Palace of Westminster (Houses of Parliament), London** (1836–68) (p.1098B). The Old Palace of Westminster was destroyed by fire in 1834, and in 1836 the design by Sir Charles Barry was selected from those submitted in the architectural competition for the New Palace. A non-Classical design had been forced upon Barry by the competition conditions, and he had obtained the expert assistance of A. W. N. Pugin for the Tudor detail of the building. Three important trends emerged from the design: the authentic Gothic detail, supplied by Pugin, reflects the antiquarian character of the contemporary Gothic Revival; the formal but not fully symmetrical planning by Barry, which had to

A. Biblioteka Raczyńskich, Poznań (1822–9). See p. 1096

B. Thorwaldsen Museum, Copenhagen (1839–48). See p. 1096

C. S. George's Hall, Liverpool (1840–54), with ground plan. See p. 1096

1. S. George's Hall
2. Crown Court
3. Nisi Prius Court
4. Sheriff's Court
5. Vice Chancellor's Court

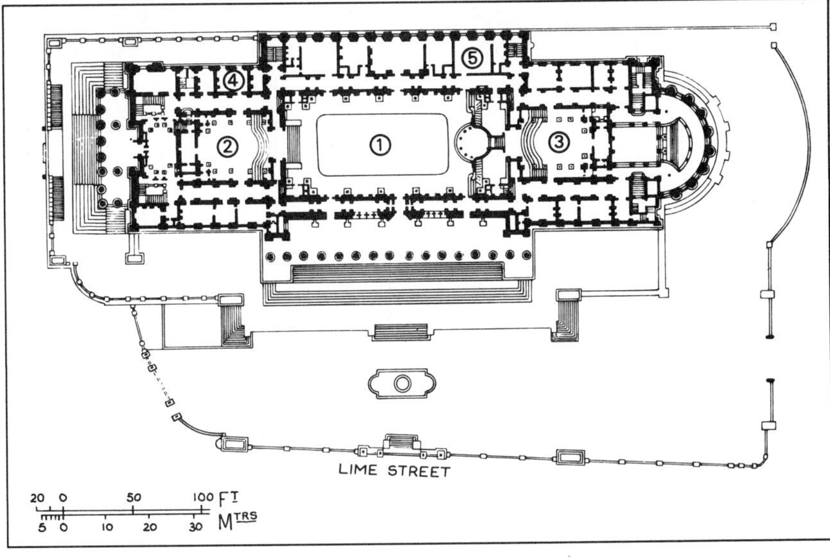

A. Old Palace, Athens (1837–41). See p. 1096

B. Palace of Westminster (Houses of Parliament), London (1836–68), with plan of principal floor. See p. 1096

1. Westminster Hall
2. S. Stephen's Hall
3. Central Hall
4. House of Commons
5. House of Peers
6. Star Chamber Court
7. Court of Cloisters
8. S. Stephen's Court
9. Judge's Court
10. Chancellor's Court
11. Royal Gallery
12. Royal Court
13. Peers' Court
14. Peers' Inner Court
15. Commons Inner Court
16. Commons Court
17. Speaker's Court

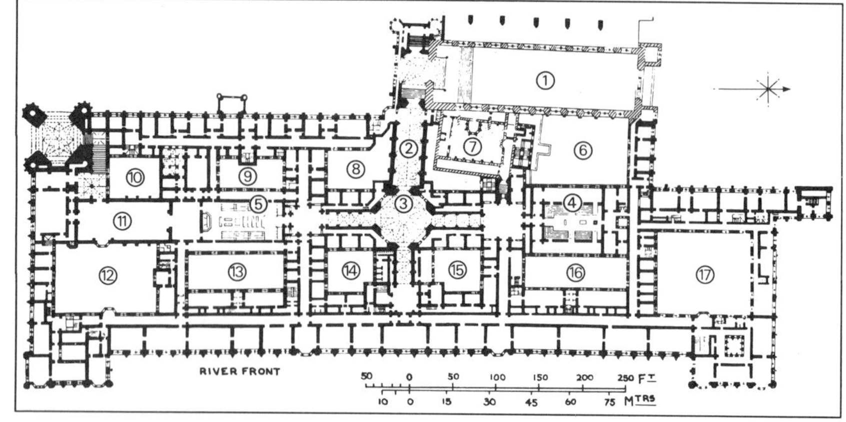

A. Fitzwilliam Museum, Cambridge (1837–47). See p. 1096

B. National Gallery of Scotland, Edinburgh (1850–4). See p. 1100

accommodate the surviving Westminster Hall, reveals the continuing potency of Classicism; and the informal, irregular grouping of the towers and skyline, especially when seen from the riverside, is eloquent testimony to the value still attached to the concept of the Picturesque. Because these three strands are so inextricably combined, the Houses of Parliament summarise the developments of several previous decades, and is significant as the first major public building of the Gothic Revival.

The formal approach from the west or landward side is through S. Stephen's Porch, which also gives access to Westminster Hall, and into the Central Hall, where a cross-axis leads south to the House of Lords and north to the House of Commons. Subsidiary suites of chambers are arranged around a series of courts. In the south-west corner the massive Victoria Tower rises 102 m (336 ft) high, and at the northern end is the Clock Tower, 96 m (316 ft) high, housing 'Big Ben'. There is a further 'Middle Tower' or spired lantern over the Central Hall, rising to 91 m (300 ft) in height. To reduce the likelihood of a repetition of the 1834 fire, the New Palace was constructed with iron joists and roofed with cast-iron plates.

The **Palace of the Congress, Madrid** (1843–50), by Narciso Pascual y Colomer (1808–70), represents the conservative tendencies of Spanish architecture at this time. A Palladian composition, the main facade is dominated by a powerful Roman Corinthian hexastyle portico which is flanked by two wings with rusticated ground floors, string courses, main cornices and low attic storeys, the general character being one of quiet dignity.

The **Central Station, Newcastle** (1847–50) (p.1101A), mostly by John Dobson (1787–1865), has an arcaded portico set in front of curved iron roofs over the platforms, and forms part of the Victorian development of central Newcastle with its handsome Classical streets. Dobson's other buildings include the **Royal Arcade, Newcastle** (1831–2; demolished 1963) (p. 1101B), and also churches and country houses which display a variety of styles – the Gothic Revival at **S. Thomas's Church, Newcastle** (1828–9), and **Beaufront Castle, Northumberland** (1837–41), and the neo-Classical at **Nunnykirk, Northumberland** (1825), and **Meldon Park, Northumberland** (1832).

The **National Gallery of Scotland, Edinburgh** (1850–4) (p. 1099B), by William Henry Playfair (1790–1857), is one of the numerous monumental Greek Revival buildings with which the city was endowed in the early decades of the nineteenth century. This, with the **Royal College of Physicians** (1844–6) by Thomas Hamilton (1785–1858), is a remarkably late example of the style for a major work. The National Gallery is in the Ionic style, while the adjacent **Royal Scottish Institution** (1822–36), also by Playfair, is a rather overladen essay in Greek Doric.

The **Caffè Pedrocchi, Padua** (1816–31) (p. 1102A), by Giuseppe Jappelli (1783–1852) and Antonio Gradenigo (1806–84), is an inventive and elegant neo-Classical design with an open, two-storey Corinthian loggia at first-floor level and, at street level, flanking twin pavilions in the Greek Doric style. Later, Jappelli designed for the building a small but elaborate neo-Gothic wing, **Il Pedrocchino** (completed 1842), an unusually early example of this style in Italy.

The **Travellers' Club, Pall Mall, London** (1829–31) (p. 1102B), by Sir Charles Barry, is one of the designs with which he initiated the Renaissance Revival and the 'palazzo' mode in England. The two-storey stuccoed facade of five regular bays is made asymmetrical by the location of the main entrance in an end bay. The storeys are divided by a deep string-course and capped by a projecting cornice. The external corners are emphasised by toothed quoins, and the windows are framed, the upper ones being made dominant by balustrades, pediments and flanking pilasters. All the Renaissance apparatus, said to be derived here from the Palazzo Pandolfini, Florence (q.v.), is deployed with refined skill.

The **Reform Club, Pall Mall, London** (1837–41) (p. 1102C), also by Sir Charles Barry, adjoins his Travellers' Club and is a similar but more imposing design: it is stone-faced, three storeys high and nine bays long, with a central entrance. The link to the Travellers' Club is managed neatly by a recessed two-storey bay. It is planned around a central saloon (in place of the Italian cortile), with rooms opening from it in such a way that the saloon and the rooms conform to axial principles. The Renaissance features are treated more confidently than before, with half-columns to the first-floor windows and a bolder cornice. The attic windows are framed by astragal mouldings and embraced in a frieze beneath the cornice.

Barry's **Athenaeum, Manchester** (1837–9), is a similar variant on the palazzo theme, which he further developed at **Bridgewater House, London** (1846–51) (p. 1103A), a town house of grand scale. It was planned on the cortile principle and was distinguished externally by a more vigorous expression of rustication (especially at the quoins) than was normal in Barry's earlier works, giving an effect of massiveness and strength.

The **Bristol Branch of the Bank of England** (1844–6) (p. 1103B) was designed by C. R. Cockerell, who was appointed architect to the Bank of England in 1833 in succession to Sir John Soane. He carried out alterations to the Bank of England, London, in 1834–35 and 1845, and also built branches at **Plymouth** (1842), **Manchester** (1844–5) and **Liverpool** (1844–7) (p. 1103C). These distinguished designs are variations on a theme which Cockerell introduced in his **Westminster Life and British Fire Office, London** (1831–2; demolished

A. Central Station, Newcastle: interior (1850). See p. 1100

B. Royal Arcade, Newcastle (1831–2). See p. 1100

A. Caffè Pedrocchi, Padua (1816–31). See p. 1100

B. Travellers' Club, Pall Mall, London (1829–31). See p. 1100

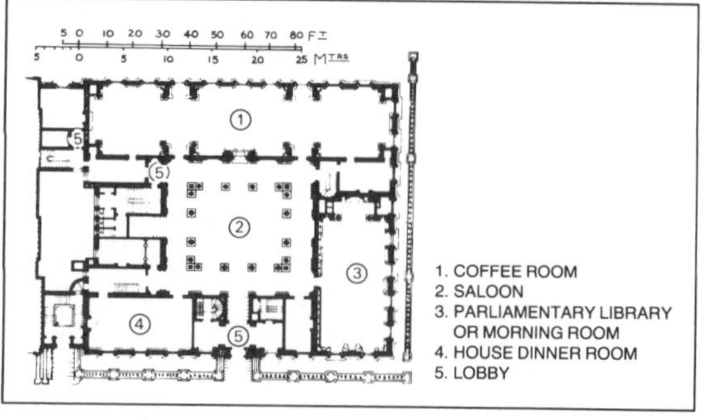

C. Reform Club, Pall Mall, London, with plan (1837–41). See p. 1100

A. Bridgewater House, London (1846–51). See p. 1100

B. Bristol Branch of the Bank of England (1844–6). See p. 1100

C. Liverpool Branch of the Bank of England (1844–7). See p. 1100

A. Clifton Suspension Bridge, Bristol (1830–63). See p. 1105

B. Entrance Screen, Euston Station, London (1835–7). See p. 1105

C. Temple Mill, Leeds (1842). See p. 1105

1908). The two lower storeys are marked by an engaged Doric portico, while a third storey separates the entablature from the pediment. Renaissance devices are employed to introduce as many windows as were necessary in these city-centre buildings. All of these elements are set within a powerful, strongly modelled, geometrical arrangement which Cockerell executed with great precision and masterly clarity.

The **Clifton Suspension Bridge, Bristol** (1830–63) (p. 1104A), designed by Isambard Kingdom Brunel (1806–59), a versatile and imaginative engineer, was carried out contrary to the recommendation of Thomas Telford (1757–1834) who, as a result of the near destruction of his recently built **Menai Suspension Bridge** (1819–26) by crosswinds, doubted the advisability of erecting a suspension bridge of this size in such an exposed position. The principal span of 214 m (702 ft) seems even more daring because of the 76 m (250 ft) deep gorge. It was characteristic of the period that Brunel sought to match the grandeur of the setting with a noble design, and the pylons (which were to have had sphinxes and hieroglyphic decoration) were of Egyptian inspiration. The bridge was delayed for lack of funds and was completed after Brunel's death using chains from another of his works, the **Hungerford Suspension Bridge, London** (1841–5).

The **Entrance Screen, Euston Station, London** (1835–7) (p. 1104B), designed by Philip Hardwick (1792–1870) as a triumphal arch in the form of a massive Greek Doric propylaeum, marked the terminus of the London and Birmingham Railway. It was destroyed in 1961/2 for the reconstruction of the station. The Greek Order chosen by Hardwick represented an already dying fashion in London, and in the later station building of 1846–9 Hardwick, assisted by his son P. C. Hardwick (1822–92), chose the Graeco-Roman style. The great hall, now demolished also, was a notable example of this style.

Temple Mill, Leeds (1842) (p. 1104C), was built as a flax-spinning factory with monumental facades by Joseph Bonomi, Junior (1796–1878), whose knowledge of Egyptian temples was employed here because of the connection between Egypt and cotton. The office wing is more ornate than the main block. The single-storey building covers almost two acres and has iron columns supporting a network of brick vaults and glass domes, a structure probably designed by the engineer, James Combe. To help maintain the humidity required for the spinning process, the roof was covered with turf on which sheep reputedly were allowed to graze.

The **Gare de l'Est, Paris** (1847–52), by François-Alexandre Duquesney (1790–1849) (p. 1106A), was one of the finest of the early railway terminals, but has been greatly altered and enlarged. Its central gable with a large semicircular window expressed the great iron-and-glass train shed behind, while two neo-Renaissance wings marked the axes of the arrival and departure platforms. A broad arcaded concourse enabled passengers to move freely from one side of the station to another. The central gable, crowned by the symbolic figure of Strasbourg, provided the focal point for Haussmann's Boulevard de Strasbourg.

King's Cross Station, London (1850–2) (p. 1106B), by Lewis Cubitt (1799–1883), consists of two arched sheds (originally one for arrivals and one for departures) expressed in the vast stock-brick arches of the facade. An Italianate clock-tower rises from the centre, and triple-arcaded porticoes originally stood below the great arches, giving a Roman scale and dignity to the unpretentious composition. The iron-and-glass sheds, each of which has a span of 32 m (105 ft), are supported on steel arches which replaced the original laminated timber arches in 1869.

The **Conservatory, Carlton House, London** (1811–12; demolished 1827–8) (p. 1107A), by Thomas Hopper (1776–1856), although pre-dating this period, illustrates the use of cast iron for structural and decorative purposes – structural in the columns and decorative in the fan-vaulting and tracery.

S. George, Everton, Liverpool (1812–14) (p. 1107B), by Thomas Rickman, and with ironwork by the ironmaster John Cragg, is one of the two churches which were built in this manner in the locality, and represents a potentially systematic use of iron for architectural purposes. The character of the Gothic design is reminiscent of the eighteenth century rather than expressive of the nineteenth century.

The **Conservatory, Chatsworth, Derbyshire** (1836–40; demolished 1920) (p. 1109A), was an early venture in iron and glass by the gardener Sir Joseph Paxton (1803–65), assisted by Decimus Burton (1800–81), in the grounds of the Duke of Devonshire's mansion. It was of unprecedented magnitude, being 84 m (277 ft) long and 37 m (123 ft) wide, rising to a height of 20.4 m (67 ft) in the centre. The arched principals were of laminated timber, and the glass was arranged in a ridge-and-furrow system which anticipated the Crystal Palace.

The **Palm House, Kew Gardens, London** (1845–7) (p. 1109B), by Decimus Burton and Richard Turner (1798–1881), has a central section similar to the Chatsworth design except that all the glass smoothly follows the double vault section and the structure is not of wood, but an ingenious combination of wrought- and cast-iron. The building is 110 m (362 ft) long, and in the centre rises to a height of 18.9 m (62 ft) and spans 32 m (106 ft).

The **Coal Exchange, Lower Thames Street, London** (1846–9; demolished 1962–3) (p. 1110A), was by J. B. Bunning (1802–63), architect to the City of London. Behind an Italian Renaissance masonry exterior was a cast-iron rotunda, its ribs supporting a glazed dome 22.5 m (74 ft) high. Cantilevered balconies gave access to offices on the upper three floors, and panels depicted coal fossils and mining scenes.

A. Gare de l'Est, Paris (1847–52). See p. 1105

B. King's Cross Station, London (1850–2). See p. 1105

A. Conservatory, Carlton House, London (1811–12; demolished 1827–8). See p. 1105

B. S. George, Everton, Liverpool (1812–14). See p. 1105

C. Library of S. Geneviève, Paris (1844–50). See p. 1105

The **Library of S. Geneviève, Paris** (design begun 1839; built 1844–50) (p. 1107C), by Labrouste, has a distinguished neo-Renaissance exterior which expresses the division between the relatively low ground floor stack rooms and offices and the long reading room above. The reading room is memorably lofty, spanned by two long barrel vaults with scrolled iron arches springing from a central line of slender cast-iron columns. A low-pitched, metal outer roof covers the full width of the building and the iron construction is disclosed by iron ties discreetly incorporated into the masonry of the facade. The building served as a model for the Boston Public Library (1887–8), designed by McKim, Mead and White.

The **Crystal Palace London** (1850–1) (p. 1111A,B), by Paxton, was one of the most remarkable buildings of the nineteenth century, and the culmination of early Victorian technology. It was designed to house the Great Exhibition in Hyde Park, and was moved to Sydenham in 1852–4. The idea of holding a great exhibition was conceived in 1849, and public subscriptions were invited. An international competition was launched in 1850, and 245 schemes were received. None was acceptable, and with limited time available all were set aside in favour of an idea of Paxton's, after an attempt to combine the best features of the more promising of the competition designs in a single official project. The working drawings were hurriedly prepared in a seven-week period after the letting of the contract in August 1850, and the structure was wholly completed nine months later on 1 May 1851, each structural component having been tested before erection.

Paxton's idea, arising from his experience at Chatsworth and elsewhere, was for a giant conservatory with a cast-iron frame and the ridge-and-furrow glazing system he had developed for the Chatsworth conservatory. In cross section the building somewhat resembled a double-aisled basilica, rising in three tiers, the lowest 124.4 m (408 ft) wide, the next (the inner aisles) 80.4 m (264 ft) and the nave or topmost 36.5 m (120 ft). However, the 'aisles' and 'nave' were divided from one another by tiered open galleries 7.3 m (24 ft) wide, so that the actual span of the 'nave' was only 22 m (72 ft), the same as its height. Symbolically, the total width was made up of fifty-one of the 2.4 m (8 ft) wide bay units, and the length was 563 m (1848 ft), this being as near to 1851 as the 8 ft units would allow. About the middle of the length a 'transept' was introduced, as a last-minute modification of the working design, to allow the enclosure of a growing tree. The transept had the same width as the nave but was barrel-vaulted.

In this colossal project of prefabricated building, requiring vast quantities of iron and glass and other materials, as well as scrupulous organisation to allow the work to be completed in so short a time, Paxton had as engineer-associates Sir Charles Fox (1810–74) and his partner, while Owen Jones (1809–74), author of the book *Grammar of Ornament* (1856), was responsible for the decoration. Changes were made when the palace was re-erected at Sydenham, the nave then being given a barrel roof, like the transepts. The entire structure was destroyed by fire in 1936.

Ludwigskirche, Munich (1829–40), by Friedrich von Gärtner (1792–1847), is modelled on Romanesque prototypes somewhat loosely interpreted, and its west end, with rose window and arcaded porch, is flanked by attenuated towers and round-arched screen arcades.

S. Vincent-de-Paul, Paris (1824; 1831–44), was designed and started by Jean-Baptiste Lepère (1761–1844), the work being taken over and completed by Hittorff (1792–1867). A five-aisled basilica in plan, the church has a fine timber roof and its inner aisles are continued around the western apse, giving a spatial effect of great power. Entered through a grand, pedimented hexastyle Ionic portico, flanked by tall towers articulated by cornices at each stage, the church is approached by elaborate and monumental external stairs.

Friedenskirche, Potsdam (1845–8), by Ludwig Persius (1803–45), a pupil of Schinkel, is a copy of an Early Christian basilica, complete with atrium and arcaded campanile. Picturesquely sited at the edge of an artificial lake, out of which the apsidal west end and one side rise sheer, the building is characterised by exceptionally refined detail.

S. Wilfrid, Hulme, Manchester (1839–42) (p. 1110C), by A. W. N. Pugin, was designed in accordance with the architect's ecclesiological principles, and was described by him in his book *The Present State of Ecclesiastical Architecture in England* (1843). It differs from earlier Gothic Revival churches (including those built with the aid of the one million pounds parliamentary grant of 1818) in having separately articulated parts – nave, aisles, and south porch, together with eastern lateral chapels and a structurally distinct chancel. Its north-west tower, an important departure from the axial planning of earlier churches, was not completed for lack of funds. Pugin did not try to conceal the cheapness of the building with decorative effects. He made a virtue of its simplicity, building in brick and choosing the plain Early English style of Gothic architecture to create a sense of massive solidity.

S. Giles, Cheadle, Staffordshire (1841–6) (p. 1110B), also by A. W. N. Pugin, is a handsome church, finely finished and as costly as S. Wilfrid, Hulme, was cheap. It has Decorated tracery, and its solid stone structure culminates in a commanding spire. There is some external ornament, but this hardly prepares one for the lavish decoration of the interior, including painted patterns on the walls, encaustic tiles and stained glass.

A. Conservatory, Chatsworth, Derbyshire (1836–40; demolished 1920). See p. 1105

B. Palm House, Kew Gardens, London (1845–7). See p. 1105

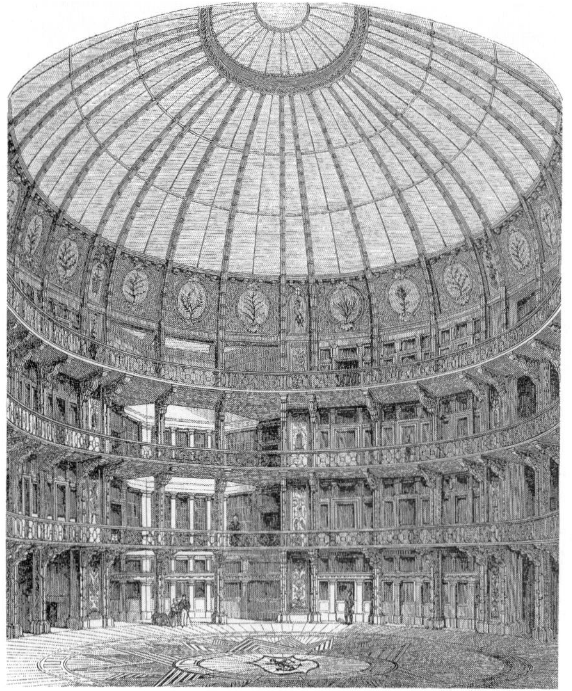

A. Coal Exchange, Lower Thames Street, London (1846–9; demolished 1962–3). See p. 1105

B. S. Giles, Cheadle, Staffordshire (1841–6). See p. 1108

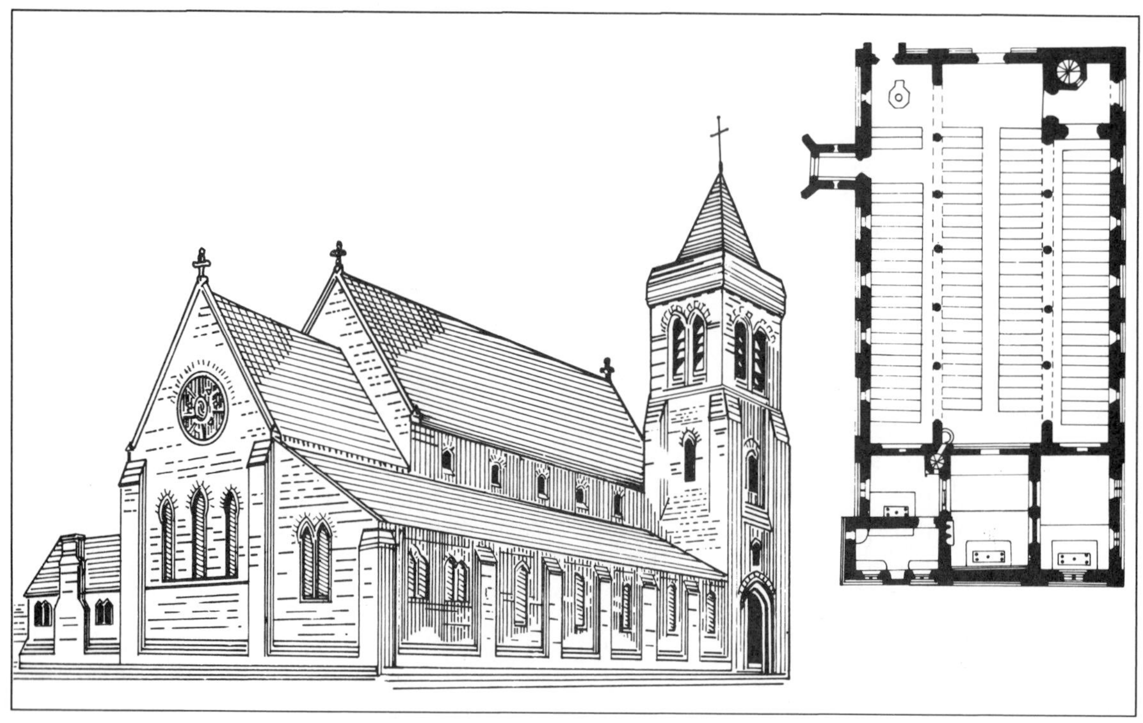

C. S. Wilfrid, Hulme, Manchester (1839–42). See p. 1108

A. Crystal Palace at completion in Hyde Park, London (1851): interior. See p. 1108

B. Crystal Palace, London: revised structure, erected (1852–4) at Sydenham, London (destroyed 1936). See p. 1108

S. Giles, Camberwell, London (1842–4) (p. 1113A), by Sir George Gilbert Scott (1811–78) and W. B. Moffatt (1812–87), was won by them in competition before Scott had set up on his own account. It is a large stone church of cruciform plan, with a tall crossing tower and spire, and shows how Scott responded to Pugin's ideas on church planning, although the details are a little mechanical. Designed in the geometrical Gothic style of the thirteenth century, it demonstrated Scott's powers and also provided a model for some of his own later churches as well as for those of fellow architects. Other comparable Gothic Revival churches are **S. Paul, Brighton** (1846–8), by Richard Cromwell Carpenter (1812–55); **S. Stephen, Rochester Row, London** (1847–50), by Benjamin Ferrey (1810–80); and **Holy Trinity, Bessborough Gardens, London** (1849–52; destroyed *c.* 1940), by J. L. Pearson.

Nikolaikirche, Hamburg (1845–63) (p. 1113B), by Sir George Gilbert Scott, was a cruciform Gothic church, much enriched with tracery and pinnacles. Its Germanic openwork spire, 147 m (482 ft) high, is almost all that survives, following an air raid in 1943.

S. Clotilde, Paris (1846–57) was designed by Franz Christian Gau (1790–1854), the first project being prepared in 1839, and completed by Théodore Ballu (1817–85). The church is in the style of French fourteenth-century Gothic, of cathedral proportions and plan, and noteworthy for the iron construction of its roof.

Osborne House, Isle of Wight (1845–51), was designed by Thomas Cubitt (1788–1855) under the direction of Prince Albert, as a private seaside residence for Queen Victoria and the royal family. Its asymmetrical plan consists of a compact pavilion block with a belvedere tower and a larger visitors' wing which is U-shaped and has a clock tower. Osborne is the most conspicuous example of the Italianate villa style in England, although it is less refined than its prototype, Barry's **Trentham Hall, Staffordshire** (1834–42; demolished 1910–12).

Harlaxton Hall, Lincolnshire (1834–55) (p. 1113C), by Anthony Salvin (1799–1881), is a prodigious building. Its boldly modelled facade and ebullient skyline of cupolas, gables and chimney stacks are quite as extraordinary as the Elizabethan houses, such as Burghley, which inspired Salvin. The interiors and some of the outbuildings were completed in a spectacular Baroque style by William Burn (1789–1870), who took over from Salvin in about 1838. At **Scotney Castle, Lamberhurst, Kent** (1835–43), Salvin created a quieter Tudor facade, expressively asymmetrical.

Zámek Hluboká, Frauenberg, near České Budějovic (Budweis), Czech Republic (1841–71), by F. Beer and D. Devorecký, is a large castellated country seat in the manner of James Wyatt's nineteenth-century houses. Vast collections are housed in an interior designed in a number of styles – Gothic, Renaissance and Baroque.

S. Marie's Grange, Alderbury, Wiltshire (1835–6), was designed by Pugin as his own house. Three main rooms on each floor formed an L-shape to which was added a stairtower on one side and a watercloset turret on the other. The generous brick walls contained recesses for shelves, and from the stone mullioned windows Pugin could see Salisbury Cathedral. The house was altered after Pugin moved to Ramsgate where he built himself another house, **The Grange** (1843–4) (p. 1114B), with **S. Augustine's Church** (1845–51) alongside.

The **Vicarage, Coalpitheath, Gloucestershire** (1844–5) (p. 1114A), an early design of William Butterfield, is a freely-planned composition of stone rubble with ashlar dressings. The window mullions are flush with the wall surface, and the construction is emphasised by relieving arches under the steep gables. Chimney breasts expressed externally add to the effect of 'Picturesque utility'. The north-east corner was added in 1863 by W. Robertson.

Rue de Rivoli (West), Paris (1811–35) (p. 1115A), by Percier and Fontaine, forms part of a larger planning scheme initiated by Napoleon I. The five-storey houses are in terrace blocks of a restrained Classical character, and are unified horizontally by elegant iron balconies at first- and third-floor levels, the continuous open arcades at street level being reminiscent of the much earlier Place des Vosges. The group was extended to the east in the same design in 1852–5, when high mansard roofs were added.

Schottenhof, Vienna (1826–32), by Joseph Kornhäusel (1782–1860), is a large housing scheme built round a series of square internal courtyards. The stuccoed street elevations have shops at ground level and rise through five main storeys, unified by shallow projecting giant Ionic pilasters, which form central pedimented 'temple fronts' to each elevation.

No. 10, Place de la Bourse, Paris (1834), a block of flats by Auguste Joseph Pellechet (1789–1871), provides an example of Parisian street architecture of the period. Stucco-faced, the seven-bay, six-storey building has a mansard roof, through which pedimented windows open onto a delicate iron balcony supported by the main cornice. At street level there are shops which, with a mezzanine floor, form a base for the facade of well-proportioned windows with carefully detailed architraves. The whole is unified horizontally by string courses.

Flats, Rue de Liège, Paris (1846–8) (p. 1114C), the first executed design of Viollet-le-Duc, is a highly original essay in the use of mediaeval detail. At street level, simple openings have shallow segmental arches, above which are bold, projecting string courses, continuous labels and cills running between the windows.

A. S. Giles, Camberwell, London (1842–4). See p. 1112

B. Nikolaikirche, Hamburg (1845–63). See p. 1112

C. Harlaxton Hall, Lincolnshire (1834–55). See p. 1112

A. The Vicarage, Coalpitheath, Gloucestershire (1844–5). See p. 1112

B. The Grange, Ramsgate (1843–4). See p. 1112

C. Flats, Rue de Liège, Paris (1846–8). See p. 1112

A. Rue de Rivoli (West), Paris (1811–35). See p. 1112

B. New Louvre, Paris (1852–7). See p. 1116

1850–70

The **New Louvre, Paris** (1852–7) (p. 1115B), initiated by Napoleon III, was designed by Ludovico Tullio Joachim Visconti (1791–1853), the work being taken over and much developed in details by Hector Martin Lefuel (1810–80) on Visconti's death. Two extensive wings, each built around twin internal courtyards, extend from either end of the west front of the Old Louvre, providing ministerial and other official accommodation. The buildings are the embodiment of the Second Empire style, incorporating late Renaissance details in facades punctuated by grand pavilions with distinctive mansard roofs. The New Louvre had considerable influence in Britain and America.

The **Town Hall, Leeds** (1853–9) (p. 1117A), by Cuthbert Brodrick (1822–1905), is a masterpiece of High Victorian Classicism. Grandiose in conception, rugged and massive in outline and opulent in detail, it asserts the independence and pride of a prosperous industrial city. The plan consists of a large public hall, rivalling that of S. George's Hall, Liverpool, and four corner pavilions containing the law courts and council chamber. The high dome and exuberant decoration suggest the influence of contemporary French architecture and the earlier English Baroque, but such elements are fully assimilated in Brodrick's accomplished design. Other notable works by Brodrick are the **Corn Exchange, Leeds** (1851–3), and the **Grand Hotel, Scarborough** (1863–7).

The **Free Trade Hall, Manchester** (1853–4) (p. 1118A), by Edward Walters (1808–72), is a powerful design in the 'palazzo' style. It differs from Barry's earlier 'palazzo' designs by its preference for bold mouldings and rich details. It was built to commemorate the success of the Anti-Corn Law League, but of the original structure only two principal elevations survive, owing to war damage. The lowest storey of the main facade forms a handsome, open arcade with massive piers and carved spandrels. The piano nobile has pedimented windows, an arcade of paired Ionic columns and tympana carving representing world trade. Above the arcade a swagged frieze is succeeded by an emphatic cornice and balustrade, and the whole facade is strongly and decisively modelled; the Renaissance cornucopia was never more generously filled. Walters designed several other excellent 'palazzo' style buildings in Manchester, mainly warehouses, His last work, the former **Manchester and Salford District Bank, Moseley Street**, of 1860, is also exceptional.

The **Foreign Office, London** (1861–73) (p. 1118B), by Sir George Gilbert Scott, is his only work in the Italian Renaissance manner. It has an almost Venetian richness, and its facade to S. James's Park (based on a sketch by M. D. Wyatt) is picturesquely composed. In the controversy of the 'Battle of the Styles' over this project, Scott was obliged to abandon his original Gothic design-although its spirit was resurrected for the Hotel at S. Pancras Station.

The **Palais de Justice, Brussels** (1866–83) (p. 1117C), by Joseph Poelaert (1817–79), stands on a height overlooking the city and builds up pyramidally to a domed tower above the central great hall. It is a gargantuan building, and although its Classical details are suitably monumental they are generally overcrowded and suggest a straining after effect which compares unfavourably with the fluent brilliance of the Opéra in Paris.

The **University Museum, Oxford** (1854–60) (p. 1119A), designed by Benjamin Woodward, (1815–61), of Deane and Woodward, showed how the Gothic Revival could be seriously employed for public buildings. The entrance block with its steep roof and central tower is reminiscent of Flemish town halls, and its subtly asymmetrical window arrangement reflects the different sizes of the ground-floor rooms. The cream-coloured stonework has contrasting bands of pink and the roofs are patterned in purple and grey-green slates. This constructional polychromy and the inventive nature of the (incomplete) window-carvings epitomise the influence of Ruskin, whose *Stones of Venice* had been published in 1851–3. Internally there is a quadrangle with a steep glass roof supported by pointed iron arches (p. 1119B), the spandrels of which are filled with delicate wrought-iron foliage. Around the quadrangle are polychrome arcades whose columns consist of geological specimens with capitals which depict various species of plants, thereby enhancing the building's didactic purpose. Alongside the main building are the chemistry laboratories, based on the plan of the mediaeval abbot's kitchen at Glastonbury in Somerset.

The **Assize Courts, Manchester** (1859–64), designed by Alfred Waterhouse, were demolished in 1959 after war damage. It was by this building, won in competition, that Waterhouse first made his name and it was said to 'unite considerable artistic merit with unusual advantages in regard to plan and internal arrangement'. It was of two storeys above a high basement, arranged more or less symmetrically around a great hall and two courtrooms. It was Ruskinian in its use of constructional polychromy, and in the hint of Venetian Gothic in its upper windows, but the French character of the high-pitched pavilion roofs showed Waterhouse's latent eclecticism.

The **Albert Memorial, London** (1863–72) (p. 1117B), by Sir George Gilbert Scott, was designed as a national memorial to Prince Albert. The seated bronze figure of the prince is placed beneath an elaborate metal-spired ciborium which stands on polished granite columns and is embellished by mosaic. The podium has a marble frieze of eminent

A. Town Hall, Leeds (1853–9). See p. 1116

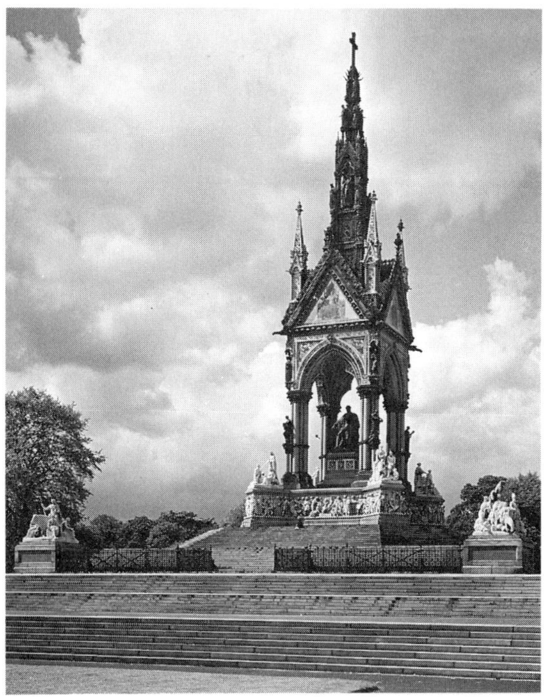

B. Albert Memorial, London (1863–72). See p. 1116

C. Palais de Justice, Brussels (1866–83). See p. 1116

A. Free Trade Hall, Manchester (1853–4). See p. 1116

B. Foreign Office, London (1861–73). See p. 1116

C. Town Hall, Manchester (1868–77). See p. 1120

A. University Museum, Oxford (1854–60). See p. 1116

B. University Museum, Oxford: interior

C. Town Hall, Congleton, Cheshire (1864–7). See p. 1120

figures from the arts, and there are symbolic groups at each corner of the monument. Scott's use of a Gothic ciborium was anticipated by Thomas Worthington (1826–1909), the designer of the **Albert Memorial, Manchester** (1862–4).

The **Town Hall, Congleton, Cheshire** (1864–7) (p. 1119C), by Edward William Godwin (1833–86), combines Italian and northern Gothic features in a way which had been first realised at the University Museum, Oxford (q.v.). It has a five-bay (originally open) arcade at street level, with eight windows lighting the formal first-floor rooms. A central tower, machicolated and battlemented, rises flush with the facade in a way reminiscent of buildings such as the Palazzo Publico at Montepulciano, while the steep roof pierced by sharp dormers suggests Flemish or perhaps French inspiration. A further High Victorian characteristic is the polychromatic detailing of walls and roof. Godwin was also responsible for the **Town Hall at Northampton** (1861–4).

The **Town Hall, Manchester** (1868–77) (pp. 1118C,1121A), by Alfred Waterhouse, is ingeniously planned on a difficult triangular site, and resolves the awkward external angles by skilful devices of projecting bays and blocks. The council chamber and main reception rooms occupy the front of the building, offices and committee rooms taking up the other two sides (with the public hall in the centre); all are reached from a ring corridor. Open arcades and different levels produce constantly changing vistas and spatial relationships. A similar spatial interest is evident in Waterhouse's **Natural History Museum, London** (1868–80), although here the facade is symmetrical and Romanesque rather than picturesquely Gothic. Terracotta, the facing material of the Natural History Museum, became a hallmark of Waterhouse's later work, especially his various buildings for the Prudential Assurance Company.

The **Royal Courts of Justice, London** (1874–82) (p. 1121C), by George Edmund Street, one of the last important buildings to be erected in the High Victorian Gothic style, is a vast, vigorously modelled composition, planned with considerable ingenuity to meet complex requirements: the courts are arranged about a huge, vaulted Gothic concourse. The design is highly personal to Street, who executed 3000 drawings by his own hand, in the face of dogged official parsimony, only to die before it was completed.

The **Opera House, Paris** (1861–74) (pp. 1121B,1122), by J.-L.-C. Garnier, shows a development of the Baroque in the New Louvre. The plan is a noteworthy example of the application of Beaux-Arts principles, its elements and spaces related and held together by a strongly controlled axial system. An enormous foyer, sumptuously enriched with brightly gilded sculpture and Baroque architectural elements, with a vaulted painted ceiling from which hang candelabra, leads to the magnificent *escalier d'honneur*, beyond which lie the auditorium and extensive stage area. Characterised throughout by opulent grandeur, the building is marked by a fine sense of architectonic control. Externally it is treated in a highly plastic, sculptural way, and makes imaginative use of a wide range of Classical details as well as some fine sculpture by J. B. Carpeaux. The main front terminates the vista along Haussmann's Avenue de l'Opéra, which was left without trees in order not to obstruct the view of Garnier's triumphant facade.

S. Pancras Hotel and Station Block, London (1865–71) (p. 1123A), by Sir George Gilbert Scott, stands in front of the huge train shed of 1864–8. It was a showpiece for the Midland Railway Company, providing extensive hotel accommodation as well as the usual booking hall and offices. It is the outstanding example of Scott's secular Gothic style, blending Italian, French and Flemish elements in a High Victorian way. The red-brick frontage rises through tiers of crowded openings with pointed arches to a steeply pitched roof serrated by jagged dormers, massive chimney stacks and soaring towers with pinnacles and spires. Other major works by Scott include **Leeds Infirmary** (1863–7) and **Glasgow University** (1864–70).

Paddington Station, London, is of interest principally for its station sheds (1852–4) designed by Isambard Kingdom Brunel and the architect Sir Matthew Digby Wyatt (1820–77), and not for the Great Western Hotel, forming its frontispiece. The sheds are of three spans totalling 72.5 m (238 ft), the centre one being wider than the others. Each of the coverings is carried on semi-elliptical wrought-iron ribs, without principals, glazed only over the central third. The three are joined together by cross vaults at two points in the length. Wyatt was responsible for the decorative aspect of the scheme, and notably the Gothic and Saracenic motifs integral within the structural members and wrought-iron screens.

S. Pancras Station, London, like Paddington, was conceived independently of the (former) Midland Hotel and offices fronting it. The train shed (1864–8) (p. 1123C), by the engineer William Henry Barlow (1812–1902) in conjunction with R. M. Ordish, is the largest and most spectacular of the High Victorian period, being a single span of 74 m (243 ft), rising 30 m (100 ft) high in a slightly pointed wrought-iron arch. The total length is 213 m (700 ft). At the base the arched vault is secured by rods 76 mm (3 in) in diameter under the platforms.

Galleria Vittorio Emanuele, Milan (1865–77), (p. 1123B), by Giuseppe Mengoni (1827–77), is a fine example of the many glass-roofed shopping arcades that have been built since the late eighteenth century, mainly in England and France. It is a large and ambitious project arranged on a cruciform plan with glass tunnel-vaulting (a feature first used by Fontaine in the Galerie d'Orléans, Paris, of

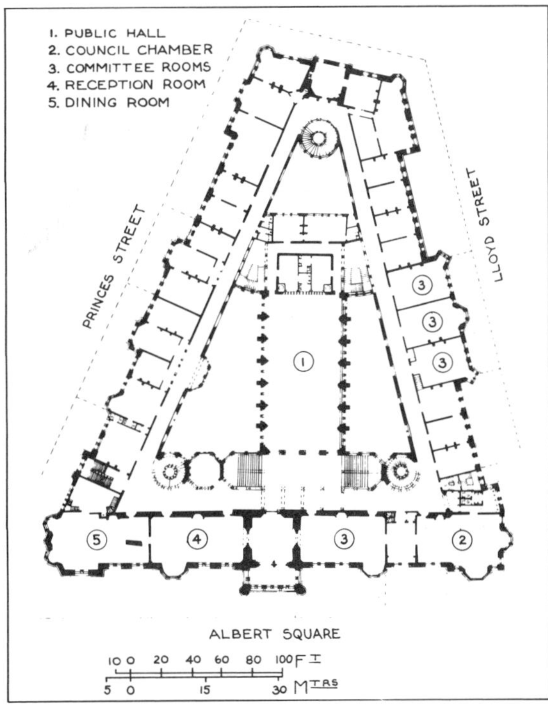

A. Town Hall, Manchester: plan. See p. 1120

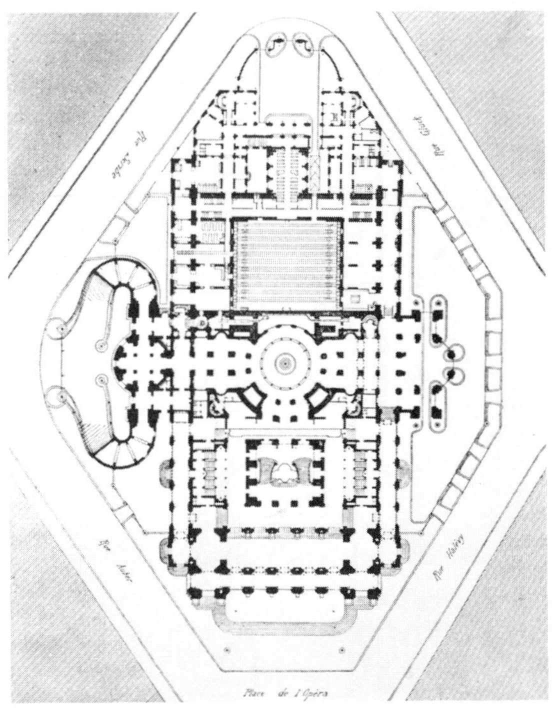

B. Opera House, Paris: ground floor plan. See p. 1120

C. Royal Courts of Justice, London (1874–82). See p. 1120

A. Opera House, Paris (1861–74): facade. See p. 1120

B. Opera House, Paris: foyer

C. Opera House, Paris: grand staircase, upper flight

A. S. Pancras Hotel and Station, London (1865–71). See p. 1120

B. Galleria Vittorio Emmanuele, Milan (1865–77). See p. 1120

C. S. Pancras Station, London: train shed (1864–8). See p. 1120

1829–31) which forms a high domed octagon at the intersection. Its internal facades, with giant pilasters embracing two of the three main storeys, have late Renaissance decoration, while the entrance from the cathedral square is treated like a triumphal arch. The **Galleria Umberto I, Naples** (1887–90), by Emanuele Rocco (born 1852), is a later, less ambitious example of the same building type.

The **Halles Centrales, Paris** (begun 1853; demolished 1971) (p. 1125A), by Victor Baltard (1805–74) assisted by Félix-Emmanuel Callet (1791–1854), were the main markets of the city, part of Haussmann's plan and connected by rail with the Gare de l'Est. The scheme consisted of six pavilions (soon extended to ten, and increased to twelve in the 1930s), laid out in a grid system with broad, covered avenues between them. The buildings were constructed of iron and glass and were completely covered, except for a boulevard which intersected the site. Storage space was provided in the vaulted cellars.

Gardner's Warehouse, Jamaica Street, Glasgow (1855–6) (p. 1125B), by John Baird I (1798–1859), with its cast-iron facades, illustrates the great popularity of the material at this time, even if it was seldom used as external cladding in Britain. Cast iron lends itself to easy repetition, and it is significant that each storey varies in this design, in which the lower ranges of arches are made progressively flatter for purely architectural reasons. A similar building, **Paisley's Warehouse** (1854–5), probably by William Spence (?1806–83), stands nearby.

The **Boatstore, Royal Naval Dockyard, Sheerness** (1858–60) (p. 1125C), by Godfrey Thomas Greene, who from 1850 to 1864 was Director of Engineering and Architectural Works to the Admiralty, is among the earliest known tiered iron-framed buildings, particularly advanced in the details of its construction. Being a utilitarian building, the external panels could be lightly infilled with sheeting. It is 64 m (210 ft) long and 41 m (135 ft) wide, arranged internally as a top-lit 'nave' running the whole length of the building, and double 'aisles' with floors on each side at each of the four storeys. The stanchions already have the 'H' section which came to be adopted regularly later on.

The **National Library, Paris** (1859–67) (p. 1126), by Pierre-François-Henri Labrouste (1801–75), shows further advances in planning and structure over the Library of S. Geneviève. The reading room is covered with a series of nine pendentive domes of terracotta, each pierced at its crown with an 'eye' providing natural top light. They are supported by slender columns and arches of cast iron, the outer columns standing close to the walls. The vaults, arch-soffits and the wall surfaces above book-stack level are enriched with delicate decoration. The stack room is top-lit and has slatted metal floors to allow light to pass to lower levels. Its central space is bridged at intervals by gangways, which link the stacks at each floor level.

The **Gare du Nord, Paris** (1861–5) (p. 1127A), by Jacques Ignace Hittorff (1792–1867), replaced a small station of 1842–7. The gable of the broad facade follows the line of the train shed's pitched iron-and-glass roof, and the outer pavilions distinguish the arrival and departure sides of the station. The architectural detail is of neo-Classical character but with some disparities of scale. The facade is crowned by the figure of Paris and eight others representing northern European cities.

Oriel Chambers, Liverpool (1864) (p. 1127B), by Peter Ellis (1804–84), is a remarkably advanced building for the period, both in construction and architectural character. It has a complete cast-iron frame, the front vertical members of which are clad in stone to form slender masonry piers; between them the horizontal members carry delicately detailed shallow oriels in each panel. There is little or no historical allusion in the forms employed, save a suggestion of collegiate Gothic in the cresting. **No. 16, Cook Street, Liverpool** (1866), also by Ellis, is of similar construction and equally original.

The **Granary, Welsh Back, Bristol** (1871–3), by Archibald Ponton and William Venn Gough (1842–1918), is the most impressive of a group of High Victorian commercial buildings in Bristol. It is of local brick, with solid piers corresponding to the corner lift-shafts, and polychrome patterns enlivening the various openings. The powerful arches at the ground floor suggest the building's massive strength, while the battlemented cornice provides a neatly decorative crest.

All Saints, Margaret Street, London (1849–59) (p. 1128A,B), by William Butterfield, marks a turning point in the Gothic Revival. It was built as a model church of the Ecclesiological Society, and in particular demonstrated the latest attitudes to urban church-building. It stands on an extremely cramped site and is approached across a small yard between the vicarage and the choir school. Brick was chosen as the building material, not as an economy (the church cost roughly twice as much as Pugin's S. Giles in Cheadle) but because of its durability and colour. The sheer red-brick walls are thus enlivened with bands and patterns of darker brick in 'constructional polychromy'. Internally, multi-coloured marble, tiles and alabaster decorate the walls and pulpit in geometrical patterns. The church attracted enormous attention, and although it had its critics it was a potent source for an entire generation of British architects. Among many other works by Butterfield are **S. Alban, Holborn, London** (1859–62; altered internally after war damage) and **Keble College and Chapel, Oxford** (1867–83), but he also designed many cottages and village schools which often assume the unobtrusive character of vernacular forms.

A. Halles Centrales, Paris (begun 1853; demolished 1971). See p. 1124

B. Gardner's Warehouse, Jamaica Street, Glasgow (1855–6). See p. 1124

C. Boatstore, Royal Naval Dockyard, Sheerness (1858–60). See p. 1124

A. National Library, Paris (1859–67): reading room. See p. 1124

B. National Library, Paris: stack room

C. National Library, Paris: detail of stacks

A. Gare du Nord, Paris (1861–5). See p. 1124

B. Oriel Chambers, Liverpool (1864). See p. 1124

C. S. Eugène, Paris (1854–5). See p. 1129

A. All Saints, Margaret Street, London (1849–59). See p. 1124

B. All Saints, Margaret Street, London: nave and chancel

C. Votivkirche, Vienna (1856–79). See p. 1129

D. Caledonia Road Free Church, Glasgow (1856–7). See p. 1129

S. Eugène, Paris (1854–5) (p. 1127C), by Louis-Auguste Boileau (1812–96), has an undistinguished exterior, largely of stone, but is remarkable for its interior in which the Gothic vocabulary of arches, vaulting and tracery has all been realised in iron. Extensive use of iron occurs also in **S. Eugène, Le Vésinet, Seine-et-Oise**(1863), by Boileau; **S. Augustin, Paris** (1860–71), by Victor Baltard (1805–74); by and **Notre-Dame-du-Travail, Paris** (1899–1901), by Zacharie Astruc (1835–1907).

The **Votivkirche, Vienna** (1856–79) (p. 1128C), by Heinrich von Ferstel (1828–83), was built as a thank-offering when an attempt on the Emperor Franz Josef's life was foiled. It is an elaborate essay in Gothic, heralded by tall, slender western towers with open belfries and crocketed steeples, and its richness is akin to Scott's Nikolaikirche in Hamburg. Also in Vienna is the Fünfhaus parish church, **Maria vom Siege** (1868–75), by Friedrich von Schmidt (1825–91), an important exponent of the Gothic Revival in Austria. It has an aisled octagonal plan above which rises a ribbed dome, Baroque in shape but mediaeval in detail. The entrance front is flanked by towers linked by flying buttresses to the drum of the dome.

The **Caledonia Road Free Church, Glasgow** (1856–7; gutted by fire, 1965) (p. 1128D), by Alexander 'Greek' Thomson (1817–75), illustrates the strength of the neo-Classical tradition in Scotland in the second half of the nineteenth century. It is an extraordinarily powerful design with an architectonic clarity reminiscent of Schinkel. The vestibule is treated as a blind podium on which stands a faultless Ionic portico. Behind this lies the church itself, lit mainly by clerestory windows, and the remainder of the wedge-shaped site is occupied by a single-storey church hall. Dominating the composition is a sheer tower, placed at one corner so as to emphasise the picturesque element which so often distinguishes Thomson's work. Thomson developed the themes of this design in two other Glasgow churches: in **S. Vincent Street** (1857–9) and **Queen's Park** (1867–9; demolished in World War II).

The **Church of S. Philip and S. James, Oxford** (1860–2) (p. 1130A), by G. E. Street, is a strongly composed cruciform building with a central broach spire and apsidal chancel. Polychromy appears in the bands of red sandstone inserted into the creamy-yellow masonry and in the alternating colours of the voussoirs. In the nave squat pillars of polished granite support the broad arches of the rough-faced walls, and the impression of solidity is continued in the plate tracery. Street, like Butterfield, was a member of the Ecclesiological Society, and among his other church commissions are **All Saints Church, Vicarage and Schools, Boyne Hill, Maidenhead** (1854–7), and **S. James-the-Less, Vauxhall Bridge Road, London** (1859–61).

S. Denys-de-l'Estrée, S. Denis, near Paris (1864–7) (p. 1130C), by Viollet-le-Duc, is comparable with work by Street and Burges in England. The stone-vaulted nave has wide, square bays lit by groups of clerestory windows, and above the western porch there is a sturdy tower, capped by a tall slated roof. Wall and vault surfaces are stencilled with coloured decoration, and generally the detailing is vigorous.

Mole Antonelliana, Turin (begun 1863), by Alessandro Antonelli (1798–1888), was initially intended as a synagogue, but was taken over for use as a municipal museum in 1876. The building is structurally audacious, especially in the great vaulted cupola covering the main mass, from which rises a tall spire-like feature, decorated with neo-Classical elements in its lower stages, making a total height for the building of 167 m (548 ft). Antonelli's cupola of **S. Gaudenzio, Novara** (begun 1840), is similar in character, with two circular Corinthian peristyles supporting a dome, above which further colonnaded tiers rise to form a steeple with a total height of 125 m (410 ft).

Red House, Bexleyheath, Kent (1859–60) (p. 1132), built by Philip Webb (1831–1915) for William Morris, took its name from the use of red brick and tiles, and represents a continuation of the simple vicarage designs by Butterfield and Street. The design is eclectic rather than pure Gothic, although the general effect of high-pitched roofs and pointed arches is Gothic in character. Nevertheless, sash windows were used for practical reasons, as were the pointed arches which span them. The planning is informal and unconventional, but met the practical needs of its owner. The elements of plan and structure are expressed in accordance with Puginian principles. The remarkable interior decoration and furnishings presage the Arts and Crafts Movement of the 1880s. Other works by Webb include **Arisaig, Inverness-shire** (1863, now much altered), and **No. 1, Palace Green, Kensington** (1868).

The **Custodian's House, Notre Dame, Paris** (1866), by Viollet-le-Duc, was built following restoration of the cathedral by Viollet-le-Duc and Jean-Baptiste-Antoine Lassus (1807–57). It has many of the characteristics of the English Gothic Revivalists' work: steep roofs, an external chimney breast and a picturesque variety of windows. However, the symmetry of the entrance wing and the uniformity of the ashlar masonry would have been considered Classical traits by Pugin or Ruskin.

Glen Andred, Groombridge, Sussex (1866–8) (p. 1133A), was one of the first examples of Norman Shaw's 'Old English' style, adapting vernacular features to the requirements of a large house. The brickwork, tile-hanging, tall chimneys and mullioned windows reflect Shaw's love of the local building traditions in the Kent and Sussex Weald. His next

A. Church of S. Philip and S. James, Oxford (1860–2). See p. 1129

B. Castell Coch, near Cardiff (1875–91). See p. 1135

C. S. Denys-de-Estrée, S. Denis, near Paris (1864–7). See p. 1129

Cardiff Castle (1868–85). See p. 1135

A. Red House, Bexleyheath, Kent (1859–60): view from south. See p. 1129

B. Red House, Bexleyheath, Kent: interior

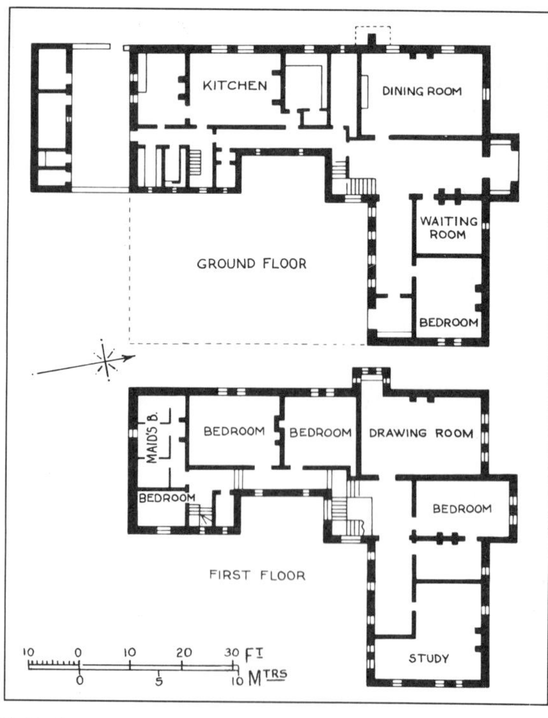

C. Red House, Bexleyheath, Kent: plan

A. Glen Andred, Groomsbridge, Sussex (1866–8). See p. 1129

B. Workers' houses, Saltaire, Yorkshire (begun 1851). See p. 1135

C. Leys Wood, Groombridge, Sussex (1868–9; mostly demolished *c.* 1955). See p. 1135

A. Alford House, London (1872; now demolished). See p. 1135

B. No. 11, Rue de Milan, Paris (*c.* 1860). See p. 1135

C. Heinrichshof, Vienna (1861–3; demolished after wartime damage). See p. 1135

houses in this vein were more romantic, with half-timbering and picturesque rooflines. Among the best examples are **Leys Wood, Groombridge** (1868–9; mostly demolished *c.* 1955) (p. 1133C), and **Grim's Dyke, near Harrow, Middlesex** (1870–2). **Crag-side, Northumberland** (1869–85), was built in stone as a concession to the rugged situation, and although Shaw's 'Old English' vocabulary may seem incongruous here, it was ideally suited to a house which was to be enlarged in stages.

Cardiff Castle (1868–85) (p. 1131) and **Castell Coch, near Cardiff** (1875–91) (p. 1130B), were reconstructed by William Burges (1827–81) for the Marquess of Bute in a fantastic and highly personal version of the Gothic Revival. The work at Castell Coch is archaeologically realistic to the point of providing a working drawbridge and portcullis, and apertures through which boiling liquids could be poured, but it also possesses magnificent formal qualities, not least in the powerful round towers with conical roofs, inspired by mediaeval illustrations. Both buildings are exotically detailed and decorated internally, and in this respect Cardiff Castle is its author's chief work. Sculptures, mural painting, painted and carved friezes, stencilled patterns and decorated tiles create an incredibly rich but never uncontrolled profusion of ornament. In these buildings the Gothic Revival was a vehicle for an unusually vivid and exuberant imagination.

Alford House, London (1872; now demolished (p. 1134A), by Sir M. D. Wyatt, was French in character, with a mansard roof, and luxuriant terracotta dressings, derived from the 'Second Empire' mode then popular.

Workers' houses, Saltaire, Yorkshire (begun 1851) (p. 1133B), by Lockwood and Mawson, form part of a model industrial township built for the textile manufacturer, Sir Titus Salt. The houses are mostly two-storeyed (consisting of living room, kitchen, and two or three bedrooms), and the neat Italianate character of the terraces is emphasised by the introduction of larger houses as corner pavilions, capped by low-pitched roofs. The workers' housing at **Akroydon, Halifax** (begun 1859), by Sir George Gilbert Scott, another product of industrial philanthropy, was composed around a domestic theme which ranges from the simple dormers and mullioned windows of the terraced cottages to the more ambitious design of the more expensive houses.

No. 15, Rue de Douai, Paris (1857–60), by Viollet-le-Duc, is an apartment house in which mediaeval forms are hinted at without violating the conventions of contemporary Parsian street architecture. The facade of clean-cut, rectangular openings has at fourth-floor level a continuous iron escape balcony carried on ponderous stone brackets. The second floor, where the windows are emphasised by heavy stone hoods, has a shorter balcony, borne on three massive corbels.

The **Boulevard de Sébastopol, Paris** (1860), is architecturally typical of Haussmann's Second Empire Paris. Above street-level shops are commonly five or six floors of flats. Despite their height, the result of exploiting the economic potential of the sites, the restrained elevations, with their judicious ornamental accents and disciplined emphasis on a regular, unifying vertical rhythm, give an excellent answer to the problem of repetitive street architecture.

No. 11, Rue de Milan, Paris (*c.* 1860) (p. 1134B), by A.-F. Mortier, represents a more opulent treatment for flats in Paris at this date. The seven-bay four-storey facade has a sumptuous array of Mannerist elements enriching its entire surface. Strongly projecting string courses unify the composition.

Heinrichshof, Vienna (1861–3; demolished after wartime damage) (p. 1134C), by Theophil Hansen, was a prosperous apartment block facing the Opera House across Vienna's Ringstrasse. It was a large, five-storey building with shops at ground level and a hierarchy of Renaissance decoration to the upper parts of the facade. The heavy cornice and regular fenestration were counteracted by corner pavilions and by a central attic storey on the axis of a glass-roofed passage which ran through the block.

1870–1900

The **Rijksmuseum, Amsterdam** (1877–85) (p. 1136A), by Petrus Josephus Hubertus Cuijpers, has a French quality about its massing and steeply pitched roofs, but its detail is derived mainly from Dutch architecture of the sixteenth century. The building is symmetrically planned, with galleries set out around two courtyards.

The **Reichstag Building, Berlin** (1884–94) (p. 1136B), by Paul Wallot (1841–1912), was built on a scale suitable for its role as a symbol of the Second Reich. Its Baroque Classicism, handled with assurance, is a little ponderous in some of the details. The building was gutted by fire in 1933, further damaged in 1945, and restored in the 1960s without the huge glazed dome which had been the climax of its silhouette.

The **Victor Emmanuel II Monument, Rome** (1885–1911) (p. 1137A), by Giuseppe Sacconi (1854–1901), was built on the slopes of the Capitol to commemorate the unification of Italy and the nation's first king. It consists of an enormous terraced platform on which stands an equestrian statue of the king, backed by an even larger, slightly concave Corinthian colonnade, supporting an elaborately decorated attic, and terminated at each end by pavilions bearing great bronze sculptural groups. The monument houses a museum of the Risorgimento.

New Scotland Yard, London (1887–90) (p. 1141A), by Richard Norman Shaw, was built on

A. Rijksmuseum, Amsterdam (1877–85). See p. 1135

B. Reichstag Building, Berlin (1884–94). See p. 1135

A. Victor Emmanuel II Monument, Rome (1855–1911). See p. 1135

B. Town Hall, Copenhagen (1892–1902). See p. 1138

the Thames Embankment as the headquarters of the Metropolitan Police. It rises from a severe base of granite to a warmer pattern of red brick with stone bands, and a cheerful variety of windows in the upper floors. The corners are softened by the 'Scottish Baronial' tourelles with helmet-like caps, and Shaw's exuberance finds final expression in the lavish Baroque flourishes at the entrance and at the gable terminals. It is an extraordinary performance in which High Victorian pomp is treated with Late Victorian levity.

The **Rylands Library, Deansgate, Manchester** (1890–9) (p. 1139), designed by Basil Champneys, is a splendid if belated example of secular Gothic. It is a much lighter and more gracious version than had been normal in the High Victorian era, reverting to the English Decorated period for inspiration, but expressing it with a topical Art Nouveau piquancy. The richly ornamented centre-piece and the great bay windows of the recessed upper stage contrast effectively with the relatively plain walls on the lower flanks, in which deep, traceried windows are set in studied asymmetry. Among Champney's other commissions is **Newnham College, Cambridge** (1875–1935), a delightful exercise in the 'Queen Anne' mode.

The **Town Hall, Copenhagen** (1892–1902) (p. 1137B), by Martin Nyrop, is a suavely eclectic design, blending mediaeval and Renaissance elements in a composition whose symmetry is counteracted by a refined bell-tower.

The **School of Art, Glasgow** (1897–1909) (p. 1140A-C), by Charles Rennie Mackintosh, is the architect's most famous work. The main building was constructed between 1897 and 1899, and its long ashlar facade is dominated by huge, north-facing studio windows disposed with subtle variations of rhythm around a more obviously asymmetrical entrance bay. Thus the direct expression of function is combined with echoes of Scottish vernacular architecture and the influence of the Arts and Crafts movement. The west wing, added in 1907–9, has a dramatic exterior with tall oriel windows which light the library whose complex and imaginative space is based on an ingenious wooden framework. Mackintosh had a wider following in Germany and Austria, particularly Vienna, than in Scotland and England, and in this respect is one of the most significant British architects of his generation.

The **Whitechapel Art Gallery, London** (1897–1901) (p. 1140D), by Charles Harrison Townsend (1851–1928), is an essay in organic geometry, remarkably free from historicism. Its facade of buff terracotta has great power. The massive, offset, semicircular entrance arch – perhaps inspired by the American architect H. H. Richardson – is balanced by an area of blank wall and contained by a band of plain windows. The facade is framed by two tapering turrets, square in plan but with rounded corners, and decorated with a deep band of stylised foliage. The recessed upper wall was to have borne a mosaic symbolising the role of art, but this was omitted for lack of funds. Many of the features of the Whitechapel Gallery were further developed by Townsend in his design for the **Horniman Museum, Forest Hill, London** (1896–1901).

The **Town Hall, Colchester** (1898–1902) (p. 1141C), by John Belcher, is a fine example of the full-blooded neo-Baroque which flourished around the turn of the century. With a powerfully modelled facade and a bold corner tower it makes maximum use of its site. The **City Hall and Law Courts, Cardiff** (1897–1906), by Lanchester and Rickards, are more spaciously arranged in a verdant civic centre and introduce a hint of Viennese Baroque. A domed council chamber is the chief feature of the city hall's facade, but the main accent is an inventive clock-tower on the building's cross-axis.

The **Stadttheater, Cologne** (1870–2) (p. 1142A), by Julius Raschdorff (1823–1914), was a building of modest dimensions destroyed in World War II. Its affinities with French Second Empire neo-Baroque were recognisable in the steep mansard roof, the dormer windows and the disposition of pavilion-like features on the otherwise plainer facades. However, the rich decoration of these 'pavilions' owed more to German Renaissance sources than to French.

The **Hoftheater (Opera House), Dresden** (1871–8; restored following bomb damage in 1945), was designed by Gottfried Semper (1803–79) to replace his earlier theatre on the same site which burned down in 1869. In contrast with the Early Renaissance clarity of Semper's first design, the Baroque tendencies are marked, for instance in the use of paired columns or the enrichment of the curving facade with a triumphal porch.

The **'Deutsches Haus' Public House, Munich** (1879; largely destroyed), by Gabriel von Seidl (1848–1913), reflected the trend towards authentic vernacular idioms, a Bavarian counterpart of the English 'Queen Anne' revival. It combined characteristic Northern Renaissance features, such as a picturesque domed corner turret and a strapwork gable, with a generally flat treatment of wall surfaces, providing an opportunity for painted decoration in the German tradition. Among Seidl's later works is the **Bavarian National Museum, Munich** (1894–99), in which the chronological arrangement of the museum's exhibits is expressed by a sequence of architectural styles, from Romanesque to nineteenth-century 'Rundbogen', dominated by a powerful centrepiece of Northern Renaissance design.

The **Maison du Peuple, Brussels** (1896–8; demolished 1965) (p. 1144A), designed by Victor Hortá for the Belgian Socialist Party, was remarkable for its skilful planning on an irregular site (a segment of a circular 'place') and for its brilliant use of glass and

Rylands Library, Deansgate, Manchester (1890–9). See p. 1138

A. School of Art, Glasgow (1897–1909): north front. See p. 1138

B. School of Art, Glasgow: the library

C. School of Art, Glasgow: west end

D. Whitechapel Art Gallery, London (1897–1901). See p. 1138

A. New Scotland Yard, London (1887–90). See p. 1135

B. Hôtel Tassel, No. 6, Rue Paul-Emile-Janson, Brussels (1892–3). See p. 1152

C. Town Hall, Colchester (1898–1902). See p. 1138

A. Stadttheater, Cologne (1870–2). See p. 1138

B. Petit Palais, Paris (1897–1900). See p. 1143

iron. Large windows lit the café and shops on the lower floors, while the iron framework of the top-floor auditorium showed how the flowing lines of Art Nouveau could be consistently and inventively exploited for structural purposes.

The **Petit Palais, Paris** (1897–1900) (p. 1142B), an art gallery by Charles-Louis Girault (1851–1932), was designed for the International Exhibition of 1900, along with the neighbouring Grand Palais and Pont Alexandre III. Its domed pavilions are characteristic of the neo-Baroque, but the more restrained Ionic colonnades introduce a Beaux-Arts discipline. It has an unusual trapezoidal plan, and the exhibition rooms are arranged around a semicircular courtyard. In two corners of the building, staircases of reinforced concrete by François Hennebique (1842–1921) spiral down from cantilevered galleries, their daring construction now concealed by subsequent enclosures.

The **Menier Chocolate Factory, Noisiel-sur-Marne** (1871–2) (p. 1145A), by Jules Saulnier (1828–1900), was a pioneer example of a full skeleton-frame in iron. It stands on massive stone piers over the river Marne, which provides power for the turbines. In the outer walls the slender iron members enclose brick panels laid in bold coloured patterns which echo the diagonal bracing of the iron frame, the effect somewhat resembling half-timber work.

The **Bon Marché, Paris**, was the pioneer department store, established in 1852 by Aristide Boucicaut. Its first purpose-built premises were greatly extended in 1876 by Louis-Charles Boileau (1837–1910) and Gustave Eiffel (1832–1923) with a spacious iron and glass structure, Classically detailed, which has now been obscured by later alterations.

The **Galerie des Machines, International Exhibition, Paris** (1889; demolished 1910) (p. 1144C), by the engineer Victor Contamin (1840–93) and the architect Charles Louis Ferdinand Dutert (1845–1906), had an unprecedented unsupported span of 114 m (375 ft). Its constituent steel principals formed four-centred arches, hinged at the apex and the base, where they tapered to their bearings in defiance of traditional aesthetic expectations. For the same exhibition, the **Eiffel Tower** (p. 1145C) was constructed as an entrance archway. At the time, this was the world's tallest structure (300 m; 985 ft), and in designing it Gustave Eiffel drew on his recent experience of building iron bridges.

Kolonáda M. Gorkého, Marianské Lázně (1884–9), by Miksch and Niedzielski, is one of the splendours of the Czech Republic spas, the colonnade at Marienbad, with a kind of hammerbeam roof, mostly constructed of cast iron.

The **Wertheim Department Store, Berlin** (1896–1904), was designed by Alfred Messel (1853–1909) in two stages. The first (1896–9) made extensive use of iron and glass, but the second part (1900–4) was of more substantial appearance externally, with tall mullioned windows lending an air of almost Gothic dignity.

The **Stock Exchange, Amsterdam** (1898–1903) (p. 1144B), the major work of H. P. Berlage, avoids any kind of monumental historicism. Inside and out, great importance is put on the qualities of the brick wall, and where stone is introduced it is flush with the brickwork. In the main hall, low arcades of segmental arches emphasise the load-bearing character of the walls, while a glass roof, neatly supported on steel trusses, lights the space and counteracts any sense of ponderousness. The same architect's **Diamond Workers' Union Building, Amsterdam** (1899–1900) (p. 1147A), has similar qualities of rational simplicity. It is again largely of brick, and the somewhat severe forms are balanced by a more varied outline.

The **Eagle Insurance Building, Birmingham** (1899–1900) (p. 1147B), by W. R. Lethaby and Joseph Lancaster Ball, highlights the predicament of the Arts and Crafts movement when faced with a commercial building in an urban situation. With historicism rejected and vernacular modes patently inappropriate, Lethaby compromised between a vague Tudor, as in the ground-floor windows, stripped Classicism, seen in the fenestration of the upper floors, and abstract patterns of primary forms, evident in the frieze. Honest intentions and nagging doubt could not be expressed more clearly than in this revealing design. Other buildings by Lethaby include **Avon Tyrell, Christchurch** (1891), **Melsetter House, Hoy, Orkney** (1898) and **All Saints, Brockhampton** (1902).

Métro Station, Place de la Bastille, Paris (1900, demolished) (p. 1145B), by Hector Guimard (1867–1942), a metal and glass structure, well illustrates the characteristics of Art Nouveau. The Métro entrances were composed from a repertoire of standard cast-iron parts, their sinuous lines giving an organic vitality to the various compositions. Whether the stations had substantial covered entrances, as in the Place de la Bastille, or merely archways with railings, their common style was quite distinctive and an important part of the Métro's identity.

The **Church of the Sacré Coeur, Paris** (begun 1875) (p. 1148A), was designed by Paul Abadie (1812–84) and was largely completed by the end of the century but not wholly finished until 1919. It stands with its cluster of white domes on the heights of Montmartre, and is one of the landmarks of Paris. The design reflects Byzantine influence by way of the mediaeval cathedral of S. Front, Périgueux.

Truro Cathedral, Cornwall (1879–1910) (p. 1148D), by J. L. Pearson, was incomplete at his death and was continued by his son. It exemplifies the architect's refined Early Gothic style, with lancet windows and sharp spires rising from square towers to give a powerful vertical emphasis. It is of granite, and the interior spaces are unified by stone vaulting,

A. Maison du Peuple, Brussels (1896–8; demolished 1965). See p. 1138

B. Stock Exchange, Amsterdam (1898–1903). See p. 1143

C. Galerie des Machines, International Exhibition, Paris (1889; demolished 1910). See p. 1143

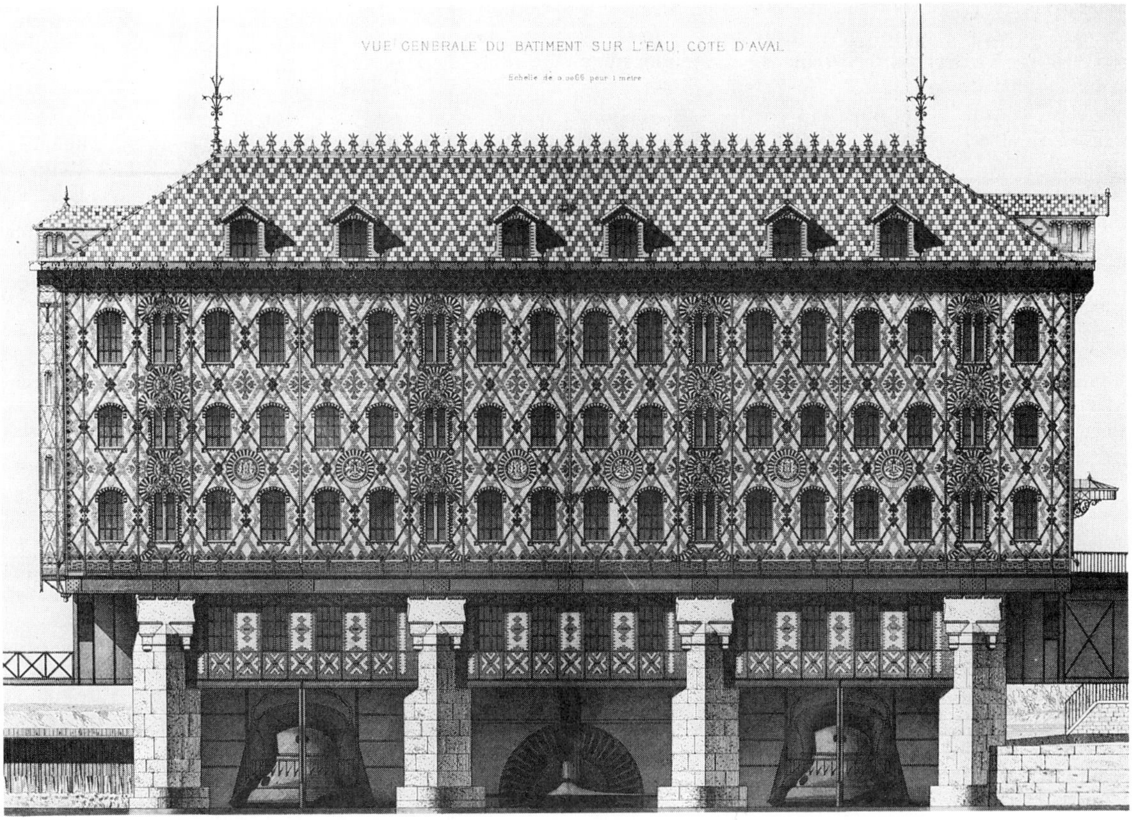

A. Menier Chocolate Factory, Noisiel-sur-Marne (1871–2). See p. 1143

B. Métro Station, Place de la Bastille, Paris (1900; demolished). See p. 1143

C. The Eiffel Tower (1887–9). See p. 1143

not often used in churches at this time. Pearson's **S. Augustine, Kilburn, London** (1871–7) (p. 1146D), is particularly notable for its slender piers and high brick vaults.

The **Church of the Sagrada Familia, Barcelona** (crypt 1882–91; chevet 1887–92; transept facade of the Nativity 1892–1930) (p. 1148B), by Antoni Gaudí, is still largely unfinished and was seen by Gaudí as the work of generations, a building which would evolve painstakingly rather than a design which was fully thought out from the beginning. The facade of the Nativity has three steeply gabled, deeply recessed porches, the outer ones corresponding to the transept aisles, dominated by four skittle-shaped openwork spires. The porches are profusely ornamented with naturalistic sculpture beneath stonework which gives the impression of soft, melting snow. The four fantastic towers are capped with enormous faceted finials, studded with broken coloured tiles. The nave was to have had a double avenue of columns, reaching up like sinewy trees to sustain a shallow vault pierced by round openings to admit shafts of daylight. The transept facade of the Passion was begun in 1960 on the basis of Gaudí's designs. Rising up to its portals are six leaning props, as tense as ligaments.

Holy Trinity, Chelsea, London (1888–91) (p. 1147C), by J. D. Sedding, is built in a free version of the Decorated and Perpendicular styles, with an elaborate west front of red brick with stone dressings. The church is decorated with furnishings and fittings by notable members of the Arts and Crafts movement, including stained glass by Burne-Jones and metalwork by Sedding's assistant, Henry Wilson (1864–1934). Amongst Sedding's other churches are **S.Clement, Boscombe, Dorset** (1871–3), and **Holy Redeemer, Clerkenwell, London** (1887–8), both of which have towers by Henry Wilson.

The **Roman Catholic Cathedral, Westminster** (1895–1903) (p. 1148C), by J. F. Bentley, is the one major English building based on the revival of Byzantine architecture. Three pendentived domes cover the length of the spacious nave and a slightly smaller dome is set over the sanctuary, beyond which lies the apse of the choir. The nave is flanked by vaulted aisles with side chapels, and short transepts with twin barrel vaults abut the easternmost dome of the nave. The grey-brown brickwork of the interior, once impressive in its plainness, is being progressively sheathed with marble and mosaic, as Bentley had intended. Externally the walls are of red brick with stone bands, and there are a number of cupola-topped turrets which echo the tall campanile that rises near the north-west angle. Among Bentley's other churches is **Holy Rood, Watford, near London** (1883–90), a sensitive Gothic design with walls of flint and stone.

S. Jean-de-Montmartre, Paris (1894; built 1897–1904) (p. 1149), is by J.-E.-A. de Baudot, a follower of Viollet-le-Duc, whose preference for Gothic and advocacy of new materials both influenced de Baudot's design. The church is built of reinforced concrete in conjuction with areas of reinforced brick-work, a hybrid system which he had already used in some houses and a school. The design is a paraphrase of a mediaeval church, with an emphasis on structural features such as rib-vaulting, but the decoration is provided by surface patterns so as not to compromise the flat surfaces of the new material.

Tampere Cathedral (1899–1907), by Lars Sonck (1870–1956), is an important example of the National Romantic movement in Finland. It has rock-faced granite masonry which recalls the primitive buildings of mediaeval Finland, and an interior decorated with symbolist wall-paintings.

Kinmel Park, Clwyd (1868–74; badly damaged by fire in 1975) (pp. 1150A, 1151A), by William Eden Nesfield, illustrates what came to be known as the 'Queen Anne' style. Many of its features derive from Wren's work at Hampton Court and other examples of the English Renaissance: red brick with stone dressings, sash windows, pilasters and segmental pediments. The mansard roofs introduce an element of the French Renaissance. However, it is not planned on the axial principles of Classical architecture, and the picturesque layout reflects Nesfield's training in the Gothic tradition.

Lowther Lodge, Kensington Gore, London (1873–5) (p. 1150C), is one of R. N. Shaw's important contributions to the 'Queen Anne' movement which – like his 'Old English' country house style – permitted freedom of planning without Gothic associations. It is notable for its ornamental brick features, including thin pilasters, cornices and fancy gables, but its syncopated composition is more Mannerist than anything known to the English Renaissance. Shaw's **Swan House, Chelsea, London** (1875–7), has a more symmetrical facade, made memorable by the unexpected conjunction of generous first-floor oriels and attenuated second-floor windows. **170 Queen's Gate, London** (1888–90) (p. 1150B), also by Shaw, is more truly akin to original seventeenth-century houses than most examples of the so-called 'Queen Anne' revival. Bay windows and picturesqueness have been quite abandoned in favour of formality and regularity.

Schloss Linderhof, near Oberammergau (1874–8) (p. 1155A), by Georg von Dollmann, was built for Ludwig II of Bavaria in South German Rococo style. It is superbly sited with delightful formal gardens and sumptuous and finely executed Rococo interiors. Another of Ludwig II's Bavarian palaces is **Herrenchiemsee** (begun 1878), an island château directly based on Louis XIV's Versailles, and also designed by Dollmann. Ludwig's most spectacular project was the mountain castle **Neuschwanstein** (1869–81), by Eduard Riedel (1813–85) and Doll-

A. Diamond Workers' Union Building, Amsterdam (1899–1900). See p. 1143

B. Eagle Insurance Building, Birmingham (1899–1900). See p. 1143

C. Holy Trinity, Chelsea, London (1888–91). See p. 1146

D. S. Augustine, Kilburn, London (1871–7). See p. 1146

A. Church of the Sacré Coeur, Paris (begun 1875). See p. 1143

B. Church of the Sagrada Familia, Barcelona: transept facade of the Nativity (1892–1930) seen from the inner side. See p. 1146

C. Roman Catholic Cathedral, Westminster (1895–1903). See p. 1146

D. Truro Cathedral, Cornwall (1879–1910). See p. 1143

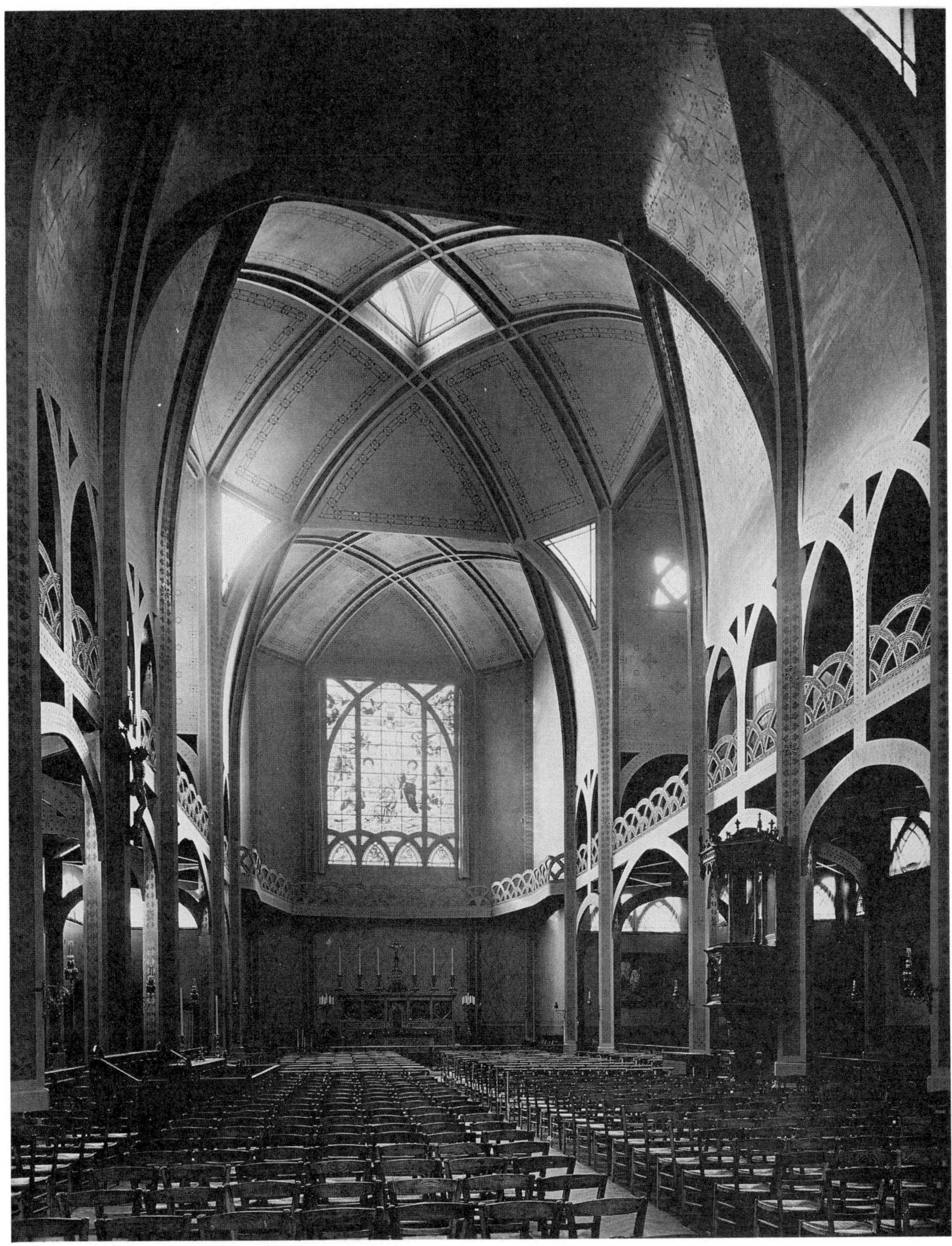

S. Jean-de-Montmartre, Paris (1894; built 1897–1904). See p. 1146

A. Kinmel Park, Clwyd (1868–74). See p. 1146

B. 170 Queen's Gate, London (1888–90). See p. 1146

C. Lowther Lodge, Kensington Gore, London (1873–5). See p. 1146

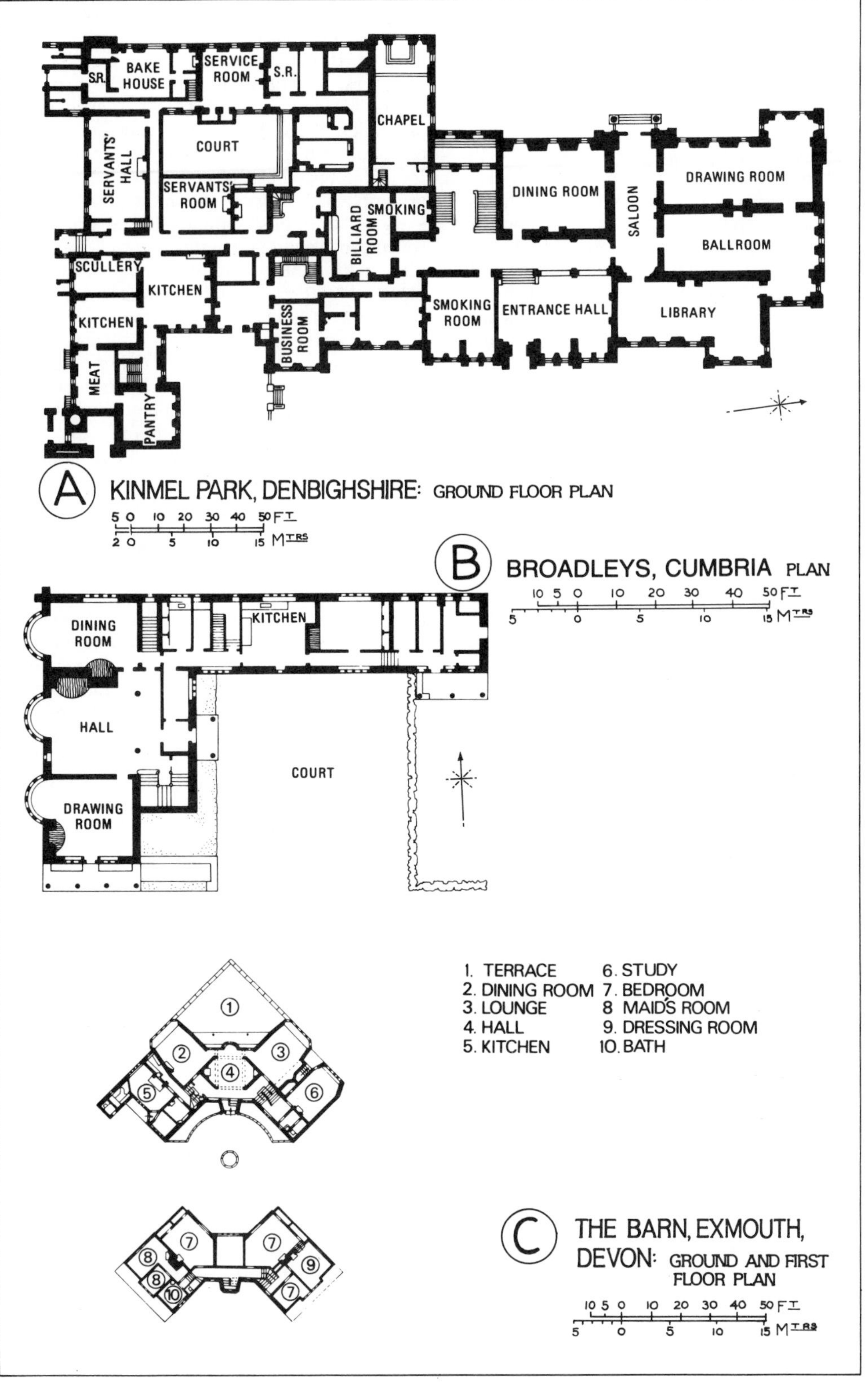
SERVICE ROOM
S.R.
BAKE HOUSE
S.R.
CHAPEL
COURT
SERVANTS' HALL
SERVANTS' ROOM
BILLIARD ROOM
SMOKING
DINING ROOM
SALOON
DRAWING ROOM
BALLROOM
SCULLERY
KITCHEN
KITCHEN
SMOKING ROOM
ENTRANCE HALL
LIBRARY
BUSINESS ROOM
MEAT
PANTRY
A KINMEL PARK, DENBIGHSHIRE: GROUND FLOOR PLAN
5 0 10 20 30 40 50 FT
2 0 5 10 15 MTRS
B BROADLEYS, CUMBRIA PLAN
10 5 0 10 20 30 40 50 FT
5 0 5 10 15 MTRS
DINING ROOM
KITCHEN
HALL
COURT
DRAWING ROOM
1. TERRACE
2. DINING ROOM
3. LOUNGE
4. HALL
5. KITCHEN
6. STUDY
7. BEDROOM
8 MAID'S ROOM
9. DRESSING ROOM
10. BATH
C THE BARN, EXMOUTH, DEVON: GROUND AND FIRST FLOOR PLAN
10 5 0 10 20 30 40 50 FT
5 0 5 10 15 MTRS

mann. It is a fantastic creation, erupting with turrets from its rocky perch, and decorated in Wagnerian spirit. Together these buildings exemplify Ludwig's passion for magnificent architectural settings, and are as indebted to stage-designers as to more conventional architects.

The **White House, Chelsea, London** (1877–9; demolished 1960s), by E. W. Godwin, was built as a studio-house for the artist J. A. M. Whistler, and was as unconventional as its owner. A large studio on the upper floor had its window facing north, and was expressed on the front of the house by a deep roof of green tiles which contrasted with the white-rendered brickwork of the wall below. The deliberate asymmetry of the windows and the plainness of the walls reflected the involvement of Godwin and Whistler in the Aesthetic movement. Although the Metropolitan Board of Works insisted that ornamental panels should be added to the facade, the design was remarkably spartan, and marked a distinct break with historical precedent.

Casa Vicens, Barcelona (designed 1878), a suburban villa, was the first major commission of Antoni Gaudí. Its stepped stalactitic forms suggest Islamic precedents, and the rubble-and-brick walling is liberally embellished with polychrome tiles. The house was greatly enlarged in 1924–7.

The **Palau Güell, Barcelona** (1885–9) (p. 1155B), by Gaudí, has a less exotic facade than the Casa Vicens, but the twin parabolic portals are a striking feature with grilles of curvilinear ironwork seeming to presage Art Nouveau. The climax of the interior is a high central room, with an organ and minstrels' gallery, which rises to a blue-tiled parabolic dome.

The Cottage, Bishop's Itchington, Warwickshire (1888–9) (p. 1153A), by Charles Francis Annesley Voysey (1857–1941), was his first house to be built and, although using traditional materials and forms, it combines them in an original and non-revivalist way. Many of the elements of Voysey's distinctly individual style of house are found here: an emphatically horizontal hipped roof, continuous ranges of mullioned windows (those at first-floor level being immediately below the eaves), white roughcast walls with sloping buttresses, and wide doors with strap hinges. Voysey enjoyed a considerable practice and his work was widely published in Britain and Germany. **Broadleys, Cumbria** (1898–9) (p. 1151B), is one of his best houses. Situated on the east side of Lake Windermere, it is planned so that the main rooms have bow windows overlooking the shore, and an east-west service wing shelters the entrance court from the north. The principal living room is a two-storey hall, a common feature of contemporary domestic planning, and a first-floor gallery links suites of bedrooms. **The Orchard, Chorley Wood, Hertfordshire** (1899–1900) (p. 1153B), the house Voysey built for his own use, epitomises his attitude to interior design, with expanses of plain colour as the setting for unstained oak furniture.

Bryanston, Dorset (1889–94) (p. 1156B), and **Chesters, Northumberland** (1890–4) (p. 1154A,B), by R. N. Shaw, both illustrate a return to Classical principles of axial design in plan and symmetry in elevation, further reinforced by the introduction of an Ionic colonnade at Chesters. Both houses are highly accomplished works attempting to continue and extend the English country-house tradition of the seventeenth and eighteenth centuries, and both make play with Gibbs surrounds (emphasising alternate blocks of stone around openings and in quoins). Bryanston has features in common with Coleshill House, Berkshire, especially in the treatment of the main block, but the contrast of red brick and Portland stone is more swaggering. Chesters incorporates an older house to which Shaw added wings to create the concave frontages to the south and west.

Hôtel Tassel, No. 6, Rue Paul-Emile-Janson, Brussels (1892–3) (p. 1141B), by Victor Horta, is often regarded as the first complete building in the fully-fledged Art Nouveau style. It is a narrow-fronted house and the main element of its generally unobtrusive facade is a segmental oriel window with steel lintels and mullions. Inside, iron is extensively used to open up the centre of the deep building, especially around the stairs and internal conservatory space. The tensile qualities of iron are extensively exploited for both structure and decoration, in free-flowing tendril-like forms which are echoed in the mosaic floor and painted wall surfaces. Among Horta's other houses in Brussels are the **Hôtel Sovay, No. 224, Avenue Louise** (1895), in which the facade is more plastic and incorporates attenuated iron columns, and the **Hôtel van Eetvelde, No. 4, Avenue Palmerston** (1895–7; extended 1898–1901), where steel stanchions are boldly employed externally. In the latter, the interior is arranged around a superb octagonal space which is ringed with slender iron columns flowing into elliptical arches and supporting a shallow glass dome.

The Barn, Exmouth, Devon (1896–7) (pp. 1151C, 1153C), by E. S. Prior, is one of the most thorough-going examples of the architecture of the Arts and Crafts movement. The plan, consisting of two diagonal arms linked by a central two-storey hall, is unusual but practical. The verandah and terrace, enclosed in the southern angle, overlook the coast-line, as do the principal rooms, which are all placed on that side of the house, with the entrance and service rooms disposed on the opposite side. The staggered floor levels are a response to the slope of the site, and Prior's passion for the organic relationship of a building to its locality is expressed in the richly textured masonry of sandstone blocks interspersed with red pebbles from the beach. The roof, originally thatched, was rebuilt with local

A. The Cottage, Bishop's Itchington, Warwickshire (1888–9). See p. 1152

B. The Orchard, Chorley Wood, Hertfordshire (1899–1900). See p. 1152

C. The Barn, Exmouth, Devon (1896–7). See p. 1152

A. Chesters, Northumberland (1890–4). See p. 1152

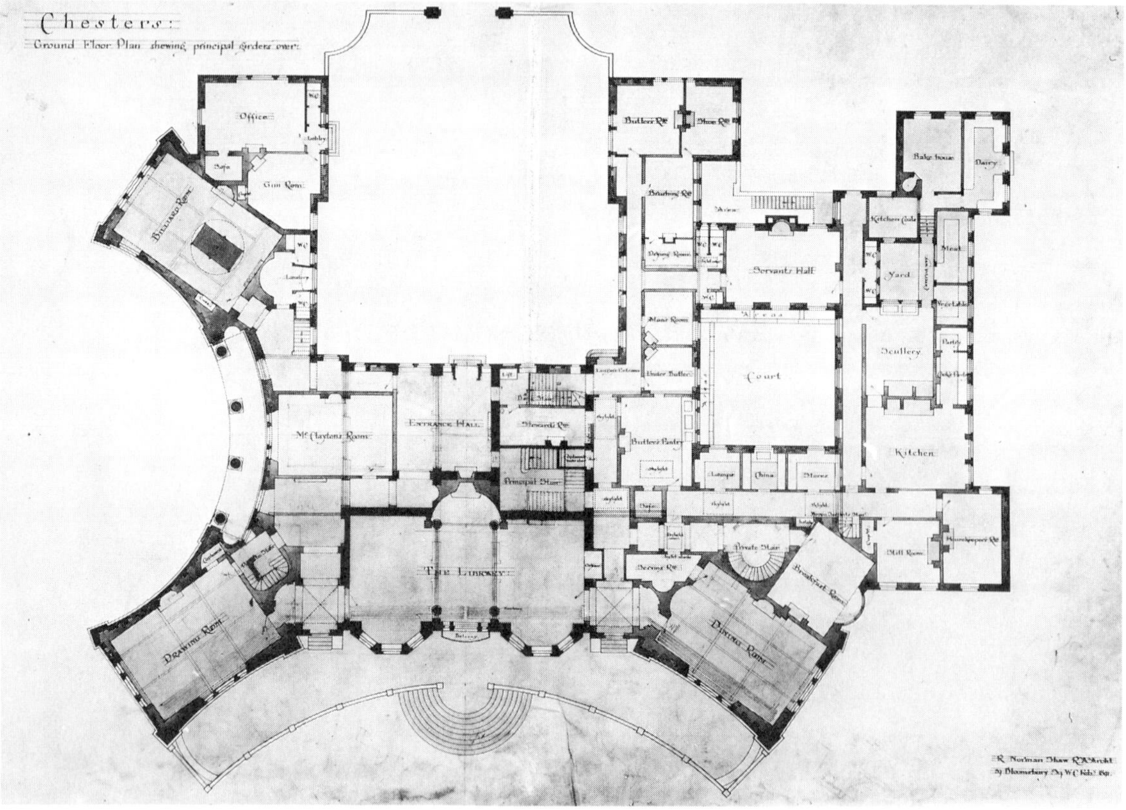

B. Chesters, Northumberland: plan of ground floor

A. Schloss Linderhof, near Oberammergau (1874–8). See p. 1146

B. Palau Güell, Barcelona (1885–9). See p. 1152

A. Deanery Garden, Sonning, Berkshire (1899–1902). See p. 1158

B. Bryanston, Dorset (1889–94). See p. 1152

A. No. 40, Linke Wienzeile (The Majolica House), Vienna (1898–9). See p. 1158

B. Poznański Factory and Housing Complex, Lódtź: factory and palace. See p. 1158

slates after a fire in 1905. Another characteristic house by Prior is **Home Place, Holt, Norfolk** (1904–6), also built on a 'butterfly' plan and constructed largely from materials excavated on site.

'Pod Jedlami', Zakopane (1897), a villa by Stanislaw Witkiewicz (1851–1915), is one of the first examples of Polish cultural self-determination, expressed through the choice of the native wooden peasant-hut style to serve as a model for a sizable holiday villa for the new intellectual bourgeoisie.

Deanery Garden, Sonning, Berkshire (1899–1902) (p. 1156A), by Sir Edwin Lutyens, demonstrates the architect's indebtedness to the Arts and Crafts movement in the sensitive use of local brick and tile, and the oak frame of the two-storey hall. The composition is less picturesque than some of Lutyens's earlier work, but not yet neo-Georgian, and the long roof of the south-west front is broken only by the hipped bay of the hall window and a strong chimney stack which rises from beside the deep-arched entrance. Deanery Garden was built for the founder of *Country Life* magazine, Edward Hudson, for whom Lutyens also restored **Lindisfarne Castle, Northumberland** (1903–4). **Tigbourne Court, Witley, Surrey** (1899–1901), is another characteristic house by Lutyens.

No. 40, Linke Wienzeile (The Majolica House), Vienna (1898–9) (p. 1157A), a block of flats by Otto Wagner, has a six-storey facade crisply punctuated by regularly-spaced windows and terminated by an emphatic cornice, a pattern known at least since Schinkel's Feilner House. Here, however, to counter the generally severe rectangular forms, the tiles which cover the facade are designed with swirling linear patterns with colourful flowers and foliage, and the ironwork of the balconies has sunflower decoration.

Poznański Factory and Housing Complex, Lódź (from 1872) (p. 1157B), was mostly designed by Hilary Majewski (1837–97). The vast textile industry of Lódź, notably cotton, was a creation of the Russian Empire close to its western borders, bringing together Western capital and expertise with a local labour force. The palace (1904) by A. Seligson, for the factory owner I. K. Poznánski, was built adjacent to the factory buildings on one side, huge blocks of workers' flats on the other. This arrangement of a well-ordered community, its elements carefully differentiated architecturally, is one of the most complete manifestations of nineteenth-century industrialism.

Part Six

THE ARCHITECTURE OF THE COLONIAL AND POST-COLONIAL PERIODS OUTSIDE EUROPE

Chapter 35
BACKGROUND

Introduction

For this part of the book the amount of background material required varies from region to region. Thus, for example, the general descriptive and locational material for Australia and New Zealand, which now appears for the first time, is more detailed than for Africa or South-east Asia, which have already received attention in Part 4, Chapter 21.

To reiterate a point made elsewhere in the book, divisions which rely upon living political and cultural movements are intended here only as convenient labels in so far as they make the architecture of towns and cities more comprehensible in the context of vastly increased building activity in the service of growing populations (see Introduction). Some of the continuities are made apparent: for example, the far-flung activities of the European maritime nations, as ship-building technology and cartographic and navigational skills improved, resulted in the diffusion of European architectural styles into the Americas, around the coasts of Africa, India and South-east Asia even in the early and middle years of the seventeenth century, when, in some cases, the motivation was trade in precious or exotic commodities, in others discovery for its own sake.

Africa

Savannah and steppe grasslands extend over more than half the African continent, stretching from the Atlantic coast of Senegal and Guinea right across to Ethiopia, roughly 2000 km (1240 miles) to the north of the equator, and almost 3000 km (1860 miles) to the south as far as the Tropic of Capricorn. Further to the north the Sahara desert extends from east to west, giving way to a fertile region along the Mediterranean coast. To the south-west of the great savannah area is the Kalahari desert, contained roughly within Botswana, and the Namib desert which extends along the Atlantic coast of South West Africa (Namibia). To the east of the Kalahari desert are the highland region of Transvaal and low-lying Mozambique, while the rest of South Africa down to the Cape of Good Hope is once again Mediterranean in character. Tropical rain forest extends along the equatorial region of the West African coast from Sierra Leone through Ghana and Nigeria, until it expands to take in the whole of the Congo basin; a smaller belt is found further south along the line of the Zambesi river.

Bisected by the equator, most of Africa is always hot. In the tropical rain forest, as the name implies, rain falls frequently and heavily, and it is always humid. Outside these areas the rainfall is normally concentrated in one short season which produces extensive flooding and soil erosion. The soil of the savannah is poor and generally infertile, leached as it is of minerals by the rainfall, and lacking in humus which is oxidised by the heat. The better-watered, lower and hotter regions support a heavier vegetation of deciduous woodland. On the upper, drier zones of eastern and southern Africa open downland provides fine grazing. The vast Sahara desert causes the Harmattan to bring dust to West Africa from November to March, but its dryness alleviates the generally humid climate.

Iron oxide is present in most tropical soils, and it was from Egypt that the use of iron penetrated into what is now Sudan, spreading gradually through the middle continental belt and then south towards the Cape of Good Hope. Copper is found in the desert of Mauritania and Niger, but to a greater extent in southern Zaire and northern Zambia. Both minerals formed part of an extensive traditional trading network, but gold and diamonds were of far greater importance, and it was the former that drew traders to the continent in the fifteenth century. Goldfields were being developed in Zimbabwe as early as the closing years of the Early Iron Age, and there was a long-established trade in gold to the towns of the Indian Ocean, and thence to Arabia or India. Equally, gold had been the most valuable product in the trans-Saharan caravan trade from West African gold-fields, principally those of Bambuk between the Senegal and Faleme rivers, of Bure in north-east Guinea, of Lobi on the edge of the tropical forest near the Volta river, and of Akan in the heart of the forest and nearest to Elmina. It was gold from the Akan mines that was exported to the trading posts set up on the coast by the Portuguese and other European powers from the fifteenth century onwards. Gold was discovered in the Transvaal, South Africa, in the 1850s; but it was not until 1886 that its extent in that region was realised and the rush began which, among other results, led to the founding of Johannesburg. The discovery of a superb white diamond of 85 carats (the Star of Africa) near the Orange river in 1869 revealed the continent's other precious natural resource – 'the rock on which the future of South Africa will be built'. Then followed the rush to the Orange Free State, the growth of Kimberley, and the success of Cecil Rhodes, who saw his diamond empire as the foundation on which to build complete British dominion in Africa.

Although European influence in the fifteenth and sixteenth centuries had atrophied, Muslim development continued along the Mediterranean coasts and had been felt in some areas of eastern Africa as the development of Ghana, Mali and Songhay continued in sub-Saharan Africa. It is important to note that the new European incursions were contemporary with developments such as these – the great Madrassa of Sultan Qaitbay in Cairo had not yet been started when the Portuguese fortified their first settlement on the west coast of Africa.

Portugal's merchant adventurers of the fifteenth and sixteenth centuries reintroduced European architecture to the African continent after the long interval since the last Byzantine outpost on the Mediterranean coast had fallen to the Muslims in AD 708. There had been an attempt by Genoese explorers to sail around Africa and reach the Indies by way of the Atlantic in 1291, but the first Europeans to succeed were the Portuguese. In 1443 Henry the Navigator reached Arguin on the southern fringe of the Sahara Desert, where the first trading post was set up. Twenty years later the Portuguese had charted the mouths of the Senegal and Gambia, and then in 1471 their navigators landed on a stretch of the West African coast which they named Elmina, 'the mine'. Gold, ivory, gems and spices were the material goal, and defensible buildings were an essential requirement in their trading activities.

It was not only in West Africa that the Portuguese established trading posts and built forts. At about the same time as they built their first castle at Elmina they had settled at Malindi on the coast of East Africa and built Fort S. Sebastian on Mozambique Island. At the end of the sixteenth century they constructed Fort Jesus close to the old Arab town of Mombasa and at a strategic point overlooking the best harbour on the coast. But by the early seventeenth century the main European trade had been taken over by the Dutch, who continued to build forts along the West African coast; and in 1650 the Dutch East India Company decided to set up a station at the Cape of Good Hope at the most southerly point of the continent.

The trading forts on the west and east coasts sometimes attracted the building of merchants' houses close by, but they were seldom colonies in the general meaning of the word. However, a colony was quickly established on the Cape, and characteristic town houses were built in Cape Town as well as homesteads or farm houses in the surrounding countryside. These were closely based on Dutch precedents. As the colony prospered, public buildings and churches were erected; and by the last quarter of the eighteenth century identifiable architects were working in Cape Town.

The Dutch East India Company was dissolved in 1793 when the Cape was occupied by the British, who handed it back to the Dutch State in 1803, but took it back in 1806. At about the same time, Napoleon's campaigns of 1789–99 in Egypt were forging a link between France and Egypt which was to result in a strong French interest in Egypt and North Africa generally. In 1830 France occupied Algeria where it imposed characteristic policies on the replanning of the old city of Algiers. In 1883 it established a protectorate over Tunisia, and twenty years later turned its attention to Morocco.

After Britain had finally taken over the Cape Colony in 1806, English architectural taste gradually modified the Dutch influence, in public buildings as well as in houses; nor was this confined to buildings. It was as a result of this influence and the insistence on driving English ways and beliefs into the Boer culture that the Afrikaners undertook the Great Trek of 1831–8 which eventually led to the foundation of the Boer Republics and, incidentally, to some distinctions between the later nineteenth-century architecture in the British colony and the new republics. But in both the buildings were often hardly distinguishable from their European counterparts, although there were some specifically South African characteristics in planning and in such external treatment as the lavish use of iron verandahs and balconies.

Meanwhile in East and West Africa mission stations were established by various European organisations throughout the nineteenth century in succession to the earlier Portuguese and Spanish missions; it was they who were largely responsible for introducing European architecture, even it had to be modified by the resources available. In building their churches and mission houses they sometimes combined national architectural characteristics with indigenous materials and methods of construction; and in developing appropriate houses for tropical countries they often displayed some ingenuity, in particular the Basel Mission.

The introduction of the railway led to a gradual diffusion of imported building materials, which had been confined at first to the coastal areas where they could easily be offloaded from ships. Missionaries introduced corrugated iron for roofing in the 1850s, and it found favour as a precaution against fire hazards. In the 1860s they set up a brick kiln in Lagos, Nigeria, and provided an alternative to the ubiquitous earth as a walling material. By the late nineteenth century there was a steady demand in such towns as Zanzibar for steel beams, cast-iron columns and brackets, and other European materials which were considered desirable embellishments of the vernacular buildings. In the prosperous South African colonies there was a much greater reliance on imported materials for walls, roofs, cast-iron verandah poles and decorative tiling; and when the prefabrication of faience facades was perfected in Britain, these too were shipped out.

The 'scramble for Africa' by most European powers in the last quarter of the nineteenth century introduced another factor. The Anglo-French agreements arising from British seizure of Egypt and the Suez Canal, the taking of a large part of central Africa by Belgium, the acquisition by Germany of parts of West and East Africa, the division of Morocco by France and Spain, were all symptomatic of the rapid growth of western European capitalism and the parallel rise of European nationalism and imperialism. In architectural terms this was often expressed in the styles chosen for the colonial buildings, such as the German government buildings in Dar-es-Salaam. In South Africa, where great wealth had been brought by the mining of gold and diamonds in the 1880s, Sir Herbert Baker's Union Buildings in Pretoria, like his later buildings in New Delhi, were symbolic of early twentieth-century imperial idealism.

The Americas

From the island bases originally secured by Columbus before the end of the fifteenth century, the Spanish pursued a policy of conquest and settlement in Central and South America. By 1600, as well as the islands of Santo Domingo and Puerto Rico, they had taken the whole of Central America as far north as the extent of present-day Mexico (Viceroyalty of New Spain), a substantial strip running the length of the west coast of South America, modern Peru and Chile (Viceroyalty of Peru), and later in Central America the Viceroyalty of New Granada (1739) and in the south the Viceroyalty of Rio de la Plata (1776). The Portuguese under their agreement with Spain limited their conquests to Brazil, and by 1600 had established their claim to an area which lay east of a line from just north of the mouth of the River Plate to the Amazon delta.

The Spanish colonists made little impression on the more easterly areas of the North American mainland, however. Their territory was limited to Florida, owing to the rival incursions, by the early years of the seventeenth century, of other European powers. The French had penetrated deeply south from the S. Lawrence down the Mississippi basin, and were on the Gulf of Mexico by 1682. The British were early on the eastern seaboard: Virginia by 1607, pilgrim fathers in New England in 1620 and more extensively after the Anglo-Dutch wars (1652–73). Their colonial settlements extended from Virginia to Nova Scotia and Newfoundland by the early eighteenth century, by which time the total population of the twelve English colonies was of the order of one-quarter of a million.

The products of the Spanish colonies in America were precious metals and cattle, of the Portuguese in Brazil sugar and other crops; apart from furs in the north, the British and French grew cotton and tobacco using slave labour in the south – some 100,000 slaves by the time of the American War of Independence. The Spanish and Portuguese relied upon Indian labour. It was autocratic control on the part of the European governments as well as unrest in the colonies themselves which led to the gradual break-up of the American colonial empires from the last quarter of the eighteenth century and through the nineteenth. This movement was initiated in the British colonies of the eastern seaboard of North America.

In 1774 representatives of the colonies met in Philadelphia as the First Continental Congress to discuss their relationship with Britain, especially with regard to taxation and trade, an event precipitated by the decision of the British government to close the port of Boston after angry colonists had refused to permit the landing of a shipment of tea on which they considered the tax unfair. The following year discontent flared up into open revolution which, with the adoption by the thirteen colonies of the Declaration of Independence, became in 1776 the American War of Independence. Peace came in 1783 and, with it, recognition of the independent status of the former colonies.

These at first formed a loose federation of separate republics, but in 1787 a constitution was drawn up whereby individuals became, for certain purposes, citizens of the federation itself and, for others, citizens of a particular state. The constitution, which remains in force today, was ratified in 1789. George Washington, the famous general of the War of Independence, was installed as first President of the United States of America in the same year.

From this point the history of the country was one of expansion. In 1803 the base area between the Mississippi and the Rockies was purchased from France (the Louisiana Purchase), and in 1819 Florida was similarly acquired from Spain. Texas was annexed in 1845 and, as a result of the ensuing war with Mexico, the south-western part of the country as far as the Californian coast was absorbed in 1848. Oregon territory in the north-west was ceded by

Britain in 1846, and small areas of Mexican territory added by the Gadsden Purchase of 1853. Finally, Alaska was bought from Russia in 1867.

Canada, which had remained loyal to Britain during the War of Independence, consisted of the four colonies of Upper and Lower Canada (both created in 1791), Nova Scotia and New Brunswick. Antagonism between Lower Canada, predominantly French, and Upper Canada led to a revolt in 1840, as a result of which Britain granted the colonies a broad constitution, providing for a parliament and the appointment of responsible ministers, the British Governor assuming a purely legal and symbolic role. With the passing of the British North American Act in 1867, the country was granted full Dominion status, which it retains within the British Commonwealth today. The Canadian Parliament and Ministries were set up at Ottawa, the national capital, on the lines of those at Westminster. To the original four provinces of Ontario (Upper Canada), Quebec (Lower Canada), Nova Scotia and New Brunswick, were added Manitoba (1870) and British Columbia (1871), former territories of the old Hudson Bay Company, and finally in 1905 the prairie provinces of Saskatchewan and Alberta.

In Latin America the viceroyalties of Spain and Portugal came to an end during the first quarter of the nineteenth century; after the failure of efforts to unite the former colonies into a federation similar to that of the USA, the subcontinent became separated into a complex of independent states, which has survived geographically unchanged to this day. During these stormy years of revolution and formation important roles were played by Simón Bolivar (1783–1830) in Colombia, Venezuela and Ecuador; by San Martin (1788–1850) in the Argentine and Peru; and by Bernardo O'Higgins in Chile. For a variety of reasons, mainly economic, the more stable countries were the Argentine, which owed much to its president General B. Mitre (1862–8) for his encouragement of railway building; Chile with its vast nitrate deposits; and Brazil. Modernisation of the last began under the Portuguese Regent (later John VI), forced by Napoleon's invasion of Portugal to move his capital to Rio de Janeiro in 1808. In 1821 John returned to Portugal and Brazil became a separate kingdom under his son, Pedro I. The latter abdicated in 1831 in favour of his infant son, who as Pedro II took over the throne in 1840. His long reign was marked by much material progress and reform, including the abolition of slavery in 1888. In 1889 an army revolt established a republic, which in 1891 adopted a federal constitution as the United States of Brazil.

Mexico obtained independence in 1821, but in 1858 was involved in bitter civil war. Supported by France, the Austrian Archduke Maximilian was installed as Emperor in 1864, but three years later, following the withdrawal of French troops, he was shot and the patriot Benito Juarez (1806–72), a Zapotec Indian, reassumed leadership of the country. But the creation of modern Mexico was left to Juarez's successor Porfirio Diaz (1830–1915), who ruled from 1876 to 1911.

Economically and socially the most advanced nation in the continent was the USA, where a sense of national identity had been reinforced by the war with Britain of 1812–14. By 1840 the country's trade was worth 250 million dollars per year, almost half being earned by the State of New York. Pennsylvania developed rapidly as its extensive coal and iron resources were exploited, but the main wealth of the country still lay in cotton, of which Louisiana's exports in 1840 were valued at 33 million dollars.

The presidency of Andrew Jackson (1829–37), a representative of the new frontier men, gave impetus to wider democratic ideals and greatly encouraged individual enterprise, while the farming prospects of the great tracts of land beyond the Alleghenies attracted increasing numbers of settlers, the westward movement being dramatically accelerated by the discovery of gold in California in 1848.

The coming to power in 1861 of an anti-slavery government under Abraham Lincoln (1809–65) brought to a head the rivalry between the more dynamic northern states and the cotton-producing southern states, with their long-established plantation system based on slavery, and kindled the tragic Civil War (1861–5), during the course of which, in 1863, slavery was abolished. The victory of the northern states, and of the union, was decisive for the future of the country and encouraged industrial development, which in turn greatly increased the rate of immigration.

Generally the period following the Civil War was one of continuing commercial expansion, an age offering great opportunities and high material rewards to individual industrialists, bankers, farmers and railway owners. This situation, clearly reflected in the architecture of the time, continued until the financial crash of 1929 and the ensuing depression. The opening-up of the country by railways was essential to development, and the continent was finally traversed by rail from coast to coast in 1869. Alexander Graham Bell's invention of the telephone in 1876 further facilitated communications across the vast country which was also linked to Europe by transatlantic cable. Finally the mass-production of the motor car between the two world wars further extended communications and movement.

As far as industry was concerned, Canada's development was much less rapid, its economy being based almost entirely on the export of timber and wheat. As in the USA, communications were of utmost importance: in 1847 improvements were completed on the S. Lawrence between Montreal and Lake Ontario, while the Canadian Pacific Railway had straddled the continent by 1885.

Like Canada, the countries of South America relied on the export of natural products rather than on manufacturing, and the opening of the Panama Canal in 1914 was of great significance in the development of the countries of the Pacific coast.

The architecture and the materials and techniques used in its realisation in the Americas by the colonists and settlers, as in other parts of the world, reflect faithfully the architecture of the corresponding periods in the home countries. From the splendid churches and cathedrals of sixteenth-century Spanish colonial cities in which masonry is used in vaulting, and Plateresque facades seem to have presented little problem, to the traditional Georgian of New England modified in the most delightful ways to meet the availability of local materials, the colonial periods seem to have established, in their various locales, architectural traditions which remained acceptable as the bases for development long after the yoke of European government became irksome. In such enormous territories the available materials varied widely, and it is of interest that good quality bricks were available in early seventeenth-century Virginia and fine glazed tiles in early eighteenth-century Mexico.

China

By the end of the fifteenth century some European powers began to seek eastward colonial expansion. The Portuguese were the first Westerners to come to the coast of Guangdong (Kwangtung) Province. They negotiated a lease of Aomen (Macao) from the local offical of the Ming dynasty in 1561. In Aomen they built fortifications and houses in the Western style – the earliest Western architecture to appear in China. In 1715 the Emperor Kang-xi (K'ang-hsi) of the Qing (Ch'ing) dynasty granted the East India Company the right to trade in Guangzhou (Canton). With the permission of the Qing government a special agency, 'Kohang', was established to take charge of the trade. Meanwhile, the Kohang constructed special buildings; the Thirteen Factories, as they were called, served as the living and trading centre for foreign merchants. After 1757 more Western merchants came to Guangzhou, among them, besides the British, the Dutch, the Americans, the Portuguese and the French. As a result the Thirteen Factories in Guangzhou were renovated and expanded many times.

During the same period Western missionaries also came to China. In 1581 Matteo Ricci, an Italian Jesuit, arrived in Guangdong by way of Aomen, and reached Beijing (Peking) in 1601. European missionaries brought with them the Catholic Christian faith as well as advanced science and technology. Roman Catholicism spread far and wide in China, and many churches appeared in different parts of the country. In the years 1745 to 1759, in the northern part of the Chang Chun Yuan (Garden of Everlasting Spring) of Yuan Ming Yuan (Garden of Perfection and Brightness), the famous imperial garden, a Western-style palace, known as Xi Yang Lou, was designed and built for the Emperor Qian-long (Ch'ien-lung) under the supervision of F. Giuseppe Castiglione, an Italian Jesuit and his colleagues who were serving in the imperial court.

The Opium War in 1840 marked the beginning of the modern history of China. The Western world succeeded at last in opening the door of ancient China with the help of its gunboats. China's 2000-year-old feudal society began to disintegrate and gradually became a semi-colonial one. After being defeated in the second Opium War of 1858, in the Sino-French war in 1884 and the Sino-Japanese War in 1894, China was compelled to sign a series of treaties, which reduced its sovereignty. Through the Nanking Treaty, signed in 1842, China opened five ports for foreign trade: Guangzhou (Canton), Xiamen (Amoy), Fuzhou (Foochow), Ningpo and Shanghai and ceded Hong Kong to Britain. By 1895, the number of open trading ports was increased to over thirty including many of the major cities along the Yangtse River, on the seacoast and even some inland and Taiwan was ceded to Japan. The foreign powers also seized many settlements and concessions in the cities of Shanghai, Tianjin (Tientsin), Hankou (Hankow) among others, and thus reduced these cities to semi-colonial status. In the following years Western-style buildings were constructed in the open ports and leased territories: these were consulates, municipal offices and trading companies, warehouses, banks, churches, schools, luxurious residences, restaurants, clubs and so on.

In the 1860s a number of bureaucrat-landlords, represented by Li Hong-zhang (Li Hung-chang), initiated the so-called 'Westernisation movement' for national defence and established munitions industries and other civil enterprises. After the Sino-Japanese War some forward-looking intellectuals led by Kang You-wei (K'ang Yu-wei) and Liang Qi-chao (Liang Ch'i ch'ao) advocated the reformation of the political system and the encouragement of Western science and technology. Supported by the Emperor Guang-xu (Kuang-hsü), they started a reform movement but were opposed by the Empress Dowager Ci-xi (Tz'u-shi) and her followers. After experiencing the Yihetuan Movement (the Boxer Uprising) and invasion by the Eight Power Allied Force, however, she was forced to change her attitude and acted in favour of reform. The educational system was altered, new schools were set up, advocating preparation for constitutional government. New governmental organs and provincial political consultative bureaux were founded. Most of the buildings constructed during this period imitated Western architectural models.

In the latter half of the nineteenth century and the early twentieth century traditional methods of building, in traditional building materials, were still maintained in most parts of China. In the trading ports and the leased territories Western building technology and more effective ways of using traditional materials were introduced, notably the wider use of load-bearing walls, timber trusses and beam and joist floors. China began to produce cement and steel at the turn of the nineteenth century in small quantities, but for some considerable time these materials were imported.

Korea

The demand by such countries as England, France, the United States, Russia, and Japan to open Korea for trade in the nineteenth century clashed with Korea's isolationist policies, and new cultural currents caused considerable confusion throughout Korean society. Taking advantage of the situation, Japan forced Korea to sign a commercial treaty in 1876, which is known as the Treaty of Kanghwa, and in 1905 a five-article protectorate treaty known as the Treaty of 1905.

Western-style architecture began to be introduced to Korea around this time. It was introduced in four ways: through foreign diplomatic missions, churches and other facilities built by foreign missionaries, commercial establishments constructed by foreign businesses, and government offices and public buildings built by the Japanese. Most of these structures were of Renaissance and Gothic styling and made of brick and cement.

There was no architectural development to speak of up to the 1910 annexation of Korea by Japan. And the Western-style buildings constructed by the Japanese after the forced opening of Korea to Japan with the 1876 signing of the Treaty of Kanghwa were poorly designed and constructed because of the relative inexperience of the Japanese architects. Moreover, Korea had little spiritual or material resources to divert to architecture as it experienced the Military Mutiny of 1882, the Kapshin *coup d'état* in 1884, the Ch'ondogyo Tonghak Rebellion in 1894, and the Sino-Japanese (1894) and Russo-Japanese (1904–5) wars.

Japan refused to train Koreans in technology after the 1910 annexation, and architecture was no exception. In the initial stages of colonial rule, Japan trained a limited number of Korean technicians in para-technical institutes. In the 1920s a small number of Koreans were given advanced architectural training but it was only after the 1930s that Korean architects were able to design works on their own.

Japan

The restoration of the Meiji Emperor brought about the political change necessary before Japan could emerge from feudalism and become a modern nation. In 1867, the fifteenth Tokugawa Shogun, renouncing his political power, abolished the feudal government and restored imperial rule. Upon establishment of the new government in 1868, lands formerly possessed by the shogunate were transferred to direct control by the new government. Between 1869 and 1871, the government also took control of the domains of the daimyo, and they were appointed prefectural governors. In this way the feudal system was replaced by the Imperial system under which the whole country was uniformly ruled. In 1873, a conscription system was adopted and the revision of land tax accomplished. Thereafter, no drastic political changes occurred for a time.

One of the factors that made the Meiji Restoration inevitable lay in the growth of commerce and industry, which had brought about the dissolution of the rural communities that had formed the economic bases of feudal government. A more direct factor, however, was the pressure exerted by the capitalist countries which, from the beginning of the nineteenth century, had forcibly sought the opening of the long-closed country. As a consequence of the commercial treaty concluded in 1858, Yokohama, Shimoda, Hakodate and Nagasaki ports were opened the following year to free trade with Russia, France, Britain and the United States. From then on, Japan was propelled toward adopting aspects of European civilisation and constrained to revise domestic policies in order to cope with the national crisis.

Even before the foundation of the new government, a policy to promote industries and build up military forces had been advanced by some feudal lords who perceived the coming crisis. The erection of blast furnaces in the 1850s, the casting of cannons, the construction of iron foundries or shipbuilding yards was undertaken. Such Western industries were developed further under the guidance of foreign engineers: the iron mill of Nagasaki was built by a Dutch engineer in 1861, and the spinning mill of Kagoshima was constructed under the direction of an American engineer in 1863. Settlements which included suitable housing, hotels, trading houses and churches for the exclusive use of foreign residents were constructed in Yokohama, Nagasaki, Hakodate and Kobe.

The new government not only inherited the policies of the feudal clans but also endeavoured anew to promote industries, to strengthen military forces and to construct public facilities nationwide. Although the buildings then required were all taken from the repertory of the traditional wooden architecture, it was necessary to construct them with Western techniques and styles. Thus the introduction of Western architecture began under the leadership of the Meiji government.

Indian Subcontinent and South-east Asia

Vasco da Gama rounded the Cape of Good Hope and sailed eastward to land at Calicut on the south-west coast of India on 20 May 1498. Primarily as Christian missions, but also with the spice trade in mind, settlements were established at Colombo in Sri Lanka (1505), and Goa on the western coast of India was taken by Albuquerque in 1510. Other Portuguese settlements were set up at Daman, Diu and Bombay, the last ceded to Britain in 1661 as part of the dowry of Catherine of Braganza; another, at Bassein, was lost to the Marathas in 1739. The Portuguese substantially held Sri Lanka until the middle of the seventeenth century, when it was taken over by the Dutch. There were Portuguese trading posts in Malacca by 1511 and in Martaban, Burma, by 1519.

The Dutch, primarily motivated by the trade in spices, formed the United East India Company (following earlier voyages to the East Indies, as they were called) in 1602. They had founded Batavia (modern Jakarta) and had gained almost complete control of Java by the end of the second decade of the seventeenth century and set about extending their grip upon other islands over the next century, even though there had been a British trading settlement on the western tip of Java since 1601.

In India and in many of the other south-east Asian countries of the period, these European incursions were made into Muslim-controlled states, and certainly the Portuguese saw their efforts in the east as an extension of their campaigns against Islam at home. Effective Hindu rule had ended with Malik Kafur's conquest of Tamil southern India and his sack of Madura. The Moghul empire burgeoned and reached its zenith under Akbar in the last quarter of the sixteenth century, and it was to his red sandstone city of Fatehpur Sikri that the first English adventurer, Thomas Newberry, came in 1585, carrying a letter from Queen Elizabeth which was completely ignored. The East India Company was founded with a charter from Elizabeth in 1600, and William Hawkins who sailed to India had better luck in his dealings with Akbar's son, Jehangir, who allowed him to set up a factory at Surat in 1608. Sir Thomas Roe followed in 1615, as accredited ambassador from James I, stayed for five years and has left a valuable account of his activities. It was the ability of the English to defeat the Portuguese at sea during these years which was at the root of the decline of Jesuit influence in India. After Jehangir's death in 1627, however, Moghul power was much reduced and the eighteenth century saw the rise of the less unified Marathas whose eventual downfall at the turn of the century opened the way to British control in India. Madras was established by 1640 on the south-east coast and Job Charnock had obtained permission to build the town of Calcutta on the Hooghly by 1690.

The French state-controlled Compagnie des Indes Orientales was not founded until 1664; Chandernagore on the Hooghly was established in 1673 and Pondicherry, 160 km (100 miles) south of Madras, in 1684. After Clive's Arcot adventure in 1751 and the capture of Pondicherry in 1761, French influence was negligible in India.

The establishment of orderly British rule stemmed from Lord North's Regulating Act of 1773 which established the governorship (over British India – Calcutta, Madras and Bombay) at Calcutta: the governor was to be assisted by four councillors. Warren Hastings was the first governor under the Act and the powers of the councillors made his task an impossible one. William Pitt changed the system in 1784, and there began in 1786 the line of great governors-general. Lord Wellesley came in 1798 when the East India Company was limited to the island of Bombay and areas of coastal territory around Madras and Calcutta, and by 1805 had expanded its activities into almost the whole of the subcontinent, and alarmed the directors by its cost. Lord Minto, appointed in 1807, outmanoeuvred the French in their last efforts to establish an eastern empire under Napoleon, and captured the Cape of Good Hope from the Dutch (as well as Java which was later returned to them). The Marquess of Hastings, who succeeded him, was responsible for the final eclipse of the Maratha confederacy and the annexation of the Deccan. A fine administrator as well as a soldier, he started extensive irrigation and road works and continued Minto's work in founding schools. In 1819 he gave Sir Stamford Raffles permission to seek a port for British trade south of Malacca, and this resulted in the establishment of Singapore. In spite of fears in London that this might cause conflict with the Dutch, Raffles's enterprise prospered. In 1826 it was joined with Penang and Malacca to form Straits Settlements, which were governed from Singapore from 1832 onwards.

Lord Amherst came next to India (1823), conquered the lower Irrawaddy basin in Burma and placed a British representative at the Burmese court. The remainder of lower Burma was annexed in 1851 in Lord Dalhousie's governorship, following the imposition of restrictions on resident British merchants, and the whole of the seaboard from Chittagong to Singapore was in British hands. Dalhousie was one of the most distinguished of the great governors-general: he began the building of railways and the installation of post and telegraph; an advanced educational system was established; some 3200 km (2000 miles) of road and 29,000 km (18,000 miles) of irrigation canals were built. He died in 1856, a year before the sepoy rising and the siege of Lucknow, and two years before the East India Company was dissolved and the act of parliament was passed which determined that India would be transferred to the Crown. Lord Canning was appointed first Viceroy.

Calcutta's influence waned and British interest was focused upon the industrial and commercial vigour of Bombay. The development of India in terms of cities, institutions and public services continued throughout the nineteenth century, but confidence in the future was nowhere better displayed than in the unbelievably rapid growth of Bombay in the second half of the century.

Lord Curzon, Viceroy from 1899 to 1905, was a man of enormous energy who wished to establish order by military means and to carry out far-reaching social reforms, but he failed to appreciate the growing spirit of nationalism or the changing social positions in a more liberally governed country. It is his statue which graces the entrance front of the Viceroy's House at New Delhi, completed some twenty-five years after his return to London.

Sri Lanka had been governed by the Dutch since 1658. There had been some contact with Kandy by the British in 1761 but it was an incident in the Anglo-French war which led to the British occupation of Trincomalee in 1795 and the eventual occupation of all the Dutch possessions on the island by 1796. The island became a crown colony in 1798; after a rebellion in Kandy the whole of Sri Lanka was annexed in 1815 and a governor was appointed, more than forty years before the appointment of the first Viceroy in India. The establishment of French rule in Indo-China dates from the same period – a treaty signed by Louis XVI in 1787.

Australia and New Zealand

Introduction

Australia is about the same size as the United States, approximately 4000 km (1250 miles) across, an island continent along with Tasmania, which is separated from the mainland by twice the distance that separates Ireland from England. New Zealand lies 1400 km (850 miles) to the east, its two islands 1500 km (930 miles) from north to south. The latitudes of Australia are comparable with those of the northern half of Africa, while those of New Zealand approach the Antarctic more closely, but no closer than the Arctic is approached by Brittany, or by the southern border of Canada. The most immediate neighbours are Papua-New Guinea and Indonesia, beyond which lies Singapore and all of South-east Asia.

White settlement in this part of the world began in the late eighteenth century, and it was entirely British. The offical landing and proclamation of possession occurred in Sydney in 1788, and in the case of New Zealand was delayed (despite earlier whaling and mission settlements) until 1840, at the Bay of Islands.

Navigators from Portugal and Holland had preceded the British but formed no settlements. French explorations occurred in much the same period as the British, but again there were no settlements, except for one brief attempt in New Zealand.

The aborigines of Australia were neither settlers nor builders. Their ancient and fascinating history, now thought to extend back at least 40,000 years, is evidently the history of nomadic hunters, consequently not an architectural topic. Their shelters were always temporary and minimal, just personal shelters of bark or of branches leaning against tree or stake.

The arrival of the Maoris in New Zealand, from somewhere to the north-east, occurred before the fourteenth century. They were more settled than the Australians and more inclined to construction, but produced no more than villages with simple houses and community halls. Old halls have not survived, but modern ones aim to reproduce them. Though admired, their influence on the architecture of the white settlers was negligible. In both countries, therefore, it is reasonable for an abridged account of nineteenth-century architecture to concentrate upon the buildings of European type, created by immigrants, in other words the architecture of the Australasian colonies.

At the other end of the period treated in this part of the book, the 1890s brought an economic recession which almost halted building for some years. In Melbourne the hiatus was complete between 1893 and 1896. In other parts of the region it was less severe and did not occur at quite the same dates, but it brought about the end of the gold era (see below).

Australian nationhood began in 1901 with federation of the former colonies, and the creation of the Commonwealth Government.

Physical Characteristics

Fertile and well-watered land is to be found throughout most of New Zealand and along the entire length of the eastern seaboard of Australia, but elsewhere the arable and temperate lands are confined to relatively small coastal areas. The dimensions of these countries are such that the climatic range is very great, from tropical north to cold south, from desert to snowy alps, and (in New Zealand) glaciers and fjords. New Zealand is earthquake-prone, some locations especially so, including the capital, Wellington.

Cities are almost all near the coasts but mining sustained a few settlements in the inhospitable interior (Kalgoorlie, Broken Hill, Mount Isa), and Alice Springs, right in the centre of Australia, was a relay station for the international telegraph route.

History

The circumstances of these colonies changed several times over. In the earliest days the Colonial Office in Britain was the supreme bureaucracy, and the construction of even quite minor buildings required permission, and design, from 'home'. Degrees of autonomy emerged, notably in mid-century when parliaments were created in each colony, but they remained legally bound to Britain and emotionally part of the Empire. In Australia that continued until the federation of the separate colonies in 1901, as States, into an independent nation, the Commonwealth of Australia. And to this day, New Zealand, each Australian State, and the federal capital at Canberra have governors appointed by the British monarch. In New Zealand there was at first considerable power in the hands of Provincial Governments (including the initiation of building work), but they were abolished in 1875 in favour of centralisation.

New Zealand's history includes armed conflicts between Maori and 'pakeha' (European settlers), especially the wars of 1861–71. Two effects were an increase in urbanisation and stimulation of the economy. In Australia's case the aborigines retaliated only in local skirmishes, and were gradually decimated by dispersion and by introduced diseases.

In both countries the oldest surviving whole buildings are significantly post-1800, such as two wings of the Sydney Civil Hospital (*c.* 1810) or houses and a stone storehouse in New Zealand's Bay of Islands area (1821 and later). Elizabeth Farm, near Parramatta, New South Wales, embodies a two-room cottage of 1793, but its well-known appearance is of later date.

The early pioneering decades bristled with problems of shipwreck and drought, and there were shortages of building supplies and craftsmen. The first Australian colonies, New South Wales and Van Diemen's Land (Tasmania), bore the official task of receiving shipload after shipload of convicts, sentenced to 'transportation', and that persisted until the 1840s. Both countries saw the future, such as it was, in terms of agricultural export, especially wool production.

Later in the nineteenth century, prosperity grew beyond earlier expectations: both countries became large suppliers of farm produce (wool, wheat, lamb, beef and butter) to Britain and other countries, and even more important, there were the gold rushes (1851–) and the subsequent wealth accruing from mineral exports.

Before the gold rushes there already existed three more colonies in the Australian continent, Western Australia (founded 1826), Victoria (unofficial settlers, 1834) and South Australia (1835). In 1859 Queensland was also created. As with Victoria in the south, Queensland was separated off from the huge territory which had at first been called New South Wales.

South Australia was the scene of the first mineral boom of all – copper was discovered in the 1840s. This was especially attractive to Welsh and Cornish emigrants. Gold rushes in the 1850s depleted the population of South Australia but it revived later as a wheat producer, first in response to the continent's much increased population, then as an exporter using the famous clipper ships.

Western Australia's early foundation was followed by various misfortunes until the 1890s, when gold was found at Kalgoorlie and drew fortune-seekers west from all over Australia and New Zealand. Kalgoorlie is situated in a hot arid location 600 km (370 miles) inland from Perth and its port, Fremantle. Perth has remained the business centre for the mineral and pastoral products in the west.

Culture

Australia and New Zealand remained primarily outposts of England, Wales, Scotland and Ireland. Some regions were dominated by a particular group such as Cornish miners, Welsh smelters or Scottish engineers. In Australia, the Irish formed a large proportion of the population, having emigrated as refugees from famine, as political exiles, or simply as servants, labourers, shopkeepers and publicans. Other groups were minor but in some locations significant – Chinese gold-diggers (Victoria), Lutheran German farmers (South Australia) and French merchants (Sydney).

Though the amalgam was remarkable and the common language had a unifying influence, in some aspects of life a degree of separation remained. The Roman Catholic church in Australia, almost wholly Irish, grew strong, and was more active and visible than the Church of England, despite the latter's connections with offical and élite activities. The Nonconformist churches were also strong. In mining districts large Methodist churches and Sunday schools were constructed. The Scottish church predominated in some farming areas. The province of Otago, New Zealand, was a settlement venture launched by the Lay Association of the Free Church of Scotland. Elsewhere in New Zealand the Church Missionary Society was effectively a founding agency. With the merchant class, Congregationalists were prominent in Hobart, Melbourne, Sydney and Adelaide.

Resources

In the early decades (1788–*c.* 1850) all the colonies of Australasia were subject to difficult, pioneering circumstances, and there were few skilled people, few tools and a lack of understanding of local materials. Australia's first professional architect, Francis Greenway, spent a great deal of time supervising the making of bricks and mortar and in instructing bricklayers, before construction of good quality could begin. Convict labour was widely used in New South Wales and Tasmania, but was usually unskilled and uncooperative.

The gold rushes brought many skilled people and created the wealth to make possible the import of whatever and whoever was needed. Once the feverish expectations of easily won alluvial gold and shallow digging gave way to deep-shaft and mechanical workings, the mining operations themselves attracted engineers and builders. From about 1865 Australian cities were almost as well equipped with building supplies and workshop facilities as any advanced country of the time, though at least six months of waiting time was involved in ordering and receiving items from 'home'.

However, the pioneering circumstances prevailed long after 1859 in the remote places untouched by the gold rush or by urban growth, and longest of all in those places out of reach of coastal shipping or the railways. The very first railway lines were under construction before the discovery of gold, and the growth of major routes continued from the late 1850s.

Building Materials and Techniques

In such extensive countries the range of building materials is wide. Some areas have dense forests of very tall trees, others have no usable wood at all. The most widespread species of timber in Australia is the eucalyptus, whose many varieties are all hardwoods, some very dense; colours vary from yellow to deep red. Early settlers found the hardness and the need for long seasoning to be serious deterrents to its use and preferred other native species such as the toon tree, which is like a soft red cedar. As a result it is now almost extinct. Timber was also imported from New Zealand, the Baltic and California.

Australian building stones define the regions distinctively – the blue-black volcanic basalt of southern Victoria, the golden sandstone of the Sydney region, or the soft grey limestones and brown-black schists of South Australia. There are also places yielding excellent granites and marbles. Clays have been available for the production of bricks almost anywhere, by farmers or by professional manufacturers, though they have varied greatly in colour and durability.

As soon as galvanised iron arrived (1850s) it was widely used. Decorative cast iron was adopted enthusiastically; at first it was imported but was soon made throughout the country, especially where the work-shops set up for mining purposes were equipped with suitable foundries.

During the period 1870–90, particularly in New South Wales and Victoria, decorative iron was popular but was displaced later by turned and fretted woodwork.

Many of the celebrated buildings of New Zealand are in timber. There was a plentiful supply of the renowned Kauri pine which was also exported to Australia in the early decades, being much easier to work than the eucalyptus hardwoods. Bricks were made and stone was available, though it was not until 1865 that the value of Oamaru limestone for fine work was recognised. Earthquakes favoured the use of timber. There are many examples of wood buildings made to look like stone, the best known being the extensive four-storey Government Offices at Lambton Quay, Wellington, by W. H. Clayton, Colonial Architect, 1874. Earthquakes have destroyed many of the country's best nineteenth-century examples: most of those in the town of Napier were demolished by the 1931 earthquake.

Chapter 36

AFRICA

The Coastal Forts

In 1481, ten years after the Portuguese first landed on the west coast of Africa, John II ordered an expedition to build a fortress at Elmina. It was given the name of São Jorge da Mina. Although constructed of stone, little of this structure, which was built in 1482, is visible in the present building. It had two storeys and was built around a courtyard, had corner towers, alternately round and square on plan, and a Great Court extending towards the sea. In its first form, it lasted for about a century but Renaissance fortifications, developed in Italy during the sixteenth century, were quickly adopted by other European princes and their engineers. Portugal was no exception, and the forts constructed on the African coast reflected the Italian treatises by such experienced engineers as Girolamo Cataneo (1564) and Galasso Alghisi (1570). The African forts were modified to take account of the materials available and were less sophisticated than their European models.

São Jorge, or Elmina Castle (pp. 1173B, 1174A), was largely reconstructed in the late sixteenth century, possibly on the advice of an Italian engineer, Filippo Terzi (1520–97), who was engaged to modernise Portuguese fortifications at home and abroad. The walls of the main block were thickened, the outer walls of the Great Court were strengthened, and additional triangular bastions were built. The fort provided a pattern for others that were built subsequently. The most important of these were the British **Cape Coast Castle** (*c.* 1674) (p. 1173A), and the Danish **Christiansborg** (1661–70), largely remodelled over the years and now the official residence of the the Ghanaian Head of State. By the end of the eighteenth century over thirty forts, castles and trading lodges had been built along the Gold Coast by nine European nations or their chartered companies.

Fort Jesus (p. 1174D) on the East African coast was designed by an Italian engineer, Joao Batista Cairato, who is described as 'Chief Architect of India' in an inscription above the main gate. Gaspar Rodriguez was in charge of the work, which was completed in 1593. In plan, it consists of a large rectangular courtyard surrounded by coral-stone curtain walls, four corner-bastions and a rectangular projection, with small angle-towers on the seaward side. Like Elmina Castle it incorporates a church in the courtyard. The Dutch had taken over the main European trade by the early seventeenth century, and they continued to construct **forts** along the West African Coast. At Elmina, for example, in 1662–6 they built one on **S. Jago** Hill to protect the former Portuguese castle which had passed into their hands in 1637 (pp. 1173C, 1174E). This was **Coenraadsburg**, and the almost square plan with four triangular corner-bastions also seems to have provided a model for later structures, for example the Brandenburg-Prussian **Gross Friedrichsburg, Princestown** (1683), the English forts at **Commenda** (1686), **Dixcove** (1692, enlarged *c.* 1750, when a large spur was constructed on the west side) (p. 1174C) and **Anomabu** (1753), and the Danish **Fort Prinsensten, Keta** (1784). Close to Christiansborg Castle a variant, a **fortified house**, was built (*c.* 1829) by Johan Emmanuel Richter (p. 1174B); this consisted of a residence placed between two courtyards surrounded by storerooms, and the whole group, contained within defensive walls and bastions, was entered through a single pedimented gateway.

Rudimentary pediments over windows and doors, sometimes filled with armorial shields, are generally the only decorative embellishments found on these severely practical buildings, although the inner face of the 1750 addition to the Dixcove Fort was unusually ambitious, with its blank arcading and coupled pilasters. The Dutch, who retained possession of their forts on the Gold Coast until 1872 when they sold them to the British, had made many alterations to the Portuguese buildings which they had taken over. It is to them that most of the Classical embellishments, such as the Doric colonnade and the segmental pedimented gateway at Elmina Castle, must be attributed. A portrait of Dirck Wilne, Director General of the North and South Coast of Africa, painted in the 1660s, indicates the quality of the gilt leather wall covering, oriental carpets and portable furnishings that were brought out from Holland to provide comfort in the Governor's apartments.

Mediterranean Sea
Tangier
Algiers
Atlas Mountains
Cairo
Qattara Depression
Nile
Persian Gulf
Red Sea
Arabian Desert
Sahara Desert
Dongola
El Ghaba
Timbuktu
Kumbi Saleh
Gambia
Niger
Meroe
Khartoum
Axum
Lalibela
Ouagadougou
Benue
Ethiopian Highlands
Yoruba States
Kumasi
Commenda
Princestown
Dixcove
Elmina Castle
Christiansborg
Accra
Cape Coast Castle
Benin
Igbo-Ukwu
Mogadishu
Dongur
Congo
Kampala
Rift Valley
Lamu
Lake Victoria
Nairobi
Mambrui
Malindi
Mombasa
INDIAN
OCEAN
Lake Tanganyika
Bagamoyo
Zanzibar
Dar-es-Salaam
Kilwa
ATLANTIC
OCEAN
Lake Nyasa
Zambesi
Blantyre
MADAGASCAR
Bulawayo
Great Zimbabwe
Pretoria
Marienburg
Johannesburg
Ladysmith
Newcastle
Freretown
Kimberley
Pietermaritzburg
Bloemfontein
0 miles 1000
Durban
Tulbagh
Graaf-Reinet
Cradock
Malmesbury
Worcester
Grahamstown
East London
Stellenbosch
Uitenhage
Cape Town
Oudtshoorn
Port Elizabeth
Cape of Good Hope
Knysna

Africa

A. Cape Coast Castle (*c.* 1674) from the east: and eighteenth-century view. See p. 1171

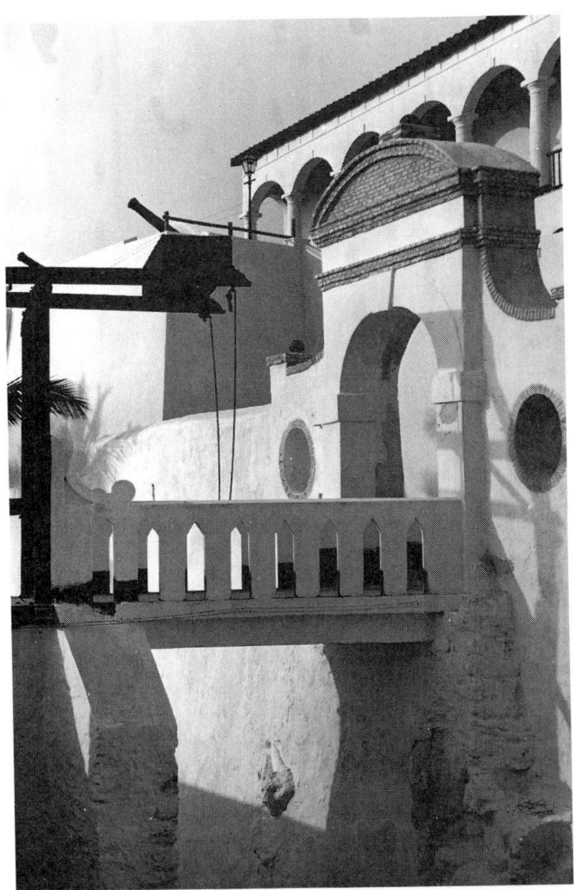

B. São Jorge or Elmina Castle (largely reconstructed in the late sixteenth century). See p. 1171

C. Fort S. Jago. See p. 1171

COLONIAL AFRICA FORTS

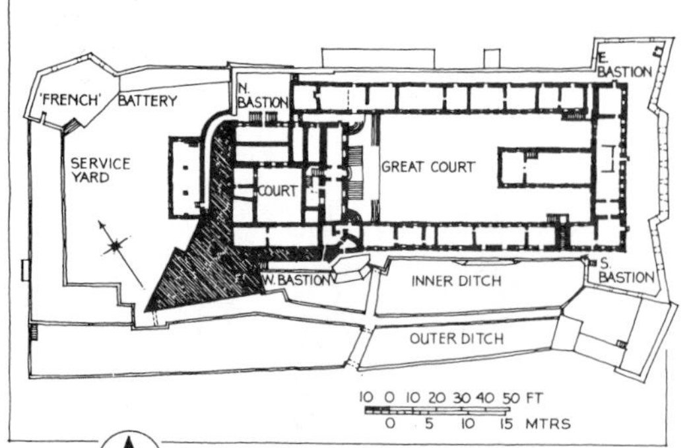

A ELMINA CASTLE

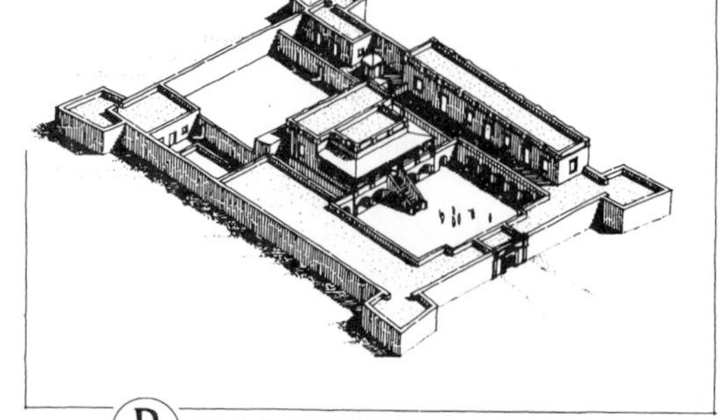

B RICHTER HOUSE

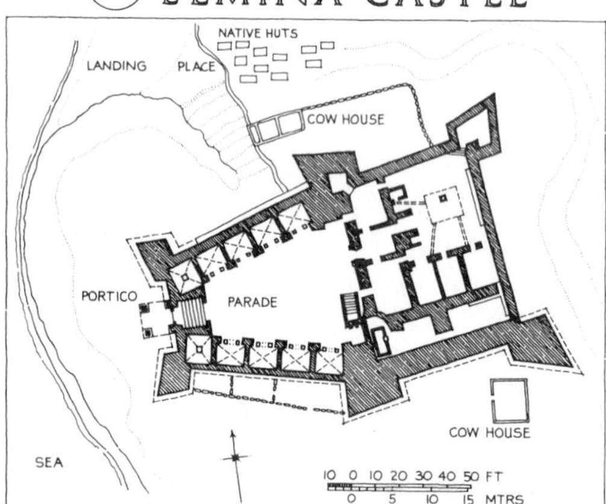

C DIXCOVE FORT

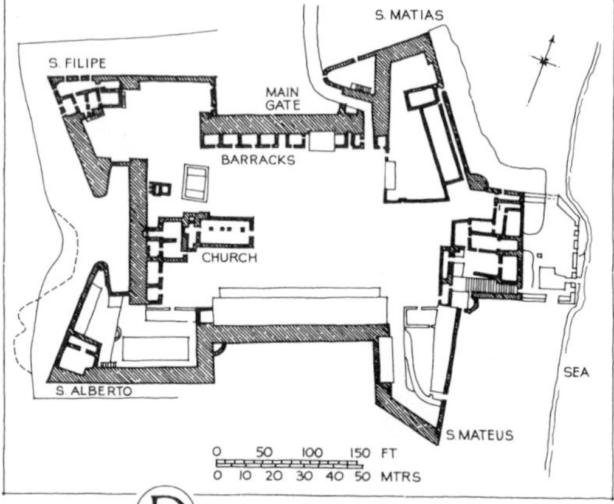

D FORT JESUS

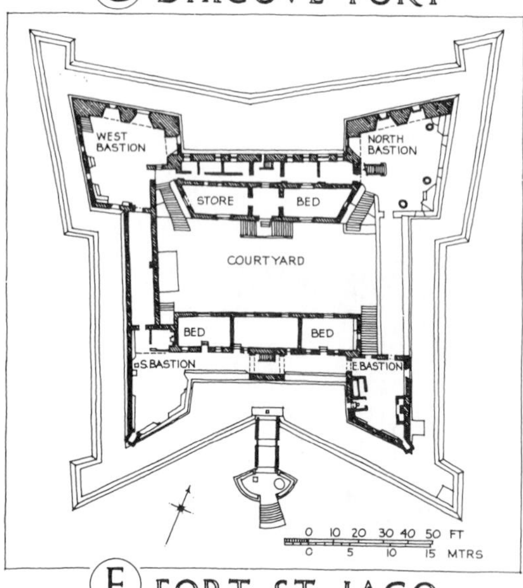

E FORT ST. JAGO

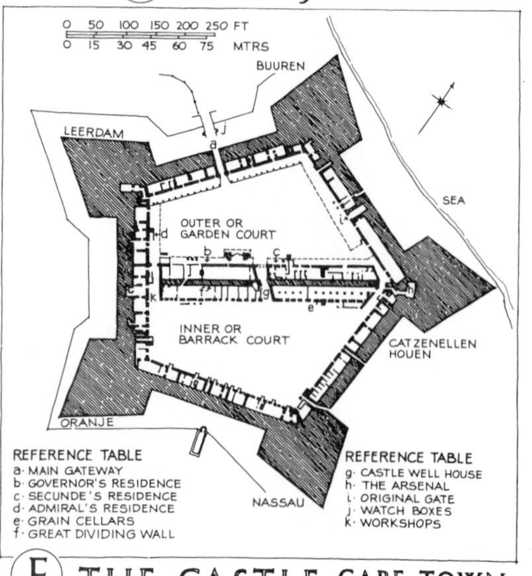

F THE CASTLE CAPE TOWN

The year after de Witt had recorded Wilne surrounded by the trappings of European civilisation, the foundation stone of a new castle was being laid more than three thousand miles to the south. The Dutch East India Company was established in 1602 when the separate companies in Amsterdam, Rotterdam, Delft, Middelburg, Hoorn and Enkhuizen united. In 1650 the new company decided to set up a station at the Cape of Good Hope where one of its ships had been driven ashore in Table Bay three years earlier. In 1652 the first Dutch ships arrived there, and an earth-built fortification with timber buildings was quickly erected. Once the station had been established, more permanent structures were needed, and a site was chosen for a **Castle**, pentagonal in plan, with a bastion named after one of the several titles of the Prince of Orange at each of the five corners (p. 1174F). Work began in 1666. This was the time when the Dutch school of military engineering had risen to a position of some importance, and the system of fortification perfected by Simon Stevin (1548–1620) was adopted by the engineer Pieter Dombaer who was responsible for the Castle. Built of stone, it was completed in 1679; three years later a gateway was added, modelled on that of Dordrecht and displaying the arms of the six founding Dutch towns.

So far there had been similarities in the setting up of trading posts in East, West and South Africa, but it was only on the Cape that a colony was quickly established. After 1657, burgher families were established behind Table Mountain to cultivate the land. Two years later it was reported that wine was pressed for the first time from the Cape grapes and that the first flowers had bloomed on the imported rose trees. From then onwards developments around the African trading forts began to take different directions.

North, West and East Africa

Portuguese expeditions to North Africa resulted in the acquisition of a number of coastal towns, including Tangier, Morocco, which was captured in 1471. Almost 200 years later it became a British possession as part of the dowry of Charles II's queen, Catherine of Braganza, and its acquisition almost led to the appointment of Christopher Wren as designer and supervisor of **Tangier's new fortifications**, but he refused the commission. Wenceslaus Hollar recorded these fortifications in 1667, but they were all destroyed when the city was abandoned in 1683. Ottoman incursions effectively ended European hopes of conquest along the North African coast until the French arrived at the end of the eighteenth century.

The Napoleonic campaigns in Egypt in 1789–99, and the publication in 1802 of Baron Dominique Vivant Denon's *Voyage dans la Basse et la Haute Egypte*, and subsequently his *Description de l'Egypte*, resulted from 1809 onwards in a European–African stylistic influence that was, for once, in reverse. Detailed archaeological surveys were beginning to offer opportunities to European designers to adopt details and forms from ancient Egyptian buildings. And although there was little time for the French themselves to undertake any building in Egypt before they departed in 1801, French scholars were to maintain a close association with Egypt. French influence was strong on Muhammid Ali, the founder of modern Egypt and the rebuilder of Alexandria. He built himself a **palace at Shubra** and laid out the long boulevard linking it with Cairo and another connecting the capital with Boulak. In 1845 work began on the construction of the rue Neuve, which cuts through the old street pattern of Cairo, and Muhammid Ali's successor, Isma'il Pasha, continued in the 1870s with the formation of the place Atabah al-Khadra and the streets radiating from it. It is said that around 400 buildings were removed in order to make way for the boulevard Muhammid Ali alone.

There was extensive construction of new buildings in **Cairo**, mostly in an Italian or Austrian classical style; but there was also a revival of interest in Arabic decoration which was used in the designs of private houses, for example, **Villa Delort** and **Villa S. Maurice** (1874) and **Villa Zogheb** (1898) and apartment buildings. The salamlik of the **Guezireh Palace** (Frantz and De Carel, 1863) is richly ornamented with Arabic details, although it was constructed of cast iron in Germany. Other examples include an elaborate public fountain at the **Babel Hadid** (C. Pantanelli, *c.* 1870), the **Khayry Bey Palace** (1870), the **Museum of Arab Art** (A. Manescalco, 1903), **Kasr el Nil Palace** (Pantanelli) and **Omar Sultan's Palace** (A. Laseiac, 1907).

The imposition of a formal pattern of open spaces and straight avenues is characteristic of French colonial development policies. In 1830 they occupied Algeria, and one of their early decrees concerned the creation of a Place du Gouvernement and the widening of a number of streets in the old city of **Algiers**. Over the next thirty years some of these ideas, which resulted in straight roads with uniform arcaded facades, were executed on the principles practised by Haussmann and others in Paris, and for similar reasons of sanitary improvement and military control. Chassériau was responsible for the long uniformity of the **Front de Mer** and for the **Opera** (1850).

There was little European building in East and West Africa during the first half of the nineteenth century, and little architectural influence, although the forts that had been built on the coasts seem to have provided models for some of the African rulers.

The **fort in Lamu**, for example, was built in 1813–21 by the liwali or governor, reputedly with the cooperation of the Sultan of Oman; its crenellated parapets, central courtyard and sturdy corner tower probably derive from European forts. So, too, did the **Stone Palace** or Aban (p. 1178A) built in 1822 by Osei Bonsu, the Asantehene, as a part of his capital Kumasi. Stone was sent up from the Elmina coast, and the ruler ordered that within this semi-fortified residence designed around a courtyard, the casing of the windows should be in gold and the doorposts and pillars were to be of ivory. The intention seems to have been both innovative and an attempt to impress European missions which were received there. At the end of the century, when the **Sultan of Zanzibar** built a new **palace**, there was little difference between its architectural character and that of the European coastal forts, although steel was used in its construction.

On the whole, traditional forms and methods of building were untouched by influences from European countries during the eighteenth and early nineteenth centuries, although the trading towns on the east coast had long been receptive to influences from Arabian and Indian ports. The Swahili **coral-stone houses** in Lamu and Zanzibar, for example, had been built as inward-looking designs around a courtyard from the fourteenth century onwards (p. 1177E). During the eighteenth century the most important of them had been richly decorated with carved plasterwork on the walls of the principal rooms and carved woodwork on the doorways. The details of this decoration suggest Iranian or Indian influence, and probably the elaborate projecting balconies in the streets of the old east-coast towns (Lamu, Zanzibar, Mogadishu, Mombasa) were also part of an imported culture from across the Indian Ocean; so too is the moulded decoration found on some nineteenth-century buildings in Mombasa which might be described as Indian-Baroque.

Portuguese and Spanish mission churches were built along the Gambia and Zaire rivers in West Africa in the sixteenth century, but of these virtually nothing remains. The first **mission station** on the East African mainland was set up in the bush north of **Bagamoyo**, Tanzania, by the French Holy Ghost Mission. Almost immediately after its establishment in 1868 a **church** was built. It was a simple coral structure with a tower crowned with corner pinnacles, and was later superseded by a more elaborate church in the French Romanesque style (1910–14) (p. 1178C). The smaller mission churches, of which relatively few survive, were usually rectangular vernacular structures, although such details as pointed or round-headed windows were often introduced as token symbols of the buildings' purpose. The remains of a stone-built church at **Niamkolo**, Zambia (1895–6), on the shore of Lake Tanganyika, illustrate the type of building, sometimes with a tower (in this case 15 m (49 ft) high), put up by the London Missionary Society under the supervision of a teacher. **Emmanuel Church at Freretown**, Kenya, was built by descendants of slaves in 1884, and this ambitious design incorporates an arcade of round-headed arches and triple lancets.

The Romanesque was a favoured style once a mission had been established and more money was available for building, as at Bagamoyo (q.v.). Presumably the characteristic heavy masonry and small windows were thought more suitable than the Gothic style to the climate and the local materials. In **Kampala**, Uganda, the White Fathers built **Rubaga Cathedral** (1912–25) with tall, twin western towers and Romanesque details, and they used a similar style for the **Cathedral at Ouagudougou**, Upper Volta, while **S. Joseph's, Zanzibar** (1896–8, M. Berangier) (p. 1178D), was modelled on the basilica of Notre-Dame de la Garde at Marseille, France. The **Roman Catholic Cathedral at Mombasa**, Kenya, is a similar but less accurate version of a Romanesque basilica. First built at the end of the nineteenth century, it was rebuilt to a design by Brother Gustave Walter in 1918. The **Anglican Cathedrals at Zanzibar** (1873–9, C. F. Hayward) and **Mombasa** (1901–5, J. H. Sinclair) combine Early English and Islamic detailing; the former has a campanile, and the latter (completed in 1905) a crossing dome and twin-domed western towers.

Many of these buildings are impressive achievements, although few were built to designs by architects. A Mr Scott, 'who had never had a single lesson even in bricklaying, much less in architecture', was responsible for the design and execution of the large brick-built **Church of Scotland Mission Church at Blantyre**, Malawi (p. 1178B), which was completed in 1895 with twin west towers and a domed crossing. However, in some cases the assistance of British architects was sought. Sir Aston Webb provided the design for **Holy Trinity Church, Accra**, Ghana (1893), and Robert Weir Schulz the low Romanesque design for **All Saints Cathedral, Khartoum**, Sudan (1909–12), in which small high-level windows only were used in an attempt to offset the effects of the African heat. Similarly, when Beresford Pite designed the **Anglican Cathedral**, the fourth on the site, **at Namirembe, Kampala**, Uganda (1913–19) he used a modified Arts and Crafts Gothic style in which small windows are set within large recessed pointed arcading. His distinctive plan for this building included triple transepts, a domed crossing and a tall western tower which was not built. Temple Moore's design for **All Saints Cathedral, Nairobi**, Kenya (1915) was not completed according to his intention. Much later, in 1938, Adrian Gilbert Scott's **All Saints Cathedral, Cairo**, Egypt was described as 'a free rendering of Ecclesiastic Classic adapted to the Egyptian climate'.

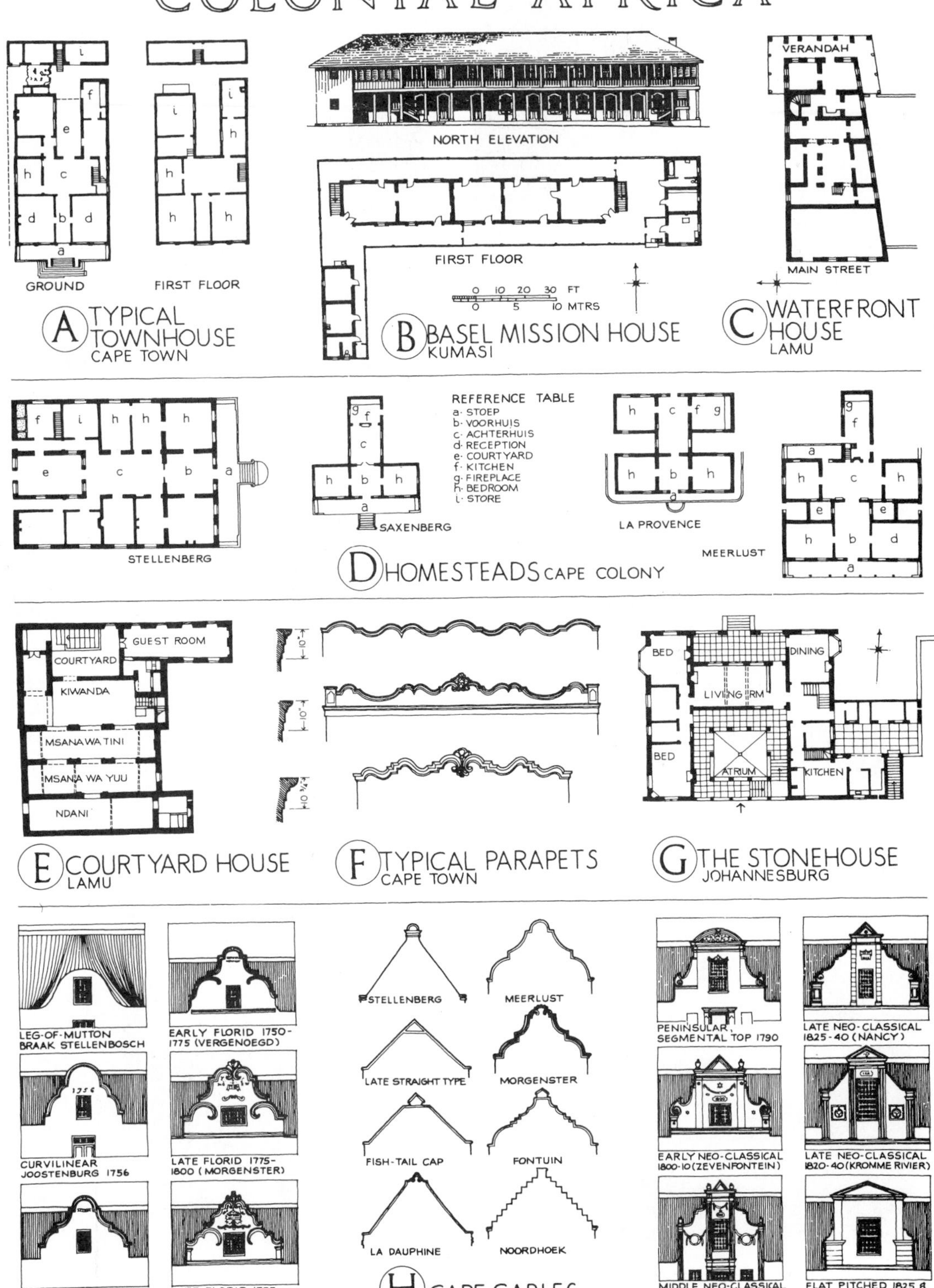
COLONIAL AFRICA
GROUND
FIRST FLOOR
A TYPICAL TOWNHOUSE CAPE TOWN
NORTH ELEVATION
FIRST FLOOR
0 10 20 30 FT
0 5 10 MTRS
B BASEL MISSION HOUSE KUMASI
VERANDAH
MAIN STREET
C WATERFRONT HOUSE LAMU
STELLENBERG
SAXENBERG
REFERENCE TABLE
a· STOEP
b· VOORHUIS
c· ACHTERHUIS
d· RECEPTION
e· COURTYARD
f· KITCHEN
g· FIREPLACE
h· BEDROOM
i· STORE
LA PROVENCE
MEERLUST
D HOMESTEADS CAPE COLONY
GUEST ROOM
COURTYARD
KIWANDA
MSANA WA TINI
MSANA WA YUU
NDANI
E COURTYARD HOUSE LAMU
F TYPICAL PARAPETS CAPE TOWN
BED
DINING
LIVING RM
BED
ATRIUM
KITCHEN
G THE STONEHOUSE JOHANNESBURG
LEG-OF-MUTTON BRAAK STELLENBOSCH
EARLY FLORID 1750-1775 (VERGENOEGD)
CURVILINEAR JOOSTENBURG 1756
LATE FLORID 1775-1800 (MORGENSTER)
EARLIEST FLORID 1750-1775 (SPIER)
LATE FLORID 1775-1800 (ZENITH)
STELLENBERG
MEERLUST
LATE STRAIGHT TYPE
MORGENSTER
FISH-TAIL CAP
FONTUIN
LA DAUPHINE
NOORDHOEK
H CAPE GABLES
PENINSULAR, SEGMENTAL TOP 1790
LATE NEO-CLASSICAL 1825-40 (NANCY)
EARLY NEO-CLASSICAL 1800-10 (ZEVENFONTEIN)
LATE NEO-CLASSICAL 1820-40 (KROMME RIVIER)
MIDDLE NEO-CLASSICAL 1810-20 (ZENITH)
FLAT PITCHED 1825 & ON (NOVA CONSTANTIA)

A. The Stone Palace, Kumasi (1822). See p. 1176

D. S. Joseph's Zanzibar (1896–98). See p. 1176

B. Church of Scotland Mission Church, Blantyre (1895). See p. 1176

C. French Mission Church, Bagamoyo (1910–14). See p. 1176

E. S. Joseph's RC Cathedral, Dar-es-Salaam (1897–1902). See p. 1180

A. The House of Wonders, Zanzibar (1883). See p. 1180

B. A coral stone-built house (now the Museum), Lamu (1892). See p. 1180

C. The Boma, Bagamoyo (1895). See p. 1180

Traditional forms of housing had evolved out of climatic considerations and the availability of materials, and their lessons were not entirely ignored by the European settlers. **Houses** built by Dutch merchants at **Elmina** in the early nineteenth century, for example, adopted a traditional courtyard plan with a formal, usually five-bayed, two-storeyed facade to the street or lagoon. But as the numbers increased and more attention was paid to precautions against malaria, more and better houses were needed in new and inland settlements. One obvious solution was to export them from England as portable structures such as J. C. Loudon had described in his *Encyclopaedia of Cottage, Farm and Villa Architecture* (1833). Although many prefabricated houses were sent out to the Colonies, they seem at first to have been of a standard design that paid no attention to the particular conditions of their location. From about the middle of the century, however, there was a more conscious effort to consider the requirements of tropical living, including the provision of ventilation and shade.

A description of Accra in 1873 refers to 'the Commandant's house ... its wide verandah denoted luxurious coolness, its wide space around it informed you that at one time or another some occupant had been assiduous to procure unpolluted air'. The genesis of the verandah is still uncertain, but as a feature of tropical dwellings it has a long history. Probably its origins can be traced from India to Portugal, and then in the fifteenth century to Portuguese settlements in Asia, whence it seems to have moved to Africa in the nineteenth century to appear in some of the first houses built by missionaries. The Basel mission was established in the hinterland of Accra in the 1840s, and in one of the first buildings the missionaries erected near Christiansborg Castle they built a verandah around some of the living rooms on the first floor. Verandahs also appeared on other houses in the same area, namely Osu. The **Sisters' Convent** in the **Bagamoyo** mission station in East Africa, built in the 1860s, is similar, while the **Brothers' House** is a more solid structure with two arcaded floors and a third verandah-floor only.

The early form of the **Basel Mission House** was developed in the second half of the century as a two-storeyed core building constructed in masonry or pisé earth and containing a single row of rooms, the whole surrounded on all four sides by a wide timber verandah supported on stone or brick piers, timber posts or cast-iron columns. In effect, it was similar to the bungalow form that had been developed in India, but raised off the ground. The living accommodation was on the first floor, the ground floor was used for storage, and there was a connecting staircase within the width of the verandah. A fine late example in **Kumasi** dates from around 1906 (p. 1177B); this incorporates first-floor spaces fitted with a system of hinged, louvred panels which can be opened or closed in various combinations to provide the maximum shade and ventilation. Variations of the verandah house may be found in most African colonial towns, and by the beginning of the present century it had become an official Colonial Office design. Examples may be seen along the late nineteenth-century waterfront in front of the old Swahili town of **Lamu** – and here it is evident also that the verandah house could be integrated with other traditional forms. One house completed in 1892 (now the Museum) presents a verandah front to the sea but retains the characteristic plan of a Swahili courtyard house at the rear (pp. 1177C,1179B).

British influence was traditionally brought to bear in East Africa through the Sultan of Zanzibar, whose **House of Wonders** (1883) (p. 1179A) incorporated technological innovations of the late nineteenth century, but in 1888 he signed a treaty with the Deutsch Ost-Afrikan Gesellschaft, and two years later he sold the coast of present-day Tanzania to the German government. The capital of the new colony was at first **Bagamoyo**, where a **Customs House** and a **Boma** were built in 1895. In designing these, the architect sent out from Germany showed an unusual understanding of and respect for local materials and conditions, but nevertheless incorporated recognisably European architectural elements. The impressive Boma (p. 1179C) is an accomplished synthesis of Swahili and European styles, and similar buildings were erected at Tanga, Mikindani and Kilwa Kvinje. In 1891 the capital was transferred to **Dar-es-Salaam**, where the first German building had been put up in 1887 for the **Berlin (Lutheran) Mission**. The new group of administrative buildings and the **Kaiserhof** (Officers' Club), dating from 1891 onwards and all Classical in style, were built with masonry lower storeys and upper floors with wide verandahs constructed of steel joists and carved timber rafters and screens, prefabricated in Germany. **Ocean Road Hospital** (1897) and the contemporary **State House** (reconstructed 1922) were similar to the earlier German buildings in that they incorporated multifoil Islamic arches. **Civil Service residences** set in the spacious landscaped Botanical Garden district are similarly hybrid in style, but the Gothic **S. Joseph's Roman Catholic Cathedral** (1897–1902) (p. 1178E) and the **Lutheran Church** (1898) are more strictly European in character. This outstanding group of buildings represents a more responsible attitude towards colonial architecture on the eve of World War I, which was to result in the partial redistribution of territories in Africa.

South Africa

After the Castle had been completed on the **Cape of Good Hope** in 1679, a number of **residences** were built within the enclosure, including that of the

Governor of the Dutch East India Company in which the Council Chamber of 1695 still exists intact. Outside the Castle walls the Company's garden was laid out as a series of parallelograms, and included a garden house which was later incorporated into **Government House** (now Tuynhuys). The early houses were single-storeyed with wattle and daub walls and thatched roofs, although some bricks were being made as early as 1654. The early country homesteads built by the burghers who were established as farmers in the colony were simply cob-walled buildings with thatched roofs, either gabled or with half-hipped ends, and floors of mud and cow dung. In plan they consisted of three rooms, and it was from these houses that the characteristic **Cape Dutch homesteads** (p. 1177D) and their manor houses developed in the middle of the eighteenth century.

These may be grouped into three main categories. There are those that are T-shaped in plan (e.g. **Saxenburg**) and those that are either H-shaped or a combination of T and H (e.g. **La Provence, Meerlust**). The third category is the U-plan, which was used for grander houses (e.g. **Stellenberg, Groot Constantia**). In each case an entrance hall (voorhuis) led into an inner hall (achterhuis) which served as dining room. Other rooms were grouped symmetrically on each side of this axis. A stoep paved with Batavian tiles ran the full length of the facade, and sometimes around the whole house to form a podium. Sometimes pillars along the stoep supported a trellised vine (e.g. **Meerlust, Morgenster, Vergelegen**); later this developed into the verandah that was a common characteristic of colonial architecture. The walls were constructed of undressed stones or sun-burnt bricks, rendered and limewashed, and the roofs were covered with reed thatching. Teak was used for the sash windows and external joinery.

Externally the two principal decorative features both derived from Dutch precedents – the central gable and the entrance doorway. As in Amsterdam, for example, there was a variety of gables – scrolled, curvilinear, pedimented, Baroque and Neo-Classical (pp. 1177H, 1182A,B, 1183A); evidently publications such as those by Philips Vingboons (1648 and 1674) provided sources for these designs up to about the end of the eighteenth century, but after that date the florid gables began to give way to Neo-Classical forms. End gables were necessary to protect the thatch, unless hipped roofs were used; before 1800 these were either straight-edged or curvilinear with a rounded top, but after that date they were more commonly pointed at the apex. The second decorative feature was the central entrance doorway, again deriving from Dutch tradition. Above the door was a tall fanlight which gave light to the entrance hall; this, too, changed from Baroque to Neo-Classical in its detailing, and teak or plaster pilasters sometimes framed the doorways.

In general these two decorative elements were less elaborate on homesteads than on town houses, but the latter differed also in one essential detail: because of the fire hazard in towns, thatched, pitched roofs were replaced by flat ones, often with a decorative parapet which was shaped, moulded or ornamented with a central pediment (p. 1177F), in some cases set on pilasters to complete a Classical facade. In plan, too, the **town houses** differed from the homesteads in the narrowness of the entrance hall, which generally led into an inner hall set at right angles to the main axis. This gave access to a courtyard – again following Dutch precedent – beyond which were the slave quarters and stores (p. 1177A). A smaller type of town house was built between 1795 and 1829 in what is now known as the Bo-Kaap (previously Malay Quarter) in Cape Town. Single-storeyed with high stoeps, these houses have simple cornices and fanlights, combining Dutch and English characteristics. The early mission churches differed little from the houses in their construction. That at **Tulbagh**, for example, was built in 1743 as a simple structure which was enlarged and given a Baroque concave-convex gable in 1795. At **Mamre**, near Malmesbury, the **church** dated 1818 (attributed to J. Melvill) is in the same tradition, with a large Baroque gable at each end, and the Rhenish **church at Stellenbosch** (1824, enlarged 1840) has an ornate Flemish-Neo-Classical gable.

The first public building erected in the colony was the **Burgher Watch House** (1716, rebuilt 1755–61, architect unknown, Johannes Struwig sculptor, restored 1917). The second and present building is a two-storeyed structure with superimposed Doric and Ionic orders, Baroque ornament and a projecting entrance porch or loggia; originally it was crowned with a balustrade (p. 1182C). Other signs of growing prosperity followed. A hospital was built in 1772, and the construction of three-storeyed brick warehouses indicated an increase in trade. In 1779 the first **Groote Kerk** (1700–4) was enlarged on a Greek cross plan with a segmental pedimented gable and pilasters. It was rebuilt *c.* 1840; only the tower now survives. The Groote Kerk contained a pulpit carved by Anton Anreith (1754–1822), who also produced one for the **Lutheran Church** (originally a warehouse) which he also refaced (1787–92) (p. 1183B) in a Classical manner. This seems to have been the model for the **Sendinggestig**, the South African Missionary Society's church (1801–3, built by J. G. Mocke, who may also have been the designer) (p. 1183C).

Anreith and Louis Michel Thibault (1750–1815) were the first identifiable architects to work in the colony. Anreith trained as a sculptor in Germany, and Thibault as an architect in Paris under Ange-Jacques Gabriel. Both arrived at the Cape as members of regiments on service, but by 1768 Anreith was master sculptor to the Dutch East India Company, and in

A. Groot Constantia: the central section of the entrance front (altered *c.* 1792). See p. 1181

B. Martin Melck House (originally the Lutheran Parsonage), Cape Town (1782). See pp. 1181, 1184

C. Burgher Watch House, Cape Town (1755–61). See p. 1181

A. The Castle, Cape Town: inner face of the entrance gateway. See p. 1181

B. Lutheran Church, Cape Town (refaced 1787–92). See p. 1181

C. Sendinggestig, Cape Town (1801–3). See p. 1181

D. The Castle, Cape Town: the Governor's Residence, 'Kat' Balcony (*c.* 1780–90). See p. 1184

1786 Thibault was appointed Inspector of the Company's buildings or, in effect, their official architect. Anreith worked in a South German late rococo style, as may be seen in his church pulpits and in the pediment of the monumental Wine Cellar at **Groot Constantia** (1791). Other works in a similar style are the teak portico and balcony (**Kat Balcony**) added to the **Governor's Residence** in the Castle (p. 1183D), and the teak verandah added in 1798 to the house, **Rust-en-Vreugd** (*c.* 1777–82), which has outstanding rococo carving in the entrance doorway (p. 1186A). Anreith probably carved the garlands on the **Martin Melck House** (1782) (p. 1182B), which was possibly his design, but certainly his style changed after Thibault's arrival in the colony. The refacing of the **Koopmans de Wet House** (*c.* 1792) with fluted pilasters and garlanded panels has been attributed to the Frenchman, but the design which most obviously betrays his French training is the old masonic **Lodge de Goede Hoop** (1803, restored 1892–3, after a fire), with its blank walls and symbolic entrance. The **Stal Plein** gateway is even more strongly reminiscent of French neo-Classicism.

Outside Cape Town, Thibault designed the **Drostdy** (court-house) at **Tulbagh** (1807), and another at **Graaff-Reinet** (1804), where he may have been responsible also for the old parsonage (*c.* 1812). Another likely commission was the remodelling (*c.* 1806) of **Rustenburg**, a house at Rondebosch which has a colonnade with a giant order. But by that date the British had taken over the colony. Thibault continued to work for the new administration, building (with Anreith) the new facade to the **Old Supreme Court** and Legislative Assembly (1811–15) and the **Customs House** (1814). He was probably responsible for extensive remodelling and additions to **Government House**, including gateways on Government Avenue, for one of which Anreith moulded plaster lionesses. The building itself shows a protracted change from Dutch to British taste. Other examples of this change may be noted in such buildings as the **Commercial Exchange** (1819, now demolished) and **Bertram House** (*c.* 1840), both in **Cape Town**, and the **Drostdy at Worcester** (W. Jones, 1823–5) (p. 1186B) with its shallow segmental bays at each end of the long facade.

The styles being revived in England at the time were adopted for important new buildings in **Cape Town**. The **Royal Observatory**, first planned in 1821 by Admiralty engineers, was built in 1825–7 to a design by Sir John Rennie (p. 1186C); the Doric portico and other Greek details were supervised by John Skirrow (later Government Architect at the Cape), who was sent out from England. In 1827–8 the Scots Presbyterians built **S. Andrew's Church** (H. W. Reveley), in which coupled Doric columns support a Doric entablature and pediment. Work began in 1830 on **S. George's Church** (later the cathedral, now demolished), in which Skirrow closely followed the model of S. Pancras, London (W. and H. W. Inwood, 1819–22) in the Ionic hexastyle portico and the western tower, which also uses references to the Tower of the Winds. The Inwoods' church had been illustrated in *The Public Buildings of London* (1825), by Britton and Pugin, and this was probably the source of the Cape Town design. There are few records of drawings being sent out from England at this time, although it may be presumed that this occurred. In 1824 a design for a marine **villa at Green Point** near Cape Town was exhibited at the Royal Academy by Thomas Willson.

Another fashionable style was the Egyptian. In 1820–1 Sir Rufane Donkin built a **pyramid** in memory of his wife at **Algoa Bay** (Port Elizabeth), and in 1839–41 the **Egyptian Building** of the **South African College** (now the University of Cape Town) was built to a design by Professor James Adamson with Colonel G. G. Lewis as architect. It has a colonnade and other details of Egyptian origin, and so has the **Gymnasium School at Paarl** (1858), in which the walls are decorated with symbolic Egyptian figures. By 1862, when the Jewish community in **Cape Town** built their **synagogue**, the Greek and Egyptian styles seem to have become confused, and both may be found in this design.

The Classical style was used for some new churches. **S. John's, Bathurst** (1829–38) is a small but distinguished design by Major Charles Cornwallis Michell, and the **Dutch Reformed Church at Uitenhage** (1820–43) incorporated pilasters, a tiered tower and spire, while that at **Cradock** (1864–7), with its tiered steeple rising above a west portico, is one of the many offspring in English-speaking countries of James Gibbs's S. Martin-in-the-Fields. When the **Groote Kerk, Cape Town**, was rebuilt between 1835 and 1841 the facade combined Classical and Gothic elements (p. 1186D); but by the time the Cradock church was being built the revived Gothic had become the general ecclesiastical style for all denominations. As early as the 1820s it had appeared in the **Pacaltsdorp Mission Church** (1822–5) and in Colonel Charles Trappes's **Dutch Reformed Church at Worcester** (1824). **S. Mary's, Port Elizabeth** (1831) and **S. Paul's, Rondebosch** (Michell, 1832–4) are other early examples, while **S. Patrick's, Grahamstown** (attributed to C. Selwyn, 1839–44) is Tudor-Gothic. By 1845 when the **Methodist Settlers' (Commemoration) Church** was built in Grahamstown, pinnacles, battlements and ogee arched windows had been incorporated; and the **Presbyterian Church, Pietermaritzburg** (1852–4, altered 1873) is a hybrid Classical-Gothic building. But it was Sophia Gray, the wife of the first Anglican Bishop of Cape Town, who provided the designs for many new churches by drawing upon her own studies and recollections of old English buildings, and making use of the current publications as well as plans and drawings brought from England (e.g. at

Stellenbosch and King William's Town she used plans made by English architects). Modifications were made to take account of the money and materials available, but the lady, who was described as 'working at her plans and drawings as if she were a qualified ecclesiastical architect', was responsible for several attractive buildings including **S. George's, Knysna** (1849–55), **S. Mark's, George** (1849–50), the **English Church at Caledon** (*c.* 1850), **S. Saviour's, Claremont** (1850–3, completed by W. Butterfield), **S. Peter's Cathedral, Pietermaritzburg** (1851–7, enlarged later) and **S. Michael and S. Andrew, Bloemfontein** (1850, replaced 1866).

The development of the Western and Eastern Cape regions in the 1820s and of towns such as Grahamstown and Port Elizabeth had consolidated the English influence on buildings as well as on life and culture generally, but the Great Trek of 1831–8 eventually led to the foundation of the Boer Republics of the Transvaal (1852) and the Orange Free State (1854). An attempt to found a third in Natal failed, and in 1842 the British occupied the colony which for five years had been the Republic of Natalia with the newly established town of Pietermaritzburg as its capital. This expansion to the north-east of the Cape Colony meant that a distinction developed between the architecture in the British colonies and the Boer republics, even if there was much common ground.

The use of the Gothic style for churches seems to have been one example of reasonable unanimity between the Boers and British, and many of those built from the 1860s onwards are often hardly distinguishable from English designs of the same date, allowing for some changes in material. In **Oudtshoorn** the elegant **Dutch Reformed Church** (K. O. Hager, 1877–80) was built by Scottish stonemasons who had already worked on the little **Belvidere Church at Knysna** which Sophia Gray designed. In Cape Town the **Metropolitan Methodist Church** (Charles Freeman, 1876–9) is in the decorated style with a nave, chancel and corner tower with spire. The same architect designed a more grandiose and less successful **Dutch Reformed Church at Graaff-Reinet** (1886), richly detailed and roofed with coloured slates laid in a pattern. In **Bloemfontein**, A. W. Wocke's **Dutch Reformed Church** was built in 1878 in a more or less Romanesque style with twin towers, and for the same denomination in **Pretoria** Klaas van Rijsse designed a **church** (1896–7) with an elaborate spire and particoloured main body. In **Grahamstown**, the **Cathedral of S. Michael and S. George** was begun in 1824 by Colonel H. M. Scott, and greatly enhanced in 1874–8 with a tower and spire designed by Sir George Gilbert Scott. His son, John Oldrid, provided the 1889 and 1909 designs for the chancel and the nave (p. 1187A). In **Durban** the Methodists built their **church** in West Street in the Early English style with aisles (R. Ridgeway, 1877), but when the Roman Catholics in that city resolved to build **S. Joseph's** in 1878 they obtained a design from an English firm, Goldie, Childe and Goldie. Their design was described as 'Gothic . . . adapted to the materials of modern, as well as colonial, production and to considerations of climate. In counteracting the heat . . . it is perfect, and to have gained this end, few people will be inclined to quarrel with the architects' free handling of the Gothic style as our fathers knew it'.

A common characteristic of all colonies was to replicate as far as possible the culture and architecture of the mother country, even when there are considerable climatic differences. But there was not necessarily a strict demarcation along national lines. For example, the **South African Museum in Cape Town** (1893–7) was the work of an architect from the Transvaal, J. E. Vixseboxse, and in the Republican style.

The **South African Library in Cape Town** (W. H. Kohler, 1857–60) was designed with a Corinthian facade based on that of Basevi's Fitzwilliam Museum at Cambridge (1836–48), and in **Durban** the **Town Hall** (P. M. Dudgeon, 1883–5) (p. 1187B) was one of several descendants of Brodrick's Leeds Town Hall (1853–8). The Leeds model, of a Classical rectangular building surrounded by a colonnaded or pilastered screen, crowned with a domed central tower, survived into the early twentieth century when Reid and Green designed **Cape Town City Hall** (1905). The prestigious image was so strong that even the modest **Port Elizabeth Town Hall** (1861) (p. 1188C) was given a domed tower (completed in 1894), in an attempt to make it conform. The Classical **Kimberley Town Hall** (Carstairs and Rogers, 1899) illustrates the importance attached to a symbolic public building, even when the town itself had been hastily built around diamond mines. **Ladysmith** and **Newcastle Town Halls** (R. Walker, 1894, and W. Lucas, 1898) continued the Classical tradition, although departing frequently from strict Classical grammar. In **Pietermaritzburg** an eclectic 'quaint blend of Tudor, Flemish and Florentine styles' was used on a large, square, brick building with a gigantic corner tower (Street-Wilson and Barr, 1891–3, reconstructed after a fire in 1898) (p. 1188A). The style of the **Town Hall at East London** (Page and Cordeaux, 1893–8) is equally eclectic. By 1903 when **Durban City Hall** was designed (Scott, Woolocott and Hudson) (p. 1187C), the Baroque style had been revived as the final architectural expression of British Imperialism.

Government buildings in the Cape and Natal generally followed English models, and were frequently the work of architects and engineers employed in the Public Works Department. The **Parliament Building in Cape Town** is a heavy but dignified brick structure with plaster dressings simulating stone (H. E. Greaves, 1875–84, enlarged 1909, 1960, 1984), a revised version of a much grander prize-winning design made by Charles Freeman (1874) with a central dome and cupolas

A. Rust-en-Vreugd, Cape Town (*c.* 1777–82, teak verandah 1798). See p. 1184

B. The Drostdy, Worcester (1823–5). See p. 1184

C. Royal Observatory, Cape Town (1825–7). See p. 1184

D. Groote Kerke, Cape Town (rebuilt 1835–41). See p. 1184

E. Parliament Building, Cape Town (1875–84). See p. 1185

A. Cathedral, Grahamstown, from NE (1824, 1874–8, 1889-1909). See p. 1185

B. Town Hall (now Post Office), Durban (1883–50). See p. 1185

C. City Hall, Durban (1903). See p. 1185

A. Town Hall, Pietermaritzburg (1891–3 reconstructed 1898). See p. 1185

B. Legislative Assembly, Pietermaritzburg (1887–9, additions 1901. See p. 1189

C. Town Hall, Port Elizabeth (1891, completed 1894). See p. 1185

(p. 1186E). The **Legislative Assembly** building in **Pietermaritzburg** (James Tibbet, 1887–9) is dominated by a two-storeyed hexastyle portico, and the first building was complemented by an addition (1901) with a copper-covered dome (p. 1188B); but the **Legislative Council** building (A. E. Dainton, 1898–1900) is French rather than English in its Classicism, especially in the square-domed roofs on the central and end pavilions. This is a characteristic also of the **Raadsaal in Pretoria** (p. 1190C), the capital of the Boer Republic of Transvaal (S. W. Wierda, 1887–90); this and the same architect's design for the facing building across Church Square, the **Palace of Justice** (1886–99) (p. 1190A), might be described as Franco-Prussian Neo-Baroque (and can be compared with the Reichstag building, Berlin, of 1884–94 by Paul Wallot). In **Bloemfontein**, the capital of the Orange Free State, the fourth and present **Raadsaal** (Lennox Canning, 1890–1) is a late neo-Classical design with an Ionic hexastyle portico linked to side-colonnades with semicircular porticoes.

Some of the architects whose work has been mentioned above built up prolific practices in their own towns or regions. Philip Maurice Dudgeon (1852–91) was born in England and arrived in Durban in 1877. Apart from the Town Hall, his work includes the **Addington Hospital** (1877), the **Alexandra Hotel** (1879), **Pietermaritzburg Town Offices** (1882), the **Masonic Temple, Kokstad** (1882), the **Standard Bank, Pietermaritzburg** (1882), the **Natal Club** (1885), **Pietermaritzburg College** (1885), and many commercial buildings and residences. Charles Freeman (1833–1911) was another Englishman who worked first for the Government in Natal, and then in **Cape Town** where he designed many buildings including the **General Post Office** (*c.* 1870), the **Standard Bank** (1880) and the **Grand Hotel** (*c.* 1885).

Other architects were C. H. Jenkyn (**Customs House, Durban**), Alfred Singleton (**Boys' Preparatory School, Girls' Model School** and an **Asylum**, all in **Pietermaritzburg**), and Sytze Wierda (**Government Buildings**, *c.* 1890; **Artillery Barracks**, 1896–8; **Staatsmodelskool**, 1895; **State Printing Works**, 1895, all in **Pretoria**). Wierda also designed the **Magistrates' Court, Potchefstroom** (*c.* 1890), the **Mental Hospital, Weskoppies** (1889), and the **Post Office** (1895) and **Telephone Tower in Johannesburg**. For the most part these architects followed the stylistic changes in Europe, and towards the end of the century an element of Art Nouveau was introduced, as well as half-timbering and Dutch gables. It is, however, the name of Sir Herbert Baker (1862–1945) that is almost synonymous with the Cape Dutch Revival which began in the late 1890s.

Trained in his uncle's office in London, and knowing the towns and buildings in Europe from first-hand study, Baker was able to offer a wider and deeper knowledge of architecture than most of his colleagues who went out to the colonies in the late nineteenth century. The 'Queen Anne' style, the 'Pont Street Dutch', the Arts and Crafts enthusiasm for vernacular buildings and traditional materials and building methods – these were the influences on Baker at the time he went to the Cape in 1892. He discovered the old homesteads, 'dignified in the ordered layout ... beautiful in the simplicity of the architecture, white walls, solid teak or green-painted shuttered windows and doors, gracefully curved gables'. He made sketches of them, some of which were published in the pioneering *Old Colonial Houses at the Cape* by Alys Trotter in 1900. He gathered together and trained a group of craftsmen who could execute the first, very English designs he made shortly after his arrival, but the rebuilding of **Groote Schuur**, a seventeenth-century barn and later a homestead destroyed by a fire shortly after Cecil Rhodes bought it in 1893, gave Baker an opportunity to work in the Cape Dutch style. He then developed this interest in four other houses at the end of the decade (**Sandhills** for himself, and **The Retreat, Welgelegen** and **The Woolsack** for Rhodes). His recognition of the quality and individuality of eighteenth-century Cape Dutch homesteads, several of which he was to restore and improve, was also a recognition that South African architecture was not simply a reflection of European models. And in his outstanding design for **Rust-en-Vrede** (1905) he demonstrated how that tradition could be developed to meet twentieth-century needs.

During the years he was in practice in **Cape Town**, Baker was responsible for commercial buildings (**Wilson and Miller**, 1899; **Rhodes**, 1902; **Marks**, 1905; **National Mutual Life Association**, 1905), and for several churches (in partnership with Francis Edward Masey, 1861–1912) which were generally basilican in plan and followed Arts and Crafts principles in the use of materials. In 1897 he was commissioned to design a **new cathedral in Cape Town** to replace John Skirrow's Greek Revival building. Cruciform in plan and Romanesque-Gothic in style, his building incorporates French, Italian and English influences, and characteristically exhibits a high standard of materials and craftsmanship. The other dominant influence on Baker's work in the Cape is that of Classical Greece and Rome; it is most apparent in the Tuscan mausoleum that is the **Kimberley Memorial** (1904) (p. 1190B) and in the Hellenic conception of the **Rhodes Memorial** (1905–8) built on the side of Devil's Peak (Table Mountain) (p. 1190E).

In 1902 Baker moved to Johannesburg where, unlike the Cape, there was no building tradition. In the 300 houses he designed in the Transvaal, he exploited several styles – English Tudor, Dutch, Mediterranean – but at the same time he encouraged good building and the correct use of materials (in the

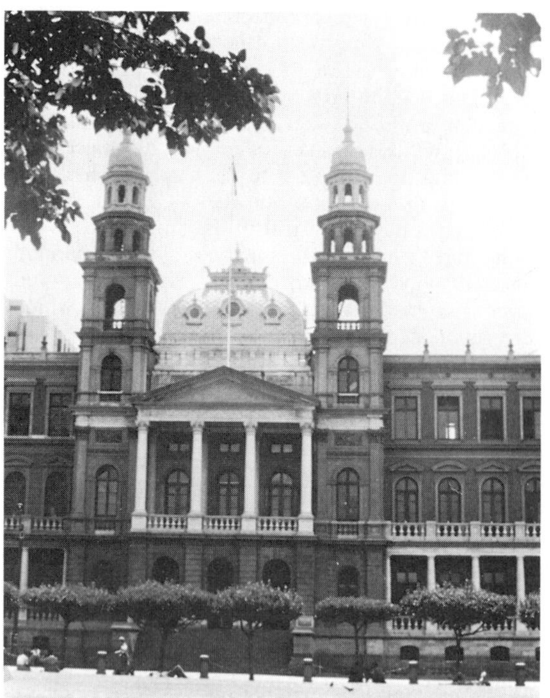

A. Palace of Justice, Pretoria (1896–9). See p. 1189

B. Kimberley Memorial (1904). See p. 1189

C. Raadsaal, Pretoria (1887–90). See p. 1189

D. Big House, Westminster (1904–5). See p. 1192

E. Rhodes Memorial, Cape Town (1905–8). See p. 1189

A. (*above*)
Union Buildings, Pretoria
(1910–12)

B. (*left*)
Union Buildings, Pretoria.
See p. 1192

small cheap houses as well as in those of the gold and diamond magnates). Eclectic though they are, his houses have been called 'the first original contributions to domestic architecture since the days of the Cape Dutch builders'. The larger houses were commonly H-shaped in plan (**Stonehouse**, 1902 (p. 1177G), **The Thatched House** and **Marienburg**, 1904 – all in **Johannesburg** – and **Government House, Pretoria**, 1905). Externally they were stone, brick or plastered; sometimes they were gabled in a Dutch or Flemish manner, and often they were crowned with elaborate chimney stacks reminiscent of Kent and Sussex manor houses. Some of them, as for example the **Big House** on the Duke of Westminster's estate in the Orange Free State (p. 1190D), are nostalgic evocations of traditional English houses and gardens, complete with luxurious stables.

Some of the Transvaal churches demonstrate what Baker called 'a primitive style of architecture', which arose out of the inherent characteristics of the available local materials (**S. John the Divine, Randfontein**, and **S. George, Cullinan**, both 1904), but in the larger churches (**S. Michael and All Angels, Boksburg**, 1911, and the partly built **S. Alban's cathedral, Pretoria**, 1905) the favoured style was a form of Romanesque. However, the early twentieth-century commissions for public buildings called for a different architectural style, and Baker's appointment in 1908 to design the **Railway Station at Pretoria** led to the adoption of a Renaissance manner which was to lead him eventually to New Delhi. A giant order of coupled Ionic columns screen the central loggia in the long, low facade which has a rusticated stone basement and Roman-tiled roof. The station stands at one end of a mile-long vista, and although impressive at a distance, it is less satisfactory in its detailing. The next Renaissance essay, which was to influence the design of official architecture in other British colonies as well as in South Africa itself until relatively recently, shows a better understanding of the subtleties of Classical design.

From the first, **Union Buildings, Pretoria** (1910–12) (p. 1191A,B), was seen as a symbol as well as an administrative necessity, and Baker selected a conspicuous hilltop overlooking Pretoria on which to erect a building that marked the post-Anglo-Boer-War union between the British Colony and the Boer Republics. His design consists of two large blocks built around courtyards and linked by a semicircular colonnaded central building; the whole is symbolic of the two nations and the four colonies (represented by two pavilions on each of the two blocks) which were being brought together in the new Union of South Africa. It was a concept deriving from the European Baroque monumental tradition of the Louvre, Versailles and the Royal Naval Hospital at Greenwich, and it was probably from this last that Baker took the idea of the two domed towers which rise above the level roofline (although there are also similarities to Sir Edwin Lutyens's unsuccessful 1907 design in the London County Hall competition). As a Classical composition it has its faults, and the Temple of Peace, which it was intended to build on the summit of the hill to resolve the obvious duality, has never been realised, but with its sweeping colonnade, descending terraces and flights of stairs, it offers majestic groupings of the major elements. As an imperial symbol it achieved what Baker intended when he wrote about the parallels between architecture, which 'within the limits of order, true science and progress' provides scope for self-expression, and British colonial rule, which conferred 'order, progress and freedom within the law to develop national civilisations on the lines of their own tradition and sentiment'.

Chapter 37

THE AMERICAS

Architectural Character

European settlers in the Americas brought with them the planning and architecture of their homelands and modified them in reference to the climate and resources of the regions in which they settled. In both Latin and North America, they began with coastal settlements or the old capitals of previous cultures and worked inwards from there. The Spaniards were the first to arrive, and defensive works on the Caribbean Islands formed the earliest permanent token of European culture in America; Santo Domingo, founded in 1496 in the Dominican Republic, is the first permanent settlement to survive. By 'The Laws of the Indies', promulgated in 1573, Philip II established a loose grid for towns, with a central open 'plaza' for public buildings and the church or cathedral, to represent ecclesiastical and secular order, and plots for sale along the side streets. This pattern, adapted from ancient town planning, pervaded the colonisation of the Americas (see Chapter 35). Early towns were fortified against attack in simple ways with earthworks and stockades. Later, when the European powers were in intensive rivalry with one another, heavier fortifications became necessary to withstand sieges.

The most important early buildings of the Catholic colonizing nations, Spain, Portugal and France, were the churches. As the monastic orders enjoyed a key role in establishing and maintaining settlements, churches and monastery buildings are the most representative constructions of sixteenth-century Latin America. They consist of a series of outbuildings which unite the European style with the pre-Hispanic tradition of worship in the open air; the huge churches with their attached cloister were preceded by an open atrium with small closed shrines or 'Indian chapels'. The quality of the structures and decoration varied in accordance with the materials, the local workforce and the backgrounds of the missionaries, who achieved works of great spatial power. They were usually built in an artisanised equivalent of contemporary European styles; due to lack of skilled labour, construction techniques were often borrowed from domestic buildings. This is most marked in the churches built by Pueblo Indians for seventeenth-century Spanish missionaries in New Mexico, where indigenous techniques of adobe and wood almost engulf the imported style. Earthquakes had also to be anticipated by construction techniques, so far as it was possible. But generally the colonial architecture of Latin America closely reflected that of Spain and Portugal. Early examples show derivation from Spanish Gothic prototypes, but Classicism made headway after 1550.

As colonisation developed, the styles of the Catholic European powers continued to be faithfully followed in their American colonies. Buildings in seventeenth-century Quebec were close in technique and style to those of northern France. Likewise, the excesses of the Baroque and Rococo styles in Spain and Portugal (see Chapter 34) were mimicked in Latin America during the eighteenth century, a period of grandeur in cities, ports and mining areas.

Dutch, German and English settlements of Protestant foundation in North America were slower to develop towns with self-conscious civic values. New Haven (1636) had a large square at the centre with streets off, but it was the plan of Philadelphia (1682–3) that set the pattern for the developed North American grid. From an early date, individual farmhouses were often the buildings of greatest interest. Northern territories, with their copious forests, offered the opportunity for carpenters to carry on the European timber-framed tradition, not only in houses but also in churches and other public buildings. In seventeenth-century New England, building followed the pattern of English heavy timber-framed prototypes with weather-boarding or shingling. Log-cabin construction seems to have been a speciality first introduced by Swedes and Germans in Delaware and Pennsylvania. In the North American South, building was quite often in brick. Though the houses are often hard to distinguish in style from counterparts of the same period in England or France, they begin after about 1660 here and in the Caribbean plantations to be planned with deep balconies or porches to allow the ventilation and protection from the sun unnecessary in Europe. Significant regional characteristics of this kind strengthened during the eighteenth century, as specialist design and crafts skills developed throughout the Americas. Professional architects, however, remained rare before the American War of Independence; the earliest well-known architects in the English North American colonies, Peter Harrison (1716–75) and Thomas Jefferson (1743–1826), were both gentlemen-amateurs.

The immediate post-colonial period in North and South America saw no attempt to dispense with European models, but there was a strong interest in the neo-Classicism then fashionable in Europe, with its intimations of independent republicanism. Jefferson, the Francophile third President of the United States, was influential in this respect. His Virginia Capitol offered a model for the many state capitols to be built in the nineteenth century, while the buildings of the University of Virginia campus foreshadowed American Beaux-Arts academicism at the end of the century. Among early professional architects in the United States, Charles Bulfinch of Boston (1763–1844) provided the basis for the handsome, Robert Adam-influenced architecture of that city during the Federal period. Boston, Philadelphia and New York all developed local variants of the English brick or stone terrace style, but unified terraces of houses were quite rare in other cities, as the ample space available made them unnecessary. The English immigrant Benjamin Latrobe (1764–1820) of Philadelphia was mainly responsible for introducing the Greek Revival, which enjoyed much success in the United States, while Pierre L'Enfant's plan for Washington (1791–2) introduced diagonal axes and other devices from European town planning to supplement the standard city grid.

In Latin America, the imposition of the neo-Classical style through the academies and military engineers reflected changes in thinking brought about by the Enlightenment, the independence of the colonies during the first decade of the nineteenth century, and the growing cultural influence of France, exercised through the work of immigrant architects such as A. J. V. Grandjean de Montigny (1776–1850) in Rio de Janeiro and C. F. Brunet-Debaines (1799–1855) in Santiago. Churches mostly remained Classical, though there were occasional flirtations with Gothic after 1850.

After 1840 the Greek Revival was increasingly ousted for churches in the United States by the English-imported Gothic Revival, championed by the New York architects Richard Upjohn (1802–78) and James Renwick Jr (1818–95). Gothic in North American secular buildings proved short-lived, having no more than a 25-year lifespan from about 1848. More popular in the United States was the picturesque or 'gardenesque' villa style associated with A. J. Davis (1803–92) and the landscapist Andrew Jackson Downing (1815–52). Their vision of picturesque variety marked the starting point for a middle-class 'Victorian' house style, usually an amalgam of French and English motifs, which developed and worked its way across the United States and Canada during the course of the nineteenth century in many shapes and forms.

At a more basic level, the primitive log-cabin construction learnt from Germans and Swedes was universal in northern and western frontier settlements where timber was plentiful up to about 1830. It then gave way to the 'balloon frame', a much-simplified version of the traditional European timber-frame. First introduced in Chicago, the balloon frame consisted of light, nailed timber sections with an external timber sheathing. It became the standard technique all over North America for anything from bungalows to the 'three-decker' houses with gables facing the street which were to become characteristic in 'streetcar suburbs' at the end of the century. Balloon framing would not have been possible without the growth of an iron industry for nail production. The middle of the nineteenth century saw a parallel growth in the use of structural and decorative cast-iron elements, often prefabricated on a large scale, notably for commercial buildings. James Bogardus (1800–74) and Daniel Badger were the pioneer fabricators, and New York City the original centre of the cast-iron buildings trade. The effect of decorative ironwork is notable in New Orleans, where from about 1850 double-decker cast-iron galleries were built in front of houses to ward off the sun instead of open single-storey arcades.

Though the Americas shared in the stylistic eclecticism of the second half of the nineteenth century, it was during this period that the United States emerged with an original architecture and architectural profession of its own and Europeans started to admire its achievement. The prime mover in this development was Richard Morris Hunt (1827–95), the first American to attend the Ecole des Beaux Arts in Paris. Hunt's own buildings were more academic than creative, but he worked conspicuously for the affluent classes of the Gilded Age and set the fashion for French methods of architectural education. His important successors Henry Hobson Richardson (1838–86), Charles McKim (1849–1909) and Louis Sullivan (1856–1924) all attended the Ecole. The first architectural school in the United States, set up at the Massachusetts Institute of Technology under W. R. Ware in 1867, followed Beaux-Arts lines; the second, at the University of Illinois, Urbana (1870), developed a German model, reflecting the different cultural character of the Mid-West.

Picturesque domestic architecture, always strong in the United States, developed on the East Coast after the American Civil War away from the gawky, French-influenced 'Stick Style' to the smoother, English-influenced 'Shingle Style', sometimes called 'Queen Anne'. This was briefly practised by Richardson, perfected in the early work of McKim, Mead and

White, W. R. Emerson and others, and ushered in a golden era for the independent American house across the continent. This achievement was to be the basis of the work of the great domestic architects of the next generation, notably Frank Lloyd Wright (1867–1959) in Chicago and Greene and Greene in Northern California (see Chapter 50). But the mature masterpieces of Richardson, the first American architect of uncontestable genius, consisted chiefly of public buildings in a Romanesque derived style of rugged power and discipline. The Richardsonian style continued to have a fleeting vogue after his death in 1886.

The last two decades of the nineteenth century were noteworthy in the United States for structural experiment and achievement. Chicago, which grew apace after a disastrous fire in 1873, and to a lesser extent New York, were important centres in the early development of the commercial skyscraper. The skyscraper was made possible by new techniques for foundations, steel-framing for superstructures, the non-load-bearing 'curtain wall' and the elevator or lift. William Le Baron Jenney (1832–1907) and Dankmar Adler (1844–1900) in Chicago were the first architects to master the techniques, while John Wellborn Root (1850–91) and Adler's brilliant partner Louis Sullivan explored formal and decorative solutions for this dramatic new building type.

After 1890, an academic strain came to the fore in the architecture of the United States. The World's Columbian Exposition of 1893 at Chicago, masterminded by Daniel Burnham (1845–1912) is commonly cited as the turning point, though the trend was visible in the sophisticated work of McKim, Mead and White before then. Public buildings assumed an increasingly Classical dress, planning schemes on axial Beaux-Arts lines found favour; houses too took on an air of symmetry and formality foreshadowing the Colonial Revival. The Beaux Arts ethos in architecture was ideologically dominant throughout the Americas at the start of the twentieth century.

Examples

The Colonial Period

Domestic Buildings

The colonial mansions of the rich in successful Spanish settlements consisted of courtyard houses on two main floors, with shops facing the street and the family rooms above, sometimes with an entresol for the slaves in between. The earliest survivor of note is the stately **House of Diego Colón, Santo Domingo** (1510–14), built in a Spanish style on two levels over a rectangular floor with a double gallery. It served as a model for other Caribbean mansions, among which the **House of Engombe, Santo Domingo** and the fortress-like **House of Cortés, Cuernavaca, Mexico** (1525–35) are noteworthy. The **House of Montejo, Mérida, Mexico** (*c.* 1549) is in the Plateresque style.

In Brazil, the most monumental residence of early date is the now-ruinous **Tower of Tatuapara** near the first city of the Portuguese colony, Bahía (formerly Salvador). Begun in 1551 and finished in 1624, it has a three-storey, brick-built central body forming a front courtyard with lower side wings over arcades. The **Saldanha House, Bahía, Brazil** (*c.* 1610, interior now burnt), like early Spanish houses, has two main floors, the lower for stores and a coachhouse, the upper for living, here also with a granary on top; there is a fine, somewhat later doorway elaborately carved in local stone with columns and caryatids.

Capen House, Topsfield, Massachusetts (1683) (p. 1196A), an excellent example of seventeenth-century New England architecture, is of heavy timber-frame construction, with first floor and gables being carried forward as 'jetties', and a central, clustered brick chimney. The house is clad in weatherboarding and has a wood shingle roof. Internal walls and partitions are faced with vertical boarding, beams are left exposed and decoration is sparse, being confined to such details as the stair balusters. Windows are small, leaded casements. The ground floor is divided into two rooms by a central brick core, incorporating two fireplaces back-to-back. At one end of the brick core is an entrance lobby, from which a staircase leads to the upper floor. Other houses of a similar character are **Whipple House, Ipswich, Massachusetts** (1639); **Scotch-Boardman House, Saugus, Massachusetts** (*c.* 1686); **Fairbanks House, Dedham, Massachusetts** (*c.* 1637); **Whitman House, Farmington, Connecticut** (1664); **Paul Revere House, Boston, Massachusetts** (*c.* 1676); **John Ward House, Salem, Massachusetts** (1684); **House of the Seven Gables, Salem, Massachusetts** (*c.* 1670).

Bacon's Castle, Surry County, Virginia (*c.* 1655) (p. 1196B) is cruciform in plan. Built in brick, with its curved Flemish gables, high clustered chimneys and Classical details in the brickwork over its entrance, the house has much in common with Jacobean examples in England. So too does **Adam Thoroughgood House, Virginia Beach, Princess Anne County, Virginia** (*c.* 1635–40), the earliest extant structure built by the Virginia colonists. It has two main rooms only and is built of brick and wood shingles with external chimneybreasts and imported window glass. **S. Nicholas Abbey, Barbados** (*c.* 1656–61) is the closest Caribbean equivalent, built of brick with stucco facing and quoins, three Jacobean gables to the front and a big chimneybreast to one side; as yet there are no verandahs. The interior is later, with a Chinese Chippendale staircase.

A. Capen House, Topsfield, Massachusetts (1683). See p. 1195

B. Bacon's Castle, Surry County, Virginia (*c.* 1655). See p. 1195

C. Westover, Charles City County, Virginia (*c.* 1730–4). See p. 1198

A. Parlange, Pointe Coupée Parish, Louisiana (1750). See p. 1198

B. Drayton Hall, South Carolina (1738–42). See p. 1198

C. Ecala Palace, Querétaro (*c.* 1785). See p. 1199

D. Casa del Alfeñique, Puebla (*c.* 1780). See p. 1199

E. S. Pedro dos Clérigos, Recife (1729–). See p. 1202

Villeneuve House, Charlesbourg, Quebec (*c.* 1700), is an example of the peasant houses of 'New France', built of whitewashed fieldstone with weatherboarded ends, small shuttered windows and a hipped roof with flared eaves rising higher than the walls (for storage space).

Abraham Ackerman House, Hackensack, New Jersey (1704), shows Dutch influence. Its roof is of the 'gambrel' or mansard type with widely projecting eaves and is covered in wood shingles, as also are the gables and dormer cheeks. The walls of the ground floor are of roughly dressed, coursed masonry. Other such houses are **Dyckman House, New York** (*c.* 1783); **Terheun House, Hackensack, New Jersey** (*c.* 1709); **Vreeland House, Englewood, New Jersey** (1818), and **Jan Ditmars House, Brooklyn, New York** (*c.* 1700). Eighteenth-century Dutch-style houses with shaped gables also exist in some numbers on the Caribbean island of **Curaçao**, notably the orange-stuccoed town houses of **Handelskade** and **Bredestraat, Willemstad**.

Parlange, Pointe Coupée Parish, Louisiana (1750) (p. 1197A), a French plantation house, has an open, colonnaded verandah running around the house on both floors, a feature providing protection from the hot sun and heavy rains of the area. The high-pitched, hipped roof is covered in shingles, and because of the dampness of the site the ground floor is constructed of brick, although the first floor is of timber. Other examples of similar character are **Connelly's Tavern, Natchez, Mississippi** (*c.* 1795) and **Keller Mansion, Saint Charles Parish, Louisiana** (*c.* 1801). This type also occurs in the West Indies. **The Deanery, Nassau, Bahamas** (*c.* 1710), is a simple, square example, with a latticed verandah and a big enveloping hipped roof; the kitchen and outhouses are separate. On a larger scale, **Clarence House, Antigua** (1786) has a stone semi-basement, a timber-framed and clad upper storey, and a colonnade of 32 columns all round forming the verandah.

Mulberry, Berkeley County, South Carolina (*c.* 1714), is a delightful farmhouse that adapts European Baroque mannerisms to practical ends by adding square pavilions for extra accommodation in the four corners of a simple centre, thus allowing ample ventilation to all the rooms. The whole is crowned by a heavy, half-hipped gambrel roof.

Westover, Charles City County, Virginia (*c.* 1730–4) (p. 1196C), one of the foremost Virginia plantation houses, was built for an owner who spent much of his career in England and so has close affinities to the English early Georgian style. It is a seven-bay structure of two storeys with further rooms in the steeply pitched hipped roof. The elaborate entrances, carved in Portland stone and therefore imported from England, are copied from plates in William Salmon's *Palladio Londinensis* (1734). The house is flanked symmetrically by two minor structures, one providing kitchen and servants' quarters, the other serving as the plantation office. There are fine interiors, of a quality ranking with the best English craftsmanship of the time. Some ceilings have applied designs, cast in composition and almost certainly also imported.

Other colonial houses of Georgian character are **Mount Pleasant, Philadelphia** (1761–2), built in stuccoed rubble, its stone details probably derived from a contemporary English pattern book such as those of Batty Langley (q.v.), with a low-pitched, lead-covered roof, truncated to form a flat terrace or deck, a feature of many American houses of this period known as a 'captain's walk'; and **Miles Brewton House, Charleston, South Carolina** (1765–9), with a fine two-storey pedimented, colonnaded porch. Similar features are to be found at **Shirley, Charles City County, Virginia** (*c.* 1769) and **Drayton Hall, South Carolina** (1738–42) (p. 1197B). Houses of this formal type in the West Indies are rarer but include **Rose Hall, near Montego Bay, Jamaica** (*c.* 1770–80), on a hillside site, with a grand centre and slightly recessed wings.

Plantation houses in the Caribbean island colonies continue in the nineteenth century to reflect the architecture of the respective mother countries. **Villa Nova, S. John, Barbados** (1833) is a handsome Regency-style villa, built of coral bricks with a low roof behind a parapet and ample verandahs. **Zevalos, Guadeloupe** (*c.* 1880) is a later French version of the plantation house encompassed with verandahs, by now constructed of pretty decorative ironwork.

In Latin America, the **House of Torre Tagle, Lima, Peru** (*c.* 1730) is a typical example of the local style of grander house built in the viceroyalty of Peru during the seventeenth and eighteenth centuries, with bedrooms on two levels round a courtyard and two box balconies with Andalusian-style lattice work. Houses in the Andean region often have corridors over the courtyard and prominent balconies and doorways, as in the **House of the Admiral** and **House of the Marqueses de Casa Concha, Cuzco, Peru**, and the **House of Diez de Medina, La Paz, Bolivia** (1775). The influence of Cuzco as the capital of the viceroyalty was felt as far away as present-day Chile (**House of the Conde del Conquista, Santiago,** 1750) and Colombia (**House of the Marqués de Valdehoyos, Cartagena**).

The **House of the Marqués de Jaral de Berrio, Mexico City** (1779–84), designed by Francisco Guerrero y Torres, is the most valuable example of the Baroque houses which led to the name 'City of Mansions' being given to the capital of New Spain. Behind a striking facade is a courtyard with stores and cellars on the ground floor and access to large bedrooms on the main floor via a magnificent flight of steps. The same architect also designed the **House of the Condes de San Mateo de Valparaiso, Mexico City** (1769–72), with its original double-flight staircase. Another important architect,

Lorenzo Rodriguez, created the **House of the Conde de San Bartolomé de Xala, Mexico City** (1764). Houses of this era in the Mexican city of **Puebla** are especially noteworthy. The **Casa de Alfeñique** (*c.* 1780) (p. 1197D) by Antonio de Santa Maria Inchaurregui is in the Chirrugueresque style with lavish sculpture; between the windows, the facade is entirely covered with tiles (*azulejos*), glazed and unglazed, in red, white and blue patterns. *Azulejos* also occur on the **House of the Conde del Valle de Orizaba, Mexico City** (1737) by Diego Durán. **The Ecala Palace, Querétaro, Mexico** (*c.* 1780) (p. 1197C) is a fine example of a Spanish colonial palace in a rich late Baroque style, with lacey wrought-iron balconies overhanging a deep, arcaded loggia; under the cornice is a frieze of blue and white tiles.

Fortifications

Military architecture was critical to the development of the American colonies. In the Caribbean, the **Castillo de la Real Fuerza, Havana, Cuba** (1558–82), by Bartolomé Sanchez represents an early model of the permanent forts built to guard Spanish possessions against piracy. It is a basic square, with triangular bastions in the corners. The widespread military work of the family dynasty of engineers, Giovanni Battista Antonelli, his son of the same name and his nephew Cristóbal de Roda (1556–1632), for the Spanish government includes the **Fortaleza de San Salvador de la Punta** and **Castillo del Morro, Havana** (1587–1630). Outstanding are the complex fortifications of **Cartagena, Colombia,** begun in the sixteenth century and culminating in **Castillo de San Felipe de Barajas** (1630–57, reconstructed *c.* 1700) (p. 1203A). Typical of later Spanish fortifications is the fine **Castillo de San Marcos, S. Augustine, Florida** (1672–95), built of shellrock to guard the first successfully established town on the North American continent (1565).

The Portuguese built more but smaller forts along the Brazilian coast. Typical are the string of forts, mostly of *c.* 1700, around **Bahía (Salvador): Santo Antônio da Barra,** designed as an irregular polygon by João and Francisco Coutinho; the hexagonal, compact **São Felipe; São Marcelo,** guarding the port; and the unmilitary-looking **Santa Maria**, with a tiny heptagonal terreplein and a pediment covered with tiles.

Remaining North American colonial fortifications are generally less impressive, but there are notable examples in Canada, including **Fort Chambly, Quebec** (1709–11), built by Josué Boisberthelot de Beaucourt, engineer-in-chief of 'New France'. The dockyards and fortifications on **Ireland Isle, Bermuda,** built up as a British naval base between 1820 and 1860 in case of war against the United States, mark the final phase of colonial fortification in the Americas.

Religious Buildings

The earliest Spanish colonial church buildings still partook of the Gothic style. Such is the **Santo Domingo Cathedral, Dominican Republic** (*c.* 1520–41), started by Luis de Moya and completed by Rodrigo Gilo de Liendo, who was responsible for the vaults with Gothic tracery which contrast with the Plateresque facade. The original portion of **Sucre Cathedral, Bolivia** (1551–61), and the **Guadalajara Cathedral, Mexico** (1571–1618), likewise have 'Gothic survival' intersecting vaults. By the time of **Cartagena Cathedral, Colombia** (1575–1612), Renaissance styles had arrived. The traditional nave and aisles are divided by an arcade with well-proportioned Tuscan columns and a round-windowed clerestory and timber roof above; only the apse is residually Gothic.

Mexico City Cathedral (1563–1667) (p. 1200A), was designed by Claudio de Arciniega (*c.* 1520–93) on an impressive scale, with double aisles to both nave and chancel, and side chapels. It mingles Baroque and more severely Classical features. The nave and transepts have barrel vaults with lunettes, while the bays of the side aisles are domed. The clustered piers of the nave are made up of four engaged Doric columns. Externally, the west facade is flanked by twin towers carried out after 1786 in a more neo-Classical taste by José Damián Ortiz de Castro and Manuel Tolsá.

Cuzco Cathedral, Peru (*c.* 1598–1654), has aisles and a nave of equal height with Gothic vaults over square Renaissance piers, deep side-chapels, and a broad, flattish facade with a Baroque centrepiece and twin towers at the ends. The old-fashioned vaulting appears to have been chosen here and elsewhere in Peru as a safeguard against earthquakes; later, builders used the *quincha* method of building simulated vaults in wood, reed and plaster. Similar is **Lima Cathedral, Peru,** begun *c.* 1596 though much rebuilt following earthquake damage. Both were probably designed by Francisco Becerra (*c.* 1545–1605).

New Spain was noted for the number of buildings constructed by the mendicant orders during the first centuries of Hispanic rule, with the aim of evangelising the indigenous peoples. The **Monastery of Tepeaca, Mexico** is one of the main sixteenth-century examples of a visibly fortified set of buildings with three roads surrounding it, sentry boxes, battlements and embrasures. The Franciscans, Augustinians and Dominicans all followed this style in the construction of their Mexican monasteries and churches, which are usually austere, single vessels with

A. Cathedral, Mexico City (1563–1667). See p. 1199

B. Monastery of San Francisco, Quito (*c.* 1630). See p. 1202

Zacatecas Cathedral Mexico (begun 1612): main doorway. See p. 1202

blank apses and high side-windows. Often there are enormous walled atria in front of the churches with a tiny chapel *(capilla posa)* in each corner. These were intended for the Indians, and mass was celebrated from an outdoor chapel or *capilla de Indios* to one side of the church. Such arrangements are found in the Mexican **Monasteries of Cuilapan, Teposcolula** and **Talmanalco.** At **Cholula, Mexico,** the *capilla de Indios* turned into a curious barrel-vaulted and arcaded structure. Features of this kind also appear in the Andean region, as in the **Church of Caquiaviri, Bolivia** (*c.* 1560), and as late as 1610–19 in the **Shrine of Copacabana, Bolivia**.

Quito, Ecuador, is one of many towns which grew up around the activities of rival monasteries, all of them keen builders. The **Monastery and Church of San Francisco** (p. 1200B), founded by Flemish monks in the mid sixteenth century on the site of an Inca palace, was a complex of great size and influence, built in a Renaissance style of stucco-covered brick with fine stone dressings and ornament. There is a large two-storey cloister with open arcades, while the church, a single nave with ceiling and side chapels encrusted with Mudejar panelling, has a rich twin-towered facade of seventeenth-century mannerist appearance. Dominicans, Augustinians and Mercedarians also built in Quito, the **Mercedarian Monastery** having a specially elegant seventeenth-century cloister with two arches above for every one below.

The Baroque style spread throughout the seventeenth-century churches of Latin America. Often it affected facades, reredoses and ornament but hardly touched the planning of churches. Examples in Central America include **Zacatecas Cathedral, Mexico** (begun in 1612 by Francisco Jiménez) (p. 1201) and **Antigua Cathedral, Guatemala** (1669–90), by Diego de Porres. Peruvian Baroque is of special richness. The Italian-influenced **Jesuit Church (Church of La Compañía), Cuzco** (1651–68) (p. 1203B), with a dome over the crossing and daringly tall towers (for such an earthquake-prone region) crowning the facade was a pace-setter in exuberance, carried on in later Jesuit work such as the facade of the **Church of La Compañía, Quito, Ecuador** (1722–65) by Father Leonardo Deubler and others. Such churches are a far cry from the hybrid or *mestizo* Baroque style found in poorer communities, like the quaint and stiff facade of **San Francisco, La Paz, Bolivia** (1744–84), or the rugged mountain churches of **Potosí, Bolivia,** notably **San Francisco** and **San Bernardo**.

Brazilian Baroque begins with the present **Bahía Cathedral** (formerly the Jesuit Church) of 1657–62. Its tall, rather blank front, of stone brought from Portugal, hides a high, wide nave covered by a coffered cylindrical vault. **São Pedro dos Clérigos, Recife** (p. 1197E), by Manuel Ferreira Jácome (1728–82), is an urban church at the back of a square; it has a polygonal plan and a prettified version of the tall stucco-and-stone facade commonplace by then, with a high scrolled gable squeezed tightly between the towers. In the gold-mining province of Minais Gerais, the delightful churches of Antônio Francisco Lisboa (or Aleijadinho) (1738–1814), a mulatto architect-sculptor of genius, include **São Francisco de Assís, Ouro Preto** (1764–76) (p. 1204A) and **São Francisco de Assís, São João del Rei** (1774), where the flanking towers are circular in plan and drawn into the body of the church, while the sculpture is exquisitely carved in *pedrasabão.* Also by Aleijadinho is the striking series of statues of prophets which line the steps leading to the church at **Congonhas do Campo** (1800–05) (p. 1204C).

The **Sanctuary, Ocotlán, Tlaxcala, Mexico** (*c.* 1745–) (p. 1204B), marks a famous pilgrimage site. Its facade is of stucco shaped into fantastic forms, with slender flanking towers covered with bright red tiles in a scale-like pattern. The interior is equally rich, much of its carving being by the Indian sculptor, Francisco Miguel. **SS. Sebastian y Santa Prisca, Taxco** (1751–8) (p. 1203C), is another Mexican church with a florid west front, twin towers and reredos and a fine dome in addition, while the energy and movement of Mexican Baroque 'in the round' is well represented by the **Cappella del Pocito, Guadalupe** (1777–91), by Antonio Guerrero y Torres, with central dome and flanking chapels.

The churches and monasteries built in North America as the Spaniards pushed northwards were simpler than those in the centre and south of the continent. **San Estevan, Acoma, New Mexico, USA** (*c.* 1629–42), is among the earliest of the churches built for Spanish missionaries in adobe by the Pueblo Indians of that region, with very plain slanting walls and twin belfry towers but a recognisably Classical pedigree. Pretty shaped gables in adobe develop at **San José, Old Laguna Pueblo** (1699–1706) while at **San Francisco, Ranchos de Taos,** built as late as 1805–15, the New Mexican adobe idiom gains a ponderous quality of mass admired for its abstraction by twentieth-century critics. The interiors of these adobe-built churches are usually ceiled flat in timber and sometimes colourfully painted.

The Mexican Baroque style worked its way north into Texas and Arizona in subdued form. The finest early Catholic church in that region is the vaulted **San José, San Antonio, Texas** (1720–31). In California, missions did not arrive until 1769 and the churches there on the whole were less ambitious. The most complete early survivor is **San Carlos Borromeo, Carmel** (1793–7), with a squat, twin-towered facade.

In the Protestant colonies of North America, the first seventeenth-century churches were far simpler than in the Catholic areas. **S. Luke's Church, Smithfield, Virginia** (1632–*c.* 1660) (p. 1205A), shows the influence of English mediaeval parish churches. Built in

A. Castillo de San Felipe de Barajas Cartagena, Colombia (1630–57, reconstructed *c.* 1700). See p. 1199

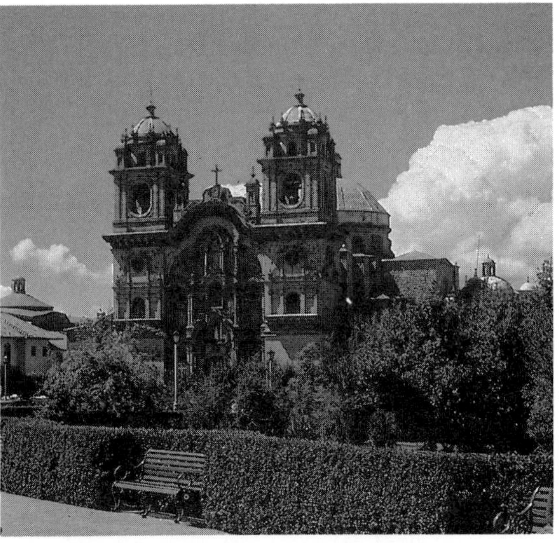

B. Church of La Compañía, Cuzco (1651–68). See p. 1202

C. SS. Sebastian y Santa Prisca, Taxco (1751–8). See p. 1202

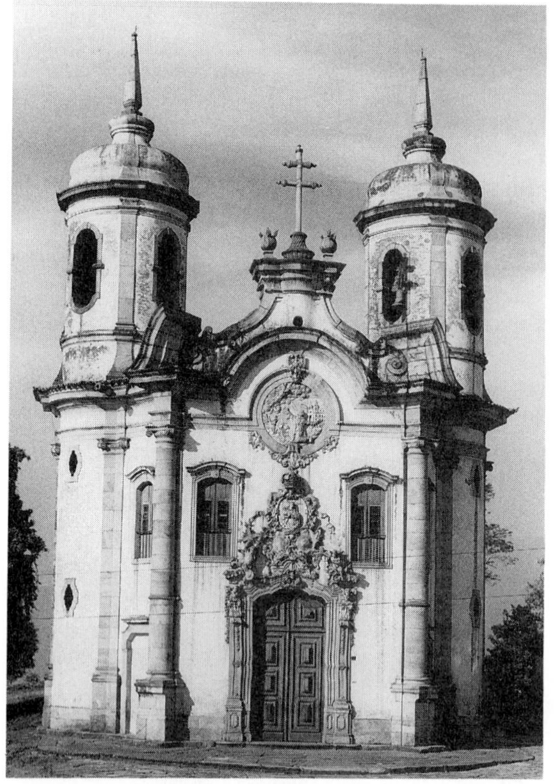

A. S. Francisco de Assís, Ouro Preto (1766–). See p. 1202

B. The Sanctuary, Octolán (*c.* 1745). See p. 1202

C. Congonhas do Campo, Brazil (1800–5). See p. 1202

A. S. Luke's Church, Smithfield, Virginia (1632–).
See p. 1202

B. Bruton Parish Church, Williamsburg, Virginia (1711–15). See p. 1206

C. William and Mary College, Williamsburg, Virginia (1695–1702). See p. 1210

D. S. Michael's Church, Charleston, South Carolina (1752–61). See p. 1206

E. King's Chapel, Boston, Massachusetts (1749–54).
See p. 1206

brick, the church consists of a simple, rectangular nave with a squat, square tower at the west end. The gables to the nave have stepped parapets, while the side walls are strengthened by stepped brick buttresses. With their crudely formed brick tracery, the windows indicate a mediaeval prototype.

Bruton Parish Church, Williamsburg, Virginia (1711–15) (p. 1205B), a simple brick structure of cruciform plan, has round-headed windows lighting the nave and transepts and an internal west gallery. The square west tower was added in 1769; this is surmounted by a timber steeple, which is a much simplified version of an English eighteenth-century spire.

S. Michael's Church, Charleston, South Carolina (1752–61) (p. 1205D), is a fully developed English colonial church in the style of James Gibbs. It has a Classical entrance portico, surmounted by an elegant timber steeple consisting of a series of diminishing octagonal drums with pilasters, entablatures and arched openings to each stage, all reminiscent of S. Martin-in-the-Fields, London (q.v.). The body of the church is of stuccoed brick; around three sides of the interior there is a gallery carried on timber Ionic columns.

King's Chapel, Boston, Massachusetts (1749–54) (p. 1205E), a stone church, considerably grander than most English colonial examples, with an unpedimented Ionic portico surmounted by a square tower (the latter uncompleted); **Christ Church, Cambridge, Massachusetts** (1759–61), built in timber; and **Touro Synagogue, Newport, Rhode Island** (1759–63), were all designed by Peter Harrison (1716–75), an English sea-captain from York.

The **First Baptist Meeting House, Providence, Rhode Island** (1774–5), **Christ Church, Philadelphia, Pennsylvania** (1727–54), and **S. Paul's Chapel, New York** (1764–6), are other important English colonial churches and show the influence of the work of Wren and, more particularly, James Gibbs through his *Book of Architecture* (1728) and his other publications (see Chapter 28).

The **Parish Church of Cap Santé, Quebec** (1754–73) is a rare example of the high, austere fieldstone churches built in French Canada before the British takeover, with twin towers, a plaster-vaulted interior and high pedimented reredos. The **Parish Church of Lacadie, Quebec** (1801), is the best surviving of a series of smaller churches built to a plan by the Abbé Pierre Conefroy, with an exuberant Baroque interior belying its date and plain external form.

Fort Amsterdam Church, Willemstad, Curaçao (1766–9), is a fine example of a church in the Dutch West Indies, raised above ground level with an oblong plan and four free-standing internal columns. Notable also is the simple **Mikve Israel Synagogue, Willemstad,** of 1732.

The Cloister, Ephrata, Pennsylvania (1740–3), is a rare surviving example of North American buildings built for a German Protestant religious community, in this case Seventh Day Baptists. It consists of two mediaeval-style, barn-like structures at right-angles to one another, of which the Sister House is built of logs concealed by clapboards, while the Prayer House has a frame structure of oak with an infilling of stone and clay, again behind clapboards.

Educational, Civic and Public Buildings

Among surviving buildings of the conquistador era in Latin America are several hospitals and schools, which were generally the responsibility of the religious orders. Among noteworthy examples are the **Hospital de Jésus, Mexico City,** founded by Hernando Cortés *c.* 1535, with a T-shaped plan; and the cruciform **Hospital de Santa Ana, Lima, Peru**.

Early government buildings include the much-altered **Palace of the Viceroys, Mexico City**, and the **Audiencia, Quito, Ecuador.** The **Governor's Palace, Santa Fé, New Mexico** (1610–14), exemplifies the nature of administrative architecture in this far-flung outpost of the Spanish Empire. A long, single-storey structure, constructed by local Indian labour in adobe brick, it is approached from the plaza of Santa Fé through an open loggia running the length of the building and terminated at each end by pavilions. The roof is flat and formed of rounded logs, supported along the loggia by tree-trunk columns.

Pure administrative architecture continued to be austere in the eighteenth-century Hispanic colonies. **La Moneda (The Mint), Potosí, Bolivia** (1759–73), the largest secular building of its era in South America, consists of barrack-like accommodation and stores in a plain, three-storey structure round a series of courtyards with inner galleries. A later version of the same building-type was **La Moneda, Santiago, Chile** (1788–99) (now the seat of the Chilean government), by the Italian-born architect Joaquín Toesca (1745–99). It covers a whole block and is divided into courtyards. The street elevations carry a heavy Doric order which marks the introduction of neo-Classicism to South America. In Mexico, neo-Classicism made its debut through the skills of Manuel Tolsá, whose **Royal School of Mining, Mexico City** (1797–1813), with a dignified main courtyard and huge staircase, is the outstanding work of its date.

The **Governmental Palace, Guadalajara, Mexico** (1751–75), by Nicholas Enriquez del Castillo and José Conique, combines a rich mixture of Churrigueresque, Baroque and neo-Mudéjar elements, while the patio of the **University, Antigua, Guatemala** (rebuilt 1763), is an important example of neo-Mudéjar design in Central America.

A. The Cabildo, New Orleans, Louisiana (1795–). See p. 1210

B. Monticello, near Charlottesville, Virginia (1770–1809). See p. 1210

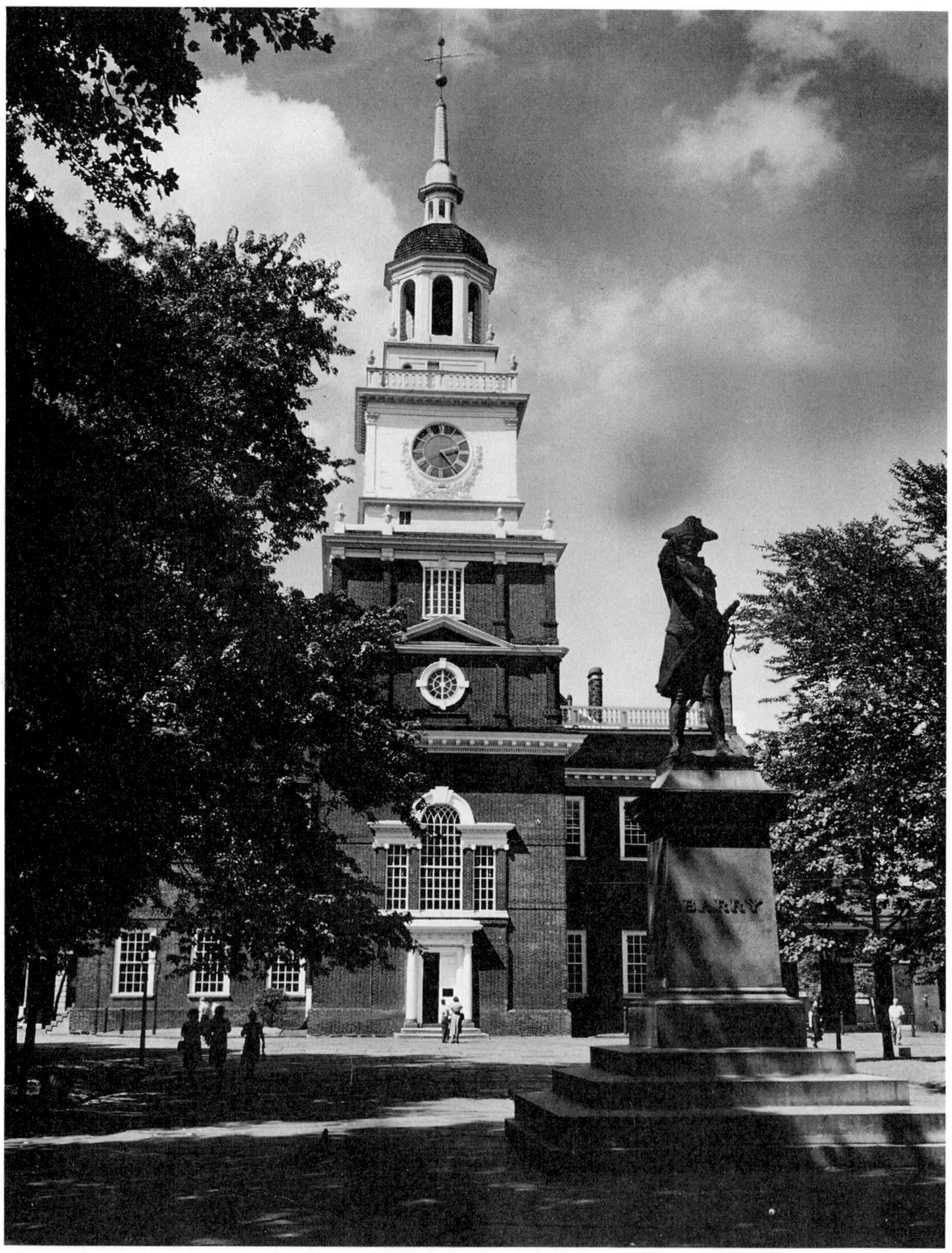

Independence Hall, Philadelphia, Pennsylvania (1731–91). See p. 1210

A. The White House, Washington, DC (1792–1829). See p. 1210

B. Belle Grove, near White Castle, Louisiana (1857). See p. 1211

C. Stoughton House, Cambridge, Massachusetts (1882–3). See p. 1211

The **Real Gabildo (Town Hall), Antigua, Guatemala** (1743–), in a more strictly Classical style favoured for colonial government buildings at this time, has arcaded loggias to both floors of its nine-bay facade.

The **Vizcáinas** (formerly Colegio de San Ignacio), **Mexico City** (1734–53), by Pedro Bueno, was a school for poor girls: the **Cabildo (Town Hall), New Orleans, Louisiana** (1795–) (p. 1207A), was built to house the Spanish administrative council during its period of control in this area. It shows the academic trend in late eighteenth-century Spanish design. The open arcaded ground floor, the arcaded first floor with its pilasters, the central pedimented feature, the weight and richness of the stone detail and the academic use of Classical motifs, relate the building closely to contemporary Spanish architecture. The mansard roof was a later addition (*c.* 1850).

The **Penitentiary, Ouro Preto, Brazil** (1784–8), by Francisco Pinto de Abreu, an example of Portuguese colonial civil architecture, combined the functions of town hall and prison; despite its purpose, it has a Rococo elegance in its facade.

The **Governor's Palace, San Antonio, Texas** (1749), built in stone, with fine wrought-iron window grilles, boasted a ballroom and grand reception rooms overlooking its internal patio, and evinces the high standard of life enjoyed by the settlers even in remote parts of the Spanish Empire.

William and Mary College, Williamsburg, Virginia (1695–1702) (p. 1205C), may have been designed by Sir Christopher Wren in his capacity of Royal Surveyor of England. If this were so, the drawings provided by Wren must have been largely diagrammatic, for records state that they were 'adapted to the Nature of the Country by the Gentlemen there'. The plan is U-shaped, the three-storey central block contained classrooms, while two projecting wings housed the college chapel and refectory. On the west side of the building, an open arcaded loggia extends between the two projecting wings. The building is Georgian in character, its central block surmounted by an elegant cupola.

Harvard University, Cambridge, Massachusetts, founded as Harvard College in 1636, is the oldest university in the USA. Nothing remains of the first buildings, constructed largely of timber, but the following are important: **Massachusetts Hall** (1718–20); **Holden Chapel** (1742–4); **Hollis Hall** (1762–3); and **Harvard Hall** (1764–6), with its pedimented gables, full cornice and comparatively massive cupola, representing an early attempt to introduce a more monumental character into North American collegiate architecture.

Other important university buildings of the colonial period include: **University Hall, Brown University, Providence, Rhode Island** (1770–1), and **Connecticut Hall, Yale University, New Haven, Connecticut** (1750–2).

Independence Hall, Philadelphia, Pennsylvania (1731–91) (p. 1208), was the scene of the signing of the Declaration of Independence on 4 July 1776. Work on the State House, as it was called, commenced in 1731, and the central block was completed by 1745. The tower with its fine steeple was built 1750–3; becoming unsound, this was demolished in 1781 and rebuilt on the original lines by William Strickland (1787–1854) in 1832. The two-storey flanking buildings, connected with the central block by arcaded links, were erected in 1736 and 1739 respectively. The buildings, essentially Georgian in character, are in brick with white stone dressings. The central block is surmounted by a balustraded roof, above which rises a tower with an elaborate timber lantern.

Carpenters Hall, Philadelphia, Pennsylvania (1770–1), built as the headquarters of the 'Carpenters Company' – the master carpenters of Philadelphia – is a simple Georgian building of cruciform plan, its four gables being treated as pediments. A timber lantern surmounts the building, in which the First Continental Congress gathered on 5 September 1774.

Province House, Halifax, Nova Scotia (1811–18), by John Merrick, a simple sturdy Classical building in stone set the pattern for other administrative buildings in Canada.

In the Caribbean, **Codrington College, S. James's Parish, Barbados** is an early foundation with a Principal's Lodge of stone in a restrained English Baroque style, *c.* 1700. The most remarkable institutional building in the region is the **Old Naval Hospital, Port Royal, Jamaica** (*c.* 1817–19), a long verandahed two-storey building largely of prefabricated iron-frame construction, the parts having been shipped out from England.

Post-colonial Period

Domestic Buildings

The **White House, Washington, DC** (1792–1829) (p. 1209A), the official residence of the presidents of the USA, was designed by James Hoban (*c.* 1762–1831), an Irish architect, in the Anglo-Irish Palladian style. After damage sustained in the War of 1812, it was restored, and considerable restoration has been carried out in the present century. The porticoes were designed by B. H. Latrobe (1807–8).

Thomas Jefferson's own house, **Monticello, near Charlottesville, Virginia**, is the most important American country house of its era (p. 1210B). It was built over a long period, between 1770 and 1809. The original work of the 1770s is Palladian, but the refashioning after 1793 was influenced by French neo-Classicism, while the plan embodies idiosyncratic requirements worked brilliantly into an arrangement of overall symmetry. The 'dependency' buildings flanking the house and linked to it by an underground 'cryptoporticus' are also of interest and ingenuity.

Tontine Crescent, Boston, Massachusetts (1793–4, demolished 1858), by Charles Bulfinch was the first example in America of speculative or 'row' housing and one of the earliest crescent-shaped urban developments to be built anywhere. Bulfinch's architecture stimulated the character of the two handsome red-brick quarters of **Beacon Hill** and **South End, Boston,** with their rows of houses with gentle bows or 'swell-fronts'. Rows of similar character can also be found in Philadelphia and New York. **Washington Square, New York**, by Town and Davis (1831, north side surviving) adopts a severer Greek idiom for the terrace, while in the brownstone **Colonnade Row, New York** (1831–3, partly surviving), by Seth Greer perhaps with A. J. Davis (1803–92), a screen of Corinthian columns rises through two storeys above a rusticated ground floor. Plain rows were also built in the form of boarding houses for migrant workers in such mill towns as **Lowell, Massachusetts** (*c.* 1825).

The development of the Federal style can be traced in the **Harrison, Gray,** and **Otis Houses** built by Bulfinch around **Beacon Hill** and **Boston Common, Boston** (1796, 1800–2, 1805–8). It was taken up with great elegance by the carpenter-architect Samuel McIntire of Salem (1757–1811) in a series of merchant houses in that seaport (e.g. **Gardner-Pingree House, Salem, Massachusetts,** 1804–5) and all over New England. The amateur William Thornton (1759–1828) designed the equally fine **Octagon House, Washington, DC** (1799–1800), a wedge-shaped house with a central bow, and **Tudor Place, Georgetown, DC** (1816), on up-to-date English villa lines, with a small centre and flanking wings.

The **Lee Mansion, Arlington, Virginia,** a house of *c.* 1802, has the first true Greek Revival portico in America, a hexastyle addition of 1820 in Paestan Doric by George Hadfield (1763–1826). A fashion for wrapping houses in the orders followed, as in **Andalusia, Pennsylvania** (1833), by Thomas Ustick Walter (1804–87). Other major Greek Revival houses include **Bowers House, Northampton, Massachusetts** (1825) by Ithiel Town; **Elmhyrst, Newport, Rhode Island** (1833) by Russell Warren; **Judge Wilson House, Ann Arbor, Michigan** (1843); and the **Wilcox-Cutts House, Orwell, Vermont** (1843), all with Ionic temple fronts. Wrap-around porticoes suited the continuously verandahed plantation houses of the Deep South, where the order was more usually Tuscan than Greek: such are the richly romantic **Oak Alley** (1837–9) and **Uncle Sam Plantation** (*c.* 1850), both in S. James's Parish, Louisiana. More typical are the **Ralph Small House, Macon, Georgia** (*c.* 1835), with a simple double-storey unpedimented hexastyle Doric portico; and **Belle Grove, near White Castle, Louisiana** (1857) (p. 1209B), a grand example with seventy-five rooms and a superb portico with the Corinthian capitals of its columns carved in cypress wood.

Greek-style houses continued all over North America on small as well as large scales. The **Jasper Collins House, Carthage, Texas** (1850), is a single-storey house with tetrastyle porticoes on no less than three of its sides. Typically, free-standing American houses of the Classical nineteenth-century type have generous hallways and stairs giving access to all the rooms from the centre of the plan.

Picturesque villa architecture shadows the Greek Revival, particularly in northern states where porticoes were less necessary. A. J. Davis set the fashion with his Tarrytown villas, notably **Lyndhurst, Tarrytown, New York** (1838, with later additions), in an English Tudor-Gothic manner. **Rotch House, New Bedford, Massachusetts** (1845) is another Davis villa in the Picturesque taste, with sharp gable, carved barge-boards and verandahs. Other styles followed on, notably Italianate and Alpine Swiss or German, an idiom suited to American timber techniques, as in **The Chalet, Newport, Rhode Island**, of 1854 by Leopold Eidlitz (1823–1908). **Olana, near Hudson, New York** (1870–91), by Calvert Vaux (1824–95) with his client, the painter Frederic Church, is Gothic with a rich Moorish overlay. The extreme of the American Picturesque was reached in the fantastic **William Carson House, Eureka, California** (1884–6), by the architect-builder brothers Samuel Newsom (1854–1908) and Joseph Newsom (1858-1930).

By then the angularity of the 'Stick Style', represented by the **Griswold House, Newport, Rhode Island** (1861), by Richard Morris Hunt, with copious external framing and bracketed gables, or the **Samuel Clemens (Mark Twain) House, Hartford, Connecticut** (1873–4), by E. T. Potter (1831–1904), had gone out of vogue on the East Coast. In its place emerged the calmer 'Shingle Style', manifest in H. H. Richardson's **Watts Sherman House, Newport, Rhode Island** (1875–6), and taken up by McKim, Mead and White in a string of delightful houses ranging from the **Ward House, Oakswood, Massachusetts** (1877–8, demolished), where the plans and elevations are still broken up in the English Picturesque manner to the wholly American **William Low House, Bristol, Rhode Island** (1887–8), entirely contained beneath a single sweeping roof of low pitch. Architects to disseminate the Shingle Style included Wilson Eyre, Bruce Price (**Pierre Lorillard House, Tuxedo Park, New York,** 1884–6), W. R. Emerson (1833–1917) (**Redwoood, Bar Harbor, Maine,** 1879) and J. L. Silsbee. More typical of suburban homes for the rich is **Glenmont (Thomas Edison's House), Llewellyn Park, New Jersey,** a deft mixture of Shingle and Stick Style motifs by H. H. Holly (1880–1).

Richardson's own domestic work became increasingly abstract. His **Stoughton House, Cambridge, Massachusetts** (1882–3) (p. 1209C), is a modest

A. (*above*)
Biltmore, Ashville, North Carolina (1890–5).
See p. 1213

B. (*left*)
Trinity Church, Boston, Massachusetts (1873–7).
See p. 1214

example, clad from head to toe in shingles. More dramatic are the **Ames Gate Lodge, North Easton, Massachusetts** (1880–1), an essay in Cyclopean masonry, and the tense **Glessner House, Chicago** (1885–7), with fortress-like street elevations in stone concealing an internal courtyard in brick and a brilliant plan.

Town-house architecture developed with aplomb in Boston and New York after the Civil War. Boston's Back Bay saw the break-up of the old row house tradition first in favour of a 'panel brick' style, then of a rich American 'Queen Anne' manner, as in the interior of the **Ames House, Dartmouth Street, Boston** (1882), by John Sturgis (1834–88). This was succeeded by the suaver French or Italian styles of architects like McKim, Mead and White, whose **Whittier House, Back Bay, Boston** (1880–3), and **Tiffany House, New York** (1882–5), digested historical references without loss of originality. By the time of their **Villard Houses, New York** (1883–5), a brownstone palazzo with Bramantesque detail, McKim, Mead and White were verging on the refined academicism of their later work. The American super-rich such as Villard and the Vanderbilts preferred academic architecture, preferably in a French taste. The **William K. Vanderbilt Mansion, Fifth Avenue, New York** (1879–82; demolished 1925), and Vanderbilt's vast country mansion, **Biltmore, Ashville, North Carolina** (1890–5) (p. 1212A), both by Richard Morris Hunt, were in the early French Renaissance chateau manner, but without the freshness that Stanford White brought to such styles. The high-rise New York apartment house was an innovation of these years: the nine-storey **The Dakota, Central Park West, New York** (1882–4), with a gabled roof line and courtyard plan, by Henry J. Hardenbergh (1847–1918) is conspicuous. Working men's lodgings began also to be built high: **Mills House (now The Atrium), Bleecker Street, New York** (1896–7), by the Beaux-Arts-trained Ernest Flagg (1857–1947) was a single men's lodging house with cubicles off linked squares with open courts for light and air, and an implied order with deep-eaved roofs to the cheap yet handsome elevations.

Strong schools of regional domestic architecture had developed in the United States by the end of the century. One was in San Francisco, where a version of the Shingle Style adapted to the temperate climate and rustic culture of Northern California emerged in the work of A. Page Brown (1859–96) (**Crocker Old People's Home, San Francisco,** 1889–90), Coxhead and Coxhead (**Carrigan House, San Anselmo,** *c.* 1892) and Willis Polk (1867–1924) (**The Bend, near McCloud** *c.* 1895). California also saw the infancy of a Pueblo or Mexican revival style, beginning with the remarkable ranch house **Hacienda del Pozo de Verona, near Sunol** by A. C. Schweinfurth (1864–1900) for William Randolph Hearst (1895–6; burnt 1969). But the most important regional centre was the so-called Prairie School, which grew up in Chicago around the personality of Frank Lloyd Wright (1867–1959). Wright's earliest house of importance was the **Charnley House, Astor Street, Chicago** (1891) in a bold, abstracted Roman style influenced by McKim, Mead and White. After some conventional Shingle Style houses in the Chicago suburbs he began to show consistent originality from the time of the **Winslow House, River Forest, Illinois** (1893), with a symmetrical, deep-eaved front showing strength, confidence and horizontality but a more complex rear elevation. Wright's lead was rapidly taken up by others, the Winslow House for instance having a clear influence on George W. Maher's **Farson House, Oak Park, Illinois** (1897). The **Studio** added to Wright's own **Oak Park, Illinois** house (1895), the **Heller House, Chicago** (1897) and the **Husser House, Chicago** (1899; demolished) all confirmed the outstanding talent of the architect who would do most to break up the nineteenth-century 'box' and catapult the free-standing house into a new era.

In Latin America, French neo-Classical influence was strong in post-colonial domestic architecture. Important was the cultural mission to Brazil led by Grandjean de Montigny in 1816. Examples in **Rio de Janeiro** include the **House of the Marquesa de Santos,** by P. J. Pézérat and the **Montigny House, Rio de Janeiro,** by Montigny himself, both of *c.* 1820. The **Itamarati Palace, Rio de Janeiro** (1841–4), by J. M. J. Rebelo, now the Brazilian Foreign Office, is a delightful villa reminiscent of buildings in Paris of a somewhat earlier date. Arched window openings extending down to floor level on both storeys encourage the free circulation of air throughout the building. In Chile, the Frenchmen Claude François Brunet-Debaines and Lucien Ambroise Hénault produced a series of elegant residences in **Santiago** (1848–80). In Argentina, the German influence strong in the nineteenth-century development of that country may be represented by the **Casa Ayersa, Buenos Aires** (*c.* 1880) by Ernesto Bunge.

Religious Buildings

Major churches in nineteenth-century Latin America after independence were generally neo-Classical in inspiration. The portico of **Buenos Aires Cathedral, Argentina** (1822), by Próspero Cartelín, follows the model of the temple front. Gothic styles became popular towards the end of the century, as in the exotic **Church of San Miguel Allende, Mexico** by Cerefino Gutiérrez (*c.* 1880). But Baroque also persisted, as in **Zamora Cathedral, Mexico** (1840–80).

The **Catholic Cathedral, Baltimore, Maryland** (1805–21), probably the most important work in

America of the English-born Benjamin H. Latrobe (1764–1820), was the first major Roman Catholic cathedral in the USA. The plan is a Latin cross with a great, coffered Pantheon-like dome more than 18 m (60 ft) in diameter over the crossing, while the nave is roofed by lesser saucer domes. Internally, the building is spacious. Externally, it has a fine pedimented portico (intended in the original design but added only in 1863), flanked by twin west towers; the main dome springs from an octagonal drum.

Early Gothic churches in the United States include Latrobe's **Christ Church, Washington, DC** (1808), and **Trinity Church, New Haven, Connecticut** (1814-17), by Ithiel Town (1784–1844). Under the influence of English ecclesiology, the style became more scholarly. This change is well represented in **New York City,** where **Trinity Church** (1839–46), by Richard Upjohn (1802–78), in English Decorated taste was an important trend-setter; **Grace Church** (1843–6) and **S. Patrick's Cathedral** (1858–79) by James Renwick (1818–1905) are also important, the latter with a west front in twin-spired French taste. Upjohn's simpler rural churches could be charming, e.g. **S. John Chrysostom, Delafield, Wisconsin** (1851–3), in bargeboarded timber with a detached belfry. English Gothic had an East Coast revival late in the century, notably in the refined work of Ralph Adams Cram (1863–1942) (**All Saints, Ashmont, Boston, Massachusetts,** 1891), and Henry Vaughan (1845–1917) (**Christ Church, New Haven, Connecticut**, 1895–8), but their cathedrals, respectively in New York and Washington, belong to the twentieth century (see Chapter 50).

H. H. Richardson built two important churches in Boston, neither in a pure Gothic style. The **Brattle Square Church** (1871–3) was his first major achievement. It has a cruciform plan and a sheer tower machicolated outwards at the top above a dramatic frieze by Bartholdi. There followed **Trinity Church** (1873–7) (p. 1212B), with west towers and porches by Shepley, Rutan and Coolidge (1894–7), a key monument of American architecture. The church has a Greek cross plan dominated by a central tower, and is linked to a parish house by a short cloister walk and open stair. The style is southern Romanesque, but applied with great power and personality in rock-faced granites with brownstone trim. Fine churches in the later Richardsonian manner include **S. Gabriel's, Chicago** (1881), by Burnham and Root, with a powerful corner tower, and **McClure Avenue Presbyterian Church, Pittsburgh** (1887), by Longfellow, Alden and Harlow, one of the firms that succeeded to Richardson's practice. Both are built in thin, high-quality Roman brickwork over a stone base.

Montreal has a spread of large churches which convey the progress and variety of nineteenth-century ecclesiastical architecture in Canada. **Notre-Dame** (1824–43), a very large early Gothic Revival building by James O'Donnell (1774–1830) and John Ostell (1813–92), has twin west towers and naive English detailing to the front. There were once double galleries internally. The **Cathedral of Mary Queen of the World** (formerly S. James) (1875–85), by Victor Bourgeau (1809–88), by contrast, was intended as a recreation of S. Peter's, Rome. Despite differences in scale and various compromises, the building is a remarkable translation of the Vatican basilica to the Canadian context. Protestant architecture, as ever, was simpler but sometimes idiosyncratic. Such is the **Sharon Temple, Holland Landing, Ontario,** a square temple for a dissident Quaker group, in three stages with a double clerestory.

Nineteenth-century synagogues in North America followed the European fashion of round-arched styles and galleried interiors. The best extant example is the **Central Synagogue, New York City** (1870–2), by Henry Fernbach (1829–83).

Educational, Civic and Public Buildings

The **State Capitol, Richmond, Virginia** (1789–98) (p. 1215A), by Thomas Jefferson, was based on the Maison Carrée, Nîmes (q.v.). An Ionic order was used but the fenestration of the 'cella' follows Palladian formulae. The building may be regarded as the first truly neo-Classical monument in the USA and had much influence on later American buildings. Classical temple forms, both Greek and Roman, were adapted for banks, schools and other buildings, and accommodation was crammed into the 'cella' in order to retain, at all costs, the external lines of the antique form.

The **State House, Boston, Massachusetts** (1795–8), by Charles Bulfinch, shows the influence of French and English neo-Classicism, particularly in the projecting central feature, with its simple arcade at entrance level and colonnaded loggia above, and in the Adam-like detail of the windows at the extremities of the main facade. The building is surmounted by a dome, a feature frequently to be incorporated in later American state capitols.

The **United States Capitol, Washington, DC** (1793–1867) (p. 1216A), seat of the United States government, has become, with its great crowning dome, one of the world's best-known buildings. The first building, erected to the designs of the amateur William Thornton, was planned on Palladian lines with a central rotunda. Thornton's work, in which he was assisted by a French architect, E. S. Hallet (1755–1825), was continued (1803–11) by Benjamin Latrobe. After the War of 1812, Latrobe was responsible for rebuilding the structure (1815–17), which had been badly damaged by the British. Charles Bulfinch continued the work which was completed in 1829. Between 1851 and 1867 additions were made by Thomas Ustick Walter (1804–88), who designed the

A. The State Capitol, Richmond, Virginia (1789–98). See p. 1214

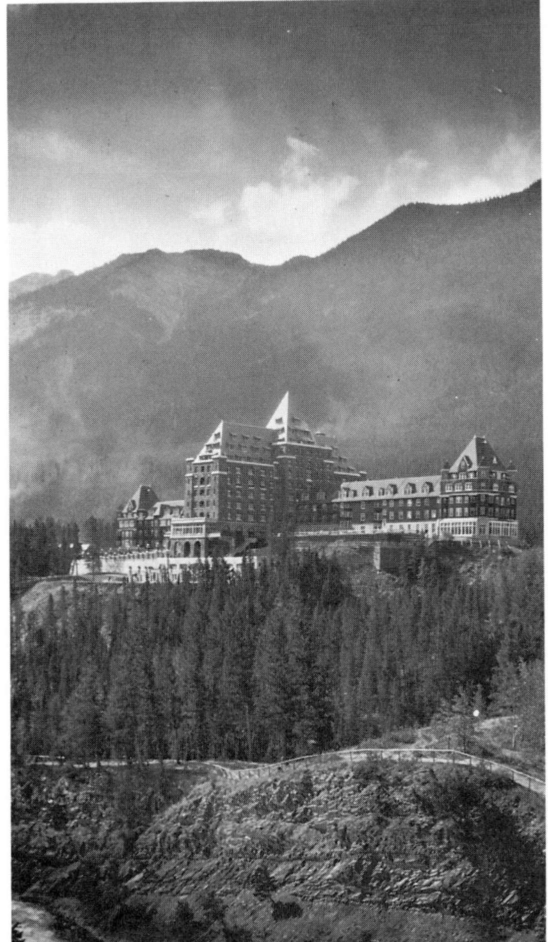

B. Banff Springs Hotel, Banff, Alberta (1886–8). See p. 1225

C. City Hall, Philadelphia, Pennsylvania (1874–1901). See p. 1217

D. Merchants' Exchange, Philadelphia, Pennsylvania (1832–4). See p. 1220

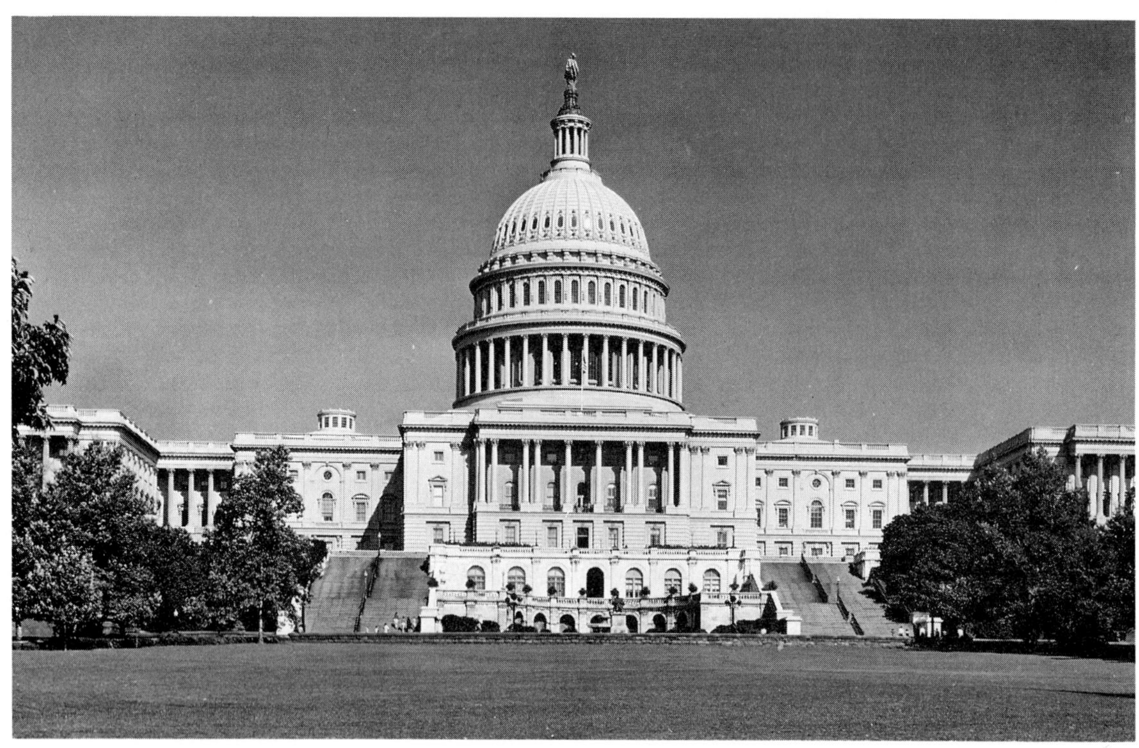

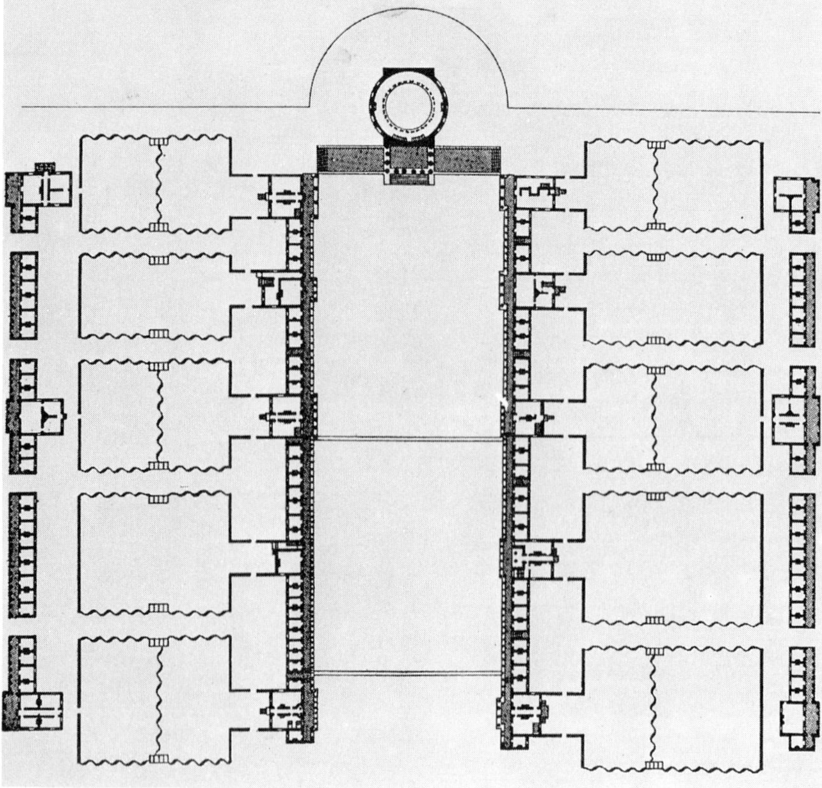

A. (*above*)
The United States Capitol, Washington, DC (1793–1867. See p. 1214

B. (*right*)
University of Virginia, Charlottesville, Virginia (1817–26): plan. See p. 1217

flanking wings and great dome and central rotunda. The latter replaced an earlier Pantheon-like dome, and was constructed largely of cast iron, with an internal diameter of 30 m (98 ft) and a total height of 68 m (222 ft).

The **University of Virginia, Charlottesville, Virginia** (1817–26) (p. 1216B), was designed by Thomas Jefferson, aided by Thornton and Latrobe, as an 'academical village'. Set in the plain overlooked by Jefferson's own home, Monticello (p. 1207B), it established a pattern for campus planning in later American universities. The plan consists of a wide, rectangular, tree-lined open space, on each of the longer sides of which are ranged five double-storey pavilions with Classical porticoes. These housed teaching staff and lecture rooms linked to one another by low colonnades from which opened the students' rooms. The central space is terminated at one end by the university library, modelled on the Pantheon, Rome. The library was burned down in the early part of the present century but its interior has now been restored. Behind the ranges of teaching and living accommodation, and separated from them by gardens, was placed the housing for slaves whom the students brought with them to the university as personal servants. Each of the buildings in the scheme was intended to illustrate some Classical work of architecture, and thus provide exemplars to the students.

Founders' Hall, Girard College, Philadelphia, Pennsylvania (1833–47), by T. U. Walter, is in the form of a giant, peripteral octastyle Corinthian temple. Its external form bears little relation to its internal planning: there are three storeys within the surrounding columns.

The **County Record Office, Charleston, South Carolina** (1822–3), the **Patent Office** (1836–40) and the **Treasury Building** (1836–42), **Washington, DC,** by Robert Mills (1781–1855), were all designed as 'fireproof' buildings, making extensive use of vaulted construction. Mills's buildings are characterised by constructional ingenuity and a vigorous and highly personal interpretation of Greek precedents. Mills also designed the **Washington Monument, Washington, DC** (designed 1836, built 1848–54; 1879–84) as a slender 170 m (555 ft) high obelisk in white granite.

The **Eastern State Penitentiary, Philadelphia** (1823–9), by John Haviland (1792–1852), was of international importance in prison planning, as the first concerted attempt to carry out 'panopticon' principles of vigilance and correction. Cell blocks were arranged radially and prisoners were held in rigid solitary confinement without any chance to communicate. Haviland's later **New York City Halls of Justice and House of Detention (The Tombs), New York** (1835–8, demolished), followed a similar plan behind a formidable Egyptian facade. In South America, these arrangements were imitated in Thomas Reed's four-armed **Bogotá Prison (now the National Museum), Colombia** (1848), and Mamede Ferreira's **Casa de Detención, Recife, Brazil** (1850–67).

The English Italianate revival had a vogue on the East Coast after the 1840s, as in the **Athenaeum, Philadelphia** (1845–7), by John Notman; or the **Customs House (now Post Office), Georgetown, DC** (1857), by Ammi B. Young.

The most complete early surviving iron building in the United States is the **Watervliet Arsenal Storehouse, New York State** (1859), constructed by Daniel Badger's ironworks, with cast-iron facades and a broad galleried interior, all of iron.

Gothic entered American public building with James Renwick's **Smithsonian Building, Washington** (1848–9), of brownstone with 'Norman' detailing and a Picturesque outline of asymmetrical towers. It assumed a Ruskinian guise with the highly Venetian and polychromatic **National Academy of Design, New York** (1862–5, demolished) by P. B. Wight (1838–1925), and reached maturity in the Philadelphia buildings of Frank Furness (1839–1912). His individualistic and wilful **Pennsylvania Academy of Fine Arts, Philadelphia** (1871–6) anticipates the force of Richardson's work; it is faced in polychromatic masonry and boasts a splendid staircase. Among many collegiate buildings in Gothic, **Memorial Hall, Harvard University, Cambridge, Massachusetts** (1870–8), by Ware and Van Brunt, may be singled out, in the decorative and colourful English idiom associated with Sir Gilbert Scott.

In Canada, the **Dominion Parliament Buildings, Ottawa** (1861–7) (p. 1218A), by Thomas Fuller (1822–98) and F. W. Stent, has an ebullient silhouette of Gothic towers, pinnacles and crestings. The interiors were largely destroyed by fire in 1916, after which the soaring neo-Gothic Pearce Tower was added by J. A. Pearson and J. O. Marchand. The development of government architecture in the Canadian provinces is well seen by the change from the charmingly picturesque **Old Legislative Building, Vancouver, British Columbia** (1859, destroyed 1957), timber-framed with brick and a deep porch, to the **New Legislative Buildings, Vancouver** (1893–8), by Francis Rattenbury (1867–1935) in a rugged Renaissance style with central dome.

Federal buildings and city halls in the United States after the Civil War generally followed an ornate French Renaissance style. The most lavish example is **Philadelphia City Hall** (1874–1901) (p. 1215C), by John McArthur (1823–90), with fine carving and a lofty central tower topped by the figure of William Penn. The **Executive Office Building** (formerly State, War and Navy Office), **Washington** (1871–88), by A. B. Mullett (1834–90), is in the same genre. The **Old Pension Building, Washington** (1883), by Montgomery Meigs (1816–92), is externally in a plainish Italian palazzo manner, but inside is a vast four-storey hall dominated by giant arcades at the ends.

A. Dominion Parliament Buildings, Ottawa, Ontario (1861–7). See p. 1217

B. Public Library, Boston, Massachusetts (1887–93). See p. 1219

These styles were put out of fashion by H. H. Richardson's Romanesque, which he developed in a fine series of small libraries (e.g. **Winn Memorial Library, Woburn, Massachusetts,** 1876–9) and railway stations (e.g. **South Framingham Station, Massachusetts,** 1883–5) and brought to final fruition in the **Allegheny County Courthouse and Gaol, Pittsburgh** (1884–7). These great granite buildings, especially the gaol, took monumental architecture to a new point of force, abstraction and virility; the interior fittings of the courthouse were as sumptuous as the exterior of the gaol was formidable.

Richardsonian public buildings include the **City Hall, Cambridge, Massachusetts** (1887), by Longfellow, Alden and Harlow, the skilfully planned **Stanford University, Palo Alto, California** (1887–1902), by Shepley, Rutan and Coolidge and, in Canada, the **City Hall, Toronto** (1890), by E. J. Lennox (1856–1933). A shift towards a purer, more academic style, already signalled by Richard Morris Hunt's **Lenox Library, New York** (1871–5, demolished), was reinforced after Richardson's death by **Boston Public Library** (1887–93) (p. 1218B), by McKim, Mead and White. This great building mixes Beaux-Arts and Italian motifs with assurance while still nodding respectfully towards Richardson's round-arched style. The front is based on Labrouste's Bibliothèque S. Geneviève, Paris (see Chapter 34). Inside, a fine staircase with murals by Puvis de Chavannes leads into the main reading room, the first Roman Renaissance interior in American architecture; in the centre is a quattrocento-style arcaded court. A later building by McKim, Mead and White, their double-galleried **Symphony Hall, Boston** (1898–1900), was the first auditorium in which the acoustics were scientifically calculated.

McKim, Mead and White's Renaissance-inspired lead was followed in Shepley, Rutan and Coolidge's **Chicago Art Institute** (1892) and became dominant after the Chicago World's Fair of 1893, where the main exhibition buildings were nearly all Classical. Among the earlier manifestations of this Beaux-Arts enthusiasm were Ernest Flagg's **Corcoran Gallery of Art, Washington** (1893–7), which has two-storey trabeated and top-lit atria behind a Labroustean facade; the **State Capitol, St. Paul, Minnesota** (1896–1903) by Cass Gilbert (1859–1934), with a Vatican-style dome; and the masterful **New York Public Library** (1897–1910), by Carrere and Hastings, one of many American buildings of the Beaux-Arts period in which Parisian Classicism of the Louis XV era is deployed on a large scale, yet with refinement.

The grandest extant railway terminus in the United states before 1900 is the **Union Station, St. Louis, Missouri** (1892–4), by Theodore C. Link and George H. Pegram, with a long Richardsonian facade and clock tower concealing crescent-shaped iron roof trusses which were the widest span in the world (186 m, 606 ft) at the time of construction.

In Latin America, the **Customs House** (1820s), **Academy of Art** and **Market Buildings** (1835–41), **Rio de Janeiro,** by the Frenchman A. J. V. Grandjean de Montigny, reflect France's international influence on public buildings. Neo-Classicism was dominant throughout the century, as in the **Parliament Building, Bogotá, Colombia** (1847–1905), by Thomas Reed; the **National Congress Building, Santiago, Chile** (1840–76), by C. F. Brunet-Debaines (1799–1855) and Hénault; or the more modest **Parliament Building, Asunción, Paraguay** (1860–80), by Alejandro Ravizza. The Italian styles favoured in Germany were common in Argentina, where several German-trained architects settled; an example is the **National Council of Education, Buenos Aires** by Carlos A. Altgelt, in an 'Italian-Munich' style. The **Plaza de Mayo, Buenos Aires,** laid out *c.* 1890 by Juan Antonio Buzchiazzo, moves towards the concept of a planned centre of government buildings, with the additions to **Government House (Casa Rosada)** (1884–1900) by Francesco Tamburini (d. 1892), and the **Parliament Building** (*c.* 1900) by Victor Meano.

Theatres were always important in Latin American architecture. Those in Brazil range from the **Teatro Santa Isabel, Recife** (1840–6), by Luis Vauthier, in the sober style championed by the French Artistic Mission to that country, to the exaggerated, plaster-gilded style of the **Teatro Amazonas, Manaos** (*c.* 1900). Uruguay has the **Teatro Solís, Montevideo** (1841–56), by Carlos Zucchi; Chile the **Teatro Municipal, Santiago** (*c.* 1873) by C. F. Brunet-Debaines and Hénault; Colombia the **Teatro Municipal, Bogotá** (1887–90), by Mariano Sanz de Santamaria; and Argentina the elegant **Teatro Colón, Buenos Aires** (1892–1906), by Francesco Tamburini. The **Teatro Juárez, Guanajuato, Mexico** (1892–1903), by Antonio Rivas Mercado, contrasts an exuberant neo-Moresque interior with a sober Classical portico.

Commercial and Industrial Buildings

The **Second Bank of the US (Old Customs House), Philadelphia, Pennsylvania** (1817–24), by William Strickland, carried out in brick and white Pennsylvanian marble, was the result of an open architectural competition. The building is rectangular in plan with octostyle Doric porticoes to the front and rear, modelled on those of the Parthenon. Internally the central banking hall, with its barrel-vaulted ceiling springing from Ionic colonnades, is particularly noteworthy.

Merchants' Exchange, Philadelphia, Pennsylvania (1832–4) (p. 1215D), by William Strickland, is in the Greek Revival style and is noteworthy for the apsidal treatment of the rear elevation and the semicircular screen of Corinthian columns rising from first-floor level through two storeys, to be crowned above the main roof by a cupola based on the Choragic Monument of Lysicrates, Athens (see Chapter 7).

Quincy Market, Boston, Massachusetts, begun in 1825 by Alexander Parris (1780–1852), was North America's foremost early market building. It consisted of a long enclosed building of great granite blocks with a central dome and end porticoes, flanked by taller red-brick warehouses and shops. Enclosed shopping arcades on the French model followed on, notably the **Providence Arcade, Providence, Rhode Island** (1828–9), by James Bucklin (1801–90) and Russell Warren (1783–1860). Here too the entrances are through granite colonnades at the two ends. The arcade is toplit, and there are elegant iron galleries from which the first-floor premises are entered.

The **Farmers' and Mechanics' Bank, Pottsville, Pennsylvania** (1830), by John Haviland, was probably the first building in America to make use of a cast-iron facade. Here iron sheets, moulded to simulate masonry, were fixed to a brick backing. Prefabricated iron units were to be used later for complete structures.

James Bogardus (1800–74) played an important part in the development of cast-iron construction, which he employed in many buildings, among them his own factory in New York (1848–9), **Laing Stores, New York** (1849), and **Harper Bros Printing Works, New York** (1854; demolished 1920). He also put forward a scheme for the **New York Exhibition Building** (1853) but this was not realised. Other buildings using the same constructional techniques were the **Penn Mutual Life Insurance Building, Philadelphia, Pennsylvania** (1850–1; demolished), by G. P. Cummings, and some particularly fine examples in the dock area of St. Louis, Missouri (*c.* 1850–*c.* 1880) (p. 1222A).

The **A. T. Stewart Store (later Wanamaker's Store), New York** (1862; burned 1956), by John Kellum (1807–71), was another noteworthy example of iron construction using prefabricated units. Elevationally the building was made up of repeated bays, and each of its five floors treated as an arcade or, in the case of the ground floor, a colonnade. Internally the building was framed with iron stanchions (cast in the form of Classical columns) and girders.

The Gothic style was not so popular for commercial structures but occasionally made a spectacular appearance, as in J. L. Silsbee's **Syracuse Savings Bank, Syracuse, New York State** (1875–6), of five storeys with two gabled Ruskinian fronts and a high tower.

Five floors remained the normal maximum in urban commercial buildings until after the Chicago fire of 1871, but were then with the help of improved elevators, new foundation techniques and 'fireproof construction' (the clothing of iron frames with terracotta or stone cladding) rapidly exceeded. Two **New York City** buildings of 1873–5 (both demolished), the **Western Union Telegraph Building** by George B. Post (1837–1913) and the **Tribune Building** by Richard Morris Hunt broke the eight-storey mark, at the price of elevational awkwardness.

Post found a better way of articulating such facades in his **New York Produce Exchange, New York City** (1881–4), of eight storeys in a round-arched palazzo manner with a two-tier system of arcading and heavy cornices, and a tower behind. It inspired two Chicago masterpieces in this manner. H. H. Richardson's seven-storey **Marshall Field Wholesale Warehouse, Chicago** (1885–7; demolished) (p. 1221A) was a powerful design with load-bearing construction to the external walls and a grid of iron columns. The elevations, of textured masonry, imparted simplified, disciplined energy to the round-arched system introduced by Post. The **Auditorium Building, Chicago** (1886–9) (p. 1221B), by Dankmar Adler (1844–1900) and Louis Sullivan (1856–1924), combined an opera house with hotel and office accommodation. Ten storeys high, it has load-bearing walls built on spread foundations. The auditorium interior is important for the development of Adler's acoustical designs for theatres and Sullivan's rich, 'organic' style of decoration, taken further in their **Schiller Theater, Chicago** (1891–2; demolished) and elsewhere.

The **Montauk Building, Chicago** (1881–2; demolished), by Daniel Hudson Burnham (1846–1912) and John Wellborn Root (1850–91) was among the first office skyscrapers to use the new spread foundations on Chicago's difficult terrain, allowing it to reach ten storeys while still using load-bearing construction. Similar methods were used for Root's masterpiece, the **Rookery Building, Chicago** (1884–5), with a fine internal atrium, and even the firm's sixteen-storey **Monadnock Building** (1889–91) (p. 1221C), with simplified bay windows and thickly battered walls. By then, however, steel skeleton construction was well established. The pioneer structures were two by William LeBaron Jenney (1832–1907): the **First Leiter Building, Chicago** (1879), in which peripheral as well as internal loads were carried by iron framing and the so-called 'Chicago' triple window first appeared between narrow brick piers; and the **Home Insurance Company Building, Chicago** (1883–5; demolished), where the stronger Bessemer steel construction was introduced.

Jenney's **Second Leiter (now Sears Roebuck) Building, Chicago** (1889–90) (p. 1222C), is among the first in which the elevations read clearly as a

A. (*right*)
Marshall Field Wholesale Warehouse, Chicago (1885–7). See p.1220

B. (*below left*)
Auditorium Building, Chicago (1886–9). See p. 1220

C. (*below right*)
Monadnock Building, Chicago (1889–91). See p. 1220

A. Cast-iron facade, St. Louis, Missouri (*c.* 1850). See p. 1220

B. Gage Building, Chicago (right) (1898–9). See p. 1225

C. Second Leiter Building, Chicago (1889–90). See p. 1220

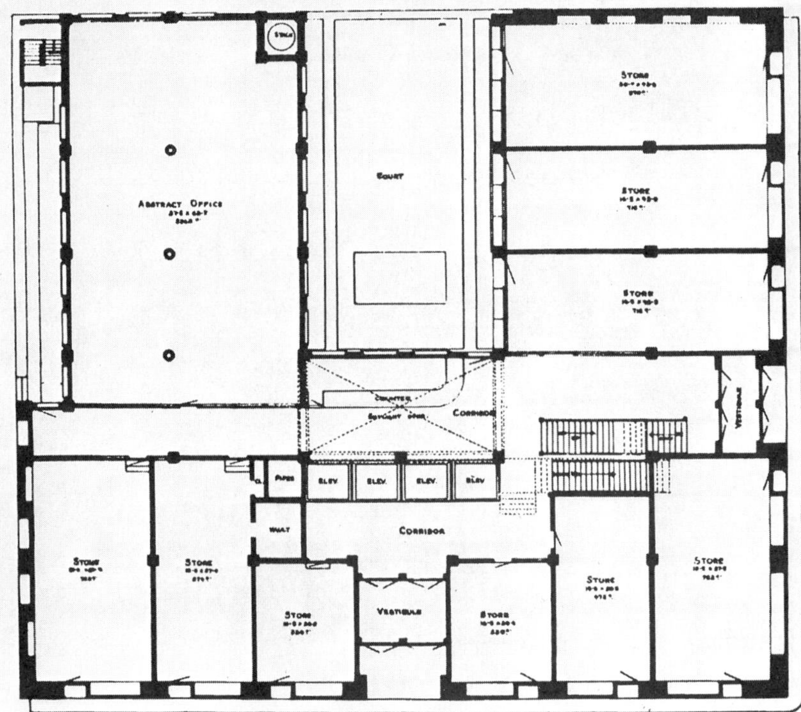

A. (*above left*)
Reliance Building, Chicago (1894–5). See p. 1225

B. (*above right*)
Schlesinger-Mayer Store, Chicago (1899–1904). See p. 1225

C. (*right*)
Wainwright Building, St. Louis, Missouri: ground floor plan. See p. 1225

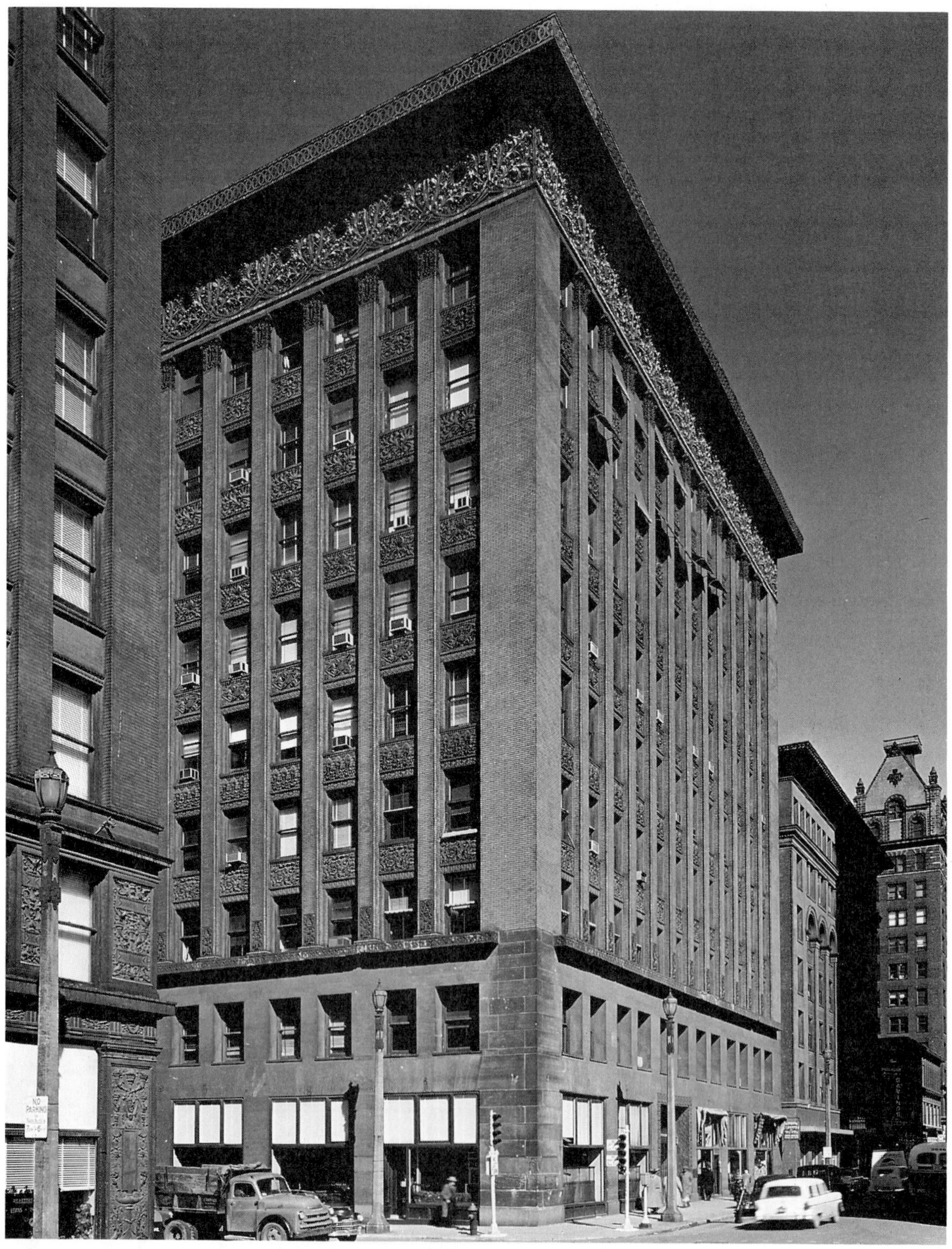

Wainwright Building, St. Louis, Missouri (1890–1). See p. 1225

sheath over a metal frame. Elevating the new tall steel-framed buildings was seen as a challenge and explored in various ways during the 1890s. The **Reliance Building, Chicago** (1894–5) (p. 1223A) by Charles B. Atwood (1849–95) of D. H. Burnham and Company retains bay windows and light terracotta detailing in Gothic over a fifteen-storey steel frame, without distinction between storeys. But the same firm's **Marshall Field Retail Store Annexe, Chicago** (1892–3), reverts, as did many later buildings, to rugged masonry cladding from top to toe, belying the steel frame behind.

The alternative was a stripped-Classical articulation of base, column and top, with passages of ornament to make up for the loss of structural surface. Such a system was worked out by Adler and Sullivan in a number of dramatic buildings. Notable are the **Wainwright Building, St. Louis, Missouri** (1890–1) (pp. 1223C, 1224), with a two-storey base, seven-storey superstructure and crowning deep frieze and cornice, and ornament deftly placed between the plain brick piers to emphasise the structure and organisation of the composition; and the taller **Guaranty (now Prudential) Building, Buffalo, New York** (1894–5). **The Gage Building, Chicago** (1898–9) (p. 1222B) consisting of lower buildings in the centre and at one end by Holabird and Roche and an eight-storey facade (later heightened) at the other end by Sullivan, shows the difference between a merely commercial approach to such fronts and Sullivan's ability to endow them with energy. Finally, the **Schlesinger-Mayer Store (now Carson, Pirie, Scott), Chicago** (1899–1904) (p. 1223B), by Sullivan, with later additions (top altered), has a base enriched with highly ornamental shop fronts while the upper parts of the facades enjoy a more horizontal articulation.

Another inventive North American building form from the 1870s onwards was the grand hotel. Urban hotels differed little in scale or style from large commercial buildings or blocks of flats; as early as 1873–4, the enormous **Palace Hotel, San Francisco, California** (demolished) by J. P. Gaynor, had already reached eight storeys. Resort hotels, however, developed into rambling, exotic structures of gigantic dimensions. Such are the **Mohonk Mountain House, New Paltz, New York** (1879–1901), by Napoleon Le Brun and James E. Ware, or the celebrated **Hotel del Coronado, Coronado Beach, California** (1887–8), by James and Merritt Reid, a picturesque, timber-built complex enclosing a one-acre open courtyard, with a dining room to seat 1000 and a circular ballroom for 1200. The firm of Bruce Price developed a domineering yet supposedly contextual idiom for resort hotels in which 'Scottish baronial' fused with the Shingle Style, as in their **Banff Springs Hotel, Alberta, in the Canadian Rockies** (1886–8, with later additions) (p. 1215B) or the **Kenilworth Hotel, Asheville, North Carolina** (1891). More sophisticated was the **Ponce de Leon Hotel, S. Augustine, Florida** (now **Flagler College**), a vivid early essay in the Spanish colonial revival style by Carrere and Hastings, 1885–7.

Mills and factories in the United States started as simple timber buildings but developed in size and complexity after independence. The pioneering structures were the cotton mills of Rhode Island, along the Blackstone River. The **Lippitt Mill, Lippitt, Rhode Island** (1809), is still of timber, but has the first known full clerestory. The **Crown and Eagle Mill, North Uxbridge, Massachusetts** (1825–9), shows the development of the granite-walled mill to hold heavy machinery, a type seen at its best in the many mills of **Fall River, Massachusetts**. The enormous mills of **Amoskeag** and **Manchester, New Hampshire,** and **Lowell** and **Lawrence, Massachusetts** have mostly, but not all gone. Architecturally more embellished are the **Ponemah Mills, Taftville, Connecticut** (1871).

Planned factory towns were important aspects of American development. Following the founding of Waltham and Lowell, Massachusetts, *c.* 1814, they attained a high degree of specialization. The most important late nineteenth-century example is **Pullman, Illinois,** laid out on a grand scale after 1880 for the paternalistic George Pullman by S. S. Beman (1853–1914).

Towards the end of the nineteenth century, reinforced concrete was introduced for American factories. The pioneer was Ernest Ransome, and his structures of greatest significance, both demolished, were the **Arctic Oil Company Building, San Francisco** (1884), and the **Pacific Coast Borax Company Building, Alameda, California** (1888–9). His four-storey **Pacific Coast Borax Building, Bayonne, New Jersey**, of 1897 survives.

In Latin America, the **Santiago Market, Chile** (1868–72), by Miguel Aldunate and the **Meat Market, Buenos Aires, Argentina** (1889), by Pedro Vasena are good examples of iron market structures. Among industrial buildings, the **Bavarian Beer Factory, Bogotá** (1888), by Alejandro Manriques is worthy of mention for its use of tiles traditional to Colombia.

Bridges

Of engineering structures that may be counted as architecture, bridges are the most important. In the United States, the two-span masonry **Carrolltown Viaduct, Baltimore** (1829), was the first significant structure on a railway, while the **Dunlap's Creek Bridge, Fayette County, Pennsylvania** (1838), is the earliest metal bridge in the country.

The great bridge engineer J. A. Roebling is principally known for the **Brooklyn Bridge, New**

York City (built by his son, Washington Roebling, 1870–83), but his early **Delaware Aqueduct, Lackawaxen, Pennsylvania** (1847–9), is a very early example of a wire-cable suspension bridge. The prototype for the Brooklyn Bridge was his **Roebling Bridge, Cincinnati, Ohio** (1856–67). The **Eads Bridge, St. Louis** (1867–74), by James Buchanan Eads is important for the width of its spans (two of 153 m (497 ft), one of 158 m (515 ft)), its cantilever construction and its early use of steel.

The small **Alvord Lake Bridge, Golden Gate Park, San Francisco** (1889), by Ernest Ransome, is the first significant reinforced concrete-arch bridge in the world.

Chapter 38

CHINA

Architectural Character

The houses built by the Portuguese in the early stages of foreign settlement in Aomen (Macao), and the Thirteen Factories in Guangzhou (Canton), erected in the eighteenth century, were two-storey buildings of mixed timber and masonry construction with arched doorways and arcaded verandahs. They were in the colonial Renaissance style adapted to the local climate.

A number of churches were built during this period and they fall into two main categories. One was Late Italian Baroque, introduced to China by the Jesuits, the other Gothic, brought in by French missionaries. A few combined Western styles with traditional Chinese features to create a unique Chinese colonial style. A number of Russian Orthodox churches in the Byzantine style also appeared in some cities from the beginning of the twentieth century onwards.

The Italian Baroque exerted great influence in China, as can be seen in the Marble Boat in Yi He Yuan (the Summer Palace), the gate of the Zoological Garden of Ten-thousand Animals, and many new shop-fronts in the city of Beijing (Peking).

The Western-style buildings in the leased territories and the sea-port cities which were opened to Westerners about the middle of the nineteenth century were mostly of two or three storeys with corrugated-iron roofing and extensive arcaded verandahs. Buildings for the foreign consulates, legations, trading companies and banks in Shanghai and Gulangyu of Xiamen (K'o long Su of Amoy), and the Legation Quarter in Beijing, were all of this type. Even now, the vestiges of such buildings remain in the former office buildings of HM Consulate-General of Great Britain in Shanghai (rebuilt in 1873).

At the beginning of the twentieth century, the European trading companies and banks began to rebuild and extend their headquarters. At first these were load-bearing masonry buildings of three to five storeys and later multi-storey buildings with steel beams enclosed in concrete. In cities such as Shanghai, Tianjin and Hankou settlements were established by several foreign countries, but in other cities by only one. Thus German influence can be noted in Qingdao (Tsingtao) or, as another example, the Russian style in Harbin. Most of the buildings were administrative or commercial, and they were usually in the Classical Revival style. There were exceptions of course – the Imperial Maritime Customs House of Shanghai (1857) looked like a Chinese Buddhist temple.

During the period of preparation for constitutional government advocated by the Qing government in its last years, many buildings commissioned by the government, including administrative offices and schools, were Western in influence and eclectic in style – usually Baroque, although some of them were decorated in the Chinese traditional way, for example the Zhong Li Yamen (the Ministry of Foreign Affairs), the Ministry for Land Forces, the Peking Station of the Peking-Fengtian (today's Liaoning) Railway and a number of provincial political consultative bureaux, all dating from the beginning of the twentieth century.

Residential buildings began to be more diversified in form. Although the traditional Chinese courtyard house retained its hold over most of China, the terrace house and the compound also appeared in large cities such as Shanghai and Tianjin to cater for the rapid growth in urban population. Early terrace houses in Shanghai and in other southern cities were mostly two-storey masonry buildings, laid out in three bays partially enclosing a small courtyard in front of the middle bay. But from the early years of the twentieth century, more compact layouts and Westernised decoration were adopted. In Qingdao, Harbin and some other northern cities, however, residential compounds were more popular. They usually consisted of a square courtyard, enclosed by some two- or three-storey timber houses connected by open corridors. Chinese details were adopted inside the house, but the street facades were mostly Western-style. In the foreign settlements within trading ports, private houses with Western-style gardens evolved by foreign consuls and managers, and adopted also by some Chinese landlords.

China did not have its own architects until the beginning of the twentieth century. Before that, all the modern buildings were designed by Westerners.

Among them, the British firms of G. J. Morrison (established 1865) and of Atkinson and Dallas (established 1898) were most prominent. The principal of the latter firm also served as an assistant engineer to the Shanghai Municipal Council. But the construction work was all done by Chinese contractors. For example, the reconstruction of the Imperial Maritime Customs House (1893) in Shanghai, although designed by a British architect, was built by a local contractor whose carpenters and masons came from the suburbs of Shanghai. Chinese craftsmen of the time played a unique role in combining Chinese craftsmanship with Western architectural design.

Although the outlook of cities such as Shanghai, Tianjin and Hankou changed considerably from the middle of the nineteenth century onwards, and in other cities Western architecture was influential to a degree, traditional Chinese architecture still flourished over vast areas of China. Just as the Qing imperial court still built its palatial architecture and imperial tombs in the traditional Chinese manner, so local authorities, landlords and others continued to follow local traditions for Buddhist temples, ancestral halls, guild houses, shops and houses. Even in the sea-ports traditional architecture maintained its popularity, although with more obvious Western details.

Examples

Xi Yang Lou (The Western-style Palace) **in Yuan Ming Yuan, Beijing** (1759), was designed by an Italian Jesuit F. Giuseppe Castiglione (1688–1766) with French Jesuits Jean Denis Attiret (1702–68) and P. Michel Benoist (1715–74) in compliance with the wishes of the Emperor Qian-long. A grand display of water cascades and a water clock with twelve sculptured animals were the centres of attraction. The buildings were in the Italian Baroque style but with some Chinese decoration. Columns and walls were generally built in white marble, some were inlaid with coloured glazed brick or plastered with pink stucco, and the roofs were finished with glazed tiles. Yuan Ming Yuan was destroyed in October 1860 by the combined forces of Britain and France: the remnants of broken columns and walls of Xi Yang Lou can be seen still on the site (p. 1229A).

The **'Thirteen Factories', Guangzhou** (1720s–1730s) (p. 1229D), now demolished, at first were two- or three-storey buildings of timber and brick with simple facades but were rebuilt in colonial Renaissance style in the latter half of the eighteenth century. After 1840, they were rebuilt again in a luxurious Revival style.

The **Catholic Church of Xuan Wu Men, Beijing** (1904) (p. 1229B), is also known as the South Church because of its location in the city. It was originally built in 1605 after Matteo Ricci (1552–1610) arrived in Beijing in 1601 and was rebuilt many times from 1650 to 1776, and the 1776 rebuilt church was destroyed by fire in 1900. The facade of the church, although displaying some traditional Chinese details, is in the strong early Jesuit Baroque style. The very earliest Catholic churches of China can be traced to 1299 and 1305 when two churches were built in Dadu, the Great Capital of the Yuan dynasty (1280–1368) (and now part of Beijing), under the supervision of an Italian priest Giovanni di Monte Corvino (1274–1328). **São Paulo in Aomen (Macao)** dates from 1602 and was also designed by a Jesuit, Carlo Spinola. None of these churches has survived, and only the remnants of a wall of the church of São Paulo remain.

The **Church of S. Francis Xavier, Shanghai** (1853) (p. 1229E), known as the Catholic Church of Dong Jia Du designed by Jean Ferrer (1819–56), a Spanish Jesuit architect, the oldest remaining church in Shanghai, and the **Church of S. Joseph, Beijing** (1905) (p. 1230A), also known as the Catholic Church at Ba Mian Chao, are both in the Baroque style. **Holy Trinity Church** (1866–9) (p. 1229C,F), also known as the Red Church because it is built in red brick, was designed by Sir George Gilbert Scott (1811–78) and William Kidner. It was the largest Christian church in Shanghai. The plan is a Latin cross, the pointed vault of the nave supported on stone piers. The east facade has an arched porch the same width as the nave, and two arcades the width of the aisles. There are stained-glass windows and a later tower (1893), which lost its spire not long after it was built.

S. Ignace Cathedral (designed by W. M. Dowdall), known as the **Catholic Church of Xu Jia Hui, Shanghai** (1896–1910) (p. 1230C), is the Cathedral of the Shanghai diocese and has a seating capacity of 2500. Also planned as a Latin cross, the nave and aisles are both groin-vaulted. The east facade, flanked by twin towers with spires 57 m (187 ft) high, bears a strong resemblance to the great French Gothic churches such as Chartres. It has three deeply recessed portals and the central doorway is divided by a pillar (cf. Reims and Laon Cathedrals); a horizontal arcaded band runs the full width of the front and is also continued around the towers. There is a rose window in the recessed wall under the gable. The external walls of brown bricks are laid on plinths of bluish-grey granite and decorated with marble carvings and mouldings.

The **Church of S. Saviour, Beijing** (1888) (p. 1230D), usually known as the Catholic Church at Xi Shi Ku, is also in the French Gothic style with a Latin-cross plan. Originally the twin towers were of two storeys, but a third was added in 1911. Steps and balustrades in Chinese style led to the portals of the church, and the main facade is flanked by sculptured lions and by two Chinese pavilions with yellow

A. The remains of the Da Shui Fa (The Great Fountains) of the Xi Yang Lou (The Western-style Palace) in Yuan Ming Yuan, Beijing (1759). See p. 1228

B. The Catholic Church of Xuan Wu Men, Beijing (1904). See p. 1228

C. Holy Trinity Church, Shanghai: east facade (1866–9). See p. 1228

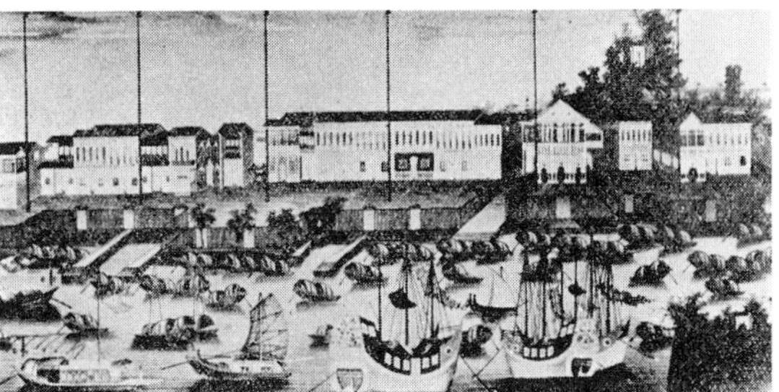

D. The 'Thirteen Factories', Guangzhou (1720s). See p. 1228

E. Church of S. Francis Xavier, Shanghai (1853). See p. 1228

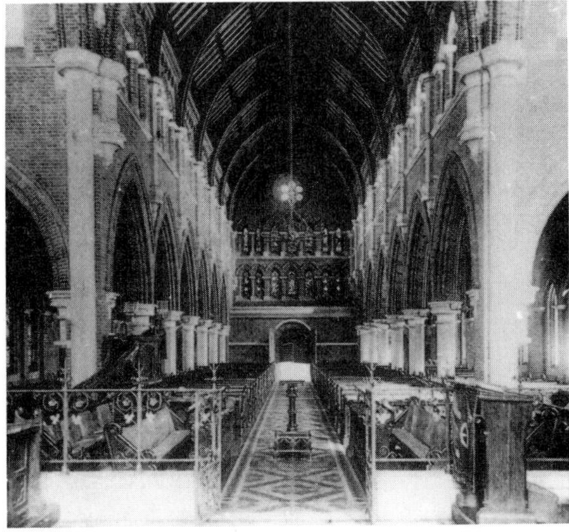

F. Holy Trinity Church, Shanghai: interior (1866–9, 1893). See p. 1228

A. Church of S. Joseph, Beijing (1905). See p. 1228

B. Orthodox Eastern Church, Shanghai (1931). See p. 1233

C. S. Ignace Cathedral, Shanghai (1896–1910). See p. 1228

D. Church of S. Saviour, Beijing (1888). See p. 1228

A. The Former British Consulate-General, Shanghai (1873). See p. 1233

B. Hôtel de Ville, French government concession, Shanghai (1862–4). See p. 1233

A. German Governor's Office, Qingdao (1905). See p. 1233

B. Old Building of the Hongkong and Shanghai Banking Corporation, Shanghai (1874–7). See p. 1233

C. The Commercial Bank of China (1897). See p. 1233

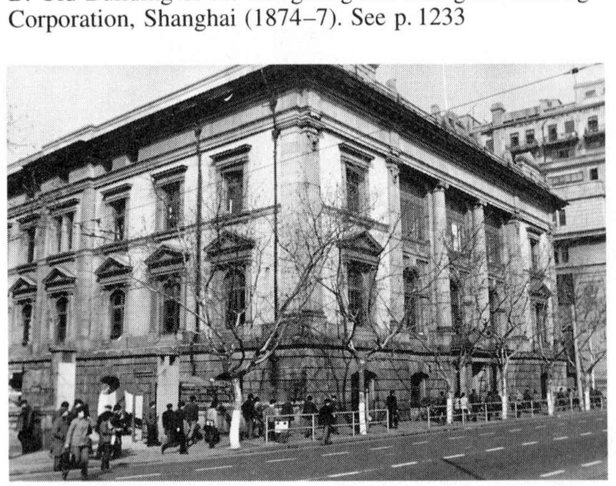

D. The Russo-Chinese Bank, Shanghai (1901). See p. 1233

E. The Shanghai Club, Shanghai (1864). See p. 1237

glazed tiles which house the tablets carved with the edict by the Qing Emperor who patronised the church. The **Chinese Episcopal Church, Beijing** (1907), on the other hand, is of timber and brick in typical Chinese traditional style, though with Western details.

S. Nicholas Russian Orthodox Church, Harbin (1900), now demolished, was octagonal in plan, with timber walls and a timber tent-shaped roof resembling those of the Russian wooden churches of the fifteenth century. The **Orthodox Eastern Church, Shanghai** (1931) (p. 1230B), although built in the 1930s, is a typical Russian church in Byzantine style which resembles the Uspensky Church (1475–9) in the Kremlin, Moscow.

The buildings for **HM Consulate-General, Shanghai** (1873) (p. 1231A), occupy a site of 2.9 ha (7.1 acres) on which the original consulate, built in 1852, once stood: it was destroyed by fire in 1870. The 1873 consulate buildings, designed by Grossman and Boyce, were placed across the west side of the compound. The business premises of the Consul-General were in the buildings facing the lawn. The Consul-General's house faces south, and on the east facade of the main building there was a centrally placed arcade with five openings. The buildings are of timber and brick in colonial Renaissance style with hipped roofs. The flat-arched and semicircular-arched windows were fitted with wooden shutters and the roofs were covered in corrugated iron. The buildings are now used for other purposes, and some of their original features have been altered by later renovations.

The **French Consulate-General, Shanghai** (1895), designed by M. J. J. Chollot, is a two-storey building in timber and brick with an attic floor under a mansard roof. With its superimposed, arcaded verandah, the architecture is of a typical colonial style relating to climate. The **German Consulate, Shanghai** (1844–5), now demolished, was a three-storeyed timber and brick building with an attic floor in a colonial Renaissance style with arcaded verandahs.

The **Hotel de Ville of the French government concession, Shanghai** (1862–4) (p. 1231B), by F. H. Knevitt, also demolished, was a two-storey axially planned building in the Renaissance style. The central section of it was crowned with a dome on an octagonal drum, and the projecting entrance, in the form of a two-storeyed triumphal arch surmounted by a pediment, was flanked by two-storeyed arcades of superimposed columns.

The **German Governor's Office, Qingdao** (1905) (p. 1232A), by Lazarowiz, a German architect, was built in the period when Qingdao was leased to Germany. It is a four-storeyed building with a symmetrical E-shaped plan. The long monumental facade, 80 m (262 ft) in length, is a German interpretation of French Classicism. Between the projections of the central entrance building and the ends of the facade there are two five-bay colonnades. The walls are granite and the mansard roof is covered with red tiles.

The two **Old Buildings of the Imperial Maritime Customs House, Shanghai** (1857 and 1893), were the predecessors of the present Customs House which stands on the same site. The 1857 building (p. 1234A) was in the form of a Chinese temple and was characteristic of the yamens (imperial offices) built at that time. It had a pailou as its gateway, flanked on both sides by a balustrade in Western style. The building was demolished in 1891, and a new Customs House (p. 1234B) by British architects J. M. Cory and M. J. Chambers was built. It was a brick building with a centrally placed five-storey clock tower 33 m (110 ft) in height. Its red brick walls with facings of green stone and the high-pitched roofs covered with red tiles recalled a British town hall in the Tudor style.

The **Hongkong and Shanghai Banking Corporation building, Shanghai** (1874–7) (p. 1232B), by William Kidner, was a three-storeyed building in the late English Renaissance style, now demolished. It had a hipped roof with bracketed eaves and a decorated cornice. The main entrance was served by a projecting semicircular porch supported by six columns with Ionic capitals. The first-floor window openings were decorated with pointed or segmental pediments, some supported by Ionic columns and some by brackets. Delicate English ironwork was introduced in the continuous balcony balustrades which ran from one end of the building to the other at first-floor level. In 1888, the semicircular porch was demolished and replaced with a grand portal with rooms at either end, and single-storey extensions were also added to both sides of the building.

The **Commercial Bank of China, Shanghai** (1897) (p. 1232C), was designed by G. J. Morrison and F. M. Gratton, a British firm of architects. The bank was established by Sheng Xuan-huai (Sheng Hsuan-huai, 1844–1916), a high official of the government (Qing dynasty). It was called the Imperial Bank of China until 1911. The building is three-storeyed with an attic floor and looks like a small, late Victorian town hall, in a Venetian free style mode with Scottish baronial overtones. The walls, originally of brick, were later plastered. Flat, segmental and semicircular arches are used in window openings from the second to ground floors respectively. Windows with pointed arches are used for the dormers, suggesting the Gothic, while the porch at the main entrance on the ground floor has a Romanesque arcade.

The **Russo-Chinese Bank, Shanghai** (1901) (p. 1232D), called the Russo-Asiatic Bank after 1910 and now used as offices, was designed by Becker and Baedecker, a German design office. This is a three-storey rendered brick building with a rusticated stone

A. Old Buildings of the Imperial Maritime Customs House, Shanghai (1857). See p. 1233

B. Old Buildings of the Imperial Maritime Customs House, Shanghai (1893). See p. 1233

A. Jardine Matheson and Co. Ltd, Headquarters building, Shanghai (1851). See p. 1237

B. Li Hong-zhang House, Shanghai (*c*. 1900). See p. 1237

A. Sheng Xuan-huai House, Shanghai (*c.* 1900). See p. 1237

B. House of an official of the French concession, Shanghai (1905). See p. 1237

C. House for a German official Qingdao (1904). See p. 1237

ground floor in the French Classical style. It has two attached giant Ionic columns flanked by pilasters facing the street on the entrance facade.

The original building for **Jardine Matheson and Co. Ltd, Shanghai** (1851) (p. 1235A), now demolished, had two storeys on a high basement. There was a low-pitched hipped roof and a colonnaded porch approached by a monumental staircase and with a balcony above it. A glassed-in verandah with a balustrade was also accessible from porch level by means of an external staircase.

The original **Shanghai Club, Shanghai** (1864) (p. 1232E), which no longer exists, was the British club in the International Settlement in Shanghai. It was a three-storey brick building with an arcaded corridor on the ground floor and colonnaded verandahs on the first and second floors, the latter surmounted over the three central bays by a pediment supported at the external angles by piers with adjacent detached columns. Even with its somewhat truncated Corinthian order, the scale and grandeur of the building place it amongst the great colonial clubs of the period.

The **Ministry of the Land Forces** of the government of the Qing Dynasty, **Beijing** (1907) designed by Shen Qi, a Chinese of obscure origin, is a group of buildings of which the main block is of two and three storeys, H-shaped on plan. The facade has superimposed arcades between square brick piers: windows have arched semicircular heads. The roof was covered originally with sheet iron and there were Baroque pediments at each end of the building with Chinese motifs in carved brickwork. Other office buildings erected at the end of the Qing dynasty in Beijing include the **Naval Ministry** (1909, also by Shen Qi), **Zhong Li Yamen** (the Ministry of Foreign Affairs, *c.* 1910) and **Da Li Yuan** (the Supreme Court, 1910).

Peking Railway Station on the Peking–Fengtian (Liaoning) line at Beijing (*c.* 1898), was in operation until the Beijing Station was erected in 1959. It consisted of a waiting hall at the centre, an office building to the north and a clock tower to the south. The segmental gable of the waiting hall had an inlaid relief sculpture of dragons and clouds until 1912, symbolising the doorway to the capital of the Qing dynasty.

Residences in Western style built around 1900 for high-ranking citizens in the big cities were situated in good localities, and had large gardens and luxurious interiors. They included the **Li Hong-zhang House, Shanghai** (*c.* 1900) (p. 1235B), in a hybrid Victorian Romanesque style, the **Sheng Xuan-huai House, Shanghai** (*c.* 1900) (p. 1236A), an imposing Beaux Arts exercise with a porch supported by a giant order, the **house of an official of the Hôtel de Ville of the French concession, Shanghai** (1905) (p. 1236B), a minor French château in the late seventeenth-century style, and the **house for a German official, at Qingdao** (1904) (p. 1236C), which is in a romantic European half-timbered style under a mansard roof.

Chapter 39

JAPAN AND KOREA

Architectural Character

This chapter covers the introduction into Japan and Korea of Western architectural styles. Although there were some Western buildings in Korea before Japanese annexation in 1910, they were few in number, and widespread development of Western architecture in Korea did not take place until the Japanese period. Thus the Japanese developments largely preceded those in Korea. Japanese architecture, dealt with here before Korean, is classified in terms of the architects and builders responsible for its design and execution: first the early work by expatriate European architects and builders, secondly buildings by mainly Japanese craftsmen, and finally the early Western-style buildings designed by Japanese architects.

The Work of Foreign Architects in Japan

In 1868 the Meiji government set up a Building and Repair Department which was to be responsible for the design of important public buildings. The government promptly invited architects and engineers from foreign countries to apply for opportunities in the Department. In the field of building, thirteen foreigners were employed by the government until 1879: seven were British, the others French, Prussian and Italian. Only three of them were qualified architects. The others were site engineers, civil engineers, masons and bricklayers. They taught the Japanese the design and building process as they understood it, in the context of buildings required by the government. Thus in the 1870s and 1880s many buildings were constructed by Japanese engineers under the guidance of foreign advisers; however, the government soon realised that in order to transfer more advanced technology to Japan, better technical education was required. Accordingly in 1871 an educational institute called Kogakuryo (School of Technology) was set up in the Ministry of Technology, and in 1873 nine Britons, including H. Dyer, came to Japan and devised a technological education system modelled on British practice. Teaching started in the same year. In 1877 the Kogakuryo was renamed the College of Technology, and the first students graduated in 1879. It became a faculty of the University of Tokyo in 1886.

Among the foreign architects was the Englishman Josiah Conder (1852–1920), who has remained a profound influence. He came to Japan in 1877 at the age of twenty-five and was immediately appointed a professor in the College of Technology, and at the same time worked for the Building and Repair Department of the Ministry of Technology. In 1888 he opened his own architectural practice in Tokyo, and until his death in 1920 he left Japan only twice for short visits to England. Of over seventy buildings he designed in Japan, only seven still remain.

Conder's ambition was to invent an architectural style suitable to the climate and traditions of Japan rather than to import European architecture. He tried to realise this idea in the museum at Ueno (q.v.), designed immediately after his arrival in the country.

The German architects who were invited to Japan in 1886 adopted an attitude quite antithetical to that of Conder. They were commissioned to plan the Diet Building and other government buildings in the central area of Tokyo. The scheme proposed by the office of Hermann Ende (1829–1907) and Wilhelm Böckmann (1832–1902) was in a magnificent neo-Baroque style. The project was never realised, because of financial difficulties and the poor condition of the soil of the site. Only two buildings, the Law Court and the Ministry of Justice, were constructed in simplified forms compared with the original design. From this time onwards, however, the solemn, dignified German style with steep roofs, towers and domes gradually permeated the work of Japanese architects.

Western-style Architecture Constructed by Japanese

It was relatively easy to transform traditional Japanese cities. The donjons in the old castle-towns had in most cases been demolished once the country had been unified. The inner compounds and the sites of retainers' houses in zones adjacent to the castles were used for government offices, schools, hospitals and the like. After the Meiji Restoration, existing timber houses were used for new purposes, but were gradually replaced by Western-style buildings. These adaptations occurred in a comparatively short time.

In the early Meiji period, responsibility for the construction of public buildings was given to Japanese artisans as well as to foreign architects. The craftsmen were originally skilled only in traditional timber architecture, but listened to the requests of foreign residents; by studying the works of foreign architects and engineers, they tried to imitate the characteristics of Western design. Thus with surprising alacrity a pseudo-Western style of timber architecture designed and constructed principally by carpenters evolved throughout Japan.

Kisuke Shimizu (1815–81), for example, a master carpenter who worked in Yokohama and Tokyo, constructed the Tsukiji Hotel (1868), the Mitsui Group Building (built in 1872 and later transferred to the First National Bank) and the Exchange Bank of the Mitsui Group (1874), which attracted public attention. These works were dubbed 'Western lies' because of their large verandahs, conspicuous roof towers and eaves adorned with cornices and balustrades – but elsewhere he did not hesitate to use huge Japanese hipped and hipped-and-gabled roofs, or walls covered with tiles.

Wooden buildings with Western characteristics in small towns, though not as eccentric as those of Kisuke Shimizu, similarly combined Western and Eastern forms. Such developments were encouraged by the spread of compulsory education. In elementary schools, for example, chairs replaced 'tatami', and it is probable that architecture combining idioms from East and West was received more favourably than the authentic Western style because of its visual familiarity.

The Work of Early Japanese Architects

After the first four students graduated from the Department of Architecture of the Imperial College of Engineering in 1879, several architects or building engineers qualified every year. Because they had to meet numerous demands they quickly took the lead in architectural practice, and their work began to appear as early as the 1880s. In the ensuing twenty-five years or so, these architects designed government offices, banks, office buildings, hospitals, universities and many imposing residences. They sought new architectural information from Conder and other foreign professors, from study abroad and from books and periodicals. Among the leaders were Kingo Tatsuno (1854–1919), Tatsuzo Sone (1852–1937), Tokuma Katayama (1853–1917), Yuzuru Watanabe (1855–1930) and Kozo Kawai (1856–1934).

Most of their buildings, at the end of the nineteenth century, embodied the architectural trends in European cities during the same period, but usually in simplified forms. They did not adhere to the style of a particular country or to any traditional style, but were inspired by the diverse predilections of the countries they visited or studied. Characteristics common to much of the work of Japanese architects of the period were: a crude, stiff appearance due to their efforts to express the dignity of a newly established regime, as well as to their own youth and immaturity; a desire to achieve the movement and spatial interpenetration of the neo-Baroque, although there were few opportunities to do so in the context of the buildings demanded of them; a predisposition to concentrate on the exterior appearance of buildings, and to neglect the harmonisation of the interior with exterior design. The last difficulty often resulted from budget limitations and from the importance given to urban landscape planning.

The Akasaka Imperial Palace was almost the sole example of a successful neo-Baroque building in Japan. Tokuma Katayama, a court architect, designed the palace, and its completion engendered confidence among Japanese architects that Japan had finally achieved the architectural standard of Europe and America. The palace was the embodiment of the ideal which the Japanese architectural world had been seeking since the Meiji Restoration – the maturing of a style once it had been transplanted from Europe.

A particular problem for Japanese architects was how to construct earthquake-proof buildings. After the Nobi earthquake (1891) in central Honshu they fully realised the weakness of brick structures, and consequently the reinforcement of brick buildings became an important subject. Furthermore, they saw the damage caused by the San Francisco earthquake in 1906, and recognised the earthquake-proof efficiency of steel and reinforced concrete framed buildings. Although buildings with steel and reinforced concrete frames had begun to be constructed in Japan around this time, it was not until the Kanto earthquake in 1923 that brick structures were completely replaced by reinforced concrete buildings.

After the completion of the Akasaka Imperial Palace, Japanese architects were at a loss for a new ideal on which to concentrate because they felt they had already mastered the techniques of Western architectural design and construction. They began to ask whether they should ignore Japanese traditional styles or through them develop a Japanese style independent of European influence. There had already been an attempt to utilise traditional wooden structures for such buildings as banks, government offices and hotels, all with Japanese roofs. Similar methods reappeared now, as the architects were eager to create a new indigenous style. These designs, however, gave an impression of regionalism, and lacked universality.

Although brick structures were replaced by reinforced concrete, the Revivalist styles which had originated in Europe in the nineteenth century continued into the 1930s and set the character of Japanese cityscapes. Such styles were applied to banks, and government and commercial office buildings. Nevertheless, the Revivalist styles in Japan seem not to have been directly inherited from Europe, and there are many traces of individuality as opposed to mere imitation. However, classical composition bore the impress of architectural details modelled on the new design movements such as Art Nouveau and the Vienna Secession.

Examples

The Work of Foreign Architects in Japan

The **Ueno Museum, Ueno, Tokyo** (1881) (p. 1241A), was one of the three buildings that Conder designed and realised immediately after his arrival in Japan. He devoted himself untiringly to the construction of two-storey brick buildings, imposing in both composition and scale. The museum was one of them, designed with arched openings suggesting Islamic architecture; he called this his 'pseudo-Saracenic style'. The museum was destroyed in the 1923 earthquake.

The first **Mitsubishi Building at Marunouchi** in the middle of **Tokyo** (1894) (p. 1241B) was the beginning of the Mitsubishi business centre. The firm conceived it as such and prohibited wooden buildings. It also set up standards to regulate the appearance and scale of the development. Josiah Conder was commissioned to design this first building and his proposal was a model expression of street architecture, adopting the terrace form with which he had been familiar in London, using exposed red brick for the exterior walls. It was demolished in 1968 to allow redevelopment of the area.

The **Tokyo Law Court Building, Kasumigaseki, Tokyo** (1896) (p. 1241C), was designed in 1887 by Ende and Böckmann, who had been responsible for the Tokyo Diet Building project (q.v.). Construction began the following year to a much altered and simplified design. It suffered war-damage in 1945 and was demolished in 1974.

Western-style Architecture Constructed by Japanese

Built as a memorial to the twenty-six Japanese martyrs who died at Nagasaki in 1597 and were canonised as saints in 1862 by Pope Pius IX, the **Oura Church, Nagasaki** (p. 1242C), was completed in 1879. The first church built in 1864 had proved to be too small and was rebuilt under the direction of Father Petitjean (1829–84) in the Gothic Revival style.

The Treaty of 1858 resulted in the opening up of the seaports, and Osaka and Tokyo became open-market cities. In 1867 foreign settlements were established at Tsukiji and in Kawaguchi, Osaka. The **Tsukiji Hotel, Tokyo** (1868) (p. 1242A), was built for foreign visitors. Although designed by an American, R. P. Bridgens, it was constructed by Kisuke Shimizu. It was a large two-storey timber hotel, 67 m (219 ft) wide by 27 m (89 ft) deep, with a tower at the centre and a long verandah facing the sea. The exterior walls were finished by a traditional method called namako-kabe: walls were covered with flat square tiles, the joints of which were filled conspicuously with white plaster to show their diagonal grid pattern. As this type of wall was fire-resistant and waterproof, it was often used in Western-style buildings of the early period. Nevertheless, the Tsukiji Hotel was lost in the 1872 holocaust that swept through the Tsukiji and Ginza areas.

Kiyoshige Tateishi, a master carpenter of Matsumoto, who had seen Western-style architecture in Tokyo and Yokohama, designed and constructed the **Kaichi School, Matsumoto** (1876) (p. 1242B). The structure is entirely of wood, but the walls are plastered with a kind of stucco. Most characteristic is the central entrance, heavily adorned with Japanese sculptural decorations.

The Work of Early Japanese Architects

Kingo Tatsuno did research in Europe before designing the Head Office of the **Bank of Japan, Nihonbashi, Tokyo** (1895) (p. 1243A). He returned home in 1889 and spent one more year refining his design. Construction began in 1890. The plan of the bank was based on that of the Palais du Luxembourg, and its elevation consists of a rusticated first storey carrying giant orders. However, there are some defects in the design resulting from subtle differences between the style itself and the form that the designer wished to create. Disparity between style and proportion was a common flaw in many European-style buildings in Japan.

Designed by Yorinaka Tsumaki and Goichi Takeda, the **Nippon Kangyo Bank Head Office, Uchisaiwaicho, Tokyo** (1899) (p. 1243B), was like several other large buildings in which the Japanese style was used in the 1890s. This did not result from a conscious effort to revive Japanese traditional construction methods and designs, but from an ambitious attempt to create a new style of wooden architecture. This office building had two floors with the wooden framework exposed on the walls, but its proportions were completely different from those found in traditional

A. Ueno Museum, Tokyo (1881). See p. 1240

B. First Mitsubishi Building, Tokyo (1894). See p. 1240

C. Tokyo Law Court Building, Tokyo (1896). See p. 1240

A. Tsukiji Hotel, Tokyo (1868). See p. 1240

B. Kaichi School, Matsumoto (1876). See p. 1240

C. Oura Church, Nagasaki (1876). See p. 1240

A. Bank of Japan, Head Office, Tokyo (1895). See p. 1240

B. Nippon Kangyo Bank Head Office, Tokyo (1899). See p. 1240

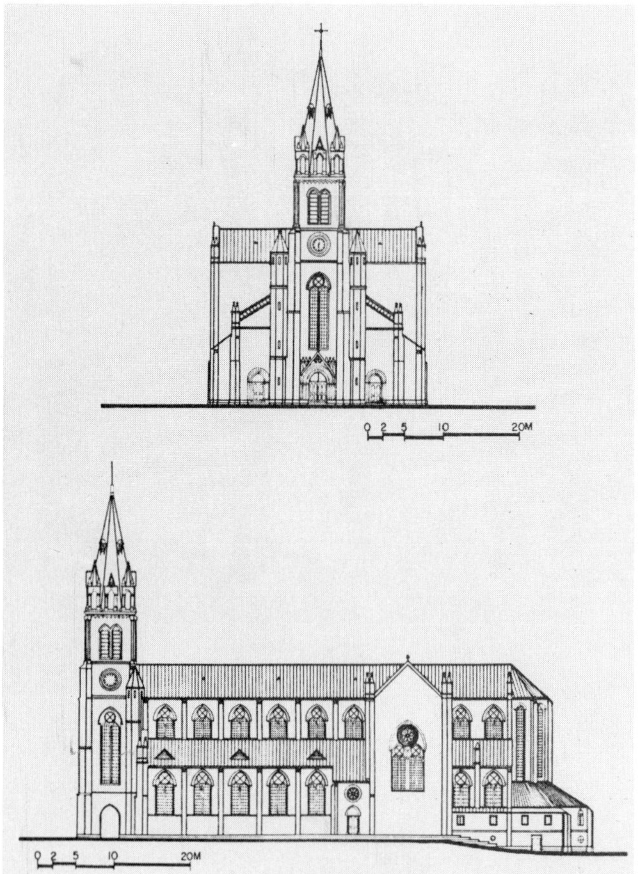

B. Bank of Korea, Namdaemunno (1912). See p. 1245

C. Seoul Railway Station (1925): main entrance. See p. 1245

A. (*above*)
Myong-dong Cathedral (1898): front and side elevations. See p. 1245

D. (*right*)
Seoul National University School of Medicine Main Building (1927): rear elevation. See p. 1245

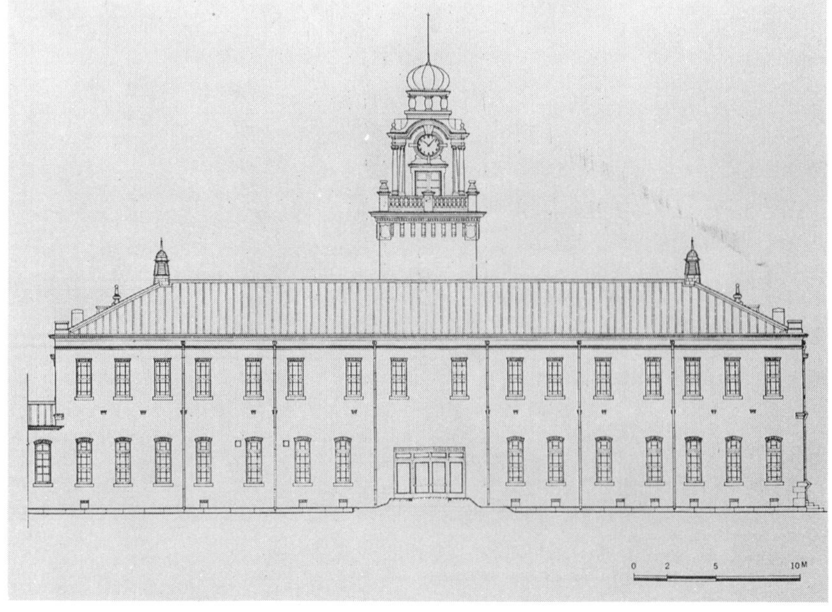

Japanese architecture. Especially characteristic was the contrast between the frame, the white walls and the openings. Ingenious fusions of Japanese and European styles were to be found in the central entrance and on the balconies. It was destroyed in 1927.

Architectural Character in Korea

The history of Western architecture in Korea corresponds to Korea's modern political history: the pre-annexation period (before 1910), the Japanese colonial period (1910–45), and the post-liberation period (after 1945).

Up to 1900 most of the Western-style buildings in Korea were either diplomatic establishments, Christian churches and facilities, or commercial buildings. Matters were not very different between 1900 and 1910, though the Korean government did build some Western-style buildings for the royal court and for government offices. It was during this period that the general public became aware of Western-style architecture.

The Japanese colonial period in Korea (1910–45) can be divided into two parts: 1910–25 and 1926–45. In the first part formalism and eclecticism were prevalent, while in the second part modernism began to appear in line with architectural trends in Japan, although Classical and other eclectic styles were followed even towards the end of the Japanese colonial period, a clear indication of how deeply formalism was rooted.

Examples

All the significant extant buildings of this period in Korea are in Seoul, and the place-names are all locations in the capital.

The architect of the two-storey brick **Student Hall at the Catholic Medical School, Myong-dong** (1890), is unknown, as are the architects of the **Sacred Heart Seminary, Wonhyoro** (1892) and the **British Embassy at Myong-dong** (1892).

Myong-dong Cathedral (p. 1244A), completed in 1898, was designed by an architect called E. Coste. It is a brick, Gothic Revival building on a Greek-cross plan with an apsidal east end and a single west-end tower with a pinnacled spire, itself flanked by octagonal towers which terminate at the level of the roof of the nave.

The **Methodist Church**, also of 1898, and the **Chongsogak Library** in the Ch'anggyonggung Palace (q.v.) are also brick buildings, the latter of two storeys, whose architects' names are no longer on record.

The **Bank of Korea, Namdaemunno** (1912) (p. 1244B), is a stone building by the Japanese architect Kingo Tatsuno (1854–1919) who also designed the Bank of Japan in Tokyo (1895) (q.v.). It is a somewhat heavy design showing German influence but with domes of an oriental flavour juxtaposed with crudely modelled pediments above two-storey pilasters.

Seoul Railway Station (p. 1244C) is an interesting north European free-style building, perhaps combining French with British models. The great arch, surmounted by a rather flat, faceted dome, is reminiscent of many French stations, though smaller in scale. It was built in 1925, and the architect is unknown.

The **Seoul National University School of Medicine, Yon-gon-dong** (p. 1244D), is a two- and three-storey building with a reinforced concrete frame, built in 1927. The main building has a Scandinavian proportion between solid and void, but the clock-tower is in a typical late free-style manner.

Chapter 40

SOUTH-EAST ASIA

South-east Asia has a long and dynamic inter-cultural architectural history which incorporates the traditions of Asia, Europe and America. With the exception of Thailand, which remained constitutionally a sovereign state, Western powers had a presence in Myanmar, Malaysia, Indo-China, Indonesia and the Philippines since the sixteenth century. But, despite varied architectural influences, indigenous building and design traditions played a formative role at all levels and phases of the region's architectural development.

Indigenous Architecture

The hot-humid zone of South-east Asia yields an abundance of tropical forests and grasslands, thus there is a major indigenous tradition of timber building. This tradition is apparent in various human settlements found in the plains, uplands, river estuaries and numerous islands throughout South-east Asia and the built-form is derived from the 'long house' and pavilions with square plans. These structures are usually piled, with an undercroft to serve as storage and shelter for animals, besides providing a natural defence against floods and enemy raids. The skills necessary in building this type of house were influential in the evolution of bungalow architecture.

In Thailand, the **Kamthieng House** (built *c.* 1844 in Chiangmei and now relocated in the grounds of the Siam Society, Bangkok), is representative of the **Lanna-thai houses** found in **Changmei, north Thailand** (p. 1247A). The platform entry is marked by a water jar. This leads to detached buildings consisting of the main house, kitchen, granary, spirit house and water storage. The main house is roofed by a pair of steeply pitched gable roofs which are connected by a valley gutter. The walls lean outwards and hang, like screens, off the posts while the column-like posts of the granary lean inwards for structural reasons.

Another house-form is the 'Central Plain type Thai house' which is found in the lowlands. Entrance to the platform is between two buildings which serve as living and sleeping quarters. Additional buildings, usually symmetrically arranged, are constructed with an enlarged platform. In **Brunei, Darussalam,** the Atap balah bumbong (pitched roof) and Atap tungkup (pyramidal roof) are evident at **Kampong Ayer** (water village), begun in the early nineteenth century. Here pantaran (open verandah) and titian (walkways) link several thousand houses (p. 1247B).

In Peninsula Malaysia, the bumbong panjang, meaning 'long gabled roof' or in the Philippines, bahay kubo, meaning cube house, represents the basic unit of an indigenous house. It is usually extended laterally to accommodate minor functions by a series of hip-rooflets. The three basic spaces of a Malay house comprises a serambi or verandah, the ibu rumah meaning the main (mother) house and the rumah dapor or kitchen.

In the Malaysian states of Malacca and Negeri Sembilan, a house-form after the style of the Hindu kingdom of Minangkabau of Sumatra was introduced during the seventeenth century. An example is the **Istana Hinggap, Negeri Sembilan** (*c.* 1865) which consists of a long serambi or verandah placed in front of the rumah ibu. The up-turn of the bumbong panjang is modest when compared to its Minangkabau precedents such as the **Minangkabau Document Centre, Padang Panjang, Sumatra** (p. 1247C), where the steeper up-turn roof and finials signify buffalo horns.

The boat-like shape in house-forms suggests the possible seafaring origins of many tribes. Saddleback roofs and extended gables are found at the Micronesian islands and Sepik region of New Guinea. Most dramatic is the house-form of the **Torajaan, Sulawesi, Indonesia**. It consists of a giant upswing gable roof which requires support by posts at both ends. It also symbolises an 'origin-house' and consists of animistic carvings including buffalo heads.

The house-forms of the **Batak Karo** and **Simalungun** in the highlands of North Sumatra are each distinguished by both the long and pyramidal roof-forms which are often ornamented with four-sided gables complete with finials shaped like buffalo heads. As with all things in nature, occupants believe that the house possesses its own vital force;

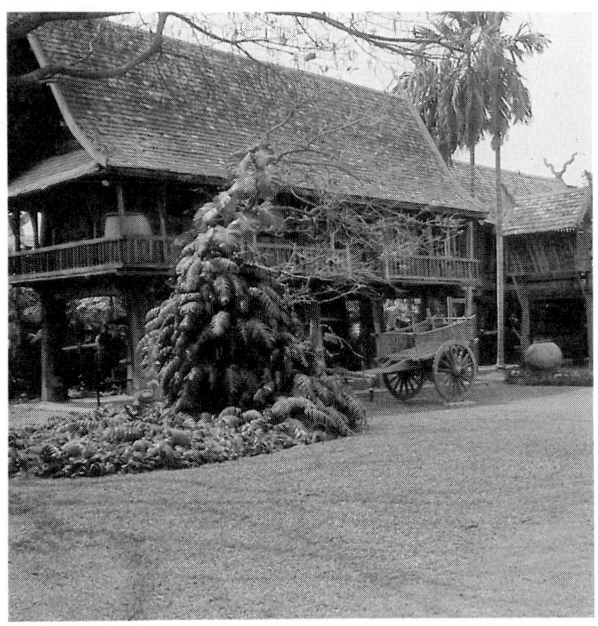

A. Kamthieng House, Bangkok, Thailand (*c.* 1844). See p. 1246

B. Kampong Ayer (water village), Brunei. See p. 1246

C. Minangkabau Document Centre, Padang Panjang, Sumatra, Indonesia. See p. 1246

this is expressed in terms of under-, middle- and upper-world.

Granary, charnel house, meeting house and viewing platform are identified with the pavilion form. This form may also incorporate a residence, shrine or adat (tradition) house as well as a granary. Examples include house-forms of the Ifugao people from Northern Luzon (Philippines); the Donggo people from Eastern Sumbawa and also locations at Alor and Kedang in Indonesia.

The Manggarains at Flores Islands, Indonesia, build circular houses with conical roof and adat houses with elliptical plans. The Balinese courtyard house is determined by beliefs in cosmology which relate influences of gods and demons with the occupant according to an Indianised heritage. The location of wall enclosures, entry and exit points are predetermined; the courtyard interior is shaped by brick platforms, gable and pyramidal roofs. The shrine, which is identified by a multi-tiered roof representing 'Mount Meru', is located at the 'holiest', north-east corner.

The Bungalow Development

The colonial bungalow, with either a flat, pyramidal or pitched roof over either a square or elongated rectangular plan, evolved from India; the one-storeyed structure has a platform with a verandah on all sides; it also may have a porte-cochere while the kitchen and service wing is detached and located at the rear. Transplanting the bungalow into South-east Asia from India has entailed its further evolution owing to other indigenous influences.

An outstanding example of an Anglo-Malayan bungalow with a transverse rectangular plan and porte-cochere, known as 'Black and White', is seen at **Green Lane, Penang** (p. 1249A). The generic-form is closely associated with the Malay house-form represented by the house belonging to a matriarch, **Che Midah, Kuala Kangsar, Perak** (*c.* 1880). The significant element here is the entrance porch which is accentuated by a short gable roof and is placed at right angles to the centre of the transverse axis. This house was demolished to make way for the rebuilding of a bungalow for the British Resident. **The Residency** retained the rectangular plan with an entrance porch, staircase and the use of stilts which had earlier appeared in Che Midah's house. It also incorporated elements from India such as verandahs surrounding all four sides of the bungalow with accompanying Anglo-Indian ornaments. This attempt to reconcile the indigenous house with forms and details symbolising colonial authority led to hybrid design.

Bungalow architecture has also absorbed Palladian ideals; this includes **The Astana, Kuching** (*c.* 1840) which was the former residence of Raja Brook of Sarawak (p. 1249D), and **Vimanmek, Bangkok, Thailand** (*c.* 1900), the Summer House of King Rama V (Chulalorngkorn).

As building frontages reduced in width for urban sites, the longitudinal plan, often double-storeyed, assumed dominance and represented a distinct development of the bungalow building type. An example is the **Syed Al-attas Mansion, Georgetown, Penang** (1875) (now the **Heritage Centre of Penang**) (p. 1249B). It consists of three bays and a porte-cochere; the extended plan which is a result of adding more rooms had earlier evolved from the square-plan bungalow.

This type of bungalow, often erected on stilts and consisting of a porte-cochere in front of a generous front verandah, was popular both as a planter's and officer's bungalow in colonial territories. An example is a bungalow, built in half-timber and brick, at the former British garrison town of **Pegu, Burma** (p. 1249C).

Deriving from the bahay kubo (Filipino indigenous hut) are such houses as the **Bahay-na-bato, Sta Rita, Pampanga, Manila**. A hybrid of Spanish and indigenous building traditions, the silang (ground floor) is used as storage and encased by stone blocks; the upper floor constitutes the house proper, including a caida (ante-room), sala (living room), comedor (dining hall), and cuarto (bedrooms) a large azotea (terrace), anda (kitchen), adjacent to which are the bano or paliguan (bath) and latrina. The second floor is made of wood, with capiz-shell glazed windows. The high-pitched nipa roof is often replaced with terra-cotta tiles.

Colonial Architecture

British Colonial architecture in the Malay peninsula began in the late seventeenth century, and was centred around two administrative subregions: which became known as the Federated Malay States (FMS) with Kuala Lumpur as the capital following the establishment of British authority in 1880, and the Straits Settlement comprising Penang, Malacca and Singapore, with Singapore as capital of the Crown Colonies. Offical architecture of the FMS generally reflected political sensitivities towards the Malay Royalty and thereby leaned towards Moorish or Anglo-Indian character for stylistic associations; the Straits Settlement, because of its Crown status, adapted British Georgian and Victorian styles.

In **Kuala Lumpur,** C. E. Spooner, the State Engineer, commissioned A. C. A. Norman, to design the former **Secretariate Building**, (now the **Bangunan Sultan Abdul Samad**) (1897) (p. 1250B). The Moorish arcades, spiralling stairs topped by castellations and 'Rajabai towers' reflect influences such as those from Bombay University Library, designed by

A. 'Black and white bungalow', Green Lane, Penang, West Malaysia (*c.* 1900). See p. 1248

B. Syed Al-attas Mansion, Penang, West Malaysia (1875). See p. 1248

C. Garrison bungalow, Pegu, Burma (*c.* 1900). See p. 1248

D. The Astana, Kuching, Sarawak, East Malaysia (*c.* 1840). See p. 1248

A. The Armenian Church, Singapore (1835). See p. 1251

B. Bangunan Sultan Abdul Samad, Kuala Lumpur, West Malaysia (1897). See p. 1248

C. Seri Carcosa Negara, Kuala Lumpur, West Malaysia (1897). See p. 1251

D. S. George's Church, Penang, West Malaysia (1817). See p. 1251

Sir George Gilbert Scott and Muir College, Allahabad, by Sir William Emerson. Spooner overruled Norman's initial preference for the neo-Classical and insisted on the use of the 'Saracenic' style because it was more in keeping with Malaysian Muslim culture and with the tropical climate. Other buildings in the city centre include the **General Post Office** (1896), the **Public Works Department** (1896), the **High Court** (1909) and the **Information Department** (1909), all designed by Norman in the same exotic manner. The **Kuala Lumpur Railway Station and Hotel** (1911) is by A. B. Hubback and in a similarly florid Saracenic manner with onion domes and Moghul chatris.

Norman's design for the British Residency **'Carcosa'** (1897) (now State House **'Seri Carcosa Negara'**) went further by combining Moorish elements with Classical, Tudor and Chinese details (p. 1250B); it exudes picturesque notions within the botanic setting of the 'Lake Gardens' and city background.

Fortifications in the Straits Settlement were always located along strategic coastlines. This included the Portuguese fort on **S. Paul's Hill, Malacca** (the Portuguese held Malacca from 1511 to 1641 with most of S. Paul's fort being demolished by the British in 1807), the former settlement at **Fort Santiago, Manila Bay, Philippines;** and British fortifications at **Fort Cornwallis, Georgetown (Penang)** (Georgetown was established in 1786) at the eastern tip opposite mainland Malaysia, and **Fort Canning, Singapore**, located alongside **Singapore River**.

The remains of a fine Portuguese church stands at the top of Residency Hill, Malacca. **S. Paul's Church** was began in 1512 and for a short time held the remains of S. Francis Xavier. Although now in ruins, the impressive stone-built pedimented facade still stands. **S. Peter's, Malacca** (1710), although built during the Dutch period of control, still mixes Portuguese Baroque details with eastern motifs, while **Christ Church, Malacca** (1750), is probably the best example of Dutch architecture in the region. The earliest surviving Dutch building in the east is the **Town Hall, Malacca** (1641–60), which is three storeys with timber louvered windows and tall gabled-ends.

During the early nineteenth century the prototype for religious buildings was the early eighteenth-century S. Martin-in-the-Field, London; the earliest of these was **S. George's Church, Penang** (1817) (p. 1250D) designed by Captain Robert Smith. The **Armenian Church, Singapore** (1835), was designed by George Drumgoole Coleman (1795–1844) (p. 1250A). The circular nave with an apse is 11 m (36 ft) in diameter and has a conical roof and lantern within a Greek-cross plan; it is lit by top vents which also diffuse natural lighting. The plan may have been derived from James Gibbs's rejected circular plan for S. Martin-in-the-Fields, possibly via S. Andrew's, Madras (q.v.). The octagonal steeple was added in 1858.

In residential architecture, Georgian villas, of the type found in contemporary India, were designed in Singapore by Coleman. The only survival is the **town house of H. C. Caldwell** (1840). It has a bow-front in the Doric astylar manner.

More overtly Victorian architecture in Singapore was ushered in by military engineers; for example Colonel Ronald Macpherson, who designed **S. Andrews Cathedral** (1862) in the Gothic style and Major John Adolphus McNair who designed **Government House (The Istana)** (1869) in an arcaded form seemingly inspired by Andrea Palladio's Renaissance Villa Emo, but with a tower and mansard roof (p. 1252A). Examples by R. A. J. Bidwell of Swan and Maclaren include the **Victoria Theatre** and **Memorial Hall** (1904), replacing the Town Hall of 1862, and **Raffles Hotel** (1897). Bidwell's design for Raffles (of which only the main facade and one wing survives) incorporated a first-floor verandah and Tuscan columns supported on a ground-floor loggia. The surviving palm court has been enlarged (p. 1252C). Also by Bidwell is the **Chassed El Synagogue, Singapore** (1905) which was inspired by Byzantine churches. The **Seri Mutiara** or **Residency, Penang** (1890), designed by Major C. A. Cameron (p. 1252D) is a hybrid wth a pediment and portico to its front portion and a bungalow-like annex at the rear.

The town plan, infrastructure and by-laws of **Singapore** (founded 1819) were developed during the 1820s according to stipulations drawn up by Sir Stamford Raffles with Lieutenant P. Jackson, the garrison engineer. These created racial enclaves or 'kampongs' that would be linked with each other by a system of commercial-residential units known as the **shop-house** (p. 1252B) set in a town grid; built after 1880 of non-inflammable materials, the ground floor was the shop which had a common 'five-footways' or verandah open to the street; the upper floors were used for storage and residence. The plan could be up to 100 ft in depth with a number of internal open courts. The Municipal Ordinance (1887) of the Straits Settlement led to the standardisation of this 'urban identity' in mainland Malaysia. It was introduced to Thailand from Singapore by Rama V (Chulalorngkorn), and imitated in other parts of South-east Asia and European concessions in coastal China.

The Royal Ordinances (1573) under Phillip II of Spain stipulated the use of arcades on a grid town plan for colonial development in the New World, including the Philippines. However, arcades were not implemented in the walled city of **Intramuros** in the metropolitan area of Manila, Philippines. Instead there was the bahay-na-bato, which is composed of stone walls at street level with top lights and vents. This feature is common to all urban buildings, including, for example, the **Universidad de Santo Tomas** (founded 1611).

A. Government House (The Istana), Singapore (1869). See p. 1251

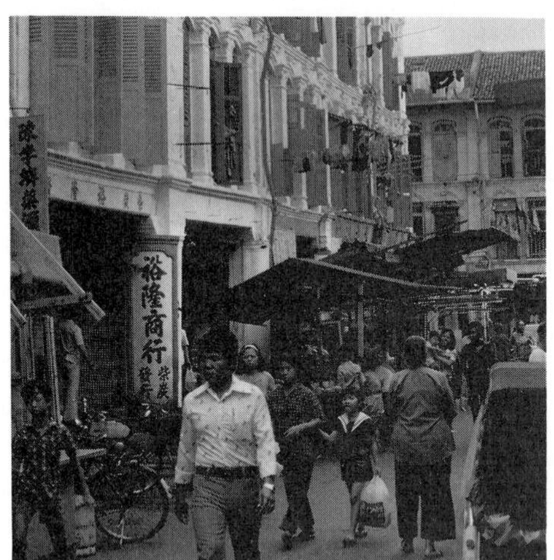

B. Shop-houses, Singapore. See p. 1251

C. Raffles Hotel, Singapore (1897). See p. 1251

D. Seri Mutiara, Penang, West Malaysia (1887). See p. 1251

E. S Pablo de los Augustinos Calzados, Manila, Philippines (1591). See p. 1255

A. Istana Bogor, Jakarta, Indonesia (1856). See p. 1255

B. The National Archives Building, Jakarta, Indonesia (*c.* 1760). See p. 1255

C. Immanuel Church, Jakarta, Indonesia (1839). See p. 1255

D. Opera House, Hanoi, Vietnam (*c.* 1900). See p. 1255

A. Pavilion, Grand Palace, Phnom-Penh, Cambodia (*c.* 1869). See p. 1255

B. Chakri Maha Prasat, Bangkok, Thailand (1872–5). See p. 1255

The Church of **S. Pablo de los Augustinos Calzados, Manila** (1591) is the only stone church in Renaissance style to survive an earthquake in 1863 (p. 1252E). The great pediment, over an arched entrance, is framed by pilasters, niches and high windows, together with a pair of towers. English Victorian-style architecture was introduced to Manila by Felix Roxas. He was the first Filipino architect to practise after working in Calcutta, Spain and London. He designed two churches in the Intramuros; namely the **Church of Santo Domingo de Manila** (1868), which features a Gothic 'skin' over a squat-like Rennaisance massing, and the **New San Ignacio Church** (1889), which has a neo-Classical facade.

Batavia (now Jakarta, capital of modern Indonesia) was named by the Dutch as the capital of Dutch East Indies in 1619. The town plan was of grid-iron type and emulated Amsterdam with canals and locks along the tributaries of the Ciliwung River. A canal gives the only access to the sea which is controlled by **Kasteel Batavia** or Fort northwards of the town. Important early Dutch buildings include the **President's Office and the Penang Gate** (1671), City Square; the **house of the Governor General** (1708) and the **Town Hall** (1710), by W. J. Van de Velde and J. Kemmer, which has a pedimented centrepiece surmounted by a cupola.

By the time Stamford Raffles arrived in Batavia in 1811 and became Lieutenant-Governor of Java (1811–15) the city was already characterised by terraced buildings in brick with verandahs set among the extensive Dutch brick warehouses. These features influenced Raffles to stipulate future building codes in Singapore, requiring terraces to include continuous verandahs. Dutch colonial architecture used high gable roofs and windows set with a giant order and occasionally with either castellations or curvilinear pediments. An example is a country house belonging to Reinier de Klerk (*c.* 1760; now the **National Archives Building, Jakarta**) (p. 1253B). The facade was originally filled with arched windows with curvilinear pediments applied to buildings forming a courtyard at the rear.

With the return of Java to the Dutch, there emerged a new attitude in architecture which is described as The Empire Style with its roots in neo-Classicism. This early nineteenth-century style is expressed best in the villas of **Weltevreden**, a garden suburb, south of Batavia. It featured the stoep, or colonnaded verandah as a living and social space. The Palladio Villa Emo form was adopted in many official buildings, such as the **Summer Palace, Bogor** (1856), (now **Istana Bogor**) (p. 1253A), and the **Hall of Justice, Jakarta** (1870, now Balai Seni Rupa). The **Immanuel Church** (1839), by J. H. Horst, was designed with a circular plan and dome; the pediment and porticos facing four directions, features straight and bow-fronts in a Doric Order (p. 1253C).

French Indo-China was forged in 1893 under the Third Republic of France. The principal buildings expressing French colonial power and taste were constructed in the major capitals of these territories, namely **Saigon, Hanoi** and **Phnom-Penh**. The planning of Saigon emulated the boulevards of Paris; by 1878, the Rue Imperiale, now Boulevard Norodom, connected the **Notre Dame Cathedral** (began 1880) by Jules Bournard, with the botanical garden at the Saigon River at one end and the palace of the governor-general at the opposite end. Georges Lhermite, the first Beaux-Arts-trained architect in Saigon, designed the **Palace** (1873) in a Palladian manner with a curved piazza. The **Saigon Theatre** (begun 1895) by Joseph-Victor Guichard and the **Hanoi Opera House** (begun 1900) (p. 1253D) are grandiose public buildings. A **cast iron pavilion, Phnom-Penh**, presented by Napoleon III to King Norodom 1st (*c.* 1869), is located between the Throne Room and the Silver Pagoda in the palace grounds (p. 1254A).

Bangkok, the modern capital of Thailand, was founded by the Kings of the Chakri dynasty in 1782, and consisted of two encircling moats and walls. It guards the entrance of the Chao Phya River which flows into the hinterland. King Rama V (Chulalongkorn) pursued and patronised European architecture and town planning; the shop-house appeared as part of an urban grain although Thai by-laws did not prescribe public-verandahs ('five-footways'). He commissioned the **Chakri Maha Prasat or Grand Palace** (begun 1872) which was designed by John Clunies (p. 1254B) in a composite Victorian and Thai pagoda style. Another commission, in the French Renaissance manner, is the **Boromaphinan Palace**, which has curved mansard roofs.

Colonial architecture and town planning in Rangoon (now Yangon), capital of former British Burma, emerged only at the end of the nineteenth century. The Burma Municipal Act of 1885 was concerned with controlling the proliferation of pukha houses or bungalows with flat roofs in the town. Commercial buildings such as **Rowe & Co.** were similarly constructed and utilise jilmils or roof awnings as a means of sun shade. Like Bangkok, there are no Burmese by-laws stipulating a uniform and continuous public verandah as in shop-houses.

Chapter 41
INDIAN SUBCONTINENT

Architectural Character

Portuguese Colonial Architecture

The Portuguese had two main objectives when they arrived in the east in the late fifteenth and early sixteenth centuries: the first was to break into trade, which at that time was the monopoly of the Arabs; the second was to convert the eastern peoples to Christianity. To these ends they established fortified settlements at strategic points along the sea routes. As Roman Catholics, the Portuguese built many churches and monasteries dedicated to saints, and even the military bastions of the forts were named after them. Many shrines and churches were built at road junctions and in the interior and were usually marked by large, conspicuous crosses. The churches, many of which were built in the sixteenth and seventeenth centuries, followed European styles, but technological and economic constraints often limited their expression to the facade only. The churches themselves were barn-like in character and constructed in indigenous materials using local techniques.

There were attempts in early churches to reproduce Gothic details, but it was not long before the effects of the Renaissance in Europe led to the development of a characteristic Portuguese Baroque style. In the colonial settlements buildings became larger in scale, their facades often heavily ornamented with oriental as well as European motifs. Religious houses such as the Franciscans, Dominicans and Capuchins stamped their own preferences upon the buildings they commissioned. As Portuguese power faded in the east, however, the architecture was debased by stylistic imitation and over-decoration.

Dutch Colonial Architecture

The Dutch sailed eastward mainly for purposes of trade, arriving in India and Sri Lanka about a century after the Portuguese. Their fortifications consisted of rampart walls encircling the settlements, which were divided into two areas, one for Europeans and the other for the indigenous population. The towns were planned with streets, drainage systems and trees, and because of the need for large numbers of dwellings within the fortified settlements, regulations were imposed upon the architectural development of streets. Some of the results can still be seen today in the form of well laid-out localities, shaded paths and vistas. The bastions of fortified towns were named after Dutch cities; in contrast to the Portuguese, each town had a simple church, sometimes with a few local motifs applied to their facades, but usually devoid of ornamentation.

The Dutch placed their warehouses for export goods in prominent positions adjacent to the harbours. Brick vaulting was the most characteristic method of construction and was also used for churches.

British Colonial Architecture

The British influence on the Indian subcontinent dated from the setting up of the East India Company (see Chapter 35). Unlike the Dutch and Portuguese, British settlers moved out of the enclosed townships, so that the scope of the economy was widened beyond basic trade to the production of capital crops and semi-processed goods suitable for the European market. This called for the provision of a comprehensive network of communications including roads and railways, as well as the establishment of provincial cities throughout the country.

The need to erect structures quickly encouraged the development of new constructional techniques: these included sophisticated prefabricated systems using cast-iron, steel and metal sheets which could be manufacturered by the new industries at home. Standard plans for common types were evolved: these were more suited to industrially manufactured components, which were used for plantation buildings and other accommodation such as that related to the new communication systems. But government and commerce alike favoured the adaptation of the prevalent European styles – in particular those of the later

Renaissance in Britain, Baroque Palladian and neo-Classical and in the nineteenth century the revival styles including Gothic. Design was influenced by the tropical climate, helping to produce local hybridised styles, as did the use of oriental motifs, sometimes giving a unique flavour to individual buildings.

Expansive civic design undertakings were implemented. Residential developments, museums, hospitals, churches, sports clubs, schools, commercial buildings including banks, administrative buildings, town halls, department stores, and communications centres with stations and post offices, were the hallmarks of British colonial development in the nineteenth century. Military buildings to house the garrisons were usually confined to cantonments on the margins of cities and townships.

Other European Colonial Settlements

Other European countries also set up trading settlements and developed colonial leanings in India and Sri Lanka, notably France and, on a smaller scale, Denmark.

Examples

Portuguese Architecture

Forts

The wealthy island port of **Goa**, originally taken by Alfonso de Albuquerque from the sultan of Bijapur in 1510, was protected from land attack by three fortifications. **Fort Aguada** (p. 1258A), on the coast of Pernem, stood on a cliff overlooking the sea, its bastions placed at strategic points related to the contours. A church and a tower provided the focus of the fort. The island **Fortalice of Cailo** and **Fort Largo** protected the mouth of the river Zuari, and the south bank of the river was protected by **Marmagoa** (p. 1258B), a fortification with prominent bastions facing the sea and with an arched entrance gate.

A fortification at the mouth of the river Mandovi protected the first capital of Portuguese India, Velha Goa – in the seventeenth century one of the most opulent cities in the world. It was laid out with a church facing onto a square, with mansions and villas arranged around minor piazzas, their windows opening onto balconies with wrought iron railings. The square fort, isolated from the main island by a canal, was entered through an arched gateway facing the waterfront. Though most of the buildings have disappeared, something of the city's splendour and romance lingers on among the ruins of Velha Goa.

Panjim, which succeeded Velha Goa as capital in the nineteenth century, was a linear town with a grid plan laid out along the sea front with high ground behind it. Other fortified towns established by the Portuguese along the west coast of India in the second half of the sixteenth century were **Diu, Bassein, Daman, Bombay**, and a little further north still, on the Gulf of Cambay, **Surat**, where the British, Dutch and French also built factories or trading lodges in the seventeenth century (p. 1258E). Similar settlements were established on the east coast on the river **Hooghly** and at **San Thome**. The posts were strongly walled enclosures containing the domestic as well as the mercantile accommodation; the degree of fortification seems to have varied with location.

On the island of Sri Lanka, the Portuguese **Fort of Colombo** was established in 1518 on lines similar to Velha Goa, with an inner fortification for administrative and military purposes, and an outer residential area. The enclosure, still known as the Fort (p. 1258D), was originally laid out by one João Baptista, an engineer commissioned to design the fortifications which consisted of fourteen bastions. There were about five hundred residential buildings with gardens in the outer part of the city. Similar **fortifications** controlled the entrance to Jaffna at **Kayts, Karaitivu** and the **Island of Hammenhiel**, and the entrance to Trincomalee harbour at **Ostenburgh** and **Sober Island**. Others, such as **Menikkadawara**, built by General Don Jeronimo d'Avesedo, were sited and constructed against attack from the interior.

Churches

At first, most of the durable buildings in the Portuguese settlements were religious in character. The missionaries saw it as their duty to convert the indigenous population to Roman Catholicism, and as soon as finance became available churches were built to simulate as nearly as possible European prototypes. This aim was often only achieved in the facades of the buildings – the accommodation for the worshippers being constructed in cheap and easily available local materials and techniques. Other early churches were little more than fortified enclosures with bastions surrounding a centrally located shrine and priests' quarters, as in the first church at **Aguada, Goa**, and at **Ratnapura**, Sri Lanka. The first Christian shrine in India was dedicated to **S. Catherine** a year after the occupation of Goa by Albuquerque. Originally constructed in mud, straw and palm leaves, it was extensively modified and rededicated in 1513, and in 1539 was inaugurated as the cathedral of the newly established diocese of Goa.

The **Church of Our Lady of the Rosary, Goa**, built in 1543, is the best surviving specimen of the early period of Portuguese church architecture. It is a

A. Fort Aguada, Goa (early seventeenth century). See p. 1257

B. Fort Marmagoa, Goa, (early sixteenth century). See p. 1257

C. Church of S. Francis of Assisi, Goa: interior. See p. 1259

D. A street in the Fort, Colombo, Sri Lanka (photographed 1968). See p. 1257

E. The British trading lodge, Surat (established 1613). See pp. 1257, 1261

hall church with nave, transept and apse. The cylindrical towers are surmounted by domes, and a two-storey box-like structure with arched portals serves as a porch with belfry above. There are Hindu and Muslim motifs in the decoration of external wall surfaces.

The **Church of S. Francis of Assisi, Goa**, begun in the pioneering early sixteenth century (1527), was rebuilt in the seventeenth century but retains its earlier facade with twin octagonal towers. The interior (p. 1258C) is vaulted and embellished with complex arrangements of coffer-like decorated square panels. The majestic simplicity of the high groin vaults is interrupted by Baroque details which include sculptured figures. Frescoed panels on the broad flat piers supporting the main vault are painted in a hybrid style using intricately combined Indian and European elements.

Se Cathedral, Goa (begun 1562, completed 1662), was by architects Ambrosio Argeiro and Julio Simayo. It combines a nave and double aisle with single-volume planning. It is rectangular in plan with an apse. The main facade with its paired flat pilasters and scroll brackets is reminiscent of Vignola's Gesù church in Rome (built about the same time). Julio Simayo also designed the **Arch of the Viceroy** and the **College of S. Paul, Goa**.

The **Basilica of Bom Jesus** (1593–1603) (p. 1260C) is the most celebrated church in **Goa**. It is cruciform in plan and has a single nave volume. The 'triumphal arch' facade has a centre bay which rises an additional storey to form a pedimented gable with ogee parapets with shell decorations either side. The Classical impression conveyed by the ground-floor facade relates comfortably to the echoes of Plateresque decoration and the Baroque forms of the upper levels. Internally there are galleries on both sides of the nave, which is vaulted. There is a gilt single-storey retable dedicated to S. Ignatius, and the southern wing of the transept houses the **Mausoleum of S. Francis Xavier**, the apostle of the Indies.

Another fine example is the **Church of S. Catejan, Goa** (1661), whose main facade seems to be a modest imitation of S. Peter's in Rome. Although the church seems to be rectangular externally, it is a Greek-cross plan, has an aisled nave ending in an apse, and four massive piers at the crossing, which is surmounted by a cupola and a lantern. The **Church of the Immaculate Conception, Panjim, Goa**, stands on a high podium approached at the west end by tiered double flights of steps, an arrangement which appeared in many Portuguese and Spanish churches of the seventeenth and eighteenth centuries and even as late as the early nineteenth century in the Americas, for example at Congonhas do Campo, Brazil (q.v.).

In **Sri Lanka** the **Church of S. Paul, Colombo**, was referred to by Antonio Rubino in 1622 as a '... church built in the Corinthian style, well proportioned and handsome'. The church no longer exists but a map of 1658 shows it as the most prominent of the nine Portuguese churches in seventeenth-century Colombo.

Dutch Architecture

The interest of the Dutch United East India Company was to lie mainly with Java and the spice islands. Sri Lanka, however, provided a useful staging post as well as a new trading base and finally came under Dutch control in 1658; it remained so until the end of the eighteenth century.

Forts

The Dutch enlarged the forts built by the Portuguese around the coasts of Sri Lanka, and where necessary established new ones. A number of comparable forts are illustrated in Chapter 36 (pp. 1171–5). There are few examples in India, though in some cases the Dutch, British and Portuguese all had warehouses within the same enclosures (for example, Surat, q.v.). The Dutch work on forts in Sri Lanka all dates from the second half of the seventeenth century. Stockaded compounds included **Tirukovil, Samanthurai** and **Kalmunai**, which were listed by Valentyn, a Dutch writer of the seventeenth century. Most of the fortified settlements were on the seaboard, but there were a few smaller square stockades on internal frontiers such as those at **Akuressa** and **Hakmana**, both moated, their garrisons housed outside the main enclosures. **Hammenhiel** and **Point Pedro** were single-bastion forts, the former with a masonry bell-tower above the entrance gate and two three-storey warehouses at the centre of the fortified enclosure.

Batticaloa, where the Dutch fleet first landed on Sri Lanka in 1602, **Kalpitya** (1667) and **Mannar** (1686) all had multi-bastion forts with churches, and the **Fort of Jaffna** had an arched gateway with a drawbridge over the moat; the enclosure was 1.6 ha (4 acres) in area and contained the commander's residence, now referred to as the King's House. The Dutch extended and consolidated the fortified townships at **Colombo** (p. 1260A), **Galle** (p. 1260B), **Trincomalee** and **Matara**. Colombo became a complete miltary town, with a hospital, schools, stores and workshops as well as various grades of residential accommodation. Galle, which by 1729 had fourteen bastions, is the best-preserved fortified township in South-east Asia (p. 1260E). The Portuguese bastions on the land side were enlarged and improved by the Dutch. The fortifications enclose about 40 ha (100 acres). There was a water gate, and access from the mainland was by means of a drawbridge through an arched entrance dating from 1669.

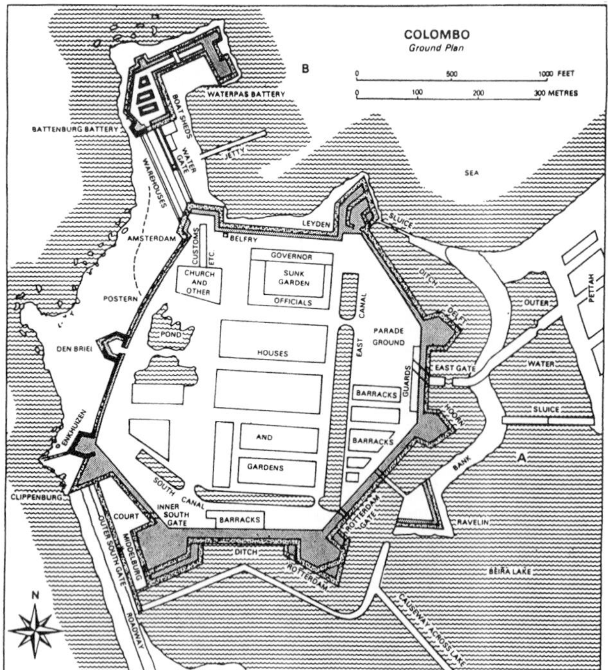

A. The Fort, Colombo (sixteenth and seventeenth centuries). See p. 1259

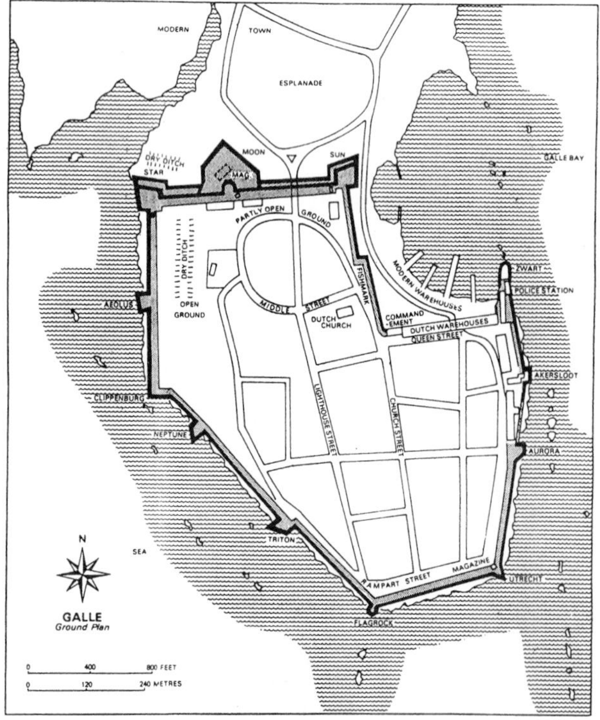

B. The Fort, Galle (sixteenth and seventeenth centuries). See p. 1259

C. Basilica of Bom Jesus, Goa (1593–1603). See p. 1259

D. Dutch church at Jaffna, Sri Lanka (1754). See p. 1261

E. The Fort, Galle: recent photograph showing stone and earth-fill construction

The Dutch church with its Baroque facade was the first Protestant church in Sri Lanka. Galle boasted a sophisticated and unique drainage system, flushed with sea water pumped by a windmill.

Churches

During the Dutch period in Sri Lanka two types of church were erected: the rural churches which combined school and meeting house, and the more formal urban churches which reflected European styles. In the former some continuity with the Portuguese period can be discerned. Simple rectangular meeting halls were roofed in local materials supported on masonry piers with half-height walls between them. There are churches of this kind at **Manner, Kalpitya** and **Ambalagonda**.

The Dutch **church at Jaffna** (dedicated 1754) (p. 1260D), was built by Martinus Leusekam on a Greek-cross plan. The arches over the doorway and windows were built with imported Dutch bricks and the walls with coral stone and rubble. The recessed square panel above the entrance doorway forms the centrepiece of the entrance facade and is surmounted by a characteristic gable with a curved outline. The windows are deeply recessed internally, with deep mullions. There were notable Dutch **churches at Galle** and **Wolfendahl, Colombo**, the former completed in 1755, the latter in 1757.

Secular Buildings

United East India Company **warehouses at Galle** were constructed as part of the main rampart walls; they were two-storey masonry buildings with massive timber-framed floors and roofs. Later buildings, such as the **warehouses at Colombo** around the old harbour, are characteristically brick-vaulted, of great length and about 9 m (30 ft) span, usually with iron tie-rods at springing level. Vaults were either single barrels or twin parallel vaults with masonry piers spanned by great arches between them. They were plastered internally and lit from circular lunettes in the crown of the vault, with lanterns covering these openings on the outside.

The typical planning grids of colonial Dutch fortress towns in Sri Lanka resulted in regular avenues with subsidiary roads crossing them at right angles. Long rows of single-storey houses had verandahs supported by rounded brick or timber columns facing onto tree-lined streets. Sometimes a timber railing fixed between the columns accentuated the urban perspectives. Entrance doors, placed centrally in the facade, gave access to the houses and to the courtyards at the rear. Louvred timber screens were placed in front of the main entrance doors to permit natural ventilation without visual intrusion, and there was a variety of carved timber fanlight grilles and ornamented lintels over openings, giving each house an air of individuality (p. 1262A). Verandahs provided shade and facilitated through ventilation to ameliorate the harsh tropical climate. Ornamental gables were turned at right angles to the line of the street in some colonial towns, of which Jaffna is one, and served as elaborate party-walls. The **Abeygunawardene Walauwa, Galle**, is a typical example of the period; it is entered through a verandah which separates the house from the street.

British Architecture

Forts and Trading Posts

The British East India Company established its first **factory at Surat** in 1613 (see p. 1258E). Many more trading stations were initiated in the next fifty years or so, some of which very quickly began to develop into settlements both within and without the fortified enclosures.

Fort S. George, Madras (originally founded in 1639) (p. 1262B), grew spectacularly throughout the seventeenth century and a second urban area was developed outside the original fortifications. On the south-east Coromandel coast of India it was to provide a stepping stone to the north-east. The fort was built with star-shaped bastions to north, south and west and was of the order of 1450 m (4250 ft) in length from north to south. The walls were comparatively low and had parapets with open embrasures. Entrance to the fort was through a water gate set into the east wall. Government offices, the arsenal and the church (S. Mary's) were within the walls.

Trade had soon moved north and east and **Fort William, Calcutta**, was built in 1696 in one of the locations – on the river Hooghly, the most westerly of the rivers of the Ganges delta – already used as a centre for the Bengal trade. It was smaller than Fort S. George but nevertheless housed within it the Governor's residence, houses for military and civilian settlers, warehouses and factories. Public buildings, including the church, were outside the walls. Fort William was rebuilt on its current site from 1757 to 1773 to the designs of Captain John Brohier.

Churches

S. Mary's Church, Fort S. George, Madras (church completed 1680, tower late eighteenth century), is one of the earliest British buildings still existing in India and was the first Anglican Church on the subcontinent. It is a simple aisled church with a gallery at one end. Heavy stone walls and roof are characteristic of the defensible location.

A. Doorway, Dutch period, Sri Lanka (eighteenth century). See p. 1261

B. Fort S. George, Madras (established 1639). See p. 1261

C. S. Andrew's Presbyterian Church, Madras (1821). See p. 1265

A. S. George's Cathedral, Madras (1816). See p. 1265

B. S. James's Church, Delhi (1836). See p. 1265

C. S. John's Church, Calcutta (1787). See p. 1265

D. S. Andrew's Church, Calcutta (1815). See p. 1265

E. S. Paul's Cathedral, Calcutta (1847) (before earthquake of 1934). See p. 1265

F. South Park Street Cemetery, Calcutta. See p. 1265

A. Constantia (La Martinière), Lucknow (1800–). See p. 1265

B. Government House, including the Banqueting Hall, Madras (1800–2). See p. 1266

S. George's Cathedral, Madras (1816) (p. 1263A), was designed and executed by Captain James Caldwell (later Sir James) (1770–1863) and Thomas Fiott de Havilland (1775–1866). Like so many colonial churches of the period, S. George's owes its style to James Gibbs's *A Book of Architecture* (1728) which had wide circulation overseas, and to designs for S. Martin-in-the-Fields, London, completed in 1726, one of the buildings included in the book. S. George's continues the incipient Palladianism of the Gibbs building, though implied Baroque movement remains in the pedimented and balustraded portico at the west end with its coupled Ionic columns, and their simple reflections in the shallower porticoes of the north and south sides. The order is repeated around the drum of the tower above the Tuscan Doric of the rusticated second storey and also in the interior colonnades of the church. The whole building gives the monolithic impression conveyed by smoothly finished chunam rendering – at S. George's carefully detailed and competently executed.

Thomas de Havilland and Caldwell were responsible also for **S. Andrew's Presbyterian Church, Madras** (1821) (p. 1262C), developed from another of Gibbs's published designs for S. Martin's, this time with a circular plan form. The result is a sophisticated and original design in the currently acceptable neo-Classical mode. The circular space is 24.5 m (82 ft) in diameter, defined by a ring of splendid Composite columns below a saucer dome. The aisles surround the central cylindrical volume outside the colonnade. The tower rises from the rectangular compartment linking the nave with the west portico, which like S. George's has coupled Ionic columns at its angles.

Two important neo-Classical churches, one late eighteenth, the other early nineteenth century, were built in Calcutta before the appearance of the Gothic Revival and the ebullience of High Victorian Gothic. **S. John's Church, Calcutta** (1787) (p. 1263C), built by James Agg (*c.* 1758–1828) after the major reconstruction of Fort William (completed 1773), was another church inspired by Gibbs's S. Martin-in-the-Fields. The tower was originally at the rear of the building, but the entrance was moved to a position below it towards the end of the eighteenth century. Additional shade from the sun was provided by adding colonnades on the north and south sides of the church in the nineteenth century. The **Presbyterian Church of S. Andrew, Calcutta** (1815) (p. 1263D), owed much to S. John's – notably its Tuscan Doric order – and returned more nearly to the London prototype. Its style and proportion were appropriate to its setting, adjacent to the Writers' Building (q.v.).

S. James's Church, Delhi (completed 1836) (p. 1263B), is a lavish and unusual example of the neo-Classical churches in India. Its founder and patron was Colonel James Skinner (of Skinner's Horse), its designer Robert Smith. The plan is a Greek cross with a dome rising from an octagonal drum with circular windows below an entablature. There are Doric porticoes with coupled columns to the north, south and west arms of the plan, with a squat tower between two of them. The crowning features of the ribbed dome are carried on scroll breackets giving it a Baroque character, strengthened by the superimposed balustrades above the entabulature and the elliptical recesses below it. The architectural effect of this seemingly small, actually spacious, church is wholly satisfying.

As well as the many neo-Classical smaller churches in cantonments and on hill stations, there were also distinguished examples in the settlements of other European countries (see p. 1274). Towards the middle of the nineteenth century picturesque Gothic began to appear, albeit slowly because it was thought unsuited to the climate. It was to retain its romantic grip for a decade or two until the appearance of buildings which demonstrated a more rigorous understanding of the principles underlying the mediaeval styles. It was maintained, for example, in **S. Peter's Church, Fort William, Calcutta** (1835): this was a Collegiate Gothic building with octagonal corner towers. But the picturesque Gothic style is best exemplified in India by **S. Paul's Cathedral, Calcutta** (completed 1847) (p. 1263E), by William Nairn Forbes (1796–1855), a military engineer. It is an impressive brick building, rendered in chunam, with a metal-framed roof. After earthquake damage the tower was rebuilt in the 1930s to a design based on the central tower of Canterbury cathedral. S. Paul's has a stained-glass west window by Burne-Jones.

It is perhaps appropriate that the more vigorous attitude to Gothic began in Bombay just before the centre of British activity in India began to move from the eastern to the western seaboard following the trauma of Cawnpore and Lucknow, and at the beginning of the imperial period. The mid-century years also marked an increase in serious consideration of the styles which might be suitable, or at least reasonably adaptable, to the climate. Henry Conybeare's **Church of S. John the Evangelist, Bombay** (1858), begun about the time S. Paul's, Calcutta, was completed, is an example. It has a high nave, a belfry and a tall broach spire. Windows are placed so as to assist cross-ventilation.

European expatriates erected impressive monuments to those of their number who died in service. Some early examples reflect local building traditions in their (Islamic and Hindu) forms. The cemeteries (p. 1263F) of the cities, hill stations and cantonments contain many fine examples of tombs in the changing architectural styles of the later eighteenth and early nineteenth centuries.

Although not built primarily as a mausoleum, it is perhaps appropriate at this point to include Claude Martin's **Constantia, Lucknow** (p. 1264A), sometimes referred to as a palace-tomb, still incomplete on his death in 1800. The building (now a boys' school, La Martinière) was conceived, probably by the enigmatic Martin himself, as a country house overlooking a lake. The two-storey building, which was approached by an impressive array of steps from the lakeside, has a squat four-storey central block surmounted by an open dome. The house has rooms at lower levels without natural light: one of these was the sepulchre which was to be occupied prematurely, before Martin could long enjoy his architecturally hybrid palace-folly with its guardian lions, mixed Composite orders and moghul pavilions. The house itself was not completed until later and the outward-curving wings were added in 1840.

Secular Buildings

Although Surat had been established over twenty years earlier, Madras (Fort S. George, q.v.) was the first centre to develop as a settlement and had pretensions to civic pride early in the eighteenth century. This development was somewhat retarded by the French capture and occupation for a few years in mid-century. The **Grand Arsenal, Madras** (1772), by Colonel Patrick Ross, mixes Classical with local forms. It preceded by a year the Regulating Act of 1773 which moved the locus of control in India to Calcutta. Nevertheless, Madras continued to grow into one of the finest of all Anglo-Indian cities. Classical buildings serving the Company lined the sea front and by 1800 a house at **Triplicane, Madras**, was being converted and enlarged as a new **Government House** by John Goldingham (1765–1849) (p. 1264B). Generally of three storeys, the house has deep colonnaded verandahs, carried on irregularly spaced coupled Tuscan columns. In the grounds, Goldingham added a free-standing **Banqueting Hall** (1802) (p. 1264B) – an octastyle Tuscan temple rising out of a single-storey terrace. An arcaded verandah with pilasters rising to a frieze with a balustrade above was added later. Buildings are faced in the white smooth chunam rendering so conducive to the execution of sharp detailing of Classical buildings.

The house in a garden compound was characteristic of the burgeoning Madras, and smaller flat-roofed private residences with Classical and Palladian detailing grew in popularity. Another of these larger semi-urban houses standing in substantial plots of land was modified to accommodate the **Madras Club** (p. 1267A) when it was founded in 1831, and many additions were made to it in various styles between this date and the end of the nineteenth century. One of them was by Robert Fellowes Chisholm (1840–1915), who designed a number of important buildings in Madras, including **university buildings** in the 1860s and **offices for the Board of Revenue** (1870). For the latter he was commissioned to modify and extend an eighteenth-century palace designed in the Islamic style. The result was a mixture of late Islamic forms, motifs and details with Victorian Gothic, in keeping with the existing turreted tower with its superimposed dome raised on an octagonal plinth. Chisholm also built in the Classical and Gothic styles, the latter exemplified in his **Post and Telegraph building, Madras** (1884) (p. 1267B).

Following the Regulating Act, the East India Company began began to turn more attention to Calcutta, which was named as the location for the seat of the new Governor General. The Company commissioned from Thomas Lyon a large new building to house its clerks – the **Writers' Building, Calcutta** (1780) (p. 1268A). It was a simple three-storey building with characteristic Georgian urban proportions, its plain lines broken only by a raised shallow central feature with Ionic pilasters. The building was much modified in the succeeding century, eventually entirely refaced in the late Victorian period and given central and end pavilions with ornate high-pitched roofs.

Government House, Calcutta (1799–1802) (p. 1268B), was designed by Captain Charles Wyatt (1758–1819), nephew of James Wyatt (q.v.). The plan is that of Robert Adam's Kedleston Hall, and the impressive gateways (p. 1268C) are based on the entrance screen of Syon House. But Charles Wyatt's Palladian house is modified to take account of the climate of Calcutta, with verandahs and a semicircular domed portico. The Governor-General's residence, **Barrackpore House** (1805–23) (p. 1269A), by Thomas Anbury (1760–1840) (later Major-General Sir Thomas), stands in a landscaped park on the east bank of the Hooghly, 22 km (14 miles) north of Calcutta, facing Serampore (under Danish control until 1845). The Tuscan-ordered building with a formal pedimented portico on one side rises one lofty storey above a ground floor with arched openings; there is a shallow attic beneath the parapeted flat roof.

Calcutta Town Hall (completed 1813) (p. 1269B), by Colonel John Garstin (1758–1820), continued in the Palladian mode – another Tuscan-columned structure facing onto the Maidan. From 1780 onwards large **town houses** evolved in the chosen residential areas such as **Chowringhee** (p. 1269C). In character they have much in common with the Nash Houses in Regent's Park, London, and continued the Palladian tradition introduced in **Warren Hastings's House at Alipur** of 1777. It was indeed not until well into the nineteenth century that the Greek Revival style was introduced, for example in the **Silver Mint, Calcutta** (1820s), by William Nairn Forbes, and continued in the 1840s in such buildings as the **Public Library, Calcutta** (1844) (originally Metcalfe Hall), by C. K. Robinson (died 1850).

The neo-Classical architecture of the eighteenth and early nineteenth centuries was more widespread, of course, than only the main centres of British

A. The Madras Club, Madras (modification from 1831 onwards). See p. 1266

B. Post and Telegraph building, Madras (1884). See p. 1266

A. The Writers' Building, Calcutta (1780). See p. 1266

B. Government House, Calcutta (1799–1802). See p. 1266

C. Government House, Calcutta: entrance screen

A. Barrackpore House, Barrackpore (1805–23). See p. 1266

B. Town Hall, Calcutta (1813). See p. 1266

C. Town houses, Chowringhee Road, Calcutta (1780–) (photographed in the nineteenth century). See p. 1266

activity in Madras and Calcutta. British Residents in other towns vied with each other to build fine, impressive government buildings. Examples were the splendid Palladian **Residency at Hyderabad**, begun in 1803 (p. 1271A), designed by Lieutenant Samuel Russell, and **Government House, Mysore** (1805) (p. 1271B), originally designed by the Resident himself, Colonel Wilks, in a Tuscan Doric style; there were later additions by de Havilland.

The full weight of mid-nineteenth-century eclecticism did not much impinge upon Indian neo-Classicism until after the transfer of power from the East India Company to the government at the end of 1858. It is exemplified in the work of Walter L. B. Granville (1819–74) who was well able to move out of the scholarly Classical style used in his fine **Post Office, Dalhousie Square, Calcutta** (1868) (p. 1272A), and immediately into the Gothic of his **High Court buildings, Calcutta** (p. 1272B), also built in the 1860s. By this time, however, interest was moving away from strife-torn upper India to the vigorous commercial centre of Bombay.

There had been an early settlement on the island of Bombay (see p. 1167), and it had consistently remained successful in trade right into the early nineteenth century, though overshadowed by the growth of wealth and power in the eastern and north-eastern regions. In the early 1860s the old walls of the fort at Bombay were finally demolished and the way was cleared for the extraordinary urban development of the next half-century or so.

The **Town Hall, Bombay** (begun 1820) (p. 1271C), by Lieutenant-Colonel Thomas Cowper (1781–1825), preceded this development. It is a distinguished Greek Revival building with a Doric order rising through two storeys above a rusticated ground floor, carrying pedimented central features on each side of the building – that on the entrance facade approached by a flight of steps the full width of the octastyle portico. Window canopies to the piano nobile were included in the original design of the building, which was completed by others after Cowper's death.

The first major urban development, **Elphinstone Circle** (p. 1273A), was designed as a deep crescent of commercial buildings with the Town Hall at its open end. It consists of individual buildings in a wide range of Renaissance and Victorian Gothic styles, mostly with arcaded verandahs or covered balconies of imported prefabricated ironwork.

There followed in Bombay during the 1870s what would have been a spectacular achievement in realising a range of major public buildings in any context (p. 1273D) – much more so in what began as little more than a trading settlement, even though a successful one. Within ten years or so Henry St Clair Wilkins (1828–96) (an engineer, later General Sir Henry) had produced the **Public Works Office** (1872), and the new **Secretariat** (1874) (p. 1273D), both typical of the contemporary High Victorian Gothic buildings being erected in London with their polychromatic arch voussoirs and spandrel panels and their high roofs; James Trubshawe had built the **Post Office** (early 1870s) (p. 1273B) and the **Telegraph Office** (1874); the **Law Courts** (1879) (p. 1273C) had been built by Lieutenant-Colonel William Augustus Fuller (1828–1902), an enginer who had worked with Wilkins, as a vast, stone, mainly four-storey building with dormer windows in a high-pitched roof, the eaves of which are not only set behind but raised above the level of a balustraded parapet – the wholly Victorian Gothic composition is symmetrical about an enormous square central tower with an overwhelming high roof, pinnacled corner turrets responding to the adjacent octagonal corner staircase towers; and last but not least in this long line of major structures, Sir George Gilbert Scott had designed and others had built **Bombay University Convocation Hall** and the **University Library** with its tower (1878) (p. 1273D). The hall is in a French Gothic style, with a balustraded apse, its windows reminiscent of the aisles of Bayeux, and the library is part-Venetian, with corner staircase towers with spiralling arcades and a very tall square clock-tower, the middle levels of which are reminiscent of Giotto's tower, Florence.

The remarkable range of secular Victorian Gothic buildings in Bombay included the **Victoria Railway Terminus** (completed 1887) p. 1277B), by Frederick William Stevens (1848–1900). Though influenced by British railway Gothic, it is a splendid and stylish building in its own right, as are the numerous small stations, also in the Gothic style, along the two Bombay lines. The Gothic precedents of the Victoria Terminus are in no way belittled by the minimal introduction of Indo-Islamic character – a reflection of Stevens's interest in linking indigenous to European forms. This was a development to continue from this time and into the twentieth century in buildings such as the **Law Courts, Madras** (1892), and the **National Art Gallery**, Madras, both by Henry Irwin (1841–1922), and later in Hyderabad and elsewhere by such architects as Vincent Jerome Esch (1876–1950).

Even during the second half of the nineteenth century, however, neo-Classical and Italianate buildings were erected. In the towns, barracks lent themselves to a simplified arcaded style, well exemplified in the **Chevron Barracks, Colombo, Sri Lanka** (early nineteenth century) (p. 1275A), and later in J. G. Smithers's **Museum**, also in **Colombo** (1876) (p. 1275B): the rusticated ground floor carries arcaded verandahs recalling those in the courtyard of the late sixteenth-century Palazzo Borghese in Rome, though the Ionic order is of less light and elegant proportions. The central entrance feature above the *porte-cochère* is pedimented and the whole building has a parapet balustrade concealing shallow pitched

A. Residency, Hyderabad (begun 1803). See p. 1270

B. Government House, Mysore (1805). See p. 1270

C. Town Hall, Bombay (1820–). See p. 1270

A. Post Office, Dalhousie Square, Calcutta (1868). See p. 1270

B. High Court, Calcutta (1860s). See p. 1270

A. Elphinstone Circle, Bombay (1860s). See p. 1270

B. Post Office, Bombay (1870s). See p. 1270

C. The Law Courts, Bombay (1879). See p. 1270

D. Nineteenth-century public buildings, Bombay. See p. 1270

roofs. A somewhat earlier; more distinguished and reminiscent example of the Italianate style in India is **Government House, Poona** (p. 1275C), with its tall tower. It was designed in the 1860s by the Bombay architect, James Trubshawe. But palazzo architecture of some distinction is to be found in town houses (p. 1275D) built well into the twentieth century in many parts of the region, usually the work of unknown architects or engineers employed by the government.

Other urban buildings which helped determine the character of towns in the late eighteenth and early nineteenth centuries were hotels and department stores. The list of hotels is long and distinguished and includes the **Grand Hotel, Calcutta** (p. 1277A), the **Taj Mahal Hotel, Bombay**, the **Coromandel Hotel, Madras**, and the **Grand Orient (now Taprobane) Hotel, Colombo** (p. 1276A). The symbolic content of the facades (aimed at raising the interest of visitors seeing the hotels for the first time, often from the sea) was considerable and varied, and it is appropriate that there are several examples, including the Taprobane, in which ground-floor arcades cover the public footpaths to provide shade: the latter examples is in the same street and adjacent to **Cargil's Department Store** (p. 1276B), which was established in 1844; the present building from the turn of the century also boasts cloistered pavements, and despite its rusticated arches, low-relief panels and segmental pedimented features at parapet level, retains a suggestion of oriental imagery. The glazed roof serves to illuminate a translucent ceiling dome to bring daylight deep into the building.

Perhaps the most widely influential building type developed in the European colonial period in India is the bungalow. The word came to be used by the British to denote any house shaded from the sun on one or more of its walls with an open-sided, roofed area called a verandah. The building type was exported to every part of the world to which the British went, as well as to Britain itself. In this region the bungalow was built in town, cantonment and hill station from the north to the far south: examples are a **bungalow in Punjab** (early nineteenth century) (p. 1276C) in the north, and a somewhat later **bungalow near Kandy, Sri Lanka** (p. 1276D). These by no means cover the historical or the stylistic range, which runs from early neo-Classical in the seventeenth and eighteenth centuries to picturesque, Gothic or merely traditional to the location, but they give an indication of the variety, examples of which are given in other chapters of this part of the book.

The integration of Islamic and Hindu architectural character with the European styles has been briefly mentioned above, and it was attempted with varying degrees of success towards the end of the nineteenth century. The building which best expresses pride in imperial achievement in India is the **Victoria Memorial, Calcutta** (completed 1921) (see Chapter 57), by Sir William Emerson (1843–1924), which also succeeds in making wholly integrated though clear references to Moghul Islamic features. For Sir Edwin Lutyen's work at New Delhi see Chapter 57).

Other European Settlements

The Danes were trading on the river Hooghly as early as 1620 and founded a settlement named **Tranquebar** and a century later **Frederiksnagore**, later renamed Serampore, near to Calcutta. Permanent buildings in the neo-Classical style were built in **Serampore**, of which the best-known is the **Church of S. Olav** (1821). Serampore was ceded to the British in 1845.

France had founded **Pondicherry**, a hundred miles south of Madras, by 1674, and **Chandernagore** in Bengal followed in 1690. Pondicherry was the main French settlement on the Coromandel coast and had a small star-shaped fort which was expanded and improved during Lenoir's governorship in the early eighteenth century. Long ramparts linked the fort to two large urban precincts. Chandernagore was a simple fortified enclave on the Hooghly, its high walls pierced by a monumental Baroque portal leading to the main administrative building on the opposite side of the compound. It was destroyed by the British in 1758. The conflict with France ended and its armies withdrew from India after the British recaptured Madras in 1761.

A. Chevron Barracks, Colombo, Sri Lanka (early nineteenth century). See p. 1270

B. Museum, Colombo, Sri Lanka (1876). See p. 1270

C. Government House, Poona (1860s). See p. 1274

D. Town house, Colombo (late nineteenth century). See p. 1274

A. Grand Orient (Taprobane) Hotel, Colombo. See p. 1274

B. Cargill's Department Store, Colombo (established 1844). See p. 1274

C. (*above*)
Bungalow, Punjab (early nineteenth century). See p. 1274

D. (*left*)
Bungalow near Kandy, Sri Lanka (mid-nineteenth century). See p. 1274

A. Grand Hotel, Calcutta. See p. 1274

B. Victoria Railway Terminus, Bombay (completed 1887): detail of elevation. See p. 1270

Chapter 42
AUSTRALASIA

Architectural Character

Australia: 1788 to 1830

After the first Government House in Sydney (1788) the amount of building in the early years was limited both by the rigours of pioneer circumstances and by the constraints imposed by the home government. Nevertheless in Macquarie Street, Sydney, two substantial pre-1820 buildings survive. They were originally wings of the first public hospital, and were built between 1810 and 1817 by an architect whose identity is uncertain. The details are simple and coarse, but they have verandahs on each of two storeys which give them a characteristic colonial appearance, although the acceptance of verandahs in Australia was not immediate.

The appearance produced by verandahs was no doubt the result of inter-colonial exchange, especially through military men who had served in India, Africa, Canada or the West Indies, and who felt that the Australian summers warranted the use of architectural features of this kind. One of them was Lieutenant John Watts, who arrived in Sydney in 1814. He had been in Jamaica and turned his hand to architectural design several times. He was responsible for the Military Hospital (1814), of which portions still survive in the premises of the National Trust of New South Wales and at Parramatta for the alternative Government House, the Lancer Barracks, and the Norman-style towers added to S. John's Church in 1818.

After the Royal Engineer Corps was established in Australia in 1835, considerable contributions to civil and military architecture were made by army officers. Their commander, Major George Barney, was responsible for many buildings: he provided the initial plans for two prisons, one at Darlinghurst, East Sydney (1835–41), still used today, and another on Norfolk Island (1835–46), long since demolished. Both prisons had cell blocks radiating from a central point.

During his term as New South Wales's Governor (1809–22), Lachlan Macquarie devoted a large portion of the state's meagre resources to the development of townships including Sydney, Parramatta and five other new settlements. Macquarie met opposition from the leading free settlers such as John Macarthur, who wanted the resources dedicated to the sheep industry, as did the home government, but he had kindled a spark of civic pride which was not extinguished when he was superseded.

Francis Greenway (1777–1837) was discovered among the convicts by Macquarie in 1814, and appointed Civil Architect. Originally from Bristol, he had been in partnership with two of his brothers, Oliver and John, in a firm of architects, builders and stonemasons. In 1812 Francis was found guilty of forging a memorandum of contract, and a death sentence was commuted to fourteen years transportation to the penal colony.

In the Sydney region Greenway led the way to higher standards with well-designed and well-built official buildings, though they were still simple and mostly of red brick. In style they are late Georgian of a domestic character. The Barracks for Convicts (1817–19) and S. James's Church (1819–24), both in Sydney, and S. Matthew's Church at Windsor (1818–20), 35 km (22 miles) from Sydney, are leading examples of his work. The effective period of Greenway's career in Sydney was very brief – from 1814 to 1822 – and greatly diminished on the departure of his patron, Governor Macquarie.

Australia: 1830 to 1850

At least two authors have used the term 'golden decade' to describe the 1830s in New South Wales, though the gold rush was not until the 1850s. Their intention is to identify the 1830s as the first and only decade between 1788 and 1850 which was sufficiently prosperous and calm to produce a series of relatively luxurious houses and other buildings. An economic recession abruptly ended the building activity and terminated the pioneer era.

Although his intention had been to set up as a sheep farmer, architect John Verge (1782–1862) was persuaded to return to his profession for a time when

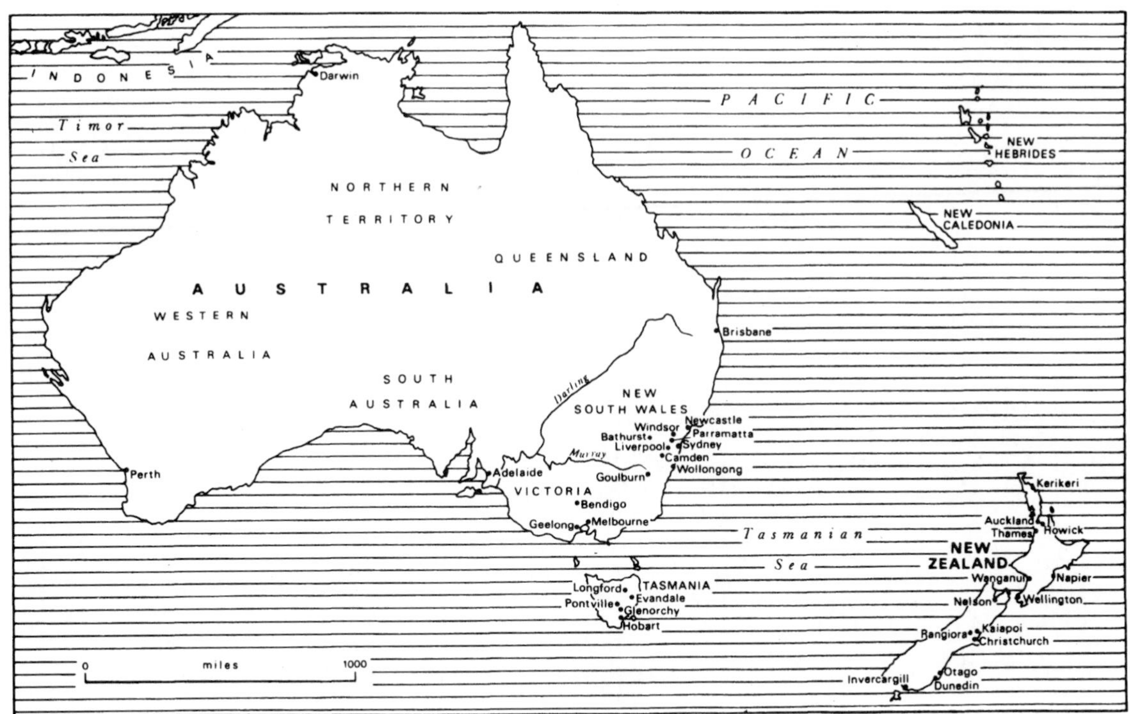

Australasia

he arrived in Australia at the end of the 1820s. Fourteen of his buildings still stand. They include early revivals of Greek, Tudor, Castellated and Chinese styles, but are primarily later Georgian with colonial additions such as verandahs. The two best-known are Elizabeth Bay House (1830s) and Camden Park (1832), the latter for John Macarthur.

Numerous homesteads exist for which no records have survived. They were sometimes designed by the owners, using books of examples, or with the help of unidentified architects. National affection for the homesteads was first awakened in 1924 by Hardy Wilson with his folio volume *Old Colonial Architecture in New South Wales and Tasmania*. Today these mostly anonymous houses are regarded as especially Australian: a single storey was preferred, and their character was often dominated by verandahs and by the steep roofs demanded by the early roofing materials.

A new Government House (p. 1280B) was constructed in Sydney in the late 1830s: the work was supervised by Lewis but designed in 1834 by Edward Blore, the British architect, who never visited Australia. This was a wholly Gothic Revival building, anticipated but not matched by Greenway's earlier stables buildings (1817) for Government House. The first true Gothic Revival practitioner in Australia was Edmund T. Blacket, who arrived in 1842 from London, with an introduction to the recently created Bishop of All Australia, William Broughton. Sydney's Anglican Cathedral, S. Andrew's, had been started by James Hume but in 1845 it was handed over to Blacket and completed by him, and was soon to be followed by other notable churches including S. Mark's, Darling Point, Sydney, begun in 1848.

In early Tasmania, the two outstanding designers were John Lee Archer (1791–1852) from Ireland, who was appointed Colonial Engineer and Architect, and James Blackburn (1803–54) an ex-convict from England, who like Greenway was transported for forgery. S. George's Church, Hobart, was begun by Archer in the Georgian manner (1837), and Blackburn added an octagonal tower in 1847. The latter also helped Lady Jane Franklin with a Greek Revival museum in Hobart in 1843.

There were also settlements in other parts of New South Wales and Tasmania, and on Norfolk Island, some 1600 km (1000 miles) to the east in the Pacific. All consisted of vernacular or simple Georgian buildings for domestic, public or commercial uses. The character of these buildings depended upon local materials. Bricks were soft, and had to be plastered over. In some regions timber or stone was available but joinery was expensive and was therefore kept

A. Elizabeth Farm, Parramatta. See p. 1289

B. Government House, Sydney (1830s). See p. 1279

simple. Roofs were sometimes covered with bark or rough thatch, but were more commonly shingled and constructed at steep pitches of 40° or more.

Sydney still reflects the early settlement patterns with streets straggling along a tiny stream leading to the harbour, or the more orderly surrounding developments of the Macquarie period. Other towns were on simple rectilinear grids, the work of official surveyors to facilitate the sale of building plots by the Crown. The exception was Adelaide, whose independent Surveyor, Colonel William Light, set out four grids related to the contours. He included six generous squares in his plan and surrounded the whole with belts of parkland.

New Zealand: before 1860

The first settlements in New Zealand predated by two decades the proclamation of its colonial status in 1840. They were missions and trading posts, usually temporary constructions, but around the Bay of Islands, for example, a few more permanent and elegant buildings appeared.

The first towns to grow after the proclamation of 1840 were Auckland (then the seat of government), Wellington and New Plymouth on the North Island, and Nelson, just across Cook Strait, on the South Island.

The history of architecture in New Zealand is similar to that of Australia, beginning with domestic scale buildings, in the late Georgian and Regency styles, followed by a variety of Classical styles for most public buildings and a mediaeval revival for ecclesiastical buildings, a few houses and, as in Britain, a few other major buildings. New Zealand was colonised two generations later than Sydney, and the impact of the Picturesque and Romantic was greater. When the seat of government was moved from Auckland to Wellington in 1865, it was to a Gothic building, later extended in the same style, albeit in timber construction. By contrast, administrative buildings in Australia were almost invariably Classical in style.

New Zealand's most distinctive and recognisable buildings are the homesteads, especially in the Canterbury, Marlborough, Hawkes Bay, Wairarapa and Manawatu districts. The earliest homesteads are often rectangular in plan with upper storeys contained within gabled roofs and naturally lit with large dormer windows. The windows of the lower storeys were occasionally casements, but more usually of double-hung sash variety. An outstanding example is Terrace Station, Canterbury (*c.* 1853 and later) (p. 1282A) by an unknown architect.

The second distinctive type of building in early New Zealand was the so-called Selwyn-style church, mostly to be found in and around Auckland. They were timber churches, the designs for which were developed jointly by Bishop Selwyn and Frederick Thatcher. They rely mainly upon clear expression of framed and braced wood construction with only limited reference to the historical styles. The finest surviving example is Old S. Paul's in Wellington (p. 1294B). There were also numerous outstanding neo-Gothic stone churches, such as First Church, Dunedin and Christchurch Cathedral, but they were related primarily to the urban growth following the gold rush, which began in 1862.

In a country which stretches more than a thousand miles from north to south and has a climate ranging from subtropical to something akin to that of northern Scotland, it is to be expected that there would be regional differences in its architecture. And the climatic differences were accentuated by the predominance of Scottish settlers in Otago in the south as well as by the range of available building materials – kauri forests in the north and limestone in the south.

Verandahs and overhanging eaves, which characterise northern houses, are less common by the time one reaches Otago, while stone buildings such as those in Christchurch, Dunedin and Oamaru are comparatively rare in the north, where stuccoed brickwork was the usual alternative to timber construction. Similarly, decorative cast iron, introduced to Dunedin by Melbourne architects following the gold boom of the 1860s and subsequently manufactured by Dunedin iron founders, is seldom found in the north. The commercial importance of Auckland, with its busy harbour, and the pastoral importance of Canterbury, Otago, Southland and Hawkes Bay contributed to the development of large country homesteads and huge woolsheds on the sheep stations.

Compared with the smaller towns of Australia, the New Zealand counterparts sometimes have an unexpected grace, conveyed by modest but charming churches, post offices, halls, banks and shops, especially when combined with a good town plan as in Feilding, or with generous tree-planting as in Cambridge.

Maori Architecture. Though it cannot be easily related to architecture derived from Europe, there were also some notable Maori buildings constructed in the nineteenth century, often combining European building methods with traditional indigenous detailing and decoration. A few churches are regarded with pride. One of these is Rangiate Church at Otaki, whose 26 m (86 ft) totara ridge beam is supported by three 12 m (40 ft) high adzed totara tree trunks. The reeded walls and decorated rafters of the interior integrate comfortably with the lancet windows which provide its daylight.

The other main building form was the whare runanga or meeting house, a long rectangular building under a low-pitched gable-ended roof with a richly decorated and carved porch at one end (p. 1282B).

A. Terrace Station homestead, Canterbury (*c.* 1853–). See p. 1281

B. Taranui Te Pokiha's house, Maketu. See p. 1281

The rafters were painted with highly developed linear patterns. Fine tukutuku weaving and carved wall panels gave distinction to the dimly lit interior. An ancestor figure frequently supported the central roof post. Numbers of these meeting houses, particularly in the areas of greater Maori population in the North Island, have been recently restored.

Sleeping houses were generally similar to the whare runanga in form but lacked the elaborate carving and painted decoration. They were also very much smaller and were sometimes built with side-porches instead of the traditional end-porch. Some very few Maori buildings, such as the prophet Rua's temple at Maungapohatu, took the form of a rotunda with a conical roof. The form was noted by early travellers to New Zealand but was built to larger sizes under European influence.

Australia: 1850–1900

In mid-century there came a dramatic agent for change – gold. In Australia the gold rushes began in 1851 and in New Zealand they began ten years later. The architectural context changed from pioneer settlements to wealthy, ambitious cities supporting many well-trained architects who had relatively easy access to building materials, skilled craftsmen and publications, despite the distance from Britain. The changes were rapid, well-funded and sometimes quite lavish, and architectural comparisons of Melbourne and Sydney with Birmingham and Leeds, or Chicago and New York, began to have some validity.

New towns created near the gold fields included the New South Wales towns of Bathurst and Goulburn, and, in Victoria, Ballarat and Bendigo. Geelong and Melbourne were Victoria's pre-gold settlements and Melbourne emerged in this period as Victoria's capital; it was the centre of government, finance and commerce, and continued its phenomenal growth until the 1890s. Characteristically, for example, a double ceremony in 1852 inaugurated both Melbourne University and the city library on a single day. Both buildings had been the subject of architectural competitions, won by F. M. White and Joseph Reed respectively. Significantly, also in Melbourne, a new Treasury building, the clearing house for gold, was built in 1857–62. The neo-Renaissance design is usually attributed to a nineteen-year-old, J. J. Clark, although Captain Charles Pasley, Colonial Architect and Engineer, may have guided the young Clark's hand. A later attribution to Clark, also much admired, is the Melbourne Mint, 1869–70, but when he moved for a while to Queensland as Colonial Architect and undertook the Treasury there in 1883, the result was less impressive.

The university in Sydney was founded in 1850 and had been accommodated temporarily in part of a school building. After the gold rush (1852), 52 ha (128 acres) just south of the township were reserved for a new campus. The initial buildings still stand and they dominated the southern approaches to Sydney until modern buildings obscured them in recent years. When it was decided that a late Tudor or an Elizabethan design was to be preferred, Edmund Blacket (1817–83) was commissioned because of his recognised skills in mediaeval revival, which had been demonstrated in several churches executed after his recent arrival from England.

Architects in Australasia after 1850 joined wholeheartedly in the eclecticism of the period. Australia's cities and leading towns were in touch with English or American towns and were equally progressive, especially considering that little was built before the gold rush of the 1850s and an abrupt end to development was brought about by financial depression in the early 1890s. The most favoured style was neo-Renaissance (of several different kinds), except for church and college buildings which were usually in the Tudor or Gothic Revival style. Both were explored and adapted from British or American models, as well as by vigorous local invention and innovation. The Australian variations of style were wide-ranging. First, there were the simple astylar buildings on palazzo models (banks and city buildings, Wardell's New South Wales Club, the Melbourne Mint and Customs building and Hunter's Hobart Town Hall). Second, the Venetian and Romanesque styles, in which were to be found the more sculptural devices of loggia, arcade, trefoil window and carved frieze (again banks and the more lavish public offices such as the Treasury at Melbourne and the Lands Department in Sydney). The Italianate style, again using palazzo models but more modern (Victorian) in its rhythmic grouping of elements; related versions (used for houses and public buildings in small towns) have broad roof-overhangs and exposed rafters or belvedere towers. The Second Empire style was distinguished by mansard or curved roofs (town halls and major hotels) and the neo-Classical version of Second Empire in which the forms are dominated by giant Classical orders (as in the Melbourne Parliament building and South Melbourne Town Hall, 1880, by Charles Webb).

Towers with clocks or viewing platforms and domes were not uncommon in public buildings of the period, and cast iron was frequently used decoratively, especially on buildings with verandahs (houses, minor hotels or public houses). The so-called Boom style emerged as a combination of these features and is associated with the 1880s and early 1890s, especially in Melbourne, which experienced a frenzied decade of property development. Two examples of the Boom style are the later stages of Sydney Town Hall, completed in 1888, and the Princess Theatre, Melbourne (1887). Finally there was neo-Baroque, of which there are only a few examples of distinction, the best being His Majesty's Theatre in Perth.

Neo-Gothic dominated the architecture of religious and educational buildings, and played a small but significant part in domestic buildings. There is only one notable example of its application in commercial buildings, a renowned group of office buildings in Collins Street, Melbourne.

On the whole, despite occasional cries of Popishness, Gothic was adopted by all denominations for church buildings. The best-known exceptions are the Congregational churches in Sydney, Adelaide and Melbourne. Blacket has already been named as the first true practitioner of neo-Gothic in Australia, but there were numerous earlier examples of churches with pointed arches from *c.* 1820 onwards. The forms of church Gothic used were usually Early English or Decorated, and this continued late into the century. High Gothic inventiveness, in the manner of Butterfield for instance, was not often employed, but one architect seems to have been sensitive to the later events of the Gothic Revival, namely ex-American J. Horbury Hunt, who built two brick Anglican Cathedrals – S. Peter's, Armidale (1875) and Christ Church, Newcastle, New South Wales (1869–94).

Butterfield himself never visited Australia, but twice provided designs for Anglican cathedrals, neither of which was completed as he intended. S. Peter's Cathedral, Adelaide (begun 1869) was completed by E. J. Woods (1904). S. Paul's, Melbourne, was begun in 1877 and progressed under local supervision until 1883, when Butterfield resigned. Joseph Reed undertook to complete it 'as Mr Butterfield intended', but no tower or spire was built until the 1930s when the cathedral was eventually completed by John Barr of Sydney.

John L. Pearson's design for the Anglican Cathedral of Brisbane is another imported Gothic design (1887, built 1901–10 and 1960–8). It has an impressive interior but is incomplete to this day.

Wardell, after Blacket the architect who produced the most important Gothic church buildings in Australia, was responsible for the two largest Catholic churches: S. Patrick's Cathedral, Melbourne, and S. Mary's Cathedral, Sydney. For S. Patrick's (1858) he used the dark Melbourne basalt with little detail or enrichment but with a chevet apsidal east end, a tall tower and a spire producing an elegance which makes an important contribution to Melbourne's urban architecture.

There was not in Australia much inclination to indulge in colourful and crafted materials, except in a few houses. Exceptions occurred in the public works of Barnet's successor, Walter Liberty Vernon, the New South Wales Colonial Architect from 1890, and in educational buildings for New South Wales designed by H. H. Kemp, for example, in whose initial buildings for Sydney Technical College (1890–3) relief panels in bright terracotta were used. The same feature was repeated in the Museum of Applied Arts and Technology, 1892. Such Schools may have helped form public expectations which were later transferred to house design. Other instances can be seen in Victoria, for example in schools by H. R. Bastow, and suburban state schools, such as Surrey Hills (1890) by J. T. Kelleher.

The architects practising in Australia were almost all British trained. An outstanding exception was J. Horbury Hunt, who arrived from Boston in 1863. Australian-born and locally articled architects were rare. One of the earliest, though late in the century, was H. Desbrowe Annear (1866–1933), born in Bendigo and trained with William Salway in Melbourne.

In the decades following the gold rushes, the architectural profession increased in numbers; a few of its leading members are mentioned below.

Joseph Reed (1823–90) of Melbourne worked in both the Classical and Gothic styles and introduced polychrome brickwork and the Italian Romanesque style. He arrived from England with the gold rush, and like other architects found the demand for his professional services overwhelming. He was a versatile architect who built up a large practice working with various partners, the first and longest-lasting of them being Frederick Barnes. Reed's buildings included Melbourne Public Library (1854) and Geelong Town Hall (1854), both in the Renaissance style, Melbourne Town Hall (1867) in Second Empire Classical, central city churches for Methodists (1858, Gothic), Baptists (1862, Classical) and Presbyterians (1873, Gothic). He completed S. Paul's Church of England Cathedral (1884–90) and with N. B. Tappin (by then Reed's partner) designed the Church of the Sacred Heart, Bendigo in 1886 (constructed 1896–1901, 1906, 1960–73).

After a European tour in 1863 he introduced polychrome brickwork, inspired by the North Italian Romanesque. His best-known building in this style is the Independent Church (1866), Collins Street, Melbourne.

James J. Barnet (1827–1904) of Sydney was the longest serving and most successful of the official architects in the Australian colonies. In his period as Colonial Architect (1862–90) New South Wales was prosperous and growing. He was a Scot who went to London at the age of sixteen and was at first apprenticed to a builder then studied drawing with W. Dyce, RA, and architecture with C. J. Richardson. He emigrated in 1854.

The architecture Barnet and his colleagues produced was competent neo-Renaissance in style, usually well built in stone. His buildings showed little inclination towards the increased complexity and use of colour typical of contemporary private architects. His successor in 1890, W. L. Vernon, seemed progressive by comparison, when he immediately introduced colourful brickwork and *fin de siècle* forms.

Barnet's leading works were: in Sydney, buildings for the Lands Department, the Colonial Secretary's Department and the General Post Office; in Goulburn, the Law Courts; in Bathurst, the administrative group – Law Courts, Post and Telegraph Offices and Lands Department. He was responsible for more than 1500 projects throughout his large territory. Public service buildings made up the heart of every country town, and provided the only permanent and careful design among private buildings, which were mainly temporary and amateur by comparison. Nineteenth-century post and telegraph offices, courts and police premises, lands and other administration offices and (after 1872) schools are still in many cases the most interesting buildings in these smaller towns.

William Wilkinson Wardell (1823–99) reached Melbourne in 1858, already experienced both as an engineer and as an architect. From 1859 he was successively Chief Architect to the Department of Works, Victoria, and Inspector General, before running a flourishing practice, chiefly carrying out ecclesiastical work, such as S. John the Evangelist, Toorak, Melbourne (1860–73), S. John's College, Sydney University (1858), S. Mary's Cathedral, Hobart (1876), and S. Mary's Cathedral, Sydney (1865). A victim of government expenditure cuts in 1878, he promptly moved to Sydney, where the Cathedral was advancing, and continued there until his death. One of his last works was the Jesuit Church of S. Ignatius, Richmond, Melbourne. In London, Wardell had met both A. W. Pugin and Cardinal Newman, who encouraged his skill in the Gothic style and under their influence he was converted to Catholicism.

John Horbury Hunt (1838–1904) came to Sydney in 1863 from Boston where he had trained under Charles Sleeper, and later under E. C. Cabot. He referred to Cabot, whose practice consisted largely of 'country houses ... in the voguish picturesque style', as his master, and work of this kind in suburb and country constitutes the major portion of Hunt's work in Australia. The largest of his many houses was Booloominbah, Armidale, in northern New South Wales, built in 1887 for the White family. The house is now the centre of the campus of the University of New England. It is rambling and solid, built in red brick with red-tiled roofs, and contains many surprising room arrangements. More modest houses in Sydney, on the other hand, are single-minded and coherent, with tall gables, wood-shingled roofs and walls in imitation of the North American shingle style of the time, which was little used in Australia. Hunt was the master of expressive timber framing and shingle finishes.

In addition to houses, Hunt was regularly involved with church buildings. The three largest were provincial Anglican Cathedrals – S. Peter's at Armidale (1871–97), Christ Church at Grafton (1874–84) and Christ Church at Newcastle (1885–95). In these he showed himself to be more closely in sympathy with High Victorian tendencies than other church designers in Australia. Perhaps his most impressive church, however, was almost his last, the Chapel for the Convent of the Sacred Heart, Rose Bay, Sydney (1895–1900). The Chapel is a simple volume with a stone ceiling formed from a single, pointed barrel vault with ribs springing from wall surfaces without column or pier. It has narrow, deeply embrasured Early English windows.

The discussion above has been concerned primarily with government buildings of various kinds and with ecclesiastical architecture, the cynosure of the best professional attention in the rapidly growing colonies of the European powers. But other building types were produced – commercial, industrial and domestic, though they were often less favoured with patronage and skill.

Banks

Although the banks and insurance companies commissioned many buildings, few of the large, head-office buildings have survived. As now, they used buildings to convey prestige, good judgement and permanence. Design was centralised in the capital cities. For example, A. M. Henderson was responsible for all the premises of the Bank of Australasia throughout Victoria. An early example was the Collins Street Bank of New South Wales, in Melbourne: the facade of this building has been incorporated into a building for Melbourne University. Built in 1854, it was designed by Reed, who used Sansovino's Library of S. Mark, Venice, as a model. In Adelaide there is a small but fine Bank of South Australia (1876–7) by Lloyd Taylor of Melbourne with E. L. Wright of Adelaide which has a rich – even crowded – facade.

Shopping Arcades

Regrettably, many of the nineteenth-century arcades have not survived. A few which have are the Royal Arcade, Melbourne (1869), by Charles Webb, the Block Arcade and Strand Arcade, Sydney (*c.* 1891), by J. B. Spencer, and the Adelaide and Gays Arcade in Adelaide (1885) by James Cumming. The largest to survive however, is the Victoria Arcade, Sydney, restored in the 1980s after fifty years of occupation as offices. The original building of 1893 by the then City Architect, George McRae (later to be State Architect), was a combination of market, hotel, offices, shops and two arcades. It is a large stone building in a style dubbed by its architect 'American Romanesque'. It is roofed with one major and sixteen minor domes, all copper clad, and its carved ornamentation is reminiscent of Louis Sullivan in the period of the Auditorium Building in Chicago, which predated the arcade by seven years or so.

Office Buildings

Few commercial office buildings in Australia were distinguished architecturally. As technology developed, buildings began to rise in height and in Melbourne in the 1880s, for example, the City Council imposed a maximum height of 40 m (132 ft). The Australia Building in Elizabeth Street, Melbourne (1886) was built to a height of 46 m (150 ft) before the limit was imposed, and remained the highest building in the town for many years. Designed by Henry Kemp in the free Classical style with a Picturesque skyline, it had an iron frame internally but the external, red-brick and granite walls were load-bearing. The lift was hydraulic, and drew upon pressure-mains installed under many streets for the purpose.

The offices for the Life Assurance Company of the United States, in George Street, Sydney (1890), was designed by Edward Raht, an American. Also in the 'American Romanesque' style, the building has a rusticated stone arch at ground-floor level, and a giant three-storey arcade carrying applied columns above.

The group of Gothic Revival commercial buildings in Melbourne includes The Rialto (1890–1) by Comely and Guillam, Olderfleet (1889–90) and the old Stock Exchange (1888–91), both by William Pitt. The inspiration for such excursions into Gothic may have been Wardell's nearby English Scottish and Australian Bank (1883–7), with its distinguished exterior and interior detailing, its Gothic banking halls and unique balconies in the Venetian style.

Hotels

In Australia the term 'hotel' is used for everything from the international grand hotel to a public house without bedrooms. Nineteenth-century Australia was rich in the former, but many of them have been lost.

The Windsor Hotel, Melbourne (1883–8) by Charles Webb is one which remains. In Sydney, while none of the grander examples have survived, during the demolition of Tattersall's Hotel its all-marble saloon bar was reconstructed on an upper floor of the new Hilton Hotel. Only the Palace Hotel survives in Perth.

The lesser old hotels, some of them little more than public houses, remain in large numbers in central areas, suburbs and country towns. Many of them have verandahs and balconies; decoration may include cast iron, turned or fretted woodwork, and occasionally coloured glass. Only a few of hundreds can be mentioned: the Botanic Hotel, Adelaide (1876–7) (p. 1287A) by M. McMullen, with its spectacular three-tier verandah of later date (1900) decorated with wrought iron; the Shamrock Hotel in Bendigo (1897), a somewhat gaunt but elaborate building with its Second Empire masonry detailing which rises three storeys above an iron-clad two-decker verandah; and the former Commercial Hotel in Quay Street, Townsville (1898), a three-decker.

Theatres

The theatre thrived in nineteenth-century Australia and ranged from troupes of entertainers in the music-halls of the gold fields, to opera and drama in the cities. One early theatre still in use is the Theatre Royal, Hobart (1837). The interior of the building is intact although the exterior has been changed. The intimacy and charm of the interior is in sharp contrast to the grandiose Princess Theatre, Melbourne (1887), designed by William Pitt in the Second Empire Boom style.

Homesteads

Homesteads have not usually been architecturally distinguished, and adopted the Georgian, Victorian and Queen Anne styles seen in the towns. They are large, single-storey and usually rambling buildings clustered around courtyards and water-wells. Occasionally notable architects were involved, especially when a family rebuilt after prosperous times. In Queensland, a distinctive house form evolved with verandahs and with the main storey raised on wooden stilts. The planning of these houses was often very open, in the interests of maximum ventilation in the tropical climate.

Other Domestic Architecture

Terraced houses were built in the earliest streets and later in the suburbs along the tram and train routes which were constructed up to the 1880s. Villas for wealthier people were also built from the earliest days in locations such as South Yarra in Melbourne, and Potts Point and Paddington, Sydney, where they could be set in spacious gardens. For the middle classes it was a little later, from the 1860s onwards, for example at Hawthorn in Melbourne. Garden suburbs followed after 1900.

Architects such as Verge, Blacket and Reed were sometimes involved in the design of early terraces and villas, but in many cases architects have not been identified for the numerous large suburban houses which testify to the post-gold-rush wealth.

In the inner suburbs of Melbourne and Sydney, terrace housing with prominent party walls and decorative cast-iron features created a highly distinctive character, for example at Carlton in Melbourne and Paddington in Sydney, which can be rivalled in few other places in the world (comparisons are made with New Orleans).

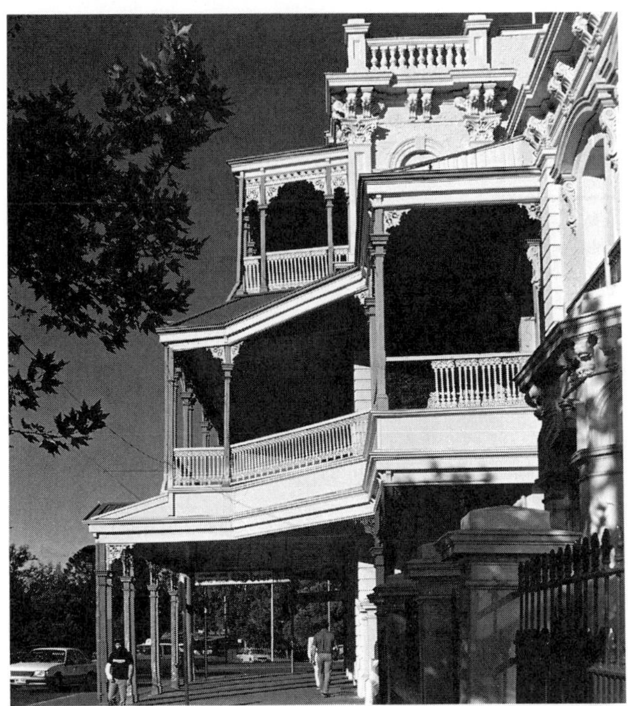

A. Botanic Hotel, Adelaide (1876–7). See p. 1286

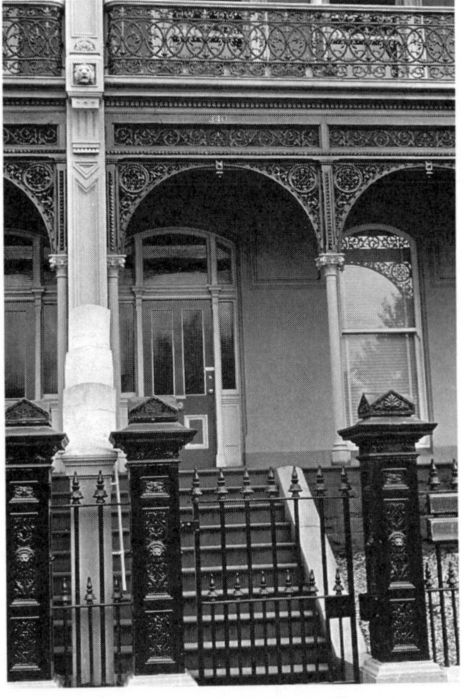

B. Terrace houses, Carlton, Melbourne. See p. 1306

C. Terrace housing, Paddington, Sydney. See p. 1306

PROVINCIAL GOVERNMENT BUILDINGS CHRISTCHURCH
PLAN A
LEGEND
a· TIMBER BLOCK 1859-61
b· STONE COUNCIL CHAMBER 1865
c· BELLAMY'S 1865
PLAN SCALE: MTR FT
B BAY WINDOW
C NORTH ELEVATION
S. MARY'S CATHEDRAL SYDNEY
PLAN D
SPIRE NOT BUILT
SCALE FOR PLAN 0 30 60 90 120 150 FT
0 15 30 45 MTR
E SECTION
F WEST ELEVATION
UNIVERSITY OF SYDNEY
PLAN G
H ORIGINAL TOWER
MTR FT
PLAN SCALE
J NORTH-EAST ELEVATION

Larger red-brick suburban villas began to appear in the free Classical and Romantic styles of British origin reminiscent of Nesfield and Norman Shaw. And in the 1880s, turning towards the United States of America, elaborate woodwork – turned, fretted and carved – began to displace the popular cast-iron decoration. Out of these pre-1900 models came a new suburban standard, the Australian Queen Anne style, at its best in 1919 in the large suburban bungalow set in a generous garden. Most distinctive of all were the imported terracotta roof tiles which appeared from 1886 onwards in Sydney, Melbourne and Launceston.

New Zealand: 1860–1900

One of New Zealand's outstanding buildings is the Canterbury Provincial Council Chamber, Christchurch (p. 1288A,B) in the High Victorian manner. The initial chamber was constructed in timber by Mountfort and Luck in 1858–60. A substantial addition in stone by Mountfort alone was completed in 1865, the interior of which is regarded as New Zealand's finest of the period. Mountfort continued as Diocesan architect through the 1870s and 1880s and his Congregational Church in Christchurch (1874–5) is an excellent example of the quality of his work. There is ample evidence of high levels of skill in Gothic Revival and Victorian eclecticism of other kinds in New Zealand. Romantic houses and country homesteads in the Gothic, Elizabethan and Manorial styles stemmed from admiration of all things English and Scottish. There was also a predominance of designs which could be achieved in wood, and which complement the dramatic, romantic landscape of New Zealand, always visible from the towns.

Nevertheless the neo-Renaissance was also exploited, one of the earliest examples being by a Melbourne architect, Leonard Terry, who designed the Bank of New Zealand in Auckland (1865–7). Other leading examples of Classical buildings are: William Mason's Exchange in Dunedin (1865, now demolished) (p. 1308B), two adjoining banks in Oamaru, one the Bank of Otago (1870) attributed to David Ross, a Melbourne architect, and the other the Bank of New South Wales (1883) by R. A. Lawson. Both of the latter have Corinthian colonnades, of Roman character and scale. The Post Office in Wellington was by Thomas Turnbull, a brick building three generous storeys in height using earthquake-resistant techniques developed earlier in San Francisco. Smaller but fine examples are the Athenaeum in Invercargill (1876, now demolished), and W. B. Armson's Bank of New Zealand, Dunedin (1883). Three Classical churches of note are the Baptist Tabernacle, Auckland (1885) by Edmund Bell, S. Paul's Presbyterian, Christchurch (*c.* 1873) by S. C. Farr, and S. Andrew's Presbyterian, Auckland, with its 1882 tower and portico by Matthew Henderson.

F. W. Petre contributed to the Gothic style with S. Joseph's Cathedral, Dunedin (1886), but then embarked on a splendid series of domed basilican churches which culminated in the Cathedral of the Blessed Sacrament in Christchurch (1905).

Examples

Australia: before 1850

Australia's earliest building of a substantial kind was the first **Government House, Sydney** (1788–9), the design of which is attributed to its bricklayer, James Bloodsworth. It contained four rooms on each of two floors, and was built of locally made bricks. Remnants of this Government House, and its many extensions, were rediscovered in 1983 beneath a building site and a street. The same early bricks were first used experimentally in a one-room cottage for Bennelong, an Aboriginal who was befriended by Governor Philip. This was Australia's first brick house, and Bennelong's name is now perpetuated as the name of the peninsula on which the Sydney Opera House stands.

Elizabeth Farm, near Parramatta (p. 1280A), was the first homestead on one of several properties owned by John Macarthur and his family. It is now seen as the prototype of many single-storey houses which followed, with high roofs and french windows opening onto verandahs. It was built originally as a two-roomed cottage in 1793, and the verandahs were added with the first of several extensions in either 1798 or 1805.

Other New South Wales homesteads from the pioneer period include **Denbigh near Narellan** (1818), **Glenfield near Liverpool** (1817) and **Kelvin near Bringelly**, thought to be pre-1809, and from the 1820s in New South Wales, **Experiment Farm** (*c.* 1820), **Rouse Hill** (*c.* 1823), **Cleveland** (*c.* 1824) and **Hobartville** (1829).

The **Civil Hospital** (between 1810 and 1817) is a building from this early period in the heart of Sydney. It is uncertain who was the architect. Referred to as the Mint, one of its later uses, it has now become a museum. There was also a **Military Hospital** designed by Lieutenant John Watts in 1814. Both hospitals had verandahs on each of their two floors. This typical tropical colonial feature is found also in the **Lancer Barracks at Parramatta** (*c.* 1820) (p. 1291A), again by Watts, who also designed **Parramatta Government House** (1800) where the portico was added and internal changes were made later, by Greenway. In association with Elizabeth

Macquarie, Watts was also involved with the Norman towers (1818) for **S. John's, Parramatta** (1804), the original designer of which is uncertain. The two-tier verandahs appear again in the later **Victoria Barracks**, in **Paddington, Sydney** (1843–8) by Major George Barney and James Gordon of the Royal Engineers.

Of the few surviving buildings from before 1825 in central Sydney, three were designed by Greenway, namely Hyde Park Barracks (1817–19), S. James's Church (1819–24) and the **Stables for Government House** (1817), while a fourth, the Courthouse, was begun by him but changed several times, both before use and after. The castellated Stables anticipated a Gothic Government House which when built was by Blore, not Greenway. There are other Greenway buildings near Sydney, at Parramatta, Windsor and Liverpool. **Hyde Park Barracks** (p. 1291D) comprises quarters for eight hundred male convicts who worked in Sydney town. There was a three-storey central block and other dormitories, within a stone-walled compound about 90 m × 60 m (300 ft × 200 ft). The plan is disarmingly simple, whilst the gateway and the compound's corner features are miniatures worthy of Dance or Soane. The end treatment of the central block, a full-width pediment with an enriched tympanum, is characteristic of Greenway, as are the window openings with double-arched heads.

Greenway's **S. James's Church, Sydney** (p. 1291B), now with later additions, is a modest but finely judged Georgian building with a tower and copper-clad spire which to this day provide an important landmark. The church has a gallery, and its full-length crypt is the only one in colonial New South Wales. The chancel was increased by one bay in 1834 by John Verge, the gallery was extended in 1846, and interior changes were made and a doorway added in 1894 by Varney Parkes.

A second church of Greenway's is **S. Matthew's Church, Windsor** (1818–20) (p. 1291C), 57 km (35 miles) out of Sydney. It has been acclaimed as his best work. Standing on a knoll overlooking the Hawkesbury Valley, its robust form makes an admirable landmark. The characteristic window forms are Greenway hallmarks.

A leading example of Verge's work is **Camden Park** (p. 1292A), **a homestead at Menangle** near Camden, New South Wales (1831–2), built for John Macarthur, one of the founders of the Australian sheep industry. The central block houses the family rooms, the servants' quarters are to the east and a bath-house to the west. The garden front has a colonnaded verandah, onto which open tall french windows. **Elizabeth Bay House** (p. 1292D), a residence on Sydney Harbour (1832, 1835–8) was also built by Verge for Alexander Macleay, Colonial Secretary and naturalist. The interior of this Regency house is notable, especially the central stair-hall, elliptical in plan and with a domed roof. The wooden portico, with iron columns, was added in the 1860s.

Other works by Verge include **Tusculum at Potts Point, Sydney** (1832), and the homestead, **Bedervale, at Braidwood near Canberra** (*c.* 1838). There are also some demolished but documented examples, such as **The Vineyard at Rydalmere** (1835).

Some fine and interesting houses and homesteads remain anonymous. One example of these is **Panshanger homestead** (p. 1292C) **near Longford**, Tasmania, built for Joseph Archer in the 1830s. Tradition has it that he obtained the plans when revisiting England in 1829, but the designer's name is not known. It is a Regency design with Doric details, and stands impressively above a river frontage.

Clarendon homestead near Evandale (*c.* 1840) is another anonymous example and represents the grandest design among the numerous colonial homesteads of Tasmania. It was built for James Cox, one of the wealthiest farmers in the colony. Its large Ionic portico (restored in 1975) rises above a semi-basement and with its concealed roof is more Classical in design than most of the colonial homesteads.

A third house of which the architect is not known is **Fernhill homestead near Mulgoa**, New South Wales (1842) (p. 1292B), built for Edward Cox, whose brother James built the Clarendon homestead described above. This is typical of the small country houses of which some fifty or so were constructed in the early colonial period (*c.* 1800–50) in New South Wales.

After Greenway and Verge, the best known early architect was Mortimer W. Lewis, Colonial Architect from 1835 to 1850. The **Courthouse at Darlinghurst, Sydney**, for which he designed the central block (*c.* 1840) is one of Australia's relatively few Greek Revival buildings.

In **Sydney**, Lewis designed the **Treasury** (*c.* 1849) in the neo-Renaissance manner. His building, a Barry-like palazzo fronting Bridge Street, was several times extended and in 1896 the Macquarie Street wing was added to accommodate the Premier's Department. The latter, by the then Colonial Architect Walter L. Vernon, has a distinctive entrance raised on Doric columns, within a large arch. The geometry is reminiscent of Soane or even of Boullée. The Treasury was converted in 1984 into a hotel. Other buildings by Lewis include the **Sydney Police Office** (1837), the **Church of S. John the Evanglist at Camden** (1840–9) in Gothic Revival style, although the attribution of the latter building to Lewis is not certain, and his own picturesque house, **Richmond Villa, in Sydney** (1849), now moved from its original site and preserved.

The **Congregational Church in Pitt Street, Sydney** (1841) by John Bibb has a monumental neo-Renaissance front with an Ionic colonnade two storeys high. **S. Peter's**, a Gothic-style church at

A. Lancer Barracks, Parramatta (*c.* 1820). See p. 1289

B. S. James's Church, Sydney. See p. 1290

C. S. Matthew's Church, Windsor (1818–20). See p. 1290

D. Hyde Park Barracks, Sydney. See p. 1290

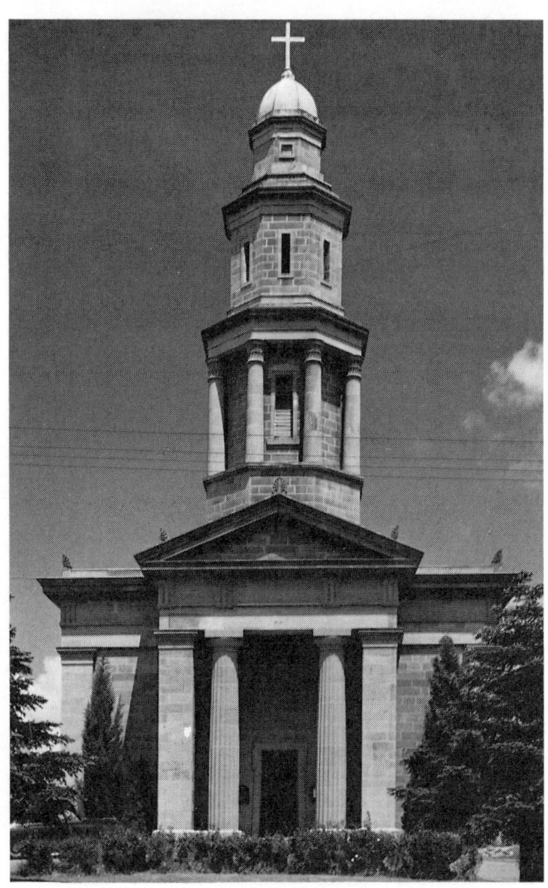

E. S. George's Church, Hobart (1837–88). See p. 1293

A. Camden Park Homestead, Menangle (1831–2). See p. 1290

B. Fernhill homestead, Mulgoa (1842). See p. 1290

C. Panshanger homestead, Tasmania (1830s). See p. 1290

D. Elizabeth Bay House, Sydney (1832, 1835–8). See p. 1290

Cook's River near Sydney, was designed by Thomas Bird about 1836.

S. George's Church, Battery Point, Hobart (1837–88) (p. 1291E) stands tall on a prominent hill, just outside central Hobart. The church itself was completed without a tower in 1838 to the design of John Lee Archer, the Colonial Architect for Van Diemen's Land. Its tapering windows are in the Regency manner, with a flavour of the Egyptian. It has a decorative plastered ceiling and still retains its enclosed pews. During the period 1841–7 a tower was added, designed by James Blackburn. Vestries by Francis Butler were added in 1862, and a striking Greek Doric portico by Robert Huckson in 1888.

There was no experienced practitioner in Gothic Revival design in Australia until the arrival in Sydney in 1842 of Blacket, who in due course was responsible for about forty churches. One of his first designs was for **Christ Church, Geelong** (1844). His first cathedral commission was to take over responsibility for **S. Andrew's Cathedral, Sydney** (1837 to *c.* 1870) (p. 1296A). A metropolitan church had been begun on another site to designs by Francis Greenway, but the work was halted in 1819 when only the foundations had been completed. S. Andrew's itself was started in 1837 by James Hume, and building progressed for five years when there was a pause because of an economic recession in the colony. The economy had improved by 1845 and Blacket was called upon to modify the design and to proceed with the work, which continued until 1870. The nave of S. Andrew's is somewhat narrow and the towers, though handsome in themselves, crowd in upon it. The Cathedral's setting was greatly enhanced in 1975 when a civic square was formed between it and the neighbouring Town Hall.

S. Mark's, Darling Point, Sydney (1847–75) (p. 1296B) was among the many churches Blacket designed as Diocesan Architect, an appointment given to him in 1847. It was one of his first, probably the best situated and now the best known. The exterior is rather severe, with tall and narrow lancet windows and shallow buttresses. An octagonal stone spire is carried on the three-storey tower. The building has a pleasing interior with timber decorations. Construction began in 1847 and the church was consecrated in 1864. The tower and spire were added in 1872–5.

One of the earliest buildings with pointed windows was the amateurish first Catholic Cathedral of Sydney, **S. Mary's**, built in the early 1820s and destroyed by fire in 1865. It was mainly designed by an Irish priest, J. J. Therry, who was Catholic Chaplain to the colony.

Early Church of England examples were **Holy Trinity, Millers Point, Sydney** (the Garrison Church), 1840–56 by Henry Ginn and others, and the more convincing **S. John's at Camden** (1840–9), supervised by Mortimer Lewis, but probably designed by John Cunningham of Liverpool, England. Others were **S. Francis' Catholic Church in Melbourne** (1841) by Samuel Jackson, **S. Peter's Anglican Church in Melbourne** (1846) by Charles Laing, and **S. John's, Newtown, Hobart** (1834–5) by John Lee Archer.

In Tasmania, James Blackburn built a number of Gothic Revival churches, the most successful of which was **Holy Trinity, Hobart** (1841–8), in the Early English manner with a large tower at the west end. He also used Romanesque forms, as in **S. Mark's, Pontville** (*c.* 1839) and **S. Matthew's, Glenorchy** (*c.* 1840).

New Zealand: before 1860

In the north, around the Bay of Islands, the **Kerikeri Church of England mission station** was set up in 1819 and **the Wesleyan mission at Hokianga River** in 1818. **Kororareka**, the principal port and trading post, dates from the mid-1820s.

The surviving buildings are at the Kerikeri mission. The **Kemp House** is a two-storey building in timber with a verandah; next to it, at the water's edge, is a stone store (1832–6), which once had a clock tower. The dressed stones for arches and quoins were prepared in Sydney, from drawings by George Clarke, a lay missionary at Kerikeri.

The governor, when installed, chose a site for his residence near to Kororareka but deliberately upstream from the town, at a place he called Russell, a name which later replaced Kororareka; the seat of government was removed in 1841 to Auckland, and twenty-four years later to Wellington.

In Auckland the official residence of the governor was at first a sixteen-room, prefabricated **Government House**, built of components made in England by the London family firm of Manning, whose main outlet in the region was to be the colony of South Australia, where numerous Manning houses were erected.

A few architects arrived with the early settlers; prominent among them were William Mason (1810–97) and Frederick Thatcher (1814–90), and a little later B. W. Mountfort (1824–98), who arrived in 1850 with the first organised settlers in Canterbury in the South Island. Mason was Governor Hobson's first Superintendent of Works, and later went into private practice. In England he had worked in Edward Blore's office and was the first architect in New Zealand to work in the Gothic Revival style. Thatcher, cleric as well as architect, was at first in New Plymouth, then undertook two hospitals in Auckland for Governor Grey, in 1846 and 1848. Later he became closely linked with the church-building activities of Bishop Selwyn, a member of the Cambridge Camden Society and an enthusiastic designer.

A. S. John's College Chapel, Auckland (1847). See p. 1295

B. Old S. Paul's Church, Wellington (1861). See p. 1295

The churches designed by Thatcher for Bishop Selwyn were organised from a studio workshop at S. John's College, West Tamaki, Auckland. They produced eight chapels which could be quickly transported and erected in various country locations. All but one, **All Saints' at Howick** (1847), are lost. At **S. John's**, however, the **College Chapel** (1847) (p. 1294A) is of similar construction. Another of their churches in **Auckland, S. Barnabas**, was built at Parnell in 1848 and moved to nearby Mount Eden in 1877, but is now somewhat overwhelmed by brick additions.

Other architects of the early period included Walter Robertson, who completed six buildings between his arrival in 1846 and his death in 1850, and H. C. Holman, who succeeded Mason as Superintendent of Works. H. C. Cridland designed a wooden church, **S. Peter's, Te Aro** (1848) and **S. Andrew's Presbyterian Church, Christchurch** (1857), which was extended by others in 1891.

In the 1850s Thatcher designed a bold, idiosyncratic tower for **Christ Church, Nelson** (1851, demolished 1887), but it is Thatcher's **Old S. Paul's Church, Wellington** (1861) (p. 1294B) which is regarded as the finest surviving example of the so-called Selwyn style. Churches by other architects apparently inspired by Selwyn include B. W. Mountfort's **S. Bartholomew, in Kaiapoi** (1854). S. Mary's pro-Cathedral, Auckland (1886) (q.v.) by Mountfort is more obviously Gothic, but still owes much to its timber construction.

In addition to Otago and Dunedin, Canterbury and Christchurch, the 1850s saw the development of townships at Wanganui, Napier, Invercargill and Nelson, the last of which had two architects in its population, Maxwell Bury and William Beatson. Bury's **Provincial Council Chambers, Nelson** (1859, demolished 1969) were Jacobean in style and were constructed in timber. Beatson designed **Nelson College** (1859), an extensive building in the Flemish manner which was destroyed by fire in 1904.

Australia: 1850–1900

Blacket resigned his post as Colonial Architect to undertake the commission for the **University of Sydney** (1854–60) (pp. 1288G–J, 1297A). His scheme envisaged a range of buildings on four sides of a grassy quadrangle (eventually completed by others), with academic accommodation on one side and the Great Hall on another. The academic wing is Tudor in style, with handsome bay windows. A central entrance is marked with a pinnacled tower. Blacket seems to have taken Westminster Hall as his model for the Great Hall, with its lofty hammer-beam roof. The walls are stone-faced brickwork, using the golden sandstone of the Sydney region which is good quality and well suited to carving.

Later Blacket churches include the **Church of S. Michael at Wollongong**, New South Wales (1858); the **Church of S. Peter, Watson's Bay**, near the entrance to Sydney Harbour (1864); the **Church of S. Stephen, Newtown, Sydney** (1871); and finally the **Cathedral Church of S. George in Perth**, Western Australia (1878).

The major offices were able to produce Gothic Revival buildings on demand; the firm of Reed and Barnes, for example, were responsible for **Wesley Church, Melbourne**, and **Scots Church, Melbourne**. They also created the fine neo-Gothic Great Hall, called **Wilson Hall**, for **Melbourne University** (1878–82), which also had an elaborate hammer-beam roof. Wilson Hall was gutted by fire in 1954 and demolished. Adjacent to the University is **Ormond College** (1879), also by Reed and Barnes, in the Scottish baronial manner.

The most innovative design by Reed and Barnes, however, was in red brick with small round arches. It was the **Independent Church, Melbourne** (Congregational Church, Collins Street) (1864) (pp. 1298, 1299A), designed immediately after Reed's return from a European trip where he studied North Italian Romanesque. It is a square plan enclosing a theatre-like auditorium set on the diagonal. Its focus – pulpit, choir and organ – is set low in one corner, its entrance high in the opposite one, and there is a rising and curving floor between them with a steeply raked, horseshoe balcony above. The balcony, and above it the ceiling, are supported on thin cast-iron columns carrying wide arches. There is a rich open-work cast-iron balustrade on the balcony.

After Blacket, the largest commissions for Gothic Revival buildings went to Wardell (q.v.). Reference has already been made to his two Roman Catholic Cathedrals, **S. Patrick's, Melbourne** (1858) (p. 1296C) and **S. Mary's, Sydney** (1865) (pp. 1288D–F, 1297B), the largest of Australia's cathedrals. The plan of S. Mary's is said to be based on Lincoln Cathedral, the interior elevation on Chartres Cathedral, and the west front on Notre Dame in Paris (q.v.). Its detail is Geometric Gothic throughout and richly decorated. The outcome is a solid massive form and a spacious interior which is, purposely, dimly lit as a refuge from the fierce sunlight. The stained glass (1881–1928, by Hardman Brothers of Birmingham) was ordered thicker and deeper in colour than usual. Although Wardell's design was followed closely, the west-end towers he had intended were not built.

Anglican cathedrals of importance include **S. Paul's, Melbourne** (Butterfield, 1880, continued in 1884 by Joseph Reed of Melbourne); **S. Peter's, Adelaide** (initially designed by Butterfield 1869–76, its nave, west end and Lady Chapel built between 1880 and 1904, by E. J. Woods of Adelaide); and others at **Hobart, Newcastle** and **Bendigo**. There are

A. S. Andrew's Cathedral, Sydney (1837–*c.* 1870). See p. 1293

B. S. Mark's, Darling Point (1847–75). See p. 1293

C. S. Patrick's Cathedral, Melbourne (1858). See p. 1295

A. University of Sydney (1854–60). See p. 1295

B. S. Mary's Cathedral, Sydney. See p. 1295

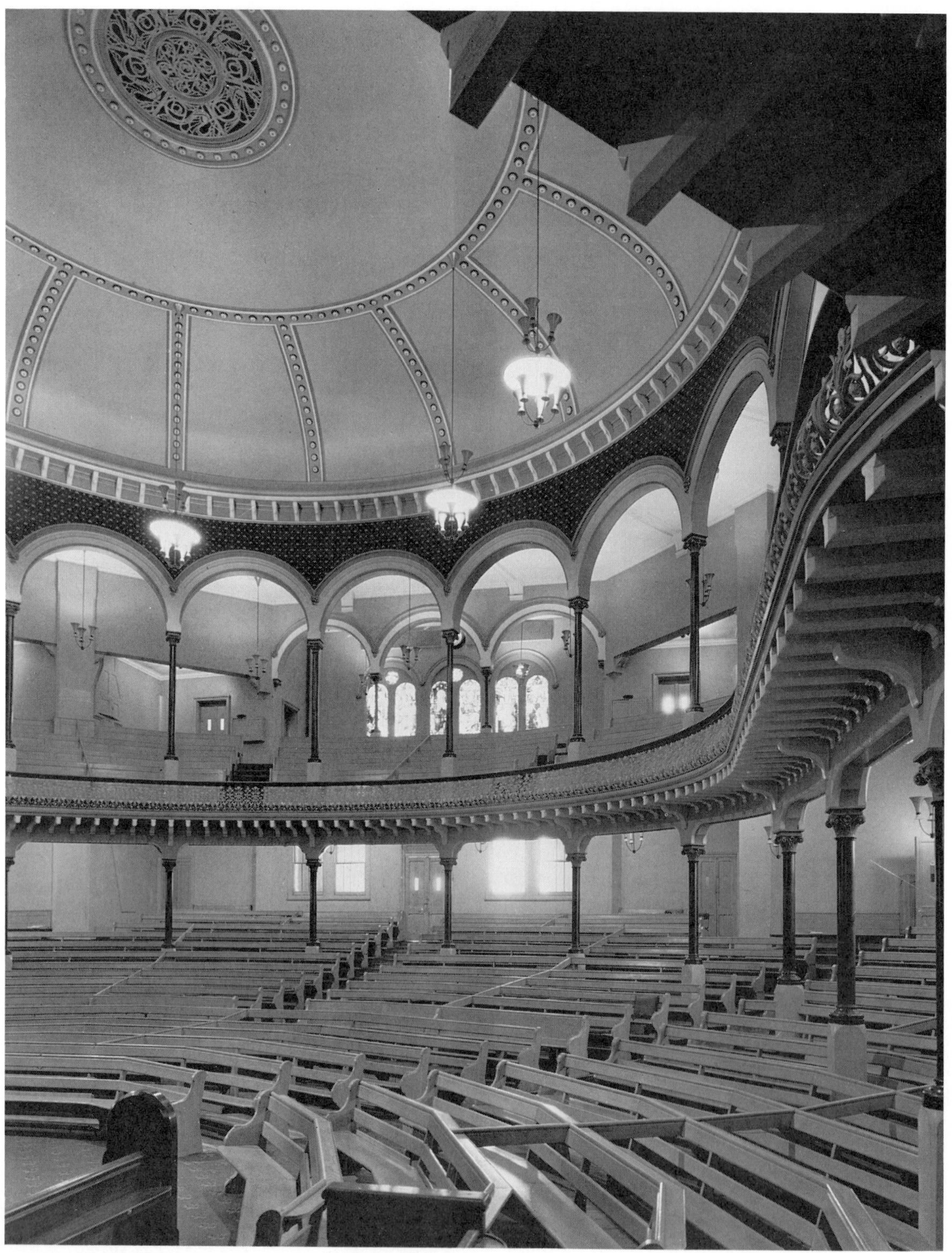

Independent Church, Melbourne: interior. See p. 1295

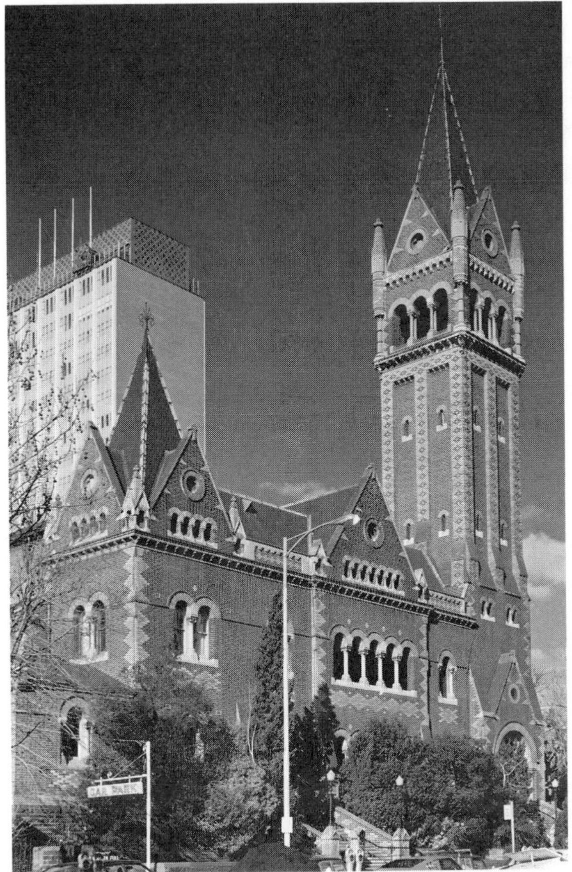

A. Independent Church, Melbourne (1864). See p. 1295

B. S. John's Cathedral, Brisbane (1887). See p. 1301

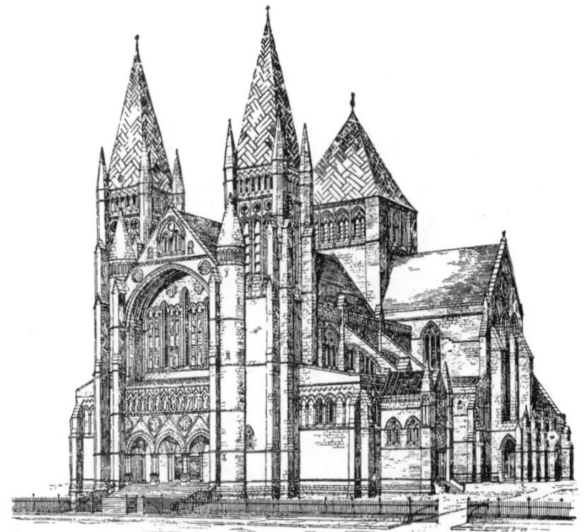

C. Frank L. Pearson's drawing to show intended completion of S. John's Cathedral, Brisbane

D. Treasury, Melbourne (1857–62). See p. 1301

A. Houses of Parliament for Victoria, Melbourne (1857–62). See p. 1301

B. Melbourne Library (1854–). See p. 1301

scores of churches in which the Gothic Revival style predominates. Classical churches also exist, for example the **Congregational Church, North Adelaide** (1860–72) by Wright and Woods with G. and E. Hamilton. In areas where Scottish settlers were numerous, such as the Western District of Victoria, Presbyterian churches are equally large and (surprisingly) Gothic in style. **S. John the Evangelist Metropolitan and Cathedral Church, Brisbane** (1887) (p. 1299B, C) is incomplete, lacking both west end and tower, but it has what is arguably Australia's finest neo-Gothic interior. The architect was John Loughborough Pearson (1817–97), who supplied the design from London. It shares with other churches he designed, such as S. Augustine's, Kilburn, London (q.v.), a curious adaptation of the triforium. In this case the arcading of the nave allows for a triforium, but there is neither floor nor vaulting at that level over the aisles. The result is a loftier and lighter interior.

The general rule that excluded neo-Gothic from public buildings was broken in the case of the **Town Hall, Perth**, Western Australia (1867–70) by Richard R. Jewell, perhaps with assistance from James Manning. The red brickwork in Flemish bond, and the tall grouped windows of white stonework, lend the building a distinctly Victorian character. There is a lofty interior with a hammer-beam roof, which was used at first as a covered market. Jewell was responsible, as Colonial Architect, for several Gothic buildings of Tudor and Flemish character, including **Government House** (1859–63) in association with the Royal Engineer Corps, **Treasury Buildings** and Bishop Hale's **Collegiate School** (1858) now referred to as The Cloisters.

Colleges preferred Gothic, usually Tudor. One example from among many is **Melbourne Grammar School** (1856, extended in 1876) by Webb and Taylor.

One of the most successful neo-Renaissance-style buildings is the **Treasury, Melbourne** (1857–62) (pp. 1299D, 1302D, E), by Clark (under Pasley). The gold rush which began in 1851 created an urgent need for such a building. It is reminiscent of the style popularised by Barry, but there is a boldness in the five-bay arcading, within which the window aedicules are deeply recessed.

At the head of the next street in Melbourne stands the **Houses of Parliament for Victoria** (1856–1930) (pp. 1300A, 1302A–C). This monumental neo-Classical building has a colonnaded front and a grand approach stairway, and there are impressive interiors, especially the two Legislative Chambers and the Library. The building is incomplete, but the absence of side and rear facades is masked by trees in the Parliament garden. An intended dome is also lacking, but even without these vital elements the building is an important example of Victorian architecture. The architects were Peter Kerr (1820–1912) and John George Knight (1826–92), commissioned after the result of a competition, won by others, was set aside. Kerr had been articled to Archibald Simpson of Aberdeen and G. F. Jones of York, and worked four years with Charles Barry on London's Parliament building before emigrating.

Begun in 1856, four years into the gold rush period, the two Chambers and the Library were completed in three years. They stood without facades and with temporary entrances for eighteen years. Knight had moved away from Victoria, and after 1866 Kerr became an officer in the Public Works Department. He resumed the Parliament project in 1877, and in the next two years completed the Queen's Hall and the Vestibule. He then continued work for the dome, which was never erected, and the grand Roman Doric colonnade which was intended to continue around the sides of the buildings. The front was completed in 1892, the year before almost all building work in the colony was suspended because of a financial collapse.

The stone used externally is a fine freestone brought at great expense from new quarries some 250 km (155 miles) from Melbourne; the local basalt was considered too dark in colour, and stone from other colonies could not be used for Victoria's Parliament buildings.

While in the Victorian Public Works Department, Kerr also had partial responsibility for Melbourne's **Law Courts, Government House, Post Office** and **Customs Office**, all buildings in the Classical style.

Sydney's first and second Government Houses have already been mentioned, and also the alternative at Parramatta. The final **Government House at Sydney** was designed in England by Edward Blore. **Government House, Hobart** (1855–8), was by William P. Kay and is Tudor Gothic in style. **Government House, Melbourne** (1871–6), the largest of them all, is an Italianate palace, a superior version of Queen Victoria's Isle of Wight house (Osborne), with a tower and a large ballroom. It was by W. W. Wardell, then Public Works architect in Victoria, assisted by J. J. Clark and Peter Kerr.

The long and productive career in Australia of Cornishman Joseph Reed (1822–90) began with the **Public Library, Melbourne** (now the State Library of Victoria) (1854–) (p. 1300B). He used a giant double-storey Corinthian portico and pilasters elevated on pedestals. The detailing of aedicules and of capitals is distinguished, as are some of the interiors. The front wing is the original building: others were added, first by Reed and Barnes and then by others. The main reading room of the library in the centre of the complex is of (1906–11) designed by Reed Smart and Tappin, a practice which was to be renamed Bates, Peebles and Smart whilst the building was under construction. See Chapter 58 for details of the extension to the reading room.

Reed and Barnes used neo-Renaissance in the Second Empire style for **Melbourne Town Hall**

PARLIAMENT: MELBOURNE
SCALE FOR SECTION
45 40 35 30 25 20 15 10 5 0 MTR
140 120 100 80 60 40 20 0 FT
DOME NOT BUILT
B ORIGINAL DESIGN W/ DOME
0 20 40 60 80 100 120 140 FT
0 10 20 30 40 MTR
A LONGITUDINAL SECTION
C PLAN
THE TREASURY: MELBOURNE
SCALE FOR PLAN
35 30 25 20 15 10 5 0 MTR
120 100 80 60 40 20 0 FT
D HALF ELEVATION
E PLAN
LANDS DEPT.: SYDNEY
SCALE FOR PLAN
0 20 40 60 80 100 120 FT
0 5 10 15 20 25 30 35 MTRS
E
F ELEVATION
G PLAN

(1867), and adapted Renaissance forms to a large-scale structure in Melbourne's **Exhibition Building** (1879–80).

Queensland was separated from New South Wales in 1859, and its new Parliament met for the first time in 1860. The **Parliament House of Queensland, Brisbane** (1865–7 and later) was designed by Charles Tiffin, Queensland's Colonial Architect from 1860 onwards.

Tiffin's building was an austere Renaissance design, without the present arcading, and had a projecting centre-bay and corners. Its roofs are prominent in the French Second Empire manner, but were of plain corrugated iron, replaced with copper in 1980. The two chambers and the stair-hall between them combine to make impressive interiors, with joinery and plasterwork of some excellence. In 1878 F. D. G. Stanley, Tiffin's successor, added Palladian arcades to link the projecting bays of the facade, providing shading and enrichment. A later Colonial Architect, H. Connolly, built a rear wing at right angles (1887–9) with an elaborate central feature with stone carvings of Queensland flora. Balconies supported on iron columns were added on the river side to both wings.

The leading neo-Renaissance public buildings of New South Wales are the work of the Colonial Architect of the day, James Barnet. His **General Post Office, Sydney** (1865–74, 1881, 1900) (p. 1304A) stands on a narrow site, 118 m (390 ft) long. The design is generally neo-Renaissance, with handsome fenestration. The arcade has short granite columns on tapered pedestals and is almost mediaeval in character. The clock tower (the building's least satisfactory feature) and an extension on Pitt Street were added in 1886. For the arcade on the latter street, Barnet commissioned carvings depicting everyday life in the arts, sciences and postal services. The top storey was added during the later 1890s.

The **Lands Department, Sydney** (1876–90) (pp. 1302F,G,1304B), also by Barnet, is an elaborate neo-Renaissance building near Circular Quay, and was for a long time a landmark for approaching ships. It was one of three major office buildings for the colonial administration in Sydney; the others were the Treasury by Lewis and the Colonial Office by Barnet.

It is a neo-Renaissance design with arcaded loggias, boldly carved doorways, a 61 m (200 ft) tower and two domes, designed in 1876 under James Barnet as Colonial Architect, assisted by William Kemp. The northern portion was built immediately, but the southern and greater part, with the tower, was delayed until 1883, when Barnet's assistant was Vicars, and completed in 1893.

The **Court House and Government Buildings, Bathurst**, New South Wales (1878–80) (p. 1304C) was another of Barnet's buildings. Bathurst, which is 250 km (155 miles) west of Sydney, was the first settlement (1815) beyond the Blue Mountains, and became a regional administration centre, with a Government House and a Bishop's Court. There is a dome over the entrance hall of the Court House. On either side of the Court building and linked to it by verandahs are the Lands Department and the Post and Telegraph offices. Stone facing is combined with bland brick pilasters which, in pale colours, create simplified Classical forms which almost anticipated the Edwardian style.

The size and high standard of the **Court House, Goulburn**, New South Wales (1887) (p. 1305B), also by Barnet, indicate expectations of city status, as was common in the wealthy inland towns of New South Wales. The copper dome of the Court House and the mix of brick and stone produce a colourful garden forecourt. The arcaded verandah is architecturally impressive and well suited to the hot inland summer.

As well as the Gothic Revival buildings for which he is justly famed, Edmund Blacket's practice also produced many neo-Renaissance commercial buildings, houses, a church and a school. The church was the **Presbyterian Church, Woolloomooloo, Sydney** (1856) and the school was **Sydney Grammar School** (also 1856), begun by Hallen and never fully completed. Most of the commercial buildings have been lost through redevelopment, but they included in Sydney the **Commercial Bank** (1850), the offices of the **Liverpool and London Insurance Co.** (*c.* 1860), and the little **Water Police Court** (1850).

Edmund Wright House, Adelaide (1876–7) (p. 1305A,D) now serves as a marriage registry, but was built originally as a bank. It began as the Bank of South Australia and later became the Australia and New Zealand Bank. Its architects were Lloyd Taylor of Melbourne with Edmund Wright of Adelaide, after whom it is now named. The building has good interiors, including a major room with impressive plasterwork which was once the banking hall but is now favoured as an auditorium for musical performances.

Additions made to Perth's government-offices complex ('the old **Treasury**') provide late Victorian examples of Classicism. The initial, Flemish-style building by Jewell (1874) (q.v.) faced Barrack Street, but was twice extended by Jewell with wings reaching S. George's Terrace. In 1889 his successor as Superintendent of Works, George Temple-Poole (1856–1934, arrived 1885) completed the Terrace front to create a new **General Post Office**, and gradually added a third storey to the group (1896–1905, four stages). It is the north wing, the **Lands Department** (p. 1305E), also by Temple-Poole (1895–6), entered from Cathedral Avenue but with one elevation to Hay Street, which is the most striking section of the complex. Its large round-arched entrance faces Blacket's cathedral, its bold

A. General Post Office, Sydney (1865–1900). See p. 1303

B. Lands Department, Sydney (1876–90). See p. 1303

C. Bathurst government buildings (1878–80). See p. 1303

A. Edmund Wright House, Adelaide (1876–7). See p. 1303

D. Edmund Wright House, Adelaide: lobbies

B. Goulburn Court House (1887). See p. 1303

C. Queen Anne style house, Parkville, Melbourne. See p. 1306

E. Lands Department, Perth (1895–6).
See p. 1303

modelling in stone enlivened further by bright red brickwork.

Some districts in Sydney which are of special interest for their terrace housing are **Paddington** (p. 1287C), **Glebe, Woolloomooloo** and **Potts Point**, and in Melbourne at **Carlton** (p. 1287B), **Parkville** (p. 1305C) and **East Melbourne**. All have some examples of distinctively Australian decorative cast iron, and especially Parkville. Paddington is a hilly district and its terraces are picturesquely arranged to respond to the topography.

A few examples from many outstanding post-1850 homesteads are: **Werribee Park**, Victoria, **Eynesbury**, Victoria, **Rupertswood**, Victoria, **Padthaway**, South Australia, **Martindale Hall**, South Australia, **Mount Pleasant (Abercrombie House)**, New South Wales, **Booloominbah**, New South Wales, **Mona Vale**, Tasmania, and **Mount Pleasant**, Tasmania. Architecturally, Werribee Park, Werribee, Victoria (1873–8) is the most distinguished. It is attributed to J. F. Fox, but there are known connections also with W. W. Wardell and J. Macvicar Anderson. The interiors are richly finished and there is a central Italianate tower. **Eynesbury**, Milton, Victoria, from the 1870s, is a more typical house, with a low, spreading, hipped roof: it is formal in plan yet in appearance nearer to the vernacular.

New Zealand: 1860–1900

Just prior to the discovery of gold, a **cathedral** was commissioned for **Christchurch** (p. 1307A). Sir George Gilbert Scott provided the design in 1859, and Robert Speechley emigrated from England in 1864 to supervise its construction; after an initial effort from 1864 to 1866 this was suspended, and Speechley returned to England. Cyril J. Mountfort was made resident architect when the building resumed in 1873. The work continued until 1881, and the transepts and chancel were eventually completed between 1894 and 1904.

Dunedin, nearest to the goldfields, benefited most from gold: an example which is evidence of the new situation is the vividly Gothic hotel in **Dunedin, the Oriental** (1863) (p. 1309A). The town attracted William Mason away from Auckland, George Mallinson from Christchurch and Danish-born Julius Toxward from Invercargill. Architects came also from Australia. They included David Ross and Robert A. Lawson of Melbourne, William H. Clayton of Launceston, Tasmania, and briefly, W. C. Vahland from Bendigo, Victoria. Another immigrant of note was the Scot, Thomas Turnbull, who had spent twenty years in Melbourne and San Francisco before reaching New Zealand. The **Post Office, Wellington** (1884) (p. 1308A) was by Turnbull. Designs from abroad were also provided from time to time, such as the **Bank of New Zealand, Auckland** (1865) (p. 1307B) by Leonard Terry of Melbourne, and the **Auckland City Art Gallery** (1887) (p. 1307C) by Grainger and D'Ebro of Melbourne, a Second Empire design, almost châteauesque.

Mason designed Dunedin's **Post Office**, which eventually became the Exchange (1865) (p. 1308B). It is neo-Renaissance in style, arcaded and with a central tower. Mason also designed the **Bank of New Zealand** (1863), the **Bank of New South Wales** (1866), a house, **Highlawn** (1863), for C. W. Richmond, and an **Exhibition Building** (1864) which later became a hospital. The last was a three-storey structure with four wings surrounding a courtyard. The detail is North Italian Romanesque and there are no less than six towers.

In partnership with Clayton, Mason moved toward High Victorian free style with the red-brick church of **All Saints** (1865). **Edinburgh House** (1865) and the **Provincial Council Chamber and Courthouse** (1865), on the site of the present Post Office at Dunedin, were also in red brick.

Lawson moved to **Dunedin** when he won a competition in 1861 for the design of the **Presbyterian First Church**, which was constructed between 1867 and 1873, and for which he also designed the Manse in 1868. **Trinity Methodist Church** (1869) followed and he was commissioned subsequently for many other churches. First Church has been described as the most impressive of all New Zealand's nineteenth-century churches, at least externally. It is built on a central island site in the heart of the city and is in a pinnacled Early English style with an impressive spire. **Knox Church** (1876) was also designed by Lawson and has a gallery designed to accommodate a large congregation.

David Ross, at first in partnership with Mason, later produced Early Victorian buildings on his own account, including a much simplified Gothic **Congregational Church** (1864) now used as a Seventh Day Adventist Church.

The career of Benjamin W. Mountfort has been referred to above. **Canterbury Provincial Government Chamber** has been nominated as his most distinguished building. Mountfort and Luck provided the first wooden building, which was later converted to offices (1858–9). Mountfort then built the stone chamber itself (1860–5). The earlier building is plain and restful in character, with undecorated wood panelling and a stone-paved perimeter corridor, 128 m (420 ft) long. The later Chamber has painted geometrical decoration, mosaic wall panels, floor tiling, and blackened, polished stone lintels and columns.

Mountfort was made Provincial Government Architect and continued in the post until 1874. His largest single work for the government was the **Sunnyside Mental Hospital**, finally completed in 1891.

He left the government post to become Diocesan Architect for the Anglican Church. He had in fact

A. Christchurch Cathedral (1864–1904). See p. 1306

B. Bank of New Zealand, Auckland (1865). See p. 1306

C. Auckland City Art Gallery (1887). See p. 1306

A. Post Office, Wellington (1884). See p. 1306

B. Exchange Building (formerly Post Office), Dunedin (1865). See p. 1306

A. Oriental Hotel, Dunedin (1863). See p. 1306

B. Stafford Place, Waimea West (*c.* 1860). See p. 1310

C. House at Parawai, near Thames (1877). See p. 1310

designed several earlier Churches, including **Kaiapoi** (1854) and **Rangiora** (1859), both constructed in timber. Now his output became prolific. Examples from these later years include the **Trinity Congregational Church, Christchurch** (1874–5), which has an unusual gabled tower and an auditorium interior with a gallery, and a wooden masterpiece, **S. Mary's pro-Cathedral, Auckland** (1886). At that time he also enlarged **Christ Church, Nelson**, into a cathedral: it had been designed originally by Thatcher in 1849 and extended by Bury in 1858.

He also carried out neo-Gothic designs at **Canterbury University** – the Clock Tower Block (1877–9) and the Hall (1882).

In the next generation F. W. Petre was responsible for a number of impressive churches, including **S. Joseph's Cathedral, Dunedin** (1886) in the Gothic style, which was followed by a series of basilican churches, culminating in the **Cathedral of the Blessed Sacrament, Christchurch** (1905).

Houses in towns and on country properties were after gold often enlarged or rebuilt. The gothicising tendencies continued, for example **Stafford Place, Waimea West** (*c.* 1860) (p. 1309B). Plainer, Italianate and verandahed forms were also common, such as **Parawai, near Thames** (1877) (p. 1309C). The architects of these two houses have not been identified.

Part Seven

THE ARCHITECTURE OF THE TWENTIETH CENTURY

Chapter 43
BACKGROUND

1900–1920

In Australia by 1900 the states which had been independently governed since the middle of the nineteenth century were about to combine to form the Commonwealth of Australia (1901); New Zealand and Canada had been unified and independent for a quarter of a century. Except for the Guianas, present-day Belize and a number of islands, therefore, Australasia and the Americas had reached their present levels of sovereignty by the turn of the century. On the other hand, in Africa and South-east Asia the European powers had only recently stabilised their colonial positions but, by comparison with the longevity of the seventeenth-century settlements (in India and Indonesia, for example), their stability was to be fragile and transient.

In the United States rapid economic development began after the Civil War and was concentrated in the north-east. The mineral wealth was tapped and there began the expansion of development away from the traditional areas of industrial activity (Boston, New England), producing urban growth in the areas south of the Great Lakes (Pittsburgh, Detroit, Chicago, Cleveland, Milwaukee) in the early years of the century. The population of the United States grew from 31 million to 92 million between 1860 and 1910. Expansion of the railways after 1870 made the movement of families westwards more feasible, a process which was encouraged by the award of hundreds of millions of acres of land to homesteaders: the number of farms trebled to 6 million and the population west of the Mississippi rose from 6 million in 1870 to 26 million in 1910. There were over 20 million immigrants between these latter dates, most of whom stayed in the north-east, providing cheap labour for the growing industries. Population growth in Canada was on a comparatively modest scale – only 3.5 million to 7 million for the whole country in the forty years or so before 1910. This was on the basis of a rapid expansion of wheat farming, once the Canadian Pacific Railway was completed in 1885. Again the wealth flowed into the eastern provinces where the highest level of urbanisation took place.

In Latin America, plans for an all-embracing South American republic having failed, there was little change from the subsistence economy of the mid-nineteenth century before about 1880, when there was a rapid increase in the levels of foreign investment, particularly in Brazil, Argentina, Chile and Mexico. The aim was to encourage the export of primary products to the industrial centres of Europe and North America. Urbanisation increased rapidly on either side of the turn of the century as the result of export trade in nitrates, coffee, rubber, meat and grain. New immigrants came to Argentina and Brazil from many European countries, but especially from Italy and Spain. Industrial growth and urbanisation produced their own problems. There was a growing urban working class dependent upon a small middle class which, as in the countries of the Industrial Revolution in Europe, was becoming rich on the export trade. The result was political unrest such as that which produced the revolution in Mexico in 1911, immediately following the despotic government of Porfirio Diaz.

These positions contrast markedly with Africa, the European 'scramble' for which took place in the thirty years or so to 1914, by which date the whole of Africa (with the exception of Ethiopia and Liberia) came under European control. Once again the motivation was the acquisition of primary products and raw materials, or strategic advantage in a European context of growing unrest related to political power and the race for industrial supremacy. The French added some 4 million square miles and 47 million people to its empire in this period (including Madagascar, Indo-China and the Pacific islands); Germany and Italy, not previously contenders for imperial power, had also entered the field. Germany acquired a million square miles and 14 million colonial subjects in South West Africa, Togoland, Tanganyika, the Cameroons and the Pacific, and Italy took Tripoli, Libya, Eritrea and Italian Somaliland; but by far the greatest proportion went to Great Britain with substantial additions in Africa during this period. Britain was also at the height of its powers in India and in control of the sea routes to the East via Suez and East Africa, as well as those through the south Pacific by way of Singapore. It is perhaps worth noting here that in the half century to 1930 or so, Indian foreign trade increased sevenfold, much of it after 1921, when protective tariffs were introduced. Here also a new middle class arose during the early part of the century – administrators as well as industrialists – but the National Congress of the day accepted British rule and it was not until after 1919 that home rule became an issue and total independence not until a decade later.

European nationalism in the second half of the nineteenth century had produced a united Italy by 1870 and a unified Germany under Bismarck by 1871. But the settlements had left each with outstanding claims. The Austro-Hungarian problem was one of those which led to confusion and conflict. Germany saw itself being surrounded by a less than friendly group of powers led by Britain, but the dénouement did not come until after the Balkan wars of 1912, when the conflict between Austria and Russia over Serbia culminated in the assassination of the Austrian Archduke Ferdinand – providing the political spark which set Europe alight in 1914. The New Industrial Revolution, as the last quarter of the nineteenth century is sometimes called, had resulted in Germany gaining ground in the heavy industrial sphere – steel production increased nearly tenfold to 13 million tons in 1910 and the country dominated also in chemicals and electricity. France, Italy and Russia all made belated attempts to catch up in the years immediately before and after 1900, and in view of the scale of armaments production in the major European countries, the stockpile of explosives was ready when the spark came.

By the time of Marshal Foch's final offensive of World War I in July 1918 Europe had poured most of its finest men and the whole of its material wealth into a useless war, undermined its own position, and virtually brought to an end European domination in world affairs. A new era of political balances had begun. Three European-based empires, the Russian, the Austro-Hungarian and the Ottoman, had disappeared, and the process of disintegration of the overseas empire was set in train. The German submarine campaign, begun early in 1917, had brought the United States into the war on the side of the Allies in April of that year. The Russian revolutions in the same year had released German troops from the eastern front, though too late to prevent the failure of the great German spring offensive of 1918. In accepting Germany's onerous terms for surrender after the October revolution (1917), Lenin was able to gain enough time to prepare his resistance to the forces ranged against him and eventually to win the civil war (1920). There followed a series of treaties by means of which he was able to win recognition for the Soviet regime before his death in 1924.

The timing also meant that the new economic policy inaugurated by Lenin had returned Russia's industrial production, sadly atrophied during the war and the subsequent civil strife, to its pre-war level. This enabled Stalin (beginning with the Five Year Plan of 1928) to realise Lenin's dream of making socialist Russia the world power it had become by the beginning of World War II in 1939.

1920–1945

Though political and economic events determine the ambience in which architecture evolves, other events in the history of ideas may be of even greater importance to its mode of evolution. Albert Einstein had published his Special Theory of Relativity in 1905, while working in the Swiss patent office in Berne; Arthur Eddington had ensured the publication of his General Theory by 1915, and was instrumental in proving its validity experimentally in 1919. A revised view of the nature of the physical universe, that time and distance are relative rather than absolute, seemed to undermine the very foundations of human perception itself. Some advocates of modernism in art and architecture were to take the theory of relativity and other conceptual advances in science as cues for a new artistic grammar of form, space and time. At the level of rhetorical inspiration and analogy this worked well, but there was no true or precise connection, as Einstein himself was keen to point out.

The period immediately following World War I was undoubtedly one of uninhibited change – in attitudes as well as ideas – and the evolution of a new architecture was an integral part of this, spurred on by the need for new buildings to support the optimism of post-war society. Many of architecture's earlier important developments had taken place in Germany, which continued as a principal milieu for its evolution. This position changed only when its exponents were unable to accept the growing political restraints of the Nazi regime. The immediate post-war period drew upon the industrial design background of the earlier twentieth-century masters such as Behrens, and by the mid-1920s developments in prefabrication, such as Gropius's house for the Werkbund Exhibition, Stuttgart (1927), had already begun to inform the architecture of the 1920s and 1930s in a way which was not to be fully realised until after 1945.

In China the Qing dynasty (in power since the middle of the seventeenth century) fell to an army mutiny and a republic was declared in 1912, but the rebels were unable to maintain control and there followed a period of internal insurrection led by provincial warlords. The country was plagued by Japanese incursions and by interference in and exploitation of the economy by European powers in the Treaty Ports. The Nationalist and Communist Parties were amalgamated for a brief period before Chiang Kai-shek's attempt to eliminate the Communists in 1927 which, although reducing their numbers in the cities, did nothing to eliminate the dual threat from growing unrest among the rural population internally and from the Japanese externally. The Communist Party re-formed (soviets were set up in the early 1930s), and in their wartime inland retreats the Nationalists were out of touch with events. In spite of American and Russian involvement, open civil war ensued in 1947 after the eclipse of the Japanese. Finally defeated in Manchuria and in the south, the Nationalists departed to Taiwan, the Communists having taken Beijing in January 1949 and inaugurated the People's Republic of China.

Forced by the Western powers after 1918 to withdraw from its foothold in China, Japan took the earliest opportunity (brought about by the impact of the depression of the early 1930s) to remedy the position and by 1937 its Chinese incursions were already causing tension with the Americans. The German successes of 1940 triggered the Japanese invasion of South-east Asia, and though it was unsuccessful, the subsequent enforced contacts with the West have probably been more instrumental in spurring Japan into the modern technological age than earlier historical events which began this process in the nineteenth century. After its defeat in World War II, Japan initiated the most energetic and diverse programme of building the country had ever seen.

The 1919–20 peace treaties had left dissatisfied minorities in many parts of Europe and there were substantial movements of refugees. Czechoslovakia was the only new country created in the treaties which could be said to be economically viable. From the mid-1920s stability seemed for a short while assured. The Locarno Treaties of 1925 settling frontier differences between France, Belgium and Germany brought Germany back into European affairs, a position also increasingly sought by the new Soviet Union. The United States enjoyed a spectacular boom, and it was during this brief, liberal breathing space that the mould of architectural modernism as it is generally understood was set in Europe. All this was broken by the Wall Street Crash of 1929, which ushered in a worldwide economic depression and the spread of Fascism, a perversion of socialist and modernist ideology hitherto confined to Italy. Among the worst-affected countries was Germany, which by 1933 had embraced Hitler and Nazism through democratic processes rather than by coercion. Here and in France architectural modernism was in retreat throughout the 1930s, as national and classical ideals came once more to the fore. Collectivist solutions to social problems were now considered acceptable even in free-enterprise countries such as the United States, where Franklin Roosevelt ushered in the New Deal. In the later 1930s political destabilisation accelerated in Spain, France, Poland and Austria, while Italy stepped up its neo-imperialist policies with its invasion of Ethiopia and take-over of Albania. The failure of Britain and France to go to the aid of the Spanish Republic in 1936 encouraged Germany to repudiate the Locarno Treaties and to enter Austria in 1938. It was only a matter of time before a non-aggression pact with Russia opened the way for Hitler's Germany to annex areas of Europe against the wishes of Britain and France, and the uneasy balance set up in 1919 collapsed into the disaster of World War II.

1945 Onwards

In spite of the well-known buildings of the Modern Movement in Europe and the Americas, those of the Constructivist movement in Russia of the 1920s and 1930s and those influenced by them, the period prior to 1945 was not notable for global acceptance of the new design genre. Whatever the reasons may have been, there was no such wide acceptance until the later 1940s, 1950s and 1960s. The term International Style (coined by Alfred Barr in 1932 for the Museum of Modern Art show of that name in New York, to denote rationalist European architecture) was widely adopted to indicate the increasing number of buildings constructed all over the world in the modernist mode. The name is important in the context of world political changes which ensued soon after 1945, because in the fifty years which have passed since World War II the practice of architecture has become more and more international. At the same time national versions and individual schools of the style soon established themselves, from the whimsical modernism of the Festival of Britain architects in the United Kingdom and the colourful panache of Mexican and Brazilian designers to the 'brutal' concrete idiom adopted all over the world by admirers of Le Corbusier. Nor were Classicism and local styles of architecture entirely overwhelmed by the modernists, though for a few years around 1960 it looked as though they might be.

The fragile structures of colonial administration and control set up in Africa and South-east Asia by the European powers over three centuries (and vastly expanded and overstretched since the last decades of the nineteenth century) could not long survive World War II. The war completed the undermining of their economic and political status, a process which had already begun by 1918. World politics had become a matter of the rise of the superpowers and the negative checks and balances of the nuclear deterrent. India was partitioned by forming a second country, Pakistan (based on the Muslim portion of the population), in 1947. The new country was originally in two parts, one of which became the independent Bangladesh in 1971. Burma and Sri Lanka were given their independence in 1948 and Indonesia (Dutch) generally in 1949, Malaysia in 1962 and Singapore in 1965; almost the whole of Africa achieved independence in the 1950s and 1960s (a few of the smaller states had to wait until the 1970s), and South Africa became a republic in 1961.

The Keynesian period of world economics was introduced in 1946 and was to produce in the following quarter of a century the highest levels of world trade ever experienced. It was based on the worldwide availability of a strong dollar and resulted in rapid and prolonged economic expansion. In world terms the 1950s and 1960s saw an unprecedented improvement in material conditions. The World Bank and the International Monetary Fund had been founded in 1944 and a decade or so later at Bandung (1955), in the wake of decolonialisation in South-east Asia and at its beginning in Africa, the idealism of a Third World uncommitted and potentially capable of future international leadership seemed an exciting innovatory ideal, though in retrospect perhaps more in the academic dreams of a Nehru than in the eventual performance of those who attended. Unrest in the newly independent countries continued through the 1970s and ranged from seizures of power by military leaders, usually with the intention of eliminating corruption, through tribal and sectarian risings to often unwarranted interventions by the great powers.

Nevertheless, from Patagonia to New Zealand, and from Alaska to Siberia, architecture was called upon to provide, on a scale never before envisaged, the facilities and amenities of economic growth, new habitation for the wartime homeless in Europe and for massive increases in the numbers of urban poor in Third World countries, the latter often requiring the installation of basic infrastructural systems, as well as education, cultural and health services and their accompanying buildings. Priorities were determined by political ideology, by the economic performance of different nations and, in poorer countries, by the availability of international loan finance. Individual homes were more affected by the twentieth-century revolution in building services and the local availability of materials than by modernism in architecture as such. Blocks of flats, offices and the more complex building types, on the other hand, required the attention of the professional engineer or architect and therefore tended to reflect the influence of Western technology and fashion in the shape of the International Style.

During the 1960s and 1970s it came to be seen as a matter of prestige that new development in a Third World country should be in the modern as opposed to an appropriate local style – that it should be constructed in imported materials with imported equipment, if it was to express adequately the aspirations of a newly successful or recently well-supported country. Thus buildings in the International Style were built everywhere in the first twenty or thirty years of development in those countries which became independent during this period. The style has to be seen in the context also of a growing number of international design consortia – often led by major American or European architects – able to offer rapid and efficient services, perhaps to overseas investors, as, for example, in the case of tourist hotels. To some degree this is now changing. Increasing numbers of indigenous architects are educated in their own country, and less susceptible to Western fashions. Local cultures are once again beginning to exert an influence upon the artefacts they produce. Expenditure on building must be seen in the context of a world economy in which, for example, the per capita GNP in 1980 in the United States was over $10,000, but in India less than $200 and in Nigeria (an oil producer) under $700.

This unbalanced economic position was exacerbated when the oil-producing countries decided to quadruple the price of oil in October 1973. It led to a general demand for a new International Economic Order in 1974. The Third World was caught in the resultant economic depression which the energy crisis precipitated. However, the shockwaves of 1973–4 also spelt the end of the optimistic phase of orthodox modernism, and the beginning of a new cultural phase in which a plurality of architectural values was once more accepted as natural and healthy. In part this was caused by the high levels of energy used in the making and running of modern buildings and their overdependence on technology, but in part also by a growing realisation of the need for global balance and diversity. Ensuing fashions have included high-tech, post-modernism, 'critical regionalism' and experiments in ecological architecture. None has been dominant, and each has been more or less dependent on strands of thought and practice previously present in European or American design between 1925 and 1975. Nevertheless, there is a consensus of a kind that buildings should be more pleasurable, accessible and human than they often were during those years.

With ever-faster means of communication, particularly for images, internationalism is a stronger force than ever in architecture today. Many designers are now able to practise across borders and continents. But the balance of that internationalism has changed. Countries such as Japan help set the fashion for the development of architecture, Western nations invite designers from round the world to participate in the prestigious competitions now fashionable, while the workforce of many well-known practices is now decidedly international in flavour. One danger is the growing separation of the conceptual phase of buildings from their production, and the elevation of individual designers into international stars, despite the fact that architecture on anything but a small scale is now always a team effort. As the twentieth century nears its end, there is no sign of a clear single pattern emerging in world architecture. The Modern Movement has failed to fulfil the utopian predictions of some of its proponents, but it has not been buried either. For the majority of contemporary architects, it remains their most significant point of reference.

Chapter 44

WESTERN EUROPE 1900 TO 1945

Introduction

The picture of European architecture throughout this period is one of stylistic variety and fertility just as broad and as confusing as had been the case during the nineteenth century. If an ideological tendency towards a common approach in the shape of the Modern Movement is increasingly apparent, it is as often belied by the practice of architecture on the ground.

In 1900 there were three main, though overlapping, currents in European architecture, one centrifugal and two centripetal. The centrifugal current was represented by nationalism, a force unleashed by the French Revolution but still working itself out at the end of the nineteenth century. It was especially strong in such expanding powers as Germany and in smaller countries of Europe like Finland, Norway and Hungary, which were only just tasting the fruits of political and cultural autonomy. Not only independent countries but also regions of countries with their own proud traditions (e.g. Scotland in Great Britain, Catalonia in Spain and Bohemia in the Austrian Empire) participated in this tendency. Local styles, materials and traditions were explored and updated in a vernacular revival, which owed much to the example of the English Gothic Revival and Arts and Crafts Movement and something also to Art Nouveau. National and vernacular motifs were particularly strong and popular in domestic architecture. They continued long after World War I and enjoyed a revival under Fascism and Nazism. But the trauma of that war turned thoughtful architects in the European democracies against nationalism and a concept of architecture rooted purely in local race or soil.

The centripetal currents were twofold, but shared the belief that civilised countries in the new century should enjoy a common language of architecture. On the one hand, there was international Classicism, at first more securely established than ever in 1900. The Classical doctrines and teaching methods of the Ecole des Beaux Arts in Paris were admired, imitated and applied in public buildings the world over. Most new European buildings and monuments of large scale built between 1900 and 1925 were Classical in style and regular in plan. The type of Classicism varied from monumental Baroque with plentiful carving to the stripped and simplified forms introduced by Otto Wagner in Vienna, Auguste Perret in Paris or Gunnar Asplund in Stockholm. Copious structural use was also beginning to be made of steel and concrete behind Classical facades; indeed, Beaux-Arts teaching encouraged this. But the concept of a living Classical language persisted, and indeed was not to be entirely eroded until World War II. Again, it was to be the endorsement of Classicism in opposition to the Modern Movement by the regimes of Fascist Italy, Nazi Germany and Stalinist Russia which sounded its final death-knell as the common language of European architecture.

The other centripetal current was the one which was to lead to what we now call 'modern architecture'. This phrase first became familiar as the title of a book of 1896 by Otto Wagner, Vienna's leading Classicist and architectural teacher. The essence of Wagner's position was not so much that architecture should have a universal style (a common call in the nineteenth century) as that it should visibly fit the purposes, habits and emotions of modern life. He was disturbed by the mismatch between the efficient planning and construction of buildings and the elaborate Classical 'dressing' of their facades. In his own later practice, Wagner sought to explore a purged and clarified language of Classicism which would have relevance and meaning to the twentieth century.

The implications of Wagner's ideas were explored in various ways by his many Viennese admirers and pupils, the *Wagnerschule*. Among these, it was to be Adolf Loos who in his writings and buildings developed the implications of a 'modern architecture' most subtly before World War I. Loos promoted an architecture of rich, simplified surfaces and open plans, as a correct setting for a clean, comfortable and efficient life for the modern middle classes of Europe. Loos himself never repudiated Classicism, but the stark exteriors of his early villas were the clearest precursors of the Modern Movement of the 1920s.

Germany's contribution to the concept of a universal style of architecture for the new century came largely out of its ambitions as an industrial power. Industrial buildings were ideal material for a purely 'functional' approach to architecture. The Deutscher Werkbund was founded in 1907 to promote links between industry and the arts. Its main instigator was Hermann Muthesius, who had championed the practical 'stylelessness' of British houses of the last quarter of the nineteenth century as pointers to the future. In 1902 Muthesius published the first tract calling for the supplanting of styles with an architecture based purely on practical purpose and the structural advances of modern engineering (*Stilarchitektur und Baukunst*, 1902). Ideas of this kind were tentatively explored in industrial buildings designed by Peter Behrens and Hans Poelzig, at heart by no means pure functionalists, but gave younger architects (notably Behrens' assistants Walter Gropius and Mies van der Rohe – and, very briefly, Le Corbusier) pause for thought. The climax of pre-war debate on this topic came at the Deutscher Werkbund Exhibition at Cologne in 1914, when Muthesius advocated 'typological studies' based on function as the way forward in architecture) but encountered bitter opposition.

The upshot of this debate emerged only in the 1920s. After a sharp but brief resurgence of highly emotional and romantic projects throughout Europe, caused in large measure by the horror of prolonged war and subsequent revolution in Russia, Germany and Hungary, the proponents of a wholly new architecture for the twentieth century settled down to develop a range of flat-roofed, freely planned styles which made candid use of the new industrialised materials and building techniques – steel, reinforced concrete, sheet glass, etc. – but allowed latitude of expression to the designer. The first fully fledged example of this 'International Style' (so christened only as late as 1932 because its advocates would not admit it to be a style) were the early French villas of Le Corbusier and the Dutch housing of J. J. P. Oud and Gerrit Rietveld.

In Germany and Russia, conditions in the early 1920s were more turbulent: less favourable for building, but more so for a revolutionary approach to architecture. Two reformed art schools, the Vkhutemas school in Moscow and the Bauhaus in Germany, became instrumental in spreading enthusiasm for a radical style of architecture. In neither was the initial approach to design purely functional. From the Vkhutemas emerged in the hands of architects such as Konstantin Melnikov the Russian variant of modern architecture known as Constructivism, which combined functionalist aspirations with a strong instinct for forceful, sculptural form. Because of circumstances in Russia, little was actually built in this manner. The Bauhaus, directed by Gropius, was of importance because it always had a strong international contingent and it encouraged publicity and controversy. In its early years at Weimar it was largely an art school with a strong 'Expressionist' streak, and indeed architecture was not formally taught. After 1925, when the Bauhaus moved to Dessau and a big German housing drive commenced, the new architecture became central to its concerns.

In the late 1920s, under the leadership of Martin Wagner and Mies van der Rohe in Berlin, Ernst May in Frankfurt and Gropius and Hannes Meyer at the Bauhaus, the austere German version of modern architecture became the dominant progressivist tendency. It was based largely on the German Modernists' approach to the large-scale programmes of state-subsidised housing then being undertaken throughout the major countries of Europe, justified chiefly on functional grounds, and identified with the search for a new objectivity or practicality (*Neue Sachlichkeit*), a phrase frequently used in the culture of the later Weimar Republic in Germany. It was soon taken up in more or less its German form in Switzerland, Czechoslovakia, Austria, Hungary and Belgium.

In France, the opposing influences of tradition and of the restless 'poet-innovator' Le Corbusier, whose powerfully influential *Vers une Architecture* was published in 1923, prevented Modernism assuming a single guise. The same was true of Italy, where perhaps the finest of all Modernist architecture before World War II was created by Giuseppe Terragni but where the Fascist regime could never quite make up its mind about the style. Here and in other countries around the Mediterranean there was no difficulty in accepting an idiom of rendered surfaces and flat roofs for ordinary houses and smaller buildings; in Greece, for instance, some fine modern schools were built in the 1930s.

The Scandinavian countries, through the example of Gunnar Asplund in Sweden and Alvar Aalto in Finland, also proved adept at taking what they wanted from Modernism and humanising the style to local circumstance. Something similar happened in Britain, though here the Modernist package arrived late, only in the 1930s, and met with dogged resistance. Only the example and ideological persistence of the emigrés Berthold Lubetkin and Walter Gropius ensured its eventual acceptance. Finally, in Russia, where many German architects went after the collapse of their national economy in 1929–30, much was expected from the Modernist vision in the way of housing and planning but very little achieved, particularly after 1934, when the political climate turned sour.

The promulgation of the international style as architectural orthodoxy depended largely on the propaganda network of CIAM, the Congrès Internationaux d'Architecture Moderne, which first met in 1928 at La Sarraz in Switzerland, with Sigfried Giedion as its secretary and propagandist. In 1929, at Frankfurt, working groups were set up to study individual problems and membership was organised on a national basis. In the 1930s CIAM was increasingly dominated by Le Corbusier; and the *Charter of Athens* agreed under his influence at its 1933 meeting refocused the Modern Movement towards broader problems of urban design. Henceforward, in the wake of the world depression of the 1930s and the rise of the dictatorships, with little Modernist architecture being built in continental Europe, CIAM adherents were increasingly concerned to come up with radical proposals for replanning old cities or laying out new ones. This approach gathered force with the Spanish Civil War of 1936–9 and the advent of a new world war in 1939, when European cities became targets for concentrated bombing. CIAM continued to meet until 1956, but its practical influence diminished in the post-war years.

Important also to Modernist thinking was the belief that architecture and technology should be integrated and that pure engineering structures such as bridges, dams, hangars and silos were the true testament to twentieth-century values. Engineer-architects like François Hennebique and Eugène Freyssinet in France, Robert Maillart in Switzerland, Pierluigi Nervi in Italy, Eduardo Torroja in Spain and Owen Williams in Britain were therefore of great significance to the development of orthodox Modernism, and images of their work were widely disseminated and admired. Reinforced concrete construction, the concrete frame, the steel frame and techniques of prefabrication and standardisation for buildings produced in large numbers (notably housing) all made great strides during this period, though by no means only in buildings designed by Modernists themselves. Indeed much of the early architecture of the Modern Movement was built with old-fashioned structural brick walls, while many Classical buildings of the period have structures of steel or concrete behind their facades.

Despite attempts to limit a definition of the Modern Movement to the 'white box architecture' of Le Corbusier, the 'New Objectivity' of the German social architects of the 1920s and the great new engineering structures, Modernism was always a broad church which developed in many different directions throughout Europe. The most easily identifiable alternative currents in new thinking were those in which feeling and subjectivity were considered paramount. They are often drawn together under the loose rubric of 'Expressionism'.

This strand in modern architectural development had its origins in the Franco-Belgian Art Nouveau and the Bavarian–Austrian *Jugendstil* of the 1890s. By 1900 Art Nouveau had lost much of its force and inventiveness but it continued for some time thereafter, most brilliantly perhaps in Russia in the hands of F. O. Shekhtel and his circle (q.v.). It was gradually extended and transformed in the work of those pupils of Otto Wagner associated with the Vienna Secession, notably Josef Maria Olbrich and Josef Hoffmann, who tried to make their architecture significant and modern by means of new kinds of ornamental and symbolic expression. After 1900 the Secessionists, along with C. R. Mackintosh in Glasgow and a number of Czech architects, worked increasingly in a blocky, cubic manner, enhanced by a rich symbolic decoration and sculpture which prevented their designs from becoming mere geometrical, objective exercises. Such symbolism proved poorly rooted in European culture and, after a brief vogue, soon lost its appeal.

The role of feeling in architecture was much discussed in German-speaking countries before and after World War I, the leading text on the subject being Wilhelm Worringer's *Abstraktion und Einfühlung* (Abstraction and Empathy), published in 1908. By World War I, Expressionism in architecture had become dissipated in various experimental and esoteric directions and had lost its universalising force. In the 1920s a middle road between 'subjective' Expressionism and 'objective' Modernism was to be found in the work of such well-known German architects as Hans Poelzig, Hugo Häring and Hans Scharoun, while many German, Dutch and Belgian modernists, notably Erich Mendelsohn, W. M. Dudok, Michel de Klerk and Henry Van de Velde, developed an architecture of expressive line, curve, volume and minimal ornament which was imitated in the 1930s all over Europe, notably for new building-types such as cinemas. Expressionism also found a natural vehicle in churches, many fine churches being built in the inter-war period with lofty concrete vaults or arches covered with a brick skin, the innovators here being Dominikus Böhm in Germany and Paul Bellot in France.

Another strand in inter-war European architecture was the rise of Art Deco, a style which can be traced back to the brilliant costumes and stage sets of the pre-1914 Ballet Russe. This colourful, decorative idiom was given a boost by the 1925 Paris Exposition des Arts Décoratifs, from which it takes its name. Art Deco proved popular for stripped Classical and 'moderne' buildings of the Expressionist variety, notably in France, and a useful counterbalance to the decorative abstinence of pure Modernism, but was practically extinct as an architectural style by 1935.

In many European countries, architectural Modernism had made only limited inroads on the dominance of Classicism for public buildings by 1930. In France, for instance, Auguste Perret's brilliant formula for cleansing and refreshing the Classical idiom by means of concrete structural technique had swept the country. Prominent urban buildings of the 1930s in Francophone cities such as Paris and Geneva tend to straddle the border between stripped Classicism and Modernism without discomfort. Other nations continued with their own versions of Classicism, and often still deployed the full panoply of the orders in important urban buildings. Sir Edwin Lutyens in his war memorials and colonial architecture for the British Empire proved the last universally acknowledged master of the grand Classical manner, though Marcello Piacentini, working in the rhetorical, neo-Roman imperial Classicism favoured in Fascist Italy of the 1920s, ran him close. Evaluation of the neo-Classicism of the 1930s dictatorships, as exemplified by Paul Troost and Albert Speer in Germany, Ivan Zholtovsky in Russia and many others, remains controversial. A wide spectrum of styles was practised, varying from literal copying of Greek and Roman forms at overblown scales to reinterpretations of Classicism as radical as those of Perret or Asplund.

For smaller buildings such as houses, particularly in colder climates and rural areas where timber construction and pitched roofs were still the norm, national traditions of architecture continued to thrive into the 1930s. Nevertheless, structure often became simpler as a result of new technology and standardisation, and decorative features were reduced or disappeared altogether. Nazi Germany attempted to revive national styles of rural architecture, but with only modest success. In other countries, a potentially fruitful convergence between vernacular traditions and Modernism was beginning to make itself felt towards the end of the 1930s, only to be interrupted in 1939 by a second, devastating world war, during which architecture was dominated by utility and almost all new structures of merit were in the engineering tradition.

In planning, this was a period when architects were unusually powerful in the shaping and extension of cities. The dominant model was that of the dispersed garden city or suburb, laid out on picturesque lines with groups of houses or flats in a landscape, and clearly demarcated zones for different activities – notably civic life, housing and industry. The concept reached early maturity in the work of Raymond Unwin at Letchworth and Hampstead Garden Suburb, and was disseminated internationally through his book *Town Planning in Practice* (1908). So-called garden cities (usually in fact only suburbs) on English lines were built all over Europe in the following thirty years, their success being most notable in northern countries (Belgium, Holland, Germany and Finland). After World War I, the constituent elements of planned suburbs tended to be blocks of flats as often as two-storey houses. This change of scale encouraged a more formal approach to planning, seen at its extreme in Le Corbusier's influential drawings for tall blocks in a generous parkland setting. In practice, blocks of flats had to be built fairly close together, and great pains were taken in the various national urban and suburban housing programmes of the 1920s to reconcile architectural formality with useful and healthy open space. In general, the English school of planning proceeded from informal housing to formal centre, while continental architect-planners worked in the reverse direction. The contrast is most manifest in the difference between the Italian new towns of the 1930s, which have compact and successful centres, but dull peripheries, and such a town as Welwyn Garden City in England, whose interest lies largely in the subtlety of its housing schemes.

Austria

The example of Otto Wagner (1841–1918) dominated the early modern period in Austrian architecture. In 1894 Wagner became professor at the Academy of Fine Arts, teaching all the foremost architects of the next generation, and in 1896 published the first edition of his *Modern Architecture*. This inaugurated an experimental period in Vienna notable for the late work of Wagner himself, for buildings by the architects of the Vienna Secession such as Josef Maria Olbrich (1867–1908) and Josef Hoffmann (1870–1956), by more eclectic designers like Jože Plečnik (1872–1957) and Max Fabiani (1865–1952), and for the austere but influential example of Adolf Loos (1870–1933).

Wagner had made his first mark as an orthodox classicist during the boom period in Vienna when the Ringstrasse was constructed (1870s-1880s). For the municipality he built railway stations on two suburban lines between 1894 and 1901 and the Nussdorf lock on the Danube (1894–8). The foremost Viennese civic building of Wagner's maturity was his **Post Office Savings Bank** (1904–12) (p. 1322A), which combines a modern structure of concrete and steel with a new form of Classical articulation for the exterior. This has a granite base with thin marble cladding above, pinned to the core of the building by conspicuous aluminium bolts forming a pattern, so as to make clear that the marble is a ceremonial dress, not a structural material. The main hall has an exposed steel frame and is covered by two skins of glass; the floor too is partly glazed. Warm air is introduced into the building through bold aluminium cylinders. Wagner's **Church Am Steinhof** (1905–7) uses similar techniques. It is covered by a double-skinned dome, makes historical references to Fischer von Erlach's Karlskirche (q.v.) and is decorated by artists of the Wiener Werkstätte, including Kolo Moser.

Olbrich's **Secession Building, Vienna** (1897–8), was the flagship building of the anti-academic movement and the high architectural point of *Jugendstil*, the Austrian counterpart to Art Nouveau. It consists of a gilded globe strewn with laurels perched boldly on top of the entrance to a large, plain gallery space. In 1899 Olbrich went to Darmstadt, Germany, at the invitation of the Grand Duke of Hesse to design buildings for his new artists' colony and the remainder of his career was spent there.

A. Post Office Savings Bank, Vienna (1904–12): main hall. See p. 1321

B. Palais Stoclet, Brussels (1905–11). See p. 1323

Josef Hoffmann was one of the founders in 1903 of the Wiener Werkstätte, a workshop which produced high-quality crafts objects for architectural settings. Hoffmann's smaller houses show admiration of English domestic work, but his larger buildings, notably the **Purkersdorf Sanatorium, Vienna** (1904), and the **Palais Stoclet, Brussels** (1905–11) (p. 1322B), combine Wagner's interest in clean, rich surfaces with cubic forms. The Palais Stoclet is centred upon a tower, with four giant figures and a small globe; its volumes are defined by a series of marble planes framed by geometrical bronze mouldings. Inside the building, Gustav Klimt designed murals in a lavish layout that connects to a formal garden and an impressive two-storey entrance hall.

Jože Plečnik was a Slovenian who worked first in Vienna and then in Prague before returning to his native country and embracing an idiosyncratic, nationalist form of classicism. Plečnik's important early Viennese works are the **Zacherlhaus** (1903–5), consisting of luxury flats over a shop and incorporating an early 'curtain wall' of polished granite topped with brooding atlantes by Franz Metzner; and the **Church of the Holy Spirit** (1910–13), which has a portico of naked concrete fronting a trabeated interior of broad span. In Prague (see Chapter 46), Plečnik creatively restored the **Hradčany Castle** for the Czech president, Jan Masaryk (1920–32) where he added a remarkable garden staircase incorporating various essays upon the primitive Ionic order, and built the **Church of the Sacred Heart, Vinohrady** (1928–32) (q.v.), an astonishing concoction of concrete Classicism. His later romantic Classical works in and around Ljubljana include many Catholic churches, the **Three Bridges** (1929–32) and the **Žale Cemetery** (1938–40). All are distinguished for their heterodox imagination and quality of craftsmanship. Plečnik's fellow countryman, Max Fabiani, was responsible in Vienna for the **Portois and Fix Store** (1898–1900, in Wagnerian mode) and the Expressionist **Urania Theatre** (1909–10). In later life he restored and built several villas in the old Slovenian town of Štanjel.

Adolf Loos was born in Brno, studied in Dresden, spent three years in America and claimed to be an Anglophile. He was a cultural critic and journalist as much as an architect. In his writings, such as *Ins Lehre Gesprochen* (Spoken into the Void) and *Trotzdem* (Nevertheless), he called for a common art of building which employed sound but not over-refined craftsmanship, and mocked the ornamentalism and preciousness of the Secession movement. Loos advocated planning rooms by volume (*Raumplan*) and insisted on flat, rich surfaces instead of meaningless ornament as the fittest setting for comfortable, efficient modern life. His **Goldmann and Salatsch Shop and Apartments** (1909–11), completing the Michaelerplatz in Vienna, was violently criticised at the time for the plainness of its exterior. His bourgeois houses, e.g. the **Scheu House, Vienna** (1912), the **Tristan Tzara House, Paris** (1927), and the **Mueller House, Prague** (1931) (see Chapter 46), combine shockingly plain elevations with plutocratic, marbled interiors. Loos's interior style influenced bourgeois apartment building throughout Europe and America in the inter-war years. In Vienna, the standard of his work was often equalled by that of Josef Frank (1885–1967), for example his **house in Wittbrangasse** (1913–14).

The greatest architectural impact upon Vienna between 1919 and 1933 resulted from the city's housing programme, under which 66,000 dwellings were built for the socialist *Gemeinde Wien* ('Red Vienna'). Some garden suburbs were laid out (e.g. **Rannersdorf**, 1921, by Heinrich Tessenow and others), but the bulk of the housing consisted of city blocks grouped round courts, with rendered elevations six to seven storeys high. The flats were small internally but there were generous community and service facilities. These blocks infiltrated the urban area in a consistent pattern. The largest complex is the combined **Karl-Marx-Hof** (p. 1325A) and **Svoboda-Hof** (1926–30), designed by Karl Ehn. Its defensive, city-wall-like appearance, more than one kilometre in length, confronts the railway. Many other architects were involved in the housing programme, including Hoffmann, Loos, Josef Frank and Peter Behrens, and the prolific partnership of H. Schmid and H. Aichinger. It provided a monumental link between the early Viennese Modernism of the pre-war years and the emerging International Style, as exemplified in the suburban **Werkbund Estate** (1930–2), Vienna's later and lesser equivalent to Stuttgart's Weissenhof Siedlung, with houses by Frank, Hugo Häring, Hoffmann, Loos, André Lurçat, Gerrit Rietveld and others. After the rise of Fascism in 1933–4, the municipal housing programme stopped. Austria then produced little first-class architecture until after World War II.

France

Fin de siècle architecture in France was dominated still by the internationally influential Classicism of the Ecole des Beaux Arts. The Beaux-Arts style of axial layout and symmetrical planning was particularly suited to the great civic statements and public buildings at which France has always excelled. Architects came from many countries to train at the Ecole, and the revived styles of Louis XIV, XV and XVI were identified with elegant architecture all over the world, specially for interiors. Charles Mewès (1860–1914), who with his partners Arthur Davis in London and Alphonse Bischoff in Cologne built Louis-XVI-style **Ritz Hotels** in **Paris** (1898), **London** (1905–6) and **Madrid** (1908–10), was one of several architects who fed the international appetite for French architecture at this time.

The festive **Pont Alexandre III,** by the engineer Louis Résal with the architects Cassien-Bernard and Cousin, one of several structures built for the **Paris Exhibition of 1900,** and the **Gare d'Orsay** (now **Musée d'Orsay**), **Paris** (1898–1900), by Victor Laloux (1850–1937), are representative examples both of the scholarly Classicism which Beaux-Arts architects brought to their work and of the ease with which they had learnt to accommodate their Classical facades and plans to iron and steel structures and interiors. Even churches, for instance Zacharie Astruc's **Notre Dame du Travail, Paris** (1899–1901), with a cheap, all-steel interior behind a plain Classical facade, sometimes followed this pattern.

'Art Nouveau' was also strong at the turn of the century in northern France. The name came from the 'Salon de l'Art Nouveau', the Paris gallery of the art dealer Samuel Bing, opened in 1895 to sell *objets d'art* from different countries in avant-garde styles including glass by Emile Galle of Nancy, textiles by the William Morris firm and furniture by Henry Van de Velde of Belgium (1863–1957). Art Nouveau therefore started as a name for the crafts, but was soon applied to the 'free' or 'organic' architecture incorporating structural and decorative ironwork, sinuous, swelling or bursting vegetable ornament and modest asymmetry which had a vogue throughout continental Europe between 1895 and 1910. Other names (e.g. *Jugendstil* or *Sezessionstil* in Germany and Austria; *Stile Floreale* or *Stile Liberty* in Italy; *Modernismo* in Spain) refer to similar tendencies. The rational strain within this current owed much to the theories of Viollet-le-Duc.

The most articulate French advocate of Art Nouveau architecture was the provocative Frantz Jourdain (1847–1935), who welcomed iron and steel construction but disdained the undecorated crudity of structures like the Eiffel Tower (q.v.). Jourdain demonstrated his ideas in his long-drawn-out rebuilding of the Paris store of **La Samaritaine** (1891–1914) (p. 1325B), in which surface decoration and advertisement adorned a rational steel structure. The style quickly became popular for the architecture of consumption, advertisement and display, as in the **Galeries Lafayette** (1906–12) and **Grand Bazar** (1906), both in Paris. Art Nouveau's most successful architect was Hector Guimard (1867–1942). His well-known stations for the **Paris Métro** (1900–12) (see Chapter 34) continue in muscular cast iron the vegetal decorative tradition begun in his apartment building, **Castel Béranger, Paris** (1894–8). But after his own **house in the Avenue Mozart, Paris** (1910), Guimard turned towards a rationalised architecture of prefabricated elements for his later apartment buildings.

Art Nouveau enjoyed much architectural popularity as a villa style for the bourgeoisie. Its strongest provincial centre of influence was Nancy, the iron-and-steel capital of Lorraine, where it was stimulated by a flourishing crafts industry and art school. A fine house in the style was the **Villa Majorelle, Nancy** (1898–1901), an early work by Henri Sauvage (1873–1932). Many French architects of the period were touched by Art Nouveau but continued to work in a variety of styles. J. Hornecker of **Nancy**, for instance, built the **Grand Théâtre** there in full classical dress, but shops in an Art Nouveau style and houses in both vernacular and Classical styles. Likewise, Samuel Bing's own architect, Louis Bonnier (1856–1946), employed an English-influenced, vernacular-revival manner for his suburban houses, for example **house for André Gide, Avenue des Sycomores, Paris** (1904–5), but refined the polychromatic brick style popular in northern France for urban buildings, like the **school in Rue Rouelle, Paris** (1908–11). Bonnier's masterpiece is his handsome **bath**, at **La Butte aux Cailles, Paris** (1920–4), with parabolic concrete vaults behind a brick facade.

The French engineering tradition in architecture, prominent in the Paris 1889 and 1900 Exhibitions, grew in strength as a result of the country's early lead in reinforced concrete, the material of the new century. The enterprising firm of François Hennebique (1842–1921) was the first to be widely successful with this technique of construction. The Hennebique system was developed in the mid-1890s for mills and factories in the Lille and Tourcoing districts and after 1900 was rapidly taken up and spread abroad through licensing. In the early years, reinforced concrete was usually exposed in factory or mill buildings where style was unimportant, but covered and given an architectural veneer in smart buildings. The main staircase of the **Grand Palais** for the 1900 Exhibition, Paris, designed in the Louis XVI style, was an early example of the use of the technique in a prominent building.

A first tentative exploration of the new architectural expression which concrete might allow was made in the church of **S. Jean de Montmartre, Paris** (1894–1904), by Anatole de Baudot (1834–1915), built in a system of concrete arches with brick infilling (see Chapter 34). Its special potential for architecture was to be consistently realised by Auguste Perret (1874–1954), an architect-engineer of Beaux-Arts background. In his early **flats in Rue Franklin, Paris** (1903–4, still in the Hennebique system) (p 1326A), the street elevation consists of a rectangular frame-and-panel arrangement. The concrete frame allows generous window space and is clearly expressed but not exposed, the surfaces being covered with decorative tiles.

Perret's architecture, built always in reinforced concrete by a construction firm he formed with his brother Gustave, soon developed towards a modern stripped and trabeated Classicism, with the material exposed on the facades. His influential **Théâtre des Champs Elysées, Paris** (1911–13) (p. 1328A), based on a scheme by Henry Van de Velde, has a vaulted

A. Karl-Marx-Hof, Vienna (1926–30). See p. 1323

B. La Samaritaine Store, Paris (1891–1914). See p. 1324

C. Villa Savoye, Poissy (1929–30). See p. 1329

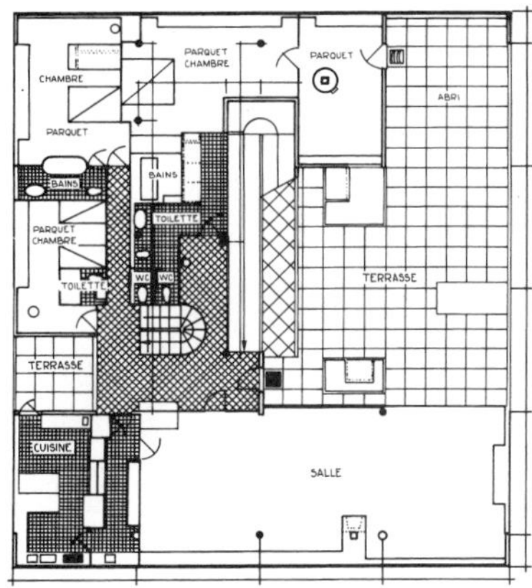

D. Villa Savoye: plan at first floor

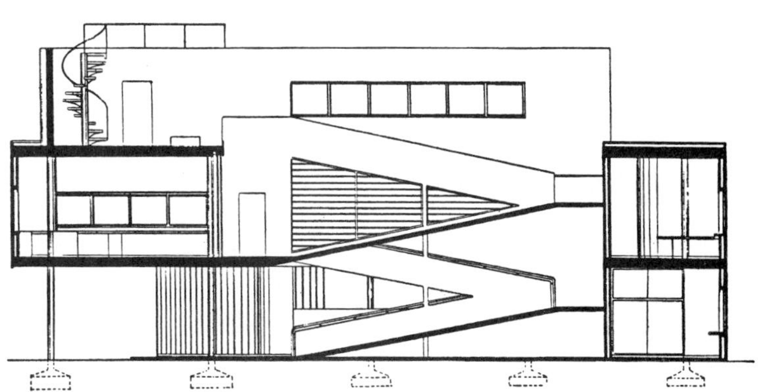

E. Villa Savoye: section

A. Flats on the rue Franklin, Paris (1903–4). See p. 1324

B. Church of Notre Dame, Le Raincy (1922–3). See p. 1327

C. Villa Savoye, Poissy (1929–30): patio. See p. 1329

D. Pavilion Suisse, Paris (1930–32). See p. 1329

auditorium, a trabeated concourse and a concrete-faced front of Doric proportions with a frieze by Antoine Bourdelle. His masterpiece is the **Church of Notre Dame, Le Raincy** (1922–3) (pp. 1326B, 1328B). This cheap building reconciles the Gothic and Classical French traditions of church architecture in naked concrete, with a frame-and-panel arrangement for the elevations, an open auditorium, shallow vaults, thin columns and a blaze of colourful glass (by Maurice Denis) in the insistent window patterning. Thereafter Perret tended to repeat himself in his churches, of which the grandest was **S. Jean, Le Havre** (1952–5). His **Atelier Esders, Paris** (1919–21), the best of his industrial buildings, had a simple, open, galleried, top-lit workplace trussed by elegant concrete arches. His public buildings became rather cerebral Classical essays in a personal programme intended to show off the versatility of concrete (e.g. **Musée des Travaux Publics, Paris,** 1936–46). Perret had great influence within France, not least on Le Corbusier.

In engineering works, concrete construction was handled with special flair by Eugène Freyssinet (1879–1962), the father of pre-stressed concrete. His most celebrated works were the **airship hangars, Orly Airport,** two gigantic parabolic sheds of 1921–3. Freyssinet assisted in many concrete-vaulted halls and factories of the inter-war years, e.g. the fine **Market Hall, Rheims,** but was primarily important as a designer of bridges. His concept of pre-stressing concrete was to allow longer and thinner spans in architecture but it remained in its infancy up to the time of World War II.

Among other important French architects of the early modern period were Henri Sauvage and Tony Garnier (1869–1948). Sauvage soon gave up designing in an Art Nouveau style and became preoccupied with the form of the urban apartment block. Beginning with colourfully clad **flats in the Rue Vavin, Paris** (1912–13), he developed a stepped section which gave good balconies, light and air throughout a building. The many stepped sections in modern architecture derive from his experiments and from dramatic sketches by the Italian Sant'Elia. Sauvage also designed the decorative **Cinéma Gambetta, Paris** (1920), and with his friend Jourdain transformed the latter's La Samaritaine Store, Paris with heavier elevations in the late 1920s. Garnier's importance belongs to the history of town planning. His *Cité Industrielle*, an ideal project begun in 1901 and published in 1917, depicts in sober tones an industrial city for 35,000 people, united by a flat-roofed, Cubic formalism and planned with rigid zoning distinctions between home and workplace, centre and suburb. The plan embodies Garnier's experience in his native Lyons, where in 1908 he was employed to lay out the market area, **Les Mouches**, of which the stepped and steel-framed **hall** (1909) had an 80 m (262 ft) span. Garnier also built a **hospital at Grange Blanche, Lyons** (1920–33), and the stripped Classical **town hall, Boulogne-Billancourt** (1931–4). Urbanism, a term arguably coined in Lyons in 1909, was further pursued there by Robert Giroud and Môrice Leroux, whose street of buildings at **Villeurbane, Les Gratte-Ciels** (1935), is a monumental composition of flats with balconies leading to a grand Art Deco town hall.

'Art Deco' in France had its roots in the exotic style of Diaghilev's Ballet Russe, but took its name from the Paris *Exposition des Arts Décoratifs* (1925). Not strictly an architectural style, it became a way of reconciling the stripped Classicism of Perret and his disciples with the decorative and crafts traditions still strong in the wake of Art Nouveau. The heavy, colourful, ceramic forms of Art Deco were popular in France for inter-war shops and cinemas. A fine example of the inter-war mixture of Classical and decorative styles is the **City Library, Toulouse**, built for a socialist municipal administration by the city architect, Jean Montariol, with reliefs of workers along the front and spangles of glass in the reading room ceiling. Public buildings of *c.* 1925–35 in France and Italy often assume such a didactic air, with ponderous symbolic programmes. Official Classicism in these years gradually became simpler and more stripped, under the influence of Perret. Such, for instance, was the architecture of Albert Laprade (1883–1978) in his **Museum of the Colonies** (now **Museum of African and Oceanic Art**) (1929) and his **Citroën Store** of the same year, and also the open-squared **Palais de Chaillot, Trocadéro, Paris**, by Azéma, Boileau and Carlu (1937).

French bourgeois houses and apartment buildings of the period, though often touched by Art Deco, mostly adhered to a quiet Classicism, with the addition of pilasters, cherubs or relief panels to assert their claims to culture. Roger Expert (1882–1955) built a specially skilful clutch of four such **villas** in the seaside town of **Arcachon** (1924–7) as well as the **French Embassy, Belgrade** (1930). Churches also remained largely traditional, their finest exponent being the Beaux-Arts-trained Benedictine monk Paul Bellot (1878–1944), whose international practice consisted mainly of brick churches influenced by Dutch and German Expressionism such as the **Prieuré Sainte-Bathilde, Vanves** (1935). Other churches of interest include the centralised **S. Louis, Vincennes** (1912), by Marrast and Droz and **S. Jeanne d'Arc, Nice** (1924), with a strong regional flavour, also by Jacques Droz.

After World War I, avant-garde French architecture was dominated by the dynamic personality of Le Corbusier (1887–1965), the Swiss-born architect, painter and polemicist. He first came to prominence through the magazine *L'Espirit Nouveau*. In 1914–15 he publicised his 'Domino' patent design, a skeletal concrete frame for mass-produced housing responding to wartime conditions. He pursued and enlarged

A. Théâtre des Champs Elysées, Paris (1911–13). See p. 1324

B. Church of Notre Dame, Le Raincy: interior

C. Maison de Verre (Dalsace House), Paris (1928–32). See p. 1329

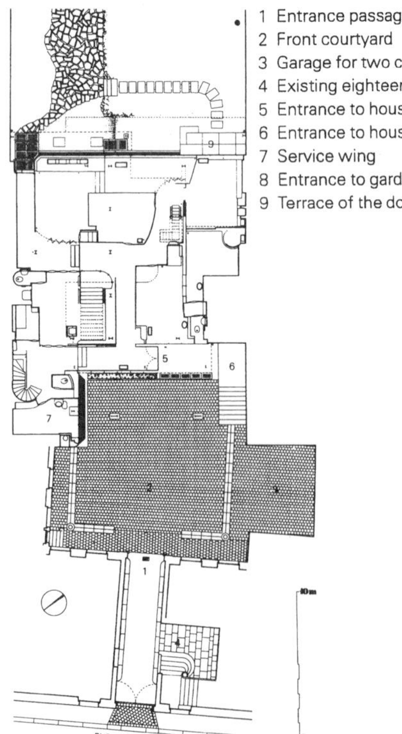

D. Maison de Verre: ground-floor plan and garden

upon the 'five points' of his theory in a stream of controversial designs and books, of which the most famous was *Vers une architecture* (Towards A New Architecture) of 1923. His early buildings were mostly artists' studios houses and suburban villas: the **La Roche-Jeanneret houses, Paris** (1924), the **Maison Planeix, Paris** (1927), the **Villa Stein, Garches** (1927) and the **Villa Savoye, Poissy** (1929–30) (pp. 1325C–E, 1326C). In these, making use of the planning freedom allowed by concrete framing, Le Corbusier pioneered the flat-roofed 'white architecture' that became synonymous with international Modernism. He broke up the elements of the house and rearranged them in carefully proportioned arrangements of square, curve and diagonal. This villa style was influenced in the first instance by Cubist painting and Dutch De Stijl designers. The houses have generous, well-windowed but chilly interiors, without clutter; at the Villa Savoye, the whole upper floor is for the first time raised up on pilotis. Le Corbusier's interest extended to the smaller house, e.g. the house for his mother at **Vevey, Switzerland** (1926), the **Maison Cook, Boulogne-sur-Seine** (1926), and most fruitfully the clever double houses he built for the garden suburb of **Pessac, Bordeaux** (1926–8). Few of his larger projects came to fruition. The most important was the **Pavillon Suisse, Paris** (1930–2) (p. 1326D). Here and in the **Salvation Army building, Paris** (1919–33), and the **Centrosoyuz Building, Moscow** (1928–34), he and his partner Pierre Jeanneret (1896–1967) explored the possibilities of curtain walling and air-conditioning. They failed to win the competitions for the League of Nations Building, Geneva (1926–7) and the Palace of the Soviets, Moscow (1931–2), but in both cases Le Corbusier's designs were widely publicised and praised. In the 1930s he spent much of his energy in abortive city-planning projects, notably for Algiers. Many of these ideas were to find an outlet in his work after 1945.

Alongside Le Corbusier and Jeanneret, mention should be made among avant-garde architects of Eileen Gray (1879–1976), Robert Mallet-Stevens (1886–1945) and Michel Roux-Spitz (1888–1957). With Jean Bacovici, Gray designed two magnificent **houses at Roquebrunne, near Nice**, taking full advantage of the Modern Movement's concern for sun and light. (The *ne plus ultra* of this fascination was the turning **solarium** devised for a clinic at **Aix-les-Bains** by Pierre Flaix, 1932.) Mallet-Stevens designed a cul-de-sac of houses (now the **Rue Mallet-Stevens**) in Paris (1926–7) which were influenced by Loos and the Dutch De Stiji designers, as well as the large **Villa Trappenard, Sceaux** (1930). He was also active as a designer of film sets and shops. Roux-Spitz occupied a midway position between Art Deco (or *Art Moderne*) and avant-garde modernism. Among his apartment buildings in Paris, **35 Boulevard des Italiens** over a Ford showroom (1931), is notable; he also built, for himself, a fine **villa at Dinard** with murals by Louis Bousquet. Lubetkin and Ginsberg's **25 Avenue de Versailles, Paris** (1930), is another major contribution to the genre of Paris apartment houses. The most famous house in Paris of the period is the **Maison de Verre** (properly **Dalsace House**) (1928–32) (p. 1328C,D), a lyrical early example of the 'machine for living' with outstanding use of glass and metal. Its designers were Pierre Chareau and the Dutchman Bernard Bijvoet.

The Paris suburbs generated many interesting projects in the inter-war period, due largely to the patronage and power of Henri Sellier, who oversaw low-cost housing on behalf of the Seine Département. New communities were created round the capital, commonly called *cités jardin* though they consisted almost entirely of brick flats with rendered elevations and public space between the blocks. They include **Le Plessis-Robinson** (1924–39) and **Châtenay-Malabry** (1931–9), where a rolling site and better architecture by Bassompierre and Rutté furnished a more congenial result. At **Drancy**, the experimentally minded Modernists Eugène Beaudouin and Marcel Lods built the **Cité de la Muette** (1931–2), the first European housing estate to include tower blocks (of fifteen storeys). At **Suresnes**, Beaudouin and Lods designed a fine **school** (1935) with single-storey pavilions, while their **Maison du Peuple, Clichy** (1938–9), was an all-steel building designed in collaboration with the influential technician Jean Prouvé (1901–1984). Another fine suburban school was the **Karl Marx School at Villejuif** (1933), the masterpiece of the Modernist André Lurçat (1894–1970).

Germany

The victories of Germany in the wars of 1866–70 led to a surge of nationalism which was far from exhausted in German architecture between 1900 and World War I. Its extreme expression was the centennial **Monument to the Battle of Leipzig**, by Bruno Schmitz with brooding sculpture by Franz Metzner, 1913. In Alsace (German territory between 1870 and 1914), **Haut-Koenigsbourg,** an ancient castle in the Vosges, was romantically reconstructed (1901–8) in German mediaeval style for Kaiser Wilhelm II by Bodo Ebhardt of Berlin (1865–1945), with striking frescoes by Léo Schnug. **Strasbourg,** the Alsatian capital, acquired fine buildings in a self-conciously German or Alsatian gabled style (**School, Rue des Pontonniers,** 1903–4) and a picturesque **garden suburb** at **Neudorf** (1912–14).

This was one of several garden suburbs for workers built on English principles at the instigation of the Anglophile Hermann Muthesius (1861–1927) to relieve the tenement-crowded German towns and cities. The movement was to some extent anticipated by Theodor Fischer (1862–1938), who had come under the influence of the picturesque town-planning theories of the Austrian Camillo Sitte while producing plans for the extension of Munich in the 1890s. Fischer's layout for the workers' village of **Gmindersdorf, Reutlingen** (1903–15), began on garden-suburb lines, but became more formal in its later stages. The first and most influential German garden suburb proper was **Hellerau, Dresden,** by Heinrich Tessenow and Richard Riemerschnied with contributions by others. It was followed by **Margaretenhöhe, Essen**, by Georg Metzendorf and **Werderau, Nuremberg,** by Ludwig Ruff.

Related but for the cultured middle classes were the celebrated **Artists Colony, Darmstadt**, founded by the Grand Duke of Hesse in 1899, with houses by Josef Olbrich and Peter Behrens (1868–1940), and the **Hohenhagen Suburb, Eppenhausen**, promoted from 1906 by Karl Osthaus of the Folkwang Museum, with houses by Behrens, Henry Van de Velde and J. L. M. Lauweriks (1864–1932). The public buildings at Darmstadt, Olbrich's **Ernst Ludwig Haus** (1901) and **Wedding Tower (Hochzeitsturm)** (1905–8) (p. 1331A), were marked by a Viennese Secessionist taste. By the time of his last building, the **Tietz Store, Düsseldorf** (1908–9), Olbrich's architecture was quietening down. In middle-class houses the same tendency can be found under the influence of Muthesius and Paul Mebes, whose elegant book *Um 1800* (Around 1800), published in 1908, drew architecture and interior decoration back towards a refined Biedermeier style. Avant-garde houses in Germany before World War I often blend English informality with a certain heaviness. Van de Velde's **Esche house, Chemnitz** (1902–3), and his **Hohenhof House, Hagen** (1906–7), for example, have weighty mansard roofs which make them less attractive than the same architect's **Weimar Art School** (1904–11) or **Chemnitz Tennis Club** (1906–8). A specially fine villa of the period was the **Remer House, Molchow See, Brandenburg** (1905–8, demolished), by the Finnish architects Gesellius, Lindgren and Saarinen.

Industrialisation was at the heart of German thinking in these years. It was against a background of concern for the relations between capitalism and culture that the Deutscher Werkbund was founded in 1907 to promote links between industry, architecture, the crafts and education. Hermann Muthesius became the Werkbund's first secretary and promoted a clear vision of its tasks; he wanted an effective, practical art of building (*Baukunst*) to replace style-mongering (*Architektur*).

The pioneering example of collaboration between German industry and architecture was the hiring of Peter Behrens by the giant industrial concern Allgemeine Elektrizitäts-Gesellschaft (AEG), at the instigation of Walther Rathenau, the cultivated son of AEG's founder. Behrens was a painter by training. His range of styles veered from *Jugendstil* to a simplified classicising architecture (as in his early-Florentine-style **Crematorium, Delstern,** 1906–7, and his Schinkelian **Cuno house, Eppenhausen,** 1910). Behrens's work for AEG began in 1907; he redesigned the company's graphics, acted as styling consultant on the mass-produced products and oversaw a building programme for the company. The most famous outcome of this work was Behrens's **AEG Turbine Hall, Berlin** (1908–9) (p. 1331C). It is both a long shed expressive of engineering and a temple to work, with powerful facades redolent of Schinkel's neo-Classicism. It proposes a romantic view of architecture, but accepts the discipline of mass-production and prefigures an interest in the design of standardised buildings and products. Similar in austere grandeur to the AEG Turbine Hall but presenting itself as an enlightened 'factory in the park' was the **Michels Silk-Weaving Mill, Nowawes, Potsdam,** of 1912 by Muthesius.

The same somewhat schizophrenic standpoint as Behrens is reflected in the early works of his two most famous assistants, Walter Gropius (1883–1969) and Mies van der Rohe (1886–1969). Gropius in about 1908–9 designed a set of flat-roofed **standardised houses** for workers on the **Golzengut** family estate in Pomerania (now in **Poland**) and then with Adolf Meyer (1881–1929) built the famous brick-and-glass facades of the **Fagus Boot Factory, Alfeld-an-der-Leine** (1911), a development of the AEG work in the direction of 'stylelessness'. Mies, with Behrens, designed the **German Embassy, S. Petersburg, Russia** (1911–12), in an extreme version of stripped Schinkelian neo-Classicism. This clash of values between an industry-based or art-based architecture came to a head at the Deutscher Werkbund exhibition in Cologne in 1914, when Muthesius proposed typological studies (Typisierung) as the basis for the future and was opposed by Henry Van de Velde, who defended the rights of the individual creative artist.

The most challenging building at this exhibition was the uneven Van de Velde's **Werkbund Theatre**, an elegantly linear composition that gave a foretaste of the streamlined style to be taken up after World War I by Erich Mendelsohn and others. Representing a natural development from Art Nouveau and *Jugendstil*, this tendency was much influenced by the 'empathy' theories of the aesthetician Wilhelm Worringer, and is most often (though unsatisfactorily) referred to as Expressionism. Until the mid-1920s there was no hard and fast distinction between Expressionism and the severer side of German Modernism. In the work of Hans Poelzig (1869–1936), an important member of the Werkbund, German Expressionism and Modernism go hand in hand. His varying idioms embraced the ponderous horizontals of the **Junkernstrasse office building,**

A. Wedding Tower (Hochzeiturm), Darmstadt (1905–8). See p. 1330

B. Einstein Tower, Potsdam (1921). See p. 1332

C. AEG Turbine Hall, Berlin (1908–9). See p. 1330

Breslau (1911), and the nervous, stepped profile of his **Chemical Factory, Posen** (now **Luban**) (1911–12), with its non-load-bearing brick facades.

Breslau (now **Wroclaw, Poland**) was an important regional centre of modern architecture. Its **Centennial Hall** by the city architect Max Berg (1870–1947) with the engineer-contractors Dyckerhoff and Widmann (1911–13) had a concrete-ribbed dome 65 m (213 ft) in diameter of epoch-making importance. In the development of concrete architecture Germany was scarcely behind France. Important early buildings in this technique included the **School of Anatomy, Munich University** (Max Littmann, 1905–7), the **Breslau Market Hall** (Heinrich Kuster, 1906–8), pioneer of the parabolic-arched style for halls and churches that spread throughout Europe between the world wars, and the concourse at **Leipzig Railway Station** (1909–11). Paul Bonatz (1877–1956) and F. E. Scholer's **Stuttgart Railway Station** (1911–28) (p. 1333A), another such building of these years, is less important for its structure than for the Schinkelesque austerity of its grand front, in which the influence of Eliel Saarinen's Helsinki Station (q.v.) is apparent.

The period directly after Germany's defeat in World War I was marked by extreme introspection and utopianism, notable in the drawings of Bruno Taut (1880–1938). A streamlined type of Modernism, in which pre-war Expressionism was related to the dynamic qualities of the modern city, was the first clear German style to emerge in the 1920s. Erich Mendelsohn (1887–1953) was its foremost proponent. His arresting **Einstein Tower, Potsdam** (1921) (p. 1331B) and **Luckenwalde Hat Factory** (1921–3) soon settled down to the smoother **Schocken Store, Stuttgart** (1926–7), and **Universum Cinema, Berlin** (1926–9). It took time for a common language of modern architecture to emerge. Among experiments in the so-called *Neues Bauen* were those of Hugo Häring (1882–1958), whose **Garkau Farm** of 1922 represented an extreme type of functionalism in which the habits and needs of the farmer, his equipment and his animals were forcibly reflected In the appearance of the buildings. Experimentalism also marked the early period of the Bauhaus, established by Gropius at Weimar in 1919 and at first more taken up with arts and crafts and with teaching theory than with architecture. Gropius and Meyer's timber-framed **houses for Adolf Sommerfeld, Berlin-Dahlem** (1920–1), are reflections of the mood and limitations of the time. Mies van der Rohe's architecture also had an emotional phase, whose principal fruit was the bricky **Liebknecht and Luxemburg Monument, Berlin** (1926, destroyed under Hitler).

German Catholic churches enjoyed a powerful and spiritual school of parabolic concrete vaults and textured brick elevations, seen at their best in the churches of Dominikus Böhm (1880–1935) (**church at Bischofsheim, near Mainz,** 1926) and Martin Weber (**S. Boniface, Frankfurt**, 1927). The development of thin concrete shells for vaults and domes by Franz Dischinger and Ulrich Finsterwalder was a highlight of German architecture and engineering during the inter-war years. It began with an experimental **dome for the Zeiss company, Jena** (1923), and was carried through in the wide-spanned and shallow-domed **Leipzig Market Hall** (1928–9) and **Frankfurt Market Hall** (1929–30). The so-called Zeiss-Dywidag patents were most extensively used in the north-light trusses of the 1930s **Volkswagen Works, Magdeburg**.

During the German economic revival of the later 1920s, an austere, functional, rather clinical, flat-roofed Modernism appeared and soon gained wide acceptance as the 'Modern' or 'International' style. It was associated with the *Neue Sachlichkeit* (New Reality or New Objectivity) movement and deployed chiefly in the great German drive for subsidised housing of 1925–30. Supported by an informal pressure and support group of Berlin architects known as Der Ring, many Modernists took jobs as city architects and gathered teams around them to build this housing. They included Fritz Schumacher (1869–1947) in Cologne, Hans Poelzig in Dresden, Bruno Taut (briefly) in Magdeburg and, most significantly, Martin Wagner (1885–1957) in Berlin and Ernst May (1886–1970) in Frankfurt. These architects were influenced by the form of the English garden city and suburb with its ample green spaces, but they built at higher densities, with more flats than houses. May's team was particularly prolific, the **Römerstadt Siedlung, Frankfurt** (1926–8), being their finest achievement, and made pioneering studies of the arrangement of the modern small dwelling, notably the kitchen. In 1930, May took members of his team to try the same methods in Russia, with very limited success. In Berlin, Martin Wagner shared out the work among many architects, including Bruno Taut (**Onkel-Toms Hütte** and **Berlin-Britz**) and Hans Scharoun and Walter Gropius (**Berlin-Siemensstadt**). The Zeilenbau concept, whereby blocks were placed in parallel disregarding the street line, with open space rather than closed courts between them for light and air, was widely taken up in the Berlin estates, having been pioneered by Theodor Fischer in his Alte Heide Estate, Munich (1919).

The most famous early manifestations of the new German housing were the **Weissenhof Siedlung, Stuttgart** (1927), organized by the Deutscher Werkbund, and the **Dessau-Törten Estate** (1926–30) by Walter Gropius and his successor at the Bauhaus, Hannes Meyer (1889–1954). Weissenhof is an individualistic estate laid out in a hesitant manner by Mies van der Rohe with flats and houses by many leading modern architects, including non-Germans; the results were mixed, the best houses being by J. J. P. Oud, Le Corbusier and Hans Scharoun.

A. Stuttgart Railway Station (1911–28). See p. 1332

B. Bauhaus Buildings, Dessau (1925–6). See p. 1334

Dessau-Törten was a small demonstration estate built after the Bauhaus had moved to Dessau in 1925; its main interest lay in the extensive use of prefabricated elements and travelling cranes in its construction. This and Gropius's **Bauhaus Buildings, Dessau** (1925–6) (p. 1333B), marked the conversion of Germany's most influential Modernist school to *Neue Sachlichkeit*. Architecture was formally taught at the Bauhaus only from 1927, but such was its prestige that it became seen in retrospect as the intellectual centre of the new style. After leaving the Bauhaus in 1928, Gropius did much to pioneer prefabricated house designs for mass-production, notably the **Hirsch copper house** (1931) but few were built. His successor, Hannes Meyer, was an extreme functionalist who believed that all architectural issues could be scientifically resolved. His most important built work (with Hans Wittwer) was the brick-faced **German Trades Union Federal School at Berlin-Bernau** (1928–30). For *Sachlichkeit* in lighter mood, Wittwer's **Airport Restaurant, Leipzig** (1930–1), a small elevated structure with a roof suspended from the centre and glass all round for viewing the planes, provides relief.

Many Modernist architects in Germany welcomed the advances of the 1920s but did not accept the stylistic reductivism of *Neue Sachlichkeit* and the housing drive. These included Poelzig, of the older generation, and Hans Scharoun (1893–1972), who built a number of houses in Berlin after 1930 that showed more relaxed and contextual possibilities for Modernism combined with free planning. Scharoun's **Schminke house, Löbau** (1932–3), with a fluid plan, diagonal stair and transparent elevations, stands for a liberal view of Modernism rare in the extreme climate of German architectural politics.

Traditional architecture with a national flavour continued strong in Germany throughout the years of the Weimar Republic. Its greatest advocates were Heinrich Tessenow, Paul Schulze-Naumburg (1869–1949) and Paul Schmitthenner (1884–1972), all of whom built housing estates of national character with pitched roofs during the 1920s. Schulze-Naumburg and Schmitthenner acquired authority during the early years of the Nazi regime from 1933, when flat-roofed Modernism was increasingly proscribed, the Bauhaus was dissolved, and many of the leading Modernists went into exile. But like most dictators, Hitler was less interested in vernacular architecture than in monumental urban Classical statements. These were efficiently provided first by Paul Troost (1878–1934) in his **House of German Art, Munich** (1933), and then by Albert Speer (1905–81), whose executed works included the **Nuremberg Parade Ground** (1934), the **Berlin Chancellery** (1938) and the smaller **studio for Josef Thorak at Baldham** (1938). Speer's Classicism combined oppressive rhetoric and inhumane scale with some clever touches of planning and detailing. His larger planning projects for Berlin, like so many monumental works planned under Nazism, were never executed. A more lasting memorial to these terrible years were the finely engineered first **autobahns**.

Switzerland

The early phases of modern architecture were manifested to advantage in Switzerland, a country known for its excellent structural technique and rich enough to be able to construct high-quality buildings. The different linguistic communities developed their own architecture. The German cantons were vigorous centres of *Neues Bauen* between the wars; more recently, attention has focused on the Italian cantons.

La Chaux de Fonds was a stimulating Swiss regional centre of art and architecture in the early years of the twentieth century. Here under the aegis of Charles L'Eplattenier (1874–1946) flourished an art school where the English small house and the Viennese *Jugendstil* were admired. The earliest houses of L'Eplattenier's famous pupil, Le Corbusier, reflect these loyalties. Before leaving for Paris, in the Villa Schwob, La Chaux de Fonds (1916), Le Corbusier had moved on to a symmetrical, almost Mannerist idiom of flat roofs, heavy cornices and brick facing.

Swiss contributions to the mainstream of twentieth-century architecture begin in **Basle** with the work of Karl Moser (1860–1936), whose work gradually loses its historicising attributes. Moser's first important work was the cruciform **S. Paul** with a grand central tower (1898–1901). There followed his fine civic **Badischer Bahnhof** of 1912–13, but his masterpiece is **S. Antonius** (1926–7), a tall concrete church influenced by Perret, with a powerful vaulted interior and perhaps the first wholly successful Modernist church tower. Basle also has excellent low-rise housing estates of which Freidorf in the suburb of **Muttenz** by Hannes Meyer (1919–21), on garden-city lines but with axial planning and a community building at the centre, is the most impressive.

Dornach, near Basle, is the home of the **Goetheanum**, the extreme statement of architectural Expressionism, here construed as the symbolic embodiment of the anthroposophical idea. A first, double-domed Goetheanum was built here in timber in 1913–14 by the teacher and mystic Rudolf Steiner with professional help from Carl Schmidt-Curtius, as the focus of Steiner's anthroposophical community. It was rebuilt after a fire in 1924–8 to a massive sculptural design worked out in models by Steiner, with restless chamfered and faceted elevations in bare concrete, ringed by a scatter of eccentric houses and structures in the same idiom. The interior of the Goetheanum is largely later.

Bridge-building in concrete was greatly advanced on both technical and aesthetic fronts by the Swiss engineer Robert Maillart (1872–1940). His range stretches from the little three-hinged **Inn Bridge, Zuoz** (1901), to the elegance of the **Arve Bridge, Vessy near Geneva** (1936), cantilevered from X-shaped, waisted supports. At the **Salginatobel Bridge** (1930) in spectacular mountain scenery, Maillart finally broke with masonry techniques and designed purely in terms of the properties of concrete. He was also the first European to build buildings in the 'flat-slab' technique, whereby wide continuous concrete floors and roofs could be constructed without supporting beams. The **Federal Grain Store, Altdorf** (1912), was the pioneer flat-slab building.

The badly managed architectural competition for the inter-war League of Nations headquarters, Geneva, dashed the hopes of many Modernists. In the event the **Palais des Nations, Geneva**, was built in 1929–37 to a mixed Classical and Modernist design made by a committee (Carlo Broggi, J. Flegenheimer, C. Lefèvre, H. P. Nénot, J. Vago). Similar in idiom was the **Bureau International du Travail, Geneva**, by Georges Epiteaux (1924–6).

The refinement of moderate Swiss Modernism is best represented by Alberto Sartoris (simple **Catholic church, Lourthier**, 1932) and by Otto Salvisberg (1882–1940). Salvisberg's early work was in Berlin. He specialised in laboratories, offices and hospitals, mostly with concrete frames, rendered elevations, crisp lines and flat roofs with deep eaves. His **Lory Hospital, Berne** (1927–9) is the best hospital of the inter-war Modern Movement. Salvisberg succeeded Moser as professor at the **Technische Hochschule, Zurich**, and there built various buildings including the **Machine Laboratory** (1930–3). Educational architecture at all levels from nursery school to university reached excellence in inter-war Switzerland. Examples include the **Catholic University of Fribourg** by Denis Honegger of Paris with Fernand Dumas (1938–41), a grand, imaginative essay in the concrete stripped Classicism championed by Perret, and the **Gewerbeschule (Industrial School), Berne** (1935–9), by Hans Brechbühler (1907–89), a former assistant of Le Corbusier.

The debates on *Neues Bauen* developed with as much force in Switzerland as in Germany and centred upon the figures of Paul Artaria (1892–1959), Hans Schmidt (1893–1972), Hannes Meyer and Alfred Roth (born 1903). The critical manifesto projects for Modernism in housing were two developments in **Zurich**: the **Neubühl Housing Estate** of 1929–32, by a variety of architects including Artaria, Schmidt and Roth, and the **Doldertal Apartments** (1936), two three-storey blocks designed as show-flats for the progressive bourgeoisie by Alfred and Emil Roth with Marcel Breuer in collaboration with the secretary of CIAM, Sigfried Giedion. Artaria and Roth took an interest in designing houses in timber, a technique too often shunned by European Modernists; the latter's small **Hélène de Mandrot House, Zurich** (1943–4), showed what could be done in the idiom.

Italy

Italy was not fully united as a country until 1870, and industrialisation on a large scale began only round the turn of the century (the Olivetti company began to manufacture typewriters in 1906, Fiat to make cars in 1916). The consequences shaped Italian architecture in contradictory ways during the first half of the twentieth century. On the one hand, Italians felt a deep need for symbols of national identity, naturally met in this history-rich country by the Classical and imperial legacy and heavily exploited under Fascism (1922–43). On the other hand, they were also keen to catch up with other nations. For many intellectuals this meant jettisoning the past; hence the iconoclastic aspects of Futurism. The somewhat schizophrenic character of Italian architecture and aggressive tone of Italian architectural debate during the period reflect these tensions. In practice they were often cleverly resolved. The dogged persistence of regionalism helps to explain the lack of any one dominant personality, school or theory.

Turin and Milan, the prosperous cities of the North, were the main centres of Italian architectural energy around 1900. They took ideas equally from Paris and Vienna. The *Stile Liberty*, otherwise *Stile Floreale* or *Arte Nuova*, was Italy's variant on Art Nouveau and *Jugendstil*. Its leading exponent was Raimondo D'Aronco (1857–1932), whose Secession-influenced pavilions were a striking success at the Turin Modern Decorative Art Exhibition of 1902. The **Palazzo Communale, Udine** (1908–32), is D'Aronco's one large permanent building in Italy; later he moved to Istanbul and built there. Italian 'Liberty' architecture often has a ponderous, Baroque exuberance, as in the work of Giuseppe Sommaruga (1867–1917). His overladen **Palazzo Castiglione, Milan** (1900–3), combines the Genoese palazzo tradition with Art Nouveau ironwork and riotous sculpture. Sommaruga's **Faccanoni Villa and Mausoleum, Sarnico** (1906–7), manifest picturesqueness, rough stonework and sheer monstrosity, while his **Hotel Tre Croci, Campo di Fiore, Varese** (1910–12), is an American-scale, Alpine hotel with separate funicular station and restaurant. The **Power Station at Trezzo D'Adda** (1906) by Gaetano Moretti (1860–1930) is perhaps the most surprising monument in the Liberty style. As grandiose but less inventive is the neo-Baroque manner represented by the **Baths, Agnano** (1911) by Giulio Ulisse Arata (1881–1962) and **Milan Railway Station** (1912–31) by Ulisse Stacchini, a butt of rationalists and futurists. In strong contrast is the **Fiat factory, Lingotto, Turin** (1917–25) (p. 1337D), by Giacomo Matté Trucco. Formed by two blocks, each is 500 m (1625 ft) made of reinforced concrete : it is the epitome of the engineered structure. The roof is a test track reached by a pair of reinforced concrete ramps. In the south, the most creative architect of the period was Ernesto Basile of Palermo (1857–1932). His Palermo villas include one for himself (1903) and the **Palazzo Belmonte, Spaccaforno** (1906), which provided a model for later seaside developments. Liberty villas on the seaside usually aspired to a lighter touch, as in G. Brega's **Villa Ruggeri, Pesaro** (1902–7).

Futurism as promoted by Marinetti and his circle in Milan was a largely literary and artistic movement which had little impact on architectural practice. However, the drawings of Antonio Sant'Elia (1888–1916) for a utopian *Città Nuova*, shown at a number of Futurist exhibitions in 1914, made a stir at the time and have enjoyed popularity since their republication in the 1950s. They consist of images of the city dominated by fast travel and new technology on the Wellsian lines intimated by Marinetti and Morasso, with high, pyloned buildings piled up above transport interchanges (a theme inspired by a sketch Sant'Elia made for Milan Railway Station).

Italy's leading architects of the 1920s were the *novecentisti* of Milan, who perfected a stylish blend of Classicism and Modernism in the period before the propaganda demands of Fascism required more rhetoric. Their work tallies in spirit with the wistful paintings of De Chirico. The outstanding *novecentista* was Giovanni Muzio (1893–1982) and the keynote building his so-called **Cà Brutta, Via Turati, Milan** (1922), an apartment block which was accused of having introduced 'Berlin syphilis' into Italy. Muzio designed the facades alone; they are decorated in a loose, whimsical, mannerist way with stripped and flattened Classical features and a mix of materials. The idiom caught on as a way of lightening the elevations of flats: Piero Portaluppi's two juxtaposed **Apartment Blocks on Via Foppa, Milan** (1928 and 1933–4), show the style giving way to the severer rationalism of the 1930s. Light, bitter-sweet Classicism is also the mark of early houses by Gio Ponti (1891–1979) (**Villa Bouilhet, Garches,** 1926) and Giuseppe Pizzigoni (**Villa Pizzigoni, Bergamo,** 1925–7). Muzio's largest work, additions to the **Catholic University, Milan** (1928 etc.), continues his interest in surface textures and his fascination with Lombardic Baroque.

Marcello Piacentini (1881–1961) was the first architect of note to be involved with Fascism. He came to the fore with his **Corso Cinema-Theatre, Rome** (1915), whose bold concrete construction and rendered facades shocked Roman conservatives. His **Victory War Memorial, Bolzano** (1925–8), in the form of an updated triumphal arch decked out with fasces, marked the debut of the so-called *Stile Littorio*, the official style (so far as there was one) of Mussolini's 'New Roman Empire'. As much a planner as an architect, Piacentini was a clever contextualist. His **Piazza della Vittoria, Brescia** (1927–32), ingeniously adapts the planning principles of Camillo Sitte to an ancient Italian town centre and the Fascist propaganda programme. Less happy was his **Via della Conciliazione, Rome,** the bland, open avenue leading up to S. Peter's and the Vatican – essentially a scheme of slum-clearance (*sventramento*) typical of Italian urban planning since Naples of the 1880s, here commandeered by Fascism for its own purposes. Piacentini also headed the planning team for **EUR (Esposizione Universale di Roma).** Though this gigantic exhibition, planned to create a whole new quarter for Rome by 1942, never came off, several of the more grandiose Fascist buildins were built, notably the **Palazzo dei Congressi** (1938) (p. 1337C) by Adalberto Libera (1903–63) and La Padula, Guerrini and Romano's **Palazzo della Civiltà Italiana**, a controversial, squared-up and rationalized version of the Colosseum.

EUR highlighted the ability of Italian architects to find common ground in official Fascist projects between the national architecture of the past and the Modernist agenda. This is shown to advantage in such projects as **Sabaudia** (1933 etc.), the best of five small new towns planned for the Pontine marshes, with a town centre lined by buildings of austere Mediterranean flat-roofed simplicity by Luigi Piccinato (1899–1983); and **Santa Maria Novella Railway Station, Florence** (1932–3) (p. 1337A), by Giovanni Michelucci (1891–1990) and others, which fits its large bulk into the periphery of historic Florence without fuss or aggression. Angiolo Mazzoni (1894–1979), a prolific designer of post offices and railway stations, was adept at this compromise, as in his circular **Agrigento Post Office,** 1931–4. It marked an accommodation of sorts between traditionalists, *novecentisti* and the radical wing of Italian Modernists, generally known as the Rationalists, who enjoyed a brief but remarkable flowering in the 1930s.

Italian rationalist architects differed from German and French contemporaries in their exacting attention to detail and superior sense of context. But they built less and argued more, notably in the pages of the magazine *Casabella.* The most talented of them was Giuseppe Terragni (1904–43) of Como. Terragni's attachment to both radical Modernism and the Fascist cause is a reminder that Italian architectural and political alignments do not fit a simple pattern. His masterpiece is the **Casa del Fascio, Como** (1933–6) (p. 1337B), a four-storey cube of assurance and discipline. It faces a built-up square in the heart of the town and is intended as a display of political and public virtue. There is an internal courtyard with a strongly articulated structure. Terragni continues his

A. Santa Maria Novella Railway Station, Florence (1932–3). See p. 1336

B. Casa del Fascio, Como (1933–6). See p. 1336

C. Palazzo dei Congressi, Esposizione Universale di Roma (EUR) (1938). See p. 1336

D. Fiat factory, Lingotto, Turin (1917–25): detail of ramp. See p. 1336

play ot solid, void, frame and wall in the single-storey **Asilo Sant'Elia nursery school** (1936–7), again with a courtyard plan. Noteworthy too are the series of Milan apartment blocks he built with Pietro Lingeri (1894–1968); their **Casa Rustici, Corso Sempione, Milan** (1933–5), achieves a balance of openness, freedom and control.

Among other rationalists, Libera's forceful **Elementary School, Piazza Raffaello, Trento** (1932), sits remarkably in its historic context. Another contextual work by Libera is the **Casa Malaparte, Capri** (1939–40), a house growing proudly out of a rocky promontory and designed with its client, the author Curzio Malaparte. The partnership of Luigi Figini (born 1903) and Gino Pollini set out on a long and fruitful collaboration with the firm of Olivetti by designing the **Olivetti offices, Ivrea** (1934–45), with a long curtain wall, and a simple, stone-walled **Nursery School** in front of a community centre (1939–41). Of buildings by architects who moved in a rationalist direction, the stylish Gio Ponti's **First Montecatini Building, Via Moscova, Milan** (1936–8), is remarkable for its beautiful exposition of absolutely flat facades in green marble and silver aluminium over an H-shaped office plan.

The career of the great Italian engineer Pierluigi Nervi (1891–1979) started in the 1930s. The concrete, criss-cross vaults which were to become a mark of his style first appear in his **Stadio Comunale, Florence** (1930–2), and in two remarkable, long-destroyed **aircraft hangars at Orvieto** (1936) and **Orbetello** (1939–41).

Britain and Ireland

British architecture pursued its empirical course between 1900 and World War II. Houses and housing commanded most attention, and were admired the world over, the garden-suburb concept meeting with widespread emulation. Churches, mostly in the Gothic tradition, were still a strong point, and urban public buildings improved in standard under a mixture of French, Scottish and American influences. Britain was the last of the major European countries to embrace Modernism wholeheartedly, but when it did so in the 1930s it produced buildings of freshness and diversity.

Urban architecture in Victorian England had enjoyed no consistency. This defect was remedied in the Edwardian period (1901–10) by a series of London projects which revealed a conversion to Beaux-Arts planning principles. They included the **Kingsway Aldwych improvement** of the London County Council (1900–25); Sir Aston Webb's new layout for **The Mall,** with **Admiralty Arch** at one end and the **Queen Victoria Memorial** and refronted **Buckingham Palace** at the other (1901–14); and the rebuilding of the **Regent Street Quadrant** by the veteran architect Norman Shaw (1831–1912) and Reginald Blomfield (1856–1942) with parts of **Piccadilly Circus** and the **Piccadilly Hotel** (1905–25) (p. 1339A). These works veer from strict adherence to French taste to the curving ingenuity of Webb's Admiralty Arch and personal monumentality of Shaw's Piccadilly Hotel and Quadrant. Collectively they sum up the style known as Edwardian Baroque.

Good examples of Edwardian Baroque civic architecture are many, as Britain lavished its imperial wealth on stone-faced town halls, galleries and theatres. Typical are the **Cardiff Civic Centre**, with a **City Hall** (1897–1906) (p. 1339B) by the Francophile partnership of H. V. Lanchester (1863–1953) and E. A. Rickards (1872–1920) and the **National Museum of Wales** (1906–9) (p. 1339C) by A. Dunbar Smith (1866–1933) and Cecil Brewer (1871–1918); and **County Hall, London** (1912–33) (p. 1340A), the riverside seat of the London County Council, by Ralph Knott (1878–1929), with a swept centre carrying a giant colonnade and a Piranesian internal courtyard. The most assured architect of Edwardian public buildings was, however, a Scot, Scotland having had a less episodic relationship with the classical tradition than England. This was Sir John Burnet (1857–1938), who trained at the Beaux Arts and first practised in Glasgow, where **McGeoch's Store, West Campbell Street** (1905–10; demolished) attested the originality and force of his Classicism. Three London buildings display Burnet's range: **General Buildings, Aldwych** (1909–10), a convex front based on the Palazzo Massimi alle Colonne; the rear of the **British Museum** (1904–14) (p. 1339D), with a giant Ionic colonnade and noble staircase round a lift shaft; and the **Kodak Building, Kingsway** (1910–11) (p. 1340B), Britain's first urban building to express its steel frame plainly and unambiguously.

The American system of stone-faced piers over a steel frame with tiers of windows and metal panels in between had already been anticipated in the Chicago-inspired **Selfridge's Store, Oxford Street** (1908–26) (p. 1339E), London's most powerful Classical building of the period. D. H. Burnham and Co. of Chicago were the principal architects for Selfridge's and Sven Bylander was the engineer; the Canadian-born Francis Swales appears to have designed the lavish colonnade along the front. On the whole, Britain was tardy in taking up the new techniques of steel-framing and concrete construction. Reinforced concrete appeared first in mills and warehouses (from 1897) but was rarely exposed in polite architecture. **Lion Chambers, Hope Street, Glasgow** (1905–6) (p. 1341A,B), by James Salmon (1874–1924) and John Gaff Gillespie (1870–1926), is constructed of Hennebique concrete with 4-inch rendered external walls, an irregular front elevation and splayed bay windows rising the full height at the back. Important

A. Piccadilly Hotel, London (1905–25). See p. 1338

B. City Hall, Cardiff (1897–1906). See p. 1338

C. National Museum of Wales, Cardiff (1906–9). See p. 1338

D. British Museum, London (1904–14). See p. 1338

E. Selfridge's Store, Oxford Street, London (1908–26). See p. 1338

A. County Hall, London (1912–33). See p. 1338

B. Kodak Building, Kingsway, London (1910–11). See p. 1338

C. Law Society, Chancery Lane, London (1903–4). See p. 1342

A. Lion Chambers, Hope Street, Glasgow (1905–6). See p. 1338

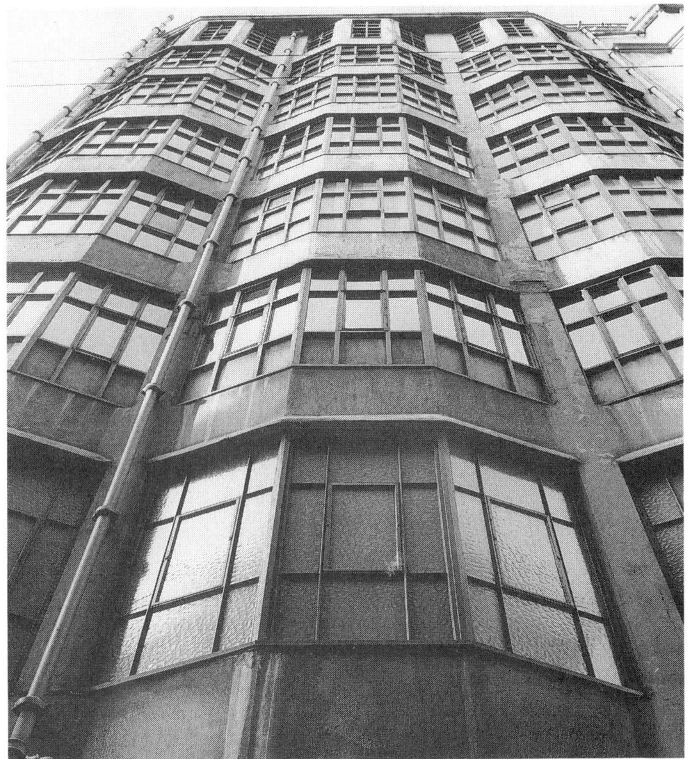

B. Lion Chambers: rear

C. Heathcote, Ilkley, Yorkshire (1905–7). See p. 1342

for getting concrete construction accepted was the **General Post Office, S. Martin-le-Grand, London**, by Sir Henry Tanner (1849–1935) of the Office of Works (1905–9), which has a Hennebique arched concrete frame faced in Edwardian Baroque stone fronts towards the main streets but rendered elevations elsewhere.

Some London architects, close in spirit to the Arts and Crafts Movement, experimented with Mannerist motifs in their office buildings. Among them were J. J. Joass (1868–1952) (**Royal Insurance Building, Piccadilly**, 1907–8) and Charles Holden (1875–1960) (**Law Society, Chancery Lane**, 1903–4, p. 1340C). On the whole, Arts and Crafts architects were not at home with conspicuous urban buildings. The **Eagle Insurance Building, Birmingham** (1899–1900) by W. R. Lethaby (1857–1931) with its complex symbolist motifs and obscurity of idiom reveals the length to which some Arts and Crafts architects would go to avoid direct allusion to historical styles.

The English Arts and Crafts Movement was at its peak in 1900. Its chief impact in architecture was upon houses; it stood for honest design, workmanship and expression of materials, rather than originality at any price; the puritanism of the Arts and Crafts attitude, endorsed by the teaching of Lethaby, C. R. Ashbee (1853–1942) and others, ensured that there was little Art Nouveau architecture in Britain. Many Arts and Crafts architects favoured a style linked to the English cottage tradition: such were C. F A. Voysey (1857–1941) and M. H. Baillie-Scott (1865–1945). Voysey clung to his idiom of roughcast walls with mullioned windows and plain timber finishes, seen at its best in his own house, **The Orchard, Chorleywood** (1900–01); Baillie-Scott's range was wider and he favoured open plans with inglenooks, as in **Tanglewood, Sollershott West, Letchworth** (1906), but his work was often sentimental. Other house-builders were less averse to historical styles. Among these were Ernest Newton (1856–1922), whose balanced houses evolve from the neo-vernacular of **Fouracre, Hartley Wintney** (1901) to the formal 'Wrennaissance' of **Luckley, Wokingham** (1907).

The most fêted of the Edwardian house architects, Sir Edwin Lutyens, (1869–1944), combined command of a range of styles with an eye for proportion and a unique sensitivity to settings, materials and textures. His best early houses were in Surrey, where he perfected a local vernacular style set off with planting and landscaping by his friend and client Gertrude Jekyll. **Deanery Gardens, Sonning** (see Chapter 34) and **Marsh Court, near Stockbridge** (1901–4) (p. 1343A,B), are in this earlier manner, with touches of formality. **Heathcote, Ilkley** (1905–7), (p. 1341C) is a consistently Classical house; it adapts the 'grand manner' of Sanmicheli and Vanbrugh to a villa of modest dimensions, built of local stone with hipped roofs and pantiles. His quieter, formally planned brick houses of the 1905–14 period such as The Salutation, Sandwich (1911), set the agenda for the gentlemanly, neo-Georgian revival of the English inter-war years.

Important British centres outside London for Arts and Crafts architecture were Birmingham, where the middle-class suburban home reached a high level, and Glasgow, where the fame of Charles Rennie Mackintosh (1868–1928) overshadows that of his contemporaries. Mackintosh's domestic masterpiece is **Hill House, Helensburgh** (1902–3) (p. 1344A), a blend of the Voysey manner with Scottish building traditions, elegant planning and an un-British obsession with perfecting the 'room as a work of art'. Sir Robert Lorimer (1864–1929) of Edinburgh rivals Mackintosh in the refinement of his simplified Scottish houses, with less inventive detailing as at **Ardkinglas near Inverary** (1907–9). Closer in spirit to Mackintosh was the practice of Edgar Wood (1860–1935) and J. H. Sellers (1861–1954) of Middleton and Manchester. Their **Christian Science Church, Victoria Park, Manchester** (1903–8), suggests an interest in Olbrich, while their **Upmeads, Stafford** (1908) (p. 1344B,C), is, for England, an early example of a house with a flat roof in concrete. The state elementary schools built by Mackintosh and by Wood and Sellers afford instructive comparison. Mackintosh's **Scotland Street School, Glasgow** (1904–6), has a conventional three-storey plan but memorable detailing, notably the glazed staircases; Wood and Sellers's **Elm Street School, Middleton** (1908–10), on a suburban site, is low but ingeniously planned with 'finger-plan' wings projecting from a hall in the centre and a hemicycle entrance in front.

The persistence of the English Gothic Revival in the twentieth century is well represented by the **Liverpool Anglican Cathedral** (1903–78) (p. 1345C) by Sir Giles Gilbert Scott (1881–1970). It is in a Free Gothic of the Decorated period with many allusions, notably to Spanish sources. It has a broad nave with central crossing, above which a dominating central tower rises between double transepts. The material is red sandstone, with concrete roofs above the vaults; the west end was curtailed and built to a revised design after Scott's death. A refined Gothic tradition was continued by many architects, among whom Temple Moore (1856–1920) and Sir Ninian Comper (1864–1960) stand out; their respective masterpieces were **S. Wilfrid, Harrogate** (1905–14) and **S. Mary, Wellingborough** (1906–30). A more radical approach to Gothic was taken by Lethaby, whose **All Saints, Brockhampton** (1901) attempts to bring the English country church up to date with such eccentricities as a pitched concrete roof covered by thatch. E. S. Prior (1852–1932) followed Lethaby's lead with more assurance in his town church of **S. Andrew, Roker, Sunderland** (1905–7) (p. 1345A,B) which has transverse concrete internal arches faced in stone, concrete purlins, and fine Arts and Crafts fittings.

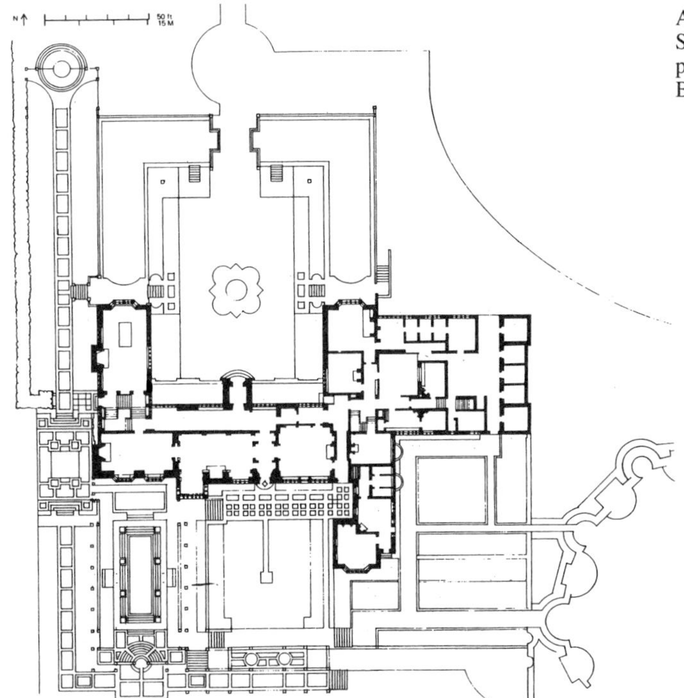

A. (*above*) Marsh Court, near Stockbridge, Hampshire (1901–4). See p. 1342
B. (*left*) Marsh Court: plan

A. Hill House, Helensburgh (1902–3). See p. 1342

B. Upmeads, Stafford (1908). See p. 1342

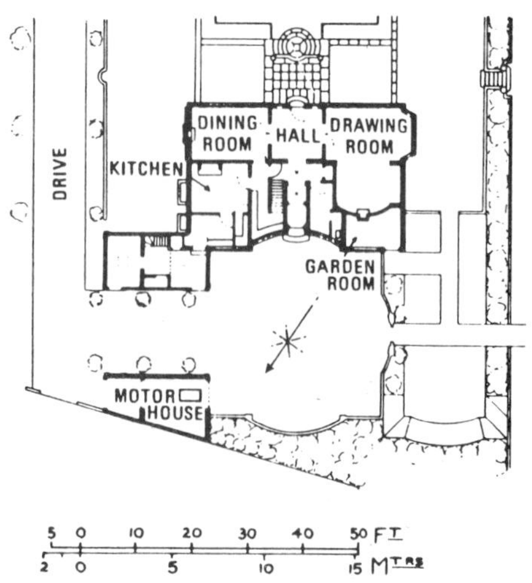

C. Upmeads: plan

A. S. Andrew, Roker, Sunderland (1905–7). See p. 1342

B. S. Andrew, Roker: interior looking east

C. Liverpool Anglican Cathedral (1903–78). See p. 1342

D. New Earswick Model Village, York (begun 1902). See p. 1346

Garden cities and suburbs were a very influential element in British Edwardian architecture. Model manufacturing suburbs with high standards of low-rise 'cottage' housing were being built at **Port Sunlight** (started 1888) and **Bournville** (started 1895) before the name of garden suburb became current. Their principles were extended in the first major commission of the architect-planners Barry Parker (1867–1941) and Sir Raymond Unwin (1853–1940), **New Earswick Model Village, York** (1902–) (p. 1345D) for the Quaker manufacturer Joseph Rowntree. New Earswick was not restricted to Rowntree's employees. It has winding streets and leafy footpaths; the cottages, arranged in short terraces with subtle relationship to the street line, are designed in a simplified vernacular spirit. Parker and Unwin were also the architect-planners for **Letchworth** (begun 1903), the pioneer project of Ebenezer Howard's garden-city movement. Howard advocated self-sufficient new towns of 30,000–35,000 with their own industry and agriculture to check the growth of cities. Since Letchworth was slow to develop, Parker and Unwin's ideas about housing layout and design were spread mainly from their faster-growing **Hampstead Garden Suburb, London** (begun 1906, with a central square and churches laid out by Lutyens). Unwin's *Town Planning in Practice* (1908) had international influence, and his concepts dominated British housing and planning throughout the 1920s. Howard's stylistic garden-city idea enjoyed a further trial at **Welwyn Garden City** (begun 1920), laid out by Louis de Soissons with a Beaux-Arts-style centre and better industrial district than Letchworth, and housing of more neo-Georgian character.

The London County Council in the years after 1900 provided cheap municipal cottage housing on lines parallel to the garden-suburb model, designed by its influential in-house Architect's Department. Of its pre-war 'cottage estates', **Totterdown Fields, Tooting** (begun 1902), and **White Hart Lane (Tower Gardens), Tottenham** (begun 1903), were the first. The Council's fire stations of these years were exceptional, 'free' Arts and Crafts statements, conspicuous among them the **Euston Fire Station** by H. F. T. Cooper (1902).

The 1920s in British architecture were dominated by the emotive Classicism of Lutyens. After New Delhi (see Chapter 57), Lutyens' most brilliant work was for the Imperial War Graves Commission (British architects indeed designing the best of the many sombre European cemeteries commemorating World War I). His **Memorial Arch to the Missing of the Somme at Thiepval, France** (1927–32), conjures a universal abstraction and power out of complex geometrical forms. **Midland Bank, Poultry, London** (1924–7) (p. 1347A), and **Britannic House, Finsbury Circus, London** (1920–4) (p. 1347B) manifest Lutyens' command of masonry detailing and his ability to adapt and vary Classicism to the height of modern urban offices without the banality of giant orders. Sir Herbert Baker (1862–1946) worked in the same modes as Lutyens but with contextual and sentimental leanings. In London, Baker's **India House, Aldwych** (1928–30), and **South Africa House, Trafalgar Square** (1935), mix Classicism with lively colonial detailing; his **Church House, Westminster** (1936–40), for the the Church of England, is in an eclectic manner layered with historical motifs and materials. Other Classicists of the period include Sir Edwin Cooper (1873–1942) and Sir Reginald Blomfield, whose refacing of the **Carlton Club, Pall Mall, London** (1921, destroyed 1940) (p. 1347C), was in a scholarly French Louis XVI idiom.

Lutyens-influenced Classicism is at its best in the civic work of E. Vincent Harris (1879–1971). Harris's circular **Central Library, Manchester** (1931–4), is overshadowed by his **Town Hall Extension** (1934–8) (p. 1348A), in a Gothic idiom to fit in with the Victorian-Gothic Manchester Town Hall; both have the Swedish overtones from the work of Östberg, Asplund and Tengbom common in British public architecture of the 1930s. **City Hall, Swansea** (1930–34), by Sir Percy Thomas (p. 1349A), the **Royal Institute of British Architects, Portland Place, London**, by G. Grey Wornum (1932–4) (p. 1349B) and the **Municipal Buildings, Norwich** (1938) by S. Rowland Pierce and C. H. James (p. 1349C) are all inspired by 'Swedish grace', with stripped Classical fronts and delicate, decorative detail. Also Swedish in part is Easton and Robertson's **Royal Horticultural Hall, London** (1926–8) (p. 1350A), with an influential stepped section carried on concrete parabolic arches.

American Beaux-Arts monumentality reaches a high point in Liverpool where the group of **Cunard Building** (begun 1913) by Willink and Thicknesse with Arthur Davis, **Royal Liver Building** (1908–10) by W. Aubacy Thomas, and **Mersey Docks and Harbour Board** (1907) by Sir Arnold Thornley overlook the Mersey with dignified pride. American and Swedish influence coalesce in the three most monumental British public buildings of the inter-war period. **S. Andrew's House, Edinburgh** (1936–9), by T. S. Tait (1882–1954) of Burnet, Tait and Lorne, is faced in severe Scottish masonry with detailing of austere perfection. **55 Broadway** (p. 1350C) for the London Passenger Transport Board (1927–9) and **Senate House** (1933–9) (p. 1348B), the headquarters of the University of London, both by Charles Holden of Adams, Holden and Pearson, adopt the New York practice of breaking back the volume and outline of high buildings as they rise; in the Broadway building the severity is alleviated with elegant reliefs. Holden also designed a brilliant series of stations for the London Underground (1924–39), notably **Clapham South** and **Tooting Broadway** on the Northern Line and **Sudbury Town, Arnos Grove** and **Cockfosters**

A. Midland Bank, Poultry, London (1924–7). See p. 1346

B. Britannic House, Finsbury Circus, London (1920–4). See p. 1346

C. Carlton Club, Pall Mall, London (1921: destroyed 1940). See p. 1346

A. Town Hall Extension, Manchester (1934–8), with Central Library (1931–4). See p. 1346

B. Senate House, University of London (1933–9). See p. 1346

A. City Hall, Swansea (1930–34). See p. 1346

B. RIBA Building. Portland Place, London (1932–4). See p. 1346

C. Municipal Buildings, Norwich (1938). See p. 1346

A. Royal Horticultural Hall, London (1926–8). See p. 1346

B. Boots factory, Beeston, Nottingham (1930–32). See p. 1351

C. 55 Broadway, London (1927–9). See p. 1346

D. Daily Express Building, Fleet Street, London (1932–3). See p. 1351

on the Piccadilly Line, in Swedish-influenced versions of Modernism.

Sweden also affected the work of the gentleman-scholar H. S. Goodhart-Rendel (1887–1959), the most individual of inter-war British architects, with a range of styles from neo-Victorian to modern. **S. Olaf's House, Hays Wharf, London,** a stone-faced building with touches of Swedish grace and Art Deco is his best secular work (1931). More consistency is found in his Gothic brick churches, notably S. Wilfrid's, Brighton (1932–4). N. F. Cachemaille-Day's **S. Saviour's, Eltham, London** (1932–3), is one of many bare brick 'Expressionist' churches influenced by German example. Sir Giles Gilbert Scott continued his fine brick churches throughout the inter-war years, but was a powerful advocate of rational structure, seen at its purest in **Waterloo Bridge, London** (1936–40).

Radical Modernism in Britain was slow to grow but sudden to flower. European developments of the 1920s were studied but little imitated during that decade. The first major breakthrough was made by the engineer-architect Sir Owen Williams (1890–1969), in his two factory buildings for **Boots, Beeston, Nottinghamshire** (1930–32 and 1935–8) (p. 1350B), his **Daily Express Building, Fleet Street, London** (1932–3, with Ellis, Clarke and Gallannaugh) (p. 1350D) and his **Empire Pool, Wembley, London** (1933–4). Williams was committed to concrete, which he used with an aplomb not seen in British architecture before. His Boots factory buildings have four-storey, top-lit interiors with glazed facades. The contrast with the showy fronts and banal interiors of fashionable industrial buildings of the time like the **Gillette Factory, Great West Road,** (1936), by Sir Banister Fletcher (1866–1953), or the **Hoover Building, Western Avenue, London** (1931–2), by Wallis, Gilbert and Partners, is striking. The Daily Express Building has an elegant curtain wall in glass and black vitrolite over a concrete frame while the Empire Pool is a cantilevered structure with idiosyncratic turrets for the counterweights.

English Modernist private houses started with such efforts as **Le Château, Silver End**, by T. S. Tait (with Frederick MacManus) (1927–8), with render over a brick structure trying to look like concrete, and prominent metal windows. **High and Over, Amersham** (1929), by Amyas Connell (1900–80), Y-shaped and symmetrical, with a roof garden, plain walls and strip glazing, was an improvement. Connell with his partner Basil Ward (1902–78) went on to establish a Corbusian 'white-box' idiom in such houses as **Alding (New Farm), Grayswood, Surrey** (1931–2), and **Saltings, Hayling Island** (1933–4). It was taken up with varying candour and commitment by many architects, ranging from the suavely eclectic Oliver Hill (**Joldwynds, Holmbury S. Mary,** 1932–4), through converts to Modernism like Maxwell Fry (**Sun House, Frognal Way, Hampstead, London,** 1935–6) to passionate believers in social Modernism like Berthold Lubetkin (1901–90) (**two bungalows at Whipsnade,** 1935–6).

In the late 1930s the prim purism of these white houses was relaxed, as in the brick-faced group of three houses in **Willow Road, Hampstead, London** (1937–9) (p. 1352A) by Ernö Goldfinger (1902–87), which attempt to bring Modernism to terms with the Georgian urban tradition, and in work by F. R. S. Yorke (1906–62) (**houses in Birmingham Road, Stratford-upon-Avon,** 1938–9). On a larger scale, **The Homewood, Esher**, by Patrick Gwynne (1938–9) reconciled Modernist white architecture with the English picturesque garden. Despite these efforts, the modern house did little to wean British loyalty from the charm of traditional domestic styles, seen at their picturesque extreme in the **Dippenhall development, Farnham, Surrey** (1921–63), by Harold Falkner (1876–1963) and the whimsical holiday village of **Portmeirion, Portmadoc, Wales** (from 1926), by Clough Williams-Ellis.

The influx of emigré architects after 1933 stimulated British Modernism. Gropius stayed only briefly, but had wide influence and with Maxwell Fry designed **Impington Village College, Cambridgeshire** (1938–40) (p. 1352B), a building of quiet assurance and refinement embodying a social vision of architecture. Lubetkin, the most dynamic of the immigrants, brought French clarity, German idealism, constructivist art, socialist planning and group-working to bear upon the projects of his firm, known as Tecton. Their major works were the luxury flats **High Point I** (1935) (p. 1353B), **High Point II** (1938), **Highgate, London,** zoo commissions in London, Dudley and Whipsnade, notably the witty, concrete-ramped **Penguin Pool, London Zoo** (1934) (p. 1354A); and **Finsbury Health Centre, London** (1938) (p. 1354B). These were the structural and aesthetic masterpieces of English Modernism.

Less creative but of technical interest is the work of the engineer-architect Wells Coates (1895–1958). His **Isokon Flats, Lawn Road, Hampstead, London** (1932–4), hide an experimental range of 'efficiency flats' behind an ugly, balconied facade; his **Palace Gate Flats, Kensington, London** (1937–9), have a clever section, matching three floors against two. **Quarry Hill Flats, Leeds,** (1935–41; demolished) by R. A. H. Livett were the first attempt to bring the technololgy of Modernism to subsidised housing on a large scale, but their welded steel structure with concrete cladding (on the French 'Mopin system') failed. On a lighter note, early Modernism in England is at its best on the seaside. The **De la Warr Pavilion, Bexhill** (1935–6) (p. 1357A), is by Erich Mendelsohn (briefly resident in Britain) and Serge Chermayeff (born1900), in an adaptation of Mendelsohn's earlier flowing style over a welded steel frame. The **Royal Corinthian Yacht Club, Burnham-on-Crouch** (1936) (p. 1353A), and the austerer **Blackpool**

A. Willow Road, Hampstead, London (1937–9). See p. 1351

B. Impington Village College, Cambridgeshire (1938–40). See p. 1351

A. Royal Corinthian Yacht Club, Burnham-on-Crouch, Essex (1936). See p. 1351

B. High Point I, Highgate, London (1935). See p. 1351

A. Penguin Pool, London Zoo (1934). See p. 1351

B. Finsbury Health Centre, London (1938). See p. 1351

Casino (1939), both by Joseph Emberton (1889–1956), also repay a visit.

Ireland had no living architectural tradition when it became independent in 1921. The administrative seat of the Irish government in Dublin was and is the Edwardian Baroque building erected for the **Dublin College of Science** (1904–13) by Sir Aston Webb and Sir Thomas Deane. **Stormont, Belfast,** the seat of the Northern Ireland executive, by Arnold Thorneley, 1927–32, is no less English, though reached down an impressive axis. A few Arts and Crafts architects had explored Irish traditions before independence, notable among them W. A. Scott (1871–1921), whose **Spiddal Church, Co. Galway** (1904–7), and **Diocesan College, Galway** (1911–12), put the blocky, stone forms of the Celtic legacy to good effect. However, independence came too late for a national tradition to develop. The most distinguished inter-war building in Ireland was the **Church of Christ the King, Turner's Cross, Cork**, by Barry Byrne of Chicago in an auditorial, Expressionist style that had little national reference. Later, Ireland made a fine contribution to the International Style in the shape of the gently curving **Dublin Airport Terminal** (1936–40) by Desmond FitzGerald (1910–87) with Dermot O'Toole (1911–71).

Holland and Belgium

The origins of modern Dutch architecture lie in the work of H. P. Berlage (1856–1934), who like Otto Wagner in Vienna fought his way through the eclecticism of the nineteenth century to the concept of a simplified, universal and rational architecture for the twentieth century. The **Amsterdam Stock Exchange** of 1897–1903 (see Chapter 34) provided the key to a national, rather puritanical style of architecture based on elegant brickwork. Berlage's own later work was influenced by Frank Lloyd Wright after an American visit in 1911. It was not completely consistent but continued the elimination of ornament and dematerialisation of the wall. Notable are his works for the Kröller-Müller family; the **De Schipborg Farm, Drenthe** (1914), the **S. Hubertus Hunting Lodge, Hoenderlo** (1916–20); and **Holland House, Bury Street, London** (1914–17). The flat-roofed **Museum Kröller-Müller, Otterlo,** by Henry Van de Velde, would have seemed remarkable if built when it was designed (1919–21) but in the event was constructed in a cut-down version in 1938.

More emotional and decorative than Berlage was the work of Willem Kromhout (1864–1940), whose **American Hotel, Amsterdam** (1899–1901, extended 1928) imaginatively exploits the mixture of brick styles fashionable at the turn of the century. The so-called 'Amsterdam School' that followed reflected both Berlage's idealism and sobriety and Kromhout's exuberance, with added dashes of Expressionism and Symbolism. The **Scheepvarthuis (Shipping Offices), Amsterdam** (1912–16), by J. M. van der Mey (1878–1949) with his assistants, P. L. Kramer (1881–1961) and Michel de Klerk (1884–1923), is an early and influential building in the manner, with jagged brick detail, sculpture and lettering over a concrete core. The Expressionist tendency abroad in Dutch architecture of this period is clear also in H. L. De Jong's **Tuschinski Cinema, Amsterdam** (1918), one of the first 'super-cinemas', with a glazed-tile facade and rich interior in proto-Art-Deco style; and J. M. Luthmann's **Radio Station, Kootwijk** (1919–22), a smoother building in mass concrete taking the form of a heavy tower with bevelled corners and a stepped profile.

Housing, however, was Holland's strength, the Dutch government having in 1901 passed a law requiring towns to plan and build for growth systematically every decade. Dutch housing traditions and the nature of the land meant that the pattern adopted was largely one of medium-rise suburban development built by public utilities; communal experiments were not infrequent. In **Amsterdam**, the most dramatic of these estates were the **Spaarndammerbuurt blocks** (1913–20) and **De Dageraad housing** (1919–22), built by socialist housing associations to the highly individualistic brick designs of the Amsterdam School architects De Klerk and Kramer. De Dageraad is part of **Amsterdam South**, a large district laid out to a plan of 1915–17 by Berlage, with perimeter blocks shielding amenable housing areas with much open space from the main roads. Two major monuments of Dutch rationalism, the **Open Air School** (1927–30) by Johannes Duiker (1890–1935) and Bernard Bijvoet, and **De Wolkenkrabber,** Europe's first multi-storey housing block (by J. F. Staal, 1927–30), fall within the confines of the plan.

Housing outside Amsterdam shunned the rhetoric of Amsterdam School Expressionism. Typical of good pre-Modernist work is the big **Vreewijk Garden Village, Rotterdam**, by M. J. Granpré Molière (1883–1972) and others (from 1913), in an English taste without communal facilities. But an early thrust towards Modernism occurred through the De Stijl group. Led by the painters Theo van Doesburg and Piet Mondrian and the architect J. J. P. Oud (1890–1963), De Stijl was influenced by French Cubism and the suburban houses of Frank Lloyd Wright. A first taste is found in the tiny oeuvre of Robert van t'Hoff (1887–1979), whose pair of juxtaposed houses in **Amersfoortsweg, Huis ter Heide**, switch from the English gabled style of **Løvdalla** (1911) to the flat-roofed, broad-eaved, concrete-built **Villa Henny** (1915), in all but its symmetry a crib from Wright. The **Schröder House, Utrecht** (1924), by Gerrit Rietveld, marks the maturity of the 'painterly' De Stijl architecture; it consists of a two-storey cube, open at first-floor level, divided into rooms elsewhere, and with the elevations developed as compositions of floating and attached planes in contrasting colours. J. J. P. Oud's **Café de Unie, Rotterdam** (1924–5; reconstructed after war damage), offers a similar play of wall surfaces combined with dashing colour and signage in capital letters.

Oud's work as Rotterdam city architect established the rationalist idiom in Dutch subsidised housing, where the fancifulness of De Stijl could not be afforded. This began with the **Spangen Estate** (1918–22), an urban area of four-storey flats round open courts built by Oud, Michiel Brinkman (1873–1925) and others in a blocky brick style straining to get away from Amsterdam School mannerisms, and came of age in the white-walled, two-storey, decentralised shops and houses with rounded ends by Oud at **Scheepvaartstraat, Hook of Holland** (1924–7), and the similar, larger **Kiefhoek Estate, Rotterdam** (1928–30), with a church also by Oud.

Dutch rationalism or *Nieuwe Bouwen* reached its zenith in three buildings marked by their high proportion of glass to wall. Bijvoet and Duiker's **Zonnestraal Sanatorium, Hilversum** (1926–31), develops Frank Lloyd Wright's horizontality into a forceful manifestation of concrete base, floor and roof, with planes of glass 'floating' in between. The **Van Nelle Factory, Rotterdam** (1925–31) (p. 1357C), by J. A. Brinkman (1902–49) and L. G. Van der Vlugt (1894–1936) with Mart Stam, is a multi-storey factory deliberately broken up into colliding elements and notable for its curtain walling over a concrete frame; while the **Bergpolder Flats, Rotterdam**, again by Brinkman and Van der Vlugt with W. Van Tijen (1932–4), were the prototype of the European multi-storey slab block for balcony-access housing, here with a steel frame and bold glazed staircase.

A middle course between the Amsterdam School and the rationalists was pursued by Willem Marinus Dudok (1884–1974), the Director of Public Works at Hilversum, whose work, rigorously conceived in three dimensions and again influenced by Wright, is the most satisfying Dutch architecture of the inter-war years. Dudok produced a garden-suburb-style plan for Hilversum and built much traditional sub-urban housing, but his main works are a series of schools and public buildings. The **Schuttersweg School, Hilversum** (1928), has a long low entrance block in Dudok's usual elegant brickwork with strips of windows, an arched porch and a beckoning, balancing two-part tower behind. **Hilversum Town Hall** (1927–31) (p. 1357B) is one of the masterpieces of modern architecture. Its balance of vertical and horizontal accent, movement and restfulness, abstraction, asymmetry and fine craftsmanship sums up the qualities of a remarkable period in Dutch architecture.

In Belgium as in Holland, domestic architecture was the country's strongest suit during the first half of the century. The talents of Horta, Hankar and others involved in the flowering of Belgian Art Nouveau during the 1890s were at their best in the Brussels town house (see Chapter 34). The style lingered on until World War I, but its masterpieces were mostly built by 1900. Horta's later work took on a more classical sensibility, beginning with the **Hotel Max Hallet, Brussels** (1903). A classical tinge is also found in the work of the unpredictable Octave Van Rijsselberghe (1853–1929), whose circular **Hotel at Westende** (1905) is the country's most surprising building of the period, with features seemingly borrowed from Ledoux. The other great innovator of Art Nouveau, Henry Van der Velde, built little in his native Belgium after 1900, but late in his career designed the **University of Ghent Library**, partly in a tower (1932–40).

The most interesting Belgian architect of the pre-modern period, Antoine Pompe (1873–1960), was self-taught as a designer. His first building, **Dr Van Neck's Clinic, Rue Waffelaerts, Brussels** (1910), with a blank, asymmetrical brick street front lit by little oriel windows at a high level, was influenced by advanced English Arts and Crafts practice and struck a note quite different from Art Nouveau. Belgium was hard hit by destruction in World War I. Afterwards, like many of his countrymen, Pompe became interested in low-cost housing and the garden-suburb movement as the answer to the major housing shortage. At **Kappeleveld Garden Suburb, Woluwe S. Lambert,** laid out by Louis Van der Swaelmen (1883–1929), Pompe contributed short terraces of partly pitched and partly flat-roofed houses, (1922–6). Other garden suburbs of the 1920s laid out by Van der Swaelmen with J. J. Eggericx (1884–1963) (e.g. **Boitsfort** and the **Cité Floréal, Brussels**) reach a standard of amenity and landscape seldom found in France or in Holland; the architecture is usually English in arrangement and inspiration.

Flat-roofed Modernism in subsidised Belgian housing arrives in the early work of Victor Bourgeois (1897–1962), e.g. his working-class flats in **Rue du Cubisme, Molenbeek,** of brick with rough concrete lintels, 1922, and **Cité Moderne, Berchem-Ste-Agathe**, of the same date. Louis de Koninck (1896–1984) built Belgian's best inter-war houses in the International Style, displaying a consistent interest in the *existenzminimum* type of dwelling. De Koninck's own house in **Avenue Fond'Roy, Brussels** (1926), is built of prefabricated blocks concealed by the usual render of 1920s Modernism but with a sophistication of servicing ahead of its date. In De Koninck's **house in Avenue Brassine, Auderghem** (1928–9), there is the same tight minimalism, but here the structure is of concrete.

A. De La Warr Pavilion, Bexhill (1935–6). See p. 1351

B. Town Hall, Hilversum (1927–31). See p. 1356

C. Van Nelle Factory, Rotterdam (1925–31). See p. 1356

Scandinavia

Scandinavian architecture showed vigour and independence throughout the first half of the twentieth century. Sweden, Denmark and Finland all made their mark on the development of Modernism; Norway, independent only from 1905, lagged a little behind.

Smaller European countries in 1900 were much preoccupied with the search for a national form of expression in architecture. In Scandinavia this took the guise of 'National Romanticism' and found clearest expression in the early Finnish work of Eliel Saarinen (1873–1950) and Lars Sonck (1870–1956). **Hvitträsk** (1901–2) by Gesellius, Lindgren and Saarinen was a little rural enclave where the architects and their families lived in stone-and-timber houses touched equally by English Arts and Crafts ideals and Karelian customs and decorative styles. The **National Museum, Helsinki** (1905–12), by the same architects in a complex Finnish mediaeval style, weaves granite, sandstone and brick together to achieve a rich texture. Sonck's **Helsinki Telephone Company Building** (1905) takes this approach to extremes in a show of Richardsonian rock-faced ruggedness. The masterpiece of the movement is Sonck's calmer **Tampere Cathedral** (1902–7), with a square plan, star-vaulted nave, low galleries and west front in simplified Gothic with towers of uneven height. By 1910 the National Romantic tendency was on the wane, as Finns hankered after middle European suavity. A precursor was Onni Tarjanne's **Takaharju Sanatorium** (1902), in a simplified *Jugendstil* style. Sonck had turned towards the disciplined orders and masonry of Classicism by the time of his **Finnish Mortgage Association Building, Helsinki** (1908). More conspicuous a signal of fresh thought was Eliel Saarinen's **Helsinki Railway Station** (1909–14), with granite elevations showing the influence of Olbrich over a reinforced concrete frame. Its monumentalism was to be taken up in station termini buildings all over Europe.

Sweden and Denmark, long independent and with their own strong architectural traditions, had less need of nationalist assertiveness. The great Swedish symbol of National Romanticism was **Stockholm City Hall** (1911–23) (p. 1359A), by Ragnar Östberg (1866–1945), a superbly sited and skilful blend of motifs from indigenous and foreign sources, including Venice, with a tapering tower as a landmark. In this richly textured and embellished building, Östberg laid the foundations of the light-handed, sensuous school of architectural decoration and ornament that came to be known as 'Swedish Grace'. Another notable Stockholm building in the National Romantic style is the **Engelbrekt Church** (1904–14) (p. 1359B) by Lars Israel Wahlman (1870–1952), with parabolic internal arches and simplified detailing. In Denmark, the famous **Grundtvig Church, Copenhagen** (1913–26) (p. 1360A) by P. V. Jensen-Klint (1853–1930), with its 'organ-pipe' gables in the stepped-brick tradition of the Baltic, is both an Expressionist gesture and a glorification of the Danish past.

'Nordic Classicim' was the prevailing architectural fashion in Sweden and Denmark between 1910 and 1930. It had its roots in those countries' post-Renaissance building traditions, where Classical and vernacular elements had long been comfortably integrated. But it was stimulated too by such German architect-authors as Mebes, Schulze-Naumburg and Tessenow and by the simple, stuccoed villas of Italy. In Sweden its foremost architects were Gunnar Asplund (1885–1940), Sigurd Lewerentz (1885– 1975) and Ivar Tengbom (1878–1968). Asplund's early buildings mostly have strong roofs, gables or pediments; his **Lister County Courthouse** (1917–21) and **Woodland Chapel, Woodland Cemetery, Stockholm** (1918–20) achieve a simple dignity without fuss or confrontation. His **Skandia Cinema, Stockholm** (1924) crossed Swedish Grace with colourful Art Deco in its interior decoration. In his masterpiece, the **Stockholm City Library** (1920–28) (p. 1361A,B) Asplund borrows the monumental primary form of circle within a square from Boullée and Ledoux and by clothing them with coloured Swedish stucco makes them friendly rather than ponderous. Lewerentz, less fertile than Asplund, produced in his **Resurrection Chapel, Woodland Cemetery, Stockholm** (1922–5) (p. 1360B,C), one of the subtlest expressions of modern Classicism, with a deep portico off centre and just detached from an austere space for prayer and reflection. Tengbom's Stockholm oeuvre starts with the **Högalid Church** (1918–23) (p. 1359C) on a hill with subtly different twin towers, and proceeds through the colonnaded **Stockholm Concert Hall** (1923–8) to his **Swedish Match Building** (1927–8), a modern Renaissance palazzo with curving courtyard and delightful sculpture by Carl Milles.

Danish Classicism of the period reveals the twin influences of Germany and the country's own neo-Classical legacy. It developed fast from Carl Petersen's **Fåborg Museum** (1912–15) to a high point in the **Copenhagen Police Headquarters** (1919–24) by Hack Kampmann (1856–1920), with Aage Rafn and Holger Jacobsen, both monumental buildings in which the discipline of Classicism is lightened and cheered up with fresh, mannered and colourful detail. Edvard Thomsen's **Øregaard School** (1922–4) and **Søndermark Crematorium** (1927–30) are further fine Danish contributions to Nordic Classicism. Finland too had a neo-Classical heritage, to which the formidable **Helsinki Parliament Building** (1927–31) by J. S. Sirén (1889–1961), with a giant order of attenuated proportions above a tall flight of steps, was a calculated response. Danish houses and housing meanwhile maintained an austere and unostentatious image, represented by the sober flats and suburban housing of Povl Baumann (1878–1963),

A. Stockholm City Hall (1911–23). See p. 1358

B. Engelbrekt Church, Stockholm (1904–14). See p. 1358

C. Högalid Church, Stockholm (1918–23). See p. 1358

A. (*above left*) Grundtvig Church, Copenhagen (1913–26). See p. 1358
B. (*above*) Resurrection Chapel, Woodland Cemetery, Stockholm: interior
C. (*left*) Resurrection Chapel, Woodland Cemetery, Stockholm (1922–5). See p. 1358

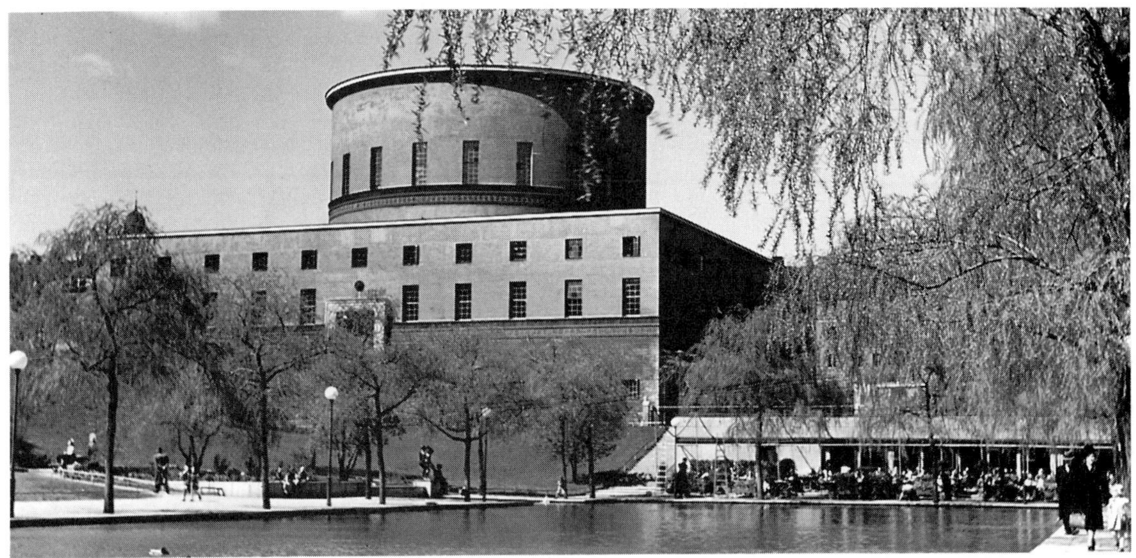

A. Stockholm City Library (1920–28). See p. 1358

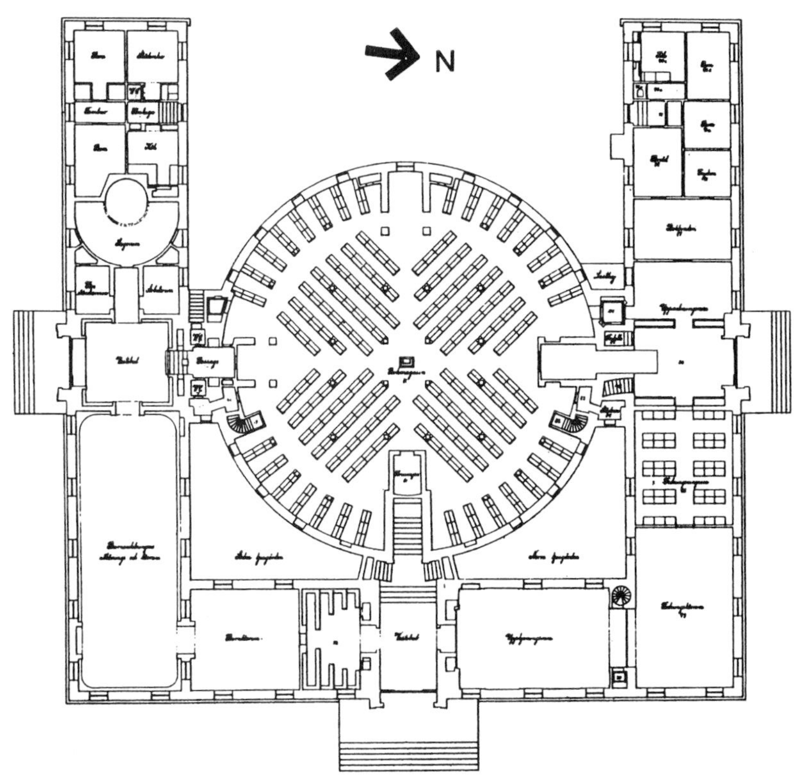

B. Stockholm City Library: plan

Ivar Bentsen, Kay Fisker (1893–1965) and the architect-planner and author Steen Eiler Rasmussen (1898–1990). Finland kept up a similar tradition, represented by the timber-built garden suburb of **Kåpylä, Helsinki** (1921–5), by Martti Välikangas.

After 1930 the leading Swedes and Finns switched to a Modernist idiom, without agony or embarrassment. Asplund's **Gothenburg City Hall extension** (1937) is a token of the success with which the change was made; the addition is tacked on to a Classical front without apology but with great subtlety. His **Woodland Crematorium, Stockholm** (1935–40) (p. 1363A), hits the midpoint between simplified neo-Classicism and monumentalised Modernism with sublime dignity and assurance. But it was in Finland and the work of Alvar Aalto, that Scandinavian Modernism developed with novelty and distinction. Aalto's earliest buildings, notably the **Working Men's Club, Jyväskylä** (1925), with a forceful blank-walled superstructure over stubby Doric columns, still adhere to Nordic Classicism. The breakthrough came with three remarkable buildings: the **Turun Sanomat Newspaper Building, Turku** (1928–9); the **Paimio Sanatorium** (1929–33) (p. 1363B); and the **Viipuri Library** (1934–5, now in Russia). These are concrete-constructed 'functionalist' buildings, yet they have a poetry, elegance and freedom of plan and section that no other European architect, including Le Corbusier, had attained at that date; they added a dimension and a humanity to the capacities of radical modernism. The **Villa Mairea, Noormarkku** (1938–9) (p. 1363C), on an L-shaped plan with walls partly plastered and partly covered with wood strip, carries Aalto's experimentation with forms and finishes into the domestic realm, blending Modernism and rusticity with unique assurance. Aalto's contemporary of nearest standing was Erik Bryggman, whose **Resurrection Chapel, Turku Cemetery** (1939–41), has an asymmetrical plan with piers along one side and light romantically pouring in behind them. It forms an apt conclusion to the exalted standard of Scandinavian funerary architecture between the two world wars.

Spain and Portugal

The liveliest centre of Spanish architectural endeavour throughout the twentieth century has been Barcelona. At the turn of the century, the strength of Catalan regional feeling made that city the most striking instance of the 'national romantic' phenomenon found all over Europe. In Catalonia this movement is known as *Modernismo*, in contrast to the often insipid academic Classicism of the *Noucentistes* as then practised in Madrid and elsewhere. Other regionalist movements were also, however, current in Spanish architecture after 1900 and persisted until the Spanish Civil War (1936–9). In Seville and the south, an elegant Mediterranean style with mildly Moorish overtones was common, as in the **Hotel Alfonso XIII, Seville,** by J. E. Muñoz and F. Urcola. In Madrid, the eclectic Manuel Maria Smith (1879–1956) practised in a variety of styles, from the romantic Spanish manner of his works for the Garay family, the **Finca Clavería, Caceres** (1913–16), and two large adjacent villas in **Calle Almagro, Madrid** (1915–17), to the flagrant Anglophilia of his **country house for the Marques de Triano, Lejona** (1915–17).

Catalan *Modernismo* had a variety of roots: in mediaeval Spanish Gothic, Spanish Baroque, Art Nouveau, traditional tile-vaulting, and the Catalan crafts tradition in metalwork, glass and ceramics. The undisputed genius of the movement, which had political and religious dimensions as well as artistic ones, was Antoní Gaudí (1856–1926). Important also were Lluis Domènech y Móntaner (1850–1923), José Puig y Cadafalch (1869–1956) and Gaudí's assistants Josip M. Jujol (1879–1949) and Francisco Berenguer (1866–1914).

Antoní Gaudí's major Barcelona project, the **Templo Expiatorio de la Sagrada Familia,** was begun in 1882; design and construction continued up to his death and beyond. His **Park Guell, Barcelona** (1900–14), shows Gaudí in light-hearted mode. It was conceived as a small garden suburb. The development was a failure, with only two houses built, but the park, graced with an array of Gaudí's strange, mosaic-clad structures, was completed. The buildings include a Greek Doric market hall that incorporates columns used in ways which the Greeks could never have imagined. The **Casa Batlló, Barcelona** (1904–6) (p. 1364B), is an example of Gaudí's mature work. He remodelled the facade of an existing house, altered the main rooms and added a new top floor and a writhing, imbricated roof. The first-floor windows are of extraordinary plasticity, in ovoid stone surounds with slender bony columns, while around the upper windows the wall surface glitters with fragments of blue and green glass. His **Casa Milá, Barcelona** (1905–10) (p. 1364C), with details by Jujol, subverts the traditional urban grid and conventional apartment-block planning. Its facade of pitted elephantine stone rises and falls in wave-like rhythms, while the iron fronts of the balconies seem tossed about like galvanised seaweed. Inside, there are virtually no right-angled corners.

Domènech y Móntaner's ideas depended more on Catalan Gothic than those of Gaudí. His two great Barcelona projects were the **Hospital of S. Paul** (1905–12) (p. 1364A) and the **Palau de la Música Catalana** (1905–9). The romantic Gothic style of the hospital seems old-fashioned for its date. It is broken up behind an imposing front into a variety of restless blocks round a large garden, each overlaid with a medley of sculpture, painting and mosaic which allow

A. Woodland Crematorium, Stockholm (1935–40). See p. 1362

B. Paimio Sanatorium (1929–33). See p. 1362

C. Villa Mairea, Noormarkku (1938–9). See p. 1362

A. (*above*) Hospital of S. Paul, Barcelona (1905–12). See p. 1362
B. (*above right*) Casa Batlló, Barcelona (1904–6). See p. 1362
C. (*right*) Casa Milá, Barcelona (1905–10). See p. 1362

the patient little peace. The concert hall is a fervent, colourful display of eclecticism with superb stained glass and quaint mosaics. Jujol's best work is found in the small town of **San Juan Despí,** where, *inter alia*, he built the multi-turreted **Torre de la Creu** (1913) and the even wilder **Can Negre** (1915) with Baroque-style painting. Berenguer was shorter-lived and therefore less prolific; his most remarkable building was a **house, chapel and gatehouse at Garraf** (*c.* 1910).

The impetus of *Modernismo* declined after 1910, but Barcelona again became the cutting edge in Spanish architecture after 1936 and the declaration of the Spanish Republic. Young architects in revolt against academicism seized the opportunity to found GATEPAC, an association of pro-Modernists with bases in both Barcelona and Madrid, but stronger in the former city, where they were led by José Lluis Sert (1902–83). Sert had worked with Le Corbusier, and his early architecture, designed mainly with José Torres-Clavé (1906–39) and J. B. Subirana, is emphatically Corbusian, notably a seven-storey **apartment block in Calle Muntaner, Barcelona** (1931), and a **Tuberculosis Clinic, Barcelona** (1935), as part of the public works programme of the republican government. But the most important GATEPAC project was the 200-unit **Sant'Andreu housing estate, Barcelona** (1934–6), consisting of six-storey maisonette blocks arranged in two continuous U-shaped ranges with balcony access. Europe's largest single block of housing built in the radical Modernist idiom before World War II, it was badly damaged during the Spanish Civil War and crudely altered thereafter.

The other remarkable Modernist achievement in Spain of the years before the Civil War were the structures of Eduardo Torroja (1899–1961) who put German skills in shell concrete to new aesthetic effect. His **Algeciras Market** (1933) has a shallow, spherical dome supported at eight peripheral points. His **Alloz Aqueduct** (1939) consists of a trough striding sculpturally across a valley on X-shaped supports. But Torroja's masterpiece was the **Zarzuela Hippodrome, Madrid** (1935), in which a series of elliptical hyperboloid canopies ripples elegantly along the top of a long, tripartite stand.

Portugal was more strongly influenced than Spain by French academicism in the early years of the century. The country's leading architect was Ventura Terra (1866–1919), a Beaux-Arts-educated figure who undertook a wide range of academic commissions (e.g. **Banco Lisboa e Açores, Lisbon,** with a rich giant order, 1906). Lisbon in these years was marked by showy but generally staid offices and flats, among the more prestigious of which were Norte Junior's **luxury apartments** on the **Avenida da Liberdade** (1915) in a late Art Nouveau manner with 'neo-Manueline' touches. **Oporto** had a more vigorous architectural culture. Here the dominant figure in both architecture and planning was Marques da Silva (1869–1947), also trained at the Ecole des Beaux Arts, who built the azulejos-lined **Railway Station** (1900–), schools, a theatre and laid out the **Avenida dos Aliados,** with the eclectic **Câmara Municipal** (1920–) by Correia da Silva as its principal building.

Radical Modernism was suspect in the conservative cultural and political milieu of Portugal. Modern architecture therefore filtered in through the sober, stripped-Classical guise of such monumental work as the large **Higher Technical Institute, Lisbon** (1927–35), by Pardal Monteiro (1897–1957), which formed the nucleus of a new quarter of the city, and the same architect's **Church of Our Lady of Fatima, Lisbon,** 1934–8. Richer than these, with strong Art Deco feeling, were the **Eden Cinema** (1930–7) and **Hotel Victória, Lisbon**, by Cassiano Branco (1898–1969).

Chapter 45

WESTERN EUROPE SINCE 1945

Introduction

Following Word War II, almost all the European countries found themselves poorer. Some, like Germany, Italy and Britain, were also physically devastated. Others such as Switzerland and Sweden – neutral during the war – suffered virtually no damage at all, and had sound economies.

In the period of post-war reconstruction architects and engineers strove to harness the industrial production techniques developed during the war for civil construction programmes after it. But the balance between expediency – easily borrowed from military culture – and the requirements of a humane environment was not an easy one to strike, and many of the 'system' building methods developed during the 1950s and 1960s in Scandinavia, France, Germany and Britain produced very dismal buildings. This was especially true when applied to the large-scale public housing developments that dominated construction in Germany, France and Britain in particular. The seemingly endless prefabrication of concrete wall panels, stacked together in rows or towers, came to symbolise a paucity of imagination, stringency of resources and the careless attitude of governments towards public housing.

Virtually all cities and towns faced rapidly increasing traffic, and while some countries were content to let the traffic take what land it wanted and to fill in the gaps with commercial architecture – Germany and Belgium being prime examples – others, like Britain and France, which wanted to plan for the motor car, looked to the United States for precedent. In the long run, however, planning proved as invidious as the *laissez-faire* approach.

In spite of a reviving interest in regionalism, mainstream architecture provided the European countries with a steady diet of international modernism throughout the 1950s and 1960s, as across Europe cities suffered extensive demolitions for road building and commercial redevelopment. Towards the end of the 1960s local objections to these massive projects increased. Paris lost Les Halles in the early 1970s, and London almost lost its equivalent, Covent Garden Market. But in the early 1970s the tide was turning. The profession of architecture was, understandably, tainted by these years of devastation. Modern was equated with ruthless exploitation in the popular mind. Architects therefore turned to history.

Historicism took many forms. The purist classicising forms of Aldo Rossi and the Italian Rational Architecture movement, and Leon Krier's town planning schemes, too often adopted formal solutions for romantic reasons, solutions quite at odds with a building's programmatic requirement. The rationale was called poetics. Others made more playful use of history. Soon the radical became conventional once more: pitched roofs and pediments were the means to approval from clients, planners and users alike.

Austria

In Austria the main concern during the 1940s and 1950s was to rebuild housing and industry; notable projects being the **Felten & Guillaume Pavilion, Vienna** (1954), by Oswald Haerdtl and the **Puchsbaumplatz Church, Vienna** (1965), by Clemens Holzmeister (1886–1983), which both demonstrated the continuation of a pre-war concern with romanticism. Roland Rainer's **Municipal Hall, Vienna** (1952–8), represents a more rational approach. This steel and concrete structure, clad in aluminium, is a fresh solution to the problem of the large (for 16,000 people) hall. Rainer realised his Garden City principles for large, low-rise housing schemes at **Puchenau, near Linz** (1966–75).

An architectural position both more historically based and more technologically dependent was established by Arbeitsgruppe 4 (Wilhelm Holzbauer, Friedrich Kurrent, Otto Leitner and Johannes Spalt; founded 1963) whose **Parish Church, Salzburg-Parsch** (1955–6), and **S. Josef's College, Salzburg** (1961), use the materials and forms of Modernism but employ them with subtle historical emphasis. Hans Puchhammer's **Widtmann House, Vienna** (1966–8), and Anton Schweighofer's **Primary School, Vienna** (1969–74), both 'white modern' in one sense, show the influence of Wagner, Loos and Frank. Friedrich

A. Abteilberg Museam, Mönchengladbach, Germany (1972–82). See p. 1368

B. Town Hall, Säynätsalo, Finland (1949–52). See p. 1369

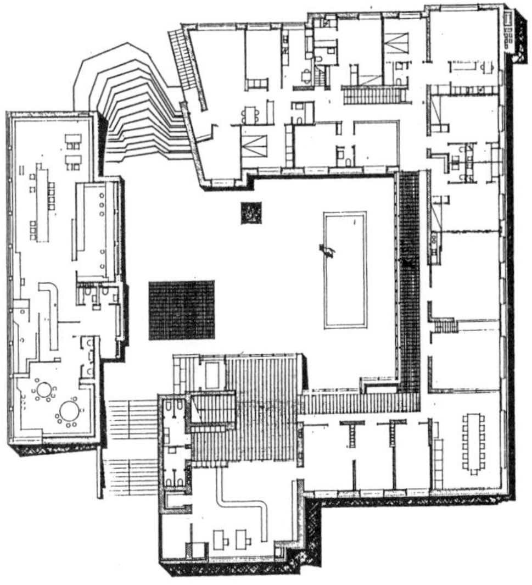

C. Town Hall, Säynätsalo: plan at courtyard level

Kurrent and Johannes Spalt's **Central Savings Bank, Vienna** (1970–4), with its three-storey volume supported by large rectangular concrete portal frames and two internal gallery levels on round columns, achieves a high standard of rational clarity and sense of place.

Gustav Peichl's (born 1928) **studios for Austria State Radio, Salzburg** (1968–72), show interest in technical and formal issues, less in historical matters. His **Satellite Transmission Station, Steiermark** (1976–9), buries all buildings under an undulating field of grass, leaving only some facades and the giant satellite dish and antennae in clear view.

The work of Hans Hollein (born 1934) is in contrast with this precision work, displaying less faith in the promise of technology and much more personality. The **Schullin jewellery store, Vienna** (1972–4), deals in a matter-of-fact manner with interior spaces and signals the luxury of the shop through an entrance composition of polished stone, chrome and brass, echoing Secessionist work. Hollein's **Austrian State Travel Bureau, Vienna** (1976–8), is similarly a plain background with fine interior details including metal palm trees and brass Indian pavilions. The **Abteilberg Museum, Mönchengladbach, Germany** (1972–82) (p. 1367A), displays Hollein's skills at a larger scale. Strong forms in differing materials are juxtaposed on a sloping site and 'eroded' at strategic points to allow entrances and connections to meet functional requirements.

A different reaction to the perfectly engineered environment – a literal eruption of protest – is the **Favoriten branch of the Zentralsparkasse der Gemeinde, Vienna** (1975–9), by Gunter Domenig (born 1934), in which it appears that the facade of metal and glass some six storeys tall has melted, and that, while still hot, has been lifted at street level into a canopy arch.

Friedensreich Hundertwasser (born 1928), whose *Mould Manifesto* of 1958 made a plea for self-build housing, whatever the cost to rationalism, eventually built a group of **Apartments, Lowengasse and Kegelgasse, Vienna** (1983–5), not self-build, but looking rather as if they might be. Curving forms, random decoration and external walls painted only 'as far as the arm will reach out of a window' make this quirky scheme enjoyable, if more a monument to than practice of Hundertwasser's ideals.

Other protesters from the 1960s include Coop Himmelblau (founded 1968: Wolf Prix, Helmut Swiczinsky and Rainer Holzer), whose protest now amounts to building rather plain sheds, knocking out a corner, and filling the gap with delicate metal and glasswork: **Funder Factory 3, S. Veit an der Glan** (1988–9); or the **roof conversion for offices, Vienna** (1983–8), where a spidery metal beak juts out over a solid older building.

Several architects maintain the 'historical thread' picked up by Arbeitsgruppe 4. Heinz Tesar's (born 1939) **Parish Church, Unternberg in Lungau-Salzburg** (1976–9), re-uses parts of an existing church in a complex of forms that is both precise and accommodating, as is the **Kleinarl Parish Church, Salzburg** (1977–86). With Herman Czech's (born 1936) **M House** (1977–80, with Ingrid Lapaine and Gustav Deutsch), the Viennese villa in the tradition of Loos is revived. The Igirien group (Werner Appelt, Eberhard Kneissel and Elsa Prochazka), follow a slightly different path, one they call 'beautiful monotony', which in practice means that their buildings all use the same motifs of arches – blind, open or windowed – and shallow pitch roofs. Their **Church and Assembly hall, Rennbahnweg** (1977) and **Church and Assembly Hall, Jedlersdorf, Vienna** (1980), are virtually the same, on the principle that against plain and repetitive architecture the individual gains emphasis.

Among the important group of architects working in Graz are the husband and wife team of Michael Szyszkowitz (born 1944) and Karla Kowalski (born 1944), best known for their **Church at Graz-Ragnitz** (1983–8). Church, meeting house, club rooms and kindergarten are arranged with deceptive informality around a market square. The gently distorted geometry of the buildings is reminiscent of Domenig, who was, in fact, Szyszkowitz's mentor.

Belgium

The dominating influence of American architecture in post-war Belgium owes something to the central position of Brussels in European politics. Brussels became the International City *par excellence* with highways and curtain wall and concrete office buildings eating away the historic fabric. The **Banque Lambert, Brussels** (1958–64), by Skidmore Owings and Merrill, a dull building of precast concrete elements, is an above-average example.

The most interesting architectural event was the **1958 World's Fair.** Buildings included the bizarre '**Atomium**' structure by A. & J. Polak, a 120 m (390 ft) high model of an iron molecule, turned into a building of nine spheres connected with tubular passages, the whole clothed not in iron but shiny aluminium. Le Corbusier made a free-plan hyperbolic paraboloid tent structure for the **Philips Pavilion**. The **West German Pavilion** was designed by Egon Eiermann and Sep Ruf as a group of eight pavilions, fully glazed on steel frames, connected by covered walkways, and immaculately detailed.

Growing dissatisfaction with the process of urban redevelopment led, in 1968, to the formation of the Atelier de Recherche et d'Action Urbaines, a multidisciplinary organisation of professionals and students which made explicit counterproposals to the mindless redevelopment plans that continued to be put forward. ARAU's interest was in preserving the viability of the central city as a residential and mixed-use environment. Historian Maurice Culot and architect Leon Krier (born 1946) were not afraid to employ traditional urban devices – squares, boulevards – to this end. The movement tended towards, and at times embraced, pastiche, and was prepared to utilise arguably obsolete physical elements of cities. Nevertheless, they achieved many successes and brought the awareness of alternative possibilities into public consciousness.

Thriving in this anti-Modernist climate was Lucien Kroll (born 1927), advocate of participative architecture, whose **Students' Residence at the Université Catholique de Louvain, Woluvé Saint-Lambert** (1969–75), exemplifies this democratic method. Aesthetic values are determined by the *ad hoc* creation process of the building, not *a priori* by the architect's tastes.

A former partner of Kroll, Charles Vandenhove (born 1927), merges the ideas of Dutch Structuralism with strong neo-Classical tendencies, both evident in his early work at the **University Clinic** (1965–86) and the **Educational Institute** (1962–72), both at **Sort Tilman, Liège**. The latter uses a 'family' of forms, executed in concrete and finely detailed brickwork. Vendenhove's interest in urban vernacular has in recent years led him towards a more open neo-Classical approach, exemplified in his later work at the University Clinic, Liège, which incorporates columns and capitals.

Finland

Eric Bryggman 's (1891–1955) timber **houses at Pansio, near Turku** (1946), and **Villa Nuuttila, Kuusisto** (1947–51), illustrate sensitivity to location and free modelling of volumes. Alvar Aalto (1898–1976), who had worked with Bryggman in the 1920s, also found himself abandoning the 'white architecture' of the pre-war period. In his **National Pensions Institution, Helsinki** (1948–56), and, above all, the **Town Hall, Säynätsalo** (1949–52) (p. 1367B), can be seen a stronger interest in 'earth' materials, brick and timber. The Säynätsalo building has offices and meeting hall arranged around a raised courtyard in a way reminiscent of mediaeval Italian hilltowns (p. 1367C). This is perhaps not accidental, as Aalto retained a strong love of both Italy and classical Greece, a love not just of form but of the humanity within the forms. The publication of these buildings and the fact that Aalto had begun to receive commissions in Germany and the United States soon made him one of the most highly regarded architects of the post-war years. The **Rautatalo Office Building** (1953–5), with a copper and glass facade, and **Cultural Centre** (1955–8), with its clam-shell curved walls and asymmetrical auditorium, both in Helsinki, show a more sophisticated manner in urban contexts, and culminated in the **Finlandia Hall** (1970–5). Aalto also built his own **summer house, Muuratsalo** (1953), a *bricolage* partly designed as a testbed of materials and techniques, his own **Studio, Munkkiniemi** (1953–5), and **Vuoksenniska Church, Imatra** (1957–9), marking a return to 'white' architecture, forming the building according to the functional requirements of the Lutheran liturgy and the demands of acoustics. The result is an asymmetrical plan and irregular massing quite at odds with pre-war functionalism.

Viljo Revell (1910–64) was in Aalto's office during the 1930s, and although his first post-war work was the sandstone and timber, broad-eaved **Rehabilitation Centre for War Invalids, Liperi** (1948), his style also varied widely, from the International style **Teollisuuskeskus Hotel and Offices, Helsinki** (1952), to the volumetric freedom of the **Meilahti School, Helsinki** (1952–3, with Osmo Sipari).

Heikki (born 1918) and Kaija (born 1920) Sirén held closer to the values of Finnish neo-Classicism: formal plan arrangements and studied sequences of volume. Their **University Chapel, Otaniemi** (1952–7), no less than their **Otsonpesä housing, Tapiola** (1959), show the romantic possibilities of conjoining formally severe architectural systems and primitive landscape.

With the planning of **Tapiola Garden City** (1953) by Otto-I Meurman, Aarne Ervi and others, close to Helsinki, a brilliant integration of town and natural surroundings was achieved in a so-called 'wooded city'. The four quarters of the town are separated by green belts. Ervi also designed the **town centre** (1954–9), as well as **housing** (1952–64), the **swimming pool** (1962) and the **Tapiola Garden Hotel** (1974). The town, whose target population of 18,000 was reached by the mid-1970s, has recently acquired a **Cultural Centre** (1990), the work of Arto Sipinen. The neo-Modern building (white rectilinear shapes, metal and glass), planned overall in terms of large cuboid volumes, fits well with the existing town, as it does with its lakeside site.

Reima (born 1923) and Raili Pietilä contributed to Tapiola with an **apartment building, Suvikumpu** (1966–9), whose irregular floor heights and window arrangements soften and humanise the building. A similar interest can be seen in the so-called **Serpent House, Helsinki** (1951), by Yrjö Lindegren, where a row of apartments snakes along a narrow plot, making semi-private open spaces and giving greater privacy and identity to individual units.

At **Kaleva Church, Tampere** (1966), the Pietiläs employed alternate vertical strips of window and curved wall to enclose the main volume of great height and have produced a building which, though it may be called 'Gothic' in respect of its proportioning and emotional impact, is entirely free of the moroseness and gloom of Germanic work such as that of Gottfried Bohm. Their **Dipoli Students' Residence, Otaniemi** (1966–7), contrasts two building masses, a rectilinear student residence and a free-form clubhouse made from random stone block. The cave-like clubhouse interior is given a ceiling of undulating concrete.

This extraordinary richness of fine individual buildings produced a reaction in the late 1960s among a number of architects who rejected the 'masterwork' conception of architecture, holding that scientifically determined systems of proportioning, together with industrialised production techniques, could answer any given building problem. The **Factory at Marimekko** (1972) by Reijo Lahtinen and Erkki Kairamo exemplifies this attitude, with its unyielding obedience to grids. But such an architecture hardly reflects the nature of Finnish society, which is not industrialised to anything like the degree of Germany or France. A modification of this approach finds industrial components combined with the traditional materials and hand finishing that characterise Finnish culture, as at Pekka Helin and Tuomo Siitonen's **Training Centre for the Metalworkers' Union, Teisko** (1976).

A continuing interest in formal solutions to architectural problems can be seen in Heikki Taskinen's **Lower Secondary School, Oulunsalo** (1983), where a wide of variety of volumes and roof forms, but made only of brick and metal, allow a large building to be visually digested with ease.

Material simplicity with volumetric complexity characterise the work of Lauri and Anna Louekari at the **Mikonkari Recreation Centre, Lohenpyrsto** (1988). The plan is a modified 'U', partly two-storey, with white-painted vertical timber siding externally, horizontal natural timber within. With scarcely a right-angle to be found in the building, this work carries echoes of the familiar with many of the disorientations one might associate with a place remembered in a dream.

France

In post-war France the demand for a large quantity of building contructed at speed meant the early introduction of industrial techniques. The **reconstruction of Le Havre** (1945–54), undertaken by Auguste Perret (1874–1954) in a neo-Classical manner, was an anachronism in both planning and stylistic terms. The neo-Classical had the advantage, however, of lending itself to the factory production of pre-cast concrete components. The same is true of Andre Lurçat's (1894–1970) **reconstruction work at Maubeuge and Saint-Denis**, carrying Beaux-Arts formalism into the factory. It is interesting that these schemes have not suffered – or perhaps caused – the social problems associated with more 'modern' developments such as the **La Sarcelle housing estate, Paris** (1959), by Boileau and Labourdette.

Le Corbusier, despite his 'machine aesthetic' and pre-war passion for vast city plans, was not at the forefront of post-war industrialised buildings nor of urban reconstruction, which was largely a continuation of the principles laid down after 1940 by Vichy regionalist planners. Le Corbusier's work from the late 1940s tends increasingly towards the handcrafted. In such works as the **Unité d'Habitation, Marseilles** (1946–52) (p. 1371A,B,D), the mere fragment of a large planning scheme, Le Corbusier preferred rough-textured concrete with a handmade quality. This development incorporating flats (with double-height living spaces and wide balconies and served by an internal 'street'), integrated with shopping (on an upper level 'street') and recreational and communal facilities on the roof, led to many direct and indirect copies throughout Europe during the following decade.

With a private commission like the **Maisons Jaoul, Neuilly-sur-Seine** (1952–6) (p. 1371C), the walls are no longer white, but concrete and brick, with wood and glass infill deeply recessed. At a time when industrialised building was becoming a reality and it was no longer necessary to 'fake' the aesthetic of industrialisation, Le Corbusier had grown interested in materiality and place.

The foremost exponent of industrialisation was Jean Prouvé (1901–84), who continued to develop his work of the 1930s on prefabricated panel systems and curtain walling. Trained as an art metal worker, Prouvé was fascinated by automotive construction techniques and aimed at an architecture of lightweight industrial components, rapid construction, and flexibility in use. In 1950, and in collaboration with architect André Sive, he designed and built **14 experimental houses at Meudon** for the Ministry of Reconstruction and Town Planning. Consisting of a lightweight steel frame and infill panels of metal, glass and wood, sitting on top of a rubblestone base, the houses contain a clever ventilation system although insulation is scanty, particularly in the metal roofs. Prouvé's **holiday house at Beauvallon** (1962) uses greater space standards to develop the open-plan layout. Here too are the 'Rousseau' panels of wood, insulation and corrugated aluminium – manufactured by Prouvé – and that trademark of 1960s industrial production, rounded corners. His **demountable school, Villejuif** (1957), represents a different type of structure, where the roof is supported on a single row of eccentric columns, while the parallel external wall skins are used as tension membranes.

Prouvé's contribution to the development of curtain walling no doubt remains his highest achievement, for although his other work was enthusiastically received, it failed, like Buckminster Fuller's in

A. Unité d'Habitation, Marseilles (1946–52). See p. 1370

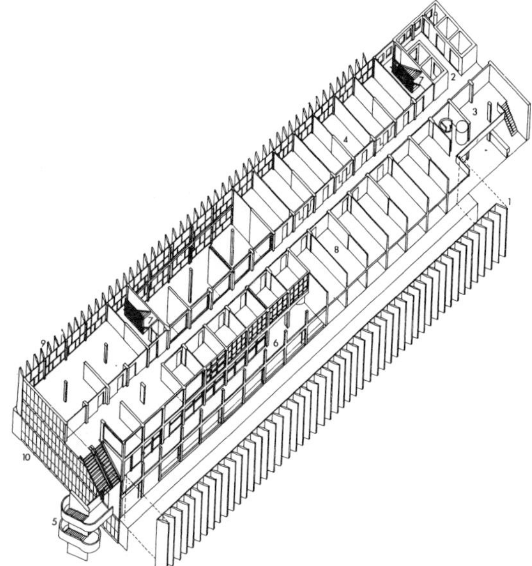

B. Unité d'Habitation: communal services floor

1 Brise-soleil
2 Hall and lifts
3 Lobby
4 Commercial premises
5 Fire escape
6 Ambulatory
7 Fire escape
8 Commercial premises
9 Brise-soleil
10 North elevation

C. (*left*) Maisons Jaoul, Neuilly-sur-Seine (1952–6). See p. 1370

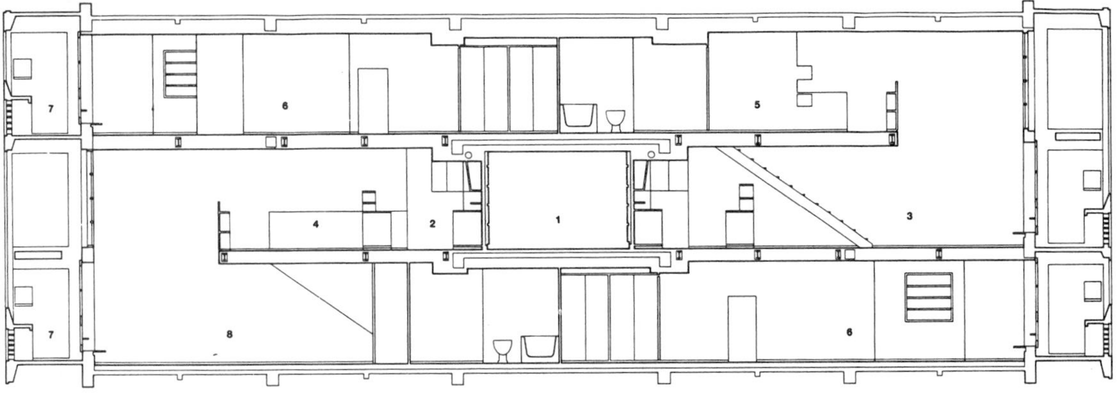

1 interior street
2 kitchen
3 dining area and living room
4 dining area and gallery
5 parents' bedroom with bathroom
6 children's bedrooms
7 balcony terrace
8 parents' bedroom and living area

D. Unité d'Habitation, Marseilles: section through typical duplex apartment

the United States, to have much direct influence on the problems it aimed to solve. Nor has time been kind to the built works, which exhibit the physical limitations of the technology of their time.

Most of the prefabrication applied to low-cost housing, involving precast concrete elements, with its in-built inflexibility, was anathema to people like Prouvé. But the building industry was geared for it. Architects attempted various formal solutions to the problem. For **Les Courtillières housing estate, Pantin** (1955–60), Emil Aillaud (born 1902) used a 2 km serpentine block, six storeys tall, around the perimeter of the site, to give local parts of his scheme some individual identity. Parking is kept outside the ring, which contains only the single-storey nursery school, an irregular plan partly roofed with an undulating concrete shell roof. At the **Weisberg estate, Forbach** (1959–63), Aillaud used a similar approach to insert fifteen eleven-storey blocks among the low-rise apartments. Mobile shuttering was used for all buildings. The inherent strength of the concrete walls meant that Aillaud was able to place window openings in an irregular fashion across the facades, which, combined with a use of brightly coloured surfaces, give this scheme a peculiarly toy-like quality.

Paul Brossard cast large random stones into the concrete elements that make up his **Les Bluets housing, Creteil** (1959–62), but the blocks of apartments remain orthogonally planned and in the end the bizarre appearance of the construction seems inadequate compensation for the bleakness of the whole.

Another attempt to come to terms with the scale of public housing schemes is seen in Ricardo Bofill's neo-Classical designs, exemplified by the concrete-built **Les Espaces d'Abraxas, Marne-la-Valle** (1978–83), with its flats arranged into a large-scale Baroque element.

In the field of cultural buildings, a wide variety of techniques was employed, from the brilliant **Musée-Maison de la Culture, Le Havre** (1957–61), by Guy Lagneau, Michel Weill, Jean Dimirijevic, and Raymond Audigier, a glazed box surrounded by mechanical solar control devices, to Robert Auzelle's more formal **Administration and Community Centre, Neufchâtel-en-Bray** (1952–61). Here, with a brief that includes law courts, a town hall and a theatre, Auzelle has given each main element a separate form and united the scheme with common materials: brick walls on a structure of concrete and steel.

The **Basilica of Pius X, Lourdes** (1956–8), represents a meeting point of architecture and the engineered somewhat akin to Nervi's buildings in Italy. Here, Eugène Freyssinet (1879–1962), Pierre Vago (born 1910) and others have created a vast underground chamber, free of columns, in plan approximating the early Christian fish symbol. The structure of prestressed concrete ribs curve to a central spine, itself curved along the chamber's 201 m (660 ft) length. The low proportions of the space reinforce the biological analogy.

Le Corbusier's **Pilgrimage church of Notre Dame-du-Haut, Ronchamp** (1950–4) (p. 1373A) contrasts sharply with the increasingly machine-produced built world. Massive battered walls pierced by tiny splayed openings, a sweeping concrete shell roof that gives a sagging ceiling within the chapel: all is handcrafted and 'one off'. This building, with its exploitation of seemingly 'primitive' and emotive forms and materials, had an enormous influence on the development of modern architecture. Le Corbusier's **Monastery of S. Marie-de-la-Tourette, Eveux-sur-l'Arbrêsle** (1957–60) (p. 1373B) a more complex building, raises the monastery cells above the site on piers to create a private world of solitude, while placing the tall chapel on the ground. All is in concrete, a beautifully organised monument to asceticism.

Commercial work of a high order was produced by Edouard Albert, a fine example of his technical skills being his **Operations Building, Orly Airport** (1958–60), where a high degree of flexible servicing was provided in an elegantly glazed four-storey 'H' planned building, with external steel frame, sealed and air conditioned against ambient noise. Paul Andreu's (born 1938) **Terminal One at Charles de Gaulle Airport, Roissy, Paris** (1967–74) (p. 1374A), is an ingeniously designed example of a centralised terminal. Circular in plan, built of boldly board-marked concrete, and organised around an open atrium crossed by transparent tubes carrying passengers, the terminal is served by seven satellites from which passengers connect with their planes. These satellites are reached by moving pavements which curve beneath the taxiway surrounding the terminal building. Cars are parked within, and on the roof of, the terminal.

Georges Candilis (born 1913), Alexis Josic (born 1921) and Shadrach Woods (1923–73), best known for their planning work at the Zone à Urbaniser en Priorité of **Le Mirail, Toulouse** (1961–77), where the 'segregationist' town-planning policies of pre-war years were rejected in favour of more integrated layouts, also produced small works of considerable refinement. Their **Artisan complex, Les Bruyères, Sèvres** (1963–5), a small group of workshops for the construction industry built in exposed concrete, could be called Brutalist but for the fact that understatement rather than exaggeration is the aesthetic rule.

The concrete shell roof held a constant fascination for the French during the 1950s and 1960s, one of the finest examples being the **covered market, Royan** (1956), by René Sarger and Louis Simon, an undulating shell of only 10 cm thickness – which might have been reduced but for weathering considerations – spanning nearly 40 m (130 ft) clear space. Briefed to build 'un ouvrage spectaculaire',

A. Pilgrimage church of Notre Dame-du-Haut, Ronchamp (1950–54). See p. 1372

B. Monastery of S. Marie-de-la-Tourette, Eveux-sur-l'Arbrêsle (1957–60). See p. 1372

A. Terminal One at Charles de Gaulle Airport, Roissy, Paris (1967–74). See p. 1372

B. Centre Nationale d'Art et de Culture Georges Pompidou, Paris (1971–7). See p. 1375

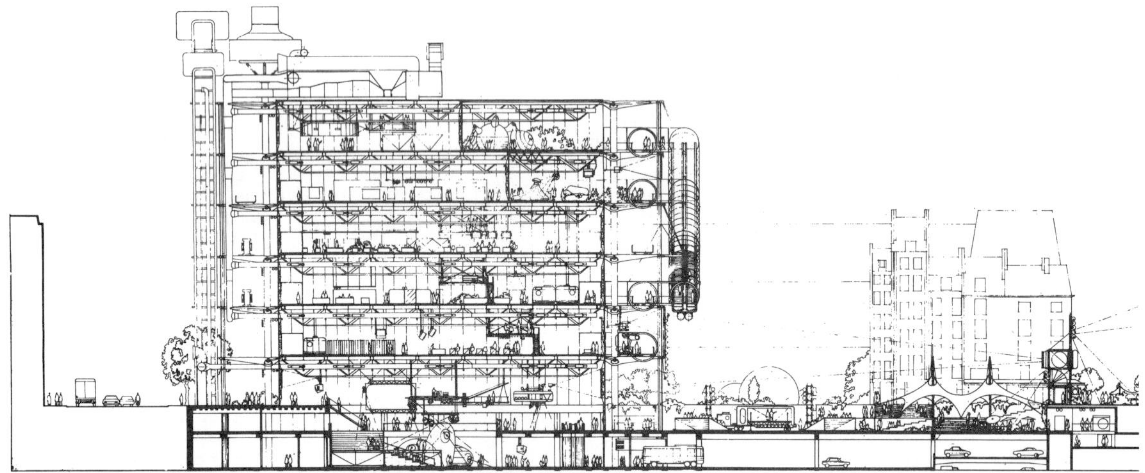

C. Centre Nationale d'Art et de Culture Georges Pompidou, Paris: section

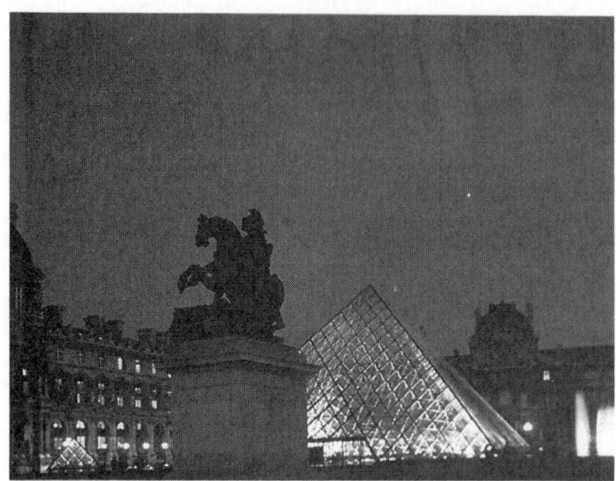

D. Glass pyramid at the Louvre, Paris (1981). See p. 1375

E. Library and Art Gallery, Nîmes (1984–93). See p. 1375

Robert Camusot, Bernard Zehrfuss (born 1911), Pier Luigi Nervi and others built the **CNIT (National Centre of Industry and Technology) exhibition hall, La Défense** (1956–8), three parabolic concrete shells on a triangular plan, making a sort of groin vault resting on only three points. Nervi and Zehrfuss also collaborated, this time with Marcel Breuer, on the **UNESCO Building, Paris** (1953–7), where the congress hall is made with a folded plate ferroconcrete structure based, apparently, on Nervi's studies of mollusc shells.

A scheme owing something to Moshe Safdie's Montreal Habitat (1965–7) (see Chapter 51) is the **Town Centre, Ivry-sur-Seine** (1970–81), by Jean Renaudie and Nina Schuch, where the compounding of small dwelling units, no two of which are alike, leads to an intricate diversity of form at the heart of the town, and to that 'organic' quality which seems to carry the conviction of mediaeval city development into the field of modern housing procurement techniques. The principle, if not the quality, was emulated in the many neighbouring Villes Nouvelles designated in 1965.

With the international success of Renzo Piano and Richard Rogers' **Centre National d'Art et de Culture Georges Pompidou, Paris** (1971–7) (p. 1374B,C), highly coloured and with all services and structure external to enclosed space, presidents and mayors began to vie with each other in sponsoring extravagant and eye-catching 'Grands Projets'. I. M. Pei's **glass pyramid at the Louvre, Paris** (1981) (p. 1374D), began the long process of reorganisation of that institution. Carlos Ott's **Opéra de la Bastille, Paris** (1989), attempts to fit an impossibly large amount of accommodation onto a cramped site, with the additional expectation of monumentality. This new interest in the grand formal gesture reaches its height with Johan Otto von Sprechelsen's **Arche de la Défense, Paris** (1989), built at the centre of the Parisian business suburb of **La Défense**, developed since 1958 to the plan of Bernard Zehrfuss. The culmination of a (nearly) straight line through the Arc de Triomphe, the new arch conveys a true sense of monumentality by depriving the viewer of any means of comparing human scale to the scale of the building. A cube whose sides measure 162 m (525 ft), the arch houses offices in its two slab sides and a gallery spanning between the two at high level. A tent structure floats above the podium.

A similar interest in the formal gesture is seen in Jean Nouvel, Pierre Soria and Gilbert Lezenes's **Arab Institute, Paris** (1983–9), housing library, administrative offices and social facilities. The south wall of this structure consists of a large number of what Nouvel calls 'modern mashrabeya work', a high-tech version of Arabic sun-shading. At the **Musée d'Orsay, Paris** (1984–6), Gaia Aulenti and others have converted a disused nineteenth-century railway station into a gallery of nineteenth-century art. One of the most satisfying of the Grands Projets is Bernard Tschumi's **Parc de la Villette** (1982–92), combining a rigorous and complex geometrical framework with a willingness to allow an autonomy of individual elements.

A significant provincial gesture towards the creation of a Parisian style 'Grand Project' is Norman Foster's **Library and Art Gallery, Nîmes** (1984–93) (p. 1374E). Sited beside the Roman Maison Carrée, Foster's transparent building, with its generous atrium, looks virtually empty. This spaciousness is achieved by placing five of this building's nine storeys below ground. The elegance of the aluminium and concrete structure is compromised by the building's roofscape where service machinery is neither properly concealed nor honestly exposed.

Recent years have seen an increasing rejection of formalism. Michel Kagan, with his **Municipal Administration Building, Paris** (1993), carries the planar language of 1930s white architecture to a new level in the development of volumetric relationships, and is superbly detailed. Bernard Huet, at **Place Stalingrade, Paris** (1989), has reclaimed a squalid scrap of land for public use without resorting to gimmickry, in an exemplary piece of urban landscaping.

Latest of the great Parisian schemes is Dominic Perrault's (born 1955) **New Paris Library.** Due for completion in 1996, it incorporates a vast podium containing reading rooms and offices, from the corners of which rise glass-clad towers for book storage.

Germany

The scale of reconstruction required in post-war Germany was unequalled in Europe, and with funding for industrial development coming from the United States, great strides were taken very quickly. Much of what was built was of indifferent quality, and there hardly seemed time for a planned approach. Apart from cities like Lübeck, where a large portion of the destroyed historic fabric was faithfully reconstructed in replica of its pre-war state, most towns proceeded on an *ad hoc* basis. Government goals were expressed in quantitative terms, and their aim of half a million new housing units a year tended towards the creation of large satellite sprawls at the edges of the larger cities.

Thoughtful architects found themselves looking for a non-ideological building style, and believed they had found it in the American curtain-wall system. Here, skin replaced structure, the expressive mass of a building was abandoned for the elegant working out of proportion on thin glass and metal skins. From Paul Schneider-Esleben's **Mannesmann office building, Dusseldorf** (1952), to Henn and Strobel's **Osram**

offices, Munich (1963–5), the style produced some exquisite buildings, finely detailed and proportioned. The limitations of the 'pretty box', however, became plain, as the boxes became larger and the variations ever more difficult to play. Helmut Hentrich and Hubert Petschnigg found one answer in the **Phoenix-Rheinrohr Building, Dusseldorf** (1957–60), where the large volume is split into three slender curtain-walled slabs.

To some architects this elegant formalism was too detached from its surroundings, making all its expressive statements in the vertical plane and giving nothing on the horizontal ground plane, where the buildings actually stood. Rolf Gutbrod, Bernard Binder and others, with the **IBM Building, Berlin** (1962), chose to express the functional components of the building to a greater degree. Here the curtain wall is replaced by a horizontal banding of precast concrete at floor levels alternating with strips of windows, and the whole nine-storey block is anchored to the ground by an angled stair block at one end. A more frantic attempt at making the facade express internal order is the **Police Headquarters, Hamburg** (1958–66), by Atmer, Marlow and others, where a heavy concrete lattice, interrupted from time to time by large internal spaces, covers the facade. It is a short step from here to the Brutalist architecture of Gunter Bock's **Sindlingen Community Centre** (1961), with its highly articulated elements wrapped in harsh concrete walls, Lenz and Muller's **Ketteler College, Mainz** (1964), a more refined use of concrete and a breaking up of the building mass into individually expressed elements; and even Gottfried Böhm's (born 1920) **Bensberg Town Hall** (1967), where, however, the desire for expression has led to the construction of a peculiar tower on top of a mighty complex of horizontal slabs, all created within the context of an old castle.

Quite different in intention is the **Friedenskirche Parish Hall, West Berlin** (1961), by Hans Muller and Georg Heinrichs, where a strict limit is set to the expressive nature of the building by the choice of a few materials and a geometrically controlled formal arrangement. Others used 'poor' materials in an undemonstrative, unpretentious way: the **Ingolstadt City Theatre** (1962–8), by Hardt-Waltherr Hamer and others, eschewed the norms of luxury finishes for cultural buildings for what must have seemed at the time the more demotic concrete and formal abstraction.

Of great significance for post-war German architecture was the work of Egon Eiermann (1904–70), who tended to see structure and detail as a way out of the stylistic conundrum. His **Blumberg Handkerchief Factory** (1949–51) may share some of the preoccupations with elegance of the curtain-wall builders, but its search for architectural value goes much deeper. Here, with a factory, every component is treated with equal architectural respect, be it a chimney or a machine shop, and all are thoroughly worked out. In the **Neckermann Export Company Building, Frankfurt am Main** (1958–60), the glass facade is screened by a secondary layer of balconies and staircases that give a richness of expression to the building without wilfulness.

Eiermann was capable of great simplicity. His **Mattheaus Kirche, Pforzheim** (1953) uses small precast concrete elements within the plainest of formal compositions, to produce a church of austere and simple dignity.

Churches provided a wonderful field of aesthetic potential in a Germany nervous of expression in the more obvious spheres of government and cultural institutions. Eiermann and Weist's **Memorial Church, Berlin** (1959–63), again uses small precast units, but here to compose mute companions to the ruined tower of an older church. Helmut Striffler's **Church on the Blumenau, Mannheim**, is an almost cubist composition, with walls of concrete bearing the imprint of their wooden formwork, slit windows, and a steep eaves-less roof. Striffler also designed the **Memorial Chapel, Dachau** (1967), also in concrete. Dieter Baumewerd's **Church of the Holy Spirit, Emmerich am Niederrheim** (1965–6), looks like an industrial building, with its great mushroom columns of differing heights. The greatest church architecture of this 'expressionist' kind was produced by Gottfried Böhm. His **Church at Neviges** (1956–68) demonstrates no evident order of structure or space. Walls and ceiling are faceted and folded like paper, but they are made of concrete. Spatially simple, the church derives a sense of complexity from the geometrical manipulation of wall and ceiling surfaces.

The festive nature of theatrical productions found expression in Adolf Abel and Rolf Gutbrod's **Stuttgart Liederhalle** (1955–6), which has a free plan of considerable interest and a plethora of architectural motifs and works by diverse artists. The result is a work that could almost define the 1950s, with its interest in maintaining visual interest at all costs.

The concern of Hans Scharoun (1893–1972) at the **Philharmonie, Berlin** (1959–63) (p. 1377A), transcended decorative treatment. This masterful auditorium in many ways resolves the relationship between audience and performers, and indeed between the individual auditor and the collective whole. What is more, the solution proposed – blocks of seating jutted out into the main body of space – is only conceivable using twentieth-century materials. The building provides a thrilling spatial experience. Similar interests can be seen in Scharoun's **School at Marl** (1968), and the **Prussian State Library, Berlin** (1967–78). The Philharmonie and Library were built close to the Berlin Wall as a gesture of faith that one day the city might be reunited and these cultural institutions stand at its centre. Joining this group, but the antithesis of Scharoun's work, is Mies van der Rohe's **New National Gallery** (1962–8) (p. 1377B,C), the last of

A. Philharmonie, Berlin (1959–63). See p. 1376

B. New National Gallery, Berlin (1962–8). See p. 1376

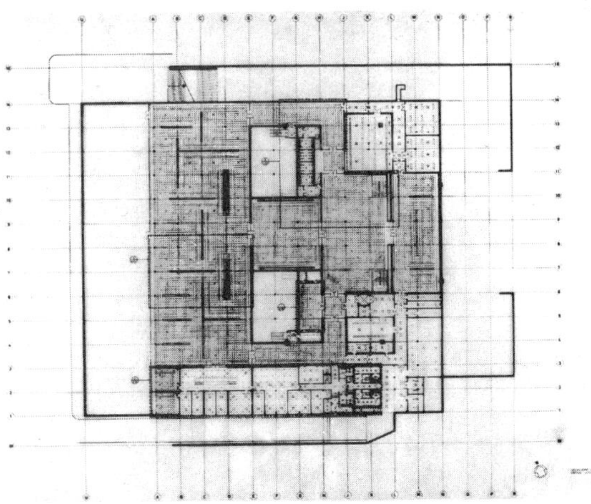

C. New National Gallery, Berlin: plan at gallery level

that master's great pavilion buildings. The gallery space within the pavilion is unitary, subdivided as necessary by movable partitions. The huge roof is held up by eight cruciform columns, the walls deeply recessed and wholly glazed. 'Service' spaces – which might be defined as any space where a person or machine has actually to perform some action – are buried in the basement, along with much of the gallery space.

The genius of Scharoun encompassed all aspects of architectural work, and his **'Romeo and Juliet' apartment blocks, Stuttgart** (1957–9), show that the principle of spatial values to lay first claim in the formation of physical reality held also in the small-scale world of housing.

Coeval with this development was the **Berlin Interbau exhibition** of 1957, intended to unite good architecture with sound urban planning – a notable want in post-war Germany. Interbau was an international affair, with Alvar Aalto, Walter Gropius, van den Boek and Bakema, Arne Jacobsen, Kay Fisker, Le Corbusier, and others invited to design housing in the Hansaviertel. Among German contributors were Eiermann and Paul Schneider-Esleben. But however good the individual buildings, the ensemble is notably suburban. No attempt was made to integrate the schemes, but rather they were isolated from one another by good landscaping, and Le Corbusier's Unité – already stripped by the planners of its recreational and commercial floors – was exiled to a site near the Olympic Stadium.

O. M. Ungers' (born 1926) **housing at Cologne-Nippes** (1957), **house at Hennef** (1960) and **housing at Cologne-Seeberg** (1965–6) brought a discipline, rationality and fascination with geometry usually associated with Dutch architecture. His use of familiar materials like brick in unusual sizes and bonds attracts fresh attention to the surface of his prismatic buildings. Ungers has been among the most consistently intellectual architects of the post-war period, although his **Skyscraper, Frankfurt am Main** (1983–5), reveals an increasing banality in the built work. Here, a parallelepiped of stone (on a steel frame) is recessed to reveal an inner box of glass (also on a steel frame), which also emerges above the top of the building.

During the 1960s several new approaches were taken to large building and planning programmes. Günter Behnisch (born 1922) achieved international fame with his **sports buildings at the Olympic Park, Munich** (1967–72), built for the 1972 Olympic Games. The tent roofs that give unity to these buildings were designed with the advice of Frei Otto (born 1925), and the complex seemed to herald an architecture in which the built environment might respond to human needs at a quicker pace than the usual 30- or 60-year building cycle. The realisation of these dreams has proven difficult to achieve. Behnisch's strong interest in organic architecture, with its close relationship to functionalism, is apparent in works like the **school at Oppelsbohm** (1966–9) and the **schools at Lorch, Wurttemburg** (1972–3), where the formality is loosened to create a building of extremely refined composition. A growing interest in technical pyrotechnics for their own sake is seen in the same architect's more recent work (**Hysolar Research Institute, University of Stuttgart**, 1987), and his **Kindergarten, Stuttgart-Luginsland** (1991), where walls and floors and seemingly every part of the building are warped and dislocated.

A different approach to providing a responsive architecture was put forward by the French firm of Candilis, Josic & Woods in their design for the **Free University, Berlin** (1966–70). Here, flexibility was offered by the provision of a horizontal 'mat' of buildings and courtyards, a deliberate rejection of the normal hierarchical buildings that typify similar institutions. The ideas were based on an unexecuted town planning project for Frankfurt-Romerburg (1963) by the same architects.

A continuation of Scharoun's tradition is seen in the work of Hermann Fehling (born 1909) and Daniel Gogel (born 1927), whose **Max Planck Institute for Educational Research, Berlin** (1965–74), and **European Southern Observatory, Garching, near Munich** (1976–80), are remarkable in their rendering of complex technical programmes into humane spatial environments, as is their **Meteorological Institute, Berlin** (1991).

In 1978 the West Berlin authorities initiated the **Internationale Bauausstellung** or **IBA**, in which once again German and foreign architects were asked to design housing for the city. But such was the shift in attitudes since Interbau that now the sites were within the city proper, and the projects either completed or replaced existing blocks of dwellings. It was recognised that planning within historic cities had, during the previous thirty years, been preponderantly interested in traffic, and that as a result many of the architectural problems had been displaced to suburban zones. The architectural results are mixed. Competitions were held for most sites, and notable blocks were designed by Herman Hertzberger (**housing at Lindenstrasse,** 1987), Aldo Rossi (**housing at Rauchstrasse,** 1988), and James Stirling and Michael Wilford (**Science Centre offices,** 1988).

James Stirling (with Michael Wilford) achieved what is arguably his best building with his **Staatsgalerie, Stuttgart** (1977–84) (p. 1379A,B,D), a remarkable fusion of inventively adapted Classical details and forms with up-to-the-minute technology. The building also posseses wit, and a plan that works. A similarly creative relationship between history and modern technology is evident in Meinhard von Gerkan's (born 1935) **Air Terminal, Stuttgart** (1980–1). Here a massive natural stone 'plinth' rakes up and bears upon it slightly Gothic steel columns that branch out into 'twigs' as they extend towards the roof.

A. Staatsgalerie, Stuttgart (1977–84). See p. 1378

B. Staatsgalerie: interior

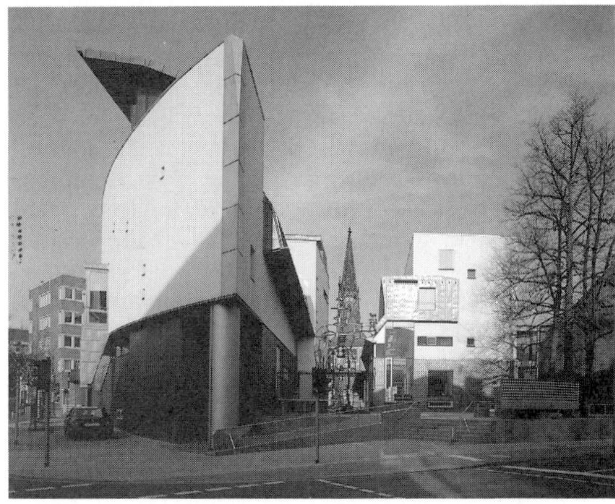

C. New City Library, Münster (completed 1993). See p. 1380

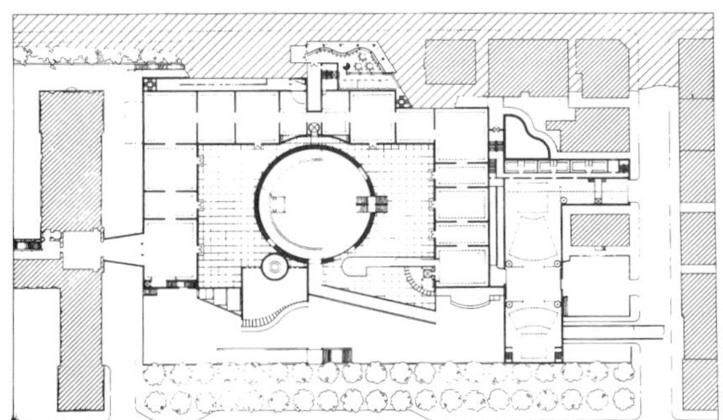

D. Staatsgalerie: plan at gallery level

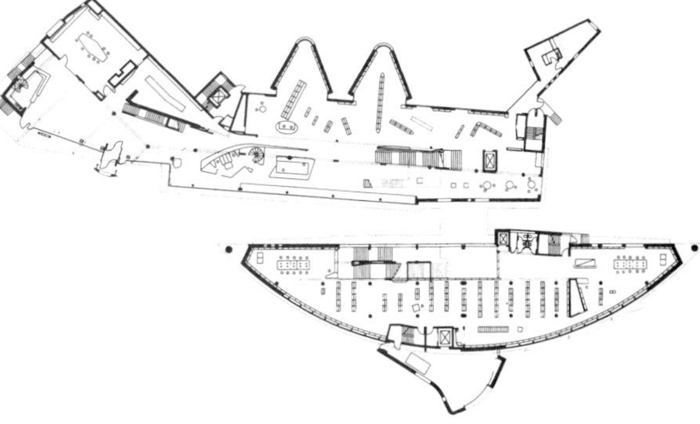

E. New City Library, Münster: plan at upper level

A very different type of relationship between history and modernity has been achieved at the **New City Library, Münster** (completed 1993) (p. 1379C,E), by Bolles-Wilson. Rather than giving the new building a formal and Classically derived plan of the sort devised by Stirling and Wilford at Stuttgart, Bolles-Wilson have created a modulated visual cacophony of angular forms, details and elevational textures. The result is striking and reveals that some of the more cerebral theories of Deconstruction can be employed in practice and with success.

Notable engineering works have also been produced, for example by Frei Otto, Dyckerhoff and Widmann, with their 208 m (676 ft) single-span concrete **Rhine Bridge, Bendorf** (1962–5), and Gerd Lomer's **Severin Bridge, Cologne** (1958–60), where the roadway is supported by twelve steel cables running from a single mast.

Communist East Germany saw a very different role for government in architecture. The building industry was under absolute state control, and the society less affluent. These facts are apparent in the process of building, with greater emphasis on prefabricated concrete elements as a means of lowering unit costs, with the poor finish of buildings, and on the emphasis on housing rather than commercial buildings. Nevertheless, there seems little to distinguish the underlying principles of architectural or urban thinking between the two societies. Communal facilities such as theatres and sports halls tended to be located centrally in towns and cities, traffic was accommodated at the expense of historic fabric, the lower-paid were housed in minimal apartments on the peripheries of cities.

Josef Kaiser's **Karl Marx Allee extension, Berlin** (1959–65), with its relentless prefabrication, is lightened by buildings like the **International Cinema** (1960–2), and is not wholly different from Berlin's **Markisches Viertel** (1962–74). The reconstruction of the **Alexanderplatz** as the focus of the former East Berlin by Joachim Nather, Roland Korn and others (1964–70) uses all the architectural idioms of its time in a mix of high- and low-rise buildings, open spaces and car parking.

Helmut Ullmann and Wofgang Scheibe's nine storey **Hotel Deutschland, Leipzig** (1965), with its sophisticated internationalism of concrete and curtain walling makes an interesting contrast to Kunz Nierade's **Opera House** (1960) in the same city. Here is an architecture not found in the West at this time, a neo-Classical affair full of self-importance.

Great Britain

As elsewhere in Europe, the end of World War II saw an almost limitless demand for housing in Britain, both in and around existing cities and at the many New Towns designated by the government between 1946 and 1972. Additionally, education reforms proposed during the war years, which raised the school-leaving age, led to an extensive schools building programme, and set the stage for a subsequent expansion of university building.

Much in public housing design was borrowed from Sweden, an informality of layout, use of natural materials like brick and timber, and a conscious cheerfulness. Herbert Tayler and David Green's **Kells Acres, Geldeston, Norfolk** (1951–2), and other developments in and around **Loddon, near Norwich**, were typical of a style much praised at the time by *The Architectural Review* under the name of the New Humanism: tiles, wavy bargeboards, white-painted windows, and a distinct sense of comfort and 'place'. Nikolaus Pevsner, in 1963, called it post-Modern. These sensibilities translated into an urban context produced the low-rise elements at the **Alton East Estate, Roehampton** (1954–6), designed by LCC architects including Oliver Cox and Rosemary Stjernstedt under Robert Matthew. Here, on a magnificent wooded site, housing, schools, shops and other facilities were to be brought together as a cohesive social whole. The picturesque atmosphere in which this scheme succeeded was not, unfortunately, available to many of its imitators.

By no means all architects subscribed to these aesthetic notions. The competition-winning **Churchill Gardens housing, London** (1946–62), by Philip Powell (born 1921) and John Hildago Moya (1920–94), set a standard for a different kind of high-density urban housing. A row of ten-storey blocks perpendicular to the Thames provides the backbone to a scheme that mixes high- and low-rise blocks, shops and communal facilities. The architecture uses modern materials plainly, and avoids any whiff of the village. Another competition produced the **Golden Lane Estate, London** (1955–62), by Chamberlin Powell & Bon, built on a bomb site on the edge of the City of London. High density here meant buildings arranged around paved courtyards, generally medium-rise buildings including a colonnade to the street with a seventeen-storey tower in the middle, and excellent facilities. A wide mix of material and methods of construction is used, from precast concrete and mosaic to brick, steel and glass.

The New Humanism was soon to be outdone by a starkly modern style of architecture having its origins in the muscular use of concrete of Le Corbusier and of his Unité in particular. The second phase of housing at Roehampton, **Alton West** (1954–63), by Bill Howell, John Killick and Colin Lucas of the LCC, is a precise contrast to the New Humanism of its adjacent predecessor. Where the earlier scheme had used brick and wood, and taken every opportunity offered by balconies and stairs for the formal play of recession and projection, this group of rigidly

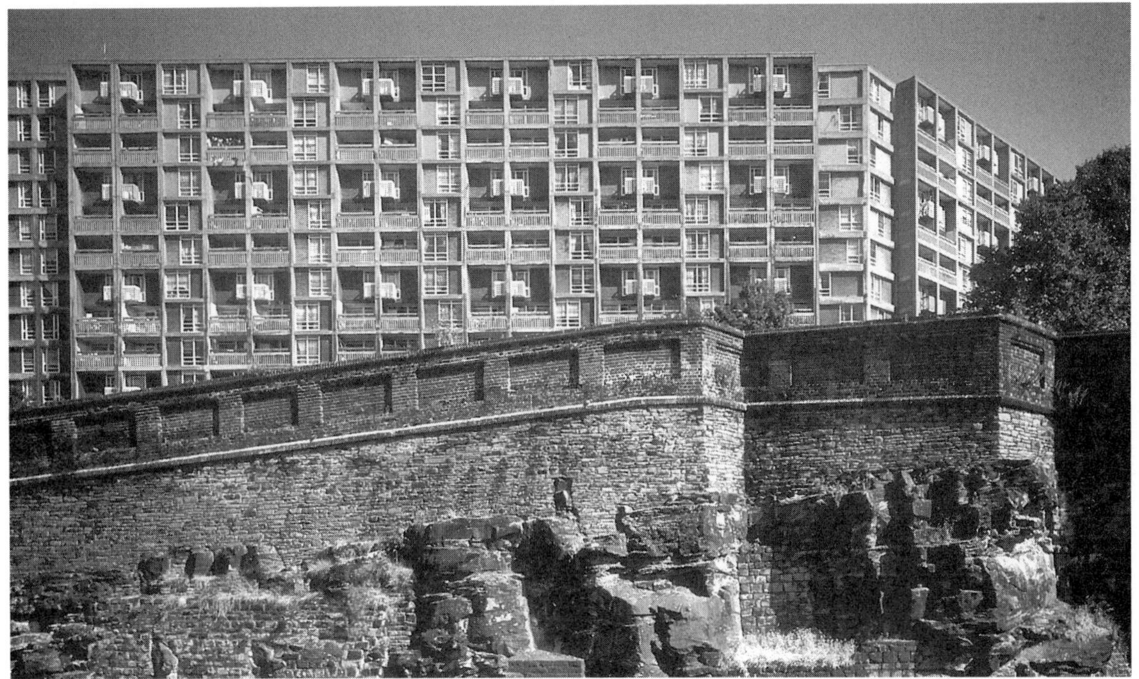

A. Park Hill, Sheffield (1955–60). See p. 1382

B. Park Hill: aerial view

C. Brunswick Centre, London (1962–70). See p. 1382

D. Alexandra Road housing, London (1970–77). See p. 1382

E. University of East Anglia, Norwich (1962–). See p. 1383

laid out blocks is insistently sheer: no concessions here to cosiness. More ruthless still is **Park Hill, Sheffield** (1955–60) (p. 1381A,B), by Jack Lynn and Ivor Smith of the City Architect's Department, and later **Hyde Park** (1962–5). Here is the New Brutalism in full flight, blocks articulated according to theory rather than site conditions. Each third level of these linked blocks, that rise as high as fourteen storeys, carries on one of its sides a 'street in the air' which provides access to the flats and is meant to accommodate children playing, milk floats delivering, and, in general terms, the life of a city street. Materials are purposely tough, and the effect is magnificent, if it isn't quite home.

It could be argued that this scheme opened the floodgates: if architects thought that harshness was the acceptable way to proceed, there was no want of construction companies to follow their lead. During the 1960s and 1970s thousands of housing units were built hurriedly and without any notion of landscaping or community. To some extent, too, the cleverer the architects became at 'solving problems', the tougher the problems they were given to solve. **Robin Hood Gardens, London** (1969–72), by Alison (1928–92) and Peter (born 1923) Smithson, is on a site isolated by appalling traffic, and the fussy and drab building conjured up to cope with the situation – which it fails to do – shows the error of depending on style to solve urban planning problems.

Tower blocks and slabs were the local governments' preferred weapon in the urban housing war, cheapness and meagre site requirements being advantages, but only seldom were the blocks well designed. **Trellick Tower, London** (1966–73), by Ernö Goldfinger (1902–87), with its sculptural form, dramatically detached lift tower and Unité-like central corridor, is one of the period's best. As towers came under criticism for their social ineptitude, other solutions were tried, including Patrick Hodgkinson's **Brunswick Centre, Bloomsbury, London** (1962–70) (p. 1381C), with its ziggurat housing blocks over shops, and Neave Browne's **Alexandra Road housing, London** (1970–7) (p. 1381D). But this architecture of bare concrete had had its day, as fashion moved back to the brick-built – or at any rate brick-faced – picturesque and irregular, for example **Lillington Gardens, London** (1968–72), by Darbourne and Darke, and the **Byker Estate, Newcastle-upon-Tyne** (1969–80), by Ralph Erskine (born 1914). The latter scheme was notable for the participation of the tenants in its design, as well as for the folksy patterning of its coloured brickwork and joinery. In recent years government has not involved itself in the construction of public housing.

The private housing market has been more traditional. Eric Lyons (1912–78) was successful during the 1950s and 1960s with the development of SPAN housing, for example **South Row, Blackheath** (1957–59). Lyons made landscaping an integral feature of his housing schemes, breaking down estates by means of courtyards and closes, and using only bricks and tiles. Even the then-neo-Brutalists James Stirling (1926–92) and James Gowan (born 1926) built private flats in stock brickwork, for example **flats at Ham Common** (1958), though this had been made intellectually respectable by Le Corbusier's Maisons Jaoul of the previous decade, and from which these flats loosely derive.

Many New Towns, remote descendants of the Garden City Movement, were designated under the New Towns Act 1946. Politically this move was unpopular: urban authorities foresaw a fall in rates revenue if their populations shifted out of town, and rural authorities regarded with horror the prospect of urban culture spoiling their bucolic way of life. Yet over thirty of these new towns were established between 1946 and the foundation of Llastisant, Glamorgan, in 1972 – the last of the line.

Occasionally striking architecture was attempted, as at **Cumbernauld** (designated 1955), by planner Hugh Wilson, which was projected to house Glasgow's overspill population. Here a mega-structure **town centre** (1960–75) was designed by Geoffry Copcutt in heroic style, but was always too isolated from the residential parts of the town to be a social success.

Milton Keynes (designated 1967), developed to a master plan by Llewelyn-Davies, Weeks, Forestier-Walker & Bor, is a new town grafted onto several old villages. It was planned as a net of roads dividing the countryside into rectangular development sectors, almost on the US model, but with a 'soft' rather than strictly orthogonal grid.

With the programme for more schools the opportunity was taken to exploit industrial production capacity and methods developed during the war. The Architect's Department of Hertfordshire (Chief Architect C. H. Aslin, 1893–1959) was responsible for the construction of over a hundred schools in ten years, and achieved exemplary results with the use of prefabricated components disposed on a fixed planning grid, while allowing a wide degree of variation in plans and somewhat less in external materials and finishes (for example, **Summerswood School, Boreham Wood** (1950–2), and **Burleigh School, Cheshunt** (1948)). The success of Aslin's **Hertfordshire Schools Programme** led to a **Consortium of Local Authorities Special Programme** (CLASP, from 1957) to develop a prefabricated school system employed with great success in the north Midlands and was highly influential. Outside the system building field was **High Lawn Primary School, Bolton** (1953), by Bernard Claydon and John Foy of the Borough Architect's Department, built as a formal series of single-storey pavilions, each with a dominating pitched roof and all linked by low connecting blocks.

This sensitivity to nature and childhood was dealt an abrupt blow by Alison and Peter Smithson in their

Smythdon Secondary School, Hunstanton, Norfolk (1949–54), using the language of Mies van der Rohe at the Illinois Institute of Technology (see Chapter 51): steel I-beams, vast sheets of glass, precision-laid wire-cut bricks. This is a raw building. Here, even the handbasin wastepipes can be seen from outside the building, behind a glass wall. This taste for toughness can be seen in two London schools: **Pimlico Comprehensive** (1970), by the GLC Architect's Department, and **Acland Burghley School** (1962), by Howell, Killick, Partridge and Amis.

Industrial building of the immediate post-war period is well represented by the **Brynmawr Rubber Factory** (1948–53) by the Architects co-partnership, a masterpiece of its kind. Offices, canteen, health clinic, and production areas were each given quite distinct expression. The main production area achieved large clear spans by means of shallow domes, with glazed spandrels, while the main office block was a strongly functional composition of concrete and glass.

During the 1960s the university population in Britain more than doubled to 220,000. Early in the decade approval was given for the 'Shakespearean Seven' new universities: Sussex, York, East Anglia, Kent, Essex, Warwick, and Lancaster, all built on greenfield sites. The **University of Sussex, Brighton** (begun 1958), designed by Sir Basil Spence (1907–76), makes good use of Le Corbusier's Maisons Jaoul as a source, with arched concrete and brick producing a monumental aspect, as Spence intended, in the Roman manner. The **University of York** (begun 1961) is, unlike Sussex, organised on the collegiate pattern. For all but a few buildings the architects, Robert Matthew, Johnson-Marshall, used a modified version of the CLASP system. This made for speedy construction, built in a high degree of flexibility for future growth, although it failed to produce aesthetically interesting results. The **University of East Anglia, Norwich** (begun 1962) (p. 1381E), whose architect was Denys Lasdun (born 1914), makes the most of a wonderful riverside site with stepped terraces of student accommodation, mitigating to some extent the harshness of its bare concrete construction.

The universities of Oxford and Cambridge have undertaken extensive building programmes since the 1950s, exploring every style from (at **Oxford**) Raymond Erith's (1904–73) **Provost's Lodgings, Queen's College** (1958–9), and Sir Albert Richardson's 1960–1 **Wolfson Building, S. Hilda's College**, both excellent neo-Georgian, to the quintessential modernism of **S. Catherine's College** (1960–4) by Arne Jacobsen (1902–71). S. Catherine's, an obsessively perfectionist ensemble of concrete and purpose-made brick, is at odds with the traditions of collegiate architecture in a way that the Smithsons' **Garden Building, S. Hilda's College** (1968–70) – stock brick and timber trellises – is not. MacCormac, Jamieson, Pritchard and Wright found an excellent balance in their **Sainsbury Building, Worcester College** (1983–6) (p. 1385B). The soft-coloured stone walls support overhanging slate roofs in a complex composition, the romantic aspects of which are reinforced by a lakeside site.

James Stirling, having designed (with James Gowan) the masterful **Engineering Laboratory Building, Leicester University** (1959–63) (p. 1384A,C) out of the 'industrial' materials of patent glazing and engineering brick, in romantically Constructivist manner, tried a variation on the theme for the **History Faculty Building, Cambridge** (1964–7) (p. 1384B,D,E). It soon became apparent that the rough-and-ready life of an engineering building was a far cry from the sophisticated environment required for the storage and reading of books, and the building has been much criticised and indeed modified as a result. No less wilful is **Harvey Court , Cambridge** (1960–2), by Sir Leslie Martin and Colin St John Wilson. This civilised residential courtyard is meant as a model of quiet enclosure for a busy city centre, but finds itself in a quiet backwater and as a result is socially ineffectual. More successful is the **Cripps Building, S. John's College, Cambridge** (1964–7), by Powell & Moya (p. 1385A), which uses the language of Modernisn (trabeated expressed construction in concrete, flat roofs) to create a romantic building tailored to its waterside site and which implies, in a subtle way, continuity with the Cambridge tradition of courtyard planning. **Churchill College, Cambridge** (1961–8), by Richard Sheppard, Robson & Partners, is also a fine design. Arranged in ten courts, the architects aimed at and achieved the intimacy of college buildings, using the then *de rigueur* brick and concrete.

The **Festival of Britain** in 1951 brought into focus co-existent dreams that have held Britain in thrall since the end of World War II: the dream of a better future and the dream of a better past. The aluminium **Dome of Discovery** by Ralph Tubbs, at 144 m (365 ft) diameter the largest dome then in existence, was all shimmering visions of the future but structurally was adventurous rather than pioneering; the **Skylon** tower, which was the competition-winning answer put forward by Powell & Moya to the Festival brief for a 'vertical feature', was a clever post-tensioned cable structure engineered by the brilliant Felix Samuely (1905–59), but the purpose of the 'monument' never developed beyond the idea of a picturesque eye-catcher: stuff of the eighteenth century. The one permanent building on the site was the **Royal Festival Hall** (1949–51) (p. 1385C) by LCC architects Sir Leslie Martin (born 1906), Robert Matthew (1908–75) and Peter Moro (born 1911). This, the first large modern building in London, has been criticised for its unresolved facade, but the interior, where public spaces flow around the elevated auditorium, is very fine.

A. Engineering Laboratory Building, Leicester University (1959–63). See p. 1383

B. History Faculty Building, Cambridge (1964–7). See p. 1383

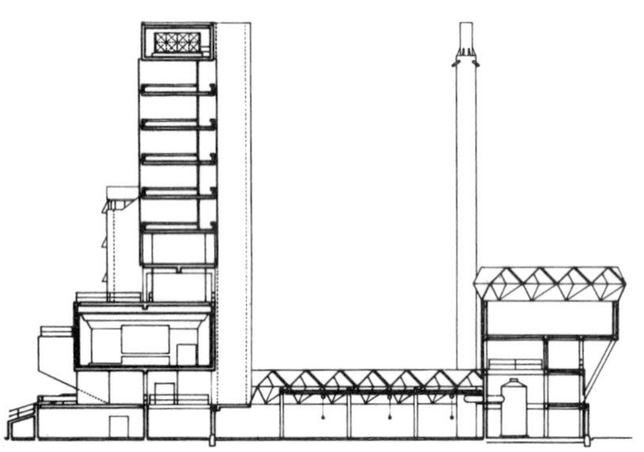

C. Engineering Laboratory Building, Leicester University: section

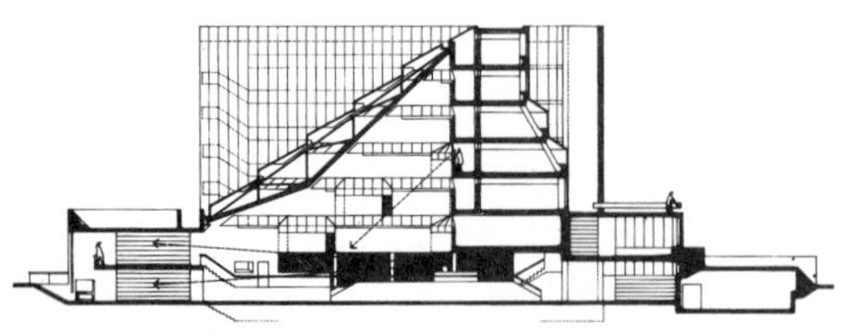

D. History Faculty Building, Cambridge: section

E. History Faculty Building, Cambridge: interior

A. Cripps Building, S. John's College, Cambridge (1964–7). See p. 1383

B. Sainsbury Building, Worcester College, Oxford (1983–6). See p. 1383

C. Royal Festival Hall, London (1949–51). See p. 1383

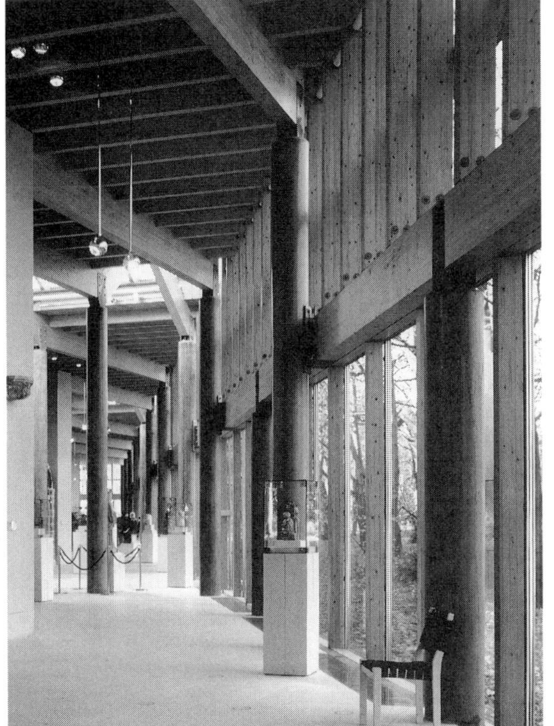

D. Burrell Collection, Glasgow (1971–83). See p. 1386

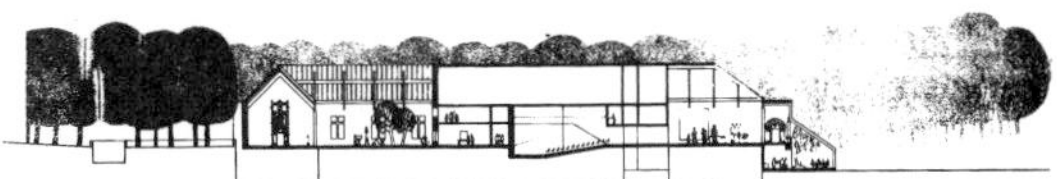

E. Burrell Collection: section

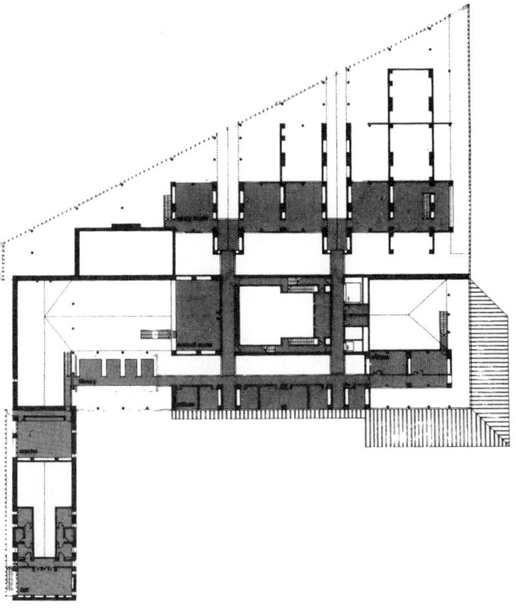

F. Burrell Collection: mezzanine plan

The colonisation of the South Bank of the Thames with cultural facilities continued with the **Queen Elizabeth Hall** (1964) and the **Hayward Gallery** (1964), Brutalist in the full sense that they make few external concessions to human comfort or the urban context. Denys Lasdun's adjacent **National Theatre** (1967–76) is a noble attempt at formal monumentality in a modern idiom. Balconies line the Thames-side front, and the two fly towers are unashamedly displayed. Yet the architect's trademark finish of bare concrete shows itself an unsuitably bleak material for such a building. A similar drift towards monumentality is seen in Sir Norman Foster's (born 1935) **Sainsbury Centre for the Visual Arts, University of East Anglia** (1978), although the declared intention is high-tech functional efficiency. The building is ostensibly single-storey, a large aluminium box with glazed ends, but as with the pavilions of Mies, the services are consigned to a vast basement. Louvres open and close to adjust light levels. The sleek appearance of this building has been compromised somewhat by recladding.

The **Clore Wing, Tate Gallery, London** (1980–7), shows the change of direction taken by Stirling's architecture. Here a concrete frame is made to hold up a thin facade of stone and brick, in a patchwork pattern that acknowledges every nuance of context. The interiors are full of spatial interest, represented best by the contrast between the formal tranquillity in the galleries and excitement in the entrance and circulation areas.

Glasgow possesses one of the finest of modern museums in the **Burrell Collection** (1971–83) (p. 1385D–F), designed by Barry Gasson, Brit Andreson and John Meunier. Mixing a high level of environmental control, much of it open to view, with robust timber and concrete structure, the architects produced a building dedicated to its purpose of display, and one that fits beautifully into its wooded site. A similar blend of high-tech and tradition is achieved at the **Mound Stand, Lord's Cricket Ground, London** (1987) (p. 1387C–E), by Michael and Patty Hopkins. A curving row of brick arches at street level is surmounted by a metal structure that is topped by a fabric tent roof, supported by masts and guy-wires. Much more wholeheartedly traditional in conception is Colin St John Wilson's **British Library, London** (started 1974), an epic compromise that has proven particularly susceptible to the vagaries by which such massive public buildings are financed in Britain.

The situation in commercial architecture parallels developments in other fields. Through the 1950s the international modern vision of curtain-wall slab blocks among superhighways prevailed, and was built in fragmentary form in cities from Glasgow to Birmingham to London. **Bracken House, London** (1956–59), designed for the *Financial Times* by Sir Albert Richardson, is a spirited exception, a building of dark-red bricks and sandstone, a personal interpretation of Georgian Classicism fused with north Italian Baroque. The building has recently (1988–90) been reconstructed by Michael Hopkins in a manner that mixes high-tech steel and glass components with nineteenth-century industrial style metal and masonry construction techniques. Another traditionalist was Howard Robertson, but his 25-storey stone-clad **Shell Building, London** (1957–62), is an attempt to reconcile traditional design with the demand for a high-rise building.

Also pursuing a blend of Modernism and tradition were Alison and Peter Smithson with their **Economist Building, London** (1964), three towers of differing scale, for residential, office and bank use, in aluminium and stone. The use of built form in the creation of public space is exemplary at a time when architects like Richard Seifert were putting up buildings such as **Centrepoint, London** (1963–6), a jazzy tower made from a kit of precast concrete parts that exploits the site only for maximum floor area and traffic management.

The issue of a building's relationship to its site boundaries reached its extreme limit with Sir Norman Foster's **Willis, Faber & Dumas offices, Ipswich** (1975) (p. 1387A,B), a three-storey building whose sheer glass walls, reflective in daylight and transparent by night, follow the irregular site boundary exactly. Sir Norman Foster's design for **Stansted Airport, Essex** (1989–91) (p. 1389) is a rational response to the requirements of air travel. But the structure transcends the merely functional. Indeed the 'structural trees' which support the roof and carry services create a powerful, romantic space with their arms branching up within an interior bathed with diffused light from roof lanterns (p. 1389A). The building is on two main levels with passengers passing at ground level and with minimal interference from arrival to departure and into the shuttle which connects with the plane. Below are services and baggage handling (p. 1389E).

At the other end of the high-tech spectrum is Foster's former partner, Sir Richard Rogers (born 1933). At the **Lloyd's Building, London** (1979–84) (p. 1388), every opportunity is taken to differentiate, not so much in spatial terms – though as a by-product this occurs – as in terms of building elements. Great twisting tubes of stairs, stacks of lavatories, pod-like meeting rooms, concrete structure, service pipes and even maintenance gantries are crowded onto the outside of the building. From the centre rises an arched roof over the atrium. The effect is highly romantic, compensating for some of the awkwardness in internal planning.

The **Broadgate Development, London** (first phase 1984–8, second phase 1988–91), aimed to use the construction of fourteen new office blocks as an opportunity to create a new urban commercial centre. Overall planning was carried out by Arup Associates, who also put up the first four buildings (architect

A. Willis Faber & Dumas Building, Ipswich (1975). See p. 1386

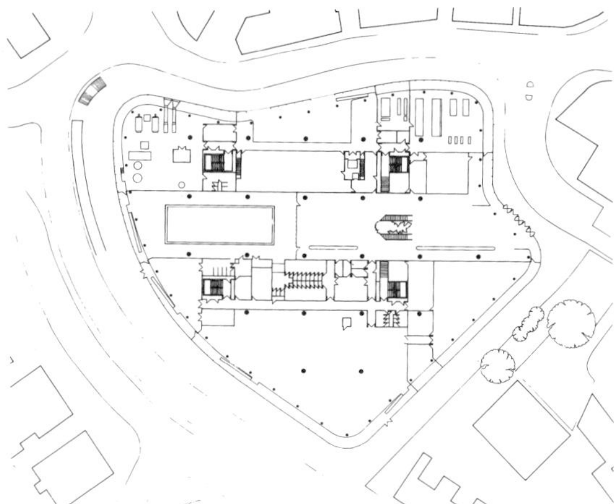

B. Willis Faber & Dumas Building: plan

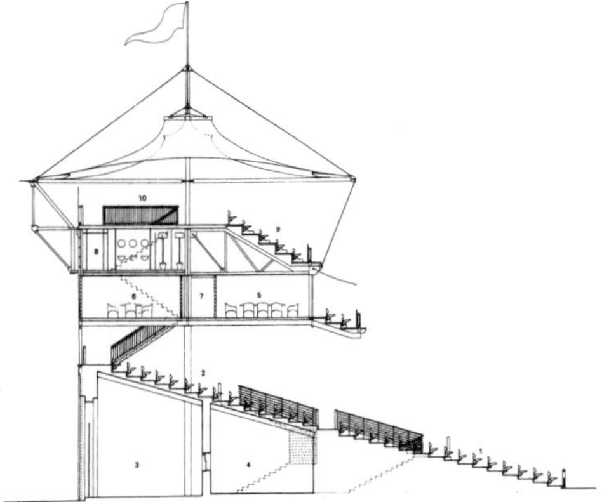

C. Mound Stand, Lord's Cricket Ground: section

D. Mound Stand, Lord's Cricket Ground, London (1987). See p. 1386

E. Mound Stand, Lord's Cricket Ground: brick arches at rear

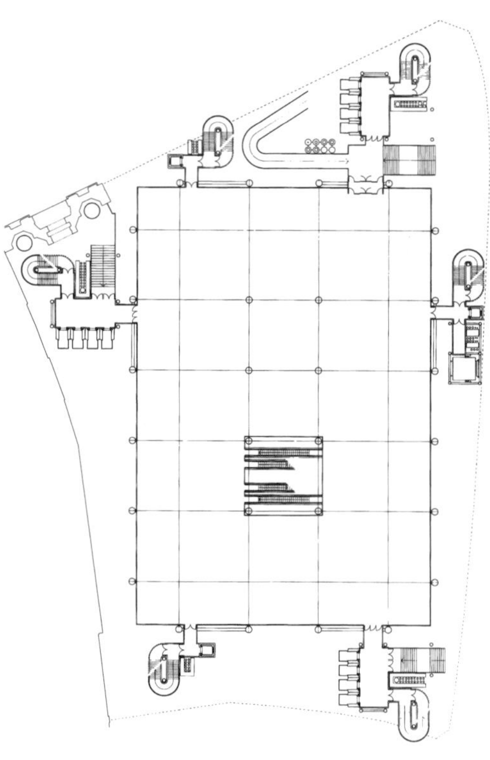

A. (*above left*) Lloyd's Building, London (1979–84). See p. 1386
B. (*above right*) Lloyd's Building: plan
C. (*right*) Lloyd's Building: section

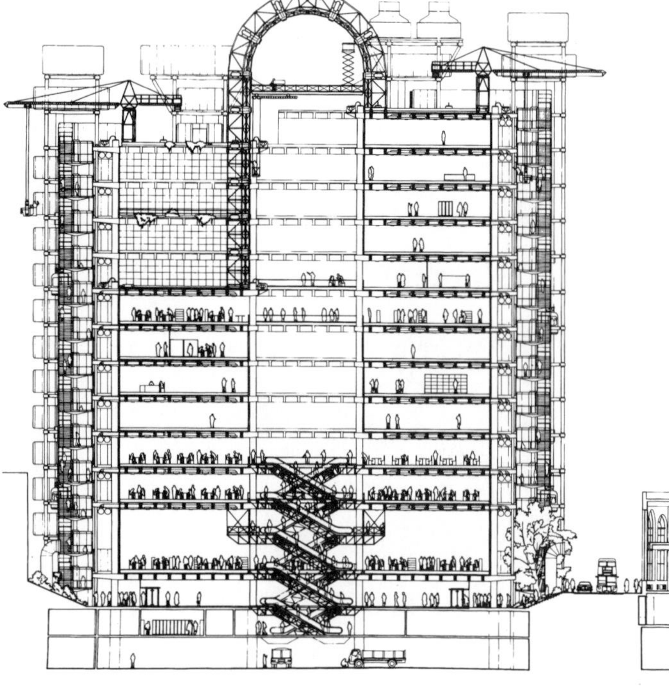

A. Stansted Airport Terminal, Essex (1986–91). See p. 1386

B. Stansted Airport Terminal: services pod

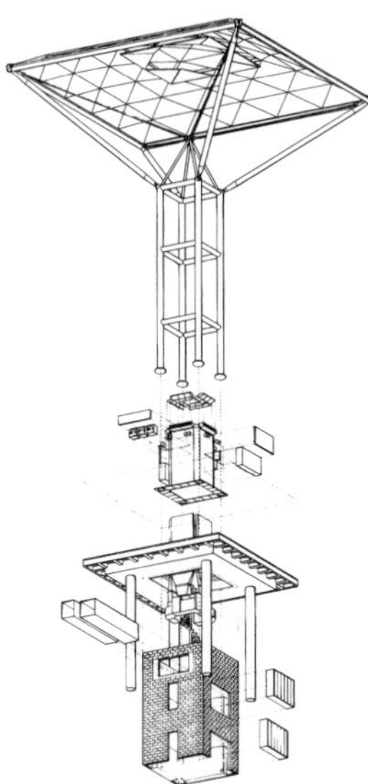

C. Stansted Airport Terminal: structural tree and services pod

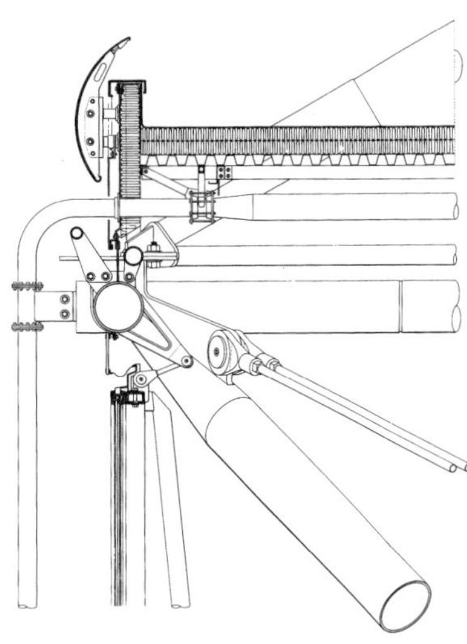

D. Stansted Airport Terminal: eaves detail

E. Stansted Airport Terminal: section showing baggage handling

Peter Fogo). The facades may be somewhat remorseless in the repetition of their simple elements (and even vulgar in the later phases in which granite cladding and pseudo-traditional stone and bronze details predominate), but there is no denying the success of the planning, with buildings centred around public squares which are thronged with people during working hours. Later phases were designed by the American firm of Skidmore, Owings and Merrill, masters of fast-track construction.

Quinlan Terry sought other means for the creation of place in his **Richmond Riverside development** (1985–8). Here rows of conventional open-plan offices have been disguised to look like a group of diverse seventeenth- and eighteenth-century Classical buildings organised around a small square and a sloping riverside garden.

This superficial approach to architectural form – selecting appropriate stylistic elements from the chest of history – has become known as Post-Modernism. The architectural principles that controlled Modernism became discomforts during the 1980s. Terry Farrell's **TV-AM Headquarters, London** (1982), with its fibreglass eggcups used as finials and giant Art Deco skeletal keystone, is an example of architecture exploiting existing sign systems, rather than trying to create them anew.

More compelling, certainly more genuinely witty and inventive essays in the Post-Modern use of history have been produced by Piers Gough and Rex Wilkinson of Campbell Zogolovitch, Wilkinson and Gough. Indeed some of their more idiosyncratic designs confirm that English eccentricity continues to flourish as a creative force. For example, there is the abruptly angular house for **Janet Street Porter, London** (1987), in which bricks lighten in colour from ground floor to parapet and concrete lintels are formed to look like logs, the Thames-side **China Wharf, London** (1988) which has a pink-painted facade composed out of parts of giant circles, and a **Craft and Design Technology studio, Bryanston School, Dorset** (1988), where external columns are rendered in the form of giant screws, emblems of one of the activities pursued within the building.

In the early 1990s the British High Tech school reached maturity, a notable example being Nicholas Grimshaw's **Eurostar Railway Terminal, Waterloo Station, London** (completed 1994). Here current developments in construction technology and materials are fully utilised to realise a late twentieth-century version of the Victorian railway shed. But the building's dramatically sinuous form, and the fact that many of its components are handcrafted, make the structure far more than a mere piece of industrialised building.

Post-war church architecture began controversially with the reconstruction of **Coventry Cathedral,** badly bombed in 1940. The competition for a new church drew proposals of extreme Modernism and traditionalism, but the winner, Basil Spence (1907–76), contrived to fall neatly between both these stools. The new building, consecrated in 1962, incorporated most of the ruins of the old, including the steeple, and refused to have its plan influenced by current trends of the liturgical movement, which argued for centralised open planning. Spence's saw-tooth walls of red sandstone give wonderful lighting while keeping the enclosed qualities of the interior.

Frederick Gibberd (1908–84) had less success with his **Roman Catholic Cathedral, Liverpool** (1960–7), a circular plan in which the outer wall is formed of ancillary rooms and side-chapels. The expression of this plan, a truncated cone surmounted by a tapering lantern, is a grand but unrefined gesture.

The Liturgical Movement's influence can be seen in **S. Paul's, Crewe** (1966), by Robert Maguire and Keith Murray. Little more than a large shed of blue brick walls and slate roof, with clerestory lighting to a central altar and baldacchino – somewhat like a barrow stall – this building reflects a growing desire in some quarters to place the Church at the centre of community life.

Gillespie, Kidd and Coia followed similar planning principles in their Roman Catholic churches in Glasgow, but with a great deal more architectural expression. **S. Benedict, Drumchapel** (1964–70, demolished 1991), and **Our Lady of Good Counsel, Dennistoun** (1964–66), were designed to be full of dramatic incident, from the geometrically extravagant copper roofs to the narrow entrances and spacious interiors, built simply in timber and brick.

Italy

Cautious and conservative ideas characterised the immediate post-war years in Italy, for example Pope Pius XII's commission to Marcello Piacentini – a favourite of the Fascist regime – to complete the **Via della Conciliazione, Rome** (1948–50); and the reconstruction of the mediaeval area of Florence destroyed by the Nazis, **Por Santa Maria.** But other ideas were also being pursued.

After the war Rationalists resurfaced, but their architecture was modified, chastened by experience. The **Monument to the victims of concentration camps, Milan** (1946), by the BBPR partnership (Gianluigi Banfi (1910–45); Lodovico Belgiojoso (born 1909), Enrico Peressutti (1908–73) and Ernesto Rogers (1909–69)), is partly a reflection of the poverty of Rationalism: when asked to deal with deep human problems rationality is insufficient. The attenuated metal cube of the monument is divided strictly according to Classical geometrical rules, abstract except at its centre, which contains a single food bowl from the camp. Mario Fiorentino's **Monument of the**

Ardeatine Caves (1944–7), near Rome, with its great travertine slab roof hovering dramatically above the ground, invokes emotional rather than intellectual response.

Large-scale reconstruction projects included **QT 8** (the eighth quarter of the Milan Triennial of 1948), planned by Bottoni, Cerutti, Gandolfi, Pollini and others, in a more or less purely Rationalist manner, but the effect is disappointingly mechanical and reductive. Luigi Figini, Gino Pollini and Gio Ponti, for the government-sponsored INA-Casa housing authority, built a scheme at **Via Harar, Milan** (1951), that shared these faults, as did the **Villa Bernabo Brea, Genoa** (1953), scheme by Luigi Carlo Daneri. These projects were put together with the long straight blocks that seemed more an attempt to tidy up the problems of social housing than to create living places.

In Rome, meanwhile, Bruno Zevi's advocacy of 'organic architecture' had an immediate effect. The work of Mario Ridolfi (1904–84) and Ludovico Quaroni (1911–87) at the **Tiburtino Quarter, Rome** (1950), also for INA, used low-rise terrace housing of a quite traditional kind – pitched roofs, wooden shutters, natural materials, and the meandering layout seen in Swedish housing schemes of the time. These experiments in what became known as 'Neo-Realism' were repeated at the **apartments, Viale Etiopia, Rome** (1950–2), by Ridolfi, Quaroni's **La Martella housing, Matera** (1950), and Mario Fiorentino's **San Basilio quarter, Rome** (1956). In the north of Italy, Ignazio Gardella's (born1905) **housing for Borsalino employees, Alessandria** (1953), equally traditional in detail but with an almost neo-Classical roof, confirmed the redirection of Rationalists to an empirical position.

Individual buildings – objects rather than community environments – proved less problematic and more open to a variety of expressive modes. The highly polished and planned works such as the **Casa del Girasole, Rome** (1951), by Luigi Moretti, an elegant apartment building with a split facade atop a recessed and rusticated base, were looked at askance by the intellectual circle. It was Giovanni Michelucci's (1891–1990) **church at Collina** (1954), simple geometrical volumes in stone; Gardella's **house on the Zattere, Venice** (1957), with its lacy balconies and rhythmically distorted fenestration; BBPR's **Torre Velasca, Milan** (1958), a high tower that solves the aesthetic problem of proximity to Milan's Duomo by jettying out the top six of its 24 floors, in a purposely mediaeval style; and Franco Albini's (1905–77) **Museum of the Treasure of San Lorenzo, Genoa** (1956), with a plan of intersecting and related circles realised in stone and concrete; these were the projects that illustrated the melding of Rationalism with a sense of context and historical continuity. Michelucci, indeed, later developed a wholly organic and expressionistic architecture at the **Church of S. Giovanni, Autostrada del Sole, Florence** (1962), influenced by the work of Hans Scharoun and Le Corbusier. In Rome Paolo Portoghesi (born 1931) took an exaggeratedly 'organic' stand with buildings like the **Casa Baldi, Rome** (1959), where the house is formed with a series of curved walls, until his architecture developed into fully developed Post-Modern, with the **Islamic Centre and Mosque, Rome** (1976–94) (p. 1392B,C).

Angelo Mangiarotti (born 1921) and Bruno Morassutti, at their **parish church, Baranzate** (1957–8), support a large concrete roof on four circular concrete columns and glaze the resulting box all round with curtain walling. The resulting volume is, both inside and out, simple and visually dynamic. The same architects' **warehouse, Padua** (1961), follows the same principle of layering several separate structural systems to create the building. One might mention in this context the **Pirelli Building, Milan** (1956–8) (p. 1392A), by Gio Ponti (1891–1979) and others, with Pier Luigi Nervi (1891–1979) as engineer. This slender tower is built on concrete 'trunks' that diminish, tree-like, as the building ascends.

Gino Valle (born 1923), working in the Venice region, has developed an architecture of concrete and glass that has remained 'rational', in that it avoids the expressive excesses of Brutalism and yet remains firmly attached to constructional technique and functional requirements. His **Zanussi Headquarters, Pordenone** (1963), is a brilliant exploitation of an unpromising site, in terms of both plan and section.

The work of Giancarlo De Carlo (born 1919) too stands apart from the main strands, and indeed political intrigues and alliances, of Italian architecture. A member of the CIAM offshoot, Team X, De Carlo broke new ground with his **Students' Residence, Urbino** (1962–6). Like Valle, De Carlo used the quintessentially modern material of concrete, and his plan making was controlled by landscape and climate as well as by social interaction. The only defect of the scheme is a certain lack of centrality and focus. De Carlo went on to do a great deal of work for the university in Urbino, with an increasing flexibility in terms of the materials he permitted himself to use and a great confidence in the handling of form. But another of his interests has been participative housing. His **Matteotti Village, Terni** (1970–5), is a complex arrangement of apartments and houses for steelworkers, planned with the help of its inhabitants. The rather picturesque results no doubt reflect the 'organic' nature of this process. De Carlo's most recent project, **housing at Mazzorbo, Venice** (1987), has increased this picturesque element, with a strong use of colour and traditional Venetian forms, quite distant from the near-Brutalist position from which he started; but not so very far, in many respects, from the Neo-realism.

Brutalism itself was not much taken up in Italy and where it was, it failed. The **Marchiondi Spagliardi**

A. Pirelli Building, Milan (1956–8). See p. 1391

B. Islamic Centre and Mosque, Rome (1976–94). See p. 1391

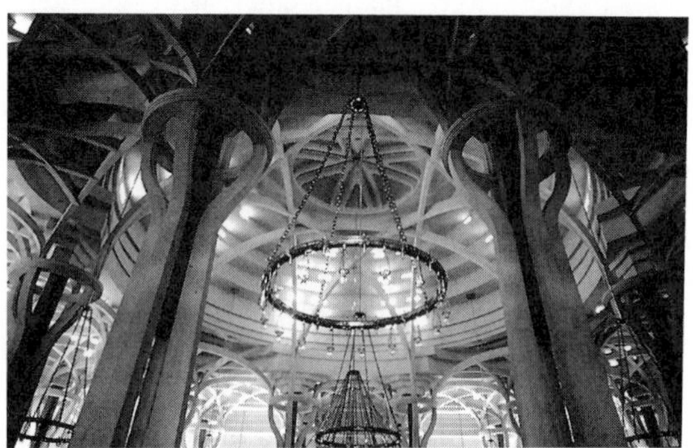

C. Islamic Centre and Mosque: interior

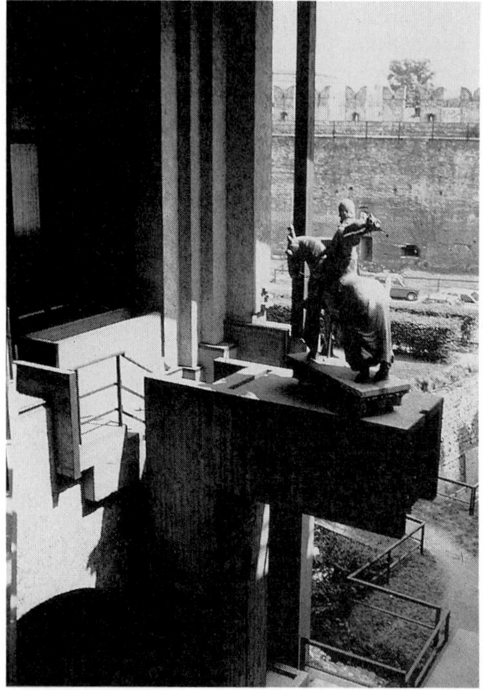

D. Museo Castelvecchio, Verona (1964): interior. See p. 1394

E. Museo Castelvecchio, Verona: extension. See p. 1394

A. Padre Pio Pilgrimage Church, S. Giovanni Rotondo, Foggia (under construction 1996). See p. 1394

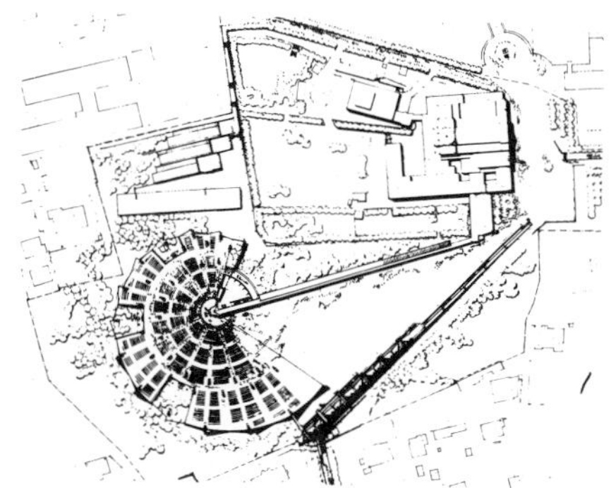

B. Padre Pio Pilgrimage Church: plan

C. Padre Pio Pilgrimage Church: section

E. Central Beheer offices, Apeldoorn (1968–72). See p. 1395

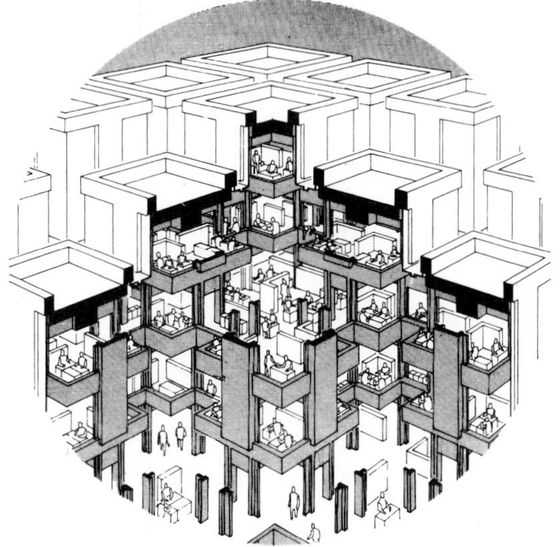

F. Central Beheer offices: section

Institute for Difficult Children, Milan (1957–9), by Vittoriano Vigano is a mostly six-storey building where almost every surface both inside and out is concrete. The suitability of the building for its purpose could hardly be farther from its mark, and is indicative of the stylistic intransigence that so infuriated people like Zevi.

The intellectual position that largely displaced neo-realism as a means of building an urban architecture, developed by Aldo Rossi (born 1931) and others during the 1960s, is a kind of formalism known, somewhat confusingly, as Rational architecture. Rossi's belief that style has nothing to do with cities, which survive on the basis of building types, allowed him to design buildings like the **housing block, Gallaratese, Milan** (1970–3), where decoration and constructional evidence are everywhere suppressed, leaving a white ghost-like building, whose long empty arcade is intentionally reminiscent of Giorgio de Chirico's paintings. Rossi's **Elementary School, Fagnano Olona** (1972), is a more complete development of the ideas, containing more functional elements. Others following Rossi's lead include Giorgio Grassi (born 1935) whose **Students' Residence, Chieti** (1979–84), is given a colonnade of diagrammatic simplicity, and Rossi's former colleague Carlo Aymonino (born 1926), who turned from a megastructure approach at **Monte Amiata housing, Gallaratese 2, Milan** (1967–70), to the more subdued formalism of his yellow brick **Liceo Scientifico, Pesaro** (1970–83), also with tall and dramatic arcades.

This was partly a reaction against the traditions of craftsmanship in building for which Italy was famous. The two modern figures who best represent that tradition, in quite different ways, are Carlo Scarpa (1906–78) and Renzo Piano (born 1937). Scarpa, a Venetian, was steeped in the rich materiality of that city's physical culture. Most of his work was restructuring existing buildings, and most was executed in or near Venice. His most important work was undertaken at the **Accademia** (1952), the **Museo Correr** (1953–60) and the **Galleria Querini Stampalia** (1961–3), all in Venice, and, above all, the **Museo Castelvecchio, Verona** (1964) (p. 1392D,E). Here his sensitivity to light, space, and the exhibits themselves, together with an intellect for detail and a love of materiality, combined to produce a building that paradoxically seems to offer a great deal more space than there is volume.

Subsequent to his collaboration with Richard Rogers on the Pompidou Centre, Paris (q.v.), the Genoese Renzo Piano has become increasingly interested in finely crafted building solutions that respond to the needs of the user and which utilise appropriate technology, so that the final result represents not a metaphor for industrial technique (as the International Style had done) but the actual use of industrial techniques and methods. His **Touring Pavilion for IBM** (1982–4) was a delightful solution to the problem of a well-built re-usable structure, of moulded polycarbonate lenses on a frame of natural wood with cast aluminium connectors. For the **San Nicola Stadium, Bari** (1987–90), use was made of precasting to create almost all elements of the structure, and the resulting building is at once elegant and honest. For the **Padre Pio Pilgrimage Church, S. Giovanni Rotondo, Foggia** (under construction 1996) (p. 1393A–C), Piano has made use of a series of huge segmental arches to create an interior to seat 10,000 people. Traditional materials and forms have been used – stone and timber, arches and domes – but the structural possibilities have been exploited to the full using the latest skills in computer-generated calculations. The **Renzo Piano Workshop, Vesima** (1990–1), designed by Piano, employs not just draughtsmen and architects but also model makers, joiners, metal forgers, and cleaning ladies, so that details can be actually made and tested before being put into production.

Continuing outside the field of architecture proper, mention must be made of the engineer Pier Luigi Nervi. Nervi has been admired because he seemed to have found a way of building that produced magnificent architecture without having to go along the road of aesthetics. Nervi himself promoted this view of the 'pure and untheoretical' engineer. His **Palazzetto dello Sport, Rome** (1956–7, with Annibale Vitellozzi), a shell dome spanning 60 m (195 ft), made of precast concrete units, and the much larger **Palazzo dello Sport** (1958–60), also in Rome, of 100 m (325 ft) diameter, are some of the highest achievements of twentieth-century engineering.

Ricardo Morandi (born1902) was another of the great engineers. He built many bridges, including the vertiginous **Polcevera autostrada viaduct, Genoa** (1965), a version in concrete of the principles used at the Firth of Forth Bridge by Baker. In **Rome** he designed the **Alitalia hangars, Fiumicino** (1970), whose roof is suspended from an asymmetrical row of masts and external tension cables.

Netherlands

While many Dutch cities favoured modest reconstruction after World War II one or two opted for more radical solutions. Under chief planner Cornelius van Traa, the historic plan of bomb-damaged Rotterdam was ignored and the city centre rebuilt so that car and pedestrian traffic were segregated, very much according to the principles of CIAM's 1933 Charter of Athens. The main feature of van Traa's plan is the **Lijnbaan shopping centre** (1949–53), for which Johannes Van den Broek (1898–1978) and Jacob Berend Bakema (1914–81) were architects. The attractive aspects of pedestrian zones drew attention away from the stultifying effect of large areas given over to car parking. The planning of the centre itself owes much to De Stijl. Van den Broek and Bakema built several similar centres during the following decade, including **Amstelveen** (1961) and **Bergen** (1962).

The return of J. J. P. Oud (1890–1963) to something like functionalism after his brief pre-war flirtation with monumental architecture is signalled by the **Bio Children's Convalescent Home, Arnhem** (1952–60). On a clearing in a wood, Oud laid out a series of functionally differing pavilions, including rectangular dormitories and circular dining hall, making this a machine for convalescence. Gerrit Rietveld (1888–1964) never abandoned the principles of De Stijl, manifest in the **house at Ilpendam** (1959), and the **Sculpture Pavilion, Arnhem** (1954 – demolished and re-erected at **Otterlo**, 1965).

In a building almost the inverse of the De Stijl type, J. Bedaux begins the **High school, Tilburg** (1961), with a rectangular plan which is then hollowed out to create courtyards, halls and lecture rooms. The exterior too is a taut face of stone, opened and varied as necessary to suit internal requirements.

Commercial work of high quality in the curtain-wall-and-concrete fashion was produced by Merkelbach, Elling and Van Eesteren during the 1950s and 1960s. Massing, detailing and above all proportioning are the critical aspects of this rectilinear architecture. The **Rijnhotel, Rotterdam** (1959), and **Administrative Buildings, Amsterdam** (1960), are excellent examples. The **IBM Laboratories, Uithoorn** (1963), by van Mourik and du Pon place laboratory and workshop buildings on the ground with a small administration block suspended above them from a concrete service core, thus giving curtain walling its truest expression as wrapping rather than structure. International companies liked these striking solutions. Another is the **Johnson Wax offices, Mijdrecht** (1967), by Maaskant, Van Dommelen, Kroos and Senf, in which the most important offices are housed in a boomerang-shaped concrete building that stands on piers in a shallow lake.

The uniformity and 'placelessness' of many large-scale redevelopments disturbed a younger generation of architects. The proposed solution, the identification and use of underlying formal architectural 'structures', on the lines of ethnological thinking, in effect meant a systematic breaking down of architectural problems into manageable parts. Important works from this period are the **Municipal Orphanage, Amsterdam** (1957–60), by Aldo van Eyck (born 1918), in which small units of accommodation are assembled into a building that remains comprehensible at an individual's level. Herman Hetzberger (born 1932), with his **Montessori school, Delft** (1967), showed a greater interest in geometrical intricacy, an interest that developed further in the **Centraal Beheer offices, Apeldoorn** (1968–72) (p. 1393D–F). This multi-storey building is organised according to a geometry of extreme complexity in order that individuals are given both privacy and spaciousness, as well as a visually rich environment. The concentration of effort on the interior space at Beheer has unfortunately left the building with no clear relationship with the buildings and spaces around it. Hertzberger's **Ministry Headquarters, The Hague** (1991), takes on these criticisms and is better integrated into the community structure. Here the building is organised as a series of towers, atrium spaces and office clusters.

Skilful massing is feature of the work of Wim Quist's **Berenplaat Waterworks** (1960–8), a series of giant concrete tanks and pump houses and the same architect's **Rijksmuseum Kröller-Müller extension, Otterlo** (1970–7), drawing on 1920s Modernism.

Rem Koolhaas (born 1944) with the Office for Metropolitan Architecture (OMA), has taken the sense of place adhered to by the Structuralists and combined it with a greater freedom of form and a richer pallette of colours – the striking colours of De Stijl – to design the **National Dance Theatre, The Hague** (Rem Koolhaas with OMA, 1980–4). With its wave-form roofs, sloping and curved ceilings and a plethora of materials, this cheaply constructed building has proven influential. The brightest product of this movement to date must be Jo Coenen's **National Architecture Institute, Rotterdam** (1992–4). Here the archive stacks, elevated onto stilts, form a long curving windowless bank against the adjacent road, while the administrative and other functions are housed in a more regular block, joined by a bridge to the archive building.

Scandinavia

In the years following the war the population shift from country to town accelerated in Scandinavian countries. Sweden in particular was quick to regulate this shift by creating planning legislation, so that communities and not mere barracks would result from new construction. Sven Markelius (1889–1972), as head of Stockholm's planning department (1944–54), brought a modified Corbusian vision to the satellite town of **Vällingby, near Stockholm** (1953–9). Twelve-storey housing towers surround a pedestrian shopping and transportation complex (1953–5, architects Sven Backström and Leif Reinius), while beyond is a variety of low-rise housing types.

Backstrom and Reinius also built the **Rosta housing estate, Orebro** (1948–52), with its three-storey housing using innovative cross-shaped plans. The spaces created by a number of these blocks tend, however, to be rather undefined, and preference was shown for the 'Greek key' planning of schemes like the **housing at Baronbackarna, Orebro** (1957), by Per-Axel Ekholm and Sidney White, a low-rise block that forms three-sided squares as it steps in and out along the site's periphery. More doctrinaire 'modern' approaches were not unknown: half-a-dozen twelve-storey slabs in parallel formation, at **Sodra Guldhelden, Gothenburg** (1959), by Svnska Riksbyggens. The ambitious project of building a million housing units in the decade 1965–75 led to an over-reliance on prefabricated buildings and system building and a drastic falling off of standards. The trend to low-rise and even single-family houses was reversed. But since the 1970s low-rise developments have again become the norm, as at the timber-clad **Nya Bruket estate, Sandviken, Gavle** (1972–80), by Ralph Erskine.

Erskine has designed industrial as well as domestic buildings. His **Cardboard Factory, Fors** (1953) is functional in terms of production process and environment, but the sculpted ventilation nacelles give the brick building a far from utilitarian appearance.

An exceptional **Community Hall, Eslov** (1957), was designed by Hans Asplund, with a series of meeting rooms built into a fan-shaped barrel-vaulted hall, and a rich geometrical and textural variety governs the whole complex. Anders Tengbom, at his **School for Industrial Work Organizers, Lidingo** (1958), uses planes of brick and glass against a wooded landscape to create an altogether cooler architecture, and this was the predominant aim of 1950s and 1960s Swedish architects. The **Art Gallery, Lund** (1957), by Klas Anshelm is another example: brick and glass planes externally, internally a section like an artist's studio, high and plain.

Peter Celsing carried this mood into church architecture in his **Church at Harlanda, Gothenburg** (1958), a group of three buildings – church, belfry and rectory – of simple massing and materials, echoed in the rectangular interior of the church itself. The person to break from this pattern was Sigurd Lewerentz (1885–1975). His churches are remarkable for obtaining maximum plasticity of form from brickwork – albeit he was generous with the mortar. His **Church of S. Mark, Skarck** (1958–60), and, above all, his **Church of S. Peter and Parish Centre, Klippan** (1962–5), show a mastery of construction allied to a deep feeling for Christian symbolism – an unusual architectural preoccupation for the time. Not a brick was cut in the making of the Klippan buildings. Ceilings are vaulted, the floor undulates like the sea, and the primitive values of Christianity are brought to the fore.

Office buildings have tended to follow the pattern set out in more moderate climates, but Neils Torp has recently designed an inwardly turning building as **headquarters for SAS** (1989), where a number of buildings connect by an indoor 'street', glazed above. The street, which does in fact contain restaurants and shops, eliminates the oppressive centrality of many atrium buildings while successfully unifying the offices.

The Danes prefer housing laid uniformly across the landscape to the formality of squares, evident either as tower blocks – **Bellahojvej, Copenhagen** (1951–4), by Dominia Architects – or as short terraces: **Bredalsparken housing estate, Hvidovrevej** (1949–59), by Svenn Eske Kristensen. Exceptions, like **Skoleparken housing, Gladsaxe** (1955), by Knud Hallberg and Jorgen Bo, are still organised according to strictly orthogonal layouts, never 'jarred' as Swedish schemes tend to be.

This interest in the possibilities of geometrical patterns, in terms both of planning and expression, is evident in the work of both Arne Jacobsen (1902–71), in the yellow-brick **Soholum housing, Klampenborg** (1950–55), and Jørn Utzon (1918–), whose L-shaped **Kingo houses, Helsingor** (1956–60), are chained to combine the density advantages of terrace housing with the spatial character of detached houses.

The superb sophistication of Jacobsen's detailing and sense of proportion are seen in the curtain-walled **Jesperson office building, Copenhagen** (1955), and in the **Munkegard School, Soborg, Copenhagen** (1952–6). The school is set out as a rigid grid of single-storey classrooms and corridors enclosing courtyards for each. The superficial ruthlessness of the plan is belied by the variety of internal and external spaces actually created within the school, and the intimacy with which each space is endowed. His last major work in Denmark was the **National Bank, Copenhagen** (1965–71), stone and glass, simple and monumental.

The intimate nature of schooling is a tradition the Danes never lost. **Hansstedt school, Copenhagen** (1954–8), by Frederick Christian Lund and Hans Christian Hansen, is laid out in two single-storey blocks, with richly expressed rooflighting and built in traditional materials. Kay Fisker's rather more complex plan for **Voldparkens school, Husum** (1951–7), achieves an equally humane result.

A more flexible planning strategy was adopted for the larger **Odense University** (1960–76) by Gunnar Krohn, Hartvig Rasmussen and Knud Holscher, where a steel frame and infill system was employed. The **School at Høje Taastrup, near Copenhagen** (1983), by Henning Larsen (born 1925) is organised as four blocks around a cloistered courtyard. In spite of the almost industrially perfect finishing of the building, its spatial arrangements together with an intelligent use of natural materials make the school a sympathetic environment.

The **Louisiana Museum, Humlebaek, Copenhagen** (1958), by Jorgen Bo and Vilhelm Wohlert is arranged as an architectural walk through the woods, where a large part of the gallery space consists of a wide corridor, glazed full height along one side, passing among the trees. Alvar Aalto's **Museum at Aalborg** (1969–73) adopts a completely opposite strategy, being a compact building with a clever system of rooflights and asymmetrical light reflectors for the gallery spaces. Hanne Kjaerholm won the commission to build the **Museum at Holstebro** (1983) in competition. The gallery consists of a series of stilted barrel vaults, glazed as required for optimum lighting and standing on round concrete columns. The exterior is clad in aluminium. The solution permits flexible use of the spaces while giving each part of the museum a strong character.

Outstanding examples of church architecture include the Roman Catholic **S. Nikolaj, Copenhagen** (1960), by Johan Otto von Spreckelsen, whose nave is oriented along the diagonal axis and given a concrete roof curved in two planes; and Jørn Utzon's **church at Bagsvaerd** (1973–6). In plan Utzon's building is laid out on a rigid grid, but in section the roof curves like billowing cloth, which, with the insertion of strip roof lights, yields a wonderful quality of light.

Spain

Without commercial and political pressure, the conservative architecture that had been the European norm in the 1930s continued to thrive in Spain until well after the end of World War II. During the early post-war period the Spanish developed something very like neo-realism, though this movement lacked the polemical fanfare it enjoyed in Italy. The **Apartments, Barcelona** (1952), by Josep Coderch have the characteristic wooden shutters, folded wall planes and brick construction that typify the style. The plans are clever but provide absolutely minimal space standards. Jose Luis Fernandez del Amo's **Caceres housing** (1954–8) follows similar lines, as does the **Esqueville housing, Seville** (1948), of Alejandro de la Sota and the **workers' housing, Calle Pallars, Barcelona** (1960), by Josep Martorell (born 1925) and Oriel Bohigas (born 1925). This last practice, with the addition of David Mackay (born 1933) from 1962, began to turn away from the earnestness of this style with the **Meridiana building, Barcelona** (1965), where a playful facade is created with an irregular disposition of canted window units. Ricardo Bofill (born 1939), whose methodological and assiduous study of plan type resulted in the **apartments at Calle Bach, Barcelona** (1963–5), a brilliant use of an awkward site, began also to make slightly fanciful gestures with his buildings, such as the patterned brickwork and fragmented wall surfaces on the **apartments, Calle Nicaragua, Barcelona** (1965). Bofill, founder of Taller de Arquitectura in 1962, gradually shifted his interest towards romantic monumentalism, and his skill in geometry lapsed into a mere repetitive procedure, for example the **Xanadu apartments, Calpe Bay** (1967). In Madrid, Francisco Saenz de Oiza (born 1918) injected a strain of Frank Lloyd Wright organic – and romantic – into the **Torres Blancas apartments** (1961–8), a tall block developed on a plan of multiple circles.

Commercial work followed a different path from housing. Francisco Cabrero's **Union Delegation Building, Madrid** (1949), is a heavy, not inelegant, structure whose square windows are recessed behind a fat masonry grid. By the mid-1960s he was building light concrete frames but still avoiding the pure curtain wall: his **Arriba newspaper building, Madrid** (1965), seems at first glance to be curtain wall, until the brick infill panels beneath the windows are noticed, and then the projecting mullions. This is Modernism at its purest in post-war Spain. Later office buildings, like the **Adriatica Building, Madrid** (1981), by Javier Carvajal, adopt the mirror-glass conventions common in Europe at the time.

Such was the change in the meaning of monumentality once the Franco dictatorship had ended that by the mid-1980s it was possible for the once-despised heroic architecture to acquire respectability – to become, actually, avant-garde. Rafael Moneo (born 1937) was able to conjure up the building methods of ancient Rome for his **Museum of Roman Art, Merida** (1980–5). Moneo has intentionally avoided iconic in favour of constructional devices, but the heroic quality of the building, with its vast brick piers and arches of thin Roman bricks, is unmistakable. His later **Airport, Seville** (1991) uses a similar arcuated construction and incorporates a spectacular departure hall roofed by a series of saucer domes carried on pendentives. Nor was Moneo on his own. Oscar Tusquets built his **housing, Mas Abello** (1990), using pilasters, pediment and cornice, detaching the building from that sense of place so dear to the neo-realists and replacing it with reference to a generalised classical grandeur. Ricardo Bofill went even farther with the **INEF Building, Barcelona** (1991), a completely, if awkwardly, Classical building.

Martorell, Bohigas and Mackay have shown another direction to richness of texture, colour and meaning in their **house in Son Vida, Majorca** (1988), where a level of inventiveness and abstraction has created an architectural language flexible enough to allow planning to follow non-Classical modes.

The work of Alberto Campo Baeza (born 1946) pursues an opposite goal, and in its re-echoing of 1930s white architecture calls up a romantic image of an age when to be modern was, it might seem, a simple thing. His **Town Hall, Fene, La Coruna** (1980), and **School, San Sebastian de los Reys, Madrid** (1983), are representative. Enric Miralles's (born 1955) **National Training Centre for Gymnastics, Alicante** (1994), reflects some of the preoccupations of Deconstuction but it is, above all, an inspired response to an irregular site and, in its modelling, the product of a lively three-dimensional spatial imagination.

The most sophisticated work of the past decade has come from the studio of Jaume Bach (born 1943) and Gabriel Mora (born 1941), whose work is of a uniformly high standard. Using simple but precise forms and the staple materials of brick and concrete they have made the **Reventos Blanc Winery, Barcelona** (1990), both functionally and formally rich. Other buildings include the **Josep Maria Jujol school, Barcelona** (1991), and the **Bellaterra railway station** (1994).

Taking over the engineer-architect's mantle from Eduardo Torroja, Santiago Calatrava (born 1951) has designed structures of great dynamism, exploiting biomorphic forms: the **Bach de Roda–Felipe II Bridge, Barcelona** (1984–7), and **Bilbao Airport** (1990–4).

In Portugal the work of Alvaro Siza (born 1933) must be mentioned. Siza, like Baeza in Spain, retains a commitment to 'classic Modernism', and is much influenced by Aalto. His **Casa Beires, Povoa do Varzim** (1973–6), consists of a white cuboid, one corner of which is missing, replaced by a sweeping glazed screen. The repercussions of this interruption throughout the plan of the house set up intriguing volumetric relationships.

Switzerland

The first post-war impulse in Swiss architecture was towards wood-built romanticism, the most telling example being the **Park Theatre, Grenchen** (1949–55), by Ernst Gisel (born 1922), a brick and timber community building of simple cubic massing with monopitch roofs, owing something to Aalto's Säynätsalo Town Hall. Regionalism was soon to take a different turn. Atelier 5 (founded 1955: Erwin Fritz, Sunwel Gerber, Rolf Hesterberg, Hans Hostettler, Alfredo Pini) looked for a way to condense housing into a small area, rather than sprawl it over the landscape. Their **Halen housing estate, near Berne** (1955–61), based loosely on Le Corbusier's unbuilt scheme for la Sainte-Baune (1948), uses long terraces of housing stepping down a sloping site, cleverly exploiting the terrain for privacy and access, and keeping the built footprint relatively small. The one similarity that remains between this scheme and Gisel's is in the open use of plain materials: here it was concrete.

Franz Füeg had a quite different approach to materials, manipulating brick and glass within a highly disciplined framework, generally of steel, in order to make them precious. His work, taking Mies as a starting point, is characterised by a strong sense of proportion and detailing. Examples are the **Metal Construction Shop, Kleinlutzel** (1958), of steel and brick, and the **Catholic Church, Meggen** (1954–66), where the steel frame is 'glazed' with translucent panels of alabaster.

Sharing this passion for a rational aesthetic were Fritz and Bruno Haller, who designed and patented several systems for constructing buildings with steel frames. Their **Factory, Munsingen** (1963), and **Technical School, Windisch** (1964–6), both demonstrate the delicacy achieved by systems that were primarily designed for internal flexibility. Ernst Gisel's **School, Engelberg** (1965–7), shows the opposite approach, a concrete building whose clever section and careful planning were expected to preclude the need for flexibility.

Following the success of Atelier 5's Halen housing, a group called Team 2000 (Ulrich Scherer and others) built **Terrace housing, Umiken, near Brugg** (1963–5), owing something to Aalto's pre-war Kauttua apartments, and Andre Studer designed **Terrace apartments,Visp**, (1964–7), both schemes exploiting steeply sloping sites in what was to become something of a modern vernacular of the 1960s and 1970s in Switzerland. Aalto himself designed the **Schonbuhl apartments, Lucerne** (1965–7), a 17-storey block with a fan-shaped plan – the intention was to give small flats the maximum view – and at its base a **shopping centre** by Alfred Roth.

A belief in individual and sculptural expression was carried into architecture by Walter Maria Förderer (born 1928–), whose **Commercial High School, S. Gallen** (1957–63, with Rolf Georg Otto and Hans Zwimpfer), focuses all main spaces onto a monumental staircase. His fraught **church of S. Nicholas, Heremence** (1963–71), is primarily an essay in self-expression. The **Roman Catholic College, Sarnen** (1964–6), by Ernst and Gottlieb Studer (with Joachim Naef), a series of sloping circular walls enclosing space like the skins of an onion, represents an attempt to bring the organic architecture of Wright to Switzerland.

The small Italian section of Switzerland, the Ticino, became the country's focus of architectural interest in the 1960s and 1970s, when younger architects found the endless refinement of a Haller or the functional reasoning of an Atelier 5 to be insufficient, even tiresome. Aurelio Galfetti (**Casa Rotalinti, Bellinzona**, 1961), Tita Carloni (**Stabio school**, 1968–74) and Luigi Snozzi (born 1932) began to reconsider the formal vocabulary of architecture, enriching their own works by reference to historical precedent. Snozzi takes on some of the formal propositions of Louis Kahn (**Casa Bianchetti, Locarno**, 1975–7; **Casa Cavalli, Verscio**, 1976–8), where a degree of autonomy is given to formal objects, quite outside the requirements of brief or function. Mario Botta (born 1943), who had worked for Le Corbusier as well as Kahn, took this process further in his series of villas and schools (**Casa Bianchi, Riva San Vitale**, 1971–2; **school at Morbio Inferiore**, 1972–7), where the formal elements are at an urban rather than domestic scale. The comparison with a town wall bastion in the **Villa Origlio** (1975) is obvious. The reversal of values is evident if one considers that convenience of plan is sacrificed to this formalism. Botta's **School at Morbio Inferiore** (1972–7) is a further exploration of these relationships.

Bruno Reichlin (born 1941) and Fabio Reinhart (born 1942), with their **Casa Tonini, Torricella** (1972–4), adapt the Palladian villa as a typological starting point, and, like Botta, systematically demonstrating the awkwardness of literal historical material in twentieth-century architecture.

North of the Alps a different relation to history was explored. Rolf Keller, with the **Parish Centre, Muttenz, near Basle** (1965–70, with Fritz Swartz), recreates the 'Gothic village', with rendered walls of irregular plan, a variety of roof shapes, and a generally comforting atmosphere which some may think results in blandness. Jacques Herzog and Pierre De Meuron, while taking maximum advantage of site and surroundings in their work, choose from a wider historical range. Their small **apartments, Helbestrasse, Basle** (1988), is a two-storey building, predominantly wood finishes on a steel frame. The larger **Schwitter Building apartments**, Basle (1990), is a concrete and glass corner building whose historical precedents quite clearly include 1960s apartment blocks.

Chapter 46

EASTERN EUROPE

Introduction

It may seem curious to maintain the distinction between West Europe and East Europe and Russia despite the fact that the ideological, political and economic barriers between these parts of Europe have been dissolved since 1989. But this barrier, which separated Russia from the West since 1917 and the Eastern and Central portions of Europe from the West since 1945, had a profound influence on the development of architecture in the region – often most significantly in terms of methods and quality of construction and types of buildings commissioned. It seems reasonable therefore to continue to reflect this distinction – relatively recent and culturally arbitrary as it may have been – even though the cause of this distinction has now been removed. While the barrier was in existence Eastern Europe and Russia acquired, through their political and social structures, a stability and distinct architectural identity and aims which were – and still are – expressed in much of the building of the period. This part of Europe was effectively almost another world, certainly another continent. As the West and East now reunite in their aspirations, and as ideas and influences – and people – once again flow freely then the architectural connections will begin to outnumber the disjunctions. By the time the next edition of this book is published it will, no doubt, be not only reasonable but essential to consider Europe once again as a single entity.

Assessing the twentieth-century architecture of Eastern Europe at this moment of political and social flux presents some substantial problems. Due to the breakdown of Communism throughout Eastern and areas of Central Europe in 1989 this part of the world has suffered – and continues to suffer – many dramatic changes. Some of these changes have affected existing borders as well as country and ethnic group boundaries. There have been a number of changes of name and identity and a move away from a largely state-controlled architecture to a new capital-based and free market construction industry. Prior to the years of oppressive controls, often imposed by outside forces (for example, in Poland and Czechoslovakia), many of the East and Central European countries had achieved significant roles in the growth of modern architecture in the 1920s and 1930s, often in tandem with developments in the other arts. Prague, Brno in former Czechoslovakia and Breslau (now Wroclaw) and Krakow in Poland were significant centres of architectural activity from the early years of this century.

The most advanced Communist society within the Eastern bloc was undoubtedly the DDR. This former Soviet satellite is dealt with in Chapter 45. However, with the seemingly endless boundary changes in and around Germany and Poland, certain 'German' buildings and the work of a number of German architects are still discussed within the context of the architecture of the adopted country.

The development of the architecture of East European countries over the last two decades of the nineteenth century right up to the late 1930s is little different from that of the rest of Europe. In many Continental countries twentieth-century architecture has been characterised by similar distinctive phases of change and development from the introduction of the various styles of design including the Belle Epoque, Viennese Secessionist, German Jugendstil, French and Belgian Art Nouveau, English Arts and Crafts, Liberty and the many versions of National Romanticism.

Definitions

From these eclectic origins there emerged in Eastern and Central Europe a radical and often avant-garde 'Modern' or Functionalist architecture. These terms need clarification as their use was often dependent on the cultural connections of Eastern Europe with other European centres such as Vienna and Paris.

The term 'Functionalism' was closely associated with the work of those architects who admired the theories of Le Corbusier and those connected after 1928 with CIAM. In the Corbusian sense Functionalism is often interchangeable with the term 'Rationalist' although this term had a more specific relationship to Italian modern architecture.

Rationalism, as a term used in architecture, derives less from any unified theory and more from the scientific humanism of the architectural theorists of the Renaissance and its use in the late nineteenth century by French and German theorists in support of their arguments for a new and 'Modern' Architecture. Otto Wagner used it as the title of his inaugural lecture at the Vienna Academy in 1894 and enshrined it in published form in his book *Moderne Architektur* published in 1896.

The more commonly used phrase to decribe the new attitudes to building design, or Modern architecture, during the 1920s and 1930s in Central and Eastern Europe was undoubtedly 'Functionalist'. The Polish architect Bohdan Lachert (1900–86) wrote in 1983 from his experience: 'The architects, realising the importance of utilitarian problems, undertook creative work which demanded that all the respective utilitarian functions of the buildings should be evident in both their exterior and interior appearance. This trend, known as *Functionalism*, was unfortunately, interpreted falsely as one rejecting all of the excessive decoration and shaping of a work of art on artistic prerequisites'.

The summary phrase 'International Style' derives from the USA. Although reputedly coined by Alfred Barr, the Director of the Museum of Modern Art (MOMA), New York, it was the architectural historian Henry-Russell Hitchcock who, with Philip Johnson, used it as the title of a book, and an exhibition at the MOMA, New York, in 1932. They defined it as a collective term for the work of the 'new pioneers'.

The term 'Modern Architecture' covered many of the recognisably pioneering modern tendencies in Europe. It is a term that indicates a shared vocabulary of forms in an architecture that has no direct reference to historical precedence and with no ornamental features but which is based on formal 'aesthetic features' such as flat roofs, white or plain thin (mostly reinforced concrete) wall surfaces and asymmetrically arranged, flexible plans.

Influences

Vienna, as the capital and cultural pivot of the Austro-Hungarian empire, played an important part in the development of twentieth-century architecture in Eastern and Central Europe. The boundaries of the empire also tended to define a cultural entity within these regions – an entity which was to a large degree shattered following the collapse of the empire in 1918. The Habsburg Empire had, largely through family connections, acquired land all over Central and Eastern Europe, extending well beyond the established boundary on the Austrian and Moravian borders to Ottoman lands. Silesia formed part of the empire until conquered by Prussia in 1742. Bohemia and Moravia were acquired in 1526 and Hungary in 1699. Vienna, the capital of Lower Austria which housed the court of the Emperor (who was the Duke of Vienna), became the cultural centre of the whole region. The city expanded enormously during the nineteenth century and its public buildings achieved internationally recognised standards of excellence.

Within the boundaries of the empire various nations reacted against the unifying influence of Vienna and sought increasingly to express their distinct identities and aspirations for political indepedence through their architecture. The consequence, the National Romantic Movement, celebrated regional, vernacular and historic traditions in preference to pan-empire or Vienna-generated styles. National Romanticism (which also found expression in countries outside Austro-Hungarian rule but within other empires, such as Finland which was under Russian rule) became a major force in European architecture in the years preceding World War I.

The Vienna Akademie, where Otto Wagner (1841–1918) taught a special Master Class from 1894, produced graduates who came from most of the surrounding countries. A number of these alumini were to become the main agents of architectural change. They included the Slovenian architect Jože Plečnik (1872–1957) and the Czech Jan Kotera (1871–1923), both of whom established reputations for inventive and original public work in Prague and who both became influential teachers of architecture.

In Prague in 1912 another movement occurred; architects acquainted with developments in French Cubist painting attempted to apply its principles to architecture and design. The result was an architecture largely free of applied ornament and similar in some ways to the crystalline projects of the architecture associated with the German Expressionist movement (1910–23). However, it never became much more than an unusual but interesting kind of angular facade treatment in the work of Josef Chochol, Josef Gocar and Pavel Janak.

The Spread of 'Modernism'

After World War I, when a number of East European countries gained their independence, a modern architecture movment was initiated by small groups of avant-garde artists, designers and architects. In Hungary there was such a group whose members published the periodical *MA* (Today) between 1916 and 1919, and Bauhaus students most whom later emigrated to West Europe and to America (Marcel Breuer (1902–81), F. Forbat (1897–1972) and Lazlo Moholy-Nagy (1895–1946)). In Czechoslovakia the artistic avant-garde was fully represented by the progressive *Devetsil* Group (initiated *c.* 1920) which was run by the theorist Karel Teige and the architect Jaromir Krejcar (1895–1949) both of whom were interested in Soviet Constructivism and French Purism.

In Poland modern architecture was initiated by the group *Blok,* formed in 1922, which had strong associations with the Soviet avant-garde. This Constructivist-orientated group contributed to the beginnings of modern architecture in Poland during the second half of the 1920s. The involvement of Polish architects, particularly the Syrkus's, in the activities of CIAM also had a stimulating effect. At the beginning of World War II an Anglo-Polish architectural axis was established through the opening up of Polish Schools of Architecture in London and Liverpool Universities.

After World War II a practical and functional modern architecture again became the dominant idiom in Eastern Europe. It continued until the beginning of the 1950s when again, as after the Fascist period, political circumstances changed and the Socialist Realism of the Soviet Union gained currency; almost all countries received a Soviet-designed Stalinist 'Palace of Culture'. After 1956 this was gradually ignored and modern architecture in many countries of Eastern Europe was able to develop more or less along the same lines as in the rest of the industrialised countries, perhaps with the most noticeable exceptions being the heavy prefabricated housing systems adopted by the Soviet Union for its own use (see Chapter 47) and for use by its satellites.

Independence and the New Boundaries

Since 1989 and the end of the Soviet Union and its domination of East and Central Europe whole countries have been renamed, new boundaries defined and some borders contested. Czechoslovakia is now divided into two with The Czech Republic (capital, Prague) to the west but including within its boundaries Bohemia, Moravia (regional capital, Brno) and Moravian Silesia. The Slovak Republic, now known as Slovakia, has as its capital Bratislava.

The former Yugoslavia has undergone more drastic change. As a federation of republics it has ceased to exist. In its stead is Bosnia Hercegovina, a complicated amalgam of ethnic and religious groups with Sarajevo as its capital; the northern state of Croatia with Zagreb as its focal city; the newly constituted Slovenia (1991) centred on Ljubljana, while Belgrade remains the capital of Serbia, the most powerful of all the former Yugoslav republics. Both Macedonia and Montenegro are separate republics.

As independent countries both Bulgaria, with its architecturally progressive capital Sofia, and Romania (capital, Bucharest) remain intact but since the demise of Communism have become democratic and increasingly market oriented. One consequence of this is that urban centres in both countries now possess examples of architecture recently fashionable in the West, notably in the Post-Modern and Deconstructivist idioms. But as with many major and historic cities in the former East Germany (for example, Leipzig, Jena and Weimar) an older urban fabric remains, neglected perhaps but not compromised. In many places this is now the subject of careful conservation, renovation and upgrading for re-use and a new life. Thus in so many places the architecture of the future is to be found embedded in the history of the past.

The Czech Republic and Slovakia (Formerly Czechoslovakia)

Czechoslovakia (now divided into The Czech Republic and Slovakia, see Introduction) was one of the first countries to adopt Modern functionalist architecture wholeheartedly. One of the key figures in its adoption was Jan Kotera (1871–23), a pupil of Otto Wagner at the Vienna Akademie. He rose rapidly to prominence in Prague where he became a professor at the School of Industrial Arts at 28 years and a local cultural leader. Kotera was determined that his kind of Modern architecture would 'catch and overtake Europe'. In 1908–12 he gave expression to his interest in the architecture of America (which he visited in 1903) with his designs for one of the earliest Frank Lloyd Wright inspired structures in Europe, the **Municipal Museum, Hradec Kralove** (1906–14) (p. 1403A,B).

Among Kotera's pupils were Josef Goĉár (1880–1945), who was later to lead the Czech Functionalist cause, Pavel Janak (1882–1945) and Josef Chochol (1880–1956), who had also studied under Wagner. They all subscribed to the Graphic Artists' Group, an association of Czech Cubists, and for that reason took a critical view of Kotera's severe rationalist architecture. They saw their work as a counteraction to the then-current Wagnerian Rationalism and demanded a more spiritual approach to architecture by 'means of the manipulation of sculptural mass'. The widely used term to describe the whole movement of Czech Cubism, 'Rondo-Cubism' (coined by Marie Bensova), is also associated with the foundation of the new Czechoslovak state in 1918.

Kotera's continuing friendship with the Slav architect Jože Plečnic (1872–1957) after they left the Wagnerschule allowed them both to keep in touch with developments in each others country. He arranged Plečnik's appointment to the chair of the School of Decorative Arts in Prague in 1910, but it was not until 1919 that any substantial architectural work in Prague was commissioned from Plečnik. Then he was

A. Municipal Museum, Hradec Kralove (1906–14). See p. 1402

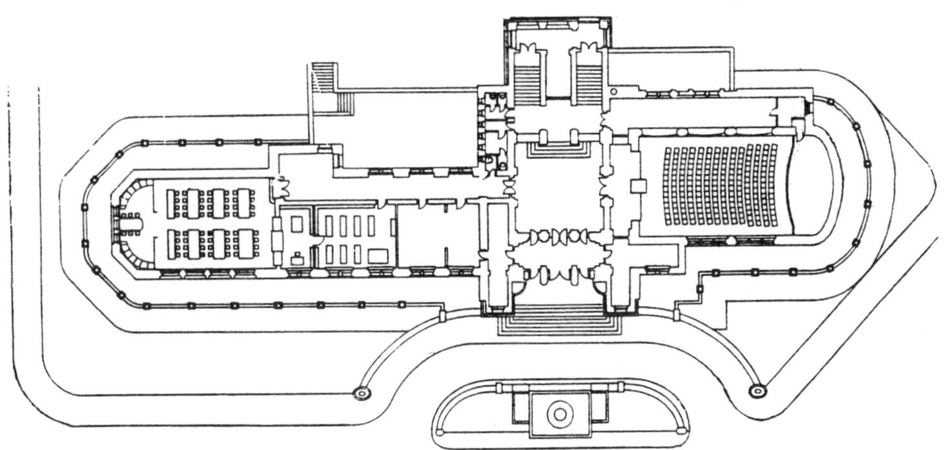

B. Municipal Museum, Hradec Kralove: plan

A. Apartment house, Neklan Street, Prague (1913–14). See p. 1405

B. Riunione Adriatica di Sicurita, Prague (1923–5). See p. 1405

C. Bull Staircase, Hradčancy Castle, Prague (1928–30). See p. 1405

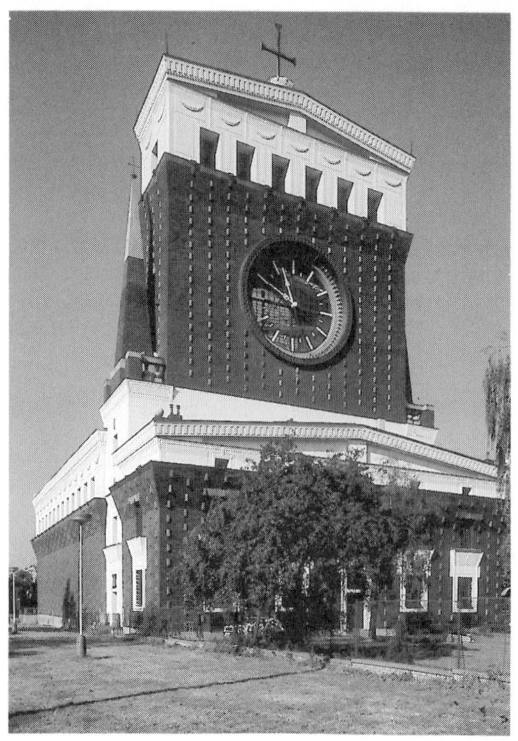

D. Church of the Sacred Heart, Vinohrady, Prague (1928–32). See p. 1405

appointed architect, by President Masaryk, to **Hradčany Castle, Prague** (1920–32). This project involved restructuring the **President's Apartment** within the castle and gave Plečnik the opportunity to display and develop his idiosyncratic brand of Modernism which combined contemporary building technology with Slavik craft traditions and a powerful, elemental, reinterpretation of antique Classicism. Plečnik's work in the castle included the creation of a triple-height colonnaded and copper-roofed entrance vestibule, called **S. Matthias Hall** (1928–30), and a top-lit **impluvium** inspired by the atria in Roman houses (1920–25). Plečnik also renovated the **Eden Garden** and the **Rampart Garden** (1921–5) which he furnished with a number of erudite and inventive Classical pavilions and belvedere and connected to the higher castle courtyard by the **Bull Staircase** (1928–30) (p. 1404C). Cut through, and rising within the eighteenth-century apartments of the castle, the staircase is an ingeniously formed and beautifully detailed design which takes the Ionic order as its central motif – Plečnik felt strongly for the Ionic for he believed that the ancient Slavs were of Ionian origin and thus the use of the Ionic was a statement about Slav national identity. Plečnik also adapted the **President's Summer Residence, Lány** (1921–30) and designed the **Church of the Sacred Heart, Vinohrady, Prague** (1928–32, commissioned 1922) (p. 1404D). This is a remarkable structure: concrete-built, clad in brick with bold and inventive Classically derived external detail and with an interior which combines traditional elements from Slavik architecture with Plečnik's own vision of Classicism.

Buhuslav Fuchs (1895–1972) studied under Kotera between 1916 and 1919 and began his architectural career in the municipal offices in Brno. In the 1920s he soon fell under the spell of Van Doesberg and the Dutch De Stijl Group but after 1927 began to look to Le Corbusier and then CIAM, of which he was a member, for inspiration. **The Avion Hotel, Brno** (1927), with its vitrolite facade and volumetric interior, was the first of a number of buildings including the **Swimming Pool, Zelena Zaba** (1935–6), the **Railway Station at Brno** (1938) and the **Czech Pavilion at the New York Fair** (1939) that demonstrate Fuchs' commitment to Modernism which was to go well into the post-war period when he taught at Brno Technical University, 1947–58.

Cubism obtained its effects largely through the creation of faceted facades and serrated roofs. The results can be clearly seen in works such as Gočár's **Baths, Bohdanec, Bohemia** (1911–12), **Sanatorium, Bohdanec** (1921–23) the grotesque overblown Baroque exterior of the **Czecholsovak Legion Bank, Prague** (1923–5), the earlier office building in **Jindrisska Street, Prague** (1920–21) and the **apartment house, Neklan Street, Prague** (1913–14) (p. 1404A), both designed by Chochol.The apartment house has four floors with a conventional ground-floor plan. Externally, inclined and angled planes dominate to produce a sense of rhythmic mobility, while the interaction of light and shade enhance the effect created by the prismatic shapes and inclined planes of the overhanging eaves and corner balconies. The consequence of this manipulation of form was to give the facade of the building the appearance of a Cubist sculpture or painting.

There is no other comparable European architecture inspired by Cubism, except perhaps the unique projects by Raymond Duchamp-Villon, for '*la maison cubiste*' in 1912. From a formal standpoint this approach to architecture can be seen as part of a general trend towards an Expressionist architecture after 1912. Duchamp-Villon, who exhibited in Prague in 1914, was published in the avant-garde magazine *Umelecky Mesicnik*.

The **Villa in Vysehrad, Prague** (1912–14), by Chochol, has facades influenced by Cubism in which hardly any of the projecting and angled surfaces of the building are parallel to the outlines of the plan. The radical form of elevational composition was seen as a way of eliminating reminiscences of historical styles.

This episode, influenced not only by Cubist paintings but also by the empathic theories of both Theodor Lipps and Wilhelm Worringer, almost faded during the years of World War I. It culminated with the erection of the **Czech Pavilion, Deutscher Werkbund exhibition, Cologne** (1914), by Otakar Novotny (1880–1959). Novotny's work was also influenced by the Dutch school led by H. P. Berlage as can be seen in his **Jan Stenc Publishing Offices, Prague** (1911–12).

After the war, at the time of the creation of an independent Czechoslovakia in October 1918, Janak and Gočár turned to a more nationalistic, folkloric and monumental architecture. Janak's interest changed from the angularity of the early cubist phase to the use of details of more obvious Classical derivation (pilasters and pediments), yet rendered in almost diagramatic forms. The results, such as the **Riunione Adriatica di Sicurita (now insurance company), Prague** (1923–5) (p. 1404B), when constructed out of concrete could be crude yet powerful. An example of Gocár's work of this period is **S. Wenceslas' Church, Prague** (1928) (p. 1406A,B), which tapers up a steep sloping site to create a stepped nave rising from a tall, slender tower and terminating in a semi-circular chancel which occupies the highest part of the site. The nave elevations are windowless with the interior being top-lit.

Later Janak and Gočár moved again towards a Modern style, the utilitarian Functionalism advocated at the first CIAM congress in 1928 in Switzerland and demonstrated in projects such as the clean detailed **Building of the former Pensions Institute, Prague** (1924–34) (p. 1406C), and the **Apartments at Pankrac, Prague** (1930), both by Karel Honzik and Josef

A. S. Wenceslas' Church, Prague (1928). See p. 1405

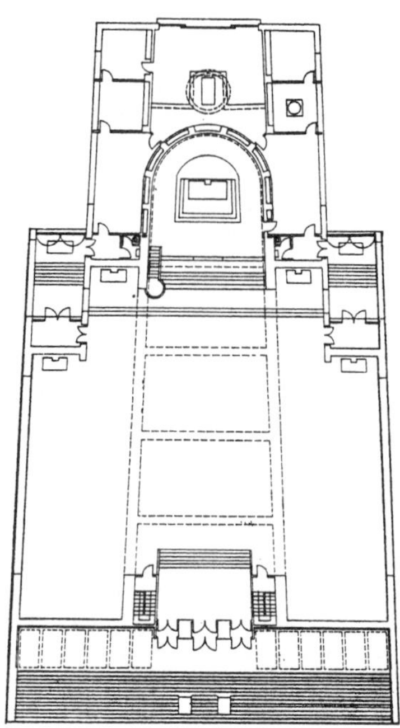

B. S. Wenceslas' Church: plan

C. Building of the former Pensions Institute, Prague (1924–34). See p. 1405

Havlicek, and those by Josef Polasek at **Kosice** (1931). This kind of Modern architecture established itself relatively quickly in Czechoslovakia due in part to contacts in France, Germany and the Netherlands as well as the influence of the Bauhaus, the Soviet Constructivists and Le Corbusier's *Vers une architecture* of 1923. In large measure, however, the Czechs made significant contributions to the new architecture themselves, through Kotera's second-generation students, Bohuslav Fuchs (1895–1972) and Adolf Bens (1894–1982), and those younger architects who rallied around the *Stavba* magazine edited by the architect Oldrich Stary (1884–1971) (and for a time by the brilliant theorist Karel Teige) which enthusiastically subscribed to the German *Neue Sachlichkeit* movement. Stary built a **house at the Werkbund exhibition** held in **Brno** in 1928 and **two more for the Werkbund exhibition, Baba, Prague**, 1932 (see below).

Teige, a close associate of Chochol, became the leader of the most radical group in Prague where, after the brief earlier interlude of Cubism, now looked towards purism and poetry as part of their new stricter, geometrical aesthetic. One of the first of the buildings in the new Modern style was the Constructivist **Trade Fair Building, Prague** (1924–8) (p. 1408A). It was won in competition by Oldrich Tyl (1884–1939), who designed the final version of the building in 1924 in collaboration with Josef Fuchs. The seven-storey building has two central slightly asymmetric halls with transverse connecting corridors between them. Around the halls are located galleries with offices, and a restaurant. Below ground are store rooms and a cinema to seat 800 people, with a separate entrance. This is a comparatively early reinforced concrete building with a tiled facade and continuous windows.

In 1927–8 the **Exhibition of Contemporary Culture** was held in **Brno**. The event acted as a stimulus for modern architecture – a completely new **exhibition area with pavilions** by Bohuslav Fuchs (1895–1972) and Kamil Roskot (1892–1945) was built and, next to it, in 1928 a small group of **model apartment houses**. These were inspired by the German Werkbund Weissenhofsiedlung in Stuttgart (q.v.). The Brno designs were more modest than Stuttgart and the result of a privately inspired initiative by two local contractors, working without subsidy. The groups of apartments were given the name **'Nový dům'** (new house) and were to be built without basements, so that technical installations and storage rooms were on the ground floor. The living area was to cover two floors, and have a terrace and a flat roof. The basic house type was intended for middle-income families and the buildings were required to have rational ground plans, built-in furniture and standard windows and doors. Most of the apartments were in fact built in reinforced concrete and in lightweight hollow concrete blocks.

Bohuslav Fuchs designed a **block of three flats** with a straight connecting staircase (p. 1408B). The first and second floors house the two-bedroom apartments. There is no terrace, but there are balconies to the second-floor rooms. Jan Višek's **block** contains **two flats with a terrace** (p. 1408C). In this case the staircase is positioned along the back of the building, allowing greater freedom in the arrangement of the rooms. The facade is plain with columns at the front and an overhanging terrace at the back. The conventional and somewhat small windows result from the use of standard frames.

The **Vesna girls' school** (1928–30) and **boarding school** (1929–30), **Brno** (p. 1409C), were original and pioneering designs. The girls' school was designed by Bohuslav Fuchs and Josef Polasek, the boarding school by Fuchs alone. The first building is a square reinforced concrete-framed block with a gymnasium attached to one side. Classrooms run the length of the building on ground and first floors, each of which also contain an examination room which may be divided off by means of a wooden partition. The entrance and the stairwell are at the back of the buildings, and in the summer the classrooms are reached by way of a continuous balcony. Large symmetrically arranged windows on the upper floor contrast with a continuous glass wall on the ground floor. The boarding school, a four-storey building, is constructed with a series of transverse walls expressed by the asymmetrical facade with deeply indented, glass-fronted balconies, the transparency creating a feeling of space. The communal facilities are on the ground floor, dormitory rooms and studio one-room flats with roof terraces above.

Four years after the model apartments were built in Brno, a **model neighbourhood,** called **'Baba'**, was built in **Prague** (1932–4). The idea came from the Czech Workers Alliance (SVAZ Ceskoslovenskeho Dila), but the realisation of the project was again dependent upon private initiatives. Any member of the Alliance could commission a design from one of the architects affiliated to it. Consequently, there was no architectural manifesto but a housing enterprise which came about in the traditional way through negotiations between client and architect. The whole project consists of thirty-three houses in four rows on a sloping site. Pavel Janak was the urban planner. The houses range from small- and medium-sized residences to large villas. The small **apartment house** by Antonin Heythum and Evzen Linhart (1898–1949) has two similar flats on both ground and first floors. Above them is a roof terrace on the south side and a third storey with an additional bedroom on the north side. The **family house** by Ladislav Zak (1900–73) has a single large ground-floor living room, with bedrooms and a partly covered roof terrace above. The facade is flat and plain with windows along its whole length. The plan arrangements of the floors produce a building

A. Trade Fair Building, Prague (1924–8). See p. 1407

B. Flats by Bohuslav Fuchs, Nový dům, Brno (1928). See p. 1407

C. Flats by Jan Višek, Nový dům, Brno (1928). See p. 1407

A. (*above*) Machnáč Sanatorium, Trenčianské Teplice (1929–32). See p. 1410

B. (*left*) Czech Pavilion, Paris Exposition (1937). See p. 1410

C. (*below*) Vesna girls' school (1928–30) (centre) and boarding school (1929–30) (right) Brno. See p. 1407

form of unusual three-dimentional structure. Another **house** was designed by the Dutchman Mart Stam, and built in his absence by J. Palicka. It is a long narrow house raised above the ground on columns. The first floor stretches the whole length of the building and has a balcony on the south side. **Stam's house** is distinguished from the others by virtue of its section and its fenestration which together produce an impression of transparency.

Jaromir Krejar's (1895–1949) **Machnáč Sanatorium, Trenčianské Teplice** (1929–32) (p. 1409A), is another fine example of functionalist architecture. The building has a T-shaped ground plan: the horizontal arm of the T houses the patients' living quarters while the vertical arm houses the communal facilities. The patients' accommodation is designed as flatlets, each with a small entrance hall, living room and balcony. The main facade of the patients' wing has a rhythm related to the windows with balconies, though the other facades are flat with continuous windows, the whole reminiscent of the early International Style of Walter Gropius's office and the Bauhaus of about the same time (for example, the Siemensstadt housing built by Gropius in Berlin between 1929 and 1930). Krejar was also responsible for the **Czech Pavilion** at the **Paris Exposition** (1937) (p. 1409B).

Czechoslovakia succeeded in becoming a magnet for Modern architects and artists. A number of buildings received worldwide publicity. They included Mies van der Rohe's (1886–1969) last European project, **Tugendhat House, Brno** (1928–30) (p. 1411A–D), Erich Mendelsohn's (1887–1953) **Bachnek Store, Ostrava** (1933–34), Adolf Loos's (1870–1933) stark, cubic **Müller House, Prague** (1928–30) (p. 1412A–C), and a number of unbuilt projects by Behrens, Breuer, Duiker, Oud and Le Corbusier. The Tugendhat House – now a national monument – is situated on a steeply sloping site. From a modest translucent single-storey street entrance front a staircase goes down into an open rectangular lower garden floor The room overlooking the garden is furnished with glass walls which can be lowered electrically into the floor.

In and around Bratislava (now the capital city of Slovakia) are located a number of buildings by Bohuslav Fuchs including **'The Green Frog' open-air pool** (1935–7) and **Hotel Morava** (1930–33).

After Prague and Brno the third most important centre of Modernism was to be found in the new industrial **'garden city' of Zlin, Moravia**, designed for the Bat'a shoe company. Kotera was the town's planning adviser until his death in 1923 when his role was taken over by his student Frantisek L. Gahura. The houses and factories for this modern city had an influence all over Europe and were developed by noted local Modern architects such as Vladimir Karfik, who had worked for Le Corbusier and Frank Lloyd Wright, and Antonin Vitak. Le Corbusier advised on the city plan for a period joining a distinguished jury for a housing competition in 1935.

Many distinguished Bat'a shops were built throughout the world in the 1930s. One of the most elegant is the narrow eight-storey concrete and glass **Bat'a Store, Prague** (1928–9) (p. 1413A,B) designed by Ludvig Kysela (1883–1960). With its prominent storey-high neon outline lettering and external night lighting the store was widely published.

The evolution of modern architecture was interrupted by World War II and a number of architects left the country due to the Nazi occupation of Czecholslovakia. These included Arnost (Arnold) Weisner (1890–1971), who was a successful architect in Brno between the wars and emigrated to England in 1939. He later taught at Liverpool University and opened a practice in that city in 1960. His buildings in Brno include the Loosian **Municipal Crematorium** (1925–30) and **Villa Neumark, Villa Hasse** and **Villa Stiassny**, all at Brno-Pisarky and built between 1928 and 1930.

After the war Socialist Realism took hold and architecture became a corollary of political development. Modern architects such as Bedrich Rozehnal (1902–84), also from Brno, were persecuted by the authorities for working independently of the state. Such a doctrinaire approach was abandoned at the end of the 1950s, from which time architecture in Czechoslovakia, as in other East European countries, began to develop along lines similar to those elsewhere in Europe.

One of the more unusual buildings constructed in the ensuing years in Czechoslovakia was the **Parliament Building Extension, Prague** (1967–9). It is the work of the GAMA Studio (Albrecht, Kaderabek and Prager), and was won in competition. One of the conditions was that the facade of the old building had to be retained, and restrictions limited the height of the new building to that of the neighbouring **National Museum**. The plan of the extension is a rectangle, 50 m × 80 m (164 ft × 262 ft), and it is two storeys high. It is carried on steel Vierendeel beams on four pylons 24 m (79 ft) high, and is above the old building. The extension has a large courtyard. The facade is mainly of glass combined with granite and marble facings. Other notable buildings of the immediate pre-1989 era include the inventive low-technology **Regatta Stadium, Racice, Roudnice** (1987), by Tomas Kulik (born 1954), Jan Louda (born 1949) and Zbysek Styblo (born 1952); the **Outdoor School, Volyne** (1989), by Ladislav Konopka (born 1933) and the well-laid-out **National Tennis Courts, Stanvice Island, Prague**, with its large **Central Tennis Grandstand** (1989) by J Kales (born 1934) and J. Novotna (born 1940).

The demise of Communism and the return to democratic principles after 1989 in the Czech Republic, and Prague in particular, provided many new

A. (*above*) Tugendhat House, Brno (1928–30). See p. 1410

B. (*left*) Tugendhat House: interior

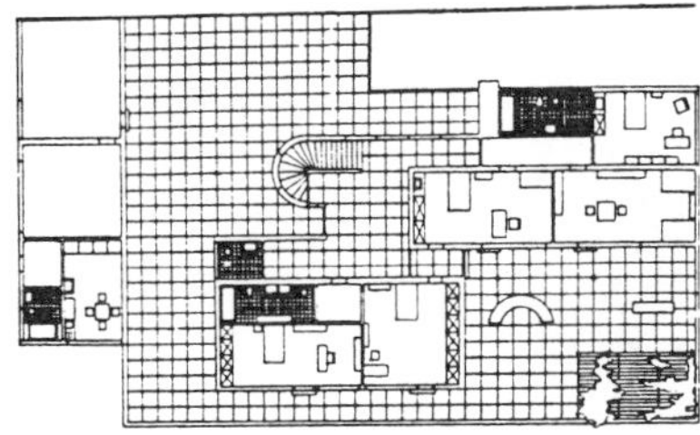

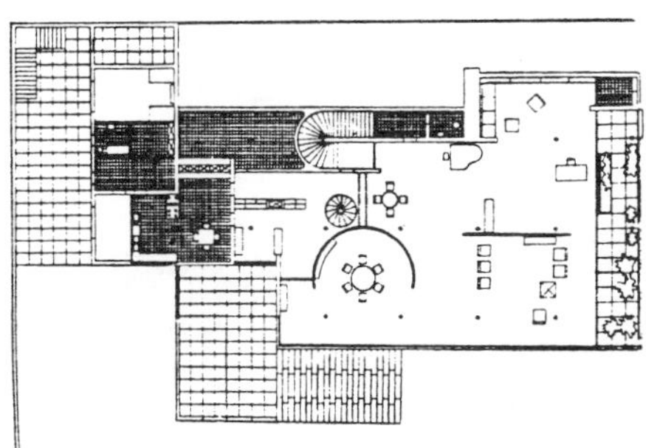

C. Tugendhat House: top, upper ground-floor plan; bottom, roof terrace plan

D. Tugendhat House: staircase

A. Müller House, Prague (1928–30). See p. 1410

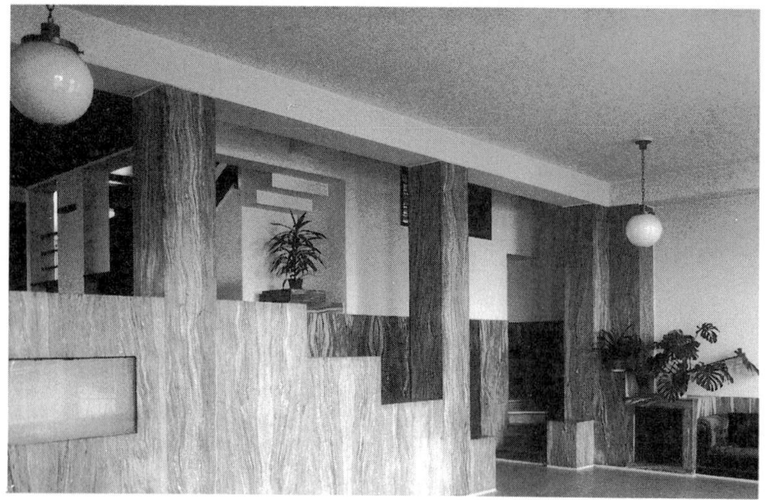

B. Müller House: first-floor reception room

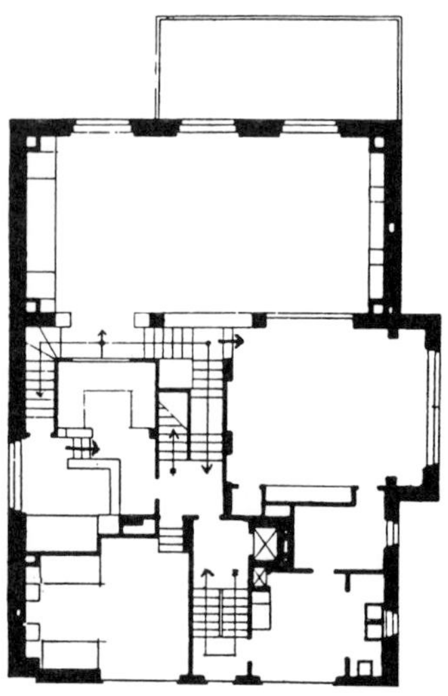

C. Müller House: first-floor plan

A. Bat'a Store, Prague (1928–9). See p. 1410

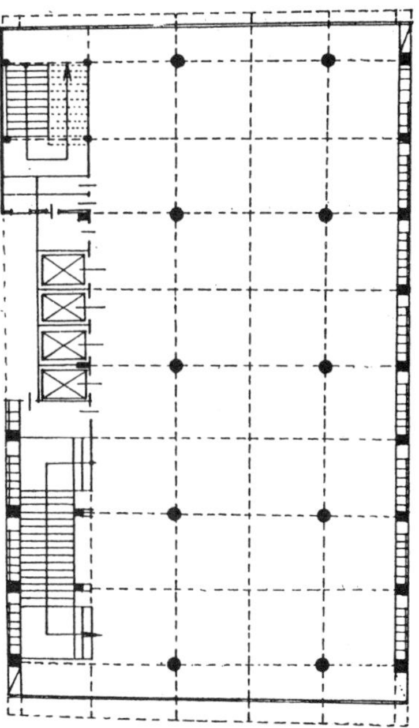

B. Bat'a Store: plan

C. Molnár's villa, Budapest (1932). See p. 1414

opportunities for architects both local and from abroad. The American-based architect Frank Gehry has produced a provocative commercial ensemble on the river in **Prague** nicknamed **'Fred Astaire and Ginger Rogers'.** Examples of a locally designed architecture influenced by Western technology and referred to as 'New Constructivist' or 'Czech Machinism' include the **CSVTS House of Technology, Brno** (1987–91), by Petr Uhlig and Zdenek Muller; the **Mazda Service Centre, Brno** (1993–4), by Jan Chlup, and the innovative use of sheet glass panels fixed to metal frames in the **Ironworks Pavilion, Trinec** (1992), by Kulik and Louda.

Hungary

Hungary developed rapidly after the Compromise of 1867 with Austria. A Settlement drawn up by Ferenc Deak turned the absolutist Austrian Empire into a dual monarchy with Hungary. That year the coronation of Franz Joseph took place in Buda and the city of Budapest (formed from Buda, Pest and Obuda) blossomed as the second capital of the Hapsburg Empire. By the turn of the century it had become the newest European metropolis. Architectural ambitions were strongly influenced by Vienna, Paris and Berlin. Examples of Secessionist design buildings as opposed to the more prevalent local national monumentalism (for example, the **Stock Exchange** of 1885 by Ignac Alpar and the neo-Gothic **Parliament Building** of 1885–1905 by Imre Steindl) were completed in the centre of the city.

The **Gresham Insurance Company building, Pest**, by Quittner and Vago (*c.* 1907) was completed some years later than the pioneering Hungarian Nationalist buildings of Odön Lechner (1845–1914). Lechner was determined to create a local 'Hungarian Style' architecture and therefore cannot be considered a mere Secessionist. He claimed 'Hungarian form did not exist, but it will now'. Lechner's **Post Office Savings Bank** (now offices) (1889–1902), **Geological Institute** (1897–99) and the **Museum of Applied Arts** (1891–96) incorporate unusual decorative elements in order to emphasise the eastern origins of the country and are finished in local non-porous and frostproof polished majolica ceramic facings.

Around the turn of the decade a more 'modern' Hungarian architecture enjoyed a short-lived vogue through the work of various architects including the talented artist and idiosyncratic designer Károly Kós (1883–1977) and Béla Lajta (1875–1920). One of Lechner's most important pupils was Dénes Györgyi (1886–1961) who designed the unusual shaped **Hungarian Pavilion** at the **International Expo, Turin**, in 1911 and some commercial buildings in Budapest before turning to a kind of Dutch Modernism with his **flats on Hanved street, Budapest** (1931) and the **Hungarian Pavilion, Brussels** (1935). Another pupil was Aladár Arkay (1868–1932) whose work shows the clear influence of Frank Lloyd Wright.

Károly Kós' (1883–1977) **Roman Catholic Church, Zebegeny** (1908–9) and various houses show a debt to the English Arts and Crafts tradition. He worked for a time with Aladár Korosfoi-Kriesch (1863–1920), the founder of a significant north **Hungarian Artists' Colony, Gödöllö**. The colony emphasised creativity, rustic living and helped to popularise the native art and crafts. The **Alatkert Pavlilion, Budapest** (1909–10), is a refreshingly witty scheme with an elongated asymmetrical plan and a witch's hat roof.

The two most celebrated Hungarian Modernists of the interwar period were the designer artist Laszlo Moholy-Nagy (1895–1946) and the architect Marcel Breuer (1902–81) who both came to international attention through the German Bauhaus and their later careers in England and the USA. The active Hungarian Modernist group (principally writers and graphic artists) who published the periodical *MA* during the years of World War I were obliged to emigrate after the political failures in Hungary in 1918–19. *MA* published the work of Theo van Doesburg (1883–1931), Jacobus Johannes Pieter Oud (1890–1963) and Vladimir Tatlin (1885–1953).

Farkas Molnár (1897–1945) who also studied at the Bauhaus became the leader of the local Modernists. His early unbuilt project, the **Red Cubist House** (1923), is almost square on plan with semi-circular projections on the ground floor. Roof terraces at both first-floor roof levels are connected with an external staircase. The contrast between the angular and round shapes, the arrangement of volumes and fine though stark detailing is in all his schemes, including the **villas at Lejto Uton, Budapest** (1932) (p. 1413C), and the **bungalow at Nyaralo, Felsogod** (1933), are characteristic of Modern Movement buildings of the early 1930s as is the reinforced concrete **Catholic Church in Budapest-Vavos-Major** by Bertalan Arkay.

Molnár also worked in collaboration with József Fischer (born 1901). Their **Sanatorium, Pestujhely** (1936) (p. 1415A), is a three-storey building on a sloping site. The facades are stark and white, divided into five bays with continuous rows of windows. Load-bearing walls carry reinfoced concrete floors and roofs. József Fischer designed the **Gyopár Hotel, Budapest** (1941) (p. 1415B), and a comparison of these two buildings illustrates the changing attitudes to design within a few years. The three-storey hotel is a curved block, divided segmentally and with an angled balcony to each room. There is an attempt to use contrasting materials in an expressive way.

By the early 1940s the avant-garde was dissipated and artists like Sandor Botnyik promoted a lyrical form of Social Realism. Gradually many of his architectural colleagues followed suit. Significant and

A. Sanatorium, Pestujhely (1936). See p. 1414

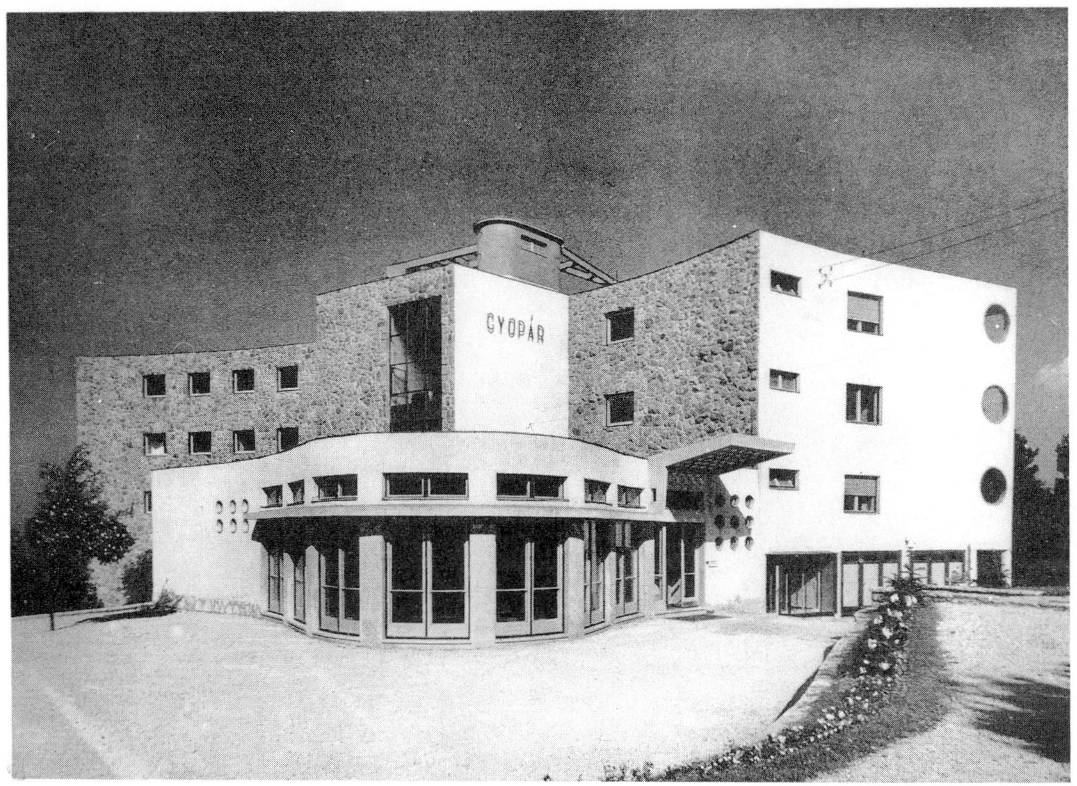

B. Gyopár Hotel, Budapest (1941). See p. 1414

B. (*above*) Lutheran Church, Siofok (1986–9). See p. 1417

C. (*below*) Hungarian Pavilion, 1992 Expo, Seville. See p. 1417

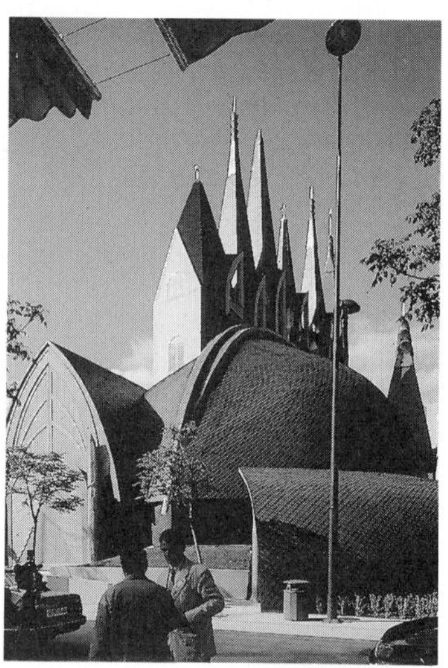

A. Roman Catholic Church, Paks (1989). See p. 1417

sometimes large works were completed during World War II, such as the **Stummer Chocolate Factory, Budapest** (1943), by the Olgyay twins, Aladár (1910–64) and Victor (1910–70) who were to achieve success in the USA in the post-war period with their work on climate controls.

Great changes occurred in Hungary in the 1960s as a direct result of the Soviet-crushed Hungarian Uprising of October 1956. Under the repressive Kádár government parts of Budapest such as Castle Hill were gradually renewed and a number of major historical monuments restored, including the **Elizabeth Bridge** which was rebuilt with American finance. The political policy was introduced partly to appease those who had revolted against the decaying condition of the city but was also an attempt to modernise the country and make it more attractive for foreign investment. Only by the 1980s did the state's influence over architecture, art and design gradually loosen.

In the early 1970s the Pécs Group led by György Csete (born 1937) attempted a reinvention of a native architecture. Inspired by Béla Bartók and Károly Kós, they called their architecture 'organic'. Their **Apartment Blocks, Paks** (1975), were condemned as superficially decorative although they stimulated a national debate on the quality of new housing and on the subject of a 'living', natural or organic architecture inspired by the ideas of Frank Lloyd Wright and Rudolf Streiner. By 1984 the anthopomorphic **Cultural Centre, Sárospatak** by Imre Makovecz (born 1935) was recognised internationally as were many of his other designs. Among Makovecz's best-known works are the traditional **Lutheran Church, Siofok** (1986–9) (p. 1416B), and the dark and amorphous **Roman Catholic Church, Paks** (1989) (p. 1416A). The **Hungarian Pavilion at the 1992 Expo, Seville, Spain** (p. 1416C), with its interpretation of village bell towers and interior composition inspired by the roots and branches of an oak tree, extended Makovecz's organic vocabulary. This pavilion confirmed his position internationally as the leader of the new Hungarian organic architectural movement.

The powerful creative works of Imre Makovecz, the collective practice of Makona, and the cooperative network of 'organic' offices are to be found in the south-west and north-east sectors of Hungary but are largely absent in cosmopolitan Budapest. There the international modes and industrial aesthetics of Post-Modernism, Neo-Functionalism and other directions characteristic of the early 1990s quickly appeared under the new political situation. Already the large-scale 'International' hotels along the Danube make Budapest look like any other European capital. The best, the darkly coloured **Forum Hotel** (1979–81), was conceived in 1970 by József Finta and others as 'a window to the Danube'. More challenging but less memorable is the **Hilton Hotel** on the crest of **Castle Hill** incorporating parts of the 1250 Dominican monastery. The **new International Trade Centre** by Finta (1989) occupies a prominent site near S. Stephen's Basilica (1851–1905).

Poland

Modern Poland emerged in 1919 after the Treaty of Versailles but its boundaries have changed significantly since and it has been subject to intense foreign pressure – first from Germany and then from the Soviet Union. This political domination has had cultural consequences, not least of which is the fact that many variations of twentieth-century architecture can now be seen in Poland.

In the former German area of what is now Western Poland there took place some of the the most important developments in early twentieth-century Modern architecture. In Wroclaw (formerly Breslau) the work of architects Hans Poelzig (1869–1936), Max Berg (1870–1947) and Hans Scharoun (1893–1972) is particularly significant. Berg was City architect and designed the spectacular and innovative **Jahrhunderthalle** (1912–13) (p. 1418A) and other buildings for the City's Centennial Exposition. The great memorial Hall, which was not completed until 1925, was designed as part of a much larger exhibition by Berg and Poelzig. It was the largest reinforced concrete structure erected anywhere in the world at that time – a huge dome rising from a cruciform plan with dramatic arches and ribs and a cupola larger than S. Peter's in Rome.

Poelzig had an office in the city from 1899 to 1916 and was Director of the Academy there from 1903 to 1916. He constructed a celebrated curved and striated office building for **Steiner and Son** (1911) that presages Mendelsohn's later store buildings in Germany. The estate of houses built in Wroclaw under the auspices of the Deutscher Werkbund gave it a residue of Modern Movement monuments. However, it is Poelzig's remarkable **Water Tower, Poznan** (formerly Posen) (1911), that shows his inventive and individualistic expressionist work at its best. This building exploited a multitude of uses, including exhibition hall and restaurant as well as water store, and it was perceived as a totemic *Gesamtkunstwerk*. Hans Scharoun, who was a professor at the Akademie fur Kunst and Kunstgewerbe in Wroclaw from 1925 to 1932, designed the fine **Apartment Block for the Werkbund Exhibition** (1929).

The **'Kaiserhaus', Poznan** (1905–10), by Franz Schwechten (1841–1924), is a vast structure which used to serve mainly as the residence of Emperor Wilhelm II when he visited the Prussian regional capital, Posen. This is one of the largest buildings in the neo-Romanesque style, which to Wilhelmine Germany carried associations of German power and

A. Jahrhunderthalle, Wroclaw (1912–13). See p. 1417

B. Three-family Terrace House, Warsaw (1928–9). See p. 1419

was linked with the Hohenstaufen Emperors around 1200. It is now used as a museum.

Among Polish *Jugendstil* buildings from around 1900 the following suggest how varied the basis of interpretation was: **The Stary Theatre, Krakow** (1903–6), by Franciszek Maczynski and Tadeusz Stryjenshi; **The Cooperative Bank, Warsaw** (1912), by J. Heurich, and **The Polski Theatre, Warsaw** (1912), by Czeslaw Przybylski.

In Poland after 1919 architecture was dominated by the first post-war generations of architects who had trained in the Architecture Department of the Warsaw Technical University. However, the older classically trained generation was responsible for a variety of buildings in the neo-Classical idiom during the inter-war years. **The Ministry of Education, Warsaw** (1927–30), by Zdzislaw Maczenski is a good example of monumental Classicism while the **Narodowa library, Warsaw** (1926), by Jan Withiewicz reflects the more modern stripped Classical tradition. Other versions of neo-Classicism are represented by the **Naradowa Museum, Krakow** (1936–9), by Boleslaw Szmidt, Janusz Juraszynski and Juliusz Dumnicki, and **Gmnach Sadow, Warsaw** (1935–9), by Bohdan Priewski.

Warsaw itself had resumed its role of capital city after 1919 and here relatively small but vociferous avant-garde radical Modern groups soon grew up. Constructivism, Art Deco, the Dutch De Stijl work and the Bauhaus all had their own special appeal in the mid-1920s and architects' projects were undoubtedly influenced by these sources. The exuberant, highly ornamented and fully glazed **Polish Pavilion at the 1925 Paris World Exposition** by Jozef Czajkowski is an example of the established links within the international decorative art trends of that time. His Modernist **Warsaw House** (1932) was clearly derived from the group of Masters' homes designed by Walter Gropius at the Bauhaus, Dessau in the mid-1920s.

A more distinctive modern local and indigenous tradition slowly developed. Initially it was largely drawn from the various synthetic art groups in Warsaw and the graduates and students of the Department of Architecture at Warsaw Technical University who were sharing the ambitions of the '*Preasens*' Group, and Modernist stalwarts such as Bohdan Lachert (1900–87), Helena Syrkns (1900–82) and Szymon Syrkus (1893–1967), Josef Szanajca and Barbara Brukalska (1899–1980) and Stanislaw Brukalski (1894–1967).

The *Praesens* group played a pioneering role in the development of modern architecture in Poland. Examples by its members included a **Three-family Terrace House, Warsaw** (1928–9) (p. 1418B), by Bohdan Lachert and Josef Szanajca.The three-storey rectangular block and each unit have a two-bay, 7 m (23 ft) frontage.The most consistent application of Le Corbusier's 'five points' are to be found in the **house designs** of Juliusz Zorawski at **3 Przyjaciol Avenue, Warsaw** (1938), and **34/6 Mickiewicza Street, Warsaw** (1937–9).

An early example of the work of Helena and Szymon Syrkus is the **Sanatorium, Warsaw** (1931) (p. 1420A), a single-storey steel-framed building. Their best-known project of the post-war period is the housing Development carried out for the **Warsaw Housing Cooperative, Kolo, Warsaw** (1947–52).

From 1927 a link with Le Corbusier was established through Szymon Syrkus and Josef Szanajca. Eventually the Polish group had a strong representation within CIAM. Its members participated in all the main meetings and showed work like the **Zoliborz WSM Estate** by the Brukaski's and Zborowski at the second CIAM Congress in Frankfurt am Main in 1929.

The influence of CIAM, and in particular of Le Corbusier, can be seen in a number of domestic commissions in Poland including the villa at **No. 9–10 Katowicka Street, Warsaw** (1928), by Lachert and Szanajca, **No. 5 Uzdrowiskowa Street, Konstancin** (1932), by the Syrkus's and **No. 12 Walecznych, Warsaw** (1900), and Brukalski's own **villa at No. 8 Niegolewskiego Street, Warsaw** (1927–9).

A good example of more local monumental Modernism with a Classical touch can be found in the impressive **Central Institute of Physical Education, Warsaw** (1928–9), designed by the Moscow-trained architect Edgar Norwerth. Here is an inventive combination of stripped Russian Classicism and Constructivist elements. Similar inventiveness in the design of public buildings can be seen in the **College of Commerce Library, Warsaw** (1928–30) (p. 1420B), designed by Jan Koszczyc-Witkiewicz but this time with a well-articulated series of generously glazed facades and a huge pyramidical reading room. **Kósciól Parafialny Zbawiciela, Warsaw** (1910–11), by Jósef Pius Dziekonski and others, is an important landmark in the regular street layout of this part of Warsaw. In its plan and decoration it mixes elements of the Baroque with those of the Polish Middle Ages and Polish Renaissance.

Oskar Sosnowski's (1880–1939) **Kósciól Niepokolanego Poczecia NMP, Parafia S.W. Jakuba, Warsaw** (1909–23), is an early work of one of the most outstanding designers of the inter-war period. It combines external brickwork of primeval roughness, usually associated with primitive early Polish Romanesque with complex Baroque internal spaces.

Due to the exodus of prominent Poles to create a provisional government in London after the Nazi invasion a Polish School of Architecture was established in Liverpool University (later transferred to London University). It was founded by its first head Boleslaw Szmidt (1908–95) a prominent architect in pre-war Poland and responsible for the **PKO Bank**

A. Sanatorium, Warsaw (1931). See p. 1419

B. (*left*) College of Commerce Library, Warsaw (1928–30). See p. 1419

C. (*above*) Seminary of the Resurrection Brothers, Krakow (1984–93). See p. 1421

(now demolished) on **Marszalkowska Street, Warsaw** (*c.* 1934). The school made a significant contribution to post-war architectural thinking in Poland, particularly in relation to housing. Oskar Hansen (born 1922), a member of Team X, carried out **housing estates** in **Slovacki, Lublin** (1960–62), that share some of the goals of English architects of that time.

After the war and throughout the country – particularly in the historic centres of cities such as Warsaw, Gdansk, Wroclaw, Krakow and Poznan – a concerted effort to reconstruct old buildings and even whole environments along historic lines was carried out. Scholarly investigations leading to precise conservation and restoration principles were followed and new buildings were inserted into city centres by adopting old forms for new uses.

The most significant post-war national initiative was the reconstruction of the **Old Town of Warsaw**. From a social, psychological, symbolic and a practical point of view the reconstruction united the nation. Work began in 1948. **The Market Place** area was completed in July 1953, under the direction of Mieczyslaw Kuzma. The detailed restoration of the Old City was completed in 1957 aided by many local architects and planners working for the city authorities. Fortunately, the Old Town had been effectively surveyed in the pre-war period by architectural students and it proved possible to relate this material to the outline ground plans which survived the total destruction of the area by the Nazis in 1944–5.

A spectacular but a less than popular intrusion into Warsaw in the immediate post-war period was the unpopular 'gift' from the former Soviet Union of a gigantic Stalinist '**People's Palace of Culture**' designed by Soviet state architects. Efforts were made by Modernist architects and planners in a national competition (1958) to obscure its visual domination of a vast area of the city through the introduction of a large new development (from 1962) of shops, apartments and offices to the eastern side of the **Marszalkowska Street**. The competition was won by Zbigniew Karpinski (1906–83) and a team which was dedicated to the furtherance of modern design (based on Western precedents) through experimental housing types and furnishings for the apartments.

After 1955 an emphasis on the industrialisation and mechanisation of construction began throughout the Communist bloc. This was begun as a direct result of Soviet Party Congress directives in which Khrushchev demanded that the academic, sentimental and decorative type of architecture should be replaced by a scientifically based approach to building. Inevitably in the Soviet world this meant heavy concrete industrialised units spread out in serrated rows with little landscaping between the blocks. Such developments (for example, the Warsaw development in **Sluzewiec** by Wlodzimierz Minich and Irena Stolarska with the **Housing estate, Sady Zoliborskie** (1958–62), by Halina Skibniewska) soon came under vigorous attack by Polish architects for their lack of humanity, trees and urbanity as well as bad planning and inhuman scale.The Poles described it later in the 1970s as development with 'a lack of socio-economic and spatial aspects'.

The renewal of transport buildings in the post-war period was more succesful (for example, the **Warsaw City Underground Station** (1963) designed by Jerzy Soltan and Zbigniew Ihnatowicz).

The new development plan for the Warsaw conglomeration, the **Warsaw Metropolitan Voivodship**, (1978), prepared under the architect planner Tadeusz Szumielewicz and his team, was intended to provide a basic model for the local authorities throughout the country. It coincided with the growth of the Solidarity Movement's revolutionary demand for freedom and autonomy. Within *Solidarnosc* radical architects demanded a voice and grew articulate about their interests in community architecture and settlements as well as ecology and green politics (disallowed in Poland). The radical viewpoints were gradually given a wider platform and Polish architects were introduced to Post-Modernism (which caught on fitfully in the years after 1980) and regional Modernist ideas. These developments incorporated a greater creative freedom for architects as individual designers largely through the numerous ecclesiastical buildings that were being erected throughout the country, in the wake of *Solidarnosc*. Somewhat paradoxically, churches represented the most interesting trend in contemporary architecture. Above all, they were not restricted by technical rules or bureaucratic procedures.

These new churches reveal an almost bewildering number of original concepts and mixtures of styles. The list of churches is enormous and ranges from the huge structural adventure of Andrej Fajan's **church, Kalisz** (1957–90), the concave roofed **church at Nowa Huta-Bienczyce,** (1967–77), by Wojciech Pietrzyk and Jan Grabaki, to the hall-like **church in Nowe Tychy** designed by Stanislaw Niemczyk (born 1943), to more bizarre excursions into a fragmented Post-Modernism as in the **Seminary of the Resurrection Brothers, Krakow** (1984–93) (p. 1420C), by Dariusz Kozlowski (born 1924) and Waclaw Stefanski's (born 1920) which has an ingeniously arranged courtyard elevation. Other churches of note include: the **church in Rudi Rysie** (1965) by Tadeusz Gawlowski and Jan Grabacki, the **church in Krakow** (1978–88) by R. Loegler and J. Czekaj, the **church in Oloza, Zakopane** (1985), by T. Gawlowski, the **church in Poznan-Winogrady** (1979–85) by J. Buszkiewicz and J. Kopydlowski and the **church in Pozan-Rataje** (1979–95) by B. and M. Eibl, S. Solryk and W. Pienkowski.

Other worthwhile schemes started before the demise of Communism in 1989 include the restoration of the old city of Elblag (begun 1980) by

R. Semka and Szczepan Baum and Associates, and the business/tourist **Forum Hotel, Krakow** (1988), designed by Janusz Ingarden. Immediate post-1989 buildings of interest include the **Centre Plaza, Warsaw**, by R. Welder and M. Karpowicz, the **Sobieski Hotel, Warsaw**, by N. Triessnig and K. Picotini and the new international **Airport Terminal Two, Warsaw**, all completed in 1992.

Bulgaria

Bulgarian independence in 1878 stimulated a search for an architecture that demonstrated national or supposedly national character, and which would help give to the new nation a distinct and stable character. The product of this quest is characterised by the combination of the type of eclectic ornamentation found in much of contemporary Europe, especially those countries heavily influenced by Art Nouveau, with multi-coloured ceramic facades, large timber roofs and other details, forms and materials inspired by indigenous traditions.

The early attempts at the development at a national style range, in the deeply multi-cultured city of Sofia, from the Neo-Byzantine, or so-called 'orthodox', forms of the **Church of the Holy Synod** (1910) by Petko Momchilov and Jordan Milanov, and Memchilov's well-articulated neo-Byzantine **Public Mineral Baths** (1910–11) to the industrially engineered but still ornamented **Covered Market** (1910) by N. Torbov and the almost Islamic roof shapes of the **Railway Station, Burgas** (1906), by N. Kostov and K. Marichkov. However, the most ambitious and certainly the most architecturally unified example of the nationalistic orthodoxy is the huge **Cathedral of S. Alexander Nevsky** (1904–12) designed by N. Pomerantzev after the death of Bogomilov.

A transitional example of the move from the eclectic Art Nouveau decorative treatment to a more restrained modern Classicism is represented by the **Odeon Hotel, Sofia** (1923), by P. Kantardzhiev. Kantardzhiev's major project for a **Children's Rehabilitation Centre, Varna** (1935), although symmetrical in plan, is a thoroughly modern essay in the Soviet Constructivist manner.

During the interwar period International Modernism exerted a strong influence on architectural attitudes in Bulgaria. The **Municipal Building, Burgas** (1927–49), by Georgi Ovcharov is a six-storey cubic building with a central atrium glazed at the top. Both exterior and interior feature simple elongated columns reflecting the Classical origins of this rational building.

But while Le Corbusier's ideas dominated the Modernist attitudes of other Balkan states, the influence of Erich Mendelsohn (1887–1953) was of greater significance in Bulgaria. Although he never found work in the country, a number of examples of apartment blocks carried out in the Mendelsohn idiom were executed in Bulgaria, principally in Sofia. These include an **office building, Moskovska Street, Sofia** (1929), by Konstantine Gechev and Peter Karasimeonov, and the **twin apartment blocks, Sofia** (1938–9), by Radoslav Radoslavov and Konstantine Dznagozov. There are also a number of commercial buildings characterised by Mendelsohn's striated glass and concrete facade treatment, particularly the inventive **Bulgaria Hotel** (1935) by Stancho Belkovski and Ivan Danchev, which incorporates a system of automatically controlled huge opening windows, and the **Slayanska Beseda Hotel, Sofia** (1935), by A. Mikhailovsky. A **block of flats, Sofia** (1935), by C. Berberov is another fine example of the Functionalist type of reinforced concrete building that dominated apartment design in the 1930s while the **Bulgarian National Bank** (1934–9), by Ivan Vassilyov and Dimiter Tsolov, shows a mature mastery of conservation techniques in the way it attaches itself to the ancient building of the **Koursham Mosque** (now the Archaelogical Museum). The bank combines Classical simplicity with elegant modern design, with the bank hall clearly expressed on the facade. A similar approach is to be found in the **Ministry of Internal Affairs, Sofia** (1936–40), by G. Ovcharov.

From the end of World War II Bulgarian architecture was dominated by the heavy buildings derived from an ideologically based Socialist Realist aesthetic. Bulgaria of all the Eastern countries remained closely aligned with Moscow during the whole of the Communist period, and thus closely followed Soviet policy.

With the Soviet satellites' growing dependence on Moscow and the increasing Soviet demands for the industrialisation of mass housing, Bulgaria witnessed a proliferation of horrendous housing estates constructed from heavy-framed prefabricated concrete units. Many of these 'communities' were produced without any real consideration for urban design and the spaces and landscaping between the blocks. They produced a repetitive and tedious architecture of soulless parallel blocks built on the theoretical foundations of what one commentator has called an 'architecture national in form and socialist in content'.

Towards the end of the 1950s a desire emerged among architects for a more creative fusion of national traditions with socialist architectural principles. Nationalism was seen as an important part of a cultural renewal process. Many architects were trained in Moscow, some as 'architect/sculptors of monuments' but most as state-employed assistant architects. As in neighbouring Romania, this meant that buildings were, on the whole, the anonymous products of state offices. Only a few schemes were individually signed. These include the sculptural **state monuments** designed by the architect Georgi

Stoilov (born 1929) at **Tolbuhin** (1964), an ambitious **Memorial House, Bouzloudja Mountain Peak** (1981), based on Thracian burial mounds, and memorials at **Gurgulyat** (1985) and **Varese** (1991).

During the1980s Western Post-Modernist theories about context and the use of historic detail were absorbed and led to such buildings as the **hotel, Veliko Tyrnova** (1981–3), by Nikola Nikolov and the **Cultural Centre, Byala Slatina** (1977–83), by Todor Khadzhistoichev and Elka Ribarova. Around the same time the Japanese architect Kisho Kurokawa won a competition to design the **new city hall, Sofia** (1983), which was not realised although his central hotel, the **Vitosha** (1980–81), was built.

Since the end of Communism in Bulgaria a gradual revitalisation of the existing building fabric of Sofia has been undertaken, often with the insertion of new shop units and offices. Overall the country has experienced great difficulties in coming to terms with the transfer to free market conditions. The forlorn Communist era peoples' housing estates which ring many Bulgarian cities have not changed much since independence, although a number of more thoughtful architects and planners are trying to lessen their leaden influence on the environment The creation of smaller units between blocks and landscaping and planting in some areas is gradually improving some of the housing stock. Much of the new investment in post-Communist building has been in renovation and rehabilitation work with new hotels and touristic buildings going up in the Black Sea resorts and in the ski centres in the mountain areas.

Romania

At the turn of the century the city of Bucharest exhibited an eclectic mix of contemporary building styles ranging from Classicist temple-like structures and *fin-de-siècle* confections to the ornamented apartment blocks of the Belle Epoque with their wrought iron balconies and filigree lift shafts. Examples include the old **Post Office Building** (now the Museum of History), **Bucharest** (1900), by Alexander Savulescu and again in the Belle-Epoque manner, the **Cantacuzino Palace, Bucharest** (1907), by D. Berindei (1871–1928), who was also responsible for the vast **Palace of Culture in Iasi** (1890–1906).The imposing **Chrissoveloni Bank** (now the State Bank), **Bucharest** (1928–30), is by the Beaux Arts-trained Gheorghe Matei Cantacuzino (1899–1960). In a later move towards Modernism Cantacuzino designed the **Romanian Pavilion, New York World Fair** (1939). He also designed two distinguished hotels, the **International Hotel, Mamaia** (1939), and **Hotel Belona, Eforie** (1940). The architect Octav Doicescu (1902–80), who specialised in modern industrial building, also designed the **Nautical Club, Snagov, Bucharest** (1934). Grigore Ionescu (born 1904) produced a number of fine Modernist buildings, including the **TB Sanatoria, Covasna** (1936), the **Emilia Institute for Pedriatrics** (1950) and the **Transport Engineering Institute** (1960), both in **Bucharest**.

From 1975 expansion and new building was to be concentrated in the central perimeter of the capital and the city's historic core restored. Other cities were considered for historic preservation including **Timisoara, Banat, Arad** and **Ploiesti**.

The Urban and Rural Systemisation Act of 1974 cleared the way for the wholesale destruction of cities and towns throughout Romania, although much urban systemisation preceded the Act by 10 years. Under the repressive dictatorship of President Ceausescu, the country's rich architectural and cultural heritage was gradually destroyed. Under this law over 80 per cent of all Romanian villages were to be demolished by the year 2000 to be replaced by 'Agro-industrial centres' with standardised state housing for the peasants. By the time Ceausescu fell in 1989 this policy, which had begun in rural areas, had not caught hold. However, over 60 towns had been or were about to be 'restructured' before his demise, including Suceara and Piatra Neami.

This destructive renewal left Romania in shock. In Bucharest much of interest was destroyed and little of interest created. The huge and hideous **Presidential Palace** (1989) set on a 2-mile 100 m (307 ft) wide boulevard that virtually bankrupted the nation survived Ceausescu's downfall and has now been opened to the public as an uncomfortable reminder of past ambitions.

Unfortunately the reconstruction and development of Bucharest since 1989 has produced no architecture of distinction. Exceptions are to be found in the expanding and potential tourist centres like Mamaia on the Black Sea and Brasov in the Transylvanian Mountains, but the work there does not reach the standard of the earlier architects such as Marcel and Julia Lancu, who built modern houses in Bucharest, for example the **Reich House** (1936), as well as a fine and distinctive **Sanatorium, Predeal** (1936).

A few reminders of Romania's prominent position in twentieth-century art and architecture circles remain. Constantin Brancusi's (1876–1957) 33 m (107 ft) high cast iron ***Endless Column*** and ***Table of Silence***, architectural sculptures from 1937, still exist in a public park near the town of Tirju-Jui, together with the **Gate of the Kiss**, benches and stools.

Former Yugoslavia

The Federal People's Republic of Yugoslavia was formally dismantled in 1989. This Communistic version of the older united Kingdom of Yugoslavia of

1918 was created at the end of World War II. It proved an uncertain alliance. Today in some of the regions that made up the People's Republic (particularly in Croatia and Bosnia-Hercegovina) a number of the major public and private buildings have been destroyed or damaged by the civil strife that has occurred subsequently.

The main cities of each of the old Republics, particularly the Serbian capital city Belgrade, the Croatian capital city Zagreb and the Slovenian capital Lubljana as well as the two major coastal cities of Split and Dubrovnik in Dalmatia (a district of Croatia), have been flourishing and independent centres of architectural thought and endeavour.

During the early part of this century the incorporation of strong local and regional characteristics were important factors in the development of the distinct environmental character of the regions and their strong urban architecture. The regions were often regarded as virtually autonomous places with the leading cities striving to be as sophisticated and progressive as the most advanced European urban centres.

After the creation of Marshall Tito's Federal Republic in 1945, which was often viewed by the West as the most open and enlightened of all the Communist states, a sense of uniformity crept into the region's architecture through the operation of the newly founded Republic Construction Design Institutes. These were set up throughout the Republic and spearheaded an ambitious national housing programme, drawing on the experience of British New Towns and on French models. These institutes also encouraged the efficient design of new factory units in a programme of rapid industrialisation, and oversaw an equally large programme of educational, commercial and archival buildings.

The pre-1945 architecture of former Yugoslavia can best be discussed within the context of the areas ancient regional boundaries which, to a large degree, reflect the post-1989 national boundaries.

Slovenia

The most important twentieth-century work here was produced by the Viennese-trained Jože Plečnik (1872–1957). After many years working in Prague Plečnik returned to his native city of Ljubljana in 1922. His principal Slovene buildings designed while based in Ljubljana include the **Chamber of Commerce, Crafts and Industry, Ljubljana**, which he restored and embellished, notably with a magnificent staircase (1924–7); a number of churches including the **Church of the Ascension, Bogojina** (1925–7), which Plečnik designed in a vernacular, almost Romanesque, idiom with internal arcades of primitive and squat Doric columns, a pitched roof and asymmetrically placed bellcote; **S. Francis, Siska, Ljubljana** (1925–31), a striking cubical building with a Doric colonnade defining a rectangular space within the building, and **S. Anthony of Padua, Belgrade** (1929–32), with a cylindrical central volume furnished with a ring of horse-shoe-shaped chapels set in the thickness of the wall. Other projects by Plečnik include the **National and University Library, Ljubljana** (1936–41), with a striking entrance elevation embellished by a single giant primitive Ionic column set against glazing and a monumental internal corridor and staircase; the **School of the Ursuline Nuns, Ljubljana** (1940–41), with a facade formed by tiers of lunettes, and the remarkable, monumentally arched **City of the Dead, Zale Cemetary, Ljubljana** (1938–40). Plečnik was also an urban planner keen on beautifying his native city, for which he produced a **masterplan** in 1928. He also designed a number of individual commercial and residential buildings in Ljubljana including the **Flat Iron Building** (1933–4), which is a powerful, extruded, Classical composition with an arcaded ground floor and a second-floor corner loggia. In 1930 Plečnik was invited to carry out a considerable amount of work on the **terraces on the banks of the river Ljubljanica** (1930–9). He also designed the ingenious Classical **Trnovo bridge over the Gradascica.**

Serbia

Here a series of designs were evolved between 1912 and 1930 for the reshaping of historic Belgrade. The 1912 Masterplan by Alban Chambon suggested a strict Classical layout and drew on Italian urban examples. It was followed by a more fluid Masterplan for the city by Rudolf Perco, Erwin Bock and Erwin Ilz. The Belgrade of the pre-war period, however, owes much more to the planning recommendations incorporated into Nikola Dubrovic's (1897–1967) award-winning urban design scheme of 1930 for the **Terazije Terrace**. It recommended the revitalisation of the whole area in a contemporary manner without the loss of historic character.

Dubrovic's own architectural work was in the Modern spirit, for example the **Grand Hotel Lopud, Dubrovnik** (1934–6), and reflected some of the principles promoted by the pro-Modern Zenit Group in Belgrade. This group, founded in the early 1920s, promoted its enthusiasm for Constructivism through the magazine *Zenit*, published in Belgrade and then Zagreb. The aesthetic of Modernism was interpreted freely in the region but a specifically Modern Movement idiom developed in Belgrade for flats, housing and commercial buildings. Milan Zlokovic (1898–1965) was a major influence during the 1920s and 1930s with his most important projects being the **Children's University Clinic, Belgrade** (1933), and his **own house, Belgrade** (1927). Zlokovic also designed the **Opel Building, Belgrade** (1930–31), the **Zica Hotel, Mataruska Banja** (1930–32), and the **Jugo-auto Building, Belgrade** (1939). In the early 1920s after a period of nationalistic classicism there was a move towards Constructivism with the formation of an avant-garde group supported by the magazine *Zenit* which was published between 1921 and 1926.

Dragisa Brasovan (1887–1965) also produced distinguished work, notably the **Yugoslav Pavilion at the Barcelona Exhibition** (1929), **the State Printing Works, Belgrade** (1933–40), the **Chamber of Commerce, Belgrade** (1939) and the **Ministry of War Air Traffic, Belgrade** (1929). Branislav Kojic (1899–1987) was also a member of the avant-garde group with his work including the **villa Djuric, Belgrade** (1933).

The Serbian Romantic – a late flowering of Expressionism which flourished between the wars – is exemplified by the work of Momir Korunovic (1883–1969) such as **Sokolski Dom-matica, Belgrade** (1929), and **Sokolana, Kumanovo** (1931).

The onslaught on Belgrade's character occurred between 1960 and 1975 when large-scale town planning activities (initially along the idealistic functionalist lines of Le Corbusier's *Plan Voisin* and *Ville Radieuse*) commenced and new settlements were constructed around Belgrade including **New Belgrade, Upper Zemun** and **Dorcol**. These new suburbs proved unpopular with the public and came in for harsh criticism at the time – criticism that eventually brought down the functionalist cause in city planning and architecture.

From 1979 to 1984 a bold new model strategy of urban design and architecture was developed by the City of Belgrade Institute for Development Planning under the architect planner Milos Perovic. Some of its recommendations have been followed and implemented in various areas within the city. As a consequence of this integrative approach there have been fewer importations of 'foreign' ideas of the type that have dominated design in other East European countries.

The aesthetic of Modernism was interpreted freely but a specific Modern Movement idiom developed in Belgrade for flats, housing blocks and offices. Milan Zlokovic (1898–1965) influenced much of this work and his own most important projects include the **Children's University Clinic, Belgrade** (1933), and his **own house, Belgrade** (1927). He also built the **Opel Building, Belgrade** (1930–31).

Croatia

The historic core of Zagreb escaped large-scale redevelopment over much of this century In the late 1920s and the 1930s most new building in the city reflected the simple cubic shapes of Modern architecture. Some fine examples of individual designs of this period include the **Villa Klaic** (1931–2) by Zlatko Neumann (1900–1969), the **Villa Meixner** (1933) by Alfred Albini (1896–1978) and the **Villa Deutsch** (1937) by Frane Cota (1898–1951). Low-cost **housing and apartment houses** in the same idiom include the **Glogoljin Brijeg colony** (1927–8) by Edo Miklos-Schreiner, **apartment buildings, Zagreb** (from 1934), by Slavko Loewy (born 1904) and an **apartment block with shops and restaurant** (1931–2) by Aleksandar Freundenreich (1892–1974) and Zvonimir Pozgaj (1900–71).

Although Zagreb has not suffered dramatic redevelopment this century the city's outer edges were drastically changed after World War II. Plans were made for Zagreb which, as in Belgrade, envisaged new areas of the city based on Le Corbusier's *Ville Radieuse*. A new **urban centre**, with large rectangular blocks set in a parkland, was designed by Bozidar Rasica (born 1912), a new **University Centre and Campus** (*c.* 1954) was designed by the architects Josip Seissel (born 1904), Dragan Boltar and Bruno Milic (born 1917) to accommodate 12000 students. The **suburb of Trngko** was developed as one of three major housing projects in the early 1960s.

In the centre of Zagreb the **Town Hall** with a courtyard plan (completed 1964) was designed by Kasimir Ostrogovic (1907–65) and the nearby **Concert Hall** (1960–73), greatly influenced by the Royal Festival Hall, London (1951), was designed by Marijan Haberle (1908–79). Also in Zagreb the **Mosa Pijade Workers' Education Centre** (1955–61) by Radovan Niksic (born 1920) and Ninoslav Kucan (born 1940) employs some of the functionalist ideas about zoning from the inter-war period with high and low blocks defining various uses.

Mausolea and public monuments by architect, artist and former mayor of Belgrade, Bogdan Bogdanovic (born 1922) show an idiosyncratic approach to the design of such specialist memorials. One of his first major designs was the monument to the **Jewish Victims of Fascism in Belgrade** (1952). Bogdanovic's later monuments can be found in other parts of former Yugoslavia, including Mostar, where he created an open spatial **'acro-necroplis'** (1965). This was followed by further symbolic archetypes including the Ledoux-inspired **liberty memorial, Ivangrad** (1977), the conical shaped towers for the **Vukovar Mausoleum** (1980) and the **Warrior's Mausoleum at Popina** (1981). Bogdanovic was also the consultant for the regionally inspired multi-domed glass-faced **National and University Library, Kosovo, Pristina** (1982), designed by a team led by Andrija Mutnjakovic.

The multi-cultural and ethnic mix of countries within former Yugoslavia can be seen in a rich variety of architectural projects that stress the continuity of traditional systems. For example, in the conservation of the entire sixteenth-century **Centre of Mostar Old Town** (1978), now badly damaged, and of the **Sherefudin's White Mosque, Fisoko, Bosnia** (1980), the design extends the architectural vocabulary of the Islamic mosque into the twentieth century. Recently, **churches in Dubrovnik, Croatia**, designed by Ivan Prtenjakin, particularly **S. Peter's, Boninovo** (1977–80), demonstrate a fresh forward-looking attitude to ecclesiastical design.

Chapter 47

RUSSIA AND THE SOVIET UNION

Introduction

Russia started the twentieth century as a single continental Empire, administratively unified but of enormous diversity in its cultural and religious traditions and in levels of economic and technological development. There were brief periods after the Bolshevik Revolution of 1917, and just before World War II, when parts of this empire enjoyed temporary independence, but for most of the period after the Bolshevik takeover was complete, those territories continued to form a single empire as the Union of Soviet Socialist Republics, formed in December 1922.

Half a century later during the 1970s and 1980s there were increasing assertions of cultural individuality in non-Russian republics of the Central Asian and Baltic periphery where strong local talent and traditions had been trampled on. Distinctive reassertions of regionalism emerged in precisely those territories which later led the political movement for national self-determination and a dissolution of the monolithic Soviet Union. Indeed architecture was a clear if modest harbinger of that political fragmentation through which the territory now comprises a number of distinct countries again for the first time in several centuries.

Being by its nature the public statement of a client's beliefs and status, archiecture has directly reflected the tensions between central power and local aspirations throughout this whole period, and the differing levels of freedom for individual building initiatives. At the same time the need to define a cultural and political identity relative to Europe and the USA has overlaid these internal tensions with outward-looking ones, between the indigenous and the international. In each phase of the twentieth century there was much in Russian and Soviet architecture that is superficially similar to contemporaneous Western work but the elements were being used in different ways and for internal social or ideological purposes.

With the economic chaos that attended political collapse after December 1991, distinctive national approaches have yet to emerge as the new countries resolve issues of their own relationships to international capital in one direction and their own ethical and cultural traditions in the other. Throughout the Soviet period, limitations on freedom to build, on economic resources and on technical skills available have meant that most architecture was shoddy and lacking rigour by Western standards. In this context, small gestures and unavoidably somewhat compromised works create a canon that must be judged with a certain relativism.

Imperial Russian Architecture

At the turn of the century the Russian Empire was in the middle of an economic boom led by rapid industrialisation. By European standards this modernisation started very late, held back, like so much in Russia, by rigid social and economic structures of an increasingly sclerotic autocracy. In the 1890s fortunes were made in heavy industry, minerals, railways and textiles but from 1900 to World War I it was consumer-goods industries that led the growth. Their markets were the expanding middle and professional classes who were a new phenomenon in Russia. The needs and social concerns of this new stratum led to the introduction of entirely new building types that were as original and unprecedented in the Russian context as the more commonly discussed 'new types' for the socialist society of the Soviet period.

Urban housing stock in Russia had historically consisted of more or less Classicised rectangular boxes, graded by size according to the owner's wealth and status in the strict Imperial 'Table of Ranks'. The new class of industrial magnates who emerged during the 1890s with a new vision of Russia as democratic and meritocratic were outside this rank system and despised it. By 1900 they were self-confidently commissioning individually designed grand villas as public statements of their autonomous power. Moscow was their centre and their main architect was Fedor Shekhtel (1859–1926). His exquisite **Riabushinsky villa, Moscow** (1900–2) (p. 1428A,B), for a member of the liberal banking and newspaper-

A. Riabushinsky villa, Moscow (1900–2): photo of 1902. See p. 1427

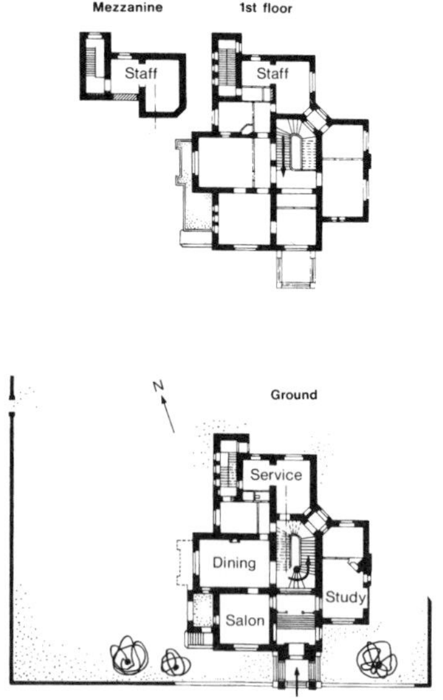

B. Riabushinsky villa: plans

C. Polovtsov House, S. Petersburg (1911–13): entrance looking towards west wing (photo 1913). See p. 1429

owning family, was Russia's finest example of the functionally free-planned home as a synthetic work of art surrounded by a garden in the European manner, though its particular decorative symbolisms were typically Russian. The vigour of this house contrasts sharply with the more static and derivative **villa for Mathilde Kshesinskaia** (1904–6) by Alexander von Gogen (1856–1914) which is its nearest equivalent in S. Petersburg.

In Russia's still-small cities it was common for a prosperous businessman to live on the same site as his business. A composite new type resulted whose best example was **P. P. Forostovsky's mansion and business premises, S. Petersburg** (1900–1), by Karl Schmidt (1866–1945). At one end of the street front is a grand porch to the owner's home; a central door is the entrance of his transportation company offices, and an arch at the other end leads to a loading yard with ramps into basement warehousing that runs under the house. The whole forms a clearly zoned but closely integrated unit. Stylistically more sober than Shekhtel's work it also has fine Art Nouveau ironwork and plays with glazed brick against matt stucco, though where the Riabushinsky house is clad in Symbolist pastels, this is in businesslike brown and grey.

The sundry variants of the free style in the 1900s were collectively known in Russia as the *Moderne*. Many elements in planning and decoration were drawn from mediaeval Russian traditions but the movement was sufficiently identified with European Art Nouveau and particularly Austro-German *Jugendstil* to have provoked a strongly nationalist hostility by about 1908–9. The result was a reassertion of the neo-Classicism characterising Russia's great Imperial period of the early nineteenth century. The grandest domestic work of this revival was the **Mansion for A. A. Polovtsov, S. Petersburg** (1911–13) (p. 1428C), by Ivan Fomin (1872–1936). In a manner appropriate to this liberal statesman the *rappel à l'ordre* simultaneously expressed a highly romantic hope that even now, Russia's Imperial order could be reinvented for the twentieth century.

Middle-class apartment housing was another new building type for Russia, and all industrial cities exploded with such development during the building boom between 1895 and World War I. Here too it was common for the owner to live on site rather than as an absent *rentier*. The owner's own mansion or grand apartment would occupy the prime position with rented accommodation surrounding it as part of the social accoutrement. Some of the architecturally most innovative examples of this type were developed by prosperous S. Petersburg architects. When the **Lidval family's apartment complex** (1899–1904) was begun, Fedor Lidval (1870–1945) was a relative unknown. Five years later the last phase of the development climaxed with an open *cour d'honneur* where the final south-facing wing was their grand family mansion containing his office, by then among the most important in the city. Lidval's mature style here is much influenced by Finnish National Romanticism, with strong granite contrasted against stucco and geometricised animal and plant forms in bas relief and in the ironwork. The **Bubyr apartment house, S. Petersburg** (1906–7), by Alexei Bubyr (1876–1919) and Nikolai Vasilev (1875–1941), was decoratively even more inventive and more boldly redolent of Lars Sonck's work in Helsinki (see Chapter 34), with birds and plants in bas relief in the granite around doors and windows.

The *Moderne* was an assertion of various cultural identities at a moment of change, but it was shortlived, and was written out of Russian architectural history through most of the Soviet period. Of great importance for the later development of Soviet urban architecture, by contrast, were the reworkings of Classicism developed by Vladimir Shchuko (1878–1939) in his adjoining **Apartment blocks for K. V. Markov, S. Petersburg** (1908–11) (p. 1430A). In the first a giant Ionic order rose five storeys from a ground-floor podium with balconies between. In the second a flatter, panelled and pilastered street facade had arched corner loggias at the setback. When historicist architecture became the approved style under Stalin twenty years later, Shchuko was at the peak of his career and these motifs became replicated on urban apartment blocks all over the Soviet Union. In the 1910s as in the 1930s, Shchuko's inventive reworkings of Classical motifs were in marked contrast to their literal use by the older Ivan Zholtovsky (1867–1959), whose magnificent **Mansion and offices for Gavril Tarasov, Moscow** (1909–12) (p. 1430D), was externally a near-exact copy of Palladio's Palazzo Thiene.

With growing affluence railways continued to expand. The most significant new termini were Shekhtel's **Yaroslavl Station, Moscow** (1902) (p. 1430B), and the **Vitebsk Station, S. Petersburg** (1902–4), by Stanislav Brzhozovsky (1863–1930s) and Semen Minash (1877–1945). Shekhtel in Moscow used the dramatic *Moderne* reinterpretation of traditional North Russian architecture he had devised the year before for Russia's pavilions at the Glasgow International Exhibition, with polychrome ceramic tiles and relief panels depicting animals and plants of the Yaroslavl region. The Vitebsk station is typical of S. Petersburg in being more urbanely European. The lightly eclectic exterior conceals an ingenious engineering solution of elevated platforms, and grand passenger spaces with Art Nouveau and *Jugendstil* motifs of finest marble and bronze.

Medical care was a growth area in all Russia's expanding cities. Moscow's outstanding new hospital

A. Markov's apartment block, S. Petersburg (1908–11): street elevation (photo *c.* 1912). See p. 1429

B. Yaroslavl Railway Station, Moscow (1902): perspective drawing by Shekhtel. See p. 1429

C. Offices and showrooms of the Moscow Trading Society, Moscow (1910) (photo from street corner, *c.* 1911). See p. 1431

D. Mansion and offices for Gavril Tarasov, Moscow (1909–12): detail of main street elevation. See p. 1429

complex was the **Morozov Children's Hospital** (*c.* 1905) by Illarion Ivanov-Shits (1865–1937) where fine *Moderne* ironwork and doorways are set against red stucco on the then-favoured 'hygienic' plan of separate pavilions. S. Petersburg's equivalent in architectural quality was the **Peter the Great Clinical Hospital** (1906–11) by Lev Ilin (1880–1942) and. Alexander Klein (1878–1961), though the architectural treatment here contrasts markedly with the stylistic freedom of the Moscow hospital. This was the most extensive application of the Petrine Revival style which used the simple somewhat Dutch elements of the city's first public buildings (notably the Twelve Colleges of 1722–41). The style expressed a patriotic romanticism officially fostered in the Russian capital between its bicentenary in 1903 and the Romanovs' tercentenary in 1913.

In the expansion and liberalisation of education Russia's finest new complex was the **Polytechnical Institute, S. Petersburg** (1899–1902), by Ernest Virrikh (1860 to after 1949). An ingenious section of broad semi-basement circulation routes under the main teaching blocks creates a closely integrated and climatically sympathetic complex, with laboratory, workshop and residential accommodation in separate pavilions around it. In its overall design and restrainedly eclectic Renaissance detailing, this was an educational complex appropriate to the world-class standards of Russian scientific and engineering education in the late-Imperial period.

By 1910 the new Moscow business classes were creating a public image for themselves with bold commercial structures, often concrete framed. The most refined were Shekhtel's **offices and showrooms of the Moscow Trading Society, Moscow** (1910) (p. 1430C), which projected an image of commerce as powerful but cultured that was appropriate to these *nouveaux riches* magnates who were major arts patrons. Equally sleek, with a boldly exposed concrete frame creating its central atrium, was Virrikh's **Department store for the Guards' Economic Society, S. Petersburg** (1908–9).

These last buildings of Imperial Russian architecture indicate the legacy of innovation inherited by the Soviet regime. They also show the quality of the tradition to which the new Russian profession can return, now that it is again free to conduct conventional architectural practice through free-market relationships and individual commissions.

During the decade after 1914, which embraced World War I, the Bolshevik Revolution and the ensuing Civil War, there was virtually no significant building activity in Russia. These years left the Soviet Union with a decimated building industry and a collapsed economy. Though nothing was built in the first post-Revolutionary years, they produced an explosion of design work that created powerful imagery of possible new architectures for the new society. As before World War I, historicist and Modernist trends developed in parallel and in mutual hostility.

Soviet Modernism

The first and most powerful architectural image of a new Soviet Modernism was the vast spiral steel structure of rotating auditoria conceived as a **Monument to the Third Communist International** in 1919 by the artist Vladimir Tatlin (1885–1953) (p. 1432A). For a new workers' parliament called **The Palace of Labour** in 1923 (p. 1432A,B) where most entries were inarticulate lumps like flattened Orthodox cathedrals, his colleagues the three Vesnin brothers, Leonid (1880–1933), Viktor (1882–1950) and Alexander (1883–1959), took third prize with a clear new spatial organisation in a stripped concrete frame that became another canonical image of Soviet Modernism.

The first opportunity for the new Soviet Union to display this architectural inventiveness abroad came in 1925. The **Soviet pavilion at the Exposition des Arts Decoratifs in Paris** (1924–5) (p. 1433A,B) by Konstantin Melnikov (1890–1974) was a dramatic split rectangle in black, red and grey timber which launched Soviet architecture onto the world scene.

When construction work resumed in Russia itself during 1924–5, the new political priorities naturally focused attention on workers' housing. The strong influence of the pre-war Garden City movement in S. Petersburg was reflected in Leningrad (as it was renamed in 1924) in a series of model low-rise developments that provided minimal family apartments with staircase access in three-to-four-storeyed blocks, pleasantly landscaped and with communal facilities. The first and most famous of these at **Tractor Street, S. Petersburg** (1925–7), by Alexander Gegello (1891–1965), Grigory Simonov (1893–1974) and Alexander Nikolsky (1884–1953), showed high densities to be compatible with healthy, human-scaled environment. It also showed how a few simplified Classical elements (giant half-arches, small details in natural stone) could bring an appropriate dignity to housing for the new 'ruling class'.

In the new capital of Moscow more theoretically inclined Modernist groups were developing. Most important were the Union of Contemporary Architects (OSA, or the Constructivists) who stressed the relationship between space and social organisation, and the Association of New Architects (ASNOVA, or the Rationalists) who stressed the relationship between abstract form and the message it conveys. Here the research into appropriate forms for socialist housing started not from garden city ideas but from the apartment block. The **Gosstrakh housing**

A. Monument to the Third Communist International, Petrograd (now S. Petersburg) (1919): side elevational drawing. See p. 1431

B. Palace of Labour, Moscow (1923): perspective. See p. 1431

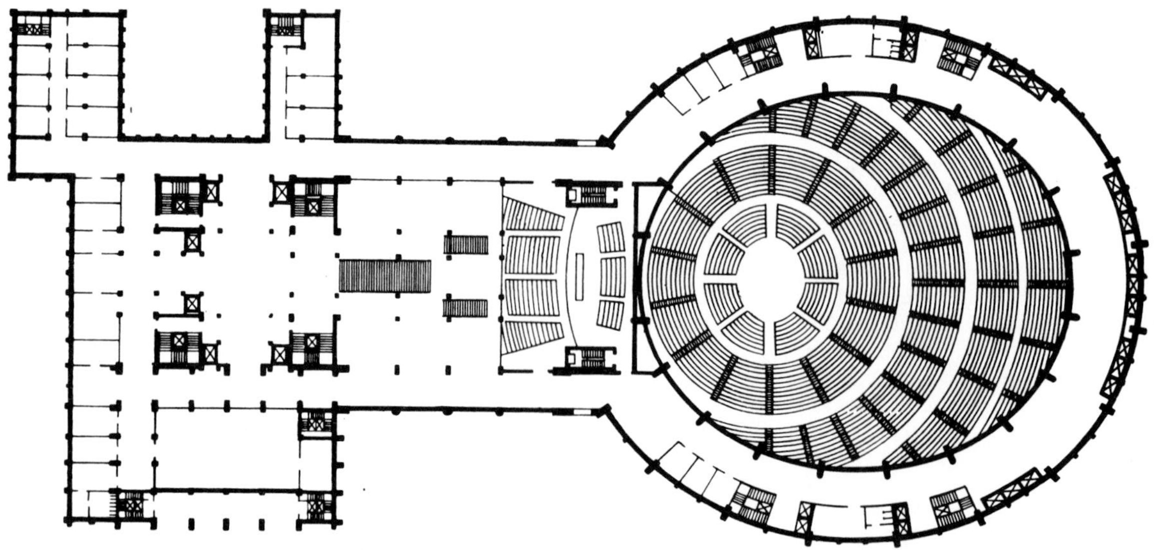

C. Palace of Labour, Moscow: second-floor plan with administrative and public facilities in cubic block (*left*); bridge element across the street (*centre*); upper level of the auditorium for workers' assemblies in oval building (*right*)

A. Pavilion of the USSR at the Exposition des Arts Decoratifs, Paris (1924–5): photo of exit. See p. 1431

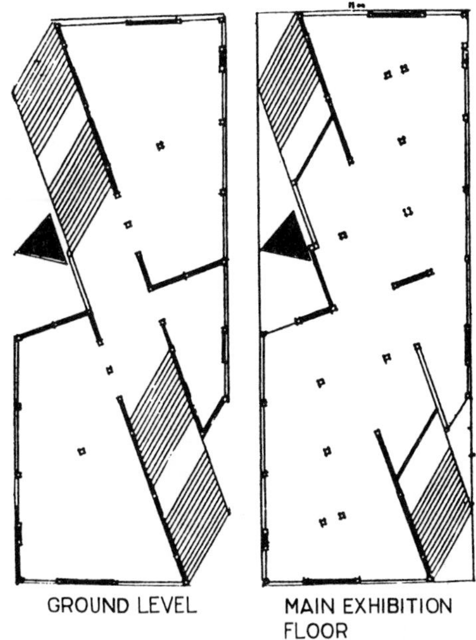

B. Pavilion of the USSR at the Exposition des Arts Decoratifs, Paris: plans

C. Semi-collective housing complex for employees of the Finance Commissariat, Narkomfin, Moscow (1928–30): perspective of original scheme. See p. 1434

D. Semi-collective housing complex for employees of Leningrad City Soviet, Leningrad (1931–4). See p. 1434

block, Moscow (1925–6), by the Vesnin brothers' younger colleague Moisei Ginzburg (1892–1946), was the first demonstration in Russia of such European Modernist elements as Corbusier's *toit-jardin* and Gropius's continuous corner windows, though the actual construction was stuccoed brickwork not a concrete frame. Apartments here also reflected European work in their minimal kitchens, maximum built-in furniture and collective facilities for single people. From this followed research by Ginzburg and his Constructivist colleagues into minimum-standard housing units that would foster time-saving (especially for women), a sharing of facilities and thus a more collectivist mentality. They drew upon European experiments like those in Frankfurt, but influence also flowed in the opposite direction when their split-sections and corridor access influenced Le Corbusier, who visited Moscow for discussions of his own **Tsentrosoyuz office building** there (designed and built 1928–36). The Soviet concept of the total living complex with semi-collectivised facilities re-emerged later as his *unité d'habitation* at Marseilles.

Within Russia the most important built demonstration of this housing research was the complex for fifty families of the Finance Commissariat, the **Narkomfin building, Moscow** (1928–30), by Ginzburg and Ignaty Milinis (1899–1942) (pp. 1433C, 1435A). This was also a demonstration project for modern concrete-framed and hollow block construction in Russian housing, and for Le Corbusier's 'Five points', notably the pilotis, the *toit jardin* and the horizontal ribbon windows. The semi-collectivised housing complex was explored with equal elegance in Leningrad by Evgeny Levinson (1894–1967) in his **Housing complex for employees of the City Soviet** (1931–4) (p. 1433D), but by drawing on the language and formal symmetries of Classicism.

Under Soviet conditions the one-family house for an individual client disappeared from the professional agenda. Except some country-house commissions for Party elite of no architectural merit, the pre-Revolutionary tradition was continued in one example only: the **Melnikov house and studio** (1927–9) built for himself by the architect of the celebrated Paris pavilion. His experimental structure of two interlocking cylinders demonstrated innovative uses of the traditional timber floor and stuccoed brickwork.

Melnikov's main contribution to the development of new Soviet building types was his sequence of Moscow workers' clubs. Of all buildings, the workers' club and the factory-kitchen had the greatest influence in developing an ideological awareness and collectivising domestic life at this time. Clubs were the focus of political education and training in such basic skills as literacy; in the later 1920s they were renamed palaces of culture to reflect an increasing emphasis on politically edifying hobbies and entertainment.

Two different spatial models for these buildings emerged. Melnikov's clubs pioneered the first, where all accommodation was integrated into a single, often highly distinctive form. Thus his **Rusakov club for Moscow municipal employees** (1927–8) (p. 1435D), was generated around the idea of one auditorium that could extend to different sizes by sliding walls into three smaller spaces cantilevered off the back. By contrast, the **Zuev club for Moscow tram workers** (1927–9) by Ilia Golosov (1883–1945) (p. 1435B,C) enclosed its auditorium within a simple rectangle of club-rooms and dramatised this by a glazed circular stair tower on the corner.

In the second planning model for clubs, which was developed by the Constructivists, accommodation was split into two buildings, one containing the auditorium and the other the club-room spaces, with a glazed linking element between. The Vesnin brothers' **Palace of Culture for the Proletarsky district of Moscow** (1930–37) was the last and largest variant on this model, though its main auditorium block was never built.

The factory-kitchen was a tool for relieving working women of family catering in the grossly overcrowded conditions of Soviet housing and each complex contained a range of different public eating facilities. Leningrad City Soviet commissioned four such complexes from the young team of Rationalist-group architects Armen Barutchev (1904–66), Isidor Gilter (1902–73), Iosif Meerzon (1900–41) and Iakov Rubanchik (1899–1948). Sleekest and most compact was their **Factory kitchen for Viborg district** (1929–30) (p. 1436A). The larger **Factory-kitchen and department store complex for Kirovsky district** (1929–31) (p. 1436B) formed the central amenity of a new workers' housing area. Their perspective of it framed by a classical building is an unusually direct insistence on Modern architecture's compatibility with the historic city.

The pre-Revolutionary innovations in office building provided technical and stylistic models for the prestige headquarters of new Soviet organisations and many competitions produced dramatic images and concepts that remained unbuilt. The purest built example of concrete frame, ribbon windows, glazed lift shafts and open-plan offices was the **Gostorg (State Trading) building, Moscow** (1925–7) (p. 1437A), though new height regulations aborted the intended tower. Here experience was joined to the new vision in a collaboration between the older Boris Velikovsky (1878–1937) and a team of young Constructivists led by Mikhail Barshch (1904–66). Russia's showpiece complex of International Style Modernism, which represented Soviet architecture in the New York exhibition of that name in 1932, was the **All-Union Electro-Technical Institute, VEI** (1928–31) (p. 1437B). This resulted from a similar collaboration, between the concrete specialist Alexander Kuznetsov (1874–1954) and young

A. Semi-collective housing complex for employees of the Finance Commissariat, Narkomfin, Moscow. See p. 1434

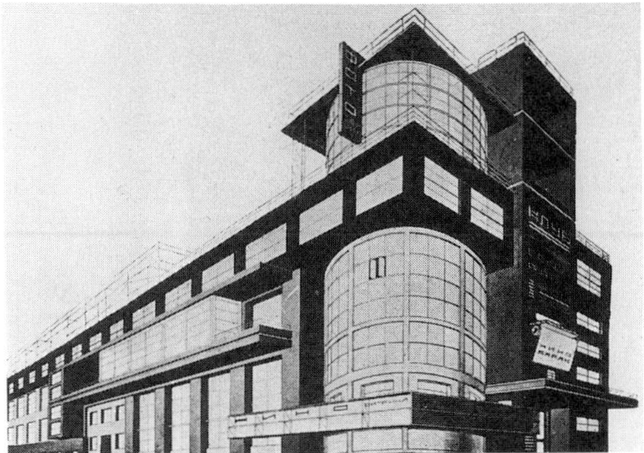

B. Zuev Club for employees of Moscow tram system, Moscow (1927–9): street corner view, perspective. See p. 1434

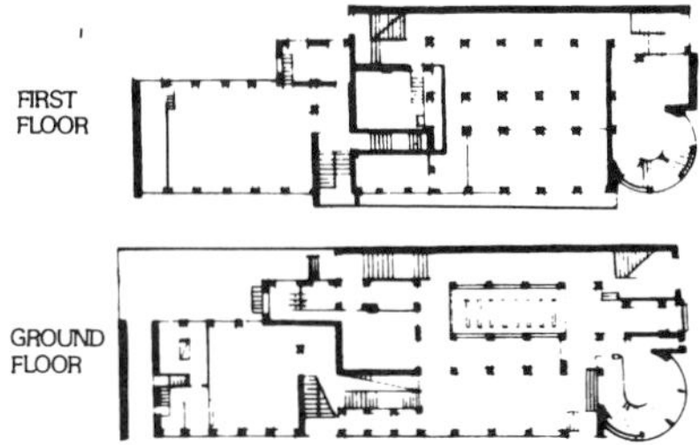

C. Zuev Club for employees of Moscow tram system: plans

D. Rusakov Club for employees of Moscow City Soviet, Moscow (1927–8) (photo from street corner, *c.* 1929). See p. 1434

A. Factory-kitchen complex for the Viborg district of Leningrad (1929–30) (photo *c.* 1931). See p. 1434

B. Factory-kitchen and department store complex for the Kirovsky district of Leningrad (1929–31). See p. 1434

A. Administrative building for the state trading organisation, Gostorg, Moscow (1925–7). See p. 1434

B. All Union Electro-Technical Institute campus, VEI, Moscow (1928–31): site photo during development (1930). See p. 1434

C. Polytechnical Institute campus, Ivanovo-Voznesensk (1927–32): perspective of main building. See p. 1438

D. Lenin State Library, Moscow (1928–9) (main design), completed 1941. See p. 1438

Constructivists Ivan Nikolaev (1901–79) and Gennady Movchan (born 1901).

With the Bolshevik Party's aesthetic and cultural policy rooted in the models of cultural continuity propounded by Marx and taken up by Lenin, other architects were exploring how the Russian Classical tradition might be reinterpreted in a Socialist architecture. Members of the pre-Revolutionary profession formulated different approaches. Thus Zholtovsky sought to apply Classicism's compositional and proportional principles to industrial architecture. Fomin offered his Red Doric as a new Order for the trabeated architecture of the concrete frame. His largest executed works in this style were the new **Polytechnical Institute campus in Ivanovo-Voznesensk** (1927–32) (p. 1437C) and two Moscow buildings, the **Dinamo complex** (1928–9) (p. 1439B) and the extension to **Moscow City Soviet** (1929–30) (p. 1439A).

As hostility to the 'ideological emptiness' of Modernism became more vicious in the later 1920s the **Lenin State Library** competition of 1928–9 produced a unified protest by the Modernist groups against reinterpretations of Classicism from the older Alexei Shchusev (1873–1949) and Shchuko. Shchuko's winning design with granite walls, marble columns and heroic bas reliefs was eventually completed in 1941 (p. 1437D). Since 1924 Shchusev had been refining his scheme in red and black marbles for the **Lenin Mausoleum** (1924–30), which is a masterly contextual insertion in Red Square (p. 1439C).

The Party finally asserted its architectural preferences through the competition for a vast **Palace of Soviets, Moscow,** during 1931–3 (p. 1439D). Modernist Soviet architects and invited Westerners including Le Corbusier, Auguste Perret and Walter Gropius were beaten by a dumpy monumental cylinder from Boris Iofan (1891–1976) that was reworked under Party instructions to become 'the world's highest building' and the podium for a statue of Lenin. Serious construction work started but was never completed. In the process of the competition, however, an architectural interpretation of the Party's Socialist Realist aesthetic was formulated. 'Critical assimilation of the heritage' meant identifying those traditional elements still considered ideologically valuable and creating a new synthesis with 'the latest achievements of technology'. The full depictive potential of painting and sculpture must be used to reinforce architecture's ideological message.

With campaigns increasing against all who were not subservient to Stalin's Party line, independent architectural groups were dissolved by decree in 1932 and replaced by a single official Union of Soviet Architects (later, Union of Architects of the USSR). All rights for an individual or a team to undertake commissions in their own name were subsequently abolished. All building design work was thereafter conducted through specialised studios within each government department, industrial trust or local authority. An Academy of Architecture brought together the professional elite and the best young architects in technical and aesthetic research, in criticism and publication of approved work and in writing ideologically 'correct' accounts of architectural history.

During the mid-1930s, individual designers and their hand were still clearly identifiable in such prestige exercises of Socialist Realism as the Moscow Metro stations or republican interpretations of the principles in Georgia, Armenia or the Ukraine. When the first Metro line opened in 1935, its stations like the **Palace of Soviets Metro station** (1931–5, later called Kropotkinskaia), by Alexei Dushkin (1903–77), were typically simple, even austere, and were criticised for not harnessing the other arts. Thus subsequent stages, typified by the same architect's **Revolution Square Metro station** (opened 1938), incorporated sculpture and mosaic pictures by leading artists to convey the political message of their name and location.

Republican seats of Soviet power like the **Armenian House of Government, Erevan** (1928–40) (p. 1440A) by Alexander Tamanian (1878–1936), the **Georgian House of Government, Tbilisi** (1938–54), by Viktor Kokorin (1886–1959) and Georgy Lezhava (1903–77) or the **Ukrainian Council of Ministers building, Kiev** (1934–8) by Fomin and Pavel Abrosimov (1900–61), represented 'critical assimilations' of local architectural traditions at a new scale. After the First Congress of Soviet Architects in 1937, real authorship was usually hidden behind a list of team members and the name of a 'chief architect'. This anonymity was further compounded by the increasing size of projects, and only started to break down during the 1970s.

The **1935 Plan for Moscow** focused attention on reshaping and technically modernising the city as 'the model capital of the world proletariat'. With all building interrupted for World War II, and massive destruction of urban fabric by the German invasion, the Academy of Architecture executed pilot studies to show how the principles of the Moscow Plan – focal ensembles, main streets realigned with heroic six- to eight-storeyed apartment blocks and offices – could be applied with nationalistic interpretation to the post -war rebuilding of war-damaged cities. Shchusev's work of 1942–3 on the **Project for rebuilding of Istra**, a small town destroyed in 1941, and others projects notably by Georgy Golts (1893–1946) (such as his proposals for Kiev (1945) (p. 1440B), established the principle that such schemes were not recreations of historic architectures but, as Socialist Realism insisted, the devising of a new synthesis of local tradition and the socialist message with new technologies at appropriate scale.

A. Extension to Moscow City Soviet (1929–30): perspective inside entrance courtyard. See p. 1438

B. Complex of administrative, commercial and housing accommodation for the Dinamo organisation, Moscow (1928–9): offices (*left*) and housing (*right*) soon after completion. See p. 1438

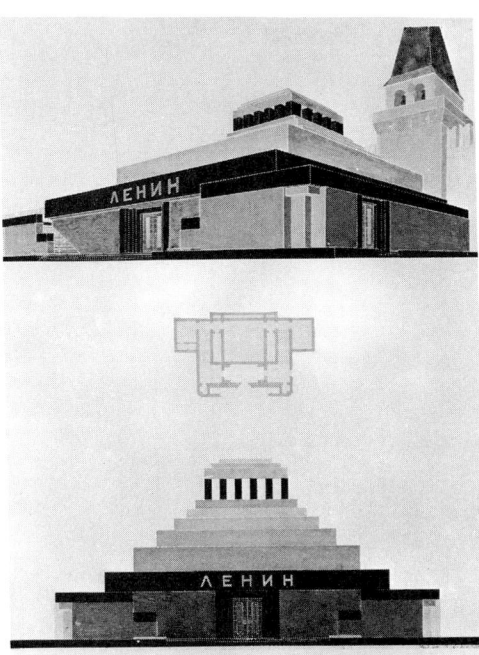

C. Lenin Mausoleum, Moscow (1924–30). See p. 1438

D. Palace of Soviets, Moscow (1933): perspective of approved scheme at penultimate stage. See p. 1438

A. House of Government of Armenian Republic, Erevan (1928–40). See p. 1438

B. Exploratory proposals for the post-war reconstruction of central Kiev (1945): perspective view towards the Dnepr River. See p. 1438

C. Ministry of Communications building at the Red Gates, Moscow (1949–53). See p. 1441

Post-World War II

Typically expressive of the Soviet victory were schemes developed from 1946 onwards for **Redevelopment of Kiev** under Alexander Vlasov (1900–62), where the central street, Kreshchatka, was a florid over-indulgence of Ukrainian Baroque; or more restrainedly, under Karo Alabian (1897–1959) for **Reconstruction of Stalingrad** (Volgograd); under Ginzburg for **Reconstruction of Sebastopol;** or under Le Corbusier's executive architect on the Tsentrosoyuz Nikolai Kolli (1894–1966), for **Reconstruction of Kalinin** (Tver).

The importance in Russian tradition of a town's overall silhouette led to the post-war embellishment of Moscow by a ring of six so-called **High Buildings** whose towers rose to 35 storeys as orientation points within the city. Though sharply distinguished in the literature from 'the exploitative skyscrapers of capitalism', pre-war New York was one influence. Meanwhile their focal locations, their relationship to standard cubic housing blocks around, and their general compositional conception derived from Russian traditions of urban church building. Their detailing, however, was highly original in its abstract reworkings of diverse historical motifs. With polychrome marble finishes inside and out, gold-topped spires, mural paintings, sculpture and high quality fittings, these were the only real Soviet legatees of pre-Revolutionary building traditions. Their functions were various. Thus enormous design teams were led by Metro veteran Dushkin for the **Ministry of Communications building at the Red Gates** (1949–53) (p. 1440C); by Rudnev for the new **Moscow University** complex (1949–53); by Arkady Mordvinov (1896–1964) for the **Ukraina Hotel** (1950–57). Replication of these forms in East European capitals where they had no traditional precedents was one of most blatant signals of post-war Soviet imperialism.

These Moscow High Buildings were Khrushchev's most explicit target in the speech denouncing Stalin's architecture which preceded by a year his denunciation of the man himself in February 1956. His speech to the Soviet Builders' Congress of December 1954 ridiculed architects as 'squanderers of the people's resources'. Several were attacked by name including Mordvinov, by then President of the Academy of Architecture. Khrushchev insisted that 'not everything was wrong with Constructivism' and decreed that Soviet architecture be redirected towards simpler forms and prefabricated construction systems as a means of tackling the housing crisis.

Further public demeaning of architectural values by the abolition of the Academy, and the increasing authority accorded to the building industry produced disorientation in the profession and launched the decline in its status which continued until the 1980s. Through the later 1950s and the 1960s Soviet architecture paralleled post-war Modernism in Europe. Massive **public housing programmes** using precast concrete elements started with relatively human-scaled blocks of five, then eight to ten storeys. As the crude craning systems permitted greater height they demanded greater distance between buildings and by the late 1970s were producing residential deserts which never received their planned amenities. Vast numbers of people were rehoused, but architects played an ever-decreasing role.

Determined to keep Moscow a showpiece of socialist progress, the planning authority under chief architect Mikhail Posokhin (1910–89) also followed Western strategies in the brutal demolition of a historic central area to insert a downtown strip, called **Kalinin Prospect** (1962–8; now New Arbat) (p. 1442A) where eight standardised housing and office towers rise from a podium of shopping, cinemas and restaurants. With large new-town construction programmes under way across the USSR, this model of a city centre was widely replicated, as was Russian high-rise housing, in climates and cultures to which it was totally unsuitable.

In the cultural liberalisation that accompanied Khrushchev's political thaw, the main one-off design projects were cinemas, sports centres, Palaces of the Arts and of Culture in old and new towns. Few were great works of architecture but many were inventive buildings of lively form and by Soviet standards were elegantly executed.

The internationalism of Western architecture at this time, with all its disregard of local difference, was also replicated within the multinational empire of the USSR. During the 1970s, protest at the manifest absurdities of uniform housing design combined with stirrings of local national feeling led to the re-emergence of embryonic national 'schools' in republics with particularly strong identities and indigenous architectural traditions – and a politically bold architect of talent to lead them. The two most important Central Asian examples were Rafael Israelian (1908–73) in Armenia and Abdulla Akhmedov (born 1929) in Turkmenia. Israelian used such projects as his **National Museum of Ethnography, Sardarapat**, completed in 1978, to reassert Armenian traditions of heavy mass, natural stone, small clean-cut apertures and bas relief decoration. As chief architect of Ashkhabad, Akhmedov revived the traditional climatic responses of deeply shaded covered areas, brises soleil, strong formal and decorative relief, use of water, most extensively in the **Turkmenian Republican Library** (1970–4) (p.1442C).

The Baltic Republic of Estonia was another seat of resentment at Russian political and cultural hegemony whose architects increasingly asserted its autonomy. With a strong Modern Movement tradition between the wars and strong cultural links to Finland, Toomas Rein (born 1940), Valve Pormeister (born 1922) and others, the so-called 'generation of the

A. Redevelopment of the historic Arbat area of central Moscow as Kalinin Prospect (1962–8). See p. 1441

B. New academic block for the Agricultural Polytechnic in Jäneda, Estonia (1974). See p. 1444

C. State Library of the Turkman Republic, Askhabad (1970–4). See p. 1441

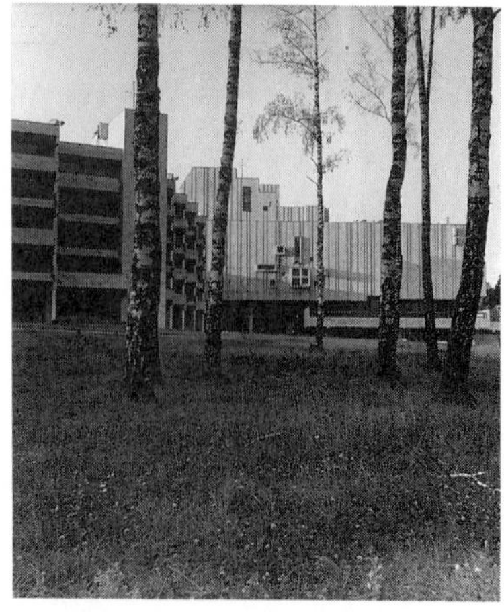

D. Voronovo country-club complex for employees of the Moscow construction industry, near Moscow (1974). See p. 1444

A. Children's Musical Theatre, Moscow (1977–80). See p. 1444

B. Bakery for Traditional Breads, Tbilisi (1986–8). See p. 1444

break', reconnected the country with those roots. Rein notably used his position as Chief Architect of Estonia's Collective Farms to build such complexes as the **Inter-Collective Farm Construction Bureau Housing, Social Centre and Kindergarten, Pärnu** (1973–8), in relaxed Scandinavian style. Pormeister's **Academic Building for the Agricultural Polytechnic, Jäneda** (1974) (p. 1442B) was in similar idiom. Almost uniquely in the Soviet Union this area preserved a flexible building industry, the tradition of small-scale community buildings of individual design, and even the habit of one-family housing. In the later 1970s and early 1980s another generation, including Leonhard Lapin (born 1947), Vilen Künnapu (born 1948), Andres Alver (born 1953), followed these pioneers into a relaxed use of natural materials and vigorous formal invention in leisure buildings and private houses whose allusions to current Western work made their allegiances clear. These architects now occupy leading positions in the free Estonia.

Best known in Russia itself for asserting these Nordic traditions of modern design informally integrated into landscape was Ilya Cherniavsky (1917–94), who was opposed by Moscow establishment but revered by frustrated colleagues for his trade union country-clubs around Moscow such as **Planernaia** (1976) and **Voronovo** (1974) (p.1442D).

Economic decline, and over-expenditure for the 1980 Olympic Games in Russia itself, led to a virtual cessation of public building projects other than mass housing during the early 1980s. A rare and distinguished exception was the **Children's Musical Theatre, Moscow** (p. 1443A) completed in 1980 by Alexander Velikanov (born 1938) and Vladimir Krasilnikov (born 1932) as a permanent home to the famous educational work of Natalia Sats. Its multifunctional auditorium and complex of storytelling spaces were designed around her techniques. After this date non-Russian Soviet republics were far more active in building than Russia itself. The **Eastern Bazaar complex, Baku** (1982), by Uruzmak Revazov (born 1929) and Pavel Yarinovsky exemplified their increasing confidence to draw upon local traditional forms.

By the early 1980s the strongest voices of protest at the stagnation and low status of architecture in the Soviet Union came from newly qualified architects and students in Moscow. Under Brezhnev and his successors the frustrated young designers developed a highly conceptual approach, reasserting humanistic and individualistic themes. When all foreign contacts were still illegal they smuggled out these projects to competitions abroad, particularly in Japan. As young design teams like Alexander Brodsky (born 1955) and Ilya Utkin (born 1955) accumulated prizes, and exhibitions in Europe and North America built an international reputation for these Soviet '**Paper architects**', they gained confidence to attack the defeatism and complacency of the professional establishment at home.

After Gorbachev took power in 1985, the growing regional independence, pressures on the Union of Architects from young professionals and the larger reforms of *perestroika* led to the re-establishing of legal means for more independent practice. The most acclaimed complex of these final Soviet years was the **Bakery for Traditional Breads, Tbilisi** (1986–8) by Vakhtang Davitaia (born 1934) (p. 1443B). On the production side it replaced the once-innovative Soviet 'bread factory' by a traditional water-driven flour mill, wood-fired ovens, and human-scaled, outward-looking working and relaxation spaces for employees. Addressing the new concept of the 'customer', the sales end formed a courtyard of raised and framed shops evoking traditional buildings of the region.

Before significant building work could be initiated under these new professional frameworks, however, they were overtaken by the larger political collapse. Precisely those nationalities of Central Asia and the Baltic who had most seriously asserted their identity through architecture were the first to declare their independence of the post-Soviet Commonwealth. With entirely new legal and social structures being evolved in parallel with free market economies the corresponding freedoms for independent architectural practice and building firms have been re-established. In the cut-throat and unstable economic conditions of the mid-1990s construction is booming as one of the few secure deposits for new money. Extensive new building work is developing in private housing, office and industrial accommodation, as well as extensive renovation and adaptation of the existing and dilapidated building stock. Much of this is still celebrating the freedom to catch up with Western Post-Modernism or simply to display wealth. The serious architectural qualities of new Russian work and any distinctive regional features of it have yet to emerge.

Chapter 48

MIDDLE EAST

At the beginning of the twentieth century the Middle East was under the cultural or political domination of Europe. The region was divided through ethnic, religious and political distinctions into three regions which were colonised by, respectively, the British, the French and the Italians. The non-colonised regions were Persia and Turkey – that is, the Ottoman Empire which by the beginning of the twentieth century had been reduced to mainland Anatolia and Thrace. But even these politically independent states were both strongly under the influence of Western ideologies.

Turkey

The Ottoman Empire's experiments in Westernisation heralded the first exercises in democracy, such as the Parliament of 1908 and the introduction of an independent press. These experiments also introduced Western values and expressions in art and architecture. All physical and cultural aspects of Turkish life were strongly influenced by Western ideas, not least because in the decades before World War I many Western architects practised in Istanbul. Many of these were German because the German Empire, in its search for spheres of influence and markets for its technological expertise and products, had pinpointed the Ottoman Empire. The construction of the Istanbul–Hijaz (i.e. Mecca in Saudi Arabia) railroad was one of the major joint projects between German industrialists and the Sultan. One of the political motivations behind this project was the Sultan's ambition to transport massive numbers of pilgrims in comfort to Mecca.

It was at this time that architecture emerged as a socially acceptable profession in Turkey. Previously it was regarded as a rather inferior, certainly not a stately, profession. The first professional architect to come from a stately background was Mimar Vedad (later Vedad Tek, 1873–1942) whose father was the Secretary General of the Palace for the last Sultan Mehmet V. After enormous effort Vedad persuaded his father to let him study architecture at the Ecole de Beaux Arts, Paris.

Vedad returned to Istanbul bearing a number of academic distinctions including the Prix de Rome. He was soon appointed chief architect to the Ministry of Post and Telegrams as well as being closely associated with the court. His position with the ministry soon presented a major opportunity which was to result in the creation of Vedad's *opus magnum*. This is the **Main Post Office, Sirkeci, Istanbul** (1909) (p. 1447A). Vedad used depressed pointed arches in traditional proportions with tiles bearing classical motifs applied to spandrels. Vedad's European architectural education is revealed by his use of semicircular Corinthian columns to clad the upper storey. The successful completion of this building established the fact that local architects could do as well as foreign architects in Istanbul.

Vedad explored the possibility of evolving a modern yet authentically Turkish architecture which would stand in opposition to the various Western architectural styles being imported into the empire – notably the Parisian *lingua franca* of neo-Classicism or eccentric Art Nouveau. This became part of the First National Movement in Architecture which endeavoured to define an architecture responsive to Turkish culture and climate. Examples are his rigidly symmetrical and large scale **Imperial Office of Land Registry, Istanbul** (1909) (p. 1448A) and the ingeniously planned, and deep-caved **House Nişantasi, Istanbul,** (1910) (p. 1448B). However, there was great professional rivalry among the few architects who were the proponents of the movement. For example, a major rival to Vedad was Kemalettin Bey (1870–1927), who had been trained as a civil engineer and was the Chief Architect of Pious Foundations. This post gave Kemalettin Bey not only the chance to design religious buildings – for example the **Bebek Mosque, Istanbul** (1913) – (p. 1448C) and to work in Ottoman dominions (he supervised the restoration of the **Masjid al-Aqsa, Jerusalem**) but also the opportunity to design large buildings using state-of-the-art construction technology. Consequently he was the first architect to utilise reinforced concrete, cast in controlled conditions, in the construction of the **Fire Victims Apartments** (Harikzedegân), (p. 1447B,C) **Istanbul** (1919–22), and the **Evkaf Apartments, Ankara** (1924).

World War I terminated the Ottoman Empire's political dominance of the region with former imperial lands being divided into kingdoms and sheikdoms with new identities as nation states. The limited economies of these new countries between the war did not allow for many major building projects. Most new buildings were realised within the traditions of the region or in vernacular derivations of imported Western styles while larger buildings were designed by expatriate architects generally working with imported technology.

In Turkey the abolition of the Sultanate and the proclamation of the Republic initiated the search for an architecture to reflect the aspirations of the new age. This search was soon concluded with the arrival of Modernism, which was favoured for it seemed to present the right 'progressive' image for the new state. This new Western architecture was imported directly from Germany, with the employment of Clemens Holzmeister (1886–1983), Bruno Taut (1880–1938), Paul Bonatz (1877–1956) and Ernst Egli (1893–1974). These architects were to have a tremendous influence, for not only were they entrusted with major commissions but also became pivotal figures in architectural education in the region. Through the influence of these Modernists, acting with the support of Kemel Ataturk (1881–1938) who was dedicated to the Westernisation of Turkey, traditionalist designers were seen as reactionary and consequently marginalised. Kemalettin was dead by this time but Vedad was denied employement and the studio he was running with Gullio Mongeri at the Academy of Fine Arts was closed.

A new generation of Turkish architects of Modernist orientation took over with one of the finer examples of the idiom being Sevki Balmumcu's (1905–1982) horse-shoes-shaped **Exhibition Hall, Ankara** (1933–34). However, this building could be anywhere in the world and would be equally appreciated in Berlin. The Viennese Clemens Holzmeister was given the commission in 1928 to design the Ankara **Administrative District**. This included the **Presidential Palace** (1932–3) and the **General Staff Building**, (1929–30) (p. 1448D). In 1938 he was appointed state architect (a job he held until 1954). His **Government Headquarters** (completed in 1934), **High Courts of Justice** (1938) and **Parliament Building** (1938–1960), all in **Ankara**, move away from the strictly modern to reflect many of motifs and architectural preoccupations of the Third Reich, including colonnaded portals and cumbersome stone detailing. In similar vein is the **State Railroad Headquarter, Ankara** (p. 1449A) designed by Bedri Uçar (1941).

Meanwhile Ernst Egli and Bruno Taut designed two influential school buildings on the main avenue of Ankara connecting the old settlement with the new city planned by another German, Hermann Jansen. The **Vocational School for Girls** (1930) and **Offices of Exchequers** (1928–30), both by Egli, display the image of uncompromising Modernism. **The Faculty of Letters** (1937) by Taut utilises some traditional regional detailing such as stone cladding laced with brick courses. The new generation of Turkish architects committed to Modernism included Seyfi Arkan (1902–1966) whose **Ùçler Apartment, Ayazpasa, Istanbul** (1935), and **Bank of Municipalities, Ankara** (1937), achieved an excellence which impressed the government and won Arkan the post of State Architect, and Emin Onat (1908–1961), who won the competition for the design of a Mausoleum for Kemal Ataturk, the **Anitkabir, Ankara** (1944–53) (p. 1449C).

World War II, in which Turkey was not involved, isolated the country from its embattled neighbours and encouraged a period of introspection. This led to a revival of interest in regional architectural traditions, pioneered by Sedad Eldam (1908–1987) and Paul Bonatz (1987–1856) who was in self-exile from Germany, and was even reflected in the work of some younger Turkish Modernist architects such as Emin Onat whose **Cenap and Residence, Ankara** (1942), broke with Modernist dogma and pioneered a revival in the use of Central Anatolian regional detail. This new interest in the creative use of history and tradition produced the **Faculty of Science, Ankara University** (1945), and the **Faculty of Arts and Letters, Istanbul University** (1944), both by Sedad Eldem, and **Housing for Government Employees (Saraçoglu Mahallesi)** (1945) and the remodelling of an exhibition hall into the **Opera House, Ankara** (1948) by Paul Bonatz (p. 1449B). These buildings, with their large eaves, tile courses in masonry and honeycomb windows challenged the orthodoxy of modernism and became the main reference points in the emerging regionalist discourse. In this period Eldem produced a rather literal interpretation of the Turkish House, inspired by a well-known mansion on the eastern bank of the Bosphorus, when designing the **Taslik Coffee House, Istanbul** (1948–50) – a project which has since become an icon of contemporary Turkish architecture.

During the post-war period Modernism was once again generally viewed as the appropriate architectural expression for the aspirations of Turkey. There was a strongly rooted tradition in Middle East countries to look to the West for exemplars and models of excellence. Therefore Modernism did not meet significant political or popular resistance. On the contrary, Modernism and Western values were generally welcomed. Quickly traditional methods of construction were abandoned and

A. Main Post Office, Sirkeci, Istanbul (1909). See p. 1445

B. Fire Victims Apartments, Istanbul (1919–22). See p. 1446

C. Fire Victims Apartments, Istanbul: courtyard

A. Land Registry, Istanbul (1909). See. p. 1445

B. House, Nişantaşi, Istanbul (1910). See p. 1445

C. Bebek Mosque, Istanbul (1913). See p. 1445

D. General Staff Building, Ankara (1929–30). See p. 1446

A. State Railroad Headquarters, Ankara (1941). See p. 1446

B. Opera House, Ankara (1948). See p. 1446

C. Anitkabir, Ankara (1944–53). See p. 1446

A. Parliament Mosque, Ankara (1985). See p. 1451

B. Turkish Language Society Building, Ankara (1972–8). See p. 1451

C. Turkish Language Society Building: atrium

D. Lassa Tyre Factory, Izmit (1975–7). See p. 1451

traditional buildings were dismissed as both culturally backward and difficult to maintain. Simultaneously the curricula of architecture schools were modelled after the German Bauhaus and thus Modernist tenets were taught as self-evident truths. Turkish modern architecture after 1950 aimed principally at importing what was perceived as the best of Western architecture and practice, mostly via the pages of architectural publications. The contemporary architecture of France, Germany and Switzerland was particularly influential with architectural practice in Turkey being dominated by a small group of architects who were prepared to do little more than copy Western prototypes. Commissions were distributed via 'competitions' in which 'competitors' and jurors were all members of the same hermetic group which was forward looking, but only towards the West.

The works of Vedad Dalokay (1927–1991) and Togrul Devres (1920–1994) are representative of the immediate post-war years. Indeed Dalokay's **Standards Institute of Turkey, Ankara** (1956), and Devres's **Etibank, Ankara** (1955–60), were seminal buildings which were much emulated during the following decades. Altug (born 1935) and Behruz Cinici (born 1932) have been among the most influential Turkish architects from the late 1960s onwards with their key projects including the **Middle East Technical University Campus** (1964–80) and additions to Holzmeister's Parliament including the **Public Relations Building** (1977), **Housing for Members of Parliament** (1982).and the **Parliament Mosque** (1985) (p. 1450A) by Behruz Cinici with his son Can (born 1962).

The more traditional regionalist approach has been pursued by Turgut Cansever (born 1926) with his **Demir Holiday Village, Bodrum** (1987), which emulates the forms of Mediterranean vernacular building, and by Cengiz Bektas (born 1934) whose **Turkish Language Society Building, Ankara** (1972–8) (p. 1450B,C) is a seminal building with an atrium plan inspired by the traditional Central Anatolian courtyard house.

Dogan Tekeli (born 1929) and Sami Sisa (born 1928) working in partnership have designed the most significant of Turkey's post-war industrial buildings, notably the **Lassa Tyre Factory, Izmit** (1975–7) (p. 1450D) and the **Halk Bankasi Headquarters, Ankara** (1983–91). the high-technology approach has been adopted and successfully adapted to local conditions by Mehmet Konuralp (born 1939) whose **Sabah Newspaper Plant and Offices, Istanbul** (1988–90), brings together all aspects of newspaper production – from journalists to printing presses – in a highly transparent construction so that the function of the building is displayed and becomes its greatest ornament and interest.

Arabic Peninsula

The post-war oil boom and the consequent economic prosperity in the region led to a vast increase in construction, particularly in cities, and the creation of types of buildings not previously known in the region. The spirit of Modernism prevailed, with a profound influence on historic cities and on vernacular building traditions.

During the 1960s Iraq became a focus of development in the Middle East, and here new architecture was dominated by Mohammed Makiya (born 1914) and Rifat Chadiriji (born 1926). Makiya established the Baghdad School of Architecture and also argued for a contemporary architecture responsive to regional building traditions and which utilised Abbasid architectural elements. His **Rafidain Bank Building, Kufa** (1968) (p. 1452A), and **Public Library, Karbala** (1969), soon became a major reference point in contemporary Arab architecture. During the high tide of Post-Modernism in the 1970s Makiya digressed from his Modern-Regionalist line into a form of 'Islamic' Post-Modernism. In this period he designed the **National Mosque, Kuwait** (1977). In this building, Makiya used forms that are germane to the Arab/Islamic heritage realised in modern materials.

Rifat Chadirji was more concerned with urban design and in creating the appropriate context for historic or cultural buildings. From the mid-1960s he developed a critical response to the dominance of 'function' in architecture which he saw as essentially a Western Modernist obsession. He argued that the functionalist view which held that structure should be the generator of plan form and of architectural expression should be replaced by pliant forms that relate more closely to the architectural and cultural traditions of the region. Two buildings by Chadirji, the **Federal Industry Offices, Baghdad** (1966), and **the Hamood Residence, Baghdad** (1972) (p. 1452B), both illustrate this theory in their use brick, vaults and plastic forms.

Given the absence of an adequately trained local architectural profession and the quantity and type of work required in the wake of the post-1970s economic boom in the Arabic Peninsula it was inevitable that Western and Japanese expertise was employed. It also now seems inevitable that Modernism was the preferred architectural language because it appeared to reflect many of the intrinsic aspirations of Islam, such as a desire for change and a belief in development and in the contemporary. And the clients of the Arabic Peninsula, since they possessed the wealth, wanted to employ the architects with the best international reputations. Quality was often sought through architectural competitions but as the winning design usually turned out to be impracticable the competition system was generally a massive waste of effort.

A. Rafidain Bank Building, Kufa (1968). See p. 1451

B. The Hamood Residence, Baghdad (1972). See p. 1451

C. Water Towers, Kuwait (1976). See p. 1453

D. Basra Hotel, Basra, Iraq (1975–81): garden courtyard. See p. 1453

E. Saudi Fund for Development Building, Riyadh (1976–81). See p. 1453

Some notable buildings were commissioned at this time, for example the **Water Towers, Kuwait** (1976) (p. 1452C), by the Scandinavian firm VVB (Sune and Joe Lindström and Stig Egnell). Located on the harbour, in assemblies of two, five or nine towers, the structures emulate palm trees in their shape and in their clusters imply the presence of oases. These structures soon became symbols not only of water – the source of life in a desert country – but also of the nation itself. The establishment of an abstract relationship between form, geographic context and heritage – pioneered by the water towers – was developed by Jørn Utzon (born 1918) in the design of the **Parliament House, Kuwait** (1985). Utzon was inspired by sails of the seafaring Kuwaiti tradition and the tents of the nomadic desert culture. The building's boldly formed reinforced concrete entrance canopy has become one of the landmarks of Kuwait.

Modernism during the 1970s and 1980s was also tempered by a concern for tradition with abstract regional references being regarded as sources of inspiration. The Architects Collaborative (TAC), a firm evolved out of the practice founded by Walter Gropius, was one of the first practices to experiment with the idea of the traditional courtyard house interpreted in a Modernist manner. Its **Basra Hotel, Basra, Iraq** (1975–81) (p. 1452D), was a seminal exploration of this transformation. The guest rooms are organised around a central courtyard and provided with wooden balconies which were inspired by traditional balconies called mashrabiyya. This solution was then developed by the New York firm Urbahn and Coile in its **Saudi Fund for Development Building, Riyadh** (1976–81) (p. 1452E), which contains within its outer walls and open galleries a cool and environmentally controlled atrium. Henning Larsen continued the idea of the courtyard house, along with other aspects of desert architecture, in his competition-winning design for the **Ministry of Foreign Affairs, Riyadh** (1985). This building includes a triangular atrium which serves as a route into the three 'wings' of the building. In the approach to these wings Larsen once again referred to tradition and employed the spatial organisation of the region's narrow urban streets (or souk) in order to give the corridors a special character. Larsen also managed to utilise the local Najdi building and design traditions, especially on the Ministry's elevation, which is clad with massive stones and pierced with small window openings, without entirely abandoning the tenets of Modernism.

Gordon Bunshaft of the US architectural practice Skidmore Owing and Merrill (SOM) designed the **National Commercial Bank, Jeddah** (1977–84) (p. 1454B), which is his last and arguably finest high-rise building. It is certainly one of the most impressive pieces of architecture in the region. In this building Bunshaft also interpreted the idea of the traditional courtyard house by incorporating three multi-storey covered spaces, each of triangular form and each with one side open at each level to offer diverse views of Old Jeddah or the lagoon, and to protect the interior from direct sunlight. Rotating the openings in the exterior wall also created a continuous funnel from the ground all the way up to the top of the building to allow hot air to rise out of the interior.

Omramia (established by architects Basem Shihabi and Nabil Fanous) was the first local architectural practice to work convincingly in the idiom of Western Modernism and then to develop the language to create a genuine new interpretation of traditional themes and symbols, notably the idea of the oasis. **Tuwaiq Palace (originally the Diplomatic Club), Riyadh** (1985) (p. 1454A), is a continuous wall-cum-building on the edge of the Diplomatic Quarter. This curvilinear building has different functions in each sector and closes around a contained space which is an oasis-like lush inner garden in striking contrast to the Virgin desert landscape outside the walls. The building incorporates fabric-covered canopies, designed by Frei Otto, which flow out beyond the facades of dark-beige Riyadh stone.

Although attempts were made during the 1970s and 1980s to give Modernism a regional flavour and to enrich it with some of the forms and symbols of the local culture there are many examples of export architecture pure and simple. Among the most extreme examples of international Modernism merely being visited upon the Arabic Peninsula are Kenzo Tange's **Royal Palaces, Jeddah** (1983) (p. 1454C), and **Yarmouk University, Irbid, Jordan** (1983), and Caudil, Rowlett and Scott's **University of Petroleum and Minerals, Dhahran** (1969–82) (p. 1454D).

The expanding economy of the region and the increasing demand for air travel ensured that the airport became a major building type during the 1970s and 1980s. Notable is the **Hajj Terminal, Jeddah** (1982) (p. 1455A), designed by SOM with Fazlur Rahman Kahn as structural engineer. This terminal made the Ottoman dream of comfortable access to pilgrimage sites by means of contemporary travel technology a reality. Located next to Jeddah Airport, the terminal has an interior with clear spans of over 50 m (160 ft) to give large open areas of floor space. This is to accommodate the pilgrims who use the terminal with their numbers reaching as high as 2 million at the same time. The tensile roof structure evokes the tradition of nomadic tents while the interior of the terminal is minimal and modern in the extreme incorporating state-of-the-art technology.

During the late 1980s the argument for a regionally responsive architecture gained momentum with clients like the Riyadh Development authority in Saudi Arabia under the leadership of Mohammed al-Sheikh, giving appointments to those local architects who were attempting to build on, rather than to ignore, regional traditions. Ali Shuaibi (born 1950), his firm

A. Tuwaiq Palace, Riyadh (1985). See p. 1453

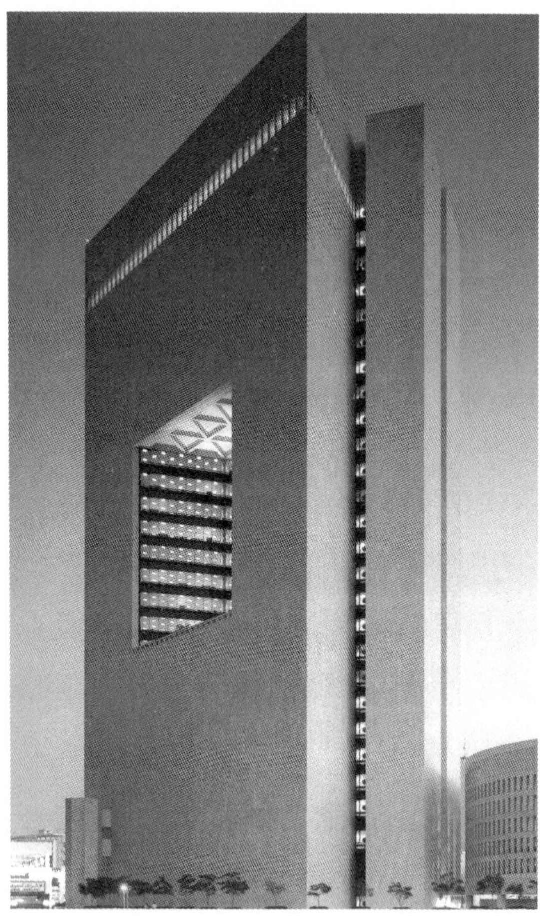

B. National Commercial Bank, Jeddah (1977–84). See p. 1453

C. Royal Palaces, Jeddah (1983). See p. 1453

D. University of Petroleum and Minerals, Dhahran (1969–82). See p. 1453

A. Hajj Terminal, Jeddah (1982). See p. 1453

B. Qatar University, Qatar (1985). See p. 1456

(BEEAH) of Saudi Arabia and Rasem Badran (born 1941) of Jordan strove to define the new regional architecture while simultaneously utilising the opportunities offered by modern technology and providing buildings that met modern standards of comfort and convenience. Shuabi designed many public buildings in Riyadh, notably the **Al-Kindi Plaza** and **Mosque** (1983–6), the **General Organisation for Social Insurance** and **Beeah Offices, Riyadh** (1985–9). Badran designed the **Justice Palace** and **Imam al-Turki Mosque, Riyadh** (1992). The designs of Badran and Shuaibi – with their anstere rectilinear forms, minaret-like towers, colonnaded walks to create protected open spaces and small windows to exclude sunlight and reduce the need for air conditioning – are fine examples of this contemporary redefinition of Najdi architecture. The architectural language devèloped by Larsen, Badran and Shuaibi has now evolved into a coherent vacabulary. Ashlar cladding cut from the dark-beige stone, local limestone and grainy stucco with finishes in matching colours give a sense of place and unity to many recently completed buildings, especially those in urban settings.

Some of the most impressive examples of the revival of traditional architectectural values can be seen in the **Corniche area of Jeddah**, a city-edge park developed in the early 1980s under the auspices of the mayor of Jeddah, Said al-Farsi. The most interesting buildings here are a series of **mosques** designed by an Egyptian architect Abdelwahed el-Wakil (born 1943), a proud disciple of Hassan Fathy. Fathy, who proclaimed the merits of traditional architecture as early as the beginning of the 1950s was regarded as one of the seminal international authorities in the 1980s when traditional values in architecture begun to be prized worldwide.

At **Jeddah** El-Wakil claimed that, historically, the architecture of the holy land of Hijaz reflected the best elements of all the architectures in the region due to the cultural interventions of the Mamluks and then the Ottomans. Therefore el-Wakil made it his aim to compose buildings incorporating the 'best' of Islamic architectural heritage. This argument secured el-Wakil a moral basis for his eclecticism. Throughout the building process el-Wakil showed a sensitivity to proportions and to the siting of the mosques which are constructed using authentic Arab (not necessarily Saudi) building technology. This has involved the use of brick with lime mortar and traditionally designed and built domes. El-Wakil's **Island Mosque**; **Miqat Mosque**; **Al-Harity Mosques**, **Jeddah**; **Quiblatain** and **Quba Mosques**, **Medina**, all built during the 1980s display an extremely consistent exploration of classical forms for mosque architecture.

Some notable buildings have been constructed in the smaller countries in the Gulf Region. Two outstanding examples are **Qatar University, Qatar** (1985) (p. 1455B), by Kamal el-Kafrawi (1931–93) which has a plan formed by a series of closely packed octagons incorporated open courts, Islamic geometic patterns and traditional forms of environmental controls and **The National Museum of Bahrain, Manama** (1988), by the Danish architects Krohn and Hartvig Rasmussen. The building is sited on the edge of a lagoon and comprises a number of display areas connected by covered circulation routes which, with pergolas, allow cool air from the lagoon to circulate through the building.

Iran

The Pahlavi dynasty which came to the throne in 1926 pursued a policy of Westernisation, even to the exclusion of a concern for the maintenance of the country's remarkable cultural and architectural heritage. During the 1930s both rationalised neo-Classicism and Modernism flourished. The wisdom of following Western practice in an almost unthinking manner was not questioned by the local architectural profession until well into the 1970s. At that time Nader Ardalan with his book *Sense of Unity* published in 1973, brought an understanding of architecture and space as conceived by Sufism and with his own architectural practice Ardalan experimented with the application of generic forms spiritual values to contemporary architecture. His **Iran Centre for Management Studies, Tehran** (1972), has radial vaulted spaces and hexagonal courtyards arranged around a large Persian garden.

Kamran Diba, and his firm DAZ, endeavoured to establish a continuity with Iran's architectural traditions while at the same time creating buildings that respond to contemporary demands and make use of new technology. His preliminary experiments at **Faculty Housing, Jondi-shapour University, Ahwaz** (1967–72), reached maturity in **Shushtar New Town, Khuzestan** (1974–80), where Diba used traditional urban patterns to create semi-open spaces and covered walkways and provided roof terraces for sleeping and food preparation as in Old Shustar. But Diba also simplified the tradition of elaborate brickwork and incorporated those technological innovations conversant with the traditions of the region. **Jondi-shapour University Mosque** (1968–73) expresses Diba's commitment to the recreation of traditional urban patterns. The Mosque was not planned or placed in isolation but integrated into the campus and plays an integral part in the pattern of pedestrian movement within the university.

Some extremely vivid architecture was produced in Iran during the 1970s. This was due partly to the influence of the Empress who had studied architecture in Paris but also to the state's economic prosperity which enabled the development of large and often ostentatious projects. The international competition for the **Tehran Public Library** (1977) placed Iran in the centre of the contemporary architectural debate while Hans Hollein's (born 1934) restoration and decoration of the **Abgineh Museum of Glass and Ceramics, Tehran**, housed in a nineteenth-century mansion (1978), was a demonstration of how new and traditional elements can be mixed successfully. Diba and Ardalan's **Museum of Contemporary Art, Tehran** (1967–76), demonstrated how traditional forms could be used in a creative, contemporary manner for the familiar wind-catcher of the region was reworked in reinforced concrete to capture light and air for the museum's interior.

A Pan-Islamic Architecture

Since the early 1980s a sustained attempt has been maintained by the Aga Khan Trust for Culture to identify and protect Islamic regional design, building, cultural and spiritual traditions and to promote their use and reflect their influence in contemporary design. The architectural and planning consequences of this initiative cannot yet be viewed in perspective but it seems clear that a number of seminal projects have emerged from this determination to reconnect with an historical continuity ruptured by decades of Western Modernism and to create a new architecture relevant to the diverse Muslim societies it serves.

Israel

Until the arrival of the early Zionist pioneers in the late nineteenth century, Israel had been culturally and socially isolated outpost of the Ottoman Empire. The history of twentieth-century architecture in Israel is dominated by European-trained architects, imported styles, and by attempts to create a particularly Jewish or Israeli style of architecture.

The most influential architect working in Israel in the early twentieth century was Alexander Baerwald (1877–1930). Baerwald, a former Prussian civil servant, who was Berlin-born and educated, was brought to Haifa to design two educational buildings, the **Technikum** (1909–13) (p. 1458) and the **Reali School** (1909–13). The **Bank Leumi, Haifa** (1925) (p. 1459A), is also by Baerwald. These buildings reflected his desire to create an appropriate modern style for Palestine, which combined European advances in planning and technology with stylistic elements of the Levant. Baerwald emigrated to Palestine in 1924, and from 1925 until his death, he served as the first professor of architecture at the Technikum.

The question of an appropriate style for Israel is one that has vexed architects for most of this century. Theodor Herzl, founder of the modern Zionist movement, had first addressed the problem in 1898, and his solution was romantic and oriental in character, deriving many of its elements from Moorish architecture. The search for an appropriate style was a recurrent theme in the architecture of **Tel Aviv** in the 1920s. It is epitomised by the **Palm House** (1922) by Y. Z. Tabatchnik, where all the decorative motifs are derived from Jewish iconography, and there is an attempt at a Jewish order of columns. It is also found, in a less overt fashion, in Joseph Minor's design for a **house for the poet H. N. Bialik** (1924–5), in much of the work of Tel Aviv's most prolific architect of the period, Yehuda Megidovitch (1886–1961), and in a very orientalising romantic manner in Alexander Levy's (1884–1942) **Pagoda House** (1925).

With the coming of the British Mandate in 1917, came C. R. Ashbee (1863–1942), who was appointed Civic Advisor by the Military Governor, Ronald Storrs. Ashbee though he did not build anything in Israel was responsible for a revival of indigenous arts and crafts, for the conservation and restoration of local monuments, and, most importantly, for Storr's edict that all buildings in Jerusalem shall be of the local stone. Among the British architects working in Palestine were Clifford Holliday (1897–1960), who designed the **S. Andrew's Church of Scotland** (p. 1459C) and the adjacent **Scottish Hospice, Jerusalem** (1927–1930), and Austen S. Barbe Harrison (1891–1976), who designed the **Governor General's House** and the **Rockefeller Museum** (1927–38) (p. 1459B) both in Jerusalem. The Rockefeller Museum must be considered the apogee of buildings Classical in origin, but Levantine in character.

The rise of Nazism in Germany saw the arrival of numerous European-trained architects in Mandate Palestine, many of whom had studied at the Bauhaus or who had worked with the acknowledged masters of the Modern Movement, and who reinforced the other European-trained architects already living and working in the country. By the 1930s, Modernism was the dominant style, and it came to symbolise the new socialist society. Kibbutz and moshav buildings were Modernist in character, as was the **new city of Tel Aviv**, which with its flat-roofed white buildings was dubbed the 'White City' by the poet Nathan Alterman.

In Jerusalem the weight of history was far stronger and an eclecticism continued well into the 1930s, in buildings such as the **Young Men's Christian Association** (1926–33) by Arthur Loomis Harmon (1879–1958) and the **King David Hotel** (1930–31) (p. 1459D) by Emile Vogt, with interiors by G. G. Hufschmid. Even the Modernism of the garden

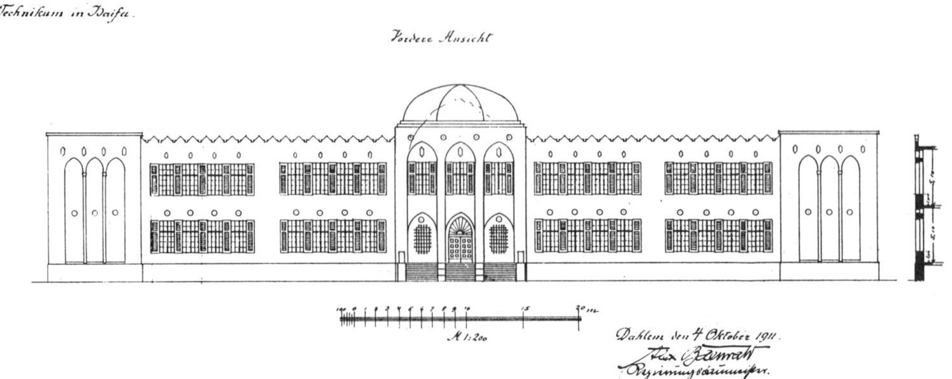

The Technikum, Haifa (1909–13); architect's drawings. See p. 1457

A. Bank Leumi, Haifa (1925). See p. 1457

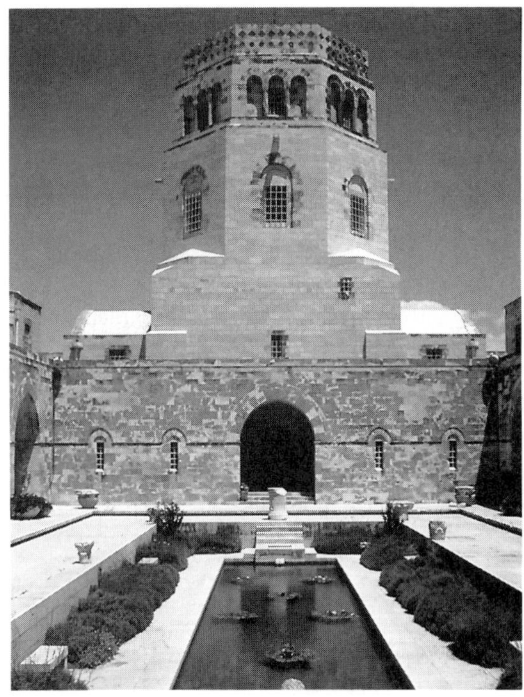

B. Rockefeller Museum, Jerusalem (1927–38). See p. 1457

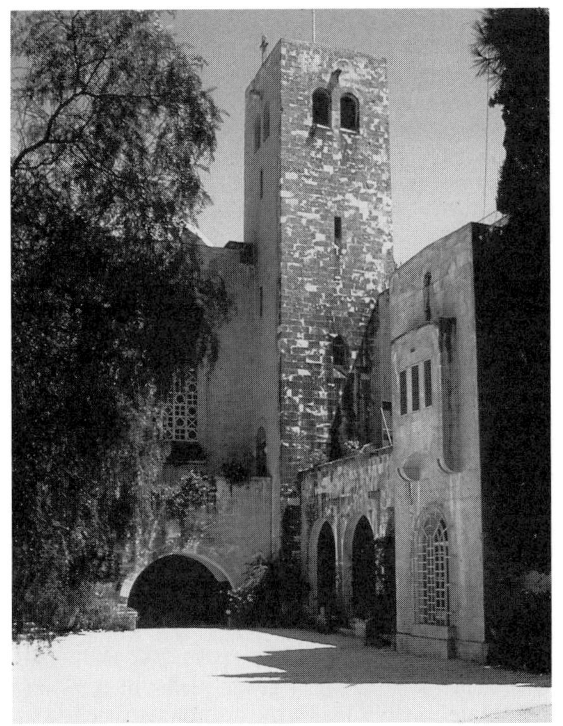

C. S. Andrew's Church of Scotland, Jerusalem (1927–30). See p. 1457

D. King David Hotel, Jerusalem (1930–31). See p. 1457

suburb of **Rechavia**, which was laid out in 1921 by Richard Kauffman (1887–1958), but which was mostly built during the 1930s, was tempered by the need to build in stone.

The planning of new settlements reflected the influence of the Social Utopianism movement rather than any eclectic attempt at an appropriate national style. Richard Kauffman was invited to Palestine by the Zionist Organisation to design rural collective settlements, the moshavim and kibbutzim. His most dramatic plan was for the **moshav of Nahalal** (1921), where he designed an elliptical plan, reminiscent in form of Filarete's ideal city of the Renaissance, with the communal buildings at the centre, surrounded by the housing, which in turn is surrounded by farmland. Kauffman's architecture, though very clearly of the Modern Movement, was adapted to suit the local climate, as can be seen in his design for a **school at Kibbutz Degania** (1930), and at the **Dead Sea Potash Works Housing** (1929), where great emphasis is laid upon the circulation of air to cool the buildings. Other distinguished kibbutz structures are the dining halls built by the Viennese-born and educated architect and artist Leopold Krakauer (1890–1954) at the **kibbutzim of Bet Alfa** (1930) and **Tel Yosef** (1933).

The best known and most influential of the émigré architects was Erich Mendelsohn (1887–1953). Mendelsohn had already visited the country in 1923, and was well known by the Jewish elite. His most important buildings were the **house and library for the Schocken family** (1934–6) (p. 1461) that he built for his former patrons from Germany in Jerusalem, the **Hadassah hospital on Mount Scopus, Jerusalem** (1936–8) (p. 1462B), the **Bank Leumi Jerusalem** (1936–39) and the **house of Chaim Weizman, Rechovot** (1936) where Mendelsohn's European Modernism is brilliantly adapted to the extreme heat of the Levant.

The dominant local, though not necessarily, locally born, architects, were Aryeh Sharon (1902–1984), Ze'ev Rechter (1899–1960), and Dov Karmi (1905–1962). In 1933, Rechter, who had studied in Rome and Paris, designed **Engle House** (p. 1462D), a very derivative Corbuserian apartment building, which was Tel Aviv's first building on piloti. It is Sharon, however, who epitomised the new architect in the socialist society. Born in Poland he emigrated to Palestine, where he lived on a kibbutz, studied at the Bauhaus (1926–9) under Walter Gropius and Hannes Meyer, for whom he worked prior to returning to Palestine in 1931. Alexander Friedman was responsible for the design of a number of apartment blocks in Jerusalem which display a fluid almost Art Deco line – for example, in **Shmuel Hanagid Street, Jerusalem** (1938–9) (p. 1462A) and in the **Hamaalot House, Jerusalem** (with Meir Rubin) (*c*.1935) (p. 1462C).

From Independence in 1948, with vast numbers of immigrants entering the fledgling state of Israel, architecture was dominated by the need to house a growing population. The white Modernism of Le Corbusier's Heroic Period was abandoned in favour of a more Brutal concrete architecture. This was a style perfectly suited to Israel with its harsh climate and lack of natural building materials. Sharon, who between 1935 and 1939, had built much cooperative workers housing in Tel Aviv, was involved in the design of some twenty new town plans, and new housing schemes grew up across the country. Among the most interesting were the schemes designed by N. Zolotov and D. Havkin for the **Ministry of Housing in Beersheba** (1960–64) and the **hillside housing, Upper Nazareth** (1955–7), designed by Sharon and Benjamin Idelson, which is distinguished by the terracing of the houses and the use of natural stone. In the 1970s, housing was again a priority and many new towns and dormitory suburbs were built, much of it having the scale and feel of a megastructure as epitomised by the **new Jerusalem Suburb of Gilo**.

An outgrowth of the housing movement was an interest in prefabrication and modularisation, and a fascination with geometry. The most extreme form of the latter can be found in the architecture of Zvi Hecker (born 1931), most particularly in his **City Hall for Bat Yam** (1959–63) designed in partnership with Alfred Neumann and Eldar Sharon, and the **Mechanical Engineering Laboratory at the Technikam, Haifa** (1964–7), executed in partnership with Neumann. Hecker's interests in housing and polyhedral geometry, which was first seen in the **Dubiner Apartment Building, Ramat Gan** (1961–3), executed with Neumann and Sharon, was carried further in the **housing in Ramot** (1972–5), where a polygonal geometry is used in plan and section.

For a period in the 1960s, the architecture of Israel was seen as being at the cutting edge of the Brutalist movement, with sculptural buildings such as the **El Al Building, Tel Aviv** (1962–5), by Dov Karmi and his son, Ram, (born 1931), and the powerful **Hilton Hotel, Tel Aviv** (1965–6), by Ze'ev Rechter's son, Yacov (born 1924) in partnership with M. Zarhi and M. Peri. This language of exposed concrete, used for both structural and decorative purposes, became the norm throughout the country, except for Jerusalem, for the better part of three decades, and came to represent the national style of the young state. Three important buildings not in this style are the **Afridar Civic Centre, Ashkelon** (1952–4), an essay in vernacular Classicism designed by Jack Barnett (born 1925), a South African architect and Rome Prize winner; the **Israel Museum** (1959–75) by Alfred Mansfield (born 1912), a gentle series of pavilions that are delicately sited on the hills of Jerusalem; and the elegant Modernist **Hebrew Union College** (1962) by Heinz Rau.

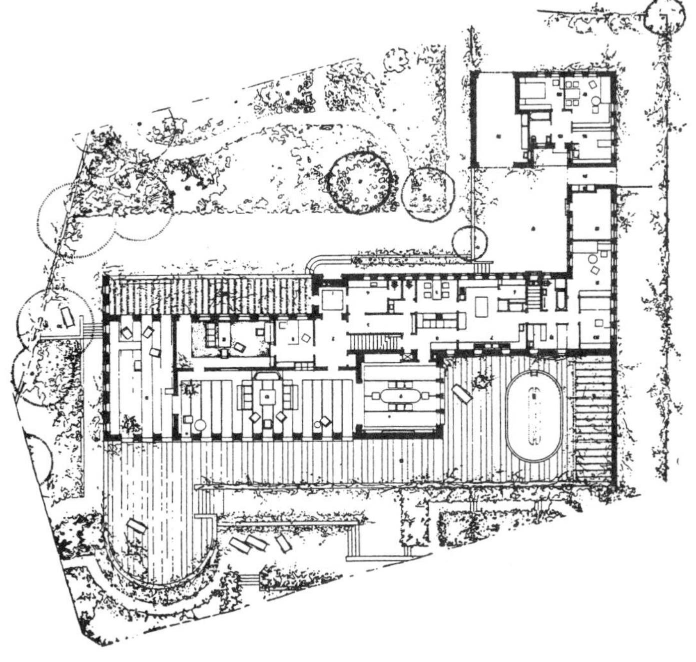

A. House and library for the Schocken family, Jerusalem (1934–6). See p. 1460

B. House for the Schocken family: plan of ground floor

A. Shmuel Hanagid Street, Jerusalem (1938–9). See p. 1460

B. Hadassah hospital on Mount Scopus, Jerusalem (1936–8). See p. 1460

C. Hamaalot House, Jerusalem (*c.* 1935). See p. 1460

D. Engle House, Tel Aviv (1933). See p. 1460

A. Jerusalem Centre for Near Eastern Studies (1986). See p. 1465

B. Supreme Court Building, Jerusalem (1986–93). See p. 1465

1 Library
2 Grand staircase
3 Atrium
4 Courtyard

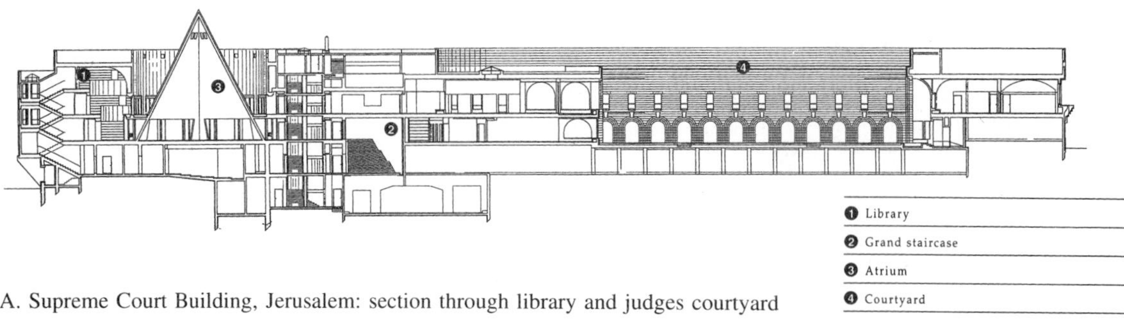

A. Supreme Court Building, Jerusalem: section through library and judges courtyard

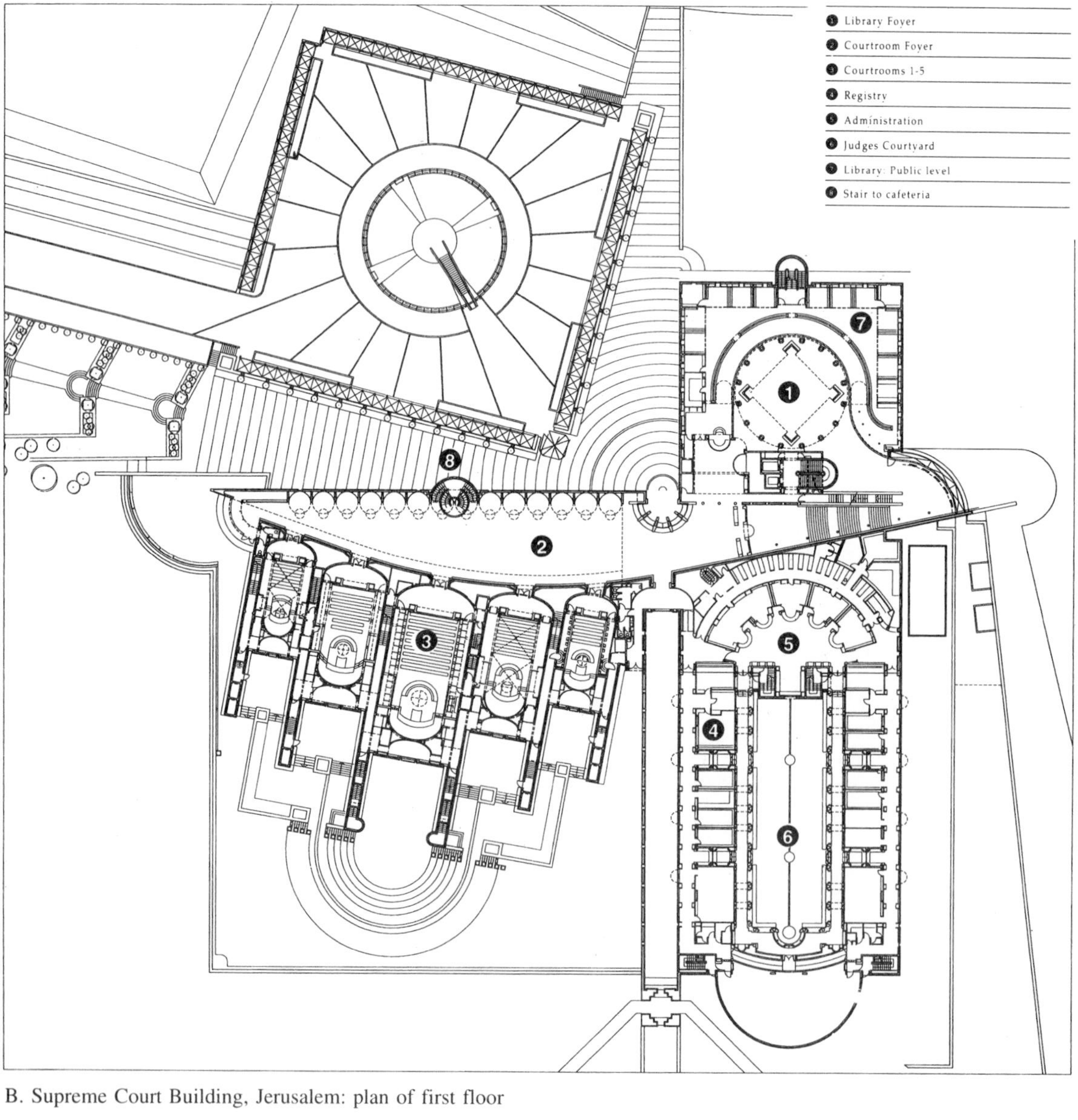

1 Library Foyer
2 Courtroom Foyer
3 Courtrooms 1-5
4 Registry
5 Administration
6 Judges Courtyard
7 Library: Public level
8 Stair to cafeteria

B. Supreme Court Building, Jerusalem: plan of first floor

The 1980s saw an emergence from the stylistic straitjacket. The two most striking buildings of recent years are in Jerusalem. The first is the **Jerusalem Centre for Near Eastern Studies** (The Mormon University) (1986) (p. 1463A) by David Reznik (born 1923), which is a terraced structure well suited to its site, with domes, arches, and courtyards obviously of the East. The second building is the new **Supreme Court Building** (1986–93) (pp. 1463B, 1464) by Ram Karmi and Ada Karmi-Melamede (born 1936), which though far more abstract and sculptural than the Jerusalem Centre owes a strong debt to history and to the *genius loci*.

Chaper 49
AFRICA

Introduction

Sir Herbert Baker's confident belief in the related qualities of architecture and colonial rule, and in an architect's mission to give outward expression to the colonist's national ideals and then to adapt them to diverse national situations, was a concept which had little chance to stand the test of time. Within a short period of seventy-five years from 1890 onwards, African empires had been founded, variously developed and lost by the major European countries. On the other hand, there were the older-established colonies and protectorates which had longer histories. Because of these circumstances there were great differences between the degrees of Europeanisation affecting the African countries. The colonies that had become well established, notably those of Britain and France, kept their architectural links with Europe, even after independence, although they were progressively more influenced by some aspects of indigenous culture. But from the beginning of the twentieth century there was a constant architectural theme, and this was the integration of cultures.

An early twentieth-century innovation was the laying-out of townships outside centres of African population for the use of colonial administrators and commercial undertakings. In 1910 the provincial and district commissioners in the Kenya province were instructed that towns should be 'laid out on more permanent lines suitable for future development', specifying land required for government purposes, nominating sites required for such buildings as markets, churches and hospitals, and indicating the position of European and Indian business quarters, European residential quarters and native location. When the northern capital of Nigeria was moved to Kaduna in 1917 the new layout was based on principles laid down by the Governor-General, Frederick John (later Lord) Lugard, and these were incorporated into his influential Townships Ordinance of 1917.

Kaduna is the work of a military mind accustomed to parade-ground discipline and the observance of a strict hierarchy; but it introduced an orderly concept of planning and spatial organisation which bore no resemblance to the African concept of organic growth around communal buildings such as religious centres, shrines and markets. The Governor's House was placed on the highest point looking down a central avenue. Below that, decreasing in size according to rank, were building plots for senior and junior officers. Avenues of trees were planted, gardens were generous, and a green belt surrounded the government residential area. There were barracks and a parade ground, a race course and a golf course, and the shops and offices were out of sight. The concept of the axial, hierarchic plan became widely established, and it was probably the source of the layout of Abuja, the new capital of Nigeria which was initiated in the 1970s.

Another important urban design was that of Heliopolis, Egypt, which was built between 1906 and 1922. This city was laid out along the lines of the British garden cities with villas and gardens.

Lugard's French contemporary, Governor-General Marshal Lyautey, was the force behind new urban plans and other innovations in colonial North Africa. When Dakar, which had been founded in 1857, was promoted to being the capital city of Senegal in 1904 it was laid out on a grid pattern. Colonial villas with Mediterranean details were built in spacious gardens, and there were clearly defined areas – an administrative centre, a business district and a port. Later, arcaded streets were added, and then more government buildings.

A French law of 1919, which became applicable to Algeria three years later, required a plan to be drawn up for the development, extension and enhancement of towns, of which Algiers was the first in Africa to be affected, although the plan was not approved until 1931. It introduced the concept of zoning, and proposed the demolition and reconstruction of the quartier de la Marine and the old Préfecture; new areas were envisaged, but at the same time an exception was made in the case of part of the old town in which there was a declared intention to preserve the authenticity and aesthetic value of the old buildings and arcaded streets on account of their picturesqueness and their quality as a living museum. Despite the imposition of colonial planning on both old and new African towns there were reciprocal influences between the two cultures, which are even more apparent in the architecture of the continent.

Architecture up to the Independence of the African States

In South Africa Sir Herbert Baker provided designs for new public buildings such as the **South African Institute for Medical Research, Johannesburg** (1912) (p. 1468A), with a series of courtyards and formal planting, colonnades linking the main wings, and a central domed tower. In **Nairobi, Kenya**, he built the **Law Courts**, the **Railway Headquarters** (1929) and **Government House** (1934–5) in a similar Wren-derived style in which standards of detailing and craftsmanship are of a high order. The **Cathedral of S. Mary and All Saints, Salisbury, Zimbabwe** (1913–38), is in his Romanesque style, with rough masonry contrasting with shallow plastered domes in the interior. Externally the most notable feature of the design is a circular campanile which was suggested by the tower of the great ruin at Zimbabwe. Baker's influence persisted in the work of his colleagues and former assistants who worked in South Africa itself and in other British colonies. Francis Massey, his partner, designed **S. James's Pro-cathedral, Maseru, Lesotho** (1905–6), and **S. John Baptist's Pro-cathedral, Bulawayo, Zimbabwe** (1910–13).

Sir Edwin Lutyens made a characteristic and distinguished addition in the English Classical tradition to Johannesburg's widely varied architecture when he designed the **Civic Art Gallery** (1911–15) as a low pantiled range with a portico and a projecting pavilion at each end. He put his point of view that in 'old countries you can use rough materials, where you find men instinctively handling it from boyhood and unconsciously weaving lovely texture into it. In a new country it is impossible to expect any help of that sort in the fabric of a building... There is in Africa no tradition on which accidents can rely, and reliance can only remain with the best thought... as concerns her architecture... You get no great poetry in a pidgin language, though you may get poetic sentiment.' His designs for the Art Gallery and for the triumphal arch of the **Rand Regiments' Memorial** (1911) bear out his conviction that where Classical architecture was designed for new countries the rules and proportions should be strictly and implicitly prescribed and followed; and he disagreed with Cecil Rhodes's theory that Classical architecture should be adapted for colonial use.

The Classical style remained in constant use in such buildings as the magnificently sited **University of Cape Town** by J. M. Solomon (1915) on the slopes of Table Mountain, the Corinthian-porticoed **Central Block of the University of the Witwatersrand, Johannesburg** by Emley and Williamson (1923), in the centre of the axially planned campus, the **University Library, Johannesburg**, by Williamson, Cowin and Powers, (1933), the **Public Library, Johannesburg** By J. Perry (1935) (p. 1469A), the **South African Reserve Bank, Cape Town**, by J. Morris (1932), and the **Land Bank, Cape Town**, by B. Mansergh (1938).

The work of Gordon Leith, a younger follower of Baker who had studied in Europe, shows the influence of contemporary Swedish neo-Classicism in such buildings as the **Railway Station, Johannesburg** (1927–32), the **City Hall, Bloemfontein** (1936), **Union Corporation Building, Johannesburg** (1938), and the **South African Reserve Bank, Johannesburg** (1938). The **National Gallery, Cape Town** by the Public Works Department (1928–9) displays a more eclectic version of Classicism and incorporates some elements drawn from the Cape Dutch style, which has remained a pervasive influence.

In other British colonies a picturesque, eclectic Mediterranean style was used, particularly for private houses. On a larger scale it can be seen in the rebuilding of **Government House, Dar-es-Salaam, Tanzania** (1922) (p. 1468D), and in later form in the 1950s in the **University of Ghana, Legon,** by Harrison, Barnes and Hubbard (p. 1468E). This is notable for its elaborate roofline and terraced campus.

At the beginning of the century there was a change of policy by the French government which suggested it was time to move away from the style of the conqueror and towards that of the protector and collaborator. In 1903 Governor Jonnard told a delegation to Alegiers, 'We are not like others, who tread down those they conquer, but we wish to walk with them, alongside them like brothers.' Between 1900 and 1914 there were several examples of the consequent neo-Arabic construction in **Algiers**, for example the **Grande Poste** by Tondoir and Voinot (1890–1900), the department stores now known as the **Galerie Algérienne** by Voinot (1902) and the **Préfecture** (1904).

In the French colonies under Marshal Lyautey's influence there was an effort to integrate two cultures, and in Fez there was a recognition of the value of the old buildings and an attempt to preserve isolated examples as well as to keep the entire structure of the medina. Himself a great admirer of traditional Moroccan architecture, as could be seen in the house he built for his own occupation at **Rabat** by H. Prost and A. Laprade (1918–20), Lyautey encouraged the incorporation of traditional forms and details into such public buildings as the **Law Courts, Casablanca,** by

A. South African Institute for Medical Research, Johannesburg (1912). See p. 1467

D. Government House, Dar-es-Salaam (1922). p. 1467

B. Administrative Buildings, Bamako (*c.* 1930). See p. 1470

C. Bank of Rome, Tripoli (mid-1930s). See p. 1470

E. University of Ghana, Legon (1950s). See p. 1467

A. Public Library, Johannesburg (1935). See p. 1467

B. Anglo-American Building, Johannesburg (1937–8). See p. 1467

C. Apartments at Casablanca (1953–4). See p. 1472

D. Housing, Rabat. See p. 1472

J. Marrast (1915), and the **Post Office, Rabat,** by J. Laforgue (*c.* 1920). The **City Hall, Casablanca,** by M. Boyer (1931) echoes the character of Moroccan palaces, especially in the arcaded courtyard: horseshoe arches are repeated along the entire length of the **Administrative Buildings, Bamako, Mali** (*c.* 1930) (p. 1468B), and they are incorporated more elegantly into the contemporary **Law Courts, Segou, Mali**. The Arabic style was still in influence in Cairo, and it was used with great success in the **Bank Misr** by A. Laseiac (1927), the **Waqfs Ministry Building** (1925) and the **American University** (1932). Religious buildings too, for example **Jamia Mosque, Nairobi** (1925–33), were faithful to tradition.

The occupation of Libya and Somalia by the Italians after World War I resulted in the founding of new **agricultural villages** based on planned centres (for example, **Oliveti** and **Mario Gioda**, designed by U. Di Segni), in which the architecture resembled that of the new towns in the Transpontine region of Italy such as Aprilia and Pontinia. A new town of **Tripoli** was planned alongside the old (by A.A. Novello and O. Cabiati), with a central piazza in which were built a **cathedral** in the Lombardic style by F. Di Fausto (1924–32), a **governor's palace** and the **Bank of Rome** by A. Limongelli (mid-1930s) (p. 1468C). The occupation of Abyssinia in 1936 produced more plans for Addis Ababa by I. Guidi and C. Valle and other towns, in which there was a clear demarcation between the European and the native districts.

To some extent the new buildings were influenced by the quality of 'mediterraneità' claimed by the Rationalist architects of the 1930s (houses in **Somalia** designed by C. A. Rava, for example), and something of the character of south Italian towns was exported abroad. The architectural style in which the new administrative buildings were designed was defined in 1936 as 'il grande spirito classico', representative of Roman civilisation. Nevertheless, modern technical resources were to be incorporated, and there were references to considering the climate and the character of the surroundings. Ottavio Cabiati wrote, 'As the Italian language is now spoken in Tripoli and Benghazi, just as in Rome, so should the Italian architectural style be used.' A so-called *Manifesto dell'architettura coloniale* (1936) written by Giovanni Pellegrini amplified this belief, and grand stripped-Classical schemes for Addis Ababa were prepared in 1939 – an imperial palace (Guidi, Vale, Ulrich and Cafiero), government offices (Guidi and Valle), and a town hall (Ceronconi) – but these remained a De Chirico-like dream of long colonnades in a sun-baked land.

The Modern Movement was making its effect felt in Africa in the early 1930s, principally in Algeria where the first *Cité Moderne* exhibition was held in 1933: but even in the highly developed South Africa the lateness of the introduction of industrialisation meant that craft traditions persisted longer than in Western Europe and the United States. Nevertheless, there were some innovations introduced from France. Auguste and Gustave Perret were working in Morocco, most notably on the **dock installations and warehouses at Casablanca**, as early as 1915: and in the 1920s they collaborated with M. J. Guiauchain on the construction of the **Palais du Gouvernement Général, Algiers**; this was designed in a Perret manner in a stripped Classical style around a *cour d'honneur*, but it also incorporated a multi-storey building. Guiauchain was the most advanced architect working in Algeria in reinforced concrete, and he also designed the **Salle Pierre Bordes**, the **Lycée du Champ de Manoeuvres** (1936), and the **Maison de l'Agriculture** (1938), all in **Algiers**. Other buildings of the 1930s, by which time the neo-Arabic style had been superseded by new ideas from France, were erected in Algiers such as the **Hôtel de Ville** and the **Foyer Civique** by L. Claro (1935) which was described as a combination of *l'art moderne et des inspirations de l'art antique*, and the **Maison des Etudiants** by C. Montaland (1933). Montaland was versatile enough to be able to design the Algerian Pavilion for the 1931 Colonial Exposition at Vincennes in the traditional Algerian style.

At that time Le Corbusier was making ambitious large-scale proposals for rebuilding the city of Algiers. In 1931 he was invited there to lecture on modern architecture and town planning; during the lectures he spoke of his concept of the city as a ribbon coastal development following the contours of the mountains. Subsequently he developed these ideas in five sets of plans from 1933 to 1942, including a residential neighbourhood which was to be linked to a skyscraper which would have dwarfed completely the picturesque old Casbah. Nothing came of these plans, nor of his proposals for a new town, **Nemours**, on the Mediterranean coast, nor for a large residential development, the **Domaine Durand, Qued Ouchaia**. *Poésie sur Alger*, published in 1950, is the only tangible result of all these ideas, but there were indirect consequences. Under French rule urban planning followed the European trends generally, as in the new town of **Berrovaghia** which was designed in 1944 by Emery and Miquel, and there were many similar residential projects, such as those at **Oran Sidi-bel-Abbes** and **Saida** by Candilis (trained in Le Corbusier's office), Josic, Woods and Pons; at **Hussein-Dey** and **Blida** by Bize and Ducollet; and another project at **Hussein-Dey** (Cité de la Montagne) by Daure and Beri.

The progress of the International Style from Europe to parts of Africa was hastened to some extent by the arrival of refugees from Nazi Germany. Steffen Ahrends, who had joined the Ernst May group in Moscow (1931–2) and then worked in his father's studio in Berlin (1932–6), emigrated to Johannesburg and built up a large practice; he is believed to have built around 500 **houses**, working all over South Africa and in Southern Rhodesia (Zimbabwe). May himself left Germany in 1934 and lived first in Tanganyika (Tanzania) and then, from 1937, in Kenya. In the 1940s he made a design for a layout of austere rendered **apartment blocks** in **Nairobi**, the **Delamere Avenue Development**, reminiscent of his earlier work as City Architect in Frankfurt; and in 1950 he designed the **Oceanic Hotel, Mombasa**, the first of many hotels to be built along the Indian Ocean coast. Wilhelm Arnold Pabst, who had trained in Berlin and worked with Mies van der Rohe, emigrated to South Africa; among his buildings in **Johannesburg** are the **Chinese Club** and **Patidar Mansions**.

Another pioneer of modern architecture, Amyas Connell, left England in 1947 and after a short stay in Tanganyika (Tanzania) he too went to Kenya. The larger projects he undertook, such as the **Aga Khan Platinum Jubilee Hospital** in the late 1950s, the **Legislative Council Building** (later the **New Parliament Buildings**) of 1955 with additions eight years later, and the **Crown Law Offices** (1960), clearly show the continuing influence of Le Corbusier on Connell's work, but they also reveal his growing interest in decoration, especially the effective use of boldly perforated walls in a repetitive design.

In South Africa, Le Corbusier was a strong influence on what he dubbed **Le Groupe Transvaal**, led by Rex Martienssen, W. G. McIntosh and Norman Hanson. Admirers successively of Dudok, Gropius and Le Corbusier, they established contact with the last, who wrote in 1936 that he was amazed 'to find something so alive in that far away spot in Africa.' He gave the group advice, telling them to 'stamp out the school (the "Corbu" school just as the Vignola school!)'; but his influence is apparent enough in such designs as **House Harris** by Hanson, Tomkin and Finkelstein (1933) and their **Suzman House** (1936), **House Stern** by Martienssen, Fassler and Cooke (1934–5) as well as Martienssen's own house. In the centre of **Johannesburg** the International Style was represented by **Peter House**, a three-storey building by Martienssen, Fassler and Cooke (1934–5), the eight-storey **Hotpoint House** by Hanson, Tomkin and Finkelstein (1934–5), **Nevada Court** by Cowin and Ellis (1938–9), and the **Twentieth-century Theatre** (1930–40) in which no fewer than five of the closely knit group collaborated. Douglass Cowin, an architect on the periphery of the group, evolved idioms that suited the local climatic conditions, and these exerted a strong influence on later domestic architecture in **Johannesburg; Casa Bedo** (1936), **Casa Miljo** (1936–37) and **House Gordon** (1938) were in a style that was to become popular.

The Dutch links with South Africa were still strong, and the brick architecture of Dudok was the source of such a design as the **Club House of the Technical College, Durban** (Ing. Jackson and Park-Ross 1938). The tall vertical blocks of **Escom House** (G. Pearse 1934) and **Van Eck House, Johannesburg**, by P. R. Cooke, succeeded by Pearse and Fassler (1936), with windows set in continuous vertical recesses, mark the first serious impact of current American architecture, and **Chrysler House, Johannesburg**, by Nurcombe and Summerley (1938) introduced the cantilevered reinforced concrete construction which made possible continuous horizontal strip glazing. In the construction of the **Anglo-American Building** (1937–8), (p. 1469B) Sir John Burnet, Tait and Lorne not only broke the general practice of concentrating all the design on the main elevation but also integrated the immediate environment in the planted forecourt on the main front.

An inherited appreciation of the quality of traditional building materials distinguished the designs of Norman Eaton, who had made a close study of Cape Dutch architecture as well as being a Rome Scholar. Among his buildings are the **Land Banks in Potchefstroom** (1940), **Pietermaritzburg** (1941–73) and **Kroonstad** (1943–4), **Netherlands Bank Buildings in Pretoria** (1946–53) and **Durban** (1961–5), the **Little Theatre, Pretoria** (*c.* 1950), and many individual houses, for example **Anderssen House, Pretoria** (1949–50). Eaton had a different viewpoint from some of his contemporaries. He believed in the possibility of an African architecture, and he wrote critically of the tendency 'for architects to use clichés which they pick up from Le Corbusier and others. This does not mean to say that the original Le Corbusier solution was not a good one, but it is senseless to pick it up and use it in Johannesburg when it has nothing to do with us and probably nothing to do with the problem in hand.'

Post-independence

Until World War II the African colonies as well as the Union of South Africa still depended to a great extent on the importation of building materials to supplement those available locally. The cessation of this supply during the war years eventually led to the setting up of industries which made South Africa self-sufficient and increasingly independent of other countries, although its architecture is international in character and closely related to European and American ideas and fashions. In 1961 South Africa became a republic, while other African countries were given independence from 1951 onwards. 'The tropical territories are the less developed areas of the world; they are inhabited by colonial or ex-colonial peoples vigorously emerging into nationhood and faced, while they do so, with the problem of assimilating European techniques and ideas of progress.' The writer in the *Architectural Review* in 1960 had no doubt that such assimilation and Westernisation was the way forward for the newly independent African states, while recognising that although 'in due course each territory will no doubt become self-sufficient architecturally, for most of them this will be a long process, and they are only now beginning to acquire their own architectural professions and architectural schools. Not till they have done, perhaps, can they expect to achieve a consistent architectural style recognisably their own.'

The implicit belief that the more developed countries in the world had a recognisably individual and consistent architectural style is open to question; but in the newly independent countries there was an inevitable reliance on European architecture as a model to be imitated in the new administrative and commercial buildings, universities and schools; almost always they were designed by European architects. The post-war building boom in Europe had firmly established the International Style (however that was interpreted) as the norm, and it was this which was being adapted and exported to Africa, often irrespective of the style's appropriateness and context.

Jane Drew, a partner in a British practice which worked extensively in West and East Africa in the 1950s and 1960s, believed that the new education buildings should be 'deliberately geometric and orderly because such a statement is required against the extreme disorder of the luxuriant forest where the forms of the trees are so jumbled up'. It was a viewpoint in the English Picturesque tradition, which was extended to incorporate the current adoption of the International Style. She amplified this by defining the character of the new architecture for Africa, which would come 'not only from the monopitch roof and long low blocks essential to a country where lifts are expensive, but from the sunbreaks, grilles and other shading but breeze-permitting devices. In some cases, particularly in blocks and balcony details, an attempt has been made to design in a way which, without in any sense copying African detail, gives a response which is African; the sunshine and moisture and heavy overcast sky and feeling of oppressive lethargy seem to call forth moulded forms which are rhythmical and strong, not spiky and elegant, but bold and sculptural. The West can really only bring Western concepts, but the Western man designing in Africa, and for Africa, is bound to be affected not only by climatic but psychological factors.'

This contemporary interpretation of the new architecture of the 1950s and 1960s sums up the current thought about design and, despite the sentiment in the final sentence, suggests why there was a mistaken disregard for local culture from which valuable lessons could have been learnt. At this time the most obvious element which distinguished designs intended for Africa from those of Europe was the brise-soleil, of which there were innumerable varied versions. There were small repeated units, creating a lace-like pattern in the **Crown Law Offices, Nairobi, Kenya,** by A. D. Connell, the larger-scale continuous rings of the curved facade of the **National Theatre and Cultural Centre, Kampala, Uganda**, by Peatfield and Bodgener, the vertically aligned movable louvres of the **Industrial Development Corporation, Accra, Ghana**, by J. Cubitt, the floor-length vertical louvres of the **British Petroleum Office, Lagos, Nigeria**, by Fry, Drew, Knight, Creamer, the equally strong horizontal louvres of the **Cooperative Bank of Western Nigeria, Ibadan**, by the same architects, and the elegant vertical triangular fins articulating the facade of the **SCIAM Ministry of Finance, Abidjan, Ivory Coast**, by J. Semichon. The **Science Buildings, Lagos University, Nigeria** (1975), **schools** at **Lagos**, and **houses** at **Ikeja**, all by Godwin and Hopwood, make dominant design elements out of the louvres.

Le Corbusier's influence remained strong in the former French colonies, especially in housing such as the **Cité de Recasement, Djennan-el-Hassan, Algeria**, by R. Simounet, and in **apartment blocks in Casablanca, Morocco** (p. 1469C), by A. Studer (1953–4) and by E. Azagury (1968). Later examples by Azagury (who also designed the **Civic Centre**, 1967) in **Rabat, Morocco** (p. 1469D), have modified the European-derived forms by incorporating courtyards and terraces which conform more to traditional North African architecture. **Housing** designed in 1962 by J. G. Halstead close to **Christiansborg Castle, Accra, Ghana** (p. 1473A) also reverts in part to a traditional courtyard house plan, as well as providing varied groupings and rooflines which respond to the local character. Julian Elliott designed houses in **Elizabethville, Katanga Province, Congo**, in the late 1950s in which he attempted to follow some principles of African housing, although these were intended for Europeans; in Zambia in the 1960s he tried to find an African solution with simple materials and forms adapted to the vegetation. Ernst May made designs in **Kampala, Uganda**, for standardised housing based on African rather than European traditions (although his **Cultural Centre, Moshi, Tanzania**, is purely European in concept). But such designs, including Jorn Utzon's endeavour to integrate individual buildings within the landscape, and his taking Berber architecture as a model (for example, **paper factory, Morocco**, 1947), were exceptional.

British architects working in Africa were inevitably influenced by current British architecture, and there were many reflections of the Festival of Britain and the New Towns, and of the rebuilding of war-damaged cities such as Coventry. The post-war churches also provided models, for example the

A. Housing at Accra, Ghana (1962). See p. 1472

B. Chapel at University College, Ibadan, Nigeria (1953–4, extended 1961–). See p. 1474

D. Algiers Cathedral, Algeria (1959–60). See p. 1474

C. Education Centre, Tit-Mellil, Morocco (1960s). See p. 1474

Chapel of the University College, Ibadan, Nigeria (p. 1473B) by G. G. Pace, (1953–4, extended 1961–2), and the **Cathedral of the Holy Cross, Lusaka, Zambia**, by Hope, Reeler and Morris (1960–70). In **Algiers** (p. 1473D) the dominating **cathedral** by P. Herbe and J. Le Couteur (1959–60), was centrally planned to accord with the revised liturgy, and is crowned by a high hyperbolic lantern, glazed at the summit.

In South Africa, although the architectural links with Britain were still strong, there was a counter-attraction in the early 1960s from the United States. The influence of Mies van der Rohe's widely admired vocabulary can be seen, for example, in the **Civic Art Museum, Pretoria**, by Burg, Lodge and Burg in association with W. G. McIntosh (1964). but perhaps the strongest impact was that of Louis Kahn, who was an inspiration for a number of young architects who studied under him at the University of Philadelphia in the 1960s. His influence can still be seen in buildings of the 1990s such as the **Library and Civic Offices, Sandton, Johannesburg**, by GAPP Architects and the **Law Centre and offices, University of Natal, Durban**, by Hallen Custers Smith.

As in Britain, the best work of the 1950s and 1960s was in educational buildings; Maxwell Fry and Jane Drew were the pioneers, and their practice built many schools and colleges in Ghana and Nigeria. Their most important design was for the **University of Ibadan, Nigeria** (1959 onwards), which incorporates a nexus of connected buildings, in which the teaching and administrative centres were surrounded by residential colleges, set on an extensive site. James Cubitt and Kenneth Scott, in partnership in the 1950s, made a large contribution to Ghana's new architecture. In the early years of the decade they began a programme of educational buildings, including the **Teachers Training Colleges** at **Berekum, Secondi, and Jasikan**, and the **Technical Institutes** at **Accra** and **Kumasi**, which are bold and precise statements constructed of steel, concrete and glass. In 1951 work began on the **College of Technology, Kumasi**, which later became the University of Science and Technology. Scott remained in Ghana for the rest of his life. His own **house** at **Accra** is an elegant Miesian design and there is a similar distinctive quality in his commercial and health buildings which contrasts with, for example, the dramatic, extrovert character of Jean-François Zevaco's **colleges** in **Morocco** (e.g. **Tit-Mellil**, p. 1473C, **Ben-Slimane**) and **schools** (**Casablanca, Quarzazate, Agadir**) of the 1960s. The rebuilding of **Agadir, Morocco**, after an earthquake in 1960 offered opportunities to a generation of largely Moroccan-born architects. Zevaco built the **Groupe Scolaire**, as well as the **Post Office** and the **Radio/TV Station**; Arsene-Henry and Honnegger were responsible for the **City Hall**, and Elie Azagury built the **Palace of Justice**.

Many of the new universities and educational buildings have been designed by or in collaboration with architects from overseas. In **Algiers** Oscar Niemeyer, Kenzo Tange, Jakob Zweifel, Devecon Oy and Skidmore, Owings and Merrill were selected to design the new universities, while Hans Munk Hansen and Vilhelm Wohlert were responsible for the **Vocational Training Centre, Ksar-el-Boukhari** (1977). In 1966 James Cubitt was commissioned to design the **University of Garyounis, Benghazi, Libya**, to accommodate 22,000 students on a 400-ha site. Julian Elliott's **University of Zambia, Lusaka** (1965 onwards), is an interesting concept in which groups of administrative and academic buildings are connected by a central library, dining room and a students' meeting hall; all are set in a dramatically landscaped campus.

A different dramatic effect is created by the enormous **University of South Africa, Pretoria**, by Brian Sandrock (1962–4) which is cantilevered out from a hilltop, and this contrasts with the geometric formalism of the **Rand Afrikaan University, Johannesburg**, by Jan van Wyk and Wilhelm O. Meyer (1967). In the late 1970s the **Ernest Oppenheimer Life Sciences Complex** was designed for the **University of Witwatersrand, Johannesburg**, in the concrete Brutalist style by Montgomerie Oldfield Kirby Elliott Grobbellaar. In the late 1980s Julian Elliott designed the **Education Building** on the **University of Cape Town** campus as a formal and dignified structure with obvious references to colonnaded courtyards of Renaissance palazzi. The **University of the Western Cape**, to which autonomy was granted in 1980, has undertaken several additions to its campus in the years following. These have been the work of various architects; Jack Barnett (the **Great Hall** and **University Centre**), Prinsloo Parker Flint Elliott and van den Heever (the **Lecture Theatre and Science Building**), and Munnik Visser Black Fish and Partners (in association with Julian Elliott). The last-named were responsible for the **Library** (1989) (p. 1475A) which has been praised for its distinctive and exciting modelling and roof geometry and for its human scale. Revel Fox and Partners devised a loosely Classical concept for the campus of the **Peninsula Technikon** (1984) at **Bellville** in the Western Cape; individual buildings are being designed according to overall guidelines, the first being completed in 1986–7. The outstanding beauty of South African landscapes is a crucial factor in architectural design, to which the best designers respond. The **Mangosuthu Technikon, Umlazi**, by Hallen Theron and Partners (1979–82) is sensitively integrated into the landscape, located on an elevated site with views over the rolling hills to the sea; and the **Research Laboratories and Library** for the National Botanical Institute at **Kirstenbosch** has been designed on a sensitive site with wide eaves

A. Library, University of the Western Cape (1989). See p. 1474

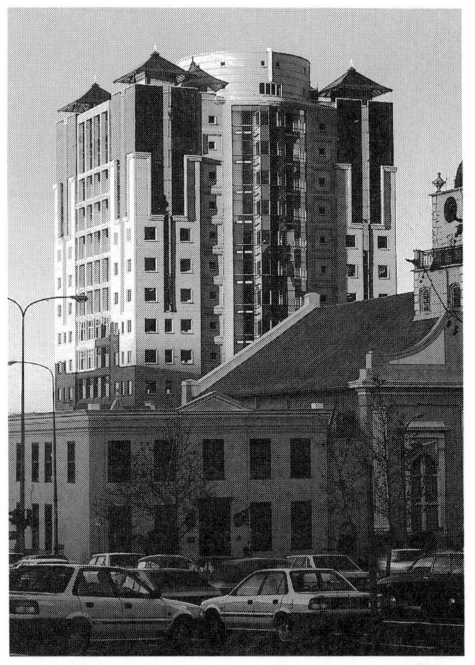

B. The Terraces, Cape Town (1980s). See p. 1477

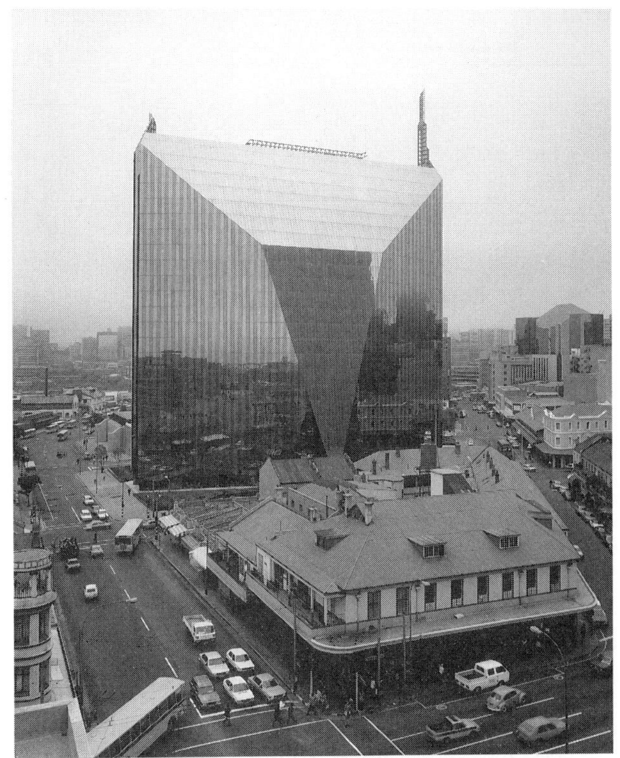

C. 11 Diagonal Street, Johannesburg (1981–3). See p. 1477

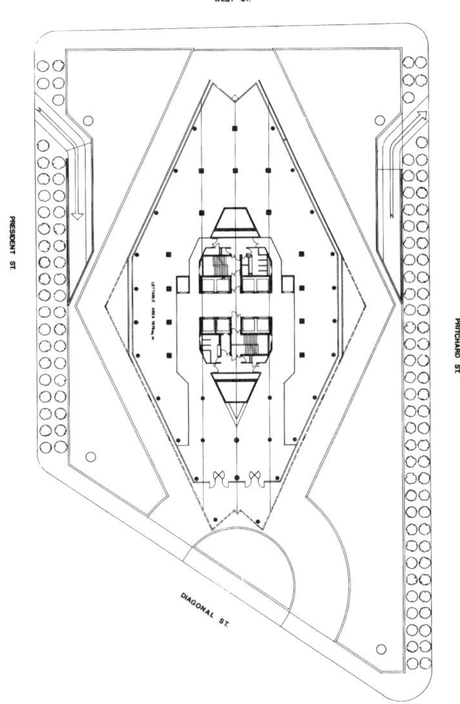

D. 11 Diagonal Street: plan of ground floor

A. Civic Art Gallery, Johannesburg (1986). See p. 1477

B. Corporate Headquarters, First National Bank, Johannesburg (1995). See p. 1477

C. Hospital, Marrakesh, Morocco (1984–5). See p. 1480

D. Corporate Headquarters, First National Bank, Johannesburg: aerial perspective from NE

over low walls by GAPP Architects (1991) in a manner sympathetic to the mountainside.

There is little to distinguish commercial buildings of the 1980s and 1990s in African Central Business Districts from those in Western cities. In general they follow the model of a multi-storey car park or retail podium beneath an office tower. They increased in size in the 1970s with such developments as the **BP Centre, Cape Town**, by Revel Fox and Partners (1971–3), the **Standard Bank Centre, Johannesburg**, by Hentrich-Petschnigg and Partners (1970) and the almost monolithic concrete **Carlton Centre, Johannesburg**, by Skidmore, Owings and Merrill (1966–72). Post-Modernism and the almost obligatory atrium are both frequently in evidence, but typical of many of the 1980s is **Ernst and Young House, Johannesburg**, by RFB Architects. **The Terraces** (p. 1475B) one of the new buildings on **Cape Town's** Foreshore by Munnik Visser Black Fish and Partners (1990), is more distinctive with its carefully detailed, unusual facades and its arresting profile with reflecting glass facings on the upper parts of the corner towers; equally distinctive is Louis Karol's **Safmarine House, Cape Town** (1992). Helmut Jahn has contributed two characteristic additions to the South African townscape, the huge glittering prism, **11 Diagonal Street, Johannesburg** (1981–3), with Louis Karol (p. 1475C,D) and the 24-storey shining tower above a retail podium, **88 Field Street, Durban** (1982–5, with Stauch Vorster), based on two interlocking octagonal forms. The new **Colosseum**, built on the site of **Johannesburg's** notable Art Deco cinema theatre by Stauch Vorster (1987), has subtle modelling and massing with reminiscences of Charles Rennie Mackintosh in the detailing, especially in the atrium. What has been described as 'a megalomaniac obsession with status symbols' led to the building in the late 1980s of the **Reserve Bank** by Burg Doherty Bryant and the **Sambou Building**, both towering above the centre of **Pretoria**; the dark mass of the latter has been likened to a 'phallic-like shaft [rising] out of the overdesigned base . . . topped off with a unique version of a mansard roof.' A quite different approach is seen in **First National Bank Building, Johannesburg** (p. 1476B,D) the largest commercial development in South Africa, due for completion in 1995. This is being undertaken by teams of architects, led by Revel Fox; unashamedly Classical revivalist and medium-rise in character with visible rooflines, it is based on what Trystan Edwards in the 1920s might have called 'good manners' and preferred to 'the unsociable skyscraper.'

As in Western countries, rehabilitation and conservation have become an important element in architectural practice in South Africa. A pioneering adaptation in the late 1970s was of the old market building in **Johannesburg** as the **Market Theatre** which retains much of its original character while serving a different use. This has been followed by other conservation/conversions of historic buildings, such as the **Supreme Court, Pietermaritzburg**, as an art gallery by Small, Pettit and Associates (1991) and the **Feather Market Hall, Port Elizabeth**, as a concert hall by Gerrie de Bruin (1993). The **Civic Art Gallery, Johannesburg** (p. 1476A), was restored by Meyer Pienaar and Partners after they had completed an extension (1986) with witty references to the work of the original architect, Sir Edwin Lutyens. The same architects have incorporated the old town hall and the Art Deco market hall into a new, formally planned **civic centre** at **Krugersdorp** (1981–6). Several historic buildings have been carefully restored for continued use, such as the **City Hall, East London**, by Rennie and Goddard, consulting architects (1993), and the **Raadsaal, Pretoria**, by Holm Jordaan Holm/Meiring Van der Lecq Rouge (1991). A new National Head Office for the National Monuments Council has been made out of an early nineteenth-century residential property in **Harrington Street, Cape Town** by Rennie and Goddard (1992–3); but the largest project of the early 1990s which incorporates conservation and new design is in Cape Town's old harbour area. A number of practices have been involved in developing the whole scheme, including the specialist consultants, Gabriel Fagan, Ivor Prinsloo, Revel Fox and Neville Dubow; Louis Karol designed the **Waterfront Retail Centre** on **Victoria Wharf**, and a warehouse (*c.* 1904) has been rehabilitated as the **Victoria and Alfred Hotel** by MLH Architects in association with Dennis Fabian and Berman as parts of the successful revitalisation of an historic area – a concept that is becoming more widely understood, in some Islamic countries as well as in South Africa. UNESCO, the Aga Khan Foundation, and a number of national governments have helped to stimulate an interest in the protection and rehabilitation of historic areas such as **Lamu** in Kenya, **Bagamoyo** and **Zanzibar** in Tanzania, the **Darb Qirmiz** in Cairo and the **Hafsia Quarter of Tunis**.

The Search for an Architectural Identity

Independence from colonial rule encouraged thought and discussion about an architectural identity in the new states which for the first half of the century had been exposed to Western influences; but there is a certain ambivalence about the thinking since Western standards still remain the ideal for many Africans, to whom an architecture with similarities to their own ethnic buildings would not represent progress.

This is not a new question, although in recent years it has acquired stronger political significance in some parts of the continent. In the 1930s Norman Eaton in South Africa claimed it was possible to develop a regional architecture, using local materials and building techniques, extending their possibilities, and creating a human environment suited to the locality. His **Greenwood House and Village, Pretoria** (1951) is an attempt to do this. Half a century later his ideas have not been forgotten; in 1982 Bannie Britz thought that what contemporary architecture needed was 'to be carefully grafted on to African contexts as Baker, Leith and Eaton had done with the respective architecture of their time.' In the 1950s Jane Drew in West Africa talked about designing 'in a way which, without in any sense, copying African detail, gives a response which is African'. James Cubitt thought that a regional aesthetic could develop, but that it would have to start with modern buildings, while the Aga Khan advised 'vernacular architecture has to be rethought because it fails to cater for contemporary aspirations, either in rural areas or the towns'.

The European countries which colonised the continent introduced new building forms, materials and techniques; but these were in relatively few towns and the majority of buildings continued to be constructed of the traditional material, earth. Since the very nature of this material and its variable strength, stability, permeability and durability call for regular maintenance and periodic renewal, it has remained the source of a continuous, living tradition which has produced most of Africa's indigenous monuments, its mosques, palaces and fortifications. Its potential capabilities may be seen in the reconstructed monuments at **Jos, Nigeria,** in the **Museum of Traditional Nigerian Art**, but Jane Drew was voicing a commonly held opinion that 'mud walls and thatched roofs' had no future. Any attempt to revive them would be either 'sentimental, political or both'; but she did make an admiring reference to the 'very inspiring mud architecture' of Northern Nigeria at Kano and Sokoto, concluding that 'the effect of such examples is problematic and rests upon the degree to which they may affect Nigerian architects'.

From time to time there have been attempts to encourage the use of earth for prestigious buildings, as in a group in Mali. The **Mosque of Djenne** was reconstructed in 1905 in its original form; the **Friday Mosque at Mopti** was enhanced by three obelisk-like minarets in 1930; and the monumental minaret of the **Friday Mosque at Mopti** was reconstructed in 1935. All three incorporate tall buttress-like elements which are both structural and decorative, as well as a characteristic spiky outline. More recently, the completion in 1972 of the **Great Mosque of Niono** (p. 1479A), as an extension of a small building dating only from 1948 has provided another example of how indigenous techniques and materials can both inspire creativity and answer a functional requirement. The work of a master-mason/architect, Lassine Minta, and a small group of helpers, it consists of a grid of columns from which spring arches supporting the earth-on-wood flat roof. Cool, calm colonnades result from the structural system and the exterior is ornamented with a vigorous phallic symbolism integrated with the plastic structure.

An even larger-scale example of the use of earth is the complete **new town, Timimoun**, built in the **Sahara Desert, Algeria**, in the 1930s. Gateways, walls, dwellings, mosques and a hotel demonstrate that the ubiquitous building material can still be used to create innovative forms derived from tradition. In **Kano, Nigeria**, the **British Council offices and library** (1940–50) (p. 1479C) were constructed of earth and decorated externally with a sophisticated version of traditional sgraffito ornament. In some cases the old forms themselves are being restored, as in Morocco, where **earth-built housing** in front of the **Fortress of Tamezmoute** has been largely rebuilt; the **Fortress of Tissergate** itself was restored for community use in 1969. In **Niamey, Niger**, the **Court of Justice** by Laszlo Mester de Parajd (1982–5) was intended to be constructed of earth, but was not because there was no guarantee that adequate regular maintenance would be provided; but it is described as 'reflecting the qualities of an ancient palace without becoming a pastiche'.

In the forefront of those architects in North Africa who have been producing work which reflects the traditional context is Hassan Fathy, the Egyptian who began as early as the 1940s (**Said House**, 1942, **Nasr House**, 1945, **Stoppleare House**, 1952) to develop an architecture which would be both relevant and responsive to local needs and cultures. In 1946 he was commissioned to design and construct a **village, New Gourna**, which has been described as 'a mixture of social realism and utopian vision.' The community was deeply involved in its development. His revived Nubian vault technology has been widely disseminated and used in places as far away as **Zimbabwe** and **Mauritania**; in the latter country Joseph Esteve adapted the techniques publicised by Fathy to shallow-domed rectangular spaces planned around public and private courtyards in his **low-cost housing** (1977), as did Fabrizio Carola in the **hospital, Kaedi**, and Philippe Glauser in the **IPD (Institut Pan-Africain pour le Developpement) University, Ouagadougou, Bourkina Faso**.

Fathy's use of mud brick construction and mediaeval forms in the villages of **New Gourna** and **New Bariz** convinced him that this was a basis for an Egyptian architecture, although in his later designs for private villas (**Riad House**, 1973 (p 1479D) **Samy House**, 1979, **Mit Rehan**, 1981, **Greiss House**, 1984) and the **presidential Rest House, Garf Husein** (1981), he used stone and fired bricks, and they show a growing preoccupation with traditional proportional systems. He has many admirers and followers, among them Ramses Wissa Wassef, who has also designed and built houses based on traditional forms, using mud bricks with which he creates domes, cubes and basic geometric forms. Several of these are at **Harrania** near

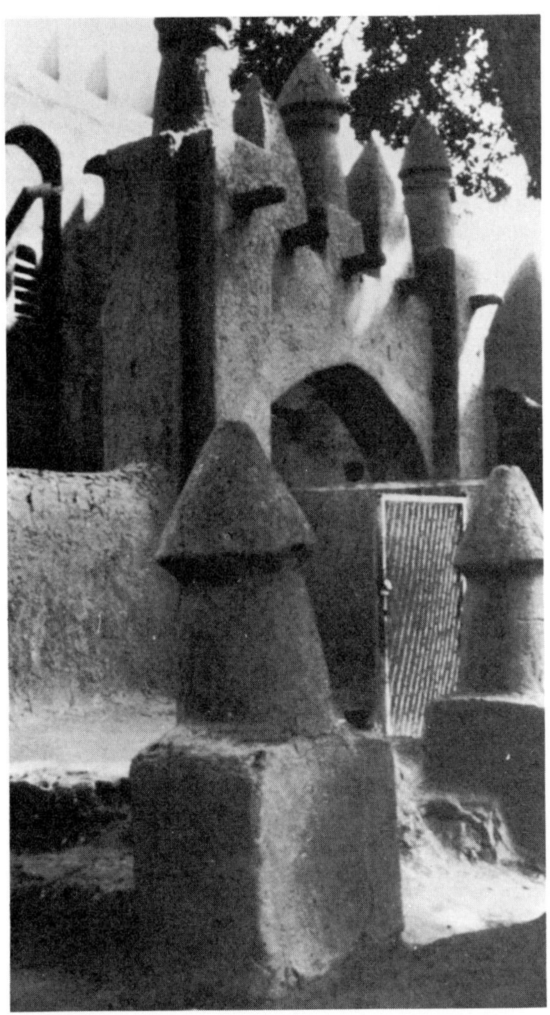

A. Great Mosque of Niono, Mali (1972). See p. 1478

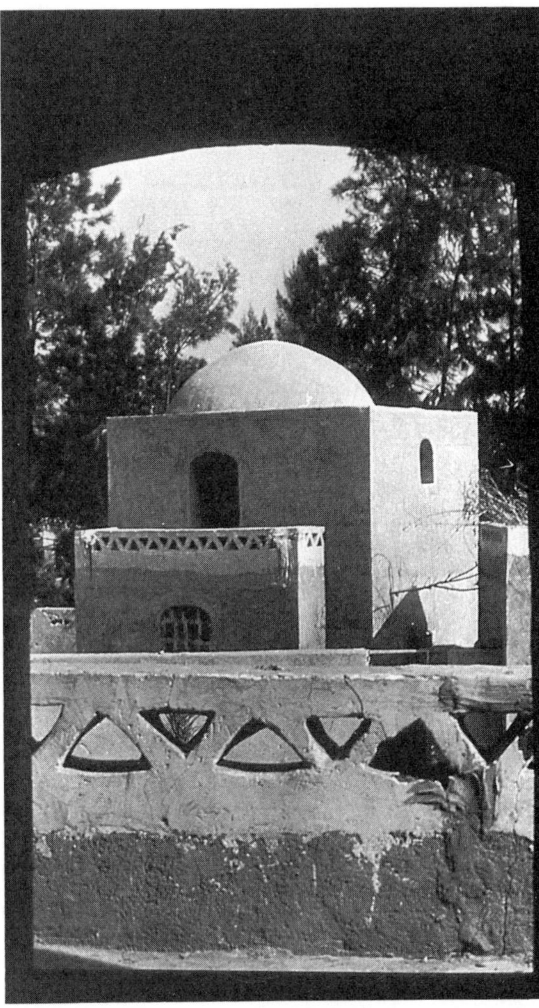

B. Wissa Wassef Arts Centre, Harrania (1950s onwards). See p. 1478

C. British Council offices and library, Kano (1940–50). See p. 1478

D. Riad House, Cairo (1973). See p. 1478

Cairo, where Wassef built a **museum and art centre** (p. 1479B), in the 1960s. Planned with courtyards and open corridors, its small, integrated galleries are domed, and there are mastabas and niches in the walls. His **Arts Centre, Giza** (1952–74), is another example of Wassef's development of traditional earth architecture, to which a **Tapestry Museum** was added in 1987–9. A younger architect who studied with Fathy and finds inspiration in traditional forms is Abdel-Wahed El-Wakil, whose designs (**Halawa House**, 1972–5, **Hamdy House**, 1978, and **Chourbaggy House**, 1984) illustrate his personal interpretation and development of Fathy's teaching. But these steps towards an Egyptian architecture based on established values and traditions are relatively minor in a country that, like most in Africa, is dominated by large foreign practices favoured by government and commercial companies.

Discussing the proposed new capital of Nigeria, **Abuja** (for which Kenzo Tange designed many of the main buildings), Omar Take expressed the view that 'People have a right to require a foreign architect to respect local traditions and cultures'. He acknowledged that 'Nigerian architecture as such is very difficult to find. Traditional buildings have been destroyed, and there is little left to study. But through Islamic architecture – the courtyards, the proportions of space, and the sequence and the articulation of spaces – we were able to work out some general principles.' It is in the Islamic countries, principally those in North Africa, that a more positive attitude to traditional forms has been developing, although it is in a description of the **Kerk Street Jami Masjid, Johannesburg**, by Muhammed Mayet with Abdel Wahed el-Wakil (1994) that one reads 'The pursuit of novelty and the disregard of traditional values and principles bring forth the loss of identity because the tradition is always greater than the individual architect'.

There are thousands of new mosques in the African Islamic countries and communities, all more or less traditional in form and decoration, but outstanding is the **mosque** at **Rabat, Morocco** (Vo Toan), built in the early 1970s as part of a group by King Hassan II in memory of his father. This marked the beginning of royal encouragement of traditional arts and crafts and the king's sponsoring of two large volumes, *Le Maroc et l'artisanat traditionnel islamique en architecture*, which are now required design sources for architects working in Morocco. External and internal details follow the traditional models, and courtyards inspired by the traditional riads, with running water and formal planting, are commonly incorporated in new buildings such as Charles Boccara's **hospital** at **Marrakesh** (1978–82) (p. 1476C), in which the detached mosque is traditional, not only in form but in the use of pisé, sun-dried bricks and eucalyptus wood. Earth construction, based on traditional forms, was used by Elie Mouyal in the **Foissac House** outside **Marrakesh** (1984–5). Riads are frequently used also in private residences, as in the house at **Casablanca** (1977–81) designed by M. Sigelmassi for his own occupation, and in Boccara's **Abtan House, Marrakesh** (1984), as well as in suburban **housing** at **Assif** on the outskirts of **Marrakesh** by Boccara 1975–83), while traditional details are incorporated with great effect into low-cost **public housing** (**Dar Lamane Housing Community, Casablanca** completed 1983) (p. 1481A).

To some extent, but without royal authority, design in **Tunisia** follows a similar line. In his **Diar El Andalous Residences**, an apartment-hotel at **Sousse** (1977–81), Serge Santelli based his design around courtyards and patios in a sequence that recalls courtyards and gardens of Arab palaces. **Sidi el-Aloui Primary School, Tunis** (p. 1481B), by Samir Hamaici (1986) is an orderly arrangement of rooms around two courtyards, discreetly enhanced by the judicious use of traditional ornament. On a more modest scale, and depending on the participation of the local population for its execution, the **Daara School, Malika**, Senegal by R. Snelder (1977–80) resembles the large, traditional family plantations in the neighbourhood, and its construction is based on traditional principles.

Hotels have offered architects an opportunity to adapt traditional forms and elements for commercial reasons; examples include the **Holiday Village Resort, M'Dig, Tetouan Province, Morocco**, by A. Faraoui and P. De Mazieres with clusters of hotel rooms placed around patios and gardens, the **Hotel Boumaine du Dades, Boumaine, Morocco**, by the same architects, which includes some characteristics of Berber architecture, and the **Serena Beach Hotel, Jumba la Mtwana, Kenya**, by Archer Associates (1975) which uses many elements of Swahili architecture and decoration as found in Lamu. Such examples of the use of traditional design elements was described by Sergio Santinelli in Tunisia in 1981 as a perpetuation of the colonial era, but it is in evidence in many sophisticated villas, apartments and hotels in Tunisia, Morocco and Egypt, and on the Kenyan coast. He perceived that architects 'have felt inclined to adapt their production to an Arab Muslim aesthetic in order to satisfy a... need on the part of the population to return to their sources... arcades, cupolas, columns and capitals of carved stone, coloured tiles and multiple irregularities of form for purely picturesque effects now cover the facades of new construction'.

The study of regional and tribal buildings has sometimes provided the more or less symbolic basic form of new architecture. André Ravereau, who studied M'Zab buildings while Director of Historic Monuments in Algeria, has emulated the local traditional plastic forms and internally oriented planning in **schools** built under his supervision in the **M'Zab region**, as well as in his **Medical Centre** in **Mali** (1976). The characteristics of traditional Ibadite architecture influenced the design for a **residence** in **Gharaia, Algeria** (1971), which Ravereau built

A. Dar Lamane Housing Community, Casablanca (completed 1983). See p. 1480

B. Sidi el-Aloui Primary School, Tunis (1986). See p. 1480

around a courtyard and based on the need to isolate the men and the women as well as to design for the hot climate. The **Solar Energy Research Centre (ONERSOL), Niamey, Niger**, by L. M. de Parajd (1981) is a physical structure inspired by traditional local architecture and building materials. Domes are used, but unlike Hausa domes (which were constructed in wood-reinforced mud) these are carried on reinforced-concrete columns; in general the considerable structure relies upon load-bearing walls of mud brick stabilised with cement.

Symbolic derivations from regional architecture have been adopted in public buildings; in the **Kenyatta Conference Centre, Nairobi, Kenya**, by K. H. Nostvik (1973) an attempt was made to adapt the form of a Musenge house to a large-scale contemporary programme; the two main elements, a 32-storey office tower and an amphitheatre conference hall, are set on a podium which houses the reception area, lecture theatre, banks and a post office in an impressive composition which seems nevertheless to have only a tenuous connection with traditional forms. At **Mmabatho**, one of the black states set up in South Africa under the old regime, Bannie Britz and Michael Scholes based their design for the **Government Square and Secretariat** (1978–83) on a Tswana town layout and a central meeting place. Technologies with a high semi-skilled labour content were appropriate, using local materials to create the bold geometric forms in brick. This permitted local people to be trained to do the work and acquire building skills once more as earlier generations had. On a smaller scale, Peter Rich has claimed that in his domestic designs of the 1980s he has been influenced by the rural dwellings of the Southern Ndebele and Bantwane in an attempt to 'define a South African architecture truly reflecting its use and location ... the clichéd patronising gesture of lifting mere style is not enough.'

Another building, the **Sonneblom Film Studios, Randpark Ridge**, in the **Transvaal** by M. and M. Bell (1993) has been described as 'exuding all the aspects we frantically search for – those of a truly Southern African architecture... flowing shapes... an ever-changing facade as shadows are cast and the sunlight moves across the African sand-coloured elevations'; but Hans Hallen pertinently observed in 1985 that 'unlike the single rooted origins of western culture, here there are a multiplicity of roots. The great Banyan tree of Milton's *Paradise Lost* – which sheltered many and had a hundred stems – is an appropriate metaphor for African architecture, which must also tell of our time and place.'

Chapter 50
NORTH AMERICA 1900 TO 1950

Architectural Character

American architecture emerged as a significant force in Western culture during the nineteenth century and the accomplishments of the modern era cannot be fully understood without careful study of North American work. The major contribution has come from the United States, not least because it became home for a number of leading European architects during the 1930s and 1940s.

In the United States, as in Europe, key developments have emanated from a few metropolitan centres: New York, Boston, Philadephia, Chicago, San Francisco, and Los Angeles. Exceptions can be found, and these six cities (and their related urban regions) have nurtured most of the country's leading architects and prestigious schools of design. The performance in each place has differed. New York has long been considered the most important city, but its role has not been supreme in the way that Paris, Vienna, or London have been for their respective countries. The existence of several centres, dissimilar in complexion and dispersed across the continent, has added to the richness and diversity of its architecture.

The abundance of land has affected American architecture in many ways, including the proliferation of low-density developments, while the abundance of natural resources has fostered the widespread and varied use of high-quality building materials. There has been almost continuous growth since 1900 necessitating enormous construction efforts and stimulating a spirit of renewal and innovation. Affluent, competitive corporations, governmental bodies, institutions, and householders have generated the demand for sophisticated buildings and often for a strong sense of architectural identity. The sanctity of free enterprise and of individual rights, and the corresponding absence of strong centralised authority, have helped to ensure that commercial and residential design is among the most innovative.

Much American architecture of the period, especially in residential districts, embodied a preference for familiar images and a dislike for those that seemed eccentric or which departed in other ways from accepted patterns. Numerous modern buildings produced in Europe and elsewhere since the turn of the century in all likelihood would not have been tolerated in the United States. Americans also tend to be more pragmatic, more concerned with improvement and implementation than with theory. Fundamentally new ideas in the formal realm of architecture have seldom originated in North America, whose architects have repeatedly looked abroad for models in developing their expressive idioms.

However, the close ties that have existed between design in Europe and the United States have long since ceased to reflect cultural servitude. American architects have sought to adapt lessons learned from other places to produce an architecture distinctly their own. New avenues of interpretation have been pursued as well: American practitioners have contributed substantially to the development of building types in all spheres. Achievements in technology – structure, materials, support systems – have enjoyed a leading position. Influences have been reciprocal, of course, and other countries have probably taken as much from American work as America has taken from them during the twentieth century.

Two major currents in design have prevailed since 1900: eclectic traditionalism and Modernism. The former began to assume an academic orientation, derived from the instructional philosophy of the Ecole des Beaux-Arts during the 1880s. This phase of eclectic traditionalism became the most significant new force in American architecture by the following decade and retained a prominent role until the 1930s. Underlying the movement was the belief that architecture is evolutionary – that change is guided by immutable principles which can be applied to all programmatic circumstances while maintaining continuity with the past. Through the application of rigorous techniques of composition architecture could also be given unity, order, and visual strength. Classicism, as it had been practised in France since the seventeenth century, lay at the heart of these ideas, and thus it is not surprising to find that many academic buildings in the United States are Classical. But the movement encompassed a much broader range of precedents from many periods and places, from the Picturesque tradition, and from vernacular as well as high-style examples. Early architecture in several American regions also provided inspiration for some academic buildings. Furthermore, academic concerns in the United States tended to ally themselves to rather than conflict with those of the Arts and Crafts movement. All these factors enhanced the sense of freedom, inventiveness, and variety.

Modernism emerged in the United States around 1900, largely through the work of Frank Lloyd Wright and his followers. Yet it did not begin to gain widespread acceptance until the mid-1920s and then in a very different form. Some of the more radical thrusts in the European avant-garde received increasing attention in the United States during the 1930s. After World War II, the country became a leader in exploring Modernism's possibilities – conceptual and expressive – and has maintained that position since.

Modernism differs from eclecticism in that, rather than seeking continuity with the past or reviving salient features of earlier periods, it emphasises newness and exploits fully the construction and design potential offered by new building materials and technology. References may be made to historical precedent by overt or oblique means, but there is a clear distinction implied between previous eras and the present. Often, too, more concern is focused on anticipating the future than on associating with the past. This outlook implies constant (and sometimes abrupt) change; revolution instead of gradual evolution. Great diversity characterises Modernism, just as it does eclecticism, but it is of another kind. Modernism has never been governed for long by one set of principles comparable to those of Classicism or the academic tradition. From its inception during the 1890s, Modernism has consisted of differing strains, some of them collective (for example, Art Nouveau, Futurism, De Stijl), others centring on the work of an individual (for example, Wright, Mies van der Rohe). Modernist rhetoric in America as elsewhere implies concordance in ideas if not always in form; however, Modernist practice resists convention and thus has always created an array of varied, frequently divergent, approaches to design. Eclecticism and Modernism have never been mutually exclusive and cross-fertilisation has occurred in many ways.

Examples

The academic phase of eclecticism came late to North America, emerging as a major force in architecture just prior to the twentieth century. Thus implanted on a continent where expediency and economic reward were portrayed as forces that had governed development for generations, this movement was cast in a revitalising spirit. Ambitious planning initiatives soon became integral to the effort. The **Court of Honor at the World's Columbian Exposition in Chicago** (1892–3) was heralded as a persuasive demonstration of how order, unity, elegance, and a vigorous allegiance to the Western cultural heritage could regenerate not only architecture but also the face of the city. The first proposal to achieve these objectives on a metropolitan scale was the 1901 **Senate Park Commission Plan for Washington, DC** (p. 1485A). Its designers, Daniel Burnham, Charles McKim, and Frederick Law Olmsted, Jr, were leading figures in the whole movement, and the former two, along with Olmsted's father, had been instrumental in shaping the Chicago Fair.

The Washington plan is based on a design prepared for the capital city in 1791 by Pierre Charles L'Enfant (1754–1825) and on the Baroque tradition in which he worked. Yet the new project reveals American adeptness at fresh interpretation. The great Mall, extending west from the Capitol, is like no previous urban space in the way it employs enormous dimensions and coherent form to reorganise the whole central precinct. This scheme combines the breadth and simplicity of Le Nôtre's palatial gardens with a sequence of focal points along the main axis like those between the Tuileries and the Place de l'Etoile in Paris. Trees and buildings join to establish clear boundaries for the eastern sector. And, while subordinated to the whole, each building is free-standing and creates a monumental focus for its immediate surroundings. Further west the layout is more in the Olmsted tradition – less formal – yet grand commemorative buildings continue to provide focus, and visual ties are always maintained with the city beyond. The Mall, its main axis terminating at its western end with the **Lincoln Memorial** (1911–22) (p. 1485C) by Henry Bacon (1866–1942), is at once subordinate to the Capitol and a great civic forum in its own right.

In addition to this civic core, the plan includes a network of parks devised to protect the natural landscape, preserve scenic vistas, provide extensive public recreation areas, and stimulate low-density residential growth. Following the example of urban park systems recently developed in Europe, and similar proposals for other United States cities, the scheme is among the most comprehensive of its era and set the standard for numerous projects in North America through the 1920s. Underlying this City Beautiful movement, as it was known, was the desire to give form and direction to the rapid development of urban areas, to make them more efficient and more attractive places. Few schemes were executed as thoroughly as in Washington, where the federal government possessed the authority to carry out so extensive a proposal. Even so, implementation took decades during which changes in planning priorities left most of the work in a fragmentary state.

While grand urban designs were executed only in fragments, an impressive array of individual public

A. Senate Park Commission Plan for Washington, DC (1901). See p. 1484

B. Sweet Briar College, Amherst County, Virginia (1901–2). See p. 1486

C. Lincoln Memorial, Washington, DC (1911–22). See p. 1484

D. Chapel and Post Headquarters, US Military Academy, West Point, New York (1903–14). See p. 1486

buildings was erected during the early twentieth century, often under the aegis of private philanthropic initiatives. McKim, Mead and White's **Boston Public Library** (1887–98) (q.v) set the example for such buildings, including **New York** City's elegant **Public Library** (1897–1911) (see Chapter 37), by Carrère and Hastings and **Metropolitan Museum of Art** (1895–1902) by Richard Morris Hunt (1827–95), and the no less sumptuous **San Francisco City Hall** (1912–15) by Bakewell and Brown. Dignified Classical buildings of this sort were introduced not only to the metropolis but in more modest forms to smaller cities and towns, embodying a new civic pride and a desire to provide a focus and give a feeling of permanence to communities across the continent.

The accelerated growth of institutions of higher learning at the turn of the twentieth century provided the other major opportunity for large-scale planning initiatives. The American campus has always had a characteristic form, with free-standing buildings, loosely organised in an open landscape, set apart from densely settled areas and constituting a community in itself. Now the need for expansion was matched by the urge to reshape the campus in a more orderly and impressive manner, generating an abundance of master plans between the 1890s and 1930s.

Cram, Goodhue and Ferguson's design for **Sweet Briar College** in rural **Virginia** (1901–2) represents these efforts at their best (p. 1485B). The buildings are placed around a large grass court, partially open to engage a panoramic view of the Blue Ridge Mountains. The plan is asymmetrical, but balanced; the building differentiated according to function, yet composed as a cohesive ensemble. The scheme's formal character is, in turn, offset by picturesque surroundings, combining civic with residential characteristics. As a diagram, the layout draws upon the French tradition; however, the buildings are more closely tied to English Classical work and to that of the early American Republic, including Thomas Jefferson's nearby University of Virginia (1817–26). These references to Classicism – local national, and European – reflect the academic concern for designing in a manner sympathetic to a given region while avoiding parochial or revivalist overtones. The Classical tradition prevailed in the design of public and institutional buildings alike. However, mediaeval sources were also employed and with equal ingenuity and inventiveness, as can be seen in Cram, Goodhue and Ferguson's scheme for the **Chapel and Post Headquarters, US Military Academy, West Point, New York** (1903–14) (p. 1485D), Day and Klauder's **dormitory buildings at Princeton University, Princeton, New Jersey** (1913–18), and James Gamble Rogers's (1867–1947) **colleges at Yale University, New Haven, Connecticut** (1916–33).

During the early twentieth century the most intense development occurred in the commercial sphere, the result of numerous singular projects rather than sweeping master plans. However, a few such undertakings did entail multi-use complexes. **Grand Central Rail Terminal, New York** (1903–13) (p. 1487), by Reed and Stem, Warren and Wetmore, set the standard. Covering 19.2 ha (48 acres), it represented the largest building programme in North America at that time. To an unprecedented degree, the ensemble was conceived as a network of interconnecting systems – railroad, subway, carriage and pedestrian – tying the terminal to offices, hotels, and other facilities. The design and the execution of so vast a scheme, where existing rail services were maintained throughout construction, marked a new high point in the technical ingenuity that had distinguished American enterprises for decades, but Grand Central, and its no less remarkable contemporary, **Pennsylvania Station**, also in New York City (1902–11, now demolished) (p. 1488A) by McKim, Mead and White, are more than engineering feats. Both utilitarian and symbolic roles as portal to the metropolis are given emphatic clarity by the terminals. Inside each building, the warren of spaces is organised as an orderly sequence. Grand Central's great concourse – vast in size, simple in form – provides the essential centrepiece for the whole complex, while it is also a mixing chamber, inducing continuous movement to all points beyond. In a characteristically American adaptation of Beaux-Arts planning principles, formal design concerns are integrated with the modern concept of architecture as an efficient container of complex functions. Perceptually, the dignified spatial procession is in command. Likewise on the exterior, the boldly scaled, heraldic elevations dominate the new urban setting – tall, dense and mechanised.

Terminal City, built using the air rights over the subterranean tracks along Park Avenue running into Grand Central Station, was planned as a catalyst for transforming mid-town Manhattan into a primary commercial centre. The development affords a good example of tall building design as it was practised between the 1890s and 1920s. Using a Classical parti – figuratively: base, shaft and capital – the elevations provide an elegant background architecture intended to bring greater cohesiveness to the metropolitan fabric. This approach to urban design stems directly from nineteenth-century work in Paris and other European centres; however, the scale, restrained sumptuousness and stringent commercial character of such precincts distinguish them as uniquely American.

Some office buildings, on the other hand, were designed as individual landmarks – conspicuous monuments to their corporate clients and to the idea of commerce, which many Americans now saw as the most significant force in society. Rising land values in city centres and the continuing demand for more profit-making space necessitated buildings of far greater dimensions than those of the decades

A. Grand Central Rail Terminal, New York (1903–13). See p. 1486

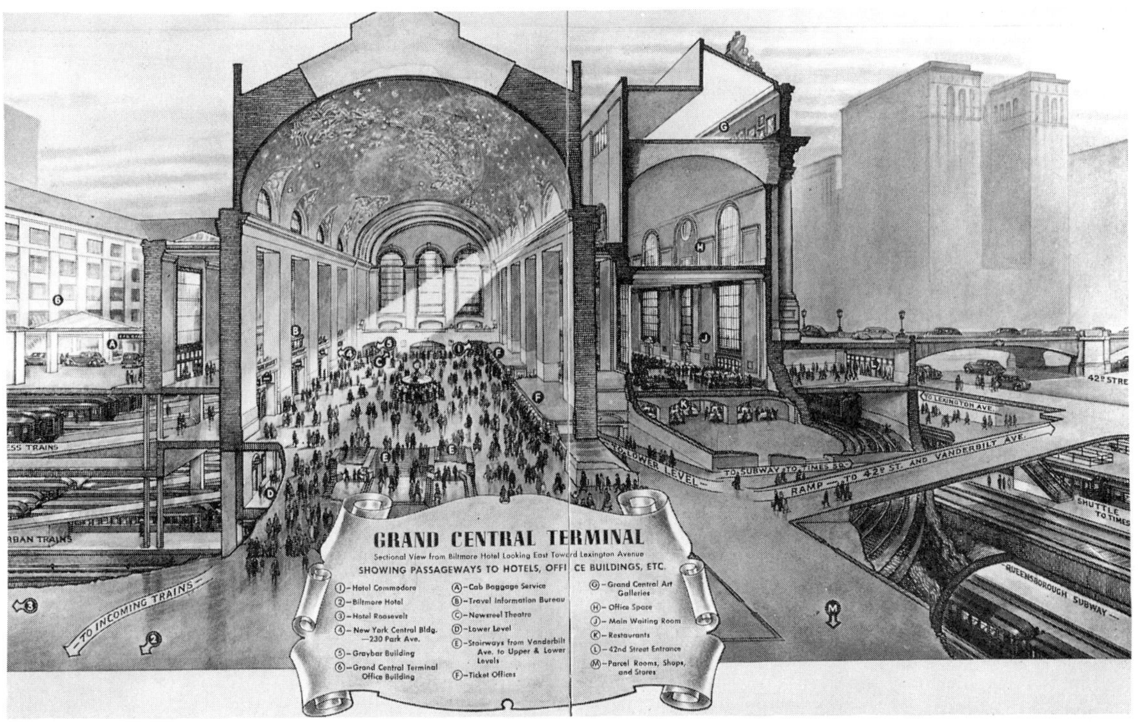

B. Grand Central Rail Terminal: section

A. Pennsylvania Station, New York (1902–11, now demolished). See p. 1486

B. Larkin Building, Buffalo, New York (1903–6, now demolished). See p. 1491

C. Woolworth Building, New York (1910–13). See p. 1489

immediately before. The resulting evolution of the skyscraper from a dense block to a soaring tower occurred in New York where the **Woolworth Building** (1910–13) was considered the exemplar (p. 1488C). This was the tallest edifice in the world until 1930 and a technical work of the first order, with portal braces integral to its steel frame and a repertoire of advanced support systems. Moulded terracotta is exploited to create a lacelike exterior envelope which, far more than the standard masonry wall plane, both suggests the structure beneath and enlivens the entire surface. The architect, Cass Gilbert (1850–1934), also brilliantly developed the mass and its composition so that the building is at once a block and a tower, conversing with its neighbours and yet standing alone as a beacon in the skyscraper forest. Comparable examples of similar date are the triangular **Fuller (Flatiron) Building** (1901–3) by D.H. Burnham & Company, the **Singer Building** (1908, destroyed 1968) by Ernest Flagg, and the **Metropolitan Life Tower** (1905–9) Le Brun & Sons. The designers of these tall buildings did attempt to evolve compositions that did not overshadow their neighbours. However, these soaring towers provoked first a popular and then a legislative reaction in New York for, it was argued, they vied for light and air, could cast whole blocks into shadow, caused street congestion and were fire-hazards. These concerns resulted in codes controlling the size and placing of towers (street facades were limited to 30 m (100 ft) and towers could occupy no more than 25 per cent of the site) and then a city ordinance in 1916 which provided for height limitations and building set-backs.

The Woolworth Building and its precinct seemed the very essence of the modern world – symbols of an era experiencing rapid, often revolutionary, change. No artificial landscape in the second decade of the twentieth century seemed to abandon traditional architectural forms and epitomise the future to the same degree. And yet the new metropolitan forms also offered potent associative links to the past through historicising details and the collective silhouette which conjured visions of ancient cities in the Near East. By contrast with Europe, where eclectic historicism was beginning to be represented as a burdensome legacy of the past, in North America it seemed to contribute to progress and a new sense of civility.

The fusion of tradition and change was conveyed with particular exuberance in cinemas, a building type new to the twentieth century. It was partly a product of American culture, and quite different in character from places designed for live performances alone. On the one hand, **Uptown Theatre, Chicago** (1924–5), by Cornelius (1861–1927) and George Rapp (1878–1942), was a utilitarian building calculated to generate high returns and arranged so as to allow high-density constructing along the prime frontage all around (p. 1490A). Long-span steel trusses enabled the auditorium to have uninterrupted sight lines; advanced air-circulating systems made the interior more comfortable than most buildings; ingenious planning induced seemingly effortless passage through large spaces squeezed into tight, irregular parcels of land. But to the audience, the 'movie palace' was foremost a purveyor of fantasy, a place where everyday life could be forgotten. The firms that specialised in such work drew from historical precedents that were emotive and often exotic, as displayed in the **Ohio Theatre, Columbus, Ohio** 1927–8) (p. 1490B), by Thomas Lamb. Flamboyant, overscaled details, indirect lighting, and extravagant colour schemes adorned billowy spaces affording a spectacle matched only by the imagination. For most people, the whole experience was new. Lavish quarters and ever more polished presentations transformed the nature of popular amusement with the theatre itself becoming a seductive agent of mass consumption.

During the latter decades of the nineteenth century advances in rail transport made long-distance travel in North America luxurious as well as an adventure, permitting mountain regions in the West to become important recreation grounds. Large hotels, many of them erected by the railroad themselves, formed an essential ingredient in stimulating this lucrative trade. The **Banff Springs Hotel in the Canadian Rockies** is among the earliest of the type and remains one of the most splendid (Chapter 37): begun in 1886 by Bruce Price, twentieth-century additions include those by William Painter (1903–14) and J.W. Orrock (1926–8). Set in isolation, it reflects the then-new concern that the Western hotel should celebrate the distinctness of its region. Banff and the expansive wooden hostelries constructed in the US National Parks became widely admired symbols of place. They engage in a dialogue with nature, but also bespeak dominance – defying their remote localities with all the comforts and much of the structured social routine found in their urban counterparts.

The free-standing, single-family house has played a central role in defining the North American landscape since the early decades of colonial settlement. Residential work of the early twentieth century continued the innovative spirit nurtured in previous decades and exhibited even greater breadth of expression. Classicism now became as influential as the Picturesque tradition in this sphere. Academic predilections were matched by those of the Arts and Crafts movement. Domestic architecture also became the initial laboratory for America's quite distinct form of Modernism. An increasingly affluent populace created ever more demand for houses designed by architects, and some of the most talented practitioners on the continent made such work a speciality. Large country houses, their more modest counterparts in suburbs, and workers' dwellings, were all subjects of professional interest. The best examples attain a high

A. (*above*) Uptown Theatre, Chicago (1924–5). See p. 1489

B. (*right*) Ohio Theatre, Columbus, Ohio (1927–8). See p. 1489

level of sophistication in their design. But, irrespective of subtleties, American houses gained most attention for their convenient plans and commodious provision. By the 1920s even relatively inexpensive residences contained support systems far more advanced than those found almost anywhere else. Like commercial buildings, the American house was both a bulwark of tradition and a modern machine.

Timberline (Smith House) near Philadelphia (1907–8), ranks among the finest country houses of the period (p. 1492C–E). Its architect, Charles Adam Platt (1861–1933), was a master at drawing upon cinquecento models and other Classical sources to create refined, elegantly proportioned designs closely related to their sites. The primary axis of a most inventive plan establishes a strong link from the entrance to the principal vista. However, all other visual connections are lateral and are arranged in a gradually expanding sequence – first inside, then on to the terrace, and finally to two formal gardens enshrouded by woods. Lacking a single focus, this dual progression implies continuous movement while, at the same time, the sense of flow is tempered by a taut, restrained vocabulary and an impressionistic use of planting.

The **Newbold House**, also near **Philadelphia** (begun 1919) (pp. 1493B, 1494B), is as creative an interpretation of Picturesque, vernacular sources as Timberline is of grand Classical ones. Here, Mellow, Meigs and Howe gave a new sense of vitality to this tradition, which had been used with such vigour by H. H. Richardson (q.v.) and others several decades earlier. It is based on a post-mediaeval manor house, and with its farm buildings forms an integrated group, but here, parts of the house reach out towards the countryside in all directions, rather than looking inwards. Each space is particularised, indoors and out, and movement is circuitous, resulting in what seems an almost random assortment of pieces. At the same time, the effect is unified through consistency in form, scale, and materials. Intricate textures are balanced by simple, abstracted masses. Underlying the whole design is the desire to avoid all references to contemporary forms of settlement, but instead to look back to a supposedly better past. The sentiment was shared by many Americans, but few people could afford to realise such an ambitiously pastoral world.

Frank Lloyd Wright (1867–1959) was no champion of the city; however, he sought to create a world of his own in its place. Rebelling against the language of the academic movement, he made an emphatic departure from all conventions, using form and space in ways that were new and with no readily perceivable ties to the past. Wright's rejection of precedent was the most pronounced of his generation, resulting in abstract designs that seemed to revolutionise the very nature of building.

His approach to design developed into a strong personal style around the turn of the century, as is evident in work such as **Willits House, Highland Park, Illinois** (1900–2) (p. 1493E). Wright's style proved equally adaptable for use with modest, compact dwellings (the **Hunt House, La Grange, Illinois**, 1907), large suburban residences (the **Coonley House, Riverside, Illinois**, 1907–9), sprawling country estates (his own **Taliesin, Spring Green, Wisconsin**, begun 1911) (p. 1493A), churches (**Unity Temple, Oak Park, Illinois**, 1904–6) (p. 1493D) (see also Chapter 37), and corporate headquarters (the **Larkin Building, Buffalo, New York**, 1903–6, demolished) (p. 1488B).

The **Robie House, Chicago** (1909–10) stands among his best early twentieth-century works and among the great achievements of Modernism (pp. 1494C,D, 1495). Responding to a long, narrow building site, Wright's characteristic interweaving of horizontal and vertical planes becomes even bolder. Horizontality predominates, making an oblique reference to the flat Illinois prairie, but the house stands in proud isolation, ignoring its suburban context. Wright did, however, share some concerns with the academic mainstream, including the pursuit of the complete unity of design. But, as with everything else, his means of dealing with these concerns was through abstraction. An insistent rectilinear geometry pervades all the parts, giving the scheme great visual strength. Inside, this penchant yields details that appear more applied and domineering. Coupled with Wright's audacious manipulation of small and large spaces in complex sequence, the effect is transcendent. The aggressive totality of Wright's work earned both admirers and critics.

Wright owed a considerable debt to the Arts and Crafts movement, with its call for simplicity, respectful use of natural materials, nature itself as a source of inspiration, and cultivation of regional character. The movement became popular shortly before 1900 in North America, where it was widely accepted by the middle class and closely associated with the spirit of progressive reform. The Arts and Crafts movement fostered individualism in design, as can be seen in a number of California buildings, such as the **First Church of Christ Scientist, Berkeley, California** (1909–11) (p. 1493E), by Bernard Maybeck (1862–1957), the **Gamble House, Pasadena** (1907–8), by Charles S. (1868–1957), and Henry M. (1870–1954) Greene (see also Chapter 37), and the **Dodge House in Los Angeles** (1914–16, demolished).

But the Arts and Crafts movement also led to broad tendencies in architecture, no more significant example of which can be found than the bungalow. While the term came from India, via Britain, the North American bungalow developed in a distinct manner under the auspices of mail-order plan companies and speculative builders (p. 1497A). Conceptually it represents a celebration of the modest house on its own terms, offering comfort, convenience, and an appealing image without the trappings of larger, more

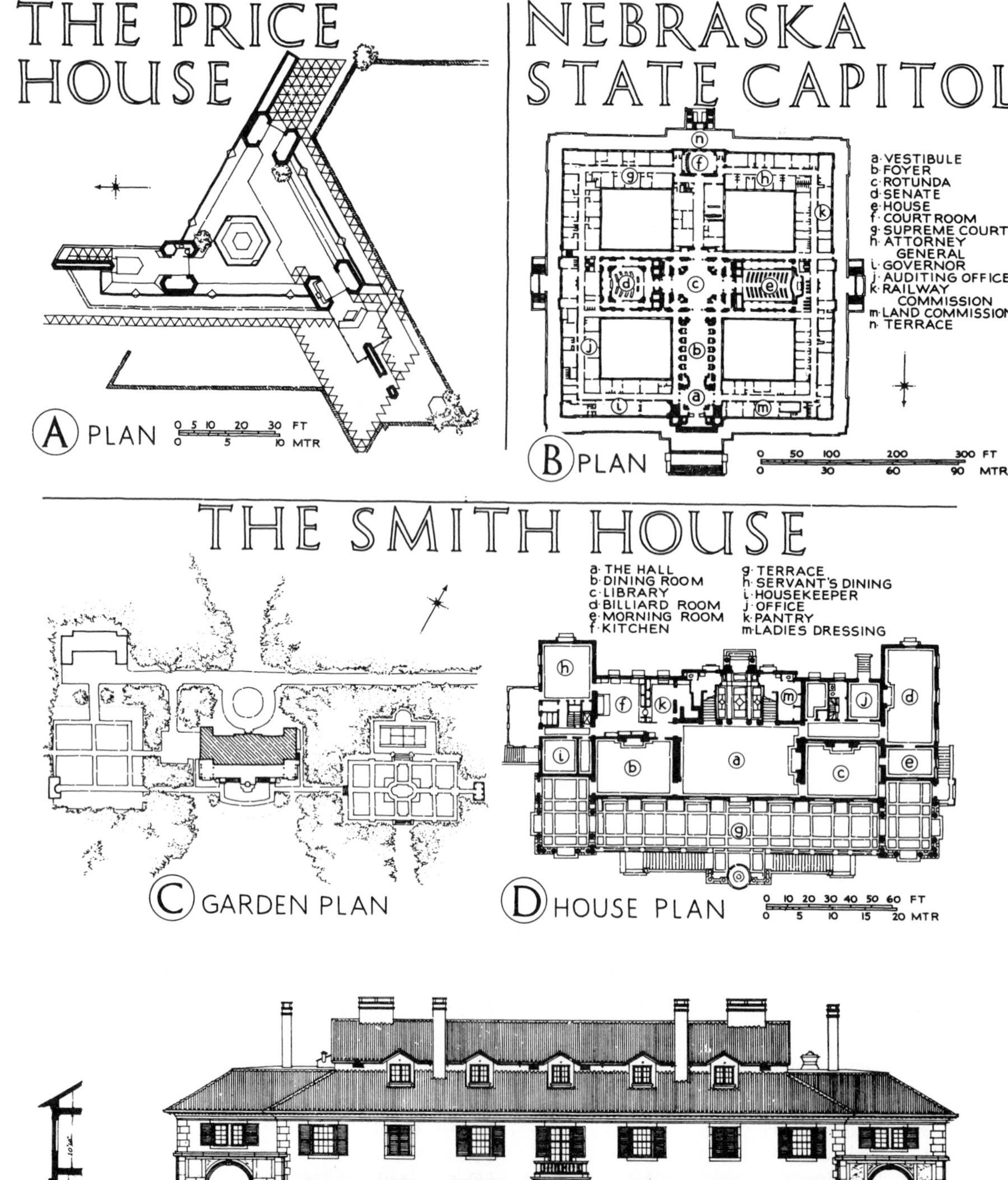

E. Timberline (Smith House), near Philadelphia (1907–8). See p. 1491

A. Taliesin, Spring Green, Wisconsin (begun 1911). See p. 1491

B. Newbold House, near Philadelphia (begun 1919). See p. 1491

C. Willits House, Highland Park, Illinois (1900–2). See p. 1491

D. Unity Temple, Oak Park, Illinois (1904–6). See p. 1491

E. First Church of Christ Scientist, Berkeley, California (1909–11). See p. 1491

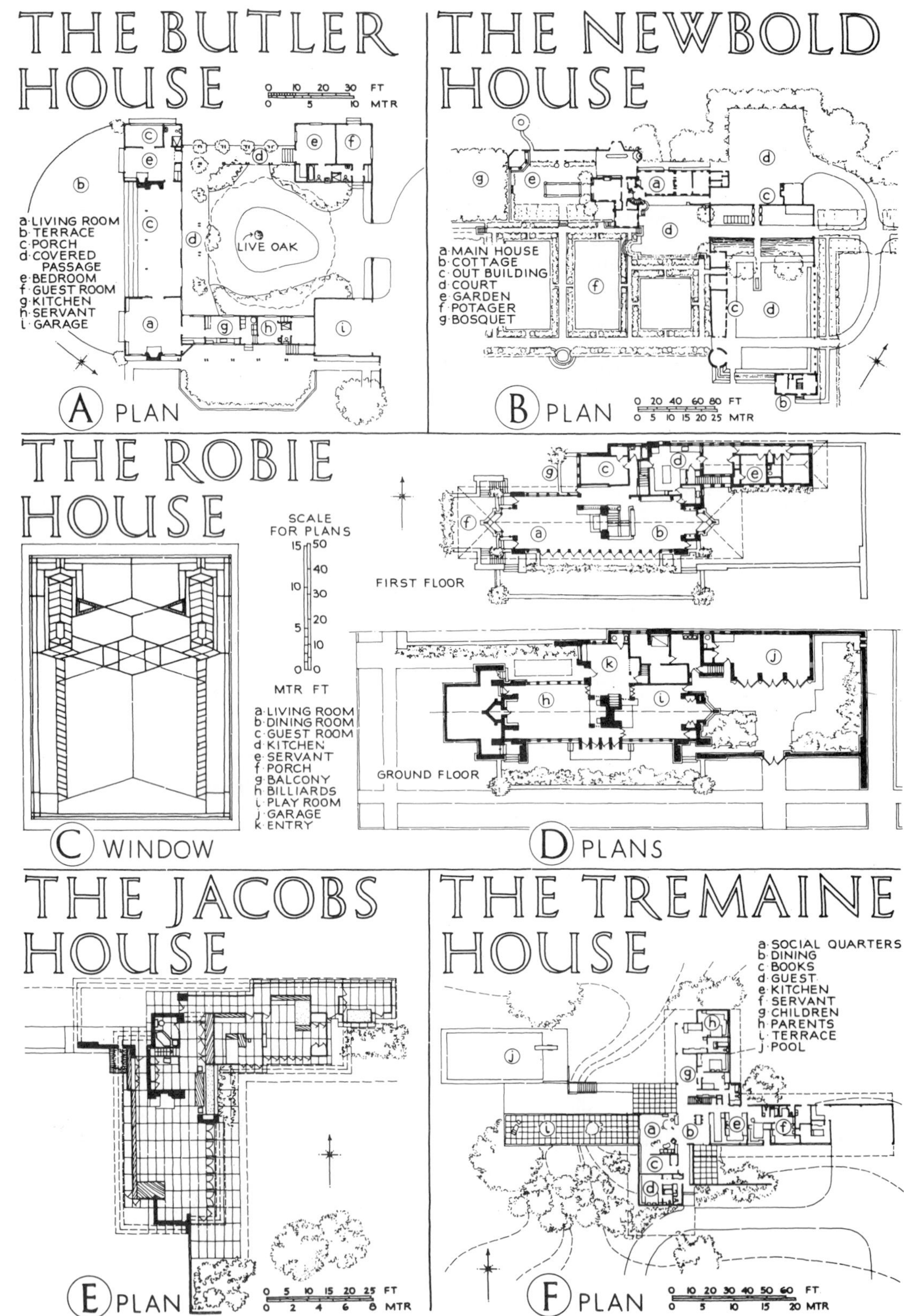
THE BUTLER HOUSE
0 10 20 30 FT
0 5 10 MTR
LIVE OAK
a·LIVING ROOM
b·TERRACE
c·PORCH
d·COVERED PASSAGE
e·BEDROOM
f·GUEST ROOM
g·KITCHEN
h·SERVANT
i·GARAGE
A PLAN
THE NEWBOLD HOUSE
a·MAIN HOUSE
b·COTTAGE
c·OUT BUILDING
d·COURT
e·GARDEN
f·POTAGER
g·BOSQUET
B PLAN
0 20 40 60 80 FT
0 5 10 15 20 25 MTR
THE ROBIE HOUSE
SCALE FOR PLANS
MTR FT
FIRST FLOOR
GROUND FLOOR
a·LIVING ROOM
b·DINING ROOM
c·GUEST ROOM
d·KITCHEN
e·SERVANT
f·PORCH
g·BALCONY
h·BILLIARDS
i·PLAY ROOM
j·GARAGE
k·ENTRY
C WINDOW
D PLANS
THE JACOBS HOUSE
E PLAN
0 5 10 15 20 25 FT
0 2 4 6 8 MTR
THE TREMAINE HOUSE
a·SOCIAL QUARTERS
b·DINING
c·BOOKS
d·GUEST
e·KITCHEN
f·SERVANT
g·CHILDREN
h·PARENTS
i·TERRACE
j·POOL
F PLAN
0 10 20 30 40 50 60 FT
0 5 10 15 20 MTR

A. Robie House, Chicago (1909–10). See p. 1491

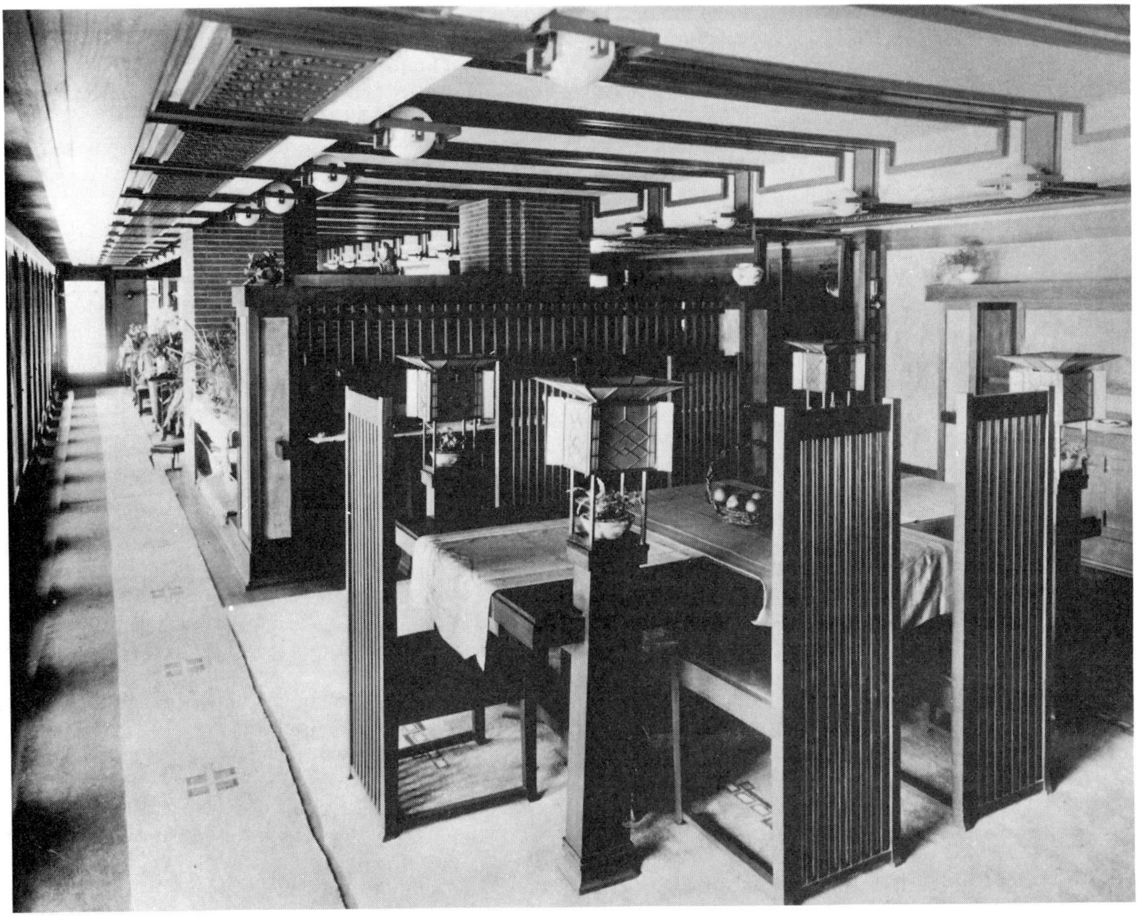

B. Robie House: dining room

pretentious residences. Many bungalows are rustic, even folksy, while seldom possessing overt historical references. Plans tended to have the main rooms on one floor and with much of the circulation and living spaces combined. Bungalows were cheap, but signified a sense of independence and financial security among the middle class, providing for domestic architecture what the Model T did for motor cars. Hundreds of thousands of Americans purchased bungalows between 1900 and the 1920s in suburbs, small towns, and rural areas. Ostensibly the type was developed in California, but it soon became ubiquitous in most North American regions.

Electrification of streetcar lines in the 1880s, and the manufacture of inexpensive motor vehicles some three decades later, encouraged low-density, small-scale growth, most of which occurred piecemeal, and was guided by little or no planning. City Beautiful initiatives, where they took hold, gave some order to this expansion, but carefully planned suburbs were the exception. One very ambitious project, the **Country Club District, Kansas City, Missouri**, and its environs, however, helped bring some change to this pattern in later years (p. 1497B). Begun in 1908 by the real estate entrepreneur J.C. Nichols (1880–1950), this residential development covers more than 6000 acres and took half a century to complete. The Nichols Company controlled all aspects of the enterprise, established regulatory covenants, and launched neighbourhood associations to ensure the district's long-term stability and appeal. Large tracts of land were reserved for parks and for a full range of communal services. As Ebenezer Howard had envisaged for the garden city, Nichols combined assets of rural and urban life on an unprecedented scale, but he also tailored his plan to the realities of the marketplace, to the existing town and American tastes. Despite the great success of this venture, few developers have possessed the same degree of commitment to one project.

By the 1920s other planning initiatives sought to restructure the very pattern of residential development. Drawing upon the garden city idea and European models, these projects called for housing clusters, communal gardens, large blocks segregating vehicles to the greatest extent possible, and, land permitting, expansive areas of peripheral open space. One result of this effort was the public housing programme inaugurated under the Roosevelt administration, which was directed at slum clearance. A more successful thrust entailed private development for people of moderate incomes. Architect Clarence Stein (1883–1975) and planner Henry Wright (1878–1936) were leading practitioners in this work and their efforts are perhaps most eloquently expressed at **Chatham Village, Pittsburgh** (begun 1931) (p. 1497C). The enclave is composed of apartments, but employs the traditional terrace form which is given an irregular configuration and is permeated by gardens and recreation areas. Americans have generally considered apartment living more a necessity than a preference. Through a complete reinterpretation of the idea, Chatham Village helped to remove this stigma. The scheme served as a prototype for numerous garden-apartment groups which became surrogates for modest free-standing houses during the lean depression years.

The appeal of early American images and a small-town atmosphere, evident at Chatham Village and in many suburban areas developed between the two world wars, was reinforced first by a reaction to the rapid rate of urban growth, then by the uncertainties of the depression. American colonial settlements were venerated owing to their physical character and because they were thought to testify to simpler, more honourable times. Besides affecting new work, this romantic perception gave added impetus to preserving remnants of the past. The most publicised and influential undertaking of this sort began in 1927 at **Williamsburg, Virginia** (p. 1497D). Funded by John D. Rockefeller, Jr, the project sought to recreate the town as it had existed over a century before, so that visitors might gain a greater understanding of colonial life. Outdoor museums, begun around the turn of the century in Scandinavia, offered some precedent for this venture, but never before had an actual community been transformed for such purposes. With extensive restoration of old buildings, reconstruction of those already lost, and the removal of later accretions, the programme brought a new level of expertise to preservation efforts in North America. At the same time, the product represents an idealised version, editing the past to perform a predetermined pedagogical role – an objective that continued to underly many preservation projects on the North American continent for several decades.

Modernism was rejected for residential design by all but a tiny segment of the populace. The assimilation of Modernism into the architectural mainstream during the 1920s and 1930s was led not by Wright or younger advocates of the avant-garde, however significant their work, but by architects schooled in the academic tradition who now believed that new avenues of exploration must be pursued if design was to retain its vitality. As in Europe, so in America efforts were made to create an architecture that broke away from the past in its modelling of form and simplification of effect, yet retained some obvious references to familiar traditions.

Among the earliest and most respected works of this genre is Bertram Goodhue's **State Capital, Lincoln, Nebraska** (1921–31) (pp. 1492B, 1498A). Goodhue (1869–1924) took the idea of an imposing block surmounted by a tower, widely used in American public buildings since the 1870s exaggerated both parts and intensified their relationship through abstracted form and bold scale. The ground-hugging base and souring tower contrast with the

A. Residential development, Los Angeles (*c.* 1910). See p. 1491

B. County Club District, Kansas City, Missouri (begun 1908). See p. 1496

C. Chatham Village, Pittsburgh (begun 1931). See p. 1496

D. Restoration/reconstruction of Williamsburg, Virginia (first phase begun 1927). See p. 1496

A. State Capitol, Lincoln, Nebraska (1921–32). See p. 1496

B. Hiawassee Dam, Cherokee Country, North Carolina (1936–40). See p. 1499

low-lying town and the plains beyond to create a strong civic character. Unity is paramount, with opposing forces balanced by stepped massing and a Beaux-Arts cross-in-square plan. Allusions to ancient Rome and the Near East, Byzantium, mediaeval Europe and native America permeate the scheme. The general effect, however, is Classicising and imparts a sense of newness as much as it pays homage to tradition. Also of this period are the more overtly modern works of Eliel Saarinen (1873–1950) who had moved to the United States in 1923 and continued his already distinguished career through such projects as the **Cranbrook School** (1924) and **Museum** (1940–43) at **Bloomfield Hills, Michigan**, and with his son Eero (1910–61), the **Tabernacle Church of Christ, Columbus, Indiana** (1939–42).

Widespread application of the approach to Modernism represented by Goodhue's work occurred in the commercial sphere, notably in skyscraper design, in which American architects continued their unrivalled leadership. Much of their inspiration came from American work, including that of Louis Sullivan, Gilbert, and Goodhue, but Eliel Saarinen's work, as well as that of the German Expressionists and contemporary French decorative designers, were also significant influences. Such diverse sources were employed to synthesise not only aspects of eclecticism and Modernism but also salient Classical and Gothic qualities. The composition of Art Deco skyscrapers, as they are now called, has a new strength and they rise as dynamic three-dimensional objects, their vertical piers leading the eye upward to varied arrangements of set-backs calculated to protect the air rights of neighbouring buildings. In these compositions such inspirational designers as Hugh Ferris made a positive virtue out of the need to set-back towers (e.g. his Zoning Envelope diagrams) while Raymond Hood, in his **Daily News Building, New York** (1929–30), gave sculptural form and character to repetitive facades by the application of the requirement for set-backs. Lavish ornament remains subordinate to bold masses which reflect the steel frame behind them. The results were considered to be the epitome of modern innovation, but they were also depicted as latter-day versions of ancient Mesoamerican pyramids and embodied a spirit of opulence and solidity inherited from their academic predecessors. New York and Chicago were the primary places where the ideal of these new soaring towers was developed; the **Chrysler Building** (1928–30) (p. 1500A) by Willian Van Alen (1883–1954), the **Empire State Building** (1929–31) (p. 1500B) by Shreve, Lamb and Harmon, and the **Board of Trade Building, Chicago** (1929–30), by Holabird and Root, are among the best-known examples. But the type was superbly employed in numerous other urban centres from the mid-1920s until the depression at the decade's end, as can be seen in the **Richfield Building, Los Angeles** (1928–30, demolished) (p. 1500C), by Morgan, Walls and Clements. During these few years Art Deco skyscrapers had a major impact on the character of large and small cities alike, offering a vivid symbol of prosperity and promise.

The consummate commercial project of the era was **Rockefeller Center New York** (begun 1929 as a way of combatting the depression) (p. 1501A). The principal architects were Reinhard and Hofmeister, with Harvey Wiley Corbett (1873–1954) and Raymond Hood (1881–1934). Encompassing nine buildings on three blocks by 1940, it was the most ambitious development since Terminal City. The plan as well as the size of the development departed from the norm. Instead of densely packed blocks, or towers, one very tall shaft, the 70-storey RCA Building, stands amid low- and medium-rise units arranged to admit unusually generous amounts of natural light. For the first time open space figures prominently in a large commercial scheme, with a pedestrian mall and plaza linking the core to Fifth Avenue. Rockefeller Centre strikes an effective balance between demands for more open development and the economic pressures for more intensive land use. The ground plan is formal, the details consistent, the sense of cohesiveness uncompromising. Contrasts in height, mass, and orientation give the design the degree of movement which provides a constant change in aspect, intensified by the fact that, despite its great size, the scale at street level is welcoming to the pedestrian. The effect is both reserved and dramatic in the best tradition of urban architecture. Drama takes the upper hand inside the buildings, especially in the theatres. Drawing upon recent French work, spaces in **Radio City Music Hall** exude an air of opulence with their slick veneers, plush furniture, and soft lighting (p. 1501B).

For generations, most American architecture that was considered progressive had been built in or near to cities. A significant break in this pattern occurred between the two world wars with the construction of huge dams and attendant hydro-electric plants in isolated areas. The most extensive such project, unprecedented in its programme to integrate the development and conservation of natural resources, was undertaken by the **Tennessee Valley Authority (TVA)**, an independent federal agency established in 1933 to regenerate an impoverished Southern region. **Dams** comprise only a part of this enterprise but are its most conspicuous artefacts (p. 1498B). Although such utilitarian structures were normally designed by engineers, architects, headed by Roland Wank (1898–1970), collaborated with engineers at all stages from the inception of the scheme. Trained in Vienna and inspired by Otto Wagner's public works, Wank sought at once to celebrate and transcend modern technology. The necessities of dam configuration thus became the basis for creating monuments, vast in scale, primal in form, rich in texture,

A. Chrysler Building, New York (1928–30). See p. 1499

B. Empire State Building, New York (1929–31). See p. 1499

C. Richfield Building, Los Angeles (1928–30, demolished). See p. 1499

A. (*above*) Rockefeller Center, New York (1929–). See p. 1499

B. (*right*) Rockefeller Center, Radio City Music Hall main lounge

spare and pragmatic in decoration. Accessible to visitors, the generator halls were seen as modern shrines, ennobling the transformation of water power into electricity which, in turn, was transforming rural life. Surrounding parks, planned for recreation, enhance the dams' civic quality. No other enterprise of the decade expressed with such forcefulness the capacity of democratic government to improve human living conditions.

A parallel in private development to TVA's co-operative spirit between architects and engineers had existed since the second decade of the century in the office of Albert Kahn (1969–1942) which achieved national prominence for its industrial buildings. Kahn organised his staff in multi-disciplinary teams to handle industrial projects from inception to construction, focusing on innovative responses to manufacturing processes, and then translating the concepts into efficient and visually integrated designs. The **Chrysler Half-Ton Truck assembly plant, near Detroit** (1937–8) is a good illustration of his mature work (p. 1503A). Inside, the need for open, flexible space and natural illumination from above is met by a novel steel truss system which also establishes the character of the building. The exterior is wrapped in a smooth, taut skin, mostly glass, which is independent of the structural frame. Covering 4.6 ha (11.5 acres), the design is rigorously holistic, yet fluid enough to permit enlargement to meet changing demands in production.

Albert Kahn's work helped to bring a new respectability to industrial architecture, but there is no indication that he considered the factory aesthetic to be appropriate for other building types. The scores of offices, institutions, houses, and even administrative units for manufacturing plants produced by the firm are all expressive of their own diverse functions. In this respect Kahn's approach reflected his roots in the academic movement and differed fundamentally from European Modernists such as Walter Gropius (1883–1969), Ludwig Mies van der Rohe (1886–1969), and Le Corbusier (1887–1965) who argued that a machine-inspired aesthetic should be universal. Like Wright, they sought a complete break from the past, not only through the elimination of historical references but also through new interpretations of form and space.

Constituting one of Modernism's most radical thrusts, what became known as the International Style attracted increasing attention in North America during the 1930s. As in Europe, however, scant demand existed for actual buildings in this idiom, and many of the early executed examples were for those who wished to support the avant-garde by building new residences.

Among the International Style's foremost exponents in North America was Richard Neutra (1892–1970). His designs enliven severe abstractness with a dramatic ardour and sensitive handling of human needs (inherited from early Modernists in his native Vienna), technical virtuosity (acquired while working on large commercial buildings in Chicago), and skill in landscape design (nurtured in his adopted home of southern California). The **Lovell House, Los Angeles** 1927–9) embodies all these attributes (p. 1503B). More than with European counterparts, the structure, a steel frame, is innovative as well as providing a basis for expression. At the same time, it is played against flat stucco bands that move into and out of the frame and extend into the garden as active sculptural counterpoints to the lush vegetation and rugged terrain. As much as any of the De Stijl group's projects, this is a formal exercise in architecture as space, defined by intersecting geometric planes; however, the effect is dramatic, and gives experiential as well as intellectual stimulus. R. M. Schindler, another Viennese, also pioneered Modernism in California. His **Philip Lovell Beach House, Newport Beach, California** (1925–6) is an astonishing display of expressed concrete construction. Its structural skeleton is composed of five fully parallel open frames which carrying two upper floors.

Neutra's later work also made a significant contribution to the effort, in both North America and abroad, to domesticate the International Style – to soften its machine imagery and cool abstractness while retaining its primary aesthetic and functional objectives. Among the most eloquent results is his **Tremaine House near Santa Barbara** (1947–8) (pp. 1494F, 1504A). The configuration is like a pinwheel, its arms reaching out into the wooded site so that a big house is seen only as a series of small-scale parts. Concrete frame and plate-glass walls are in sharp contrast to the abundant vegetation, but they remain subordinate to the overall effect. The design's rational qualities are further mollified by precise, yet serene, interiors. Neutra's concern for refining Modernism's humanistic qualities was shared by a number of colleagues, especially in California, which was the location of much of the avant-garde domestic architecture of the mid-twentieth century. The rich variety of solutions may be judged by comparing his houses with those of William Wurster (1895–1972). Trained in the academic tradition, Wurster began in the 1930s the attempt to reconcile that legacy with Modernism. His **Butler House** (1934–6), a weekend retreat near the California coast, borrows from the region's early Hispanic and Yankee architecture to create a throroughly novel design (pp. 1494A, 1504B). Reflecting the Modernist penchant for spatial freedom, the main precincts of the house are linked together only by a series of covered walkways and a living porch that becomes the principal room. The plan is more or less symmetrical and its organisation implies axiality, but movement is peripheral and unguided by a strong focal point. Despite such unorthodoxies, the Butler house does not look 'new' in the way so much Modernist architecture does, including a far more

A. (*right*) Chrysler Half-Ton Truck assembly plant, near Detroit (1937–8). See p. 1502

B. (*below* Lovell House, Los Angeles (1927–9). See p. 1502

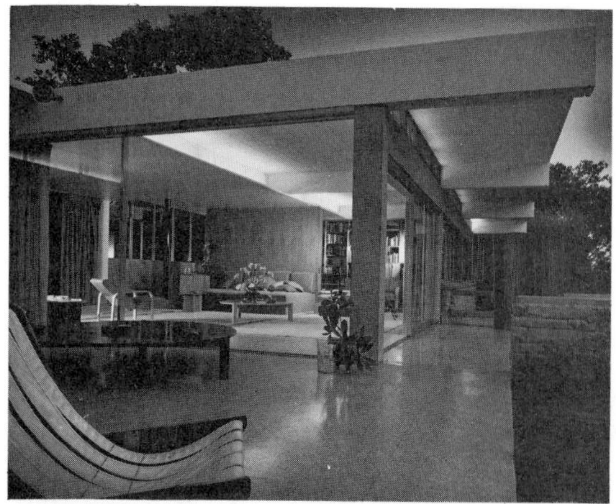

A. Tremaine House, near Santa Barbara (1947–8). See p. 1502

B. Butler House, Pasatiempo, California (1934–6). See p. 1502

C. Falling Water, Pennsylvania (1936–9). See p. 1505

elaborate East Coast counterpart, Frank Lloyd Wright's **Falling Water**, in rural western **Pennsylvania** (1936–9) (p. 1504C). Instead, Wurster offers evocative associations with a pastoral world. Few architects have produced work that is at once so innovative and so reassuring. As a result, Wurster enjoyed a degree of popularity seldom attained by Modernists.

The Houses of Bruce Goff (1904–1982) also strike a sympathetic chord at the popular level, but otherwise could not be more unlike those of his California contemporaries. Working in the American heartland, he created uninhibited, arresting designs that manifest the notions of luxury among the region's populace. Goff drew from Wright, from the Expressionists, and many other sources, but by the 1940s had developed a highly personal approach, trying to ensure that each scheme should not be based upon any other that had gone before. An early example is his **Graves House, Los Angles** (1919), which has a continuous perimeter space, containing living and sleeping areas, wrapped around a service core. Externally the house is strongly horizontal with a low-pitched roof, podium and verandas on four sides. Goff's **Bartman House, Fern Creek, Kentucky** (1941), is equally thoughtful though, with its flat roof and simple detailing, it is conceived in a very different language.

The **Price House** in eastern **Oklahoma** (1956–8) exhibits his independent style (pp. 1492A, 1506A). Poised at the edge of a knoll, the dwelling eludes all predictable images of 'house', offering instead improbably mixed metaphors rendered in equally improbable materials: a great tent of gold and anodised aluminium bracketed by free-form walls of coal and blue glass cullet; a machine of the future wrought from the petrified remains of a prehistoric past. Inside lies one expansive room, wrapped in plush carpet and goose feathers, affording the sense of total escape requested by the client. An underlying geometry controls this exoticism while remaining visually unobtrusive. Goff shared Neutra's and Wurster's belief that human activities are principal determinants of architectural character; however, the results are often closer to Wright's in their demand for full human participation.

Although most of their clients were affluent, Modernist architects were concerned about addressing the needs of a much broader audience. The 1930s and the immediate post-war years witnessed numerous new approaches to the design of low- and moderate-cost dwellings intended to improve domestic life generally. Frank Lloyd Wright's **Usonian Houses**, which evolved from his Utopian project for **Broadacre City**, are among the best-known examples (pp. 1494E, 1506B). As in the popular bungalow, the plan is arranged for economy and convenience: the dining room becomes an alcove bridging the living area and compact kitchen; the garage becomes a carport; the basement is eliminated. Technical innovation now figures prominently as well, with heat supplied through pipes laid in the concrete floor and most walls consisting of prefabricated wood sandwich panels. But while the site is suburban, and the Broadacre City concept entails one unending suburb, the layout implies a rural location where the house stands free. The street front becomes the 'rear', with all major rooms oriented to the opposite side. This reversed arrangement reflects what was becoming a widespread desire for privacy from motor traffic and for informal living patterns, but the approach is also typically Modernist in its treatment of the house as a visually independent unit rather than as part of a community. A companion project of similar date if different function is Wright's **Johnson Wax Administration Building, Racine, Wisconsin** (1936–9). Here Wright almost reinvented Modernism, avoiding all direct reference to the European modern tradition, to produce a streamlined building utilising pioneering materials and construction techniques. The building is internalised with the focus being the imposing columnar hall for clerks and typists.

After 1945 houses by Wright and other Modernists were promoted by the popular as well as the professional press, and aspects of their work have had a greater influence on the mainstream of residential design and indeed upon the development of Modernism than is generally believed, and not only in America but in Europe and elsewhere. The pristine minimalism of Mies van der Rohe elicted much attention through work such as the **Farnsworth House, Plano, Illinois** (1945–51) (p. 1507), and the retreat of his disciple, Philip Johnson (1906–), his **house in New Canaan Connecticut** (1945–9) (p. 1508). Among the most noteworthy attempts to reinterpret this aesthetic for suburban middle-class residences was the Case Study House programme (1945–62) in California, exemplified in works such as **Charles Eames's** (1907–78) own **house, Pacific Palisades** (1945–50) (p. 1506C), and Craig Ellwood's (1922–) **Case Study House No. 16, Bel Air** (1951–2). Equally abstract designs, though more evocative of the vernacular dwelling, were pursued by other architects, including Wright himself, for example his **Friedman House, Pleasantville, New York** (1948–50). With projects such as the **Robinson House at Williamstown, Massachusetts** (1946–7), Gropius's protégé, Marcel Breuer (1902–81) emerged as a leading practitioner in this vein on the East Coast. Similarly, Neutra's former employee, Harwell Hamilton Harris (1903–) developed his own regional style for dwellings in the West, as can be seen in the **Johnson House, Los Angeles** (1948–51). Another Gropius student, Carl Koch (born 1912), was one of the few architects successfully to apply Modernist principles to a mass-produced, **prefabricated system** for constructing houses inaugurated as **Techbuilt** in 1953.

A. Price House, Bartlesville, Oklahoma (1956–8). See p. 1505

B. Herbert Jacobs House, Madison, Wisconsin (1936–7). See p. 1505

C. House at Pacific Palisades, California (1945–50). See p. 1505

D. Levittown, near Philadelphia (1951–7). See p. 1509

A. Farnsworth House, Plano, Illinois (1945–51). See p. 1505

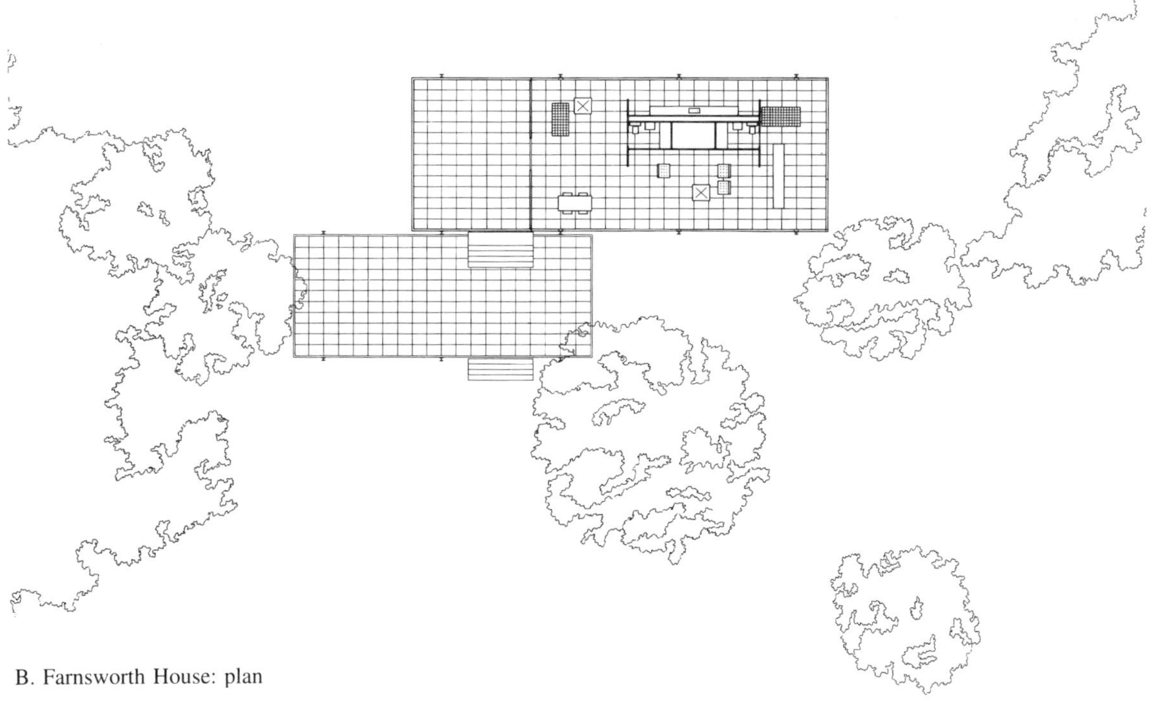

B. Farnsworth House: plan

A. House at New Canaan, Connecticut (1945–9). See p. 1505

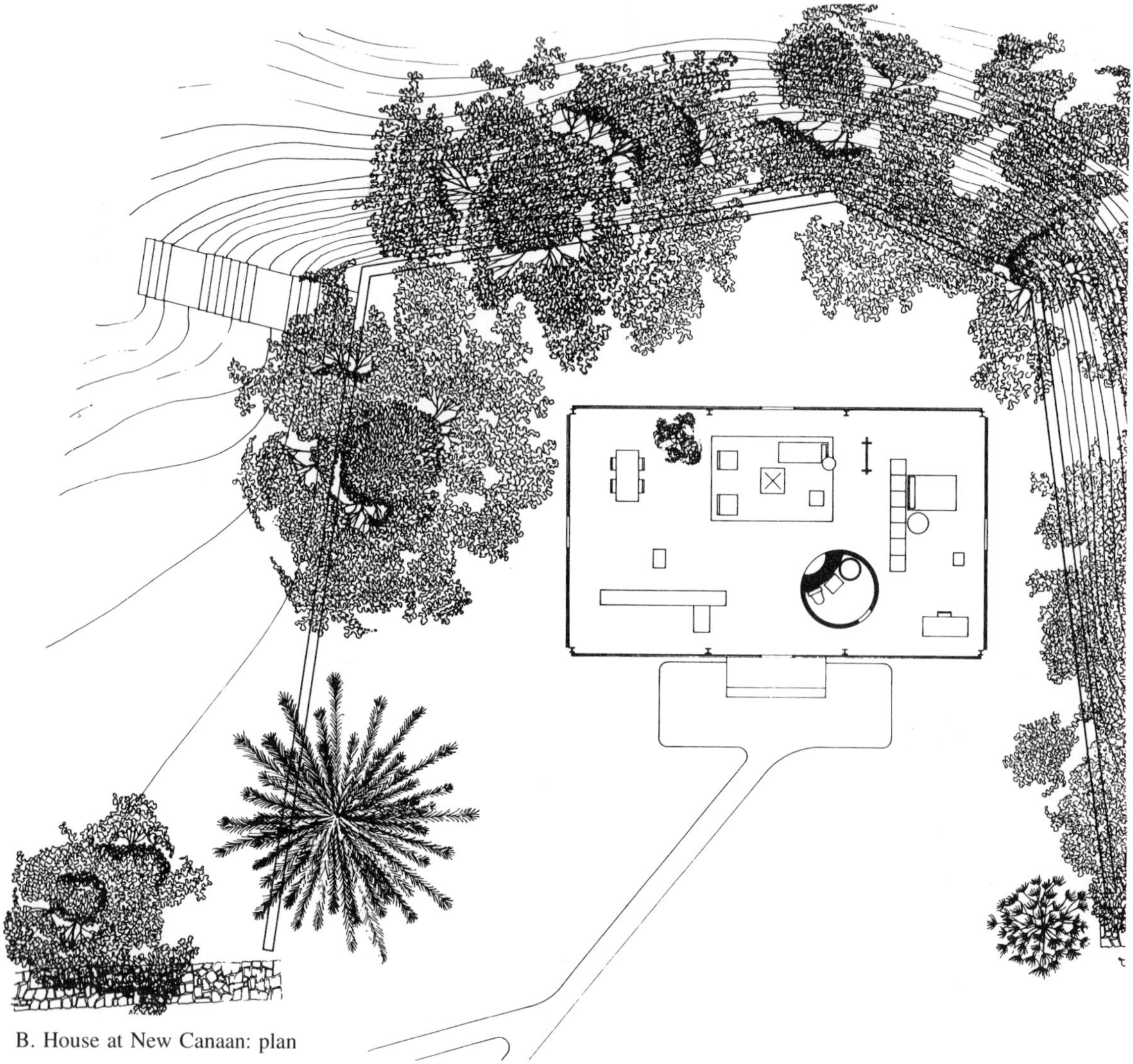

B. House at New Canaan: plan

Yet most Americans rejected a complete departure from the conventional idea of 'house'. The major force in residential design remained builders and, increasingly, developers, both of whom operated on a larger scale than in previous decades. Demand swelled owing to an acute housing shortage. Many more Americans could now afford to purchase a house because of federally financed long-term loans and mortgage insurance. Among the most remarkable post-war residential developments is **Levittown, near Philadelphia** (1951–7) – a new community comprising some 16,000 houses, along with shopping centres, schools, churches and other facilities (p. 1506D). Comparable in size to the Country Club District in Kansas City, it took only about six years to build, a feat made possible by Levitt & Sons' comprehensive organisational structure, standardisation of plans and building components, and adaptation of assembly line techniques on the site. The houses themselves owe a debt to Wright and Marcel Breuer, among others, but they also retain traditional features and impart a sense of community. Levittown is an updated garden city with parkways, winding streets, and large tracts of open space, but also with each site conceived as its own park. The project thus fused collective planning ideals with the American taste for self-identity. Ample precedent for this balance existed in suburbs occupied by the well-to-do; the Levitts brought it to the working class. The development epitomised a new generation of residential growth which transformed the metropolitan fringe between the 1940s and 1960s.

While most residential design has continued to retain ties to the past, commercial architecture has persisted in embracing new tendencies in Modernism. The International Style enjoyed its first widespread adaptation in North America with a new building type, the motor vehicle service station. During the depression, a number of oil companies sought to bolster sales by capitalising on Modernism's connotations of a better future rendered through functional planning and technology. The public responded, welcoming on the highway what would have been considered alien at home. The contribution of Texaco to this phenomenon was among the most influential. Walter Dorwin Teague (1883–1960), one of a new breed of industrial designers who specialised in giving objects a streamlined image, was commissioned to design standardised station types that would advertise a nationwide network of consistently good products and efficient service. Creating a distinct appearance and reinforcing it through repetition was a device calculated to attract customers. **Texaco's** new building campaign helped to establish a model for competitors and to generate an archetypal **service station** design which lasted until the 1950s. By that time, too, other companies were pursuing this approach, and while the images have changed the basic strategy remains, leaving a decisive imprint on the North American landscape.

Modernism assumed some of its most ebullient forms in the design of urban retail establishments, where individuality rather than standardisation was the basic objective. Inspired by European counterparts and by some of the more adventurous work at recent exhibitions, American shop design acquired a spirited character of its own during the late 1930s. Victor Gruenbaum (Gruen after 1941) (1903–80), who had trained in Vienna under Peter Behrens, was a principal figure in this specialised field. The **Grayson Store, Seattle** (1940–1) reveals his ingenuity. The front is a seemingly dematerialised billboard employing graphics, walls of glass, special lighting effects, and plastic forms to capture the eye of motorist and pedestrian alike. At ground level, minimal differentiation exists between the recessed display area and the sales room so as to lure customers inside. As with the cinema, the store is a part of the show, but now overt advertising and a dazzling repertoire of abstract elements are the primary ingredients.

American cities did not become the main proving ground for new forms of skyscraper design with which exponents of the International Style had been experimenting since the 1920s. Most of these projects remained on paper, although Howe and Lescaze's **Philadelphia Saving Fund Society Building, Philadelphia** (1929–32), is a major exception, rising during the depression as a potent emblem of what this form of Modernism could achieve on a large scale. Post-war prosperity induced financial institutions, manufacturers, hotel chains and a host of other operations to seek a new corporate image, much as the depression had fostered this impulse in the retail trade. By the mid-1950s, the vertical slab wrapped in glass, often denoting its structure, replaced the Art Deco tower as a symbol of business enterprise and prestige. The more or less continuous growth of commercial city-centres since then has led to a transformation in the character and scale of the urban skyline. Through such work the United States has had what is perhaps its greatest impact on architecture abroad. Two seminal designs are **Lever House** (1951–2) (see Chapter 51) and the **Seagram Building** (1954–8) (see Chapter 51), which stand opposite each other in **Manhattan, New York City** (see Chapter 37). The Seagram Building was anticipated by Mies's slightly earlier pair of apartments towers at **Nos 845–60 Lake Shore Drive, Chicago** (1948–51) (Chapter 51). The similarity between these projects, despite their different functions, is significant for it reveals Mies's conviction that architectural solutions transcended functional requirements and thus could be employed to suit a variety of needs.

The desire to create a universal architecture is also evident in Mies's smaller buildings. His master plan for the **Illinois Institute of Technology,**

Chicago (1939–40) called for more or less similar units arranged in a large, open superblock – the whole carefully balanced, yet without the traditional focus – as if one of Albert Kahn's automatic assembly plants were Classicised and set in a park. The most prominent and elegant building in the complex, **Crown Hall** (1950–6) houses the architecture school; however, it, too, possesses oblique industrial allusions, with one large space, supported by an external steel frame and enveloped in plate glass, comprising the essence of the conception.

The continued vitality of Wright; the emergence of younger Americans as diverse in their work as Wurster, Goff, and Skidmore, Owings and Merrill; the immigration of Neutra, Gruen, Mies, Gropius, and Breuer among others, made the United States an undisputed leader in Modernism after World War II. The riches of talent brought to bear during this period carried with them a dialectical tension over the existing state and future course of Modernism – an exchange that continues today, albeit with modified concerns. The controversy has been fuelled by the fact that while Modernism fosters pluralistic expression, architects and critics alike have sought coherence – not necessarily in terms of the International Style as canonised by the Americans, largely on the basis of European examples in the 1930s, but as clear parameters for the form and content of architecture. One of the outcomes of this dilemma has been the tendency to experiment among younger architects who began to come into their own around the time that the Seagram Building – a consummate statement of Modernist resolve – was completed in the late 1950s.

Chapter 51

NORTH AMERICA SINCE 1950

Introduction

The United States of America has been the richest and most powerful country in the world throughout the second half of the twentieth century. In such a well-developed industrialised society the presumed determinants of architectural form – climate, geography, available building materials, traditional methods of construction, customary patterns of use, conventional iconographic programmes, and so on – operate with diminished force. Climate can be modified artificially, land can be settled or abandoned with impunity, materials can be imported, new techniques can be invented and new worlds of significance and meaning can be created. America builds what it wants to build. In these circumstances, architecture, traditionally the mirror of a society's priorities and preoccupations, sometimes presents a distorted image.

Arguably, the buildings that most clearly represent the history of America over the last 50 years are those that stand on the periphery of architecture's territory. The ruined, deserted and dangerous ghettos of cities like Chicago and Detroit speak more eloquently than downtown skyscrapers of the true economic state of a society in which expanding wealth has been accompanied by increasing poverty. Even for middle-class Americans, the most important buildings are not churches or palaces, universities or hospitals, but pattern-book suburban homes and out-of-town shopping malls. Military bases, missile silos and nuclear bunkers constitute the architectural remains of the Cold War. The upsurge of rebellious youth in the liberated 1960s and 1970s is symbolised by the makeshift, self-build domes of Drop City in Colorado, while the increasing effectiveness of American technology in those decades is best represented by the more sophisticated geodesic domes of Richard Buckminster Fuller. Perhaps the true monument of the Apollo Space programme and the landing of a man on the moon on 21 July 1969 is not the National Air and Space Museum in Washington, DC, but the huge Vehicle Assembly Building at Cape Kennedy. The clearest architectural expression of the powerful communication and entertainment industries is not the AT&T Building in New York, or even a Hollywood film studio, but the cartoon city of Disneyland. The permanent built symbol of increasing personal mobility might be a cloverleaf junction of the Los Angeles freeway system. And what, on American soil, is the architectural outcome of the war in Vietnam? Only a slice cut into the ground in a Washington park and a list of names carved in black granite. None of these structures quite counts as architecture in the traditional sense.

Architecture flourishes in America nevertheless, not only as an established and respected profession working on behalf of the nation's most important government and business institutions but also as an intellectual discourse. American architects participate in architectural debate every bit as much as their counterparts in Europe or Japan. Like all architects in the West, they have struggled over this period to resolve the polarities of abstraction and figuration, tradition and invention, purity of form and diversity of context. They have also struggled with two conflicting traditions: European Modernism, represented by immigrants like Mies van der Rohe and Walter Gropius, and its American equivalent, represented by Louis Sullivan and Frank Lloyd Wright. Over the last 50 years these traditions have been combined, transformed, restated and, lately, challenged by Post-Modernism in all its multifarious forms. The built examples that follow are chosen to illustrate the progress of this debate and to represent the still-thriving cultural institution known as American architecture.

Examples

Progressive American architecture of the 1950s was dominated by the influence of European immigrants such as Walter Gropius and Mies van der Rohe, who had been teaching at Harvard and the Illinois Institute of Technology respectively since1938. Educationally it might be argued that Gropius had the greater influence – his students included Philip Johnson, Paul Rudolph and I. M. Pei – but in architectural practice it was Mies who led by example, most notably his design for the IIT campus itself (from 1940). The IIT buildings created a new architectural language which combined the American virtues of simplicity and practicality, represented by the pre-war factories of Albert Kahn, with the authority and intellectual seriousness of the European Modernist tradition. It was an architecture of 'almost nothing', which achieved a monumental grandeur by reducing the building to its essential components. In general terms function, in the sense of human use, was less important than structure, which usually took the form of an exposed steel frame.

In the twin 26-storey towers of Mies's **Lake Shore Drive Apartments, Chicago** (completed in 1951) (p. 1513A), steel remains the dominant material, even though the structural frame itself is encased in insulation for fireproofing. I-section steel 'pilasters' attached to the external wall divide the 21-foot structural bays into four sub-bays, creating an impression of solidity when the wall is viewed at an oblique angle.

A year later, the influence of the spare, rectilinear Miesian aesthetic was already evident in the 21-storey office tower of **Lever House, New York** (1951–2) (p. 1513B), designed by Gordon Bunshaft of Skidmore, Owings and Merrill. There are, however, some important differences. Mies's emphasis on the frame has given way to an emphasis on the skin – a curtain wall of aluminium and glass with pale-green spandrel panels, wrapped around the structure and concealing it from view. The wall is a two-dimensional grid, emphasising neither mullions nor transoms. In fact the idea of the curtain wall as a smooth skin was not unprecedented. In 1948, the Italian immigrant architect Pietro Belluschi had completed a 12-storey office slab for the **Equitable Savings and Loan Association in Portland, Oregon,** with a smooth curtain wall of green glass and polished sheet aluminium. But whereas in both the Belluschi building and the Lake Shore Drive Apartments the structural columns are at the perimeter and rise uninterrupted through the whole height of the building, at Lever House they are set back so that the tower appears as a box on stilts. At street level a low, flat podium block – the horizontal equivalent of the tower – hovers over an open plaza, maintaining the building line of the street. This tower/podium combination was to be enormously influential, becoming the model for countless imitations all over the world for the next twenty years.

When Mies himself was called upon to design an office tower for Joseph E. Seagram and Sons on a site almost opposite Lever House, he could not help but be influenced in his turn by Bunshaft's masterpiece. Like the Lake Shore Drive Apartments, the **Seagram Building** (completed in 1958) (p. 1514A,B) stands four-square on perimeter columns. Above ground level, however, the columns and floor beams are masked by the uniform pattern of the curtain wall with its regular rhythm of I-section pilasters. The ruggedness of Lake Shore Drive seems to have been tempered by the sleekness of Lever House. The Seagram Building also generously donates a public plaza to the city, but here there is no podium block to obscure the view of the elegantly proportioned monolith which, though it is actually T-shaped on plan, stands aloof from the street like a classical monument. It too created progeny all over the world, sometimes as single towers, sometimes as groups of towers and slabs, all wearing the same uniform. An example of the latter is the **Toronto-Dominion Centre, Toronto, Canada** (completed in 1971), by John B. Parkin Associates, with Mies as consultant.

Le Corbusier only ever built one building in America – the **Carpenter Visual Arts Centre, Harvard** (completed 1964) – but his influence was felt nevertheless in another New York tower, the **United Nations Secretariat** (completed in 1950) (p. 1513C). The building was designed by Harrison and Abramovitz, working with a team of international consultants which included Le Corbusier. Glass curtain walls on the two main faces of the tower are framed by masonry-clad flank walls giving it a strongly directional quality. There are echoes here of early Le Corbusier buildings like the Pavillon Suisse of 1931 and the Ministry of Education in Rio of 1935, designed in collaboration with Lucio Costa and Oscar Niemeyer, the latter also a member of the UN team.

But of all the European masters it was Mies who dictated the terms under which American capitalism adopted and adapted the language of European Modernism. After the success of Lever House, Gordon Bunshaft and SOM went on to design several very accomplished buildings in the Miesian idiom for the glorification of government and big business clients. Until the 1950s banks had sought to convey messages of permanence and security by housing themselves in solid, stone-clad structures decked out with columns, entablatures and pediments. SOM's relatively small, four-storey building on a corner site in 5th Avenue, New York, for the **Manufacturers Hanover Trust Company** (1954) is a systematic denial of every aspect of this tradition. Enormous sheets of plate glass are all that separate the double-height banking hall from the street, and the ceiling is a vast plane of light opening up the whole interior to view. To complete this reversal of expectations, the massive round steel door of the vault is placed just behind the curtain wall facing the street – and is left open.

Whereas Mies's use of the universal I-section steel member might be said to symbolise in a general way the productivity of American industry, SOM's use of immaculate stainless steel cladding in the **Inland Steel Building, Chicago** (1958), has a more obvious and less lofty aim – to show off the client's product. Nevertheless, this is another fine variation on the

A. Lake Shore Drive Apartments, Chicago (completed 1951). See p. 1512

B. Lever House, New York (1951–2). See p. 1512

C. United Nations Secretariat (right), New York (completed 1950). See p. 1512

A. (*left*) Seagram Building, New York (completed 1958). See p. 1512

B. (*below*) Seagram Building: plan of ground floor

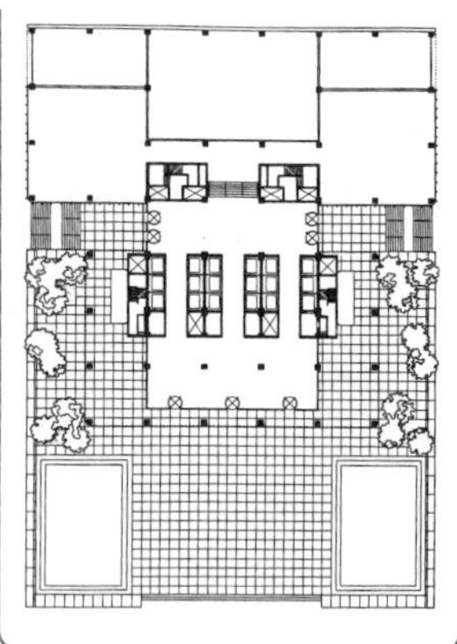

Miesian formula. Service elements are housed in a separate linked tower and the 18 m (60 ft) wide office floors are completely uninterrupted by internal columns.

Eero Saarinen's first works were carried out in partnership with his father, the Finnish architect Eliel Saarinen, who had been an exponent of the National Romantic Style before his emigration to the USA in 1923. Eero Saarinen cannot, therefore, be characterised as a child of Mies. Nevertheless, when he took over his father's practice in 1950 and began work on a huge $100 million dollar project for a **Technical Centre for General Motors, Warren, Michigan,** he designed a wide, low-rise complex spread over a 990-acre site that bears some resemblance to the IIT campus. The site plan, including the large lake in the centre, is strictly rectilinear with the exception of the circular 'styling dome' and a near-spherical tripod water tower which stands in the lake. Most of the buildings are two- or three-storey flat-roofed boxes with steel frames and curtain-wall facades. Unlike Mies, who was mainly interested in the monumental potential of technology, Saarinen genuinely sought to bring advanced, factory-based techniques to building construction. Working with the designers at General Motors, he developed prefabricated sandwich panels for curtain-walling, luminous ceilings made of translucent plastic pans, and neoprene gasket jointing systems. This was the beginning of what would later be called 'technology transfer'.

The new steel-framed architecture was not restricted to buildings for commerce and industry. The **Californian Case Study House programme**, which was commissioned by the influential Los Angles-based magazine *Arts and Architecture* under the editorship of John Entenza and had included the **Eames House** of 1949 (see Chapter 50), continued throughout the 1950s with a series of elegant single-storey, steel-framed houses designed by Rafael Soriano, Craig Ellwood and Pierre Koenig. Here the monumental overtones of steel construction as practised in New York and Chicago gave way to a more relaxed West Coast manner in which the apparent flow of space between exterior and interior was made real by the use of large sliding glass walls. Ellwood's **1129 Miradero Road, Beverley Hills** (1957), and Koenig's **1635 Woods Drive, Los Angles** (1959), are typical of this phase of the programme. The Koenig house is the more spectacular. Perched on a plateau high above the city, it has an L-shaped plan embracing an outdoor swimming pool. The thin steel deck roof spans 6 m (20 ft) between beams, and cantilevers 2 m (7 ft) out over the adjacent terraces, blurring the distinction between inside and outside. Houses such as this paid lip service to the idea of industrialised production, but the steel frame was used more for its slenderness and openness than for structural efficiency or speed of assembly.

In house design, the influence of Frank Lloyd Wright remained strong among those architects that resisted the European Modernist orthodoxy. Bruce Goff, who had been in independent practice since the early 1930s, designed a series of individualistic houses which took the concept of 'organic architecture' further than Wright ever did. The **Bavinger House, Norman, Oklahoma** (1955), for an artist client, is an *ad hoc* assemblage of recycled industrial components and natural materials picked up on the site. A spiralling roof, suspended from a central steel mast made from oil-well drilling pipes, is combined with an enclosing wall of sandstone boulders that seems to grow out of the ground. Inside, the living spaces are circular platforms hovering in a single unified space that is more like a natural landscape than a designed interior. Goff's pupil, Herb Greene, introduced a consciously figurative element to the style in his **Prairie House, Norman, Oklahoma** (1962). Its monolithic form, clad in feather-like timber boards and shingles, provokes various animal metaphors, including a mother hen protecting her chicks, the interpretation favoured by the architect.

Meanwhile, Frank Lloyd Wright himself had produced a masterpiece of organic architecture, the **Guggenheim Museum, New York**, facing Central Park (p. 1516A). It was completed in 1959, six months after the architect's death, though it had been on the drawing board since 1943. Given the opportunity at last to build in the middle of America's greatest city, Wright chose to ignore the regularity and uniformity of the Manhattan street grid and assert his individuality in an inward-looking building. A tapered drum encloses a high, top-lit space, surrounded by a spiral pedestrian ramp on the outer wall on which the works of art are displayed. With characteristic boldness, Wright reinvents the art gallery building-type, converting the traditional episodic promenade from picture to picture and room to room into a single, continuous spatial experience. The Guggenheim's direct precursor is Wright's V. C. Morris gift shop, San Francisco (1948), but it is possible to trace its ancestry back to the beginning of the century in the rectilinear but equally unified interiors of the Unity Temple in Oak Park and the Larkin Building in Buffalo (see Chapter 50).

Not only did it take 16 years to navigate the Guggenheim design through the complexities of the New York building regulations and bring it to successful completion but it also took 27 years to realise another of Wright's organic designs, the S. Mark's Tower project of 1929. This was finally built in 1956 as the **H. C. Price Tower, Bartlesville, Oklahoma**. Like a tree, it is based on the principle of the cantilever – the vertical cantilever of the main structure corresponding to the trunk, and the horizontal cantilevers of the floors corresponding to the branches. The tower is basically square on plan, but this regular geometry is disrupted by the cruciform

A. Guggenheim Museum, New York (completed 1959). See p. 1515

B. Dulles International Airport, Washington, DC (1958–62). See p. 1517

concrete core which is set at an angle of 60°. The various permutations of triangular, rhomboidal and rectilinear grids, and the alternation of single- and double-height floors, are all clearly expressed on the exterior to create a complex, angular form, in concrete, glass and copper. It could hardly be more different from the sleek monoliths of Mies van der Rohe. Indeed, the overlaying of different geometries might be said to prefigure, in a controlled way, the Deconstructivist manner of the 1980s.

In the new designs that Wright produced in the last phase of his long career, formal and structural inventiveness gave way to a superficial image making that critics have tended to dismiss as mere kitsch. The **Marin County Civic Centre, San Rafael, California,** completed by Wright's associates in 1964, takes the circle at its geometric motif, but lacks the unity and integrity of the Guggenheim. Long low wings, radiating from a central shallow dome, have arcaded facades that echo the form of a Roman aqueduct but, being non-load-bearing, are devoid of structural logic.

In the early 1960s the Miesian tradition, though far from exhausted, began to be challenged by a new Expressionism and a different kind of monumentality. It became clear, for example, that the Miesian manner of Eero Saarinen's Technical Centre for General Motors was only one aspect of an architectural philosophy that sought to match style with function in an Expressionistic way. Saarinen had already experimented with curved, organic forms in the **Kresge Auditorium, Massachusetts Institute of Technology** (1950–5), and the **David Ingalls Ice Hockey Rink, Yale University** (1956–9). The former is roofed by a section of a sphere resting on three points, and the latter by a tent-like structure of steel tension cables supported by a parabolic reinforced concrete spine. Saarinen used steel tension cables again in the sweeping catenary roof structure of **Dulles International Airport, Washington, DC** (1958–62) (p. 1516B), but the definitive statement of his Expressionist period is the **TWA Terminal, Idlewild (now John F. Kennedy) Airport, New York** (1956–62) Four concrete shell roofs linked by strips of glazing spring from massive sculptural Y-shaped columns. Glass curtain walls are curved on plan and raked in section as if being stretched upwards by the billowing roof. Inside, form and space seem to be in constant flowing movement. The austere abstraction of the 1950s has been rejected in favour of an almost literal representation of an enormous bird alighting on the airport tarmac.

But organic curved forms were only one aspect of the new expressive freedom that was characteristic of the early 1960s. Paul Rudolph's **Architecture School, Yale University** (completed in 1964) (p. 1518A) showed the influence of Le Corbusier's 'Brutalist' post-war style, epitomised by the Monastery at La Tourette completed four years previously. Rudolph had trained under Gropius and Marcel Breuer at Harvard. But in the Yale School, where he was chairman from 1958 to 1965, he rejected the technocratic, collaborative approach of Gropius and broke through into a personal language of dramatically contrasting cubic forms in heavy 'ridge hacked' concrete. The basically rectangular building is surrounded by varied clusters of boldly articulated service towers rising to different heights. Formal complexity outside is matched by a spatial complexity inside. Though this is only a seven-storey building there are no fewer than 37 different floor levels. Criticised for its formalism and for its functional shortcomings, the Yale Architecture School nevertheless had many imitations. Kallmann, McKinnel and Knowles' **Boston City Hall** (1968) refers even more obviously to La Tourette with its projecting upper floors, while John M. Johansen's **Clark University Library, Worcester, Massachusetts** (completed 1969), seems to acknowledge both Boston and Yale as its parents.

Alongside these attempts to carry forward the work of 'form givers' (to use Philip Johnson's phrase) like Mies van der Rohe and Le Corbusier, there flourished a less intellectually demanding monumental tradition represented by architects like Minoru Yamasaki, Edward Durrell Stone and Philip Johnson himself. The **Lincoln Centre for the Performing Arts, New York** (1962–6) (p. 1518B), is typical of the style. Three box-like buildings, the **Metropolitan Opera House** (1966) by Wallace Harrison, the **Philharmonic (now Avery Fisher) Hall** by Max Abramovitz (1962) and the **New York State Theatre** (1964) by Philip Johnson and Richard Foster, face a large open plaza. The axial, symmetrical arrangement is reminiscent of the Campidoglio in Rome, with a fountain in place of the statue of Marcus Aurelius. The front facades of the three buildings are equipped with vaguely Classical open colonnades, arcuated in the case of the dominant opera house. The most interesting of the three is Johnson's theatre, which has a high entrance hall surrounded by galleries on three levels and reached via a pair of operatic staircases. The paving is travertine, the balustrades are bronze and the ceiling is gold leaf. When the building was opened critics were shocked that the architect who introduced Mies van der Rohe to America should have reverted to such an overtly Classical style and such an over-rich pallette of materials.

Edward Durrell Stone's **John F. Kennedy Centre, Washington, DC** (completed 1971), also adopts the superficial neo-Classical style, though here the auditoria are all subsumed into a single block and share a gigantic foyer, 194 m (630 ft) long and six storeys high. Minoru Yamasaki, who had worked with Harrison and Abramovitz, developed his own version of the style, wrapping his buildings in fine-textured, perforated screens. In the **World Trade Centre, New York** (completed in 1973). A Gothic version of this

A. (*above*) Architecture School, Yale University (completed 1964). See p. 1517

B. (*right*) Lincoln Center for the Performing Arts, New York (1962–6). See p. 1517

C. US Pavilion, Expo 67, Montreal. See p. 1519

D. Habitat, Expo 67, Montreal. See p. 1519

device is applied to a pair of gigantic skycrapers, turning them into featureless monoliths when viewed from a distance.

By 1967 many architects and engineers, encouraged by the prevailing mood of technological confidence in the glory years of the space age, had become interested in the design of 'megastructures' that transcended the traditional boundaries of architecture. **Expo 67 in Montreal** provided the opportunity to experiment with these new ideas. Frei Otto's **German Pavilion** created an amorphous enclosure with a net of steel cables supported by raking steel struts, while the design of the **US Pavilion** (p. 1518C) was entrusted to the inventor/architect Richard Buckminster Fuller, who took the opportunity to demonstrate the principle of what he called 'tensegrity structures' in a vast geodesic dome. More influential than both of these, however, was the housing complex called **Habitat** (p. 1518D), designed by Moshe Safdie, a young Israeli architect trained at McGill University in Montreal. Habitat was conceived not as a building but as a building system, applying the principles of industrial production to the problem of mass housing. Each dwelling was a prefabricated concrete box weighing 90 tons, lifted into position on a supporting concrete frame by specially designed cranes. But it was the indeterminate, proliferating form, with open terraces and elevated walkways, that caught the imagination of Safdie's contemporaries.

Ironically, the influence of the arch-technologist Buckminster Fuller was felt most directly not in the factories and building sites of the mainstream construction industry but in the various 'alternative' self-built communes that sprang up in the south-western deserts, of which **Drop City, Colorado** (founded in 1965), was the first. The geodesic dome, completely disassociated from its traditional masonry equivalent, turned out to be the ideal form for houses assembled from salvaged timber, second-hand corrugated metal sheeting and the roofs of scrapped cars.

Another kind of alternative settlement was proposed by the Italian-born architect, Paolo Soleri, who had been an apprentice in Frank Lloyd Wright's Taliesin West studio. Soleri's visionary urban projects were, however, very different from Wright's. In contrast to the wide open spaces of Broadacre City, with 4000 square metres of land for each family, Soleri's 'arcologies' (architecture plus ecology) were vast megastructures housing up to 6 million people at high density. In 1964 work started in the desert on a built prototype called **Arcosanti, near Scottsdale, Arizona**, not far from Taliesin West, and has continued slowly ever since, though the settlement is unlikely ever to achieve its original target population of 15,000.

The 1960s was the decade of space travel, flower power and alternative architecture, but it was also the decade which saw the emergence into maturity of America's own 'form giver' – Louis I. Kahn. In Kahn's work the compositional discipline of the Beaux-Arts tradition and the abstraction of the Modernist tradition are combined to create an architecture which is monumental in a far deeper and more poetic sense than that of his neo-Classical contemporaries – Stone, Johnson and Yamasaki. Kahn sought architectural equivalents of archetypal human institutions by asking the question 'what does the building want to be?' He was not interested in the flowing, ambiguous spaces of European Modernism but instead strove for clarity and definition by reviving the solid wall and the contained room. In his buildings symmetry and axiality serve the functional programme rather than any purely aesthetic motive.

Born in 1901, Kahn was already 50 when he got his first major commission, the **Yale University Art Gallery**. But it is in the **A. N. Richards Medical Laboratories, Philadelphia** (phase one completed 1961) (p. 1520A,B), that we find the first clear demonstration of one of the cornerstones of Kahn's architectural theory: the distinction between 'served' and 'servant' spaces. The laboratories themselves are housed in seven-storey towers, each floor of which is an uninterrupted square room. These are the served spaces, mostly glazed, with cantilevered, column-free corners. Attached to them are the 'servant' towers in contrasting solid brickwork, containing either air ducts or staircases. The arrangement arose from the functional demands of highly serviced, flexible laboratories, but it was the simplicity and expressiveness of its forms – the way that the flank walls of the servant towers continued high above the roofline, for example – that appealed to new generation of young architects.

In the **Salk Institute, La Jolla, California** (1959–65) (p. 1520C,D) on an elevated site overlooking the Pacific, Kahn once again tackled the problem of the highly serviced laboratory. Like the Richard Laboratories, the Salk Institute has large flexible spaces served by towers at the perimeter, but this time the servant spaces extend horizontally between the laboratory floors, taking advantage of the space created by the storey-height concrete Vierendeel trusses that span right across the building. There are two parallel buildings on either side of a paved court. Individual studies for the scientists occupy the facades facing the court. This mixture of large, almost industrial spaces for collaborative working and small intimate spaces for private contemplation is typical of the way Kahn's architecture gives form to the hierarchies of human use. In early versions of the plan the court was treated as a landscaped garden, but Kahn became disatisfied with this design and decided to consult the Mexican architect Luis Barragán. Barragán's solution was simple. The court, he said, should be completely free of vegetation so as not to obscure its dramatic spatial relationship with the Pacific horizon.

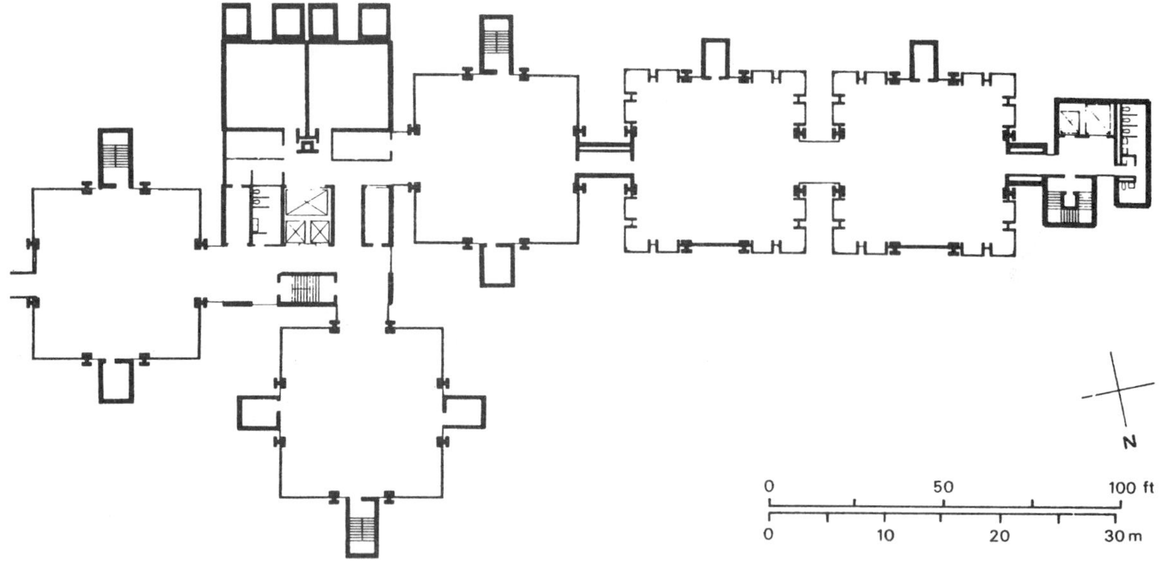

A. Richards Medical Research Laboratories: plan of first floor

B. Richards Medical Research Laboratories, Philadelphia (completed 1961). See p. 1519

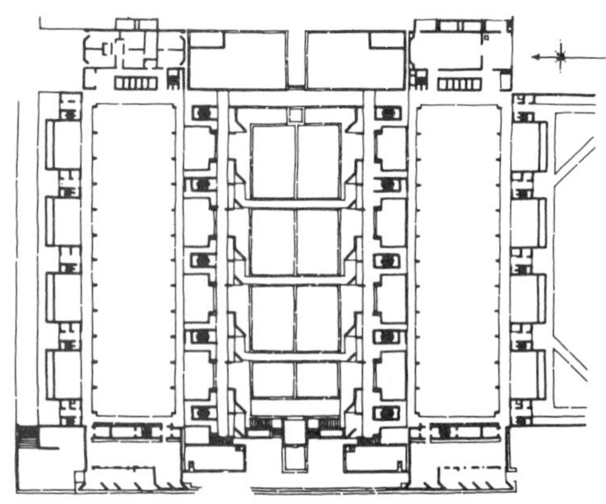

C. Salk Institute: plan

D. Salk Institute, La Jolla, California (1959–65). See p. 1519

Kahn's combination of Modernist abstraction and Beaux-Arts symmetry is perhaps clearest in the **Kimbell Museum of Fine Art, Fort Worth, Texas** (completed in 1972). Set on a sloping site, a large semi-basement storage area is surmounted by a single-storey building containing the galleries themselves. Six parallel 'barrel vaults' (actually curved concrete long-span beams incorporating longitudinal skylights) alternate with servant bays to form an abstract matrix which is adapted to accommodate different gallery configurations and ancillary spaces. The auditorium, for example, is formed by simply raking the floor under one of the vaults and its adjacent servant bay. But whereas a true Modernist might have dispersed these linear elements in a fragmented, functionally differentiated, composition, Kahn confines them within a basically symmetrical rectangular plan.

Kahn also worked on the larger, urban, scale in a series of **projects for Philadelphia**. In his 1955 plan for the midtown area of the city he attempted to reconcile the conflicting demands of pedestrians and motor traffic by proposing a new urban artefact called a 'dock', consisting of a cylindrical multi-storey car park surrounded by 18-storey apartment and office buildings. The project was not realised.

The mainstream Modernist tradition developed during the 1960s in corporate and government buildings in the centres of the big cities. In 1968 Kevin Roche, an Irishman who had studied under Mies at IIT and who, with John Dinkeloo, had taken over Eero Sarrinen's practice upon his death in 1961, completed the **office building for the Ford Foundation, New York** (p. 1522A–D). Sited next to a small public park, the building is relatively modest in both size and architectural demeanour. What made it one of the most influential American buildings of the 1960s was the generosity of its plan which gives over most of the site to an internal garden, open to the public and separated from the street only by a ten-storey high glass screen. This was the forerunner of a new building type: the 'atrium' office building.

Perhaps the best of the Miesian skyscrapers of the 1960s is **Chicago City Hall (Richard Daley Center)** (completed 1965) by Jaques Brownson of C.F. Murphy Associates. In his early career, Murphy himself had worked with D. H. Burnham, of Burnham and Root, and he therefore represents a direct link between the pioneering Chicago School of the late nineteenth century and the European Modernism of Mies. Chicago City Hall is a simple monolith of glass and Corten oxidised steel presenting itself, like the Seagram Building, to an open plaza. What is most impressive, however, is the way that its sheer size is mastered by its architectural scale. It contains courtrooms as well as offices and its floor-to-floor dimension is therefore unusually high, but this is balanced by the breadth of the structural bay – an unprecedented 15 m (49 ft) by 26 m (87 ft). It is this expansiveness of proportion that gives the building its power and presence – a clear, resonant bass note in the architectural clamour of downtown Chicago.

Five years later, Bruce Graham of SOM's Chicago office completed the **John Hancock Center** (1965–70) (p. 1523A,B), an enormous tapering tower containing a mixture of business and residential accommodation. Here the external structural steel cross-bracing mediates between the human scale of the individual floors and the sublime scale of the building as a whole. For a short while the John Hancock Centre was the tallest building in Chicago, but it was soon overtaken by another SOM giant, the **Sears Tower** (completed 1974) (p. 1523C), and still the tallest building in the world. However, its composite form – a cluster of smaller towers rising to different heights – lacks the solidly confident stance of its stablemate and rival.

In Washington, DC, the mid-1970s saw the completion of two museums, the **East Building of the National Gallery of Art** by I. M. Pei (p. 1524A,B) and the **National Air and Space Museum** by Helmut, Obata and Kassabaum, which share certain characteristics despite the very different nature of the objects exhibited in them. Both are adjacent to The Mall and appropriately monumental in scale, with plain, stone-clad volumes linked by glazed atriums. The East Building is an extension to the original neo-Classical gallery by John Russell Pope, completed in 1941, and is clad in pink marble from the same Tennessee quarries. Its plan, however, has none of the formality or symmetry of the older building, but is based on a triangular geometry arising from the trapezoidal shape of the site. At its heart is a three-storey high, glass-roofed atrium which drew criticism at the time because of its resemblance to the architecture of shopping centres. For the National Air and Space Museum, the shopping-centre comparison is even more apt. HOK had designed gallerias in Houston and Dallas and thought of the museum as a similar design problem: to display objects to the best advantage to the largest possible number of people. For a while after its opening it was said to be the most popular museum in the world.

The origins of the covered shopping mall as a building type can be traced back to the early 1950s and specifically to the **Northland Shopping Center, Detroit** (completed 1954) (p. 1524C) by Victor Gruen. Situated on the outskirts of the city, the centre was designed almost exclusively for the car-owning public. The inward-looking complex sits in a sea of car parking – a self-contained shopping city divorced from any urban context. The type proved to be so successful that it quickly became the norm for large-scale shopping developments all over the USA, with ultimately disastrous consequences for the social and economic wellbeing of American cities.

However, new building types like out-of-town shopping centres were an effect rather than a cause

A. (*left*) Office building for the Ford foundation: interior

B. Office building for the Ford Foundation, New York (completed 1968). See p. 1521

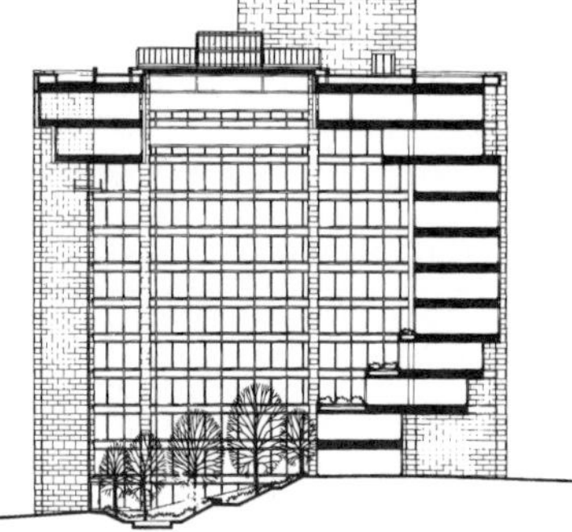

C. Office building for the Ford Foundation: section

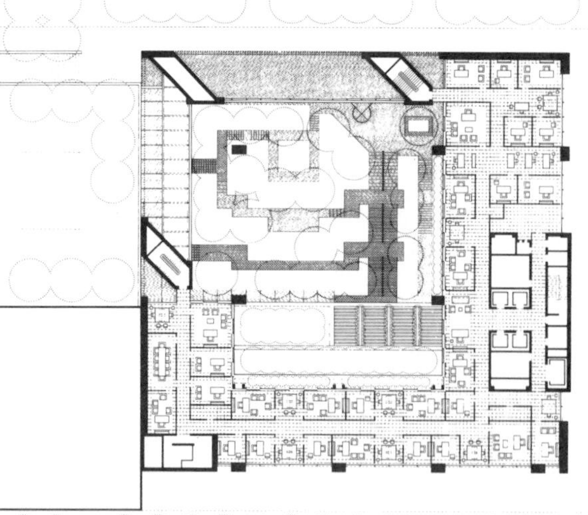

D. (*left*) Office building for the Ford Foundation, New York: plan of ground floor

A. John Hancock Center, Chicago (1965–70).
See p. 1521

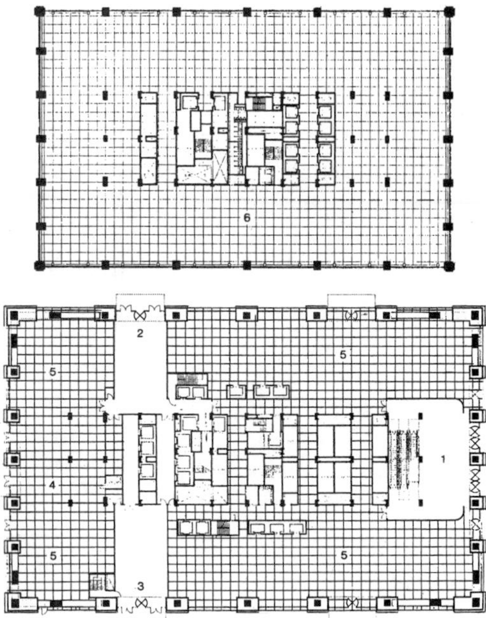

B. John Hancock Center: plans. (*Top*) Typical upper office floor. (*Above*) Street level. 1 office lobby, 2 restaurant lobby, 3 apartment lobby, 4 car lobby, 5 shops, 6 office area, 7 restaurant

C. Sears Tower, Chicago (completed 1974).
See p. 1521

A. East Building of the National Gallery of Art, Washington, DC (completed 1975). See p. 1521

B. East Building of the National Gallery of Art: atrium

C. Northland Shopping Center, Detroit (completed 1954). See p. 1521

of the slow disintegration of urban life in the United States. The so-called GI Bill, which offered cheap mortgages to war veterans, boosted home ownership and encouraged sprawling suburban developments, while the Federal sponsorship of a new Interstate Highway network encouraged car ownership and population movement, breaking the traditional bonds of proximity and community that hold cities together. The city centres were bequeathed to the poor, and the decaying urban fabric became a problem to be solved by slum clearance and comprehensive redevelopment.

By the early 1960s, however, opposition to this process was growing. In her book *The Death and Life of the Great American Cities*, published in 1961, journalist and urban theorist Jane Jacobs vehemently attacked the suburbanisation of America and the starvation of the communal life of cities. For the first time the vision of a Modernist Utopia, to be brought about by comprehensive redevelopment and functional zoning, was seriously questioned. Jacobs saw cities not as productive machines but as delicate social and economic organisms. As she saw it, the traditional street, with its rich mixture of uses – residential, industrial and commercial – was vital to the health and wellbeing of the urban population. Far from improving the lives of their inhabitants, massive Modernist redevelopments like the **Pruitt Igoe housing project, St Louis**, by Minoru Yamasaki, were becoming centres of delinquency and vandalism and slowly killing the city. And the authorities were beginning to listen. In 1972, just 17 years after its completion, the social fabric of Pruitt Igoe was finally declared beyond repair and the buildings were dynamited. It was this event, according to the critic Charles Jencks, that marked the death of Modernism.

But small-scale, piecemeal adaptations of the kind advocated by Jane Jacobs were not the only possible means of urban regeneration. An alternative strategy was to build a mixed-use version of the self-contained, out-of-town shopping complex right in the centre of the city. In the late 1960s and early 1970s the architect and developer John Portman built just such a complex in downtown Atlanta. The **Peachtree Center** includes office buildings, shopping centres and two large luxury hotels, one of which, the Hyatt Regency, is built around a 23-storey atrium. This was the first a series of similar Portman hotels in San Francisco, Los Angeles, Chicago and Detroit. It was Portman who first developed the full dramatic potential of the high internal atrium, treated as a quasi-external public space, fully landscaped, with shops and restaurants and the obligatory glazed wall-climber lifts. Externally, Portman's buildings are often monumental, symmetrical compositions of cylindrical towers clad in reflective glass curtain-walling. In them, the Miesian Modernist tradition is allied with the powerful forces of commercial real estate development.

Portman's developments demonstrated that the enclosed shopping centre form could be applied on a large scale to urban as well as suburban sites. The idea was adopted in cities all over North America. In Canada, for example, the **Eaton Centre, Toronto** (completed 1981), by Bregman and Hamann and the Ziedler Partnership, covers five city blocks. A 274 m (890 ft) long glass-roofed mall, with shops on three levels, slices through the centre of the development, imitating, on an even grander scale, nineteenth-century European precedents like the Galleria in Milan.

Already by the late 1960s the Modernist orthodoxy was under attack, not just from critics, sociologists, urban theorists and an increasingly vociferous general public, but also from within the profession itself. In 1966, the architect Robert Venturi, who had worked with Saarinen and Kahn, published a book called *Complexity and Contradiction in Architecture* in which he attacked what he saw as the over-simplification of form in the Modernist tradition, and especially its Miesian branch. Mies's 'Less is more' was countered by Venturi's 'Less is a bore'. Citing examples from the Mannerist and Baroque architecture of the sixteenth and seventeenth centuries, Venturi argued that traditional concerns like meaning and symbolism had been neglected by Modernist architects, who had concentrated on function and abstraction. According to Venturi, Mies's architecture achieved an elegant simplicity only by ignoring the unresolved conflicts and ambiguities of real life. Instead of an exclusive architecture of 'either or', Venturi proposed an inclusive architecture of 'both and'. He took up the theme again in *Learning from Las Vegas*, published in 1972 and written with his wife, Denise Scott Brown and his partner Steven Izenour. The book attacked the elitism of the Modernist tradition and urged architects to come to terms with the architectural manifestations of popular culture.

Venturi had already begun to put his ideas into practice in buildings like the **Vanna Venturi House, Philadelphia** (1962) (p. 1526A–D), built for his mother, and the **Guild House old people's home, Philadelphia** (1965). The latter is a symmetrical, six-storey building and basically Classical in feel. Far from being grand or monumental, however, it strives to be ordinary, domestic and approachable and is only saved from complete banality by the subtle use of understatement and irony. Its plain brick walls and standard manufacturer's windows are ornamented by glazed tiles on the ground floor, standing for a rusticated base, a thin string course at high level, representing the entablature, and a segmental arch which emphasises the centre like a pediment. The composition is crowned by an outsize, imitation television aerial to symbolise the main activity taking place within.

In his project for a **National Football Hall of Fame** (1967), Venturi simultaneously demonstrated

A. Vanna Venturi House, Philadelphia (1962). See p. 1525

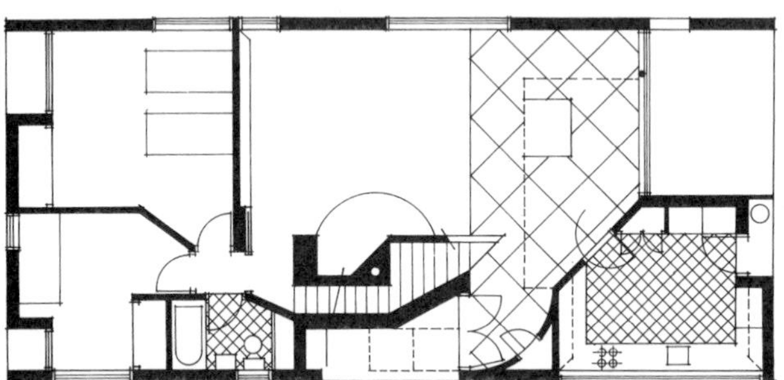

B. Vanna Venturi House: plan of ground floor

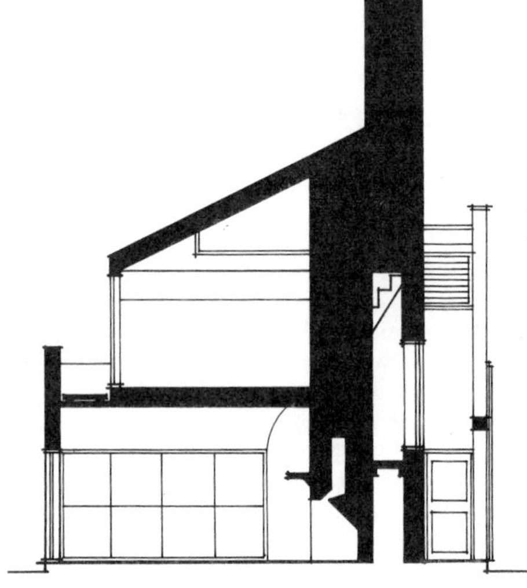

C. Vanna Venturi House: section

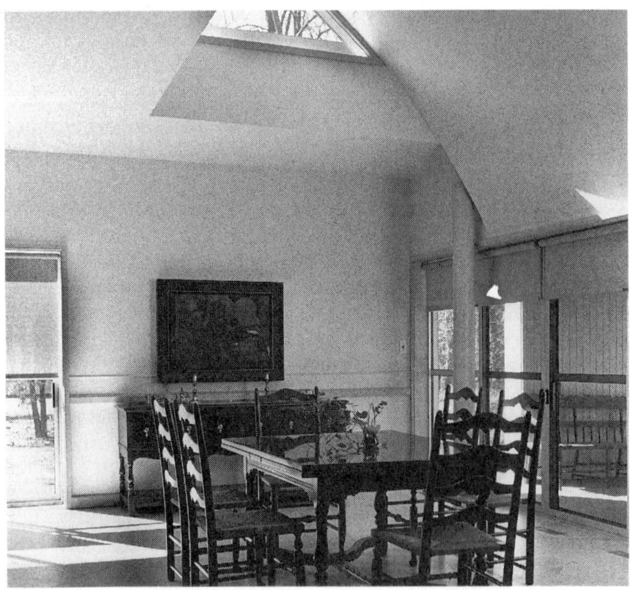

D. Vanna Venturi House: interior

E. Piazza Italia, New Orleans (1975). See p. 1527

his acceptance of popular culture and his rejection of modernist slogans like 'form follows function'. The proposed building is what Venturi calls a 'decorated shed'. A large, two-dimensional advertising billboard takes the place of a conventional facade, dwarfing the barrel-vaulted exhibition building behind. The **Fire Station, Columbus, Indiana** (1966), also has a flat, billboard-like front facade, this time demonstrating the principle of 'both and': both symmetrical (in profile) and asymmetrical (in the pattern of window and door openings).

Charles Moore also experimented with anti-Modernist ideas in the 1960s. Like Venturi, he resisted the exclusivity of mainstream Modernism and sought an accommodation between his buildings and their settings, both physical and cultural. The **Sea Ranch Condominium**, a modest group of second homes built in 1966 on rugged coastal cliffs north of San Francisco, became one of the most influential American buildings of the decade. It is a loose assemblage of timber-clad, pitched-roofed forms which recall the American vernacular tradition of rural agricultural and small-scale industrial structures. Critics at the time called it 'mineshaft modern'.

By 1975, Moore had so far departed from the Modernist tradition that he could contemplate the revival of Classical ornament, albeit in a purely monumental structure - the **Piazza Italia, New Orleans** (p. 1526E), built for the Italian community of the city and dedicated to S. Joseph. The piazza takes the form of a circular fountain, in which is inscribed a map of Italy, anchored by a triumphal arch and a Corinthian colonnade. But this is a new kind of monumentality, designed not to impress or intimidate but to entertain and amuse. Column capitals are of stainless steel, mouldings are picked out in neon and the whole composition has the character of an opera stage set. A figurative, communicative architectural style, striving to speak the language of American popular culture, was by now well established and had begun to be known as Post-Modernism.

Michael Graves was perhaps the foremost exponent of the Post-Modernist style throughout the 1980s. He first came to prominence in the early 1970s as a member of the so-called New York Five, with Peter Eisenman, Charles Gwathmey, John Hejduk and Richard Meier. To quote Arthur Drexler's preface to the book *Five Architects* published in 1975: 'Historically they are continuing what Gropius and Breuer (and before them Richard Neutra) began with their first houses in the United States: the development through small scale residential work of a teachable vocabulary of forms, but this time without some of the doctrinaire restrictions of the German pre-occupation with "Functionalism".' Graves's **Hanselmann House** (1967), illustrated in the book, is a mannerist reinterpretation of pre-war Modernist themes, recalling especially Le Corbusier's Purist villas. But already there were signs of a change taking place in Graves's ideology. He began to talk and write enthusiastically about the figurative, associative and anthropomorphic aspects of architecture, and of the importance of myth and ritual. A preoccupation with symmetry and 'centredness' began to show itself in projects like the **Fargo Moorhead Cultural Centre Bridge** (1977) which used abstracted Classical motifs like keystones and columns to create a new monumentality reminiscent of the eighteenth-century French neo-Classicist Claude-Nicolas Ledoux.

In 1980 Graves won a competition to design new **municipal offices for the City of Portland, Oregon** (p. 1528A,B), and the building became an icon of the Post-Modernist style. Occupying the whole of a roughly square city block, the economical, box-like form of the Portland Building is decorated with giant pilasters rising through seven storeys from a stepped podium and supporting four-storey keystones picked out in red. On the sides of the building, the capitals of the pilasters are decked out in petrified ribbon garlands. In the original scheme, a monumental female figure, 'Portlandia', crowned the main entrance. Such explicit monumentality created much controversy at the time and was fiercely criticised by the Modernist old guard but Graves continued to develop his Post-Modern Classical style in a succession of public and commercial buildings, including the **Humana building, Louisville, Kentucky**, and the **Library at San Juan Capistrano, California** (both completed in 1982). In the latter building, a low-rise, courtyard complex, Graves responded to the local planning guidelines which required new buildings to follow the indigenous Spanish Mission style. But there is evidence also of the influence of European neo-rationalists like Aldo Rossi and especially of the vernacular Classicism of Leon Krier, who had taught with Graves at Princeton in the late 1970s. By the end of the 1980s, critical enthusiasm for Post-Modernism was beginning to wane. When, in 1987, Graves designed **two hotels at Walt Disney World, Florida**, one decorated with swans the other with dolphins, all talk of myth and ritual was abandoned and they were described simply as 'entertainment architecture'.

Meanwhile in New York, Philip Johnson, by now firmly established as the 'Dean' of American architecture, had decided to exert his considerable influence in the Post-Modernist cause. His new headquarters for the **AT&T Telephone Company** (completed in 1984) (p. 1528C) had been the subject of much controversy ever since its design had first been published in 1978. The reason for the controversy was not so much the form of the building itself, or its effect on the Manhattan skyline, but the fact that this obviously Classical skyscraper, topped by a broken pediment like a Chippendale highboy, had been designed by the man who made his name promoting the International Style. Until now, despite evidence to the contrary,

A. Municipal offices for the City of Portland, Oregon (1975). See p. 1527

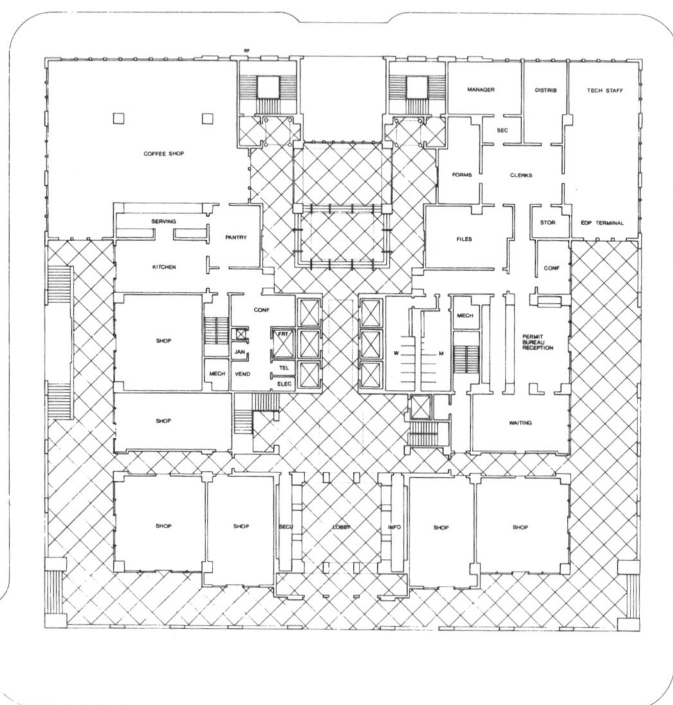

B. Municipal offices for the City of Portland: plan of first floor

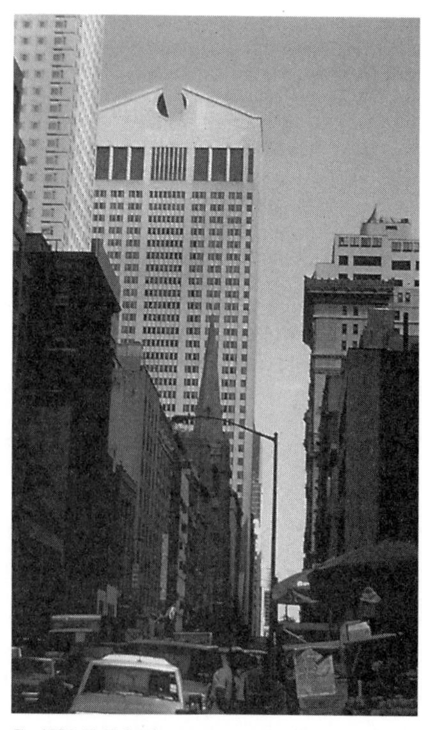

C. AT&T Telephone company Headquarters, New York (completed 1984). See p. 1527

such as the basically neo-Classical New York State theatre in the Lincoln Centre, it had been assumed that Johnson was a Modernist at heart. If even Johnson had deserted the cause, then it seemed that Modernism really was beyond hope.

There were those, however, who remained true to the Modernist cause, prominent among them Richard Meier. Meier, like Graves, had made his name in the 1960s designing single houses, like the **Smith house, Darien, Connecticut** (1965–7), which revived the formal language of 1920s Modernism. Unlike Graves, however, Meier remained unaffected by the renewed interest in Classicism and continued to develop his refined Modernist style in larger public buildings such as the **Atheneum, New Harmony, Indiana** (completed 1974), and the **Bronx Development Center, New York** (completed 1976). The **High Museum of Art, Atlanta** (completed in 1983) (p.1530A,B) is typical of many museums that Meier designed in the 1980s, though most of them were in Europe. The building is basically square on plan, but with one corner removed and replaced by a quadrant-shaped top-lit atrium. A switch-back pedestrian ramp follows the curve of the quadrant but, unlike the ramp in Frank Lloyd Wright's Guggenhein Museum to which it specifically refers, this ramp is remote from the works of art themselves which are displayed in conventional rectangular galleries. Like most of Meier's museums, the building itself is the major work of art on display – a picturesque composition of abstract forms, clad externally in white enamelled steel panels. Form, space and light are more important than function, structure or technology. The **Getty Center, near Santa Monica, California** (p. 1530C), a cliff-top museum campus nearing completion in 1995, promises to be the culmination of Meier's museum building career.

Where Meier's Modernism is essentially conservative and pragmatic, Peter Eisenman's architecture is exploratory and intellectually challenging. Once again the one-off house is the starting point, often represented by conceptual paper projects like the enigmatically named **Fin d'Ou T hou S** of 1985. In it, grids, planes and volumes undergo a series of formal transformations according the rules of an internalised architectural game. The aim of the project is to undermine the traditional frames of reference – function, structure, tradition – against which architecture is commonly measured, and to challenge the assumed unity of the subject or individual observer. But Eisenman played conceptual games even in his built houses. **House VI, Cornwell, Connecticut** (completed 1972), for example, contains a staircase that cannot be climbed. Eisenman is the foremost American exponent of the style known as Deconstructivism, derived from the philosophy of Jaques Derrida and celebrated in an exhibition (supported by Philip Johnson) at the New York Museum of Modern Art in 1988.

In the 1980s, Eisenman began to build on a large scale for public and commercial clients in Germany, Japan and America. Like the conceptual house projects, the **Wexner Center for the Visual Arts, Ohio State University, Columbus**, plays intellectual games with abstract grids, in this case the existing planning grids of the University and the City of Columbus, which happen to be set at slightly different angles. A central circulation spine marked by an open steel frame follows the city grid, slicing through the space between two existing auditoria which follow the university grid. Most of the new spaces connected by this spine, including an arts library, a gallery and a film theatre, are underground. Their roofs form 'wracked plinths' which, in Eisenman's own words, 'obscure the traditional anthropocentric horizontal plane'. The archaeological aspect of the use of 'found' grids is emphasised by a curious, almost Post-Modern feature: the recreation in fragmentary form of an old fortress-like armoury building which once stood at the entrance to the site.

The California-based architect Frank Gehry is sometimes bracketed with the Deconstructivists because of a superficial similarity between his richly inventive, informal compositions and the more overtly intellectual work of his East Coast and European contemporaries. Gehry does not, however, feel any need to justify his architecture by reference to philosophical ideas. Ironically, his preoccupations are more purely architectural and urbanistic. **Gehry's own house, Santa Monica** (1978), built on a suburban street corner, sums up many of the preoccupations he was later to develop in larger buildings: first, his acceptance of the reality of the existing urban context, in this case a completely conventional 1920s pattern-book house; second, his formal and spatial playfulness, partially concealing the house with a complicated assemblage of ramps, angled walls and tilted glass cubes; and third, his use of ordinary, cheap industrial building materials like chain link fencing, plywood and corrugated steel. Gehry's architecture is relaxed, inclusive and opportunistic. His **office building for the Chiat Day advertising agency, Los Angles** (completed 1986), places two completely contrasting wings, one curved, white and boat-like, the other rugged, copper-clad and tree-like, on either side of the main entrance. When the adventurous clients asked for an even more striking image to mark their presence, Gehry had no qualms about straddling the entrance with a monumental pair of Claes Oldenburg binoculars.

But it was the **Loyola Law School,** built in the early 1980s on a site in a run-down and dangerous area of Los Angeles, that established Gehry's reputation. Making a virtue of a limited budget, he placed the offices and classrooms in a straightforward, three-storey stuccoed block, but then animated

A. The High Museum of Art, Atlanta (completed 1983). See p. 1529

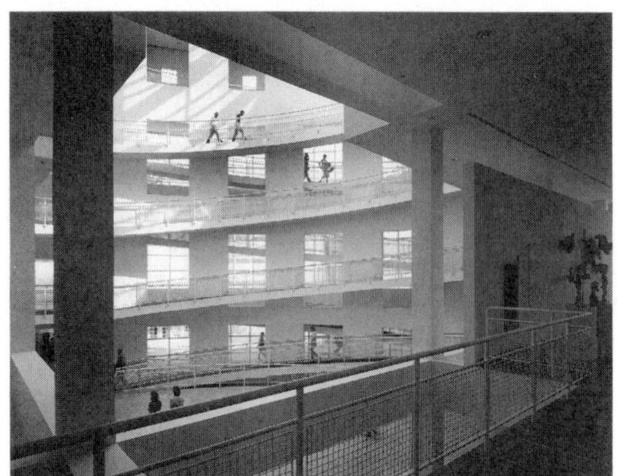

B. The High Museum of Art: atrium

C. Getty Center, near Santa Monica, California (under construction 1995). See p. 1529

D. Disney Concert Hall, Los Angeles (under construction 1995). See p. 1531

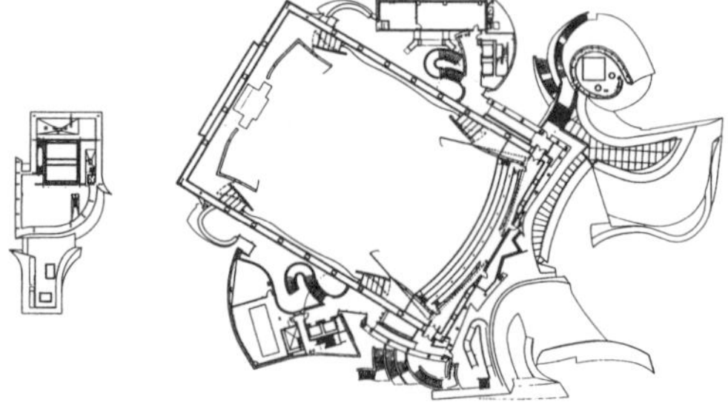

E. Disney Concert Hall: plan at balcony level

it (and saved money) by placing the main stair externally in the middle of the block. The remaining functions – a lecture theatre, a chapel and an 'instructional hall' – occupy free-standing structures in front of the main block, so that they create a miniature urban plaza (though enclosed by a security fence). Simple honorific devices – a pair of fat concrete columns, a portico of galvanised metal and a campanile in plywood and glass – confirm the monumental intentions in a typically playful and understated way.

Gehry continues to exercise his unique architectural sensibility in ever larger projects, such as the **Disney Concert Hall, Los Angeles** (under construction in 1995) (p. 1530D,E). His work takes on the figurative concerns of Post-Modernism without its regressive tendencies and the inventiveness of Modernism without its moralising elitism. It accepts the world as it is and yet remains optimistic about the future. It is unconventional, but approachable, non-intellectual but fundamentally serious. It is these qualities that make it typically American.

Chapter 52
LATIN AMERICA

Introduction

Dominating the understanding of twentieth-century Latin American architecture are images of fantastic shell structures, concrete frames and sculpted curved and concrete forms. These exotic interpretations represent the assimilation of the products of European Modernism of the late 1920s and 1930s into the architecture of more stable and economically developed countries like Brazil, Mexico and Venezuela from the mid-1930s onwards. This image, however, represents only a fragment of a history which has been generated through a complex relationship between the dual concepts of modernity and tradition, and between the desire to both emulate Western prototypes and to develop and assert national identity.

One of the explanations for Latin America's largely Eurocentric perspective is its peripheral status within the economic world system. The Latin American countries had been politically independent for around seventy years by the turn of the twentieth century. Dependence was maintained, however, through more subtle means. From 1880 onwards this took the form of the development of the export–import growth trade system, whereby Latin American countries fed the European demand for raw materials and food while providing a passive market for imported manufactured goods. An architectural example of this is the anonymously designed **De Chopo Museum, Mexico City** (p. 1533A) which was prefabricated in France in 1899, and then assembled in Mexico City in 1910.

This positioning of the new countries of Latin America within the global division of labour implied by the export–import system helped to maintain Europe's position at the centre of economic control while, at the same time rendering them susceptible to the instabilities of an unpredictable market. Resistance took the form of the first Pan-American conference in 1889 in pursuit of a dream of unity and a strong world presence which began with Bolivar at the time of liberation. This attempt to initiate a hemisphere-wide allegiance marked the New World's struggle to change the balance of world power, and a relationship between the north and the south which would subtly shift over the century had begun. The promotion of free-trade essential to the practice of the export–import system was accompanied by the adoption of liberalism, and the present century subsequently began with the renewed overlaying of one cultural system upon another, superficially similar but in fact fundamentally different in character.

1900–29

The twentieth century began with the legacy of Latin America's colonial past still dominant within its cities. The setting for the Classical buildings of the previous century for a while remained poised around the grids which emanated from the Plaza Mayor, centre of urban power form Quito to Buenos Aires. The notion of style which gained validity during the nineteenth century was a predominant factor in architectural design of this period, attached as it was to associations of taste and power inherent in such models as French Academicism and the Beaux-Arts tradition. **The Palace of Fine Arts, Mexico City** (1904–34) (p. 1533B), by Adamo Boari, Frederico Mariscal, R. Alvarez and Espinosa, is an example of the use and mix of Classical styles in this way. The relationship with colonial architecture was ambiguous, however, and while superficially derived from European styles the romantic and eclectic Neo-colonial movement, founded between 1914 and 1916 by José Mariano Carneiro da Cuna and Ricardo Severo in Brazil, was rooted in nationalist ideologies and intended as a challenge to the dominance of European culture. It inspired a new interest in the history of Latin American art and architecture initiated by the Argentinean Martin Noel. Ephemeral European styles such as Art Nouveau, which influenced the design of the **Mairinque Station, São Paulo** (1907), by V. Dubugras, were briefly admired. They remained influential in some countries, like Colombia, into the 1930s as is illustrated by the **Red Cross Building, Bogota** (1934), by Alberto Manrique Martin (1890–1983).

A. De Chopo Museum, Mexico City (1910). See p. 1532

B. Palace of Fine Arts, Mexico City (1904–34). See p. 1532

C. Argentinian Pavilion, Seville Expo (1929). See p. 1534

D. Peruvian Pavilion, Seville Expo (1929). See p. 1534

E. Argentinian Pavilion, Seville Expo: entrance

Beginning to manifest itself at the same time was a developing awareness of the formal possibilities of the multiple layers of history. Created by the superimposition of different cultural systems in Latin America over the centuries they were not solely confined within the narrow boundaries of the relatively recent influence of Europe. Other factors as disparate as the indigenous Empires of the Incas of the Andes, the Mexican Aztecs and Mayans, and the African populations of Brazil and the Caribbean also emerged as important references. This shift can be seen in the work of Manuel Amabilis (1883–1966), for example, which changed in direction from an eclectic French Classicism to a philosophic and aesthetic exploration of pre-Hispanic Mayan architecture. His **Mexican Pavilion** for the **Feria Iberoamericana de Sevilla of 1929** is an example both of the self-representation of a Latin American country in Europe and the use of indigenous motifs which were to become an expression of national difference in subsequent years. Similar tendencies can be seen in the buildings of other countries such as the **Peruvian Pavilion** (p. 1533D by Manuel Piqueras Cotoli and the **Argentinian Pavilion** (p. 1533C,E) by Martin Noel.

The Mexican Revolution of 1910 and the overthrow of Porfirio Diaz left in its wake a country eager to liberate itself from its immediate past in order to meet the demands of a new social and political state. José Villagran Garcia (1901–82) was the first to interpret the architectural ideals of the European avant-garde, specifically those of Le Corbusier and the Bauhaus. His **Hygiene Institute**, **Tabuca** (1925), in which he collaborated with students such as Juan O'Gorman (1905–82), is described as the first Mexican Functionalist building, to be followed by the **Tuberculosis Sanatorium** (1929). His approach was that of the 'integralista' school which was based upon a belief in the close relationship between art and science, truth and logic. O'Gorman, who also trained as a painter under the muralist Diego Rivero, represented the radical camp of the early rationalists. Their belief in an architecture of pure engineering with no inherent aesthetic was expressed in his utilitarian structures of the 1920s and 1930s. His work was beginning to manifest an ambiguity, however, which is illustrated in his bright-blue **house for Diego Rivero** and **house for Frida Khalo, Mexico City** (1931–2). Rationalist in form, these houses were painted a colour commonly used as a protection against evil spirits. In later years he was to react against what he perceived to be the aesthetic poverty of this early work.

A continuous influx of European people and imported values into Latin America at the beginning of the century acted as a catalyst for change in a continent where new social relations, opportunities and technological possibilities were becoming apparent. In some Latin American countries the generation and dissemination of Modernist ideas happened almost concurrently with developments in Europe. In Brazil, for example, interest in these new tendencies was initiated by the Modern Art Week in São Paulo, 1922, organised by Ricardo Severo. It took off a year later with the arrival in Brazil of the Russian Gregori Warchavchick (1896–1972). His *Manifesto of Functional Architecture*, 1925, which was heavily influenced by the early work of Le Corbusier (1887–1965), prepared the ground for the turn towards the global concepts of Rationalism and Formalism being generated in Europe and the United States. This was balanced by an awareness of the particularity of local traditions, technologies and landscapes, combined with a developing perception of the need for environmental control, especially sunlight, initiated by Alexandre Albuquerque, which was to become increasingly important. The majority of the remaining countries of Latin America were slower in general in taking up the ideals adopted by Mexico and Brazil, and the work that was to come out of these two countries was to capture the imagination of the world for the next fifty years.

1930–69

The great worldwide depression of the 1930s highlighted the dependent and vulnerable role of peripheral economies like those of Latin America. An instinct for self-preservation acted as a catalyst for change, and a system of import-substituting industrialisation, the equivalent of a minor industrial revolution in a principally agricultural economy, replaced the export–import model as the new economic structure. In initiating the growth of national manufacturing industries the new system had profound social and political effects, creating new definitions and roles for the middle and new working classes. Industrialisation also provoked urban growth. Sao Paulo's population grew from 200,000 in 1890 to 9 million in 1985, for example, while the overall populations of each country increased rapidly – Brazil from 18 million in 1900 to a forecast 178 million by the end of the century and Mexico from 13.5 million to a forecast 110 million people in the same period.

In Brazil the reaction took the form of the revolution of Getulio Vargas in 1930 which prepared the ground for a whole series of Modernist projects. This was largely due to the substantial support given by the ruling classes and the state to the avant-garde, whose imagery and ideals symbolised the notions of progress and change, the assimilation of technology and industrialised techniques and hence growing prosperity which they were keen to propagate. The subject of a competition in the early 1930s the **Ministry of Education and Health** (now the Palace of Culture), **Rio de Janeiro** (1937–42) (p. 1536A), was one of the first of these. Overriding the rejection by the jury of all the proposals made by the Modernists the minister in charge, Gustavo Capanema, offered the commission to Lúcio Costa (1902–). This was a man in whom the complexity of the relationship between Modernism and identity in the history of Latin American architecture was apparent. Combined with his championing of the Functionalism of Le Corbusier as a way forward for his country was a desire to assimilate the traditions of Brazil's Portuguese colonial architectural heritage into an architecture appropriate to the technology and society of the twentieth century. This interest was to form the foundations of the particular Brazilian synthesis of international Modernism and regional traditions which was to become so influential.

Costa's team on the Ministry of Health and Education consisted of architects previously refused in the competition, among them Jorge Machado Moreira (1904–), Affonso Eduardo Reidy (1909–64) and Oscar Niemeyer (1907–). Le Corbusier, who had visited Latin America once before on a lecture tour in 1929, was invited to Rio for three weeks in 1936 to act as consultant. The building became very influential as the first example of a Corbusier-influenced project in Brazil despite substantial changes made to the design subsequent to his involvement. Many later office buildings all over Latin America exploited the architectural effect of the brise-soleil which was devised as a solution to problems of solar control. The carefully proportioned grids of the **Retiro Odontologico, Havana** (1953), by Quintana Simonetti are derived from this device, while its potential is developed in the **Nazarenas Building, Lima** (1953), by Enrique Seoale Ros, and Luis Miguel Morea's **Esso Building, Buenos Aires** (1951). **Havana** is the site of two important buildings of this type, the **United States of America Embassy** (1952) designed by Harrison and Abramovitz and the **Office of the Comptroller** (1952–4) by Achiles Capablanca y Graupera (1907–) (p. 1537A) which combines Corbusian features of the early 1930s with the brise-soleil system.

The Ministry of Health and Education, along with the **Brazilian Pavilion, New York's World Fair** (1939), is significant because it is one of the first interjections of Oscar Niemeyer into the architectural scene, soon to become the best-known Brazilian architect outside his own country thanks to the publication in 1943 of the book *Brazil Builds* by The Museum of Modern Art, New York, and *The Works of Oscar Niemeyer* by Stamo Papadaki in 1950. The exterior surroundings of the Ministry of Education and Health were the work of the landscape architect Roberto Burle Marx (1909–93), who was to have a major influence on the designed landscapes of Brazil for the next fifty years. His exuberant projects used almost exclusively Brazilian flora – a passion developed from the work of Nina Warchavchik and Victor Brecheret, pioneers in the field of exotic landscape gardening at this time Burle Marx also worked on the gardens of the Corbusian **Santos Dumont Airport, Rio de Janeiro** (1940) (p. 1536C), the result of a competition won by Marcelo, Martin and Mauricio Roberto.

While the influence of Corbusier was extensive in Latin America, other European influences were also apparent. The **Art Palacio Cinema, Recife** (1938), by the São Paulo Modernist Rino Levi (1901–65) influenced by Erich Mendelsohn is an example of this diversity, as is the **Faculty of Engineering, University of the Republic, Montevideo** (1940), by Julio Vilamajo, which is reminiscent of Perret's churches. The work of Ludwig Mies van der Rohe and Walter Gropius were especially influential in the design of many of the tall buildings going up as a result of the accelerating growth of Latin American cities. The **Polar Building, Caracas** (1953–4), by M. Vegas Pacheco and José Miguel Galia (1926–) and the 182 m (590 ft) high **Torre Latino Americano, Mexico City** (1957), by Augusto Alvarez are concrete-framed buildings derived from the work of Mies. Another Miesian design is the **Office Building, Calle de Niza, Mexico City** (1953), by Juan Sordo Madaleno where the black and white grid of the facade is no more than a curtain wall to a concrete-framed building. This aesthetic was not appropriate to the climate of Latin America, however, where high levels of solar radiation prohibit the use of smooth glass facades, while at the same time the steel required was often too expensive. In Mexico City, however, where earthquakes are a constant threat, the use of steel made economic sense.

Europe was not the only outside influence in Latin America during the first half of the century. In Buenos Aires, for example, large office buildings of the 1930s took the shape of massive stepped forms clad in stone reminiscent of Manhattan of the early twentieth century. This can be seen, for example, in the **Safino Building** (1932) by Walter Möll and the **Kavanagh Building** (1934) by Sanchez, Lagos and De La Torre. Geographically closer to North America the countries of Central America such as Puerto Rico tended to have more links with the architecture being produced there. These were made through the channels of education, apparent in the **Caribe Hilton Hotel, San Juan** (1947–9), by Torro, Ferrer, and Torregrosso, and by emigration during the Great Depression. Henry Klumb, a German American and pupil of Frank Lloyd Wright who moved to Puerto Rico in 1943, was an example of the latter. Klumb's work included buildings for the University of Puerto Rico.

Experiments exploring the structural properties and formal capabilities of reinforced concrete generated some of the most exciting and innovative buildings of the 1940s and 1950s in Latin America. Not only was

A. Ministry of Education and Health (now the Palace of Culture, Rio de Janeiro (1937–42). See p. 1535

B. Central Library, National University of Mexico (1953). See p. 1540

C. Santos Dumont Airport, Rio de Janeiro (1940). See p. 1535

A. (*left*) Office of the Comptroller, Havana (1952–4). See p. 1535

B. (*below*) S. Francisco Chapel, Pampulha (1943). See p. 1538

C. (*bottom*) Palace of Sport, Mexico City (1968). See p. 1538

the material suitable to the climate but it was also compatible with available resources, which consisted principally of cheap mass labour. In Brazil the Communist Oscar Niemeyer's friendship with the mayor of Belo Horizonte, Juscelino Kubitscheck, helped win him commissions for a series of buildings in Pampulha including the **Casino** (1942), and the **S. Francisco Chapel** (1943) (p. 1537B). This building was an experiment by Niemeyer in pushing forward the limits of free-form concrete construction, and the curved and folded slab of the chapel is a single architectural element which forms both roof and wall. The exterior of the church is adorned with murals of 'azulejos' (traditional Portuguese painted and glazed ceramic tiles) admired by Le Corbusier and designed by Candido Portinari. Other structures exploring the possibilities of reinforced concrete parabolic shells are the **Church of La Purisma, Monterry, Mexico** (1947), by Enrique de la Mora (1907–78), **Cabaret Tropicana, Havana** (1952), by Max Borges and the **Primary School and Gymnasium, Pedregulho, Rio de Janeiro** (1948–50) by Affonso Eduardo Reidy, who was concerned with 'social architecture' on an urban scale and built several public housing complexes of which Pedregulho was one.

The Spanish engineer Félix Candela (born 1910) who emigrated to Mexico in 1939 made a substantial contribution to the development of parabolic concrete shell structures. He constructed his first laminated structures in 1944, working with his brother Antonio in their firm Cubiertas Ala. In 1952 he constructed the **Cosmic Ray Pavilion** for the **University of Mexico** (p. 1539C) extraordinary for the thickness of its roof which had to be a maximum of 15 mm in order for cosmic rays to penetrate. He developed his system of parabolic concrete structures for a variety of functions through a process of calculation, intuition and practice, constantly improving their cost-efficiency. Critical of the arbitrary forms and flamboyant scale of projects such as Brasilia, Candela's work pursued fluidity of form, efficiency and purity in structural terms which can be seen in many of his smaller buildings such as the **Medallia Milagrosa, Mexico City** (1954–5) (p. 1539D). Candela's best-known later buildings include the **Palace of Sport** built for the Mexican Olympics of 1968 (p. 1537C) which has a copper-plated geodesic roof, and underground stations such as **Candelaria Station** (1966–8).

Reinforced concrete was not the only cost-effective material being experimented with and in Uruguay the engineer Eladio Dieste (born 1917) created some extremely plastic forms, developing his original construction techniques from traditional brick technology. In 1959 he constructed the **Atlantida Church, Montevideo** (p. 1539A), in which his brick vaulting system is used both vertically and horizontally to create an impressive sculptural composition and subtly lit interior space. The **Warehouse** for **Talleres Electricos, Montevideo**, built a year later is another example of his extraordinary structural logic at work.

Despite the enthusiastic assimilation of European avant-garde ideals the current of national awareness apparent at the beginning of the century continued to be a major factor in the architecture of many Latin American countries, as can be seen in the work of Emilio Hart in Peru and Raul Lerena in Uruguay. In Argentina the Casas Blancas group combined a critical appraisal of the work of Le Corbusier with a regionalist anti-rationalism inspired by Christianity and colonial building, in their search for a national expression for modern architecture. Their radical stance caused them to be culturally ostracised for over twenty years. The **Church of our Lady Fatima, Buenos Aires** (1957–9), designed by Eduardo Ellis and Claudio Caveri, the group's main theorist, is its best-known building, with its purist form and concern with simplicity, traditional construction and climatic validity. Another team with very different methods but a similar desire to evolve an architecture with a national identity by interpreting the transformation of European culture that had taken place in Latin American was the Valparaiso Group. Started by the Chilean architect Alberto Cruz and the Argentinian poet Godofredo Lommi in Chile in 1952 its first intentions were to develop a new knowledge of Chile and its landscape through exploration facilitated by an extended journey. The group later settled to become the Cooperativa Amereida.

A similar resistance to the cultural hegemony of Europe was apparent in the ambivalent attitude towards Modernism in Mexico, the contradictions of which led André Breton, the French surrealist writer who lived in Mexico during the 1940s, to describe it as the world's most surrealist country. Continuing the Mexican interest in its own history and architectural traditions was the architect Luis Barragán (1902–88). Barragán created a position for himself that allowed him to develop a personal architecture which he described as 'emotional architecture', characterised by simple massive forms, solid walls with small openings, bold colours (derived from folklore) and traditional materials. Texture and the use of light and water were essential elements in the composition of his domestic-scale architecture.

Barragán designed and built several residential developments, unusual in their sensitive relationship with the natural landscape. The most famous is **El Pedregal** (1950), where creative use of topography and exploitation of location was also inherent in **two houses** by Francisco Artigas (born 1916) built in 1953 and 1956. El Pedregal was followed by other schemes such as **los Clubes** (1963–4) in which he explored more fully his 'emotional architecture' aesthetic. Barragán was influenced by a wide range of sources including the Moorish architecture of southern Spain. With Jesus Reyes Ferreira and the sculptor

A. (*left*) Atlantida Church, Montevideo (1959). See p. 1538

B. (*above*) Torres de Ciudad Satelite, Mexico City (1957). See p. 1540

C. Cosmic Ray Pavilion, University of Mexico (1952). See p. 1538

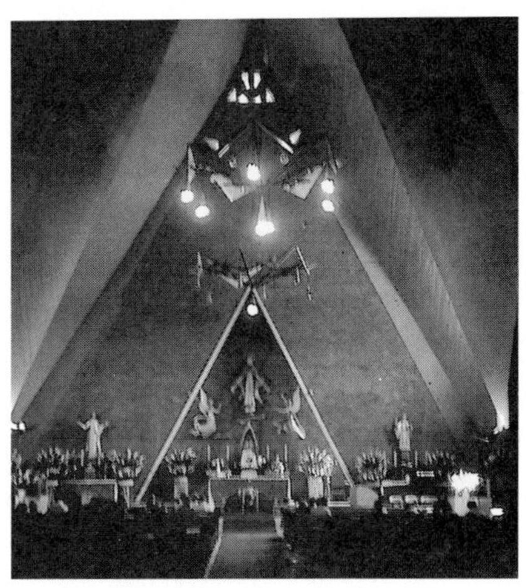

D. Medallia Milagrosa, Mexico City (1954–5). See p. 1538

Mathias Goeritz he designed the **Torres de Ciudad Satelite, Mexico City** (1957) (p. 1539B). Understood as being symbolic of the move towards a national expression these five brightly coloured and functionless towers of between 30 and 50 m (97 and 162 ft) high create a very powerful image.

In 1953 Juan O'Gorman, returning from his ten-year break from architecture with a new 'regional' style generated from his interpretation of the ornamental richness of Mexican Baroque, constructed his **Central Library, National University of Mexico, Mexico City** (1953) (p. 1536B). The building acts as the support for an enormous, brightly coloured and textured mosaic covering twelve floors of book stacks which depicts the history of ideas in Mexico. The long, low block from which it rises is cut into symbolic relieves, contrasting with the mural. The **Olympic Stadium** (1951–2) (p. 1541A) by Augusto Pérez Palacios (1909–) with Raul Salinas Moro and Jorge Bravo Jimenez which is also part of the University campus makes several references to pre-Hispanic Mexican history. Surrounded by massive embankments its construction and scale are reminiscent of pre-Colombian models, while the lava facings of the curved concrete retaining walls are conducive of Aztec imagery, complemented by the Rivero paintings on the entrance front depicting Indian themes. The tendency for history to permeate the present within Mexican architecture is continued in the work of Pedro Ramirez Vazquez (born 1919). His **National Museum of Anthropology and History, Chapultepec Park, Mexico City** (1964) (p. 1542), combines modern construction techniques and materials with historical reference. This is illustrated, for example, in its impressive covered plaza which is supported by a huge fountain-column which provides both relief from the heat while depicting images of Mexican history.

The plan for the **University City, Mexico** (1947) was designed by Mario Pani (1911–93) and Enrique del Moral who led a team which included the young architects Abraham Zabludovsky (born 1924) and Teodoro de Leon (born 1926). Influenced by the visit to Mexico by Hannes Meyer of the Bauhaus in 1939, at the encouragement of Enrique Yanez (born 1908), it marked the end of the direct influence of European Modernism in Mexico and the emergence of the new national consciousness, latent in Mexican architecture since Amabilis. The Catalan José Luis Sert was another influential European figure who carried out several major town planning exercises, among them were the **Motor City, Rio de Janeiro** (1943–5), and a **master plan for Chimbote, Peru** (1948). Sert's most important project, with P. L. Wiener, was the **master plan for Bogota** (1951–3), developed following the preliminary pilot plan with Le Corbusier and Ritter.

The City University, Caracas, Venezuela, illustrates a further alternative method of assimiliating the ideals of modernist planning into the Latin American landscape. The majority of the buildings were designed by the Ecole des Beaux-Arts-trained Venezuelan architect Carlos Raúl Villanueva (1900–75) who, like Niemeyer, was searching for a regional independence within the modern international panorama. A series of distinguished buildings set in a Venezuelan landscape, showing **Rectorate Offices and Hall of Honour** (1952) where the scale is large and the climate is demanding, the University is the exhibition ground for a remarkable range of works of modern art which, unlike its Mexican counterpart, originate from both Europe and North and South America. Linked by a system of sculptural concrete covered walkways providing communal areas of rest and shade the **Great Auditorium** (p. 1541B) and the associated **Cubierta Plaza** (1952–3) act as the focal point and the main expression of Villanueva's belief in the synthesis of the arts. The open-sided but covered space of the Cubierta Plaza is divided by solid 'floating' panels which provide the backdrops for murals and mosaics, sculptures and relief panels by contemporary artists. These include murals by the French painter Fernand Léger and Victor Vasarely, and sculptures by Jean Arp and Antoine Pevsner. The acoustic design of the auditorium was by Robert Newman in collaboration with the sculptor Alexander Calder, whose 'Cloud Shepherd' dominates the principal space. Another building on the Campus which illustrates Villanueva's fascination with the possibilities of reinforced concrete is the **Olympic Stadium** (1950–51) (p. 1543A).

Villanueva was an architect involved in trying to provide solutions to some of the urban and social problems of his country. The entry of Venezuela into the world market following the discovery of oil at the bottom of Lake Maracaibo in 1917 initiated a process of industrialisation and urbanisation which created as much poverty as wealth. The **Banco Obrero de Venezuela** (Workers' Bank of Venezuela, or the State Housing Authority), for whom Villanueva acted as architect, was set up to tackle slum clearance and the housing problems of the poorest. His redevelopment of **El Silencio, Caracas** (1941), is the best known and most widely criticised of these slum clearance programmes which also includes the **Urbanisacion 23 de Enero, Caracas** (1955). Villanueva, funded by the Banco Obrero, also tacked the problems created by the monotonous rows of prefabricated units which made up the 'company compounds' of the oil companies. He designed solutions such as the **General Rafael Urdareta Settlement** (1943) which became prototypes for subsequent low-cost neighbourhoods. The influence of Le Corbusier was apparent in his work as it was in many of the large-scale housing projects of the 1940s and 1950s in Latin America which were subsequently to become influential as successful interpretations in response to local problems, particularly in the adaption of scale.

A. Olympic Stadium, Mexico (1951–2). See p. 1540

B. Great Auditorium, City University of Caracas (1952–3). See p. 1540

A. National Museum of Anthropology and History, Mexico City (1964): fountain-column. See p. 1540

B. National Museum of Anthropology and History, Mexico City: entrance square

C. National Museum of Anthropology and History, Mexico City: umbrella

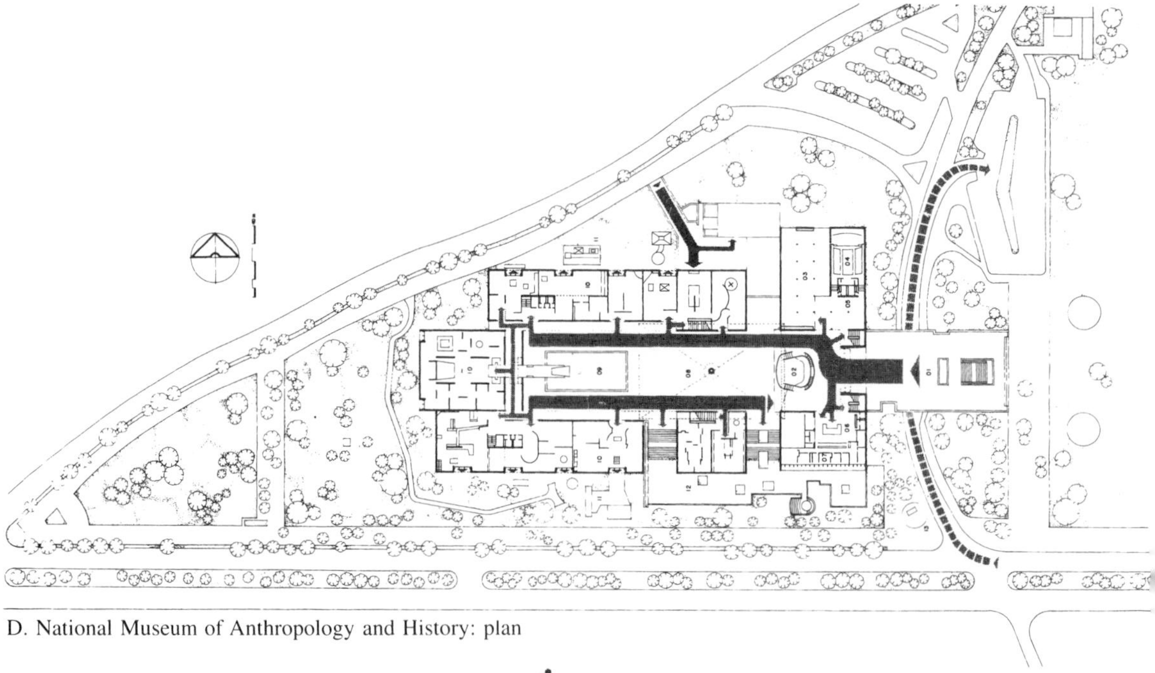

D. National Museum of Anthropology and History: plan

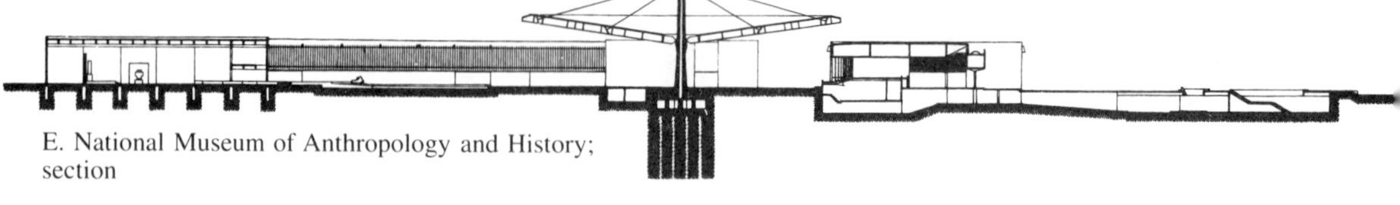

E. National Museum of Anthropology and History; section

A. Olympic Stadium, City University of Caracas (1950–51). See p. 1543

B. (*left*) National Congress Building, Brasilia (1960). See p. 1545

C. The Itamarati Palace, Brasilia (1958). See p. 1545

D. The Cathedral, Brasilia (1970). See p. 1545

A. The Berlingieri House, Punta Ballena (1947–8). See p. 1545

B. School of Architecture and Urbanism, São Paulo (1958). See p. 1545

The **Unidad de Habitacion, Cerro Grande, Caracas** (1951–4), and the forty-eight blocks of the **Cerro Piloto Housing Development, Caracas** (1954), by Guido Bermudez (born 1925) for which Villanueva acted as consultant are examples of this.

In Brazil at the end of the 1950s the government was preparing for the biggest and most expensive quest for the utopian dream attempted in Latin America during the twentieth century. **Brasilia** was the ultimate political statement of Niemeyer's friend Kubitscheck, now president of Brazil, who was to use $2 billion of foreign loans to fulfil his election slogan of 'More Food, More Power, More Transportation'. In 1957 a competition jury selected Lúcio Costa's master plan and the rapid development of Brazil's new capital city, which was to replace Rio de Janeiro, began. The plan is clear and simple, with two principal axes crossing at about the one-third point of the longer of the two. This long axis, known as the Monumental Axis, acts as the main spine of the city around which the plan is structured. The city has a spatial quality that alienates by its exaggerated scale. Its landscape, composed of artificial lakes and the sinuous curves now characteristic of Burle Marx, was designed as a backdrop for the huge sculptural forms of Niemeyer's collection of public buildings. The best known is possibly the **National Congress Building** (p. 1543B) completed in 1960, the year of the inauguration of the new city. This building closes the main vista at the tip of the cross and forms the main feature of the **Square of the Three Powers** which is flanked by the **Ministry of Justice** and the **Itamarati Palace** (1958) (p. 1543C). Another unmistakable image of Brasilia is Niemeyer's **Cathedral** (p. 1543D) completed in 1970.

In 1955 Clorindo Testa (1923–) started to construct his **Government Offices, La Pampa, Argentina** (1955–73), which made many formal references to Le Corbusier's Secretariat Building, Chandigarh, of 1951 (q.v.) reinforcing Corbusier's assertions of the internationality of his architecture. Testa was one of the first exponents of the Latin American assimilation of Le Corbusier's later work. This link was woven, however, with the work of Amacio Williams (born 1913) and the Austral Group which was influential throughout the 1940s and 1950s in Argentina, one of the most important projects being the **House at Mar del Plata** (1945). Testa's former **Bank of London, Buenos Aires** (1956–66) designed with the organisation SEPRA, is the best known of his powerful concrete constructions along with the **National Library, Buenos Aires**, designed in 1962, initiated in 1971 and one third complete in 1981. Another early example is the **Berlingieri House, Punta Balena, Uruguay** (1947–8) (p. 1544A) by Antonio Bonet (born 1913). In Brazil the main representative of Brutalism is Joao Vilanova Artigas (1915–85) known for his **School of Architecture and Urbanism, São Paulo** (1958) (p. 1544B) the powerful building incorporating a block suspended from two huge concrete beams. The **Museum of Art, São Paulo** (1957) by Lina BoBardi (born 1914) is also important. In Chile the delicate balance between the international and the local is subtly explored in the **Chapel of Las Condes, Santiago** (1965), by Father Gabriel Guarda where the Corbusian antecedent is combined with references to pre-Hispanic formal massing also explored in Emilio Duhart's **United Nations Building, Santiago** (1966), and the **Columbarium, Montevideo** (1961), by Nelson Bayardo. A Peruvian example of this tendency is the **Crushed Oats Factory, Lima**, by F. Cooper Llosa and E. Nicolini. By the end of the 1960s the immutable ideals of Modernism were losing their relevance in a rapidly changing and unstable world. The architectural discourse of Latin America subsequently found itself in the throes of a complex and self-conscious search for a new regional identity, and with the advent of the age of communication the ambivalence inherent throughout its relationship with the West from the beginning of the century began to take on a new meaning.

1970–95

The 1970s was a decade in which the impetus of import-substituting growth which had defined the major economies of Latin America stagnated. Following a series of military coups countries like Argentina (1966), Brazil (1964) and Chile (1973) became lands under the control of beaurocratic-authoritarian state systems, whose anti-political and anti-inflationary policies imposed strict cultural and economic restraints. By the 1980s democracy had been universally reinstated. Concurrent with this, however, was a long-term economic crisis in many countries, especially Argentina, Brazil and Mexico, and, of course, countries of perennial poverty like Bolivia. This was induced by a phenomenal foreign debt which had increased from $27 billion in 1970 to $231 billion in 1980 for Latin America as a whole.

Despite this the architectural field gained strength from a number of sources. The education of the poor and poorest in the age of democracy acted as an important catalyst for action among architects trained during the 1980s in such countries as Argentina, Peru, Columbia and Chile. This younger generation of designers began to generate a resistance to the traditional institutions and definitions of architecture, organising themselves under the title 'Movimiento Viviendista'. Occurring at the same time was the development of a theoretical discourse within the more established intellectual boundaries of the architectural field. Guided by such voices as Marina Waisman, Roberto Segre, Enrique Browne and Ramon Gutierrez it was principally concerned with questions of identity and regional consciousness.

Enrique Browne's identification of the new 'spirit of place' that is critical of the Modernist preoccupation with the 'spirit of the time' is part of a tendency which is not only confined to Latin America, being apparent in the work of Alvaro Siza in Portugal and Mario Botta in Switzerland (q.v.). In Mexico this current manifests itself in what has been defined as the **Regionalist Movement**. Rooted in the work of Luis Barragán and developing his idea of 'emotional architecture' it finds expression in the architecture of Ricardo Legoretta (born 1929) who was first noted for his series of **Hotel 'Camino Real'** buildings in **Mexico City** (1968), **Cancun** (1975) and **Ixtapa** (1981). Legoretta's work is important not least in its development of this architectural, aesthetic and philosophy from a domestic to a larger scale, as in his **Renault Factory, Gomez Palacio, Durango** (1984) (p. 1547A,B). Situated in the desert it is the ochre colour of earth containing at its centre a courtyard space of water-cooled air. His domestic buildings are more rooted in the vernacular. In the **Weekend House, Valle de Bravo** (1973), traditional timber construction techniques were used to form a roof plane sweeping down a hillside.

During the last ten years the concept of 'emotional architecture' has continued to develop in Mexico and is expressed in such buildings as the **Pablo Neruda Building, Guadalajara**, by Alejandro Zohn and the **Casa Habitacion, Guadalajara** (1992), by Hugo Gonzalez Jimenez. Rereadings of Mexico's history are also being developed from alternative roots, however, and a different attitude to time and place can be seen in the Film Studios, San Angel, Mexico City (1993), by Enrique Norten and Bernardo Gomez of TEN Arquitectos, and the two market buildings in Dino Suarez and San Antonio Abud, Mexico City (1992), by Sanchez Arquitectos.

Developing from the assimilation of the later work of Le Corbusier into Latin American architecture in the 1960s is another tendency apparent in Mexico during the 1970s, exemplified by the work of Abraham Zabludovsky and Teodoro Gonzalez de Leon. The **Rufino Museum, Mexico** (1975), was designed to house an extensive collection of pre-Columbian art. Formally derived from a simple geometry of interlocking angled masses it is approached by the huge flat plane of a sculpture garden. This shaping of the landscape into large-scale monumental contours is even more important in the **Mexican Embassy, Brasilia** (1973), where the earth berms suggest the elemental geometric massing of pre-Hispanic ceremonial forms. The **Cultural Centre of Velasco, Cuba** (1964–91), by Walter Betancourt also uses pre-Hispanic forms and motifs, which simultaneously acknowledge this tendency while holding memories of the early twentieth-century Expo pavilions. This search for Cuban cultural identity was shared with Betancourt's peers Antonio Quintana, Joaquin Galvan and Fernando Sallnas. In Argentina this thread can be read as beginning with Amancio Williams, continuing through the work of Clorinda Testa to culminate in buildings by Solsona, Vinoly, Santos, Manteola and Sanchez Gomez, such as the **Telivisora Color, Buenos Aires** (1978), and the **Prourban offices, Buenos Aires** (1983).

A Brazilian counterpart can be found in the work of Lina Bobardi, most notably the **Sports Complex, Pompeia Factory, São Paulo** (1977), which is a series of large concrete elements. Niemeyer's later work in Brazil, following his semi-exile in Europe, continues to develop a Modernist concern for abstract form within a monumental landscape. This is true of both his **Latin American Memorial, São Paulo** (1989), which is intended to represent the idea of Latin American cultural unity, and the **Contemporary Art Museum, Niteroi** (1991).

The **Chilean Pavilion, Seville Expo 1992** (p. 1547C) by German de Sol and José Cruz, which held at its centre a piece of Chilean iceberg, can be compared with the pavilions of the 1929 Expo in Seville in which national identity was generally expressed through imagery and historic references. But it is the use of timber which makes the 1992 pavilion especially interesting, for this choice reflects a growing interest in the use of indigenous building materials and techniques. An example of the use and reinterpretation of traditional materials are the projects of Eduardo Rojas in **Chiloe, Chile**, and Severiano Porto's **Centre for the Protection of the Environment, Maneus** (1983–8).

Joao Filgueiras Lima (born 1932) approaches the construction of architecture from a different angle in the **Isolada do Alto da Boa Vista School, Boa Vista, Brazil** (1985). The school is composed of a modular system of prefabricated components which have the advantages of being both cheap and quickly constructed. This system, although widely used in other parts of the world from the 1960s onwards for these reasons, is relatively new in Latin America, where unpredictable demand prohibited the constant and therefore cost effective fabrication of these elements. The **Government Buildings**, **Bahia** (1985), is his best known work. Prefabricated, its most striking features are the two huge steel trusses from which the main auditorium is suspended, liberating the space within. Frutas Vivas in Venezuela also exploits the aesthetic of this technique in his sophisticated **'Arbor para vivir'** houses in **Caracas** like the **House for Dr Martin** (1975–9) and the later **Casa Gisela Adjiman** (1988). In 1991 Vivas started to apply his ideas on a larger scale, specifically in the development project in the **Barrio 'Los Erasnos'**, an immense undertaking intending to rehouse over 450 families. This approach to technology is very different from that of his fellow Venezuelan Jimmy Alcock, whose experiments with

A. Renault Factory, Durango (1984); interior. See p. 1546

B. Renault Factory, Durango: exterior

C. Chilean Pavilion, Seville Expo 1992. See p. 1546

D. 'El Parque', Bogota (centre right of photograph) (1965–70). See p. 1549

A. (*left*) Uruguay Centre, La Paz, Bolivia (1988–90). See p. 1549

B. Gezzi House, Lima (1984). See p. 1549

C. Gezzi House, Lima: interior

D. Gezzi House, Lima

colonial typologies are represented by his brick building for the **Caracas Country Club** (1987–9).

The **Residence for Distinguished Guests, Cartagena de Indies** (1981) by Rogelio Salmona (born 1929) seeks to evoke a sense of national identity by making references to local history and construction traditions. Salmona has also concerned himself with the urban problems created by the rapidly expanding population. He designed several large housing schemes, the best known being the towers of **'El Parque', Bogota** (1965–70) (p. 1547D).

Control of the chaos being created in phenomenally expanding cities became an important preoccupation in the architectural profession. The solutions took various forms, ranging from self-build programmes initiated by some governments to help improve conditions in the peripheral shanty towns surrounding most major cities to the work of architects like Miguel Angel Roca (1940–) in **Argentina** and **Bolivia.** Roca's substantial contributions to the city of **Cordoba** in the west of Argentina range from a series of mass housing projects like the **Santo Domingo Complex** (1971–5) to strong architectural statements in such spaces as the **Plaza de Armas** (1988) in which he expresses his belief that the insertion of fragments into a city is more valid than the total plans of modernist projects like Brasilia. In **La Paz, Bolivia**, Roca worked with several squatter settlements constructing infrastructural elements such as the **Uruguay Centre** (1988–90) (p. 1548A) and **La Florida Park** (1989).

Juvenal Baracco (born 1940) refers to his home capital of **Lima** as 'Courtesan City'. This description emphasises the parallel between buying up old ideas at cheap rates, such as television soap operas, or of reproducing them cheaply and belatedly (both of which are common tendencies in Third World countries) with the acquisition of dated and alien architectural styles and using them out of context. As a challenge to this inappropriate importation of ideas which dilute national cultural identity it continues the resistance shown to this type of superimposition found throughout the history of Latin America. Baracco has designed several houses which attempt to reflect and reinforce rather than ignore or destroy the fragile traditional housing typology and nomadic living patterns. For example, the **Gezzi House, Lima** (1984) (p. 1548B–D), experiments with materials and fluidity of space both as an enclosed element and as a functional entity influenced by ideas from pre-Columbian desert dwellings. A similar interest in a nomadic past had generated the attempts by the Valparaiso Group to define territories and delimit boundaries by a series of mapping. These were developed in the works of the Cooperativa Amereida, which constructed its **'Ciudad Abierta', Valparaiso**, during the course of the 1980s. Experimenting with materials and construction techniques in its buildings and utopian ideals in its programmes the group brought to praxis the poetic precedent set by the Valparaiso Group in two works, the **'Travesia' a Santiago** (1988) and the **'Travesia' a la Pampa** (1990).

Chapter 53
CHINA

Architectural Character

1900 to 1950

Steel-framed structures were used in Shanghai from 1916 onwards, originally for eight- to ten-storey buildings, but by the 1930s for up to twenty-four storeys. Reinforced concrete frames were introduced in the 1920s in buildings up to ten storeys in height. Urban developments of the period including banks, commercial premises, clubs, post offices and customs houses were mainly in the Classical Revival style, but higher buildings soon reflected the influence of the Chicago school – massing was simple and decoration was Art Deco in character. By the 1940s the International Style had appeared in Shanghai, and some other cities.

The first buildings referred to as 'Chinese Classical' were the work of foreign architects. They were normally load-bearing masonry buildings, Classical in feeling but with large Chinese concave roofs, often covered with coloured glazed tiles. Missionary schools, hospitals, and libraries were usually designed in this way in such cities as Beijing, Shanghai, Nanjing, Guangzhon and some provincial capitals.

The first conventionally qualified Chinese architects returned to China in the 1920s after being educated in Europe and America. Some of them had started their professional careers abroad and were soon playing an important role in the development of architecture in China. At first they were more at ease with the Western Classical Revival but, under the 'National Rejuvenation' movement initiated by the Nanjing National Government at that time, some of them began the revival of Chinese traditional monumentality, and designed a number of major buildings, such as government offices, auditoria, museums and libraries, in this manner. Others adopted the flat roofs of the International Style while decorating their buildings with Chinese details and motifs. The office buildings commissioned by the Manchu regime in the 1930s in Changchun were by Japanese architects and usually combined Western eclecticism with the Japanese style of the period.

In the 1930s and 1940s houses became more comfortable and their forms more Westernised. Terrace houses with small gardens and multi-storeyed apartment houses appeared, and high-quality private houses with gardens in various styles were built for officials and men of wealth in cities such as Shanghai, Nanjing and Tianjin. But from this time, in spite of the influence of some of the old houses, traditional Chinese architecture as a whole tended to decline.

In this period, a number of architectural practices operated by foreign and native architects were established in the large cities. Among the foreign firms were Palmer and Turner (established in 1912 by a British architect, G. L. Wilson), Hazzard and Phillips (managed by American architect Elliott Hazzard), Leonard, Veysseye, and Kruze, a French architectural practice, and those founded in the nineteenth century, such as R. B. Moorhead (which was reorganised later and called Spense, Robinson and Partners), and Atkinson and Dallas. There were also influential consultants, such as American architect Henry K. Murphy (1877–1954), architectural consultant to the National Government, and L. E. Hudec (1893–1958), a Hungarian architect and a significant figure in the International Style. The most representative Chinese architectural firms who were active in Nanjing and Shanghai were Kwan, Chu and Yang, and Allied Architects. The most influential individuals were Zhuang Jun (T. Chuang, 1888–1990), Lü Yan-zhi (1894–1929), Dong Da-you (Dayu Doon, 1899–1973), Yang Ting-bao (T. P. Yang, 1901–82, a member of the practice Kwan, Chu and Yang), Zhao Shen (Shen Chao, 1898–1978), Tong Jun (Chuin Tung, 1900–83), and Chen Zhi (B. Chih Chen, 1902–). All were members of the Allied Architects practice.

In 1929, the Society for Research in Chinese Architecture was established in Beiping (Peiping), as Beijing was called from 1928 to 1949. Under the direction of architects and architectural historians Liang Si-cheng (Liang Su-Che'ng, 1901–72) and Liu Dun Zhen (1897–1968), the Society carried out a series of investigations and studies on ancient Chinese architecture which were of great value to the development of the subject. The Society also played an active role in exploring and disseminating traditional Chinese architectural precedents in the hope of enhancing and promoting the quality of architectural design in China. At this time there were two architectural magazines, *The Chinese Architect* and *The Builder*, both first published in 1932 in Shanghai, continuing until the outbreak of the war of resistance against Japan. Also in the 1920s, a formal architectural education system came into being in China. At the end of the 1940s, there were ten and more university departments of architecture, the most prominent being those of the Central University in Nanjing, the Tsinghua University in Beiping and S. John's University in Shanghai.

1950 to the Present

In the 1950s, the development of architecture in mainland China developed in the context of urgent post-war reconstruction. At that time, the main building materials were masonry and concrete or reinforced concrete. Owing to the lack of steel, brick and timber, and even rammed earth, were used as structure materials. To save steel and cement, prestressed reinforced concrete and shell structures were also used. Although construction was still largely handcrafted, the prefabrication and field-assembling of standardised elements were experimented with and partially adopted. As part of the post-war recovery process many new factory buildings were erected. In the new industrial bases and large cities also, a vast number of workers' homes were built in response to solve the sudden need for housing. At the same time, in many large cities, especially in the capital Beijing, various types of public buildings were also built.

At the beginning of the 1950s, most of the new public buildings reflected the influence of the so-called International Style of the Modern Architecture, which had been accepted in the main cities since the 1940s, before the revolution. From 1953, in response to an ardent patriotism aroused by the founding of a new China and the influence of the Soviet revivalism, a so-called 'National Style' emerged. This style found abundant expression because of the many large-scale construction programmes then underway. The main character of the National Style is a large curved roof inspired by old Chinese palaces. Beijing was the centre of the style and the style prevailed, for Modern Architecture was severely criticised and rejected as an expression of bourgeois culture. From 1955, the 'National Style' was subject to nationwide criticism because of its expense. From then on a large number of public buildings were simply constructed of brick and reinforced concrete and decorated with Chinese details. The major public structures built to celebrate the tenth anniversary of new China in 1959 are of this kind. During the 1960s, much attention was paid to the problem of economy and technology. Suspension cable structures and space-frame structures were used for large-span buildings, but the ordinary public buildings and mass housing remained economical in construction and simple in form with little decoration. It is not until the 1970s that the southern part of China, especially Guangzhou, began to break away from this monotony of expression. Attempts were made to create modest buildings within simplified Chinese landscape design, to enrich new buildings with Chinese traditional character and to relate buildings in specific regional traditions.

Since the end of the 1970s, China's 'open-door policy' has stimulated architectural development to an unprecedented degree. Constructions in cities and towns have boomed and buildings of high quality have emerged. Taking housing as an example, there is an average of 127 million m^2 built each year since 1980, and the floor areas of new houses built in 1980–90 made up 72 per cent of the total areas of that built since the establishment of the People's Republic.

Architects benefit from the easier political atmosphere of the new era. Free from the ideological yoke, they are able to pursue the courses they desire and to indulge in open academic debate. As a result of the 'open-door policy', Chinese architects can now renew friendships and come into contact with their colleagues all over the world. Books and theoretical monographs on famous architects are translated into Chinese, and international academic exchanges take place in conferences both abroad and in China. All these developments have broadened the horizons of Chinese architects and have played an active role in urging them to evolve a contemporary Chinese architecture. The consequence has been a large number of public buildings with rational layout, good function and organisation and utilising progressive technology. However, the forms and styles of these buildings are diverse. Some are neo-Chinese Classicism, some are vernacular or regional in character, while others are neo-Modern or reflect the influence of Post-Modernism. In housing, the International Style still prevails, but enriched in composition and form.

Since the 1980s, young architects have played an important role in the modernisation of Chinese architecture. They have remained in their own country but have kept in touch with international architectural developments and have obtained new information mostly from architectural publications. Architects from Taiwan and Hong Kong have begun to take part in construction projects in mainland China, and have introduced a certain amount of Western expertise. Exchanges of scholars and specialists between the mainland and Hong Kong constantly take place, and architects on both sides of the Taiwan Straits have held an annual conference since 1989 with the aim of encouraging the evolution of a new Chinese architecture. Foreign architects and architectural firms are also now regularly invited to practise in China. Their work has introduced new means of architectural expression and prompted the modernisation of Chinese architecture. Architectural education has also developed greatly in recent years. In order to enhance the quality of architectural design and to enable architects to meet the new demands put upon them by the changing world, Architects Registration will be carried out in China and the first experimental Registration Examination was undertaken in 1994.

Examples

1900 to 1950

The **Hongkong and Shanghai Banking Corporation Building, Shanghai** (1921–3) (p. 1553A), by Palmer and Turner, and used as government offices from the 1950s to the mid-1990s, is a five-storey building of reinforced concrete construction, and approximately square in plan. Symmetrical on the ground floor, it has a circular lobby which leads to the main hall clad in Italian marble. The facade is Classical Revival in character, built in solid granite, rusticated to first-floor level. Above the triple-arched main entrance a Corinthian colonnade rises through three storeys, above which is a steel-framed dome carried on a two-level drum, the treatment of which is reminiscent of the Pantheon.

Other bank buildings such as the **Mercantile Bank of India, Shanghai** (1916), originally called the Union Building, the first steel-framed structure in Shanghai, **Banque de L'Indo-Chine, Shanghai** (1911), and the **Yokohama Specie Bank, Shanghai** (1924), were also designed by Palmer and Turner and are in the Classical Revival style. All of them were later used for purposes other than banking.

The **Continental Bank, Beijing** (1924) (p. 1553B), was designed by Bei Shou-tong (1875–1945) and Guan Song-sheng (S. S. Kwan, 1892–1961), two of the earliest of China's qualified architects. The former studied architecture in Germany; the latter, who was the leading member of the Kwan, Chu and Yang practice, studied in America. Now used as the central office of the Bank of China, it is one of the earliest examples of Western Classical architecture designed by Chinese architects. Other bank buildings designed by Chinese architects are the **Shanghai Chinese Bankers Association Building, Shanghai** (1924), by Guo Yang-mo (Y. M. Ko, 1895–1975), the **Yien Yieh Commercial Bank, Tianjin** (1925), by Shen Li-yuan, (1890–1951), who studied in Italy, and the **Bank of Communications, Qingdao** (1932), by Zhuang Jun. All are members of the first generation of qualified architects in China.

The last of the **Jardine Matheson Company buildings, Shanghai** (1922) (p. 1554A), designed by Stewardson and Spence, was afterwards used as the seven-storey offices for the Shanghai Foreign Trade Corporation. It is in the Classical Revival style, is symmetrical and its two lowest storeys are in heavily rusticated granite. The central part of the facade has a colonnade of granite composite columns, rising from second- to fourth-floor level.

Shanghai Customs House (1925–7) (p. 1553C), by Palmer and Turner, is steel-framed and of eight storeys. A tower with a four-faced clock was placed centrally at the front of the building. The heavily corbelled eaves resemble an entablature, and Greek Doric columns framing the entrance give the building a strong Classical base.

Shanghai Post Office Building, Shanghai (1924), by Stewardson and Spence, is a reinforced concrete structure of five storeys. A colonnade of bluish-grey polished granite Corinthian columns makes the main facade monumentally Classical. A grand marble staircase leads to a marble-clad business hall on the first floor. The office building of the **North China Daily News, Shanghai** (1924) (p. 1554B), was designed by Lester, Johnson and Morriss, a British practice established by Henry Lester (1840–1926) in 1913. It has nine storeys – the central entrance marked by imposing Roman Doric columns with a marble entablature – surmounted by two towers.

The **Shanghai Club, Shanghai** (1909–11) (p. 1554C), by Tarrant and Morriss, built on the site of an earlier club (1864), is now a hotel. It has five storeys with an attic floor. Six Ionic columns rise through two storeys beginning at second-floor level. Pedimented windows and two pavilions convey a sense of movement. The building for **Club Concordia, Shanghai** (1905–7, demolished 1936), by Becker and Baedecker, German architects, had three storeys with an attic floor. Towers of different shape and height, steep roofs and rich decoration recall the early German Renaissance.

Tsinghua College, Beijing (1911), (p. 1554D), part of today's Tsinghua University, is in a simplified Renaissance style, with a mansard roof over the entrance. The auditorium, built in 1920 (p. 1554E) by Murphy and Dana of New York, has a Greek-cross plan and is covered by a dome on an octagonal drum. Here the Classical character of the campus generally is conveyed by four Ionic columns rising through two storeys at the entrance.

There are many buildings of the 1920s and 1930s designed by foreign architects in Chinese traditional forms. They include the **University of Nanking, Nanjing** (1917–29), now Nanjing University, designed by Perkins Fellows and Hamilton Architects (PFHA) of Chicago, the **Yenching University, Beijing** (1917–29), now Beijing University, and **Ginling College for Girls, Nanjing** (1921–3), both designed by Henry K. Murphy. Although basically in the

A. Hongkong and Shanghai Banking Corporation Building, Shanghai (1921–3). See p. 1552

B. Continental Bank, Beijing (1924). See p. 1552

C. Shanghai Customs House (1925–7). See p. 1552

A. Jardine Matheson Company building, Shanghai (1922). See p. 1552

B. Office building of the North China Daily News, Shanghai (1924). See p. 1552

C. Shanghai Club, Shanghai (1909–11). See p. 1552

D. Tsinghua College, Beijing (1911). See p. 1552

E. Auditorium of Tsinghua College, Beijing (1920). See p. 1552

Chinese style, they are constructed by Western techniques. Other stylistically comparable buildings are the **Wuhan University, Wuhan** (1929–35), by F. H. Kales (1899–1979), an American architect, the **Peking Union Medical College and Hospital, Beijing** (1919–25), the first phase of buildings (1919–21) by Shattuck and Hassey of Chicago, the second (1925), by another American, C. W. Anner, and the **National Library of Peiping, Beiping** (1929–31) (p. 1556C), by the Danish architect, V. Leth-Moller, now the Branch of the National Library of China in Beijing.

The earliest building group in Chinese traditional form designed by a Chinese architect is **Sun Yet-sen's Mausoleum, Nanjing** (1926–31) (p. 1556A), by Lü Yan-zhi who had worked with Henry K. Murphy on the design of Ginling College for Girls. It is situated at the foot of the Purple Mountain and covers an area of over 8 ha (20 acres). A stone pailou is used for its entrance, from which a path leads towards the mausoleum gate and to the tablet pavilion. At the top of a grand staircase of 290 steps, divided into eight flights, there is the platform on which the Memorial Ceremonial Hall with the coffin chamber is located. The Hall is in white marble and is covered with a roof of blue glazed tiles in traditional Chinese style. **Sun Yet-sen's Memorial Hall at Guangzhou** (1928–31) is also by Lü Yan-zhi, but after his death in 1929 it was completed by Li Jin-pei (Poy G. Lee, born 1900). The hall is octagonal in plan with three extended porches and has a capacity of 4700. The three porches and the stage are in the palatial Chinese style with pillars of purple stone and roofs of blue glazed tiles. The central hall is covered with an octagonal roof in similar style.

Other buildings designed by Chinese architects are the **Office Building of Municipality of Greater Shanghai, Shanghai** (1931–3), designed by Dong Da-you (1899–1973), and now used as an assembly hall for the Shanghai Physical Culture Institute. It is a four-storey building in the traditional Chinese style of the Qing dynasty (1644–1911). The **Central Museum, Nanjing** (1937) (p. 1556B), designed by Xu Jing-zhi, (G. D. Su) and Li Hui-bo (Wei P. Lei), consultant architect Liang Si-cheng, is now the Museum of Jiangsu Province. The main gallery (flanked by two wings, forming an H-shaped plan) follows the design of a Buddhist hall of the Liao dynasty (904–1125). The **Shanghai Library** and the **Shanghai Museum** (1934–5), both designed by Dong Da-you, have plans of symmetrical layout in three storeys, and central features consisting of pavilions of traditional Chinese shape.

The office building of the **Ministry of Foreign Affairs** in the National Government, **Nanjing** (1934), designed by Allied Architects, is an early attempt to develop new Chinese architecture without curved roofs. Its facade has three horizontal divisions as it might have in Western Classical composition. The ground floor is treated as a pedestal with decorated mouldings resembling xu-mi-zhuo (a kind of decorated platform in traditional Chinese architecture), and the top floor as an entablature with dougong. The porch is decorated with Chinese details.

There were many other buildings in which architects tried to develop a new national style. These include: the **National Hall, Nanjing** (1935) (p. 1557A), by Xi Fu-quan (F. G. Ede, 1903–83) and Li Zhong-kan, where the first National Congress of the National Government was held in 1946, the **Jiangwan Stadiums, Shanghai** (1931–5), by Dong Da-you, the **Jen Li Company, Beiping** (1932), designed by Liang Si-cheng, a shop with its front and interior decorated with the details in the style of Tang (618–907), Song (960–1279), and Qing (1644–1911), dynasties, the **Bank of Communications, Beiping** (1931), by Yang Ting-bao, and other buildings in the Chinese tradition, for instance the **Central Athletic Stadiums** (1931–3) and the **Central Hospital** (1932), both at **Nanjing**, designed by Kwan, Chu and Yang.

Theatres were built in Shanghai in the 1930s and early 1940s in the then popular International Style. The facade of the **Grand Theatre** (1933) (p. 1557B), by L. E. Hudec, was faced in vertical and horizontal slabs, lining up with large windows, and a square translucent glass tower stood at the centre of an asymmetrical composition. The **Majestic Theatre** (1941), by Fan Wen-zhao, (Robert Fan, 1893–1979), with its Art Deco decoration, the **Metropol Theatre** (1933), by Allied Architects, and the **Paramount Ballroom** (now a cinema) (1931–3), by Yang Xi-qiu (S. J. Young, 1899–1978) were all in the International Style.

The **Voh Kee Building, Nanjing** (1946–8), by Li Hui-bo and Wang Tan, the **Out-patient Department of the Hospital** attached to **Peking University, Beiping** (1946), by Zhang Bo, and **Talien Railway Station, Dalian** (1937), by Japanese architects, Sotaro Oda and Yashiharu Kobayashi, were all simple in form.

There was also an active hotel-building period in Shanghai in the 1920s and 1930s, presaged perhaps by the **Palace Hotel, Shanghai** (1906) (p. 1557C), by Walter Scott, a British architect, which is one of the earliest multi-storey buildings in China, and one of the first to install lifts. The facade, designed in Renaissance Style, is faced with light yellow ceramic tiles decorated with red ceramic bands. The window openings have flat or round arches, some of them with pediments. Originally there were two turrets and a roof garden on the top floor, which were later demolished. **Sassoon House, Shanghai** (1929) (p. 1557D) by Palmer and Turner (now the Peace Hotel), housed the office of E. D. Sassoon and Company and the Cathay Hotel. The hotel contained suites which were decorated in the Chinese, English, French, Italian, Spanish and Indian styles, and the

A. Sun Yet-sen's Mausoleum, Nanjing (1926–31). See p. 1555

B. Central Museum, Nanjing (1937). See p. 1555

C. National Library of Peiping, Beiping (1929–31). See p. 1555

A. National Hall, Nanjing (1935). See p. 1555

B. The Grand Theatre, Shanghai (1933). See p. 1555

C. The Palace Hotel, Shanghai (1906). See p. 1555

D. Sassoon House, Shanghai (1929). See p. 1555

A. The Cathay Mansions, Shanghai (1929). See p. 1560

B. Central Office of the Bank of China, Shanghai (1936). See p. 1560

C. Broadway Mansions, Shanghai (1930–4). See p. 1560

D. Sassoon Villa, Shanghai (1932). See p. 1560

A. Muller House, Shanghai (1936). See p. 1560

B. Zhou House, Shanghai (1930). See p. 1560

manager's living quarters on the top floor in Tudor style. The exterior is clad in granite with Art Deco motifs.

The **Cathay Mansions** (now the Jinjiang Hotel), **Shanghai** (1929) (p. 1558A), by Algar and Co. a British firm, is steel-framed and thirteen storeys high, its facades in brick with granite trim. The **Park Hotel, Shanghai** (1931–4), by L. E. Hudec, is a steel-framed structure of twenty-four storeys, 86 m (282 ft) high. The facade is clad in reddish-brown facing brick in Georgian style with some Art Deco decorations, the lower part in polished black granite. The composition is reminiscent of the skyscraper style of the period. **Broadway Mansions** (1930–4) (p. 1558C), by B. Flazer, now the Shanghai Mansions, is an early example of mixed development. It is a hotel, office and apartment block of twenty-two storeys with Art Deco motifs. **Picardie Apartments, Shanghai** (1934), now called Hengshan Apartments, by Minutti and Co., a French firm, has a reinforced concrete frame. The central part is of fifteen storeys flanked by two wings of eight and nine storeys.

The **Central Office of the Bank of China, Shanghai** (1936) (p. 1558B), was designed by Palmer and Turner in collaboration with Lu Qian-shou (H. S. Luke, 1904–91). The east block is a steel-frame tower-like structure, seventeen storeys high clad in granite and with a pyramidal dougong roof and glazed tile bands in the traditional Chinese manner. The west block of four storeys is in reinforced concrete.

Other high-rise buildings, such as the house for the **Young Men's Christian Association (YMCA), Shanghai** (1931) (now the YMCA Hotel), designed by Li Jin-pei, Fan Wen-zhao and Zhao Shen and the building of the **Sun Company, Shanghai** (1936) (later Shanghai's First Department Store), by Kwan, Chu and Yang, although simple in form, are decorated with Chinese details.

The **Sassoon Villa** (1932) (p. 1558D), by Palmer and Turner, is a British half-timber house; the **Muller House** (1936) (p. 1559A) is a romantic Scandinavian design. The **Wu House** (1935–7), by L. E. Hudec, is a four-storey house in the modern idiom as is the **Zhou House** (1930) (p. 1559B), and there are houses in Western Classical Revival, American Colonial, traditional Chinese, British and Spanish styles, reflecting the influences of foreign residents and the aesthetic inclination of Chinese officials and rich people living in **Shanghai**, the most cosmopolitan of seaport cities.

1950 to the Present

In the early 1950s, Professor Liang Si-cheng (1901–72), an earnest advocate of the so-called 'National Style', postulated that the key feature of the National Style of Chinese architecture is the profile of its roofs: a form derived from traditional palace architecture. In consequence a large number of buildings, mainly in Beijing but in other cities as well, were erected in the National Style with large and curved roofs. These were mainly governmental office buildings, guest houses for receiving foreign visitors, cultural exhibition centres and buildings located close to historic sites. As typical examples, there are the **Friendship Guest-house** (1954) (p. 1561A), the **Sanitorium of Asian-African Students** (1954), both designed by Zhang Bo, the **San Li He Office Building** (1955), designed by Zhang Kai-ji and the **Di An Men Hostel** (1955), by Chen Deng-ao. All of them were built in Beijing, and the last is located at the two sides of Di An Men Street which is the axis of Beijing from the rear gateway of the Imperial City. The **Municipal Auditorium, Chongqing (Chungking)** (1951–3), by Zhang Jia-de, is another example. The central part of the facade of the auditorium is a reproduction of Tain An Men, the main gate of the Imperial City (q.v.) in Beijing and its central dome, a steel-framed one with three layers of eaves, looks like the Qi Nian Dian of the Temple of Heaven (Tiantan Shrine, q.v.) in Beijing. Other examples around 1960 were the **Cultural Palace of the Nationalities** (1958–9) (p. 1561B), also by Zhang Bo, and the **National Art Gallery** (1960–2) by Dai Nian-ci (1920–91), both in Beijing. The Cultural Palace of the Nationalities, with a fifteen-storey tower containing multi-storey exhibition halls at its centre, was the first high-rise building in the National Style.

The National Style was also evoked in a more contemporary manner characterised by cubical blocks of concrete decorated with Chinese details, such as the **Xinqiao Hotel, Beijing** (1954), by Zhang Bo. This building is a typical example of the attempt to achieve a National Style without recourse to the use of large roofs. Other examples in Beijing were the **Beijing Planetarium** (1957), by Zhang Kai-ji, the **Office Building of Ministry of Construction (MOC)** (1955) by Gong De-shun, and the **Capital Theatre** (1955) by Lin Le-yi (1916–88). Because this type of National Style was economical to construct it was favoured throughout China, for example the **People's Theatre, Xi 'an** (1954), by the Northwest China Institute of Architectural Design, the **Gymnasium at Changchun** (1954), by Ge Ru-liang (1926–89), and the **Guangzhou Gymnasium, Guangzhou** (1957), by Lin Ke-ming. Also of this type are the **Great Hall of the People** (1959) (p. 1562A) designed by Zhao Dong-ri and Zhang Bo, the **Museum of Chinese History** (1959), by Beijing Municipal Institute of Architectural Design, which form two sides of Tian An Men Square and the **Memorial Hall of Chairman Mao** (1977) (p. 1562B) forming the south side of the Square, all of which echo Western composition with colonnades decorated with Chinese details.

A. The Friendship Guesthouse, Beijing (1954). See p. 1560

B. Cultural Palace of the Nationalities, Beijing (1958–9). See p. 1560

A. The Great Hall of the People, Beijing (1959). See p. 1560

B. The Memorial Hall of Chairman Mao, Beijing (1977). See p. 1560

There were some International Style buildings erected in the 1950s, such as a group of **Exhibition Halls in the Local and Special Products of South China Exhibit, Guangzhou** (1951), by Xia Chang-shi and his colleagues, the **Peace Hotel, Beijing** (1952), by Yang Ting-bao (1901–82), the **Beijing Children's Hospital, Beijing** (1952), by Hua Lan-hong (Leon Hoa), the **Hospital of Tongji Medical University, Wuhan** (1952–5) (p. 1564A), by Feng Ji-zhong, and the **Wen Yuan Lou**, a classroom block in Tongji University, **Shanghai** (1953), by Huang Yu-lin (1927–53) and Ha Xiong-Wen (1907–81). Some of them incorporated a limited use of traditional details.

During the 1960s and 1970s communication buildings pioneered functional design and simple forms, such as the **Beijing Telegraph Building** (1958) (p. 1564B) by Lin Le-yi, the **CAAC Building, Beijing** (1960), by the Beijing Municipal Institute of Architectural Design, the **Terminal Building of Hangzhou Airport** (1971) by the Zhejiang Provincial Institute of Architectural Design, the **Terminal Building of Urumqi Airport** (1973) by the Design Office of the Building Department Xinjiang Uygur Autonomous Region and the **Lanzhou Railway Station** (1978) by the Gansu Provincial Institute of Architectural Design. At the same period, many gymnasiums and sports buildings were constructed, such as the **Beijing Workers' Gymnasium** (1961) (p. 1564C) by Xiong Ming. This has a concrete frame with a double-layered radiating suspended-cable roof 94 m (368 ft) in diameter. This type of structure was adopted in China for the first time. The **Beijing Workers' Stadium** (1959) was designed by the Beijing Municipal Institute of Architectural Design which also designed the **Capital Gymnasium, Beijing** (1968), roofed by a steel space-frame. The **Wutaishan Gymnasium, Nanjing** (1975) (p. 1564D) by the Jiangsu Provincial Institute of Architectural Design and the Southeast University, the **Shanghai Gymnasium** (1975) and **Swimming Pool** (1983), by Wang Ding-zeng and Wei Dun-shan, all have space-framed roofs over octagonal, circular or hexagonal plans.

The **Kuangquan Hotel, Guangzhou** (1964) (p. 1565A), also known as the Mineral Spring Resort, by Mo Bo-zhi, was the first complex to develop planning traditions by combining landscape with buildings to create an elegant effect of organic interpenetration of interior with exterior space. The extension of **Eastern Hotel, Guangzhou** (1973), by the Guangzhou Municipal Institute of Architectural Design, and the **Baiyuan Hotel, Guangzhou** (1976), by the Guangzhou Municipal Planning Bureau, were also designed in this way.

Since the 1980s, construction in China has rapidly increased to reflect the economic expansion spurred by political reformation and the 'open-door' policy. In consequence, hotels, commercial and financial complexes, cultural centres and sports buildings have been erected in many cities throughout the country. Initially joint venture projects were designed by foreign architects to introduce new architectural ideas, but the Chinese architectural profession has begun to make major contributions after experiencing depression for almost twenty years. The **Jianguo Hotel, Beijing** (1982), by Clement Chen and Associates from San Francisco, is the first joint Sino-American project in China and the first to incorporate modest Post-Modern idioms. The **Great Wall Hotel, Beijing** (1980–4), designed by Becket International, USA, is another Sino-American joint venture. It has twenty-two storeys, is clad in reflective glass and has glass-enclosed scenic lifts, both motifs used here in China for the first time. The **Jinling Hotel, Nanjing** (1980–3), by Palmer and Turner, Hong Kong, 111 m (356 ft) high and thirty-seven-storeys with a rotating restaurant at the top, was also a first in China. On the dilapidated site of an eighteenth-century garden of the Qing dynasty (1644–1911), I. M. Pei and Partners have designed and built the **Xiangshan Hotel, Xiangshan** (the Fragrant Hill), a suburb of Beijing (1980–2) (p. 1565B). This is Pei's first work in mainland China, and is a series of two- and four-storey buildings forming some ten large and small courtyards with Chinese landscape features. The building's walls are white and decorated with dark-grey brick mouldings in the manner of the Tang dynasty (618–907), an historic style which lingers on in the vernacular tradition of South-east China. **Longbai Hotel, Shanghai** (1982), by Zhang Yao-zeng, is situated in the western suburb of Shanghai, just at the west of the former Sassoon Villa (q.v.). It has a pound with rockeries and flower beds extending from the exterior to the interior. The exterior wall is finished with brown facing brick and the sloped parapet is finished with red bricks to harmonise with the old Villa. The **White Swan Hotel, Guangzhou** (1980–3), by She Jun-nan and Mo Bo-zhi, faces the Zhujiang River. It is thirty-four storeys high with a Chinese-style garden at its west end and an interior garden with rockeries and falling water in the atrium.

Since the mid-1980s pluralism has begun to characterise current Chinese architecture. Buildings situated in historic cities or historic sites are in traditional idiom expressed in a contemporary manner. The **Queli Hotel, Qufu, Shandong Province** (1985) (p. 1566A), by Dai Nian-ci and Fu Xiu-rong, is located in the centre of Qufu with the Confucian Temple to its right and the Confucian Mansion at its rear. It has a multiple-court layout with two-storied buildings, matching the Confucian complex. The central interest of the building complex is an atrium covered by a traditional crossed gabled-and-hipped roof which, seen from the exterior, is clearly a modern groin vault. **Tanghua Hotel, Xi'an** (1988) (p. 1566B), by Zhang Jin-qiu, close to the Tang dynasty Greater Wild Goose Pagoda (q.v.), tries to reflect the context and architectural traditions of Xi'an, once the capital of the flourishing Tang dynasty.

A. The Hospital of Tongji Medical University, Wuhan (1952–5). See p. 1563

B. The Beijing Telegraph Building (1958). See p. 1563

C. The Beijing Workers' Gymnasium, Beijing (1961). See p. 1563

D. Wutaishan Gymnasium, Nanjing (1975). See p. 1563

A. Kuangquan Hotel, Guangzhou (1964). See p. 1563

B. Xiangshan Hotel, Beijing (1980–2). See p. 1563

A. Queli Hotel, Qufu, Shangdong Province (1985). See p. 1563

B. Tanghua Hotel, Xi'an (1988). See p. 1563

C. Beijing International Hotel, Beijing (1988). See p. 1567

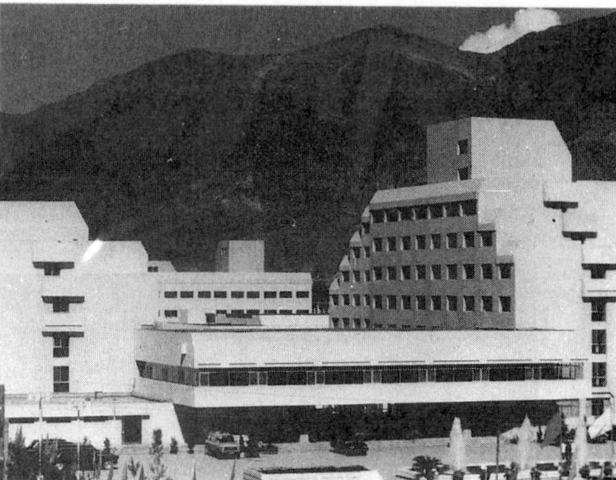

D. Lhasa Hotel, Lhasa (1985). See p. 1567

E. Huating Sheraton Hotel, Shanghai (1986). See p. 1567

Architects working in the region with minority nationalities in old cities or in mountainous regions in many instances take native national and vernacular styles. The **Xinjiang Guesthouse, Urumqi** (1985), by Gao Qing-lin, has a series of pointed arches on its facade and a pair of water towers linked with a latticed pointed arch reflecting a style of local Islamic architecture. **Juci Hotel, Kuqa of Xinjiang Uygur Autonomous Region** (1993), by Wang Xiao-dong, tried to combine the imagery of the Buddhist grottos built in Juci with present local Islamic architecture. Other examples are the **Bamboo Hotel, Jinghong, Xishuangbanna Dai Autonomous Prefecture** (1984), by Yunnan Provincial Institute of Architectural Design, and **Jiuzhaigou Hotel, Nanping, Aba Tibetan Autonomous Prefecture** (1988), by Southwest China Institute of Architectural Design. The former is built of concrete imitating the local bamboo-piled house of the Dai region and the latter is inspired by the stone barbican houses of Tibet. The **Bamboo Grove Hotel, Suzhou** (1987), a joint design by Kumagai Design Ltd of Hong Kong and Suzhou Municipal Institute of Architectural Design, is a four- and five-storey building complex with whitewashed walls and sloping roof of black tiles to be in harmony with the context of the old city. The **Wuyi Mountain Villa, Chong'an, Fujian Province** (1984), by Qi Kang and Lai Ju-kui, situated in the scenic area of the Wuyi Mountain reflects the characteristics of the locality.

In addition there is a contemporary architecture which favour allusionism and symbolism. For example, **Lhasa Hotel, Lhasa** (1985) (p. 1566D), by Jiangsu Provincial Institute of Architectural Design, is composed of white geometrical cubes trimmed with some Tibetan canopies and demonstrates the consequences of combining Modern architecture with traditional details from the nearby Potala Palace. **Epanggong Hotel, the Hyatt, Xi'an** (1990), by Liang Yin-tain combines two square towers diagonally spaced on a broad podium, the lower part of the towers slanting towards the podium alluding to the curved roof of the Chinese palaces, and the broad podium to the so-called high platform building in the Qin and Han dynasty 2000 years ago. **Beijing International Hotel, Beijing** (1988) (p. 1566C), by Lin Le-yi and **Wuzhou Hotel (the Intercontinental Hotel)** in the **Eleventh Asian Games Athletic Village in Beijing** (1990), by Song Rong, are other examples combining simplified features from varied Chinese traditional sources within modern construction. On the other hand, **Huating Sheraton Hotel, Shanghai** (1986) (p. 1566E), by the East China Institute of Architectural Design, **Jing'an Hilton Hotel, Shanghai** (1987), by AP Architects Ltd of Hong Kong and the Shanghai Municipal Institute of Architectural Design, **Jinjiang Tower, Shanghai** (1989), by Wong and Tung International Ltd of Hong Kong and the Shanghai Municipal Institute of Architectural Design, are all thoroughly modern.

Recently constructed office/apartment complexes are mainly modern in style. **Beijing International Building** (1984) by the Beijing Municipal Institute of Architectural Design, an early expression of the commercial building type in China, looks somewhat like Lever House in New York built more than thirty years ago. Other more recent examples are the **Shenzhen International Trade Centre, Shenzhen** (1985), by Hubei Provincial Institute of Architectural Design, **Shanghai Centre** (1990), by John Portman and Associates, **China World Trade Centre, Beijing** (1990), by Sobel and Roth from the USA, **Jing Guang Centre, Beijing** (1990), by Nihon Sekkei Inc. and Kumatani Ltd both from Japan, **Guangdong International Building, Guangzhou** (1992) by the Guangdong Provincial Institute of Architectural Design. Among these, the podium of Shanghai Centre has a facade alluding to Chinese traditional wood structures. The China World Trade Centre has a sunken garden surrounded by an office tower, an international guest-house and an exhibition hall, all of which aim to evoke the quality of the traditional courtyard house.

The Jing Guang Centre, with a 208 m (683 ft) high fan-shaped plan main tower and the Guangdon International Building, with a 198.4 m (651 ft) square plan main tower are currently the tallest buildings in China. Both of them have aluminium alloy curtain walls with mirror-glass and granite clad podiums.

During the 1980s, many exotically designed cultural buildings were constructed. The **Shaanxi Historical Museum, Xi'an** (1991) (p. 1568A), by Zhang Jin-qiu, with a symmetrical layout and reinforced concrete structure, gives a new expression to the bold and monumental manners of Tang dynasty palaces. The **Museum of Nanyue King's Tomb, Guangzhou** (1989), by Mo Bo-zhi, situated on the site of the original Nanyue King's tomb built in about 120 BC contains an exhibition hall and an attached grave chamber. The style of the museum is neo-Modern but combines this with certain references to the region vernacular traditions. The **Dinosaur Museum in Zigong, Sichuan Province** (1986) by the Southwest China Institute of Architecural Design, built on the site where the fossils of dinosaurs were found, preserves the excavation site and incorporates a pavilion containing a piece of huge stone to imply the dinosaurs' environment in remote times. The **Memorial Museum to the Big Massacre Victims in Nanjing** (1985), by Qi Kang, is situated on the site of one of the massacre sites carried out during the invasion of the area by the Japanese army in December 1937. The complex has an exhibition hall, a memorial park and a sunken pavilion containing the victims' remains. The main building, enclosed with greenish-white marble standing on a grey platform, is

A. Shaanxi Historical Museum, Xi'an (1991). See p. 1567

B. Chinese Painting Research Institute, Beijing (1984). See p. 1569

C. Fujian Provincial Academy of Painting, Fuzhou (1991). See p. 1569

D. The National Library of China, Beijing (1987). See p. 1569

E. Huaxia Art Centre, Shenzhen (1991). See p. 1569

a clean-cut geometrical form to express the solemnity of the place.

The **Chinese Painting Research Institute, Beijing** (1984) (p. 1568B), by Shen Ji-ren, comprises a group of two- and three-storey exhibition buildings and about fifty studios, all set within gardens. The buildings have grey brick exterior wall and grey tile pitched roofs in a style influenced by vernacular dwellings in North China. There are zigzag covered pathways to connect the buildings around a pond which includes an old Lamaist pagoda originally situated on the north-east of the site. The **Fujian Provincial Academy of Painting, Fuzhou** (1991) (p. 1568C), by Huang Han-min, is a group of three- and five-storey buildings surrounding an open court with ponds. The partly decorated parapets covered with blue tiles and the trapezium-shaped concave roofs above the entrance give the building a local flavour. The **Yan-Huang Art Gallery, Beijing** (1991), by Liu Li, includes an entrance hall, a central exhibition hall, a two-storey exhibition hall, a single-storey conference hall and seminar rooms. The exhibition halls and conference hall are covered with trundated pyramidal roofs finished with greenish-purple glazed tiles. The **International Exhibition Centre, No. 2–5 Halls, Beijing** (1985), by Chai Pei-yi, includes four square exhibition halls with three connecting halls in between as entrances. They are Modern in structure and form, but with flourishes of Post-Modern decoration. **The National Library of China, Beijing** (1987) (p. 1568D), by the MOC Institute of Architectural Design and Northwest China Institute of Architectural Design, covers a 7.42 ha (18.33 acre) site, has a floor area of 140,000 m^2 (1,507,094.5 ft^2) and contains a collection of 20 million books. It has 88 reading rooms, two symmetrical bookstack towers surrounded by reading rooms on its lower floors and three courtyards with a Chinese-style landscape. Its milky grey exterior walls and blue glazed hipped roofs give the building a strong flavour of the Han dynasty (206BC–220). The **New Building of the Library of Tsinghua University, Beijing** (1991), by Guan Zhao-ye, situated on the west of the former library buildings built in 1919, designed by Henry K. Murphy, and its extension in 1931, designed by Yang Ting-bao, is an outstanding example of the successful reconciliation between a rational functional new building and its historic neighbours.

The **Huaxia Art Centre, Shenzhen** (1991) (p. 1568E), by Gong De-shun, is a multi-purpose arts and cultural complex, including a theatre, a dance hall, a gymnasium and shops. It is a building that for the first time in China contains a central open space as a means of providing inner communications and of spatial organization. The space is sheltered by a triangular-shaped down-sloping space-frame covered by glass. The **Performance and Conference Centre of Shenzhen University, Shenzhen** (1988), by Liang Hong-wen, is a multi-purpose complex built on a hillside. The grand auditorium is a semi-open hall sheltered by a space-frame roof supported by eight large concrete pillars and enclosed by walls of different heights calculated to keep out sunlight and improve acoustics. In addition, the whole complex is carefully crafted to fit in with its context and respond to the climate of south China. **The Fangta Yuan (Square Pagoda Park), Songjiang County, Shanghai** (1987) (p. 1570B), planned and designed by Feng Ji-zhong, is a new park built around a nine-storey square pagoda built in the Song dynasty (907–1279). The two entrance gateways on the east and the north are sheltered by sloping roofs of grey tiles of traditional type but built with lightweight steel trusses. The ends of the trusses under the eaves are reminiscent of the romantic rhythm of the Chinese dougong (corbel bracket, q.v.).

A large number of sports buildings have been constructed in many Chinese cities in recent years. In Beijing, as part of the Eleventh Asian Games of 1990, more than ten sports buildings were renovated or extended and twenty new ones built. The most spectacular is the **National Olympic Centre** (1990) (p. 1570A), planned and designed by Ma Guo-xin and his colleagues in the Beijing Municipal Institute of Architectural Design. It incorporates a General Gymnasium, a Natatorium, a Track and Field Stadium and a Field Hockey Ground. The General Gymnasium is a stretched hexagonal in plan. It has two towers, 60 m (197 ft) or 70 m (230 ft) high, at its latitudinal ends. Between the towers are cables to suspend a pair of concave shell roofs. Other examples of this building type are the **Shenzhen Gymnasium, Shenzhen** (1985), by Xiong Cheng-xin and Liang Ying-tian, the **Dalian Gymnasium, Dalian** (1988), by the North-east China Institute of Architectural Design, the **Tianhe Sports Centre, Guangzhou** (1987), by the Guangdong Provincial Institute of Architectural Design and the **Gymnasium for Wrestling and Judo, Tangshan, Hebei Province** (1991), by Tianjin University.

The construction of schools, hospitals, sanitoriums, offices, department stores, shopping malls, railway stations, airports and bus terminals has rapidly expanded in recent decades and reflects the same spirit of pluralism that characterises other building types. The **Teaching Buildings in the Minhang Branch of the Jiaotong University, Shanghai** (1988), by the Shanghai Municipal Institute of Architectural Design, the **Science Building in Tongji University, Shanghai** (1994), by Wu Lu-sheng, the **Stomatological Hospital of Beijing Medical University, Beijing** (1985), by the Beijing Municipal Institute of Architectural Design are all elegant, simple functionalist buildings, and the last is more in the Modern style. The **Lake Tai Santorium for Xinjiang Petroleum Workers, Wuxi, Jiangsu Province**, by Lu Ji-wei (1985) (p. 1570C) is composed of several groups of two-storey houses for convalescents

A. National Olympic Centre, Beijing (1990). See p. 1569

B. Fangta Yuan, Shanghai (1987). See p. 1569

C. Lake Tai Sanatorium for Xinjiang Petroleum Workers, Wuxi (1985). See p. 1569

D. Ju'er Hutong New Courtyard House, Beijing (1989–92). See p. 1571

and service buildings scattered on the hillside facing Lake Tai. They are in harmony with the natural scenery, and the buildings are influenced by the vernacular house in South Yangtze. The **East China Electric Power building, Shanghai** (1987), by Luo Xin-yang, located along the East Nanjing Road, a busy street in downtown Shanghai, is an example of contemporary urban design incorporating a twenty-four-storey office tower, which turns 45° against the street, leaving space for a small plaza with a fountain. The building's red facing brick walls and vertical glass windows relate it to its urban context.

The **Terminal Building of Dunhuang Airport** (1985), by Liu Chun-han, is situated on the Gebi Desert close to the world-famous Dunhuang Caves. The passenger hall has a glass-roofed inner court, forming an atrium. Its yellowish-brown external walls with irregular small openings and niches are reminiscent of the inner court of an adobe block house and of the grottoes of Dunhuang Caves. The building's design is an attempt to combine the local Silk Road culture with the modern architecture. Combining local culture with modernity characterises many newly completed shopping buildings, such as the **Wumaci Shopping Street, Oufu, Shandong Province** (1989), by Southeast University, the **Xiuyifang Shopping Street, Xiaoshan, Zhejiang Province** (1991), by the Hangzhou Municipal Institute of Architectural Design. There are also many other shopping malls built in many cities which are in the style of the ancient timber building tradition. Although some of them are well laid out, such as **Fuzimiao Shopping Street, Nanjing** (1987), by Southeast University, this approach seems to be excessively abused.

The large amount of residential development that has taken place in the last decade has improved living conditions of city dwellers. Also the appearance of housing development has changed with the stereotyped monotonous form of former years being replaced by an architecture of greater diversity and regional character. Experimentation with the development of middle-class housing has begun, for example the **Liulitun Residential Area, Beijing** (1993), planned and designed by the Beijing Institute of Textile Industry, the **Kang-le Residential Quarter, Shanghai** (1992), by the Shanghai Municipal Institute of Architectural Design, and the **Experimental Well-to-do Housing in Shiziazhuang, Hebei Province** (1993), by the China Development Centre of Construction Technology. Particularly interesting schemes are the **Terrace Garden Housing, Beijing** (1985–7), by Lü Jun-hua which is low rise and high density, and creates an interesting layout using standardised building construction, and the **Ju'er Hutong New Courtyard House, Beijing** (1989–92) (p. 1570D), planned, designed and supervised by Professor Wu Liang-yong, Tsinghua University. This is part of a successful experimental project which combines new houses with the rehabilitation of courtyard houses in the old city. Responding to the principle of organic renewal, old buildings that are still in sound condition and with historic value are retained, those in average condition renovated, or extended as necessary, and those badly dilapidated are replaced by new courtyard houses designed for this project. This helps to preserve the neighbourhood's cultural atmosphere and establishes an organic structure for the old city's fabric. Since old houses still represent a large percentage of city dwellings, this project offers an effective and culturally sensitive model for the solution to China's housing shortage. For this achievement, Professor Wu won the ARCASIA 1992 Gold Medal Award and the World Habitat Award 1992 on World Habitat Day 1993.

Chapter 54
JAPAN AND KOREA

Introduction

Japan is a country that delights in opposites. From the bullet trains and electronic billboards of its cities to the antiquated imagery of kimonos and sumo, in Japan the old and the new, the ascetic and luxurious, the indigenous and foreign, all exist without apparent contradiction in a state of paradoxical equilibrium. For architects, though, it is the very landscape of Japan that provides the central dichotomy. The traditional vision of Japan, of a bucolic scenery of patchwork fields and villages, still informs both Western and Eastern images of the Orient, and is one that has habitually formed the basis for all Japanese aesthetics. In marked contrast to this pastoral ideal, however, are the encroaching realities of an increasingly urbanised society. Of Japan's 120 million population over 60 per cent live in dense urban areas, the vast proportion of which include the conglomerative cities of Tokyo, Osaka, Yokohama and Nagoya, forming a uniform environment for all architectural expression.

A capacity to hold opposites, therefore, is part of what makes Japan's cultural and architectural landscape unique. This very particular place has been created, in part, by the pressures of space and a need to make constriction work. But beyond the limitations of geography, it is Japan's relationship to history that has created a society so different from that of the West. Rather than developing in a linear progression from past, via present, to future, the simultaneous coexistence of opposing ideological and historical moments in Japan has produced a society where time no longer eradicates things past and where, as a result, nothing appears ever to go away. It is this multi-layering of history, and of a progress without apparent synthesis, that has provided, and continues to provide, the backdrop against which all architecture and life in Japan is played out.

1868–1945

Although the absorption of a number of historical moments can be characterised as something unique to Japan, the multifarious nature of its modern life indicates that not everything in Japan derives from things Japanese alone. Indeed this current receptivity to a plurality of cultural influences has many historical precedents. Prior to the self-enforced isolation of its Edo Period (1603–1868) Japan had always been a country quick to recognise the accomplishments of other, more developed societies, borrowing in particular the cultural and scientific advances from Korea and China during the T'ang and Sung dynasties in the ninth and thirteenth centuries. Following the reopening of its borders in 1868, Japan once again looked to the West, but this time beyond its immediate neighbours towards the distant civilities of Europe. The Meija Era (1868–1912), which initiated this renewed expansive outlook, propagated the slogan Bunmei Kaika – Civilisation and Enlightenment – which idealised a European model as modernisation increasingly became synonymous with Westernisation.

Alongside the technological imports of industrialisation, a Western architecture and art also came to be seen as equally significant elements in Japan's overall reconstruction. Desperate to break away from the polished but stifling craftsmanship of the Edo period, specialists such as the Englishman Josiah Conder (1852–1920) (see Chapter 39) helped to structure new schools of architectural instruction (notably the Industrial College at Tokyo University). Not only did this educational process open the whole of European architectural history to imitation, but it also precipitated an extraordinary stylistic eclecticism, in which the Classical, Gothic and other styles proliferated. Conder's own work in Japan encouraged such diversity, with the elaborate Baroque styling of his brick and stone **Villa at Takanawa for the Iwasaki Family, Tokyo** (1908, rebuilt 1964) (p. 1573A) and the almost Borrominiesque **Mitsui Family Club, Mita, Tokyo** (1913) (p. 1574D). However, it was the Japanese architect Tokuma Katayama whose **Akasaka Imperial Palace Hotel, Tokyo** (1909) (p. 1573B) best represented this pre-war eclecticism. Built for Japan's Crown Prince, and at the time Japan's largest building, the palace mimics various Western architectures both aesthetically and

A. Villa at Takanawa for the Iwasaki Family, Tokyo (1908: rebuilt 1964). See p. 1572

B. Akasaka Imperial Palace Hotel, Tokyo (1909). See p. 1572

A. Tokyo National Museum (1938). See p. 1576

B. Central Telegraph Office, Tokyo (1926). See p. 1576

C. Central Post Office, Tokyo (1931). See p. 1576

D. Mitsui Family Club, Tokyo (1913). See p. 1572

A. Japanese Pavilion, Paris Exposition of 1937. See p. 1576

B. Museum of Modern Art, Kamakura (1951). See p. 1577

technically; incorporating a Versailles-inspired facade, an American-made steel frame, Norwegian marble, a classical eighteenth-century-style French interior and even traditional Japanese decorative motifs.

The Kanto earthquake of 1923, in which many of Tokyo's traditional timber buildings were destroyed, re-emphasised to the Japanese the structural limitations of an Oriental architecture; a perception illustrated by the survival of Frank Lloyd Wright's **Imperial Hotel, Tokyo** (1916–22, demolished 1968), in which concrete piles cross-braced by floor slabs clearly worked to good effect. Ironically, the rich decoration of the Imperial Hotel's wood and oya stone carvings, together with the detail and character of Wright's other buildings in Japan (notably the **Jiyu Gakuen School, Tokyo**, of 1921), encouraged the Japanese to question the value of all things Western. Supporting Wright in this regard was the work of his Czech assistant Antonin Raymond (1860–1976), who after the completion of the Imperial Hotel settled in Japan to establish his own architectural practice. Significant among the buildings that Raymond produced were the **Architect's Own House, Tokyo** (1923); the **Rising Sun Petroleum Company Headquarters** (1929); **Tokyo Golf Club** (1930); and the **Reader's Digest Offices, Tokyo** (1949 with Ladislav Rado, demolished 1964) which introduced the Japanese to exposed reinforced concrete as a new material capable of combining a greater structural rigidity with the ability to express a more obviously Japanese aesthetic sensibility. Raymond was very influential in helping the Japanese to formulate their own modern architecture, particularly through his role as a teacher and by the training his office offered young architects such as Kunio Maekawa. Bruno Taut also made a significant contribution to the development of a Japanese Modernism. In his book *Houses and People of Japan* (1938) Taut drew the attention of designers to the importance of Japan's architectural heritage, celebrating in particular the **Grand Shrine of Ise** (rebuilt every twenty years), the simple but stunning **Katsura Palace, Kyoto** (1750), and the traditional tatami mat as a forerunner to modular planning.

Faced with these conflicting ideologies, by the 1920s the emerging generations of architects were divided between two distinct architectural approaches: the first ultimately embraced a modern European style, while the second, although favouring new design technologies, was derivative of a Japanese spirit. The former centred around a group of students at Tokyo Imperial University and founders of the Japanese Secession. As virtually the first formal acknowledgement of the International style in Japan, the Secessionists abandoned any notion of historical style in declaring their rejection of the academic architecture of the past. Among its first supporters were Sutemi Horiguchi, Mayumi Takizawa, Mamoru Yamada and Kikuchi Ishimoto. Influenced by the publication of the French *L'Esprit Nouveau* and German *Internationale Architektur*, as well as the increased use of exposed reinforced concrete, the group progressed from the expression of Yamada's **Central Telegraph Office, Tokyo** (1926) (p. 1574B) to the more rational lines of Ishimoto's **Asahi News Press Building, Tokyo** (1927), Tetsuro Yoshida's **Central Post Office, Tokyo** (1931) (p. 1574C), and Togo Murano's **Sogo Store, Osaka** (1932). But significantly it was in Europe, with the **Japanese Pavilion, Paris Exposition** of 1937 (p. 1575A) that key elements of the Secession found their full expression. Here, Junio Sakakura, who had worked in Le Corbusier's atelier for a number of years, used the new materials of glass, steel and concrete, with a delicacy previously unseen within the International Style.

However, despite the growing confidence of Japanese Modernism, the Imperialistic politics and increasing nationalism within Japan meant that the Japanese traditionalists had a greater, more immediate impact. Typified by Hitoshi Watanabe's **Tokyo National Museum** (1938) (p. 1574A) an 'Imperial Court Style' of brick building overlaid with heavy oriental ornamentation became the required architectural standard. Under governmental edicts demanding 'a Japanese style founded in Oriental taste', Japan's modern architectural movement collapsed, as the country became devoured by the nationalistic militarism of World War II. However, this style and Japan's expansionist policies were not without their influence on the younger generation of architects that was to flourish after the war, for example Kenzo Tange's **Daitoa Kensetsn Memorial project** (1942) and his **Japanese-Chinese Culture Centre** (1943), or Kunio Maekawa's **Japanese Cultural Centre, Bangkok** (1943).

1945–75

In the wake of its defeat in 1945 most of Japan's cities were, with the exceptions of Kyoto and Kanazawa, very badly damaged and in some cases totally destroyed by the fires and bombs of war. As millions of people found themselves without homes or shelter, the need for architectural reconstruction became as urgent as the country's political regeneration. In response to demands for an immediate urban solution, Japan's rebirth as a democratic society provided architects with the opportunity for an unguarded assimilation of a Western replanning strategy, as the traditional and indigenous were once again rejected as reactionary and obsolete.

Acting as one of a number of public examples of this new spirit of regeneration was Le Corbusier's **National Museum of Western Art, Tokyo** (1955–9) (p. 1578A). Built as a variation of his Museum of

Unlimited Growth model of 1939, the museum represented a fundamentally Western aesthetic vision, through both the art it exhibited and the architecture which enclosed it. Although designed by Le Corbusier, the building was executed by the Japanese architects Kunio Maekawa and Junio Sakakura. The latter had earlier followed his Paris Pavilion with the Le Corbusier-inspired **Museum of Modern Art, Kamakura** (1951) (p. 1575B). The grand public project also remained the definitive architectural subject for Maekawa, whose **Metropolitan Festival Hall, Tokyo** (1961) (p. 1579A) containing Oriental decorative motifs, followed standard Corbusian practice in the boldness of its board-marked concrete and sculptural masses.

Reacting against the hurried Westernisation of these immediate post-war years, a new generation of young architects began to look ever more sympathetically towards aspects of Japan's own architectural culture. Led by Kenzo Tange, and exemplified by his **Hiroshima Peace Centre** (1949–55) (p. 1578C), this new architecture attempted to integrate the language of Le Corbusier's *béton brut* with that of traditional Japanese post and beam construction. By the late 1950s, this pattern of design had crystallised into a distinct 'New Japanese Style', as exemplified by Tange's **Kagawa Prefectural Office Building, Takamatsu** (1955–8) (p.1578B) and later, with the more structurally dynamic forms of his **National Gymnasium**, for the **Tokyo Olympics** (1964) (p. 1580A). But beyond Tange's concerns for a new individual building style, the mass destruction of Japan's existing urban fabric presented an opportunity to him, and others, fully to indulge in the Corbusian theory that the architect should be concerned not simply with the design of buildings within the city but with the design of the city itself.

The first of such attempts to overcome the absence of any urban planning tradition in Japan was Tange's own **1960 Plan of Tokyo** – an innovative scheme proposing a linear extension to the city over Tokyo Bay and forming a vast new civic axis along which extended growth and change would be possible. Fuelled partly by Tange's urban studies unit URTEC, and more generally by Japan's economic expansion of the 1960s, shortage of land and consequent escalating land values, the Tokyo Plan became the generator of a succession of similarly megapolitan proposals, which shared the spirit of Le Corbusier's *Ville Radieuse* in presenting visions of continuous urban growth through an advanced technology. Prominent among such schemes were those of a newly formed group of young architects inspired by the World Design Conference in Tokyo, 1960, four designers, Kisho Kurokawa, Fumihiko Maki, Kiyonori Kikutake, Masato Otaka, and the critic Noboru Kawazoe, eager to impress the assembled architects, including Louis Kahn and Alison and Peter's Smithson, published a set of radical new proposals in a manifesto entitled *Metabolism*. In exploring alternative solutions to the city, the Metabolists held that architecture should not be static but be capable of undergoing metabolic change; an architecture of technological organisms that could live and grow by discarding its outdated parts and regenerating newer, more viable elements. Recalling Futurist statements about modern cities of moving and variable parts, the Metabolist proposals also mirrored those of their London-based contemporaries, Archigram. Analogous to the **Walking Cities** and **Plug-in-City** projects of Archigram's Ron Herron and Peter Cook in 1964, these ideas found expression in Japan in the various urban utopias of Kikutake's **Ocean City Project** (partly realised in his **Aquapolis, Okinawa**, 1975) Kurokawa's **Helix City** (1961) and Otaka's **Artificial-Housing Land Program**. Together with the **Space City Project** (1963) (p. 1581D) of Arata Isozaki, who, although outside the Metabolist Group had played a key role in the development of Tange's 1960 Tokyo Plan, these urban schemes represented a new stage in Japan's architectural evolution. Filled with the optimism of an unquestioning faith in technology, and encouraged by Japan's continuing economic boom the city remained the definitive object of architectural design and provider of an experimental context for bold and dynamic images of the architectural future.

With the oil crisis of 1973, however, Japan's economic advances came to an end, and also the hopes and dreams for a new urbanism. Technology, previously idealised with an unthinking veneration, was looked upon with renewed scepticism, as congestion polluted the modern city. In this shifting climate, ironically the Metabolists had proved too inflexible to survive. Those projects that were realised, including Tange's **Yamanashi Communications Centre** (1967) (p. 1580B), Kurokawa's **Takara Beautillion** at the **Osaka Expo** (1970) (p. 1581A) and **Nagakin Capsule Tower, Tokyo** (1972) (p. 1581B) existed solely as isolated, unchanging monuments to change. As faith in technology was rejected, so too was Metabolism.

Amid this growing disillusion, the future of the city was becoming an increasingly important issue. As Kenzo Tange and others had recognised, in Japan there was no precedent for planning of the European type. Rather than a coherent, perspectival placing of parts along the radiates of an urban core, Japanese cities have traditionally been composed of urban elements layered on top of, or alongside, one another, producing a seemingly random spatial arrangement structured not by the idea of centre but by that of depth. Those planning strategies that were designed to restrict urban growth had always failed, notably the collapse of Japan's National Development Law of 1956, as 2 million people occupied the intended green-belt and so sabotaged the whole idea of plan, control and restraint.

A. National Museum of Western Art, Tokyo (1955–9). See p. 1576

B. Kagawa Prefectural Office Building, Takamatsu (1955–8). See p. 1577

C. Hiroshima Peace Centre (1949–55). See p. 1577

A. Metropolitan Festival Hall, Tokyo (1961). See p. 1577

B. Metropolitan Festival Hall, Tokyo: detail of exterior

C. Metropolitan Festival Hall, Tokyo: wall of auditorium

A. National Gymnasium, Tokyo (1964). See p. 1577

B. Yamanashi Communications Centre (1967). See p. 1577

A. Takara Beautillon, Osaka Expo (1970). See p. 1577

B. Nagakin Capsule Tower, Tokyo (1972). See p. 1577

C. Hillside Terrace Housing, Tokyo (1969–79). See p. 1582

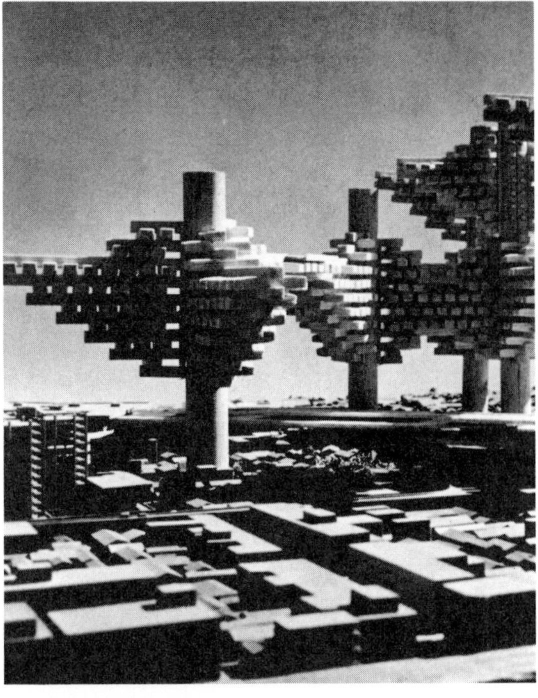

D. Space City Project (1963). See p. 1577

1975–85

Allied to Japan's resistance to rational urban planning, the pressing limitations of its territorial area during rapid commercial expansion of the 1970s had a substantial influence upon the character of Japanese architecture. With less than 30 per cent of its mountainous terrain suitable for human habitation, and an elevenfold increase in land prices between 1960 and 1980, the economics of construction meant that the grand megapolitan gestures of Tange, Kurokawa and Isozaki were no longer financially viable. As the value of one square foot of land in Tokyo in 1985 soared towards £15,000, the city was increasingly recognised not as a controllable artifice but as an irrational, often hostile environment no longer subject to an overriding design.

Among the architects of the mid-1970s, Fumihiko Maki was the first to express this more pragmatic attitude towards the city. Although a founder member of the group that had launched Metabolism, Maki did not share the exuberant utopian speculations of Kikutake and Kurokawa. Recalling the formal language of his teacher at Harvard, Josâ Luis Sert, Maki's building in **Tokyo**, with the **Hillside Terrace Housing** (1969–79) (p. 1581C) and **Kyoto**, with the **National Museum of Modern Art** (1978) display a more reciprocal relationship between urban elements and their organising system, between the part and the whole.

Fundamental to this new-found appreciation of the heterogeneities inherent in Japanese life was a shift away from technology to consumerism as the ideological base for both architecture and culture as a whole. As practically every segment of the built environment became transformed into an advertisable and marketable commodity, designers became increasingly seduced by the instantaneous power of the image. First illustrated by Minoru Takeyama's extravagantly coloured **Ni-Ban-Kan offices, Tokyo** (1970) (p. 1583B) buildings celebrated the diversities of the modern city as architecture began to enjoy the popular, playful and profitable.

In recognition of the cosmopolitan nature of Japan's cities, historical images, referring to a multitude of eclectic sources, also started to appear. Principal among designers using such motifs was Arata Isozaki. Accredited with the label, 'Post-Modern', Isozaki's work during the 1970s and 1980s, in contrast to his earlier designs, displayed a fondness for foreign architectures both past and present; reflected in the Ledoux-inspired **Gunma Prefectural Museum of Fine Arts** (1974) (p. 1583C) and **Kitakyushi Central Library** (1975). But it was at the **Tsukuba Centre, Ibaraki** (1983) (p. 1585A) that Isozaki fully indulged in the Mannerism of Post-Modernity. A star-shaped square at the centre of the building recalls Michelangelo's Campadoglio in Rome, while portals further echo the Classicism of Ledoux. Together with acknowledgements to the villas of Palladio, the temples of Kyoto, Constructivism, and the Viennese School of Hoffman and Wagner, Isozaki's Tsukuba building created an architecture that freely borrows from tradition, both Japanese and the Western.

Significantly, this approach of explicitly quoting from previous architectures became the definitive style for a number of museum-based projects, a tendency which suggests that the external styling of a museum should in some way mirror the historical range of its exhibits. Notable among those who embraced this architecture was Kisho Kurokawa, Metabolism's most ardent disciple, who in the **Saitama Prefectural Museum of Art** (1978–82) (p. 1583A) turned to a more historicist approach, subtler and less dramatic. Similar designs by other younger architects have included the historical abstractions of Hiromi Fuji's **Ushimado International Arts Festival Centre** (1985), and Osamu Ishiyama's more obviously eclectic **Chohachi Art Museum, Matsazaki** (1986).

As the opportunity for large-scale development passed into Japan's immediate architectural history, architects relinquished their roles as progenitors of social systems. With this abdication, a generational hierarchy of diminishing building scale became firmly entrenched. To the oldest generation of architects and established design corporations were reserved the largest, most prestigious public commissions, such as Tange's governmental buildings and the universities and new towns of the firm Nikken Sekkei. The second generation of Kurokawa, Isozaki and Maki were restricted to the municipal institutions of libraries, museums and theatres. Unable to launch their careers under the aegis of a national urban project, the emerging third generation were forced to find expression within the confines of small-scale design. But in being restricted to the introspections of the private and the personal, these young architects could achieve a conceptual freedom denied to those with larger, public projects.

The building type which conformed most clearly to these preconditions of scale was the private house. The modern dwelling of the 1970s and 1980s took on a new position of social significance. As progressive commercialisation continued to break down Japan's ingrained values and institutions, the house became established as a ready symbol for the enduring strength of the traditional Japanese family. Although its social function remained secure, the freedom allowed to new designers precipitated an energetic architectural questioning of what a home could look like. Analogous to the Los Angeles Case Study houses of Ellwood, Eames and Koenig in the 1940s and 1950s a succession of distinct and original urban structures each attempted to reinvent the form and character of the modern house. As with the architects of the 1920s, the ambivalence still felt by many

A. Saitama Prefectural Museum of Art (1978–82). See p. 1582

B. Ni-Ban-Kan offices, Tokyo (1970). See p. 1582

C. Gunma Prefectural Museum of Fine Arts (1974). See p. 1582

Japanese towards questions of East and West, urban and rural, polarised the course of this domestic architecture between ideologies of rejection and those of consent. Within the former category existed a group of architects who although recognising the heterogeneities implicit within urbanity, attempted to shut out the chaos and disorder of the contemporary Japanese city with an architecture of uncompromising visual purity.

The architect who, through both his building and writing, played a significant role in the evolution of such a style was Kazuo Shinohara. His early work, for example the **House at Kugayama, Tokyo** (1954), and the **House in White, Tokyo** (1966), was characterised by the theoretical abstraction of traditional Japanese construction. Believing that, as a private building, a house should not be expected to participate within the city as a whole, Shinohara's later 'existential' architecture expressed this conviction with uncommunicative exterior concrete facades. Typified by the stark walls and limited openings of the **Uehara House, Tokyo** (1976) (p. 1585B,C) Shinohara's central conviction that 'I create negative space as a protest against frenzied movement about me' was to have a profound influence upon subsequent generations of Japanese architects.

Probably the most significant architect to have emerged from within this tradition is Tadao Ando. Over the last twenty years Ando has produced a succession of houses, which offer a level of finish and detail unprecedented in concrete construction. First and most powerfully illustrated by his **Row House, Sumiyoshi, Osaka** (1976) (p. 1586B–D) Ando's architecture creates rigid boundaries between inside and outside, linked, in this instance, only by an external staircase along which one has to pass in moving between rooms. Devoid of the luxuries of heating and cooling systems, together with decor, this is an architecture of denial. Ando's concern throughout is purely one of simplification and enrichment; an apparently contradictory synthesis that allies him to a Buddhist way of building. Ando's **Koshino House, Osaka** (1979–81, studio added 1983) (p. 158A), illustrates this approach: two parallel concrete-built volumes on a sloping rural site are linked by an underground corridor. The blocks are separated by an almost urban courtyard with steps. The shorter block contains living quarters, including a double-height space, with the longer block containing bedrooms. In both buildings the entry of light is manipulated to create extraordinarily serene spaces.

Although Ando's work seems to represent an explicitly anti-urban architecture, buildings such as his **Rokko Housing Project, Hyogo** (1983) (p. 1586A), **Nakayama House, Nara** (1985), and **Kidosaki House, Tokyo** (1986), all contain, paradoxically, elements which confirm the value of urbanism in the creation of architectural images. All these houses are, like the Kashino House, structured around courtyards, as analogous to city squares, and feature diminutive bridges and street-like connecting walkways. Adopting a similar strategy, Hiroshi Hara's **Reflection House, Machida** (1974), consists of a central 'street' linking a reflecting sequence of rooms.

The introverted character of these houses is also partly a response to Japanese housing regulations which, keen to increase the amount of direct natural light, stipulate that 40 per cent of a building's site must be left open. In order to maintain a necessary level of privacy, the standard response by architects has been to leave the core of their buildings empty, creating a central courtyard. An extreme example is Toyo Ito's **U-House, Tokyo** (1976), in which a pair of curving concrete walls turn their back on the street in enclosing a vacant space for the meditative appreciation of nature. Noting this intrinsically Japanese structural approach, the Englishman David Chipperfield has adopted a similar strategy in his own work in Japan. At the **Gotoh Museum, Tokyo** (1989), and the **Design Centre, Kyoto** (1991), the space or void onto which the building looks, be it a light well or a terrace, appears to be attributed a significance and value equal to that of the solid of the building itself. Left with the undeniable visual power of some hermetic object, this is an architecture in which the house and building is totally absorbed within itself, and where self-expression, in retreat from an imposing society, journeys inward: the Zen way of building.

During the 1980s, the speculative formalism characterised in the houses of Ando, Ito and Hara was replaced by a less symbolic architecture, less conceptual, and seemingly easier to live in. With this progression came an apparent architectural maturity in which the avant-garde's defensive reaction of withdrawal was superseded by a willingness to confront the city on its own terms. Rather than concealing an alternative, idealised city within the impenetrable boundaries of the house, architects successively looked to a more reciprocal relationship with urbanity, in which the house, embracing the realities of the city, opens up to the diversity of its immediate streets and neighbourhood.

This architecture also introduced an increased sense of physical and structural freedom. Expressed principally through its materials, ferrous elements, surfaces and structures, including corrugated and perforated aluminium sheets, mesh-wire screens and slim metal frames, started to appear as the new building standard. By renewing an interest in industrial elements, both high and low tech, architects could reinterpret the rice paper screens and partitions of traditional Japanese construction with tensile and membrane structures, to achieve a new architectural ephemerality.

Responsible most directly for the development of this approach, were the architects Toyo Ito and Itsuko Hasegawa. Alongside Issei Sakamoto, Ito and Hasegawa in the early 1970s were known collectively as the

A. Tsukuba Centre Building, Ibaraki (1983). See p. 1582

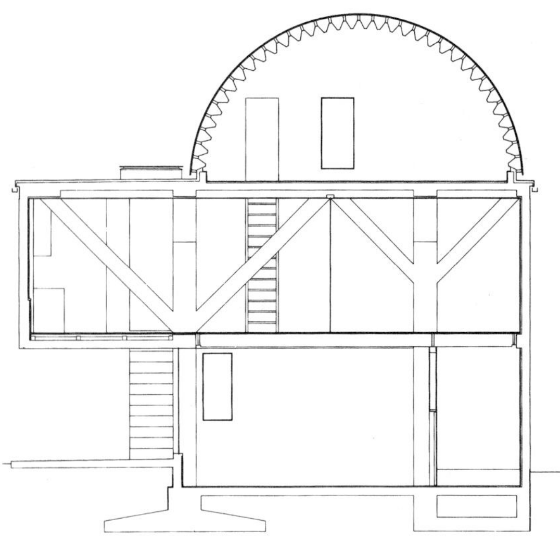

B. Uehara House, Tokyo: section

C. Uehara House, Tokyo (1976). See p. 1584

A. Rokko Housing Project, Hyogo (1983). See p. 1584

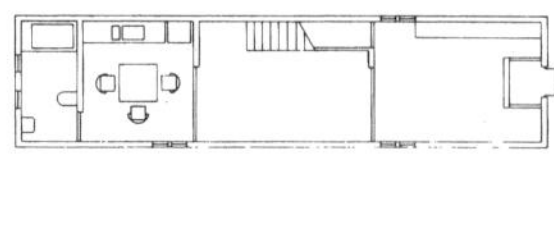

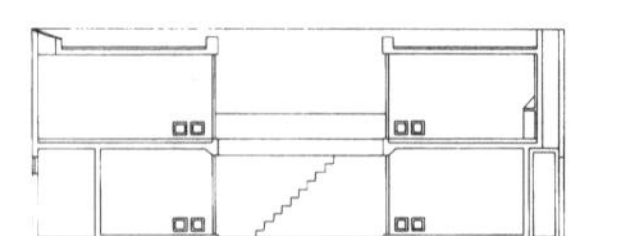

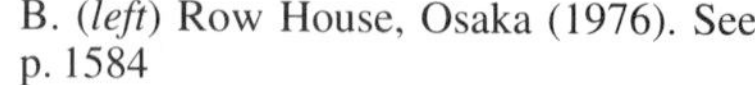

B. (*left*) Row House, Osaka (1976). See p. 1584

C. (*above*) Row House, Osaka: interior

D. (*right*) Row House, Osaka: plan, section and axonometric

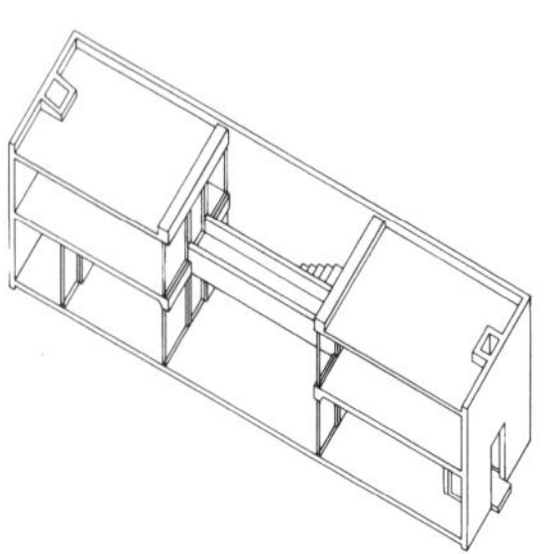

A. Tower of Winds, Yokohama (1986). See p. 1588

B. Truss Wall House, Tokyo (1993). See p. 1588

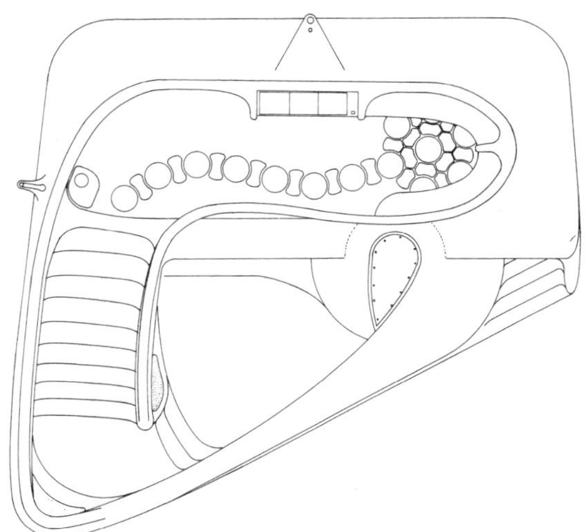

C. Truss Wall House, Tokyo: plan

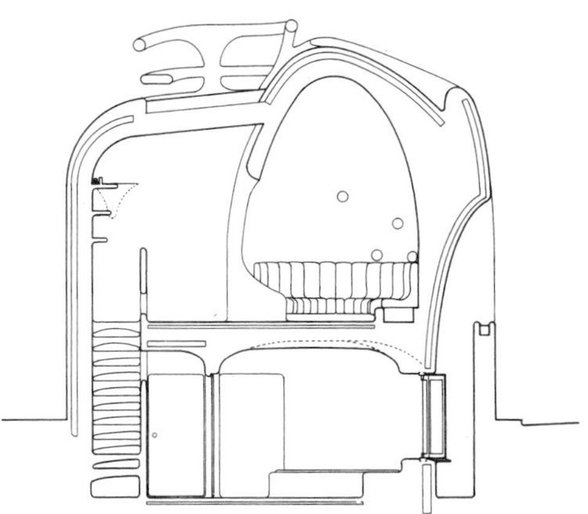

D. Truss Wall House, Tokyo: section

'Shinohara School', in reference to their teacher and principal architectural influence. Adopting Shinohara's powerful but reclusive aesthetics, they each produced designs of similar style and scale, typified by Ito's rigidly insular U-House of 1976. But as Shinohara moved incessantly towards artistic abstraction, his students lost faith in an architecture progressively detached from the intricacies of life. Criticising their former designs for overindulging in the self-consciousness of the architect, they sought to reacquaint themselves with an architecture of real-life spaces.

Best illustrating this newly expansive ideal is Toyo Ito's own house, the **Silver Hut** (1984). Situated in the Tokyo suburb of Nakano, the house offers a complete contrast to his previous domestic model, the U-House, immediately behind which the Silver Hut is sited. Rather than an architecture of concrete roof and walls, Ito uses a series of lightweight barrel vaults, bolted together above a grid of slender columns, to form a lattice canopy of triangulated pieces, which can be left open or closed with its retractable canvas covering. Breaking the regularity of this prefabricated system, asymmetrically placed openings destroy any sense of a uniform facade as the distinction between inside and outside is blurred. Using aluminium and steel, Itsuko Hasegawa has produced buildings of equally informal effect. In the **Tokyo houses at Nerima** (1986) and **Higashitamagawa** (1987) coloured perforated screens soften the boundary between public and private realms, while floodlit, their undulating silhouettes dramatise the banalities of night-time suburbia.

Influencing the directions taken by younger designers, such as Kazuyo Sejima and her **Platform Houses, Katsura** (1989), and **Kitakoma-Gun** (1990), Ito and Hasegawa have also extended their architecture beyond the confines of domestic design into the public arena. At the **Shonandai Cultural Centre, Fujisawa** (1990), Hasegawa's use of varying forms and explorable spaces appeared particularly suited to a new building eager to emphasise its accessibility. Ito too, at the **Tower of Winds, Yokohama** (1986) (p. 1587A), has offered a more public display of his architecture. Placed over a ventilation shaft he positioned a metal and glass cylinder, filled with a multitude of different lighting systems. Lighting up individually in response to the variances of time, noise and wind, this structure visualises the previously invisible becoming in the process a kind of monument to the immaterial.

1985–96

As Japan's cities have regained their momentum for change, more recent architectural expression has steadily become polarised between large-scale, corporate constructions and smaller, artistically considered and innovative buildings. Within the dominant majority of the former, Kenzo Tange has remained the key figure. But in buildings such as **Tokyo's new City Hall**, (1991) his designs, however refined, has lost their sculptural vitality. With little trace of his previous demands for a modern interpretation of traditional building remaining this is a monumental architecture devoid of place, equally at home in the cities of Berlin, Dallas, or Dubai. As a counterpoint to Tange and others is the conceptualist minority of Shinohara, Ando and Ito, building the modern interpretation of the house. Negating the precedence of form and the necessities of function, their architecture repositions its own parameters beneath the ideologies of artistic abstraction; redefining in the process Japan's understanding of art, away from the practice of creating beautiful objects, to the realisation of introspective visions and ideas. For example, Ando's **Church on the Water, Hokkaido** (1985–8) (p. 1590), with minimal means creates a memorable fusion between architecture, the elements and the landscape. The church, formed by two overlapping squares rendered in the simplest of terms, sits on a lake edge with the wall behind the alter being formed entirely of glass. This massive window offers a spectacular view of the mountainous landscape and, like a traditional shoji screen, the glass wall can slide open to emphasise the connection between the church interior and nature.

Providing some sense of identity, of difference, young architects have continued to produce idiosyncratic and innovative variations to the house as a kind of aesthetic calling-card for their architectural ambitions. Examples are the wildly esoteric **Truss Wall house, Tokyo** (1993) (p. 1587B–D) and **Soft and Hairy house, Tsukuba** (1994), by the Scottish–Japanese practice, Ushida Findlay. Similarly expressive work over the last ten years, including Shin Takamatsu's industrialised **Ark Dental Clinic, Nishima** (1984), Atsushi Kitagawara's surrealist **RISE Cinema, Tokyo** (1986), and the Dada-inspired **Crystal Light Building, Tokyo** (1987), by Masahara Takasaki, has offered varied and compelling evidence of the continued commitment by Japanese patrons to commission an intellectualised architecture as art.

Significantly, this period has also witnessed the accumulating introduction of foreign architectural practices. Before the mid-1980s, the cost of importing Western designers prohibited their use, but as the value of the yen soared against the dollar, the fees charged by overseas architects achieved a parity with Japan's own. At the same time, the dramatic increase in land prices meant that construction costs constituted, at most, only 10 per cent of the total architectural investment. By attracting distinguished American and European designers, the Japanese could increase the value of these investments by increasing the value of the architecture.

Among the first architects to be imported in this way were the Frenchman Philippe Starck and

A. Koshino House, Hyogo (1979–81, 1983). See p. 1584

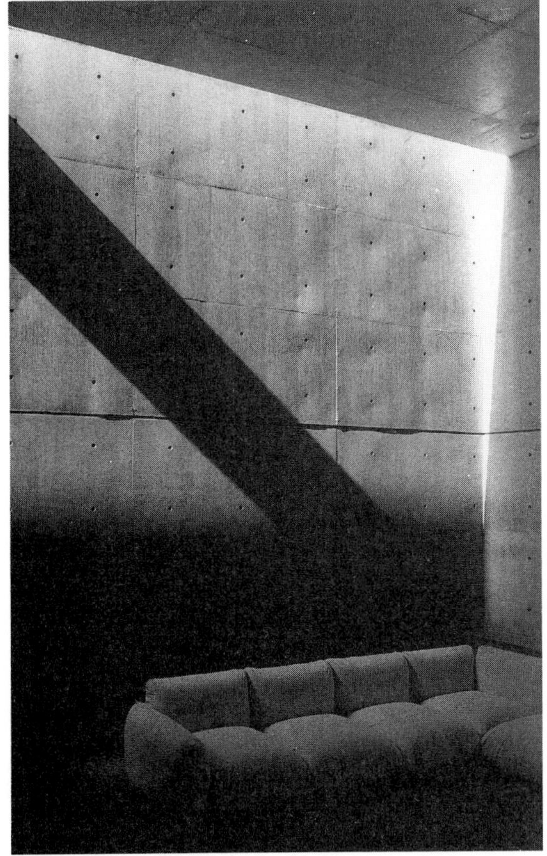

B. Koshino House, Hyogo: interior

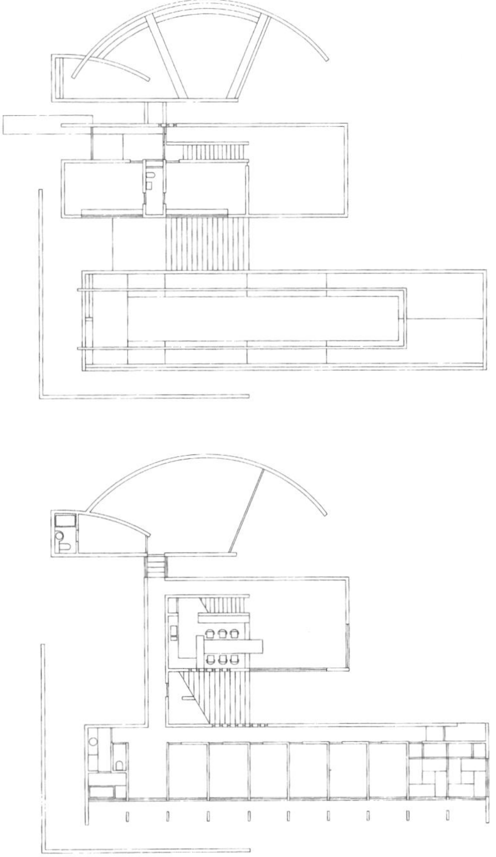

C. Koshino House, Hyogo: ground- and first-floor plans

A. Church on the Water, Hokkaido (1985–8). See p. 1588

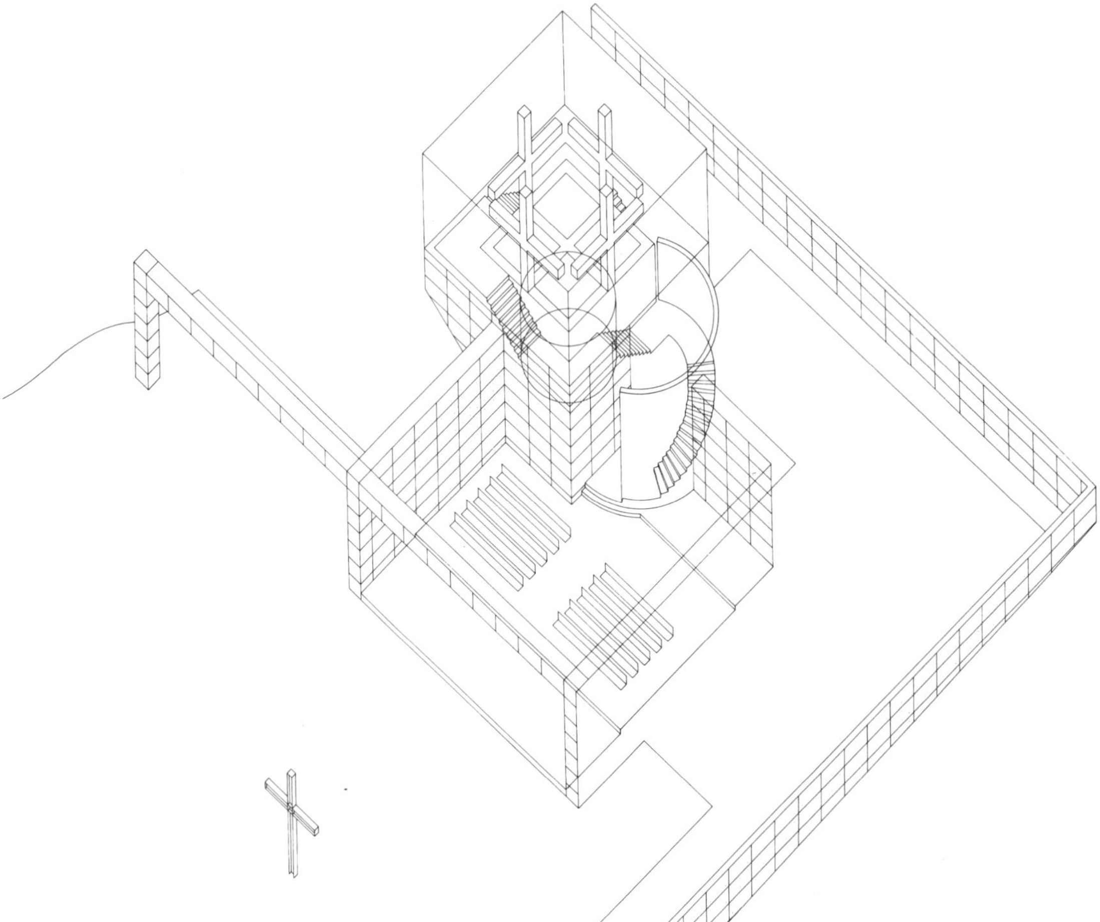

B. Church on the Water, Hokkaido: perspective

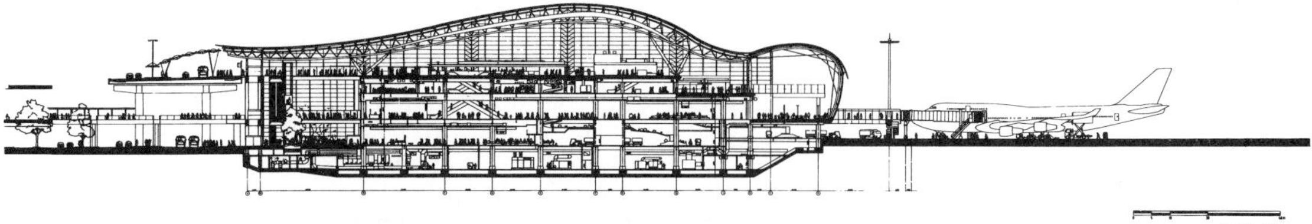

A. Kansai International Airport Terminal: section

B. Kansai International Airport Terminal (1988–94). See p. 1592

C. Nani Nani Building, Tokyo (1989). See p. 1592

D. L'Arcadi Noé Building, Sapporo (1988). See p. 1592

Englishman Nigel Coates. At the **Flamme d'Or building, Tokyo** (1989), built for the Asahi beer firm, Starck produced a distinct and exuberantly eccentric structure as a kind of habitable logo for a company eager to promulgate its corporate identity. Equally distinct, his **Nani Nani Building, Tokyo** (1989) (p. 1591C) constitutes a ribbed 'flask' of offices, coated in copper sheets, and designed to react and change colour over the succeeding decade. But, given the pressures of Tokyo fashion the building is unlikely to last that long. Responding to these fluidities of style, the bars and restaurants of Nigel Coates also offer areas of indulgence to society nostalgic for a culture not its own. At the **Caffé Bongo, Tokyo** (1986), **Bohemian Jazz Club, Tokyo** (1986), and **L'Acardi Noé building, Sapporo** (1988) (p. 1591D), the encrustations of a modern European baroque blur the distinction between high and low culture, and provide a shock of the old to a country where everything is new.

Renzo Piano, the architect of **Kansai International Airport Terminal** (1988–94) (p.1591A,B) may have been hired for his European pedigree but Kansai appears to have distinctly Japanese ancestry. As the late twentieth-century incarnation of the 1960s megapolitan projects of Tange, Kurokawa, and Kikutake, Kansai realises previously fantastical ideas for a city extended onto artificial oceanic platforms. With its mile-long terminal building, constructed upon a man-made island in the middle of Osaka Bay, Piano's architecture perhaps heralds a return to the technological heroism of the 1960s.

In addition to Piano, Coates and Starck, Japan has recently experienced the incursion of a number of other significant foreign architectural practices. Although provided with opportunities to experiment denied them at home, the appearance of buildings by Aldo Rossi (**Hotel II Pallazzo, Fukuoka**, 1989), Peter Eisenman (**Koizumi Lighting Theatre, Tokyo**, 1990) and Sir Norman Foster (**Century Tower, Tokyo**, 1991) ostensibly owes more to current architectural taste in Japan. Seeing the real cachet in building as not so much the architecture as the architect, Japanese patrons have increasingly sought to deal in architecture as a collectible item. Design in this way has become valued as never before. But ignoring the traditional criteria of value in architecture, for example the ergonomics of form, function and use, means that architecture is in danger of being valued merely in terms of fashion and potential profit.

Conclusion

The scale and rapidity at which this architectural turnover has occurred in Japan is revealed by the fact that over 25 per cent of Tokyo was completely rebuilt during the first half of the 1990s. Taken to its natural conclusion, this speed of development after twenty years would produce a complete and distinct city, different in every way from its previous incarnation, except name. The result of seeing architecture as product, therefore, has created a perpetual demand for the new. With the abandonment of any notion of permanence, buildings are dictated by economic incentives and the law of diminishing returns, so that their existence is solely dependent upon their novelty. In this way, the processes of building, demolition and reconstruction have become synonymous with one another, with little room for conservation. Clearly illustrated in 1968, the apparent irrelevance of architectural preservation in modern Japan accelerated the demolition of Frank Lloyd Wright's luxurious Imperial Hotel, barely 45 years after it was first opened. By giving priority to space over time (of a building's site rather than its age), old buildings are seemingly attributed a significance and value inferior to that of new ones, as Japan continues to look to the future as providing a greater sense of reassurance than the past.

Throughout these vicissitudes of construction, the only fixed and permanent features of Japan's urban landscape are the neon signs that illuminate its night sky. It is one of the ironies of modern Japan that these two-dimensional advertising signs and slogans resonate with an impact greater than that of the three-dimensional structures onto which they are attached. Manifest through this enduring imagery is the ascendancy of a purely visual order of things. Reflected not simply by advertisers but also by architects designing successively bizarre and surreal facades, urban life is increasingly predicated upon the idea of surface rather than that of depth. In this way, the medium of the architectural message in Japan has steadily become subsumed beneath the message itself. As buildings progressively become transformed into billboards, the most vivid and lasting impression of Japan at the end of the twentieth century is of a country that has delighted in opposites but whose culture and iconography are uniformly coming to represent the same thing.

South Korean Architecture of the Post-war period

Post-war architecture in Korea can be characterised by the wafer-thin residential slab block with south-facing living rooms and access corridors and kitchens to the north and by the commercial tower block of utterly anonymous type. However, the need to create accommodation to house the Olympic Games, held in Seoul in 1988, encouraged a revival in the art of architecture in South Korea. A number of the key Olympic buildings were won by international competition and not designed by Korean architects but the promise of the Olympics stimulated an increased interest in high-quality architecture in Korea while the presence of a number of exemplary Olympic buildings clearly raised standards and provided models to emulate.

One of the most successful buildings completed in 1988 is the **Olympic Village, Seoul**, designed by United States-based architects Woo and Williams. The building, which was selected via a competition held in 1984, covers 57 ha (143 acres) and incorporates buildings of stepped profile and sited to simulate the appearance of a giant amphitheatre within the landscape. The plan radiates, fan-like, from a central glass-vaulted atrium building. Two courses of water run between the radiating blocks. The village contains 5540 units which, after the Olympics, were put to permanent residential use. The atrium has become a shopping centre. The flats, 70 per cent of which are duplexes, have sun-capturing two-storey living rooms – a device inspired by the form of traditional village houses. The buildings are constructed of concrete clad with stucco which gives them a superficial similarity to much traditional Korean architecture.

A number of Olympic Games stadia are of interest, including the **Gymnasic Stadium, Seoul** (1988), by David H. Geiger. Inspired by Buckmaster Fuller's dome structure, the stadium is an elegant conception with a fabric membrane covering.

Significant non-Olympic architecture includes the **National Museum of Modern Art, Seoul** (1987), by Tai Soo Kim, which sprawls on a hillside site and incorporates a series of courts, and a Guggenheim Museum-like (q.v.) ramped drum; the **Seoul Opera House** (1985–93) by Seok Chul Kim which has a circular form with key spaces defined by overlapping segments of circles; the **Seoul Metropolitan Airport** (started 1993) by C.W. Fentress and J.H. Bradburn which incorporates a three-quarter mile concourse, and the **Kim Whanki Museum, Seoul** (1993), by K. S. Woo which possesses minimalist white interiors, top-lit and barrel vaulted cubical galleries calculated to display Whanki's abstract paintings to advantage.

Chapter 55
SOUTH-EAST ASIA

Introduction

Though the different countries which comprise South-east Asia have distinct cultural histories, they also have a number of key factors in common which continue to shape the course of development. Most important of these is a shared linguistic culture, based on the broad spread of the Indonesian/Malay language, or variants of it, throughout (Thailand excepted) most of the region. In addition, there are the importance of the nuclear family in peasant society and the related high status of women, the cultural complexity generated by the assimilation of successive imported religions from India, China, and the Middle East, and the impact of Western colonialism. Finally, there have been the shared post-colonial experiences of independence and nationalism, which are still working their way through, and the parallel search for national and regional identities.

Consequently, the architecture of South-east Asia reflects a complex overlaying of different cultures until the middle of the twentieth century, often creating a unique synthesis of imported and local elements, mediated by the tropical climate. By contrast, the latter half of the century has seen much of this multi-cultural heritage eroded by global economic and cultural forces, as well as by mechanised technologies of climate control, producing a homogenised architecture little different from other parts of the world. In the last decade, however, a small number of architects scattered throughout the region have sought to find a middle way between modernity and tradition, leading to an architecture more reflective of both the local climate and South-east Asian culture.

Regional Vernacular

While the dominant forces shaping South-east Asian architecture in the twentieth century have been those of colonialism and nationalism, vernacular dwelling forms continued to be built well into the second half of the century, and still influence current forms of building. The timber-framed, **house-on-stilts** is the archetypal building form of South-east Asia and variants can be found throughout the region, and even beyond, in other countries lying on the Pacific Rim. Usually built as single-family units grouped in random village clusters, or **kampongs**, the detached, raised form reflects both the indigenous social structure and the need to protect the occupants from snakes and tropical floods. The free-standing arrangement also maximises cooling air movement around and through the framed structures, which have floor-to-ceiling openable shutters providing light and ventilation. The high, pitched roofs of palm tree leaves, or atap, have wide-spreading eaves which shade the walls and throw off rainwater, while gable vents allow rising warm air to escape. Most variants, like the typical **Malay house** (p. 1595A), employ sophisticated methods of prefabrication and dry assembly of the hardwood frame and other components, enabling their owners to take down their houses when required and reassemble them elsewhere (see Chapter 40). Examples of colonial domestic architecture are also so common and widespread as to constitute a regional vernacular. Often, the process of adaptation to the tropical climate and other needs involved significant cross-cultural exchanges, resulting in a hybrid architecture (p. 1595B).

Singapore

Singapore benefited greatly from the interwar export boom of rubber and tin through its harbour, boosted by the developed world's new infatuations with the motor car and tinned foods. A building boom followed, producing a new spate of ostentatious public works, as well as improvements in public services and infrastructure, carried out by the city's own Public Works Department, similar to Kuala Lumpur's. The **Municipal Building** on the **Padang** (1926–9) (p. 1595C) by F. D. Meadows, the **General Post Office** (1928) by Keys and Dowdeswell, and the **Edward VII School of Medicine** (1927) by the same firm, were among the last neo-Classical buildings to be built in Singapore,

A. Malay house-on-stilts. See p. 1594

B. Colonial villa, Penang (1938). See p. 1594

C. Municipal Building, Singapore (1926–9). See p. 1594

D. The Supreme Court, Singapore (1937–9). See p. 1596

and signalled the twilight of the colonial era. All three structures are somewhat ponderous horizontal compositions and feature the giant Doric order and colonnades. The **Hongkong & Shanghai Bank** (1925), by Swan and MacLaren, was a much lighter, though uneven design, and had 'modern' balconies slotted in between the columns of the upper three-storey facade. The **Supreme Court** (1937–9) (p. 1595D), by F. Dorrington Ward, was the last building in Singapore to be designed in the Imperial manner. The inflated scale, cramped proportions and classical facade stuck over a steel-framed box all betray the confusions of this transitional period. By comparison, the earlier **Railway Terminus** (1932), by the PWD, is a self-assured exercise in modern building engineering, and was said to be influenced by Eliel Saarinen's Helsinki Station. The impressive booking hall, with its exposed reinforced concrete arches, clearly points ahead, while the bold arches and heroic sculptures of the entrance colonnade have something of the original Roman spirit in them. In 1937 a new airport was built at **Kallang** to handle the growing civil air traffic. The steel-framed **Terminal Building** exhibited all the streamlined features of the early Modern Movement, including cantilevered roofs and balconies and full-height strip windows. It was followed in 1939 by the **Cathay Building**, by Frank Brewer, Singapore's first high-rise building, and a portent of the city's future pattern of growth.

The fall of Singapore to the Japanese in 1942, as with the fall of Hong Kong, had a traumatic effect on the colony, which endured long after the eventual Allied victory and hastened independence in the following decade. Soon after the war the Hong Kong-based firm of Palmer and Turner also established a branch office in Singapore and were responsible for a number of significant buildings of the time. **MacDonald House** (1949), built for the Hongkong & Shanghai Bank, was the first postwar high-rise structure, and has a Modern, clean-cut brick facade, surmounted by tiled-roofed apartments for the Bank's employees. The **Bank of China Building** (1954) resembles more the architects' earlier high-rise architecture in Hong Kong and Shanghai, and makes a solid impression with its stone-clad, vertical facade elements. Ethnic Chinese architects also began to make their mark in this period, and the contemporary **Asia Insurance Building** (1954), by Ng Keng Siang, presents an unambiguous Modern expression by comparison with the previous work, made up of projecting horizontal window canopies and a 'streamline' corner tower. Similarly, the **Singapore Rubber House** (1960), by Swan and MacLaren, is an accomplished exercise in a tropicalised International Style and marks both the firm's and Singapore's transition from colonial to post-colonial architecture.

Independence in 1957 brought a brief union with Malaysia until 1959. Then Singapore went its own way, led by the charismatic Lee Kuan Yew and his People's Action Party (PAP). The previous economic booms had resulted in a rapid expansion in Singapore's population, creating severe problems of overcrowding in the Chinese and other non-European sectors of the city. In 1927 the colonial government set up the Singapore Improvement Trust and built a number of International Style model housing estates before and after World War II, such as the **Prinsep Court Flats** (1949). However, though well designed in themselves, they barely scratched the surface of the problem. In 1960 the Housing and Development Board (HDB) was established to create a series of **new towns**, based on European models, which would supply sufficient housing and workplaces outside the main city to relieve congestion, and also provide for the future growth of the population. As with the similar programme in Hong Kong, a shortage of land, coupled with the persuasions of orthodox Modernists trained in Europe, compelled HDB architects and planners to adopt **high-rise housing** solutions in imitation of Western solutions. Again, as with the Hong Kong programme, the first of these provided only for the most basic needs and were designed to minimal space requirements. Standards quickly improved, however, and successive generations of new towns in the 1970s and 1980s added improvements in community facilities and landscaping. **Pasir Rif New Town** (p. 1597A), in the north-eastern end of the Island, is typical of the late 1980s generation and consists of several neighbourhoods further divided into precincts of four to eight residential blocks of 100 to 120 families each. A secondary hierarchy of community services interconnected by pedestrian pathways is distributed throughout the town, with major facilities gathered in the town centre, and minor or frequently used services in the precinct centres. To date, twenty new towns have been or are in the process of being completed, housing a staggering 87 per cent of the population, of whom 81 per cent own their own flat, thanks to various government loan schemes.

Parallel with its housing programme, the Singapore government oversaw a heavy programme of public and private investment aimed at transforming the Island economy from colonial dependency to post-colonial self-sufficiency. Conscious of the Island's limited size and resources, Singapore's leaders devised a bold and astute development strategy aimed at encouraging maximum foreign capital, backed up by government investment in infrastructure and education.

By the mid-1970s, Singapore was known as one of the 'Four Tigers', or elite nations emulating Japan and spearheading the fast-growing Asian Pacific economy (the other original 'Tigers' are Hong Kong, Taiwan and South Korea). A large number of multinational companies set up regional headquarters in the city, sprouting office towers and other commercial buildings in the centre and transforming the Singapore

A. Pasir Rif New Town (*c.* late 1980s). See p. 1596

C. Woh Hup Complex: section (1974). See p. 1598

D. Ardmore Condominium (1984). See p. 1598

B. OCBC Centre, Singapore (1976). See p. 1598

skyline. Many of these were designed by well-known foreign architects, who were often favoured over local architects by both government and private clients, not only for their experience in high-rise architecture and other complex briefs but also for the international prestige which was assumed to accrue to their works, and therefore to their clients. They include the **OCBC Centre** (1976) (p. 1597B), **Raffles City** (1985), and the **Gateway Project** (1986), all by I. M. Pei, the **Nanyang Institute of Technology** (1986), the **OUB Centre** (1986), and **Singapore Indoor Stadium** (1989) by Kenzo Tange, and the **Pavilion International Hotel** (1983) and **Marina Square** (1985) hotel complexes, by John Portman. Of this group, Pei's OCBC Centre is the most striking design, comprising a reinforced concrete suspended structure of twin service cores, between which three equal batches of floors are hung from giant girders.

More generally, Singapore's commercial architecture of the 1970s and early 1980s is indistinguishable from that in the West. While part of the blame rests on the indifference of foreign architects to the tropical climate and other conditions, local architects hardly varied in their approach at this time. The **Comcentre** (now Telecoms) (1978), by BEP Architects, is marginally more responsive to the climate, insofar as the glazed fenestration is recessed between floors, which project between twin service cores like Pei's OCBC Centre. Neither was the fashion for Western models restricted to commercial buildings. **Jurong Town Hall** (1970), by Team 3 International, is a Brutalist composition in reinforced concrete with cantilevered upper floors shading the floors below. In the same spirit, the **Subordinate Courts** (1974), by Kumpulan Architects, strongly resembles Denys Lasdun's National Theatre complex in London, particularly in the overlapping terraces and pyramidal massing centred on the service core. Marking the apogee of this Brutalist phase is the mixed-use **Woh Hup Complex** (1974) (p. 1597C), by Design Partnership (DP) Architects. Comprising a stepped 'ziggurat' of apartments mounted over a shopping centre podium and internal 'street', the design was strongly influenced by avant-garde Japanese and European 'megastructure' projects of the previous decade.

While Western fashions remained in the ascendency, a small number of local architects cherished the notion of a different approach. The **National University of Singapore, Kent Ridge** (1973–7), by the PWD, based on a master plan by the Dutch architect Joshua van Embden, is a landmark in the development of a modern tropical regionalism, and created almost a complete concrete frame and brick vernacular in itself which has been widely imitated since. Most of the three- to five-storey buildings, which are carefully planned to fit into the contours of the green and hilly site west of the city, have overhanging tiled roofs and cantilevered balconies which provide shade and circulation, in the manner of many colonial-era schools. They are linked together with one- and two-storey covered passageways, which provide all-weather pedestrian circulation throughout the campus.

New approaches also began to emerge in the private housing sector, particularly in the development of apartment towers. Beginning with **Ardmore Condominium** (1984) (p. 1597D), by Moshe Safdie, with Regional Development Consortium, a local firm, they created a distinctive, tropicalised high-rise architecture, matching the similar experiments taking place in Kuala Lumpur over the same period. In the Ardmore scheme, Safdie's familiar preference for terraced dwelling forms is translated into two sculpted tower blocks, each deeply incised with shaded, double-height 'skycourts' and slotted terraces. Clearly inspired by their collaboration with Safdie, Regional Development Consortium soon after produced **Balestier Point** (1986), a staggered block of terraced apartments mounted over a shopping centre. Paul Rudolph's **Grange Road Condominium** followed in 1987 (p. 1599A) and has a similar articulated form produced by the solid projections of the bedrooms, which are cantilevered out beyond the main building frame or 'megastructure', to help shade the more open living spaces and terraces. A recent addition to the series is Tang Guan Bee's **Abelia Condominium** (1994) (p. 1599B). Like its forebears, it has maisonettes planned around double-height open 'skycourts', but has a lighter, mostly glazed fenestration, relying on sunscreens and luxuriant hanging vegetation to provide shading. Excellent as these designs are, a consequence of Singapore's development as a high-rise city has been the destruction of most of the city's original low-rise urban fabric and shop-houses. The **Villa Chancery Condominium** (1986), by William Lim, is a rare exercise in terraced courtyard housing modelled on the shop-house type, and suggests how similar patterns might be revived.

Innovations are now also taking place in other building forms, sometimes in unexpected places. **Tampines Community Centre** (1992) (p. 1599C), by William Lim, with partner Mok Wei Wei, is one of several recent projects commissioned from local private firms by the government as part of a more liberal building programme. With its colourful collage of assorted shapes and sizes, bound together by the strict order of the perimeter circulation frame – a modern translation of the traditional 'five-foot way' – the Centre has been described as a metaphor for Singapore's multi-cultural but disciplined society. The **Bukit Batok Mosque** by HDB Architect Liu Thai Ker, with its innovative reinterpretation of Islamic themes, and the **Crescent Girls' School** (1994), by the PWD architect Phan Pit Li, with its multiple references to Aldo Rossi and Post-Modernism as well as colonial architecture, both demonstrate that, given the opportunity, government designers are capable of equally creative approaches. Lastly,

A. Grange Road Condominium, Singapore (1987). See p. 1598

B. Abelia Condominium, Singapore (1994). See p. 1598

C. Tampines Community Centre, Singapore (1992). See p. 1598

D. Institute of Education, Bishan (1994). See p. 1600

the **Institute of Education** (1994) (p. 1599D) at **Bishan**, by Tenggara II, demonstrates the maturity of contemporary Singaporean architecture with a convincing reinterpretation of tropical regionalism in steel and concrete. Comprising two linear classroom blocks facing each other across a gently curved, verdant 'street', the design adapts a number of practical features from regional building traditions, including overhanging roofs, cantilevered balconies for shade and circulation, and narrow functional spaces to ensure effective cross-ventilation.

Despite the increasing availability of proven local talent, at the end of the century the Singapore government continued to favour better-known overseas architects for major projects, as demonstrated in the mid-1990s by the choice of Stirling Wilford as principal designers for **Temasek Polytechnic**, and for the **Singapore Arts Centre**, both in collaboration with DP Architects. The former, with its tight urban scale and horseshoe-shaped central block and plaza, is a recognisable product of the Stirling Wilford stable. The latter project, prominantly sited close to the Padang overlooking Singapore harbour, is a more controversial, abstract design. Comprising a cluster of five public auditoria and supporting facilities, the main buildings have a variable, double-skin cladding which, while protecting the enclosed functional spaces, also obscure their purpose.

Malaysia

With the chief infrastructure and adminstrative buildings in the Capital, Kuala Lumpur, completed by *c.* 1910, there was relatively little public activity during the interwar years. With some exceptions, notably the New Delhi style **Johore State Government Building**, **Johore Bahru** (1939) (p. 1601A) by the ubiquitous firm of Palmer and Turner, the choice of styles also settled down in line with more conventional European fashions of the period. The neo-Classical **Coliseum Theatre, Hotel and Restaurant**, **Kuala Lumpur** (1920) (architect unknown), is distinguished for its recessed upper storey and colonnade of paired columns. By contrast, both the **Overseas Chinese Banking Corporation Building** (1926–7), by the Danish engineers Sehested and Neilsen, and the **Hotel Majestic** (1932) (architect unknown), both in **Kuala Lumpur**, boast clean lines and large glazed windows. Unsurprisingly, the former was originally designed as a department store. The **Anglo-Oriental Building** (1936) (architect unknown), had Art Deco details and strong horizontal lines emphasised by thin-edged, projecting window canopies. The vertical, 'streamline' corner entrance treatment is reminiscent of Art Deco cinemas of the period.

The Anglo-Oriental Building confirmed the arrival of Modern architecture in Kuala Lumpur. The post-war years were marked by enthusiastic acceptance of the new forms, spurred on by the declaration of Independence in 1957, and ensuing national programmes of modernisation. Early exercises, like the glass-clad **Federal House** (1954), by the PWD, differed little from European models. However, a renewed appreciation of traditional building forms and climate control techniques, plus a continued lack of mechanical systems of air-conditioning, combined to produce a 'tropicalised' Modernism, not unlike similar post-war movements in India and Africa. These often took the shape, as with the concrete-framed and louvred **British Council** (1956), by the PWD, of a modified interpretation of traditional roof forms, window shutters, and so on, in modern materials. The **National Mosque** (1956), also by the PWD, is a contemporary reinterpretation of Middle Eastern traditions of mosque building, adapted to the tropical climate. On occasion, as with the **National Museum** (1963), by Ho Kok Hoe, expressions of national identity led to imitations of traditional forms at inflated scales, with odd results.

By contrast, a number of architects adopted a robust Modernism based on a late Corbusian vocabulary of fairfaced reinforced concrete, piloti, and brise-soleil. They involve a number of large projects in **Kuala Lumpur**, such as the **University of Malaya** (1959–75), by Palmer and Turner with the PWD, and various other foreign and local firms. Individual structures designed in this fashion include the **University Hospital and Medical Faculty** (1964–6), by James Cubitt. Another tribute to Le Corbusier, the **Kuala Lumpur General Hospital** (1966–8), by Wells and Joyce in association with John Harris, is one of the most successful post-war exercises of its kind in adapting Modern architecture to the tropics. The low-rise, human scale, the consistent logic of structure and planning, as well as the skilful use of brise-soleil and other climate-control techniques, all contribute to its special quality. The first International Style tower buildings in Kuala Lumpur also emerged in the late 1950s. Generally, like the **Federal Hotel** (1957), by Goh Hock Guan, the **Malaysian Parliament Building** (1963), by the PWD, and the **American International Assurance Building** (1964) (p. 1601B), by John Graham and Co., with Palmer and Turner, they employed various forms of concrete or metal sunscreen to protect their walls from the intense sun and glare. The **National Electricity Board Building** (1966), by their own Architects Department, takes another step in using a load-bearing, reinforced concrete sunscreen.

The widespread availability of mechanical air-conditioning and relatively cheap energy in the late 1960s and 1970s encouraged architects to ignore climate as a significant design factor, with the result that, by the 1980s, Kuala Lumpur's rapidly

A. Johore State Government Building, Johore Bahru (1939). See p. 1600

B. American International Assurance Building, Kuala Lumpur (1964). See p. 1600

C. Dayabumi Tower, Kuala Lumpur (1981). See p. 1602

D. Menara Mesiniaga Tower, Kuala Lumpur (1992). See p. 1602

expanding central business district was indistinguishable from any other such places in the world. A few architects attempted to modify the standard tower type by using forms which carried additional cultural meaning. The **Bumiputra Bank** (1972), by Kumpulan Akitek, combines a functionalist office tower with a separate public banking hall in the form of a traditional Malay House, in deference to its mainly native Malay (Bumiputra) customers. The **Tabung Haji Tower** (1980), by Hijas Kasturi, has an unusual waisted cylindrical form further distinguished by five large circular (non-structural) columns, symbolising the 'Five Pillars of Wisdom' of Islam, while the **Dayabumi Tower** (1981) (p. 1601C), by BEP with MAA, also makes reference to Malaysia's links with the Islamic world with a plan and sunscreen patterned on Islamic ornamental traditions common to the Middle East and elsewhere.

The return of the sunscreen in the Dayabumi Tower marked a renewed concern among Malaysian architects with climate control, though it generally remains a minority interest. The **Plaza Atrium** (1983), in the capital's Golden Triangle district, by Hamzah and Yeang, is one of a series of experiments by its architects to develop a high-rise, 'bioclimatic' architecture appropriate to the tropics, based on rational principles of climate control. Partly inspired by shophouse arcades, the upper floors on one corner of the Plaza Atrium are stepped back under a canopy roof, leaving the corner exposed like a portion of a giant arcade. The architects' highly original approach is best exemplified by the **Menara Mesiniaga Tower** (1992) (p. 1601D), an office tower situated near Kuala Lumpur International Airport, and the **MBF Tower** (1994), a residential and mixed-use building in **Georgetown, Penang**. Both towers are distinguished by exposed 'megastructure' frames, recessed 'skycourts', free-standing, naturally ventilated service cores, and a variety of sunscreen devices, combining international and regional influences in a free and creative manner.

Other building types have also undergone various transformations, as their architects wrestled with the problems of reconciling modern imperatives with cultural traditions. The hybrid architecture of Jimmy Lim belongs to a Pacific-wide tradition of timber-framed building, and is inspired by Frank Lloyd Wright and the Australian Sydney School – some of whom were Lim's teachers – as well as by Malay, Chinese and colonial vernaculars. The **Salinger House, Bangai** (1986) (p. 1603A), raised off the ground in the midst of a rubber plantation, typifies Lim's domestic designs. The concrete-framed **Impiana Resort**, **Pahang** (1993), on the east coast, by the same architect, is modelled on the raised timber structures of South-east Asian fishing villages, so as to minimise disturbance of the landscape, as well as the danger of floods. Also designed to minimise disturbance of the natural surroundings, the **Datai Resort**, **Langkawi Island** (1993) (p. 1603B), by Kerry Hill, an Australian architect based in Singapore, is carefully sited several hundred yards inland from the coastline in a clearing high in the dense tropical forest. Built from local stone and timbers felled in the process of clearing the site, the impression is that of the remnants of a recently uncovered civilisation, part village, part temple-platform.

There are signs, too, of more adventurous approaches. The **Golf Club**, **Johore Bahru** (1994), by Tenggara II, is a steel and concrete construction of colliding planes, angles and drums, based on a fragmented, circular composition, not unlike contemporary 'deconstructivist' compositions in the West. Ruslan Khalid's research centre for the **Malaysian Institute for Microelectronic Systems (MIMOS)**, **Kuala Lumpur** (1995), also has a dynamic plan and 'high-tech' image in keeping with its purpose. At the same time, the lightweight, framed construction, curved 'umbrella' roofs and various forms of sun-shading all reflect climatic considerations. The 'floating', hyperbolic paraboloid shell roof of the new **Kuala Lumpur International Airport Terminal**, by Kisho Kurokawa, now under construction, was also inspired by traditional Malay roof forms, as well as by images of tropical rain forests. Other major infrastructure projects under construction include the **Customs Immigration and Quarantine Complex**, **Johore Bahru**, by Group Design Partnership, with UK engineers Battle McCarthy. Situated on the Malaysian side of the new causeway link with Singapore Island, the giant concrete arched structure promises to be one of the most dramatic new landmarks in the region. Also due for completion by 1996 and 1997 respectively, the twin **Petronas Towers** (p. 1603C), by Cesar Pelli, for Malaysia's premier oil-based company, and the **Telecom Tower** (p. 1603D), by Hijjas Kasturi, present dramatically different visions of Kuala Lumpur's future as the growing capital of one of the region's most prosperous and modern countries. At 454 m (1476 ft), the 88-storey Petronas Towers will be the tallest structure in the world (the first time since 1891 that the record has been held by a building outside North America) and is part of an immense new 'city within a city' in the heart of Kuala Lumpur. Aside from token formal gestures – the plan is based on Islamic designs – it presents a powerful symbol of the country's, and the region's, rising status and ambitions. By contrast, the Telecom Tower is situated in an outlying suburb of the city and is planned as part of a strategy for decentralised expansion along the Klang Valley. At 55 storeys, the curvacious tower is a relatively modest and graceful response to the city's need for growth. Partly inspired, like Kurokawa's project, by tropical green imagery, the tower comprises two tapering facades overlapping like the growing leaves of a bamboo shoot. Other features include 'sky gardens'

A. Salinger House, Bangai (1986). See p. 1602

B. Datai Resort, Langkawi Island (1993). See p. 1602

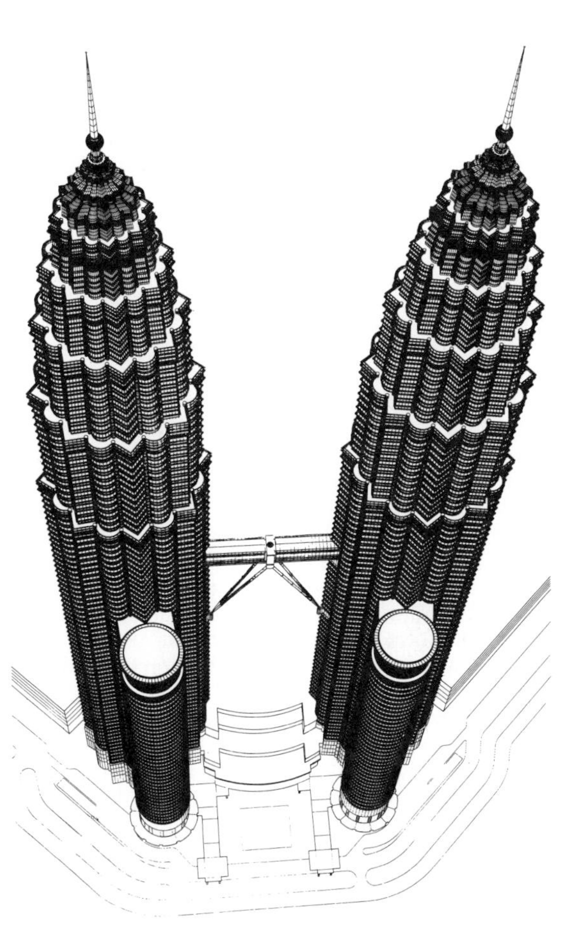

C. Petronas Towers, Kuala Lumpur: aerial perspective (completion 1996). See p. 1602

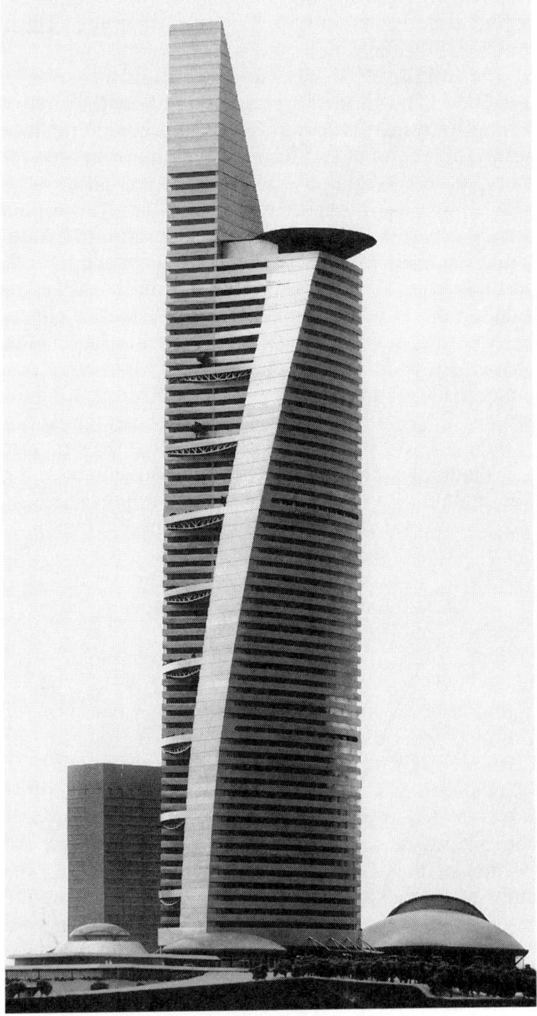

D. Telecom Tower, Kuala Lumpur: model (completion 1997). See p. 1602

every sixth floor, and a host of technical innovations in keeping with its description as one of Malaysia's first 'intelligent' buildings.

Indonesia

Following the pattern of colonial architecture in Malaysia and Singapore, architects in the former Dutch East Indies relied heavily on imported European models for their public buildings, clubs and churches. However, the experience of World War I and its aftermath compelled Dutch settlers to become less reliant on Europe and to reassess their local commitments. The result was that, from the 1920s on, a number of colonial architects began to look increasingly inwards for cultural sustenance and inspiration, leading to original developments in public architecture quite apart from anything else in the region at the time.

The Institute of Technology, **Bandung** (1920) (p. 1605A), by Henri Maclaine Pont, was the first of a series of remarkable buildings, based on meticulous study of regional traditions, which attempted to incorporate indigenous features in a new way. Maclaine Pont's main sources were the timber houses-on-stilts of the Minangkabau region in **Sumatra**, with their distinctive peaked, suspended roofs, and the Javanese kratons, or royal palaces. Like the palaces, the ITB, as it is known, consists of a cluster of pavilions set around small courtyards and interconnected with shaded colonnades with stout columns made of uncut stone. The multi-layered roofs provide for ventilation in the gaps between the layers, as well as in their high peaks, while the open structure at ground level provides further free movement of air. The main hall, or Aula, is especially impressive, and has an exposed structure of giant parabolic beams of laminated wood, bound with iron clamps. In 1925 Maclaine Pont began experimenting with small tensile roofs based on the Sumatran type, going on to develop a hybrid 'Indonesian Gothic' for large spans of up to 25 m (81 ft), out of a combination of suspended wire 'roofnets' and timber arches. These ingenious experiments (which were later noted by the German tensile engineer Frei Otto) led to the **Catholic Church, Pohsarang, Java** (1937), Maclaine Pont's last work in the region. The hilltop site is treated as a series of stepped walled courtyards and gateways, rising up towards the church in the fashion of the Hindu temple-platforms of Java. The main body consists of a large, five-cornered cupola, made up of giant bent timber rafters converging on a key-piece at the apex, between which is suspended a composite 'roofnet' of steel cables and lattice timber frameworks, supporting clay roof tiles. Overhead windows with overlapping, open panes of glass ensure adequate light and ventilation at the apex. The cupola, like the ancilliary structures, was originally completely open at ground level in the fashion of the indigenous pendopo, or open-pillared hall, commonly used for dance and dramas. It has since been walled in, to the detriment of the design.

The theme of the open pendopo also occurs in the **Folk Theatre**, **Semarang** (*c.* 1930) and again at the **Sonobudoyo Museum, Yogyakarta** (1935), both by Thomas Karsten, a former associate of Maclaine Pont. For the museum, Karsten based his plan, just as Maclaine Pont had done with his Institute of Technology, on that of the princely kraton, with its courtyards and linked open pavilions. A large, pillared hall, or pendopo, capped by a layered pyramidal roof, leads via a colonnaded link into the enclosed exhibition spaces. The extraordinary work of these two innovative architects ranks with the highest achievements of Western Arts and Crafts designers and went far towards establishing a twentieth-century architecture based on indigenous idioms and local structural and symbolic elements.

Despite (or perhaps because of) the depth of their researches, Maclaine Pont's and Karsten's example was mostly ignored in the post-war headlong rush to imitate the latest Western fashions. It was not until 1962, with the **Tandjung Sari Resort**, **Bali**, by Wija Wawo Runtu, that a similar attempt was made to draw directly on indigenous traditions. Starting as an extension to the architect's own house, the resort now comprises 29 bunglows clustered around the original building. The **Bali Hyatt Hotel**, **Sanur** (1973), by Palmer and Turner, followed, and though much is lost in the inflated scale of the open, timber-framed pavilions, the sympathetic ambiance captured by buildings and landscaping together, has been widely imitated by resort builders throughout South-east Asia. Other notable examples of the genre, also in **Bali**, include the **Club Med** (1988), by Noelle Janet and Christian Demoncy, the **Amandari Resort** (1989), by Peter Muller, and the **Amanusa Resort** (1992), by Kerry Hill. All these resorts project the image of a complete settlement, either a self-contained village, or, in the case of the Amanusa, a temple-platform complex not unlike Hill's Datai resort in Malaysia, and draw heavily on local idioms in both plan and detail.

A similar movement can be traced in upper-income residential architecture, producing a growing number of fine houses based on indigenous idioms, sometimes blended with colonial or modern themes. An example of the traditional approach is the **Giusti House** at **Sanur**, **Bali** (1980), by Rodulfo Giusti de Marle, which is planned as a loose group of open-framed, thatch-roofed pavilions. The three-storey, steel-framed **Abidin House**, **Jakarta** (1988), by Ismeth Abidin, presents a more contemporary, hybrid approach. **Kampung Kali Cho-de**, **Yogyakarta** (1985), by Yousef B. Mangunwijaya, shows that regional idioms are equally valid at the opposite end

A. The Institute of Technology, Bandung (1920). See p. 1604

B. Said Naum Mosque, Jakarta (1797). See p. 1606

C. Dharmala Building, Jakarta: architect's sketch (1982). See p. 1606

D. Science Museum, Bangkok (1977). See p. 1606

of the housing spectrum. Based on a raised 'A'-framed timber structure with bamboo floors and walls of plaited split-cane, the simple but functional architecture is enlivened with colourful wall paintings by the residents, aided by local art students.

Aside from hotel and residential buildings, however, there are relatively few positive exemplars of contemporary building types in the country, especially in comparison with developments in Malaysia and Singapore. The work of Suyudi, Indonesia's most prominent first-generation, mainstream Modernist, is represented best by the 'winged' **Conference Hall, Jakarta** (*c.* 1965), inspired by Eero Saarinan's TWA Terminal. Representing the regional approach, the **Said Naum Mosque, Jakarta** (1977) (p. 1605B), by Hariyanto Sudikontoro and Atelier 6, is a modern variant of the traditional pyramidal mosque, itself based on the pendopo, and demonstrates the continued cultural relevance of local typologies. Designed in the same spirit, the **Citra Niagra Urban Development, Samarinda** (1986), by Antonio Ismael, PT Triaco and PT Griyantara, is an attempt to create a shopping centre based on local social patterns and building forms. The **Dharmala Building, Jakarta** (1982) (p. 1605C) by Paul Rudolph, is a rare example of a tropicalised tower, partly inspired by indigenous idioms, and like the architect's Grange Road tower in Singapore, features shady overhangs and open terraces on every floor.

Thailand

Thailand is unique in being the only country in South-east Asia not to have been colonised by any Western power, its royal rulers having retained their autonomy by cunningly playing off the competing imperial powers against each other. Nevertheless, by the turn of the century, normal trade and related cross-cultural exchanges had already left their architectural mark, often producing hybrid styles not unlike those which characterised colonial architecture in the region (see Chapter 40). **Government House, Bangkok** (*c.* 1910), originally built by King Rama VI as the residence for a favoured aide, presents a relatively consistent exercise in Gothic eclectism by the Italian architect Annebale Rigotti, and incorporates elaborate stone window tracery. The Gothic mansion known as **Ban Phitsanuloke** (*c.* 1910) also by Rigotti, was built in a similar style by the same King for another aide, and is capped with Gothicised 'Moghul' chatris and a dome over an octagonal tower. Compared with these previous designs, the **British Embassy** (*c.* 1920), which is credited to Sir Edward Lutyens, is a relatively modest and sedate work, and includes such familiar colonial features as shady arcades, and an imposing entrance portico and other neo-Classical details. The **Prasit House** (1909), built by Phraya Attakarn Prasit, who served as Attorney General of Siam under Kings Rama V and Rama VI, likewise demonstrates a relatively restrained and functional approach.

Such evidence suggests that political independence in itself does not therefore guarantee cultural independence. Certainly, the course of Modern architecture in Thailand after World War II is hardly any different from that of the newly independent countries, and early leading Modernists actively conversed with fellow Modernists elsewhere. The **School for the Blind, Bangkok** (1973), by Sumet Jumsai, with its shuttered concrete structure, pilotis and brise-soleil, owes as much, for example, to the work of Le Corbusier as some of the post-war projects in Kuala Lumpur described above. Similar models inspired the sculptured forms of the **Science Museum, Bangkok** (1977) (p. 1605D), by the same architect, who has been among the most influential of his generation. **Thammasat University, Rangsit** (1980), also by Jumsai, represents the first of several sharp changes of direction by the architect. The master plan is modelled on the ancient temple city of Angkor Thom in Cambodia, and is organised around a monumental axis and a complex network of canals and storage lakes which drain and ornament the site. The main buildings, which are arranged in clusters of square modules, each with its own central courtyard, have red-tiled, pitched roofs and are raised off the ground, providing shaded, breezy spaces underneath for dining, informal study and recreation. In stark contrast, the **Nation Building, Bangkok** (1990), has giant 'computer circuit' side elevations, clearly intended to advertise the client's involvement in modern communications.

Jumsai's uninhibited, inclusive approach is repeated in the work of other leading Thai practices, reflecting both the recent impact of Post-Modern liberalism as well as the catholic tastes of earlier generations of Thai architects and clients. Plan Architect, for example, work on a typically broad front. The mixed-use **Baan Ton Sak Complex, Bangkok** (1988), lies at the traditional end of the firm's work, and consists of a cluster of one- to three-storey, raised pavilions of shops and residences arranged around a courtyard and linked with inter-connecting decks in the fashion of the indigenous Central Plains Cluster House. The **Ruk-Look Kindergarten, Bangkok** (1988) comprises an irregular pile of assorted shapes and spaces which look as though they have been assembled out of a toy-kit, while the **Pridi Banomyong Institute, Bangkok** (1993), is a Post-Modern reinterpretation of classical themes. The concrete-framed **Tiptus House, Bangkok** (1983), by Boonywat and Tiptus, comprises a cluster of three raised pavilions linked by an upper decked courtyard, and is modelled on the indigenous Cluster House type. In contrast to these informal designs, the **Sala Rajakarunja Memorial Museum**,

Khao Lahn, **Trat** (1992), by Tiptus, with Bundit Chulasai, Vira Sachakul, and Chaiboon Sirithanawat is an abstract, monumental work in the form of a semi-underground bunker, symbolising the desperate plight of the Cambodian refugees it honours. The more extreme aspects of Thai Post-Modernism are represented by the **Jareemart apartment block**, **Bangkok** (1986) by Ong Ard – a bizarre mixture of neo-Classical confections and curtain walling, topped by a penthouse in the form of a temple.

The scale of recent redevelopment and expansion in Bangkok has brought the city's infrastructure to the point of collapse. A solution long advocated but only now being put into action is to channel future growth into a number of mini-cities on the outskirts of the capital. The spectacular speed and scale of these new projects, like **Muang Thong Thani**, a privately sponsored development for 250,000 people by the Australian architects Robert Nation and Karl Fender, have no precedents in the West. What they presage for the quality of urban life and architecture in Thailand is yet uncertain.

The Philippines

In 1898, after 300 years of Spanish rule, American forces moved into the weakened colony, imposing their own special brand of Imperial rule for the next 50 years. As with other Western empires, the culture of the occupying power soon left its mark on that of the occupied, sometimes with unexpected results.

In 1904, the American architect Daniel H. Burnham was brought to the Philippines to survey and prepare development plans for the capital city, **Manila**, and **Baguio**, another major urban centre. As a renowned enthusiast for the Beaux Arts School and architect for the 1893 Chicago Exposition, Burnham might have been expected to pursue his enthusiasm in the colony, as Western architects have done throughout the region. Instead, impressed with the indigenous architecture and dwellings, as well as with the Spanish colonial churches, which had been adapted to local conditions, Burnham suggested they be taken as appropriate models for development. Among those architects influenced by Burnham's recommendation was the American architect William E. Parsons, whose works include the **Philippine General Hospital**, **Manila** (1910). A product of mixed sources, the building has a neo-Classical pediment and pillasters framing the projecting entrance, from which stretch two equal wings, each with a steeply pitched roof with spreading eaves modelled on indigenous forms. While American architects like Parsons were searching for ways to learn from regional traditions, local architects, who were mostly educated in America in the Beaux Arts Graeco-Roman tradition at this time, were producing more orthodox designs in the same style. The **Legislative Building**, **Manila** (1918–20), and the **Manila Post Office** (1926), both by Juan Arellano, are typically overbearing buildings, each fronted by giant, double-storey colonnades, not unlike public works of the same period in Singapore. The Art Deco, **Metropolitan Theatre**, **Manila** (*c.* 1930), also by Arellano, demonstrates a lighter, more open approach, and includes an attached, two-storey group of arcaded shop-houses in the same style. Also in the same open spirit, the **Legarda Elementary School**, **Manila** (1900), by Tomas Mapua, is an elegant adaptation of the French chateau in timber, and has wide, shuttered window openings distributed beneath a steep, mansard roof.

Similar struggles for an appropriate expression characterise architecture after World War II, intensified by post-independence introspection and experimentation. They were led by two local architects, Leandro V. Locsin, and Francisco Manosa, whose different approaches encapsulate between them many of the key issues and problems which have faced post-war architects throughout South-east Asia. Of the two, Locsin's early work is characterised by an uncompromising modernity, which nevertheless also projects a uniquely personal interpretation of what may be called the 'post-colonial dilemma': the search for regional identity in a modern global culture. His best-known and most powerful work is the **Theatre for the Performing Arts** (1969) (p. 1608A), part of the **Cultural Centre of the Philippines**, **Manila**, for which he also prepared the masterplan and designed a number of other key buildings. Comprising a raised, horizontal slab and podium containing foyers and circulation spaces, fronting a taller rectangular block housing the main auditorium, the sculptured composition is dominated by the dramatic, gravity-defying foyer slab, hovering over the reflective pool below on a 12 m (39 ft) cantilever of reinforced concrete. In the **Philippine International Convention Centre** (1976), which Locsin designed as part of the same cultural complex, the architect employed an equally daring concept of 'floating' slabs, a visual effect achieved by the use of dark solar glass to conceal the concrete-framed structure, so that the heavier, visible sections seem to hang in space without any visible means of support. In his more recent work in **Brunai**, at the **Istana Nural Iman** (1984), or 'Palace of Religious Light', **Bandar Seri Begawan**, for the Sultan of Brunai, Locsin strove for a more direct expression of regional culture, with sweeping, layered roofs modelled on indigenous dwellings.

Francisco 'Bobby' Manosa has concentrated on the development of an appropriate residential architecture, occasionally stretching to hotel and resort developments. The government-sponsored **Tahanang Pilipono** (1981), or 'Coconut Palace', as it is popularly known, was designed both as a temporary residence for artists and as a showcase for the

A. Theatre for the Performing Arts, Manilla (1969). See p. 1607

B. San Miguel Building, Manilla (1984). See p. 1609

versatile uses of the coconut tree, which include 200 by-products, including a wide range of building and finishing materials. The flamboyant result, which suggests the work of a tropical Gaudí, is both a visual feast and a convincing exercise in appropriate technology. Adopting a similar but more restrained approach for his own residence, the **Filipino House, Alabang** (1982), the architect used local materials and finishes throughout. Comprising two linked, timber-framed pavilions, the larger, raised pavilion contains the living spaces, which focus onto a full-height atrium, while the bedrooms and other private spaces are gathered into the smaller pavilion. The largest, and most used area, is the open zaguan, or family space, beneath the main pavilion. Occupying the conceptual ground somewhere between Locsin's abstract compositions and Monosa's homages to tradition is the **San Miguel Building, Manila** (1984) (p. 1608B), by José Manosa. Designed in the form of a terraced ziggurat, this unusual, eight-storey office building makes effective use of well-planted overhangs on all sides to create a convincing image of a modern 'hanging garden', appropriate to a future 'tropical city'.

Chapter 56
HONG KONG

Introduction

The British Crown Colony of Hong Kong was the last addition to the Far Eastern Empire and has its origins in one of the seamier episodes in colonial history. By 1840 mounting trade disputes between Britain and the Chinese Imperial Government came to a head over opium imports into China, in which the London-based East India Company had a major and profitable share. British victory in the ensuing Opium Wars resulted in the permanent concession of Hong Kong Island in 1842, together with unlimited trading rights. The adjacent Kowloon Peninsula was ceded in 1860, giving Britain full control over the magnificent enclosed harbour.

The new colony prospered rapidly, and on 1 July 1898 the adjoining New Territories on the Chinese mainland were leased for 99 years, adding much-needed land for the expanding population. Local manufacturing industries sprang up and trade became increasingly diversified, though the Hong Kong authorities retained their monopoly over opium processing as late as the 1930s. By the time of the Japanese invasion in 1941 the population of Hong Kong had grown to 1.7 million, the vast majority of whom were Chinese migrants.

From the outset, building in the colony has been shaped by two primary factors: shortage of buildable land due to the Island's steep topography, and an explosive population growth fed by continuous migration from the troubled mainland. Initially, the main growth of the city was restricted to a narrow strip along Victoria Bay (now the Harbour), which has been steadily added to by a series of land-reclamation projects, which are still being extended. The chief local building form consisted of typical Chinese **terraced shop-houses** of two and three storeys, made of plastered Canton brick walls, timber floors, and timber roofs finished with clay tiles. Streets were narrow and poorly ventilated, over-crowding was common and water supply and sanitary conditions were rudimentary. In 1903 the British Government implemented new building and health regulations, resulting in some limited improvements in basic conditions. The Housing Commission of 1923 recommended further improvements, including land-use control, and encouraged building development on Kowloon Peninsula to take the pressure off Hong Kong Island. Few of its recommendations were implemented, however, and the situation remained unresolved until after World War II.

Examples

By contrast with the generally poor state of housing and infrastructure in the first half century, the relative high quality of major public and commercial building over the same period produced a number of works of distinction. Many of these were designed by the expatriate firm of Palmer and Turner, and it is accurate to say that the history of Hong Kong architecture over this period is largely synonymous with the history of this one practice. Founded by William Salway in 1868, the firm of architects and engineers is one of the oldest in the world. By the end of the nineteenth century they were already responsible for a number of key public buildings. As with other parts of the Empire, colonial clients generally favoured imported styles from Europe, modified to a greater or lesser extent for local needs and often freely mixed with motifs from other parts of the Empire. Notable early works included the **Chartered Bank** (1878), in Venetian Gothic style, and the elegant neo-Classical **Beaconsfield Arcade** (1880), a mixed-use structure combining a ground-floor shopping arcade with upper floors of offices set back behind slender paired columns. In 1883 the firm was joined by Clement Palmer. Arthur Turner, a structural engineer, joined the firm a year later. Palmer's first job was for the **Hongkong and Shanghai Bank** (1883), for which he provided a domed, neo-Baroque design, the first of many buildings for the same client. In 1897 Palmer crowned his career with the **Hong Kong Club**, an eclectic composition with a rustic base, superimposed orders, colonnaded attic and towers that mix Baroque and Moghal elements (p. 1611A). The building was regarded as a symbol of the colony until it was demolished in 1981, by then

A. The Hong Kong Club (1897, demolished 1981). See p. 1610

B. The Choi Hung Estate (1962). See p. 1612

C. The Hongkong & Shanghai Bank (1935). See p. 1612

D. The Supreme Court (1912). See p. 1612

overshadowed by its taller neighbours. Another notable landmark from the same era is the **Supreme Court** (1912) (p. 1611D), by the London architects Aston Webb and E. Ingress Bell. Its most distinctive features are a tall dome raised over a central attic, and a two-story shaded colonnade of Ionic columns. In 1985 it was converted for use as the Legislative Council Chambers. All the above buildings were erected close together in the heart of the city, in what was later called the **Central District**.

Palmer's retirement in 1907 brought the local fashion for Renaissance styles, which he favoured, to an end, to be replaced by more modern conceptions and materials. The post-war economic depression severely affected construction activity, however, and most of Palmer and Turner's energies during this period were concentrated in Shanghai, where conditions were more favourable (see Chapter 53). The situation changed dramatically in 1933 with their second commission for a new headquarters for the **Hongkong & Shanghai Bank** (1935) (p. 1611C). Conscious of its prestige as the premier bank in the region, the Chief Manager requested the architects to 'build the best building possible regardless of cost'. A landmark in South-east Asian architecture, the Art Deco design incorporated a number of advanced technical features. High tensile steel not previously used outside North America was used in the stone-clad frame. Its main tower, 68 m (220 ft) high, made it the tallest building of its time between Cairo and San Francisco. It was serviced by high-speed lifts, concealed panel heating and air-conditioning, all then rare in Asia. Firmly looking to the future, it even had provision on the roof for a landing pad for autogiros. Among its more conventional attractions the building included a barrel-vaulted banking hall covering more than an acre and an elaborate wall mosaic.

The Japanese occupation brought an abrupt end to Hong Kong's reviving fortunes, and no new building of consequence emerged until the 1950s. However, the most important force to shape post-war Hong Kong architecture was not a private firm of architects but a group of public authorities. By that time the growing population problem, exacerbated by a steady flood of illegal immigrants fleeing deteriorating conditions in China, was refocusing the colonial government's attention on the chronic housing situation. Up to 1953, housing had been left to private enterprises, who mostly concentrated on multi-storey tenement houses for those who could afford them. With the available housing stock filled to capacity, the rest spilled over into the increasingly numerous squatter settlements on the urban fringes in a pattern typical of most Third World cities. The disastrous squatter fire in Kowloon's Shek Kip Mei district in December of that year, which made 53,000 people homeless overnight, forced the government's hand, compelling them to take a more active role in housing provision.

The first coordinated programme of government housing focused on resettling the squatters. Space standards were minimal, and were based on 2.23 square metres per adult. The earliest form of **mass housing** consisted of six- and seven-storey concrete-framed 'H'-shaped blocks, comprising back-to-back single-room units accessed from open communal balconies. Shared toilets and washrooms were grouped in the central wing on each floor. The formation of the Hong Kong Housing Authority in 1954 to provide accommodation for middle-income families and the easing of restrictions on density to encourage more private initiatives combined to further ease the problem. However, a 1961 Census showed that over half a million households throughout the Colony were still living in wholly inadequate conditions. As a result, the Public Works Department undertook a major programme of urban redevelopment and low-cost housing, transforming Hong Kong over the next decade from a dense, low-rise city of four to five storeys to a high-rise one of over twenty storeys. The new, higher blocks were a considerable improvement on earlier models and had lifts and self-contained units with their own toilets. A few estates, like the **Choi Hung Estate** (1962) (p. 1611B), by Palmer and Turner, were commissioned from private architects to help raise design standards. Space standards, however, remained minimal and densities were as high as 8000 persons per hectare. It was apparent that redevelopment of the existing urban area alone could not meet Hong Kong's needs. Consequently, in 1972 Hong Kong embarked on a long-term development programme in the **New Territories** of nine new towns, with the aim of providing sufficient new housing and support facilities for 1.8 million people. Each, Like **Sha Tin New Town**, was to have its own character and community facilities and were connected to each other and to Hong Kong Island by a new Mass Transit Railway system. By the mid-1980s all were in various stages of development and are still growing.

Over the same period, Hong Kong's burgeoning economy and escalating land values were having their own effects in the commercial sector, resulting in a mushrooming of high-rise office and hotel building concentrated in the Central District of Hong Kong. As pioneers in the field of tall building, Palmer and Turner continued to set the pace in the early post-war years. The stone-clad **Bank of China** (1950) came first, followed by the **Chartered Bank** (1959), both of which harked back to the earlier Hong Kong & Shanghai Bank. A change in partners brought about a change in approach, however, resulting in the **Hong Kong Hilton** (1962) (p. 1615A), an 'L'-shaped tower block in the International Style covered with sunscreens and mounted on a curved podium.

Increasing competition from both local and foreign architects in the 1970s and 1980s have since overshadowed Palmer and Turner's remarkable achievements, though they remain one of the largest and

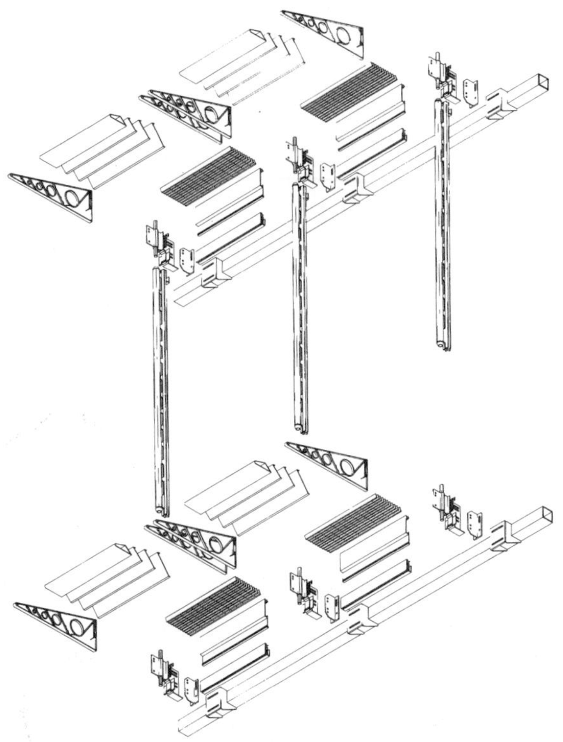

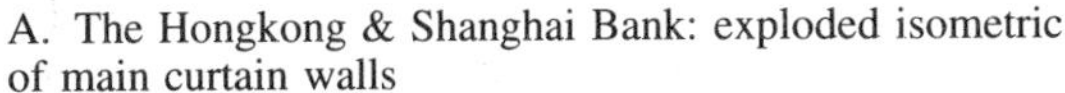

A. The Hongkong & Shanghai Bank: exploded isometric of main curtain walls

B. The Hongkong & Shanghai Bank (1986). See p. 1616

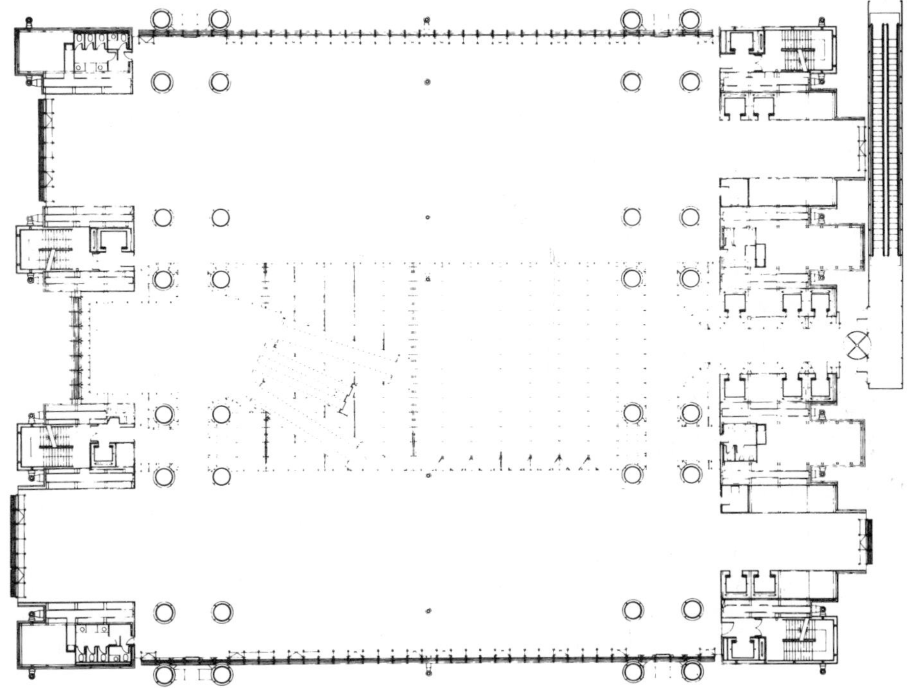

C. The Hongkong & Shanghai Bank: first-floor banking hall

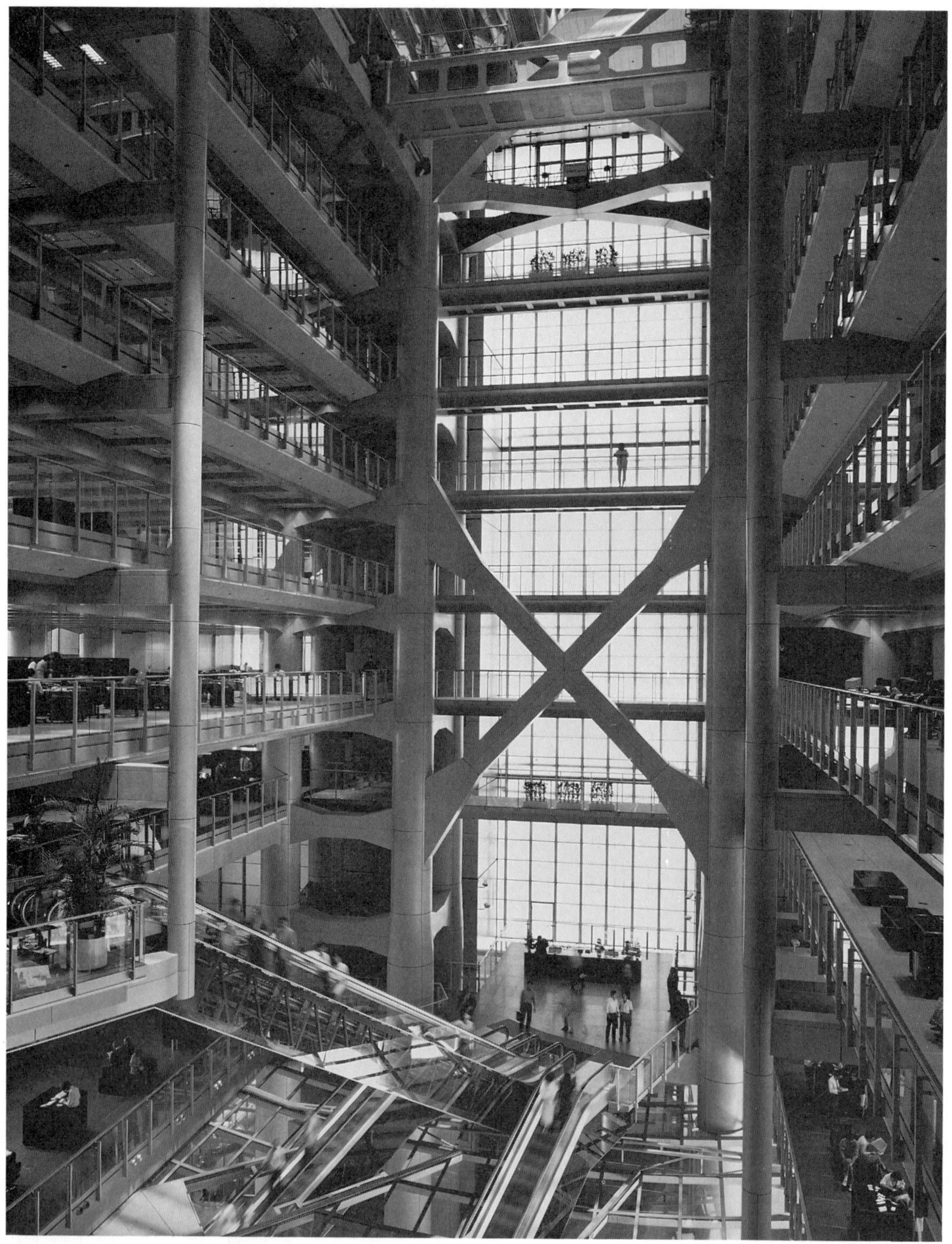

The Hongkong & Shanghai Bank: interior. See p. 1616

A. The Hong Kong Hilton (1962). See p. 1612

C. The Lippo Centre (1988). See p. 1616

B. The Bank of China Tower (1990). See p. 1616

busiest firms in the region. In 1979 they lost out to the British architect Sir Norman Foster in a limited competition for a new headquarters for the **Hongkong & Shanghai Bank** (pp. 1613A–C, 1614), thus finally ending a most enduring and fruitful architect–client relationship.

The tradition continued in other ways, however, and the Bank's new management were no less demanding of their new architects than of their predecessors. Completed in 1986, the new headquarters, which occupies the same site as its predecessors, represents the cutting edge of architectural design and technology, much of which is borrowed from other advanced construction industries. Noteworthy 'technology transfers' include: a suspended steel floor structure inspired by bridge-building techniques to provide maximum usable space and flexibility; aluminium cladding made by industrial robots; removable floor panels made of a lightweight aluminium sandwich construction similar to the floor panels in Boeing aircraft; moving escalators between intermediate floors, and not least, a rotating, computer-controlled 'sunscoop' beaming natural daylight straight into an eight-storey atrium (p. 1614). Despite the international nature of the technologies employed, the design for the Bank also achieves a convincing regional expression, most of all in its exaggerated expressed structure and transparent spatial qualities, both typical of East Asian traditions.

The Hongkong & Shanghai Bank provides a potent symbol for an Asian-Pacific resurgence to bolster local confidence, which has undergone a series of setbacks. On 19 December 1984 the British government concluded an agreement with the Peking (Beijing) government to hand back the New Territories on expiry of the lease in 1997, together with Hong Kong Island, which would hardly be viable as a state on its own. Economic liberalisation within China, though potentially positive, added to the general climate of political and economic uncertainty. Confidence has slowly returned, however, as the business community observed the growing effects of the Chinese reforms and began to take advantage of them.

The late 1980s and early 1990s saw a surge in investment in new building and infrastructure as the population learnt to live with the idea of a future coupled to mainland China. The **Lippo Centre** (1988) (p. 1615C), by Paul Rudolph, in the **Central District**, is a notable landmark for its twin octagonal towers and faceted glass walls. The dominant new structure in the area, however, is I. M. Pei's 70-storey **Bank of China Tower** (1990) (p. 1615B). The asymmetrical geometry and visible cross-bracing provides an original and effective solution to the hurricane-force wind loads the structure has to cope with, as well as a striking profile fit to match the natural backdrop of The Peak mountain. The latest tower to break the Hong Kong skyline is **Central Plaza, Wanchai** (1992), designed by the local firm of Ng Chun Man and Associates. At 374 m (1215 ft) it is the second-tallest building in Asia. With its decorative glazed facade, colonnaded podium and pyramidal top, reminiscent of the Empire State Building, it presents a relatively conservative image in the Post-Modern manner of current American high-rise architecture. The medium-rise **Hong Kong University of Science and Technology** (1992), by Simon Kwan, overlooking **Port Shelter**, is built on a similar impressive scale, and is virtually a small city by itself. Composed of three basic geometries, semi-circle, square and triangle, the style and skilful site planning bear strong resemblances to the work of the America architect Richard Meier. Among Palmer and Turner's work, the **Hong Kong Science Museum** (1990) (p. 1617A), **Tsimshatsui**, stands out as an exuberant display of form in the contemporary Japanese manner. Other major current building and infrastructure projects include **new rail stations**, at **Kowloon**, for both the MRT and the main line railway into China, by Terry Farrell and Sir Norman Foster respectively, and Foster's **Passenger Terminal** at **Chek Lap Kok**, Hong Kong's new airport. Farrell's project includes a large-scale commercial development above and below ground and all projects express their functions with graceful examples of modern architectural engineering. The closing of the existing airport in Kowloon in 1997 on completion of Chek Lap Kok will also release a vast tract of land for **redevelopment** in **Kowloon Peninsula**, which will eventually provide much-needed open green space for the crowded city.

Both Ng Chun Man's Central Plaza and Simon Kwan's University demonstrate the increasing professional success of ethnic Chinese architects in Hong Kong, and also the general tendency to imitate Western fashions. It might be argued that this is reflective of the colonial history of Hong Kong in itself, but post-colonial developments elsewhere (see Chapter 55) suggest that this may only be a temporary condition, and that the ending of British ties may encourage Hong Kong architects to look for alternative sources of inspiration closer to home. A few architects have already taken significant steps in this direction. As a founding member of Asia Planning and Architectural Collaboration (APAC), a regional thinktank, Tao Ho has been a leading exponent of Asian Modernism since the late 1960s. His **Hong Kong Arts Centre, Wanchai** (1977), was specifically created to encourage interaction between Eastern and Western art forms and is influenced by both Western and Japanese Modern Movements. Since then, his practice has been actively exploring the possibilities for a regional architecture, both in Hong Kong and in China. Chung Wah Nan has taken a traditional approach to the same problem, and in keeping with the basic function of columbarium – a peaceful place for remembrance – has modelled the **Bo Fu Ancestral Worship Hall** (1985), **Shatin**, on

A. The Hong Kong Science Museum (1990). See p. 1616

B. The Environmental Friendly Housing Development, Tseung Kwan O: model. See p. 1618

C. The Upper Peak Tram Terminus: model. See p. 1618

the Chinese Tang/Song style. Working in an equally sensitive but more abstract fashion, Rocco Yim has carefully tailored his **youth hostel** (1988) to its natural site on **Tai Mo Shan**, Hong Kong's tallest mountain. In the same vein, his 29-unit residential development at **Belleview Place** (1988), seems to rise straight out of its steep site on the rocky slopes above **Repulse Bay**. On a larger scale, his slender, cruciform design for the **Tregunter Tower C,** situated mid-way up **The Peak**, is an elegant solution to high-rise residential architecture, and maximises both views and natural ventilation. Looking into the near future, Anthony Ng's project for the **Environmental Friendly Housing Development, Tseung Kwan O** (p. 1617B), due for completion in 1997, promises, as its name implies, to be Hong Kong's most advanced exercise yet in regional high-rise housing design. In addition to its distinctive stepped profile, which echoes that of the surrounding mountains, the project incorporates a number of 'green' features, such as planted screen walls, an integrated 'cooling strategy' combining natural ventilation and other measures, solar water heating, and wind turbines powering water features and outdoor lighting.

All these architects are currently heavily engaged with new projects in China, which can be expected to have reciprocal effects in time on their work in Hong Kong. Paradoxically, the most recent project to express regional aspirations is Terry Farrell's striking design for the **Upper Peak Tram Terminus** (p. 1617C), now under construction. Situated high on the crest of The Peak, its main feature is a curved 'Bowl' containing restaurants and other public spaces, suspended over a solid podium. Reminiscent of traditional Chinese architecture, the dramatic silhouette provides a powerful symbol of Hong Kong's future orientation.

Chapter 57
INDIAN SUBCONTINENT

Introduction

The nations of India, Pakistan, Nepal, Sri Lanka and Bangladesh share similar economic and environmental conditions, and similar historic and folk traditions; together they possess a distinct architectural identity. By the turn of the century, allegiance to European influences of the eighteenth and nineteenth centuries had created a common colonial tradition. The later post-independence work that emerged in the twentieth century drew on many sources including Post-colonialism, Modernism, the International Style, regionalism, and the local vernacular tradition.

For most regions of South Asia the century began under colonial rule. The influences of imperialism were reflected in the architecture of the imperial capital at Delhi, the Residencies, the numerous public and administrative buildings, the domestic architecture of bungalows, and the development of an Indo-Saracenic style. After independence, this region began to draw on the idea of linguistic and cultural identity to redefine the sovereign state. Emerging from a colonial past, it became necessary for it to construct emblems that conspicuously suggested its new status. The invitations to Le Corbusier and Louis Kahn to create new architectural symbols for a nascent nationalism shaped much of the architecture of the early Post-independence period.

Indian Prime Minister Jawaharlal Nehru's allegiance to the Western industrial model made India's future development dependent upon a universal technology. Chandigarh, like the Bhakra Nangal Dam or the Rourkela Steel Plant, was consistent with the nation's dedication to change. The new 'temples of the twentieth century' – the industries, housing, public institutions – were all built by the public sector, under single bureaucratic control. In such a grand national enterprise, architecture assumed a secondary position. According to democratic socialism, it was more important to create buildings that set common standards and conformed to an established norm than to foster individual expression. Even the development of towns was intrinsically related to their value as models of development, Alongside the citadels of government, the symbolic centres of power, created equally powerful symbols of industry and progress. The steel town of Jamshedpur, the railway town of Chittaranjan, the company town of Modinager existed to make explicit the messages of their peculiar purpose; central to the theme of nation building were ideas on business enterprise and economic development.

Whether the subcontinent's Modernism captured much of the credo and optimism of its European source is difficult to say. The mixed heritage of colonialism and the European Modernism of Le Corbusier were not broad enough in scope or design to fully express the aspirations of countries independently emerging with their own localised forms of nationalism – a nationalism tainted by poverty and unemployment.

Rapidly increasing populations, the growth of urban centres, chronic unemployment, marginalised economies and unstable political situations have, during the last 50 years, created a new set of priorities cutting across national boundaries. Increasing urbanisation has necessitated large, designed commercial zones within the uncontrolled sprawl of the city; expanding industry has created burgeoning facilities for commerce and trading; growing pressure on urban land has congested city centres, and led to commercial enterprises that have given a new scale to public space and urban architecture. The governments of the subcontinent's various countries have, in line with twentieth-century aspirations, taken responsibility for the provision of schools, universities, offices and infrastructure.

Yet, in the background of the Modernism of the 1950s and 1960s, a vernacular imagery has persisted, a regional industrial ideal. The autonomy of regions and locales, the more pressing needs of clients intent on individual expression, now manifest themselves in forms and materials that speak of a more localised identity. The growing awareness of the necessity for people's involvement in building has also contributed to the integration of local ideals into the professional processes of design and construction.

The Colonial Presence

At the beginning of the century, after almost 300 years of British rule on the Indian subcontinent, imperial rulers felt compelled to commemorate the empire in stone. The idea for a **Memorial to Queen Victoria, Calcutta** (1906–21) (p. 1621A) by William Emerson (1843–1924) came to Lord Curzon who decreed that, as a grand gesture of their gratitude, the Indian princely states would contribute the funds for its construction. Built on a high plinth at the edge of the Maidan, a vast central city space, the building served its monumental purpose well. The central feature of the plan, a huge chamber containing a marble bust of the Empress, is surmounted by a lofty dome.

With the British government's decision in 1911 to shift the capital to Delhi, the **Viceroy's House (now the Rashtrapati Bhavan), Central Vista, Delhi** (1912–1930) (pp. 1621B, 1622B), by Sir Edwin Lutyens (1869–1944) was designed as a grand civic gesture, indicating its imperial intent in the raised location on Raisina hill. The **Central Secretariat** (p. 1623A) and the nearby circular **Parliament House, Delhi** (1930), by Sir Herbert Baker (1862–1946) were both designed alongside to reinforce the axiality of the 2 km tree-lined **Central Vista** (p. 1622A). The Viceroy's House represents a subtle synthesis of indigenous motifs and forms with European Classical traditions, and the successful fusion gives the building an architectural significance that transcends its initial role as an imperial monument. The same fusion of forms are found inside the Viceroy's House. The focus of the main floor is the Durbar, or Coronation Hall, located under the central dome and surrounded by a number of state apartments adjacent to the three main drawing rooms. The building also houses the state dining room, ballrooms and numerous guest suites. Opposing the Viceroy's House, at the other end of the Central Vista, is the commemorative arch of the **All-India War Memorial (India Gate)** (completed 1931) (p. 1623C) and the **King George V Memorial** (both by Lutyens).

The main axis of the New Delhi plan, the Central Vista, is bisected by a main cross axis and, in the Baroque tradition, these major axes form the framework for a matrix of diagonal roads of lesser scale which radiate from circuses and octagons of various scales and importance. Different types and scales of housing are segregated into separate quarters and non-residential uses are generally confined to the north-eastern portion of the plan which adjoins Old Delhi. Important buildings and points of historical interest in the old city – for example, the Red Fort – are linked visually to the key buildings in New Delhi by diagonal vistas. The plan was evolved by a Town Planning Committee established in 1912 whose members included John Brodie, the City Engineer of Liverpool and Sir Edwin Lutyens as architectural adviser with Henry Lanchester as consultant.

The large green in front of Lutyens' India Gate is ringed by an octagonal roadway. The four major junctions of the octagon are occupied by princely houses, all designed by Lutyens with central dome and flanking wings. The common butterfly plan was partly the outcome of the urban sequence. Of the four, **Baroda House** (1920) and **Hyderabad House** (*c.* 1920) (p. 1623D) are the most noteworthy.

Robert Tor Russell (1888–1972), Chief Architect to the Government of India, working in the shadow of Lutyens, aligned his buildings to respect the wishes of the master planner. The 335 m (1090 ft) diameter circus, that constitutes **Connaught Place, Delhi** (1928–31) (p. 1623B), by R. T. Russell and W. H. Nicholls , with its concentric colonades links New Delhi, with radial axes, to the more informal plan of Old Delhi. Russell also designed the **Flagstaff House (Teen Murti), Delhi**, (1930) (p. 1624A), the residence of the Commander-in-Chief. One of the finest domestic buildings of the period in India, it was to become the prototype for large bungalows throughout the country.

New Delhi contains a rewarding mixture of lesser government and domestic buildings, mostly designed in a simple Classical manner responsive to climate and the traditions of tropical design. Thus verandahs, deep porches and high-level and aligned windows for cross-ventilation become dominant motifs, rendered in classical form and detail. A notable example is the **middle-category housing in Ferozshah Road, New Delhi** (*c.* 1925) (p. 1624B) by W.H. Nicholls. Delhi also possesses one of the most remarkable churches of the twentieth century – **S. Martin's Garrison Church** (1928–30) (p. 1624C) by A. G. Shoosmith is a monumental, cubical brick-built composition of immense, elemental power and presence. Other important churches which flank the urban sequences in New Delhi are the semi-Palladian, Lutyenesque **Cathedral Church of Redemption** (began 1928), and the **Catholic Church of the Sacred Heart** (1934) (p. 1624D), both by Henry Medd (1892–1977).

Among the colonial architects practising in Bombay, George Wittet demonstrates a stylistically more wilful appreciation of Indian architecture than his Delhi counterparts. **The Prince of Wales Museum, Bombay** (1905), mixes elements from both the Indian and European traditions, and Hindu brackets and Moghul arches are combined in a plan of classical symmetry. But unlike much of the city's delicate nineteenth-century Gothic architecture, of which F. W. Steven's Victoria Terminus (q.v.) and the City Town Hall are prime examples, Whittet's facade is of an unrelenting monumentality. He later adapted a similar design of the **Gateway of India, Bombay** (completed 1927), the commemorative arch built to mark the visit of King George V to India in 1911. A strange blend of sixteenth-century ornament, detail

A. Memorial to Queen Victoria, Calcutta (1906–21). See p. 1620

B. Viceroy's House (Rashtrapati Bhavan), Delhi (1912–30). See p. 1620

A. The Viceroy's house and Central Secretariat Buildings, Delhi (1912–30). See p. 1620

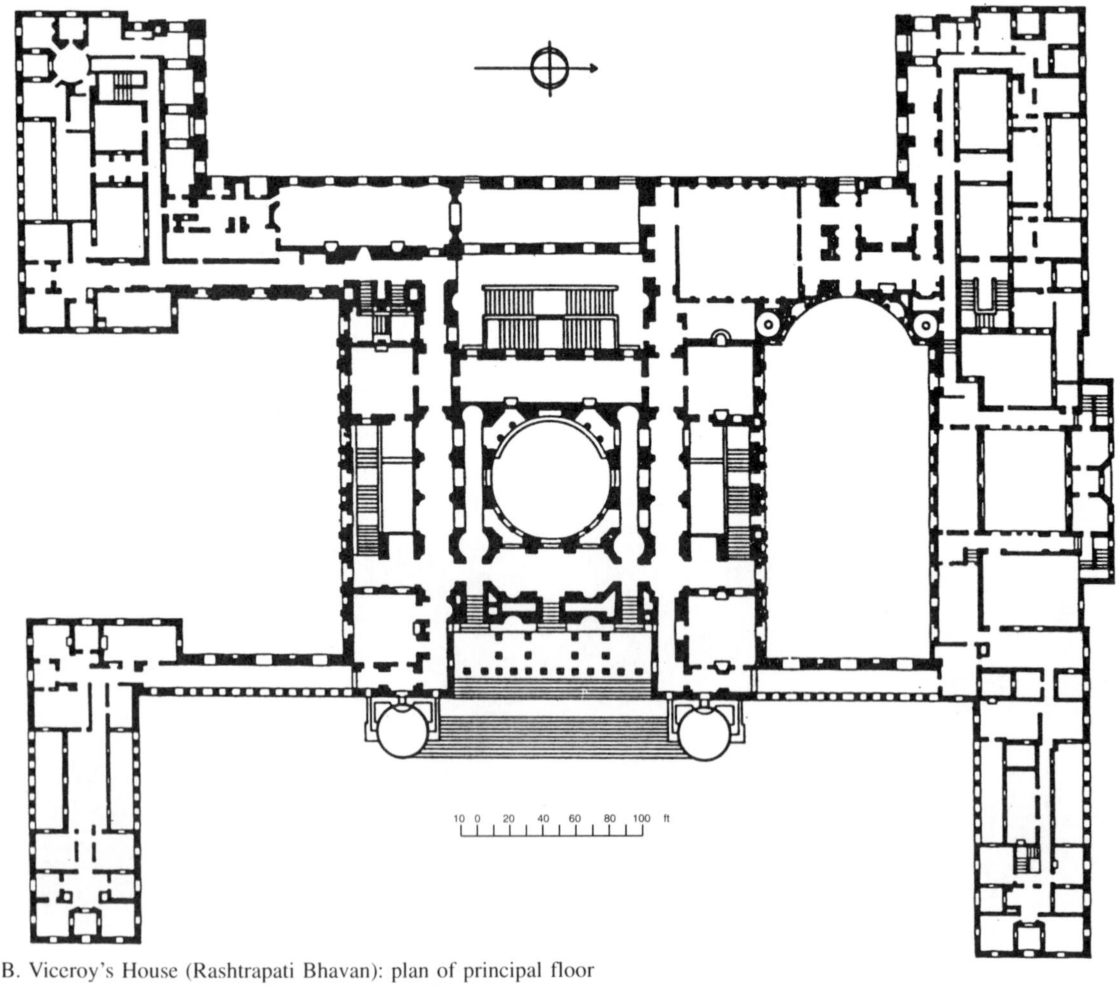

10 0 20 40 60 80 100 ft

B. Viceroy's House (Rashtrapati Bhavan): plan of principal floor

A. Central Secretariat, Delhi (completed 1930). See p. 1620

B. Connaught Place, Delhi (1928–31). See p. 1620

C. All India War Memorial (India Gate) (completed 1931). See p. 1620

D. Hyderabad House, Delhi (*c.*1920). See p. 1620

A. Flagstaff House, Delhi (1930). See p. 1620

B. Middle-category housing, New Delhi (*c.* 1925). See p. 1620

C. S. Martin's Garrison Church, New Delhi (1928–30). See p. 1620

D. Catholic Church of the Sacred Heart, New Delhi (1934). See p. 1620

and planning, the triple arch resembles a provincial city gate, the prominent central arch framed in engaged turrets, the lesser arches infilled with a delicate stone lattice. This Indo-Saracenic hybrid presented a convenient medium by which to establish a new colonial presence in an alien land. The **Taj Mahal Hotel, Bombay** (1903), by W. Chambers was built alongside it, adjacent to the Yacht Club in 1903. The hotel's seven-storey waterside elevation presents a great profusion of classical and Gujarati elements.

Outside the main cities, major twentieth-century colonial architecture can be found in **Lucknow**, notably Henry V. Lanchester's (1863–1953) **Council Chamber** (1928) and the **Post and Telegraph Building** (with Rodeck) (1931–2). Lanchester also designed the **Umaid Bhawan Palace**, **Jodhpur** (1929–44), which is his best work in India. Also impressive is the **Lalitha Mahal Palace, Mysore** (1930), by E. W. Fritchley which is a loose and elongated essay upon S. Paul's Cathedral, London.

If the colonial period had one major overriding influence on the country's post-independence architecture, it was in the setting up of the 'Public Works Department'. The PWD was designated the awesome task of providing the architectural and engineering infrastructure that would make administering such a vast country possible. From the long span of **Howrah Bridge**, **Calcutta** (1943), by Hubert Shirley-Smith and one of the PWD's most ambitious engineering endeavours is visible the **Howrah Station** (1900–08) by Halsey Ricardo (1854–1928), a great, sprawling Romanesque-cum-Moorish pile of brick, whose facade flanks the river. Its symbolic importance, however, cannot be over-emphasised, for the building was a persistent reminder of imperialism's physical spread, its vast road and rail network stretching across the country from this first railhead.

Modernism and India

After independence from British rule in 1947, Jawaharlal Nehru's government initiated the construction of **Chandigarh**, the new state capital of the Punjab. The master plan (1950), by Le Corbusier, envisaged a grid-iron city plan which reflects the key principles of Modernist town planning enshrined in the CIAM 'Charter of Athens' of 1933. Le Corbusier also designed the major administrative buildings . The combination of Modernist monuments and city plan was a turning point in the development of post-independence Indian modern architecture. If Chandigarh symbolised a certain detachment from India, it was intentional and indeed desirable. Democracy had finally come to India, and Chandigarh, according to Nehru, was to give it physical expression.

Le Corbusier's **Capital Complex buildings**, the **Assembly** (1955–60) (p. 1626A), the **High Court** (1952–6) (p. 1627A), and the **Secretariat** (1952–6) (p. 1626B) have an interrelated but separate presence in the heart of the city, against the monumental backdrop of the Himalayas. **Neighbourhood Sectors** were designed by Maxwell Fry and Jane Drew. Realising the new architecture in reinforced concrete, Le Corbusier borrowed certain sculptural forms and cultural and climatic elements from the Indian tradition. Although the shapes of screen walls and pergolas were changed to suit his own exposed concrete aesthetic, their incorporation into Modernist forms began to influence the architects of the independent nation. Pierre Jeanneret was responsible for the execution of Le Corbusier's projects at Chandigarh and for the design of numerous minor buildings in the new capital – all of which display a great empathy with indigenous design and building traditions; for example, the mix of building types in **Peon village** including housing (1952–3), and **Gandhi Bhavan** (1959–61).

Besides the Capital Commissions at Chandigarh Corbusier also designed the **Mill Owners Association Building**, **Ahmedabad** (1953–6) (p. 1627B), and two important residences, the **Shodan Villa** (1953–6) and the **Sarabhai Villa** (1953–6), both of which used pivoted doors and parallel walls as a measure of integration with the surrounding landscape.

After partition, the University Senate decided to commission an integrated campus for the **Punjab University** (previously situated in Lahore) in the newly planned city of Chandigarh. Though the first master plan was prepared by J. K. Chowdhury (born 1918), who subsequently designed its **Chemical Engineering and Technology blocks**, the campus plan was revised in 1958 by Pierre Jeanneret (1896–1967) and Bhanu Mathur, who designed and supervised the execution of the campus.

The campus is situated at the north-east end of Chandigarh adjoining the **Post Graduate Institute of Medical Research**, the **Punjab Engineering College**, and the **College of Architecture**, which together constitute the educational belt of the city. The plan comprises an academic complex built around an inner core consisting of the **Library, Student Centre, Fine Arts Museum** and the **Gandhi Bhavan**. The main teaching facility of the **Engineering College** (1950–53) designed by architect J. K. Chowdhury is a three-storeyed rectangle connected vertically by free-standing staircases and projecting the individual laboratories beyond its ground-floor face. In layout it typifies many of the institutions being built in the country at the time on rectangular grid plans across flat – often undistinguished – terrain, and connected by covered walkways.

The commission for the **Haryana Agricultural University, Hissar** (1970–77), also went to Chowdhury when an improved farming technology was considered imperative to the national economy. Museums, workshops, exhibition halls, and lecture

A. The Assembly, Chandigarh (1955–60). See p. 1625

B. The Secretariat, Chandigarh (1952–6). See p. 1625

A. The High Court, Chandigarh (1952–6). See p. 1625

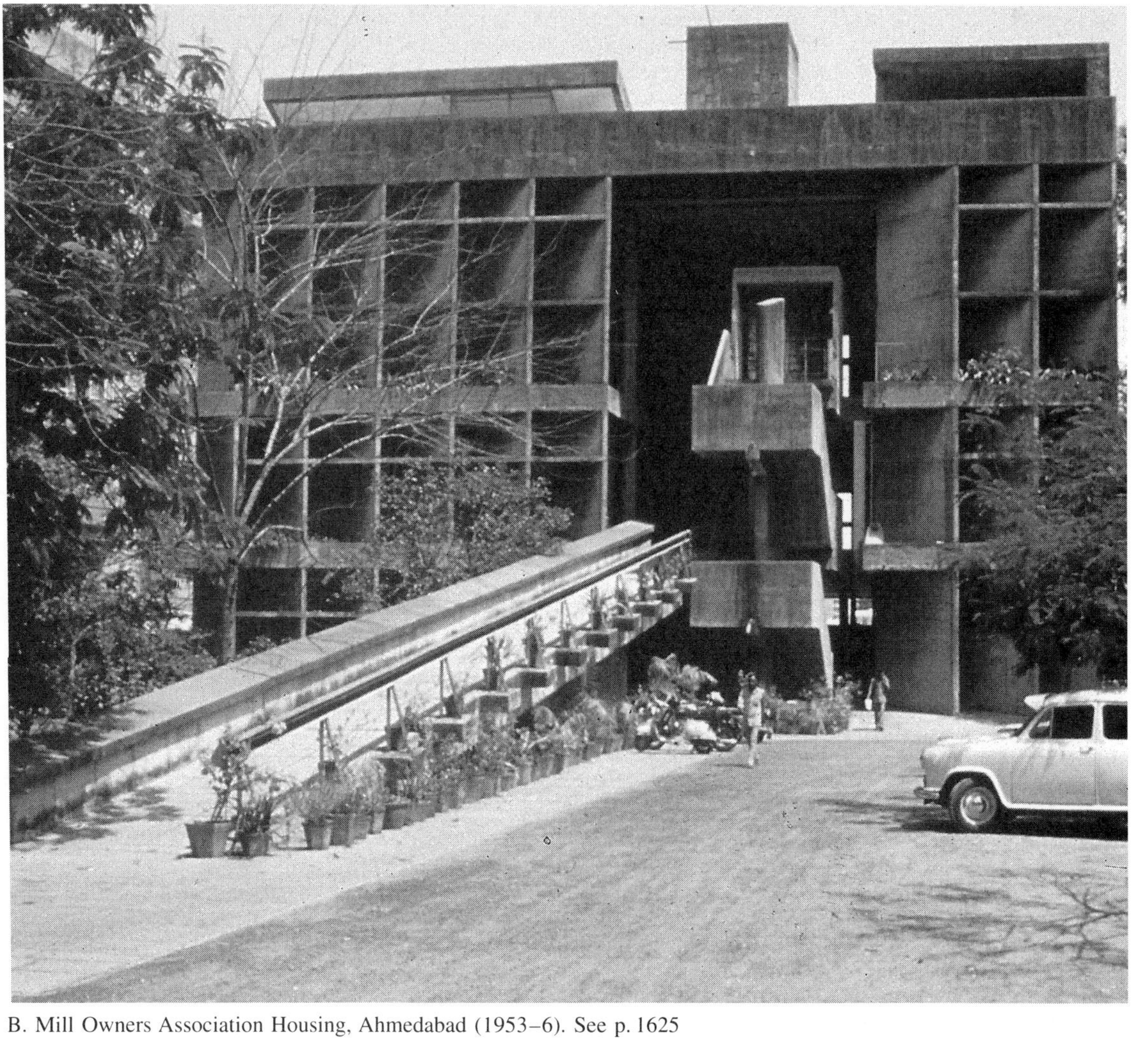

B. Mill Owners Association Housing, Ahmedabad (1953–6). See p. 1625

theatres create a setting conducive to an exchange of ideas between urban teacher and rural benefactor, and vice versa. Likewise, the Punjab Government's Compulsory Education Scheme created a sudden demand for school facilities. The **Higher Secondary School, Chandigarh** (1959–60), by Jeet Malhotra (born 1929), a linear, exposed brick building with corbelled openings, was one of the 14 schools built under the programme.

One of the more memorable buildings on the campus is the **Fine Arts Museum**, **Punjab University, Chandigarh** (1969), by Bhanu Mathur, a sandstone-faced cubical building, one of the earliest expressions of the minimalist modern tradition in India. Interconnected square rooms around a central court ensure uninterrupted movement around the exhibits. Such spatial variation was originally conceived by Charles Correa (born 1930) at the **Gandhi Smarak Sangrahalaya, Sabarmati Ashram, Ahmedabad** (1958–63). The building, modularly conceived as a series of open pavilions on a continuous grid of brick piers, is topped by concrete-supported terracotta tile roofs. Architectural elements punctuate the sequence of exhibits on Mahatma Gandhi.

In addition to the buildings inspired by Le Corbusier there are, throughout India, buildings constructed during the 1940s and 1950s that reveal the versitility of Modernism when executed with sensitivity to the demands of different climates and cultures. Notable examples include the **Golconde House** (1936–48), **Aurobindo Ashram, Pondicherry**, by Antonin Raymond, and the **TB Association Building**, Delhi (1950–52), by Walter George.

The early effects of the International style were apparent in the pioneering works of architects such as Habib Rahman, (born 1916) whose distinctive architectural imprint could be felt even in the highly bureaucratised environment of the PWD in the 1950s and 1960s, and A. P. Kanvinde (born 1916), who had studied under Walter Gropius.

Rahman, as senior architect with the central public works department, designed public buildings, memorials and housing across India, including the fourteen-storey **New Secretariat, Calcutta** (1949–54) (p. 1629A), at the time of its construction one of the earliest high-rises in the city. His exhibition building for the **Rabindra Bhavan, Delhi** (1959–61) (p. 1629B), has a stretched pentagonal plan following the curve of the traffic circle. The exhibition galleries have windows, shielded by 'jalis', to provide a glare-free light for the interiors.

Since its establishment in the 1960s, the government-owned firm, PEPAC (Pakistan Environmental Planning and Architectural Consultants), has controlled some of the major public commissions in Pakistan. PEPAC's high standards of design and construction are visible in the **Frontier House, Islamabad**, several urban cinema halls, and other structures built by the HHBFC (Housing and House Building Finance Corporation) in Islamabad. While the government has maintained a rigorous control over major public commissions, several foreign-trained Pakistani architects in the past two decades have left a creditable legacy of privately financed works. Notable among the projects are **House for Commodore Haq, Karachi**, by Yasmeen Lari, **Workers' Housing, Kot**, and the **Al Hamra Arts Council Building**, **Lahore**, by Kamal Khan Mumtaz. In the **Rivaz Garden Flats, Lahore**, and the **Shakir Ali Auditorium**, **Lahore**, Nayyar Ali Data uses concrete and brick in a restrained yet dramatic way, in simple planes combined with precast jalis.

Unlike India and Pakistan, Sri Lanka remained unaffected in the early years of independence by the growth and resurgence of Modernism on the subcontinent. While architecture in other countries in the region were influenced by the growing industrial activity and the dominating presence of Le Corbusier and later by the ideas of Louis Kahn (1901–74), Sri Lankan public architecture developed an intrinsically traditional vocabulary.

British colonial legacies in Sri Lanka, **Torrington House** (1915) and the **New Town Hall** (1927), both in **Colombo**, remain symbolic presences. After independence, an increased national awareness appeared in buildings that exemplified local tradition, specifically in the **Independence Commemoration Monument** (1953) by Wynn Jones which is capped with a hipped Kandyan roof. Similar examples of the period, incorporating Sri Lankan roof features, are the **Peradeniya University** (1931) by Shirely de Alwis.

Minnette de Silva's work in the 1950s and 1960s accepted the growing presence of a Modernist idiom and sought newer architectural applications. Her early houses include the **Split Level House, Kandy** (1951), the **Senanayake Flats** (1954), each with carport and roof garden, and the **Peiris House** (1953), a structure assembled under a floating slab of concrete. Only in her later work did something of the local island tradition intervene. **The Sigiriya Tourist Complex** (1970) is composed of cottages with mud walls, while the **Second Peiris House** (1965) is organised around a traditional courtyard.

Though most Indian architects embraced the readily available vocabulary of Modernism, adaptation of the style to local conditions became necessary. A case in point is C. S. H. Jhabvala's (born 1920) design for **Kirorimal College, Delhi University** (1954), which is rambling and elongated in response to the shape of the pre-existing excavation for brick clay which characterised the site.

Buildings on sites contained within boundary walls – a characteristic of the academic complexes conceived in the 1950s and 1960s – generally had architectural programmes unrelated to their surroundings. The **Guru Nanak University**, **Amritsar** (1970–78) (p. 1629C), by Jasbir and Rosemary Sachdev forms the focus of the campus with other

A. New Secretariat, Calcutta (1949–54). See p. 1628

B. Rabindra Bhavan, Delhi (1959–61). See p. 1628

C. Guru Nanak University, Amritsar (1970–78). See p. 1628

D. Indira Gandhi Stadium, Delhi (1980–82). See p. 1631

A. Premabhai Hall, Ahmedabad (1956–72). See p. 1631

B. Nehru Pavilion, Delhi (1971–2). See p. 1631

C. Hindustan Motors Factory, Hosur (1975). See p. 1632

buildings located on the four corners of the rectangle. With a more dispersed layout, the **Jawaharlal Nehru University's** campus plan, by C. P. Kukreja (born 1938), was developed on a even larger scale along arterial roads. In the master plan, the academic complex comprises the nucleus of the campus. It is situated on a large, central, undulating plateau, overlooking a disused quarry.

Several buildings specific to education, but independent of the campus plan, have emerged in response to specialised artistic and scientific imperatives. The **School of Architecture, Navrangpura, Ahmedabad** (1966–8), by B. V. Doshi (born 1927), includes facilities for fine arts, exhibitions and library and is accommodated between parallel walls of exposed brick oriented north–south to reduce sunlight and create natural breezeways. Achyut Kanvinde's design for the **Nehru Science Centre, Bombay** (1976–80), also evolved out of standardised units of structure and space which, used in varying configurations, created variety within the complex. It is an idea that Charles Correa explores in two of his projects, both housing distinctly different functions.

At the **Bharat Bhawan, Bhopal** (1975–81), by Charles Correa, the facilities are housed within a landscape of courts and terraces whose layout invites exploration. Correa chose similarly to create his own sequences and methods for defining religious progression in the **Salvacao Church, Bombay** (1974–7). Here sequences of light and shadow, one of the primary considerations in church design, are used in a series of interconnected courts and rooms, drawing the visitor to the darker epicentre of the church sanctum. In both buildings the elemental qualities of space and light are reinforced by the rough-cut stone, exposed concrete surfaces, beams and concrete shells.

Many of the commercial buildings of post-Lutyens New Delhi were built not only to assert an independence from the colonial tradition but also to make effective structural statements that set them apart aesthetically. The primary consideration of 'structuralism' was the expression of the buildings' engineering framework as the only form of ornament. The curving 18-storey concrete tower of the **New Delhi Civic Centre, Sansad Marg, Delhi** (1956–83), by Kuldip Singh (born 1934), along with some of its neighbours, such as the **LIC Centre** (1975–88) by Correa, and the **DLF Centre** (1990) by Ranjit Sabhiki (born 1935) has redrawn the skyline of the central business district of the city. These more recent landmarks with their marble and granite floors, their pillared hallways and their reflecting glass curtain walls, stand out in isolation as towering citadels of commerce

The tendency to 'structuralism' was unabated in the 1970s, being most pronounced in public halls and exhibition buildings. Two major works at the time, the **Hall of Nations, Delhi** (1972), by Raj Rewal (born 1934) and the **Sher-e-Kashmir Stadium, Srinagar** (1984), by Kanvinde, Rai and Chowdhury, demonstrate construction methods for an innovative concrete space frame. The two buildings look similar, but the Srinagar stadium is a single-layered truss, while the Rewal building is an *in situ* concrete frame.

A number of other noteworthy stadia were built during the 1982 Asiad at Delhi. Among these are Jasbir and Rosemary Sachdev's **Weight-lifting Arena, Siri Fort** and Satish Grover's (born 1940) roofless **Swimming Stadium, Talkatora** (1979–82). Structurally, the most impressive was the 25,000 capacity **Indira Gandhi Indoor Stadium, Inderprastha, Delhi** (1980–82) (p. 1629D), by Sharat Das, with its periphery of eight concrete pylons supporting a latticed steel girder roof with a central clerestory dome. The eight slip-form pylons of pre-stressed concrete also contain the services and staircases for the building. Though the building asserts its monumental presence along the river Jamuna, a more conscious and studied urban response is B. V. Doshi's **Premabhai Hall, Teen Darwaza, Ahmedabad** (1956–72) (p. 1630A). Embracing the street with its extensive upper cantilever, the structure complements the historic city gate nearby.

While architecture has traditionally not shaped the growth of urban commerce in the major metropolises, in the last two decades municipal authorities have been propelled into earmarking city land for planned office complexes. The **Nehru Place District Centre, Delhi** (1975), by Rattan Singh and V. V. Bodas, was one of the first commercial complexes to be conceived and built in Delhi on a grand scale. It envisaged 98 multi-storeyed blocks of shops-cum-offices with recreational facilities, cinema sites, hotels and a cultural complex with open-air theatres, museums, libraries and art galleries.

In India, commemorating a public figure has often produced monuments that relied on the notion of deification. The **Mahatma Gandhi Smarak, Rajghat, Delhi** (1956), by Vanu Buta (born 1922) projects the honesty and simplicity of Gandhi's life in its elemental geometry. A ramped entrance, an enclosing court and a square memorial slab are symbolic of the life and death of Mahatma Gandhi. Subtle changes in elevation and the open enclosure containing a granite slab create a prayerful mood. Raj Rewal achieves a similar reverse monumentality at the **Nehru Pavilion, Pragati Maidan, Delhi** (1971–2) (p. 1630B), in a two-storey structure buried under a grassy embankment conceived internally as a traditional temple ambulatory.

Industrial Building

Corporate architecture is relatively new to India; only in recent years have companies become aware of the need for an architectural image to project and promote their corporate ideals. For the **United Breweries Headquarters, Bangalore** (1979), Romi Khosla (born 1941) inserted all administrative functions within a four-storey, fully glazed core building with a detached octagonal outer shell as a novel means of environmental control. Traditional sun shields, developed as design features, inspired the projecting concrete lattice frame at the **Hindustan Motors Factory, Hosur, Tamil Nadu** (1975), by Chandavarkar (born 1928) and Thackar (born 1923) (p. 1630C). Two recent large-scale projects, though dissimilar in design, display internal structural relationships that would not be possible in smaller complexes or individual structures. One is the **Bharat Diamond Bourse** by B. V. Doshi which, on the scale of a small township, brings most of the activities of the diamond trade under one roof. The other on a similarly grand scale is the integrated campus plan for the **Jawaharlal Nehru Naval Academy, Ezhimala**, by Satnam, Namita & Associates which follows the natural contours of the land on a 2300-acre site along a Western Ghats peninsula. Both these projects were due to begin on-site in 1995.

Religious Symbolism

Ecclesiastical architecture in India has maintained a distinctive cultural identity. Largely unaffected by industrialisation, the stylistic nuances and symbols peculiar to Christian, Sikh, Hindu, Muslim or Jain beliefs still persist. Contemporary use of traditional religious symbols, however, goes hand in hand with the mix of styles and of traditional and modern materials and methods of construction. The **Dakshin Delhi Kalibari Temple** (1986–8), by Sumit and Suchitra Ghosh, is traditionally designed, using the 'Bengal roof', while the conoid superstructure of the temple is made of concrete. The **Delhi Orthodox Diocesan Centre** (1984) by Ramu Katakam (born 1944), headquarters of the Metropolitan Delhi Diocese of the Syrian Christian Church (Jacobite) in India, with its dome and sloped profiles clad in local Dholpur stone is reminiscent of similar structures in the Middle East. By contrast, the new **Baha'i Temple, Delhi** (1982), by Fariburz Sahba utilises a unique roof structure to symbolise the universal nature of the Bahai religion. The main structure of the temple takes the form of a massive circle of concrete shells that simulate the unfolding petals of the lotus. The inner petals, form the dome of the structure and are supported by a system of ribs, which in turn, are held in position by a set of radial beams.

Laurie Baker's (born 1917) **S. John's Cathedral, Tiruvella** (1977) (p. 1633A,B), built entirely of locally available granite and brick with jackwood trusses that span walls and rise to a central skylight, combines the internal organisation of a Greek cross with the external appearance of a Hindu temple. When Christianity first came to India, the local architecture that developed resembled the 'Bamboo' style used by the Hindus in their religious buildings. **S. Mary's Cathedral, Varanasi** (1990–93) (p. 1633C–E), by A. G. K. Menon (born 1941) is conceived with a multi-faceted plan-form depending on simple geometric elements; it has a sloping, tiled roof, and traditional jalis.

Kahn and the Institution

Louis Kahn's preoccupation with silence and light gave a form and order to his buildings. For his two major projects on the subcontinent, the **Indian Institute of Management (IIM), Ahmedabad** (1963–74) (p. 1634A–C), and the **Citadel of the Assembly, Dhaka, Bangladesh** (begun 1967) (see below), his search for that order culminated in layered assemblages of brick and concrete walls which moderated the harsh climate. Location and culture affected both the housing of activities within his buildings, as well as outer architectural form. The 65-acre campus of the Institute of Management in Ahmedabad is divided into three parts: the institution – library, offices and classrooms on a U-shaped plan; the surrounding dormitories – units of student cells separated by courts; and the teacher's residences – linked bungalows around garden courts defining the periphery of the complex. All buildings are oriented to take advantage of the prevailing winds, while lightwells, courts and loggias help to minimise sun penetration. The housing for the institute was designed to reflect this distillation in specific architectural elements: loggias, which keep windows in deep shadow; the clustering of services – kitchen, WCs; and stairs bays of equal width between load-bearing brick walls, spanned by concrete slabs and relieved by arches and parapet ties.

Anant Raje (born 1929), the natural inheritor of Kahn's Indian legacy, carried on the brick vocabulary for the IIM's additions after Kahn's death in 1974 – for example, the **Dining Halls**, **Housing** (1975–80) and the **Mathai Centre** (1994), an auditorium and office complex. Another institutional project, the **Jawaharlal Nehru Industrial Development Bank of India, Hyderabad** (1992), by Charles Correa, has a stepped landscaped court as the institute's main feature.

Raje's particular design approach to his independent work suggests the kind of monumentality found in the mediaeval ruins of central India. The government-sponsored project for the **Indian Institute of Forest Management, Bhopal** (begun 1984), houses facilities for teaching, seminars, residence and recreation, and was expressly set up to promote a more ecologically sound programme for forestry. On a

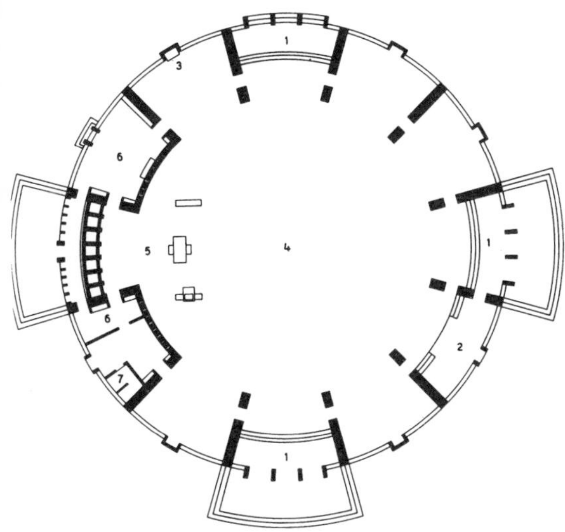

1 PORCH
2 BAPTISTRY
3 CHAPEL
4 THE NAVE
5 SANCTUARY
6 SACRISTRY
7 TOILET

0 2 4 8 32 ft

A. (*above*) S. John's Cathedral, Tiruvella: ground-floor plan

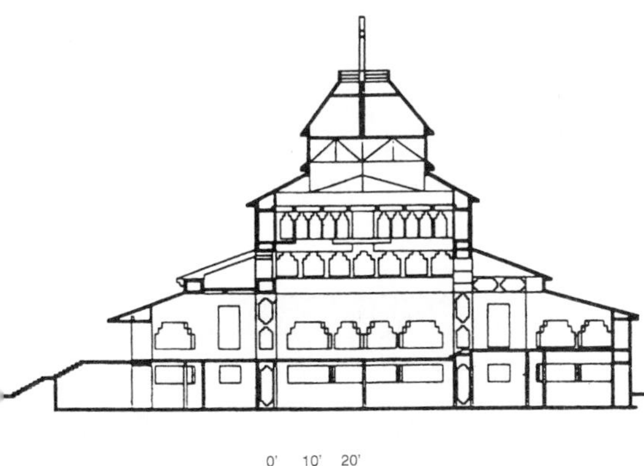

C. S. Mary's Cathedral, Varanasi: section

B. S. John's Cathedral, Tiruvella (1977). See p. 1632

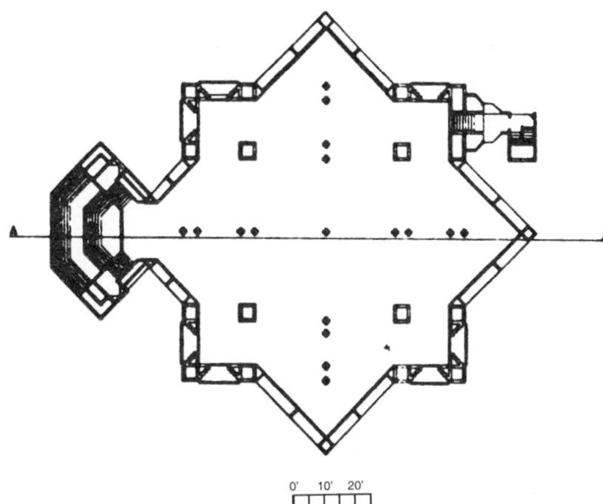

D. S. Mary's Cathedral, Varanasi: lower ground-floor plan

E. S. Mary's Cathedral, Varanasi (1990–93). See p. 1632

A. Indian Institute of Management, Ahmedabad (1963–74). See p. 1632

B. Indian Institute of Management, Ahmedabad: administration offices

C. Indian Institute of Management, Ahmedabad: main entrance

D. Indian Institute of Management, Bangalore (1977–85). See p. 1635

E. Entrepreneurship Development Institute, Ahmedabad (begun 1985). See p. 1635

rocky site overlooking the lakes of Bhopal, the institute creates a combination of building and landscape that sets off the terrain and the surrounding vistas. The administration, accounts and related offices are grouped around the main arrival court, while classrooms, seminar rooms, library and auditorium cluster about a more contained academic court, with adjacent dormitories. The geometry is one of fusion and collision, about an orthogonal axis, an idea first realised by Raje at the **Indian Statistical Institute, Delhi** (1970–76), along with Kanvinde and Rai, where the diverse functions of the offices, classrooms and residences were skilfully manipulated into a single unified plan. The volumetric alignments and deflections of the plan of the **Entrepreneurship Development Institute, Ahmedabad** (begun 1985) (p. 1634E), by Bimal Patel (born 1956) are, as in Raje's designs, meant to give visual emphasis to the special areas of the institute.

The dominating theme in much of B. V. Doshi's institutional work is also that of land and building interaction. The **Indian Institute of Management, Bangalore** (1977–85) (p. 1634D), by Stein, Doshi and Bhalla was conceived as a city where, guided by the topography of the site, 'there are movements and transitions which overlap, creating a pattern of crossroads'. The site of Doshi's **Gandhi Institute of Labour Studies, Ahmedabad** (1980–84) (p. 1636A), permits minor complexes to move away in a studied but informal manner, creating a series of three courts defined by long and low barrel-vaulted buildings. **Sangath, Ahmedabad** (1979–81) (p. 1636B), designed by Doshi as his office, provides a setting conducive to discourse, meeting and the exchange of ideas, somewhat like the carefully articulated indoor outdoor spaces of the **India International Centre, Delhi** (1960–62) (p. 1637A), by J. A. Stein.

Two important scientific institutes that exploit the undulations of their sites are the **National Institute of Immunology, Delhi** (1983–94) (p. 1637B) by Raj Rewal, and the **Sitaram Bhartia Institute for Science and Research** (1988–91) by S. Ghosh and Associates. These consist of extensive research facilities and housing for faculty, students and staff. Grouped along the rocky slopes of the site with internal courts, these buildings together define a series of landscaped quadrangles forming a kind of citadel of scientific ideas. Of similar form is Rewal's **Centre of Education and Training, Delhi** (1986–89).

Changes in school curricula and the development of more open and instinctive attitudes to teaching and learning began first to affect the conventional linear form of schools. The design for the **Mirambika School, Delhi** (1987), by Sanjay Prakash (born 1958) proposed a series of chamfered but linked octagons to form open courts. The chief merit of the **Modern School, Vasant Vihar, Delhi** (1954–84) (p. 1637C), by Jasbir and Rosemary Sachdev is also the fragmented quality of the layout, where ramps, stairs, courts, classrooms and passages are perceived as individual but connected entities. In a plan open to constant sensory influence, the court, its related classroom, and the surrounding landscape become integral to the development of the child. Similarly noteworthy is the U-shaped plan of Romi Khosla's **School for Spastic Children, Delhi** (1982), and the **Classrooms and Lecture Theatres** (1969–71), **Jodhpur University, Jodhpur** (p. 1638A,B,D), by Uttam C. Jain (born 1934), which are organised like a street in a desert town. Closed and shaded, the classrooms and theatres are built in locally dressed stone and make extensive use of traditional masonry crafts. Jain's similarly skilled manipulation of building elements in the more tropical landscape of Bombay is seen in the sprawling complex of the **Indira Gandhi Institute of Development Research** (begun 1985).

A studious appreciation of traditional forms has given rise to a number of programatically diverse buildings. Two of Charles Correa's projects rely on mythological concepts for their architectural ideas. The **Vidhan Bhavan, Bhopal** (begun 1980), containing the State Assembly Building for the Government of Madhya Pradesh, contains buildings within buildings, buildings within gardens, courts within buildings. The nine divisions of the circle are each used for its own explicit purpose; the four corner segments house the Vidhan Parishad (Upper House), the Vidhan Sabha (Lower House), the library and the combined hall, while the five central segments form the entrances, offices, public reception area and banquet hall in an open garden setting. Correa's other project, a city museum, the **Jawahar Kala Kendra, Jaipur** (1990), set up as a multi-disciplinary arts facility, is based on the Navagraha, the 9 square mandalas described in Hindu religious texts. The external elevations of the windowless sandstone walls rise two storeys to protect an internal world of cavities and voids, of domed halls and flat-roofed galleries, offices and restaurants. While the Jaipur museum was still under construction, Correa started on his commission for the **Inter-University Centre for Astronomy and Astrophysics (IUCAA), Pune** (1988–92), an architectural realisation of different notions of the cosmos. The library, faculty offices, lecture halls and student facilities are organised around a *kund*, an open-air theatre. Larger-than-life figures within the *kund* represent four scientists: Aryabhata, Newton, Galileo and Einstein.

Correa's modernistic **British Council Building, Delhi** (1986–92), containing library, auditorium, art gallery and conference rooms, symbolises growth, with its vast banyan tree-shaped mural by Howard Hodgkin. Opposite is the 23-floor **Amba Deep Towers, Delhi** (1990) (p. 1638C), by C. P. Kukreja (born 1939) grouped around an eight-storeyed atrium. Ceramic tiles with patterned bands and repetitive multicoloured elements borrowed from an Islamic tradition are distinctively used on its street facades.

A. Gandhi Institute of Labour Studies, Ahmedabad (1980–84). See p. 1635

B. Sangath, Ahmedabad (1979–81). See p. 1635

A. India International Centre, Delhi (1960–62). See p. 1635

B. National Institute of Immunology, Delhi (1983–94). See p. 1635

C. Modern School, Vasant Vihar, Delhi (1975–85). See p. 1635

A. Jodhpur University, Jodhpur (1969–71). See p. 1635

C. Amba Deep Towers, Delhi (1990). See p. 1635

B. Jodhpur Univeristy, Jodhpur: cluster of four lecture theatres

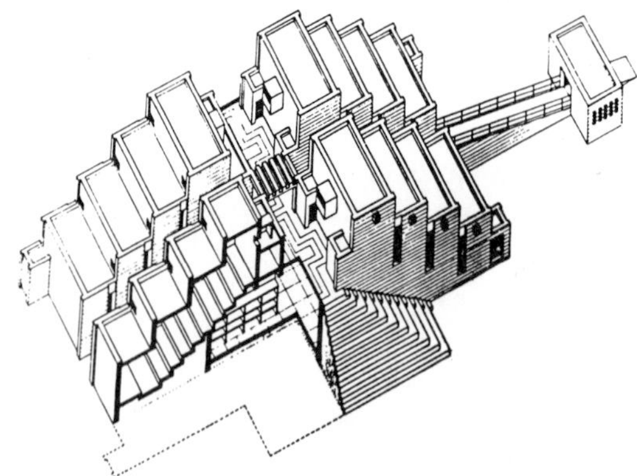

D. Jodhpur University, Jodhpur: axonometric of lecture theatre building

National Expression

Architecture as a national symbol expresses ideas that come to represent a time and so suggest the nationalist intent of the government in power. Louis Kahn's **Capital Complex (Sher-e-Bangla Nagar, Dhaka)** the **Citadel of the Assembly** (begun 1967) (p. 1640A) is a vast symmetrical congregation of concrete structures outside the city, and was the consequence of a growing nationalism in the eastern half of Pakistan that could not be easily contained by the power elite based in Islamabad in West Pakistan. The citadel comprises the main **Legislative Assembly Building** and **Mosque** in exposed concrete with marble string courses, and a secondary grouping across an artificial lake of the **Supreme Court** and **Hostels** (p. 1640B,C) in exposed brickwork.

Realised at a time when the nation state of Bangladesh had just come into being, the Assembly's architecture left its mark on the national psyche as a symbol of the new freedom. Similarly, with the elections in Sri Lanka in 1977 the decision to design a new symbolically appropriate Parliament building marked a shift in national politics. Kotte, an undeveloped area within Colombo's environs, became the site for the **New Parliamentary Complex, Sri Jayawardenepura** (1982). A series of pavilions spanning an artificial lake, the new parliamentary 'island' complex is approached across a great causeway and forecourt.

On a more subdued scale, national symbols also appear in the design of Delhi's Embassy buildings. The **Finnish Embassy, Delhi** (1964–86), by Reima Pietila (born 1923) derives its profiles from the northern landscapes of his own country, Finland. Irregular concrete roofs resemble winter snow sculptures. By contrast, the **Belgian Embassy, Delhi** (1983), by Satish Gujral has a more traditional brick exterior and a Beaux-Arts interior. Symmetrical in layout on a central axis, the catacomb-like public spaces are separated from the garden- oriented private offices above. Also prominent among the city's diplomatic buildings is the **United States Embassy**, by Edward D. Stone.

Housing

In the low-cost project for **Belapur Housing, New Bombay** (1986 onwards) (p. 1641B), Correa capitalised on the imagination of the residents by allowing them to build, extend or change their houses to suit their own needs and finances. Materials and technology were kept deliberately simple – plastered brick walls and tile roofs – while essential services lined the boundary walls. Higher land values in Bombay's prime residential district led, however, to Correa creating the 32-storey luxury **Kanchanjunga Apartments, Bombay** (1975–83) (p. 1641C). The tower has a square plan, but the corners are recessed to provide each unit with a balcony which offers a cool sitting area, a sea view and a geometric pocket to catch prevailing winds which are then channelled inside.

Two private group housing projects, the high-density, low-rise **Tara Group Housing, Alaknanda, Delhi** (1975–8), by Correa and the **Yamuna Apartments, Delhi** (1975) (p. 1641A), by The Design Group, both stagger dense housing around an unfolding community space. The grouping of two- and three-bedroom duplexes one above the other in step-backs and cantilevers provides covered verandahs and open terraces overlooking the street. This guarantees the openness so often absent in high-density living while reconciling the private home with the shared spaces of community life.

The traditional idea of the street as a key component of urban life began to be reflected in the individual private housing schemes in several north Indian cities. The **Asian Games Village, Delhi** (1980–82) (p. 1641D), by Raj Rewal with its 700 dwelling units, and the **Housing, Chandershekharpur, Bhubaneshwar** (begun 1986), by S. K. Das (born 1952) both simulate the traditional 'mohalla', an urban agglomeration common to the north Indian city. Here, public and private spaces are linked by narrow pedestrian streets intersected by gateways and bridges. In the **Atira Staff Housing project, Ahmedabad** (1982), by Anant Raje, this narrow, traditional street – an idea that Rewal used earlier in his design for the **French Embassy Quarters, Delhi** (1968–9) – expresses hierarchies of space and sequence, in which clusters of apartments are organised around more contained family courts and roof terraces. The Scheme for the **Bhopal Gas Victims, Bhopal** (1990), by M. N. Joglekar of HUDCO has a larger clusters of units. Four basic modules of five units form a single-entry, closed condominium, with a central open space shared by all the residents.

Though most of these housing projects use conventional technologies, some actually exploit financial constraints to evolve structural innovations, as in the **Industrial Housing, Vysenkere** (1983) (p. 1644A), by Kamu Iyer and in the **Low-cost Housing, Rajkot** (1990), by Kulbushan and Meenakshi Jain. The latter has a system of jack arches spanning concrete ribs, and a limited roof span over a single narrow volume.

In matters of cost-effectiveness and structural inventiveness the work of the Development Alternatives is particularly noteworthy. Both their **Headquarters Building** and the **Circular Exhibition Structure, Central Vista, Delhi**, are designed entirely as composites employing low-cost materials. Using brick-vaulted roofs, nubian vaults, mud domes, flat-tile roofs, adobe or composite mud and brick walls, the architects project in their works their socially conscious goals.

A. Citadel of the Assembly, Dhaka (begun 1967). See pp. 1632, 1639

B. Secretaries' Hostels, Dhaka (1968). See p. 1639

C. Hostels for Members of the National Assembly, Dhaka (1968). See p. 1639

A. Yamuna Apartments, Delhi (1975). See p. 1639

B. Belapur Housing, New Bombay (1986–). See p. 1639

C. Kanchanjunga Apartments, New Bombay (1975–83). See p. 1639

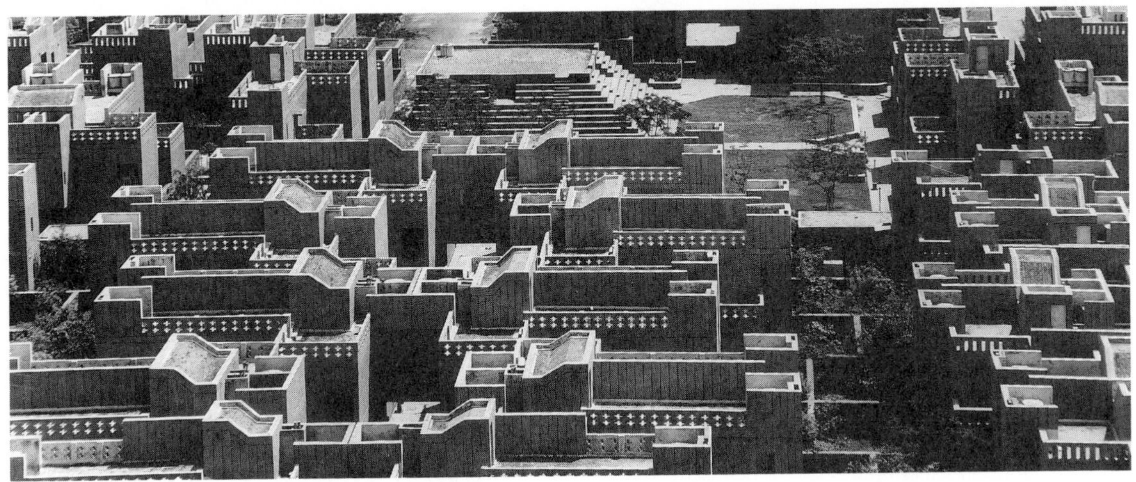

D. Asian Games Village, Delhi (1980–82). See p. 1639

The New Regionalism

In many recent projects, the expression of a local image has acquired a special importance. An urban vernacular is simulated at the **Cidade de Goa Hotel, Panaji, Goa** (1978–82), by Charles Correa. A composition of cubical forms shifting along the base of a hill, the hotel's 100 rooms are organised like a small Portuguese settlement. At the **Kala Akademi, Panaji, Goa** (1973–83), Correa exuberantly integrates mural painting with architecture. At the **Kovalam Beach Resort, Kerala** (1969–74), Correa reinforces the character of the site by dispersing the hotel structure down the rocks.

Several recent hotel designs combine elements from colonial and local traditions, with modern adjustments. Influences of the colonial architecture of Calcutta are visible in the **Taj Bengal Hotel, Calcutta** (1990), by The Design Group. At Agra, the Islamic tradition of Fatehpur Sikri and the Agra Fort prompted the adoption of Mughal design principles for the **Hotel Mughal Sheraton, Agra** (1974–77), by ARCOP Design Group. Revathi (born 1955) and Vasant (born 1946) Kamath's similarly repackaged traditional rural architecture for the **Tourist Village, Mandava, Rajasthan**. As in their **Artisans' Housing project, Madipur, Delhi** (1983), for displaced artisans and in the stone and mud structure for the **Community Centre, Maheshwar** (1991), the Kamaths worked directly with craftspeople to evolve design details then engaged local masons, carpenters and stone workers to execute and finish the building.

Contemporary structures frequently draw inspiration from historical buildings. One which assimilates vernacular elements and echoes them in new materials is the **Kalakshetra Theatre, Madras** (1978–84), by D. Appukuttan Nair (born 1923). This design attempts to perpetuate the time-honoured interaction of actor and audience. Such ideas have found ready acceptance with Trivandrum-based architect Laurie Baker, whose major projects include the **Chitralekha Film Studios** (1974–6) (p. 1643A) and the **Nalanda Institute** (1973) (p. 1643B,C) both in **Trivandrum**, and the **Corpus Christi School, Kottayam** (1972). Baker's largest project, the **Centre for Development Studies, Trivandrum (CDS)** (1971) (p. 1643D,E), achieves a certain rational randomness on a sloped hill site, with the logistics of the placement of the centre's buildings, including classrooms, housing and amphitheatre, being determined by the gradients. The design of the circulating corridor in the nearby **Women's Hostel building** (1987) at the CDS incorporates in its outer wall of latticed brickwork all the basic amenities for hostel living: low seats, kitchen counters, built-in tables, ironing boards and work areas. The most recent addition to the campus is an unusual, double-wall building of intersecting circles for the **Campus Computer Centre** (1971). By scaling and assembling similar elements to suit the function of each project, Baker has devised different building types.

The first museum constructed wholly from carved wooden pieces salvaged from demolished havelis (traditional courtyard houses) was the **Calico Museum of Textiles, Ahmedabad** (1980), by the Sarabhai Foundation. An important aspect of Baker's own cost-reduction methods for home building is a similar re-use of material from demolished sites. In the **Leela Menon House** (1973–4), and the **Narayanan residence**, (1972–3), both designed in the early 1980s, much of the woodwork was saved from older family houses. Door frames, timber columns, traditional brackets were merely re-incorporated.

Baker's commissioned houses show the same spirit that went into the making of his own home, **The Hamlet, Nalanchira** (from 1970), on an uneven, sloping tract of land. The house has grown organically with rooms, porches, verandahs, walks and bridged connections built in accordance with the changing requirements of Baker's own family.

Recent Sri Lankan work that parallels Baker's in its concern for local imagery and sense of history is that of Geoffrey Bawa. His early works of note include the **S. Bridget's Montessori School** (1964) and the **Farm School, Hanwella** (1966). These projects have been dubbed 'regional vernacular', but this is an oversimplification because the materials of many of his buildings reflect the international vernacular tradition as much as local design. The **Bentota Beach Hotel** (1969) is a wood-frame building set within rough, stone rubble walls. The **Bishop's College Extension** (1963) is open-plan, with external concrete screens.

Bawa's architecture with its blend of traditional ideas and Modernist simplifications defies classification. But all his works demonstrate an environmental breadth of design. One of the few projects undertaken by Geoffrey Bawa in India, the **Madurai Club, Madurai** (1974), responds to the natural vistas of the site with stone slab floors, rough-hewn stone pillars, and rubble walls with timber rafters and clay-tile roofs. The plan of the **Triton Hotel, Ahungalla** (1981), was largely shaped by the site, a long, narrow beachfront. The recreational nature of the building encouraged its almost total integration with the surroundings.

The **Textile Printing Workshop, New Okhla Industrial Development Area (NOIDA), Uttar Pradesh** (1984), by Vasant and Revathi Kamath houses the traditional activity of hand printing in a structure generically residential, a courtyard house. The factory plan, with a stone-clad court and sloped terracotta roofs, is appropriately traditional in spirit, textile dyeing having traditionally been a household activity. At **Nrityagram, Bangalore** (1987) (p. 1644B), by Gerard de Cunha (born 1955) the building form was influenced by the traditions of

A. Chitralekha Film Studios, Trivandrum (1974–6). See p. 1642

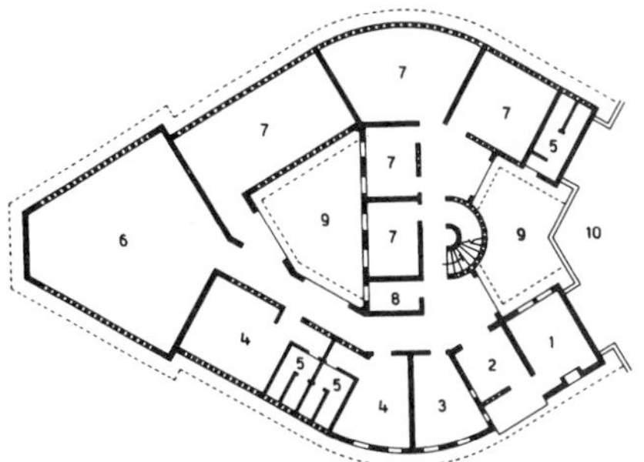

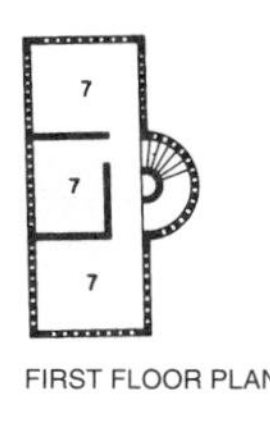

B. Nalanda Institute, Trivandrum: plans

C. Nalanda Institute. Trivandrum (1973). See p. 1642

D. Centre for Development Studies, Trivandrum (1971). See p. 1642

E. Centre for Development Studies, Trivandrum: detail of exterior

A. Industrial Housing, Vysenkere (1983). See p. 1639

B. Nrityagram, Bangalore (1987). See p. 1642

C. Path Bhavan Girl's Hostel, Santiniketan (1979–85). See p. 1645

training and development of the classical dance form. Abundant stone and brick were used to produce a hybrid structure of composite walls, open and pavilion-like, allowing assemblies of student hostels around practice and performance halls. The architect, like his mentor Laurie Baker, uses an overall site plan, but improvises on the site, assembling and reworking individual details in relation to the materials and conditions of the place.

Community centres in different parts of the country, built with available skills and materials, have an intrinsically local identity. Both the **Path Bhavan Girls' Hostel**, **Santiniketan** (1979–85) (p. 1644C), by Dulal Mukherjee (born 1940), and the **Community Mental Health Centre, Bangalore** (1983), by Kamu Iyer rely on low, dignified profiles of simple, repeating volumes, in accord with the surrounding vernacular. A crucial element in designing of **Mother and Child Care Centre**, **Bagnam Village, West Bengal** (1979), by Ashish M. N. Ganju (born 1942) was the participation of the local people. Available brick, timber and hardware was used with simple construction technology and local skills to erect a large, multipurpose hall with a pitched tile roof on wooden rafters. Learning by doing was an idea also explored at S. K. Das's **Campus for GRAM, Nizamabad, Andhra Pradesh**. The architecture of the campus was intended to inspire self-help and promote popular architecture in the region. The campus consists of an administrative block, a clinic with a few beds for minor treatment, a dairy, a training hall, a hostel and some staff housing.

Two places that have captured the spirit of the ethnic marketplace are the **Dilli Haat** (1992–3) by Pradeep Sachdeva, an ambitious layout of cottage industries atop a covered city drain, and Charles Correa's **Crafts Museum, Pragati Maidan Exhibition Complex** (1975–91). Both display and market Indian handicrafts.

Note

In 1995 the name of Bombay was changed to Mumbai. To be consistent with earlier chapters, Bombay is used here.

Chapter 58

OCEANIA

Australia, New Zealand, Papua New Guinea and the Smaller Islands of the South Pacific

Architectural Character

Australia

Australia was proclaimed a nation in 1901 when the colonial states were federated. During the following decades, although the historical styles persisted, the tendency in commercial architecture was towards more severe forms. By the end of the nineteenth century a Romanesque-based style, influenced by the contemporary architecture of Chicago, had appeared in strictly utilitarian buildings, but by the second decade of the twentieth century high rusticated bases and giant round arches brought an imposing scale to a wide range of building types. They were added to the more conservative architecture derived from that of the Victorian period, usually built in red brick and enlivened by plasterwork bands and cream-painted details. Art Nouveau reached Australia early in the century, primarily in the form of decorative motifs, but no notable buildings in that style were produced.

The first tall building, Culwalla House, Sydney, by Spain and Cosh, was completed in 1910. It stood 52 m (170 ft) high and was still in load-bearing brick construction – steel technology was still in its infancy and production limited. Concern over fire risk resulted in the introduction of building height limits in all cities. The limit was 45.7 m (150 ft) in Sydney and 40.2 m (132 ft) in Melbourne. Uniform height limits were retained in Australian cities until the end of the 1950s.

In domestic architecture the lively red-brick Queen Anne revival, with its varied roof forms and decorative timber work, was succeeded by the darkly toned California Bungalow. Architects' houses were romantically inspired by the work of Americans, such as Greene and Greene, while the simpler versions that reached Australia through builders' catalogues were rapidly accepted throughout the country.

Further romantic influences came from Walter Burley Griffin, who arrived from Chicago after winning the 1912 competition for the planning of the new capital of Australia at Canberra. Griffin was a member of the so-called Prairie School, and his work was not widely appreciated at the time but its merits were rediscovered in the 1950s.

A reawakened interest in Australia's early colonial buildings contributed to a neo-Georgian revival. This probably was partly inspired by Sir Edwin Lutyens' later buildings, notably his bungalows for New Delhi (1913–30). Slightly later, Leslie Wilkinson introduced an architecture inspired by Mediterranean models, which he thought suitable for the climate. By the 1930s commercial buildings were showing the influence of Art Deco and the Gothic skyscraper style of New York. Australia also produced a large number of fine, confident buildings which reflected in their horizontal banding and streamlined curves the architecture of Eric Mendelsohn. Brick and glass blocks figured prominently in such buildings as factories and warehouses. Outstanding were the new hospitals with balconies at each floor level.

The early modern buildings were solid in appearance and stocky in form, owing more to the work of architects such as Dudok than to buildings of the International Style. Functionalism was advocated but not fully understood. Melbourne was the centre of progressive thinking in the 1930s and produced the first convincing buildings in the white aesthetic of the Modern Movement, but architectural leadership soon passed to Sydney, where the first pure examples of the International Style appeared.

After the years of austerity following Word War II, Australia entered a period of growth and prosperity. Air-conditioned curtain-wall buildings were built and in 1957 in Sydney and Melbourne the limits on building height were lifted. The 117 m (383 ft) high AMP Building, Sydney (1957–61), by Peddle, Thorp and Walker, was the first of the high-rise towers. Curtain-walls proved unsuitable for the climate, however, and for most subsequent tall buildings in the warmer states more solid cladding materials or sun-shielding devices were used.

The international nature of the new urban architecture was countered in Sydney by a romantic regional movement. The initial concepts were inspired by traditional Japanese architecture and the organic theories of Frank Lloyd Wright, and later by the bungalow style, the brick buildings of Alvar Aalto and the New Brutalism of France and Britain. The architecture of this 'Sydney School' was mainly a domestic style in brick and tile that blended in form, colour and texture with the sloping bushland sites and influenced architecture throughout Australia for more than a decade.

Regional concerns remain a strong force in Australian architecture. Some current work is consciously revivalist, drawing mostly on the nineteenth-century vernacular. In rural areas, buildings are often framed in lightweight timber or steel with corrugated steel for roof- and wall-cladding. Although these buildings are clearly contemporary in their imagery, their roots in the traditional homesteads and barns are evident, while in the cities the nineteenth-century terrace house provides the most suitable model.

In the late 1970s the quality of urban life became a major focus. Nineteenth-century inner-city housing was renovated for low-income and more affluent groups. Recycling of the existing building stock for aesthetic, economic and heritage reasons became widespread. In the 1980s the central waterfront areas of the major cities, notably Circular Quay and Darling Harbour, Sydney, and the river frontages in Brisbane and Melbourne, underwent extensive upgrading to enhance public amenity. At the same time the suburbs – where most Australians live in detached, single-family dwellings – received long-overdue attention. Robert Venturi's writings contributed to the attitudes underlying this architecture, which is found mainly in Melbourne. It is a distinct, vigorous, suburban style carried out in two-tone brickwork and with parapet walls.

Recent decades witnessed an increased appreciation of the traditional lightweight temporary structures of the Aborigines, and their sensitivity to the fragility of the land. Australian architects exhibited a growing concern with ecological and energy issues in projects of a significant scale, such as the proposals for the Olympic Games 2000 in Sydney. Further, they have become increasingly conscious of Australia's location in Oceania and its relationship with Asia. This has meant closer cultural exchange and design commissions from neighbouring countries contributing to an acknowledgment of the importance of the region as a whole.

New Zealand

In the first half of the twentieth century the architecture of New Zealand was conservative, and technological developments had little immediate impact. Timber was most widely used for small buildings but reinforced concrete was used increasingly in commercial buildings of five or more storeys. The steel commercial buildings of S. and A. Luttrell were exceptional. The most accomplished of their works was the Trentham Grandstand (1923).

British ideas and styles were influential, especially the Arts and Crafts Movement: there is a high craft quality in the best small and medium-sized buildings inspired by Shaw, Webb, Voysey and Lutyens, whose later Classicism also had its effect. Although these traditions persisted into the later 1930s, houses also show the influence of the California Bungalow which was introduced after 1910. The Spanish Mission Style was not widely accepted in New Zealand but some fine examples of institutional and church architecture were built. The Italian Romanesque style found favour for churches, which were usually constructed in high-quality brickwork, often with blind arcades under the eaves. The town centres of Napier and Hastings, destroyed in the earthquake of 1931, were rebuilt in a unique restrained Art Deco style.

The Modern Movement came late to New Zealand. The first significant steps in this direction were taken by the Government Housing Construction Department (founded in 1936) in several blocks of apartments. They were flat-roofed, white buildings with regular fenestration.

During the 1950s a more consciously regional attitude to domestic architecture emerged in the Auckland area, stimulated by the work of Vernon Brown, whose houses after 1945 were of simple, timber-framed construction with mono-pitched roofs and weatherboarded walls stained to a dark colour.

Group Architects, a collaborative formed in Auckland in 1949 and led by W. D. Wilson, sought to design inexpensive lightweight houses which would combine functionalist principles with regional character. By the mid-1950s post-and-beam houses with spacious open living areas were being built in other parts of the country – notably the J. A. Beard House in Karori, Wellington (1955), and the Bishop House, Waipukuran, Hawke's Bay (1956), by John Scott. On the whole, commercial architecture was undistinguished, although Massey House, Wellington (1952), by Plischke and Firth, is an exception.

The modern movement thrived in the 1960s and concrete remained the favoured material for large structures. With the return of Sir Miles Warren in the later 1950s, after a period with the London County Council, Christchurch emerged as an important centre of innovative architectural development. He introduced New Brutalism, and with Peter Beaven led a school which produced many spirited buildings.

Beaven's work, in particular, exhibited regional characteristics.

It was also in the 1960s that Ian Athfield and Roger Walker rebelled against the restrictive regulations and conformity of architectural practice in New Zealand to produce a new and original architecture based on the New Zealand architectural heritage itself. Through the 1980s and 1990s little commercial architecture of note was produced and the house generally remained the testing ground for invention. Accomplished examples of a romantic vernacular-inspired architecture, such as the corrugated steel barn-like Eskdale School Hall, Hawkes Bay (1992), by Paris Magdalinos, continued to be built though the influence of international movements was evident. Significant examples include the austere, geometrical Jenner House, Auckland (1985), by Ross Jenner which exhibits affiliations with Rationalism, and the National Bank, Newton Branch, Auckland (1993), by Andrews Scott Cotton – a highly eclectic building with primarily Constructivist overtones.

Maori-European culture has found little expression in architecture, although some building types such as the meeting house evolved in the nineteenth century to meet new needs. These have been developed further in the twentieth century as the culture gains strength and assurance.

Papua New Guinea and the Smaller Islands of the South Pacific

While there is diversity in the architecture of the South Pacific as a whole, the twentieth-century buildings of the islands belong to a few distinct categories. The traditional buildings of the islands, now rapidly disappearing, are constructed in local materials (usually vegetation), and are highly responsive to climatic conditions. The building forms emphasise steeply pitched roofs with wide overhangs to give protection from sun and rain. Walls allow through-breezes or are non-existent, though in cooler mountainous regions, such as New Caledonia, adobe walls are used. Raised timber floors are common, as in the Solomon Islands and Kiribati, although there are notable exceptions in the 'fale' of Samoa and the 'bure' of Fiji, which are built on raised earthen banks. The buildings are usually simple, but high points of ingenuity and creativity are sometimes reached, as in the ceremonial structures of Papua New Guinea.

Colonial architecture, here as elsewhere, reflected European architecture of the countries of origin and was rarely elaborate. The single-storey bungalow style with pitched roof and wide verandahs, introduced to the Pacific area in the nineteenth century, was continued well into the twentieth. The Nuku'alofa Club, Tonga (1914), is typical. Such buildings with verandahs were normal for the houses of expatriates, for example the German verandah houses of Samoa. In addition, the buildings left behind by the occupying forces of World War II have become part of the legacy of the islands.

Settlers from Asia also played a part in shaping and influencing the patterns of development, but towards the end of the century Asian development companies, who often brought their own resources, including labour, were having a negative impact through inappropriately scaled and designed buildings such as the Chinese-designed Government Office Buildings, Apia (1994). Such international modern architecture of commerce and tourism is often air-conditioned and makes few concessions to climate and context. Traditional buildings now often serve as sources of motifs for pastiche. The lack of durability of traditional materials (in some islands also a shortage of supply) and the desire to follow modern practices has resulted in the use of such materials as corrugated iron and asbestos-cement sheeting and has produced inappropriate designs in relation to comfort. The increasing urbanisation has meant the move from the traditional village to either government-built suburbs or squatter areas. Countering such tendencies are attempts to revive the logic of past practices and to build an appropriate regional architecture from first principles. While currently most trained architects are not of the indigenous races this situation is slowly changing.

Examples

Australia

Office Buildings

City Mutual Life Assurance Society Building, Sydney (1936) (p. 1649A), by Emil Sodersten (1901–61), shows the influence of American Art Deco. It is a powerfully massed block with a monumental corner entrance and stepped-back facades. The doorway is framed in polished black granite enriched with patterned metallic panelling. The high entrance foyer contains a sweeping plaster ceiling which is carried like a canopy on fluted columns.

The ICI Building, Melbourne (1957) (p. 1649B), by Bates, Smart and McCutcheon, was one of the first air-conditioned, modular, steel-framed, curtain-wall buildings in Australia. Other examples include the **MLC Building, North Sydney** (1957), by the same architects and **Unilever House, Sydney** (1957), by Stephenson and Turner.

Australia Square, Sydney (1961–7) (pp. 1649C, 1650A), by Harry Seidler (born 1923) and Associates, combines a rectangular slab block containing offices,

A. City Mutual Life Assurance Society Building, Sydney (1936). See p. 1648

B. ICI Building, Melbourne (1957). See p. 1648

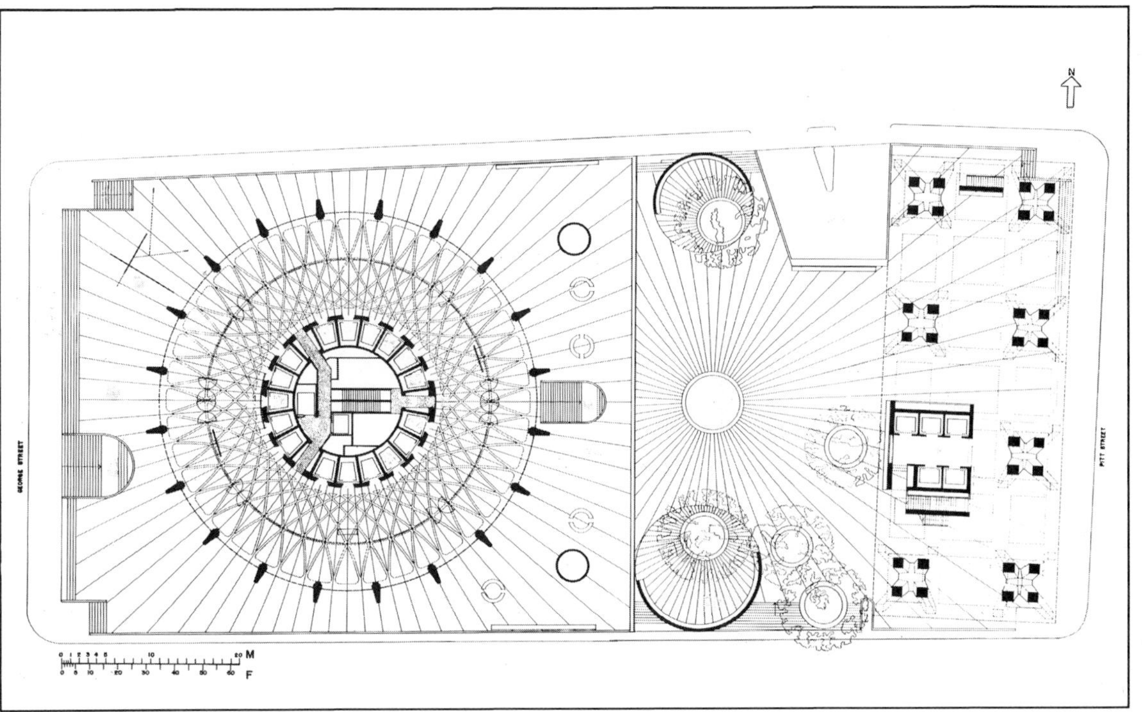

C. Australia Square, Sydney (1961–7): plan showing upper and lower plazas. See p. 1648

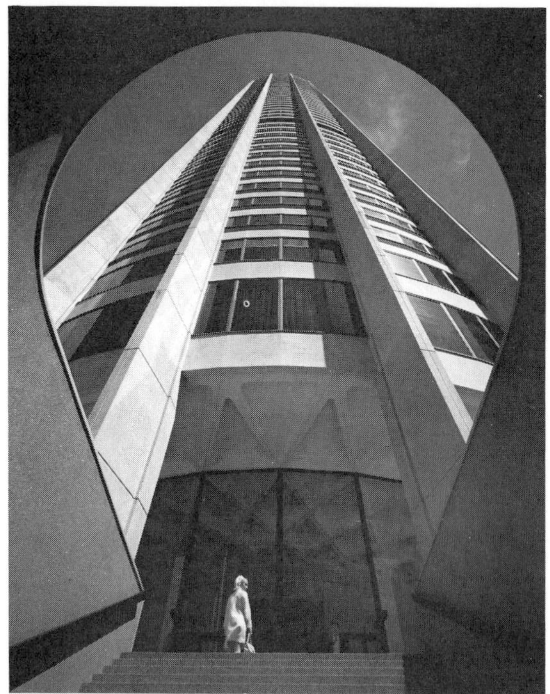

A. Australia Square, Sydney (1967–7). See p. 1648

B. American Express Tower, Sydney (1976). See p. 1652

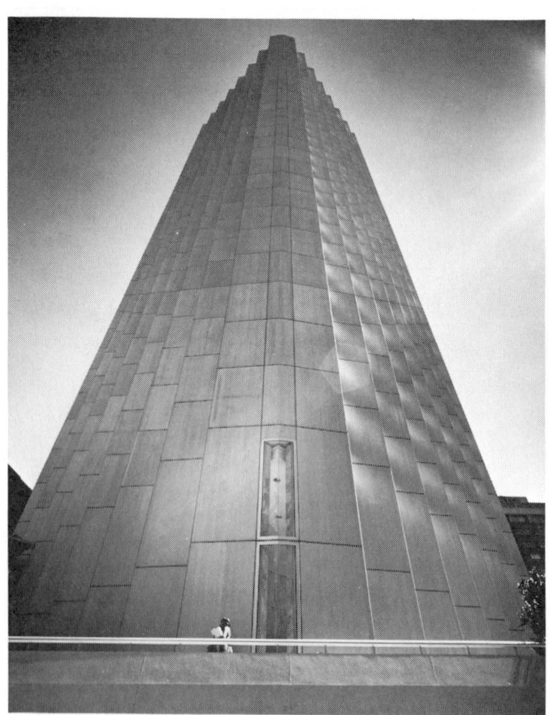

C. Allendale Square, Perth (1976). See p. 1652

D. The Mercy Hospital, Melbourne (1935, 1938). See p. 1652

A. Drummond Street Office, Melbourne (1987). See p. 1652

B. 1 Collins Street, Melbourne (1983). See p. 1652

C. Governor Phillip Tower, Sydney (1994). See p. 1652

raised on V-shaped pilotis, with a circular tower block, with a pleasant public plaza between them. Nervi was the consulting engineer. The **MLC Centre, Sydney** (1978), is a larger urban development by Seidler and includes a concrete-framed eight-sided tower, 244 m (800 ft) high, as well as restaurants, theatres and shops. Seidler's **Riverside Centre, Brisbane** (1986), furthers the geometrical and structural principles of his preceding work, and invigorates the waterfront with a spacious public plaza and quay.

American Express Tower, Sydney (1976) (p. 1650B), by John Andrews (born 1933) International, an *in-situ* concrete building, is triangular in plan. The glass walls are protected from the sun by polycarbonate panels supported on external aluminium space-frames. Bars, restaurants, and the arrangement of seating and trees add to the dynamic quality of the architecture. **Allendale Square, Perth** (1976) (p. 1650C), by Cameron, Chisholm and Nicol, has a square tower sheathed in aluminium and turned at 45 degrees to the street. It is faceted to present blank walls to the least favourable aspects.

The **Cameron Offices, Belconnen**, Australian Capital Territory (1976), by John Andrews International, houses 4000 government office workers, and is planned to serve also as a pedestrian pathway for the town. It consists of an elevated mall above which are special-use spaces. Branching from this are three-storey general offices planned around deep garden-courtyards. Other office buildings of this kind are the **Benjamin Offices, Belconnen** (1980), by McConnel Smith and Johnson and the **McLaughlan Offices, Canberra** (1980), by Daryl Jackson Evan Walker.

The **Edmund Barton Offices, Canberra** (1974), by Harry Seidler and Associates is a purist exercise in structural clarity. The office floors enclose two large courtyards. The building has an heroic scale appropriate to its setting at the edge of the Parliamentary Triangle.

Drummond Street Office, Melbourne (1987) (p. 1651A), by Ashton and Raggatt is a speculative development in a heritage area. This building uses historically evocative elements which overlie, yet reveal, the mundane structure behind in order to offer a critique on the developer's requirements and the strictures of conservation policy.

1 Collins Street, Melbourne (1983) (p. 1651B), by Denton Corker Marshall exemplifies the increasing concern for the historic urban environments. The building addresses the site corner with the taller of its two stepped towers, and the neutral grey surface of precast concrete panels provides a refined but unobtrusive background to the earlier buildings. Internally the design creates a subtle spatial transition from the nineteenth-century entry to the high-rise office tower. Denton Corker Marshall's **Governor Phillip Tower, Sydney** (1994) (p. 1651C), stands on the historic site of the first Government House. It is an elegant building that combines stainless steel and zinc wall sheeting with sandstone and granite panels. Its roof profile, extending in stainless steel the 12-metre grid of the facades, provides an arresting geometrical landmark by day and night. At ground level the building incorporates a museum and plaza displaying the archeology of the first historic building, and encloses a courtyard edged by retained terrace houses.

Public Buildings

The **Main Reading Room of Melbourne Public Library**, now the State Library of Victoria (1906–11), by Bates, Peebles and Smart, is an early example of the use of reinforced concrete. The octagonal dome has sixteen ribs and spans 35 m (115 ft). When built it was the largest dome of its kind in the world. An annulus with flying buttresses surrounds the central octagon giving to the interior an overall diameter of 41 m (134 ft). The floor of the Reading Room is 35 m (115 ft) below the lantern.

The **Anzac War Memorial, Sydney** (1934), by C. Bruce Dellit (1900–42), is the foremost example of Art Deco in the country with symmetrically stepped forms and rich decorative and symbolic motifs.

The **Mercy Hospital, Melbourne** (1935, 1938) (p. 1650D), by Stephenson and Meldrum, is one of several hospitals influenced by Alvar Aalto's Paimio Sanatorium (see Chapter 44), which Sir Arthur Stephenson (1890–1967) had visited.

The **Olympic Swimming Pool, Melbourne** (1956), by John and Phyllis Murphy, Borland and McIntyre, which seats 6000, is an expressive building in which function, structure and form are closely related. The logic of the design was readily comprehended through the glass walls of the building.

The **High Court of Australia** (competition 1972 – completed 1980) (p. 1653A), and the **Australian National Gallery, Canberra** (competition 1968 – completed 1982) (p. 1653C), by Edwards Madigan Torzillo and Briggs, stand adjacent to each other on the lakeside in the Parliamentary Triangle. Broad concrete walls, cantilevers and large areas of glass make for wilful, dramatic architecture. The High Court building contains a 24 m (79 ft) high Public Hall. The triagrid roofs of the National Gallery establish a geometric order that is followed throughout the building.

The **Parliament House of Australia, Canberra** (international competition 1979 – completed 1988), by Mitchell Giurgola Thorp, stands on Capital Hill at the hub of Walter Burley Griffin's plan (1912). It is a low-profile building which is topographically related to the hilltop and integrated with the geometry of the city plan. The cross-axes of the symmetrical composition are aligned with Griffin's land and water axes. Grassed ramps, which pass over the building, visually extend the axes of the diagonal avenues approaching the site.

A. High Court of Australia, Canberra (1980). See p. 1652

B. State Theatre, Sydney (1929). See p. 1655

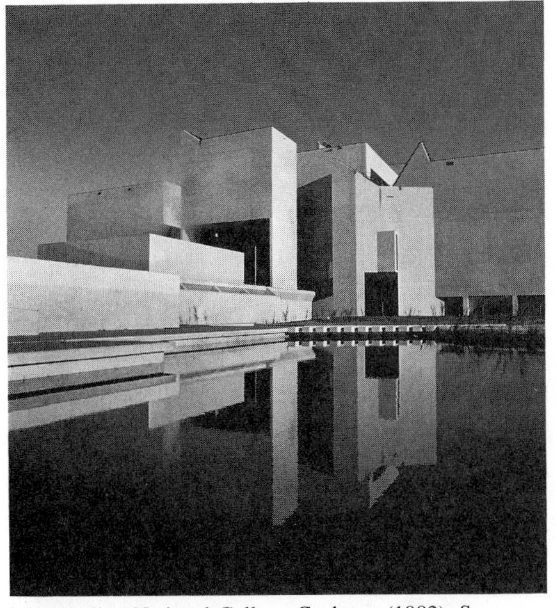

C. Australian National Gallery, Canberra (1982). See p. 1652

D. Festival Centre, Adelaide (1977). See p. 1655

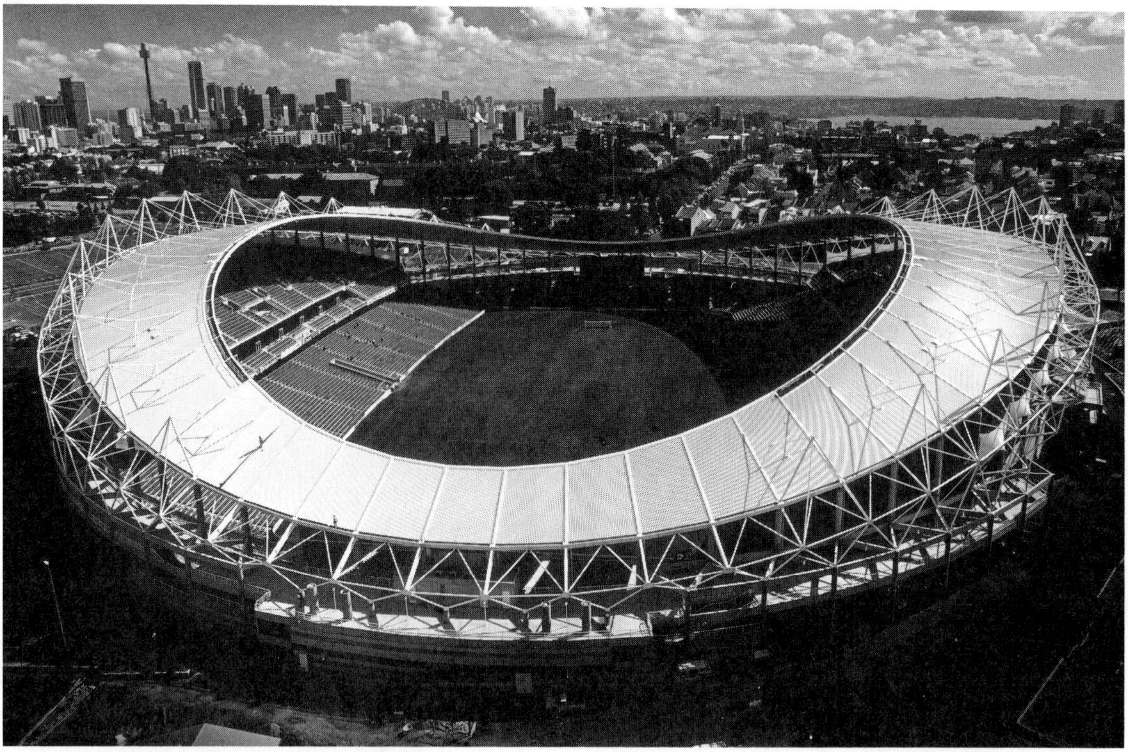

A. Sydney Football Stadium (1988). See p. 1655

B. National Athletics Stadium, Bruce (1974). See p. 1655

Outward-curving walls divide the plan into a central zone containing the public rooms and the executive accommodation and enclaves containing the House of Representatives and the Senate. The central Meeting Hall is celebrated by means of a huge flag on a 65 m (213 ft) high stainless-steel flagpole. It is an orderly, Classical composition which draws its inspiration from the natural and man-made features of its setting.

The **Swimming Training Halls, Bruce**, Australian Capital Territory (1982), by Daryl Jackson (born 1937) Architects, is one of a group of sports buildings by Jackson which forms a part of the National Sports Centre. The curved, stepped levels of the roof allow natural light into the pool area and help to relate the building to the soft contours of the surrounding hills.

The **Sydney Football Stadium** (1988) (p. 1654A) by Philip Cox (born 1939) and Partners, is one of five major steel structures completed by the firm in that year. These are refined and exuberant buildings that combine advanced technology with a fanciful romanticism that derives inspiration from context. Cox's seminal building of this type is the **National Athletics Stadium, Bruce** (1974) (p. 1654B), a steel tension structure subtly related to banked-earth forms. Cox's major Olympic buildings such as the **Aquatic Centre, Sydney** (1994) provide further refinement in technolgical development and the generation of expressive form.

Churches and Education Buildings

S. Andrew's Presbyterian Church, Brisbane (1907), by C. D. Payne, is an austere, strongly massed brick building. Simplified Romanesque elements suggest the early influence of America, notably the severe style of H. H. Richardson. **Newman College, University of Melbourne** (1917) (p. 1656A), by Walter Burley Griffin (1876–1937) (in association with Augustus Fritsch), is a heavy, stone building with student rooms around a courtyard. The circular refectory has a concrete ribbed dome. A historic atmosphere is suggested by leaded windows, heavy piers and particularly low storey heights. But the building is strikingly original in its massing, and in the geometry of some of its elements such as window surrounds.

Tamrookum Church, Beaudesert, Queensland (1915) (p. 1655B), by Robin Dods (1868–1920), is dramatically sited on the knoll of a hill in the midst of rolling pastureland. It combines the simple forms of 'village' church architecture with the Queensland timber tradition. Typical of Dods' architecture is his consideration of climate, exemplified here by wide roof-overhangs and french doors opening from the aisles on to generous verandahs.

The **Church of the Resurrection, Keysborough, Melbourne** (1976), by Edmond and Corrigan, is one of a group of church buildings designed for a large site in a new suburb. The two-coloured brickwork, the porch with its verandah and the bay windows are in sympathy with the character of the suburbs in which it stands.

Theatres and other Cultural Buildings

The **Capitol Theatre, Melbourne** (1924), by Walter Burley Griffin (in association with Peck and Kemper), contains Griffin's decorative masterpiece – the illuminated prismatic plaster ceiling. And a few years later the **State Theatre, Sydney** (1929) (p. 1653B), by Henry E. White (1877–1952) (to sketch designs by John Eberson), is a grand 'picture palace' which seats over 2500 people. It forms part of a vertical shopping and office block. Predominantly French Baroque in style, its interiors are moulded in fibrous plaster.

A comparatively early 'high-tech' building, the **Sidney Myer Music Bowl, Melbourne** (1959), by Yuncken, Freeman Brothers, Griffiths and Simpson, is supported by twin steel masts cased in glass fibre. The plywood roof-covering is bolted to secondary transverse cables.

The **Sydney Opera House, Sydney** (p. 1656C), was the subject of an international competition in 1957 and was completed 1973. The competition was won by Jørn Utzon (born 1918). The engineers were Ove Arup and Partners, and Hall, Todd and Littlemore handled the work as architects after 1966. It is composed of two major sections, the solid podium which contains small theatres, exhibition rooms and the service areas and the symphony hall, opera theatre and restaurant which are housed under the white, vaulted roofs poised on the podium. The vaults are formed on pre-cast concrete ribs which follow a curvature of common radius. Monumental stairs lead from the forecourt to the podium. Despite the narrowness of the site, Utzon placed the major auditoria side by side. To achieve this, normal theatre planning is reversed and the stages are placed closest to the entrance, and lounges ideally located overlooking the harbour to the north. The **Victorian Art Centre, Melbourne** (1961–85), by Sir Roy Grounds (1905–81), the **Festival Centre, Adelaide** (1977) (p. 1653D), by Hassell and Partners, and the **Queensland Cultural Centre, Brisbane** (1982–7) by Robin Gibson (born 1930) and Partners, are other notable cultural centres of this period.

Brambuk Living Cultural Centre, Halls Gap (1990), by Gregory Burgess (born 1945) serves as a focus for Aboriginal activities in the area. It is located in a dramatic valley that strongly influenced the sensitive siting, orientation and form. The building is composed of a massive central stone fireplace with an encircling ramp that serves as the fulcrum for the surrounding organic composition of exhibition spaces and ceremonial grounds and gardens. The structure is

A. Newman College, University of Melbourne (1917). See p. 1655

B. Tamrookum Church, Beaudesert (1915). See p. 1655

C. Sydney Opera House (1973). See p. 1655

of stone, consolidated earth and timber, with interior reed screens utilizing traditional weaving techniques.

Domestic Buildings

Eryldene, Sydney (1914) (p. 1658A), designed by W. Hardy Wilson (1881–1955) for E. G. Waterhouse, the Professor of Botany at Sydney University, is a harmonious example of the neo-colonial revival. Wilson was Australia's first architectural historian, and Eryldene, with its overtones of chinoiserie, together with his own house **Purulia** (1916), are the finest examples of his simple, symmetrical reinterpretation of early colonial forms.

Belvedere, Sydney (1919), by Alexander Stuart Jolly (1887–1957), is an Australian adaptation of the California Bungalow with dark, stained timbers and white walls. Its simple horizontal forms are sheltered by broad, sweeping roofs and deep porches with heavy pylons. More picturesque examples, such as **The Cobbles**, Sydney (1919), by S. G. Thorp (1887–1967), provided the models for domestic architecture of the 1960s.

Greenway, Sydney (1923, south-east wing 1951) (p. 1659A) was the residence of Leslie Wilkinson (1882–1973), who came to Australia from England in 1918 to take up the first Chair of Architecture. It is the first of many houses in which he sought to demonstrate the appropriateness of the features of Mediterranean architecture for the climate of Australia. Wilkinson substituted pergolas and vaulted loggias for the traditional Australian overhanging eaves and verandahs. His many buildings for the University of Sydney, such as the **Physics Building** (1926) (p. 1659B), with R. Keith Harris, are related in style to his domestic work.

The designs for **Stanhill Flats, South Melbourne** (1942–50) (p. 1660A), by Frederick Romberg (1913–92), were ready by 1943 but war delayed the construction. Romberg, of German background, moved to Melbourne in 1939 and his early buildings were fundamental to the establishment of modern architecture in Australia. Stanhill welds together the taut, lightweight aesthetic of the International Style with the plastic forms typical of early Mendelsohn. Stanhill Flats was preceded by Romberg's **Newburn Flats, Melbourne** (1941), one of the first buildings with external concrete walls made directly from the formwork.

The **Rose Seidler House, Sydney** (1949) (p. 1658B), by Harry Seidler, one of three stylistically related houses designed by Seidler for a large bushland site in an outer suburb of the city, is a white, flat-roofed building with the main rooms elevated and supported on a stone core and on slender pipe columns. The nearby **Rose House** (1950) and **Marcus Seidler House** (1951) are of more interest structurally. The **Harry Seidler House, Sydney** (with Penelope Seidler) (1967), develops further the spatial, structural and formal qualities of the early houses.

The **Hamill House, Sydney** (1948) is one of four houses in Maytone Avenue, Killara, designed by Sydney Ancher (1904–79) between 1945 and 1951. It shows a typical adaptation of the modern architecture of Europe to Australian sites and conditions. **The houses of Robin Boyd** (1919–71), on the other hand, are notable for a structural approach to design and the positive use of open space. The **Boyd House, Melbourne** (1957), is divided into two double-level sections placed at either end of the site. The roofs are carried on suspension cables which span the courtyard between them. Other examples include the **Featherston House, Melbourne** (1967), and the **Richardson House, Melbourne** (1954); they are typical of the exploratory architecture which was evolved in Melbourne in the 1950s and 1960s. The **Grounds House, Melbourne** (1952) and the house at **Frankston, Victoria** (1953), by Sir Roy Grounds, share similar characteristics with the Boyd houses.

The **Johnson House, Sydney** (1963), by R. N. (Peter) Johnson (born 1923), is an example of the romantic architecture of the Sydney School. It is a rugged building of highly textured clinker bricks and dark-stained unplaned timbers exposed inside and outside. The colours and textures blend with the suburban bushland site. The **Woolley House, Sydney** (1962), by Ken Woolley (born 1933), provides a further rugged example of the work of the Sydney School.

The **Musgrave House, Brisbane** (1973), by John Dalton (born 1927) and Associates, is one of many houses in which Dalton demonstrated that the traditional ways of building in the hot climate of Queensland could be adapted to modern design. Window openings to control sun, traditional ceiling fans, verandahs and pergolas all contribute to an architecture which is responsive to climate.

The **Tent House, Eumundi** (1991) (p. 1662A), by Gabriel Poole (born 1934) is located on an isolated site in coastal mountains. The building is typical of Poole's Queensland work in its reductivist aesthetic and minimal enclosure. It has a simple rectangular plan and consists of an elevated platform supporting a steel framed pavilion with fabric roof and walls that can be rolled up to open the interior to the environment.

The **Short House, Kempsey, New South Wales** (1975) (three bays added 1981), by Glenn Murcutt (born 1936), consists of a linked pair of light, timber-framed pavilions with corrugated steel roofs. Baffled rooflights and louvred windows help create an interior with some of the character of the traditional verandah. The simple plan and the line of the building exterior are characteristic of Murcutt's rural houses which include the well-sited **Magney House, Bingie Bingie** (1984). Murcutt's **Marika-Alderton House, Nhulunbuy** (1994), and the **Kakadu Visitor Infor-**

A. Eryldene, Sydney (1914). See p. 1657

B. Rose Seidler House, Sydney (1949). See p. 1657

A. (*above*)
Greenway, Sydney:
south-east wing (1951).
See p. 1657
B. (*right*)
Physics Building, University
of Sydney (1926).
See p. 1657

A. Stanhill Flats, south Melbourne (1942–50). See p. 1657

B. The Woolley House, Paddington, Sydney (1981). See p. 1663

C. Forbes Street Houses, Woolloomooloo, Sydney (1979). See p. 1663

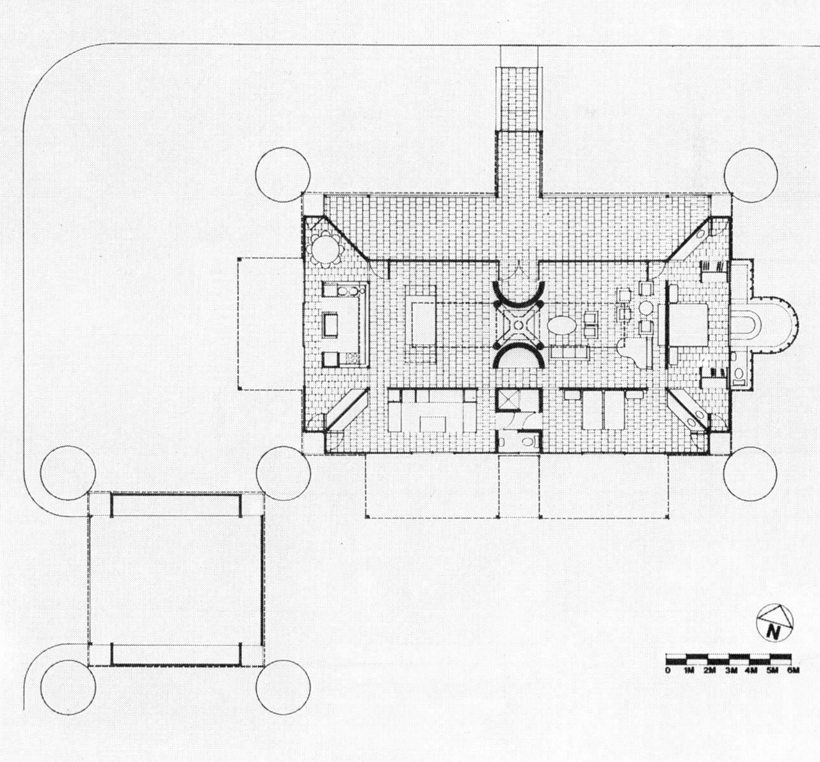

The Andrews House,
Eugowra, New South Wales
(1980): exterior and plan
See p. 1663

A. Tent House, Eumundi (1991). See p. 1657

B. Yulara (1984). See p. 1663

C. Athan House, Monbulk (1988). See p. 1663

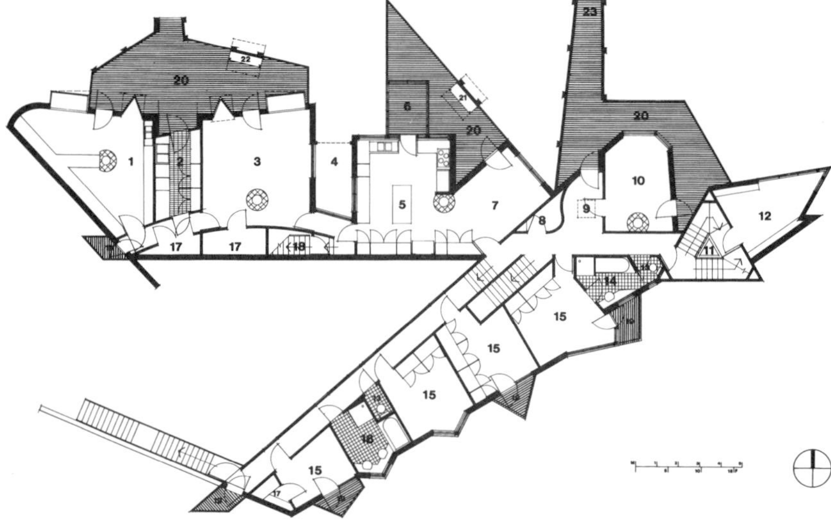

D. (*right*) Athan House: first-floor plan. 1 Studio, 2 laundry, 3 living room, 4 aviary, 5 kitchen, 6 greenhouse fernery, 7 dining room, 8 cloak room, 9 entry foyer, 10 parlour, 11 stairwell, 12 library, 13 toilet, 14 en suite, 15 bedroom, 16 bathroom, 17 storage, 18 cellar, 19 balcony, 20 decking, 21 breakfast seat, 22 artist's seat, 23 entry bridge, 24 winter garden

mation Centre and Park Headquarters (1994) (in association with Troppo Architects), are in the tropical areas of the Northern Territory and were influenced by Aboriginal traditions and building practices. Both buildings consist of open, climatically responsive, lightweight pavilions with adjustable enclosures. **The Andrews House, Eugowra, New South Wales** (1980) (p. 1661), by John Andrews, is a prefabricated steel-framed building with wall and roof cladding of corrugated steel. It extends the formal qualities and sound climatic design features of the traditional homestead but creates a new dramatic image. The **Jackson House and Stables, Shoreham, Victoria** (1978), by Daryl Jackson, are of weathered, silver-grey timbers and corrugated steel. Rustic timber buildings of this kind are found in the work of many Melbourne architects.

The **Woolley House, Paddington, Sydney** (1981) (p. 1660B), by Ken Woolley, is built on a steep, narrow site in an inner-city suburb and rises turret-like from the ground, which is below street level. The curved corrugated-steel roof and the oversized Victorian chimney stack were derived from the surrounding architecture.

The **Forbes Street Houses, Woolloomooloo, Sydney** (1979) (p. 1660C), by Philip Cox and Partners, are terrace houses designed to be compatible with the neighbouring nineteenth-century housing. These are a part of the Woolloomooloo Scheme of public low-income housing in which renovated terrace houses are combined with infill houses and walk-up apartments.

The tourist township of **Yulara** (1984) (p. 1662B), also by Cox, is in the very fragile, arid red lands of central Australia near Ayers Rock. This striking group of buildings is built along a spine following a dune and is notable for its sympathetic visual and ecological response to the site.

Athan House, Monbulk (1988) (p. 1662C,D), by Edmond and Corrigan extends the architects' typical language of the suburbs to a rural setting with the idea of the building as a series of houses facing a nominal 'street'. The plan is splintered on two levels, and vibrant colours and various materials and textures add to the dynamic composition of fractured forms.

New Zealand

Office Buildings

Massey House, Wellington (1952), by Plischke and Firth, a seven-storeyed office building, is an early New Zealand example of curtain-wall construction. The building is refined in its detail and in the lively patterning of the facades. Ernest Plischke (born 1903) migrated from Austria to New Zealand in 1939 and introduced an accomplished and disciplined architecture based on the International Style.

Public Building

The **Railway Station, Dunedin** (1904), by Sir George Troup (1863–1941), is in a bold eclectic style, its facades enriched with geometric patterns of contrasting materials. The booking hall contains fine Art Nouveau majolica tiled panels. In contrast, the **Railway Station, Wellington** (1937), by Gray Young, Morton and Young, presents a flat neo-Georgian facade relieved only by a projecting Doric portico. The copper-vaulted booking hall is large in scale and was probably inspired by Pennsylvania Station, New York.

The **Lyttelton Road Tunnel Authority Administration Building, Christchurch** (1963), by Peter Beaven (born 1925), provides for the collection of tolls, and the administration and servicing of the tunnel connecting Christchurch to its port at Lyttelton. It is a Brutalist *in-situ* concrete building with a curved sculptured form suggesting strength and monumentality in a stark landscape. Beaven's personal and often wilful architecture inspired those who sought an architectural expression rooted in the New Zealand landscape and vernacular traditions.

Christchurch Town Hall and Civic Centre (1972) by Warren and Mahoney was the winning scheme in a competition. It is a restrained and rational design containing a fine auditorium with outstanding acoustical control.

Wellington Library (1992), by Ian Athfield (born 1940), is a stately yet whimsical building with a principal facade of precast concrete panels supported on low arches pierced by a lofty entrance portal embellished with Nikau Palm columns of copper and lead with steel fronds that support a bridging truss. The Nikau Palms continue as a colonnade flanking the side facade. A sinuous glass wall edges the redeveloped **Wellington Civic Square** (1992) from which access is available to a mezzanine level passage with shops and coffee-bars providing views, but not entry, into the library. Colourful finishes and carpets, neon signage, and imaginative metal elements and details enliven the extensive interior space.

Stables Complex, Auckland Trotting Club (1991), by Adams Langley Architects, is a direct solution that consists of two curved halls each with precast concrete perimeter walls that contrast with independent gently curved roofs that cantilever from steel columns towards the central axis. A continuous gap between the independent arcs of the roofs allows for natural light and ventilation.

Churches and Educational Buildings

Christ's College, Christchurch (founded 1850), the **Hare Memorial Library** (1916) and the **Memorial Dining Hall** (1925) by Cecil Wood (1878–1947)

A. Auckland Grammar School (1916). See p. 1665

B. University College, Auckland (1921). See p. 1665

C. Civic Theatre, Auckland (1929). See p. 1665

represent the best of the historical revival architecture. Wood was a nephew of Norman Shaw and an exponent of the English Free Style.

Auckland Grammar School (1916) (p. 1664A), by R. Aitkinson Abbott (1883–1954), is a fine representative example of the Spanish Mission Style with a symmetrical facade with bold arches. **University College, Auckland** (1921) (p. 1664B), by Roy Alston Lippincott and Edward Billson, is an arresting building combining solidly massed wings of rusticated stone and concrete with a fanciful Gothic central entrance hall surmounted by a fretted and incised concrete clock tower. The architecture is undoubtedly inspired by that of Lippincott's brother-in-law and associate in Australia, Walter Burley Griffin (q.v.).

Futuna Chapel, Marist Fathers Retreat House, Wellington (1961), by John Scott (1924–92), is a spatially complex building, though maintaining the simple geometric discipline of a square plan surmounted by a symmetrical roof with crossed ridges. Between the ridges the roof planes are folded forming hips and valleys. The quality of the light admitted by the coloured acrylic windows combines with the elusive spatial effect to create a distinctive and moving atmosphere in the building. In his **All Saints Church, Ponsonby, Auckland** (1959), Dick Toy (1911–95) adapted the gable roof form and the plan of the traditional Maori's shelter to Christian architecture. Toy was an influential romantic who taught at the University of Auckland.

Cinemas

The **Civic Theatre, Auckland** (1929) (p. 1664C), by Bohringer, Taylor and Johnson (of Melbourne), is a grand atmospheric theatre on an Indian theme. The decorative facades, which have friezes with Greek figures and incised panels between fluted columns, culminate in an angled clock tower which accentuates the corner site on which it stands.

Domestic Buildings

26 Heriot Row, Dunedin (1905), by Basil Hooper (1877–1960), is typical of the large picturesque houses influenced by English architects such as Webb and Voysey. The bay window, leaded lights and rearing chimney stacks add a romantic flavour to the simple asymmetrical wings under slate gabled roofs. The persistence of the Arts and Crafts tradition can be seen also in the 'English Cottages' of the 1920s designed and built by James Walter Chapman-Taylor (1878–1958).

The **Raynor House, Auckland** (1913 or 1916), by Roy Keith Binney (1886–1957), clearly shows the influence of Lutyens, under whom Binney studied before beginning practice in Auckland in 1912. Built of bluestone (lower storey) and dark-stained shingles (upper storey) it is a robust building sheltered by a dominant roof with projecting rafters. The varied fenestration, which includes tall bow windows for the stairwell, derives from Lutyens. There are similar details in the **Binney House, Auckland** (1911), which combines the romantic and Classical aspects of Lutyens' work.

Stoneways, Auckland (1926) (p. 1666A), which combines Classical proportions with picturesque crafted features, was the home of William H. Gummer (1885–1966) who had worked for Lutyens and for Burnham in Chicago, before establishing in 1923 a highly successful practice with C. R. Ford. The **Dilworth Building, Auckland** (1927), and the **Domain Winter Gardens, Auckland** (1914–29), are among Gummer's finest non-domestic designs.

Berhampore Flats, Wellington (1938–40) (p. 1666B), by the Government's Housing Construction Department, of which Francis Gordon Wilson (1900–59) was Chief Architect, are of domestic scale with two- and three-storeyed blocks arranged around a central square containing a circular community hall. They were the first high-quality housing introduced by the Department and are evidently influenced by modern European architecture. They are asymmetrical with undecorated white facades, flat roofs and balconies. **State Flats, Auckland** (1947), designed by Ernest Plischke, are a further example of the work of the Housing Construction Department. They resemble the Weissenhof Housing in Stuttgart (1927).

The **Rotherham House, Devonport** (1951), by Bruce Rotherham (born 1927) of Group Architects, is an early example of the romantic domestic architecture of Auckland in the 1950s and 1960s. It is a single-volume space interrupted by a fireplace and a curved stairway that leads to a mezzanine which extends the full width of the house. It combines textured, dark materials with external walls made up of industrial glazing.

In designing the **Pattison House, Waipawa** (1967), John Scott drew his inspiration from the site and the nearby seismic fault line, in that the spatial characteristics of the house arise from its structure. His **Ngamatea House, Hawkes Bay** (1990), is a cavernous, enveloping building of warm natural materials that is sheltered by a spreading pyramidal roof. The house merges with the hillocks of the site and the two arms of the plan embrace a sheltered courtyard.

The **Athfield House, Wellington** (1965), by Ian Athfield, is by contrast a social and architectural statement of considerable originality on a steep site overlooking the town. The house has been extended in various ways over two decades and grows naturally up the hillside. The plastered sculptural curved forms diminish the distinction between walls, roofs and chimneys. Another and particularly poetic example of

A. Stoneways, Auckland (1926). See p. 1665

B. Berhampore Flats, Wellington (1938–40). See p. 1665

C. The Cox House, Petone, Wellington (1978). See p. 1668

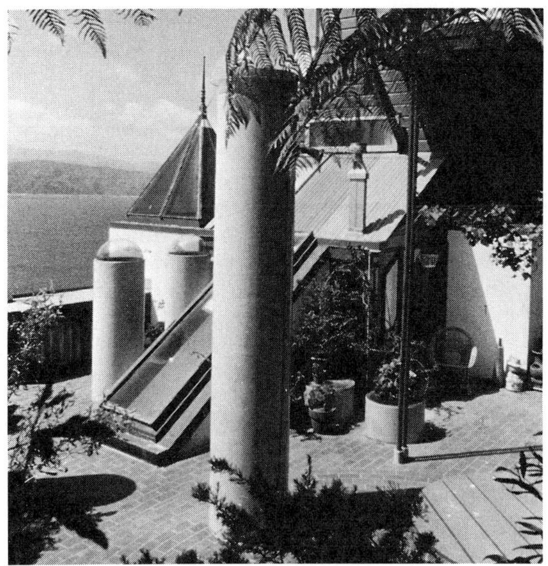

A. The Britten House, Wellington (1974). See p. 1668

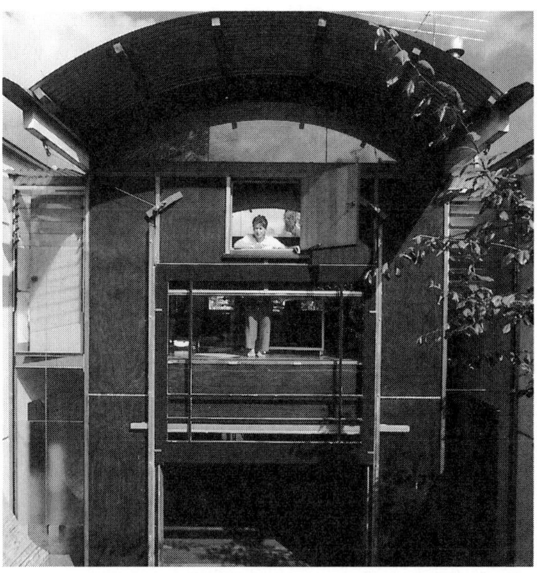

B. The Mitchell/Stout House, Auckland (1990). See p. 1668

C. Nuku'alofa Club, Nuku'alofa, Tonga (1914). See p. 1668

D. Conference Centre, Suva, Fiji (1994). See p. 1668

E. The Raun Raun Theatre, Goroka, Papua New Guinea (1982). See p. 1668

Athfield's architecture is the **Cox House, Petone, Wellington** (1978) (p. 1666D), where a variety of vernacular forms become sculptural objects in the open green farmland.

The **Britten House, Wellington** (1974) (p. 1667A), by Roger Walker (born 1942), combines multiple geometric shapes in a variety of unexpected ways. The various elements of the building – box-like forms with circular windows, pyramidal and pitched roofs (often more than 45 degrees) – step up a steep hillside overlooking Wellington. Spaces are distributed on eight levels in a highly personal and picturesque manner. Walker's **Wellington Club** (1972), now demolished, was a visually powerful building that combined a strong Brutalist aesthetic with a roofscape of towers and pyramidal shapes.

The **Gibbs House, Auckland** (1984), by David Mitchell (born 1941), is unrelated to contemporary trends in the architecture of New Zealand. Its precise angled planes and clearly cut openings produce a lucidity reminiscent of Le Corbusier's houses. **The Mitchell/Stout House, Auckland** (1990) (p. 1667B), with Julie Stout (born 1958), which is a multilevel and spatially complex townhouse on a steep site, reverts to a picturesque timber romanticism.

The **Congreve House, Auckland** (1992), by Pip Cheshire (born 1950) of Jasmax, is a sophisticated and austere composition of abstract, sculptural elements in rough and polished concrete brick. The simple orthogonal plan is loosely organised along an axis that relates the tripartite scheme of house, courtyard and pool, and controls vistas from the cliff-edge site.

Papua New Guinea and the Smaller Islands of the South Pacific

The **Ceremonial House, Paiyembit, Palimbei Village, Sepik River, Papua New Guinea** (1978), shows the continuation of traditional building practices using local materials for ceremonial buildings. Longhouses in the region housed entire villages and were up to 180 m (590 ft) in length. The last surviving example in Isago Village, Aramia River (1959), was destroyed by fire. A replica has been built at the Gogodola Cultural Centre, Balimo (1973).

The **Nuku'alofa Club, Nuku'alofa, Tonga** (1914) (p.1667C), built to plans by H. Monk, is a bungalow of timber construction. With its weatherboard siding, corrugated-iron roof and raised verandah it is typical of the many climate-conscious buildings erected by Europeans in this as in other tropical regions.

The **Raun Raun Theatre, Goroka, Papua New Guinea** (1982) (p. 1667E), by Rex Addison and Paul Frame, is a column-free timber-pole structure 18 m (59 ft) high with intersecting, conical kunai thatched roofs. The design owes much to the traditional village round house. The **Coffee Industries Board Offices and Warehouse, Goroka, Papua New Guinea** (1982), also by Rex Addison, combines a richly textured and modelled timber-framed, shingle-roofed office building, with an auditorium clad in stone and a steel-framed warehouse. The jutting roofs and the baffled and screened facades of the office building make a lively response to the problems of climate.

The **South Pacific Bureau for Economic Cooperation (SPEC) Forum Secretariat, Suva, Fiji** (1976–94), by Architects Pacific, consists of a series of modern buildings with short cross-axes, and steep triple-pitched roofs, oversailing gables and eaves which reflect indigenous Fijian architecture. The gables of the major buildings in the group are enlivened by Fijian paintings. The **Conference Centre** (1994) (p. 1667D) relates to the earlier structures and incorporates an authentic thatched Polynesian 'fale'. A water-blasted plaster finish containing sea shells gives the walls the appearance of sandy beaches. Architects Pacific's **Headquarters for the South Pacific Commission, Noumea, New Caledonia** (competition 1992 – completed 1995), is imbued with Pacific Ocean metaphors. The navigation chart of the Marshall Islands underlies the site planning, and canoe construction informs the structural design and form of the main building, the Conference Centre. The principal wall consists of a stitched coconut wood panel assembled using traditional canoe building techniques. Huge operable vertical louvres of white 'masi' (tapa cloth) control the light. Reflections from outside water pools evoke images of the Pacific Ocean.

Radio Station, Honiara, Solomon Islands (1981) (p. 1669A), by Ancher Mortlock and Woolley, responds to the tropical conditions by placing the heavy-walled sound-sensitive parts of the building along one side of a courtyard and protecting the remainder of the lighter-weight buildings with hinged lattice shutters of local hardwood. The perimeter offices are one room deep with access from the verandah surrounding the courtyard. The shutters are designed to stand at different angles according to aspect, and bolted flat they serve as storm shutters.

Maoto Fono, the Legislative. Assembly Building, **Ti-afau, Apia, Western Samoa** (1971) (p. 1669C), by the Public Works Department at Apia, is a circular building with a heavy projecting overhang and a domed roof clad in shingles. The old fono from which its form was derived is preserved on the same site. The latter, a thatched building, was reconstructed in 1975 (p. 1669B).

The **Parliament House of Papua New Guinea, Port Moresby** (1984) (p. 1669D), by the Papua New Guinea Government Architect (design architect Cecil Hogan, born 1926) with Peddle Thorp and Harvey, unites three buildings under one embracing roof. Surrounding water pools refer to the seas around the country. The central block containing the Great Hall

A. Radio Station, Honiara, Solomon Islands (1981). See p. 1668

B. Old Fono, Apia, Western Samoa (reconstructed 1975). See p. 1668

C. Maoto Fono, Apia, Western Samoa (1971). See p. 1668

D. Parliament House of Papua New Guinea, Port Moresby (1984). See p. 1668

E. Parliament of Fiji, Suva (1992). See p. 1670

is symbolically derived from the 'haus tambaran' of the Sepik River region while the round building housing entertainment facilities is characteristic of the 'haus raun' of the Highlands. Decorative elements are based on the diverse artistic traditions of the nineteen provinces. Native timbers including structural glulam beams are used throughout.

With the ending of colonial rule for many of the countries in the region further Parliament buildings were completed in the 1990s, including those for Vanuatu and the Solomon Islands. Of note is the **Parliament of Fiji, Suva** (1992) (p. 1669E), by Vitia Architects with the Fijian Government Architect, which is based on a Fijian village and planned as a series of structures with short cross-axes for natural cooling. The Vale ni Bose Lawa housing the Legistative chamber is based on the 'bure kalou' and stands on a ceremonial 'yavu' (stone platform) and is sheltered by a high, steep pyramidal roof with upturned eaves. Decorative structural binding, woven mats, 'masi', and carvings derived from Fijian implements and ornaments enhance the interiors.

Lae Lodge, Lae, Papua New Guinea (1950), a guest house and hostel, has a raised floor and wide verandahs typical of early Australian building in the islands and in the northern regions of Australia itself. It is timber-framed with timber siding and a main roof clad in corrugated galvanised iron. This language and the logic of traditional living patterns and crafts persist as the basis for much of the more responsive housing such as **Asiawe Village Stage II, Lae** (1991), by Niugini Pacific Consultants (design architect, Rahim Milani (born 1941), and Pacific Architecture's houses on **Bougainville** (1990) and **New Britain** (1992).

BIBLIOGRAPHY

PART 1 The Architecture of Egypt, the Ancient Near East, Asia, Greece and the Hellenistic Kingdoms

Chapter 2 Prehistoric

ALDRED, C. *Egypt to the End of the Old Kingdom.* London, 1965.

ANATI, E. *Palestine Before the Hebrews.* London, 1963.

BAUMGARTEL, E. J. *The Cultures of Prehistoric Egypt.* Oxford, 1955.

BURNEY, C. *The Ancient Near East.* New York, 1977.

CHILDE, V.G. *New Light on the Most Ancient East.* London, 1958 (reprinted).

DAVID, R. *The Ancient Egyptians: Religious Beliefs and Practices.* London, 1982.

HAYES, W. C. *Most Ancient Egypt.* Chicago, 1964.

LAMPL, P. *Cities and Planning in the Ancient Near East.* London, 1970.

LLOYD, S. *The Archaeology of Mesopotamia.* London, 1978.

—. *Early Highland Peoples of Anatolia.* London, 1967.

MELLAART, J. *Catal Huyuk.* London, 1967.

—. *The Earliest Civilisations of the Near East.* London, 1965.

—. *The Neolithic of the Near East.* London, 1975.

MOOREY, P. R. S. *The Origins of Civilisation.* Oxford, 1979.

OATES, D. and OATES, J. *The Rise of Civilisation.* Oxford, 1976.

REDMAN, C. L. *The Rise of Civilisation.* San Francisco, 1978.

TRIGGER, B.G. *Ancient Egypt: a Social History.* Cambridge, 1983.

UCKO, P. J. *Man, Settlement and Urbanism.* London, 1972.

WOLFF, W. *Early Civilizations: Egypt, Mesopotamia, the Aegean.* London, 1989.

Chapter 3 Egypt

ALDRED, C. *The Development of Egyptian Art.* London, 1952.

ARNOLD, D. *Building in Egypt: Pharaonic Stone Masonry.* Oxford, 1991.

BADAWY, A. *A History of Egyptian Architecture.* 3 vols. Giza (Vol.1) and Berkeley, 1954–68.

BREASTED, J. H. *A History of Egypt.* New York, 1905.

BRITISH MUSEUM. *An Introduction to Ancient Egypt* (Guide to Collections). London, 1979.

CARTER, H. and MACE, A. C. *The Tomb of Tut-ankh-Amen.* 3 vols. London, 1923–33.

DAVIES, W. V. (Ed.). *Egypt and Africa: Nubia From Prehistory to Islam.* London, 1991.

DRIOTON, E. and LAUER, J. P. *Sakkarah: the Monuments of Zoser.* Cairo, 1939.

DRIOTON, E. and VANDIER, J. *Les Peuples de l'orient méditerranéen (l'Egypte).* Paris, 1952.

EDWARDS, I. E. S. *The Pyramids of Egypt.* New edn, Harmondsworth, 1985.

EMERY, W. B. and OTHERS. *Great Tombs of the First Dynasty.* 3 vols. London, 1949–58.

FAIRMAN, H. W. 'Town Planning in Pharaonic Egypt', *Town Planning Review,* vol. xx, no.1. 1949.

—. 'Worship and Festivals in an Egyptian Temple', *Bulletin of the John Rylands Library,* vol. 37, no.1. 1954.

FAKHRY, A. *The Pyramids.* Chicago, 1969.

FIRTH, C. M., QUIBELL, J. E. and LAUER, J. P. *The Step Pyramid.* Cairo, 1935.

GARDINER, A. H. *The Temple of King Sethos I at Abydos.* Vols. i-iii. London and Chicago, 1933–8.

—. 'Les grandes découvertes archéologiques de 1954', *La Revue de Caire,* vol. xxxiii, no. 175, Numéro Spécial.

GORRINGE, H. H. *Egyptian Obelisks.* New York, 1882.

HART, G. *Pharaohs and Pyramids: a Guide Through Old Kingdom Egypt.* London, 1991.

HODGES, P. *How the Pyramids Were Built*. Shaftesbury, 1989.
HORNUNG, E. *The Valley of the Kings: Horizon of Eternity*. New York, 1990.
IVERSON, I. *The Canon and Proportion in Egyptian Art*. 2nd ed. Warminster, 1975.
KAMIL, J. *Luxor: a Guide to Ancient Thebes*. 3rd edn, London, 1983.
KEMP, B. J. *Ancient Egypt: Anatomy of a Civilization*. 2nd edn, London, 1991.
KIELLAND, E. C. *Geometry in Egyptian Art*. Oslo, 1987.
LANGE, K. and HIRMER, M. *Egypt*. 4th edn, 1968.
MEHLING, M. (ED.). *Egypt*. Oxford, 1990. *Monuments of Egypt: the Napoleonic Edition: the Complete Archaeological Plates from La Description de l'Egypte*. Princeton and London, 1987.
NAVILLE, E. and CLARKE, G. SOMERS. *The XIth Dynasty Temple at Deir el-Bahari*. Parts I and II. London, 1907, 1910.
PETRIE, W. M. FLINDERS. *Egyptian Architecture*. London, 1938.
PORTER, B. and MOSS, R. L. B. *Topographical Bibliography of Ancient Egyptian Hieroglyphic Texts, Reliefs, and Painting*. 7 vols. Oxford, 1927–51; amplified 2nd edn, 1960–4.
REISNER, G. A. *The Development of the Egyptian Tomb down to the Accession of Cheops*. Cambridge, Mass., and London, 1935.
SETON-WILLIAMS, V. Egypt. 3rd edn, London, 1993.
SMITH, W. STEVENSON. *The History of Egyptian Sculpture and Painting in the Old Kingdom*. London, 1946; 2nd edn, 1949.
—. *The Art and Architecture of Ancient Egypt*. Harmondworth, 1958. Revised by W. K.Simpson, 1981.
STEINDORFF, G. and SEELE, K.C. *When Egypt Ruled the East*. Chicago, 1942; revised edn, 1957.
UPHILL, E. P. *The Temples of Per Ramesses*. Warminster, 1984.
WOLDERING, I. *Egypt: the Art of the Pharaohs* (Art of the World series). London, 1963.

Chapter 4 The Ancient Near East

AKURGAL, E. *The Birth of Greek Art*. London, 1968.
ALKIM, U. B. *Anatolia I*. Geneva, 1970.
ARIK, R. O. *Les Fouilles d'Alaca Hüyük*. Ankara, 1937.
BELL, E. *Early Architecture in Western Asia*. London, 1924.
BITTELL, K. *Boğazköy-Hattušas*. Berlin, 1952.
—. *Hattusha: The Capital of the Hittites*. New York, 1970.
BOTTA, P. E. and FLANDIN, E. *Monuments de Ninive*. 5 vols. Paris, 1849–50.
BURNEY, C. A. and LANG, D. M. *The Peoples of the Hills*. London, 1971.
CONTENEAU, G. *Everyday Life in Babylon and Assyria*. Trans. K. R. and A. R. Maxwell-Hyslop. London and New York, 1954.
—. *Manuel d'archéologie orientale*. 4 vols. Paris, 1947.
CURTIS, J. E. (Ed.). *Fifty Years of Mesopotamian Discovery*. London, 1983.
DIEULAFOY, M. *L'Art antique de la Perse*. 5 vols. Paris, 1884–9.
DOWNEY, S. B. *Mesopotamian Religious Architecture: Alexander Through the Parthians*. Princeton and London, 1988.
FERGUSSON, J. *The Palaces of Nineveh and Persepolis Restored*. London, 1851.
FORBES, T. B. *Urartian Architecture*. British Archaeological Reports. Oxford, 1983.
FRANKFORT, H. *The Art and Architecture of the Ancient Orient*. Harmondsworth, 1954, Rev. edn, 1970.
—. *The Birth of Civilisation in the Near East*. London, 1954.
GHIRSHMAN, R. *Iran*. Harmondsworth, 1961.
—. 'Report on the Ziggurat at Tchoga-Zanbil', *Illustrated London News*, 8 September 1956.
GURNEY, O. R. *The Hittites*. 2nd edn, Harmondsworth, 1961.
HASPELS, C. H. E. *The Highlands of Phrygia: Sites and Monuments*. 2 vols. Princeton, 1971.
KELLER, W. *The Bible as History*. London, 1956.
KEMPINSKI, A. and REICH, R. (Eds). *The Architecture of Ancient Israel: from the Prehistoric to the Persian Periods*. Jerusalem, 1992.
KENYON, KATHLEEN M. *Archeology in the Holy Land*. London, 1965, 1969.
—. *Digging up Jerusalem*. London, 1974.
—. *Royal Cities of the Old Testament*. London, 1971.
KUBBA, S. A. A. *Mesopotamian Architecture and Town Planning from the Mesolithic to the End of the Proto-historic Period, C.10,000–3,500 B.C.* Oxford, 1987.
LAMPL, PAUL. *Cities and Planning in the Ancient Near East*. London, 1970.
LAYARD, A. H. *Monuments of Nineveh*. 2 vols. London, 1849.
—. *Nineveh and its Palaces*. 2 vols. London, 1849.
LEICK, G. *A Dictionary of Ancient Near Eastern Architecture*. London, 1988.
LLOYD, S. *Early Highland Peoples of Anatolia*. London, 1967.
—. *Ruined Cities of Iraq*. 3rd edn, London, 1946.
LLOYD, S. AND MELLAART, J. *Beycesultan I-II*. London, 1962–5.
LOUD, G. *Khorsabad*. 2 vols. Chicago, 1936–8.
LUSCHAN, F. and OTHERS. *Ausgrabungen in Sendschirli*. 5 vols. Berlin, 1893–1943.
MACQUEEN, J. G. *Babylon*. London, 1964.
MALLOWAN, M. E. L. *Nimrud and its Remains*. 2 vols. London, 1966.
MELLAART, J. 'Notes on the Architectural Remains of Troy I and II', *Anatolian Studies*, ix, 1959.

NYLANDER, C. *Ionians in Pasargadae*. Stockholm, 1971.

OATES, D. 'Early Vaulting in Mesopotamia', in *Architectural Theory and Practice: Essays Presented to W. F. Grimes*. London, 1973.

OLMSTEAD, A. T. *History of the Persian Empire: Achaemenid Period*. Chicago, 1948.

PARROT, A. *Archéologie mésopotamienne*. 2 vols. Paris, 1946–53.

—. *Mari-Capitale fabuleuse*. Paris, 1974.

—. *Mission archéologique de Mari II: Le Palais. 1. Architecture. 2. Peintures. 3. Documents et Monuments*. Paris, 1958–9.

—. *Ziggurats et Tour de Babel*. Paris, 1949.

PERROT, G. and CHIPIEZ, C. *History of Art in Chaldea and Assyria, Persia, Phrygia and Judaea*. 5 vols. London and New York, 1884–92.

PLACE, VICTOR. *Ninive et l'Assyrie*. 3 vols. Paris, 1867–70.

PUCHSTEIN, O. *Boghazköy: die Bauwerke*. Leipzig, 1912.

RUSSELL, J. M. *Sennacherib's Palace Without Rival at Nineveh*. Chicago, 1991.

SAFAR, F., MUSTAFA, M. A. and LLOYD, S. *Eridu*. Baghdad, 1983.

SCHMIDT, E.F. *Persepolis I*. Chicago, 1953.

SINCLAIR, T. A. *Eastern Turkey: an Architectural and Archaeological Survey*. 3 vols. London, 1987–90.

SMITH, S. *Alalakh and Chronology*. Brochure. London, 1940.

SPIERS, R. P. *Architecture East and West*. London, 1905.

STRONACH, D. *Pasargadae*. Oxford, 1978.

TEXIER, C. *L'Arménie, la Perse et l Mésopotamie*. 2 vols. Paris, 1842–52.

WILBER, D. N. *Persepolis – The Archaeology of Parsa, Seat of the Persian Kings*. London, 1969.

WOOLLEY, SIR C. L. *A Forgotten Kingdom*. Harmondsworth, 1953.

—. *Ur of the Chaldees*. Harmondsworth, 1954.

WRIGHT, G. E. *Biblical Archaeology*. Philadelphia and London, 1957.

YADIN, Y. *The Art of Warfare in Biblical Lands*. London, 1963.

Chapter 5 Early Asian Cultures

AGRAWAL, D. P. *The Archaeology of India*. London, 1982.

ALLCHIN, B. and R. *The Rise of Civilisation in India and Pakistan*. Cambridge, 1982.

CHANG, K. C. *The Archaeology of Ancient China*. New Haven, 1963.

CHENG, TE-K'UN. *Archaeology in China. Vol. 1: Prehistoric China. Vol. 2: Shang China. Vol. 3: Chou China*. Cambridge, 1959–63.

RAWSON, J. *Ancient China*. London, 1980.

TRIESTMAN, J. *The Prehistory of China*. New York, 1972.

WATSON, W. *China Before the Han Dynasty*. London, 1961.

WHEELER, R. E. M. *Civilisations of the Indus Valley and Beyond*. New York, 1966.

—. *The Indus Civilisation. (Cambridge History of India)*. Cambridge, 1968.

Chapter 6 Greece

Chapter 7 The Hellenistic Kingdoms

ADAM, J. P. *L'Architecture militaire grecque*. Paris, 1983.

ASHMOLE, B. *Architect and Sculptor in Classical Greece*. London, 1972.

BEAN, G. E. *Aegean Turkey: an Archaeological Guide*. London, 1966.

—. *Lycian Turkey*. London, 1978.

—. *Turkey Beyond the Maeander*. London, 1971.

—. *Turkey's Southern Shore: an Archaeological Guide*. 2nd edn, London, 1979.

BERVE, H., GRUBEN, G. and HIRMER, M. *Greek Temples, Theatres and Shrines*. London, 1963.

BETANCOURT, PHILIP. *The Aeolic Style in Architecture*. Princeton, 1977.

BIEBER, M. *The History of the Greek and Roman Theatre*. London and Princeton, 1961.

BLEGEN, C. W. *Troy and the Trojans*. London, 1966.

BOARDMAN, J. *The Parthenon and its Sculptures*. London, 1985.

BRONEER, O. *Isthmia. Vol. 1: Temple of Poseidon*. Princeton, 1971.

BROWN, A. *Arthur Evans and the Palace of Minos*. Oxford, 1983.

BURFORD, A. *The Greek Temple Builders at Epidaurus*. Liverpool, 1969.

CADOGAN, G. *Palaces of Minoan Crete*. London, 1976.

CARY, M. *The Geographical Background of Greek and Roman History*. Oxford, 1949.

CHITHAM, R. *The Classical Orders of Architecture*. London, 1985.

COOK, J. M. *The Greeks in the East*. London, 1962.

COOK, R. M. *The Greeks till Alexander*. London, 1961.

COOPER, F. A. *The Temple of Apollo at Bassai*. London, 1978.

COULTON, J. J. *The Architectural Development of the Greek Stoa*. Oxford, 1976.

—. *Greek Architects at Work*. London, 1977.

DINSMOOR, W. B. *The Architecture of Ancient Greece*. 3rd edn, London, 1950.

DINSMOOR, W. B. JR. *The Propylaia to the Athenian Akropolis. Vol.1: The Predecessors*. Princeton, 1980.

DOXIADIS, C. E. *Architectural Space in Ancient Greece*. Cambridge, Mass., 1972.

FINLEY, M. I. *The Ancient Greeks*. London,1963.

GARDNER, R. W. *The Parthenon: its Science of Forms*. Washington, DC, 1973.

GRAHAM, J. W. *The Palaces of Crete*. Rev. edn, Princeton and London, 1987.
HANDLER, S. *Architecture on the Roman Coins of Alexandria*. AJA 75 (1971) 57f. for the Hellenistic Serapaion.
HEGE, W. and RODENWALDT, G. *The Acropolis*. Oxford, 1957.
HEYDEN, A. A. M. VAN DER and SCULLARD. H. H. (Eds). *Atlas of the Classical World*. London, 1960.
HENNER VON HESBERG. *Konsolengeisa des Hellenismus und der frühen Kaiserzeit*. RM Suppl. 24. Mainz, 1980.
HODGE, A. T. *The Woodwork of Greek Roofs*. Cambridge, 1960.
HOPPER, R. J. *The Acropolis*. London, 1971.
HUTCHINSON, R. W. *Pre-Historic Crete*. Harmondsworth, 1962.
LAWRENCE, A. W. *Greek Aims in Fortification*. Oxford, 1979.
—. *Greek Architecture*. 4th edn, Harmondsworth, 1983.
LYTTELTON, M. *Baroque Architecture in Classical Antiquity*. London, 1974.
MALLWITZ, A. *Olympia und seine Bauten*. Munich, 1972.
MARTIENSSEN, R. D. *The Idea of Space in Greek Architecture*. Witwatersrand, 1958.
MARTIN, R. *Living Architecture: Greek*. London, 1967.
—. *Manuel d'architecture grecque*. Vol.1. Paris, 1965.
—. *L'Urbanisme dans la Grèce antique*. Paris, 1956.
MATZ, F. *Crete and Early Greece*. London, 1962.
MERTENS, D. *Der Tempel von Segesta*. Mainz, 1984.
MILLER, S. *The Prytaneion*. Berkeley and Los Angeles, 1978.
ONIANS, J. *Bearers of Meaning: the Classical Orders in Antiquity, the Middle Ages and the Renaissance*. Princeton and London, 1988.
ORLANDOS, A. K. *Les Matériaux de construction et la technique architecturale des anciens grecs*. Paris, 1966.
PALAGIA, O. *The Pediments of the Parthenon*. Leiden, 1993.
PATON, J. M. and STEVENS, G. P. *The Erechtheum*. Cambridge, Mass., 1927.
PENDLEBURY, J. D. S. *A Handbook to the Palace of Minos, Knossos*. London, 1955.
QUENNELL, M. and QUENNELL, C. H. N. *Everyday Things in Ancient Greece*. 2nd edn, London, 1954.
ROBERTSON, D. S. *A Handbook of Greek and Roman Architecture*. 2nd edn, Cambridge, 1943.
ROUX, G. *L'Architecture de l'Argolide*. Paris, 1961.
SCRANTON, R. L. *Greek Architecture*. London, 1968.
YIGAL SHILOH. *The Proto-Aeolic Capital and Israelite Ashlar Masonry*. QEDEM Vol.II. Hebrew University of Jerusalem, 1979.
SPIERS, R. P. *The Orders of Architecture*. London, 1926.
STEELE, J. *Hellenistic Architecture in Asia Minor*. London, 1992.
STOBART, J. C. *The Glory that was Greece*. 4th edn, London, 1964.
TAYLOR, W. *Greek Architecture*. London, 1971.
TAYLOUR, W. *The Mycenaeans*. London, 1965.
THOMPSON, H. A. and WYCHERLEY, R. E. *The Agora at Athens: the History, Shape and Uses of an Ancient City Center*. Princeton, 1972.
TOMLINSON, R. A. *Greek Sanctuaries*. London, 1976.
TRAVLOS, J. *Pictorial Dictionary of Ancient Athens*. London and New York, 1971.
WINTER, F. E. *Greek Fortifications*. London, 1971.
WOODHEAD, A. G. *The Greeks in the West*. London, 1962.
WYCHERLEY, R. E. *How the Greeks Built Cities*. 2nd edn, London, 1962.

PART 2 The Architecture of Europe and the Mediterranean to the Renaissance

Chapter 9 Prehistoric

ATKINSON, R. J. C. *Stonehenge*. Harmondsworth, 1960 (1979 printing with revisions).
BURDAJEWICZ, M. *The Aegean Sea Peoples and Religious Architecture in the Eastern Mediterranean at the Close of the Late Bronze Age*. Oxford, 1990.
CHIPPINDALE, C. *Stonehenge Complete*. London, 1983.
CLARK, J. G. D. *Prehistoric Europe*. London, 1952
COLES, J. M. and HARDING, A. F. *The Bronze Age in Europe: an Introduction to the Prehistory of Europe c.2000–700 BC*. London, 1979.
COLLIS, J. *The European Iron Age*. London, 1984.
CUNLIFFE, B. *Iron Age Communities in Britain*. London, 1974.
DANIEL, G. E. *The Megalith Builders of Western Europe*. London, 1963.
—. *The Prehistoric Chamber Tombs of France*. London, 1960.
FAGERSTROM, K. *Greek Iron Age Architecture: Developments through Changing Times*. Gothenburg, 1988.
FORDE-JOHNSTON, J. *Prehistoric Britain and Ireland*. London, 1976.
GIMBUTAS, M. *Iron Age Cultures in Central and Eastern Europe*. The Hague, Paris, London, 1965.
—. *The Prehistory of Eastern Europe*. Cambridge, Mass., 1965.
GUILANE, J. *La Préhistoire française*. 2 vols. Paris, 1976.
KLEIN, R. G. *Ice Age Hunters of the Ukraine*. Chicago and London, 1973.
MILISAUSKAS, S. *European Prehistory*. London, 1978.
MORGAN, W. N. *Prehistoric Architecture in Micronesia*. London, 1989.
MUIR, R. and WELFARE, H. *The National Trust Guide to Prehistoric and Roman Britain*. London, 1983.

PERICOT GARCIA, L. *The Balearic Islands*. London, 1972.

PHILLIPS, P. *The Prehistory of Europe*. Harmondsworth, 1981.

PIGGOTT, S. *Ancient Europe: from the Beginnings of Agriculture to Classical Antiquity*. Edinburgh, 1965.

SAVORY, H. N. *Spain and Portugal: the Prehistory of the Iberian Peninsula*. London, 1968.

SIMPSON, D. D. A. *Economy and Settlement in Neolithic and Early Bronze Age Britain and Europe*. Leicester, 1971.

TRINGHAM, R. *Hunters, Fishers and Farmers of Eastern Europe 6000–3000 BC*. London, 1971.

WINTER, N. A. *Greek Architectural Terracottas from the Prehistoric to the End of the Archaic Period*. Oxford, 1993.

WYMER, J. *The Paleolithic Age*. London and Sydney, 1982.

Chapter 10 Rome and the Roman Empire

ADAM, J.-P. *Roman Building: Materials and Techniques*. London, 1994.

AURIGEMMA, S. *Villa Adriani*. Rome, 1962.

BARTON, I. (Ed.). *Roman Public Buildings*. Exeter, 1989.

BOETHIUS, A. *Etruscan and Early Roman Architecture*. 2nd edn, Harmondsworth, 1978.

—. *The Golden House of Nero*. Ann Arbor, 1960.

BRODRIBB, G. *Roman Brick and Tile*. Gloucester, 1987.

CLARKE, J. R. *The Houses of Roman Italy, 100 B.C. – A.D. 250: Ritual, Space and Decoration*. Berkeley, 1991.

COARELLI, M. (Ed.). *Etruscan Cities*. London, 1975.

COZZO, G. *The Colosseum, the Flavian Amphitheatre*. Rome, 1971.

DE LA BEDOYERE, G. *The Buildings of Roman Britain*. London, 1991.

GAZZOLA, P. *Ponti romani*. 2 vols. Florence, 1963.

GRANT, M. *The Roman Forum*. London, 1970.

HAMEY, L. A. *The Roman Engineers*. Cambridge, 1981.

HANSON, J. A. *Roman Theatre-Temples*. Princeton, 1959.

HEINTZE, H. VON. *Roman Art*. London, 1990.

HENIG, M. (Ed.). *Architecture and Architectural Sculpture in the Roman Empire*. Oxford, 1990.

JOHNSON, S. *Late Roman Fortifications*. London, 1983.

KAHLER, H. *Rome and her Empire*. London, 1963.

KRAUS, T. and MATT, L. VON, *Pompeii and Herculaneum*. New York, 1975.

LICHT, K. DE F. *The Rotunda in Rome*. Jutland Archaeological Society Publications VIII, Copenhagen, 1968.

LUCIANI, R. *The Colosseum: Architecture, History and Entertainment in the Flavian Amphitheatre, Ancient Rome's Most Famous Building*. Novara, 1990.

MACDONALD, W. L. *The Architecture of the Roman Empire. Vol. 1: An Introductory study. Vol. 2: An Urban Appraisal*. New Haven and London, 1965–86.

—. *The Pantheon*. London, 1976.

MACDONALD, W. and PINTO, J. *Hadrian's Villa and its Legacy*. New Haven and London, 1995.

MACREADY, S. and THOMPSON, F. H. (Eds). *Roman Architecture in the Greek World*. London, 1987.

MARTA, R. *Tecnica costruttiva romana (Roman Building Techniques.)* 2nd edn, Rome, 1991.

MCKAY, A. *Vitruvius: Architect and Engineer: Buildings and Building Techniques in Augustan Rome*. London, 1978.

MEIGGS, R. *Roman Ostia*. 2nd edn, Oxford, 1973.

NASH, E. *Pictorial Dictionary of Ancient Rome*. 2nd edn, 2 vols. London, 1968.

NIELSEN, I. *Thermae et Balnea: the Architecture and Cultural History of Roman Public Baths*. Aarhus, 1990.

RAGETTE, F. *Baalbek*. London, 1980.

RICHARDSON, L. *Pompeii: an Architectural History*. Baltimore, 1988.

RIVOIRA, G. T. *Roman Architecture*. Oxford, 1925.

ROBERTSON, D. S. *A Handbook of Greek and Roman Architecture*. 2nd edn, Cambridge, 1943.

SEAR, F. *Roman Architecture*. Rev. edn, London, 1989.

VITRUVIUS. *De Architectura*. 2 vols. Cambridge, Mass., 1945.

WARD-PERKINS, J. B. *Roman Architecture*. New York, 1977 (reprinted 1988).

—. *Roman Imperial Architecture*. 2nd (integrated) edn. Harmondsworth, 1981.

—. *Studies in Roman and Early Christian Architecture*. London, 1994.

WHEELER, R. E. M. *Roman Art and Architecture*. London, 1964.

WHITE, M. L. *Building God's House in the Roman World: Architectural Adaptation Among Pagans, Jews and Christians*. Baltimore, 1990.

Chapter 11 The Byzantine Empire

BUTLER, H. C. *Early Churches in Syria*. Princeton, 1929.

CORBO, V. C. *Il Santo Sepulcro di Gerusaleme*. Jerusalem, 1981.

CROWFOOT, J. W. *Early Churches in Palestine*. London, 1941.

DEMUS, O. *Byzantine Mosaic Decoration*. London, 1947.

FORSYTH, G. H. and WEITZMANN, K. *The Monastery of Saint Catherine at Mount Sinai: the Church and Fortress of Justinian*. Ann Arbor, 1968.

GALEY, J. *Sinai and the Monastery of St.Catherine*. Cairo, 1985.

GANDOLFO, F. *Le Basiliche armene: IV-VII secolo*. Rome, 1982.

GRABAR, A. *Byzantium from the Death of Theodosius to the Rise of Islam (The Arts of Mankind)*. London, 1966.

—. *Martyrium: recherches sur le culte des reliques et l'art chrétien antique*. 3 vols. Paris, 1943–46.

HETHERINGTON, P. *Byzantine and Medieval Greece: Churches, Castles and Art of the Mainland and the Peloponnese*. London, 1991.

HODDINOT, R. F. *Early Byzantine Churches in Macedonia and Southern Serbia*. London, 1963.

HUTTER, I. *Early Christian and Byzantine*. London, 1988.

KRAUTHEIMER, R., CORBETT, S., FRAZER, A.K. and FRANKL, W. *Corpus Basilicarum Christianarum Romae*. 5 vols. Vatican City, 1937–77.

KRAUTHEIMER, R. *Early Christian and Byzantine Architecture*. Rev. edn, Harmondsworth, 1981.

—. *Rome, Profile of a City, 312–1308*. Princeton, 1980.

—. *Three Christian Capitals*. Berkeley and Los Angeles, 1983.

MAINSTONE, R. J. *Hagia Sophia: Architecture, Structure and Liturgy of Justinian's Great Church*. London, 1988.

MANGO, C. *Byzantine Architecture*. New York, 1976.

MARK, R. and CAKMAK, A. H. (Eds). *Hagia Sophia from the Age of Justinian to the Present*. Cambridge, 1992.

MATHEWS, T. F. *The Byzantine Churches of Istanbul: a Photographic Survey*. University Park, Pa., 1976.

—. *The Early Churches of Constantinople: Architecture and Liturgy*. University Park, Pa, 1971.

MEPISASHVILI, R. and TSINTSADZE, V. *The Arts of Ancient Georgia*. London, 1979.

MILBURN, R. *Early Christian Art and Architecture*. Aldershot, 1988.

MULLER-WEINER, W. *Bildlexikon zur Topographie Istanbuls*. Tübingen, 1977.

PLANT, R. *Architecture of the Tigre, Ethiopia*. Worcester, 1985.

RODLEY, L. *Byzantine Art and Architecture: an Introduction*. Cambridge, 1994.

—. *Cave Monasteries of Byzantine Cappadocia*. Cambridge, 1985.

RUGGIERI, V. *Byzantine Religious Architecture (582–867): its History and Structural Elements*. Rome, 1991.

SINCLAIR, T. A. *Eastern Turkey: an Architectural and Archaeological Survey*. 3 vols. London, 1987–90.

STYLIANOU, A. and STYLIANOU, J. *The Painted Churches of Cyprus: Treasures of Byzantine Art*. London, 1985.

SWIFT, E. H. *Roman Sources of Christian Art*. New York, 1951.

VAN NICE, R. L. *St. Sophia in Istanbul: an Architectural Survey*. Washington, 1965.

WARD-PERKINS, J. B. *Studies in Roman and Early Christian Architecture*. London, 1994.

—. 'The Italian Element in Late Roman and Early Mediaeval Architecture', *Proceedings of the British Academy*, vol. 33, 1947, pp. 163–94.

WHARTON, A. J. *Art of Empire: Painting and Architecture of the Byzantine Periphery: a Comparative Study of Four Provinces*. University Park, Pa and London, 1987.

YARWOOD, D. *The Architecture of Europe. Vol. 1: The Ancient Classical and Byzantine World, 3000 B.C. – A.D. 1453*. London, 1992.

Chapter 12 Early Russia

AINALOV, D. *Geschichte der russischen Monumentalkunst*. Berlin and Leipzig, 1932–3.

ALPATOV, M. and BRUNOV, N. *Geschichte der altrussischen Kunst*. Augsburg, 1932.

BRUMFIELD, W. C. *A History of Russian Architecture*. Cambridge, 1993.

DEROKO, A. *Monumentalna i dekorativna arhitektura u serdnjovekovnoj Serbji*. Belgrade, 1953.

FAENSEN, H. and IVANOV, V. *Early Russian Architecture*. London and New York, 1975.

GRABAR, A. *Die Mittelalterliche Kunst Osteuropas*. Baden-Baden, 1968.

GALITZINE, G. *Imperial Splendour: Palaces and Monasteries of Old Russia*. London, 1991.

GIPPENREITER, V. *Old Russian Cities*. London, 1991.

HAMILTON, G. H. *The Art and Architecture of Russia*. 3rd (integrated) edn, Harmondsworth, 1983.

IONESCU, G. *Istoria arhitecturii in Romania*. Bucharest, 1963–4.

Istorija russkoj architektury, Kratkij kurs. Moscow, 1956.

KRAUTHEIMER, R. *Early Christian and Byzantine Architecture*. Harmondsworth, 1979.

MANGO, C. *Byzantine Architecture*. Milan, 1974.

MILLET, G. *L'Ancien art serbe: les églises*. Paris, 1919.

—. *L'art byzantin chez les slaves*. Paris, 1930–2.

MARODINOV, N. *Starobulgarskoto izkustvo*. Sofia, 1959.

MIJATJEV, K. *Arhitekturata v srednovekovna Bulgarija*. Sofia, 1965.

NICKEL, H. *Osteuropäische Baukunst des Mittelalters*. Leipzig, 1981.

OPOLOVNIKOV, A. V. and OPOLOVNIKOVA, Y. *The Wooden Architecture of Russia: Houses, Fortifications, Churches*. London, 1989.

PETKOVIC, V. P. *Pregled crkvenih spomenika kroz povesnicu Srpskog naroda*. Belgrade, 1950.

RAPPOPORT, P. A. *Drevnerusskaja architektura*. Moscow, 1970.

SAS-ZALOZIECKY, W. *Die byzantinische Baukunst in den Balkanländern*. Munich, 1955.

VORONIN, N. N. *Zodčestvo severo-vostočnoj Rusi*. Moscow, 1961–2.

WHARTON, A. J. *Art of Empire: Painting and Architecture of the Byzantine Periphery: a Comparative Study of Four Provinces*. University Park, Pa and London, 1987.

Chapter 13 Early Mediaeval and Romanesque

CLAPHAM, A. W. *Romanesque Architecture in Western Europe*. Oxford, 1936.

CONANT, K. J. *Carolingian and Romanesque Architecture, 800–1200*. 3rd edn, Harmondsworth, 1974.

FOCILLON, H. *Art of the West in the Middle Ages*. 2 vols. Vol.1: *Romanesque Art*. 2nd edn, London and New York, 1969.

FRANKL, P. *Die Frühmittelaterliche und Romanische Baukunst*. Potsdam, 1926.

GREENE, J. P. *Medieval Monasteries*. Leicester, 1992.

HELIOT, P. *Du Carolingien au Gothique (IXe-XIIIe S.)*. Paris, 1966.

HOLLANDER, H. *Early Medieval*. London, 1990.

HUBERT, J. *L'Art pre-Roman*. New edn. Chartres, 1974.

KUBACH, H. E. *Romanesque Architecture*. New York, 1975.

KUNSTLER, G. (Ed.). *Romanesque Art in Europe*. London, 1969.

LETHABY, W. R. *Mediaeval Art*. 1904. Revised and edited by D.Talbot Rice. London, 1949.

MOORE, C. H. 'Romanesque Architecture', *Journal RIBA*, 3rd series, vol. xxi, 1913–14.

PORTER, A. K. *Mediaeval Architecture: its Origins and Development*. 2nd edn, New York, 1966.

—. *Romanesque Sculpture of the Pilgrimage Roads*. 3 vols. New York, 1966.

PUIG Y CADAFALCH, J. *La Géographie et les origines du premier art roman*. Paris, 1935.

RADDING, C. M. *Medieval Architecture, Medieval Learning: Builders and Masters in the Age of Romanesque and Gothic*. New Haven and London, 1992.

SAALMAN, H. *European Architecture, 600–1200*. 2nd edn. New York and London, 1968.

TIMMERS, J. J. M. *Handbook of Romanesque Art*. London, 1969.

YARWOOD, D. *The Architecture of Europe*. Vol. 2: *The Middle Ages, 650–1550*. London, 1992.

ZARNECKI, G. *The Monastic Achievement*. London, 1972.

—. *Romanesque*. London, 1989.

ZODIAQUE 'La Nuit des Temps' Series. 60 volumes on Romanesque Architecture by Region.

Italy

ARATA, G. U. *L'Architettura arabo-normanna in Sicilia*. Milan, 1914.

ARSLAN, W. *L'Architetettura romanica veronese*. Verona, 1939.

CARLI, E. (Ed.). *Il Duomo di Pisa: il Battistero, il Campanile*. Florence, 1989.

CESILU, C. *Architettura romanica genovese*. Milan, 1945.

CUMMINGS, C. A. *A History of Architecture in Italy*. 2 vols. 2nd edn, New York and London, 1928.

DECKER, H. *Romanesque Art in Italy*. London, 1958.

GOY, R. J. *The House of Gold: Building a Palace in Medieval Venice*. Cambridge, 1992.

GURLITT, C. *Denkmäler der Kunst in Dalmatien*. 2 vols. Berlin, 1910.

KRONIG, WOLFGANG. *The Cathedral of Monreale and Norman Architecture in Sicily*. Palermo, 1965.

MAGNI, M. C. *Architettura romanica comasca*. Milan, 1960.

MARTIN, C. and ENLART, C. *L'Art roman en Italie*. Paris, 1912–24.

NORWICH, J. J. *The Normans in the South: 1016–1130*. London, 1967.

PORTER, A. K. *The Construction of Lombard and Gothic Vaults*. New Haven and London, 1911.

—. *Lombard Architecture*. 4 vols. New York, 1967. (reprint).

RICCI, C. *Romanesque Architecture in Italy*. London, 1925.

SALMI, M. *L'Architettura romanica in Toscana*. Milan and Rome, 1927.

VENTURI, A. *Storia dell'arte italiana*. Vols 2 and 3. Milan, 1902–4.

France

ARMI, C. E. *Masons and Sculptors in Romanesque Burgundy: the New Aesthetic of Cluny III*. University Park, Pa, and London, 1983.

AUBERT, M. *et al. L'Art roman en France*. Paris, 1961.

AUBERT, M. *Romanesque Cathedrals and Abbeys of France*. London, 1966.

AUBERT, M. and VERRIER, J. *L'Architecture française des origines à la fin de l'époque romane*. Paris, 1947.

BAUM, J. *Romanesque Architecture in France*. 2nd edn, London, 1928.

COLAS, RENÉE *Le Style roman en France*. Paris, 1927.

DESHOULIÉRES, F. *Élements datés de l'art roman en France*. Paris, 1936.

ENLART, C. *L'Architecture religieuse en France*. Paris, 1902.

EVANS, J. *Romanesque Architecture of the Order of Cluny*. Cambridge, 1938.

GANTNER, J. and POBÉ, M. *Romanesque Art in France*. London, 1956.

HEITZ, C. *L'Architecture religieuse carolingienne*. Paris, 1980.

HORSTE, K. *Cloister Design and Monastic Reform in Toulouse: the Romanesque Sculpture of La Daurade*. Oxford, 1992.

HUDSON, E. W. 'The Beginnings of Gothic Architecture and Norman Vaulting', *Journal RIBA*, 3rd series, vol. ix, 1902.

LASTEYRIE, R. DE. *L'Architecture religieuse en France à l'époque romane*. 2nd edn, Paris, 1929.

MARKHAM, V. R. *Romanesque France*. London, 1929.

MARTIN, C. *L'Art roman en France*. Paris, 1912.

MICHEL, A. *Histoire de l'art*. Paris, 1905. Vol. 1, pt 1 (for a contribution from C. Enlart on Romanesque).

PORTER, A. K. *Medieval Architecture*. 2 vols. New York and London, 1909.

REY, R. *L'Art roman et ses origines* (Archéologie pré-Romane et Romane). Toulouse and Paris, 1945.

RUPRICH-ROBERT, V. M. C. *L'Architecture normande aux XIe et XIIe siècles*. Paris, 1884–9. Farnborough, 1971 (reprint).

UHLER, F. *France romane*. Neuchatel and Paris, 1952.

VIOLLET-LE-DUC, E. E. *Dictionnaire raisonné de l'Architecture française du XIe au XVIe siècle*. 10 vols. Paris, 1858–68.

WATSON, K. *French Romanesque and Islam: Andalusian Elements in French Architectural Decoration, c. 1030–1180*. Oxford, 1989.

Central Europe

BERIDSE, W. and NEUBAUER, E. *Die Baukunst des Mittelalters in Georgien vom 4. bis zum 18. Jahrhundert*. Vienna, 1981.

BUSCH, H. *Germania Romanica*. Vienna and Munich, 1963.

DAVIES, J. G. *Medieval Armenian Art and Architecture: the Church of the Holy Cross, Aght'amar*. London, 1991.

GOSS, V. P. *Early Croatian Architecture: a Study of the Pre-Romanesque*. London, 1987.

GRODECKI, L. *Architecture ottonienne*. Paris, 1958.

HAUPT, A. VON. *Die Baukunst der Germanen von der Völker-wanderung bis zu Karl dem Grossen*. Leipzig, 1909. 3rd edn, Berlin, 1935.

HEITZ, C. *L'Architecture religieuse carolingienne*. Paris, 1980.

HORN, W. and BORN, E. *The Plan of St Gall: a Study of the Architecture & Economy of, & Life in a Paradigmatic Carolingian Monastery*. Berkeley, Calif., 1979.

JANTZEN, H. *Ottonische Kunst*. Munich, 1947.

LEHMANN, E. *Der frühe deutsche Kirchenbau*. Berlin, 1938.

LEUSCHNER, P. *Romanische Kirchen in Bayern*. Pfaffenhofen, 1981.

OSWALD, R., SCHAEFER, L. and SENNHAUSER, H. R. *Vorromanische Kirchenbauten. Katalog der Denkmäler bis zum Ausgang der Ottonen*. 3 vols. Munich, 1966–71.

SCHUTZ, B. and MÜLLER, W. *Deutsche Romanik: die Kirchenbauten der Kaiser, Bischofe und Kloster*. Freiburg, 1989.

SWIECHOWSKI, Z. *Romanesque Art in Poland*. Warsaw, 1983.

WAGNER-RIEGER, R. Mittelalterliche Architektur in Österreich. S. Polten, 1988.

Spain and Portugal

BEVAN, B. *Mudéjar Towers of Aragon*. London, 1929.

DODDS, J. *Architecture and Ideology in Early Medieval Spain*. University Park, Pa, and London, 1990.

GAILLARD, G. *Les Débuts de la sculpture romane espagnole*. Paris, 1938.

—. *Premiers essais de sculpture monumentale en catalogne aux Xe et XIe siècles*. Paris, 1938.

KING, G. G. *Mudéjar*. London, 1927.

—. *Pre-Romanesque Churches of Spain*. London, 1924.

—. *The Way of Saint James*. London, 1920.

POLLEY, G. H. *Spanish Architecture and Ornament*. Boston, 1919.

PORTER, A. K. *Spanish Romanesque Sculpture*. London, 1928.

PUIG Y CADAFALCH, J. *L'Architectura románica a Catalanya*. Barcelona, 1919–21.

WATSON, W. C. *Portuguese Architecture*. London, 1908.

WHITEHILL, W. M. *Spanish Romanesque Architecture of the Eleventh Century*. Oxford and London, 1941.

Holy Land

BOASE, T. S. R. *Castles and Churches of the Crusading Kingdom*. London, 1967.

DESCHAMPS, P. *Le Château de Saone*. Paris, 1935.

—. *Les Châteaux des Croisés en Terre Sainte. Le Crac des Chevaliers*. 2 vols. Paris, 1934.

—. *Terre Sainte Romane*. Zodiaque Series 'La Nuit des Temps', Vol. 21. La Pierre-qui-Vive, 1964.

FEDDEN, R. and THOMPSON, J. *Crusader Castles*. London, 1957.

KENNEDY, H. *Crusader Castles*. Cambridge, 1994.

LAWRENCE, T. E. *Crusader Castles*. New edn, with introduction and notes by Denys Pringle. Oxford, 1988.

MÜLLER-WIENER, W. *Castles of the Crusaders*. London, 1966.

PERNOUD, R. *In the Steps of the Crusaders*. London, 1959.

Britain and Ireland

BATSFORD, H. and FRY, C. *Cathedrals of England*. London, 1936.

BILSON, J. 'The Architecture of the Cistercians with Special Reference to some of their Earlier Churches in England', *Archaeological Journal*, vol. LXVI, 1909, pp. 185–280.

BOASE, T. S. R. *English Art: 1100–1216*. Oxford, 1953.

BROWN, G. B. *The Arts in Early England: Vol. 2, Anglo-Saxon Architecture*. 2nd edn, London, 1925.

BROWN, R. A. *English Castles*. London, 1976.

CLAPHAM, A. W. *English Romanesque Architecture After the Conquest*. Oxford, 1934.

—. *English Romanesque Architecture Before the Conquest*. Oxford, 1930.

—. *Romanesque Architecture in England*. London, 1950.

COX, J. C. *English Church Fittings*. London, 1933.

—. *Parish Churches of England*. London, 1937 and other editions.

CROSSLEY, F. H. *The English Abbey*. London, 1935.

CRUDEN, S. *The Scottish Castle*. London, 1960.

—. *Scottish Medieval Churches*. Edinburgh, 1986.

DUNBAR, J. G. *Historic Architecture of Scotland*. 2nd edn, London, 1978.

FERGUSSON, P. *Architecture of Solitude: Cistercian Abbeys in Twelfth-Century England*. Princeton and London, 1984.

FERNIE, E. C. *The Architecture of the Anglo-Saxons*. London, 1983.

GILYARD-BEER, R. *Abbeys*. London, 1958.

HARVEY, J. H. *Cathedrals of England and Wales*. London, 1974.

HENRY, F. *Irish Art*. 3rd edn, London, 1965.

HEWETT, C. A. *English Cathedral and Monastic Carpentry*. Chichester, 1985.

KAHN, D. *Canterbury Cathedral and its Romanesque Sculpture*. London, 1991.

LITTLE, B. *Architecture in Norman Britain*. London, 1985.

MORRIS, R. *Cathedrals and Abbeys of England and Wales: the Building Church, 600–1540*. London, 1979.

NORTON, C. and PARK, D. (Eds). *Cistercian Art and Architecture in the British Isles*. Cambridge, 1986.

PEVSNER, N. *et al. The Buildings of England*. Harmondsworth, 1951.

PLATT, C. *The Abbeys and Priories of Medieval England*. London, 1984.

—. *The Architecture of Medieval Britain: a Social History*. New Haven and London, 1990.

—. *The Castle in Medieval England and Wales*. London, 1982.

ROWLEY, T. *The Norman Heritage, 1055–1200*. London, 1983.

STOLL, R. *Architecture and Sculpture in Early Britain (Celtic, Saxon, Norman)*. London, 1966.

TAYLOR, H. M. and TAYLOR, J. *Anglo-Saxon Architecture*. Vols 1 and 2. Cambridge, 1965.

WEBB, G. F. *Architecture in Britain in the Middle Ages*. 2nd edn, Harmondsworth, 1965.

WOOD, M. *Norman Domestic Architecture*. London, 1974.

ZARNECKI, G. *English Romanesque Sculpture, 1066–1140*. London, 1951.

—. *Later English Romanesque Sculpture, 1140–1210*. London, 1953.

Scandinavia

ALNAES, E. *et al. Norwegian Architecture Throughout the Ages*. Oslo, 1950.

BUGGE, A. *Norwegian Stave Churches*. Oslo, 1953.

FABER, T. *A History of Danish Architecture*. Copenhagen, 1978.

GRAHAM-CAMPBELL, J. and KIDD, D. *The Vikings*. London, 1980.

HAHR, A. *Architecture in Sweden*. Stockholm, 1938.

LINDHOLM, D. *Stave Churches in Norway*. London, 1970.

SANTAKARI, E. *Keskiajan Kivikirkot – The Medieval Stone Churches of Finland*. Helsinki, 1979.

TUULSE, A. *Scandinavia Romanica*. Vienna, 1968.

Chapter 14 Gothic

General

DEUCHLER, F. *Gothic*. London, 1989.

GIMPEL, J. *The Cathedral Builders*. Salisbury, 1983.

GRODECKI, L. and BRISAC, C. *Gothic Stained Glass, 1200–1300*. London, 1985.

MARK, R. *Light, Wind and Structure: the Mystery of the Master Builders*. Cambridge, Mass. and London, 1990.

France

AUBERT, M. *L'Architecture française à l'époque gothique*. Paris, 1943.

AUBERT, M. and GOUBERT, S. *Cathédrales et trésors gothiques en France*. Paris, 1958.

BARANDARD, A. *La Cathédrale de Chartres dans tous ses états*. Paris, 1982.

BASDEVANT, D. *L'Architecture française*. Paris, 1971.

BAUDOT, A. DE and PERRAULT-DABOT, A. *Les Cathédrales de France*. 2 vols. Paris, 1905–7.

BONY, J. *Les Cathédrales gothiques en France du nord*. Paris, 1951.

—. *French Gothic Architecture of the 12th and 13th Centuries*. Berkeley, Calif. and London, 1983.

BOWIE, T. (Ed.). *The Sketchbook of Villard de Honnecourt*. Bloomington, Ind., 1959 and 1968. Several other illustrated commentaries on this album of annotated drawings by a thirteenth-century architect have been published in French, English and German.

BRANNER, R. *Burgundian Gothic Architecture*. London, 1960.

—. *The Cathedral of Bourges and its Place in Gothic Architecture*. New York and London, 1989.

—. *Gothic Architecture*. New York and London, 1961.

CALI, F. and MOLINIER, S. *L'ordre ogival*. Paris, 1963.

COLOMBIER, P. DU. *Les chantiers des cathédrales*. Paris, 1953.

CROSBY, S. M. *The Royal Abbey of Saint-Denis from its Beginnings to the Death of Suger, 475–1151*. New Haven and London, 1987.

DEMOUY, P. *Notre-Dame de Reims: la cathédrale royale*. Paris, 1986.

ERLANDE-BRANDENBOURG, A. *The Cathedral: the Social and Architectural Dynamics of Construction*. Cambridge, 1994.

—. *Notre-Dame De Paris*. Paris, 1991.

FAVIER, J. *The World of Chartres*. London, 1990.

FITCHEN, J. *The Construction of Gothic Cathedrals*. Oxford, 1961.

FOCILLON, H. *Art d'Occident, le Moyen Age roman et gothique*. Paris, 1938 and 1965.

FRANKL, P. *Gothic Architecture*. Harmondsworth, 1962.

GRODECKI, L. *Suger et l'architecture monastique*. Paris, 1948.

KURMANN, P. *La Façade de la cathédrale de Reims: architecture et sculpture des portails: étude archéologique et stylistique*. Paris, 1987.

LASTEYRIE, P. DE. *Histoire de l'architecture religieuse en France à l'époque gothique*. Paris, 1926.

LAVEDAN, P. *French Architecture*. Harmondsworth, 1956.

LEFRANÇOIS-PILLION, L. *Maîtres d'oeuvre et tailleurs de pierres des cathédrales*. Paris, 1949.

MÂLE, E. *L'Art religieux au XIIe et au XIIIe siècles en France*. 2 vols. Paris, 1910 and 1922. English editions of 13th-century volume: London, 1913 and 1961, New York, 1958.

MURRAY, S. *Beauvais Cathedral: Architecture of Transcendence*. Princeton and London, 1989.

RECHT, R. (Ed.). *Les Batisseurs des cathédrales gothiques*. Strasbourg, 1989.

SALET, F. *L'art gothique*. Paris, 1963.

SIMSON, O. VON. *The Gothic Cathedral*. 2nd edn, London, 1962.

VIOLLET-LE-DUC, E. *Dictionnaire raisonné de l'architecture française du XIe au XVIe siècles*. Paris, 1854–68.

WEST, G. H. *Gothic Architecture in England and France*. London, 1927.

WORRINGER, W. *Form in Gothic*. London, 1957.

Great Britain

BARLEY, M. W. *The English Farmhouse and Cottage*. London, 1961.

BATSFORD, H. and FRY, C. *The Greater English Church*. London, 1940.

BLOXHAM, M. H. *Introduction to English Church Architecture*. London, 1913.

—. *Gothic Architecture in England*. London, 1905.

—. *The Principles of Gothic Ecclesiastical Architecture*. London, 1849.

BONY, J. *The English Decorated Style*. Oxford, 1979.

BOWMAN, H. and CROWTHER, J. S. *The Churches of the Middle Ages*. Manchester, 1894.

BRANDON, R. and J. A. *Analysis of Gothic Architecture*. Edinburgh, 1903. (1st edn 1847)

—. *Open Timber Roofs of the Middle Ages*. London, 1849.

—. *Parish Churches*. 2 vols. London, 1851.

BRAUN, H. *English Abbeys*. London, 1971.

—. *Parish Churches*. London, 1970.

BRITTON, J. *Architectural Antiquities*. London, 1807–26.

—. *Cathedral Antiquities*. 13 vols. 1817–35.

BRUNSKILL, R. W. *Illustrated Handbook of Vernacular Architecture*. 2nd edn, London, 1978.

CLARK, G. T. *Mediaeval Military Architecture in England*. 2 vols. London, 1884.

COCKE, T. and KIDSON, P. *Salisbury Cathedral: Perspectives on the Architectural History*. London, 1993.

COLDSTREAM, N. *The Decorated Style: Architecture and Ornament, 1240–1360*. London, 1994.

COOK, G. H. *The English Cathedral through the Centuries*. London, 1957.

—. *English Collegiate Churches*. London, 1959.

—. *Mediaeval Chantries and Chantry Chapels*. London, 1947.

CORMACK, P. *English Cathedrals*. London, 1984.

CROSSLEY, F. H. *English Church Craftsmanship*. London, 1941.

—. *English Church Monuments: AD 1150–1550*. London, 1921.

FERGUSSON, P. *The Architecture of Solitude*. Princeton, 1984.

FERNIE, E. *An Architectural History of Norwich Cathedral*. Oxford, 1993.

FRANKL, P. *The Gothic: Literary Sources and Interpretations Through Eight Centuries*. Princeton, 1960.

GARDNER, S. *A Guide to English Gothic Architecture*. Cambridge, 1922.

GARNER, T. and STRATTON, A. *The Domestic Architecture of England During the Tudor Period*. 2 vols. London, 1929.

GODFREY, W. H. *The Story of Architecture in England*. London, 1928.

GREENE, J. P. *Medieval Monasteries*. Leicester, 1992.

HARVEY, J. H. *English Mediaeval Architects: a Biographical Dictionary down to 1550*. Rev. edn, Gloucester, 1984.

—. *Gothic England*. 2nd edn, London, 1948.

—. *Henry Yevele*. 2nd edn, London, 1946.

—. *The Perpendicular Style*. London, 1978.

HEWETT, C. A. *English Cathedral and Monastic Carpentry*. Chichester, 1985.

HOWARD, F. E. and CROSSLEY, F. H. *English Church Woodwork*. 2nd edn, London, 1927.

KNOOP, D. and JONES, G. P. *The Mediaeval Mason*. Manchester, 1933.

LEEDY, W. *Fan Vaulting*. London, 1980.

LETHABY, W. R. *Westminster Abbey and the King's Craftsmen*. London, 1906.

MERCER, E. *English Vernacular Houses*. London, 1975.

PALEY, F. A. *A Manual of Gothic Mouldings*. London, 1845–1902 (many editions)

PARKER, J. H. *An Introduction to the Study of Gothic Architecture*. 13th edn, Oxford, 1900.

PEVSNER, N. and METCALF, P. *The Cathedrals of England*. 2 vols. Harmondsworth, 1985.

PLATT, C. *The Abbeys and Priories of Medieval England*. London, 1984.

PUGIN, A. C. *Specimens of Gothic Architecture*. 2 vols. London, 1821.

PUGIN, A. C. and A. W. N. *Examples of Gothic Architecture*. London, 1836–8.

PUGIN, A. W. N. *A Treatise on Chancel Screens and Rood Lofts*. London, 1851.

RICKMAN, T. *Gothic Architecture*. Oxford and London, 1881.

ROBOTTOM, J. *Castles and Cathedrals, 1066–1500*. Harlow, 1991.

SALZMAN, L. F. *Building in England down to 1540*. Oxford, 1952.

SCOTT, G. G. *History of English Church Architecture*. London, 1881.

—. *Lectures on Mediaeval Architecture*. 2 vols. London, 1879.

SHARPE, E. *Architectural Parallels*. London, 1848.

—. *Mouldings of the Six Periods of British Architecture*. London, 1871–4.

—. *Rise and Progress of Decorated Window Tracery in England*. 2 vols. London, 1849.

—. *Seven Periods of British Architecture*. London, 1881.

SMITH, E. AND COOK, O. *English Cathedrals*. London, 1989.

STATHAM, H. H. (Ed.). *Cathedrals of England and Wales*. London, 1898. (The 'Builder' series, with large-scale plans.)

SWARTOUT, R. E. *The Monastic Craftsman*. Cambridge, 1932.

THOMPSON, A. HAMILTON. *English Monasteries*. Cambridge, 1913.

—. *The Ground Plan of the English Parish Church*. Cambridge, 1911.

—. *Historical Growth of the English Parish Church*. Cambridge, 1913.

TIPPING, H. A. *English Homes*. Period I, 1066–1485; Period II, 1485–1558. London, 1921–37.

TRACY, C. *English Gothic Choir-Stalls, 1200–1400*. Woodbridge, 1987.

VALLANCE, A. *Greater English Church Screens*. London, 1947.

—. *Old Crosses and Lychgates*. London, 1933.

WICKES, C. *Spires and Towers of the Mediaeval Churches of England*. 3 vols. London, 1853–9.

WILSON, C. *The Gothic Cathedral: the Architecture of the Great Church, 1130–1530*. London, 1990 (1992 printing with revisions).

WOOD, M. E. *The English Mediaeval House*. London, 1965.

Germany and Central Europe

BRUCHER, G. *Gotische Baukunst in Österreich*. Salzburg, 1990.

CROSSLEY, P. *Gothic Architecture in the Reign of Casimir the Great: Church Architecture in Lesser Poland, 1320–1380*. Cracow, 1985.

DEHIO, G. *Geschichte der deutschen Kunst, II*. Berlin and Leipzig, 1921.

—. *Handbuch der deutschen Kunstdenkmäler*. 5 vols. Berlin, 1927–35.

—. *Dehio-Handbuch: die Kunstdenkmäler Österreichs*. 4th and 5th edns 1954–8.

EYDOUX, H. B. *L'architecture des églises cisterciennes en Allemagne*. Paris, 1952.

HAHN, H. *Die frühe Kirchenbaukunst der Zisterzienser*. Frankfurt, 1957.

HARVEY, J. *The Gothic World*. London, 1950.

HOOTZ, R. (Ed.). *Deutsche Kunstdenkmäler*. 7 vols. Darmstadt, 1958–62.

LÜBKE, W. *Ecclesiastical Art in Germany During the Middle Ages*. Edinburgh, 1873.

MAROSI, E. *Die Anfänge der Gotik in Ungarn: Esztergom in der Kunst des 12.-13. Jahrhunderts*. Budapest, 1984.

STURGIS, R. and FROTHINGHAM, A. L. *A History of Architecture*. Vols iii and iv. New York, 1915.

SWOBODA, K. M. *Peter Parler: der Baukünstler und Bildhauer*. Vienna, 1943.

Low Countries

DESSART, CHAS (Ed.). *Images de Belgique*. 7 vols.

—. *Pierres flammandes*. Edition des Deux Mondes. Paris.

FOCKEMA, ANDREAE, TERKUILE and OZINGA. *Duizend jaar bouwen in Nederland*. Vol. 1. Amsterdam, 1948.

—. *Guide to Dutch Art*. Ministry of Education, Arts and Science. The Hague, 1953.

LAURENT, M. *L'Architecture et la sculpture en Belgique*. Paris and Brussels, 1928.

LUYKX, T. *Atlas culturel et historique de Belgique*. 1954.

MEISCHKE, R. *Die gothische bouwtraditie: studies over opdrachtgevers en bouwmeesters in de Nederlanden*. Amersfoort, 1988.

TIMMERS, J. J. M. *A History of Dutch Life and Art*. Amsterdam and London, 1959.

VRIEND, J. J. *De Bouwkunst van ons land*. 3 vols. Amsterdam, 1942.

Spain and Portugal

AZCARATE, J. M. *Arte gotico en Espana*. Madrid, 1990.

BALBAS, L. T. *Arquitectura gótica* (Ars Hispaniae VII). Madrid, 1952.

BEVAN, B. *History of Spanish Architecture*. London, 1938.

BOOTON, H. W. *Spain*. Newcastle upon Tyne, 1963.

CALVERT, A. F. *Spain*. 2 vols. London, 1924.

DURLIAT, M. *Art catalan*. Paris, 1963.

GALANTE GOMEZ, F. J. *Elementos del gotico en la arquitectura Canaria*. Las Palmas de Gran Canaria, 1983.

HARVEY, J. The Cathedrals of Spain. London, 1957.

LAMBERT, E. *L'art gothique en Espagne aux 12e et 13e siècles*. Paris, 1931.

LAMPÉREZ Y ROMEA, V. *Historia de la arquitectura cristiana española*. 2nd edn, Madrid, 1930.

LAVEDAN, P. *L'Architecture gothique religieuse en Catalogne*. Paris, 1935.

LOZOYA, J. DE CONTRERAS, MARQUÉS DE. *El Arte gotico en España*. Barcelona, 1935.

—. *Historia del arte hispanico*. Madrid, 1940.

MARTINEZ FRIAS, J. M. *El Gotico en Soria: arquitectura y escultura monumental*. Salamanca, 1980.

RAHLVES, F. *Cathedrals and Monasteries of Spain*. Paris, 1965. London, 1966.

SANTOS, R. DOS. *O estilo manuelino*. Lisbon, 1952.

STREET, G. E. *Account of Gothic Architecture in Spain*. London, 1874. Revised edition with notes by G. G. King, London, 1914.

STURGIS, R. and FROTHINGHAM, A. L. *A History of Architecture*. Vol. iii. New York, 1915.

UNAMUNO, M. DE. *Por Tierras de Portugal y España*. Madrid, 1941.

WASHBURN, O. *Castles in Spain*. Mexico City, 1957.

WEISMÜLLER, A. A. *Castles from the Heart of Spain*. London, 1967.

Italy

ARGAN, G. C. *L'Architettura del Duecento e Trecento*. Florence, 1936.

CUMMINGS, C. A. *A History of Architecture in Italy from the Time of Constantine to the Dawn of the Renaissance*. 2 vols. New edn, 1928.

FRANKLIN, J. W. *The Cathedrals of Italy*. London, 1958.

JACKSON, T. G. *Gothic Architecture in France, England and Italy*. 2 vols. London, 1915.

NESFIELD, E. *Specimens of Mediaeval Architecture*. London, 1862.

POPE-HENNESSY, J. *Italian Gothic Sculpture*. London, 1955.

PORTER, A. KINGSLEY. *Lombard Architecture*. 4 vols. New Haven, Conn., 1915–17.

—. *Mediaeval Architecture*. 2 vols. New York and London, 1909.

ROMANINI, A. M. *L'Architettura gotica in Lombardia*. 2 vols. Milan, 1964.

RUSKIN, J. *Stones of Venice*. 3 vols. London, 1851–3.

STREET, G. E. *Brick and Marble in the Middle Ages*. London, 1874.

TOESCA, P. *Storia dell'arte italiana: Il Medioevo*. Vol. 2. Turin, 1927.

—. *Storia dell'arte italiana: il Trecento*. Turin, 1951.

WAGNER-RIEGER, R. *Die italienische Baukunst zu Beginn der Gotik*. Graz and Cologne, 1956–7.

WHITE, J. *Art and Architecture in Italy: 1250–1400*. Rev. edn. Harmondsworth, 1970.

PART 3 The Architecture of Islam

Chapter 16 Seleucid, Parthian and Sassanian

Chapter 17 Architecture of the Umayyad and Abbasid Caliphates

Chapter 18 Local Dynasties of Central Islam and Pre-Moghul India

Chapter 19 Safavid Persia, the Ottoman Empire and Moghul India

Chapter 20 Vernacular Building and the Paradise Garden

AKURGAL, E. *The Art and Architecture of Turkey*. Oxford, 1980.

ARDALAN, N. and BAKTIAR, L. *The Sense of Unity*. London, 1973.

ASHER, C. B. *Architecture of Mughal India*. Cambridge, 1992.

ASLANAPA, O. *Turkish Art and Architecture*. London, 1971.

BARRUCAND, M. *Moorish Architecture in Andalusia*. Cologne, 1992.

BEGLEY, W. E. and DESAI, Z. A. *Taj Mahal: the Illumined Tomb: an Anthology of Seventeenth Century Mughal and European Documentary Sources*. Cambridge, Mass., and London, 1989.

BEHRENS-ABOUSEIF, D. *Islamic Architecture in Cairo: an Introduction*. Leiden, 1989.

BLAIR, S. S. and BLOOM, J. M. *The Art and Architecture of Islam, 1250–1800*. New Haven and London, 1994.

BLOOM, J. M. *Minaret: Symbol of Islam*. Oxford, 1989.

BOSWORTH, C. E. *The Islamic Dynasties*. Edinburgh, 1967.

BOURGET, S. J. *Coptic Art*. London, 1971.

BRAND, M. and LOWRY, G. D. (Eds). *Fatehpur-Sikri*. Bombay, 1987.

BROOKES, J. *Gardens of Paradise: the History and Design of the Great Islamic Gardens*. London, 1987.

BROWN, P. *Indian Architecture*. Bombay, 1942.

BURCKHARDT, T. *The Art of Islam: Language and Meaning*. London, 1976.

BURGOYNE, M. H. *Mamluk Jerusalem: an Architectural Study*. London, 1987.

BUTLER, A. J. *The Ancient Coptic Churches of Egypt*. London, 1986.

COSTA, P. M. *Studies in Arabian Architecture*. Aldershot, 1994.

CRESWELL, K. A. C. *A Bibliography of the Architecture, Arts and Crafts of Islam*. Cairo, 1962 and 1973.

—. *Early Muslim Architecture*. Parts I, II and III. Oxford, 1932–68.

—. *The Early Muslim Architecture of Egypt*. Oxford, 1952.

—. *A Short Account of Early Muslim Architecture*. Revised and supplemented by James W. Allan. London, 1989.

ELDEM, S. H. *Turk Evi: Osmanli Donemi (Turkish Houses: Ottoman Period)*. 2 vols. Istanbul, 1984–87.

ETTINGHAUSEN, R. *From Byzantium to Sasanian Iran and the Islamic World*. Leiden, 1972.

ETTINGHAUSEN, R. and GRABAR, O. *The Art and Architecture of Islam, 650–1250*. New Haven and London, 1987.

FREELY, J. and BURELLI, A. M. *Sinan: Architect of Suleyman the Magnificent and the Ottoman Golden Age*. London, 1982.

FRISHMAN, M. and KHAN, H. U. (Eds). *The Mosque: History, Architectural Development and Regional Diversity*. London, 1994.

GASCOIGNE, B. *The Great Moghuls*. London, 1971.

GHIRSHMAN, R. *Iran, Parthians and Sassanians*. London, 1962.

GIBB, H. A. R. *Mohammedanism*. New York, 1972.

GODARD, A. *The Art of Iran*. New York, 1965.

GOLOMBEK, L. and WILBER, D. *The Timurid Architecture of Iran and Turan*. Princeton and London, 1988.

GOODWIN, G. *A History of Ottoman Architecture*. London, 1971.

—. *Islamic Spain*. London, 1990.

—. *Sinan: Ottoman Architecture and its Values Today*. London, 1993.

GRABAR, O. *The Formation of Islamic Art*. 2nd edn, revised and enlarged, New Haven and London, 1987.

—. *The Great Mosque of Isfahan*. London, 1990.

GREENLAW, J. P. *The Coral Buildings of Suakin*. London, 1976.

GROVER, S. *The Architecture of India*. New Delhi, 1981.

GRUBE, E. J. *The World of Islam*. London, 1969.

GUILLAUME, A. *Islam*. Harmondsworth, 1960.

HAKIM, S. B. *Arabic Islamic Cities – Building and Planning Principles*. London, 1986.

HAMBLY, G. and SWAAN, W. *Cities of Moghul India*. London, 1968.

HAMILTON, R. W. *Khirbat al-Mafjar, An Arabian Mansion in the Jordan Valley*. Oxford, 1959.

—. *Structural History of Aksa Mosque*. Oxford, 1949.

HARDING, G. L. *The Antiquities of Jordan*. London, 1959.

HASAN, S. M. *Muslim Monuments of Bangladesh*. 2nd rev. edn, Dacca, 1980.

HAURANI, A. H. and STERN, S. M. *The Islamic City*. Oxford, 1970.

HELMS, S. *Early Islamic Architecture of the Desert: A Bedouin Station in Eastern Jordan*. Edinburgh, 1990.

HERDEG, K. *Formal Structure in Islamic Architecture of Iran and Turkistan*. New York, 1990.

HERRMANN, G. *The Iranian Revival*. Oxford, 1977.

HERZFELD, E. *Iran in the Ancient East*. Oxford, 1941.

HILL, D. and GRABAR, O. *Islamic Architecture and its Decoration*. London, 1964.

HILLENBRAND, R. *The Art of the Seljuks in Iran and Anatolia*. Costa Mesa, USA, 1982.

—. *Islamic Architecture*. Edinburgh, 1994.

—. *Islamic Art, Form, Function and Meaning*. Edinburgh, 1992.

HITTI, P. K. *Capital Cities of Arab Islam*. London, 1973.

HOAG, J. *Islamic Architecture*. New York, 1977.

—. *Western Islamic Architecture*. New York, 1963.

HOLT, P. M., LAMBTON, A. K. S. and LEWIS, B. (Eds). *The Cambridge History of Islam*. 2 vols. Cambridge 1970.

HRBAS, M. and KNOBLOCH, E. *The Art of Central Asia*. London, 1965.

HUTT, A. *Iran*. 2 vols. London, 1977.

—. *Islamic Architecture: North Africa*. London, 1977.

HUTT, A. (Ed.). *Arab Architecture: Past and Present*. Durham, 1983.

HYLAND, A. D. C. *The Arab House*. Newcastle upon Tyne, 1986.

JAIRAZBHOY, R. A. *An Outline of Islamic Architecture*. Bombay, 1972.

KIEL, M. *Studies on the Ottoman Architecture of the Balkans*. Aldershot, 1990.

KING, G. R. D. *The Historical Mosques of Saudi Arabia*. London, 1986.

KOCH, E. *Mughal Architecture: an Outline of its History and Development (1526–1858)*. Munich and London, 1991.

KUHNEL, E. *Islamic Art and Architecture*. London, 1966.

KURAN, A. *The Mosque in Early Ottoman Architecture*. Chicago and London, 1968.

—. *Sinan: the Grand Old Master of Ottoman Architecture*. Washington, DC, and Istanbul, 1987.

LAPIDUS, I. M. *Muslim Cities in the Later Middle Ages*. Cambridge, 1967.

LEHRMANN, J. *Earthly Paradise: Garden and Courtyard in Islam*. London, 1980.

MAYER, L. A. *Islamic Architects and their Works*. Geneva, 1956.

MICHELL, G. *Architecture of the Islamic World*. London, 1978.

MICHELL, G. (Ed.). *The Islamic Heritage of Bengal*. Paris, 1984.

MICHELL, G. and DAVIES, P. *The Penguin Guide to the Monuments of India*. London, 1989.

MOYNIHAN, E. B. *Paradise as a Garden in Persia and Moghul India*. London, 1980.

NASR, S. H. *Islamic Science*. London, 1976.

—. *Science and Civilisation in Islam*. Cambridge, 1968.

NATH, R. *History of Mughal Architecture*. New Delhi, 1982–.

NICHOLSON, L. *The Red Fort, Delhi*. London, 1989.

O'KANE, B. *Timurid Architecture in Khurasan*. Costa Mesa, Calif., 1987.

PACCARD, A. *Traditional Islamic Craft in Moroccan Architecture*. Saint-Jorioz, 1980.

PAPADOPOULO, A. *Islam and Muslim Art*. London, 1980.

PARKER, R. and SABIN, R. *Islamic Monuments in Cairo: a Practical Guide*. 3rd edn revised and enlarged by Caroline Williams. Cairo, 1985.

PETRUCCIOLI, A. *Fatehpur Sikri*. Berlin, 1992.

POPE, A. U. *Persian Architecture*. London, 1965.
POPE, A. U. and ACKERMANN, P. *A Survey of Persian Art*. Oxford, 1939.
PRUSSIN, L. *Hatumere: Islamic Design in West Africa*. Berkeley and London, 1986.
RICE, D. TALBOT. *Islamic Art*. London, 1965.
RICE, T. TALBOT. *The Seljuks in Asia Minor*. London, 1961.
ROGERS, M. *The Spread of Islam*. London, 1976.
ROWLAND, B. *The Art and Architecture of India: Buddhist, Hindu, Jain*. 3rd edn, Harmondsworth, 1967.
RUSSELL, D. *Mediaeval Cairo and the Monasteries of the Wadi Natrun*. London, 1962.
SALAM-LIEBICH, H. *The Architecture of the Mamluk City of Tripoli*. Cambridge, Mass., and London, 1983.
SAVORY, R. M. (Ed.). *Islamic Civilization*. Cambridge, 1995.
SCERRATO, U. *Islam*. London, 1976.
SEHERR-THOSS, S. and H. *Design and Colour in Islamic Architecture*. Washington, 1968.
SERJEANT, R. B. and LEWCOCK, R. *San'a: an Arabian Islamic City*. London, 1978.
STEVENS, R. *The Land of the Great Sophy*. London, 1971.
TALIB, K. *Shelter in Saudi Arabia*. London, 1984.
TILLOTSON, G. H. R. *Mughal India*. London, 1990.
UNSAL, B. *Turkish and Islamic Architecture in Seljuk and Ottoman Times*. London, 1959.
WARREN, J. and FETHI, I. *Traditional Houses in Baghdad*. Horsham, 1993.
WILBER, D. N. *The Architecture of Islamic Iran: The Il-Khanid Period*. Princeton, 1955.

PART 4 The Architecture of the Pre-colonial Cultures outside Europe

Chapter 22 Africa

BEGUIN, J. P. *L'Habitat au Cameroun*. Paris, 1952.
BIDDER, I. *Lalibela, the Monolithic Churches of Ethiopia*. London, 1959.
BOURDIER, J.-P. *African Spaces: Designs for Living in Upper Volta*. New York and London, 1985.
BOURGEOIS, J.-L. *Spectacular Vernacular: a New Appreciation of Traditional Desert Architecture*. Salt Lake City, 1983.
CLARK, J. D. *The Prehistory of Southern Africa*. Harmondsworth, 1959.
DAVIDSON, B. *Africa, the History of a Continent*. London, 1972.
DAVIES, W. V. (ED.). *Egypt and Africa: Nubia from Prehistory to Islam*. London, 1991.
DENYER, S. *African Traditional Architecture*. London, 1978.
FAGAN, B. M. *Southern Africa During the Iron Age*. London, 1965.
HULL, R. W. *African Cities and Towns Before the European Conquest*. New York, 1976.
KIRKMAN, J. S. *Men and Monuments on the East African Coast*. London, 1964.
KOBISHCHANOV, Y. M. *Axum*. Pennsylvania and London, 1979.
OLIVER, P. *Shelter in Africa*. London, 1971.
OLIVER, R. A. and FAGAN, B. M. *Africa in the Iron Age*. Cambridge, 1975.
PHILLIPSON, D. W. *African Archaeology*. Cambridge, 1965.
PRUSSIN, L. *Hatumere: Islamic Design in West Africa*. Berkeley and London, 1986.
SCHWERDTFEGER, F. W. *Traditional Housing in African Cities*. New York and Chichester, 1982.
SHAW, T. *Nigeria, its Archaeology and Early History*. London, 1978.
SHINNIE, M. *Ancient African Kingdoms*. London, 1965.
SHINNIE, P. L. *Meroe, a Civilisation of the Sudan*. London, 1967.
SIRAVO, F. and PULVER, A. *Planning Lamu: Conservation of an East African Seaport*. Paris, 1989.
SUMMERS, R. *Ancient Ruins and Vanished Civilisations of Southern Africa*. Cape Town, 1971.
—. *Zimbabwe*. Johannesburg, 1963.
WALTON, J. *African Village*. Pretoria, 1956.
WILLETT, F. *African Art*. London, 1971.

Chapter 23 The Americas

ABRAMS, E. M. *How the Maya Built their World: Energetics and Ancient Architecture*. Austin, 1994.
ALCINA FRANCH, J. *Pre-Columbian Art*. New York, 1983.
ANDREWS, G. *Maya Cities*. Norman, Okla, 1975.
BUSHNELL, G. H. S. *Peru*. 2nd edn, London, 1963.
CASO, A. *The Aztecs: People of the Sun*. Norman, Okla, 1958.
CASPARINI, G. and MARGOLIES, L. *Inca Architecture*. Bloomington, Ind., and London, 1980.
CASTEDO, L. *Historia del arte iberoamericano*. Madrid, 1988.
HAMMOND, N. *Ancient Maya Civilisation*. New Brunswick, NJ, 1982.
HARDOY, J. E. *Pre-Columbian Cities*. New York and Toronto, 1973.
HEMMING, J. *Monuments of the Incas*. Boston, 1982.
HEYDEN, D. and GENDROP, P. *Pre-Columbian Architecture of Mesoamerica*. New York, 1975.
HYSLOP, J. *Inka Settlement Planning*. Austin, 1990.
KUBLER, G. *The Art and Architecture of Ancient America: the Mexican, Maya and Andean Peoples*. 3rd (integrated) edn, Harmondsworth, 1984.
LANNING, E. P. *Peru Before the Incas*. Englewood Cliffs, NJ, 1967.
MARQUINA, I. *Arquitectura prehispanica*. Mexico, 1964.

MASON, J. A. *The Ancient Civilisations of Peru*. Harmondsworth, 1956.

MATOS MOCTEZUMA, E. *The Great Temple of the Aztecs: Treasures of Tenochtitlan*. London, 1988.

MORELY, S. J. and BRAINERD, G. W. *The Ancient Maya*. 3rd edn, Stanford, Calif., 1956.

MORGAN, W. L. *Prehistoric Architecture in the Eastern United States*. Cambridge, Mass., and London, 1980.

MORRIS, C. and THOMPSON, DONALD E. *Huanuco Pampa: An Inca City and its Hinterland*. London, 1985.

POLLOCK, H. E. D. 'Architecture of the Maya Lowlands', in *Handbook of Middle American Indians*. vol. 2, London, 1965.

PROSKOURIAKOFF, T. *An Album of Maya Architecture*. 2nd edn, Norman, Okla, 1963.

PROTZEN, J.-P. *Inca Architecture and Construction at Ollantaytambo*. New York and Oxford, 1993.

ROBERTSON, D. *Pre-Columbian Architecture*. New York, 1963.

STIERLIN, H. *Living Architecture: Mayan*. New York and London, 1964.

—. *Living Architecture: Ancient Mexican*. New York, 1968.

THOMPSON, J. E. S. *The Rise and Fall of Maya Civilisation*. 2nd edn, Norman, Okla, 1966.

TOWNSEND, R.F. (Ed.). *The Ancient Americas: Art from Sacred Landscapes*. Chicago, 1992.

VAILLANT, G. C. *The Aztecs of Mexico*. Harmondsworth, 1950.

Chapter 24 China

BEIJING SUMMER PALACE ADMINISTRATION OFFICE and QINGHUA UNIVERSITY DEPARTMENT OF ARCHITECTURE. *Summer Palace*. Beijing, 1981.

BOERSCHMANN, E. *Die Baukunst and religiöse Kultur der Chinesen*. Berlin, 1911.

—. *Chinesische Architektur*. 2 vols. Berlin, 1926.

BOYD, A. *Chinese Architecture and Town Planning, 1950 BC-AD 1911*. London, 1962.

BUSSAGLI, M. *Oriental Architecture*. London, 1989.

CHAMBERS, W. *Designs of Chinese Buildings*. London, 1757.

CHAN, C. *Imperial China*. London, 1991.

CHANG, CHAO-KANG and BLASER, W. *Architectures de Chine*. Lausanne, 1988.

CHI, TSUI. *A Short History of Chinese Civilisation*. London, 1942.

DE SILVA, A. *Chinese Landscape Painting*. London, 1967.

ECKE, G. *Chinese Domestic Furniture*. Hong Kong, 1962.

FUGL-MEYER, H. *Chinese Bridges*. Shanghai, 1937.

GRATTAN, F. M. *Notes Upon the Architecture of China*. London, 1894.

HEWLEY, W. M. (Ed.). *Chinese Folk Design*. Berkeley, 1949.

HILDEBRAND, H. *Der Tempel Ta-Chüeh-sy bei Peking*. Berlin, 1897.

INSTITUTE OF THE HISTORY OF NATURAL SCIENCES, CHINESE ACADEMY OF SCIENCES. *History and Development of Ancient Chinese Architecture*. Beijing, 1986.

JOHNSTON, R. S. *Scholar Gardens of China: a Study and Analysis of the Spatial Design of the Chinese Private Garden*. Cambridge, 1991.

JONES, O. *Examples of Chinese Ornament*. London, 1867.

KESWICK, M. *The Chinese Garden: History, Art & Architecture*. 2nd rev. edn, London, 1986.

KNAPP, R. G. *The Chinese House: Craft, Symbol and the Folk Tradition*. Hong Kong and Oxford, 1990.

LATOURETTE, K. S. *The Chinese Civilisation*. New York, 1941.

LIANG SSU-CH'ENG. *Annotations on Ying Zao Fa Shi*. Beijing, 1984.

—. *A Pictorial History of Chinese Architecture: a Study of the Development of its Structural System and the Evolution of its Types*. Cambridge, Mass., and London, 1984.

—. *Qing Structural Regulations*. Beijing, 1934, 2nd edn, 1981.

LI CHIEH. *Ying-tsao Fa Shih* (Building methods and patterns; the Sung Manual of Architecture.) First produced in 1103; reproduced in colour 1925; printed in smaller format in Shanghai, 1957.

LIU DUN ZHEN (Ed.). *Garden in Suzhou*. Beijing, 1979.

—. *A History of Ancient Chinese Architecture*. Beijing, 1980.

LIU, L. G. *Chinese Architecture*. London, 1989.

MIRAMS, D. G. *Brief History of Chinese Architecture*. Hong Kong, 1940.

MÜNSTERBERG, O. *Chinesische Kunstgeschichte*. 2 vols. Esslingen, 1910–12.

NEEDHAM, J. *Science and Civilisation in China*. Cambridge, 1954–.

PALEOLOGUE, M. *L'Art chinois*. Paris, 1887.

PIRALOZZI-T'SERSTEVENS, M. *Living Architecture: Chinese*. Fribourg and London, 1972.

PRIP-MOELLER, J. *Chinese Buddhist Monasteries*. Copenhagen and London, 1937; Hong Kong, 1967.

QUIAN YUN (Ed.). *Classical Chinese Gardens*. Hong Kong, 1982.

QINGHA UNIVERSITY. DEPARTMENT OF ARCHITECTURE. *Historic Chinese Architecture*. Beijing, 1985.

SCHWARTZ, D. *The Great Wall of China*. London, 1990.

SICKMAN, L. and SOPER, A. *The Art and Architecture of China*. Rev. edn, Harmondsworth, 1971.

SIREN, O. *The Gardens of China*. New York, 1949.

—. *The Imperial Palaces of Peking*. 3 vols. Paris, 1926.

—. *The Walls and Gates of Peking*. London, 1924.

SKINNER, R. T. F. (translator). *Types and Structural Forms in Chinese Architecture. General Account of the Chinese House. Ming Dynasty House in Hui-chou*. Peking, 1957.

SPEISER, W. *Art of the World: China*. London, 1962.

STEIN, M. A. *Ruins of Desert Cathay*. 2 vols. London, 1912.

TIANJIN UNIVERSITY DEPARTMENT OF ARCHITECTURE AND CHENGDE CULTURAL RELICS ADMINISTRATION. *Ancient Architecture of Chengde: the Architectural Art of the Imperial Summer Villa and Waibamiao*. Hong Kong, 1982.

TOKIWA, D. and SEKINO, T. *Buddhist Monuments in China*. Tokyo, 1930.

VITALI, R. *Early Temples of Central Tibet*. London, 1990.

WATSON, W. *Archaeology in China*. London, 1960.

—. *China Before the Han Dynasty*. London, 1961.

WU, N. I. *Chinese and Indian Architecture*. London and New York, 1963.

YU ZHUOYN (Ed.). *Palaces of the Forbidden City*. London, 1984.

Chapter 25 Japan and Korea – see Chapter 39

Chapter 26 Indian Subcontinent

ACHARYA, P. K. *A Dictionary of Indian Architecture*. London, 1927.

—. *Manasara Architecture and Sculpture*. London, 1933–4.

Annual Reports of the Archaeological Survey of Ceylon.

Annual Reports of the Archaeological Survey of India, 1902–30.

ARSHI, P. S. *The Golden Temple: History, Art and Architecture*. New Delhi, 1989.

BANNERJEE, N. R. *Nepalese Architecture*. New Delhi, 1980.

BAREAU, A. *La vie et l'organisation des communautés bouddhiques modernes du Ceylan*. Pondicherry, 1957.

BARTHOUX, J. *Les Fouilles de Hadda*. Paris, 1930.

BASHAM, A. L. *The Wonder that was India*. New York, 1959.

BASNAYAKE, H. T. *Sri Lankan Monastic Architecture*. Delhi, 1986.

BATLEY, C. *Indian Architecture*. London, 1934.

BELL, H. C. P. *Archaeological Survey of Ceylon*. Plans and Plates. Annual Reports, 1892–1912.

BLAIR, K .D. *4 Villages: Architecture in Nepal: Studies of Village Life*. Los Angeles, 1983.

BROWN, P. *Indian Architecture: Buddhist and Hindu*. Bombay, 1959.

—. *Indian Architecture: Islamic*. Bombay, 1959.

BURROW, S.M. *Buried Cities of Ceylon*. London, 1906.

BURGESS, J. *Ancient Monuments, Temples and Sculptures of India*. London, 1911.

Cambridge History of India. 6 vols, 1922.

CAVE, H. W. *Ruined Cities of Ceylon*. London, 1900.

CHANDRA, P. (Ed.). *Studies in Indian Temple Architecture*. New Delhi, 1975.

CODRINGTON, K. DE B. *Ancient India*. London, 1926.

COHN, W. *Indische Plastik*. Berlin, 1923.

COOMARASWAMY, A. K. *History of Indian and Indonesian Art*. New York, 1927.

—. *Mediaeval Sinhalese Art*. London, 1908.

CUNNINGHAM, A. *Archaeological Survey of India*. 23 vols. (2 vols, Cunningham only, 1762–5). Simla and Calcutta, 1871–87.

DE FOREST, L. *Indian Domestic Architecture*. Boston, 1885.

DEHEJIA, V. *Early Buddhist Rock Temples*. London, 1972.

DEVENDRA, D. T. *Guide to Yapahuwa*. Colombo, 1951.

FERGUSSON, J. *Architecture of Ahmedabad*. London, 1866.

—. *History of Indian and Eastern Architecture*. 2 vols. Revised by J. Burgess and R. P. Spiers. London, 1910.

—. *Illustrations of the Rock-cut Temples of India*. London, 1845.

—. *Picturesque Illustrations of the Ancient Architecture of Hindoustan*. London, 1948.

FISHER, R. E. *Buddhist Art and Architecture*. London, 1993.

FOUCHER, A. *L'Art gréco-buddhique du Ghandara*. 2 vols. Paris, 1942.

GANGOLY, O. C. *Indian Architecture*. 2nd edn, Calcutta, 1946.

GEIGER, W. (translator). *The Mahawamsa and the Chulawamsa*. Colombo, 1953.

—. *The Mediaeval Period in Ceylon Culture*. Wiesbaden, 1960.

GHOSH, S. P. *Hindu Religious Art and Architecture*. Delhi, 1982.

GODAKUMBURA, C. E. *Administration Report of the Archaeological Commissioner, 1963–64*. Colombo, 1965.

GOONETILEKE, H. A. I. *A Bibliography of Ceylon*. 2 vols. Zug, 1970.

GRISWOLD, A. B. *Siam and the Sinhalese Stupa*. Colombo, 1964.

GUPTA, S. P. *The Roots of Indian Art: a Detailed Study of the Formative Period of Indian Art and Architecture Third and Second Centuries B.C.: Mauryan and Late Mauryan*. Delhi, 1980.

HACKIN, J. *Diverses recherches archéologiques en Afghanistan*. Paris, 1961.

—. *Indian Art in Tibet and Central Asia*. London, 1925.

HALLET, S. L. and SAMIZAY, R. *Traditional Architecture of Afghanistan*. New York, 1980.

HARDY, A. *Indian Temple Architecture: Form and Transformation*. New Delhi, 1995.

HARLE, J. C. *The Art and Architecture of the Indian Subcontinent*. 2nd edn, New Haven and London, 1994.

HAVELL, E. B. *The Ancient and Mediaeval Architecture of India*. London, 1915.

HERDEG, K. *Formal Structure in Indian Architecture*. New York, 1990.

History of Ceylon From the Earliest Times to 1505. Vol. 1 (in two parts). Colombo, 1959–60.

HOCART, A. M. *Memoirs of the Archaeological Survey of Ceylon*. Vols 1 and 2. Colombo, 1924–6.

HULUGALLA, H. A. J. *Ceylon Yesterday – Sri Lanka Today*. Colombo, 1975.

HUNTINGTON, S. L. (with contributions by J. C. Huntington) *The Art of Ancient India: Buddhist, Hindu, Jain*. New York, 1985.

JEST, C. *Monuments of Northern Nepal*. Paris, 1981.

KAK, R. C. *Ancient Monuments of Kashmir*. London, 1933.

KNOX, R. *An Historical Relation of Ceylon*. London, 1681. Glasgow, 1911.

KRAMRISCH, S. *The Hindu Temple*. Delhi, 1948, 1986.

KORN, W. *The Traditional Architecture of the Katmandu Valley*. Katmandu, 1976.

LA ROCHE. *Indische Baukunst*. 6 vols. Berlin, 1921–2.

LE BON, G. *Les Monuments de l'Inde*. Paris, 1893.

LEVI, S. *Le Népal*. 3 vols. Paris, 1905–8.

LIBERA DALLAPICCOLA, A. (Ed.). *The Stupa: its Religious, Historical and Architectural Significance*. Wiesbaden, 1980.

MAJUMDAR, R. C. *The History and Culture of the Indian People*. Vols 1–5. Bombay, 1951–7.

MARSHALL, J. *Memoirs of the Archaeological Survey of India*. Vols 1–40.

—. *Taxila*. 3 vols. Cambridge, 1951.

MEISTER, M. W. (Ed.). *Encyclopaedia of Indian Temple Architecture*. Vol. 1, Pt 1, *South India, Lower Dravidadesa 200 B.C.–A.D. 1324*. 2 vols. New Delhi and Philadelphia, 1983

—. (Ed.) with DHAKY, M. A. *Encyclopaedia of Indian Temple Architecture*. Vol. 1, Pt 2, *South India, Upper Dravidadesa A.D. 550–1075*. 2 vols. New Delhi and Philadelphia, 1986

—. (Ed.) with DHAKY, M. A. and DEVA, K. *Encyclopaedia of Indian Temple Architecture*. Vol. 2, Pt 1, *North Indian, Foundations of North Indian Style* c. *250 B.C.–A.D. 100*. 2 vols. New Delhi and Princeton, 1988

—. (Ed.) with DHAKY, M. A. *Encyclopaedia of Indian Temple Architecture*. Vol. 2, Pt 2, *North India, Period of Early Maturity* c. *A.D. 700–900*. 2 vols. New Delhi and Princeton, 1991.

MICHELL, G. *The Hindu Temple: an Introduction to its Meaning and Forms*. New York, 1977.

MICHELL, G. and DAVIES, P. *The Penguin Guide to the Monuments of India*. London, 1989.

MITTON, G. E. *The Lost Cities of Ceylon*. London, 1928.

MORELAND, W. H. and CHATTERJEE, A. C. *A Short History of the Indian People*. London, 1936.

MUMTAZ, K. K. *Architecture in Pakistan*. Singapore, 1985.

MURTY, K. S. *Handbook of Indian Architecture*. New Delhi, 1991.

OLDFIELD, H. A. *Sketches from Nepal*. 2 vols. London, 1880.

PARANAVITANA, S. *The Stupa in Ceylon*. Colombo, 1946.

PARKER, H. *Ancient Ceylon*. London. 1910.

RATHNASARA, T. *Bauddha Stupa*. Colombo, 1967.

RAY, A. *Villages, Towns and Secular Buildings in Ancient India: 150 BC–AD 350*. 1964.

ROWLAND, B. *The Art and Architecture of India: Buddhist, Hindu, Jain*. Rev. edn, Harmondsworth, 1971.

SENEVIRATNA, A. and POLK, B. *Buddhist Monastic Architecture in Sri Lanka: the Woodland Shrines*. New Delhi, 1992.

SMITH, V. A. *A History of Fine Art in India and Ceylon*. 2nd edn, revised by K. de B. Codrington. Oxford, 1930.

SMITHERS, J. G. *Architectural Remains, Anuradhapura*. Colombo, 1894.

SNELLGROVE, D. L. and RICHARDSON, H. *Cultural History of Tibet*. London, 1968.

SOUNDARA RAJAN, K. V. *Cave Temples of the Deccan*. New Delhi, 1981.

—. *Indian Temple Styles: The Personality of Hindu Architecture*. New Delhi, 1972.

—. *Temple Architecture in Kerala*. Trivandrum, 1974.

SRINIVASAN, K. R. *Temples of South India*. New Delhi, 1972.

STARZA, O. M. *The Jagannatha Temple at Puri: its Architecture, Art and Cult*. Leiden, 1993.

STEIN, M. A. *Ruins of Desert Cathay*. 2 vols. London, 1912.

STILL, J. *Ancient Capitals of Ceylon*. 1907.

SZABO, A. and BARFIELD, T. J. *Afghanistan: an Atlas of Indigenous Domestic Architecture*. Austin, 1991.

TADGELL, C. *The History of Architecture in India: from the Dawn of Civilization to the End of the Raj*. London, 1990.

TILLOTSON, G. H. R. *The Rajput Palaces: the Development of an Architectural Style, 1450–1750*. New Haven and London, 1987.

TURNER, L. J. B. *Kandy: Historical Sketch*. Colombo, 1924.

VOLWAHSEN, A. *Living Architecture: Indian*. 2 vols. London and Fribourg, 1969.

Chapter 27 South-east Asia

General

BUSSAGLI, M. *Oriental Architecture*. London, 1989.

DUMARCAY, J. *The House in South-East Asia*. Singapore, 1987.

—. *The Palaces of South-East Asia: Architecture and Customs*. Singapore, 1991.

FISHER, R. E. *Buddhist Art and Architecture*. London, 1993.

RAWSON, P. *The Art of Southeast Asia: Cambodia, Vietnam, Thailand, Laos, Burma, Java, Bali*. London, 1967.

WATERSON, R. *The Living House: an Anthropology of Architecture in South-East Asia*. Singapore, 1990.

Burma

AUNG, U HTIN. *Folk Elements in Burmese Buddhism*. London, 1962.

BEYLIE, L. DE. *Prome et Samara*. Paris, 1907.

COLLIS, M. *The Land of the Great Image*. London, 1943.

DUROISELLE, C. *Guide to Mandalay Palace*. Calcutta, 1931.

GRISWOLD, A. B., KIM, C. and POTT, P. H. *Burma, Korea, Tibet*. London, 1964.

HALL, D. G. *Burma*. London, 1950.

HARVEY, G. E. *History of Burma*. London, 1925.

LUCE, G. H. *The Greater Temples of Pagan*. Rangoon, 1970.

MURARI, K. *Cultural Heritage of Burma*. New Delhi, 1985.

O'CONNOR, V. C. SCOTT. *Mandalay and other Cities of the Past in Burma*. London, 1907.

PICHARD, P. *The Pentagonal Monuments of Pagan*. Bangkok, 1991.

ROWLAND, B. *The Art and Architecture of India: Buddhist, Hindu, Jain*. Rev. edn, Harmondsworth, 1971.

STRACHAN, P. *Pagan: Art and Architecture of Old Burma*. Whiting Bay, 1989.

TIN, U PE MAUNG and LUCE, G. H. *The Glass Chronicle*. London, 1923.

YULE, H. *Narrative of the Mission to the Court of Ava in 1855*. London, 1858.

Other sources include the *Annual Reports* and *Memoirs* of the Archaeological Survey of India; The *Reports* of the Superintendant, Archaeological Survey of Burma; the *Journal of the Burma Research Society*; the *Bulletins de l'École française d'Extrême Orient*.

Cambodia

BRIGGS, L. P. *The Ancient Khmer Empire*. Philadelphia, 1951.

COEDÈS, G. *Inscriptions du Cambodge*. 6 vols. Hanoi and Paris, 1937–54.

FINOT, L., GOLOUBEW, V., COEDÈS, G., *et al*. *Le Temple d'Angkor Vat*. 7 vols. Paris, 1929–32.

GITEAU, M. *Histoire du Cambodge*. Paris, 1957.

GLAIZE, M. *Les monuments du Groupe d'Angkor*. Paris, 1963, and Saigon, 1944.

GROSLIER, B. P. *Angkor, hommes et pierres*. Grenoble, 1968.

—. *Art and Civilisation of Angkor*. New York, 1957.

—. *Art of the World*. London, 1962.

MALLERET, L. *L'Archéologie du Delta du Mékong*. 3 vols. Paris, 1959–60.

PORÉE-MASPERO, G. AND E. *Traditions and Customs of the Khmers*. New Haven, 1953.

RÉMUSAT, G. DE CORAL. *L'Art Khmer: les grandes étapes de son évolution*. Paris, 1912, 1940.

RIMBOUD, M. *Angkor: the Serenity of Buddhism*. London, 1993.

'S.O.S. Angkor', *UNESCO Courier*. December, 1971.

SRIVASTAVA, K. M. *Angkor Wat and Cultural Ties with India*. New Delhi, 1987.

STERN, P. *Les monuments khmers du style du Bayon et Jayavarman VII*. Paris, 1965.

STIERLIN, H. *Angkor*. Fribourg, 1970.

WALES, H. G. QUARITSCH. *Towards Angkor*. London, 1937.

Thailand

BROMAN, B. M. *Old Homes of Bangkok: Fragile Link*. Bangkok, 1984.

COEDÈS, G. *Archaeological Discoveries in Siam*. Vol. 4 of *Indian Art and Letters*. London, 1930.

EMBREE, J. F. and DOTSON, L. O. *Bibliography of the Peoples and Culture of Mainland South-East Asia*. New Haven, 1950.

FICKLE, D. H. *Images of the Buddha in Thailand*. Singapore, 1989.

GRAHAM, W. *Siam: a Handbook*. 2 vols. London, 1924.

GRISWOLD, A. B. 'The Architecture and Sculpture of Siam: A Handbook to the Arts', Catalogue of the Exhibition in the USA, 1960–2.

—. *Siam and the Sinhalese Stupa*. Colombo, 1964.

HUTCHINSON, E. W. *Reconstitution d'Ayuthya au temps de Phaulkon*. Saigon, 1946.

LE MAY, R. *Buddhist Art in Siam*. London, 1938.

LOUBÈRE, M. DE LA. *A New Historical Relation of the Kingdom of Siam*. Paris, 1962, London, 1963.

MOUHOT, H. *Voyage dans les royaumes de Siam, de Cambodge, de Laos*. Paris, 1968.

RINGIS, R. *Thai Temples and Temple Murals*. Singapore, 1990.

ROWLAND, B. *The Art and Architecture of India: Buddhist, Hindu, Jain*. Rev. edn, Harmondsworth, 1971.

SALMONY, A. *La Sculpture du Siam*. Paris, 1925.

SMITHIES, M. *Old Bangkok*. Singapore, 1986.

WELLS, K. E. *Thai Buddhism: its Rites and Activities*. Bangkok, 1939.

WOOD, W. A. R. *A History of Siam*. Bangkok, 1933.

Indonesia and the Malay Archipelago

COEDÈS, G. *The Indianized States of South-East Asia*. Honolulu, 1968.

COOMARASWAMY, A. K. *History of Indian and Indonesian Art*. New York, 1927.

COVARRUBIAS, M. *Island of Bali*. New York, 1937.

DAWSON, B. and GILLOW, J. *The Traditional Architecture of Indonesia*. London, 1994.

FRÉDÉRIC, L. *Sud-Est Asiatique: ses temples, ses sculptures*. Paris, 1964.

GANGOLY, O. C. *The Art of Java*. Calcutta, 1928.
HALL, D. G. E. *A History of South-East Asia*. London, 1964.
HARRISON, B. *South-East Asia: a Short History*. London, 1954.
HEEKEREN, H. R. VAN. *The Bronze Age of Indonesia*. The Hague, 1958.
—. *The Stone Age of Indonesia*. The Hague, 1958.
HEINE-GELDERN, R. VON. Introduction: Catalogue of the Exposition of 'Indonesian Art'. New York, 1948.
KROM, H. J. *Barabudur: Archaeological Description*. The Hague, 1927.
LIM JEE YUAN. *The Malay House: Rediscovering Malaysia's Indigenous Shelter System*. Pulau Pinang, 1987.
LOEB, E. M. and HEINE-GELDERN, R. VON. *Sumatra: its History and People*. Vienna, 1935.
MAY, R. LE. *The Culture of South-East Asia*. London, 1954.
MIKSIC, J. *Borobudur: Golden Tales of the Buddhas*. London, 1990.
MOORHEAD, F. J. *A History of Malaya and her Neighbours*. London, 1957.
ROWLAND, B. *The Art and Architecture of India: Buddhist, Hindu, Jain*. Rev. edn, Harmondsworth, 1971.
TWEEDIE, M. W. F. *Prehistoric Malaya*. Singapore, 1955.
WAGNER, F. A. *Indonesia*. London, 1959.
WALES, H. G. QUARITSCH. *Pre-History and Religion in South-East Asia*. London, 1957.
WINDSTEDT, R. *The Malays*. London, 1953.
WITH, K. *Java*. The Hague, 1920.
ZIMMER, H. *The Art of Indian Asia*. New York, 1955.
—. *Myths and Symbols in Indian Art and Civilization*. New York, 1946.
ZOETE, B. DE. and SPIES, W. *Dance and Drama in Bali*. 2nd edn, London, 1952.

PART 5 The Architecture of the Renaissance and Post-Renaissance in Europe and Russia

Chapter 28 Background

BENEVOLO, L. *The Architecture of the Renaissance*. 2 vols. London, 1978.
BLUNT, A. *Baroque and Rococo Architecture and Decoration*. London, 1978.
CLARK, K. *The Art of Humanism*. London, 1983.
DE FUSCO, R. *L'Architettura del Quattrocento*. Turin, 1984.
HONOUR, H. *Neo-Classicism*. Harmondsworth, 1968.
MIDDLETON, R. and WATKIN, D. *Neo-Classical and 19th Century Architecture*. New York, 1980.
MURRAY, P. *Renaissance Architecture*. New York, 1971.
NORBERG-SCHULZ, C. *Late Baroque and Rococo Architecture*. New York, 1974.
Palladio e la sua eredità nel mondo. Exhibition catalogue. Vicenza, 1980.
PLUMB, J. H. *The Pelican Book of the Renaissance*. New edn, Harmondsworth, 1964.
SMITH, C. *Architecture in the Culture of Early Humanism: Ethics, Aesthetics and Eloquence, 1400–1470*. New York, 1992.

Chapter 29 Italy

ACKERMAN, J. S. *The Architecture of Michelangelo*. 2nd edn, Harmondsworth, 1986.
—. *Palladio*. Harmondsworth, 1966.
ACTON, H. *Tuscan Villas*. London, 1973.
ARGAN, G. C. *Michelangelo Architect*. London, 1993.
AMES-LEWIS, F. *The Draftsman Raphael*. New Haven and London, 1986.
BARBIERI, F. *Vincenzo Scamozzi*. Vicenza, 1952.
BASSI, E. *Palazzi di Venezia*. 2nd edn, Venice, 1978.
BATTILOTTI, D. *Le Ville de Palladio*. Milan, 1990.
BATTISTI, E. *Brunelleschi*. London, 1981.
BLUNT, A. *Borromini*. Harmondsworth, 1979.
—. *A Guide to Baroque Rome*. London, 1982.
—. *Neapolitan Baroque and Rococo Architecture*. London, 1975.
—. *Sicilian Baroque*. London, 1968.
BORSI, F. *Alberti*. London, 1978.
—. *Bernini*. New York, 1984.
—. *Bramante*. Venice, 1989.
BORSI, S. *Giuliano da Sangallo: i disegni di architettura e dell'antico*. Rome, 1985.
BOUCHER, B. *Andrea Palladio: the Architect in his Time*. New York, 1994.
—. *The Sculpture of Jacopo Sansovino*. New Haven and London, 1991.
BRIZIO, A. M. *L'Architettura barocca in Piedmonte*. Turin, 1953.
BRUSCHI, A. *Bramante*. London, 1977.
BURCKHARDT, J. *The Architecture of the Italian Renaissance*. English trans. by J. Palmes, Ed. P. Murray. London, 1985.
BURNS, H. *Andrea Palladio 1508–1580. The Portico and the Farmyard*. Exhibition catalogue, Arts Council of Great Britain, London, 1975.
BURROUGHS, C. *From Signs to Design: Environmental Process and Reform in Early Renaissance Rome*. Cambridge, Mass., and London, 1990.
CARPEGGIANI, P. and TELLINI PERINA, C. *Giulio Romano a Mantova: una nuova estravagante maniera*. Mantua, 1987.
CEVESE, R. *Ville della Provincia di Vicenza*. 2 vols. Milan, 1971.
COFFIN, D. *The Villa in the Life of Renaissance Rome*. Princeton, 1979.
CONNORS, J. *Borromini and the Roman Oratory*. Cambridge, Mass., and London, 1980.
COSGROVE, D. *The Palladian Landscape: Geographical Change and its Cultural Representations in Sixteenth-century Italy*. Leicester, 1993.

DE FEO, V. *Andrea Pozzo: architettura e illusione*. Rome, 1988.

DONATI, C. *Carlo Maderno*. Lugano, 1957.

FIORE, F.P. and TAFURI, M. (Eds). *Francesco di Giorgio architetto*. Milan, 1993.

FOSSI, M. *Bartolomeo Ammannati*. Naples, 1967.

FRANCK, C. L. *The Villas of Frascati: 1550–1750*. London, 1966.

FROMMEL, C. L. *Der römische Palastbau der Hochrenaissance*. Tübingen, 1973.

FROMMEL, C. L., RAY, S. and TAFURI, M. *Raffaello architetto*. Milan, 1984.

FURNARI, M. *Atlante del Rinascimento: il disegni dell'architettura da Brunelleschi a Palladio*. Naples, 1993.

GAZZOLA, P. *Michele Sanmicheli*. Exhibition catalogue. Venice, 1960.

GINORI LISCI, L. *The Palazzi of Florence: their History and Art*. Florence, 1985.

GIOVANNONI, G. *Antonio da Sangallo il Giovane*. 2 vols. Rome, 1959.

GOLDTHWAITE, R. *The Building of Renaissance Florence*. Baltimore, 1980.

GRITELLA, G. *Juvarra: l'architettura*. Modena, 1992.

HERSEY, G. L. *Architecture, Poetry and Number in the Royal Palace at Caserta*. Cambridge, Mass. and London, 1983.

—. *High Renaissance Art in St Peter's and the Vatican: an Interpretive Guide*. Chicago, 1993.

HEYDENREICH, L. H. and LOTZ, W. *Architecture in Italy 1400–1600*. Harmondsworth, 1974.

HIBBARD, H. *Bernini*. London, 1965.

—. *Carlo Maderno and Roman Architecture, 1580–1630*. London, 1971.

—. *Michelangelo*. 2nd edn, Harmondsworth, 1985.

—. *Palazzo Borghese*. Rome, 1962.

HOLBERTON, P. *Palladio's Villas: Life in the Renaissance Countryside*. London, 1990.

HOWARD, D. *The Architectural History of Venice*. London, 1980.

HUSE, N. and WOLTERS, W. *The Art of Renaissance Venice: Architecture, Sculpture, and Painting, 1460–1590*. Chicago and London, 1990.

JAMES, G. *The Italian Garden*. New York, 1991.

JARZOMBEK, M. *On Leon Battista Alberti: his Literary and Aesthetic Theories*. Cambridge, Mass., and London, 1989.

KEMP, M. *Leonardo da Vinci: the Marvellous Works of Nature and Man*. London, 1981.

KLOTZ, H. *Filippo Brunelleschi: the Early Works and the Medieval Tradition*. London, 1990.

LAZZARO, C. *The Italian Renaissance Garden: from the Conventions of Planting, Design and Ornament to the Grand Gardens of Sixteenth-Century Central Italy*. New Haven and London, 1990.

LETAROUILLY, P. M. *Student's Letarouilly Illustrating the Renaissance in Rome*. London, 1948.

LIEBERMAN, R. *Renaissance Architecture in Venice*. London, 1982.

LOTZ, W. *Studies in Italian Renaissance Architecture*. Cambridge, Mass., 1977.

MACANDREW, J. *Venetian Architecture of the Early Renaissance*. Cambridge, Mass., 1980.

MACK, C. R. *Pienza: the Creation of a Renaissance City*. Ithaca, 1987.

MANETTI, A. *Life of Brunelleschi*. Translator C. Enggass. University Park, Pa, and London, 1970.

MASSON, G. *Italian Gardens*. London, 1961.

—. *Italian Villas and Palaces*. London, 1966.

MATTEUCCI, A. M. *Carlo Francesco Dotti e l'architettura bolognese del Settecento*. 2nd edn, Bologna, 1969.

MEEK, H. A. *Guarino Guarini and his Architecture*. New Haven and London, 1988.

MILLER, N. *Renaissance Bologna: a Study in Architectural Form and Content*. New York, 1989.

MILLON, H. A. and MAGNAGO LAMPUGNANI, V. (Eds). *The Renaissance from Brunelleschi to Michelangelo: the Representation of Architecture*. London, 1994.

MURARO, M. *Venetian Villas: the History and Culture*. New York, 1986.

MURRAY, L. *Michelangelo: his Life, Work and Times*. London, 1984.

MURRAY, P. *The Architecture of the Italian Renaissance*. Rev. edn, London, 1986.

NOEHLES, K. *La Chiesa di SS. Martino e Luca nell'opera di Pietro da Cortona*. Rome, 1970.

PINTO, J. A. *The Trevi Fountain*. New Haven and London, 1986.

POLEGGI, E. *Strada Nuova*. Genoa, 1968.

POMMER, R. *Eighteenth-Century Architecture in Piedmont*. New York, 1967.

PORTOGHESI, P. *Francesco Borromini*. 2nd edn, Milan, 1984.

—. *Guarino Guarini*. Milan, 1956.

—. *Roma barocca*. 2nd edn, Rome, 1973.

PUPPI, L. *Andrea Palladio*. London, 1975.

—. *Michele Sanmicheli architetto: opera completa*. Rome, 1986.

PUPPI, L. (Ed.). *Architettura e utopia nella Venezia del Cinquecento*. Milan, 1980.

PUPPI, L. *et al*. *Longhena*. Milan, 1982.

ROBISON, A. *Piranesi: Early Architectural Fantasies: a Catalogue Raisonné of the Etchings*. Washington, DC, 1986.

ROVERE, L., VITALE, V. and BRICKMANN, A. E. *Filippo Juvarra*. Milan, 1957.

SAALMAN, H. *The Cupola of S. Maria del Fiore*. London, 1980.

—. *Filippo Brunelleschi: the Buildings*. London, 1993.

SATKOWSKI, L. *Giorgio Vasari: Architect and Courtier*. Princeton and London, 1993.

SEMENZATO, C. *L'Architettura di Baldassare Longhena*. Padua, 1954.

SHEPHERD, J. C. and JELLICOE, G. A. *Italian Gardens of the Renaissance*. London, 1925. (Reprinted 1986.)

SPAGNESI, G. (Ed.). *Antonio da Sangallo il Giovane: la vita e l'opera*. Rome, 1986.

TAFURI, M. *Sansovino*. Padua, 1969.

—. *Venice and the Renaissance*. Cambridge, Mass., and London, 1989.

TAVERNOR, R. *Palladio and Palladianism*. London, 1991.

THORNTON, P. *The Italian Renaissance Interior 1400–1600*. London, 1991.

TRAGER, P. and SCULLY, V. *The Villas of Palladio*. Boston, Mass., 1986.

VARRIANO, J. *Italian Baroque and Rococo Architecture*. New York, 1986.

WADDY, P. *Seventeenth-Century Roman Palaces: Use and the Art of the Plan*. New York, 1990.

WALCHER CASOTTI, M. *Il Vignola*. 2 vols. Trieste, 1960.

WILTON-ELY, J. *Piranesi as Architect and Designer*. New York and London, 1993.

WITTKOWER, R. *Architectural Principles in the Age of Humanism*. 5th edn, London, 1988.

—. *Art and Architecture in Italy, 1600–1750*. Rev. edn. Harmondsworth, 1973.

—. *Studies in the Italian Baroque*. London, 1975.

WÖLFFLIN, H. *Renaissance und Barock*. English trans. London, 1964.

Chapter 30 France, Spain and Portugal

France

Alexandre-Theodore Brogniart 1739–1813: architecture et decor. Paris, 1986.

ANDROUET DU CERCEAU, J. *Les Plus excellents bastiments de France*. Paris, 1576–9. (Reprinted 1988.)

ARNEVILLE, M.-B., D'. *Parcs et jardins sous le Premier Empire: reflets d'une societé*. Paris, 1981.

BABELON, J.-P. *Demeures parisiennes sous Henri IV et Louis XIII*. Paris, 1991.

BALLON, H. *The Paris of Henri IV: Architecture and Urbanism*. New York, 1991.

BASDEVANT, D. *L'Architecture française*. Paris, 1971.

BAUBION-MACKLER, J. *French Royal Gardens: the Designs of Andre Le Nôtre*. New York, 1992.

BERGER, R. B. *Antoine Le Pautre*. New York, 1979.

BERGER, R. W. *A Royal Passion: Louis XIV as Patron of Architecture*. Cambridge, 1994.

—. *The Palace of the Sun: the Louvre of Louis XIV*. University Park, Pa, and London, 1993.

—. *Versailles: the Chateau of Louis XIV*. University Park, Pa, and London, 1985.

BIVER, M.-L. *Le Paris de Napoléon*. Paris, 1963.

BLOMFIELD, R. *A History of French Architecture, 1494–1661*. 2 vols. London, 1921.

BLONDEL, J. F. *L'Architecture française* (the 'Grand Blondel'). 4 vols. Paris, 1752–6.

BLUNT, A. *Art and Architecture in France, 1500–1700*. Harmondsworth, 1953. 2nd edn, 1973.

—. *François Mansart*. London, 1941.

—. *Philibert de l'Orme*. London, 1958.

BOULLÉE, E.-L. *Etienne-Louis Boullée: l'architecte visionnaire et neoclassique*. Textes réunis et presentés par J.-M. Perouse de Montclos. Paris, 1993.

BOURGET, P. *Les Architectures baroques en France*. Paris, 1993.

BRAHAM, A. *The Architecture of the Enlightenment*. London, 1980.

BRAHAM, A. and SMITH, P. *François Mansart*. London, 1973.

CHASTEL, A. *Culture et demeures en France au XVIe siécle*. Paris, 1989.

COOPE, R. *Salomon de Brosse*. London, 1972.

DEBRIE, C. *Nicolas Blasset: architecte et sculpteur ordinaire du roi, 1600–1659*. Paris, 1985.

DENNIS, M. *Court and Garden: from the French Hotel to the City of Modern Architecture*. Cambridge, Mass., and London, 1986.

DESHAIRS, L. *Le Petit Trianon et le Grand Trianon*. 2 vols. Paris, 1909–.

ELEB-VIDAL, M. and DEBARRE-BLANCHARD, A. Architectures de la vie priveé: maisons et mentalités xviie-xixe siecles. Brussels, 1989.

ERIKSEN, S. *Early Neo-Classicism in France*. London, 1974.

FELS, E. FRISCH, COMTE DE. *Jacques-Ange Gabriel*. Paris, 1912, 1924.

FRANCE-LANORD, A. *et al. Germain Boffrand 1667–1754: l'aventure d'un architecte indépendant*. Paris, 1986.

GALLET, M. *Paris Domestic Architecture of the Eighteenth Century*. London, 1972.

GALLET, M. and BOTTINEAU, Y. *Les Gabriel*. Paris, 1982.

GANAY, E. DE. *Châteaux de France*. Paris, 1948–50.

GÉBELIN, F. *Les Châteaux de la Loire*. Paris, 1927.

—. *Les Châteaux de la Renaissance*. Paris, 1927.

—. *Le Style Renaissance en France*. Paris, 1942.

GEYMUELLER, H. VON. *Die Baukunst der Renaissance in Frankreich*. Stuttgart, 1898–1901.

HAUTECOEUR, L. *L'Architecture française de la Renaissance à nos jours*. Paris, 1941.

—. *Histoire de l'architecture classique en France*. 7 vols., sixteenth century to 1900, some of which have been revised. Paris, 1943–65.

HERRMANN, W. *Laugier and Eighteenth-Century French Theory*. London, 1962.

—. *The Theory of Claude Perrault*. London, 1973.

JACQUES, A. and MOUILLESEAUX, J.-P. *Les Architectes de la liberté*. Exhibition catalogue, Paris, 1990.

JACQUIN, E. (Ed.). *Les Tuileries au XVIIIe siècle*. Paris, 1990.

JESTAZ, B. *Le Voyage d'Italie de Robert de Cotte*. Paris, 1966.

KALNEIN, W. VON. *Architecture in France in the Eighteenth Century*. New Haven and London, 1995.

KAUFFMANN, F. *Architecture in the Age of Reason*. Cambridge, Mass., 1955.

KIMBALL, F. *The Creation of the Rococo*. Philadelphia, 1943.

KRAFFT ET RANSONNETTE. *Plans ... des plus belles Maisons ... construites à Paris, etc*. Paris, *c*. 1810.

LAMBELL, R. *French Period Houses and their Details*. London, 1992.

LAVEDAN, P. *French Architecture*. Harmondsworth, 1956.

LAVIN, S. *Quatremère de Quincy and the Invention of a Modern Language of Architecture*. Cambridge, Mass., and London, 1992.

LEDOUX, C.-N. *Architecture de C.-N. Ledoux*. Paris, 1847. Reprinted 1983.

—. *Unpublished projects*. Berlin, 1992.

MCCORMICK, T. J. *Charles-Louis Clérisseau and the Genesis of Neo-Classicism*. New York, 1990.

MADEC, P. *Boullée*. Paris, 1986.

MINGUET, P. *France baroque*. Paris, 1988.

NEUMAN, R. *Robert de Cotte and the Perfection of Architecture in Eighteenth-Century France*. Chicago and London, 1994.

NOLHAC, P. DE. *La Création de Versailles*. Paris, 1925.

—. *Histoire du château de Versailles*. Paris, 1911–18.

—. *Versailles and the Trianons*. London, 1906.

PEROUSE DE MONTCLOS, J.-M. *Etienne-Louis Boullée: l'architecte visionnaire et neoclassique*. (Includes an annotated version of Boullée's *Architecture. Essai sur l'art*). Paris, 1993.

—. *Histoire de l'architecture française de la Renaissance à la Révolution*. Paris, 1989.

PETZET, M. *Soufflots Sainte-Geneviève und der französische Kirchenbau des 18. Jahrhunderts*. Berlin, 1961.

PICON, A. *Claude Perrault 1613–1688 ou la curiosité d'un classique*. Paris, 1988.

—. *French Architects and Engineers in the Age of Enlightenment*. Cambridge, 1992.

RAVAL, M. *C.-N. Ledoux*. Paris, 1945.

REUTERSWÄRD, P. *The Two Churches of the Hôtel des Invalides*. Stockholm, 1965.

ROSENAU, H. *Boullée's Treatise on Architecture*. 1953.

SZAMBIEN, W. *J.-N.-L. Durand, 1760–1834*. Paris, 1984.

TADGELL, C. *Ange-Jacques Gabriel*. London, 1978.

THOMSON, D. *Renaissance Paris: Architecture and Growth, 1475–1600*. London, 1984.

VIDLER, A. *Claude-Nicolas Ledoux: Architecture and Social Reform at the End of the Ancien Régime*. Cambridge, Mass., and London, 1990.

—. *The Writing of the Walls: Architectural Theory in the Late Enlightenment*. Princeton and London, 1987.

VILLARI, S. *J. N. L. Durand (1760–1834): Art and Science of Architecture*. New York, 1990.

WALTON, G. *Louis XIV's Versailles*. Harmondsworth, 1986.

WARD, W. H. *Architecture of the Renaissance in France, 1495–1830*. 2 vols. London, 1926.

—. *French Châteaux and Gardens in the Sixteenth Century*. London, 1969.

WHITEHEAD, J. *The French Interior in the Eighteenth Century*. London, 1992.

WOODBRIDGE, K. *Princely Gardens: the Origins and Development of the French Formal Style*. London, 1986.

Spain and Portugal

BEVAN, B. *History of Spanish Architecture*. London, 1938.

BONET CORREA, A. *La Arquitectura en Galicia durante el siglo XVII*. Madrid, 1966.

—. *Art baroque en Andalousie*. Paris, 1978.

BYNE, A. and STAPLEY, M. *Provincial Houses in Spain*. New York, 1925.

CALZADA, A. *Historia de la arquitectura espanola*. Barcelona, 1933.

CHAMOZO LAMAS, M. *La Arquitectura barroca an Galicia*. Madrid, 1955.

CHUECA GOITIA, F. *Andrés de Vandelvira*. Madrid, 1954.

—. *Arquitectura del siglo XVI* (Ars Hispaniae, Historia Universal del Arte Hispanico, Vol. 11). Madrid, 1953.

CHUECA GOITIA, F. and MIGUEL, C. *La Vida y las obras del arquitecto Juan de Villanueva*. Madrid, 1959.

FRANCA, J.-A. *Une Ville des Lumières, la Lisbonne de Pombal*. Paris, 1965.

GALLEGO Y BURIN, A. *El barroco granadino*. Milan, 1956.

HARVEY, J. *The Cathedrals of Spain*. London, 1957.

KUBLER, G. *Arquitectura española, 1600–1800* (Ars Hispaniae, Historia Universal del Arte Hispanico, Vol. 14). Madrid, 1957.

—. *Building the Escorial*. Princeton, 1982.

—. *Portuguese Plain Architecture: between spices and diamonds, 1521–1706*. Middleton, Conn., 1972.

KUBLER, G. and SORIA, M. *Art and Architecture in Spain and Portugal*. Harmondsworth, 1959.

LEES-MILNE, J. *Baroque in Spain and Portugal*. London, 1960.

LOPEZ MARTINEZ, C. *El Arquitecto Hernan Ruiz en Seville*. Seville, 1949.

MARTIN GONZALEZ, J. J. *La Arquitectura domestica de renacimento en Valladolid*. Valladolid, 1948.

PEREDA DE LA REQUERA, M. *Bartolome de Bustamente*. Santander, 1950.

—. *Rodrigo Gil de Hontañon*. Santander, 1951.

REESE, T. F. *The Architecture of Ventura Rodriguez*. 2 vols. Garland, 1972.

ROSENTHAL, E. *The Cathedral of Granada*. Princeton, 1961.

SITWELL, S. *Spanish Baroque Art*. London, 1931.

SMITH, R. C. *The Art of Portugal, 1500–1800*. London, 1968.
—. *Nicolau Nasoni, arquitecto do Porto*. Lisbon, 1966.
VILLIERS-STUART, C. M. *Spanish Gardens*. 1929.
WYATT, SIR M. DIGBY. *An Architect's Note-book in Spain*. 1872.

Chapter 31 Austria, Germany and Central Europe

AURENHAMMER, H. *J. B. Fischer von Erlach*. London, 1973.
BERGDOLL, B. *Karl Friedrich Schinkel: an Architecture for Prussia*. New York, 1994.
BIALOSTOCKI, J. *The Art of the Renaissance in Eastern Europe: Hungary, Bohemia, Poland*. Oxford, 1976.
BOURKE, J. *Baroque Churches of Central Europe*. 2nd edn, London, 1962.
BRUSATIN, M. and PIZZAMIGLIO, G. *The Baroque in Central Europe: Places, Architecture and Art*. New York, 1992.
BURROUGH, T. H. B. *South German Baroque: an Introduction*. London, 1956.
CHARPENTRAT, P. *Living Architecture: Baroque*. Fribourg and London, 1967.
DEHIO, G. *Dehio-Handbuch: die Kunstdenkmäler Österreichs*. 4th and 5th edns, Vienna, 1954–8.
—. *Handbuch der deutschen Kunstdenkmäler*. Berlin, 1927.
FEUER-TOTH, R. *Renaissancebaukunst in Ungarn*. Budapest, 1981.
FISCHER VON ERLACH, J. B. *Entwurf einer historischen Architektur*. Vienna, 1721.
FORSSMANN, E. *Karl Friedrich Schinkel: Bauwerke and Baugedanken*. Zurich, 1981.
FRANZ, H. G. *Bauten und Baumeister der Barockzeit in Böhmen*. Leipzig, 1962.
Friedrich Gilly. Exhibition catalogue, Berlin Museum, 1984.
GIERSBERG, H.-J. *Friedrich als Bauherr: Studien zur Architektur des 18. Jahrhunderts in Berlin und Potsdam*. Berlin, 1986.
GRIMSCHITZ, B. *Johann Lucas von Hildebrandt*. 2nd edn, Vienna, 1959.
GUBLER, H.-M. *Der Vorarlberger Barockbaumeister Peter Thumb 1681–1766: ein Beitrag der süddeutschen Barockarchitektur*. Sigmaringen, 1972.
HANFSTAENGL, E. *Die Brüder Asam*. Munich, 1955.
HARRIES, K. *The Bavarian Rococo Church: Between Faith and Aestheticism*. New Haven and London, 1983.
HECKMANN, H. *Matthaus Daniel Pöppelmann und die Barockbaukunst in Dresden*. Stuttgart, 1986.
HEDERER, O. *Leo von Klenze*. Munich, 1964.
HEMPEL, E. *Baroque Art and Architecture in Central Europe*. Harmondsworth, 1965.
—. *Geschichte der deutschen Baukunst*. 2nd edn, Munich, 1956.
HITCHCOCK, H.-R. *German Renaissance Architecture*. Princeton, 1981.
—. *German Rococo: the Zimmermann Brothers*. London, 1968.
—. *Rococo Architecture in Southern Germany*. London and New York, 1968.
KADATZ, H.-J. and MUZKA, G. *Georg Wenzeslaus von Knobelsdorff: Baumeister Friedrichs II*. 2nd edn, Munich, 1985.
Karl Friedrich Schinkel. Exhibition catalogue, Berlin, Schloss Charlottenburg, 1981.
KLINGENSMITH, S. J. *The Utility of Splendor: Ceremony, Social Life and Architecture at the Court of Bavaria, 1600–1800*. Chicago and London, 1993.
KRAUS, H. *Die Schlosskapellen der Renaissance in Sachsen*. Berlin, 1970.
KUNOTH, G. *Die historische Architektur Fischers von Erlach*. Düsseldorf, 1956.
LANDOLT, H. and SEEGER, T. *Schweizer Barockkirchen*. Frauenfeld, 1948.
LIEB, N. *Die Fugger und die Kunst*. 2 vols. Munich, 1952, 1958.
—. *Johann Michael Fischer: Baumeister und Raumschopfer im späten Barock Süddeutschlands*. Regensburg, 1982.
LIEB, N. and DIEDL, F. *Die Vorarlberger Barockmeister*. Munich and Zurich, 1960.
LORENTZ, S. and ROTTERMUND, A. *Neoclassicism In Poland*. Warsaw, 1986.
LORENZ, H. *Johann Bernhard Fischer von Erlach*. Zurich, 1992.
—. *Liechtenstein Palaces in Vienna from the Age of the Baroque*. New York, 1985.
POWELL, N. *From Baroque to Rococo*. London, 1959.
PRATT, M. *The Great Country Houses of Central Europe: Czechoslovakia, Hungary, Poland*. New York, 1991.
PUNDT, H. G. *Schinkel's Berlin*. Cambridge, Mass., 1972.
RAVE, P. O. *Karl Friedrich Schinkel*. Berlin, 1981.
REUTHER, H. *Balthasar Neumann*. Munich, 1983.
—. *Die Kirchenbauten Balthasar Neumanns*. Berlin, 1960.
SAUERMOST, H. J. *Die Asams als Architekten*. Munich, 1986.
SEDLMAYER, H. *Johann Bernhard Fischer von Erlach*. Vienna, 1976.
—. *Österreichische Barockarchitektur*. Vienna, 1930.
SNODIN, M. (Ed.). *Karl Friedrich Schinkel: a Universal Man*. New Haven and London, 1991.
VALDENAIRE, A. *Friedrich Weinbrenner: sein Leben und seine Bauten*. 2nd edn, Karlsruhe, 1926.
VILIMKOVA, M. and BRUKCER, J. *Dientzenhofer: eine bayerische Baumeisterfamilie in der Barockzeit*. Rosenheim, 1989.
WAGNER, H. *Bayerische Barock- und Rokokokirchen*. Munich, 1983.

WATKIN, D. and MELLINGHOFF, T. *German Architecture and the Classical Ideal, 1740–1840*. London, 1987.

Chapter 32 The Low Countries and Britain

The Low Countries

ACKERE, J. VAN. *Baroque and Classic Art In Belgium (1600–1789): Architecture, Monumental Art*. Brussels, 1972.

BURKE, G. L. *The Making of Dutch Towns*. London, 1956.

FOCKEMA ANDREAE, S. J. *et al. Duizend jaar bouwen in Nederland*. Vol. 2. Amsterdam, 1957.

GERSON, H. and TER KUILE, E. H. *Art and Architecture in Belgium, 1600–1800*. Harmondsworth, 1960.

GUILLERMO, J. *Dutch Houses and Castles*. London, 1990.

HAAN, H. DE and HAAGSMA, I. *The House Erasmus Built: a Profile of Dutch Architecture*. Utrecht, 1990.

HITCHCOCK, H.-R. *Netherlandish Scrolled Gables of the 16th and Early 17th Centuries*. New York, 1978.

KUYPER, W. *Dutch Classicist Architecture*. Delft, 1980.

MINGUET, P. *Baroque et rococo en Belgique*. Liège, 1987.

MINISTRY OF EDUCATION, ARTS AND SCIENCES. *Guide to Dutch Art*. The Hague, 1953.

OTTENHEYM, K. *Philips Vingboons (1607–1678) Architect*. Zutphen, 1989.

OZINGA, M. D. *De Protestansche kerkenbouw in Nederland*. Amsterdam, 1929.

PARENT, P. *L'Architecture aux Pays-Bas méridionaux aux XVI-XVIII siècles*. Paris and Brussels, 1926.

PLUYM, W. VAN DER. *Vijf eeuwen binnenhuis en meubels in Nederland*. Amsterdam, 1954.

ROSENBERG, J., SLIVE, S. and TER KUILE, E. H. *Dutch Art and Architecture, 1600–1800*. Harmondsworth, 1966.

TERWEN, J. J. and OTTENHEYM, K. A. *Pieter Post (1608–1669) Architect*. Zutphen, 1993.

TIMMERS, J. J. M. *A History of Dutch Art and Life*. Amsterdam and London, 1959.

VANDEVIVERE, I. and BOUCHER, H. *Renaissance Art in Belgium: Architecture, Monumental Art*. Brussels, 1973.

VERMEULEN, F. A. J. *Handboek tot de geschiednis der nederlandsche bouwkunst*. 4 vols. The Hague, 1928.

VRIEND, J. J. *De Bouwkunst van ons land*. Amsterdam, 1949.

WATTJES, J. G. *Amsterdams bouwkunst en stadsschoon 1305–1942*. Amsterdam, 1948.

WEISSMAN, A. W. *Geschiednis der Nederlandsche Bouwkunst*. Amsterdam, 1912.

YERBURY, F. R. *Old Domestic Architecture in Holland*. London, 1924.

Britain

AIRS, M. *The Making of the English Country House, 1500–1640*. London, 1975.

BARNARD, T. and CLARK, J. (Eds). *Lord Burlington: Architecture, Art and Life*. London, 1995.

BEARD, G. *Georgian Craftsmen*. London, 1966.

—. *The Work of John Vanbrugh*. London, 1986.

BINNEY, M. *Sir Robert Taylor: from Rococo to Neo-classicism*. London, 1984.

BOLD, J. *John Webb: Architectural Theory and Practice in the Seventeenth Century*. Oxford, 1989.

BOLD, J. and CHANEY, E. (Eds). *English Architecture Public and Private: Essays for Kerry Downes*. London, 1993.

BOLD, J. and REEVES, J. *Wilton House and English Palladianism: Some Wiltshire Houses*. London, 1988.

BOLTON, A. T. *The Architecture of Robert and James Adam*. 2 vols. London, 1922.

BROWN, R. (Ed.). *The Architectural Outsiders*. London, 1985.

CHANCELLOR, E. B. *The Lives of the British Architects from William of Wykeham to Sir William Chambers*. London, 1909.

CLARK, K. *The Gothic Revival*. 2nd edn, London, 1950.

CLIFTON-TAYLOR, A. *The Pattern of English Building*. 4th edn, London, 1987.

COLVIN, H. *A Biographical Dictionary of British Architects, 1600–1840*. 3rd edn, New Haven and London, 1995.

CORNFORTH, J. and FOWLER, J. *English Decoration in the Eighteenth Century*. London, 1974.

CRAIG, M. *Dublin, 1660–1860*. Rev. edn, London, 1992.

CROOK, J. M. *The Greek Revival*. London, 1972.

CRUICKSHANK, D. *A Guide to the Georgian Buildings of Britain and Ireland*. London, 1985.

CRUICKSHANK, D. and WYLD, P. *Georgian Town Houses and Their Details*. London, 1990. Rev. edn of *London: the Art of Georgian Building*. London, 1975.

CURL, J. S. *Classical Architecture: an Introduction to its Vocabulary and Essentials, with a Select Glossary of Terms*. London, 1992.

—. *Georgian Architecture*. Newton Abbot, 1993.

DALE, A. *James Wyatt, Architect 1746–1813*. Oxford, 1936.

DAVIS, T. *The Architecture of John Nash*. London, 1960.

—. *The Gothick Taste*. London and Vancouver, 1974.

—. *John Nash*. London, 1966.

DOWNES, K. *The Architecture of Wren*. 2nd edn, London, 1988.

—. *English Baroque Architecture*. London, 1966.

—. *Hawksmoor*. London, 1959.

—. *Sir Christopher Wren: the Design of St. Paul's*

Cathedral. London, 1988.
—. *Sir John Vanbrugh: a Biography*. London, 1987.
—. *Vanbrugh*. London, 1977.
FAULKNER, T. and GREG, A. *John Dobson: Newcastle Architect, 1787–1865*. Newcastle upon Tyne, 1987.
FLEMING, J. *Robert Adam and his Circle*. London, 1962.
FRIEDMAN, T. *James Gibbs*. London, 1984.
GIFFORD, J. *William Adam, 1689–1748: a Life and Times of Scotland's Universal Architect*. Edinburgh, 1989.
GIROUARD, M. *Life in the English Country House*. London, 1978.
HARRIS, J. *The Architect and the British Country House, 1620–1920*. Washington, D.C., 1985.
—. *The Palladian Revival: Lord Burlington, His Villa and Garden at Chiswick*. New Haven and London, 1994.
—. *Sir William Chambers*. London, 1970.
—. *William Talman: Maverick Architect*. London, 1982.
HARRIS, J. and HIGGOTT, G. (Eds). *Inigo Jones: Complete Architectural Drawings*. New York, 1989.
HILL, O. and CORNFORTH, J. *English Country Houses, 1625–1865*. London, 1966.
HINDE, T. *Capability Brown: the Story of a Master Gardener*. London, 1986.
HOWARD, M. *The Early Tudor Country House: Architecture and Politics, 1490–1550*. London, 1987.
HUNT, J. D. *William Kent: Landscape Garden Designer: an Assessment and Catalogue of his Designs*. London, 1987.
HUNT, J. D. and WILLIS, P. (Eds). *The Genius of the Place: the English Landscape Garden, 1620–1820*. Cambridge, Mass., and London, 1975 (1988 printing with corrections).
HUSSEY, C. *English Country Houses*. 3 vols. London, 1955–8 (1986 reprint).
—. *English Gardens and Landscapes 1700–1750*. London, 1967.
—. *The Picturesque*. London 1927, reprinted 1967.
KING, D. *The Complete Works of Robert and James Adam*. Oxford, 1991.
LEACH, P. *James Paine*. London, 1988.
LISCOMBE, R. W. *William Wilkins, 1778–1839*. Cambridge, 1980.
MACAULAY, J. *The Classical Country House in Scotland, 1660–1800*. London, 1987.
MANSBRIDGE, M. *John Nash: a Complete Catalogue*. Oxford, 1991.
MARKUS, T. A. *Buildings and Power: Freedom and Control in the Origin of Modern Building Types*. London, 1993.
MARKUS, T. A. (Ed.). *Order in Space and Society: Architectural Form and its Context in the Scottish Enlightenment*. Edinburgh, 1982.
MCCARTHY, M. *The Origins of the Gothic Revival*. New Haven and London, 1987.
MCPARLAND, E. *James Gandon: Vitruvius Hibernicus*. London, 1984.
MORLEY, J. *Regency Design, 1790–1840: Gardens, Buildings, Interiors, Furniture*. London, 1993.
MOWL, T. *Elizabethan and Jacobean Style*. London, 1993.
MOWL, T. and EARNSHAW, B. *John Wood: Architect of Obsession*. Bath, 1988.
ORRELL, J. *The Theatres of Inigo Jones and John Webb*. Cambridge, 1985.
PARISSIEN, S. *Palladian Style*. London, 1994.
—. *Regency Style*. London, 1992.
PEVSNER, N. *et al. The Buildings of England*. Harmondsworth, 1951–.
PILCHER, D. *The Regency Style*. London, 1947.
RAMSEY, S. C. *Small Houses of the Late Georgian Period*. 2 vols. London, 1919–23.
RICHARDSON, A. E. *Monumental Classic Architecture in Great Britain and Ireland*. London, 1914 (1982 reprint).
RICHARDSON, A. E. and EBERLEIN, H. D. *The Smaller English Country House, 1660–1830*. London, 1925.
ROBINSON, J. M. *The Wyatts. an Architectural Dynasty*. Oxford, 1979.
RYKWERT, J. and RYKERT, A. *The Brothers Adam: the Men and the Style*. London, 1985.
SCHUMANN-BACIA, E. *John Soane and the Bank of England*. Harlow, 1991.
SEKLER, E. *Wren and his Place in European Architecture*. London, 1956.
SMALL, T. and WOODBRIDGE, C. *Houses of Wren and Early Georgian Periods*. London, 1928.
STILLMAN, D. *English Neo-Classical Architecture*. London, 1988.
STROUD, D. *Capability Brown*. 3rd edn, London, 1975.
—. *George Dance the Younger*. London, 1970.
—. *Henry Holland*. London, 1950.
—. *Humphrey Repton*. London, 1962.
—. *Sir John Soane, Architect*. London, 1984.
STUTCHBURY, J. *The Architecture of Colen Campbell*. Manchester, 1967.
SUMMERSON, J. *Architecture in Britain, 1530–1830*. 9th edn, Harmondsworth, 1993.
—. *The Architecture of the Eighteenth Century*. London, 1986.
—. *Georgian London*. New edn, London, 1988.
—. *Inigo Jones*. Harmondsworth, 1966.
—. *The Life and Work of John Nash, Architect*. London, 1980.
—. *Sir Christopher Wren*. London, 1983.
—. *Sir John Soane*. London, 1952.
TAVERNOR, R. *Palladio and Palladianism*. London, 1991.
THURLEY, S. *The Royal Palaces of Tudor England: Architecture and Court Life, 1460–1547*. New Haven and London, 1993.
TURNER, R. *Capability Brown and the Eighteenth-century English Landscape*. London, 1985.

—. *Vitruvius Britannicus*, by Campbell, Woolfe and Gandon. 6 vols. London, 1715–71.

WATKIN, D. *Athenian Stuart*. London, 1982.

—. *The Life and Work of C. R. Cockerell*. London, 1974.

—. *Thomas Hope and the Neo-Classical Idea*. London, 1968.

WHIFFEN, M. *Stuart and Georgian Churches*. London, 1947–8.

—. *Thomas Archer: Architect of the English Baroque*. New edn, Los Angeles, 1973.

WHINNEY, M. *Renaissance Architecture in England*. London, 1952.

WILLIS, P. *Charles Bridgeman and the English Landscape Garden*. London, 1977.

WILSON, M. I. *William Kent: Architect, Designer, Painter, Gardener, 1685–1748*. London, 1984.

WILTON-ELY, J. *The Mind and Art of Giovanni Battista Piranesi*. London, 1978.

WITTKOWER, R. *Palladio and English Palladianism*. London, 1974.

WORSLEY, G. *Classical Architecture in Britain: the Heroic Age*. New Haven and London, 1995.

WREN SOCIETY. Publications, vols I-XX. London, 1924–43.

YOUNGSON, A. J. *The Making of Classical Edinburgh, 1750–1840*. Edinburgh, 1966 (1993 reprint with corrections).

Chapter 33 Russia and Scandinavia

Russia

AKADEMIIA ARKHITEKTURY SSSR. *Russkoe zodchestvo: pamyatniki arkhitektury X-XX vekov*. 7 vols. Moscow, 1953–7.

—. *Istoriia Russkoi arkhitektury*. 2nd edn, Moscow, 1956.

ALFEROVA, G. V. *Russkiye goroda XVI-XVII vekov*. Moscow, 1989.

BERTON, K. *Moscow: an Architectural History*. London, 1977.

BRUMFIELD, W. C. *Gold in Azure: One Thousand Years of Russian Architecture*. Boston, Mass., 1983.

—. *A History of Russian Architecture*. Cambridge, 1993.

CRACRAFT, J. *The Petrine Revolution in Russian Architecture*. Chicago, 1988.

EVSINA, N. A. *Arkhitekturnaja teorija v Rossii XVIIIv*. Moscow, 1975.

GALITZINE, G. *Imperial Splendour: Palaces and Monasteries of Old Russia*. London, 1991.

GALKINA, E. N. (Ed.). *Country Estates Around Moscow: From the History of Russian Estate Culture of the 17th, 18th and 19th Centuries*. Moscow, 1979.

GOSLING, N. *Leningrad: History, Art and Architecture*. New York, 1965.

GRIMM, G. G. *Arkhitektor Andeian Zakharov*. Moscow, 1940.

HAMILTON, G. H. *The Art and Architecture of Russia*. 3rd edn, Harmondsworth, 1983.

KENNETT, A. *The Palaces of Leningrad*. London, 1975.

SARABIANOV, D. V. *Russian Art from Neoclassicism to the Avant-Garde: Painting, Sculpture, Architecture*. London, 1990.

SCHMIDT, A. *The Architecture and Planning of Classical Moscow: a Cultural History*. Philadelphia, 1989.

VORONIN, N. N. (Ed.) *Palaces and Churches of the Kremlin*. London, Prague and Moscow, 1965.

Scandinavia

ABRAHAMSEN, H. *Building in Norway*. Oslo, 1959.

ALNAES, E. *et al. Norwegian Architecture*. Oslo, 1950.

ANDERSSON, H. O. and BEDOIRE, F. *Stockholms byggnader*. Stockholm, 1977.

BROCHMANN, O. *Copenhagen*. Copenhagen, 1970.

BUGGE, A. *Norwegian Stave Churches*. Oslo, 1953.

BUGGE, G. and NORBERG-SCHULZ, C. *Stav og laft. 1: Norge*. Oslo, 1969.

CORNELL, H. *Den Svenska konstens historia*. 2 vols. Stockholm, 1944–6.

DAHLBERG, E. *Suecia antiqua et hodierna*. Stockholm, 1716.

DI NISCEMI, M. *Manor Houses and Castles of Sweden: a Voyage Through Five Centuries*. Woodbridge, 1988.

DONNELLY, M. C. *Architecture in the Scandinavian Countries*. Cambridge, Mass. and London, 1992.

FABER, T. *A History of Danish Architecture*. Copenhagen, 1978.

GROTH, H. *Neoclassicism in the North: Swedish Furniture and Interiors, 1770–1850: with a Catalogue of Furniture Types and Styles and Notes on the Architects, Artists and Craftsmen*. London, 1990.

HAHR, A. *Architecture in Sweden*. Stockholm, 1938.

JORGENSEN, L. B. and PORPHYRIOS, D. *Neoclassical Architecture in Copenhagen and Athens*. London, 1987.

JOSEPHSON, R. *Nicodème Tessin*. Paris and Brussels, 1930.

KAVLI, G. *Norwegian Architecture Past and Present*. Oslo, 1958.

LANGBERG, H. *Danmarks bygningskultur*. Copenhagen, 1955.

LUNDBERG, E. *Svensk bostad*. Stockholm, 1942.

NORDIN, E. *Swedish Timber-churches*. Stockholm, 1965

PAULSSON, T. *Scandinavian Architecture*. London, 1958.

RICHARDS, J. M. *A Guide to Finnish Architecture*. London, 1966.

—. *800 Years of Finnish Architecture*. Vancouver, 1978.

SKORGAARD, J. *A King's Architecture: Christian IV and His Buildings*. London, 1973.

SLOTHOUWER, D. F. *Bouwkunst der nederlandsche Renaissance in Denemarken*. Amsterdam, 1924.

THURAH, L. DE T. *Den danske Vitruvius*. Copenhagen, 1749.

VREIM, H. *Norsk trearkitektur*. Oslo, 1947.

Chapter 34 Post-Renaissance Europe

ALDRICH, M. *Gothic Revival*. London, 1994.

ALLIBONE, J. *Anthony Salvin: Pioneer of Gothic Revival Architecture*. Cambridge, 1988.

ASLIN, E. *The Aesthetic Movement: Prelude to Art Nouveau*. London, 1969.

ATTERBURY, P. and WAINWRIGHT, C. (Eds). *Pugin: a Gothic Passion*. New Haven and London, 1994.

BARRE-DESPOND, A. and TISE, S. *Jourdain: Frantz, 1847–1935, Francis, 1876–1958, Frantz-Philippe, 1906–1990*. New York, 1991.

BARRY, A. *The Life and Works of Sir Charles Barry, R.A., F.R.S.* London, 1867.

BARTHES, R. *La Tour Eiffel*. Paris, 1961.

BASSEGODA NONELL, J. *Modernisme a Catalunya: arquitectura*. Barcelona, 1988.

BEENKEN, H. *Schöpferische Bauideen der deutschen Romantik*. Mainz, 1952.

BEŇSOVÁ, M. *Česká Architektura v Proménách Dvou Století*. Prague, 1984.

BOASE, T. S. R. *English Art, 1800–1870*. London, 1959.

BOHLE-HEINTZENBERG, S. and HAMM, M. *Ludwig Persius: Architekt des Königs*. Berlin, 1993.

BORISOVA, E. A. and STERNIN, G. *Russian Art Nouveau*. New York, 1988.

BORSI, F. and GODOLI, E. *Vienna 1900: Architecture and Design*. London, 1986.

BORSI, F. and PORTOGHESI, P. *Victor Horta*. London, 1991.

BROOKS, M. W. *John Ruskin and Victorian Architecture*. New Brunswick, 1987.

BROWNLEE, D. B. *The Law Courts: the Architecture of George Edmund Street*. New York, 1984.

BRUMFIELD, W. C. *The Origins of Modernism in Russian Architecture*. Berkeley, Calif., 1991.

CHADWICK, G. F. *The Works of Sir Joseph Paxton, 1803–1865*. London, 1961.

CHEMETOV, P. and MARREY, B. *Architectures a Paris, 1848–1914*. Paris, 1984.

CLARK, K. *The Gothic Revival*. 3rd edn, London, 1962.

COLE, D. *The Work of Sir Gilbert Scott*. London, 1980.

COLLINS, G. R. and BASSEGODA NONELL, J. *The Designs and Drawings of Antonio Gaudí*. 2 vols. Princeton, 1982.

COLLINS, P. *Changing Ideals in Modern Architecture 1750–1950*. London, 1965..

COLVIN, H. *A Biographical Dictionary of British Architects 1600–1840*. 3rd edn, New Haven and London, 1995.

CONWAY, H. *People's Parks: the Design and Development of Victorian Parks in Britain*. Cambridge, 1991.

COOPER, J. *Victorian and Edwardian Furniture and Interiors from the Gothic Revival to Art Nouveau*. London, 1987.

CRAWFORD, A. *C. R. Ashbee: Architect, Designer and Romantic Socialist*. New Haven and London, 1985.

—. *Charles Rennie Mackintosh*. London, 1995.

CROOK, J. M. *Dilemma of Style: Architectural Ideas from the Picturesque to the Post-Modern*. London, 1987.

—. *The Greek Revival*. London, 1973.

—. *William Burges and the High Victorian Dream*. London, 1981.

CUMMING, E. and KAPLAN, W. *The Arts and Crafts Movement*. London, 1991.

CUNNINGHAM, C. and WATERHOUSE, P. *Alfred Waterhouse, 1830–1905: Biography of a Practice*. Oxford, 1992.

CURL, J. S. *Victorian Architecture*. Newton Abbot, 1990.

DAL CO, F. *Figures of Architecture and Thought: German Architecture Culture, 1880–1920*. New York, 1990.

DAVEY, P. *Arts and Crafts Architecture*. Rev. edn, London, 1995.

DELHAYE, J. *La Maison du Peuple de Victor Horta*. Bruxelles, 1987.

DIERKENS-AUBRY, F. *Art Nouveau in Belgium: Architecture and Interior Design*. Paris, 1991.

DIXON, R. and MUTHESIUS, S. *Victorian Architecture*. London, 1978.

DREXLER, A. (Ed.). *The Architecture of the Ecole des Beaux-Arts*. New York, 1977.

DYOS, H. J. and WOLFF, M. (Eds). *The Victorian City*. 2 vols. London, 1973.

EASTLAKE, C. L. *A History of the Gothic Revival*. London, 1872. Reprinted 1978, edited by J. M. Crook).

FARR, D. *English Art, 1870–1940*. Oxford, 1979.

FAWCETT, J. (Ed.). *Seven Victorian Architects*. London, 1976.

FELLOWS, R. *Edwardian Architecture: Style and Technology*. London, 1995.

FERGUSSON, J. *History of the Modern Styles of Architecture*. 2 vols. 3rd edn, revised by R. Kerr. London, 1891.

FERRIDAY, P. (Ed.). *Victorian Architecture*. London, 1963.

FRAMPTON, K. *Modern Architecture, 1851–1945*. New York, 1983.

FROHLICH, M. *Gottfried Semper*. Zurich, 1991.

GEIST, J. R. *Arcades: the History of a Building Type*. Cambridge, Mass., and London, 1983.

GERE, C. and WHITEWAY, M. *Nineteenth Century design: from Pugin to Mackintosh*. London, 1993.

GERETSEGGER, H. and PEINTNER, M. *Otto Wagner*. London, 1971.

GERMANN, G. *The Gothic Revival in Europe and Britain*. London, 1972.

GIEDION, S. *Space, Time and Architecture*. Cambridge, Mass., 1941; London, 1967 and other editions.

GIROUARD, M. *Sweetness and Light: the 'Queen Anne' Movement 1860–1900*. Oxford,1977.

—. *The Victorian Country House*. 2nd edn, London and New Haven, 1979.

GOODHART-RENDEL, H. S. *English Architecture since the Regency: an Interpretation*. London, 1953. (Reprinted 1989.)

GROMORT, G. *Small Structures: French Architecture of the Early Nineteenth Century*. New York, 1986.

Guimard. Exhibition catalogue, Paris, 1992.

HAWKES, D. (Ed.). *Modern Country Homes in England: the Arts and Crafts Architecture of Barry Parker*. Cambridge, 1986.

HEARN, M. F. (Ed.). *The Architectural Theory of Viollet-le-Duc: Readings and Commentary*. Cambridge, Mass. and London, 1990.

HERRMANN, W. *Gottfried Semper: in Search of Architecture*. Cambridge, Mass. and London, 1984.

HITCHCOCK, H. R. *Architecture, Nineteenth and Twentieth Centuries*. 4th edn, Harmondsworth, 1977.

—. *Early Victorian Architecture*. 2 vols. London, 1954.

HOBHOUSE, H. *Thomas Cubitt: Master Builder*. London, 1971.

HOWARTH, T. *Charles Rennie Mackintosh and the Modern Movement*. 2nd edn, London, 1977.

HUSSEY, C. *The Life of Sir Edwin Lutyens*. London, 1953.

JACKSON, F. *Sir Raymond Unwin: Architect, Planner and Visionary*. London, 1985.

JENKINS, F. I. *Architect and Patron*. London, 1961.

KAUFMANN, E. *Von Ledoux bis le Corbusier*. Vienna, 1933.

KAYE, B. *The Development of the Architectural Profession in Britain*. London, 1960.

KOHLMAIER, G. and SARTORY, B. VON. *Houses of Glass: a Nineteenth-Century Building Type*. Cambridge, Mass. and London, 1986.

LETHABY, W. R. *Philip Webb and his Work*. London, 1935.

LONG, H. C. *The Edwardian House: the Middle-Class Home in Britain, 1880–1914*. Manchester, 1993.

LOYER, F. *Architecture of the Industrial Age, 1789–1914*. Geneva, 1983.

—. *Dix ans d'Art Nouveau: Paul Hankar architecte*. Brussels, 1991.

—. *Paris Nineteenth Century: Architecture and Urbanism*. New York, 1988.

LOZE, P. *Belgian Art Nouveau: from Victor Horta to Antoine Pompe*. Ghent, 1991.

MACAULAY, J. *The Gothic Revival*. Glasgow, 1975.

MACLEOD, R. *Style and Society: Architectural Ideology in Britain 1835–1914*. London, 1971.

MADSEN, S. T. *Art Nouveau*. London, 1967.

—. *Sources of Art Nouveau*. Oslo and and New York, 1956.

MCFADZEAN, R. *The Life and Work of Alexander Thomson*. London, 1979.

MEAD, C. *Charles Garnier's Paris Opera: Architectural Empathy and the Renaissance of French Classicism*. New York, 1991.

MEEKS, C. L. *Italian Architecture, 1750–1914*. New Haven and London, 1966.

—. *The Railroad Station*. New Haven, 1956.

MESNIL, C. *Victor Horta: un maitre de l'Art Nouveau: sa vie, son oeuvre*. Braine-l'Alleud, 1990.

MIDDLETON, R. (Ed.). *The Beaux-Arts and Nineteenth Century Architecture*. London, 1982.

MIGNOT, C. *Architecture of the Nineteenth Century in Europe*. New York, 1984.

MILLER, M. *Raymond Unwin: Garden Cities and Town Planning*. Leicester, 1992.

MILOBEDZKI, A. *Zarys dziehów architektury w Polsce*. Warsaw, 1968.

MORAVANSZKY, A. *Die Architektur der Jahrhundertwende in Ungarn und ihre Beziehungen zu der Wiener Architektur der Zeit*. Vienna, 1983.

MUTHESIUS, H. *The English House*. English edn, London, 1979.

—. *Stilarchitektur und Baukunst: Wandlungen der Architektur im XIX Jahrhundert*. Mülheim-Ruhr, 1902

MUTHESIUS, S. *Art, Architecture and Design in Poland*. Königstein im Taunas, 1994.

—. *The English Terraced House*. New Haven and London, 1982.

—. *The High Victorian Movement 1850–1870*. London and Boston, 1972.

NAYLOR, G. *The Arts and Crafts Movement: a Study of its Sources, Ideals and Influence on Design Theory*. London, 1971.

NERDINGER, W. (Ed.). *Friedrich von Gärtner: ein Architektenleben, 1791–1847*. Munich, 1992.

NUTTGENS, P. (Ed.). *Mackintosh and his Contemporaries in Europe and America*. London, 1988.

PEVSNER, N. *Pioneers of Modern Design from William Morris to Walter Gropius*. London, 1936, Harmondsworth, 1960 and other editions.

—. *A History of Building Types*. London and Princeton, 1976.

POLANO, S. *Hendrik Petrus Berlage: Complete Works*. London, 1987.

PORT, M. H. (Ed.). *The Houses of Parliament*. New Haven and London, 1976.

PUGIN, A. W. N. *Contrasts, or a Parallel Between the Noble Edifices of the Fourteenth and Fifteenth Centuries*. Salisbury, 1836. (1841 edition reprinted 1969.)

QUINEY, A. *John Loughborough Pearson*. New Haven and London, 1979.

RAGON, M. *Histoire mondiale de l'architecture et de l'urbanisme modernes*. Vol. 1: *Idéologies et pionniers, 1800–1910*. Paris, 1971.

RÉAU, F. L. *L'Oeuvre du Baron Haussmann*. Paris, 1954.
RHEIMS, M. *Hector Guimard*. New York, 1988.
RICHARDS, J. M. *The Functional Tradition in Early Industrial Buildings*. London, 1958.
—. *A Guide to Finnish Architecture*. London, 1966.
RICHARDS, J. M. and PEVSNER, N. (Eds). *The Anti-Rationalists*. London, 1973.
RICKMAN, T. *An Attempt to Discriminate the Styles of English Architecture*. 4th edn, London, 1835.
RUBENS, G. *William Richard Lethaby: his Life and Work, 1857–1931*. London, 1986.
RUSKIN, J. *The Seven Lamps of Architecture*. London, 1849.
—. *The Stones of Venice*. 3 vols. London, 1851–3.
SAINT, A. *Richard Norman Shaw*. New Haven and London, 1976.
SCHEZEN, R. and HAIKO, P. *Vienna, 1850–1930: Architecture*. New York, 1992.
SCHILD, E. *Zwischen Glaspalast und Palais des Illusions*. 2nd edn, Brunswick and Wiesbaden, 1983.
SERVICE, A. *Edwardian Architecture: a Handbook to Building Design in Britain, 1890–1914*. London, 1977.
SERVICE, A. (Ed.). *Edwardian Architecture and Its Origins*. London, 1950.
SIMMONS, J. *St Pancras Station*. London, 1968.
SIMPSON, D. *C. F. A. Voysey: an Architect of Individuality*. London, 1979.
SINGER, C. *et al. A History of Technology*. Vols 4 and 5. London, 1958.
STAMP, G. and GOULANCOURT, A. *The English House, 1860–1914: the Flowering of English Domestic Architecture*. London, 1986.
STAMP, G. and MCKINSTRY, S. (Eds). *'Greek' Thomson*. Edinburgh, 1994.
STANTON, P. *Pugin*. London, 1971.
STRATTON, M. *The Terracotta Revival: Building Innovation and the Image of the Industrial City in Britain and North America*. London, 1993.
STREET, A. E. *Memoir of George Edmund Street, R.A.* New York, 1972 (reprint of 1888 edition).
SUMMERSON, J. *Heavenly Mansions*. London, 1949.
—. *Victorian Architecture: Four Studies*. New York, 1970.
SWEENEY, J. J. and SERT, J. L. *Antoni Gaudí*. 2nd edn, London, 1970.
THOMPSON, P. *William Butterfield*. London, 1971.
VAN ZANTEN, D. *Designing Paris: the Architecture of Duban, Labrouste, Duc and Vaudoyer*. Cambridge, Mass., and London, 1987.
VIOLLET-LE-DUC, E. *Entretiens sur l'architecture*. Paris, 1858–72.
WATKIN, D. *The Life and Work of C. R. Cockerell*. London, 1974.
WEDGWOOD, A. *A. W. N. Pugin and the Pugin Family*. Catalogue of Architectural Drawings. London (Victoria and Albert Museum), 1985.
WILKES, L. and DODDS, G. *Tyneside Classical*. London, 1964.
ZADOR, A. *Revival Architecture in Hungary: Classicism and Romanticism*. Budapest, 1985.
ZEITLER, R. *Die Kunst des 19. Jahrhunderts*. Berlin, 1966.

PART 6 The Architecture of the Colonial and Post-colonial periods outside Europe

Chapter 36 Africa

Books

BEGUIN, F. *Arabisances: decor architectural et trace urbain en Afrique du Nord, 1830–1950*. Paris, 1983.
CHIPKIN, C. M. *Johannesburg Style: Architecture & Society, 1880s-1960s*. Cape Town, 1993.
DE BOSDARI, C. *Cape Dutch Houses and Farms*. Cape Town, 1971.
FRANSEN, H. and COOK, M. *The Old Buildings of the Cape*. Cape Town, 1980.
—. *The Old Houses of the Cape*. Cape Town, 1965.
GREIG, D. *Herbert Baker in South Africa*. Cape Town, 1970.
KEARNEY, B. *Architecture in Natal, 1824–1893*. Cape Town, 1973.
KEATH, M. *Herbert Baker: Architecture and Idealism, 1892–1913: the South African Years*. Gibraltar, 1992.
LAWRENCE, A. B. *Trade Castles and Forts of West Africa*. London, 1963.
LEWCOCK. R. *Early Nineteenth-Century Architecture in South Africa*. Cape Town, 1963.
OBHOLZER, A. M., BARAITSER, M. and MALHERBE, W. D. *The Cape House and its Interior: an Inquiry into the Sources of Cape Architecture and a Survey of Built-in Early Cape Domestic Woodwork*. Stellenbosch, 1985.
PEARSE, G. E. *The Cape of Good Hope 1652–1833*. Pretoria, 1956.
—. *Eighteenth-Century Architecture in South Africa*. Cape Town, 1968.
PICTON-SEYMOUR, D. *Victorian Buildings in South Africa*. Cape Town, 1977.
RENNIE, J. *The Buildings of Central Cape Town*. Cape Town, 1978.
WALTON, J. *Homesteads and Villages of South Africa*. Pretoria, 1965.

Reports and Articles

AALUND, F. 'Zanzibar Old Stone Town'. *Monumentum*, vol. 26, no. 2, 1983.
GHAIDAN, U. *Lamu: a Study in Conservation*. Nairobi, 1976.
—. *Lamu: a Study of the Swahili Town*. Nairobi, 1975.
ISAKA, A. *Area Conservation for Traditional Buildings in Ghana*. Unpublished thesis, University of York, 1982.

WATSON, T. N. 'Bagamoyo, Tanzania'. *Monumentum*, vol. 25, no. 1, 1982.
—. 'Conservation Report on Bagamoyo'. Bury St Edmonds, 1979.

Chapter 37 The Americas

ADAMS, W. H. *Jefferson's Monticello*. New York, 1983.
ALEXANDER, R. L. *The Architecture of Maximilian Godefroy*. Baltimore, 1974.
ANGULO, D. *Planos de monumentos arquitectónicos de América y Filipinas, en el Archivo General de Indias*. Seville, 1939.
ANGULO, D., MARCO DORTA, E. and BUSCHIAZZO, M. *Historia del arte hispanoamericano*. Barcelona, 1974.
ARANGO, S. *Historia de la arquitectura en Colombia*. Bogotá, 1989.
AXELROD, A. (Ed.). *The Colonial Revival in America*. New York, 1985.
BAKER, P. R. *Richard Morris Hunt*. Cambridge, Mass., 1980.
BARDI, P. M. *Historia da arte brasiliera*. Sao Paulo, 1978.
BAYÓN, D. *Sociedad y arquitectura colonial sudamericana*. Barcelona, 1974.
BAYÓN, D. AND MARX, M. *History of South American Colonial Art and Architecture: Spanish South America and Brazil*. New York, 1992.
BAZIN, G. *L'Architecture religieuse baroque au Brésil*. Paris, 1956.
BENAVÍDEZ, A. *La Arquitectura en el Virreynato del Perú y la Capitan#dia General de Chile*. Santiago, 1945.
BERCHEZ, J. *Arquitectura mexicana de los siglos XVII y XVIII*. Mexico City, 1992.
BLASER, W. (Ed.). *Chicago Architecture: Holabird & Root 1880–1992*. Basel, 1992.
BRIDENBAUGH, C. *Peter Harrison, First American Architect*. Chapel Hill, 1949.
BRUEGMANN, R. *Holabird & Roche, Holabird & Root: An Illustrated Catalog of Works*. New York and London, 1991.
BURY, J. *Arquitetura e arte no Brasil colonial*. Sao Paulo, 1991.
BUSCHIAZZO, M. *La Arquitectura en la República Argentina, 1810–1930*. Buenos Aires, 1969.
—. *Historia de la arquitectura colonial en Iberoamérica*. Buenos Aires, 1961.
CARROTT, R. *The Egyptian Revival*. Berkeley, Calif., 1978.
Centros Históricos. América Latina. Coordinator R. Gutierrez. Bogotá, 1990.
CONDIT, C. W. *The Chicago School of Architecture*. Chicago and London, 1964.
—. *The Rise of the Skyscraper*. Chicago, 1952.
CUMMINGS, A. L. *The Framed Houses of Massachusetts Bay, 1625–1725*. Cambridge, Mass., 1974.
DONOGHUE, J. *Alexander Jackson Davis: Romantic Architect, 1803–1892*. New York, 1982.
EARLY, J. *The Colonial Architecture of Mexico*. Albuquerque, 1994.
ETZEL, E. *O Barroco no Brasil*. Sao Paulo, 1974.
FERNÁNDEZ, M. *Arquitectura y gobierno virreinal*. Mexico, 1985.
FITCH, J. M. *American Building: the Historical Forces that Shaped it*. New York, 1966.
FORMAN, H. C. *Architecture of the Old South; the Mediaeval Style, 1585–1850*. Cambridge, Mass., 1948.
FRASER, V. *The Architecture of Conquest: Building in the Viceroyalty of Peru, 1535–1635*. Cambridge, 1990.
GALLAGHER, H. M. P. *Robert Mills, Architect of the Washington Monument, 1781–1855*. New York, 1935.
GASPARINI, G. *América, barroco y arquitectura*. Caracas, 1972.
—. *La arquitectura colonial en Venezuela*. Cararacas. 1965.
GILCHRIST, A. A. *William Strickland, Architect and Engineer, 1788–1854*. Philadelphia, 1950.
GISBERT, T. and DE MESA, J. *Arquitectura andina, 1530–1830*. La Paz, 1985.
GIURIA, J. *La arquitectura en el Paraguay*. Buenos Aires, 1950.
—. *La arquitectura en el Uruguay*. Montevideo, 1955.
GOSNER, P. *Caribbean Georgian: the Great and Small Houses of the West Indies*. Washington, DC, 1982.
GOWANS, A. *Building Canada*. Toronto, 1966.
GRROSS, P. *Arquitectura en Chile*. Santiago de Chiles, 1988.
GUTIÉRREZ, R. *Arquitectura y urbanismo en Iberoamérica*. Madrid, 1983.
—. *Evolución urban#distica y arquitectónica del Paraguay*. Asunción, 1978.
—. *Tipologías de las Misiones Jesuíticas*. Buenos Aires, 1982.
HAMLIN, T. F. *The Architecture of H. H. Richardson and his Times*. New York, 1936 and 1965.
—. *Benjamin Henry Latrobe*. New York, 1955.
—. *Greek Revival Architecture in America*. New York, 1944 and 1964.
HANDLIN, D. P. *American Architecture*. New York and London, 1985.
—. *The American Home; Architecture and Society, 1815–1915*. Boston, 1979.
HARDOY, J. E. *La Ciudad en América Latina*. Buenos Aires, 1972.
—. *Historia urbana de Iberoamerica*. Coordinator M. L. Cerrillos. 3 vols. Madrid, 1987.
HITCHCOCK, H.-R. *Architecture: Nineteenth and Twentieth Centuries*. 4th edn, Harmondsworth and Baltimore, 1977.
HOFFMAN, D. *The Architecture of John Wellborn Root*. Baltimore, 1973.

JENKINS, B. S. *William Thornton: Small Star of the American Enlightenment*. San Luis Obispo, Calif., 1982.

JOHNSTON, F. B. and WATERMAN, T. T. *The Early Architecture of North Carolina*. Chapel Hill, 1941.

JORDY, W. H. *American Buildings and their Architects*. Vols 3 and 4. New York, 1970–73.

KATZMAN, I. *Arquitectura del siglo XIX en México*. Mexico, 1973.

KELEMEN, P. *Baroque and Rococo in Latin América*. New York, 1951.

KELLY, J. F. *The Early Domestic Architecture of Connecticut*. New Haven, 1948.

KENNEDY, R. G. *Greek Revival America*. New York, 1989.

KIMBALL, F. *Domestic Architecture of the American Colonies and of the Early Republic*. New York, 1922, reprinted 1966.

—. *Thomas Jefferson, Architect*. Boston, 1916, Repr. 1968.

KIRKER, H. *The Architecture of Charles Bulfinch*. Cambridge, Mass., 1969.

KUBLER, G. and SORIA, M. *Art and Architecture in Spain and Portugal and their American Dominions, 1500–1800*. Baltimore, 1959.

LARSON, G. A. and PRIDMORE, J. *Chicago Architecture and Design*. New York, 1993.

LISCOMBE, R. W. *Altogether American: Robert Mills, Architect and Engineer, 1781–1855*. New York, 1994.

LOUNSBURY, C. R. (Ed.). *An Illustrated Glossary of Early Southern Architecture and Landscape*. New York, 1994.

LUJÁN MUÑOZ, L. *Síntesis de la arquitectura de Guatemala*. Guatemala, 1968.

MCKIM MEAD & WHITE. *The Architecture of McKim, Mead & White In Photographs, Plans and Elevations*. New York and London, 1990.

MAITLAND, L. *Neoclassical Architecture in Canada*. Ottawa, 1984.

MAZA, F. DE LA. *El Arte colonial como expresión histórica de México*. Mexico, 1965.

MESA, J. and GISBERT, T. *Monumentos de Bolivia*. La Paz, 1992.

MONTECINOS, H. *et al*. *Arquitectura de Chile*. Santiago, 1976.

MORRISON, H. *Early American Architecture*. New York, 1952.

—. *Louis Sullivan, Prophet of Modern Architecture*. New York, 1935, 1952 and 1962.

NEWCOMB, R. *Architecture in Old Kentucky*. Urbana, Ill., 1953.

—. *Spanish Colonial Architecture in the United States*. New York, 1937.

NEWTON, R. H. *Town and Davis, Architects*. New York, 1942.

NICOLINI, A. R., SILVA, M. and MARTÍNEZ, E. *El Patrimonio arquitectónico de los Argentinos*. Buenos Aires, 1982.

O'GORMAN, J. F. *The Architecture of Frank Furness*. Philadelphia, 1973.

—. *H. H. Richardson: Architectural Forms for an American Society*. Chicago, 1987.

—. *Three American Architects: Richardson, Sullivan and Wright, 1865–1915*. Chicago, 1991.

PALM, E. W. *Los monumentos arquitectónicos de la Española*. Ciudad Trujillo, 1955.

—. *El Patrimonio arquitectónico de los Argentinos*. 4 vols. Buenos Aires, 1982–7.

PIERSON, W. H. *American Buildings and their Architects*. Vols 1 and 2. New York, 1970–73.

ROTH, L. M. *McKim, Mead & White, Architects*. London, 1984.

SCHUYLER, M., JORDY, W. and COE, R. (Eds). *American Architecture and Other Writings*. Cambridge, Mass., 1961.

SCULLY, V. J. *American Architecture and Urbanism*. New York and London, 1969.

—. *The Shingle Style and the Stick Style*. New York, 1971.

SOUSA, A. *Arquitectura neoclásica brasiliera: um reexame*. Sao Paulo, 1994.

STEIN, S. R. (Ed.). *The Architecture of Richard Morris Hunt*. Chicago, 1986.

SULLLIVAN, L. H. *The Autobiography of an Idea*. New York, 1956 and earlier editions.

TALLMADGE, T. *Architecture in Old Chicago*. Chicago, 1941.

THOMAS, G. E., LEWIS, M. J. and COHEN, J. A. *Frank Furness: the Complete Works*. Princeton and London, 1991.

TOUSSAINT, M. *Arte colonial en México*. Mexico, 1962.

TWOMBLY, R. *Louis Sullivan: his Life and Work*. Chicago, 1987.

UPJOHN, E. *Richard Upjohn: Architect and Churchman*. New York, 1939.

VAN RENSSELAER, M. G. *Henry Hobson Richardson and his Works*. Boston, 1888, reprinted 1969.

VARGAS, J. M. *Historia del arte ecuatoriano*. Quito, 1963.

WAISMAN, M. *Arquitectura colonial argentina*. Buenos Aires, 1987.

WATERMAN, T. T. *The Dwellings of Colonial America*. Chapel Hill, 1950.

—. *Domestic Colonial Architecture in Tidewater Virginia*. New York, 1932.

—. *The Mansions of Virginia*. Chapel Hill, 1946.

WEISS, J. *La arquitectura colonial cubana*. La Havana, 1979.

WETHEY, H. *Art and Architecture in Peru*. Cambridge, 1949.

WHIFFEN, M. *The Eighteenth Century Houses of Williamsburg: a Study of Architecture and Building in the Colonial Capital of Virginia*. Rev. edn, Williamsburg, Va, 1984.

—. *The Public Buildings of Colonial Williamsburg*. Williamsburg, 1958.

WHITE, T. (Ed.). *Philadelphia in the Nineteenth Century*. Philadelphia, 1953.

WILSON, R. G. *McKim, Mead & White, Architects*. New York, 1983.

ZUKOWSKY, J. *Chicago Architecture, 1872–1922: Birth of a Metropolis*. Munich, 1987.

Chapter 38 China

ADAM, M. *Yuen ming yuen, L'Oeuvre Architecturale des Anciens Jésuites au XVIII Siècle*. Peking, 1936.

CHEN CONG-ZHOU and ZHANG MING. *Shanghai Jindai Jianzhu Shigao (A Historical Draft of Shanghai Modern Architecture)*. Shanghai, 1988 (Chinese edition).

EDITORIAL BOARD OF THE CHINESE ARCHITECTURAL HISTORY. *A Brief History of Chinese Architecture*. Book Two. Beijing, 1962 (Chinese edition).

INSTITUTE OF CHINESE MODERN ARCHITECTURE AND JAPANESE INSTITUTE OF ASIAN MODERN ARCHITECTURE. The Architectural Heritage of Modern China, Tianjin. Tokyo, 1989 (Chinese and Japanese edition with English summary).

MURAMATSU SHIN. *Shanghai, 1842–1949*. Tokyo, 1991 (Japanese edition).

PREPARATORY COMMITTEE OF THE CHINESE YUAN MING YUAN INSTITUTE. *Yuan Ming Yuan*. Vol. 1. Beijing, 1981 (Chinese edition).

TENG GU. *The Remains of the Western Style Palace of Yuan Ming Yuan*. Shanghai, 1933 (Chinese edition).

WANG SHAO-ZHOU. *A Pictorial Handbook of Chinese Modern Architecture*. Shanghai, 1989 (Chinese edition).

—. *Shanghai Modern Architecture*. Nanjing, 1989 (Chinese edition).

WANG SHAO-ZHOU AND CHEN ZHI-MIN. *Li-long, Lane Houses in Shanghai*. Shanghai, 1987 (Chinese edition).

WANG TAN and FUJIMORI, TERUNOBU. *The Architectural Heritage of Modern China, Beijing*. Beijing, 1993 (Chinese edition).

—. *The Architectural Heritage of Modern China, Chongqing*. Beijing, 1993 (Chinese edition).

—. *The Architectural Heritage of Modern China, Guangzhou*. Beijing, 1992 (Chinese edition).

—. *The Architectural Heritage of Modern China, Harbin*. Beijing, 1992 (Chinese edition).

—. *The Architectural Heritage of Modern China, Kunming*. Beijing, 1993 (Chinese edition).

—. *The Architectural Heritage of Modern China, Lushan*. Beijing, 1993 (Chinese edition).

—. *The Architectural Heritage of Modern China, Nanjing*. Beijing, 1992 (Chinese edition).

—. *The Architectural Heritage of Modern China, Qingdao*. Beijing, 1992 (Chinese edition).

—. *The Architectural Heritage of Modern China, Wuhan*. Beijing, 1992 (Chinese edition).

—. *The Architectural Heritage of Modern China, Xiamen*. Beijing, 1993 (Chinese edition).

—. *The Architectural Heritage of Modern China, Yantai*. Beijing, 1992 (Chinese edition).

YANG BING-DE. *Chinese Modern Cities and their Architecture, 1840–1949*. Beijing, 1993 (Chinese edition).

Chapter 39 Japan and Korea

ABE, K. 'Meiji Architecture', in Ueno Naoteru (Ed.), *Japanese Arts and Crafts in the Meiji Era*. Tokyo, 1958.

ALEX, W. *Japanese Architecture*. New York, 1963.

BLASER, W. *Japanese Temples and Tea Houses*. New York, 1956.

CHANG, KYUNG HO. *A Study of Structural Styles of Korean Wooden Constructions and their Characteristics*. Tokyo National Research Institute of Cultural Properties, 1983.

COALDRAKE, W. 'Edo Architecture and Tokugawa Law', *Monumenta Nipponica*, vol. 36, no. 3, 1981, pp. 235–84.

—. *The Way of the Carpenter: Tools and Japanese Architecture*. New York, 1990.

DREXLER, A. *The Architecture of Japan*. New York, 1966.

FUKUYAMA, T. *Heian Temples: Byodo-in and Chuson-ji*. New York and Tokyo, 1976.

FUKUYAMA, T. and AKIYAMA, T. *Report of the Institute of Art Research: Study on the Octagonal Hall of Eizanji; the Architecture and Painting of the Nara Period*. Kyoto, 1951.

HAKWON-SA. *Korea: its Land, People and Culture of All Ages*. Seoul, 1960.

HALL, J. W. *Japan from Prehistory to Modern Times*. Tokyo, 1984.

HASHIMOTO, F. *Architecture in the Shoin Style*. Tokyo, New York and San Francisco, 1981.

HAYASHIYA, T., NAKAMURA, M. and HAYASHIYA, S. *Japanese Arts and the Tea Ceremony*. New York and Tokyo, 1974.

HIRAI, K. *Feudal Architecture in Japan*. New York and Tokyo, 1974.

INAGAKI, E. 'Revolt and Conformity in Architecture', *This is Japan*, no. 10, 1963.

INOUE, M. *Space in Japanese Architecture*. New York, 1985.

ITO, T. *The Elegant Japanese House: Traditional Sukiya Architecture*. New York and Tokyo, 1969.

—. *Traditional Domestic Architecture of Japan*. New York and Tokyo, 1972.

ITO, T. and FUTUGAWA, Y. *Traditional Japanese Houses*. New York, 1983.

ITO, T. and NOVOGRAD, P. 'The Development of Shoin-style Architecture', in *Japan in the Muromachi Age*. Berkeley and London, 1977.

ITO, T., *et al. Katsura*. Tokyo, 1983.

JAPAN ARCHITECT (Ed.). *A Guide to Japanese Architecture*. New edn, Tokyo, 1984.

JOE, W. J. *Traditional Korea: a Cultural History*. Seoul, 1972.

KIM, CHOUNG KI, HWANG, SU YONG and CHUNG, YOUNG HO. *The Arts of Korea: Architecture, VI.* Seoul, 1974.

KIM, WON YONG. *Recent Archaelogical Discoveries in the Republic of Korea.* Tokyo, 1983.

KIRBY, J. B. *From Castle to Teahouse: Japanese Architecture of the Momoyama Period.* Tokyo and Rutland, Vt., 1962.

KOREAN NATIONAL COMMISSION FOR UNESCO. *A Study of Traditional Culture in Korea.* Seoul, 1973.

LEE, KI-BAIK. *A New History of Korea.* Translated by E. W. Wagner and E. J. Shultz. Seoul, 1984.

MCCLAIN, J. L. *Kanazawa: a Seventeenth-Century Japanese Castle Town.* New Haven and London, 1982.

MINISTRY OF CULTURE AND INFORMATION. *The Ancient Arts of Korea.* Seoul, 1974.

MORSE, E. *Japanese Homes and their Surroundings.* 1896 (reprinted, Tokyo and Rutland, Vt, 1972).

MURAMSATSU, T. 'Ventures into Western Architecture', in Yamada Chisaburo (Ed.). *Dialogue in Art: Japan and the West.* Tokyo and New York, 1976.

NISHI, K. and HOZUMI, K. *What is Japanese Architecture?* Tokyo, New York and San Francisco, 1985.

ODATE, T. *Japanese Woodworking Tools: Their Traditional Spirit and Use.* Newtown, Conn., 1984.

OKAWA, N. *Edo Architecture: Katsura and Nikko.* New York and Tokyo, 1975.

OOKA, M. *Temples of Nara and their Art.* New York and Tokyo, 1973.

OTA, H. (Ed.). *Japanese Architecture and Gardens.* Tokyo, 1972.

PAINE, R. T. and SOPER, A. *The Art and Architecture of Japan.* Harmondsworth, 1975.

PARENT, M. N. 'A Reconsideration of the Role of Horinji in the History of Japanese Architecture', *The Japan Architect*, January-July, 1975.

—. *The Roof in Japanese Buddhist Architecture.* New York and Tokyo, 1983.

—. 'Yamadadera: Tragedy and Triumph', *Monumenta Nipponica*, vol. 39, no. 3, 1984, pp. 307–31.

—. 'Yamadadera: Excavations 1984', *Monumenta Nipponica*, vol. 40, no. 2, 1985, pp. 209–19.

SADLER, A. L. *A Short History of Japanese Architecture.* 1941 (reprinted, Tokyo and Rutland, Vt, 1963).

SANSOM, G. *A Short Cultural History of Japan.* Stanford, 1952.

SOPER, A. *The Evolution of Buddhist Architecture in Japan.* New York, 1978.

STEWART, D. B. *The Making of a Modern Japanese Architecture: 1868 to the Present.* Tokyo, 1988.

SUZUKI, K. *Early Buddhist Architecture in Japan.* Tokyo, New York and San Francisco, 1980.

UEDA, A. *The Inner Harmony of the Japanese House.* Tokyo, 1990.

WATANABE, Y. *Shinto Art: Ise and Izumo Shrines.* New York and Tokyo, 1974.

Chapter 40 South-east Asia

BEAMISH, J. and FERGUSON, J. *A History of Singapore Architecture: the Making of a City.* Singapore, 1985.

DE JESUS, M. Q. *The Philippines.* Manila, 1981.

FORAN, W. R. *Malayan Symphony.* Plymouth, 1935.

GRETCHEN, M. *Pastel Portraits.* Singapore, 1984.

KLASSEN, W. *Architecture in the Philippines: Filipino Building in a Cross-Cultural Context.* Cebu City, 1986.

KLEIN, W. *Burma.* Singapore, 1981.

LEE KIP LIN. *The Singapore House, 1819–1942.* Singapore, 1988.

SHEPPARD, H. A. M. *Malayan Forts.* Kuala Lumpur, 1961.

VAN DE WALL, V. I. *Onde hollandsche bouwkunst in Indonesie.* Antwerp, 1942.

Chapter 41 Indian Subcontinent

ALLEN, C. *Plain Tales from the Raj.* London, 1975.

AZEVEDO, C. DE. *Arte christã na India Portuguesa.* Lisbon, 1959.

BALDAEUS, P. *A True and Exact Description of the Great Island of Ceylon.* Translator Pieter Brohier. Maharagama, 1980.

BARLOW, G. *The Story of Madras.* London, 1921.

BENCE-JONES, M. *Palaces of the Raj.* London, 1973.

BINHAM, P. M. *History of the Public Works Department, Ceylon, 1796–1896.* 3 vols. Colombo, 1922.

BROHIER, R. L. *Links between Sri Lanka and the Netherlands.* Colombo, 1978.

BROHIER, R. L. and PAULUSZ, J. H. O. *Land, Maps and Surveys, etc.* 2 vols. Colombo, 1951.

CLARKE, B. *Anglican Cathedrals Outside the British Isles.* London, 1958.

DAVIES, P. *Splendours of the Raj: British Architecture in India, 1600 to 1947.* London, 1985.

DE QUEYROZ, F. *The Temporal and Spiritual Conquest of Ceylon.* Translator S. G. Perera. 3 vols. Colombo, 1930.

DODWELL, H. H. *The Cambridge History of India.* Vol. 5, Cambridge, 1929.

DOSHI, S. 'Goa – An Encounter', *Marg*, vol. XXXV, no.3. Bombay.

DOSSAL, M. *Imperial Designs and Indian Realities: the Planning of Bombay City, 1845–1875.* Bombay, 1991.

EVENSON, N. *The Indian Metropolis: a View Towards the West.* New Haven and London, 1989.

FERRACUTI, G. *Goa: memoria e immagine: architettura e citta dell'India Potoghese.* Milan, 1991.

GREIG, D. *The Reluctant Colonists: Netherlanders Abroad in the 17th and 18th Centuries.* Assen, 1987.

GUPTA, S. *Architecture and the Raj (Western Deccan 1700–1900).* Delhi, 1984.

HEYDT, J. W. *Heydt's Ceylon.* Translator R. Raven-Hart. Colombo, 1952.

HUTT, A. *Goa: A Traveller's Historical and Architectural Guide.* Buckhurst Hill, 1988.

KING, A. D. *Colonial Urban Development*. London, 1976.

LLEWELLYN-JONES, R. *Fatal Friendship: the Nawabs, the British and the City of Lucknow*. Delhi, 1985.

MARTYN, M. 'Georgian Architecture in Calcutta', *Country Life*, vol. civ, 3 December 1948.

METCALF, T. R. *An Imperial Vision: Indian Architecture and Britain's Raj*. Berkeley, Calif., 1989.

MICHELL, G. *The Royal Palaces of India*. London, 1994.

MORRIS, J. *Stones of Empire: Buildings of the Raj*. Oxford, 1983.

MUKHERJI, S. C. *The Changing Face of Calcutta: an Architectural Approach*. Calcutta, 1991.

MUMTAZ, K. K. *Architecture In Pakistan*. Singapore, 1985.

MUNASINGHE, H. *Transformation of Colonial Urban Space in Sri Lanka with Special Reference to the Port City of Galle*. Espoo, 1992.

MUTHIAH, S. *Madras Discovered*. Madras, 1981.

NELSON, W. A. *Dutch Forts in Sri Lanka*. Edinburgh, 1984.

NILSSON, S. *European Architecture in India, 1750–1850*. London, 1968.

NUNES, J. *The Monuments in Old Goa*. Delhi, 1979.

PIERIS, P. E. *Ceylon: the Portuguese Era*. Colombo, 1914.

POTT, J. *Old Bungalows in Bangalore*. London, 1977.

REIMERS, E. *Constantine De Sa's Maps and Plans of Ceylon (1624–1618)*. Colombo, 1929.

TADGELL, C. *The History of Architecture in India from the Dawn of Civilization to the End of the Raj*. London, 1990.

THAPAR, R. *Penguin History of India, Vol. 1*. Harmondsworth, 1970.

TILLOTSON, G. H. R. *The Tradition of Indian Architecture: Continuity, Controversy and Change since 1850*. New Haven and London, 1989.

TINDALL, G. *City of Gold: the Biography of Bombay*. London, 1982.

TOY, S. *The Strongholds of India*. London, 1957.

VAN DE WALL. *Oude hollandsche bouwkunst in Indonesie*. Antwerp, 1942.

WOODFORD, P. *Rise of the Raj*. London, 1978.

WRIGHT, G. *The Politics of Design in French Colonial Urbanism*. Chicago and London, 1991.

Chapter 42 Australasia

ANDREWS, B. *Gothic in South Australian Churches*. Adelaide, 1984.

APPERLY, R, IRVING, R. and REYNOLDS, P. *A Pictorial Guide to Identifying Australian Architecture: Styles and Terms from 1788 to the Present*. North Ryde, 1989.

AUSTRALIAN COUNCIL OF NATIONAL TRUSTS. *Historic Homesteads of Australia*. 2 vols. Melbourne, 1976.

—. *Historic Houses of Australia*. Melbourne, 1974.

—. *Historic Places of Australia*. 2 vols. Melbourne 1979.

—. *Historic Public Buildings of Australia*. Melbourne, 1971.

AUSTRALIAN HERITAGE COMMISSION. *The Heritage of Australia, the Illustrated Register of the National Estate*. South Melbourne, 1981.

COX, P. and LUCAS, C. *Australian Colonial Architecture*. East Melbourne, 1978.

DE JONG, U. *William Wilkinson Wardell, 1823–1899, his Life and Work*. Clayton, 1983.

DREW, P. *Veranda: Embracing Place*. Pymble, NSW 1992.

ELLIS, M. H. *Francis Greenway: his Life and Times* 2nd edn, Sydney, 1953.

FEARNLEY, C. *Colonial Style: Pioneer Buildings of New Zealand*. Auckland, 1986.

FREELAND, J. M. *Architect Extraordinary: the Life and Work of John Horbury Hunt, 1838–1904*. Melbourne, 1970.

—. *Architecture in Australia*. Melbourne, 1968.

HERMAN, H. *The Blackets: an Era of Australian Architecture*. Sydney, 1969.

—. *The Early Australian Architects and their Work* Sydney, 1954.

HODGSON, T. *Looking at the Architecture of New Zealand*. Wellington, 1990.

HOWELLS, T. and NICHOLSON, M. (Eds). *Towards the Dawn: Federation Architecture in Australia 1890–1915*. Sydney, 1989.

KINGSTON, D. *Early Colonial Homes of the Sydney Region, 1788–1838*. Kenthurst, 1990.

LANE, T. and SERLE, J. *Australians at Home: a Documentary History of Australian Domestic Interiors from 1788 to 1914*. Melbourne, 1990.

MURPHY, J. and NORRIS, K. *The Most Useful Art. Architecture in Australia, 1788–1985*. Sydney, 1985.

NEW ZEALAND HISTORIC PLACES TRUST. *Historic Buildings of New Zealand, North Island*. Auckland, 1979.

—. *Historic Buildings of New Zealand, South Island*. Auckland, 1983.

ROBERTSON, E. G. *Decorative Cast Iron in Australia*. South Yarra, Vic., 1984.

SALMOND, J. *Old New Zealand Houses, 1800–1940*. Auckland, 1986.

SHAW, P. *New Zealand Architecture from Polynesian Beginnings to 1990*. Auckland, 1991.

STACPOOLE, J. *Colonial Architecture in New Zealand* Wellington, 1976.

STACPOOLE, J. and BEAVEN, P. *Architecture, 1820–1970 in New Zealand*. Wellington, 1972.

PART 7 The Architecture of the Twentieth Century

Chapter 44 Western Europe 1900–1945

Chapter 45 Western Europe since 1945

BAIRATI, E. AND RIVA, D. *Il Liberty in Italia*. Bari, 1985.

BANHAM, R. *The Age of the Masters*. London, 1975.

—. *The Architecture of the Well-Tempered Environment*. 2nd edn, London, 1984.

—. *A Concrete Atlantis: U.S. Industrial Building and European Modern Architecture, 1900–1925*. Cambridge, Mass., and London, 1986.

—. *Theory and Design in the First Machine Age*. London, 1972.

BEHRENDT, W. C. *Modern Building*. London, 1938.

BELLUZZI, A. and CONFORTI, C. *Architettura italiana 1944–1984*. Bari, 1985.

BENEVELO, L. *History of Modern Architecture*. 2 vols. London, 1971.

BORSI, F. *The Monumental Era: European Architecture and Design, 1929–1939*. London, 1987.

BRUNETTI, F. *Momenti di architettura italiana contemporanea*. Florence, 1990.

BUCH, J. *A Century of Architecture in The Netherlands 1880–1990*. Rotterdam, 1994.

CASTEX, J., DEPAULE, J.-C. and PANERAI, P. *Formes urbaines: de l'Îlot à la Barre*. Paris, 1977.

CHASLIN, F. *Les Paris de François Mitterrand: histoires des grands projets architecturaux*. Paris, 1985.

COLLINS, P. *Concrete: The Vision of a New Architecture*. London, 1959.

CONRADS, U. *Modern Architecture in Germany*. London, 1962.

—. *Programmes and Manifestoes on 20th Century Architecture*. London, 1970.

CREESE, W. L. *The Search for Environment: the Garden City*. New Haven and London, 1966. Expanded edn, Baltimore, 1992.

CURTIS, W. J. R. *Modern Architecture since 1900*. 2nd edn, London, 1987.

DAL CO, F. *Figures of Architecture and Thought: German Architecture Culture, 1880–1920*. New York, 1990.

DANNATT, T. *Modern Architecture in Britain: Selected Examples of Recent Building*. London, 1959.

DELEVOY, R., CULOT, M. and LOO, A. VAN. *Le Cambre 1928–1978*. Brussels, 1979.

DOORDAN, D. *Building Modern Italy: Italian Architecture, 1914–1936*. New York, 1988.

DUNSTER, D. *Key Buildings of the Twentieth Century. Vol. 1: Houses 1900–1945*. London, 1985.

EMANUEL, M. (Ed.). *Contemporary Architects*. 3rd edn, New York and London, 1994.

ETLIN, R. A. *Modernism in Italian Architecture, 1890–1940*. Cambridge, Mass., and London, 1991.

FANELLI, G. *Architettura, edilizia urbanistica Olanda 1917–1940*. Florence, 1978.

FELDMEYER, G. *The New German Architecture*. New York, 1993.

FRANCISCONO, M. *Walter Gropius and the Creation of the Bauhaus in Weimar*. Chicago, 1971.

GLANCEY, J. *New British Architecture*. London, 1989.

GRAY, A. S. *Edwardian Architecture. A Biographical Dictionary*. London, 1985.

GROPIUS, W. *The New Architecture and the Bauhaus*. London, 1935.

GUBLER, J. *Nationalisme et Internationalisme dans l'Architecture Moderne de la Suisse*. Lausanne, 1975.

HITCHCOCK, H.-R. *Architecture: Nineteenth and Twentieth Centuries*. 4th edn, Harmondsworth, 1977.

HUSSEY, C. *The Life of Sir Edwin Lutyens. London, 1953.*

JAFFE, H. L. C. *De Stijl*. London, 1970.

JOEDICKE, J. *Architecture since 1945*. London, 1969.

BLUNDELL JONES, P. *Hans Scharoun*. London, 1995.

JULIEN, R. *Histoire de l'architecture moderne en France*. Paris, 1984.

KNOBEL, L. *The Faber Guide to Twentieth Century Architecture: Britain and Northern Europe*. London, 1985.

KOPP, A., BOUCHER, F. and PAULY, D. *L'Architecture de la reconstruction en France, 1945–1953*. Paris, 1982.

LAMPUGNANI, V. M. (Ed.). *Encyclopaedia of 20th-Century Architecture*. London, 1986.

LANE, B. M. *Architecture and Politics in Germany, 1918–1945*. Cambridge, Mass. and London, 1968.

LASDUN, D. *Architecture in the Age of Scepticism*. London, 1985.

LESNIKOWSKI, W. *The New French Architecture*. New York, 1990.

LUCAN, J. *France: architecture 1965–1988*. Paris, 1989.

MIERAS, J. P. and YERBURY, F. *Dutch Architecture of the Twentieth Century*. London, 1926.

MOFFETT, N. *The Best of British Architecture 1980 to 2000*. London, 1993.

MONNIER, G. *Histoire critique de l'architecture en France 1918–1950*. Paris, 1990.

NAYLOR, G. *The Bauhaus*. London, 1968.

Nordic Classicism. Exhibition catalogue, Museum of Finnish Architecture, 1982.

NORBERG-SCHULZ, C. *Modern Norwegian Architecture*. Oslo, 1986.

OKKONEN, I. *Suomalainen Arkkitehtuuri 1900-luvulla – Finnish Architecture in the 20th century*. Helsinki, 1985.

OVERY, P. *De Stijl*. London, 1991.

PEHNT, W. *Expressionist Architecture*. London, 1973.

PEVSNER, N. *Pioneers of Modern Design*. Harmondsworth, 1972.

POOLE, S. *The New Finnish Architecture*. New York, 1992.

RICHARDS, J. M. and PEVSNER, N. (Eds). *The Anti-Rationalists*. London, 1973.

SARTORIS, A. *Éncyclopédie de l'architecture nouvelle*. 3 vols. Milan, 1954–7.

SCHREIBER, M. *Deutsche Architektur nach 1945: vierzig Jahre Moderne in der Bundesrepublik*. Stuttgart, 1986.

SHARP, D. *Modern Architecture and Expressionism*. London, 1966.

—. *Sources of Modern Architecture: a Critical Bibliography*. 2nd edn, London, 1981.

—. *Twentieth Century Architecture: a Visual History*. Rev. ed. London, 1991.

SMITH, G.E. KIDDER. *The New Architecture of Europe*. Harmondsworth, 1966.

STIMPSON, M. F. *A Field Guide to Landmarks of Modern Architecture in Europe*. Englewood Cliffs, NJ, and London, 1985.

TAFURI, M. *History of Italian Architecture, 1944–1985*. Cambridge, Mass., and London, 1989.

TAFURI, M. and DAL CO, F. *Modern Architecture*. London, 1980.

TAUT, B. *Modern Architecture*. London, 1929.

TROY, N. J. *The De Stijl Environment*. Cambridge, Mass., and London, 1983.

TZONIS, A. and LEFAIVRE, L. *Architecture in Europe since 1968: Memory and Invention*. London, 1992.

VOGT, A. M. *Architektur 1940–1980*. Frankfurt, 1980.

WEBB, M. *Architecture in Britain Today*. London, 1969.

WHITTICK, A. *European Architecture in the Twentieth Century*. London, 1974.

WIT, W. DE (Ed.). *The Amsterdam School: Dutch Expressionist Architecture 1915–1930*. New York and London, 1983.

YERBURY, F. R. *Modern European Buidings*. London, 1928.

ZABALBEASCOA, A. (Ed.). *The New Spanish Architecture*. New York, 1992.

ZUKOWSKY, J. (ED.). *The Many Faces of Modern Architecture: Building in Germany between the World Wars*. Munich and London, 1994.

Chapter 46 Eastern Europe

AMAN, A. *Architecture and Ideology in Eastern Europe during the Stalin Era: an Aspect of Cold War History*. New York, 1992.

BOERSMA, T. (Ed.). *Imre Makovecz, Hongaars Architect*. Rotterdam, 1989.

BURKHARDT, F., EVENO, C. and PODRECCA, B. *Jože Plečnik*. Cambridge, Mass., 1989.

CZERNER, O. and LISTOVSKI, H. *The Polish Avant-Garde. Architecture and Town Planning, 1918–1939*. Warsaw, 1981.

DOSTAL, O., PECHAR, J. and PROCHÁZKA, V. *Modern Architecture in Czechoslovakia*. Prague, 1967.

DVORSZKY, H. (Ed.). *Hungarian Organic Architecture*. Venice, 1991.

GERLE, J., KOVACS, A. and MAKOVECZ, I. *Hungarian Turn of the Century Architecture*. Budapest, 1990.

GIURESCU, D. C. *The Razing of Romania's Past*. London, 1990.

GYÖRGYI, D. *New Hungarian Architecture*. Budapest, 1935.

KASER, M. and ZIELINSKI, J. G. *Planning in Eastern Europe*. London, 1970.

KUBOVA, A. *L'Avant-garde architecturale en Tchecoslovaquie, 1918–1939*. Liège, 1992.

KULTERMANN, U. *Zeitgenössische Architektur in Osteuropa*. Cologne, 1985.

KUNNAPU, L. *Estonian Architecture: the Building of a Nation*. Helsinki, 1992.

MAJOR, M. *Geschichte der Architektur*. Vol. 3. East Berlin, 1984. (Hungary)

MARGOLIUS, I. *Cubism in Architecture and Applied Arts*. Newton Abbot, 1979.

—. *Prague: a Guide to 20th Century Architecture*. London, 1994.

MEZEI, O. *Molnár Farkas*. Budapest, 1987.

MIHÁLY, K. *Bohuslav Fuchs*. Berlin, 1986.

MLADENNOVIC, I. *Eleven Outstanding Yugoslav Architects*. Belgrade, 1986.

MORAVANSZKY, A. *Die Architektur der Jahrhundertwende in Ungarn und ihre Beziehungen zu der Wiener Architektur der Zeit*. Vienna, 1983.

—. *Die Erneuerung der Baukunst: Wege zur Moderne in Mitteleuropa 1900–1940*. Salzburg, 1988.

MUTHESIUS, S. *Art, Architecture and Design in Poland*. Königstein im Taunus, 1994.

OLSZEWSKI, A. K. *Polish Art and Architecture*. Warsaw, 1989.

SLAPETA, V. *Bat'a: Architektura a Urbanismus 1910–50*. Zlin, 1991.

—. *Czech Functionalism, 1918–38*. London, 1987.

SVACHA, R. (Ed.). *Czech Avant-garde Art, Architecture and Design of the 1920s and 30s*. Oxford, 1990.

SZAFER, T. P. *New Polish Architecture*. Warsaw, 1981.

SZAFER, T. P. *Contemporary Polish Architecture*. Warsaw, 1988.

SZENDRÖI, J. *Ungarische Architektur, 1945–1970*. Budapest, 1978.

TEIGE, K. and KROHA, J. *Avantgardni architektura* (reprint). Prague, 1969.

TIBOR, B. and MIHALY, K. *Odön Lechner*. Budapest, 1981.

Chapter 47 Russia and the Soviet Union

BELOV, M., COOKE, C., HATTON, B. *et al*. *Nostalgia of Culture: Contemporary Soviet Visionary Architecture*. Architectural Association Text Six. London, 1988.

BOWN, MC. C. and TAYLOR, B. *Art of the Soviets: Painting, Sculpture and Architecture in a One-Party State, 1917–1992*. Manchester, 1993.

BRUMFIELD, W. C. *The Origins of Modernism in Russian Architecture*. Berkeley, Calif., 1991.

COHEN, J-L. *Le Corbusier and the Mystique of the USSR: Theories and Projects for Moscow, 1928–1936*. Princeton, 1992.

COOKE, C. 'Fedor Osipovich Shekhtel: an Architect and his Clients in Turn of the Century Moscow.' *Architectural Association Files*, No. 5. London, 1984.

—. *Russian Avant-Garde*: *Theories of Art, Architecture and the City*. London, 1995.

—. 'Socialist Realist Architecture: Theory and Practice', in: Cullerne, M. and Taylor, B. (Eds), *Art of the Soviets*. Manchester, 1993.

COOKE, C. and KUDRIAVTSEV, A. (Eds). *Uses of Tradition in Russian and Soviet Architecture*. Architectural Design Profile, no. 68, London, 1987.

FRENCH, R. A. *Plans, Pragmatism and People: the Legacy of Soviet Planning for Today's Cities*. London, 1995.

HUDSON, H. D. *Blueprints and Blood: the Stalinization of Soviet Architecture, 1917–1937*. Princeton and London, 1994.

IKONNIKOV, A. *Russian Architecture of the Soviet Period*. London and Moscow, 1988.

—. *Soviet Architecture of Today*. Leningrad, 1975.

KHAN-MAGOMEDOV, S. O. *Pioneers of Soviet Architecture: the Search for New Solutions in the 1920s and 1930s*. London and New York, 1987.

KOPP, A. *L'Architecture de la Période Stalinienne*. Grenoble, 1978.

—. *Constructivist Architecture in the USSR*. London, 1985.

—. *Town and Revolution*. London, 1970.

LODDER, C. *Russian Constructivism*. New Haven and London, 1983.

MILNER, J. *Vladimir Tatlin and the Russian Avant-Garde*. New Haven and London, 1983.

RYABUSHIN, A. V. and SMOLINA, N. WITH QUILICI, V. *Landmarks of Soviet Architecture, 1917–1991*. New York, 1992.

SENKEVITCH, A. *Soviet Architecture, 1917–1962.: a Bibliographical Guide to Source Material*. Charlottesville, 1974.

SHVIDOVSKY, O. A. *Building in the USSR, 1917–1932*. London, 1971.

STARR, S. F. *Melnikov: Solo Architect in a Mass Society*. Princeton, 1978.

TARKHANOV, A. and KAVTARADZE, S. *Stalinist Architecture*. London, 1992.

Chapter 48 Middle East

ABEL, C. 'Work of El-Wakil', *Architectural Review*, vol. 180, no. 1077, November 1986.

AL-BAYATI, B. *Basil Al-Bayati, Architect*. London, 1988.

AL-KHAIL, I. 'New Architectural Trends in Saudi Arabia', *Albenaa*, vol. 10, October/November 1990.

—. 'The Architectural Renaissance in Saudi Arabia', *Alam Albenaa*, no. 97, 1989.

—. 'Architecture in the Gulf: the United Arab Emirates', *Albenaa*, no. 59, April/May 1991.

ARDALAN, N. and BAKHTIAR, L. *The Sense of Unity*. Chicago, 1973.

BOZDOGAN, S., OZKAN, S. and YENAL, E. *Sedad Eldem: An Architect in Turkey*. Singapore, 1987.

CHARIRJI, R. *Concepts and Influences: Towards a Regionalised International Architecture*. London, 1986.

CINICI, A. and B. *architectural works*. ankara, 1975.

'CONTEMPORARY ARAB ARCHITECTURE IN IRAQ', no. 68, april 1986.

DIBA, D.'Iran and Contemporary Architecture', *Mimar*, no. 38, March 1991.

DIBA, K. *Buildings and Projects*. Stuttgart, 1981.

EL-FATTAH, T. M. A. 'Architecture in Egypt', *Albenaa*, no. 57, December/January 1990/1.

FATHY, H. *Architecture for the Poor*. Chicago, 1972.

GERÇEK, C. (Ed.). *Cengiz Bektas: Mimarlik Calismalari*. Ankara, 1979.

GERÇEK, C. (Ed.). *Sevki Vanli: Architectural Works*. Ankara, 1977.

HOLOD, R. and EVIN, A. *Modern Turkish Architecture*. Philadelphia, 1984.

ILBERT, I. and VOLAIT, M. 'Neo-Arabic Renaissance in Egypt, 1870–1930', *Mimar*, no. 13, July/September 1984.

KULTERMANN, U. 'Contemporary Arab Architecture: the Architects of Egypt', *Mimar*, no. 4, April/June 1982.

—. 'Contemporary Arab Architecture: the Architects of Saudi Arabia', *Mimar*, no. 16, April/June 1985.

LEVIN, M. *White City: International Style Architecture in Israel*. Tel Aviv, 1984.

MAKIYA, K. *Post-Islamic Classicism: a Visual Essay on the Architecture of Mohammad Makiya*. London, 1991.

RAN, A. 'The Architecture of Israel', *Architecture of Israel*, no. 1, January 1988.

SHUAIBI, A. (Ed.). *Beeah: Architectural Experiment*. Riyadh, 1989.

TANYELI, U. *et al.* 'Contemporary Art and Architecture of Turkey', *SD*, no. 346, July 1993.

TEKELI, D. and SISA, S. (Eds). *Dogan Tekeli and Sami Sisa: Architectural Works, 1954–1974*. Istanbul, 1973.

STEELE, J. 'Hassan Fathy', *Architectural Monographs*, no. 13, 1988.

Chapter 49 Africa

Books

ALLIN, C. H. *Norman Eaton: Architect*. Cape Town, 1975.

BORALEVI, A. 'Le città dell'impero': urbanista fascista in Etiopia, 1936–41', *Urbanista fascista*. Milan, 1980.

CANTACUZINO, S. (Ed.). *Architecture in Continuity.* New York, 1985.

CHIPKIM, C. M. *Johannesburg Style: Architecture and Society 1880s-1960s.* Cape Town, 1993.

DETHIER, J. *Down to Earth.* London, 1983.

FRY, E. M. and DREW, J. *Tropical Architecture in the Dry and Humid Zones.* New York, 1964.

GREIG, D. *A Guide to Architecture in South Africa.* Cape Town, 1971.

—. *Herbert Baker in South Africa.* Cape Town, 1970.

HARROP-ALLIN, C. *Norman Eaton: Architect.* Cape Town, 1975.

HERBERT, G. *Martiensson and the International Style.* Cape Town, 1975.

HITCHINS, S. (Ed.). *Fry, Drew, Knight, Creamer.* London, 1978.

HOLOD, R. and RASTORFER, S. (eds). *Architecture and Community.* New York, 1983.

KEATH, M. *Herbert Baker: Architecture and Idealism, 1892–1913.* Cape Town, 1992.

KULTERMANN, U. *New Architecture in Africa.* London, 1963.

—. *New Directions in African Architecture.* London, 1969.

LYAUTEY, P. *Lyautey l'africain.* Paris, 1953.

REITANI, G. 'Politica territoriale e urbanistica in Tripolitania, 1920–40', *Urbanista fascista.* Milan, 1980.

RICHARDS, J. M. (Ed.). *New Buildings in the Commonwealth.* London, 1961.

RICHARDS, J. M., SERAGELDIN, I. and RASTORFER, D. *Hassan Fathy.* London, 1985.

VAN DER WAAL, G.-M. *From Mining Camp to Metropolis: the Buildings of Johannesburg 1886–1940.* Pretoria, 1987.

Reports, Journals and Articles

ABEL, C. 'Work of El-Wakil,' *Architectural Review,* vol. 180, no. 1077, November 1986.

Architectural Association Journal, Special Issue, 'Connell, Ward and Lucas 1927–39', November 1956.

Architectural Review, Special Issue: South Africa, vol. 197, no. 1177, March 1995.

L'architecture d'aujord'hui. Special issues: Morocco. 1949, 1952.

BORAKEVI, A. 'Le 'Citta dell'Impero': urbanista fascista in Etiopia, 1936–41', *Storia Urbana,* no. 8, 1979.

FRY, E. M. 'African Experiment', *Architectural Review,* vol. 113, no. 677, May 1953.

HERBERT, G. 'Le Corbusier and the South African Movement', *Architectural Association Quarterley,* January/March 1972.

HUET, B. 'The Modernity in a Tradition: the Arab-Muslim Culture of North Africa', *Mimar,* no. 10, October/December 1993, pp. 49–56.

ILBERT, I. and VOLAIT, M. 'Rethinking Colonial Architecture: Neo-Arabic Renaissance in Egypt 1870–1930', *Mimar,* no. 13, July/September 1984 pp. 26–34.

JATTA, A. *et al.* 'Africa: Planning, Architecture Images', *Controspazio,* vol. 15, no. 1, January. March, 1984, pp. 2–91.

KULTERMANN, U. 'Contemporary Arab Architecture the Architects of Algeria, Tunisia and Libya' *Mimar,* no. 9, 1983, pp. 59–65.

—. 'Contemporary Arab Architecture: the Architects of Egypt', *Mimar,* no. 4, (April/June 1982).

LOCK, M. *Kaduna: A Survey and Plan of the Capital Territory.* London, 1967.

—. *Reading the Contemporary African City*: A Seminar in Dakar, 1982.

—. *Mimar.* Special issue: Morocco. no. 22, October. December 1986.

Reading the Contemporary African City. Architectural Transformations in the Islamic World Seminar Series. 7, Singapore. 1983.

PRINSLOO, I. *et al.* 'Towards Appropriate Architecture for Southern Africa', *Architecture SA,* no. 22, November/December 1982, pp. 15–68.

TAYLOR, B. B. 'Demythologising Colonial Architecture', *Mimar,* no. 13, 1984, pp. 16–26.

Chapter 50 North America 1900–1950

Chapter 51 North America since 1950

AMERICAN INSTITUTE OF ARCHITECTS. *American Architecture of the 1980s.* Washington, DC, 1990.

BALFOUR, A. *Rockefeller Center.* New York, 1978.

BANHAM, R. *The Architecture of the Well-Tempered Environment.* 2nd edn, Chicago and London, 1985.

—. *A Concrete Atlantis: U.S. Industrial Building and European Modern Architecture, 1900–1925.* Cambridge, Mass., and London, 1986.

—. *Megastructure; Urban Futures of the Recent Past.* New York, 1976.

BENEVELO, L. *History of Modern Architecture.* 2 vols. Cambridge, Mass., and London, 1971.

BREEZE, C. *New York Deco.* New York, 1993.

BROOKS, H. A. *The Prairie School; Frank Lloyd Wright and his Midwest Contemporaries.* Toronto, 1972.

BUSH, D. *The Streamline Decade.* New York, 1975.

CAWKER, R. and BERNSTEIN, W. *Contemporary Canadian Architecture: the Mainstream and Beyond.* Revised and expanded edn, Ontario, 1988.

CHENEY, S. *The New World Architecture.* New York, 1930.

CLARK, R. J. *et al. Design in America: the Cranbrook Vision 1925–1950.* New York, 1983.

COLLINS, P. *Concrete: the Vision of a New Architecture.* New York, 1959.

CONDIT, C. W. *American Building Art; the Twentieth Century.* New York, 1961.

—. *The Chicago School of Architecture.* Chicago, 1964.

—. *Chicago, 1910–1929*. Chicago and London, 1973.

—. *Chicago, 1930–1970*. Chicago, 1974.

—. *The Port of New York*. 2 vols. Chicago and London, 1980, 1981.

CURTIS, W. J. R. *Modern Architecture Since 1900*. 2nd edn, London, 1987.

DE LONG, D. *The Architecture of Bruce Goff; Buildings and Projects 1916–1974*. 2 vols. New York, 1977.

EDGELL, G. H. *The American Architecture of Today*. New York, 1928.

FRAMPTON, K. *Modern Architecture: a Critical History*. 2nd edn, New York and London, 3rd edn, 1992.

GEBHARD, D. *Schindler*. New York, 1971.

—. and NEVINS, D. *200 Years of American Architectural Drawing*. New York, 1977.

GEBHARD, D. and VON BRETON, H. *L. A. in the Thirties*. Santa Barbara and Salt Lake City, 1975.

GEIST, J. F. *Arcades*. Cambridge, Mass., 1983.

GIEDION, S. *Space, Time and Architecture*. 5th edn, Cambridge, Mass., 1979.

GOLDBERGER, P. *The Skyscraper*. New York, 1981.

GOWANS, A. *Building Canada*. Toronto, 1966.

—. *Images of American Living*. Philadelphia, 1964.

HAMLIN, T. F. *Forms and Functions of Twentieth-Century Architecture*. 4 vols. New York, 1952.

HANDLIN, D. P. *American Architecture*. New York and London, 1985.

—. *The American Home; Architecture and Society 1815–1915*. Boston, 1979.

HANKS, D. A. *The Decorative Designs of Frank Lloyd Wright*. New York, 1979.

HAYS, K. M. and BURNS, C. *Thinking the Present: Recent American Architecture*. Princeton and London, 1990.

HEGEMANN, W. and PEETS, E. *The American Vitruvius: American Architects' Handbook of Civic Art*. New York, 1921.

HEYER, P. *American Architecture: Ideas and Ideologies in the Late Twentieth Century*. New York and London, 1993.

HILDEBRAND, G. *Designing for Industry: the Architecture of Albert Khan*. Cambridge, Mass., 1974.

HINES, T. S. *Burnham of Chicago, Architect and Planner*. New York, 1974.

—. *Richard Neutra and the Search for Modern Architecture*. New York, 1982.

HITCHCOCK, H.-R. *Architecture: Nineteenth and Twentieth Centuries*. 4th edn, Harmondsworth, 1977.

—. *In the Nature of Materials; the Buildings of Frank Lloyd Wright*. New York, 1942.

HITCHCOCK, H.-R. and JOHNSON, P. *The International Style*. New York, 1932.

HITCHCOCK, H.-R. and SEALE, W. *Temples of Democracy: the State Capitols of the U.S.A.* New York, 1976.

JACOBUS, J. *Twentieth-Century Architecture, 1940–65*. London, 1966.

JANDL, H. W. (Ed.). *The Technology of Historic American Buildings*. Washington, DC, 1983.

JENCKS, C. *Modern Movements in Architecture*. 2nd edn, Harmondsworth, 1985.

JORDY, W. H. *American Buildings and their Architects*. Vols 3 and 4. New York, 1970–3.

KAUFMANN, E. (Ed.). *The Rise of an American Architecture*. New York, 1969.

KIMBALL, F. *American Architecture*. New York, 1928.

KING, A. (Ed.). *Buildings and Society*. London, 1980.

KLOTZ, H. and SABAU, L. (Eds). *New York Architecture, 1970–1990*. Munich, 1989.

KRINSKY, C. H. *Rockefeller Center*. New York, 1978.

LANCASTER, C. *The American Bungalow*. New York, 1985.

LEBLANC, S. *20th Century American Architecture: 200 Key Buildings*. New York, 1993.

LIEBS, C. *Main Street to Miracle Mile: American Roadside Architecture*. Boston, 1985.

LONGSTRETH, R. *On the Edge of the World; Four Architects in San Francisco at the Turn of the Century*. New York and Cambridge, Mass., 1983.

MACRAE-GIBSON, G. *The Secret Life of Buildings: an American Mythology for Modern Architecture*. Cambridge, Mass., and London, 1985.

MCCALLUM, I. *Architecture USA*. New York, 1959.

MCCOY, E. *Five California Architects*. New York, 1960.

—. *New Directions in American Architecture*. Revised edn, New York, 1977.

MEEKS, C. L. V. *The Railroad Station*. New Haven, 1956.

MORGAN, K. *Charles Platt; the Architect as Artist*. New York and Cambridge, Mass., 1985.

NAYLOR, D. *American Picture Palaces*. New York, 1981.

OLIVER, R. *Bertram Grosvenor Goodhue*. New York and Cambridge, Mass., 1983.

ROBINSON, C. and BLETTER, R. H. *Skyscraper Style: Art Deco New York*. New York, 1975.

ROTH, L. M. *A Concise History of American Architecture*. New York, 1979.

—. *McKim, Mead and White, Architects*. New York, 1983.

ROTH, L. M. (Ed.). *America Builds: Source Documents in American Architecture and Planning*. New York and London, 1983.

SCULLY, V. *American Architecture and Urbanism*. New York and London, 1969.

—. *Frank Lloyd Wright*. New York, 1960.

—. *Louis I. Kahn*. New York, 1965.

—. *Modern Architecture*. Revised edn, New York, 1974.

—. *The Shingle Style Today*. New York, 1974.

SEARING, H. (Ed.). *In Search of Modern Architecture*.

New York and Cambridge, Mass., 1982.
—. *New American Art Museums*. Berkeley, 1982.
SEARING, H. and REED, H. H. *Speaking a New Classicism: American Architecture Now*. Northampton, Mass., 1981.
SMITH, H. K. *Frank Lloyd Wright; a Study in Architectural Content*. Englewood Cliffs, NJ, 1966.
SPAETH, D. *Mies van der Rohe*. New York, 1985.
STEIN, C. S. *Toward New Towns for America*. Cambridge, Mass., 1971.
STERN, R. A. M. *George Howe*. New Haven, 1975.
STERN, R. A. M., GILMARTIN, G. and MASSENGALE, J. M. *New York 1900: Metropolitan Architecture and Urbanism, 1890–1915*. New York, 1983.
STERN, R. A. M., GILMARTIN, G. and MELLINS, T. *New York 1930: Architecture and Urbanism Between the Two World Wars*. New York, 1987.
STILGOE, J. *Metropolitan Corridor: Railroads and the American Scene*. New Haven, 1983.
TEMKO, A. *Eero Saarinen*. New York, 1962.
TURNER, P. V. *Campus; an American Planning Tradition*. New York and Cambridge, Mass., 1984.
WHITESON, L. *Modern Canadian Architecture*. Edmonton, 1983.
WILSON, R. G. *et al. The American Renaissance, 1876–1917*. New York, 1979.
WILSON, R. G. and ROBINSON, S. K. (Eds). *Modern Architecture in America: Visions and Revisions*. Ames, Iowa, 1991.
WOODBRIDGE, S. (Ed.). *Bay Area Houses*. New York, 1976.
WRIGHT, G. *Building the Dream; a Social History of Housing in America*. Cambridge, Mass., 1981.
ZUKOWSKY, J. *et al. Chicago and New York: Architectural Interactions*. Chicago, 1984.
ZUKOWSKY, J. (Ed.). *Chicago Architecture, 1872–1922: Birth of a Metropolis*. Chicago and Munich, 1987.
—. *Chicago Architecture and Design, 1923–1993: Reconfiguration of an American Metropolis*. Chicago and Munich, 1993.

Chapter 52 Latin America

AMBASZ, E. *The Architecture of Luis Barragán*. New York, 1976.
ALTEZOR FUENTES, C. *Arquitectura urbana en Costa Rica: exploracion historica, 1900–1950*. Costa Rica, 1986.
AMARAL, A. *Arte y arquitectura del modernismo brasileno (1917–1930)*. Caracas, 1978.
BULLRICH, F. *New Directions in Latin American Architecture*. New York, 1969.
CASTEDO, L. *Historia del arte iberoamericano*. Madrid, 1988.
CETTO, M. L. *Modern Architecture in Mexico*. Stuttgart and London, 1961.
FABER, C. *Candela: the Shell Builder*. New York and London, 1963.
HITCHCOCK, H.-R. *Latin American Architecture since 1945*. New York, 1955.
IRIGOYEN, A. and GUTIERREZ, R. *Nueva arquitectura Argentina: pluralidad y coincidencia*. Bogota, 1990.
LOPEZ RANGEL, R. *La Modernidad aquitectonica mexicana: antecedentes y vanguardias, 1900–1940*. Azcapotzalco, 1989.
MINDLIN, H. *Modern Architecture in Brazil*. Rio de Janeiro and Amsterdam, 1956.
MOYA TASQUER, R. and PERALTA, E. *Arquitectura contemporanea: 20 arquitectos del Ecuador*. Quito, 1990.
MYERS, I. E. *Mexico's Modern Architecture*. New York, 1952.
NOELLE, L. M. *Arquitectos contemporaneos de Mexico*. Mexico, DF, 1989.
RIGAU, J. *Puerto Rico 1900: Turn-of-the-century Architecture in the Hispanic Caribbean*. New York, 1992.
SALDARRIAGA ROA, A. *Arquitectura y cultura en Colombia*. Bogota, 1986.
SPADE, R. *Oscar Niemeyer*. London and New York, 1971.
TOCA FERNANDEZ, A. (Ed.). *Nueva arquitectura en America Latina: presente y futuro*. Naucalpan, 1990.
TOCA FERNANDEZ, A. and FIGUEROA, A. *Mexico: nueva arquitectura*. Naucalpan, 1991.
UNDERWOOD, D. K. *Oscar Niemeyer and the Architecture of Brazil*. New York, 1994.

Chapter 53 China

ACADEMY OF BUILDING RESEARCH. *The Memorial Hall of Chairman Mao*. Beijing, 1978 (Chinese edition).
—. *New China Builds*. Beijing, 1976.
—. *Ten Years of Chinese Architecture*. Nanjing, 1959 (Chinese edition).
ARCHITECTURAL SOCIETY OF CHINA. *Architectural Journal*. Beijing, 1953–1994.
CHEN BAO-SHENG. *Chinese Architecture, 1949–1989*. Shanghai, 1992 (Chinese edition with English translation).
CHEN CONG-ZHOU and ZHANG MING. *Shanghai Jindai Jianzhu Shigao* (A Historical Draft of Shanghai Modern Architecture). Shanghai, 1988 (Chinese edition).
EDITORIAL BOARD OF CHINA BUILDING ALMANAC. *China Building Almanac 1984–1985*. Beijing, 1985. (Chinese edition)
—. *China Building Almanac 1986–1987*. Beijing, 1988 (Chinese edition).
—. *China Building Almanac 1988–1989*. Beijing, 1990 (Chinese edition).
—. *China Building Almanac 1990–1991*. Beijing, 1992 (Chinese edition).
THE EDITORIAL BOARD OF 'CHINA BUILDING INDUSTRY' ALMANAC. *China Building Industry Almanac*

1992–1993. Beijing, 1994 (Chinese edition).

EDITORIAL BOARD OF CHINESE ARCHITECTURAL HISTORY. *A Brief History of Chinese Architecture*, Book Two. Beijing, 1962 (Chinese edition).

FU ZHAO-QING. *New Architecture of Chinese Traditional Style*. Taibei, 1991 (Chinese edition).

GONG DE-SHUN, ZOU DE-NONG and DOU YI-DE. *An Outline of Modern Chinese Architectural History (1949–1985)*. Tianjin, 1989 (Chinese edition).

INSTITUTE OF CHINESE MODERN ARCHITECTURE and JAPANESE INSTITUTE OF ASIAN MODERN ARCHITECTURE. *The Architectural Heritage of Modern China, Tianjin*. Tokyo, 1989 (Chinese and Japanese edition with English summary).

MURAMATSU, SHIN. *Shanghai, 1842–1949*. Tokyo, 1991 (Japanese edition).

MURPHY, H. K. *'Chinese' Architecture in China*. Berkeley and Los Angeles, 1946.

SU, GIN DJIH. *Chinese Architecture, Past and Contemporary*. Hong Kong, 1964.

WANG SHAO-ZHOU. *Shanghai Modern Architecture*. Shanghai, 1989 (Chinese edition).

—. *A Pictorial Handbook of Chinese Modern Architecture*. Shanghai, 1989 (Chinese edition).

WANG SHAO-SHOU and CHEN ZHI-MIN. *Li-long, Lane Houses in Shanghai*. Shanghai, 1987 (Chinese edition).

WANG TAN and FUJIMORI, TERUNOBU. *The Architectural Heritage of Modern China, Beijing*. Beijing, 1993. (Chinese edition).

—. *The Architectural Heritage of Modern China, Chongqing*. Beijing, 1993 (Chinese edition).

—. *The Architectural Heritage of Modern China, Guangzhou*. Beijing, 1992 (Chinese edition).

—. *The Architectural Heritage of Modern China, Harbin*. Beijing, 1992 (Chinese edition).

—. *The Architectural Heritage of Modern China, Kunming*. Beijing, 1993 (Chinese edition).

—. *The Architectural Heritage of Modern China, Lushan*. Beijing, 1993 (Chinese edition).

—. *The Architectural Heritage of Modern China, Nanjing*. Beijing, 1992 (Chinese edition).

—. *The Architectural Heritage of Modern China, Qingdao*. Beijing, 1992 (Chinese edition).

—. *The Architectural Heritage of Modern China, Wuhan*. Beijing, 1992 (Chinese edition).

—. *The Architectural Heritage of Modern China, Xiamen*. Beijing, 1993 (Chinese edition).

—. *The Architectural Heritage of Modern China, Yantai*. Beijing, 1992 (Chinese edition).

WRIGHT, A. *Twentieth Century Impressions of Hong Kong, Shanghai, and other Treaty Ports of China: Their History, People, Commerce, Industries and Resources*. London, 1908.

XIAO MO. *Chinese Architecture 1980–1989*. Beijing, 1991 (Chinese edition).

YANG BING-DE. *Chinese Modern Cities and Their Architecture 1840–1949*. Beijing, 1993 (Chinese edition).

YAO QIAN and GU BING. *Sun Yet-sen Mausoleum*. Beijing, 1981 (Chinese edition with English translation).

Chapter 54 Japan and Korea

BARTHES, R. *Empire of Signs*. Translator Richard Howard. New York, 1989.

BOGNAR, B. *Contemporary Japanese Architecture: its Development and Challenge*. New York, 1985.

—. *The New Japanese Architecture*. New York, 1990.

BOYD, R. *New Directions in Japanese Architecture*. London and New York, 1968.

BURUMA, I. *A Japanese Mirror. Heroes and Villains in Japanese Culture*. London, 1985.

FAWCETT, C. *The New Japanese House: Ritual and Anti-Ritual Patterns of Dwelling*. London and New York, 1980.

FRAMPTON, K. and KUDO, K. (Eds). *Nikken Sekkei: Building Modern Japan 1900–1990*. New York, 1990.

FRIEDMAN, M. (Ed.). *Tokyo: Form and Spirit*. Minneapolis, 1986.

A Guide to Japanese Architecture. Edited by *The Japan Architect*. Tokyo, 1984.

GREENBIE, B. B. *Space and Spirit In Modern Japan*. New Haven and London, 1988.

—. *The Japan Architect*. (1965–).

KESTENBAUM, J. (Ed.). *Emerging Japanese Architects of the 1990s*. New York and Oxford, 1991.

KUROKAWA, K. *New Wave Japanese Architecture*. London, 1993.

—. *Rediscovering Japanese Space*. New York, 1988.

RICHARDS, J. M. *An Architectural Journey in Japan*. London, 1963.

ROSS, M. F. *Beyond Metabolism: the New Japanese Architecture*. New York, 1978.

STEWART, D. B. *The Making of a Modern Japanese Architecture. 1868 to the Present*. New York, 1868.

SUZUKI, H., BANHAM, R. and KOBAYASHI, K. *Contemporary Architecture in Japan, 1958–1984*. London and New York, 1985.

TATE GALLERY LIVERPOOL. *A Cabinet of Signs: Contemporary Art from Post Modern Japan*. 1989.

TEMPEL, E. *New Japanese Architecture*. London, 1969.

Chapter 55 South-east Asia

ABEL, C. 'Regional Transformations', *The Architectural Review*, vol. CLXXX, no. 1077, November 1986.

—. 'Localisation Versus Globalisation' and other articles. Special issue on South-east Asia, *The Architectural Review*, vol. CXCVI, no. 1171, September 1994.

ARCASIA. *Contemporary Architecture in Asia*. Seoul, 1994

BEAMISH, J. and FERGUSON, J. *A History of Singapore*

Architecture. Singapore, 1985.

BROMAN, B. M. *Old Homes of Bangkok*. Bangkok, 1984.

DUMARCAY, J. *The House in South-East Asia*. Singapore, 1987.

GHOSE, R. (Ed.). *Design and Development in South and Southeast Asia*. Hong Kong, 1990.

KHOO, S. N. *Streets of George Town Penang*. Penang, 1993.

KLASSEN, W. *Architecture in the Philippines*. Cebu City, 1986.

KULTERMANN, U. 'Architecture in South-East Asia 1: Thailand', *Mimar* No. 20 April- June 1985.

—. 'Architecture in South-East Asia 2: Indonesia', *Mimar*, no. 21, July- September, 1986.

—. 'Architecture in South-East Asia 3: Singapore', *Mimar*, no. 23, March 1987.

LIM, H. K. *The Evolution of the Urban System in Malaya*. Kuala Lumpur, 1978.

LIM, J. W. *The Malay House*. Penang, 1987.

MORRIS, J. *et al. Architecture of the British Empire*. London, 1986.

NASIR, A. H. *Mosques of Peninsula Malaysia*. Kuala Lumpur, 1984.

OSBORNE, M. *Southeast Asia*. Sydney, 1979.

PEREZ III, R. D. *An Essay on Philippine Architecture*. Manila, 1989.

PERTUBUHAN AKITEK MALAYSIA, *Guide to Kuala Lumpur Notable Buildings*. Kuala Lumpur, 1976.

—. *Post-Merdeka Architecture*. Kuala Lumpur, 1985.

POWELL, R. *The Asian House*. Singapore, 1993.

—. *Innovative Architecture of Singapore*. Singapore, 1989.

TAN, H. B. *Tropical Architecture and Interiors*. Singapore, 1994.

WOLTERS, O. W. *History, Culture and Region in Southeast Asian Perspectives*. Singapore, 1982.

WONG, A.K. and YEH, S.H.K. *Housing a Nation*. Singapore, 1985.

YEANG, K. *The Architecture of Malaysia*. Singapore, 1994.

—. *Bioclimatic Skyscrapers*. Berlin, 1994

Chapter 56 Hong Kong

ABEL, C. 'A Building for the Pacific Century', *The Architectural Review*, vol. CLXXIX, no. 1070, April 1986.

BONAVIA, D. *Hong Kong 1997*. Bromley, 1985.

CHUNG WAH NAN. *Contemporary Architecture in Hong Kong*. Hong Kong, 1989.

JEONG-KEUN LEE (Ed.). *Contemporary Architecture in Asia*. Seoul, 1994.

LAMBOT, I. (Ed.). *Norman Foster: Buildings and Projects, Vol. 3: 1978–1985*. Hong Kong, 1989.

LAMPUGNANI, V. M. (Ed.). *Hong Kong Architecture*. Munich and New York, 1993.

MARSHALL, J. G. *et al.* (Eds). *Rising High in Harmony*. Hong Kong, 1993.

PURVIS, M. *Tall Storeys*. Hong Kong, 1985.

Chapter 57 Indian Subcontinent

Architectural Review, special issue: indian identity, vol. clxxxii, no. 1086, August 1987.

BAHGA, S., BAHGA, S. and BAHGA, Y. *Modern Architecture In India: Post-independence Perspective*. New Delhi, 1993.

BHATT, V. and SCRIVER, P. *Contemporary Indian Architecture. Vol. 1: After the Masters*. Ahmedabad, 1990.

CURTIS, W. *Modern Architecture in Indian Tradition: Balkrishna V. Doshi*, Ahmedabad, 1987.

DAVIES, P. *Splendours of the Raj: British Architecture in India 1660 to 1947*. London, 1968.

IRVING, R. G. *Indian Summer: Lutyens, Baker and Imperial Delhi. New Haven and London, 1981.*

NILSSON, S. The New Capitals of India, Pakistan and *Bangladesh*. Lund, 1973.

RICHARDS, J. M. *New Buildings in the Commonwealth*. London, 1961.

TAYLOR, B. B. *Geoffrey Bawa*. Singapore, 1986.

Chapter 58 Oceania

BOYD, R. *Australia's Home, its Origins, Builders and Occupiers*. Ringwood, Australia, 1968.

FREELAND, J. M. *Architecture in Australia: a History*. Melbourne, 1968.

HODGSON, T. *Looking at the Architecture of New Zealand*. Wellington, 1990.

IRVING, R. (Ed.). *The History and Design of the Australian House*. Melbourne, 1985.

JAHN, G. *Contemporary Australian Architecture*. Basel and Roseville, 1994.

JOHNSON, D. L. *Australian Architecture 1901–1951: Sources of Modernism*. Sydney, 1980.

MITCHELL, D. and CHAPLIN, G. *The Elegant Shed: New Zealand Architecture since 1945*. Auckland, 1984.

OGG, A. *Architecture in Steel: the Australian Context*. Red Hill, ACT, 1994.

PAROISSIEN, L. and GRIGGS, M. (Eds). *Old Continent, New Building*. Sydney, 1983.

PEGRUM, R. *Details In Australian Architecture*. Canberra, 1984.

—. *Details In Australian Architecture*. Vol. 2. Canberra, 1987.

SHAW, P. *New Zealand Architecture: from Polynesian Beginnings to 1990*. Auckland, 1991.

STACPOOLE, J. and BEAVEN, P. *New Zealand Art: Architecture 1820–1970*. Wellington, 1972.

TAYLOR, J. *Australian Architecture Since 1960*. 2nd edn, Red Hill, ACT, 1990.

GLOSSARY

Abbreviations

(Isl) refers mainly to Islamic buildings. (Bud) refers mainly to Buddhist buildings. (Hind) refers mainly to Hindu buildings. Terms relating specifically to Japanese architecture and construction are explained within the relevant chapters.

Abacus. A slab forming the crowning member of a capital. In Greek Doric, square without chamfer or moulding. In Greek Ionic, thinner with ovolo moulding only. In Roman Ionic and Corinthian, the sides are hollowed on plan and have the angles cut off. In Romanesque, the abacus is deeper but projects less and is moulded with rounds and hollows, or merely chamfered on the lower edge. In Gothic, the circular or octagonal abacus was favoured in England, while the square or octagonal abacus is a French feature.

Ablaq (Isl). Alternating courses of masonry in contrasting colours.

Abutment. Solid masonry which resists the lateral pressure of an arch.

Acanthus. A plant whose leaves, conventionally treated, form the lower portions of the Corinthian capital.

Acropolis. Most ancient Greek cities were built on hills, the citadel on the summit being known as the acropolis, containing the principal temples and treasure-houses.

Acroteria. Blocks resting on the vertex and lower extremities of the pediment to support statuary or ornaments.

Adobe. Sun-dried (i.e. unbaked) brick, often used as the core of a wall behind a facing of stone bricks.

Adyton or **adytum**. The most sacred room of a Greek temple. Usually approached from the naos by a doorway.

Aedicule. A small temple-like arrangement, originally limited to shrines, which became a common motif in the Classical system: columns or pilasters carry a pedimented entablature and enframe a niche or window. The term 'tabernacle' sometimes is used to convey a similar meaning. In Hindu architecture an image or representation of a building (or shrine) used as an architectural element.

Agora. The Greek equivalent of the Roman forum, a place of open-air assembly or market.

Aisles. Lateral divisions parallel with the nave in a basilica or church.

Alabaster. A very white, fine-grained, translucent, gypseous mineral, used to a small extent as a building material in the ancient Middle East, Greece, Rome the Eastern Empire of Byzantium and, nearer to our own day, by certain Victorian architects for its decorative qualities (and biblical associations). In Italy a technique was evolved many centuries ago (and still survives) of treating alabaster to simulate marble while there seems little doubt that in the past marble was often mistakenly described as alabaster.

Alae. Small side extensions, alcoves or recesses opening from the atrium (or peristyle) of a Roman house.

Alpa vimana (Hind). Basic form of shrine in south Indian temple architecture.

Alure. An alley, walk or passage. A gallery behind a parapet.

Amalaka (Hind). 'Myrobolan fruit'; ribbed crowning member in north Indian temples.

Ambo. A raised pulpit from which the Epistle and the Gospel were read in a Christian church.

Ambry or **aumbry**. A cupboard or recess in a church to contain sacred vessels.

Ambulatory. The cloister or covered passage around the east end of a church, behind the altar.

Amorino. Diminutive of Amor, the Roman god of love, identified with the Greek Eros. Amorini were usually represented by Renaissance artists as cherubs.

Amphi-antis. A temple with columns between antae (i.e. a recessed portico) at both ends. None such survives.

Amphi-prostyle. A temple with a portico at both ends.

Ancones. Consoles on either side of a doorway supporting a cornice. Also, projections left on blocks of stone such as drums of columns for use in hoisting and setting in position.

Annulet. A small flat fillet encircling a column. It is repeated several times under the ovolo or echinus of the Doric capital.

Anta. A pilaster terminating the side wall of a Greek temple, with base and capital differing from those of adjacent columns; also seen in Egyptian temples. *See* **Pilaster**.

Antefixae. Ornamental blocks, fixed vertically at regular intervals along the lower edge of a roof, to cover the ends of tiles.

Anthemion. A honeysuckle or palmette ornament of several varieties, in cornices, neckings of Ionic capitals and elsewhere in Greek and Roman architecture.

Antiquarian. The phase in western European Renaissance architecture, *c.* 1750–1830, when renewed inspiration was sought from ancient Greek and Roman and from mediaeval architecture. Its more specific manifestations were the **Greek** and **Gothic Revivals** (q.v.), both continuing further into the nineteenth century.

Apodyterium. A room for undressing in a Roman bath-house.

Apophyge. The cavetto or concave sweep at the top and bottom of the column shaft connecting it with the fillet.

Apse. The circular or multangular termination of a church sanctuary, first applied to a Roman basilica. The apse is a Continental feature, and contrasts with the square termination of English Gothic churches.

Apteral. A temple without columns on the sides.

Arabesque. Surface decoration, light and fanciful in character, much used by Arabic artists, in elaborate continuations of lines. Applied also to the combination of flowing lines interwoven with flowers, fruit and figures as used by Renaissance artists.

Araeostyle. A term used when the space between two columns is more than three diameters.

Arcade. A range of arches supported on piers or columns, attached to or detached from the wall.

Arch. A structure of wedge-shaped blocks over an opening, so disposed as to hold together when supported only from the sides.

Arch-braced roof. *See* **Collar-braced roof**.

Architrave. The beam or lowest division of the entablature, which extends from column to column. The term is also applied to the moulded frame round a door or window.

Archivolt. The mouldings on the face of an arch, and following its contour.

Arcuated. A building, building system or style of architecture, of which the principal constructive feature is the arch (e.g. Roman). *See also* **Trabeated**.

Arris. The sharp edge formed by the meeting of two surfaces.

Art Nouveau. A decorative movement in European architecture, heralded in the 1880s and flourishing 1893–1907, characterised by flowing and sinuous naturalistic ornament and avoidance of historical architectural traits. *See also* **Jugendstil, Stile Liberty**.

Asbestos. A fibrous mineral, which has high resistance to fire but is hazardous to health.

Ashlar. Masonry of smooth squared stones in regular courses, in contradistinction to rubble work.

Astragal. A small semicircular moulding, often ornamented with a bead or reel. Torus is the name applied to large mouldings of similar section.

Astylar. A treatment of a facade without columns.

Atlantes. Carved male figures serving as pillars, also called Telamones.

Atrium. An apartment in a Roman house, forming an entrance hall or court, the roof open to the sky in the centre. Sometimes the rim of the roof aperture (compluvium) was supported by four or more columns. In Early Christian and later architecture, a forecourt.

Attic. A term first applied in the Renaissance period to the upper storey of a building above the main cornice; also applied to rooms in a roof.

Attic base. A base to a Classic column, so named by Vitruvius, and formed of upper and lower torus and scotia joined by fillets; it is the most usual of all column bases.

Aumbry. *See* **Ambry**.

Aureole. A quadrangular, circular, or elliptic halo or frame surrounding the figure of Christ, the Virgin, or certain saints. Also known as the mandorla or vesica piscis (q.v.). When a circular halo envelops only the head, it is called a nimbus.

Azulejos. Tile covering for walls used during the eighteenth century in Latin America.

Bab (Isl). Gateway.

Bailey. Open area or court of a fortified castle.

Baldac(c)hino. A canopy supported by columns, generally placed over an altar or tomb, also known as a 'cibonum'.

Ball-flower. The ornament of Decorated Gothic architecture, possibly from a flower form or a horse bell.

Balloon frame. A method of light timber framing, long established in the United States for domestic buildings, in which the corner posts and studs (intermediate posts) are continuous from cill to roof plate, the joists carried on girts (ties) spiked to, or let into, the studs, and all these elements secured by simple nailing.

Baluster. A pillar or column supporting a handrail or coping, a series forming a balustrade.

Bangaldar roof (Hind). Roof with curved ridge and eaves, used in later Indian temples.

Baptistery. A separate building to contain a font, for the baptismal rite.

Bar tracery. *See* **Tracery.**

Barbican. An outwork of a mediaeval castle, of which the object was to protect a drawbridge or the entrance.

Barge board. A board fixed to the verge of a pitched roof.

Baroque. A term applied to Renaissance architecture beginning in Italy in the early seventeenth century with characteristic non-Roman expression, rich, bold and full of movement.

Barrel vault. A continuous vault of semicircular section, used at most periods and in many countries from Roman times to the present. Also called a tunnel vault, wagonhead vault, or wagon vault.

Bartizan. A small, overhanging turret.

Bas-relief. Carving in low or shallow relief, on a background

Base. The lower portion of any structure or architectural feature.

Basement. The lowest stage of a building; also an underground storey.

Basilica. A hall, with nave and aisles for the administration of justice.

Basse-cour or **base court**. An inferior court or service yard, generally at the back of a house.

Bath stone. Oolite building stone, not confined to the area of Bath, Somerset, used throughout English architectural history.

Batter. A wall with an inclined face.

Battlement. A parapet having a series of indentations or embrasures, between which are raised portions known as merlons

Baulk-tie. A tie-beam joining the wall posts of a timber roof and serving also to prevent walls from spreading. *See* **Tie-bar.**

Bays. Compartments into which the nave or roof of a building is divided. The term is also used for projecting windows.

Bayt or **beyt** (Isl). A house or a building.

Bead. A small cylindrical moulding often carved with an ornament resembling a string of beads. *See* **Astragal**.

Beak-head. A Romanesque enrichment like a bird's head and beak.

Begunets. An ornamental string course of bricks on-edge laid in a triangular pattern.

Belfry. A term generally applied to the upper room in a tower in which the bells are hung, and thus often to the tower itself.

Bell capital. The solid part, core, or drum of a capital, especially of the Corinthian and Composite Orders or of a Corinthianesque character in French and English Gothic. So-called 'bell' capitals, moulded and without foliate ornament, occur frequently in the mediaeval ecclesiastical architecture of both countries.

Belvedere. A roofed but open-sided structure affording an extensive view, usually located at the roof-top of a dwelling but sometimes an independent building on an eminence in a landscape or garden.

Bema. A raised stage reserved for the clergy in Early Christian churches; it forms the germ of the transept when expanded laterally in later architecture.

Bhumija (Hind). One of the later, composite modes of Nagara (north Indian) temples.

Billet. A Norman moulding of short cylinders or square pieces at regular intervals.

Bipedales. Tiles, 2 ft square, used by the Romans for bonding masonry.

Bird's beak. A moulding used in Greek architecture, which in section is thought to resemble the beak of a bird.

Bit-hilâni. Syrian porched house.

Boss. A projecting ornament at the intersection of the ribs of ceilings, whether vaulted or flat. The term is also applied to the carved ends of weather mouldings of doors and windows.

Bouleuterion. A Greek Senate building or council house.

Bowtell. A Romanesque convex moulding (usually three-quarters of a circle in section) applied to an angle – a form of roll moulding. Pointed bowtell is a roll moulding in which two faces meet in a blunt arris.

Brace. In framed structures, a subsidiary member placed near and across the angle of two main members in order to stiffen them, as in carpentry roofs.

Brace-moulding. *See* **Bracket moulding.**

Bracket. A projecting member to support a weight, generally formed with scrolls or volutes; when carrying the upper members of a comice, brackets are generally termed modillions or consoles. *See also* **Ancones**.

Bracket moulding (also called 'brace' or 'double ogee'). A late Gothic moulding consisting of two ogee mouldings with convex facings adjoining, resembling a printer's 'brace' or bracket.

Branch tracery. A form of tracery characteristic of German Gothic, suggesting the branches of a tree.

Brise-soleil. A screen to break the glare of sunshine upon windows. In recent architecture such screens often take the form of **louvres** (q.v.), and are usually made a permanent and effective part of the architecture.

Broach spire. An octagonal spire rising without a parapet above a tower, with pyramidal forms at the angles of the tower, as in Early English churches.

Broch. Vernacular term for a primitive Scottish fort.

Brownstone. A brown sandstone found in New Jersey, Connecticut, Pennsylvania and elsewhere. A popular building material in the nineteenth century in New York and the eastern United States.

Buttress. A mass of masonry built against a wall to resist the pressure of an arch or vault. A flying buttress is an arch starting from a detached pier and abutting against a wall to take the thrust of the vaulting.

Byzantine architecture. The style evolved at Constantinople (Byzantium, now Istanbul) in the fifth century, and still the style of the Eastern or Greek Church.

Cable. A Norman moulding enrichment like a twisted rope.

Caen stone. A building stone from Caen, Normandy, sometimes used in the construction of English mediaeval buildings, despite difficulties of transport.

Caisson. *See* **Coffers.**

Caldarium or **calidarium**. A chamber with hot water baths in a Roman baths building.

Camber. Slight rise or upward curve of an otherwise horizontal structure.

Cames. Slender strips of lead, grooved at the sides for the reception of pieces of glass, in casement, stained glass and other types of window.

Campanile. An Italian name for a bell-tower, generally detached from the main building.

Cancelli. Low screen walls enclosing the choir in Early Christian churches, hence 'chancel' (q.v.).

Canephorae. Sculptured female figures bearing baskets on their heads.

Cantoria. In the Renaissance the term was generally used to denote a singers' gallery, often elaborately carved, in a major church.

Capital. The crowning feature of a column or pilaster.

Caravanserai (Isl). An inn or extensive enclosed courtyard for travellers arriving in a town.

Carrara marble. A snow-white marble from the Carrara district of Tuscany, although the band of rock also extends far to the north of this area. It was the favoured medium of Michelangelo. It was known to the Romans as Luna.

Caryatids. Sculptured female figures used as columns or supports.

Casemate. A vaulted chamber contrived in the thickness of a fortress wall, usually with embrasures for defence. The term is often applied nowadays to other forms of armoured enclosure (e.g. gun-turret). Hence 'casemated', meaning strongly fortified.

Casement. A wide hollow used in late Gothic, so called as it encased bunches of foliage.

Casement window. A window of which the opening lights are hinged at the side and open in the manner of a door.

Casino. A summer- or garden-house of ornamental character.

Cast-iron. Iron shaped by pouring into moulds. Cast-iron was used to a rapidly increasing extent in building works from the late eighteenth century (e.g. the Iron Bridge, Coalbrookdale) until superseded by steel in the mid-nineteenth.

Castellation. Fortifying a house and providing it with battlements.

Caulicoli. The eight stalks supporting the volutes in the Corinthian capital.

Cavetto. A simple concave moulding.

Cella. The chief apartment of a temple, where the image of a god stood.

Cenotaph. A sepulchral monument to a person buried elsewhere.

Chaines. Vertical strips of rusticated masonry rising between the horizontal string-mouldings and cornice of a building, and so dividing the facades into bays or panels. A popular mode of wall ornamentation in French seventeenth-century domestic architecture.

Chaitya hall. A Buddhist barrel-vaulted hall of worship.

Chajja (Hind). Stone canopy consisting of widely overhanging eaves, in Indian architecture.

Chamfer. A diagonal cutting-off of an arris formed by two surfaces meeting at an angle. Hollow chamfer, the same but concave in form, like the cavetto.

Chancel. The space for clergy and choir, separated by a screen from the body of a church, more usually referred to as the **choir.**

Chantry. A small chapel, usually attached to a church, endowed with lands or by other means, for the maintenance of priests to sing or say mass for whomever the donor directs.

Chapels. Places for worship, in churches, in honour of particular saints. Sometimes erected as separate buildings.

Chapter house. The place of assembly for abbot, prior and members of a monastery, often reached from the cloisters. In England, it was usually polygonal on plan, with a vault resting on a central pillar, but sometimes oblong.

Chatravalli (Bud). The umbrella ornament above a **stupa** (q.v.); sometimes crowned with a gilded finial.

Chattri (Isl). Pavilion or kiosk with a parasol shaped domed roof.

Chevet. A circular or polygonal apse when surrounded by an ambulatory, off which are chapels.

Chevron. A zigzag moulding used in Romanesque architecture, and so called from a pair of rafters, which gave this form.

Choir. *See* **Chancel**.

Chunam. A kind of stucco containing burnt and ground seashells, and able to take polish resembling marble: used for rendering buildings in India over brick construction.

Churrigueresque. An expression of Spanish Baroque architecture and sculpture associated with the Churriguera family of artists and architects, characterised by a lavish, even fantastic, but not inharmonious, decorative exuberance. In architecture a recurrent feature was the richly garlanded spiral column.

Ciborium. *See* **Baldacchino**.

Cimborio. The Spanish term for a lantern or raised structure above a roof admitting light into the interior.

Cinquefoil. In tracery an arrangement of five foils or openings, terminating in cusps.

Cladding. An outer veneer of various materials applied to a building facade.

Classical. The architecture originating in ancient Greece and Rome, the rules and forms of which were largely revived in the Renaissance in Europe and elsewhere.

Classicism, a Classical idiom or style.

Claustra. A term sometimes used in the late nineteenth and early twentieth centuries to describe panels, pierced with geometrical designs, as employed by the French architect Auguste Perret in certain of his reinforced concrete buildings.

Clepsydra. A water-clock or instrument for measuring time by the discharge of water through a small opening.

Clerestory, clere-story, clearstory or **clear-storey**. An upper stage in a building with windows above adjacent roofs; especially applied to this feature in a church.

Cloisters. Covered passages round an open space or garth, connecting the church to the chapter house, refectory, and other parts of the monastery. They were generally south of the nave and west of the transept, probably to secure sunlight and warmth.

Coemeteria. Underground burial places, in ancient Rome often taking the form of vaults each containing a number of interments in funerary receptacles.

Coffers. Sunk panels, caissons or lacunaria formed in ceilings, vaults, and domes.

Collar-braced roof. A logical development of the cruck-type timber frame (*see* **Crucks**) in which the principal rafters are raised upon walls (instead of rising from the ground) and linked close to the ridge by a short tie-beam (also called a collar-beam) to form an A-shaped truss or collar. When this collar is additionally stiffened underneath by braces extending from the principal rafters, the roof is described as arch-braced.

Collar-purlin. A purlin (longitudinal member) laid centrally and stiffening the collars (*see* **Collar-braced roof**) of an open timber-framed roof, and supported by a crown-post rising from a tie-beam. If the roof was long, more than one crown-post (and, therefore, more than one tie-beam) might be needed.

Column. A vertical support, generally consisting of base, circular shaft, and spreading capital.

Compartment. A division or separate part of a building or of an element of a building (*see* **Bays** and **Severy**).

Compluvium. A quadrangular opening in the atrium of a Roman house, towards which the roof sloped so as to throw the rainwater into a shallow cistern or impluvium in the floor.

Composite. *See* **Order**.

Concrete. A mixture of water, sand, stone and a binder (today generally Portland cement). The Romans used pozzolana in place of sand, and lime. **Reinforced concrete**, is concrete with a reinforcement of steel rods or mesh (often bamboo in eastern countries). **Prestressed concrete** is concrete in which cracking (an inherent characteristic) and tensile force are counteracted by compressing it. Two principal methods are applied to achieve this, post-tensioning and pre-tensioning, both using bars or wires. Prestressed concrete is reliable and relatively economical for large spans (e.g. for factory buildings). In recent decades **pre-cast concrete**, in which various concrete elements are cast on-site or in a factory before assembly, has been much used for many building types. In **board-marked concrete**, made fashionable by Le Corbusier, a supposedly pleasing effect is created by leaving the marks of the wood shuttering on the exposed concrete. Among the many other methods of treating a concrete surface is **bush-hammering** (usually on surfaces cast *in situ*), by which a roughened, 'rusticated' appearance is attained with the aid of a bush hammer, a mechanically operated percussive tool.

Conoid. Having the form of a cone. The term is usually applied to the lower part of a mediaeval vault where the ribs converge against the outer wall and form an approximation of an inverted half-cone or half-pyramid.

Console. *See* **Bracket**.

Coping. The capping or covering to a wall.

Corbel. A block of stone, often elaborately carved or moulded, projecting from a wall, supporting the beams of a roof, floor, vault or other feature.

Corbel table. A plain piece of projecting wall supported by a range of corbels and forming a parapet, generally crowned by a coping.

Corbie gable or **crow-step gable**. A gable with stepped sides.

Corinthian. *See* **Order**.

Cornice. In Classic or Renaissance architecture, the crowning or upper portion of the entablature, also used for any crowning projection.

Coro. In Spanish churches the choir, usually occupying two or more bays of the nave, the *Capilla Mayor* (comprising sanctuary, high altar and presbytery) filling the east end. Rejas (q.v.) often served as dividing screens.

Corona. The square projection in the upper part of a cornice, having a deep vertical face, generally plain, and with its soffit or under-surface recessed so as to form a 'drip', which prevents water from running down the building.

Corps de logis. That part of a substantial house which forrns a self-contained dwelling, i.e. without the service quarters (*communs*), stables, etc.

Cortile. The Italian name for the internal court, surrounded by an arcade, in a palace or other edifice.

Cosmati. The name given to craftsmen in mosaic and marble working in Rome in the twelfth to fourteenth centuries, many of whom belonged to a family of that name. Hence **Cosmato work**.

Cour d'honneur. The finest, most handsome, court of a chateau or other great house, where visitors were formally received.

Cove, coving. A large hollow, forming part of an arch in section, joining the walls and ceiling of a room. Often decorated with coffering or other enrichment.

Credence table. A small table or shelf near the altar, on which the Eucharistic elements were placed.

Crenellation. An opening in the upper part of a parapet. Furnished with 'crenelles', or indentations. In Britain, a licence to crenellate was necessary before houses could be fortified.

Crepidoma The steps forming the base of a columned Greek temple.

Cresting. A light repeated ornament, incised or perforated, carried along the top of a wall or roof.

Crocket. In Gothic architecture a projecting block or spur of stone carved with foliage to decorate the raking lines formed by angles of spires and canopies.

Croisée. (1) Transept; (2) the French term for the type of casement window preferred for the last three centuries in France; (3) *croisée d'ogives* = intersecting ribs of a vault. Rarely used in English.

Cross vault or **groin vault.** Vaults characterised by arched diagonal arrises or groins, which are formed by the intersection of two barrel vaults.

Crossing. Area at the intersection of nave, chancel and transepts.

Crow-step gable. *See* **Corbie gable**.

Crown-post. A post standing upright on the tie beam of a timber roof and by means of struts or braces giving support to a central collar-purlin and adjacent rafters but not reaching the apex of a roof as in the case of a king-post (q.v.).

Crucks. Pairs of timbers, arched together and based near the ground, erected to form principals for the support of the roof and walls of timber-framed small houses: in use in the western half of England until the sixteenth century or later.

Crypt. A space entirely or partly under a building; in churches generally beneath the chancel and used for burial in early times.

Crypto-porticus. A passageway wholly or mainly below ground.

Cubiculum. A bedroom in a Roman house, but sometimes used in a less specific sense to denote other rooms.

Cunei. The wedge-shaped sections into which seats are divided by radiating passages in ancient theatres.

Cupola. A spherical roof, placed like an inverted cup over a circular, square or multangular apartment. *See* **Dome**.

Curtain wall. The logical outcome of skeleton frame construction, in which the external walls serve no load-bearing purpose, but are suspended on the face of a building like a curtain. Not to be confused with the curtain wall of mediaeval military architecture, denoting a defensive (usually outer) wall linking towers and gatehouses.

Cushion capital. A cubiform capital, the angles being progressively rounded off towards the lowest part.

Cusp. The point formed by the intersection of the foils in Gothic tracery.

Cyma, cymatium. *See* **Sima, Simatium**.

Dado. The portion of a pedestal between its base and cornice. A term also applied to the lower portions of walls when decorated separately.

Dais. A raised platform at the end of a mediaeval hall, where the master dined apart from his retainers: now applied to any raised portion of an apartment.

Decastyle. A portico of ten columns.

Deconstruction. A philosophic/semiological approach to reassesssing texts that acquired an architectural meaning during the 1980s, mainly due to the writings of the philosopher Jacques Derrida. The architectural consequence of the application of the theories of deconstruction was the apparent fragmentation of buildings forms, the rejection of the right-angle and curve in favour of the sharp acute angle and a general reversal or at least questioning of all principles of design and construction conventionally believed to be axiomatic.

Decorated. The style of English Gothic architecture prevalent during the fourteenth century.

Demi-columns. Columns semi-sunk into a wall.

Dentils. Tooth-like blocks in Ionic and Corinthian cornices.

Diaconicon. The vestry, or sacristy, in Early Christian churches.

Diaper. A term probably derived from tapestry hangings of Ypres, and applied to any small pattern, such as lozenges or squares, repeated continuously over the wall surface.

Diastyle. A term used when the space between two columns is three diameters.

Diazoma. A horizontal passage dividing upper and lower levels of seats in an ancient theatre or amphitheatre.

Die. The part of a podium or pedestal between its cap-mould and base.

Dipteral. A temple having a double range of columns on each of its sides.

Distyle in antis. A portico with two columns between antae.

Diwan or **divan** (Isl). Formal reception chamber smoking room.

Dodecastyle. A portico of twelve columns (rare).

Dog-tooth. An ornament resembling a row of teeth especially occurring in Early English buildings.

Dome. A convex covering, usually hemispherical or semi-elliptical over a circular or polygonal space. *See also* **Cupola**.

Domical vault. Segmental masonry shells rising to a common apex over a polygonal, usually square, ground plan.

Donjon. *See* **Keep**.

Doric. *See* **Order**.

Dormer. A window in a sloping roof, usually that of a sleeping-apartment, hence the name.

Dosseret. A deep block sometimes placed above a Byzantine capital to support the wide voussoirs of the arch above.

Dou. The notched timber block supporting the next higher bracket in the Chinese structural system employing multiple bracket arms, **gong** (q.v.).

Double cone moulding. A characteristic Romanesque motif, formed by the continuous horizontal juxtaposition of cones, alternately base to base and vertex to vertex.

Dravida (Hind). Architectural language of south Indian temple architecture

Dripstone. In Gothic architecture, the projecting moulding over the heads of doorways, windows and archways to throw off rain; also known as 'hood moulding' or, when rectangular, a 'label'.

Dromos. A long, uncovered narrow passage leading to an underground tholos or chamber tomb.

Drum. The upright part below a dome or cupola, in which windows might be placed to light the central area of a building.

Dutch gable. A shaped gable surmounted by a pediment.

Early English. The style of English Gothic architecture prevalent during the thirteenth century.

Eaves. The lower part of a roof projecting beyond the face of the wall.

Echinus. The convex or projecting moulding, resembling the shell of a sea-urchin, which supports the abacus of the Greek Doric capital; sometimes painted with the egg and dart ornament.

Egg and dart or **egg and tongue**. Alternating oval (*see* **Ovolo**) and pointed motifs, originating in Greece and widely applied to mouldings in the Renaissance

Elizabethan. A term applied to English Early Renaissance architecture of the period 1558–1603.

Embattled. Furnished with battlements: occasionally applied to an indented pattern on mouldings.

Embrasure. An opening in a parapet between two merlons; the inward splaying of a door or window

Encaustic. The art of mural painting in any way in which heat is used to fix the colours. **Encaustic tiles**. Ornamental tiles of different clays, producing colour patterns after burning. Used in the Middle Ages and revived in the 19th century.

Entresol. See Mezzanine.

English bond. Brickwork with alternate courses of stretchers and headers.

Enneastyle. A portico of nine columns.

Entablature. The upper part of an Order of architecture, comprising architrave, frieze and cornice, supported by a colonnade.

Entasis. A swelling or curving outwards along the outline of a column shaft, designed to counteract the optical illusion which gives a shaft bounded by straight lines the appearance of curving inwards.

Ephebeion (**ephebeum**). A room connected with an ancient Greek or Roman gymnasium, or with the gymnasium element of a baths building.

Eustyle. A term used when the space between two columns is 2¼ diameters.

Exedra. In Greek buildings a recess or alcove with raised seat where the disputations of the learned took place. The Romans applied the term to any semicircular or rectangular recess with benches, and it is also applied to an apse or niche in a church.

Extrados. The outer curve of an arch.

Facade. The face or elevation of a building.

Faience. Glazed earthenware, often ornamented, used for pottery or for building. Originally made at Faenza in Italy from about 1300.

Fan vault. Vaulting peculiar to the Perpendicular period, in which all ribs have the same curve, and resemble the framework of a fan.

Fascia. A vertical face of little projection, usually found in the architrave of an Order. The architrave of the Ionic and Corinthian Orders is divided into two or more such bands. Also, a board or plate covering the end of roof rafters.

Feretory. A shrine for relics designed to be carried in processions.

Fielded panels. Panels of which the surface is raised to the same plane as that of the enclosing frame.

Fillet. A small flat band between mouldings to separate them from each other; also the uppermost member of a cornice.

Finial. The upper portion of a pinnacle, bench end, or other architectural feature.

Flamboyant. Tracery in which the bars of stonework form long wavy divisions like flames.

Flèche. A slender wooden spire upon a roof.

Flemish bond. Brickwork with alternate headers and stretchers in the same course.

Fluting. The vertical channelling on the shaft of a column.

Flying buttress. *See* **Buttress**.

Foil. The small arc openings in Gothic tracery separated by cusps. Trefoil, quatrefoil, cinquefoil, etc., signify the number of foils.

Folded slab. A development of the reinforced concrete thin slab, which has both aesthetic and structural advantages in spanning large halls and buildings of similar type, while also facilitating the provision of good natural and artificial lighting. So called because in section the resultant ribbed roof assumes the form of pleats or folds.

Formeret. In a mediaeval vault, the half-rib against the wall, known in Britain as the 'wall rib'.

Formwork. Temporary casing of woodwork, within which concrete is moulded.

Fortalice. A small fortification, often a tower.

Forum. The public open space, for social, civic or market purposes, found in every Roman town.

Fresco. The term originally applied to painting on a wall while the plaster is still wet, but is often used for any wall painting not in oil colours.

Fret. An ornament in Classical or Renaissance architecture consisting of an assemblage of straight lines intersecting at right angles, and of various patterns. Sometimes called the **key pattern**.

Frieze. The middle division of the Classical entablature. *See* **Zoophorus**.

Frigidarium. An apartment in a Roman baths building equipped with a large, cold bath.

Gable. The triangular portion of a wall, between the enclosing lines of a sloping roof. In Classical architecture it is called a pediment.

Gadroon. One of a series of convex curves, like inverted fluting, used as an ornamental border.

Galilee. A porch used as a chapel for penitents, etc., in some mediaeval churches.

Gallery. A communicating passage or wide corridor for pictures and statues. An internal and external feature in mediaeval buildings. An upper storey for seats in a church.

Garbhagriha (Hind).'Womb-house'; the sanctum, holy of holies in Indian temples..

Gargoyle. A projecting water-spout grotesquely carved to throw off water from the roof.

Gavaksha (Hind). 'Cow eye'; horseshoe arch gable motif in Indian temple architecture.

Georgian. British Late Renaissance architecture of the period 1714–1830.

Glyph. A carved vertical channel. *See* **Triglyphs.**

Glyptotheca. A building to contain sculpture.

Gong. In Chinese structure the bow-shaped or cranked bracket arms: the lower and shorter brackets support the upper longer ones at their end points on shaped blocks, **dou** (q.v.).

Gopura (Hind). (Sanskrit equivalent of Tamil gopuram), barrel-roofed south Indian temple gateway.

Gorge cornice. The characteristic hollow-and-roll moulding of an Egyptian cornice. Also found in Persian architecture.

Gothic. The name generally given to the pointed style of mediaeval architecture prevalent in Western Europe from the thirteenth to the fifteenth centuries.

Gothic Revival. A manifestation first evident in the mid-eighteenth century, but belonging principally to the nineteenth. The countries most affected were Britain, France and Germany and, less strongly, the USA.

Greek Revival. Like the Gothic Revival, this had its beginnings in the mid-eighteenth century. In England it culminated in the 1820s and had concluded by 1840 (later in Scotland), while in France it similarly was at its most evident in the early nineteenth century. In Germany it endured to the mid-nineteenth century. In the USA it was the especially characteristic of the architecture of the period 1815–60.

Groin. The curved arris formed by the intersection of vaulting surfaces.

Groin vault. *See* **Cross vault.**

Guilloche. A circular interlaced ornament like net work, frequently used to ornament the 'torus' moulding.

Guttae. Small cones under the triglyphs and mutules of the Doric entablature.

Gymnasium (**gymnasion**). In ancient Greece, a place for physical exercises and training, larger than the palaestra (q.v.).

Gynaeceum. The women's apartments in a Greek (or Roman) house; also the women's gallery in a Byzantine church.

Hagioscope. An oblique opening in a mediaeval church wall giving a view of the altar, sometimes known as a 'squint'.

Half-timber building. A building of timber posts, rails and struts, and interspaces filled with brick or other material, and sometimes plastered.

Hall church. Church in which nave and aisles are of, or approximate to, equal height.

Hall-keep. Early type of keep, rectangular in form, in which the great hall and private bed-chamber were placed side by side.

Hammam (Isl). Bath.

Hammer-beam roof. Late Gothic form of roof without a direct tie.

Hara (Hind). Chain or necklace of pavilions in Indian temple architecture.

Harem or haram (Isl). Private quarters of a house; sanctuary of a mosque.

Hecatompedon. The name given to the naos of the Parthenon, Athens, inherited from a former temple of 566 BC upon the site, of which the length was exactly 100 Doric feet (1 Doric foot = 12.88 in) and the width 50 Doric feet.

Helix. One of the 16 small volutes (helices) under the abacus of a Corinthian capital.

Helm. Bulbous termination to the top of a tower, found principally in central and eastern Europe.

Helm roof. Type of roof in which four faces rest diagonally between the gables and converge at the top.

Hemicycle buttress. Half-moon-shaped buttress, sometimes very large, often masked by other masonry or designed to perform utilitarian tasks additional to its purely structural purpose, widely used by the Romans.

Henostyle-in-antis. A portico with one column between antae.

Heptastyle. A temple having seven columns on the front.

Hermes. A Greek deity. A bust (Hermes, Herm or Term) on a square pedestal instead of a human body used in Classical times along highways and to mark boundaries, and decoratively in Roman and Renaissance times.

Heroum. In Greek architecture, a small shrine or chapel dedicated to a semi-deified person or to the memory of a mortal.

Hexastyle. A portico having a row of six columns.

Hieron. The sacred enclosure surrounding a temple.

Hippodrome. In ancient Greece, a course for horse and chariot racing, the equivalent of the Roman circus.

Honeysuckle ornament. *See* **Anthemion**.

Hood moulding. *See* **Dripstone**.

Hoop-tie principle. A method developed in the Renaissance period, by which a pieced ring of timber, or a metal chain or hoop, binds the lower part of a dome or cupola to prevent splitting outwards or to minimise the burden on external buttresses having a similar purpose.

Hypaethral. A building or temple without a roof or with a central space open to the sky.

Hypocaust. A system of ducts by which heat from the furnace was distributed throughout the building.

Hypogeum. In ancient times, all parts of a building underground.

Hypostyle. A pillared hall in which the roof rests on columns. applied to the many-columned halls of Egyptian temples.

Hypotrachelion. The channels or grooves beneath the trachelion at the junction of the capital and shaft of a column. *See* **Trachelion.**

Iconostasis. A screen between nave and chancel of a Byzantine church.

Imbrex. In Classical architecture, a roofing cover tile over the joint between flat or hollow tiles.

Imbrication. An overlapping, as of one row of scalloped roofing tiles breaking joint with the next.

Impluvium. In Greek and Roman houses, a shallow tank under the compluvium, or opening in the roof of an atrium.

Impost. The member, usually formed of mouldings, on which an arch rests.

In antis. A covered colonnade at the entrance to a building is 'in antis' if recessed. *See* **Prostyle.**

Incrustation. The facing of a wall surface, generally marble, with a decorative overlay. An Italian, predominantly Venetian, craft.

Indent. A notch.

Indented moulding. A moulding cut in the form of zigzag pointed notches.

Intarsia. In furniture, a decorative inlay of various materials in another, usually wood.

Inter-columniation. The space between the columns.

Intrados. The inner curve of an arch.

Ionic. *See* **Order**.

Insula. A block of flats in a Roman town.

Irimoya gable. A traditional type of Japanese gable, placed vertically above the end walls and marked by roofs of varying pitch.

Iwan (Isl). Roofed or vaulted hall (or recessed area of a room) open at one end.

Jacobean. English Early Renaissance architecture of the period 1603–25.

Jali (Hind). Net pattern grille.

Jambs. The sides of doors and windows. The portion exposed outside the window-frame is the 'reveal'.

Jami' masjid (Isl). Congregational mosque.

Jarookha (Hind). Projecting aedicular balcony.

Jubé. The French equivalent of the English rood screen between nave and chancel.

Jugendstil. The movement in Germany contemporary with **Art Nouveau** (q.v.).

Kalasa (Hind). *See* **Sikhara**.

Kapota (Hind). Curved moulding, usually as a cornice, in Indian temple architecture.

Keel moulding. A moulding like the keel of a ship formed of two ogee curves meeting in a sharp arris; used rounded in form in the fifteenth century. The word 'keel' is also applied to the ogee form of arch.

Keep. The inner great tower or donjon of a castle.

Key pattern. *See* **Fret.**

Keystone. The central stone of a semicircular arch, sometimes sculptured.

Khan (Isl). Urban **caravanserai** (q.v.), inn for travellers arriving in a town.

Kheker cresting. A decorative motif used by the Egyptians.

Kibla or **qibla** (Isl). In a mosque the direction of Mecca: the kibla wall is marked by the **mihrab** (q.v.).

King-post. A vertical post extending from the ridge to the centre of the tie-beam below.

Kiosk. A light, open pavilion.

Knapped flint. A traditional East Anglian craft of splitting flints, so that they present a smooth black surface on a wall face. The arrangement of knapped flints in patterns is sometimes called 'flushwork'.

Kokoshniki. Ornamental or blind gables, ogee shaped or semicircular, most often in two or three tiers around the dome of a Byzantine church.

Kreshchaty vault. Method of vaulting a domed cruciform church without pillars, with a kind of basket vault over the arms of the cross, and segments of domical vaulting over the corner cells.

Kuta (Hind). 'Peak': in north Indian temple architecture a pavilion with a pointed spire or shikhara; in south Indian temple architecture a square (occasionally circular, octagonal or stellate) pavilion, with domical roof.

Kuta-stambha (Hind). Pillar form (usually embedded, as a pilaster) crowned by a **kuta** (q.v.).

Label. *See* **Dripstone**.

Laconicum. A dry sweating room in a Roman baths building.

Lacunaria. *See* **Coffers.**

Lancet arch. A sharp pointed arch, chiefly in use during the Early English period.

Lantern. A construction, such as a tower, at the crossing of a church, rising above the neighbouring roofs and glazed at the sides.

Lararium. A room or niche in a Roman house, in which the effigies of the household gods (lares) were placed.

Later. A Roman unburnt brick

Laths. *See* **Stambhas.**

Latina (Hind). The basic unitary mode of Nagara (north Indian) shrine.

Lavabo. Ritual washing-basin for celebrant; monastic washing-trough.

Leaf and tongue. In Greek architectural ornament, a conventional motif of the sima reversa.

Lesene. An undecorated pilaster without base or capital.

Lich or **lych gate**. A covered gateway to a churchyard, forming a resting-place for a coffin where a portion of the burial service is often read.

Lierne. A short intermediate rib in Gothic vaulting which does not rise from the impost and is not a ridge rib.

Linenfold. A type of relief ornament, imitating folded linen, carved on the face of individual timber panels. Popular in the late fifteenth and the sixteenth centuries.

Lintel. The horizontal timber or stone, also known as the architrave, that spans an opening.

Loculi. Recesses for corpses in Roman burial vaults.

Loggia. A gallery behind an open arcade or colonnade.

Long and short work. In Anglo-Saxon building, a method of laying the quoins or angles, in which the stone slabs are superposed vertically and horizontally in alternate courses.

Louvre. A series of inclined slats in a vertical frame, allowing ventilation without admitting rain or direct sunlight; a roof ventilator embodying the principle. Sometimes applied to roof ventilators in general.

Lucarne. A window in a sloping roof. *See also* **Dormer.**

Luna marble. *See* **Carrara**.

Lunette. A semicircular window or wall-panel let into the inner base of a concave vault or dome. *See* **Thermal Window**.

Machicolation. A projecting wall or parapet allowing floor openings, through which molten lead, pitch, stones etc., were dropped on an enemy below.

Madrassa or **madrassah** (Arabic or Persian) or **Medrese** (Turkish). Collegiate mosque, theological college.

Maeander. Running ornament in the form of a **fre** (q.v.) or key pattern.

Makara (Bud). A type of stone console-shaped balustrade, usually at either end of a short flight of external steps.

Maksura or **maqsura** (Isl). The sanctuary in an early mosque enclosed by a wooden latticed screen or pierced stonework.

Mandapa (Hind). The hall, usually pillared, in Indian architecture.

Mandorla. *See* **Aureole**.

Mannerism. A term coined originally to describe the characteristics of the work of some sixteenth century Italian architects whose work was less rigidly governed by the stylist rules; later applied more widely to other similar European Renaissance buildings.

Mansard roof. A roof with steep lower slope and flatter upper portion, named after Mansart. Also known as a 'gambrel' roof.

Marquise. A projecting canopy over an entrance door, often of metal and glass.

Masjid (Isl). District mosque.

Masjid-I Jum'a (Isl). Friday mosque.

Masons' mitre. The treatment in masonry and sometimes in joinery for mouldings meeting at right angles,when the diagonal mitre thus formed does not coincide with the joint, but is worked on the face of the one piece which is carried straight through and simply butts on the other.

Mastaba. An ancient Egyptian, rectangular, flat topped, funerary mound, with battered (sloping) sides, covering a burial chamber below ground.

Mathematical tiles. Brick tiles designed to imitate facing bricks.

Maydan or **meydan** (Isl). Ceremonial open space or square.

Meander fret. *See* **Maeander.**

Mediaeval. A term taken to comprehend the Romanesque and Gothic periods of architectural development.

Megaron. The principal room of an early Anat olian or Aegean house.

Merlon. The upstanding part of an embattled parapet, between two 'crenelles' or embrasure openings.

Metope. The space between Doric triglyphs sometimes left open in ancient examples; afterward applied to the carved slab.

Mezzanine. An intermediate floor formed within a lofty storey.

Mihrab (Isl). Niche oriented towards Mecca.

Minabar. The pulpit of a mosque.

Minaret. A slender tower, rising above (or other wise connected with) a mosque, from which the muezzin (crier) calls the faithful to prayer.

Misericord. A hinged seat, made to turn up to afford support to a standing person, with the underside frequently grotesquely carved.

Mitre. The term applied, especially in joinery, to the diagonal joint formed by the meeting of two mouldings at right angles.

Modillion. *See* Bracket.

Module. A measure of proportion, by which the parts of a Classical Order or building are regulated, being usually the diameter of a column immediately above its base, which is divided into sixty parts or minutes.

Monopteral. A temple, usually circular, consisting of columns only.

Mosaic. Decorative surfaces formed by small cubes of stone, glass and marble; much used in Hellenistic, Roman and later times for floors and wall decoration.

Motte. The earthen conical mound of a castle; usually has a related **bailey**, thus a courtyard or ward.

Mouldings. The contours given to projecting members.

Mudéjar. A Spanish Moslem under Christian rule. A vernacular style of Spanish architecture, particularly of Aragon and Castile, of twelfth and sixteenth centuries, blending Muslim and Christian characteristics; its influence survived into the seventh century. **Neo Mudéjar** is a perpetuation or revival of features of the style in the sixteenth to nineteenth centuries in Latin America.

Mulaprasada (Hind). Main shrine of a Nagara (north Indian) temple.

Mullions. Vertical members dividing windows into different numbers of lights.

Multivallate. Having more than one wall or rampart.

Muqarnas (Isl). Small-scale ornamental corbelled brackets and niches forming concave three-dimensional segments decorating (especially) the soffits of arches or vaults: also called stalactites.

Mushrabiyah (Isl). Window with lattice-work screen of elaborately turned or carved wood to admit air and light without loss of privacy.

Mushroom construction. A system of reinforced concrete construction without beams, in which the floor-slabs are directly supported by columns flared at the top.

Mutules. Projecting inclined blocks in Doric cornices, derived from the ends of wooden beams.

Nagara (Hind). Architectural language of north Indian temple architecture.

Nail-head. A Romanesque motif, carved in the form of a small pyramidal stud or nail-head.

Naos. The principal chamber in a Greek temple, containing the statue of the deity.

Narthex. A long arcaded entrance porch to a Christian basilican church, originally allocated to penitents.

Naumachia. A lake for the exhibition of sea fights, encircled by seats for spectators; sometimes refers to the spectacle itself.

Nautilus shell. A decorative motif used by the Greeks, especially for the spiral of the Ionic volute.

Nave. The western limb of a church, as opposed to the choir; also the central aisle of the basilican, mediaeval, or Renaissance church, as opposed to the side aisles.

Necking. The space between the astragal of the shaft and the commencement of the capital proper in the Roman Doric.

Necropolis. A burial ground.

Newel. (1) The central shaft of a circular staircase; (2) also applied to the post into which the handrail is framed.

Niche. A recess in a wall, hollowed like a shell, for a statue or ornament.

Nimbus. *See* **Aureole**.

Nook-shaft. A shaft set in the angle of a pier, a respond, a wall, or the jamb of a window or door.

Norman. The style, also termed English Romanesque, of the eleventh and twelfth centuries.

Nymphaeum. A building in Classical architecture for plants, flowers and running water, ornamented with statues.

Obelisk. A tall pillar of square section tapering upwards and ending in a pyramid.

Octastyle. A portico with a range of eight columns.

Odeion. A building, resembling a Greek theatre, designed for musical contests.

Oecus. The main room of a Greek house, the successor of the megaron.

Ogee. A moulding made up of a convex and concave curve. Also an arch of similar shape.

Ogival. The traditional term in France for Gothic architecture. Not commonly used today.

Opaion. A Greek term for a clerestory or top light.

Opisthodomos. The rear porch of a temple.

Opus. A work.

Opus Alexandrinum. Mosaics inlaid in a stone or marble paving.

Order. An Order in architecture comprises a column, with base (usually), shaft and capital, the whole supporting an entablature. The Greeks recognised three Orders: Doric, Ionic and Corinthian. The Romans added the Tuscan and the Composite (the latter also known as Roman), while using the Greek Orders in modified form. The Greek **Doric Order** is unique in having no base to the column. The capital is plain; the shaft fluted. The **Ionic Order** is lighter, more elegant, than the Doric, with slim columns, generally fluted. It is principally distinguished by the volutes of its capital. The **Corinthian Order** has a bell-shaped capital, from which eight acanthus stalks (caulicoli) emerge to support the modest volutes. The shaft is generally fluted. The **Tuscan Order** resembles the Doric but has a very plain entablature. The shaft is properly unfluted. The **Composite** (or **Roman**) **Order** combines the prominent volutes of the Ionic with the acanthus of the Corinthian on its capital, and is thus the most decorative. The shaft may be fluted or plain.

Ordinates. Parallel chords of conic section (in relation to the bisecting diameter) describing an ellipse; a principle followed by Renaissance builders to adjust cross-vaults of equal height, but unequal span.

Ordonnance. The disposition of the parts of the building.

Oriel. A window corbelled out from the face of a wall by means of projecting stones.

Orthostats. Courses of large squared stones at the base of a wall.

Osiris pillars. Pillars incorporating the sculptured figure of Osiris, Egyptian God of Death and Resurrection.

Ovolo. A convex moulding much used in Classics and Renaissance architecture, often carved with the egg and dart or egg and tongue.

Pai-lou. A Chinese ceremonial gateway, erected in memory of an eminent person. Also found in Japan.

Palaestra. A public building for the training of athletes.

Palladian motif. An arched opening flanked by two smaller, square-headed openings.

Palm vaulting. Similar to **fan vaulting** (q.v.).

Palmette. *See* **Anthemion**.

Panel. A compartment, sunk or raised, in walls, ceilings, doors, wainscoting etc. *See also* **Coffer**.

Panjara (Hind). 'Cage'; representation of a pavilion with a horseshoe gable as its roofing element, in south Indian temple architecture.

Papyrus. Aquatic plant used by the Egyptians for a great variety of purposes, including the construction of primitive 'reed' huts. A recurrent motif in Egyptian architectural sculpture.

Parabolic vaulting. A thin shell covering, normally of reinforced concrete, of parabolic section (i.e. a shape made by cutting a cone parallel to one edge). Such structures are comparatively light, and not subject to tensional stresses under conditions of uniform loading. *See* **Shell vaulting**.

Parapet. The portion of wall above the roof-gutter, sometimes battlemented. Also applied to the same feature, rising breast-high, in balconies, platforms and bridges.

Parclose. A screen enclosing a chapel, as a shelter from draughts, or to prevent distraction to worshippers; also the screen around a tomb or shrine.

Pargetting (**pargeting**, **parging**). Extemal ornamental plasterwork having raised, indented or tooled patterns; used from Tudor times onwards chiefly in East Anglia and the south-east of England.

Pastas or **prostas**. A vestibule in front of a Greek house, with a part of one side open to a forecourt.

Pastophoria. Rooms of apses to the north and south of the main altar in Byzantine churches for use of the clergy and where vestments, etc. are kept or where the altar of preparation or offerings stands.

Paterae. Flat circular ornaments which resemble the Classical saucers used for wine in sacrificial libations.

Patio. A Spanish arcaded or colonnaded courtyard.

Pavilion. A prominent structure, generally distinctive in character, marking the ends and centre of the facade of a major building. A similarly distinctive building linked by a wing to a main block. An ornamental building in a garden.

Pavimentum. A pavement formed by pieces of tile marble, stone, flint or other material set in cement and consolidated by beating down with a rammer.

Pedestal. A support for a column, statue or vase. It usually consists of a base, die and cornice or cap mould.

Pediment. In Classical architecture, a triangular piece of wall above the entablature, enclosed by raking cornices. In Renaissance architecture used for any roof end, whether triangular, broken or semicircular. In Gothic, such features are known as gables.

Pele-towers. Small square towers of massive construction, built in the border country between England and Scotland until the late Middle Ages.

Pendant. An elongated boss projecting downward or suspended from a ceiling or roof.

Pendentive. The term applied to the triangular curved overhanging surface by means of which a circular dome is supported over a square or polygonal compartment.

Pentastyle. A temple front of five columns.

Peribolus. The enclosing wall or colonnade surrounding a temenos or sacred enclosure, and hence sometimes applied to the enclosure itself.

Peripteral. A term applied to an edifice surrounded by a single range of columns.

Peristyle. A range of columns surrounding a court or temple.

Perpendicular. A phase of English Gothic evolved from the Decorated style, and prevalent during the fifteenth and sixteenth centuries.

Perron. A landing or platform outside the portal of a domestic or public building, approached in a dignified way by a single or double flight of steps.

Phamsana (Hind). Mode of Indian temple with pyramidal superstructure of tiered eaves-mouldings.

Piano nobile. The principal floor of an Italian palace, raised one floor above ground level and containing the principal social apartments.

Piazza. A public open place, surrounded by buildings: may vary in shape and in civic purpose.

Picturesque. The term is used in a specialised sense to describe one of the attitudes of taste towards architecture and landscape gardening in the late eighteenth and early nineteenth centuries (*c.* 1785–1835); buildings and landscape were to have the controlled informality of a picture.

Pier. A mass of masonry, as distinct from a column, from which an arch springs, in an arcade or bridge; also applied to the wall between doors and windows. The term is sometimes given to a pillar in Gothic architecture.

Pilaster. A rectangular feature in the shape of a pillar, but projecting only about one-sixth of its breadth from a wall, and the same design as the Order with which it is used. *See* **Anta.**

Pilotis. Posts on an unenclosed ground floor carrying a raised building.

Pinacotheca. A building to contain painted pictures.

Pinnacle. In Gothic architecture, a small turret-like termination on the top of buttresses, parapets, or elsewhere, often ornamented with bunches of foliage called crockets.

Piscina. A stone basin in a niche near the altar, to receive the water in which the priest rinses the chalice. Also applied to the tank or fountain in Roman baths.

Pisé. Clay or earth mixed with gravel used for building by being rammed between boards which are removed as pisé hardens.

Plate tracery. *See* **Tracery.**

Plateresque. A phase of Spanish Architecture of the later fifteenth and early sixteenth centuries, an intricate style named after its likeness to silver-work.

Plinth. The lowest square member of the base of a column; also applied to the projecting stepped or moulded base of any building.

Plough-share twist. The irregular or winding surface in a vault, where the wall ribs, owing to the position of the clerestory windows, start at a higher level than the other ribs.

Podium. A continuous pedestal; also the enclosing platform of the arena of an amphitheatre.

Polychromy. A term originally applied to the art of decorative painting in many colours, extended to the colouring of sculpture to enhance naturalism, and very loosely used in an architectural context to describe the application of variegated materials to achieve brilliant or striking effects. As such, it is a characteristic of the High Victorian phase and of **Art Nouveau** (q.v.).

Poppy-head. The ornamental termination of a bench-end, frequently carved with fleur-de-lis, animals or figures.

Porphyry. A hard rock, red or purple in colour, used as a building stone or for sculpture, especially by the Egyptians, Greeks and Romans.

Portcullis. A heavy lattice grating of timber or iron, sliding in vertical grooves in the jambs of a portal of a defended building.

Portico. A colonnaded space forming an entrance or vestibule, with a roof supported on at least one side by columns.

Porticus. In mediaeval architecture a vestibule, any colonnade as part of a church, a non-columnar side space or adjunct opening from the main body of a building but not actually a vestibule.

Posticum. The Latin term for the rear porch of a temple. *See* **Opisthodomos**.

Post-Modernism. A term which describes an architectural style or theory that is a criticism of orthodox modernism. The usual physical manifestation of this approach is an eclectic style mixing decorative elements of different periods, especially those of Western classical origin. These elements, robbed of their traditional meanings, are usually placed out of context and scale and used with an ironic intent. Post-Modernisn arose in the early 1970s and was passé within a decade.

Prakara (Hind). Enclosure wall of an Indian temple compound.

Prato marble. A green marble from the district of Prato in Tuscany..

Presbytery. The space at the eastern end of a church for the clergy, but often applied to the whole sanctuary.

Pronaos. The part of a temple in front of the naos, often synonymous with portico.

Propylaeum (pl. **propylaea**). An important entrance gateway or vestibule, in front of a sacred enclosure.

Proscenium. In ancient Greek theatres, a colonnade standing in front of the scene building (*skene*), the top of which eventually became the stage (*logeion* = a speaking place): thus all of the stage works in front of the ornamental back-stage. Nowadays, the term means only the frontispiece of the stage.

Prostyle. An open portico of columns standing in front of a building.

Prothesis. That part of a church where the credence table (q.v.) stands

Prytaneion (**prytaneum**). The public hall and state dining room of a Greek city.

Pseudo-dipteral. A temple which is planned as a dipteral building, i.e. two columns in depth around the naos, but from which the inner range is omitted.

Pseudo-peripteral. A temple lacking a pteroma and having the flank columns attached to the temple walls.

Pteroma. The space between the lateral walls of the naos of a temple and the peristyle columns.

Pulpitum. A stone gallery or **rood loft** (q.v.) over the entrance to the choir of a cathedral or church.

Pulvinated. A term applied to a frieze whose face is convex in profile.

Pumice. Igneous rock derived from volcanic lava. As a building stone, it was used by the Romans and, later, is present in Byzantine and Romanesque work: it had the advantage of extreme lightness.

Purbeck marble. A fine hard limestone from Purbeck, Dorset.

Purlin. A horizontal beam in a roof, resting on the principal rafters and supporting the common rafters and roof covering.

Pycnostyle. A term given when the space between two columns is 1½ diameters.

Pylon. A term applied to the mass of masonry with a central opening, forming a monumental entrance to Egyptian temples.

Qasr (Isl). A castle, palace or mansion.

Quadrangle. A broad enclosure or court, defined by buildings.

Quadriga. A four-horsed chariot, in sculptured form, often surmounting a monument.

Quadripartite vaulting. A vault in which each bay is divided by intersecting diagonal ribs into four parts.

Quatrefoil. In tracery, a panel divided by cusps into four openings.

Quincunx. An arrangement of five objects, one at each corner of a square, the other at the crossing of its diagonals.

Quirk. A sharp V-shaped incision in a moulding, such as that flanking the Norman bowtell.

Quoin. A term generally applied to the corner stones at the angles of buildings and hence to the angle itself.

Rampart. Defensive earthen bank surrounding a castle, fortress or fortified city. May have a stone parapet.

Rath. Hindu rock-cut temple, especially in south India.

Rebate. A rectangular sinking, channel or groove cut longitudinally in a piece of timber to receive the edge of another, or a recess in the jambs of an opening to receive a door or window.

Recursive. Repeating the same abstract organising principle, or design idea.

Reeding. A series of convex mouldings of equal width, side by side: the inverse of fluting. The fluting of the lower third of column shafts was sometimes infilled with reeds to strengthen them.

Refectory. The dining-hall in a monastery, convent or college.

Regula. The short band, under the triglyphs, beneath the tenia of the Doric entablature, and to which the guttae are attached.

Reja. An ornate iron grille or screen, a characteristic feature of Spanish church interiors.

Reliquary. A light portable receptacle for sacred relics.

Renaissance. The term applied to the reintroduction of Classical architecture all over Europe, in the fifteenth and sixteenth centuries.

Rendering. Plaster or stucco applied to an external wall; a first coat of plaster internally.

Repoussé work. Ornamental metalwork, hammered into relief from the reverse side.

Reredos. The screen, or ornamental work, rising behind the altar.

Respond. A half-pillar at the end of an arcade

Retable. A ledge or shelf behind an altar for holding vases or candles The Spanish **retablo** is a sumptuously ornate form of reredos.

Retro-choir. The parts of a large church behind the high altar.

Reveal. The surface at right angles to the face of a wall, at the side of an opening cut through it; known as a 'splay' when cut diagonally. Especially applied to the part outside the window-frame.

Rib. A projecting-band on a ceiling, vault or elsewhere.

Ribat (Isl) Fortified monastery.

Ridge. The apex of a sloping roof, running from end to end.

Ringhiera. A balcony on the main front of an Italian mediaeval town hall from which decrees and public addresses were delivered.

Riwaq (Isl). Colonnade, portico, aisle, usually one side of a courtyard; colonnaded or arcaded hall of a mosque.

Rococo. A term applied to a type of Renaissance ornament in which rock-like forms, fantastic scrolls and crimped shells are worked up together in a profusion and confusion of detail often without organic coherence, but presenting a lavish display of decoration.

Roll moulding. A plain round moulding. In mediaeval architecture, sometimes known as the **bowtell** (q.v.).

Romanesque. The sty!e of architecture prevalent in western Europe from the ninth to the twelfth centuries.

Rood loft. A raised gallery over the **rood screen**, a name given to the chancel screen when it supports the 'rood' or large cross erected in many churches in mediaeval times. Reached by stairs in the chancel wall it was also used as a gallery for minstrels and singers on festival days.

Rose window. *See* **Wheel window**.

Rostrum. The plural 'rostra' denoted the raised tribune in the Forum Romanum, from which orators addressed the people, and was so called because decorated with the prows of ships taken in war, as were **rostral columns**.

Rotonda. A round building.

Rubble. Stone walling of rough, undressed stones.

Rustication. A method of forming stonework with roughened surfaces and recessed joints, principally employed in Renaissance buildings.

Sahn (Isl). Courtyard of a mosque.

Sanctuary. A holy or consecrated place. The most sacred part of a church or temple.

Sarcophagus. Richly carved coffin.

Sash window. A double-hung, usually wooden, glazed frame (or sash), designed to slide up and down in grooves with the aid of pulleys.

Säteri roof. A form of hipped roof, interrupted by a smaller vertical part sometimes provided with windows. This low perpendicular break forms a middle portion between the lower part of the roof and its considerably smaller continuation above the break. It is characteristic of the great houses of the Swedish nobility and gentry of the seventh and eighteenth centuries.

Scena. The back scene of an ancient theatre.

Scholae. Places of leisure, which to the Classical mind meant places for learned conversation or instruction; hence 'lecture rooms of the philosophers'.

Scotia. The concave moulding between two torus mouldings in the base of a column, throwing a deep shadow.

Screen. A partition or enclosure of iron, stone or wood, often carved; when separating choir from nave, it is termed the choir screen. *See* **Chancel**.

Scroll moulding. A moulding resembling a scroll of paper, the end of which projects over the other part.

Section. The representation of a building cut by a vertical plane, so as to show the construction.

Sedilia. The seats for the priests, generally of masonry, in the south wall of the chancel.

Severy. A compartment or bay of a vault.

Sexpartite vaulting. A vault where each bay is divided into parts by the intersection of two diagonal ribs and one transverse rib.

Sgraffito. A method of decoration by which an upper coat of white stucco is partially cut away to expose a dark undercoat and so form a design.

Shaft. The portion of a column between base and capital; also applied in mediaeval architecture to a small column, as in a clustered pier, supporting a vaulting rib.

Shala (Hind). Representation of a barrel-vaulted pavilion in south Indian temple architecture.

Shastra (Hind). An Indian canonical text.

Shastric (Hind). Pertaining to the shastras.

Shekhari (Hind). One of the later composite modes of Nagara temple.

Shell vaulting. A thin curved plate-like form of roofing, generally of reinforced concrete and often of striking elegance, widely used nowadays for spanning large halls. *See* **Parabolic vaulting**.

Shikhara (Hind). Superstructure or 'spire' of a north Indian temple.

Shingle style. The cladding of external walls with shingles (wooden tiles) over a timber frame.

Shrine. A sacred place or object, e.g. a receptacle for relics.

Sikhara (Hind). The pyramidal roof form of a Hindu temple; either over the shrine or gateways. Usually elaborately sculptured with human and animal figures.

Sima. A moulding with an outline of two contrary curves – either the cyma recta or cyma reversa.

Simatium. The crowning member of a cornice generally in the form of a sima.

Soffit. The ceiling or underside of any architectural member.

Solar. A mediaeval term for a private chamber on the upper floor.

Space frame. A frame which is three-dimensional and stable in all directions.

Span. The distance between the supports of an arch, roof or beam.

Spandrel. The triangular space enclosed by the curve of an arch, a vertical line from its springing, and a horizontal line through its apex. In modern architecture, an infill-panel below a window-frame in a curtain wall.

Specus. The duct or channel of a Roman aqueduct, usually rectangular in section and lined with a water proofing of successive coatings of a hydraulic cement, and covered by stone slabs or by arched vaults.

Spere (also **speer** or **spur**). A fixed timber screen, sometimes elaborately carved, shielding the entr ances of mediaeval houses and large halls. When directly attached to a roof-principal, the resultant structure became a **spere-truss**.

Spina. The spine wall down the centre of an ancient hippodrome or circus.

Spire. The tapering termination of a tower in Gothic or Renaissance architecture, which was the result of elongating an ordinary pyramidal or conical roof.

Splay. The diagonal surface formed by the cutting away of a wall, as when an opening is wider inside than out or conversely.

Springer. The lowest unit or voussoir of an arch, occurring just above the springing line.

Squinch. A small arch, bracket or similar device built across each angle of a square or polygonal structure to form an octagon or other appropriate base for a dome or spire. Sometimes known as a **squinch arch**.

Stalls. Divisions with fixed seats for the clergy and choir, often elaborately carved, with projecting elbows, 'misericords' and canopies.

Stambhas. Free-standing monumental pillars, characteristic of Buddhist architecture. Also called **laths.**

Stanchion. A vertical steel support. Cast-iron was used until relatively cheap steel became available.

Starling. The pointed mass of masonry projecting from the pier of a bridge, for breaking the force of the water, hence known as a 'cutwater'.

Steeple. The term applied to a tower crowned by a spire.

Stele. An upright slab forming a Greek tombstone or carrying an inscription.

Stellar vault. A vault in which the ribs compose a star-shaped pattern.

Stepped gable. A gable with stepped sides, especially characteristic of the Netherlands.

Stijl, de. A short-lived geometric-abstract movement in Holland (1917–31), which had a lasting influence on the development of modernist architecture and of industrial design.

Stile Liberty. In Italy the contemporary equivalent of **Art Nouveau** (q.v.), named after the London store.

Stilted arch. An arch having its springing higher than the line of impost mouldings, to which it is connected by vertical pieces of walling or stilts.

Stoa. In Greek architecture, a portico or detached colonnade.

Storey. The space between two floors.

Strapwork. A type of relief ornament or cresting resembling studded leather straps, arranged in geometrical and sometimes interlaced patterns; much used in the early Renaissance architecture of Britain and the Low Countries.

String course. A moulding or projecting course running horizontally along the face of a building.

Stuart. A term applied to English Late Renaissance architecture of the period 1625–1702.

Stucco. A fine quality of plaster, much used in Roman and Renaissance architecture for ornamental modelled work in low relief. In Britain, it was extensively employed in the late eighteenth and early nineteenth centuries as an economical medium for the modelling of external features, in lieu of stone.

Stupa (Bud). An earth mound, usually dome shaped, forming a sacred Buddhist monument. Often faced with brickwork and/or rendered and painted white. Early examples were surrounded by a stone ceremonial fence with thoranas (q.v.) at the cardinal points.

Stylobate. In Classical architecture, the upper step forming a platform on which a colonnade is placed. Collectively, the three steps of a Greek Doric temple constitute a crepidoma.

Sudatorium. The sweating room in a Roman baths building.

Systyle. A term used where the space between two columns is two diameters.

Tabby. A form of concrete made from oyster shells.

Tabernacle. A recess or receptacle – usually above an altar – to contain the eucharistic Host; also applied to a niche or arched canopy. 'Tabernacle work' is the name given to elaborately carved niche and canopy work.

Tablet-flower. A variation of the ball-flower ornament of Decorated Gothic architecture in the form of a four-petalled open flower.

Taenia or **tenia.** A flat projecting band capping the architrave of a Doric entablature.

Tauf. Arabic for packed mud walling. The mud is mixed with straw to prevent cracking, and is laid by hand in courses. Each layer is left to dry before the next is added.

Tegula. The Latin term for a large flat tile.

Telamones. *See* **Atlantes.**

Temenos. A sacred precinct in which stood a temple or other sanctuary.

Tempera. In painting, the same as distemper.

Tempietto. A small temple. The term is usually reserved for Renaissance and later buildings of an ornamental character, compact circular or temple-like structures erected in the parks and gardens of country houses, although the most famous instance is Bramante's chapel in the cloisters of S. Pietro in Montorio, Rome.

Tepidarium. An apartment in a Roman baths building equipped with warm baths.

Terracotta. Earth baked or burnt in moulds for use in construction and decoration, harder in quality than brick.

Tessera. A small cube of stone, glass or marble, used in making mosaics.

Tetrastyle. A portico of four columns.

Thermal window. Semi-circular window, usually furnished within a pair of mullions, derived from widows set with barrel or groin vaults in Roman Baths, particularly in the Baths of Dioclesian, thus also called Dioclesian window. *See* **Lunette**.

Tholos. The dome (cupola) of a circular building, hence the building itself.

Thorana (Bud). Ceremonial gateway through the fence of a **stupa** (q.v.). Resembles a Chinese pai-lou or a Japanese torii.

Thrust. The force exerted by inclined rafters or beams against a wall, or obliquely by the weight of an arch, vault or dome.

Tie-bar. A beam, bar or rod which ties parts of a building together, and is subjected to tensile strain. Sometimes of wood, but usually of metal. Tie-bars are especially notable in Byzantine, Italian Gothic and Renaissance architecture to stiffen arcades or to contain the outward thrust of vaults.

Tie-beam. Normally the lowest member of a roof truss, extending from wall-plate to wall-plate and primarily intended to prevent the walls from spreading. A secondary function may be to carry a king-post or crown-post.

Tierceron. An intermediate rib between the main ribs of a Gothic vault.

Torii. The characteristic entrance gateways to Shinto temples, comprising upright posts supporting beams.

Torus. A large convex moulding, used principally in the bases of columns. *See* **Astragal**.

Trabeated. A style of architecture such as the

Greek, in which posts and beams form the main constructive features. *See also* **Arcuated**.

Tracery. The ornamental patternwork in stone, filling the upper part of a Gothic window; it may be either 'plate' or 'bar' tracery. **Plate tracery** appears to have been cut out of a plate of stone, with special reference to the shape of the lights, whereas **bar tracery** was designed principally for the pleasing forms produced by combinations of geometrical figures. It is also applied to work of the same character in wood panelling.

Trachelion. The neck of a Greek Doric column, between the annulets and the grooves or hypotrachelion.

Transept. The part of a cruciform church, projecting at right angles to the main building.

Transoms. The horizontal divisions or cross-bars of windows.

Transverse rib. A rib which extends at right angles to the wall across a bay or other vaulted space.

Travertine stone. A calcareous deposit from springs, yellowish in colour, used since Roman times as a building stone, especially in Italy where there are large accumulations. In modern architecture, often seen as a decorative facing material, in thin panels.

Trefoil. In tracery, a panel divided by cusps into three openings.

Triangulation. The principle of the design of a roof-truss, in which every panel or space enclosed by its members is triangular.

Tribune. Platform inside a church, usually raised on columns and overlooking the interior; originally a raised platform in a Roman basilica, sometimes in a semicircular addition to the end of the building, thus also used as an alternative name for the apse in a basilican church.

Triclinium. A Roman dining room with couches on three sides.

Triforium. A shallow passage above the arches of nave and choir in a mediaeval church but below the clerestory and opening into the nave; sometimes called a triforium gallery when floored above the aisle vaults.

Triglyphs. Blocks with vertical channels which form a distinguishing feature in the frieze of the Doric entablature.

Tristyle-in-antis. A portico having three columns between antae.

Trussed-rafter roof. A form of roof composed of pairs of rafters, closely spaced and without a ridge piece. To contain the outward thrust, the rafters were joined by collars and further stiffened by braces.

Tudor. A term applied to English Late Gothic architecture of the period 1485–1558.

Tufa. A building stone of rough or cellular texture, of volcanic or other origin (travertine may be described as calcareous tufa).

Tunnel vault. *See* **Barrel vault**.

Turkish triangles (Isl). Small-scale faceted corbelling built up to serve the same purpose as a pendentive (q.v.) or for decorative purposes in the same way as muqarnas (q.v.).

Turrets. Small towers, often containing stairs, and forming special features in mediaeval buildings.

Tuscan. *See* **Order**.

Tympanum. The triangular surface bounded by the sloping and horizontal cornices of a pediment; also the space enclosed between the lintel and the arch of a mediaeval doorway.

Unctuaria. Rooms for oils, unguents, and various forms of treatment in Roman public baths.

Undercroft. In mediaeval architecture, vaulted chambers upon which the principal rooms are sometimes raised.

Vakif (Isl). Financial or property trust.

Valabhi (Hind). Type of north Indian shrine with wagon-roof.

Vault. An arched covering in stone or brick over any building.

Velarium. A great awning drawn over Roman theatres and amphitheatres to protect spectators against the sun.

Vesica piscis. A pointed oval form, so called from its shape. *See* **Aureole**.

Vestibule. An ante-room to a larger apartment of a building.

Vihara. A Buddhist monastery.

Vimana (Hind). Main shrine of a Dravida (south Indian) temple.

Vine ornament. Variations on the theme of the vine-leaf, a characteristic motif of the Gothic Decorated style.

Volute. The scroll or spiral occurring in Ionic, Corinthian and Composite capitals.

Voussoirs. The truncated wedge-shaped blocks forming an arch.

Wakf (Isl). *See* **Vakif**.

Wagon or **wagonhead vault.** *See* **Barrel vault**.

Waqf (Isl). Charitable endowment.

Wave moulding. A typical moulding of the Decorated period consisting of a slight convexity flanked by hollows.

Weathering. The slope given to offsets to buttresses and the upper surfaces of cornices and mouldings, to throw off rain.

Westwork. A multistorey gallery at the west end of some German and Netherlandish churches, surmounted by towers or turrets.

Wheel (or **rose**) **window.** A circular window, whose mullions converge like the spokes of a wheel.

Zakomara. Semicircular gable usually corresponding to the shape of the vault in a Byzantine church, but sometimes used in a purely ornamental manner.

Ziggurat or **ziqqarat.** A high pyramidal staged tower, of which the angles were oriented to the cardinal points, which formed an important element in ancient Mesopotamian temple complexes. the number of stages rose from one to seven in the course of time, and in the Assyrian version the stages were developed into a continuous inclined ramp, circulating the four sides in turn.

Zigzag. *See* **Chevron.**

Zoophorus. A frieze in which reliefs of animals are introduced.

Among the many sources consulted in revising and extending this glossary, the following works have been of especial value:

AHLSTRAND, J. R. and others. *Architektutermen*. Lund, 1969.

HARRIS, J. and LEVER, J. *Illustrated Glossary of Architecture:* 850–1830. Rev. edn, London, 1969.

LONGMORE, J. and MURAD, F. *A Glossary of Arabic Architectural Terms.* Bartlett School of Architecture and Planning, University College London, 1980.

SCOTT, J. S. *The Penguin Dictionary of Building.* 3rd edn, Harmondsworth, 1984.

—. *The Penguin Dictionary of Civil Engineering.* 3rd edn, Harmondsworth, 1980.

INDEX

Page references in italics are to illustrations

Individual buildings are indexed under identifiable names where appropriate and also generally under location (e.g. town)